ST. JAMES GUIDE TO
HORROR, GHOST & GOTHIC WRITERS

Twentieth-Century Writers Series
(now St. James Guide to Writers Series)

Twentieth-Century Children's Writers
Twentieth-Century Romance & Historical Writers
Twentieth-Century Western Writers
Twentieth-Century Young Adult Writers

St. James Guide to Crime & Mystery Writers
St. James Guide to Fantasy Writers
St. James Guide to Horror, Ghost & Gothic Writers
St. James Guide to Science Fiction Writers

ST. JAMES GUIDE TO
HORROR, GHOST & GOTHIC WRITERS

FIRST EDITION

WITH A PREFACE BY
DENNIS ETCHISON

EDITOR
DAVID PRINGLE

ST. JAMES PRESS
AN IMPRINT OF GALE

DETROIT • NEW YORK • TORONTO • LONDON

David Pringle, *Editor*

Laura Standley Berger, *Project Coordinator*

Joann Cerrito, Dave Collins, Nicolet V. Elert, Miranda Ferrara,
Kristin Hart, Margaret Mazurkiewicz, Michael J. Tyrkus,
St. James Press Staff

Peter M. Gareffa, *Managing Editor, St. James Press*

Mary Beth Trimper, *Production Director*
Shanna Heilveil, *Production Assistant*

Cynthia Baldwin, *Product Design Manager*
Pamela Galbreath, *MacIntosh Artist*

The paper used in this publication meets the minimum
requirements of American National Standard for Information Sciences—
Permanence Paper for Printed Library Materials, ANSI Z39.48-1984.

ISBN 1-55862-206-3
Printed in the United States of America

St. James Press is an imprint of Gale

10 9 8 7 6 5 4 3 2 1

CONTENTS

PREFACE

The Darker Side

by Dennis Etchison

Welcome to the *St. James Guide to Horror, Ghost & Gothic Writers.* I'm sure I need not convince you of the value of this book since you are already holding it in your hands, an admission of curiosity about the dark and unseemly side of literature and perhaps of life.

Charles H. Jackson, the author of *The Lost Weekend,* once published a collection of short stories entitled *The Sunnier Side,* as a response to readers who claimed he was interested only in gloomy and sordid matters. I can't recall any of those stories now, but I remember *The Lost Weekend.* It has outlasted his more cheerful work, and not only because of the Oscar-winning film made from it, with the indelible image of a bat devouring a rat on the wall during Ray Milland's bout with delirium tremens, but because it is a deeply disturbing book that speaks to us from a place of authentic knowledge rather than from the imagination of an author merely trying to entertain.

Which is not to shortchange the importance of imagination. That has more to do with a novel's value than adherence to literal truth. I have no idea how much of Charles Jackson's narrative came from personal struggle and how much from research; for all I know he may have been stone cold sober his entire life. Stephen Crane's *The Red Badge of Courage* and Dalton Trumbo's *Johnny Got His Gun,* both masterpieces, were written by men too young to have experienced the horror of the wars they described, just as Nabokov sang the anguished praises of his Lolita without reference to a real-life nymphet in his bed.

By the same token, pain and suffering are certainly not the only subjects worthy of great art. To say that would be to deny centuries of love sonnets, adventures, mysteries and the comedies of Shakespeare. And as for the ability to entertain, it is no small achievement, as Preston Sturges demonstrated so movingly in the greatest of all his films, *Sullivan's Travels.*

And yet *The Lost Weekend* remains more memorable than the equally well-written stories in *The Sunnier Side.* Why?

A moment ago I used the phrase *authentic knowledge.* By this I mean something more than reportage. A factually accurate account will have meaning to others only if it is illuminated by the prism of understanding. Ray Bradbury's short stories are not loved for the documentary information they contain but for the quality of the prose and their wisdom about the human heart and soul. The incidents portrayed, whether realistically or in wildly metaphorical terms, are deeply particular to the author's life and profoundly universal. This is the starting point for great art, whether we are speaking of *Remembrance of Things Past* or *The Rosy Crucifixion* or the bright and dark jewels laid before us by the writers under consideration here.

Still, the question remains:

Why the darker side?

I know that horror's appeal is peculiar to certain readers; if it were otherwise I would not have to spend so much time defending the virtues of this field and spreading the word. It may have to do with early childhood experiences and an acquired association between fear and pleasure, or with genetics and personality types, or simply with an adolescent attraction to anything that shocks our parents and polite society, or all of these things, or none.

For myself, I'd prefer to think that this literature's power derives from its predilection for addressing the fundamental questions of life and death, the drama that does not need to be melodramatized. As a writer I can tell you that this has advantages and a downside. One is able to establish a sense of weight and impending significance early on if the reader knows he is dealing with primal issues. Such a story requires less buildup to launch, so to speak, assuming that the writing throughout is skillful enough to sustain the tension. The problem is that this also requires a greater degree of attention to style, mood and the connotative aspects of language than is found in most fiction, and that the better you do your job the more the reader is likely to expect an extraordinary payoff at the end—something larger, deeper and truer, justifying the trust that has been extended to you.

In that respect a fine horror story may well be the most difficult form of writing extant, excepting poetry. Because it is about the Greater Truth, it ultimately calls for nothing less than *authentic knowledge,* or at least an intimation of it, the kind of understanding of one's characters and their problems that can only come from personal insight. This is something that is not easy to fake. As a result the best work in this field tends to demonstrate both an extraordinary stylistic control and a degree of personal honesty and self-revelation that is sometimes as stark and terrifying as the subject matter. And that, I believe, is why *The Seven Who Were Hanged* or *The Turn of the Screw* will last longer than popular novels of manners and relationship, which approach life more obliquely and timidly.

It is a kind of writing that entertains with the grace and imagination we seek in any fiction but that offers something more than distraction and amusement. It calls us, readers and practitioners alike, to confront rather than evade the most important questions, the which than which there is no whicher. A tall order, but worth the effort.

EDITOR'S NOTE

This work was conceived as the second of a two-volume set, the first of which is the now-published *St. James Guide to Fantasy Writers*. Hence the omission from the present volume of certain writers who some readers might expect to find here; F. Anstey, J. M. Barrie, Peter S. Beagle, Angela Carter, G. K. Chesterton, John Collier, Stephen R. Donaldson, Lord Dunsany, E. R. Eddison, Jack Finney, Paul Gallico, Alan Garner, William Goldman, H. Rider Haggard, Barbara Hambly, Russell Hoban, Robert E. Howard, Garry Kilworth, Rudyard Kipling, Henry Kuttner, Tanith Lee, David Lindsay, George MacDonald, Brian Moore, Robert Nathan, E. Nesbit, Barry Pain, Mervyn Peake, John Cowper Powys, E. Hoffmann Price, Darrell Schweitzer, Thorne Smith, James Stephens, Sheri S. Tepper, Mark Twain, E. Charles Vivian, Karl Edward Wagner, Manly Wade Wellman, Robert Westall, Oscar Wilde, Charles Williams, Gene Wolfe, Jane Yolen, and several others, many of whom have written at least some ghostly or horrific fiction, were covered in *St. James Guide to Fantasy Writers*.

This book endeavors to avoid comment on "pure" fantasy fiction, i.e., tales of magic, heroic fantasies, sword-and-sorcery adventures, humorous fantasies, adult fairy tales, animal fantasies, *Arabian-Nights* tales and *chinoiserie*, timeslip romances, fantastic allegories or fabulations, and the like, even though some overlaps of coverage are inevitable. It concentrates instead on those types of fiction which may be labelled as horror novels, dark fantasies, ghost stories, gothic novels, tales of terror, supernatural fictions, occult fantasies, black-magic stories, psychological thrillers, tales of unease, *grand-guignol* shockers, creepy stories, shudder-pulp fictions, *contes cruels*, uncanny stories, macabre fictions and weird tales. Although the emphasis is mainly on adult fiction, several children's horror-writers who are popular with adults are also included.

Of course, there is no such as thing as "purity" in the matter of literary genres, least of all in a field as protean as the horrific, the ghostly, and the gothic. Nevertheless, "horror" as a perceived type of modern fiction, regarded by most readers as quite distinct from fantasy and science fiction, is here to stay. Indeed, over the past twenty-five years horror has been one of the most popular of publishers' categories, and its origins may be traced back through the 18th and 19th centuries (if not a good deal further), to Horace Walpole, Mrs. Radcliffe, E. T. A. Hoffmann, Mary Shelley, Edgar Allan Poe, J. Sheridan Le Fanu, Bram Stoker, and many others; but it is only since the huge success of Stephen King's novels, coming hard on the heels of Ira Levin's *Rosemary's Baby* (1967) and William Peter Blatty's *The Exorcist* (1971), that horror has become a widely recognized marketplace genre. Since then, it has produced a large number of highly praised (and in some cases best-selling) practitioners, most of whom have entries herein.

Following the established St. James Press style, each entry consists of a brief biography (where the facts have been available), a complete list of works, and a signed critical essay. In addition, living authors were invited to comment on their own work. Original British and United States editions of all books have been listed, and series titles have been indicated for horror, ghost and gothic publications. Entries include notations of film/media adaptations, and of critical studies; other critical materials appear in the Reading List of secondary works on horror fiction and film at the back of the volume. Name, nationality, and title indexes enable users to access author entries by author name, including pseudonyms, nationality, and book title.

ACKNOWLEDGEMENTS

I would like to thank everyone who contributed to this book, from Jack Adrian to Gary Westfahl, and not forgetting several of the entrants themselves who took time to provide facts or to write short statements about their work. In particular, I would like to give thanks to my two advisers, Mike Ashley and Brian Stableford. Each has a prodigious knowledge of the field, and each has added greatly to this volume; however, neither should be blamed for any errors or omissions—those are the editor's responsibility.

—David Pringle

ADVISERS

Mike Ashley   Brian Stableford

CONTRIBUTORS

Jack Adrian

Mike Ashley

Ramsey Campbell

Gary Couzens

Peter Crowther

Don D'Ammassa

Paul Di Filippo

Stefan Dziemianowicz

Peter T. Garratt

Chris Gilmore

John Grant

Lawrence Greenberg

Rhys Hughes

Will Johnstone

S. T. Joshi

Ann Kennedy

Cosette Kies

Joel Lane

David Langford

Adam Meyer

David Mathew

Sean McMullen

Chris Morgan

Pauline Morgan

Steve Paulsen

David Pringle

Nicholas Royle

Andy Sawyer

Darrell Schweitzer

Brian Stableford

Lisa Tuttle

Jeff VanderMeer

Gary Westfahl

Tom Winstead

LIST OF ENTRANTS

Peter Ackroyd
Robert Aickman
Conrad Aiken
Joan Aiken
W. Harrison Ainsworth
Grant Allen
Kingsley Amis
V. C. Andrews
Michael Arlen
Robert Arthur
Cynthia Asquith
Gertrude Atherton
Peter Atkins
Jonathan Aycliffe

Denys Val Baker
Nancy Baker
Scott Baker
J. G. Ballard
Iain Banks
Maurice Baring
Clive Barker
Charles Beaumont
William Beckford
Neil Bell
Peter Benchley
Stephen Vincent Benét
E. F. Benson
R. H. Benson
Ambrose Bierce
Anne Billson
Margaret Bingley
Charles Birkin
Campbell Black
John Blackburn
Algernon Blackwood
Caroline Blackwood
William Peter Blatty
Christopher Blayre
Robert Bloch
Jay R. Bonansinga
Guy Boothby
Douglas Borton
Elizabeth Bowen
Marjorie Bowen
Randall Boyll
Ray Bradbury
M. E. Braddon
Scott Bradfield
Gary Brandner
Chaz Brenchley
Joseph Payne Brennan
Alan Brennert
Poppy Z. Brite
David Britton
J. W. Brodie-Innes
Owen Brookes

D. K. Broster
Rhoda Broughton
Charles Brockden Brown
Edward Bryant
John Buchan
Edward Bulwer-Lytton
John Burke
Arthur J. Burks
Mark Burnell
A. M. Burrage
William S. Burroughs

Michael Cadnum
Jack Cady
Arthur Calder-Marshall
Ramsey Campbell
Lisa W. Cantrell
Bernard Capes
Jonathan Carroll
David Case
Hugh B. Cave
Mark Chadbourn
Robert W. Chambers
Fred Chappell
Suzy McKee Charnas
R. Chetwynd-Hayes
Joseph Citro
Mary Higgins Clark
Simon Clark
Douglas Clegg
Leonard Cline
Nancy A. Collins
Robin Cook
Dennis Cooper
A. E. Coppard
Basil Copper
Matthew J. Costello
Sean Costello
Mary Elizabeth Counselman
John Coyne
F. Marion Crawford
Gary Crew
John Keir Cross
Aleister Crowley
Peter Crowther

Roald Dahl
Brian D'Amato
Don D'Ammassa
Les Daniels
M. P. Dare
Robertson Davies
Ron Dee
Frank De Felitta
Walter de la Mare
August Derleth
Charles Dickens

Isak Dinesen
Thomas M. Disch
Joe Donnelly
John Douglas
Terry Dowling
Arthur Conan Doyle
H. B. Drake
Daphne du Maurier
Katherine Dunn

Max Ehrlich
Bret Easton Ellis
Harlan Ellison
P. N. Elrod
Guy Endore
Elizabeth Engstrom
Dennis Etchison
Ken Eulo

J. Meade Falkner
John Farris
Dion Fortune
Christopher Fowler
John Fowles
Mary E. Wilkins Freeman
Mark Frost

Neil Gaiman
Stephen Gallagher
Ray Garton
R. Murray Gilchrist
Charlotte Perkins Gilman
William Godwin
William Golding
John Gordon
Ed Gorman
Charles L. Grant
Alasdair Gray
Stephen Gresham

G. M. Hague
William H. Hallahan
Alex Hamilton
W. A. Harbinson
Joanne Harris
M. John Harrison
Steve Harris
Thomas Harris
L. P. Hartley
W. F. Harvey
Rick Hautala
Julian Hawthorne
Nathaniel Hawthorne
H. F. Heard
Lafcadio Hearn
James Herbert
Robert Hichens
Susan Hill
William Hjortsberg
William Hope Hodgson

James Hogg
Nancy Holder
Robert Holdstock
Tom Holland
Gordon Honeycombe
Robert Hood
Clemence Housman
Rhys Hughes
Violet Hunt
Shaun Hutson
Christopher Hyde

Shirley Jackson
Carl Jacobi
W. W. Jacobs
G. P. R. James
Henry James
M. R. James
Peter James
K. W. Jeter
Graham Joyce

Jeanne Kalogridis
Susan Kay
Marvin Kaye
Victor Kelleher
David H. Keller
Rick Kennett
Jessie Douglas Kerruish
Gerald Kersh
Jack Ketchum
Nancy Kilpatrick
Stephen King
Russell Kirk
T. E. D. Klein
Nigel Kneale
Harry Adam Knight
Kathe Koja
Jeffrey Konvitz
Dean Koontz
Jerzy Kosinski

Alexander Laing
Terry Lamsley
Joel Lane
Joe R. Lansdale
Marghanita Laski
Margery Lawrence
Stephen Laws
Richard Laymon
Ben Leech
Vernon Lee
J. Sheridan Le Fanu
Fritz Leiber
Jeremy Leven
Ira Levin
D. Francis Lewis
M. G. Lewis
Thomas Ligotti
David L. Lindsey

Bentley Little
Frank Belknap Long
Robert Lory
H. P. Lovecraft
James Lovegrove
Tim Lucas
Brian Lumley

Dorothy Macardle
Arthur Machen
Simon Maginn
Richard Marsh
David Martin
George R. R. Martin
Elizabeth Massie
Graham Masterton
Richard Matheson
Richard Christian Matheson
Charles R. Maturin
Robert R. McCammon
Michael McDowell
Ian McEwan
Patrick McGrath
Kenneth McKenney
Clare McNally
John Metcalfe
Richard B. Middleton
Rex Miller
Marlys Millhiser
Mary L. Molesworth
Brent Monahan
Thomas F. Monteleone
A. R. Morlan
David Morrell
Mark Morris
W. C. Morrow
A. N. L. Munby
H. Warner Munn

Yvonne Navarro
Andrew Neiderman
E. Nesbit
Kim Newman
Hume Nisbet
Robert Nye

Joyce Carol Oates
Elliott O'Donnell
Mrs. Oliphant
Oliver Onions
Vincent O'Sullivan

Jessica Palmer
T. L. Parkinson
Norman Partridge
Tom Piccirilli
Christopher Pike
Edgar Allan Poe
John Polidori
Petru Popescu

Mrs. Campbell Praed
Thomas Peckett Prest
K. & Hesketh Prichard
John Pritchard
Kathryn Ptacek

Arthur Quiller-Couch
Seabury Quinn

Ann Radcliffe
Herman Raucher
Garfield Reeves-Stevens
G. W. M. Reynolds
Daniel Rhodes
Anne Rice
Phil Rickman
Mrs. J. H. Riddell
Tod Robbins
Alan Rodgers
Sax Rohmer
L. T. C. Rolt
Adrian Ross
Marilyn Ross
Theodore Roszak
Victor Rousseau
Nicholas Royle
Ray Russell
W. Clark Russell
John Russo
Alan Ryan
R. R. Ryan
James Malcolm Rymer

Fred Saberhagen
Jeffrey Sackett
David St. Clair
Saki
Sarban
Al Sarrantonio
John Saul
Peter Saxon
David J. Schow
Michael Scott
Walter Scott
David Seltzer
Nick Sharman
Mary Shelley
Lucius Shepard
M. P. Shiel
John Shirley
Anne Rivers Siddons
David B. Silva
Dan Simmons
Iain Sinclair
May Sinclair
Isaac Bashevis Singer
Curt Siodmak
David J. Skal
John Skipp and Craig Spector
Michael Slade

William M. Sloane
Clark Ashton Smith
Guy N. Smith
Lady Eleanor Smith
Martin Cruz Smith
Michael Marshall Smith
S. P. Somtow
William Browning Spencer
Brian Stableford
Robert Stallman
Eric Stenbock
Robert Louis Stevenson
Fred Mustard Stewart
R. L. Stine
Bram Stoker
Tim Stout
J. Michael Straczynski
Peter Straub
Whitley Strieber
Theodore Sturgeon
Gerald Suster

Michael Talbot
Bernard Taylor
Lucy Taylor
Melanie Tem
Steve Rasnic Tem
Thomas Tessier
Paul Theroux
D. M. Thomas
Rosemary Timperley
Peter Tonkin
Peter Tremayne
Thomas Tryon

James Turner
Lisa Tuttle
John Updike

Steve Vance
Jeff Vandermeer
E. H. Visiak
H. Russell Wakefield
Robert W. Walker
Horace Walpole
Hugh Walpole
Elizabeth Walter
Donald Wandrei
Ian Watson
Robert Weinberg
Fay Weldon
H. G. Wells
Eudora Welty
Edith Wharton
Dennis Wheatley
Henry S. Whitehead
Leslie H. Whitten
Mary Williams
Chet Williamson
J. N. Williamson
Colin Wilson
F. Paul Wilson
Ken Wisman
Bari Wood
Stuart Woods
T. M. Wright

Chelsea Quinn Yarbro

Steve Zell

FOREIGN-LANGUAGE WRITERS

Michel Bernanos
Mikhail Bulgakov
Dino Buzzati
Jacques Cazotte
Umberto Eco
Hanns Heinz Ewers
Nikolai Gogol
Stefan Grabinski
E. T. A. Hoffmann
Joris-Karl Huysmans
Franz Kafka
Pierre Kast
Gaston Leroux

Guy de Maupassant
Gustav Meyrink
Thomas Owen
Milorad Pavic
Horacio Quiroga
Jean Ray
Maurice Renard
Claude Seignolle
Fyodor Sologub
Eugène Sue
Patrick Süskind
Comte de Villiers de l'Isle Adam

ST. JAMES GUIDE TO
HORROR,
GHOST & GOTHIC
WRITERS

A

ACKROYD, Peter

Nationality: British. **Born:** London, 5 October 1949. **Education:** St. Benedict's, Ealing, 1960-67; Clare College, Cambridge, 1968-71; Yale University, New Haven, Connecticut (Mellon fellow), 1971-73. **Career:** Literary editor, 1973-77, and joint managing editor, 1978-81, the *Spectator*, London. Since 1986 chief book reviewer, the *Times*, London. **Awards:** Maugham award, 1984; Whitbread award, for biography, 1985, for fiction, 1986; Royal Society of Literature Heinemann award, for non-fiction, 1985; *Guardian* Fiction prize, 1985. Fellow, Royal Society of Literature, 1984. H.D.L.: Exeter University, 1993. **Agent:** Anthony Sheil Associates, 43 Doughty Street, London WC1N 2LF, England. Lives in London.

HORROR, GHOST AND GOTHIC PUBLICATIONS

Novels

Hawksmoor. London, Hamish Hamilton, 1985; New York, Harper, 1986.
First Light. London, Hamish Hamilton, and New York, Grove Weidenfeld, 1989.
The House of Doctor Dee. London, Hamish Hamilton, 1993.
Dan Leno and the Limehouse Golem. London, Sinclair Stevenson, 1994; as *The Trial of Elizabeth Cree*, New York, Doubleday, 1995.

OTHER PUBLICATIONS

Novels

The Great Fire of London. London, Hamish Hamilton, 1982; Chicago, University of Chicago Press, 1988.
The Last Testament of Oscar Wilde. London, Hamish Hamilton, and New York, Harper, 1983.
Chatterton. London, Hamish Hamilton, 1987; New York, Grove Press, 1988.
English Music. London, Hamish Hamilton, 1991; New York, Knopf, 1993.
Milton in America. London, Sinclair Stevenson, 1996.

Poetry

London Lickpenny. London, Ferry Press, 1973.
Country Life. London, Ferry Press, 1978.
The Diversions of Purley and Other Poems. London, Hamish Hamilton, 1987.

Other

Notes for a New Culture: An Essay on Modernism. London, Vision Press, and New York, Barnes and Noble, 1976.
Dressing Up: Transvestism and Drag: The History of an Obsession. London, Thames and Hudson, and New York, Simon and Schuster, 1979.

Ezra Pound and His World. London, Thames and Hudson, and New York, Scribner, 1981.
T. S. Eliot. London, Hamish Hamilton, and New York, Simon and Schuster, 1984.
Dickens. London, Sinclair Stevenson, and New York, Harper Collins, 1990.
Blake. London, Sinclair Stevenson, 1995.

Editor, *PEN New Fiction*. London, Quartet, 1984.
Editor, *The Picture of Dorian Gray*, by Oscar Wilde. London, Penguin, 1985.
Editor, *Dickens' London: An Imaginative Vision*. London, Headline, 1987.

*　　*　　*

Murders occur in the vicinity of a number of London churches, all of which date from the early 18th century and from the same architectural team. Nicholas Hawksmoor, an experienced detective, is called in to investigate. The first three victims, two young boys and a mentally-ill derelict, seem to have little in common: but all have been strangled, and on none of bodies have any forensic clues been left. Horror fans will not be surprised to learn that the murders parallel earlier, sacrificial deaths which took place when the churches were originally built (or rebuilt following damage in the Great Fire of London.) The main architect, Nicholas Dyer, a former protegé of Sir Christopher Wren, was before that a survivor of the Great Plague, who had seen his parents die and had later been taken up by a group whose occult practices verged on devil-worship.

However typical this might seem of the horror genre, Peter Ackroyd's most celebrated novel, *Hawksmoor*, was not marketed as horror but as a literary novel. (It won the Whitbread prize and the Guardian Fiction prize.) It revolves round a literary conceit that in the real 18th-century world there was an architect called Nicholas Hawksmoor who built many churches in London. It has many of the classic differences of the literary from the genre novel. The writing is lively and vigorous, especially in the sections told from Nicholas Dyer's 18th-century viewpoint. The descriptions are vivid, and the evocations of the world-view of a period which nurtured the seeds of our own but differs from it in so many essentials are convincing. There is a good deal of intelligent discussion and speculation. However, compared to a genre novel the plot is back-to-front and the pace at times funereally slow. This especially applies to the Dyer passages, in which the faithful retention of authentic 18th-century spelling eventually loses its appeal.

The novel in fact starts with a lengthy passage in Dyer's voice, which essentially tells the reader what is happening and about to happen. Nicholas Hawksmoor, the detective, doesn't appear until halfway through, and we then see him searching for solutions which we already know. Possibly Ackroyd, as chief book reviewer for the London *Times*, feels it is beneath his dignity to provide his readers with a mystery to work out for themselves, whodunit style. Which is a pity, because to this reader the many excellent passages would be more enjoyable if laid out in a more populist manner.

Juxtapositions of present and past are very common in Ackroyd's work, as are mischievous mixtures of all kinds. He has written the *Last Testament* of Oscar Wilde, and an "alternative-universe" novel in which the Puritan poet John Milton went to America to escape the Stuart Restoration and founded a colony. In *Chatterton*, based around the late-18th-century boy wonder who committed suicide after certain of his literary "discoveries" were exposed as fakes, we again have a dual narrative, Chatterton's own viewpoint alternating with those of modern characters. *English Music* starts briefly in 1992: Tim Harcomb, its elderly protagonist, recalls his childhood in the 1920s. In those days he had to act as a sometimes reluctant assistant to his father, a medium and healer who attempts to contact the spirits of the dead: later Tim also has visions of fictional or semi-fictional characters. In the first of these he encounters Alice (from Wonderland) and characters from Bunyan's *Pilgrim's Progress*.

Ackroyd's first novel, *The Great Fire of London*, is not primarily about the historical fire which does feature in *Hawksmoor*, but about an effort to make a film of Dickens's *Little Dorrit* in modern London. (Ackroyd was born in London, and has written much about his fascination for the city: like his fellow literary horror novelist Iain Sinclair, he makes the city not just a setting, but a theme, a preoccupation, almost a character in most of his novels.)

Ackroyd uses a more conventional structure in *First Light*, a horror mystery with comic elements. Fire in a woodland reveals the existence of a hitherto unknown and unresearched prehistoric burial mound. It is surrounded by a neolithic stone circle, and there is speculation that the tumulus is the burial place of an early astronomer who designed the circle. A team of archaeologists gets to work: meanwhile, modern astronomers in the same area continue to study the heavens. There are no gross horrors, but throughout there are small mysteries which convey a sense of unease. The main characters are all oddballs in whose eccentricities Ackroyd seems to revel: the scientists seem always like outsiders, the locals, who have a personal interest in the tomb and the underground passages it conceals, unconvincing rustic yokels. The pace is again rather slow, often interrupted by entertaining digressions, but it at least seems to be going somewhere and indeed is.

The use of a wild mix of variegated elements is not a habit for which Ackroyd makes any apology; indeed, in his essay in the *New Worlds* 50th-anniversary souvenir issue (November 1996), originally prepared as a London Weekend Television lecture, he actively defends himself, claiming the inheritance of "Cockney Visionaries" like Blake, Dickens and Turner. He believes that London has a certain ongoing exuberance of spirit, and notes the odd continuity of certain traditional but unorganized activities in particular areas of the city: some streets have always housed brothels over the centuries, he says, while others have contained the homes of political revolutionaries or the meeting-places of esoteric groups.

Perhaps the most typical of Ackroyd's novels is *Dan Leno and the Limehouse Golem*. This brings the real-life music-hall star Leno, a supremely popular and versatile figure in his day, and a personality much admired by Ackroyd, into contact with "the Golem," a Jack-the-Ripper-type murderer who one assumes is fictitious. To Ackroyd, Dan Leno symbolizes "all the life and energy and variety of the city itself." The ill-matched protagonists are linked by a woman who admires Leno, but marries a man we learn is the killer.

Ackroyd is not a typical horror writer, and I dare say many enthusiasts for his work would hastily revise their opinions were

it to be so marketed. He is not necessarily a better novelist than writers like Kim Newman (also known as Jack Yeovil) who do similar things while remaining more explicitly part of the genre. But I think horror readers will find Ackroyd's mix of unease and brutality with more playful elements well worth exploring.

—Peter T. Garratt

AICKMAN, Robert (Fordyce)

Nationality: British. **Born:** London, 27 June 1914; grandson of horror writer Richard Marsh (q.v.). **Education:** Highgate School, London. **Career:** Worked for a literary agency, London; drama and film critic for various newspapers; director, Willow Wren Canal Transport Services Ltd.; founder, Inland Waterways Association; chairman, various opera and ballet companies. **Awards:** World Fantasy award for best short story, 1975. **Died:** 27 February 1981.

HORROR, GHOST AND GOTHIC PUBLICATIONS

Novels

The Late Breakfasters. London, Gollancz, 1964.
The Model. New York, Arbor House, 1987; London, Robinson, 1988.

Short Stories

We Are for the Dark: Six Ghost Stories, with Elizabeth Jane Howard. London, Cape, 1951.
Dark Entries. London, Collins, 1964.
Powers of Darkness. London, Collins, 1966.
Sub Rosa: Strange Tales. London, Gollancz, 1968.
Cold Hand in Mine: Eight Strange Tales. London, Gollancz, 1976; New York, Scribner, 1977.
Tales of Love and Death. London, Gollancz, 1977.
Painted Devils: Strange Stories. New York, Scribner, 1979.
Intrusions: Strange Tales. London, Gollancz, 1980.
Night Voices. London, Gollancz, 1985.
The Unsettled Dust. London, Mandarin, 1990.
The Wine-Dark Sea. New York, Arbor House, 1988; abridged edition, London, Mandarin, 1990.

Other

Editor, *The Fontana Book of Great Ghost Stories*. London, Fontana, 1964.
Editor, *The Second Fontana Book of Great Ghost Stories*. London, Fontana, 1966.
Editor, *The Third Fontana Book of Great Ghost Stories*. London, Fontana, 1966.
Editor, *The Fourth Fontana Book of Great Ghost Stories*. London, Fontana, 1967.
Editor, *The Fifth Fontana Book of Great Ghost Stories*. London, Fontana, 1969.
Editor, *The Sixth Fontana Book of Great Ghost Stories*. London, Fontana, 1970.
Editor, *The Seventh Fontana Book of Great Ghost Stories*. London, Fontana, 1971.

Editor, *The Eighth Fontana Book of Great Ghost Stories*. London, Fontana, 1972.

OTHER PUBLICATIONS

Other

Know Your Waterways. N.p., 1955.
The Attempted Rescue. London, Gollancz, 1966.
The River Runs Uphill: A Story of Success and Failure. Burton-on-Trent, Staffordshire, Pearson, 1986.

*   *   *

Robert Aickman published eleven collections of short stories, but these volumes contain only a total of 48 tales. This is a relatively small body of work, but it is not Aickman's quantity of output but his exceptional gifts as a writer—a prose style of impeccable fluidity, urbanity and elegance; a high sensitivity to those nuances and details productive of a weird scenario; a keen insight into all aspects of human psychology, not merely those touching upon the strange; and some very powerful weird conceptions that do not require copious, or any, bloodletting for their effectiveness—that distinguish him. The chief quality of Aickman's tales is, however, simply their indefinableness: some are ghost stories, although hardly conventional ones; in others it is difficult even to specify what makes them horrific in the utter absence of supernatural manifestations. Perhaps the subtitle Aickman himself used for most of his collections—"strange stories"—is as precise a definition as one can have.

Aickman evolved a distinctive theory of weird fiction, most compactly expressed in *The Second Fontana Book of Great Ghost Stories*, which he edited: ". . . the ghost story must be distinguished both from the mere horror story and from the scientific extravaganza . . . the ghost story draws upon the unconscious mind, in the manner of poetry; . . . it need offer neither logic nor moral; . . . it is an art form of altogether exceptional delicacy and subtlety . . ." The most problematical assertion here is the notion that the ghost story must offer "neither logic nor moral." Aickman clearly practised this principle, and for many readers the events in Aickman's tales are narrated so obliquely as to appear confusing; moreover, the lack of "logic" sometimes gives the impression that the weird effect is unmotivated. Aickman's stories appear to be full of symbols meant to reach "the unconscious mind"; but that symbolism is at times very obscure and, I believe, related to personal symbols that conveyed meaning for Aickman but which he was perhaps not entirely successful in conveying to others. Nevertheless, Aickman was such a skilled writer that one can enjoy his work even if one does not fully understand it.

Many of Aickman's tales involve journeys, reflecting his own fondness for travel. These journeys can be as seemingly mundane as going across town to a beauty shop ("No Stronger Than a Flower") or hiking in the north of England ("The Trains") and as exotic as islands off the coast of Greece ("The Wine-Dark Sea") or Finland ("The Houses of the Russians"). Whatever the case, the unfamiliarity of the setting gradually allows the characters to perceive (as one of them, in "Hand in Glove," states) that "There's something very wrong with almost everything." One of Aickman's strangest stories ("The Hospice") involves a travelling salesman forced to lodge in a roadside inn, where he meets a bizarre group of individuals all eating voraciously and is finally driven away in a hearse.

Just as nearly all of Aickman's stories involve a journey into the unfamiliar, so do they almost all involve a sexual tension between the protagonist (usually male, but on a surprising number of occasions female) and an alluring figure of the opposite sex. The title of a late collection, *Tales of Love and Death*, could serve for almost any of his volumes. "Letters to the Postman" involves a naive postman attempting to help a woman who claims to have married someone she does not know and is half-confined in a house. "The Swords" features a carnival act in which men plunge swords, seemingly without effect, into a woman's body (the symbolism of this action does not need to be belaboured). Later a young man is offered a chance to have a sexual encounter with her, but the result is far from satisfying.

Perhaps two of Aickman's most powerful tales are "Ringing the Changes" and "Meeting Mr. Millar," which unite many or all of the important themes running through his work. In the former, a newly married couple travels to a small coastal town in England for their honeymoon, only to discover that the frequent ringing of church bells throughout the town is for a very ominous purpose: "They're ringing to wake the dead." It would require a long commentary to trace the seamless way in which Aickman builds up the cumulative suspense in this story; and the spectacular climax—where the dead (if that is who they are) are only *heard*, never seen—is a master-stroke of suggestiveness. In "Meeting Mr. Millar" a starving writer moves into a cheap flat; the large apartment below him seems occupied by a company that does not seem to engage in much actual business. After several inconclusive encounters with the singularly colourless manager of the company, the writer hears a disturbing suggestion from another tenant: "It just struck me for one moment that you might have seen into the future. All these people slavishly doing nothing. It'll be exactly like that one day, you know, if we go on as we are." It is not entirely clear how seriously we are to regard this suggestion, but the tale's odd twists and turns all seem to work, achieving a cumulative power in no way marred by the lack of an explanation.

Aickman also wrote two novels—*The Late Breakfasters*, which, aside from a few ghostly effects, turns out surprisingly to be a sensitive and poignant story of lesbianism, and the posthumously published *The Model*, a charming but ultimately insubstantial quasi-fairy tale set in Tsarist Russia. His first autobiography, *The Attempted Rescue*, is a poignant human document; his second, *The River Runs Uphill*, is largely concerned with his work on the Inland Waterways Association, an early environmentalist concern devoted to preserving England's inland rivers from destruction and pollution. Neither of them discusses his weird writing to any significant degree. In addition, there are among his papers two entire collections of unpublished short stories, and it is hoped that they will soon be made available to the public.

—S. T. Joshi

AIKEN, Conrad (Potter)

Nationality: American. **Born:** Savannah, Georgia, 5 August 1889. **Education:** Middlesex School, Concord, Massachusetts; Harvard University, Cambridge, Massachusetts (president, *Harvard Advocate*), 1907-10, 1911-12, A.B. 1912. **Family:** Married 1) Jessie

McDonald in 1912 (divorced 1929), one son and two daughters, the writers Jane Aiken Hodge and Joan Aiken; 2) Clarissa M. Lorenz in 1930 (divorced 1937); 3) Mary Hoover in 1937. **Career:** Contributing editor, *The Dial*, New York, 1916-19; American correspondent, *Athenaeum*, London, 1919-25, and London *Mercury*, 1921-22; lived in London, 1921-26 and 1930-39; instructor, Harvard University, 1927-28; London correspondent, *New Yorker*, 1934-36; lived in Brewster, Massachusetts, from 1940, and Savannah after 1962. Fellow, 1947, and consultant in poetry, 1950-52, Library of Congress, Washington, D.C. **Awards:** Pulitzer Prize, 1930; Shelley Memorial award, 1930; Guggenheim fellowship, 1934; National Book award, 1954; Bollingen prize, 1956; Academy of American Poets fellowship, 1957; American Academy Gold Medal, 1958; Huntington Hartford Foundation award, 1960; Brandeis University Creative Arts award, 1967; National Medal for Literature, 1969. **Member:** American Academy, 1957. **Died:** 17 August 1973.

Horror, Ghost and Gothic Publications

Short Stories

Among the Lost People. New York and London, Scribner, 1934.
The Short Stories of Conrad Aiken. New York, Duell, 1950.
The Collected Short Stories of Conrad Aiken. Cleveland, World, 1960; London, Heinemann, 1966.

Play

Mr. Arcularis (earlier version entitled *Fear No More*) (produced Provincetown, Massachusetts, 1949). Cambridge, Massachusetts, Harvard University Press, 1957; London, Oxford University Press, 1958.

Poetry

The Jig of Forslin: A Symphony. Boston, Four Seas, 1916; London, Secker, 1921.

Other Publications

Novels

Blue Voyage. London, Howe, and New York, Scribner, 1927.
Gehenna. New York, Random House, 1930; London, John Rodker, 1931.
Great Circle. New York, Scribner, and London, Wishart, 1933.
King Coffin. New York, Scribner, and London, Dent, 1935.
A Heart for the Gods of Mexico. London, Secker-Richards Press, 1939.
Conversation; or, Pilgrims' Progress. New York, Duell, 1940; as *The Conversation,* London, Rodney Phillips and Green, 1948.
The Collected Novels of Conrad Aiken. New York, Holt Rinehart, 1964.

Short Stories

Bring! Bring! and Other Stories. London, Secker, and New York, Boni and Liveright, 1925.
Costumes by Eros. New York, Scribner, 1928; London, Cape, 1929.

Poetry

Earth Triumphant and Other Tales in Verse. New York, Macmillan, 1914.
Turns and Movies and Other Tales in Verse. Boston, Houghton Mifflin, 1916.
Nocturne of Remembered Spring and Other Poems. Boston, Four Seas, 1917.
The Charnel Rose, Senlin: A Biography, and Other Poems. Boston, Four Seas, 1918.
The House of Dust: A Symphony. Boston, Four Seas, 1920.
Punch: The Immortal Liar. New York, Knopf, 1921.
Priapus and the Pool and Other Poems. Cambridge, Massachusetts, Dunster House, 1922.
The Pilgrimage of Festus. New York, Knopf, 1923.
(Poems), edited by Louis Untermeyer. New York, Simon and Schuster, 1927.
Prelude. New York, Random House, 1929.
Selected Poems. New York, Scribner, 1929.
John Deth, A Metaphysical Legend, and Other Poems. New York and London, Scribner, 1930.
Preludes for Memnon. New York, Scribner, 1931.
The Coming Forth by Day of Osiris Jones. New York, Scribner, 1931.
Landscape West of Eden. London, Dent, 1934; New York, Scribner, 1935.
Time in the Rock: Preludes to Definition. New York and London, Scribner, 1936.
And in the Human Heart. New York, Duell, and London, Staples Press, 1940.
Brownstone Eclogues and Other Poems. New York, Duell, 1942.
The Soldier. New York, New Directions, 1944; London, Editions Poetry, 1946.
The Kid. New York, Duell, 1947; London, Lehmann, 1948.
The Divine Pilgrim. Athens, University of Georgia Press, 1949.
Skylight One: Fifteen Poems. New York, Oxford University Press, 1950; London, Lehmann, 1951.
Collected Poems. New York, Oxford University Press, 1953.
A Letter from Li Po and Other Poems. New York, Oxford University Press, 1955.
The Flute Player. Privately printed, 1956.
Sheepfold Hill: 15 Poems. New York, Sagamore Press, 1958.
Selected Poems. New York, and London, Oxford University Press, 1961.
The Morning Song of Lord Zero: Poems Old and New. New York, Oxford University Press, 1963.
A Seizure of Limericks. New York, Holt Rinehart, 1964; London, W.H. Allen, 1965.
The Clerk's Journal: An Undergraduate Poem, Together with a Brief Memoir of Dean LeBaron Russell Briggs, T.S. Eliot, and Harvard, in 1911. New York, Eakins Press, 1971.
Collected Poems 1916-1970. New York, Oxford University Press, 1971.

Other

Scepticisms: Notes on Contemporary Poetry. New York, Knopf, 1919.
Ushant: An Essay (autobiography). New York and Boston, Duell-Little Brown, 1952; London, W.H. Allen, 1963; illustrated edition, New York, Oxford University Press, 1971.

A Reviewer's ABC: Collected Criticism from 1916 to the Present.
Cleveland, World, 1958; London, W.H. Allen, 1959; as *Collected Criticism,* New York, Oxford University Press, 1968.

Cats and Bats and Things with Wings (juvenile). New York, Atheneum, 1965.

Tom, Sue and the Clock (juvenile). New York, Macmillan, and London, Macmillan, 1966.

Editor, *Modern American Poets.* 1922; revised edition, 1927; revised edition, as *Twentieth Century American Poetry,* 1945; revised edition, 1963.

Editor, *Selected Poems of Emily Dickinson.* 1924.

Editor, *American Poetry 1671-1928: A Comprehensive Anthology.* 1929; revised edition, as *A Comprehensive Anthology of American Poetry,* 1944.

Editor, with William Rose Benét, *An Anthology of Famous English and American Poetry.* 1945.

*

Bibliography: *Aiken: A Bibliography (1902-1978)* by F. W. and F. C. Bonnell, 1982; *Aiken: Critical Recognition 1914-1981: A Bibliographic Guide* by Catherine Kirk Harris, 1983.

Manuscript Collection: Harvard University, Cambridge, Massachusetts.

Critical Studies: *Aiken: A Life of His Art* by Jay Martin, Princeton, New Jersey, Princeton University Press, 1962; *Aiken* by Frederick J. Hoffman, New York, Twayne, 1962; *Conrad Aiken* by Reuel Denney, Minneapolis, University of Minnesota Press, 1964; *Lorelei Two: My Life with Aiken* by Clarissa M. Lorenz, Athens, University of Georgia Press, 1983; *The Art of Knowing: The Poetry and Prose of Aiken* by Harry Marten, Columbia, University of Missouri Press, 1988; *Aiken: Poet of White Horse Vale* by Edward Butscher, Athens, University of Georgia, Press, 1988; *Aiken: A Priest of Consciousness* edited by Ted R. Spirey and Arthur Waterman, New York, AMS Press, 1989.

*   *   *

Conrad Aiken was a prolific and well-known American writer who is best known for his highly acclaimed poetry, but he also wrote novels, short fiction and criticism during his long and productive career. The eldest of three sons, he was orphaned in 1900 when his physician father killed his mother then committed suicide. In 1911 he entered Harvard, becoming a classmate of T. S. Eliot, writing for the *Harvard Monthly and Advocate*, resigned to go to Italy, returned and married Jessie McDonald, then honeymooned in Europe for a year before settling in Cambridge, Massachusetts. By means of an independent income, he was free to pursue literature as a career. During the First World War he claimed that he was in an "essential industry" because of being a poet, and was granted an exemption for this very reason. He was in fact awarded the Pulitzer Prize for his poetry in 1929.

Aiken wrote few short stories and novels, but these show diverse influences, ranging from James Joyce to the then newly developing practice of psychoanalysis. His horror is subtle, with sinister undercurrents running below a tranquil, mundane surface, and even his prose is Modernist yet romantic. The pity is that he did not write more works in this vein.

"The Vampire" (1914) and the vampire narrative of *The Jig of Forslin* are both lush, erotic ballads on the theme of vampiric seduction. The female vampires of these works are intensely alluring rather than horrific, and if they are dangerous as well it is the danger of a beautiful psychopath.

> And this we heard: "Who dies for me,
> He shall possess me secretly,
> My terrible beauty he shall see,
> And slake my body's flame."
> ("The Vampire," verse 7)

The vampire in *The Jig of Forslin* is somewhat more direct, and she rather stylishly uses a golden pin to draw the blood of her lover. He feigns sleep as she caresses him, but at the critical moment he tears open her web of allure and drives her away. Later he returns with a priest and lays the vampire to rest. The narrators in both works are willing to flirt with the beautiful and powerful creatures, yet there is no question that surrender is ever contemplated. The vampires are treated rather like symbolist paintings, being appreciated but not embraced.

Aiken's most famous short stories, "Mr. Arcularis" (1931) and "Silent Snow, Secret Snow" (1932), are both outstanding horror pieces (and have been reprinted in many genre anthologies, commencing with such titles as Dashiell Hammett's *Creeps by Night* [1931] and Herbert A. Wise and Phyllis Fraser's *Great Tales of Terror and the Supernatural* [1944]). The theme running through these tales is one of the real and the surreal co-existing, where death is the solid reality and life is the transcendent dream. Human imagination is used here by Aiken to gradually separate his protagonists from the world, as they progress from alienation, through psychosis to death. Some of this may be related to the tragic events of his childhood, which Aiken may have come to terms with by blotting out the excruciating reality with constructs of his own imagination.

In "Mr. Arcularis" the man of the title leaves hospital after a successful operation that has saved his life. His friend Harry drives him to the docks, and he leaves on a voyage to Britain to convalesce. Mr. Arcularis is middle aged, but has the prospect of many years of life ahead of him as a result of the operation, even though it has left him feeling so weak. Aboard the ship he meets Miss Dean, who has a light romance with him in spite of her being much younger. He also begins sleepwalking, walking further and further through the ship each night, and getting closer to a coffin being taken to Ireland for burial. Mr. Arcularis becomes progressively colder, and the ship appears to make practically no headway, he even fancies that he has travelled to the stars and back in his dreams. The cold grows more intense—and the story curves back upon itself to before its beginning as the surgeon loses the fight to save Mr. Arcularis on the operating table.

The theme of "Silent Snow, Secret Snow" is that of the whiteout of a snowstorm that obscures the world and disorients those travelling through it. Paul, a young boy, uses the white-out effect of snow to sponge out the external world, until he exists only in a blankness within his own mind. Each morning he can hear the postman's boots in the distance, but as the snow begins to fall, the boots become muffled. Metaphorical walls are approaching, walls to shut out the world which are measured by the diminishing distance at which he can first hear the boots each morning. Paul's parents are worried, for while he is intelligent and compliant, he is growing more withdrawn and dreamy. Finally he dashes away to his room midway through an examination by the family doctor, shouts that he hates his mother, then surrenders to the peace, remoteness, cold and sleep of the snow within his mind.

The mechanism that Paul uses to escape may have been related to Aiken's childhood methods of coping with the real-life horror of the death of his parents, while his language has much of the opulent horror and hysteria of his earlier vampire poems. Aiken's horror walks close beside the mundane of scientific medicine, comfortable houses, cars and ships like floating palaces, reminding the reader that the death in the age of romanticism is the same death that is present in the age of *art deco*.

—Steven Paulsen & Sean McMullen

AIKEN, Joan (Delano)

Nationality: British. **Born:** Rye, Sussex, 4 September 1924; daughter of the writer Conrad Aiken. **Education:** Wychwood School, Oxford, 1936-40. **Family:** Married 1) Ronald George Brown in 1945 (died 1955), one son and one daughter; 2) Julius Goldstein in 1976. **Career:** Worked for the BBC, 1942-43; information officer, then librarian, United Nations Information Centre, London, 1943-49; subeditor and features editor, *Argosy,* London, 1955-60; copywriter, J. Walter Thompson, London, 1960-61. **Awards:** *Guardian* award for children's literature, 1969; Mystery Writers of America Edgar Allan Poe award, 1972. **Agent:** A. M. Heath, 79 St. Martin's Lane, London, WC2N 4AA; or, Brandt and Brandt, 1501 Broadway, New York, New York 10036, USA. **Address:** The Hermitage, East Street, Petworth, West Sussex GU28 0AB, England.

Horror, Ghost and Gothic Publications

Novels

Castle Barebane. London, Gollancz, and New York, Viking Press, 1976.
The Shadow Guests. London, Cape, and New York, Delacorte Press, 1980.
The Moon's Revenge. London, Cape, and New York, Knopf, 1987.
Voices. London, Hippo, 1988; as *Return to Harken House,* New York, Delacorte Press, 1988.
The Haunting of Lamb House. London, Cape, 1991; New York, St. Martin's Press, 1993.
The Cockatrice Boys. London, Gollancz, and New York, Tor, 1996.

Short Stories

The Windscreen Weepers and Other Tales of Horror and Suspense. London, Gollancz, 1969.
The Green Flash and Other Tales of Horror, Suspense, and Fantasy. New York, Holt Rinehart, 1971.
A Bundle of Nerves: Stories of Horror, Suspense, and Fantasy. London, Gollancz, 1976.
A Touch of Chill: Stories of Horror, Suspense, and Fantasy. London, Gollancz, 1979; New York, Delacorte Press, 1980.
A Whisper in the Night: Stories of Horror, Suspense, and Fantasy. London, Gollancz, 1982; New York, Delacorte Press, 1984.

A Goose on Your Grave. London, Gollancz, 1987.
A Foot in the Grave, illustrated by Jan Pienkowski. London, Cape, 1989; New York, Viking, 1991.
Give Yourself a Fright: Thirteen Tales of the Supernatural. New York, Delacorte Press, 1989.
A Fit of Shivers. London, Gollancz, 1990.
A Creepy Company. London, Gollancz, 1993; revised edition, New York, Dell, 1995.
The Winter Sleepwalker and Other Stories. London, Cape, 1994.

Other Publications

Novels

The Kingdom and the Cave. London, Abelard Schuman, 1960; New York, Doubleday, 1974.
The Wolves of Willoughby Chase. London, Cape, 1962; New York, Doubleday, 1963.
Black Hearts in Battersea. New York, Doubleday, 1964; London, Cape, 1965.
The Silence of Herondale. New York, Doubleday, 1964; London, Gollancz, 1965.
The Fortune Hunters. New York, Doubleday, 1965.
Nightbirds on Nantucket. London, Cape, and New York, Doubleday, 1966.
Trouble with Product X. London, Gollancz, 1966; as *Beware of the Bouquet,* New York, Doubleday, 1966.
Hate Begins at Home. London, Gollancz, 1967; as *Dark Interval,* New York, Doubleday, 1967.
The Ribs of Death. London, Gollancz, 1967; as *The Crystal Crow,* New York, Doubleday, 1968.
Night Fall. London, Macmillan, 1969; New York, Holt Rinehart, 1971.
The Embroidered Sunset. London, Gollancz, and New York, Doubleday, 1970.
The Whispering Mountain. London, Cape, 1968; New York, Doubleday, 1969.
The Cuckoo Tree. London, Cape, and New York, Doubleday, 1971.
Died on a Rainy Sunday. London, Gollancz, and New York, Holt Rinehart, 1972.
The Butterfly Picnic. London, Gollancz, 1972; as *A Cluster of Separate Sparks,* New York, Doubleday, 1972.
Midnight Is a Place. London, Cape, and New York, Viking Press, 1974.
Voices in an Empty House. London, Gollancz, and New York, Doubleday, 1975.
Last Movement. London, Gollancz, and New York, Doubleday, 1977.
The Five-Minute Marriage. London, Gollancz, 1977; New York, Doubleday, 1978.
Go Saddle the Sea. New York, Doubleday, 1977; London, Cape, 1978.
The Smile of the Stranger. London, Gollancz, and New York, Doubleday, 1978.
The Lightning Tree. London, Gollancz, 1980; as *The Weeping Ash,* New York, Doubleday, 1980.
The Stolen Lake. London, Cape, and New York, Delacorte Press, 1981.
The Young Lady from Paris. London, Gollancz, 1982; as *The Girl from Paris,* New York, Doubleday, 1982.

Bridle the Wind. London, Cape, and New York, Delacorte Press, 1983.

Foul Matter. London, Gollancz, and New York, Doubleday, 1983.

Mansfield Revisited (sequel to *Mansfield Park* by Jane Austen). London, Gollancz, 1984; New York, Doubleday, 1985.

Dido and Pa. London, Cape, and New York, Delacorte Press, 1986.

Deception. London, Gollancz, 1987; as *If I Were You,* New York, Doubleday, 1987.

The Erl King's Daughter. London, Heinemann, 1988.

The Teeth of the Gale. London, Cape, and New York, Harper, 1988.

Blackground. London, Gollancz, and New York, Doubleday, 1989.

Jane Fairfax (sequel to *Emma* by Jane Austen). London, Gollancz, and New York, St. Martin's Press, 1990.

Is. London, Cape, 1992; as *Is Underground,* New York, Delacorte Press, 1992.

Morningquest. London, Gollancz, 1992; New York, St. Martin's Press, 1993.

Eliza's Daughter (sequel to *Sense and Sensibility* by Jane Austen). London, Gollancz, and New York, St. Martin's Press, 1994.

Cold Shoulder Road. London, Cape, 1995.

The Jewel Seed. London, Hodder and Stoughton, 1997.

Short Stories

All You've Ever Wanted and Other Stories. London, Cape, 1953.

More Than You Bargained For and Other Stories. London, Cape, 1955; New York, Abelard Schuman, 1957.

A Necklace of Raindrops and Other Stories. London, Cape, and New York, Doubleday, 1968.

A Small Pinch of Weather and Other Stories. London, Cape, 1969.

Armitage, Armitage, Fly Away Home. New York, Doubleday, 1968.

Smoke from Cromwell's Time and Other Stories. New York, Doubleday, 1970.

All and More (omnibus; includes *All You've Ever Wanted, More Than You Bargained For*). London, Cape, 1971.

The Kingdom under the Sea and Other Stories (retellings). London, Cape, 1971.

A Harp of Fishbones and Other Stories. London, Cape, 1972.

All But a Few. London, Penguin, 1974.

Not What You Expected: A Collection of Short Stories. New York, Doubleday, 1974.

The Faithless Lollybird and Other Stories. London, Cape, 1977; New York, Doubleday, 1978.

The Far Forests: Tales of Romance, Fantasy, and Suspense. New York, Viking Press, 1977.

Tale of a One-Way Street and Other Stories. London, Cape, 1978; New York, Doubleday, 1979.

Up the Chimney Down, and Other Stories. London, Cape, and New York, Harper, 1984.

The Last Slice of Rainbow and Other Stories. London, Cape, 1985; New York, Harper, 1988.

Past Eight O'Clock: Goodnight Stories. London, Cape, 1986.

Fiction for Children

Arabel's Raven. London, BBC Publications, 1972.

The Escaped Black Mamba. London, BBC Publications, 1973.

The Bread Bin. London, BBC Publications, 1974.

Tales of Arabel's Raven. London, BBC Publications, 1972; as *Arabel's Raven,* New York, Doubleday, 1974.

Mortimer's Tie. London, BBC Publications, 1976.

Mice and Mendelson, music by John Sebastian Brown. London, Cape, 1978.

Mortimer and the Sword Excalibur. London, BBC Publications, 1979.

The Spiral Stair. London, BBC Publications, 1979.

Arabel and Mortimer (omnibus; includes *Mortimer's Tie, The Spiral Stair, Mortimer and the Sword Excalibur).* London, Cape, 1980; New York, Doubleday, 1981.

Mortimer's Portrait on Glass. London, Hodder and Stoughton, 1981.

The Mystery of Mr. Jones's Disappearing Taxi. London, Hodder and Stoughton, 1982.

Mortimer's Cross. London, Cape, 1983; New York, Harper, 1984.

The Kitchen Warriors. London, BBC Publications, 1983.

Fog Hounds, Wind Cat, Sea Mice. London, Macmillan, 1984.

Mortimer Says Nothing and Other Stories. London, Cape, 1985; New York, Harper, 1987.

The Shoemaker's Boy. New York, Simon and Schuster, 1991.

The Midnight Moropus. New York, Simon and Schuster, 1993.

Hatching Trouble. London, BBC Publications, 1993.

Plays

Winterthing, music by John Sebastian Brown (produced Albany, New York, 1977). New York, Holt Rinehart, 1972; included in *Winterthing, and The Mooncusser's Daughter,* 1973.

Winterthing, and The Mooncusser's Daughter, music by John Sebastian Brown. London, Cape, 1973; *The Mooncusser's Daughter* published separately, New York, Viking Press, 1974.

Street, music by John Sebastian Brown (produced London, 1977). New York, Viking Press, 1978.

Moon Mill (produced London, 1982).

Television Plays: *The Dark Streets of Kimballs Green,* 1976; *The Apple of Trouble,* 1977; *Midnight Is a Place* (serial), from her own story, 1977; *The Rose of Puddle Fratrum,* 1978; *Armitage, Armitage, Fly Away Home,* from her own story, 1978.

Poetry

The Skin Spinners. New York, Viking Press, 1976.

Other

The Way to Write for Children. London, Elm Tree, 1982; New York, St. Martin's Press, 1983.

Translator, *The Angel Inn,* by Contessa de Segur. London, Cape, 1976; Owings Mills, Maryland, Stemmer House, 1978.

*

Film Adaptations: *The Wolves of Willoughby Chase,* 1989; *Black Hearts in Battersea* (TV serial), 1996.

*   *   *

Joan Aiken is a prolific writer, having produced more than 30 books for adults and over 60 for children. She is also the kind of writer that is difficult to categorize, as even her fantasy novels—

such as the "James III" series of alternate-England adventures beginning with her most famous title, *The Wolves of Willoughby Chase*—have dark overtones and disturbing passages. Her writing that is describable as supernatural horror or gothic rather than fantasy covers the range of her output, including novels and a very large number of stories.

She was born and spent her early years in the ancient town of Rye in Sussex and has used her knowledge to great effect in the novel *The Haunting of Lamb House*. Lamb House is a real place built in 1723 by one of Rye's leading families and is now owned by the National Trust. The first part of the novel is told from the point of view of Toby Lamb, the crippled son of James Lamb, the house's builder. It begins on the day he learns that his sister, Alice, is to be sent away to be a surrogate daughter to relatives in Tunbridge Wells. On that day he also sees a strange man in the garden. The apparition, he is told, is the ghost of a Frenchman who was hanged for daring to fall in love with a local girl. The story goes that anyone who sees the Frenchman's ghost will be cursed to live for a long time but will never gain his heart's desire. Toby would have liked to have become a writer but the only thing he managed to produce was the chronicle of his childhood.

This part of the book is written in the straightforward, engaging style typical of much of Aiken's work. Traumatic events, such as the death of Toby's brother, Moses, are related in a matter-of-fact way as they would be remembered when the narrator is separated from them by the distance of time. Others, such as what really happened to Alice when she was sent from home, are only alluded to but in such a way that the reader is able to interpret the underlying horror from the meagre clues. It is skilfully done.

Lamb House was the home of the writer Henry James for many years. The second part of *The Haunting of Lamb House* is an account of his time there. During the renovations after a fire in his study, Toby Lamb's manuscript is uncovered. James considers it too simplistic for publication but wants to rewrite it. He is put off publication, first by his brother who suggests that descendants of the Lamb family might object to his highlighting the more sordid aspects of the tale, then by his friend Edith Wharton who tells him that his characters are too shallow. James, though, has seen parallels between his and Toby's life and feels that Toby's spirit is still around, and when publication of the manuscript seems to be receding little ghostly happenings begin to occur. This part of the book has a Jamesian flavour to the style and includes many actual quotations cleverly placed within the text.

The third part is from the point of view of E. F. Benson, who also lived at Lamb House and is best known for his "Mapp and Lucia" novels set in Tilling (a very loosely disguised Rye). He has known Henry James and knows about Toby Lamb's chronicle though he has never seen it and its whereabouts cannot be traced. It is in this section that the strongest supernatural presence is felt. Here again the style is different, chosen to imitate Benson's own. Overall, the approach chosen for this novel is highly effective.

Some of Aiken's children's novels also use supernatural themes, for example *The Shadow Guests*. Cosmo Curtoys has returned home from Australia to live with a cousin after his mother and elder brother go missing. He discovers that his family lies under a curse. The eldest son is doomed to die in battle and his mother soon afterwards. During the week Cosmo spends a miserable time at boarding school in Oxford but spends the weekends in the countryside on the edge of the estate that was once his family's ances-

tral home. He meets ghosts of his ancestors who seem real to him but invisible to everyone else. The first ones are benevolent, temporary friends but the later ones are concerned with killing him, in the forlorn hope of ending the curse for them. In the book, Aiken does what she is good at—painting credible pictures of capable young people. She also draws on her own childhood as she, too, had an unhappy experience of boarding-school life in Oxford. *The Cockatrice Boys* on the other hand draws much of its effect from the darker side of fantasy. Nasty, mythological beasts such as cockatrices, manticores and gorgons kill a high percentage of Britain's population. The horror, as in many of Aiken's short stories, is very understated because of the audience it is aimed at. What cannot be side-stepped is the fact that a very large number of people die horribly.

Aiken's short stories have been collected into a number of volumes, some aimed at children, others at adults. The main difference between them is the age of the principal characters—those written for children having young people as protagonists. In all cases the best of them are short and subtle. Because the horror is understated, the reader is brought up short as she realizes exactly what has happened. An example is "Dead Language Master," which appears in both *The Windscreen Weepers* and *A Bundle of Nerves*, in which a class of boys torment their Latin master to the extent that he decides to commit suicide. However, as he prepares to leave the school for the last time, his chief tormentor is inadvertently shut in the boot of his car. The horror of the situation is increased not only because the details are left to the reader's imagination but also because you cannot be sure that what you imagine is what happened. Similarly, in "Marmalade Wine" (again collected in both the above volumes) it is not what is said, but what is assumed that creates the horror. Here, a man with a penchant for exaggeration meets a retired surgeon in the woods and because he claims to be able to predict the future his host takes steps to prevent him leaving.

Some of the chills are of a supernatural origin, as in "The Windscreen Weepers" from the collection of the same name. When a girl arrives looking for somewhere to stay at the estate of an eccentric old lady she brings with her her grandmother's tale of the invisible weepers who sob and cry around a car's windscreen when a death is nigh. The narrator thinks he hears something as she leaves, to become a victim of a road accident. This story also has another sub-text, the clues to which are placed delicately—the eccentric lady is looking for the reincarnation of the poet Coleridge. The narrator, asked to leave for breaking her rules, is an artist by the name of Taylor Samuel. One of the best of this kind of story is "As Gay as Cheese" (in *Windscreen Weepers* and *A Bundle of Nerves*). It is brilliantly subtle and tells of a barber who knows about people's lives by touching their hair. We are given the images he perceives from doing the hair of a honeymoon couple, and the author leaves the imagination to do the rest.

Aiken's ghosts can be friendly, such as the one in "Miss Spitfire" (from *A Whisper in the Night*) who lands a hijacked plane, or nasty as in "Power Cut" (from *A Touch of Chill*) where the ghost of a vengeful son haunts the cottage his parents inhabit. Whether she is dealing with terror arising from human nature or involving supernatural elements each story succeeds in being different from the rest and never is the horror allowed to overpower the story.

—Pauline Morgan

AINSWORTH, W(illiam) Harrison

Nationality: British. **Born:** Manchester, 4 February 1805. **Education:** Manchester Grammar School; articled to a Manchester solicitor, 1821-24; studied law in London, 1824-26. **Family:** Married 1) Anne Frances Ebers in 1826 (separated 1835), three daughters; 2) second marriage in 1878. **Career:** Editor, *The Boetian*, 1824; publisher in London, 1826-28; lawyer, early 1830s; editor, *Bentley's Miscellany*, London, 1839-41; editor and publisher, *Ainsworth's Magazine*, 1842-54, *New Monthly Magazine*, 1845-70, and *Bentley's Miscellany*, 1854-68, all London; lived in Brighton, Sussex, from 1853. **Died:** 3 January 1882.

HORROR, GHOST AND GOTHIC PUBLICATIONS

Novels

Rookwood: A Romance. 3 vols., London, Bentley, 1834; 2 vols., Philadelphia, Carey, 1834.
Windsor Castle: An Historical Romance. London, Colburn, 1843.
The Lancashire Witches. 3 vols., London, Colburn, 1849; 1 vol., New York, Stringer and Townsend, 1849.
Auriol: Fragment of a Romance. London, Chapman and Hall, 1850; as *Auriol; or, The Elixir of Life*, London, Routledge, 1865.
Stanley Brereton. London and New York, Routledge, 1881.

OTHER PUBLICATIONS

Novels

Sir John Chiverton, with J. P. Aston. London, Ebers, 1826.
Crichton. 3 vols., London, Bentley, 1837; 2 vols., New York, Harper, 1837.
Jack Sheppard. 3 vols., London, Bentley, 1839; 2 vols., Philadelphia, Lea and Blanchard, 1839.
The Tower of London. (13 monthly parts) London, Bentley, 1840; 1 vol., Philadelphia, Lea and Blanchard, 1841.
Guy Fawkes; or, The Gunpowder Treason. 3 vols., London, Bentley, 1841; 1 vol., Philadelphia, Lea and Blanchard, 1841.
Old Saint Paul's: A Tale of the Plague and the Fire. (12 monthly parts) London, Cunningham, 1841.
The Miser's Daughter. London, Cunningham and Mortimer, 1842.
Saint James's; or, The Court of Queen Anne. 3 vols., London, Mortimer, 1844; 1 vol., New York, Colyer, 1844.
James the Second; or, The Revolution of 1688. London, Colburn, 1848.
The Star-Chamber. 2 vols., London, Routledge, 1854; 1 vol., New York, Routledge, 1873.
The Flitch of Bacon; or, The Custom of Dunmow. London and New York, Routledge, 1854.
The Spendthrift. London and New York, Routledge, 1857.
Mervyn Clitheroe. N.p., 1858.
Ovingdean Grange. London, Routledge, 1860.
The Constable of the Tower. London, Chapman and Hall, 1861.
The Lord Mayor of London; or, City Life in the Last Century. London, Chapman and Hall, 1862.
Cardinal Pole; or, The Days of Philip and Mary. London, Chapman and Hall, 1863.
John Law the Projector. London, Chapman and Hall, 1864.

The Spanish Match; or, Charles Stuart at Madrid. London, Chapman and Hall, 1865.
The Constable de Bourbon. London, Chapman and Hall, 1866.
Old Court. London, Chapman and Hall, 1867.
Myddleton Pomfret. London, Chapman and Hall, 1868.
Hilary St. Ives. London, Chapman and Hall, 1870.
The South-Sea Bubble. N.p., 1871.
Talbot Harland. London, Dicks, 1871.
Tower Hill. N.p., 1871.
Boscobel; or, The Royal Oak. London, Tinsley, 1872.
The Good Old Times: The Story of the Manchester Rebels of '45. London, Tinsley, 1873.
Merry England; or, Nobles and Serfs. London, Tinsley, 1874.
The Goldsmith's Wife. London, Tinsley, 1875.
Preston Fight; or, The Insurrection of 1715. London, Tinsley, 1875.
Chetwynd Calverley. London, Tinsley, 1876.
The Leaguer of Lathom. London, Tinsley, 1876.
The Fall of Somerset. London, Tinsley, 1877.
Beatrice Tyldesley. London, Tinsley, 1878.
Beau Nash; or, Bath in the Eighteenth Century. London and New York, Routledge, 1879.

Short Stories

December Tales, with others. London, Whitaker, 1823.

Poetry

Poems by Cheviot Tichburn. London, Arliss, 1822; as *The Maid's Revenge, and A Summer Evening's Tale, with Other Poems*, n.p., 1823; as *Works of Cheviot Tichburn*, n.p., 1825.
Monody on the Death of John Philip Kemble. N.p., 1823.
A Summer Evening Tale. N.p., 1825.
Letters from Cockney Lands. London, Ebers, 1826.
May Fair. N.p., 1827.
Ballads: Romantic, Fantastical, and Humorous. London and New York, Routledge, 1855; revised edition, n.p., 1872.
The Combat of the Thirty, from a Breton Lay of the Fourteenth Century. London, Chapman and Hall, 1859.

Other

Consideration on the Best Means of Affording Immediate Relief to the Operative Classes in the Manufacturing Districts. N.p., 1826.

Editor, *Modern Chivalry; or, A New Orlando Furioso*, by Catherine Gore. N.p., 1843.

*

Bibliography: *A Bibliographical Catalogue of the Published Novels and Ballads of Ainsworth* by Harold Locke, 1925.

Critical Studies: *Ainsworth and His Friends* by S. M. Ellis, 2 vols., n.p., 1911; New York, Garland, 1979; *The Newgate Novel 1830-1837: Bulwer, Ainsworth, Dickens and Thackeray* by Keith Hollingsworth, Detroit, Wayne State University Press, 1963. *Ainsworth* by George J. Worth, n.p., 1972.

* * *

Harrison Ainsworth was one of the first Victorian writers to set out with the intention of making a living from his pen by catering to evident popular taste. Although he immediately selected the historical novel as his genre he was almost certainly following the example of Edward Bulwer (who was yet to become Lord Lytton) rather than the more distant precedent set by Sir Walter Scott. Like Bulwer—in whose footsteps he belatedly followed as the editor of the *New Monthly Magazine*—Ainsworth decided that the criminals of the past offered far more scope for melodrama than honest folk; his first major novel, *Rookwood*, features among its subplots the career of Dick Turpin and is the work which brought to final formulation the legend of that notorious highwayman. The supernatural aspects of the novel are, however, focused on the curse which afflicts the family of the novel's eponymous hero and the ominous signs which embody its threats and visitations.

Jack Sheppard features the exploits of two other legendary criminals—the second is Jonathan Wild, already elevated to mock-heroic status by Henry Fielding's satire—which Ainsworth extended in similar fashion. The anti-hero of *Guy Fawkes* is by no means a common criminal but his exploits are dealt with in similarly lurid fashion, with equally scant regard for historical accuracy; if the real Fawkes ever met the famous occultist John Dee he certainly did not embark upon the remarkable collaborative endeavours that Ainsworth credits to the two of them.

Windsor Castle is a tale of the court of Henry VIII, which includes the fates of the much-married king's first three wives. A Gothic element is added by means of the symbolic figure of Herne the Hunter, who has become the Devil's instrument as a result of a pact made in the distant past. This amalgamation of pagan and Christian folklore was, in its way, as influential as Ainsworth's portrayal of Turpin; the horned master of the Devil's crew became a key image in Margaret Murray's scholarly fantasies reinterpreting the European witch-persecutions as attempts by the Church to suppress covert pagan cults.

Murray must also have taken inspiration from Ainsworth's luridly credulous interpretation of Thomas Potts' account of the trial of the witches of Pendle, *The Lancashire Witches*. This remains his most famous work and the only one still widely read today. The intrinsic interest of its subject matter makes up for the difficulties caused by the extensive use of Lancashire dialect (although this is itself a point of interest for linguists; Ainsworth, who was born and brought up in Manchester, was one of very few writers of the era who experimented with the rendition of that dialect). Ironically, Potts—the clerk of the court which hanged the witches, on the highly fanciful evidence of young Jennet Device—is featured in the novel as a corrupt lawyer who is roused to take action against the witches when their leader, Alice Nutter, uses her magic to win a dispute over land-boundaries with his client. Alizon Device (the name is pronounced as Davis), whose indiscreet cursing precipitates the actual trial, here becomes a virtuous heroine whose trials and tribulations at the hands of her vicious relatives reach their climax in the sensational Sabbat scene.

Not long after writing *Windsor Castle* Ainsworth had begun serialization in his own magazine—which he published between 1842 and 1853, after a stint as editor of *Bentley's Miscellany*—of a novel called *Revelations of London*. This was to have been a pure Gothic novel, in much the same vein as Charles Maturin's *Melmoth the Wanderer*, but the serialization was rudely terminated in 1845 and Ainsworth never went back to it. It was reprinted five years later as *Auriol*, still in its incomplete form, with the plot abruptly short-circuited by the already-hoary device of having its hero awaken from a dream. The eponymous hero is gifted with eternal youth by the elixir of life discovered by his grandfather, whose monopoly he shares with the old alchemist's laboratory assistant. In order to maintain his unnatural perfection, however, he must offer sacrifices to the Devil at ten-year intervals under the tutelage of the sinister Rosicrucian Rougemont—a standardized Gothic villain.

One can only speculate as to why Ainsworth became dissatisfied with *Auriol*. Its abandonment may well have been prompted by adverse reader response but it is possible that he felt uncomfortable with it anyway because the bulk of its action is set in the recent past, allowing no scope for the antiquarian divertissements with which he was wont to flesh out his more notable works. It is certainly the case that his repetitive and dispirited later works made increasing but invariably ineffective use of contemporary settings. *Stanley Brereton*, the last of them, derives no excitement at all from its formularized demonic tempter and its lacklustre ghost.

Almost all of Ainsworth's non-supernatural works contain slight Gothic elements and some of those set in London—especially *The Tower of London* and *Old St. Paul's*—foreshadow the melodramatic literary panoramas of Eugene Sue and G. W. M. Reynolds. Ainsworth was neither as versatile as Bulwer nor as prolific as G. P. R. James but he made a significant contribution nevertheless to the early development of English popular fiction. His plots are rambling and sometimes cluttered with irrelevances, but that was by no means uncommon in a day when the standard forms of popular fiction were the three-decker novel and the weekly serial. Abridged editions of several of his best-known works were produced in the early twentieth century for reissuing in the cheapest hardcover formats, including a version of *Windsor Castle* entitled *Herne the Hunter*; although they are not "authentic" these may be the manifestations of his work least likely to try the patience of modern readers.

—Brian Stableford

ALLEN, (Charles) Grant (Blairfindie)

Pseudonyms: Cecil Power; Olive Pratt Rayner; Martin Leach Warborough. **Nationality:** British. **Born:** Alwington, near Kingston, Ontario, Canada, 24 February 1848. **Education:** Private, in New Haven, Connecticut; Collège Impérial, Dieppe, France; King Edward's School, Birmingham, England; Merton College, Oxford (Senior Classical Postmastership), 1867-70, B.A. (honours) 1871. **Family:** Married Miss Jerrard in 1873 (second marriage); one son. **Career:** Professor of philosophy, Government College, Spanish Town, Jamaica, 1873-76; tutor in Oxford, 1877; worked on the *Gazetteer of India*, Edinburgh, 1878; staff member, *Daily News*, London, 1879; lived in Surrey from 1880. **Died:** 28 October 1899.

HORROR, GHOST AND GOTHIC PUBLICATIONS

Novels

Kalee's Shrine, with May Cotes. Bristol, Arrowsmith, 1886; New York, New Amsterdam, 1897; as *The Indian Mystery*, New Amsterdam, 1902.

The Great Taboo. London, Chatto and Windus, 1890; New York, Harper, 1891.

Short Stories

Strange Stories. London, Chatto and Windus, 1884.
The Beckoning Hand and Other Stories. London, Chatto and Windus, 1887.
Ivan Greet's Masterpiece. London, Chatto and Windus, 1893.
Twelve Tales, with a Headpiece, a Tailpiece, and an Intermezzo. London, Richards, 1899.

OTHER PUBLICATIONS

Novels

Philistia (as Cecil Power). London, Chatto and Windus, 3 vols., and New York, Harper, 1 vol., 1884.
Babylon. London, Chatto and Windus, 3 vols., and New York, Appleton, 1 vol., 1885.
For Maimie's Sake. London, Chatto and Windus, and New York, Appleton, 1886.
The Sole Trustee. London, SPCK, 1886.
A Terrible Inheritance. London, SPCK, 1887; New York, Crowell, n.d.
In All Shades. London, Chatto and Windus, 3 vols., and Chicago, Rand McNally, 1 vol., 1888.
This Mortal Coil. London, Chatto and Windus, 3 vols., and New York, Appleton, 1 vol., 1888.
The White Man's Foot. London, Hatchards, 1888.
The Devil's Die. London, Chatto and Windus, 3 vols., and New York, Lovell, 1 vol., 1888.
The Tents of Shem. London, Chatto and Windus, 3 vols., and Chicago, Rand McNally, 1 vol., 1889.
Dr. Palliser's Patient. London, Mullen, 1889.
The Jaws of Death. London, Simpkin Marshall, 1889; New York, New Amsterdam, 1897.
A Living Apparition. London, SPCK, 1889.
Wednesday the Tenth. Boston, Lothrop, 1890; as *The Cruise of the Albatross; or, When Was Wednesday the Tenth?*, 1898.
Recalled to Life. Bristol, Arrowsmith, and New York, Holt, 1891.
What's Bred in the Bone. London, Tit-Bits, and Boston, Tucker, 1891.
Dumaresq's Daughter. London, Chatto and Windus, 3 vols., and New York, Munro, 1 vol., 1891.
The Duchess of Powsland. London, Chatto and Windus, 3 vols., and New York, Munro, 1 vol., 1892.
The Scallywag. London, Chatto and Windus, 3 vols., and New York, Cassell, 1 vol., 1893.
Michael's Crag. London, Leadenhall Press, and Chicago, Rand McNally, 1893.
Blood Royal. London, Chatto and Windus, and New York, Cassell, 1893.
An Army Doctor's Romance. London, Tuck, 1893.
At Market Value. London, Chatto and Windus, 2 vols., and Chicago, Neely, 1 vol., 1894.
The British Barbarians: A Hilltop Novel. London, Lane, and New York, Putnam, 1895.
The Woman Who Did. London, Lane, and Boston, Roberts, 1895.
Under Sealed Orders. London, Chatto and Windus, 3 vols., 1895; New York, New Amsterdam, 1 vol., 1896.

A Splendid Sin. London, White, 1896; New York, Buckles, 1899.
Tom, Unlimited: A Story for Children (as Martin Leach Warborough). London, Richards, 1897.
The Type-Writer Girl (as Olive Pratt Rayner). London, Pearson, 1897; as Grant Allen, New York, Street and Smith, 1900.
Linnet. London, Richards, 1898; New York, New Amsterdam, 1900.
The Incidental Bishop. London, Pearson, and New York, Appleton, 1898.
Rosalba: The Story of Her Development (as Olive Pratt Rayner). London, Pearson, and New York, Putnam, 1899.

Short Stories

The General's Will and Other Stories. London, Butterworth, 1892.
The Desire of the Eyes and Other Stories. London, Digby Long, 1895; New York, Fenno, 1896.
A Bride from the Desert. New York, Fenno, 1896.
Moorland Idylls. London, Chatto and Windus, 1896.
An African Millionaire. London, Richards, and New York, Arnold, 1897.
Miss Cayley's Adventures. London, Richards, and New York, Putnam, 1899.
Hilda Wade, completed by Arthur Conan Doyle. London, Richards, and New York, Putnam, 1900.
The Reluctant Hangman and Other Stories of Crime, edited by Tom and Enid Schantz. Boulder, Colorado, Aspen Press, 1973.

Other

Physiological Aesthetics. London, King, 1877; New York, Appleton, 1878.
The Colour-Sense: Its Origin and Development: An Essay in Comparative Psychology. London, Trubner, and Boston, Houghton Osgood, 1879.
Anglo-Saxon Britain. London, SPCK, and New York, Young, 1881.
The Evolutionist at Large. London, Chatto and Windus, 1881; revised edition, 1884.
Vignettes from Nature. London, Chatto and Windus, 1881; New York, Fitzgerald, 1882.
The Colours of Flowers, as Illustrated in the British Flora. London and New York, Macmillan, 1882.
Colin Clout's Calendar: The Record of a Summer, April-October. London, Chatto and Windus, 1882; New York, Funk and Wagnalls, 1883.
Biographies of Working Men. London, SPCK, 1884.
Charles Darwin. London, Longman, and New York, Appleton, 1885.
Common Sense Science. Boston, Lothrop, 1887.
A Half-Century of Science, with T. H. Huxley. New York, Humboldt, 1888.
Force and Energy: A Theory of Dynamics. London, Longman, 1888; New York, Humboldt, 1889.
Falling in Love, with Other Essays on More Exact Branches of Science. London, Smith Elder, 1889; New York, Appleton, 1890.
Individualism and Socialism. Glasgow, Scottish Land Restoration League, 1890(?).
Science in Arcady. London, Lawrence and Bullen, 1892.
The Tidal Thames. London, Cassell, 1892.
Post-Prandial Philosophy. London, Chatto and Windus, 1894.
In Memoriam George Paul Macdonell. London, Lund, 1895.

The Story of the Plants. London, Newnes, 1895; as *The Plants*, New York, Review of Reviews, 1909.

The Evolution of the Idea of God: An Inquiry into the Origins of Religions. London, Richards, and New York, Holt, 1897.

Paris. London, Richards, 1897; New York, Wessels, 1900; revised edition, 1906.

Florence. London, Richards, 1897; New York, Wessels, 1900; revised edition, 1906.

Cities of Belgium. London, Richards, 1897; New York, Wessels, 1900; as *Belgium: Its Cities*, Boston, Page, 2 vols., 1903.

Venice. London, Richards, 1898; New York, Wessels, 1900.

Flashlights on Nature. New York, Doubleday, 1898; London, Newnes, 1899.

The European Tour: A Handbook for Americans and Colonists. London, Richards, and New York, Dodd Mead, 1899.

The New Hedonism. New York, Tucker, 1900.

Plain Words on the Woman Question. Chicago, Harman, 1900.

In Nature's Workshop. London, Newnes, and New York, Mansfield, 1901.

County and Town in England, Together with Some Annals of Churnside. London, Richards, and New York, Dutton, 1901.

Evolution in Italian Art, edited by J. W. Cruickshank. London, Richards, and New York, Wessels, 1908.

The Hand of God, and Other Posthumous Essays. London, Watts, 1909.

Editor, *The Miscellaneous and Posthumous Works of H. T. Buckle*, abridged edition. London, Longman, 2 vols., 1895.

Editor, *The Natural History of Selborne*, by Gilbert White. London, Lane, 1900.

Translator, *The Attis of Caius Valerius Catullus.* London, Nutt, 1892.

*   *   *

During the early years of his career Grant Allen certainly thought of himself as a writer of horror stories. The preface to *The Beckoning Hand and Other Stories* apprises the reader of his ambition to "make your flesh creep" and recommends *Strange Stories* as "every bit as gruesome." Most modern readers would, however, consider his work in this vein to be marginal to the horror genre. He was an enthusiastic propagandist for free thought and science and was extremely loath to use the supernatural as a means of generating dramatic tension.

The three items in *Strange Stories* which deal with seemingly supernatural phenomena, "The Mysterious Occurrence in Piccadilly," "New Year's Eve among the Mummies" and "Our Scientific Observations of a Ghost," are satirical pieces taking a loftily ironic view of the mistaken beliefs of spiritualists and psychic researchers. In the later collection only two stories stoop to the employment of supernatural devices. The title story equips a Haitian *femme fatale* with the alluring magic of "vaudoux" (voodoo) and then uses her increasingly desperate deployment of it to bring about her destruction. "The Two Carnegies" employs an impossibly exact hereditary destiny to shape the lives of unlucky twins, posing intricate problems when they become rivals for the hand of a girl. Whereas "The Beckoning Hand" is a horror story through and through, however, "The Two Carnegies" is too wrapped up in the fascination of its central premise to be disturbing.

Most of the stories in these two collections do contain a distinct horrific element, but it is a naturalistic kind of horror. Allen evidently felt that only things which might actually occur ought to be reckoned truly scary. Some of his early tales are unrelenting *contes cruels* while others include episodes in which the protagonists are briefly consigned to terrifying situations of various kinds and then mercifully delivered therefrom. Although these situations are resolutely non-supernatural they are far from mundane, usually being set in far-flung parts of the world where local customs may seem horribly alien even when they are innocuous. Allen's keen interest in the insights and theories of the nascent science of anthropology informed many his tales, importing into his accounts of men cursed by exotic obsessions or unfortunate atavisms—the most notable examples are "The Reverend John Creedy" and "John Cann's Treasure"—a distinctive repulsive shudder. Women who marry exotic foreigners, as in "Olga Davidoff's Husband," are held to be asking for trouble, and even women who intend to marry morally anaesthetized colonialists may put undue stress on their more scrupulous English lovers, as revealed by the chilling manuscript which comprises "The Search Party's Find."

Allen's early potboiler *Kalee's Shrine*, written for Arrowsmith's famous series of "shilling shockers," is one of several 19th-century accounts of the Thugs, whose murderous exploits in the service of the goddess Kali alarmed and fascinated the English imperialists who took charge of the Indian subcontinent. The protagonist of the story is an English girl consecrated by her native governess to the goddess, who is given the power to possess her while she sleeps. The story's hero is, however, the doctor who interprets her condition in terms of hypnotism and somnambulism—by which means he effects a cure. "The Dead Man Speaks" similarly imposes a quasi-scientific explanation upon traditional superstition, while *The Great Taboo* offers a much more elaborate account of primitive belief and ritual inspired by the earliest editions of James Frazer's *The Golden Bough.*

The Great Taboo tells the story of two castaways among the savages of the Pacific island of Boupari, whose cannibal inhabitants worship the bloodthirsty god Tu-Kila-Kila. Modern anthropologists have banished the key elements of *The Great Taboo* and "The Beckoning Hand" to the wilderness of unfortunate error, but they became staple elements of pulp fiction and Hollywood movies, reflecting Western anxieties about the supposed dark heart of primitive culture. Allen's versions of this modern myth is remarkable only for the level of their theorization, but for precisely that reason they offers an unusually accurate measure of the depth and dimensions of the horror infusing crude racism. The horrific aspects of Allen's work became noticeably less pronounced as time went by, and by 1893 he seems to have abandoned his ambition to make the reader's flesh creep in favour of producing quirky love stories of the kind best beloved by popular magazine editors. The racist elements of his work were also softened, although this must have reflected a change of heart rather than editorial pressure. The title story of *Ivan Greet's Masterpiece* is the last of his extended *contes cruels*, this time set in Jamaica, but it acquires an extra dimension of tragedy by virtue of the sympathetic treatment afforded to its black heroine. The same collection contains the most conventional of all Allen's ghost stories, "Pallinghurst Barrow," although the author carefully leaves open the possibility that it was all a delusion brought on by tincture of cannabis (which was widely rumoured in those days to be a powerful hallucinogen).

The most interesting of Allen's marginally supernatural stories is perhaps "Wolverden Tower" in *Twelve Tales*, in which local superstition is represented as underpinning rather than undermining

Christian impositions. The eponymous tower is part of a church, but the local hagwife insists that the ancient dead resting in its vaults require a most un-Christian human sacrifice to make the edifice fast. A much more straightforward species of horror is featured in the disaster story "The Thames Valley Catastrophe," which Allen did not include in any of his collections, although it often crops up in anthologies of early science fiction.

Although *The Desire of the Eyes* is listed in Everett Bleiler's *Checklist of Science-Fiction and Supernatural Literature*, the original Digby Long edition contains no supernatural stories or *contes cruels*; the two reprinted short stories attributed to it in Bleiler's *Guide to Supernatural Fiction* must have been added by the U.S. publisher.

—Brian Stableford

AMIS, (Sir) Kingsley (William)

Pseudonyms: Robert Markham; Lt.-Col. William "Bill" Tanner. **Nationality:** British. **Born:** London, 16 April 1922. **Education:** City of London School; St. John's College, Oxford, M.A. in English. **Military Service:** Served in the Royal Corps of Signals, 1942-45. **Family:** Married 1) Hilary Ann Bardwell in 1948 (marriage dissolved, 1965), two sons, including the writer Martin Amis, and one daughter; 2) the writer Elizabeth Jane Howard in 1965 (divorced, 1983). **Career:** Lecturer in English, University College, Swansea, Wales, 1949-61; visiting fellow in Creative Writing, Princeton University, New Jersey, 1958-59; fellow in English, Peterhouse, Cambridge, 1961-63; visiting professor, Vanderbilt University, Nashville, Tennessee, 1967. **Awards:** Maugham award, 1955; *Yorkshire Post* award, 1974; John W. Campbell Memorial award, 1977; Booker prize, 1986. Honorary Fellow, St. John's College, 1976. C.B.E. (Commander, Order of the British Empire), 1981. Knighted, 1990. **Died:** 22 October 1995.

HORROR, GHOST AND GOTHIC PUBLICATIONS

Novel

The Green Man. London, Cape, 1969; New York, Harcourt Brace, 1970.

Short Stories

Collected Short Stories. London, Hutchinson, 1980; revised edition, 1987.
Mr. Barrett's Secret and Other Stories. London, Hutchinson, 1993.

OTHER PUBLICATIONS

Novels

Lucky Jim. London, Gollancz, and New York, Doubleday, 1954.
That Uncertain Feeling. London, Gollancz, 1955; New York, Harcourt Brace, 1956.
I Like It Here. London, Gollancz, and New York, Harcourt Brace, 1958.

Take a Girl Like You. London, Gollancz, 1960; New York, Harcourt Brace, 1961.
One Fat Englishman. London, Gollancz, 1963; New York, Harcourt Brace, 1964.
The Egyptologists, with Robert Conquest. London, Cape, 1965; New York, Random House, 1966.
The Anti-Death League. London, Gollancz, and New York, Harcourt Brace, 1966.
Colonel Sun: A James Bond Adventure (as Robert Markham). London, Cape, and New York, Harper, 1968.
I Want It Now. London, Cape, 1968; New York, Harcourt Brace, 1969.
Girl, 20. London, Cape, 1971; New York, Harcourt Brace, 1972.
The Riverside Villas Murder. London, Cape, and New York, Harcourt Brace, 1973.
Ending Up. London, Cape, and New York, Harcourt Brace, 1974.
The Alteration. London, Cape, 1976; New York, Viking Press, 1977.
Jake's Thing. London, Hutchinson, 1978; New York, Viking Press, 1979.
Russian Hide-and-Seek: A Melodrama. London, Hutchinson, 1980.
Stanley and the Women. London, Hutchinson, 1984; New York, Perennial Library, 1988.
The Old Devils. London, Hutchinson, 1986; New York, Summit, 1987.
The Crime of the Century. London, Dent, 1987; New York, Mysterious Press, 1989.
Difficulties with Girls. London, Hutchinson, and New York, Summit, 1988.
The Folks That Live on the Hill. London, Hutchinson, and New York, Summit, 1990.
We Are All Guilty (for children). London, Reinhardt, and New York, Viking, 1991.
The Russian Girl. London, Hutchinson, 1992; New York, Viking, 1994.
You Can't Do Both. London, Hutchinson, 1994.
The Biographer's Moustache. London, HarperCollins, 1995.

Short Stories

My Enemy's Enemy. London, Gollancz, 1962; New York, Harcourt Brace, 1963.
Penguin Modern Stories 11, with others. London, Penguin, 1972.
Dear Illusion. London, Covent Garden Press, 1972.
The Darkwater Hall Mystery. Edinburgh, Tragara Press, 1978.

Plays

Radio Plays: *Touch and Go,* 1957; *Something Strange,* 1962; *The Riverside Villas Murder,* from his own novel, 1976.

Television Plays: *A Question about Hell,* 1964; *The Importance of Being Harry,* 1971; *Dr. Watson and the Darkwater Hall Mystery,* 1974; *See What You've Done* (*Softly, Softly* series), 1974; *We Are All Guilty* (*Against the Crowd* series), 1975.

Poetry

Bright November. London, Fortune Press, 1947.
A Frame of Mind. Reading, Berkshire, University of Reading School of Art, 1953.
(Poems). Oxford, Fantasy Press, 1954.

A Case of Samples: Poems 1946-1956. London, Gollancz, 1956; New York, Harcourt Brace, 1957.
The Evans Country. Oxford, Fantasy Press, 1962.
Penguin Modern Poets 2, with Dom Moraes and Peter Porter. London, Penguin, 1962.
A Look Round the Estate: Poems 1957-1967. London, Cape, 1967; New York, Harcourt Brace, 1968.
Wasted, Kipling at Bateman's. London, Poem-of-the-Month Club, 1973.
Collected Poems 1944-1979. London, Hutchinson, 1979; New York, Viking Press, 1980.

Recordings: *Kingsley Amis Reading His Own Poems,* Listen, 1962; *Poems,* with Thomas Blackburn, Jupiter, 1962.

Other

Socialism and the Intellectuals. London, Fabian Society, 1957.
New Maps of Hell: A Survey of Science Fiction. New York, Harcourt Brace, 1960; London, Gollancz, 1961.
The Book of Bond, or Every Man His Own 007 (as Lt.-Col. William "Bill" Tanner). London, Cape, 1965.
The James Bond Dossier. London, Cape, and New York, New American Library, 1965.
Lucky Jim's Politics. London, Conservative Political Centre, 1968.
What's Become of Jane Austen? and Other Questions. London, Cape, 1970; New York, Harcourt Brace, 1971.
On Drink. London, Cape, 1972; New York, Harcourt Brace, 1973.
Rudyard Kipling and His World. London, Thames and Hudson, 1975; New York, Scribner, 1976.
An Arts Policy? London, Centre for Policy Studies, 1979.
Every Day Drinking. London, Hutchinson, 1983.
How's Your Glass? London, Weidenfeld and Nicolson, 1984.
The Amis Collection: Selected Non-Fiction 1954-1990. London, Hutchinson, 1990.
Memoirs. London, Hutchinson, and New York, Summit, 1991.

Editor, with James Michie, *Oxford Poetry.* Oxford, Blackwell, 1949.
Editor, with Robert Conquest, *Spectrum [1-5]: A Science Fiction Anthology.* London, Gollancz, 5 vols., 1961-65; New York, Harcourt Brace, 5 vols., 1962-67.
Editor, *Selected Short Stories of G.K. Chesterton.* London, Faber, 1972.
Editor, *Tennyson.* London, Penguin, 1973.
Editor, *Harold's Years: Impressions from the New Statesman and The Spectator.* London, Quartet, 1977.
Editor, *The New Oxford Book of Light Verse.* London and New York, Oxford University Press, 1978.
Editor, *The Faber Popular Reciter.* London, Faber, 1978.
Editor, *The Golden Age of Science Fiction.* London, Hutchinson, 1981.
Editor, with James Cochrane, *The Great British Songbook.* New York, Pavilion-Joseph, 1986; London, Faber, 1988.
Editor, *The Amis Anthology: A Personal Choice of English Verse.* London, Hutchinson, 1988.
Editor, *The Pleasures of Poetry: From His Daily Mirror Column.* London, Cassell, 1990.
Editor, with others, *The Best Winners of the Booker Prize.* San Francisco, California, Mercury House, 1991.
Editor, *The Amis Story Anthology: A Personal Choice of Short Stories.* London, Hutchinson, 1992.

*

Film Adaptations: *Lucky Jim,* 1957; *Only Two Can Play,* 1961, *That Uncertain Feeling* (TV serial), 1986, from the novel *That Uncertain Feeling; Take a Girl Like You,* 1969; *The Green Man* (TV serial), 1991; *Stanley and the Women* (TV serial), 1991; *The Old Devils* (TV serial), 1992.

Bibliography: *Kingsley Amis: A Checklist* by Jack Benoit Gohn, Kent, Ohio, Kent State University Press, 1976: *Kingsley Amis: A Reference Guide* by Dale Salwak, Boston, Hall, and London, Prior, 1978.

Manuscript Collection (verse): State University of New York, Buffalo.

Critical Studies: *Kingsley Amis* by Philip Gardner, Boston, Twayne, 1981; *Kingsley Amis* by Richard Bradford, London, Arnold, 1989; *Kingsley Amis: An English Moralist* by John McDermott, London, Macmillan, 1989; *Kingsley Amis in Life and Letters* edited by Dale Salwak, London, Macmillan, 1990; *Kingsley Amis: Modern Novelist* by Dale Salwak, London, Macmillan, 1992.

*   *   *

Kingsley Amis was best known as a writer of comic and satirical novels, the keynote being set by the great success of his first book *Lucky Jim.* Despite the sunniness of its humour, this novel led to his being grouped with Colin Wilson and others as a 1950s left-wing social rebel or "Angry Young Man" (a label unhelpfully invented by journalists). Over the years Amis moved politically to the right while still producing comedy in the same polished vein. Later mainstream honours included the Booker Prize for *The Old Devils* and a 1990 knighthood. "Respectable" admirers of the straight novels have tended to downplay this author's lifelong fondness for genre fiction. Such enthusiasm became apparent in his affectionate 1960 survey of science fiction, *New Maps of Hell,* and in works which explored the popular genres: sf, crime, espionage, war, and supernatural fiction.

His great supernatural achievement is the partly comic ghost story *The Green Man.* Initially it would seem that the comedy must be at odds with any true horrific *frisson* . . . but Amis is expert at conveying a certain moral chill that undercuts the fun. Several of his boozy, lecherous, quipping anti-heroes are clearly whistling in the dark. Taking examples from two of the most extravagantly funny novels, Patrick in *Take a Girl Like You* is regularly convulsed by icy fears of death, while Jake in *Jake's Thing* can be seen as slowly withdrawing from all human contact into a kind of private damnation. And the ostensible spy story *The Anti-Death League* conceals a bitter tirade against the injustice and cruelty of God.

The Green Man takes its name from an old coaching inn—now also a slightly pretentious restaurant—owned by the likeable but reprehensible Maurice Allington, who is flirting with alcoholism and a master plan to lure both wife and mistress into bed for a threesome. One of the inn's minor attractions is the legend of a not very exciting ghost, which Maurice boredly recites to despised customers. Then he sees certain things himself; and his father dies of a stroke while apparently also experiencing a vision. Maurice's self-confidence is shaken, leaving him open to fears of madness and to an assault from the past.

Gradually it emerges that the 17th-century Dr. Thomas Underhill, a sexual predator who used both faked and real wizardry to dominate his young female prey, had made plans to circumvent death and hopes—with our hero's aid—to return. He has chosen his victim cunningly: projected hallucinations resonate with the terror of *delirium tremens*, while Maurice's difficulty in recalling revealing conversations with the shade of Underhill may be no more than alcoholic memory loss. As the doctor smugly informs him, "Not to remember is your quality."

Worse is waiting. The real Green Man is an appalling golem or forest elemental which the wizard was accustomed to conjure from the local woods. Underhill's return to life will be *via* possession of his living contact's body. And he already has carnal plans for Maurice's adolescent daughter. . . .

Ironically echoing the Dennis Wheatley plot-turn of all too convenient divine intervention, Amis permits Maurice an interview with God in the unspectacular (though briefly grisly) form of a pale young man. The chill arises not so much from the casual explanation that the terrifying Underhill is a minor "security" problem which Maurice is expected to deal with single-handed, as from this dialogue's dismaying implications of a deity with scant emotional interest in his creation, and of an inescapable afterlife which is too bleakly alien for even God to describe.

Nevertheless, earthy realism is maintained by Amis's fine control of language and diction, and of the sense that life's comedy continues even while bad smells seep in from the metaphysical outside. On the real-life level, Maurice's hoped-for *ménage à trois* gives him a splendidly farcical come-uppance.

At last, in a scene of considerable horror, the powerful and repulsive Green Man walks again. Acting on information received, Maurice is able to use the forms of religion against the golem and Underhill—not devoutly but as game-rules where appropriate offensive and defensive points are scored by the cross, by consecrated ground, and by the ritual of exorcism into which he cajoles a reluctant and decidedly agnostic vicar. ("The spirit killeth, but the letter giveth life.") With evil routed, all has in theory ended well. However, Maurice's peep into the theological abyss and his increased self-knowledge have not brought contentment but a complexly bitter spiritual aftertaste. It is on this discomforting note that *The Green Man* ends.

Amis has also produced shorter relevant works. "Who or What Was It?" (*Collected Short Stories*) is an entertaining tall tale, originally a radio broadcast, in which Amis himself claims to have stumbled into a situation uncannily duplicating his own creation in *The Green Man*: an audaciously implausible denouement was meant to establish the story as incontrovertibly fictional—yet several people were fooled. The 1980 vampire novella "To See the Sun" (*ibid*), told in traditional epistolary manner, has a typically charming but unreliable English traveller enjoying an extramarital fling with an exotic female vampire in 1925 Dacia; there are several effective ironies, including the man's explanation to this lover that vampire legends arose from hallucinations caused by ergot poisoning, and the emerging fact that despite her condition she possesses a far greater sense of honour . . . leading to the self-sacrifice implied in the title. Another seeming spy-story, "The House on the Headland" (*ibid*), develops Gothic elements as mysterious doings prove to hinge on teratophilia—the morbid love of deformity. "A Twitch on the Thread" (*Mr. Barrett's Secret*), a glum story of moral downfall, uses the legendary psychic affinity of twins to cast a cold or perhaps merely sophistical light on the value of religious experience.

Kingsley Amis made a significant contribution to every genre in which he worked. Although *The Green Man* is his sole book-

length tale of the supernatural, its disquieting sophistication and the deepening of its darkness by contrasting veins of light comedy make it a major 20th-century horror story.

—David Langford

ANDREWS, V(irginia) C(leo)

Nationality: American. **Born:** Portsmouth, Virginia, 1933. **Education:** Attended schools in Portsmouth, Virginia. **Career:** Worked as a fashion illustrator, commercial artist, portrait artist, and gallery exhibitor; later a bestselling novelist. **Died:** 19 December 1986.

HORROR, GHOST AND GOTHIC PUBLICATIONS

Novels (series: Casteel-Tatterton Saga; Cutler Family; Dollenganger Family; Landry Family)

Flowers in the Attic (Dollenganger Family). New York, Pocket, 1979; London, Fontana, 1980.
Petals on the Wind (Dollenganger Family). New York, Pocket, and London, Piatkus, 1980.
If There Be Thorns (Dollenganger Family). New York, Pocket, and London, Piatkus, 1981.
My Sweet Audrina. New York, Poseidon Press, and London, Piatkus, 1982.
Seeds of Yesterday (Dollenganger Family). New York, Poseidon Press, and London, Piatkus, 1984.
Heaven (Casteel-Tatterton). New York, Poseidon Press, and London, Collins, 1985.
Dark Angel (Casteel-Tatterton). New York, Poseidon Press, and London, Collins, 1986.
Garden of Shadows (Dollenganger Family), with Andrew Neiderman (uncredited). New York, Pocket, and London, Collins, 1987.

Novels by Andrew Neiderman writing as V. C. Andrews

Fallen Hearts (Casteel-Tatterton). New York, Pocket, and London, Collins, 1988.
Gates of Paradise (Casteel-Tatterton). New York, Pocket, and London, Collins, 1989.
Web of Dreams (Casteel-Tatterton). New York, Pocket, and London, Collins, 1990.
Dawn (Cutler Family). New York, Pocket, 1990; London, Simon and Schuster, 1991.
Ruby (Landry Family). New York, Pocket, 1991; London, Simon and Schuster, 1994.
Secrets of the Morning (Cutler Family). New York, Pocket, and London, Simon and Schuster, 1991.
Twilight's Child (Cutler Family). New York, Pocket, and London, Simon and Schuster, 1992.
Midnight Whispers (Cutler Family). New York, Pocket, 1992; London, Simon and Schuster, 1993.
Darkest Hour (Cutler Family). New York, Pocket, 1993; London, Simon and Schuster, 1994.
Pearl in the Mist (Landry Family). New York, Pocket, and London, Simon and Schuster, 1994.

All That Glitters (Landry Family). New York, Pocket, and London, Simon and Schuster, 1995.
Hidden Jewel (Landry Family). New York, Pocket, 1995; London, Simon and Schuster, 1996.
Tarnished Gold (Landry Family). New York, Pocket, and London, Simon and Schuster, 1996.
Melody. New York, Pocket, 1996; London, Simon and Schuster, 1997.

*

Film Adaptation: *Flowers in the Attic*, 1987.

*   *   *

The novels of V. C. Andrews (published in Britain as by Virginia Andrews) are family sagas involving gutsy heroines, huge fortunes, rambling mansions, passionate love-affairs, and leaps across the social divide. Yet the tinge of psychological grotesqueness and melodrama in her first series, beginning with *Flowers in the Attic*, ensured interest from horror readers. *Flowers*, and its sequels *Petals on the Wind*, *If There be Thorns* and *Seeds of Yesterday*—there is also a "prequel," *Garden of Shadows*—are modern Gothic novels of betrayal and fatal attraction. They are also modern fairy tales—if by "fairy tale" we understand such stories as "Hansel and Gretel" in which a loving brother and sister are betrayed by their wicked stepmother and maltreated by a witch. Andrews's stories follow this pattern, adding the similar motifs of family curses and obsessive love between forbidden blood-lines to create a world in which Hansel and Gretel are lovers as well as siblings.

Andrews belongs firmly to the non-supernatural brand of Gothickry, although there are hints of brooding metaphysical clouds operating a malevolent destiny. Apart from the hints of ESP in her most macabre novel, *My Sweet Audrina*, however, all supernatural events—even the ghosts pacing Farthinggale Manor in her second sequence consisting of *Heaven*, *Dark Angel* and the posthumous *Fallen Hearts*, *Gates of Paradise* and *Web of Dreams*—are metaphorical imagery (or actual characters). The horror, the grotesquerie and the melodrama arise out of her characters and the situations in which she places them.

Born in Portsmouth, Virginia, V. C. Andrews used a Southern-state setting for much of her fiction, which deals in such quintessentially Southern concepts as lineage, beautiful women, and dark secrets (though not race: there is only one black American in her books, significantly a kindly but comic servant). She attributed the lurid plots of her books to imagination and early reading (the Bible, science fiction and fantasy, fairy tales and Edgar Allan Poe) rather than experience, although a fanatically religious grandparent, artistic talent, and the frustrations of metaphorical and actual confinement (she used a wheelchair after contracting arthritis due to a fall) are among components of her life found in her fiction. She worked for many years as a commercial artist and portrait painter and one of her main themes could be how the illusion of beauty masks a particularly ugly and cruel world.

The *Flowers in the Attic* sequence starts with the removal of the four blonde and beautiful Dollenganger children to their mother's ancestral home after their father's death. Corrine Foxworth has been disinherited because of her marriage to her half-uncle Christopher (the children's father) and can only be welcomed back into the family if she keeps secret the fact that there are

children. Only Corrine's mother knows of the children, and they are hidden in an attic to be brought down at the death of their grandfather Malcolm. This temporary expedient lasts for several years, and in this pressure-cooker all sorts of emotions begin to simmer. Not surprisingly, given all these influences, teenage Cathy and Chris find sexual tensions growing between them. As payment for transgressing their grandmother's rules of modesty and purity, Chris is whipped, Cathy's hair is cut off, and on one occasion the children are starved to the point where, in one of the book's most memorable passages, Chris offers his blood to keep the others alive. This is not typical romantic fiction, even by the standards of the decadent 1980s.

The single image of four young children imprisoned in an attic under the totalitarian regime of a "witch" while their beautiful mother gradually forgets about them (her later remarriage makes their eventual disclosure even more of a potential embarrassment) is still perhaps Andrews's best creation: a lurid picture of environment versus heredity as Chris and Cathy struggle with their sexual feelings for each other. The rest of the sequence works out the initial situation through the lives of Cathy and Chris. If *Flowers in the Attic* is "Hansel and Gretel," *Petals on the Wind* is "Snow White." The children escape and are taken in by a kindly doctor, Paul Schofield, who supports them and finances Chris's ambition to go to medical school and Cathy's to be a ballerina. But there are more sexual entanglements for Cathy, not least with Paul himself and Julian, a brilliant dancer whom Cathy eventually marries and by whom she has a son, Jory. Cathy is also determined to revenge herself on her mother, and after Julian's death sets out to seduce her stepfather Bart, by whom she has a child. The final confrontation results, *Jane Eyre*-like, in a fire, death and insanity.

The popularity of the series owes a great deal to its theme of "forbidden love." There is an ambiguity at the heart of the relationship between Cathy and Chris. In themselves they are tragic innocents: the abuse depicted in the sequence is the neglect and ill-treatment of the children, the claustrophobic atmosphere of the attic, yet at the root of this is their own parents' incest which is itself a tragic meeting of innocents. Thus there is a murky fog at the moral centre of the saga. Cathy and Chris are never really free of the tag of "Devil's Spawn." Parallel with this is Virginia Andrews's constant restating of the theme that victims of life can rise above whatever fate throws at them. Her heroines are beaten but never broken: like Little Orphan Annie they find protectors but remain fighters. Unlike Orphan Annie, they are sexually exploited—but often managed to do their own share of sexual exploitation. There is a great deal of rather obvious masochism above and beyond the clear instances involving physical persecution, but it is a masochism which works through to a histrionic resolution. "I have been deprived," declaims another of Andrews's heroines, Heaven Leigh Casteel, in *Dark Angel*, "starved, beaten, burned, humiliated, and shamed, and still I find life rewarding."

Virginia Andrews's second series is more titillating than shocking, although Tony Tatterton is a suitably nasty villain, with his ambiguous (both evil and feeble) character and his multi-generational incestuous obsessions. Often, however, we are restating themes, characters and incidents found in the first series, while the increasingly-useful device of a car crash feels less like the Persecuting Hand of Fate and more like an author desperate for a way of moving a stalled plot along. Tatterton is powerful as a sinister magician-manipulator, buying and selling affection and lusting after his pawns; on the other hand a villain whose excuse for incest is "I just got confused" is soap-operatic rather than Satanic. Gothickry treads a thin line between the baroque and the bathetic: in *Fallen Hearts* we have no doubt about on which side of the divide the book falls. In fairness, three out of the five volumes of this series are by another hand (said to be that of horror novelist Andrew Neiderman), and obviously written to conform to readers' expectations of the themes and structure of the first series, increasingly becoming pastiche.

The third series, the Cutler Family saga beginning with *Dawn*, and the fourth series, the Landry saga beginning with *Pearl*, efface the author as original creator almost completely: they are linked to Virginia Andrews (whose name is trademarked) only by "inspiration" and the two series reflect both the structure (each four volumes and a prequel) and the specific incidents of the previous sequences.

Flowers in the Attic apart, Andrews's most interesting book is her only singleton, *My Sweet Audrina*, another paranoid fairy tale in which a young girl is kept secluded by her parents. Combining the archetypes of "Cinderella," "Rapunzel" and "Red Riding Hood," *Audrina* links transgression to sexuality. The narrator is forbidden to go into the surrounding woods because exactly nine years before she was born her sister was "spoiled" there by boys and died. Her life is a memorial to the "First and best Audrina" after whom she was named, and she lives a life curiously dislocated in time and identity, with the image of her dead sister constantly before her as a model into which her father is apparently trying to mould her. There are the usual convoluted relationships, but the cast-list is more grotesquely inventive, including a multiple-amputee ex-Olympic skater who is the mother of Audrina's lover and also for a time the lover of her father. There is also another sister, Sylvia, whose potentially homicidal tendencies are just this side of the paranormal. All Virginia Andrews's novels offer reversals of fortune and dramatic changes of circumstance and cast list, but *My Sweet Audrina*, with sudden deaths, departures, returns, and people whose roles in the course of events are more fundamental and sinister than we or Audrina think, does so more than most.

These novels demand to be read as scorchingly intense psychological horror-soaps. They are, perhaps, examples of hothouse kitsch, written to an obsessive formula and full of artificially composed dialogue in which characters sermonize rather than speak. Nevertheless the underlying motifs are openly cited too often to allow us to doubt that these tales of inter-family persecution and abuse, arbitrary reversals, struggles against half-supernatural assailants and, above all, heroines are interpretations for the modern world of the tales collected (and bowdlerized) by scholars like the Brothers Grimm. They recall the original function of folk tales as warning stories showing the perilous nature of the world to (especially) young girls. Fate, though, can be taken in hand and defeated. Andrews's range of literary skill may be narrow, but in those stories indisputably hers she is undeniably a compelling and disturbing writer—made so precisely because of her deliberate reinterpretation of the old folk motifs in terms of their nearest contemporary equivalent, the high-society soap opera.

—Andy Sawyer

ARLEN, Michael

Nationality: British; emigrated to England, 1901; naturalized as Michael Arlen, 1922. **Born:** Dikran Kouyoumdjian, in Rustchuk, Bulgaria, 16 November 1895. **Education:** Malvern College, Worcestershire; studied medicine at the University of Edinburgh, 1913. **Military Service:** Served as Civil Defence public relations officer in the West Midlands, 1940-41. **Family:** Married Atalanta, daughter of Count Mercati, in 1928; one son and one daughter. **Career:** Staff member, *Ararat: A Searchlight on Armenia*, London, 1916, and columnist, the *Tatler*, London, 1939-40; lived in Cannes, 1928-39, and in New York City after 1945. Friends with the writer D. H. Lawrence and satanist Philip Heseltine. **Died:** 23 June 1956.

HORROR, GHOST AND GOTHIC PUBLICATIONS

Novel

Hell! Said the Duchess: A Bed-Time Story. London, Heinemann, and New York, Doubleday, 1934.

Short Stories

These Charming People. London, Collins, 1923; New York, Doran, 1924; selection, as *The Man with the Broken Nose and Other Stories*, Collins, 1927.
May Fair, in Which Are Told the Last Adventures of These Charming People. London, Collins, and New York, Doran, 1925; selection, as *The Ace of Cads and Other Stories*, Collins, 1927.
Ghost Stories. London, Collins, 1927; New York, Arno Press, 1976.

OTHER PUBLICATIONS

Novels

The London Venture. London, Heinemann, and New York, Dodd Mead, 1920.
Piracy: A Romantic Chronicle of These Days. London, Collins, 1922; New York, Doran, 1923.
The Green Hat: A Romance for a Few People. London, Collins, and New York, Doran, 1924.
Young Men in Love. London, Hutchinson, and New York, Doran, 1927.
Lily Christine. New York, Doubleday, 1928; London, Hutchinson, 1929.
Men Dislike Women: A Romance. London, Heinemann, and New York, Doubleday, 1931.
Man's Mortality. London, Heinemann, and New York, Doubleday, 1933.
Flying Dutchman. London, Heinemann, and New York, Doubleday, 1939.

Short Stories

The Romantic Lady. London, Collins, and New York, Dodd Mead, 1921.
Babes in the Wood. London, Hutchinson, and New York, Doubleday, 1929.
The Ancient Sin and Other Stories. London, Collins, 1930.
A Young Man Comes to London. Privately printed, 1931.
The Short Stories. London, Collins, 1933.

The Crooked Coronet and Other Misrepresentations of the Real Facts of Life. London, Heinemann, and New York, Doubleday, 1937.

Plays

Dear Father (produced London, 1924; revised version, as *These Charming People*, produced New York, 1925).
Why Shelmerdene Was Late for Dinner, adaptation of his story "The Real Reason Why Shelmerdene Was Late for Dinner" (produced London, 1924).
The Green Hat, adaptation of his own novel (produced Detroit, London, and New York, 1925). New York, Doran, 1925.
The Zoo, with Winchell Smith (produced Southsea and Pittsburgh, 1927). New York and London, French, 1927.
Good Losers, with Walter Hackett (produced London, 1931). London, French, 1933.

Screenplay: *The Heavenly Body*, with others, 1943.

*

Film Adaptations: *A Woman of Affairs*, 1928, *Outcast Lady* (*A Woman of the World*), 1934, both from the novel *The Green Hat*; *Golden Arrow*, 1936; *The Gay Falcon*, 1941, from his short story.

Critical Study: *Michael Arlen* by Harry Keyishian, Boston, Twayne, 1975.

*   *   *

Michael Arlen loved to tell the tale of how, while touring in the Near East after World War II, he was shown what purported to be the grave of the "great Armenian writer" Dikran Kouyoumdjian. (Although born in Bulgaria, Kouyoumdjian/Arlen was descended from Armenian Jews.) The English tourist was, of course, far too polite to point out that he was the man in question—and in any case, he no longer was. He had made every possible effort to naturalize himself, cultivating English manners as well as the English language—but he wisely adopted the stereotyped role of the cynical outsider, wittily critical of the *haut monde* whose periphery he inhabited by virtue of being the youngest son of a successful Manchester-based merchant.

Arlen was careful to borrow the sentimentality as well as the wit and snobbery of Oscar Wilde's plays. His biggest bestseller was *The Green Hat*, a slightly racy novel which waxed mawkish about the sad fate of the naughty flapper who was its heroine, and thus achieved the reputation of being a profoundly immoral book. The supernatural stories intermingled with mundane materials in *These Charming People* and *May Fair* are set in exactly the same milieu as *The Green Hat*, detailing the uneasy predicament of a very particular social class, whose members were trying—desperately but hopelessly—to recover the gaiety and calculated decadence of the 1890s. In much the same way that their real-world equivalents could never entirely escape the memory and legacy of the Great War, Arlen's characters constantly encounter discomfiting reminders of the various kinds of nastiness they are trying so hard to forget. In such tales as "The Ancient Sin" the nastiness is sudden and brutal, but the dutifully formulaic haunted-house story "The Gentleman from America" is more typical of his method in delivering the message by a less direct route. The

hauntings in such stories are sometimes dissolved, but never disarmed, by apologetic rationalization.

The narrator of "The Ancient Sin"—who poses as a man relating an authentic anecdote—also features in "The Loquacious Lady of Lansdowne Passage" and "The Battle of Berkeley Square." The latter, which records a remarkable case of sympathetic pregnancy, was not reprinted in *Ghost Stories*. Nor was "The Revolting Doom of a Gentleman Who Would not Dance With His Wife," whose jocular title fails to conceal an equally uneasy contemplation of the burdens of matrimony. Their omission does not, however, result from scrupulousness of definition; "The Ghoul of Golders Green"—one of the two stories original to *Ghost Stories* and the longest of Arlen's weird tales—is certainly not a ghost story, although it addresses issues of uncomfortable sexuality which are essentially similar to those touched on in the omitted stories. "The Prince of the Jews," a tale of naked envy whose sexual symbolism cries out for Freudian decoding, is Arlen's most extreme, and perhaps most interesting, endeavour in this eccentrically risqué vein.

Hell! Said the Duchess may have been conceived as a similar tale but its inflation to novel length required a dramatic change of tone, its fundamental unease being buried under thick layers of contrived jocularity. This bizarre story invites interest today primarily as a pioneering exercise in the "slasher" genre, in that it features the exploits of a female serial killer—inevitably nicknamed Jane the Ripper—who takes delight in mutilating her victims. A bumbling detective suspects the beautiful Lady Dove, whose mildly hedonistic behaviour has generated a faint whiff of scandal, but contemporary readers who had read *The Green Hat* would have had no difficulty at all in identifying the true culprit; nor would such readers have been in the least surprised to discover the absurd motive behind the murders. The lubricious comedy with which this plot is fleshed out must, however, have seemed direly inappropriate to those same contemporary readers—although modern cinema-goers thoroughly educated to the notion that mass murder can be screamingly funny might be able to relate to it far better. The story was probably conceived as a parodic version of Arthur Machen's classic Decadent fantasy "The Great God Pan," with a casually satirical tilt at popular detective thrillers thrown in for good measure.

Arlen was a relentless borrower of other writers' ideas, although he was certainly not slavish in his use of them (*Man's Mortality*, a scientific romance admittedly based on Rudyard Kipling's "With the Night Mail" and "As Easy as A.B.C.," is so much more elaborate than its models that it easily ranks as his most interesting work). If he is compared to his models he seems conspicuously second-rate, but that is not the most interesting way to look at his work. What gives his fiction a distinct and peculiar edge is the viewpoint of his narrators, all of whom are trying with all their might to put into practice Oscar Wilde's advice that one should never speak disrespectfully of Society lest one should reveal oneself as a person who can't get into it.

Whenever they encounter something unpleasant the instinct of Arlen's heroes is to react forcefully, but they dare not; they must capitulate with the rules which define certain things as unchallengeable simply by establishing them as unmentionable. All disturbing supernatural encounters must be fitted into that category, even if they are only the result of error or delusion. The archetypal Arlen tale of the uncanny, with the title that best sums up his approach, is the second of the two tales original to *Ghost Stories*: "The Smell in the Library." The odour in question turns out not to be supernatural after all—probably not, at any rate—but it simply won't go away.

—Brian Stableford

ARTHUR, Robert (Andrew)

Pseudonyms: Andrew Fell, Anthony Morton, Jay Norman, John West, Mark Williams. **Nationality:** American. **Born:** Fort Mills, Corregidor Island, Philippines, 10 November 1909. **Education:** William and Mary College; University of Michigan. **Family:** Married the writer Joan Vatsek. **Career:** Editor, Munsey Publications, 1930-1934; editor, Street and Smith, Dell, and Fawcett, 1935-1941; producer and director, Mutual Broadcasting System; co-wrote and directed *The Mysterious Traveler* and *Adventure into Fear* radio series, 1943-1952; freelance writer. **Awards:** Edgar Allan Poe award for best radio drama, 1949 and 1952. He should not be confused with the movie producer Robert Arthur Feder, who used the alias "Robert Arthur" and also was born in 1909 but died in 1986. **Died:** 1 May 1969.

HORROR, GHOST AND GOTHIC PUBLICATIONS

Short Stories

Ghosts and More Ghosts. New York, Random House, 1963.

Other

Editor, *Davy Jones's Haunted Locker.* New York, Random House, 1965.
Editor, *Monster Mix.* New York, Dell Books, 1968.
Editor, *Thrillers and More Thrillers.* New York, Random House, 1968.

Other (as anonymous editor for Alfred Hitchcock)

Stories for Late at Night. New York, Random House, 1961; London, Reinhardt, 1962; in 2 vols. as *12 Stories for Late at Night*, New York, Dell, 1962, and *More Stories for Late at Night*, New York, Dell, 1962; as *Stories for Late at Night, Part One*, London, Pan, 1964, and *Stories for Late at Night, Part Two*, London, Pan, 1965.
Alfred Hitchcock's Haunted Houseful. New York, Random House, 1961; London, Reinhardt, 1962.
Alfred Hitchcock's Ghostly Gallery. New York, Random House, 1962; London, Reinhardt, 1966.
Stories My Mother Never Told Me. New York, Random House, 1963; London, Reinhardt, 1964; in 2 vols. as *Stories My Mother Never Told Me*, New York, Dell, 1966, and *More Stories My Mother Never Told Me*, New York, Dell, 1966; as *Stories My Mother Never Told Me, Part I*, London, Pan, 1966, and *Stories My Mother Never Told Me, Part II*, London, Pan, 1967.
Alfred Hitchcock's Monster Museum. New York, Random House, 1965; abridged edition, London, Collins, 1973; revised edition, Random House, 1982.
Alfred Hitchcock's Witches' Brew. New York, Dell, 1965; as *Alfred Hitchcock's Witch's Brew*, New York, Random House, 1977.

Stories Not for the Nervous. New York, Random House, 1965; London, Reinhardt, 1966; in 2 vols. as *Stories Not for the Nervous*, New York, Dell, 1966, and *More Stories Not for the Nervous*, New York, Dell, 1966; as *Stories Not for the Nervous, Book One*, London, Pan, 1968, and *Stories Not for the Nervous, Book Two*, London, Pan, 1969.
Stories That Scared Even Me. New York, Random House, 1967; London, Reinhardt, 1967; in 2 vols. as *Scream Along With Me*, New York, Dell, 1970, and *Slay Ride*, New York, Dell, 1971; as *Stories That Scared Even Me, Part One*, London, Pan, 1970, and *Stories That Scared Even Me, Part Two*, London, Pan, 1970.
Spellbinders in Suspense. New York, Random House, 1967; London, Reinhardt, 1972; abridged edition, Random House, 1982.
A Month of Mystery. New York, Random House, 1969; London, Reinhardt, 1970; in 2 vols. as *Dates With Death*, New York, Dell, 1972, and *Terror Time*, New York, Dell, 1972; as *A Month of Mystery, Book One*, London, Pan, 1972, and *A Month of Mystery, Book Two*, London, Pan, 1972.

OTHER PUBLICATIONS

Novels

The Case of the Murderous Mice. New York, Tower, 1933.
The Glass Bridge. New York, Scribner, 1958.
Somebody's Walking Over My Grave. New York, Ace, 1961.
The Mystery of the Man Who Evaporated. New York, Random House, 1963.
The Secret of Terror Castle. New York, Random House, 1964; London, Collins, 1967.
The Mystery of the Stuttering Parrot. New York, Random House, 1964; London, Collins, 1967.
The Mystery of the Whispering Mummy. New York, Random House, 1965; London, Collins, 1968.
The Mystery of the Green Ghost. New York, Random House, 1965; London, Collins, 1968.
The Mystery of the Vanishing Treasure. New York, Random House, 1966; London, Collins, 1968.
The Secret of Skeleton Island. New York, Random House, 1966; London, Collins, 1968.
The Mystery of the Fiery Eye. New York, Random House, 1967; London, Collins, 1969.
The Mystery of the Silver Spider. New York, Random House, 1967; London, Collins, 1969.
The Mystery of the Screaming Clock. New York, Random House, 1968; London, Collins, 1969.
The Mystery of the Talking Skull. New York, Random House, 1969; London, Collins, 1970.

Short Stories

Mystery and More Mystery. New York, Random House, 1966.

Other

Editor, *Spies and More Spies.* New York, Random House, 1967.

*   *   *

Robert Arthur moved in a number of genres, especially crime, mystery and science fiction as well as light fantasy and the macabre. Because he did much of his later work for radio, especially *The Mysterious Traveler* series, his published work is less readily available, much of it tucked away in pulp and slick magazines of the 1930s and 1940s and little of it published in book form. Towards the end of his life he became best known for a series of children's novels involving three teenagers who go on to form the Jupiter Jones detective agency. The popularity of the series resulted in it being continued after his death by other writers, some of whom, especially M. V. Carey, have made the books increasingly more bizarre, occasionally involving the supernatural. Arthur kept his books strictly in the rationalized mystery mode but he wasn't averse to introducing scenes of menace and mock-supernatural. The first in the series, *The Secret of Terror Castle*, had all the appropriate gothic trappings as the three investigators (by which name the series became known) search for an authentic haunted house. The series utilized the Alfred Hitchcock name as the introducer of each book and it consequently reflects the macabre quirkiness of Hitchcock's own predilections at which Arthur was adept.

Before channelling his creative energies towards the teenage readership, Arthur had specialized in the short story (and its equivalent half-hour radio script), with the emphasis on clever ideas, story-twists, and surprise (often shock) endings. In the realms of ghost and horror fiction his stories fall into two primary categories: the shock-horror story with a sharp twist, and the slick fantasy or ghost story, reminiscent of Lord Dunsany and Stephen Vincent Benét, some with frightening elements but often light-hearted.

His shock-horror stories were ideally suited to the sardonic vein of Alfred Hitchcock, with whom Arthur worked on a number of television shows as well as ghost-editing some of his anthologies. One of his most effective stories in this vein was "Footsteps Invisible" (*Argosy*, 1940) where an explorer and Egyptologist is haunted by an invisible demon and the sound of footsteps, the latter making it an ideal story for radio. Perhaps more typical of the dark humour in many of Arthur's stories is "The Jokester" (*Mysterious Traveler*, 1952). Bradley, who works in a morgue, is something of a practical jokester and frightens his elderly assistant by pretending to be one of the corpses and coming alive. Later Bradley is killed in a bar brawl, though his consciousness remains alive. However he finds it impossible to influence his dead body and ends up locked in the morgue.

Arthur's best stories in this category are his psychological thrillers, which often turn upon an issue of possession, either psychically or through a mental affliction. "Death is a Dream" (*Alfred Hitchcock's Mystery Magazine*, 1957) tells of a man with a split personality whose *alter ego* exists only in his dreams. A psychiatrist seeks to cure him but succeeds only in demonstrating that the *alter ego* really exists. A similar mood prevails in ". . . Said Jack the Ripper" (*Alfred Hitchcock's Mystery Magazine*, 1957) where the proprietor of a Chamber of Horrors museum becomes possessed by the waxworks and repeats their crimes. Arthur had used a parallel theme in "The Knife" (*Mysterious Traveler*, 1951), where the knife of Jack the Ripper takes control of its new owners and continues to murder, "The Vengeful Pearls of Madame Podaire" (*Argosy*, 1940), where the pearl necklace of an Haitian witch throttles its wearer, and "The Mirror of Cagliostro" (*Fantastic*, 1963), where the mirror of the medieval magician continues to exert an influence through the centuries.

Arthur's lighter fantasies are seldom so menacing, and though they can occasionally cause a shudder, their main purpose is to amuse and fascinate. His best stories are those narrated by

Murchison Morks, which are similar to Lord Dunsany's Joseph Jorkens series. The first of these was "Postmarked for Paradise" (*Argosy*, 1940; also known as "Postpaid to Paradise") in which a rare stamp becomes a passport to El Dorado. Others include "Wilfred Weem, Dreamer" (*Argosy*, 1941; also known as "Just a Dreamer") in which everything Weem dreams comes into existence while he sleeps, and its counterpart "Obstinate Uncle Otis" (*Argosy*, 1941), where Morks's uncle becomes so stubborn, following an accident, that anything he chooses not to believe in ceases to exist. Many of Arthur's fantasies are wish-fulfilment, almost the mirror image of his horror stories where he seeks release rather than entrapment. "The Flying Eye" (*Argosy*, 1940) tells of a camera which captures on film the desires of the model, not their real image. In "The Wall" (*Unknown*, 1942) a prisoner on death row is able to paint a doorway in his cell through which he can escape. However in "Gateway" (*Unknown*, 1940) one of life's losers is allowed the choice of staying in this world or entering another, but cannot make up his mind. Generally, Arthur's protagonists succeed in mastering their occasional powers, and his best story in this vein is "Satan and Sam Shay" (*Elk's Magazine*, 1942), a delightful fantasy in which the devil tries to get his own powers back on Sam who beat him three times in a bet. This is probably Arthur's most successful story.

Although Arthur liked to dabble with the supernatural in his fiction he wrote very few genuine ghost stories, which makes it all the more surprising that his one collection of fantasies is entitled *Ghosts and More Ghosts*. "The Haunted Trailer" (originally "Death Thumbs a Ride," *Weird Tales*, 1942) where a caravan becomes haunted by a party of tramps, is his most effective ghost tale. Here Arthur manages to balance very successfully the heightened atmosphere of the ghost story alongside his lighter vein of standard characters.

Most of Arthur's stories are clever but slight, the kind that you read as an aperitif rather than the main course. When he chose he was adept at convincing psychological insight and when he combined this with a first-person narrative he could produce some startling shock stories. Generally, though, he preferred the idea-story with the twist ending which worked well on radio and was fun to read but soon forgotten.

—Mike Ashley

ASQUITH, (Lady) Cynthia

Nationality: British. **Born:** Mary Evelyn Charteris, in Wiltshire, 27 September 1887. **Family:** Married Herbert Asquith in 1910. **Career:** Private secretary to the playwright J. M. Barrie, 1918-37. **Died:** 31 March 1960.

HORROR, GHOST AND GOTHIC PUBLICATIONS

Short Stories

This Mortal Coil. Sauk City, Wisconsin, Arkham House, 1947; revised as *What Dreams May Come*, London, Barrie, 1951.

Other

Editor, *The Ghost Book.* London, Hutchinson, and New York, Scribner, 1927.

Editor, *The Black Cap*. New York, Scribner, and London, Hutchinson, 1928.
Editor, *Shudders*. New York, Scribner, and London, Hutchinson, 1929.
Editor, *When Churchyards Yawn*. London, Hutchinson, 1931.
Editor (anonymously), *My Grimmest Nightmare*. London, Allen and Unwin, 1935.
Editor, *The Second Ghost Book*. London, Barrie, 1952.
Editor, *The Third Ghost Book*. London, Barrie, 1956.

*   *   *

There is a quietness and a restraint characterizing Cynthia Asquith's small output of stories. "God Grante That She Lye Stille" is probably the best known, having been often anthologized. These are mostly ghost stories, all supernatural except for "The Lovely Voice," and they contain almost no horror elements. Her ghosts are disagreeable, even dangerous, and one of her supernatural beings is Death himself, in "The Follower," yet there is no terror. She mentions the word in that story; she even has its protagonist die of fear (as do other characters, in other stories), but she is throughout too well bred to make the reader feel terror.

Dreams, nightmares and disturbed sleep are a continuing theme. In "Who is Sylvia?", dream and reality are confused in Susan Small's frantic letters. Lionel Furze, the protagonist of "From What Beginnings?", is bothered by a recurring dream of a man he abuses for no good reason. Felicity, in "In a Nutshell," relives, in almost nightly nightmares, the moment when her awkwardness led to her husband's death; she is dogged by guilt. Her son, Roy, tells her: "Dreams are often the result of someone else thinking very intently about you—very often someone dead." In "The White Moth," Joyce Legge, the young woman who is an overnight poetic success and is extremely embarrassed by the whole business, is afraid to go to sleep for fear of producing more poems through automatic writing. In "God Grante That She Lye Stille," it is Margaret Clewer, a young woman of 22 and last of the family line, who is terrified of sleeping in case her ancestor, Elspeth Clewer, should take over her body.

Because these stories were written during the 1930s and 1940s and reflect that era (or even a slightly earlier decade), they seem old-fashioned today. The dialogue and relationships tend to be very formal. The reasonably well-off characters all have servants, so that maids, gardeners and chauffeurs are frequently mentioned. This is reminiscent of the stories of E. F. Benson and H. Russell Wakefield, many of which have the same rather dated feel. Only occasional references, such as travelling by the London Underground system in "The White Moth," have much relevance to today.

Asquith's settings are, at least in her longer stories, well described with considerable atmosphere, though a good proportion are large country houses. All of the settings are English except in the case of "The Lovely Voice," set in a French hotel at the edge of a forest. She brings in a number of different professions very convincingly, including acting, nursing (in several stories) and publishing. The majority of the stories employ female narrators, and their emotions are strikingly put across. Yet she is an accomplished narrator from the male point of view, too, as in "God Grante That She Lye Stille," where the young woman's doctor tells the story, and in "The Corner Shop." The stories are well rounded. The prose is polished and allusive without ever requiring the reader to stop and think.

Indeed, her stories are generally rather too straightforward. The plots rarely hold any surprises, because she tends to put in too many injudicious clues early on. For example, Mrs. Deane's visitor in "The Follower" is obviously not the psychoanalyst she is expecting; he is clearly wearing a mask to prevent her from recognizing him, and not for the reason given. Again, in "The Corner Shop," only the narrator seems unable to spot that the old man with such cold hands must be dead. And in "The Lovely Voice" Asquith makes it clear from the start that beautiful people can commit murder. She could have done with a little of the subtlety of Walter de la Mare or Robert Aickman, and perhaps if she had written longer supernatural material she would have made it more subtle.

In the telling, Asquith often uses the device of a tale told to the narrator. This was a popular approach of the period, and it generally succeeds in her stories, though in "Who is Sylvia?" it is done as just two letters from Susan to Joan, describing a long period of time and various changing emotions; a longer series of shorter letters or else a different approach would have been advisable.

One of her favourite plot devices is coincidence, especially history repeating itself. In "From What Beginnings" it is an astonishing coincidence that both the patient and his surgeon should have come to this country from Geelong in Australia. In "One Grave Too Few" we have the recurrent deaths of pregnant women from fear at Greystock Manor. In "The Playfellow," Claud Halyard has already lost his niece Daphne (aged ten) in a fire at Lichen Hall, and now his daughter Hyacinth (also ten and very similar in looks) is threatened by another fire at the house. Once again he is ineffective in his rescue efforts. This plot is repeated in "In a Nutshell," when Felicity, having failed to prevent her husband dying of a heart attack, later fails to prevent her son going the same way.

Almost all of Asquith's characters are passive. Events happen to them while they watch and react. None of them seem to be in control of their surroundings.

Asquith was probably more important to the field of supernatural fiction as an anthologist than as a writer. During the 1930s she prised good new stories out of some of the best writers of the period. L. P. Hartley, Algernon Blackwood, Arthur Machen, Walter de la Mare and Elizabeth Bowen are all represented in her anthologies. Indeed, Hartley was particularly grateful to her for the help she gave him; he dedicated his collection of horror tales *The Travelling Grave* to her. She tended to include a story of her own in each of her anthologies. In *The Ghost Book* her story "The Corner Shop" appears as by C. L. Ray, the only time she used a pseudonym for fiction.

—Chris Morgan

ATHERTON, Gertrude (Franklin)

Pseudonym: Frank Lin. **Nationality:** American. **Born:** Gertrude Horn in San Francisco, California, 30 October 1857. **Education:** Private schools in California and Kentucky. **Family:** Married George H. Bowen Atherton in 1876 (died 1887). After 1887 travelled extensively and lived in Europe; in later life returned to San Francisco. Trustee, San Francisco Public Library; member, San Francisco Art Commission. President, American National Academy of Literature, 1934; chair of letters, League of American Pen

Women, 1939; president, Northern California Section of P.E.N. **Awards:** International Academy of Letters and Sciences of Italy Gold Medal. D.Litt: Mills College, Oakland, California, 1935; LL.D.: University of California, Berkeley, 1937. Chevalier, Legion of Honor, 1925; honorary member, Institut Litteraire et Artistique de France. **Died:** 14 June 1948.

HORROR, GHOST AND GOTHIC PUBLICATIONS

Novel

Black Oxen. New York, Boni and Liveright, and London, Murray, 1923.

Short Stories

The Bell in the Fog and Other Stories. New York, Harper, and London, Macmillan, 1905.
The Foghorn. Boston, Houghton Mifflin, 1934; London, Jarrolds, 1935.

OTHER PUBLICATIONS

Novels

What Dreams May Come (as Frank Lin). Chicago, Belford Clarke, 1888; as Gertrude Atherton, London, Routledge, 1889.
Hermia Suydam. New York, Current Literature, 1889; as *Hermia, An American Woman*, London, Routledge, 1889.
Los Cerritos: A Romance of the Modern Times. New York, Lovell, 1890; London, Heinemann, 1891.
A Question of Time (includes *Mrs. Pendleton's Four-in-Hand*). New York, Lovell, 1891; London, Gay and Bird, 1902.
The Doomswoman. New York, Tait, 1893; London, Hutchinson, 1895.
A Whirl Asunder. New York, Stokes, and London, Cassell, 1895.
His Fortunate Grace. New York, Appleton and London, Bliss Sands, 1897.
Patience Sparhawk and Her Times. London and New York, Lane, 1897.
American Wives and English Husbands. New York, Dodd Mead, and London, Service and Paton, 1898; revised edition, as *Transplanted*, Dodd Mead, 1919.
The Californians. London and New York, Lane, 1898.
The Valiant Runaways. New York, Dodd Mead, 1898; London, Nisbet, 1899.
A Daughter of the Vine. New York, Lane, and London, Service and Paton, 1899.
Senator North. New York and London, Lane, 1900.
The Aristocrats, Being the Impressions of Lady Helen Pole During Her Sojourn in the Great North Woods. New York and London, Lane, 1901.
The Conqueror, Being the True and Romantic Story of Alexander Hamilton. New York and London, Macmillan, 1902.
Heart of Hyacinth. New York, Harper, 1903.
Rulers of Kings. New York, Harper, and London, Macmillan, 1904.
The Travelling Thirds. New York and London, Harper, 1905.
Rezanov. New York, Authors and Newspapers Association, and London, Murray, 1906.

Ancestors. New York, Harper, and London, Murray, 1907.
The Gorgeous Isle: A Romance: Scene, Nevis, B.W.I., 1842. New York, Doubleday, and London, Murray, 1908.
Tower of Ivory. New York, Macmillan, and London, Murray, 1910.
Julia France and Her Times. New York, Macmillan, and London, Murray, 1912.
Perch of the Devil. New York, Stokes, and London, Murray, 1914.
Mrs. Balfame. New York, Stokes, and London, Murray, 1916.
The White Morning: A Novel of the Power of the German Women in Wartime. New York, Stokes, 1918.
The Avalanche: A Mystery Story. New York, Stokes, and London, Murray, 1919.
The Sisters-in-Law: A Novel of Our Time. New York, Stokes, and London, Murray, 1921.
Sleeping Fires. New York, Stokes, 1922; as *Dormant Fires*, London, Murray, 1922.
The Crystal Cup. New York, Boni and Liveright, and London, Murray, 1925.
The Immortal Marriage. New York, Boni and Liveright, and London, Murray, 1927.
The Jealous Gods: A Processional Novel of the Fifth Century B.C. (Concerning One Alcibiades). New York, Liveright, 1928; as *Vengeful Gods*, London, Murray, 1928.
Dido, Queen of Hearts. London, Chapman and Hall, 1929.
The Sophisticates. New York, Liveright, and London, Chapman and Hall, 1931.
Golden Peacock. Boston, Houghton Mifflin, 1936; London, Butterworth, 1937.
Rezanov and Dona Concha. New York, Stokes, 1937.
The House of Lee. New York, Appleton Century, 1940; London, Eyre and Spottiswoode, 1942.
The Horn of Life. New York, Appleton Century, 1942.

Short Stories

Before the Gringo Came. New York, Tait, 1894; revised edition, as *The Splendid Idle Forties: Stories of Old California*, New York and London, Macmillan, 1902.

Plays

Screenplay: *Don't Neglect Your Wife*, with Louis Sherwin, 1921.

Other

California: An Intimate History. New York, Harper, 1914; revised edition, New York, Boni and Liveright, 1927.
Life in the War Zone. New York, System Printing, 1916.
The Living Present (essays). New York, Stokes, and London, Murray, 1917.
Adventures of a Novelist. New York, Liveright, and London, Cape, 1932.
Can Women Be Gentlemen? Boston, Houghton Mifflin, 1938.
Golden Gate Country. New York, Duell, 1945.
My San Francisco: A Wayward Biography. Indianapolis, Bobbs Merrill, 1946.

Editor, *A Few of Hamilton's Letters, Including His Description of the Great West Indian Hurricane of 1772.* New York, Macmillan, 1903.

*

Film Adaptation: *Black Oxen*, 1924.

Bibliography: "A Checklist of the Writings of and about Gertrude Atherton" by Charlotte S. McClure, in *American Literary Realism* 1870-1910, Spring 1976.

Critical Studies: *Gertrude Atherton* by Joseph Henry Jackson, New York, Appleton Century, 1940; *Gertrude Atherton*, Boise, Idaho, Boise State University, 1976, and *Gertrude Atherton*, Boston, Twayne, 1979, both by Charlotte S. McClure.

*   *   *

Gertrude Atherton was a prolific novelist, highly regarded in her day. Like her contemporaries Henry James and Edith Wharton she was prepared to dabble in weird fiction for the sake of dramatizing the burdensome nature of certain legacies carried over from the past into the present, and for metaphysical speculation of an earnest and painstakingly refined variety.

Atherton's earliest supernatural story, "Death and the Woman," was initially published in *Vanity Fair* in 1892. A loyal and dutiful wife waiting by her husband's deathbed hears the footsteps of Death approaching and throws herself into the dying man's arms so that she may be carried way with him. Almost as relentlessly Victorian is "The Striding Place" (1896)—an oft-anthologized story reprinted in both the above-cited collections—in which a man hypothesizes that although the soul must usually linger in the body after death, were he to "dissever" himself too quickly when his own time comes he would surely yield to the temptation of hastening to investigate the mysteries of space. When his body is recovered after drowning it is faceless, although the singularity of the instance would surely make it insufficient to constitute any kind of proof of his theory.

The more effective stories in *The Bell in the Fog* are "Death and the Countess" and the title story. "Death and the Countess" concerns a hapless priest who can hear the spirits of the dead—still attendant upon their buried bodies—lamenting their fate in the local cemetery. The incredibility of this testimony prevents his being believed when he further testifies that he has also heard the far less eloquent agony of a woman buried alive. "The Bell in the Fog" concerns a wealthy American who buys an English stately home and becomes fascinated by the portrait of a young girl which hangs in a gallery there. He writes what he imagines to be her story but subsequently finds that he has been misled; then he becomes convinced that he has rediscovered her in the person of an actual child living on the estate—who believes, correctly, that she too is doomed to die young. The moral of the story appears to be that although Americans may buy English estates they can never reclaim the heritage that goes with them.

The theme of "The Bell and the Fog" is further expanded in the novella "The Eternal Now," which is longer than the other three items in *The Foghorn* put together. Here the wealthy American has a French name, Simon de Brienne, and he becomes fascinated by the life of a similarly-named ancestor who lived in the 14th century. In pursuit of this fascination he hosts a costume ball, requiring the guests to masquerade as inhabitants of the year 1358. The ball provides him with the bridge to the past which he has so ardently desired, but he finds himself on the wrong side in a political struggle and is condemned to die by being lowered into an iron pot full of boiling oil. By way of preparation de Brienne is forced to watch his friend subjected to the same ordeal—which instantly reduces the unlucky man to the status of a "mindless primitive"—and the story ends with a brief ironic reflection on the fatuity of believing that all of history is contained within a single Eternal Moment. The novella was probably inspired by Henry James's incomplete novel *The Sense of the Past* (1917), in which Atherton had presumably seen the strong influence of "The Bell in the Fog," and the cruel ending might be read as a sly admonition to the older writer.

Black Oxen also recovers a motif from "The Bell in the Fog," but handles it very differently. A New York socialite and newspaper columnist becomes fascinated by a beautiful woman who is the living image of Mary Ogden, a society belle transplanted to Europe 30 years before following her marriage to a Hungarian count. The protagonist pursues his fascination with an assiduity which combines love-sickness with the dogged determination expected of an American newshound, but when he asks her to marry him it is she who insists that he must know the truth about her. She *is* May Ogden, rejuvenated in Vienna by the effect of X-rays on her endocrine glands—a revelation which naturally results in her ostracism by the vain but aging *doyennes* of New York society and eventually sends her back to the waiting arms of another European nobleman. Mrs. Atherton was in her mid-60s when she wrote it, and might conceivably have read Marie Corelli's intensely self-indulgent romance of rejuvenation *The Young Diana* (1918), written when Miss Corelli was 63 (although she only admitted to 55), but if the novel is an ironic reply cast in the same mould as "The Eternal Now" it certainly keeps its tongue-in-cheek quality well hidden.

Atherton had insufficient interest in the morbid and the peculiar to be a first-rate writer of supernatural fiction. Her work in that vein is studiously recherché, its horrific quality always compromised by calculatedly jarring notes. Even "Death and the Countess" is lightened—and weakened—by the introduction of a railway whose hooting trains are mistaken by the entombed dead for the last trump. If her work in this vein was intended as mockery it is far too subtle; if not, it is not nearly earnest enough. If, however—as seems more than likely—she could never quite make up her mind exactly what she intended or wanted to do, she might be reckoned to have recorded that awkward hesitation with perfect accuracy.

—Brian Stableford

ATKINS, Peter

Nationality: British. **Born:** Liverpool, 1955. **Career:** Actor and musician; freelance screenwriter and novelist from 1987. Lives in Los Angeles, California.

HORROR, GHOST AND GOTHIC PUBLICATIONS

Novel

Morningstar, or The Vampires of Summer. London, HarperCollins, 1992.
Big Thunder. London, HarperCollins, 1997.

Plays

Screenplays: *Hellbound: Hellraiser II*, 1988; *Hell on Earth: Hellraiser III*, 1992; *Fist of the North Star*, 1995; *Hellraiser: Bloodline*, 1996.

Other

The Hellraiser Chronicles, with Clive Barker and Stephen Jones. London, Titan, 1992.

*   *   *

Even when he is not writing a screenplay, Atkins uses a style which is extremely filmic, full of detailed close-ups, fast-moving action and jump cuts between scenes.

Morningstar combines supernatural and non-supernatural horror. It is both more and less than a novel about killing vampires. Morningstar, also known as the Matador, also known as Jonathan Frost, is a respected and successful businessman in contemporary San Francisco. But this is just a cover for his mission in life: to seek out and kill vampires all over the world. In a 30-year period he has staked some 300 of them. This would seem to be a laudable vocation, yet throughout the novel Frost is portrayed as the bad guy, as the killer without mercy or a soul. And it is Frost who is himself killed, in a swift but very unpleasant manner, in the novel's over-the-top finale.

The Morningstar soubriquet comes from the fact that this word is found written in blood and excrement next to the remains of each victim. It makes the San Francisco authorities believe that they have a serial killer at work in their city—though they know that each victim has also been staked. But Frost thinks of himself as the Matador, making his kills by (normally) luring the vampires one by one to his penthouse suite and there engaging them in hand-to-hand combat, slashing them with a knife until they bleed and blunder around bull-like. And it is under his real name of Jonathan Frost that he contacts a journalist and relates his story.

The journalist, who is young, struggling and not well known, yet capable of writing prose as purple as anybody else in the city, is Dovovan Noon. It is he alone to whom Frost unburdens himself. The bargain is that Noon is allowed to write and sell the story only once Frost is dead, so that somebody else will be inspired to take up Frost's mission of killing vampires.

Frost's story is that he is British, born in Liverpool during World War II and raised there and on a cousin's farm in North Wales. One night, when he is 18, he watches his cousin's daughter, the beautiful 16-year-old Laura (whom he lusts after), having sex with a swarthy young man. During sex, the young man bites Laura's neck and she bleeds heavily and apparently dies. Jonathan and the farmer chase the young man. In a bizarre scene, the young man stabs the farmer to death and Jonathan pierces the young man through the neck with a stake. Back at the farmhouse, Jonathan finds Laura seemingly still alive, but he is convinced that she is a vampire and, with one swing of the spade he just happens to be holding, he cuts off her head. So begins his anti-vampire crusade.

The vampires that he has killed have been old and young, rich and poor, black and white. They have not been bothered in the least by sunlight or crosses or garlic, but a stake through the heart and the spilling of most of their blood has stopped them rising from the dead. Frost is sure of himself, and he even demonstrates the killing of a vampire to Noon, beginning with a knife-slash which cuts away the vampire's top lip, displaying the typical vampiric fangs. But this is the only evidence the reader, or Noon, is offered.

If Frost is shown as the bad guy and Noon as the independent observer, the side of good is personified in Shelley Masterton, a typical Jewish young woman living in San Francisco. Her best friend Chris Tempest has been one of the Morningstar victims, not because she was a vampire but because she saw Frost at work. Chris returns, contacting Shelley via dreams and plotting an involved scheme of revenge. Shelley and the teenage son of another Morningstar victim have sex, calling into being a woman who might well be the goddess Astarte. In any case, this unnamed woman has godlike powers and, besides conjuring up a thunderstorn and an earthquake, pulls down a star from the sky and burns all the flesh off Frost's head.

Atkins is a talented writer, capable of lyrical passages and graphic horror, and the novel itself is probably ideal for being turned into an empty-headed Hollywood movie, being stuffed with over-the-top scenes and wisecracking dialogue. As a novel, it has two major drawbacks, besides being a stylistic pot-pourri. One is that it is completely implausible throughout. The other is that Atkins seems to go out of his way to build up minor characters, showing the reader too many scenes which have no relevance to the main thrust of the plot. And the corollary of this is that he fails to come to terms with the fascinating nub of his story: is Frost actually killing vampires or is he a deluded psychotic who believes he sees vampires about him? Besides lacking the necessary philosophical depth, this novel fails to bring its characters to life and, especially, to make the reader care about them.

In the same vein is Atkins's first published story, "Here Comes a Candle," in *Fear* for November-December 1988. It tries to make a point about the necessity for nursery rhymes to retain their raw, frightening qualities, and it does so with the reformist protagonist finding his wife's disembodied head fastened to the wall and dripping blood, while the protagonist himself is attacked by an axe-wielding dwarf. Now that's the way to make a point! Another of his stories is "Aviatrix," a cleverly written fear-of-flying piece which combines an international flight, a recurrent dream about flying in an open biplane with a female pilot and, predictably, the crashing of an airliner. Atkins has also written comic-book scripts.

—Chris Morgan

AYCLIFFE, Jonathan

Pseudonym for Dennis MacEoin. **Other Pseudonym:** Daniel Easterman. **Nationality:** British. **Born:** Belfast, 26 January 1949. **Education:** Royal Belfast Academical Institution; Trinity College, Dublin, MA in English Literature, 1971; University of Edinburgh, MA in Persian and Arabic, 1975; King's College, Cambridge, PhD in Persian studies, 1979. **Family:** Married Beth MacEoin. **Career:** Lecturer, University of Fez, Morocco, 1979-80; lecturer in Islamic Studies, University of Newcastle, 1981-86; honorary fellow, Centre for Middle East and Islamic Studies, Durham University; freelance writer since 1986. **Address:** c/o HarperCollins Publishers, 77-85 Fulham Palace Road, London W6 8JB, England.

HORROR, GHOST AND GOTHIC PUBLICATIONS

Novels

Naomi's Room. London, HarperCollins, 1991.
Whispers in the Dark. London, HarperCollins, 1992.

The Vanishment. London, HarperCollins, 1993.
The Matrix. London, HarperCollins, 1994.
The Lost. London, HarperCollins, and New York, HarperPrism, 1996.

OTHER PUBLICATIONS

Novels as Daniel Easterman

The Last Assassin. London, Hodder and Stoughton, and New York, Doubleday, 1984.
The Seventh Sanctuary. London, Grafton, and New York, Doubleday, 1987.
The Ninth Buddha. London, Grafton, 1988; New York, Doubleday, 1989.
Brotherhood of the Tomb. London, Grafton, 1989; New York, Doubleday, 1990.
Night of the Seventh Darkness. London, HarperCollins, 1991.
Name of the Beast. London, HarperCollins, 1992.
The Judas Testament. London, HarperCollins, 1994.
Day of Wrath. London, HarperCollins, 1995.
The Last Judgement. London, HarperCollins, 1996.

Other as Dennis MacEoin

Islam in the Modern World, with Ahmad al-Shahi. N.p., n.d.
The Sources for Early Basic Doctrine and History. N.p., n.d.
A People Apart: The Baha'i Community of Iran in the Twentieth Century. N.p., n.d.
New Jerusalems: Reflections on Islam, Fundamentalism and the Rushdie Affair (as Daniel Easterman). London, Grafton, 1992.

*   *   *

Jonathan Aycliffe is the lesser-known pseudonym of the academic Dennis MacEoin, who has published a string of bestsellers as Daniel Easterman; these latter books could be regarded as the thinking person's airport thrillers, since in general they are charged with a vigorous imagination and a sense that they are trying to convey more than is visible on the surface. Indeed, some of them like *Day of Wrath*, which is concerned with terrorism, and *The Judas Testament*, in which an original manuscript by Christ is discovered and reveals him to be no loving prophet of peace, could be regarded as of sideline horror interest, in that Easterman is not afraid to confront the human nightmare: brutality, its consequences and importantly its origins in greed or bigotry.

The Aycliffe books are all much shorter than the Easterman ones, but in their own way are even harder-hitting in their depiction of the human condition, although here the concentration is on other psychological states, notably guilt. One has the feeling that they were designed to be read in a sitting, and certainly it is hard to read them otherwise, because they are very difficult to put down: Aycliffe is adept at creating a dramatic sense of atmosphere, accumulating his effects in such a fashion that even the smallest detail may convey a profound chill. Furthermore, they differ from most entertainments of their kind in that there is generally no typical resolution: Aycliffe's protagonists usually stare into the jaws of Hell, advance with seeming reluctance towards the nightmare landscape, and are at the last seen stepping with either willingness or trepidation into it.

The earlier novels comprise a recreation of the British ghost story in the tradition of M. R. James. *Naomi's Room* has as its protagonist the father of a child, Naomi, whom he lost track of in the crowds of the famous London toy-store Hamleys. Later she was discovered murdered. Then she returns, as a ghost, to share his home, occupying the attic. In this book the expression of guilt is the most extreme for, not only is the father certain that in a sense he was the murderer, he feels additional guilt because the child he once loved above all else now repels and terrifies him. Then he discovers that the house is possessed (as he himself becomes) by a figure who is probably Jack the Ripper, and contains other ghosts. Finally he finds himself driven to perform vile acts of rape and murder. The book is undoubtedly flawed (there are plot hiccups, as if Aycliffe changed his mind about its direction as he was writing), but it is certainly powerful.

In *Whispers in the Dark* Aycliffe adopts a traditional strategy. The novel starts with a letter from one contemporary character to another saying that he's discovered a hellish memoir, which he is forwarding herewith, and finishes with the addressee writing back to say that he has read the journal (there is also a journal within the journal) and discovered that the evil lives on: "I'll see you in a few days, John. In the meantime, please do something for me. Keep your bedroom door locked at night. Tightly." The bulk of the book comprises the memoir of Charlotte Metcalf who was born into a well-to-do family but who, on the death of her father, was plunged into the workhouse and all its cruelties, then evicted from there into a world that possessed only emptiness. As she tries to seek out her remaining family members, her mother and her brother, she discovers all the pains of persecution. Some of this is at the hands of spectral beings, but very much more terrifying is the historically accurate depiction of the sins human beings could commit upon each other in what is often regarded as the golden period of Queen Victoria's final glorious years. This is an excellent ghost story; it is also an excellent and perceptive novel. Again the theme of guilt appears: the multiply-abused Metcalf, as an old woman, still cannot entirely shake herself free of the nonsensical conviction that she was responsible for her own sufferings.

The Vanishment is a contemporary novel. Writer Peter Clare and artist Sarah Clare, their marriage on the rocks, rent the remote Petherick House high on a cliff in Cornwall, hoping to sort things out. The locals make gloomy remarks about the house, as locals do in ghost stories, but the Clares have no time for such superstitions. Soon, however, Sarah vanishes. . . . The rest is a confection of haunting, possession and ancient evils some of which prove to be not so ancient, because we discover that Peter became a writer only after his release from a prison term served for, in madness, killing his own daughter. Once again Aycliffe handles his effects with skill, playing tricks with the reader's perceptions: none of his narrators can be trusted to reveal the whole truth about themselves except gradually.

The Matrix is a less approachable book. Set in Scotland, it sees the widower Andrew Macleod take up an academic post at Edinburgh University, where he carries out research into the ideas and rituals of magic. Unfortunately, he begins to lose his scholarly distancing from his subject matter and falls under the spell of a sort of Scottish Aleister Crowley (who in fact did live in Scotland for a while). Although it is to be admired for its scholarship, *The Matrix* somehow lacks the frissons one expects from Aycliffe.

The Lost is a bit different, since it relates less to M. R. James than to Bram Stoker. The style is epistolary, very much as was

Stoker's *Dracula*, although much more readably so; it is revealed to us that none of the characters is quite (or at all) whom the others thinks s/he is. Throughout Aycliffe's work, it is hard to find such a personage as a totally trustworthy narrator. Young Michael Feraru, a Briton of Romanian descent, goes to post-Communist Romania to reclaim his family's property, and discovers he is owner of not only Castel Vlaicu but also a horrific family tradition: the Vlahuta, never truly die, instead continuing to exist as soul-eaters (*strigo*). . . . The most fascinating part of this sometimes confused book is the way in which Aycliffe studies the changing personality of his central character, who evolves from a simple prep-school master to become a quite ruthless Romanian aristocrat. He has an affair with his Romanian lawyer, never realizing that she does not love him but just likes having sex with him; in the end he betrays her in a most vile way, continuing the Vlahuta family habit. There are many scarinesses but also pathos as we watch him head towards his spiritual doom, which he regards, in his altered state, as a triumph.

The Aycliffe books, despite their intense readability, present us with a challenge: scary entertainments they might be, viewed on one level, but they also require us to re-evaluate ourselves.

—John Grant

B

BAKER, Denys Val

Pseudonym: David Eames. **Nationality:** British. **Born:** Poppleton, Yorkshire, 24 October 1917. **Education:** A boarding school in Sussex. **Family:** Married Jess Margaret Bryan in 1948; two sons and four daughters. **Career:** Journalist, 1935-41; freelance writer from 1941; editor and publisher, *The Cornish Review*, 1949-53 (revived in the 1960s); proprietor, St. Hilary Pottery, Cornwall. Lived in various homes in Cornwall for most of his career. **Died:** July 1984.

HORROR, GHOST AND GOTHIC PUBLICATIONS

Short Stories

Worlds without End. London, Sylvan Press, 1945.
The Return of Uncle Walter. London, Sampson Low, 1948.
The Strange and the Damned. New York, Pyramid, 1964; London, Brown Watson, 1966.
Strange Journeys. New York, Pyramid, 1969.
The Face in the Mirror. Sauk City, Wisconsin, Arkham House, 1971.
The Secret Place and Other Cornish Stories. London, Kimber, 1977.
At the Sea's Edge and Other Stories. London, Kimber, 1979.
The Girl in the Photograph and Other Stories. London, Kimber, 1982.
At the Rainbow's End and Other Stories. London, Kimber, 1983.
The Tenant and Other Stories. London, Kimber, 1985.

Other

Editor, *One and All.* London, Museum Press, 1951.
Editor, *Haunted Cornwall.* London, Kimber, 1973.
Editor, *Stories of the Macabre.* London, Kimber, 1976.
Editor, *Stories of the Night.* London, Kimber, 1976.
Editor, *Stories of Horror and Suspense.* London, Kimber, 1977.
Editor, *Stories of the Occult and Other Tales of Mystery.* London, Kimber, 1978.
Editor, *Stories of the Supernatural.* London, Kimber, 1979.
Editor, *Stories of Fear.* London, Kimber, 1980.
Editor, *Cornish Ghost Stories.* London, Kimber, 1981.
Editor, *Ghosts in Country Houses.* London, Kimber, 1981.
Editor, *When Churchyards Yawn.* London, Kimber, 1982.
Editor, *Ghosts in Country Villages.* London, Kimber, 1983.
Editor, *Stories of Haunted Inns.* London, Kimber, 1983.
Editor, *Phantom Lovers.* London, Kimber, 1984.
Editor, *Haunted Travellers.* London, Kimber, 1985.

OTHER PUBLICATIONS

Novels

The White Rock. London, Sylvan Press, 1945.
The More We Are Together. London, Sampson Low, 1947.
The Widening Mirror. London, Sampson Low, 1949; revised edition, as *Frances*, London, Kimber, 1985.
The Title's My Own (as David Eames). London, Bles, 1955.
As the River Flows. Aylesbury, Buckinghamshire, Milton House, 1974.
A Company of Three. Aylesbury, Buckinghamshire, Milton House, 1974.
Don't Lose Your Cool, Dad. Aylesbury, Buckinghamshire, Milton House, 1975.
Barbican's End: A Novel of Cornwall. London, Kimber, 1979.
Rose: A Novel of Cornwall. London, Kimber, 1980.
Karenza: A Novel of Cornwall. London, Kimber, 1980.
One Summer at St. Merry's. London, Kimber, 1984.

Short Stories

The Flame Swallower and Other Tales from Cornwall. London, Lake, 1963.
Bizarre Loves. London, Brown Watson, 1966.
The Woman and the Engine Driver. Zennor, Cornwall, United Writers, 1972.
A Summer to Remember: Cornish Stories. London, Kimber, 1975.
Echoes from the Cornish Cliffs. London, Kimber, 1976.
Passenger to Penzance and Other Stories from Cornwall. London, Kimber, 1978.
Thomasina's Island: A Novella of Cornwall and Other Short Stories. London, Kimber, 1981.
The House on the Creek and Other Stories of Cornwall. London, Kimber, 1981.
Martin's Cottage: A Novella of Cornwall and Other Stories. London, Kimber, 1983.
A Work of Art and Other Stories. London, Kimber, 1984.

Play

Cornwall for the Cornish. N.p., Porthmeor Press, 1964.

Other

Britain Discovers Herself. N.p., Johnson, 1950.
Paintings from Cornwall. N.p., Cornish Library, 1950.
How to be an Author. London, Harvill Press, 1952.
The Pottery Book, with Jess Val Baker. London, Cassell, 1959.
Britain's Art Colony by the Sea. N.p., Ronald, 1959.
How to be a Parent. London, Boardman, 1960.
The Minack Theatre. N.p., Ronald, 1960.
Pottery Today. Oxford, Oxford University Press, 1961.
The Sea's in the Kitchen. N.p., Phoenix House, 1962.
The Door is Always Open. N.p., Phoenix House, 1963.
Pottery for Profit and Pleasure (as David Eames). London, Museum Press, 1963.
The Young Potter. London, Kaye and Ward, 1963; as *Fun with Pottery,* 1975.
We'll Go Round the World Tomorrow. London, John Baker, 1965.
To Sea with Sanu. London, John Baker, 1967.
Adventures Before Fifty (omnibus). London, John Baker, 1969.
Life Up the Creek. London, John Baker, 1971.
The Petrified Mariner. London, Kimber, 1972.
An Old Mill by the Stream. London, Kimber, 1973.

Timeless Land: Creative Spirit in Cornwall. Bath, Adams and Dart, 1973.
Spring at Land's End. London, Kimber, 1974.
Sunset over the Scillies. London, Kimber, 1975.
A View from the Valley. London, Kimber, 1976.
The Wind Blows from the West. London, Kimber, 1977.
It's a Long Way to Land's End. London, Kimber, 1977.
All This and Cornwall Too. London, Kimber, 1978.
A Family for All Seasons. London, Kimber, 1979.
As the Stream Flows By. London, Kimber, 1980.
The Spirit of Cornwall. London, Allen, 1980.
A Family at Sea. London, Kimber, 1981.
Let's Make Pottery. London, Warne, 1981.
Upstream at the Mill. London, Kimber, 1981.
The Waterwheel Turns: A Retrospect. London, Kimber, 1982.
Summer at the Mill. London, Kimber, 1982.
Family Circles. London, Kimber, 1983.
Down a Cornish Lane. London, Kimber, 1983.
A Mill in the Valley. London, Kimber, 1984.
When Cornish Skies Are Smiling. London, Kimber, 1984.
My Cornish World. London, Kimber, 1985.
Cornish Prelude. London, Kimber, 1985.

Editor, *Writers of Today.* London, Sidgwick and Jackson, 1948.
Editor, *The Ways of Love.* London, New English Library, 1969.
Editor, *The Dreams of Love.* London, New English Library, 1969.
Editor, *Cornish Harvest.* London, Kimber, 1974.
Editor, *Stories of the Sea.* London, Kimber, 1974.
Editor, *Stories of Country Life.* London, Kimber, 1975.
Editor, *Cornish Short Stories.* London, Penguin, 1976.
Editor, *Personal Choices: An Anthology.* London, Kimber, 1977.
Editor, *Twelve Stories by Famous Women Writers.* London, Allen, 1978.
Editor, *Women Writing.* London, Allen, 1979.
Editor, *The Sea Survivors.* London, Allen, 1979.
Editor, *A View from Land's End: Writers Against a Cornish Background.* London, Kimber. 1982.
Editor, *Women Writing: An Anthology.* London, Sidgwick and Jackson, 1980.
Editor, *Something Special.* London, Crescent, 1986.

*

Critical Study: "Denys Val Baker" by Tim Scott, in *Book and Magazine Collector* (London) no. 78, September 1990.

*   *   *

Denys Val Baker was a prolific and versatile author, with about a hundred books published. He lived in western Cornwall for much of his life, and the county's landscape and people are very important to his fiction and non-fiction. In this respect he was following in the tradition of Sir Arthur Quiller-Couch and Daphne du Maurier, while the ghost-story writer Mary Williams was a close contemporary of his.

Quite a few of Val Baker's many short stories and novelettes contain at least slight supernatural elements. One problem is that his fiction is subtle, so that, as with Walter de la Mare or Robert Aickman, the reader is sometimes left wondering whether the effect suggested is meant to be supernatural or merely a subjective feeling. Another problem with Val Baker's supernatural stories is

that they are thinly spread throughout his many collections, right from the bizarre "Passenger to Liverpool" in his first collection, with only the Arkham House volume *The Face in the Mirror* making any attempt to bring them together.

In fact, "The Face in the Mirror" (also published as "A Strange Story") is a good place begin examining his fiction, because it is typically subtle, though leaning more towards horror than is general for him. On the surface it describes, in the first person, how a man who is having an afternoon shave in a barber's shop sees another man staring menacingly at him in the mirror, and is so disturbed that he leaves quickly and runs away through the shops and streets of the town. But wherever the narrator goes, the staring man—with sunken eyes, protruding teeth and a balding head—follows. At length the narrator attacks his pursuer and tries to throttle him. Waking in hospital with neck injuries, he finds that *he* is the ugly, balding man. The sense of blind panic is well conveyed; the narrator is so gripped by his need to escape that he never considers why the other man is pursuing him, nor does he think to call on the assistance of a policeman (despite bumping into one). Val Baker's intention is not to suggest some implausible fantasy scenario of exchanged personalities, but to demonstrate mental imbalance, the hysterical effects of paranoia.

Quite a few of Val Baker's stories feature ghosts, though these assume original forms. In "The Visitation" it is a ghost car which regularly drives one way through a small village. The car and its driver are seen differently by everyone. To Tilly, an ugly teenage girl, they represent some kind of hope, the only uplifting moment of her days. And the car is, indeed, the means of her escape: she runs out under its wheels and is killed, after which the car, which does not stop, is never seen again. In "The Haunting of Angela Prendergast," a youngish spinster comes to realize that something supernatural has become active in the "large rambling house" in which she lives. Far from being frightened, she welcomes its attentions, taking more care with her appearance and encouraging it to visit her in bed.

This leads on to a whole body of stories which are concerned with sexual obsession, and which Val Baker wrote throughout his life. Most of these stories do not concern us, but in some the obsession is so extreme that the explanation must be either a mental imbalance or a manifestation of the supernatural. The novelette "The Girl in the Photograph" shows how a middle-aged man (who moves with his wife to western Cornwall, so that he can paint) finds a photo of people who lived in their house, an old mill, over 60 years before and falls in love with one of them, a young woman. Clearly he is haunted by her face, though not in the supernatural sense. As he has a portion of the original photograph secretly enlarged and tries to discover more about her, his behaviour becomes more extreme and irrational. He tries to strangle his wife, and he comes to believe that the young woman is still out there and returns his love.

In the sharply bizarre story "Masks" a man and a woman, strangers to each other, try on a series of rubber masks he has bought, their apparent personas changing with each different face. The sexual obsession is there, but tinged with horror. Whereas in "The Girl" a teenage boy falls in love with a teenage girl who, with her parents, moves into a neighbouring house. He will not or cannot speak to her, but he watches. With each passing night he finds the courage to go further: looking through the window of her bedroom, entering her room to stand and admire, bending over her in bed, lying beside her, touching her breasts as she sleeps. The girl wakes and accepts him as a lover, but the only reasonable explanation is that he is a ghost.

Val Baker was a smooth and passably entertaining writer, though there is an old-fashioned ring to his later stories, with characters supposedly in the 1980s uttering dialogue straight out of the 1930s.

As an anthologist, Val Baker was prolific though unadventurous. Most of the volumes contain British ghost stories, particularly set in Cornwall and reprinting post-1950 stories, with one or two original tales per book.

—Chris Morgan

BAKER, Nancy

Nationality: Canadian. **Born:** 1959. **Career:** Journalist.

HORROR, GHOST AND GOTHIC PUBLICATIONS

Novels

The Night Inside. Toronto, Viking Canada, and New York, Fawcett Columbine, 1993; London, Signet Creed, 1995.
Blood and Chrysanthemums. Toronto, Viking Canada, and New York, Fawcett Columbine, 1994; London, Signet Creed, 1995.

*   *   *

Nancy Baker served her apprenticeship working on one of Canada's leading woman's magazines and her style shows great competence. Her books are contemporary vampire novels set in Canada. The first, *The Night Inside*, also has mystery and thriller elements.

Ardeth Alexander is a university research student of the blue-stocking variety—dependable and unadventurous. She and two others have been doing some, apparently unconnected, research for a corporation by the name of Armitage. It seems a coincidence that one of them was killed while high on drugs and, a short while later, the second is the victim of a gay killing. The deaths seem unconnected until Ardeth is abducted on her regular morning walk. Instead of being killed she is locked in a basement cell in what used to be an asylum for the insane. The man in the next cell looks like an elderly tramp but when Ardeth is forced to put her arm through the bars of his cell he drinks her blood.

To take her mind from the boredom of incarceration and away from the thoughts of what is likely to happen to her, Ardeth talks to the vampire. She is also shown what happens in the asylum. It is being used as a venue for pornographic movies and the vampire's hunger makes him the ideal means of turning them into erotic snuff movies. Ardeth realizes that she has no way out. She will die. In desperation she persuades Rozokov, the vampire, to change her. Her dead body is taken to the woods and when she revives as a vampire she is able to help him escape.

Alone in Toronto, Ardeth now has to learn how to survive as a vampire. To begin with, she takes too much from her victims and they die, but gradually she learns to take just enough to keep herself fed and to induce forgetfulness in them. But Toronto is dangerous in other ways. Not only is her sister searching for her but the people who snatched her in the first place are still hunting Rozokov. Although they are not yet aware that she is like him now, they are sure she knows where he is. The book then develops into an all-action thriller with her sister, Sara, being kidnapped

and her freedom being offered in exchange for Ardeth and Rozokov and the subsequent rescue and demise of the "bad guys" and razing of their headquarters.

This is one of those wish-fulfilment, nice vampire novels which lacks the horror of Stoker's *Dracula* or Le Fanu's story "Carmilla," both of which get passing references. *The Night Inside* dwells more on the sensual aspect of vampirism, suggesting that vampires are romantic creatures, to be loved, not feared. This theme is continued in *Blood and Chrysanthemums*, its sequel.

The second novel begins with Ardeth and Rozokov together in Banff, a tourist town in central Canada. They survive mostly by drinking the blood of elks although that of humans is preferable, the difference being like that between water and wine—you don't need to drink wine but it tastes so much better. They part acrimoniously after Rozokov unfaithfully drinks the blood of a local (female) doctor while Ardeth is abstemiously resisting the lure of a good-looking climber. She returns to Toronto, leaving Rozokov in Banff.

Enter the Japanese, in the guise of Lisa Takara, a remnant from *The Night Inside*. In that volume she was a scientist forced to work for the corporation that had been hunting the vampires. Back in Japan she is harassed by the man who sent her. Yamagata is *yakusa*, the Japanese equivalent of the Mafia, and he doesn't believe her story because his boss, Sadamori Fujiwara, is a vampire. Both want to know the truth, but for different reasons. Yamagata wants to be a vampire, Fujiwara wants to meet another of his own kind.

Interspersed with the main thrust of the volume are a series of stories from Fujiwara's life. The diary containing them has been left for Rozokov in the hope that he will be intrigued enough to want to meet the author. They do intrigue and they are the part of this novel that lifts it out of the ordinary, partly because it looks at the attitudes of a different culture, and partly because it brings across the loneliness of losing those you care for but staying young for a thousand years—survival is not too difficult for a Japanese samurai where obedience is expected and the eccentricities of your superiors are ignored if you want to live.

These books do not add anything to the vampire myth. In fact, except for their need to drink blood and their aversion to sunlight (it will not kill them though it is very uncomfortable for them) Baker's vampires are very ordinary. Yes, they are stronger than mortals and can mesmerize their victims in the way a weasel hypnotizes a rabbit before it strikes, and induce forgetfulness, but they are capable of the same emotions and go by the same moral code as they had before they became vampires. We are told that the relationship between Ardeth and Rozokov is intensely sexual but except for one episode in *The Night Inside* this aspect is played down. They seem more like an old married couple, going to sleep in each other's arms, rather than passionate lovers.

Baker's plots are internally consistent but her characters lack the edge of bizarreness that would make these vampire novels really stand out from the rest.

—Pauline Morgan

BAKER, Scott (MacMartin)

Nationality: American. **Born:** 1947. Has lived for many years in Paris, France. **Awards:** World Fantasy award for short story, 1985.

HORROR, GHOST AND GOTHIC PUBLICATIONS

Novels

Nightchild. New York, Berkley, 1979; revised edition, New York, Pocket, 1983.
Dhampire. New York, Pocket, 1982; revised as *Ancestral Hunger,* New York, Tor, 1995.
Webs. New York, Tor, 1989.

OTHER PUBLICATIONS

Novels

Symbiote's Crown. New York, Berkley, 1978.
Firedance. New York, Tor, 1986; London, Arrow, 1987.
Drink the Fire from the Flames. New York, Tor, 1987; London, Arrow, 1988.

*   *   *

Quite a few very talented writers have failed to achieve the fame and respect they deserve because they have spread their work across several genres. William Kotzwinkle and the late Angela Carter are two of the best examples. Scott Baker is another, though he goes further than most and tends to allow each of his novels or stories to include elements of horror, fantasy and science fiction. It is very difficult to decide which of these predominates in his work—perhaps fantasy, since the two "Ashlu" novels, *Firedance* and *Drink the Fire from the Flames,* concerned with shamanistic magic and the gradual accretion of personal power, represent his finest achievement to date.

Baker has not always chosen the most propitious subject matter for his horror novels; nor has he always tackled his plots and characters in a way that would make them easy for the reader to follow or enjoy. Obviously he expects rather too much of his readers; or, to put it another way, he can be too oblique for his own good.

Dhampire takes a much-used theme, the battle for control of a family after its head dies, and complicates it cleverly with much fine detail of magic ritual, supernatural power and physical torture. It is also an exercise in Baker's favourite plot progression: the gradual accretion of power by somebody who begins as a normal human being and ends up with god-like abilities. David Bathory is a 29-year-old American who is just another cocaine addict and breeder of dangerous snakes. He knows that among his ancestors is supposed to be Vlad the Impaler, but he has never noticed anything unusual about the present members of the family—perhaps because he has been out of touch for twelve years, perhaps because he was too naive or drugged to spot anything when he did live at home.

Now his wife dies of snake-bite and, a few days later, his father dies. In between these two events, David has met and made love to a strange young woman, Dara, who has an affinity with snakes and wears a large gold bracelet featuring an Indian Naga, a nine-headed cobra. Dara disappears and, it turns out a bit later, is a sister he knew nothing about. Returning home for his father's funeral, David is soon made aware of the supernatural ambience. His older brother Michael and his Uncle Stephen are both dhampires, that is, capable of controlling their undead (vampire) ancestors. Both of them augment their powers regularly through sex magic, which means forced intercourse (usually anal) with other members of the family. Michael has captured Dara, and he and Stephen (who pretends to want to help David) are fighting each other for control of the whole family—especially the generations of the undead. The only hope for David seems to be that his maternal grandparents (present for the funeral) possess Naga magic.

The fine details of the plot are extremely complex and fast-moving, too much so for reader enjoyment, since David's feelings and reactions are often ignored. What the reader must do is to surrender to Baker's fascination for magic ritual, and enjoy the novel on that basis. While many of the tortures and injuries with which David is afflicted seem too remote to make the reader sympathetic, there is one almost too terrible to describe. Stephen forces David to be inhabited by a familiar (produced for him by a demon) in the shape of a segmented worm, six inches long. It is called Monteleur, and it burrows its way into David; he can communicate with it and feel it moving around inside him. After many setbacks, when all seems lost, David manages to acquire enough power to control the others.

The plot of *Nightchild* is similar is some ways. Once again, the protagonist starts out powerless and ends up hugely powerful, effectively godlike, but the setting is an alien planet and the basis of the power is technological. That the novel can be classified as horror is largely due to the vanquished priests of the Temple of Night being described as vampires by their enemies. Lozan is an orphan brought up on the planet Nosferatu. Being intelligent, he is promised to the priesthood, but testing reveals him to be a half-human symbiote, a Lha, capable of developing enormous mental powers. Some of the scenes of the execution of the defeated priests and the obtaining of information from other Lha involve the absorption of life-force, which is analogous to drinking a person's blood.

Once again, the plot is complex and, though clever, not always clear. At the end it fails to satisfy; it is difficult to feel sympathy for somebody who is a composite male/female being with superpowers.

Webs is another highly original novel. It seems easy to understand: Brian Gerard is a fairly ordinary college lecturer in Florida; he gets mixed up with large spiders and with Karen, a young and attractive arachnologist. Only gradually do the supernatural forces which have been affecting Gerard throughout become clear, and the book ends in a complicated and paradoxical manner. This is certainly not just another giant-spider horror-adventure yarn.

Baker's uncollected short stories tend to be more easily understood: they are unforgettable gems. Many have science-fiction elements along with the horror. "The Lurking Duck" (in *Omni*, 1982) has a girl of eleven describing how she captures a murderous mechanical duck from a local lake and uses it to kill her disabled father. And yet, the "duck" is too clever and variable to be just a device. Truly amazing is "Full Fathom Deep" (in *Interzone*, 1995), which portrays how Thomas and his wife Katy have changed from being Greenpeace activists for whale conservation into dedicated and determined whale-killers, because of the feeling of supernatural exaltation they experience whenever a school of whales is wiped out. Another wonderful tale which should have won an award, but did not, is "Nesting Instinct" (in *The Architecture of Fear* edited by Kathryn Cramer and Peter D. Pautz, 1987); and one which did was "Still Life with Scorpion" (in *Asimov's SF Magazine*, 1984)—it gained a 1985 World Fantasy Award for best short story.

—Chris Morgan

BALLARD, J(ames) G(raham)

Nationality: British. **Born:** Shanghai, China, 15 November 1930. **Education:** Cathedral School, Shanghai; Lunghua Civilian Assembly Centre (Japanese-run prison camp for European civilians), Shanghai, 1942-45; Leys School, Cambridge, 1946-49; King's College, Cambridge, 1949-51; University of London, 1951-52. **Military Service:** Served in the Royal Air Force, 1954-55 (stationed in Canada). **Family:** Married Helen Mary Matthews (died 1964); one son and two daughters. **Career:** Contributor of short stories to British science-fiction magazines from 1956; editorial assistant, *The Baker*, London, 1956-57; assistant editor, *Chemistry and Industry*, London, 1957-61; freelance writer from 1961. **Awards:** *Guardian* Fiction prize, 1984; James Tait Black Memorial prize, 1985. **Agent:** Margaret Hanbury, 27 Walcot Square, London SE11 4UB.

HORROR, GHOST AND GOTHIC PUBLICATIONS

Novels

Crash. London, Cape, and New York, Farrar Straus, 1973.
Concrete Island. London, Cape, and New York, Farrar Straus, 1974.
High-Rise. London, Cape, 1975; New York, Holt Rinehart, 1977.
The Unlimited Dream Company. London, Cape, and New York, Holt Rinehart, 1979.
The Day of Creation. London, Gollancz, 1987; New York, Farrar Straus, 1988.
Running Wild (novella). London, Hutchinson, 1988; New York, Farrar Straus, 1989.
Rushing to Paradise. London, Flamingo, 1994; New York, Picador, 1995.

Short Stories

The Four-Dimensional Nightmare. London, Gollancz, 1963; revised edition, 1974; as *The Voices of Time*, London, Dent, 1984.
The Terminal Beach. London, Gollancz, 1964; New York, Carroll and Graf, 1987.
The Day of Forever. London, Panther, 1967; revised edition, 1971.
The Disaster Area. London, Cape, 1967.
The Overloaded Man. London, Panther, 1967; revised as *The Venus Hunters*, London, Granada, 1980.
Vermilion Sands. New York, Berkley, 1971; expanded edition, London, Cape, 1973, and New York, Carroll and Graf, 1988.
Low-Flying Aircraft and Other Stories. London, Cape, 1976.
Myths of the Near Future. London, Cape, 1982.
War Fever. London, Collins, 1990; New York, Farrar Straus, 1991.

OTHER PUBLICATIONS

Novels

The Wind from Nowhere. New York, Berkley, 1962; London, Penguin, 1967.
The Drowned World. New York, Berkley, 1962; London, Gollancz, 1963.

The Burning World. New York, Berkley, 1964; revised as *The Drought*, London, Cape, 1965.
The Crystal World. London, Cape, and New York, Farrar Straus, 1966.
Hello America. London, Cape, 1981; New York, Carroll and Graf, 1988.
Empire of the Sun. London, Gollancz, and New York, Simon and Schuster, 1984.
The Kindness of Women. London, HarperCollins, and New York, Farrar, Straus, 1991.
Cocaine Nights. London, Flamingo, 1996.

Short Stories

The Voices of Time and Other Stories. New York, Berkley, 1962.
Billenium. New York, Berkley, 1962.
Passport to Eternity. New York, Berkley, 1963.
Terminal Beach. New York, Berkley, 1964.
The Impossible Man and Other Stories. New York, Berkley, 1966.
Why I Want to Fuck Ronald Reagan. Brighton, Unicorn Bookshop, 1968.
The Atrocity Exhibition. London, Cape, 1970; as *Love and Napalm: Export USA*, New York, Grove Press, 1972; expanded edition published under original title, San Francisco, Re/Search, 1990; revised, London, Flamingo, 1993.
Chronopolis and Other Stories. New York, Putnam, 1971.
The Best of J. G. Ballard. London, Futura, 1977.
The Best Short Stories of J. G. Ballard. New York, Holt Rinehart, 1978.
News from the Sun. London, Interzone, 1982.
Memories of the Space Age. Sauk City, Wisconsin, Arkham House, 1988.

Other

A User's Guide to the Millennium: Essays and Reviews. London, HarperCollins, and New York, Picador, 1996.

*

Film Adaptations: *Empire of the Sun*, 1987; *Crash*, 1996.

Bibliography: *J. G. Ballard: A Primary and Secondary Bibliography* by David Pringle, Boston, Hall, 1984.

Critical Studies: *Earth is the Alien Planet: J. G. Ballard's Four-Dimensional Nightmare* by David Pringle, San Bernardino, California, Borgo Press, 1979; *Re/Search: J. G. Ballard* edited by V. Vale and Andrea Juno, San Francisco, Re/Search, 1984; *J. G. Ballard* by Peter Brigg, Mercer Island, Washington, Starmont House, 1985; *Out of the Night and Into the Dream: A Thematic Study of the Fiction of J. G. Ballard* by Gregory Stephenson, Westport, Connecticut, Greenwood Press, 1991.

* * *

Although he has never been published as a generic horror writer, there have been several attempts to co-opt some of J. G. Ballard's novels into the horror field. In an appendix to his critical survey *Danse Macabre* (1981) Stephen King listed *Concrete Island* and *High-Rise* among his hundred favourite horror books, with the former asterisked as a "particularly important" title. In his collection of interviews *Faces of Fear* (1985) Douglas E. Winter included a similar appendix, "The Best of Horror Fiction," which listed Ballard's *Crash*, *Concrete Island* and *High-Rise*. In his anthology *Splatterpunks: Extreme Horror* (1991) Paul M. Sammon likewise cited *Crash* as an early example of the sub-genre, "splatterpunk," which he was endeavouring to establish. Latterly one of the horror cinema's leading writer-directors, David Cronenberg, has made a powerful movie from his own script based on that same novel of Ballard's.

Sometimes referred to by Ballard's critics as "the urban disaster trilogy," *Crash*, *Concrete Island* and *High-Rise* are not linked in any formal sense. What the three books have in common is that they are set in present-day London or its suburbs and describe very localized "disasters" that befall small groups of characters (Ballard's earlier science-fiction novels, such as *The Drowned World*, were set in the future and involved disasters on a global scale; and he was to return to this futuristic, large-scale mode in *Hello America*). The "disaster" in *Crash* is, of course, the automobile accident—or rather, the "autogeddon" which is not so much accidental as deliberately sought by the characters for their sexual fulfilment. *Concrete Island* also begins with a car-smash, but is mainly about the physical and psychological marooning of its characters on a piece of waste ground between city freeways. *High-Rise* is about the multi-storey apartment block of the title, a mini-city whose inhabitants perversely set about destroying their environment. In all three novels the horror resides not so much in the bizarre events—although these are certainly horrific, and frequently violent—but in the "welcoming" attitudes of the central characters, the ways in which they *collaborate* with the unpleasantness. These people are embodiments of what may be termed Ballard's Burden: the suspicion that we have created an urban world of metal and concrete and media overload which is specifically *designed* to indulge all our worst instincts.

Ballard has dealt in similar themes throughout his novel-writing career, but there are at least four later works which are particularly amenable to a reading as "horror." *The Unlimited Dream Company* is his one overtly supernatural novel, a posthumous fantasy somewhat on the lines of William Golding's *Pincher Martin* (1956); its protagonist, dead in chapter one but seemingly reborn, is in effect a ghost. Unlike Golding's marooned sailor, however, Ballard's hero lives out his afterlife on the home ground of contemporary London's suburbia. *The Day of Creation* can be read as a phantasmagoric study in delusion: set in Africa, it involves the mysterious appearance of a new river which the protagonist imagines he has created; the subsequent life and death of the river is described with haunting intensity. *Running Wild* is a slim novella cast as a murder mystery; again, the horror arises from the way in which the apparently "perfect" suburban environment becomes a nightmare of entrapment. In *Rushing to Paradise* Ballard turns once more to an exotic setting, a South Sea island which becomes the private domain of a messianic leader who sets about killing her followers. In Ballard's novels, although the emphasis of the narrative is always on some lushly-described environment, there is no escape from the perversities of the human soul.

Ballard has written over 120 short stories which collectively form a very important part of his *oeuvre*. It is surprising that so few of these have found their way into standard anthologies of horror, the supernatural and the weird (on the other hand, scores of his stories have been anthologized as science fiction,

a genre with which he is identified still by most readers). The few exceptions are "Manhole 69" (1957), which Edmund Crispin reprinted in his *Best Tales of Terror* (1962); "Track 12" (1958), which Alex Hamilton included in *Best Horror Stories 3* (1972); "The Watch-Towers" (1962), which Christopher Evans placed in *Mind at Bay: Eleven Horror Stories* (1969); "Now Wakes the Sea" (1963), which Hugh Lamb included in *Star Book of Horror No. 1* (1975); "The Screen Game" (1963), which Peter Haining reprinted in *The Hollywood Nightmare: Tales of Fantasy and Horror from the Film World* (1970); "Prisoner of the Coral Deep" (1964), which D. M. Mitchell saw fit to include in *The Starry Wisdom: A Tribute to H. P. Lovecraft* (1994); and "A Host of Furious Fancies" (1980), which Michele Slung put in her anthology of sex-horror, *Shudder Again* (1993).

Others of Ballard's short stories that have not been reprinted in a horror context, but which belong to the field, include: "Now: Zero" (1959), about a man who discovers the power to wish people to death; "Zone of Terror" (1960), a *doppelgänger* tale; "The Last World of Mr. Goddard" (1960), about a man who presides, god-like, over a miniature town in a box; "The Overloaded Man" (1961), about a disaffected husband who learns to "switch off" aspects of reality, including, ultimately, his wife; "Mr. F. is Mr. F." (1961), about a husband who regresses to his wife's womb; "The Thousand Dreams of Stellavista" (1962), a hi-tech haunted-house story; "The Man on the 99th Floor" (1962), about murderous or self-destructive urges implanted by hypnotism; "The Reptile Enclosure" (1963), about the lemming-like compulsion of sunbathers to immerse themselves in the sea; "Minus One" (1963), about a mysterious disappearance in a mental hospital; "The Sudden Afternoon" (1963), about a switch of identities; "Time of Passage" (1964), a time-reversal story; "The Lost Leonardo" (1964), about Ahasuerus the Wandering Jew—one of Ballard's most delightful tales of the supernatural; "The Delta at Sunset" (1964), about a sick man's obsession with apparitions of snakes on a beach; "The Gioconda of the Twilight Noon" (1964), a small masterpiece about a temporarily-blinded man's ghostly visions; "The Recognition" (1967), about a shabby circus which exhibits human beings in a cage; "The Air Disaster" (1975), a devastatingly ironic story about the exhuming of corpses from peasants' graves in order to fulfil the macabre demands of a reporter in search of a newsworthy disaster; "The Sixty Minute Zoom" (1976), about a murderous amateur-movie maker in a Spanish holiday resort; "The Smile" (1976), about a man who "marries" a female doll, or mannequin; "The Dead Time" (1977), one of the author's most powerful tales, about a boy's ferrying of corpses in post-war China; "Having a Wonderful Time" (1978), about a sunny resort which becomes a prison camp; "Motel Architecture" (1978), about a recluse obsessed with possible intruders; "Report on an Unidentified Space Station" (1982), a Kafka-esque fable about an ever-expanding artificial environment; and "The Enormous Space" (1989), about a man who immures himself in his suburban home.

All of these stories are to be found in one or another of the Ballard collections listed above, with the single exception of "The Recognition," which, unaccountably, has yet to appear in any of the author's books. A large collection which brought together the best of J. G. Ballard's short horror fictions would be a rich volume indeed.

—David Pringle

BANKS, Iain (Menzies)

Also writes as Iain M. Banks. **Nationality:** British. **Born:** Dunfermline, Fife, Scotland, 16 February 1954. **Education:** North Queensferry Primary School; Gourock Primary School; Gourock High School; Greenock High School; Stirling University, 1972-75, B.A. in English with philosophy and psychology. **Family:** Married Ann Blackburn in 1992. **Career:** Vacation jobs as hospital porter, estate worker, pier porter, road worker, dustman, gardener; a year as testing technician for British Steel; expediter-analyzer, IBM, Greenock, Scotland, 1978; solicitor's clerk, London, 1980-84; freelance writer. **Agent:** Mic Cheetham, 138 Buckingham Palace Road, London SW1W 9SA. **Address:** c/o Little, Brown, Brettenham House, Lancaster Place, London WC2E 7EN, England. Lives in Fife.

HORROR, GHOST AND GOTHIC PUBLICATIONS

Novels

The Wasp Factory. London, Macmillan, and Boston, Houghton Mifflin, 1984.
Walking on Glass. London, Macmillan, 1985; Boston, Houghton Mifflin, 1986.
The Bridge. London, Macmillan, 1986; New York, St. Martin's Press, 1989.
Espedair Street. London, Macmillan, 1987.
Canal Dreams. London, Macmillan, 1989; New York, Doubleday, 1991.
The Crow Road. London, Little Brown, and New York, Scribner, 1992.
Complicity. London, Little Brown, 1993; New York, Doubleday, 1995.
Whit, or Isis Among the Unsaved. London, Little Brown, 1995.
A Song of Stone. London, Abacus, 1997.

OTHER PUBLICATIONS

Novels (as Iain M. Banks)

Consider Phlebas. London, Macmillan, 1987; New York, St. Martin's Press, 1988.
The Player of Games. London, Macmillan, 1988; New York, St. Martin's Press, 1989.
The State of the Art (novella). Willimantic, Connecticut, Ziesing, 1989.
Use of Weapons. London, Orbit, 1990; New York, Bantam, 1992.
Against a Dark Background. London, Orbit, and New York, Bantam, 1993.
Feersum Endjinn. London, Orbit, 1994; New York, Bantam, 1995.
Excession. London, Orbit, 1996.

Short Stories

The State of the Art (includes the 1989 novella plus additional stories). London, Orbit, 1991.

*   *   *

Few novelists can have erupted onto the literary scene amid such controversy as did Iain Banks with his first-published novel, *The Wasp Factory*, in 1984. The book was widely reviled by many reviewers on the grounds of its violence and sadism; a few critics recognized that a distinctive new voice had been added to British literature—or, more specifically, a new *Scottish* voice, for, like Alasdair Gray and many others, Banks refuses to conform to the English literary tradition. More recently, his voice has been echoed by writers such as Ken MacLeod (beginning with *The Star Fraction*, 1995) and Ian Maitland (beginning with *Cathedral*, 1992).

The critics who protested about *The Wasp Factory* had clearly never read any of the standard genre horror novels that, quite likely, their kids had read, for there is little to object about in the novel, which—although laced with delicious dark humour and a sense of the surreal—is a quite serious study of childhood psychopathy. Its central character commits mayhem and murder and, in between, enjoys torturing wasps in a specially devised gadget (the "wasp factory" of the title). Perhaps what unsettled the critics so much was that Banks, through his skill as a writer, made his readers begin to sympathize with and even like this character.

Banks had written several science-fiction novels before the publication of *The Wasp Factory*. Revised versions of these—plus further works of science fiction—have since been published under the slightly altered signature "Iain M. Banks." They are of mixed standard, *Consider Phlebas*, *The Player of Games* and *Feersum Endjinn* probably being the best; the first two of these could have originated from an author in any country, but the third exhibits a linguistic playfulness which is again very Scottish.

Banks is not a complacent author: with each new book he experiments. Sometimes the experiment fails—and he is refreshingly honest about those failures. *The Bridge*—one of his most intricate (and funniest) books—combines the obsessions of Sword and Sorcery with the Forth Rail Bridge, whose structure, in very convoluted fashion, is adopted as the structure of the book. This is one of his finest works. *The Crow Road* is, after *The Wasp Factory*, a further examination of the traumas of having to live through that dreadful period of life known as "childhood": it begins with the memorable sentence, "It was the day my grandmother exploded," the explosion being a literal one as it happens while she is being cremated. *The Crow Road* is Banks's most complicated novel (and his longest, aside from some of his science-fiction work), with most of the action being depicted in flashback from that traumatic funeral.

Complicity is certainly his most horrific book. In this novel a Scottish eremite exacts horrible revenge on people who have committed crimes but got away with them; it is not a comfortable book, and is made even less so by its superficial construction as a work of detection. It is more difficult here, however, to sympathize with the central character, who is a muckraking journalist, drug addict and sexual masochist—his masochism is played off effectively against the murderer's sadism, but somehow the mixture fails to gel.

No one could dispute that Banks is one of the most important writers currently working in the English language—although he has yet to be fully recognized in the United States. Each new book of his deservedly goes straight to the top of the British bestseller lists. And yet there must be some small reservations. Because he has become a cult author of astonishing proportions (most cult authors are known to a discerning few, but Banks is known to a discerning many), there is a reticence on the part of publishers to curb his occasional excesses. His best books are major literary events; his slightest (including some of his science fiction) are very slight indeed. That said, his constant inventiveness and his playfulness with language make his books unrelentingly enjoyable.

In early 1997 Banks was again involved in controversy when he remarked in public that he saw little wrong in the use of the drug Ecstasy.

—John Grant

BARING, Maurice

Nationality: British. **Born:** London, 27 April 1874. **Education:** Eton College; Trinity College, Cambridge. **Military Service:** Served in the Royal Flying Corps during World War I: Major. **Career:** Worked in the Foreign Office, 1898-1904; journalist and war correspondent, 1904-14; poet, travel-writer and novelist. **Awards:** Chevalier of the French Legion of Honour. **Died:** 14 December 1945.

Horror, Ghost and Gothic Publications

Short Stories

Orpheus in Mayfair and Other Stories and Sketches. London, Mills and Boon, 1909.
The Glass Mender and Other Stories. London, Nisbet, 1910; as *The Blue Rose Fairy Book*, New York, Dodd Mead, 1911.
Half a Minute's Silence and Other Stories. London, Heinemann, and New York, Doubleday Page, 1925.

Other Publications

Novels

Passing By. London, Secker, 1921.
Overlooked. London, Heinemann, and Boston, Houghton Mifflin, 1922.
C. London, Heinemann, and New York, Doubleday Page, 1924.
Cat's Cradle. London, Heinemann, 1925; New York, Doubleday Page, 1926.
Daphne Adeane. London, Heinemann, 1926; New York, Harper, 1927.
Tinker's Leave. London, Heinemann, 1927; New York, Doubleday Doran, 1928.
Comfortless Memory. London, Heinemann, 1928; as *When They Love*, New York, Doubleday Doran, 1928.
The Coat without Seam. London, Heinemann, and New York, Knopf, 1929.
Robert Peckham. London, Heinemann, and New York, Knopf, 1930.
In My End Is My Beginning. London, Heinemann, and New York, Knopf, 1931.
Friday's Business. London, Heinemann, 1932; New York, Knopf, 1933.
The Lonely Lady of Dulwich. London, Heinemann, and New York, Knopf, 1934.
Darby and Joan. London, Heinemann, 1935.

Short Stories

Lost Diaries. London, Duckworth, and Boston, Houghton Mifflin, 1913.

Plays

Gaston de Foix and Other Plays. London, Richards, 1903.
Desiderio. Oxford, Blackwell, 1906.
Proserpine: A Masque. Oxford, Blackwell, 1908.
The Grey Stocking and Other Plays. London, Constable, 1911.
Palamon and Arcite: A Play for Puppets. Oxford, Blackwell, 1913.
Manfroy: A Play in Five Acts. London, privately published, 1920.
His Majesty's Embassy and Other Plays. London, Heinemann, and Boston, Little Brown, 1923.

Poetry

Hildesheim: Quatre Pastiches. Paris, Lemerre, 1899; London, Heinemann, 1924.
The Black Prince and Other Poems. London and New York, Lane, 1903.
Fifty Sonnets. London, privately printed, 1905.
Sonnets and Short Poems. Oxford, Blackwell, 1906.
The Collected Poems of Maurice Baring. London and New York, Lane, 1911; enlarged edition, London, Heinemann, and New York, Doubleday Page, 1925.
Poems 1914-1917. London, Secker, 1918; enlarged edition, as *Poems 1914-1919*, 1920.
Poems 1892-1929. London, privately printed, 1929; as *Selected Poems*, London, Heinemann, 1930.

Other

With the Russians in Manchuria. London, Methuen, 1905.
A Year in Russia. London, Methuen, 1907; revised edition, London, Methuen and New York, Dutton, 1917.
Russian Essays and Stories. London, Methuen, 1908.
Dead Letters. London, Constable, and Boston, Houghton Mifflin, 1910.
Landmarks in Russian Literature. London, Methuen, 1910; New York, Macmillan, 1912.
Diminutive Dramas. London, Constable, and Boston, Houghton Mifflin, 1911.
The Russian People. London, Methuen, 1911.
Letters from the Near East, 1909 and 1912. London, Smith Elder, 1913.
What I Saw in Russia. London, and New York, Nelson, 1913.
An Outline of Russian Literature. London, Williams and Norgate, 1914; New York, Holt, 1915.
Round the World in Any Number of Days. Boston, Houghton Mifflin, 1914; London, Chatto and Windus, 1919.
In Memoriam: Auberon Herbert. Oxford, Blackwell, 1917.
R.F.C., H.Q., 1914-1918. London, Bell, 1920; as *Flying Corps Headquarters, 1914-1918*, London, Heinemann, 1930.
The Puppet Show of Memory. London, Heinemann, and Boston, Little Brown, 1922.
A Triangle: Passages from Three Notebooks. London, Heinemann, 1923; New York, Doubleday Page, 1924.
Punch and Judy, and Other Essays. London, Heinemann, and New York, Doubleday Page, 1924.

Catherine Parr; or, Alexander's Horse. Chicago, Old Tower Press, 1927.

French Literature. London, Benn, 1927.

Cecil Spencer. London, privately printed, 1928.

Lost Lectures; or, The Fruits of Experience. London, Davies, and New York, Knopf, 1932.

Sarah Bernhardt. London, Davies, 1933; New York, Appleton Century, 1934.

Unreliable History. London, Heinemann, 1934.

Have You Anything to Declare? London, Heinemann, 1936; New York, Knopf, 1937.

Editor, *English Landscape.* London, Milford, 1916.

Editor, *The Oxford Book of Russian Verse.* Oxford, Clarendon Press, 1924.

Editor, *Algae: An Anthology of Phrases.* London, Heinemann, 1928.

Translator, *Thoughts on Art and Life*, by Leonardo da Vinci. Boston, Merrymount, 1906.

Translator, *Translations: Ancient and Modern.* London, Secker, 1918.

Translator, *Last Days of Tsarskoe Selo*, by Count Paul Benckendorff. London, Heinemann, 1927.

Translator, *Fantasio: A Comedy in Two Acts*, by Alfred Musset. New York, Pleiad, 1929.

Translator, *Russian Lyrics.* London, Heinemann, 1943.

*   *   *

Maurice Baring was the dedicatee of Vernon Lee's collection *For Maurice: Five Unlikely Stories* (1927) but the youthful enthusiasm for Decadent fantasies which inspired Lee's gesture was not widely exhibited in his own literary work. Although one of his novels, *Daphne Adeane*, is identified as a ghost story in Everett Bleiler's *Checklist of Science-Fiction and Supernatural Literature* it is actually devoid of any supernatural content. Baring's contribution to the horror and fantasy genres was restricted to a relatively small number of short stories, but a few of these make up in quality what they lack in quantity.

The stories in *Orpheus in Mayfair and Otherf Stories* are various in tone and theme but the title story may be regarded as typical of Baring's supernatural fiction. The hostess of a cosy upper-middle-class house party is let down by the person supposed to be providing the music and somehow—the mechanism is unclear—Orpheus is recruited to fill the breach. His songs induce visions, climaxing with a glimpse of the Underworld where the unlucky genius gave his greatest performance. For the narrator, that revelatory moment constitutes a curious amalgam of authentic awe, plaintive nostalgia for the lost glories of Greek myth, and the sad awareness that his fellow-guests are utterly blind to the beauties and profundities of Orphic excess. Even the outrightly comic version of the same plot which is presented in "A Luncheon Party," featuring Shakespeare instead of Orpheus and an ill-judged diabolical bargain as mechanism, is not without an element of appreciable tragedy, and although Baring wrote nothing with a tenth of the fervour of "Winthrop's Adventure" in *For Maurice* it is evident that he inherited something of Vernon Lee's intense fascination with the dangerous allure of the gaudy past.

A similar encounter with a figure displaced from Greek myth is featured in "The Island," while "The Ikon" features a syncretically-inclined collector of antiquities, but the collection's best work along these lines is "The Flute Player's Story," in which the curse of Marsyas falls upon everyone unlucky enough to be inspired by Apollo. In "Venus" the author's ironic wordplay substitutes a lush vision of the planet's imagined surface for a direct revelation of the goddess herself, but the protagonist's gradual slide into the deadly grip of the supernatural remains a punctilious reflection of the dictum that whom the gods destroy they first make mad.

Baring's fascination with the notion that music—or some equivalent artistic endeavour—has the potential to offer a gateway to supernatural enlightenment is further displayed in several historical fantasias which combine sentimental lightness with an element of the *conte cruel*; these include "Jean Francois," "The Flute of Chang Liang," "Fete Galante," "The Spider's Web," "Russalka" and "The Star." It is arguable, however, that the most horrific tale in *Orpheus in Mayfair* is the brutally unadorned historical story "Edward II: At Berkeley Castle"—but the reader has to know what the masked men intend to do with the red-hot iron, because the prevailing standards of decency made explicit description impossible. The most conventional tale is certainly "The Shadow of a Midnight," a thoroughly orthodox account of a premonitory vision.

The most wholehearted fantasies in *Orpheus in Mayfair* are couched as mock folk tales. "Dr. Faust's Last Day" and "The Conqueror" are parables which require an adult reading but "The Old Woman" is unashamedly couched as a children's story. The collection was followed by *The Glass Mender and Other Stories*, which consists of tales explicitly designed for children. This intention effectively rules out *conte cruel* endings but some of the inclusions—especially "The Story of Vox Angelica and Lieblich Gedacht" and "The Ring"—deploy quasi-Gothic motifs and offer darker suggestions to adult readers, as of course do many authentic folk tales.

Fifteen of the tales included in *Orpheus in Mayfair* were reprinted in *Half a Minute's Silence and Other Stories*, including nine of the supernatural pieces. Among the new items added to the later volume are a horrified (but not particularly horrific) account of the loss of the great library at Alexandria, "Habent Sua Fata Libelli," and the dour non-supernatural *conte cruel* "The Brass Ring." By the time the later book was issued Baring had become a highly reputable writer of naturalistic fiction and—like many others who attained such heights—had apparently come to regard supernatural fiction as something best put away along with things authentically childish. Lovers of imaginative fiction are bound to regard this as something of tragedy; had he continued to produce work in the vein of *Orpheus in Mayfair* Baring could certainly have distinguished himself as a writer of delicately ironic horror stories.

—Brian Stableford

BARKER, Clive

Nationality: British. **Born:** Liverpool, 5 October 1952. **Education:** University of Liverpool. **Career:** Illustrator, actor, playwright and novelist; director and executive producer of motion pictures. **Awards:** British Fantasy award for short story, 1985, and for film, 1988; World Fantasy award for collection, 1985. Has lived in Los Angeles, California, since 1991.

HORROR, GHOST AND GOTHIC PUBLICATIONS

Novels

The Damnation Game. London, Weidenfeld and Nicolson, 1985; New York, Putnam, 1987.
Weaveworld. London, Collins, and New York, Poseidon Press, 1987.
Cabal: The Nightbreed. London, Fontana, 1989.
The Great and Secret Show: The First Book of the Art. London, Collins, 1989.
The Hellbound Heart (novella). London, Fontana, 1991.
Imajica. London and New York, HarperCollins, 1991.
The Thief of Always: A Fable. London and New York, HarperCollins, 1993.
Everville: The Second Book of the Art. London and New York, HarperCollins, 1994.
Sacrament. London and New York, HarperCollins, 1996.

Short Stories

Clive Barker's Books of Blood, Volume One. London, Sphere, 1984; New York, Berkley, 1986.
Clive Barker's Books of Blood, Volume Two. London, Sphere, 1984; New York, Berkley, 1986.
Clive Barker's Books of Blood, Volume Three. London, Sphere, 1984; New York, Berkley, 1986.
Clive Barker's Books of Blood, Volume Four. London, Sphere, 1985; as *The Inhuman Condition: Tales of Terror*, New York, Poseidon Press, 1986.
Clive Barker's Books of Blood, Volume Five. London, Sphere, 1985; as *In the Flesh: Tales of Terror*, New York, Poseidon Press, 1986.
Clive Barker's Books of Blood, Volume Six. London, Sphere, 1985; as *Cabal*, New York, Poseidon Press, 1988.

Plays

Incarnations: Three Plays. New York, HarperPrism, 1995; London, HarperCollins, 1996.
Forms of Heaven: Three Plays. New York, HarperPrism, 1996.

Screenplays: *Underworld*, 1985; *Rawhead Rex*, 1987; *Hellraiser*, 1987; *Nightbreed*, 1990.

Other

Clive Barker Illustrator, edited by Steve Niles. Forestville, California, Eclipse, 1990.
Clive Barker's Nightbreed: The Making of the Film. London, Fontana, 1990.
Clive Barker's Shadows in Eden, edited by Stephen Jones. Lancaster, Pennsylvania, Underwood Miller, 1991.
The Nightbreed Chronicles. London, Titan, 1991.
Pandemonium: The World of Clive Barker, edited by Michael Brown. Forestville, California, Eclipse, 1991.

*

Film Adaptations: *Hellraiser*, 1987, from his novella *The Hellbound Heart*; *Rawhead Rex*, 1987, from his short story of the same title; *Nightbreed*, 1990, from his novella *Cabal*; *Candyman*, 1992, from his short story "The Forbidden"; *Lord of Illusions*, 1995, from his short story "The Last Illusion."

Critical Studies: *Clive Barker: Mythmaker for the Millennium* by Suzanne J. Barbieri, Stockport, Lancashire, British Fantasy Society, 1994; *Clive Barker's Short Stories: Imagination as Metaphor in the Books of Blood and Other Works*, by Gary Hoppenstand, Jefferson, North Carolina, McFarland, 1994; *Writing Horror and the Body: The Fiction of Stephen King, Clive Barker, and Anne Rice* by Linda Badley, Westport, Connecticut, Greenwood Press, 1996.

Theatrical Activities:
Director: **Films**—*Hellraiser*, 1987; *Nightbreed*, 1990; *Lord of Illusions*, 1995. Executive Producer: *Hellbound: Hellraiser 2*, 1988; *Candyman*, 1992; *Hellraiser III: Hell on Earth*, 1992; *Candyman 2: Farewell to the Flesh*, 1995; *Hellraiser: Bloodline*, 1995.

*   *   *

Clive Barker is probably the most talented British writer working in the horror genre today. It is therefore a shame that most of his works display his true quality only spasmodically, and that in several of his novels he has chosen to mix genres almost indiscriminately, with fantasy, general fiction, science fiction, literary fiction, crime fiction and even historical fiction being included alongside (or instead of) the horror.

His debut with *Books of Blood* was startling, vivid and audacious; unfortunately it was also overpraised. The 28 stories (and some brief framing material) in six volumes show that Barker is willing to write about anything, however gross or untouchable, with spirit and panache. Indeed, some of the stories are multilayered and original at the same time as being disgustingly strewn with dismembered body parts: literary splatterpunk was born here. Outstanding stories here are "Dread," the only completely nonsupernatural piece in the set, about using psychological torture to make people do the thing they most dread, and "Jacqueline Ess: Her Will and Testament," in which a woman discovers an ability to kill men using only the power of her mind. Some others of the stories, by contrast, are clichéd and unconvincing. The symbolism with which Barker tries to deepen most of the stories is occasionally too obvious (and occasionally too obscure to be clear), and his tendency to go right over the top in order to drive home his horror message is wearying, resulting in a never-ending atrocity exhibition.

When Barker's first novel, *The Damnation Game*, was published (in between the third and fourth volumes of stories) it showed up his weaknesses more sharply than his strengths. Despite some poetic phrases (for Barker has always been noted for his pretty turns of trope) and a few unforgettable images—a woman skinned and boned, yet able to move around and answer the telephone; a fat man, dead for months from a broken neck and pierced by knives, gradually decomposing but still murderous—the book is most notable for being a rambling thriller about gambling. The ambition is great, involving a wide range of settings, times and characters (alive and dead), while the execution falters a little.

The novella *The Hellbound Heart* (which formed the basis of his own film, *Hellraiser*, followed by three sequels produced but not scripted by Barker) is arguably his most successful piece of horror fiction because it is subtly told, magnificently well-sustained in terms of tone, and pared down to an economical length with not a superfluous word. The story is simple: Frank, seeking the ultimate in sensual pleasure, achieves it through contact with supernatural creatures called the Cenobites, but discovers that it is too painful to bear. He is trapped in another dimension just a step away from an unused room in his brother's house. His brother's wife, Julia, tries to help him by luring men to the room and killing them, so that Frank can use the blood and tissue to rebuild his own body and escape.

Cabal, which was published in the U.S. in one volume with the *Books of Blood VI*, is a dark and depressing short novel, set in Canada, and dealing heavily with Midian, city of the living dead. Dreamlike in its style but also full of atrocity, it includes some sparkling ingredients yet is disappointing overall. There are too many ideas and subplots inserted as throwaways and not integrated into the rest of the action. At times it seems as if Barker is trying to include as many taboo subjects as possible. At other times he deals delicately with a tussle for a human soul between death and love. And it seems not to be a complete story: the sequel has not yet appeared.

A sharp and fascinating contrast to his horror works so far mentioned is *The Thief of Always*, a short novel aimed mostly at children. Much of the action is a good-versus-evil fable concerning ten-year-old Harvey, persuaded to visit the marvellous Holiday House, which provides everything a child could want. This is an updated version of the fairy tale about a mortal visiting fairies, and finding that a year has passed back home for every day spent with the creatures of magic. But Harvey is faced with horrors as well as magic. Not only does he escape, to discover that 31 years have passed in the outside world while he is still aged ten, but he finds the strength and resourcefulness to return and destroy the house and its supernatural inhabitants, so releasing all the other children trapped there. While the plot is probably fine for a younger reader (but too simplistic for adults), the metaphorical style ("The great grey beast February had eaten Harvey Swick alive") is surely too much for many children to cope with.

All of Barker's big novels, *Weaveworld*, *The Great and Secret Show*, *Imajica*, *Everville* and *Sacrament*, contain horror elements, yet none is primarily a horror novel due to the preponderance of fantasy or science-fiction ideas. For example, both *The Great and Secret Show* and *Everville* have groups of demons (and demon-hunters) roaming around, but both are partly concerned with Quiddity, another continuum just a few paces away through a cleft in time and space—a very familiar concept to readers of science fiction. Both also contain considerable (and convincingly written) sections of general fiction, while *Everville* includes scenes of early settlers edging across America in wagons in 1848. It is this variety and its accompanying tumescence which have spoiled most of his recent creations. He is trying to include so many disparate themes and groups of characters and subplots in each that unevenness is inevitable. And too many scenes are overlong, so that the book as a whole becomes more a trial of stamina for the reader than a pleasure.

Sacrament, his most recent novel, is an excellent piece of writing, closer to general or literary fiction than anything else Barker has written. It includes the adventures of a photographer in northern Canada, a childhood in a Yorkshire village and a sensitive picture of gay life in San Francisco, yet at the heart of it all are two amazing and dangerous fantasy characters, Rosa McGee and Jacob

Steep, who kill with little reason and may be immortal. And at the end, worth waiting for, is Domus Mundi, the House of the World, a terrifying creation of mind and matter. There are shafts of horror here, but it is good to see that Barker no longer feels it necessary to aim at ultimate gross-out nastiness every time in order to keep his audience.

Since the *Books of Blood* Barker has written relatively few stories, though they have appeared in prestige markets and several have been of note. "Lost Souls" is a deliberately laid-back and loosely connected story about a search for a demon in Manhattan. "Coming to Grief" is the gentle tale (set in Barker's native Liverpool) of a woman returning to her home for the first time in 18 years, to arrange her mother's funeral, and managing to come to terms with a terrible childhood fear (which stands, symbolically, for the whole of childhood).

—Chris Morgan

BEAUMONT, Charles

Pseudonym (later legally adopted name) of Charles Leroy Nutt. **Other Pseudonyms:** Keith Grantland (joint pseudonym with John E. Tomerlin). **Nationality:** American. **Born:** Chicago, Illinois, 2 January 1929. **Education:** High-school dropout. **Military Service:** Served in the United States Army for a few months. **Family:** Married Helen Louise Brown in 1949; two sons and two daughters. **Career:** Radio writer, actor, illustrator, animator and screenwriter. **Awards:** Jules Verne award, 1954; *Playboy* award, for nonfiction, 1961; Horror Writers of America Bram Stoker award (posthumous), 1989. **Died:** 21 February 1967.

Horror, Ghost and Gothic Publications

Short Stories

The Hunger and Other Stories. New York, Putnam, 1957; abridged as *Shadow Play*, London, Panther, 1964.
Night Ride and Other Journeys. New York, Bantam, 1960.
The Magic Man—and Other Science-Fantasy Stories. Greenwich, Connecticut, Fawcett, 1965; London, Fawcett, 1966.
The Edge. London, Panther, 1966.
Best of Beaumont, edited by Christopher Beaumont. New York, Bantam, 1982.
Charles Beaumont: Selected Stories, edited by Roger Anker. Arlington Heights, Illinois, Dark Harvest, 1988; as *The Howling Man*, New York, Tor, 1992.

Plays

Screenplays: *Burn, Witch, Burn* (*Night of the Eagle*), with Richard Matheson and George Baxt, 1962; *The Premature Burial*, with Ray Russell, 1962; *The Haunted Palace*, 1963; *7 Faces of Dr. Lao*, 1964; *The Masque of the Red Death*, with R. Wright Campbell, 1964; *Brain Dead*, with Adam Simon, 1990.

Television Plays: episodes of *Twilight Zone*, *One Step Beyond* and *Alfred Hitchcock Presents*.

Other

Editor, with William F. Nolan as anonymous co-editor, *The Fiend in You*. New York, Ballantine, 1962.

OTHER PUBLICATIONS

Novels

Run from the Hunter (with John E. Tomerlin as Keith Grantland). New York, Fawcett, 1957; London, Boardman, 1959.
The Intruder. New York, Putnam, 1959; London, Muller, 1960.

Short Stories

Yonder: Stories of Fantasy and Science Fiction. New York, Bantam, 1958.

Plays

Screenplays: *Queen of Outer Space*, with Ben Hecht, 1958; *The Intruder* (*The Stranger*), 1962; *The Wonderful World of the Brothers Grimm*, with David P. Harmon and William Roberts, 1962; *Mister Moses*, with Monja Danischewsky, 1965.

Television Plays: episodes of *Naked City, Thriller, Four Star Playhouse, Damon Runyon Theatre, The D.A.'s Man, Markham, Have Gun—Will Travel, Wanted—Dead or Alive, Route 66* and other series.

Other

Remember? Remember? New York, Macmillan, 1963.

Editor, with William F. Nolan, *Omnibus of Speed: An Introduction to the World of Motor Sport*. New York, Putnam, 1958; London, Stanley Paul, 1961.
Editor, with William F. Nolan, *When Engines Roar*. New York, Bantam, 1964.

*

Film Adaptation: *The Intruder* (*The Stranger*), 1962.

Bibliography: *The Work of Charles Beaumont: An Annotated Bibliography and Guide* by William F. Nolan, San Bernardino, California, Borgo Press, 1986, 2nd edition, 1990.

*   *   *

Charles Beaumont's attitude toward weird fiction is summed up in his pithy introduction to the anthology *The Fiend in You*. There, he writes about the new monster riding the crest of the contemporary horror wave: "He doesn't wear an opera cape or shaggy shirt or a white bedsheet; he doesn't rattle chains or moan; he doesn't sleep in a coffin; yet he is the most terrifying monster of all. He's called The Mind." Beaumont elaborated this idea in terms of what he called "the slumbering fiend in you," that part of the reader's consciousness aroused by horror stories. The stories that Beaumont had in mind, however, were not those built around traditional Gothic horrors, but ones being turned out by a

circle of writers that included Ray Bradbury, Richard Matheson, Ray Russell, William F. Nolan, and himself: dark fantasies featuring modern characters caught up in situations that resonated with the reader's personal experience.

Beaumont's career as a writer began in 1951, just when the pulp magazines that had sustained the weird fiction market for decades began disappearing from the newsstands. Although he ultimately contributed to the digests that replaced the pulps, a significant amount of his writing—his macabre fiction in particular—appeared first in *Playboy*, *Rogue* and other titles in the burgeoning men's-magazine market. These magazines catered to a more adult audience than the pulps had, and the fiction that appeared in them tended to be more sophisticated and less bound by the clichés of genre. Furthermore, they allowed writers to explore candid subjects hitherto taboo in genre magazines.

Beaumont responded to the greater latitude these markets permitted with stories in which elements of crime, fantasy and science fiction served as vehicles for themes more commonly associated with the literary mainstream: alienation, social conformity, the quest for personal meaning. In his tales of horror, he replaced the usual supernatural forces that threaten from outside with forces that destabilize the individual and the community from within: ennui, discontent, and the death of dreams. One of the most formidable menaces in his fiction is the banality of average existence. In his tale "The Vanishing American," a meek man who holds down an uninspiring office job discovers that the predictable routine of his home and work life is slowly rendering him invisible: "The process of disappearing was set into action every time he brought his pay check home and turned it over to Madge, every time he kissed her, or listened to her vicious unending complaints, or decided against buying that novel, or punched the adding machine he hated so." In "The New People," the ordinary is a catalyst for the diabolical. The protagonist discovers too late that he and his family have moved into a neighbourhood whose members are so jaded by the mundane ease of their lives that they resort to deviant and deadly games to alleviate their boredom. Were it not for the comic edge to much of his writing, these and other of his stories might have earned Beaumont a reputation as the angry young man of the postwar horror generation.

Beaumont was fascinated by the possibility that pathology festered beneath the most normal facades. "Why, every city has its neighbourhoods just like ours," observes one of the malefactors in "The New People." "We're not really that unique." Many of his stories are character studies of individuals who find themselves goaded to extreme behaviours that seem entirely out of character. Repressed sexuality proves a hidden reservoir of personal darkness that engulfs the protagonists of several of his most powerful macabre tales. "The Dark Music" features a spinsterly schoolteacher who punishes her students for having the same passionate impulses that she herself indulges in a secret tryst with a satyr. In "The Hunger," an unmarried woman whose youth is fading hopes to avoid the life lived by her puritanical sisters by becoming the victim of a sexual predator. The title character of "Miss Gentibelle" is a woman so traumatized by a failed romance that she forces her young son to dress as a girl and inflicts cruel punishments on him as means of striking back at the man whom she feels has betrayed her sexually.

In Beaumont's tales, strong emotion proves as disorienting and dislocating a force as the supernatural. Many of his darkest tales feature no supernaturalism or a fantasy element that is ambiguous at best. Some are studies of psychopathology that barely qualify as horror in the usual sense. In "Black Country," he suggests the supernatural possession of a white trumpet-player by the spirit of his black mentor through the rhythm of the jazzy narrative. "Night Ride" offers a portrait of the devil incarnate in its rendering of a manager whose job is to keep his band members miserable so that they'll always have painful experiences to transform into their blues-driven music. His novel *The Intruder* is a non-supernatural tale of race relations in the American South during the Civil Rights movement, but its study of a rabble rouser who draws out the prejudices of seemingly tolerant townspeople to serve a scheme of his own sinister design merits comparison to Shirley Jackson's "One Ordinary Day with Peanuts," Richard Matheson's "The Distributor," and other tales of paranoia that border on the fantastic.

Beaumont never completely forsook the traditional themes of horror fiction, and wrought untraditional variations on them in some of his best-known stories. In "The Jungle," he imagined the incongruity of an ancient native curse working itself out in a near-future society. "Blood Brother" and "Place of Meeting" are both vampire tales, but the former is a comic reflection on the practical difficulty of being a vampire in modern times and the latter a sardonic doomsday tale that uses vampiric immortality as a sounding board for humankind's endless capacity for self-destruction. The Devil makes appearances in "The Devil, You Say?" a screwball fantasy on the dark side of small-town life, and "The Howling Man," which ends with a meditation on the banality of evil in Hitler's Germany. Several of these stories were adapted for Rod Serling's television programme *The Twilight Zone*, to which Beaumont was the second most prolific contributor after Serling himself. Indeed, television adaptations of Beaumont's work were as important as his stories for keeping his memory alive following his tragic death from Alzheimer's disease at the age of 38. Through both, he became one of the most important, if largely unsung influences on dark fantasy fiction of the 1970s and 1980s.

—Stefan R. Dziemianowicz

BECKFORD, William

Pseudonym: Jacquetta Jenks. **Nationality:** British. **Born:** Fonthill, Wiltshire, 29 September 1760; son of an ex-Lord Mayor of London. **Education:** Private. **Family:** Married Lady Margaret Gordon in 1783 (died 1786); two daughters. **Career:** Inherited great wealth at the age of nine; lived in France and elsewhere on the continent of Europe for much of his early adult life; wrote his fiction in French; art collector and dilettante; owner of Fonthill Abbey; member of Parliament; obliged to sell Fonthill in 1822, he spent his last two decades in Bath. **Died:** 2 May 1844.

HORROR, GHOST AND GOTHIC PUBLICATIONS

Novel

An Arabian Tale, from an Unpublished Manuscript, translated by Samuel Henley. London, Johnson, 1786; as *Vathek*, London, Clarke, 1816; as *The History of the Caliph Vathek*, London, Sampson Low, 1868.

Short Stories

The Episodes of Vathek, translated by Frank Marzials. London, Swift, 1912.
The Vision: Liber Veritatis. London, Constable, 1930.
Vathek and Other Stories: A William Beckford Reader, edited by Malcolm Jack. London, London, Pickering and Chatto, 1993.

OTHER PUBLICATIONS

Novel

Azemia (as Jacquetta Jenks). 1797.

Other

Biographical Memoirs of Extraordinary Painters. 1780.
Dreams, Waking Thoughts, and Incidents. 1783; revised edition, as *Italy, with Sketches of Spain and Portugal*, 1834.
Modern Novel Writing; or, The Elegant Enthusiast. 1796.
Recollections of an Excursion to the Monasteries of Alcobaca and Batalha. 1835.
Life at Fonthill, 1807-22, edited by Boyd Alexander, London, Hart Davis, 1957.

*

Critical Studies (selection): *The Life and Letters of William Beckford* by Lewis Melville, 1910; *The Life of William Beckford* by John W. Oliver, 1932; *The Caliph of Fonthill* by H. A. N. Brockman, 1956; *England's Wealthiest Son: A Study of William Beckford* by Boyd Alexander, London, Centaur Press, 1962; *Beckford of Fonthill* by Brian Fothergill, London, Faber, 1979.

*   *   *

The blanket attachment of the label "Gothic" to the sensational fiction which became fashionable as the 18th century neared its *fin de siècle* had as much to do with William Beckford's architectural exploits at Fonthill Abbey and Horace Walpole's erection of Strawberry Hill as with the contents of the fantasies on which their literary fame is founded. The gaudy Oriental narrative apparatus of *Vathek* is in many ways unlike the gloomy Germanic stock-in-trade of *The Castle of Otranto*, which provided a blueprint for many of the imitative "horrid novels" which followed in their wake. The critic in search of parallels between *Vathek* and the typical Gothic extravaganza can find a few—a spectacularly defiant and charismatic villain, a submerged but darkly obsessive interest in perverse sexuality, and a diabolical bargain which ultimately leads to damnation—but the fact remains that Beckford's is a highly idiosyncratic production which differs from the run-of-the-mill Gothics not merely in the overblown exoticism of its Arabic setting but also in the near-comic grotesquerie of its manner.

Vathek owes an obvious debt to *The Arabian Nights*, which had been translated into French by Antoine Galland in the early part of the 18th century. A more direct inspiration, however, was the satirical *contes philosophiques* of Voltaire, whom Beckford met in Paris in 1777—although *Vathek* is no more typical of the genre of *contes philosophiques* than it is of the Gothic genre. Voltaire subjected his corrosive sarcasm and phantasmagorical imagination to a discipline which Beckford did not try to imitate; he aimed instead for excess, thus anticipating another writer of elaborately-extended *contes philosophiques*: the Marquis de Sade. Five years before Sade published *Justine*—which may be regarded as his own version of Voltaire's *Candide*, carrying the related argument that there is nothing in Nature to deny the powerful the right to indulge themselves to the full in the perverse pleasure of perpetrating horrors—Beckford had sent forth his eponymous Caliph on a similar quest.

Having contrived a massacre of innocents to seal a bargain with the diabolical Giaour—a decision sanctioned and prompted by his venal mother Carathis—Vathek is provided with an alluring but dim-witted consort in Nouronihar, in whose company he sets off for the Halls of Eblis to claim the ultimate prize. Whereas the great pioneer of diabolical bargains, Faust, had bargained with the devil for enlightenment, pleasure and profit, Vathek—who already possesses all that—has no option but to ask for more. He has to aspire to some final and absolute indulgence, even though he cannot imagine what it might be.

The fate which eventually claims Vathek may appear to pay lip service to the psychological terrorism of priestly morality but in fact it bursts the petty bounds of that sort of retributive justice. So far has he transcended the limits of earthly evil that even the archfiend Eblis has no torture to fit his crime. Vathek can only be self-condemned to a Hell of his own: the realization that his boundless desires must remain forever unsatisfied. This revelation is symbolized by the essentially ineffective fire which can sear but never consume his desirous heart, leaving all the yearnings of the flesh intact while it mocks their hopeless ambition for fulfilment. It is arguable that this image has never been surpassed in the two centuries during which a veritable legion of later writers has delved deep in search of the ultimate horror.

Beckford had inherited property worth a million pounds from his erratic father, including the neo-Gothic monstrosity of Fonthill Abbey, which had the habit of being burnt to the ground and falling down, only to rise each time like a phoenix, more grandiosely than before. Until a shortage of ready money forced him to sell the Abbey (before its famous tower came crashing down for the last time) Beckford furnished it with everything he might desire and indulged himself as far as practicality would permit. No one was ever as well-placed to dream such a dream as Vathek—certainly not poor Sade, entombed within the Bastille while he doggedly ploughed his way through the co-prophiliac enumerations of *The 120 Days of Sodom*—and it is not surprising that modern critics have found much of the author's own life and personality in the novel. Whether or not his mother could have recognized herself in Carathis, or his cousin's wife Louisa in Nouronihar, the scathing parodies evidently seemed appropriate to Beckford.

The last paragraph of *Vathek* assures us that "the humble and despised Gulchenrouz" (who serves to introduce a note of homoerotic paedophilia into the unruly pattern of Vathek's lusts) has gone to a very different place, where he will pass "whole ages in the undisturbed tranquillity and the pure happiness of childhood." This is not, however, a sop to conventional morality; the passage is sarcastic in the best Voltairean tradition, arguing that Paradise is a place fit only for children: perfect bliss for the ignorant and eternal peace for the mindless. The final irony of Vathek's paradoxical damnation is that there is, after all, no alternative that anyone blessed with freedom of desire could possibly want. The fact that this sarcasm

survived the text's translation from the original French by the Reverend Samuel Henley—who published it in apparent defiance of the author's wishes—must be regarded as a fortunate consequence of the clergyman's own ignorance.

Beckford wrote *Vathek* at the age of 22; after its premature publication he often claimed to be working on a series of tales to be interpolated into the narrative but when they failed to materialize they were thought not to exist, until versions of three of them turned up 50 years after his death. Unfortunately, the two completed tales offer routine and—if the Marzials translation can be trusted—disappointingly earnest accounts of sin and damnation, while the third is unfinished. They were probably penned when Beckford was a good deal older, wiser, sadder and duller than he had been at 22. Clark Ashton Smith provided an ending of sorts for the last episode, but even such master of Decadent excess as he could not recapitulate the magnificent blasphemy of the original. Another incomplete work belatedly found among Beckford's papers was "The Vision," a phantasmagoric romance seemingly written when he was 17, involving a journey into a strange subterranean world whose inhabitants involve the dwarfish and degenerate remnants of the races which ruled the Earth in antediluvian times. It includes an early version of the Nouronihar of *Vathek* but is far less cynical and not remotely as magnificent.

—Brian Stableford

BELL, Neil

Pseudonym for Stephen Southwold. **Other Pseudonyms:** S. H. Lambert; Paul Martens; Miles. **Nationality:** British. **Born:** Stephen Henry Critten, in Southwold, Suffolk, 1887; adopted the name Stephen Southwold. **Education:** St. Mark's College, Chelsea, London. **Military Service:** Served in the British Army, World War I. **Family:** Married in 1928; two sons and one daughter. **Career:** Journalist; freelance novelist. **Died:** 5 June 1964.

HORROR, GHOST AND GOTHIC PUBLICATIONS

Novels

Precious Porcelain. London, Gollancz, and New York, Putnam, 1931.
The Disturbing Affair of Noel Blake. London, Gollancz, and New York, Putnam, 1932.
Death Rocks the Cradle: A Strange Tale (as Paul Martens). London, Collins, 1933.
Portrait of Gideon Power (as S. H. Lambert). London, Jarrolds, 1944.

Short Stories

Mixed Pickles: Short Stories. London, Collins, 1935.
Alpha and Omega. London, Hale, 1946.
Who Walk in Fear. London, Alvin Redman, 1953.
The Captain's Woman and Other Stories. London, Alvin Redman, 1955.

OTHER PUBLICATIONS

Novels

The Seventh Bowl (as Miles). London, Partridge, 1930; as Neil Bell, London, Collins, 1934.

The Gas War of 1940 (as Miles). London, Partridge, 1931; as *Valiant Clay* as Neil Bell, London, Collins, 1934.

Life and Andrew Otway. London, Gollancz, 1931; New York, Putnam, 1932.

The Marriage of Simon Harper. London, Gollancz, 1932.

The Lord of Life. Boston, Little, Brown, and London, Collins, 1933.

Bredon and Sons. London, Collins, 1934.

The Truth About My Father (as Paul Martens). London, Collins, 1934; as Neil Bell, London, Collins, 1936.

Winding Road. Boston, Little, Brown, and London, Collins, 1934.

The Days Dividing. Boston, Little, Brown, and London, Collins, 1935.

The Son of Richard Carden. Boston, Little, Brown, and London, Collins, 1935.

Crocus. London, Collins, 1936; New York, Doubleday, 1937.

Strange Melody. New York, Doubleday, and London, Collins, 1936.

Pinkney's Garden. London, Collins, and New York, Doubleday, 1937.

The Testament of Stephen Fane. London, Collins, 1937.

One Came Back. London, Collins, 1938.

The Abbot's Heel. London, Collins, 1939.

Love and Julian Farne. London, Collins, 1939.

Not a Sparrow Falls. London, Collins, 1939.

So Perish the Roses. London, Collins, and New York, Macmillan, 1940.

Desperate Pursuit. London, Collins, 1941.

Tower of Darkness. London, Collins, 1942.

Peek's Progress. London, Collins, 1942.

Cover His Face: A Novel of the Life and Times of Thomas Chatterton. London, Collins, 1943.

Child of My Sorrow. London, Collins, 1944.

The Handsome Langleys. London, Eyre and Spottiswoode, 1945.

A Romance in Lavender. London, Hale, 1946.

Life Comes to Seathorpe. London, Eyre and Spottiswoode, 1946.

Forgive Us Our Trespasses. London, Eyre and Spottiswoode, 1947.

The Governess at Ashburton Hall. London, Eyre and Spottiswoode, 1948.

Immortal Dyer. London, Alvin Redman, 1948.

Scallywag. London, University of London Press, 1949.

Who Was James Carey? London, Eyre and Spottiswoode, 1949.

I am Legion. London, Eyre and Spottiswoode, 1950.

The Inconstant Wife (as Stephen Southwold). London, Hale, 1950.

The Dark Page. London, Eyre and Spottiswoode, 1951.

Flowers of the Forest. London, Eyre and Spottiswoode, 1952.

One of the Best. London, Eyre and Spottiswoode, 1952.

Custody of the Child. London, Eyre and Spottiswoode, 1953.

Many Waters. London, Eyre and Spottiswoode, 1954.

Luke Branwhite. London, Eyre and Spottiswoode, 1955.

All My Days. London, Eyre and Spottiswoode, 1956.

The Endless Chain. London, Alvin Redman, 1956.

What No Woman Knows. London, Eyre and Spottiswoode, 1957.

Thy First Begotten. London, Alvin Redman, 1957.

Love and Desire and Hate. London, Alvin Redman, 1957.

The Black Sheep. London, Alvin Redman, 1958.

Mrs. Rawleigh and Mrs. Paradock. London, Alvin Redman, 1958.

At the Sign of the Unicorn. London, Alvin Redman, 1959.

Simon Dale. London, Alvin Redman, 1959.

My Brother Charles. London, Alvin Redman, 1960.

The Narrow Edge. London, Alvin Redman, 1961.

13 Piccadilly. London, Alvin Redman, 1961.

Weekend in Paris. London, Alvin Redman, 1962.

I Paint Your World. London, Alvin Redman, 1963.

The Story of Leon Barentz. London, Alvin Redman, 1963.

This Time for Love. London, Alvin Redman, 1964.

Short Stories

The Smallways Rub Along. London, Collins, 1938.

Spice of Life. London, Collins, 1941.

The House at the Crossroads. London, Alvin Redman, 1946.

Ten Short Stories. N.p., 1948.

Three Pair of Heels. London, Alvin Redman, 1951.

The Secret Life of Miss Lottinger. London, Alvin Redman, 1953.

Forty Stories. London, Alvin Redman, 1958.

Corridor of Venus. London, Alvin Redman, 1960.

Village Casanova and Other Stories. London, Alvin Redman, 1961.

The Ninth Earl of Whitby. London, Alvin Redman, 1966.

Books for Children (as Stephen Southwold)

In-Between Stories. New York and London, Longmans, 1923.

Twilight Tales. London, Faber and Gwyer, 1925.

Listen Children!: Stories for Spare Moments. London, Harrap, and New York, Dodd, Mead, 1926.

The Children's Play-Hour Book. New York and London, Longmans, 1927

Once-Upon-a-Time Stories. London, Collins, 1927

Ten-Minute Tales. London, Longmans, 1927.

Listen Again, Children! London, Harrap, 1928.

Yesterday and Long Ago. London, Collins, 1928.

The Book of Animal Tales. New York, Crowell, 1929.

Man's Great Adventure. London and New York, Longmans, 1929.

Happy Families. New York and London, Longmans, 1929.

Fiddlededee: A Medley of Stories. N.p., 1930.

Hey, Diddle Diddle. London, Collins, 1930.

The Hunted One and Other Stories. N.p., 1930.

The Jumpers. N.p., 1930.

Tales Quaint and Queer. London, Collins, 1930.

The Last Bus and Other Stories. N.p., 1930.

The Welsh Rabbit and Other Stories. N.p., 1930.

Tick-Tock Tales. London, Phillips, 1930.

The Longest Lane and Other Stories. N.p., 1930.

True Tales of an Old Shellback. London and New York, Longmans, 1930.

The Sea Horses and Other Stories. N.p., 1930.

Tales of Forest Folk and Other Stories. N.p., 1930.

Three by Candlelight and Other Stories. N.p., 1930.

The Old Brown Brook. London, University of London Press, 1931.

Fairy Tales. N.p., 1931.

Once Upon a Time. N.p., 1931.

Forty More Tales. London, Collins, 1935.

More Animal Stories. London, Harrap, 1935.

The Tales of Joe Egg. London, Collins, 1936.

Tell Me Another. London, Longmans, 1938.

Now for a Story. London, Harrap, 1938.
Now for More Stories! N.p., 1938.

Other

My Writing Life. London, Alvin Redman, 1955.

Editor (as Stephen Southwold), *Old Gold: A Book of Fables and Parables.* London, Dent, 1926.

*   *   *

Neil Bell was the first of several pseudonyms invented by Stephen H. Critten, and the one he used most frequently, although the one he adopted as his "real" name was Stephen Southwold. It was because he hated and despised his father—for reasons elaborately described in the quasi-autobiographical sections of several of his novels—that he preferred to call himself after his birthplace, and the legacy of his harsh upbringing infected his worldview so considerably as to give almost all of his work a cynical cutting edge. Had magazine editors not found such early *contes cruels* as "Slip" and "Sovvy's Babe" too repellent to be publishable—leaving him to put them in print himself in *Mixed Pickles*—he might have become England's premier writer in that genre, but he softened his work in the interests of professionalism. In the same collection, the messianic fantasy "The Facts About Benjamin Crede" brings its saintly flier crashing down to earth, while the delusional fantasies "The Spider" and "The Mirror" both end in humiliating fatality, but the occasional supernatural tales dotted about his later collections are decidedly anaemic by comparison.

Although they are not nearly as nasty-minded as the scientific romances he published as "Miles," Bell's two early novels of artificially-disordered personality, *Precious Porcelain* and *The Disturbing Affair of Noel Blake*, are noteworthy for the development of a subtler kind of horror. In each case a series of peculiar but not initially menacing manifestations disturb the tranquil life of onlookers, with steadily increasing violence, until the perspective shifts and the individual responsible can give a chilling account of his personal disintegration. The "Paul Martens" novel *Death Rocks the Cradle* is far less sophisticated in narrative terms—Bell's autobiography *My Writing Life* admits that it was a potboiler knocked out in a fortnight—but it contains a strikingly garish vision of the nightmarish land of Salabria, where degenerates are encouraged to indulge their unhealthy appetites so that an elite of sadists can savour the agonies and indignities of their subsequent medical treatment.

The success of *Bredon and Sons* persuaded Bell to put aside imaginative fiction in favour of narrative realism, punctuated by occasional ventures into historical romance. It was not until his career began to decline that he was tempted back to horror fiction in earnest, although the "S. H. Lambert" novel *Portrait of Gideon Power* is a curious psychological case-study of a man whose capacity for selfless heroism is intricately intertwined with his capacity for dispassionate sadism. The novel takes the form of "evidence" offered at the Seat of Judgment by people who all knew the eponymous enigma reasonably well but reached very different assessments of his moral worth; the fantasized format requires the reader to consider the hypothesis that good and evil are not as easily separable as Christian doctrine tacitly supposes.

Among Bell's later story-collections the one which includes the highest proportion of supernatural stories is *Alpha and Omega*, the most interesting being "Strange Encounter," an unusual tale of reincarnation. Most of his short work from the 1950s is, however, calculatedly trivial and casually sarcastic. Such brutal *contes cruels* as the title-story of *The Captain's Woman* have none of the subtlety and devastating simplicity of "Slip" or "Sovvy's Babe." The scientific romance *Life Comes to Seathorpe* reproduces the narrative pattern of *Precious Porcelain* and *The Disturbing Affair of Noel Blake* but is far more interested in the implications of its central premise than the disturbing nature of the problematic manifestations. One late book by Bell which did aspire to break new ground, however, was the collection of three novellas *Who Walk in Fear*, which is prefaced by an essay on horror fiction.

Only the first of the three tales, "Culver Island," has any fantastic element. It tells the story of a group of castaways on a desert island who are menaced by giant crabs, detailing the manner in which possession of their one and only firearm becomes the key to power within the group. As in Bell's early disaster story *The Lord of Life*, the microcosm of society formed by the isolated company is ruled by the politics of envy and administered by the threat of violence—with the inevitable result that the crabs only have to wait for their meal to be delivered to them. "The Mate of the S.S. Vega" is also about castaways, who extend their lives while drifting in a small boat by resorting to cannibalism; the survivors are rescued from the boat but not from the habit acquired during their ordeal. "Thirty-six Hours" is a kind of tale which has since become very common, in which the handsome stranger who seems to be the man of the heroine's dreams turns out to be a serial killer, but it was exceptional in its day. Earnestly fascinated literary analyses of sexual psychosis are now so familiar that Bell's story will inevitably seem crude to contemporary readers but 1953 was the year of the first "Hank Janson" obscenity trial, which spearheaded a significant moral panic about sex and sadism in popular fiction. "Thirty-six Hours" was a daring endeavour for a respectable middlebrow novelist and it broke new ground in the stratum of the literary marketplace in which Bell operated.

Like many other British writers of the inter-bellum period, Bell found horror fiction unprofitable and gave it up after several significant early endeavours—but he was one of those who could never rid himself of the jaundiced world-view which gave rise to such material, and he went back to it when he could. Had he lived in a different era, he would certainly have indulged his bent much more fully, but we can only speculate as to what he might have produced had his propensity for literary cruelty ever been let off the bit.

—Brian Stableford

BENCHLEY, Peter (Bradford)

Nationality: American. **Born:** New York, 8 May 1940; son of novelist Nathaniel Benchley and grandson of humorist Robert Benchley. **Education:** Harvard University, A.B. (cum laude), 1961. **Military Service:** U.S. Marine Corps Reserve, 1962-63. **Family:** Married Wendy Wesson in 1964. **Career:** Reporter, *Washington Post*, Washington, D.C., 1963; associate editor, *Newsweek*, New York City, 1964-67; staff assistant to the President of the

United States, 1967-69; freelance writer and television news correspondent, from 1969. Host of television series, *Expedition Earth*, ESPN; host/narrator/writer of more than a dozen wildlife/adventure television shows. **Agent:** International Creative Management, 40 West 57th St., New York, NY 10019, USA.

Horror, Ghost and Gothic Publications

Novels

Jaws. New York, Doubleday, 1974.
The Deep. New York, Doubleday, 1976.
The Island. New York, Doubleday, 1979.
The Girl of the Sea of Cortez. New York, Doubleday, 1982.
Beast. New York, Random House, and London, Hutchinson, 1991.
Three Complete Novels (omnibus; includes *Jaws, The Girl of the Sea of Cortez, Beast*). New York, Random House Value Publishing, 1993.
White Shark. New York, Random House, and London, Hutchinson, 1994.

Plays

Screenplays: *Jaws*, with Carl Gottlieb, 1975; *The Deep,* with Tracy Keenan Wynn, 1977; *The Island,* 1980.

Other Publications

Novels

Jonathan Visits the White House (for children). New York, McGraw, 1964.
Q Clearance. New York, Random House, 1986.
Rummies. New York, Random House, 1989.

Other

Time and a Ticket. Boston, Houghton Mifflin, 1964.
Ocean Planet: Writing and Images of the Sea. New York, Abrams/ Times Mirror Magazines/Smithsonian Institution, 1995.

*

Film Adaptations: *Jaws*, 1975; *The Deep*, 1977; *The Island*, 1980; *Beast* (television film), 1996; *White Shark* (television film), 1998.

* * *

Since some physiological evidence, like an infant swimming reflex and webbed fingers, indicates that prehistoric humans once lived in the water, the ocean should be a place that evokes primordial emotions, just as suitable a setting for horror as the shadowy forests that were our other ancient home. Perhaps that explains why people of the past often avoided swimming in the ocean. During the last century, however, seashore swimming emerged as a characteristic pastime of the idle rich, and to this day remains an activity associated with wealth and leisure time. A horror story about the sea, then, might necessarily become a story about social classes and economic distinctions.

Thus, Peter Benchley's *Jaws* may read today like a novel obsessed with materialism for reasons other than that it was originally accompanied by an immense promotional hoopla leading to four films, an amusement-park ride, innumerable items of merchandise, and the eventual emergence of its homicidal white shark as a cultural icon. In Bram Stoker's *Dracula*, nobody worried about how an army of vampires preying upon London might dampen the British economy; but in *Jaws*, the economic impact of the shark, more than the relatively few deaths it causes, is everyone's dominant concern. The humble residents of Amity desperately require a large influx of summer visitors to stay alive; whenever police chief Martin Brody wants to close the beaches because of shark attacks, he is opposed by business interests who fear a disastrous loss of income; and, while the shark rips open the submerged social divisions in Amity, it also divides Brody from his wife, since the appearance of shark scientist Matthew Hooper reawakens in Ellen a longing for the privileged life she abandoned to marry the proletarian Martin. The true horror of *Jaws* is that it exposes just how miserable it is to be a poor person dependent upon rich people; and it is remarkable that Benchley, himself the scion of a distinguished literary family, displays so much sympathy for the sorts of people who waited on him as he grew up living in comfort like Amity's tourists. Unfortunately, Benchley seems unaware that these issues are central to his narrative, since *Jaws* ends abruptly and unsatisfactorily with the killing of the shark, which eliminates the immediate threat but does not heal the larger social and personal wounds the shark inflicted.

Benchley's next three novels, while about the sea, are only tangentially related to horror and largely lack the substantive undercurrents that animated *Jaws*. *The Deep* has a few horrific touches—a brief shark attack, a Bermudan villain who employs voodoo fetishes—but is basically an adventure novel, with wealthy honeymooners joining a veteran seaman to explore the intermingled wrecks of an old pirate ship and a World War II vessel filled with explosive shells and morphine ampoule. *The Island* features a reporter investigating disappearances in the Bermuda Triangle who discovers descendants of pirates living on an undiscovered island. And *The Girl of the Sea of Cortez*, gently describing a young Mexican girl's love for and desire to protect the sea, comes alive in a conclusion that reverses the emotional dynamics of *Jaws*, as readers root for a gigantic manta ray who rises out of the depths to attack fishermen. Because the chief villain, the girl's brother, is killing fish simply to earn money so he can move away, there appears again a conflict between commerce and idealism, now alloyed to a heightened ecological awareness.

After going ashore for two unheralded novels—*Q Clearance*, a political comedy about a presidential speech-writer, and *Rummies*, the story of an alcoholic who discovers shady dealings at a rehabilitation facility—Benchley visibly attempted to recapture the essence of his greatest triumph with *Beast*, where a giant sea squid repeatedly attacks residents of Bermuda. Judged solely in terms of writing skill, it is superior to *Jaws*, including some involving chapters from the perspective of the squid and featuring Whip Darling, the most persuasive of Benchley's crusty old tars. Yet it lacks the thematic unity of its precursor; though Benchley haphazardly aims at various targets—obdurate bureaucrats, unscrupulous fishermen, a manipulative media mogul, an incompetent government scientist—none of these occupy his attention long enough to have any impact; as a result, *Beast* provides a series of exciting encounters with a sea monster, but little more.

While *Beast* maintained the realistic atmosphere of *Jaws*, Benchley next lurched into science fiction with the bizarre *White Shark*. Flatly summarized, its premise seems laughable: near the end of World War II, a Nazi scientist develops a prototype for the Ultimate Weapon—an amphibious human, something like a half-man, half-shark—which is also a programmed killing machine. Smuggled out of the collapsing Third Reich on a U-Boat, it inexplicably survives in a locked chamber when the submarine sinks off the Atlantic, then is accidentally released to terrorize the New England town of Waterboro. When, after several animals and humans are slaughtered, its true nature is revealed by a surviving assistant to the scientist, it is hard to avoid mental pictures of the old *Saturday Night Live* sketches about "land sharks" or the television cartoon heroes *Street Sharks*. Yet this ludicrous threat is oddly juxtaposed with Benchley's most effective setting and characters to date; apparently happy to return to the United States after four sea novels set further south, the author conveys the atmosphere of New England more successfully than in *Jaws*, and he offers his most fully developed and resonant characters, including Simon Chase, an idealistic ocean scientist; Max, the twelve-year-old son he is finally bonding with after a divorce; Elizabeth, a deaf but empathic girl whom Max has a crush on; and Amanda Macy, a wealthy scientist studying at Simon's struggling research institute. And uniting the characters is a common desire to defend the sea against the encroachment of greedy and thoughtless exploiters, the theme that surfaced in *The Girl of the Sea of Cortez* and might have been even more effective here if the problem being confronted did not provoke giggles. One wishes that Benchley had employed this cast in a different novel.

The sea continues to intrigue and terrify the human race, and Benchley probably should be praised for his efforts to develop the sub-genre of the seagoing horror novel with no true prototypes to guide him. He has at least identified the necessary ingredients—a deep knowledge of and respect for the sea, a primeval predatory menace, attentiveness to developed settings and characters, and a strong socioeconomic sub-text—and he remains clearly capable of putting all the pieces together to produce a genuine masterpiece. In the meantime, readers can sporadically enjoy the imperfect successes he has so far achieved.

—Gary Westfahl

BENÉT, Stephen Vincent

Nationality: American. **Born:** Bethlehem, Pennsylvania, 22 July 1898; brother of the writer William Rose Benét. **Education:** Hitchcock Military Academy, Jacinto, California, 1910-11; Summerville Academy; Yale University, New Haven, Connecticut (chairman, *Yale Literary Magazine*, 1918), 1915-18, 1919-20, A.B. 1919, M.A. 1920; the Sorbonne, Paris, 1920-21. **Family:** Married Rosemary Carr in 1921; one son and two daughters. **Career:** Worked for the State Department, Washington, D.C., 1918, and for an advertising agency, New York, 1919; lived in Paris, 1926-29; during 1930s and early 1940s was an active lecturer and radio propagandist for the liberal cause. Editor, Yale Younger Poets series. **Awards:** Poetry Society of America prize, 1921; Guggenheim fellowship, 1926; Pulitzer Prize, 1929, 1944; O. Henry award, 1932, 1937, 1940; Shelley Memorial award, 1933; American Academy gold medal, 1943. Litt.D.: Yale University, 1937. Member, 1929, and vice-president, National Institute of Arts and Letters. **Died:** 13 March 1943.

HORROR, GHOST AND GOTHIC PUBLICATIONS

Short Stories

The Devil and Daniel Webster. New York, Farrar and Rinehart, 1937.
Thirteen O'Clock: Stories of Several Worlds. New York, Farrar and Rinehart, 1937; London, Heinemann, 1938.
Johnny Pye and the Fool-Killer. Weston, Vermont, Countryman Press, and London, Heinemann, 1938.
Tales before Midnight. New York, Farrar and Rinehart, 1939; London, Heinemann, 1940.
The Last Circle: Stories and Poems. New York, Farrar Straus, 1946; London, Heinemann, 1948.

Plays

The Devil and Daniel Webster, adaptation of his own story, music by Douglas Moore (produced New York, 1939). Opera version published New York, Farrar and Rinehart, 1939; play text published New York, Dramatists Play Service, 1939.
All That Money Can Buy (*The Devil and Daniel Webster*), with Dan Totheroh, in *Twenty Best Film Plays*, edited by John Gassner and Dudley Nichols. New York, Crown, 1943.

Screenplay: *All That Money Can Buy* (*The Devil and Daniel Webster*), with Dan Totheroh, 1941.

OTHER PUBLICATIONS

Novels

The Beginning of Wisdom. New York, Holt, 1921; London, Chapman and Dodd, 1922.
Young People's Pride. New York, Holt, 1922.
Jean Huguenot. New York, Holt, 1923; London, Methuen, 1925.
Spanish Bayonet. New York, Doran, and London, Heinemann, 1926.
James Shore's Daughter. New York, Doubleday, and London, Heinemann, 1934.

Short Stories

The Barefoot Saint. New York, Doubleday, 1929.
The Litter of Rose Leaves. New York, Random House, 1930.
Short Stories: A Selection. New York, Farrar and Rinehart, 1942.
O'Halloran's Luck and Other Short Stories. New York, Penguin, 1944.

Plays

Five Men and Pompey: A Series of Dramatic Portraits. Boston, Four Seas, 1915.
Nerves, with John Farrar (produced New York, 1924).
That Awful Mrs. Eaton, with John Farrar (produced New York, 1924).
The Headless Horseman, music by Douglas Moore (broadcast 1937). Boston, Schirmer, 1937.
Elementals (broadcast 1940-41). Published in *Best Broadcasts of 1940-41*, edited by Max Wylie, New York, McGraw Hill, 1942.

Freedom's Hard Bought Thing, adaptation of his own story (broadcast 1941). Published in *The Free Company Presents*, edited by James Boyd, New York, Dodd Mead, 1941.

Nightmare at Noon, in *The Treasury Star Parade*, edited by William A. Bacher. New York, Farrar and Rinehart, 1942.

A Child Is Born (broadcast 1942). New York, Farrar and Rinehart, 1942.

They Burned the Books (broadcast 1942). New York, Farrar and Rinehart, 1942.

We Stand United and Other Radio Scripts (includes *A Child Is Born, The Undefended Border, Dear Adolf, Listen to the People, Thanksgiving Day—1941, They Burned the Books, A Time to Reap, Toward the Century of Modern Man, Your Army*). New York, Farrar and Rinehart, 1945.

Screenplays: *Abraham Lincoln*, with Gerrit Lloyd, 1930; *Cheers for Miss Bishop*, with Adelaide Heilbron and Sheridan Gibney, 1941.

Radio Plays: *The Headless Horseman*, 1937; *The Undefended Border*, 1940; *We Stand United*, 1940; *Elementals*, 1940-41; *Listen to the People*, 1941; *Thanksgiving Day—1941*, 1941; *Freedom's Hard Bought Thing*, 1941; *Nightmare at Noon*, 1942; *A Child Is Born*, 1942; *Dear Adolf*, 1942; *They Burned the Books*, 1942; *A Time to Reap*, 1942; *Toward the Century of Modern Man*, 1942; *Your Army*, 1944.

Poetry

The Drug-Shop; or, Endymion in Edmonstoun. New Haven, Connecticut, Yale University Press, 1917.

Young Adventure. New Haven, Connecticut, Yale University Press, 1918.

Heavens and Earth. New York, Holt, 1920; London, Heinemann, 1928.

The Ballad of William Sycamore 1790-1880. New York, Hackett, 1923.

King David. New York, Holt, 1923.

Tiger Joy. New York, Doran, 1925.

John Brown's Body. New York, Doubleday, and London, Heinemann, 1928.

Ballads and Poems 1915-1930. New York, Doubleday, 1931; London, Heinemann, 1933.

A Book of Americans, with Rosemary Benét. New York, Farrar and Rinehart, 1933.

Burning City. New York, Farrar and Rinehart, 1936; London, Heinemann, 1937.

The Ballad of the Duke's Mercy. New York, House of Books, 1939.

Nightmare at Noon. New York, Farrar and Rinehart, 1940.

Listen to the People: Independence Day 1941. New York, Council for Democracy, 1941.

Western Star. New York, Farrar and Rinehart, 1943; London, University of London Press, 1944.

Other

The Magic of Poetry and the Poet's Art. Chicago, Compton, 1936.

A Summons to the Free. New York, Farrar and Rinehart, and London, Oxford University Press, 1941.

Selected Works. New York, Farrar and Rinehart, 2 vols., 1942.

America. New York, Farrar and Rinehart, 1944; London, Heinemann, 1945.

From the Earth to the Moon (letter). Privately printed, 1958.

Selected Poetry and Prose, edited by Basil Davenport. New York, Rinehart, 1960.

Selected Letters, edited by Charles A. Fenton. New Haven, Connecticut, Yale University Press, 1960.

Stephen Vincent Benét on Writing: A Great Writer's Letter of Advice to a Young Beginner, edited by George Abbe. Brattleboro, Vermont, Stephen Greene Press, 1964.

Editor, with others. *The Yale Book of Student Verse 1910-1919*. New Haven, Connecticut, Yale University Press, 1919.

Editor, with Monty Woolley. *Tamburlaine the Great*, by Christopher Marlowe. New Haven, Connecticut, Yale University Press, 1919.

*

Film Adaptation: *All That Money Can Buy* (*The Devil and Daniel Webster*), 1941.

Bibliography: By Gladys Louise Maddocks, in *Bulletin of Bibliography 20* (Boston), September 1951 and April 1952.

Manuscript Collection: Beinecke Library, Yale University, New Haven, Connecticut.

Critical Studies: *Stephen Vincent Benét: My Brother Steve* by William Rose Benét, New York, Farrar and Rinehart, 1943; *Stephen Vincent Benét: The Life and Times of an American Man of Letters* by Charles A. Fenton. New Haven, Connecticut, Yale University Press, 1958; *Stephen Vincent Benét* by Parry Stroud, New York, Twayne, 1962.

*   *   *

Despite the suggestive titles of his first two story collections only a minority of Stephen Vincent Benét's short fiction is supernatural, and much of that consists of adapted folk tales which are light in tone even when they deal with traditionally horrific materials. He first shot to fame as a poet, winning the first of two Pulitzer Prizes for his quintessentially American epic *John Brown's Body*, and when he diverted his efforts to prose he set out to write in a line of literary descent rooted in the work of Washington Irving. Benét's interest in fantastic fiction assumed a quasi-anthropological gloss when he deployed real and imagined folklore as a means of obtaining a special insight into the character and manners of emergent American society. The adversaries faced by his most famous folk-hero, the lawyer Daniel Webster, are presented in caricature—but they have a serious side too because they illuminate authentic threats to the American dream.

In "The Devil and Daniel Webster" the lawyer comes to the aid of Jabez Stone, a farmer who has made a deal with the Devil—whose Hellish consequences he desperately wants to escape. The Devil is Americanized as a heartlessly efficient businessman, Mr. Scratch, and the jury which he calls to hear Webster's case is compounded out of the greatest villains of American history—but they remain Americans through and through, infused with a glorious pioneer spirit which encourages them to look beyond the conventional bounds of good and evil in reaching their verdict. Adapted to the stage and as an opera, the story formed the basis of a memorable Hollywood dark-fantasy film in 1941 (also released as *All That Money Can Buy*), co-scripted by Benét and starring Walter Huston as Mr. Scratch.

The monster Samantha in "Daniel Webster and the Sea Serpent" becomes menacing through lovesickness, but the threat is defused by means of the draft which draws her into the American navy, charged with keeping the British fleet at bay. In addition to the two Daniel Webster tales (a third, "Daniel Webster and the Ides of March," was not reprinted), *Thirteen O'Clock* contains a New-Worldly revisitation of an Old-Wordly folk tale, "The King of the Cats," in which the seductive conductor Mr. Tibault is successfully banished by the American hero—but the fascinating girl who roused his jealousy disappears too, leaving him to marry a native of Chicago. A much more earnestly horrific story is, however, "By the Waters of Babylon," which imagines an America delivered to desolation by the collapse of civilization.

The three classic fantasies in *Tales before Midnight* are headed by "Johnny Pye and the Fool-Killer," in which Death is distinctively personalized as an item of Americana much as the Devil was in the first Daniel Webster story. His phantom footsteps are heard every time Johnny is endangered by a hucksterish scam—which is, of course, all too often in a land overfull of men whose first item of faith is that there's a sucker born every minute. "O'Halloran's Luck" transplants a leprechaun to America to look after the Irish immigrants, while the hero of "Doc Mellhorn and the Pearly Gates," like Daniel Webster before him, takes it upon himself to challenge the pre-set boundaries of good and evil in order to minister to the sick in Hell.

Benét's later fantasies, written in the three years preceding his premature death and collected in *The Last Circle*, are mostly dispirited revisitations of ground already covered. This is not surprising, given that he was crippled by arthritis and suffered a bout of mental illness, not to mention the distractions of writing radio scripts to assist the war effort and trying to revive his career as a poet. The protagonist of "The Minister's Books" is corrupted by Old World magic, but there is no Daniel Webster to come to his aid when payment for his acquisitions falls due. The ultimate huckster, Phineas T. Barnum, fails to obtain any advantage from an angel he wins from a farmer in "The Angel Was a Yankee." "The Land Where There Is No Death" is a pointless extrapolation of the riddle posed by Johnny Pye's fool-killer. "William Riley and the Fates," "The Danger of Shadows" and "The Gold Dress" are more orthodox weird tales whose relative sobriety makes them less suspenseful as well as less lively than the author's earlier endeavours. "The Danger of Shadows"—which adopts a restrained version of the motif most famously employed by Adalbert von Chamisso's *Peter Schlemihl* and Hans Christian Andersen's "The Shadow"—is, however, far the most pessimistic, and hence the most harrowing, of all Benét's tales.

The only purely horrific notes which Benét struck in his work are to be found in his poetry. The first volume of his *Selected Works* include a whole section devoted to "Nightmares and Visitants," but even the darkest of the items set beneath that rubric is no dourer in mood and implication than some of those grouped under the heading "Creatures of Earth," especially "Ghosts of a Lunatic Asylum." Benét seems to have taken the view that the editors of popular periodicals would not tolerate unrelieved bleakness in the stories they bought, but the world-view of his poetry is unadulterated by diplomacy and is, in consequence, occasion-

ally unalleviated by hope. *The Last Circle* closes with a cruelly unvarnished "Little Testament," which he refused to publish when he wrote it in 1941, because he thought it might serve him best as an epitaph. He was right.

—Brian Stableford

BENSON, E(dward) F(rederic)

Nationality: British. **Born:** Shropshire, 24 July 1867; brother of the writers A. C. Benson and R. H. Benson. **Education:** Marlborough College (editor of the *Marlburian*); King's College, Cambridge (exhibitioner 1888, scholar 1890, Wortz Student, Prendergast and Craven Student), first-class honours degree 1891. **Career:** Member of the staff of the British School of Archaeology, Athens, 1892-95, and the Society for the Promotion of Hellenic Studies, in Egypt, 1895; full-time writer from 1895. Lived in Lamb House, Rye, East Sussex, during the latter part of his life; Mayor of Rye, 1934-37. Honorary Fellow, Magdalene College, Cambridge, 1938. **Died:** 29 February 1940.

HORROR, GHOST AND GOTHIC PUBLICATIONS

Novels

The Luck of the Vails. London, Heinemann, 1901.
The Image in the Sand. London, Heinemann, and Philadelphia, Lippincott, 1905.
The Angel of Pain. Philadelphia, Lippincott, 1905; London, Heinemann, 1906.
The House of Defence. Toronto, Macleod and Allen, and New York, Authors and Newspapers Association, 1906; London, Heinemann, 1907.
Across the Stream. London, Murray, and New York, Doran, 1919.
Colin. London, Hutchinson, and New York, Doran, 1923.
Colin II. London, Hutchinson, and New York, Doran, 1925.
The Inheritor. London, Hutchinson, and New York, Doubleday, 1930.
Ravens' Brood. London, Barker, and New York, Doubleday, 1934.

Short Stories

The Room in the Tower and Other Stories. London, Mills and Boon, 1912; New York, Knopf, 1929.
Visible and Invisible. London, Hutchinson, 1923; New York, Doubleday, 1924.
"And the Dead Spake—"; and, The Horror-Horn. New York, Doran, 1923.
Expiation, and Naboth's Vineyard. New York, Doran, 1924.
Spinach, and Reconciliation. New York, Doran, 1924.
The Face. New York, Doran, 1924.
The Temple. New York, Doran, 1925.
A Tale of an Empty House, and Bagnell Terrace. New York, Doran, 1925.
Spook Stories. London, Hutchinson, 1928.
The Step. London, Marrot, 1930.
More Spook Stories. London, Hutchinson, 1934.
The Horror Horn: The Best Horror Stories of E. F. Benson. London, Panther, 1974.

The Tale of the Empty House and Other Ghost Stories. London, Black Swan, 1986.
The Flint Knife: Further Spook Stories, edited by Jack Adrian. Wellingborough, Northamptonshire, Equation, 1988.
Desirable Residences and Other Stories, edited by Jack Adrian. Oxford, Oxford University Press, 1991.
The Collected Ghost Stories of E. F. Benson, edited by Richard Dalby. London, Robinson, and New York, Carroll and Graf, 1992.
The Technique of the Ghost Story and Three Short Stories, edited by Jack Adrian. Harleston, Hermitage, 1993.
Fine Feathers and Other Stories, edited by Jack Adrian. Oxford, Oxford University Press, 1994.

OTHER PUBLICATIONS

Novels

Dodo: A Detail of Today. London, Methuen, 2 vols., 1893.
The Rubicon. London, Methuen, 2 vols., 1894.
The Judgment Books. London, Osgood McIlvaine, 1895.
The Babe B.A. New York, Putnam, 1896; London, Putnam, 1897.
Limitations. London, Innes, 1896.
The Vintage. London, Methuen, 1898.
The Money Market. Bristol, Arrowsmith, 1898.
The Capsina. London, Methuen, 1899.
Mammon and Co. London, Heinemann, 1899.
The Princess Sophia. London, Heinemann, 1900.
Scarlet and Hyssop. London, Heinemann, 1902.
The Book of Months. London, Heinemann, 1903.
An Act in a Backwater. London, Heinemann, 1903.
The Relentless City. London, Heinemann, 1903.
The Valkyries: A Romance Founded on Wagner's Opera. London, Dean, 1903.
The Challoners. London, Heinemann, 1904.
Paul. London, Heinemann, 1906.
Sheaves. London, Stanley Paul, 1907.
The Blotting Book. London, Heinemann, 1908.
The Climber. London, Heinemann, 1908.
A Reaping. London, Heinemann, 1909.
Daisy's Aunt. London, Nelson, 1910.
The Osbornes. London, Smith Elder, 1910.
Margery. New York, Doubleday, 1910; as *Juggernaut,* London, Heinemann, 1911.
Account Rendered. London, Heinemann, 1911.
Mrs. Ames. London, Hodder and Stoughton, 1912.
The Weaker Vessel. London, Heinemann, 1913.
Thorley Weir. London, Heinemann, 1913.
Dodo's Daughter: A Sequel to Dodo. New York, Century, 1913; as *Dodo the Second,* London, Hodder and Stoughton, 1914.
Arundel. London, Unwin, 1914.
The Oakleyites. London, Hodder and Stoughton, 1915.
David Blaize. London, Hodder and Stoughton, 1916.
Mike. London, Cassell, 1916.
The Freaks of Mayfair. London, Foulis, 1916.
Mr. Teddy. London, Unwin, 1917.
An Autumn Sowing. London, Collins, 1917.
David Blaize and the Blue Door (for children). London, Hodder and Stoughton, 1918.
Up and Down. London, Hutchinson, 1918.

Robin Linnet. London, Hutchinson, 1919.
Queen Lucia. London, Hutchinson, 1920.
Dodo Wonders. London, Hutchinson, 1921.
Lovers and Friends. London, Unwin, 1921.
Miss Mapp. London, Hutchinson, 1922.
Peter. London, Cassell, 1922.
David of King's. London, Hodder and Stoughton, 1924.
Alan. London, Unwin, 1924.
Rex. London, Hodder and Stoughton, 1925.
Mezzanine. London, Cassell, 1926.
Pharisees and Publicans. London, Hutchinson, 1926.
Lucia in London. London, Hutchinson, 1927.
Paying Guests. London, Hutchinson, 1929.
Mapp and Lucia. London, Hodder and Stoughton, 1931.
Secret Lives. London, Hodder and Stoughton, 1932.
Travail of Gold. London, Hodder and Stoughton, 1933.
Lucia's Progress. London, Hodder and Stoughton, 1935; as *The Worshipful Lucia,* New York, Doubleday, n.d.
All About Lucia (omnibus; includes *Queen Lucia, Miss Mapp, Lucia in London, Mapp and Lucia*). New York, Doubleday, 1936.
Trouble for Lucia. London, Hodder and Stoughton, 1939.

Short Stories

Six Common Things. London, Osgood McIlvaine, 1893.
A Double Overture. Chicago, Sergel, 1894.
The Countess of Lowndes Square and Other Stories. London, Cassell, 1920.
The Male Impersonator. London, Elkin Matthews, 1929.

Plays

Aunt Jeannie. N.p., 1902.
Dodo: A Detail of Yesterday, from his own novel (produced 1905).
The Friend in the Garden (produced 1906).
Westward Ho!, music by Philip Napier Miles, from the novel by Charles Kingsley (produced 1913).
Dinner for Eight (produced 1915). N.p., 1915.
The Luck of the Vails, from his own novel (produced 1928).

Other

Sketches from Marlborough. Privately printed, 1888.
Daily Training, with Eustace Miles. London, Hurst and Blackett, 1902.
Cricket of Abel, Hirst and Shrewsbury, with Eustace Miles. London, Hurst and Blackett, 1903.
Mad Annual, with Eustace Miles. London, Grant Richards, 1903.
A Book of Golf, with Eustace Miles. London, Hurst and Blackett, 1903.
Diversions Day by Day, with Eustace Miles. London, Hurst and Blackett, 1905.
English Figure-Skating. London, Bell, 1908.
Skating Calls. London, Bell, 1909.
Winter Sports in Switzerland. London, George Allen, 1913.
Deutschland uber Allah. London, Hodder and Stoughton, 1917.
Crescent and the Cross. London, Hodder and Stoughton, 1918.
The White Eagle and Poland. London, Hodder and Stoughton, 1918.
Poland and Mittel-Europa. London, Hodder and Stoughton, 1918.
The Social Value of Temperance. True Temperance Association, 1919.

Our Family Affairs 1867-1896. London, Cassell, 1920.
Mother. London, Hodder and Stoughton, 1925.
Sir Francis Drake. London, Bodley Head, 1927.
The Life of Alcibiades. London, Benn, 1928.
From Abraham to Christ (lecture). N.p., 1928.
Ferdinand Magellan. London, Bodley Head, 1929.
As We Were: A Victorian Peepshow. London, Longman, 1930.
As We Are: A Modern Review. London, Longman, 1932.
Charlotte Bronte. London, Longman, 1932.
King Edward VII. London, Longman, 1933.
The Outbreak of War, 1914. London, Peter Davies, 1933.
Queen Victoria. New York and London, Longman, 1935.
The Kaiser and English Relations. London, Longman, 1936.
Queen Victoria's Daughters. New York, Appleton Century, 1938;
    as *Daughters of Queen Victoria*, London, Cassell, 1939.
Final Edition: An Informal Autobiography. London, Longman, 1940.

Editor, *Henry James: Letters to A. C. Benson and Auguste Monod.*
London, Elkin Matthews, 1930.

*   *   *

Two essential—even crucial—facts should be understood about the writer E. F. Benson. First, he *was* a writer. He was a professional wordsmith who made a good deal of his living from his pen, and a good living too. To be sure, he possessed a useful income on the side from various judicious investments made throughout his career, but to all intents and purposes the income from his writing largely kept him in the style to which, from the 1890s onwards, he had become accustomed, and was thus immensely important to him.

Secondly, although he wrote well over 70 weird and macabre tales, and a number of novels in which, to a greater or lesser extent, the supernatural played a part, he had no pressing need to do so. Nor, indeed, was it a particularly wise choice of genres to write in. Ghost stories were by no means every editor's, and certainly not every reader's, cup of tea, and in any case there were other, more modish, genres to conquer. Benson might not have had the cruciverbial mind for creating detective fiction (he was a poor plotter), but if he had wanted to write genre fiction alongside his society and social comedies, given his undoubted capacity for hard work and in-depth research (as evidence his many biographies), then historical fiction (hugely popular during that period) would have brought home the bacon rather better than "spook" stuff.

Of course, he was a naturally prolific writer, pouring out what seemed to be an endless stream of novels about high society, novels about heroic and self-sacrificing young men, and the brilliant series of comic camp satires featuring the two warring she-dragons, Miss Mapp and Mrs. Lucas (the extravagantly absurd Lucia). Yet still, although it was a well-established rule of publishing that the writing of weird fiction in general was neither a paying proposition nor a sensible career option (even Algernon Blackwood had other writing strings to his bow), Fred Benson's pen drove across the page, conjuring up horrors by the score, on occasion for months at a time.

Thus for Benson it can only have been the case that writing stories about the supernatural was a quite deliberate—even a necessary—act, although, perhaps significantly, whenever he wrote about his endeavours in this direction (e.g. in his last volume of autobiography, *Final Edition*), he was brief and dismissive,

downplaying their role in his general *oeuvre*. What is clear, however, is that for Benson ghost stories were almost an escape into, as it were, reality—or at any rate weird fiction became a genre in which he might say or write things that would certainly have raised an eyebrow, if nothing else, if they appeared in his mainstream fiction.

As a consequence, Benson's "spook stories" (the phrase seems to have originated in a mildly contemptuous reference by his friend/enemy Sir Edmund Gosse—typically, Benson shamelessly appropriated it for the titles of his last two collections) can surely be read on two quite separate and distinct levels: as supremely horrible tales about supremely horrible beings, but also, for their author, as a kind of catharsis. Certainly a good many obsessions are paraded through his "spook" *oeuvre*, again and again—ghastly women and giant slugs (and who knows?—to Benson these two may well have seemed indistinguishable, one from the other) merely the most obvious.

It has always been difficult to reconcile Benson's surface affection for some women (not many) with his loathing of the gender in general that seems clearly to be expressed in so many of his weird tales—whatever the evidence to the contrary offered by those who declare stoutly that Benson had no dark side to his character, however many examples (in letters, for instance; in his mainstream novels and stories) of Benson the amiable old codger and friend-of-the-female. To be sure, there are wicked and dreadful male revenants in his stories—the trouble is, they are simply not as explicitly nasty or threatening as the women.

In the literary sense, of course, so long as Benson's strong bias is recognized for what it is, there is not much inherently wrong with it. Indeed, this tension gives an extra, and interesting, edge to his best work. To put it another way, his sexual orientation has given weird literature some of its most terrifying tales.

In general, women in his stories do fare badly. They figured as many things: as vampires—Mrs. Stone in "The Room in the Tower," and the eponymous Mrs. Amworth (whose final demise is so graphically described); as murderesses—Mrs. Ayton in "The Top Landing," the dreadful, hulking Mrs. Labson in "The Corner House" ("I felt," remarks the horrified narrator, "that I had looked upon something hellish"); as Satanists—Mrs. Ray in "The Sanctuary" (perhaps the most overtly and lasciviously homo-erotic story Benson ever wrote, and probably never, unlike the bulk of his short weird fiction, published in a magazine prior to its collection in book form); as witches—the terrible Mrs. Penarth in "The Wishing Well" (the germ for Benson's most bizarre novel, *Raven's Brood*); as non-human monsters—the fiendish Yeti-like creature, with "withered and pendulous breasts," and "a fathomless bestiality" in its eyes in "The Horror Horn"; as human caricatures—the unfortunate Mrs. Gabriel, whose freshly dead corpse is utilized in the most gruesome way in "And the Dead Spake . . ."; even as the reincarnation of "the worst being that ever lived" (Judas Iscariot), who is virtually unkillable, in "The Outcast." And if they are not the chief characters then they are the victims—strangled, throats slit, walled up, shoved over cliffs—who in most cases return to wreak a terrible vengeance.

But perhaps Benson's most horrific—one might almost say most vindictive—tale is "The Face," in which the blameless heroine is carried off into outer darkness for absolutely no reason whatsoever. That is, her abduction by a long-dead horror is entirely causeless, and motivated by sheer malevolence. Despite (perhaps because of) its author's sadism—not too strong a word, under the circumstances—"The Face" in fact is a little masterpiece of tension and terror.

Yet Benson also had a saving comic streak, which resulted in some of the funniest ghost stories in the language. There is certainly something attractively robust, even Dickensian, about tales such as "Mr. Tilly's Séance," "Thursday Evenings," "The Psychical Mallards" and the hilarious "Spinach" (in most of which Benson launches himself, pig's-bladder-on-a-stick flailing, at psychic charlatans and psychical research societies).

In the main his weird novels are best left alone. *Colin* and *Colin II* constitute the interminable saga of the descendant of a man who sold his soul to the Devil. *The Angel of Pain* is a broodingly homoerotic paean to pantheism. *Across the Stream*, it has now been determined, owes rather too much to its author's younger brother Hugh's *The Necromancers* (1909). Only *The Image in the Sand* has merit—as a highly readable Edwardian thriller concerning Ancient Egyptian horrors re-awakened in the twentieth century (foreshadowing to a certain extent Sax Rohmer's *Brood of the Witch-Queen*).

—Jack Adrian

BENSON, R(obert) H(ugh)

Nationality: British. **Born:** 18 November 1871; brother of the writers A. C. Benson and E. F. Benson. **Education:** Eton College; Trinity College, Cambridge. **Career:** Ordained a priest in the Church of England, 1895; converted to the Roman Catholic faith, 1903; Private Chamberlain to His Holiness Pius X, 1911. **Died:** 19 October 1914.

HORROR, GHOST AND GOTHIC PUBLICATIONS

Novels

Lord of the World. London, Pitman, 1907; New York, Dodd Mead, 1908.
The Necromancers. London, Hutchinson, 1909; St. Louis, Herder, 1909.
The Dawn of All. London, Hutchinson, 1911; St. Louis, Herder, 1911.

Short Stories

The Light Invisible. London, Isbister, 1903.
A Mirror of Shalott. London, Pitman, 1907.
Ghosts in the House, with A. C. Benson, edited by Hugh Lamb. Chester, Ash-Tree Press, 1996.

OTHER PUBLICATIONS

Novels

By What Authority? London, Isbister, 1904.
The King's Achievement. London, Pitman, 1905.
The Queen's Tragedy. London, Pitman, 1906.
The Sentimentalists. London, Pitman, 1906; New York, Benziger, 1906.
The History of Richard Raynal, Solitary. London, Pitman, 1907.

The Conventionalists. London, Hutchinson, 1908.
A Winnowing. London, Hutchinson, 1910; St. Louis, Herder, 1910.
None Other Gods. London, Hutchinson, 1910; St. Louis, Herder, 1910.
Come Rack! Come Rope! London, Hutchinson, 1912.
The Coward. London, Hutchinson, 1912.
An Average Man. London, Hutchinson, 1913.
Oddsfish. London, Hutchinson, 1914.
Initiation. London, Hutchinson, 1914.

Plays

A Mystery Play in Honour of the Nativity of Our Lord. London, Longman, 1908.
The Cost of a Crown. London, Longman, 1910.
The Maid of Orleans. London, Longman, 1911.
The Upper Room. London, Longman, 1914.

Poetry

Old Testament Rhymes. London, Longman, 1913.
Poems. London, Burns and Oates, 1914.

Other

The Conversion of England. London, Catholic Truth Society, 1906; St. Louis, Herder, 1906.
The Death-Beds of "Bloody Mary" and "Good Queen Bess." London, Catholic Truth Society, 1906.
The Religion of the Plain Man. London, Burns and Oates, 1906.
Infallibility and Tradition. London, Catholic Truth Society, 1907.
Mysticism. London, Sands, 1907; St. Louis, Herder, 1907.
Papers of a Pariah. London, Smith Elder, 1907.
The Holy Blissful Martyr Saint Thomas of Canterbury. London, Macdonald and Evans, 1908.
Non-Catholic Denominations. London, Longman, 1910.
Christ in the Church (essays). London, Longman, 1911.
Spiritualism. London, Catholic Truth Society, 1911.
A Child's Rule of Life. London, Longman, 1912.
The Friendship of Christ (sermons). London, Longman, 1912.
Confessions of a Convert. London, Longman, 1913.
Optimism. London, Catholic Truth Society, 1913.
Paradoxes of Catholicism. London, Longman, 1913.
Lourdes. London, Manresa Press, 1914; St. Louis, Herder, 1914.
Catholicism. London, Catholic Truth Society, 1914.
Loneliness. London, Hutchinson, 1915.
The Spiritual Letters of Monsignor R. Hugh Benson to One of His Converts. London, Longman, 1915.
Sermon Notes, edited by the Reverend C. C. Martindale. London, Longman, 1917.

Editor, *A Book of the Love of Jesus.* London, Isbister, 1904.
Editor, *Vexilla Regis: A Book of Devotions.* London, Longman, 1914.

*

Critical Studies: *Memoirs of a Brother* by A. C. Benson, London, Smith Elder, 1915; *The Life of Monsignor Robert Hugh Benson* by the Reverend C. C. Martindale, London, Longman, 1916; *The*

Bensons: A Victorian Family by Betty Askwith, London, E. F. Benson Society, 1994 (originally published as part of *Two Victorian Families*, London, Chatto and Windus, 1971).

*   *   *

R. H. Benson, who was always known as Hugh, was the youngest child of the remarkable Benson family, the children of Edward White Benson who became Archbishop of Canterbury in 1882. Benson's elder brothers included the essayist Arthur C. Benson and the novelist and biographer E. F. (Fred) Benson, both of whom also produced supernatural stories, especially Fred. All three were insatiable writers. Although both Arthur and Fred were more prolific, Hugh's output was far from modest. He concentrated on his role in the church, writing many books and booklets as propaganda for the Roman Catholic faith, to which he converted amidst much scandal in 1895. Hugh may be perceived as a spoilt child, since he was the youngest. Certainly he was headstrong and rather selfish, following his own chosen route in life regardless of the effect that it may have had on others. Once he had converted to Catholicism he became an ardent, sometimes violent preacher, which established his fame but which also earned him constant notoriety.

Because Hugh did whatever he wanted, it meant that he had no concern over exploring dubious areas of research. He attended séances, experimented with drugs and had an overly morbid fear of death, and all of this gives an added conviction to his supernatural fiction. Such verisimilitude is constantly challenged by Hugh's desire to proselytize which weighs down some of his work, but genuine moments shine through. Unlike Fred's "spook" stories, however, which were almost always intended to frighten and even repulse, Hugh's are more in the mood of expositions, where the narrators explore a religious or mystical theme and the story emerges by way of example or anecdote.

His short fiction is generally more accessible than his novels. These consist of two volumes of work: *The Light Invisible* and *A Mirror of Shalott*. They have added interest because the first was written before his conversion to Catholicism but when he clearly had doubts so that the views expressed are almost those of an apologist. Both books take a similar form. The first is a series of episodes told by a Catholic priest. The second are stories related by each of a convention of priests at Rome. Many may be based on real narrations Benson had heard, and therefore may hold a kernel of truth. The best-known story from the first volume is "The Traveller," where the ghost of one of Thomas Becket's murderers seeks to expiate for his crime through the confessional. "Consolatrix Afflictorum" is a pleasing if overly sentimental story told in the form of a letter. A child, aged seven, loses his mother. He had been devoted to her and after her death enters a period of illness and mental decline. He pleads to see his mother again and is rewarded when her spirit visits him over several days and nurses him through his illness. At last she stops coming, and the child witnesses a vision of the Virgin Mary. The other stories mostly take the form of visions or attempts to explain spiritual experiences. For instance, "The Watcher" tells of the narrator, when young, having gone hunting. In his anger at not shooting anything he kills a thrush and his immediate feeling of guilt is accompanied by the mocking laughter of a demon-like figure lurking in the undergrowth. "In the Convent Chapel" is a similar lesson in humility when the priest, who felt contempt for an unlettered nun, has a mystical vision showing her spiritual attraction.

The stories in *A Mirror of Shalott* are rather more conventional, though no less intense in Benson's desire to explore the religious experience. The stories tell mostly of hauntings, possession or visions. They are all very personal, with the other priests at the convention sometimes challenging the narrator to prove his case. A single example may suffice in "Father Girdlestone's Tale" which reads almost like a story from one of the *Lives of the Saints*. Girdlestone is sent by his bishop to establish a new parish in south Wales. Evidently the devil tries to stop the venture, as from the outset Girdlestone finds himself subject to a psychic onslaught from beyond which increases the more he persists, leading to visions and delusions. Girdlestone believes he may almost have to admit defeat but it is when the devil believes he has succeeded that he lets his guard down and God delivers his blow. The story has a genuine atmosphere and climax, demonstrating Benson's ability to create an evocative atmosphere whilst still delivering his apostolic message.

It is regrettable that Benson wrote no more short stories. He devoted his energies to a mass of novels and pamphlets, many of the latter in the form of sermons and essays. Two of his novels are quasi-science fiction, inasmuch as they are set in the future and consider the fate of mankind. *The Lord of the World* is an apocalyptic novel set a century hence. It considers the increased materialism of the world (much of Benson's future vision is remarkably accurate) and the decline in religion to the point where it becomes outlawed. This sets the scene for the final cataclysmic battle between the Church and the Antichrist. At the end we are left to believe that God intervenes, destroying not only the Antichrist but the Earth in the final Armageddon. *The Dawn of All* was written as an antidote to the first book, looking ahead 60 years and projecting what might happen if the opposite events occurred, leading to a harmonized religious (i.e. Roman Catholic) society. The book, however, is not a utopia, as friction still exists between the Catholic world-government and petty socialist states. In his desire to promote the benefits of the Catholic church Benson also unwittingly reminds us of many of the past follies of the church, and thus his message becomes double-edged. If one sets Benson's overbearing propaganda aside, the books are both fascinating and harsh visions of the future.

Two of his mainstream historical novels may be recognized as almost gothic in treatment: *By What Authority?* and *Come Rack! Come Rope!*—in which Benson explored the persecution of the Catholic church during the reformation. Neither would have been out of place amongst the "shilling shockers" of the mid-Victorian period, except that Benson only sought to sensationalize in order to promote his pro-Catholic message. Two other novels, *The Sentimentalists* and *The Conventionalist*, are explorations of religious experience that become deeply personal and mystical, almost bordering on the supernatural with the main protagonists' efforts to come to terms with their beliefs.

Benson's best novel of the supernatural, however, is *The Necromancers*. It tells of a young man whose fiancée dies before their marriage. He joins a group of spiritualists in the hope of regaining her, only to find himself possessed by an evil spirit. Benson was very anti-spiritualist and used the novel to warn people against dabbling with the unknown. Since he firmly believed in the spirit world, and by all accounts had experienced hauntings, his conviction comes across. It is a powerful novel with many atmospheric scenes.

R. H. Benson was a celebrity in his day and his books sold well, though he is now the least known of the three literary brothers. However, because he was unable to tame his religious zeal in his fiction it makes his interpretation of the supernatural perhaps the most convincing of all of their work, though the least horrifying. With R. H. Benson you are forced to interpret the events rather than experience them, and then to make up your mind.

—Mike Ashley

BIERCE, Ambrose (Gwinnet)

Pseudonym: Dod Grile. **Nationality:** American. **Born:** Horse Cave Creek, Meigs County, Ohio, 24 June 1842. **Education:** A high school in Warsaw, Indiana; Kentucky Military Institute, Franklin Springs, 1859-60. **Military Service:** Served in the 9th Indiana Infantry of the Union Army during the Civil War, 1861-65: Major. **Family:** Married Mollie Day in 1871 (separated 1888; divorced 1905); two sons and one daughter. **Career:** Printer's devil, *Northern Indianan* (anti-slavery paper), 1857-59; U.S. Treasury aide, Selma, Alabama, 1865; served on military mapping expedition, Omaha to San Francisco, 1866-67; night watchman and clerk, United States Sub-Treasury, San Francisco, 1867-78; editor and columnist ("Town Crier"), *News Letter,* San Francisco, 1868-71; lived in London, 1872-75: staff member, *Fun,* 1872-75, and editor, *Lantern,* 1875; worked in the assay office, U.S. Mint, San Francisco, after 1875; associate editor, *Argonaut,* 1877-79; agent, Black Hills Placer Mining Company, Rockervill, Dakota Territory, 1880-81; editor and columnist ("Prattle"), *Wasp,* San Francisco, 1881-86; columnist, San Francisco *Examiner,* 1887-1906, and New York *Journal,* 1896-1906; lived in Washington, D.C., 1900-13: Washington correspondent, New York *American,* 1900-06; columnist, *Cosmopolitan,* Washington, 1905-09; travelled in Mexico, 1913-14; served in Pancho Villa's forces and is presumed to have been killed at the Battle of Ojinaga. **Died:** (probably 11 January) 1914.

HORROR, GHOST AND GOTHIC PUBLICATIONS

Short Stories

Tales of Soldiers and Civilians. San Francisco, Steele, 1891; as *In the Midst of Life,* London, Chatto and Windus, 1892; revised edition, New York, Putnam, 1898; as *Eyes of the Panther,* London, Cape, 1928.
Can Such Things Be? New York, Cassell, 1893; expanded edition, New York, Boni and Liveright, 1924; London, Cape, 1926.
Fantastic Fables. New York and London, Putnam, 1899.
Ghost and Horror Stories of Ambrose Bierce, edited by Everett F. Bleiler. New York, Dover, 1964.

OTHER PUBLICATIONS

Short Stories

The Fiend's Delight (as Dod Grile). London, Hotten, 1872; New York, Lyster, 1873.
Nuggets and Dust Panned Out in California (as Dod Grile). London, Chatto and Windus, 1873.

Cobwebs from an Empty Skull (as Dod Grile). London, Routledge, 1874.
The Dance of Death, with Thomas A. Harcourt. San Francisco, Keller, 1877; revised edition, 1877.
A Son of the Gods, and A Horseman in the Sky. San Francisco, Elder, 1907.
Ten Tales. London, First Editions Club, 1925.
Battlefields and Ghosts. N.p, 1931.
The Complete Short Stories of Ambrose Bierce, edited by Ernest Jerome Hopkins. New York, Doubleday, 1970.
Stories and Fables, edited by Edward Wagenknecht. Owings Mill, Maryland, Stemmer House, 1977.
The Best of Ambrose Bierce. Secaucus, New Jersey, Castle, 1984.

Poetry

Black Beetles in Amber. New York, Western Authors, 1892.
Shapes of Clay. San Francisco, Wood, 1903.
An Invocation. San Francisco, Book Club of California, 1928.
A Vision of Doom, edited by Donald Sidney-Fryer. West Kingston, Rhode Island, Grant, 1980.

Other

The Cynic's Word Book. New York, Doubleday, 1906; London, Bird, 1907; as *The Devil's Dictionary,* 1911; revised edition, by Ernest Jerome Hopkins, as *The Enlarged Devil's Dictionary,* New York, Doubleday, 1967.
The Shadow on the Dial and Other Essays, edited by S. O. Howes. San Francisco, Robertson, 1909; revised edition, as *Antepenultimata* (in *Collected Works 11*), 1912.
Write It Right: A Little Black-List of Literary Faults. New York, Neale, 1909.
Collected Works, edited by Walter Neale. Washington, D.C., Neale, 12 vols., 1909-12.
The Letters of Ambrose Bierce, edited by Bertha Clark Pope. San Francisco, Book Club of California, 1922.
Twenty-One Letters of Ambrose Bierce, edited by Samuel Loveman. Cleveland, Ohio, Kirk, 1922.
Selections from Prattle, edited by Carroll D. Hall. San Francisco, Book Club of California, 1936.
The Collected Writings of Ambrose Bierce. New York, Citadel Press, 1946.
The Sardonic Humor of Ambrose Bierce, edited by George Barkin. New York, Dover, 1963.
Satanic Reader: Selections from the Invective Journalism, edited by Ernest Jerome Hopkins. New York, Doubleday, 1968.
Skepticism and Dissent: Selected Journalism, 1898-1901, edited by Lawrence I. Berkove. Ann Arbor, Michigan, Delmas, 1986.
The Devil's Advocate: An Ambrose Bierce Reader, edited by Brian St. Pierre. San Francisco, Chronicle, 1987.

Translator, with Gustav Adolph Danziger, *The Monk and the Hangman's Daughter,* by Richard Voss. Chicago, Schulte, 1892; London, Cape, 1927.

*

Bibliography: *Ambrose Bierce: A Bibliography* by Vincent Starrett, Philadelphia, Centaur Bookshop, 1929; in *Bibliography of American Literature* by Jacob Blanck, 1955; *Ambrose Bierce:*

Bibliographical and Biographical Data edited by Joseph Gaer, 1968.

Critical Studies (selection): *Ambrose Bierce: A Biography* by Carey McWilliams, New York, Boni, 1929; *Ambrose Bierce: The Devil's Lexicographer*, Norman, University of Oklahoma Press, 1951, and *Ambrose Bierce and the Black Hills,* Norman, University of Oklahoma Press, 1956, both by Paul Fatout; *Ambrose Bierce* by Robert A. Wiggins, Minneapolis, University of Minnesota Press, 1964; *The Short Stories of Ambrose Bierce: A Study in Polarity* by Stuart C. Woodruff, University of Pittsburgh Press, 1965; *Ambrose Bierce: A Biography* by Richard O'Connor, London, Gollancz, 1968; *Ambrose Bierce* by M. E. Grenander, New York, Twayne, 1971; *Critical Essays on Bierce* edited by Cathy N. Davidson, Boston, Hall, 1982, and *The Experimental Fictions of Bierce: Structuring the Ineffable* by Davidson, Lincoln, University of Nebraska Press, 1984; *Ambrose Bierce: The Making of a Misanthrope* by Richard Saunders, 1985.

*   *   *

In a literary career that spanned almost 50 years, Ambrose Bierce distinguished himself as perhaps the most notable American journalist of the 19th century, writing thousands of editorial articles, totalling several million words, for a variety of newspapers and magazines in San Francisco and London. But since the vast majority of this work is not currently available, Bierce has instead achieved renown as one of Poe's most able successors in tales of psychological and supernatural horror.

As a short-story writer, Bierce is chiefly known for two volumes, *Tales of Soldiers and Civilians* and *Can Such Things Be?*. The contents of both collections were shuffled on successive reprints, and as gathered in his *Collected Works* they reveal an interesting dichotomy: virtually all the tales in the former volume (now bearing the title *In the Midst of Life*) are what would now be termed psychological suspense, while virtually all those in the latter are supernatural.

The distinguishing feature of all Bierce's work is satire—and satire of a mordant, biting, even malicious variety. It was the infusion of satire in his journalism that made him countless enemies and branded him "The Wickedest Man in San Francisco," and it is satire that adds a pungency to his supernatural tales and actually creates horror in many of his stories of the macabre. Bierce's unrelenting pessimism and misanthropy ("this is a world of fools and rogues, blind with superstition, tormented with envy, consumed with vanity, selfish, false, cruel, and cursed with illusions—frothing mad!" he wrote in "To Train a Writer") impelled him to devise scenarios in which characters are helplessly placed in appalling positions by what appear to be the sardonic twists of fate.

The war stories in *Tales of Soldiers and Civilians* can in large measure be considered horror tales because (although Bierce himself served in the Civil War and clearly drew upon his experiences for these works) the war setting is frequently irrelevant to the tales' import. To be sure, the crazy kind of heroism we find in such tales as "A Son of the Gods" could only be exhibited in war; but the intolerable situation in which a soldier finds himself in "One of the Missing" (he is rendered physically immobile while caught in the collapse of a house, with his rifle pointing directly at his head) is not materially different from that of "The Man and the Snake," in which a man is rendered psychologically paralysed by what he fancies to be a dangerous snake in his room (it is a

toy). The "soldier" story "A Tough Tussle" and the "civilian" story "A Watcher by the Dead" both play upon every person's fear and detestation of the proximity of a corpse.

Bierce also enlivens his war stories with elements of fantasy and pseudo-supernaturalism. His most celebrated tale, "An Occurrence at Owl Creek Bridge," features a man who thinks he has escaped from an execution by hanging and returned to his wife at his plantation, but this is merely a drawn-out hallucination occurring in the split second prior to his death. An air of dreamlike fantasy pervades "Chickamauga," in which a little boy sees the pitifully mangled survivors of one of the bloodiest battles of the Civil War.

Bierce's supernatural tales are perhaps less effective than his tales of psychological horror. Many of them are simple stories of revenge ("The Middle Toe of the Right Foot," "The Night-Doings at 'Deadman's'"), while in others the climax is merely the confirmation that what was taken to be a living person is in fact a ghost or apparition. By far his best supernatural tale is "The Death of Halpin Frayser," a wildly hallucinatory account of a man who engaged in incestuous relations with his mother, then killed her, only to be dispatched by her reanimated corpse. "The Moonlit Road" mingles horror and pathos in its tale of a man who murders his wife in the false belief that she was being unfaithful to him. The tale is narrated successively by the man's son, the man himself, and the spirit of the wife (channelled "through the medium Bayrolles"); each of these characters only knows a portion of the scenario, but by the end the reader knows the whole of it.

Two stories in *Can Such Things Be?* are landmarks of what can only be called proto-science-fiction. The lesser of them is "Moxon's Master," in which a mechanical chess-playing machine harrowingly develops human emotions (the entity on one occasion moves a chess piece "with a slow, uniform, mechanical and, I thought, somewhat theatrical movement of the arm"). Far superior is "The Damned Thing," a powerfully cosmic tale in which a character appeals to science to explain the existence of an invisible entity ("'I am not mad; there are colors that we cannot see. And, God help me! the Damned Thing is of such a color!'").

A variety of miscellaneous tales round out Bierce's corpus of weird writing. Satire is at the forefront in the four tales of "The Parenticide Club," whose events—to say nothing of their cheerfully irreverent narration—border upon the sadistic. Various odd events—perhaps put forth as "real" occurrences—are related in several other story-cycles: "Bodies of the Dead" (included only in the first edition of *Can Such Things Be?*), "The Ways of Ghosts," "Soldier-Folk," "Some Haunted Houses," and "Mysterious Disappearances."

No reader should overlook a handful of stories (mostly found in the first volume of Bierce's *Collected Works*) that might best be termed political fantasies. Among these are his two longest works of fiction, "Ashes of the Beacon" and "The Land Beyond the Blow," both of which are merciless satires on American political institutions. The former tale (which Bierce considered his finest fictional work) is a monograph by a "future historian" of the year 4930 relating the demise of the American republic, while the latter is a sprawling Swiftian satire in which a traveller voyages to a succession of imaginary realms and reports on the social and political conditions he finds there. These and other stories lend credence to the view that Bierce gained—or, at least, augmented—his cynicism and misanthropy by witnessing the "game of politics," where folly, hypocrisy, and duplicity are certainly on ever-present display.

Bierce's horrific satire—or satiric horror—may have laid the groundwork for such later writers as L. P. Hartley and Roald Dahl, but his achievement was unique. As masterful a craftsman of the short story as Poe; gifted with a rapier-sharp wit, a prose style of exceptional clarity and conciseness, and an imagination that peopled the untenanted wilderness of the American West with the grotesque spectres of a failed American dream, Bierce put a capstone on his own horrific achievement by disappearing from the face of the earth in late 1913. His small corpus of fiction continues to mock us with its sardonic and skeletal grin.

—S. T. Joshi

BILLSON, Anne

Nationality: British. **Born:** Southport, Lancashire, 1954. **Career:** Journalist and film critic for *The New Statesman, The Times, The Sunday Telegraph* and other periodicals, London; novelist. **Address:** c/o Macmillan Publishers Ltd., 25 Eccleston Place, London SW1W 9NF, England. Lives in London.

HORROR, GHOST AND GOTHIC PUBLICATIONS

Novels

Dream Demon (novelization of screenplay). London, New English Library, 1989.
Suckers. London, Pan, and New York, Atheneum, 1993.
Stiff Lips. London, Macmillan, 1996.

OTHER PUBLICATIONS

Other

The Screen Lovers. New York, St. Martin's Press, 1988.
My Name is Michael Caine. N.p, n.d.

*   *   *

Anne Billson is a clever and extremely witty writer, perhaps the wittiest currently working in the horror genre. The first of her three novels, *Dream Demon*, is a film tie-in, so it would be unfair to blame her for the inanity of the plot; she has made a tolerably good job of converting the script into a readable and occasionally amusing novel.

Rich young Diana Markham is preparing to marry Oliver, an RAF officer, and the novel follows a week in her life. She moves into a ground-floor flat in the house her father has given her as a wedding present. Almost at once, she takes a dislike to its cold, threatening basement. She begins having problems with nightmares, which seem very realistic, warping the world she knows into scenes that upset and disgust her. As a high-society bride, she is considered newsworthy and is bothered by two unscrupulous and obnoxious reporters, journalist Paul Lawrence and a photographer named Peck. Diana only manages to escape them with help from a young American woman, Jenny, who knees Peck in the groin. In the flat, Diana discovers that Jenny has come over to England to

seek out her roots; she was brought up in the house Diana now owns, and has survived a fire which killed her parents.

From this point on, events get nastier, more complicated and even less credible. Diana and Jenny make several visits to the basement, which grows larger all the time and is sometimes a dream and sometimes not; it seems to hold all the people who have ever lived in the house. In fact, reality and dream have become mixed, with extremely unpleasant things happening every time Diana falls asleep. Diana and Jennie are threatened by an assortment of nightmares including a psychotic child, a mirror-image world, and a maimed and bloated version of Peck.

In the real world, Oliver and a therapist "friend" of Diana's scheme to get Diana locked up and separated from her fortune. But Diana works out how to control her dreams; she uses her powers to rid herself of these nuisances by marooning them in her dreamworld. And then the whole novel is revealed as a dream.

By contrast, *Suckers* is a joy to read. Yuppie vampires are gradually taking over London; they wear black and drink pints of blood at their local bar. This is all conveyed with terrific pace and humour, though it has its serious side, with murders, dismemberments and other shocks. The story is most wittily narrated by Dora, a Creative Consultant for advertising agencies (which means she makes up survey results and fudges research). When she and her friend Duncan (for whom she has long nurtured an unrequited passion) were menaced by a vampire named Violet 13 years before, Duncan killed her, Dora had a fingertip bitten off, and Duncan and Dora dumped parts of Violet's body all round London. Now Violet is back, with corporate muscle, heading a large organization which is taking control of advertising and the media.

The novel is very sharp and cleverly told, full of only slightly exaggerated details of the worst aspects of living in London in the early 1990s. Dora describes yuppie parties, the perils of apartment existence, the problems of being a penniless and pretentious art student, and the reality of the advertising industry. The book is intended partly as a satire on contemporary advertising, where everything is false, everything is hyped and everybody is drunk, drugged and having affairs. Information provision is brilliant, even though the book resembles a sequel for its first few chapters. Only towards the end, when the vampires succeed too quickly and armageddon time arrives for London, does credibility slip, though the furious pace increases in an attempt to compensate.

It is Dora herself who is the main attraction here. She is cynical, vindictive, streetwise to the point of criminality, and almost completely amoral, yet the reader, male or female, cannot help but sympathize with her plight and support her wholeheartedly in her battle against life's problems. Wit and humour in the face of even the worst of horrors—but a complete avoidance of the farce which crept into *Dream Demon*—make her an original and superior heroine in an outstanding example of the usually clichéd vampire sub-genre.

Stiff Lips, which pretends to be very laid-back and almost unplotted, is a brilliantly subtle novel concerned partly with dangerous ghosts. It is set in contemporary London, which is entertainingly described, particularly in a large house in Notting Hill split into four flats. The main story is narrated by Clare, a single twentysomething artist. She is plump and mousey, wears glasses and is very gauche, but she is a determined social climber, trying to keep up with the rich and graceful Sophie (an old schoolfriend) and to get herself a worthwhile man. Sophie moves into the middle flat in this house and Clare (some weeks later) unofficially takes over the long-empty top floor.

Sophie's flat is haunted by the music of a long-defunct 1960s rock group, the Drunken Boats, who used to live there, while Clare's is haunted by Robert Jamieson, who cut his own throat in the bathroom 12 years before. Yet Robert still seems to inhabit the building. Letters arrive for him on a regular basis, Sophie has an affair with him and, later, Clare may also be having an affair with him.

Clare, in her narration, is generally clear and sure of what is happening, but she is often proved to be wrong by what others say to her. This subjectivity/objectivity axis is most wonderfully exploited by Billson, providing good surprises for the reader. A equally well used theme is communication, or the lack of it. Two down-market friends of Clare's are Dirk and Lemmy (the whole novel is full of the most marvellous minor characters) and Lemmy's lines of dialogue almost always sound like gibberish to Clare. "Bandung travolta yabba dabba Sophie's pad," he says. But Dirk is always there to translate.

Gradually Clare realizes that Robert is exceedingly nasty, good in bed perhaps but mad, bad and dangerous to know. The events build up to a set-piece Halloween party at the house, when blood must be spilt to quiet the place down for another 12 years. Not only does Clare survive, for she is the narrator, but she gets the man she most wants.

This is a novel of the highest quality, no less deep and horrific for being amusingly told. Billson is certainly an author to watch.

—Chris Morgan

BINGLEY, Margaret

Nationality: British. **Born:** 1947. **Address:** c/o Piatkus Books, 5 Windmill St., London W1P 1HF, England.

HORROR, GHOST AND GOTHIC PUBLICATIONS

Novels

The Devil's Child. London, Piatkus, 1983; New York, Popular Library, 1987.
The Waiting Darkness. London, Piatkus, 1984.
Children of the Night. London, Piatkus, 1985; New York, Popular Library, 1989.
After Alice Died. London, Piatkus, 1986; as *After Alice,* New York, Popular Library, 1989.
The Unquiet Dead. London, Piatkus, 1987; as *Deadtime Story,* New York, Popular Library, 1990.
Seeds of Evil. London, Piatkus, 1988; New York, Carroll and Graf, 1989.
Village of Satan. London, Piatkus, 1990.
Gateway to Hell. London, Piatkus, 1991.

*   *   *

The child as monster is a theme that has been such a prevalent one in modern horror fiction that it has become an overworked cliché. Classic tales such as Ray Bradbury's "The Small Assas-

sin," the possessed child of William Peter Blatty's *The Exorcist,* Stephen King's demonic "Children of the Corn" and the devil's offspring in *The Omen* and *Rosemary's Baby,* would seem to have covered the possibilities quite thoroughly. Horror fiction tends to be a conservative, ingrown genre, however, and many of its writers draw on the success of other stories to produce their own work, attempting to find a new twist for an old tale.

Margaret Bingley is one such writer, whose small but respectable body of horror fiction concentrates very heavily on that single theme, the child controlled by an evil, external force. *Devil's Child* could almost have been the sequel to *Rosemary's Baby.* Shortly after giving birth, Laura begins to suspect that there's something wrong with her infant son Edward. He's just too well behaved, never crying, never laughing, always solemn and alert. Eventually Laura realizes that her son can read the minds of people around him, and insinuate himself into their thoughts, even seize control of their will and make puppets of their bodies. Edward can turn people into toys, or weapons he can use against those who displease him. When she realizes that her son is a menace to the entire world, Laura tries to kill him, but of course it's far too late by then. She ends up institutionalized and Edward is free to grow up, and into whatever it is that he is to become. This pessimism about our ability to defeat evil is often present in novels of demonic children, perhaps because the corruption of youth, our only immortality, is so depressing a subject that it is hard to imagine good triumphing.

Children of the Night uses the same theme but on a smaller scale. Judith marries Marc while on an emotional rebound from the death of her first husband. Marc's obsession with his dead wife is a source of friction, but Judith is patient, hoping that he'll get over her loss with the passage of time. And Marc's five young sons seem to be admirable children as well, until their dark powers begin to manifest themselves. People who annoy the boys are very likely to turn up missing, permanently. Judith comes to fear her foster sons, but her unexpected pregnancy preoccupies her thoughts. And then her own child is born and for a while he seems perfectly normal, her shield against the strangeness of the rest of the family. Unfortunately Laurence grows a strange tooth, characteristic of his half-siblings, and she realizes that he is not a human being either, but a mutant like the others. The climax strongly resembles that of *Devil's Child.* Judith tries unsuccessfully to kill her baby, although in this case she is killed by the other boys rather than simply thwarted. In both books there is no hint of salvation; the monsters win.

After Alice Died is a story of ghostly possession. Allan is haunted by the wraith of a mysterious woman named Alice, whom he never met in life. Although no one else can see her, Allan never doubts his own sanity because Alice is able to affect the lives of others, in one instance causing his wife Julie to fall down a staircase, with a subsequent miscarriage. What follows is a sometimes confused mix of sex and the supernatural. Julie and Alice had a brief, lesbian affair in their youth, and Alice was subsequently murdered by Julie's half brother, Richard. Allan and Julie have a child, Melissa, whose personality is supplanted by that of Alice. Once again the characters fail to overcome the evil with which they are faced. Julie dies, Allan commits suicide, and Richard ends up in an insane asylum.

The Unquiet Dead involves an entire community filled with demonically possessed youngsters. A small English town is plagued by a series of mishaps and fatalities, all engineered by the local children. Amy discovers that her husband Carlo holds a strange power over these children, and that together they are responsible for a series of unexplained deaths. Ultimately her own child becomes a victim, and in the aftermath Amy thinks she has destroyed Carlo and his followers forever. But once again Bingley deflates our final chapter hopes, this time by having Carlo's spirit possess the body of Amy's new husband.

Bingley's best novel is *Seeds of Evil*. Meg has twin children after being impregnated artificially by an anonymous sperm donor. As the twins begin to grow, Meg suspects that there is something evil about them. Their eyes don't look entirely human, and they seem to share a secret relationship even more intense than that usually displayed between twins. When Ashley enters their lives, he professes love for Meg, but she suspects that he is actually the father of the twins, more interested in them than in his new wife.

The plot thickens as we discover Ashley has been doing genetic engineering and spreading his altered seed to a variety of women, hoping to be father to a race of superhuman, but soulless creatures. Unfortunately, a contagious disease kills most of his children, and Meg suspects that one survivor, Ophelia, is actually a cold blooded killer. But Meg is no luckier than Bingley's other protagonists, and she dies trying to kill Ophelia, while Ashley lives to raise a new crop of mutant children.

Although Bingley demonstrates most of the virtues of a good suspense writer, she seems mired artistically in a single plot, with minor variations. Her protagonists are so ineffectual that the reader knows from the outset that evil will prevail, and with that certainty, there's little suspense to hold our attention. If Bingley is to be anything other than a minor footnote in modern horror, she will need to explore new themes, and stop telegraphing her endings.

—Don D'Ammassa

BIRKIN, Charles (Lloyd; 5th Baronet Birkin)

Nationality: British. **Born:** Nottingham, 24 September 1907. **Career:** Editor with the publishing house of Philip Allan, London, in the 1930s. Succeeded to the baronetcy in 1942. **Died:** 9 November 1986.

HORROR, GHOST AND GOTHIC PUBLICATIONS

Short Stories

Devil's Spawn. London, Philip Allan, 1936.
The Kiss of Death. London, Tandem, 1964; New York, Award, 1969.
The Smell of Evil. London, Tandem, 1965; New York, Award, 1969.
Where Terror Stalked and Other Horror Stories. London, Tandem, 1966.
My Name Is Death and Other New Tales of Horror. London, Panther, 1966; New York, Award, 1970.
Dark Menace. London, Tandem, 1968.
So Pale, So Cold, So Fair. London, Tandem, 1970.
Spawn of Satan. New York, Award, 1971.

Other

Editor (anonymously), *Creeps.* London, Allan, 1932.
Editor (anonymously), *Shivers.* London, Allan, 1932.
Editor (anonymously), *Shudders.* London, Allan, 1932.
Editor (anonymously), *Horrors.* London, Allan, 1933.
Editor (anonymously), *Nightmares.* London, Allan, 1933.
Editor (anonymously), *Quakes.* London, Allan, 1933.
Editor (anonymously), *Terrors.* London, Allan, 1933
Editor (anonymously), *Monsters.* London, Allan, 1934.
Editor (anonymously), *Panics.* London, Allan, 1934.
Editor (anonymously), *Powers of Darkness.* London, Allan, 1934.
Editor (anonymously), *Thrills.* London, Allan, 1935.
Editor (anonymously), *Tales of Fear.* London, Allan, 1935.
Editor (anonymously), *The Creeps Omnibus.* London, Allan, 1935.
Editor (anonymously), *Tales of Dread.* London, Allan, 1936.
Editor (anonymously), *Tales of Death.* London, Allan, 1936.
Editor, *The Tandem Book of Ghost Stories.* London, Tandem, 1965.
Editor, *The Tandem Book of Horror Stories.* London, Tandem, 1965.

*   *   *

In an output of just over one hundred stories written between the early 1930s and the late 1970s, Birkin concentrated on non-supernatural horror. His tales feature grotesque means of death, murderous madmen, torture, cannibalism, sex with lepers, embalmed corpses kept by people who love them, and similar accounts of nastiness. It should not be supposed that his stories are mere catalogues of atrocity; in fact they are mostly well-developed accounts of character interaction against a wide variety of atmospheric backgrounds. The *grand guignol* elements are frequently only to be found in the last page or two.

One of his very best stories is "The Finger of Fear," about Cornelia Jamieson, a rich but miserly spinster of 70. She is reclusive (and an alcoholic) and is becoming gradually more eccentric. An elderly couple, the Tomlins, act as servants at her large, isolated country house. The Tomlins' grandson, six-year-old Peter, lives with them. Miss Jamieson's meanness includes dismantling things in order to send only the broken component in for repair with Mr. Tomlin when he makes his monthly trip to the nearest market town for supplies. When Peter becomes very ill with an abscessed tooth, Miss Jamieson will not allow him to be taken for treatment—but she cuts off his head and sends that in a box as a component for repair.

Birkin's stories contain many demented murderers. In "Some New Pleasures Prove" it is an escaped maniac (Birkin's term), a convicted mass murderer, who has broken into a lonely cottage and killed the woman living there. When Laura, who has run out of petrol, calls at the cottage, the murderer at first treats her with civility. But then, when it is clear that she has identified him, he sends her up to the bedroom which contains the dead woman's scattered remains. Laura escapes by pretending to be a ghost, but the first person she meets is the dead woman's husband, on his way home. Laura is hysterical, but the husband insists upon taking her to his cottage, where his wife will surely be able to help her. In "Fine Needlework" the madman is a relative of an old French family, supposedly kept safely under lock and key in a room at the family chateau, but using secret passageways to roam the building and kill two visitors for the most bizarre of reasons. Birkin used the theme so often that it would have become a cliché due to his efforts alone.

A very memorable story is "The Hitch," in which the attractive painted lampshade brought back as a souvenir from a holiday in Germany, and featuring Neptune and some seahorses, turns out to be the tattooed skin of a German Jew, the victim of Nazi atrocity. In fact, several of Birkin's stories are concerned with Nazi Germany. "Green Fingers" is about Hilde's garden in wartime Germany; she always grows the very best flowers, fruit and vegetables in the area, unaware that her soil is being fertilized with the bodies of victims from the nearby concentration camp.

Equally unforgettable is "The Kiss of Death," set on a plantation in the East Indies soon after World War II. The youngish and still attractive Lady Sylvia Nicholson is just visiting her brother. At night a man enters her room and, in total darkness, they make love. She believes it to be Philip Dewhurst, a handsome American, but it is in fact an old flame of hers, who is now suffering from leprosy. An earlier version of the theme is to be found in Birkin's "Shelter," first published in 1934, and set in Brazil.

Birkin's settings are mostly British, though some stories are contemporary (to the 1930s or 1960s) while others are period pieces. "The Orphanage" is about the starvation, slavery and abuse which occurred in English orphanages in the 1860s. And a tale of rape and mass murder set around 1904 is "The Godmothers." "The Terror on Tobit" (later retitled "My Name is Death") is a very atmospheric supernatural piece set among the Scilly Islands, off Cornwall, while "The Three Monkeys" is Irish. One very strange story, clearly set deeply in rural Sussex, is "Havelock's Farm." This, which appeared in Birkin's 1936 collection, is obviously a satire on *Cold Comfort Farm* by Stella Gibbons, first published in 1932.

When he set his stories abroad, Birkin chose locations all over the world, though always places he had visited. Jamaica features in "The Kennel," in which a woman who has betrayed her plantation-owner common-law husband, and has had a child by a casual lover, is kept in a kennel with her baby. She is fed on a meat broth which, it is made clear to her, has been made out of the body of her baby's father.

"The Mouse Hole" is set among members of the French resistance during World War II. Several other stories are set in France, including "The Belt," "Parlez Moi d'Amour" and "Paris Pilgrimage," the last two among the foreign artists living there. The protagonist of "Hosanna" is a young bearded Briton, hitch-hiking across France, who is given a lift and lodging for the night by an artist who tells him how much he resembles Jesus, and then crucifies him. There is a Greek setting to "So Pale, So Cold, So Fair," in which a British tourist sells all his blood and ends up "just an empty shell," and a Cypriot setting in "A Low Profile"; Birkin lived in Cyprus for four years.

It would be untrue to suggest that Birkin wrote no supernatural stories. Most of his collections include at least one, with incubi and succubi in "Malleus Maleficarum," zombies in "Ballet Négre," murderous ghosts in "'Is Anybody There?'" and a pair of cursed cufflinks in "The Road."

Birkin was important as an anthologist of ghost and horror tales, especially during the 1930s; he put a story of his own into almost every anthology he edited, usually under the pseudonym Charles Lloyd. He also wrote occasional horror verse, such as "Au Claire de Lune," reprinted in *The Eleventh Pan Book of Horror Stories*.

—Chris Morgan

BLACK, Campbell

Pseudonyms: Thomas Altman; Campbell Armstrong; Jeffrey Campbell. **Nationality:** British. **Born:** Glasgow, in 1944. **Education:** University of Sussex, Brighton. **Career:** Editor in a publishing house, London, late 1960s; moved to the USA, 1971; creative writing tutor, State University of New York; latterly, a freelance writer, living in Arizona, Scotland and Ireland.

HORROR, GHOST AND GOTHIC PUBLICATIONS

Novels

Brainfire. New York, Morrow, 1979; London, Joseph, 1980; as Campbell Armstrong, New York, Harper, 1990.
Dressed to Kill (novelization of screenplay). New York, Bantam, and London, Arrow, 1980.
The Homing, with Jeffrey Caine (as Jeffrey Campbell). New York, Putnam, 1980.
Raiders of the Lost Ark (novelization of screenplay). New York, Ballantine, and London, Corgi, 1981.
Letters from the Dead. New York, Villard, 1985; London, Grafton, 1987.
The Wanting. New York, McGraw Hill, 1986; London, Mandarin, 1991.
The Piper. New York, Pocket, 1986; London, Mandarin, 1992.

Novels as Thomas Altman

Kiss Daddy Goodbye. New York, Bantam, 1980.
The True Bride. New York, Bantam, 1982; London, Severn House, 1986.
Black Christmas. New York, Bantam, 1983; London, Corgi, 1984.
Dark Places. New York, Bantam, 1984; London, Corgi, 1985.
The Intruder. New York, Bantam, 1985.

OTHER PUBLICATIONS

Novels

Assassins and Victims. London, Macmillan, 1969; New York, Harper's Magazine Press, 1970.
The Punctual Rape. London, Macmillan, 1970; New York, Lippincott, 1971.
Death's Head. London, Collins, and New York, Lippincott, 1972.
The Asterisk Destiny. New York, Morrow, 1978; London, Joseph, 1979.
Mr. Apology. New York, Ballantine, 1984.

Novels as Campbell Armstrong

Jig. London, Hodder and Stoughton, 1987.
Mazurka. London, Hodder and Stoughton, 1988.
Mambo. London, Hodder and Stoughton, 1990.
Agents of Darkness. London, Hodder and Stoughton, 1991.
Concert of Ghosts. London, Hodder and Stoughton, 1992.
Jigsaw. London, Hodder and Stoughton, 1994.
Heat. London, Doubleday, 1996.
Silencer. London, Doubleday, 1997.

Plays

Television Play: *Death's Head*, 1971.

*   *   *

Campbell Black moved to horror fiction after beginning his career as a writer of spy thrillers, an unusual progression in some ways. It was not as great a leap as it might seem, however, because some of Black's early novels blended international espionage with the fantastic, anticipating to some extent the trend that would later develop in the popular television series *The X-Files*. In *The Asterisk Destiny*, for example, we know that there's a secret government base in Arizona which has attracted the attention of a number of spies. Two investigators suspect that there is a UFO at the site, but they ultimately learn that it is a fake one, created by the US Government in order to frighten the Russians. *Brainfire* has a similar feel but contains more legitimate horror elements. This time the Russians have a secret project, one designed to locate and put to use genuine psychic powers. They find an elderly woman who can kill with the power of her mind and test her abilities by means of several assassinations, all in preparation for the greatest target of all, the President of the United States. Both novels are reasonably conventional thrillers wrapped around a mystery. Although both novels are basically adventure stories in a contemporary setting, there are enough hints of the fantastic to make Black's subsequent move to horror fiction not entirely surprising.

Most of Black's novels continued to be mundane suspense fiction, though the mood of *Kiss Daddy Goodbye* and *The True Bride*, both written under the name Thomas Altman, made them of interest to horror fans. Even more pronounced in macabre atmosphere was *Black Christmas*, also as by Altman, which pitted a small-town sheriff against a serial killer with a grudge, a man who specifically stalks and slaughters women who are friends of the protagonist. Although the form is that of a traditional murder mystery, the ferocity of the killer and the pervasive atmosphere of imminent danger resembles that of other serial-killer stories which fit more properly into the horror genre.

Black also did the novelization of the movie *Raiders of the Lost Ark*, which is essentially an adventure story, but which contains elements of the supernatural, specifically the Ark of the Covenant which contains unspecified disembodied spirits. The story is reminiscent of the occult adventures of Seabury Quinn, C. S. Cody and others, a form that has fallen out of favour with modern readers. Another film novelization, *Dressed to Kill*, concerned a deranged serial killer, and is more successful in prose form because it does not rely as much on the visual pyrotechnics of *Raiders*. All of these novels were well-written, as plausible as can be expected given their fantastic nature, and entertaining, but up to this point Black had still not produced anything that could genuinely be labelled horror fiction except a minor collaboration with Jeffrey Caine, *The Homing* (as Jeffrey Campbell).

That changed with *Letters from the Dead*. Two single mothers and their children decide to spend a vacation in a long-abandoned house in a remote area as a way to clear their minds of past problems and gain a fresh start. Shortly after arriving, one of the teenagers begins to feel strange fears about the contents of a closet, in which he later discovers an Ouija board. While his mother hears inexplicable and unintelligible voices in the night, Tommy tells Lindy about the game and they decide to try it out. Lindy gets

spooked the very first time they receive what appears to be an intelligent reply to a question, but Tommy is fascinated by now and convinces her to try again. What follows is a better-than-average haunted-house story, effective because Black takes the time to flesh in the small plot details that lead inevitably to the climactic scene. The teenagers try to discover the identity of "Roscoe," who speaks to them from beyond the grave, as well as the identity of a second spirit who begs them for protection from Roscoe. Meanwhile their mothers begin to notice subtle but disturbing events taking place around them, unaware of the fact that the children are being enticed toward making a human sacrifice to appease a man long dead.

The Wanting is a supernatural child-in-jeopardy novel. The Untermeyers and their 12-year-old son move into a summer house in northern California, hoping for peace and quiet. An elderly couple living nearby make them welcome, and are particularly solicitous of the boy, Denny. At first, everything seems all right, but then the parents begin to notice changes in their son, as if he were developing a new personality. The mother begins to suspect their neighbours, particularly after discovering evidence that they are actually even older than they appear. The revelation that the couple are able to live by supplanting the personalities of children when their own bodies begin to fail is pretty well telegraphed, but Louise Untermeyer is an interesting, credible character and her systematic unravelling of the mystery and ultimate reaction to her discovery are convincing enough to hold the reader's interest.

The Piper, published in the same year as *The Wanting*, proved to be Black's last real horror novel, and since then he has concentrated on crime thrillers under the further pseudonym of Campbell Armstrong. The old, pre-Armstrong, Campbell Black wrote solid, well-crafted novels that drew on familiar plot-lines, but which were memorable because of his excellent grasp of pacing, his straightforward prose, and a sure hand at creating sympathetic and plausible characters. Had he produced a larger body of work in the field, he might well have achieved the respected status in horror that he has since enjoyed in suspense, but he seems uncommitted to a single genre, and the future course of his career is therefore unpredictable.

—Don D'Ammassa

BLACKBURN, John (Fenwick)

Nationality: British. **Born:** Corbridge on Tyne, Northumberland, 26 June 1923; brother of the writer Thomas Blackburn. **Education:** Haileybury College, 1937-40; Durham University, B.A. 1949. **Military Service:** Served as a radio officer in the merchant navy, 1942-45. **Family:** Married Joan Mary Clift in 1950. **Career:** Worked as a lorry driver, schoolmaster in London, 1949-51, and Berlin, 1951-52; director, Red Lion Books, London, 1952-59; also ran a book shop with his wife in Richmond, Surrey. **Died:** 1993.

HORROR, GHOST AND GOTHIC PUBLICATIONS

Novels

A Scent of New-Mown Hay. London, Secker and Warburg, and New York, Mill, 1958.

A Ring of Roses. London, Cape, 1965; as *A Wreath of Roses,* New York, Mill, 1965.
Children of the Night. London, Cape, 1966; New York, Putnam, 1969.
Nothing But the Night. London, Cape, 1968.
Bury Him Darkly. London, Cape, 1969; New York, Putnam, 1970.
Blow the House Down. London, Cape, 1970.
For Fear of Little Men. London, Cape, 1972.
Devil Daddy. London, Cape, 1972.
Our Lady of Pain. London, Cape, 1974.
The Cyclops Goblet. London, Cape, 1977.

OTHER PUBLICATIONS

Novels

A Sour Apple Tree. London, Secker and Warburg, 1958; New York, Mill, 1959.
Broken Boy. London, Secker and Warburg, 1959; New York, Mill, 1962.
Dead Man Running. London, Secker and Warburg, 1960; New York, Mill, 1961.
The Gaunt Woman. London, Cape, and New York, Mill, 1962.
Blue Octavo. London, Cape, 1963; as *Bound to Kill,* New York, Mill, 1963.
Colonel Bogus. London, Cape, 1964; as *Packed for Murder,* New York, Mill, 1964.
The Winds of Midnight. London, Cape, 1964; as *Murder at Midnight,* New York, Mill, 1964.
The Flame and the Wind. London, Cape, 1967.
The Young Man from Lima. London, Cape, 1968.
The Household Traitors. London, Cape, 1971.
Deep Among the Dead Men. London, Cape, 1973.
Mister Brown's Bodies. London, Cape, 1975.
The Face of the Lion. London, Cape, 1976.
Dead Man's Handle. London, Cape, 1978.
The Sins of the Father. London, Cape, 1979.
A Beastly Business. London, Hale, 1982.
A Book of the Dead. London, Hale, 1984.
The Bad Penny. London, Hale, 1985.

*

Manuscript Collection: Mugar Memorial Library, Boston University.

*   *   *

Horror fiction has had considerable difficulty defining itself in recent years. One school of thought maintains that some element of the supernatural must be present to differentiate between horror fiction and a simple "thriller." Others would include such work as William Goldman's *Magic,* Michael Slade's *Ghoul,* and *The Silence of the Lambs* by Thomas Harris despite their lack of a fantastic element simply because their tone is so akin to the genre. Horror and science fiction frequently overlap as well, rationalized monsters including aliens from outer space, horrible mutations, and other scientifically explained dangers. John Blackburn is one of a handful of writers who plant themselves firmly in the no man's land where all three forms overlap, refusing to pigeonhole themselves into a narrowly defined niche.

If horror is a mood rather than a theme, then Blackburn was writing horror with his very first novel, a spy thriller titled *A Scent of New-Mown Hay,* the first in a short-lived series about General Kirk of British Intelligence. In that novel, a demented scientist has bred a deadly fungus whose distinctive aroma warns of the disease it carries. Primarily a novel of espionage, the story is punctuated with distinctly horrific scenes and the climax, involving an animated, human-sized fungus, is every bit as chilling as a supernatural manifestation.

Children of the Night is set in rural England, a small village plagued by mysterious events. There are rumours of a mysterious group called the Children of Paul and the village history is checkered with unexplained deaths and disasters. An outsider asks an innocent question and is assaulted for his trouble. Incensed, he decides to find out the truth, oblivious to the real danger confronting him, although the reader has been forewarned that there's a sinister presence hovering over the village.

The Children of Paul are apparently a human mutation that appeared 700 years earlier. They are a race of troglodytes who spend most of their lives hidden in caverns near the village. Although their bodies have become misshapen, it is their minds that are most altered. They possess the power of telepathy, the ability to read minds, and can actually change the thoughts of ordinary human beings, forcing them to kill each other or perform other services. Eventually, of course, the protagonist finds a way to insulate himself from their influence and cause their destruction, but only after nearly destroying the entire local population.

Perhaps the most effective of Blackburn's sf/horror thrillers is *Bury Him Darkly.* Martin Railstone was a 17th-century writer and artist who produced a small body of work which attracts the nearly fanatic interest of a contemporary society of admirers. In a provision of his will, Railstone entrusted his tomb, estate, and the balance of his artistic work to the Church of England, which has steadfastly refused all requests to open the vault. Railstone, in the clergy's opinion, was a debauched madman and probably an insane satanist, who believed that he could kill simply by touching people. But there are others interested in investigating the remains, including a German biologist who suspects Railstone's "disease" was something more sinister, and an historian who believes Railstone possessed a significant religious artefact, possibly the authentic Holy Grail.

Through a series of manoeuvres, legal and otherwise, various attempts are made to breach the fortified vault. The results are startling. Primitive but still effective traps seriously injure one man, and another dies of heart failure after hearing uncanny laughter from within the tomb. Although readers might expect a vampire or other supernatural creature at this juncture, Blackburn explains everything in scientific terms, and ultimately Railstone's mummified body is found and examined and a trunk full of treasures removed.

Which is when things really start to fall apart. The artefact is not the Grail; in fact, no one knows exactly what it is, although clearly it was meant as some kind of container. More startling is an examination of its structure, revealing an alloy harder than diamond and literally millions of years old. The artefact is of extraterrestrial origin, and it has carried to Earth the biological heritage of an extinct species, one which obtained immortality by engineering a micro-organism that could convert living tissue into an analogue of its own species. The last section of the novel is a restrained but suspenseful version of the Authorities vs. the Blob, marred slightly by the *deus ex machina* ending of having the alien creature allergic to another version of itself. That cavil notwithstanding, this is a nicely crafted, often surprising, and definitely gripping thriller.

For Fear of Little Men also uses science fiction to explain the extraordinary. The setting is a small Welsh village where the local people avoid a nearby mountain. Even animals refuse to inhabit its slopes. Once again Blackburn uses outsiders as the fulcrum of the plot, and their investigations reveal an ancient race of parasitic creatures who occupy human hosts as part of their patient plan to unleash a world destroying plague. Blackburn leaves their origin shrouded in mystery, but hints that they may be aliens from outer space rather than some terrestrially spawned menace.

An infrequent short story writer, Blackburn has written two of some interest. "Drink to Me Only" presents a ruthless egotist who has succeeded in life largely due to the intercession of his doting sister, who possesses the evil eye, the ability to cause misfortune for his enemies. But her insistence of monopolizing his time has become irksome, and when she is kidnapped and blindfolded, unable to use her powers, he demands that the kidnappers send him proof that they really have her under their control—and asks for her eyes. "The Final Trick" involves a bumbling amateur magician who finally manages to perform a trick that amazes his instructor, but to do so he must actually kill his assistant.

Blackburn's novels have not enjoyed wide popularity in the U.S., probably because they do not fit easily into established marketing stereotypes. Despite that handicap, his reputation as a reliable source of suspenseful, often horrifying fiction seems assured.

—Don D'Ammassa

BLACKWOOD, Algernon (Henry)

Nationality: British. **Born:** Shooters' Hill, Kent, 14 March 1869. **Education:** Moravian School, Germany; Wellington College; Edinburgh University. **Career:** Staff member, *Canadian Methodist Magazine*, Toronto; hotel proprietor and farmer in Canada; reporter, New York *Evening Sun* and New York *Times;* private secretary to James Speyer, New York; returned to England in 1899, and worked briefly in the dried-milk business; full-time writer, 1908-51; appeared on television, 1947-51. **Awards:** Television Society Silver Medal, 1948. C.B.E. (Commander, Order of the British Empire), 1949. **Died:** 10 December 1951.

HORROR, GHOST AND GOTHIC PUBLICATIONS

Novels (series: LeVallon)

Jimbo: A Fantasy. London and New York, Macmillan, 1909.
The Human Chord. London, Macmillan, 1910; New York, Macmillan, 1911.
The Centaur. London and New York, Macmillan, 1911; New York, Macmillan, 1912.
Julius LeVallon. London, Cassell, and New York, Dutton, 1916.
The Bright Messenger (LeVallon). London, Cassell, 1921; New York, Dutton, 1922.

Short Stories

The Empty House and Other Ghost Stories. London, Nash, 1906; New York, Vaughan, 1915.
The Listener and Other Stories. London, Nash, 1907; New York, Vaughan and Gomme, 1914.
John Silence, Physician Extraordinary. London, Nash, 1908; Boston, Luce, 1909.
The Lost Valley and Other Stories. London, Nash, 1910; New York, Vaughan and Gomme, 1914.
Pan's Garden. London and New York, Macmillan, 1912.
Ten Minute Stories. London, Murray, and New York, Dutton, 1914.
Incredible Adventures. London and New York, Macmillan, 1914.
Day and Night Stories. London, Cassell, and New York, Dutton, 1917; as *Tales of the Mysterious and Macabre,* London, Spring, 1968.
The Wolves of God and Other Fey Stories, with Wilfred Wilson. London, Cassell, and New York, Dutton, 1921.
Tongues of Fire and Other Sketches. London, Jenkins, 1924; New York, Dutton, 1925.
Ancient Sorceries and Other Tales. London, Collins, 1927.
The Dance of Death and Other Tales. London, Jenkins, 1927; New York, Dial Press, 1928.
Strange Stories. London, Heinemann, 1929; New York, Arno Press, 1976; abridged as *The Best Supernatural Tales of Algernon Blackwood,* New York, Causeway, 1973.
Full Circle. London, Mathews and Marrot, 1929.
Short Stories of To-Day and Yesterday. London, Harrap, 1930.
The Willows and Other Queer Tales. London, Collins, 1932.
Shocks. London, Grayson, 1935; New York, Dutton, 1936.
The Tales of Algernon Blackwood. London, Secker, 1938; New York, Dutton, 1939.
Selected Tales: Stories of the Supernatural and the Uncanny. London, Penguin, 1942.
Selected Short Stories of Algernon Blackwood. New York, Armed Services, 1945.
The Doll and One Other. Sauk City, Wisconsin, Arkham House, 1946.
Tales of the Uncanny and Supernatural. London, Nevill, 1949; Secaucus, Castle Books, 1974.
In the Realm of Terror. New York, Pantheon, 1957.
Selected Tales. London, Baker, 1964; as *Tales of Terror and the Unknown,* New York, Dutton, 1965; as *The Insanity of Jones and Other Stories,* London, Penguin, 1966.
Tales of the Mysterious and Macabre. London, Hamlyn, 1967; Secaucus, Castle Books, 1974.
Ancient Sorceries and Other Stories. London, Penguin, 1968.
Best Ghost Stories, edited by E. F. Bleiler. New York, Dover Publications, 1973.
Tales of Terror and Darkness. London, Hamlyn, 1977.
Tales of the Supernatural, edited by Mike Ashley. Woodbridge, Suffolk, Bookmasters, 1983.
The Magic Mirror: Lost Supernatural and Mystery Stories, edited by Mike Ashley. Wellingborough, Northamptonshire, Thorsons, 1989.
A Mysterious House. Edinburgh, Tragara Press, 1987.

Plays

The Crossing, with Bertram Forsyth (produced London, 1920).
The Halfway House, with Elaine Ainley (produced London, 1921).

White Magic, with Bertram Forsyth (produced Toronto, 1921).
Max Hensig, with Kinsey Peile (produced London, 1929).

Radio Plays: *Told in a Mountain Cabin,* 1942; *Running Wolf,* 1944; *In a Glass Darkly,* 1945.

Other Publications

Novels

The Education of Uncle Paul. London, Macmillan, 1909; New York, Holt, 1910.
A Prisoner of Fairyland: The Book That "Uncle Paul" Wrote. London and New York, Macmillan, 1913.
The Extra Day. London and New York, Macmillan, 1915.
The Wave: An Egyptian Aftermath. London, Macmillan, and New York, Dutton, 1916.
The Promise of Air. London, Macmillan, and New York, Dutton, 1918.
The Garden of Survival. London, Macmillan, and New York, Dutton, 1918.
Dudley and Gilderoy: A Nonsense. London, Benn, and New York, Dutton, 1929.
The Fruit Stoners: Being the Adventures of Maria among the Fruit Stoners. London, Grayson, 1934; New York, Dutton, 1935.

Fiction for Children

Sambo and Snitch. Oxford, Blackwell, and New York, Appleton, 1927.
Mr. Cupboard. Oxford, Blackwell, 1928.
By Underground. Oxford, Blackwell, 1930.
The Parrot and the Cat. Oxford, Blackwell, 1931.
The Italian Conjuror. Oxford, Blackwell, 1932.
Maria—of England—in the Rain. Oxford, Blackwell, 1933.
Sergeant Poppett and Policeman James. Oxford, Blackwell, 1934.
How the Circus Came to Tea. Oxford, Blackwell, 1936.
The Adventures of Dudley and Gilderoy, adapted by Marion B. Cothren. New York, Dutton, and London, Faber, 1941.

Plays

The Starlight Express, with Violet Pearn, adaptation of the story *A Prisoner in Fairyland* by Blackwood (produced London, 1915).
Karma: A Re-incarnation Play, with Violet Pearn. London, Macmillan, and New York, Dutton, 1918.
Through the Crack, with Violet Pearn (produced London, 1920). London and New York, French, 1920.

Radio Plays: *It's About Time,* 1945; *The Secret Society,* 1947.

Other

Episodes Before Thirty (autobiography). London, Cassell, 1923; New York, Dutton, 1924; as *Adventures Before Thirty,* London, Cape, 1934.

*

Critical Studies: "Algernon Blackwood: Novelist and Mystic" by Stuart Gilbert, *Transition,* July 1935; "Algernon Blackwood" in *The Supernatural in Fiction* by Peter Penzoldt, London, Peter Nevill, 1952; "A Study of Algernon Blackwood" by Derek Hudson, *Essays and Studies #14,* London, John Murray, 1961; "The Visionary Ghost Story: Algernon Blackwood" in *Elegant Nightmares* by Jack Sullivan, Athens, Ohio University Press, 1978; *Blackwood's Books* by John Robert Colombo, Toronto, Hounslow Press, 1981; *Algernon Blackwood: A Bio-bibliography* by Michael Ashley, Westport, Connecticut, Greenwood Press, 1987; "Algernon Blackwood: The Expansion of Consciousness" in *The Weird Tale* by S. T. Joshi, Austin, University of Texas Press, 1990.

*   *   *

By the time of his death Algernon Blackwood had become well known to the British radio and television audiences for his regular short-story spots. As most of these focused on ghostly or bizarre incidents Blackwood became known as "the Ghost Man," and he is still remembered primarily as a ghost-story writer. In fact ghost stories, as traditionally defined, make up only a small part of Blackwood's output. His thesis was more one of the expanded consciousness and how, through a closer affinity with the world about us, the individual may form a wider perception of reality and a communion with Nature. This communion included ghosts, but Blackwood was more interested in the spirits of Nature and the majority of his best stories are those which consider their impact upon the individual who, either through training or by accident, suddenly finds his world under siege from beyond.

Blackwood's earliest stories were more traditional in content. Those in *The Empty House* are mostly conventional ghost stories, although even here Blackwood uses his wide experience of the world to introduce more original features. "A Haunted Island" (*Pall Mall,* 1899), for instance, has a remote Canadian island haunted by the vengeful spirit of an American Indian; and "A Case of Eavesdropping" (*Pall Mall,* 1900) describes a New York lodging room where a murder is spectrally re-enacted in the empty room next door. "The Strange Adventures of a Private Secretary in New York" is very untypical of Blackwood's work and betrays a heavy gothic influence in portraying its narrator's experiences in a remote rambling old house. Although his second volume of stories, *The Listener,* contained further ghost stories, it was evident that Blackwood was striving to portray these more as spiritual afflictions than simple hauntings. "The Listener" itself is about a room haunted by the spirit of a leper, whilst "The Woman's Ghost Story" reveals how an accursed spirit can be saved by love.

Both these early collections also contained stories which were more typical of the two directions that Blackwood's fiction would take. The first of these are the stories developed from his knowledge of the occult. He was a student of arcane lore and for many years a member of the Hermetic Order of the Golden Dawn. "With Intent to Steal" is a powerful story of the vengeful spirit of a black magician, while "Smith: An Episode in a Lodging House" depicts the perils of interfering with the unknown. Both of these stories serve as precursors to Blackwood's third book, which would also prove his most successful, *John Silence: Physician Extraordinary.* Silence is a doctor who seeks to cure people of psychic rather than physical afflictions. His years of study throughout the world provide him with a formidable knowledge of the spiritual realm. Blackwood had originally intended to explore these

themes in a series of essays but he was convinced by his publisher to convert them into fiction. Some of these conversions work
better than others and the stories are inconsistent in their plotting
and structure, but at their best they pack considerable power. "A
Psychical Invasion" is an extremely effective haunted-house story
bearing some similarity to Bulwer Lytton's "The Haunted and the
Haunters." "Ancient Sorceries" explores the influence of witchcraft over a French village. "The Nemesis of Fire," which is the
closest Blackwood comes to modelling Silence on Sherlock Holmes,
features a fire elemental. "The Camp of the Dog" is an exploration of lycanthropy as a psychic affliction, whilst "Secret Worship" is a macabre study of the cumulative impact of years of
malignity, a concept Blackwood revisited in "The Damned."

Blackwood chose not to return to the character of John Silence,
although a story written at this time, "A Victim of Higher Space"
(*Occult Review*, 1914), subsequently appeared in print. He did produce one further novel which revolved solely around his arcane
knowledge, and that was *The Human Chord*. A clergyman brings
together a group of individuals capable of perfect pitch in order
that the union of their tonalities can speak the name of God and
invoke the Holy Spirit. Blackwood's interest in the occult soon
waned as he was not looking for hermetic knowledge but a deeper
mystical understanding of the realities of human and spiritual experience.

It was this understanding of the world beyond human understanding that began to power his greater fiction and represents
the second main strand of his work. This was also evident in his
early stories, especially "The Willows" in *The Listener* and "The
Wendigo" in *The Lost Valley*, both still regarded by many as among
his best work. Both of these stories show how individuals entering remote areas of the world—the less accessible parts of the
river Danube in the first, and the forests of northern Canada in
the second—become aware of vast forces at work, way beyond
the comprehension of man. These forces are not necessarily malign to humanity, but our presence amongst them places us in danger. In "The Wendigo" the spirit force of Nature saps man of his
own psychic energies, leaving just a shell.

By 1910 Blackwood was reaching the peak of his creative abilities. His work over the next two to three years showed an intense
marriage of his mystical and hermetic knowledge and his personal
experiences in the wild places of the world. Some of the stories in
Pan's Garden and *Incredible Adventures* might almost be seen as
Nature Gothic, a form of which Blackwood is the only true master. In *Pan's Garden* nature is shown as all-powerful but generally benign provided mankind keeps its place. Stories including
"The Man Whom the Trees Loved" and "The Temptation of the
Clay" demonstrate that man can never defeat Nature but may work
with it to a great symbiotic benefit or be ejected. The stories in
Incredible Adventures, however, are more sinister. In "A Descent
into Egypt," a companion piece to "Sand" in *Pan's Garden*,
Blackwood endeavours to portray the unimaginable immensity of
power accumulated over the aeons and how man can become over-
powered by the manifestation of Time. "The Regeneration of Lord
Ernie" shows how a psychically withdrawn child can be re-ener-
gized by contact with Nature, although the body and soul may be
incapable of containing the energies released.

These shorter pieces are further workings of themes contained
in Blackwood's two most important novels: *The Centaur* and *Julius
LeVallon*. Blackwood regarded *The Centaur* as his favourite novel,
though he appreciated it had less commercial appeal than his earlier work. It is blatantly self-indulgent, but there was no other

way in which Blackwood could attempt to explore the affinity
between a psychically sensitive man and the spirit of Mother Earth
which culminates in a mystical revelation of the Garden of Eden.
This novel, which may be the ultimate in genuine *super-natural*
fiction, otherwise defies classification, since it is not gothic, ghost
or horror. It is a product of a pantheistic world-view uniting visions and concepts culled from years of mystical study and communion. *Julius LeVallon*, which was written at the same time
(around 1910) but not published until 1916, has more sinister overtones. It is really a precursor to a later novel, *The Bright Messenger*, which Blackwood did not complete until after the war, by
which time his own perceptions had changed.

What Blackwood wanted to explore was the consequences of a
human body inhabited by an elemental spirit. *Julius LeVallon*,
which concentrates on the circumstances leading up to the conception of the child, is essentially an occult novel, developing upon
forbidden practices in the ancient past. It introduces another of
Blackwood's fascinations, the concept of reincarnation, which features in many of his stories. But central to the novel is
Blackwood's portrayal of the battle between Nature and the attempts by mankind, through arcane knowledge, to have power of
it, in this case an air elemental. Since, as Blackwood has shown in
other stories, Nature will always prevail, LeVallon's efforts are
doomed from the start, but that does not stop the reader's sympathies with him and the other characters, especially his wife. In
LeVallon, whose character was modelled on one of the same influences who inspired John Silence, a Hindu student whom
Blackwood befriended at Edinburgh University, Blackwood creates one of his most believable individuals, which is always difficult when Blackwood's fiction seeks to demonstrate the insignificance of man against the immensity of the cosmic. Blackwood found
this difficult to carry through into *The Bright Messenger* which becomes little more than an adaptation of the post-war society novel,
where the primary character happens to be a Nature Boy.

Blackwood was unable to recapture the power of these works
in his later fiction. The effects of the First World War, of his pla-
tonic love relationships, and simply of getting old, began to cripple
Blackwood's imagination. Later excursions into the cosmic, such
as *The Wave*, which seeks to re-explore love through an eternity
of reincarnation, and *The Promise of Air*, which may have been a
dry run for *The Bright Messenger* as it also tries to explore the
evolution of man's spirit from earth-bound toward the freedom of
the air, become over-burdened with sentiment and theory, and offer precious little character or story.

The best of Blackwood's later writings are those written for or
about children. Blackwood discovered that his explorations of
wonder were more attuned to a child's imagination than an adult's.
Ever since his first novel, *Jimbo*, Blackwood had made occasional
forays into the minds of children. *Jimbo* has its genuine moments
of horror in its portrayal of the mind of an unconscious child seeking to escape from the house in which it finds itself trapped, but
in later works Blackwood eschewed the horrific for the magic of
wonder, so that *The Education of Uncle Paul*, *A Prisoner in Fairyland* and *The Extra Day* show how man may be freed from the
bondage of adulthood by an affinity with the child's power of
imagination. With *Sambo and Snitch* and later books, Blackwood
shifted entirely to stories for children, and only one longer work,
The Fruit Stoners, endeavours to capture the wonder of his earlier books about children: the Big House in which young Maria
finds herself has some gothic trappings, but the story is primarily
an exploration of the loss of childhood innocence.

At his peak, in the works written between 1906 and 1914, Blackwood was the most powerfully original voice in supernatural fiction. His invocations of mankind's place within the cosmic were an inspiration to many, ranging from C. S. Lewis to H. P. Lovecraft, but he explored avenues which few could follow, leaving his voice individualistic and inimitable. This degree of specialism has resulted in Blackwood's best work becoming marginalized in favour of his more traditional and conventional outings. The time is long overdue for a rediscovery of the real spirit of Blackwood's cosmic consciousness.

—Mike Ashley

BLACKWOOD, Caroline (Maureen)

Full name Lady Caroline Hamilton-Temple-Blackwood. **Nationality:** British. **Born:** Northern Ireland, 16 July 1931; daughter of the Marquis and Marchioness of Dufferin and Ava. **Education:** Attended a boarding school in England. **Family:** Married 1) the painter Lucian Freud (divorced); 2) Israel Citkovitz, three daughters (one deceased); 3) the poet Robert Lowell in 1972 (died 1977), one son. **Awards:** Higham award, 1976. **Address:** c/o Macmillan Publishers Ltd., 25 Eccleston Place, London SW1W 9NF, England.

HORROR, GHOST AND GOTHIC PUBLICATIONS

Novels

Great Granny Webster. London, Duckworth, and New York, Scribner, 1977.
The Fate of Mary Rose. London, Cape, and New York, Summit, 1981.

OTHER PUBLICATIONS

Novels

The Stepdaughter. London, Duckworth, 1976; New York, Scribner, 1977.
Corrigan. London, Heinemann, 1984; New York, Viking, 1985.

Short Stories

For All That I Found There (includes essays). London, Duckworth, 1973; New York, Braziller, 1974.
Good Night Sweet Ladies. London, Heinemann, 1983.

Other

Darling, You Shouldn't Have Gone to So Much Trouble (cookbook), with Anna Haycraft. London, Cape, 1980.
On the Perimeter (on the Greenham Common nuclear protest). London, Heinemann, 1984; New York, Penguin, 1985.
In the Pink: Caroline Blackwood on Hunting. London, Bloomsbury, 1987.
The Last of the Duchess. London, Macmillan, 1995.

*   *   *

Caroline Blackwood specializes in writing about grotesque characters; all her novels contain them. This is not necessarily to say that these characters are gothic or are horrific, yet the dividing line is fine between these states of being.

Great Granny Webster is a slim literary novel with intermittent Gothic elements. An unnamed great-granddaughter narrates family anecdotes covering the previous three generations. Great Granny Webster herself is met at the beginning of the book when our narrator, a 14-year-old schoolgirl, is staying with her for a couple of months. The period is 1948, and the place is Hove, near Brighton, but Great Granny makes no concessions to the 20th century, rejecting change, enjoyment, humour, responsibility, friends and most things that cost money. She lives frugally with one maidservant, doing nothing all day except sit upright in an uncomfortable wooden chair. She does not read or relish conversation. Her only outings are a drive in a hired Rolls Royce each afternoon to take the sea air. She is a Scottish widow of about 80, waiting for death. All her great-granddaughter can do is to sit and read.

And at the end of the novel we see her buried, 15 years later. She has left her complete fortune to the Society for Euthanasia. The narrator and the extremely elderly servant watch as the white ashes are poured from an urn into the grave.

Even more Gothic is Grandmother Dunmartin, Great Granny's daughter, who married an Irishman with a large, crumbling house in Ireland, and then went mad. Dunmartin Hall in the 1930s seems little different from The Lodge in Charles Maturin's *Melmoth the Wanderer* in 1820. The roof lets more water in than it keeps out, the house is always cold, the food is uneatable, most of the servants do not know what to do (in particular, the cooks cannot cook and cannot understand French, and always produce the same dreadful food, yet they participate in an astonishing daily ritual of menu writing and menu approval), and there is no money for the payment of bills. Even Mervyn Peake's Gormenghast, though much larger, shares some features with Dunmartin Hall.

By contrast, *The Fate of Mary Rose* is a non-supernatural murder mystery, full of unconvincing characters—though all of them are grotesques. A six-year-old girl has been raped and murdered in a village in Kent, and the reactions to this crime bring the narrator's two relationships—with his wife in the village and his mistress in London—to crisis point. Even allowing for the fact that this narrator, Rowan Anderson, a relatively emotionless male chauvinist and an alcoholic, his attitudes are peculiar and detract from the credibility of the situation. He has married his wife, Cressida, solely because he made her pregnant on their first and only date, and their daughter Mary Rose is now the same age as the murdered girl. While Cressida and Mary Rose live in the village, Rowan visits them only for occasional nights, spending almost all his time in his London flat, where his long-term mistress, Gloria, often visits him.

The murder causes Cressida to become irrationally fearful for Mary Rose's safety, and also irrationally obsessed by the murder itself, to the extent that she begins to neglect her daughter. Gloria is upset by Rowan's uncaring attitude towards the murder, and this is a final straw which leads her to end their relationship. Rowan is concerned only that he got very drunk on the night of the murder and seems to have no alibi. The novel is suggesting that he may be the killer, until a neighbour's evidence late on in the story provides that alibi—yet he is such a bigoted and unreliable narrator that the reader must wonder if his account should be believed.

In its later stages the plot seems to escape from Blackwood's control, becoming a frantic and ever less credible series of journeys and phone calls between the village and London, culminating in Rowan kidnapping his daughter for her own good. The horror elements come not from the murder details but from the irrationality of Cressida, who talks her way past police to visit the blood-spattered murder scene, repeatedly indoctrinates her daughter with details of the crime as a warning, and visits the sorrowing parents to help them relive the murder. Her oddities may originate from her upbringing, though this is never made clear.

Scarcely less grotesque are the characters in *Corrigan*, even though this cannot be classified as horror or gothic. Corrigan himself is a wheelchair-bound cripple who travels around England as a fund-raiser for St. Crispins, an institution which helps the disabled. (He is eventually revealed as a trickster, not disabled at all.) He persuades widowed Mrs. Blunt to help him, and while Mrs. Blunt herself is not a grotesque, her cook/cleaner Mrs. Murphy certainly is; she is astonishingly noisy and clumsy around the house, serves fat as a sauce, and rides a motorbike. And there is Mrs. Blunt's married daughter, Nadine, who is totally ungrateful and unfeeling towards her mother, and who is married to a male chauvinist who is unfeeling towards her.

—Chris Morgan

BLATTY, William Peter

Nationality: American. **Born:** 7 January 1928. **Education:** Brooklyn Preparatory School, New York; Georgetown University, Washington, D.C. **Military Service:** Served in the U.S. Air Force. **Career:** Contributor of articles to the *Saturday Evening Post* in the 1950s; novelist and screenwriter; latterly also a producer and director in Hollywood. **Awards:** Academy Award for best screenplay, 1974; Golden Globe award for best screenplay, 1981.

HORROR, GHOST AND GOTHIC PUBLICATIONS

Novels

The Exorcist. New York, Harper and Row, 1971; London, Blond and Briggs, 1972.
Legion. New York, Simon and Schuster, and London, Collins, 1983; as *Exorcist III: Legion,* New York, Pocket, 1990.

Plays

Screenplays: *The Exorcist,* 1973; *The Exorcist III,* 1990.

OTHER PUBLICATIONS

Novels

Which Way to Mecca, Jack? New York, 1959; London, Gibbs and Phillips, 1961.
John Goldfarb, Please Come Home! New York, 1962; London, Gibbs and Phillips, 1963.
I, Billy Shakespeare. New York, Doubleday, 1965.

Twinkle, Twinkle, "Killer" Kane! New York, 1966; London, Futura, 1975; revised as *The Ninth Configuration,* New York, Harper and Row, 1978.
Demons Five, Exorcists Nothing. New York, Donald Fine, 1996.

Plays

Screenplays: *The Man from the Diner's Club,* 1963; *A Shot in the Dark,* 1964; *John Goldfarb, Please Come Home!,* 1965; *Promise Her Anything,* 1966; *What Did You Do in the War, Daddy?,* 1966; *Gunn,* 1967; *The Great Bank Robbery,* 1969; *Darling Lili,* 1970; *The Ninth Configuration,* 1980.

Other

I'll Tell Them I'll Remember You. New York, Harper and Row, 1973.
William Peter Blatty on The Exorcist, from Novel to Film. New York, Bantam, 1974.

*

Film Adaptations: *John Goldfarb, Please Come Home!,* 1965; *The Exorcist,* 1973; *The Ninth Configuration,* 1980; *The Exorcist III,* 1990, from the novel *Legion.*

*   *   *

The fame that William Peter Blatty achieved when *The Exorcist* became a bestseller was certainly not expected and, in some ways, not wholly desired by its author. Having written several comic novels that attracted virtually no attention, Blatty produced a work that not only brought him celebrity but helped to initiate the entire modern horror movement. But Blatty does not wish to be regarded as a "horror writer"; rather, he wrestles in alternately comic and serious ways with the problems of good and evil within a specifically Roman Catholic framework. Blatty is not merely a writer who happens to be Catholic; he is, like Arthur Machen, ardently striving to convert his readers to Catholicism and rid them of the godless secularism that he feels is undermining modern society. His novels are platforms from which he openly debates—through characters who are transparent vehicles for the views he is advocating or disputing—the existence of God, the soul, and the afterlife, and the nature of good and evil. But Blatty is neither a sufficiently acute philosopher to discuss these matters with any depth or persuasiveness, nor a sufficiently adept storyteller to integrate these discussions adequately into the fabric of his works.

The Exorcist, however, is a remarkable piece of work. Blatty has taken an actual case of exorcism (which he somewhat credulously assumes proves the actual existence of transcendent forces) and weaved a novel in which Father Damien Karras expels the demon Pazuzu from a little girl, Regan, by taking it into his own body and then killing himself. This conclusion is meant by Blatty to be seen as a triumph and a vindication: Karras's eyes are "filled with peace" as he is found dying on the steps down which he has fallen. It is difficult to read the novel without thinking of the tremendously successful film made from it; but the film lacks much of the spiritual earnestness that fills the book, and it is no surprise that Blatty has repudiated it. (Blatty's involvement with the film is now the subject of a rather lame satirical novel, *Demons Five, Exorcists Nothing.*) It is worth noting that Blatty's charmingly zany psychological novel, *Twinkle, Twinkle, "Killer" Kane!*, anticipates some of the themes, characters and scenarios found in *The Exorcist*, although neither this novel nor its later re-write—*The Ninth Configuration*—can be regarded as weird in any meaningful sense.

The singular—and, for Blatty, bitter—irony in all this is that in *The Exorcist* (both the book and the film), there is such a compound of gruesome horror, sex, violence and sacrilege that it becomes very easy to bypass Blatty's preaching and relish his work for the pleasant shudders it provides. (It is this that made Stephen King once come up to Blatty and say, "You know, in a way, you're my father.") In spite of the oceans of blood and gore that have been spilled in books and movies in the last two or three decades, many portions of *The Exorcist* retain their power to shock, especially a scene where Regan battles in vain with the demon that is possessing her and tormentedly performs obscene acts with a crucifix. Such passages are powerful and convincing, even to unbelievers, because Blatty's own sense of horror and outrage (he has well learned the age-old dictum that a writer must scare himself before he can scare others) is so evident in them.

Legion is a purported sequel to *The Exorcist*, but is so burdened with tedious and simple-minded religious philosophizing that the plot—a potentially interesting one involving the resumption of a serial killer whose victims were all involved in the earlier exorcism—never has a chance to get underway. A minor character in *The Exorcist*, William F. Kinderman, here assumes the role of Father Karras, and whenever he is not engaged in windy proselytizing he is a competent detective who learns that the demon in Karras' body was not killed with Karras' death; in sardonic irony, it had actually revived the priest's body, escaped from his coffin just prior to his burial, and, although it is now confined in a psychiatric ward, still commits murders by possessing the minds of other inmates and having them do his dirty work for him. *Legion* would be, without its theological baggage, a powerful supernatural detective story; as it is, the core of the plot (which, Blatty's worries to the contrary, would have been sufficient to convey his theological message to intelligent readers) is simply not given adequate attention or related as adeptly as it could have been. The film version of this novel, titled *The Exorcist III*, was written and directed by Blatty, and it is far superior to the novel: as an experienced scenarist Blatty knows much about the pacing of films, and he has removed much of the theology and focused his attention on the actual story-line. As a result, a tense but surprisingly restrained horror film has been produced. Even the confrontations between Kinderman and the demon in the psychiatric ward gain power through crisp dialogue and dramatic lighting effects; and the ending of the film is far more potently cataclysmic than the novel.

As early as 1985 Blatty reported that he was at work on a "suspense thriller with a theological theme" that will be "much bigger in scope and size" than either of his two previous works; but this book does not appear to be soon forthcoming. If Blatty is to continue writing theological horror tales, he must learn not to broadcast his message bluntly through long-winded disquisitions by his characters but to allow his theme to emerge by means of the scenario. But if *Legion* and his other post-*Exorcist* novel, *The Ninth Configuration*, are any indication, he has yet to learn this basic rule of the writer's craft.

—S. T. Joshi

BLAYRE, Christopher

Pseudonym for Edward Heron-Allen. **Other Pseudonym:** Nora Helen Warddel. **Nationality:** British. **Born:** London, 17 December 1861. **Education:** Harrow School. **Military Service:** Served with the Staff Intelligence Department of the War Office during World War I. **Family:** Married 1) Marianna Lehmann in 1891; 2) Edith Pepler in 1903; one daughter. **Career:** Admitted as a Solicitor of the Supreme Court, 1884. Lived in the United States, 1886-89; gave frequent lectures on protozoology. Editor, with E. Polonaski, *Violin Times*, London, 1893-1907. Fellow, Royal Society, 1919. **Died:** 28 March 1943.

HORROR, GHOST AND GOTHIC PUBLICATIONS

Novel

The Princess Daphne: A Novel (with Selina Delaro, as Edward Heron-Allen). London, Drane, 1885; Chicago, Belford Clarke, 1888.

Short Stories (series: University of Cosmopoli)

A Fatal Fiddle (as Edward Heron-Allen). Chicago, Belford Clarke, 1890.
The Purple Sapphire and Other Posthumous Papers, Selected from the Unofficial Records of the University of Cosmopoli. London, Philip Allan, 1921; expanded edition, as *The Strange Papers of Dr. Blayre*, 1932; New York, Arno Press, 1976.
The Cheetah Girl (Cosmopoli). London, privately printed, 1923.
Some Women of the University, Being a Last Selection from the Strange Papers of Christopher Blayre (Cosmopoli). London, Stockwell, 1934.

OTHER PUBLICATIONS (AS EDWARD HERON-ALLEN)

Novel

The Romance of a Quiet Watering-Place (as Nora Helen Warddel). Chicago, Belford Clarke, 1888.

Short Stories

Kisses of Fate. Chicago, Belford Clarke, 1888.

Poetry

The Love-Letters of a Vagabond. London, Drane, 1889.
The Ballads of a Blasé Man. Privately printed, 1891.

Other

De Fidiculis Opusculum. Privately printed, 9 vols., 1882-1941.
Chiromancy; or, The Science of Palmistry, with Henry Frith. London, Routledge, 1883.
Codex Chiromantiae. Privately printed, 3 vols., 1883-86.
Violin-Making, As It Was and Is. London, Ward Lock, 1884; Boston, Howe, 1901.

A Manual of Cheirosophy. London, Ward Lock, 1885.
Practical Cheirosophy: A Synoptical Study of the Science of the Hand. New York and London, Putnam, 1887.
De Fidiculis Bibliographia, Being an Attempt Towards a Bibliography of the Violin and All Other Instruments with a Bow. London, Griffith Farran, 2 vols., 1890-94.
Prolegomena Towards the Study of Chalk Foraminifera. London, Nichols, 1894.
Some Side-lights upon Edward FitzGerald's Poem "The Rubá'iyát of Omar Khayyám." London, Nichols, 1898.
Nature and History at Selsey Bill. Selsey, Sussex, Gardner, 1911.
Selsey Bill: Historic and Prehistoric. London, Duckworth, 1911.
The Vistors' Map and Guide to Selsey. Selsey, Sussex, Gardner, 1912.
The Foraminifera of the Clare Island District, Co. Mayo, Ireland, with Arthur Earland. Dublin, Clare Island Survey, 1913.
Protozoa (report for the 1910 Antarctic expedition), with Arthur Earland. Privately printed, 1922.
Barnacles in Nature and Myth. London, Oxford University Press, 1928.
The Gods of the Fourth World, Being Prolegomena Towards a Discourse upon the Buddhist Religion. Privately printed, 1931.
The Parish Church of St. Peter on Selsey Bill, Sussex. Privately printed, 1935.

Editor, *Edward FitzGerald's Rubá'iyát of Omar Khayyám, with the Original Persian Sources.* London, Quaritch, 1899.
Editor, *The Second Edition of Edward FitzGerald's Rubá'iyát of Omar Khayyám.* London, Duckworth, 1908.
Editor, with Arthur Earland, *The Fossil Foraminifera of the Blue Marl of the Côtedes Basques.* Manchester, Literary and Philosophical Society, 1919.
Editor, *Memoranda of Memorabilia,* by Madame de Sévigné. Privately printed, 1928.
Editor, *The Further and Final Researches of Joseph Jackson Lister upon the Reproductive Process of Polystomella Crispa (Linné).* Washington, D.C., Smithsonian Institution, 1930.
Editor and translator, *A Fool of God: The Mystical Works of Bába Táhir.* London, Octagon Press, 1979.

Translator, *The Science of the Hand,* by C. S. d'Arpentigny. London, Ward Lock, 1886.
Translator, *The Rubá'iyát of Omar Khayyám.* London, Nichols, 1898.
Translator, *The Lament of Bába Táhir.* London, Quaritch, 1902.
Translator, *Quatrains of Omar Khayyám.* London, Mathews, 1908; revised edition, 1908.
Translator, *The Rubá'yát of Omar Khayyám the Poet: The Literal Translation of the Ousley Manuscript.* London, Lane, 1924.

*   *   *

Edward Heron-Allen is one of those fascinating people who lurk at the edges of orthodox weird and fantastic fiction. Despite his remarkable productivity, his wide range of interests, and his contribution to reference works in his day, there is much still not known about him. As a result various pseudonymous works are attributed to him that may not be his work at all. He was secretive about his "alternative" output and it was only the researches of collector George Medhurst in 1941 that identified Heron-Allen as the author behind the alias Christopher Blayre. Since then Heron-

Allen has become one of the suspects for other unconfirmed pseudonymous writings during his period of active writing, though suggestions that he also wrote as Dryasdust and M. Y. Halidom remain to be proved and, indeed, the writing in those volumes does not generally compare with Heron-Allen's. Nevertheless it is very likely that he wrote more fiction than his bibliography covers and his full contribution to weird and science fiction remains to be assessed.

Heron-Allen's range of interests is phenomenal and his ability to write authoritatively on them demonstrates his credentials as a polymath. Besides his passion for violins, and his interests in marine biology, ancient Persian literature, Buddhism and paleontology he was also a devotee of the occult. Amongst some of his archive material are papers where he signed himself "necromancer," probably in fun, but there is no denying his interest in the dark side of nature as evidenced in his fiction. It was his early fascination for fortune-telling and the inevitability of fate that resulted in his first books, *Chiromancy; or, The Science of Palmistry* and the short story collections *Kisses of Fate* and *A Fatal Fiddle.* These collections were published while Heron-Allen was resident in the United States and it is possible that some of the stories appeared earlier in the exceedingly rare *Belford's Magazine.* Those in *Kisses of Fate* are not fantastic, but have strong undertones of the supernatural in how Heron-Allen traces the lives of three individuals.

The workings of fate are more overt in *A Fatal Fiddle* where Heron-Allen introduces his knowledge of the violin and traces the impact a violin has on a series of lives through to after-death in the final story, "Autobiography of a Disembodied Spirit." Throughout the book Heron-Allen explores how the essence, almost the soul of the violin, possesses its owner. Interestingly, a couple of other stories featuring violins appeared soon after Heron-Allen's: "The Ensouled Violin" by Helena Blavatsky and *The Lost Stradivarius* by J. Meade Falkner, and it is interesting to speculate whether Heron-Allen's book exerted any influence. Certainly his knowledge of chiromancy and divination influenced Oscar Wilde who consulted Heron-Allen on the matter for his story "Lord Arthur Savile's Crime." Heron-Allen moved among the literary circle of the 1890s and may have offered his advice to other writers of that creative decade. His only other credited weird fiction of this period was *The Princess Daphne,* which is also about possession and concerns a woman capable of projecting her personality into another's and draining them of their life force, a form of psychic vampirism.

For the next 30 years Heron-Allen seems to have confined himself to his academic writings and pursuits, though it is to this period that the possible pseudonymous writings as Dryasdust and M. Y. Halidom belong. Tempting though it is to find a connection with these books, the writing is very different and there is none of the expert knowledge that Heron-Allen delighted in peppering through his fiction.

With *The Purple Sapphire* and the later Blayre books we are on much safer ground. Here you can tell that Heron-Allen was indulging himself in wild extravaganzas at the expense of some of his academic colleagues. The stories are written as if they are manuscripts by professors at the fictional library of the University of Cosmopoli in the year 1952. They are strong on ideas, but rather superficially written as if Heron-Allen was himself dabbling in whimsy. *The Purple Sapphire* contains eight stories. Three of them are classifiable as science fiction, though they still have moments of horror. "Aalila" has a scientist contact a woman from Venus and, through matter transmission, bring her to Earth, though it ends in both their deaths. Its sequel "The Cosmic Dust" explores how life may have been transmitted through interplanetary space by dust spores. "The Blue Cockroach" tells of the effects of the bite of a rare insect which acts as an aphrodisiac. This story may have seemed a little risqué at the time but clearly not as much as "The Cheetah Girl," which was removed from the book at the last moment, probably for fear of prosecution under the obscenity laws of the time. This story, which was certainly bold for its day, concerns the sexually aroused female offspring of the cross between a woman and a cheetah. Heron-Allen arranged for it to be printed privately in a small limited edition, but it has never been commercially published.

The remaining stories in *The Purple Sapphire* are weird or supernatural. The title story about an accursed jewel is perhaps the least original. Both "The Demon," about a woman dying of cancer whose life is prolonged by a demonic agent, and "Purpura Lapillus," about another malignant growth, are slight. More atmospheric are "The Thing That Smelt" which tells of a house haunted by a cat-like creature invoked by a bogus medium, and "The Book" about a haunted library. A second edition of the book, published as *The Strange Papers of Dr. Blayre*, added four more stories. "The Man Who Killed the Jew" is about an incompetent doctor who kills the Wandering Jew. "Mano Pantea" is about a charm that protects its owner. "The Mirror That Remembered" is borderline science fiction and tells of a mirror that reflects the past. Best of them all is the tongue-in-cheek "The House on the Way to Hell." After death the librarian at the University finds himself in Hell as the curator of the library of unfinished projects.

Heron-Allen completed one final volume of stories, *Some Women of the University*, which he published privately in 1934. They are generally less successful stories which Heron-Allen had left over when he completed *Strange Papers*. "Zum Wildbad," involving vampires and lesbianism in Austria, is perhaps the most effective. The other three are slight, although "Passiflora Vindicta Wrammsbothame" is a tongue-in-cheek tale about a tropical plant which takes on human qualities.

His joint interests in science and the occult gave Heron-Allen a fertile imagination with which he created some ingenious stories but they were never quite matched by his skills as a writer. Nevertheless some of his pieces, especially "The Cheetah Girl" and "The Cosmic Dust," were ahead of their time.

—Mike Ashley

BLOCH, Robert (Albert)

Pseudonym: Collier Young. **Nationality:** American. **Born:** Chicago, Illinois, 5 April 1917. **Education:** Attended public schools in Maywood, Illinois and Milwaukee. **Family:** Married 1) Marion Holcombe, one daughter; 2) Eleanor Alexander in 1964. **Career:** Copywriter, Gustav Marx Advertising Agency, Milwaukee, 1943-53. **Member:** Mystery Writers of America (president, 1970-71). **Awards:** Guest of Honour, World Science Fiction Convention, 1948, 1973; Evans Memorial award, 1959; Hugo award, 1959; Ann Radcliffe award, 1960, 1966; Mystery Writers of America Edgar Allan Poe award, 1960; Trieste Film Festival award, 1965; Guest of Honour, Bouchercon I, 1971; Convention du Cinéma Fantastique de Paris prize, 1973; World Fantasy Convention award, 1975; World Science Fiction Convention Lifetime Career award, 1985; Horror Writers of America Bram Stoker award, 1990; World Hor-

ror Convention Grandmaster award, 1991. **Died:** 23 September 1994.

HORROR, GHOST AND GOTHIC PUBLICATIONS

Novels (series: Psycho)

The Scarf. New York, Dial Press, 1947; as *The Scarf of Passion,* New York, Avon, 1948; revised edition, New York, Fawcett, 1966; London, New English Library, 1972.
The Kidnapper. New York, Lion, 1954.
Spiderweb. New York, Ace, 1954.
The Will to Kill. New York, Ace, 1954.
Shooting Star. New York, Ace, 1958.
Psycho. New York, Simon and Schuster, 1959; London, Hale, 1960.
The Dead Beat. New York, Simon and Schuster, 1960; London, Hale, 1961.
Firebug. Evanston, Illinois, Regency, 1961; London, Corgi, 1977.
The Couch (novelization of screenplay). New York, Fawcett, 1962.
Terror. New York, Belmont, 1962; London, Corgi, 1964.
The Star Stalker. New York, Pyramid, 1968.
The Todd Dossier (as Collier Young). New York, Delacorte Press, and London, Macmillan, 1969.
It's All in Your Mind. New York, Curtis, 1971.
Night-World. New York, Simon and Schuster, 1972; London, Hale, 1974.
American Gothic. New York, Simon and Schuster, 1974; London, W. H. Allen, 1975.
Strange Eons. Browns Mills, New Jersey, Whispers Press, 1979.
There Is a Serpent in Eden. New York, Zebra, 1979; as *The Cunning Serpent,* 1981.
Psycho II. New York, Warner, and London, Corgi, 1982.
The Night of the Ripper. New York, Doubleday, 1984; London, Hale, 1986.
Unholy Trinity: Three Novels of Suspense (omnibus; includes *The Scarf, The Dead Beat, The Couch*). Santa Cruz, California, Scream Press, 1986.
Lori. New York, Tor, 1989.
Screams (omnibus; includes *The Will to Kill, Firebug, The Star Stalker*). Los Angeles, California, Underwood Miller, 1989.
Psycho House. New York, Tor, 1990; London, Hale, 1995.
The Jekyll Legacy, with Andre Norton. New York, Tor, 1990.

Short Stories

Sea-Kissed. London, Utopian, 1945.
The Opener of the Way. Sauk City, Wisconsin, Arkham House, 1945; London, Spearman, 1974; selection, as *House of the Hatchet,* London, Panther, 1976.
Terror in the Night and Other Stories. New York, Ace, 1958.
Pleasant Dreams—Nightmares. Sauk City, Wisconsin, Arkham House, 1960; London, Whiting and Wheaton, 1967; as *Nightmares,* New York, Belmont, 1961.
Blood Runs Cold. New York, Simon and Schuster 1961; London, Hale, 1963.
More Nightmares. New York, Belmont, 1962.
Yours Truly, Jack the Ripper: Tales of Horror. New York, Belmont, 1962; as *The House of the Hatchet and Other Tales of Horror,* London, Tandem, 1965.
Atoms and Evil. New York, Fawcett, 1962; London, Muller, 1963.
Horror-7. New York, Belmont, 1963; London, Corgi, 1965.

Bogey Men. New York, Pyramid, 1963.

Tales in a Jugular Vein. New York, Pyramid, 1965; London, Sphere, 1970.

The Skull of the Marquis de Sade and Other Stories. New York, Pyramid, 1965; London, Hale, 1975.

Chamber of Horrors. New York, Award, 1966; London, Corgi, 1977.

The Living Demons. New York, Belmont, 1967; London, Sphere, 1970.

Dragons and Nightmares. Baltimore, Mirage Press, 1969.

Bloch and Bradbury, with Ray Bradbury. New York, Tower, 1969; as *Fever Dream and Other Fantasies,* London, Sphere, 1970.

Fear Today—Gone Tomorrow. New York, Award, 1971.

The Best of Robert Bloch. New York, Ballantine, 1977.

Cold Chills. New York, Doubleday, 1977; London, Hale, 1978.

The King of Terrors. New York, Mysterious Press, 1977; London, Hale, 1978.

The Laughter of a Ghoul: What Every Young Ghoul Should Know. West Warwick, Rhode Island, Necronomicon Press, 1977.

Out of the Mouths of Graves. New York, Mysterious Press, 1979; London, Hale, 1980.

Such Stuff as Screams Are Made Of. New York, Ballantine, 1979; London, Hale, 1980.

Mysteries of the Worm: All the Cthulhu Mythos Stories of Robert Bloch. New York, Zebra, 1981; revised and expanded edition, Oakland, California, Chaosium, 1993.

Twilight Zone: The Movie (novelizations of screenplays). New York, Warner, and London, Corgi, 1983.

Out of My Head. Cambridge, Massachusetts, NESFA Press, 1986.

Lost in Time and Space with Lefty Feep, edited by John Stanley. Pacifico, California, Creatures at Large, 1987.

Midnight Pleasures. New York, Doubleday, 1987.

The Selected Stories of Robert Bloch. Los Angeles, California, Underwood Miller, 3 vols., 1987.

Fear and Trembling. New York, Tor, 1989.

Yours Truly, Jack the Ripper (short story). Eugene, Oregon, Pulphouse, 1991.

The Skull of the Marquis de Sade (short story). Eugene, Oregon, Pulphouse, 1992.

Early Fears (omnibus; includes *The Opener of the Way* and *Pleasant Dreams—Nightmares*). Minneapolis, Fedogan and Bremer, 1994.

Plays

Screenplays: *The Couch,* with Owen Crump and Blake Edwards, 1962; *The Cabinet of Caligari,* 1962; *Strait-Jacket,* 1964; *The Night Walker,* 1964; *The Psychopath,* 1966; *The Deadly Bees,* with Anthony Marriott, 1967; *Torture Garden,* 1967; *The House That Dripped Blood,* 1970; *Asylum,* 1972; *The Amazing Captain Nemo,* with others, 1979.

Radio Plays: *Stay Tuned for Terror* series (39 scripts), 1944-45.

Television Plays: *The Cuckoo Clock, The Greatest Monster of Them All, A Change of Heart, The Landlady, The Sorcerer's Apprentice, The Gloating Place, Bad Actor,* and *The Big Kick,* in *Alfred Hitchcock Presents,* 1955-61; *The Cheaters, The Devil's Ticket, A Good Imagination, The Grim Reaper, The Weird Tailor, Waxworks, Till Death Do Us Part,* and *Man of Mystery,* in *Thriller,* 1960-61; scripts for *Lock-Up,* 1960, *I Spy,* 1964, *Run for Your Life,* 1965, *Star Trek,* 1966-67, *Journey to the Unknown,* 1968, and *Night Gallery,* 1971; *The Cat Creature,* 1973; *The Dead Don't Die,* 1975; *Beetles,* 1987.

Other

Editor, with Martin Harry Greenberg, *Psycho-Paths.* New York, Tor, 1991.

Editor, with Martin Harry Greenberg, *Monsters in Our Midst.* New York, Tor, 1993.

OTHER PUBLICATIONS

Novels

Ladies' Day; and, This Crowded Earth. New York, Belmont, 1968.

Sneak Preview. New York, Paperback Library, 1971.

Other

The Eighth Stage of Fandom: Selections from 25 Years of Fan Writing, edited by Earl Kemp. Chicago, Advent, 1962.

The First World Fantasy Convention: Three Authors Remember, with Fritz Leiber and T. E. D. Klein. West Warwick, Rhode Island, Necronomicon Press, 1980.

The Robert Bloch Companion: Collected Interviews 1969-86, edited by Randall D. Larson. Mercer Island, Washington, Starmont House, 1989.

Once Around the Bloch: An Unauthorized Biography. New York, Tor, 1993.

Editor, *The Best of Fredric Brown.* New York, Ballantine, 1977.

*

Film Adaptations: *Psycho,* 1960, from the novel (*Psycho II,* 1983, *Psycho III,* 1986, and *Psycho IV: The Beginning,* 1990, unrelated to Bloch's later novels *Psycho II* and *Psycho House*); *The Skull,* 1965, from the story "The Skull of the Marquis de Sade" in *The Skull of the Marquis de Sade and Other Stories.*

Bibliography: *The Complete Robert Bloch: An Illustrated, Comprehensive Bibliography* by Randall D. Larson, Sunnyvale, California, Fandom Unlimited Enterprises, 1986.

Manuscript Collection: University of Wyoming Library, Laramie.

Critical Study: *Robert Bloch* by Randall D. Larson, Mercer Island, Washington, Starmont House, 1986.

*   *   *

Few weird-fiction writers have had careers as long or as significant as Robert Bloch's. Bloch's writing spanned seven decades of the 20th century, and his fiction helped to shape most of the major trends in weird fiction that occurred during this interval.

Bloch's first professionally published story, "The Feast in the Abbey," appeared in the January 1935 issue of *Weird Tales* when he was just 17. One of the most auspicious debuts in modern weird fiction, this Gothic shocker featured a climax so memorable that it was copied many times by others writers and was lampooned by Bloch himself years later in "The Closer of the Way." It was the consummate pulp horror tale and its atmosphere and orchestration showed the influence of Edgar Allan Poe, as well as

H. P. Lovecraft with whom Bloch had been corresponding since 1933. Most of the fiction Bloch published between 1935 and 1938 falls within or on the periphery of the Cthulhu Mythos, the shared world of cosmic mythologies and extra-dimensional monsters that Lovecraft and his cronies created in pulp magazines throughout the 1920s and '30s. Bloch fell in with the spirit of this group, contributing the forbidden books of occult knowledge *De Vermiis Mysteries* by Ludvig Prinn and the *Cultes de Goules* of Comte d'Erlette (a play on the name of Lovecraft protegé August Derleth) and incorporating proper names and references dropped in the fiction of other members of the Lovecraft circle much as they mentioned those Bloch invented for his own stories. Bloch's "The Shambler from the Stars" remains one of the finest example of the good humour and camaraderie that characterized the fiction of the first generation of mythos writers. His account of a "mystic dreamer of New England" destroyed by an invisible monster inspired Lovecraft, it obvious model, to dispose of one "Robert Blake" in his weird classic, "The Haunter of the Dark."

Derivative though Bloch's mythos stories were, they differed in significant respects from those of other writers. Several, including as "The Faceless God," "The Brood of Bubastis" and "Fane of the Black Pharaoh," featured Egyptian themes, and showed a deliberate effort to link Lovecraft's mythology to other myth patterns, rather than simply appropriate those Lovecraft had invented. More important, Bloch's tale were usually character- rather than phenomena-driven. The protagonists of "The Opener of the Way," "The Creeper in the Crypt," "The Secret of Sebek," "The Eyes of the Mummy" and many of Bloch's other Lovecraftian tales are not the usual faceless scholars done in by their thirst for forbidden knowledge, but self-serving, petty opportunists with distinctly unpleasant personalities who get their well-deserved comeuppance, often in spectacularly gruesome physical ways. Bloch's early tales show an understanding of human nature lacking even in Lovecraft's fiction.

Bloch never completely put the Cthulhu Mythos and the lessons it taught behind him, and returned to it periodically, most notably in "Notebook Found in a Deserted House," the story that completes the collaborative "Shambler" trilogy, and *Strange Eons*, a rare novel-length work of Mythos fiction that managed both to evoke the cosmic horrors intrinsic to this vast and influential body of writing as well as reflect on its uniqueness as a literary phenomenon. After Lovecraft's death in 1937, however, Bloch broadened the scope of his fiction to include more conventional horror themes, including voodoo ("Mother of Serpents"), revenge ("The Mandarin's Canaries"), demonic possession ("Fiddler's Fee"), and black magic ("Return to the Sabbat"). In 1939, he broke new ground with "The Cloak," the story of a man who discovers that a rented Halloween costume endows him with vampiric cravings impossible to satisfy in polite company but difficult to suppress. Self-consciously modern and deliberately comic, the story launched Bloch's reputation as the most capable writer since Ambrose Bierce to see the comic possibilities inherent in the horrible. The comic strain that crept into much of Bloch's writing was a natural outgrowth of his understanding of the craft of horror fiction: the well-told horror story, like the well-told joke, depended for its impact upon perfect timing and a punch-line that grabbed the audience.

Bloch's humorous approach to horror is most noticeable in his tall tales of Lefty Feep, a perennial loser cut from the same cloth as Damon Runyon's comic low-lifes whose encounters with supernatural beings end as slapstick deflations of traditional horrors. A subtler type of black comedy can be found in the clever riffs on classic horror themes that Bloch pulled off in "The Man Who Cried 'Wolf'," "The Bogy Man Will Get You," and other stories published in *Weird Tales* throughout the 1940s. Tales from this period show Bloch purging his prose of the purple excesses typical of his Lovecraftian stories for a sleek, economic style appropriate for their modern characters and settings and perfect for setting up sharp O. Henry-type twist endings. "Catnip," "Hungarian Rhapsody" and similar efforts conclude with sardonic final sentences that cap their events like a perfect punch line.

During this interval Bloch's fiction also began to reflect his growing preoccupation with human psychopathology. For any other writer who cut his teeth on the cosmic horrors of the Lovecraft mythos, this interest in the anthropomorphic might have seemed incongruous, but Bloch had, almost from the outset, framed the hidden horrors of Lovecraft's universe in terms of the hidden motives of its all too human victims. As early as 1938, Bloch had tried to get inside the mind of a pyromaniac in his story "Slave of the Flames." "Waxworks," published the following year, was fundamentally a crime story dressed with supernatural trimmings, and "The Strange Flight of Richard Clayton," a study of the psychological effects of isolation outfitted as science fiction. "Your Truly, Jack the Ripper," published in 1943, remains one of Bloch's most popular stories, a study of the sociopath mentality that suggests serial killings that span a century are the ritual sacrifices one man offers to dark gods who award him immortality. From this point on, Bloch's stories often fused the supernatural and the psychological. "Enoch" extrapolated the idea of the madman who hears voices into the account of a man driven to murder at the urging of a demonic familiar. "One Way to Mars," "Lucy Comes to Stay," and "The Real Bad Friend" all feature characters whose damaged psyches create personal perceptions of reality so warped and fragmented that they border on the supernatural.

Bloch's novels from the 1950s and '60s helped to break down the walls separating the horror and crime genres with their skilful refurbishings of classic horror themes for contemporary tales of psychological terror. *The Scarf*, which is narrated by a young man turned into a serial strangler by a childhood trauma, reads like one Poe's tales of the rational lunatic updated for the age of juvenile delinquency. *The Deadbeat* and *Spiderweb* portray the psychoanalyst-patient relationship in the same terms, respectively, as the exorcist and the possessed, and the sorcerer and his apprentice. *Firebug*, whose protagonist cannot be sure that he is not the culprit setting fatal fires during periods when he blacks out, reads like nothing so much as a reworking of the theme of *Dr. Jekyll and Mr. Hyde* (to which Victorian classic Bloch later wrote a sequel, *The Jekyll Legacy*, with Andre Norton). In all of these novels, Bloch uses his psychopaths as springboards for more sweeping commentaries on the societies that nurture them.

His *Psycho* trilogy is his most powerful examination of the social ills and evils that inculcate sociopathic behaviour. *Psycho*, which gave the world Norman Bates, is one of the most credibly-realized literary treatments of the split personality and the horrifying accommodations it makes to achieve psychic balance. Its sequels are more direct responses to the impetus that drove Bloch to write *Psycho* in the first place: the need to understand how a character like Norman (who was based on real-life mass-murderer Ed Gein) could have live unnoticed as a normal person in his community. *Psycho II* holds up a mirror to American culture in 1980s and reflects an image of a society so depraved in its values that sociopathy seems a natural response. In *Psycho House* he takes this idea one step farther, suggesting that it is the world outside the asylum that has become dangerously psychotic.

As the arc of the *Psycho* trilogy suggests, Bloch was not one to avoid using his fiction to express opinions. His later fiction in particular is laced with stinging criticism of society and the corrupted values that he felt contributed toward a desensitizing to violence and the horrors of real life. Bloch was not a moralist so much as an ironist who must have found it intriguing that of all the horrors he explored in his life, the one that earned him his biggest audience was the one whose features most closely resembled theirs.

—Stefan Dziemianowicz

BONANSINGA, Jay R.

Nationality: American. **Career:** Screenwriter and maker of short films. **Address:** c/o Warner Books, Inc., 1271 Avenue of the Americas, 9th Floor, New York, NY 10020, USA.

HORROR, GHOST AND GOTHIC PUBLICATIONS

Novels

The Black Mariah. New York, Warner, 1994.
Sick. New York, Warner, and London, Orion, 1995.

*   *   *

Sometimes timing can make or break a writer's career independent of his or her actual abilities. Stephen King would undoubtedly have become a major figure in the horror field sooner or later, but his fortuitous arrival just as *Rosemary's Baby* and *The Exorcist* had shocked and entertained moviegoers certainly provided a welcome initial impetus. Jay Bonansinga's debut novel, *The Black Mariah*, would under ordinary circumstances have been another major event, and in fact the novel was well received by readers and reviewers, and was optioned for a movie version almost immediately. Unfortunately, strong parallels between that story and the subsequently-released hit film *Speed* may have derailed, temporarily at least, a major new horror talent.

The central device of *The Black Mariah* is simple and direct. Lucas Hyde and his partner Sophie Cohen are cross-country truckers who make the mistake of answering a call for help which they hear on their CB radio. The caller offended an elderly woman with demonic powers and has been cursed to drive at high speed for the rest of his short life. If he slows down, his body heat begins to rise toward the point of spontaneous combustion. When Lucas and Sophie try to help the man, they earn the enmity of the same elderly sorceress who brought about the original curse, even though their intervention is unsuccessful. Only partly satisfied by the death of her initial target, the sorceress now pursues the would-be Samaritans in her dark limousine, having transferred the curse to her first victim's benefactors. Lucas and Sophie shed their scepticism very quickly, as every attempt to slow down causes their body temperatures to rise uncomfortably.

Their subsequent adventures are tautly suspenseful, high adventure rather than traditionally horrific but just as gripping as

they struggle to find ways to maintain their speed, acquire new fuel, and figure out how to lift the curse before their time finally runs out. They pick up a companion along the way, a young man who believes them insane until he sees what happens the first time they actually slow down. The final confrontation is satisfying and evolves logically from the story, and the relationship between the two main characters, a tough but unhappy black man and a cynical Jewish woman, adds a level of complexity to their characters which provides greater texture to the novel. Bonansinga clearly understands that readers must find an element of vulnerability in his characters in order to feel any vicarious thrill from their perilous situation.

Bonansinga's second novel, *Sick*, is equally interesting, this time taking a conventional horror theme and driving it in very unconventional directions. Sarah is an exotic dancer who seeks medical help after a series of headaches becomes frighteningly persistent. The doctors discover that there's a growth inside her head, possibly a tumour, but can offer little explanation when their subsequent plans to operate become unnecessary. The tumour, it appears, has vanished from her body, apparently absorbed into healthy body tissue. The explanation doesn't satisfy Sarah, who believes something sinister is happening inside her head.

Then Sarah's tattoos begin to grow, extending their thin webbing all over her body. At the same time, a serial killer who calls himself the Escape Artist begins prowling the city, choosing victims from among Sarah's friends, killing them and wrapping their bodies in chains and ropes. The police suspect that Sarah is responsible, particularly after she admits to having visions of the Escape Artist at work, and perhaps memories of something similar from her forgotten childhood. The reader may well suspect that Sarah is indeed the killer, but the truth ends up being more complex than that. Sarah's psyche has absorbed the essence of an evil legend, and her body physically transforms into the Escape Artist until eventually Sarah and a friendly police officer banish the Escape Artist forever. But something of his legacy lives on, and the final paragraphs reveal that Sarah is not as much a victim as we might think. The novel is masterfully done, embraces a unique and frightening series of images and events, and deserves to be recognized as a significant event in horror publishing.

Bonansinga has also written a handful of short horror stories. Of these "Big Bust at Herbert Hoover High" is the most interesting, an offbeat sendup of "B"-movie themes. A sex obsessed teenager is magically transformed into one of a young girl's breasts after lusting after her body. "Black Celebration" is a fairly interesting blend of horror and rock 'n' roll. Two vampires find each other through a computer dating service in "The Need" and discover true love. The stories are competently done but lack the power of the two novels, both of which are among the very best modern horror has produced. Bonansinga's talent is clearly extraordinary enough that his work should continue to appear even during the periodic waning of popularity for the genre as a whole.

—Don D'Ammassa

BOOTHBY, Guy (Newell)

Nationality: Australian. **Born:** Adelaide, 13 October 1867. **Career:** Private secretary to the mayor of Adelaide; unsuccessful playwright; moved to Britain, 1894, and became a farmer, dog-breeder and freelance writer. **Died:** 26 February 1905.

HORROR, GHOST AND GOTHIC PUBLICATIONS

Novels (series: Dr. Nikola)

A Bid for Fortune, or Dr. Nikola's Vendetta. London, Ward Lock, and New York, Appleton, 1895; as *Enter Dr. Nikola!*, Hollywood, California, Newcastle, 1975.
Doctor Nikola. London, Ward Lock, and New York, Appleton, 1896; as *Dr. Nikola Returns*, Van Nuys, California, Newcastle, 1976.
The Lust of Hate (Nikola). London, Ward Lock, and New York, Warwick House, 1898.
Doctor Nikola's Experiment. London, Hodder and Stoughton, and New York, Appleton, 1899.
Pharos, the Egyptian. London, Ward Lock, and New York, Appleton, 1899.
"Farewell, Nikola." London, Ward Lock, and Philadelphia, Lippincott, 1901.
The Curse of the Snake. London, White, 1902.

Short Stories

The Lady of the Island. London, Long, 1904.

OTHER PUBLICATIONS

Novels

In Strange Company. London, Ward Lock, and New York, Neely, 1894.
A Lost Endeavour. London, Dent, and New York, Macmillan, 1895.
The Marriage of Esther. London, Ward Lock, and New York, Appleton, 1895.
The Beautiful White Devil. London, Ward Lock, 1896; New York, Appleton, 1897.
Sheilah McLeod. London, Skeffington, and New York, Stokes, 1897.
Across the World for a Wife. London, Ward Lock, 1898.
The Fascination of the King. London, n.p., 1898.
Love Made Manifest. London, Ward Lock, and New York, Stone, 1899.
A Maker of Nations. New York, Appleton, 1899; London, Ward Lock, 1900.
The Red Rat's Daughter. London, Ward Lock, 1899; New York, New Amsterdam, 1900.
A Sailor's Bride. London, White, 1899.
Long Live the King. London, Ward Lock, and New York, Stone, 1900.
The Woman of Death. London, Pearson, 1900.
A Cabinet Secret. London, White, and Philadelphia, Lippincott, 1901.
A Millionaire's Love Story. London, White, and New York, Buckles, 1901.
My Indian Queen. London, Ward Lock, and New York, Appleton, 1901.
My Strangest Case. New York, Page, 1901; London, Ward Lock, 1902.
The Mystery of the Clasped Hands. London, White, and New York, Appleton, 1901.
The Childerbridge Mystery. London, White, 1902.

The Kidnapped President. London, Ward Lock, and New York, Munro, 1902.
Connie Burt. London, Ward Lock, 1903.
The League of the Twelve. London, White, 1903.
A Queer Affair. London, White, 1903.
A Two-Fold Inheritance. London, Ward Lock, 1903.
A Bid for Freedom. London, Ward Lock, 1904.
A Bride from the Sea. London, Long, 1904.
A Consummate Scoundrel. London, White, 1904.
A Desperate Conspiracy. London, White, 1904.
An Ocean Secret. London, White, 1904.
A Brighton Tragedy. London, White, 1905.
In Spite of the Czar. London, Long, 1905.
The Race of Life. London, Ward Lock, and New York, Buckles, 1906.
A Stolen Peer. London, White, 1906.
The Man of the Crag. London, White, 1907.

Short Stories

Bushigrams. London, Ward Lock, 1897.
Billy Binks, Hero, and Other Stories. London, Chambers, 1898.
A Prince of Swindlers. London, Ward Lock, 1900; as *The Viceroy's Protegé*, New York, New Amsterdam, 1903.
Uncle Joe's Legacy, and Other Stories. London, White, 1902.
The Countess Londa. London, White, 1903.
The Crime of the Under-Seas. London, Ward Lock, 1905.
For Love of Her. London, Ward Lock, 1905.
A Royal Affair and Other Stories. London, White, 1906.

Other

On the Wallaby. N.p., 1894.

*   *   *

Guy Boothby was one of many writers to benefit from the fierce competition for readers which animated the British magazine market of the 1890s. The flood of money enabled the emergence of an entire generation of professional writers, while the pressure to increase popular appeal favoured an unprecedentedly feverish melodrama. Boothby, who came to England from Australia in 1894, had the fluency to maintain reasonably prolific production and a flair for garish imagery, but his fluency seemingly depended on making up his plots as he went and he rarely managed to produce coherent explanations of the vividly enigmatic scenes which kept them in motion and maintained their suspense. His most successful books were the series of novels featuring Doctor Nikola, begun with *A Bid for Fortune*, and their success was at least partly based on the fact that Nikola was never called upon to offer a full explanation of his motives or his methods—nor, indeed, to bring his ongoing quest for the secret of immortality to any explicit conclusion.

The Nikola series was original in one significant respect: its central character was not the hero of the series but its villain. In this sense the novels harked back to the Gothic novels of a century before, but the cat-loving and soft-voiced Nikola is a far more urbane figure than the diabolical villains of Gothic fiction. He represents a further stage in the remodelling process begun by Wilkie Collins in the archetypal post-Gothic thriller *The Woman in White*; like Collins's Fosco he is a foreigner, but he is much more securely adjusted to Victorian manners and fashions. His mesmeric talents and occult interests are cast in a quasi-Theosophical mould rather than the Rosicrucian mould favoured by Bulwer-Lytton, and it is entirely appropriate that his quest should be narrowly focused on the elixir of life rather than some pompously intellectual enlightenment. His most notorious successor, Sax Rohmer's Fu Manchu, was even more down-to-earth—as befitted a genius of the twentieth century—but Nikola was capable of being charming in a manner that would have been quite impossible for Fu Manchu.

When Boothby became more imaginatively adventurous he showed a distinct tendency to lose the logical threads of his plots as he struggled manfully to unravel the mysteries located at their heart. He never could make up his mind exactly who or what the eponymous anti-hero of *Pharos, the Egyptian* was supposed to be. Pharos is certainly very old, but it remains stubbornly unclear whether the mummy which the hero has inherited from his father is his ancestor or another version of himself. At any rate, possession of the mummy brings the hero into dangerously intimate contact with Pharos, with various unfortunate effects (including a literal plague) which last until mysterious but awesome powers arbitrarily step in to put a stop to his nefarious activities. *The Curse of the Snake* was the least successful of Boothby's occult thrillers, although it is by far the most interesting. The ending leaves the marvellously creepy beginning frustratingly unexplained, but the sinister and curiously demanding snake which the hero eventually inherits from a false friend is a much more efficient plot-lever than Pharos's mummy or the various enigmatic objects which Dr. Nikola becomes avid to seize in case they hold the key to his quest. As in *Pharos, the Egyptian* much of the narrative tension derives from the fact that the hero and the villain are intimates, the villain concealing his malevolence behind a mask of amiability. Although the hero of the Nikola novels never gets close enough to the occultist to count him as a friend there is often a similar ambivalence in the way Nikola treats him.

Considering that Boothby could never be considered a subtle writer there is a curious slyness about the manner in which such adversaries as Nikola and Pharos function; it is notable, too, that the heroes who oppose them never accomplish much by their own efforts, their fortunes always remaining subject to casual whims of fate. The idiosyncratic paranoia extrapolated in these horror stories is thus doubly disrespectful of literary convention—an unusual trait in an unashamed hack, which might require some special explanation were anyone to become sufficiently interested in what is, after all, conspicuously second-rate work. Boothby's exotic thrillers use their formal supernatural apparatus in a relatively discreet fashion—suggesting that if he had not been forced to equip his extraordinary villains with extraordinary motives he might not have bothered with the supernatural at all—but once he has invoked such devices he does reveal a rather peculiar attitude in the manner of their display.

Boothby's short fiction includes a few trivial tales of the supernatural, the best of which is "A Professor of Egyptology" in *The Lady of the Island*—a romance of reincarnation which follows *Pharos, the Egyptian* in trying to cash in on the contemporary vogue for stories about mummies. Like many other writers of the period, however, he found that the editors of the magazines became increasingly suspicious of outré materials as the 1890s wore on and he readily fell in with the trend, sometimes using humour as an apologetic device when his plots strained credulity too far.

—Brian Stableford

BORTON, Douglas

Nationality: American. **Born:** 1960. **Career:** Screenwriter and novelist.

HORROR, GHOST AND GOTHIC PUBLICATIONS

Novels

Manstopper. New York, Onyx, 1988.
Dreamhouse. New York, Onyx, 1989.
Deathsong. New York, Onyx, 1989.
Kane. New York, Onyx, 1990.

OTHER PUBLICATIONS

Novel

Shadow Dance. New York, Signet, 1991.

*   *   *

There is an unfortunate pressure on writers of any genre to repeat successful devices and techniques and to avoid experimentation. If a particular theme, or setting, or other plot element strikes a chord with readers, the writer often seeks to exploit that fact in future work. Although in the short term this seems to satisfy the desires of readers, in the long term it tends to constrict writers into a narrowly focused career and discourages them from doing the kind of innovative writing that might result in an even more satisfying work later on. Horror fiction is not an exception to this rule.

Although he had previously written for the screen, Douglas Borton made his first appearance as a novelist in 1988 with *Manstopper*. The 1970s had seen a rash of novels in which one animal or another became a menace to society—dogs, cats, crabs, earthworms, birds, slugs, ants, spiders. Although that vein of material appeared to have been mined to capacity, Borton returned to it on a smaller scale in this novel, in which four fiercely intelligent, highly trained attack dogs have banded together to prey on the residents of a small town. And prey is the right word, because the dogs have developed a taste for human flesh. The novel is presented as virtually a duel between the protagonists and the dogs, whose intelligence we eventually discover may be close to that of human beings. Although the dogs are destroyed, Borton hints that their dangerous intelligence has not entirely disappeared from the gene pool.

Borton's second novel was entirely different, derived at least in part from Borton's experiences with Hollywood. *Dreamhouse* is a haunted house story, but a very untraditional one. Matthew Wilde is a horror-film genius who builds himself an enormous mansion fitted with many of the tricks of his trade. Wilde's self-indulgence is meant to be a source of amusement, but instead he has created a nexus around which the spirits of the unhappy dead can gather and break through the barriers between their world and our own. Nightmares occur to the residents every night, sometimes even when they're awake. Phantom figures shed their skin or transform into other shapes, and these manifestations can interact with the real world and actually kill the people who see them. Those resident in the house gradually lose the ability to distinguish between artificial tricks, genuine manifestations, and reality itself. The parade of horrors continues in cinematic fashion, until the house itself is destroyed. Some of the individual encounters are effectively drawn, but others verge on the ludicrous. The novel draws too heavily on cinematic conventions and stale clichés, and lacks the close plotting of *Manstopper*.

Borton returned to sharper form with his third novel, *Deathsong*. Billie Lee Kidd, a country-and-western singer, writes a new song and adds it to her act, unaware that she has recreated an ancient piece of music which has supernatural significance. Shortly thereafter, people around her begin to die under mysterious circumstances, in each case shortly after hearing a mysterious, chilling singing that resembles Billie Lee's song. And sometimes when Billie sings, she finds herself substituting other words, words from a language no longer spoken on Earth.

Her only chance of surviving against an evil cult attracted to her aura of power is to master the magic of the tune herself, find a way to turn it into a weapon she can wield against her enemies. She must also prevent the return to Earth of a Lovecraftian monster from beyond the stars. She ultimately triumphs, as do the protagonists of all of Borton's novels, but even in victory she recognizes that at best she has only delayed the inevitable, and that sooner or later the monstrous being she has thwarted will have its way with Earth.

This persistent but veiled pessimism was manifested most distinctly in Borton's fourth, and most recent, horror novel. *Kane* is set in a small, dying town in a remote part of California. As the novel opens, there are only 23 remaining residents, and some of them are thinking of leaving. But then Kane comes to town, a mysterious, powerfully built man, and a ruthless killer. At first no one suspects what's happening, but then it becomes obvious that Kane is systematically killing everyone left in Tuskett, and that he doesn't intend to let anyone escape. In the first half of the book, Kane might be mistaken for a purely mundane madman, but as the survivors rally against him we discover that he's more than human, a killing machine that can only be stopped when it is totally destroyed. Kane is death personified, and Borton makes certain we understand that death is unpleasant, uncaring and unstoppable.

Borton switched to more conventional subjects for his next novel and his only subsequent horror fiction has been at shorter length. "Voivode" was one of several stories that appeared from various authors hinting that dictator Ceaucescu of Romania was actually a reincarnation of Dracula, or rather Vlad Tepes. Also of interest is "Venice, CA." Borton's career in horror to date is of too limited a duration to provide meaningful indicators of his potential, but his willingness to explore different settings and themes in every book is promising and his ability to create credible and likable characters is above average. If he returns to the form, his subsequent work is likely to be innovative.

—Don D'Ammassa

BOWEN, Elizabeth

Nationality: Irish. **Born:** Dublin, 7 June 1899. **Education:** Down House School, Kent. **Family:** Married Alan Charles Cameron in 1923 (died, 1952). **Awards:** Black Memorial Prize, 1970. D.Litt., Trinity College, Dublin, 1948; Oxford University, 1956. Honorary member, American Academy of Arts and Letters, C.B.E. (Commander, Order of the British Empire). 1948. Companion of Literature, Royal Society of Literature, 1965. **Died:** 22 February 1973.

HORROR, GHOST AND GOTHIC PUBLICATIONS

Short Stories

Encounters: Stories. London, Sidgwick and Jackson, 1923; New York, Boni and Liveright, 1926.
Joining Charles. London, Constable, and New York, Dial Press, 1929.
The Cat Jumps and Other Stories. London, Gollancz, 1934.
The Demon Lover and Other Stories. London, Cape, 1945; as *Ivy Gripped the Steps and Other Stories,* New York, Knopf, 1946.

OTHER PUBLICATIONS

Novels

The Hotel. London, Constable, 1927; New York, Dial Press, 1928.
The Last September. London, Constable, and New York, Dial Press, 1929.
Friends and Relations. London, Constable, and New York, Dial Press, 1931.
To the North. London, Gollancz, 1932; New York, Knopf, 1933.
The House in Paris. London, Gollancz, 1935; New York, Knopf, 1939.
The Heat of the Day. London, Cape, and New York, Knopf, 1949.
A World of Love. London, Cape, and New York, Knopf, 1955.
The Little Girls. London, Cape, and New York, Knopf, 1964.
Ewa Trout; or, Changing Scenes. New York, Knopf, 1968; London, Cape, 1969.

Short Stories

Ann Lee's and Other Stories. London, Sidgwick and Jackson, and New York, Boni and Liveright, 1926.
Look at All Those Roses: Short Stories. London, Gollancz, and New York, Knopf, 1941.
Selected Stories. Dublin, Fridberg, 1946.
Stories. New York, Knopf, 1959.
A Day in the Dark and Other Stories. London, Cape, 1965.

Other

Bowen's Court. London, Longman, and New York, Knopf, 1942.
English Novelists. London, Collins, and New York, Hastings House, 1942.
Seven Winters. Dublin, Cuala Press, 1942; as *Seven Winters: Memories of a Dublin Childhood,* London and New York, Longman, 1943.
Anthony Trollope: A New Judgement. New York and London, Oxford University Press, 1946.
Why Do I Write: An Exchange of Views Between Elizabeth Bowen, Graham Greene and V. S. Pritchett. London, Marshall, 1948.
Collected Impressions. London, Longman, and New York, Knopf, 1950.

The Shelbourne: A Centre of Dublin Life for More Than a Century. London, Harrap, 1951; as *The Shelbourne Hotel,* New York, Knopf, 1951.
A Time in Rome. London, Longman, and New York, Knopf, 1960.
After-Thought: Pieces about Writing. London, Longman, 1962; with *Seven Winters,* New York, Knopf, 1962.
The Good Tiger (juvenile), New York, Knopf, 1965.

Editor, *The Faber Book of Modern Stories.* London, Faber, 1937.
Editor, *Stories,* by Katherine Mansfield. New York, Knopf, 1956; as *34 Short Stories,* London, Collins, 1957.

*　　*　　*

Many of Elizabeth Bowen's short stories are ghost or horror stories, and nearly all of the stories she wrote during the Second World War—which many consider to be her best and most lasting work—contain a strong element of the supernatural.

Of her earlier stories, "The Storm," "The Back Drawing-Room" and "Foothold" are perhaps of most interest. All are ghost stories which work both to unsettle expectations, and to comment upon human social relationships. In "The Storm" an ill-matched married couple are on holiday in Italy where they each have separate ghostly experiences. The woman, frightened at first, rationalizes it away; the man, unaware at first, becomes convinced he's had a special spiritual encounter. The woman believes she will win her husband away from God even as he believes he can save her soul. In "The Back Drawing-Room" the divisive political situation in Ireland gives an added bite and emotional significance to what would otherwise be a conventional anecdote about a man entering a house he later learns was burnt down two years earlier. The influence of Henry James is strongly evident in "Foothold," an oblique, allusive psychological portrait of a married couple and their old friend, Thomas. Visiting their home, Thomas learns it is haunted by a ghost they call Clara, an unthreatening figure which Janet but not her husband Gerard has seen. Janet confides in Thomas that her life has changed in the new house: she feels, uncomfortably, that she has "more room" somehow "underneath" the surface. Thomas too senses Janet is changing; he believes that the ghost has managed to reach Janet where he and Gerard have failed. In a Henry James story this would all be ambiguous supposition, however Bowen allows Thomas as well as Janet to have a glimpse of Clara.

Bowen dealt in horror and gruesomeness as well as ghosts. In "Look at All Those Roses," the air is super-charged with menace during a woman's visit to an isolated country house where murder may have once been committed. "The Cat Jumps" is perhaps Bowen's nastiest tale, a powerfully effective horror story about a party of rational minded, thoroughly modern bright young things coming under the influence of a past crime—the particularly brutal murder of a wife by her husband.

The Demon Lover is Bowen's wartime short-story collection. There is an hallucinatory quality to all of the stories; the image of London as a ghost-city recurs, and time itself seems to be breaking down, confusing past and present in the absence of any sure future. The title story is perhaps her most striking and chilling tale of all. In it, a woman has come up from the country to pick up some things from her London house, closed during the bombings, and finds a letter waiting for her. Years before she had been forced by her fiancé to plight a "sinister troth." He had been killed during the First World War, but now, he writes in the letter, "the

day we said" has arrived and he is coming for her. She leaves the house and gets a taxi. But as the taxi drives off, the driver turns to look at her, and as she begins to scream, "the taxi, accelerating without mercy, made off with her into the hinterland of deserted streets."

"The Happy Autumn Fields" is less sinister but equally compelling in its marriage of the themes of love and death. Asleep in a bombed house, a young woman dreams she is someone else, a member of a large, Edwardian family in the country, and when she wakes finds the present, with the house collapsing around her, curiously unreal.

The third great story from this collection is "Mysterious Kor," an atmospheric, hallucinatory story about the longing for peace and privacy in the midst of wartime London. With nowhere to go to be alone with her lover, Pepita fantasizes that London is really the long-dead city of Kor, a place without time, where they can have eternity together.

"The Cheery Soul," "Green Holly" and "Pink May" are lighter fare, creepy yet humorous rather than frightening ghost stories, all given a particular edge and individuality by the setting of wartime deprivation, paranoia and forced cheerfulness. In the first story the ghost is a drunken cook; in the second, an unintelligent, romantic woman returns after death to haunt the sexually frustrated group billeted in the house where a man once killed himself for her love; and in the third the ghost exists perhaps only in the conscience of an adulterous woman.

After the war Bowen wrote one final ghost story, "Hand in Glove," a deliberately old-fashioned tale about impoverished gentlewomen seeking husbands in the early years of this century. It is competently done, but lightweight; the notion of a murderous glove lurking in a locked trunk is hard to take seriously.

—Lisa Tuttle

BOWEN, Marjorie

Pseudonym for Gabrielle Margaret Vere Campbell Long. **Other Pseudonyms:** Robert Paye; George Preedy; Joseph Shearing; John Winch. **Nationality:** British. **Born:** Hayling Island, Hampshire, 29 October 1886. **Family:** Married 1) Zeffrino Emilio Costanzo in 1912 (died 1916), one son; 2) Arthur L. Long in 1917, two sons. **Died:** 23 December 1952.

HORROR, GHOST AND GOTHIC PUBLICATIONS

Novels

Black Magic: A Tale of the Rise and Fall of Antichrist. London, Alston Rivers, 1909.
The Haunted Vintage. London, Odhams Press, 1921.
Julia Roseingrave (as Robert Paye). London, Benn, 1933.
The Fetch (as Joseph Shearing). London, Hutchinson, 1942; as *The Spectral Bride,* New York, Smith and Durrell, 1942.

Short Stories

Curious Happenings. London, Mills and Boon, 1917.
Dark Ann and Other Stories. London, Lane, 1927.

The Devil Snar'd (as George Preedy). London, Benn, 1932.
The Last Bouquet: Some Twilight Tales. London, Lane, 1932.
Dr. Chaos, and The Devil Snar'd (as George Preedy). London, Cassell, 1933.
The Bishop of Hell and Other Stories. London, Lane, 1949.
Kecksies and Other Twilight Tales. Sauk City, Wisconsin, Arkham House, 1976.

Other

Editor, *Great Tales of Horror.* London, Lane, 1933.
Editor, *More Great Tales of Horror.* London, Lane, 1935.

OTHER PUBLICATIONS

Novels

The Viper of Milan. London, Alston Rivers, and New York, McClure Phillips, 1906.
The Glen o'Weeping. London, Alston Rivers, 1907; as *The Master of Stair*, New York, McClure Phillips, 1907.
The Sword Decides! London, Alston Rivers, and New York, McClure, 1908.
The Leopard and the Lily. New York, Doubleday, 1909; London, Methuen, 1920.
I Will Maintain. London, Methuen, 1910; New York, Dutton, 1911; revised edition, London, Penguin, 1943.
Defender of the Faith. London, Methuen, and New York, Dutton, 1911.
God and the King. London, Methuen, 1911; New York, Dutton, 1912.
Lovers' Knots. London, Everett, 1912.
The Quest of Glory. London, Methuen, and New York, Dutton, 1912.
The Rake's Progress. London, Rider, 1912.
The Soldier from Virginia. New York, Appleton, 1912; as *Mister Washington*, London, Methuen, 1915.
The Governor of England. London, Methuen, 1913; New York, Dutton, 1914.
A Knight of Spain. London, Methuen, 1913.
The Two Carnations. London, Cassell, and New York, Reynolds, 1913.
Prince and Heretic. London, Methuen, 1914; New York, Dutton, 1915.
Because of These Things. . . . London, Methuen, 1915.
The Carnival of Florence. London, Methuen, and New York, Dutton, 1915.
William, By the Grace of God—. London, Methuen, 1916; New York, Dutton, 1917; abridged edition, Methuen, 1928.
The Third Estate. London, Methuen, 1917; New York, Dutton, 1918; revised edition, as *Eugénie*, London, Fontana, 1971.
The Burning Glass. London, Collins, 1918; New York, Dutton, 1919.
Kings-at-Arms. London, Methuen, 1918; New York, Dutton, 1919.
Mr. Misfortunate. London, Collins, 1919.
The Cheats. London, Collins, 1920.
Rococo. London, Odhams Press, 1921.
The Jest. London, Odhams Press, 1922.
Affairs of Men (selections from novels). London, Cranton, 1922.
Stinging Nettles. London, Ward Lock, and Boston, Small Maynard, 1923.
The Presence and the Power. London, Ward Lock, 1924.

Five People. London, Ward Lock, 1925.
Boundless Water. London, Ward Lock, 1926.
Nell Gwyn: A Decoration. London, Hodder and Stoughton, 1926; as *Mistress Nell Gwyn*, New York, Appleton, 1926.
Five Winds. London, Hodder and Stoughton, 1927.
The Pagoda: Le Pagode de Chanteloup. London, Hodder and Stoughton, 1927.
The Countess Fanny. London, Hodder and Stoughton, 1928.
The Golden Roof. London, Hodder and Stoughton, 1928.
Dickon. London, Hodder and Stoughton, 1929.
The English Paragon. London, Hodder and Stoughton, 1930.
The Devil's Jig (as Robert Paye). London, Lane, 1930.
Brave Employments. London, Collins, 1931.
Withering Fires. London, Collins, 1931.
The Shadow on Mockways. London, Collins, 1932.
Dark Rosaleen. London, Collins, 1932; Boston, Houghton Mifflin, 1933.
Passion Flower. London, Collins, 1932; as *Beneath the Passion Flower* (as George Preedy), New York, McBride, 1932.
Idlers' Gate (as John Winch). London, Collins, and New York, Morrow, 1932.
I Dwelt in High Places. London, Collins, 1933.
Set with Green Herbs. London, Benn, 1933.
The Stolen Bride. London, Lovat Dickson, 1933; abridged edition, London, Mellifont Press, 1946.
The Veil'd Delight. London, Odhams Press, 1933.
The Triumphant Beast. London, Lane, 1934.
Trumpets at Rome. London, Hutchinson, 1936.
A Giant in Chains: Prelude to Revolution—France 1775-1791. London, Hutchinson, 1938.
God and the Wedding Dress. London, Hutchinson, 1938.
Mr. Tyler's Saints. London, Hutchinson, 1939.
The Circle in the Water. London, Hutchinson, 1939.
Exchange Royal. London, Hutchinson, 1940.
Today Is Mine. London, Hutchinson, 1941.
The Man with the Scales. London, Hutchinson, 1954.

Novels as George Preedy

General Crack. London, Lane, and New York, Dodd Mead, 1928.
The Rocklitz. London, Lane, 1930; as *The Prince's Darling*, New York, Dodd Mead, 1930.
Tumult in the North. London, Lane, and New York, Dodd Mead, 1931.
The Pavilion of Honour. London, Lane, 1932.
Violante: Circe and Ermine. London, Cassell, 1932.
Double Dallilay. London, Cassell, 1933; as *Queen's Caprice*, New York, King, 1934.
The Autobiography of Cornelius Blake, 1773-1810, of Ditton See, Cambridgeshire. London, Cassell, 1934.
Laurell'd Captains. London, Hutchinson, 1935.
The Poisoners. London, Hutchinson, 1936.
My Tattered Loving. London, Jenkins, 1937; as *The King's Favourite* (as Marjorie Bowen), London, Fontana, 1971.
Painted Angel. London, Jenkins, 1938.
The Fair Young Widow. London, Jenkins, 1939.
Dove in the Mulberry Tree. London, Jenkins, 1939.
Primula. London, Hodder and Stoughton, 1940.
Black Man—White Maiden. London, Hodder and Stoughton, 1941.
Findernes' Flowers. London, Hodder and Stoughton, 1941.
Lyndley Waters. London, Hodder and Stoughton, 1942.

Lady in a Veil. London, Hodder and Stoughton, 1943.
The Fourth Chamber. London, Hodder and Stoughton, 1944.
Nightcap and Plume. London, Hodder and Stoughton, 1945.
No Way Home. London, Hodder and Stoughton, 1947.
The Sacked City. London, Hodder and Stoughton, 1949.
Julia Ballantyne. London, Hodder and Stoughton, 1952.

Novels as Joseph Shearing

Forget-Me-Not. London, Heinemann, 1932; as *Lucile Cléry*, New York, Harper, 1932; as *The Strange Case of Lucile Cléry*, Harper, 1941.
Album Leaf. London, Heinemann, 1933; as *The Spider in the Cup*, New York, Smith and Haas, 1934.
Moss Rose. London, Heinemann, 1934; New York, Smith and Haas, 1935.
The Golden Violet: The Story of a Lady Novelist. London, Heinemann, 1936; New York, Smith and Durrell, 1941; as *Night's Dark Secret* (as Margaret Campbell), New York, New American Library, 1975.
Blanche Fury; or, Fury's Ape. London, Heinemann, and New York, Harrison Hilton, 1939.
Aunt Beardie. London, Hutchinson, and New York, Harrison Hilton, 1940.
Laura Sarelle. London, Hutchinson, 1940; as *The Crime of Laura Sarelle*, New York, Smith and Durrell, 1941.
Airing in a Closed Carriage. London, Hutchinson, and New York, Harper, 1943.
The Abode of Love. London, Hutchinson, 1945.
For Her to See. London, Hutchinson, 1947; as *So Evil My Love*, New York, Harper, 1947.
Mignonette. New York, Harper, 1948; London, Heinemann, 1949.
Within the Bubble. London, Heinemann, 1950; as *The Heiress of Frascati*, New York, Berkley, 1966.
To Bed at Noon. London, Heinemann, 1951.

Short Stories

God's Playthings. London, Smith Elder, 1912; New York, Dutton, 1913.
Shadows of Yesterday: Stories from an Old Catalogue. London, Smith Elder, and New York, Dutton, 1916.
Crimes of Old London. London, Odhams Press, 1919.
The Pleasant Husband and Other Stories. London, Hurst and Blackett, 1921.
Seeing Life! and Other Stories. London, Hurst and Blackett, 1923.
The Seven Deadly Sins. London, Hurst and Blackett, 1926.
The Gorgeous Lover and Other Tales. London, Lane, 1929.
Sheep's-Head and Babylon, and Other Stories of Yesterday and Today. London, Lane, 1929.
Old Patch's Medley; or, A London Miscellany. London, Selwyn and Blount, 1930.
Bagatelle and Some Other Diversions (as George Preedy). London, Lane, 1930; New York, Dodd Mead, 1931.
Grace Latouche and the Warringtons: Some Nineteenth-Century Pieces, Mostly Victorian. London, Selwyn and Blount, 1931.
Fond Fancy and Other Stories. London, Selwyn and Blount, 1932.
The Knot Garden: Some Old Fancies Re-Set (as George Preedy). London, Lane, 1933.
Orange Blossoms (as Joseph Shearing). London, Heinemann, 1938.

Plays as George Preedy

Captain Banner (produced London, 1929). London, Lane, 1930.
A Family Comedy, 1840 (as Marjorie Bowen). London, French, 1930.
The Question. London, French, 1931.
The Rocklitz (produced London, 1931).
Rose Giralda (produced London, 1933).
Court Cards (produced London, 1934).
Royal Command (produced Wimbledon, Surrey, 1952).

Screenplay: *The Black Tulip* (as Marjorie Bowen), 1921.

Other

Luctor et Emergo, Being an Historical Essay on the State of England at the Peace of Ryswyck. Newcastle upon Tyne, Northumberland Press, 1925.
The Netherlands Display'd; or, The Delights of the Low Countries. London, Lane, 1926; New York, Dodd Mead, 1927.
Holland, Being a General Survey of the Netherlands. London, Harrap, 1928; New York, Doubleday, 1929.
The Winged Trees (for children). Oxford, Blackwell, 1928.
The Story of the Temple and Its Associations. London, Griffin Press, 1928.
Sundry Great Gentlemen: Some Essays in Historical Biography. London, Lane, and New York, Dodd Mead, 1928.
William, Prince of Orange, Afterwards King of England, Being an Account of His Early Life. London, Lane, and New York, Dodd Mead, 1928.
The Lady's Prisoner (for children). Oxford, Blackwell, 1929.
Mademoiselle Maria Gloria (for children). Oxford, Blackwell, 1929.
The Third Mary Stuart, Being a Character Study with Memoirs and Letters of Queen Mary II of England 1662-1694. London, Lane, 1929.
Exits and Farewells, Being Some Account of the Last Days of Certain Historical Characters. London, Selwyn and Blount, 1930.
Mary, Queen of Scots, Daughter of Debate. London, Lane, 1934; New York, Putnam, 1935.
The Scandal of Sophie Dawes. London, Lane, 1934; New York, Appleton Century, 1935.
Patriotic Lady: A Study of Emma, Lady Hamilton, and the Neapolitan Revolution of 1799. London, Lane, 1935; New York, Appleton Century, 1936.
The Angel of Assassination: Marie-Charlotte de Corday d'Armont, Jean-Paul Marat, Jean-Adam Lux: Three Disciples of Rousseau (as Joseph Shearing). London, Heinemann, and New York, Smith and Haas, 1935.
Peter Porcupine: A Study of William Cobbett 1762-1835. London, Longman, 1935; New York, Longman, 1936.
William Hogarth, The Cockney's Mirror. London, Methuen, and New York, Appleton Century, 1936.
Crowns and Sceptres: The Romance and Pageantry of Coronations. London, Long, 1937.
The Lady and the Arsenic: The Life and Death of a Romantic, Marie Capelle, Madame Lafarge (as Joseph Shearing). London, Heinemann, 1937; New York, A.S. Barnes, 1944.
This Shining Woman: Mary Wollstonecraft Godwin 1759-1797 (as George Preedy). London, Collins, and New York, Appleton Century, 1937.

Wrestling Jacob: A Study of the Life of John Wesley and Some Members of His Family. London, Heinemann, 1937; abridged edition, London, Watts, 1948.

World's Wonder and Other Essays. London, Hutchinson, 1938.

The Trumpet and the Swan: An Adventure of the Civil War (for children). London, Pitman, 1938.

The Debate Continues, Being the Autobiography of Marjorie Bowen, by Margaret Campbell. London, Heinemann, 1939.

Ethics in Modern Art (lecture). London, Watts, 1939.

Child of Chequer'd Fortune: The Life, Loves, and Battles of Maurice de Saxe, Maréchal de France (as George Preedy). London, Jenkins, 1939.

Strangers to Freedom (for children). London, Dent, 1940.

The Life of John Knox (as George Preedy). London, Jenkins, 1940.

The Life of Rear-Admiral John Paul Jones 1747-1792 (as George Preedy). London, Jenkins, 1940.

The Courtly Charlatan: The Enigmatic Comte de St. Germain (as George Preedy). London, Jenkins, 1942.

The Church and Social Progress: An Exposition of Rationalism and Reaction. London, Watts, 1945.

In the Steps of Mary, Queen of Scots. London, Rich and Cowan, 1952.

Editor, *Some Famous Love Letters.* London, Jenkins, 1937.

*　　＊　　＊　　＊*

Marjorie Bowen was the best-known of several pseudonyms employed by the prolific Mrs. Long. Although it was mostly employed for historical fiction it was also attached to almost all her supernatural fiction. Her work under other names tends to be fully rationalized although it often deals with the history of witchcraft and alleged hauntings. Her work as Bowen was more obviously commercial than the fiction she produced under other names, which often became more intense and more painstakingly detailed. Her work as George Preedy included a good deal of commercial non-fiction but she also attached that name to two non-supernatural but nevertheless strikingly macabre novellas, which were eventually united in one volume (the second and less interesting had previously appeared in a separate edition).

Although, like most of her contemporaries, she found writing supernatural fiction unprofitable, Bowen maintained a lifelong interest in the outré. She edited two of the best and most wide-ranging representative anthologies of horror fiction, including her own translations of several obscure French and German tales. Much of her historical fiction—and, for that matter, much of her historical non-fiction—is intensely interested in superstition and magical impostures. *The Poisoners*, the Preedy book she wrote about the great scandal in pre-Revolutionary Paris which introduced the world to the mythology of the Black Mass, was a considerable inspiration to contemporary lifestyle fantasists eager to revive such theatrics. Although *The Cheats* is included in the Bleiler *Checklist of Science-Fiction and Supernatural Fiction* by mistake, several of the historical novels signed with the Bowen name, most notably *Five Winds* and *The Veil'd Delight*, make use of their superstitious elements in a quasi-Gothic fashion. *The Shadow on Mockways* is a vivid and unusual melodrama the critical and commercial failure of which may have dissuaded her from further experiments in Grand Guignol.

Black Magic is an outrightly supernatural historical fantasy based on the Medieval legend of Pope Joan. This had been discussed in Sabine Baring-Gould's *Curious Myths of the Middle Ages* in the same chapter as the mythology of the Antichrist; Bowen took the hint and casually conflated the two myths into a zestful story of a transvestite sorceress who comes close to bringing down the political edifice of Christendom, failing only by virtue of the fact that her lover and intended consort suffers a belated fit of conscience. The hero's attraction to a female in male disguise (whom the text insistently calls "he") recalls the passion of Ambrosio in Matthew Gregory Lewis's *The Monk*. Although stylistically rough-hewn by comparison with Bowen's best work, *Black Magic* remains a classic of neo-Gothic fiction. *The Haunted Vintage* is another *femme fatale* story, whose hero is fascinated by a strange girl imprisoned in an asylum. She turns out to be unhuman, but not unduly menacing. The novel is more smoothly written than *Black Magic* and perhaps more effective in its own quieter fashion, but because it lacks the uninhibited bombast of the earlier novel it could not recapitulate its popular success.

The Last Bouquet was the first of Bowen's story-collections to be wholly dedicated to weird fiction, but most of her others contain a decent proportion of such tales. Her personal favourites were reassembled in *The Bishop of Hell*, which overlaps somewhat with the eclectic Arkham House collection *Kecksies*—whose contents she also nominated, although its publication was delayed until long after her death.

"Kecksies" is the most spectacularly blatant of all her horror stories, in which the Devil reanimates a corpse so that it might seek vengeance by means of rape. It remains one of the classic twentieth-century horror stories, but Bowen was rarely so brutal in her choice of motifs. She had a particular fondness for rather delicate stories in which the repressed desires of patient spinsters find paradoxical expression in oblique hauntings; "The Last Bouquet" and "The Crown Derby Plate" are both of this kind. *The Fetch* is a more extensive and minutely detailed study of a similar ilk, but with a male protagonist whose folly is exploited by cunning females. The painstaking manner of its analysis of the way in which individual anxiety may be built up into a collective conspiracy—with tragic consequences—removes it from the horror genre more decisively than the earlier *Julia Roseingrave*, which offered a similar analysis of witch-hunting. Another Shearing story of some interest to lovers of the outré is *The Abode of Love*, which includes accounts of the rituals of an eccentric religious sect. The other novel written under the Paye pseudonym, *The Devil's Jig*, is also of marginal interest.

Another of Bowen's best short stories, "Florence Flannery," features a treacherous female burdened by a curse whose climax is decidedly unusual. A few of her ghost stories and posthumous fantasies, including "Dark Ann," are straightforwardly sentimental but even when she set out to write in a lighter vein she always liked to add a final cruel twist, as she does in "They Found my Grave" (published under the Shearing signature). Supernatural short stories which draw profitably upon the author's historical researches include "The Fair Hair of Ambrosine," set in Revolutionary France, and "The Housekeeper," set in the reign of Queen Anne. Both are tales of ironically punished murder, as are "The Avenging of Anne Leete" and "Half-Past Two." "Raw Material" is a more unusual story in the same general vein, in which the ghost seeks a different kind of compensation. "The Tallow Candle" is based—as were many of the writings published under the Shearing pseudonym—on a matter of actual (if not entirely reliable) historical record.

The world-view contained in Bowen's multifarious work is difficult to encapsulate by any neat summary; she was a writer of many facets, some of which seemed to belong to strikingly different psychological formations. She was capable of evoking a mood of haunting sadness, which deeply regretted the violence and injustice of the world, but she was also capable of taking a voyeuristic delight in contemplation of that same violence and injustice. She would have been a less interesting writer were she not capable of such transformations, although her deep-seated ambivalence must have made her readers feel uncomfortable on occasion. A definitive collection of her supernatural fiction is long overdue and it is a great pity that so many of her novels are extremely difficult to find. She is one of the most important twentieth-century writers of weird fiction and her works in that vein deserve a wider audience.

—Brian Stableford

BOYLL, (James) Randall

Nationality: American. **Born:** 1962. **Address:** c/o Pocket Books, 1230 Avenue of the Americas, New York, NY 10020, USA.

HORROR, GHOST AND GOTHIC PUBLICATIONS

Novels (series: Darkman)

After Sundown. New York, Charter, 1989; London, Corgi, 1991.
Wes Craven's Shocker (novelization of screenplay). New York, Berkley, and London, Corgi, 1990.
Darkman (novelization of screenplay). New York, Jove, and London, Titan, 1990.
Mongster. New York, Berkley, 1991.
Chiller. New York, Jove, 1992.
The Hangman (Darkman). New York, Pocket, 1994.
The Price of Fear (Darkman). New York, Pocket, 1994.
The Gods of Hell (Darkman). New York, Pocket, 1994.
In the Face of Death (Darkman). New York, Pocket, 1995.
Demon Knight (novelization of screenplay). New York, Pocket, 1995.

*   *   *

The rise in popularity of horror fiction following the success of Stephen King and others brought a flood of new writers into the field, many of whom had nothing to contribute except inferior imitations of existing works. But there came as well a handful of genuinely original writers who brought imagination and a gift for shocking images and suspenseful plots. One of the most promising of these was Randall Boyll.

Boyll's debut novel was *After Sundown.* A bare outline of the plot indicates nothing of particular merit. A handful of people are snowbound in a mountain hut, where they discover that the previous occupants, a band of religious fanatics led by a cruel and domineering leader, have perished but not entirely abandoned the area. In fact, their spirits remain active and vindictive, and they have no intention of allowing the newcomers to leave. If anyone is to escape alive, they must uncover the dark secret that died with the cult and banish their influence from the world of the living. What makes this haunted house variant so effective is a combination of good characterization and some truly bizarre imagery, particularly the sequence in which phantom trees are summoned up to block egress from the cabin. Boyll's manifestation of the chief villain is particularly effective and he takes great care to humanize his characters so that the reader can feel a reflection of their terror.

Boyll's next original work, *Mongster*, was not nearly as effective, primarily because the tone alternates between horror and twisted humour, never quite achieving the right balance. An abused child learns the location of an ancient treasure rumoured to be guarded by a powerful supernatural force. He unwisely allows others to discover that he possesses this knowledge and in due course finds himself being pursued by two ruthless men intent upon acquiring the keys to both wealth and supernatural power. In order to preserve his own life, the boy must find a way to raise the dead to do his bidding. There's also a particularly repulsive creature who may or may not be subject to the boy's will. Once again Boyll uses strong images to reinforce the suspense, but in this case the plot is less controlled and the overall tone disjointed.

Boyll returned to his previous good form with his next novel, *Chiller*, to date his most effective work. Peter Kaye is a fugitive sought by the FBI after he kidnaps the dead but still conscious body of his daughter from an experimental clinic. Kaye races cross country, trying to control his own panic and soothe his daughter, who doesn't understand why she has to be packed in ice cubes and why her body continues to decompose. Although this could have been the vehicle for thinly veiled dark humour, Boyll opts for absolute seriousness, and the effect is intensely unsettling. The reader must decide whether Kaye's quest to preserve his daughter's consciousness, if not her life, is worthwhile, or whether he is himself a monster for prolonging her unnatural state. Far and away Boyll's best novel, which makes his subsequent transition to media-related fiction even more unfortunate.

Early in his career, Boyll was chosen to do the novelization of a pretty good horror film, *Wes Craven's Shocker.* This story of a condemned criminal who makes a pact with an evil force so that his life is preserved as a form of electricity even makes a good transition to the printed page. Boyll would also write the novelization of the first "Tales from the Crypt" film, *Demon Knight*, a rather monotonous story about a handful of people besieged by a horde of demons. In this case, the absence of visual effects reduces the novel to tedium. But the largest sap on Boyll's creative talents began when he novelized the story of dark revenge, *Darkman.*

Darkman is a blend of hero-pulp and comic-book action. The protagonist is maimed and left for dead by criminals, so he becomes a master of disguise and prowls the night searching for those who injured him. The film was popular enough to spawn sequels, and Boyll has to date written an additional four original adventures, all of which include marginal horror elements. In *The Hangman*, Darkman destroys an evil gang preying on young people. In *The Price of Fear* there's another criminal organization, but there's also a supernatural creature stalking the city, both of which must be defeated if Darkman is to survive. A pseudo-satanic cult seeking the secret of immortality provides the menace in *The Gods of Hell.* Darkman's gift for disguise comes in particularly handy this time as it allows him to infiltrate the organization and find out the secret identities of its members. Most recently, Darkman returned in *In the Face of Death.* The plot edges toward science fiction, with a rogue CIA agent intent upon stealing the secret of

Darkman's ability to impersonate others. The agent plans to replace the President and use that position to secure for himself dictatorship over the entire country. The Darkman books are good adventure novels as well as marginal horror, but for the most part they lack the intense imagery of Boyll's earlier, less derivative work. It would be unfortunate if he abandoned original material entirely because of the success of this series.

—Don D'Ammassa

BRADBURY, Ray(mond Douglas)

Nationality: American. **Born:** Waukegan, Illinois, 22 August 1920. **Education:** Los Angeles High School, graduated 1938. **Family:** Married Marguerite Susan McClure in 1947; four daughters. **Career:** Full-time writer from 1943. President, Science-Fantasy Writers of America, 1951-53. Member of the Board of Directors, Screen Writers Guild of America, 1957-61. **Awards:** O. Henry prize, 1947, 1948; Benjamin Franklin award, 1954; American Academy award, 1954; Boys' Clubs of America Junior Book award, 1956; Golden Eagle award, for screenplay, 1957; Ann Radcliffe award, 1965, 1971; Writers Guild award, 1974; Aviation and Space Writers award, for television documentary, 1979; Gandalf award, 1980; Nebula Grand Master, 1988; Bram Stoker Life Achievement award, 1989. D.Litt.: Whittier College, California, 1979. **Agent:** Harold Matson Company, 276 Fifth Avenue, New York, NY 10001. **Address:** c/o Bantam, 666 Fifth Avenue, New York, NY 10103, USA. Lives in Los Angeles.

HORROR, GHOST AND GOTHIC PUBLICATIONS

Novels

Dandelion Wine. New York, Doubleday, and London, Hart Davis, 1957.
Switch on the Night (for children). New York, Pantheon, and London, Hart Davis, 1955.
Something Wicked This Way Comes. New York, Simon and Schuster, 1962; London, Hart Davis, 1963.
The Halloween Tree (for children). New York, Knopf, 1972; London, Hart Davis MacGibbon, 1973.

Short Stories

Dark Carnival. Sauk City, Wisconsin, Arkham House, 1947; abridged edition, London, Hamish Hamilton, 1948; abridged edition, as *The Small Assassin,* London, Ace, 1962.
The October Country. New York, Ballantine, 1955; London, Hart Davis, 1956.

OTHER PUBLICATIONS

Novels

Fahrenheit 451. New York, Ballantine, 1953; London, Hart Davis, 1954.
Death Is a Lonely Business. New York, Knopf, 1985; London, Grafton, 1986.

A Graveyard for Lunatics: Another Tale of Two Cities. New York, Knopf, and London, Grafton, 1990.
Green Shadows, White Whale. New York, Knopf, and London, HarperCollins, 1992.

Short Stories

The Martian Chronicles. New York, Doubleday, 1950; as *The Silver Locusts,* London, Hart Davis, 1951.
The Illustrated Man. New York, Doubleday, 1951; London, Hart Davis, 1952.
The Golden Apples of the Sun. New York, Doubleday, and London, Hart Davis, 1953.
A Medicine for Melancholy. New York, Doubleday, 1959.
The Day It Rained Forever. London, Hart Davis, 1959.
R is for Rocket (for children). New York, Doubleday, 1962; London, Hart Davis, 1968.
The Machineries of Joy. New York, Simon and Schuster, and London, Hart Davis, 1964.
The Vintage Bradbury. New York, Random House, 1965.
S is for Space (for children). New York, Doubleday, 1966; London, Hart Davis, 1968.
Twice Twenty Two (omnibus). New York, Doubleday, 1966.
I Sing the Body Electric! New York, Knopf, 1969; London, Hart Davis, 1970.
Bloch and Bradbury, with Robert Bloch. New York, Tower, 1969; as *Fever Dreams and Other Fantasies,* London, Sphere, 1970.
(Selected Stories), edited by Anthony Adams. London, Harrap, 1975.
Long after Midnight. New York, Knopf, 1976; London, Hart Davis MacGibbon, 1977.
The Best of Bradbury. New York, Bantam, 1976.
To Sing Strange Songs. Exeter, Devon, Wheaton, 1979.
The Stories of Ray Bradbury. New York, Knopf, and London, Granada, 1980.
The Last Circus, and The Electrocution. Northridge, California, Lord John Press, 1980.
Dinosaur Tales. New York, Bantam, 1983.
A Memory of Murder. New York, Dell, 1984.
The Toynbee Convector. New York, Knopf, 1988; London, Grafton, 1989.
The Smile. Mankato, Minnesota, Creative Education, 1991.
Quicker Than the Eye. New York, Avon, 1996.

Plays

The Meadow, in *Best One-Act Plays of 1947-48,* edited by Margaret Mayorga. New York, Dodd Mead, 1948.
The Anthem Sprinters and Other Antics (produced Los Angeles, 1968). New York, Dial Press, 1963.
The World of Ray Bradbury (produced Los Angeles, 1964; New York, 1965).
The Wonderful Ice-Cream Suit (produced Los Angeles, 1965; New York, 1987; musical version, music by Jose Feliciano, produced Pasadena, California, 1990).
The Day It Rained Forever, music by Bill Whitefield (produced Edinburgh, 1988). New York, French, 1966.
The Pedestrian. New York, French, 1966.
Christus Apollo, music by Jerry Goldsmith (produced Los Angeles, 1969).

The Wonderful Ice-Cream Suit and Other Plays (includes *The Veldt* and *To the Chicago Abyss*). New York, Bantam, 1972; London, Hart Davis, 1973.

The Veldt (produced London, 1980).

Leviathan 99 (produced Los Angeles, 1972).

Pillar of Fire and Other Plays for Today, Tomorrow, and Beyond Tomorrow (includes *Kaleidoscope* and *The Foghorn*). New York, Bantam, 1975.

The Foghorn (produced New York, 1977).

That Ghost, That Bride of Time: Excerpts from a Play-in-Progress. Glendale, California, Squires, 1976.

The Martian Chronicles, adaptation of his own stories (produced Los Angeles, 1977).

Fahrenheit 451, adaptation of his own novel (produced Los Angeles, 1979).

Dandelion Wine, adaptation of his own story (produced Los Angeles, 1980).

Forever and the Earth (radio play). Athens, Ohio, Croissant, 1984.

On Stage: A Chrestomathy of His Plays. New York, Primus, 1991.

Screenplays: *It Came from Outer Space*, with David Schwartz, 1952; *Moby-Dick*, with John Huston, 1956; *Icarus Montgolfier Wright*, with George C. Johnston, 1961; *Picasso Summer* (as Douglas Spaulding), with Edwin Booth, 1972.

Television Plays: *Shopping for Death*, 1956, *Design for Loving*, 1958, *Special Delivery*, 1959, *The Faith of Aaron Menefee*, 1962, and *The Life Work of Juan Diaz*, 1963 (all *Alfred Hitchcock Presents* series); *The Marked Bullet* (*Jane Wyman's Fireside Theater* series), 1956; *The Gift* (*Steve Canyon* series), 1958; *The Tunnel to Yesterday* (*Trouble Shooters* series), 1960; *I Sing the Body Electric!* (*Twilight Zone* series), 1962; *The Jail* (*Alcoa Premier* series), 1962; *The Groom* (*Curiosity Shop* series), 1971; *The Coffin*, from his own short story, 1988 (UK).

Poetry

Old Ahab's Friend, and Friend to Noah, Speaks His Piece: A Celebration. Glendale, California, Squires, 1971.

When Elephants Last in the Dooryard Bloomed: Celebrations for Almost Any Day in the Year. New York, Knopf, 1973; London, Hart Davis MacGibbon, 1975.

That Son of Richard III: A Birth Announcement. Privately printed, 1974.

Where Robot Mice and Robot Men Run Round in Robot Towns: New Poems, Both Light and Dark. New York, Knopf, 1977; London, Hart Davis MacGibbon, 1979.

Twin Hieroglyphs That Swim the River Dust. Northridge, California, Lord John Press, 1978.

The Bike Repairman. Northridge, California, Lord John Press, 1978.

The Author Considers His Resources. Northridge, California, Lord John Press, 1979.

The Aqueduct. Glendale, California, Squires, 1979.

The Attic Where the Meadow Greens. Northridge, California, Lord John Press, 1980.

Imagine. Northridge, California, Lord John Press, 1981.

The Haunted Computer and the Android Pope. New York, Knopf, and London, Granada, 1981.

The Complete Poems of Ray Bradbury. New York, Ballantine, 1982.

Two Poems. Northridge, California, Lord John Press, 1982.

The Love Affair. Northridge, California, Lord John Press, 1983.

Other

The Autumn People (comic-book adaptations). New York, Ballantine, 1965.

Tomorrow Midnight (comic-book adaptations). New York, Ballantine, 1966.

Teacher's Guide: Science Fiction, with Lewy Olfson. New York, Bantam, 1968.

Mars and the Mind of Man. New York, Harper, 1973.

Zen and the Art of Writing, and The Joy of Writing. Santa Barbara, California, Capra Press, 1973.

The Mummies of Guanajuato, photographs by Archie Lieberman. New York, Abrams, 1978.

Beyond 1984: Remembrance of Things Future. New York, Targ, 1979.

About Norman Corwin. Northridge, California, Santa Susana Press, 1979.

The Ghosts of Forever, illustrated by Aldo Sessa. New York, Rizzoli, 1981.

Los Angeles, photographs by West Light. Port Washington, New York, Skyline Press, 1984.

Orange County, photographs by Bill Ross and others. Port Washington, New York, Skyline Press, 1985.

The Art of Playboy (text by Bradbury). New York, van der Marck Editions, 1985.

Zen in the Art of Writing (essays). Santa Barbara, California, Capra Press, 1990.

Yestermorrow: Obvious Answers to Impossible Futures (essays). Santa Barbara, California, Capra Press, 1991.

*

Film Adaptations: *Fahrenheit 451*, 1966; *The Illustrated Man*, 1969; *The Martian Chronicles*, 1980 (TV mini-series); *Something Wicked This Way Comes*, 1983.

Manuscript Collection: Bowling Green State University, Ohio.

Critical Studies: *The Ray Bradbury Companion* (includes bibliography) by William F. Nolan, Detroit, Gale, 1975; *The Drama of Ray Bradbury* by Benjamin P. Indick, Baltimore, T-K Graphics, 1977; *The Bradbury Chronicles* by George Edgar Slusser, San Bernardino, California, Borgo Press, 1977; *Ray Bradbury* edited by Joseph D. Olander and Martin H. Greenberg, New York, Taplinger, and Edinburgh, Harris, 1980; *Ray Bradbury* by Wayne L. Johnson, New York, Ungar, 1980; *Ray Bradbury and the Poetics of Reverie: Fantasy, Science Fiction, and the Reader* by William F. Toupence, Ann Arbor, Michigan, UMI Research Press, 1984; *Ray Bradbury* by David Mogen, Boston, Twayne, 1986; *Ray Bradbury* by William F. Toupence, Mercer Island, Washington, Starmont House, 1989.

* * *

In Ray Bradbury's midwestern gothic tale "The Jar," a group of rustics gathers nightly at the house of a neighbour to speculate on the identity of a pickled thing in a jar. Although they never arrive at a satisfactory answer, they never grow tired of their repetitive small talk. "When you said the same thing night after night in the deep summer," writes Bradbury, "it always sounded different. The crickets changed it. The frogs changed it. The thing in the jar changed it." This simple observation on the power of peripheral details to influence perception can be read as an allusive commentary on Bradbury's personal approach to the weird tale.

The basic content of Bradbury's weird fiction, most of which was published in the pulp magazine *Weird Tales* between 1942 and 1948, differs little from that of the work of his colleagues. His stories are stuffed with the imagery of death and abound with characters confronting their mortality in unexpected and sometimes horrible ways. Bradbury, however, had a talent for finding fresh perspectives from which to ponder mankind's preoccupation with the grave. In "The Scythe," he transformed the grim reaper of legend into an ordinary American farmer racking up the world's death toll as he mows his field. In "Skeleton," he gave a sardonic twist to a stock prop of gothic horror by making a man afraid of his own skull and bones. In his prose poem "The Maiden," he likened the action of a guillotine blade to the kiss of an enraptured lover. He even narrated the murder mystery "It Burns Me Up!" from the corpse's point of view.

Bradbury wrought variations on traditional horror themes not only by approaching them from imaginative tangents, but by careful attention to narrative craft. In a field where purple prose and cheap shock tactics had been the order of the day, he stood apart as a natural prose stylist who could sum up a situation memorably with an evocative image or metaphor. He applied his subtle lyricism to the most macabre subject matter, and as a result was able to persuade readers that a travelling carnival of freaks perfectly expressed the panorama of life in *Something Wicked This Way Comes*, or that a family with their throats slit would look very much like "The Smiling People."

Probably the best example of how consciously Bradbury fine-tuned his writing to achieve a desired weird effect is his story "The Wind." When it first appeared in a 1943 issue of *Weird Tales* it was a routine pulp thriller about a man who incurs the wrath of a wind elemental. Bradbury revised the story for inclusion in his first collection, *Dark Carnival*, in 1947, streamlining the prose to a sleek economy and shifting the point of view from the hysterical victim to a friend who listens to the man's pleas for help over a telephone. The displaced action and detached viewpoint of this version create the discomfiting feeling one would have if stuck in a house being savagely buffeted by a windstorm.

The term that best describes what Bradbury brought to bear on his fiction is a sense of enchantment. He used it to cut traditional gothic horrors down to size so that they could be woven into the fabric of ordinary life and to invest the most mundane situations with eerie potential. Through its transformational power, the quiet rural towns and middle-class people of his stories become tools for probing a human condition touched by wonder. Genuine episodes of the supernatural in his stories are often matched by the experiences of characters in the grip of emotions so strong they seem to torque events into the uncanny. "The Lake" and "Reunion," for example, are both poignant stories of love that endures after death. In the former, a dead playmate reawakens the affections of the man who once loved her by leaving a sand castle for him on the beach where she drowned decades before. In the latter, an orphaned boy achieves a similar rapport with his dead family simply by recreating them in his imagination from the smell and feel of clothing and other effects they handled in their lifetimes.

There is no ostensible supernatural element in either "The Jar" or "The Next in Line." Nevertheless, their accounts of deteriorating marriages escalating toward disaster convey a sense of eerie menace as events culminate around symbols that crystallize their

moods of dread: respectively, a jar containing a freak-show attraction and a catacomb filled with mummies. Counterbalancing these tales of horrors spawned from the everyday is the whimsical series that includes "Homecoming," "Uncle Einar," "The Traveller," and "The April Witch." All of these tales feature an extended family of vampires, werewolves and other supernatural beings who live unobtrusively among humans and who express emotional needs no different than those of their mortal neighbours.

The fantastic, whether dark or light, is always lying in wait for the vulnerable in Bradbury's fiction. Not surprisingly, children figure prominently in his stories. In rare instances, such as "The Small Assassin" and "Let's Play 'Poison'," they are "strange little improbabilities who cause death" by manipulating adult presumptions of their innocence. More often, though, they are genuine *naïfs* who access the supernatural unselfconsciously through their as-yet unspoiled imaginations. They resurrect the dead with a simple wish in "The Emissary," and abolish death entirely in "Bang! You're Dead" and "The Ducker" by treating it as a game of make-believe. Bradbury's adults, on the other hand, are rendered vulnerable through their lack of innocence. They have lost the youthful romance that can preserve life in "The Screaming Woman," and are obsessively preoccupied with their own mortality in "The Dead Man." In *Something Wicked This Way Comes*, these "tired men and women whose faces were dirty with guilt, unwashed of sin, and smashed like small windows by life that hit without warning, ran, hid, came back and hit again" are susceptible to the worst horror of all: disillusionment so strong that it propels them into satanic bargains to regain the promise of their youth.

The conviction that life is chock full of marvels waiting to reveal themselves has shaped virtually all of Bradbury's writing. *Dandelion Wine*, *Something Wicked This Way Comes*, *Death is a Lonely Business*, *A Graveyard for Lunatics* and *Green Shadows, White Whale* span the genres from mainstream to mystery fiction and integrate loosely to serve as his fictional autobiography in which windows on the fantastic are perpetually opening. Together with the weird tales collected in *Dark Carnival* and *The October Country*, they represent Bradbury's lifetime effort to map the borderland that is the setting for all of his fiction: the point where the banality of the fantastic and the magic of everyday life collide.

—Stefan R. Dziemianowicz

BRADDON, M(ary) E(lizabeth)

Pseudonyms: Aunt Belinda; Babington White. **Nationality:** British. **Born:** London, 4 October 1835. **Family:** Married the publisher John Maxwell in 1874 (but had lived with him since 1860); seven children, including the writer W. B. Maxwell. **Career:** Actress, 1857-1860; magazine editor, and author of more than 80 novels. **Died:** 4 February 1915.

HORROR, GHOST AND GOTHIC PUBLICATIONS

Novels

Gerard; or, the World, the Flesh and the Devil. London, Simpkin Marshall, 1891; as *The World, the Flesh and the Devil*, New York, Lovell, 1891.
The Conflict. London, Simpkin Marshall, 1903.

Short Stories

Ralph the Bailiff and Other Tales. London, Ward Lock, 1862; revised and enlarged, 1867.
Weavers and Weft and Other Tales. London, Maxwell, 1877; New York, Harper, 1877.

OTHER PUBLICATIONS

Novels

Three Times Dead; or, The Secret of the Heath. London, Clark, 1860; New York, Dick and Fitzgerald, 1864(?); revised as *The Trail of the Serpent; or, The Secret of the Heath*, London, Ward Lock, 1866.
The Lady Lisle. London, Ward Lock, 1862; New York, Dick and Fitzgerald, 1863.
Lady Audley's Secret. London, Tinsley, 1862; New York, Dick and Fitzgerald, 1863.
The Captain of the Vulture. London, Ward Lock, 1862; as *Darrell Markham, or The Captain of the Vulture*, New York, Dick and Fitzgerald, 1863.
Aurora Floyd. London, Tinsley, and New York, Harper, 1863.
Eleanor's Victory. London, Tinsley, and New York, Harper, 1863.
John Marchmont's Legacy. London, Tinsley, 1863; New York, Harper, 1864.
Henry Dunbar: The Story of an Outcast. London, Maxwell, 1864; as *The Outcast; or, The Brand of Society*, New York, Dick and Fitzgerald, 1864.
The Doctor's Wife. London, Maxwell, and New York, Dick and Fitzgerald, 1864.
Only a Clod. London, Maxwell, and New York, Dick and Fitzgerald, 1865.
Sir Jasper's Tenant. London, Maxwell, and New York, Dick and Fitzgerald, 1865.
The Lady's Mile. London, Ward Lock, 1866; New York, Dick and Fitzgerald, 1867.
What is This Mystery? New York, Hilton, 1866; as *The Black Band*, London, Vickers, 1877.
Circe (as Babington White). London, Ward Lock, 1867.
Rupert Godwin. London, Ward Lock, and New York, Dick and Fitzgerald, 1867.
Birds of Prey. London, Ward Lock, and New York, Harper, 1867.
Charlotte's Inheritance. London, Ward Lock, and New York, Harper, 1868.
Diavola. New York, Dick and Fitzgerald, 1867; as *Run to Earth*, London, Ward Lock, 1868.
Dead-Sea Fruit. London, Ward Lock, and New York, Harper, 1868.
The White Phantom. New York, Williams, 1868.
The Factory Girl. New York, De Witt, 1869(?).
Oscar Bertrand. New York, DeWitt, 1869(?).
The Octoroon; or, the Lily of Louisiana. New York, DeWitt, 1869.
Fenton's Quest. London, Ward Lock, and New York, Harper, 1871.
The Lovels of Arden. London, Maxwell, 1871; New York, Harper, 1872.
Robert Ainsleigh. London, Maxwell, 1872; as *Bound to John Company; or, The Adventures and Misadventures of Robert Ainsleigh*, New York, Harper, 1876.
To the Bitter End. London, Maxwell, 1872; New York, Harper, 1875.
Strangers and Pilgrims. London, Maxwell, and New York, Harper, 1873.
Lucius Davoren; or, Publicans and Sinners. London, Maxwell, 1873; as *Publicans and Sinners; or, Lucius Davoren*, New York, Harper, 1874.
Taken at the Flood. London, Maxwell, and New York, Harper, 1874.
Lost for Love. London, Chatto and Windus, 1874; New York, Harper, 1875.
A Strange World. London, Maxwell, and New York, Harper, 1875.
Hostages to Fortune. London, Maxwell, and New York, Harper, 1875.
Dead Men's Shoes. London, Maxwell, and New York, Harper, 1876.
Joshua Haggard's Daughter. London, Maxwell, 1876; New York, Harper, 1877.
An Open Verdict. London, Maxwell, and New York, Harper, 1878.
Vixen. London, Maxwell, and New York, Munro, 1879.
The Cloven Foot. London, Maxwell, and New York, Harper, 1879.
The Story of Barbara. London, Maxwell, 1880; as *Barbara*, New York, Harper, 1880.
Just as I Am. London, Maxwell, and New York, Harper, 1880.
Asphodel. London, Maxwell, and New York, Munro, 1881.
Flower and Weed. New York, Harper, 1882.
Mount Royal. London, Maxwell, and New York, Harper, 1882.
The Golden Calf. London, Maxwell, and New York, Lovell, 1883.
Married in Haste. London, Maxwell, 1883; New York, Munro, 1887.
Phantom Fortune. London, Maxwell, and New York, Harper, 1883.
Under the Red Flag. New York, Harper, 1883.
Ishmael. London, Maxwell, and New York, Munro, 1884.
Wyllard's Weird. London, Maxwell, and New York, Harper, 1885.
Cut By the County. New York, Munro, 1885; London, Maxwell, 1886.
One Thing Needful. London, Maxwell, and New York, Harper, 1886.
Mohawks. London, Maxwell, and New York, Harper, 1886.
The Good Hermione (as Aunt Belinda). London, Maxwell, 1886.
Like and Unlike. London, Spencer Blackett, and New York, Munro, 1887.
The Fatal Three. London, Simpkin Marshall, and New York, Lovell, 1888.
The Day Will Come. London, Simpkin Marshall, and New York, Munro, 1889.
One Life, One Love. London, Simpkin Marshall, 1890.
The Venetians. London, Simpkin Marshall, and New York, Harper, 1892.
All Along the River. London, Simpkin Marshall, 1893.
The Christmas Hirelings. London, Simpkin Marshall, 1893; New York, Harper, 1894.
Thou Art the Man. London, Simpkin Marshall, 1894.
Sons of Fire. London, Simpkin Marshall, 1895.
London Pride. London, Simpkin Marshall, 1896; as *When the World Was Younger*, New York, Fenno, 1897.
Under Love's Rule. London, Simpkin Marshall, 1897.
In High Places. London, Hutchinson, 1898.
Rough Justice. London, Simpkin Marshall, 1898.
His Darling Sin. London, Simpkin Marshall, and New York, Harper, 1899.
The Infidel. London, Simpkin Marshall, and New York, Harper, 1900.
A Lost Eden. London, Hutchinson, 1904.

The Rose of Life. London, Hutchinson, and New York, Brentano's, 1905.

The White House. London, Hurst and Blackett, 1906.

Dead Love Has Chains. London, Hurst and Blackett, 1907.

Her Convict. London, Hurst and Blackett, 1907.

During Her Majesty's Pleasure. London, Hurst and Blackett, 1908.

Our Adversary. London, Hutchinson, 1909.

"Beyond These Voices." London, Hutchinson, 1910.

The Green Curtain. London, Hutchinson, 1911.

Miranda. London, Hutchinson, 1913.

Mary. London, Hutchinson, 1916.

Short Stories

Dudley Carleton; or, The Brother's Secret and Other Tales. New York, Dick and Fitzgerald, 1864.

Milly Darrell, and Other Tales. London, Maxwell, 1873; New York, Carleton, 1877; as *Meeting Her Fate*, New York, Carleton, 1881.

In Great Waters and Other Tales. Leipzig, Tauchnitz, 1877.

My Sister's Confession and Other Stories. New York, Worthington, 1879.

Flower and Weed and Other Tales. London, Maxwell, 1884.

Under the Red Flag and Other Tales. London, Maxwell, 1886.

Poetry

Garibaldi, and Other Poems. London, Bosworth and Harrison, 1861.

Plays

Loves of Arcadia (produced London, 1860).

Griselda (produced London, 1873).

The Missing Witness. London, Maxwell, 1880.

Dross; or, The Root of Evil. London, Maxwell, 1882; New York, De Witt, 1884(?).

Marjorie Daw: A Household Idyll in Two Acts. London, Maxwell, 1882; New York, De Witt, 1885.

Married Beneath Him. London, Maxwell, 1882.

Other

Boscastle, Cornwall, and English Engadine. Launceston, Cater, 1881.

Editor, *Put to the Test*, by Ada Buisson. London, Maxwell, 1865.

Editor, *The Summer Tourist.* London, Ward, Lock and Tyler, 1871.

*

Film Adaptations: *Lady Audley's Secret*, 1906, 1908, 1912, 1915, 1920; *Her Better Lesson*, 1912, 1915, from the novel *Aurora Floyd*.

Manuscript Collections: Houghton Library, Harvard University, Cambridge, Massachusetts; University of Texas, Austin.

Critical Studies: *Time Gathered* by W. B. Maxwell, New York and London, Appleton-Century, 1938; *Things Past* by Michael

Sadleir, London, Constable, 1944; introduction to *Lady Audley's Secret* by Norman Donaldson, New York, Dover, 1974; *A Literature of Their Own* by Elaine Showalter, Princeton, New Jersey, Princeton University Press, 1977; *Sensational Victorian: The Life and Fiction of Mary Elizabeth Braddon* by Robert Lee Wolff, New York, Garland, 1979; *The Maniac in the Cellar: Sensation Novels of the 1860s* by Winifred Hughes, Princeton, New Jersey, Princeton University Press, 1980.

*   *   *

Mary Braddon was one of the most prolific of the Victorian lady novelists. She thought nothing of producing two or three three-decker novels year after year whilst also raising a sizable family of children (seven of her own and five step-children), assisting her husband in his publishing enterprise and editing the magazines *Temple Bar* and *Belgravia*. All of this might suggest that her work was repetitive and superficial, but although she did occasionally repeat the formula of her most successful novel, *Lady Audley's Secret*, to much financial gain, she was more original and creative than her critics would credit her. Along with Wilkie Collins and Bulwer Lytton she became the darling of the sensation novel of the mid-Victorian era. Although this was a descendant of the Gothic novel, and the staple diet of the yellowback books that sold in profusion at railway bookstalls, the novels are not Gothic other than in their heightened atmosphere of murder, mystery and dread. They sought to thrill rather than horrify and scarcely ever resorted to the supernatural. Their relevance to this volume is thus only of associational interest.

The profusion of Braddon's work, much of it published anonymously in her early days, especially the magazine fiction, makes it difficult to identify her complete output of ghost and horror stories. It is likely that she produced more than she is credited with, though she chose not to publish a single volume dedicated to these tales. The earliest collection of any significance was *Ralph the Bailiff and Other Tales* which was later reissued with additional stories. It contains two of Braddon's most reprinted stories: "The Cold Embrace" (*Welcome Guest*, 1860) and "Eveline's Visitant" (*Belgravia*, 1867). The first is an obvious derivative of the second-generation Gothic fiction then prevalent in Britain. It tells of a German art student who becomes haunted by the spirit of his betrothed who committed suicide after he deserted her. The story is written with remarkable originality for the period, using pointed statements and changes in narrative to heighten the atmosphere of imminent dread. "Eveline's Visitant" has another sense of immediacy about it, even though the story is set in the past. The narrator's cousin is killed by him in a duel but the spirit returns to haunt the narrator's wife, who falls in love with the ghost. In both these stories Braddon decided to abandon the obvious gothic trappings that the story settings might otherwise demand to allow the events to have a more natural, and ultimately more unsettling effect. For someone who would make her name for the sensationalism of her plots and story delivery, Braddon sought the opposite in her early ghost stories. It is interesting to compare "Eveline's Visitant" with the novel *The Conflict* written over 30 years later though with a similar plotline. Here Braddon, evidently needing to produce another potboiler, uses the similar theme of spectral revenge but with less finesse so that the frisson of horror is lost.

Most of Braddon's ghost stories explore the relationship between young lovers and the inevitable ghostly consequences when one of them dies. This desire for union through eternity and fear of separation must reflect some image of Braddon's own life. In 1860, when only 25, she had fallen in love with the publisher John Maxwell and had moved in with him even though his wife was still alive but hopelessly insane in an asylum. The two were unable to wed until after the wife's death 14 years later. This threat of separation and insanity was probably behind her story "The Mystery at Fernwood" (*Temple Bar*, 1861), written soon after they met. It is more in the mood of her later novels. Set in a reputedly haunted mansion in Yorkshire, a young woman's interest in the house's secretive past inadvertently lets loose the idiot brother of her betrothed who promptly murders his brother. The story drops hints along the way, but Braddon is discerning in her use of tension to allow the ending to come as a violent shock. Braddon drew upon her experiences upon the stage in a further story of love beyond the grave, "Her Last Appearance" (*Belgravia*, 1876), where an actress dies but returns for one last appearance for her betrothed.

Braddon was also interested in the consequences of fate. "At Chrighton Abbey" (*Belgravia*, 1871) explores a further relationship between two young lovers, but the young girl witnesses a portent of her fiancé's death as the consequence of the inevitable family curse. In "Sir Hanbury's Bequest" (*Belgravia*, 1874), a young squire finds himself reliving episodes from a dream about one of his ancestors.

One of Braddon's best stories is "Good Lady Ducayne" (*The Strand*, 1896) an atmospheric vampire story written just before the publication of *Dracula*. It demonstrates that despite having written nearly 70 books by then she was still able to invoke original ideas and sustain a mounting mood of dread. Although she repeated this time and again in her novels, she never produced a successful horror or supernatural novel. The closest she came was with *Gerard; or, the World, the Flesh and the Devil*, where she adapts the Faust theme for a society novel. Gerard, a young author on the verge of suicide, meets the charismatic Justin Jermyn, a manifestation of the devil who secures for Gerard the love of a beautiful woman, despite his betrothal to another. In the end Gerard loses both his women and meets his just deserts. It's a weak novel, but is suggestive of one that Braddon needed to write to explore her own life and relationships.

It is probable that Braddon had no more than a passing interest in the supernatural, finding that there were enough horrors in real life, especially in the darkness of the human soul, to need the addition of spectral elements. Her use of ghosts, therefore, is usually only to emphasize everlasting love, or retribution from beyond the grave. By using it sparingly, the examples from her work tend to remain fresh and exciting.

—Mike Ashley

BRADFIELD, Scott (Michael)

Nationality: American. **Born:** California, 1955. **Education:** University of California, Ph.D. in American literature. **Career:** University teacher of English, on an intermittent basis; at University of Connecticut since 1989; contributor of short stories and reviews to many magazines and journals, including *Ambit, Interzone, The Listener, The New Statesman, Omni* and *The Times Literary Supplement*. Spends part of his time in London, England.

HORROR, GHOST AND GOTHIC PUBLICATIONS

Novels

The History of Luminous Motion. London, Bloomsbury, and New York, Knopf, 1989.
What's Wrong with America. London, Picador, and New York, St. Martin's Press, 1994.
Animal Planet. New York, Picador, 1995; London, Picador, 1996.

Short Stories

The Secret Life of Houses. London, Unwin Hyman, 1988; expanded as *Dream of the Wolf*, New York, Knopf, 1990.
Greetings from Earth: New and Collected Stories. London, Picador, 1993; New York, Picador, 1996.

OTHER PUBLICATIONS

Other

Dreaming Revolution: Transgression in 19th Century American Literature. N.p., 1987; revised as *Dreaming Revolution: Transgression in the Development of American Romance*, n.p., n.d.

*   *   *

Scott Bradfield is a satirical fabulist whose inclination toward dark fantasy is nicely balanced by his sly comic talents. His short fiction and three novels never stray far from our modern world, a place rendered in vibrant neon colors and gritty textures, populated with struggling, mostly lower-middle-class figures who exhibit extremes of both selfish and selfless behaviour. Yet this mimetic venue, a land of deep despair and tenuous hope so recognizable as our own, generally proves as disturbingly, alluringly horrifying as any supernatural realm.

Greetings from Earth: New and Collected Stories (which incorporates in its entirety the earlier collections, *The Secret Life of Houses* and *Dream of the Wolf*) provides a good introduction to Bradfield's characteristic themes and angles of attack. In "The Dream of the Wolf," average joe Larry Chambers finds his life being swamped by nightly dreams of wolfhood, a destiny he comes to embrace—the first instance in Bradfield's work of the powers of fantasy and delusion to remake reality, usually for the worse. A non-sensationalistic coolness of tone and an authorial certainty that his deft prose is having its intended effect both conduce toward a subtle horror that will be seen as typical of Bradfield's non-splattering fiction.

"The Darling" tells the story of young Dolores Starr, by every measure a pampered pet of a girl who nonetheless turns cruel killer. This Blochian revelation of the buried murderer lurking in most citizens will resurface in *What's Wrong with America* and elsewhere, providing many chills and much black comedy. In "Ghost Guessed," milquetoast Kenneth Millar (the actual name of crime writer Ross MacDonald, and a clue to a certain California lineage Bradfield shares) finds himself saddled with a nagging ghost who brings out Millar's worst side. A hallucinatory doppelganger comes between husband and wife in "The Other Man," proving once again that ultimate terror is cerebral. As a character in "The Wind Box" says, "The mind has special powers all its own." "Closer to You" is reminiscent of Richard Matheson's "Born of Man and Woman" in its depiction-from-inside of a "special child." The title of "The Secret Life of Houses," might almost serve as Bradfield's statement of purpose. Not only will he show us the shocking hidden doings of people who feel themselves safely concealed behind their walls, but he will also exteriorize their fears and desires, investing inanimate objects with a kind of Poe-like or Ballardian malignancy.

Bradfield specializes in points-of-view that privilege the traditionally dispossessed and powerless members of society. He is particularly adept at getting into the psyches of his female characters ("The Last Man That Time"; "Hey Hey Hey"; "The Promise"), children ("In the Time of the Great Dying"; "The *Flash!* Kid"), and animals ("Dazzle"; "The Parakeet and the Cat"). We will see Bradfield perched on these powerful coigns of vantage in his novels, like some wise gargoyle.

The History of Luminous Motion is perhaps Bradfield's most impactful novel. Deriving directly from "Hey Hey Hey" in its portrait of a hapless mother and precocious child adrift in an uncaring world, this book carries the themes and potential for disaster of that story as far as humanly possible. Narrated in the first person by eight-year-old Phillip Davis, the book eschews the realistic speech and observational powers of a child for the vocabulary and insights of a punk Rimbaud. With affinities to Gunter Grass's *The Tin Drum* (1959) and Ian McEwan's *The Cement Garden* (1978), foreshadowing the movie *Kids* (1995), the novel is a phantasmagoric voyage through the minefields of contemporary U.S. West Coast culture.

In the first portion of the novel, titled "Motion," self-educated, Oedipal Phillip performs his first murder, that of his Mom's latest lover, propelling mother and son onto the endless urban highway and making his Mom wax philosophical: "The history of motion is that luminous progress men and women make in the world alone." Such portentous pronouncements generally mark the descent into hell for many of Bradfield's victim/perpetrators, and such is the case here.

After relocating and settling into surface normality, Phillip finds bad companions in the shape of the slightly older Rodney and Beatrice, slipping into theft and drunkenness. His father resurfaces in his life, but falls afoul of Phillip's deadly ire. Eventually caught and brought to justice, Phillip remains at book's end a clear unrepentant brother to the Alex of Anthony Burgess's *A Clockwork Orange* (1962).

What's Wrong with America, despite its all-embracing title, is not a scattershot rant, but maintains a narrower focus on one individual's quandry. Elderly Emma O'Hallahan, a kind of longstifled Edith Bunker figure, has, at novel's start, already killed her horrid husband Marvin and planted him in the back yard. Inspired by this blow for liberation, she decides to begin keeping a journal, which Bradfield's skill renders as a flawlessly in-character farrago that manages both to advance the plot and to damn with sweetness the most lamentable aspects of modern culture: television, New Age self-help rituals, parent-child bonding among them. Besieged by hallucinations, remorse and the practical implications of her act, Emma gradually dissolves into a desperation that proves in climax to be surprisingly salutary. This novel would have been a perfect text for Hitchcock to film, although conveying Emma's unique voice onscreen might have proved impossible even for that master.

Bradfield's most recent book, *Animal Planet*, is the least horrific of his novels, concentrating instead on straight satire. Talking animals, led by a lazy troublemaker named Charlie the Crow, manifest themselves in the contemporary world. Blitzed by the media and politicians, the animals gradually fall into the role once occupied by African-American slaves, objects of human lust and cruelty. As in Native American tales, the animals are portrayed in a near-surrealistic manner, sometimes seeming small and clawed and beaked and furred, at other times—within the same scene even—they assume human proportions and features. Any horror in this book is the common carnage of the abbatoir, where animals are sacrificed every day.

Master of a cutting, edgy, economical prose style, expert at provoking groans, grimaces and grins in equal measures, Bradfield strides boldly forward on the trail of psychological horror blazed by such pioneers as Robert Bloch and Jim Thompson.

—Paul Di Filippo

BRANDNER, Gary (Phil)

Pseudonyms: Nick Carter; Phil Garrison; Clayton Moore; Lee Davis Willoughby. **Nationality:** American. **Born:** Saulte Ste. Marie, Michigan, 31 May 1933. **Education:** Grant High School, Portland, Oregon; Bellingham High School, Bellingham, Washington; University of Washington, 1951-55, B.A. in journalism. **Family:** Married 1) Paula Moon in 1958 (divorced 1963); 2) Barbara Grant Nutting in 1979 (divorced 1983); 3) Martine Frances Wood in 1988. **Career:** Worked in public relations for Bethlehem Steel; television scriptwriter; worked briefly in advertising agency, Los Angeles, California; technical writer, Douglas Aircraft, 1959-60, and North American Aviation, 1960-66; manager, Litton Industries, 1966-67, and ITT Gilfillan, 1967-68; freelance technical writer and author of fiction from 1969. **Awards:** Academy of Science Fiction, Fantasy and Horror Films Saturn award, 1981, 1988.

HORROR, GHOST AND GOTHIC PUBLICATIONS

Novels (series: Howling)

The Howling. New York, Gold Medal, 1977; London, Hamlyn, 1978.
The Howling II. New York, Gold Medal, 1978; as *Return of the Howling*, London, Hamlyn, 1979.
Walkers. New York, Gold Medal, 1980; as *Death Walkers*, London, Hamlyn, 1980.
Hellborn. New York, Gold Medal, 1981; London, Hamlyn, 1981.
Cat People (novelization of screenplay). New York, Gold Medal, and London, Sphere, 1982.
Quintana Roo. New York, Gold Medal, 1984; as *Tribe of the Dead.* London, Hamlyn, 1984.
The Brain Eaters. New York, Gold Medal, and London, Hamlyn, 1985.
The Howling III. New York, Gold Medal, 1985; as *The Howling III: Echoes*, London, Hamlyn, 1985.
Carrion. New York, Gold Medal, 1986; London, Severn House, 1991.
Cameron's Closet. New York, Gold Medal, 1987; as *Cameron's Terror*, London, Severn House, 1988.
Floater. New York, Gold Medal, 1988.
Doomstalker. New York, Gold Medal, 1989; London, Severn House, 1990.

Plays

Screenplays: *Howling II: Stirba—Werewolf Bitch*, with Robert Sarno, 1984; *Cameron's Closet*, 1989.

OTHER PUBLICATIONS

Novels

Saturday Night in Milwaukee. New York, Curtis, 1973.
The Death's Head Conspiracy, with Robert Colby (as Nick Carter). New York, Award, 1973.
Wesley Sheridan (as Clayton Moore). New York, Berkley, 1974; London, Star, 1976.
The Aardvaark Affair. New York, Zebra, 1975; London, New English Library, 1976; as *The Big Brain*, London, Severn House, 1991.
The Players. New York, Pyramid, 1975; London, Hamlyn, 1979.
The Beelzebub Business. New York, Zebra, 1975; London, New English Library, 1976.
London. New York, Pocket, 1976.
Billy Lives! New York, Manor, 1976.
Offshore. Los Angeles, Pinnacle, 1978; London, Hamlyn, 1982.
The Sterling Standard. New York, Popular Library, 1980.
A Rage in Paradise. New York, Playboy, 1981.
The Express Riders (as Lee Davis Willoughby). New York, Dell, 1982.

Fiction for Children

The Good Luck Smiling Cat (as Phil Garrison). Belmont, California, Pitman, 1984.
The Disappearing Man (as Phil Garrison). Belmont, California, Pitman, 1984.
Dressed Up for Murder. Belmont, California, Pitman, 1986.
The Wet Goodbye. Belmont, California, Lake, 1986.
The Experiment. Belmont, California, Lake, 1987.
Mind Grabber. Belmont, California, Lake, 1987.

Other

Vitamin E: Key to Sexual Satisfaction. Los Angeles, Nash, 1971.
Living Off the Land. Los Angeles, Nash, 1971.
Off the Beaten Track in London. Los Angeles, Nash, 1972.

Editor (anonymously), *Illusions.* Belmont, California, Lake, 1988.
Editor (anonymously), *Claws & Feathers.* Belmont, California, Lake, 1989.

*

Film Adaptations: *The Howling*, 1981; *Howling IV: The Original Nightmare*, 1988, from his novel *The Howling*; *From the Dead of Night* (TV mini-series), 1989, from his novel *Walkers*; *Cameron's Closet*, 1989.

Bibliography: *The Work of Gary Brandner* by Martine Wood, San Bernardino, California, Borgo Press, 1995.

*   *   *

One of the more prolific horror writers, Gary Brandner is best known for his werewolf story, *The Howling*, and the series of at least six cheap films that derived from it. Although the original novel and its two sequels (the latter of which are not the inspiration for the several cinematic sequels, although ironically the movie *Howling IV* was based on Brandner's original novel in the series, the plot of which had been largely abandoned in the first film) represent some of Brandner's best work, it is unfortunate that he has become so identified with that theme that the best of his other horror fiction is largely ignored.

Brandner's first flirtation with horror was in his offbeat espionage series featuring a hero known as the Big Brain. In *The Beelzebub Business* Colin Garrett's extraordinary mental powers lead him to investigate an exclusive political club where he discovers that a charismatic and mentally gifted villain is using the pretence of satanism to recruit traitors into his spy network. The device of superimposing a supernatural motif on a mundane contemporary setting seemed to please Brandner, who then produced *The Howling*.

Even with the flood of horror fiction that has been published in the last two decades, there are very few novels of lycanthropy that stand out. *The Howling* is one of these, partly because Brandner constructed a tight, suspenseful plot, partly because he hit upon a novel idea. There's a colony of werewolves living right within human society, led by a prominent scientist whose influence helps protect their idiosyncratic lifestyles. A tough-minded reporter discovers the truth, but only after her husband has been seduced and infected with lycanthropy. Although the colony is destroyed, some of its members survive.

Brandner's two sequels bear little relationship to the string of movies that followed. *The Howling II* follows two of the adult survivors of the destruction of the werewolf colony as they seek revenge against those who destroyed their fellow shapechangers, particularly the protagonist of the first novel. *The Howling III* deals with a lycanthropic child who may still have the choice of remaining ostensibly human, or letting the lycanthropic abilities emerge. Both of these are suspenseful novels in their own right, though neither matches the impact of the first volume. Brandner's skill and reputation for novels of lycanthropy probably explain his selection as novelizer for the remake of the classic *Cat People*, a moody atmospheric piece which was not really suited for Brandner's writing style.

Walkers is less original but still disturbing. Joana is clinically dead but recalled to life, and tries to return to her home and friends. Unfortunately, there are those among the dead who resent her escape, and they manifest themselves in the real world to hunt her down. Unlike most stories with this theme, the protagonist triumphs. There's more mystery than horror in *Hellborn*. Although there's a demon from hell as chief villain, the plot involves more speculation about which of the human characters hosts the intruder than any genuine supernatural manifestations. It is not one of the author's more suspenseful, or successful works. Brandner investigates another common horror theme in *Quintana Roo*, which is much more of an adventure novel than his other work. An expedition to the Yucatan runs into unexpected trouble when they discover that the local inhabitants practice a form of zombification, and resent the presence of outsiders.

The Brain Eaters is science fiction as well as horror. The title refers to a form of parasite which lodges in the human brain and alters emotional responses, turning its hosts into berserk maniacs. At first the violent incidents are scattered, but as the parasites multiply a pattern emerges as the contagion spreads throughout the world. Eventually the U.S. and the Soviet Union team up to find an antidote, although Brandner leaves us with hints that it may not have been totally effective. *Carrion* is a modern twist on the zombie story, and one of Brandner's most successful works. A fake magician discovers that he possesses a genuine supernatural talent. To provide an air of authenticity to his act, he briefly studies genuine voodoo rituals. Subsequently, during a supposedly staged effort to raise the dead, he actually succeeds. Unfortunately, he lacks the knowledge or ability to control those he has brought back and his resurrectees are soon rotting, soulless but animate hulks. Even worse, they possess an insensate rage against the living, particularly the person who disturbed their death sleep.

Another notable book is *Cameron's Closet*. Cameron is a young boy with that familiar dread of a creature that lurks secretly in his closet, emerging only when the adults are gone. His belief is buttressed by his father's insistence that the human mind encompasses the power to alter reality. Efforts to convince him otherwise fail, particularly after his fear becomes so great that it literally gives birth to a murderous creature. Cameron overcomes his own fears and harnesses his mental abilities to banish the creature in a chilling climax. Less successful is *Floater*. A cruel prank by a group of children results in the death of one of their number, but their victim's mind continues to exist on the astral plane. Twenty years later, the disembodied spirit decides to take revenge on his old enemies in a standard hack-and-slash horror plot. Similarly, *Doomstalker* follows a predictable course of mayhem as a police officer discovers that the demonic creature that killed his father has returned and is stalking and slaughtering his friends one by one.

Brandner also wrote several short stories of merit, of which the best are "Julian's Hand," "Mark of a Loser," "Old Blood," "The Price of the Demon," and "To Have and To Hold." Perhaps as a consequence of the uncertain state of the horror market, he has been absent from the field for the past several years.

—Don D'Ammassa

BRENCHLEY, Chaz

Pseudonym: Carol Trent; Daniel Fox. **Nationality:** British. **Born:** Oxford, 1959. **Education:** St. Andrews University, Scotland. **Address:** c/o Hodder Headline, 338 Euston Road, London NW1 3BH, England. Lives in Newcastle upon Tyne.

HORROR, GHOST AND GOTHIC PUBLICATIONS

Novels

The Samaritan. London, Hodder and Stoughton, and New York, St. Martin's Press, 1988.
The Refuge. London, Hodder and Stoughton, and New York, St. Martin's Press, 1989.
The Garden. London, Hodder and Stoughton, 1990.
Mall Time. London, Hodder and Stoughton, 1991.
Paradise. London, Hodder and Stoughton, 1994.
Dead of Light. London, Hodder and Stoughton, 1995.
Dispossession. London, Hodder and Stoughton, 1996.
Light Errant. London, Hodder and Stoughton, 1997.

OTHER PUBLICATIONS

Novels

Time Again (as Carol Trent). London, Fontana, 1983.
The Thunder Sings (for children). Leeds, Arnold Wheaton, 1988.
The Fishing Stone (for children). Leeds, Arnold Wheaton, 1988.
The Dragon in the Ice (for children). Leeds, Arnold Wheaton, 1988.

Short Stories

Blood Waters. Newcastle upon Tyne, Flambard, 1996.

*   *   *

Along with Derek Raymond, Jack Curtis, David Bowker and others, Chaz Brenchley mingles horror fiction with crime fiction. All of Brenchley's horror novels involve crime elements (mostly serial killers) and only the two most recent include the supernatural. His horror short stories have mostly appeared under the pseudonym Daniel Fox; his many stories in crime and other genres are generally under the Chaz Brenchley name. He is highly regarded for his grittily realistic present-day novels, each featuring a few carefully planned peaks of horror. Brenchley is a fine writer who deserves to be more widely known.

The most outstanding of his novels are *The Garden* and *Dispossession*, both set in a lightly fictionalized Newcastle upon Tyne. In *The Garden* he invents an organization, the Sherpas, which is a self-help group for people who have had a close relative murdered—and there have been several unsolved murders in the area. Under the aegis of this, Steph Anderson (a widow in her early 20s) begins visiting Alice Armstrong, an elderly spinster whose twin brother Edward has been murdered. Since retirement, Alice and Edward had lived together in an isolated house on the moors. Now Alice has been joined by Brian, her nephew, a simpleton in his 40s. Steph helps mainly by working to restore Alice's garden. The other protagonist, besides Steph, is Laurie Powell, a young executive with a video-making firm. The only connection between Steph and Laurie is that Brian is given a part-time job with the firm.

When Laurie's gay lover is found murdered, with a machete, like some of the other victims, Laurie is initially suspected of this, and of a similar murder which occurs soon after in the premises beneath the firm. There are many twists in this engrossing and ingenious tale. The horror is both physical (several nasty scenes) and psychological. Gay and straight relationships are very sensitively handled. The atmosphere of dread and despair is cleverly sustained via winter weather, the bleak moors (and even bleaker streets of Newcastle), and the mental states of people whose loved ones have become murder victims. Here, as in all his novels, there is no happy ending.

Dispossession has young lawyer Jonty Marks waking up after a serious car crash to find that not only does he have three months' memories missing, but during that period he seems to have broken all the habits of his brief lifetime. He has left his long-term partner and suddenly got married to somebody else whom he does not know (she is Chinese); he is freelancing for the area's most powerful crooked businessman instead of working for a legal firm; his clothes, make of car and personal habits have nearly all altered. Information which might answer the questions is on a floppy disc which he cannot access because he cannot remember the password. And somebody seems to be trying to kill him.

All this, told in the first person and developing at a fast pace, would be enough to make an entertaining thriller. But to this admittedly clichéd mix Brenchley has added a wild card: a fallen angel. Luke resembles a handsome young man, but he has not changed in ten years. He does not actually possess a pair of wings, though he can fly; he just hates to do so. He has superhuman strength (and deals very unpleasantly with several people who deserve it and one who does not). In fact, Luke can never be relied upon to behave in a human manner; he remains a frightening and enigmatic character, helping occasionally as Jonty tries to sort out his life.

Brenchley's own favourite amongst his novels is *Paradise*, set in a fictional Newcastle suburb of that name. The subject matter is partly religious, a gospel church taken over by a charismatic new preacher who may sometimes be able to work miracles (through the power of God). He creates much religious fervour and attracts many converts, though this causes its own problems when the Christ Commando is formed—a uniformed example of muscular Christianity at its worst. And when they come into conflict with local land developers and hoodlums, it is difficult to know who is good and who is evil; atrocities are committed by all sides. There is an enormous cast of characters, too many dealt with too shallowly despite the thickness of the book. However, two stand out: Rachel, who is half of the teenage love interest, and Vinnie, who breeds pit-bull terriers and specializes in injuring people. This is an entertaining and well-sustained novel, perhaps a little light on horror.

Without doubt, *Dead of Light* is Brenchley's cleverest book, at least in terms of style and wit. It tells the story of a family with varying supernormal powers. The Macallans run the city where they live (another fictionalized Newcastle) but there are quarrels within the family and somebody is trying to exterminate them: members die in a great variety of gruesome ways. The narrator, Ben, believes that he has little of the family power, and he tries to live a normal life outside the family; but he is wrong in his belief and he finds that the family needs him. Many of the chapter titles are excellent puns, such as "L'après-midi d'un Anglophone" and "Fissures of Men." A sequel, *Light Errant*, will be published late in 1997.

The other three novels are workmanlike though less original, written to please publishers or average horror readers rather than having anything different to say. *The Samaritan* describes the exploits of a man who counsels lonely and desperate people, arranges to meet them, then kills them very unpleasantly. In *The Refuge* homeless teenagers are offered a secret and safe house to stay in, in a London suburb, but journalistic exposés, aborted drug deals and the actions of a serial killer who needs to protect himself by killing a witness all conspire to upset the smooth running of the house. *Mall Time* describes the havoc caused by one well-armed madman in a large shopping mall. All three books are, to a certain extent, weakened by the participation of too many characters, most rather shallowly developed, though Brenchley has a knack for putting across teenagers.

Brenchley writes powerful and quirky short stories. Although *Blood Waters* is published as a crime collection it contains much physical and psychological horror, including the sharp and memorable novelette "My Cousin's Gratitude." The stories as by Daniel Fox, among them "High-Flying, Adored" in *Dark Voices 4* (1992) and "How She Dances" in *Dark Voices 5* (1993), are all clever and unusual, mostly with impressive subtexts.

—Chris Morgan

BRENNAN, Joseph Payne

Nationality: American. **Born:** Bridgeport, Connecticut, 20 December 1918. **Military Service:** U.S. Army, 1943-45. **Family:** Married Doris Philbrick in 1970. **Career:** Technical services specialist, Yale University Library, from 1941 to retirement; poet and short-story writer; editor and publisher, the poetry journal *Essence*, and the small-press *Macabre* magazine, 1957-76, and Macabre House publishing imprint. **Awards:** Poetry Society of America Leonora Speyer Memorial award for poetry. **Died:** 1990.

HORROR, GHOST AND GOTHIC PUBLICATIONS

Novel

Act of Providence, with Donald Grant. West Kingston, Rhode Island, Grant, 1979.
Evil Always Ends. West Kingston, Rhode Island, Grant, 1982.

Short Stories (series: Lucius Leffing)

Nine Horrors and a Dream. Sauk City, Wisconsin, Arkham House, 1958.
The Dark Returners. New Haven, Connecticut, Macabre House, 1959.
Scream at Midnight. New Haven, Connecticut, Macabre House, 1963.
The Casebook of Lucius Leffing. New Haven, Connecticut, Macabre House, 1973.
Stories of Darkness and Dread. Sauk City, Wisconsin, Arkham House, 1973.
The Chronicles of Lucius Leffing. West Kingston, Rhode Island, Grant, 1977.
The Shapes of Midnight. New York, Berkley, 1980.
The Borders Just Beyond. West Kingston, Rhode Island, Grant, 1986.
The Adventures of Lucius Leffing. Hampton Falls, New Hampshire, Grant, 1990.

Poetry

Hearts of Earth. N.p., 1950.
The Humming Stair. N.p., 1953.
The Wind of Time. N.p., 1961.
Nightmare Need. Sauk City, Wisconsin, Arkham House, 1964.
Death Poems. N.p., 1974.
Edges of Night. N.p., 1974.
An Evening Advances. N.p., 1978.
Webs of Time. N.p., 1979.
Creep to Death. West Kingston, Rhode Island, Grant, 1981.
Sixty Selected Poems. Amherst, New York, New Establishment Press, 1985.
Look Back on Laurel Hills. Minneapolis, Minnesota, Jwindz, 1989.

Other

A Select Bibliography of H. P. Lovecraft. N.p., 1952; expanded as *H. P. Lovecraft: A Bibliography*, Washington, Biblio Press, 1952.
H. P. Lovecraft: An Evaluation. New Haven, Connecticut, Macabre House, 1955.

* * *

Joseph Payne Brennan is unusual among modern horror writers for having built a distinguished reputation from mostly noncommercial work. His first four horror stories appeared in *Weird Tales* between 1952 and 1953, only months before the magazine's demise deprived him of a professional market for any further such fiction. While many of his colleagues jumped ship to the flourishing crime and science-fiction magazines, or sublimated their taste for horror in mainstream fiction with a dark edge, Brennan took the opposite tack, creating the small-press magazine *Macabre* and book imprint Macabre House to publish most of the horror fiction he wrote in 1950s and 1960s. Working for the small press gave Brennan the freedom to write whatever he chose, but also appears to have limited the scale of his efforts. Until the horror revival of the 1970s provided him with more publishing outlets, very few of his stories ran to more than several thousand words in length. Brennan's name quickly became associated with stories built around a single idea and developed in the minimum number of words necessary to create a horrific effect.

Brennan's *Weird Tales* stories are representative of all his horror writing, which evolved little over the course of his career. They are simple tales of average human beings confronting the supernatural. "Slime," although his best known work, is in some ways his least characteristic: it features a formidable supernatural menace—a hulking ball of ocean slime that clearly inspired "The Blob" of film fame—which rampages through a seaside town for 10,000 words. Most of Brennan's other horror tales are subtler and shorter. "Slime," however, shows Brennan at the top of his form, building a powerful sense of the uncanny through shifts in the viewpoint between the mindless monster and the horrified human beings unfortunate enough to cross its path. His description of the monster's sensory impressions crudely draws attention to his talents as a poet. Brennan had begun publishing poetry as far back as 1940, and his volumes *Nightmare Need* and *Creep to Death* rank as high watermarks of modern macabre verse. His more atmospheric stories are laced with poetic images and several read like narrative expansions of poetic moments, among them the sublime "Mr. Octbur," a prose poem of delicate beauty all the more remarkable for the simplicity of its language.

In contrast to the terrors of the Unknown evoked in "Slime," two of Brennan's other *Weird Tales* stories, "The Green Parrot" and "The Calamander Chest," are simple ghost stories. In the former, a good samaritan assists an elderly woman in a fruitless search for an escaped house pet and finds out later that she is the ghost of a woman who died during a similar search years before. In the latter, a man falls under the influence of a haunted talisman and dies the same way its previous owner did. Both stories elaborate a theme that unites much of Brennan's weird fiction, the unnatural survival of the past into the present. Sometimes, as in "Black Thing at Midnight" and "On the Elevator," Brennan's representations of the past are malignant and inimical to the existence of those living in the present. In most of his stories, though, he portrays the past as an endlessly repeating cycle that occasionally overlaps the present and overtakes the incautious. Brennan's masterpiece in this vein is "Canavan's Back Yard," first published in his debut collection *Nine Horrors and a Dream*, about a man who discovers that his distorted perception of his backyard stretching off endlessly into the distance is literally a glimpse into the past, and an event that has left the land eternally cursed.

Brennan's fondness for using the past as a vehicle for supernatural horror was rooted in his genuine nostalgia for New England history. Many of his tales are set in his native New Haven, Connecticut, a town that inspired him in much the same way that Providence, Rhode Island, inspired H. P. Lovecraft (an early and important influence on Brennan's writing). Brennan's characters are frequently mouthpieces for his anger at the soulless modernization of New Haven and several of his most provocative dark fantasies draw their power from his strong emotions for the town's quaint past. "The House on Hazel Street" features an elderly gentleman whose memories of the town's better days permit time travel into the past. In "The House at 1248" and "Episode on Cain Street," New Havens of the past and present are fatal to those who attempt to cross from one to the other. The title character of "Mr. Octbur" is a magical personification of old New Haven who is hopelessly lost in the present, while "In the Very Stones" crystallizes the dismembering of the town's past in images of ghostly body parts glimpsed in the older neighbourhoods. In "The Peril That Lurks Among the Ruins," a demon lures the narrator with a soothing vision of the town as he remembers it from his childhood.

Nearly all of Brennan's stories are set in rural towns where the supernatural erupts through the fabric of daily life. Juniper Hill, the setting for more than a half dozen of his weird tales, is host to a variety of horrors, including a self-confessed lycanthrope in "The Diary of a Werewolf," a satanic wager in "The Mail for Juniper Hill," and a Lovecraftian monstrosity in "The Willow Platform." The prevalence of so many bizarre episodes in "an isolated Connecticut village with scarcely fifty inhabitants" might make Juniper Hill seem a sister city to Lovecraft's monster-infested Arkham, but Brennan's town is more the prototype for Charles L. Grant's Oxrun Station, Stephen King's Castle Rock, and other milieus of modern dark fantasy where horror evolves from anxieties and tensions of small-town life. Brennan makes it clear, for example, in "The Corpse of Charlie Rull," that the "viciousness and hatred" of a reanimated corpse that terrorizes Juniper Hill are due to a catalysis of toxic chemicals with "the negative emotions which had smouldered throughout a lifetime of frustration and bitterness." Even when not particularly sympathetic, Brennan's characters earn reader identification. Who has read his gem "Levitation" and not felt horror for the man doomed to ascend through space eternally following a botched carnival trick?

Although his forte was the tale of rural horrors, Brennan tried his hand at all types of fantasy writing: Cthulhu Mythos fiction in "Forringer's Fortune" and "The Feaster from Afar," science fiction in "The Dump" and "Vampires from the Void," even sword-and-sorcery in "Queen of the Dead" and "Oasis of Abomination." Some of his best horror tales are non-supernatural suspense stories, including "The Pavilion" and "The Disappearance," both of which dress basic crime scenarios with the trappings of horror fiction. His three dozen adventures of Lucius Leffing, a Sherlockian detective in modern times, span the length of his career and are an interesting footnote to his horror writing. Leffing began life as a psychic detective, but after his third escapade Brennan felt compelled to minimize the supernatural content of the stories to ensure their acceptance in the mystery/detective magazines. With the revival of the horror market in the 1980s, Leffing turned ghostbuster once again—a career move that mirrors Brennan's own resurrection in the horror mainstream following his years of self-exile in the small press.

—Stefan R. Dziemianowicz

BRENNERT, Alan

Pseudonym: Michael Bryant. **Nationality:** American. **Born:** Englewood, New Jersey, 30 May 1954. **Education:** William Paterson State College, 1972-73; California State University, Long Beach, B.A. 1978; graduate student, University of California, Los Angeles, 1977-78. **Family:** Married Paulette Klaus in 1996. **Career:** Story editor, *Buck Rogers in the Twenty-Fifth Century,* 1979-80; executive story consultant, *Twilight Zone,* 1985-87; producer, *L.A. Law,* 1991-92; freelance writer, from 1978. **Awards:** Nebula Award for short story, 1991; second place, Theodore Sturgeon Memorial award for short story, 1991; Emmy award, producer, for drama series, 1991; People's Choice award, producer, for drama series, 1992. **Agent:** Howard Morhaim Literary Agency, 175 Fifth Avenue, Suite 709, New York, NY 10010, USA.

HORROR, GHOST AND GOTHIC PUBLICATIONS

Novels

City of Masques. Chicago, Playboy Press, 1978.
Kindred Spirits. New York, Tor, 1984.
Time and Chance. New York, Tor, 1990.

Short Stories

Her Pilgrim Soul, and Other Stories. New York, Tor, 1990.
Ma Qui, and Other Phantoms. Eugene, Oregon, Pulphouse, 1991.

Plays

Weird Romance: Two One-Act Musicals of Speculative Fiction, with David Spenser. New York, Samuel French, 1993.

Television Plays: episodes of *Darkroom,* 1983; *The Twilight Zone,* 1985-87 ("Her Pilgrim Soul," "A Message from Charity," "Wong's Lost and Found Emporium," "The Star," "Shatterday," "Healer" [as Michael Bryant], "One Life, Furnished in Early Poverty," "Quarantine," with Philip DeGuere and Steven Bochco, "I of Newton," "Dead Run," "A Small Talent for War," with Carter Scholz, "Voices in the Earth," "Time and Teresa Golowitz," "The Cold Equations"); *The Outer Limits,* 1995-97 ("The Second Soul," "Dark Matters," "The Refuge," "Falling Star" [as Michael Bryant], "Heart's Desire").

Other

Editor (anonymously), with Martin H. Greenberg, *New Stories from the Twilight Zone.* New York, Avon, 1991; as *The New Twilight Zone: 21 Tales by the Greatest Sci-Fi and Dark Fantasy Writers of Our Time,* New York, MJF Books, 1996.

OTHER PUBLICATIONS

Graphic Novels

"To Kill a Legend." *Detective Comics,* no. 500 (March, 1981).
"Paperchase." *Brave and the Bold,* no. 178 (September, 1981).

"Time, See What's Become of Me . . ." *Brave and the Bold,* no. 181 (December, 1981).
"Interlude on Earth-Two." *Brave and the Bold,* no. 182 (January, 1982).
"Promises." *Daredevil,* no. 192 (March, 1983).
"The Autobiography of Bruce Wayne." *Brave and the Bold,* no. 197 (April, 1983).
"Should Auld Acquaintance Be Forgot." *Christmas with the Superheroes,* no. 2 (1989).
"Unfinished Business." *Secret Origins,* no. 50 (August, 1990).
Batman: Holy Terror, illustrated by Norm Breyfogle. New York, Warner, 1991.

Plays

Television Plays: episodes of *The New Adventures of Wonder Woman,* 1977-79; *Buck Rogers in the Twenty-Fifth Century,* 1979-80; *L.A. Law; China Beach; Simon & Simon; The Mississippi.*

*

Critical Study: "Spotlight: Alan Brennert" by John Peel, in *Into the Twilight Zone: The Rod Serling Programme Guide* by Jean-Marc and Randy Lofficier, London, Virgin, 1995.

*   *   *

Alan Brennert believes in ghosts. Not literally, perhaps, but he recognizes that most people's lives are perpetually haunted by images of "phantoms": the people we've lost touch with, the people we've never met, the people we no longer are, the people we may or may not become. And while conveying this philosophy in fiction logically leads Brennert to forms of the ghost story, the results are rarely horrific, for his spirits are usually benign, ready to help characters better understand themselves and possibly gain a second chance in life.

These concerns surface only fitfully in Brennert's first and weakest novel, *City of Masques,* where unscrupulous film producer Patricia Dalmatton employs a science-fictional brainwashing technique to transform actors into physical and mental duplicates of the celebrities they are portraying on screen, like James Dean, John Kennedy and Charles Manson. While the plot generally unfolds with predictably horrifying consequences, as some people lose the ability to distinguish between their real and fictional selves—a man who adopts the Superman persona leaps off a building to his death, the Manson figure becomes a crazed cult-leader himself—Brennert refreshingly refuses to make his novel a parable about the importance of Being True to One's Self; instead, he suggests that a strong psychic identification with iconic popular figures may sometimes be beneficial, a way to help people recognize their real personalities. Thus, protagonist Marnie is ultimately strengthened by her brief sojourn in Dalmatton's aggressive personality.

After focusing on television (which remains his principal occupation), Brennert returned to the novel with *Kindred Spirits,* about a lonely man and woman who both attempt suicide on Christmas. While their bodies lie comatose at the same hospital, their spirits meet, become friends and lovers, and teach each other how to relate to other people and to enjoy life again. Returning to their bodies, they awaken and develop satisfying relationships with other partners, only vaguely recalling their ghostly existence.

Though the novel is not without cloying moments, especially in the opening chapters chronicling the characters' cloistered, miserable lives, Michael and Ginny soon transcend self-pity to emerge as convincing characters, and their final happiness seems fully earned.

Brennert's masterpiece, however, is surely *Time and Chance*, about an aspiring actor who faced a painful decision: to stay in his home town and marry his pregnant girlfriend, or abandon her to go to New York and pursue his ambitions. In one world, Rick Cochrane stayed behind to become a husband, father, and insurance worker; in another world, Richard Cochrane became a moderately successful, though lonely, stage and television actor. When they somehow cross paths, they agree to exchange worlds and lives, Rick gaining an acting career, Richard gaining a family. After adjusting to their new lives, they meet again and realize they must return to their old worlds; but each contrives to re-adjust his life to accommodate his unfulfilled desires: Rick quits his job to act in a repertory company, Richard plans to reconcile with an ex-lover. Impressive because Brennert so persuasively portrays both theatre life and small-town life, the novel also intriguingly resists easy interpretation. Though its structure of alternating chapters suggests a neat parallelism—each man has something and lacks something, but manages to keep what he has while gaining a semblance of what he lacked—the beginnings and endings of the men's lives are hardly similar: before the meeting, Rick's life was falling apart due to simmering rage and frustration, while Richard was only mildly unhappy; and Rick entirely changes his life, while Richard only *might* change his life. This suggests that *Time and Chance* is really Rick's story, Richard being a friendly doppelganger who validates Rick's initial focus on family and shows him how to accommodate his ambitions; yet Richard's fame, wealth and glamorous lifestyle seemingly make him the focus of attention and the more attractive character. The novel thus may function as a Rorschach test revealing its readers' priorities in their own life-choices: some will see Rick's domestic bliss as the better alternative; others will prefer Richard's conspicuous success.

Brennert may be better known for his short stories, though the award-winning "Ma Qui" is oddly not one of his best, a conventional cautionary tale about dead American soldiers trapped in the grim afterlives of Vietnamese superstition. More innovative is "Her Pilgrim Soul," based on his remarkable *Twilight Zone* script about a physicist whose laboratory hologram is visited by a baby ghost who rapidly grows up before his eyes to become a valued companion; she finally reveals that she was his wife in a previous lifetime, who died prematurely, and that she returned to live her life with him again to provide what he missed and eliminate his unresolved anger. Other noteworthy stories include two haunting visions of Earth's far future: "Ghost Story" (*Ma Qui*), where the degenerate dregs of humanity uncomprehendingly observe holographic images of the people who long ago abandoned Earth, and "Voices in the Earth" (*Her Pilgrim Soul*, also based on a *Twilight Zone* script), where workers about to demolish the dead planet Earth confront their ancestors' ghosts, who do not wish to lose their home. Other stories involve figures from myths and legends: "Sea Change" (*Her Pilgrim Soul*), where a modern man encounters a Siren, immortal and still enchanting listeners with her voice; "Cradle" (*Magazine of Fantasy and Science Fiction*, January 1995), describing a female vampire's efforts to have a child; and "The Man Who Loved the Sea" (*Fantasy and Science Fiction*, September 1995), about a man who experiences a strange romance with a water spirit.

"Echoes" (*Fantasy and Science Fiction*, May 1997), perhaps his best story, describes a young girl suddenly afflicted with vivid images of all the people she might have been or might become; eventually, she adjusts to their presence, realizes she must make her own choices in life, and breaks away from parental influence to follow her own path. This poignant story about recognizing, reconciling with, and learning from the phantoms that surround a person brilliantly epitomizes the characteristic concerns of Brennert's fiction.

A different side of Brennert's character appears in his graphic novel *Holy Terror*. Granted the freedom to envision an entirely different universe for Batman, Brennert places the masked avenger in a dystopian America ruled by religious zealots which systematically imprisons and tortures its nascent superheroes like Superman, Flash, and Aquaman—a grim scenario that recalls the embittered, revisionist Superman of his story "Steel" (*Her Pilgrim Soul*). How strange it is that a man who offers such reassuring and gentle spirits in his adult fiction should craft such chambers of horrors for his childhood heroes.

—Gary Westfahl

BRITE, Poppy Z.

Nationality: American. **Born:** New Orleans, 1967. **Education:** Attended the University of North Carolina, Chapel Hill. **Family:** Lives with two partners in New Orleans. **Career:** Various short-term jobs, including artist's model and exotic dancer; contributor of short stories to *Horror Show* magazine and elsewhere from 1985; freelance novelist from 1991; has appeared in an erotic underground film, *John Five*, 1992. **Agent:** Richard Curtis Associates, 171 East 74th Street, New York, NY 10021, USA.

HORROR, GHOST AND GOTHIC PUBLICATIONS

Novels

Lost Souls. New York, Delacorte, 1992; London, Penguin, 1994.
Drawing Blood. New York, Delacorte, 1993; London, Penguin, 1994.
Exquisite Corpse. London, Orion, and New York, Simon and Schuster, 1996.

Short Stories

Swamp Foetus. Baltimore, Maryland, Borderlands, 1993; London, Penguin, 1995.

Other

Editor, with Martin H. Greenberg. *Love in Vein: Twenty Original Tales of Vampire Erotica.* New York, HarperPrism, 1994; London, Voyager, 1995.
Editor, with Martin H. Greenberg. *Love in Vein II.* New York, HarperPrism, 1996.

*   *   *

Every *fin de siècle* brings forth writers whose self-appointed mission is to celebrate the decadence of the dying century by testing the boundaries of expression and toleration. The fascination with cruelty and monstrousness incarnate in precedents laid down by the Marquis de Sade at the end of the 18th century has been recapitulated and reexamined as each subsequent century has drawn to its close. If extremism in devotion to this cause may be taken as a warrant of literary significance, then Poppy Z. Brite is one of the central figures of the 20th century's *fin de siècle*. Her horror fiction attempts to test limits that have never been tested before, despite the difficulty of discovering any such limits in an era when literary censorship is dead and buried.

As is typical of *fin de siècle* chroniclers, Brite likes to strike outrageous poses; her closest analogue a century ago would have been the Parisian "Amazon" Rachilde, dubbed "Madame Salamandre" by her friend and fellow poseur Jean Lorrain. Brite has posed for publicity photographs naked above the waist save for a strategically-placed ferret, and she delights in describing herself as a homosexual male whose "present incarnation" happens to be in a female body. Her first novel, *Lost Souls*, is set within the relentlessly morbid subculture of American "Goths": a lifestyle fantasy to which the author was for a while committed.

Lost Souls encapsulates the typical neo-Gothic fascination with music that combines maudlin lyrics with a driving rock beat, providing a respectful account of the eponymous band and its visionary lyricist Ghost. The plot of the novel, inevitably, is a detailed account of the particular existentialist angst associated with vampiric undeath—an obsession which the Goth subculture embraced wholeheartedly when it appointed Anne Rice as its primary literary voice. Rice's languorously erotic accounts of the centuries-long career of the vampire Lestat already display a conscientiously Decadent Romanticism, but Brite's novel casually shears away every last vestige of Romantic sentiment in order to isolate and extrapolate the nihilistic and sado-masochistic elements of the Decadent sensibility. She gives these elements sharp expression in the kind of vividly lyrical passages which can only be occasional, cushioned by a more restrained but still faintly luxurious narrative as if they were gems set on a velvet cloth.

Drawing Blood moves away from the explicit supernaturalism of *Lost Souls*, its horrific materials being based in the paranoid intimacy of madness and hallucination. The son of a comic-book artist—the sole survivor of a night of terror in which his father murdered his mother and brother before committing suicide—returns to the scene of the crime in the hope of understanding what happened and why. This quest is continually sidelined by his involvement in a homosexual love affair—whose evolution is tracked in graphic detail—but its climax, which involves a dangerous journey into a nightmarish private dream-world, cannot be avoided. Again, the strength of the novel lies in its continual efflorescences of brittle and darkly luminous descriptive prose.

Exquisite Corpse eschews supernaturalism altogether, even in terms of hallucination. The insanity of its principal characters—an American serial killer loosely based on Jeffrey Dahmer and a British serial killer loosely based on Dennis Nilsen—is wholly conscious and deliberate. Both men have forged an unbreakable experiential link between sex and murder, and their eventual meeting is charged to an unprecedented degree with erotic desire and homicidal ambition. The fury of their combined energies inevitably threatens to overwhelm and extirpate the characters who serve as their "innocent" counterparts, whose victim status is as extremely exaggerated as their own predatory status. In spite of its ostensible naturalism this is easily the most bizarre of Brite's works, and by virtue of its ostensible naturalism it is perhaps the most disturbing. Its key passages are dressed with the same vivid lyricism as those of its predecessors, constituting a stylistic, if not a moral, glorification of the alleged ecstasies of murder and cannibalism. The novel's insistent linkage of homoerotic lust with extremes of violence and insanity might seem to interested readers to be a curiously repugnant, if not outrightly malign, expression of the author's admitted obsession with male homosexuality.

Brite's early short stories, collected in *Swamp Foetus*, include a number of tales linked to *Lost Souls*, some of them featuring the members of the band. "The Sixth Sentinel" makes the most effective use of the author's New Orleans background. "His Mouth Will Taste of Wormwood" is an exercise in literary Decadence so calculatedly archetypal that it would probably qualify as a parody were it not for the fact that Decadent prose is so artificial and so ornate as to leave no further room for satirical exaggeration. "Calcutta, Lord of Nerves" and "The Ash of Memory, the Dust of Desire" are far more subtle and far more powerful; they are Brite's best works and are among the outstanding horror stories of their period. The former displays remarkable descriptive flair in the depiction of its exotic location, and a brilliantly vivid imagination in equipping that scenario with a distinctive population of zombies; it undoubtedly owes a debt to Dan Simmons's *Song of Kali* but is even more striking than its model. "The Ash of Memory, the Dust of Desire" is a calm *conte cruel* which brings American urban desolation into sharp focus with devastating effect.

As the 20th century approaches its end it becomes increasingly difficult to find boundaries as yet unbreached and disgusting images as yet undisplayed. Nothing can now be deemed "unthinkable" and there is no taboo which has not been subject to literary transgression—and thus to a glut of hypothetical analysis. Perhaps there is a certain desperation in the lengths to which *Exquisite Corpse* goes in the hope of striking a horrific chord which has not been sounded before, but Brite's undeniable power as a writer is no mere reflection of her willingness to wallow in an ooze of nastiness that has barely been stirred by previous visitors. It is the remarkable clarity of her finest prose passages, rather than the calculated murkiness of her themes, that recommends her for special consideration. Her descriptions sometimes attain a breathtaking precision as well as a hectic gaudiness, combining brilliant colour and dark emotive effect in a way that few writers of horror fiction have ever been able to achieve.

—Brian Stableford

BRITTON, David

Nationality: British. **Born:** 1945. **Career:** Writer and bookshop proprietor; founder, with Michael Butterworth, Savoy Books and Savoy Records publishing companies, Manchester, England.

HORROR, GHOST AND GOTHIC PUBLICATIONS

Novels

Lord Horror. Manchester, Savoy, 1989.
Motherfuckers: The Auschwitz of Oz. Manchester, Savoy, 1996.

Graphic Novels

Lord Horror, illustrated by Kris Guidio. Manchester, Savoy, 2 parts, 1989.

Lord Horror: Hard Core Horror, illustrated by Kris Guidio. Manchester, Savoy, 5 parts, 1990.

Meng & Ecker, illustrated by Kris Guidio. Manchester, Savoy, 9 parts, 1989-95; new edition, with new material, as *The Adventures of Meng & Ecker*, Manchester, Savoy, 1997.

Reverbstorm, illustrated by John Coulthart. Manchester, Savoy, 4 parts, 1994-95.

OTHER PUBLICATIONS

Other

Editor, with Michael Butterworth, *The Savoy Book*. Manchester, Savoy, 1978.

Editor, with Michael Butterworth, *Savoy Dreams*. Manchester, Savoy, 1984.

*   *   *

It is rare nowadays for literary works to be deemed so objectionable as to warrant legal suppression, but David Britton—veteran of a long war waged against his bookshops by the Greater Manchester Police's Obscene Publications Squad—has proved to be an exception. Although a seizure order against the novel *Lord Horror* was eventually thrown out on appeal, very few copies survived to be returned to the author/publisher and the same appeal court ordered that copies of the comic *Meng & Ecker* seized at the same time were to be destroyed.

Lord Horror actually made his debut on a 12" single released by Savoy Records in 1986, where he featured as lead vocalist for the "The Savoy-Hitler Youth Band" on a stirring rendition of Bruce Springsteen's "Cadillac Ranch" superimposed on the backing-track of New Order's "Blue Monday" (his voice was supplied by P. J. Proby, who also "played" Lord Horror on a number of other single releases, although he was replaced by Bobby Thompson on a hectic version of Iggy Pop's "Raw Power.") The record's sleeve featured a caricature of James Anderton, then the chief constable of Greater Manchester, his head exploding amid a tattered halo of hateful obscenities; the lettering on the other side overlaid photographs taken during the liberation of Dachau. This illustration sufficed to get the record banned, and a new phase in the conflict between Britton and his *bête noire* was joined.

The novel version of *Lord Horror* is a complex work which includes among its many characters a chief constable named James Appleton, whose viciously anti-Semitic dialogue is derived by substituting the word "Jew" for the word "homosexual" (and various equivalent terms) in public pronouncements which had been made by Anderton.

The character of *Lord Horror* is remotely based on William Joyce, who broadcast German propaganda to the British people throughout World War II and was nicknamed "Lord Haw-Haw" by his listeners. Britton's Lord Horror proudly wears the glamour of Fascism, and exhibits the prejudices and aspirations fundamental to Nazism. The characterization is calculated to excite revulsion and the plot of the novel employs grotesque shock tactics to put such attitudes in the pillory. The imagery of the story borrows from comic-strip art and the philosophical *weltanschauung* of Schopenhauer, attempting through such odd juxtapositions to heighten the reader's sense of the awful absurdity of the polite veneer which hides the politics of genocide. Britton's Hitler—a quaintly pathetic figure whose inconvenient delusions of grandeur are symbolized by his incredibly expansive penis, Old Shatterhand—is not monstrous in himself, but the monstrousness of his career and its legacy are exhibited in no uncertain terms.

The first *Lord Horror* comic is a slapstick patchwork, as is the first issue of its companion, *Meng & Ecker*, which features the adventures of two minor characters from the novel, Lord Horror's "creep boys." Subsequent issues of *Meng & Ecker* followed the same unrepentantly gross formula as the first, but Lord Horror was diverted to present the five-part graphic novel *Hard Core Horror*, subtitled "The Romance of Lord Horror and Jessie Matthews." (Jessie Matthews was a singer and actress who became the principal British musical star of the 1930s.) This parodic tale of absurdly star-crossed lovers is played out against the background of Oswald Mosley's Fascist Movement and the outbreak of World War II, with some interpolated commentary by Horror's "brother," James Joyce. The vivid graphics by Kris Guidio reach their climax in an extraordinary rendition of the imagery of the holocaust.

The various Lord Horror recordings were eventually rereleased as a CD album called *Savoy Wars*. These included the CD single *Reverbstorm*, whose title was also applied to an as-yet-incomplete graphic novel starring Lord Horror, this time phantasmagorically illustrated by John Coulthart. The text supplied by Britton to the earlier episodes was drawn from *Motherfuckers*, a more combative novel than *Lord Horror* which moves Meng and Ecker to centre-stage, presumably in response to the fact that the courts had continued to wage war on the *Meng & Ecker* comic while grudgingly liberating the novel. The spirit of the Holocaust is here incarnate in Dr. Mengele, who separated Siamese twins Meng and Ecker in the course of one of his experiments in Auschwitz. "Lord Horror," the text explains, "was Auschwitz made myth."

Neither *Lord Horror* nor *Motherfuckers* is pornographic in the sense that it could be employed for titillation, but they are seriously discomfiting works. Their humour is scabrous, but occasionally brilliant, and their grossness is flamboyant, but always repulsive. They refuse to treat the horrific as if it were something far removed from the everyday lives of living people, permanently relegated to the past or the less civilized parts of the world or the realms of fantasy. The narrative links which they forge between genocidal violence, the politics of hate and sanitized matinée idols, cute cartoon characters, academic philosophy, the streets of Manchester and domestic untidiness are intended to taunt readers with the allegation that the veneer of politeness which masks civil society is both thin and brittle.

The ad for *Motherfuckers* in *The Adventures of Meng & Ecker* boasts that it "stands four-square in a tradition which embraces de Sade, Lautréamont, Céline, Burroughs and Bataille" and claims as its English ancestors "the Gothic, Lewis Carroll, William Hope Hodgson, Jonathan Swift and J. G. Ballard." At least some of those writers would, indeed, recognize their influence on the book, and at least three might actually approve of the extension of their ideas (although the Marquis de Sade is one of those who probably would not). The extremism of their method makes the two novels remarkable, and their association with Lord Horror's other manifestations—which feature some excellent music and some astonishing artwork—assimilates them to a multi-media enterprise which is in perfect harmony with the contemporary *zeitgeist.* Even if the forces of law and order manage to prevent them from reaching a large audience today they, may one day be regarded as landmark works.

—Brian Stableford

BRODIE-INNES, J(ohn) W(illiam)

Nationality: British. **Born:** 1848. **Career:** Lawyer, turned to writing late in life; dabbled in occultism; friend of the horror novelist Bram Stoker (q.v). **Died:** 1923.

HORROR, GHOST AND GOTHIC PUBLICATIONS

Novels

Morag the Seal. London, Rebman, 1908.
Old as the World: A Romance of the Western Islands. London, Rebman, 1909.
For the Soul of a Witch: A Romance of Badenoch. London, Rebman, 1910.
The Devil's Mistress. London, Rider, 1915.

OTHER PUBLICATIONS

Novels

The Tragedy of an Indiscretion. London and New York, Lane, 1916.
The Golden Rope. London and New York, Lane, 1919.

*   *   *

J. W. Brodie-Innes was a Scottish lawyer who became fascinated with the unusually rich history of witch trials that his native country provided. He was sufficiently carried away by it to take an increasing interest in occult matters, and in later life he became peripherally involved with various occult societies, including the Order of the Golden Dawn and the Theosophical Society. The supernatural fiction he published in his sixties grew out of this involvement.

Credulity is often a disadvantage to the writer of supernatural fiction but Brodie-Innes retained sufficient detachment to use his fiction as a means of exploring possibilities rather than laying down dogmas. The hero of *Morag the Seal* is a solicitor whose investigation of the phenomena with which he is confronted when he undertakes a business trip to the Highlands is admirably rational. In this case the central folkloristic motif—the belief that certain women can transform themselves into seals—is "explained" by reference to psychic phenomena. Morag's real talent is the ability to induce strange dreams by means of telepathy—a possession which Brodie-Innes evidently thought more likely, but which many readers will probably find less interesting. *Old as the World* is a more orthodox work dealing with notions of reincarnation which had already been the subject of a tediously rich abundance of popular fiction. It is, however, enlivened by quasi-anthropologi-

cal speculations regarding the religion of the Druids and the possible persistence of Druid lore through the centuries.

The most interesting of Brodie-Innes's novels are the two which drew most copiously on his historical researches. Both were based on actual reported cases—the second, that of Isabel Gowdie, was one of the most famous Scottish witch-trials—and both feature the thesis that women locked into unhappy marriages are ripe for seduction by the devil. In *For the Soul of a Witch* the wife in question is Beatrix Dunbar, who refuses to consummate the marriage forced upon her by the Church and "goes to the bad." Her dearest friend, Elspet Simpson, is a much more complex and interesting figure who lives a double life; she has been initiated into devil-worship by one Dr. Finn and granted shape-shifting powers rather more robust than Morag the Seal's. (Finn is presumably based on the "Dr. Fian" appointed as chief scapegoat by the investigators of the North Berwick witches, who attained great celebrity by claiming that they had mounted a magical attack on King James VI, which the king was persuaded to take seriously.) Finn's opposite number on the side of virtue is not a Churchman but—as might be expected by readers of *Old as the World*—a Druid. One of the last survivors of that discipline, he must practise his benevolent magic in secret for fear of being tarred with the same brush as Finn's acolytes.

The Devil's Mistress takes the melodrama of *For the Soul of a Witch* much further. Thanks to the vivid fecundity of her confessions—which must have been greatly assisted by the fact that she was one of the few literate women charged with witchcraft—Isabel Gowdie attained greater celebrity than any other Scottish witch. Under torture she was not content, as most of her contemporaries were, simply to admit all the charges laid against her. She produced in addition an extraordinarily elaborate account of her seduction by the devil and her fabulous exploits in his service, which drew upon a wide range of literary and folkloristic sources—thus providing ideal material to a novelist keenly interested in the reinterpretation of witch mythology in the specific context of Scottish folklore.

Like the modern day "reformed witches" who produce confessional literature for the edification of devout Christians, Gowdie was not content to be a member of the rank and file; she declared that she had been the Devil's mistress and queen of all her kind, periodically disappearing with her lover into fairy mounds where time passed at a different pace, allowing her and her lover to play lively games with elf-shot. Brodie-Innes weaves all of this into a melodramatic plot which also involves a male witch with Royalist sympathies. In his version Gowdie repents of her wickedness and redeems herself by good works before being delivered to the fire. The novel is dedicated to Bram Stoker, who had died three years before, and was probably a conscious attempt to duplicate the runaway success of *Dracula*; it certainly demonstrates Brodie-Innes's acceptance of the fact that successful stories of the supernatural ought not to aim for likelihood.

It was not long after the publication of *The Devil's Mistress* that Margaret Murray began to delve into the records of witch trials in the construction of her classic scholarly fantasy *The Witch-Cult in Western Europe*, which proposed that witches were actually the last practitioners of a secret pagan cult driven underground by heresy-hunters. Murray's thesis—which became increasingly preposterous in further volumes—drew a great deal of its inspiration from the Gowdie confessions. The idea that witches were organized into 13-strong covens with a male leader who represented the Devil in their rituals, is entirely Gowdie's invention, and the more general notion that witch lore and fairy mythology are intricately intertwined is heavily indebted to her confessions. We can, of course, only speculate as to the role which Brodie-Innes's reformulation of the materials in question might have played in influencing Murray's thought, but the parallels between their theories are certainly intriguing.

Brodie-Innes was not an accomplished prose stylist and his plots are rather confused but he deployed his specialist knowledge with unusual care, exploiting its inherent fascination to the full. Although it is certainly not to be numbered among the more plausible fictionalized accounts of historically-based "case studies" in witchcraft, *The Devil's Mistress* remains one of the most interesting novelizations of the Scottish witch-panic.

—Brian Stableford

BROOKES, Owen

Pseudonym for Dulan Friar Whilberton Barber. **Other Pseudonyms:** David Fletcher; Robert Rush. **Nationality:** British. **Born:** Reading, Berkshire, 11 October 1940. **Education:** Leamington College for Boys; Leeds University, 1958-59. **Family:** Married Paddy Kitchen in 1968; one stepson. **Career:** Editor, Calder and Boyars, London, 1963-68, Charles Skilton, London, 1968-72; executive councillor, Writers Guild of Great Britain, London, mid-1970s; tutor, Morley College, London, 1976-78, City Literature College, 1978-79. **Awards:** Thomas R. Coward Memorial award, 1974. **Died:** 7 October 1988.

HORROR, GHOST AND GOTHIC PUBLICATIONS

Novels

The Widow of Ratchets. New York, Holt Rinehart and Winston, 1979; London, Fontana, 1980.
Inheritance. New York, Holt Rinehart and Winston, and London, Hutchinson, 1980.
The Gatherer. New York, Holt Rinehart and Winston, 1983; London, Futura, 1985.
Deadly Communion. New York, Holt Rinehart and Winston, 1984; London, Futura, 1985.
Forget-Me-Knots. New York, Holt Rinehart and Winston, 1985; London, Futura, 1986.

OTHER PUBLICATIONS

Novels as David Fletcher

A Lovable Man. London, Macmillan, 1974; New York, Coward McCann, 1975.
A Respectable Woman. London, Macmillan, and New York, Coward McCann, 1975.
Accomplices. London, Macmillan, 1976.
Don't Whistle "Macbeth." London, Macmillan, 1976.
The Marriage Ring, with Paddy Kitchen (novelization of television script). London, Allen, 1976.
Only Children. London, Macmillan, 1977.
Raffles (novelization of television script). London, Pan, and New York, Putnam, 1977.

A Crime for the Family. London, Macmillan, 1978.
Beasts. London, Macmillan, 1980.
The Touch (as Owen Brookes). London, Macdonald, 1981.
Rainbow in Hell. London, Macmillan, 1983.
Rainbows End in Tears. London, Macmillan, 1984.
On Suspicion. London, Macmillan, 1985.
The Accident of Robert Luman. London, Macmillan, 1988.
A Wagon-Load of Monkeys. London, Macmillan, 1988.
Dismal Ravens Crying. London, Macmillan, 1989.

Novels as Robert Rush

The Birthday Treat. London, Macdonald, 1981.
The Birthday Girl. London, Macdonald, 1983.

Other

Three Canterbury Tales (for children). London, Blackie, 1966.
Pornography and Society. London, Skilton, 1972.
The Horrific World of Monsters (for children). London, Marshall Cavendish, 1974.
Unmarried Fathers (interviews). London, Hutchinson, 1975.

Editor, *Concerning Thomas Hardy: A Composite Portrait from Memory,* by J. Stevens Cox. London, Skilton, 1968.
Editor, *One Parent Families.* London, Davis Poynter, 1975.
Editor, with Giles Gordon, *Members of the Jury.* London, Wildwood House, 1976.

*　　*　　*

The novel and film versions of *Rosemary's Baby* achieved great success partly because of the vicarious thrill of believing that satanists could exist unsuspected right among us and partly because of the heavily sexual overtones of that story. It is no coincidence that the neo-Gothic mysteries of the 1970s frequently featured mysterious cults, witches' covens and similar plot devices. Ira Levin gave the theme a legitimacy it had previously lacked, and it wasn't just genre writers who adopted it for their own purposes. Owen Brookes is the pseudonym of a mainstream writer who used that byline to explore the possibilities of the subtle sexuality of horror.

The first novel to appear under the Owen Brookes byline was *The Widow of Ratchets.* Lyndsay Dolben is a young American woman who travels to England to meet her new husband, only to discover that he has been killed in an automobile accident just prior to her arrival. In a state of near shock, she travels to his home town, Ratchets, to attend his funeral and wind up his affairs. But within days of her arrival, she senses that there is something wrong in Ratchets. The local populace seems to have an unhealthy obsession with traditional behaviour, and some of the traditions are rather unorthodox.

Adding to her unease are persistent dreams in which she is raped by a mysterious figure in the garb of a priest. Her subsequent experiences seduce her into sympathy with the coven, but later she learns that there are factions within the group and that she is a pawn in the battle between them. Even more startling, her husband isn't dead after all but actually a prisoner of the witches, who are led by his own brother. Brookes resolves the conflicts after a deadly confrontation and explains away the apparently supernatural elements in what appears to be a rational manner. But just as we're convinced that there's really nothing supernatural involved, we learn that at least one of the witches is a genuine shape-changer who has used various guises to influence the protagonist all through the story. This is an intensely atmospheric novel with romantic overtones that loses some of its focus at the climax, chiefly because of the contrived surprise ending.

Inheritance makes no pretence of explaining the fantastic elements away but rather emphasizes them heavily. Regina is a bitter and lonely woman, effectively cut off from intercourse with the rest of her community. She lives with her son and several foster children, children with unusual powers. One has psychokinesis, the ability to move objects through force of will, one can read minds and implant thoughts in others, and two can astrally project themselves. Regina nurses old hurts, and now that she has the power to strike back, she begins to exact her revenge, using the gifted children as her tools. Although the story owes much to Stephen King's *Carrie*, Brookes has reworked the idea into a much more complex story that is satisfying both as a straight supernatural thriller, and as a commentary on the terrible ways that emotional breakups can leave scars on the people involved.

The Gatherer contains some of the most frightening scenes in Brookes's work, even though this is the one novel that includes no genuinely supernatural occurrences. A rural English farming community is home to legends of the Gatherer, a giant scarecrow that supposedly stalks the fields searching for those who have sinned. Although no one admits believing in such a creature, there's an uneasiness about the town, particularly when people start disappearing, and when abandoned scarecrows are found in the same area where they were last seen.

The plot develops quickly, and the reader is led to believe that there actually is an oversized monster prowling the countryside, although Brookes eventually reveals the truth—a mentally deranged man is killing people and arranging the scarecrows after the fact. His actions are effectively disguised by the complicity of his family in some of the murders. The mundane resolution somewhat softens the impact of the final chapters, but there are a number of genuinely chilling scenes along the way.

Brookes's fourth horror novel was *Deadly Communion*. Stephen Cole is a hospital administrator who suspects that his wife has been unfaithful, although he has no actual proof. Shortly after his suspicions are roused, he begins to experience intense headaches, during which he erupts into fits of frightening rage, rage so intense that he begins to fear that he is losing his sanity. Cole himself takes a lover, who turns out to be a psychic who explains the truth to him. He has become mentally linked with the mind of a serial killer.

Cole and his mistress decide to use their unique abilities to track down the killer. Brookes employs a standard plot-twist on this theme, and the serial killer becomes aware of the link, making Cole and his son Mark prospective murder victims themselves. Although the story is, in terms of plot, the least interesting of Brookes's novels, it is on the other hand very tightly controlled and focused, and the relationships among the characters are the most complex and believable in his work. After one more book, *Forget-Me-Knots*, Brookes left the horror field. His novels were certainly well above average, but in the absence of a larger body of work it seems unlikely that he will be remembered as more than a footnote in modern horror.

—Don D'Ammassa

BROSTER, D(orothy) K(athleen)

Nationality: British. **Born:** 1877. **Education:** Cheltenham Ladies' College, Gloucestershire; St. Hilda's College, Oxford, M.A. **Career:** Contributor to magazines from the early 1900s; novelist. Lived in Battle, Sussex. **Died:** 7 February 1950.

HORROR, GHOST AND GOTHIC PUBLICATIONS

Short Stories

A Fire of Driftwood. London, Heinemann, 1932.
Couching at the Door. London, Heinemann, 1942.

OTHER PUBLICATIONS

Novels

Chantemerle, with Gertrude Winifred Taylor. London, Murray, and New York, Brentano's, 1911.
The Vision Splendid, with Gertrude Winifred Taylor. London, Murray, 1913; New York, Brentano's, 1914.
Sir Isumbras at the Ford. London, Murray, 1918.
The Yellow Poppy. London, Duckworth, 1920; New York, McBride, 1922.
The Wounded Name. London, Murray, 1922; New York, Doubleday, 1923.
Mr. Rowl. London, Heinemann, and New York, Doubleday, 1924.
A Jacobite Trilogy. London, Penguin, 1984.
  The Flight of the Heron. London, Heinemann, 1925; New York, Dodd Mead, 1926.
  The Gleam in the North. London, Heinemann, 1927; New York, Coward McCann, 1931.
  The Dark Mile. London, Heinemann, 1929; New York, Coward McCann, 1934.
Ships in the Bay! London, Heinemann, and New York, Coward McCann, 1931.
Almond, Wild Almond. London, Heinemann, 1933.
World under Snow, with G. Forester. London, Heinemann, 1935.
Child Royal. London, Heinemann, 1937.
The Sea Without a Haven. London, Heinemann, 1941.
The Captain's Lady. London, Heinemann, 1947.

Poetry

The Short Voyage and Other Verses. Privately printed, 1950.

Other

The Happy Warrior. London, Cayme Press, 1926.

*

Film Adaptation: *The Flight of the Heron* (television serial), 1976.

* * *

Viewed dispassionately, it is difficult not to come to the conclusion that Dorothy Broster was one of the great schizophrenics of literature. A writer of popular historical novels with a solid grounding in reality—that were, indeed, as starkly down-to-earth and unfanciful as one could get—at the same time she demonstrated a talent for not merely the macabre, but the intriguingly macabre.

While neither attaining anything like the roaring bestsellerdom of Rafael Sabatini, say, or Georgette Heyer (whose publishers' most worrying problem was working out whether to print 60,000 copies of a first edition, or 100,000-plus), nor, it must be said, blessed with the immense fecundity and diversity of view of Marjorie Bowen, nevertheless Broster flourished as a successful historical novelist during the inter-war years, bought in highly satisfactory quantities by the public as well as the circulating libraries, and even modestly rated by the critics (the often brutal *Times Literary Supplement* rarely gave her a less than easy ride).

Her scope was by no means wide-ranging. The 17th and 18th centuries seemed to suit her. There were brief excursions into other times, other cultures: some successful, others not. *Child Royal* dealt convincingly with the harried childhood of Mary, Queen of Scots; in the early *The Vision Splendid*, written with her friend Gertrude Taylor, however, a leaden love story does nothing to cheer up a tale revolving around the Oxford Movement. She was far more comfortable in Europe (or, rather, France) during that period of ferocious upheaval bracketed roughly by the bread-riots in Paris in the mid-1780s and the immediate aftermath of Napoleon's return from Elba, or the Britain (or, rather, the Scotland) of 1745 (give or take a decade or so for the purposes of the plot). Her themes encompassed the usual: love and revenge, hatred and conspiracy, families torn asunder by the sweeping, unstoppable tides of great movements, great wars (her first book, *Chantemerle*, also written with Gertrude Taylor, chillingly depicts the gradual estrangement of two kinsmen, both Royalists, set against the bloody uprisings in La Vendée during the 1790s).

What is generally regarded as her masterpiece in the historical mode is the "Jacobite Trilogy." This remarkable sequence, in three long, densely structured, densely plotted, and (despite the liberal use of dialect) utterly riveting novels, *The Flight of the Heron*, *The Gleam in the North* and *The Dark Mile*, evokes the excitement and the tragedy of the Rebellion of 1745 and its fearsome aftermath, through the adventures of Ewen Cameron of Ardroy, his friends and kinsmen (one of whom, Dr. Archie Cameron, a cousin, is ignobly executed at Tyburn). Throughout, the storytelling is assured and unshowy, the characterization as crisp as can be, and some of the set-pieces constitute truly bravura performances: Broster's description of the tension and atmosphere generated on the eve of Culloden, for instance, is dramatic scene-setting of a high order.

Even so, as atmospheric as it is, it is not macabre. It is simply compelling descriptive writing. In fact there is little or nothing Broster wrote up until the early 1930s that prepares the reader for the stories she began to spin during that last decade before the war.

This is not to say she wrote no weird fiction before the 1930s. Like most popular writers of the period, she tried her hand at the genre, probably her earliest effort "All Souls' Day" in 1907, in *Macmillan's Magazine*. In the early 1900s she was also placing occasional stories with its stablemate *Temple Bar*, but these were straight historical tales (and though their author was only in her early 20s, less excitable and rather more convincing than what was emanating from the pen of the Baroness Orczy at the same time.)

"All Souls' Day," in which a murderer and evil-doer returns from the dead to save one of his would-be victims, is certainly

more than a competent effort: there are touches of irony which lift the story well out of the general ruck of late-Victorian/Edwardian ghostsmiths' wares. It also features touches of religious feeling (Broster seems to have been a Catholic in her younger days), although these get badly out of hand in another story, "The Crib," in which the Virgin Mary, for no identifiable reason, appears beside the Christmas crib in a small suburban parish church. Redemption is a recurring theme.

Both of these tales were collected in *A Fire of Driftwood*, a mixture of pure historical stories (mainly French Revolution) and those with, to a greater or lesser extent, elements of the supernatural. Of the rest of these latter, "The Promised Land" leans towards weird-free Grand Guignol (a put-upon elderly spinster murders her crass and appalling cousin and then goes quietly, then loudly, mad), while in "The Window" the eponymous object, set in the decaying wall of an old, derelict chateau, traps one whose ancestor betrayed a friend to the *sans-culottes*, who promptly butchered all in the house. Both are conspicuously better than all but one of the rest, and read as though they were written not in the 1900s, or even the early 1920s, but around the time (February 1932) *A Fire of Driftwood* was actually published. The best tale, "Clairvoyance," is absolutely contemporary—almost hot off the presses—since it first appeared in mid-December 1931 (in the January 1932 issue of *Nash's Pall Mall Magazine*), and is a *tour de force* of horror: at a weekend house-party a psychically receptive young girl takes up a Japanese samurai sword possessed by the malign spirit of a centuries-old warrior and goes berserk, slaughtering her fellow guests in an orgy of bloody violence.

These three stories stand out in *A Fire of Driftwood*, and point to the quite different direction in which Broster, for some unknown, unguessed-at reason, suddenly seems to be heading. Crucially, especially in "The Promised Land" and "Clairvoyance," there is no softening of the climax, no redemption. No religion.

Broster's final short-story volume, the hugely elusive *Couching at the Door*, is a pure masterwork, one of the most satisfying weird collections of the century. There are five stories. One, "The Pavement," is non-weird but still effectively chilling. An obsessed and selfish old woman (when and under precisely what circumstances, one idly wonders, did Broster's mother die?) smashes to smithereens a priceless Roman floor-tessellation (of which she is part-custodian) to stop HM Office of Works' "men in suits" taking it over.

Of the rest, "Couching at the Door" itself is her most famous, and most reprinted, short work—the tale of a decadent poet (part Wilde, part Dowson, part Swinburne, with the merest touch of Henry James—the fussy writing—and a good deal of Crowley) who goes too far in some kind of diabolic orgy in Prague. Clearly a prostitute has been sacrificed to Lucifer, but Broster ingeniously, yet always delicately, hints at so much more, something far more lasciviously revolting (or, indeed, revoltingly lascivious) that one is tempted to wonder if some kind of sea-change has not taken place within her own psyche. There is certainly no hint of religiosity in the story—or any of the stories. Marchant, the poet, is pursued by—of all things (yet still far more dreadfully plausible than any amount of "crumpled linen")—an animated feather boa (the street-walker's) which becomes more and more malevolent as the tale progresses.

"From the Abyss" features "dual-" or "split-personality"—quite literally, since one of the protagonists, after a fearful car-smash in the Alpes Maritimes, becomes two, each of which is searching for the other. "Juggernaut" features a haunted bath-chair—the only real commonplace thing in the entire volume—but the story is lifted by the needle-point characterization, lashings of irony, and a finale in which the driven murderer rushes eagerly, almost obsessively (Broster really is excellent on obsession) to his doom. On the surface a simple tale of a haunting in a small Worcestershire village, "The Pestering," in which there are some authentically creepy passages, is in fact far more complex, and ought to have achieved classic status decades ago. Against that is the genuine rarity of the first (and sole, thus far) edition of the book—only the anthologist Richard Dalby appears to have reprinted the story—and its length: "The Pestering" is a novella, and at over 20,000 words takes up rather more than a third of the volume.

Dorothy Broster has been sadly neglected, rarely appearing in encyclopedias or reference works, except as "mentions" or in footnotes or a few paragraphs focusing on *Couching at the Door* and precious little else. Yet she is a significant and sophisticated creator of weird fiction, with a beguiling style (in sum: E. M. Delafield crossed with E. F. Benson, a potent mix) and a perfect grasp of the essentials of the form. The mystery of her own "dual-personality"—and that seemingly sudden change of approach at a comparatively late stage in her life (her mid-50s)—will probably never be adequately explained. Whatever the reason, it has given the weird fiction aficionado some priceless stories.

—Jack Adrian

BROUGHTON, Rhoda

Nationality: British. **Born:** Segrwyd Hall, near Denbigh, 29 November 1840. **Education:** Private. **Family:** None. **Career:** Writer, 1862-1920; lived with her sister for much of her life, in Wales, Oxford and London. **Died:** 5 June 1920.

HORROR, GHOST AND GOTHIC PUBLICATIONS

Short Stories

Tales for Christmas Eve. Leipzig, Tauchnitz, 1872; London, Bentley, 1873; expanded as *Twilight Stories*, 1879; New York, Transatlantic, 1948.
Strange Dream and Other Stories. New York, Ogilvie, 1881.
Betty's Visions and Mrs. Smith of Longmains. London, Routledge, and New York, Lovell, 1886.
Rhoda Broughton's Ghost Stories and Other Tales of Mystery and Suspense, edited with an introduction by Marilyn Wood. Stamford, Paul Watkins, 1995.

OTHER PUBLICATIONS

Novels

Cometh Up as a Flower. London, Bentley, and New York, Appleton, 1867.
Not Wisely But Too Well. London, Tinsley, 1867; New York, Appleton, 1868.
Red as a Rose Is She. London, Bentley, and New York, Appleton, 1870.

Good-Bye, Sweetheart. London, Bentley, and New York, Appleton, 1872.
Nancy. London, Bentley, 1873; New York, Appleton, 1874.
Joan. London, Bentley, and New York, Appleton, 1876.
Second Thoughts. London, Bentley, and New York, Appleton, 1880.
Belinda. London, Bentley, and New York, Appleton, 1883.
Doctor Cupid. London, Bentley, and New York, Munro, 1886.
Alas. London, Bentley, and New York, United States Book Company, 1890.
A Widower Indeed, with Elizabeth Bisland. London, Osgood McIlvaine, and New York, Appleton, 1891.
Mrs. Bligh. London, Bentley, and New York, Appleton, 1892.
A Beginner. London, Bentley, and New York, Appleton, 1894.
Scylla or Charybdis? London, Bentley, and New York, Appleton, 1895.
Dear Faustina. London, Bentley, and New York, Appleton, 1897.
The Game and the Candle. London, Macmillan, and New York, Appleton, 1899.
Foes in Law. London and New York, Macmillan, 1900.
Lavinia. London and New York, Macmillan, 1902.
A Waif's Progress. London, Macmillan, 1905.
Mamma. London, Macmillan, 1908.
The Devil and the Deep Sea. London, Macmillan, 1910.
Between Two Stools. London, Stanley Paul, 1912.
Concerning a Vow. London, Stanley Paul, 1914.
Thorn in the Flesh. London, Stanley Paul, 1917.
A Fool in Her Folly. London, Odhams, 1920.

Short Stories

Jerry and Other Stories. Philadelphia, Lippincott, 1889.

*

Biography: *Rhoda Broughton: Profile of a Novelist* by Marilyn Wood, 1993.

*   *   *

Rhoda Broughton was another of that brigade of Victorian women writers who turned their hand to the occasional ghost story. In Broughton's case few of these stories have been reprinted and it is only with the recent research of Marilyn Wood and the publication of *Rhoda Broughton's Ghost Stories and Other Tales of Mystery and Suspense* that we can at last enjoy a special talent.

Broughton was not as prolific as her fellow female wordsmiths, certainly not in the league with Mary Braddon or Mary Molesworth, but this was because Broughton was a cautious and careful writer who did not waste words. She was much annoyed when her publishers insisted that her first two novels be extended in length to comply with the current demands of three-decker novels. Broughton acquiesced but felt that the increased wordage spoiled the stories and there is no doubt that the additional padding is noticeable and slows the pace at which Broughton had intended the novel to flow.

It was probably for this reason that Broughton soon turned to the short-story form to demonstrate that considerable impact can be conveyed with the limited use of words. Her ghost stories are noticeably shorter than those of her contemporaries but they do not suffer from any reduced atmosphere or plot development. If anything, their shortness has helped maintain their freshness. Her first ghost story, "The Truth, the Whole Truth and Nothing But the Truth" (*Temple Bar*, 1868) is remarkable in that it takes the form of an exchange of six letters between two ladies. One of them has recently moved into a flat only to discover that it is reputedly haunted. She never sees the ghost herself but the letters describe the effect that seeing it has upon others in the household, driving them mad or, in one case, causing them to drop dead. Evidently the ghost was too horrible to describe and Broughton wastes no words trying to do so. She may well have learned this approach from her uncle (by marriage), J. Sheridan Le Fanu, who encouraged her in her writing.

"The Man With the Nose" (*Temple Bar*, 1872) is a very strange story and requires more than one reading to sense its full effect. Elizabeth and the narrator are to be married and will spend their honeymoon on a trip along the Rhine. Before their marriage, while Elizabeth is on holiday, she visits a theatrical mesmerist who hypnotizes her. Thereafter she has a series of dreams or visions which to her are very real, though no one else sees them. In each dream she is visited by a man about whom she can remember nothing except his large nose. During their honeymoon Elizabeth disappears and is never seen again. The story's ending has a double whammy when we learn that the events described occurred 20 years ago and that the husband is still searching for her.

"Poor Pretty Bobby" (*Temple Bar*, 1872) is a more traditional ghost story about a young sailor who is barred from ship but succeeds in getting on board only to be drowned. His clammy body visits the woman he loves and it is only later she discovers this was a portent of his death. "Behold It Was a Dream!" (*Temple Bar*, 1872) captures in a phrase all that is bad about many horror and supernatural stories. Fortunately Miss Broughton does not fall into that trap. Her dreams are not sudden revelations at the end, but are premonitions of the terrible fate that will befall the narrator's friends. These four stories plus the mystery spoof "Under the Cloak" (*Temple Bar*, 1873) were collected as *Tales for Christmas Eve*, better known under its subsequent title of *Twilight Stories*, a core Victorian volume.

It was some years before Miss Broughton returned to the ghost story and this time it was with a volume of two novelettes published under their combined title, *Betty's Visions and Mrs. Smith of Longmains*. This volume is very rare and does not appear to be in any public collection in Britain and is in only a single public library in the United States. Both stories concern themselves with prevision. "Betty's Visions" takes over from where "Behold It Was a Dream!" ended. Betty is psychic and, as a child, has occasional visions that presage death in the family. As she grows older these deaths come closer. Her final vision occurs as she is about to give birth and she realizes that she and the child will die. It is effectively told (apart from the annoying habit of Victorian women swooning), made all the more powerful by being related in the present tense, giving an immediacy to the action. "Mrs. Smith of Longmains" is a clever story. The female narrator has a compulsive urge to visit Mrs. Smith even though she only knows her distantly and neither family has been on particularly good terms. The narrator has a dream in which she witnesses Mrs. Smith being killed though the murderer's face remains unclear. The narrator is convinced it is Mrs. Smith's old butler. When she reaches the house and is admitted amongst some consternation she is surprised to find a new butler. However nothing untoward happens and, feeling foolish, the narrator returns home the next day. It is over a year before the narrator discovers that a murder had happened

elsewhere and that her visit to Mrs. Smith had saved her life. Not included in this volume, but related by theme, was "What It Meant" (*Temple Bar*, 1881), another story of prevision where the warnings of doom take a variety of forms, all seemingly real, but in fact supernatural in provenance.

All of these stories retain a freshness and vivacity that is typical of Broughton's better work. She had an engaging sense of humour that comes through in many incidental episodes, and she had a gift for describing people living normal lives in natural surroundings, so that you can imagine the world that goes on about them and, particularly in "Mrs. Smith of Longmain," life continuing after the story. It is this that keeps Rhoda Broughton's stories refreshingly alive to the modern-day reader when the work of many of her contemporaries in this field have become staid and predictable. At least four stories: "The Truth, the Whole Truth and Nothing But the Truth," "The Man With the Nose," "Betty's Visions" and "Mrs. Smith of Longmains" should be regarded as classics of the genre.

—Mike Ashley

BROWN, Charles Brockden

Nationality: American. **Born:** Philadelphia, Pennsylvania, 17 January 1771. **Education:** The Friends' Latin School, Philadelphia, 1781-86; studied law in the office of Alexander Wilcocks, Philadelphia, 1787-92, but never practised. **Family:** Married Elizabeth Linn in 1804; three sons and one daughter. **Career:** Lived in New York and was associated with the Friendly Society there, 1798-1801: editor of the society's *Monthly Magazine and American Review*, 1799-1800; returned to Philadelphia, and worked in his brother's importing business, 1800-06, and as an independent trader, 1807-10. Editor, *Literary Magazine*, 1803-07, and *American Register*, 1807-10. **Died:** 21 February 1810.

HORROR, GHOST AND GOTHIC PUBLICATIONS

Novels

Wieland; or, The Transformation: An American Tale. New York, Caritat, 1798; London, Colburn, 1811.
Ormond; or The Secret Witness. New York, Caritat, 1799; London, Colburn, 1811.
Arthur Mervyn; or, Memoirs of the Year 1793. Part 1, Philadelphia, Maxwell, 1799, part 2, New York, Hopkins, 1800; London, Lane and Newman, 1803.
Edgar Huntly; or, Memoirs of a Sleep-Walker. Philadelphia, Maxwell, 1799; London, Lane and Newman, 1803.

Short Stories

Carwin the Biloquist and Other American Tales and Pieces. London, Colburn, 1822.

OTHER PUBLICATIONS

Novels

Clara Howard. Philadelphia, Dickins, 1801; as *Philip Stanley; or, The Enthusiasm of Love*, 2 vols., London, Lane, Newman, 1807.

Jane Talbot. Philadelphia, Conrad, 1801; London, Lane, Newman, 1804.

Novels. 7 vols., Boston, Goodrich, 1827.

Memoirs of Stephen Calvert, edited by Hans Borchers. Frankfurt-am-Main, Lang, 1978.

The Novels and Related Works, edited by Sydney J. Krause. 6 vols., Kent, Ohio, Kent State University Press, 1977-86.

Other

Alcuin: A Dialogue. New York, Swords, 1798.

An Address to the Government on the Cession of Louisiana to the French. Philadelphia, Conrad, 1803.

Monroe's Embassy. Philadelphia, Conrad, 1803.

An Address on the Utility and Justice of Restrictions upon Foreign Commerce. Philadelphia, Conrad, 1809.

The Rhapsodist and Other Uncollected Writings, edited by Harry R. Warfel. 1943.

Translator, *A View of the Soil and Climate of the United States of America,* by C. F. Volney. Philadelphia, Conrad, 1804.

*

Bibliography: In *Bibliography of American Literature* by Jacob Blanck, New Haven, Connecticut, Yale University Press, 1955-91; "A Census of the Works of Brown" by Sydney J. Krause and Jane Nieset, in *Serif 3,* 1966; *Charles Brockden Brown: A Reference Guide* by Patricia L. Parker, Boston, Hall, 1980.

Critical Studies: *The Life of Charles Brockden Brown* by William Dunlap, 2 vols., n.p., 1815, as *Memoirs of Brown,* n.p., 1822; *Charles Brockden Brown: American Gothic Novelist* by Harry R. Warfel, Gainesville, University of Florida Press, 1949; *Charles Brockden Brown: Pioneer Voice of America* by David Lee Clark, Durham, North Carolina, Duke University Press, 1952; *Charles Brockden Brown* by Donald A. Ringe, New York, Twayne, 1966; *Rational Fictions: A Study of Charles Brockden Brown* by Arthur G. Kimball, McMinnville, Oregon, Linfield Research Institute, 1968; *Critical Essays on Charles Brockden Brown* edited by Bernard Rosenthal, Boston, Hall, 1981; *The Coincidental Art of Charles Brockden Brown* by Norman S. Grabo, Chapel Hill, University of North Carolina Press, 1981; *Charles Brockden Brown: An American Tale* by Alan Axelrod, Austin, University of Texas Press, 1983; *A Right View of the Subject: Feminism in the Works of Charles Brockden Brown and John Neal* by Fritz Fleischmann, Erlangen, Palme and Enke, 1983; *Conspiracy and Romance: Studies in Brockden Brown, Cooper, Hawthorne and Melville* by Robert Levine, Cambridge and New York, Cambridge University Press, 1989; *The Godwinian Novel: The Rational Fictions of Godwin, Brockden Brown, Mary Shelley* by Pamela Clemit, Oxford, Clarendon Press, and New York, Oxford University Press, 1993; *The Apparition in the Glass: Charles Brockden Brown's American Gothic* by Bill Christophersen, Athens, University of Georgia Press, 1994.

*   *   *

In America in the eighteenth century, writing was not considered to be a serious profession. Even so, Brown left his job as a lawyer in the early 1790s and became the nation's first full-time professional writer. Of his four Gothic novels, the first, *Wieland,* is regarded as a masterpiece.

It is easy to see that Brown was drawing on the work of Ann Radcliffe (*The Mysteries of Udolpho* was published four years earlier) and M. G. Lewis (*The Monk* appeared only two years earlier), but he was also a great originator. He substituted American settings and he brought in psychological horror to replace the flimsy and worn-out supernatural elements, founding a school of American Gothic writing that was to influence Poe, Hawthorne, Melville and many others right up to the present day. Although not much read in England, Brown's novels were very influential upon Mary Shelley (his four Gothic novels were said to be among her six favourite books) and were read by John Keats and Sir Walter Scott.

The Wielands are a dysfunctional family; their tale of woe is described in retrospect by Clara, its last surviving member. The elder Wieland is a German immigrant and religious mystic who has settled in Pennsylvania, where he dies as a result of spontaneous combustion. After his wife's death, their two children, Theodore and Clara, are looked after by family friend Catharine Pleyel who, in the fullness of time, becomes Theodore's wife, and they start a family. When Catharine's brother Henry also comes to Pennsylvania from Germany, Clara falls in love with him and, despite his having a fiancée back in Germany, the four are briefly happy.

But the enigmatic Carwin appears, and relationships unravel. He is at once discernible as the serpent in this particular Eden. Soon after his arrival, disembodied voices begin to cause trouble. They announce that Henry's fiancée has died in Germany; they make the suggestion that Clara is having a love affair with Carwin. Henry returns to Germany to discover that the voices lied: his fiancée is well, and he decides to remain there and marry her. Then the voice speaks to Theodore, telling him to kill his wife and children.

Theodore has always been unstable and subject to religious hysteria. Now he becomes convinced that this is the voice of God, which must be obeyed. He is pushed over the edge and carries out these terrible acts. At his trial for murder he is able to explain, calmly and rationally, how he has done the bidding of the voice, luring Catharine to Clara's house on a pretext and strangling her, then accounting for their two children. He is sent to an asylum, but escapes and returns to the Pennsylvania estate, bent on killing his sister, on the same evening that Carwin confesses to Clara that the voices are all the result of his own talent for ventriloquism. Carwin throws his voice a last time to insist that Theodore must not kill Clara, so Theodore commits suicide by cutting his throat, while Carwin sets off alone into the virgin forests of Pennsylvania and is not seen again. Eventually, Henry's wife dies in Germany and he returns to marry Clara.

The Gothic plot is traditionally and almost ludicrously melodramatic, yet the characters are all more than they appear. Clara, in particular, is an anti-Gothic heroine, who develops during both the dramatic events and the later recollection and interpretation of them. She is initially fearful that the mental instability of her father and brother will come upon her as well—especially in view of the voices she hears. Later she is able to be strong, to conquer her fear of self, admit that she has been manipulated by tricks and learn to be stronger in the future, even though she may for ever suffer from guilt. Theodore turns from a well raised young man with some religious mania into a complete psychopath, with very little persuading, yet he is to be seen as a victim, like his wife and children. On the other hand, Carwin the mysterious infiltrator is delighted with the power of his ability. He is a force for evil, encouraging the seeds of chaos to sprout within the Wielands, though his intentions and his true identity remain unknown.

Brown's second novel, *Arthur Mervyn*, is a plot-driven tale mainly set in Philadelphia during an outbreak of yellow fever. Mervyn himself, who narrates, is a young man from the country, sucked into crime by a forger named Thomas Welbeck. After Welbeck's apparent death Mervyn returns to the country, taking with him (unknowingly) a fortune in cash, the proceeds of Welbeck's crimes. Mervyn finds a farm on which he can live happily, even falling for Eliza, the farmer's daughter. But Welbeck is not really dead. Mervyn discovers the money and burns it. Returning to Philadelphia on business, Mervyn contracts yellow fever but is helped by a kindly doctor. Back on the farm, yellow fever has claimed all except Eliza. But questions are asked about Mervyn's honesty. Have events occurred in the way he has narrated? There is a final confrontation with a dying Welbeck before the happy ending, with Mervyn getting married, though not to Eliza.

There are some fine scenes here of Mervyn wandering the dark and infected streets of Philadelphia—a learning process for an *ingenue*. His sickness with yellow fever is intended to symbolize an attack of conscience. Welbeck and the doctor are both father-figures, for good and evil, replacing the one from whom Mervyn ran away.

Ormond utilizes the same setting of Philadelphia's yellow fever plague, but here the eponymous protagonist is neither a hero nor simply untrustworthy, but an unredeemable villain. He terrorizes the beautiful Constantina Dudley, after having had her father killed, holding her captive and threatening rape. But she defeats him (and the oppression he symbolizes) by stabbing him.

In *Edgar Huntley* the setting becomes more peculiarly American than ever, while preserving the convolutions of a Gothic plot. It is an epistolary novel with scenes by night and twilight in a haunted forest inhabited by ghostly-seeming Indians. Dreams, nightmares and the act of sleepwalking all figure in what is, for most of its length, a strange and confusing story. None of these three later novels possesses the authority or originality of *Wieland*.

—Chris Morgan

BRYANT, Edward (Winslow, Jr.)

Nationality: American. **Born:** White Plains, New York, 27 August 1945. **Education:** University of Wyoming, Laramie (General Motors scholar; Ford Foundation fellow), B.A. in English 1967, M.A. 1968. **Career:** Disk jockey, KYCN-Radio, 1961-63; broadcaster, disk jockey, and news director, KOWB-Radio, Laramie, 1965-66; worked as rancher and in a stirrup buckle factory, 1966-68; shipping clerk, Blevins Manufacturing, 1968-69; columnist ("The Screen Game"), *Cthulhu Calls*, Powell, Wyoming, 1973-77; reviewer of horror novels for *Twilight Zone* and *Mile High Futures*; monthly book reviewer for *Locus* magazine from 1989; full-time writer from 1969. **Awards:** Nebula award for short story, 1978, 1979; International Horror Guild Living Legend award, 1997. **Agent:** William Morris Agency, 1325 Avenue of the Americas, New York, NY 10019. **Address:** c/o Locus Publications, 34 Ridgewood Lane, Oakland, CA 94661, USA.

HORROR, GHOST AND GOTHIC PUBLICATIONS

Short Stories

Among the Dead and Other Events Leading to the Apocalypse. New York, Macmillan, 1973.
Wyoming Sun. Laramie, Wyoming, Jelm Mountain, 1980.
Particle Theory. New York, Pocket Books, 1981.
Night Visions 4, with Dean R. Koontz and Robert R. McCammon. Arlington Heights, Illinois, Dark Harvest, 1987; as *Night Visions: Hardshell*, New York, Berkley, 1988.
Trilobyte: An Easter Treasure, with *The Shadow on the Doorstep*, by James P. Blaylock. Seattle, Washington, Axolotl, 1987.
Neon Twilight. Eugene, Oregon, Pulphouse, 1990.
The Man of the Future. Arvada, Colorado, Roadkill Press, 1990.
The Cutter. Eugene, Oregon, Pulphouse, 1991.
Fetish. Eugene, Oregon, Pulphouse, 1991.
Darker Passions. Arvada, Colorado, Roadkill Press, 1992.
The Thermals of August. Eugene, Oregon, Pulphouse, 1992.

OTHER PUBLICATIONS

Novels

Phoenix Without Ashes: A Novel of the Starlost, with Harlan Ellison. New York, Fawcett, 1975; Manchester, Savoy, 1978.
Cinnabar. New York, Macmillan, 1976; London, Fontana, 1978.

Plays

Radio Play: *Breakers,* 1979.

Television Play: *The Synar Calculation*, with Edward Hawkins, 1973.

Other

Editor, *2076: The American Tricentennial.* New York, Pyramid, 1977.

*

Bibliography: *Edward Bryant Bibliography*, Los Angeles, Swigart, 1980.

Theatrical Activities:
Actor: **Films**—*Flesh Gordon*, 1974; *The Laughing Dead*, 1989.

*   *   *

Like his friend and one-time mentor Harlan Ellison, Edward Bryant specializes almost exclusively in short fiction and has gradually shifted from science fiction to horror. Yet Bryant seems a gentler soul, lacking Ellison's volcanic temperament and flair for self-advertisement; thus, while his stories may offer little in the way of pyrotechnics, they often manifest a quiet, understated strength. What is most striking in Bryant's horror fiction is that his characters rarely seem terrified, or even surprised, by the terrors they confront; instead, they calmly deal with them, then prepare themselves for another day's work.

In one early story, "Among the Dead," a character notes that his journal "would make a tremendous beginning for a horror story"; and in fact, Bryant's science-fiction stories of the 1970s frequently take the form of nightmarish, near-future dystopias. In a story written for Ellison's anthology *Again, Dangerous Visions* (1971), "The 10:00 Report Is Brought to You By . . .," producers of news programmes desperate for ratings begin to pay criminals to commit violent crimes for their cameras. Similar horror stories in his collection *Among the Dead and Other Events Leading to the Apocalypse* include the title story, about three survivors of a biological war who survive by eating cryogenically preserved human bodies; "Shark," featuring a woman who willingly participates in a hushed-up experiment that transforms her into a shark; "The Human Side of the Village Monster," where an inventor trying to survive in an overpopulated, underfed New York breeds giant cockroaches to serve as meat; and "Tactics," describing a future election where cold-blooded murder has become a commonplace political strategy.

Also in *Among the Dead* are horror stories with present-day or unspecified locales: "The Hanged Man," an explicit tribute to Edgar Allan Poe's "The Cask of Amontillado," featuring a man who hangs another man by his feet to torture him; "Adrift on the Freeway," in which a man theorizes that a mysterious increase in abandoned cars is due to attacks by invisible carnivorous birds; and the surrealistic "Dune's Edge," where five people are trapped in a strange realm where they feel compelled to climb an immense dune, always unsuccessfully. Noteworthy horror stories in his second collection, *Particle Theory*, are "Teeth Marks," involving a ghost haunting the home of the politician earlier seen in "Tactics"; "Strata," where the complex emotions of a reunion of high-school friends lead to a vision of an immense, prehistoric sea monster; "Stone," about a self-destructive rock singer modeled on Janis Joplin who sings in concerts while hooked to electrodes that convey all her sensations to the audience; and "giANTS," where a scientist attempts to defeat a coming onslaught of vicious ants by breeding them to grow huge and die because of the square-cube law.

The 1970s also brought Bryant's two experiments with the novel. First, he adapted Ellison's script for the pilot episode of the series *The Starlost*, about a young man who discovers that he is living in a generation starship, as a novel, *Phoenix without Ashes*. By the standards of either author, the novel is undistinguished, and projected additional novels in a Starlost series never appeared. Bryant then published *Cinnabar*, generally called a novel though it might better be regarded as a collection of eight linked stories sharing the setting of Cinnabar, a strange, far-future city somehow existing at "the focal point of all time." Avowedly influenced by, and more than slightly reminiscent of, J. G. Ballard's *Vermilion Sands* series, the stories are colourful but unremarkable; a few are related to horror, like "Jade Blue," about a boy neglected by his parents, then sexually abused by a housekeeper, who is then nurtured by a "catmother" and perhaps healed by a device that alters time. (A ninth Cinnabar story, "Waiting in Crouched Halls," later surfaced in *Neon Twilight*.)

In the 1980s and 1990s, Bryant generally focused on pure horror stories, though he did contribute a solid science-fiction story set in Fred Saberhagen's Berserker universe, "Pilots of the Twilight," in *Neon Twilight*, where one genocidal dreadnought is amazingly destroyed by the telepathic powers of a seemingly primitive alien race. One of his memorable contributions to horror is the character Angie Black, a usually reticent but lethally effective witch. In "Dark Angel" (in *Dark Forces: New Stories of Suspense and Supernatural Horror*, edited by Kirby McCauley, 1980), a vengeful Angie arranges for the man who once made her pregnant and abandoned her to himself become pregnant, though her magic does not provide him with a birth canal for the baby; in "Haunted" (in *Night Visions 4*), a woman calls Angie to deal with the apparent ghost of her former lover; and in the novella *Fetish*, Bryant's most striking longer work, Angie comes into conflict with a man whose magical powers more than match hers, though she manages to defeat him by using a trick set up by a movie stuntwoman. Such unusually strong female characters have virtually become a Bryant trademark, as seen in two other stories: "Predators" (in *Night Visions 4*), in which a new man in an apartment complex harasses a female neighbour until she reveals her sharp teeth and claws and slaughters him; and "While She Was Out" (in *Splatterpunks: Extreme Horror*, edited by Paul M. Sammon, 1990), featuring a woman shopper, cornered by four rowdy youths intent on rape and murder, who takes a toolbox out of her car trunk and proceeds to methodically kill them all.

Three other noteworthy horror stories in *Night Visions 4* are "The Baku," where Japanese victims of the atomic bombs haunt one bomber pilot (Hiroshima and Nagasaki also figure in the stories "Jody after the War," in *Among the Dead*, and "The 'Hibakusha' Gallery," in *Particle Theory*); "Frat Rat Bash," about the grim aftermath of a brutal fraternity initiation; and "Buggage," featuring a man taken over by a small army of insects who inhabit his body, keep him healthy, and plan to "colonize" other people.

Despite a flurry of small-press publications in the 1990s, Bryant remains a rather marginalized figure, like most writers who do not produce novels, and he may be best known to recent horror fans for his consistently excellent reviews of horror novels in *Locus* magazine. In the introduction to *Neon Twilight*, Bryant notes incredulously that "There are apparently those, for god's sake, who only think of me as an sf *critic*"; yet he characteristically fails to become indignant or upset about this. So, if circumstances ever conspire to turn Bryant into a full-time critic, he will no doubt placidly accept that fate, just as his characters placidly accept their own horrible fates.

—Gary Westfahl

BUCHAN, John (1st Baron Tweedsmuir of Elsfield)

Nationality: British. **Born:** Broughton Green, Peeblesshire, 26 August 1875. **Education:** Hutchison Grammar School, Glasgow; University of Glasgow; Brasenose College, Oxford (scholar, 1895; Stanhope prize, 1897; Newdigate prize, 1898; President of the Union, 1899), B.A. (honours) 1899; Middle Temple, London, called to the Bar, 1901. **Military Service:** Served on the Headquarters Staff of the British Army in France, as temporary Lieutenant Colonel, 1916-17; Director of Information under the Prime Minister, 1917-18. **Family:** Married Susan Charlotte Grosvenor in 1907; three sons and one daughter. **Career:** Private secretary to the High Commissioner for South Africa, Lord Milner, 1901-03; director, Nelson publishers, London, from 1903, and Reuters, London, 1919; Conservative Member of Parliament for the Scottish Universities, 1927-35; Lord High Commissioner, Church of Scotland, 1933, 1934; Governor-General of Canada, 1935-40; privy councillor, 1937; curator, Oxford University Chest, 1924-30; president, Scottish History Society, 1929-33; bencher, Middle Temple, 1935; chancellor, University of Edinburgh, 1937-40; Justice of the Peace, Peeblesshire and Oxfordshire. **Awards:** James Tait Black Memorial prize, 1929. D.C.L.: Oxford University; LL.D.: University of Glasgow; University of St. Andrews; University of Edinburgh; McGill University, Montreal; University of Toronto; University of Manitoba, Winnipeg; Harvard University, Cambridge, Massachusetts; Yale University, New Haven, Connecticut; D. Litt.: Columbia University, New York; University of British Columbia, Vancouver; McMaster University, Hamilton, Ontario. Honorary Fellow, Brasenose College, Oxford. Companion of Honour, 1932; created Baron Tweedsmuir, 1935; G.C.M.G. (Knight Grand Cross, Order of St. Michael and St. George), 1935; G.C.V.O. (Knight Grand Cross, Royal Victorian Order), 1939. **Died:** 11 February 1940.

HORROR, GHOST AND GOTHIC PUBLICATIONS

Novels

The Dancing Floor. London, Hodder and Stoughton, and Boston, Houghton Mifflin, 1926.
Witch Wood. London, Hodder and Stoughton, and Boston, Houghton Mifflin, 1927.
The Gap in the Curtain. London, Hodder and Stoughton, and Boston, Houghton Mifflin, 1932.

Short Stories

Grey Weather: Moorland Tales of My Own People. London, Lane, 1899.
The Watcher by the Threshold and Other Tales. Edinburgh, Blackwood, 1902; augmented edition, New York, Doran, 1918.
The Moon Endureth: Tales and Fancies. Edinburgh, Blackwood, and New York, Sturgis, 1912.
The Runagates Club. London, Hodder and Stoughton, and Boston, Houghton Mifflin, 1928.

OTHER PUBLICATIONS

Novels

Sir Quixote of the Moors, Being Some Account of an Episode in the Life of the Sieur de Rohaine. London, Unwin, and New York, Holt, 1895.
John Burnet of Barns. London, Lane, and New York, Dodd Mead, 1898.
A Lost Lady of Old Years. London, Lane, 1899.
The Half-Hearted. London, Isbister, and Boston, Houghton Mifflin, 1900.
Prester John. London, Nelson, 1910; as *The Great Diamond Pipe,* New York, Dodd Mead, 1911.
Salute to Adventurers. London, Nelson, and Boston, Houghton Mifflin, 1915.
The Thirty-Nine Steps. Edinburgh, Blackwood, 1915; New York, Doran, 1916.
The Power-House. Edinburgh, Blackwood, and New York, Doran, 1916.

Greenmantle. London, Hodder and Stoughton, and New York, Doran, 1916.
Mr. Standfast. London, Hodder and Stoughton, and New York, Doran, 1919.
Huntingtower. London, Hodder and Stoughton, and New York, Doran, 1922.
Midwinter: Certain Travellers in Old England. London, Hodder and Stoughton, and New York, Doran, 1923.
The Three Hostages. London, Hodder and Stoughton, and Boston, Houghton Mifflin, 1924.
John Macnab. London, Hodder and Stoughton, and Boston, Houghton Mifflin, 1925.
The Courts of the Morning. London, Hodder and Stoughton, and Boston, Houghton Mifflin, 1929.
Castle Gay. London, Hodder and Stoughton, and Boston, Houghton Mifflin, 1929.
The Blanket of the Dark. London, Hodder and Stoughton, and Boston, Houghton Mifflin, 1931.
A Prince of the Captivity. London, Hodder and Stoughton, and Boston, Houghton Mifflin, 1933.
The Free Fishers. London, Hodder and Stoughton, and Boston, Houghton Mifflin, 1934.
The House of the Four Winds. London, Hodder and Stoughton, and Boston, Houghton Mifflin, 1935.
The Island of Sheep. London, Hodder and Stoughton, 1936; as *The Man from the Norlands,* Boston, Houghton Mifflin, 1936.
The Long Traverse. London, Hodder and Stoughton, 1941; as *Lake of Gold,* Boston, Houghton Mifflin, 1941.
Sick Heart River. London, Hodder and Stoughton, 1941; as *Mountain Meadow,* Boston, Houghton Mifflin, 1941.

Short Stories

Ordeal by Marriage: An Eclogue. London, R. Clay, 1915.
The Path of the King. London, Hodder and Stoughton, and New York, Doran, 1921.
The Best Short Stories of John Buchan, edited by David Daniell. London, Joseph, 2 vols., 1980-82.

Play

Screenplay: *The Battles of Coronel and Falkland Islands,* with Harry Engholm and Merritt Crawford, 1927.

Poetry

The Pilgrim Fathers. Oxford, Blackwell, 1898.
Poems, Scots and English. London, Jack, 1917; revised edition, London, Nelson, 1936.

Other

Scholar Gipsies. London, Lane, and New York, Macmillan, 1896.
Sir Walter Raleigh. Oxford, Blackwell, 1897.
Brasenose College. London, Robinson, 1898.
The African Colony: Studies in the Reconstruction. Edinburgh, Blackwell, 1903.
The Law Relating to the Taxation of Foreign Income. London, Stevens, 1905.
A Lodge in the Wilderness. Edinburgh, Blackwood, 1906.

Some Eighteenth Century Byways and Other Essays. Edinburgh, Blackwood, 1908.

Sir Walter Raleigh (for children). London, Nelson, and New York, Holt, 1911.

What the Home Rule Bill Means (speech). Peebles, Smythe, 1912.

The Marquis of Montrose. London, Nelson, and New York, Scribner, 1913.

Andrew Jameson, Lord Ardwall. Edinburgh, Blackwood, 1913.

Britain's War by Land. London, Oxford University Press, 1915.

Nelson's History of the War. London, Nelson, 24 vols., 1915-19; as *A History of the Great War,* 4 vols., 1921-22.

The Achievement of France. London, Methuen, 1915.

The Future of the War (speech). London, Boyle Son and Watchurst, 1916.

The Purpose of War (speech). London, Dent, 1916.

These for Remembrance. Privately printed, 1919; London, Buchan and Enright, 1987.

The Island of Sheep, with Susan Buchan (as Cadmus and Harmonia). London, Hodder and Stoughton, 1919; Boston, Houghton Mifflin, 1920.

The Battle-Honours of Scotland 1914-1918. Glasgow, Outram, 1919.

The History of the South African Forces in France. London, Nelson, 1920.

Francis and Riversdale Grenfell: A Memoir. London, Nelson, 1920.

A Book of Escapes and Hurried Journeys. London, Nelson, 1922; Boston, Houghton Mifflin, 1923.

The Last Secrets: The Final Mysteries of Exploration. London, Nelson, 1923; Boston, Houghton Mifflin, 1924.

The Memoir of Sir Walter Scott (speech). Privately printed, 1923.

Days to Remember: The British Empire in the Great War, with Henry Newbolt. London, Nelson, 1923.

Some Notes on Sir Walter Scott (speech). London, Oxford University Press, 1924.

Lord Minto: A Memoir. London, Nelson, 1924.

The History of the Royal Scots Fusiliers (1678-1918). London, Nelson, 1925.

The Man and the Book: Sir Walter Raleigh. London, Nelson, 1925.

Two Ordeals of Democracy (lecture). Boston, Houghton Mifflin, 1925.

Homilies and Recreations. London, Nelson, 1926; Freeport, New York, Books for Libraries, 1969.

To the Electors of the Scottish Universities (speech). Glasgow, Anderson, 1927.

The Fifteenth—Scottish—Division 1914-1919, with John Stewart. Edinburgh, Blackwood, 1926.

The Causal and the Casual in History (lecture). Cambridge, University Press, and New York, Macmillan, 1929.

What the Union of the Churches Means to Scotland. Edinburgh, McNivern and Wallace, 1929.

Montrose and Leadership (lecture). London, Oxford University Press, 1930.

The Revision of Dogmas (lecture). Ashridge, Wisconsin, Ashridge Journal, 1930.

Lord Rosebery 1847-1930. London, Oxford University Press, 1930.

The Novel and the Fairy Tale. London, Oxford University Press, 1931.

Sir Walter Scott. London, Cassell, and New York, Coward McCann, 1932.

The Magic Walking-Stick (for children). London, Hodder and Stoughton, and Boston, Houghton Mifflin, 1932.

Julius Caesar. London, Davies, and New York, Appleton, 1932.

The Massacre of Glencoe. London, Davies, and New York, Putnam, 1933.

Andrew Lang and the Border (lecture). London, Oxford University Press, 1933.

The Margins of Life (speech). London, Birkbeck College, 1933.

The Principles of Social Service (lecture). Glasgow, Glasgow Society of Social Service, 1934(?).

The Scottish Church and the Empire (speech). Glasgow, Church of Scotland Commission on Colonial Churches, 1934.

Gordon at Khartoum. London, Davies, 1934.

Oliver Cromwell. London, Hodder and Stoughton, and Boston, Houghton Mifflin, 1934.

Men and Deeds. London, Davies, 1935; Freeport, New York, Books for Libraries, 1969.

The King's Grace 1910-35 (on George V). London, Hodder and Stoughton, 1935; as *The People's King,* Boston, Houghton Mifflin, 1935.

An Address [The Western Mind]. Montreal, McGill University, 1935.

Address [A University's Bequest to Youth]. Toronto, Victoria University, 1936.

Augustus. London, Hodder and Stoughton, and Boston, Houghton Mifflin, 1937.

The Interpreter's House (speech). London, Hodder and Stoughton, 1938.

Presbyterianism Yesterday, Today, and Tomorrow. Edinburgh, Church of Scotland, 1938.

Memory Hold-the-Door. London, Hodder and Stoughton, 1940; as *Pilgrim's War: An Essay in Recollection,* Boston, Houghton Mifflin, 1940.

Comments and Characters, edited by W. Forbes Gray. London, Nelson, 1940; Freeport, New York, Books for Libraries, 1970.

Canadian Occasions (lectures). London, Hodder and Stoughton, 1940.

The Clearing House: A Survey of One Man's Mind, edited by Lady Tweedsmuir. London, Hodder and Stoughton, 1946.

Life's Adventure: Extracts from the Works of John Buchan, edited by Lady Tweedsmuir. London, Hodder and Stoughton, 1947.

Editor, *Essays and Apothegms,* by Francis Bacon. London, Scott, 1894.

Editor, *Musa Piscatrix.* London, Lane, and Chicago, McClurg, 1896.

Editor, *The Compleat Angler,* by Izaak Walton. London, Methuen, 1901.

Editor, *The Long Road to Victory.* London, Nelson, 1920.

Editor, *Great Hours in Sport.* London, Nelson, 1921.

Editor, *Miscellanies, Literary and Historical,* by Archibald Primrose, Earl of Rosebery. London, Hodder and Stoughton, 1921.

Editor, *A History of English Literature.* London, Nelson, 1923; New York, Ronald Press, 1938.

Editor, *The Nations of Today; A New History of the World.* London, Hodder and Stoughton, and Boston, Houghton Mifflin, 12 vols., 1923-24.

Editor, *The Northern Muse: An Anthology of Scots Vernacular Poetry.* London, Nelson, 1924.

Editor, *Modern Short Stories.* London, Nelson, 1926.

Editor, *Essays and Studies 12.* Oxford, Clarendon Press, 1926.

Editor, *South Africa.* London, British Empire Educational Press, 1928.

Editor, *The Teaching of History*. London, Nelson, 11 vols., 1928-30.

Editor, *The Poetry of Neil Munro*. Edinburgh, Blackwood, 1931.

*

Film Adaptations: *The Thirty-Nine Steps*, 1935, 1959, 1978; *The Three Hostages* (TV movie), 1977; *Huntingtower* (TV serial), 1978.

Bibliography: *John Buchan: A Bibliography* by Archibald Hanna, Jr., Hamden, Connecticut, Shoe String Press, 1953; by J. Randolph Cox, in *English Literature in Transition* (Tempe, Arizona), 1966-67; *The First Editions of John Buchan: A Collector's Bibliography* by Robert G. Blanchard, Hamden, Connecticut, Archon, 1981.

Manuscript Collections: National Library of Scotland, Edinburgh; Edinburgh University Library; Douglas Library, Queen's University, Kingston, Ontario.

Critical Studies: *Clubland Heroes: A Nostalgic Study of Some Recurrent Characters in the Romantic Fiction of Dornford Yates, John Buchan and Sapper* by Richard Usborne, London, Constable, 1953; *John Buchan* by Janet Adam Smith, London, Hart Davis, 1965; *The Interpreter's House: A Critical Assessment of John Buchan* by David Daniell, London, Nelson, 1975; *John Buchan and His World* by Janet Adam Smith, London, Thames and Hudson, 1979; *John Buchan: A Memoir* by William Buchan, London, Buchan and Enright, 1982.

*   *   *

John Buchan became such a paragon of all the manly virtues after a sojourn in South Africa during which he turned into a dedicated Imperialist that he became rather uncomfortable with some of his earliest literary endeavours. Although he was never remotely Decadent he was, for a while, something of an aesthete and his first collection of tales and sketches, *Grey Weather*, was issued in John Lane's Arcady Library with a figure of Pan on the cover. Two of the stories—including "A Journey of Little Profit," whose protagonists carouse with the lightly-disguised Devil—had actually appeared in Lane's notorious *Yellow Book*, along with a third that was never reprinted. Another item in the collection, "Prester John," invoked a myth which—reformulated in quasi-Imperialistic fashion—supplied the title of one his best early novels. Buchan never abandoned the dignified pastoralism of these early stories but he did repent of their tacit paganism and was content in the later part of his career, when they might have been profitably reprinted, to let them perish by neglect.

The Watcher by the Threshold contains some similar materials, including the allegorical "The Rime of True Thomas" and the deftly bleak "The Outgoing of the Tide," but the collection is leavened by more generalized antiquarian interests and the other tales have conscientiously artificial plots. The title story wonders whether neuralgia—popularly considered by non-sufferers to be an imaginary affliction—might be a demonic affliction shared by the protagonist and the Byzantine emperor Justinian. "Basilissa" is a tale of premonitory dreams involving a Greek enchantress. The fine novella "No-man's Land" is an interesting development of the notion that our world co-exists with others hidden in parallel.

Alongside more mundane items *The Moon Endureth* features the best of Buchan's visionary fantasies. In "The Grove of

Ashtoreth" an unlucky Englishman falls under the sway of the goddess when he happens upon her last surviving shrine in the African wilderness; he is liberated by a friend who dutifully obliterates the magic—but not without a twinge of regret. In "Space" a mathematician who discovers a way of penetrating the fourth dimension in his sleep is dissuaded from its further exploration by the enigmatically menacing presences which lurk there. Buchan was himself dissuaded from further excursions in the supernatural; in 1914, while anxiously awaiting a summons to active service, he wrote *The Thirty-Nine Steps*, a "shilling shocker" extolling—by courtesy of its redoubtable hero Richard Hannay—all the virtues which would be needed to sustain the English through the Great War. It became a great favourite in the trenches and he never looked back, his work as a conscientious propagandist seemingly insulating him from any realization that the horrors of the war had made a hollow mockery of his jingoistic protestations.

When Buchan briefly revisited his early interests in the 1920s he produced three more books of some relevance to the horror genre. *The Dancing Floor* is another visionary fantasy based in Greek folklore, whose first phases are reasonably compelling. Unfortunately, the climax to which the hero is drawn by his premonitory dreams is a routine last-minute rescue in which the heroine must be saved from the silly pagans who intend to make a human sacrifice of her. *Witch Wood* is a historical novel in which a congregation of stern Scottish Protestants, who believe that those who will enjoy the rewards of Heaven are already selected and that good works count for naught, decide that since their salvation cannot be withheld they may as well enjoy the rewards of self-indulgence while they remain on earth. They adopt the trappings of devil worship as a means to this end, but receive no actual aid from the Devil.

More interesting than either of these novels is the short story collection *The Runagates Club*, which employs the apologetic framework of a dining club whose much-travelled members exchange tall tales. Richard Hannay's contribution is "The Green Wildebeest," a well-executed story about the violation of a native shrine in the Transvaal at the turn of the century. Another shrine to a forgotten god, this time in the context of Celtic mythology, is unwisely violated in "The Wind in the Portico." "Sule Skerry," "Tendebant Manus" and "Full Circle" are all tales of subtle hauntings, told with a delicacy which Buchan rarely bothered to bring to his hurriedly-penned novels.

Buchan's last supernatural work was *The Gap in the Curtain*, an atypically thoughtful study of predestination. The guests at a country house party are enabled by an unconventional scientist to catch a glimpse of an issue of the *Times* dated a year ahead. Some try to take advantage of what they read there while others are convinced that it cannot come true but ingenious fate cheats them all. The idea on which the story is based is a variant of J. W. Dunne's then-fashionable theory of premonitory dreams, which also inspired J. B. Priestley's "time plays"; the sharply contrasting attitudes of the two writers reflect the differences in their politics as well as their backgrounds.

Buchan always had far more important things to do than write fiction, which became an occasional pastime that he affected to regard as a mere sop to the masses who doted on his thrillers. It may well be, however, that his imaginative works are more revealing than he supposed; the way in which certain key themes keep cropping up is certainly intriguing. Such was his assessment of his own worth that he regarded the Governor-Generalship of

Canada as a mere consolation-prize, so he presumably clung stead-fastly to the notion that fate had cheated him until the day he died. Also, he probably never quite contrived to shake off the guilty suspicion that the neuralgia which plagued him all his life was psychosomatic, perhaps inflicted by some mysterious in-dwelling demon whose neglected but not entirely impotent shrine he had unwittingly contrived to violate.

—Brian Stableford

BULWER-LYTTON, Edward (George Earle; 1st Baron Lytton of Knebworth)

Nationality: British. **Born:** London, 25 May 1803. **Education:** Dr. Ruddock's School, Fulham, London; Dr. Hooker's School, Rottingdean, Sussex; with a Mr. Wallington, Ealing, London, 1818-20; Trinity College, Cambridge (pensioner), 1822, and Trinity Hall, Cambridge (fellow-commoner; Chancellor's Medal for verse, 1825), 1822-25, B.A. 1825, M.A. 1833. **Family:** Married Rosina Doyle Wheeler in 1827 (separated 1836); one daughter and one son. **Career:** Travelled between London and Paris, 1825-27; settled at Woodcot House, near Pangbourne, Berkshire, and contributed to magazines, including *Books of Beauty, Keepsakes* and *Quarterly Review*, 1827-29; moved to London, 1829; editor, *New Monthly Magazine*, London, 1831-33; Liberal Member of Parliament for St. Ives, Cornwall, 1831, and for Lincoln, 1832-41; active lobby-ist for stronger copyright laws and for the removal of taxes on literature; co-publisher, *The Monthly Chronicle*, London, 1841; succeeded to the family estate at Knebworth, 1843; travelled abroad, 1849; Tory Member of Parliament for Hertfordshire, 1852-66; Sec-retary for the Colonies, 1858-59. Lord Rector of the University of Glasgow, 1856, 1858. **Awards:** Knighted in 1837; LL.D., Cambridge University, 1864; created Baron Lytton, 1866. **Died:** 18 January 1873.

HORROR, GHOST AND GOTHIC PUBLICATIONS

Novels

Asmodeus at Large. Philadelphia, Carey, 1833.
Zanoni. 3 vols., London, Saunders and Otley, 1842; 1 vol., New York, Harper, 1842.
A Strange Story. London, Low, Marston, and New York, Harper, 1862.

Short Stories

The Pilgrims of the Rhine. London, Saunders and Otley, and New York, Harper, 1834.
The Student. 2 vols., London, Saunders and Otley, 1835; 1 vol., New York, Harper, 1836.
The Haunted House, and Calderon the Courtier. New York, Lovell, 1882.
The Haunted and the Haunters. London, Blackwood, 1859; Chicago, Rajput, 1911.

OTHER PUBLICATIONS

Novels

Falkland. London, Colburn, 1827; New York, Harper, 1830.
Pelham; or, The Adventures of a Gentleman. 3 vols., London, Colburn, 1828; 2 vols., New York, Harper, 1828.
The Disowned. 4 vols., London, Colburn, 1828; 2 vols., New York, Harper, 1829.
Devereux. 3 vols., London, Colburn, 1829; 2 vols., New York, Harper, 1829.
Paul Clifford. 3 vols., London, Colburn, 1830; 2 vols., New York, Harper, 1830.
Eugene Aram. 3 vols., London, Colburn and Bentley, 1832; 2 vols., New York, Harper, 1832.
Godolphin. 3 vols., London, Bentley, 1833; 2 vols., Philadelphia, Carey, 1833.
The Last Days of Pompeii. 3 vols., London, Bentley, 1834; 2 vols., New York, Harper, 1834.
Rienzi, the Last of the Roman Tribunes. 3 vols., London, Saunders and Otley, 1835; 2 vols., New York, Harper, 1836.
Ernest Maltravers. 3 vols., London, Saunders and Otley, 1837; 2 vols., New York, Harper, 1837.
Alice; or, The Mysteries. 3 vols., London, Saunders and Otley, 1838; 2 vols., New York, Harper, 1838.
Night and Morning. 3 vols., London, Saunders and Otley, 1841; 2 vols., New York, Harper, 1841.
The Last of the Barons. 3 vols., London, Saunders and Otley, 1843; 1 vol., New York, Harper, 1843.
Lucretia; or, The Children of the Night. 3 vols., London, Saunders and Otley, 3 vols., 1846; 1 vol., New York, Harper, 1846
Harold, the Last of the Saxon Kings. 3 vols., London, Bentley, 1848; 1 vol., New York, Harper, 1848.
The Caxtons: A Family Picture. 3 vols., Edinburgh, Blackwood, 1849; 1 vol., New York, Hurst, 1849.
My Novel; or, Varieties in English Life. 1 vol., New York, Harper, 1852; 4 vols., Edinburgh and London, Blackwood, 1853.
What Will He Do With It? 4 vols., London, Blackwood, 1859; 1 vol., New York, Harper, 1859.
The Coming Race. Edinburgh, Blackwood, and New York, Felt, 1871; as *Vril: The Power of the Coming Race,* Blauvelt, New York, Steiner, 1972.
Kenelm Chillingly. 3 vols., Edinburgh, Blackwood, 1873; 1 vol., New York, Harper, 1873.
The Parisians. 4 vols., London, Blackwood, 4 vols., 1873; 1 vol., New York, Harper, 1874.

Plays

The Duchess de la Valliére. London, Saunders and Otley, 1836; New York, Harper, 1837.
Richelieu. London, Saunders and Otley, and New York, Harper, 1839.
Money. London, Saunders and Otley, 1840; New York, Taylor, 1845.

Poetry

Ismael: An Oriental Tale. London, Hatchard, 1820.
The Siamese Twins: A Satirical Tale of the Times. London, Colburn and Bentley, and New York, Harper, 1831.

The New Timon. London, Colburn, and Philadelphia, Carey and Hart, 1846.
King Arthur. London, Colburn, and New York, Hurst, 1849.

Other

England and the English. London, Bentley, and New York, Harper, 1833.
The Life, Letters and Literary Remains of Edward Bulwer, Lord Lytton, edited by Edward Robert Bulwer-Lytton. New York, Harper, 1883.

*

Critical Studies: *Edward Bulwer, First Baron of Knebworth* by T. H. S. Escott, London, Routledge, 1910; *The Life of Edward Bulwer, First Lord Lytton* by Victor A. G. Lytton, Second Earl of Lytton, London, Macmillan, 2 vols., 1913; *The Newgate Novel 1830-1837: Bulwer, Ainsworth, Dickens and Thackeray* by Keith Hollingsworth, Detroit, Wayne State University Press, 1963; *Edward Bulwer-Lytton: The Fiction of New Regions* by Allan C. Christensen, Athens, Georgia, University of Georgia Press, 1976; *The Victorian Novel before Victoria: British Fiction During the Reign of William IV, 1830-37* by Elliot Engel and Margaret F. King, New York, St. Martin's Press, 1984.

*   *   *

Edward Bulwer, as he then was, took to writing novels in the late 1820s when his family cut off their financial support because he had married against his mother's wishes. He quickly discovered that mildly scandalous novels of high society and lurid crime stories sold well, but when he became the editor of the *New Monthly Magazine* in the early 1830s he felt free to use its pages to indulge his more exotic tastes. It was there that he published the satirical *Asmodeus at Large,* based on Alain René le Sage's *The Devil on Two Sticks,* in which the amiable demon who had exposed the follies and hypocrisies of Paris visits London and waxes lyrical on all manner of political and philosophical issues; the closing stages of the tale became exceedingly strange, replete with ominous imagery of dubious implication. "The Tale of Kosem Kesamim," which is interpolated into the novel in some reprinted versions, is a bombastic Faustian fable. The tales and sketches reprinted as *Pilgrims of the Rhine* are fantastic without being horrific but those gathered into *The Student* include the Byronically gloomy tale of "Monos and Daimos" and the nasty-minded "Manuscript found in a Madhouse." The latter became the prototype for an entire sub-genre of horror fiction.

Bulwer's most successful early work, the historical novel *The Last Days of Pompeii,* employs a quasi-Gothic villain in the person of Arbaces, the lustful priest of Isis—who eventually kidnaps the heroine, as all good Gothic villains are bound to do. The story also features an old witch who lives in a cave on the slopes of Vesuvius, brewing potions while the volcano hubbles and bubbles away. Bulwer's honest fascination with the heterodox occult philosophy of Arbaces was to be extended and much exaggerated in several of his later novels. Similarly enigmatic figures play a peripheral role in some of his other historical novels, including *Ernest Maltravers* and its sequel *Alice; or, The Mysteries.*

In 1841 Bulwer began a serial version of a rather light-hearted occult novel called *Zicci* but left it incomplete and began again in a different vein, producing the much more earnest *Zanoni,* which quickly became established as a classic Rosicrucian romance. The eponymous anti-hero is a supernaturally gifted immortal of Chaldean origin who vies with the artist Glyndon for the love of the heroine while allowing his associate Mejnour to guide Glyndon towards occult enlightenment. Glyndon's progress is interrupted when reckless disobedience leads him to an uncomfortable encounter with the fearsome Dweller of the Threshold. Zanoni's powers ebb away as his commitment to the heroine grows, and he loses her after his own fateful confrontation with the same demon. In the climax, however, Zanoni has a chance to redeem himself by taking the heroine's place when she is condemned to the guillotine by the Revolutionary Tribunal in Paris. Charles Dickens borrowed the redemptive denouement but left the occult claptrap strictly alone, whereas Madame Blavatsky imported Bulwerian occultism wholesale into her own account of *The Secret Doctrine* and paid no attention whatsoever to what Sidney Carton deemed the "far, far better thing."

Zanoni caught the mood of the times well enough to give rise to speculation that Bulwer might be a Rosicrucian initiate—a rumour which he never tried over-strenuously to discourage although he was always careful to assert that he remained conscientiously sceptical about all matters supernatural. His second occult romance was the novella "The Haunters and the Haunted," initially published in *Blackwood's* in 1859. It describes the frightful apparitions which plague two friends in a house which is eventually torn down—at which point a hidden room containing a vessel full of "magnetic fluid" is discovered. Many reprints of the story (which often use the alternate title "The House and the Brain") end at this point but the full-length version introduces the immortal magician whose will-power conjured up the apparitions, who proceeds to employ the hapless narrator as a medium. The story caused something of a sensation; the various manifestations plaguing the haunted house have been copied far too many times for sensible enumeration, but Marie Corelli ploughed her usual lone furrow by utilizing the second part of the story—or perhaps the amended version of it contained in *A Strange Story*—as the basis for *The Soul of Lilith.*

A Strange Story is more of a thriller than a metaphysical romance but Bulwer could never resist the temptation to dress up his fanciful excursions with ponderous and murky allegorical implications. The materialistic doctor Allen Fenwick becomes engaged to the neurasthenic Lilian, and then finds himself at odds with the charming occultist Margrave, who wants to use her as a medium. Margrave is in pursuit of the secret of immortality, as is Sir Philip Derval, who returns from the East in search of the murderer of his mentor—but Derval is murdered himself and Fenwick is fitted up for the crime. Margrave contrives his release, inevitably demanding a price—but when, after much delay, he finally gets around to claiming his due he comes woefully unstuck because the powers he releases are too strong. No doubt the novel would have made more sense had Bulwer ever made up his mind what sense it was supposed to make, but he never quite did—and he was never one to delay publication once he had enough pages to make a three-decker.

Given that *A Strange Story* remains something of a mess it was perhaps rather immoderate of Bulwer to forbid his son to sully *The Ring of Amasis*—a florid occult romance which his son wrote at about the same time—with the family name (it appeared in 1863 under the pseudonym Owen Meredith, although once Baron Lytton was safely dead it was reprinted under the proud signature of the Earl of Lytton). The problem was, in part, that Bulwer never could decide once and for all how serious he was about matters occult—or, if he were serious, exactly what sort of seriousness was involved. Viewed dispassionately, his three occult romances fail just as dismally in literary terms as they do in terms of metaphysical acuity, but the fascination they reflect was certainly infectious in their day, and they remain grotesquely ambivalent classics of post-Gothic supernatural fiction.

We can only wonder what Bulwer might have accomplished had he clung fast to the political and intellectual heresies which he gladly embraced while he was at odds with his redoubtable mother, instead of beating a rapid retreat to unorthodox but dull conservatism as soon as he inherited the family fortune—but he never was cut out to be an Arbaces, let alone a Zanoni, and the fate to which he eventually delivered poor Margrave looks suspiciously like sour grapes.

—Brian Stableford

BURKE, John (Frederick)

Pseudonyms: Jonathan Burke; Owen Burke; Harriet Esmond (in collaboration with his wife); Jonathan George; Joanna Jones; Robert Miall; Sara Morris; Martin Sands. **Nationality:** British. **Born:** Rye, Sussex, 8 March 1922. **Education:** Holt High School, Liverpool. **Military Service:** Royal Air Force, Royal Electrical and Mechanical Engineers, and Royal Marines, 1942-47: Sergeant. **Family:** Married 1) Joan Morris in 1941 (divorced 1963), five daughters; 2) Jean Williams in 1963, two sons. **Career:** Associate editor, 1953-56, and production manager, 1956-57, Museum Press, London; editorial manager, Books for Pleasure Group, London, 1957-58; public relations and publications executive, Shell International Petroleum, London, 1959-63; story editor, Twentieth Century-Fox, London, 1963-65; director, Lom Associates Ltd., literary agency, London, 1965; freelance writer since 1966. **Awards:** Rockefeller Foundation Atlantic award, 1949. **Agent:** David Higham Associates Ltd., 5-8 Lower John Street, Golden Square, London W1R 4HA; or, Harold Ober Associates, Inc., 425 Madison Avenue, New York, NY 10017, USA.

HORROR, GHOST AND GOTHIC PUBLICATIONS

Novels (series: Dr. Caspian)

The Outward Walls (as J. F. Burke). London, Laurie, 1952.
Dr. Terror's House of Horrors (novelization of screenplay). London, Pan, 1965.
Dracula: Prince of Darkness (novelization of screenplay). London, Pan, 1967.
The Devil's Footsteps (Dr. Caspian). London, Weidenfeld and Nicholson, and New York, Coward McCann, 1976.
The Black Charade (Dr. Caspian). London, Weidenfeld and Nicholson, and New York, Coward McCann, 1977.
Ladygrave (Dr. Caspian). London, Weidenfeld and Nicholson, and New York, Coward McCann, 1978.

Short Stories

The Hammer Horror Omnibus 1 (novelizations of screenplays). London, Pan, 1966.

The Hammer Horror Omnibus 2 (novelizations of screenplays). London, Pan, 1967.

Other

Editor, *Tales of Unease*. London, Pan, 1966.
Editor, *More Tales of Unease*. London, Pan, 1969.
Editor, *New Tales of Unease*. London, Pan, 1976.

OTHER PUBLICATIONS

Novels as J. F., John or Jonathan Burke

Swift Summer. London, Laurie, 1949.
Another Chorus. London, Laurie, 1949.
These Haunted Streets. London, Laurie, 1950.
Chastity House. London, Laurie, 1952.
Dark Gateway. London, Panther, 1953.
The Echoing Worlds. London, Panther, 1954.
Twilight of Reason. London, Panther, 1954.
Pattern of Shadows. London, Panther, 1954.
Hotel Cosmos. London, Panther, 1954.
Deep Freeze. London, Panther, 1955.
Revolt of the Humans. London, Panther, 1955.
The Poison Cupboard. London, Secker and Warburg, 1956.
Pursuit Through Time. London, Ward Lock, 1956.
Corpse to Copenhagen. London, Amalgamated Press, 1957.
Echo of Barbara. London, Long, 1959.
Fear by Instalments. London, Long, 1960.
A Widow for the Winter (as Sara Morris). London, Barker, 1961.
Teach Yourself Treachery. London, Long, 1962.
Deadly Downbeat. London, Long, 1962.
The Twisted Tongues. London, Long, 1964; as *Echo of Treason*, New York, Dodd Mead, 1966.
Only the Ruthless Can Play. London, Long, 1965.
The Weekend Girls. London, Long, 1966; New York, Doubleday, 1967; as *Goodbye, Gillian*, New York, Ace, n.d.
Gossip to the Grave. London, Long, 1967; as *The Gossip Truth*, New York, Doubleday, 1968.
The Suburbs of Pleasure. London, Secker and Warburg, and New York, Delacorte Press, 1967.
Someone Lying, Someone Dying. London, Long, 1968.
Rob the Lady. London, Long, 1969.
Four Stars for Danger. London, Long, 1970.
The Killdog (with George Theiner, as Jonathan George). London, Macmillan, and New York, Doubleday, 1970.
Dead Letters (as Jonathan George). London, Macmillan, 1972.
Expo 80. London, Cassell, 1972.
The Figurehead (as Owen Burke). London, Collins, and New York, Coward McCann, 1979.

Novelizations of Plays, Screenplays or Television Scripts

The Entertainer. London, Four Square, 1960.
Look Back in Anger. London, Four Square, 1960.
The Angry Silence. London, Hodder and Stoughton, 1961.
Flame in the Streets. London, Four Square, 1961.
The Lion of Sparta. London, Pan, 1961; as *The 300 Spartans*, New York, Signet, 1961.
The Boys. London, Pan, 1962.

Private Potter. London, Pan, 1962.
The Man Who Finally Died. London, Pan, 1963.
The World Ten Times Over. London, Pan, 1963.
Guilty Party. London, Elek, 1963.
A Hard Day's Night. London, Pan, and New York, Dell, 1964.
The System. London, Pan, 1964.
That Magnificent Air Race. London, Pan, 1965; as *Those Magnificent Men in Their Flying Machines*, New York, Pocket, 1965.
The Power Game. London, Pan, 1966.
The Trap. London, Pan, 1966.
The Jokers (as Martin Sands). London, Pan, 1967.
Maroc 7 (as Martin Sands). London, Pan, 1967.
Privilege. London, Pan, and New York, Avon, 1967.
Till Death Us Do Part. London, Pan, 1967.
Chitty Chitty Bang Bang. London, Pan, 1968.
Smashing Time. London, Pan, 1968.
Moon Zero Two. London, Pan, 1969.
The Smashing Bird I Used to Know. London, Pan, 1969.
All the Right Noises. London, Hodder and Stoughton, 1970.
Strange Report. London, Hodder and Stoughton, 1970.
UFO 1-2 (as Robert Miall). London, Pan, 2 vols., 1970-71.
Dad's Army. London, Hodder and Stoughton, 1971.
Jason King (as Robert Miall). London, Pan, 1972.
Kill Jason King! (as Robert Miall). London, Pan, 1972.
The Protectors (as Robert Miall). London, Pan, 1973.
The Adventurer (as Robert Miall). London, Pan, 1973.
Luke's Kingdom. London, Fontana, 1976.
The Prince Regent. London, Fontana, 1979.
The Bill [*2, 3, 4*]. First two vols., London, Methuen, 1985-87; last two vols., London, Mandarin, 1989-90.
The Fourth Floor. London, Methuen, 1986.
King and Castle. London, Methuen, 1986.

Novels as Harriet Esmond

Darsham's Tower. New York, Delacorte Press, 1973; as *Darsham's Folly*, London, Collins, 1974.
The Eye Stones. London, Collins, and New York, Delacorte Press, 1975.
The Florian Signet. London, Collins, and New York, Fawcett, 1977.

Novels as Joanna Jones

Nurse is a Neighbour. London, Joseph, 1958.
Nurse on the District. London, Joseph, 1959.
The Artless Flat-Hunter. London, Pelham, 1963.
The Artless Commuter. London, Pelham, 1965.

Short Stories as Jonathan Burke

Alien Landscapes. London, Museum Press, 1955; as *Exodus from Elysium*, Australia, 1965.

Plays

Screenplay: *The Sorcerers*, with Michael Reeves and Tom Baker, 1967.

Television Plays: *Safe Conduct*, 1965; *Calculated Nightmare*, from his own story, 1970; *Miss Mouse*, from his own story, 1972.

Radio Plays: *The Prodigal Pupil*, 1949; *The Man in the Ditch*, 1958; *Across Miss Desmond's Desk*, 1961.

Other

The Happy Invaders: A Picture of Denmark in Springtime, with William Luscombe. London, Hale, 1956.
Suffolk. London, Batsford, 1971.
England in Colour. London, Batsford, and New York, Hastings House, 1972.
Sussex. London, Batsford, 1974.
An Illustrated History of England. London, Collins, 1974; New York, McKay, 1976.
English Villages. London, Batsford, 1975.
South East England (for children). London, Faber, 1975.
Suffolk in Photographs, photographs by Anthony Kersting. London, Batsford, 1976.
Czechoslovakia. London, Batsford, 1976.
Historic Britain. London, Batsford, 1977.
Life in the Castle in Mediaeval England. London, Batsford, and Totowa, New Jersey, Rowman and Littlefield, 1978.
Life in the Villa in Roman Britain. London, Batsford, 1978.
Look Back on England. London, Orbis, 1980.
The English Inn. London, Batsford, and New York, Holmes and Meier, 1981.
Musical Landscapes. Exeter, Webb and Bower, and New York, Holt Rinehart, 1983.
Roman England. London, Weidenfeld and Nicolson, 1980.
The Illustrated History of Music. London, Sphere, 1988.
A Traveller's History of Scotland. London, Murray, 1990.

Editor, *Beautiful Britain.* London, Batsford, 1976.

Translator, *The West Face*, by Guido Magone. London, Museum Press, 1955.
Translator, *The Spark and the Flame*, by F. B. Muus. London, Museum Press, 1957.
Translator, with Eiler Hansen, *The Moon of Beauty*, by Jorgen Andersen-Rosendal. London, Museum Press, 1957.
Translator, with Eiler Hansen, *The Happy Lagoons: The World of Queen Salote*, by Jorgen Andersen-Rosendal. London, Jarrolds, 1961.

*   *   *

John Burke's early writing career, in the 1950s, concentrated on science-fiction novels, under the name Jonathan Burke. From the 1960s he has written a small number of horror novels and about 45 novelizations of films and TV series covering all genres. In all, he has written more than 120 books, fiction and non-fiction. His short horror stories have appeared regularly in British anthologies since the mid-1960s, and he has edited a couple of horror anthologies.

Dr. Terror's House of Horrors is a film novelization, too brief to achieve atmosphere or credibility. It is a collection of five stories, each a prophecy by the mysterious Dr. Schreck and based on the Tarot's Major Arcana. The doctor, whose name means "terror," is travelling by train in a compartment with five other men (all strangers) who ask him to reveal their futures.

Each future is disastrous, featuring a horror cliché. Jim Dawson, a Scottish architect, learns that he will be hunting werewolves and will be killed by them. Bill Rogers will try to protect his wife and daughter from a dangerous and swiftly-growing plant, but the suggestion is that the plant will prevail in the end. Trumpeter Biff Bailey is due to visit the West Indies and become a victim of a voodoo god. Franklyn Marsh, who is a noted art critic, famous for feuds with artists (and a total sceptic where fortune-telling is concerned), will be blinded by the disembodied hand of one of his artist victims. And Bob Carroll, a medical doctor from the U.S., will return home with a new bride and quickly become mixed up with vampires.

For each fortune the next card may be consulted to offer an alternative, which is always Death. At the end of the book the five men discover that their train has crashed, they are already dead, and Dr. Schreck is Death personified.

For the same reasons, the novelization of *Dracula: Prince of Darkness*, plus the eight other Hammer horror films which Burke converted into novellas in two volumes, are shallow and relatively unconvincing; each needs more space for development and some freedom from the clichés of the genre.

Fortunately, Burke is a much better writer when not novelizing somebody else's screenplay. His Dr. Caspian series consists of three convincing and fast-paced supernatural horror novels set in the 1880s. In *The Devil's Footsteps* much of the action occurs in the Norfolk village of Hexney, where an odd series of deep footprints (or hoofprints) has appeared, and seems to be advancing day by day. They resemble backwards-facing arrowheads, all in a direct line, and not made by any known creature. Dr. Alexander Caspian, a stage magician with contempt for the supernatural, comes to investigate. Also staying in the village is Bronwen Powys, a young photographer.

The superstitious nature of the villagers is evidenced by the way Bronwen is treated when a boy she has photographed is later found drowned—she is turned out of her lodgings and only Caspian's assistance prevents her from being hounded out of the village. Caspian calculates that the line of prints, when complete, will form a pentacle of lines around the village. Also, Caspian discovers that the village suffers from an ungodly heritage of ceremonies and rites, due partly to witchcraft trials there in the 17th century, while Bronwen (the seventh daughter of a seventh daughter) realizes that she can receive Caspian's thoughts.

The two of them leave Hexney (though not without some difficulty), yet Bronwen is drawn back to the village by a stone placed in her luggage. She believes herself to be the intended sacrifice in a ghastly ritual, but it is actually Caspian who is to be the sacrifice; her part is just to call him, using her talent. In the end, the presence of outsiders (a train stranded by floods) is enough to counterbalance the belief of the villagers and enable the pentacle to be broken.

The novel is full of entertaining scenes, particularly Caspian and Bronwen's mental love-making as they lie in separate rooms at the village's inn, and the way that all Christian things within the village church (altar, font, statues) have been veiled in black and the rector has taken a short holiday, handing over his parish to a priest of the devil. In the two later books Caspian and Bronwen (now his wife) act as psychic detectives, hiring themselves out to investigate and combat the powers of darkness. These two main characters are sharply drawn throughout, though other characters in the series tend to be either ciphers or stereotypes.

Burke's short horror stories are always entertaining, though they have improved over the years. All are set in the present day, with

about two thirds being supernatural. The early story "Party Games," from 1965, cleverly shows how some children remain outsiders, loathed by their contemporaries. Simon attends Ronnie's birthday party uninvited (he is the sort of unemotional and too-clever child whom nobody would invite to anything) and is admitted by Ronnie's mother partly because he has brought a present for Ronnie. The *grand guignol* ending (Ronnie's father is killed and parts of him are passed around as a party game) is logical, since Simon has no father and wants to deprive the hated Ronnie of the person he most adores, though not persuasive, since a boy of his age (eight or ten) is unlikely to be able to kill and partly dismember an adult. Similarly, "A Comedy of Terrors," about a film special-effects designer, is very nasty, showing him skinning his girlfriend alive just so that he can learn how to fake it in his next film, yet not particularly credible. And the vengeance of her brother is just a little too easily achieved.

"Casualty" is a very clever piece which turns out to be about a ghost trying to persuade a baby not to be born because life is not worth it. "Lucille Would Have known" concerns a group of middle-aged and elderly people who often gather to go on coach trips and how Lucille, their organizer, now dead, takes revenge upon Madge, who could have saved her. A wonderfully subtle and terrifying story is "The Loiterers," which is reminiscent of Robert Aickman's work. Bernard meets Elizabeth at a dinner party hosted by their mutual friends. He pursues her, though she is reluctant, and falls in love with her. But she is death to fall in love with, and Bernard's ghost joins all the others loitering outside her flat, while the crass and loudmouthed Neil (the married host from the dinner party) carries on an affair with Elizabeth without being affected. And the best of Burke's tales is probably the most recent, "One Day You'll Learn," from 1992. It features a mother from hell, who is awful enough to her son, daughter-in-law and granddaughter while she is alive, always persecuting her son for her own mistakes, but much, much more terrible after she dies.

—Chris Morgan

BURKS, Arthur J.

Pseudonym: Esther Critchfield. **Nationality:** American. **Born:** 13 September 1898. **Military Service:** Served in the U.S. Army: Lieutenant. **Career:** Prolific contributor of stories to pulp magazines, and in particuar *Weird Tales* from 1924. **Died:** 1974.

HORROR, GHOST AND GOTHIC PUBLICATIONS

Novels

The Great Amen. New York, Egmont Press, 1938.
The Great Mirror. London, Gerald Swan, 1952.
The Casket. Lakemont, Georgia, Tarnhelm Press, 1973.

Short Stories

Look Behind You! Buffalo, New York, Shroud, 1954.
Black Medicine. Sauk City, Wisconsin, Arkham House, 1966.

*

Critical Study: *The Shudder Pulps* by Robert Kenneth Jones, West Linn, Oregon, Fax, 1975.

*   *   *

Arthur J. Burks wrote tens of millions of words for the pulps, yet it is hardly surprising that few of them are read today. Burks was the consummate pulpsmith, a writer who could produce on demand and who often placed ten or more stories per month in a variety of magazines that spanned the horror, science fiction, mystery, adventure, western and romance genres. By necessity much of his writing was generic, built around basic plots and stock characters that could be shaped to fit the needs of a given market. His name endures in the annals of weird fiction primarily because he knew how to create a powerful atmosphere of dread in his stories in lieu of compelling plots.

Burks's earliest and best weird fiction appeared in *Weird Tales*, where he emerged as one of editor Farnsworth Wright's first "discoveries." "Thus Spake the Prophetess," published in the November 1924 issue under the pseudonym Estil Critchie (a byline Burks transformed into "Esther Critchfield" when writing for the love pulps), was the first of nearly a dozen stories for the magazine that he set in Haiti and the Dominican Republic. Purportedly drawn from his experiences while a marine stationed overseas, they are basic adventure tales leavened with incidents of horror. Burks pandered to reader tastes for the exotic, portraying the islands as lands of enchantment where magic is not uncommon. Eager to portray his settings as pregnant with mysterious possibilities, he filled his stories with cultural stereotypes endemic to the pulps, particularly his rendering of natives. The islands were, as he wrote in "Black Medicine," "back country jungles which had never known the touch of a white man's foot, and in which ebony people, blacker even than the 'raven tresses of midnight,' stalked silently on bare splay feet, red-rimmed eyes searching the jungle, broad nostrils twitching like those of a questing feline—searching forever for answers to strange questions which no white man had ever asked and no white man may ever answer." Although his depictions of blacks as brutal savages are difficult to digest today, they were integral to his portrait of an island culture shaped by primitive superstitions rooted in occult truths.

As Robert Kenneth Jones points out in *The Shudder Pulps*, most of Burks's stories were mood pieces. They are filled with disembodied voices, ghostly faces at the window, burning eyes glimpsed in the dark, dogs howling eerily in the distance, and curses that portentously foreshadow the outcome of events. Burks was a master at deploying these clichés effectively in suspenseful narratives surprisingly free of the purple prose that most of his colleagues used to liven things up. He could build a sense of supernatural menace, even when nothing supernatural was happening, as in "Voodoo" and "Black Medicine," both of which are little more than descriptions of gruesome voodoo rituals, and he could tease the reader with ambiguous treatments of the uncanny, as in "Daylight Shadows" and "Faces," which use dream and hallucination to rationalize their bizarre manifestations. The best of his island tales, "Three Coffins," is typical of all Burks's weird fiction: native labourers in a construction crew believe themselves cursed when they discover that the cargo of a boat ferrying them to a remote island contains three empty coffins. The white bosses scoff at superstitious interpretations of their every misfortune as a harbinger of doom, but eventually each dies mysteriously and is

shipped home in one of the coffins. The late discovery of a native plot to scuttle the construction project fails to explain all of the strange events, leaving open the possibility of actual supernatural intervention.

Burks wrote on a variety of common and uncommon themes in his other weird stories. "Invisible Threads" concerns a team of vigilantes who use their astral projections to bring criminals to justice, "Asphodel" a field of flowers nourished on human blood, and "When the Graves Were Opened" the horrifying implications of a biblical prophecy. He even wrote a horror story about writing a horror story in "Something Toothsome," which satirizes his legendary ability to turn the most unlikely object into the subject of a story. In this tale, a writer is framed for murder through an elaborate plot for a crime story that he himself concocts from a dental mould in a doctor's office. When writing at shorter length Burks tended to emphasize mood over plot. "The Place of Pythons," for example, is a stream-of-consciousness story that relates the narrator's transformation (or imagined transformation) into a predatory snake as it takes place. Longer stories allowed him to fill out his narrative with history and local colour, as in the novella "Guatomzein the Visitant," where a resurrected king of the Aztecs avenging the slaughter of his people regales his victims with memories of Mexico's ancient past.

In his best weird tales, Burks simply piled weird incidents one on top of the other before offering an anticlimactic explanation for them. The narrator of "The Ghosts of Steamboat Coulee" witnesses a series of inexplicable visions before discovering that he has strayed into a haunted canyon. In "The Bells of Oceana" a ship is menaced by spectral manifestations and disappearances that end abruptly once it passes beyond a certain latitude. "The Room of Shadows" abounds with weird transformations and apparent plot contradictions that make sense only when a change in the narrative point of view is revealed in the closing paragraphs.

By the mid-1930s, Burks had shifted his weird fiction writing almost entirely to *Dime Mystery*, *Horror Stories*, *Terror Tales* and other shudder pulps. These magazines, which specialized in tales of luckless heroes and heroines subjected to an endless series of weird menaces and torments that prove to have a logical (if far-fetched) explanation, were perfectly suited to Burks's "scare first, plot later" style of storytelling. Shudder-pulp stories tended to be formulaic and undistinguished, but Burks occasionally put an interesting supernatural spin on their events, as in "Six Doors to Horror," or spiced up stories like "Murder Brides" with hints of taboo sexuality.

Burks briefly revived his weird fiction career in the 1950s with a handful of stories for *Weird Tales* and *Look Behind You!*, a collection of previously unpublished short stories. Except for "Black Harvest of Moraine," a tale of an ancient life-form liberated by the melting of an underground glacier, these stories are unremarkable hodpodges of horror, fantasy and science fiction. Burks's best work remains the stories he wrote early in the century, when expectations for and expert practitioners of the pulp weird tale were fewer.

—Stefan Dziemianowicz

BURNELL, Mark

Nationality: British. **Born:** 1964. **Address:** c/o Hodder Headline plc, 338 Euston Road, London NW1 3BH, England.

HORROR, GHOST AND GOTHIC PUBLICATIONS

Novels

Freak. London, Hodder and Stoughton, 1994.
Glittering Savages. London, Hodder and Stoughton, 1995.

* * *

Several young British horror novelists have emerged during the 1990s. Burnell is neither the best nor the worst of these, displaying some talent and promising greater things to come. He is capable of creating excellent scenes but has not so far achieved the consistency which is necessary to a novelist. Both *Freak* and *Glittering Savages* are flawed novels; while the former contains a single very good idea handled poorly, the latter is a mostly unconvincing version of hackneyed themes, despite some sporadically attractive writing.

Christian Floyd, the protagonist and narrator of *Freak*, is a young and very successful city trader working in London, a high-living yuppie with a BMW and a live-in girlfriend. One night, leaving work late, he rescues a young woman from an attack by three men in an underground carpark. There is a lot of blood around, but he leaves before an ambulance arrives. Not wishing to become involved, he dumps his own bloodstained clothes and has his car cleaned. He finds that he has no wounds, so the blood must not have been his own. Not until the young woman, Gabriella, comes to his office to thank him a day or two later does he realize that she was seriously wounded by a knife in the attack and that he healed her wounds.

A week later, Christian does the same thing again. He has left a boring charity dinner and is going home with a casual pick-up called Julia (this marks his break-up with girlfriend Katy), when they encounter a blind man in the apartment block where she lives. Christian feels compelled to try and heal him. The old man's eyes bleed and Christian himself bleeds from his hands, feet and side. This healing is a success; the old man can at once see again.

Nobody, including Christian, can believe what they have seen. He feels himself to be an ordinary person with no religious beliefs. Yet what he has done—or appears to have done—alters his life permanently. Only Gabriella is prepared to accept him and put herself out by helping him. When he is quickly beset by the media and a lunatic fringe church, she outwits or fights off his attackers. She does this not simply out of gratitude but because she has fallen in love with him.

The first third of the book is exciting and surprising, then it descends into farce and cliché, as Christian allows an agent to look after his interests (and his safety). The rest of the plot is all too predictable, including hostile crowds, TV chat shows and a face-to-face confrontation between Christian and his religious persecutor, Louis, who comes in waving a gun around.

The irony of Christian's position, with regard to his name, his new found power and his lack of belief, is too obvious to be spelt out, yet Burnell does spell it out, and too much space is taken up with discussions about stigmata and whether Christian's power must be God-given or could have come from Satan. The book continues to move along well, but it holds no more surprises and becomes more of a light-hearted thriller than genre horror.

Glittering Savages is much more of a genre horror novel, yet this is part of its problem; in it Burnell tries to imitate the big, multi-plotted splatterpunk novels which have littered the genre in recent years, and he fails even to come up to their low standards. Though published second, it seems as though it may have been written first.

It is, by classification, a superwoman story. Rachel is over 200 years old, has remained young and beautiful for all that time, and possesses superhuman senses and powers of strength and speed. She also has the ability to assimilate the memories and skills of anybody she kills (just so long as she drinks some of their blood and rips out their heart). Now she has spotted Robert, fallen in love more deeply than ever before, murdered several people around him, and infected him with her own superhuman blood so that he will die and be reborn as a superman.

There is one scene notable for its gratuitous violence, where Rachel and the (still only human) Robert are attacked by a quartet of youthful attackers on the London underground. Quick as a flash, Rachel despatches them, throwing one out through a window, crushing another's fist into pulp with her own, and then ripping out hearts by punching her fist through breastbones in a display that bravely defies all scientific possibilities.

The rest of the plot is complex, though this is just a means of padding out the book, involving the police, a vampire-hunter who has travelled over from the US and the sister of one of Rachel's earlier victims. None of these elements do much to help credibility, which goes out of the window at about the same time as the attacker on the underground train. The fact that the plot complexity (to say nothing of the shifts in viewpoint from paragraph to paragraph) only serves to dilute the novel's focus might be important if that focus contained any originality. And the fact that most of the characters, in turn, pour out their sad life histories, does nothing to make the reader care what happens to any of them.

Even so, the novel has its good points. The setting, a very hot summer in contemporary London, is well captured, with excellent small details presumably taken from life. A few scenes are written with great panache, especially one where the almost-dead Robert is revitalized by a quick taste of Rachel's blood and the two of them engage in a bout of love-making in an alley full of trash as the summer heat breaks and torrential rain pours down.

Perhaps, in a future book, Burnell will manage to bring it all together—the sympathetic protagonist and grabbingly original idea as in *Freak*, together with the broad span, fine setting and horrific sharpness of *Glittering Savages*—and add in some credible plotting to come up with a novel of high quality. The ability is there.

—Chris Morgan

BURRAGE, A(lfred) M(cLelland)

Pseudonym: Ex-Private X. **Nationality:** British. **Born:** Hillingdon, Middlesex, 1 July 1889; son of the writer Alfred Sherrington Burrage; nephew of the writer Edwin Harcourt Burrage. **Military Service:** British Army, during World War I. **Career:** Professional writer from the age of 16, initially for juvenile weekly papers, later for a wide range of fiction magazines. **Died:** 18 December 1956.

HORROR, GHOST AND GOTHIC PUBLICATIONS

Novel

Seeker to the Dead. London, Swan, 1942.

Short Stories

Some Ghost Stories. London, Palmer, 1927.
Someone in the Room (as Ex-Private X). London, Jarrolds, 1931.
Between the Minute and the Hour, edited by Anthony Skene. London, Jenkins, 1967.
Warning Whispers, edited by Jack Adrian. Wellingborough, Northamptonshire, Equation, 1988.
Unpaying Guests, edited by Jack Adrian. Chester, Cheshire, Ghost Story Society, 1989.
Intruders: New Weird Tales, edited by Jack Adrian. Chester, Cheshire, Ash-Tree Press, 1995.
The Occult Files of Francis Chard: Some Ghost Stories, edited by Jack Adrian. Chester, Cheshire, Ash-Tree Press, 1996.
Someone in the Room: Strange Tales Old and New, edited by Jack Adrian. Ashcroft, British Columbia, Ash-Tree Press, 1997.

OTHER PUBLICATIONS

Novels

For the Honour of the Team! (for children). London, Aldine, 1910.
The Cad of the College (for children). London, Aldine, 1912.
The Hope of Her Heart. London, Newnes, 1922.
The Golden Barrier. Dundee, Leng, 1925.
Poor Dear Esmé. London, Newnes, 1925.
The Smokes of Spring. London, John Long, 1926.
Courtland's Crime. London, John Long, 1928.
Don't Break the Seal. London, John Long, 1946.

Other

War is War (as Ex-Private X). London, Gollancz, 1930.

*   *   *

In the general short-story line A. M. Burrage was a writer of prodigious fecundity. He wrote not simply scores—which would have been prolific enough, even in the great days of the British popular fiction magazine, such as the *Grand, Strand, Novel, London, Windsor, Royal, New, 20-Story, Premier, Red Storyteller, Happy* together with *Pearson's* and *Cassell's*—but hundreds. His grand total, from the time he started, around 1905, through to the Second World War, when he virtually ceased to write, must run to well over a thousand stories, a good two-thirds of which almost certainly have followed a precise formula: boy meets girl, boy has row with girl, boy makes it up with girl, wedding bells. Burrage was a dab-hand at that plot and could ring the changes on it endlessly and inventively. He had a rich and lively imagination, and although he had his own pet sub-plots, pet incidents, pet plot-confrontations, he wasn't the writer to return to them time and again to the exclusion of some new and ingenious gimmick dreamed up on the spur of the moment.

But, excellent of their type as they undeniably are, it is not for his romances—which, depending upon the requirements of individual editors, could be frothy, jolly, comic, farcical, moving, sentimental, nostalgic, tear-inducing, even starkly tragic—that A. M. Burrage has been remembered (and by a few celebrated) over the years. Burrage has been remembered because he wrote superlative tales of the supernatural.

He was lucky with his editors, two in particular—Isabel Thorne and David Whitelaw—having an immense influence on his artistic development, not only in the realms of the weird and the uncanny, but in the far tougher world of mainstream popular fiction as well. Burrage began writing for a living at the age of 16, due to his father's sudden death, and had thus to become sole wage-earner for his mother, sister and an aunt. This had a profound effect upon his view of the world, and certainly coloured his writing and his attitude towards writing. Authority figures who were *simpatico* were (metaphorically speaking) welcomed as allies in what he saw as a lone-handed battle against almost overwhelming odds.

Isabel Thorne, chief editor of Shurey's Publications (a small but bustling off-Fleet Street concern), oversaw two regular outlets for short fiction, *Yes or No* and *The Weekly Tale-Teller*. She took Burrage's early stories (for adults; he was already a prolific contributor to the school-story papers of the juvenile market), gave him advice, and selflessly steered him in the direction of better-paying rivals. She had a fondness for weird fiction, as did Burrage. David Whitelaw was then (immediately prior to the Great War) editor of the prestigious *London Magazine*, at this time arguably even ahead of the *Strand Magazine* in terms of influence, literary and illustrative quality, and, crucially, circulation. He too was an enthusiast for ghost stories, the weirder the better (he thought them "easy to write," a view of which Burrage later disabused him). Burrage's first contribution to the *London* was a light romance of the type that would, a decade later, bring him in over a thousand a year, net, at a time when the average annual income was still only roughly £180. His second, in 1913, was a weird, "The Chalk-Pit" (*Intruders*)—and in the 20 years from 1913-33 (when the magazine ceased publication) he wrote over 30 tales of the strange and supernatural for Whitelaw and his successors.

These contributions to the *London* later formed the basis of his two celebrated weird-story collections, *Some Ghost Stories* (recently reprinted together with a previously uncollected "psychic detective" series, and other rare work, as *The Occult Files of Francis Chard: Some Ghost Stories*) and *Someone in the Room* (recently reprinted, together with a number of previously uncollected stories, as *Someone in the Room: Strange Tales Old and New*). Two further, posthumous, volumes, *Warning Whispers* and *Intruders*, both of which collect a mass of previously unpublished material, offer even more evidence of his talents in the weird-fiction field.

As befitted a professional writer—a man who earned his living (however precarious at times that living could be) by his pen, and had of necessity to keep turning material out and not just, somewhat pathetically, "wait for inspiration"—Burrage took his plots from everywhere and everything. A half-heard conversation . . . something in the morning paper . . . an incident in the street . . . a gloomy face on a tram. He had served throughout the Great War, and in the 1920s found that this experience proved a useful jumping-off point for some of his finest weird tales. The interestingly named A. M. Bainbridge in "The Lady of the Chateau" (*Intruders*) has a peculiar experience on a scouting expedition, while in "Orders from Brigade" (*Intruders*) a revenant saves a company from destruction by the German guns. In one of the Francis Chard tales, "The Soldier," the psychic sleuth discovers not a haunted house but a haunted couple, fleeing from a betrayed husband whom died in the muck and blood of the trenches. Serrald, in "The Shadowy Escort" (*Someone in the Room*) is pursued in horribly relentless fashion by the enemy he left to die in No Man's Land. Burrage's war masterpiece, however, is undoubtedly "The Recurring Tragedy" (*Warning Whispers*), in which a British Army general suddenly recalls his past life as the man who spurned with his boot the crucifix-laden Christ.

Like E. F. Benson, he was fond of the old-fashioned "cut-throat" razor as a means of hurling both murder victims (e.g. the silently screaming maid in "The House of Unrest" in *Someone in the Room*) and suicides (e.g. the tragic butler in "Wine of Summer" in *Intruders*) into the ceaseless loom. Gypsy curses and malevolence, though politically incorrect today, made for some memorably horrific tales—such as "Furze Hollow" (*Some Ghost Stories*) and the brilliant and unusual "Between the Minute and the Hour," in which Burrage plays with the concept of time (for insulting an old gypsywoman Trimmer finds that, near the midnight hour, his house becomes somehow displaced in time, until at the end he seems to be trapped in the Middle Ages, pursued then dragged down by ravening wolves). The story was originally published (in the *Premier Magazine*) in 1922, long before J. W. Dunne's radical theories about time-shifts, "dimensional movement" and so on had gained general currency with the publication of *An Experiment with Time* (1927). One story which was clearly influenced by Dunne, however, was "The Affair at Paddock Cross," in which the narrator has a car-smash, then finds himself back in the 1750s dallying with another man's wife, is shot in a duel, then re-awakens in the 1920s and finds himself in precisely the same romantic, but dangerous, situation, from which he flees in horror.

Burrage was never much interested in mere hauntings, and his ghosts were by no means all malignant. The poor shade in "The Pace Maker" (*Intruders*) is doomed to plod alongside the champion runner on the cinder-track and off it; the ghost in "The Protector" (*The Occult Files of Francis Chard*) is a benign spirit, bent on warning the authorities of an impending outbreak of meningitis; in the splendid "For the Local Rag" (*Warning Whispers*) the spook merely appears to the hard-headed newspaperman Dorby to prove that there are indeed "more things in heaven and earth."

Even so Burrage's *oeuvre* has its full mead of horrors. The vengeful militia from another time in "The Green Scarf" (*Some Ghost Stories*), for instance; the crouching, bestial shadow in "The Little Blue Flames" (*Warning Whispers*); "The Intruder" itself, slowly descending the stairs (*Intruders*); the beast from the dawn of time in "In the Waters Under the Earth" (*Intruders*); the suffocating mass of hair in the brilliant "The Acquittal" (*Warning Whispers*); the thing with the cloven feet in "Mr. Garshaw's Companion" (*Someone in the Room*); the couple of "dingy waxworks" waiting . . . waiting . . . in "Corner Cottage" (*Intruders*).

The list is long, the variety infinite—the manner of telling invariably spellbinding. Burrage was a born storyteller who knew precisely how to utilize each and every one of the 6,000-or-so words in the average magazine short story to gain the effect he was aiming at. He succeeded with novella-length tales as well—as "The Lady of Graeme" (*Intruders*) and "The House by the Crossroads" (*The Occult Files of Francis Chard*) perfectly testify. He was perhaps less happy with anything longer. In his one full-length weird novel, *Seeker to the Dead* (black magic, necromancy and vampirism) there are more *longueurs* than gripping horror sequences (although when they arrive they are certainly effective enough).

But it is in his short fiction that A. M. Burrage truly triumphs. His purpose, as he once said, was to give the reader "a pleasant shudder"—a worthwhile enough aim. More often than not, however, he afforded his readers some very unpleasant shudders indeed.

—Jack Adrian

BURROUGHS, William S(eward)

Pseudonym: William Lee. **Nationality:** American. **Born:** St. Louis, Missouri, 5 February 1914. **Education:** John Burroughs School and Taylor School, St. Louis; Los Alamos Ranch School, New Mexico; Harvard University, Cambridge, Massachusetts, A.B. in anthropology 1936; studied medicine at the University of Vienna; Mexico City College, 1948-50. **Military Service:** Served in the U.S. Army, 1942. **Family:** Married 1) Ilse Herzfeld Klapper in 1937 (divorced 1946); 2) Jean Vollmer in 1945 (died 1951), one son (deceased). **Career:** Worked as a journalist, private detective, and bartender; later a full-time writer. Painter: exhibitions at Tony Shafrazi Gallery, New York; October Gallery, London, 1988; Kellas Gallery, Lawrence, Kansas, 1989. Lived for many years in Tangier and New York City; lived latterly Lawrence, Kansas. **Awards:** American Academy award, 1975. **Died:** 2 August 1997.

HORROR, GHOST AND GOTHIC PUBLICATIONS

Novels

The Naked Lunch. Paris, Olympia Press, 1959; London, Calder, 1964; as *Naked Lunch,* New York, Grove Press, 1962.
The Soft Machine. Paris, Olympia Press, 1961; New York, Grove Press, 1966; London, Calder and Boyars, 1968.
The Ticket That Exploded. Paris, Olympia Press, 1962; revised edition, New York, Grove Press, 1967; London, Calder and Boyars, 1968.
Dead Fingers Talk. London, Calder, 1963.
Nova Express. New York, Grove Press, 1964; London, Cape, 1966.
The Wild Boys: A Book of the Dead. New York, Grove Press, 1971; London, Calder and Boyars, 1972; revised edition, London, Calder, 1979.
Cities of the Red Night. London, Calder, and New York, Holt Rinehart, 1981.
The Place of Dead Roads. New York, Holt Rinehart, 1983; London, Calder, 1984.
The Western Lands. New York, Viking, 1987; London, Picador, 1988.

OTHER PUBLICATIONS

Novels

Junkie: Confessions of an Unredeemed Drug Addict (as William Lee). New York, Ace, 1953; London, Digit, 1957; complete edition, as *Junky,* London, Penguin, 1977.
Blade Runner: A Movie. Berkeley, California, Blue Wind Press, 1979.
Port of Saints. Berkeley, California, Blue Wind Press, 1980; London, Calder, 1983.
Queer. New York, Viking, 1985; London, Picador, 1986.

Short Stories

Exterminator! New York, Viking Press, 1973; London, Calder and Boyars, 1974.
Short Novels. London, Calder, 1978.

Early Routines. Santa Barbara, California, Cadmus, 1981.

The Streets of Chance. New York, Red Ozier Press, 1981.

Interzone, edited by James Grauerholz. New York, Viking, and London, Picador, 1989.

Ghost of Chance, illustrated by George Condo. New York, Library Fellows of the Whitney Museum of American Art, 1991.

Junky's Christmas and Other Stories. London, Serpents Tail, 1994.

Play

The Last Words of Dutch Schultz (film script). London, Cape Goliard Press, 1970; New York, Viking Press, 1975.

Other

The Exterminator, with Brion Gysin. San Francisco, Auerhahn Press, 1960.

Minutes to Go, with others. Paris, Two Cities, 1960; San Francisco, Beach, 1968.

The Yage Letters, with Allen Ginsberg. San Francisco, City Lights, 1963.

Roosevelt after Inauguration. New York, Fuck You Press, 1964.

Valentine Day's Reading. New York, American Theatre for Poets, 1965.

Time. New York, "C" Press, 1965.

Health Bulletin: APO-33: A Metabolic Regulator. New York, Fuck You Press, 1965; revised edition, as *APO-33 Bulletin,* San Francisco, Beach, 1966.

So Who Owns Death TV?, with Claude Pelieu and Carl Weissner. San Francisco, Beach, 1967.

The Dead Star. San Francisco, Nova Broadcast Press, 1969.

Ali's Smile. Brighton, Unicorn, 1969.

Entretiens avec William Burroughs, by Daniel Odier. Paris, Belfond, 1969; translated as *The Job: Interviews with William S. Burroughs* (includes *Electronic Revolution*), New York, Grove Press, and London, Cape, 1970.

The Braille Film. San Francisco, Nova Broadcast Press, 1970.

Brion Gysin Let the Mice In, with Brion Gysin and Ian Somerville, edited by Jan Herman. West Glover, Vermont, Something Else Press, 1973.

Mayfair Academy Series More or Less. Brighton, Urgency Press Rip-Off, 1973.

White Subway, edited by James Pennington. London, Aloes, 1974.

The Book of Breeething. Ingatestone, Essex, OU Press, 1974; Berkeley, California, Blue Wind Press, 1975; revised edition, Blue Wind Press, 1980.

Snack: Two Tape Transcripts, with Eric Mottram. London, Aloes, 1975.

Sidetripping, with Charles Gatewood. New York, Strawberry Hill, 1975.

The Retreat Diaries, with *The Dream of Tibet,* by Allen Ginsberg. New York, City Moon, 1976.

Cobble Stone Gardens. Cherry Valley, New York, Cherry Valley Editions, 1976.

The Third Mind, with Brion Gysin. New York, Viking Press, 1978; London, Calder, 1979.

Roosevelt after Inauguration and Other Atrocities. San Francisco, City Lights, 1979.

Ah Pook Is Here and Other Texts (includes *The Book of Breeething, Electronic Revolution*). London, Calder, 1979; New York, Riverrun, 1982.

A William Burroughs Reader, edited by John Calder. London, Picador, 1982.

Letters to Allen Ginsberg 1953-1957. New York, Full Court Press, 1982.

New York Inside Out, photographs by Robert Walker. Port Washington, New York, Skyline Press, 1984.

The Burroughs File. San Francisco, City Lights, 1984.

The Adding Machine: Collected Essays. London, Calder, 1985; New York, Seaver, 1986.

Tornado Alley. Cherry Valley, New York, Cherry Valley Editions, 1988.

The Cat Inside. New York, Viking, 1992.

Everything Is Permitted: The Making of Naked Lunch, edited by Ira Silverberg. New York, Grove Weidenfeld, 1992.

The Letters of William S. Burroughs: 1945-1959, edited by Oliver Harris. New York, Viking, and London, Picador, 1993.

My Education: A Book of Dreams. New York, Viking, 1994.

*

Film Adaptation: *Naked Lunch,* 1991.

Bibliography: *William S. Burroughs: A Bibliography 1953-1973* by Joe Maynard and Barry Miles, Charlottesville, University Press of Virginia, 1978; *William S. Burroughs: A Reference Guide* by Michael B. Goodman and Lemuel B. Coley, New York, Garland, 1990.

Critical Studies: *William Burroughs: The Algebra of Need* by Eric Mottram, Buffalo, Intrepid Press, 1971, revised edition, as *The Algebra of Need,* London, Boyars, 1991; *Contemporary Literary Censorship: The Case History of Burroughs' Naked Lunch* by Michael B. Goodman, Metuchen, New Jersey, Scarecrow Press, 1981; *With William Burroughs: A Report from the Bunker* edited by Victor Bokris, New York, Seaver, 1981, London, Vermilion, 1982; "William Burroughs Issue" of *Review of Contemporary Fiction* (Elmwood Park, Illinois), vol. 4, no. 1, 1984; *William Burroughs* by Jennie Skerl, Boston, Twayne, 1985; *Literary Outlaw: The Life and Times of William S. Burroughs* by Ted Morgan, New York, Holt, 1988, London, Bodley Head, 1991; *William S. Burroughs at the Front: Critical Reception 1959-1989* edited by Jennie Skerl and Robin Lydenberg, Carbondale, Southern Illinois University Press, 1991; *William Burroughs: El Hombre Invisible: A Portrait* by Barry Miles, London, Virgin, 1992, and New York, Hyperion, 1993.

*   *   *

Although in no sense a genre author, William S. Burroughs was possibly the greatest horror writer of the century. The book which established his reputation, *The Naked Lunch* (the definite article was dropped for the American edition), is a Menippean Satire—loosely referred to by the world at large as a "novel"—which consists of scores of short "routines" (Burroughs's term) strung together non-consecutively but unified by recurring patterns of imagery and obsession. The horror resides in the subject-matter, drug-addiction with its attendant ways of life and all their consequences, and in the remarkable clarity with which Burroughs views his nightmare world of drop-outs, criminals and addicts. The book expands far beyond the comparatively narrow world of addiction, however, becoming a satire on politics, business, medicine, sexual relationships and power-relations in general. Burroughs's ear for "dialogue" is beyond compare, his phrase-making hauntingly evocative; and, above all, he is relentlessly, grotesquely funny.

All Burroughs's subsequent major works are Menippean Satires in the same sense—loose, fantastic, apparently formless but at the same time razor-sharp, dissections of the follies of the mid-to-late 20th-century western world. They are full of parody, pastiche and quotation, intermixed with an astonishing realism founded on personal experience. *The Soft Machine, The Ticket That Exploded* and *Nova Express* (*Dead Fingers Talk* was a re-editing of material from the other books) employ much of the same matter as *The Naked Lunch* but further complicate it by use of the "cut-up" technique, a species of automatic writing *cum* concrete poetry which Burroughs later abandoned. Because of their cut-up nature, these are Burroughs's most difficult works (any new reader is recommended to begin with *The Naked Lunch* and then jump to the later books, such as *Cities of the Red Night*, before returning to these earlier fictions), but nevertheless they contain some superb horror imagery and characterizations.

The blurb on the first British paperback edition of *Nova Express* described the book as "an hallucinatory interplanetary cops and robbers game with the Nova Police on one side and the Nova Mob (among whom, Izzy the Push, Hamburger Mary and the Subliminal Kid) on the other." Clearly, all of American pop culture—and much of its high culture—is grist to Burroughs's word-mill. Science-fiction horror has its place there, along with the private-eye novel, the superhero comic, the western, and the shapeless beat "confession" (*à la* Jack Kerouac, a one-time close friend of Burroughs's). The basic idea is that there is a group of entities called the Nova Mob and that their purpose is to take control of this planet by manipulating the strings of addiction—not just drug addiction, but the human dependence on sex, on violence, on language itself. They are in cahoots with "the all-powerful boards and syndicates of the earth," and they offer us the Garden of Delights, Immortality, Cosmic Consciousness, and the Best Ever in Drug Kicks. But as Burroughs's spokesman says: "*Listen*: Their Garden of Delights is a terminal sewer . . . Their Immortality Cosmic Consciousness and Love is second-run grade-B shit— Their drugs are poison designed to beam in orgasm Death and Nova Ovens—."

Pitted against the Nova conspiracy are the good guys, Inspector J. Lee (a surrogate of Burroughs himself) and the Nova Police. They offer nothing but "total austerity and total resistance." Their object is to expose the Nova criminals who, by extension, are all the forces of capitalism and bureaucratic control, and "to occupy The Reality Studio and retake their universe of Fear Death and Monopoly . . ." The bulk of the book consists of an avalanche of metaphors which in differing ways—amusing, horrific, enlightening, disgusting—give power to this straightforward message. There is a tumble of brilliant and disturbing images, and a continuous rhetoric of subversive outrage interspersed with hilarious routines which feature the most bizarre characters—for instance, Uranian Willy, the Heavy metal kid, who visits a café where "two Lesbian Agents with glazed faces of grafted penis flesh sat sipping spinal fluid through alabaster straws."

We are introduced to the Insect Brains of Minraud, and to the Venusian Fish People: "The green boy-girl . . . squirmed towards the controller with little chirps and giggles—The controller reached down a translucent hand felt absently into the boneless jelly caressing glands and nerve centres—The green boy-girl twisted in spasms of ingratiation—." We are taken on a tour of the Amuse-

ment Gardens, and of the Biologic Courts: "Swarming with terminal life forms desperately seeking extension of cancelled permissos and residence certificates . . . Holding up insect claws, animal and bird parts, all manner of diseases and deformities . . ." These vivid ramblings, with their own special grammar, are more than crazed hallucinations. They amount to an alternative mythology of our time, deployed in a moral cause. They convince us that Burroughs, much loved and much imitated by poets and punk musicians, as well as by some horror and science-fiction writers, was the leading demonologist of his era.

Cities of the Red Night, opening volume in the late "trilogy" completed with *The Place of Dead Roads* and *The Western Lands*, was received as his most significant book since *The Naked Lunch*, and described as some kind of masterpiece by critics as various as Peter Ackroyd, Christopher Isherwood and Ken Kesey. This may have been due to the fact that it was his most straightforward and linear narrative to date, less fragmentary than *Nova Express*. Nevertheless, it is still a novel of disparate parts: strands of story interweave, each surging into prominence then fading away, without any clear beginning, middle and ending to the whole. But then one does not expect the conventional from Burroughs: he is one of those who "transmit their reports at midnight from the dark causeways of our own spinal columns" (in J. G. Ballard's memorable words).

The cities of the title are called Tamaghis, Ba'dan, Yass-Waddah, Waghdas, Naufana and Ghadis. Once centres of civilization and learning, they are imagined as existing a hundred millennia ago in the area which is now the Gobi Desert. A cosmic catastrophe turns the sky red and causes genetic mutations. Up until now all people have been black, but red, yellow and white skins begin to appear for the first time, and civil strife ensues: "The women, led by an albino mutant known as the White Tigress, seized Yass-Waddah, reducing the male inhabitants to slaves . . . The Council in Waghdas countered by developing a method of growing babies in excised wombs . . . Many strange mutants arose as a series of plagues devastated the cities . . . Finally, the cities were abandoned and the survivors fled in all directions, carrying the plagues with them." But these cities do not exist merely in historical fantasy: they are symbolic places, to be visited in dreams—and possibly they still endure, except that now they have names like New York, London, Moscow, Tokyo, Paris, Shanghai.

The vivid scraps of narrative leap from past to present to future: "Ba'dan is the oldest spaceport on planet Earth and like many port towns has accreted over the centuries the worst features of many times and places. Riffraff and misfits from every corner of the galaxy have jumped ship here or emigrated to engage in various pernicious and parasitic occupations . . ." Intermingled with the parable of the cities are an 18th-century story of boy pirates who fight the Spanish and attempt to found a womanless utopia; a present-day tale of a private eye, Clem Snide, who investigates murder and is drawn into the contemplation of ancient mysteries; a 1920s story about the travels of Farnsworth, a stiff-upper-lipped District Health Officer and not-so-secret drug addict; and more, in parodic, menacing or elegiac veins.

Characters recur from earlier Burroughs books, as do the usual obsessions with drugs, death by hanging, and homosexuality. The imagery is both haunting—"Smell of the salt marshes, slivers of ice at dawn, catwalks, towers, and wooden houses over the water where white-furred crocodiles lurk . . ."—and wildly, grossly comedic: "The subtlest assassins among them are the Dream Killers or Bangutot Boys. They have the ability to invade the REM sleep of the target, fashion themselves from the victim's erection, and grow from his sexual energy until they are solid enough to strangle him." In the end, when all the revels are ended, the author seems to speak in his own voice: "I have blown a hole in time with a firecracker. Let others step through . . . A nightmare feeling of foreboding and desolation comes over me as a great mushroom-shaped cloud darkens the earth. A few may get through the gate in time."

—David Pringle

C

CADNUM, Michael

Nationality: American. **Born:** 3 May 1949. **Career:** Poet and novelist. **Awards:** Creative Writing Fellowship from the National Endowment for the Arts; *Poetry Northwest*'s Helen Bullis Prize; Owl Creek Book Award. Lives in Northern California.

HORROR, GHOST AND GOTHIC PUBLICATIONS

Novels

Nightlight. New York, St. Martin's Press, 1990.
Sleepwalker. New York, St. Martin's Press, 1991.
Saint Peter's Wolf. New York, Carroll and Graf, 1991; London, Arrow, 1992.
Calling Home. New York, Viking Press, 1991.
Ghostwright. New York, Carroll and Graf, 1992.
Breaking the Fall. New York, Viking, 1992.
The Horses of the Night. New York, Carroll and Graf, 1993.
Skyscape. New York, Carroll and Graf, 1994.
Taking It. New York, Viking Press, 1995.
The Judas Glass. New York, Carroll and Graf, 1996.
Zero at the Bone. New York, Viking Press, 1996.

OTHER PUBLICATIONS

Novel

Ella and the Canary Prince. N.p., Cobblestone Press, n.d.

Poetry

Long Afternoons. N.p., 1986.
Invisible Mirror. Chicago, Ommation Press, 1987.
Foreign Springs. Bakersfield, California, Amelia, n.d.
By Evening. N.p., 1992.
The Cities We Will Never See. Canton, Connecticut, Singular Speech Press, 1994.

*   *   *

Michael Cadnum is one of those almost-special writers, a poet of note, and a solidly second-rank horror writer who has not yet had his big book, which will win awards and raise him to the front rank. But it may come along at any time. The signs are all there.

His first novel, *Nightlight*, has many genuinely eerie moments, toys with the supernatural, then ends abruptly, without quite getting as interesting as it could have, the most intriguing character having been kept virtually offstage all the way to the end. *Ghostwright* is a more assured performance, with a genuine ability to build suspense through surprising plot developments. It concerns a writer stalked by his old collaborator, who might be back from the dead.

The Horses of the Night has a soft opening, without much tension. The first scene introduces a couple of symbols which are invoked again in the close-up, but otherwise accomplishes nothing dramatically. It takes a few chapters to seriously involve the reader. But the first thing we notice in any Cadnum novel is that he writes dialogue uncommonly well. His characters are capable of conversing at one level while battling one another in the subtext. His narrative is often lyrical, with strikingly apt descriptions. As many critics have remarked, Cadnum's poetry has enriched his prose.

Inevitably, we start reaching for comparisons. The first one that springs to mind—and stays—is Jonathan Carroll, which is unfair to Cadnum, because he is not Carroll, and his intentions are different. Yet he has much of Carroll's stylishness (though lacking Carroll's whimsy), and he writes about the same sort of people: the very rich, successful, artistic, old-money set with odd names. The hero's name is Stratton Fields, or "Strater" to his friends, scion of a leading San Francisco family, seemingly set in life, a dilettante architect whose life and finances aren't nearly as secure as they seem on the surface.

Stratton makes a Faustian bargain with Something, a phantom, a hallucination . . . . People who were in Stratton's way start dying. Circumstances force him to embrace the situation aggressively, rather than flee from it. He climbs to the top of the ladder of success/fame/revenge, toward a seemingly inevitable Faustian overreacher's fall. (The title is from Marlowe: *Run slowly, slowly, horses of the night*—meaning the horses of Time, drawing the fatal hour near.) We seem, at this point, to be on the verge of something extraordinary. Cadnum's characterizations ring true. His story-telling is rich and satisfying. He seems, if not another Jonathan Carroll, a talent of that magnitude.

Yet often there is a falling off toward the end of a Cadnum novel. Some books, which seem to be supernatural throughout, suddenly produce mundane explanations, not always convincingly. People conveniently tell all or go mad, and the story furiously wraps itself up like an over-tied parcel. The author's hand is too evident, with entirely too much plot-string visible. Stratton's Faustian bargain gives way to a happy ending for no thematically compelling reason, and *The Horses of the Night* sinks down to the level of just another thriller.

Saint Peter's Wolf, on the other hand, is unambiguously supernatural, and might, in a weird way, have been jokingly entitled *The Joy of Lycanthropy*. Another economically upscale San Francisco protagonist, this one a psychologist and antiques expert, loses his wife and much of his medical practice to a rival (an ostensible friend), and then acquires a set of wolf teeth set in silver, a beautiful, alluring, accursed object, which quite literally brings out the beast in Dr. Byrd. The inevitable night rampages follow. He crosses a moral line when, in wolf form, he deliberately murders his rival, rather than merely attacking prey. A convoluted, exciting plot spins out, complete with a crazed werewolf-hunter, romance with a female werewolf, and several less melodramatic elements. The hero loses touch with his son, then with humanity, as he evolves into something else, becoming a true fusion of man and beast, as centaurs were. It is not surprising, the protagonist remarks, that centaurs in Greek myth were seen as wise beings, and were often the mentors of heroes. The transcendent werewolf is a force of nature, something urban, human civilization cannot understand. Unlike Larry Talbot in the movie *The Wolf Man*, for whom his condition is a terrible curse, Dr. Byrd has ambiguous feelings toward his lycanthropy. At times, even at first, he enjoys it. It enriches his work. He discovers a new, more vivid world of sensory experience unknown to normal humans. But then guilt sets in. He resolves to turn himself in to the authorities, who, officially, don't believe him, and unofficially want him destroyed. The reader's sympathies shift from the humans to the werewolves. The title refers to the legend that Saint Peter envied God's creation, and got permission to create one animal by himself, something which would be as magnificent as humankind but not as holy. The result was the wolf.

Skyscape is more clearly psychological, about a painter suffering creative block, who takes a cure from a celebrity psychologist out in the desert. The question is: which of these men is actually insane?

Mainstream critics are often puzzled by Cadnum, trying to classify his horror novels (including *Saint Peter's Wolf*, with its explicit violence and a rape scene) as Young Adult; but such books as *Breaking the Fall* and *Calling Home* actually do have adolescent protagonists and the categorization becomes meaningful, even if parents and librarians are disturbed by these stories of, as one critic put it, "good kids doing evil things." In *Calling Home*, the teen protagonist has accidentally killed his best friend. He begins to feel himself possessed by the dead boy's spirit and begins to impersonate him over the phone to the boy's frantic parents. Once this has begun, it becomes harder and harder to stop, as the lie (or the ghost) consumes him. *Breaking the Fall* is about a youth drawn into crime by a charismatic friend.

In all of these works, Cadnum shows himself to be a fine stylist and a gripping, elegant writer with a good sense of subtle character nuance. Probably what prevents them from truly breaking out is that they're not quite imaginative enough. Even *Saint Peter's Wolf* does not entirely, in a way that the reader can feel, transcend its subject matter. Edward Bryant described *Sleepwalker* (about archaeologists and reanimated mummies) as "slightly creepy, slightly musty, and slightly slight." But if the time comes when we can look back on all these as mere early works, then Michael Cadnum will have arrived as a master.

—Darrell Schweitzer

CADY, Jack (Andrew)

Pseudonym: Pat Franklin. **Nationality:** American. **Born:** Columbus, Ohio, 20 March 1932. **Education:** University of Louisville, Kentucky, B.S. 1961. **Military Service:** U.S. Coast Guard, 1952-56; petty officer, 2nd class. **Career:** Auctioneer; social-security claims representative, U.S. Department of Health, Education, and Welfare; truck driver; tree high-climber; landscape foreman; assistant professor of English, University of Washington, Seattle, 1968-72; visiting writer, Knox College, Galesburg, Illinois, 1973; visiting writer, Clarion State College, Clarion, Pennsylvania, 1974; co-owner, Cady-Robson Landscaping, Port Townsend, Washington, from 1974; editor and publisher, *Port Townsend Journal*, 1974-76; visiting writer, Sitka Community College, Alaska, 1977-78; freelance writer from 1978. **Awards:** *Atlantic Monthly* "First" award, 1965, for short story; National Council for the Arts, National Literary award, 1971, for short story; Washington Governor's award for short fiction, 1972, for collection; University of Iowa Press, Iowa award for short fiction, 1972, for collection; World Fantasy award, 1993, for collection; Nebula award, 1994, for short story. **Address:** c/o St. Martin's Press, 175 Fifth Avenue, New York, NY 10010, USA. Lives in Port Townsend, Washington.

HORROR, GHOST AND GOTHIC PUBLICATIONS

Novels

The Well. New York, Arbor House, 1980.
The Jonah Watch: A True-Life Ghost Story in the Form of a Novel. New York, Arbor House, 1981.
McDowell's Ghost. New York, Arbor House, 1982.
Inagehi. Seattle, Broken Moon Press, 1994.
The Off Season: A Victorian Sequel. New York, St. Martin's Press, 1995.

Novels as Pat Franklin

Dark Dreaming. New York, Diamond, 1991.
Embrace of the Wolf. New York, Diamond, 1993.

Short Stories

The Burning and Other Stories. Iowa City, University of Iowa Press, 1973.
Tattoo and Other Stories. N.p., Circinatum, 1978.
The Sons of Noah and Other Stories. Seattle, Washington, Broken Moon Press, 1992.

OTHER PUBLICATIONS

Novels

The Man Who Could Make Things Vanish. New York, Arbor House, 1983.
Street. New York, St. Martin's Press, 1994.

*   *   *

Jack Cady's roots are in mainstream literature. His career has cautiously edged toward the fantastic without branding him a genre writer. He is certainly not a "horror writer" *per se*, any more than was Joseph Conrad (to whom he is sometimes compared), which only goes to show the meaninglessness (outside of marketing considerations) of such terms. (Some horror-fiction reference books have entries on Joseph Conrad.) His lyrical, deeply textured fictions often border on the strange and bizarre, whether they step all the way over the line into the openly fantastic or not. Cady's work has been published in *Best American Short Stories* (1966, 1969, 1970, 1971) and in *The Atlantic Monthly* and *The Yale Review*, although he has probably reached a wider audience in *The Magazine of Fantasy and Science Fiction* and *Omni*.

The story which initially brought him to the attention of the horror community was the masterful novella, "By Reason of Darkness," which appeared in Douglas Winter's anthology *Prime Evil* in 1988. Here we see all of Cady's strengths: the intense imagery; the well-realized, off-kilter characters who bond together in something beyond ordinary friendship (arguably, every member of the cast is insane); and the poetic language which, in addition to the subject matter (ex-servicemen haunted by what they did while running rogue in the jungles of Vietnam) has caused this story, especially, to be compared to Conrad's "The Heart of Darkness." But it is also a ghost story, and a story of forgiveness and revenge. With the unreliability of the narrator (who seems the sanest of the bunch), the ghosts may or may not be objectively real. They are none the less frightening. The American sequences in "By Reason of Darkness" are set in the far Northwest, an area Cady knows well. It always seems to be raining in Cady stories. He makes excellent (sometimes symbolic) use of misty, muddy landscapes.

At this point, horror fans researched back and discovered that Cady's work had contained ghostly elements for some time. *The Well* is a fine haunted-house novel. *The Jonah Watch* and *McDowell's Ghost* also contain supernatural elements. *The Man Who Could Make Things Vanish* is borderline science fiction, about a man with special powers battling a sinister corporation a few years in the future from the date of the book's publication.

"The Night We Buried Road Dog" is the second Cady novella that particularly stands out, but it defines him differently, drawing comparisons to R. A. Lafferty, Terry Bisson, or even Mark Twain. It is a tall tale in the classic American tradition, about a man obsessed with the cars of the 1940s and '50s (a classical American obsession), who even operates a cemetery for such vehicles. There are ghosts aplenty, of both human and machine, and a mysterious Kilroy-like character whose graffiti in roadside rest-stops leads the protagonist on a wild chase and ultimately to the unveiling of a tragic mystery. The tone of the story shifts flawlessly from comedy to something bordering on terror; it is certainly eerie throughout, and even comprehensible to readers who don't know their automobile models and brands as well as the characters do.

Street is science fiction. *Inagehi* is haunting and ghostly, evoking the Cherokee country of North Carolina as vividly as any of Cady's earlier descriptions of Washington State, and makes effective and compassionate use of Native American lore. *The Off Season* is a supernatural comedy with a serious core—like all of Cady's novels, a rich book, but it is closer to Charles Finney's fantastical *The Circus of Dr. Lao* than to actual horror. It's about a thoroughly and imaginatively haunted tourist resort in Washington State. Resemblances to Port Townsend, where the author presently lives are, he assures us, intentional.

Cady is one of those writers whose career weaves in and out of the horror and gothic field. But to read only some of the stories, which fit this or that definition of horror or fantasy, is to miss a lot.

—Darrell Schweitzer

CALDER-MARSHALL, Arthur

Pseudonym: William Drummond. **Nationality:** British. **Born:** Wallington, Surrey, 19 August 1908. **Education:** Hertford College, Oxford, B.A. 1930. **Family:** Married Violet Nancy Sales in 1934; two daughters. **Career:** Schoolmaster, Denstone College, Staffordshire, 1931-33; full-time novelist, biographer and screenwriter from 1933. Fellow, Royal Society of Literature. **Died:** 1992.

HORROR, GHOST AND GOTHIC PUBLICATIONS

Novels

The Fair to Middling. London, Hart Davis, 1959.
The Scarlet Boy. London, Hart Davis, 1961.

OTHER PUBLICATIONS

Novels

At Sea. London, Cape, 1934.
Dead Centre. London, Cape, 1935.
Pie in the Sky. London, Cape(?), 1937.
A Man Reprieved. London, Cape(?), 1949.
Occasion of Glory. London, Cape, 1955.
The Man from Devil's Island. London, Hart Davis, 1958.

Novels as William Drummond

Midnight Lace (novelization of screenplay). London, Pan, 1960.
Victim (novelization of screenplay). London, Corgi, 1961.
Life for Ruth (novelization of screenplay). London, Corgi, 1962.
Night Must Fall (novelization of screenplay). London, Fontana, and New York, Signet, 1964.
Gaslight (novelization of play by Patrick Hamilton). New York, Paperback Library, 1966; London, Arrow, 1967.

Other

The Magic of My Youth. London, Hart Davis, 1951.
No Earthly Command. London, Hart Davis, 1957.
Havelock Ellis. London, Hart Davis, 1959.
Lone Wolf: The Biography of Jack London. London, Methuen, 1961.
The Enthusiast. London, Faber, 1962.
The Innocent Eye. London, Allen, 1963.

Editor, *Selected Writings*, by Tobias Smollett. London(?), Falcon Press, 1951.
Editor, *The Bodley Head Jack London.* London, Bodley Head, 2 vols., 1963-64.

*   *   *

Arthur Calder-Marshall's early literary work is all naturalistic, although *At Sea*, which describes the ordeal of a honeymoon couple swept out to sea in a small boat, is a horror story of sorts. A religious element enters into such works as *Occasion of Glory*, set against the background of the ritual reenactments of Christ's crucifixion at Acotitlan in Mexico, but it remains dutifully free of any taint of miraculous intervention. It was not until his literary career entered a distinct second phase that he became interested in the employment of supernatural apparatus. As with many other writers, it was in framing work for a juvenile audience that he initially found it natural to dabble in the fantastic, and, again as with many others, he then seems to have thought it a shame to leave such rich resources entirely to the use of the young.

Although *The Fair to Middling* was written and marketed as a children's book it is set squarely in the tradition of such classics of weird fiction as Charles G. Finney's *The Circus of Dr. Lao* and Ray Bradbury's *Something Wicked This Way Comes*. Like those predecessors it concerns a travelling show that brings magic to a small town, allowing certain inhabitants a once-in-a-lifetime opportunity to confront squarely their hopes and fears, and thus make crucial choices as to how they will live the remainder of their lives.

In this instance the characters in need of moral rearmament are the patron, staff and pupils of the Alderman Winterbottome's School for Incapacitated Orphans. Most of their "incapacities" are minor but nevertheless have the potential to create untold misery. Some, like the facially-disfigured music teacher and her talented but partially-sighted pupil, only need to be reconciled to their respective fates by Monsieur Volte-Face the Fairdresser and Mr. Madderwort of the Gothick House, but others need sharper lessons. The personnel of the fair includes O. L. D. Scratch, the Universal Provider, who offers a tempting contract dated "Burnsday the Hate-th of Remember" that must be refused if safety is to be maintained. The other allegorical regions over which O. L. D. Scratch presides include Turmoil City and the Amazement Park, but the fair is not entirely Hellish. Small miracles are available to those whose need is authentic and whose ambitions are modest. In this allegorical account of the world, the fashion in which the meek can "inherit the earth" is hedged around with minimizing codicils, but the world remains well worth inheriting in spite of them.

Although it is a Christian allegory there is nothing particularly pious about *The Fair to Middling*; it offers an intriguingly respectful account of the seductiveness of evil without resorting to undue psychological terrorism in spelling out the penalties of sinful self-indulgence. Even so, its clever wit carefully fails to conceal the darker undercurrent which lurks beneath the surface. The novel is, as might be expected, dedicated to the author's two daughters—one of whom, then ten years old, became the actress Anna Calder-Marshall. When the author returned, after writing another book for children (a biography of Jack London), to the production of adult fiction, he carried over the elements of fantasy and allegory from *The Fair to Middling* into *The Scarlet Boy*. The latter novel contains a good deal of material about childhood, but its reflections are those of an adult looking back into his own past rather than those of a parent looking forward to his children's future. It is, in consequence, an authentically disturbing tale of the revenant dead.

Although the blurb for *The Scarlet Boy* insists that it is not a ghost story, it is difficult to locate it convincingly under any other heading, but it is also a tale of unusual psychic sensitivity—and in its handling of both these themes it is an orthodox religious fantasy. As the elusive but determinedly unquiet spirit of a boy who committed suicide becomes increasingly troublesome to the living—especially to the sensitive—the plot moves inexorably towards a formal exorcism. The real point of the story, however, is not so much the suspicion that the unsettled dead may return to pester the gifted, as it is the conviction that unsettling memories are far better confronted than repressed—an item of faith which decisively unites the novel with its juvenile predecessor.

The Scarlet Boy appeared a year before Ray Russell's *The Case Against Satan*, a lurid tale of exorcism given wide distribution by the Catholic Book Club, and ten years before William Peter Blatty's even-more-lurid *The Exorcist*, but it ought not to be reckoned an anticipation of their meretricious concerns or melodramatic methods. Calder-Marshall's novel is far less garish, and the demons who are called upon to take the blame for what has happened in the penultimate chapter are not the external paragons of malevolence favoured by Russell and Blatty; they are less obviously malign forces working much more intimately within the human heart. As in *The Fair to Middling*, there is a suggestion in the final chapter that good is active too, and that small visitations of a kinder sort may be available to the needy and the faithful. Both novels are among the most interesting and most cleverly-constructed examples of reverent Christian fantasy.

—Brian Stableford

CAMPBELL, (John) Ramsey

Pseudonyms: Carl Dreadstone; E. K. Leyton; Jay Ramsay. **Nationality:** British. **Born:** Liverpool, 4 January 1946. **Education:** St. Edward's College, 1957-62. **Family:** Married Jenny Lynne Chandler in 1971; one daughter and one son. **Career:** Clerical officer, Inland Revenue, Liverpool, 1962-66; librarian, Liverpool Public Libraries, 1966-73; film reviewer, BBC Radio Merseyside, from 1969; freelance writer from 1973. **Member:** British Fantasy Society (president, 1972-73). **Awards:** British Fantasy award, including 1978, 1981, 1988, 1989; World Fantasy award for short story, 1978, 1980; *Liverpool Daily Post and Echo* award for literature, 1984; World Fantasy award for anthology, 1991; Horror Writers of America Bram Stoker award for collection, 1994. **Agent:** Carol Smith, 22 Adam and Eve Mews, Kensington High Street, London W8 6UJ, England; or, Pimlico Agency, Box 20447, 1539 First Avenue, New York, NY 10028, USA.

HORROR, GHOST AND GOTHIC PUBLICATIONS

Novels

The Doll Who Ate His Mother. New York, Bobbs Merrill, 1976; revised edition, London, Century, 1987.
The Face That Must Die. London, Star, 1979; restored text, Los Angeles, Scream Press, 1983, and London, Futura, 1990.
To Wake the Dead. London, Millington, 1980; revised edition, as *The Parasite*, New York, Macmillan, 1980, and London, Granada, 1985.
The Nameless. London, Macmillan, 1981; revised edition, London, Panther, 1985.
Incarnate. New York, Macmillan, 1983; London, Granada, 1984; revised edition, London, Futura, 1990.
Claw (as Jay Ramsay). London, Macdonald, 1983; as *Night of the Claw*, New York, Tor, 1985; as *The Claw* by Ramsey Campbell, London, Warner, 1992.
Obsession. New York, Macmillan, and London, Granada, 1985.
The Hungry Moon. New York, Macmillan, 1986; London, Century, 1987.
The Influence. New York, Macmillan, and London, Century Hutchinson, 1988.
Ancient Images. London, Legend, and New York, Macmillan Scribner, 1989.
Midnight Sun. London, Macdonald, 1990; New York, Tor, 1991.
Needing Ghosts (novella). London, Legend, 1990.
The Count of Eleven. London, Macdonald, 1991; New York, Tor, 1992.

The Long Lost. London, Headline, 1993; New York, Tor, 1995.
The One Safe Place. London, Headline, 1995; New York, Tor, 1996.
The House on Nazareth Hill. London, Headline, 1996.

Novels as Carl Dreadstone

The Bride of Frankenstein (novelization of screenplay). New York, Berkley, 1977; London, Star, 1978.
The Wolfman (novelization of screenplay). New York, Berkley, 1977; London, Star, 1980.
Dracula's Daughter (novelization of screenplay). New York, Berkley, 1977; as E. K. Leyton, London, Star, 1980.

Short Stories

The Inhabitant of the Lake, and Less Welcome Tenants. Sauk City, Wisconsin, Arkham House, 1964.
Demons by Daylight. Sauk City, Wisconsin, Arkham House, 1973.
The Height of the Scream. Sauk City, Wisconsin, Arkham House, 1976.
Through the Walls. Rochdale, Lancashire, British Fantasy Society, 1981.
Dark Companions. New York, Macmillan, 1982; with differing contents, London, Fontana, 1982.
Watch the Birdie: A Story. Runcorn, Cheshire, Pardoe, 1984.
Slow. Round Top, New York, Footsteps Press, 1985.
Cold Print. Santa Cruz, California, Scream Press, 1985; expanded edition, New York, Tor, 1987; further expanded edition, London, Headline, 1993.
Black Wine, with Charles L. Grant, edited by Douglas E. Winter. Niles, Illinois, Dark Harvest, 1986.
Dark Feasts: The World of Ramsey Campbell. London, Robinson, 1987.
Ghostly Tales. Mount Olive, North Carolina, Cryptic Publications, 1987.
Medusa. Round Top, New York, Footsteps Press, 1987.
Scared Stiff: Tales of Sex and Death. Los Angeles, Scream Press, 1987.
Waking Nightmares. New York, Tor, 1991; London, Little Brown, 1992.
Alone with the Horrors: The Great Short Fiction of Ramsey Campbell, 1961-1991. Sauk City, Wisconsin, Arkham House, 1993; London, Headline, 1994.
Two Obscure Tales. West Warwick, Rhode Island, Necronomicon Press, 1993.
Strange Things and Stranger Places. New York, Tor, 1993.
Der Reisefuhrer/The Guide (text in German and English). Bellheim, Germany, Phantasia, 1994.
Far Away and Never. West Warwick, Rhode Island, Necronomicon Press, 1996.

Other

The Core of Ramsey Campbell: A Bibliography & Reader's Guide, with Stefan Dziemianowicz and S. T. Joshi. 1995.

Editor, *Superhorror.* London, Allen, 1976; as *The Far Reaches of Fear*, Allen, 1980.
Editor, *New Tales of the Cthulhu Mythos.* Sauk City, Wisconsin, Arkham House, 1980; London, Grafton, 1988.
Editor, *New Terrors.* London, Pan, 2 vols., 1980; New York, Pocket, 1984.

Editor, *The Gruesome Book* (for children). London, Piccolo, 1983.
Editor, *Fine Frights: Stories that Scared Me.* New York, Tor, 1988.
Editor, with Stephen Jones. *Best New Horror [1-5].* London, Robinson, and New York, Carroll and Graf, 1990-94.
Editor, *Uncanny Banquet.* London, Little Brown, 1992.
Editor, with Martin H. Greenberg. *Horror Writers of America Present Deathport.* New York, Pocket, 1993.

*

Critical Study: *Ramsey Campbell* by Gary William Crawford, Mercer Island, Washington, Starmont House, 1988.

Ramsey Campbell comments:

I began writing horror fiction before I reached my teens. Readers wishing to be appalled may seek out the result, *Ghostly Tales.* At 14 I chanced upon a collection of tales by H. P. Lovecraft and determined to model my writing on his. Having done so to the extent of my first published book, I set out to sound like myself. Underlying that ambition was the one I've had for as long as I've been writing fiction—to repay some of the pleasure the field has given me.

By pleasure I mean terror, certainly to begin with. I first encountered this in children's fiction: "Rupert's Christmas Tree," an eerie tale in a British children's annual, and the scenes involving the goblin animals in *The Princess and the Goblin.* The reticence of all this material was presumably meant to keep the young reader from being too frightened, but as far as I was concerned at four and five years old the various scenes showed just enough to suggest far worse. I soon had the same experience with M. R. James as well as Lovecraft, and Fritz Leiber too, that master of the urban supernatural tale. Several anthologies also shaped my attitude to the genre, in particular *Best Horror Stories* (1957), edited by John Keir Cross, and *Great Tales of Terror and the Supernatural* (1947, but encountered by me some 12 years later), edited by Wise and Fraser. Crucially, both books anthologized mainstream writers—in Cross we find Angus Wilson, Kipling, Faulkner and Melville; Wise and Fraser include Balzac, Hardy, Hemingway, Coppard and others—and persuaded me there was no reason to regard horror fiction at its best as cut off from the mainstream. That has been my principle ever since.

It led me to appreciate more varied kinds of terror: Thomas Hinde's first-person accounts of madness (*The Day the Call Came, The Investigator*); Beckett's claustrophobic psychological landscapes (*The Unnameable, How It Is*); the horribly comical murder of Quilty in *Lolita*; in films, the unnerving dislocations of *Last Year in Marienbad* and *Muriel*, and the aching barrenness of the streets at the end of Antonioni's *The Eclipse.* . . . All these helped convince me in my teens that terror was far larger and more diverse than the genre specializing in it, though that isn't in any way to repudiate the latter. I'm for largeness and variety, and that's why I continue to write in the field—because I haven't found its limits. It can encompass comedy and tragedy, it's capable of functioning as satire and social comment, it stretches from psychological terror to visionary horror, to which I should like to see more of a return. It can also be a lot of fun.

Now and then conflict erupts in the field, usually between practitioners of graphic horror and those who favour restraint, as though both approaches haven't always been valid. Such squabbles are amusing to watch, but ultimately as unrewarding as the 1940s spectacle of Raymond Chandler and John Dickson Carr savaging each other's work. The point is surely not how graphic a piece of fiction is but whether it enriches the imagination rather than dulling it, if not actually taking its place. The best fiction in the genre achieves its effects by careful and imaginative use of language, and has always sought to convey more than horror, whether it's awe or lyricism or the frisson subtlety brings. Don't settle for less. Though pulp fiction produced some masters of horror, most of it was mediocre or (often much) worse, and the same proportions are to be found in recent writing in the field. History will judge, but contemporary readers will be rewarded by doing so too.

*   *   *

Although he has only a fraction of the popular appeal of Stephen King or Clive Barker, Ramsey Campbell is likely to be remembered as the leading horror writer of his generation, and perhaps the most significant writer in the field since Lovecraft. His unflinchingly bleak vision, his richly allusive style and his chilling analysis of abnormal psychology are certainly not best-seller material; but his very bountiful output—hundreds of short stories and nearly a score of novels—already represents a substantial contribution to weird fiction, even though Campbell may be only at the midpoint of his career.

Campbell's earliest writings are pastiches of Lovecraft, collected in *The Inhabitant of the Lake and Less Welcome Tenants*. Although derivative, they are written with such verve and enthusiasm as to be superior to much work of their kind; and some of the later tales already reveal Campbell's gradual surmounting of the Lovecraft influence. Indeed, Campbell has confessed that, "Having imitated Lovecraft, I rejected him with all the obstreperousness of a fanzine contributor determined to make a name for himself at the expense of his betters."

This declaration of independence is signalled by "The Cellars" (written in 1965), a gritty tale of a man luring a woman into the catacombs in Campbell's native Liverpool, and as startling a contrast to Lovecraft's asexual "cosmicism" as could be imagined. Two further early stories—"Cold Print" (written in 1966-67) and "The Franklyn Paragraphs" (written in 1967)—are masterful fusions of the Lovecraft influence and Campbell's developing originality of conception and style.

The end result of this early experimentation is *Demons by Daylight*. This landmark volume could be said to have almost single-handedly ushered in the modern age in horror fiction, and its 14 stories—in their focus on human relationships, their evocation of the squalor of urban decay, their oblique narration, and their nebulous, indirect and nearly incomprehensible horrific climaxes—are encapsulations of nearly all Campbell's later work. Campbell points to Fritz Leiber as an influence in his use of the urban setting, and to Vladimir Nabokov in his selection of words that suggest and evoke rather than state.

Abandoning Lovecraftian cosmicism (except in such a "visionary" novel as *Midnight Sun*, a gripping story of a man who attempts to usher in the return of a nebulous ice creature that will overwhelm the planet), Campbell places the emphasis on an intense concentration on individual consciousness, to the degree that much of his work approaches stream-of-consciousness. Love, sexuality, and gender confusion play a key role in many of Campbell's early tales, as they do even more explicitly in a later volume, *Scared Stiff: Tales of Sex and Death*, containing tales written over a long period. The complex interrelationship between dream and reality that we find in so many of

Campbell's *Demons by Daylight* stories is elaborated upon in *Incarnate*, one of the longest and most challenging of his novels. The short novel *Needing Ghosts* is a bizarre, surrealistic fantasy capable of a variety of interpretations or of no interpretation at all; its atmosphere of crazed nightmarishness is unique in Campbell's work.

Campbell has had only mixed success in the novel form, and his earlier novels are often weak and insubstantial. But *The Face That Must Die* (written 1976-77, published in a truncated form in 1979, and in unabridged form in 1983) still ranks among his best: this uncompromising story of a deranged serial killer forces us to inhabit the killer's mind, so that we come to understand the twisted logic by which his paranoia leads him to suspect enemies at every turn. A much later novel, *The Count of Eleven*, returns to the serial killer topos, but does so in a twistedly *comic* way that makes it a tour de force.

The Face That Must Die is one of Campbell's most exhaustive treatments of the horrors of the city, and it complements a number of short stories written at this time. Campbell is the poet of urban squalor and decay; only he can instil horror in the commonest objects of our daily existence: plastic bags ("In the Bag"), garbage ("Litter"), a raincoat ("Old Clothes"). One of Campbell's most horrifying stories, "Mackintosh Willy" (included in *Dark Companions*, one of his best collections), tells of the loathsome death of a derelict in a bicycle shelter and his resurrection as he terrorizes a gang of boys who have mutilated his corpse. "The Man in the Underpass" is another magnificent tale of the dangers of a pedestrian underpass, that distinctively British topographical landmark which has exercised a great fascination for Campbell. "The Depths" provides a sort of philosophical justification for Campbell's emphasis on the horrors of the city. Its premise—an author finds that if he does not frantically write down his horrible nightmares of violence and sadistic crime, they come true in actuality—is a thinly veiled metaphor for the indifference to society's ills that typifies middle-class urban life.

Children have become the focus of Campbell's more recent novels and tales—understandably so, as he has watched his own two children grow from infancy to adolescence. *Obsession* focuses on the lives of four teenagers who appear to cast some supernatural wishes but suffer unexpected repercussions in later years. *The Influence* is a straightforward psychic possession novel in which the spirit of an old woman occupies the body of her own grandniece. In the non-supernatural novel *The One Safe Place* the plight of an American family subject to violence from a lower-class British clan is keenly depicted, but the emphasis is laid on the fate of a hapless American boy who is kidnapped, drugged, and nearly killed.

In some of his more recent works Campbell gave the impression of abandoning the supernatural altogether, but he has returned to it in subtle fashion in two of his best novels, *The Long Lost*—in which an elderly woman from Wales proves to be a preternaturally aged "sin-eater" attempting to divest herself of the sins she has accumulated—and *The House on Nazareth Hill*, one of the finest modern treatments of the haunted house theme as well as a searing portrayal of domestic conflict.

Campbell deserves some note as an anthologist. Aside from co-editing the first five volumes of the *Best New Horror* series, he has produced a number of distinctive original and reprint anthologies (of which the most notable is *Uncanny Banquet*). He has also been a significant and charitable promoter of his fellow-writers.

If Campbell's cheerlessly dark vision robs him of immediate popularity, it (along with his impeccable craftsmanship and powerful imagination) should ultimately grant him a high, perhaps unassailable, place in the literature of the supernatural.

—S. T. Joshi

CANTRELL, Lisa W.

Nationality: American. **Born:** 1945. **Awards:** Horror Writers of America Bram Stoker award, 1988. **Address:** c/o Tor Books, 175 Fifth Avenue, New York, NY 10010, USA.

HORROR, GHOST AND GOTHIC PUBLICATIONS

Novels

The Manse. New York, Tor, 1987.
The Ridge. New York, Tor, 1989.
Torments. New York, Tor, 1990.
Boneman. New York, Tor, 1992.

* * *

Although the majority of readers of horror fiction are women, the majority of writers in the genre are male. This disparity is clearly not a function of talent, or lack of a taste for the gruesome, as some of the most effective writers in the field are women. Lisa Cantrell is a case in point. *The Manse* won the Bram Stoker award from the Horror Writers Association as the year's best first novel. It's a haunted-house story of almost relentless ferocity, paced very much like a motion picture but with a richness of detail all its own. The Manse is an oversized, abandoned house transformed every Halloween into a House of Horrors, a charity event organized by the local community. It's all good fun until one year, when the special effects turn out to be more than just illusions. Unbeknown to the latest team of organizers, the Manse has a terrible history, and the minor frights of the past several years have provided increments of terror to free the powers trapped within its walls. This Halloween they can alter reality, bring inanimate statues to deadly life, turn kudzu vines into malevolent death traps, cause electronic devices to turn themselves on even when disconnected from all power sources, and manifest themselves in other, always deadly, fashions. And one by one, they isolate and kill those who venture inside the Manse. With relentless inevitability, the visitors fall prey to the manifestations of the Manse until a fire breaks out fortuitously and burns the building to the ground. Even then, we discover, the evil atmosphere lingers, residing in the very ground beneath the ruins. Cantrell's carnival of horrors was an impressive first effort filled with well-constructed scenes that gave life to its very simple plot.

Torments is a direct sequel. The owners of the site where the Manse was destroyed are planning to build a housing project, but the restless spirits that inhabit the land don't take kindly to being disturbed. Strange figures stalk the night, people disappear, and the border between reality grows increasingly blurred. One woman discovers that it is up to her to confront her own fears and face down the evil that threatens anyone who ventures onto the cursed property. The plot is much stronger this time with better characterization, but the individual scenes lack the impact of the first novel.

Therwe's a similar setting in *The Ridge*, another cursed house. In this instance, several people are killed in rather gruesome fashion—their bodies quite literally explode—while they are present in an old house that was apparently built on a nexus point where supernatural forces can leak over from another reality into our world. One person survives the tragedy, a young girl who seems unwilling or unable to explain what happened.

The logical suspect in the deaths is Nick Vears, the girl's father, who is in fact a professional killer, though he is innocent in this instance. Nick is put in the awkward position of having to solve the crime himself before the police track him down. His investigations lead to a strange artifact and a deadly supernatural secret, from which he only escapes when his daughter displays a surprising psychic ability. All three of these novels share the theme of evil connected to a physical location, the lingering effects of old evil visited on the innocent.

Where *The Ridge* was a skilfully executed horror novel with overtones of a crime story, *Boneman* is just the opposite, a crime novel with overtones of horror. A seasoned police detective is investigating the murders of several drug dealers when he begins to hear stories of the Boneman. The latter is a charming, talented voodoo practitioner who is using fear and some zombie assistants to carve out his own criminal empire. The investigation is further complicated by the state authorities, who have assigned the case to Jackie Swann, one of their operatives, and given her jurisdiction superseding the local law enforcement agencies. Eventually the two team up, both convinced that the stories of zombie servants are tales made up specifically to frighten rival gangs.

They discover differently when they finally begin to penetrate the shield of mystery shrouding the Boneman's operation. When dead men can make telephone calls and corpses decompose literally in the blink of an eye, it makes it difficult to adhere to official police procedures. *Boneman* works better as a crime novel than as horror, however, not just because the supernatural elements are almost incidental to the plot, but also because there is little effort to make these sequences frightening. They provide disconcerting and innovative difficulties for the protagonists, but have little effect on the overall tone of the novel.

Cantrell is also the author of several shorter pieces. One of the most interesting of these is "Cruising," in which a dead boy and his phantom car return seeking vengeance against the girl who scorned him. "The Nana's House" is a building that absorbs evil over a period of many years, so much evil in fact that when a brutal fugitive from the law shelters there, his psychic baggage overloads the house which subsequently manifests its stored evil and overwhelms him. In "Juice," vampires have multiplied and taken control of the world, and humans have become their servants. And in "Arc Light," the best of her short fiction, a welder is so terrified of a creature he imagines waits in the dark for him that he destroys his own face so that he cannot see it.

Like many of the new horror writers who emerged in the late 1980s, Cantrell has had little published in the 1990s. An overly expanded horror field has drawn back, leaving many talented writers stranded by the tide. It would be unfortunate if someone with Cantrell's demonstrated skills were to remain silent.

—Don D'Ammassa

CAPES, Bernard (Edward Joseph)

Nationality: British. **Born:** 1854. **Career:** Varied employment, of which little is now known; editor, *Theatre* magazine, late 1870s; journalist and novelist. **Died:** 1918.

HORROR, GHOST AND GOTHIC PUBLICATIONS

Short Stories

At a Winter's Fire. London, Pearson, 1899.
From Door to Door: A Book of Romances, Fancies, Whimsies and Levities. Edinburgh, Blackwood, 1900.
Plots. London, Methuen, 1902.
Loaves and Fishes. London, Methuen, 1906.
Bag and Baggage. London, Constable, 1913.
The Fabulists. London, Mills and Boon, 1915.
The Black Reaper, edited by Hugh Lamb. London, Equation, 1989.

OTHER PUBLICATIONS

Novels

The Mill of Silence. New York, Rand, 1897; London, Long, 1902.
The Lake of Wine. London, Heinemann, 1898.
Adventures of the Comte de la Muette During the Terror. Edinburgh, Blackwood, and New York, Dodd Mead, 1898.
Our Lady of Darkness. Edinburgh, Blackwood, and New York, Dodd Mead, 1899.
Joan Brotherhood. London(?), n.p., 1900.
Love Like a Gypsy. London, Constable, 1901.
The Secret in the Hill. London, Smith Elder, 1903.
The Extraordinary Confessions of Diana Please. London, Methuen, 1904.
The Vanishing Cheques. London, Daily Mail, 1904.
A Jay of Italy (Bembo). London, Methuen, and New York, Dutton, 1905.
A Rogue's Tragedy. London, Methuen, 1906.
The Great Skene Mystery. London, Methuen, 1907.
The Love Story of St. Bel. London, Methuen, 1909.
Jemmy Abercraw. London, Methuen, and New York, Brentano, 1910.
Why Did He Do It? London, Methuen, and New York, Brentano, 1910.
The Will and the Way. London, Murray, 1910.
The House of Many Voices. London, Unwin, 1911.
The Pot of Basil. London, Constable, 1913.
The Green Parrot. London, Smith Elder, 1918.
Where England Sets Her Feet. London, Collins, 1918.
The Mystery of the Skeleton Key. New York, Doran, 1918; as *The Skeleton Key*, London, Collins, 1919.

Short Stories

Historical Vignettes. London, Fisher Unwin, and New York, Stokes, 1910.
Gilead Balm, Knight Errant. London, Unwin, and New York(?), Baker, 1911.

*   *   *

Bernard Capes turned to writing in middle age, having already tried his hand at several very various careers. He regarded it as one more trade to be tried and was unashamedly professional in his approach. His first success was with a historical romance and he quickly observed that the most popular genre in the marketplace was detective fiction, so those were the areas on which he concentrated when writing novels. Many of his short stories are mundane thrillers and romances, but he did take advantage of the relative acceptability of supernatural elements in short fiction. Perhaps he did so simply because such devices allowed him a convenient extra turn of the melodramatic screw, but it is probable that—as with many late Victorian and Edwardian writers of ghost stories—these seemingly arbitrary elements gave his private sentiments their freest expression.

The supernatural stories in Capes's earliest collections are relatively tentative. The most effective items in *At a Winter's Fire* are "The Vanishing House," in which an itinerant band of musicians plays outside a ghostly mansion although only one of them has the courage to drink from the cup offered in return, and "The Moon Stricken," a delusional fantasy recapitulating the common idea that the moon might be the abode of lost souls, which first appeared in the *Cornhill* magazine in 1896. "Dark Dignum" and "An Eddy on the Floor" are conventional tales of malevolent revenants. The posthumous influence in "William Tyrwhitt's 'Copy'" is less menacing, and "The Black Reaper" is an oddly hopeful allegory about the plague of 1665. Of the six stories designated "fantasies" in *From Door to Door*—which do not entirely justify that appellation—the most effective are the historical *conte cruel* "The Sword of Corporal Lacoste" and the delusional fantasy "The Cursing-Bell." "The Meek Shall Inherit the Earth" is more ironic than horrific.

A few of the stories in *Plots* are more elaborately and more idiosyncratically developed. "The Accursed Cordonnier" is a long story offering a rather rambling but oddly unsettling account of the Wandering Jew, here employed as a figure of outright menace. "The Devil's Fantasia," in which a stray piece of sheet music turns out to be half of a duet to be played with the Devil, is even more unsettling, and is possessed of a neatness that Capes often did not bother to contrive. "The Green Bottle" is a simple but seemingly heartfelt tale of a trapped soul. "The Plot of the Fearful Head" is a dispiritedly straightforward deployment of a standard motif. The title item is merely a collection of story ideas the author never used, although it had sold to the *Cornhill*—the most prestigious of Capes's numerous markets—in 1900.

Loaves and Fishes includes "The Ghost-Leech," a bizarre tale of phantom rugby whose living fullback stands to collect a reward—perhaps a premonition of the game's eventual professionalization—accomplished "over the dead bodies" of the Rugby Union's "old guard." "The Jade Button" also features a supernatural bounty that comes with an ironic price tag attached. "Poor Lucy Rivers" is an eccentrically sentimentalized tale of a haunted typewriter. The most disturbing items in the collection are, however, "A Ghost-Child," a subtle tale of phantom impregnation, and the *conte cruel* "A Gallows-bird." Capes's ghosts continued to exercise subtle ingenuity in relatively novel ways in *Bag and Baggage*. "Tony's Drum," returned from the battle in which the youthful signaller was killed, proves unexpectedly obliging. "John Field's Ghost" makes up for the failures which drove its living counterpart to suicide. Again, these are supplemented by a tale of exotic conception in the curious moral fantasy "The Hamadryad."

Capes's last collection, *The Fabulists*, contains a greater proportion of supernatural stories than any other, but they are disappointingly slight and formulaic, mostly involving brief appearances by phantoms or the supernatural reenactment of crimes. The best of them are "The Thing in the Forest," which features a werewolf, and the quaint account of "The Blue Dragon," about a minuscule refugee from a china tea service.

Hugh Lamb's introduction to his eclectic collection of 12 of the above-mentioned stories quotes the opinion of Robert Aickman that some few of Capes's supernatural tales reveal "the author's desperate frustration, an all too familiar property of the trade." Aickman suggests that the introductions to "The Green Bottle" and "An Eddy on the Floor" must offer insights into the author's own misery as well as the plights of the characters in the stories. If this is true there might be grounds for reading a story like "John Field's Return" (which was not considered for inclusion in *The Black Reaper* because no copy of *Bag and Baggage* was available to the editor) as a comment on the author's past failures and frustrated hopes. Whether or not one would then want to read some special significance into "A Ghost-Child" and "The Hamadryad" would, of course, be a matter of inclination; we do not know enough about Capes's life to draw any firm conclusions. Lamb does note that Capes's uncle was prominent in the Oxford Movement, but the extent to which his own Catholic faith was lost in later life is not a matter of record.

Capes's fiction is often careless and sometimes crude, but this was a failure—or perhaps a refusal—to exercise a capacity for stylishness that he undoubtedly possessed. It seems likely that he was a one-draft writer who thought it unprofitable to waste time in careful revision. His fertile imagination sometimes combined fruitfully with his historical researches, and occasionally worked on its own to produce memorable imagery and curiously touching resolutions. There remain enough interesting stories in his *oeuvre* to fill another eclectic collection the equal of *The Black Reaper*.

—Brian Stableford

CARROLL, Jonathan (Samuel)

Nationality: American. **Born:** New York(?), 1949; son of television playwright and screenwriter Sidney Carroll. **Family:** Married; one son. **Career:** Journalist, teacher, novelist and screenwriter. Has lived in Vienna, Austria, for many years. **Awards:** World Fantasy award, 1988; British Fantasy award, 1991; Horror Writers of America Bram Stoker award for best collection, 1996. **Agent:** David Higham Associates, 5-8 Lower John Street, Golden Square, London, W1R 4HA, England.

HORROR, GHOST AND GOTHIC PUBLICATIONS

Novels

The Land of Laughs. New York, Viking Press, 1980; London, Hamlyn, 1982.
Voice of Our Shadow. New York, Viking Press, 1983; London, Arrow, 1984.
Bones of the Moon. London, Century, 1987; New York, Arbor House, 1988.

Sleeping in Flame. London, Legend, 1988; New York, Doubleday, 1989.
A Child Across the Sky. London, Legend, 1989; New York, Doubleday, 1990.
Black Cocktail (novella). London, Legend, 1990; New York, St. Martin's Press, 1991.
Outside the Dog Museum. London, Macdonald, 1991; New York Doubleday, 1992.
After Silence. London, Macdonald, 1992; New York Doubleday, 1993.
From the Teeth of Angels. London, HarperCollins, and New York Doubleday, 1994.

Short Stories

The Panic Hand (a version with differing contents originally published in German as *Die Panische Hand*, 1989). London, HarperCollins, 1995; New York, St. Martin's Press, 1996.

OTHER PUBLICATIONS

Plays

Screenplays: *The Joker,* date unknown; plus others, not divulged.

* * *

Although only a few of them overlap substantially in terms of their *dramatis personae* all of Jonathan Carroll's novels are set in a distinctive narrative space whose deceptively close resemblances to the reader's world usually break down with the abrupt introduction of some unexpected fantastic motif. These unceremonious intrusions of the supernatural can seem jarring, although they often serve the purpose of rendering brutally explicit a creeping but numinous unease which has possessed the plot since its inception. Carroll has standardized a strategy whereby his books grip the reader with their easy narrative manner and sentimental accounts of rewarding emotional relationships, then spring transformative narrative ambushes which remove everything into a new and exotic context.

The uneasily-allied protagonists of *The Land of Laughs* investigate the background of a writer whose tales they loved as children, and find that the small town where he lived and died is still in the grip of his too-powerful imagination. That grip is far more oppressive than his heart-warming works had implied, although its tightness and sternness both derive from the capacity that his fantasies had to provide an avenue of escape for alienated readers. The protagonist of *Voice of Our Shadow* is befriended by a happily married couple and inconveniently falls in love with the wife. The sudden death of the husband does not serve to make the situation any less complicated; instead, its further development releases a torrent of pent-up guilt left over from the protagonist's troubled relationship with his bullying brother. Penitent though he is for all his past sins, the luckless young man can find no release from the merciless oppression of his long-dead sibling.

Bones of the Moon is the least downbeat of Carroll's fantasies, striking the most delicate balance between unease and sentimentality. Its heroine—whose ordinary hopes and ambitions have already been fulfilled—finds a certain solace in her vivid dreams of an imaginary world called Rondua, but they become increasingly disturbing and eventually impact dramatically on her everyday existence. As with several of Carroll's later works the focal point of the disturbance is a child whose advent is eagerly anticipated but strangely ominous. *Sleeping in Flame*—which shares some of the same characters—is similar in several ways, this time featuring a male protagonist who becomes increasingly aware of paranormal powers after falling in love and fathering a child. The "explanation" ultimately provided for his peculiar heritage can hardly help but seem ill-fitting, but its strident discordance is clearly deliberate, given that the parallel devices deployed in the novella *Black Cocktail* and *Outside the Dog Museum* are just as casually alien to the surfaces of the stories. Another protagonist similarly afflicted with burdensome near-godlike powers is featured in the short story "The Sadness of Detail."

The protagonist of *A Child Across the Sky* is a film director who once fell in love with Cullen James, the protagonist of *Bones of the Moon*, and briefly shared her dreams of Rondua. He is impelled by the mysterious death of a close friend into a search for a crucial scene missing from the last of four horror movies—perhaps because it was never shot—made by the friend in question. He is aided by the filmmaker's no-longer-imaginary childhood playmate, who also claims to be an angel and likes to manifest herself in the guise of a paradoxically pregnant nine-year-old girl. *A Child Across the Sky* is the most complicated of all Carroll's works, and the most nakedly horrific; the conscientiously nasty-minded double-twist ending is the most effective of all his climaxes. Another imaginary friend who becomes disturbingly real is featured in "Mr. Fiddlehead," the story which opens the collection *The Panic Hand*.

Outside the Dog Museum is surreal from the very beginning, featuring an acclaimed architect pursued by an enigmatic Sultan who wants him to design a billion-dollar dog museum. When an earthquake kills the original client, the Sultan's son and heir transfers the project from the Arabian desert to the Austrian alps. When the architect is finally drawn into the construction process, however, he finds that the erection's true nature and purpose are even stranger than he imagined.

After Silence is much more naturalistic than its immediate predecessors, although it includes a careful reference to Cullen James having no purpose other than to establish that the novel belongs to the same fictitious world. It tells the story of a cartoonist who falls in love with a single parent whose past contains an ugly secret, but nothing very untoward happens until he decides, out of love for her and the child that is not really hers, to keep the secret—thus taking on a burden of guilt which corrodes his life and mind exactly as the life and mind of the protagonist of *Voice of our Shadow* were corroded. *After Silence* is the most reflective of Carroll's novels, replete with philosophical reveries and aphoristic observations, but its protagonist is as unreliable a narrator as any of his predecessors and if his blithe failure to unravel the appeal of his own cartoons does not suffice to make the point, the final phase of the story comprehensively undermines the credibility of his earlier self-analyses.

The central tenet of Carroll's *oeuvre* seems to be that if that which people imagine were somehow to become real, its actuality would be nightmarish no matter how innocent the initial process of imagination seemed to be. His characters are usually nice and fundamentally honest people who always try to do their best, sometimes in very difficult circumstances, but cannot ever escape the insidious and cruel assaults of conscience. His curiously seductive but calculatedly perverse narratives imply that no one is authentically pure in heart, and that love—however ecstatic or

true—not only cannot save us from the effects of our spiritual pollution but is likely to bring them out more fully.

By the gruesome standards of modern horror fiction Carroll is extraordinarily subtle, but that gives his work a peculiar effectiveness which is his alone. His narrative voice is original and distinctive—and quite probably inimitable—and the ruminations of his characters, however unreliable they may be as narrators, are possessed of real depth as well as endless fascination.

—Brian Stableford

CASE, (Brian) David (Francis)

Nationality: American. **Born:** Gloversville, New York, 22 December 1937. **Education:** State University of New York, Albany, 1956; Endicott College, Beverly, Massachusetts, 1959. **Family:** Married Valerie Priest; three children. **Career:** Full-time writer; is said to have written more than 300 books under 17 pseudonyms, mostly pornography and including some westerns. Lived in England and Greece after 1960. **Agent:** Richard Curtis Associates, 171 East 74th Street, New York, NY 10021, USA.

<small>HORROR, GHOST AND GOTHIC PUBLICATIONS</small>

Novels

Fengriffen: A Chilling Tale. New York, Hill and Wang, 1970; as *And Now the Screaming Starts . . .*, London, Pan, 1973.
Wolf Tracks. New York, Belmont Tower, 1980.
The Third Grave. Sauk City, Wisconsin, Arkham House, 1981.

Short Stories

The Cell: Three Tales of Horror. New York, Hill and Wang, 1969; as *The Cell and Other Tales of Horror.* London, Macdonald, 1969.
Fengriffen and Other Stories. London, Macdonald, 1971.

<small>OTHER PUBLICATIONS</small>

Novels

Plumb Drillin'. New York Stein and Day, 1975; London, W. H. Allen, 1976; as *Gold Fever*, New York, Belmont, 1982.
The Fighting Breed. New York, Zebra, 1980.
Guns of Valentine. New York, Ace, 1982.

*

Film Adaptations: *And Now the Screaming Starts . . .*, 1973, from his story "Fengriffen"; *Scream of the Wolf*, 1974, from his story "The Hunter."

*   *   *

David Case quickly established a reputation as a fine and promising horror writer with his two collections, each of three long stories. His two horror novels, published some ten years later, did not add sufficiently to that reputation, and since that time he has written in other genres, producing only a handful of horror tales over more than 25 years.

"The Cell," which is supposed to be the first story Case wrote, is narrated in diary form by a werewolf. He thinks of himself as an ordinary married man with a progressive disease, against which he struggles to maintain his normality. He will not seek professional help for his lycanthropy but has a subterranean cell constructed in which he spends one night a month, to save his wife and the world from harm. Yet, as the story progresses, his psychological peculiarities become clear—he feels little or no responsibility for the murders he has committed—and his unpleasant demise seems justified.

In the same collection were "The Hunter" and "The Dead End." "The Hunter," later filmed as *Scream of the Wolf*, suggests a werewolf explanation to serial killings on Dartmoor, though the eventual explanation is non-supernatural. The horror comes from the nature of the injuries: severe lacerations to the body of each victim and the head cleanly chopped off and missing. The story focuses on two elderly big-game hunters, one called in by the police to track the supposed animal killer, and the other, his long-time rival, who lives nearby. "The Dead End" is much more unusual, being set in and around Ushuaia, which is the most southerly town in the world, in Tierra del Fuego. While the one-man museum expedition from London to follow up reports of a primitive ape-man may require considerable suspension of disbelief by the reader, the atmospheric descriptions of the desolate countryside and the peculiar characters who have chosen to live there make fascinating reading. The chemical mutation explanation nicely combines science fiction and horror, not to mention a whole string of clichés (the world's strongest man, a mad scientist with a secret laboratory, a beautiful naked woman who offers herself to the narrator, and a terrible fear of mutated genes) in a very memorable story.

"Fengriffen," which was filmed as *And Now the Screaming Starts . . .*, is Case's only period piece. While the period is never specified, it must be about 1870. This is a fine novella, full of Gothic and supernatural elements, yet narrated by Dr. Pope, a psychologist who tries to employ rationality and the scientific method to account for what seems to be madness in Catherine, the young wife of Charles Fengriffen. Fengriffen House is a forbidding mansion on moorland, somewhere in England. For twelve generations it has been occupied by the Fengriffen family, who are now subject to a curse because of the inexcusable behaviour of the grandfather of the present master. Perhaps 50 or 60 years earlier Henry Fengriffen claimed the "right of the first night" with the bride of one of his gamekeepers, raping her and maiming her husband, Silas. Silas's curse is upon the next virgin bride of the Fengriffens, which is Catherine. She claims to have been visited in bed by an incubus—which turns out to be the spirit of Silas. While the descriptions are too thin and Dr. Pope's role is perhaps too passive, the story contains some excellent scenes.

In *Fengriffen and Other Stories* are the novelettes "Strange Roots" and "Among the Wolves." The former is a strange and rather lop-sided tale about the artificial creation of werewolves, while the latter is a more subtle piece concerning a series of apparently senseless murders perpetrated to support the theory that only the fittest deserve to survive.

Case's later stories are shorter and less memorable. "A Cross to Bear" consists of two "told tales," one concerning a steamship voyage up a South American river, involving the delivery of a new priest to a mission, the presence of jaguar-men, and the practice of ripping out and burning the hearts of the dead. "The War is Over" describes atrocities just after a war has ended, and is applicable to almost any post-war locale.

Wolf Tracks is yet another attempt at a werewolf story. This time the setting is Toronto, where a serial killer is biting his way through the necks and faces of (mainly) young women at the rate of one a day. The police seem to spend their time hesitating and trying to score points off each other, while the other male characters all meet in a bar and get drunk. The novel is an easy read, though not a satisfying one. For some reason Case adopts a simplistic and deliberately repetitive style (rather reminiscent of Richard Brautigan's, though lacking the poetic touch and inventive genius of Brautigan). The result is that all characterization is limited and flat. The dialogue is natural but often lacks direction or entertainment. In an attempt to inject pace, Case presents the story in four-page chapters, which rarely allow for the development of atmosphere. The only interesting character is a female expert on wolves, called N. V. Cronski, who plays only a small part. It seems likely that some scenes and characters are unsuccessful attempts at humour.

The Third Grave is a more entertaining novel. It reads like an offbeat version of a pulp-magazine story from the 1930s, complete with clichéd characters and plot situations. In fact the plot, partly about mummys' curses, is convoluted and never credible, but the pace carries the reader through. Despite the shortcomings of these two novels it is a shame that Case has not devoted much of his energy towards horror fiction over the last 17 years, especially at novelette length, which seems to be his forte.

—Chris Morgan

CAVE, Hugh B(arnett)

Nationality: American. **Born:** Chester, England, 11 July 1910; emigrated to the United States as a child. **Career:** Full-time writer from the age of 18; prolific contributor to pulp magazines from 1929; contributor to slick magazines, such as *Cosmopolitan* and *Good Housekeeping*, in later years; lived in Haiti and Jamaica for many years after World War II. **Awards:** World Fantasy award for collection, 1978; Horror Writers of America Life Achievement award, 1991. Lives in Oak Harbor, Washington State.

HORROR, GHOST AND GOTHIC PUBLICATIONS

Novels

Legion of the Dead. New York, Avon, 1979.
The Nebulon Horror. New York, Dell, 1980.
The Evil. New York, Charter, 1981.
Shades of Evil. New York, Charter, 1982.
Disciples of Dread. New York, Tor, 1988.
The Lower Deep. New York, Tor, 1990.
Lucifer's Eye. New York, Tor, 1991.

Short Stories

The Witching Lands. N.p., 1962.
Murgunstrumm and Others, illustrated by Lee Brown Coye. Chapel Hill, North Carolina, Carcosa House, 1977.

The Corpse Maker, edited by Sheldon Jaffery. Mercer Island, Washington, Starmont House, 1988.
Death Stalks the Night. Minneapolis, Minnesota, Fedogan and Bremer, 1995.
Bitter/Sweet. West Warwick, Rhode Island, Necronomicon Press, 1996.

OTHER PUBLICATIONS

Novels

Run, Shadow, Run. London, Hale, 1968.
The Voyage (for children). New York, Macmillan, and London, Collier, 1988.
Conquering Kilmarnie. New York, Macmillan, and London, Collier, 1989.
The Wild One (for children). N.p., n.d.

Poetry

The Sacred Cave and Other Poems. Cupertino, California, Omega Cat Press, 1992.

Other

Haiti: High Road to Adventure. N.p., 1952.
Four Paths to Paradise: A Book About Jamaica. N.p., n.d.
Magazines I Remember. Chicago, Tattered Pages Press, 1994.

*

Critical Study: *Pulp Man's Odyssey: The Hugh B. Cave Story* by Audrey Parente, Mercer Island, Washington, Starmont Press, 1988.

*   *   *

Hugh Cave's long and distinguished career as a weird-fiction writer spans most of the twentieth century and the enduring appeal of his tales of horror and the supernatural is attributable to his mastery of the fundamentals of good storytelling: plot, atmosphere and character. Cave's career can be divided into two phases, the first involving his work for the pulps, to which he contributed prolifically beginning in 1929. Although a generalist who published regularly in the detective, western and adventure magazines, he showed an early aptitude for horror fiction when "The Corpse on the Grating," a tale of medical terror about a scientifically reanimated corpse, appeared in the February 1930 issue of *Astounding Stories*. A grim and suspenseful story coloured more by Gothic darkness than the scientific enlightenment typical for science fiction at that time, it is essentially a science-fiction variation on the zombie theme, and thus a foreshadowing of interests Cave would explore in his fiction years later.

Between 1931 and 1933, Cave placed a dozen stories with the weird-fiction pulps *Ghost Stories, Strange Tales* and *Weird Tales*. Their themes are the familiar stuff of pulp horror fiction: weird scientific experiments ("The Affair of the Clutching Hand," "The Strange Case of No. 7"), vengeance from beyond the grave ("Dead Man's Belt"), the fatal family curse ("The Ghoul Gallery"), shape-shifting ("The Cult of the White Ape"), the haunted mansion

("The Door of Doom") and so forth. Cave, however, was adept at finding a new angle or approach to ideas long-mired in cliché. "The Crawling Curse," for example, concerns a murderer stalked by a disembodied hand animated by black magic. Cave diverts this well-known horror theme from its usual predictable treatment with an inventive twist that has the hand dressing a corpse with the murderer's clothing, forcing him to seek out the body or die by slow putrefaction of his own flesh. "The Isle of Dark Magic," in which a bereaved man animates a statue of his dead lover through black magic, ends with an unforeseen complication in which the magic spell he uses also unexpectedly resurrects the woman's corpse.

The variety and freshness Cave could bring to a horror theme are most evident in the four vampire tales he published between 1932 and 1936. "The Brotherhood of Blood" concerns a woman's hereditary curse of vampirism and a love triangle in which a rejected suitor engineers her and her lover's doom. "The Prey of the Nightborn" also involves a different love triangle, with two female vampires, one good and one evil, fighting for the soul of a mortal victim. In "Stragella," a vampire *femme fatale* uses a derelict ship as a secret fortress from which to launch nightly assaults on the mainland. "Murgunstrumm" features vampire lounge lizards whose idea of night life differs considerably from that of the victims they pick up at a local roadhouse.

"Murgunstrumm" is Cave's best-known story and a prime example of his storytelling prowess. He swirls an atmosphere thick with dread around the decrepit New England inn where events take place. His descriptions of its labyrinthine interior and sinister innkeeper are portentous without being overblown, and they invest every corner of the building with a sense of unseen menace. The mounting hysteria of his characters as their efforts to escape grow increasingly desperate contributes to the suspense, and the pacing of the story is relentless, building through one false climax after another to an exciting finale.

Narrative skills of this kind served him well when in the mid-1930s Cave decamped from the weird fiction pulps to write for *Horror Stories, Terror Tales, Spicy Mystery Stories* and other shudder pulps whose selections generally evoked a mood of supernatural terror for events inevitably revealed as the work of human malefactors. Owing to his proficiency at this type of story, a liberal sampling of which fills his collections *Murgunstrumm and Others* and *Death Stalks the Night*, Cave was one of the writers most responsible for shaping the shudder-pulp sensibility, which transformed rural American towns into Gothic landscapes, local powerbrokers into megalomaniacal fiends, and ordinary men and women into paragons of imperilled virtue.

The second phase of Cave's weird fiction writing begins with his "rediscovery" in the 1970s, following years spent in Haiti and Jamaica. Stories he wrote during this interval, a representative selection of which can be found in his collection *The Witching Lands*, are set largely in the West Indies and were published mostly in the slick-paper magazines. Although noticeably devoid of supernatural content, they are nevertheless imbued with a sense of magic and mystery through their descriptions of the exotic islands and their psychologically rich portraits of travellers, expatriate Americans and average West Indian natives whose dreams and superstitions leaven their daily experiences.

Cave's weird fiction since the mid-1970s, much of which runs to novel length, shares the setting and spirit of these stories. His West Indies are, as he writes in *The Lower Deep*, a land of mystery where "the impossible was merely improbable. And the improbable happened all the time." Voodoo is rampant among the natives, but it is "not what the stick-a-pin-in-a-doll writers said it was." In *Legion of the Dead*, the first of his contemporary horror novels, he makes a distinction between voodoo as practised in the islands and popular western conceptions of voodoo as equivalent to black magic. "Voodoo," says one native practitioner, "is good and decent, a combination of healing and religion which for years has sustained our barefoot people in their poverty and sickness, giving them the strength to go on and a faith that a better world awaits them. Those others, the practitioners of witchcraft, are something else altogether."

Cave takes pains to differentiate the voodoo *houngan*, or priest, from the *bocor*, or sorcerer, and frequently portrays voodoo as a system of mystical faith frustratingly misunderstood by the prejudiced western mind. In *The Lower Deep*, for example, American visitors to the island of St. Joseph blame a series of seemingly supernatural events on voodoo when, as it turns out, voodoo has actually been invoked to protect people from the real perpetrators. Zombies appear in some of these stories (most notably in his short masterpiece, "The Place of No Return") but Cave frequently uses them to demystify the mythology surrounding them: although he doesn't dispute that zombies may actually be reanimated corpses, he suggests that many so-called zombies are the slaves of evil-minded men who dominate them through knowledge of folk medicine and manipulation of superstitious fears.

The supernatural evils that fill Cave's novels are ultimately metaphors for examining the evil that men do. In *Legion of the Dead* and *Disciples of Dread*, repressive political regimes and terrorist movements recruit sorcerers to serve them. However, as a freedom fighter in *Legion of the Dead* remarks about a zombie army mobilized by a petty dictator, "the zombies are not our real enemy. They are already dead—just being used by that evil man. The real enemy is the man himself." A *bocor* named Margal epitomizes human evil in *The Evil* and *Shades of Evil* by using mind-control to rob his victims of their will. In *Shades of Evil* and *The Nebulon Horror*, both of which are set in Florida, the evil of island practitioners of black magic is measured by its impact on susceptible Americans who have brought its taint back across the ocean with them.

The most powerful antidote to evil in these novels is basic human goodness. It brings men and women together, breaks down cultural barriers to unite foreigners and natives with a common objective, and in *The Lower Deep* and *Lucifer's Eye* leads to heroic feats of self-sacrifice. Cave's heroes and heroines are men and women responding to extraordinary challenges of basic moral convictions. That they inevitably triumph is a measure of Cave's optimism, and perhaps a gauge of why, in a field where trends come and go, much of Cave's fiction seems timeless.

—Stefan Dziemianowicz

CHADBOURN, Mark

Nationality: British. **Family:** Married Elizabeth Chadbourn; two children. **Career:** Journalist. **Awards:** Best New Author award, *Fear* magazine. **Address:** c/o Gollancz, The Cassell Group, Wellington House, 125 Strand, London WC2R 0BB, England. Lives in Leicestershire.

HORROR, GHOST AND GOTHIC PUBLICATIONS

Novels

Underground. London, Piatkus, 1993.
Nocturne. London, Gollancz, 1994.
The Eternal. London, Gollancz, 1996.
Scissorman. London, Gollancz, 1997.

OTHER PUBLICATIONS

Other

Testimony. London, Vista, 1996.

* * *

Despite his winning of *Fear* magazine's Best New Author Award for *Underground*, Mark Chadbourn's first two novels might well have been written by different people. *Underground* follows the formula typical of many second-rate horror novels, whereas *Nocturne* not only rises above the mundane in approach and subject matter but somewhere between the two publication dates Chadbourn learned how to write.

Underground is set in the British Midlands, an area with a long history of coal-mining. Mike Leary is a trouble-shooter for the Coal Board and has been sent to Colthorpe colliery to investigate their abysmal accident record. He knows there is a hidden agenda—his immediate boss would love to see him foul up, and a scapegoat is needed for when they announce the closure of the pit. He quickly realizes that the incidents cannot be straight accidents because the details don't tally, especially with standard safety procedures. We quickly realize there is something nasty down the pit. From then on the story becomes largely predictable. The miner who breaks ranks and offers to tell Leary about what is happening is obviously going to be the next victim. When Leary's family arrive you can be certain that they will be threatened. As well as being cyphers rather than well-rounded personalities, many of the lesser characters are clichés. Among them are the seedy newspaper reporter, the angry union man, the academic with the key information and the bluff pit manager who sympathizes with the miners because he was one himself. Naturally, as this is horror, there are lots of corpses produced in gruesome ways. Any spark of originality must lie with the threat itself, as in times of crisis the spirits of the dead solidify and claim others.

Nocturne, on the other hand, drags the reader along with its sense of mystery. David Easter wakes up on a street car in New Orleans and cannot remember how he got there. Two months of memories are missing. The narrative follows David as he tries to make sense of what has happened. He has a hotel room booked and paid for, a return ticket from England and sufficient travellers' cheques for his immediate needs. He is a jazz fan who works in a record shop and lives in a dingy London flat, and this is the one place in all the world he wanted to visit. In his wallet he finds a dog-eared photograph of a woman he doesn't recognize but instinctively knows is important to him. As a starting point he decides to try to find her, hoping that that is why he has come to New Orleans. Gradually the mystery unravels as he comes closer to the woman and his memory starts to dribble back. Just as New

Orleans seems to be a nexus of cultures, voodoo, jazz, French and American, so the novel becomes a nexus of ideas involving a mafia-like krewe (normally these are societies that organize the floats for the Mardi Gras), a legendary lost record and the supernatural—disconcertingly for David, he finds he can see the dead and they appear to want something from him.

Although Chadbourn is apparently very familiar with both landscapes, New Orleans comes across as a much sharper, more real place than Colthorpe, peopled with the living. Although the village of Colthorpe is fictitious, its antecedents are not. There are real places in the same part of the country that are very similar. Also, David Easter is directly threatened, in fact he deliberately puts himself in danger at times, while Mike Leary always seems to be an accidental victim. The biggest flaw in *Nocturne* is in the development of David's character. Can love really change a shallow, apparent loser into the determined and positive personality who will not take "go away" for an answer in New Orleans?

The Eternal returns to the comfortable English countryside, to a village not far from Colthorpe. Like Colthorpe, it and most of its inhabitants have a vagueness about them, as if Chadbourn is afraid they will be recognized by the real residents of the West Midlands. It is like a canvas in which one or two characteristics are painted in detail in each of the figures and the rest is left blurred. The beginning does not particularly inspire. Annie Boulton gets chatting to a stranger on the train home for Christmas. When it is derailed she sees the stranger systematically kill the trapped passengers. Despite a broken leg, she manages to flee and survive. Six months later the stranger turns up in Annie's village and starts turning it inside out, exposing all the nasty things that actually go on behind closed doors. Although it has a lot of good things going for it, *The Eternal* does not have the impact of realism present in *Nocturne*. Death and violence are more common in big cities and excite no more than a paragraph on the back page, The number of deaths that occur in a few days in Annie's village would produce worldwide banner headlines, so immediately marking the account as fiction.

The best horror always makes one harbour the suspicion that it could happen. Chadbourn's non-fiction book, *Testimony*, attempts to do just this, being a factual account of events in a haunted house. Stylistically, *Testimony* is poor and another author might have been tempted to detail all the possible, and unlikely, explanations for the recorded phenomena, but it does what was intended—to record in their own words what the people involved experienced.

Chadbourn is a writer who shows his potential when he expands his horizons and is less effective when using more traditional, parochial approaches.

—Pauline Morgan

CHAMBERS, Robert W(illiam)

Nationality: American. **Born:** Brooklyn, New York, 26 May 1865. **Education:** Art Students' League, New York; Ecole des Beaux Arts and Academie Julien, Paris. **Family:** Married Elsa Vaughn Moller in 1898; one son. **Career:** Illustrator for *Life*, *Truth* and *Vogue*, New York; novelist. **Member:** National Institute of Arts and Letters. **Died:** 16 December 1933.

HORROR, GHOST AND GOTHIC PUBLICATIONS

Novels

The Slayer of Souls. New York, Doran, and London, Hodder and Stoughton, 1920.

Short Stories

The King in Yellow. Chicago, Neely, and London, Chatto and Windus, 1895; abridged as *The Mask, and Other Stories*, Racine, Wisconsin, Whitman, 1929.
The Maker of Moons. New York, Putnam, 1896.
The Mystery of Choice. New York, Appleton, 1897.
The Tree of Heaven. New York, Appleton, 1907; London, Constable, 1908.
The King in Yellow and Other Horror Stories, edited by E. F. Bleiler. New York, Dover, 1970.

OTHER PUBLICATIONS

Novels

In the Quarter. Chicago, Neely, 1894; London, Chatto and Windus, 1895.
The Red Republic: A Romance of the Commune. New York, Putnam, 1895; London, Nash, 1903.
The King and a Few Dukes. New York, Putnam, 1896; London, Greening, 1906.
Lorraine. New York, Harper, 1897.
Ashes of Empire. New York, Stokes, and London, Macmillan, 1898.
The Cambric Mask. New York, Stokes, 1899; London, Macmillan, 1900.
The Conspirators. New York, Harper, 1899.
Outsiders: An Outline. New York, Stokes, 1899; London, Richards, 1900.
Cardigan. New York, Harper, and London, Constable, 1901.
The Shining Band. London, Ward Lock, 1901.
The Maids of Paradise. New York, Harper, 1902; London, Constable, 1903.
The Maid-at-Arms. New York, Harper, and London, Constable, 1902.
Iole. New York, Appleton, 1905; London, Constable, 1906.
The Reckoning. New York, Appleton, and London, Constable, 1905.
The Fighting Chance. New York, Appleton, 1906; London, Constable, 1907.
The Tracer of Lost Persons. New York, Appleton, 1906; London, Murray, 1907.
The Firing Line. New York, Appleton, 1908.
Some Ladies in Haste. New York, Appleton, and London, Constable, 1908.
The Danger Mark. New York, Appleton, 1909.
Special Messenger. New York, Appleton, 1909; London, Laurie, 1910.
Ailsa Page. New York, Appleton, and London, Newnes, 1910.
The Adventures of a Modest Man. New York, Appleton, and London, Newnes, 1911.
The Common Law. New York, Appleton, 1911.
The Streets of Ascalon: Episodes in the Unfinished Career of Richard Quarren Esq. New York, Appleton, 1912; London, Newnes, 1915.

The Business of Life. New York, Appleton, 1913; London, Newnes, 1915.

Between Friends. New York, Appleton, 1914.

Athalie. New York, Appleton, 1915; London, Pearson, 1927.

The Girl Philippa. New York, Appleton, 1916.

Barbarians. New York, Appleton, 1917.

The Dark Star. New York, Appleton, 1917.

The Restless Sex. New York, Appleton, 1918; London, Pearson, 1928.

In Secret. New York, Doran, and London, Hodder and Stoughton, 1919.

The Moonlit Way. New York, Appleton, 1919.

The Crimson Tide. New York, Appleton, 1919.

The Little Red Foot. New York, Doran, and London, Hodder and Stoughton, 1921.

The Flaming Jewel. New York, Doran, 1922.

Eris. New York, Doran, and London, Hodder and Stoughton, 1923.

The Talkers. New York, Doran, 1923; London, Unwin, 1925.

America; or, The Sacrifice: A Romance of the American Revolution. New York, Grosset and Dunlap, 1924.

The Mystery Lady. New York, Grosset and Dunlap, 1925; London, Cassell, 1926.

Marie Halket. London, Unwin, 1926; New York, Appleton Century, 1937.

The Men They Hanged. New York, Appleton, 1926.

The Drums of Aulone. New York, Appleton, 1927.

Beating Wings. London, Cassell, 1928; New York, Appleton Century, 1930.

The Rogue's Moon. New York, Appleton, 1928; London, Cassell, 1929.

The Sun Hawk. New York, Appleton, and London, Cassell, 1929.

The Rake and the Hussy. New York, Appleton, 1930.

The Painted Minx. New York, Appleton, 1930.

Gitana. New York, Appleton, 1931.

War Paint and Rouge. New York, Appleton, 1931.

Whistling Cat. New York, Appleton, 1932.

Whatever Love Is. New York, Appleton Century, 1933.

Secret-Service Operator. New York, Appleton Century, 1934; as *Spy Number 13*, London, Philip Allan, 1935.

The Young Man's Girl. New York, Appleton Century, 1934.

The Gold Chase. New York, Appleton Century, 1935.

Love and the Lieutenant. New York, Appleton Century, 1935.

The Girl in Golden Rags. New York, Appleton Century, 1936.

The Fifth Horseman. New York, Appleton Century, 1937.

Smoke of Battle. New York, Appleton Century, 1938.

Short Stories

The Haunts of Men. New York, Stokes, and London, Bowden, 1899.

In Search of the Unknown. New York, Harper, 1904; London, Constable, 1905.

A Young Man in a Hurry, and Other Short Stories. New York, Harper, 1904; London, Constable, 1905.

The Gay Rebellion. New York, Appleton, 1913.

Police!!! New York, Appleton, 1915.

The Better Man. New York, Appleton, 1916.

Fiction for Children

Outdoorland. New York, Harper, 1902.

Orchard-land. New York, Harper, 1903.

River-land. New York, Harper, 1904.

Forest-land. New York, Appleton, 1905; as *Hide and Seek in Forest Land,* New York, Appleton, 1909.

Mountain-land. New York, Appleton, 1906.

The Younger Set. New York, Appleton, and London, Constable, 1907.

Garden-land. New York, Appleton, 1907.

The Green Mouse. New York, Appleton, 1910.

Blue-bird Weather. New York, Appleton, 1912.

Japonette. New York, Appleton, 1912.

The Hidden Children. New York, Appleton, 1914.

Quick Action. New York, Appleton, 1914.

Anne's Bridge. New York, Appleton, 1914.

Who Goes There. New York, Appleton, 1915.

The Laughing Girl. New York, Appleton, 1918.

The Happy Parrot. New York, Appleton, and London, Cassell, 1929.

Poetry

With the Band. New York, Stone and Kimball, 1896.

*   *   *

In pursuit of his early ambition to be a painter Robert W. Chambers set out for Paris, and lived there while the Decadent Movement was at its height. One of the key influences on Decadent prose fiction was Edgar Allan Poe, whose works had been translated by the movement's spiritual forefather Charles Baudelaire. It is not entirely surprising, therefore, that Chambers' first book included, ahead of several innocuous stories of life and love in Paris, a group of Poesque fantasies heavily infected with the Decadent sensibility. Four of the five stories were linked together by references to an imaginary text called *The King in Yellow*: a drama set in the imaginary land of Carcosa (a locale borrowed from the most attentive literary descendant Poe then had in his homeland, Ambrose Bierce) which is so intense and malign that it drives its readers mad.

The longest of these remarkable tales, "The Repairer of Reputations," is set in a future America which has, in political terms, gone to the bad. The shortest, "In the Court of the Dragon," is a tale of undefinable supernatural pursuit. "The Mask" is a parable of artistic endeavour in which a sculptor works all too literally "from life." "The Yellow Sign" is a marvellously creepy tale of nightmares become real which is one of the finest horror stories ever written and a foundation stone of the modern genre. The fifth story, which does not refer to the imaginary text, is "The Demoiselle d'Ys," a timeslip romance based on prototypes penned by Theophile Gautier, which outshines its models in delicacy and dramatic effect.

The King in Yellow—particularly the dimly glimpsed text-within-the-text—established a landmark in the history of American supernatural fiction; it was a key influence on H. P. Lovecraft and the *Weird Tales* "school" whose linchpin Lovecraft became. The volume was reprinted several times and its best stories were widely anthologized, but Chambers never did anything like them again. Having abandoned painting to work as a professional writer his work became increasingly trivial; although his historical novels are not without merit the fluffy romantic comedies he churned out in quantity were resolutely mindless. He did not give up imaginative fiction, nor were his later short stories in that vein entirely without flair, but they were relentlessly formulaic and annoyingly casual.

The tales of expeditions in search of exotic life-forms contained in *In Search of the Unknown* and its sequel *Police!!!* are interesting in their own right, but with the exception of "A Matter of Interest"—which was reprinted from *The Mystery of Choice*—they are not at all horrific. It was as if Chambers simply could not find his way back to the nightmarish milieu of his first stories, thus encouraging the speculation that they might have been based on actual nightmares which did not recur once he had attained full maturity. *The Mystery of Choice* does retain a few fugitive echoes of the dark mood of the *King in Yellow* stories. "The Messenger" is a tale of supernatural vengeance whose conscientiously Gothic method is conspicuously artificial. "The White Shadow" fails ignominiously to recapture the mood of "The Demoiselle d'Ys," although "Passeur" and "The Key to Grief" come a little closer.

A longer story of supernatural romance, probably cobbled together from an aborted novel, had earlier appeared as the title-story of *The Maker of Moons*. It appears to be an attempt to relocate a Gautieresque sensibility within the framework of a pulpish thriller (of a kind which Sax Rohmer was later to make his own). An Oriental sorcerer heading a diabolical secret society is opposed by Secret Service agents, providing an action-adventure context for the hero's romance. The grotesque unworkability of the project is not helped by the invocation of a further apologetic device, in which the tale becomes a tissue of romantic fancies spun by a husband to entertain his wife. Chambers did, however, make a better fist of an essentially similar project in *The Slayer of Souls*, which is not ineffective if one can overlook the preposterous suggestion that Kurdistan borders China. It reconstructs the Yezidees as a secret society bent on world domination by occult means.

Chambers employed supernatural devices (some of them excused by science-fictional jargon) in several matchmaking fantasies, of which *The Tracer of Lost Persons* is the most blatantly absurd, by virtue of being the only dating-agency story ever penned which fixes up a client with a mummy. He also invoked extra-sensory perception in his sentimental romance *Athalie*. Apart from *The Slayer of Souls*, however, the only book he wrote after 1900 into which he attempted to introduce a note of supernatural horror was *The Tree of Heaven*, a collection of stories linked by a device introduced in the first of them, "The Carpet of Belshazzar." The carpet in question is patterned with cartouches whose decoded symbols offer ominous prophecies. The other stories painstakingly work out the gloomy fates imposed on those present at the fateful dinner when the carpet's secret is revealed. There is, as usual, a romantic connection between the book's narrator and the fey girl whose awareness of previous incarnations allows her to perceive the carpet's evil nature. The tales are so weak and contrived that Everett Bleiler did not deign to note their existence—although he certainly knew of them—when compiling his eclectic collection of Chambers' best weird tales for Dover.

It might conceivably have been the case that Chambers' subsequent failure to produce anything remotely comparable to the classic fantasies of *The King in Yellow* was a matter of inclination. He probably made more money out of his frothy romances and gained a better contemporary reputation from his historical novels than he could have achieved as a writer of weird tales, although his posthumous reputation is entirely based on that first book. It does seem, however, that he occasionally tried to recapture something of the magic that had affected him in Paris; delicious Gautieresque female phantoms continued to haunt his output, and he did attempt to introduce a note of true horror into the most lurid of his melodramas. The abysmal depth of his failure and the desperation of his apologies suggests that he really could not do it—that he had completely lost whatever spark of the imagination it was that flared so brilliantly into "The Yellow Sign" and "The Demoiselle d'Ys," and that he deeply regretted the loss. His readers have every right to regret it too.

—Brian Stableford

CHAPPELL, Fred (Davis)

Nationality: American. **Born:** Canton, North Carolina, 28 May 1936. **Education:** Duke University, Durham, North Carolina, B.A. 1961, M.A. 1964. **Family:** Married Susan Nicholls; one son. **Career:** Since 1964 teacher of English, University of North Carolina, Greensboro. **Awards:** Sir Walter Raleigh prize, 1972; North Carolina award, 1980; Bollingen prize, 1985; World Fantasy awards, 1992, 1994; T. S. Eliot prize, 1993. **Agent:** Rhoda Weyr, 151 Bergen Street, New York, NY 14416, USA.

HORROR, GHOST AND GOTHIC PUBLICATIONS

Novel

Dagon. New York, Harcourt Brace, 1968.

Short Stories

More Shapes Than One. New York, St. Martin's Press, 1991.
The Lodger. West Warwick, Rhode Island, Necronomicon Press, 1993.

OTHER PUBLICATIONS

Novels

It Is Time, Lord. New York, Atheneum, 1963.
The Inkling. New York, Harcourt Brace, 1965.
The Gaudy Place. New York, Harcourt Brace, 1972.
I Am One of You Forever. Baton Rouge, Louisiana State University Press, 1985.
Brighten the Corner Where You Are. New York, St. Martin's Press, 1989.

Short Stories

Moments of Light. Los Angeles, New South, 1980.

Poetry

The World Between the Eyes. Baton Rouge, Louisiana State University Press, 1971.
River. Baton Rouge, Louisiana State University Press, 1975.
The Man Twice Married to Fire. Greensboro, North Carolina, Unicorn Press, 1977.
Bloodfire. Baton Rouge, Louisiana State University Press, 1978.

Awakening to Music. Davidson, North Carolina, Briarpatch Press, 1979.
Earthsleep. Baton Rouge, Louisiana State University Press, 1980.
Driftlake: A Lieder Cycle. Emory, Virginia, Iron Mountain Press, 1981.
Midquest. Baton Rouge, Louisiana State University Press, 1981.
Castle Tzingal. Baton Rouge, Louisiana State University Press, 1985.
First and Last Words. Baton Rouge, Louisiana State University Press, 1988.
C. Baton Rouge, Louisiana State University Press, 1993.
Spring Garden: New and Selected Poems. Baton Rouge, Louisiana State University Press, 1995.

Other

The Fred Chappell Reader. New York, St. Martin's Press, 1987.
Plow Naked: Selected Writings on Poetry. Ann Arbor, University of Michigan Press, 1993.

*

Manuscript Collection: Duke University, Durham, North Carolina.

*   *   *

Fred Chappell's contributions to weird fiction are inseparable from his work in the literary mainstream. A celebrated poet and distinguished writer of fiction in the southern regionalist tradition, Chappell weaves elements of fantasy and horror into stories that have helped to broaden the literary horizons of the weird tale.

His best known work of weird fiction, *Dagon,* is both a serious novel of ideas and one of the few attempts at visionary horror in the Lovecraftian vein to succeed at novel length. The story, as he observes in "Remarks on *Dagon,*" his address at the H. P. Lovecraft Centennial Conference in 1990, was conceived as "a short novel . . . with overtones of moral philosophy, and to use as reference points colonial American history, the story of Samson as found in the Bible, and the artificial mythology developed by H. P. Lovecraft and his circle." Set in the contemporary American South, *Dagon* chronicles the tragic downfall of Peter Leland, a Methodist minister who has retreated to his family homestead to complete a scholarly treatise entitled *Remnant Pagan Forces in American Puritanism.* Leland's thesis is that the worship of the Philistine fertility god Dagon persists metaphorically in modern times, encoded in the "endless irrational productivity" of our consumer culture. While working on the book, he becomes obsessed with Mina Morgan, the sexually voracious daughter of a sharecropper who lives on his family's land. Pretentious and repressed, Leland fails to see that Mina is the flesh-and-blood embodiment of the crude appetites he is studying and to which he is slowly succumbing. On impulse, he murders his wife and seeks refuge with the Morgans. Psychologically broken, he submits to voluntary sexual enslavement by Mina and is reduced to a bestial level.

Chappell insinuates a minimum of Lovecraftian references into the story, dropping an occasional reference or image that only readers intimately familiar with Lovecraft's mythology would recognize. Indeed, there is more Faulkner than Lovecraft in this tale of violent passion, madness and degeneracy. Nevertheless, Leland emerges as the quintessential Lovecraftian protagonist whose world view is shattered by the unpalatable truths he uncovers. In one of his last lucid moments, Leland complains how "The things that happen more and more don't mean anything, and I can't make them mean anything." Like Lovecraft's characters, he is discomposed by the revelation that morality, religious faith and other systems of belief are flimsy security blankets people use to shield themselves from the chaos of existence. The story's climax, in which Leland appears to become one with the void that has opened up before him, is in some ways more audacious than any in Lovecraft, who typically leaves his characters teetering on the edge. A unique fusion of the southern Gothic and the tale of cosmic horror, *Dagon* is also the rare instance of a tale in the Lovecraft tradition whose philosophical foundations are as rigorously thought out as those of Lovecraft's fiction.

In his shorter fiction, Chappell effortlessly assimilates influences as diverse as pulp fiction of the 1930s, French symbolist poetry, contemporary academic criticism and prewar horror films to wreak challenging variations on familiar weird-fiction themes. "Weird Tales" is a cosmic conspiracy story built from Lovecraft's brief encounter with the poet Hart Crane, suggesting that Crane's "suicide" in 1932 and Lovecraft's death at the height of his creative powers in 1937 were engineered by the "invisible alien forces" both men exposed through their writings. This serves to link Lovecraft's vision of a universe in entropic decline to Crane's critiques in verse of the stultifying effects of cultural philistinism. "The Adder," a revisionist treatment of the book of forbidden knowledge, has Lovecraft's dreaded *Necronomicon* corrupting a volume of Milton shelved next to it, turning the poet's transcendent verse into bawdy doggerel.

Few of Chappell's stories are as calculatedly horrific as *Dagon,* or "Ember," a tale of murder and supernatural vengeance set in rural North Carolina. Most are gentle fantasies punctuated with tidbits of history and local colour and peopled with simple characters whose plain-spokenness contrasts sharply with the marvels they encounter. "Miss Prue" features a fickle spinster who continues to put off suitors even after they have died and returned as ghosts. In "Linnaeus Forgets," a magic plant that is its own self-contained universe underscores the shortcomings of a scientist's rigid classification scheme for our world's flora and fauna. "Mankind Journeys Through the Forest of Symbols" is a deadpan account of the absurdities that might have followed the materializing of a symbolist poem in the middle of a country road. Chappell's World Fantasy award-winning tale, "The Lodger," takes a comic poke at a number of literary and academic concerns in its portrait of a mild-mannered university librarian who becomes possessed by the spirit of a wretched decadent poet and attempts to exorcise him by indulging in excesses of banality.

Very little of Chappell's lyric verse can be described as weird, although several of his poems draw from the same reservoir of imagery as his fantastic fiction. "Burning the Frankenstein Monster: Elegiac Letter to Richard Dillard" and "Weird Tales" (not to be confused with his short story of the same name) use the cinematic adaptation of *Frankenstein* and the heyday of the pulp weird tale, respectively, to comment on the creative process. "Castle Tzingal," a cycle of poems narrated by a sentient homunculus, a mad king, and other persons who live within the confines of a Gothic castle, is a Poe-esque study of the depraved spirit that ranks as one of Chappell's darkest fantasies.

—Stefan Dziemianowicz

CHARNAS, Suzy McKee

Nationality: American. **Born:** New York City, 22 October 1939. **Education:** New York High School of Music and Art; Barnard College, New York, B.A. in economic history 1961; New York University, M.A.T. in social studies (secondary teaching). **Family:** Married Stephen Charnas in 1968; two stepchildren. **Career:** Peace Corps English and history teacher, Girls' High School, Ogbomoso, Nigeria, 1961-62; lecturer in Economic History, University of Ibadan, Ife, Nigeria, 1962-63; English-History Core Teacher, New Lincoln School, New York, 1965-67; worked for Community Mental Health organization, New York, 1967-69. Instructor, Clarion West Writers Workshop (Seattle), 1984, 1986 and Clarion Writers Workshop (Michigan), 1987; Chair, Archive Project Committee, National Council of Returned Peace Corps Volunteers, 1986-88; instructor, Southwest Writers Workshop, University of New Mexico, Taos, summer 1993. Since 1969, freelance writer. **Awards:** Nebula award, for novella, 1980; Hugo award, for short story, 1990; Gigamesh award (Spanish), for best fantasy stories, 1990; Aslan award, Mythopoeic Society, best children's book, 1993. **Member:** Science Fiction and Fantasy Writers Association, Horror Writers of America, Authors Guild, Dramatists Guild. **Agent:** Jennifer Lyons, Joan Davis Agency, Writers House, 21 W. 26th St., New York, NY 10010. **Address:** 212 High St. NE, Albuquerque, NM 87102, USA.

HORROR, GHOST AND GOTHIC PUBLICATIONS

Novels

The Vampire Tapestry. New York, Simon and Schuster, 1980; London, Women's Press, 1992.
The Bronze King. Boston, Houghton, 1985.
Dorothea Dreams. New York, Arbor House, 1986.

OTHER PUBLICATIONS

Novels

Walk to the End of the World. New York, Ballantine, 1974; London, Gollancz, 1979.
Motherlines. New York, Berkley, 1979; London, Gollancz, 1980.
The Silver Glove. New York, Bantam, 1988.
The Golden Thread. New York, Bantam, 1989.
The Kingdom of Kevin Malone. San Diego, Harcourt, 1993.
The Furies. New York, Tor, 1994; London, Women's Press, 1995.

Short Stories

Listening to Brahms. Eugene, Oregon, Pulphouse, 1991.
Moonstone and Tiger Eye. Eugene, Oregon, Pulphouse, 1992.

Play

Vampire Dreams, adaptation of "Unicorn Tapestry" (produced 1990).

*

Critical Study: *Suzy Charnas, Joan Vinge, and Octavia Butler* by Richard Law, with others, San Bernardino, California, Borgo Press, 1986.

* * *

Some of the best of modern horror fiction has been produced by writers who are not specifically identified with the field. William Goldman, John Farris, Joyce Carol Oates, George R. R. Martin and others have all made their reputations in other areas of literature and all have created major works of horror fiction as well. Suzy McKee Charnas is another such writer, the majority of whose work has been science fiction or fantasy. But she is also the author of one of the most original and highly regarded vampire novels of all time.

The Vampire Tapestry is an episodic novel about Dr. Edward Weyland, a dream researcher who is also a vampire. In the opening segment, Weyland himself explains his nature, in theoretical terms, explaining why a vampire's bite could not be contagious, how a "real" vampire would be designed by nature to achieve a balance with his prey. In part two, Weyland is seriously injured and convalesces in a private home, while his uneasy host confronts a satanist with confused ideas about the vampire's nature. It's in this section that we first realize that the terms "predator" and "prey" aren't as clear cut as we might have thought, because the satanist eventually imprisons Weyland, hoping to somehow draw a kind of mystical power from his being.

Weyland consults a psychoanalyst in part three, a woman who predictably believes his vampirism to be no more than a delusion, although she is fascinated by the aura of power he exudes. Weyland confesses that he is unique, that he has found no evidence that any other vampires exist, and that he thinks of humans simply as his food source, lower beings with whom he has no interest in sex or other forms of interaction, though there are hints subsequently that he might not be quite as distanced as he would like to believe. Their interchanges are witty, clever and pointed, with Weyland sometimes assuming the role of interrogator in what is certainly the strongest section of the novel.

In the final segments, Weyland relocates to the southwestern United States, where we learn more of his own unique psychology. He is neither cruel nor kind; although he avoids killing his victims whenever possible, it is for practical reasons—the risk of discovery. Weyland is, in fact, a tremendously lonely figure, the only one of his species, unaging, his nightmares filled with human images. Pursued by his old enemy the satanist, Weyland finally disposes of him and then sheds his present identity, hibernating in preparation for a new career after he wakens years in the future. Although there have been numerous attempts to write stories from the vampire's point of view in recent years, most notably by Anne Rice, none rival *The Vampire Tapestry*'s straightforward, intelligent treatment.

There are also horror overtones in *The Bronze King*, the opening volume of a fantasy trilogy for younger readers. Tina discovers that she may have to save the world from an evil power from another dimension that manifests itself in the form of a gigantic serpent, strange street-gang members and other shapes. These overtones did not carry over into subsequent volumes.

Dorothea Dreams is more properly horror fiction, although the tone is very different. Dorothea is an artist who is struggling to deal with the imminent death of an old friend when she begins to dream of a previous life. Just as Dorothea begins to learn how to deal with her ghost, criminals break into her home and hold Dorothea and her friend prisoner. Charnas's unconventional story of the supernatural is crisp, insightful, and thought provoking.

Three short stories are also of note. "Advocates," written in collaboration with Chelsea Quinn Yarbro, is set in a world where vampires have become the rulers of humankind. But these are conventional vampires, and Weyland has awakened to find himself no less alone than before. And now that humans are carefully tended food animals, he can no longer prey on them easily, so instead he takes the blood of the ruling class, a type just as foreign to him as is the human race.

A much better tale is "Evil Thoughts." Fran is a woman approaching middle age who is uncertain of her charming, but considerably younger lover. She moves to the small town where he lives in order to be closer to him, but the change seems to cause more problems than it solves. The income from her freelance job decreases sharply, one of the neighbours seems to be certifiably insane, and worst of all she has begun to notice signs of aging when she looks into the mirror. Fran also discovers an unsettling patch of mushrooms in her lawn. No matter how many times she destroys them, they always seem to have grown back the following morning. And her crazy neighbour insists that they are a manifestation of her evil thoughts. As the season turns, Fran's deterioration becomes more evident. Her moods are unpredictable, she quarrels with her lover, and the obsession with signs of aging increases. With the first frost, most of the mushrooms die, and she finally succeeds in destroying the last of them. But with no outlet, where are her evil thoughts going now? The resolution is deliberately ambiguous; either the evil has lodged within her own body, causing changes to her appearance, or perhaps she has just convinced herself that this is the case. An understated, quietly effectively and distinctly disturbing story.

Also of interest is a very non-horrific vampire story, "Now I Lay Me Down to Sleep," in which a disembodied spirit becomes a vampire temporarily in order to learn how to become a guardian angel. Charnas is neither a predictable nor a prolific writer, and it's impossible to guess the direction she will take next. We can be assured however that whenever she writes in the horror genre, she will produce superior work of lasting interest.

—Don D'Ammassa

CHETWYND-HAYES, R(onald Henry Glynn)

Pseudonym: Angus Campbell. **Nationality:** British. **Born:** Isleworth, Middlesex, 30 May 1919. **Education:** Hanworth School. **Career:** Showroom manager in the furnishing trade, London; freelance writer since 1973. **Awards:** British Fantasy Society special award, 1989; Horror Writers of America Life Achievement award, 1989.

HORROR, GHOST AND GOTHIC PUBLICATIONS

Novels (series: Clavering Grange)

The Dark Man. London, Sidgwick and Jackson, 1964; as *And Love Survived,* New Yorka, Zebra, 1979.

Dominique (novelization of screenplay). London, W. H. Allen, and New York, Belmont, 1979.
The Awakening (novelization of screenplay). London, Magnum, 1980.
The Partaker: A Novel of Fantasy. London, Kimber, 1980.
The King's Ghost (Clavering). London, Kimber, 1985; as *The Grange,* New York, Tor, 1985.
The Haunted Grange (Clavering). London, Kimber, 1988.
The Curse of the Snake God. London, Kimber, 1989.
Kepple. London, Hale, 1992.
The Psychic Detective. London, Hale, 1993.

Short Stories

The Unbidden. London, Tandem, 1971.
Cold Terror. London, Tandem, 1973.
The Elemental. London, Fontana, 1974.
Terror by Night. London, Tandem, 1974.
The Monster Club. London, Severn House, 1975.
The Night Ghouls, and Other Grisly Tales. London, Fontana, 1975.
Tales of Fear and Fantasy. London, Fontana, 1977.
The Cradle Demon, and Other Stories of Fantasy and Terror. London, Kimber, 1978.
The Fantastic World of Kamtellar: A Book of Vampires and Ghouls. London, Kimber, 1980.
Tales of Darkness. London, Kimber, 1981.
Tales from Beyond. London, Kimber, 1982.
Tales from the Other Side. London, Kimber, 1983; as *The Other Side,* New York, Tor, 1988.
A Quiver of Ghosts. London, Kimber, 1984.
Tales from the Dark Lands. London, Kimber, 1984.
Ghosts from the Mists of Time. London, Kimber, 1985.
Tales from the Shadows. London, Kimber, 1986.
Tales from the Haunted House. London, Kimber, 1986.
Dracula's Children. London, Kimber, 1987.
The House of Dracula. London, Kimber, 1987.
Tales from the Hidden World (Clavering). London, Kimber, 1988.
Hell Is What You Make It. London, Hale, 1994.
Shudders and Shivers. London, Hale, 1995.
The Vampire Stories of R. Chetwynd-Hayes. N.p., Transylvania Press, 1996.

Other

Editor, *Cornish Tales of Terror.* London, Fontana, 1970.
Editor (as Angus Campbell), *Scottish Tales of Terror.* London, Fontana, 1972.
Editor, *Welsh Tales of Terror.* London, Fontana, 1973.
Editor, *The Ninth Fontana Book of Great Ghost Stories.* London, Fontana, 1973.
Editor, *The Tenth Fontana Book of Great Ghost Stories.* London, Fontana, 1974.
Editor, *The Eleventh Fontana Book of Great Ghost Stories.* London, Fontana, 1975.
Editor, *The First Armada Monster Book.* London, Armada, 1975.
Editor, *Gaslight Tales of Terror.* London, Fontana, 1976.
Editor, *The Twelfth Fontana Book of Great Ghost Stories.* London, Fontana, 1976.
Editor, *The Second Armada Monster Book.* London, Armada, 1976.
Editor, *The Thirteenth Fontana Book of Great Ghost Stories.* London, Fontana, 1977.

Editor, *The Third Armada Monster Book*. London, Armada, 1977.
Editor, *Doomed to the Night: An Anthology of Ghost Stories*. London, Kimber, 1978.
Editor, *The Fourteenth Fontana Book of Great Ghost Stories*. London, Fontana, 1978.
Editor, *The Fourth Armada Monster Book*. London, Armada, 1978.
Editor, *The Fifteenth Fontana Book of Great Ghost Stories*. London, Fontana, 1979.
Editor, *The Fifth Armada Monster Book*. London, Armada, 1979.
Editor, *The Sixteenth Fontana Book of Great Ghost Stories*. London, Fontana, 1980.
Editor, *The Seventeenth Fontana Book of Great Ghost Stories*. London, Fontana, 1981.
Editor, *The Eighteenth Fontana Book of Great Ghost Stories*. London, Fontana, 1982.
Editor, *The Nineteenth Fontana Book of Great Ghost Stories*. London, Fontana, 1983.
Editor, *The Twentieth Fontana Book of Great Ghost Stories*. London, Fontana, 1984.

OTHER PUBLICATIONS

Novels

The Man from the Bomb. London, Badger, 1959.
The Brats. London, Kimber, 1979.

Other

Editor, *Tales of Terror from Outer Space*. London, Fontana, 1975.

*

Film Adaptations: *From Beyond the Grave*, 1973; *The Monster Club*, 1981.

*   *   *

Relatively unknown to readers in the United States, R. Chetwynd-Hayes is one of Britain's most prolific writers of ghost and horror tales. The quality of his work is variable, extending to cover all the major supernatural themes and subjects within the genre, though too often in a traditional and routine manner. This tends to obscure the fact that at his best he is a fine writer, capable of producing gripping and wonderfully atmospheric stories at all lengths. Sometimes he brings elements of humour and even farce into his stories, a bold move which either works brilliantly or not at all.

He is best known as a writer of ghost stories, and his major work here is the Clavering Grange series of two novels and about a dozen stories, written during the 1980s. Clavering Grange is a fictional stately home in the county of Kent, built at the end of the 12th century on "tainted ground"—the site of a massacre. It is occupied by the Sinclair family for 700 years and suffers persistent hauntings by dangerous ghosts, including banshees and ghouls. The Clavering stories are set in various historical periods and the present day. *The King's Ghost* is set in the 1590s and narrated by Miles Harrington, a young man of noble birth who begins by aiding the Sinclairs, discovers the terrible secrets of Clavering's ghosts, and ends up being knighted by Queen Elizabeth I. *Tales From the Hidden World* contains four Clavering sto-

ries set at various times during the 20th century and featuring different groups of characters. *The Haunted Grange* is a novel covering recent decades and including the demolition of Clavering Grange; but will this only serve to release more of its supernatural inhabitants?

Another series concerns the psychic detectives Francis St. Clare and Frederica Masters. Masters is the one with the psychic powers, while St. Clare is rich and has expertise in the occult. Their dangerous encounters with the spirit world are humorously told; they include the novel *The Psychic Detective* and stories "The Astral Invasion" and "The Cringing Couple of Clavering" (which is also a Clavering Grange tale).

Chetwynd-Hayes has written two volumes of linked stories concerning the three "wives" of Bram Stoker's Dracula, and their children. While Stoker failed to name the wives, Chetwynd-Hayes calls them Barbushka, Marikova and Nanaskya. The family's exploits are related in *Dracula's Children* and *The House of Dracula*. Humour is added through the coining of silly names for various descendants who are only half, a quarter or an eighth vampire: Vamlings, Mocks and Shadmocks.

These names, together with many others sounding even less likely, were used in Chetwynd-Hayes's best-known book, *The Monster Club*, which was filmed in 1981. This concerns various cross-bred monsters with, for example, the progeny of a vampire and a werewolf being a werevamp, of a werewolf and a ghoul being a weregoo, and of a vampire and a ghoul being, naturally enough, a vamgoo. And if a werevamp and a weregoo were to mate they would produce a shaddy, and so on. The basic premise of the book is that such monsters have their own London club, where all are accepted and are equal, and the book is a linked collection of five stories centred around the club. The author's "basic rules of Monsterdom," given in the book, are: Vampires sup; Werewolves hunt; Ghouls tear; Shaddies lick; Maddies yawn; Mocks blow; Shadmocks only whistle. Some of this is very entertaining, though occasionally the humour seems forced.

A few of Chetwynd-Hayes's very earliest stories show the influence of H. P. Lovecraft, particularly "No One Lived There," an atmospheric first-person piece with the narrator writing down his feelings about a long-abandoned house he has entered by chance after his car has run out of petrol, where giant rats are menacing him and his pen is running dry.

Essentially, Chetwynd-Hayes is a writer of short stories about haunted houses: many of his stories, from earliest to latest, have tackled this theme. Quite often the result has been entertaining, if not very original. In some instances this is tackled with a robust humour, for example in "The Night Watch," which suggests that ghosts keep watch for the spirits of the dead and help them on their way. In other cases the ghosts are very dangerous to the living, as in the case of "Something Comes in from the Garden," where the attractive young woman who is invited in by Robert and Edna, and who chats with their children, is shown to be a catalyst who causes Robert to kill his wife. (Chetwynd-Hayes's stories feature many husbands and wives killing their spouses.) And in yet other stories the house is haunted by a monster, never human, such as the huge and terrible creatures in "The Sloathes." Or perhaps the ghost is embodied within an object rather than haunting the house as a whole, as in "The Chair."

In his better stories the ghosts are combined in some way with horror: in any case, this is what most readers seem to demand today. There is no better example of this than "Moving Day," which was reprinted in Karl Edward Wagner's *The Year's Best Hor-*

ror Stories: XVI. Here the youngish narrator lives with his three very ancient great-aunts, who are very concerned (some might say obsessed) with graveyards and their inhabitants. For his 35th birthday, they buy him his own burial plot. And after the eldest dies, the build-up of tension leading first to her burial and then to her "moving day" is extremely well conveyed.

But perhaps his most successful tales eschew both ghosts and humour to concentrate on horror. "The Jumpity-Jim" is a terrifying period piece about a teenage girl sent as a servant to a grand house of ill repute, while "The Cradle Demon" shows the early development of a most unnatural new-born baby. They show Chetwynd-Hayes at his finest, truly deserving his "prince of chill" nickname.

Apart from his own fiction, Chetwynd-Hayes has edited numerous volumes of other writers' ghost and horror stories. In particular, he took over the *Fontana Book of Great Ghost Stories* series from Robert Aickman and edited volumes 9 to 20. He has always been a cautious editor, preferring traditional ghost stories, and he has always included a story of his own in every anthology.

Chetwynd-Hayes has used the pseudonym Angus Campbell for one anthology and for several of his stories, particularly in the Armada Monster Book series. Apart from the film made of *The Monster Club*, three of his early stories were assembled as the 1973 film *From Beyond the Grave*.

—Chris Morgan

CITRO, Joseph (A.)

Nationality: American. **Address:** c/o Twilight Publishing Co., 18 Oaktree Lane, Sparta, NJ 07871, USA. Lives in Vermont.

HORROR, GHOST AND GOTHIC PUBLICATIONS

Novels

Shadow Child. New York, Zebra, 1987.
Guardian Angels. New York, Zebra, 1988.
The Unseen. New York, Warner, 1990.
Dark Twilight. New York, Warner, 1991.
Deus X. Sparta, New Jersey, Twilight, 1994.

*   *   *

New England has long been a popular setting for horror stories, and it's no coincidence that a number of major genre writers have lived in that area, including Stephen King, Rick Hautala, Peter Straub and, of course, H. P. Lovecraft. Joseph A. Citro, whose setting of choice is rural Vermont, cites Lovecraft as a powerful influence on his own writing, and certainly his own depictions of decaying cultures and secret subsets of quasi-humankind echo Lovecraftian themes. Puritanism was at its strongest in New England, and there are echoes of Jonathan Edwards and the Salem witch trials that survive to the modern day and which have influenced many modern horror writers. Citro is clearly a regional writer, setting almost all of his fiction in his native Vermont, and he draws on his familiarity with that setting to create a plausible background for his imaginative efforts.

Citro made his debut with *Shadow Child.* Eric Nolan returns as an adult to the small town where his brother disappeared during their childhood. To his surprise, he discovers that there have been more disappearances since, a steady attrition of the children of the area. His nephew Luke, only four years old, wonders if his uncle will understand why he fears the strange voices he hears during the night. They are both fated to discover the truth, that the missing children have been recruited into a tribe of primitive creatures who live secretly in the forests of Vermont. In the sequel, *Guardian Angels,* four years have passed and people have convinced themselves that the horror is over. Will Crockett and his parents arrive unaware of the tragic history that preceded them, and Will is blamed for a series of minor incidents around the house that he knows are not his fault before he is able to waken people to the truth.

The Unseen is a variation of that same theme. This time the creatures prowling in the darkness are reportedly large, hairy brutes that convince some people that the wendigo has returned, predicting death to any who hear its cry. Ultimately we learn that the lurkers are descendants of runaway slaves, perfectly human, but who have evolved their own culture and exist separate from the modern world, reacting violently to any intrusion from the outside. The premise seems somewhat implausible, but Citro does a good job of making the situation seem credible given the remoteness of some portions of Vermont.

Citro's next novel was *Dark Twilight.* Harrison Allen is travelling around Vermont gathering folk tales when he hears the stories of a Loch Ness-type monster living in one of the local lakes. Intrigued he pursues his investigations, trying to remain objective, but is increasingly drawn by the possibility that there might be some truth behind the legend. When someone subsequently makes secretive visits to his rented cabin, he wonders if it's a casual prowler or someone trying to find out what he's doing and why. The visitor also leaves odd objects lying about, objects which appear to have no meaning. He is also troubled by the sound of a woman sobbing at night. We ultimately learn that one of his neighbours is the last member of a cult of spiritualists whose activities are the cause of the current disturbances. The ending is rather confused, involving a family of telepaths, the mating of humans with creatures from another plane of existence, with a parting reference to the surviving dinosaur in the lake. It's an unsatisfactory conclusion to what is otherwise a well constructed story.

Deus X was very different from Citro's previous novels. At a secret government project, observers watch a condemned criminal mysteriously die after a series of convulsions. In the Vermont forest, a hunter is transfixed by the appearance of what he believes to be an angel. An elderly man lies in a strange coma in Quebec and in Boston a psychologist wonders if demonic possession might be possible after all. There is something taking control of people's bodies, something with extraordinary powers that might originate in Hell or, it is suggested, from outer space. The resolution, that one man is psychically linked with a supercomputer that can actually alter reality, provides the build-up for an earthshaking climax, but by this point Citro may well have lost his readers, overwhelmed by too many random events with nothing to unify them into a coherent plotline.

Citro is also an occasional short story writer. Of these the best is "Kirby." Kirby is a young boy who befriends the protagonist, a boy who doesn't get along with his other peers, protecting him from his enemies, playing with him when he's lonely. But no one knows much about Kirby; he's from the next town over and doesn't talk much about his life. In a satisfyingly unsettling climax, the protagonist discovers that his friend is a shape-changing creature and not human at all. The "Soul Keeper" is a crazed religious fanatic who imprisons a man in his attic, which he claims to be Heaven. When the prisoner attempts to escape, he is judged to be damned and condemned to the basement, presumably Hell. Citro's short stories are better controlled than his novels, and at either length he is at his best when writing about rural Vermont, which he depicts in a convincing, almost affectionate fashion.

—Don D'Ammassa

CLARK, Mary Higgins

Nationality: American. **Born:** New York City, 24 December 1929. **Education:** Attended Villa Maria Academy, Ward Secretarial School, and New York University; Fordham University, B.A. (summa cum laude), 1979. **Family:** Married 1) Warren F. Clark in 1949 (died 1964); 2) Raymond Charles Ploetz, 1978 (marriage annulled); children: Marilyn, Warren, David, Carol, Patricia. **Career:** Remington Rand, New York City, advertising assistant, 1946; stewardess for Pan American Airlines, 1949-50; radio scriptwriter and producer for Robert G. Jennings, 1965-70; Aerial Communications, New York City, vice-president, partner, creative director, and producer of radio programming, 1970-80; David J. Clark Enterprises, New York City, chairman of the board and creative director since 1980. Chairman, International Crime Writers Congress, 1988. **Awards:** New Jersey Author award, 1969, 1977 and 1978; Grand Prix de Litterature Policière (France), 1980; honorary doctorate, Villanova University, 1983. **Member:** Mystery Writers of America (president, 1987; member of board of directors), American Academy of Arts and Sciences, American Irish Historical Society (member of executive council). **Agent:** Eugene H. Winick, McIntosh and Otis, Inc., 475 Fifth Ave., New York, NY 10017. **Address:** 210 Central Park South, New York, NY 10019, USA.

HORROR, GHOST AND GOTHIC PUBLICATIONS

Novels

Where Are the Children? New York, Simon and Schuster, and London, Talmy Franklin, 1975.
A Stranger Is Watching. New York, Simon and Schuster, and London, Collins, 1978.
The Cradle Will Fall. New York, Simon and Schuster, and London, Collins, 1980.
A Cry in the Night. New York, Simon and Schuster, 1982; London, Collins, 1983.
Stillwatch. New York, Simon and Schuster, and London, Collins, 1984.
Weep No More, My Lady. New York, Simon and Schuster, and London, Collins, 1987.
While My Pretty One Sleeps. New York, Simon and Schuster, and London, Century, 1989.
Loves Music, Loves to Dance. New York, Simon and Schuster, 1991.
All Around the Town. New York, Simon and Schuster, 1992.
I'll Be Seeing You. New York, Simon and Schuster, 1993.

Remember Me. New York, Simon and Schuster, 1994.
Let Me Call You Sweetheart. New York, Simon and Schuster, 1995.
Silent Night. New York, Simon and Schuster, 1995.
Moonlight Becomes You. New York, Simon and Schuster, 1996.
Pretend You Don't See Her. New York, Simon and Schuster, 1997.

Short Stories

The Anastasia Syndrome and Other Stories. New York, Simon and Schuster, 1989; London, Century, 1990.

OTHER PUBLICATIONS

Novel

Murder in Manhattan, with Thomas Chastain and others. New York, Morrow, 1986.

Short Stories

Death on the Cape and Other Stories. London, Arrow Books, 1993.
The Lottery Winner. New York, Simon and Schuster, 1994.

Other

Aspire to the Heavens: A Biography of George Washington (for children). New York, Meredith Press, 1969.

Editor, *Murder on the Aisle: The 1987 Mystery Writers of America Anthology.* New York, Simon and Schuster, 1987.
Editor, *Bad Behavior.* New York, Harcourt Brace, 1995.

*

Film Adaptations: *A Stranger Is Watching,* 1982; *The Cradle Will Fall,* 1984 (television movie); *A Cry in the Night,* 1985; *Where Are the Children?,* 1986; *Stillwatch,* 1987 (television movie).

* * *

Mary Higgins Clark is a hugely successful writer of "romantic suspense" and mystery novels. She has been called America's Queen of Suspense, as well as the Queen of Thrillers. Not specifically a horror writer, Clark's generally mimetic tales are built from common settings, situations and themes. Her stories generally feature three basic elements: average people thrust into extraordinary circumstances, a mystery, and life-or-death consequences. Her characters are familiar—average American people who usually can be identified easily by the reader, people who have had their normally comfortable circumstances turned on end. Her novels also feature women in jeopardy, and have reestablished the rules for that particular sub-genre of crime fiction.

With recurring themes, and familiar, if not familial, characters, Clark has built her reputation and her audience with her handling of plot. Clark's books are released and marketed in the mainstream (and generally end up topping most of the bestseller lists), despite sharing a neo-Gothic aesthetic found in much of the horror world. Her plots are sometimes byzantine, written to a level of detail in which the most insignificant-seeming item is raised to internal importance. A misplaced key, a midnight fax, a coincidental meeting—everything comes into play, much as in many contemporary mystery novels. The stakes are high: women and children are at risk, are being exploited, and may die. This fundamental ingredient of her work is effective for her detailed and careful storytelling. Her point-of-view characters are generally presented in a close, subjective manner, allowing for the emotional and psychological aspects of her suspenseful plotting. This, and the plots themselves, have been the strength of her work.

Where Are the Children?, Clark's second book following a failed historical biography, established many of the themes that would follow in her work. In this book, the heroine is a woman with a tragic past, who has spent several years rebuilding her life. She has relocated, remarried, and started a new family, after having lost her husband and two children and then suffering the accusation that she murdered them. Just as she was beginning to put the past behind her, her new children, again a boy and a girl, disappear. Simultaneously, the old accusations resurface, printed on the front page of the local paper in her new hometown. With a little coincidence, a little luck, and some amateur detective work, it is discovered that her first husband didn't really die, and is a psychopath out for revenge.

The Cradle Will Fall introduced what would become another Clark theme in the setting of a medical thriller. The heroine, a young, recently widowed prosecutor, has an accident and is put in the hospital. Looking out the window of her hospital room while mildly sedated, she sees a body put into a trunk, and is later compelled to find out whether what she saw actually took place. The ensuing plot also relies heavily on coincidence in the solving of its mystery, which involves uncovering a couple of doctors who have developed a method of implanting aborted fetuses into women who cannot conceive. In this, unlike many other Clark novels, the antagonist, a doctor, is known throughout, but his methods are kept from view. A climactic ending featuring the doctor's suicide wraps up literally dozens of loose ends.

A Cry in the Night is more directly gothic, placing the heroine and her children in a cloistered, unfamiliar, and faraway setting. The protagonist, recently divorced, is swept off her feet by a wealthy artist, who takes her and her two children from New York to his childhood farm in a rural Minnesota community. He quietly and systematically shuts her off from the world, and after a short period of bliss, things turn quickly for the worse. She and her children are haunted by terrible nightmares, and the strange, unyielding nature of her new husband comes to light—somewhat. She discovers that he was attracted to her because she closely resembles his deceased mother. When her ex-husband is murdered nearby, she is accused. Her new husband absconds with her children, and the race is on. Drawing from elements in Robert Bloch's *Psycho*, this is one of Clark's most successful stories.

The themes of resemblance and fetal tampering return in *I'll Be Seeing You*. The heroine, working as a reporter, sees a woman in the morgue that could be her twin. She is also doing a seemingly unrelated story on a successful in-vitro fertilization clinic, where doctors are having tremendous success with the freezing of fertilized eggs. Also, her father is missing and presumed dead. In her pursuit of these three mysteries—her father, the clinic, the identity of the dead woman—she finds that all are related to one another. The story also ends with the suicide of one of the doctors involved. *I'll Be Seeing You* is as complex as any of Clark's plots, maybe more so, but relies on coincidence in its conclusion.

The Lottery Winner is somewhat a change of pace for Clark, a collection of stories based on the recurring characters Alvirah and Willy Meehan, a couple who, late in life, won the lottery. Willy is still a plumber, but Alvirah has left her work as a maid (as first seen in *Weep No More, My Lady*) to become an amateur sleuth. These stories are fun and funny, lighter than Clark's normal fare, but still containing ample amounts of mystery and mayhem. Another collection of short work, *The Anastasia Syndrome and Other Stories*, features a rare tale (the title story) in which horror of a non-mimetic nature is explored. A doctor successfully conducts experiments connecting people spiritually to the last moments of a dead person's life. A parallel tale of two cultures ensues, with one of Clark's rare downbeat endings.

Whether from a serial killer, as in *Loves Music, Loves to Dance*, or a close friend, or a new husband, or a relentless hitman as in *Pretend You Don't See Her*, Clark's heroines are always at risk, but always seem to find the resources to win.

Mary Higgins Clark is very active in education, both as a trustee of Fordham University and as a member of the Board of Regents at St. Peters College. She is also active in the Literacy Volunteers. Besides being a repeat *New York Times* bestselling author, she has recently been awarded with a degree, Doctor of Literature, *honoris causa*, by Seton Hall University. At least five of her novels have been turned into films, two for television, and three for theatrical release.

—Tom Winstead

CLARK, Simon

Nationality: British. **Born:** Wakefield, West Yorkshire, 20 April 1958. **Education:** Hemsworth High School; Whitwood Mining and Technical College. **Family:** Married; two children. **Career:** Worked in local government; fulltime writer from 1993. **Address:** c/o Hodder Headline, 338 Euston Road, London NW1 3BH, England.

HORROR, GHOST AND GOTHIC PUBLICATIONS

Novels

Nailed By the Heart. London, Hodder and Stoughton, 1995.
Blood Crazy. London, Hodder and Stoughton, 1995.
Darker. London, Hodder and Stoughton, 1996.
King Blood. London, Hodder and Stoughton, 1997.

Short Stories

Blood & Grit. Sheffield, BBR Books, 1990.
Annabelle Says, with Stephen Laws. Stockport, British Fantasy Society, 1995.

*   *   *

Simon Clark is comparatively new to the field of horror fiction. Thus far he has had four novels published and around 40 short stories. Although he rings the changes in each story there is a definite pattern to his work which suggests some deep-rooted feelings and fears within the author. Throughout Clark's work is the strong feeling of pursuit, with the pursued often in ignorance of what is happening until too late. Several early stories show how easily victims become so without realizing it. "... Beside the Seaside, Beside the Sea ..." (*Back Brain Recluse*, 1985) has a horror emerge from the sea in the likeness of a young girl. A young girl is also the lure in "Salt Snake" (*Peeping Tom*, 1993) where the sea again appears to create the pit of madness in which the villainous victims meet their doom.

The sea, and the lure of water, is central to Clark's first novel, *Nailed By the Heart*. Here a husband and wife and their young son, seek a complete change of life and settle in a small coastal village with the idea of converting an old sea-fort into a hotel. Unfortunately this is the site where an ancient god begins to revive from its slumber, bringing with it the long-drowned occupants of a sunken ship. Small incidents, initially focused around the young son, David, whose defences are easier to breach, gather pace until the full force of the horror is unleashed on David's parents.

In *Blood Crazy* Clark turned the approach around. This time the horror happens up-front, perhaps the most horrific concept of all—parents throughout the world killing their children. The image of a parent who turns out not to be kissing its child but eating its face is an especially powerful one. Children are forced to fight for their own survival and before long there are only a few isolated retreats of children under siege from the adults. The answer to this mad apocalypse is a long time coming, and not entirely convincing. Clark conjectures that the children have become the victims of the next stage of mental evolution, which happens overnight. Adults suddenly become aware that their children have changed and have taken the next step in this evolution. It becomes a fight for survival between parents and offspring. Clark uses the concept of a cosmic consciousness as the force that triggers evolutionary change.

After novels of two extremes, Clark's next two settle into the middle ground, utilizing concepts from both, and creating imagery and style similar to the works of Stephen King. In *Darker* the story again revolves about the pursuer and the pursued. We are back with the small family—a husband, wife and two children. They find themselves jerked into a nightmare by a stranger seeking help. Soon they, and others, are at the mercy of a force so powerful that it can scarcely be imagined. Again Clark conjures up a remarkable scene where a fleeing girl finds she is not alone, as all of the wild animals in the countryside are similarly fleeing from the great unknown. The fourth novel, *King Blood*, is very similar. A small family becomes enmeshed with a mysterious stranger and before long they and others have become refugees fleeing from an enemy which is as much inside themselves as outside.

In each of these novels, and in many of his short stories, Clark is exploring one of our deepest, innermost fears—that of confrontation and becoming the victim of something we cannot control. His horrors might be construed as a manifestation of life itself, the life of the late twentieth century where other forces—commercial, political, medical, economical—dictate the trends. Clark has taken this fear and focused it on the standard family, utilizing the imagery of horror to represent these many uncontrollable forces pitted against us. For this reason, despite the occasional lapses in characterization and dialogue that make some scenes less convincing than others, Clark's stories and novels have considerable appeal because they relate to the universal dread of absolute uncontrollable power.

—Mike Ashley

CLEGG, Douglas

Nationality: American. **Born:** Virginia, 1958. **Education:** Washington and Lee University, B.A. in English literature. **Address:** c/o Bantam Doubleday Dell Publishing Group, Inc., 1540 Broadway, New York, NY 10036, USA. Lives in California.

HORROR, GHOST AND GOTHIC PUBLICATIONS

Novels

Goat Dance. New York, Pocket, 1989.
Breeder. New York, Pocket, 1990.
Neverland. New York, Pocket, 1991.
Dark of the Eye. New York, Pocket, 1994.
The Children's Hour. New York, Dell, 1995.

*   *   *

The best writers in any field earn their reputation not by creating new ideas with every book but rather by looking at old ideas in new and creative ways, by turning concepts inside out and discovering possibilities that have been previously overlooked. They also people their fiction with characters who are more than just reprises of standard horror figures—the obvious victim, the threatened child, the resourceful man, the menaced but perky woman. Douglas Clegg displayed both varieties of talent with his debut novel, *Goat Dance*, and has been demonstrating his growing craftsmanship with each subsequent title.

Goat Dance deals with a strange sort of demonic possession, a young girl apparently drowned but somehow returned to life. Her family suspects that there is another presence inside her now, an evil creature that has used her as a bridge to enter our world. The usurper is the Eater of Souls, a nebulous entity comparable to the devil himself, and his influence begins to seep through the community, bringing death and destruction. In a series of brilliantly constructed scenes delivered with first-rate prose, Clegg created a truly memorable monster whose power can only be challenged by those willing to make a terrible personal sacrifice. The novel also includes one of the best climactic battles in modern horror.

His follow-up novel, *Breeder,* was not as successful. In form, it's a haunted-house variation with some odd twists. The Heards move into a new home in which the sounds of a crying child and other inexplicable events leave their nerves on edge. There's a cult planning to use Rachel Heard as a breeding machine, burying her alive after inserting a malevolent, inhuman foetus into her womb. The closing chapters are riveting but the story loses a great deal of its impetus along the way because it takes too long for the real menace to become obvious. Clegg returned to good form in *Neverland.* The title refers to a small, decrepit building on an island where two young boys fall under the influence of an evil entity. One manages to resist, but the other becomes a secretive killer. There's considerably more emphasis on the psychological side of horror this time, augmented by the telepathic abilities of some of the characters.

Dark of the Eye bears some superficial resemblance to Stephen King's *Firestarter*. Hope Stewart loses an eye in a terrible accident, but in return she gains the power to heal with a touch, and perhaps to harm as well. Her father wants to subject her to a scientific study and at least one determined government agent wants to kill her, so her mother kidnaps the child and tries to escape from both parties. Although much of the novel involves the subsequent chase, Hope's powers develop in unpredictable ways, and her ultimate revenge against her tormentors is nicely handled.

The Children's Hour's protagonist is a successful writer who returns with his new family to the town where he grew up, and a past that he has never quite understood. During his childhood, he miraculously survived what should have been a fatal accident. At the same time, a young girl disappeared, a child who reappears mortally wounded 13 years later, but no further advanced in age. After various adventures and tragedies, the writer confronts a malevolent, vampiric creature imprisoned in an abandoned mine, a creature that absorbs the personalities and memories of its victims. Clegg reinvents the vampire legend from the ground up, and the result is a blend of cunning and repulsiveness. *The Children's Hour* is noticeably superior to any of his previous novels.

Clegg is also a prolific short story writer. In "The Mysteries of Paris" a man with a paranoid fear that someone near him is a serial killer confronts his terror when it proves to be true. A dying man confronts the lovelessness of his life is "O, Rare and Most Exquisite." "The Cabinet-Maker's Wife" discovers that her husband is a necrophiliac who kills women before being unfaithful with them—one of Clegg's most powerful stories. A nice elderly man systematically kills his wife and nine children in "Damned, If You Do." "The Five" is ostensibly about a young child obsessed with the disappearance of five kittens who believes they are living inside the walls of her home, but it's actually about a more subtle form of child abuse.

"The Fruit of Her Womb" uses an old plot device, the couple who discover their new home was the scene of ghastly murders in the past, but enriches it with strange imagery. A small town loses the grace of God in "The Ripening Sweetness of Late Afternoon" after one of its number causes two deaths. Each night, malevolent angels descend to seize the unwary and subject them to eternal torment, until one day the man responsible, a failed preacher, returns to make atonement. A curious writer unwisely tries to track down a legendary killer in "White Chapel," a remote part of Asia, and finds him at last, ageless, possessing the power of a mysterious goddess, convinced that pain is a gift ultimately desired by his victims. "Ice Palace" refers to a fraternity hazing ritual in which young men are imprisoned naked inside a shell of ice. When the idea is used to cover up a murder, it has unexpected results.

Douglas Clegg has become one of the more highly regarded of modern horror writers because of his innovative ideas, thorough understanding of the psychology of his characters, and an intelligent, well-crafted prose style. His demonstrated ability to write equally well at varying lengths assures him continued prominence in the field.

—Don D'Ammassa

CLINE, Leonard (Lanson)

Pseudonym: Alan Forsyth. **Nationality:** American. **Born:** Detroit, Michigan, 1893. **Education:** Attended a Jesuit high school in Montreal; University of Michigan, degree 1910. **Career:** Author and journalist; staff member on the *Detroit News*, 1916-22; mainstream short story published in *The Best Short Stories of 1923*; imprisoned for manslaughter. **Awards:** Pulitzer Prize for articles about the Ku Klux Klan, published in *The Baltimore Sun*. **Died:** 1929.

HORROR, GHOST AND GOTHIC PUBLICATIONS

Novel

The Dark Chamber. New York, Viking Press, 1927.

Short Stories

The Lady of Frozen Death and Other Stories. West Warwick, Rhode Island, Necronomicon Press, 1992.

OTHER PUBLICATIONS

Novels

God Head. N.p., 1925; as *Ahead the Thunder,* London, n.p., 1927. *Listen, Moon!* N.p., 1926.

Poetry

Poems. N.p., 1914. *Afterwalker.* N.p., 1930.

*　*　*

Leonard Cline's *The Dark Chamber* is one of those novels—like H. B. Drake's *The Shadowy Thing* or Gerald Biss's *The Door of the Unreal*—which is now remembered almost solely for what H. P. Lovecraft said about it in *Supernatural Horror in Literature*, and of interest more for how it may have influenced Lovecraft than for its own merits.

It must be admitted that *The Dark Chamber* continues to have admirers, and that it has enjoyed one modern paperback reprinting from Popular Library (undated edition, about 1970), which tried to package it as a women's Gothic, carefully concealing the fact that the protagonist is male. Indeed, but for the hero's gender, the book has much in common with formula Gothics. The hero, a musician, is summoned to the remote country estate of a wealthy eccentric, Richard Pride, who wants to use the hero's talents as part of an obsessive effort to recall every single instant of his own memory. There are sinister servants, threats, budding and frustrated love affairs, and passages of deep purple prose, all of which may well defeat the modern reader well before the big payoff: Pride's efforts succeed beyond wildest expectations and his attempts to recapture the past recede well beyond his own lifetime, beyond the earliest history of the human species, back, as Lovecraft put it, "to still more unimaginable deeps of primal time and entity." Pride, having become less than entirely human, is found with his throat ripped out, destroyed by his own ferocious German shepherd dog, Tod (German = Death), which he, in turn, has killed just as savagely. In concept, at least, the novel prefigures Paddy Chayevsky's *Altered States* and any number of reversion-to-the-primitive tales.

Lovecraft was effusive in his praise of the novel's "extremely high" artistic stature and devotes a long paragraph to it. Considering that much of the foreground plot has to do with complicated romantic hugger-mugger, it becomes significant that *all* Lovecraft describes is Pride's experiment, reversion, and death, elements which manage to be ignored for long stretches in the actual novel. Lovecraft was attracted more to what was implied by the material than what is actually there: the sweeping vistas of remote time; mankind's kinship, not with the angels, but with the beast; the stark horror of pre-human ancestry; etc. All of this resonates clearly with Lovecraft's philosophy of mechanistic materialism, and with his own fiction, from "Arthur Jermyn" through "The Shadow Out of Time." His own closest approach to the material, "The Rats in the Walls" (1923) predates Cline by four years, so the relationship is one of affinity, not influence.

Cline's life and career were tragic. He began with a volume of poetry, then progressed to novels, one of which, *God Head*, drew a great deal of critical acclaim and was compared to Dostoevsky. Unfortunately, he drank to excess, which may have ended both his marriages. In a drunken argument, he killed his friend Wilfred Irwin with a shotgun. A much-publicized trial followed, during which Cline pleaded guilty of manslaughter. He served less than a year in prison, but died of heart failure, probably the result of alcoholism, at the age of 35.

During the last year of his life, Cline found himself in desperate financial straits and turned to deliberate hackwork, writing a number of weird and mystery stories under the pseudonym of Alan Forsyth. He was under no illusions about the merit of this material and asked his heirs not to include any of the Forsyth material in any posthumous collection. Cline remarked in a letter to his daughter that Forsyth "as an artist could walk under a mole's belly with a silk hat on."

The supernatural and horrific works of Alan Forsyth were aimed at the lowest level of the pulps, mostly at *Ghost Stories*, a "true confession" magazine comparable to a modern supermarket tabloid. The stories pretended to be true and were often bylined "as told to." Anything resembling literary merit was strictly discouraged. While enthusiasts of lurid pulp trash might enjoy such efforts as "Shuffle-Thump, in the Dark," the tragedy of these stories is that (as Cline himself noted) many of them contain material which could have benefited from better treatment. Here was a genuinely intelligent, literate writer forced to pander to the lowest possible level. The great shame is that he did not attempt to write for *Weird Tales*, which would have allowed him considerably greater freedom.

—Darrell Schweitzer

COLLINS, Nancy A(verill)

Pseudonym: Nanzi Regalia. **Nationality:** American. **Born:** Arkansas, 1959. **Family:** Married underground filmmaker Joe Christ. **Career:** Has written comic-strip continuity for DC Comics. **Awards:** Horror Writers of America Bram Stoker award for first novel, 1990. **Address:** c/o White Wolf Publishing, 735 Park North Blvd., Suite 128, Clarkston, GA 30021, USA. Lives in New York.

Horror, Ghost and Gothic Publications

Novels (series: Sonja Blue)

Sunglasses after Dark (Sonja Blue). New York, Onyx, 1989; London, Futura, 1990.

Tempter. New York, Onyx, 1990; London, Futura, 1991.
In the Blood (Sonja Blue). London, Kinnell, 1991; New York, Roc, 1992.
Wild Blood. London, New English Library, 1993.
Paint it Black (Sonja Blue). London, New English Library, 1995.
Midnight Blue: The Sonja Blue Collection (omnibus; contains *Sunglasses after Dark, In the Blood, Paint it Black*). Clarkston, Georgia, White Wolf, 1995.
Walking Wolf: A Weird Western. Clarkston, Georgia, White Wolf, 1995.
A Dozen Black Roses. Clarkston, Georgia, White Wolf, 1996.

Short Stories

Love Throbbing Bob (as Nanzi Regalia). Berkeley, California, Dark Carnival Press, 1990.
The Tortuga Hill Gang's Last Ride: The True Story. Arvada, Colorado, Roadkill Press, 1991.
Cold Turkey. Holyoke, Massachusetts, Crossroads Press, 1992.
Nameless Sins. N.p., 1994.

Other

Editor, with Martin H. Greenberg and Edward E. Kramer, *Dark Love.* New York, Roc, and London, Hodder and Stoughton, 1995.
Editor, with Edward E. Kramer, *Forbidden Acts.* New York, Avon, 1995.

Other Publications

Novel

The Fantastic Four: To Free Atlantis. New York, Boulevard, 1995.

*   *   *

Add the name of Sonja Blue to the list of fictional hero-villains who appear in long-running series. If the message on the back of some of Nancy A. Collins's paperbacks is true, Sonja Blue is "wild, wicked, weird . . . the sharpest vampire yet." Where other genres (detective fiction, for example) often have long-running characters that are forces for good, one of the important points about horror fiction is that it celebrates the dark side—the forbidden, the taboo—and the book-to-book characters tend to be forces for darkness, or at the very least, unconventionality. Rex Miller's Chaingang; Thomas Harris's Hannibal Lecter: and now Nancy Collins's sexy, bolshy vampire—Sonja Blue.

Sonja's first appearance was in the award-winning *Sunglasses after Dark.* We see, in fact, from even this early on, that she is not entirely evil, although her ways are certainly contrary to those of the humans whose world she now inhabits. Sonja Blue is in prison, and we get to understand her through a mixture of first-person narrative and third-person depositions about her behaviour as a captive. From the start there is little doubt about Sonja's potential abilities: "He always saves me for last," she says of one of the warders. "I guess it's because he's scared of me. I don't blame him. I'm scared of me too." Sonja has already killed a different warder—Kalish—in a manner that makes clear in our minds Sonja's attitude at this stage to murder; the killing has strongly sexual overtones in that she strips his body before drinking from his neck. Simultaneously, the second warder, Claude, has both nothing and everything to be afraid of; Sonja is not looking to hurt him, but how would he know that? As it is, Sonja decides that she would like to leave prison now: "She'd had enough of this place, with its endless drugs and intravenous feedings." Having left, Sonja has cause to save Claude while on the outside—just to show him, and the readership, that she is a nicer breed of vampire. However, the way that Sonja saves her erstwhile captor creates psychological problems with Claude that he will carry with him to his grave: "After that, Claude was never able to look at the old tomcat in quite the same way, just as he could not look at Sonja Blue without sensing the feline sadism lurking below her surface, waiting for a mouse."

Collins excels at ripe descriptions of downtown, rundown areas—the sorts of place that a vampire such as Sonja likes to frequent. As Sonja herself puts it: "The porn shops, titty bars, and adult cinemas are all very busy, like maggots in a corpse . . . It's my element." But what makes her walks around downtown special is more than simply forcing us to stare at ugliness; we are made to feel and smell it too, through the sensitive faculties of one of the undead. We smell with Sonja the "roasting flesh and burning hair" of a pyrotic who happens to be nearby. Sonja's senses are best tuned to the place where inner-city dives meet a sort of twilight fantasy realm that most of us can neither see nor imagine: the pool bars we can experience and the Ramones music at deafening volumes we can hear; but there is more to Collins's world than a vampire on our streets—she makes us believe in the shadowland too, where many otherworlders live among us, breathing and smiling, in camouflage, but interacting with us all on a daily basis.

Sonja Blue was not always Sonja Blue; nor, more intriguingly, is she only Sonja Blue. Once upon a time she was mortal—a lady named Denise. In London, with its characters often speaking would-be authentic gorblimey Cockney, Denise is introduced into the cult of vampirism by a character called Morgan. Shortly afterwards, as if being dead is not bad enough, she falls into the employ of Joey—an insecure and violent London pimp. Given the travesty of her existence thus far it is hardly surprising that Sonja turns to thorough forms of retribution to punish misdemeanours. Joey she eventually kills, and then pushes a blind man's cane up his bottom, emphasizing once more Sonja's attitude to the twin impulses of sex and death. The story of how Sonja comes to America is told, and from the reader's point of view, part of the reason why the series seems so fresh is the existence of several well-realized international settings.

Why Sonja is not only Sonja is simple. There is another important plot hook that will stay with the Sonja Blue series for as long as the theme of her sexuality will: that of the Other. The Other is a feat of vampiric imagination; an invisible, amorphous entity that lives in Sonja's psyche and says hello from time to time. The Other is able to take a stroll around the dreams of potential victims.

By the second in the Sonja Blue series, *In the Blood*, Sonja is well and truly ready to punish Morgan for his having made her a vampire in the first place—Morgan being as important a thread through the epic as Sonja herself, and a different angle on what we perceive as evil. Compared even to Sonja, Morgan is a very dark character indeed.

One of the confrontations between Sonja and Morgan takes place in a library that has been taken straight from one of a thousand old British movies or Agatha Christie stories. Even the aris-

tocratic persona of Morgan fits in nicely. "The voice was familiar although it lacked the upper-class British accent it had possessed when she'd first heard it in 1969." It is retribution time: "The Other thought that it would be a really good idea to pluck Morgan's eyes out and use his head for a bowling ball. Sonja agreed, but continued to fight the rage boiling inside her." In case it is not clear to the reader by now, Sonja Blue is a psychologically divided vampire. That said, even Sonja cannot be calm for long, and shows a winning way with put-downs; she says to Morgan: "Cut the routine, dead boy! You know why I'm here."

Showing that not only physical cities (with or without extra dimensions perceptible only to the select) are eligible for the Collins touch, the highlighting conflict of *In the Blood* occurs in the amazing Place Between Places—a partly physical, partly mental terrain which Sonja and Morgan share for the purposes of conflict. On an ethereal level there are hallucinations for the combatants to go through—Lovecraftian images of tentacles bursting from chests—while on the physical plane the violence is considerably stronger than fisticuffs.

"Lord Morgan, late of the Inquisition and the Gestapo, lay on the floor of his car and contemplated the dreadful sickness that humans called Love," is written near the end of *In the Blood*. It is a fitting omen for the presiding sentiment of *Paint it Black*, the next Sonja Blue novel. *Paint it Black* is not only the most unusual book in the series; it is also Collins's most experimental novel. And, as is the nature of experiments, some of it works, and some of it does not. Arguably, in fact, *Paint it Black* does not qualify for the term "novel" in the traditional sense at all; it is a scrapbook of interconnecting diary snippets and vignettes. Multiple voices, cross-indexed and occasionally overlapping, tell the story ostensibly of Sonja's (and the Other's) continuing struggles with their maker while also providing a curt and ugly parable of Love at the end of the 20th century. Maybe "warning" is a better word, for this is Collins's bleakest yet: this is the Dark Age of Love. Without resorting to unnecessary explanation, it should be clear enough to say, in the atmosphere of disease in which we live, that this is partly a book about what happens when you fall in love with the wrong person. The rape scene and its consequences alone are new ways of looking at love and manipulation.

Paint it Black unfortunately has its faults. The fact that Blue and Morgan go into such detail is one of them. If Morgan has been keeping a journal for 700 years why would he comment on how he hasn't been afraid of the arrival of dawn since before the steam engine? Such a fact should be made clear to the reader, of course, but not in this way; his journals on occasion do not read like journals. There should be another way of imparting information, even the old-fashioned utilization of the third-person omniscient narrator, which exists elsewhere in the book anyway and would not have seemed at all out of place. Elsewhere, Sonja's line in hyperbolic simile is sometimes a trifle overdone, given that she has not used such off-the-wall comparisons before (perhaps we are to take these outbursts as evidence of her growing in maturity or confidence). For example: "Chaz yowls like a baby dropped in a vat of boiling oil and disappears in a swirl of dust and ectoplasm, leaving me alone with Judd's phone number still clenched in one fist." It is Raymond Chandler crossed with early Clive Barker, or with Skipp and Spector, and something of an acquired taste.

Minor quibbles, perhaps, for *Paint it Black* also sees some of Collins's best writing and most bizarre tongue-through-cheek black humour. In this novel's world of shape-shifting and sado-masochism, Sonja has got involved with a young man named Judd, much to the disgust of Judd's ex-girlfriend. Swiftly and messily the ex-girlfriend's protests are silenced: Sonja bats the woman's head off with a stolen church crucifix and then throws her dismembered corpse to the alligators that populate the swamps around New Orleans. One of the most shocking scenes is that of Sonja killing Judd and then dismembering him: "Judd is in the trunk, divvied up into six garbage bags, just like Kitty. At least it was fast. My hunger was so intense, I drained him within seconds . . . Maybe part of him knew I was doing him a favor."

The Other in this novel invades real-space and real-time during moments of Sonja's distress; to use analogies from other fictional works, the appearances of the Other are like sudden bionic episodes, or like the Incredible Hulk breaking free of its mild-mannered host. Sonja ends up, as we all knew she would, in a fight with her *alter ego* that is worthy of Robert Louis Stevenson, complaining to the Other that, "You've ruined everything for me." Trying to starve the Other of blood by locking herself in an industrial freezer does not work ("Face it, sweetmeat, I'm here and there's nothing you can do to get rid of me!") and what is interesting is that Sonja's ongoing battle with Morgan has become almost incidental; the battle of wills is much more intriguing.

Collins does more than write Sonja Blue, as her bibliography shows, and she should not be burdened by Sonja Blue unnecessarily, as has been the case with other authors and their fictional creations (Sir Arthur Conan Doyle was shackled by his public's demands for more Sherlock Holmes stories, for example). There are many other strings to Collins's bow. *Wild Blood* is her were-creatures novel and *Tempter* confirms her fascination with scavengers and the maladjusted in a story of voodoo, which as Ti Alice, a priestess therein is keen to point out that it, "ain't all wringin' chicken necks and burning Fast Money candles, baby." Furthermore, she writes occasional non-fiction too, with the Swiftian skill of making uncomfortable arguments sound more reasonable than they might from the lips of others. In the magazine *SF Eye* (issue 14) Collins discusses neonatal technology and how doctors fight to save the life of a baby that has been born three months early. Miscarriages are sad, is her argument, but natural: the female body's way of avoiding possible future damage to the child. All of the babies that are saved change the shape of Western civilization.

Whether we believe what she has to say or not, we cannot help but admire her willingness to have her voice heard. If the essay reads like science fiction/horror, then it is because there is plenty about the modern world that on reflection makes the horrifically fantastical hinterland of the inner cities seem not so far away after all.

—David Mathew

COOK, Robin

Nationality: American. **Born:** New York, 4 May 1940. **Education:** Wesleyan University, B.A., 1962; Columbia University, M.D., 1966; postgraduate study at Harvard University. **Military Service:** U.S. Navy, 1969-71; became lieutenant commander. **Family:** Married Barbara Ellen Mougin in 1979. **Career:** Resident in general surgery, Queen's Hospital, Honolulu, 1966-68; resident in ophthalmology, Massachusetts Eye and Ear Infirmary, 1971-75, and staff member since 1975 but currently on leave; clinical instructor at Harvard Medi-

cal School, from 1972. **Agent:** William Morris Agency, 1325 Avenue of the Americas, New York, NY 10019. **Address:** 6001 Pelican Bay Blvd., Naples, FL 33963-8166; or c/o G. P. Putnam's Sons, 51 Madison Ave., New York, NY 10010-1603, USA.

HORROR, GHOST AND GOTHIC PUBLICATIONS

Novels

Coma: A Novel. Boston, Little Brown, and London, Macmillan, 1977.
Brain. New York, Putnam, and London, Macmillan, 1981.
Fever. New York, Putnam, and London, Macmillan, 1982.
Godplayer. New York, Putnam, and London, Macmillan, 1983.
Mindbend. New York, Putnam, and London, Macmillan, 1985.
Outbreak. New York, Putnam, and London, Macmillan, 1987.
Mortal Fear. New York, Putnam, and London, Macmillan, 1988.
Mutation. New York, Putnam, and London, Macmillan, 1989.
Harmful Intent. New York, Putnam, and London, Macmillan, 1990.
Vital Signs. New York, Putnam, and London, Macmillan, 1991.
Blindsight. New York, Putnam, and London, Macmillan, 1992.
Terminal. New York, Putnam, and London, Macmillan, 1993.
Fatal Cure. New York, Putnam, and London, Macmillan, 1994.
Acceptable Risk. New York, Putnam, and London, Macmillan, 1995.
Contagion. New York, Putnam, and London, Macmillan, 1995.
Invasion. New York, Putnam, and London, Macmillan, 1997.
Chromosome 6. New York, Putnam, and London, Macmillan, 1997.

OTHER PUBLICATIONS

Novels

The Year of the Intern. New York, Harcourt Brace Jovanovich, 1972.
Sphinx. New York, Putnam, and London, Macmillan, 1979.

*

Media Adaptations: Films—*Coma,* 1978; *Sphinx,* 1981; *Mutation,* 1990. Television—*Robin Cook's Virus,* adapted from the novel *Outbreak,* 1995; *Robin Cook's Invasion,* 1997.

Critical Study: *Robin Cook: A Critical Companion* by Lorena Laura Stookey, Westport, Connecticut, Greenwood Press, 1996.

*   *   *

Vulnerable people placed under the control of powerful, mysterious and potentially malevolent forces. The scenario seems the essence of horror; it is also the situation faced by all citizens of a modern society who become seriously ill. The surprise, then, is not that a sub-genre of medical horror exists, but that it was mastered and popularized by a relatively recent author, Robin Cook.

Of course, while there have long been doctors represented in horror fiction (ranging from Mary Shelley's *Frankenstein* and Robert Louis Stevenson's *Strange Case of Dr. Jekyll and Mr. Hyde* to Michael Crichton's *The Terminal Man*), the last 20 years have proved an especially auspicious era to marry the field of medicine to horror literature. With the disappearance of the house call, patients today always confront doctors on their home turf, and modern hospitals and clinics, filled with arcane technology, strange poly-syllabic potions, and murmurs of incomprehensible acronyms and jargon, are infinitely more alienating than the homey doctors' offices of Norman Rockwell paintings. Increasing numbers of lawsuits and disputes about insurance coverage have made the doctor-patient relationship more and more adversarial, and there are legitimate concerns about granting ever-increasing amounts of money, resources and power to doctors, who are all too human and eminently fallible. Robin Cook, who worked as an ophthalmologist in hospitals for several years, brilliantly validates and exploits all of these anxieties, resentments and worries.

Consider *Coma*, his first horror novel and one of his best. Despite signs of inexperience—a slow, expository beginning and a few improbable plot twists—Cook effectively chronicles medical student Susan Wheeler's efforts to uncover a sinister scheme at Boston Memorial Hospital: patients of desirable tissue-types are deliberately driven into an irreversible coma so that their organs can be harvested and sold on the black market. Along with its relentless pace and an almost-surprising final revelation, *Coma* succeeds largely because its author is manifestly used to working in hospitals and is conversant with their daily routines, varied personalities and petty politics, making the story seem completely plausible. Cook's medical background proved helpful to horror in another way: at one point, the heroine keeps a pursuer from opening a door by stabbing him in the hand with a pair of scissors. A routine moment in most horror novels, Cook's version is more impressive: "The point of the scissors struck between the knuckles of the second and third fingers. The force of the blow carried the blades between the metacarpal bones, shredding the lumbrical muscles and exiting through the back of the hand. . . . A small arterial pumper squirted blood in short pulsating arcs onto the opaque plastic floor, forming a pattern of red polkadots." Medical knowledge also helped Cook to create the novel's most haunting image, the cadavers hanging suspended in air, which is "the best method of . . . totally preserving the skin and minimizing nursing care," as determined by research in "orthopedics" and "burn treatment."

Coma set the pattern for several other Cook novels: a major hospital on the East Coast as the setting; a series of apparently random and inexplicable deaths, only gradually viewed as related to each other; a dedicated but marginalized doctor who sets out to find the explanation behind these deaths, even though he encounters vigorous opposition from other doctors who later are usually revealed to be working hand in hand with some evil corporation or Health Maintenance Organization (one of Cook's favourite targets); and the final revelation of a convoluted scheme to profit from the deaths. Accompanying the death or punishment of the perpetrators is a little polemic about the need for caution about certain lines of medical research and/or a plea for more vigilant policing of doctors' activities, sometimes followed by a list of references to substantiate that the danger depicted in the novel is real. (While Cook apparently remains on the staff of Massachusetts Eye and Ear Infirmary, on permanent leave, one has to wonder how popular Cook is among his former colleagues.)

An excellent novel following this formula is *Godplayer*, which engrossingly depicts a brilliant surgeon, increasingly unbalanced because of illegally garnered prescription drugs, who decides to systematically murder those patients who are unlikely to ever again be productive members of society and who therefore, by his logic, are only wasting precious medical resources. Also memorable is *Mortal Cure*, where the discovery of a drug that radically acceler-

ates the process of death is exploited by a sinister company that goes by the incongruous name of the Good Health Plan. HMOs take it on the chin again in the meticulous and suspenseful *Contagion*, where this time they generate profitable deaths by taking advantage of a virus left over from the World War I pneumonia epidemic and preserved in an frozen Eskimo dwelling; fortunately, idealistic Dr. Jack Stapleton manages to figure out the problem.

Cook is less successful with the other type of medical novel he produces—the story of a medical research centre which unwisely plunges into some ill-advised project which predictably leads to frightening consequences—since he seems less familiar with this sort of setting and since the horrors he concocts to be unleashed by these establishments tend towards the implausible. In *Mutation*, for example, readers are asked to believe that the apparently ordinary twelve-year-old son of a scientist, created as a part of an experiment, is actually a super-genius who has managed to secretly construct his own fully-equipped research laboratory within his father's facility to carry out his own radical and loathsome experiments. Also straining credulity is *Acceptable Risk*, where an apparently ideal designer drug turns out to have one unfortunate little side-effect on the researchers who test it out: they are unknowingly transformed into feral monsters who stalk the countryside every night. The frustrating thing about *Acceptable Risk* is that it incorporates an intriguing sub-plot about efforts to research the Salem witch hunts and possibly link those events to an undiagnosed substance causing mental instability; in this case, the obligatory inclusion of horror-story elements spoiled what otherwise might have been a quietly gripping story about historical research.

Although Cook is always careful to include more thrills than lectures, he still runs the risk, like any polemicist, of becoming shrill and repetitive in warning about the dangers of unrestrained doctors and profit-hungry hospitals. Then again, given our society's ongoing fascination with medical matters and continuing support for extensive medical research, there may always arise new concerns and perils to provide Cook with fresh material for terrifying fiction leavened with argument. Overall, while neither a versatile writer nor an impressive stylist, Cook is still very good at what he does, which is all that patients want from a doctor, and all that many readers want from a novelist.

—Gary Westfahl

COOPER, Dennis

Nationality: American. **Born:** 1952. **Career:** Founder of *Little Caesar* (a poetry magazine) and Little Caesar Press; organizer of visual arts shows and creator of performance pieces. Lives in New York City.

HORROR, GHOST AND GOTHIC PUBLICATIONS

Novels

Frisk. New York, Grove Weidenfeld, 1991.

Short Stories

Wrong. New York, Grove Weidenfeld, 1992.

OTHER PUBLICATIONS

Novels

Closer. New York, Grove Weidenfeld, 1989.
Jerk. New York(?), Artspace, 1992.
Try. New York, Grove Atlantic, 1994.
Guide. New York, Grove Atlantic, 1997.

Graphic Novel

Horror Hospital Unplugged, with Keith Mayerson. N.p., Juno, 1996.

Poetry

He Cried. N.p., n.d.
The Missing Men. N.p., n.d.
The Tenderness of the Wolves. N.p., n.d.
Idols. N.p., n.d.
Tiger Beat. N.p., n.d.
The Dream Police (Selected Poems, 1969-1993). New York, Grove, 1994.

*

Film Adaptation: *Frisk*, 1995.

* * *

Known for his exploration of explicitly gay themes, Dennis Cooper has, in several of his works, mixed in streaks and tones of black (and red) enough to colour them horrific. His writing is terse, even abrupt, and also full of unexpected metaphors that segue to and from sharply observed physical details. The knife-edgy juxtaposition of the concrete and the abstract, the tangible and the imagined in Cooper's descriptions gives them an intensity that can be ruthlessly unsettling. The focus in his darker works is on the inner pain that isolation causes, and the isolation that the inflicting of pain creates. Thought must result in action; the body must be acted upon, affected enough in turn to (further) unhinge the mind that first conceived the action. For Cooper the body exists to experience what the mind must discover. His stories can read more like blow-by-blow accounts of the often unpredictable twists and turns his characters put themselves and each other through to fulfil their lust to understand, their understanding of (blood) lust.

In the title story of his collection *Wrong*, Cooper's first protagonist, Mike, sequentially murders four men he randomly picks up thinking, "Once you've killed someone, life's shit." Ultimately he kills himself. There is no reason for Mike's homicides other than the momentary need to see someone lifeless; there's no other possible end than to see himself the same way. The murders are described so quickly and so matter-of-factly that casual killing seems nothing out of the ordinary. The second protagonist, George, frequently thinks of death; imagines himself dead. A chance sexual encounter leaves him that way, but he then sees himself dead from across the room where his partner killed him. Now a ghost, he subsequently visits the one man he felt something for while alive and fails to communicate with him. The two scenarios of a man who randomly dispenses death to others, then kills himself, and one who imagines death and is then killed are parallel; both are

wrong because both men ultimately see themselves dead for no apparent reason, then die; neither one is fulfilled.

The violence that defines Cooper's work as horrific is always linked to sex. The inevitability of brutal sex is the same as that of the lethal violence that sex—brutal or not—leads to. The "little death" of orgasm for Cooper is actual death, the sexual release his darker characters must have. The killer in "A Herd," Ray, carefully selects and stalks high-school students for his victims, furtively, repeatedly watching them disrobe before he corners them alone, drugs them, brings them to his basement, straps them down, kisses them, has sex with them, covers their faces with a mask, mutilates them, kills them. The God he imagines himself becoming, occasionally, is evolving from the weak, scared man he knows himself to be: "when Ray wasn't horny or couldn't be, he was worthless. He thought about suicide." The God he sees himself as is also a man who imagines the boys he's killed returning from the dead to destroy him. They are the herd he fears but cannot stop wanting when he sees them not yet dead. In the end, God sleeps; the killer darkens his room. But the deaths will continue because the boys are the flock he must communicate with, in his own way—and because Ray is still alive; because God has not (yet) committed suicide.

Frisk, Cooper's only (so far) venture into the horrific in novel form, also makes use of the edgy abrupt prose the author relentlessly builds his characters with. In addition the power of the work is hugely intensified by the narrator's voice which is first-person omniscient. Scenes without Dennis, the narrator, are depicted in detail immediately followed by his entrance, as though he knew everything that happened before he arrived—or for that matter everything that could happen at any time. This clearly gives the feeling that all characters are invented not by the author, but by the narrator—or that the author is the narrator, and vice versa. Dennis is, right from the outset, fascinated by lethal sex as evidenced by a series of photographs he examines at the age of 13 which show a young naked mutilated boy, presumably dead.

But he does not know why he feels the way he does, "everything I do is based on an urge that I don't understand." He has sex with various partners and imagines killing them, or mutilating them, crushing their skulls. Emotional depth does not figure in his behaviour, "love's what you feel for someone you don't know very well, if at all." What he does understand is his ever-momentary need to unify sex and death, "someone else dying was strictly a sexual fantasy." This "someone else" is a man or a boy he must either have had sex with or been strongly attracted to, enough to want sex with, "you fascinate me so much that in a perfect world I'd kill you to understand the appeal."

In the novel's most intense chapter, "Numb," Dennis relates how, after moving to Amsterdam, he and two like-minded gay German men find Dutch boys and lure them to the windmill Dennis lives in. There, after engaging in ferocious sex, the three men slaughter their victims. The author spares no detail of this murderous activity, methodically listing every perverse step of the way for each of the several boys they kill. This chronicling takes the form of a letter Dennis writes to his former lover back in the U.S., saying, "I'm writing to the Julian I imagine you to be" (this is the only spot in the novel where the author hints at the labile author-narrator relationship he has constructed).

Ultimately these perversions are seen to be completely fabricated when Julian arrives and finds no evidence of any wrongdoing. But Dennis has shown himself to be a character likely capable of what he described in the previous chapter. The darkness of Cooper's work is made all the more so by this subtle, nasty device; the narrator-author seems likely to burst forth directly from the pages of the book and find the person he needs to slaughter.

A 1995 film version of *Frisk* was only partially successful in capturing the true blackness of what the novel so effectively portrays.

—Lawrence Greenberg

COPPARD, A(lfred) E(dgar)

Nationality: British. **Born:** Folkestone, Kent, 4 January 1878; moved with his family to Brighton, 1883. **Education:** Lewes Road Boarding School, Brighton, 1883-87; left school at age nine; apprenticed to a tailor in Whitechapel, London, 1887-90; later trained as an accountant in his own time. **Family:** Married 1) Lily Annie Richardson in 1905 (died); 2) Winifred May de Kok, one son and one daughter. **Career:** Had worked as a paraffin vendor's assistant, auctioneer, cheesemonger, soap-agent, and carrier, in Brighton by the time he was 20; thereafter office boy and clerk; moved to Oxford, 1907; Confidential Clerk, Eagle Ironworks, Oxford, 1907-19; freelance writer from 1919. **Died:** 13 January 1957.

Horror, Ghost and Gothic Publications

Short Stories

Adam and Eve and Pinch Me. Waltham St. Lawrence, Berkshire, Golden Cockerel Press, 1921; expanded edition, New York, Knopf, 1922.
Clorinda Walks in Heaven: Tales. Waltham St. Lawrence, Berkshire, Golden Cockerel Press, 1922.
The Gollan. Privately printed, 1929.
Crotty Shinkwin. Waltham St. Lawrence, Berkshire, Golden Cockerel Press, 1932.
Fearful Pleasures. Sauk City, Wisconsin, Arkham House, 1946; revised edition, London and New York, Peter Nevill, 1951.

Other Publications

Short Stories

The Black Dog and Other Stories. London, Cape, and New York, Knopf, 1923.
Fishmonger's Fiddle: Tales. London, Cape, and New York, Knopf, 1925.
The Field of Mustard: Tales. London, Cape, 1926; New York, Knopf, 1927.
Silver Circus: Tales. London, Cape, 1928; New York, Knopf, 1929.
Count Stefan. Waltham St. Lawrence, Berkshire, Golden Cockerel Press, 1928.
The Hundredth Story. Waltham St. Lawrence, Berkshire, Golden Cockerel Press, 1931.
Pink Furniture: A Tale for Lovely Children with Noble Natures. London and New York, Cape, 1930.
Nixey's Harlequin: Tales. London, Cape, 1931; New York, Knopf, 1932.

Cheefoo. Croton Falls, New York, Spiral, 1932.
Dunky Fitlow: Tales. London, Cape, 1933.
Ring the Bells of Heaven. London, White Owl, 1933.
Emergency Exit. New York, Random House, 1934.
Polly Oliver: Tales. London, Cape, 1935.
Ninepenny Flute: Twenty-One Tales. London, Macmillan, 1937.
Tapster's Tapestry. London, Golden Cockerel Press, 1938.
You Never Know, Do You? and Other Tales. London, Methuen, 1939.
Ugly Anna and Other Tales. London, Methuen, 1944.
Selected Tales. London, Cape, 1946.
The Dark-Eyed Lady: Fourteen Tales. Lodnon, Methuen, 1947.
The Collected Tales of A. E. Coppard. New York, Knopf, 1948.
Lucy in Her Pink Jacket. London and New York, Peter Nevill, 1954.

Poetry

Hips and Haws. Waltham St. Lawrence, Berkshire, Golden Cockerel Press, 1922.
Pelagea and Other Poems. Waltham St. Lawrence, Berkshire, Golden Cockerel Press, 1926.
Yokohama Garland and Other Poems. Philadelphia, Centaur Press, 1926.
Collected Poems. London, Cape, and New York, Knopf, 1928.
Easter Day. London, Ulysses Bookshop, 1931.
Cherry Ripe. Windham, Connecticut, Hawthorne House, 1935.

Other

Rummy: The Noble Game, with Robert Gibbings. Waltham St. Lawrence, Berkshire, Golden Cockerel Press, 1932; Boston and New York, Houghton Mifflin, 1933.
It's Me, O Lord! (autobiography). London, Methuen, 1957.

Editor, *Songs from Robert Burns.* Waltham St. Lawrence, Berkshire, Golden Cockerel Press, 1925.

*

Bibliography: *The Writings of A. E. Coppard* by Jacob Schwartz, 1931, 1975, Folcroft, Pennsylvania, Folcroft Library Editions.

Critical Studies: *A. E. Coppard: His Life and His Poetry* by George Brandon Saul (dissertaition), University of Pennsylvania, 1932; *Remarks on the Style of A. E. Coppard* by A. Jehin, Buenos Aires, Argentine Association of English Culture, 1944.

*   *   *

A. E. Coppard was primarily noted for his short stories of rural life. These are often compared to and associated with the tales of H. E. Bates, which also share the strong influence of Thomas Hardy and similarly contemplate everyday tragedies with a crystal clear but mutely sympathetic eye. Unlike Bates, however, Coppard had a strong interest in the fantastic, which he deployed in numerous stories ranging from the whimsical to the earnestly allegorical. The element of horror in his work is rarely brutal, but many of his mercurial and oddly plaintive fantasies are authentically disturbing. His work did not fit into any readily available category, and a good deal of it first appeared in small editions produced by private presses, but it is a notable facet of that quintessentially British genus of weird fiction whose leading practitioner was Walter de la Mare. The American and later British editions of *Adam and Eve and Pinch Me*—which combine the contents of the author's first two Golden Cockerel Press volumes—form what is perhaps the strongest of all Coppard's collections, and the one with the highest proportion of imaginative fiction. The oft-anthologized title story is a sentimental fantasy of anticipation in which a man sees his children playing happily with a sibling as yet unborn. "Clorinda Walks in Heaven" is a fine posthumous fantasy in which a dead spinster meets the husbands of her previous incarnations and finds that none of them lives up to her unfulfilled ideal. "The Elixir of Youth" is a parable about the granting of wishes whose precise moral remains tantalizingly elusive—a characteristic shared by many of Coppard's surreal fables. "Piffingcap," about a weird shaving mug, and the historical fantasy "The King of the World" are more straightforward if still a little evasive, but "Marching to Zion" is very enigmatic indeed. It follows the allegorical journey of three protagonists whose actions and encounters obliquely echo the Christian Mysteries.

None of Coppard's later collections contains more than a few fugitive fantasies—it was as if he deliberately spread them thinly to avoid the risk of their attracting overmuch attention—but the great majority of them are gathered, along with "Adam and Eve and Pinch Me," "Clorinda Walks in Heaven" and "The Elixir of Youth," into the eclectic Arkham House collection *Fearful Pleasures*. Most are mock folk tales with allegorical superimpositions, after the fashion of German *kunstmarchen*.

The Irish setting of "The Elixir of Youth" is revisited in "The Gollan" and "Crotty Shrinkwin." The eponymous anti-hero of the first story is physically powerful and mentally weak; when a leprechaun offers to grant his wishes he is quite incapable of turning the gift to his advantage. The eponymous hero of the second tale is a fisherman whose anchor becomes entangled near an ominous island, which inverts itself to reveal magical landscape whose residue of Eden is not at all welcoming. The sarcastic pessimism of these stories is further elaborated in the story of "Simple Simon," who unwittingly smuggles a ration of sins into Heaven in the lining of coat given to him by an unorthodox philosopher. The village idiot in "Rocky and the Bailiff" is far luckier in his magical dabblings but never gets the credit for his good work. "Jack the Giant-Killer"—Coppard's contribution to the notable anthology *The Fairies Return*, issued by Peter Davies in 1934—is an uninhibited satire in which Jack avails himself of modern aids to dispatch the hapless giants.

Explicit horrors are featured in "Old Martin," in which the last person buried in a village cemetery is bound to serve her predecessors until Judgement Day and begs her living relatives for release, "The Homeless One," in which an attempted suicide is tormented by a neighbour who might be the Wandering Jew, and the supernatural revenge story "Cheese." Most of Coppard's tales of ghosts and mental disturbance are, however, far more elliptical. "Polly Morgan" is witness to her aunt's apparent congress with a spirit lover and eventually finds herself in the same boat. "The Bogie Man" who afflicts a female thief is a teasing imp whose monstrousness is contained in the anxiety of his beholder. Those of his fantasies which introduce a note of erotic promise (never fulfilled and usually betrayed) are more frankly ironic; these include "The Drum," "Ahoy, Sailor Boy" and the farcical "The Kisstruck Bogie." The excellent but very marginal "Jove's Nectar" in *Ninepenny Flute* is similar in kind. The Peter Nevill edition

of *Fearful Pleasures* omits "Adam and Eve and Pinch Me" but adds "The Tiger," a *conte cruel* set in a menagerie, and "The Gruesome Fit," a fine tale in which a pathetic murder's guilty conscience is externalized as an angry and penetrative wind.

Although Coppard's non-supernatural stories are rarely as harrowing as Bates's most extreme *contes cruels*, he was more consistent in examining the darker side of rural life. It is arguable that such tales of injustice as "The Poor Man" and such accounts of everyday cruelty as "The Watercress Girl" and "Arabesque: The Mouse" are more horrific than his fantasies, and the latter has been reprinted more than once in anthologies of horror stories. His grotesque folk tales and awkward fables do, however, constitute a unique and highly effective contribution to the less travelled by-ways of English literature. If one were to judge by the contents of the *Collected Tales* which he assembled in 1948 it would seem that he did not think very highly of them himself—only a handful of the 38 stories contained therein are fantasies—but it may well be that he thought it politic to concentrate there on works more likely to obtain critical approval. Had he not been keenly interested in his weird tales he surely could not have written so many, or written them so well.

—Brian Stableford

COPPER, Basil

Nationality: British. **Born:** London, 5 February 1924. **Education:** Grammar school and a private commercial college. **Family:** Married Annie Renée Guerin. **Career:** Journalist for 30 years, including 14 years as news editor with a Kent county newspaper. **Member:** Crime Writers Association (chairman, 1981-82). **Address:** Stockdoves, South Park, Sevenoaks, Kent TN13 1EN, England.

HORROR, GHOST AND GOTHIC PUBLICATIONS

Novels

The Great White Space. London, Hale, 1974; New York, St. Martin's Press, 1975.
The Curse of the Fleers. London, Harwood Smart, 1976; New York, St. Martin's Press, 1977.
Necropolis. Sauk City, Wisconsin, Arkham House, 1980; London, Sphere, 1981.
The House of the Wolf. Sauk City, Wisconsin, Arkham House, 1983.
Into the Silence. London, Sphere, 1983.
The Black Death. Minneapolis, Fedogan and Bremer, 1991.

Short Stories

Not after Nightfall. London, New English Library, 1967.
From Evil's Pillow. Sauk City, Wisconsin, Arkham House, 1973.
When Footsteps Echo: Tales of Terror and the Unknown. London, Hale, and New York, St. Martin's Press, 1975.
And Afterward, the Dark: Seven Tales. Sauk City, Wisconsin, Arkham House, 1977.
Here Be Daemons: Tales of Horror and the Uneasy. London, Hale, and New York, St. Martin's Press, 1978.

Voices of Doom. London, Hale, and New York, St. Martin's Press, 1980.

Other

The Vampire: In Legend, Fact, and Art. London, Hale 1973; Secaucus, New Jersey, Citadel Press, 1974.
The Werewolf: In Legend, Fact, and Art. London, Hale, and New York, St. Martin's Press, 1977.

OTHER PUBLICATIONS

Novels

The Dark Mirror. London, Hale, 1966.
Night Frost. London, Hale, 1966.
No Flowers for the General. London, Hale, 1967.
Scratch on the Dark. London, Hale, 1967.
Die Now, Live Later. London, Hale, 1968.
Don't Bleed on Me. London, Hale, 1968.
The Marble Orchard. London, Hale, 1969.
Dead File. London, Hale, 1970.
No Letters from the Grave. London, Hale, 1971.
The Big Chill. London, Hale, 1972.
The Phantom. New York, Avon, 1972.
The Phantom and the Scorpia Menace. New York, Avon, 1972.
The Phantom and the Slave Market of Mucar. New York, Avon, 1972.
Strong-Arm. London, Hale, 1972.
A Great Year for Dying. London, Hale, 1973.
Shock-Wave. London, Hale, 1973.
The Breaking Point. London, Hale, 1973.
A Voice from the Dead. London, Hale, 1974.
Feedback. London, Hale, 1974.
Ricochet. London, Hale, 1974.
The High Wall. London, Hale, 1975.
Impact. London, Hale, 1975.
A Good Place to Die. London, Hale, 1975.
The Lonely Place. London, Hale, 1976.
Crack in the Sidewalk. London, Hale, 1976.
Tight Corner. London, Hale, 1976.
The Year of the Dragon. London, Hale, 1977.
Death Squad. London, Hale, 1977.
Murder One. London, Hale, 1978.
A Quiet Room in Hell. London, Hale, 1979.
The Big Rip-Off. London, Hale, 1979.
The Caligari Complex. London, Hale, 1980.
Flip-Side. London, Hale, 1980.
The Long Rest. London, Hale, 1981.
The Empty Silence. London, Hale, 1981.
Dark Entry. London, Hale, 1981.
Hang Loose. London, Hale, 1982.
Shoot-Out. London, Hale, 1982.
The Far Horizon. London, Hale, 1982.
Trigger-Man. London, Hale, 1983.
Pressure-Point. London, Hale, 1983.
Hard Contract. London, Hale, 1983.
The Narrow Corner. London, Hale, 1983.
The Hook. London, Hale, 1984.
You Only Die Once. London, Hale, 1984.

Tuxedo Park. London, Hale, 1985.
The Far Side of Fear. London, Hale, 1985.
Snow-Job. London, Hale, 1986.
Jet-Lag. London, Hale, 1986.
Blood on the Moon. London, Hale, 1986.
Heavy Iron. London, Hale, 1987.
Turn Down an Empty Glass. London, Hale, 1987.
Bad Scene. London, Hale, 1987.
House-Dick. London, Hale, 1988.
Print-Out. London, Hale, 1988.

Short Stories

The Dossier of Solar Pons. Los Angeles, Pinnacle, 1979.
The Further Adventures of Solar Pons. Los Angeles, Pinnacle, 1979.
The Secret Files of Solar Pons. Los Angeles, Pinnacle, 1979.
Some Uncollected Cases of Solar Pons. Los Angeles, Pinnacle, 1980.
The Exploits of Solar Pons. Minneapolis, Fedogan and Bremer, 1993.
The Recollections of Solar Pons. Minneapolis, Fedogan and Bremer, 1996.

* * *

Although the majority of Basil Copper's output has been in the hard-boiled detective field, with over 50 novels featuring Los Angeles private eye Mike Faraday, his soul is in the mist-enshrouded age of the late Victorian and Edwardian era, or a timeless 1920s that nostalgia has created. These are the settings for many of his stories and novels. Copper is a great emulator, rather in the vein of his mentor August Derleth. He is able to reproduce accurately the pace, mood and approach of the work of authors he admires, particularly H. P. Lovecraft, Mickey Spillane, Arthur Conan Doyle and Derleth himself. This is not to detract from Copper's creative abilities—he can produce excellent original material—rather it is a demonstration of his flexibility within the field. He is made of the same material as many of the writers for the pulp magazines who could switch moods as the markets required. It was this ability that enabled him to produce so many books within a relatively short space of time. In the horror field, Copper's work falls loosely into three categories. There are his stories which emulate the work of H. P. Lovecraft; there are those which are Victorian gothics, and there are his own individual stories.

The influence of Lovecraft and, for that matter, Edgar Allan Poe is best demonstrated in *The Great White Space*, which describes an expedition beyond the Plain of Darkness in search of the home of the Old Ones. The same mood is evoked in *Into the Silence*, exploring a vast cavern deep under Cornwall. The first of these forms part of the Lovecraft-Derleth extended Cthulhu Mythos, whilst the second creates Copper's own underground world with considerable similarity to Lovecraft's cavernous depths. Both novels are similar in structure and development to Lovecraft's major works such as *At the Mountains of Madness*. Copper superbly captures the timelessness of Lovecraft's 1920s and 1930s when individuals, usually university professors, explored little-known parts of the globe. The books start with that apprehension and excitement of entering the unknown checked to some degree by a more leisurely academic pace and reserve until events begin to snowball out of control and menaces from Earth's distant past are unearthed. Several of Copper's short stories are in a similar vein, but probably none better than "The Knocker in the Portico" (*Dark Things*, 1971), a title reminiscent of Lovecraft's "The Thing on the Doorstep" but in denouement more like his "The Outsider" mixed with Poe's "The Fall of the House of Usher." The story is told in the form of a series of diary entries in which the narrator comes steadily under the influence of the mysterious Dr. Spiros. The narrator's house takes on a sinister aspect, with a frequent and maddening knocking sound. Only at the end does the narrator realize that he is in an asylum for the insane. The narrator's great-grandson, who discovers the diary, also starts to hear the knocking.

Copper's works of Victorian/Edwardian fiction are best exemplified by *Necropolis*, a wonderful emporium of a novel in which a private investigator, looking into the death of a client's father, unearths foul deeds in the depths of the massive Brookwood Cemetery. The novel is set in the same atmospheric London as Sherlock Holmes: in fact Inspector Lestrade is one of the characters and there are several cross-references to Holmes's cases. Copper succeeded in recreating this atmosphere in his later novels, *The House of the Wolf* and *The Black Death*, though neither of these had the gothic extravagance of *Necropolis*.

Although August Derleth's Solar Pons stories were set in the 1920s, they had much the same atmosphere as Victorian/Edwardian London, and Copper chose to emphasize this when he continued the series after Derleth's death. If anything Copper made them more like Conan Doyle's original Holmes stories than Derleth's own pastiches. Copper's stories are longer than Derleth's and they ooze atmosphere, so that the dense fogs of London drip from the pages. Almost all of Copper's versions feign the bizarre and supernatural, although none of them venture beyond our ken. "The Adventure of the Crawling Horror" from *The Secret Files of Solar Pons* is one such example. Pons and Parker are called in to investigate a glowing corpse that crawls out of the marshes near Grimstone Manor in Kent. Copper develops the story along supernatural lines until the inevitable rational denouement. This does not come as an anti-climax because it is a test of Copper's ingenuity to explain his bizarre manifestation in an acceptable and logical way. They are *bona fide* modern examples of gothic fiction at its best.

Although his novels are bravura examples of fantastic adventure and gothic extravaganza, to find the real Basil Copper one needs to explore his short fiction, particularly in his early collection *Not After Nightfall* where Copper narrated in his own voice. This collection contains what is arguably Copper's best short story, "The Janissaries of Emilion," in which a visionary is killed by a product of his own dreams. Copper's first short story was "The Spider" (*The Fifth Pan Book of Horror Stories*, 1964), a straightforward study in terror. It was followed by "Camera Obscura" (*The Sixth Pan Book of Horror Stories*, 1965), about revenge from the grave. Both of these stories are written from a personal perspective on terror. Copper likes to bring the reader into the narrator's mind and follow the gradual mental degradation amidst rising fright. More powerful, however, was "The Grey House," a vivid haunted-house story which presages Stephen King's *The Shining* in its evocation of possession. Another powerful story from this period, one which demonstrates Copper's interest in and knowledge of the cinema, was "Amber Print" in which two collectors discover an unknown and, it transpires, haunted print of *The Cabinet of Dr. Caligari*.

There was a period in the early 1970s when Copper was becoming recognized as one of Britain's premier horror writers, and stories like "The Academy of Pain" and "The House By the Tarn" added to this reputation. Unfortunately dwindling markets limited Copper's output, but the occasional outpourings of his typewriter (Copper refuses to upgrade to a computer) became more polished as a result, losing some of that repetitiveness that was becoming apparent in his later collections. "Wish You Were Here" (*Horror for Christmas*, 1992), for instance, is a long haunted-house story where Copper uses the space to gradually develop the sense of wrongness until the final explosive denouement. Because he is able to bring to the story his wide experience of horror fiction and his ability to create an almost Victorian atmosphere he is able to produce a modern-day ghost story which packs the punch of a century of supernatural fiction.

Basil Copper remains the most complete traditionalist working in the field of horror fiction today.

—Mike Ashley

COSTELLO, Matthew J(ohn)

Nationality: American. **Born:** 1948. **Career:** Computer-game scenarist and novelist. **Address:** c/o Twilight Publishing Co., 18 Oaktree Lane, Sparta, NJ 07871, USA. Lives in New York State.

HORROR, GHOST AND GOTHIC PUBLICATIONS

Novels

Sleep Tight. New York, Zebra, 1987.
Beneath Still Waters. New York, Berkley, 1989.
Child's Play 2 (novelization of screenplay). New York, Jove, 1990.
Midsummer. New York, Diamond, 1990.
Child's Play 3 (novelization of screenplay). New York, Jove, 1991.
Wurm. New York, Diamond, 1991.
Darkborn. New York, Diamond, 1992.
Garden. Sparta, New Jersey, Twilight, 1993.
The Seventh Guest, with Craig Shaw Gardner. New York, Prima, 1995.
Mirage, with F. Paul Wilson. London, Headline, 1996.

OTHER PUBLICATIONS

Novels

Revolt on Majipoor: A Crossroads Adventure in the World of Robert Silverberg's Majipoor (as Matt Costello). New York, Tor, 1987; London, Orbit, 1990.
Robert Heinlein's Glory Road: Fate's Trick (as Matt Costello). New York, Tor, 1988.
Guardians of the Three, Volume Three: The Wizard of Tizare. New York, Bantam, 1989.
Time of the Fox. New York, Roc, 1990.
Hour of the Scorpion. New York, Roc, 1991.
Day of the Snake. New York, Roc, 1992.
Homecoming. New York, Berkley Publishing Group, 1992.
seaQuest DSV: The Fire Below. New York, Ace, and London, Millennium, 1994.

Other

How To Write Science Fiction. New York, Paragon House, 1992.

*   *   *

Matthew Costello made his debut with *Sleep Tight*, a competent but not groundbreaking novel about a small town menaced by the Tall Man, a mysterious figure who haunts the dreams of the local children. After a string of disappearances, nightmares, and other events, the protagonists realize it isn't just overactive imaginations at work and later discover that an ancient being has opened a portal into our universe and is about to hatch a brood of creatures to conquer the world. This overt nod to H. P. Lovecraft is amusing, but only the final chapters foreshadow the much tighter writing and more suspenseful plots that would appear in Costello's later work.

Beneath Still Waters is a far better novel, featuring an entire ghostly town sunk under the small lake created by a new flood-control project. Years after the dam is completed, cracks begin to appear in the structure, divers disappear mysteriously in the drowned town, and even the local plant life seems to take on a sinister personality. Costello's modern ghost story is filled with creepy scenes, particularly those set underwater as divers try to figure out just what's going on and encounter a still inhabited community. This is certainly Costello's most terrifying vision, the effect is even greater because the horrors are described in such matter-of-fact fashion.

Costello, who also has written interesting several science-fiction novels, drew on both genres for his next effort, *Midsummer*. An Antarctic expedition is disrupted by a series of murders, each apparently the result of a psychotic episode. The sole survivor is evacuated to the mainland where he is kept under surveillance by the government, which suspects he has been exposed to some previously unknown contagion. The authorities are correct, because the scientists were infected by a parasite that spreads from one person to another, seizing control of the nervous system, turning each of its hosts into a maniacal killer. The survivor is in fact a carrier and the parasite begins to spread through the small town where he is living, giving rise to a fresh wave of murders. And even after the outbreak seems to have been finally contained, Costello hints that the government will not be content to leave the source in Antarctica uninvestigated, and that it is only a matter of time until the parasite is free again.

Darkborn is a more conventional horror story. A group of teenagers jokingly attempt to conjure up a demon, and during the ceremony one of their number dies tragically. Although the fatality is dismissed as an accident and gradually fades from their memories, many years later they discover that they did in fact succeed in summoning an evil creature into the world. Not only that, the demon is still around, and all of their lives are in jeopardy unless they can find a way to send it back to Hell. Their only chance may lie in mentally journeying back through time to prevent the ceremony from ever taking place.

Wurm rivals *Beneath Still Waters* as Costello's most terrifying novel, although its mood is entirely different. It strongly resembles *Midsummer* in its basic premise. There's another parasite, this one living in the remote depths of the ocean until inadvertently brought to the surface by scientists. The creatures seize control of human bodies and turn them against one another, breeding and spreading themselves with incredible speed. Panic seizes the world as the parasites reach major cities. The military finally establishes something approaching control, since the parasites cannot stray far from the coastline, but in the final chapter we discover that they have mutated, and that they may be able to spread overland.

The shudders are more visceral and more explicit, torn bodies, repulsive creatures, more emphasis on the physical and visceral than the intellectual. Costello proves himself equally adept with a fast-paced action format, and was interested enough in his theme to write a short sequel to *Wurm* in 1993. *The Garden* depicts a world in chaos. The parasites can now move overland, infect people at will, and the world is descending into chaos. It's a logical development of the original story, with a couple of interesting plot twists, but doesn't really match the original novel.

Costello is perhaps best known for having written the basic story for the computer game *The Seventh Guest* and its sequel *The Eleventh Hour*. With Craig Shaw Gardner, he later wrote a novel based loosely on the first game. *The Seventh Guest* is a haunted-house tale. Stauf was a brilliant but twisted toymaker whose toys sapped the lives of the children who owned them. As a final act of revenge against a world he despises, Stauf invites a group of characters to visit his house, which is filled with tricks, traps and puzzles. One of their number holds the key to survival for all, but he may not realize his own powers.

An occasional short-story writer, Costello has written of a vampire trapped on the *Titanic* in "Deep Sleep," of Frankenstein's monster on display in a Coney Island museum in "My Coney Island Baby," of zombies among us in "Corporate Takeover," and werewolves in "Nick of Time." His most interesting shorts are "Abuse" and "Unfortunate Obsession," both of which deal with murderous impulses, one born of sexual intensity, the other of guilt. Costello also wrote the novelizations of the horror movies *Child's Play 2* and *Child's Play 3*.

Costello has demonstrated himself to be a flexible writer who is just as at ease writing science fiction or straight suspense as he is in the horror field. His short stories are competent but rely heavily on plot tricks and surprises, unlike his novels which frequently derive their greatest strength from terrifying imagery. *Beneath Still Waters* is filled with unsettling scenes. *Wurm*, though less subtle, is powerfully written and genuinely frightening.

—Don D'Ammassa

COSTELLO, Sean

Nationality: American. **Address:** c/o Pocket Books, 1230 Avenue of the Americas, New York, NY 10020, USA.

HORROR, GHOST AND GOTHIC PUBLICATIONS

Novels

Eden's Eyes. New York, Pocket, 1989.
The Cartoonist. New York, Pocket, 1990.
Captain Quad. New York, Pocket, 1991.

*   *   *

One of the marks of a superior writer in any genre, but particularly in horror fiction, is the ability to hold the reader's attention even when it appears that we know exactly what is happening and what is yet to occur. Sean Costello's first novel, *Eden's Eyes*, was remarkable not only because it managed to do so, but because the author has more than a few tricks up his sleeve and manages some genuine surprises in the closing chapters.

The basic plot is not particularly new. Eden Crowell was an unpleasant young man whose death provides some benefit to others when his father agrees to several organ transplants, most notably his eyes. Eden's mother, a religious fanatic, is outraged and driven to insanity by the loss of her son, whom she refuses to believe is really dead. She kills her husband and one of the doctors and vows to track down the recipients of various parts of her son's body. A young child and a homeless man, both organ recipients, are brutally murdered, their bodies literally torn apart, the implants missing from the scene. The major protagonist is Karen Lockhart, the beautiful young woman who received Eden's eyes, and who gets glimpses of the murders in her dreams, as though those dead eyes were present in the room when the murders were done. Her doctors have her half-convinced that these visions are hallucinations originating in her guilt about recovering the ability to see at the expense of Eden Crowell's life, but Karen cannot accept the explanation. The details she remembers from the dreams are too close to actual physical evidence found at the murder scenes.

Costello provides a triple threat to build the suspense. Eden's mother is obviously a murderer, quite capable of the mutilations. Less obvious is Eden himself, dead but perhaps risen to reclaim his missing organs, an explanation that would account for Karen's uncanny visions. And finally there's an obsessed but rejected admirer determined that Karen will be his or belong to no one at all. He is prepared to remove her eyes by force, convinced that her rejection of him resulted from her ability to see how ugly he is. Costello makes excellent use of misdirection and an entire sequences of climaxes to wind up the action. A very impressive first novel whose promise was reflected in Costello's second novel, *The Cartoonist*.

A group of young scientists are driving around after drinking excessively when they accidentally strike and kill a young child. Terrified that this will jeopardize their careers and convinced that there are not witnesses to the accident, the three men conceal the body and make a pact never to speak of the incident again. Years pass and it appears that they've gotten away with it, but justice will not be denied. Now a successful psychiatrist, the driver is called upon to treat an aging, senile patient who draws pictures of terrible events and tragedies that have not yet occurred. Gradually the doctor becomes convinced that his patient actually sees the future, and transforms what he perceives into the drawings. When the cartoonist draws a caricature of the doctor's family, dead, he is desperate to discover a way to avert their fate, unaware that his long-concealed crime is actually the key to their survival. And is the Cartoonist seeing the future, or perhaps shaping it? Is this all a coincidence, or does the Cartoonist actually know about his doctor's long-concealed crime, and has he used his unique power to exact a terrible retribution?

What makes *The Cartoonist* particularly memorable is the protagonist's characterization. Despite his inexcusable crime, the doctor is basically a decent person who succumbed to weakness at a critical moment. The Cartoonist, who seems to feel justified in claiming an eye for an eye, is undeniably a villain, but like Eden Crowell's mother, motivated by what he sees as justice and balance rather than some innate desire to do evil. The tension and contradictions within the viewpoint character lend an extra depth to the novel which avoids the stereotypes of most similar stories.

Costello's third and most recent novel is *Captain Quad*. Peter Gardner seems to have everything going for him. He's handsome, an accomplished athlete and musician, gifted with a remarkable intelligence. Then a motorcycle accident leaves him paralyzed from the neck down, confined to a bed for the rest of his life. Or is he? As his anger turns to insanity, Gardner turns in upon himself, developing his mental powers until he achieves the impossible. He can astrally project himself out of his body and travel the world at will, invisible and unstoppable.

Gardner turns his anger against those around him, his alcoholic mother, his ex-fianceé, his brother, and his doctor. When his brother becomes romantically involved with the woman he still hopes to possess physically, Gardner's murderous rage overcomes his discretion and he manifests himself, warning his brother that he faces something no longer entirely human. When he finally gathers the courage to act, it's too late; Gardner has found a way to continue to exist independent of his physical body, even if that paralyzed shell should be destroyed. A darker, more pessimistic novel that Costello's previous novels.

Captain Quad was the last novel to appear by Costello, who has not written any short fiction in the genre. Highly regarded by many of his fellow writers, Costello's career seems to have been cut short by the genre's waning American popularity in the 1990s.

—Don D'Ammassa

COUNSELMAN, Mary Elizabeth

Nationality: American. **Born:** Birmingham, Alabama, 19 November 1911. **Family:** Married in 1941. **Career:** Poet and short-story writer, mainly for pulp magazines. **Died:** 3 May 1994.

HORROR, GHOST AND GOTHIC PUBLICATIONS

Short Stories

Half in Shadow. London, Consul, 1964; revised edition, Sauk City, Wisconsin, Arkham House, 1978.

Poetry

The Face of Fear and Other Poems. N.p., 1984.

*   *   *

In the introduction to the American edition of her collection *Half in Shadow*, Mary Elizabeth Counselman articulates her personal philosophy of fantasy. "Fantasy is man's magic key to the creaking door of that Other World that is the misty, imaginary, spiritual counterpart of what some choose to call 'broad daylight' in our workaday experience." This is not a terribly sophisticated idea on which to base an aesthetic of fantasy writing, yet it sums up the simplicity that is the hallmark of Counselman's fiction, and that has helped to keep her weird tales in circulation long after the markets for which they were originally written have disappeared.

Counselman's fiction began appearing in *Weird Tales* in 1933, where she would publish sporadically for almost 20 years. Her first stories were competent if unremarkable efforts indistinguishable from other fare filling the magazine's back pages. "The Accursed Isle" in the November 1933 issue showed a bit more ambition. A suspenseful tale in the "and then there were none" vein, it tells of a group of castaways whose numbers are depleted nightly by an anonymous murderer in their midst. Only two survivors are left by the time a rescue ship appears, and Counselman plays on reader expectations that the killer's identity will out—up to the final words of the narrative.

With her next tale, Counselman hit her high-water mark as a fantasist. "The Three Marked Pennies" (1934) is a puzzle story set in an quiet rural town whose citizens awaken one morning to find anonymously posted signs announcing a strange contest: Three pennies, each marked with a triangle, square or circle, will be circulated in the town's money. On a designated day, the people who possess the coins will be given "gifts" symbolized by the specific markings: a fortune in money, a cruise around the world, or death. The story ends with the coins in the hands of the three people least likely to benefit from their respective rewards, but not before weeks of guessing and speculation among the townsfolk as to which coin symbolizes what fate reveals that they are not the community united by common beliefs and values that they once thought they were. Terse and sardonic, "The Three Marked Pennies" proved one of the most popular stories ever published in *Weird Tales* and has since become Counselman's most reprinted work.

Counselman never duplicated the success of "The Three Marked Pennies," even when she wrote a follow-up tale featuring one of its characters, "The Web of Silence," and another puzzle story, "The Devil's Lottery," which reprises its plot virtually scene by scene. Nevertheless, certain key elements of the story can be found in almost all of her writing. Counselman's characters are invariably just plain folk whose mundane lives do not admit the possibility of the fantastic. "Mark, Jeb, and I—children of the Depression and the Second World War—were not inclined to believe anything we couldn't see or touch" observes the narrator of "The Green Window." Their encounters with the uncanny are usually quiet, personal experiences touched off by an inconsequential event. "Such little, little things can light the fuse of disaster, can't they?" reflects the heroine of "The Breeze and I" (1947), who finds herself endowed with the power to control the wind after muttering a few phrases found in an obscure book. "A word, a right-turn at some intersection, a cigarette stub tossed into a dry gutter, a foolish harmless little joke." The outcome of these experiences are, as a character in "Drifting Atoms" puts it, a sobering appreciation of "how close we are to the weird and the unbelievable even in the most ordinary settings."

In many of Counselman's stories, the supernatural is rendered ambiguously and its explanation is of secondary importance to the human dramas it catalyses. "The Three Marked Pennies," "The Devil's Lottery" and "The Web of Silence" explain away, or never explain at all, the phenomena that disturb the peace of their small towns and rupture the bonds that have hitherto joined their people together. The tone of narration in "The Breeze and I" suggests that the narrator is a madwoman who only thinks she has developed the magic powers that have ruined her, and it is not impossible that the malefactors of "The Bonan of Balaweda" and "Night Court" are motivated by feelings of personal guilt rather than the ghosts of their victims. When the supernatural is not ambiguous, Counselman's favoured manifestations are ghosts. The spirit of family members protect and sustain their survivors in "The House of Shadows" and "Mommy," and a ghost town warns a newly married couple of impending disaster in "Twister." No

doubt Counselman was thinking of these stories when she wrote "Most of my 'ghoulies and ghosties and long-legged beasties' are allies and not enemies of humankind, working to aid my protagonists rather than to sneak up and pounce on them in the darkness." In fact, in just as many of her tales the supernatural expresses itself malevolently or becomes a dangerous tool in the hands of evil people.

Most of Counselman's stories are set in towns that might be found anywhere in America, but a handful depend on the atmosphere and local colour of her native South for their power. "Seventh Sister" and "The Unwanted" are sentimental dark fantasies built around backwoods superstitions. "The Tree's Wife" draws on a staple of southern folklore, the multi-generational hillbilly family feud, while "The Shot Tower Ghost" is based on a legend from the American Civil War. "Parasite Mansion" is a brooding southern Gothic replete with a decaying plantation, a degenerate family with skeletons in the closet and an imprisoned heroine.

Although most of Counselman's horror and fantasy stories— and her poems—appeared in *Weird Tales*, she also contributed to the mystery and detective pulps and placed a few borderline fantasies in *Jungle Stories*. The fiction and verse she wrote in the post-pulp years for August Derleth's Arkham House anthologies and the small press is indistinguishable in theme and style from her work for the pulps. Her total weird fiction legacy amounts to only some three dozen stories, each a fair representative of her simple but by no means artless craft.

—Stefan Dziemianowicz

COYNE, John (P.)

Nationality: American. **Born:** 10 October 1937. **Education:** St. Louis University; Western Michigan University, M.A. in English. **Family:** Married Judy Wederholt. **Career:** Volunteer in the Peace Corps; freelance writer from 1971; has also written nonfiction on the subject of alternative education.

HORROR, GHOST AND GOTHIC PUBLICATIONS

Novels

The Legacy (novelization of screenplay). New York, Berkley, and London, Coronet, 1979.
The Piercing. New York, Putnam, 1979.
The Searing. New York, Putnam, 1980.
Hobgoblin. New York, Putnam, 1981.
The Shroud. New York, Berkley, 1983.
The Hunting Season. New York, Macmillan, 1987.
The Fury. New York, Warner, 1989.
Child of Shadows. New York, Warner, 1990.

OTHER PUBLICATIONS

Novel

Brothers and Sisters. New York, Penguin, 1985.

*   *   *

John Coyne has threatened to become one of the major writers in the genre right from the outset of his career, but he has never quite managed to achieve the level of popularity that would make him a serious rival of King, Koontz, Straub and others. His debut novel, *The Legacy*, was actually a film novelization, the expansion of a story by Jimmy Sangster, and a much better work than the mediocre film upon which it is based. Six people are invited to the remote home of a rich but dying man who promises to make one of them the heir to all of his wealth and occult power. But one by one the guests begin to die, each in a different way, until only two survive. Despite the straightforward, simplistic plot, Coyne manages to create and maintain a genuinely suspenseful atmosphere throughout. His first original novel, *The Piercing,* appeared that same year and was a far superior work. Betty Sue is an unlikely saint, but she manifests stigmata every week, so predictably that the events become a national sensation, covered by live television. Millions of people believe her to be touched by God, but organized religions dismiss her as a fake. One priest, however, believes that the effects are genuine, but that they are inspired by Satanic rather than angelic forces, and sets out to prove his theory. A haunting, disturbing novel with an intelligent and richly complex storyline and a satisfyingly thrilling ending.

Coyne followed up with *The Searing*, an even less predictable work. The small community of Renaissance Village is the setting for a very bizarre phenomenon; each evening every woman in the town simultaneously experiences a moment of extreme sexual pleasure. The downside is that at the same time, someone or something is claiming the lives of local infants. The key is an autistic child who is the conduit through whom an extraterrestrial force is working in Renaissance Village. The science-fictional explanation of what's actually happening is disappointingly unconvincing after an excellent buildup. *Hobgoblin* has another interesting premise. Scott Gardiner is a classic nerd, so wrapped up in fantasy role-playing games that he sometimes has difficulty distinguishing reality from imagination. In fact, Scott believes that the various monsters from his game are real, and he begins seeing them at home and at school, even though they're invisible to everyone else. To convince everyone he's telling the truth, Scott organizes a Halloween party, an event at which everyone, and everything, will take off its mask. Where *The Searing* floundered toward the end, *Hobgoblin* picks up speed steadily and concludes with a series of well-realized shocks and thrills.

The Shroud is a partial reprise of *The Piercing*. This time the manifestation is of a brooding man in funeral garb, who appears mysteriously to a troubled young priest. Is this the figure of Jesus Christ, a miracle of some similar variety, or is it a temptation sent by the minions of Hell? The implications grow more complex as the priest seeks the truth, which threatens to undermine the stability of the entire church. The protagonist of *The Hunting Season* is a young woman recently married, who moves to the remote community of Mad River Mountain. There she hopes to diplomatically investigate the ingrown culture of that region, only to discover that it holds secrets far more bizarre and dangerous than she suspected. Dwarflike humans live concealed in the woods, and the man she loves has fallen prey to a communal madness that may claim all their lives. *The Hunting Season* is Coyne's strongest novel, controlled, intelligent, and nicely resolved.

The Fury, on the other hand, was very disappointing. Jennifer Winters is outwardly the perfect urban professional, attractive, intelligent, and self confident. But she conceals a dark secret. When angered, she falls into a rage born of primitive racial memories, and her response to aggression is brutal and deadly. Jennifer is the reincarnation of an ancient hunter, and she eventually is locked in combat with another of her kind in an anachronistic duel to the death. Unfortunately, the plot this time is painfully contrived. Muggers and other villains just happen to cross her path frequently enough to provide several deaths and dismemberments. By the time she gets to her real enemy, the reader is likely to be jaded by the destruction and uninterested in the survival of either party.

Child of Shadows was a return to better form. Melissa is a jaded social worker who can no longer stand the hopelessness of the inner city. She rescues Adam, a feral child who lives in the subway system, and takes him to a remote area of North Carolina. There she sets out to make a new life for the two of them, but many of her neighbours resent outsiders, and their fears are bolstered by a series of murders and mutilations. Is Adam responsible? And if so, could his influence be affecting Melissa's personality as well?

Coyne has also written a number of good shorter works. "Snow Man" looks inside the mind of a Peace Corps volunteer who can't quite see the viewpoint of his students. Jealousy and lust lead to disaster in Africa in "The Ecology of Reptiles." In "Flight," a man kidnaps his infant son from his wife (or does he?), and falls into the hands of an insane man who believes that the baby isn't really human (and he might not be). "The Crazy Chinaman" features an unhappy man who commits suicide over and over again, to the dismay of his companions. A city man tries to beat back the encroachment of a virulent fungus in "A Cabin in the Mountains," the best of Coyne's short stories. Although the shorter pieces are interesting, John Coyne is clearly more at home with the novel.

—Don D'Ammassa

CRAWFORD, F(rancis) Marion

Nationality: American. **Born:** Bagni di Lucca, Tuscany, Italy, 2 August 1854; son of the sculptor Thomas Crawford. **Education:** privately educated in Rome, 1860-66; at St. Paul's School, Concord, New Hampshire, 1866-69; privately in Hatfield Broad Oak, Essex, England, 1870-73; Trinity College, Cambridge, 1873; Technische Hochschule, Karlsruhe, Germany, 1874-76; University of Heidelberg, 1876; University of Rome, 1878. **Family:** Married Elizabeth Berdan in 1884; two daughters and two sons. **Career:** Correspondent, London *Daily Telegraph,* late 1870s; editor, *Indian Herald,* Allahabad, 1879-80; convert to Roman Catholicism, 1880; full-time writer from 1881; lived in Boston, 1881-83, Rome, 1883-84, and Sorrento, Italy, after 1885. **Died:** 9 April 1909.

HORROR GHOST, AND GOTHIC

Novel

The Witch of Prague: A Fantastic Tale. London and New York, Macmillan, 3 vols., 1891.

Short Stories

The Upper Berth. London, Unwin, and New York, Putnam, 1894.
Man Overboard! New York and London, Macmillan, 1903.

Uncanny Tales. London, Unwin, 1911; as *Wandering Ghosts*, New York, Macmillan, 1911; expanded edition, as *For the Blood Is the Life*, Clarkston, Georgia, White Wolf, 1996.

The Dead Smile. West Warwick, Rhode Island, Necronomicon Press, 1986.

OTHER PUBLICATIONS

Novels

Mr. Isaacs: A Tale of Modern India. London and New York, Macmillan, 1882.

Doctor Claudius: A True Story. London and New York, Macmillan, 1883.

To Leeward. 2 vols., London, Chapman and Hall, 1883; 1 vol., Boston, Houghton, Mifflin, 1884; revised edition, New York and London, Macmillan, 1893.

A Roman Singer. Boston, Houghton, Mifflin, and London, Macmillan, 1884.

An American Politician. London, Chapman and Hall, and Boston and New York, Houghton, Mifflin, 1884.

Zoroaster. London and New York, Macmillan, 1885.

A Tale of a Lonely Parish. London and New York, Macmillan, 1886.

Saracinesca. 3 vols., Edinburgh and London, Blackwood, 1887; 1 vol., New York, Macmillan, 1887.

Marzio's Crucifix. London and New York, Macmillan, 1887.

Paul Patoff. London and New York, Macmillan, 1887.

With the Immortals. London and New York, Macmillan, 2 vols., 1888.

Greifenstein. London and New York, Macmillan, 1889.

Sant' Ilario. London and New York, Macmillan, 1889.

A Cigarette-Maker's Romance. London and New York, Macmillan, 1890.

Khaled: A Tale of Arabia. London and New York, Macmillan, 2 vols., 1891.

The Three Fates. London and New York, Macmillan, 1892.

Don Orsino. London and New York, Macmillan, 1892.

The Children of the King. London and New York, Macmillan, 1893.

Pietro Ghisleri. London and New York, Macmillan, 1893.

Marion Darche: A Story without Comment. London and New York, Macmillan, 1893.

Katharine Lauderdale. London and New York, Macmillan, 1894.

Love in Idleness. 1894.

The Ralstons. London and New York, Macmillan, 1895.

Casa Braccio. London and New York, Macmillan, 1895.

Adam Johnstone's Son. London and New York, Macmillan, 1896.

Taquisara. London and New York, Macmillan, 1896.

A Rose of Yesterday. London and New York, Macmillan, 1897.

Corleone. London and New York, Macmillan, 1897.

Via Crucis: A Romance of the Second Crusade. London and New York, Macmillan, 1899.

In the Palace of the King: A Love Story of Old Madrid. London and New York, Macmillan, 1900.

Marietta: A Maid of Venice. London and New York, Macmillan, 1901.

Cecilia: A Story of Modern Rome. New York and London, Macmillan, 1902.

The Heart of Rome: A Tale of the "Lost Water." London and New York, Macmillan, 1903.

Whosoever Shall Offend. London and New York, Macmillan, 1904.

Soprano: A Portrait. London and New York, Macmillan, 1905; as *Fair Margaret,* New York and London, Macmillan, 1905.

A Lady of Rome. London and New York, Macmillan, 1906.

Arethusa. London and New York, Macmillan, 1907.

The Little City of Hope: A Christmas Story. London and New York, Macmillan, 1907.

The Primadonna: A Sequel to Soprano. London and New York, Macmillan, 1908.

The Diva's Ruby: A Sequel to Soprano and Primadonna. London and New York, Macmillan, 1908.

The White Sister. London and New York, Macmillan, 1909.

Stradella: An Old Italian Love Tale. London and New York, Macmillan, 1909.

The Undesirable Governess. London and New York, Macmillan, 1910.

Novels. London and New York, Macmillan, 30 vols., 1919.

Plays

Doctor Claudius, with Harry St. Maur, from the novel by Crawford (produced 1897). London and New York, Macmillan, 1883.

Francesca Da Rimini (produced 1902). New York and London, Macmillan, 1902.

The Ideal Wife, from a work by M. Prage (produced 1912).

The White Sister, with Walter Hackett, from the novel by Crawford. New York, Dramatists, 1937.

Other

Our Silver. N.p., 1881.

The Novel: What It Is. New York and London, Macmillan, 1893.

Constantinople. New York, Scribners, 1895.

Bar Harbor. N.p., 1896.

Ave, Roma Immortalis: Studies from the Chronicles of Rome. 2 vols., New York and London, Macmillan, 1898; revised edition, 1902.

The Rulers of the South: Sicily, Calabria, Malta. 2 vols., New York and London, Macmillan, 1900; as *Southern Italy and Sicily,* and *The Rulers of the South,* London and New York, Macmillan, 1905.

Salve Venetia: Gleanings from Venetian History. 2 vols., New York and London, Macmillan, 1905; as *Venice, The Place and the People,* New York, Macmillan, 1909.

*

Critical Studies: *My Cousin Crawford* by Maud Howe Elliott, 1934; *F. Marion Crawford* by John Pilkington, Jr., 1964; *The American 1890s: Life and Times of a Lost Generation* by Lorzer Ziff, 1966; *An F. Marion Crawford Companion* by John C. Moran, Westport, Connecticut, Greenwood Press, 1981.

*   *   *

Although F. Marion Crawford was in his day a best-selling writer of historical novels, he is now known, if at all, for some very grim and compelling supernatural tales posthumously collected in *Wandering Ghosts*. These tales were written over a 20-year period, from as early as 1885 to around 1908; but the mere fact that Crawford never made the effort to collect them himself appears to indicate his belief that they occupied an insignificant place in his corpus.

In addition to his short stories, Crawford is the author of two fantasy novels, *Zoroaster* and *Khaled: A Tale of Arabia*, as well as a supernatural novel, *The Witch of Prague*. Although each have their flaws, they are all striking works that do not deserve the obscurity into which they have fallen.

Zoroaster purports to be an historical novel about the life of the religious leader Zoroaster (Zarathustra), who probably lived in the sixth century B.C.; but in reality the work is a sort of historical fantasy, with many of the facts (or legends) about Zoroaster's life knowingly discarded in order to present a stirring and dramatic chronicle of love and faith. The novel focuses on the presence of Zoroaster in the court of Belshazzar, and the complicated emotional tangles involving him, his beloved Nehushta, Belshazzar, and his wife Atossa, who loves Zoroaster but is spurned by him and connives his destruction. But the true merits of *Zoroaster* lie not in its convoluted plot but in its fluid, melodic prose style: it is, in effect, a novel-length prose poem, and in this regard can take its place with the work of Oscar Wilde, Walter Pater and Lord Dunsany.

Khaled is a delightful fable of a spirit from the Islamic heaven who, because of some misdeed, is forced to occupy a human form and, before his mortal death, win the love of the princess Zehowah, to whom he is betrothed, in order to attain an immortal soul. As with *Zoroaster*, the novel focuses around a love triangle, this time involving Khaled, Zehowah and the servant girl Almasta; and, like the earlier novel, the prose-poetic style of *Khaled* redeems its somewhat melodramatic plot.

Crawford clearly put more effort into the lengthy novel *The Witch of Prague*. This is the very convoluted story of Unorna, the witch of Prague, and her sardonic partner Keyork Arabian, who attempt to extend the bounds of human life, perhaps indefinitely, through the power of hypnotism. The two have kept an aged man under hypnosis for years in the hope that this process, plus the replacement of his old blood with the blood of a younger man, will rejuvenate him. Although this plot sounds suspiciously like that of Poe's "Facts in the Case of M. Valdemar," the handling is deft, and the then relatively new discipline of psychology is treated almost as if it were tantamount to witchcraft. But the novel becomes bogged down in a love element that takes attention away from the central supernatural phenomenon, in spite of some spectacular hallucination scenes. The fundamental metaphor behind hypnotism—loss of identity or individuality—is probed interestingly, and lends substance to an otherwise drawn-out and melodramatic novel.

But Crawford will occupy a niche in weird fiction largely on the strength of his short stories. The best known of them is "The Upper Berth" (1886), a classic of the first rank that tells of the loathsome entity that haunts a cabin in a passenger ship. The gradual accumulation of horrific details—the porthole that refuses to stay closed; the air of musty dampness in the room; the fact that we never get a good look at the doomed occupant of the upper berth, who leaps to his death on the first night out—creates an intensely potent atmosphere. Less histrionic, and actually quite affecting, are "The Doll's Ghost," in which an aged doll-repairer falls in love with a doll brought to his shop, and "Man Overboard!", another sea-horror tale in which the ghost of a drowned man returns at his twin brother's wedding.

"The Dead Smile" (1899) is, in its atmosphere of horrific gloom, one of the most grippingly terrifying tales ever written, although its "surprise" ending—a man and a woman engaged to be married prove to be brother and sister—is fairly obvious from the start. The very title signals the loathsome perversion of the good that is at the heart of the tale: just as a smile is ordinarily an indication of happiness, so is a "dead smile" suggestive of the grinning of a skeleton and a symbol for the near-incest that is warded off at the story's conclusion. As an instance of lurid, "oh-my-God" horror, "The Dead Smile" has rarely been surpassed. "For the Blood Is the Life" (1905), on the other hand, is merely a confused story of vampirism in which the supernatural premise is seriously flawed. A young woman in Italy is killed by two robbers as she sees them burying their treasure in a mound, and they hurl her body into the pit along with their ill-gotten prize; but in some inexplicable fashion the woman becomes one of the undead, and repeatedly drains the blood of her still-living lover. "The Screaming Skull" (1908) is a weak account of a strange murder and its supernatural revenge.

An uncollected tale that has recently been reprinted, "The King's Messenger" (1907), tells of a dinner party in which one seat is unoccupied; a young woman awaits this guest, and indeed longs for him. Finally he comes: he is Death, and the woman seeks him because she wishes to commit suicide. The entire tale becomes a *double entendre*, as everything the woman says about the expected guest takes on another meaning under the bland conventionality of her words. "The King's Messenger" is an unrecognized jewel of weird fiction.

—S. T. Joshi

CREW, Gary

Nationality: Australian. **Born:** Brisbane, Queensland, 23 September 1947. **Education:** Queensland Institute of Technology, Certificate in Engineering Drafting 1970; Queensland University, B.A. 1979; M.A. (Literature) 1985. **Family:** Married Christine Joy Willis in 1970; two daughters and one son. **Career:** Civil and mechanical engineering design draughtsman 1963-73; high school English teacher, 1974-83; head of English, Aspley and Albany Creek Schools, 1984-90; freelance writer and part-time lecturer in creative writing and publishing, Queensland University of Technology, from 1990. **Awards:** Australian Children's Book of the Year (Older Readers), 1991; Alan Marshall prize for Children's Literature, 1991; NSW Premier's award for children's literature, 1991; Arts Council Senior Literature Fellowship, 1994; Australian Children's Book of the Year (Older Readers), 1994; National Children's Book award, 1994; Australian Picture Book of the Year, 1994 and 1995; "Hungry Mind" Children's Book of Distinction (U.S.), 1996. **Agent:** Franny Kelly, 25 Panorama Crescent, Toowoomba, Queensland 4350, Australia.

HORROR, GHOST AND GOTHIC PUBLICATIONS

Novels

Strange Objects. Melbourne, Reed, and New York, Simon and Schuster, 1990.
No Such Country. Melbourne, Reed, and New York, Simon and Schuster, 1992.

Short Stories

The Bent Back Bridge. Melbourne, Lothian, 1995.
The Barn. Melbourne, Lothian, 1996.
The Well. Melbourne, Lothian, 1996.

Fiction for Children

The Watertower, illustrated by Steven Woolman. Adelaide, ERA, 1994.
Caleb, illustrated by Steven Woolman. Adelaide, ERA, 1996.
The Figures of Julian Ashcroft, illustrated by Hans De Haas. St. Lucia, UQP, 1996.

Other

Editor, *Dark House.* Melbourne, Mammoth, 1995.

OTHER PUBLICATIONS

Novels

The Inner Circle. Melbourne, Reed, and London Reed, 1986.
The House of Tomorrow. Melbourne, Reed, 1988.
Angel's Gate. Melbourne, Reed, and New York, Simon and Schuster, 1993.
Inventing Anthony West. St. Lucia, UQP, 1994.
The Blue Feather, with Michael O'Hara. Melbourne, Reed, 1997.

Fiction for Children

Tracks, illustrated by Gregory Rogers. Melbourne, Lothian, 1992; and New York, Gareth Stevens, 1996.
Lucy's Bay, illustrated by Gregory Rogers. St. Lucia, UQP, 1992.
First Light, illustrated by Peter Gouldthorpe. Melbourne, Lothian, 1993; New York, Gareth Stevens, 1996.
Gulliver in the South Seas, illustrated by John Burge. Melbourne, Lothian, 1994.
The Lost Diamonds of Killiecrankie, illustrated by Peter Gouldthorpe. Melbourne, Lothian, 1995.
Bright Star, illustrated by Anne Spudvilas. Melbourne, Lothian, 1997.

* * *

Gary Crew comes from a mainstream literary background and is recognized as one of Australia's leading writers for young adults, but even so much of his work has horror or Gothic elements. Crew's novels, short stories and picture books often challenge traditional children's story-telling techniques and subjects, and demonstrate his ability to transcend age and genre boundaries. His young-adult novels are frequently cross-over books which can be enjoyed by both teenagers and adults, while his picture books are often aimed at teenage readers.

Crew's first foray into horror was the remarkable novel *Strange Objects*. This book broke new ground in teenage fiction in Australia when it became the first horror novel of any kind to win major literary recognition in that country, including prizes such as the NSW Premier's Literary Award, the NSW State Literary Award, and the prestigious Children's Book of the Year for Older Readers.

Strange Objects begins when a modern-day teenager, Steven Messenger, finds a cache of gruesome relics—an iron pot, a leatherbound journal and a mummified human hand—from the wrecked real-life Dutch vessel *Batavia* which struck uncharted rocks of the coast of Western Australia on 4th June 1629. The Batavia's tale was drenched in blood when over 120 of the shipwreck victims were murdered by fellow survivors. Four months after finding the relics Steven Messenger mysteriously disappears without a trace from outside an isolated roadhouse on the central Western Australian coast. The mystery deepens when Messenger's personal journal is mailed to the Institute of Maritime Archaeology in Perth. As with all of Crew's work the story structure is extremely tight, even when he is working outside traditional techniques. This tale is told with the presentation of 34 items called "The Messenger Documents" which include Messenger's own writings, newspaper articles, police reports, letters and journal extracts, all of which form a gripping multi-layered narrative of intrigue, horror and mystery. *Strange Objects* is arguably one of the best Australian horror novels yet published, and although it was originally published for children, it was later re-released in an adult edition.

Crew followed *Strange Objects* with a borderline horror novel with Gothic undertones called *No Such Country*. It is set in an imaginary Australian small town called New Canaan which is cut off from the rest of the world by sea and swamp. The book is described as a "tale of old guilt, superstition and ghastly secrets" and begins when a series of peculiar events happen which become known to the townsfolk as "signs." *No Such Country* can be categorized as magic realism, but few reviewers (if any) have recognized it as such.

After *No Such Country* Gary Crew wrote a novel which was loosely related to the horror genre. *Angel's Gate*, won the 1994 Australian Children's Book Council Book of the Year Award for Older Readers and the 1994 National Children's Book Award. It is a novel which explores the dark side of humankind. On the surface it is a compelling story of murder in a small rural community, on another level, however, there is an undercurrent of suspicion and mystery pervading a story of alienation and the search or identity.

Crew was the series editor for the "After Dark" series of horror novellas published by Lothian Books. Three of the books are written by Crew. *The Bentback Bridge* is based on his short story "Sleeping Over at Lola's" which tells of a lonely girl who is lured to an isolated old bridge at night by the promise of friendship. *The Barn* is really a fantasy tale with minimal horror. *The Well* is a ghost story about loss, and secrets long denied.

Picture books are another field in which Crew enjoys significant success and continues to experiment and break new ground. His horror/mystery/science-fiction picture book, *The Watertower*, which is illustrated with striking pictures by Adelaide artist Steven Woolman, belongs to a new niche in children's literature, that of the picture book for nine-to-fifteen year old readers. According to Crew it is "based on the notion that children, especially older boys, still love looking at pictures, but are generally intellectually insulted by the childish fare (in both print text and visual text) that they are served up." *The Watertower* was judged by the Children's Book Council of Australia to be the best of the 70 books entered into the picture book category in 1995. The judges described it as a book of "landmark significance which breaks new ground in its unity of text, picture and book design." This is now the fourth time that Gary Crew has won this prestigious award, making him something of a phenomenon in Australian children's publishing.

Crew and Woolman collaborated on a second picture book called *Caleb*, which is more macabre and Gothic than truly horrific. *Caleb* is difficult to categorize, crossing the genre boundaries of science fiction, mystery and dark fantasy. It is set around about 1890, and tells of a 15-year-old scientific child prodigy named Caleb van Dorrn who has been elevated into university because of his fantastic knowledge of entomology. The story is told in a Victorian voice, through the eyes of Caleb's room-mate Stuart Quill. Caleb is a peculiar young man who is actually the son of a very famous entomologist who has disappeared, and little by little, by tracking issues such as evolution and how species survive or don't the reader realizes late in the piece that Caleb is actually in the process of evolving himself, or metamorphosing, and is following the same path as his father and his father before him. Woolman's black-and-white and sepia illustrations are well suited to the tale. Crew's horror picture books are greatly enhanced by the close collaboration between author and artist. In *The Figures of Julian Ashcroft*, for example, the colourful illustrations by Hans De Haas become darker both in tone and subject as the story nears its haunting conclusion.

Gary Crew's horror fiction is not restricted to books alone. Although not a prolific short-story writer he has written a handful of fine horror stories which have been published in a variety of anthologies. "Sleeping Over at Lola's" (which is the basis of his book *The Bentback Bridge*) appeared in *Spine-Chilling: Ten Horror Stories* (1992) edited by Penny Matthews. "Face to Stony Face" appeared in *The Lottery* (1994) edited by Lucy Sussex. "A Breeze off the Esplanade," although not strictly horror, is a darkly disturbing tale which appeared in *Nightmares in Paradise* (1995) edited by Robyn Sheahan, an anthology of stories by Queensland writers which explores the downside of "tropical paradise." "The Staircase," probably Crew's best horror story to date can be found in *Dark House*, a collection of horror stories edited by Crew himself. Three-quarters of the stories in this anthology were recommended in the Datlow and Windling *Year's Best Horror and Fantasy* anthology.

There remains little doubt that Gary Crew is a writer of great talent. His horror fiction is rich in symbolism and metaphor, and whatever genre Crew chooses to write in he explores important human themes such as the search for identity, the mystery of life, the awe of the universe and the mortality of humankind.

—Steven Paulsen and Sean McMullen

CROSS, John Keir

Pseudonyms: Stephen MacFarlane; Susan Morley. **Nationality:** British. **Born:** Carluke, Lanark, Scotland, 19 August 1914. **Family:** Married; one son. **Career:** Worked as insurance clerk, hobo and travelling entertainer prior to 1937; writer for the British Broadcasting Corporation in the drama, variety, features, and *Children's Hour* departments, writing and producing radio plays, including adaptations of stories and books, 1937-46; freelance writer from 1946; co-writer of BBC radio serial *The Archers*, 1962-67. **Died:** 22 January 1967.

HORROR, GHOST AND GOTHIC PUBLICATIONS

Short Stories

The Other Passenger: 18 Strange Stories. London, Westhouse, 1944; Philadelphia, Lippincott, 1946; abridged as *Stories from The Other Passenger*, New York, Ballantine, 1961.

Other

Editor, *Best Horror Stories*. London, Faber, 1957.
Editor, *Best Black Magic Stories*. London, Faber, 1960.
Editor, *Best Horror Stories 2*. London, Faber, 1965.

OTHER PUBLICATIONS

Novels

Mistress Glory (as Susan Morley). New York, Dial Press, 1948; as *Glory*, as John Keir Cross, London, Laurie, 1951.
Juniper Green. London, Laurie, 1952; as Susan Morley, New York, Dial Press, 1953.

Novels for Children

Studio J Investigates: Spy Story for Children. London, Lunn, 1944.
The Angry Planet: An Authentic First-Hand Account of a Journey to Mars in the Spaceship "Albatross". London, Lunn, 1945; New York, Coward McCann, 1946.
Jack Robinson. London, Lunn, 1945.
The Owl and the Pussycat. London, Lunn, 1946; as *The Other Side of Green Hills*, New York, Coward McCann, 1947.
The Man in Moonlight. London, Westhouse, 1947.
The White Magic. London, Westhouse, 1947.
Blackadder: A Tale of the Days of Nelson. London, Muller, 1950; New York, Dutton, 1951.
The Flying Fortunes in an Encounter with Rubberface! London, Muller, 1952; as *The Stolen Sphere: A Journey and a Mystery*, New York, Dutton, 1953.
SOS from Mars. London, Hutchinson, 1954; as *The Red Journey Back: A First-Hand Account of the Second and Third Martian Expeditions by the Space-Ships "Albatross" and "Comet"*, New York, Coward McCann, 1954.
The Dancing Tree. London, Hutchinson, 1955.
Elizabeth in Broadcasting. London, Chatto and Windus, 1957.
The Sixpenny Year: A Country Adventure. London, Hutchinson, 1957.

Novels for Children as Stephen MacFarlane

The Blue Egg. London, Lunn, 1944.
Detectives in Greasepaint. London, Lunn, 1944.
Lucy Maroon: The Car That Loved a Policeman. London, Lunn, 1944.
Mr. Bosanko and Other Stories. London, Lunn, 1944.
The Strange Tale of Sally and Arnold. London, Lunn, 1944.
The Story of a Tree. London, Lunn, 1946.

Plays

Radio Plays: *The Kraken Wakes,* from the novel by John Wyndham; *The Archers* series, with others, 1962-67; *The Brockenstein Affair*, from a work by George R. Preedy, 1962; *The Free Fishers,* from the novel by John Buchan, 1964; *Bird of Dawning,* from the novel by John Masefield, 1965; *Be Thou My Judge,* from a work by James Wood, 1967; *The Green Isle of the Great Deep*, 1986.

Television Play: *She Died Young,* 1961.

Other

Aspect of Life: An Autobiography of Youth. London, Selwyn and Blount, 1937.
Editor, *The Children's Omnibus.* London, Lunn, 1948.

*   *   *

To modern readers, especially those on the western side of the Atlantic, John Keir Cross is a distant, elusive figure. His extensive work for the BBC radio network is forgotten and essentially untraceable; his books are all long out of print and difficult to locate; his best-remembered works in America—the science-fiction novels for children *The Angry Planet, The Stolen Sphere* and *The Red Journey Back*—are undistinguished and convey little in the way of a personal voice; and the available biographical information is sketchy, so that, for example, one learns that he had a wife and son only by reading an anecdote in *Best Black Magic Stories*. On the basis of such data, one could construct many different pictures of Cross, but the most romantic scenario would be that he was a quietly frustrated man, dutifully working on routine projects to support himself and his family while tormented by the grander ambitions he never revealed and could never fulfil.

Thus envisioned, Cross would be much like the characters who inhabit *The Other Passenger*, his collection of stories that constitute the major reason why he should be remembered today. Although Cross divides his stories into ten "Portraits" and eight "Mysteries," they all are character-driven and all centre on something mysterious. Examining ordinary people at various levels of British society—aristocrats, working-class merchants and teachers, artists and musicians—Cross finds them filled with their own quiet frustrations, suppressed longings and unanswered questions. They are usually impelled to some bold action to satisfy their desires, yet the resulting events or revelations are invariably unpleasant. Thus, while stories often lack an overt horrific element or atmosphere, they present and endorse the underlying ethos of horror: stay where you are, ask no questions, make no changes, or suffer the consequences.

While congruent in mood, the forms of Cross's cautionary tales vary. Some completely lack fantastic elements: "Hands," "Amateur Gardening" and "Couleur de Rose" depict frustrated people who are driven to murder and then make little effort to avoid arrest. "The Last of the Romantics" is the ironic tale of a man who regularly goes to a restaurant, orders two cups of tea, and hangs one of them from a lamp chain; it turns out that he is a hangman once forced to execute the woman he loved. In "Liebestraum" an older man commits suicide when he learns that the 16-year-old girl he loves has other suitors. "Cyclamen Brown" describes a female singer who always wears a mask because she was scarred by a jealous lover; "Another Planet" involves a woman who goes insane when her lover is executed; "Valdemosa" is a vignette about Frederick Chopin and George Sand's dreary sojourn in Majorca; and "Absence of Mind" involves a woman named Maud Carpenter who believes she shoplifted a valuable pendant, though she actually purchased it.

Other stories involve overtly macabre features or apparent supernatural events, though everything is eventually explained. "Miss Thing and the Surrealists" features an artist who is arrested when his lover discovers that the female body parts in his eccentric studio are not wax, but pieces of the woman he murdered, and "Music, When Soft Voices Die" describes a wealthy man who apparently murdered his wife and her lover and made their skulls into African drums. In "The Glass Eye" a lonely woman falls in love with a handsome ventriloquist, only to discover that the "ventriloquist" is actually a dummy while the "dummy" is a misshapen dwarf. "The Little House" features a greedy couple who move the coffin of their recently deceased daughter out of the house to earn an extra pound by renting her room. And in "The Lovers" a none-too-bright electrician believes he has seen the ghost of a customer's wife, but in reality the husband, a taxidermist, merely stuffed and preserved her body and left it sitting in one room.

Of the four unquestionably supernatural stories, "Petronella Pan" singularly veers toward science fiction in describing a mother, obsessed with her beautiful baby, who uses her husband's research into longevity to successfully halt her baby's growth, so that she can continue to take him to baby shows even as his mind matures. In "Clair de Lune" a man visiting an estate encounters a ghost who tells him, puzzled, that "It is not you they are waiting for." When another guest, afflicted by a hereditary tendency to commit suicide, finally kills himself, the visitations stop. "Esmerelda" is another tale of an ordinary man driven to murder—this time, his repulsive wife—but he abandons plans to flee after an eerie visit from the beautiful daughter he dreamed of but never had. The final story, "The Other Passenger," about a man who commits suicide because he is haunted by reports of a strange doppelganger appearing in different places and being seen by his friends, presents what Cross wishes to serve as the volume's unifying conceit: that each person always feels constantly accompanied by an "unexplained presence," a strange "Other Passenger"; yet the metaphor seems inadequate to describe all the misgivings afflicting his characters.

What is most striking about these stories is their deliberate and self-conscious artlessness; narrators regularly apologize for rambling on about unimportant things, not stating things clearly, and not being able to fully explain the events they recount. Through this style, more than his statements, Cross conveys the message that life is full of unknowns and uncertainties, making all of our lives like little horror stories—as also suggested by this comment in "Absence of Mind": "people as trivial as Mrs. Carpenter are, in their own way, as tragic victims of the Other Passenger as Dr. Faustus or George Gordon, Lord Byron."

Over a decade after *The Other Passenger* appeared, Cross returned to horror as editor of three anthologies. One of them, *Best Black Magic Stories*, features another typical Cross story, "Mothering Sunday," about a cold, disturbing young man who is apparently the son of a magically animated snowman, while the "Introduction" and "Envoi" relate a true story that might have been offered as fiction: the night after Cross's unsuccessful attempt to ritually summon the Devil on live radio, his son was attacked by a large and vicious rat—coincidence? or the Devil responding to that summons according to his own schedule? Like his pathetic, mystified characters, Cross cannot be sure.

—Gary Westfahl

CROWLEY, Aleister

Pseudonym: Master Theiron. **Nationality:** British. **Born:** Edward Alexander Crowley, in Leamington, Warwickshire, 12 October 1875. **Education:** Cambridge University. **Family:** Married

Rose Kelly (divorced). **Career:** Inherited wealth and travelled widely; occultist, and reputed "black magician"; member, Hermetic Order of the Golden Dawn, 1898-1908; founded various similar organizations; author of copious self-published occult writings. **Died:** 1 December 1947.

HORROR, GHOST AND GOTHIC PUBLICATIONS

Novel

Moonchild: A Prologue. London, Mandrake Press, 1929.

Short Stories

The Stratagem and Other Stories. London, Mandrake Press, 1929; expanded edition, Brighton, East Sussex, Temple Press, 1990.

OTHER PUBLICATIONS

Novel

Diary of a Drug Fiend. London, Collins, 1922; New York, Dutton, 1923.

Poetry

Songs of the Spirit. London, K. Paul, 1898.
Tannhauser: A Story of All Time. London, K. Paul, 1902.
The Argonauts. Foyers, Society for the Propagation of Religious Truth, 1904.
Orpheus: A Lyrical Legend. Foyers, Society for the Propagation of Religious Truth, 2 vols., 1905.
Ambergris. N.p., 1910.

Other

Magick in Theory and Practice (as Master Theiron). Paris (by subscription only), 1929.
The Confessions of Aleister Crowley. London, Mandrake Press, 2 vols., 1929.

*

Critical Studies: *The Great Beast: The Life of Aleister Crowley* by John Symonds, London, Rider, 1951; *The Magical World of Aleister Crowley* by Francis King, London, Arros, 1977; *Aleister Crowley: The Nature of the Beast* by Colin Wilson, Wellingborough, Northamptonshire, Aquarian Press, 1987; *King of the Shadow Realm* by John Symonds, London, Duckworth, 1989.

*   *   *

Edward Crowley, who preferred to call himself Aleister, was a rebel against the stern Protestantism of his wealthy parents, who were members of the Plymouth Brethren. He spent his considerable inheritance on travel, high living and bombastic self-decoration. Unlike most such rebels, however—who could be reasonably content with aggressive agnosticism and a mildly scandalous lifestyle—Crowley was determined in his apostasy to an unprec-

edented extreme. He cultivated by degrees a new and exceedingly exotic species of satanic Paganism, which established him as the most flamboyant exponent of 20th-century lifestyle fantasy. He took a positive delight in such sobriquets as "the most evil man in the world" and "the Great Beast," and became an inspiration to subsequent generations of desperate outsiders. In 1898 Crowley joined the Hermetic Order of the Golden Dawn and attempted to take it over, eventually abandoning the resultant splinters in 1908 to form his own Argentinum Astrum, whose creed and ritual he was able to organize from scratch (with the alleged aid of his tutelary spirit Aiwass), incorporating various kinds of sexual intercourse into its ceremonies. His copious writings in association with this mission are among the foundation-stones of modern occultism. Like all dedicated lifestyle fantasists Crowley drew considerable inspiration from literary sources—many of which he listed with tongue-in-cheek annotations in the Curriculum for would-be initiates of the Argentinum Astrum in *Magick in Theory and Practice.* He thought very highly of his own poetic endeavours, almost all of which embraced occult or mythological themes, but his work in that vein invites discussion under the heading of fantasy rather than horror. His prose work makes more use of the conventional apparatus of horror fiction, although he would not have regarded himself as a writer of horror stories.

Crowley's most substantial work of prose fiction was *Moonchild,* a *roman à clef* including characters based on his acquaintances in the Golden Dawn, including W. B. Yeats and Arthur Machen. The plot concerns two societies of rival magicians who become actively opposed by virtue of an experiment to incarnate the eponymous supernatural being. The early phases of the story, which spare no effort in poking fun at Crowley's ex-collaborators, are more amusing than horrific, and it seems that the author could not take the antics of the characters—no matter that they included a thinly-disguised version of himself—at all seriously. Reality eventually intrudes upon the occult games in the form of World War I, at whose outbreak the hero shows unexpected sensitivity in deciding that lifestyle fantasy, however serious its intent and however profound its potential, really ought to be put away for the duration.

The later novel *Diary of a Drug Fiend,* which has no supernatural content although it contains a similarly vain self-portrait, has a few deft touches of horror in its analysis of the discomfiting phenomena of addiction (based, of course, in experience). Crowley's two-volume autobiography is an interesting exercise combining self-aggrandizement with a certain measure of fanciful but not unrevealing self-analysis, and might be classified by cynical critics as a work of occult fiction with many interesting Gothic touches.

Three shorter items are assembled in *The Stratagem and Other Stories,* but two of them are disappointingly mundane as well as unhorrific. The third, however—and by far the most impressive—is "The Testament of Magdalen Blair," which is very definitely a horror story. The psychically gifted Mrs. Blair is able to observe the slow death of her husband and the disintegration of his personality caused by the "demon" of Bright's disease. The progress of the disease is recorded in scrupulously horrible detail, and death does not put an end to the flow of information—which eventually reveals that the soul's reunion with the Universal Consciousness is far from paradisal. The novelette is one of the most extreme literary formulations of Decadent sensibility and entitles Crowley to a place of honour in the great tradition of horror fiction—but it must be admitted nevertheless that his primary importance within that tradition was as an example to others.

Crowley contributed a substantial legacy to the work of writers who knew him (and mostly took against him). He provided the primary model for 20th-century portraits of the black magician, freely acknowledged as the source of the miscellaneous anti-heroes and villains of Edgar Jepson's *No. 19*, Somerset Maugham's *The Magician*, H. Russell Wakefield's "He Cometh and He Passeth By!", Dennis Wheatley's *The Devil Rides Out* and numerous similar figures featured in the work of Arthur Machen, Dion Fortune and Elliot O'Donnell (to name but a few). Those who knew him best (Machen, Jepson and Fortune) tended to be more sympathetic to his poses and delusions than those who took an instant dislike to him (Maugham and Wheatley) but the evident success of his aspiration to be the Great Beast is measurable in the authentic charisma possessed by all these characters and the real sense of danger encapsulated in their portrayal. Crowley's lifestyle fantasy remains a constant source of inspiration to many of today's unorthodox thinkers, receiving abundant homage not merely in fiction but also scholarly fantasy and Gothic rock music. Without his own input 20th-century horror fiction would have lost very little, but without his inspiration it would almost certainly be less colourful and less sensational, and perhaps noticeably less prolific.

—Brian Stableford

CROWTHER, Peter

Nationality: British. **Born:** Leeds, Yorkshire, 4 July 1949. **Education:** Leeds Grammar School; Leeds College of Technology, 1966-68. **Family:** Married Nicky Hassam in 1976; two sons. **Career:** Computer operations manager, Leeds Permanent Building Society, 1968-80; publications editor, Leeds Permanent, 1980-87; head of communications, Leeds Permanent, 1987-95; since 1995, freelance writer, editor and communications consultant. **Agent:** Susan Gleason Associates, 325 Riverside Drive, New York, NY 10025, USA.

HORROR, GHOST AND GOTHIC PUBLICATIONS

Novel

Escardy Gap, with James Lovegrove. New York, Tor, 1996.

Short Stories

Forest Plains. Eugene, Oregon, Hypatia Press, 1996.
The Longest Single Note and Other Strange Compositions. Baltimore, Maryland, CD Publications, 1998.

Other

Editor, *Narrow Houses*. London, Little Brown, 1992; New York, Warner, 1994.
Editor, *Touch Wood: Narrow Houses, Volume 2*. London, Little Brown, 1993; New York, Warner, 1996.
Editor, *Blue Motel: Narrow Houses, Volume 3*. London, Little Brown, 1994; Atlanta, Georgia, White Wolf, 1996.
Editor, *Heaven Sent: An Anthology of Angel Stories*. New York, DAW, and London, Creed, 1995.

Editor, with Ed Kramer, *Tombs*. Atlanta, Georgia, White Wolf, 1995.
Editor, with Ed Kramer, *Dante's Disciples*. Atlanta, Georgia, White Wolf, 1996.
Editor, *Destination Unknown*. Atlanta, Georgia, White Wolf, 1997.

*   *   *

The world of Peter Crowther is a world of incursions. You're carrying on your life much as usual when something sinister erupts into it. How do you react? Badly, most often—not that reacting with courage, grace or dignity is very likely to save you. It's bleak comfort for the reader or the characters that virtue may have been its own reward. Such is the case with three of his quietest and most effective stories, "All We Know of Heaven," "The Longest Single Note" and "Cankerman." All are set in the environment of a classic middle-class nuclear family, and in all the central character does what must be done because it's *right*—without hope of reward, and in all cases with the serious risk (in the last amounting to certainty) of a fearful punishment. They offer an austere form of uplift which not all readers will be able to share.

Not that all the characters are virtuous, or even innocent; "In Country" begins with the only real character committing a series of sordid and brutal murders, then segues into his Vietnam experiences with the effect that he commits a whole lot more, which may be regarded as real or (legitimately, but less convincingly) as the hallucinations of a madman. The danger with such writing is that, because it eschews moral purpose, there is really nothing to look at but the blood and guts, about which there is nothing new to be said and whose inherent appeal is limited. More successful, though with equally little moral purpose are "Head Acres" and "Rustle." Both succeed because they display Crowther's characteristic virtues, which are control of tone and originality of thought.

"Head Acres" is written as the diary of a clever but exceedingly inexperienced university freshman who admits nonsense into the core of his being, simultaneously on three levels: he embraces uncritically some of the most extreme propositions of Jungian psychology; he looks for, and soon perceives, significance in some of the most pretentious rock-&-pop of his time; and he adopts the belief (attributed to Australian Aborigines) that it is possible to "sing things into existence," from which it's a short step to believing he can do it himself. The entries skilfully document his rapid descent into schizophrenia, as the "pathways" he has "sung" about his flat first enrich, then constrict his inner life as he loses control of them. On the way he certainly kills a down-and-out, but the extent to which the circumstances of the death are as described in the journal is left deliberately vague. The whole story hinges on the larger, related question of whether the student's hallucinations are affecting reality as well as his mind.

"Rustle" is more conventional in form but quite as original in concept. A number of prostitutes have vanished without trace from a small area in a short time, and careful analysis of their last known movements leads to the apartment of a reclusive, inadequate bachelor. A cardboard box found in his possession contains sufficient clobber for eleven women. Open-and-shut; just apply the third degree until he leads them to the bodies. His story, that a door appears from time to time and demands to be fed a woman, is hardly to be taken seriously—either he believes it himself, in which case he's psycho, or he doesn't, in which case he's pretending . . . except that there's something a bit odd about the clothes . . . and how come he manages to hang himself in his cell? And with a pink bra! No real explanation is ever furnished, but the sense of a malign counter-reality overlapping our own comes across very forcefully.

The sense of incursion is especially well suited to the eponymous small town of *Escardy Gap*, the sort of smug, ultra-folksy Midwestern rural community where everyone knows everyone else which gave rise to the epigram that "God made the country, Man made the city, and the Devil made the small town." Thither rides Jeremiah Rackstraw, a senior minion of the Devil, a-visiting his handiwork.

He rides in style, with what he describes as one each of the Furies, the Fates and the Hesperides fetchingly disguised as Graces to adorn the engine of his carnival train. Other members of his entourage having, by a combination of personal charm and moral blackmail, insinuated themselves into the lives of the populace, set about the predictable mayhem, each in his/her own special way. It's handled as more than usually imaginative black farce with some fine bravura passages: the one which takes four pages to tell how a pipe is filled and lit deserves to be adopted as a model of suspense-writing.

Most importantly the authors address a nagging wrongness found in almost all genre horror but very little fantasy, however dark: that the evil incursion is unsought and unearned. Horrid as the folk are, with their cracker-barrel wisdom, Mom's pie, regular churchgoing and long evenings gossiping in the porch, they deserve nothing worse than to be left to get on with it. While the real world is full of injustice, the supernatural should effect a certain symmetry between what is sown and what is reaped. The Mayor expresses that forcefully enough to Rackstraw, only to be told that for all the torture and murder there is neither rationale nor justice, only the exercise of malign whimsy.

It's a grim and gruesome message, the more so as, though the book uses multiple viewpoints, the most important is that of Josh, aged 12-going-on-13. Can Josh save the town? No, actually. Can he even save himself? Yes, but only by escaping out of the story entirely into the frame within which it's written—which explores an entirely different set of American clichés, and adds little until the book is almost over, where it's used to parallel the main text in a way that is certainly mannered, but clever enough to get away with it.

In the space of a few years Crowther has become a notable anthologist in the horror and dark-fantasy fields; and, in addition to the collected short stories described above, many other shorter tales by him have appeared in magazines and anthologies—so no doubt more collections will follow his first. Projected for future publication is a sequel to *Escardy Gap*, also with James Lovegrove, provisionally entitled *Unfinished Business*.

—Chris Gilmore

D

DAHL, Roald

Nationality: British. **Born:** Llandaff, Wales, 13 September 1916. **Education:** Repton School. **Military Service:** Royal Air Force, fighter pilot, 1939-42: Wing Commander; assistant air attaché in Washington, D.C., 1942-45. **Family:** Married 1) the actress Patricia Neal, 1953 (divorced, 1983), four daughters and one son; 2) Felicity Ann Crosland, 1983. **Career:** Shell Oil Co., London, England, member of eastern staff, 1933-37, member of staff in Dar-es-Salaam, Tanzania, 1937-39; writer. Host of a series of half-hour television dramas, *Way Out*, during early 1960s. **Awards:** Edgar award, Mystery Writers of America, 1954, 1959, and 1980; New England Round Table of Children's Librarians award, 1972, and Surrey School award, 1973; Surrey School award, 1975, and Nene award, 1978; Surrey School award, 1978, and California Young Reader Medal, 1979; Federation of Children's Book Groups award, 1982; Massachusetts Children's award, 1982; *New York Times* Outstanding Books award, 1983; Whitbread award, 1983; West Australian award, 1983; World Fantasy Convention Lifetime Achievement award, 1983; Federation of Children's Book Groups award, 1983; *Boston Globe/Horn Book* nonfiction honor citation, 1985; International Board on Books for Young People awards for Norwegian and German translations, both 1986; Smarties award, 1990. **Died:** 23 November 1990.

HORROR, GHOST AND GOTHIC PUBLICATIONS

Novel

My Uncle Oswald. London, Joseph, 1979; New York, Knopf, 1980.

Short Stories

Someone Like You. New York, Knopf, 1953; London Secker and Warburg, 1954; revised edition, London, Joseph, 1961.
Kiss, Kiss. New York, Knopf, and London, Joseph, 1960.
Twenty-Nine Kisses from Roald Dahl. London, Joseph, 1969.
Selected Stories. New York, Random House, 1970.
Switch Bitch. New York, Knopf, and London, Joseph, 1974.
Roald Dahl's Tales of the Unexpected. New York, Vintage, 1979.
Taste and Other Tales. London, Longman, 1979.
A Roald Dahl Selection: Nine Short Stories, edited and introduced by Roy Blatchford, photographs by Catherine Shakespeare Lane. London, Longman, 1980.
More Tales of the Unexpected. London, Penguin and Joseph, 1980; as *Further Tales of the Unexpected,* Chivers, 1981.
Two Fables. London, Viking, 1986; New York, Farrar Straus, 1987.
A Second Roald Dahl Selection: Eight Short Stories, edited by Helene Fawcett. London, Longman, 1987.
Ah, Sweet Mystery of Life. London, Cape, 1988; New York, Knopf, 1989.
The Collected Short Stories of Roald Dahl. London, Joseph, 1991.

Other

Editor, *Roald Dahl's Book of Ghost Stories.* New York, Farrar Straus, 1983.

OTHER PUBLICATIONS

Novel

Sometime Never: A Fable for Supermen. New York, Scribner, 1948.

Short Stories

Over to You: Ten Stories of Flyers and Flying. New York, Reynal, 1946.

Fiction for Children

The Gremlins. New York, Random House, 1943.
James and the Giant Peach: A Children's Story. New York, Knopf, 1961; London, Allen and Unwin, 1967.
Charlie and the Chocolate Factory. New York, Knopf, 1964; revised edition, 1973; London, Allen and Unwin, 1967.
The Magic Finger. New York, Harper, 1966; London, Puffin, 1974.
Fantastic Mr. Fox. New York, Knopf, 1970.
Charlie and the Great Glass Elevator: The Further Adventures of Charlie Bucket and Willy Wonka, Chocolate-Maker Extraordinary. New York, Knopf, 1972; London, Allen and Unwin, 1973.
Danny: The Champion of the World. New York, Knopf, 1975.
The Wonderful World of Henry Sugar and Six More. New York, Knopf, and London, Cape, 1977.
The Enormous Crocodile. New York, Knopf, 1978.
The Complete Adventures of Charlie and Mr. Willy Wonka (omnibus; contains *Charlie and the Chocolate Factory* and *Charlie and the Great Glass Elevator*). London, Allen and Unwin, 1978.
The Twits. London, Cape, 1980; New York, Knopf, 1981.
George's Marvellous Medicine. London, Cape, 1981; New York, Knopf, 1982.
The BFG. New York, Farrar Straus, 1982.
The Witches. New York, Farrar Straus, 1983.
The Giraffe and Pelly and Me. New York, Farrar Straus, 1985.
The Roald Dahl Omnibus. New York, Hippocrene Books, 1987.
Matilda. New York, Viking Kestrel, 1988.
Esio Trot. New York, Viking, 1990.
The Dahl Diary. London, Puffin Books, 1991.
The Minpins. New York, Viking, 1991.
The Vicar of Nibbleswicke. New York, Viking, 1992.
My Year. New York, Viking Children's, 1994.

Poetry for Children

Roald Dahl's Revolting Rhymes. London, Cape, 1982; New York, Knopf, 1983.
Dirty Beasts. New York, Farrar Straus, 1983.
Rhyme Stew. London, Cape, 1989; New York, Viking, 1990.

Plays

Screenplays: *You Only Live Twice,* with Jack Bloom, 1967; *Chitty Chitty Bang Bang,* with Ken Hughes, 1968; *The Night-Digger,* adapted from *Nest in a Falling Tree* by Joy Crowley, 1970; *Willie Wonka and the Chocolate Factory,* adaptation of *Charlie and the Chocolate Factory,* 1971; *The Lightning Bug,* 1971.

Other

Boy: Tales of Childhood. New York, Farrar Straus, 1984.
Going Solo. New York, Farrar Straus, 1986.
Memories with Food at Gipsy House, with Felicity Dahl. New York, Viking, 1991.

*

Film Adaptations: *36 Hours,* adaptation of the short story "Beware of the Dog," 1964; *Willie Wonka and the Chocolate Factory,* 1971; *The Witches,* 1990; *James and the Giant Peach,* 1996; *Matilda,* 1996.

Critical Studies: *Pied Pipers: Interviews with the Influential Creators of Children's Literature* by Justin Wintle and Emma Fisher, London, Paddington Press, 1975; *Now Upon a Time: A Contemporary View of Children's Literature* by Myra Pollack Sadker and David Miller Sadker, New York, Harper, 1977; *Roald Dahl* by Chris Powling, London, Hamish Hamilton, 1983; *Roald Dahl* by Alan Warren, Mercer Island, Washington, Starmont House, 1988, revised as *Roald Dahl: From The Gremlins to The Chocolate Factory,* San Bernardino, California, Borgo Press, 1994; *Roald Dahl: A Biography* by Jeremy Treglown, London, Faber, 1994.

*   *   *

Roald Dahl achieved best-selling success in two separate literary veins: short stories written for adults, and many short novels written for children. In both cases, he freely (though far from exclusively) used horrific and supernatural themes.

The most characteristic of Dahl's adult stories echo the approaches of three literary predecessors: O. Henry's predilection for twist-in-the-tail endings, John Collier's slick-magazine sophistication with its accompanying poison barbs, and something of the wit and irony of Saki. The early collection of war stories *Over to You* is not without its gruesome passages, but *echt* Dahl emerges in the three collections *Someone Like You, Kiss Kiss* and *Switch Bitch,* all of them rich in shockers. Later compilations like *Tales of the Unexpected*—famous for having spawned a similarly titled TV series—tend to rearrange the stories from these collections, though occasionally with some new material added.

Dahl's comic-horrific range runs from black comedy to Grand Guignol excess, though the latter is often implied and not depicted. Straightforward murder is the exception rather than the rule, although the famous "Lamb to the Slaughter" (*Over to You*) still delights with its brilliant disposal of a murder weapon—roasted and eaten by the police—and the title character of "The Landlady" (*Kiss Kiss*) is a pleasantly sinister serial killer. Virtuosity kills the cat in "Edward the Conqueror" (*Kiss Kiss*), who convincingly proves to be a reincarnation of Liszt and—like Saki's Tobermory—too great an embarrassment to be let live.

Several stories produce their *frisson* through mutilation and deformity. "Man from the South" (*Someone Like You*) features a repeated bet with a Cadillac staked against the amputation of a finger; "Skin" (*Someone Like You*) pays homage to Saki's gentler "The Background", with the hapless protagonist being tattooed with an artistic masterpiece for which connoisseurs might kill and flay; "The Sound Machine" (*Someone Like You*) shudders to the dreadful cry of an axe-wounded tree, made audible by the eponymous device; all that doctors can save of William in "William and

Mary" (*Kiss Kiss*) is a disembodied brain and eye, now impotent against the small revenges of long-downtrodden wife Mary. More subtly, "Royal Jelly" (*Kiss Kiss*) hints at a disquieting bee-like transformation after over-indulgence in the title's universal panacea.

Occasionally Dahl's fiction betrays the slight strainedness of an author aware that he is expected to be unexpected, as in "Pig" (*Kiss Kiss*). There is high comedy in this saga of a born vegetarian chef who eventually, inadvertently, discovers the blasphemous Joy of Pork; however, his "punishment" in a slaughterhouse is just too inconsequential and incredible, and disappoints. But avoiding the most-anticipated surprise is effective in "The Soldier" (*Someone Like You*), where the reader at first rejects the viewpoint character's madness and assumes a plot against him, and in "The Neck" (*Someone Like You*), whose blackly comic build-up to a crime of passion actually gains force by halting on the brink. "Mr. Hoddy" (*Someone Like You*) eschews twists altogether and simply presents a splendidly revolting fantasy of how a maggot-farm might be run, related with escalating inventiveness by a man who fails to notice his prospective father-in-law's less than enthusiastic reactions.

Unsane delusions seem to take on solid reality in "The Wish" (*Someone Like You*), where a child's fantasy of snakes in the carpet develops—as it were—fangs; and in "Georgy Porgy" (*Kiss Kiss*), which is amusingly knowing about sexual repression, and whose harried clergyman protagonist believes himself literally swallowed up by a predatory woman. From his refuge in her duodenum (commanding interesting views of the pylorus and pancreatic duct), he scoffs at the alternative views of reality proposed by his frequent white-coated visitors. . . .

The four stories in *Switch Bitch* use the highly charged material of borderline-pornographic sex as their basis for fantastication, horror and comic excess. Of special note are two tales of Uncle Oswald, a bedroom athlete whose memoirs "make Casanova read like a parish magazine." "The Visitor" shows him as a traveller with an almost morbid awareness of the pitfalls of disease in the Middle East; after a daring sexual fling he finds he may well have been exposed to something worse than even he had imagined. The uproarious "Bitch" strays towards science fiction with the development of the ultimate aphrodisiac scent, for which Oswald has appalling plans which go very nearly as appallingly wrong. His exploits continue at book length in *My Uncle Oswald,* which extensively and perhaps a little repetitively rings the changes on aphrodisiac themes (the imagined Sudanese Blister Beetle being infinitely more potent than Spanish Fly). Besides such gruesome asides as a discussion of Australian farmers' castration techniques, the novel repeatedly hints at the horror of being unable to control one's own drug-aroused body—but largely defuses the unpleasantness by dwelling instead on its comic side.

Although the relevance to horror and gothic fiction is perhaps marginal, Dahl's parallel success as a writer for children owes much to a transplanting of his adult shockers' lively ruthlessness and amorality into the juvenile context. For example, in *Charlie and the Chocolate Factory,* the child visitors to Willy Wonka's fantastical confectionery-works are all (except hero Charlie himself) subjected to grotesque humiliations and transformations by way of retribution for character flaws. Particularly disquieting is the unreliable Mr. Wonka's lack of concern for the victims: when one greedy lad falls into the machinery, Wonka's chief fear is that this inclusion may spoil the flavour of the strawberry chocolate fudge. The eponymous adult villains in *The Witches* are plotting to turn all the world's children into mice, and there is a sense of genuine creepiness and menace here.

Dahl's exuberant storytelling enthusiasm and sense of the macabre have translated well into visual media. Notable examples are the TV series *Roald Dahl's Tales of the Unexpected* and the successful movie adaptations of the above-mentioned children's novels (as well as others).

—David Langford

D'AMATO, Brian

Nationality: American. **Born:** In Grand Rapids, Michigan; the son of the novelist Barbara D'Amato. **Education:** Yale University, New Haven, Connecticut. **Career:** Artist and writer. **Address:** c/o Bantam Doubleday Dell Publishing Group, Inc., 1540 Broadway, New York, NY 10036, USA. Lives in New York.

HORROR, GHOST AND GOTHIC PUBLICATIONS

Novel

Beauty. New York, Delacorte, 1992; London, HarperCollins, 1993.

* * *

Beauty is the first and (so far) only novel by the young New York artist, Brian D'Amato. It comes across as a combination of *Frankenstein* and *American Psycho*. Not only does its protagonist, who is also a young New York artist like D'Amato, create a monster which eventually tries to harm him, but that protagonist (while not a serial killer) is very much like Patrick Bateman in Bret Easton Ellis's *American Psycho*. *Beauty* is an obsessive novel about an obsessive character.

Jamie Angelo is a fairly well-known artist, with exhibitions in important New York galleries. At only 29 he is becoming rich and mixing with the upper echelons of the art world. His major obsession is with facial beauty. He is concerned with keeping his own face flaw-free and delaying the onset of ageing; he has always dated women with the most perfect faces; and, as a lucrative sideline, he improves the look of people's faces with a radical new approach to plastic surgery. This last is a secretive business, because Angelo is not medically trained and is thus breaking the law; yet he works wonders, partly due to a new artificial skin still in development called PCS 10, and mostly due to his artistic feelings for shapes and colours. Even allowing for his arrogance as he describes in detail the techniques of planning and operating, he is very talented and achieves excellent results. The novel describes every stage in an operation on Penny Penn, a movie actress who was a contemporary of Angelo at Yale and who already has crow's-feet and incipient eye-bags.

But making the faces of movie stars look young again is not enough for Angelo. He dreams of creating the most beautiful female face in the world. Then he meets Jaishree, a young performance artist of Indian descent; they have an affair and eventually but quite naturally, after some months of knowing each other, Angelo persuades her to let him redesign her face completely. His preparations are amazingly thorough. He uses photos of Jaishree

from all angles, he makes plaster casts of her face, and he uses a computer to superimpose photos of actresses, models and images from antiquity. He also redesigns her in terms of clothes (she must dress in saris to stress her Indianness) and persuades her to use the name Minaz. The operation goes smoothly and a career in modelling and acting swiftly blossoms for Minaz, though this takes her away from him, and their relationship falters.

Then, after only a few months, Angelo's three high-profile clients, Minaz, Penny Penn and another actress, Virginia Feiden, all develop cancers within the facial grafts. Civil and criminal law cases are imminent, Minaz confronts Angelo (bringing with her some bodyguards to beat him up), and Angelo has to liquidate some of his considerable assets and go into hiding in a rural location on Lake Michigan. While Angelo cannot at first think what has gone wrong, it seems that one of the two medical research experts who created PCS 10, Dr. Karl Vanders, has deliberately sabotaged batches of the material in order to discredit Angelo and gain control of the process. The final plot twists, in which Angelo tries to revenge himself on Vanders by giving all his tapes and notes of the operations to a rival medical expert, and by physical assault, and is himself given the face of a devil, are melodramatic.

The outstanding elements of the novel are Angelo's character, the overwhelming obsessions of both him and the book with beauty, and the audacious use of convincing background material.

Angelo is a complex and wholly convincing person: talented, peculiar and contradictory. He needs regular visits to a psychiatrist. He is moody, with occasional bouts of rage (directed mostly towards TV screens) and depression. He is almost as obsessed with style and designer labels as Bateman in *American Psycho*, and, like Bateman, he gives the reader firm and detailed advice on skin care. While not likeable, Angelo is certainly fascinating and mercurial. (But most of the characters here seem to be warped; Angelo's first substantial conversation with Jaishree is on the subject of the efficacy of pain-killer pills.) His relationship with Jaishree is believably handled, though they are the only two fully rounded characters in the book.

Throughout the novel is the recurring motif of beauty becoming the beast. (This is, of course, the way of nature; however beautiful are the young, they gradually wither—Angelo cannot bear to look at the old and ugly; they are beasts to him—and die.) Penny Penn is ageing at 29. One of Angelo's pictures shows a series of plaster balls ranging from perfect to wrinkled. When Angelo tries to prevent this natural process by his advanced surgical techniques, the result is eventually more beastlike than ever, with the three cancer-suffering women looking grotesquely ugly. And, at the end of the book, Angelo himself receives a beastlike face to replace his own beauty.

The book's obsession with beauty means that D'Amato gives his readers more detail than they would ever want about PCS 10, about Angelo's ideas on artists' abilities to represent faces, detailing Angelo's collection of beautiful things, his 4,000-square-foot loft living-space, the facial flaws of former girlfriends, the "lumpy and bad-looking" underclass.

There is much verisimilitude in D'Amato's New York settings: the small details of loft life, the streets and subways, exhibition openings, smart restaurants. But, via Angelo, he is also a name-dropper. Jodie Foster and Cher get mentioned in passing. One of the minor characters (a photographer) is on the phone to Julia Roberts. Models Naomi Campbell and Linda Evangelista are taking part in a catwalk show with Minaz. Real magazines and TV shows are mentioned as interviewing Minaz. And as for the welter of galleries, artists and agents mentioned, well, some of them may be real. Presumably D'Amato can get away with using real people like this because he is not (normally) disparaging about them and because he has cunningly set his novel marginally in the future: it was first published in 1992, is set in 1993-94.

While some descriptions seem overlong and the major plot elements are never surprising, the fine detail is often fascinating, with witty dialogue and thoughtful observations. For a first novel it is all surprisingly fluent and polished. If *American Psycho* is the novel of the uncaring late 1980s, then *Beauty* is the novel of the early 1990s, which are apparently gentler and more caring but also hypocritical and overlaid with artificiality. It may be that D'Amato has put everything he knows into the book and will never write another, but there is so much quality here that a follow-up is worth waiting for.

—Chris Morgan

D'AMMASSA, Don(ald Eugene)

Nationality: American. **Born:** 24 April 1946. **Education:** Michigan State University, B.A. **Military Service:** U.S. Army, 1968-71; served in the Vietnam war. **Family:** Married Sheila D'Ammassa in 1968; one son. **Career:** Production Control Manager and Vice President, Taunton Silversmiths, 1971-92; Computer Network Administrator, Air Products and Chemicals, from 1993; contributor of short stories to many small-press magazines; book-reviewer, *Science-Fiction Chronicle* and other publications; contributor to many reference books. **Address:** 323 Dodge Street, East Providence, RI 02914, USA. **Online Address:** dammassa@ix.netcom.com.

HORROR, GHOST AND GOTHIC PUBLICATIONS

Novel

Blood Beast. New York, Pinnacle, 1988.

Short Stories

Twisted Images. West Warwick, Rhode Island, Necronomicon Press, 1995.

*   *   *

Don D'Ammassa is primarily a short-story writer, and his sole novel, *Blood Beast*, actually consists of separate stories interwoven against a common theme and background. The novel traces the lives of several characters from childhood to maturity, each of whom is subliminally influenced by an enigmatic gargoyle mounted on the side of an abandoned library. Although the supernatural nature of the gargoyle is not explicitly shown until the closing chapters, its influence pervades the novel as each of its followers competes to perform acts of evil that will distinguish them above their fellows. Ultimately we are shown that human evil is more insidious than the supernatural, a theme that shows up repeatedly in D'Ammassa's work. The novel is set in the mythical town of Managansett, Rhode Island, which is the background for the majority of his short fiction.

The best of D'Ammassa's work deals with mental disorders. The protagonist of "Misadventures in the Skin Trade" is a narcissistic man who believes that a jealous rival has literally stolen his skin and replaced it with an inferior variety. An elderly recluse in "Context" believes that someone else is living in his house, an alternative version of himself who made all the right decisions where he chose the opposite paths. In "Friday Nights at Home" a woman becomes so obsessed with her duties to her family that she serves them bits of meat carved from her own body. A popular singer kills the people she loves in order to be inspired by her grief in "Inspiration," and a vindictive and cruel businessman is literally haunted by visions of people he has mistreated in "Present in Spirit."

For the most part, D'Ammassa avoids the more visceral brands of horror. *Twisted Images*, a novelette published as a chapbook, blends Oriental legends with life in small-town New England. A young man living in his first apartment discovers that the ornate mirror in his bedroom is a gateway to another world, which he inadvertently opens with disastrous results. In "Passing Death," a detective is puzzled when a series of unlikely culprits all insist on confessing to murders that don't appear to have taken place, all of which have the same victim. An unprepossessing woman moves into an apartment building in "Sneak Thief" and subsequently acquires the talents of her neighbours, while they lose their own abilities. Similarly, the menace in "Expectations" is a mysterious figure that absorbs the lives and sorrows of its victims until it encounters a tragedy so great that it is overwhelmed.

A resident of the smallest state of the Union, Rhode Island, D'Ammassa has made the occasional nod toward his famous compatriot and precursor, H. P. Lovecraft. "The Dunwich Gate" is a pastiche, "Bad Soil" a more contemporary tale, and "Shadow Over R'Lyeh" a spoof. Of more interest are "Dark Providence," which suggests Lovecraft may have drawn his inspiration from an alternative universe, and "The Managansett Horror," wherein Lovecraft is himself the protagonist pitted against an insane and psychically gifted fan.

Although humour and horror rarely mix well, D'Ammassa has played with genre themes with some success. "The Daylight Vampire" can only appear during the day, injects fluid into his victims, and sleeps in a well-lit room at night. A dead President is revived as a zombie for political purposes in "Corruption in Office." Witches have regular offices and a professional licensing association in "Hair Apparent," and vampire cows menace a small town in "Milk Curdling Horror."

D'Ammassa draws on his experiences in Vietnam for the moody "The Guard Tower." In "Kaleidoscope" the protagonist discovers that by changing the pattern in an antique kaleidoscope, he alters the lives of people around him. "All Flesh is Clay" is an unconventional vampire story in which one of the undead is revived when a sculptor selects clay from his grave site. A young woman discovers that a stone statue has been killing her enemies in "Scylla and Charybdis." A creature dwelling in a claustrophobic system of underground passages provides the threat in "A Tight Situation." Other stories of interest include the traditional ghost stories "Kites" and "Remnants," and the tale of a repulsive man who can draw people into his own dreams in "Forever in My Thoughts." A shape-changing creature is featured in "Moloch's Furnace," and in "The Splicer" a film fan can psychically alter the images appearing on the screen. "Jack the Martian" is an interesting hybrid dealing with the first serial killer on Mars, who turns out to be a mass hallucination made real.

D'Ammassa is a prolific book-reviewer and critic, with a wide knowledge of the field, and has contributed many entries to the present volume. As a writer of fiction he is of less note, although he shows an admirable persistence. A few of his short stories are memorable, while the majority could be described as competent but undistinguished. His single novel, although interesting, is not noteworthy enough to form the basis for a lasting reputation. Whether or not he will emerge as a significant writer at shorter length remains to be seen.

—David Pringle

DANIELS, Les(lie Noel, III)

Nationality: American. **Born:** Danbury, Connecticut, 1943. **Education:** Brown University, Providence, Rhode Island; B.A. in English; M.A. 1968. **Career:** Composer, performer and freelance writer. **Address:** c/o Tor Books, Tom Doherty Associates, Inc., 175 Fifth Ave., 14th Floor, New York, NY 10010, USA.

HORROR, GHOST AND GOTHIC PUBLICATIONS

Novels (series: Don Sebastian in all titles)

The Black Castle: A Novel of the Macabre. New York, Scribner, 1978.
The Silver Skull: A Novel of Sorcery. New York, Scribner, 1979.
Citizen Vampire. New York, Scribner, 1981.
Yellow Fog. West Kingston, Rhode Island, Grant, 1986; expanded edition, New York, Tor, 1988; London, Raven, 1995.
No Blood Spilled. New York, Tor, 1991; London, Raven, 1996.
The Don Sebastian Vampire Chronicles (omnibus; includes *The Black Castle, The Silver Skull, Citizen Vampire*). London, Raven, 1994.
White Demon. Forthcoming.

Other

Living in Fear: A History of Horror in the Mass Media. New York, Scribner, 1975; as *Fear: A History of Horror in the Mass Media*, London, Paladin, 1977.

Editor, *Dying of Fright: Masterpieces of the Macabre.* New York, Scribner, 1976.
Editor, with Diane Thompson. *Thirteen Tales of Terror.* New York, Scribner, 1977.

OTHER PUBLICATIONS

Other

Comix: A History of Comic Books in America. New York, Outerbridge and Dienstfrey, 1971.
Marvel: Five Fabulous Decades of the World's Greatest Comics. New York, Abrams, and London, Virgin, 1991.
DC Comics: Sixty Years of the World's Favorite Comic Book Heroes. New York, Abrams, and London, Virgin, 1995.

*   *   *

After having written *Living in Fear*—a remarkably comprehensive history of horror in all its forms from antiquity to the present—and compiled a noteworthy anthology, *Dying of Fright*, Les Daniels took to writing horror fiction himself. His six novels (one of them, *White Demon*, forthcoming) are stated by the author to form two trilogies, although in reality they are a kind of march through history on the part of their protagonist, the forbidding vampire Don Sebastian de Villenueva. The hallmark of these works is the intermingling of genres, notably the supernatural tale, the historical novel, the mainstream novel and the detective story—a fusion Daniels has accomplished with panache.

Daniels' first novel, *The Black Castle*, takes place in 1496. But this is not merely a vampire tale set in the midst of the Spanish Inquisition: the historical "background" ultimately comes to dominate the work, and the real horror becomes not Sebastian but the Inquisition itself—as the lengthy and painfully precise depictions of the Inquisition's dungeons and torture procedures, as well as a spectacular *auto-da-fé* where living heretics are burned and dead ones exhumed and their rotting skeletons put to the torch, clearly establish. This becomes the dominant theme in all Daniels' fiction: the horrors of real life far exceed those of even so redoubtable a figure as Sebastian.

With *The Silver Skull* we not only leap ahead a century but are also transferred to a new continent, as Sebastian becomes enmeshed in the horror and barbarism of Aztec rites in Mexico, and the savage fighting between Aztecs and Spaniards that would ultimately lead to the former's extirpation. Sebastian in this novel begins to make it clear that his interest lies not so much in drinking blood as in absorbing knowledge: "I am less concerned with the health of these people than with their knowledge. The magic that brought me here exceeds anything I have ever experienced, and I would know more of it." Throughout the rest of the series he will become more and more a detached and cynical observer of events rather than a participant.

Citizen Vampire, perhaps the best of Daniels' novels, continues the contrast of real vs. supernatural horror. Sebastian, finding himself amidst the chaos of the French Revolution, takes a decided back seat to such grisly realities as the invention of the guillotine, the storming of the Bastille, and the vicious revenge of the working classes upon the hapless and outraged aristocracy. Sebastian, speaking to a lady's maid who seeks nothing but the destruction of her hated mistress, sums up his view of the Revolution: "To me, you are the revolution. Impulsive, angry, vengeful, rushing righteously toward a destiny that even you cannot imagine."

Yellow Fog, first published as a novelette and expanded into a full-length novel two years later, is probably Daniels' most successful attempt at the intermingling of genres. Here we have a little of the historical novel (the bulk of the work takes place in England in 1847), a little of the supernatural novel (the ubiquitous Sebastian), a little of the detective story (the ex-Bow Street runner Samuel Sayer, who is on the track of Sebastian as a private detective, as is the newly formed Scotland Yard), and a little of the mainstream novel in its careful delineation of character. Again, the most horrific scene is a very natural one: one character's hideous murder of his mistress, who fails to die promptly but instead wanders about her room in a bloody daze.

No Blood Spilled takes us to India, where Sebastian has gone to pursue his quest for knowledge—specifically, knowledge of the nature of death. In the earlier novels, Sebastian had become increasingly weary of suffering the indignity of periodic resurrection, and began to devote himself to the pursuit of utter extinction. Here, as a result, he comes to Calcutta to penetrate the mysteries of Kali, the Hindu goddess of death. He is pursued by the maniacal Reginald Callender (from *Yellow Fog*), who escapes from the madhouse in which he has been confined and vows to hunt down Sebastian and despatch him for causing the death of his fiancée. Callender actually becomes a little more interesting than Sebastian: the latter, in fact, does not even make much of an appearance in the novel, while the former wavers between cringing sycophancy and a surprisingly dogged tenacity.

No Blood Spilled continues the now well-established Daniels formula of contrasting natural and supernatural horror, with a subtle suggestion that the former may be the more loathsome of the two. While Sebastian's thirst for blood is certainly depicted with verve, the many natural horrors usurp our attention: nightmarish accounts of the madhouse in which Callender is placed (reminiscent of Maturin's *Melmoth the Wanderer* but actually derived—as many of Daniels' historical details are—from thorough research); the savagery of the Indian rite of suttee (the burning alive of a man's wife after his death); the vileness of teeming and impoverished Calcutta, where beggar children are intentionally mutilated by their family so as to appear more pitiable; and the viciousness of the Thugs, those assassins and worshippers of Kali who have been almost eradicated by the British but who can still be found on the underside of Anglo-Indian society. The novel, however, seems to lack the searching philosophical reflections of Sebastian on his anomalous state, reflections that make Daniels' novels far more than mere exercises in bloodletting.

The complex and enigmatic figure of Sebastian is clearly Daniels' greatest accomplishment, although praise must also be extended to the richness of historical setting, the elaborate interweaving of genres, and in general the whole conception of a vampire stalking through history (a conception he clearly derived independently of his more celebrated contemporary Anne Rice). What further innovations we may look for in subsequent works, it is difficult to tell. Will Sebastian in fact reach the contemporary world? If so, what will he make of a time when bloodletting has reached proportions even he has never seen in his trek across four centuries and two continents? A more significant query, perhaps, is whether Daniels himself can avoid repetitiveness in the somewhat narrow and confining sub-genre he has created for himself, and whether he allows himself to become so typecast as a "vampire novelist" that he cannot direct his talents to other weird themes.

—S. T. Joshi

DARE, M(arcus) P(aul)

Nationality: British. **Born:** Leicester, England, 22 July 1902. **Education:** Wyggeston Boys' School, Leicester. **Career:** Journalist, 1920-40; bookdealer, 1947-62. **Died:** August 1962.

HORROR, GHOST AND GOTHIC PUBLICATIONS

Short Stories

Unholy Relics. London, Edward Arnold, 1947; New York, Longmans Green, 1947; expanded as *Unholy Relics and Other Uncanny Tales*, Ashcroft, British Columbia, Ash-Tree Press, 1997.

OTHER PUBLICATIONS

Other

Ayleston Manor and Church. Leicester, Backus, 1924.
Charnwood Forest and Its Environs. Leicester, Backus, 1925.
Notes Upon a Prehistoric Contracted Burial Discovered at Leire. Leicester, Thornley, 1926.
Old Time Lawkeepers. Lincoln, Lincolnshire Chronicle, 1927.
The Cemeteries of Roman Leicester, in the light of recent discoveries, 1922-1928. Leicester, Thornley, 1928.
Bradgate, Groby and the Story of Lady Jane Grey. Leicester, privately published, 1931.
The Church of St. John the Evangelist, Carlton-in-Lindrick. Carlton-in-Lindrick, The Church, 1936.
Indian Underworld: A First-hand Account of Hindu Saints, Sorcerers and Superstitions. London, Rider, 1938; New York, Dutton, 1940.
The Church of St. Mary the Virgin, Bottesford, Leicester, and Its Monuments. Gloucester, British Publishing Company, 1947.

*

Critical Study: "M. P. Dare (1902-62)" by Geoffrey K. Nelson, in *Ghosts & Scholars*, #10, 1988.

*   *   *

M. P. Dare was a devoted antiquarian and book enthusiast, and something of a rogue as he was imprisoned for fraud on more than one occasion. But he wrote enough stories to fill a small volume, *Unholy Relics*, which, because of its comparative rarity, has become one of the more sought-after items produced by that circle of imitators of M. R. James, known colloquially as the James Gang. Not all of the stories are worth the effort. Dare had neither the skill nor style of James in creating either an atmosphere of horror or that frisson of anticipation that comes from knowing his monstrous demons must soon be unleashed; neither did he have the emulative skills of A. N. L. Munby, L. T. C. Rolt or R. H. Malden. But he did have considerable antiquarian knowledge to make the background to his stories convincing, and they have occasional incidents of sudden shock that are momentarily pleasing.

In total Dare published 13 stories. They all relate to the antiquarian adventures of Gregory Wayne and Alan Granville. Some of them, such as "The Haunted Drawers," are based on Dare's experiences during his own researches, and they come across as matter-of-fact accounts rather than constructed stories. The better stories are those where Dare relies more on his imagination. These include the title story, "Unholy Relics," where Wayne is locked in a cathedral crypt overnight. He uses this as an opportunity to plunder the relics of two English saints who are buried there, but when he opens the tomb he is attacked by a horde of skeletons who guard it. The denouement is highly charged, with a good atmosphere. "A Nun's Tragedy" is equally effective. The two companions investigate a priory where a nun had been walled up alive for her misdemeanour. The spirit of the nun haunts the crypt and is extremely vindictive towards those who disturb her. Both "The Beam" and "Fatal Oak" are similar to M. R. James's "The Stalls of Barchester Cathedral," as they depend upon wood which had previously been part of a gibbet exerting the evil influence of those hanged from it. "The Beam" has the best effect, when a hairy green ghostly arm emerges from the beam during their investigation. "The Demoniac Goat" is a tale of witchcraft rather than hauntings and concerns a dead clergyman who practises black magic. The other stories are interesting but less effective.

Dare's stories are suited best for completists of antiquarian ghost stories. They have a homely feel, with the relationship between Wayne and Granville similar to that between Holmes and Watson, and Dare does his best to create moments of real horror. At times he takes this perhaps a step too far, but overall his stories are a pleasurable addition to the sub-genre.

—Mike Ashley

DAVIES, (William) Robertson

Nationality: Canadian. **Born:** Thamesville, Ontario, 28 August 1913. **Education:** Upper Canada College, Toronto; Queen's University, Kingston, Ontario; Balliol College, Oxford, 1936-38, B.Litt. 1938. **Family:** Married Brenda Mathews in 1940; three daughters. **Career:** Teacher and actor, Old Vic Theatre School and Repertory Company, London, 1938-40; literary editor, *Saturday Night,* Toronto, 1940-42; editor and publisher, Peterborough *Examiner,* Ontario, 1942-63. From 1960 professor of English, from 1962 Master of Massey College, and from 1981 founding master, University of Toronto. Governor, Stratford Shakespeare Festival, Ontario, 1953-71. **Awards:** Ottawa Drama League prize, 1946, 1947; Dominion Drama Festival prize, for play, 1948, 1949, for directing, 1949; Leacock medal, 1955; Lorne Pierce medal, 1961; Governor-General's award, for fiction, 1973; World Fantasy Convention award, for fiction, 1984; City of Toronto Book award, 1986; Canadian Authors' Association award, for fiction, 1986; Banff Centre award, 1986; Foundation for the Advancement of Canadian Letters award, 1986, 1990; Toronto Arts Lifetime Achievement award, 1986; U.S. National Arts Club Medal of Honor, 1987 (first Canadian recipient); Molson prize, 1988; Canadian Conference of the Arts diploma, 1988; Scottish Arts Council Neil Gunn International fellowship, 1988. LL.D.: University of Alberta, Edmonton, 1957; Queen's University, 1962; University of Manitoba, Winnipeg, 1972; University of Toronto, 1981; University of Prince Edward Island, Charlottetown, 1989. D.Litt.: McMaster University, Hamilton, Ontario, 1959; University of Windsor, Ontario, 1971; York University, Toronto, 1973; Mount Allison University, Sackville, New Brunswick, 1973; Memorial University of Newfoundland, St. John's, 1974; University of Western Ontario, London, 1974; McGill University, Montreal, 1974; Trent University, Peterborough, Ontario, 1974; University of Lethbridge, Alberta, 1981; University of Waterloo, Ontario, 1981; University of British Columbia, Vancouver, 1983; University of Santa Clara, California, 1985; Trinity College, Dublin, 1990; Oxford University, 1991; University of Wales, 1995. D.C.L.: Bishop's University, Lennoxville, Quebec, 1967. LL.D.: University of Calgary, Alberta, 1975. D.H.L.: Rochester University, Rochester, New York, 1983; Dowling College, New York, 1992; Loyola University, Chicago, 1994; D.S.L.: Thornloe University, Sudbury, Ontario, 1988; Diplome honoris causa: Royal Conservatory of Music, Toronto, 1994. Fellow, Balliol College, Oxford, 1986, and Trinity College, Toronto, 1987. Fellow, Royal Society of Canada, 1967, and Royal Society of Literature, 1984; honorary

member, American Academy, 1981 (first Canadian elected). Companion, Order of Canada, 1972; Order of Ontario, 1988. **Died:** 2 December 1995.

HORROR, GHOST AND GOTHIC PUBLICATIONS

Novels

Fifth Business. Toronto, Macmillan, and New York, Viking Press, 1970; London, Macmillan, 1971.
The Manticore. Toronto, Macmillan, and New York, Viking Press, 1972; London, Macmillan, 1973.
World of Wonders. Toronto, Macmillan, 1975; New York, Viking Press, 1976; London, W.H. Allen, 1977.
The Rebel Angels. Toronto, Macmillan, 1981; New York, Viking Press, and London, Allen Lane, 1982.
The Deptford Trilogy (omnibus; includes *Fifth Business, The Manticore, World of Wonders*). Toronto and London, Penguin, 1983.
What's Bred in the Bone. Toronto, Macmillan, and New York, Viking, 1985; London, Viking, 1986.
The Lyre of Orpheus. Toronto, Macmillan, and London, Viking, 1988; New York, Viking, 1989.
The Cornish Trilogy (omnibus; includes *The Rebel Angels, What's Bred in the Bone, The Lyre of Orpheus*). Toronto and London, Penguin, 1991.
Murther and Walking Spirits. Toronto, McClelland and Stewart, New York, Viking, and London, Sinclair Stevenson, 1991.
The Cunning Man. Toronto, McClelland and Stewart, 1994; New York and London, Viking Penguin, 1995.

Short Stories

High Spirits: A Collection of Ghost Stories. Toronto and London, Penguin, 1982; New York, Viking Press, 1983.

OTHER PUBLICATIONS

Novels

Tempest-Tost. Toronto, Clarke Irwin, 1951; London, Chatto and Windus, and New York, Rinehart, 1952.
Leaven of Malice. Toronto, Clarke Irwin, 1954; London, Chatto and Windus, and New York, Scribner, 1955.
A Mixture of Frailties. Toronto, Macmillan, London, Weidenfeld and Nicolson, and New York, Scribner, 1958.
The Salterton Trilogy (omnibus). Toronto and London, Penguin, 1986.

Plays

A Play of Our Lord's Nativity (produced Peterborough, Ontario, 1946).
Overlaid (produced Peterborough, Ontario, 1947). Included in *Eros at Breakfast and Other Plays,* 1949.
The Voice of the People (produced Montreal, 1948). Included in *Eros at Breakfast and Other Plays,* 1949.
At the Gates of the Righteous (produced Peterborough, Ontario, 1948). Included in *Eros at Breakfast and Other Plays,* 1949.

Hope Deferred (produced Montreal, 1948). Included in *Eros at Breakfast and Other Plays,* 1949.

Fortune, My Foe (produced Kingston, Ontario, 1948). Toronto, Clarke Irwin, 1949.

Eros at Breakfast (produced Ottawa, 1948). Included in *Eros at Breakfast and Other Plays,* 1949.

Eros at Breakfast and Other Plays. Toronto, Clarke Irwin, 1949.

At My Heart's Core (produced Peterborough, Ontario, 1950). Toronto, Clarke Irwin, 1950.

King Phoenix (produced Peterborough, Ontario, 1950). Included in *Hunting Stuart and Other Plays,* 1972.

A Masque of Aesop (for children; produced Toronto, 1952). Toronto, Clarke Irwin, 1952; in *Five New One-Act Plays,* edited by James A. Stone, London, Harrap, 1954.

A Jig for the Gypsy (produced Toronto and London, 1954). Toronto, Clarke Irwin, 1954.

Hunting Stuart (produced Toronto, 1955). Included in *Hunting Stuart and Other Plays,* 1972.

Leaven of Malice, adaptation of his own novel (as *Love and Libel,* produced Toronto and New York, 1960; revised version, as *Leaven of Malice,* produced Toronto, 1973). Published in *Canadian Drama* (Waterloo, Ontario), vol. 7, no. 2, 1981.

A Masque of Mr. Punch (for children; produced Toronto, 1962). Toronto, Oxford University Press, 1963.

Centennial Play, with others (produced Lindsay, Ontario, 1967). Ottawa, Centennial Commission, 1967.

Hunting Stuart and Other Plays (includes *King Phoenix* and *General Confession*), edited by Brian Parker. Toronto, New Press, 1972.

Brothers in the Black Art (televised 1974). Vancouver, Alcuin Society, 1981.

Question Time (produced Toronto, 1975). Toronto, Macmillan, 1975.

Pontiac and the Green Man (produced Toronto, 1977).

Television Play: *Brothers in the Black Art,* 1974.

Other

Shakespeare's Boy Actors. London, Dent, 1939; New York, Russell and Russell, 1964.

Shakespeare for Young Players: A Junior Course. Toronto, Clarke Irwin, 1942.

The Papers of Samuel Marchbanks (revised editions). Toronto, Irwin, 1985; New York, Viking, 1986; London, Viking, 1987.

The Diary of Samuel Marchbanks. Toronto, Clarke Irwin, 1947.

The Table Talk of Samuel Marchbanks. Toronto, Clarke Irwin, 1949; London, Chatto and Windus, 1951.

Renown at Stratford: A Record of the Shakespearean Festival in Canada 1953, with Tyrone Guthrie. Toronto, Clarke Irwin, 1953.

Twice Have the Trumpets Sounded: A Record of the Stratford Shakespearean Festival in Canada 1954, with Tyrone Guthrie. Toronto, Clarke Irwin, 1954.

Thrice the Brinded Cat Hath Mew'd: A Record of the Stratford Shakespearean Festival in Canada 1955, with Tyrone Guthrie. Toronto, Clarke Irwin, 1955.

A Voice from the Attic. New York, Knopf, 1960; revised edition, New York and Toronto, Penguin, 1990.

The Personal Art: Reading to Good Purpose. London, Secker and Warburg, 1961.

Marchbanks' Almanack. Toronto, McClelland and Stewart, 1967.

Stephen Leacock. Toronto, McClelland and Stewart, 1970.

What Do You See in the Mirror? Agincourt, Ontario, Book Society of Canada, 1970.

The Revels History of Drama in English 6: 1750-1880, with others. London, Methuen, 1975.

One Half of Robertson Davies: Provocative Pronouncements on a Wide Range of Topics. Toronto, Macmillan, 1977; New York, Viking Press, 1978.

The Enthusiasms of Robertson Davies, edited by Judith Skelton Grant. Toronto, McClelland and Stewart, 1979; London, Viking, 1990.

Robertson Davies, The Well-Tempered Critic: One Man's View of Theatre and Letters in Canada, edited by Judith Skelton Grant. Toronto, McClelland and Stewart, 1981.

The Mirror of Nature (lectures). Toronto, University of Toronto Press, 1983.

Conversations with Robertson Davies, edited by J. Madison Davis. Jackson, University Press of Mississippi, 1989.

Reading and Writing (lectures). University of Utah Press, 1994.

Editor, *Feast of Stephen: An Anthology of Some of the Less Familiar Writings of Stephen Leacock.* Toronto, McClelland and Stewart, 1970; as *The Penguin Stephen Leacock,* London, Penguin, 1981.

*

Bibliography: By John Ryrie, in *The Annotated Bibliography of Canada's Major Authors 3* edited by Robert Lecker and Jack David, Downsview, Ontario, ECW Press, 1981.

Manuscript Collection: National Archives, Canada.

Critical Studies: *Robertson Davies* by Elspeth Buitenhuis, Toronto, Forum House, 1972; *Conversations with Canadian Novelists 1* by Silver Donald Cameron, Toronto, Macmillan, 1975; *Robertson Davies* by Patricia A. Morley, Agincourt, Ontario, Gage, 1977; "Robertson Davies Issue" of *Journal of Canadian Studies* (Peterborough, Ontario), February 1977; *Robertson Davies* by Judith Skelton Grant, Toronto, McClelland and Stewart, 1978; *Here and Now 1* edited by John Moss, Toronto, NC Press, 1979; "The Master of the Unseen World" by Judith Finlayson, in *Quest* (Toronto), vol. 8, no. 4, 1979; *Studies in Robertson Davies's Deptford Trilogy* edited by Robert G. Lawrence and Samuel L. Macey, Victoria, British Columbia, English Literary Studies, 1980; *The Smaller Infinity: The Jungian Self in the Novels of Robertson Davies* by Patricia Monk, Toronto, University of Toronto Press, 1982; in *Canadian Writers and Their Work* edited by Robert Lecker, Jack David, and Ellen Quigley, Downsview, Ontario, ECW Press, 1985; *Robertson Davies* by Michael Peterman, Boston, Twayne, 1986; *Robertson Davies: Man of Myth* by Judith Skelton Grant, Toronto, Penguin, 1994.

Theatrical Activities:

Actor: **Plays**—Lord Norfolk in *Traitor's Gate* by Morna Stuart, London, 1938; Stingo in *She Stoops to Conquer* by Oliver Goldsmith, London, 1939; Archbishop of Rheims in *Saint Joan* by Shaw, London, 1939; roles in *The Taming of the Shrew* by Shakespeare, London, 1939.

*   *   *

Robertson Davies achieved international acclaim as one of Canada's most distinguished novelists, while in genre circles he is also highly regarded as one of those "borderline" authors whom enthusiasts for horror and the supernatural will almost invariably enjoy. Davies's last eight novels—including the two trilogies which are his finest work—increasingly use fantastical and supernatural elements in a rich literary stew of gamy grotesquerie and obscure erudition.

Such material is relatively muted and ambiguous in the remarkable Deptford Trilogy, comprising *Fifth Business*, *The Manticore* and *World of Wonders*. The first book's narrator is fascinated by the exotic lore of magic and saints, and believes his life to have been saved in World War I by a miracle involving a "simple" woman from his home town: a belief which shapes his destiny. At the climax, a spectacular stage-magic performance features an oracular Brazen Head whose cryptic pronouncement—perhaps by chance, perhaps not—ringingly summarizes the hidden side of a recently ended life. *The Manticore* begins as a tale of one harried man's psychoanalysis, in which the Jungian archetypes seem to develop a disturbing life beyond mere symbols; it culminates in a potent shamanic ordeal or rite of passage. *World of Wonders*, the artfully framed but relatively realistic autobiography of a stage conjurer, repeatedly invokes "Merlin's laugh"—the terrible and ironic laughter of the seer who knows what happens next.

Attendant spirits appear in the subsequent Cornish Trilogy, though those in the title of the initial *The Rebel Angels* are metaphorical. This is an unusual campus novel revolving around Rabelais, Romany lore, the Tarot, the therapeutic virtue of filth, and a crossbreeding of modern science and alchemy, with a memorable denouement mingling low sexual comedy and Grand Guignol. Preceding it in time, *What's Bred in the Bone* deals with the life of Francis Cornish, artist, connoisseur and spy, whose legacy motivates the other books. His deepest secrets are known only to the frame-story's spirits: the Lesser Zadkiel, Angel of Biography, and the Daimon Maimas who patiently twists Cornish's life to force out the one great painting which he has in him—at whatever cost in suffering. The presiding spirit of *The Lyre of Orpheus* is the voluble shade of E. T. A. Hoffmann himself, caught in Limbo until his unscored opera *Arthur of Britain: or, The Magnanimous Cuckold* can be completed and performed. Indeed the wealth of the Cornish Foundation is turned to just this end, but—in a repeated phrase of Hoffmann's own—"the lyre of Orpheus opens the door of the underworld." As the opera takes shape, murky stuff comes welling up into the mundane world and its episodes of comedy. Again the Tarot points the way; a curse is laid, and seems to work; the Arthurian glamour may or may not have enabled a man to attain a woman's bed in the semblance of her own husband (as, in Malory, Uther came to Ygraine with Merlin's aid, and Lancelot to Elaine). At last Hoffmann is freed and can say farewell.

Another impotent watcher from the afterlife narrates *Murther and Walking Spirits*—having been murdered in the first paragraph. Now he finds himself shackled to the oblivious murderer, a critic colleague who is blandly attending a movie festival. The narrator does not see the same films as his mortal companion, but intense vignettes of his ancestors' lives, an ancestry which in its ultimate Welsh roots parallels Davies's own. We are reminded that for all his cosmopolitan erudition, Davies firmly identified himself as a Canadian—one who, by analogy with the Matter of Britain or of Rome, was feeling his way towards the Matter of Canada. (The tough, memorable childhood sequences in *Fifth Business* and *What's*

Bred in the Bone also point in this direction.) Again, at the close, the captive finds a kind of freedom by reconciliation with what might be his soul or Jungian anima.

The doctor who is the title character of Davies's final novel *The Cunning Man* practises a highly unorthodox rather than a supernatural brand of healing. He leads an unlikely life of strange episodes (such as being pitchforked without warning into judging a Best Halitosis contest). Throughout, his viewpoint is coloured by a boyhood bout of scarlet fever and how, it seems, he was saved from death by the medicine woman Mrs. Smoke with her totemic snakes, whose tepee shook mysteriously through the long winter night while she wrestled or pretended to wrestle with things unknown. Mysticism and medical common sense alternate in *The Cunning Man*—and from time to time exchange their masks.

These last two books, though enjoyable, lack the great cumulative force of the trilogies. All eight novels are linked by crossover characters, with the murder of *Murther and Walking Spirits* forming a mystery subplot in *The Cunning Man*. The next book which Davies did not live to write might have completed a third trilogy which again would have been more than the sum of its parts.

Shorter supernatural fiction is assembled in the uneven but amusing *High Spirits*, whose 18 stories were read aloud as annual Christmas entertainments at Massey College in the University of Toronto, during Davies's period as Master. Naturally the fictionalized college proves a magnet for ghosts and prodigies, including Satan, the shade of Einstein, a carnivorous bust of Dickens, a monstrous college cat built by a student Frankenstein, and all the 200 or so saints who were demoted to mere legends by Pope Paul VI.

Davies's most notable contribution to horror/Gothic criticism is the 1976 lecture series "Masks of Satan," addressing the concept of Evil as portrayed in literature, from the grand old days of melodrama through ghost stories to the 20th-century novel. The sequence is collected in *One Half of Robertson Davies*, which also discusses "Insanity in Literature" and offers jocular advice to modern architects on the need for haunted houses with secret passages and oubliettes.

A writer of great and surely lasting stature, Robertson Davies saw life and literature in the round, with their horrific, grotesque and supernatural aspects as facets of the whole—necessary facets.

—David Langford

DEE, Ron(ald David)

Pseudonym: David Darke. **Nationality:** American. **Born:** 1957.

HORROR, GHOST AND GOTHIC PUBLICATIONS

Novels

Boundaries. Port Washington, New York, Ashley, 1979.
Brain Fever. New York, Pinnacle, 1989.
Blood Lust. New York, Dell, 1990.
Dusk. New York, Dell, 1991.
Descent. New York, Dell, 1991.
Blood. New York, Pocket, 1993.
Blind Hunger (as David Darke). New York, Pinnacle, 1993.
Shade (as David Darke). New York, Zebra, 1994.

Succumb. New York, Pocket, 1994.
Horrorshow (as David Darke). New York, Zebra, 1994.
Last Rites (as David Darke). New York, Zebra, 1996.

Short Stories

The Turning. N.p., Simulacran Press, 1993.
Sex & Blood. Leesburg, Virginia, TAL Publications, 1994.

*   *   *

Ron Dee's first horror novel was an interesting but rather predictable medical psychothriller. The protagonist of *Brain Fever* awakens one day to find himself in an unfamiliar body, called by an unfamiliar name, with a life history that doesn't match anything in his memory. He worries about his sanity, then suspects a plot, which ultimately proves to be the correct solution. His personality has been transplanted into another body as part of an unethical and highly illegal medical experiment, the author of which views him as little more than a test animal with no rights of his own. Although the plot itself broke no new ground, Dee's portrayal of the mental state of his hero was powerfully dramatic and effective.

Blood Lust was the first of several vampire novels Dee would write, a subject that dominates most of his subsequent work. A charming newcomer arrives in a suburb of St. Louis, and a mysterious transformation stirs the entire community. The vampiric curse spreads rapidly and in traditional fashion, though Dee adds a strong erotic element. His hero is a minister whose strength slips for a time, and he is briefly seduced by one of the vampires before regaining his self control for an exciting confrontation. *Dusk*, a sequel, was a significantly better. There's a coven of vampires living in a ghost town near the Mexican border, but some of their recent victims are less circumspect than they ought to be. They travel to Dallas on a killing spree, but their contempt for their prey and their inexperience causes them to become too brazen, endangering not only themselves, but their older brethren as well. The minister and his wife return to help the authorities destroy the wayward predators and track them back to their hidden colony. There are several extremely effective scenes in the novel, most notably an amusing encounter between black vampires and white racists.

Descent abandoned vampires in favour of ghosts, but not the usual spirits of the departed. A young woman appears to be suffering from a form of mental illness, insists that she is somehow in contact with the dead, sees things invisible to others, even feels their presence physically. Although some of the individual sequences are quite effective, *Descent* is inconsistent in its mood and occasionally too vague to maintain its hold. Dee returned promptly to vampires with *Blood*, which was nearly as well written as *Dusk* and has an even more interesting focus. This time the plot involves a new wonder drug developed by a secret government project which cures people of terminal diseases. That sounds fine, except that those treated have subsequently turned into undead killers because the serum was developed from vampire blood. Obviously, government employees aren't bright enough to have anticipated this possibility. Two intrepid independent investigators are suspicious of the wave of vampire-like killings and uncover the truth, only to find themselves targeted for death by both the living and the dead.

In 1993, Dee reinvented his career as David Darke, but without abandoning his fascination with vampires. In *Blind Hunger* Patty Hunsacker is a recently widowed blind woman whose life takes an apparent turn for the better when her husband's previously unsuspected twin brother shows up. He promptly moves in, promising to take care of her, but seems oddly reticent at times, and Patty suspects that something strange and unpleasant is happening in his room, from which she occasionally hears odd sounds. She's right, of course, since the "brother" is actually her dead husband, risen from the grave. Scarlett Shade is a popular vampire novelist in *Shade*, an often amusing look at one aspect of the writing profession. Scarlett's novels are particularly authentic because she actually is one of the undead, and when some of her more persistent fans insist upon meeting her in private, there's an obvious sequel planned for them.

A television horror-show host slaughters a family, then dies live in front of the cameras in *Horrorshow*. Twenty years later, his evil spirit returns from the dead to celebrate the anniversary of that first bloodbath with a new one, this time using the television medium to implant homicidal impulses in his viewers and send them out to murder their family and friends. Old evil returns as well in *Last Rites*. A circle of friends who dabbled ineffectively with satanism in their youth is reunited in maturity and tempted to try again. But this time they're more successful, literally raising the dead to do their bidding. Except that it never quite works out that way, and the revived dead insist on a price greater than they had expected to pay. Both *Horrorshow* and *Last Rites* owe much in their concept to filmed horror, although neither is hobbled by the predictable shallowness of that genre. Dee's vampire novels remain his strongest, most memorable work, but his other horror fiction is well plotted and heavily atmospheric.

Dee has also written a number of short stories, of which the best and most disturbing is "Genderella." A young gay boy with a crush on a straight friend is able to magically alter his body to that of a girl. But the magic reverses itself at precisely midnight, and catches them in the middle of the act of sex, causing their bodies to be permanently joined with particularly chilling consequences. Dee explores vampirism again in "A Matter of Style" and "Soulmates." Other stories of interest include "Jet Lag," "Dealer's Choice," "A Little Night Music" and "Stomach Trouble." Dee is predominantly a niche writer, specializing in vampires, but through choice rather than limited ability. His other horror fiction is of sufficiently high quality to have established his reputation independently, and novels like *Dusk* and *Blood* are notable vampire novels in an era when stories of the undead frequently reach the bestseller lists.

—Don D'Ammassa

DE FELITTA, Frank (Paul)

Nationality: American. **Born:** New York City, 1921. **Family:** Married Dorothy De Felitta; one son and one daughter. **Career:** Documentary filmmaker, screenwriter, director and novelist. Lives in Hollywood, California.

HORROR, GHOST AND GOTHIC PUBLICATIONS

Novels

Audrey Rose. New York, Putnam, 1975; London, Collins, 1976.
The Entity. New York, Putnam, 1978; London, Collins, 1979.

For Love of Audrey Rose. New York, Warner, and London, New English Library, 1982.
Golgotha Falls: An Assault on the Fourth Dimension. New York, Simon and Schuster, and London, New English Library, 1984.
Funeral March of the Marionettes. London, New English Library, 1990.

OTHER PUBLICATIONS

Novels

Oktoberfest. New York, Doubleday, 1973; London, Collins, 1974.
Sea Trial. New York, Avon, and London, Gollancz, 1980.

Plays

Screenplays: *Zero Population Growth*, with Max Ehrlich, 1971; *The Savage Is Loose*, with Max Ehrlich, 1974; *Audrey Rose*, 1977; *The Entity*, 1981.

*

Film Adaptations: *Audrey Rose*, 1977; *The Entity*, 1981.

Theatrical Activities:
Director: **Films**—*The Two Worlds of Jennie Logan* (television movie), 1979; *Dark Night of the Scarecrow* (television movie), 1981; *Killer in the Mirror* (television movie), 1986; *Scissors*, 1991.

*   *   *

Frank De Felitta, who, rather engagingly, has incorporated himself as "Penny Dreadful, Inc.," served his apprenticeship as an author of horror fiction by writing films. (Two of his screenplays, the science-fictional *Zero Population Growth* and the curious robinsonade-cum-sex drama *The Savage Is Loose*, have been novelized by his co-screenwriter, Max Ehrlich—the former movie under the title *The Edict*.) Those movies both appeared in the early 1970s, before De Felitta's foray into print with the ground-breaking *Audrey Rose*. It is probable that the screenplays helped to teach De Felitta something of the art of novel-writing; certainly the first novel is a solid, cinematically-detailed piece of work, a fact no doubt that eased its passage onto the big screen a few years later.

Audrey Rose was published as a sibling to William Peter Blatty's *The Exorcist* (1971), which had been a popular addition to the canon of paranormal literature. The first comparison between the two volumes is the obvious one: both have a young girl being possessed by the soul of someone or something else. The title of Blatty's book suggests that the exorcist himself—the man who will try to rid little Regan of her unwelcome visitor—is the star of the show, the force for good. Implicit, therefore, is that there is a force for evil to be countered: that which changes Regan into a cursing, violent other-worlder, with a neck as twistable as a rubber band and a habit of projectile-vomiting. Here the two novels differ: Audrey Rose is the star of De Felitta's book, and she has already passed away. Audrey Rose died in a burning car wreck before the novel's opening credits, and she is introduced to the reader by her father; the father has started to pester a family because he believes that the family's 12-year-old girl, Ivy, is the reincarnation of Audrey. Audrey's spirit is not a force for evil, how-

ever; Audrey Rose does not want to haunt anybody. Indeed, her manifestations in Ivy's life are marked by personal pain and suffering as she re-enacts her last moments in the car, beating her hands against a scalding window pane. *Audrey Rose* is a rarity in the horror genre: there is not an evil force, *per se*, to fight. The two girls in question—the inhabiter and the inhabitee—are innocents, slogging against the sheer unfairness of the Hindu concept of reincarnation and its consequent absence of choice.

Horror fiction lends itself to sequels, of course, in the sense that a character believed dead can be brought back to life. But when the trope on display is that of soul-displacement, even this carry-on clause seems unnecessary. In De Felitta's novels, once a soul is tormented it stays tormented. Seven years after *Audrey Rose* came the story's culmination, in *For Love of Audrey Rose*. The Templetons are back, but the family is in pieces, their first daughter Ivy (and Audrey, naturally) believed dead and gone. The father, Bill, is an obsessive nervous wreck who cannot forgive his wife for finally believing Audrey's father's theory of karma-substitution and testifying to the effect. The novel leans more heavily than before on Eastern philosophy and lore. It is as powerful and cold as the story's first volume; and by the book's final pages one feels the possibility that even this might not be the end of the metapsychological saga.

The most important thing with Frank De Felitta is to hold your breath and fall for the initial premise. Once that has been done, you are in for an excellent time. *The Entity*, for example, is a different slant on the idea of possession; the novel sees a woman who is habitually sexually assaulted by a creature that might (or might not) come from her own id. But it is *Funeral March of the Marionettes*—De Felitta's least typical novel—that is probably his most successful.

Funeral March of the Marionettes is a playful, postmodern non-supernatural horror story that refers subtly to his own earlier work, as well as to staple horror fare by other novelists and, more importantly, horror filmmakers. In this equivalent of the type of games played by Georges Perec (among others), we see a text about people's reactions to thrilling and violent films; the ironic touch is that the references that De Felitta makes throughout to other works will only be appreciated by those of its readership who like (or at least watch) thrilling and violent films. To a certain extent the book is a critique of everybody who reads, writes or watches horror. It is about artistic responsibilities and moral passivity or laxity, the way that horror-viewers have become numb to gruesome material and now use the real world as a cinema screen on which to watch acts of ever more alarming atrocity. After the discovery of a murder: "People made way, but what infuriated Santomassimo was that they gobbled Mars Bars and Snickers and tossed the wrappers into the gutter, like they were watching a film. Someone slurped Coke through a straw, peering at what action there was right through the ambulance window. Santomassimo even thought he saw a hand with gleaming, yellowed, buttered popcorn." Voyeurism, De Felitta seems to be arguing, is the new pornography; images of sight and spying are present throughout. And the killer lets voyeurism eat away at rational common sense.

The title refers to the musical composition by Gounod—which happens to be the theme tune for the TV show, *Alfred Hitchcock Presents*. As well as the novel being De Felitta's homage to Hitchcock, the killer is also enamoured of Hitch's work and chooses to murder his victims using variations on techniques from some of the films: dive-bombing one victim with an explosive-laden toy plane, for example, or electrocuting one person in the shower. The detective, Santomassimo, enlists the help of Professor Quinn, who teaches a college course called "Hitch-500" and who suggests that Hitchcock's humour was a form of cruelty; Santomassimo goes one step further: "My Aunt Rosa saw *The Ten Commandments* eight times. . . Every time she waited for the miracles. It was an obsessive, hypnotic kind of thing. Sometimes I wonder if it should be legal." Successful both as a novelist and as a filmmaker, De Felitta knows the power of art as a manipulative influence, and the narrator even implies that the very process of filmmaking is cruel. Quite how literally we can take this as a comment straight from the horse's mouth is moot, but the novel certainly has a tone of shocked acceptance at the way entertainment has gone. But neither the narrator nor De Felitta can resist the power of storytelling; perhaps such devotion to the darkness of the human soul is the greatest horror of all.

—David Mathew

de la MARE, Walter

Pseudonym: Walter Ramal. **Nationality:** British. **Born:** Charlton, Kent, 25 April 1873. **Education:** St. Paul's Cathedral Choristers' School, London (founder, *Choristers Journal,* 1889). **Family:** Married Constance Elfrida Ingpen in 1899 (died 1943); two sons and two daughters. **Career:** Clerk, Anglo-American Oil Company, London, 1890-1908; reviewer for the *Times, Westminster Gazette, Bookman,* and other journals, London. **Awards:** Royal Society of Literature de Polignac prize, 1911; James Tait Black Memorial prize, for fiction, 1922; Library Association Carnegie medal, 1948; Foyle Poetry prize, 1954. D.Litt.: Oxford, Cambridge, Bristol, and London universities; LL.D.: University of St. Andrews. Honorary Fellow, Keble College, Oxford. Granted Civil List pension, 1908; Companion of Honour, 1948; Order of Merit, 1953. **Died:** 22 June 1956.

HORROR, GHOST AND GOTHIC PUBLICATIONS

Novel

The Return. London, Arnold, 1910; New York, Putnam, 1911; revised edition, London, Collins, and New York, Knopf, 1922.

Short Stories

The Riddle and Other Stories. London, Selwyn and Blount, 1923; as *The Riddle and Other Tales,* New York, Knopf, 1923.
Ding Dong Bell. London, Selwyn and Blount, and New York, Knopf, 1924.
Two Tales: The Green-Room, The Connoisseur. London, Bookman's Journal, 1925.
The Connoisseur and Other Stories. London, Collins, and New York, Knopf, 1926; abridged as *The Nap and Other Stories,* London, Nelson, 1936.
On the Edge: Short Stories. London, Faber, 1930; New York, Knopf, 1931.
Seven Short Stories. London, Faber, 1931.
A Froward Child. London, Faber, 1934.
The Wind Blows Over. London, Faber, and New York, Macmillan, 1936.

Best Stories of Walter de la Mare. London, Faber, 1942.
The Collected Tales of Walter de la Mare, edited by Edward Wagenknecht. New York, Knopf, 1950.
A Beginning and Other Stories. London, Faber, 1955.
Ghost Stories. London, Folio Society, 1956.
Some Stories. London, Faber, 1962.
Eight Tales. Sauk City, Wisconsin, Arkham House, 1971.

OTHER PUBLICATIONS

Novels

Henry Brocken: His Travels and Adventures in the Rich, Strange, Scarce-Imaginable Regions of Romance. London, Murray, 1904; New York, Knopf, 1924.
Memoirs of a Midget. London, Collins, 1921; New York, Knopf, 1922.

Short Stories

Lispet, Lispett, and Vaine. London, Bookman's Journal, 1923.
At First Sight. New York, Crosby Gaige, 1928.
The Picnic and Other Stories. London, Faber, 1941.

Fiction for Children

The Three Mulla-Mulgars, illustrated by Dorothy P. Lathrop. London, Duckworth, 1910; New York, Knopf, 1919; as *The Three Royal Monkeys; or, The Three Mulla-Mulgars,* London, Faber, 1935.
Story and Rhyme: A Selection from the Writings of Walter de la Mare, Chosen by the Author. London, Dent, and New York, Dutton, 1921.
Broomsticks and Other Tales, illustrated by Bold. London, Constable, and New York, Knopf, 1925.
Miss Jemima, illustrated by Alec Buckels. Oxford, Blackwell, 1925; Poughkeepsie, New York, Artists and Writers Guild, 1935.
Old Joe, illustrated by C. T. Nightingale. Oxford, Blackwell, 1927.
The Dutch Cheese and the Lovely Myfanwy, illustrated by Dorothy P. Lathrop. New York, Knopf, 1931.
The Lord Fish and Other Tales, illustrated by Rex Whistler. London, Faber, 1933.
The Old Lion and Other Stories, illustrated by Irene Hawkins. London, Faber, 1942.
Mr. Bumps and His Monkey, illustrated by Dorothy P. Lathrop. Philadelphia, Winston, 1942.
The Magic Jacket and Other Stories, illustrated by Irene Hawkins. London, Faber, 1943.
The Scarecrow and Other Stories, illustrated by Irene Hawkins. London, Faber, 1945.
The Dutch Cheese and Other Stories, illustrated by Irene Hawkins. London, Faber, 1946.
Collected Stories for Children, illustrated by Irene Hawkins. London, Faber, 1947.
A Penny a Day, illustrated by Paul Kennedy. New York, Knopf, 1960.

Play

Crossings: A Fairy Play, music by C. Armstrong Gibbs, illustrated by Randolph Schwabe (produced Hove, Sussex, 1919; London, 1925). London, Beaumont Press, 1921; New York, Knopf, 1923.

Poetry

Songs of Childhood (as Walter Ramal). London, Longman, 1902; New York, Garland, 1976; revised edition, as Walter de la Mare, Longman, 1916, 1923.

Poems. London, Murray, 1906.

A Child's Day: A Book of Rhymes, illustrated by Carine and Will Cadby. London, Constable, 1912; New York, Holt, 1923.

The Listeners and Other Poems. London, Constable, 1912; New York, Holt, 1916.

The Old Men. London, Flying Fame, 1913.

Peacock Pie: A Book of Rhymes. London, Constable, 1913; New York, Holt, 1917.

The Sunken Garden and Other Poems. London, Beaumont Press, 1917.

Motley and Other Poems. London, Constable, and New York, Holt, 1918.

Flora, drawings by Pamela Bianco. London, Heinemann, and Philadelphia, Lippincott, 1919.

Poems 1901 to 1918. London, Constable, 2 vols., 1920; as *Collected Poems 1901 to 1918,* New York, Holt, 2 vols., 1920.

The Veil and Other Poems. London, Constable, 1921; New York, Holt, 1922.

Down-Adown-Derry: A Book of Fairy Poems, illustrated by Dorothy P. Lathrop. London, Constable, and New York, Holt, 1922.

Thus Her Tale: A Poem. Edinburgh, Porpoise Press, 1923.

A Ballad of Christmas. London, Selwyn and Blount, 1924.

The Hostage. London, Selwyn and Blount, 1925.

St. Andrews, with Rudyard Kipling. London, A. and C. Black, 1926.

(Poems). London, Benn, 1926.

Alone. London, Faber, 1927.

Selected Poems. New York, Holt, 1927.

Stuff and Nonsense and So On, illustrated by Bold. London, Constable, and New York, Holt, 1927; revised edition, London, Faber, 1946.

The Captive and Other Poems. New York, Bowling Green Press, 1928.

Self to Self. London, Faber, 1928.

A Snowdrop. London, Faber, 1929.

News. London, Faber, 1930.

Poems for Children. London, Constable, and New York, Holt, 1930.

To Lucy. London, Faber, 1931.

The Sunken Garden and Other Verses. Birmingham, Birmingham School of Printing, 1931.

Two Poems. Privately printed, 1931.

The Fleeting and Other Poems. London, Constable, and New York, Knopf, 1933.

Poems 1919 to 1934. London, Constable, 1935; New York, Holt, 1936.

Poems. London, Corvinus Press, 1937.

This Year, Next Year, illustrated by Harold Jones. London, Faber, and New York, Holt, 1937.

Memory and Other Poems. London, Constable, and New York, Holt, 1938.

Two Poems, with Arthur Rogers. Privately printed, 1938.

Haunted: A Poem. London, Linden Press, 1939.

Bells and Grass: A Book of Rhymes, illustrated by Rowland Emett. London, Faber, 1941; New York, Viking Press, 1942.

Collected Poems. New York, Holt, 1941; London, Faber, 1942.

Time Passes and Other Poems, edited by Anne Ridler. London, Faber, 1942.

Collected Rhymes and Verses, illustrated by Berthold Wolpe. London, Faber, 1944.

The Burning-Glass and Other Poems, Including The Traveller. New York, Viking Press, 1945.

The Burning-Glass and Other Poems. London, Faber, 1945.

The Traveller. London, Faber, 1946.

Two Poems: Pride, The Truth of Things. London, Dropmore Press, 1946.

Rhymes and Verses: Collected Poems for Children, illustrated by Elinore Blaisdell. New York, Holt, 1947.

Inward Companion. London, Faber, 1950.

Winged Chariot. London, Faber, 1951.

Winged Chariot and Other Poems. New York, Viking Press, 1951.

O Lovely England and Other Poems. London, Faber, 1953.

The Winnowing Dream. London, Faber, 1954.

Selected Poems, edited by R. N. Green-Armytage. London, Faber, 1954.

The Morrow. Privately printed, 1955.

Poems, edited by Eleanor Graham, illustrated by Margery Gill. London, Penguin, 1962.

(Poems), edited by John Hadfield. London, Vista Books, 1962.

A Choice of de la Mare's Verse, edited by W. H. Auden. London, Faber, 1963.

Envoi. Privately printed, 1965.

The Complete Poems of Walter de la Mare, edited by Leonard Clark and others. London, Faber, 1969; New York, Knopf, 1970.

The Collected Poems of Walter de la Mare. London, Faber, 1979.

The Voice, edited and illustrated by Catherine Brighton. London, Faber, 1986; New York, Delacorte Press, 1987.

Other

M. E. Coleridge: An Appreciation. London, The Guardian, 1907.

Rupert Brooke and the Intellectual Imagination (lecture). London, Sidgwick and Jackson, and New York, Harcourt Brace, 1919.

Some Thoughts on Reading (lecture). Bembridge, Isle of Wight, Yellowsands Press, 1923.

Some Women Novelists of the 'Seventies. London, Cambridge University Press, 1929.

The Printing of Poetry (lecture). London, Cambridge University Press, 1931.

The Early Novels of Wilkie Collins. London, Cambridge University Press, 1932.

Lewis Carroll. London, Faber, 1932.

Early One Morning in the Spring: Chapters on Children and on Childhood as It Is Revealed in Particular in Early Memories and in Early Writings. London, Faber, and New York, Macmillan, 1935.

Poetry in Prose (lecture). London, Oxford University Press, 1936; New York, Oxford University Press, 1937.

Arthur Thompson: A Memoir. Privately printed, 1938.

An Introduction to Everyman. London, Dent, 1938.

Stories, Essays, and Poems, edited by M. M. Bozman. London, Dent, 1938.

Pleasures and Speculations. London, Faber, 1940; Freeport, New York, Books for Libraries Press, 1969.

Private View (essays). London, Faber, 1953; Westport, Connecticut, Hyperion, 1979.

Walter de la Mare: A Selection from His Writings, edited by Kenneth Hopkins. London, Faber, 1956.

Other for Children

Told Again: Traditional Tales, illustrated by A. H. Watson. Oxford, Blackwell, 1927; as *Told Again: Old Tales Told Again,* New York, Knopf, 1927; as *Tales Told Again,* London, Faber, and Knopf, 1959.

Stories from the Bible, illustrated by Theodore Nadejen. London, Faber, and New York, Cosmopolitan, 1929.

Letters from Mr. Walter de la Mare to Form Three. Privately printed, 1936.

Animal Stories, Chosen, Arranged, and in Some Part Re-Written. London, Faber, 1939; New York, Scribner, 1940.

Selected Stories and Verses, edited by Eleanor Graham. London, Penguin, 1952.

Molly Whuppie, illustrated by Errol Le Cain. London, Faber, and New York, Farrar Straus, 1983.

Editor, *Come Hither: A Collection of Rhymes and Poems for the Young of all Ages,* illustrated by Alec Buckels. London, Constable, and New York, Knopf, 1923; revised edition, 1928.

Editor, with Thomas Quayle, *Readings: Traditional Tales Told by the Author,* illustrated by A. H. Watson and C. T. Nightingale. Oxford, Blackwell, 6 vols., 1925-28; New York, Knopf, 1 vol., 1927.

Editor, *Desert Islands and Robinson Crusoe.* London, Faber, and New York, Fountains Press, 1930; revised edition, Faber, 1932.

Editor, *Poems,* by Christina Rossetti. Newtown, Wales, Gregynog Press, 1930.

Editor, *The Eighteen-Eighties: Essays by Fellows of the Royal Society of Literature.* London, Cambridge University Press, 1930.

Editor, *Tom Tiddler's Ground: A Book of Poetry for the Junior and Middle Schools.* London, Collins, 3 vols., 1932; New York, Knopf, 1 vol., 1962.

Editor, *Old Rhymes and New, Chosen for Use in Schools.* London, Constable, 2 vols., 1932.

Editor, *Behold, This Dreamer! Of Reverie, Night, Sleep, Dream, Love-Dreams, Nightmare, Death, The Unconscious, The Imagination, Divination, The Artist, and Kindred Subjects.* London, Faber, and New York, Knopf, 1939.

Editor, *Love.* London, Faber, 1943; New York, Morrow, 1946.

*

Bibliography: In *L'Oeuvre de Walter de la Mare: Une Aventure Spirituelle* by Luce Bonnerot, Paris, Didier, 1969.

Manuscript Collections: Syracuse University, New York; Temple University, Philadelphia; University of Chicago; King's College, Cambridge.

Critical Studies (selection): *Walter de la Mare: A Critical Study* by Forrest Reid, London, Faber, and New York, Holt, 1929; *Walter de la Mare: An Exploration* by John Atkins, London, Temple, 1947; *Walter de la Mare* by Kenneth Hopkins, London, Longman, 1953; *Tea with Walter de la Mare* by Russell Brain, London, Faber, 1957; *Walter de la Mare* by Leonard Clark, London, Bodley Head, 1960, New York, Walck, 1961; *Walter de la Mare* by Doris Ross McCrosson, New York, Twayne, 1966; "On the Edge: Walter de la Mare," in *Night Vistors: The Rise and Fall of the English Ghost Story* by Julia Briggs, London, Faber, 1977.

* * *

Walter de la Mare was a poet and critic with a keen appreciation of the supernatural—or, to use his own favourite term, the preternatural—who wrote some of the finest oblique tales of the macabre of the 20th century. Not for him an eldritch and unremitting parade of the hideous, the ghastly, the deliberately gruesome, although all such appear in his work. His talent was for rendering the familiar, in the words of T. S. Eliot (celebrating the older poet's 75th birthday) "suddenly strange." And de la Mare's "strange" is by no means the "strange" of the workaday horror hack; it is often stranger by far than that.

De la Mare rarely, if ever, used the supernatural as an end in itself; as a revelation in the finale to give the reader an ugly moment or two. Almost his sole essay in this direction is the late story "Bad Company" (*A Beginning and Other Stories*), in which the narrator is lured by an old man to an old deserted house in which the old man's corpse is "awaiting company." This comes as a signal shock to those looking for the typical de la Mare ellipsis, the ending which seems to be missing certain vital ingredients—even, simply, certain words—that would make sense of an otherwise baffling experience. In this, it might be said that de la Mare's best stories are like life: unnerving, and hopelessly perplexing.

All events in stories of the supernatural are, in their way, more or less inexplicable, events in de la Mare's stories even more inexplicable than most. Obsession comes into it, strongly. The rage-filled Fruit-Merchant in "The Tree" (*The Riddle and Other Stories*) spends what remains of his life buying up the gorgeous paintings of his hated brother, agonizingly aware that he can only ever purchase the cheaper ones, yet still frantically, obsessively, buying. In "The Green Room" (*On the Edge*), Alan's obsession is to reveal the genius of the sad poetess-suicide by publishing her unpublished work. Yet when this is achieved the vision he is vouchsafed is by no means the vision he thinks he is going to see. Far from it.

There are rather more sinister obsessions, those of Messrs Bloom and Kempe a good deal worse than most. In "Mr. Kempe" (*The Connoisseur*), the main character's obsession is to discover what happens immediately after death, or, rather, to capture the precise moment when life is transformed into death. To this end, he utilizes a camera, but his photographs of falling climbers are such that the narrator has to flee rather than look at them closely. Bloom, too, in "A Recluse" (*On the Edge*), does more than just dabble in the occult. His house, "Montresor" (with a tip of de la Mare's hat to Poe), is not merely haunted . . . "it was infested"— and Bloom's invaders are beginning to get out of hand.

Not that some horrific explosion of violence, psychic or otherwise, will occur. At his best de la Mare has a featherlight touch. He brushes the back of the reader's neck as a light wind thrums on an Aeolian harp, softly and hintingly. At times one is not entirely sure that one is indeed dealing with the supernatural. His most famous, and most reprinted, strange tale, "Seaton's Aunt," can, to an extent, be read in two quite distinct ways—as a perfectly moral piece of mainstream fiction about an elderly woman, rather disagreeable and dominating and cantankerous; or, as a tale of a powerfully evil presence who obsessively pursues her hapless nephew, draining him of his life-force.

And what of "All Hallows" (*The Connoisseur*)?—arguably one of the finest "strange tales" in the literature. What on earth—or in Hades—is going on inside, or beneath, this vast, lorn edifice? The dean's verger believes he knows—but, after all, what is there to see, to experience, to hear? The trembling of taut canvas high amongst the flying buttresses, the eddying of fog "like flowing milk," the abyssal rumblings and grindings from far below, the vulturine aspect of a statue of St. Mark . . . the maunderings of an old man. Yet although de la Mare was by no means a man of orthodoxy, this extraordinarily embattled cathedral is clearly a metaphor for the world as he saw it. When faith has gone, as the old verger grimly puts it, "the seas are in"—the cathedral, the world, is about to be overwhelmed by evil, by "Satan himself."

"All Hallows" is on the large, indeed the vast, scale. Much of de la Mare's work is limned on a far smaller, even domestic, canvas. The consumptive Alice in "The Looking-Glass" (*The Riddle*) is told that the garden outside her bedroom is haunted; dying, she realizes the ghost is none other than herself; little Emmeline's experiences in "What Dreams May Come" (*The Wind Blows Over*) are nightmarish enough, but in the end bed-bound (though not perhaps entirely safely bed-bound, since a nurse is watching over her); another sick child, Philip in "The Guardian" (*A Beginning*), glancing sideways, catches glimpses of a "dark, small and stunted" figure crouching in wait; "Alice's Godmother" is the terrifying tale of a young girl who is offered incredible things by her strange old godmother—who lives in a be-shadowed old house in an enormous park—but flees from them all, probably wisely; in the powerful "Strangers and Pilgrims" (*Ding Dong Bell*) a man in black, towards evening, comes from the direction of the sea looking for a grave that is increasingly implied to be his own.

In the main, the style is clearly that of a poet, sharp and lucid; although there is something ominously Pinteresque about a good deal of the dialogue, descriptive passages, soliloquies, these last often broken up and disjointed—*fractured*—almost in the naturalistic manner of Joyce (although it is doubtful that de la Mare would have much appreciated either the fire and brimstone of Joyce as a young man, or his mature self, clawing into life's midden with both bare hands). Another writer with whom de la Mare does have an odd affinity is Samuel Beckett: in the work of both death is a central, an abiding, concern, at times to the exclusion of all else. The critic Julia Briggs has argued plausibly that rather than a late Romantic, de la Mare should be considered an early Modern.

His novels all certainly bear striking witness to his vivid, singular, awkward imagination. *Henry Brocken* is a *conte fantastique* in which the hero journeys to a land unknown to mapmakers wherein reside those who were never born and will never die: Lucy Gray (Wordsworth), La Belle Dame Sans Merci, Lemuel Gulliver, Jane Rochester (née Eyre), Annabel Lee (Poe). *Memoirs of a Midget* (for which, in 1922, de la Mare won the prestigious James Tait Black Memorial Prize) is the at times farcical, at times enormously moving tale of "Miss M," so tiny she can almost stand in one's hand.

The Return (which gained for its author the de Polignac Prize) is de la Mare's most elaborate essay in the preternatural, a story laden with ambiguities, but a story, too, which grips the imagination. Arthur Lawford goes to sleep beside the crumbling gravestone of Nicholas Sabathier, a 17th-century Huguenot suicide, and awakes not with his mind taken over (the obvious cliché) but his face, now transformed into the wolfish features of Sabathier. *The Return* is a journey of self-revelation for Lawford, almost a "pilgrim's progress," as he discovers who accepts him, who denies (his wife takes the latter course); who can understand his terrible predicament, who alleviate the crawling horror of being "taken over," of being slowly eclipsed by another. Most commentators have accepted that after Lawford's psychic trials and tribulations he returns to his wife. Another reading of the text might very well determine quite the opposite.

Virtually nothing about Walter de la Mare is straightforward or clear-cut; there are no cheap and easy resolutions. That is precisely why, as a writer, he fascinates so. He writes, as it were, not of something rushing towards us, gabbling and gobbling, but of something just glimpsed, momentarily, at the peripheries of one's vision. The kind of glimpse that, at its worst, can truly raise the hairs at the back of the neck.

—Jack Adrian

DERLETH, August (William)

Pseudonyms: Stephen Grendon; Tally Mason. **Nationality:** American. **Born:** Sauk City, Wisconsin, 24 February 1909. **Education:** St. Aloysius School; Sauk City High School; University of Wisconsin, Madison, B.A. 1930. **Family:** Married Sandra Winters in 1953 (divorced 1959); one daughter and one son. **Career:** Editor, Fawcett Publications, Minneapolis, 1930-31; editor, *The Midwesterner*, Madison, 1931; lecturer in American regional literature, University of Wisconsin, 1939-43; owner and co-founder (with Donald Wandrei, 1939-42), Arkham House Publishers (including the imprints Mycroft and Moran, and Stanton and Lee), Sauk City, 1939-71; editor, *Mind Magic*, 1931; literary editor and columnist, *Madison Capital Times*, 1941-71; editor, *The Arkham Sampler*, 1948-49, *Hawk and Whippoorwill*, 1960-63, and *The Arkham Collector*, 1967-71, all Sauk City. **Awards:** Guggenheim fellowship, 1938; *Scholastic* award, 1958; Midland Authors award, for poetry, 1965; Ann Radcliffe award, 1967. **Died:** 4 July 1971.

HORROR, GHOST AND GOTHIC PUBLICATIONS

Novels

The Lurker at the Threshold, with H. P. Lovecraft. Sauk City, Wisconsin, Arkham House, 1945; London, Gollancz, 1948.
The Trail of Cthulhu. Sauk City, Wisconsin, Arkham House, 1962; London, Spearman, 1974.
The Beast in Holger's Woods (for children). New York, Crowell, 1968.

Short Stories

Someone in the Dark. Sauk City, Wisconsin, Arkham House, 1941.
Something Near. Sauk City, Wisconsin, Arkham House, 1945.
Not Long for This World. Sauk City, Wisconsin, Arkham House, 1948.
The Survivor and Others, with H. P. Lovecraft. Sauk City, Wisconsin, Arkham House, 1957.
The Mask of Cthulhu. Sauk City, Wisconsin, Arkham House, 1958; London, Consul, 1961.
Lonesome Places. Sauk City, Wisconsin, Arkham House, 1962.
Mr. George and Other Odd Persons (as Stephen Grendon). Sauk City, Wisconsin, Arkham House, 1963; as *When Graveyards Yawn*, London, Tandem, 1965.
Colonel Markesan and Less Pleasant People, with Mark Schorer. Sauk City, Wisconsin, Arkham House, 1966.
The Shadow Out of Time and Other Tales of Horror, with H. P. Lovecraft. London, Gollancz, 1968; abridged edition, as *The Shuttered Room and Other Tales of Horror*, London, Panther, 1970.

The Watchers Out of Time and Others, with H. P. Lovecraft. Sauk City, Wisconsin, Arkham House, 1974.
Harrigan's File. Sauk City, Wisconsin, Arkham House, 1975.
Dwellers in Darkness. Sauk City, Wisconsin, Arkham House, 1976.

Other

Editor, with Donald Wandrei, *The Outsider and Others,* by H. P. Lovecraft. Sauk City, Wisconsin, Arkham House, 1939.
Editor, with Donald Wandrei, *Beyond the Wall of Sleep,* by H. P. Lovecraft. Sauk City, Wisconsin, Arkham House, 1943.
Editor, with Donald Wandrei, *Marginalia,* by H. P. Lovecraft. Sauk City, Wisconsin, Arkham House, 1944.
Editor, *Sleep No More: Twenty Masterpieces of Horror for the Connoisseur.* New York, Farrar and Rinehart, 1944; abridged edition, London, Panther, 1964.
Editor, *The Best Supernatural Stories of H. P. Lovecraft.* Cleveland, World, 1945; revised edition, as *The Dunwich Horror and Others,* Sauk City, Wisconsin, Arkham House, 1963.
Editor, *Who Knocks? Twenty Masterpieces of the Spectral for the Connoisseur.* New York, Rinehart, 1946; abridged edition, London, Panther, 1964.
Editor, *The Night Side: Masterpieces of the Strange and Terrible.* New York, Rinehart, 1947; London, New English Library, 1966.
Editor, *The Sleeping and the Dead.* Chicago, Pellegrini and Cudahy, 1947; as *The Sleeping and the Dead* and *The Unquiet Grave,* London, New English Library, 2 vols., 1963-64.
Editor, *Dark of the Moon: Poems of Fantasy and the Macabre.* Sauk City, Wisconsin, Arkham House, 1947.
Editor, *Night's Yawning Peal: A Ghostly Company.* Sauk City, Wisconsin, Arkham House, 1952; London, Consul, 1965.
Editor, *The Shuttered Room and Other Pieces by H. P. Lovecraft and Divers Hands.* Sauk City, Wisconsin, Arkham House, 1959.
Editor, *Fire and Sleet and Candlelight: New Poems of the Macabre.* Sauk City, Wisconsin, Arkham House, 1961.
Editor, *Dark Mind, Dark Heart.* Sauk City, Wisconsin, Arkham House, 1962; London, Mayflower, 1963.
Editor, *When Evil Wakes: A New Anthology of the Macabre.* London, Souvenir Press, 1963.
Editor, *Over the Edge.* Sauk City, Wisconsin, Arkham House, 1964; London, Gollancz, 1967.
Editor, *At the Mountains of Madness and Other Novels,* by H. P. Lovecraft. Sauk City, Wisconsin, Arkham House, 1964; London, Gollancz, 1966.
Editor, *Dagon and Other Macabre Tales,* by H. P. Lovecraft. Sauk City, Wisconsin, Arkham House, 1965; London, Gollancz, 1967.
Editor, with others, *The Dark Brotherhood and Other Pieces,* by H. P. Lovecraft and others. Sauk City, Wisconsin, Arkham House, 1966.
Editor, *Travellers by Night.* Sauk City, Wisconsin, Arkham House, 1967.
Editor, *Tales of the Cthulhu Mythos,* by H. P. Lovecraft and others. Sauk City, Wisconsin, Arkham House, 1969.
Editor, *The Horror in the Museum and Other Revisions,* by H. P. Lovecraft. Sauk City, Wisconsin, Arkham House, 1970; abridged edition, London, Panther, 1975.
Editor, *Dark Things.* Sauk City, Wisconsin, Arkham House, 1971.

Novels

Murder Stalks the Wakely Family. New York, Loring and Mussey, 1934; as *Death Stalks the Wakely Family,* London, Newnes, 1937.
The Man on All Fours. New York, Loring and Mussey, 1934; London, Newnes, 1936.
Three Who Died. New York, Loring and Mussey, 1935.
Sign of Fear. New York, Loring and Mussey, 1935; London, Newnes, 1936.
Still Is the Summer Night. New York, Scribner, 1937.
Wind over Wisconsin. New York, Scribner, 1938.
Restless Is the River. New York, Scribner, 1939.
Sentence Deferred. New York, Scribner, 1939; London, Heinemann, 1940.
Bright Journey. New York, Scribner, 1940.
The Narracong Riddle. New York, Scribner, 1940.
Evening in Spring. New York, Scribner, 1941.
Sweet Genevieve. New York, Scribner, 1942.
The Seven Who Waited. New York, Scribner, 1943; London, Muller, 1945.
Shadow of Night. New York, Scribner, 1943.
Mischief in the Lane. New York, Scribner, 1944; London, Muller, 1948.
No Future for Luana. New York, Scribner, 1945; London, Muller, 1948.
The Shield of the Valiant. New York, Scribner, 1945.
Fell Purpose. New York, Arcadia House, 1953.
Death by Design. New York, Arcadia House, 1953.
The House on the Mound. New York, Duell, 1958.
The Hills Stand Watch. New York, Duell, 1960.
The Shadow in the Glass. New York, Duell, 1963.
Mr. Fairlie's Final Journey. Sauk City, Wisconsin, Mycroft and Moran, 1968.
The Wind Leans West. New York, Candlelight Press, 1969.

Short Stories

Place of Hawks. New York, Loring and Mussey, 1935.
Any Day Now. Chicago, Normandie House, 1938.
Country Growth. New York, Scribner, 1940.
"In Re: Sherlock Holmes": The Adventure of Solar Pons. Sauk City, Wisconsin, Mycroft and Moran, 1945; as *Regarding Sherlock Holmes,* New York, Pinnacle, 1974; as *The Adventures of Solar Pons,* London, Robson, 1975.
Sac Prairie People. Sauk City, Wisconsin, Stanton and Lee, 1948.
The Memoirs of Solar Pons. Sauk City, Wisconsin, Mycroft and Moran, 1951.
Three Problems for Solar Pons. Sauk City, Wisconsin, Mycroft and Moran, 1952.
The House of Moonlight. Iowa City, Prairie Press, 1953.
The Return of Solar Pons. Sauk City, Wisconsin, Mycroft and Moran, 1958.
The Reminiscences of Solar Pons. Sauk City, Wisconsin, Mycroft and Moran, 1961.
Wisconsin in Their Bones. New York, Duell, 1961.
The Adventure of the Orient Express. New York, Candlelight Press, 1965; London, Panther, 1975.
The Casebook of Solar Pons. Sauk City, Wisconsin, Mycroft and Moran, 1965.

Praed Street Papers. New York, Candlelight Press, 1965.
The Adventure of the Unique Dickensians. Sauk City, Wisconsin, Mycroft and Moran, 1968.
A Praed Street Dossier. Sauk City, Wisconsin, Mycroft and Moran, 1968.
A House Above Cuzco. New York, Candlelight Press, 1969.
The Chronicles of Solar Pons. Sauk City, Wisconsin, Mycroft and Moran, 1973; London, Robson, 1975.

Poetry

To Remember, with *Salute Before Dawn,* by Albert Edward Clements. Hartland Four Corners, Vermont, Windsor, 1931.
Hawk on the Wind. Philadelphia, Ritten House, 1938.
Elegy: On a Flake of Snow. Muscatine, Iowa, Prairie Press, 1939.
Man Track Here. Philadelphia, Ritten House, 1939.
Here on a Darkling Plain. Philadelphia, Ritten House, 1941.
Wind in the Elms. Philadelphia, Ritten House, 1941.
Rind of Earth. Prairie City, Illinois, Decker Press, 1942.
Selected Poems. Prairie City, Illinois, Decker Press, 1944.
And You, Thoreau! New York, New Directions, 1944.
The Edge of Night. Prairie City, Illinois, Decker Press, 1945.
Habitant of Dusk: A Garland for Cassandra. Boston, Walden Press, 1946.
Rendezvous in a Landscape. New York, Fine Editions Press, 1952.
Psyche. Iowa City, Prairie Press, 1953.
Country Poems. Iowa City, Prairie Press, 1956.
Elegy: On the Umbral Moon. Forest Park, Illinois, Acorn Press, 1957.
West of Morning. Francestown, New Hampshire, Golden Quill Press, 1960.
This Wound. Iowa City, Prairie Press, 1962.
Country Places. Iowa City, Prairie Press, 1965.
The Only Place We Live. Iowa City, Prairie Press, 1966.
By Owl Light. Iowa City, Prairie Press, 1967.
Collected Poems, 1937-1967. New York, Candlelight Press, 1967.
Caitlin. Iowa City, Prairie Press, 1969.
The Landscape of the Heart. Iowa City, Prairie Press, 1970.
Listening to the Wind. New York, Candlelight Press, 1971.
Last Light. New York, Candlelight Press, 1971.

Recordings: *Psyche: A Sequence of Love Lyrics,* Cuca, 1960; *Sugar Bush by Moonlight and Other Poems of Man and Nature,* Cuca, 1962; *Caitlin,* Cuca, 1971.

Other

The Heritage of Sauk City. Sauk City, Wisconsin, Pioneer Press, 1931.
Consider Your Verdict: Ten Coroner's Cases for You to Solve (as Tally Mason). New York, Stackpole, 1937.
Atmosphere of Houses. Muscatine, Iowa, Prairie Press, 1939.
Still Small Voice: The Biography of Zona Gale. New York, Appleton Century, 1940.
Village Year: A Sac Prairie Journal. New York, Coward McCann, 1941.
Wisconsin Regional Literature. Privately printed, 1941; revised edition, 1942.
The Wisconsin: River of a Thousand Isles. New York, Farrar and Rinehart, 1942.
H. P. L.: A Memoir (on H. P. Lovecraft). New York, Abramson, 1945.

Oliver, The Wayward Owl (for children). Sauk City, Wisconsin, Stanton and Lee, 1945.
Writing Fiction. Boston, The Writer, 1946.
Village Daybook: A Sac Prairie Journal (for children). Chicago, Pellegrini and Cudahy, 1947.
A Boy's Way: Poems (for children). Sauk City, Wisconsin, Stanton and Lee, 1947.
Sauk County: A Centennial History. Baraboo, Wisconsin, Sauk County Centennial Committee, 1948.
It's a Boy's World: Poems (for children). Sauk City, Wisconsin, Stanton and Lee, 1948.
Wisconsin Earth: A Sac Prairie Sampler (selection). Sauk City, Wisconsin, Stanton and Lee, 1948.
The Milwaukee Road: Its First 100 Years. New York, Creative Age Press, 1948.
The Country of the Hawk (for children). New York, Aladdin, 1952.
The Captive Island (for children). New York, Aladdin, 1952.
Empire of Fur: Trading in the Lake Superior Region (for children). New York, Aladdin, 1953.
Land of Gray Gold: Lead Mining in Wisconsin (for children). New York, Aladdin, 1954.
Father Marquette and the Great Rivers (for children). New York, Farrar Straus, 1955; London, Burns and Oates, 1956.
Land of Sky-Blue Waters (for children). New York, Aladdin, 1955.
St. Ignatius and the Company of Jesus (for children). New York, Farrar Straus, and London, Burns and Oates, 1956.
Columbus and the New World (for children). New York, Farrar Straus, and London, Burns and Oates, 1957.
The Moon Tenders (for children). New York, Duell, 1958.
The Mill Creek Irregulars (for children). New York, Duell, 1959.
Wilbur, The Trusting Whippoorwill (for children). Sauk City, Wisconsin, Stanton and Lee, 1959.
Arkham House: The First Twenty Years—1939-1959. Sauk City, Wisconsin, Arkham House, 1959.
Some Notes on H. P. Lovecraft. Sauk City, Wisconsin, Arkham House, 1959.
The Pinkertons Ride Again (for children). New York, Duell, 1960.
The Ghost of Black Hawk Island (for children). New York, Duell, 1961.
Walden West (autobiography). New York, Duell, 1961.
Sweet Land of Michigan (for children). New York, Duell, 1962.
Concord Rebel: A Life of Henry D. Thoreau. Philadelphia, Chilton, 1962.
Countryman's Journal. New York, Duell, 1963.
The Tent Show Summer (for children). New York, Duell, 1963.
Three Literary Men: A Memoir of Sinclair Lewis, Sherwood Anderson, Edgar Lee Masters. New York, Candlelight Press, 1963.
The Irregulars Strike Again (for children). New York, Duell, 1964.
Forest Orphans (for children). New York, Ernest, 1964; as *Mr. Conservation,* Park Falls, Wisconsin, MacGregor, 1971.
Wisconsin Country: A Sac Prairie Journal. New York, Candlelight Press, 1965.
The House by the River (for children). New York, Duell, 1965.
The Watcher on the Heights (for children). New York, Duell, 1966.
Wisconsin (for children). New York, Coward McCann, 1967.
Vincennes: Portal to the West. Englewood Cliffs, New Jersey, Prentice Hall, 1968.
Walden Pond: Homage to Thoreau. Iowa City, Prairie Press, 1968.
Wisconsin Murders. Sauk City, Wisconsin, Mycroft and Moran, 1968.
The Wisconsin Valley. New York, Teachers College Press, 1969.

Thirty Years of Arkham House: A History and a Bibliography 1939-1969. Sauk City, Wisconsin, Arkham House, 1970.
The Three Straw Men (for children). New York, Candlelight Press, 1970.
Return to Walden West. New York, Candlelight Press, 1970.
Love Letters to Caitlin. New York, Candlelight Press, 1971.
Emerson, Our Contemporary. New York, Crowell Collier, 1971.

Editor, with R. E. Larsson, *Poetry Out of Wisconsin.* New York, Harrison, 1937.
Editor, *Strange Ports of Call.* New York, Pellegrini and Cudahy, 1948.
Editor, *The Other Side of the Moon.* New York, Pellegrini and Cudahy, 1949; abridged edition, London, Grayson, 1956.
Editor, *Something About Cats and Other Pieces,* by H. P. Lovecraft. Sauk City, Wisconsin, Arkham House, 1949.
Editor, *Beyond Time and Space.* New York, Pellegrini and Cudahy, 1950.
Editor, *Far Boundaries: 20 Science-Fiction Stories.* New York, Pellegrini and Cudahy, 1951; London, Consul, 1965.
Editor, *The Outer Reaches: Favorite Science-Fiction Tales Chosen by Their Authors.* New York, Pellegrini and Cudahy, 1951; as *The Outer Reaches* and *The Time of Infinity,* London, Consul, 2 vols., 1963.
Editor, *Beachheads in Space.* New York, Pellegrini and Cudahy, 1952; London, Weidenfeld and Nicolson, 1954; abridged edition, as *From Other Worlds,* London, New English Library, 1964.
Editor, *Worlds of Tomorrow: Science Fiction with a Difference.* New York, Pellegrini and Cudahy, 1953; London, Weidenfeld and Nicolson, 1954; abridged edition as *New Worlds for Old,* London, New English Library, 1963.
Editor, *Time to Come: Science-Fiction Stories of Tomorrow.* New York, Farrar Straus, 1954; London, Consul, 1963.
Editor, *Portals of Tomorrow: The Best Tales of Science Fiction and Other Fantasy.* New York, Rinehart, 1954; London, Cassell, 1956.
Selected Letters, by H. P. Lovecraft. Sauk City, Wisconsin, Arkham House, 5 vols., 1965-76.
Editor, *A Wisconsin Harvest.* Sauk City, Wisconsin, Stanton and Lee, 1966.
Editor, *New Poetry Out of Wisconsin.* Sauk City, Wisconsin, Stanton and Lee, 1969.

*

Bibliography: *100 Books by August Derleth,* Sauk City, Wisconsin, Arkham House, 1962; *August Derleth: A Bibliography* by Alison M. Wilson, Metuchen, New Jersey, Scarecrow Press, 1983.

Manuscript Collection: State Historical Society of Wisconsin Library, Madison.

*   *   *

August Derleth is one of the most controversial and contradictory figures in modern weird fiction. The second most published contributor to *Weird Tales,* the legendary pulp magazine that shaped the course of American weird fiction in the 20th century, he admitted in introductions to his collected stories that most of his fiction for the magazine was mediocre. A ground-breaking editor and publisher who played a vital role in establishing the liter-

ary reputation of H. P. Lovecraft, he is considered by many scholars to have distorted Lovecraft's aesthetic principles through the way he promoted Lovecraft's legacy.

Derleth's first professionally published tale, "Bat's Belfry," appeared in *Weird Tales* in 1926, when he was only 17 years old. The account of a man who discovers that the English estate he has moved into is infested with vampires, it was a competent if unremarkable tale for a writer so young. The same could be said for most of the stories that Derleth wrote for *Weird Tales* over the next ten years. The majority were minor exercises of no more than several thousand words, not enough space in which to build up realistic characters, work complications into plots or create the atmosphere of menace crucial to memorable weird fiction. A typical Derleth story from this period features a character new to a locale who encounters uncanny phenomena that are the supernatural residue of some past event, or who is warned by the cautious not to indulge in activities certain to bring supernatural repercussions, but does, and suffers the consequences.

In the introduction to his collection *Not Long for this World,* Derleth dismissed these early efforts as magazine "filler," "a short story, usually of no consequence, which is used to take up the slack space between the major stories and the advertising pages." They helped to establish his name in *Weird Tales,* where he appeared some years as often as two out of every three issues, but Derleth had little regard for them himself. He refrained from including any in his first two collections of stories, and most of those published prior to 1930 have never been reprinted since.

Derleth tackled a variety of horrors in these early tales, including tortures of the Inquisition ("The Coffin of Lissa"), scientific experiments run amok ("The Tenant"), and shape-shifting ("The Captain is Afraid"), but his favourite theme was the ghost or spectral presence. His ghosts could be vengeful ("Melodie in E Minor"), sentimental ("The Lilac Bush"), incarnations of the ancient past ("Old Mark"), or disembodied presences with no known history ("The Three-Storied House"). The stories tended to be formulaic and repetitive, not only in terms of structure but sometimes their plots: "A Dinner at Imola" and "The Portrait," both published within a year of each other, feature men who kill an enemy by burning a candle shaped in their effigy. Years later, Derleth recycled elements from some of these works in his more ambitious fictions.

Derleth's tales from the 1930s and '40s, written under his own name and the pseudonym Stephen Grendon, show greater maturity and technical proficiency. His models, as he notes in the introduction to his first weird-fiction collection, *Someone in the Dark,* were M. R. James and Mary E. Wilkins-Freeman, and there is indeed more of the genteel ghost-story tradition than pulp shocker about them. Their greater length gave him more room in which to develop an appropriately eerie mood.

Two haunted-house stories from this period, "The Shuttered House" and "The Panelled Room," stand out precisely because Derleth orchestrates their events gradually to suitably disturbing climaxes. Derleth also showed a knack for the biter-bit story, which he sometimes wrote as deadpan black comedy. "Pacific 421," in which a greedy heir schemes to blame the death of his miserly stepfather on a legendary ghost train and then discovers that the locals are not as superstitious as he thought, is one of his best weird tales.

Derleth was one of H. P. Lovecraft's young protegés and saw his first pastiche of Lovecraft's fiction, "The Lair of the Star Spawn," published in *Weird Tales* in 1932. With the publication of "The Return of Hastur" in 1939, he began devoting considerable energy to longer stories in which he shaped the broad underlying philosophies of Lovecraft's fiction into the rigid framework of what he dubbed "the Cthulhu Mythos." The Mythos, as defined by Derleth, was the shared world of shunned towns, books of occult lore and monstrous entities that Lovecraft, Derleth, Clark Ashton Smith, Robert E. Howard, Robert Bloch and other well-known *Weird Tales* writers had playfully traded around in their fiction. In his opinion, the cosmic horrors that Lovecraft had evoked as metaphors for the limits of human understanding had their parallels in traditional religious representations of Good and Evil, and could be grouped into hierarchies of elementals. Virtually the sole writer in the Lovecraft tradition at this time, Derleth almost singlehandedly shape perceptions of Lovecraft's contribution to the weird tale for a generation of readers.

Many of Derleth's Cthulhu Mythos stories deliberately echo Lovecraft's writing. Each is filled with terrors and mysteries peculiar to its plot, but most conform to a simple pattern that Derleth repeated in story after story: a man comes into possession of a house, often a family home, and his investigations into a curse hanging over it or strange events that occur there reopen a gateway (usually established by a relative from the past) to evil entities anxious to gain a foothold in our world. This describes the basic plot of "The Return of Hastur," "The Whippoorwills in the Hills," "Beyond the Threshold," "The House in the Valley," and other stories Derleth collected in *Something Near* and *The Trail of Cthulhu*. The predictability of these such tales, and their anti-climactic finales which usually re-establish the very order Lovecraft worked to undermine, is even more pronounced in the five interconnected novellas that Derleth fashioned into *The Trail of the Cthulhu*. Each describes the means by which its hero is recruited by an enigmatic occultist to serve as a foot soldier in the war against Lovecraftian monstrosities.

With the publication of the novel *The Lurker at the Threshold* in 1948, Derleth embarked on a series of so-called "posthumous collaborations" with H. P. Lovecraft in which he purportedly completed story fragments found among Lovecraft's papers. These "fragments" were often no more than a plot germ of one or two sentences which Derleth fleshed out into stories that reshuffled elements from Lovecraft's best-known works. *Lurker* bears a striking resemblance to Lovecraft's *The Case of Charles Dexter Ward*, "The Shadow out of Space" to his "The Shadow out of Time," and "The Shuttered Room" to both "The Dunwich Horror" and "The Shadow over Innsmouth." Derleth wrote 16 of these stories between 1948 and 1961.

Derleth's Mythos tales and posthumous collaborations helped to sustain interest in Lovecraft's writing at a time when his work had little recognition, and created a simple template for the Lovecraft pastiche that scores of later writers, among them Ramsey Campbell and Brian Lumley, would use when writing stories set in Lovecraft's universe. Unfortunately, their notoriety eclipsed interest in Derleth's non-Lovecraftian fiction from the 1940s on, when he was arguably writing his best weird tales. A trio of his stories from this time concerned with the dark side of childhood imagination—"The Lonesome Place," "A Room in a House" and "Mr. George" (published under the Stephen Grendon pseudonym)—are superior efforts of their type, and his sardonic vampire tale "'Whom Shall I Say is Calling?'" merits comparison to Robert Bloch's fantasy classic "The Cloak." Derleth's writing in the 1950s and early 1960s shows the benefits he enjoyed writing for magazines other than *Weird Tales* and more demanding editors than he knew in the pulps. It was at this time, however, that he virtually gave up weird-fiction writing to concentrate on editing

and running Arkham House, the publishing company he had founded with Donald Wandrei in 1939 with the primary of objective of publishing Lovecraft's fiction.

It was as an editor and publisher that Derleth made his most significant contribution to weird fiction. When he expanded the scope of Arkham House's publishing ambitions beyond the preservation of Lovecraft's work, he helped to introduce the fiction of Robert E. Howard, Clark Ashton Smith, Donald Wandrei and other pulp colleagues to new generations of readers. *Sleep No More*, *The Sleeping and the Dead*, *Who Knocks?*, and the many anthologies he assembled in the 1940s and '50s were seminal mixtures of pulp and classic horror fiction. Derleth brought out first story-collections by Robert Bloch, Ray Bradbury and Fritz Leiber, and was instrumental in exposing the fiction of L. P. Hartley, Cynthia Asquith, William Hope Hodgson, and other British writers to American audiences under the Arkham House imprimatur. It is well known that much of the fiction Derleth churned out after 1939 was designed to raise money for his publishing programme. In so far as his stories helped to subsidize Arkham House and ensure its continued survival, they may be among the most under-appreciated weird tales of the 20th century.

—Stefan Dziemianowicz

DICKENS, Charles (John Huffam)

Nationality: British. **Born:** Landport near Portsmouth, Hampshire, 7 February 1812. **Education:** Attended a school in Chatham, Kent; worked in a blacking factory, Hungerford Market, London, while his family was in Marshalsea debtor's prison, 1824; attended Wellington House Academy, London, 1824-27, and Mr. Dawson's school, Brunswick Square, London, 1827. **Family:** Married Catherine Hogarth in 1836 (separated 1858), seven sons and three daughters; possibly had a son by Ellen Ternan. **Career:** Clerk in a law office, London, 1827-28; shorthand reporter, Doctors' Commons, 1828-30, and in parliament for *True Son*, 1830-32, *Mirror of Parliament*, 1832-34, and *Morning Chronicle*, 1834-36; contributor, *Monthly Magazine*, 1833-34 (as Boz, 1834), and *Evening Chronicle*, 1835-36; editor, *Bentley's Miscellany*, 1837-39; visited the U.S., 1842; lived in Italy, 1844-45; appeared in amateur theatricals from 1845, and managed an amateur theatrical tour of England, 1847; editor, London *Daily News*, 1846; lived in Switzerland and Paris, 1846; founding editor, *Household Words*, London, 1850-59, and its successor, *All the Year Round*, 1859-70; gave reading tours of Britain, 1858-59, 1861-63, 1866-67, and 1868-70, and the U.S., 1867-68; lived in Gad's Hill Place, near Rochester, Kent, from 1860. **Died:** 9 June 1870.

HORROR, GHOST AND GOTHIC PUBLICATIONS

Novels

A Christmas Carol, in Prose: Being a Ghost Story of Christmas. London, Chapman and Hall, 1843; Philadelphia, Carey and Hart, 1844.

The Chimes: A Goblin Story of Some Bells that Rang an Old Year Out and a New Year In. London, Chapman and Hall, 1844; Philadelphia, Carey and Hart, 1845.

The Cricket on the Hearth: A Fairy Tale of Home. London, Bradbury and Evans, 1845; New York, Harper, 1846.

The Haunted Man and the Ghost's Bargain: A Fancy for Christmas-Time. London, Bradbury and Evans, 1848; New York, Harper, 1849.

Christmas Books (omnibus). London, Chapman and Hall, 1852; as *Christmas Stories*, New York, Appleton, 1868.

The Mystery of Edwin Drood. London, Chapman and Hall, 1870 (6 monthly parts); Boston, Fields, Osgood, 1870.

Short Stories

The Complete Ghost Stories of Charles Dickens, edited by Peter Haining. London, Joseph, and New York, Watts, 1982.

The Signalman and Other Ghost Stories. Stroud, Gloucestershire, Alan Sutton, 1990.

Charles Dickens' Christmas Ghost Stories, edited by Peter Haining. London, Hale, 1992; New York, St. Martin's Press, 1993.

OTHER PUBLICATIONS

Novels

The Posthumous Papers of the Pickwick Club. London, Chapman and Hall, 1836-37 (20 monthly parts); Philadelphia, Carey, 1836-37.

Oliver Twist; or, The Parish Boy's Progress. London, Bentley, 3 vols., 1838; Philadelphia, Lea and Blanchard, 1839.

The Life and Adventures of Nicholas Nickleby. London, Chapman and Hall, 1838-39 (20 monthly parts); Philadelphia, Lea and Blanchard, 1839.

The Old Curiosity Shop. London, Chapman and Hall, and Philadelphia, Lea and Blanchard, 1841.

Barnaby Rudge: A Tale of the Riots of 'Eighty. London, Chapman and Hall, and Philadelphia, Lea and Blanchard, 1841.

The Life and Adventures of Martin Chuzzlewit. London, Chapman and Hall, 1843-44 (20 monthly parts); New York, Harper, 1844.

The Battle of Life: A Love Story. London, Bradbury and Evans, 1846; New York, Harper, 1847.

Dealings with the Firm of Dombey and Son, Wholesale, Retail, and for Exportation. London, Bradbury and Evans, 1846-48 (20 monthly parts); New York, Wiley, 1846-48 (19 monthly parts).

The Personal History of David Copperfield. London, Bradbury and Evans, 1849-50 (20 monthly parts); Philadelphia, Lea and Blanchard, 1851.

Bleak House. London, Bradbury and Evans, 1852-53 (20 monthly parts); New York, Harper, 1853.

Hard Times, for These Times. London, Bradbury and Evans, and New York, McElrath, 1854.

Little Dorrit. London, Bradbury and Evans, 1855-57 (20 monthly parts); Philadelphia, Peterson, 1857.

A Tale of Two Cities. London, Chapman and Hall (8 monthly parts), and Philadelphia, Peterson, 1859.

Great Expectations. London, Chapman and Hall, 3 vols., and Philadelphia, Peterson, 1861.

Our Mutual Friend. London, Chapman and Hall, 1864-65 (20 monthly parts); New York, Harper, 1865.

Short Stories

Sketches by "Boz" Illustrative of Every-Day Life and Every-Day People. London, Macrone, 3 vols., 1836-37; Philadelphia, Carey, 1837.

Master Humphrey's Clock (includes two serialized novels, *The Old Curiosity Shop* and *Barnaby Rudge*). London, Chapman and Hall, 1840-41 (88 weekly parts).

The Uncommercial Traveller. London, Chapman and Hall, 1860; New York, Sheldon, 1865.

The Lamplighter's Story; Hunted Down; the Detective Police; and Other Nouvellettes. N.p., 1861.

The Uncommercial Traveller and Additional Christmas Stories. Boston, Ticknor and Fields, 1868.

Hunted Down: A Story, with Some Account of Thomas Griffiths Wainewright, the Poisoner. London, Hotten, and Philadelphia, Peterson, 1870.

Plays

O'Thello (produced 1833). In *Nonesuch Dickens,* London, Nonesuch Press, 1937-38.

The Village Coquettes, music by John Hullah (produced 1836). London, Bentley, 1836.

The Strange Gentleman (produced 1836). London, Chapman and Hall, 1837.

Is She His Wife? or, Something Singular (produced 1837). Boston, Osgood, 1877.

Mr. Nightingale's Diary, with Mark Lemon (produced 1851). N.p., 1851.

The Lighthouse, with Wilkie Collins, from the story "Gabriel's Marriage" by Collins (produced 1855).

The Frozen Deep, with Wilkie Collins (produced 1857). 1866; in *Under the Management of Mr. Dickens: His Production of the Frozen Deep*, edited by R. L. Brannan, Ithaca, New York, Cornell University Press, 1966.

No Thoroughfare, with Wilkie Collins and Charles Fechter, from the story by Dickens and Collins (produced 1867). New York, DeWitt, 1867.

The Lamplighter. N.p., 1879.

Other

American Notes for General Circulation. 2 vols., London, Chapman and Hall, 1842; 1 vol., New York, Harper, 1842.

Pictures from Italy. London, Bradbury and Evans, 1846; as *Travelling Letters: Written on the Road,* New York, Wiley and Putnam, 1846.

Works (Cheap Edition). 17 vols., London, Chapman and Hall, 1847-67.

A Child's History of England. 3 vols., London, Bradbury and Evans, 1852-54; 2 vols., New York, Harper, 1853-54.

Speeches Literary and Social, edited by R. H. Shepherd. N.p., 1870; revised edition, as *The Speeches 1841-1870*, 1884.

Speeches, Letters, and Sayings. N.p., 1870.

Letters, edited by Georgina Hogarth and Mamie Dickens. 3 vols., N.p., 1880-82; revised edition (Pilgrim Edition), edited by Madeline House, Graham Storey, and Kathleen Tillotson, 1965-.

The Mudfog Papers. N.p., 1880.

Plays and Poems, edited by R. H. Shepherd. 2 vols., London, Allen, 1885.

To Be Read at Dusk and Other Stories, Sketches, and Essays, edited by F. G. Kitton. N.p., 1898.

Miscellaneous Papers, edited by B. W. Matz. 2 vols., N.p., 1908.

The Life of Our Lord (for children). New York, Simon and Schuster, 1934.

Nonesuch Dickens, edited by Arthur Waugh and others. 23 vols., London, Nonesuch Press, 1937-38.

Speeches, edited by K. J. Fielding. Oxford, Clarendon, Press, 1960.

Uncollected Writings from Household Words, 1850-1859, edited by Harry Stone. Bloomington, Indiana University Press, 2 vols., 1968; London, Lane, 1969.

Household Words: A Weekly Journal, 1850-1859, edited by Anne Lohrli, Toronto and Buffalo, University of Toronto Press, 1974.

The Public Readings, edited by Philip Collins. Oxford, Clarendon Press, 1975.

Dickens on America and the Americans, edited by Michael Slater. Austin, University of Texas Press, 1979.

Dickens on England and the English, edited by Malcolm Andrews. New York, Barnes and Noble, 1979.

Book of Memoranda, edited by Fred Kaplan. New York, New York Public Library, 1981.

The Portable Dickens, edited by Angus Wilson. New York, Viking, 1983.

Selected Letters, edited by David Paroissien. Boston, Twayne, 1985.

A December Vision: Social Journalism, edited by Neil Philip and Victor Neuburg. New York, Continuum Press, 1986.

Dickens' Working Notes for His Novels, edited by Harry Stone. Chicago, University of Chicago Press, 1987.

The Oxford Illustrated Dickens. 21 vols., Oxford and New York, Oxford University Press, 1987.

Editor, *The Pic Nic Papers*. 3 vols., 1841.

*

Film Adaptations (selection): *The Chimes*, 1914, from the novella; *The Mystery of Edwin Drood*, 1914, 1935, 1993, from the novel; *A Christmas Carol*, 1908, 1914, 1938, 1951, 1971, *Scrooge*, 1913, 1935, 1970, *An American Christmas Carol*, 1979, *Mickey's Christmas Carol*, 1983, all from the novella *A Christmas Carol*.

Bibliography: *The First Editions of the Writings of Dickens* by John C. Eckel, 1913, revised edition, 1932, 1972, New York, Haskell; *A Bibliography of the Periodical Works of Dickens* by Thomas Hatton and Arthur H. Cleaver, 1933, 1973, New York, Haskell; *A Bibliography of Dickensian Criticism 1836-1975* by R. C. Churchill, New York, Garland Press, 1975; *The Cumulated Dickens Checklist 1970-1979* by Alan M. Cohn and K. K. Collins, Troy, New York, Whitston, 1982; *The Critical Reception of Dickens 1833-1841* by Kathryn Chittick, New York, Garland Press, 1989.

Manuscript Collections: Beinecke Rare Book and Manuscript Library, Yale University; Berg Collection, New York Public Library; Dickens House, London; Free Library of Philadelphia; Huntington Library, San Marino, California; Pierpont Morgan Library, New York.

Critical Studies (selection): *Dickens: A Critical Introduction* by K. J. Fielding, London and New York, Longmans, 1958, revised 1965; *The Dickens Critics* edited by George H. Ford and Lauriat Lane, Jr., Westport, Connecticut, Greenwood Press, 1961; *From Copyright to Copperfield: The Identity of Dickens* by Alexander Welsh, Cambridge, Massachusetts, Harvard University Press, 1987; *Reader's Guide to Dickens* by Philip Hobsbaum, New York, Farrar, 1973; *Dickens and His Publishers* by Robert Patten, Oxford, Clarendon Press, and New York, Oxford University Press, 1978; *Dickensian Melodrama: A Reading of the Novels* by George J. Worth, Lawrence, University of Kansas Press, 1978; *A Reformer's Art: Dickens' Picturesque and Grotesque Imagery* by Nancy K. Hill, Athens, Ohio University Press, 1981; *Dickens: A Biography* by Fred Kaplan, New York, Morrow, 1988; *Dickens* by Peter Ackroyd, New York, Harper, 1990; *Dickens and the 1830's* by Kathryn Chittick, New York, Cambridge University Press, 1990; *A Dickens Glossary* by Fred Levit, New York, Garland, 1990.

*   *   *

Charles Dickens made a crucial contribution to the development of British supernatural fiction. Both as a writer and as an editor he played a major role in establishing the "Christmas ghost story" as an institution. His reason for doing so was that supernatural fiction had come under attack, especially from educationalists who thought it injurious to the intellectual development of children; he was prepared to argue that it was not injurious at all, but he was careful also to cultivate the fallback position that once a year, on the nation's favourite holiday, a certain amount of extra indulgence might be permitted. Without his championship of the form it is doubtful that so many eminent Victorian writers would have dabbled in the production of ghost stories, and the niche to which such academic dabblers as M. R. James fitted their production of horror stories would not have been available.

At the age of five Dickens had been delivered to the care of a 13-year-old nursemaid named "Mercy" Weller, who delighted in telling him bloodcurdling tales. Two of the finest—"Captain Murderer" and "The Devil's Bargain"—he later preserved for posterity in an article reprinted in *The Uncommercial Traveller*, and if they can be taken as fair representations of her narrative style they establish that Miss Weller had a fine flair for the melodramatic. This youthful exposure to the warp and weft of horror fiction taught him a useful lesson in narrative suspense which he never forgot, and most of his popular novels include terrifying episodes like Pip's first meeting with Magwitch in *Great Expectations* and Oliver's nocturnal encounters with Fagin and Bill Sikes in *Oliver Twist*. Dickens' early ghost stories are mostly comedies in the light vein of the anecdotes featured in *The Pickwick Papers*, which includes the tale of "The Bagman's Uncle," but he often sharpened their comedy with a spice of horror. *Pickwick* contains one authentic horror story in "The Madman's Manuscript"—and "The Story of the Goblins Who Stole a Sexton," from the same source, became the seed of *A Christmas Carol*, the most famous of all nineteenth-century ghost stories.

Although it is a moral allegory, *A Christmas Carol* does make judicious use of horror as an instrument, especially in the scene where the second of the three spirits who visit Ebenezer Scrooge draws back his opulent robe to reveal personifications of Ignorance and Want—"Man's feral children." Those feral children are tacitly present throughout the nightmarishly stark vision of future possibility experienced by Trotty Veck, the hapless hero of *The Chimes*, with which Dickens hoped to "strike a great blow for the poor." He admitted failure when he felt compelled to add strong doses of comforting sentimentality to his next two Christmas books, *The Cricket on the Hearth* and the non-supernatural *The Battle of Life*, but the last of the five, *The Haunted Man and the Ghost's Bargain*, is an authentic horror story. The protagonist, having fallen prey to dispiriting self-pity, accepts the offer of a sinister doppelganger to banish his woes if he will agree to infect others with the same anaesthesia. When he does so he finds that he is destroying the power of empathy which enables the unfortunate to comfort and assist one another, and he has to enlist his saintly housekeeper to counter the plague.

The batches of tales which Dickens compiled for the Christmas supplements to *All the Year Round* rarely indulged in supernaturalism, and when they did he usually allowed other writers to provide it, but two of them provided a home for his most famous horror stories. "Doctor Marigold's Prescriptions," the 1865 supplement, included "The Trial for Murder," in which the ghost of a murdered man becomes a 13th juror in order to make certain that justice is done. "Mugby Junction," the 1866 supplement, included "The Signalman," which is sometimes reprinted as "No. 1 Branch Line: The Signalman" although the preface has no significance outside the original context. "The Signalman" is one of the finest of all tales of premonitory apparitions, exhibiting a devastatingly effective sense of irony in its account of the luckless signalman's failure to make advantageous use of his warnings and their ultimate betrayal of his confidence.

Although "The Signalman" was the last explicit tale of the supernatural that Dickens wrote, his increasingly close association with Wilkie Collins (performances of whose play "The Frozen Deep" afforded him the opportunity to make intimate contact with the young actress who became his long-term mistress) was correlated with an increase in the grotesque and outre aspects of his work. *Our Mutual Friend* is replete with subtle quasi-Gothic touches, which became even more prominent in *The Mystery of Edwin Drood*. The hypnotically gifted John Jasper is a typical toned-down Gothic villain, carefully adapted to Victorian sensibilities. Whether or not the mystery would have deepened into explicitly supernatural form we can only guess, but the completed novel would probably have qualified as a horror story in any case, just as Collins's *The Woman in White* does. Like the classic "horrid novels" of the Gothic heyday the story obtains most of its emotional charge from the threat which the villain poses to the heroine's chastity: a threat which is deftly and slyly heightened in all kinds of sinister ways.

Had Dickens indulged his interest in the supernatural more freely he would undoubtedly be reckoned one of the great pioneers of modern horror fiction, but he was so restrained that he must be reckoned an amiable uncle rather than an actual progenitor. "The Signalman" is, however, a classic and *The Haunted Man and the Ghost's Bargain* deserves more careful attention from readers and critics than it tends to receive.

—Brian Stableford

DINESEN, Isak

Pseudonym for Karen Christentze Blixen-Finecke, Baroness Blixen of Rungstedlund. **Other Pseudonym:** Pierre Andrézel. **Nationality:** Danish. **Born:** Karen Christentze Dinesen in Rungsted, Denmark, 17 April 1885. **Education:** Oxford University, England;

Royal Academy, Copenhagen. **Family:** Married Baron Blor Blixen-Finecke in 1914 (divorced 1921). **Career:** Managed a coffee plantation in British East Africa (Kenya), with her husband, 1913-21, and on her own, 1921-31; contributor of short stories and journalism to many publications, from 1907. **Awards:** Ingenio e Arti Medal, Denmark, 1950; Henry Nathansen Memorial Fund, 1951; The Golden Laurels, 1952; Hans Christian Andersen prize, 1955; Danish Critics' prize, 1957. **Member:** American Academy of Arts and Letters; Danish Academy. **Died:** 7 September 1962.

HORROR, GHOST AND GOTHIC PUBLICATIONS

Short Stories

Seven Gothic Tales. New York, Smith and Haas, and London, Putnam, 1934.
Winter's Tales. London, Putnam, 1942; New York, Random House, 1943.
Last Tales. London, Putnam, 1957.
Anecdotes of Destiny. London, Michael Joseph, 1958.

OTHER PUBLICATIONS

Novel

The Angelic Avengers (as Pierre Andrézel). London, Putnam, 1946.

Short Stories

Ehrengard. London, Michael Joseph, 1963.
Carnival: Entertainments and Posthumous Tales. N.p., 1977.

Other

Out of Africa. London, Putnam, 1937.
Shadows on the Grass. London, Michael Joseph, 1961.
Isak Dinesen: Letters from Africa, 1914-1931, edited by Frans Lasson. London, Weidenfeld, and Chicago, University of Chicago Press, 1981.

*

Critical Studies: "Modern Perceptions of the Barbaric" in *The Literature of Terror* by David Punter, London, Longman, 1980; *Isak Dinesen: The Life of Karen Blixen* by Judith Thurman, London, Weidenfeld, 1982.

Film Adaptations: *The Immortal Story*, 1968, from the short story; *Out of Africa*, 1985.

*   *   *

Nowadays, Isak Dinesen is better known as an author under a form of her real name, Karen Blixen, and as the "heroine"—as played by Meryl Streep—of the successfully filmed autobiographical volume *Out of Africa*. But she wrote a considerable number of short stories and novellas under the Dinesen pseudonym, many of which were published in magazines during the 1930s and 1940s and collected in four principal volumes. Almost all of these stories are historical romances; only a few are gothic horror. (One of her late tales, a fable set in Macao about an old man who tries to make a fantastic legend come true, also formed the basis of a notable short film, Orson Welles's *The Immortal Story*.)

Despite either suffering translation from her native Danish (in the case of the earliest material only) or else written in English as her second language, Dinesen's stories are smooth, polished and erudite. They are also very subtle and often rather too slow in their development for the demands of readers in the 1990s, which accounts for Dinesen being out of fashion today. Also, the amount of horror in her tales is slight and is mixed with wit and with other facets of the gothic, such as romanticism, wild settings and fanciful plots.

Among the most gothic of all her stories are "The Dreamers" and "Echoes," both concerned with Pellegrina Leoni, formerly the greatest diva in the world during the early years of the 19th century. Her story is a sad one: during a performance of *Don Giovanni* in Milan, the opera house burns down and Pellegrina is injured when a burning beam falls on her. She is robbed of her singing voice and her shadow, and is left with a scar running from ear to collar-bone. As far as she is concerned, Pellegrina is dead, and she wanders through Europe under different names, scarcely ageing for decades, having frequent love affairs with younger men but resisting their attempts to form a permanent relationship. In "Echoes" she reaches a small town in the mountains above Rome, where she discovers a choirboy with her voice, whom she trains. But he does not trust her motives and eventually runs away from her.

"The Dreamers" catalogues several of her affairs. The story's English narrator, Lincoln Forsner, has discovered her calling herself Olalla and working as a prostitute in Rome, and has fallen in love with her. But one of his friends knows her as Madame Lola, a milliner and revolutionary, working in Lucerne, and another recognizes her as Madame Rosalba, a rich widow whom he falls for and pursues in Saumur (France). There is a wonderfully gothic scene where these three friends pursue her up a snowy mountainside, first by coach and then on foot. To maintain her independence from these lovers and to prevent her real identity being revealed, Pellegrina leaps over a cliff. Eventually, after explanations and a tearful farewell, she dies of her injuries.

Dinesen makes almost no attempt to explain or justify any of her supernatural elements. In "The Monkey," for example, the prioress of a convent changes places with her pet monkey simply because Dinesen wanted to explore the differences between the advice that a prioress and a monkey would give to a young man seeking a wife. In the story the complete explanation is given as "Strange powers were out tonight." The result is a light-hearted fantasy in which Boris, a high-born young army officer, asks the prioress, who is also his aunt and godmother, for advice. He is told who to try—the rich, young and statuesque Athena Hopballehus. But when she turns him down, the further advice is to invite her to a meal at the convent, get her drunk and leap on her, which Boris does even though Athena knocks out two of his teeth. So compromised is Athena (and so naive) that she is manoeuvred into agreeing to marry Boris. Then the prioress manages to regain possession of her own body in a spectacular metamorphosis, leaving three surprised people and a whining monkey.

More horrific—and, indeed, much more in the gothic tradition—are two stories which turn upon mistaken relationships, "A Country Tale" and "The Caryatids." "A Country Tale" is a nature-

versus-nurture story, in which a wet nurse has exchanged her own new-born baby for the son of a wealthy landowner, for reasons of revenge. Her own baby grows up to be a kind and considerate gentleman, while the landowner's real son is wild, always in trouble and now about to be executed for murder. The nurse comes and tells the gentleman who he really is. He does not believe her, but visits the condemned man in prison anyway. Both realize that, even if the story were true, nothing can be done about it.

"The Caryatids," whose title refers to the statues of women who help to support the roof of some Greek buildings and hence by implication those women who uphold the family tradition, is an unfinished story about innocent incest. A young husband and father discovers from an old bundle of love letters that his wife is also his half-sister. It is knowledge to be kept to oneself. A similar point is made in "The DeCats Family," in which the family name is kept spotless, with the remainder of the family behaving correctly so long as one black sheep maintains his devotion to sin.

Magic with just a touch of horror is the basis for "The Sailor Boy's Tale." When a young sailor-boy climbs the mast of a barque to release a falcon caught in the rigging, he has no idea that this is an incarnation of a Lapp witch. And when, at least a couple of years later, he kills a troublesome Russian seaman, the witch repays his help.

Dinesen's gothic stories are spread throughout her collections, and each gothic story contains a romantic plot, just like her other stories.

—Chris Morgan

DISCH, Thomas M(ichael)

Pseudonyms: Thom Demijohn; Leonie Hargrave; Cassandra Knye. **Nationality:** American. **Born:** Des Moines, Iowa, 2 February 1940. **Education:** Cooper Union, New York, and New York University, 1959-62. **Career:** Part-time checkroom attendant, Majestic Theatre, New York, 1957-62; copywriter, Doyle Dane Bernbach Inc., New York, 1963-64. Since 1964, freelance writer and lecturer; since 1987, theatre critic for *The Nation*. **Member:** Member of the board, National Book Critics Circle, 1988-91; secretary, 1989-91. **Awards:** O. Henry prize, 1975; John W. Campbell Memorial award, 1980. **Address:** Box 226, Barryville, NY 12719, USA.

HORROR, GHOST AND GOTHIC PUBLICATIONS

Novels

The House That Fear Built (with John Sladek, as Cassandra Knye). New York, Paperback Library, 1966.
Clara Reeve (as Leonie Hargrave). New York, Knopf, and London, Hutchinson, 1975.
The Businessman: A Tale of Terror. New York, Harper, and London, Cape, 1984.
The M.D.: A Horror Story. New York, Knopf, 1991; London, HarperCollins, 1992.
The Priest: A Gothic Romance. London, Millennium, 1994; New York, Knopf, 1995.

Short Stories

Getting into Death: The Best Short Stories of Thomas M. Disch. London, Hart Davis MacGibbon, 1973; revised edition, New York, Knopf, 1976.

The Silver Pillow: A Tale of Witchcraft. Willimantic, Connecticut, Ziesing, 1987.

OTHER PUBLICATIONS

Novels

The Genocides. New York, Berkley, 1965; London, Whiting and Wheaton, 1967.

Mankind Under the Leash: Being a True and Faithful Account of the Great Upheavals of 2037. . . . New York, Ace, 1966; as *The Puppies of Terra,* London, Panther, 1978.

Echo Round His Bones. New York, Berkley, 1967; London, Hart Davis, 1969.

Black Alice (with John Sladek as Thom Demijohn). Garden City, New York, Doubleday, 1968; London, W. H. Allen, 1969.

Camp Concentration. London, Hart Davis, 1968; Garden City, New York, Doubleday, 1969.

The Prisoner (novelization of television series). New York, Ace, 1969; London, Dobson, 1979; as *The Prisoner: I Am Not a Number!,* London, Boxtree, 1992.

334. London, MacGibbon and Kee, 1972; New York, Avon, 1974.

On Wings of Song. New York, St. Martin's Press, and London, Gollancz, 1979.

Neighboring Lives, with Charles Naylor. New York, Scribner, 1980; London, Hutchinson, 1981.

Triplicity (omnibus; includes *Echo Round His Bones, The Genocides,* and *The Puppies of Terra*). Garden City, New York, Doubleday, 1980.

Short Stories

One Hundred and Two H-Bombs and Other Science Fiction Stories. London, Compact, 1966; expanded as *White Fang Goes Dingo and Other Funny S.F. Stories,* London, Arrow, 1971; original version revised as *One Hundred and Two H-Bombs,* New York, Berkley, 1971.

Under Compulsion. London, Hart Davis, 1968; as *Fun with Your New Head,* Garden City, New York, Doubleday, 1971.

The Early Science Fiction Stories of Thomas M. Disch. Boston, Gregg Press, 1977.

Fundamental Disch. New York, Bantam, 1980; London, Gollancz, 1981.

The Man Who Had No Idea: A Collection of Stories. London, Gollancz, 1982.

Ringtime: A Story. West Branch, Iowa, Toothpaste Press, 1983.

Torturing Mr. Amberwell. New Castle, Virginia, Cheap Street, 1985.

The Brave Little Toaster (for children). Garden City, New York, Doubleday, and London, Grafton, 1986.

The Tale of Dan De Lion: A Fable. Minneapolis, Coffee House Press, 1986.

The Brave Little Toaster Goes to Mars (for children). Garden City, New York, Doubleday, 1988.

Plays

Ben Hur (produced New York, 1989)
The Cardinal Detoxes (produced New York, 1990).

Poetry

Highway Sandwiches, with Marilyn Hacker and Charles Platt. Privately printed, 1970.

The Right Way to Figure Plumbing. New York, Basilisk Press, 1971.

ABCDEFG HIJKLM NPOQRSt. UVWXYZ. London, Anvil Press Poetry, 1981.

Burn This. London, Hutchinson, 1982.

Orders of the Retina. West Branch, Iowa, Toothpaste Press, 1982.

Here I Am, There You Are, Where Were We. London, Hutchinson, 1984.

Yes, Let's: New and Selected Poems. Baltimore, Maryland, Johns Hopkins University Press, 1989.

Dark Verses and Light. Baltimore, Maryland, Johns Hopkins University Press, 1991.

Haikus of an AmPart. Minneapolis, Minnesota, Coffee House Press, 1991.

The Hawk and the Metaphor. N.p., Aralia Press, 1993(?).

The River's Snowing on the House. Barryville, New York, Disch, 1993.

Other

The Castle of Indolence: On Poetry, Poets, and Poetasters. New York, Picador, 1995.

Editor, with Robert Arthur, *Alfred Hitchcock's Stories That Scared Even Me.* New York, Random House, 1967.

Editor, *The Ruins of Earth: An Anthology of Stories of the Immediate Future.* New York, Putnam, 1971; London, Hutchinson, 1973.

Editor, *Bad Moon Rising.* New York, Harper, 1973; London, Hutchinson, 1974.

Editor, *The New Improved Sun: An Anthology of Utopian S-F.* New York, Harper, 1975; London, Hutchinson, 1976.

Editor, with Charles Naylor, *New Constellations: An Anthology of Tomorrow's Mythologies.* New York, Harper, 1976.

Editor, with Charles Naylor, *Strangeness: A Collection of Curious Tales.* New York, Scribner, 1977.

*

Film Adaptation: *The Brave Little Toaster,* 1987.

Bibliography: *Thomas M. Disch: A Preliminary Bibliography* by David Nee, Berkeley, California, Other Change of Hobbit, 1982; *A Checklist of Thomas M. Disch* by Christopher P. Stephens, Hastings-on-Hudson, New York, Ultramarine, 1991.

Manuscript Collection: Beinecke Library, Yale University.

Critical Study: *The American Shore: Meditations on a Tale of Science Fiction by Thomas M. Disch—"Angouleme"* by Samuel R. Delany, Elizabethtown, New York, Dragon Press, 1978.

* * *

The work of Thomas M. Disch spans several different media as well as several different genres. Although his most significant contributions to the horror genre are the three late novels *The Businessman*, *The M.D.* and *The Priest* the roots of his interest extend all the way back to the beginning of his career and sideways into such endeavours as his libretti for Gregory Sandow's musical compositions based on "The Fall of the House of Usher" and *Frankenstein*.

The earliest novels Disch signed with his own name were all science fiction, but *The Genocides*—in which colonizing aliens turn the entire Earth into a monoculture farm, reducing the last surviving members of the unheeded human race to the status of root parasites—is a horror story too; significantly, it is set in a region close to that of his later horror novels: the agricultural heartland of the U.S., extending northwards from Disch's home state of Iowa towards the twin cities of Minneapolis-St. Paul. The earliest of his pseudonymous novels, written in collaboration with John Sladek, was *The House That Fear Built*, signed Cassandra Knye. This was an experiment in the then-popular genre of "Gothic romance," which consists of formulaic love stories emotionally heightened by a sense of threat whose literary origins can be found in such Gothic extravaganzas as Mrs. Radcliffe's *Mysteries of Udolpho* and J. Sheridan Le Fanu's *Uncle Silas*. Disch's interest in the mechanics and method of this type of story were much more elaborately displayed in the elegant pastiche *Clara Reeve*, signed Leonie Hargrave, which opens with the interment of the heroine's mother in Highgate Cemetery in 1850, and follows her through the many misadventures which befall her in the wake of her marriage to her cousin Niles. The novel is equipped with a stereotypical Gothic villain, in the form of Niles' enigmatic valet Manfredo, but toys cleverly with genre habits and expectations in placing a more sinister guiding hand behind him.

A recurrent theme which is particularly noticeable in Disch's early short fiction is the desperate difficulty of establishing a secure identity in a mercurially hostile world. The prominence of such a theme is unsurprising in the work of a homosexual writer—as, perhaps, is a parallel preoccupation with the corrosive and destructive aspects of sexual attraction. He wrote several stories which describe people who become lost, captive within such ominously vacuous spaces as the staircase in "Descending," the graveyard in "Let Us Quickly Hasten to the Gate of Ivory," and "The Asian Shore" of Istanbul, but the nightmarish edge of such stories is sometimes blunted by the tacit assumption that a certain bliss might be found in oblivion. A much more elaborate and unalleviated analysis of existential angst is, however, provided by such later stories as "Getting into Death"—whose dying heroine has devoted her career to the production of detective fiction as "B. C. Millar" and Gothic romances as "Cassandra Knye"—and "The Joycelin Shrager Story."

A similar pessimism possesses the linked stories gathered in *334*, a compelling vision of near-future New York in which the struggles of the various characters, however courageous, are painful exercises in futility. The young hero of *On Wings of Song*, who begins life in rural Iowa but ultimately moves to New York (as Disch did), is far more adventurous in his attempts literally to rise above the awful banality of life on Earth—and the evils to which it is subject by courtesy of the oppressive morality of the "undergoders"—but finds himself similarly cursed.

The introspective mood of this mid-period fiction was decisively broken by *The Businessman*, in which Disch—not for the first time, but with a new verve and intensity—turned his corrosive scepticism outwards. The element of horror becomes far more vivid in this novel because it is mostly inflicted, with vengeful black humour, upon the callous and hypocritical Bob Glandier. As a man long used to making executive decisions, Glandier anticipates no problems in completing the expeditious murder of his wife, but her ghost will not let him rest. Much attention is, in the meantime, paid to the sad plight of other recruits to the ranks of the unquiet dead—including the poet John Berryman—who are equally haunted after their own peculiar fashion.

The M.D. is a much more sustained exercise in the same vein, following the career of Billy Michaels, who is given a magical caduceus by an enigmatic supernatural being who is initially manifest as Santa Claus but prefers the guise of the Roman god Mercury. The caduceus has the power to heal all diseases save for those carried by the genes, but it must be constantly recharged with power by inflicting illnesses of a like kind; it is a redistributor rather than an alleviator of pain and suffering, but possession of it nevertheless confers great power upon its user. While Billy is a small boy it is unsurprising that his experiments with the device go so badly awry, but it is when he becomes a man that a fully mature and truly profound irresponsibility sets in. *The M.D.* is perhaps Disch's best novel to date, superimposing a powerful and telling allegory on a finely-detailed account of the myriad curses afflicting everyday life.

The cool, thoroughgoing and essentially clinical analysis of *The M.D.* contrasts somewhat with the tone of *The Priest*, which is a pure hymn of hate—but that might conceivably have as much to do with fitting method to subject as with the depth of Disch's own feelings. Religious men had always had a bad press in Disch's work, but even the scathing assaults on the undergoders of *On Wings of Song* and Billy Michaels's fanatical son Judge in *The M.D.* seem pale beside this demolition of the endemic hypocrisies of the Catholic faith—in particular, the attitude of the Church to the legions of homosexuals and paedophiles which it (allegedly) attracts into its ranks. The principal villain of the piece, Father Patrick Bryce, is cast by guilt into a Hell of personal disintegration which—among other indignities—hurls him back in time to the war of extermination fought by 13th-century Inquisitors against the Cathars. Some of the apparatus of his hallucinations is borrowed from the writings of sf writer-turned-cult leader A. D. Boscage, who is a combination of L. Ron Hubbard and Whitley Strieber—two more of Disch's pet hates.

The Priest justifies its subtitle by including a Gothic monstrosity of a shrine where pregnant teenagers are held captive, tortured and occasionally murdered by an assortment of mad clergymen and their lay associates. Attentive as ever to matters of tradition, Disch thus recovers an extends a rich tradition of anti-clericalism which was earlier carried forward from M. G. Lewis's Gothic classic *The Monk* by such works as Eugene Sue's *The Wandering Jew*. Even more than *Clara Reeve*, by virtue of its unrepentant modernity, *The Priest* deserves consideration as the purest Gothic novel of the 20th century.

—Brian Stableford

DONNELLY, Joe

Nationality: British. **Born:** 1950. **Career:** Journalist, Glasgow, Scotland. **Address:** c/o Michael Joseph Ltd., Penguin Books, 27 Wrights Lane, London W8 5TZ, England.

HORROR, GHOST AND GOTHIC PUBLICATIONS

Novels

Bane. London, Barrie and Jenkins, 1989.
Stone. London, Barrie and Jenkins, 1990.
The Shee. London, Ebury Press, 1991.
Still Life. London, Century, 1993.
Shrike. London, Century, 1994.
Havock Junction. London, Century, 1995.
Incubus. London, Michael Joseph, 1996.
Twitchy Eyes. London, Michael Joseph, 1997.

*   *   *

All of Joe Donnelly's novels share common themes. They are graphic, contemporary novels with a very high body count induced by a supernatural element which has been hanging around for a very long time.

Most of the novels are set in Scotland (the exception being *The Shee*, which has an Irish setting), in and around the fictional town of Levenford which lies about 20 miles north of Glasgow. The action in his first novel, *Bane*, takes place in the coastal village of Arden. Journalist Nick Ryan has just returned to the place where he grew up intending to write novels. Close by is a hill called Ardhmor. One summer he and two friends were found under a rock fall on the hill. Of those one has the mind of a ten year-old, the other has also just returned to the village with her young daughter. This is the start of a "bad summer," one where a lot of nasty things happen in the area and the events, like those in 1961, begin with the disappearance of a boat.

Beneath the hill the Cu Saeng is awake and reaching out to create havoc. This monster was called from the pits of hell many centuries before to repel the viking invaders. However it had never been banished, only confined under Ardhmor, trapped by walls of water, bone, wood and stone. As the walls are breached by roadworks and archaeologists it becomes more powerful. Only Nick and his friends have the power to banish it by dint of their ancestry. The vast numbers of deaths (many described in bloody detail) occur when the village is cut off from the outside world and are the effect of infection from ergot of rye.

Stone is set only 15 miles from Levenford. Alan Crombie, who was born there, brings his family to live in the house he has just bought. What he doesn't know at the time is that it was built within and partly from a ring of standing stones. These, planted thousands of years before, ring a place of power, a gateway to the low roads (which Donnelly equates to ley lines, being routes to other places and/or roads to hell). By uprooting the stones, the original builder of the house partially opened the gate. As gates are two way, not only can people disappear through them (as some of the earlier occupants of the house seem to have done) but other things can come through. Instead of confining the action to the house and the immediate environs, Donnelly sends out monsters to ravage the country side and heap up the bodies.

His third book, *The Shee*, is a diversion, being set in Ireland, though it has elements in common with *Bane*. The morrigan is freed from her prison when archaeologists break into the tomb where she is trapped and it is her activities that account for the many gruesome deaths. The main character, who has to banish the monster, is Sean McCullain a photographic journalist from Skye. At the height of the action the coastal village of Kilgallen, where everything takes place, is cut off from the outside world. Like Nick Ryan in *Bane*, Sean McCullain is beset by nightmares.

Still Life takes us back to the Levenford area. The journalist here is Martin Thornton who is following up a story he won an award for when a young woman was paralysed in a shooting incident. The woman, Caitlin Brook, is the one having dreams. The deaths are caused by an ancient stand of trees. People have always tended to keep away from the wood but now the trees are eating those who stray within their bounds. Again Donnelly is using an aspect of celtic mythology to create his monster. The ancient oak at the centre of this woodland glade is also a node where ley lines meet, another gateway to the low roads. It is from this tree that Cerunos will emerge to accept the sacrifice of a virgin on midsummer's day—this was also the crucial date for culmination of the events in *Stone*. Sheila Garvie, who instigates the events in the village (which doesn't actually get cut off but plant growth does make the lane to it very difficult to find), is the high priestess who has been around for centuries.

Levenford itself is the site of the events in *Shrike*. This time the ancient evil is released by a seance and is responsible for the deaths. Again dreams play an important part in the story but this time the main character is a policeman whose job it is to catch the murderer.

Havock Junction takes us onto the low roads. Patsy Havelin has rescued her children from Kerron Vaunche who, like Sheila Garvie in *Still Life*, is long-lived but needs a ritual killing to renew her youth. This time it is Patsy's daughter. The ritual, to be effective, must be conducted at the winter solstice at the meeting place of ley lines which this time is in the cellars of a house in Scotland. As she flees, Patsy finds herself beset by all the nasty things which haunt the roads and chased by Vaunche who wants the children back.

The monster of *Incubus* does not have its roots in Celtic mythology but is ancient, perhaps being the real reason why Herod ordered the deaths of all children under three in Biblical times. The creature has a very long period of development when it appears as a baby, feeding off women by stimulating them to perpetual lactation. It has been passed between several "mothers," each feeding it for a number of years before the action in this novel takes place. Now it is undergoing rapid maturation and the body count rises. As in *Shrike*, the lead characters are the police, who at one point visit Levenford during the hunt for the missing woman who is now the creature's "mother" but is unlike the other novels as by the end the threat has not been totally removed.

Donnelly uses a number of different approaches for his stories and the action is always fast but often it takes too long for the for the crucial point in the novel to be reached. He tends to repeat information, especially in *Shrike* and *Incubus* where the same event is related from more than one viewpoint. Dreams, which feature in so many of the books, have the effect of rehashing what we have already been told. Many of the characters are introduced merely for the purpose of killing them in a gruesome manner and frequently at the height of a sexual experience. Even the main characters don't come across as real people and much of the writing is woolly. Deaths are described in intimate detail whereas crisper prose would have heightened the terror. The only subtleties are the oblique references to events in earlier novels, for example, the policewoman in Incubus remembers the body on the steeple in Levenford as she drives past.

—Pauline Morgan

DOUGLAS, John

A pseudonym. **Nationality:** British. **Born:** 1955. **Address:** c/o Hodder Headline plc, 338 Euston Road, London NW1 3BH, England.

HORROR, GHOST AND GOTHIC PUBLICATIONS

Novels

The Late Show. London, Hodder and Stoughton, 1994.
Cursed. London, Hodder and Stoughton, 1995.
Hard Shoulder. London, Hodder and Stoughton, 1996.
Zoo Event. London, New English Library, 1997.

* * *

John Douglas writes the kind of supernatural horror fiction in which the cause of the manifestation seems to have no rational explanation. It is merely there to cause problems and kill people. However, each of his novels has a very different approach. Douglas packs his novels with incident and energy but each one has its flaws.

The first two novels are set in the fictitious town of Ollington—situated in central England, just north of the Midlands, and one of those places that can change its character as knowledge of the town evolves between novels. In *The Late Show* it has the appearance of being a small town with very little to occupy an evening. Even the cinema is dying. In *Cursed* it has opened out and boasts a university campus (probably of the newer variety converted from a humble polytechnic). *Hard Shoulder* takes place on the M6, a motorway which runs most of the length of the western side of England.

Bill Anders (in *The Late Show*) is depressed: nobody seems to appreciate the old movies these days. Modern films are violent or are made to titillate and have no soul. His old-fashioned cinema is loosing out to the multi-screen complexes in nearby towns. As a result it is due to close and be replaced by a supermarket. In a last-ditch attempt to save it he is persuaded to put on an all-night horror programme. But something nasty has woken up and promises him his dearest wish. Unfortunately, it lies. Nearly 200 people turn up for the showing, but as the first reel starts to roll so does the horror. The first punter dies by being attacked and absorbed by piles of Anders's hoarded film magazines. His friend, fleeing the room, finds himself on an endless staircase which is gradually eaten by black nothingness. Later, a youth is dragged into a poster which acquires his face, a girl is devoured by a toilet, and another is roasted by a hand-dryer turned flamethrower. Handles from doors disappear, as do the doors themselves, trapping the customers in the cinema. Some are crushed by a moving washroom wall or attacked by a firehose. The most bizarre death must be of the girl, a virgin, who is sexually assaulted by a conglomeration of old chewing gum before being smothered by it.

The whole thing is an exercise in finding as many different ways as possible of killing people nastily, and as such goes way over the top. After a while it gets a tad tedious. The entity that has caused all the mayhem doesn't seem to have any real origin—it has just been there, waiting—and is never really defeated. It just retreats to carry on waiting.

Cursed cannot be regarded as anything but a comedy. Leonard Halsey is killed in his hotel room and gets to haunt the person who found his body. Imagine having the ghost of a fat slob, dressed only in his underpants, always in your presence, including the bathroom. And you are told that he won't go away until you have killed the person who killed him. That is the situation Duncan Cantrill finds himself in. In desperation to get rid of Leonard, Duncan agrees to hunt down the killer. The problem is, Leonard doesn't know who it is. He joined a black magic circle simply for the sex and only knows the names of a couple of the other participants, both of whom wind up dead. Every lead Duncan follows up seems to have a corpse at the end of it, and following behind is Chief Inspector Chater who begins to suspect that Duncan is either the killer or out of his skull, probably both. The haunting is one supernatural aspect in this novel; the other is the killing agent which appears as a very cold, very hungry Black Wind capable of ripping a horse to pieces and strangling people. The wind is directed to its victim by a method reminiscent of "Casting the Runes" by M. R. James, the message being passed to the victim secretly but written on paper in a runic form. The assumption is that the Black Wind has been called up by the leader of the coven but it is never really explained why.

Hard Shoulder is a more interesting book. Ronald's daughter died in a car accident and in the last photographs taken of her he sees a white truck. Convinced that it caused her death, Ronald starts cruising the M6 motorway hunting for it. He takes photographs of crashes and sees the truck in all of them. No one else can. Douglas paints a realistic portrait of a man with an obsession that is slowly destroying him. The other principal character is 16-year-old Cally. When she gets upset enough to hate someone, she dreams of a train. The object of her hatred dies. Trapped in a mental hospital, she is experimented on by the unscrupulous doctor in charge. She resolves to escape but to take with her an autistic man who she believes will be tortured when her disappearance is discovered. Inevitably, Cally and Ronald meet as it will take a combination of their individual problems to resolve the situation for both of them. The supernatural elements here are explained better though there are still some inconsistencies, and the book is quite enjoyable.

—Pauline Morgan

DOWLING, Terry

Nationality: Australian. **Born:** Terence William Dowling, in Sydney, Australia, 21 March 1947. **Education:** Boronia Park Public School, Sydney, 1952-59; Hunters Hill High School, Sydney, 1960-64; Sydney Teachers' College, 1965-66; B.A. (honours) and M.A. (first class honours), University of Sydney, 1970-76. **Military Service:** Australian Infantry, 1968-69. **Career:** Communications lecturer, from 1976; freelance journalist, from 1976; contributor of short stories to Australian science-fiction and mainstream magazines and overseas publications, from 1982; guest performer on ABC's *Mr. Squiggle & Friends*, 1978-86, and ABC science programmes; genre reviewer for *The Australian*, from 1989; assistant editor and currently co-editor (with Dr. Van Ikin) of *Science Fiction: A Review of Speculative Literature*. **Awards:** Nine Ditmar awards for Australian science fiction; William Atheling, Jr., award for science-fiction criticism; Readercon award for collection, 1991, and for short story, 1993; Aurealis award for novel, 1996. **Agent:** Richard Curtis Associates, 171 East 74th Street, New York, NY 10021, USA. **Address:** 11 Everard Street, Hunters Hill, NSW 2110, Australia.

HORROR, GHOST AND GOTHIC PUBLICATIONS

Short Stories

An Intimate Knowledge of the Night. Adelaide, Aphelion, 1995.
The Man Who Lost Red. Sydney, MirrorDanse, 1995.

OTHER PUBLICATIONS

Short Stories

Rynosseros. Adelaide, Aphelion, 1990; New York, Science Fiction Book Club, 1993.
Wormwood. Adelaide, Aphelion, 1991.
Blue Tyson. Adelaide, Aphelion, 1992.
Twilight Beach. Adelaide, Aphelion, 1993.

Other

Editor, with Richard Delap and Gil Lamont, *The Essential Ellison: A 35-Year Retrospective*, by Harlan Ellison. Omaha, Nebraska, Nemo Press, 1987.
Editor, with Van Ikin, *Mortal Fire: Best Australian SF.* Sydney, Hodder and Stoughton, 1993.

*   *   *

Terry Dowling is one of Australia's most respected and awarded science-fiction writers. His sf short stories are lyrical and exotic, and demonstrate the influences of writers such as J. G. Ballard, Ray Bradbury, Jack Vance and Cordwainer Smith. Dowling's interest in horror has been evident in his work from the beginning, and in recent years he has achieved considerable success in the horror field. While his non-sf horror work is perhaps more accessible to some readers than his multi-layered sf, a careful analysis of his science fiction reveals that fear and haunting have also played a role there, often taking new and unexpected forms. His stories invariably have an undercurrent of darkness brought on by intense seeing, making use of dark deeds and of phantoms, monsters and alarming images and situations, even if scientifically produced. Indeed, four of his first six professional story sales can easily be viewed as horror, because of their explorations of fear, fright and darkness.

On this topic Dowling says of his own work, "Most of my tales concern mystery, new states of awareness, the nature of perception, obsession and transcendence, often using fear, moments of illuminating encounter, the conventions of quest and sleuthing to achieve these things." In short, Dowling is a natural for the horror form, with much of his fiction carefully conceived with the perceptual intensity of a horror vision. Rarely interested in the blood and gore of so much modern horror, however, Dowling prizes *inquietude*, the disquiet or unease prized by the Surrealists, creating situations of intense focus which allow the reader to see the world with "new eyes."

Dowling likes to re-work the standards, giving them a new spin and devising new explanations, such as the nature of ghosts in "The Bullet That Grows in the Gun" and "The Daemon Street Ghost-Trap." Much of his work walks the fine line between sanity and insanity, as in "The Gully," "Beckoning Nightframe" and "Scaring the Train," where he explores our ability to haunt ourselves. At the same time, Dowling demonstrates great genre versatility. "The Bullet That Grows in the Gun," for instance, appeared in both *Urban Fantasies* and *Omega Science Digest*, while what is set up as a traditional killer-on-the-prowl horror tale, "Fear-Me-Now," appeared in the cross-genre crime anthology *Crosstown Traffic*, then made Gardner Dozois's *Year's Best* Recommended Reading list as science fiction. Similarly his Tom Rynosseros tale "The Maiden Death" in Peter Crowther's *Destination Unknown* anthology would not have been out of place in *Weird Tales*.

Dowling's Tom Rynosseros tales (collected in *Rynosseros*, *Blue Tyson* and *Twilight Beach*), tell of a bizarre future Australia where huge sand-ships ply a landscape peopled by the Ab'O tribes of the interior. While these tales are surrealistic and futuristic, the following stories all include horror elements: "Shatterwrack at Breaklight" tells of a phantom lover; "What We Did to The Tyger" includes a curse; "The Only Bird in Her Name" is about a shape-shifting "vampire"; "Marmordesse" tells of a burial custom gone wrong; "Going to the Angels" is a tale of genocide; "A Song to Keep Them Dancing" is about a genetically-bred death creature; "Stoneman" has a contest with Death; "Dreaming the Knife" is a story of revenge; in "Totem" bizarre life experiments kill someone; "Sailors Along the Soul" is either about mirages or ghosts; "Nights at Totem Rule" is a haunted-house tale of hallucinations or ghosts; "A Whisper from the Voice at the Vanishing Point" is also about mirages or ghosts; "The Green Captain's Tale" is a tale of possession; "Fear-Me-Now" is about a serial killer; "A Woman Sent Through Time" includes phantoms; "The Maiden Death" is a monster story.

Dowling's Wormwood tales (collected in *Wormwood*) tell of a future world invaded by the Nobodoi, a powerful alien race against whose rule the few remaining humans struggle to survive. A number of these stories, too, include horror elements. "The Man Who Walks Away Behind the Eyes," which won the 1983 Ditmar Award for Best Australian science fiction, is a tale of revenge. "Housecall" is monster story about a deadly domain. "For As Long As You Burn," which won the 1988 Ditmar Award for Best Australian long fiction, is a tale of monstrous sex. "Nobody's Fool" is about a monstrous and deadly world. "A Deadly Edge Their Red Beaks Pass Along" is about a deadly creature.

It is with his stand-alone horror stories, however, where Dowling has allowed himself free reign, that his best work in the genre has appeared. "The Bullet That Grows in the Gun" is a small masterpiece, a tale of quiet horror which explores the idea that reality is an echo of our own expectations, what Dowling describes as function following form. It won the 1986 Ditmar Award for best Australian short fiction. "The Quiet Redemption of Andy the House," also a Ditmar Award-winner even though it was first published in a mainstream literary magazine, is a haunting story of a man trying to hold on to sanity. The first horror story to bring Dowling international recognition was "The Daemon Street Ghost-Trap" from the anthology *Terror Australis* (1993), a ghost story, of an unusual sort, which evokes a 19th-century atmosphere and was reprinted in the Ellen Datlow and Terri Windling *Year's Best Fantasy and Horror: 7th Annual Collection.* Similarly, the brilliant

"Scaring the Train," a story about a juvenile prank of scaring train-drivers which turns into something more nightmarish, was included in both the Datlow and Windling *Year's Best Fantasy and Horror: 9th Annual Collection* and the Stephen Jones and Ramsey Campbell *Best New Horror 7*.

Much of Dowling's straight horror, including the above-mentioned stories, are collected in *An Intimate Knowledge of the Night*, which won the 1996 Aurealis Award. On one level it is a collection of Dowling's horror tales which are not linked to the sf worlds of Tom Tyson and Wormwood, and can be read independently of each other; but on another level, because of the thematic linking material in which Dowling "the author" keeps being interrupted as he writes by telephone calls from an ex-mental patient named Raymond, the book uses the stories to create a larger canvas which further explores sanity and the nature of reality and perception.

Similar themes are explored to chilling effect in Dowling's most recent horror story, "Beckoning Nightframe," which was selected for inclusion in the Datlow and Windling *Year's Best Fantasy and Horror: 10th Annual Collection*. This story forms part of a forthcoming horror book called *Blackwater Days*, a closely linked collection of stories set in a mental hospital in the Hunter Valley outside Sydney and concerning various strange events which befall Dr. Dan Truswell. If "Beckoning Nightframe" is an indication of the quality of the other stories in the book, *Blackwater Days* will take Dowling's tales deeper into the horror maze of insanity and the perception of reality.

—Steven Paulsen and Sean McMullen

DOYLE, (Sir) Arthur Conan

Nationality: British. **Born:** Edinburgh, 22 May 1859. **Education:** Hodder School, Lancashire, 1868-70, Stonyhurst College, Lancashire, 1870-75, and the Jesuit School, Feldkirch, Austria (editor, *Feldkirchian Gazette*), 1875-76; studied medicine at the University of Edinburgh, 1876-81, M.B. 1881, M.D. 1885. **Military Service:** Served as senior physician at a field hospital in South Africa during the Boer War, 1899-1902; knighted, 1902. **Family:** Married 1) Louise Hawkins in 1885 (died 1906), one daughter and one son; 2) Jean Leckie in 1907, two sons and one daughter. **Career:** Practised medicine in Southsea, Hampshire, 1882-90; full-time writer from 1891; stood for Parliament as Unionist candidate for Central Edinburgh, 1900, and tariff reform candidate for the Hawick Burghs, 1906. Member, Society for Psychical Research, 1893-1930 (resigned). **Awards:** LL.D.: University of Edinburgh, 1905. Knight of Grace of the Order of St. John of Jerusalem. **Died:** 7 July 1930.

HORROR, GHOST AND GOTHIC PUBLICATIONS

Novels

The Mystery of Cloomber. London, Ward and Downey, 1888; New York, Fenno, 1895.
The Hound of the Baskervilles. London, Newnes, and New York, McClure, 1902.
The Land of Mist. London, Hutchinson, and New York, Doran, 1926.

Short Stories

The Captain of the Polestar and Other Tales. London, Longman, 1890; New York, Munro, 1894.
The Parasite. London, Constable, 1894; New York, Harper, 1895.
Round the Red Lamp, Being Facts and Fancies of Medical Life. London, Methuen, and New York, Appleton, 1894.
Round the Fire Stories. London, Smith Elder, and New York, McClure, 1908.
Tales of Terror and Mystery. London, Murray, 1922; as *The Black Doctor and Other Tales of Terror and Mystery* (selection). New York, Doran, 1925.
The Conan Doyle Stories. London, Murray, 1929.
The Maracot Deep and Other Stories. London, Murray, and New York, Doubleday, 1929.
The Best Supernatural Tales of Arthur Conan Doyle, edited by E. F. Bleiler. New York, Dover, 1979.
The Best Horror Stories of Arthur Conan Doyle, edited by Martin H. Greenberg and Charles G. Waugh. Chicago, Academy, 1988.
The Supernatural Tales of Sir Arthur Conan Doyle, edited by Peter Haining. Slough, Berkshire, Foulsham, 1988.

OTHER PUBLICATIONS

Novels

A Study in Scarlet. London, Ward Lock, 1888; Philadelphia, Lippincott, 1890.
Micah Clarke. London, Longman, and New York, Harper, 1889.
The Firm of Girdlestone. London, Chatto and Windus, and New York, Lovell, 1890.
The Sign of Four. London, Blackett, 1890; New York, Collier, 1891.
The White Company. London, Smith Elder, 3 vols., 1891; New York, Lovell, 1 vol., 1891.
The Doings of Raffles Haw. London, Cassell, and New York, Lovell, 1892.
The Great Shadow. New York, Harper, 1892.
The Great Shadow, and Beyond the City. Bristol, Arrowsmith, 1893; New York, Ogilvie, 1894.
The Refugees. New York, Longman, 3 vols., 1893; New York, Harper, 1 vol., 1893.
The Stark Munro Letters. London, Longman, and New York, Appleton, 1895.
Rodney Stone. London, Smith Elder, and New York, Appleton, 1896.
Uncle Bernac: A Memory of Empire. London, Smith Elder, and New York, Appleton, 1897.
The Tragedy of Korosko. London, Smith Elder, 1898; as *Desert Drama*, Philadelphia, Lippincott, 1898.
A Duet, with an Occasional Chorus. London, Grant Richards, and New York, Appleton, 1899; revised edition, London, Smith Elder, 1910.
Sir Nigel. London, Smith Elder, and New York, McClure, 1906.
The Lost World. London, Hodder and Stoughton, and New York, Doran, 1912.
The Poison Belt. London, Hodder and Stoughton, and New York, Doran, 1913.
The Valley of Fear. New York, Doran, 1914; London, Smith Elder, 1915.

Short Stories

Mysteries and Adventures. London, Scott, 1889; as *The Gully of Bluemansdyke and Other Stories*, 1892.

The Adventures of Sherlock Holmes. London, Newnes, and New York, Harper, 1892.

My Friend the Murderer and Other Mysteries and Adventures. New York, Lovell, 1893.

The Memoirs of Sherlock Holmes. London, Newnes, 1983; New York, Harper, 1894.

The Great Keinplatz Experiment and Other Stories. Chicago, Rand McNally, 1894.

The Exploits of Brigadier Gerard. London, Newnes, and New York, Appleton, 1896.

The Man from Archangel and Other Stories. New York, Street and Smith, 1898.

The Green Flag and Other Stories of War and Sport. London, Smith Elder, and New York, McClure, 1900.

Hilda Wade (completion of book by Grant Allen). London, Richards, and New York, Putnam, 1900.

Adventures of Gerard. London, Newnes, and New York, McClure, 1903.

The Return of Sherlock Holmes. London, Newnes, and New York, McClure, 1905.

The Last Galley: Impressions and Tales. London, Smith Elder, and New York, Doubleday, 1911.

His Last Bow: Some Reminiscences of Sherlock Holmes. London, Murray, and New York, Doran, 1917.

Danger! and Other Stories. London, Murray, 1918; New York, Doran, 1919.

Tales of Adventure and Medical Life. London, Murray, 1922; as *The Man from Archangel and Other Tales of Adventure.* New York, Doran, 1925.

Tales of Long Ago. London, Murray, 1922; as *The Last of the Legions and Other Tales of Long Ago.* New York, Doran, 1925.

Tales of Pirates and Blue Water. London, Murray, 1922; as *The Dealings of Captain Sharkey and Other Tales of Pirates.* New York, Doran, 1925.

Tales of the Ring and Camp. London, Murray, 1922; as *The Croxley Master and Other Tales of the Ring and Camp,* New York, Doran, 1925.

The Case-Book of Sherlock Holmes. London, Murray, and New York, Doran, 1927.

The Conan Doyle Historical Romances. London, Murray, 2 vols., 1931-32.

The Field Bazaar. Privately printed, 1934; Summit, New Jersey, Pamphlet House, 1947.

The Professor Challenger Stories. London, Murray, 1952.

Great Stories, edited by John Dickson Carr. London, Murray, and New York, London House and Maxwell, 1959.

Strange Studies from Life, Containing Three Hitherto Uncollected Tales, edited by Peter Ruber. New York, Candlelight Press, 1963.

The Annotated Sherlock Holmes, edited by William S. Baring-Gould. New York, Potter, 2 vols., 1967; London, Murray, 2 vols., 1968; as *The Annotated Sherlock Holmes: The Four Novels and Fifty-Six Short Stories Complete,* New York, Wings Books, 1992.

The Adventures of Sherlock Holmes (facsimile of magazine stories). New York, Schocken, 1976; as *The Sherlock Holmes Illustrated Omnibus,* London, Murray-Cape, 1978.

Sherlock Holmes: The Published Apocrypha, with others, edited by Jack Tracy. Boston, Houghton Mifflin, 1980.

The Best Science Fiction of Arthur Conan Doyle, edited by Charles G. Waugh and Martin H. Greenberg. Carbondale, Southern Illinois University Press, 1981.

The Final Adventures of Sherlock Holmes, edited by Peter Haining. London, W.H. Allen, 1981.

The Edinburgh Stories. Edinburgh, Polygon, 1981.

Uncollected Stories, edited by John Michael Gibson and Roger Lancelyn Green. London, Secker and Warburg, and New York, Doubleday, 1982.

The Best of Sherlock Holmes. London, Dent, 1992.

Plays

Jane Annie: or, The Good Conduct Prize, with J. M. Barrie, music by Ernest Ford (produced London, 1893). London, Chappell, and New York, Novello Ewer, 1893.

Foreign Policy, adaptation of his story "A Question of Diplomacy" (produced London, 1893).

Waterloo, adaptation of his story "A Straggler of 15" (as *A Story of Waterloo,* produced Bristol, 1894; London, 1895; as *Waterloo,* produced New York, 1899). London, French, 1907; in *One-Act Plays of To-Day,* 2nd series, edited by J. W. Marriott, Boston, Small Maynard, 1926.

Halves, adaptation of the story by James Payne (produced Aberdeen and London, 1899).

Sherlock Holmes, with William Gillette, adaptation of works by Doyle (produced Buffalo and New York, 1899; Liverpool and London, 1901).

A Duet (A Duologue; produced London, 1902). London, French, 1903.

Brigadier General, adaptation of his stories (produced London and New York, 1906).

The Fires of Fate: A Modern Morality, adaptation of his novel *The Tragedy of Korosko* (produced Liverpool, London, and New York, 1909).

The House of Temperley, adaptation of his novel *Rodney Stone* (produced London, 1910).

The Pot of Caviare, adaptation of his story (produced London, 1910).

The Speckled Band: An Adventure of Sherlock Holmes (produced London and New York, 1910). London, French, 1912.

The Crown Diamond (produced Bristol and London, 1921). Privately printed, 1958.

It's Time Something Happened. New York, Appleton, 1925.

Poetry

Songs of Action. London, Smith Elder, and New York, Doubleday, 1898.

Songs of the Road. London, Smith Elder, and New York, Doubleday, 1911.

The Guards Came Through and Other Poems. London, Murray, 1919; New York, Doran, 1920.

The Poems of Arthur Conan Doyle: Collected Edition (includes play *The Journey*). London, Murray, 1922.

Other

The Great Boer War. London, Smith Elder, and New York, McClure, 1900.

The War in South Africa: Its Cause and Conduct. London, Smith Elder, and New York, McClure, 1902.

Works (author's edition). London, Smith Elder, 12 vols., and New York, Appleton, 13 vols., 1903.

The Fiscal Questions. Hawick, Roxburgh, Henderson, 1905.

An Incursion into Diplomacy. London, Smith Elder, 1906.

The Story of Mr. George Edalji. London, Daily Telegraph, 1907.

Through the Magic Door (essays). London, Smith Elder, 1907; New York, McClure, 1908.

The Crime of the Congo. London, Hutchinson, and New York, Doubleday, 1909.

Divorce Law Reform: An Essay. London, Divorce Law Reform Union, 1909.

Sir Arthur Conan Doyle: Why He Is Now in Favour of Home Rule. London, Liberal Publication Department, 1911.

The Case of Oscar Slater. London, Hodder and Stoughton, 1912; New York, Doran, 1913.

Divorce and the Church, with Lord Hugh Cecil. London, Divorce Law Reform Union, 1913.

Great Britain and the Next War. Boston, Small Maynard, 1914.

In Quest of Truth, Being Correspondence Between Sir Arthur Conan Doyle and Captain H. Stansbury. London, Watts, 1914.

To Arms! London, Hodder and Stoughton, 1914.

The German War. London, Hodder and Stoughton, 1914; New York, Doran, 1915.

Western Wanderings (travel in Canada). New York, Doran, 1915.

The Outlook on the War. London, Daily Chronicle, 1915.

An Appreciation of Sir John French. London, Daily Chronicle, 1916.

A Petition to the Prime Minister on Behalf of Sir Roger Casement. Privately printed, 1916.

A Visit to Three Fronts: Glimpses of British, Italian, and French Lines. London, Hodder and Stoughton, and New York, Doran, 1916.

The British Campaign in France and Flanders. London, Hodder and Stoughton, 6 vols., 1916-20; New York, Doran, 6 vols., 1916-20; revised edition, as *The British Campaigns in Europe 1914-18,* London, Bles, 1 vol., 1928.

The New Revelation; or, What Is Spiritualism? London, Hodder and Stoughton, and New York, Doran, 1918.

The Vital Message (on spiritualism). London, Hodder and Stoughton, and New York, Doran, 1919.

Our Reply to the Cleric. London, Spiritualists' National Union, 1920.

A Public Debate on the Truth of Spiritualism, with Joseph McCabe. London, Watts, 1920; as *Debate on Spiritualism,* Girard, Kansas, Haldeman Julius, 1922.

Spiritualism and Rationalism. London, Hodder and Stoughton, 1920.

The Wanderings of a Spiritualist. London, Hodder and Stoughton, and New York, Doran, 1921.

Spiritualism: Some Straight Questions and Direct Answers. Manchester, Two Worlds, 1922.

The Case for Spirit Photography, with others. London, Hutchinson, 1922; New York, Doran, 1923.

The Coming of the Fairies. London, Hodder and Stoughton, and New York, Doran, 1922.

Three of Them: A Reminiscence. London, Murray, 1923.

Our American Adventure. London, Hodder and Stoughton, and New York, Doran, 1923.

Our Second American Adventure. London, Hodder and Stoughton, and Boston, Little Brown, 1924.

Memories and Adventures. London, Hodder and Stoughton, and Boston, Little Brown, 1924.

Psychic Experiences. London and New York, Putnam, 1925.

The Early Christian Church and Modern Spiritualism. London, Psychic Bookshop, 1925.

The History of Spiritualism. London, Cassell, 2 vols., and New York, Doran, 2 vols., 1926.

Pheneas Speaks: Direct Spirit Communications. London, Psychic Press, and New York, Doran, 1927.

What Does Spiritualism Actually Teach and Stand For? London, Psychic Bookshop, 1928.

A Word of Warning. London, Psychic Press, 1928.

An Open Letter to Those of My Generation. London, Psychic Press, 1929.

Our African Winter. London, Murray, 1929.

The Roman Catholic Church: A Rejoinder. London, Psychic Press, 1929.

The Edge of the Unknown. London, Murray, and New York, Putnam, 1930.

Works (Crowborough edition). New York, Doubleday, 24 vols., 1930.

Strange Studies from Life, edited by Peter Ruber. New York, Candlelight Press, 1963.

Arthur Conan Doyle on Sherlock Holmes. London, Favil, 1981.

Essays on Photography, edited by John Michael Gibson and Roger Lancelyn Green. London, Secker and Warburg, 1982.

Letters to the Press: The Unknown Conan Doyle, edited by John Michael Gibson and Roger Lancelyn Green. London, Secker and Warburg, and Iowa City, University of Iowa Press, 1986.

The Sherlock Holmes Letters, edited by Richard Lancelyn Green. London, Secker and Warburg, 1986.

Editor, *D. D. Home: His Life and Mission,* by Mrs. Douglas Home. London, Paul Trench Trubner, and New York, Dutton, 1921.

Editor, *The Spiritualist's Reader.* Manchester, Two Worlds Publishing Company, 1924.

Translator, *The Mystery of Joan of Arc,* by Léon Denis. London, Murray, 1924; New York, Dutton, 1925.

*

Film Adaptations (selection): *The Hound of the Baskervilles,* 1921, 1931, 1939, *The Scarlet Claw,* 1944 (also released as *Sherlock Holmes and the Scarlet Claw*), 1959, 1978, 1983, *Sherlock Holmes and the Baskerville Curse* (animated), 1984, all from the novel *The Hound of the Baskervilles.*

Bibliography: *A Bibliographical Catalogue of the Writings of Sir Arthur Conan Doyle* by Harold Locke, Tunbridge Wells, Kent, Webster, 1928; *The World Bibliography of Sherlock Holmes and Dr. Watson* by Ronald Burt De Waal, Boston, New York Graphic Society, 1975; *A Bibliography of A. Conan Doyle* by Richard Lancelyn Green and John Michael Gibson, Oxford, Clarendon Press, 1983.

Manuscript Collection: Humanities Research Center, University of Texas, Austin.

Critical Studies (selection): *The Private Life of Sherlock Holmes* by Vincent Starrett, New York, Macmillan, 1933, London, Nicholson and Watson, 1934, revised edition, Chicago, University of Chicago Press, 1960, London, Allen and Unwin, 1961; *Conan Doyle: His Life and Art* by Hesketh Pearson, London, Methuen, 1943, New York, Walker, 1961; *The Life of Sir Arthur Conan Doyle* by John Dickson Carr, London, Murray, and New York, Harper, 1949; *In the Footsteps of Sherlock Holmes* by Michael Harrison, London, Cassell, 1958, New York, Fell, 1960, revised edition, Newton Abbot, Devon, David and Charles, 1971, New York, Drake, 1972; *The Man Who Was Sherlock Holmes* by Michael and Mollie Hardwick, London, Murray, and New York, Doubleday, 1964; *Conan Doyle: A Biography* by Pierre Nordon, London, Murray, 1966, New York, Holt Rinehart, 1967; *A Sherlock Holmes Commentary* by D. Martin Dakin, Newton Abbot, Devon, David and Charles, 1972; *A Biography of the Creator of Sherlock Holmes* by Ivor Brown, London, Hamish Hamilton, 1972; *Sherlock Holmes in Portrait and Profile* by Walter Klinefelter, New York, Schocken, 1975; *The Sherlock Holmes File* by Michael Pointer, Newton Abbot, Devon, David and Charles, 1976; *Sir Arthur Conan Doyle's Sherlock Holmes: The Short Stories: A Critical Commentary* by Mary P. De Camara and Stephen Hayes, New York, Monarch, 1976; *The Adventures of Conan Doyle: The Life of the Creator of Sherlock Holmes* by Charles Higham, London, Hamish Hamilton, and New York, Norton, 1976; *The Encyclopedia Sherlockiana* by Jack Tracy, New York, Doubleday, 1977, London, New English Library, 1978; *Conan Doyle: A Biographical Solution* by Ronald Pearsall, London, Weidenfeld and Nicolson, 1977; *Sherlock Holmes and His Creator* by Trevor H. Hall, London, Duckworth, 1978, New York, St. Martin's Press, 1983; *Conan Doyle: Portrait of an Artist* by Julian Symons, London, G. Whizzard, 1979; *Sherlock Holmes: The Man and His World* by H. R. F. Keating, London, Thames and Hudson, and New York, Scribner, 1979.

Who's Who in Sherlock Holmes by Scott R. Bullard and Michael Collins, New York, Taplinger, 1980; *The International Sherlock Holmes* by Ronald Burt De Waal, Hamden, Connecticut, Shoe String Press, and London, Mansell, 1980; *A Sherlock Holmes Compendium* edited by Peter Haining, London, W. H. Allen, 1980; *Sherlock Holmes in America* by Bill Blackbeard, New York, Abrams, 1981; *Sherlock Holmes: A Study in Sources* by Donald A. Redmond, Montreal, McGill-Queen's University Press, 1982; *The Quest for Sherlock Holmes: A Biographical Study of the Early Life of Sir Arthur Conan Doyle* by Owen Dudley Edwards, Edinburgh, Mainstream, 1982, Totowa, New Jersey, Barnes and Noble, 1983; *A Study in Surmise: The Making of Sherlock Holmes* by Michael Harrison, Bloomington, Indiana, Gaslight, 1984; *Arthur Conan Doyle* by Don Richard Cox, New York, Ungar, 1985; *The Complete Guide to Sherlock Holmes* by Michael Hardwick, London, Weidenfeld and Nicolson, 1986; *Sherlock Holmes: A Centenary Celebration* by Allen Eyles, London, Murray, 1986; *Elementary My Dear Watson: Sherlock Holmes Centenary: His Life and Times* by Graham Nown, New York, Ward Lock, 1986; *The Unrevealed Life of Doctor Arthur Conan Doyle: A Study in Southsea* by Geoffrey Salvert, Horndean, Hampshire, Milestone, 1987; *Arthur Conan Doyle* by Jacqueline A. Jaffe, Boston, Twayne, 1987; *The Quest for Sir Arthur Conan Doyle: Thirteen Biographers in Search of a Life* edited by Jon L. Lellenberg, Carbondale, Southern Illinois University Press, 1987; *The Real World of Sherlock Holmes: The True Crimes Investigated by Arthur Conan Doyle* by Peter Costello, New York, Carroll and Graf, 1991; *Critical Essays on Sir Arthur Conan Doyle* edited by Harold Orel, New York, G. K. Hall, 1992; *I Remember the Date Very Well: A Chronology of the Sherlock Holmes Stories of Arthur Conan Doyle* by John Hall, Studio City, California, Players Press, 1993; *Encyclopedia Sherlockiana: An A-to-Z Guide to the World of the Great Detective* by Matthew E. Bunson, New York, Macmillan, 1994.

*   *   *

As with his detective stories and science fiction, Arthur Conan Doyle regarded his forays into weird fiction as hack writing, and much of his work in that vein is relentlessly conventional. His earliest fictional endeavours include "The American's Tale" (1880), about a man-eating plant, "The Silver Hatchet" (1883), about an accursed object whose custodians become homicidal, and "The Captain of the 'Polestar'" (1883), about strange apparitions seen from a ship becalmed in the Arctic ice. The third, which draws on Doyle's own experiences at sea, foreshadows the work of William Hope Hodgson; it is arguable that Doyle never produced another horror story to equal its eeriness or its conviction, although it lacks the stylistic polish of his later work.

The Captain of the "Polestar" and Other Tales also contains the oft-reprinted "The Great Keinplatz Experiment," a comical identity-exchange fantasy written—like many others—in the wake of F. Anstey's *Vice Versa*, "John Barrington Cowles," a straightforward account of a *femme fatale* with mesmeric powers, and "The Ring of Thoth," one of many late Victorian fantasies about unquiet mummies which add a little love interest to their creepy manifestations. As with other writers of the period, Doyle found that editors became less interested in weird fiction as the 1890s progressed and none of his later collections contains as high a proportion of such material.

The Mystery of Cloomber is a tale of supernatural revenge in which fortress walls and perpetual vigilance prove inadequate to secure a military man from the justice meted out by three Buddhist priests. Apparently modelled on the work of Wilkie Collins, the plot never becomes gripping and exhibits a grotesque misunderstanding of the nature of Eastern culture and religion. The novella *The Parasite* is a more leisurely revisitation of the theme of "John Barrington Cowles," with the important extra twist that the mesmerically talented medium Mrs. Penelosa is not physically attractive. When she begins her pursuit of the hero he is horrified, and his horror grows by slow degrees as the exercise of her powers trashes his life. The story preceded Doyle's conversion to Spiritualism by many years, and it is highly unlikely that its willingness to acknowledge the power of Mrs. Penelosa's mediumistic talents reflected an actual willingness to believe, any more than the earlier novel's attribution of magical menace to Buddhist priests reflected an authentic anxiety.

Round the Red Lamp includes the best of Doyle's *contes cruels*, "The Case of Lady Sannox," and two weird tales which had seen first publication in 1892. "Lot No. 249" is another account of a hyperactive mummy, this time guided by an amateur magician who is eventually persuaded to end his experiments. "The Los Amigos Fiasco" is more striking, by virtue of its novel premise; the citizens of the town in question are very proud of their new electric chair until they discover that far from dispatching a murderer with due expedition it supercharges him with unholy energy. "De Profundis," written in the same year, was for some reason not collected until 1911, when it appeared in *The Last Galley*. Another story set at sea, it involves a premonitory vision whose implication is partly misleading.

After 1892 Doyle wrote no more weird fiction for some years, but *Round the Fire Stories* includes three items first published in

1899-1900. "The Brown Hand" is a quietly effective ghost story. "The Leather Funnel" is a neat account of an object cursed by evil association. "Playing with Fire" is another tale of Spiritualism gone bad, in which the manifestations conjured up at a seance are more ominous than was expected. Shortly afterwards he wrote the Sherlock Holmes novel that makes the most prolific and most productive use of an element of horror, *The Hound of the Baskervilles*—which remains the classic of its hybrid kind.

"The Silver Mirror" in *The Last Galley* is another story of an object infected by association, and "How it Happened" in *Danger! and Other Stories* another in which the communication received from the Other Side by a medium is ironically unwelcome. The latter was first published in 1913, not long before the outbreak of the Great War—in which Doyle lost his son and became so desperate for consoling news that he embraced Spiritualism wholeheartedly. *The Last Galley* and *Danger! and Other Stories* each contain a science-fictional monster story of greater interest than any of their tales of the supernatural. "The Terror of Blue John Gap" wonders whether there might be an extension of the biosphere beneath the earth's surface, while the excellent "The Horror of the Heights" adds an extra stratum of life to the upper atmosphere.

Credulity regarding the supernatural is not normally conducive to the writing of good weird fiction, and it is arguable that the two novels Doyle produced under the influence of his new-found Spiritualist faith are far below the standard of his best work, but the fact that he was now able to take the notion of haunting more seriously seems to have worked to the advantage of "The Bully of Brocas Court" (1921), reprinted in *Tales of the Ring and the Camp*. This account of a sadistic phantom boxer is conspicuously nastier than his other tales in the same vein.

The Land of Mist is not really a horror story, but rather a fearful exercise in self-examination, in which the brashly arrogant Professor Challenger (an admitted exaggeration of aspects of Doyle's own character) is humbled by encounters with the supernatural in the wake of his wife's death. The short novel *The Maracot Deep*, on the other hand, is an out-and-out fantasy in which a Challenger-like adventurer winds up in Atlantis and unwisely disturbs the slumbering spirit of the Lord of the Dark Face. Doyle seemingly lost patience with it when he was only part-way through and he put the plot out of its misery when it was only three-quarters complete; the book version had to be filled out by a couple of late Professor Challenger stories, the relatively slight "The Disintegration Machine" and the ludicrously melodramatic "When the World Screamed."

Doyle was never sufficiently interested in weird fiction to become a first-rank contributor to the genre; he usually regarded horror as a kind of spice which could be casually added to workaday stories whenever required. On the rare occasions when he did bring his full and formidable story-telling talents to bear on he project of making his readers' flesh creep, however, he produced some very effective tales.

—Brian Stableford

DRAKE, H(enry) B(urgess)

Nationality: British. **Born:** 1894. **Career:** Novelist and educator; professor of English, Keijo Imperial University, Tokyo; also taught in Korea. **Died:** 1963.

HORROR, GHOST AND GOTHIC PUBLICATIONS

Novels

The Remedy. London, Lane, 1925; as *The Shadowy Thing*, New York, Burt, 1928.
Cursed Be the Treasure. London, Lane, 1926; New York, Burt, 1928.
Hush-a-by Baby. London, Falcon Press, 1952; as *Children of the Wind*, Philadelphia, Lippincott, 1954.

OTHER PUBLICATIONS

Novels

The Schooner California. New York, Harper, 1927.
The Children Reap. New York, Vanguard, 1929.
Slave Ship. New York, Universal, 1936.
Chinese White. London, Falcon Press, 1950.
The Book of Lyonne. N.p., 1952.
The Woman and the Priest. London, Davies, 1955.

Other

Korea of the Japanese. London, Lane, 1930; New York, Dodd Mead, 1930.
An Approach to English Literature for Students Abroad. London, Oxford University Press, 5 vols., 1939-50.
The Oxford English Course for Secondary Schools. London, Oxford University Press, 1957.

*   *   *

H. B. Drake is one of several authors now vaguely canonical because H. P. Lovecraft mentioned him in *Supernatural Horror in Literature*, wherein it is charitably stated that *The Shadowy Thing* "summons up strange and terrible vistas." The novel concerns one Avery Booth, an evil hypnotist of the Svengali or even Dracula mould, who quite early in the course of things causes a spirit to pass into a schoolboy, who grows up, goes mad, and has to be shot by the hero in an extraordinarily lurid sequence which makes the treatment of Renfield in Stoker's *Dracula* positively sensitive in comparison. For this and other outrages, there is eternal enmity between the narrator and Avery Booth.

The plot settles down to romance, vaguely following *Dracula* in the sense that Booth is largely an unseen force, luring female members of the cast offstage for undoubtedly vile ends. Things become slightly more interesting as the villain makes some effort to reform, but, alas, the pig-headed hero pushes him further into wickedness. Booth absconds with the hero's fiancée, then is killed in World War I, but returns to possess the body of the hero's brother-in-law and work further evil, most of it concerning the ladies. He is finally defeated by the narrator's sister, Blanche, whose mediumistic powers equal his own, the difference being, presumably, that her heart is pure.

While Drake was by no means a technically incompetent writer, the modern reader is unlikely to make it through *The Shadowy Thing*, with its stereotyped characters (including a taciturn, kilt-wearing, ever-faithful Scottish retainer inevitably named Jock), extraordinarily naive view of hypnotism (which was, at the time, still linked with the occult in the vulgar imagination), and complete absence of adult psychology. The hero hates Avery Booth because he is evil. He is evil because the hero says so. There is no sense of what this evil consists of (other the an ability to manipulate others) or why Booth has such powers. You just can't trust a charismatic fellow who can kill a raging bull by staring at it.

The "strange and terrible vista" which intrigued Lovecraft occurs right at the outset, with the hint that, in the midst of hypnotism, some alien from "outside" might slip into the subject's body, eventually displacing the original personality. Otherwise, *The Shadowy Thing* is significant primarily as the source for Lovecraft's own "The Thing on the Doorstep," which handles the same premise far better.

Drake's other novels are of marginal interest. *Cursed Be the Treasure* is primarily an adventure story. There's a curse in it, all right, but the supernatural element is at best extremely tangential. *Hush-a-by Baby* features twin poltergeists, the spirits of babies dead at birth.

H. B. Drake also wrote a few supernatural short stories; two which have been reprinted in anthologies are the Korean-flavoured "Yak Mool San" (1949) and "Noel" (1950), both originally published in the *London Mystery Magazine*. Bibliographer and critic E. F. Bleiler reports that Drake's memoirs of his days in Korea are more interesting than his fiction.

—Darrell Schweitzer

du MAURIER, Daphne

Nationality: British. **Born:** London, 13 May 1907; daughter of the actor-manager Sir Gerald du Maurier; granddaughter of the writer George du Maurier. **Education:** Attended schools in London, Meudon, France, and Paris. **Family:** Married Lieutenant-General Sir Frederick Arthur Montague Browning in 1932 (died 1965); two daughters and one son. **Career:** Freelance writer, 1931-89. **Awards:** National Book award, 1938; Dame Commander, Order of the British Empire, 1969; Mystery Writers of America Grand Master award, 1977. Member, Royal Society of Literature (fellow). **Died:** 19 April 1989.

Horror, Ghost and Gothic Publications

Novels

Rebecca. London, Gollancz, and New York, Doubleday, 1938.
Castle d'Or, with Arthur Quiller-Couch. London, Dent, and New York, Doubleday, 1962.
The House on the Strand. London, Gollancz, and New York, Doubleday, 1969.

Short Stories

The Apple Tree: A Short Novel and Some Stories, London, Gollancz, 1952; as *Kiss Me Again, Stranger: A Collection of Eight Stories, Long and Short*, New York, Doubleday, 1953; as *The Birds, and Other Stories*, London, Pan, 1977.
The Breaking Point: Eight Stories. London, Gollancz, and New York, Doubleday, 1959; as *The Blue Lenses, and Other Stories*, Penguin, 1970.

Not after Midnight and Other Stories. London, Gollancz, 1971; as *Don't Look Now*, New York, Doubleday, 1971.
Echoes from the Macabre: Selected Stories. London, Gollancz, 1976; New York, Doubleday, 1977.
Classics of the Macabre. London, Gollancz, and New York, Doubleday, 1987.

Other Publications

Novels

The Loving Spirit. London, Heinemann, and New York, Doubleday, 1931.
I'll Never Be Young Again. London, Heinemann, and New York, Doubleday, 1932.
The Progress of Julius. London, Heinemann, and New York, Doubleday, 1933.
Jamaica Inn. London, Gollancz, and New York, Doubleday, 1936.
Frenchman's Creek. London, Gollancz, 1941; New York, Doubleday, 1942.
Hungry Hill. London, Gollancz, and New York, Doubleday, 1943.
The King's General. London, Gollancz, and New York, Doubleday, 1946.
The Parasites. London, Gollancz, 1949; New York, Doubleday, 1950.
My Cousin Rachel. London, Gollancz, 1951; New York, Doubleday, 1952.
Mary Anne. London, Gollancz, and New York, Doubleday, 1954.
The Scapegoat. London, Gollancz, and New York, Doubleday, 1957.
The Glass-Blowers. London, Gollancz, and New York, Doubleday, 1963.
The Flight of the Falcon. London, Gollancz, and New York, Doubleday, 1965.
Rule Britannia. London, Gollancz, 1972; New York, Doubleday, 1973.
Four Great Cornish Novels (omnibus). London, Gollancz, 1978.

Short Stories

Happy Christmas. New York, Doubleday, 1940.
Come Wind, Come Weather. London, Heinemann, 1940; New York, Doubleday, 1941.
Spring Picture. London, Todd, 1944.
London and Paris. London, Vallencey Press, 1945.
Early Stories. London, Todd, 1954.
The Treasury of du Maurier Short Stories. London, Gollancz, 1960.
The Rendezvous, and Other Stories. London, Gollancz, 1980.

Plays

Rebecca (produced London 1940; New York, 1945), London, Gollancz, 1940; New York, Dramatists Play Service, 1943.
The Years Between (produced Manchester, 1944; London, 1945), London, Gollancz, 1945; New York, Doubleday, 1946.
September Tide (produced London, 1948), London, Gollancz, 1949; New York, Doubleday, 1950.
My Cousin Rachel, edited by Diana Morgan. New York, Dramatists Play Service, 1990.

Screenplay: *Hungry Hill*, with Terence Young and Francis Crowdry, from her own novel, 1947.

Television Play: *The Breakthrough*, 1976.

Other

Gerald: A Portrait. London, Gollancz, 1934; New York, Doubleday, 1935.

The du Mauriers. London, Gollancz, and New York, Doubleday, 1937.

The Infernal World of Branwell Brontë. London, Gollancz, 1960; New York, Doubleday, 1961.

Vanishing Cornwall, photographs by Christian Browning. London, Gollancz, and New York, Doubleday, 1967.

Golden Lads: Sir Francis Bacon, Anthony Bacon and Their Friends. London, Gollancz, and New York, Doubleday, 1975.

The Winding Stair: Francis Bacon, His Rise and Fall. London, Gollancz, 1976; New York, Doubleday, 1977.

Growing Pains: The Shaping of a Writer, London, Gollancz, 1977; as *Myself When Young: The Shaping of a Writer.* New York, Doubleday, 1977.

The "Rebecca" Notebook, and Other Memories. New York, Doubleday, 1980; London, Gollancz, 1981.

Enchanted Cornwall: Her Pictorial Memoir. London, Viking Penguin, 1992.

Editor, *The Young George du Maurier: A Selection of His Letters, 1860-1867.* London, Davies, 1951; New York, Doubleday, 1952.
Editor, *Best Stories,* by Phyllis Bottome. London, Faber, 1963.

*

Film Adaptations: *Jamaica Inn,* 1939, 1985 (TV serial); *Rebecca,* 1940, 1979 (TV serial), 1997 (TV serial); *Frenchman's Creek,* 1944; *Hungry Hill,* 1947; *My Cousin Rachel,* 1953; *The Scapegoat,* 1959; *The Birds,* 1963; *Don't Look Now,* 1973.

Critical Studies: *Daphne: The Life of Daphne du Maurier* by Judith Cook, London, Bantam, 1991; *The Private World of Daphne du Maurier* by Martyn Shallcross, New York, St. Martin's Press, 1992; *Daphne du Maurier* by Margaret Forster, London, Chatto and Windus, 1993.

* * *

The author of 17 novels as well as works of biography, history, and volumes of short stories, Daphne du Maurier is best remembered as the author of *Rebecca.* Her seventh book, and her greatest bestseller on publication in 1938, *Rebecca* went on to be made as a notable film by Alfred Hitchcock (1940, starring Joan Fontaine and Laurence Olivier), was adapted by du Maurier for the stage, and has also been adapted for television more than once. Along with *Jane Eyre* by Charlotte Brontë (with which it was unfavourably compared by reviewers on first publication) it can be seen as the template for the modern gothic romance which flourished in the 1960s and 1970s.

Although not a ghost story, *Rebecca* does concern a psychological haunting. The unnamed narrator is a poor and timid young woman who marries a wealthy widower, Maxim de Winter. His feelings for her seem paternal more than passionate, and she assumes that he has never stopped loving his dead wife, Rebecca, whose spirit still seems to inhabit Manderley, the de Winters' old house in Cornwall. He never speaks of her, but the new wife often hears how superior was the first Mrs. de Winter from the sinister servant, Mrs. Danvers. The narrator's fears and fantasies

dominate the book, as her feelings distort reality, but eventually we learn that Max had never loved Rebecca, and indeed grew to hate her. A cruel, egotistical woman who was skilled at convincing others of her goodness, she tormented and taunted her husband into killing her when she learned she had a fatal illness.

Within a month of publication 45,000 copies sold in Britain, and it was also an instant success in the U.S. Over the years it has continued to sell and to appeal to new generations of readers. The story, with its tight focus on the internal life of the narrator, in which dreams, fantasies and fears have more power than external reality, and du Maurier's psychologically accurate examination of jealousy, has an emotional grip which has made it an indisputable contemporary classic.

Other of du Maurier's novels included elements of the grotesque and psychological suspense. In *My Cousin Rachel* she returned to the theme of jealousy, this time as experienced by a male narrator, examining how a man may be manipulated and driven nearly to madness by a woman. It was hugely successful—initially selling even more copies than *Rebecca* in the first months of publication, although it did not, over time, catch the public imagination quite as firmly as the earlier book.

Because she was usually perceived—inaccurately—as a "romantic novelist," the publication in 1952 of *The Apple Tree,* a collection of macabre and occasionally violent short stories, shocked the reviewers. In the title story, a man becomes convinced that his hated wife has been reincarnated as an apple tree; his attempts to destroy the tree results finally in his own demise. Even more shocking to the attitudes of the time must have been "Kiss Me Again, Stranger" and "The Little Photographer"—two short stories in which sexually assertive women take pleasure from men before killing them. Also included in this collection was "The Birds," a tense and terrifying tale of nature turning on humanity, which was to become famous as the basis for another film by Alfred Hitchcock in 1963.

In the late 1950s, du Maurier began to take an interest in the supernatural. She wrote a series of short stories all concerned with "breaking points" at a time when she felt herself to be nearing a nervous breakdown. The stories, which proved useful therapy for her in exploring fears and paranoid fantasies, were published in *The Breaking Point* in 1958. Among the stories are "The Pool," about a young girl who glimpses a magical world one night in the woods, only to find it has been barred to her forever when she passes through puberty. This was based on an experience du Maurier described having had herself in the woods around her home in Cornwall. In the morning, she began menstruating, for the first time in years, and realized she had not yet passed through menopause. In "The Blue Lenses" a woman sees everyone around her as having the head of an animal. After this hallucination is explained as the result of a pressure on her optic nerve, which is corrected, she sees humans around her—but she sees herself in the mirror with the head of a defenceless, hunted deer.

In 1970 she wrote another series of short stories, published as *Not After Midnight.* Of these the best-known is "Don't Look Now," a frightening and mysterious tale set in Venice, involving psychic twins and a murderous dwarf, which became the basis for a fine horror film by Nicholas Roeg starring Donald Sutherland and Julie Christie in 1973. The collection also included "The Breakthrough," about the attempt to tap into the source of energy released when someone dies, and "The Way of the Cross," a novella about a group of tourists each of whom meets the fate he most fears.

Although many of her short stories concerned the supernatural, only one of her novels, *The House on the Strand*, is a ghost story. In it, the main character takes an experimental drug in order to travel back in time to the 14th century. There he is no more than a ghost, able to observe but not to interact, but gradually he becomes more and more disillusioned with his own times and more and more drawn to Isolda, the woman of the 14th century whose life he haunts.

Daphne du Maurier also completed a novel left unfinished by Sir Arthur Quiller-Couch, *Castle d'Or*, a mystical love story in which two young people in 19th-century Cornwall are drawn by spiritual forces to re-enact the story of Tristan and Isolde.

—Lisa Tuttle

DUNN, Katherine

Nationality: American. **Born:** 1945.

Horror, Ghost and Gothic Publications

Novel

Geek Love. New York, Knopf, 1989.

Other Publications

Novels

Attic. New York, Warner, 1970.
Truck. New York, Warner, 1971.

*   *   *

Although Katherine Dunn's first two novels, *Attic* and *Truck*, received widespread acclaim, she has become inextricably linked to her Gothic third novel *Geek Love*, much as author Mark Helprin has become synonymous with his only fantasy, *Winter's Tale*. *Attic* and *Truck* contain horrific, even at times surreal, images, but are clearly mainstream novels. *Geek Love* breaks from this tradition; it displays a mimetic approach to character development but embraces, without apology, elements of the grotesque.

In part, the book's artistic success depends upon its risky structure: two strands (past and present) that alternate chapters, each strand offering insight into the other. Much like the novel's Siamese twins, the two stories intertwine to form one cohesive narrative. This double storyline forces the reader to continually re-evaluate the characters and to reassess Dunn's slant on morality.

Both strands have the same narrator: Olympia Binewski, an albino hunchback dwarf. The present-day story relates Olympia's attempts to save her daughter (born normal but for a small tail) from the perverse machinations of Ms. Lick, a rich "philanthropist" with severe sado-masochistic proclivities. The other story relates Olympia's upbringing by her parents, Aloysius and Lil Binewski. Chief among Olympia's siblings is the "flipper boy" Arturo, who eventually gains control of the circus and creates a cult of self-mutilating "normals" known as the Arturans or "the

Admitted." (The Jonestown massacre, and the resultant furore about cults, gave Dunn the idea for Arturo's character and eventual demise.)

In its grotesqueries, in its commentary on the meaning of "freak" versus "normal," *Geek Love* belongs to that peculiar yet often transcendent subgenre, the circus novel, examples of which include Charles G. Finney's *The Circus of Dr. Lao* (1935), Ray Bradbury's *Something Wicked This Way Comes* (1962), Angela Carter's *Nights at the Circus* (1984) and Tom DeHaven's *Freaks Amour* (1979). *Geek Love* most resembles *Freaks Amour* (even sharing a synonymous title), a book in which hideously mutated human beings attempt to find their way in a treacherous "normal" world. Like DeHaven, Dunn demonstrates the senselessness of judging a person by appearance—in both books "normals" act like freaks and "freaks" act normal. The basic humanity of Dunn's position plays against the blatant horrors of her set-pieces.

Dunn's book also belongs to two legitimate Gothic traditions: the Southern United States Gothic novel, with its inbred, backwoods gentry, its trashy, almost trailer-park mentality, and the more staid, rarefied Gothic represented by Mary Shelley's *Frankenstein*. The book's special genius is to embed the *Frankenstein* plot within a Southern Gothic tale of power and betrayal. In a sense, the Binewskis' circus is Gothic-to-go, bringing the required atmosphere of decay and gloom to even the brightest, most wholesome towns.

Dunn's take on the *Frankenstein* mythos reflects a uniquely American mentality, for the part of the mad scientist is played by Aloysius, the "mad" father, who with perverse Yankee ingenuity, decides to breed freaks—his sons and daughters—by using illicit drugs on his wife, a willing participant. Aloysius's experiments do not serve the designs of pure science, and they are not intended to develop the perfect human being, but, rather, the uniquely *imperfect* human being, in order that his circus make more money. Ironically enough, Al and Lil treat their children well—once they are born.

In the present-day sections, the monstrous "normal" Ms. Lick plays the mad scientist role. She entices women to mutilate themselves by offering money or an education. Ostensibly, Lick desires to free these women from dependence on their looks, so that they will no longer be objects in a male-dominated world. At the same time, she derives great pleasure from the mutilations.

These commentaries on society run like a hidden vein of satire throughout the book. Dunn's exploration of the utter mercilessness of science when applied by human beings provides a needed counterpoint to her sometimes repetitive lesson that the true monsters are often hidden behind handsome faces with charming smiles.

Despite the strangeness of *Geek Love*, the book contains moments as autobiographical as those in the more accessible *Attic* and *Truck*. Dunn clearly used her own alienation as a child to create the character of Olympia. The book's working title was "Toad," her nickname in grade school ("I was an ugly kid with a deep, huge voice," she writes in the essay that serves as an afterword to the American trade paperback edition), and like Olympia, Dunn worked as the Story Lady at a radio station. Dunn's ability to transfer these experiences to Olympia—and thus allow Olympia to escape the one-dimensional nature of many Gothic protagonists—makes the book much more human and therefore more successful.

However, it would be a mistake to dismiss the more horrifying aspects of *Geek Love* as less real to the author. As she commented in a *Publishers' Weekly* interview: "I've been accused all my life of being preoccupied with the bizarre, the macabre, the violent. But they are actual parts of the world I see. The writers I like most (Gunter Grass, Gabriel Garcia Marquez) tend to confront the aspect of life they're dealing with. . . . The things most destructive to you are the things you must confront. Otherwise, they'll come up on you . . . and whack you on the head when you're not looking." (10 March 1989, pp. 66-7)

The complexity of *Geek Love* has made it a modern Gothic classic, but also doomed it to relative obscurity within the horror genre. In retrospect, *Geek Love* is like any Frankenstein experiment—largely unrepeatable, despite the use of familiar ingredients. It is no less magnificent an achievement because of its eccentricity.

—Jeff VanderMeer

E

EHRLICH, Max (Simon)

Nationality: American. **Born:** Springfield, Massachusetts, 10 October 1909. **Education:** University of Michigan, Ann Arbor, B.A. **Family:** Married 1) Doris Rubinstein in 1940 (divorced), two daughters; 2) Margaret Druckman in 1980. **Career:** Reporter, *Knickerbocker Press* and *Evening News*, both Albany, New York, and *Republican* and *Daily Press*, both Springfield; radio and television writer; novelist and screenwriter. Member of the copyright and screen committees, Writers Guild of America West. **Died:** February 1983.

HORROR, GHOST AND GOTHIC PUBLICATIONS

Novels

The Reincarnation of Peter Proud. Indianapolis, Bobbs Merrill, . 1974; London, Allen, 1975.
The Cult. New York, Simon and Schuster, 1978; London, Mayflower, 1979.
Reincarnation in Venice. New York, Simon and Schuster, 1979; as *The Bond*, London, Mayflower, 1980.

OTHER PUBLICATIONS

Novels

The Big Eye. New York, Doubleday, 1949; London, Boardman, 1951.
Spin the Glass Web. New York, Harper, 1952; London, Corgi, 1957.
First Train to Babylon. New York, Harper, and London, Gollancz, 1955; as *Dead Letter*, London, Corgi, 1958; as *The Naked Edge*, London, Corgi, 1961.
The Takers. New York, Harper, and London, Gollancz, 1961.
Deep is the Blue. New York, Doubleday, and London, Gollancz, 1964.
The High Side. New York, Fawcett, 1969.
The Savage is Loose (novelization of screenplay). New York, Bantam, 1974.
The Edict (novelization of screenplay). New York, Doubleday, 1971; London, Panther, 1984.
Naked Beach. Chicago, Playboy Press, 1979; London, Mayflower, 1980.
The Big Boys. Boston, Houghton Mifflin, 1981.
Shaitan. New York, Arbor House, 1981; London, Severn House, 1982.

Plays

Screenplays: *Zero Population Growth*, with Frank De Felitta, 1971; *The Reincarnation of Peter Proud*, 1974; *The Savage is Loose*, with Frank De Felitta, 1974.

Television Plays: *The Apple* (*Star Trek* series), plus plays or episodes for *Studio One*, *The Defenders*, *The Dick Powell Show* and *Winston Churchill* series.

Radio Plays: episodes of *The Shadow*, *Mr. and Mrs. North*, *Sherlock Holmes*, *Nick Carter*, *The Big Story* and *Big Town* series.

*

Film Adaptations: *The Naked Edge*, from the novel *First Train to Babylon*, 1961; *The Reincarnation of Peter Proud*, 1974.

* * *

Max Ehrlich specializes in showing how the ordinary well-off American citizen reacts to extraordinary circumstances—which are made to seem plausible and even commonplace. The horror is subtle and understated; the message is: this could happen to you. His novels are slick and readable, though not of the highest quality.

Most novels do not seem dated after barely quarter of a century, though *The Reincarnation of Peter Proud* is one which does. Something written, set and published in 1974 could very easily be either as true today as then or else acceptable as a part of the 1970s. Unfortunately, Ehrlich sets out not only to tell a story but to give the reader a guided tour of the occult areas that were opening up in the early 1970s and were still known, or believed in, by a relative few, such as clairvoyance, hypnotic regression, reincarnation and even horoscopes. These and dream research are explained in what now seems to be a patronizing tone, spoiling the early part of the book.

Peter Proud, a Los Angeles college associate professor aged 27, is being troubled by what seem to be vivid dreams. The same ten small incidents recur often, including one in which he swims out into the middle of a lake at night, rather drunk, and is followed (in a boat) and clubbed insensible by a beautiful woman called Marcia, so that he drowns. None of the scenes in these dreams is at all familiar to him. His live-in girlfriend finds the dreams upsetting, and Proud himself is made ill by them. He finds himself unable to concentrate on anything, performing his job badly and becoming irritable; he also suffers from a hip pain without any medical explanation.

The plot takes the form of a detective story, in which Proud hunts for an explanation to his dreams, though from fairly early on (even apart from the presence of the title) there is a suggestion that these are memories of a previous incarnation. When he is tested by a dream researcher, the electro-encephalograph shows that his vivid dreams are not dreams at all. And when he is given regression hypnosis Dr. Hall Bentley, a parapsychologist, it seems that the "dreams" may be memories of a past life, though his subconscious refuses to reveal details. He is hypnotized to forget the "dreams" and seems to be cured.

Then he sees one of the scenes from his "dreams" in a TV documentary and sets off to find the place. He makes trips to New England and eventually, after much legwork, locates the city (Riverside), the lake (Lake Nipmuck) and the identity and current address of Marcia. The man whose memories he has been "dreaming" was named Jeffrey Chapin, who died of drowning in Lake Nipmuck in 1946, fifteen days before Proud was born. Marcia, Jeffrey's wife and killer, is still a widow; in her early 50s, she is now an alcoholic. But Proud falls in love with Ann, her daughter, just a few weeks older than himself. Marcia instinctively dislikes him and, in the end, recognizes him as a reincarnation of her husband and kills him, too, shooting him as he swims by night in Lake Nipmuck.

At its best this is an exciting thriller with entertaining supernatural elements, though it does contain overlong explanatory passages. It was filmed from Ehrlich's own screenplay in 1974. *Reincarnation in Venice*, which was retitled *The Bond* in Britain, was an unsatisfactory sequel with a very similar plot.

The Cult is an unusual and sometimes entertaining novel which tries to give a balanced view of cult religions, and whether it is ever justified for family members to "kidnap" and de-programme young adults who have joined such cults. This, too, is more of a thriller; Ehrlich tries to suggest that supernatural forces are at work, that the master of the cult, Souls For Jesus, may be divine, and that the arch de-programmer may be the Devil. But it turns out that this is merely the author's playfulness, enabling him to feature a phone call from "the Devil" to "His Divinity, the Messenger of God."

The plot shows how the Reed family kidnap their son Jeff, who has been an SFJ member for some months and is fully indoctrinated, and pay John Morse (also known as "the Devil") to de-programme him in the same harsh manner in which he was programmed, by subjecting him to an almost continuous barrage of convincing argument without allowing him much food or sleep. (Both the SFJ and Morse use quotations from the Bible to back up their arguments.) Jeff returns to normal and accepts his family again, but is recaptured by the cult and reprogrammed. The Reeds and Morse are put on trial for kidnapping and false imprisonment, and Morse is convicted as two cult members were planted in the jury.

Although the novel begins well and contains some exciting scenes, it gradually loses focus and ends unsatisfactorily. The personal bad feeling between Morse and the SFJ's master, Buford Hodges, is fascinating though relatively underdeveloped. Nor is the story of Jeff or of his family carried through as the reader would wish. The moral seems to be that the cult, however corrupt and damaging, is powerful enough to win and to go on winning, and this can be seen as an horrific warning.

—Chris Morgan

ELLIS, Bret Easton

Nationality: American. **Born:** Los Angeles, 7 March 1964. **Education:** Bennington College, Vermont, B.A. 1986. **Agent:** International Creative Management, 40 West 57th Street, New York, NY 10019, USA.

Horror, Ghost and Gothic Publications

Novel

American Psycho. New York, Vintage, and London, Picador, 1991.

Other Publications

Novels

Less Than Zero. New York, Simon and Schuster, 1985; London, Pan, 1985.

The Rules of Attraction. New York, Simon and Schuster, 1987; London, Picador, 1988.
The Informers. New York, Knopf, and London, Picador, 1994.

*   *   *

American Psycho is the cult novel about the 1980s which combined yuppie behaviour with grotesquely detailed descriptions of serial killings and, unsurprisingly, caused a furore in literary circles. Ellis was highly regarded as a literary writer from his two previous novels, so it was inevitable that many well-placed reviewers would read *American Psycho* and be disgusted by it, call for it to be banned—unaware that it is only slightly more gruesome than many other works in the horror genre.

In fact, this is not intended as genre horror, but as a satire on the 1980s. It is, in particular, a condemnation of yuppie behaviour and attitudes, a bitterly clever opening up for inspection of the whole yuppie ethos. That is, essentially, the worship of materialism, practised via conspicuous consumption, an unhealthy obsession with the latest fashions in clothes and food, a burning desire to possess a slim and fit body, and a general disregard for people. And it is this ethos, presented in enormous detail, only slightly exaggerated from the truth, which is as worrying (and disgusting) as the serial-killer plot which is woven into it.

Patrick Bateman narrates the story. He is 27, a Harvard graduate who is now a Wall Street executive, handsome, well tanned and narcissistic, who works out every day at the Xclusive Gym to ensure that his body carries no fat. Yet he comes from a rich family and need not hold down a job; he works as a matter of principle, because he believes so strongly that everybody should have a job and that the economic system would be worse off without him. Not only does he dress exceptionally well, following fashion, he is obsessive enough about clothes and accessories (for men and women) to be able to recognize their designers and retailers at a glance; not only must each item look trendy and match the rest, but it must be expensive. The same approach is adopted to food: each lunchtime and evening (and sometimes for breakfast or brunch, too) Patrick goes out with a group of colleagues or acquaintances to eat. They try desperately to get reservations at the newest and trendiest of restaurants, where they eat tiny portions of unusual foods costing hundreds of dollars and drink too much alcohol (trendy brands only). Then they move on to clubs where they hope to buy small bags of cocaine and to pick up attractive women.

Bateman's attitudes about people are the key to understanding the book. His icon is the multi-billionaire Donald Trump. He dislikes blacks and gays, but most of all he detests street beggars because they are not working. Often he berates them for their idleness, sometimes he tantalizes them by seeming to offer money then pocketing it again, and occasionally he punishes them. About women he has conflicting feelings: for sexual purposes (or even for ogling) he is only interested in young "hardbodies" (those with fit, beautiful, fatless bodies), but they should preferably be blonde with "big tits"; he has no compunctions about cheating on Evelyn, his regular girlfriend; although willing to talk to women, he firmly believes that they have no intelligent conversation and little intellect; he sees all women as prostitutes, meaning that he does not expect sex without paying money, either as a straight fee or in the form of a meal out, and he believes that prostitutes get what they deserve (including violence and death); he needs them yet he never loves them.

For his male colleagues, Bateman has a greater or lesser degree of contempt, sometimes veiled and occasionally tinged with respect. They are what passes for friends in his world, yet his reason for being with them is to show off (his expensive clothes, possessions, knowledge), to insult them, to win arguments. Ellis has a running gag throughout the novel about these men mistaking each other for somebody' else: this is partly an endorsement of the yuppie obsession with products rather than people, partly an acknowledgement of their interchangeable appearance—Armani suits, slicked back hair and non-prescription glasses—and partly an attempt by Ellis to add subjectivity and fallibility to Bateman's narration.

Bateman is also a serial killer. There is no clue as to how long this has been going on or what the total body count is (though at one point he makes a confession to his lawyer in an extensive telephone message of "thirty, forty, a hundred murders"; the lawyer assumes it all to be a joke). His reasons for killing seem to be twofold, either that the victims deserve to die, or for sexual excitement. In both cases they are connected to a lack of control and, to some extent, to the effects of alcohol and drugs. So, he stabs a beggar in both eyes, cuts the throat of a child at the zoo, shoots a street musician and a taxi driver; these are spur-of-the-moment crimes, unplanned though not unprepared for. He often carries knives and handguns in his executive briefcase.

His sexual murders are very different. The victims may be either high-class prostitutes or middle-class female acquaintances, or one of each, since he seems to prefer pairs of women. He tries to get them having sex with each other (which turns him on) before he has sex—vaginal, oral and anal—with both. Then he assaults them, doing some physical damage, and if they are lucky he will let them go. On other occasions he tortures them to death in a multitude of appallingly painful and degrading ways. He cares nothing for their suffering, nor does he seem to suffer any guilt or remorse for his crimes. Most worrying of all, perhaps, is that he gets away with it.

It is not that he is particularly clever at selecting his victims or disposing of their bodies, just that he is, in general, not suspected, or that the victims seem not to be missed. And he often films the sex and killings on a camcorder; he is turned on by porn and horror videos.

A curious exception is when he kills Paul Owen, a senior executive working for the same firm; he puts a message on Owen's answering machine about going to England, and several other people claim to have seen Owen in England, even to have lunched with him. Ellis's motive here is unclear. Is he just persevering with the misidentification gag mentioned earlier, or is he trying to suggest that Bateman is a fallible narrator, even a liar? It could be that some of his murders (though not all of them) are illusory—just wishful thinking. Whatever the rationale behind it, this adds mystery to the plot. The story is told is a great number of shortish, named but unnumbered sections, which are only loosely connected; in particular, the passing of time between sections is rarely made clear, and the sections may not even be in chronological order, which further emphasizes the subjectivity (and fallibility) of the narrative.

Overall, this is a fascinating novel, outrageous in many respects. The clothing details and vapid conversations quickly become tiresome, yet the obnoxious characters and their obsessive self-regard remain breathtaking in their so-credible awfulness. Ellis is a very clever writer and *American Psycho* is a book which cannot be ignored.

—Chris Morgan

ELLISON, Harlan (Jay)

Nationality: American. **Born:** Cleveland, Ohio, 27 May 1934. **Education:** Attended Ohio State University, Columbus, 1953-55. **Military Service:** Served in the United States Army, 1957-59. **Family:** Married 1) Charlotte Stein in 1956 (divorced); 2) Billie Joyce Sanders in 1960 (divorced); 3) Lory Patrick in 1965 (divorced); 4) Lori Horowitz in 1976 (divorced); 5) Susan Toth in 1986. **Career:** Editor, *Rogue* magazine, 1959-60; founding editor, Regency Books, Evanston, Illinois, 1961-62; freelance writer and lecturer from 1962; editor, Harlan Ellison Discovery Series, 1975-78; president, Kilimanjaro Corporation, from 1979; creative consultant, *Twilight Zone*, 1986; host, *Sci-Fi Buzz*, the Sci-Fi Channel, from 1993; conceptual consultant, *Babylon 5*, from 1993. Vice-president, Science Fiction Writers of America, 1965-66 (resigned). **Awards:** Nebula award, 1965, 1969, 1977; Writers Guild of America award, for TV play, 1965, 1967, 1973; Hugo award, 1966, 1968, 1969, 1972 (for editing), 1974, 1975, 1978, 1986; *Locus* award, 1970, 1972 (2 awards), 1973, 1974, 1975, 1977, 1978, 1982, 1984, 1985 (2 awards), 1988 (2 awards); Jupiter award, 1973, 1977; Mystery Writers of America Edgar Allan Poe award, 1974, 1988; British Fantasy award for short story, 1979; Horror Writers of America Bram Stoker award, for collection, 1988, for nonfiction, 1990, for short story, 1996, for Lifetime Achievement, 1996; International Silver Pen award for journalism, 1988; World Fantasy Award, for collection, 1989, for Lifetime Achievement, 1993. **Agent:** Richard Curtis Associates, 171 East 74th Street, New York, NY 10021. **Address:** c/o The Kilimanjaro Corporation, 3484 Coy Drive, Sherman Oaks, CA 91423, USA.

HORROR, GHOST AND GOTHIC PUBLICATIONS

Short Stories

Ellison Wonderland. New York, Paperback Library, 1962; as *Earthman, Go Home,* 1964; revised edition, with original title, New York, Bluejay, 1984.

Paingod and Other Delusions. New York, Pyramid, 1965; revised edition, 1975.

I Have No Mouth and I Must Scream. New York, Pyramid, 1967; revised edition, New York: Ace, 1983.

From the Land of Fear. New York, Belmont, 1967.

Love Ain't Nothing But Sex Misspelled: Twenty-Two Stories. New York, Trident Press, 1968; revised edition, New York, Pyramid, 1976.

The Beast That Shouted Love at the Heart of the World. New York, Avon, 1969; abridged edition, London, Millington, 1976; revised edition, New York, Bluejay, 1984; further revised, Baltimore, Borderlands Press, 1994.

Over the Edge: Stories from Somewhere Else. New York, Belmont, 1970.

Partners in Wonder, with others (collaborations). New York, Walker, 1971.

Alone Against Tomorrow: Stories of Alienation in Speculative Fiction. New York, Macmillan, 1971; in 2 vols. as *All the Sounds of Fear* and *The Time of the Eye,* London, Panther, 1973-74.

Approaching Oblivion: Road Signs on the Treadmill Toward Tomorrow. New York, Walker, 1974; London, Millington, 1976.

Deathbird Stories: A Pantheon of Modern Gods. New York, Harper, 1975; London, Millington, 1977; revised edition, New York, Bluejay, 1984; further revised, Norwalk, Connecticut, Easton Press, 1991.

No Doors, No Windows. New York, Pyramid, 1975; revised edition, Baltimore, Borderlands Press, 1991.

Strange Wine: 15 New Stories from the Nightside of the World. New York, Harper, 1978.

The Illustrated Harlan Ellison, edited by Byron Preiss. New York, Baronet, 1978; abridged edition, New York, Ace, 1980.

The Fantasies of Harlan Ellison (omnibus; includes *Paingod and Other Delusions* and *I Have No Mouth and I Must Scream*). Boston, Gregg Press, 1979.

All the Lies That Are My Life. San Francisco, Underwood-Miller, 1980.

Shatterday. Boston, Houghton Mifflin, 1980.

Stalking the Nightmare. Huntington Woods, Michigan, Phantasia Press, 1982.

The Essential Ellison: A 35-Year Retrospective, edited by Terry Dowing with Richard Delap and Gil Lamont. Omaha, Nebraska, Nemo Press, 1987.

Angry Candy. Boston, Houghton Mifflin, 1988.

Footsteps. Round Top, New York, Footsteps Press, 1989.

Dreams with Sharp Teeth: A Three-Volume Omnibus (omnibus; includes *I Have No Mouth and I Must Scream, Deathbird Stories* and *Shatterday*). New York, Quality Paperback Book Club, 1991.

Mefisto in Onyx. Shingletown, California, Ziesing, 1993.

Mind Fields: The Art of Jacek Yerka, the Fiction of Harlan Ellison. Beverly Hills, California, Morpheus International, 1994.

Edgeworks: The Collected Ellison. White Wolf, 3 vols., 1996-97.

Slippage: Precariously Poised, Previously Uncollected Stories. Shingletown, California, Ziesing, 1997.

Graphic Novels

Harlan Ellison's Chocolate Alphabet, illustrated by Larry S. Todd. Berkeley, California, Last Gasp Eco-Funnies, 1978.

Demon with a Glass Hand, illustrated by Marshall Rogers. New York, DC Comics, 1986.

Night and the Enemy, illustrated by Ken Steacy. Norristown, Pennsylvania, Comico, 1987.

Vic and Blood: The Chronicles of a Boy and His Dog, illustrated by Richard Corben. New York, St. Martin's Press, 1989.

Harlan Ellison's Dream Corridor Special. Milwaukie, Oregon, Dark Horse Comics, 1995.

Other Publications

Novels

Rumble. New York, Pyramid, 1958; revised edition as *Web of the City,* 1975.

The Man with Nine Lives, bound with *A Touch of Infinity.* New York, Ace, 1960.

The Juvies. New York, Ace, 1961.

Rockabilly. Greenwich, Connecticut, Fawcett, 1961; London, Muller, 1963; revised edition as *Spider Kiss,* New York, Pyramid, 1975.

Doomsman, bound with *Telepower* by Lee Hoffmann. New York, Belmont, 1967; bound with *The Thief of Thoth* by Lin Carter, New York, Belmont Tower, 1972.

Phoenix without Ashes: A Novel of the Starlost, with Edward Bryant. Greenwich, Connecticut, Fawcett, 1975; Manchester, Savoy, 1978.

The City on the Edge of Forever (novelization of TV play). New York, Bantam, 1977.

Short Stories

The Deadly Streets. New York, Ace, 1958; London, Digit, 1959; revised edition, New York, Pyramid, 1975.

Sex Gang (as Paul Merchant). Evanston, Illinois, Nightstand, 1959.

A Touch of Infinity, bound with *The Man with Nine Lives.* New York, Ace, 1960.

Gentleman Junkie and Other Stories of the Hung-Up Generation. Evanston, Illinois, Regency, 1961; revised edition, New York, Pyramid, 1975.

Run for the Stars, bound with *Echoes of Thunder* by Jack Dann and Jack C. Haldeman II. New York, Tor, 1991.

Plays

The City on the Edge of Forever (televised, 1967). Published in *Six Science Fiction Plays,* edited by Roger Elwood, New York, Pocket Books, 1976.

Harlan Ellison's Movie. Westminister, Maryland, Mirage Press, 1990.

I, Robot: The Illustrated Screenplay. New York, Warner, 1994.

Screenplay: *The Oscar,* with Russell Rouse and Clarence Greene, 1966.

Television Plays: episodes of *Cimarron Strip, Ripcord, Route 66, The Young Lawyers, The Untouchables, The Alfred Hitchcock Hour, Voyage to the Bottom of the Sea, The Flying Nun* and *The Man from U.N.C.L.E.* series; *Who Killed Alex Debbs?* [*Purity Mather?, Andy Zygmunt?, Half of Glory Lee?*] (*Burke's Law* series), 1963-65; *Soldier* and *Demon with a Glass Hand* (*The Outer Limits* series), 1963-64; *The City on the Edge of Forever* (*Star Trek* series), 1967; *The Special Dreamers* (program aired on KCET Los Angeles in 1971); episodes of *The Starlost,* 1973; *Logan's Run,* 1975; *Twilight Zone,* 1985-89; *Babylon 5,* 1994.

Other

Memos from Purgatory. Evanston, Illinois, Regency, 1961.

The Glass Teat: Essays of Opinion on Television. New York, Ace, 1970.

The Other Glass Teat: Further Essays of Opinion on Television. New York, Pyramid, 1975.

The Book of Ellison, edited by Andrew Porter. New York, Algol Press, 1978.

Sleepless Nights in the Procrustean Bed: Essays, edited by Marty Clark. San Bernardino, California, Borgo Press, 1984; London, Xanadu, 1990.

An Edge in My Voice. Norfolk, Virginia, Donning, 1985; revised edition, 1987.

Harlan Ellison's Watching. Los Angeles, Underwood-Miller, 1989.

The Harlan Ellison Hornbook (essays). Westminster, Maryland, Mirage Press, 1990.

Editor, *Dangerous Visions.* Garden City, New York, Doubleday, 1967; New York, Berkley, 3 vols., 1969; London, Bruce and Watson, 2 vols., 1971.

Editor, *Nightshade and Damnations*, by Gerald Kersh. Greenwich, Connecticut, Fawcett, 1968.

Editor, *Again, Dangerous Visions.* Garden City, New York, Doubleday, 1972; New York, Signet, 2 vols., 1973; London, Millington, 1976.

Editor, *Medea: Harlan's World.* Huntington Woods, Michigan, Phantasia Press, 1985.

Recordings: *Blood!*, with Robert Bloch, Alternate World, 1976; *Harlan! Harlan Ellison Reads Harlan Ellison*, Alternate World, 1976.

*

Film Adapations: *A Boy and His Dog*, 1975; "Djinn, No Chaser," episode of television series *Tales from the Darkside*, 1984; "Shatterday" and "One Life Furnished in Early Poverty," episodes of television series *Twilight Zone*, 1985.

Bibliography: *Harlan Ellison: A Bibliographical Checklist* by Leslie Kay Swigart, Dallas, Williams, 1973; partial second edition, Long Beach, California, Libra Aurore, 1981.

Critical Studies: *Harlan Ellison: Unrepentant Harlequin* by George Edgar Slusser, San Bernardino, California, Borgo Press, 1977; "Harlan Ellison Issue" of *Fantasy and Science Fiction* (New York), July 1977; *The Book of Ellison* edited by Andrew Porter, New York, Algol Press, 1978; "Harlan Ellison" by Curtis C. Smith, in *Supernatural Fiction Writers: Fantasy and Horror*, Vol. 2, edited by E. F. Bleiler, New York, Scribner, 1985; "Rogue Knight: Harlan Ellison in the Men's Magazines" by Gary K. Wolfe, *Foundation* no. 44, Winter 1988-89; *The Book on the Edge of Forever: An Enquiry Into the Non-Appearance of Harlan Ellison's The Last Dangerous Visions* by Christopher Priest, Seattle, Washington, Fantagraphics, 1994; "Harlan Ellison" in "Extracts from *The Biographical Encyclopedia of Science Fiction Film*" by Gary Westfahl, *Foundation*, no. 64, Summer 1995.

*　　*　　*

Since Harlan Ellison rejects the label of "science fiction" for his works, and since "fantasy" seems far too gentle a word for his ferocious creativity, perhaps he is best considered a horror writer, though he does not officially publish in that category. Certainly no writer of his generation has produced so many variegated and horrifying visions of a world gone wrong—whether it is contemporary Las Vegas, the bowels of a crazed giant computer, or a far-future metropolis—and few writers have delineated their nightmares with such visceral impact. When Roger Zelazny, introducing "Pretty Maggie Moneyeyes" in *Nebula Award Stories Three*, said Ellison "is about to punch you in the belly," he perfectly conveyed the elemental power that animates his finest stories.

And if nothing else, Ellison represents a horror to any would-be epitomizer. For over 40 years, he has worked with bewildering energy in every conceivable medium, including fiction, nonfiction, film, television, comic books and spoken-word recordings. A quintessentially postmodern writer, he has eschewed longer forms to focus on brief bursts of creativity—stories, essays, columns,

reviews, introductions—published in innumerable prominent and obscure venues, many of which were later assembled and reassembled in sometimes satisfying, sometimes unsatisfying collections. Whenever one of these collages comes back into print, Ellison may remove or add a story or two, add another new introduction or afterword, or tinker once again with a story's prose, making it that much harder to locate a given work or choose its definitive text. One reason Ellison does not receive the critical attention he merits is surely that scholars are frightened off by the amount of work even a cursory study would demand.

Still, patterns must be perceived, pigeonholes constructed, and common threads followed in order to make some sense of Ellison's kaleidoscopic career, no matter how unsatisfactory these are. What must be considered his horror fiction can be roughly sorted into three stages: in his first years as a struggling science-fiction writer, Ellison's frightening scenarios characteristically occurred on the far-flung worlds of space empires; in the 1960s, his best fiction typically depicted future dystopias on Earth; and since the early 1970s, he has most often found his terrors in the here and now of modern American society. And the more Ellison has circled closer to home, the more impressive his output has become.

Ellison's first story, "Glow Worm" (in *The Essential Ellison*—all stories here except where noted), has been ridiculed, but this science-fictional take on Mary Shelley's *The Last Man*—a single man survives the death of Earth because an experiment has given him an unwelcome immortality that also makes him glow—features the first appearance of the archetypal Ellison hero, the lonely, alienated victim; only his whiny passivity separates him from his more resourceful successors. Of several space adventures where Earth battles evil aliens called the Kyben—five featured in *Night and the Enemy*—the two best are *Run for the Stars*, where a desperate drug addict, implanted with a deadly bomb as a tactic to delay Kyben invaders, turns against his own people to lead a band of renegade Kybens to Earth, and "Life Hutch," where the robot running a tiny outpost designed as a refuge inexplicably turns on an arriving spaceman and attempts to kill him. The Kyben also figure in Ellison's best television episode, "Demon with a Glass Hand," where a man pursued by Kyben agents through a deserted building is guided by his robotic hand, which finally reveals that he is a robot himself, carrying the data that will someday resurrect the human race. Other early stories include "Deeper Than Darkness" (in *Alone Against Tomorrow*), where a man with the ability to mentally start fires receives a repugnant assignment—to make the star of an alien race go nova—which he fortunately evades to start a new life as a wandering Minstrel, and "Paingod" (in *Deathbird Stories*), where a powerful being charged with distributing pain throughout the galaxy enters the body of a human sculptor and learns to accept the beautiful necessity of his assignment.

In the 1960s, while becoming a successful television writer, Ellison attracted critical attention with "'Repent, Harlequin!' Said the Ticktockman," where complaints about a growing societal obsession with punctuality engender the depiction of a futuristic dystopia where being late is punished by having that much time subtracted from your lifespan; an anarchic spirit easily identifiable with Ellison himself valiantly but unsuccessfully resists the system. A similar but grimmer story, "The Prowler in the City at the Edge of the World," casts Jack the Ripper in the role of ineffectual reformer, removed from 19th-century England to provide violent entertainment for residents of a well-ordered future city. Going more than a little over the top, "I Have No Mouth, and I

Must Scream" depicts an immense, all-powerful computer which has destroyed all humanity save a handful of people it keeps alive for repetitive, vindictive torture. "A Boy and His Dog," perhaps the definitive post-holocaust horror story, features a scrappy survivor who escapes a sterile underground society and keeps his telepathic canine companion alive by calmly feeding a girlfriend to his dog. And Ellison's most compelling apocalyptic vision is "The Deathbird," a savage redaction of Christian theology in which God, a vengeful lunatic, is finally killed along with the world He crafted by an Adam who survived ages of misery to become the last man on Earth; the story effectively incorporates seemingly autobiographical passages about a man who puts a beloved sick dog out of his misery, and about an adult son who does the same for his dying mother. The story, in a way, functions as a bridge between the extravagant inventiveness of his early career and the heightened realism of his later fiction.

Ellison's early efforts to imaginatively examine the world around him included "Shattered like a Glass Goblin," in which hippie drug addicts are gradually transformed into monsters, and "Pretty Maggie Moneyeyes," where a down-and-out man in Las Vegas is sucked into a slot machine by the spirit of the woman who came to inhabit it. "Croatoan" (in *Strange Wine*) is the haunting story of a man who arranges for a girlfriend to have an abortion, flushes the fetus down the toilet, then goes into the sewers to search for it, discovering a civilization of surviving fetuses who accept him as "father." In "Shatterday" (in *Shatterday*), a thoughtless man finds his life gradually taken over by a doppelganger who is far more deserving of it. Other stories apparently represent Ellison recalling and reconsidering the experience of childhood: in "One Life, Furnished in Early Poverty," a character much like Ellison literally travels back in time to meet himself as a child; "Jeffty is Five" poignantly pictures a child who always remains five years old, ensconced in an idyllic world of radio programmes, comic books and movies; and in "Adrift Just Off the Islets of Langerhans," considered his greatest story by critic George Slusser, the legendary Wolfman, seeking help for his condition, goes to a scientist who miniaturizes him for a fantastic voyage into his own body where he locates, at the heart of his being, a Howdy Doody button. The story's unusual spirit of reconciliation suggests a coming to terms with certain demons, as might also be construed from a reading of "Strange Wine," where a man grieving for his dead daughter and paralyzed son suspects that he is really an alien, sent to live in human form as a punishment; he learns he is right, except that life on Earth is actually regarded by aliens as a privilege and pleasure. In explicitly rejecting any portrayal of human life as endless pain, the story seems a refutation, or at least a reconsideration, of previous stories like "Paingod" and "The Deathbird."

All in all, the 1970s are clearly Ellison's finest decade, an era of excellent new stories and the assembling of two fine collections, *Alone Against Tomorrow* and *Deathbird Stories*, that perfectly encapsulate the best of his earlier work. If his career in the 1980s and 1990s seems less spectacular, reasons include a series of health problems limiting his productivity and an increasing predilection for non-fiction. But he remained capable of compelling work: *All the Lies That Are My Life*, a thinly disguised autobiography; "Grail," describing a man's long and obsessive quest for a mysterious artefact promising True Love; "Paladin of the Lost Hour" (*Twilight Zone* magazine, 1985), also a *Twilight Zone* script, featuring a dying man with a stopped watch that controls the fate of the world; and "The Avenger of Death" (*Omni*, 1988), about a

man who sets out to kill all the agents of Death, only to learn that he is actually the son of Death, about to enter the family business. Another epiphany of sorts occurred with the gritty, involving *Mefisto in Onyx*, where a man with the unsettling ability to read minds is asked to confront and probe the mind of a condemned serial killer; after a few plot twists, he realizes he is locked in battle with another spirit capable of leaping from mind to mind whose past lives include a stint as Jack the Ripper.

Another recent story, "The Man Who Rowed Christopher Columbus Ashore," earned Ellison a long-coveted place in the *Best American Short Stories* series. Ellison's hundreds of published stories are not all gems, and his ventures into some conventional forms—humorous vignettes, stories about the Devil, ghost stories—are usually disappointing. But history judges writers by their hits, not their misses, and future historians looking for superior writing, and for some insights into the horrors of the human condition in the late 20th century, would be well advised to read Ellison's stories.

—Gary Westfahl

ELROD, P(atricia) N(ead)

Nationality: American. **Address:** c/o Ace Books, 200 Madison Avenue, New York, NY 10016, USA. Lives in Texas.

HORROR, GHOST AND GOTHIC PUBLICATIONS

Novels (series: Jonathan Barrett; Vampire Files)

Bloodlist (Vampire Files). New York, Ace, 1990.
Lifeblood (Vampire Files). New York, Ace, 1990.
Bloodcircle (Vampire Files). New York, Ace, 1990.
Art in the Blood (Vampire Files). New York, Ace, 1991.
Fire in the Blood (Vampire Files). New York, Ace, 1991.
Blood on the Water (Vampire Files). New York, Ace, 1992.
I, Strahd. Lake Geneva, Wisconsin, TSR, 1993.
Red Death (Barrett). New York, Ace, 1993.
Death and the Maiden (Barrett). New York, Ace, 1994.
Death Masque (Barrett). New York, Ace, 1995.
Dance of Death (Barrett). New York, Ace, 1996.
Jonathan Barrett, Gentleman Vampire (omnibus; includes *Red Death, Death and the Maiden, Death Masque, Dance of Death*). New York, Guild America, 1996.

Other

Editor, with Martin H. Greenberg. *The Time of the Vampires*. New York, DAW, 1996.

*   *   *

Ever since Bram Stoker's *Dracula* first appeared, vampire stories have been a major part of the horror genre, and during the last several years they have flourished even when horror as a whole has slipped in popularity. Writers such as Anne Rice, Chelsea Quinn Yarbro and Les Daniels have built their careers almost exclusively on vampire fiction. P. N. Elrod is another of these, with nearly a dozen novels and a half-dozen short stories all dealing with the undead. But Elrod has also taken up another popular modern trend, the vampire as hero, with two well-received series.

The first of these was The Vampire Files, a contemporary mystery series with a vampire as the detective. In the opener, *Bloodlist*, Jack Fleming is an up-and-coming reporter who dallies with the wrong woman and is turned into a vampire. He doesn't realize that until later, when he survives a bullet wound that should have killed him outright. But once he comes to terms with his new existence, he discovers that it has its good points, and he sets out to track down the man who tried to kill him. In *Lifeblood* Fleming discovers some of the bad parts of being one of the undead. One group of humans is convinced he's an evil monster and are determined to track him down and destroy him, while another sees vampirism as the key to personal immortality for themselves. For a while, it's not clear which is the greater menace. Elrod maintains a light hand throughout this series, but the ironically humorous aspects are at their best in this title. Fleming sets out to find the vampire who converted him in *Bloodcircle*, convinced now that despite everything he is in love with her. His efforts cause conflict with another vampire, and he eventually is called upon to solve an unconventional murder mystery.

Art in the Blood is even more of a standard detective story, this one involving the murder of a promising young artist and the intrigue that takes place in the world of high finance. The vampire under-story is less interesting this time, more of a distracting gimmick than a genuine plot device. A gang of art thieves are the adversaries in *Fire in the Blood*, a return to Elrod's previous form. The series came to an apparent close with *Blood on the Water*, wherein a major crime lord becomes aware of Fleming's continued success at evading his enemies and puts pressure on him to reveal the nature of the secret "equipment" he must be using to stay alive. At the same time, Fleming finds his own bloodlust becoming more powerful and fears that he may no longer be able to control the darker side of his new nature. The six books are well written and enjoyable in a light-hearted way, but there is very little outright horror in any of them, other than the nature of their protagonist.

Elrod was considerably more ambitious, and consequently more interesting, with her second vampire series. In *Red Death*, Jonathan Barrett travels to England in 1773 where he is bitten by a vampire. Upon his return to America, he finds the colonies in rebellion and is subsequently killed in combat. But the vampire taint is in his blood and he rises from the dead to an uneasy existence concealing his politics from his enemies and his vampirism from his friends. Barrett returns in *Death and the Maiden*, reunited with his family, still leading a precarious existence in revolutionary America. After adjusting to his new way of life, Barrett follows the same path as Jack Fleming, searching for the mysterious woman who first made him what he is. But when he returns to London, she has disappeared. He remains in London for the third and fourth volumes, *Death Masque* and *Dance of Death*, eventually discovering that he has fathered a young boy, and that some of his enemies plan to use the child as a lever against him. The Barrett series is much richer in detail and characterization than the Fleming books, and even though Barrett is, like Fleming, a benevolent vampire, his nature is considerably darker.

I, Strahd is a solo novel set in the shared "Ravenloft" universe of TSR books. A brutal noble of that mysterious realm makes an unholy pact in order to remove a rival and win the woman he loves, only to discover that as a consequence he has lost his soul and become a vampire. It's the darkest of Elrod's novels by far, but the protagonist is much harder to identify with and the setting never seems real enough for the story to succeed.

Elrod has also written a number of short stories about vampires, including "A Night at the (Horse) Opera," in which Jack Fleming helps Harpo Marx out of a tight spot. In "The Wind Breathes Cold" Quincey Morris awakens following his death at the hands of Dracula's minions to find that he is himself a vampire. Dracula, who survived after all, convinces him that they are not necessarily evil just because of their changed natures. Elrod also co-edited *The Time of the Vampires*, which includes her own "The Devil's Mark," wherein vampires decide to end the life of the Witch-Finder General before he stirs up too much trouble.

Elrod is well established as a significant writer of vampire novels, but for the most part these have been light adventure or mystery stories and not horror fiction as the term is normally understood. She seems more interested in character development and a crisp, straightforward plot than in suspense or a strong sense of atmosphere. Given her success to date, it seems unlikely that she will greatly alter her approach.

—Don D'Ammassa

ENDORE, (Samuel) Guy

Nationality: American. **Born:** New York, 4 July 1900. **Education:** Columbia University, New York, A.B., 1923, M.A., 1925. **Family:** Married Henrietta Portugal in 1927; two daughters. **Career:** Translator, novelist, and screenwriter. **Died:** 12 February 1970.

HORROR, GHOST AND GOTHIC PUBLICATIONS

Novel

The Werewolf of Paris. New York, Farrar and Rinehart, 1933; London, Long, 1934.

Plays

Screenplays: *Mark of the Vampire*, with Bernard Schubert, 1935; *Mad Love*, with P. J. Wolfson and John L. Balderston, 1935; *The Raven*, with David Boehm, 1935; *The Devil Doll*, with Tod Browning, Garrett Fort, and Erich von Stroheim, 1936.

Other

Translator, *Alraune* by Hanns Heinz Ewers. New York, Day, 1929.

OTHER PUBLICATIONS

Novels

The Man from Limbo. New York, Farrar and Rinehart, 1930; London, Gollancz, 1931.
Methinks the Lady—. New York, Duell Sloan, 1945; London, Cresset Press, 1947; as *Nightmare*, New York, Dell, 1956.

Babouk. N.p., n.d.
Detour at Night. New York, Simon and Schuster, 1959; as *Detour Through Devon*, London, Gollancz, 1959.
Satan's Saint: A Novel About the Marquis de Sade. N.p., 1965.

Plays

Screenplays: *The League of Frightened Men*, 1937; *Carefree*, 1938; *The Story of G. I. Joe*, 1945; *The Vicious Circle*, 1948; *Johnny Allegro*, 1949; *He Ran All the Way*, 1951; *Captain Sindbad*, 1963.

Other

Casanova: His Known and Unknown Life. N.p., 1929.
The Sword of God. N.p., 1931.
King of Paris. N.p., 1956.

*

Film Adaptations: *Whirlpool*, 1949, from the novel *Methinks the Lady—*; *The Curse of the Werewolf*, 1961, from the novel *The Werewolf of Paris*.

*   *   *

Guy Endore hung around Columbia College for nine years collecting various degrees but never pursued any of the professions for which he trained, preferring to support himself with his pen. He began as a translator from French and German, his work in that field including a bravura version of Hanns Heinz Ewers' classic Decadent horror story *Alraune*. He diversified into biography and novel-writing, but quickly moved on to Hollywood in the interests of making a better living. There he assisted in turning a couple of classic horror novels into schlock-horror films, helping to adapt A. Merritt's *Burn, Witch, Burn!* as *The Devil Doll* and redrafting Maurice Renard's *The Hands of Orlac* as *Mad Love*. His choice of subjects for biographical analysis always tended to the sensational (ranging from Casanova to the Marquis de Sade) but his novels, although consistently unusual, were also conspicuously literary. Like Ben Hecht, who also scripted a number of routine horror films, he seems to have regarded his prose fiction not merely as a refuge for unashamed self-indulgence but as a means of trumpeting the fact that he was, after all, a man of great intelligence, wide learning and cunning wit.

From *The Man from Limbo*, a conscientiously Jewish novel about a man who invents an imaginary adventure so intense that he has to live it rather than merely write it down, to *Detour at Night*, a brilliantly harrowing tale of frustrated ambition and erotic desire, Endore's novels never descended to any ordinary level. *The Man from Limbo* is partly an homage to Robert Louis Stevenson and *Detour at Night* is partly an acknowledgement of the emotional force of genre romance, but in recomplicating the basic formulas he was deploying he transformed them dramatically. His murder mystery, *Methinks the Lady—*, is one of the classics of that genre, although purists look at it askance because all the detective work is carried out by means of careful Freudian analysis; it effortlessly upstages Ben Hecht's *The Florentine Dagger*—as it was, perhaps, intended to do.

Given all this, it is not surprising that when Endore set out to write a horror novel he set out to make it a horror novel like no other, more perverse and more subtly unsettling than all the rest—

although he did accept some influence from Ewers, particularly from *Vampire*, the third in the "Frank Braun" sequence whose second volume he had translated so vividly. *The Werewolf of Paris* is perhaps entitled to be considered *the* werewolf novel, just as *Dracula* is *the* vampire novel, although it assertively inverts the underlying assumption of formulaic monster stories by preserving the essential innocence of its central character and indicting the world which contains him for its intolerable monstrousness. He preserved it from cinematic adaptation for 28 years but eventually allowed it to be turned into the schlock-horror film *Curse of the Werewolf*; either he was past caring by then or felt compelled to bow to the irony of the situation.

The Werewolf of Paris opens with the observation that the Latin word for wolf was once the root of the festival of Lupercalia and is still preserved in *lupanar*, one of many French terms for a brothel. It proceeds to tell the story of Bertrand Caillet, the physically-stigmatized bastard son of a disreputable priest, who begins to exhibit lycanthropic tendencies in adolescence. The enlightened liberal who is the teller of his tale takes him in hand and tries to educate him in self-control, but the power of Bertrand's sexual urges defies containment until he finds a self-sacrificing partner willing to let him dine on her blood. By then, alas, he has been drafted into the National Guard during the siege of Paris, which began in September 1870 and was followed by the bloody Spring of the Commune.

In such evil circumstances Bertrand finds it far too easy to scavenge for other meat, and he is eventually caught (there is, in fact, an actual case on record of a "Sergeant Bertrand" who was charged with murder, necrophilia and cannibalism before being committed to an asylum). As the narrator observes, however, what is one wolfman among so many? Had not Paris in 1871 become the exclusive territory of wild and uncontrollable beasts? Is Bertrand to be despised on account of physiological honesty, while the deceptive creatures who maintain their human masks remain altogether admirable? The story-teller admits that he is not as liberal as he once was, and has begun to drift back to the comforting embrace of religious faith.

Purist fans of supernatural horror fiction may complain that *The Werewolf of Paris* is neither supernatural enough nor horrific enough, because Bertrand's condition is too suffocatingly cloaked in ambiguity. The whole point of the exercise is, however, to blur the boundaries between the human and the inhuman, the natural and the unnatural. Although it was never offered up as a sacrificial lamb to Hollywood (the movie eventually made of it was a British-made Hammer film) it might well have had an influence on the cinematic mythology of werewolves. Stuart Walker's imitatively titled *Werewolf of London* (1935) and George Waggner's *The Wolf Man* (1941), although scripted without any acknowledged reference to pre-existing texts, make their central characters tortured victims of fate rather than archetypes of evil. It was, however, left to filmmakers of a much later era to offer more robust metaphors implying that the human world is full enough of wolfish tendencies regardless of the relative scarcity of manifest werewolves.

Endore's occasional exercises in short fiction have never been collected but they include a few notable horror stories. His science fiction story "The Day of the Dragon" (1934) anticipates *Jurassic Park* with its account of a biological engineer who recreates the dinosaurs of old but cannot keep them in safe confinement. The Talmudic fantasy "Lazarus Returns," in Dennis Wheatley's *A Century of Horror* (1935), is a more orthodox but effective tale of a young man who makes an unhealthy bargain with an obnoxious aged relative and pays the inevitable horrid penalty. Endore's Haiti-set novel *Babouk* is not without its horrific moments but it is essentially a novel of social protest in which voodoo plays a very marginal role.

—Brian Stableford

ENGSTROM, Elizabeth

Nationality: American. **Born:** 1951. **Career:** Contributor of short stories to *The Magazine of Fantasy and Science Fiction* and various small-press magazines. **Address:** c/o Tor Books, Tom Doherty Associates, Inc., 175 Fifth Avenue, 14th Floor, New York, NY 10010, USA. Lives in Eugene, Oregon.

HORROR, GHOST AND GOTHIC PUBLICATIONS

Novels

When Darkness Loves Us. New York, Morrow, 1985.
Black Ambrosia. New York, Tor, 1988.

Short Stories

Nightmare Flower. New York, Tor, 1992.

OTHER PUBLICATIONS

Novel

Lizzie Borden. New York, Tor, 1991.

* * *

Some of the most effective modern horror fiction ignores the traditional supernatural themes of ghosts, vampires, demons and the like, in favour of investigating the intricacies of the human mind. In the hands of a skilful writer, a journey through the tormented thoughts of a serial killer, or a harried housewife driven to insanity, or a frustrated lover can be just as terrifying as dripping fangs or things that go bump in the night. In order for such a story to be effective, the writer must have superior skills of characterization and an ability to interpolate the darker side of human experience. Elizabeth Engstrom is a writer who, like Shirley Jackson, has made bizarre psychological twists her specialty, and she has produced some remarkable stories as the result.

Her first horror novel was *When Darkness Loves Us*, a dark fable that reads like a modern fairy tale with a perverse twist. Sally Ann is a young woman who stumbles into a cavern and is lost underground in a series of tunnels she fancies are inhabited by the spirits of the dead. Twenty years later, impossibly, she returns to the surface world only to discover that her husband has remarried and now has several children with his new wife. Sally kidnaps the youngest of her ex-husband's children and carries her away to the underground world, and that child is the central character in the ensuing chain of dark strangeness. An unconventional and unusually effective blend of rural realism and the surreal.

Black Ambrosia is more realistic but equally bizarre. Angelina is a young girl who leaves home to see the world, and almost immediately gets picked up by two prospective rapists. Their attack wakens some hidden vein of violence in Angelina, who attacks and drinks the blood of one of the men. This convinces her that she's a vampire, and although she adopts an outwardly conventional lifestyle thereafter, she stalks victims during the hours of darkness, killing them and drinking their blood, convinced she is bringing them the gift of eternal life and love rather than simply butchering them. Her vampirism is entirely in her mind; there is in fact nothing supernatural at all in the novel. But that doesn't make it any less effective. In fact, the plausibility makes the situation even more unnerving and Angelina's madness is one of the most convincing characterizations to occur in a horror novel.

Engstrom has written a considerable number of short horror stories, most of which were collected in *Nightmare Flower*. In "The Fog Knew Her Name" an unhappy, overweight woman encounters a genuine shapechanger and discovers a strange new future for herself as the catalyst by which other couples find happiness. "Elixir" is an odd variation of the vampire story. A troubled man becomes convinced that his ability to see colors will go away if he doesn't drink fluids from the body of a prostitute with whom he's become infatuated. When she balks at his marriage proposal, he drugs and imprisons her until her resistance breaks down, but with the birth of their child, his obsession takes a bizarre new twist.

"Nightmare Flower" contains some particularly vivid scenes. A man and his wife buy a new home and begin cultivating a garden in their yard. The husband becomes obsessed with an oversized flowering plant after sniffing its addictive pollen. The relationship between himself and his wife deteriorates rapidly, and ultimately he feeds his newborn son to the plant. Even the realization that he has become the plant's servant doesn't dissuade him from considering repeating that terrible act just for the chance of another whiff of the pollen. The protagonist of "Rivering" uses portions of the anatomies of the dead to fish their souls from a river. In "The Jeweler's Thumb Is Turning Green," a man discovers a woman's finger slowly growing within the fabric of his new, handmade wallet. After making inquiries to learn the identity of the wallet's creator, he begins to lose control of his own body. Eventually he discovers that the wallet was made by a murderous artist who recently died, and who is now slowly returning to life by pre-empting his own. A woman has a highly detailed snake tattooed on her body in "Genetically Predisposed." The snake has a life of its own and can leave her body to hunt living prey. It can also reproduce, much to the dismay of her boyfriend. "Project Stone," a short novel, explores the consequences of a secret project to build a community in which the transmission of a soothing subliminal sound helps to ease tensions. Unfortunately, the sound turns out to be addictive, and when some of the experimental subjects try to leave, they discover they cannot survive beyond its influence.

Much of Engstrom's short horror also avoids fantastic content. "Will Lunch Be Ready on Time" is set in the remote, rural America that is featured in much of Engstrom's work. Police respond to reports of a violent attack at a primitive household, but the eldest child tells them everything is all right. After they've departed, we discover that her brother has killed their drunken father, and that his body is in the larder waiting to be cooked. A gentler variant can be found in "Grandma's Hobby," wherein an elderly woman whose hobby is canning turns her husband's body into jelly for later consumption. "The Old Woman Upstairs" examines the tension between generations, when a woman finally loses patience with the difficulties of dealing with her elderly mother, and hastens her death. A group of friends swap horror stories one night in "The Final Tale," after which each of the authors meets his or her fate in much the same fashion as the story they told.

Other stories of interest include "Quiet Meditation," "Seasoned Enthusiast," "Spice" and "The Night of a Hawaiian Sky." Engstrom has also written a novel about the murderer Lizzie Borden, which is of peripheral interest to horror readers.

—Don D'Ammassa

ETCHISON, Dennis (William)

Pseudonym: Jack Martin. **Nationality:** American. **Born:** Stockton, California, 30 March 1943. **Education:** Attended Los Angeles State College and the University of California, Los Angeles. **Family:** Married Kristina Etchison. **Career:** Many part-time jobs, including a three-and-a-half year stint as a filling-station attendant in Malibu, California; contributor of short stories to numerous magazines and anthologies since the early 1960s; full-time writer since 1976; teaches creative writing part-time at University of California extension, Los Angeles. Lives in Los Angeles. **Awards:** British Fantasy award for short story, 1981, 1986 and 1994; World Fantasy award for short story, 1982, and for anthology, 1993.

HORROR, GHOST AND GOTHIC PUBLICATIONS

Novels

The Fog (novelization of screenplay). New York, Bantam, and London, Corgi, 1980.
Halloween II (novelization of screenplay; as Jack Martin). New York, Zebra, 1981.
Halloween III: Season of the Witch (novelization of screenplay; as Jack Martin). New York, Zebra, 1982.
Videodrome (novelization of screenplay; as Jack Martin). New York, Zebra, 1983.
Darkside. New York, Charter, 1986; London, Futura, 1987; revised edition, Chicago, Airgedlamh Publications, 1996.
Shadowman. New York, Abyss, 1993; London, Raven, 1994.
California Gothic. New York, Abyss, and London, Raven, 1995.
Double Edge. New York, Dell, 1996.

Short Stories

The Dark Country. Santa Cruz, California, Scream Press, 1982; London, Futura, 1988.
Red Dreams. Santa Cruz, California, Scream Press, 1984; London, Futura, 1988.
The Blood Kiss. Los Angeles, Scream Press, 1988.
The Dark Country (story). Eugene, Oregon, Pulphouse, 1991.

Other

Editor, *Cutting Edge*. New York, Doubleday, 1986; London, Macdonald, 1988.

Editor, *Masters of Darkness*. New York, Tor, 1986.
Editor, *Masters of Darkness II*. New York, Tor, 1988.
Editor, *The Complete Masters of Darkness* (omnibus). Lancaster, Pennsylvania, Underwood Miller, 1991.
Editor, *Masters of Darkness III*. New York, Tor, 1991.
Editor, *Lord John Ten: A Celebration*. Northridge, California, Lord John Press, 1988.
Editor, *MetaHorror*. New York, Abyss, 1992.

*

Critical Study: "Dennis Etchison," in Douglas E. Winter, *Faces of Fear*, London, Pan, 1990.

*   *   *

In Dennis Etchison's story "Deadspace," a would-be Hollywood producer sits by a pool at a hotel, waiting for a phone call from the actor whom he hopes to sign to the movie deal that will make or break his career. A series of encounters takes place while he waits: he tells a woman swimming in the pool about the movie, entitled *Is Anybody There?*; he is reminded by the bartender that it is November 2, the Day of the Dead; and he exchanges small talk with a woman who has spent the last few years caring for her terminally ill husband. The phone call never comes, and the story ends on a haunting note of despair.

The tale is quintessential Etchison. None of its individual moments are distinctly horrific, but all contribute to the cumulating sense of dread that builds throughout the narrative. Each features a carefully chosen symbol or metaphor that prefigures the bleak ending: the plaintive unanswered question in the movie title, the candy skull on the bar that is part of the Day of the Dead festivities, the grotesquely misshapen invalid wheezing out his final breaths beside his wife. The story ends not with a shock, but with an quietly disturbing revelation whose impact transcends the spare and subtle prose used to express it—an example of what Etchison refers to, in his tale "Drop City," as an attempt to "use words to get beyond words."

In the introduction to Etchison's collection *The Dark Country*, Ramsey Campbell calls him "a poet of loneliness and alienation." Many of Etchison's most powerful stories are set in isolated, out-of-the-way places, or along familiar byways visited only infrequently after hours. "The Late Shift" takes place at an all-night convenience store, where the disinterest and detachment of the staff approximates the mindlessness of zombies. The narrator of "Sitting in the Corner, Whimpering Quietly" overhears the horrible outcome of a domestic drama while washing clothes at an all-night laundromat. One of Etchison's favourite settings is the highway, whose openness reflects the aimlessness and lack of direction of the people who travel it. "It Only Comes Out of Night" takes place at an abandoned rest-stop that may be the stomping ground of a serial killer. "The Scar" climaxes with an explosion of violence at a roadside diner. In "The Olympic Runner," a long-distance car-trip culminates in the unravelling of unstable family bonds. These settings are natural milieus in which one would expect horrors to flourish, unseen and unregulated. But more important for Etchison's fiction, they are places whose darkness and vacancy mirror the spiritual emptiness of the characters who chance upon them. Sometimes, this emptiness is so overwhelming that it actually transforms familiar environments into wastelands of the soul. "Deathtracks" ends with the indelible image of a television pollster who has just interviewed a family grieving over the loss of their son, walking past . . .

> . . . other isolated houses on the block, ghostly living rooms turning to flickering beacons of cobalt blue against the night. The voices from within were television voices, muffled and anonymous and impossible to decipher unless one were listening too closely, more closely than life itself would seem to want to permit, to the exclusion of all else, as to the falling of a single blade of grass or the unseen whisper of an approaching scythe. And it rang out around him then, too, through the trees and into the sky and the cold stars, the sound of the muttering and the laughter, the restless chorus of the dead, spreading rapidly away from him across the city and the world.

In Etchison's earliest published stories, many of which were written for science-fiction markets, the alienated are actually aliens, extraterrestrials who either live miserable lives incognito among human beings ("A Walk in the Wet") or as fifth columns infiltrating their adopted civilization ("Wet Season"). His few overtly supernatural tales feature people set apart from the rest of humanity by their wild talents: precognitive dreams in "The Graveyard Blues" and shape-shifting in "The Nighthawk." Most of Etchison's characters, however, are ordinary people who have suffered a loss so significant that it has knocked them from their familiar orbit and left them disoriented and vulnerable. Describing the motive that drives the protagonist of "Deadspace" to his rendezvous with failure, he writes "Once, a long time ago, someone had taken from him something irreplaceably valuable. He couldn't remember what it was. And no one would admit it." In "Call 666," a man struggling to regain stability after his divorce fantasizes that "Sometimes, for a few minutes in the morning, it was as if he had never met her, had not lost so much already." The shut-in young boy who may be prone to uncontrollable physical transformation in "The Nighthawk" looks "like someone who had something terribly valuable to give away but could hardly remember where he had hidden it."

It is easy to identify, at least on a superficial level, what characters in Etchison's stories have lost: a son in "Deathtracks," a wife's affections in "Not from Around Here," basic dignity in "The Chair," and personal identity in "Drop City." On a deeper level, these characters are victims of a society that has lost its capacity for empathy and communication. Like the character in "Call 666," who discovers a telephone service that recruits the disgruntled to perform anonymous contracts killings, they inhabit a world where matters of life and death are handled with chilling remoteness. In the triptych of stories comprised of "The Machine Demands a Sacrifice," "Calling All Monsters," and "The Dead Line," Etchison uses the harvesting of organs from donors maintained on life-support to symbolize the impersonality of a world that reduces life to a clinical process. "There is a machine outside my door," he writes in "The Dead Line." "It eats people, chews them up and spits out only what it can't use."

The roots of this dark view of the world can be traced to the failed promise of the counter-cultural revolution of the 1960s, a recurrent motif in Etchison's stories. The majority of his protagonists are men and women who find that the idealism of their youth has not prepared them for the broken dreams and unfulfilled promise of their adult lives. "Don't you ever wonder what happened to our generation?" asks a disillusioned character in the novel

Shadowman. "The best and the brightest, all the things they were going to do. . . . Now they're driving cabs, washing dishes, pumping gas. There's a generation, a whole nation that disappeared, millions of them. They're still here, but they're invisible. What they had to offer, it's all wasted."

Etchison's first three novels comprise an informal trilogy concerned with the debased forms counter-cultural ideals have assumed in contemporary times. In *Darkside*, the hippy movement's belief in spiritual transcendence is perverted into the mystical neardeath experiences that a suicide cult peddles to teenagers smitten with 1960s nostalgia. In *Shadowman*, the once glamorized dropout mentality of the youth culture has led to the creation of Box City, "an army of dropouts, turning tail and running for the hills, growing into some kind of alien nation cut off from the real world." *California Gothic* features a serial killer who appears to have literally risen from the ashes of the radical underground and who represents that classic horror theme, the unnatural survival of the past into the present. For Etchison's characters, the death of the 1960s represents a sort of personal death in life. Writing to a horror author whose work resonates with his feelings, the protagonist of "Talking in the Dark" reflects, "It seems to me that the things we learned up until now, the really important things, and I can tell we've had many of the same experiences (the Sixties, etc.), when it came time to live them, the system balked. And we're dying." Small wonder that the monster whose image Etchison evokes most frequently is the zombie.

Etchison's fiction abounds with film references and often features characters who work in the film industry. Names of wholly imaginary horror movies such as *American Zombie II* and *Is Anybody There?* and fictional employees of the trade including Jack Martin (the pseudonym under which Etchison wrote novelizations of the *Halloween* films and David Cronenberg's *Videodrome*) are dropped in several of his stories, joining them together in an informal Hollywood mythos. Film provides a template for the fragmented and artificial lives many of his characters lead. In *Double Edge*, a novel in which the heroine's life increasingly begins to resemble the teleplay she has written about the Lizzie Borden murders, he writes "In L.A., everything was separate and compartmentalized, like scenes in a movie, even friendship. It was possible to know someone for months . . . without ever being privy to any of the players in other scenes. Lives could be played out according to the schedule on the call sheet with no overlap."

Film and real life mirror one another in other stories as well. "The Blood Kiss" intercuts an account of a screenwriter's struggles to survive professionally with excerpts from her film script about an attack of flesh-eating zombies. Hollywood's dog-eat-dog climate is evoked literally in "The Dog Park" (a.k.a. "A Little Known Side of Elvis"), which juxtaposes the networking of film hopefuls at a park to the savaging of their pets in the background. Nevertheless, film can only go so far in reflecting reality. As a character in *California Gothic* acknowledges, cinematic horrors pale in comparison to the horrors we tolerate as a culture on a daily basis:

> I'm living in a horror movie, all right. Only the horror doesn't have anything to do with necrophilia or black masses or crosses hung upside down, or with vampires who can't swim or zombies who work in sugar cane fields and can't stop shambling off cliffs when some guy with a jawbreaker accent says so. No, this is real life. It was running out all around him, the footprints of assassins and neofascists and government officials with secret closets

full of tutus, private armies training in ships named after the wives of oilmen, of drunken presidents in bed with the mob and cartels that slice up the world and stick FOR SALE signs on the pieces; while the real kings of the earth lie moldering in their graves, their brains stolen away in the night and their bullet wounds altered to match storybook plots that would be laughed out of any pre-school classroom. And all this while the billions sweat and grow old like the living dead, their lifeblood sucked dry by the takers of souls who need our labor to feed a hunger for power without end. The undead? What a cheapjack explanation for so much misery. There is more than enough to account for it all without falling back on the unnameable. It's already here. The trick is to see it and not flinch—there's no future in denial. It as simple, and as enormous, as that.

This then is the real horror Etchison wrestles with in his fiction: the discovery that once we have turned off the film projector and the thrills it has provided, there is a deeper and more dangerous darkness to face.

—Stefan Dziemianowicz

EULO, Ken

Nationality: American. **Born:** Newark, New Jersey, 17 November 1939. **Education:** Attended the University of Heidelberg, 1961-64. **Family:** Married, three sons. **Career:** Playwright, director, and novelist. Director of Playwrights Forum and O'Neill Playwrights; artistic director of Courtyard Playhouse, New York; member of Actors Studio Playwriting Workshop; staff writer for Paramount, 1988—. **Address:** 14633 Valley Vista Blvd., Sherman Oaks, California 91403. **Agent:** Mitch Douglas, International Creative Management, 40 West 57th St., New York, New York 10019, USA.

HORROR, GHOST AND GOTHIC PUBLICATIONS

Novels (series: Chandal)

The Brownstone (Chandal). New York, Pocket, 1980.
The Bloodstone (Chandal). New York, Pocket, 1981.
The Deathstone (Chandal). New York, Pocket, 1982.
Nocturnal. New York, Pocket, 1983; London, Coronet, 1985.
The Ghost of Veronica Gray. New York, Pocket, 1985.
The House of Caine. New York, Tor, 1988.

*   *   *

Unlike most genres, horror fiction has generally avoided the series novel. There have been a few exceptions, most notably those involving vampires, but for the most part the form makes continuing stories impossible. If the reader knows that the protagonist is going to survive into the next book, it robs the current work of much of its potential suspense. It is surprising therefore that Ken Eulo's first three horror novels comprise a trilogy of adventures focusing on a single character.

The Brownstone is a blend of the traditional haunted house and satanic-cult stories. Justin and Chandal are a young couple who find the perfect apartment, rented to them by two elderly women who seem friendly and perfectly sensible, at least until they've lived there a while. Then Chandal begins to hear voices when no one is around, and notices odd inconsistencies in the behaviour of their two landladies. And Justin is also affected by the strange atmosphere of the Brownstone, taking up photography as a hobby, something for which he had never shown any particular previous interest. Then the visions come, ghostly figures forming in the air, accompanied by the putrid smell of death, and Chandal is inspired to investigate the building's past. Ultimately she learns that her husband has been seduced by a cult that plans to steal her body and use it to house an evil spirit. Although the plot holds few surprises, the novel stands out because of its intensity and Eulo's talent for gruesome description.

Chandal returns in *The Bloodstone*, a novel of possession. Two years have passed and she is under a psychiatrist's care, having forgotten her role in the burning of the Brownstone and the death of her husband and the two elderly women in the fire. A mysterious pendant appears in her purse after she moves back to New York City, the agency by which a supernatural force seeks to gain control of her body, giving her the power to literally reshape her physical form. Her new husband thinks Chandal's problems are a form of psychosis, but he learns otherwise when she reveals inexplicable knowledge of terrible events that happened in their home years earlier.

The Deathstone brought the series to a close, this time changing locale to a small town. Seven more years have passed and Chandal now has a daughter. The family is taking a vacation in the mountains when an accident temporarily strands them in a town filled with people from the same cult that has plagued Chandal's life. This time they send a spirit to possess her daughter, led by an inhuman creature who wants all three of their lives. This was the weakest of the trilogy, and Eulo wisely turned to another set of characters for his next novel.

His fourth book, *Nocturnal*, made use of an overly familiar plot, although Eulo manages to provide some new thrills. Rose Carpenter has the powers of clairvoyance and precognition; she can catch glimpses of other people's lives, and foresee their futures. Her dream visions take a bad turn when she begins to tap into the mind of an insane serial rapist and killer. Unfortunately, and predictably, the link works both ways, and the killer becomes aware of her vicarious participation in his crimes. The killer begins stalking Rose's friends, claiming two of them before turning his attention to Rose herself. There's a pretty good mystery plot, with some surprising twists, and hints of an evil force directing events from the background. The ending, despite a rousing climax, is somewhat dissatisfying; we're left not entirely certain that the villains have been dealt with, but for the most part *Nocturnal* is a workmanlike horror novel.

The Ghost of Veronica Gray reprises many of the themes Eulo had already used. Dorothy is a weak-willed young woman who falls under the influence of the ghost in the title, an uneasy spirit who lives in the house next door. The young man who once loved Veronica is dead, an apparent suicide, and Dorothy begins to believe that there are virtues to be found on the other side, that death can become a form of immortality. But ultimately Dorothy discovers that Veronica murdered the dead man, and that she in turn has been manipulated to commit a similar crime. Dorothy's tragic end is much less effective because she has been portrayed as such a gullible, weak-willed individual that it is difficult to care about her fate. As always, Eulo delivers a well-written novel, but this time the plot contains no surprises, and the characters aren't interesting enough to hold our attention.

His most recent, and best, novel is *The House of Caine*. This time the evil takes the form of vampires, a small town dominated by the undead. The Vietnam War is underway when Robert Martin returns to Millhouse to confront the vampires that have transformed his friends and family into their own kind. Initially alone, Martin gathers a small group of allies in his campaign to destroy the evil of the House of Caine forever. Eulo's vampires aren't the troubled or sympathetic creatures that dominate much of modern horror fiction; they're the old fashioned, thoroughly evil and re-

pulsive variety, and they dissolve spectacularly when finally staked or exposed to the sunlight. There's nothing particularly surprising in this novel either, but this is the best-paced and most exciting of his plots, the characters are well drawn, and the suspense is almost unbroken.

Eulo has been silent for the past eight years, so it seems unlikely that he will return to the horror genre. None of his novels were sufficiently successful to establish him as a important writer in the genre, although they are all entertaining and competently done. As a writer, he seemed content to produce well-crafted imitations rather than original work, and that was probably the factor limiting his success.

—Don D'Ammassa

F

FALKNER, J(ohn) Meade

Nationality: British. **Born:** Wiltshire, 8 May 1858. **Education:** Marlborough School; Oxford University, B.A. in history 1882. **Career:** Private tutor to the children of Sir Andrew Noble, and later private secretary to the latter; worked for Armstrong, an armaments company, rising to become its chairman, 1915-21; librarian, Durham Cathedral. **Died:** 22 July 1932.

HORROR, GHOST AND GOTHIC PUBLICATIONS

Novel

The Lost Stradivarius. Edinburgh, Blackwood, 1895.

OTHER PUBLICATIONS

Novels

Moonfleet. London, Arnold, 1898.
The Nebuly Coat. London, Arnold, 1903.

Poetry

Poems. London, Westminster Press, 1935(?).

Other

Handbook for Travellers in Oxfordshire. London, Murray, 1894.
A History of Oxfordshire. London, Murray, 1899.
Handbook for Berkshire. N.p., Stanford, 1902.
Bath in History and Social Tradition. London, Murray, 1918.

*

Film Adaptations: *Moonfleet,* 1955, 1984 (TV serial).

*   *   *

John Meade Falkner was the son of a clergyman of good family, which guaranteed him a decent education at Marlborough and Oxford but then cast him adrift in the world to look after his own financial future. He was lucky enough to secure a position as tutor to the sons of a partner in a firm of munitions manufacturers, and luckier still to be offered a position within the firm, but his subsequent rise within its ranks must have been a reflection of ability. Buoyed up by the business generated by the Great War the company thrived, becoming the greater part of the amalgamated Armstrong Whitworth, and Falkner became its chairman. On retiring from business, however, he took up an unpaid post as librarian of Durham Cathedral—he had always been a keen book-collector and connoisseur of libraries—and became a noted scholar in the field of ecclesiastical history. Along the way he wrote three novels, seemingly without any commercial motive, although they were unashamed entertainments; it is typical of the man that when he accidentally left the unfinished manuscript of a fourth on a train he flatly refused to submit himself to the risk of such a disappointment again and never wrote another word of fiction.

All of Falkner's novels are mysteries. The most successful at the time was the second, *Moonfleet,* a historical adventure story involving smugglers, a gentleman pirate and the search for a hidden diamond. Clearly influenced by Robert Louis Stevenson, it seems to have been an attempt to write a classic "boys' book."

The third, *The Nebuly Coat,* is a much more recherché mystery story involving investigations of a more antiquarian nature, whose principal setting—a decaying church—is unsettling without being literally haunted. The novel whose reputation has increased most steadily since the author's death, however, is the first, which was belatedly recognized as one of the classic Victorian ghost stories. *The Lost Stradivarius* is one of several notable 19th-century tales in which the spirit of the past preserved in music is extended by literary device to encompass more active spirits.

The central character of the story—which is told by his sister—is a student at Oxford who one day plays a duet with a friend, following an obscure and anonymous score of Italian origin. The spectre of a man in 18th century dress subsequently appears, vanishing into a wall which turns out to be hollow; in the covert thus revealed the student discovers a violin bearing two labels. One of these labels, dated 1704, proclaims it to be the work of Antonio Stradivarius at the height of his powers; the other bears the inscription *Porphyrius philosophus.* The behaviour of the young man then becomes gradually erratic, much to the distress of his sister and her close friend, the girl who loves him. He becomes obsessively devoted to the music of the violin, eventually travelling to Naples, where he becomes involved in pagan rites of a very un-Victorian nature. His sister, meanwhile, recognizes the ghost he described to her in a portrait of one of her friend's ancestors, who was the black sheep of the family. It becomes gradually clear—although the final pieces do not fall into place until the young man is dead—that the ancestor in question had progressed from an apprenticeship served in Sir Francis Dashwood's Hellfire Club to the serious study of neo-Platonic magic (to which thaumaturgical tradition the philosopher Porphyry reputedly belonged). He had then achieved a kind of Satanic Revelation—a profound visionary experience facilitated and heightened by sinister music—which the possessed protagonist has recapitulated.

Falkner's sojourn at Oxford presumably overlapped that of the notorious Count Stenbock (who was born a year later, in 1859), and even if he never actually met the infamous count he must have been familiar with rumours of Stenbock's occult pretensions and decadent lifestyle. Perhaps Falkner read "Viol d'Amor" in Stenbock's *Studies of Death*—which was published a year before *The Lost Stradivarius*—and perhaps not, but if there was no direct influence the two stories certainly draw on the same legendary sources of inspiration. As the loyal son of a clergyman, Falkner was fully committed in opposition to the allure of *fin de siècle* occultism and aestheticism, but there is no sign in *The Lost Stradivarius* of the horrified piety of such writers as Robert Hugh Benson, nor even the suspiciously excessive fascination of Montague Summers. In spite of the fact that it is conveyed through the voice of a very proper Victorian maiden the narration is calm and studied, a virtuoso exercise in telling understatement. The unusual and intriguing notion of the Satanic Revelation is handled with all due gravity.

It is possible that Falkner came to regret his own subtlety, especially when he saw the public reaction to the hysterical excesses of Bram Stoker's *Dracula*, and thus made a determined effort to insert more colour into *Moonfleet*, but he was by nature a calm and thoughtful man and *The Lost Stradivarius* is a masterpiece of its own restrained kind. He might, had he so determined, have become a notable writer of good-quality popular fiction, but he preferred to reserve his work in that vein as a kind of recreation, and to cultivate success and prestige in other fields (which he doubtless considered far more worthy). Even so, he must have cared about his novels, perhaps more deeply than he could bring himself to admit, else he could never have given them up in the way he did. *The Lost Stradivarius* is the work of an authentic artist, not a dilettante dabbler.

—Brian Stableford

FARRIS, John

Pseudonym: Steve Brackeen. **Nationality:** American. **Born:** Missouri, 1936. **Family:** Married Mary Ann Farris; one son. **Career:** Novelist (first book published at age 19), screenwriter and occasional film director. **Address:** c/o Tor Books, 175 Fifth Avenue, New York, NY 10010, USA. Lives in Atlanta, Georgia.

HORROR, GHOST AND GOTHIC PUBLICATIONS

Novels

The Fury. Chicago, Playboy Press, 1976; London, Macdonald, 1977.
All Heads Turn When the Hunt Goes By. Chicago, Playboy Press, 1977; London, Macdonald, 1978; as *Bad Blood*, London, Gollancz, 1989.
Catacombs. New York, Delacorte, 1981; London, New English Library, 1982.
The Uninvited. New York, Delacorte, 1982; London, New English Library, 1983.
Son of the Endless Night. New York, St. Martin's Press, and London, New English Library, 1985.
Wildwood. New York, Tor, 1986; London, New English Library, 1987.
The Axman Cometh. New York, Tor, 1989; London, New English Library, 1990.
Fiends. Arlington Heights, Illinois, Dark Harvest, 1990; London, Grafton, 1991.

Short Stories

Scare Tactics. New York, Tor, 1988; London, New English Library, 1989; expanded edition, New York, Tor, 1989.

Plays

Screenplays: *Dear Dead Delilah*, 1972; *The Fury*, 1977.

OTHER PUBLICATIONS

Novels

The Corpse Next Door. New York, Graphic, 1956.
Harrison High. New York, n.p., 1959; London, Ace, 1961.
The Long Light of Dawn. New York, n.p., 1962.
When Michael Calls. New York, Trident Press, 1967; London, New English Library, 1970.
King Windom. New York, Trident Press, 1967.
The Captors. New York, Trident Press, 1969; London, New English Library, 1971.
The Trouble at Harrison High. New York, Pocket, 1970.
Happy Anniversary, Harrison High. New York, Pocket, 1973.
Sharp Practice. New York, Simon and Schuster, 1974; London, Weidenfeld and Nicolson, 1975.
Shatter. London, Allen, 1980; New York, Popular Library, 1981.
Minotaur. New York, Tor, and London, New English Library, 1985.
Nightfall. New York, Tor, 1987; London, Severn House, 1988.
Sacrifice. New York, Tor, 1994.
Dragonfly. New York, Tor, 1995; London, Severn House, 1997.

Novels as Steve Brackeen

The Body on the Beach. N.p., Mystery House, 1957.
Baby Moll. New York, Crest, 1958; London, Gold Medal, 1959.
Danger in My Blood. New York, Crest, 1959.
Delfina. New York, Gold Medal, 1962; London, Muller, 1963.
The Guardians. New York, Holt Rinehart, 1964; London, Hale, 1966.

*

Film Adaptations: *When Michael Calls*, 1969 (TV movie); *The Fury*, 1977.

Theatrical Activities:
Director: **Film**—*Dear Dead Delilah*, 1972.

*   *   *

Whenever a writer produces a novel that strikes a popular chord with readers, other novelists are tempted try to imitate that success. The runaway popularity of Stephen King and, initially, supernatural horror in general, caused a number of writers of mainstream fiction to jump on the bandwagon. Many of these were quickly and mercifully forgotten, but at least one author, John Farris, produced a significant body of memorable work before following the trend away from fantasy-horror and toward more mundane thrillers.

His best-known foray into the genre is science fiction as well as horror. *The Fury*, subsequently filmed, concerns two siblings who have psychic powers, and who are ruthlessly exploited by an evil man who sees them as a tool to securing personal power for himself. Sharp-edged weapons have a bad habit of turning in one's hand, however, and the villain is suitably dealt with and the brother and sister reunited after a series of thrills and chills that owe more to the spy novel than the gothic horror tradition.

The memorably-titled *All Heads Turn When the Hunt Goes By* is more identifiably supernatural fiction (and earned an entry in *Horror: 100 Best Books*, edited by Kim Newman and Stephen

Jones). Farris draws on African folklore for this story of a southern family entangled with black magic and old secrets. Regarded by some critics as Farris's finest work, it was also one of the first modern horror novels to explicitly examine the sexuality implicit in most horror themes. His next, the Rider Haggard-ish *Catacombs*, concerns ghastly things brought to light by an archaeological expedition to Mount Kilimanjaro, East Africa.

The Uninvited is a superior treatment of a familiar theme: Barry Brennan is a young woman so disturbed by the death of her fiancé that she retreats into depression and solitude. One night she discovers that her lover is alive again, though he seems to have no memory, limited personality, and is clearly emotionally disturbed. As the days pass, he begins to recover more of his faculties, but only when someone close to Barry dies, surrendering their life-force to enhance his own. Barry's ultimate discovery of the consequences of a love grown twisted into something evil climaxes an excellent, chilling story of the supernatural.

Farris drew upon actual events as the inspiration for his next horror novel, *Son of the Endless Night*. In a small town in Vermont, a serial killer pleads innocent by reason of demonic possession. Although the authorities are ready to dismiss the claim as nonsense, there is mounting evidence indicating that the defendant may be telling the truth after all. *Wildwood* is the name of an old country estate, whose past is filled with bizarre events and strange legends. The property's history is investigated by a man who discovers that one of his oldest friends may have lost his sanity while living there, imagining the forests to be filled with sinister, misshapen creatures who watch over the cursed estate. As the story unfolds, we discover that the old friend has evidence backing his claim about inhuman creatures, and that an ancient Indian magic has survived the advent of the White Man and may be about to reassert dominion over the country. Monsters and magic notwithstanding, the most terrifying sequences are those in which we begin to question the sanity of the protagonist in this fine blend of psychological and supernatural horror.

The Axman Cometh is a tighter, though less ambitious work. The protagonist lost her entire family to an insane killer who disappeared shortly after the crime. She eventually recovers from the nervous breakdown that followed the murders, and subsequently attempts to build a new life for herself under a new identity. But she cannot escape her memories of the past, and in fact her unconscious mind helps to regenerate the killer, initially a conscious effort to deal with her past, but later an actual danger when the murderer assumes physical form. Unsettling and suspenseful, *The Axman Cometh* is essentially *The Uninvited* with its central premise reversed, a woman menaced by the object of her hatred rather than the object of her love.

Fiends is perhaps Farris's best horror novel to date. A humanoid but clearly inhuman body is found, apparently a relic of a long-ago age. This leads to the discovery of an entire colony of creatures, somewhat resembling vampires, whom we learn were created at the same time as the human race, but who were refused God's grace and have been living in darkness ever since. Farris portrays his monsters as intelligent and even admirable in some ways, despite being undeniably evil, and their charming grace makes them even more effective as antagonists.

Most of Farris' shorter horror fiction, including the short novels "horrorshow" and "The Guardians: A Novel," were collected in *Scare Tactics*. In "horrorshow" a strange young man who claims to be able to remember past lives is accused of a brutal murder. Through astral projection, he is able to discover the truth and bring the real culprit to justice. An egotistic and generally unpleasant writer summons a physical muse to help him with his work in "The Odor of Violets," and discovers that he has been assigned the personal muse that he deserves, a foul-smelling, repulsive creature. A ghostly ice-cream truck dispenses rough justice in "I Scream. You Scream. We All Scream for Ice Cream." First published separately under the pseudonym Steve Brackeen in 1964, "The Guardians" is a non-supernatural suspense thriller about an old family enmity that leads to a series of murder attempts.

As the popularity of supernatural horror fiction has waned in the United States, Farris has switched to other themes, but it seems likely that he will return to the genre when the market regains its health. With a generous handful of horror novels (which earned him much peer praise, from Stephen King, Peter Straub and others), he proved himself capable of writing gripping, often unusual stories which took familiar themes in unfamiliar directions.

—Don D'Ammassa

FORTUNE, Dion

Pseudonym of Violet Mary Firth. **Other Pseudonym:** V. M. Steele. **Nationality:** British. **Born:** Llandudno, Wales, 6 December 1890. **Education:** Schools in Llandudno and Weston-super-Mare; University of London. **Family:** Married Thomas Penry Evans in 1927. **Career:** Lay psychoanalyst, 1913-14; established the Fraternity of the Inner Light, 1927; writer and mystic. **Died:** 8 January 1946.

HORROR, GHOST AND GOTHIC PUBLICATIONS

Novels

The Demon Lover. London, Noel Douglas, 1927.
The Winged Bull: A Romance of Modern Magic. London, Williams and Norgate, 1935; New York, Kyle, 1935.
The Goat-Foot God. London, Williams and Norgate, 1936.
The Sea Priestess. London, Inner Light, 1938.
Moon Magic. London, Aquarian Press, 1956.

Short Stories

The Secrets of Dr. Taverner. London, Noel Douglas, 1926.

OTHER PUBLICATIONS

Novels as V. M. Steele

The Scarred Wrists. London, Stanley Paul, 1935.
Hunters of Humans. London, Stanley Paul, 1935.
Beloved of Ishmael. London, Stanley Paul, 1935.

Poetry as Violet Mary Firth

Violets. Weston-super-Mare, Mendip Press, 1904.
More Violets. London, Jarrold, 1905.

Other

The Esoteric Philosophy of Love and Marriage. London, Rider, 1923.
Esoteric Orders and Their Work. London, Rider, 1928.
Sane Occultism. London, Rider, 1929.
The Training and Work of an Initiate. London, Rider, 1930.
Mystical Meditations Upon the Collects. London, Rider, 1930.
Spiritualism in the Light of Occult Science. London, Rider, 1931.
Psychic Self Defence: A Study in Occult Pathology and Criminality. London, Rider, 1931.
Through the Gates of Death. London, Inner Light, 1932.
The Mystical Qabalah. London, Williams and Norgate, 1935.
Practical Occultism in Daily Life. London, Williams and Norgate, 1935.
The Cosmic Doctrine. London, Inner Light, 1949.
Applied Magic. London, Aquarian Press, 1962.
Aspects of Occultism. London, Aquarian Press, 1962.
The Magical Battle of Britain. Bradford-on-Avon, Golden Gates Press, 1994.

Other as Violet Mary Firth

Machinery of the Mind. London, Allen and Unwin, 1922.
The Psychology of the Servant Problem. London, Daniel, 1925.
The Soya Bean. London, Daniel, 1925.
The Problem of Purity. London, Rider, 1928.
Avalon of the Heart. London, Muller, 1934.

*

Critical Studies: *The Story of Dion Fortune* by Carr Collins and Charles Fielding, Dallas, Texas, Star and Cross, 1985; *Priestess: The Life and Magic of Dion Fortune* by Alan Richardson, London, Aquarian Press, 1987, as *The Magical Life of Dion Fortune*, London, Aquarian Press, 1991.

*   *   *

Violet Mary Firth was a psychic and student of the occult. She formed the Fraternity of the Inner Light as an off-shoot of the Order of the Golden Dawn and adopted as her motto within these organizations the phrase *Deo Non Fortuna* which she conflated into the pseudonym Dion Fortune for all her writings on psychic matters after 1922. She used fiction as one medium in which to express her more romantic occult ideals, and though they may be enjoyed as fiction the reader gains a better judgment of these works by understanding Firth's own views. Interestingly, her own Society has progressed from Firth's original basis. When they reprinted her works in the 1980s they made the point that "many of the ideas then expressed are not now necessarily acceptable." Clearly in the fiction of Dion Fortune we are dealing with a set of very personal and idiosyncratic views and values.

Her first work of fiction was a series of stories for the *Royal Magazine* that, with several new stories, were collected together as *The Secrets of Dr. Taverner.* Taverner is an occult detective and Firth drew heavily for his character, and probably his adventures, from an adept whom she knew in the Golden Dawn. The stories are rather more simplistic than the John Silence stories by Algernon Blackwood which were their spiritual forebears. Firth was still learning the art of fiction writing and these essays in

occult adventure betray her inexperience. They are more fascinating for their concepts than as stories. The years immediately after World War I saw a massive increase in interest in spiritualism, and Firth responded to that demand. The War had not only disturbed people's mental attitudes but also the spiritual balance of the world. In the first story, "Blood-Lust," Firth sought to imply some occult provenance for some of the War's horrors by depicting a soldier possessed by the spirit of a vampire. Other stories deal with reincarnation, psychic revenge and, in particular, the spiritual continuum. Despite their superficiality as stories they hold a fascination for Firth's ideas.

Soon after these stories Firth made her first attempt at a novel. *The Demon Lover* suffers again from poor characterization but this hardly matters when set against the breathless pace and scale of Firth's vision. Lucas is an adept of the black arts who uses a folklore society as a front for his occult pursuits. He draws into his activities Veronica Mainwaring, a medium. It later transpires that these two had been unfulfilled lovers in a past incarnation. Lucas uses Veronica to spy into the occult realm and for these indiscretions he is killed, though his earthly body remains as a vampire. It is only through Veronica's love that Lucas is allowed to return to life.

Firth reworked these themes of unrequited love, reincarnation and psychic experimentation in her next two novels. *The Winged Bull* tells of the mystic Ted Murchison who endeavours to help restore the psychic balance within Ursula, sister of the magician Brangwyn. Ursula, however, is under the influence of the black magician Hugo Astley and the novel explores Murchison's efforts to sustain Ursula despite her dislike for him. *The Goat-Foot God* is one of her best works. It tells of the gradual spiritual fulfilment of Hugh Paston who, through occult studies, begins to unite with the spirit of a medieval monk and pantheist. Both of these books teem with ideas but are weak as novels because of Firth's inconsistent writing and characterization.

Her final two occult novels are part of a sequence. *The Sea Priestess* and *Moon Magic* tell of the development of Lilith Le Fay Morgan, the priestess of the revived cult of an ancient goddess. In the first book Morgan uses as her agent Maxwell who becomes psychically alert in her presence and has visions of their past lives. He becomes her priest and must make a spiritual sacrifice so that she can unite with the goddess. In the second novel Morgan seeks out a new priest, a neurologist—Dr. Malcolm. The story follows much the same pattern as the first though it is more unified as a whole and the most complete of Firth's novels.

What emerges most strongly from Firth's occult novels is her own conviction. All of the novels have strong sexual undertones which only impress Firth's deep desire for spiritual union. As a consequence the message and vision in her books overcome the unequal writing to provide works of interest for any student of the occult.

—Mike Ashley

FOWLER, Christopher

Nationality: British. **Born:** 1953. **Career:** Television scriptwriter; director, The Creative Partnership (film promotion company), London; short-story writer and novelist. **Agent:** Serafina Clarke Agency, 98 Tunis Rd., London W12 7EY, England.

HORROR, GHOST AND GOTHIC PUBLICATIONS

Novels

Roofworld. London, Century Hutchinson, and New York, Ballantine, 1988.
Rune. London, Century, 1990; New York, Ballantine, 1991.
Red Bride. London, Little Brown, 1992; New York, Roc, 1993.
Darkest Day. London, Little Brown, 1993.
Spanky. London, Warner, 1994.
Psychoville. London, Warner, 1995.

Short Stories

City Jitters. London, Sphere, 1986; New York, Dell, 1988; revised edition, London, Warner, 1992.
More City Jitters. New York, Dell, 1988; London, Sphere, 1996.
The Bureau of Lost Souls. London, Century, 1989; New York, Ballantine, 1991.
Sharper Knives. London, Warner, 1992.
Flesh Wounds. London, Warner, 1995.

OTHER PUBLICATIONS

Other

How to Impersonate Famous People. N.p., n.d.
The Ultimate Party Book: The Illustrated Guide to Social Intercourse, illustrated by Stuart Buckley. London, Unwin, 1985.

* * *

Christopher Fowler specializes in the Urban Nightmare. His novels and short stories are largely set in contemporary cities (usually London) and deal with the nasty things that people do to each other. The stories often culminate in one or more gory deaths and the novels are splattered with them. In most of his work supernatural elements tend to be peripheral.

His first novel, *Roofworld*, could be regarded as a thriller set among the rooftops of London. Robert Linden is attempting to trace the author of a book in order to discuss a possible option for a TV series, only to find she has been murdered by an intruder. In trying to contact her next-of-kin he is dropped into a battle between the last remnants of what was a thriving community living on the roofs of London's higher buildings and a rival gang intending to eradicate them. The attention of the police is drawn to the skyline by a series of horrific murders in which the victims appear to drop from the sky, as Chymes (the villain) disposes of the opposition. DCI Hargreave is put in charge of the case. The resulting book takes on the persona of a fast-paced detective novel with elements of farce, a tiny hint of the supernatural, and a feeling that a lot of the basics of the situation have been glossed over.

Rune, Fowler's next novel, can be regarded as a homage to M.R. James. The ideas from "Casting the Runes" have been brought up to date, with the runes being passed to the unwitting victim via modern technology. Again detective thriller and horror have been combined in a London setting. A series of murders is initially dismissed as freak accidents but suspicions are aroused when it is noticed (both by Harry Buckingham, son of the first victim, and

the police) that all the victims have business connections. The demon summoned by the runes is controlled by a large business corporation intent on intimidating smaller rivals.

Red Bride has its roots in the Caribbean although the story begins and ends in London. Again there are two strands. There is John Chapel, new to the film PR business, who meets and is entranced by one of his clients, Ixora De Corizo, to the extent that he loses first his family, then his job. The other strand is the detective thriller as gory bodies start turning up. The first police assigned to the case are soon replaced by Ian Hargreave (from *Roofworld*), now promoted to Chief Inspector. The trail leads him in John Chapel's direction, especially as Ixora seems to have known all of the victims. A supernatural element is introduced when we learn that Ixora's parents were drowned off St. Lucia and that when she walked from the sea apparently unharmed three days later it was locally believed that she had made a pact with the devil.

Darkest Day follows a similar pattern with a London setting, gory murders and a team of police on the perpetrator's tail, but *Spanky* is an attempt to break out of the formula Fowler has created for himself. Martyn Ross is one of life's failures. Everything about him is mediocre. Then he meets Spanky. Spanky is a demon and promises to make Martyn's dreams come true—but without harming anyone. In a short space of time Martyn gets a new wardrobe, a new flat, promotion, sexual charisma, and his family is set back on an even keel. Everything is perfect until Spanky sends in his bill. Once he discovers what Spanky requires in return for his help—the use of his body—Martyn refuses, and battle for possession ensues. Everything Martyn has gained is taken away, and people start dying as Spanky carries out his threats in an attempt at intimidation. As the novel is told by Martyn in first-person it can be read in two ways. Either everything recounted is true, or it is all in his mind; either it is a supernatural story or it is a psychological thriller depicting the disintegration of his sanity. Whichever version is preferred by the reader is immaterial as this novel has a quality not found in Fowler's earlier work. It is sharp, fresh and nicely observed. The changes in Martyn's situation and character are well-paced and believable within the context.

Fowler achieves similar excellence in *Psychoville*. This again falls into two halves. In the first, Billy March and his family are rehoused from inner London to a new housing estate. However hard they try, they do not fit in and what was a comfortable, if penurious, family life disintegrates in the face of hostility from the neighbours. The characterizations and the sequence of events are all very believable. The horror here is psychological and chilling because these are attitudes that we all recognize. The second part takes place ten years later. When a young couple take up residence in a house on the same street where Billy used to live, people begin to die. The body count rises as vengeance is extracted for the perceived harm caused to Billy and his family. To some extent the violence goes way over the top, but it demonstrates the ways in which minds can be warped by circumstance and the depths to which human beings can sink.

Fowler is also a prolific writer of short stories, most of which feature the same kind of urban violence as his novels. They have appeared in a wide variety of magazines and anthologies as well as being collected in, so far, five volumes.

His first-published book was *City Jitters* which was a collection of stories linked to each other by the adventures of Paul Norris, an English businessman who is stranded in New York overnight on his way to Florida for a holiday. Everything that can possibly go wrong, does, but each episode is used as an introduction to a story. For example, being nearly run down by a car leaving an underground car-park is the introduction to "Left Hand Drive" in which a driver finds himself going deeper and deeper into a car-park in an attempt to find the way out. *More City Jitters* reprises the format, this time with Norris stranded on a broken elevator, and the conversations of those trapped with him serve as the introductions to the stories. In both these volumes the stories tend to be too short to develop the characters, and certainly in the first volume the fact that the stories are mostly set in London detracts from the effect Fowler is trying to create—it makes London scary rather than New York.

The Bureau of Lost Souls contains a couple of stories reprinted from *More City Jitters* and is tentatively linked by the title story which is also printed last. A young man is sent by an employment agency to a new job in which he finds that he is processing the souls of the newly deceased, deciding their final destination. Some of the files deal with characters who have died horribly in earlier stories in the volume.

As in the novels, the deaths in the stories are largely gory, sometimes predictable and sometimes more shocking because they are sudden. The longer stories are more satisfying because Fowler is able to develop the characters and situations, and later stories are better as he has become more skilful at handling his material. In all his work he shows the nastier side of human nature, and the best demonstrates how the minds of apparently normal people can degenerate. The horror is that atrocities can be committed by anyone and you may not suspect them until it is too late.

—Pauline Morgan

FOWLES, John (Robert)

Nationality: British. **Born:** Leigh-on-Sea, Essex, 31 March 1926. **Education:** Bedford School, 1940-44; Edinburgh University, 1944; New College, Oxford, B.A. (honors) in French 1950. **Military Service:** Served in the Royal Marines, 1945-46. **Family:** Married Elizabeth Whitton in 1956. **Career:** Lecturer in English, University of Poitiers, France, 1950-51; teacher at Anargyrios College, Spetsai, Greece, 1951-52, and in London, 1953-63. **Awards:** Silver Pen award, 1969; W. H. Smith Literary award, 1970; Christopher award, 1981. **Address:** c/o Jonathan Cape Ltd, 20 Vauxhall Bridge Road, London SW1V 2SA, England.

HORROR, GHOST AND GOTHIC PUBLICATIONS

Novels

The Collector. London, Cape, and Boston, Little Brown, 1963.
The Magus. Boston, Little Brown, 1965; London, Cape, 1966; revised edition, London, Cape, 1977; Boston, Little Brown, 1978.
A Maggot. London, Cape, and Boston, Little Brown 1985.

OTHER PUBLICATIONS

Novels

The French Lieutenant's Woman. London, Cape, and Boston, Little Brown, 1969.
Daniel Martin. London, Cape, and Boston, Little Brown, 1977.
Mantissa. London, Cape, and Boston, Little Brown, 1982.

Short Stories

The Ebony Tower: Collected Novellas. London, Cape, and Boston, Little Brown, 1974.

Plays

Don Juan, adaptation of the play by Molière (produced London, 1981).
Lorenzaccio, adaptation of the play by Alfred de Musset (produced London, 1983).
Martine, adaptation of a play by Jean Jacques Bernard (produced London, 1985).

Screenplay: *The Magus,* 1968.

Poetry

Poems. New York, Ecco Press, 1973.
Conditional. Northridge, California, Lord John Press, 1979.

Other

The Aristos: A Self-Portrait in Ideas. Boston, Little Brown, 1964; London, Cape, 1965; revised edition, London, Pan, 1968; Boston, Little Brown, 1970.
Shipwreck, photographs by the Gibsons of Scilly. London, Cape, 1974; Boston, Little Brown, 1975.
Islands, photographs by Fay Godwin. London, Cape, 1978; Boston, Little Brown, 1979.
The Tree, photographs by Frank Horvat. London, Aurum Press, 1979; Boston, Little Brown, 1980.
The Enigma of Stonehenge, photographs by Barry Brukoff. London, Cape, and New York, Summit, 1980.
A Brief History of Lyme. Lyme Regis, Dorset, Friends of the Lyme Regis Museum, 1981.
A Short History of Lyme Regis. Wimborne, Dorset, Dovecote Press, 1982; Boston, Little Brown, 1983.
Land, photographs by Fay Godwin. London, Heinemann, and Boston, Little Brown, 1985.
Lyme Regis Camera. Stanbridge, Dorset, Dovecote Press, 1990; Boston, Little Brown, 1991.

Editor, *Steep Holm: A Case History in the Study of Evolution.* Sherborne, Dorset, Allsop Memorial Trust, 1978.
Editor, with Rodney Legg, *Monumenta Britannica,* by John Aubrey. Sherborne, Dorset Publishing Company, 2 vols., 1981-82; vol. 1, Boston, Little Brown, 1981.
Editor, *Thomas Hardy's England,* by Jo Draper. London, Cape, and Boston, Little Brown, 1984.
Translator, *Cinderella,* by Charles Perrault. London, Cape, 1974; Boston, Little Brown, 1975.

Translator, *Ourika,* by Claire de Durfort. Austin, Texas, Taylor, 1977.

*

Film Adaptations: *The Collector,* 1965; *The Magus,* 1968; *The French Lieutenant's Woman,* 1981; *The Ebony Tower,* 1984 (TV movie).

Bibliography: "John Fowles: An Annotated Bibliography 1963-76" by Karen Magee Myers, in *Bulletin of Bibliography* (Boston), vol. 33, no. 4, 1976; *John Fowles: A Reference Guide* by Barry N. Olshen and Toni A. Olshen, Boston, Hall, 1980; "John Fowles: A Bibliographical Checklist" by Ray A. Roberts, in *American Book Collector* (New York), September-October 1980; "Criticism of John Fowles: A Selected Checklist" by Ronald C. Dixon, in *Modern Fiction Studies* (Lafayette, Indiana), Spring 1985.

Manuscript Collection: University of Tulsa, Oklahoma.

Critical Studies: *The Fiction of John Fowles: Tradition, Art, and the Loneliness of Selfhood* by William J. Palmer, Columbia, University of Missouri Press, 1974; *John Fowles: Magus and Moralist* by Peter Wolfe, Lewisburg, Pennsylvania, Bucknell University Press, 1976, revised edition, 1979; *Etudes sur The French Lieutenant's Woman de John Fowles* edited by Jean Chevalier, Caen, University of Caen, 1977; *John Fowles* by Barry N. Olshen, New York, Ungar, 1978; *John Fowles, John Hawkes, Claude Simon: Problems of Self and Form in the Post-Modernist Novel* by Robert Burden, Würzburg, Königshausen & Neumann, and Atlantic Highlands, New Jersey, Humanities Press, 1980; *John Fowles* by Robert Huffaker, New York, Twayne, 1980; "John Fowles Issue" of *Journal of Modern Literature* (Philadelphia), vol. 8, no. 2, 1981; *Four Contemporary Novelists* by Kerry McSweeney, Montreal, McGill-Queen's University Press, 1982, London, Scolar Press, 1983; *John Fowles* by Peter J. Conradi, London, Methuen, 1982; *Fowles, Irving, Barthes: Canonical Variations on an Apocryphal Theme* by Randolph Runyon, Columbus, Ohio State University Press, 1982; *The Timescapes of John Fowles* by H. W. Fawkner, Rutherford, New Jersey, Fairleigh Dickinson University Press, 1983; *Male Mythologies: John Fowles and Masculinity* by Bruce Woodcock, Brighton, Harvester Press, 1984; *The Romances of John Fowles* by Simon Loveday, London, Macmillan, 1985; "John Fowles Issue" of *Modern Fiction Studies* (Lafayette, Indiana), Spring 1985; *The Fiction of John Fowles: A Myth for Our Time* by Carol M. Barnum, Greenwood, Florida, Penkevill, 1988; *The Art of John Fowles* by Katherine Tarbox, Athens, University of Georgia Press, 1988; *Form and Meaning in the Novels of John Fowles* by Susana Onega, Ann Arbor, Michigan, UMI Research Press, 1989; *John Fowles: A Reference Companion* by James R. Aubrey, New York, Greenwood Press, 1991; *Point of View in Fiction and Film: Focus on John Fowles* by Charles Garard, New York, P. Lang, 1991; *John Fowles's Fiction and the Poetics of Postmodernism* by Mahmoud Salami, Rutherford, Fairleigh Dickinson University Press, 1992; *Something and Nothingness: The Fiction of John Updike and John Fowles* by John Neary, Carbondale, Southern Illinois University Press, 1992; *Understanding John Fowles* by Thomas C. Foster, Columbia, University of South Carolina Press, 1994.

* * *

John Fowles's richly and sensually textured prose has established him firmly as a "literary" writer. But his fondness for games with metaphorical mirrors and labyrinths—and often, an underlying sense of the allegorical—gives much of his work an exotic imaginative flavour . . . straying beyond realistic narration towards magic realism and the borderlands of the supernatural.

His first published novel *The Collector* is a psychological thriller which leans strongly towards horror with its tale of understated obsession and the banality of evil. The appallingly unimaginative narrator is a collector of butterflies (a hobby with disturbing associations of impalement and the killing-bottle) who, thanks to a football pool win, is able to extend his fantasies by kidnapping and imprisoning a young woman whom he has decided he loves. She is an intelligent, lively art student; he is a philistine and not particularly bright; her small intellectual victories cannot alter the basic captor/captive situation, from which her ultimate pathetic death is the only release. At the finale—delicately prefiguring the later vogue for serial-killer horror—we see the collector toying with the idea of a repeat performance: "this time it won't be love, it would just be for the interest of the thing and to compare them." This is a most disquieting work.

Fowles's long second novel *The Magus* was actually drafted before *The Collector*—initially as a complex and ambiguously supernatural story in the vein of Henry James's *The Turn of the Screw,* as Fowles himself tells us. Its working title was *The Godgame,* this being the elaborate and fantastical psychodrama into which the manipulating "magus" Conchis lures the young narrator Nicholas Urfe. Urfe is something of a hollow man, a restless philanderer who escapes the coils of his latest soured love affair by coming to work on the Greek island of Phraxos. This is the millionaire Conchis's island, with shades and echoes of *The Tempest:* Conchis is a capricious Prospero commanding strange masques and apparent revenants; the role of Miranda is filled by a woman (in fact, twins) whose real nature is concealed beneath multiple layers of deception; there is even a Caliban, a seemingly brutish black bodyguard masked as Anubis.

Nothing on Phraxos is what it seems. Conchis overwhelms Nicholas with mysteries; with magical appearances and disappearances; with scenes from the past, including electrifying episodes from the island's days of Nazi occupation; with shifting explanations of events—timeslips, occult manifestations, madness and delusion—which invariably conceal further, hidden traps. The moves of the godgame extend beyond Conchis's estate and even beyond Phraxos: newspapers from England cannot be trusted, and ordinary-seeming characters in London also dance to the Conchis strings. Nicholas's and the reader's rationalizations of the seeming supernatural are themselves unsatisfactory, for although any individual incident can be explained away (and many, if not all, are), it seems incredible that even a Prospero with a millionaire's resources and an extensive troupe of supporting actors could or would ever go to such trouble. It *must* be magic. But then one remembers that stage magicians also rely on the audience following such patterns of thought. . . .

For its victim, the ramifying paranoia of the godgame is in the end subtly flattering: Conchis has thought Nicholas somehow worth all this colossal effort. (As Fowles has remarked, *The Magus* exploits adolescent longings.) Finally Nicholas is released or breaks free from Conchis's script, to write his own again—almost literally so in the book's first version, although the 1977 revision makes this point a trifle less obviously. The book is a haunting and absorbing magic-show, no less alluring on repeated reading.

Distant echoes of the godgame appear in Fowles's third and perhaps most acclaimed novel *The French Lieutenant's Woman*, in the form of the author's intrusive presence and overt exercise of capricious power over events. His fifth novel *Mantissa* might be said to invert the situation as a goddess-game, since here the author hero is no longer the all-manipulating Prospero but the subject of extraordinary and frequently erotic manipulations by his personified Muse. She is in fact the muse Erato, once the patron goddess of love poetry but now—according to Fowles—the most appropriate muse to watch over and inspire the modern novel. Who is actually in control: Erato with her many guises and millennia of ribald experience, or the barely-disguised Fowles who thinks he is writing the book? Ibsen equated life with a battle against trolls; in *Mantissa*, Fowles shows the artistic process as an uninhibited wrestle with spirits in the solipsistic corridors of the imagination.

Despite much underlying allegory about the nature of creativity and inspiration, *Mantissa* seems poorly regarded . . . partly owing to brevity, and partly perhaps because its farcical sex-comedy and welter of literary in-jokes are regarded by some as being of lesser worth than the more solemn narratives expected from this author.

A later and stranger novel, *A Maggot*, has a dense 18th-century historical setting and re-invokes something of *The Magus*'s sense of layered secrets concealing a possible ultimate revelation that may be too much for the mind to bear. Its deep oddness emerges with slow, cumulative power from a kind of protracted detective investigation of a disappearance. The visionary revelation is indeed extraordinary and utterly disorienting, and in this book's slight reworking of history it leads to the founding of the evangelical sect known as the United Society of Believers in Christ's Second Appearing, alias the Shakers. But what the 18th-century woman at the heart of the story can interpret only as prophetic visions (and her lawyer interrogator only as blasphemy or insanity) would seem—to 20th-century eyes—to suggest contact with travellers from the future, making the story "only" science fiction. Is such a modern categorization of *A Maggot*'s central narrative tangle—of an account filtered through veils of emotive memory and brutal legal examination—actually any more valid than the contemporary supernatural view whereby the mystery becomes a Mystery? A certain haunting doubt lingers.

John Fowles remains one of the least predictable and most re-readable of major modern authors.

—David Langford

FREEMAN, Mary E(leanor) Wilkins

Nationality: American. **Born:** Randolph, Massachusetts, 31 October 1852. **Education:** Brattleboro High School, Holyoke Female Seminary, South Hadley, Massachusetts, 1870-71; Glenwood Seminary, West Brattleboro, 1871. **Family:** Married Charles M. Freeman in 1902 (died 1923). **Career:** Brought up in Randolph, then in Brattleboro, Vermont; returned to Randolph, 1883; lived in Metuchen, New Jersey, after 1902. **Awards:** American Acad-

emy Howells Medal, 1925. **Member:** American Academy, 1926. **Died:** 13 March 1930.

HORROR, GHOST AND GOTHIC PUBLICATIONS

Short Stories

The Wind in the Rose-Bush and Other Stories of the Supernatural. New York, Doubleday, Page, and London, Murray, 1903.
Collected Ghost Stories. Sauk City, Wisconsin, Arkham House, 1974.

OTHER PUBLICATIONS

Novels

Jane Field. London, Osgood, McIlvaine, 1892; New York, Harper, 1893.
Pembroke. New York, Harper, and London, Osgood, McIlvaine, 1894.
Madelon. New York, Harper, and London, Osgood, 1896.
Jerome, a Poor Man. New York and London, Harper, 1897.
The Heart's Highway: A Romance of Virginia in the Seventeenth Century. New York, Doubleday, Page, and London, Murray, 1900.
The Portion of Labor. New York and London, Harper, 1901.
The Debtor. New York and London, Harper, 1905.
"Doc" Gordon. New York and London, Authors and Newspapers Association, 1906.
By the Light of the Soul. New York and London, Harper, 1907.
The Shoulders of Atlas. New York and London, Harper, 1908.
The Butterfly House. New York, Dodd, Mead, 1912.
The Yates Pride. New York and London, Harper, 1912.
An Alabaster Box, with Florence Morse Kingsley. New York and London, Appleton, 1917.

Short Stories

A Humble Romance and Other Stories. New York, Harper, 1887; as *A Far-Away Melody and Other Stories,* Edinburgh, Douglas, 1890.
A New England Nun and Other Stories. New York, Harper, and London, Osgood, McIlvaine, 1891.
Silence and Other Stories. New York and London, Harper, 1898.
The People of Our Neighborhood. Philadelphia, Curtis, 1898; as *Some of Our Neighbours,* London, Dent, 1898.
The Love of Parson Lord and Other Stories. New York and London, Harper, 1900.
Understudies. New York and London, Harper, 1901.
Six Trees. New York and London, Harper, 1903.
The Givers. New York and London, Harper, 1904.
The Fair Lavinia and Others. New York and London, Harper, 1907.
The Winning Lady and Others. New York and London, Harper, 1909.
The Copy-Cat and Other Stories. New York and London, Harper, 1914.
Edgewater People. New York and London, Harper, 1918.

Fiction for Children

Goody Two-Shoes and Other Famous Nursery Tales, with Clara Doty Bates. Boston, Lothrop, 1883.
Decorative Plaques (verse), designs by George F. Barnes. Boston, Lothrop, 1883.
The Cow with Golden Horns and Other Stories. Boston, Lothrop, 1884(?).
The Adventures of Ann: Stories of Colonial Times. Boston, Lothrop, 1886.
The Pot of Gold and Other Stories. Boston, Lothrop, and London, Ward, 1892.
Young Lucretia and Other Stories. New York, Harper, and London, McIlvaine, 1892.
Comfort Pease and Her Gold Ring. New York, Revell, 1895.
Once Upon a Time and Other Child-Verses. Boston, Lothrop, 1897; London, Harper, 1898.
The Green Door. New York, Moffat, Yard, 1910; London, Gay and Hancock, 1912.

Play

Giles Corey, Yeoman. New York, Harper, 1893.

Other

The Infant Sphinx: Collected Letters, edited by Brent L. Kendrick. 1985.

*

Bibliography: In *Bibliography of American Literature* by Jacob Blanck, New Haven, Yale University Press, 1955-91.

Critical Studies: *Mary Wilkins Freeman* by Perry D. Westbrook, 1967, revised edition, New York, Twayne, 1988; *The Infant Sphinx: Collected Letters of Mary Wilkins Freeman* edited by Brent L. Kendrick, Metuchen, New Jersey, Scarecrow Press, 1985; *A Web of Relationship: Women in the Short Fiction of Mary Wilkins Freeman* by Mary R. Reichardt, Jackson, University of Mississippi Press, 1992.

*   *   *

Mary Wilkins Freeman—who did not marry until she was 50 and published most of her books under her maiden name—was a prolific writer noted for her careful and unassuming evocations of life in rural New England. She received some critical acclaim towards the end of her career but her reputation declined thereafter as the simplicity and directness that were the hallmarks of her style fell somewhat out of fashion. The straightforwardness and seeming innocence of her story-telling manner do, however, serve to provide her ghost stories with a useful gloss of credibility which has made them more resistant than her other work to the changing tide of critical opinion. The innocence is only seeming, for her accounts of the long-lingering effects of old hatreds show a keen sensitivity to, and a careful understanding of, the awkward workings of human emotion. Although their literary mannerisms are quite distinct, Wilkins Freeman shares with such American ghost-story writers as Edith Wharton and Henry James and the British writer Mrs. Oliphant a penetrating interest in the enduring tensions of family life.

The most famous and most frequently reprinted of Wilkins Freeman's supernatural stories is "Luella Miller," in which a sick woman soaks up the energy of all those who attend to her needs, as if she were some kind of psychic vampire. Even death does not free her victims from their servitude, but it is the pressing need of her physical and emotional dependence rather than any obvious kind of power which destroys their lives and makes their spirits captive. Great-Aunt Harriet in "The Southwest Chamber" is a more actively malign presence, who stamps her personality on her surroundings so powerfully as to change the reflections cast by others in her mirror, but her influence survives her in much the same demanding way.

As is only to be expected—all the more so given that she remained so long a spinster—Wilkins Freeman is much gentler in her presentation of the ghosts of children. In "The Wind in the Rose-Bush" little Agnes, who died of neglect, is glimpsed by the child protagonist at play in her garden, and her phantom presence is most consistently maintained by the stirring of roses of the bough. "The Lost Ghost" is even more sentimental, featuring a similarly neglected ghost-child whose bewilderment and loneliness are finally set aside when she is taken in hand by the ghost of a kindly old lady.

The hauntings in "The Vacant Lot" and "The Shadows on the Wall" are more orthodox, both involving resentful manifestations whose disturbances rake over the coals of past misdemeanours. These complete the slender set of six stories assembled in *The Wind in the Rose-Bush*, which was the author's own choice of her best supernatural tales—although she may have felt compelled to ignore two that had previously been collected in *A Humble Romance and Other Stories.* "A Far-Away Melody" is a straightforward account of a premonition of death, but the atypical "A Symphony in Lavender" is an atmospheric tale of a disturbing dream, which introduces a deft symbolism in its use of various flowers that is reminiscent of the strategies of some *fin de siècle* French writers. These two stories and three others were added to the contents of *The Wind in the Rose-Bush* to make up the Arkham House *Collected Ghost Stories.* "A Gentle Ghost" is not a supernatural story, though, and is in consequence somewhat weaker than "A Lost Ghost," with which it has much in common.

"The Jade Bracelet" is an unusually melodramatic but thoroughly orthodox tale of an accursed object, but the remaining story in the Arkham House collection, "The Hall Bedroom," is considerably more interesting. Edward Wagenknecht, introducing the book, points out the similarity of its plot to that of "The Southwest Chamber," but also observes that in this instance the situation is employed to set up a series of metaphysical speculations more imaginatively adventurous than anything else the author produced. "The Hall Bedroom" demonstrates that Wilkins Freeman was capable of far greater versatility than the bulk of her work exhibits, but she was restrained—as were many of the writers of her period—by an excessive critical regard for literary naturalism. She lived up to those expectations well enough to win the William Dean Howells Gold Medal, but it is arguable that her occasional fantasies offer a deeper insight into her own emotions and sensibilities than her naturalistic works. Although Wilkins Freeman only wrote enough supernatural stories to fill a single volume the volume in question is an important and worthwhile contribution to the tradition of American supernatural fiction.

—Brian Stableford

FROST, Mark

Nationality: American. **Born:** 1953. **Career:** Screenwriter, film director and novelist. **Family:** Married. **Address:** c/o William Morrow and Company, Inc., 1350 Avenue of the Americas, New York, NY 10019, USA. Lives in Los Angeles and upstate New York.

HORROR, GHOST AND GOTHIC PUBLICATIONS

Novels

The List of Seven. New York, Morrow, and London, Random House, 1993.
The Six Messiahs. New York, Morrow, and London, Random House, 1995.

OTHER PUBLICATIONS

Other

Welcome to Twin Peaks: An Access Guide, with David Lynch and Richard Saul Wurman. New York, Pocket Books, 1991.

Plays

Screenplays: *The Believers,* 1987; *Storyville,* 1992.

Television Plays: episodes of *Hill Street Blues* and *Twin Peaks.*

*

Theatrical Activities
Director: **Film**—*Storyville,* 1992. Executive Producer: Film—*Twin Peaks: Fire Walk With Me,* with David Lynch, 1992; **Television**—*Twin Peaks* series, with David Lynch, 1989-91.

*   *   *

While Mark Frost's introduction to novel-writing was unorthodox, it cannot be said that he landed without a splash. After writing scripts for the prototypically gritty TV cop show, *Hill Street Blues,* Frost took a diagonal leap and co-created (with David Lynch) the weird soap opera, *Twin Peaks.* In itself this is worthy of note. Frost had moved from the real to the surreal in what was to be the first step on a spiral of weirdness that would lead to his first novel, *The List of Seven. Twin Peaks* was a soap opera that seemed to be anti-soap opera, not to mention anti-television, anti-horror, anti-life. Not only did the series mark a radical development of its other creator's movies *Blue Velvet* and *Wild at Heart,* it was a series in praise of American Gothic—where the demons forming the soul of the small town's life were accepted and revered. Twin Peaks the town is situated (fictionally, and forever) in the Pacific Northwest of America, and the peace of the town is shattered when Laura Palmer, a seemingly normal young lady, is murdered. "Who killed Laura Palmer?" became as vital a cry and as tragic a commentary on the power of TV on our lives as "Who shot JR?" had been a decade or so earlier.

For the first time the magical balance of Twin Peaks is held up for micro-inspection, and to some extent, micro-introspection. The town had been swinging along in the salubrious give-and-take of accepted bizarrenesses; but murder is more than even Twin Peaks is prepared to put up with, and with the arrival of the investigators comes a spotlight to show up the place's faults.

Thus we, the outside world, see the investigative leads that arrive via ESP, or dreams involving midgets; see the local sheriff Harry S. Truman and his tearful deputy Andy Brennan; the dwarf who talks backwards, the Lady with the Log, the murderer possessed by a demon named Bob. By the time the series had played out its early curious quirks and had become another creature altogether—namely, the movie *Twin Peaks: Fire Walk with Me* (1992; directed by David Lynch), Mark Frost was in the process of moving on to full-length prose fiction and another loud round of applause.

Metafictionally and with a nod to the postmodern—drawing attention to other novels and works—both *The List of Seven* and *The Six Messiahs* are written from the point of view of Sir Arthur Conan Doyle. But these are not Sherlock Holmes tales. Of course, a writer building upon the structure created by another is not new; to great effect Kim Newman has worked in this format, as has the American writer, Howard Waldrop. There is a train-spottery type of "what-if?" inquiry to be made when discussing the possibilities of famous people thrown into situations that one knows never occurred. More than anything else, Frost's novels demand of their audience a huge intake of breath and suspension of belief. Doyle was not the most ubiquitous of 19th-century writers, perhaps, but he was one of whom enough is known for the reader to understand that Mark Frost's *List of Seven* and *Six Messiahs* are fictional, set in alternative universes.

The idea is to build into what one knows of Doyle and of 19th-century England (in the first book) and America (in the second). In the first of the novels a thus-far failing novelist is to be observed; in fact, in the time before *The Dark Brotherhood* was written, Doyle here is being accused of plagiarism. This is Arthur Conan Doyle updated and refreshed—the smart-aleck rhetoric often held at bay, the insecurities showing. It is clear that Sherlock Holmes was Doyle's Superman; Doyle himself, being pursued, for example, after Black Mass scenes on Christmas Day, 1884, is a long way from achieving Holmes's cool—or, for that matter, Holmes' implied gay tendencies; Doyle is seduced by a woman and shows no regret at this having been the case. The most important matter to note, perhaps, though, is that these novels are not strictly detective stories: they are metaphysical suspense tales, often surreal and disturbing.

Of Frost's two novels, *The Six Messiahs* is the greater artistic achievement. The character of Doyle is more fully rounded, possibly because the author does not have to try as hard this time to recreate authentic 19th-century inner London. *The Six Messiahs* takes place on Doyle's book-signing tour of the States. Doyle, at this point, has killed off Holmes (his "Baker Street Frankenstein") in order to concentrate on his real work. The fans are not happy. But Doyle is content to do a signing tour of the U.S. anyway, little knowing of course that with a nod to the more ridiculously coincidental episodes of Sherlock Holmes, Doyle himself will be travelling on the ship across the water with six people sharing the same religious-tinted dream of a black tower and a river of blood. Needless to say, it is not long before Doyle is scheming for his life. In *The Six Messiahs* Doyle is more interesting, largely because of the picture of him as a dissatisfied serious novelist; a man who was not happy to be a pulpster. The scenes with Doyle in America—confronting a new-found land—are rich in cinematic detail, and the eerie scenes of a newly birthed religion are most effective of all. It would be good to see Doyle the novelist in the next volume struggling with the inner conflict of commerce versus art; or perhaps struggling with the reality of his own mortality.

—David Mathew

G

GAIMAN, Neil (Richard)

Nationality: British. **Born**: Portchester, 10 November 1960. **Education**: Ardingly College, 1970-74; Whitgift School, 1974-77. **Family**: Married Mary McGrath in 1985; one son, one daughter. **Career**: Miscellaneous journalist, London, from the early to mid-1980s; comics writer from 1987; occasional novelist and television writer. Moved to the United States in 1992. **Awards**: Mekon award, 1988; Eagle award, 1988, 1990; World Fantasy award, 1992.

HORROR, GHOST AND GOTHIC PUBLICATIONS

Novels

Good Omens: The Nice and Accurate Prophecies of Agnes Nutter, Witch, with Terry Pratchett. London, Gollancz, 1990; revised edition, New York, Workman, 1990.
Neverwhere. London, BBC Books, 1996.

Short Stories

Angels & Visitations: A Miscellany. Minneapolis, Minnesota, DreamHaven, 1993.

Graphic Novels (series: The Sandman)

Violent Cases, illustrated by Dave McKean. London, Titan, 1987; Northampton, Massachusetts, Tundra, 1991.
The Doll's House, illustrated by Mike Dringenberg and others (Sandman). New York, DC Comics, and London, Titan, 1990.
Preludes and Nocturnes, illustrated by Mike Dringenberg and others (Sandman). New York, DC Comics, and London, Titan, 1991.
Dream Country, illustrated by Kelley Jones and others (Sandman). New York, DC Comics, 1991; London, Titan, 1992.
The Books of Magic, illustrated by John Bolton and others. New York, DC Comics, 1991.
Black Orchid, illustrated by Dave McKean. London, Titan, and New York, DC Comics, 1991.
Season of Mists, illustrated by Kelley Jones and others (Sandman). New York, DC Comics, and London, Titan, 1992.
Signal to Noise, illustrated by Dave McKean. London, Gollancz, 1992.
A Game of You, illustrated by Shawn McManus and others (Sandman). New York, DC Comics, and London, Titan, 1993.
Fables and Reflections, illustrated by Bryan Talbot and others (Sandman). New York, DC Comics, 1993; London, Titan, 1994.
Miracleman: Book 4: The Golden Age, illustrated by Mark Buckingham. N.p., 1993.
Death: The High Cost of Living, illustrated by Chris Bachalo and others (Sandman). New York, DC Comics, and London, Titan, 1994.
Brief Lives, illustrated by Jill Thompson and others (Sandman). New York, DC Comics, and London, Titan, 1994.

The Tragical Comedy or Comical Tragedy of Mr. Punch: A Romance, illustrated by Dave McKean. London, Gollancz, 1994.
World's End, illustrated by Michael Allred and others (Sandman). New York, DC Comics, and London, Titan, 1995.
The Kindly Ones, illustrated by Marc Hempel and others (Sandman). New York, DC Comics, and London, Titan, 1996.

Play

Television Serial: *Neverwhere*, 1996.

Other

Editor, with Edward E. Kramer. *The Sandman Book of Dreams*. New York, HarperPrism, and London, Voyager, 1996.

OTHER PUBLICATIONS

Other

Duran, Duran: The First Four Years of the Fab Five. New York, Proteus, 1984.
Don't Panic: The Official Hitch Hiker's Guide to the Galaxy Companion. London, Titan, 1988; revised as *Don't Panic: Douglas Adams & The Hitchhiker's Guide to the Galaxy*, with David K. Dickson, London, Titan, 1993.

Editor, with Kim Newman, *Ghastly Beyond Belief*. London, Arrow, 1985.
Editor, with Stephen Jones, *Now We Are Sick*. Minneapolis, Minnesota, DreamHaven, 1991.
Editor, with Alex Stewart, *Temps, Volume 1*. London, Roc, 1991.

*   *   *

During the 1980s, Neil Gaiman, along with several of his countrymen—notably Alan Moore—brought a new relevance to that most traditional of American literary forms, the comic book. But where, with his groundbreaking treatment of DC Comics' Swamp Thing character, Moore worked within both the science-fictional and fantasy veins, Gaiman approached the medium by concentrating on the latter, imbuing his work with mythical and Gothic undertones.

Unlike most of the work produced by Moore, Gaiman's writing, while, at times, equally horrific and black, is filled with optimism. The first time this really showed itself was in a three-issue comic-book series from DC Comics entitled *Black Orchid*.

Black Orchid was a re-working of a character from the dim-and-distant past of DC Comics, home of Superman and Batman, but, unlike those world-famous caped vigilantes, Black Orchid had always been distinctly second-division. Gaiman and illustrator Dave McKean, the team chosen to produce the mini-series, had already worked together on *Violent Cases*, a self-contained *bete noir* produced by Titan Books in 1987. Mixing together extremes in depravity and gentility, Gaiman touched on some of the topics Moore had already flirted with in the watershed *Swamp Thing* and yet made them his very own, in a story which, ultimately, dwelt on the collective sentience of plants and the remarkable resilience of the human spirit.

His excursions into prose *without* visual accompaniment are restricted to one collaborative novel—a hilarious send-up of horror fiction, *Good Omens*, written with Terry Pratchett—a number of short stories, many of which are gathered into the collection *Angels & Visitations*, and the horror-fantasy novel *Neverwhere*, about a magical "London Below," which was also conceived as a serial for BBC Television. But it is, rightly, the Sandman for which Gaiman is most renowned and which, for the purposes of this book, is most appropriate for discussion.

The Sandman was another forgotten character from the vaults of DC Comics, but it really isn't even worth considering the earlier incarnation. Gaiman's version of the Sandman has the character as one of the Endless, a group of omniscient entities who have existed since the dawn of time. The Sandman himself is the Lord of Dreams, a gangling, pale man with a shock of coal-black hair, who rules The Dreaming, a surreal world which co-exists with reality but to which people can gain access when they are asleep. The rest of the Endless—Death, Inaction, Madness, Desire, Destruction and Destiny—make occasional appearances in the storylines. Death, the most frequently featured of these "support characters," is portrayed as a neo-punkish young woman for whom the shepherding of souls at the moment of their release is simply a job. Nevertheless, she brings to the task and to each of her charges a gentle understanding.

When the story unfolds, the pasty-faced, emaciated, wire-haired Sandman has been held in captivity for a human lifetime. On his release, he must find his sand-pouch, his helmet and his dream jewel—all of which have been stolen during his incarceration (thus neatly explaining why the earlier character with the same name was so completely different)—and then he must track down his missing helpers. In his quest, he visits Hell to battle the demon which stole his helmet; seeks out a young girl who has become fatally addicted to the sand in his pouch; and battles an embittered sociopath, Doctor Destiny, who has unleashed from the Sandman's ruby the full psychotic power of dreams onto an unsuspecting world.

In the course of his time writing the magazine (he has now ceased regular scripting of *Sandman*, although occasional one-off stories and mini-series are anticipated) Gaiman has truly revolutionized the power of the medium, effortlessly warping the action between asylums and dolls' houses, and including *en route* a motel where all the serial killers in America are holding a convention, a pub in London where the Sandman arranges to meet an immortal friend every century, and an English hillside in 1593 where, during the final performance of the Faery folk for humankind, we learn the "true" story of William Shakespeare's *A Midsummer Night's Dream*. Not surprisingly, this last story won the World Fantasy Award for best short story of 1991—the first time a comic book has won a non-comics award for a short story.

Occasionally, like any writer intent on expanding rather than on simply milking his chosen field, Gaiman misses the mark and becomes a little self-indulgent. But when he's on form (which is most of the time) he is without peer. The various volumes of collected Sandman stories, for instance, are almost uniformly excellent and any one of them would make a good starting point for those readers who, while well-versed in the field of Gothic prose literature, have yet to discover the rare but powerful joy inherent in a great comic book.

Gaiman went on to relate the adventures of his character and the experiences of those with whom the Sandman comes into contact for several years. Bravely (and, perhaps, wisely) he elected to leave the title—at least as permanent writer—while it was on a high. It is to DC's equal credit that they have (so far) not even tried to replace him on the book.

But the Gaiman voice, so rich in nostalgia and the downright weird, has continued undimmed. In his latest (at the time of this writing) non-series graphic novel, *Mr. Punch*, again with frequent collaborator Dave McKean, Gaiman centres on a young boy's encounters with a mysterious puppeteer, strange relatives and a woman whose work involves dressing up as a mermaid. It is, of course, the revered (in the right hands . . . feared in the wrong ones) rite-of-passage story, a sequence of events in which, in this case, the protagonist learns about mortality, loss and madness. It is an impressive work, rich not only in freshness and originality but also in compassion, Gaiman's hallmark and an increasingly rare commodity in the slam-bang, fisticuffs-and-fatalities worldscapes depicted in 1990s comic books.

The collective impact is literally breathtaking, writer and artist working together like the finest, most practised vaudeville act to produce a visual spinning-top of timing and imagery, intrigue and betrayal, illusory perception and cold reality. *Mr. Punch*'s first-person narrative looks back on the time when the protagonist was a young boy, sent to stay with his grandparents by the seaside while his mother produces a sister for him. With enviable simplicity and clarity, the words and pictures portray first, the strange world of out-of-season Southsea, with its empty beaches and run-down pier arcades, and, ultimately, a gradual breakdown of sanity leading to a lonely death and the slow awakenings of comprehension.

The vast majority of Gaiman's published works—certainly his short stories and his graphic novels—are heady mixtures of the everyday and the obscure. Managing to be salutary, evocative and entertaining at the same time is a trick that few can pull off. In this respect, his blending of poetic prose, marvellous invention and artistic vision has assured him of his place in the vanguard of modern-day dark fantasists.

—Peter Crowther

GALLAGHER, Stephen

Pseudonyms: Stephen Couper; John Lydecker. **Nationality:** British. **Born:** Salford, Lancashire, 1954. **Education:** University of Hull, B.A. in drama and English, 1975. **Family:** Married; one daughter. **Career:** Worked for various north-of-England television companies, including Yorkshire Television and Granada Television, 1975-80; freelance scriptwriter and novelist from 1980. **Address:** c/o Bantam Press, Transworld Publishers Ltd., 61-63 Uxbridge Rd., London W5 5SA, England. Lives in Blackburn, Lancashire.

HORROR, GHOST AND GOTHIC PUBLICATIONS

Novels

Chimera. London, Sphere, and New York, St. Martin's Press, 1982.
Follower. London, Sphere, 1984.

Valley of Lights. London, New English Library, 1987; New York, Tor, 1988.

Oktober. London, New English Library, 1988; New York, Tor, 1989.

Down River. London, New English Library, 1989; New York, Tor, 1990.

Rain. London, Hodder and Stoughton, 1990.

The Boat House. London, Hodder and Stoughton, 1991.

Nightmare, with Angel. London, Hodder and Stoughton, and New York, Ballantine, 1992.

Red, Red Robin. London, Bantam Press, and New York, Ballantine, 1995.

Plays

Television Plays: *Chimera* (serial), 1991; *Here Comes the Mirror Man* and *Prophecy* (*Chillers* series), 1995.

Radio Plays: *The Babylon Run,* 1979; *The Humane Solution,* 1979; *An Alternative to Suicide,* 1979; *A Resistance to Pressure,* 1980; *Chimera,* 1985; *The Kingston File,* 1987; *By the River, Fontanebleau,* 1988; *The Wonderful Visit,* from the novel by H. G. Wells, 1988; *The Horn,* 1989; *Life Line,* 1993.

OTHER PUBLICATIONS

Novels

The Last Rose of Summer (novelization of radio script). London, Corgi, 1978; revised as *Dying of Paradise* (as Stephen Couper), London, Sphere, 1982.

Silver Dream Racer (novelization of screenplay; as John Lydecker). London, Futura, 1980.

Saturn 3 (novelization of screenplay). London, Sphere, 1980.

The Ice Belt (novelization of radio script; as Stephen Couper). London, Sphere, 1983.

Dr. Who and the Warrior's Gate (novelization of television script; as John Lydecker). London, W. H. Allen, 1982.

Dr. Who: Terminus (novelization of television script; as John Lydecker). London, W. H. Allen, 1983.

Plays

Television Plays: *Dr. Who: Warrior's Gate,* 1981; *Dr. Who: Terminus,* 1983; *Moving Targets* (*Rockliffe's Folly* series), 1988; *Assassins, Inc., Down Among the Dead Men, Stealth, Pulse, Schrodinger's Bomb, The Bureau of Weapons, A Cage for Satan, Blaze of Glory, The Revenge Effect* and *Renegades* (*Bugs* series), 1995-97.

Radio Plays: *The Last Rose of Summer,* 1978; *Hunters' Moon,* 1979.

*

Film Adaptation: *Chimera* (television serial), 1991.

*   *   *

Stephen Gallagher is one of the most competent of British horror writers; the only question is whether the excellent and very

satisfying novels he has written, particularly since the late 1980s, should be classified as horror. That he is not better known is due to his compulsion to write something different all the time. He began with science-fiction novels, moved on to science-fictional horror, and finally to non-supernatural novels with a crime content and relatively little horror. Always an impeccable researcher, he has been unafraid of using American and European settings, with convincing results. His ultimate goal has always been to write for the media, and after several radio plays adapted from his own stories, he has recently written TV scripts for horror and science-fiction series.

There is no doubt about *Chimera* being horror. Although it resembles a superior crime thriller, focusing on both police procedure and upon the non-police characters caught up in the aftermath of multiple murder, its central subject matter is the creation of a human-monkey hybrid, which equates to a reworking of *Frankenstein.* This chimera, given the name of Chad and hidden away in a small government-funded research establishment in Cumbria, fails to be either a human being or a monkey, though it seems to possess near-human intelligence. Before the novel begins, Chad has gone berserk and wiped out all the staff there, at the Jenner Clinic. But the police know nothing about the research; they believe they are hunting a human killer. Hennessy, a senior civil servant from the Home Office, who is fully aware of the situation, closes down the police investigation and brings in a military team.

The way in which different government agencies squabble, try to suppress the truth, and attempt murder to prevent publicity, makes the novel resemble a proto-*X-File.* The main character is Peter Carson, a writer who unwittingly gets involved when he is asked by a female acquaintance on the Jenner Clinic staff to visit her in Cumbria. It is his feeling that a cover-up is in operation and his dissatisfaction over the way the police have treated everybody that make him investigate further, leading to revelations and more tragedy. The working relationships between police officers on the case are very well handled, and the whole novel has a gritty realism which has come to be recognized as Gallagher's trademark.

His next three novels all contain supernatural ingredients and are set in Norway, the United States, and Switzerland respectively. The central idea in *Valley of Lights,* set convincingly in Phoenix, Arizona, is another horror treatment of a science-fiction idea—a creature which can possess and control other minds. The narrator is a police sergeant who knows this and yet, familiarly, cannot persuade anybody else to believe him. In *Oktober* (which Gallagher has just scripted for a TV mini-series) the author is back with unethical scientific research, this time into the creation of a dream-controlling drug. The ideas may not be particularly original, but the details of character and event make these novels work.

Down River marks a shift away from the supernatural. It is a horror thriller about a corrupt English policeman, Johnny Mays. He uses his position to obtain anything he wants, letting nobody obstruct him. The plot comes down to a personal struggle between Mays and his more honest patrol-car partner, Nick Frazier, all made more difficult and more poignant because they have been friends since their schooldays. Once again, the details are wonderfully convincing. Johnny keeps a grudge book in which he writes down even the smallest of actions against him, all to be avenged in due course. The significance of this is that Johnny has become convinced that Nick has betrayed him—and the fact that Johnny seems to be dead gives Nick no peace of mind at all. Apart from its exciting and surprising plot, the novel opens out into an examination of people's roots: can they ever be returned to or re-captured? And it is hauntingly set against decaying urban land-scapes in an unnamed city in the north of England.

Another murder thriller with police-procedural elements is *Nightmare, with Angel*, Gallagher's finest achievement to date. Here he creates a very believable ten-year-old girl, Marianne, who lives unhappily with her father in an isolated coastal house on Morecombe Bay, Cumbria. Marianne misses her mother, left be-hind when they moved from Germany suddenly, a few years be-fore, and her father begrudges her because she reminds him too much of the mother. Being bilingual and an outsider, Marianne has no friends of her own age, but she tries to befriend a middle-aged man, Ryan, who once saved her from drowning and who scav-enges anything saleable from the beach. Ryan knows that he must not become friends with her, because he murdered another little girl when he was a teenager, and served a long sentence in a men-tal hospital for the crime. Against his better judgement he allows Marianne to persuade him to accompany her to Germany in search of her mother, with the police and Marianne's father following on behind.

The central relationship, in which Marianne's trust is justified and Ryan (who is clever but clearly not completely sane) becomes fiercely protective towards the only person he has ever been able to love, is superbly handled, without sentimentality or too much soul-searching. The plot twists are many and varied, with much excitement and a few horrific scenes. All the characters and the German settings are effortlessly and convincingly portrayed.

Red, Red Robin, set in various parts of the United States, is much more obviously a horror novel, being the uncovering of a serial killer—with more police-procedural material. Ruth Lasseter is lucky to escape the murderous intentions of a date who turns into a stalker. But the perpetrator, though believed dead, turns up again, just like Johnny Mays. Gallagher paints a very sympathetic picture of the effect that violent crime has upon surviving vic-tims, and he mounts a breathtaking finale in the atmospheric bayou area of Louisiana.

In addition to the novels, Gallagher is noted for his unusual and often unclassifiable short stories, which tend to be just a little more horrific and supernatural than his books, and very different from each other. For example, "Life Line" (in *Dark Fantasies*, 1989) deals with premium-rate phone lines that might put you in touch with the dead; "The Drain" (*Fantasy Tales #4*, 1990) is the terrifying tale of a childhood expedition that goes wrong; "The Visitors' Book" (in *Darklands*, 1991) is an unsettling study of events at a house rented for a week in the summer; and "In Gethsemene" (in *Heaven Sent*, 1995) is Gallagher's only historical piece, about the rivalry between a stage magician and a medium. A collection of these stories seems deserved and overdue.

—Chris Morgan

GARTON, Ray

Pseudonym: Joseph Locke. **Nationality:** American. **Born:** Redding, California, 1962. **Family:** Married Dawn Garton. **Ad-dress:** c/o Bantam Doubleday Dell Publishing Group, Inc., 1540 Broadway, New York, NY 10036, USA. Lives in Anderson, Cali-fornia.

HORROR, GHOST AND GOTHIC PUBLICATIONS

Novels

Seductions. New York, Pinnacle, 1984.
Darklings. New York, Pinnacle, 1985.
Invaders from Mars (novelization of screenplay). New York, Pocket, and London, Grafton, 1986.
Live Girls. New York, Pocket, 1987.
Crucifax Autumn, Arlington Heights, Illinois, Dark Harvest, 1988; abridged as *Crucifax*, New York, Pocket, 1988.
Warlock (novelization of screenplay). New York, Avon, 1989.
Trade Secrets. Shingletown, Connecticut, Ziesing, 1990.
Lot Lizards. Shingletown, Connecticut, Ziesing, 1991.
The New Neighbor. Lynbrook, New York, Charnel House, 1991.
Dark Channel. New York, Bantam, 1992.
1-900-Killer. New York, Bantam, 1994.
Biofire. New York, Bantam, 1996.
Shackled. New York, Bantam, 1997.

Novels as Joseph Locke (series: Blood and Lace)

The Nightmares on Elm Street, Parts 4 & 5 (novelizations of screenplays). New York, St. Martin's Press, 1989.
Kill the Teacher's Pet. New York, Bantam, 1991.
Petrified. New York, Bantam, 1991.
Kiss of Death. New York, Bantam, 1992.
Game Over. New York, Bantam, 1993.
Vengeance. New York, Bantam, 1994.
Vampire Heart (Blood and Lace). New York, Bantam, 1994.
Deadly Relations (Blood and Lace). New York, Bantam, 1994.

Short Stories

Methods of Madness. Arlington Heights, Illinois, Dark Harvest, 1990.
Pieces of Hate. Baltimore, Maryland, CD Publications, 1995.

Other

In a Dark Place: The Story of a True Haunting (with others). New York, Villard, 1992.

*   *   *

Ray Garton has effectively had three separate careers as a hor-ror writer, one as a novelizer of motion pictures, one as the au-thor of several highly regarded original horror novels, and another as "Joseph Locke," the byline for several noticeably above-average young-adult horror novels. Novelizations rarely attract much attention; they are generally very closely tied to the film and don't provide their authors much room to add their own ma-terial or touches. Garton's treatment of *Warlock* is essentially that, a faithful rendition of the film about a sorcerer who is recreated in the 20th century with all of his powers intact. The same is true of *The Nightmares on Elm Street*, which consists of the fourth and fifth episodes in the series, fortunately the two most inven-tive and interesting of the films. Although Garton does a work-manlike job with both of these, it is only with *Invaders from Mars*, the Tobe Hooper remake about Martians secretly kidnapping and reprogramming humans from their underground base, that he appears to have added something of his own. Garton's adaptation manages to blend the paranoia of the basic concept with some of the zaniness of Hooper's treatment.

His original novels are, obviously, far more interesting. *Seductions* is, as its title might suggest, a highly erotic horror novel. There are hidden among us a number of beautiful people who are willing to fulfill our every fantasy, people so attractive and sensual that it doesn't seem possible they could be human. And of course they aren't. They are instead a totally inhuman creature, capable of regenerating from almost any injury, with the ability to alter their shape to entice victims. Although their origin is never clearly explained, they seem to be a prehistoric species the remnants of which live underground except when they emerge to feed.

Darklings inverts that concept. Ordinary human beings are infiltrated by physical manifestations of evil which influence them to commit horrible crimes, murder, cannibalism, and worse. The ultimate origin is an incredibly evil man whose dead body was found to contain a mass of tentacles, and whose spawn has broken free to steal into the bodies of others. Filled with gruesome deeds and a really nasty monster, *Darklings* deserves far wider recognition than it has received.

Live Girls is a vampire novel, but enlivened by Garton's superior ability to set scenes and his gift for building tension. An unemployed man with no prospects decides to console himself in a disreputable night club, but the girl he meets there is more than he bargained for. Initially in thrall to her powers, he eventually finds the strength to break free and fight back. There's a great deal of overt sexuality, as is common in vampire stories, and Garton takes advantage of the psychological links between sex and death to underscore his theme. There's a strong sexual element in *Crucifax* as well. Mace is a charismatic figure whose arrival in the San Fernando Valley causes consternation and exaltation. He becomes the centre of a new cult, adored by his followers but hated by others who recognize that he is corrupting the young and innocent. But even they don't realize the depth of his evil, for Mace is not a human being at all. Garton was unhappy about the editing of this novel by its original publisher, and an unexpurgated version appeared in a limited-edition hardcover as *Crucifax Autumn*.

Dark Channel is also concerned with a cult, but this time one ostensibly dedicated to peace and love. Although some complain that their loved ones have been lured or kidnapped, there seems to be no evidence supporting that position until a news reporter disappears and another investigator discovers the truth. There's a demon at the center of the cult. Although just as suspenseful as Garton's other work, the climax is considerably less powerful and the explanation of what's been happening lacks the originality of his previous novels. *Lot Lizards* is a return to the vampire story, this time using truck stops as the setting. As with all of Garton's novels, there is a strongly erotic element made more effective by finely realized characters and situations, but this time the element of suspense is rather flat.

Garton's popular young-adult horror novels were all written as by Joseph Locke. Although aimed at younger readers, Garton was somehow able to avoid the worst of the restrictions imposed on that form. His stories never talk down to his audience as do so many others in that field, nor do they incorporate the blatantly bad plotting and background development that is so common with lesser writers. He also manages to incorporate more overt violence than usual, although never gratuitously. *Kill the Teacher's Pet*, for example, is about a teacher with a deadly hobby, and *Kiss*

of Death is a short but satisfying werewolf story, littered with mutilated corpses, creepy events, and a well defined cast of characters. *Game Over* uses the tired old supernatural video game theme, but even in this case, Garton provides some new twists and turns. *Vampire Heart* and its companion novel, *Deadly Relations*, are obviously about vampires. Eric's new girlfriend Sabrina isn't one, but there's a history of bloodlust in her family as the two of them discover in the first book. And in the second, old rivalries come to the boiling point and Eric and Sabrina find themselves fighting for their lives.

Garton is also a frequent short-story writer. A young boy blackmails a child molester and killer in "Sinema," eventually forcing him to murder his repressive mother. A dead musician returns for one more performance in "Weird Gig." Two child-abusers come to a horrible, if well-deserved, end in the short novel, "Dr. Krusadian's Method." "The Picture of Health" is an erotic twist on the story of Dorian Gray. "The Other Man" looks at marital infidelity on the astral plane. Other stories of interest include "Shock Radio" and "Hair of the Dog." Garton is a reliable source of high-quality horror fiction.

—Don D'Ammassa

GILCHRIST, R(obert) Murray

Nationality: British. **Born:** Sheffield, Yorkshire, 6 January 1868. **Education:** Sheffield Grammar School. **Family:** None. **Career:** Worked for the *National Observer*, London, 1890s; novelist and short-story writer. **Died:** 4 April 1917.

HORROR, GHOST AND GOTHIC PUBLICATIONS

Short Stories

The Stone Dragon and Other Tragic Romances. London, Methuen, 1894.

OTHER PUBLICATIONS

Novels

Passion the Plaything. London, Heinemann, and New York, Lovell, 1890.
Hercules and the Marionettes. London, Bliss, 1894.
A Peakland Faggot. London, Richards, 1897.
The Rue Bargain. London, Richards, 1898.
Willowbrake. London, Methuen, 1898.
Nicholas and Mary. G. Richards, 1899.
The Courtesy Dame. London, Heinemann, and New York, Dodd Mead, 1900.
The Labyrinth. London, Heinemann, 1902.
Natives of Milton. London, G. Richards, 1902.
Beggars's Manor. London, Heinemann, 1903.
The Abbey Mystery. London, Ward Lock, 1908.
The Gentle Thespians. London, Milne, 1908.
The Two Goodwins. London, Milne, 1908.
Pretty Fanny's Way. London, Everett, 1909.

The First Born. London, Laurie, 1911.
Willowford Woods. London, Ward Lock, 1911.
Damosel Croft. London, Paul, 1912.
The Secret Tontine. London, Long, 1912.
Roadknight. London, Holden, 1913.
Weird Deadlock. London, Long, 1913.
The Chase. London, White, 1914.
Under Cover of Night. London, Long, 1914.
Honeysuckle Rogue. London, Westall, 1917.

Short Stories

Lords and Ladies. London, Hurst, 1903.
Good-Bye to Market. N.p., Moorlands, 1908.
A Peakland Faggot: The Collected Short Stories of R. Murray Gilchrist. London, Faber and Gwyer, 1926.

Other

The Peak District. London, Blackie, 1911.
The Dukeries. London, Blackie, 1913.
Scarborough and Neighborhood. London, Blackie, 1914.

*   *   *

R. Murray Gilchrist was one of the first recruits to the English Decadent Movement, but no other writer put it behind him quite so emphatically as he did once the trials of Oscar Wilde had brought the word "decadence" into disrepute. Gilchrist was "discovered" by W. E. Henley, then the editor of the *National Observer*, who was the least willing of several poets who had the Decadent label slapped upon them by the Movement's ardent propagandist, Arthur Symons. Henley took advantage of his editorial privilege to launch a particularly cruel demolition of Wilde on the day after his conviction, which took the form of a hymn of hate against "decadence"; Gilchrist seemingly took this so much to heart that he spent the rest of his career producing heart-warming stories about the charming simplicity of Derbyshire yokels, reproducing their dialect with such phonetic exactitude as to render his work effectively unreadable by future generations. Before the Wilde trials of 1895, however, Gilchrist had produced one book in a very different kind of exotic language, which Everett Bleiler once described as "probably as close to Beardsley in prose as one can get."

Only five of the 14 stories in *The Stone Dragon and Other Tragic Romances* are supernatural, and less than half of the rest are orthodox *contes cruels*, but the collection does possess a kind of unity. This was not the only collection of "tragic romances" to be produced in the 1890s—the term had earlier been used in quasi-generic fashion by "Fiona MacLeod" (William Sharp)—but the tragic romances of the Celtic Twilight were myth-like constructions displaying Tragedy in the grandest possible manner. Gilchrist's stories are historical romances of a less extravagant kind, and his tragedies operate on a personal scale. The impression given by Gilchrist is that all romance is tragic, and that its tragedy is mercurial, perverse and intimate.

The climaxes of the most effective stories in the collection are moments of individual revelation which obliterate illusion and destroy hope. It matters little whether the supernatural elements of the stories are literal as well as symbolic, as they are in two of the *National Observer* stories, "Witch In-Grain" and "The Basilisk";

the point is that Fate itself is set against the hopes of those who seek solace in love. Moments of ecstasy may still be found, but they belong to a world of fantasy; the protagonist of "The Return," who finds his old sweetheart so wonderfully welcoming, awakes to find himself stretched out on her suicide's grave. More often, the dead stand in the way of the living, casting a dark shadow over their aspirations, as the phantom Cuthbert does in "Midsummer Madness."

In the first and longest story in the collection the stone dragon never comes to life; is function is to preside with adamantine hardness over the death of Rachel, one of the two women between whom the hero must choose. There is also a symbolic dragon—this time incorporated into a seal—in "The Manuscript of Francis Shackleby," which features a similarly fatal web of fate. The shorter stories in the volume are formed like poems in prose; the shortest of them all is the magnificently pointed "Roxana Runs Lunatick," although "Witch In-Grain" is only a little longer and the final item in the book, the stately "The Pageant of Ghosts," is a remarkably economical summation of all that has gone before. "The Lost Mistress" is effectively a triptych of prose-poems, and the accounts of "The Writings of Althea Swarthmoor" and "Excerpts from Pliny Witherton's Journal also a letter of Crystalla's" consist of documents of an extraordinarily flamboyant morbidity. The whole is, however, considerably greater than the sum of its parts; there is no other book in the English language quite like this one.

Gilchrist is forgotten now, but he was not without influence in his day. *The Stone Dragon and Other Tragic Romances* is almost certainly to be counted among the influences on M. P. Shiel, whose *Shapes in the Fire* must surely have borrowed a little from its example. Gilchrist's later work, which endeavoured to trap and record the vanishing spirit of the rural Peak District, attracted admiration from other "regional" writers, including Eden Phillpotts, who introduced a posthumous omnibus collection of Gilchrist's Peakland tales. That omnibus, *A Peakland Faggot*, contains only one story which has anything in common with Gilchrist's early work, and it serves to set that work in a very different context. In "The Panicle" a middle-aged woman tells the young man who is courting her daughter an extraordinarily vivid horror story about a monstrous parasite which has to be driven from the body of a young woman by roasting—but the tale is a test, and the young man's willingness to believe it is taken as plain evidence of his unworthiness as a potential husband. The message is clear: if Romance is essentially tragic, wise folk ought not to let it into their lives—or, indeed, into their literary endeavours. On the other hand, if Murray Gilchrist had stuck to the exploratory work of *The Stone Dragon* instead of lending himself to the strenuous cultivation of Derbyshire dialect, he might well warrant more than an abrupt footnote in the history of English literature.

—Brian Stableford

GILMAN, Charlotte (Anna) Perkins (Stetson)

Nationality: American. **Born:** Hartford, Connecticut, 3 July 1860. **Family:** Married 1) Walter Stetson in 1884 (divorced), one daughter; 2) George Houghton Gilman in 1900. **Died:** 17 August 1935.

HORROR, GHOST AND GOTHIC PUBLICATIONS

Short Stories

The Yellow Wallpaper. Boston, Small Maynard, 1899.
The Charlotte Perkins Gilman Reader: The Yellow Wallpaper and Other Fiction, edited by Ann J. Lane. New York, Pantheon, 1980.
The Yellow Wallpaper and Other Writings, edited by Lynne Sharon Schwartz. New York, Bantam, 1989.
"The Yellow Wall-Paper" and Selected Stories of Charlotte Perkins Gilman, edited by Denise D. Knight. Newark, Delaware, University of Delaware Press, 1994.
The Yellow Wall-Paper and Other Stories, edited by Robert Schulman. Oxford, Oxford University Press, 1995.

OTHER PUBLICATIONS

Novels

What Diantha Did. New York, Charlton, 1910; London, Unwin, 1912.
The Crux. New York, Charlton, 1911.
Moving the Mountain. New York, Charlton, 1911.
Herland. New York, Pantheon, and London, Women's Press, 1979.
Benigna Machiavelli. Santa Barbara, California, Bandanna Books, 1994.

Short Stories

Herland and Selected Stories, edited by Barbara H. Solomon. New York, Signet, 1992.

Poetry

In This Our World. Oakland, California, McCombs and Vaughan, 1893; London, Unwin, 1895.
Suffrage Songs and Verses. New York, Charlton, 1911.

Other

A Clarion Call to Redeem the Race! Mt. Lebanon, New York, Shaker Press, 1890.
Women and Economics. Boston, Small Maynard, 1898; London, Putnam, 1905.
Concerning Children. Boston, Small Maynard, 1900; London, Putnam, 1901.
The Home, Its Work and Influence. New York, McClure Phillips, 1903; London, Heinemann, 1904.
Human Work. New York, McClure Phillips, 1904.
The Punishment that Educates. Cooperstown, New York, Crist Scott, 1907.
The Man-Made World; or, Our Androcentric Culture. New York, Charlton, and London, T. F. Unwin, 1911.
His Religion and Hers: A Study of the Faith of Our Fathers and the Work of Our Mothers. New York and London, Century, 1923.
The Living of Charlotte Perkins Gilman (autobiography). New York, Appleton-Century, 1935.
Charlotte Perkins Gilman: A Nonfiction Reader, edited by Larry Ceplair. New York, Columbia University Press, 1991.

The Diaries of Charlotte Perkins Gilman, edited by Denise D. Knight. Charlottesville, Virginia, University Press of Virginia, 1994.
A Journey from Within: The Love Letters of Charlotte Perkins Gilman, 1897-1900, edited by Mary A. Hill. Lewisburg, Pennsylvania, Bucknell University, 1995.

*

Critical Study: *Charlotte Perkins Gilman: The Woman and Her Work* by Sheryl L. Meyering, Ann Arbor, Michigan, UMI Research Press, 1989; *To "Herland" and Beyond: The Life and Work of Charlotte Perkins Gilman* by Ann J. Lane, New York, Pantheon, 1990.

*   *   *

A socialist feminist writer and lecturer of the early 20th century, best known for *Women and Economics* and for the utopian novel *Herland,* Charlotte Perkins Gilman wrote only one horror story, "The Yellow Wallpaper," but it is one of the lasting classics of the genre.

One of the first pieces of fiction she wrote, it was rejected by the *Atlantic Monthly* for, as the editor wrote to her, "I could not forgive myself if I made others as miserable as I have made myself!" In her posthumously published autobiography Gilman wrote, "The story was meant to be dreadful, and succeeded. I suppose he would have sent back one of Poe's on the same ground." It was published by the *New England Magazine* in January 1892, and subsequently published as a short book, as well as being reprinted in many anthologies.

Based on her own experiences with depression, and the "rest cure" treatment she received from the fashionable specialist in women's nervous disorders, Dr. S. Weir Mitchell, which came close to driving her mad, "The Yellow Wallpaper" is narrated by a woman who is kept in seclusion by her well-meaning physician husband, ordered to "rest" for her health. She becomes obsessed by the hideous, patterned yellow wallpaper of her bedroom, eventually catching glimpses of a woman "creeping" behind it, struggling to escape, and finally coming to believe that she herself has escaped from the pattern, and is content to creep endlessly around the room, mindlessly content.

Gilman wrote all her fictions with a didactic purpose, and "The Yellow Wallpaper," although so different in other ways (the only story without a happy ending, and probably the most intensely personal she ever wrote) also had its non-literary purpose, according to Gilman. Readers have always responded to the powerfully captured image of madness, the inherent creepiness of the woman who creeps behind the hideous pattern. It became an immediate classic of the macabre (William Dean Howells and H. P. Lovecraft were among the many who praised it), but was only rediscovered as a specifically feminist story—demonstrating the cost to women of enforced passivity and confinement, of letting others control their lives—after its reprinting by The Feminist Press in 1973.

Never one to see herself as a writer of high literature, nor to be content with merely providing a powerfully spooky read, Gilman explained that the "real purpose" of the story was "to reach Dr. S. Weir Mitchell, and convince him of the error of his ways." Although he did not respond to the copy she sent him, years later she was told by a friend of a friend of his that he had changed his treatment since reading "The Yellow Wallpaper." In her autobiography she wrote, "If that is a fact, I have not lived in vain."

—Lisa Tuttle

GODWIN, William

Pseudonym: Edward Baldwin. **Nationality:** British. **Born:** Wisbech, Cambridgeshire, 3 March 1756. **Education:** Hoxton College, London. **Family:** Married 1) the writer Mary Wollstonecraft in 1797 (died 1797), two children, including the writer Mary Wollstonecraft Shelley; 2) Mary Jane Clairmont in 1801, one son, and one son and one daughter from a previous marriage. **Career:** Preacher, Yarmouth and Lowestoft, 1777; minister, Ware, Hertfordshire, 1778-79, and Stowmarket, Suffolk, 1779-82; prolific contributor, *English Review, New Annual Register* and *Political Herald*, 1780s; wrote three anonymous hack novels in the space of a year, 1784, but then abandoned fiction for a decade; became a celebrated political philosopher and novelist, 1790s; bookseller and publisher (and pseudonymous author) of children's books from 1805; suffered poverty in later life. **Died:** 7 April 1836.

HORROR, GHOST AND GOTHIC PUBLICATIONS

Novels

Things as They Are; or, The Adventures of Caleb Williams. London, Crosby, 3 vols., 1794; Baltimore, Rice, 1795; as *Caleb Williams*, edited by David McCracken, London, Oxford University Press, 1970.
St. Leon: A Tale of the Sixteenth Century. London, Robinson, 4 vols., 1799; Alexandria, Virginia, Thomas, 1801.

OTHER PUBLICATIONS

Novels

Italian Letters; or, The History of Count de St. Julian (anonymous). London, Robinson, 1784.
Damon and Delia: A Tale (anonymous). London, Hookham, 1784.
Imogen: A Pastoral Romance, from the Ancient British (anonymous). London, Lane, 1784.
Fleetwood; or, The New Man of Feeling. London, Phillips, 3 vols., 1805.
Mandeville: A Tale of the Seventeenth Century in England. Edinburgh, Constable, 3 vols., 1817.
Cloudesley: A Novel. London, Colburn, 3 vols., 1830.
Deloraine. London, Bentley, 3 vols., 1833.

Plays

Antonio: A Tragedy in Five Acts. N.p., 1800.
Faulkener: A Tragedy. N.p., 1807.

Other

Sketches of History in Six Sermons. London, Cadell, 1784.
History of the Internal Affairs of the United Provinces from the Year 1780 to the Commencement of Hostilities in June 1787. London, Robinson, 1787.
The English Peerage; or, a View of the Ancient and Present State of the English Nobility. London, Robinson, 3 vols., 1790.

An Enquiry Concerning Political Justice, and Its Influence on General Virtue and Happiness. London, Robinson, 2 vols., 1793; 2nd edition, 1796; 3rd edition, 1798.
The Enquirer: Reflections on Education, Manners and Literature. London, Robinson, 1797; revised edition, 1823.
Memoirs of the Author of a Vindication of the Rights of Woman. London, Johnson and Robinson, 1798.
Life of Geoffrey Chaucer . . . including Memoirs of John of Gaunt . . . with Sketches of England in the Fourteenth Century. London, Phillips, 2 vols., 1803.
Essay on Sepulchres. London, Miller, 1809.
The Lives of Edward and John Philips. London, Longman, 1815.
Letter of Advice to a Young American. London, Godwin, 1818.
Of Population. London, Longman, 1820.
History of the Commonwealth of England. London, Colburn, 4 vols., 1824-28.
Thoughts on Man, His Nature, Productions, and Discoveries. London, Effingham Wilson, 1831.
Lives of the Necromancers. London, Mason, 1834.
Essays, Never Before Published, by the Late William Godwin. London, King, 1873.

Other for Children as Edward Baldwin

Fables, Ancient and Modern. London, Godwin, 2 vols., 1805.
The History of England. London, Godwin, 1806.
The Pantheon; or, Ancient History of the Gods of Greece and Rome. London, Godwin, 1806.
History of Rome. London, Godwin, 1809.
Outlines of English Grammar. London, Godwin, 1810.
Outlines of English History . . . for the Use of Children from Four to Eight Years of Age. London, Godwin, 1814.
History of Greece. London, Godwin, 1822.

Editor, *Posthumous Works of the Author of a Vindication of the Rights of Woman.* London, Johnson, 4 vols., 1798.

*

Manuscript Collections: Forster Collection of the Victoria and Albert Museum, London; Bodleian Library, Oxford.

Critical Studies: *William Godwin: A Biographical Study* by George Woodcock, London, Porcupine Press, 1946; *A Fantasy of Reason: The Life and Thought of William Godwin* by Don Locke, London, Routledge, 1980; *William Godwin* by Peter H. Marshall, New Haven, Connecticut, Yale University Press, 1984; *The Godwins and the Shelleys: The Biography of a Family* by William St. Clair, New York, Norton, and London, Faber, 1989.

*   *   *

William Godwin was one of the foremost social and political theorists of his day, perhaps the most influential English importer of the French philosophy of progress and the aesthetic doctrines of Romanticism. He was the husband of the pioneering feminist Mary Wollstonecraft and the father of Mary Shelley. He turned to novel writing in a spirit of experiment, desiring to dramatize and popularize some of the theses laid out in *An Enquiry Concerning the Principles of Political Justice*. Although the novel nowadays known as *Caleb Williams* is set in the present and has no supernatural embellishments it nevertheless borrowed many elements of the fashionable Gothic fiction which was rapidly approaching the height of its popularity (Mrs. Radcliffe's *The Mysteries of Udolpho* was issued in the same year).

Although the plan for *Caleb Williams* was designed back-to-front, beginning with the persecution and then constructing its rationale, the novel had perforce to be written (and has, of course, read) forwards. The eponymous hero's misfortunes begin when he finds proof that his employer, the seemingly-benevolent but secretive Fernando Falkland, once committed murder. When he confesses his discovery Caleb unleashes upon himself a sustained campaign of persecution from which no escape seems to be possible, no matter how hard he tries. In the course of this harassment Falkland comes to seem an altogether paradoxical figure—an important prototype of the smoothest and most enigmatic kind of Gothic villain. The account of Caleb's imprisonment and exile is a calculated indictment of the British criminal justice system, whose horrific element is a powerful spice, but the novel is primarily fascinating for the remarkable sense of paranoia developed therein. This was, of course, partly a product of the artifice by which Godwin conducted his step-by-step explanation of the source of Caleb's predetermined troubles. (*Caleb Williams* must have been one of the earliest novels to be planned out in scrupulous detail before a word was written rather than made up as the author went along.)

Caleb Williams includes a number of philosophical dialogues in which the criminals into whose company Caleb is thrust explain and justify their predatory lives, providing a kind of gloss on the lurid accounts of criminal activity provided by such ever-popular agencies as broadside ballads and the Newgate Calendar. As well as providing a template for the sub-genre of "political Gothics," therefore, it laid down a useful precedent for the crime-fiction genre subsequently developed by Bulwer Lytton and Harrison Ainsworth. It was a great success, to the extent that the publishers reinstated in the later editions of 1795 the combative preface they had not dared to print in 1794.

In the apologetic preface to an 1831 edition of his second novel, *St. Leon*, Godwin observed that he had been urgently solicited to follow up the success of his first, but had long remained in a state of "diffidence and irresolution" for lack of a new idea. What he eventually produced was a longer and far more orthodox Gothic tale following the adventures of a dissolute French nobleman, who takes to farming after gambling away his inheritance but loses everything to a caprice of nature. After giving shelter to a fugitive alchemist, however, he obtains the secret of the philosophers' stone, which enables him to make gold from base metal and prolong his youth indefinitely. Alas, these gifts alienate him from his family and, by measured degrees, from society in general, so that be becomes an unhappy outcast eternally bothered by suspicion, envy and exploitation. The plot presumably contains an element of wish-fulfilment fantasy—Godwin was notoriously inept with money, perpetually on the brink of financial ruin—and also, not surprisingly, an element of sour grapes in its firm assertion that happiness cannot be bought.

St. Leon prompted a sharp satire in *St. Godwin: A Tale of the Sixteenth, Seventeenth and Eighteenth Century* (1800) by "Count Reginald de Saint Leon" (Edward du Bois)—which pioneered the sub-genre of Gothic parody carried forward by the comical *Tales*

of Terror (falsely attributed to its target, Matthew Gregory Lewis)—but it failed to recapitulate the success of its predecessor. It is, however, a significant novel in several respects. In its flirtation with Rosicrucian mysticism it anticipates Bulwer Lytton's *Zanoni* and further compounded the influence of Godwin on that writer (whose *Eugene Aram* was based on a case which Godwin had contemplated using as the basis for a book). It also provided inspiration for the explanatory phase of *Frankenstein* which Mary Shelley composed, *Caleb Williams*-fashion, as a prelude to the scene established as a focal point by her famous dream. Although the idea of the elixir of life had always had something of a bad press in admonitory literary fantasies, it was *St. Leon* which provided the definitive account of the downside of extended life—a sceptical account whose main features continue to recur in many 20th-century works by writers blithely unaware of the precedent. Charles Maturin's *Melmoth the Wanderer* is a much more powerful work, but it owes a considerable debt to the inspiration of *St. Leon*. *Caleb Williams* is certainly the better-written as well as the more philosophically interesting of Godwin's novels, but it is a pity that the later novel has almost vanished from sight while the earlier has been so carefully preserved.

Godwin's political ideas were radical in their day, and might seem equally radical today were they not so oddly ill-mixed. He contrived to be both a puritan of sorts and an anarchist of sorts, although such a combination now seems oxymoronic. His utopian faith in progress played a significant role in the inspiration of T. R. Malthus's essays on population, which set out to prove them illusory, and Malthus's criticisms have worn much better than the hopes they sought to devastate, but Godwin's ardent championship of rationalism still entitles him to a place of privilege in the intellectual hierarchy of the Enlightenment. He deserves credit for writing the only two Gothic novels which were solidly and stridently aligned on the side of Reason rather than set anxiously against it.

—Brian Stableford

GOLDING, (Sir) William (Gerald)

Nationality: British. **Born:** St. Columb Minor, Cornwall, 19 September 1911. **Education:** Marlborough Grammar School; Brasenose College, Oxford, B.A. 1935. **Military Service:** Served in the Royal Navy, 1940-45. **Family:** Married Ann Brookfield in 1939; one son and one daughter. **Career:** Writer, actor and producer in small theatre companies, 1934-40; schoolmaster, Bishop Wordsworth's School, Salisbury, Wiltshire, 1945-61; visiting professor, Hollins College, Virginia, 1961-62. **Awards:** James Tait Black Memorial prize, 1980; Booker prize, 1980; Nobel Prize for Literature, 1983. M.A.: Oxford University, 1961; D.Litt.: University of Sussex, Brighton, 1970; University of Kent, Canterbury, 1974; University of Warwick, Coventry, 1981; the Sorbonne, Paris, 1983; Oxford University, 1983; LL.D.: University of Bristol, 1984. Honorary Fellow, Brasenose College, 1966. Fellow, 1955, and Companion of Literature, 1984, Royal Society of Literature. C.B.E. (Commander, Order of the British Empire), 1966. Knighted, 1988. **Died:** 19 June 1993.

HORROR, GHOST AND GOTHIC PUBLICATIONS

Novels

Lord of the Flies. London, Faber, 1954; New York, Coward McCann, 1955.
Pincher Martin. London, Faber, 1956; as *The Two Deaths of Christopher Martin,* New York, Harcourt Brace, 1957.
The Spire. London, Faber, and New York, Harcourt Brace, 1964.

OTHER PUBLICATIONS

Novels

The Inheritors. London, Faber, 1955; New York, Harcourt Brace, 1962.
Free Fall. London, Faber, 1959; New York, Harcourt Brace, 1960.
The Pyramid. London, Faber, and New York, Harcourt Brace, 1967.
Darkness Visible. London, Faber, and New York, Farrar Straus, 1979.
Rites of Passage. London, Faber, and New York, Farrar Straus, 1980.
The Paper Men. London, Faber, and New York, Farrar Straus, 1984.
Close Quarters. London, Faber, and New York, Farrar Straus, 1987.
Fire Down Below. London, Faber, and New York, Farrar Straus, 1989.
To The Ends of the Earth (omnibus; includes *Rites of Passage, Close Quarters, Fire Down Below*). London, Faber, 1991.
The Double Tongue. London, Faber, and New York, Farrar Straus, 1995.

Short Stories

The Scorpion God: Three Short Novels. London, Faber, 1971; New York, Harcourt Brace, 1972.

Plays

The Brass Butterfly, adaptation of his story "Envoy Extraordinary" (produced London, 1958). London, Faber, 1958; Chicago, Dramatic Publishing Company, n.d.

Radio Plays: *Miss Pulkinhorn,* 1960; *Break My Heart,* 1962.

Poetry

Poems. London, Macmillan, 1934; New York, Macmillan, 1935.

Other

The Hot Gates and Other Occasional Pieces. London, Faber, 1965; New York, Harcourt Brace, 1966.
Talk: Conversations with William Golding, with Jack I. Biles. New York, Harcourt Brace, 1970.
A Moving Target (essays). London, Faber, and New York, Farrar Straus, 1982.

Nobel Lecture. Leamington Spa, Warwickshire, Sixth Chamber, 1984.
An Egyptian Journal. London, Faber, 1985.

*

Film Adaptations: *Lord of the Flies*, 1963, 1990.

Bibliograpy: *William Golding: A Bibliography* by R. A. Gekoski and P. A. Grogan, London, Deutsch, 1994.

Critical Studies (selection): *William Golding* by Samuel Hynes, New York, Columbia University Press, 1964; *William Golding: A Critical Study* by James R. Baker, New York, St. Martin's Press, 1965; *The Art of William Golding* by Bernard S. Oldsey and Stanley Weintraub, New York, Harcourt Brace, 1965; *William Golding* by Bernard F. Dick, New York, Twayne, 1967; *William Golding: A Critical Study* by Mark Kinkead-Weekes and Ian Gregor, London, Faber, 1967, New York, Harcourt Brace, 1968; *William Golding* by Leighton Hodson, Edinburgh, Oliver and Boyd, 1969, New York, Putnam, 1971; *The Novels of William Golding* by Howard S. Babb, Columbus, Ohio State University Press, 1970; *William Golding: The Dark Fields of Discovery* by Virginia Tiger, London, Calder and Boyars, and Atlantic Highlands, New Jersey, Humanities Press, 1974; *William Golding* by Stephen Medcalf, London, Longman, 1975; *William Golding: Some Critical Considerations* edited by Jack I. Biles and Robert O. Evans, Louisville, University Press of Kentucky, 1978; *Of Earth and Darkness: The Novels of William Golding* by Arnold Johnston, Columbia, University of Missouri Press, 1980; *A View from the Spire: William Golding's Later Novels* by Don Crompton, Oxford, Blackwell, 1985; *William Golding: The Man and His Books: A Tribute on His 75th Birthday* edited by John Carey, London, Faber, 1986, New York, Farrar Straus, 1987; *William Golding: A Structural Reading of His Fiction* by Philip Redpath, London, Vision Press, 1986; *The Novels of William Golding* by Stephen Boyd, Brighton, Sussex, Harvester Press, and New York, St. Martin's Press, 1988; *William Golding* by James Gindin, London, Macmillan, and New York, St. Martin's Press, 1988; *William Golding Revisited: A Collection of Original Essays* edited by B. L. Chakoo, New Delhi, Arnold, 1989; *The Modern Allegories of William Golding* by L. L. Dickson, Tampa, University of South Florida Press, 1990; *William Golding* by Kevin McCarron, Plymouth, England, Northcote House, 1994.

*   *   *

William Golding was one of Britain's few recipients of the Nobel Prize for Literature in recent decades. His first novel, *Lord of the Flies,* always remained his best known—it is a set text in many British schools—and has been filmed twice. Ostensibly a "desert-island story," about the adventures of boy-castaways, it takes its cue from R. M. Ballantyne's Victorian boys' book *The Coral Island* (1858), reversing many of the values and perspectives of that minor imperial classic. It is also, marginally, a science-fiction novel (the air-crash which maroons the schoolboys on their idyllic island has been caused by a World War III aerial battle) but the original framing narrative about a near-future global war was trimmed away in the editing process which transformed Golding's lengthy manuscript into the tight psychological thriller that we know. From our present perspective, we may view it more usefully as a horror novel: a chillingly memorable treatment of the "beast within." Certainly the narrative rises to a horrifying pitch, as the boys revert to primitive ways and begin to hunt each other down. Humanity's fallen nature, our ever-present capacity for evil—symbolized here by the ghastly totem of a pig's head on a stick (the "lord of the flies" of the title)—was to remain Golding's principal theme throughout his distinguished career.

That theme is very evident in his second and perhaps greatest book, *The Inheritors*—although this profoundly moving tale, about the death of the last family of Neanderthals at the hands of the incoming Cro-Magnons (i.e. ourselves) some 30,000 years ago, is clearly a work of science fiction rather than supernatural or psychological horror. It was in his third novel, *Pincher Martin*, that Golding was to make his closest pass by the supernatural—and thereby to achieve his most extreme tale of terror.

The story begins: "He was struggling in every direction, he was the centre of the writhing and kicking knot of his own body. There was no up or down, no light and no air." Although it opens like yet another adventure story, *Pincher Martin* may be read as a Posthumous Fantasy—that is, a tale not so much of the afterlife as of the very moment of death. This useful label was coined by the critic John Clute; in his review of J. G. Ballard's *The Unlimited Dream Company* (*Foundation* no. 19, June 1980), Clute wrote: "What I'd like to designate the posthumous fantasy, though a better term may well be forthcoming, closely resembles stories like Ambrose Bierce's 'An Occurrence at Owl Creek Bridge,' or Conrad Aiken's 'Mr. Arcularis,' stories where men at the literal point of death escape into an imagined alternative to that death, only gradually to realize that this dream world is fading out, generally to the tune of some insistent horrifying rhythm, perhaps that of the failing heart." Golding's novel fits this paradigm exactly.

Its protagonist, Lieutenant Christopher Martin (known as "Pincher" to his naval fellows), is a British sailor who is on the point of drowning in the Atlantic Ocean. This is during World War II, and his ship has just been torpedoed by a German U-boat. We seem to enter Martin's consciousness and to follow his thoughts and feelings in minute detail as he struggles against the cold sea. For the first 20 pages of the novel he is adrift, flailing madly, gulping salt water, his mind a confusion of memories, hopes and regrets. No rescue comes, but he spies a small scrap of land, a solitary rock strewn with seaweed, and it proves to be his (temporary) salvation. He hauls himself ashore on this "single point of rock, peak of a mountain range, one tooth set in the ancient jaw of a sunken world, projecting through the inconceivable vastness of the whole ocean"—and there he remains for the duration of the novel: a man alone, symbol of all the terror of the human condition.

Little happens, but the writing is extraordinarily vivid. As in other books by Golding, we become privileged voyeurs, spying on God's preternaturally bright creation. It is as though we are witnessing everything through the effects of a mind-enhancing drug. We follow poor Pincher Martin as he climbs to the summit of his barren islet, as he searches for food and drink and shelter, and as he stares into the abyss of himself. He is a sort of pared-down, minimal Robinson Crusoe. He holds imaginary conversations with old acquaintances, fights off madness, and suffers occasional de-

lusions of grandeur: "'I am Atlas. I am Prometheus.' He felt himself loom, gigantic on the rock." But in the end he can find no peace, no heavenly grace. The entire hallucination of survival by naked will-power crumbles, and he reverts to what he is: a drowning sailor, soon to be dead.

Much of Golding's work is allegorical in nature and takes the form of the historical novel, or science fiction, or (as in the case of *Pincher Martin*) metaphysical fantasy. Another of his finest novels is *The Spire*, which concerns the driving obsession of a medieval churchman who wishes to build a 400-foot cathedral spire—ostensibly to the greater glory of God, but possibly to the advantage of the Devil. Like *Pincher Martin*, but more in terms of psychological horror than of the supernatural, it deals with the ever-present problem of the evil which dwells in the human heart.

Golding was one of the century's most powerful writers. His "messages" may seem simple, even simplistic, when summarized in bald critical outline, but in fact they are always complexly articulated and stunningly realized on the page. He was a writer who unveiled inward abysses for our contemplation.

—David Pringle

GORDON, John (William)

Nationality: British. **Born:** Jarrow, County Durham, 19 November 1925. **Education:** Wisbech Grammar School, Cambridgeshire. **Military Service:** Royal Navy, 1943-47. **Family:** Married Sylvia Ellen Young in 1954; one son and one daughter. **Career:** Reporter, 1947-49, and sub-editor, 1949-51, *Isle of Ely and Wisbech Advertiser*; chief reporter and sub-editor, *Bury Free Press*, Bury St. Edmunds, Suffolk, 1951-58; sub-editor, *Western Evening Herald*, Plymouth, 1958-62; sub-editor and columnist, *Eastern Evening News*, Norwich, 1962-73; sub-editor, *Eastern Daily Press*, Norwich, 1973-85. **Address:** 99 George Borrow Road, Norwich, Norfolk NR4 7HU, England.

HORROR, GHOST AND GOTHIC PUBLICATIONS

Novels

The Giant under the Snow. London, Hutchinson, 1968; New York, Harper, 1970.
The House on the Brink. London, Hutchinson, 1970; New York, Harper, 1971.
The Ghost on the Hill. London, Kestrel, 1976; New York, Viking Press, 1977.
The Waterfall Box. London, Kestrel, 1978.
The Edge of the World. London, Hardy, and New York, Atheneum, 1983.
The Quelling Eye. London, Bodley Head, 1986.
The Grasshopper. London, Bodley Head, 1987.
Ride the Wind. London, Bodley Head, 1989.
Blood Brothers. London, Signpost, 1989.
Secret Corridor. London, Blackie, 1990.
Gilray's Ghost. London, Walker, 1995.

Short Stories

The Spitfire Grave and Other Stories. London, Kestrel, 1979.
Catch Your Death and Other Ghost Stories, illustrated by Jeremy Ford. London, Hardy, 1984.
The Burning Baby and Other Ghosts. London, Walker, 1992; New York, Candlewick, 1993.

OTHER PUBLICATIONS

Other

Ordinary Seaman (memoir). London, Walker, 1992.

*   *   *

John Gordon writes fantasy, ghost and supernatural stories, aimed at—or at least marketed for—young-adult audiences but of considerable general interest. He has a well-developed ability to convey a sense of uncanny menace, which extends also to those Gordon books which are more readily classified as fantasy.

For example, his first novel *The Giant under the Snow* offers a conventional-seeming conflict of children (under the aegis of a good witch who grants the power of flight) against a magic-wielding warlord who long ago invaded England in a longship. But although this is a children's rather than a young adult story, the warlord's "leather men" minions—faceless, mummified but fearfully agile—are most effectively horrid. Also disquieting is the revelation that danger centers not in the wild woods but in the modern city where the children live and which the warlord has made his own. Far from representing safety, the city's walls are menacing occult barriers. Outside, the giant of the title is both a burial mound and an elemental force of English landscape, a Green Man who at the climax rises and walks. *Ride the Wind* is a slightly less inventive sequel in which the killed warlord returns.

Gordon's second novel *The House on the Brink* established him as an expert in creating serious unease through spare descriptions and laconic dialogue. The woman living in the lonely fenland house is apparently being persecuted or stalked by something resembling an old, black, wet log—inanimate, but inexorably moving or being moved through the countryside, its trail exuding an aura of dislocation and wrongness which rises from the pages like a stench. Investigation by two younger characters (who prove to have a trace of psychic sensitivity) slowly shifts the focus of wrongness from the log to the widowed woman whose neurotic obsessions about good and evil are being projected on to the bleak fen landscape, and who herself is unknowingly moving the thing by night. The finale unravels complex knots of emotion. Supernatural influence is not, however, dispelled, for the sinister log which has catalysed the action proves to be a sea-changed, mummified corpse that links with grim local legends of King John and the Wash.

The Ghost on the Hill repeats the previous book's precise handling of early, painful teenage relationships and also darker adult ones. A university boy and his still all too attractive and flirtatious mother return to the village of her birth, where a small cruelty of her own adolescence once had deadly consequences. An ambiguous witch-figure lurks, seemingly attended by dark birds. The newcomers' presence disrupts the village's emotional balance, and ultimately their Midsummer's Eve party generates an intensity of guilt and shame that wakes the ghost—though not with the expected vengefulness. Torrid adolescent emotion, complicated by rustic-English class barriers, likewise structures *The Waterfall Box . . .* whose alchemical McGuffin, created by a past magus and sought by an unpleasant modern one, provides a *deus ex machina* finale rather than genuinely informing the story as a whole.

The Edge of the World is more of a fantasy, in which slightly younger children penetrate "just beyond the edge of things" into an alternate Norfolk of hideous deserts. With its horrific but implausible monsters—insectile with horse-skull heads, riding flying machines—this place seems a routinely clichéd fantasyland. But there are hints that it's a country of the mind, opened up or even created by old hatred and jealousy, and containing a palace which in English history was planned but never built. *The Quelling Eye* is another quirky supernatural thriller which makes use of the old superstition of the Evil Eye and plays ambiguously with the notion of human transformation into bird form, and the resulting power of flight. Two children experience being carried off by an oversized hawk . . . but this central episode seems to occur in a "dreamtime" outside the realm of common sense. *The Grasshopper* is a straight novel told with interesting obliqueness, with one tiny knot of mystery at its core: the secret of how the title's giant, and perhaps impossible, leaping automaton may be ridden.

Most recently, *Gilray's Ghost* ambitiously combines a strange and eclectic variety of narrative elements. There is supernatural horror, grimmer than ever and leading to actual deaths. The story revolves around the pyramidal tomb of a very nasty revenant who legendarily preys on young girls, and who whenever blood is spilled can possess both boys and men with a killing frenzy. Two sinisterly eccentric modern occultists plan to summon him for their own purposes. But, as in *The Grasshopper*, there's also a vein of comedy, sexual and otherwise: when the occultists plot to obtain their victim's body fluid for the ritual, we expect bloodshed and then find her merely maneuvered into using a bedroom chamber-pot. Science fiction enters the mix with the extraordinary and clownish Gilray himself. His weird (and sometimes distressingly babyish) conversation is largely the jargon of his homeland in the 22nd century; his walking-stick is crammed with advanced microelectronics; and his journeying through time has provided foreknowledge of tragedy. The villains meet a suitably grisly come-uppance. As a whole, though, the book does not quite seem to jell.

The author's fine short supernatural stories, collected in *The Spitfire Grave*, *Catch Your Death* and *The Burning Baby*, feature a range of interesting and often strikingly memorable manifestations, hauntings and apparitions. An example is the Burning Baby itself, a blazing and vengeful spirit to which a murdered girl gives birth in fire. *Catch Your Death* was deservedly recommended as a highlight collection of 1984 in Stephen Jones's and Kim Newman's *Horror: 100 Best Books* (1988).

John Gordon, as he has said himself, writes best about borderlands. East Anglia's fen country, where he lives and where water and land interpenetrate with almost fractal complexity, is his favourite setting. The similarly confused border between child and adult sexuality is his most effective generator of tension, both natural and supernatural—for adolescent turmoil is also legendarily the power-source for poltergeists.

—David Langford

GORMAN, Ed(ward Joseph)

Pseudonym: Daniel Ransom. **Nationality:** American. **Born:** Cedar Rapids, Iowa, 29 November 1941. **Education:** Coe College, Iowa, 1962-65. **Family:** Married Carol Gorman in 1982; one son and one stepson. **Career:** Worked in advertising as a writer and freelance writer, 20 years; since 1989 full-time writer. Co-founder and editor, *Mystery Scene* magazine. **Awards:** International Horror Critics Guild award; Private Eye Writers of America Shamus award; Western Writers of America Spur Award. **Agent:** Matt Bialer, William Morris Agency, 1325 Avenue of the Americas, New York, NY 10019. **Address:** 3601 Skylark Lane SE, Cedar Rapids, Iowa 52403, USA.

HORROR, GHOST AND GOTHIC PUBLICATIONS

Novels (series: Robert Payne)

I, Werewolf (for children). Boston, Little Brown, 1992; London, Fantail, 1993.
Shadow Games. London, Blake, 1993.
Wolf Moon. New York, Fawcett, 1993.
Blood Moon (Payne). New York, St. Martin's Press, 1994; as *Blood Red Moon*, London, Headline, 1994.
Cold Blue Midnight. London, Headline, 1995; New York, St. Martin's Press, 1996.
Hawk Moon (Payne). London, Headline, 1995; New York, St. Martin's Press, 1996.
Black River Falls. London, Headline, 1996.
Runner in the Dark. London, Headline, 1996.
Cage of Night. Atlanta, Georgia, White Wolf, 1996.

Novels as Daniel Ransom

Daddy's Little Girl. New York, Zebra, 1985.
Toys in the Attic. New York, Zebra, 1986.
Night Caller. New York, Zebra, 1987.
The Forsaken. New York, St. Martin's Press, 1988.
The Babysitter. New York, St. Martin's Press, 1989.
Nightmare Child. New York, St. Martin's Press, 1990.
The Serpent's Kiss. New York, Dell, 1992.
The Long Midnight. New York, Dell, 1993.

Short Stories

Prisoners and Other Stories. Baltimore, Maryland, CD Publications, 1992.
Dark Whispers. Eugene, Oregon, Mystery Scene Press, 1993.
Cages. Los Gatos, California, Deadline Press, 1995.
Moonchasers and Other Stories. New York, Forge, 1996.

Other

Editor, with Martin H. Greenberg, *Stalkers*. Arlington Heights, Illinois, Dark Harvest, 1989; London, Severn House, 1991.
Editor, with Martin H. Greenberg, *Predators*. New York, Roc, and London, Severn House, 1993.
Editor, with Martin H. Greenberg, *Night Screams*. New York, Roc, 1996.

OTHER PUBLICATIONS

Novels

Rough Cut. New York, St. Martin's Press, 1985; London, Hale, 1987.
New, Improved Murder. New York, St. Martin's Press, 1986.
Murder Straight Up. New York, St. Martin's Press, 1986.
Murder in the Wings. New York, St. Martin's Press, 1986.
Guild. New York, Evans, 1987; Bath, Avon, Chivers, 1989.
Murder on the Aisle. New York, St. Martin's Press, 1987.
The Autumn Dead. New York, St. Martin's Press, 1987; London, Allison and Busby, 1989.
Death Ground. New York, Evans, 1988; Bath, Avon, Chivers, 1990.
Several Deaths Later. New York, St. Martin's Press, 1988.
Blood Game. New York, Evans, 1989; Bath, Avon, Chivers, 1991.
Grave's Retreat. New York, Doubleday, 1989.
A Cry of Shadows. New York, St. Martin's Press, 1990.
Night Kills. New York, Ballantine, 1990.
Night of Shadows. New York, Doubleday, 1990.
What the Dead Men Say. New York, Evans, 1990.
Dark Trail. New York, Evans, 1991.
The Night Remembers. New York, St. Martin's Press, 1991.
The Sharpshooter. New York, Fawcett, 1994.
The Marilyn Tapes (as E. J. Gorman). New York, Forge, 1995.
The First Lady (as E. J. Gorman). New York, Forge, 1995.

Short Stories

The Best Western Short Stories of Ed Gorman, edited by Bill Pronzini and Martin H. Greenberg. Athens, Ohio University Press, 1992.
Gunslinger, and Nine Other Action-Packed Stories of the Wild West, edited by Martin H. Greenberg and Bill Pronzini. New York, Barricade Books, 1995.

Other

Editor, *Westeryear*. New York, Evans, 1988.
Editor, with Robert J. Randisi and Martin H. Greenberg, *Under the Gun*. New York, New American Library, 1990.
Editor, with Martin H. Greenberg, *Cat Crimes [II, III]*. New York, Fine, 1991-92.
Editor, with Martin H. Greenberg, *Invitation to Murder*. Arlington Heights, Illinois, Dark Harvest, 1991.
Editor, *Dark Crimes: Great Noir Fiction from the '40s to the '90s*. New York, Carroll and Graf, 1991.
Editor, with Martin H. Greenberg, *Solved*. New York, Carroll and Graf, 1991.
Editor, with Martin H. Greenberg, Larry Segriff, and Jon L. Breen, *The Fine Art of Murder: The Mystery Reader's Indispensable Companion*. New York, Carroll and Graf, 1993.
Editor, with Martin H. Greenberg. *Danger in D.C.: Cat Crimes in the Nation's Capital*. New York, Fine, 1993.
Editor, *Dark Crimes 2: Modern Masters of Noir*. New York, Carroll and Graf, 1993.
Editor, with Martin H. Greenberg and Bill Munster, *The Dean Koontz Companion*. New York, Berkley, and London, Headline, 1994.

Editor, with Martin H. Greenberg, *Feline and Famous: Cat Crimes Goes Hollywood*. New York, Fine, 1994.

Editor, *A Modern Treasury of Great Detective and Murder Mysteries*. New York, Carroll and Graf, 1994; London, Hale, 1995.

Editor, *Woman on the Beat: Stories of Women Police Officers*. New York, Gramercy Books, 1995.

Editor, with Martin H. Greenberg, *Cat Crimes Takes a Vacation*. New York, Fine, 1995.

Editor, with Larry Segriff and Martin H. Greenberg, *Murder Most Irish*. New York, Barnes and Noble, 1996.

*   *   *

Ed Gorman remains one of America's best-kept literary secrets, walking the narrow lines which separate a whole host of literary fields—western, crime, suspense, private eye, mystery, and even the occasional horror story. He made what reputation he has—and even that is grossly inadequate when one considers the quality of his work and the sheer quantity of it—primarily through a steady stream of novels and short stories which touch heavily on police-procedural and private-detective fiction, and psychological suspense. But these are merely the vehicles for what he really wants to talk about: people.

Gorman's people live in the constant shadow of "making it": they can see the towering twin monoliths of success and happiness but such luxuries remain forever out of their reach. And in his slow unfolding of their lives, Gorman has them take on three-dimensional qualities to an extent which puts him at the forefront of his field. Characters in Gorman's fiction are flawed and believable. He recognizes that the boundaries and touchstones which commonly denote goodness and badness are almost impossible to define, and he possesses that rare quality to be able to make his readers understand even the most heinous crime without necessarily condoning it. In short, the good guys have *off* days while the dyed-in-the-wool despicable villains have the occasional *on* one. There's God and the Devil in us all.

His short work, particularly his exemplary collections *Prisoners*, *Cages* and *Moonchasers*, introduces readers to the innumerable men and women, youths and children, who populate the American dream—past, present and future: the bars and the streets, the bus terminals and the dust-blown highways, the city tenements and the small-town front porches, and the isolated wilderness *between* the towns. Here are saints and sinners, killers and saviours . . . each containing just a few of their opposite's attributes: most notably, a young boy in an undetermined future who attempts to sell his deformed sister in order to give money to his mother so she can buy food ("Cages") and, in an equally futuristic setting, a "bounty hunter" who makes his living by rounding up empathic children and selling them to down-at-heel medics so that, simply by tethering the unfortunate children to patients, the doctors may perform intricate invasive surgery without anaesthetic ("Survival"). The pain must go somewhere, however, and it comes as no surprise that the children come off worst.

In "The Brasher Girl" (the inspiration for his novel *Cage of Night*), a creature travels to Earth from the depths of space and hides in an old well, there to exert its murderous will over anyone who happens by. In other stories, a 19th century executioner revisits a small town to do a job—and to experience once more an all-too-brief slice of his own salvation in the arms of a favourite whore ("Deathman"); a Confederate soldier in the closing stages of the American Civil War discovers an expression on a wounded man's face that calls into question everything they're fighting for ("The Face"); a man who contracted AIDS following a one-night-stand liaison away from home sets out to kill the woman who tainted him . . . and then confess all to his wife and children ("The Long Silence After"); and, in one of the most criminally unrecognized short stories of the past 20 or 30 years, a young itinerant worker becomes embroiled in a rooming-house dispute between an old man and his wife-beating neighbour ("Render Unto Caesar").

This ability to make the reader empathize—even sympathize—with his antagonists is Gorman's stock in trade. He carries it to even greater effect in his longer work, with the ensuing unpleasantness ever more graphically detailed, though never gratuitous. Nevertheless, one novel was considered by his agent to be so unremittingly bleak that Gorman was recommended he tone it down for publication. The result, *Shadow Games*, is a maelstrom of malicious evil and perverse manipulation that never lets up until the final few pages. The book is a fine testament to effort and determination—on the part of both Gorman and the novel's protagonist—and a savage indictment of the manipulative powers of the entertainment media.

Gorman's blurring of the differences and similarities between his pro- and antagonists reaches its most eloquent level in *The Marilyn Tapes*, a striking combination of political intrigue and mean-streets sassiness, which borrows elements from all the field's sub-genres. The novel features the most callous and inventive murderer since the serial killer in Lawrence Block's *The Long Walk* who Scotch-tapes his bound victim's mouth and nose and watches her suffocate slowly—except Gorman's killer is a *she* and works for the FBI.

Over the 1990s Gorman has been devoting more attention to dialogue—for which he has an unerring ear—honing his craft ever further while continuing to unleash quality work at a prolific rate. He has developed a mesmerizing cinematographic quality in his writing by using short chapters to heighten the speed and intensity of the action, particularly in a novel's denouement (most notably in *The Marilyn Tapes* and *Cold Blue Midnight*, where some chapters are less than one page in length). This attention to visual detail is borne out by the fact that several of his works have now been optioned for either TV or movie treatments. Not surprising: the puzzle is simply the time it's taken for people—both those in the entertainment industry and those browsing the book stores—to recognize Gorman's storytelling and characterization abilities.

Gorman is a voyeur: he watches, he sees and he remembers. In *Prisoners*, he prefaces each of the stories with a personal recollection as to what prompted him to write the tale. His brief intro to "The Long Silence After" is perhaps the most enlightening: "We kill so many people off in our stories that I worry we have no sense of real death, or the true spiritual cost of dying. In this story, I wanted to give death at least a little dominion."

—Peter Crowther

GRANT, Charles L(ewis)

Pseudonyms: Felicia Andrews; Steven Charles; Lionel Fenn; Simon Lake; Deborah Lewis; Geoffrey Marsh. **Nationality:** American. **Born:** Newark, New Jersey, 12 September 1942. **Education:** Trinity College, Hartford, Connecticut, B.A. 1964. **Military Service:** Served in the United States Army Military

Police, 1968-70: Bronze Star. **Family:** Married Debbie Voss in 1973; one son and one daughter. **Career:** English teacher, Toms River High School, New Jersey, 1964-70, Chester High School, New Jersey, 1970-72, and Mt. Olive High School, New Jersey, 1972-73; English and history teacher, Roxbury High School, New Jersey, 1974-75. Since 1975, freelance writer. Executive secretary, Science Fiction Writers of America, 1973-77. **Awards:** Nebula award, 1976, 1978; World Fantasy award, for nonfiction, 1980, for editing, 1983. **Agent:** Howard Morhaim Literary Agency, 175 Fifth Avenue, Suite 709, New York, NY 10010, USA.

HORROR, GHOST AND GOTHIC PUBLICATIONS

Novels (series: Oxrun Station; X-Files)

The Curse (as C. L. Grant). Canoga Park, California, Major, 1977.
The Hour of the Oxrun Dead. New York, Doubleday, 1977.
The Sound of Midnight (Oxrun). New York, Doubleday, 1978.
The Ravens of the Moon. New York, Doubleday, 1978; London, Sidgwick and Jackson, 1979.
The Last Call of Mourning (Oxrun). New York, Doubleday, 1979.
Quiet Night of Fear. New York, Berkley, 1981.
The Grave (Oxrun). New York, Popular Library, 1981.
The Bloodwind (Oxrun). New York, Popular Library, 1982.
The Soft Whisper of the Dead (Oxrun). West Kingston, Rhode Island, Donald Grant, 1982.
The Nestling. New York, Pocket, 1982; London, Hamlyn, 1983.
Night Songs. New York, Pocket Books, 1984.
The Tea Party. New York, Pocket Books, 1985; London, Raven, 1995.
The Long Night of the Grave (Oxrun). West Kingston, Rhode Island, Donald Grant, 1986.
The Orchard (Oxrun). New York, Tor, 1986; London, Macdonald, 1989.
The Pet. New York, Tor, 1986; London, Futura, 1987.
For Fear of the Night. New York, Tor, and London, Futura, 1988.
Dialing the Wind (Oxrun). New York, Tor, 1988.
In a Dark Dream. New York, Tor, 1989; London, New English Library, 1990.
Stunts. New York, Tor, 1990: London, New English Library, 1991.
Fire Mask (for children). New York, Bantam, 1991.
Something Stirs. New York, Tor, 1991; London, New English Library, 1992.
Raven. New York, Tor, and London, New English Library, 1993.
Jackals. New York, Tor Forge, 1994; London, New English Library, 1995.
Goblins (X-Files). New York, HarperPrism, 1994; London, HarperCollins, 1995.
Whirlwind (X-Files). New York, HarperPrism, and London, HarperCollins, 1995.
The Black Carousel (Oxrun). New York, Tor, 1995.

Novels as Felicia Andrews

River Witch. New York, Jove, 1979.
Moon Witch. New York, Jove, 1980.
Mountain Witch. New York, Jove, 1980.

Novels as Steven Charles (for children; series: Private School in all titles)

Nightmare Session. New York, Archway, 1986; London, Lightning, 1990.
Academy of Terror. New York, Archway, 1986; London, Lightning, 1990.
Witch's Eye. New York, Archway, 1986; London, Lightning, 1990.
Skeleton Key. New York, Archway, 1986; London, Lightning, 1990.
The Enemy Within. New York, Archway, 1987.
The Last Alien. New York, Archway, 1987.

Novels as Lionel Fenn (series: Diego; Kent Montana; Quest for the White Duck)

Blood River Down (Quest). New York, Tor, 1986.
Web of Defeat (Quest). New York, Tor, 1987.
Agnes Day (Quest). New York, Tor, 1987.
The Seven Spears of the W'dch'ck (Montana). New York, Tor, 1988.
Kent Montana and the Really Ugly Thing from Mars. New York, Ace, 1990.
Kent Montana and the Reasonably Invisible Man. New York, Ace, 1991.
Kent Montana and the Once and Future Thing. New York, Ace, 1991.
The Mark of the Moderately Vicious Vampire (Montana). New York, Ace, 1992.
668: The Neighbor of the Beast (Montana). New York, Ace, 1992.
Once Upon a Time in the East (Diego). New York, Ace, 1993.
By the Time I Get to Nashville (Diego). New York, Ace, 1994.
Time: The Semi-Final Frontier (Diego). New York, Ace, 1994.

Novels as Simon Lake (for children; series: Midnight Place in all titles)

Daughter of Darkness. New York, Bantam, 1992.
Something's Watching. New York, Bantam, 1993.
He Told Me To. New York, Bantam, 1993.
Death Cycle. New York, Bantam, 1993.

Novels as Deborah Lewis

Voices out of Time. New York, Zebra, 1977.
Eve of the Hound. New York, Zebra, 1977.

Novels as Geoffrey Marsh (series: Lincoln Blackthorne in all titles)

The King of Satan's Eyes. New York, Doubleday, 1984.
The Tail of the Arabian, Knight. New York, Doubleday, 1986.
The Patch of the Odin Soldier. New York, Doubleday, 1987.
The Fangs of the Hooded Demon. New York, Tor, 1988.

Short Stories

Tales from the Nightside: Dark Fantasy. Sauk City, Wisconsin, Arkham House, 1981; London, Futura, 1988.
A Glow of Candles and Other Stories. New York, Berkley, 1981.

Nightmare Seasons (Oxrun). New York, Doubleday, 1982; London, Futura, 1989.

Black Wine, with Ramsey Campbell; edited by Douglas E. Winter. Arlington Heights, Illinois, Dark Harvest, 1986.

The Dark Cry of the Moon (Oxrun). West Kingston, Rhode Island, Donald Grant, 1986.

Other

Editor, *Shadows [1]-10.* New York, Doubleday, 10 vols., 1978-87; vol. 1 as *Shadows II,* London, Headline, 1987; *Shadows 4* as *Shadows,* London, Headline, 1987.

Editor, *Nightmares.* Chicago, Playboy, 1979.

Editor, *Horrors.* New York, Playboy, 1981.

Editor, *Terrors.* New York, Playboy, 1982.

Editor, *The Dodd, Mead Gallery of Horror.* New York, Dodd Mead, 1983; as *Gallery of Horror,* London, Robson, 1983.

Editor, *Fears.* New York, Berkley, 1983.

Editor, *Midnight.* New York, Tor, 1985.

Editor, *The Chronicles of Greystone Bay:*
The First Chronicles of Greystone Bay. New York, Tor, 1985.
Doom City. New York, Tor, 1987.
The SeaHarp Hotel. New York, Tor, 1990.
In the Fog: The Final Chronicle of Greystone Bay. New York, Tor, 1993.

Editor, *Night Visions 2: All Original Stories.* Arlington Heights, Illinois, Dark Harvest, 1985; as *Night Visions: Dead Image,* New York, Berkley, 1987; as *Night Terrors,* London, Headline, 1987.

Editor, *After Midnight.* New York, Tor, 1986.

Editor, *The Best of Shadows.* New York, Doubleday, 1988.

Editor, *Final Shadows.* New York, Doubleday, 1991.

OTHER PUBLICATIONS

Novels

The Shadow of Alpha. New York, Berkley, 1976.
Ascension. New York, Berkley, 1977.
Legion. New York, Berkley, 1979.

Other

Editor, *Writing and Selling Science Fiction,* by the Science Fiction Writers of America. Cincinnati, Writer's Digest, 1976.

*   *   *

Although he began as a science-fiction writer (with three novels, 1976-79), Charles L. Grant has long been one of the mainstays of the horror field, with over 40 books published under half a dozen different bylines. There are also elements of the supernatural in the gothic romances he wrote under the name Deborah Lewis and romances as Felicia Andrews. He has long been characterized as the master of quiet horror, his work generally far more subtle and less inclined to the extremes to which the horror genre has sometimes been inclined.

Grant's first horror novel, *The Curse,* is an otherwise forgettable story of Indian magic and revenge that is noteworthy only because it demonstrated immediately the author's gift for creating likable, believable characters and placing them in extraordinary situ-

ations. *The Hour of the Oxrun Dead* introduced Grant's fictional Connecticut town, Oxrun Station. The protagonist is the wife of a police officer who was savagely murdered and mutilated. She discovers that he had run afoul of a mysterious cult that demands human sacrifices. In *The Sound of Midnight* a group of children play mysterious games that are recreations of ancient rituals to a still viable, malevolent entity. A young woman returns to her home town in *The Last Call of Mourning,* and during her visit her father apparently dies. But he's back a short while later, insisting she imagined the entire thing, and other residents of Oxrun Station seem to have similarly cheated death. A private investigator tries to track down a missing body in *The Grave* and discovers that an evil force is hunting him in turn. An unhappy woman attempts to put her life back together in *The Bloodwind,* but there's an evil presence in town that cloaks itself in the wind, and it has marked her as its next victim. These five early novels with a common setting all juxtapose the supernatural with suburbia, and Grant's careful restraint and understatement made them particularly effective in contrast to the work of most of his peers.

The Nestling was significantly more ambitious and moved to Wyoming. A rural community is already torn by internal dissension when new problems arise in the form of a winged predator that chooses victims from both sides of the dispute. A much longer novel than anything Grant had written previously, *The Nestling* provided ample room for a large cast of credible characters. *Night Songs* is set on a remote island and the evil originates under the ocean, but the effect is the same, a community menaced by an external danger, forced to set aside its own differences in order to survive.

There's a haunted house in *The Tea Party,* but not the conventional sort. Winterrest has an evil life of its own, can even change its shape to confound its victims. A young boy escapes death at the hands of a serial killer in *The Pet,* and discovers that even worse things hide in the darkness. Grant returned to Oxrun Station for *The Orchard,* in which a series of grotesque deaths and other bizarre phenomena spread out from an orchard to infect the nearby town. *For Fear of the Night* is a nicely controlled ghost story, more traditional than most of Grant's work. So also is *In a Dark Dream,* a particularly effective story that poses a delicate problem for a police officer after the release of a psychopathic killer. On the one hand he is sworn to uphold the law, but on the other, his daughter is experiencing precognitive visions of the man's future, which threatens both their lives. *Stunts* takes place around a Halloween season during which a madman plots his revenge.

Strange music disturbs the lives of four residents of Oxrun Station in *Dialing the Wind,* the weakest of Grant's later novels. A group of outcasts mourn the death of their leader in *Something Stirs,* but then grow horrified when a series of killings provides evidence that his spirit has returned from the grave to exact revenge on his enemies. *The Black Carousel,* also set in Oxrun Station, is an episodic novel about supernatural events surrounding the arrival of a travelling carnival and their effects on the local residents. It is one of Grant's best efforts and one of the outstanding works in the entire horror genre.

Grant also wrote three more conventional Oxrun Station novels for the specialty publisher, Donald Grant. *The Soft Whisper of the Dead* involves a vampire, *The Dark Cry of the Moon* features a werewolf, and a mummy stalks the Connecticut woods in *The Long Night of the Grave.* Although ostensibly pastiches, all three novels benefit from Grant's restrained treatment of the familiar horror cliches. As Lionel Fenn, Grant lampooned various horror themes in *The Mark of the Moderately Vicious Vampire, Kent Montana and the Reasonably Invisible Man, 668: The Neighbor of the Beast* and *Kent Montana and the Once and Future Thing.*

Grant wrote a number of young-adult horror novels as well, only one of which, *Fire Mask,* appeared under his own name. Avoiding the usual condescension of the form, Grant produced a tight thriller about a family curse involving spontaneous combustion. As Simon Lake he wrote four similar works. An evil monster preys on teenagers in *Something's Watching,* the new girl in town is a witch in *Daughter of Darkness,* a ghostly motorcyclist claims victims in *Death Cycle,* and an evil magician seizes control of children's minds in *He Told Me To.* As Steven Charles, Grant wrote the six-volume "Private School" series, in which a group of teenagers learns that aliens have replaced their teachers as part of their plan to invade Earth. The premise may be a bit forced but it certainly isn't comical as Grant chronicles the long struggle to thwart the invaders' plans. His young-adult fiction is particularly impressive because Grant doesn't write down to his audience, and provides stories that are engaging enough for adult readers as well.

Grant has also written two enjoyable X-Files novels, *Goblins* and *Whirlwind,* and a substantial body of short fiction, much of which is excellent. Some of the best stories appear in *Nightmare Seasons* and *Tales from the Nightside,* but many others remain uncollected. Of particular note are "Ellen, in Her Time" and "Come Dance With Me on My Pony's Grave." In addition to his career as a writer, Grant is one of the most respected editors in the field, most notably for the *Shadows* and *Greystone Bay* series of anthologies. Both as writer and editor, Grant has had a significant impact on the shape of modern horror fiction, and will likely be remembered as one of the major talents in the field.

—Don D'Ammassa

GRAY, Alasdair (James)

Nationality: Scottish. **Born:** Glasgow, 28 December 1934. **Education:** Whitehill Senior Secondary School, 1946-52; Glasgow Art School (Bellahouston travelling scholarship, 1957), 1952-57, diploma in mural painting and design 1957. **Family:** Married 1) Inge Sorensen in 1962 (divorced 1970), one son; 2) Morag McAlpine in 1991. **Career:** Art teacher, Lanarkshire and Glasgow, 1958-61; scene painter, Pavilion and Citizens' theatres, Glasgow, 1961-63; freelance painter and writer, Glasgow, 1963-76; artist recorder, People's Palace Local History Museum, Glasgow, 1976-77; writer-in-residence, Glasgow University, 1977-79. Since 1979, freelance writer and painter. **Address:** Dog and Bone Books, 175 Queen Victoria Drive, Glasgow G14 9BP, Scotland.

Horror, Ghost and Gothic Publications

Novels

Lanark: A Life in Four Books. Edinburgh, Canongate, and New York, Harper, 1981.
Poor Things. London, Bloomsbury, 1992; New York, Harcourt Brace, 1993.

Short Stories

Unlikely Stories, Mostly. Edinburgh, Canongate, 1983; New York, Penguin, 1984.
Ten Tales Tall and True. London, Bloomsbury, 1993; New York, Harcourt Brace, 1994.

Other Publications

Novels

1982, Janine. London, Cape, and New York, Viking, 1984.
The Fall of Kelvin Walker: A Fable of the Sixties. Edinburgh, Canongate, 1985; New York, Braziller, 1986.
Something Leather. London, Cape, 1990; New York, Random House, 1991.
McGrotty and Ludmilla; or, The Harbinger Report. Glasgow, Dog and Bone, 1990.
A History Maker. Edinburgh, Canongate, 1994; New York, Harcourt Brace, 1995.

Short Stories

The Comedy of the White Dog. Glasgow, Print Studio Press, 1979.
Lean Tales, with Agnes Owens and James Kelman. London, Cape, 1985.
Mavis Belfrage: A Romantic Story, with Five Shorter Tales. London, Bloomsbury, 1996.

Plays

Jonah (puppet play; produced Glasgow, 1956).
The Fall of Kelvin Walker (televised 1968; produced on tour, 1972).
Dialogue (produced on tour, 1971).
The Loss of the Golden Silence (produced Edinburgh, 1973).
Homeward Bound (produced Edinburgh, 1973).
Tickly Mince (revue), with Tom Leonard and Liz Lochhead (produced Glasgow, 1982).
The Pie of Damocles (revue), with others (produced Glasgow, 1983).

Radio Plays: *Quiet People,* 1968; *The Night Off,* 1969; *Thomas Muir of Huntershill* (documentary), 1970; *The Loss of the Golden Silence,* 1974; *The Harbinger Report,* 1975; *McGrotty and Ludmilla,* 1976; *The Vital Witness* (on Joan Ure), 1979.

Television Plays and Documentaries: *Under the Helmet,* 1965; *The Fall of Kelvin Walker,* 1968; *Triangles,* 1972; *The Man Who Knew about Electricity,* 1973; *Honesty* (for children), 1974; *Today and Yesterday* (3 plays; for children), 1975; *Beloved,* 1976; *The Gadfly,* 1977; *The Story of a Recluse,* 1986.

Poetry

Old Negatives: Four Verse Sequences. London, Cape, 1989.

Other

Self-Portrait (autobiography). Edinburgh, Saltire Society, 1988.
Why Scots Should Rule Scotland. Edinburgh, Canongate, 1992.

*

Manuscript Collections: Scottish National Library, Edinburgh; Hunterian Museum, Glasgow University.

Theatrical Activities:
Actor: **Television**—*The Story of a Recluse,* 1986.

Critical Studies: *The Arts of Alasdair Gray* edited by Crawford and Naion, Edinburgh, Edinburgh University Press, 1991; *Scottish Fantasy Literature: A Critical Survey* by Colin Manlove, Edinburgh, Canongate, 1994.

*   *   *

"Only horror films and fairy stories tell the truth about the worst things in life, the moments when hands turn into claws and a familiar face becomes a living skull." So believes the liquor-sodden Jock MacLeish, protagonist of Alasdair Gray's *1982, Janine,* in his worst moments. While it is tempting—and perhaps even accurate—to ascribe this sentiment also to MacLeish's creator, based on the variety of Beckett-like, existential tortures Gray's characters undergo, to do so would be to paint only half the picture. Gray's love of life, his delight in the simple pleasures of family, drink, love, art and landscape, his comic exuberance, his continued belief in the possibility of mankind's self-improvement in the face of a bumbling history—all these traits neatly counterbalance his moments of dour pessimism.

A Scotsman intimately entwined in a literary love-hate relationship with his frustrating nation, Gray came late to the novel and short story, publishing his first book, *Lanark,* only when near 50. (In this respect, as well as in a certain shared foxy-grandfather tone, he resembles the science-fiction writer R. A. Lafferty, another fabulist who blossomed in mid-life.) Gray's formal training was in the visual arts, a fact reflected in the supremely witty drawings that adorn all his books (Gray's illustratory inspirations, among others, seem to be Blake, Artzybasheff and anonymous Native American artisans), and in the bursts of inventive typography that mirror in concrete form various thematic and narrative concerns.

Gray's early literary work included scriptwriting stints (although some of the stories in his first collection bear copyrights extending as far back as 1951). These early experiences in the marketplace of ideas led perhaps to the wry observation in *Lanark:* "There were two kinds [of story]. One kind was a sort of written cinema, with plenty of action and hardly any thought. The other kind was about clever, unhappy people, often authors themselves, who thought a lot but didn't do very much." The fact that Gray has been able to fuse and transcend these simplistic categorizations in his own books is a testament to his drive and talents.

First and foremost among Gray's books is *Lanark,* a novel so buttressed with five decades of deep living and keen observation that it seems more the culmination of a career than the beginning of one. Through a skewed chronology, two life stories are unrolled, seemingly separate yet ultimately linked.

In our familiar world—Glasgow in the 1940s and 1950s, to be precise—precocious, antisocial art student Duncan Thaw reaches a brief peak of accomplishment in young adulthood, then commits suicide. After death, he finds himself memoryless in a surreal, Boschian afterworld, whose chief city is the grim grey metropolis of Unthank. Thaw's major problem is an inability to love, a failure to connect with other people, and an unhealthy reliance on an inner fantasy program. These flaws continue to plague him in the afterlife, but in the

end, by assuming the mantle of spokesman for Unthank, although he hates the city, he redeems his second chance.

Gray is an eminently *conscious* writer, incorporating allusions to and actual snippets of resonant older texts as homage. He forestalls critics by providing handy mocking roadmaps to his thefts within the books themselves. Readers will find *Lanark* to be influenced by writers as various as George MacDonald, Wyndham Lewis and James Joyce. Not mentioned, however, yet quite relevant, are Charles Finney for his *The Unholy City* (1937), Maurice Sendak, and the demiurgic James Branch Cabell. Additionally, *Lanark* in retrospect is plainly a harbinger of Terry Gilliam's film *Brazil* (1985).

Following this massive assault of a first book came the more subtle *Unlikely Stories, Mostly.* As fine a collection as nearly any Borges or Calvino volume, it looks more and more with the passage of time like one of the century's seminal assortments of fabulist tales. Employing parody, satire and realism, Gray offers us everything from the Tolkienish "The Star" to the Monty-Pythonesque "The Great Bear Cult." Central to the book is "The Comedy of the White Dog," which invokes a little-known (perhaps original with Gray) animal archetype in a quietly horrifying Ovidian tale of metamorphosis.

Two of Gray's succeeding texts opted more for realism than horrific fantasy, yet remain of interest for their irrepressible storytelling brio that flouts typical mimetic conventions.

The Fall of Kelvin Walker is Jerzy Kosinski's *Being There* (1970) as seen through J. P. Donleavy's mordant gaze. The atrociously amoral title character arrives in London from Scotland and proceeds to climb the ladder of success, becoming a television star and conservative commentator, only to meet his predestined Freudian doom. Gray gets off many sharp zingers on selfish reactionary politicians and the monied classes, his own politics being of a William Morris socialist bent. The final effect of the short book is amusing but slight.

1982, Janine is a much more substantial work, and seems to mark the end of the first phase of Gray's writing—a phase where autobiography and metafictional tricks were prominent. The reader finds himself floating on the turbulent stream-of-consciousness of the fortyish Jock MacLeish, alcoholic "security system installer." In a single night's boozy ramblings, we learn MacLeish's entire sorry life story. He is trapped in an Unthank-like existence right here on our mortal globe. Like Duncan Thaw, his tragic flaws are an inability to open his heart (traceable, Gray always asserts, to scarring resulting from the common unthinking cruelties inflicted during childhood) and a subsequent unhealthy use of fantasy as a crutch. At once erotic, hilarious and evocative of real pity, this novel reads like a conflation of Russ Meyer, Nicholson Baker and Stanislaw Lem. MacLeish's ultimate epiphany offers a hard yet not unpromising path out of his problems.

The dustjacket of *Ten Tales Tall and True* advertises a mix of "social realism, sexual comedy, science fiction [and] satire," and the book itself delivers precisely that. However, the sheer Borgesian brilliance of conceits found in *Unlikely Stories, Mostly* is missing, and the collection, though assured, seems thinner, less of an essential brick in the edifice of postmodern literature.

The tale of Frankenstein's monster lies at the heart of both horror and science fiction. In *Poor Things,* Gray cleverly shows that not all changes have yet been rung on the themes and forms of Mary Shelley's classic. And it is with this book and the following one that Gray begins to exhibit a more "objective" style and subject matter, withdrawing his authorial presence from centre stage.

Poor Things—which might profitably be slotted into the growing "steampunk" genre—tells how the Caliban-like Victorian-era genius Godwin Baxter makes himself a chimeric wife out of the corpse of a drowned woman and the foetus she was carrying, only to lose her love to his best friend. This vitally female creation, christened Bella, becomes the kind of naive-yet-wise observer of Victorian society that Michael Valentine Smith was for modern times in Robert A. Heinlein's *Stranger in a Strange Land* (1961). Identified explicitly with Scotland as a nation and with Jesus, Bella is both an emblematic figure and engagingly real person. That she gets to have the last word over her narrator-husband, Archie McCandless, illustrates Gray's characteristic privileging of woman as the wiser, more reality-connected sex.

Gray's most recent book, *A History Maker*, continues this theme. In the 23rd century, a pastoral matriarchy rules the globe, its easy, non-competitive existence made possible by advanced, wealth-producing biotechnology accessible to all. War has been ritualized into a deadly game, and utopia seems to have been realized. Yet seeds of this civilization's destruction await, to be watered by the selfish actions of one Wat Dryhope, the eponymous doer of big deeds. Flavours of Ursula Le Guin, John Crowley, Edgar Pangborn, Huxley and Shakespeare make this novel a toothsome, fully satisfying dish.

Over the course of almost two decades, the multi-talented Gray, like Sinbad, has sailed among many fantastic isles. From early lands almost too exuberant and complicated to be contained in books, to more recent, quieter climes more favourable to old bones, Gray has brought us the heady legends of many faraway places that are really our own backyards.

—Paul Di Filippo

GRESHAM, Stephen (Leroy)

Nationality: American. **Born:** 1947.

<small>HORROR, GHOST AND GOTHIC PUBLICATIONS</small>

Novels

Moon Lake. New York, Zebra, 1982.
Half Moon Down. New York, Zebra, 1985.
Dew Claws. New York, Zebra, 1986.
The Shadow Man. New York, Zebra, 1986.
Midnight Boy. New York, Zebra, 1987.
Night Touch. New York, Zebra, 1988.
Abracadabra. New York, Zebra, 1988.
Runaway. New York, Zebra, 1988.
Demon's Eye. New York, Zebra, 1989.
Blood Wings. New York, Zebra, 1990.
The Living Dark. New York, Zebra, 1991.

<small>OTHER PUBLICATIONS</small>

Novel

Rockabye Baby. New York, Zebra, 1984.

* * *

During the 1980s, Zebra books and its Pinnacle imprint published a significant number of new horror writers. Among those who found a home there were Rick Hautala, Ronald Kelly, Joseph Citro, Ruby Jean Jensen, and J. N. Williamson. Although most of the better Zebra horror writers eventually moved on to other publishers, a few remained loyal through the early 1990s, when there was a general contraction of the horror field leaving the midlist writers scrambling for new publishers. One promising writer who fell into this category was Stephen Gresham.

Gresham's debut was *Moon Lake*, a highly atmospheric novel about a young couple who decide to spend their honeymoon at a remote mountain lake. Shortly after arriving, they begin noticing oddities about the area; the vegetation is just a bit too thick and the insects make strange, unnatural sounds. There is a presence in the lake that reaches out to place thoughts and visions into the minds of those close by. *Moon Lake* was a nicely contrived eerie atmosphere, and an auspicious debut novel. *Half Moon Down* wasn't nearly as successful. A small Alabama town is all but destroyed by a devastating tornado, a storm which one young survivor is convinced was unnatural, not a random act of nature but a weapon wielded by Satan himself. Young Ronnie's battle with the demonic Windkiller has a few good moments, but there are other times when the storyline seems to just plod along.

Dew Claws has a very similar plot to *Half Moon Down* but is much more skilfully handled. Jonathan is recovering from the terrible death of the rest of his family, all lost to a treacherous swamp in what others mistakenly believe to be an accident. But the boy knows the truth, that a hungry presence lives in the murky interior of the bogs, and that it has lately emerged searching for the one victim that escaped its grasp. The book is genuinely spooky, with much better characterization than Gresham's earlier novels, and a more convincing plot. Another youngster is menaced in *The Shadow Man*. The evil this time is a sort of boogeyman for the age of data-processing, because he first materializes on the boy's computer screen. Naturally his parents don't believe him when he insists the Shadow Man is in the house, but once inside his computer, it becomes real in an entirely new way.

The *Midnight Boy* is a 13-year-old armed with the power to sometimes foresee the future. That comes in handy when a serial killer begins claiming victims from among the town's children. The protagonist's prescient visions of future crimes offer one possible way of saving his own life and bringing the killer to justice, but only if he himself isn't killed beforehand. There's another 13-year-old in *Runaway*, one of Gresham's less interesting works. His rich parents don't have much use for him, so Mark runs away and finds sanctuary at Redemption House, supposedly a home for wayward children. But it turns out that the reputedly benevolent people running Redemption House are insane, visiting bizarre punishments on those who break the rules. The monsters are all human this time, and the story takes too long to develop and often loses focus.

Night Touch carries the message that everything good has its price. Adam is 15 years old and blind, and has few friends. His unhappiness changes when he is visited by a mysterious man who claims to have seen an occult symbol on Adam's hand. As a consequence, he gives Adam the power to "see" without eyes, a weird sixth sense that allows him to function as though he had no impairment. But there's a catch. In order to pay for the gift he has received, Adam must cause the death of others, friends as well as enemies. There's a child protagonist in *Abracadabra* as well, but this time it's a teenaged girl. A group of professional magicians experimented with the genuine occult early in their careers. Although they abandoned their studies, they kept a magical skeleton key as a memento, and that key has fallen into the hands of a precocious youngster. Shortly thereafter, the magicians begin to die, one by one, all under mysterious circumstances. The survivors conclude, rightly, that the girl has somehow caused a sleeping presence to awaken, seeking prey from among those who abandoned it long ago. *Abracadabra* is one of Gresham's most successful books, cleverly plotted and skilfully paced.

There's another demonic force surrounding a decrepit tavern in *Demon's Eye*. Three families decide to pool their resources and restore the building, but as the work proceeds, their children begin to act strangely, insisting that they are not alone in the building, and that someone else is responsible for the misdeeds of which they are accused. Eventually the dumb adults realize the truth as well, but even though the reader will know what's happening long before they do, Gresham has provided enough surprises and plot twists to ensure the story remains interesting. We see the vampiric attacks of *Blood Wings* through the eyes of another young boy,

this time set against the backdrop of the swampland of Florida. This is an occasionally interesting vampire variation that opens well but fails to maintain its early promise. Good intentions go awry in *The Living Dark* when a woman with magical powers creates a spectral wolf to protect her children, but fails to banish it prior to her own death. Although dormant, it suddenly wakens and begins claiming human victims while one man who believes himself responsible tries to discover the nature of its existence so that it can be banished back to a spiritual plane.

Gresham may have limited his appeal by using children as viewpoint characters a few times too often. Novels like *Dew Claws* and *Abracadabra* demonstrated considerable ability and the potential for more significant work, but Gresham seemed reluctant to try a fresh approach and that probably limited his audience. He is also the author of a handful of entertaining shorter pieces, most notably "The Drabbletails," "Once Upon a Darkness" and "Wolf in the Memory," but is clearly more adept at greater length.

—Don D'Ammassa

H

HAGUE, G(raeme) M(alcolm)

Nationality: Australian. **Born:** Rawtenstall, England, 12 November 1959. **Education:** Various state primary and high schools in Western Australia. **Military Service:** Six months' apprenticeship in the Royal Australian Navy until voluntary discharge. **Career:** Local government clerk, car air-conditioning fitter, confectionary salesman, manager of electronics store, white-goods salesman, vehicle workshop manager, turf-farm farmhand, ten years as a sound engineer/theatre technician, and 15 years as a professional musician touring Australia. Contributor of articles to *The Australian Newspaper*, *Australian Playboy*, *Mode Magazine*, *She Magazine*, *The RACQ*, *Sonics*, *Connections* and various other trade publications. **Agent:** Selwa Anthony Author Management, 10 Loves Avenue, Oyster Bay, Sydney 2225, Australia.

HORROR, GHOST AND GOTHIC PUBLICATIONS

Novels

Ghost Beyond Earth. Sydney, Pan Macmillan Australia, 1993.
A Place to Fear. Sydney, Pan Macmillan Australia, 1994.
Voices of Evil. Sydney, Pan Macmillan Australia, 1996.
The Devil's Numbers. Sydney, Pan Macmillan Australia, 1997.
Missing Pieces. Sydney, Random House Australia, 1997.

OTHER PUBLICATIONS

Other

Recording: *Quick or the Dead*, with Antony Kliszewski and Billy Butler, 1994.

*   *   *

G. M. Hague is a relative newcomer on the Australian horror scene who arrived with the 1993 "blockbuster" horror novel, *Ghost Beyond Earth*. It was generally well received, and established Hague's place in the Australian market. The book was packaged to look like a Dean Koontz novel, but Hague's work probably owes more to James Herbert than Koontz. Hague has gone on to publish another four "epic"-style books, all of which, except for the crime/horror novel *Missing Pieces*, use traditional supernatural-horror motives such as ghosts and demons in a horror-thriller format.

Ghost Beyond Earth is Hague's most successful novel. It is a near-future science-fiction horror story which weaves several strands into an effective tale. A large portion of the novel is set aboard the orbiting space station *Freedom* which houses the cryogenically stored bodies of wealthy people awaiting a cure for their various forms of terminal illness. But things begin to go wrong as preparations are being made to revive one of *Freedom*'s silent passengers. A crew member dies, the ghost of a young girl who is terrorizing a family on Earth is seen on the space station, and a priest is visited by a demon. The main characters are believable, and some of the scenes, particularly those aboard the space station, are truly chilling. The various threads come together and resolve themselves satisfactorily in what stands as a competent horror thriller and a promising debut novel.

Hague's second novel, *A Place to Fear*, did not entirely fulfil the promise of the first book. Its main weakness is that the novel is overly long, although this is probably the fault of the publisher wanting to produce "big" books rather than entirely the author's fault. *A Place to Fear* is another science-fiction horror novel which tells of an Australian outback sugarcane town targeted by aliens planning to invade Earth, plus ghosts, zombies and conspiracy. The book lacks the plot and character originality of *Ghost Beyond Earth*, and the pace is slowed by unnecessary extraneous material.

Voices of Evil, which followed, moved away from futuristic science-fictional concepts and delved into history. The novel switches between Australia of the 1990s and the Middle East in 1915. In contemporary Australia a married couple, Brendan and Gwen, inherit an ancient amulet, but it turns out to be the link to a spirit that drives its victims to suicide. The amulet also affords protection for its carriers, however, as a similarly tormented ANZAC soldier, Hamilton, finds out back in 1915. Hague's idea is that traumatic events become "imprinted" on the fabric of our dimensions, and under some circumstances timelines can co-exist. After several suicides around him, Brendan journeys to Gallipoli. In 1915 the amulet's spirit failed to protect Hamilton, who was killed by the Turks before he could be induced to suicide. Thus the long-dead Hamilton is still the rightful owner of the amulet, which he "takes" back from Brendan and traps it in 1915. As with most of Hague's work, one has the impression that a fine 250-page novel has been padded out to 600 or so pages and thus had a lot of its impact and pace diluted.

In *The Devil's Numbers* Hague again uses demons and ghosts to wreak mayhem on unsuspecting victims. The novel begins with a very effective preface set some centuries ago in which a young boy is being schooled in the three R's by a recluse/necromancer living in a isolated wood. The boy unwittingly opens a "door" for an evil demon when he burns a page of arithmetic and is killed by the demon. The ghost of the boy is then seen to appear at various times in history, in a WWI German U-Boat, a modern luxury cruise liner, and a jet fighter. His appearance manifested by certain combinations of numbers. Yet again, the book is longer than it should have been and some of the computer science is rubbery, but the unpadded sections show Hague can write well when he sets his mind to it.

Hague's most recent effort, *Missing Pieces*, is another thriller-style horror novel, except this time the horror is human rather than supernaturally based. The story begins with somebody leaving severed body parts in elevators around Sydney. First a cut-off finger, then a hand, then a whole arm (it becomes obvious they come from different victims) and the novel develops into a kind of whodunnit race, before somebody finds a decapitated head, which of course they do. The sub-plot involves an armed robber kidnapping a pretty young woman who he considers killing and dismembering in a copy-cat attempt to get equal tabloid space.

The market in which Hague has established himself has a definite preference for "doorstop" novels, so perhaps the blame for Hague's books carrying more padding than they should can be shared with publishers who are concerned with giving readers a feeling of value for money when they heft a book rather than when they begin to read it. At his best, Hague writes pacey thrillers with strong characterization and dialogue, and original ideas. One suspects, however, while the market continues to force him to write "big" books he will never write a great novel, although there is evidence in his writing to indicate he is capable of producing quality horror fiction.

—Steven Paulsen and Sean McMullen

HALLAHAN, William H(enry)

Nationality: American. **Born:** Brooklyn, New York. **Education:** Temple University, Philadelphia; degrees in journalism and English. **Awards:** Mystery Writers of America Edgar Allan Poe Award for novel, 1978. **Address:** c/o William Morrow and Company, Inc., 1350 Avenue of the Americas, New York, NY 10019, USA.

Horror, Ghost and Gothic Publications

Novels

The Search for Joseph Tully. Indianapolis, Bobbs Merrill, 1974; London, Macmillan, 1975.
Keeper of the Children. New York, Morrow, 1978; London, Gollancz, 1979.
The Monk. New York, Morrow, and London, Gollancz, 1983.

Other Publications

Novels

The Dead of Winter. Indianapolis, Bobbs Merrill, 1972; London, Sphere, 1979.
The Ross Forgery. Indianapolis, Bobbs Merrill, 1973; London, Gollancz, 1977.
Catch Me, Kill Me. Indianapolis, Bobbs Merrill, 1977; London, Gollancz, 1979.
The Trade. New York, Morrow, and London, Gollancz, 1981.
Foxcatcher. New York, Morrow, and London, Gollancz, 1986.
Tripletrap. New York, Morrow, 1989.

*   *   *

The borderline between horror fiction and more conventional thrillers is frequently blurred, and it is not surprising that authors associated with one form frequently cross over and produce good, even exceptional work, in the other. William Goldman and Peter Straub are perhaps the best examples of writers who have excelled in multiple forms. This flexibility allows them to weather the varying popularities of specific forms because their essential writing skills remain independent of specific themes or story lines. Will-

iam H. Hallahan, though less well known, is another writer who has written both crime novels and supernatural horror. He received an Edgar award for his mystery novel *Catch Me, Kill Me*, and given the quality of his work in the horror field, it is surprising that he is so generally overlooked.

The Search for Joseph Tully is the story of Peter Richardson, a perfectly ordinary man who persistently dreams of a strange rushing sound, and who knows instinctively that someone or something is planning to kill him. His efforts to figure out what is happening include consultation with a clairvoyant and an excommunicant of the Catholic church who believes the sound is important. Elsewhere, a mysterious Englishman arrives in America to search for someone named Joseph Tully, or more specifically for his descendants. As the searcher comes closer, Richardson begins to experience memories that don't seem to be his own, as though he were remembering something from a past life. Which is in fact the case.

The suspense and mystery build as the Englishman tracks Tully's descendants, and as he comes closer to Richardson, the latter's visions grow more frequent and intense. It is the very fact that Hallahan builds the suspense by such small, logical increments that makes the novel so chilling. There is a clear focus in the distance toward which the two plotlines are progressing on a collision course. The revelation that Richardson is in fact the reincarnation of Joseph Tully, and that the Englishman is similarly a reborn enemy, doesn't come as much of a surprise, but foreknowledge in this case doesn't diminish the suspense, or the very effective climax.

Hallahan's next novel, *Keeper of the Children*, was quite different, relying more on physical adventure and less on psychological suspense. Benson is happily married and content with his life until his 14-year-old daughter Renni is kidnapped by a cult. In this case, it isn't merely a question of brainwashing. The charismatic cult leader has psychic powers and can literally reshape the personality imprinted in the human mind and impose his own will, turning his followers into slaves. Benson initially tries conventional means to recover his daughter, including asking the government to deport the man back to Vietnam. Unfortunately, this attracts the attention of his enemy, who can also bring life to inanimate objects. Toys and scarecrows become deadly weapons when they can be made to wield knives and other weapons and sent into the homes of the unwary.

After confronting a malevolent doll, Benson acknowledges that he's facing the supernatural and decides to confront it directly by learning to leave his body in spirit form and confront the villain on the astral plane. After receiving training in the mystic arts, Benson manages to accomplish astral projection, although his soul is tethered to his physical self by a slender, visible cord that must never be severed if he is to return. In that mysterious other universe, he will eventually confront and defeat his adversary and rescue his daughter. The scenes of astral projection are vivid and creepy, but Benson's rapid acquisition of mental powers adequate to defeat the Buddhist mystic come too easily and too quickly to be entirely plausible. There's a lot of good writing in the novel, but the resolution is dissatisfying.

Hallahan's third and most recent horror novel was *The Monk*. Brendan Davitt lives his entire life under an aura of dread. Premonitions of a disastrous struggle trouble his dreams, psychics insist that his soul is doomed, and scientists are unable to explain unusual characteristics of his body chemistry. Although everyone seems to feel his destiny is not his own, Brendan is determined to make a normal life for himself, alongside the girl he loves.

The novel tackles events on a spectacular scale. The climax involves no less than a major confrontation between the powers of Heaven and the minions of Satan, both of whom work through the instruments of ordinary human lives. Through Brendan's efforts the world is saved and Satan thwarted on Earth, but there's an interesting postscript in which the forces of Hell invade Heaven itself and discover that God has made the firmament forever inaccessible to them. Interesting though this speculation might be, the brief scene trivializes the forces of evil by making them seem quite mundane, and it robs the book of much of its impact.

Hallahan wrote one short story of note, a clever tale of ghostly possession titled "The New Tenant." An ambitious but dead businessman possesses the body of his ex-partner after the latter marries the widow, determined to spend more years with the woman he loves. But the displaced spirit of his partner takes control of the woman's body in turn.

After an interval of more than a decade since his last horror novel, it seems unlikely that Hallahan will emerge as a significant writer in the genre, although *The Search for Joseph Tully* in particular is one of the more successful novels of that form.

—Don D'Ammassa

HAMILTON, Alex(ander John)

Pseudonym: Donald Speed. **Nationality:** British. **Born:** Bristol, 5 November 1930; grew up mainly in South America. **Education:** Oxford University, B.A. **Family:** Married the writer Stephanie Nettell; two sons. **Career:** Journalist, travel-writer, novelist, short-story writer and anthologist.

HORROR, GHOST AND GOTHIC PUBLICATIONS

Short Stories

Beam of Malice: Fifteen Short, Dark Stories. London, Hutchinson, 1966; New York, McKay, 1967.
Flies on the Wall. London, Hutchinson, 1972.

Other

Editor, *The Cold Embrace, and Other Stories.* London, Corgi, 1966.
Editor (as Donald Speed), *My Blood Ran Cold.* London, Corgi, 1966.
Editor, *Splinters: A New Anthology of Modern Macabre Fiction.* London, Hutchinson, and New York, Walker 1968.
Editor, *Best Horror Stories 3.* London, Faber, 1972.
Editor, with Giles Gordon. *Factions.* London, n.p., 1974.

OTHER PUBLICATIONS

Novels

As If She Were Mine. London, New Authors Ltd., 1962.
Wild Track. London, Hutchinson, 1963.
Town Parole. London, Hutchinson, 1964.
The Dead Needle. London, Hutchinson, 1969.

* * *

A contributor to four volumes of the long-running series *The Pan Book of Horror Stories*, Alex Hamilton is a short-story writer for connoisseurs of the form. The first of his three novels, *As If She Were Mine*, was published by New Authors Ltd., a Hutchinson list which also included M. John Harrison among its debut novelists. It was in his short stories, however, as well as in his work as an anthologist, that Hamilton indulged his affection for and fascination with the macabre.

"The Attic Express" is probably Hamilton's best-known tale. The vividly rendered story of a railway modeller and bossy parent who shrinks to the scale of the model railway in his attic, it appeared in *The 4th Pan Book of Horror Stories* (1963), edited by Herbert van Thal, and was later included in Hamilton's very fine first collection, *Beam of Malice*. Its effectiveness lies in the author's inventiveness and imagination, and in the depth of detail he comes up with in response to the challenge of the story's premise. The level of his success is measured by the fact that, as you read the story, it becomes less a tale about a man who has shrunk to tiny proportions and more about a frightening world in which there are life-size, faceless plastic figures on station platforms, and swimming pools are filled not with water but with glass. A world, indeed, where a man's son, operating the railway as instructed, is in charge of his father's fate.

Hamilton appeared in the very next volume of van Thal's classic series, in 1964, with "The Words of the Dumb," in which an animal impersonator communicates rather better with the creatures in the zoo than with his own wife. This story, too, was reprinted in *Beam of Malice* and is fairly typical of that collection: in most of the stories, bourgeois order is first undermined then destroyed, and in the destruction usually there lies a moral—it needn't have happened this way. But to reduce the stories to a social/moral framework would be to ignore a bold imagination at work. "Breakaway" is the diary of a man marooned on an iceberg which has broken free of the polar icecap. In "End of the Road," an ordinary drive in the country turns into a nightmare journey to hell, open roads morphing into dead ends around the next blind bend.

Both these latter stories graced other landmark anthology series. "Breakaway," although it had already appeared in *Beam of Malice*, was chosen by the estimable Dr. Christopher Evans for *Mind at Bay* (1969). A psychologist and co-author of a theory of dreaming, Evans described "Breakaway" as "a horror story with a two-pronged assault, playing not only on the theme of the remorseless disintegration of the apparently indestructible, but also on that of the condition of utter human loneliness." Evans was proud to present in his sequel volume, *Mind in Chains* (1970), an original story, "Below the Shadow," which is one of Hamilton's most extraordinary and most effective tales of complete breakdown. A bitterly ironic and wonderfully sly account of thought-control, it playfully manipulates the reader's own patterns of thought.

"End of the Road" appeared for the first time in John Burke's excellent 1966 anthology *Tales of Unease*, which three years later gave rise to *More Tales of Unease* and another Hamilton story, "The Flies on the Wall," a superbly affecting study of paranoia—and yet is it? Perhaps the figures in the play Harman attends with his wife's attractive American girlfriend really are acting out scenes from his life. The dreamlike atmosphere soon becomes nightmarish as Harman is forced on to the stage and the implications of the story—that its real theme is actually the fear of women—do produce a genuine sense of unease.

Hamilton didn't just contribute to anthologies, he also edited a few. Notable among the projects he put his name to were *The Cold Embrace*, macabre stories by women, including a then 22-year-old Shena Mackay; *Splinters*, all-original stories by writers not normally associated with the macabre, including Anthony Burgess, Derwent May and William Trevor; and *Factions*, for which the two editors (Hamilton shared the honours with Giles Gordon) asked distinguished authors, including Robert Nye, Michael Moorcock and Brian Aldiss, to create fictions about real 20th-century figures who obsessed or intrigued them.

As Hamilton moved into the world of journalism (at the time of publication of *Beam of Malice* he was a Smithfield offal trader, but married to literary critic Stephanie Nettell) he wrote less fiction, and what stories he did publish reflected his growing interest in travel. "Dead Men Walk" in Peter Haining's anthology *The Clans of Darkness* (1971) is about a journalist sent to do a colour piece in Orkney. "You can bring out the darkness a bit if you want," his editor tells him, but dead men walking is a bit darker than the paper bargained for. "The Loadstar," first published in James Hale's *The Midnight Ghost Book* (1978), is set on a cruise ship which puts in at Caracas. It would have been no surprise to followers of Hamilton's fiction when he became a broadsheet travel editor. These days he is best known for compiling the annual paperback fast-seller chart for *The Guardian* newspaper—which, given the large numbers of formulaic, second-rate books muscling into the chart, shows that he has not lost his taste for the disturbing and the horrifying.

—Nicholas Royle

HARBINSON, W(illiam) A(llen)

Nationality: British. **Born:** Belfast, 1941. **Education:** National Certificate in Mechanical Engineering. **Military Service:** Royal Australian Air Force; telegraphist. **Family:** Married; two children. **Career:** Began writing short stories and articles for a variety of magazines while serving in the Air Force and stationed in Australia, Thailand and Malaysia; circulation manager, later copyeditor, Stonehart Publications, London; chief associate editor, *Men Only* and *Club International*, London; freelance writer. **Address:** c/o New English Library, Hodder Headline plc, 338 Euston Rd., London NW1 3BH, England. Lives in London.

Horror, Ghost and Gothic Publications

Novels (series: Projekt Saucer)

Genesis (Projekt Saucer). London, Corgi, 1980; New York, Dell, 1982.
Revelation. London, Corgi, 1982.
Otherworld. London, Corgi, 1984.
The Light of Eden. London, Corgi, 1987; as *Eden*, New York, Dell, 1987.
Dream Maker. London, Sphere, 1991; New York, Walker, 1992.
Inception (Projekt Saucer). New York, Dell, 1991; London, New English Library, 1994.
Phoenix (Projekt Saucer). London, New English Library, 1995.
Millennium (Projekt Saucer). London, New English Library, 1995.

Other Publications

Novels

The Running Man. Sydney, Horwitz, 1967; New York, Award, 1970.
Death of an Idol. Sydney, Horwitz, 1969.
Instruments of Death. London, Corgi, 1973; as *None But the Damned*, New York, n.p., n.d.
Knock. London, n.p., n.d.
No Limit for Charlie. London, Panther, 1977.
The Oil Heist. London, Corgi, 1978.
The Lodestone (as Allen Harbinson). London, Sphere, 1989.

Plays

Radio Play: *Astronaut*, 1977.

Other

The Illustrated Elvis. London, Joseph, 1975; New York, Grosset and Dunlap, 1976.
Charles Bronson. London, W. H. Allen, 1976.
George C. Scott. London, n.d.
Evita! A Legend for the Seventies. London, Star Books, 1977.
The Life and Death of Elvis Presley. London, Joseph, 1977.
Beauty and the Beast: An Illustrated Biography of Klaus and Nastassja Kinski. London, n.d.
Projekt UFO: The Case for Man-Made Flying Saucers. London, Boxtree, 1995.

*   *   *

Long before we realized the skies were getting dark, before we started to hope that the truth is out there, even before we learned to trust no one, there was W. A. Harbinson, working away at his mammoth "Projekt Saucer" series. Of course, flying saucers have been in and out of the news since the late 1940s, but when Harbinson published *Genesis*, the first of the series (though not chronologically: there's a prequel) in 1980, science-fiction and horror writers had been quiet about them for some years.

Harbinson gives us the full range of recently described saucer experiences: abductions, experiments on abductees, strange sexual aspects, and of course secret conspiracies going all the way to the top. Indeed, at times it seems that anyone who knows too much is likely to be stopped by interference with his car electrics on a lonely road, whisked away, and unlike run-of-the-mill abductees, never seen again.

In some of the volumes, such as the recent *Millennium*, there is a satisfying sense of mystery: however Harbinson always makes it clear that the reader should lean towards the view that saucers result from a vast, weird, but not alien or unnatural conspiracy, originating right here on Earth, among scientists who, according to the afterword of *Millennium*, did at one time try to develop a saucer-shaped aircraft. This seems to me about the least likely explanation for UFOs, and it doesn't help that the plot for *Genesis* is given away in the blurb in the back of one of Harbinson's other novels, *The Light of Eden*. Nor does the spelling of "Projekt" make it hard to guess the nationality of at least some of the conspirators.

In *The Light of Eden* itself, a very different take on the UFO phenomenon crosses with Harbinson's other preoccupation, with dramatic quasi-religious events. Moving masses of darkness, possibly black holes and often associated with UFO phenomena, appear at sacred sites such as Glastonbury. Not only do individuals disappear, but whole landscapes: Glastonbury itself vanishes and is replaced by an area of marsh. (This is not a comic novel in the tradition of *Blackpool Vanishes*: it's at least meant to be horrific.) Most of the people involved are never seen again, but some come back. One man, Jack Schul, an American con-man and card-shark, is transported from near Glastonbury to a location in Southern Iraq, near the supposed site of the Garden of Eden. He has no idea how he got there. He is examined by Frances Devereux, an English doctor (and daughter of a psychic and a vanished father), and Laurence, an innocent, religious, American medical student. Soon one of the dark masses appears and they are transported to an Eden-like landscape where Schul plays the role of the Serpent. Clearly, Frances is Eve: she has at times been promiscuous, but although strongly attracted to Schul she is reluctant to sleep with him because his ruthless personality repels her. Presumably Laurence is meant to represent Adam: he too desires Frances, but his religious background means he holds back until she gives in to Schul. Eventually, Frances and Laurence kill Schul and escape to England, where Frances at last seduces Laurence. Later Laurence is absorbed by a dark mass which scientists are trying to study at Stonehenge and Frances begins an affair with her psychiatrist (or a psychologist—Harbinson irritatingly uses the terms as if they were interchangeable). Later, she feels impelled to return to the site of Eden . . .

Harbinson has written a variety of non-UFO novels, for instance *Dream Maker*, a futuristic piece in which environmental degradation is at last having a seriously disastrous effect on the atmosphere and the ozone layer, and *Otherworld*, in which a woman photographer and journalist travels to the Amazon to try to meet the Yano, an elusive Indian tribe dedicated to the powers of darkness. However, an unidentified flying, or rather landing, object does feature in *Revelation*, another book in which Harbinson's preoccupations cross-fertilize. Here the protagonist is Kate Hirshfield, an Americanized, non-Zionist, Jewish doctor working in Jerusalem some time in the very near future. Israelis and Arabs are at each others throats, things can only get worse, when instead they get stranger. Bright stars appear in the sky, there is a mighty storm, earthquakes begin and something crashes onto the Mount of Olives . . . and where the Chapel of the Ascension has just been destroyed, they find a glowing, rectangular object. As usual Harbinson has blended those of our fears and desires which stem from the past with those which look to the future, in a typical package of horrific possibilities.

—Peter T. Garratt

HARRIS, Joanne

Nationality: British. **Address:** c/o Arrow Books, Random House, 20 Vauxhall Bridge Rd., London SW1V 2SA, England.

HORROR, GHOST AND GOTHIC PUBLICATIONS

Novels

The Evil Seed. London, Warner, 1992.
Sleep, Pale Sister. London, Arrow, 1994.

*   *   *

Both of Joanne Harris's novels use Pre-Raphaelite images for their inspiration. The artists of this period were regarded by some as gothic revivalists as many of their themes took ideas from the gothic tradition in art and literature. To this Harris has added supernatural elements.

Her first book, *Evil Seed*, begins with an extract from a study written by one of the main characters. It describes in detail Dante Gabriel Rossetti's painting, "Proserpine." A member of the Pre-Raphaelite brotherhood, he depicted the goddess with the pomegranate she has just bitten into in her hand. It is a delicate, sensitive portrait and an obvious influence on Joanne Harris. This picture is vitally important to the book because Ginny is "Proserpine," and so is Rosemary.

In 1948, Daniel Holmes, a young art scholar living in Cambridge, pulls Rosemary Ashley from the river. She is a beautiful, fragile red-head, the image of his Blessed Damosel (whom he is tracing through the works of the Pre-Raphaelites) and he is instantly smitten with her. Unfortunately, he is taken ill after his dip in the river and on recovering finds that his best friend, Robert, has been captivated by Rosemary. Robert plans to marry her. Half the novel is written by Daniel much later, towards the end of his life, and details the events that began that day on the river bank.

Interleaved with this narrative is the present day story of Alice Farrell. Alice is an artist, a young woman of Cambridge, tending to plumpness. Unexpectedly, her ex-lover, Joe, rings her and asks if she can put up his new girlfriend for a while. He sees Ginny as a shy, delicate girl who needs protecting. Alice discovers she is anything but that but initially explains her odd behaviour as drug-related, especially as Ginny admits to having been a patient at Fulbourne, the mental hospital where Daniel Holmes spent his last years.

As both stories unfold, the links between them become more and more apparent. Rosemary is dead. But Ginny is Rosemary; and the woman in the pictures that Alice is hardly aware of having painted. When Alice discovers Daniel's diary in Ginny's room she begins to piece together the horror that hides behind Ginny's lies. Something old and dark has returned to Cambridge as Daniel's story repeats itself with Paul now as the victim, as it has done for centuries.

This is not a vampire novel; Ginny is more like the Beast Within incarnate but, like a vampire, she brings to the surface desires better left submerged. Joanne Harris has cleverly woven together her two plot strands though the emphasis on the horror of the events is diminished by much of it taking place off stage. Some of the plot is telegraphed by the introduction, a problem that does not arise in her second novel, *Sleep, Pale Sister*.

This novel is set entirely in 1881 and is told from the point of view of each of the principal characters in turn so that we have different interpretations of the same event but without tedious repetition. Henry Chester is an artist on the fringes of the Pre-Raphaelite Brotherhood—celebrities such as Holman Hunt and William Morris attend his exhibitions. He is obsessed with the idea of joining that elite. He is also obsessed with Effie. She was only a child when he first started to use her as a model for his paintings. Then he married her and became obsessed with keeping her pure, something which was in direct opposition to the reality of marriage. Moses Harper, who faintly despised Chester, set out to seduce Effie. When Fanny Miller comes on the scene, the atmosphere of the novel changes. From being a tale of Victorian hang-ups it becomes one of possession, revenge and death. Fanny has been watching Chester. She believes that he was responsible for her daughter, Marta's death ten years previously, but without proof who would take notice of the accusations of a brothel keeper? Instead, she plans to take from him what he prizes most, Effie. At this point you can choose as to whether Marta's ghost has been hanging around waiting to possess a suitable host or if Fanny uses narcotics and mesmerism to shape Effie's behaviour. The possibilities are deftly handled, the characters realistic and the writing atmospheric. Again, the horror is in the situation and is implied or off-stage.

In both these books Harris shows a deep understanding of human nature. In *The Evil Seed* it shows in Daniel Holmes's obsession with Rosemary, and in Alice's suspicion of the woman Joe has chosen as her replacement and who he expects her to look after. In *Sleep, Pale Sister* it is the dichotomy of Victorian values possessed by Henry Chester. On one hand his wife must be pure, innocent and submissive, having no sexual desires whatsoever, yet he can go weekly to a brothel and demand virtual children as his bed-partners. The idea that Effie should take a lover is alien to his thought-processes. Any stereotyping of the characters can be regarded as part of the sub-genre in which Harris has chosen to write and is neatly offset by the original elements in the books.

—Pauline Morgan

HARRIS, Steve

Nationality: British. **Born:** 1957(?). **Address:** c/o Gollancz, The Cassell Group, Wellington House, 125 Strand, London WC2R 0BB, England. Lives in Basingstoke, Hampshire.

HORROR, GHOST AND GOTHIC PUBLICATIONS

Novels

AdventureLand. London, Headline, 1990; as *The Eyes of the Beast*, New York, n.p., 1993.
Wulf. London, Headline, 1991.
The Hoodoo Man. London, Headline, 1992.
Angels. London, Headline, 1993.
Black Rock. London, Gollancz, 1996.
The Devil on May Street. London, Gollancz, 1997.

* * *

Steve Harris writes big, thick books populated with losers. Contemporary settings are invaded by the supernatural, leaving corpses in its wake (varying in number from a mere handful to whole towns).

Basingstoke is an English suburban town, no different from many others within a train-ride from the centre of London, yet Harris seems to have a grudge against it. In *AdventureLand*, one hot summer a child goes missing at a touring funfair. Its next stop is Basingstoke. Dave Carter, one of the local but less violent teenagers of the town goes with friends to the fair. Two of them disappear during a ghost train ride. As Dave and his girlfriend, Sally, discover, the ghost train is a doorway into another dimension and for some reason Dave has been chosen as the best person to cross over and stop the evil which is threatening to break into the real world. During part of his journey Dave finds himself in a largely deserted, alternate Basingstoke which crumbles around him.

The village that suffers Harris's depredations in *Wulf* lies within easy reach of Basingstoke but has that useful facility (to horror writers) of being easily cut off from the outside world. As in *AdventureLand*, the hero is a put-upon teenager, aided by his girlfriend, but this time his personal enemies are adults, including his drunken father. The village of West Waltham is triply cursed; there is a field, called God's Teardrop, on which nothing will grow and from which the supernatural element of the novel emanates: a local farmer's wife put the brains of a cow infected with Bovine Spongiform Encephalopathy (BSE) into a communal pie four years earlier and an inordinate number of social misfits seem to live in the village. Something from the field has triggered BSE in the human population of the village and the undesirables go on a rampage, killing everyone they can. Admittedly, *Wulf* was written before the European "beef crisis" of 1996 when BSE in cows was blamed for the upsurge in cases of Croizfeld-Jacob Disease (CJD), the human equivalent of the disease, but the symptoms were well-known from other studies. Here, the BSE element not only complicates the plot but makes it appear outdated. In the end, people die but nothing is really resolved.

The Hoodoo Man is more believable because it concentrates on one element for its effect. Danny Stafford is shot by his brother at the age of five and a piece of bone is lodged in his pineal gland. As a result he sometimes has visions of events that have either taken place or will occur. All of them are violent. Since Danny spent most of his childhood and early adult life in Basingstoke some of the violence inevitably happens in or near the town. Gradually, Danny learns that he can influence the events he predicts, not to the extent of preventing them, but more to lessening their impact. All this merely leads up to the main thrust of the plot which is that Danny's mind latches onto that of a serial killer and he spends periods of time, sometimes weeks, not being aware of his own actions, as he sees the killer's actions as if he was actually committing them.

It always seems to take Harris a very long time to get to the nub of his plots, complicating the reader's view by a lot of extraneous material. This is especially the case with *Angels*. It is a very long way through the book before we begin to know what is going on. Big-time car-thief Paul Dekker starts having dreams about a dead girl and midnight phone calls from someone he thinks is her. Then people start dying, nastily. When one of them is his mother and the police suspect him, he flees the country. It is on a Greek island that he finds the dead girl, Katie, and kills two men who won't stay dead. He attempts to take her back to Cambridge, England, where, she tells him, the problem started. It came about because H. Tyler tried to develop the ultimate virtual-reality system and tapped into another dimension. He tried to bring an angel through into this dimension using Katie as a conduit and instead tapped into an evil force. The plot itself is extremely slight and merely a vehicle for car-chases and deaths across Europe. At one point an Italian town is cataclysmically destroyed, killing upwards of 9,000 people.

All four of these books are extremely long (*Angels* is the worst) and would have benefited by the axe being taken to the wordage rather than to the trees which provided the paper they are printed on. It is also interesting to note that there was a gap of three years and a change of publisher before Harris's next book appeared. *Black Rock* is actually a very readable, though flawed, novel. After she throws out her editor lover, Sarah-Jane Dresden discovers the first few chapters of a novel which she assumes he has left behind deliberately. It begins the story of Snowdrop Dresden who goes to the isolated house, Black Rock, near Tintagel to sell a new computer system to the owner and falls in love with him. What intrigues and worries Sarah-Jane are the similarities to her own life—almost as if someone is trying to rewrite it. As she gets sucked into the plot impossible things seem to happen and she finds herself fighting for her own identity as she discovers the fine line between reality and fiction. Where the plot falters is in the premise behind the events. The perpetrator is tapping into another dimension, possibly connected with ley lines, by feeding it with the pain of tortured human beings. The power he gets out makes him god-like.

When Harris follows a straightforward plot line his writing can be very effective but he tends to make situations over-complicated by adding spurious dimensions. All his books have supernatural elements and although the nature of the supernatural is such that it may not have a rational explanation, Harris has a tendency to use it as a graft to get his plot out of trouble. *The Hoodoo Man* is the exception to this as the supernatural element not only has a rational explanation (even if it is reminiscent of Stephen King's *The Dead Zone*) and the same idea is a constant from start to finish without any suggestion that the rules are changing as you read on. Harris also tends to fall back on the idea of other dimensions into which he can insert his characters or have things coming out of. What Harris does do well is paint thumbnail sketches of bizarre characters. Unfortunately, almost all his characters, though realistic, have problems of some kind and most of his protagonists are unlikeable, giving the reader little to identify with. Only *Black Rock* contains personalities which approach a semblance of normality and whom the average reader might like to cultivate as friends.

—Pauline Morgan

HARRIS, Thomas

Nationality: American. **Born:** Jackson, Mississippi, 1940. **Education:** Baylor University, B.A. 1964. **Family:** Has a daughter, Anne. **Career:** Reporter, Waco *News-Tribune*; general assignment reporter and night editor, Associated Press, New York City, 1968-74; full-time writer since 1974. **Awards:** Horror Writers of America Bram Stoker award for best novel, 1989. **Address:** c/o St. Martin's Press, 175 Fifth Ave., New York, NY 10010, USA.

Horror, Ghost and Gothic Publications

Novels

Red Dragon. New York, Putnam, 1981; London, Bodley Head, 1982; as *Manhunter*, New York, Bantam, 1986.
The Silence of the Lambs. New York, St. Martin's Press, and London, Heinemann, 1988.

Other Publications

Novel

Black Sunday. New York, Putnam, and London, Hodder and Stoughton, 1975.

*

Film Adaptations: *Black Sunday*, 1977; *Manhunter*, from his novel *Red Dragon*, 1986; *Silence of the Lambs*, 1991.

* * *

Thomas Harris is not your usual best-selling author. In the first place, in contrast to the mechanical regularity of Judith Krantz, Sidney Sheldon and especially Stephen King, Harris has written only three novels in about 15 years; in the second place, his spare, tight, but rather colourless style is leagues away from the floridity, tawdriness and plain bad writing of the Danielle Steels of the world. In his two best and most representative novels, Harris straddles the thin boundary between suspense and horror; readers will have to decide for themselves whether he ultimately lands in the former or latter mode.

Black Sunday is a mere potboiler, with a preposterous premise—terrorists wish to blow up the Super Bowl from a blimp—and stereotypical characters. It has only one point of interest: early on, a portion of a chapter is devoted to a psychological history of one of the terrorists from infancy onward, supplying the inner motives for his actions and desires. It is written in a clinical, almost emotionless manner, but it nevertheless provides the necessary psychological motivation for the entire novel.

Harris developed this idea in an ingenious way in *Red Dragon*. The premise of this novel is the attempt by Will Graham, a semi-retired FBI agent, to hunt down a serial killer by adopting the mind-set of the criminal. Graham has an unusual sensitivity to other people's minds (it must be emphasized that this idea is not presented as in any way supernatural or occult, and Graham is nothing like the "psychic detectives" of Algernon Blackwood, William Hope Hodgson, and others), and the FBI, stumped in the matter, feel that this may be the only way to capture the killer. It is not entirely clear whether Graham really does solve the case, or any part of it, by entering the criminal's mind rather than by merely interpreting the physical evidence more thoroughly than others have; but Harris in any event presents Graham's method as a "new" technique in detection.

The killer in *Red Dragon*, Francis Dolarhyde, was an orphan who was raised by a hideous and tyrannical grandmother who made fun of his speech impediment and who once threatened to cut off his penis with scissors when she found him as a young boy exposing himself to a little girl. Throughout the novel Dolarhyde pretends to have self-tormenting conversations with his deceased grandmother, and he fancies that it is the grandmother who is urging him to kill a young blind woman, Reba McClane, who has taken a romantic interest in him. (The resemblance of all this to Robert Bloch's *Psycho* is surely not accidental.) But Graham apparently uses his psychic link with the killer to track him down and have him put away.

The Silence of the Lambs has now perhaps exceeded the acclaim of *Red Dragon*, a result of the success of the 1990 film version. If *Silence* lacks the gripping and monomaniacal intensity of its predecessor, it is overall a finer work—in fullness of characterization, in intricacy of plot, and in cumulative suspense. Once again much of the action revolves around the mechanics of tracking down the serial killer; and here the evidence ranges from death's-head moths (found in the victims' throat) to anomalous triangular markings found on the back of one victim. As in *Red Dragon*, several of the murders have already occurred, and much attention is given to rescuing the killer's latest victim, who has been abducted but is not murdered immediately.

Dr. Hannibal Lecter, who was merely a sort of sardonic commentator in *Red Dragon* (his capture and imprisonment was Graham's greatest victory in police work), plays a much larger role in *The Silence of the Lambs*, virtually orchestrating the events even though he spends much of the novel behind bars. Lecter really is one of the more delightfully evil figures in recent literature, and his knowledge of psychiatry allows him to play the most exquisite games of mental torture upon his various targets. While there is something of the Gothic villain in Lecter, he could just as well be considered a Moriarty figure. In this case, however, the Sherlock Holmes figure is not Will Graham but Clarice M. Starling, a trainee in the FBI Academy. She has been chosen to interrogate Lecter so as to produce a psychological profile of serial killers, but—because she finds that Lecter appears to know much about the serial killer known as Buffalo Bill—she becomes enmeshed in the case and ultimately helps to solve it. The sensitive portrayal of Starling is one of the quiet triumphs of this novel.

The gripping mental battle between Lecter and Starling actually ends up relegating the actual murderer to the background, and we learn relatively little about the motivations of Buffalo Bill, who is ultimately identified as one Jame Gumb. It turns out that Gumb is profoundly confused sexually: he is not homosexual, nor does he truly fit the psychological model of the transsexual; for that reason he has been turned down for a sex-change operation, and so he resorts to killing women. Why? He wishes to make an entire suit *out of women's skin*, since this will be the closest he will ever come to being a woman. So he takes various pieces of skin from each of his victims: the back from one, the thighs from another, and so on. This, certainly, is exceptionally perverse, but Harris' presentation of it is so indirect (this, in fact, is the clue to the killings, and so cannot be fully revealed until the end) as to rob it of much of its potential horror. This is not a criticism: it only suggests that Harris' *prime* goal in the novel is detection, not horror.

What is interesting is that the film version of *The Silence of the Lambs* is actually much more horrifying (and, accordingly, much less of a detective story) than the novel. An early scene, in which Starling must confront Lecter in his heavily guarded cell in a madhouse, is presented in the film as something out of *Melmoth the Wanderer*: we seem suddenly transported out of the present and into the horrors of the Inquisition. There is nothing like this in the novel. Jame Gumb's home in the film is a Gothic castle with a stone-encircled well in which he keeps his hapless victim. This is not to say that the film is unfaithful to the novel in these and other particulars; perhaps it is merely drawing out hints that were only implicit in Harris' work.

Harris's two novels are certainly among the more successful works of popular fiction in recent years, even though he succumbs to various conventions of popular fiction—abundance of dialogue, stereotypical conflict of good and evil, occasionally contrived plot-twists, an abundance of technical knowledge of certain matters (especially forensics) that is meant to impress the reader—that

may lower his standing as an artist. It is certainly not his fault that lesser writers have attempted to match not so much his skill as his commercial success in the portrayal of serial killers, a trope that has already become so hackneyed as to be a source of amusement or tedium rather than horror.

—S. T. Joshi

HARRISON, M(ichael) John

Pseudonyms: Ron Fawcett; Gabriel King. **Nationality:** British. **Born:** Warwickshire, 26 July 1945. **Education:** At schools in England. **Career:** Groom, Atherstone Hunt, Warwickshire, 1963; student teacher, Warwickshire, 1963-65; clerk, Royal Masonic Charity Institute, London, 1966; literary editor and reviewer, *New Worlds,* 1968-75; regular contributor, *New Manchester Review,* 1978-79. **Awards:** Boardman Tasker award, 1989. **Agent:** Anthony Sheil Associates, 43 Doughty Street, London WC1N 2LF, England.

Horror, Ghost and Gothic Publications

Novels

The Course of the Heart. London, Gollancz, 1992.
Signs of Life. London, Gollancz, and New York, St. Martin's Press, 1997.

Short Stories

The Ice Monkey and Other Stories. London, Gollancz, 1983.

Other Publications

Novels

The Committed Men. London, Hutchinson, and New York, Doubleday, 1971.
The Pastel City. London, New English Library, 1971; New York, Doubleday, 1972.
The Centauri Device. New York, Doubleday, 1974; London, Panther, 1975.
A Storm of Wings. London, Sphere, and New York, Doubleday, 1980.
In Viriconium. London, Gollancz, 1982; as *The Floating Gods,* New York, Pocket Books, 1983.
Climbers. London, Gollancz, 1989.
The Wild Road, with Jane Johnson (as Gabriel King). London, Arrow, 1997.

Short Stories

The Machine in Shaft Ten and Other Stories. London, Panther, 1975.
Viriconium Nights. New York, Ace, 1984; revised edition, London, Gollancz, 1985.

Graphic Novel

The Luck in the Head, illustrated by Ian Miller. London, Gollancz, 1993.

Other

Fawcett on Rock (ghost-written as by Ron Fawcett). N.p., 1987.

* * *

The importance of M. John Harrison's contribution to the supernatural horror genre is all the more remarkable given its small volume. Harrison's writing combines an exceptional thematic richness with a measured intensity of style that carries absolute conviction. His themes are not easy to sum up. They encompass elements of Gnostic mysticism, complex geographical knowledge and both organic and emotional pathology. A typical Harrison story begins with an obsessed individual or group of individuals, develops through a vividly evoked urban or natural landscape, reaches towards an overarching statement about the human condition— and then snaps back into the ordinariness of its origins. Harrison has pointed to the influence of Arthur Machen; he shares Machen's ability to see the everyday and the transcendent within a single framework, and to bind them together in supernatural images which are at once grotesque and awesome.

Harrison's abilities were reflected in his first novel, *The Committed Men*: a grim, sardonic post-apocalypse narrative in which a group of survivors undertake a futile quest among the distorted relics of English culture. A key passage involves a ruined office block where ageing civil servants live out an insane ritual of bureaucracy, dressed in rotting suits and papier-mâché masks. Several key Harrison themes emerge here: quests, rituals, relics, madness. The lyrical aspect of this novel would fuel his "Viriconium" cycle of fantasy novels and short stories; the bleak and realistic aspect would fuel his supernatural horror stories.

The collection *The Machine in Shaft Ten* included what is still the finest Harrison story, "Running Down." The narrator, Egerton, describes his friendship with a bitter and "comically accident-prone" man called Lyall. Through a dismal career, an unhappy marriage and an involvement with far-right politics, Lyall's accident-proneness develops into a violent personal entropy: "Everything I touch falls to pieces." Egerton visits him in a rural cottage which he has reduced to an appalling state of disorder. As Britain undergoes a fascist takeover, Lyall's house burns down and he climbs manically up the steep face of Pavey Ark; as he reaches the summit, an earth tremor causes it to collapse. Egerton's final comment is chilling: "It might have been averted perhaps . . . but it seems as futile to judge myself on that account as to be continually interpreting and reinterpreting the moment at which I was forced to realize that one man's raw and gaping self-concern had brought down a mountain."

"Running Down" was reprinted in *The Ice Monkey*, an astonishing collection which prompted Ramsey Campbell to comment: "M. John Harrison is the finest British writer now writing horror fiction and by far the most original." In the title story, an unvoiced resentment and a half-hearted piece of magic combine to cause a fatal accident. In "The New Ray" an extreme treatment for terminal illness serves only to generate helpless effigies of the patient. Continuing the theme of failed or misapplied magic, "The Incalling" describes a sordid ritual undertaken by a man dying of cancer; it traps him in a surreal cycle of repetition, but doesn't save his life. "The Quarry" describes the shared sensuality of a disabled couple in order to suggest how a damaged identity might be repaired through transcendence. In "Egnaro" the narrator observes a friend's obsessive quest for a secret country left off the maps, but hinted at in obscure fragments of cultural detritus. Finally, he sees that "If Egnaro is the substrate of mystery which underlies all daily life, then the reciprocal of this is also true, and it is the exact dead point of ordinariness which lies beneath every mystery." The reader may notice that "Egnaro" is "orange" spelt backwards. Harrison's irony mediates between the bleak pessimism on the surface of his writing and the compassion at its heart.

Two later stories reflect Harrison's growing preoccupation with ritual magic. "The Great God Pan" (in *Prime Evil* edited by Douglas E. Winter, 1988), which takes its title from a Machen story, describes the strange apparitions experienced by three people in the aftermath of a ritual which they cannot remember. In one remarkable passage, the narrator looks out of his friend's kitchen window to see a huge white chrysalis shape composed of two angelic figures, making love. His friend's only explanation is: "There's no limit to suffering. They follow me wherever I go." Equally disturbing, "GIFCO" (in *Metahorror* edited by Dennis Etchison, 1992) has a narrator working in the service of a person who is never described. Under directions from Gifco, he helps to abduct a young girl and deliver her to an empty house. Later, he returns to the house to find photographs of the girl undressed and a woman who resembles his wife. Going home, he finds his wife missing; she has written the message GIFCO LEAVE US ALONE. In the middle of this ominous narrative is a breathtaking vision: driving into London with the girl, the narrator sees the Polytechnic of North London covered in giant roses and wild animals. Miracles happen, but only at a price.

These two stories and "The Quarry" appear in altered form as episodes in *The Course of the Heart*, a brief but richly textured novel described by Harrison as a "metaphysical thriller." It follows the lives of three characters: the male narrator and his friends Pam and Lucas, who as students underwent a magical ritual under the direction of a mystic called Yaxley. This experience opened up to them a sacred domain of "fullness" or Pleroma, which stays with them in the form of recurrent apparitions—such as the "white couple" described above—and as an overarching sense of loss. Drawn together by fear and longing, Pam and Lucas create a shared historical myth of "the Coeur": a secret country of variable location which mediates between the world and the Pleroma. The narrator tries to get Yaxley's help, and is coerced into assisting with a pointless (yet somehow potent) ritual involving the rape of a pubertal girl. Yaxley is a faux Aleister Crowley: he has Crowley's arrogance and perversity, but none of his charisma. After this episode, the narrator retreats to the countryside, where he experiences erotic visions of a "green woman."

The novel's conclusion is both grim and poetic. Pam becomes terminally ill with cancer. Lucas weaves her life into the story of the Coeur, which he tells to her in the hope that it will prevent her death. When the narrator visits her in hospital, he sees her staring at a TV screen; on it, he sees the white couple. After Pam's death, Lucas becomes insane with grief; the narrator meets Lucas's own recurrent spectre, a violent dwarf. Later, the sight of snowflakes becoming rose petals leads the narrator into a redemptive vision of "the goddess"; later still, his wife is killed in an inexplicable car crash. *The Course of the Heart* is a brilliant use of supernatural themes to explore human mortality and loss. It portrays a heaven as corruptible and arbitrary as the world.

Four recent stories show Harrison's continuing preoccupation with the imagery of loss and transformation. In "The Dead" (with Simon Ings; in *The Sun Rises Red* edited by Chris Kenworthy, 1992) the souls of dead people are reborn as birds from the wombs of living women: birth and mortality become indistinguishable. In "Anima" (*Interzone* no. 58, 1992) a man spends his life trying to recapture an adolescent experience of seeing—and making love to—a woman made of light. "The East" (*Interzone* no. 114, 1996) is a quiet, haunting story about how political changes have turned Eastern Europe into a lost territory, a myth. "Isobel Avens Returns to Stepney in the Spring" (in *Little Deaths* edited by Ellen Datlow, 1994) is a sensuous treatment of the partial transformation of a woman into a bird through genetic science. This story is the basis of Harrison's latest novel, *Signs of Life*; its combination of scientific, natural, erotic and religious imagery reflects the creative scope of one of horror fiction's most powerfully imaginative authors.

—Joel Lane

HARTLEY, L(eslie) P(oles)

Nationality: British. **Born:** Whittlesey, Cambridgeshire, 30 December 1895. **Education:** Harrow School; Balliol College, Oxford University, B.A. 1922 (co-editor, *Oxford Outlook*). **Military Service:** Served in World War I, 1916-18. **Family:** None. **Career:** Fiction reviewer for *Spectator*, *Week-end Review Weekly Sketch*, *Time and Tide*, *The Observer* and *Sunday Times*, all London, 1923-72. Clark Lecturer, Trinity College, Cambridge, 1964. Lived quietly in Somerset, but spent much time in Venice, Italy. **Awards:** James Tait Black Memorial Prize, 1948; Heinemann award, 1954; Companion of Literature, Royal Society of Literature, 1972. C.B.E. (Commander, Order of the British Empire), 1956. **Died:** 13 December 1972.

HORROR, GHOST AND GOTHIC PUBLICATIONS

Short Stories

Night Fears, and Other Stories. London, Putnam, 1924.
The Killing Bottle. London, Putnam, 1932.
The Travelling Grave, and Other Stories. Sauk City, Wisconsin, Arkham House, 1948; London, Barrie, 1951; as *Night Fears and Other Supernatural Tales*, 1993.
The White Wand and Other Stories. London, Hamilton, 1954.
Two for the River and Other Stories. London, Hamilton, 1961.
The Collected Short Stories of L. P. Hartley. London, Hamilton, 1968; New York, Horizon Press, 1969.
Mrs. Carteret Receives and Other Stories. London, Hamilton, 1971.
The Complete Short Stories of L. P. Hartley. London, Hamilton, 1973.

OTHER PUBLICATIONS

Novels

Simonetta Perkins (novella). London and New York, Putnam, 1925.

The Shrimp and the Anemone. London, Putnam, 1944; as *The West Window*, New York, Doubleday, 1945.

The Sixth Heaven. London, Putnam, 1944; New York, Doubleday, 1945.
Eustace and Hilda. London, Putnam, 1947.
The Boat. London, Putnam, 1949, and New York, Doubleday, 1950.
My Fellow Devils. London, Barrie, 1951.
The Go-Between. London, Hamilton, 1953; New York, Knopf, 1954.
A Perfect Woman. London, Hamilton, 1955; New York, Knopf, 1956.
The Hireling. London, Hamilton, 1957; New York, Rinehart, 1958.
Eustace and Hilda: A Trilogy (omnibus; includes *The Shrimp and the Anemone, The Sixth Heaven, Eustace and Hilda*). London, Putnam, 1958.
Facial Justice. London, Hamilton, 1960; New York, Doubleday, 1961.
The Brickfield. London, Hamilton, 1964.
The Betrayal. London, Hamilton, 1966.
Poor Clare. London, Hamilton, 1968.
The Love-Adept: A Variation on a Theme. London, Hamilton, 1969.
My Sister's Keeper. London, Hamilton, 1970.
The Harness Room. London, Hamilton, 1971.
The Collections. London, Hamilton, 1972.
The Will and the Way. London, Hamilton, 1973.

Other

The Novelists' Responsibility: Lectures and Essays. London, Hamilton, 1967; New York, Hillary House, 1968.

*

Film Adaptations: *The Go-Between*, 1971; *The Hireling*, 197?; *Eustace and Hilda* (television serial), 1977-78.

Critical Studies: *L. P. Hartley* by Paul Bloomfield, London, Longman, 1962, revised edition, 1970; *L. P. Hartley* by Peter Bien, London, Chatto and Windus, 1963; *Wild Thyme, Winter Lightning: The Symbolic Novels of L. P. Hartley* by Anne Mulkeen, Wayne State University Press, 1974; *L. P. Hartley* by Edward T. Jones, Boston, Twayne, 1978.

* * *

L. P. Hartley occupies a distinctive position in the realm of weird literature. A noted British novelist, Hartley also wrote more than 60 short stories scattered through six collections. While by no means a majority of these stories are weird, a representative proportion of them deal with crime, violence and psychological terror, occasionally crossing over into the genuinely supernatural. A few of Hartley's best tales are of a form now termed "nonsupernatural horror" or "psychological suspense," and he can be seen as a precursor of this now prominent sub-genre.

In his introduction to Cynthia Asquith's *Third Ghost Book* (1955), Hartley made an important pronouncement: "The ghost-story writer's task is the more difficult [than the detective writer's], for not only must he create a world in which reason doesn't hold sway, but he must invent laws for it. Chaos is not enough. Even ghosts must have rules and obey them." Hartley goes on to say that the modern ghost manifests itself in all manner of ways not given to his sheeted predecessor: "Like women and other depressed classes, they have emancipated themselves from their disabilities . . ." In order for a tale to be convincing, therefore, it must utilize some sort of internal logic for the supernatural (short of explaining it away altogether) and extreme subtlety in the depiction of weird effects. Hartley practises what he preaches, and finds that the most effective and subtle way to suggest the supernatural is through a focus on the psychologies of his characters. Both his supernatural and his non-supernatural tales are much concerned with the analysis of aberrant mental states, and in many instances we are not certain until the very end whether or not the supernatural actually comes into play; in some tales this uncertainty is not, and is not intended to be, resolved.

Some of Hartley's tales of crime can be dispensed with quickly, for there is nothing either weird or horrific about them, however accomplished they may be. "The Island" involves a murder and a love triangle, and is told with superb indirection. "The Killing Bottle"—a somewhat long-winded crime story which contains a hideous description of the death of a butterfly in a killing bottle—is somewhat closer to the horrific.

Hartley's first genuinely supernatural tale, "A Visitor from Down Under" (written for Cynthia Asquith's first *Ghost Book*, 1926), is also one of his best. This is one of many stories of supernatural revenge (Rumbold has killed his colleague in Australia, presumably for gain, and the colleague comes back to avenge his murder), and Hartley's rapier-sharp wit is also on display in the punning title (the dishevelled man who hunts down Rumbold in his elegant London hotel is indeed from Australia, but is also from some other place "down under"). Another masterful tale of this kind is "Podolo," a deceptively simple story of a woman who goes to an island off the coast of Italy, kills a cat, and is herself killed by some loathsome but nebulous entity. "W. S.," which appeared in Asquith's *Second Ghost Book* (1952), is a Doppelgänger story, but its resolution is somewhat obvious. A much better tale of this type is the late "Fall In at the Double," whose title is also a pun: a man is nearly killed when ghosts of brutalized soldiers pounce upon him instead of the ghostly colonel standing next to him.

Another masterwork is "The Travelling Grave." Like several others, it relies on a clever use of graveyard humour in which his characters talk at cross-purposes in some particularly hideous context. Here, Richard Munt has developed a penchant for collecting coffins, but his friend Valentine Ostrop, one of the guests invited to spend a weekend with him, is unaware of this predilection, and by misunderstanding the dialogue of the other guests assumes that Munt collects baby perambulators. One exchange ("You keep them empty?" "Yes, that is, most of them are") is especially piquant. This is an entirely non-supernatural tale, but pungent satire raises it to the level of horror.

"The Cotillon," although a supernatural tale, contains more of this talking at cross-purposes. A woman who has just jilted a man finds him at her party skulking about in a sort of death-mask. They confront each other; he pulls a revolver. "'I was always an empty-headed fellow,' he went on, tapping the waxed covering [of his mask] with his gloved forefinger, so that it gave out a wooden hollow sound—'there's nothing much behind this. No brains to speak of, I mean. Less than I used to have, in fact.'" In fact, Henry is a ghost; he had blown his brains out earlier that evening.

A number of Hartley's best tales are so unclassifiable that they must be placed in the weird only by default. Here the supernatural may or may not come into play, and yet the stories develop

such an atmosphere of the odd that they present an excellent case for the extension of the weird to encompass tales of psychological terror. "Night Fears"—in which a night watchman encounters a strange derelict who repeatedly torments him psychologically and finally kills him—is among the best of these. Other tales are perhaps too nebulous for detailed analysis: "Home, Sweet Home," a strange, dreamlike tale of a couple who return to their long-deserted home and find the ghosts of disturbed children who had been interred there; "The Shadow on the Wall," perhaps a conscious nod to the story of a similar title by Mary E. Wilkins-Freeman, in which a woman has a peculiar encounter in her bath with a man who may be a ghost; "Conrad and the Dragon," a twisted fairy tale; "Feet Foremost" and "Monkshood Manor," stories of supernatural curses; "Three, or Four, for Dinner," a somewhat obvious tale of a man who returns from the dead. All these tales testify to Hartley's pervasive interest in the weird, an interest that must be regarded as central to his entire literary work.

Hartley's *Complete Short Stories* collects the stories in all Hartley's collections (some of whose contents overlap), but omits ten stories (none of them truly weird) from the early *Night Fears*. There are at least three additional uncollected stories, but only one of these is weird—"The Sound of Voices," published posthumously in *The Seventh Ghost Book* (1973) and very likely Hartley's last short story.

—S. T. Joshi

HARVEY, W(illiam) F(ryer)

Nationality: British. **Born:** Yorkshire, 1885. **Education:** Quaker schools at Bootham, York, and Leighton Park, Reading; Balliol College, Oxford. **Career:** Qualified as a doctor but never practised; Warden, Fircroft Working Men's College 1920-25; freelance writer. **Died:** 4 June 1937.

HORROR, GHOST AND GOTHIC PUBLICATIONS

Short Stories

Midnight House and Other Tales. London, Dent, 1910.
The Beast With Five Fingers and Other Tales. London, Dent, 1928.
Moods and Tenses. Oxford, Blackwell, 1933.
Midnight Tales, edited by Maurice Richardson. London, Dent, 1946; as *The Beast With Five Fingers: Twenty Tales of the Uncanny*, New York, Dutton, 1947.
The Arm of Mrs. Egan and Other Stories. London, Dent, 1951; as *The Arm of Mrs. Egan and Other Strange Stories*, New York, Dutton, 1952.

OTHER PUBLICATIONS

Novels

The Mysterious Mr. Badman. London, Pawling and Ness, 1934.
Caprimulgus (for children). London, Constable, 1936.
Mr. Murray and the Boococks. London, Nelson, 1938.

Short Stories

The Misadventures of Athelstan Digby. London, Swarthmore Press, 1920.

Other

Quaker Byways. Weybridge, Surrey, Friends Book Centre, 1929.
John Rutley of Dublin, Quaker Physician. London, privately printed, 1934.
We Were Seven. London, Constable, 1936.

*

Film Adaptation: *The Beast With Five Fingers*, 1946; *August Heat*, n.d.

* * *

It may be too easy to see in W. F. Harvey's horror fiction something of the tragedy and inner resentment of the man himself. Poor health ruined Harvey's intended career as a doctor, and a heroic rescue during the First World War left him a semi-invalid. Although he spent some years lecturing in and promoting the growing adult-education movement he was forced to retire from this and eke out a living by writing. Although Harvey always remained outwardly pleasant and mild his stories bubble with an undercurrent of malice and vengeance, and it may be that it served as therapy. However he was also an intensely religious man with a Quaker upbringing and this stoicism was almost certainly a greater solace in his life than his fiction, so it is dangerous to read too much into his stories.

Harvey wrote two of the most reprinted of all short horror stories, "The Beast With Five Fingers" and "August Heat," both of which have been filmed or adapted for television. "The Beast With Five Fingers" was originally written for *The New Decameron* series of anthologies in 1919 and then revised for its inclusion in the eponymous collection. The first version is superior, as the introduction allows us a better glimpse of Adrian Borlsover and it lacks the unnecessary epilogue Harvey added for the second printing. Adrian Borlsover is depicted as a friendly uncle to young Eustace. He is an invalid with a weak body who subsequently goes blind. His hands compensate for his blindness so much so that rumour has it he can detect the colour of an object by his touch. Towards the end of his life his right hand begins to write automatically, most of its output rubbish. When Borlsover dies he bequeaths his right hand to Eustace. Eustace is initially unaware that the hand is in a box he is sent and when something unnoticed escapes from the box he believes it to be a rat. Unlike his uncle, the hand has become malign, increasingly so after Eustace's treatment of it, and ultimately the hand kills Eustace. Harvey felt he needed to add an epilogue to explain why the hand should have become malignant, suggesting that it (and Borlsover) had become possessed by the spirit of an evil ancestor. Harvey was not the first to use the idea of a disembodied hand, but his image of the hand scuttling around in the dark like a rat or a scorpion is particularly strong and has made the story a classic.

"August Heat" is a very different type of story and in construction more effective. While sketching, an artist finds himself drawing the picture of a murderer in the dock. Later that day he goes for a walk and encounters a stonemason who is the exact image of the man he has drawn. The mason, similarly under impulse, has carved a grave stone bearing the artist's name and birth date, plus that day's date in August as his date of death. The story ends with the two men conversing surrounded by the stonemason's implements. The remarkable coincidence in the story is suggestive of a death-portent. The workings of fate and the inevitability of death were common themes in Harvey's fiction. In the stories "Peter Levisham," "Across the Moors," "Ghosts and Jossers," "Midnight House" and others, the individuals involved, often the narrators, receive either direct or coded messages about their fate but none seem able to affect it. Only in "Six to Six-Thirty" does a psychic phone-call prevent a murder.

The other theme strong in Harvey's work is that of the *femme fatale*. She is not necessarily a beautiful woman, more likely the opposite, but she is an obsessive dominating woman who, like fate, seeks to influence or control individuals' lives and ultimately drain the life-force from them. These characters appear in "Miss Avenel," where she is a psychic vampire, "Miss Cornelius," where she is a witch who invokes poltergeist activity, "Mrs. Ormerod," where she is an even more malevolent psychic vampire, as Mrs. Egan in "The Arm of Mrs. Egan," where the woman places a curse on her doctor following the death of her daughter, and as the Jekyll-and-Hyde like Mrs. Hollis in "The Flying Out of Mrs. Barnard Hollis," where her opposing spirit-selves become disembodied and engage in violent struggles. In all of these stories the women may initially be perceived as benign, just as Adrian Borslover in "The Beast With Fiver Fingers," but their malevolence emerges once they are wronged.

Behind all of these stories is a more basic theme of possession, and this is perhaps at the root of most of Harvey's writing. It is possible that Harvey convinced himself that the lack of control over one's own body was because it was in some way possessed by another. He may have thought this about his own condition, and he almost certainly witnessed it in the mood-swings of others. He titled one of his books *Moods and Tenses*, and in his introductory narrative to the stories, "The Double Eye," explores again the idea of parts of the body having a life of their own, independent of the brain or the heart. He pursues the concept of "the Evil Eye" suggesting that the visual organ can become "possessed" and exert an influence. In this episode the narrator is both an artist and a short-story writer whose work reflects differing aspects of his mind: there are "left-hand" works and "right-hand" ones.

Harvey used the theme of possession, in the form of lingering malignancies, in several stories, but none better than in "The Ankardyne Pew." This story has been likened to the work of M. R. James, but this is primarily because of its antiquarian aspects, and to some degree because of the gradually developed atmosphere. The story features another of Harvey's mysterious old ladies, Miss Ankardyne, who has lived all her life in a house possessed of some evil residuum that manifests itself in the sound of birds. It transpires that the chapel had once been used as a cockpit.

A brief word should be given to Harvey's other fiction. *The Misadventures of Athelstan Digby* is a volume of connected short stories which are essentially humorous but become increasingly bizarre in tracing through the investigations of a detective. Digby returns in the murder mystery *The Mysterious Mr. Badman*. *Caprimulgus* is a much overlooked and very enjoyable children's fantasy. Children create from their imagination a supernatural being with whom they then have adventures.

Harvey was a skilled writer who wrote with an artistic and poetic vision. The grotesqueness of some of his stories is balanced by a strain of humour that pervades others of his tales and perhaps gives us a glimpse of a man who was a remarkable survivor despite all that life threw at him.

—Mike Ashley

HAUTALA, Rick

Nationality: American. **Born:** Richard Henry Hautala, in 1949. **Family:** Married; three children. Lives in Maine.

HORROR, GHOST AND GOTHIC PUBLICATIONS

Novels

Moondeath. New York, Zebra, 1980.
Moonbog. New York, Zebra, 1982.
Night Stone. New York, Zebra, 1986.
Little Brothers. New York, Zebra, 1988.
Moonwalker. New York, Zebra, 1989.
Winter Wake. New York, Warner, 1989.
Dead Voices. New York, Warner, 1990.
Cold Whisper. New York, Zebra, 1991.
Dark Silence. New York, Zebra, 1992.
Ghost Light. New York, Zebra, 1993.
Twilight Time. New York, Zebra, 1994.
Shades of Night. New York, Zebra, 1995.
Beyond the Shroud. Clarkston, Georgia, White Wolf, 1996.
The Mountain King. Baltimore, Maryland, CD Publications, 1996.

*   *   *

The state of Maine has been the setting for many of Stephen King's popular horror novels, but he isn't the only writer to successfully marry the small-town atmosphere of northern New England with supernatural horror. With over a dozen novels in print, Rick Hautala has established himself as a steady source of powerful, suspenseful novels, although he has often moved away from the supernatural in favour of more mundane terrors.

His first novel was *Moondeath*, set in a small New Hampshire town bedeviled by a werewolf. Although the plot is fairly straightforward, lycanthropy with a hint of witchcraft, the novel stands out because of the evocative settings and a sizable cast of credible characters. Though relatively crude by Hautala's later standards, the book remains readable and frequently chilling. *Moonbog* turned up the intensity considerably, but without resorting to demons or other monsters. A serial killer specializing in children haunts the bogs of a small New England town, until finally brought to justice in a particularly fierce finale.

The *Night Stone* is a haunted-house story with some unusual twists. Beth is disturbed by her parents' decision to move to the old house in Maine, but somewhat mollified by the discovery of a doll which she senses has some secret property. Her subsequent dreams are filled with frightening images and her parents begin to act strangely as Beth and her family discover they are in the grip of an angry supernatural force. Hautala drew upon local legend

for *Little Brothers*, a major leap forward from his earlier work. The title refers to supposedly mythical creatures from Indian legends, diminutive humanoids who emerge periodically to slaughter and devour people. The protagonist is a young boy who witnessed the killing of his family, and who fears that he is slated to be on the next menu.

Moonwalker transfers a common horror theme, the zombie, from its usual setting and imposes it on the New England countryside with startling effectiveness. The town of Dyer has been plagued by disappearances, but the local people won't talk about the matter, nor are they willing to speak of the silent figures that labour in the village fields. An outsider dares to break the silence and finds himself ranged against an army of the walking dead. Hautala avoids the obvious devices popularized in recent films and concentrates instead on building an eerie atmosphere and a sense of mystery. *Winter Wake* is a more conventional ghost story. John Carlson brings his family to a small island off the coast of Maine, the place where he grew to manhood, hoping to find peace. But instead the family is troubled by the spirit of a dead woman who blames John for the wreckage of her life and who has returned from the dead to exact revenge. Hautala's strongest characterizations yet made this a major milestone in his career.

Witchcraft and the power of the dead also figure prominently in *Dead Voices*. Elizabeth is despondent after the accidental death of her young daughter Caroline and leaves her husband, returning to her home town in a desperate effort to find a sense of peace. Her respite is short-lived, however, because a sorceress determined to acquire power over the dead is raising corpses to do her bidding. When Caroline's body rises from the grave, host to a demonic spirit jealous of the living, Elizabeth is called upon to find a core of strength to save her daughter's soul.

Cold Whisper is the most inventive of Hautala's novels. Sarah's imaginary friend Tully is a bit too accommodating. Whenever she wishes that something bad would happen to someone with whom she's angry, Tully makes sure she gets her wish. Eventually horrified, Sarah repudiates Tully, hoping that he will fade away with time. But years later, a killer rapist murders her mother and threatens her life, and Sarah must once again turn to the dark side of herself to save her own life.

In *Dark Silence*, an old mill is home to a throng of angry ghosts, still resentful of their treatment while living. Brian Fraser returns to his home when his mother dies, unaware of the fact that she used her psychic powers to keep the revenants under control. Now that she's gone, they are free to spread their influence through the town and exact a terrible revenge. *Ghost Light* is also a ghost story, although it's almost incidental to the plot. The protagonist steals her brother-in-law's children when she realizes he is a killer. During the subsequent cross-country chase, the children have visions of a mysterious lady, a ghost who has returned to protect them.

Hautala switched largely to conventional devices of suspense after *Ghost Light*. *Twilight Time* is a darkly introspective novel of murder and revenge; there are scenes that are reminiscent of his horror fiction, particularly those involving the protagonist's descent toward multiple-personality disorder, but for the most part it's a standard suspense novel. *Shades of Night* is a psychological ghost story, a woman tormented by strange dreams filled with ghostly figures, dire warnings and the menacing figure of an unknown man. He returned to more overt supernatural elements with *Beyond the Shroud*. The protagonist is dead throughout the novel, his spirit wandering on an eerie other level of existence where the ghost of his daughter implores him to help prevent the murder of his widow. Unfortunately, it is very difficult for him to interact with the world of the living, and there are bizarre creatures threatening him in the world of the dead. The difficulties involved in thwarting the insane killer create a fascinating puzzle, and Hautala's world of the dead is distinctly unsettling.

Hautala writes occasional short fiction, though not as successfully as with his novels. Stories worth noting include "The Back of My Hands," "Cousin's Curse" and "Getting the Job Done." His major strengths are clearly as a novelist, and most of the tension in his work derives from the emotions of his characters rather than the physical events in which they participate.

—Don D'Ammassa

HAWTHORNE, Julian

Nationality: American. **Born:** Boston, 22 June 1846; son of the novelist Nathaniel Hawthorne. **Education:** Lowell Scientific School, Harvard; trained as a hydrographic engineer in Dresden, Germany. **Career:** Worked briefly for the New York Dock Department; lived in England for many years, where he established himself as a novelist; worked for the *Spectator*, London; lived in California in later life, and wrote for pulp magazines. **Died:** 14 July 1934.

HORROR, GHOST AND GOTHIC PUBLICATIONS

Novels

Idolatry: A Romance. Boston, Osgood, and London, King, 1874.
Archibald Malmaison. New York, Funk and Wagnalls, and London, Bentley, 1879.
The Professor's Sister: A Romance. Chicago, Belford Clarke, 1888; as *The Spectre of the Camera*, London, Chatto and Windus, 1888.

Short Stories

The Laughing Mill and Other Stories. London, Macmillan, 1879.
Ellice Quentin and Other Stories. London, Chatto and Windus, 1880.
Yellow-Cap. London, Longmans Green, 1880.
Prince Saroni's Wife, and The Pearl Shell Necklace. London, Chatto and Windus, 1882; New York, Funk and Wagnall, 1884.
David Poindexter's Disappearance and Other Tales. New York, Appleton, 1888; expanded edition, London, Chatto and Windus, 1888.
Kildhurm's Oak; A Strange Friend. New York, Burt, 1889.
Constance, and Calbot's Rival. New York, Appleton, 1889.
Six-Cent Sam's. St. Paul, Minnesota, Price McGill, 1893; as *Mr. Dunton's Invention and Other Stories*, Springfield, Massachusetts, Merriam, 1896.

Other

Editor, *Doctor Grimshawe's Secret: A Romance*, by Nathaniel Hawthorne. Boston, Houghton Mifflin, and London, Longmans Green, 1883.
Editor, *The Lock and Key Library; Classic Mystery and Detective Stories.* 10 vols., New York, Review of Reviews, 1909.

OTHER PUBLICATIONS

Novels

Bressant. New York, Appleton, and London, King, 1873.
Garth. New York, Appleton, and London, Bentley, 1877.
Mrs. Gainsborough's Diamonds. New York, Appleton, 1878; London, Chatto and Windus, 1879.
Sebastian Strome. London, Bentley, 1879; New York, Appleton, 1880.
Dust. Boston, Houghton Mifflin, 1882; London, Chatto and Windus, 1883.
Fortune's Fool. New York, Osgood, and London, Chatto and Windus, 1883.
Beatrix Randolph. New York, Osgood, and London, Chatto and Windus, 1884.
Love—or a Name. Boston, Ticknor and Fields, and London, Chatto and Windus, 1884.
Miss Cadogna. London, Chatto and Windus, 1885.
Noble Blood. New York, Appleton, 1885.
John Parmelee's Curse. New York, Cassell, 1886.
An American Penman. New York, Cassell, 1887; London, Cassell, 1888.
The Great Bank Robbery. New York, Cassell, 1887; London, Cassell, 1888.
A Tragic Mystery. New York, Cassell, 1887; London, Cassell, 1888.
A Dream and a Forgetting. Chicago, Belford Clarke, 1888; London, Chatto and Windus, 1888.
Another's Crime. New York, Cassell, 1888; London, Cassell, 1889.
Section 558; or, The Fatal Letter. New York and London, Cassell, 1888.
Pauline. Chicago, U.S. Book Company, 1890.
A Messenger from the Unknown. New York, Collier, 1892.
An American Monte Cristo. London, Allen, 1893.
A Fool of Nature. New York, Scribner, and London, Downey, 1896.
Love is a Spirit. New York, Harper, 1896.

Short Stories

The Trial of Gideon; and, Countess Almara's Murder. New York, Funk and Wagnall, 1886.

*   *   *

Julian Hawthorne's bibliography is extraordinarily complex. Although born in the US, to which nation he returned in later years, he was long resident in London and he frequently rearranged and retitled (and sometimes rewrote) his works for their English and American publications. He began publishing short fiction in 1870, much of his early work—notably "Otto of Roses" (1871), more effectively revised as "The Rose of Death" (1876)—consisting of weird tales. Even works which were supposedly naturalistic frequently contained baroque embellishments. His first novel, *Bressant*, briefly involves a ghost but is not nearly as strange as the conscientiously Gothic and oddly effective *Idolatry*, whose tortuous but non-supernatural plot involves two fateful rings. The vivid visionary fantasy "The New Endymion" (1879) offers a modern version of a Greek myth popular with the Romantics. The four fantasy novellas collected in *Yellow-Cap*, ostensibly written for children, include the notable dark allegory "Calladon." In his use of these various outré materials Julian was, of course, following precedents set by his famous father Nathaniel Hawthorne, but his work was much more pedestrian no matter how hard he tried to be adventurous.

Julian Hawthorne's most notable weird novels are the dual personality story *Archibald Malmaison* and the metaphysical fantasy *The Professor's Sister*. The former uses its rather peculiar motif to neatly cruel effect; the luckless hero undergoes an abrupt and complete personality-change, involving a dramatic increase in his intellectual powers, which is reversed many years later with tragic consequences. The latter is a hectic account of the Eternal Triangle which includes an intriguing account of artificially suspended animation. His most wholehearted and most satisfactory horror stories were, however, confined to shorter lengths. *David Poindexter's Disappearance and Other Stories* includes the best of them, "Ken's Mystery," which is a frequently reprinted timeslip romance set in Ireland, involving a magic ring and a female vampire.

A feverishly melodramatic novella in which a tree becomes the agent of a family curse, "Kildhurm's Oak," appeared in *Ellice Quentin and Other Stories* before being reprinted in *Kildhurm's Oak; A Strange Friend*, whose second item is a marginal fantasy. The title novella of *The Laughing Mill and Other Stories* is an elaborate but non-horrific ghost story which was reprinted as the second item in *Prince Saroni's Wife, and The Pearl Shell Necklace*. One of the other stories accompanying "The Laughing Mill" in the 1879 collection, which became the second element in *Constance, and Calbot's Rival*, is an eccentric but engaging antiquarian romance in which a manuscript is strangely affected when droplets of the elixir of life are spilled upon it. "Constance" is a long novella involving spiritualism and ghosts, which has more romance in it than horror and which eventually peters out in dispirited fashion.

The *femme fatale* story "Sinfire" has no supernatural content and never manages to inject any force into its account of a metaphorical family curse. Like all the "complete novels" published in *Lippincott's Magazine* it was designed to facilitate extraction and binding as a do-it-yourself book, and is sometimes listed as one; so is the routine visionary fantasy "The Golden Fleece," one of many tales of hidden treasure penned by the younger Hawthorne. Both stories are marginal with respect to the author's contributions to the horror genre. His last story collection, *Six-Cent Sam's*, uses the familiar device of a club whose members take turns telling tall tales; the inclusions are essentially trivial although "The Unseen Man's Story," about living mummies, is not without interest.

Julian Hawthorne's literary career was interrupted after the turn of the century by a jail term which he served for his (probably unwitting) involvement in a land speculation fraud; he then moved to California, where he wrote for newspapers and tried to write for the movies but found it impossible to publish books. The best of his subsequent fantasies, and one of the best of all his horror stories, is "The Delusion of Ralph Penwyn" (1909), an atypically economical tale of hallucinatory paranoia. Towards the end of his writing life he did a good deal of work for pulp magazines owned by Frank A. Munsey; this included a series of spiritualist romances featuring the psychically gifted Martha Klemm, which are on the borderline of the "psychic detective" sub-genre. The series included "Absolute Evil" (1918), "Fires Rekindled" (1919) and the novel "Sara Was Judith?" (1920). His last published works included "The Jewels of Nobleman Jack" (1921), a bizarre adventure story involving an unnaturally clever chimpanzee.

Julian Hawthorne edited a notable series of anthologies, initially issued as *Library of the World's Best Mystery and Detective Stories* and much expanded as *The Lock and Key Library; Classic Mystery and Detective Stories*, which included many translations of important supernatural stories from various European languages. They have been productively mined by many subsequent anthologists. He also cobbled together a quasi-Gothic novel from miscellaneous documents left behind by his father, *Doctor Grimshawe's Secret*, which had earlier been organized by other hands into the rather different *Septimius* (1872) and *The Dolliver Romance* (1876).

Had he not worked in the shadow of his much more able father Julian Hawthorne's endeavours might have been viewed more sympathetically, but he was doomed to disappoint everyone who knew what his surname signified. Had he not had such a famous name to exploit he might have found it harder to break into print himself, but the advantage ultimately became a curse. His best short stories are not far short of first-rate and most of his weird fiction is of some interest but the bulk of his production was, alas, lacklustre hackwork which always seemed to his fiercest critics to be a nasty stain on the family escutcheon. The total neglect into which his work has fallen is, however, decidedly unjust. An eclectic collection of his supernatural fiction is long overdue and might serve as a crucial aid to the redemption of his reputation.

—Brian Stableford

HAWTHORNE, Nathaniel

Nationality: American. **Born:** Nathaniel Hathorne in Salem, Massachusetts, 4 July 1804. **Education:** Samuel Archer's School, Salem, 1819; Bowdoin College, Brunswick, Maine, 1821-25. **Family:** Married Sophia Peabody in 1842; two daughters and one son. **Career:** Lived with his mother in Salem, writing and contributing to periodicals, 1825-36; editor, *American Magazine of Useful and Entertaining Knowledge*, Boston, 1836; weigher and gager, Boston Customs House, 1839-41; invested in the Brook Farm Commune, West Roxbury, Massachusetts, and lived there, 1841-42; lived in Concord, Massachusetts, 1842-45, 1852, and 1860-64; surveyor, Salem Customs House, 1846-49; lived in Lenox, 1850-51, and West Newton, 1851, both Massachusetts; U.S. Consul, Liverpool, England, 1853-57; lived in Italy, 1858-59, and London, 1859-60. **Died:** 19 May 1864.

HORROR, GHOST AND GOTHIC PUBLICATIONS

Novels

The Scarlet Letter: A Romance. Boston, Ticknor, Reed and Fields, 1850; London, Johnston and Hunter, 1851.

The House of the Seven Gables: A Romance. Boston, Ticknor, Reed and Fields, and London, Bohn, 1851.

The Marble Faun. Boston, Ticknor and Fields, 1860; as *Transformation; or, The Romance of Monte Beni*, London, Smith Elder, 1860.

Septimius: A Romance, edited by Una Hawthorne and Robert Browning. London, Henry King, 1872; as *Septimius Felton; or, The Elixir of Life*, Boston, Osgood, 1872.

Dr. Grimshaw's Secret: A Romance, edited by Julian Hawthorne. Boston, Houghton Mifflin, and London, Longmans, Green, 1883.

Short Stories

Twice-Told Tales. Boston, American Stationers Company, 1837; revised and enlarged edition, Boston, Munroe, 1842; London, Kent and Richards, 1849.
Mosses from an Old Manse. New York and London, Wiley and Putnam, 1846; revised and enlarged edition, Boston, Ticknor and Fields, 1854.
The Snow-Image and Other Twice-Told Tales. Boston, Ticknor, Reed and Fields, and London, Bohn, 1851.
The Dolliver Romance and Other Pieces, edited by Sophia Hawthorne. Boston, Osgood, 1876.

OTHER PUBLICATIONS

Novels

The Blithedale Romance. 2 vols., London, Chapman and Hall, 1852; 1 vol., Boston, Ticknor, Reed and Fields, 1852.
Pansie: A Fragment. London, Hotten, 1864.

Short Stories

Fanshawe: A Tale. Boston, Marsh and Capen, 1828.
The Celestial Rail-Road. Boston, Wilder, 1843; London, Houlston and Stoneman, 1844.
Fanshawe and Other Pieces. Boston, Osgood, 1876.
The Ghost of Dr. Harris. N.p., 1900.

Other

Grandfather's Chair: A History for Youth. Boston, E.P. Peabody, 1841, revised edition, Boston, Tappan and Dennet, 1842.
Famous Old People, Being the Second Epoch of Grandfather's Chair. Boston, E.P. Peabody, 1841.
Liberty Tree, with the Last Words of Grandfather's Chair. Boston, E.P. Peabody, 1841.
Biographical Stories for Children. Boston, Tappan and Dennet 1842; London, Sonnenschein, 1898; republished as *True Stories from History and Biography*, n.p. 1851.
A Wonder-Book for Girls and Boys. Boston, Ticknor, Reed and Fields, and London, Bohn, 1851.
Life of Franklin Pierce (campaign biography). Boston, Ticknor, Reed and Fields, 1852; London, Routledge, 1853.
Tanglewood Tales for Girls and Boys, Being a Second Wonder Book. London, Chapman and Hall, and Boston, Ticknor, Reed and Fields, 1853.
Our Old Home: A Series of English Sketches. 1 vol., Boston, Ticknor, Reed and Fields, 1863; 2 vols., London, Smith, Elder, 1863.
Passages from the American Note-Books, edited by Sophia Hawthorne, 2 vols. Boston, Ticknor, Reed and Fields, and London, Smith, Elder, 1868.
Passages from the English Note-Books, edited by Sophia Hawthorne. 2 vols. Boston, Fields, Osgood, 1870, and London, Strahan, 1870.
Passages from the French and Italian Note-Books, edited by Una Hawthorne, 2 vols. London, Strahan, 1871; Boston, Osgood, 1872.

*

Film Adaptations: *House of the Seven Gables*, 1910, 1940; *The Scarlet Letter*, 1926, 1934, 1973, 1979 (television movie), 1986 (television serial), 1995.

Bibliography: *Hawthorne: A Descriptive Bibliography* by C.E. Frazer Clark, Jr., Pittsburgh, University of Pittsburgh Press, 1978; *Hawthorne and the Critics: A Checklist of Criticism 1900-1978* by Jeanetta Boswell, Metuchen, New Jersey, Scarecrow Press, 1982.

Critical Studies (selection): *Hawthorne* by Henry James, 1879; *Hawthorne: A Biography* by Randall Stewart, Hamdon, Connecticut, Archon, 1948; *Hawthorne* by Mark Van Doren, Westport, Connecticut, Greenwood Press, 1949; *Hawthorne's Fiction: The Light and the Dark,* 1952, revised edition, 1964, and *Hawthorne's Imagery,* 1969, both by Richard Harter Fogle, both published by Norman, University of Oklahoma Press; *Hawthorne: A Critical Study,* 1955, revised edition, 1963, Cambridge, Massachusetts, Harvard University Press, and *The Presence of Hawthorne,* Baton Rouge, Louisiana State University Press, 1979, both by Hyatt H. Waggoner; *Hawthorne's Tragic Vision* by Roy R. Male, Austin, University of Texas Press, 1957; *Hawthorne: An Introduction and Interpretation,* New York, Barnes and Noble, 1961, and *Hawthorne: A Biography,* New York, Oxford University Press, 1980, both by Arlin Turner; *Hawthorne* by Terence Martin, New York, Twayne, 1965, revised edition, 1983; *The Sins of the Fathers: Hawthorne's Psychological Themes* by Frederick Crews, New York, Oxford University Press, 1966; *Hawthorne: A Collection of Critical Essays* edited by A. N. Kaul, Englewood Cliffs, New Jersey, Prentice-Hall, 1966; *Twentieth-Century Interpretations of The Scarlet Letter* edited by John C. Gerber, Englewood Cliffs, New Jersey, Prentice-Hall,1968; *Plots and Characters in the Fiction and Sketches of Hawthorne* by Robert L. Gale, Hamden, Connecticut, Archon, 1968; *Hawthorne, Transcendental Symbolist* by Marjorie Elder, Athens, Ohio University Press, 1969; *The Recognition of Hawthorne: Selected Criticism since 1828* edited by B. Bernard Cohen, Ann Arbor, University of Michigan Press, 1969; *Hawthorne as Myth-Maker: A Study in Imagination* by Hugo McPherson, University of Toronto Press, 1969; *Hawthorne: The Critical Heritage,* New York, Barnes and Noble, 1970, and *Hawthorne: A Collection of Criticism,* New York, McGraw Hill, 1975, both edited by J. Donald Crowley; *The Pursuit of Form: A Study of Hawthorne and the Romance* by John Caldwell Stubbs, Urbana, University of Illinois Press, 1970; *Hawthorne's Early Tales: A Critical Study* by Neal F. Doubleday, Durham, North Carolina, Duke University Press, 1972; *The Shape of Hawthorne's Career* by Nina Baym, Ithaca, New York, Cornell University Press, 1976; *Hawthorne: The Poetics of Enchantment* by Edgar A. Dryden, Ithaca, New York, Cornell University Press, 1977; *Rediscovering Hawthorne* by Kenneth Dauber, Princeton, New Jersey, Princeton University Press, 1977; *Hawthorne and the Truth of Dreams* by Rita K. Gollin, Baton Rouge, Louisiana State University Press, 1979; *A Reader's Guide to the Short Stories of Hawthorne* by Lea B.V. Newman, Boston, G. K. Hall, 1979; *Hawthorne: The English Experience 1853-1864* by Raymona E. Hull, Pittsburgh, University of Pittsburgh Press, 1980; *Hawthorne in His Times* by James R. Mellow, Boston, Houghton Mifflin, 1980; *The*

Productive Tension of Hawthorne's Art by Claudia D. Johnson, University of Alabama Press, 1981; *Hawthorne: New Critical Essays* edited by A. Robert Lee, London, Vision Press, and Totowa, New Jersey, Barnes and Noble, 1982; *Family Themes in Hawthorne's Fiction* by Gloria C. Erlich, New Brunswick, New Jersey, Rutgers University Press, 1984; *The Province of Piety: Moral History in Hawthorne's Early Tales* by Michael J. Colacurcio, Cambridge, Massachusettes, Harvard University Press, 1984, and *New Essays on The Scarlet Letter* edited by Colacurcio, New York, Cambridge University Press, 1985; *Hawthorne's Secret: An Un-told Tale* by Philip Young, Boston, D. R. Godine, 1984; *Critical Essays on Hawthorne's Short Stories* edited by Albert J. von Frank, Boston, G. K. Hall, 1991; *Salem Is My Dwelling Place: A Life of Nathaniel Hawthorne* by Edwin Haviland Miller, Iowa City, University of Iowa Press, 1991; *Contexts for Hawthorne: The Marble Faun and the Politics of Openness and Closure in American Literature* by Milton R. Stern, Urbana, University of Illinois Press, 1991; *The Office of the Scarlet Letter* by Sacvan Bercovitch, Baltimore, Johns Hopkins University Press, 1991; *The Production of Personal Life: Class, Gender, and the Psychological in Hawthorne's Fiction* by Joel Pfister, Stanford, California, Stanford University Press, 1991; *The Critical Response to Nathaniel Hawthorne's The Scarlet Letter* edited and introduced by Gary Scharnhorst, New York, Greenwood Press, 1992; *Nathaniel Hawthorne: A Study of the Short Fiction* by Nancy Bunge, New York, Twayne, 1993.

*   *   *

Nathaniel Hawthorne and Edgar Allan Poe were the two founding fathers of modern American imaginative fiction. Writing a generation after Charles Brockden Brown had introduced the Gothic sensibility into American fiction, they were the writers who pioneered its distinctive evolution. Their short fiction was sometimes scathingly comical but it was the aesthetic response of horror, and the emotions associated with it, that were their chief stock-in-trade. Both were preoccupied with the mechanics of conscience but where Poe tended to the feverish, hounding his characters to insanity, Hawthorne was always clinical, subjecting the mental processes of his characters to a minute dissection which rarely permitted them the luxury of taking leave of their senses. His works include some of the most acute and most challenging moral allegories ever produced.

The fabular tales included in the first version of *Twice-Told Tales* are mostly tentative, but they include "The Prophetic Pictures," in which a painter captures the fates as well as the faces of his subjects, and "Dr. Heidegger's Experiment," in which a modest elixir of life reveals as it revives. The tales added to the second edition include a quartet collectively entitled "Legends of the Province-House," which features three rationalized ghost stories.

Mosses from an Old Manse is Hawthorne's best collection, including his finest works. "Young Goodman Brown" yields to temptation and discovers that his community is riddled with secret diabolism; his life is ruined by the awareness that his wife is as corrupt as the rest. In "The Birthmark" a scientist who tries to erase a slight flaw in his wife's complexion obliterates her entirely. In "Rappaccini's Daughter" a young student falls in love with a girl raised in a garden of poisons, but his attempt to counter the infection she has suffered in consequence goes tragically awry.

"The Celestial Railroad" traverses the landscape of Bunyan's *Pilgrim's Progress*. "The New Adam and Eve" survey the world devastated by Divine Judgment and accept that it would be better not to set the tragedy in train again. The augmented edition also contains "Feathertop," in which an animated scarecrow mirrors the plight of many humans but is driven to despair by the sight of his own reflection.

The Snow-Image and Other Twice-Told Tales is slighter and, on average, more sentimental than its predecessors. In the title story the children who animate the image by means of their imagination cannot sustain its activity against the scepticism of their parents. However, "Ethan Brand"—also known as "The Unpardonable Sin" and subtitled "A chapter from an Abortive Romance"—is much darker and more enigmatic, refusing to provide a full description of the unpardonable sin which the labourer-turned-showman claims to have discovered after a long search. "The Devil in Manuscript" is a similarly elusive account of the perils of authorial arrogance.

The Scarlet Letter is a classic of American literature, a psychological melodrama about the cruel and unusual punishment of a sin committed out of love. The heroine, who lives in a colonial town akin to that inhabited by "Young Goodman Brown," gives birth to a child while her husband is away, seemingly lost in the wilderness. She is instructed to wear an embroidered A (for "adulteress") which declares her a scarlet woman, but she will not name her lover so that he might share her punishment. When her husband returns, demonized by his long sojourn in the dark heart of the continent, he takes up the thread of this inquiry, adding greatly to the torment suffered by the clergyman he (rightly) believes to be responsible. There is no account of the war between puritanical moralism and natural inclination which can be reckoned more meticulous or more powerful.

The House of the Seven Gables has never been ranked anywhere nearly as high as its predecessor, and on the surface it is a much more orthodox American Gothic romance in which a monstrous house—symbolic, of course, of the family whose home it is—infects all who dwell within it with creeping corruption. It is a far more elaborate and clinical account of hereditary decadence than Poe's "Fall of the House of Usher," but in this instance the scrupulousness of the analysis does not work to the advantage of the allegory. The novel was, however, a key influence on the Lovecraftian school of horror fiction, and its dogged fascination with the grim symbolism of the ominous edifice has obvious parallels in the imagery of Hollywood.

The novel usually known nowadays as *The Marble Faun*, after the symbolic sculpture which is its centrepiece, is even more dispiriting, in its way, than *The House of the Seven Gables*—but not inappropriately, given that its subject is "the demon of weariness" (a puritanized variant of the thoroughly Catholic sin of *accidie*). It is, however, a novel with a more upbeat thrust than either of its predecessors, carefully containing the hope that a human being's fall into corruption, however inevitable, might be the prelude to some kind of rejuvenative rise. Hawthorne fails to carry this hope through to any firm conviction, but he seems to have been troubled by his own failure. At his death he left behind no less than three incomplete, and sharply contrasted, drafts of a novel about the elixir of life, which he had tried and failed to shape to his own satisfaction. One was published as *Septimius* and *Septimius Felton*, another as *The Dolliver Romance*, and bits of all three were cobbled together by his son Julian Hawthorne into *Dr.*

Grimshawe's Secret. As with other nineteenth-century romances about the elixir of life, Hawthorne's is deeply unconvinced about the value of such a possession and anxious about the effect that obsession with its discovery might have on its seekers, but the author was unable to find his way to any sturdy conclusion.

As is only befitting in an honest puritan, however dubious his puritanism may have become, Hawthorne looked back at his own work with conscientious modesty. The preface to the 1851 edition of *Twice-Told Tales* judges that they are "flowers that blossomed in too retired a shade" and suggests that the book "requires to be read in the clear, brown, twilight atmosphere in which it was written" lest its message fade away entirely beneath the harsh light of scepticism. In the prefaces to *The Scarlet Letter* and *The House of the Seven Gables*, however, the sarcasm of this self-effacement becomes manifest as he refuses to mend his ways in the face of criticisms. In the latter he observes that the author "considered it hardly worth his while . . . relentlessly to impale the story with its moral, as with an iron rod—or rather, as by sticking a pin through a butterfly" lest he deprive it of life and cause it "to stiffen in a ungainly and unnatural attitude." This was a difficulty which afflicted all his work: how to write sharp and scrupulous moral fantasies of a distinctively modern character, without suffocating the product with over-conspicuous artifice. His achievement was to explore artifices of many different kinds, and to bring the great majority of them to a very vital kind of life.

—Brian Stableford

HEARD, H(enry) F(itzgerald)

Pseudonym: Gerald Heard. **Nationality:** British. **Born:** London, 6 October 1889. **Education:** Gonville and Caius College, Cambridge, B.A. (honours) in history 1911, graduate work 1911-12. **Career:** Worked with the Agricultural Cooperative Movement in Ireland, 1919-23, and in England, 1923-27; editor, *Realist,* London, 1929; Lecturer, Oxford University, 1929-31; science commentator, BBC Radio, London, 1930-34; settled in the United States, 1937; visiting lecturer, Washington University, St. Louis, 1951-52, 1955-56; Haskell Foundation Lecturer, Oberlin College, Ohio, 1958. **Awards:** Bollingen grant, 1955; British Academy Hertz award. **Died:** 14 August 1971.

Horror, Ghost and Gothic Publications

Novel

The Black Fox: A Novel of the "Seventies" (as Gerald Heard). London, Cassell, 1950; New York, Harper, 1951.

Short Stories

The Great Fog and Other Weird Tales. New York, Vanguard Press, 1944; revised edition, London, Cassell, 1947; as *The Great Fog: Weird Tales of Terror and Detection,* Garden City, New York, Sun Dial Press, 1946.
The Lost Cavern and Other Tales of the Fantastic. New York, Vanguard Press, 1948; London, Cassell, 1949.

Other Publications

Novels

A Taste for Honey. New York, Vanguard Press, 1941; London, Cassell, 1942; as *A Taste for Murder,* New York, Avon, 1955.
Reply Paid: A Novel. New York, Vanguard Press, 1942; London, Cassell, 1943.
Murder by Reflection. New York, Vanguard Press, 1942; London, Cassell, 1945.
Doppelgängers: An Episode of the Fourth, the Psychological, Revolution, 1997. New York, Vanguard Press, 1947; London, Cassell, 1948.
The Notched Hairpin. New York, Vanguard Press, 1949; London, Cassell, 1952.

Short Stories

Gabriel and the Creatures (as Gerald Heard). New York, Harper, 1952; as *Wishing Well: An Outline of the Evolution of the Mammals Told as a Series of Stories about How the Animals Got Their Wishes,* London, Faber, 1953.

Other as Gerald Heard

Narcissus: An Anatomy of Clothes. London, Kegan Paul, and New York, Dutton, 1924.
The Ascent of Humanity: An Essay on the Evolution of Civilization. London, Cape, and New York, Harcourt Brace, 1929.
The Emergence of Man. London, Cape, 1931; New York, Harcourt Brace, 1932.
Social Substance of Religion: An Essay on the Evolution of Religion. London, Allen and Unwin, and New York, Harcourt Brace, 1931.
This Surprising World: A Journalist Looks At Science. London, Cobden Sanderson, 1932.
Those Hurrying Years: An Historical Outline 1900-1933. London, Chatto and Windus, and New York, Oxford University Press, 1934.
Science in the Making. London, Faber, 1935.
The Source of Civilisation. London, Cape, 1935; New York, Harper, 1937.
The Significance of the New Pacifism, with *Pacifism and Philosophy,* by Aldous Huxley. London, Headley, 1935.
Exploring the Stratosphere. London, Nelson, 1936.
Science Front 1936. London, Cassell, 1937.
The Third Morality. London, Cassell, and New York, Morrow, 1937.
Pain, Sex and Time: A New Hypothesis of Evolution. New York, Harper, and London, Cassell, 1939.
The Creed of Christ: An Interpretation of the Lord's Prayer. New York, Harper, 1940; London, Cassell, 1941.
A Quaker Meditation. Wallingford, Pennsylvania, Pendle Hill, 1940(?).
The Code of Christ: An Interpretation of the Beatitudes. New York, Harper, 1941; London, Cassell, 1943.
Training for the Life of the Spirit. London, Cassell, 2 vols., 1941-44; New York, Harper, 1 vol., n.d.
Man the Master. New York, Harper, 1941; London, Faber, 1942.
A Dialogue in the Desert. London, Cassell, and New York, Harper, 1942.

A Preface to Prayer. New York, Harper, 1944; London, Cassell, 1945.

The Recollection. Stanford, California, Delkin, 1944.

The Gospel According to Gamaliel. New York, Harper, 1945; London, Cassell, 1946.

Militarism's Post-Mortem. London, P.P.U., 1946.

The Eternal Gospel. New York, Harper, 1946; London, Cassell, 1948.

Is God Evident? An Essay Toward a Natural Theology. New York, Harper, 1948; London, Faber, 1950.

Is God in History? An Inquiry into Human and Pre-Human History in Terms of the Doctrine of Creation, Fall, and Redemption. New York, Harper, 1950; London, Faber, 1951.

Morals since 1900. London, Dakers, and New York, Harper, 1950.

The Riddle of the Flying Saucers. London, Carroll and Nicholson, 1950; as *Is Another World Watching?.* New York, Harper, 1951; revised edition, New York, Bantam, 1953.

Ten Questions on Prayer. Wallingford, Pennsylvania, Pendle Hill, 1951.

The Human Venture. New York, Harper, 1955.

Kingdom Without God: Road's End for the Social Gospel, with others. Los Angeles, Foundation for Social Research, 1956.

Training for a Life of Growth. Santa Monica, California, Wayfarer Press, 1959.

The Five Ages of Man: The Psychology of Human History. New York, Julian Press, 1964.

Editor, *Prayers and Meditations.* New York, Harper, 1949.

*   *   *

Gerald Heard (as his earliest books were signed) was a successful journalist and broadcaster in the UK between the wars, who wrote a number of book-length essays extending a sprawling patchwork of evolutionary science, history, social philosophy, psychology and religion (the last two heavily tempered by fashionable pseudoscience and mysticism). In 1937 he emigrated to California, where he spent the rest of his life; most of his American publications were signed H. F. Heard, although his British publishers retained the signature more familiar to English readers. His fiction was distributed across four popular genres—crime fiction, science fiction, weird fiction and children's fantasy—although his reputation as a modern sage saved his productions from the stigmatization of genre packaging. He brought a distinctively dogged philosophical adventurousness to all of his work, even his didactic animal fable *Gabriel and the Creatures.*

An element of horror enters into some of Heard's crime novels by virtue of the bizarre ways in which murder is committed therein. *A Taste for Honey* features killer bees, while *Reply Paid* and *Murder by Reflection* both involve the cruel deployment of harmful radiation. The third novel is quite unlike its predecessors; it does not feature the unnamed but easily recognisable Great Detective who unravels the earlier mysteries and its denouement involves a very different kind of retribution. *The Notched Hairpin,* which belatedly completed the Holmesian trilogy, features a much more trivial instrument of death but follows the example of *Murder by Reflection* in laying out an intense study of the psychology of homicide.

Both of Heard's short-story collections mix weird tales with science fiction. The most significant horror story in *The Great Fog and Other Weird Tales* is the novella "Dromenon," in which the restoration of an old church enables a curious antiquary to fathom the true and startling nature of early Christian worship by reproducing its inspiring context: a disturbing combination of architecture, light and music. "The Swap" is an unusually sober identity-exchange story and "The Cat 'I Am'" an account of an unusual haunting. "The Crayfish" is yet another tale of unusual murder. The downbeat "Despair Deferred. . . ?", whose theme overlaps that of "Dromenon" although it has no supernatural content, was replaced in the UK edition of the book by an unusually concise *conte cruel* about the Inquisition, "Vindicae Flammae," and the mystically inclined scientific romance "Eclipse."

The Lost Cavern contains four novellas. The title story is an excellent account of the discovery of a population of giant intelligent bats. "The Cup" is a fine and highly unusual story about an art forger who locates the Holy Grail in a little church and plans to substitute a fake, but is forced into a change of heart and mind when he witnesses an unsuccessful attempt by inchoate forces of evil to disconcert and dispossess the relic's custodian. "The Chapel of Ease" is a more subdued account of a haunted church, stretched far beyond its natural length by the compulsive verbosity to which the author was always prone.

There is a considerable element of horror in the mystical scientific romance *Doppelgängers,* whose confusions of identity recall such Gothic classics as James Hogg's *Confessions of a Justified Sinner,* but the main thrust of the work is the development of a highly idiosyncratic theory of progressive social evolution. Heard's purest and most traditional horror story was his last novel, *The Black Fox.* Its central character is a Victorian Anglican clergyman and Islamist who is passed over for promotion and is tempted to deploy an Islamic magical formula to curse the preferred candidate; he has no real expectation of success but the man does indeed sicken and die, leaving his murderer to be haunted and harassed by the demons he has invoked. These externalized manifestations of conscience drive the luckless scholar to mental breakdown, forcing his sister to seek assistance from a Sufi mystic; unfortunately, the only exorcism the Sufi can contrive requires a sacrificial victim. Although the novel is wordy and perhaps overly pretentious it builds up considerable tension by virtue of its implacably earnest treatment of its central theme and the serious attention it pays to fundamental issues of theology.

The uncollected stories which Heard contributed to various magazines and anthologies are markedly lighter in tone than those in his collections but still carry a certain chilling frisson. "The Collector" (1951) features an aesthetically-sensitive giant squid and "The Marble Ear" (1952) is a variant on the classic theme of how best to employ a gift of three wishes. "B + M - Planet 4," in Raymond J. Healy's *New Tales of Space and Time* (1951), is an interplanetary fantasy about humanoids in thrall to giant bees and "Cyclops," in Kendell Foster Crossen's *Future Tense* (1952), is a post-holocaust story every bit as ambivalent as the author's science-fiction classic "The Great Fog," which provided the prototype for many later tales of benign catastrophe by other hands.

Many of the concerns which fascinated Heard seem dated now; his psychological theories are way behind the times and his theological investigations may appear murky and tedious to contemporary readers. He was certainly an original thinker, but his harshest critics would doubtless assert that the manner of his thought was unduly convoluted and its rewards unfortunately meagre. Even at his most relaxed he was not easily readable, but he does not deserve the total neglect into which his work has fallen. When he deployed his talents to best effect, as he did in "Dromenon," "The

Lost Cavern" and "The Cup," he produced first-rate stories that are markedly unlike the standard products of their genres. An eclectic collection of his best short fiction could bring together some extraordinary and fascinating works.

—Brian Stableford

HEARN, (Patricio) Lafcadio (Tessima Carlos)

Nationality: Irish (but took Japanese citizenship in 1891 and changed name to Koizumi Yakumo). **Born:** Santa Maura, Greece, 27 June 1850; brought up in Dublin. **Education:** St. Cuthbert's College, Ushaw, County Durham, England, 1863-66; Petits Precepteurs, Yvetot, near Rouen, France, 1867. **Family:** Married Setsuko Koizumi in 1891; three sons. **Career:** Lived in Paris, 1869, and New York, 1869-71; worked at various jobs in Cincinnati, 1872; proofreader, Robert Clarke Company, then staff member, *Trade List* weekly, and reporter, Cincinnati *Enquirer*, 1873-76, and Cincinnati *Commercial*, 1876-77; co-founder, *Ye Giglampz* satirical journal, Cincinnati, 1874; assistant editor, New Orleans *Item*, 1877-81; staff member, New Orleans *Times-Democrat*, 1881-87; lived in Martinique and wrote for *Harper's*, 1887-89; moved to Japan, 1890; teacher, Ordinary Middle School, Matsue, 1890-91, and Government College, Kumamoto, 1891-94; worked for Kobe *Chronicle*, 1894-95; professor of English literature, Imperial University, Tokyo, 1896-1903; English teacher, Waseda University, 1904. **Died:** 26 September 1904.

HORROR, GHOST AND GOTHIC PUBLICATIONS

Short Stories

Stray Leaves from Strange Literature. Boston, Osgood, 1884; London, Paul Trench Trubner, 1889.
Some Chinese Ghosts. Boston, Roberts, 1887.
In Ghostly Japan. Boston, Little Brown, and London, Sampson Low, 1899.
Shadowings. Boston, Little Brown, and London, Sampson Low, 1900.
Kwaidan: Stories and Studies of Strange Things. Boston, Houghton Mifflin, and London, Kegan Paul, 1904.
Fantastics and Other Fancies, edited by Charles Woodward Hutson. Boston, Houghton Mifflin, 1914.
Karma and Other Stories, edited by Albert Mordell. New York, Boni and Liveright, 1918; London, Harrap, 1921.

Other

Out of the East: Reveries and Studies in New Japan. Boston, Houghton Mifflin, and London, Osgood McIlvaine, 1895.

OTHER PUBLICATIONS

Novels

Chita: A Memory of Last Island. New York, Harper, 1889.
Youma: The Story of a West-Indian Slave. New York, Harper, 1890.

Short Stories

Barbarous Barbers and Other Stories, edited by Ichiro Nishizaki. Tokyo, Hokuseido Press, 1939.
The Romance of the Milky Way and Other Studies and Stories. Boston, Houghton Mifflin, and London, Constable, 1905.

Other

Two Years in the French West Indies. New York, Harper, 1890.
Gleanings in Buddha-Fields: Studies of Hand and Soul in the Far East. Boston, Houghton Mifflin, 1894; London, Harper, 1897.
Glimpses of Unfamiliar Japan. Boston, Houghton Mifflin, and London, Osgood McIlvaine, 2 vols., 1894.
Kokoro: Hints and Echoes of Japanese Inner Life. Boston, Houghton Mifflin, and London, Osgood, McIlvaine, 1896.
Exotics and Retrospectives. Boston, Little Brown, 1898; London, Sampson Low, 1899.
A Japanese Miscellany. Boston, Little Brown, and London, Sampson Low, 1901.
Kotto, Being Japanese Curios, with Sundry Cobwebs. New York and London, Macmillan, 1902.
Japan: An Attempt at Interpretation. New York and London, Macmillan, 1904.
Letters from the Raven, Being the Correspondence of Hearn with Henry Watkin, edited by Milton Bronner. New York, Brentano's, 1907; London, Constable, 1908.
The Japanese Letters, edited by Elizabeth Bisland. Boston, Houghton Mifflin, 1910; London, Constable, 1911.
Leaves from the Diary of an Impressionist: Early Writings, edited by Ferris Greenslet. Boston, Houghton Mifflin, 1911.
Editorials from the Kobe Chronicle, edited by Merle Johnson. N.p., 1913; edited by Makoto Sangu, 1960.
Writings. Boston, Houghton Mifflin, 16 vols., 1922.
Essays in European and Oriental Literature, edited by Albert Mordell. New York, Dodd Mead, and London, Heinemann, 1923.
Creole Sketches, edited by Charles Woodward Hutson. Boston, Houghton Mifflin, 1924.
An American Miscellany: Articles and Stories Now First Collected, edited by Albert Mordell. New York, Dodd Mead, 2 vols., 1924; as *Miscellanies: Articles and Stories Now First Collected*, London, Heinemann, 1924.
Occidental Gleanings: Sketches and Essays Now First Collected, edited by Albert Mordell. New York, Dodd Mead, and London, Heinemann, 2 vols., 1925.
Some New Letters and Writings, edited by Sanki Ichikawa. Tokyo, Kenkyusha, 1925.
Editorials, edited by Charles Woodward Hutson. Boston, Houghton Mifflin, 1926.
Facts and Fancies, edited by R. Tanabe. N.p., 1929.
Essays on American Literature, edited by Sanki Ichikawa. Tokyo, Hokuseido Press, 1929.
Gibbeted: Execution of a Youthful Murderer, edited by P. D. Perkins. N.p., 1933.
Spirit Photography, edited by P. D. Perkins. N.p., 1933.
Letters to a Pagan, edited by R. B. Powers. N.p., 1933.
Letters from Shimane and Kyushu. N.p., 1935.
American Articles, edited by Ichiro Nishizaki. Tokyo, Hokuseido Press, 4 vols., 1939.
Buying Christmas Toys and Other Essays, edited by Ichiro Nishizaki. Tokyo, Hokuseido Press, 1939.

Literary Essays, edited by Ichiro Nishizaki. Tokyo, Hokuseido Press, 1939.

The New Radiance and Other Scientific Sketches, edited by Ichiro Nishizaki. Tokyo, Hokuseido Press, 1939.

Oriental Articles, edited by Ichiro Nishizaki. Tokyo, Hokuseido Press, 1939.

An Orange Christmas. N.p., 1941.

Selected Writings, edited by Henry Goodman. New York, Citadel Press, 1949.

Children of the Levee, edited by O. W. Frost. N.p., 1957.

Japan's Religions: Shinto and Buddhism, edited by Kazumitsu Kato. N.p., 1966.

Manuscripts and Letters, edited by Hojin Yano and others. N.p., 1974.

The Buddhist Writings, edited by Kenneth Rexroth. Santa Barbara, California, Ross-Erikson, 1977.

Writings from Japan, edited by Francis King. N.p., 1984.

Editor, *La Cuisine Creole: A Collection of Culinary Recipes.* New York, Coleman, 1885.

Translator, *One of Cleopatra's Nights,* by Theophile Gautier. New York, Worthington, 1882.

Translator, *Gombo Zhebes: Little Dictionary of Creole Proverbs.* New York, Coleman, 1885.

Translator, *The Crime of Sylvestre Bonnard,* by Anatole France. New York, Harper, 1890.

Translator, *Japanese Fairy Tale* series. New York, Boni and Liveright, 5 vols., 1898-1922.

Translator, *The Temptation of St. Anthony,* by Gustave Flaubert. N.p., 1910.

Translator, *Japanese Lyrics.* N.p., 1915.

Translator, *Saint Anthony and Other Stories,* by Guy de Maupassant, edited by Albert Mordell. N.p., 1924.

Translator, *The Adventures of Walter Schnaffs and Other Stories,* by Guy de Maupassant, edited by Albert Mordell. N.p., 1931.

Translator, *Stories,* by Pierre Loti, edited by Albert Mordell. N.p., 1933.

Translator, *Stories,* by Émile Zola, edited by Albert Mordell. N.p., 1935.

Translator, *Sketches and Tales from the French,* edited by Albert Mordell. N.p., 1935.

*

Bibliography: *Hearn: A Bibliography of His Writings* by F. R. and Ione Perkins, 1934; in *Bibliography of American Literature* by Jacob Blanck, 1963.

Critical Studies: *Life and Letters* by Elizabeth Bisland, Boston, Houghton Mifflin, 2 vols., 1906; *Lafcadio Hearn's American Days* by Edward Larocque Tinker, New York, Dodd Mead, 1924; *Lafcadio Hearn* by Marcel Robert, 2 vols., 1950-51; *Young Lafcadio Hearn* by O. W. Frost, 1958; *Lafcadio Hearn* by Elizabeth Stevenson, New York, Macmillan, 1961; *An Ape of Gods: The Art and Thought of Lafcadio Hearn* by Beongcheon Yu, Detroit, Wayne State University Press, 1964; *Discoveries: Essays on Lafcadio Hearn* by Albert Mordell, 1964; *Lafcadio Hearn* by Arthur E. Kunst, New York, Twayne, 1969; *Lafcadio Hearn and His German Critics: An Examination of His Appeal* by Kathleen M. Webb, 1984; *Wandering Ghost: The Odyssey of Lafcadio Hearn* by Jonathan Cott, New York, Knopf, 1991; "Cultural Translator: Lafcadio Hearn" by Hephzibah Roskelly in *Literary New Orleans: Essays and Meditations,* edited by Richard S. Kennedy, 1992.

*   *   *

Hearn's cosmopolitan background and lack of parental guidance or support made him a rolling stone for over half his life, and it was not until he settled in Japan after 1890 that he found a home. Although of European origin, with strains in his blood that could draw him to many nations, he spent the first half of his adult life in the United States where he had been despatched penniless and with no contacts in 1869, abandoned by his mother. This lack of any family attachment gave Hearn an inferiority complex which was made worse by his appearance. He regarded himself as deformed, especially since he had become blinded in one eye and the other eye had swollen to compensate. Most portraits of him are in profile. The result was an intensely introverted individual who sought solace in books and study, but who was adaptable to any culture about him, and became most drawn to those who accepted him for what he was. He was employed as a reporter for various newspapers in Cincinnati and later New Orleans throughout the 1870s and 1880s, frequently being fired because of his non-conformity. Nevertheless his persistence with what most interested him—which was usually local custom and folklore—gradually earned him a respectable reputation and by the late 1880s he had established himself with the quality magazines, most notably *Harper's.*

The direction of Hearn's interests and the nature of his writing is only too evident from his earliest titles. His first book was a translation of several stories by Théophile Gautier, *One of Cleopatra's Nights,* where Hearn revelled in the romantic bohemianism and the florid style. *Stray Leaves from Strange Literature* selected further esoterica from English and French legends, whilst *Some Chinese Ghosts* drew upon Oriental fable and folklore. At the same time Hearn was producing a considerable amount of reportage which studied the local Creole and Negro legends, items which were only posthumously collected as *Fantastics.* These last items, which are frequently only short sketches or mood pieces, continued to reflect the exotic romanticism of Gautier and Baudelaire, and we can see in Hearn's idealization of other cultures a wistful escapism. "The Vision of the Dead," for instance, has a Creole man united with the spirit of his dead lover; "The Fountain of Gold" tells of a Conquistador who survived for centuries in an idyllic valley with a beautiful lover but who dies when he leaves; "Hereditary Memories" tells of a man's visions of a beautiful Oriental city which a doctor diagnoses as a memory inherited from his father's days in India.

The best of these stories are those in *Some Chinese Ghosts,* which remains one of Hearn's most rewarding collections. Again there is the wistful longing for peace and love, as well as the search for perfection. Tales like "The Soul of the Great Bell," in which a bellmaker seeks to cast the perfect bell which can only be achieved if a virgin is incorporated into the metal, and which is achieved by the self-sacrifice of his daughter, and "The Tale of the Porcelain God" in which a potter has to sacrifice himself in order to achieve the perfect pot, reveal Hearn's longing for the ideal, whilst "The Legend of Tchi-Niu" is a story of filial duty suggestive of Hearn's own longing for his lost childhood and parentage. The most popular story from *Some Chi-*

nese Ghosts, if the number of reprintings is any guide, is "The Story of Ming-Y," about a love affair between a Chinese scholar and the ghost of a long-dead courtesan.

Hearn's exoticism was tempered when, in 1887, Harper's sent him to the Caribbean to write about life in the West Indies. He remained there for two years out of which came not only Two Years in the French West Indies, a book which gave considerable reportage of West Indian obeah and voodoo customs, but Hearn's only novel-length works. Neither of these are supernatural, but they demonstrate a transition in Hearn's writing from moments of quiet beauty and reflection to ones of savagery and barbarity. The first was Chita, a very moving novel about the sole survivor of a small island that was destroyed in a tidal wave in 1856. Hearn succeeds in creating not only a sentimental attitude towards the young girl, but an almost pantheistic mood in portraying the elements, particularly the sea, devouring the island. Youma is quite different. It is set on Martinique at the time of the slave insurrection of 1848 and traces the devotion of a young slave girl to her mistress amidst scenes of considerable brutality.

After Hearn's return from the West Indies we find a greater realism entering his works, though that yearning for love and perfection remains. Some of this poured out of him in the personalized story "Karma" (Lippincott's, 1890) where we find a narrator searching and eventually being reunited with a lost love. In 1890 Hearn was sent to Japan by Harper's. He never returned. He settled down, married, and found work as a teacher. His reputation remained in the West and he became something of an interpreter of Eastern cultures for the Western reader. Over the next 14 years his works shifted from rather uncertain attempts at understanding Japanese life and tradition, to a recognition of the inevitable change in the east and the loss of past values. Hearn wrote a dozen books about Japanese life, much of this nonfiction, mood sketches, or retellings of legends and folklore. The works closest to literary fiction are those in In Ghostly Japan, Shadowings and particularly Kwaidan (the word means "Weird Tales"). Several of the latter were subsequently adapted by Japanese filmmakers for the cinema.

Kwaidan was a collection of stories that Hearn had collected from readings of old Japanese literature, or from discussion with local peasants and farmers. In at least one story, "Riki-Baka" ("Riki the Fool"), the episode of bad karma was directly experienced by Hearn. These tales, written when Hearn had become strongly imbued with Japanese culture, contain his best work. They portray a world which Hearn originally regarded as something of a fairyland but in which, as he had become more familiar with it, he could see a close association between the Japanese way of life, their land and their traditions—to a far greater degree than in the "civilized" West. As a result you encounter people who live with respect for ghosts who are recognized as part of the world about them. "Yuki-Onna" ("Snow Woman") is arguably the most effective of all these stories. A young man, Minokichi, trapped by the snow, is befriended by a snow demon, who spares his life provided he never reveals the facts about her. Later he marries a young girl, unaware that she is a transformation of the snow demon. For ten years Minokichi keeps his secret but one evening he reveals it. The demon disappears and Minokichi only narrowly escapes with his life. In several of the stories Hearn reproduces quite grotesque scenes with an almost reckless acceptance of reality. "Jikininki," for instance, tells of a priest who has been punished for his gluttony and has become a monster that feeds on corpses; "The Story of Mimi-Nashi-Hoichi" (or "Hoichi the Earless") is

about a blind story-teller who is requested to perform before a company of ghosts. Although a priest protects his body he forgets his ears and these are pulled off by the ghosts who would otherwise have devoured him. Evil demons abound in such stories as "Mujina" and "Rokuro-Kubi," whilst others, including "Diplomacy" and "Riki-Baka" are concerned with revenge from the grave.

Yet, within all these terrors, Hearn has not lost his yearning for perfection. Examples of his earlier tales remain. "The Dream of Akinosuké" tells of a young soldier-farmer who is lured away to fairyland where he spends several blissful years married to a beautiful princess. When she dies he returns to earth only to find that he has been away but a few moments and that his fairyland was simply an anthill. In both "The Story of Aoyagi" and "Jiu-Roku-Zakura" ("The Cherry Tree of the Sixteenth Day") the samurai protagonists performs deeds of self-sacrifice in order to save the spirits of the trees.

Throughout Hearn's fables, fairy tales and ghost stories we find a writer delighting in the exotic and the bizarre, as much because as an outcast himself he felt a closer affinity with other worlds, but also because it afforded him an escapist perspective. Within these worlds he sought to rationalize his own lot in life which often emerged as a vision of the ideal. Although Hearn had his moments of happiness, especially in Japan, he also recognized happiness could not last for ever. He was preparing to return to the United States, after a growing disillusionment with the changing culture of Japan, when he died of a heart attack aged only 54.

—Mike Ashley

HERBERT, James

Nationality: British. **Born:** London, 8 April 1943. **Education:** St. Aloysius College, and Hornsey College of Art, both London. **Family:** Married Eileen O'Donnell in 1968; three daughters. **Career:** Typographer, John Collings Advertising, London, 1963-66; art director, Group Head, and associate director, Ayer Barker Hegemann International, London, 1966-67. **Agent:** Bruce Hunter, David Higham Associates, 5-8 Lower John Street, London W1R 4HA, England; or, Claire Smith, Harold Ober Associates, 40 East 49th Street, New York, NY 10017, USA.

HORROR, GHOST AND GOTHIC PUBLICATIONS

Novels (series: David Ash; Rats)

The Rats. London, New English Library, 1974; New York, New American Library, 1975; reprinted as Deadly Eyes, New American Library, 1983.
The Fog. London, New English Library, and New York, New American Library, 1975.
The Survivor. London, New English Library, 1976; New York, New American Library, 1977.
Fluke. London, New English Library, 1977; New York, New American Library, 1978.
The Spear. London, New English Library, 1978; New York, New American Library, 1980.
The Lair (Rats). London, New English Library, and New York, New American Library, 1979.

The Dark. London, New English Library, and New York, New American Library, 1980.

The Jonah. London, New English Library, and New York, New American Library, 1981.

Shrine. London, New English Library, 1983; New York, New American Library, 1984.

Domain (Rats). London, New English Library, 1984; New York, New American Library, 1985.

Moon. London, New English Library, 1985; New York, Crown, 1986.

The Magic Cottage. London, Hodder and Stoughton, 1986; New York, New American Library, 1987.

Sepulchre. London, Hodder and Stoughton, 1987; New York, Putnam, 1988.

Haunted (Ash). London, Hodder and Stoughton, and New York, Putnam, 1988.

Creed. London, Hodder and Stoughton, 1990.

Portent. London, Hodder and Stoughton, 1992; New York, HarperPrism, 1996.

The Ghosts of Sleath (Ash). London, HarperCollins, 1994; New York, HarperPrism, 1995.

'48. London, HarperCollins, 1996.

Graphic Novel

The City: The Rats Saga Continues, illustrated by Ian Miller. London, Pan, 1994.

Other

James Herbert's Dark Places: Locations and Legends, with photographs by Paul Barkshire. London, HarperCollins, 1993.

*

Film Adaptations: *The Rats,* 1980; *The Survivor,* 1982; *Fluke,* 1995; *Haunted,* 1995.

Critical Study: *James Herbert: By Horror Haunted* edited by Stephen Jones, London, New English Library, 1992.

* * *

James Herbert is one of a handful of British horror writers who have been successful on both sides of the Atlantic. With more than 15 published novels, many of them bestsellers, Herbert has used both scientific and supernatural themes as the basis for his stories. He began in a small way, with paperback-originals. His first published novel, *The Rats,* was one of a wave of nature-gone-mad novels that flooded the bookstores in the 1970s. A single rat has mutated under the streets of London, and her ever-growing brood consists of oversized, remarkably intelligent creatures who work cooperatively and have a taste for human blood. In Herbert's second novel, *The Fog,* a plague is released from a chamber underground and spreads in yellow clouds across the surface of the Earth above. Any humans who wander into the affected area are turned into crazed maniacs who kill and mutilate each other.

Herbert turned to the supernatural in *The Survivor.* The protagonist is the only passenger to live through a spectacular air crash, and the circumstances of his survival seem unlikely in the extreme. In the aftermath, he starts to hear voices, and people

begin dying, a chain that will continue until he tracks down the person responsible for the disaster and then rejoins the dead with whom he belongs. *Fluke* was another change of pace, using a horror theme as the basis for a low-key mystery. A dead man is reincarnated in the body of a stray dog, in which form he tracks down his original family and investigates the circumstances of his own death.

The Spear blends horror with espionage. An investigator searching for a missing secret agent discovers the existence of a neo-Nazi cult which has tapped into a genuine supernatural source of power. Unless they are exposed and eliminated, they could unleash a new era of world-wide conflict, this time armed with demonic powers. Herbert returned to his mutated rats for *The Lair,* a less ambitious thriller that depends more on gruesome death and mutilation than genuine suspense. *The Dark* closely resembles *The Fog* in its individual scenes, humans driven mad by an external force, but this time the source is occult, and Herbert proves himself much more effective at creating characters and setting scenes than in his earlier novels.

The most original novel of Herbert's early career is *The Jonah.* Jim Kelso is a police officer who leads a particularly lonely life. Terrible things happen to anyone who gets close to him. Through most of the book we are led to suspect that Kelso himself is responsible, that he commits these crimes during blackouts, but eventually we learn that he has a deformed, undead twin who is jealous of Kelso's comparatively normal life. A young deaf, mute girl becomes a miracle worker in *Shrine,* and her power to heal the sick seems a blessing to most. But the power comes from the devil rather than God, and eventually the people around her are called upon to pay a terrible price for their health.

Domain completed Herbert's rat trilogy, this time starting with a nuclear war that destroys most of civilization. The survivors have to deal with the usual troubles in the aftermath, but the mutant rats, more intelligent than ever, emerge as a viable contender for domination of what remains of the Earth. Although more interesting than its two predecessors, this is still the weakest of Herbert's later novels. In *Moon,* a troubled man retreats to a remote island where he has visions of terrible crimes committed elsewhere. The psychic link to the killer proves to work both ways, unfortunately, and the protagonist discovers that he is being stalked within his supposed haven.

The Magic Cottage is an unconventional haunted-house story, the most atmospheric and restrained of Herbert's novels. *Sepulchre* recombines several previous themes, featuring a psychic living in a remote part of England whose activities inadvertently waken an evil, occult force. There's another house filled with ghosts in *Haunted,* one of Herbert's best novels. David Ash, a sceptical psychic investigator, is hired to find out the truth about strange sightings in an old house, and he is transformed by the experience, the most complexly drawn of Herbert's protagonists.

James Creed is a photographer who suddenly discovers he can take pictures of things that are not there, or at least aren't visible to the eye, in *Creed.* The scale of events is much grander in *Portent,* in which a series of disasters—earthquakes, volcanoes, and so forth—are warnings of an imminent battle between the forces of good and evil. We see all this through the eyes of several disparate individuals who are called upon to play a part in the climactic battle. Investigator of the psychic David Ash returns in Herbert's more recent novel, *The Ghosts of Sleath,* wiser now but still not prepared for the scale of the haunting of an entire village, a haunting in which even ghosts can be the victims. In *'48,* an alternative-history horror novel, the narrative takes place in a 1948 that never was, after Hitler has devastated Britain with a plague known as the Blood Death.

Herbert's short story, "Breakfast," is a chilling but very brief look at a woman whose grief is so great that she cannot accept the death of her children. It is evident however that Herbert is much more at ease, and more effective, at novel length. By now his books "have sold more than 37 million copies worldwide," according to his publishers' publicity, making him Britain's nearest equivalent, in terms of popularity if not of literary merit, to America's Stephen King. Although his tales tend to involve more action than atmosphere, he has proven himself capable of writing strongly-plotted, suspenseful work, and his characterization has improved steadily during his career.

—Don D'Ammassa

HICHENS, Robert (Smythe)

Nationality: British. **Born:** Speldhurst, Kent, 14 November 1864. **Education:** Clifton College, Bristol; Royal College of Music, London; London School of Journalism. **Career:** Music critic, the *World*. Fellow, Royal Society of Literature, 1926. **Died:** 20 July 1950.

HORROR, GHOST AND GOTHIC PUBLICATIONS

Novels

Flames: A London Phantasy. London, Heinemann, and Chicago, Stone, 1897.
The Dweller on the Threshold. London, Methuen, and New York, Century, 1911.
Harps in the Wind. London, Cassell, 1945; as *The Woman in the House*, Philadelphia, Macrae Smith, 1945.

Short Stories

Bye-Ways. London, Methuen, and New York, Dodd Mead, 1897.
Tongues of Conscience. London, Methuen, and New York, Stokes, 1900.
The Black Spaniel and Other Stories. London, Methuen, and New York, Stokes, 1905.

OTHER PUBLICATIONS

Novels

The Green Carnation (published anonymously). London, Heinemann, and New York, Appleton, 1894.
After Tomorrow, and The New Love. New York, Merriam, 1895.
An Imaginative Man. London, Heinemann, and New York, Appleton, 1895.
The Londoners: An Absurdity. London, Heinemann, and Chicago, Stone, 1898.
The Daughters of Babylon, with Wilson Barrett. London, Macqueen, and Philadelphia, Lippincott, 1899.
The Slave. London, Heinemann, and Chicago, Stone, 1899.

The Prophet of Berkeley Square: A Tragic Extravaganza. London, Methuen, and New York, Dodd Mead, 1901.
Felix: Three Years of a Life. London, Methuen, 1902; New York, Stokes, 1903.
The Garden of Allah. London, Methuen, and New York, Stokes, 1904.
The Women with the Fan. London, Methuen, and New York, Stokes, 1904.
The Call of the Blood. London, Methuen, and New York, Harper, 1906.
Barbary Sheep. New York, Harper, 1907; London, Methuen, 1909.
A Spirit in Prison. London, Hutchinson, and New York, Harper, 1908.
Bella Donna. London, Heinemann, and Philadelphia, Lippincott, 1909.
The Knock on the Door. London, Heinemann, and Philadelphia, Lippincott, 1909.
The Fruitful Vine. London, Unwin, and New York, Stokes, 1911.
The Way of Ambition. London, Methuen, and New York, Stokes, 1913.
In the Wilderness. London, Methuen, and New York, Stokes, 1917.
Mrs. Marden. London, Cassell, and New York, Doran, 1919.
The Spirit of the Time. London, Cassell, and New York, Doubleday, 1921.
December Love. London, Cassell, and New York, Doran, 1922.
After the Verdict. London, Methuen, and New York, Doran, 1924.
The God Within Him. London, Methuen, 1926; as *The Unearthly*, New York, Cosmopolitan, 1926.
The Bacchante and the Nun. London, Methuen, 1927; as *The Bacchante*, New York, Cosmopolitan, 1927.
Dr. Artz. London, Hutchinson, and New York, Cosmopolitan, 1929.
On the Screen. London, Cassell, 1929.
The Bracelet. London, Cassell, and New York, Cosmopolitan, 1930.
The First Lady Brendon. London, Cassell, and New York, Doubleday, 1931.
Mortimer Brice: A Bit of His Life. London, Cassell, and New York, Doubleday, 1932.
The Paradine Case. London, Benn, and New York, Doubleday, 1933.
The Power to Kill. London, Benn, and New York, Doubleday, 1934.
"Susie's" Career. London, Cassell, 1935; as *The Pyramid*, New York, Doubleday, 1936.
The Sixth of October. London, Cassell, and New York, Doubleday, 1936.
Daniel Airlie. London, Cassell, and New York, Doubleday, 1937.
The Journey Up. London, Cassell, and New York, Doubleday, 1938.
Secret Information. London, Hurst and Blackett, and New York, Doubleday, 1938.
That Which Is Hidden. London, Cassell, 1939; New York, Doubleday, 1940.
The Million: An Entertainment. London, Cassell, 1940; New York, Doubleday, 1941.
Married or Unmarried. London, Cassell, 1941.
A New Way of Life. London, Hutchinson, and New York, Doubleday, 1942.
Veils. London, Hutchinson, 1943; as *Young Mrs. Brand*, Philadelphia, Macrae Smith, 1944.
Incognito. London, Hutchinson, 1947; New York, McBride, 1948.
Too Much Love of Living. Philadelphia, Macrae Smith, 1947; London, Cassell, 1948.

Beneath the Magic. London, Hutchinson, 1950; as *Strange Lady*,
 Philadelphia, Macrae Smith, 1950.
The Mask. London, Hutchinson, 1951.
Nightbound. London, Cassell, 1951.

Short Stories

The Folly of Eustace and Other Stories. London, Heinemann, and
 New York, Appleton, 1896.
The Hindu. New York, Ainslee, 1917.
Snake-Bite and Other Stories. London, Cassell, and New York,
 Doran, 1919.
The Last Time and Other Stories. London, Hutchinson, 1923; New
 York, Doran, 1924.
The Streets and Other Stories. London, Hutchinson, 1928.
The Gate of Paradise and Other Stories. London, Cassell, 1930.
My Desert Friend and Other Stories. London, Cassell, 1931.
The Gardenia and Other Stories. London, Hutchinson, 1934.
The Afterglow and Other Stories. London, Cassell, 1935.
The Man in the Mirror and Other Stories. London, Cassell, 1950.

Plays

The Medicine Man, with H. D. Traill (produced London, 1898).
 New York, De Vinne Press, 1898.
Becky Sharp, with Cosmo Gordon-Lennox, adaptation of the novel
 Vanity Fair by Thackeray (produced London, 1901; as *Vanity
 Fair,* produced New York, 1911).
The Real Woman (produced London, 1909).
The Garden of Allah, with Mary Anderson, adaptation of the novel
 by Hichens (produced New York, 1911; London, 1920).
The Law of the Sands (produced London, 1916).
Black Magic (produced London, 1917).
Press the Button! (produced London, 1918).
The Voice from the Minaret (produced London 1919; New York,
 1922).

Screenplay: *Bella Donna,* with Ouida Bergère, 1923.

Other

The Coastguards Secret (for children). London, Sonnenschein, 1886.
Homes of the Passing Show, with others. London, Savoy Press,
 1900.
Egypt and Its Monuments. London, Hodder and Stoughton, and
 New York, Century, 1908; as *The Spell of Egypt,* London,
 Hodder and Stoughton, 1910; New York, Century, 1911.
The Holy Land. London, Hodder and Stoughton, and New York,
 Century, 1910.
The Near East. London, Hodder and Stoughton, and New York,
 Century, 1913.
Yesterday: The Autobiography of Robert Hichens. London, Cassell,
 1947.

*

Film Adaptations: *Bella Donna,* 1934; *Temptation,* 1935, from
the novel *Bella Donna*; *The Garden of Allah,* 1936.

*   *   *

Robert Hichens's first aspiration was to pursue a career in music but he was diverted into journalism. In the early 1890s he was commissioned to write a series of articles about the various species of occultists flourishing in *fin de siècle* London and he was later to turn this research to good effect in producing supernatural fiction. He was also much affected by a tour of the Nile which he undertook in the company of Lord Alfred Douglas, which provided fuel for his phantasmagoric novel of delusion and marital betrayal *An Imaginative Man.*

"A Reincarnation" (1895), reprinted in *The Folly of Eustace,* is one of several tales Hichens wrote involving the apparent transmigration of souls between human and animal bodies, this example involving a cat seemingly reincarnate in its murderer's wife. Lord Frederick Hamilton, editor of the *Pall Mall Magazine,* was sufficiently impressed by it to commission Hichens to write up a plot of his own in the novella "A Tribute of Souls," about a taxing diabolical bargain. Unfortunately, Hamilton found Hichens' next submission, "The Cry of the Child," too nasty-minded to stomach, let alone print. This harrowing tale of a man haunted by the ghostly cries of a child he allowed to die of neglect eventually became the keystone of Hichens' best collection, the aptly-named *Tongues of Conscience.* This was, however, preceded by the more sedate *Bye-Ways*—which reprinted "A Tribute of Souls" alongside the enigmatic novella "The Charmer of Snakes," in which a man loses his wife to the seductive music of a snake-charmer, who seemingly transforms her into a huge white snake—and the novel *Flames.*

Flames is a remarkable work in which the effortlessly moral Valentine Cresswell desires to feel the temptations which afflict and torment his imperfect friend Julian Addison; he proposes that they attempt a magical exchange of souls. The experiment goes awry and Valentine's body is possessed by the soul of an evil occultist named Marr, whose sly influence threatens to corrupt Julian irredeemably. Julian's damnation is eventually averted by virtue of the assistance of a wise counsellor and the self-sacrifice of a tart with a heart of gold. The strength of this rather preposterous story lies in its elaborate description, couched in vividly melodramatic metaphors, of the temptations sent to try the worth of the unlucky Julian.

There is no other account of the Victorian moral sensibility under stress quite as feverish as *Flames,* and Hichens never attained such fervour again, save perhaps in the most heightened passages of his famous bestseller *The Garden of Allah.* His later work is far more clinical and much more tedious, afflicted by a tendentious verbosity that robs all but a few of his stories of their narrative force. While it was still new, though, this painstaking clinicality of attitude enabled him to produce one authentic masterpiece of horror fiction, when he expanded "The Man Who Was Beloved," a story originally published in *Pearson's Magazine,* into "How Love Came to Professor Guildea" for reprinting in *Tongues of Conscience.* The positivist professor is fond of explaining to his only friend, a priest, that he has no room in his well-ordered life for emotion or affection—but he then becomes the object of the slavish infatuation of a moronic phantom whose fawning attitude is revealed by the mimicry of a pet parrot, to which she is uniquely visible. This pioneering tale of a stalker from beyond exploits an intimate species of horror which no previous tale had contrived to tap so effectively. The obsessions featured in the remaining tales in the collection are far from anodyne, but cannot begin to compare with the raw brutality of "The Cry of the Child" and "How Love Came to Professor Guildea"; the best of them is the atypically subtle "Sea-Change."

The Garden of Allah is not a horror story, although its plot is heavily laden with sinister omens. Its heroine journeys into the African desert in search of spiritual renewal but the man who seems to offer it turns out to be a renegade monk and she feels compelled to send him back to servitude, even though she will have to bring up their child alone. Two other tales of private haunting set in the same milieu, "The Desert Drum" and "The Figure in the Mirage," were reprinted in *The Black Spaniel and Other Stories*, whose title novella is a woefully unconvincing tale of a dog which might or might not be possessed by the soul of a dead vivisectionist.

The Dweller on the Threshold revisits the theme of *Flames*. A timid curate is hoping to gain an infusion of spiritual strength from his gifted superior but, as before, the experiment goes awry. The donation leads to the senior's gradual enfeeblement and the eventual usurpation of his position by the "doppelgänger" he has created. Hichens wrote a third and even more enigmatic version of the same plot in "The Sin of Envy," in *The Gardenia and Other Stories*, in which both parties to the exchange suffer equally—although it is not at all clear exactly what has been transferred from one to the other.

None of Hichens' later collections features a preponderance of weird fiction; like "The Sin of Envy," his three other novellas of note stood alone in collections of mundane fiction. "The Lost Faith," in *Snake-Bite and Other Stories*, is the story of a faith-healer who loses her power—after the fashion of the witches of legend—when she falls in love. "The Villa by the Sea," in *The Last Time*, is a straightforward tale of a haunted house. The title-story of *The Man in the Mirror* is a much more interesting account of a portraitist trying to paint his own doppelgänger, with fateful consequences. Hichens' final fantastic novel, *Harps in the Wind*, is a curious romance in which a courtship encouraged by visions is also made more difficult by its supernatural component.

Hichens never quite made up his mind where he stood on the matter of fashionable occultism, and his perpetual uncertainty in the face of apparently supernatural phenomena eventually became a weakness robbing his horror stories of any real bite. He did make up his mind where he stood on matters of morality, putting all temptation behind him and quite probably remaining celibate unto death, but that conviction did not work to the advantage of his work either once he had exhausted the fervour of his dilemma in *Flames* and "How Love Came to Professor Guildea." The strange psychology of his work remains, however, a fascinating case study for psychoanalysts of every theoretical stripe.

—Brian Stableford

HILL, Susan (Elizabeth)

Nationality: British. **Born:** Scarborough, Yorkshire, 5 February 1942. **Education:** Grammar schools in Scarborough and Coventry; King's College, University of London, B.A. (honours) in English 1963. **Family:** Married the writer and editor Stanley Wells in 1975; three daughters (one deceased). **Career:** Since 1963, full-time writer: since 1977, monthly columnist, *Daily Telegraph,* London. Presenter, *Bookshelf* radio programme, 1986-87. **Awards:** Maugham award, 1971; Whitbread award, 1972; Rhys Memorial prize, 1972. Fellow, Royal Society of Literature, 1972, and King's College, 1978. **Address:** Longmoor Farmhouse, Ebrington, Chipping Campden, Greater London GL55 6NW, England.

HORROR, GHOST AND GOTHIC PUBLICATIONS

Novels

The Woman in Black: A Ghost Story. London, Hamish Hamilton, 1983; Boston, Godine, 1986.
The Mist in the Mirror. London, Sinclair Stevenson, 1992.
Mrs. de Winter (sequel to *Rebecca* by Daphne du Maurier). London, Sinclair Stevenson, and Thorndike, Maine, Thorndike Press, 1993.

Other

Editor, *Ghost Stories.* London, Hamish Hamilton, 1983.
Editor, *The Walker Book of Ghost Stories.* London, Walker, 1990; as *The Random House Book of Ghost Stores,* New York, Random House, 1991.

OTHER PUBLICATIONS

Novels

The Enclosure. London, Hutchinson, 1961.
Do Me a Favour. London, Hutchinson, 1963.
Gentleman and Ladies. London, Hamish Hamilton, 1968; New York, Walker, 1969.
A Change for the Better. London, Hamish Hamilton, 1969.
I'm the King of the Castle. London, Hamish Hamilton, and New York, Viking Press, 1970.
Strange Meeting. London, Hamish Hamilton, 1971; New York, Saturday Review Press, 1972.
The Bird of Night. London, Hamish Hamilton, 1972; New York, Saturday Review Press, 1973.
In the Springtime of the Year. London, Hamish Hamilton, and New York, Saturday Review Press, 1974.
Air and Angels. London, Sinclair Stevenson, 1991.

Short Stories

The Albatross and Other Stories. London, Hamish Hamilton, 1971; New York, Saturday Review Press, 1975.
The Custodian. London, Covent Garden Press, 1972.
A Bit of Singing and Dancing. London, Hamish Hamilton, 1973.
Lanterns Across the Snow (novella). London, Joseph, 1987; New York, Potter, 1988.
Listening to the Orchestra. Ebrington, Gloucestershire, Long Barn Books, 1996.

Plays

Lizard in the Grass (broadcast 1971; produced Edinburgh, 1988). Included in *The Cold Country and Other Plays for Radio,* 1975.

The Cold Country and Other Plays for Radio (includes *The End of Summer, Lizard in the Grass, Consider the Lilies, Strip Jack Naked*). London, BBC Publications, 1975.

On the Face of It (broadcast 1975). Published in *Act 1,* edited by David Self and Ray Speakman, London, Hutchinson, 1979.

The Ramshackle Company (for children; produced London, 1981).

Chances (broadcast 1981; produced London, 1983).

Radio Plays: *Taking Leave,* 1971; *The End of Summer,* 1971; *Lizard in the Grass,* 1971; *The Cold Country,* 1972; *Winter Elegy,* 1973; *Consider the Lilies,* 1973; *A Window on the World,* 1974; *Strip Jack Naked,* 1974; *Mr. Proudham and Mr. Sleight,* 1974; *On the Face of It,* 1975; *The Summer of the Giant Sunflower,* 1977; *The Sound That Time Makes,* 1980; *Here Comes the Bride,* 1980; *Chances,* 1981; *Out in the Cold,* 1982; *Autumn,* 1985; *Winter,* 1985; *I'm the King of the Castle,* 1990.

Television Play: *Last Summer's Child,* 1981, from the story "The Badness Within Him."

Other (for children)

One Night at a Time. London, Hamish Hamilton, 1984; as *Go Away, Bad Dreams!,* New York, Random House, 1985.

Mother's Magic. London, Hamish Hamilton, 1986.

Suzy's Shoes. London, Hamish Hamilton, 1989.

I Won't Go There Again. London, Walker, 1990.

Septimus Honeydew. London, Walker, 1990.

Stories from Codling Village. London, Walker, 1990.

The Collaborative Classroom, with Tim Hill. Portsmouth, Hampshire, Heinemann, 1990.

Beware, Beware, with illustrations by Angela Barrett. Cambridge, Massachusetts, Candlewick Press, and London, Walker, 1993.

The Christmas Collection, with illustrations by John Lawrence. Cambridge, Massachusetts, Candlewick Press, and London, Walker, 1994.

The Glass Angels. London, Walker, 1991. Cambridge, Massachusetts, Candlewick, 1992.

White Christmas. London, Walker, and Cambridge, Massachusetts, Candlewick, 1994.

King of Kings. Cambridge, Massachusetts, Candlewick, 1993; London, Walker, 1994.

Can It Be True? A Christmas Story. London, Hamish Hamilton, and New York, Viking Kestrel, 1988.

A Very Special Birthday. London, Walker, 1992.

Other

The Magic Apple Tree: A Country Year. London, Hamish Hamilton, 1982; New York, Holt Rinehart, 1983.

Through the Kitchen Window. London, Hamish Hamilton, 1984.

Through the Garden Gate. London, Hamish Hamilton, 1986.

Shakespeare Country, photographs by Rob Talbot. London, Joseph, 1987.

The Lighting of the Lamps. London, Hamish Hamilton, 1987.

The Spirit of the Cotswolds, photographs by Nick Meers. London, Joseph, 1988.

Family. London, Joseph, 1989; New York, Viking, 1990.

Crown Devon: The History of S. Fielding and Co. Stratford Upon Avon, Jazz, 1993.

Editor, *The Distracted Preacher and Other Tales,* by Thomas Hardy. London, Penguin, 1979.

Editor, with Isabel Quigly, *New Stories 5.* London, Hutchinson, 1980.

Editor, *People: Essays and Poems.* London, Chatto and Windus, 1983.

Editor, *The Parchment Moon: An Anthology of Modern Women's Short Stories.* London, Joseph, 1990; as *The Penguin Book of Modern Women's Short Stories,* 1991.

Editor, *Contemporary Women's Short Stories.* London, Joseph, 1995.

*

Film Adaptation: *The Woman in Black* (TV movie), 1989.

Manuscript Collection: Eton College Library, Windsor, Berkshire.

Critical Study: *Susan Hill: I'm the King of the Castle* by Hana Sambrook, London, Longman, 1992.

* * *

Susan Hill is well known in Britain as the author of literary novels and short stories. Her ventures into the genre of ghost stories seem almost to be an anomaly for her, yet these novels are as carefully written as all her others. She holds very strong views on the writing of ghost stories, which she regards as almost a lost art, and which she lays down in her excellent introduction to her *Ghost Stories* anthology. A ghost story, she says, must contain a ghost (the "spirit of some person, now dead, or else an embodiment of an evil force, or a strong emotion, such as distress or terror") not a monster or shape-changer or anything science-fictional. And, of course, it must be a supernatural story, with the phenomenon never explained away. She recognizes the difficulty of writing such a story today without being laughed at.

In both *The Woman in Black* and *The Mist in the Mirror* she tries hard to practise what she preaches. So both are pastiches of the Victorian ghost story, set, respectively, in about the first and third decades of the 20th century. Both are narrated in the first person and feature the frequent appearance of particular ghosts which distress the narrator while also leading him on to a certain course of action. There are other parallels between the two books, in terms of plot, setting and characters, though these are separate novels with no common characters.

The narrator of *The Woman in Black* is a young solicitor, Arthur Kipps, who is sent to a flat, coastal part of the north of England to attend the funeral of one of the firm's clients, Mrs. Drablow, and to sort out her papers. At the poorly-attended funeral he notices a woman in an old-fashioned dress and bonnet, her face thin and very white—but when he mentions her it upsets the estate agent who is assisting him, and he will say nothing about her.

Kipps goes to the deceased woman's home, the lonely Eel Marsh House, across Nine Lives Causeway, which is regularly inundated by the tide and set among dangerous quicksands. This empty Gothic habitation is most wonderfully described, even though Hill is building on the clichés of the genre. The house itself is cold and forbidding, unaccountably noisy at night, with a locked room in which something seems to be moving; the island also contains a family graveyard with the woman in black occasionally to be seen in it; the whole area is subject to sudden sea-frets which prevent access or escape; the month is a stormy November with short days and long nights; the local people will say nothing about Mrs. Drablow or her house but are clearly disturbed by the subject.

Another ghostly visitation, which Kipps hears more than once, is a pony and trap which goes astray from the causeway in a fret, being sucked into the marsh to the accompaniment of a child's anguished cries. The locked room (which mysteriously opens itself) is a nursery. The dead child was the six-year-old illegitimate son of Mrs. Drablow's sister, drowned with his nanny some 60 years before. And the woman in black is revealed as the boy's mother, who died of a wasting disease some 50 years before. The locals dread her because, each time she is seen, a child dies.

The effect upon Kipps of these ghosts and the atmosphere which accompanies them is to cause a nervous collapse. He is rescued from the house by a local landowner, Samuel Daily, whom he has met on the train, and who befriends and gives him lodging. A couple of years later, when Kipps has recovered, returned to London, married his fiancée and they have a young baby son, he sees the ghost of the woman in black again. It presages a terrible pony-cart accident in which his wife and son are killed.

In *The Mist in the Mirror* the narrator is James Monmouth, orphaned at an early age and raised abroad, who has spent 20 years travelling the world and now returns to Britain for the first time since childhood, as a man of 37. He wants to research the life of the late Conrad Vane, a similar traveller from some decades earlier. Everyone to whom he mentions Vane tries to dissuade him, hinting at dark deeds best not spoken.

But Monmouth perseveres. He has little money and no known family or friends in Britain, yet he is a gentleman. From the beginning of his time in Britain he catches glimpses of a young boy, thin and miserable, and sometimes hears him crying, but is unable to approach the youngster or discover what is wrong. Only gradually does he come to realize that this is a ghost.

He hopes to obtain information about Vane from Alton School (a thinly disguised portrait of Britain's most renowned school, Eton College) which Vane attended. In the train *en route* Monmouth meets Lady Viola Quincebridge, who invites him to her family home for the impending Christmas holiday and acts as his benefactor (in the same way as Samuel Daily helped Arthur Kipps). At Alton he discovers a link between Vane and his own family. After Christmas he travels to Scotland and finds Kittiscar Hall, the seat of the Monmouth family, together with a recently deceased Miss Monmouth, presumably an aunt and his only relative. Despite the house being neglected and having a bad name locally, he returns there after the funeral, whereupon he is attacked by the dangerous ghost of Conrad Vane and is lucky to escape with his life. The ghost of the young boy is assumed to be an ancestor who died at the hands of Vane while they were both at Alton School.

The Woman in Black does manage to be truly menacing in places, due to Hill's fine atmospheric descriptions, but *The Mist in the Mirror* is less successful in this respect, since both Vane's sudden presence in the chapel at Kittiscar and Monmouth's survival are somewhat brief and contrived. Hill proves that it is possible, though not easy, to write successful ghost stories today.

While a few of Hill's other novels and most of her stories contain elements which are tragic, harrowing or bizarre, scarcely any fall into the present genre. *Mrs. de Winter* must be mentioned here; it is a commissioned sequel to Daphne du Maurier's *Rebecca* and

contains slight ghostly and gothic elements. Also of some relevance is *I'm the King of the Castle*, which contains childhood brutality. The only story of hers to be reprinted in a horror anthology (one of Denys Val Baker's) is "Friends of Miss Reece." This describes a young boy's view of a nursing home run by his aunt, where his mother also works. One of the nurses seems to be sexually abusing him, and she also murders a patient who is too much trouble.

—Chris Morgan

HJORTSBERG, William (Reinhold)

Nationality: American. **Born:** New York City, 23 February 1941. **Education:** Dartmouth College, B.A. 1962; Yale School of Drama, 1962-63; Stanford University, 1967-68. **Family:** Married Marian Souidee Renken in 1962; one daughter and one son. **Career:** Teacher, St. Croix, Virgin Islands, 1963-64, 1966-67; freelance writer. **Awards:** Wallace Stegner Creative Writing fellowship, 1967-68; *Playboy* Editorial award for short story, 1971.

HORROR, GHOST AND GOTHIC PUBLICATIONS

Novels

Falling Angel. New York, Harcourt Brace Jovanovich, 1978.
Nevermore. New York, Atlantic Monthly Press, and London, Orion, 1994.

OTHER PUBLICATIONS

Novels

Sometimes Horses Don't Come Back. New York, Random House, 1963.
Alp. New York, Simon and Schuster, 1969.
Gray Matters. New York, Simon and Schuster, 1971.
Symbiography. Fremont, Michigan, Sumac Press, 1973.
Toro! Toro! Toro! New York, Simon and Schuster, 1974.

Short Stories

Tales & Fables. Los Angeles, Sylvester and Orphanos, 1985.

*

Film Adaptation: *Angel Heart*, 1987, from the novel *Falling Angel*.

*   *   *

Aside from a science fiction/crime novel, *Gray Matters*, William Hjortsberg is of interest to readers of genre fiction on the strength of two quite different novels, *Falling Angel* and *Nevermore*. Of these, the former is by far the more interesting and is as clever a fusion of the hard-boiled crime story with the tale of supernatural horror as any novel in recent years.

Falling Angel is seen through the eyes of Harry Angel, a private detective in New York City. Sometime in the year 1959 he takes on a case put to him by the enigmatic Louis Cyphre, who wishes Angel to locate a man named Jonathan Liebling. Under the name Johnny Favorite, Liebling had attained spectacular success as a crooner in the early years of World War II; but he was seriously injured during an air raid in Tunisia in 1943, where he was performing in a troop show. Cyphre, who "gave Johnny some help at the start of his career" that involved some type of "contract," is most anxious to know whether Johnny is still alive. At last accounts he was at a private hospital in Poughkeepsie. Angel doggedly pursues the rather cold trail, coercing from a doctor at the hospital the information that two individuals, a man and a woman, took Johnny (who was suffering from amnesia) away years before. Shortly after Angel interviews the doctor, the latter is found dead—whether by murder or suicide is unclear.

Further investigation by Angel reveals much of interest, especially the fact that Johnny was involved in voodoo rites in connection with a black woman, Evangeline Proudfoot, who was Johnny's mistress even though he was engaged to a rich society girl, Margaret Krusemark, whose father is a wealthy shipping magnate. Angel manages to hunt down Evangeline's daughter, Epiphany (now herself a voodoo priestess), along with Krusemark and her daughter, gathering further information in the process. Suspicious deaths, however, continue to pile up: a black musician who had played with Johnny is murdered in a revolting fashion shortly after Angel interviews him; Margaret Krusemark, an astrologer, is killed in her apartment; and Epiphany, frightened at the series of murders, takes refuge in Angel's own office, eventually engaging in a torrid affair with him.

Meanwhile Angel begins to wonder what Cyphre's role in all this is. The matter gains new significance when Angel observes that his client performs as "Dr. Cypher" at an obscure circus on 42nd Street and gives lectures in Harlem as el Çifr; in one such lecture he makes clear allusion to the three murders that have been committed, even though some details have not been made public by the police. Can Cyphre himself be the murderer?

With continued diligence Angel finds the truth. Johnny Favorite had sold his soul to the devil in exchange for fame as a crooner; but he hoped to outwit the devil by performing an elaborate rite involving the switching of his soul with that of a soldier that he and Evangeline had kidnapped on Times Square one New Year's Eve. But before he could complete the job he was shipped overseas and came back as an amnesiac. Louis Cyphre is none other than Lucifer; and the soldier involved in the rite is none other than Harry Angel. We are led to understand that Angel himself, under Cyphre's guidance, committed the three murders.

Falling Angel is a suspenseful novel that masquerades as a crime story until close to the cataclysmic conclusion. There is perhaps only one tip of the hat to the supernatural prior to the end, when Cyphre reveals knowledge of a dream that Angel had just had; but beyond this we appear to be dealing only with the superficial paraphernalia of the weird—voodoo, devil worship, predictions of the future, and the like. Hjortsberg's tough-guy first-person narrative, clearly modelled on the prose of Raymond Chandler, effectively carries forward the deception.

The film version of the novel, *Angel Heart* (1987), written and directed by Alan Parker, takes some liberties with the plot but otherwise adheres faithfully to the novel's premises. Much of the film takes place in New Orleans, as Krusemark is now postulated as a wealthy Louisiana businessman. This transference of setting certainly enhances the voodoo atmosphere, although we are therefore deprived of a powerful scene in the novel in which Angel witnesses a hideous black mass performed by Krusemark in the bowels of the New York subway system. (In spite of statements to the contrary on various editions of *Falling Angel*, Hjortsberg was not involved in the making of the film.)

Nevermore is a sad falling off from the bracing dynamism of *Falling Angel*. Here we are dealing with what might be called an historical novel with crime and supernatural episodes. The setting is again New York, but the year is 1923; and the novel displays the friendly rivalry of Sir Arthur Conan Doyle (now the great champion of spiritualism) with Harry Houdini, spiritualism's great foe. In the midst of vignettes relating to Conan Doyle's lecture tour and Houdini's escape acts, the novel concerns itself with a series of crimes that newspaper writers (including Damon Runyon) deem the "Poe murders" because each is committed in the manner of a story by Poe. It becomes evident that all the victims are connected in some fashion to Houdini, and he himself believes that the perpetrator might well be one Opal Crosby Fletcher, a young socialite who engages in séances and other occult practices under the name Isis. Fletcher ends up seducing Houdini and also manages to convince him, during a séance, that he has communicated with his dead mother. (Why Houdini subsequently persists in his scepticism about spiritualism becomes an unresolved mystery.) Conan Doyle is pressured by the press to attempt to solve the case, and he seeks assistance from the spirit of Edgar Allan Poe, who appears at odd moments whenever Conan Doyle is in a city where Poe once resided. Both Conan Doyle and Houdini are on separate occasions kidnapped by the murderer, but each manages to escape with remarkable ease. Finally Houdini deduces the true perpetrator and teams up with Conan Doyle to capture him.

Nevermore leaves much to be desired: its prose is stilted and lacks the hard resonance of *Falling Angel*; Hjortsberg's period setting becomes heavy-handed and overwhelming, as he cannot resist the temptation to throw in all the historical research he has accumulated; and the supernatural manifestation—the sporadic appearance of the spirit of Poe—proves to have no bearing on the central plot, as Poe provides no appreciable assistance in solving the murders. Hjortsberg is to be praised for not attempting merely a rewrite of *Falling Angel*, but he has chosen an unwieldy subject that strains credulity, failing to produce either a satisfying mystery story or an engaging tale of the supernatural.

—S. T. Joshi

HODGSON, William Hope

Nationality: British. **Born:** Blackmore End, Essex, 15 November 1877. **Career:** Apprentice seaman, 1891-95; officer in the Mercantile Marine: lieutenant; founder and teacher, W. H. Hodgson's school of Physical Culture, Blackburn, Lancashire, 1899-1901. **Military Service:** Joined University of London Officer Training Corps, 1914; commissioned in Royal Field Artillery, 1915; left service because of injury, 1916; recommissioned, 1917, and died at Ypres. **Awards:** Royal Humane Society Medal, 1898. **Died:** 17 April 1918.

HORROR, GHOST AND GOTHIC PUBLICATIONS

Novels

The Boats of the Glen Carrig. London, Chapman and Hall, 1907; New York, Ballantine, 1971.
The House on the Borderland. London, Chapman and Hall, 1908; New York, Ace, 1962.
The Ghost Pirates. London, Stanley Paul, 1909; Westport, Connecticut, Hyperion Press, 1976.
The Night Land. London, Nash, 1912; Westport, Connecticut, Hyperion Press, 1976.
The House on the Borderland and Other Novels (omnibus). Sauk City, Wisconsin, Arkham House, 1946.

Short Stories

The Ghost Pirates, A Chaunty, and Another Story. New York, Reynolds, 1909.
Carnacki, The Ghost Finder, and a Poem. New York, Reynolds, 1910.
Carnacki, The Ghost Finder. London, Nash, 1913; augmented edition, Sauk City, Wisconsin, Mycroft and Moran, 1947.
Deep Waters. Sauk City, Wisconsin, Arkham House, 1967.
Out of the Storm: Uncollected Fantasies, edited by Sam Moskowitz. West Kingston, Rhode Island, Grant, 1975.
Demons of the Sea. West Warwick, Rhode Island, Necronomicon Press, 1992.
The Haunted Pampero. West Kingston, Rhode Island, Grant, 1993.
Terrors of the Sea. West Kingston, Rhode Island, Grant, 1996.

OTHER PUBLICATIONS

Short Stories

Men of the Deep Waters. London, Nash, 1914.
The Luck of the Strong. London, Nash, 1916.
Captain Gault, Being the Exceedingly Private Log of a Sea-Captain. London, Nash, 1917; New York, McBride, 1918.

Poetry

Poems, and The Dream of X. London, Watt, and New York, Paget, 1912.
Cargunka and Poems and Anecdotes. London, Watt, and New York, Paget, 1914.
The Calling of the Sea. London, Selwyn and Blount, 1920.
The Voice of the Ocean. London, Selwyn and Blount, 1921.
Poems of the Sea. London, Ferret Fantasy, 1977.

*

Bibliography: By A. L. Searles, in *The House on the Borderland and Other Novels*, Sauk City, Wisconsin, Arkham House, 1946.

Critical Study: *William Hope Hodgson: Voyages and Visions*, edited by Ian Bell, privately printed, 1987.

*   *   *

William Hope Hodgson ran away to sea at a tender age and found the experience terrible, but he stuck at it for some years before deciding that he could make a more adequate living as a writer. He dabbled in popular fiction of several kinds but his most effective work was that which reprocessed the terrors of his experiences at sea, in which the world's oceans became a vast and malign wilderness inhabited by all manner of monsters. He played a major role in establishing the mythology of the Sargasso Sea: a weed-infested region of the Atlantic in which sailing ships might get stuck for months or years (although it was eventually rendered harmless and desolate by the passage of powerful steamships).

The Sargasso-set "From the Tideless Sea," the earliest of the scary sea stories collected in *Deep Waters*, uses giant man-eating crabs as its figures of menace, while "The Mystery of the Derelict" employs unnaturally large rats, but Hodgson's most impressive tales in this vein deploy more bizarre imagery. *The Boats of the Glen Carrig* offers a whole spectrum of inimical life-forms, including predatory molluscs and evil fungi. A fungus which transforms the flesh of its eaters into its own substance is the deceptive menace described in his most famous exercise of this kind, "The Voice in the Night." In "The Shamraken Homeward-Bounder" the arch of red cloud assumed by the crew to be the gate of Heaven is similarly deceptive, as are the mass of "red hair" which sits on the head of the petrified master of "The Stone Ship" and the bleeding mould which infests "The Derelict." Hodgson reprinted a few stories of this kind alongside more mundane materials in such contemporary collections as *Men of the Deep Waters* but most languished in periodicals or among the author's papers until the Arkham House collection *Deep Waters* brought the bulk of them together.

The best of Hodgson's stories in this vein is the fine novel *The Ghost Pirates*, the only one of his book-length narratives to constitute a coherent crescendo of gathering menace. The significantly named *Mortzestus* is prone to slip into a grey area which is in the margins of our world and another, where it becomes vulnerable to invasion by the monstrous inhabitants of the other world. The only man on board who is capable of understanding this becomes the sole survivor when—after a wonderfully eerie glimpse of the ships of the other world sailing below the surface of the ocean—these invaders overwhelm the unlucky ship.

The idea of a marginal region separating our world from others plays an even more significant part in Hodgson's most famous novel, *The House on the Borderland*. The enigmatic house described in this strange patchwork is clearly symbolic of the mind of its inhabitant. Hodgson's preface—which is unfortunately omitted from most modern paperback editions of the book—advises the reader that the story contains such an allegory, and hence of the human mind in general. The narrator of the story-within-the-story describes two phases of the house's invasion by mysterious forces and repulsive entities, separated by a remarkable visionary sequence in which the inhabitant of the house witnesses the death of the Earth in the far future, visits the shores of the Sea of Sleep and catches a glimpse of the symbolic "central suns" around which the whole universe revolves, which offer a further allegory of life and death.

The last novel which Hodgson published, although it may have been the first to be written, was another visionary fantasy, in which an 18th-century Englishman stricken by grief after the death of his beloved experiences a dream-odyssey across the face of *The Night Land*: a far future in which the last remnants of mankind await extinction, besieged in their last two Redoubts by huge monsters. The hero, who journeys from one Redoubt to the other in order to rescue the heroine, must rely on the bounty of the Earth Current to revive her after she is killed with their goal in sight. The calculatedly archaic style of this very long novel has proved a severe test to many of its readers, and some prefer the drastically shortened version released (apparently to secure US copyright) as *The Dream of X*. Even some of those who cannot abide its artificiality, however, concur with those who do not mind it in the estimation that its account of the phantasmagoric journey is an achievement without equal, and that the text is a masterpiece of sorts.

Among the purely commercial works that Hodgson wrote in order to support his poetry and his visionary extravaganzas is a series of "psychic detective stories," which were collected as *Carnacki the Ghost-Finder*. The items published in Hodgson's lifetime were inventive and engaging but calculatedly trivial; however, one of the unsold stories added to the Mycroft & Moran edition, "The Hog," develops into yet another visionary fantasy in which the meta-empirical realm is revealed to be dark and hostile, populated by degraded and malevolent entities whose porcine attributes mock human ambition. This was the recurrent note resonating within all Hodgson's most effective work, resoundingly struck by two of the stories that still remained to be collected in *Out of the Storm*. The title story is the most elementary of all Hodgson's scary sea stories, in which the tempestuous ocean embodies a malign blight visited upon all human endeavour, while "Eloi, Eloi, Lama Sabachthani" describes how a man who seeks enlightenment by duplicating the conditions of Christ's crucifixion experiences a very nasty revelation. An unusually assiduous determination to scrape the bottom of the barrel produced three further assemblages of the dregs of Hodgson's production, but none contain anything of real interest. Even at his best, Hodgson was inclined to awkwardness—apart from *The Ghost Pirates* and a handful of short stories none of his narratives is as carefully constructed and as smoothly flowing as one might wish—but his was the awkwardness of a man groping in the dark for an effect and a revelation that no one else had ever achieved. He looked at the world with an inquiring eye trained as no eye had ever been trained before, and glimpsed horrific possibilities which he did his level best to describe and evaluate. It would be a great pity if recent attempts to rescue his dreariest hackwork and aborted projects were to detract from his status as a writer of unique vision and powerful effect.

—Brian Stableford

HOGG, James

Nationality: British. **Born:** Ettrick, Selkirkshire, Scotland, November 1770. **Education:** A few months' formal schooling. **Family:** Married Margaret Phillips in 1820. **Career:** Labourer and cowherd from childhood; shepherd, from 1788; poet from 1793; befriended by Sir Walter Scott, whom he assisted in the collection of ballads; farmer from 1807; bankrupt, 1809; editor and publisher, *The Spy* (weekly), Edinburgh, 1810-11; contributor to *Blackwood's Edinburgh Magazine* and other publications; granted a farm, Altrive Lake, Yarrow, by the Duke of Buccleuch, 1815. **Died:** 30 November 1835.

HORROR, GHOST AND GOTHIC PUBLICATIONS

Novels

The Brownie of Bodsbeck and Other Tales. Edinburgh, Blackwood, 1818.
The Private Memoirs and Confessions of a Justified Sinner (published anonymously). London, Longman, 1824.

Short Stories

Winter Evening Tales. London, Oliver and Boyd, 1820.
The Shepherd's Calendar. Edinburgh, Blackwood, 1829.
Tales and Sketches of the Ettrick Shepherd, edited by D. O. Hill. N.p., 1837.
Selected Stories and Sketches, edited by Douglas S. Mack. Edinburgh, Scottish Academic Press, 1982.

OTHER PUBLICATIONS

Novels

The Three Perils of Man. London, Longman, 1822.

Short Stories

The Three Perils of Woman. London, Longman, 1823.
Altrive Tales. London, Cochrane, 1832.
Tales of the Wars of Montrose. London, Cochrane, 1835.

Poetry

Scottish Pastorals. Privately printed, 1801.
The Mountain Bard. Edinburgh, Constable, 1807.
The Forest Minstrel. Edinburgh, Constable, 1810.
The Queen's Wake. Edinburgh, Goldie, 1813.
The Pilgrims of the Sun. Edinburgh, Blackwood, 1815.
Mador of the Moor. Edinburgh, Blackwood, 1816.
The Poetic Mirror. London, Longman, 1816.
Poetical Works. Edinburgh, Constable, 4 vols., 1822.
Queen Hynde. Edinburgh, Blackwood, and London, Longman, 1825.
Songs, by the Etrrick Shepherd. Edinburgh, Blackwood, 1831.
Selected Poems, edited by Douglas S. Mack. Oxford, Clarendon Press, 1970.
Selected Poems and Songs, edited by David Groves. Edinburgh, Scottish Academic Press, 1986.

Other

The Shepherd's Guide. Edinburgh, Constable, 1807.
Familiar Aecdotes of Sir Walter Scott. New York, n.p., 1834; as *The Domestic Manners and Private Life of Sir Walter Scott*, London, n.p., 1834.
The Works of the Ettrick Shepherd, edited by Thomas Thompson. London, Blackie, 2 vols., 1876.
Memoir of the Author's Life, edited by Douglas S. Mack. Edinburgh, Scottish Academic Press, 1972.

*

Critical Studies: *James Hogg* by G. B. S. Douglas, 1899; *The Ettrick Shepherd* by E. C. Batho, 1927; *Life and Letters of James Hogg* by Allen Lang Strout, Lubbock, Texas, Texas Tech Press, 1946; *James Hogg: A Critical Study* by A. L. Simpson, 1962; *James Hogg* by Douglas Gifford, Edinburgh, Ramsay Head Press, 1976; *James Hogg* by Nelson C. Smith, Boston, Twayne, 1980.

* * *

When James Hogg became a regular contributor to *Blackwood's Magazine* the author of the conversational column "Noctes Ambrosianae"—who signed himself "Christopher North" although his real name was John Wilson—took to referring to him, in jocular fashion, as "the Ettrick Shepherd." Hogg had, indeed, once worked as a shepherd and he had perforce to tolerate his travesty as a pugnacious, hard-drinking county bumpkin, but he was undoubtedly put out by the firmness with which the nickname stuck. Were the dead really capable of spinning in their graves he might well have been rotating furiously throughout the latter part of the 19th century as edition after edition of his variously selected works appeared as *The Ettrick Shepherd's Tales* or some variant thereof. He might even have been able to take some consolation from the fact that the bulk of his work was utterly forgotten once the 20th century had dawned, leaving his continued celebrity solely dependent on one novel whose separate editions were never cursed by the attachment of the nickname: *The Private Memoirs and Confessions of a Justified Sinner*, usually featured in collections of his tales in a truncated version as "The Private Memoirs and Confessions of a Fanatic" and also reprinted as *The Suicide's Grave* and *The Confessions of Justified Sinner*.

At the beginning of his literary career Hogg assisted Walter Scott in the collection of border ballads, and he spent the rest of that career in the shadow of the more accomplished writer, whose biography he wrote in an off-handedly uncharitable spirit which offended many of Scott's closer friends. He and Scott took different sides, politically and doctrinally, in their accounts of Scottish history—a distinction made very clear by contrasting *The Brownie of Bodsbeck* with *Old Mortality*. Hogg's addition of the brownie served to give sympathizers with the rival (aristocratic and Anglican) cause an extra critical stick to wield against him, but the evocation of the household spirit and its firm alliance with the Calvinistically-inclined common people does make a point. "The Brownie of the Black Hags" serves a similar allegorical purpose, as do most of Hogg's other borrowings from the rich folklore of the Scottish borders.

Much of Hogg's supernatural fiction is interesting today only as a quasi-anthropological record of local superstitions. Relatively few of his shorter productions qualify as authentic horror stories; when elements of Christian doctrine overlay more traditional materials, as they do in "Dreadful Story of Macpherson," "The Witches of Traquair" and "George Dobson's Expedition to Hell," they are usually supplemented by a softening irony. The most orthodoxly horrific of his ghost stories is the novella "Weldean Hall," usually subsumed with lesser items under the rubric of "Country Tales and Apparitions." Another of his more interesting novellas, "The Hunt of Eildon," is more folkloristic fantasy than horror, offering an entertaining vision of a romantically fantasized Medieval Scotland; the briefer "Mary Burnet" is similar in spirit. "The Renowned Adventures of Basil Lee" is more straightforwardly historical, although it veers towards the supernatural in its later phases. When Hogg ventured further afield than the territory he knew most intimately, as he did in "A Tale of Good Queen Bess: Her Jealousy of a Successor," his supernatural devices became more conventionally—and more ponderously—Gothic. "The Mysterious Bride," a neatly orthodox ghost story set in Ireland, is perhaps his most engaging tale set on foreign soil.

The book nowadays known as *The Confessions of a Justified Sinner* is generally acknowledged as one of the great Gothic novels. The sinner in question is Robert Wringham, whose murder of his half-brother George Colwan is twice described, first from an objective viewpoint as a kind of "case study" and then from within, as a highly problematic "confession." Wringham's attempt to deny responsibility for the murder is twofold. On the one hand, he seeks to excuse the benefit he derives from his kinsman's death by reference to the Calvinistic doctrine of predestination; he claims that he is one of the Elect, and is thus guaranteed not only a place in Heaven but a greater moral entitlement to the family inheritance than Colwan—whose damnation is allegedly obvious by virtue of the unfortunate and violent circumstances of his conception. On the other hand, he tries to deny the crime altogether by attributing it to an evil doppelgänger named Gil-Martin, who may be the Devil in disguise or merely an imaginary projection of his own evil impulses.

Wringham is eventually driven to despair and suicide, not so much by guilt as by the impossibility of deciding what has actually occurred. The reader is left in the same dubious condition, uncertain as to whether Gil-Martin is to be construed as an external or an internal demon. Such hesitation between supernatural and psychological interpretations is what the theorist Tzvetan Todorov considers to be the defining feature of the genre of *le fantastique* (the Fantastic), which bridges the otherwise separable genres of *le merveilleux* (the Marvel Tale) and *l'inconnu* (Tales of the Uncanny).

Like Nathaniel Hawthorne, whose account of *The Scarlet Letter* similarly uses the historical past as an arena for the careful exemplary analysis of the enigmatic workings of conscience, Hogg evidently felt that the central issue of Protestant philosophy still retained all of its urgency—and like Hawthorne, he preserved a strong sense of scalding irony in his narrative account of its insistent pressure. John Buchan was later to examine the same question of predestination within a specifically Scottish context in *Witch Wood*, but never managed to transcend the limitations of earnest simplicity; Hogg burst those bounds in a spectacular fashion unmatched by anything else in his extensive *oeuvre*. *The Confessions of a Justified Sinner* is "tidied up" in some heavily edited and bowdlerized versions, which may read a little better than the original but are markedly less effective than the raw original. As modern psychology has developed the notions of repression and the unconscious the story has come to seem increasingly insightful and profound, and it is one of those rare and precious works in which a seemingly mediocre writer far exceeded his apparent potential.

—Brian Stableford

HOLDER, Nancy

Nationality: American. **Born:** Los Altos, California, 1953; lived in Japan for three years as a child. **Family:** Married Wayne Holder; one daughter. **Career:** Contributor of short stories to many magazines and anthologies; author of at least 15 romantic novels under pseudonyms (not divulged). **Awards:** Horror Writers of America Bram Stoker Award for short story, 1991, and for novel, 1995. Lives in San Diego, California.

HORROR, GHOST AND GOTHIC PUBLICATIONS

Novels

Making Love, with Melanie Tem. New York, Dell, 1993.
Dead in the Water. New York, Dell, 1994; London, Raven, 1995.
Witch-Light, with Melanie Tem. New York, Dell, 1996.

Short Stories

The Ghosts of Tivoli. Eugene, Oregon, Pulphouse, 1992.
Cannibal Dwight's Special Purpose. Arvada, Colorado, Roadkill Press, 1992.

*   *   *

There are many who believe that the natural form for horror is the short story, that it is difficult to maintain an atmosphere of suspense and terror at novel length. Not surprisingly, the horror short remains a very popular form, although at present most new tales are published in the small press rather than in mass-market editions. It is therefore always a pleasant surprise to discover that a writer has made a reputation by writing superior short fiction. Although in recent years Nancy Holder has turned to the novel, the substantial body of fascinating, idiosyncratic short stories that she has written has already established her as a major name in modern horror.

Holder's stories are powerful, stylish, and frequently rely more on the intensity of the imagery and language than the plot itself. Many like "Moving Night" are snapshots of terror, in this case a young and troubled boy frightened by what appears to be the animate furniture in his room. In other cases, the supernatural content might almost be a dream, as with "Blood Gothic," in which a woman obsessed with vampirism seems to imagine a vampire lover as the cause of her waning health, and resorts to a vampiric attack in an attempt to renew her life. A drug-user hallucinates the horrible aftermath of an airplane crash in the decidedly creepy "Bring Me the Head of Timothy Leary."

Holder often uses traditional horror devices, but in untraditional ways. An American tourist in Japan reveals herself as a vampire to her local lover in "Cafe Endless: Spring Rain," and their ensuing tryst is both erotic and unsettling. Two young boys resort to cannibalism in "Cannibal Cats Come Out Tonight," their secret crime a strong bond that unites them until they are stranded without food and driven to consider each other as prospective prey. A young girl escapes death at the hands of an animate scarecrow during the Civil War in "Strawman."

Sometimes her inspiration comes from decidedly untraditional sources of horror, such as the tormented mermaid lover of "I Hear the Mermaids Singing." A woman faced with imminent blindness confronts what might be the Devil himself in "Glass Eyes." A gay couple runs up against a local superstition against saving anyone from drowning in "Down to the Sea," but one of them returns from the dead, after a fashion, to help his lover. "We Have Always Lived in the Forest" is a surreal tale of a woman living in the woods with her young children, whom she periodically eats, until a refugee from a nearby town interferes with her life.

In "The Beard" a woman whose dead husband used her as camouflage to conceal his homosexuality paints nude portraits under his name, and imagines—or does she?—that his decaying body makes love to her. A possessive man mourns his wife to extremes in "The Sweetest Rain": convinced that he can communicate with her ghost, he abandons the rest of his family to feed his private grief, and only discovers years later that due to a mixup at the cemetery, he has been communicating with the wrong spirit, concealing the wrong mummified body in his home. A dead woman is frozen for generations in an ice house in "O Love, Thy Kiss," but when a particularly hot summer comes and the ice begins to melt, the protagonist discovers a journal entry that indicates she will return to life if thawed.

Holder's only solo novel to date, *Dead in the Water*, draws on an honoured but largely forgotten tradition of horror tales set at sea. Few writers have used the theme since William Hope Hodgson was writing one terrifying story after another set on the ocean, but Holder proved herself equal to the task. A disparate group of tourists and crew members find themselves on the *Morris*, an elderly, substandard freighter departing from California. They soon discover this will be a voyage like no other, that the dead will walk again, the spirits of the departed will mesh with the minds of the living, and the border between reality and hallucination is about to break down. Holder proved herself capable of maintaining a sense of imminent doom and brooding evil at novel length with this work, which also benefits from its original imagery and well constructed plot.

With Melanie Tem, Holder collaborated on two other novels. *Making Love* is a superb work in which a frustrated woman imagines the perfect lover in such detail that she brings him to life. Pleased with her creation, she teaches the trick to others, and everything seems to be going perfectly until the created beings discover that they have desires of their own, and that these don't necessarily coincide with those of their creators. A clever idea developed thoughtfully and with terrifying implications. Also worthwhile, though less impressive, is *Witch-Light*. Valerie is a young woman who comes to visit her estranged father in his Mexican retreat when she learns that he is quite ill. Shortly after arriving, she becomes romantically involved with a male witch, a charming but mildly sinister man who is at once feared and respected by his neighbours. Valerie hopes that his magic will help her father, but fails to realize until it is almost too late that his intentions toward her are deadly.

Other short stories of note include "Shift," "Woman's Little Wound," "Dancer in the Hall of Mirrors," "In Search of Anton La Vey," "Bird on a Ledge" and "Ami Amet Deli Pencet." Holder's short fiction is rarely predictable, often presented from a non-realistic point of view, fabulous rather than conventionally narrative. Her gift for creating unusual situations and deftly creating unique characters is likely to ensure her continued popularity within the genre.

—Don D'Ammassa

HOLDSTOCK, Robert (Paul)

Pseudonyms: Robert Black; Ken Blake; Chris Carlsen; Steve Eisler; Robert Faulcon; Richard Kirk. **Nationality:** British. **Born:** Hythe, Kent, 2 August 1948. **Education:** University College of

North Wales, Bangor, 1967-70, B.Sc. (honours) in applied zoology 1970; London School of Hygiene and Tropical Medicine, 1970-71, M.Sc. in medical zoology 1971. **Career:** Research student, Medical Research Council, London, 1971-74. Since 1974, freelance writer. **Awards:** British Science Fiction Association award, 1985; World Fantasy award, 1985, 1993. **Agent:** A. P. Watt Ltd., 26-28 Bedford Row, London WC1R 4HL, England. **Address:** 54 Raleigh Road, London N8 0HY, England.

HORROR, GHOST AND GOTHIC PUBLICATIONS

Novels (series: Mythago)

Legend of the Werewolf (novelization of screenplay; as Robert Black). London, Sphere, 1976.
The Satanists (novelization of screenplay; as Robert Black). London, Futura, 1978.
Necromancer. London, Futura, 1978; New York, Avon, 1980.
Mythago Wood. London, Gollancz, 1984; New York, Arbor House, 1985.
Lavondyss: Journey to an Unknown Region (Mythago). London, Gollancz, 1988; New York, Morrow, 1989.
The Fetch. London, Orbit, 1991; as *Unknown Regions*, New York, Roc, 1996.
The Hollowing (Mythago). London, HarperCollins, and New York, Roc, 1993.
Merlin's Wood, or The Vision of Magic (Mythago). London, HarperCollins, 1994.
Ancient Echoes. London, Voyager, and New York, Roc, 1996.

Novels as Robert Faulcon (series: Night Hunter in all books)

Night Hunter. London, Arrow, 1983; New York, Charter, 1987.
The Talisman. London, Arrow, 1983; New York, Charter, 1987.
The Ghost Dance. London, Arrow, 1984; New York, Charter, 1987.
The Shrine. London, Arrow, 1984; New York, Charter, 1988.
The Hexing. London, Arrow, 1984; New York, Charter, 1988.
The Labyrinth. London, Arrow, 1987; New York, Charter, 1988.
The Stalking (omnibus; includes *Night Hunter, The Talisman*). London, Arrow, 1987.
The Ghost Dance (omnibus; includes *The Ghost Dance, The Shrine*). London, Arrow, 1987.
The Hexing and The Labyrinth (omnibus). London, Legend, 1989.

Short Stories

The Bone Forest (Mythago). London, Grafton, 1991.

OTHER PUBLICATIONS

Novels

Eye Among the Blind. London, Faber, 1976; New York, Doubleday, 1977.
Earthwind. London, Faber, 1977; New York, Pocket Books, 1978.
Shadow of the Wolf (as Chris Carlsen). London, Sphere, 1977.
Swordsmistress of Chaos (with Angus Wells, as Richard Kirk). London, Corgi, 1978.

A Time of Ghosts (as Richard Kirk). London, Corgi, 1978.
The Bull Chief (as Chris Carlsen). London, Sphere, 1979.
The Horned Warrior (as Chris Carlsen). London, Sphere, 1979.
Lords of the Shadows (as Richard Kirk). London, Corgi, 1979.
Cry Wolf (novelization of television script; as Ken Blake). London, Sphere, 1981.
Where Time Winds Blow. London, Faber, 1981, and New York, Pocket Books, 1982.
The Untouchables (novelization of television script; as Ken Blake). London, Sphere, 1982.
Operation Susie (novelization of television script; as Ken Blake). London, Sphere, 1982.
Bulman (novelization of television script). London, Futura, 1984.
The Emerald Forest (novelization of screenplay). New York, Zoetrope, and London, Penguin, 1985.
One of Our Pigeons is Missing (novelization of television script). London, Futura, 1985.

Short Stories

In the Valley of the Statues. London, Faber, 1982.
Elite: The Dark Wheel. Cambridge, Acornsoft, 1984.

Other

Alien Landscapes, with Malcolm Edwards. London, Pierrot, 1979.
Space Wars: Worlds and Weapons (as Steve Eisler). London, Octopus, 1979.
The Alien World: The Complete Illustrated Guide (as Steve Eisler). London, Octopus, 1980.
Tour of the Universe, with Malcolm Edwards. London, Pierrot, and New York, Mayflower, 1980.
Magician, with Malcolm Edwards. Limpsfield, Surrey, Dragon's World, 1982.
Realms of Fantasy, with Malcolm Edwards. Limpsfield, Surrey, Dragon's World, 1983.
Lost Realms, with Malcolm Edwards. Limpsfield, Surrey, Dragon's World, and Topsfield, Massachusetts, Salem House, 1985.

Editor, *Encyclopedia of Science Fiction.* London, Octopus, 1978.
Editor, with Christopher Priest, *Stars of Albion.* London, Pan, 1979.
Editor, with Christopher Evans, *Other Edens.* London, Unwin Hyman, 3 vols., 1987-89.

* * *

Although he is more often thought of as a fantasy writer, Robert Holdstock has also written horror novels, both under his own name and pseudonyms. However, all of his work shares common themes and takes a similar approach to the supernatural, mingling high fantasy, psychological exploration and nightmare terrors in the same book. To classify individual works as "pure" fantasy or "pure" horror is difficult, if not impossible; usually the distinction was made by the publisher to suit the perceived audience, and readers may have a different perception. To give an example, *Mythago Wood*, the award-winning fantasy novel which began the sequence for which Holdstock is perhaps best known, was selected by Michael Moorcock as his choice in Stephen Jones and Kim Newman's *Horror: 100 Best Books*. Certainly, there are dark elements and frightening moments in *Mythago Wood*, which is already recognized as a modern classic of British fantasy; like Alan Garner, Robert Holdstock delves deep into myth, magic, primitive religion and prehistoric, sometimes even prehuman, belief systems in his fantasy, exploring that mysterious, shadowy ground where ghost stories, fairy tales and heroic fantasy all originate.

In *Mythago Wood* Holdstock created Ryhope Wood, a patch of primeval English woodland which is unchartably large on the inside, and where time works differently. Once inside the woods a visitor will meet "mythagos," or myth-images from the collective unconscious, which may be heroes or monsters. Some are recognizably the archetypes underlying story-figures such as King Arthur or Robin Hood, but the older ones, from mankind's most distant past, can be terrifyingly inhuman. In *Lavondyss* and *The Hollowing* other characters enter the mythic internal landscape of the wood for often terrifying adventures on their way to self-discovery and/or reconciliation with their families.

Holdstock began his career as a science-fiction writer, and in his first horror novel (apart from a couple of minor movie novelizations), *Necromancer*, as well as in those which followed, a scientific, or pseudo-scientific, attitude is maintained towards the supernatural: the process of measuring and monitoring immaterial forces or dream journeys is often described at length, and there are nearly always some characters for whom the paranormal is a profession.

Throughout the 1970s and 1980s Holdstock wrote a number of pseudonymous works. Of these, the most significant is the six-novel "Night Hunter" series published under the name of Robert Faulcon. In the first book, Dan Brady (a researcher into the paranormal in the employ of the Ministry of Defence) is attacked and his family abducted by animal-masked satanists. His determination to save his wife, Alison, and their two children actually brings him back from the dead, and once he has recovered from the ordeal he begins to study magical arts, turning himself into an expert as he pursues the mysterious Arachne. More than simply satanists, Arachne is revealed eventually to be a group determined to use all forms of magic ever devised; gathering and storing in the minds of especially gifted "Accumulators" the spirits, ghosts and demonic forces of the past for some huge occult purpose. Throughout six volumes, Dan Brady pursues them to a final confrontation in an underground labyrinth constructed by a spiritual descendant of Daedalus. In the penultimate volume, *The Hexing*, Dan is reunited with Alison, and they learn that she has been a priestess in many past lives, and continues to function as the home of the goddess when the situation demands. In the conclusion, *The Labyrinth*, the Bradys are able to call upon their own strength and also upon ancient powers to defeat Arachne and save civilization.

Themes and images which appear in the Robert Faulcon novels are returned to, and more richly developed, in novels which appeared under Holdstock's own name. Some of the plot elements of *Ancient Echoes* are foreshadowed—in particular, the chthonic forces, the revival of an ancient city, and rituals linking humans and animals. The tree-like creatures which appear in *The Labyrinth* seem to have escaped from Ryhope Wood.

Jack Chatwin in *Ancient Echoes* has had visions of another world since childhood. When he is having his dream-like experiences observers can see him "shimmer" and hear echoes of the sounds he hears—which may be a parallel world, or from some time in humanity's distant past. Instead of entering a magical wood, Jack goes inside himself to find the mythic landscape, but instead of being dreams the characters he meets are real enough to enter our world and pose a threat to his family. In Holdstock's work the

ancient past is still alive; the hold that past events and personalities can have on contemporary individuals, even when they are long lost to conscious recollection, is a major theme, obsessively explored.

Besides recurring themes, there are recurring characters in Holdstock's work, and one whose presence seems to mark a work as "horror" rather than "fantasy," is Francoise Jeury, the French psychic investigator who can "read" inanimate objects. Introduced as a major character in *Necromancer*, she returns for a small but recurring role in the "Night Hunter" series, and again—as the only character able to provide trustworthy answers—in *The Fetch*.

The Fetch centres on young Michael Whitlock, born with a psychic power: he can "fetch" objects from other times and places. Neither space nor time is an obstacle to his apportational ability. An adopted child, he feels himself to be a disappointment to his parents, and attempts to buy his father's love by bringing him valuable artefacts. But no one understands the extent of his power, or the danger that it poses, until the discovery that Michael's "imaginary friend" Chalk Boy is really a ghost, and that there is a source of power in an ancient shrine near their house.

In addition to the novels, Holdstock has also written short stories, in which elements of horror and the supernatural mingle with fantasy and humour, just as they do in the longer works. Probably the closest to a traditional horror story is "Scarrowfell," a spooky tale of a traditional festival held annually in an English village. Told from a child's point of view, the mystery is well maintained until the end, with its inevitable sacrifice to an embodied spirit. "The Boy Who Jumped the Rapids" is a prehistoric ghost story. These and other stories are collected in *The Bone Forest*.

—Lisa Tuttle

HOLLAND, Tom

Nationality: British. **Born:** 1967. **Education:** Oxford University; doctorate in English literature. **Family:** Married Sadie Holland. **Address:** c/o Little, Brown and Company (UK), Brettenham House, Lancaster Place, London WC2E 7EN, England. Lives in London.

HORROR, GHOST AND GOTHIC PUBLICATIONS

Novels

The Vampyre: Being the True Pilgrimage of George Gordon, Sixth Lord Byron. London, Little Brown, 1995; as *Lord of the Dead: The Secret History of Lord Byron*, New York, Pocket, 1996.
Supping with Panthers. London, Little Brown, 1996.
Deliver Us from Evil. London, Little Brown, 1997.

*   *   *

The male version of the modern literary vampire is the direct descendant of the maiden-despoiling villain of John Polidori's novelette *The Vampyre*. Polidori had briefly served as Byron's doctor and confidant and was present when Byron read horror stories to Shelley and Mary Godwin at the Villa Diodati, but he became so deeply embittered once Byron could tolerate his company no longer that he decided to follow the example set by Lady Caroline Lamb and write a vitriolic condemnation of his former friend in fictional form. He even borrowed the name which Lady Caroline had given to the hero of her own novel, *Glenarvon*, and so the father-figure of the modern vampire became "Lord Ruthven."

Perhaps inadvertently, Polidori's caricature communicated not merely his intensely envious hatred of Byron but also the vivid charisma which had occasioned that envy. Thus, the monster which Polidori stitched together from mixed and ill-fitting images and emotions became the beneficiary of a marvellous synergy, which paved the way for Bram Stoker's *Dracula* and all those who came after him, including the ultra-Byronic heroes featured in revisionist vampire novels by Chelsea Quinn Yarbro and many others. It was perhaps inevitable that someone would eventually elect to take this process full circle to its logical terminus, writing a historical novel in which Lord Byron really does become a vampire, but there is reason to be grateful that the job was taken on by a writer as adequate to the task as Tom Holland (who should not be confused with the American horror-movie screenwriter and director of the same name, born 1943).

Holland's *Vampyre* is no straightforward revision of Polidori's, although the novel further acknowledges the contribution of its predecessor, in slyly ironic fashion, by having its hero adopt for the purposes of his posthumous career the pseudonym credited to him by his slanderers. It is, in fact, a flamboyant tour-de-force of revisionist vampire fiction, which outshines its model as easily and as magnificently as the noble poet outshone his envious associate. As well as providing an infinitely more interesting adventure in the wilds of Eastern Europe, Holland carefully recomplicates the predicament of the undead in a manner truly befitting a hero who, if not mad or bad, certainly becomes exceedingly dangerous to know. Polidori becomes a vampire too, but his conspicuous lack of innate nobility inevitably makes him a much inferior kind of vampire.

The two key issues which revisionist vampire fiction habitually addresses are the matter of out-growing the predatory need for blood to become authentically immortal and the matter of vampire origins—which is reducible, at its simplest, to a quest for the "primal vampire" who set in train the process of infection which converted all the rest. Holland establishes a distinctive stance in respect of both questions, ingeniously sharpening the horns of the vampire's moral dilemma by making eternal youth dependent on incestuous predation, and conflating various myths of terrifying but fecund mother-goddesses to the dramatization of the question of origins. The plot of *The Vampyre*, which first raises these issues, is neatly intricate and zestfully melodramatic, liberally spiced with atmospheric sub-climactic confrontations. The author makes clever use of his scholarly researches, fleshing out Byron's modified character with considerable artistry. The groundwork laid here is cleverly put to further use, and further developed, in *Supping with Panthers*, which is set in the *fin de siècle* period of the 19th century.

Byron's role in *Supping with Panthers* is important but peripheral. Bram Stoker is a more active character, his adventure providing an extraordinarily elaborate basis for the novel he eventually writes, but the primary protagonist of the novel is John Eliot, a medical man who once studied (alongside Arthur Conan Doyle) under Joseph Bell at Edinburgh and inherited from him the same expertise in deduction that Doyle attributed to Sherlock Holmes. Eliot first encounters vampirism in the far reaches of the British Raj, and continues his researches into the "disease" in Whitechapel, with the assistance of Byron. The British Empire's intrusion into the secret stronghold of vampirism has, however, caused a reaction; the godlike progenitor of the plague of undeath travels to London to win back the independence of her tiny realm. In his capacity as stand-in for Sherlock Holmes, Eliot becomes involved in the attempt to save a politician from her insidious pressure—but he falls prey to her supernatural seductiveness himself, with horrible consequences.

Like its predecessor, *Supping with Panthers* has an intricate plot which moves with grace and alacrity—this despite its appropriation of the multi-documentary format of *Dracula*. Its conscientiously Decadent deployment of the marvellous *femme fatale* and her deceptively sinister companion is done with great style and its climactic passages carry a considerable erotic charge. Although the novel has inevitable overlaps with Kim Newman's parallel *fin de siècle* text *Anno Dracula* it is very different in tone, being more homage than caricature, but it is no mere pastiche or assembly of pastiches. Holland brings a thoroughly modern sensibility and knowledgeability to the reconstruction of the late Victorian era and the delineation of its characters, and he draws on all the expertise which 20th-century writers have accumulated in the course of designing slick and suspenseful thrillers. *Supping with Panthers* is, in consequence, a brilliantly sophisticated but blithely unashamed exercise in popular fiction.

The series begun by *The Vampyre* and *Supping with Panthers* will presumably be continued in due course, and may well build into the most impressive of the many sustained exercises in vampire revisionism which have been initiated since the mid-1970s. At any rate, Holland—who was still in his twenties when *Supping with Panthers* was published—seems assured of a highly successful literary career.

—Brian Stableford

HONEYCOMBE, Gordon

Nationality: British. **Born:** 1936. **Career:** Journalist; newscaster, Independent Television News, London; freelance writer.

HORROR, GHOST AND GOTHIC PUBLICATIONS

Novels

Neither the Sea nor the Sand. London, Hutchinson, 1969; New York, Weybright, 1970.
Dragon under the Hill. London, Hutchinson, and New York, Simon and Schuster, 1972.

Plays

Screenplay: *Neither the Sea nor the Sand*, with Rosemary Davies, 1972.

OTHER PUBLICATIONS

Novels

Adam's Tale. London, Hutchinson, 1974.

Other

Red Watch. London, Hutchinson, 1976.
The Murders of the Black Museum, 1870-1970. London, Hutchinson, 1982.
The Year of the Princess. London, M. Joseph, 1982.
Selfridges: Seventy-Five Years. London, Park Lane, 1984.

*

Film Adaptation: *Neither the Sea nor the Sand*, 1972.

*   *   *

In the famous story "The Monkey's Paw" by W. W. Jacobs, the parents of a recently deceased young man wish for him to return to them; he does, but by implication he has not returned to life and is a member of the walking dead; he is too horrible to be faced. Gordon Honeycombe's novel *Neither the Sea nor the Sand* dispenses with the magic of three wishes but reuses the idea by substituting the power of love.

Annie Robins, a shy and awkward librarian, meets Hugh Dabernon on a beach in St. Ouen's Bay on the island of Jersey, where he lives and she is visiting—a solitary holiday. They quickly fall in love and become completely devoted to each other. They exchange rings but do not bother with a marriage ceremony, a frowned-upon novelty in the 1960s. Together they set up house on Jersey; he works at the airport and she, too, gets a job there. They take an out-of-season holiday to Cape Wrath at the northwest tip of Scotland, living in a caravan and sharing the beauty of the scenery. During an exuberant chase on the beach there, he drops dead. The local doctor diagnoses heart failure, with no need for a post mortem; the local farmer's wife who rented them the caravan seems more concerned about them not being married than about Hugh's death.

When Annie wakes during the night—she has been sedated for shock—she goes to the caravan, where Hugh's body lies. She stands over him, vocalizing her love for him and saying his name. Then she goes to sit on rocks overlooking the sea, and he gets up and comes to her. He is neither a ghost nor alive. He is, to use the convenience of a cliché, a zombie, unable to speak or act of his own volition except that he always looks towards her.

In the morning, Annie gets Hugh into their hired car and and drives him to the airport at Glasgow. The doctor and the farmer and his wife accept that some sort of mistake has occurred; he could not have been dead at all. Annie and Hugh fly back to Jersey, return to their house. But this is no longer a sanctuary from the rest of the world, or the love nest it was. She cannot accept that Hugh is dead, but neither can she decide what should be done to help him, and only gradually does the horrific nature of it all become clear to her. She phones his elder brother, George, who arrives drunk, but not too drunk to see that Hugh is dead, and tries to take him away by car, presumably to begin the process of doctor, undertaker, burial. Hugh causes the car to crash, and George is killed. Hugh returns to her and she is temporarily happy. The scene between Annie and George comes close to being black comedy, and the reader is reminded of certain plays by Joe Orton.

But by morning the process of bodily decomposition has begun. Part of Annie's mind realizes that Hugh is dead and tries to send him away to die properly. However, the power of love is too strong. She is found on the seashore, suffering from pneumo-

nia and, just like her lover, unable to speak or make decisions for herself. She is institutionalized. For more than six months she acts like a zombie, while Hugh remains undiscovered in a bedroom of their house, not wholly dead, but decomposing. The coincidence of a burglar visiting the house and the anniversary of Hugh and Annie's first meeting causes the authorities to become involved and the loving couple to make their separate ways to the beach where they first met. Together they are, presumably, swept out to sea.

So an unsentimental love story becomes a grotesque tragedy. The gradual deterioration of Hugh's body is not avoided. The novel includes some grossly unpleasant scenes. For example, Hugh's leg has been badly gashed in the car crash and, when Annie tries to repulse him in the morning, the pooling blood in his slipper splashes across the bedroom. Seven months later, once his eyes have liquefied and he is being consumed by maggots, he loses a hand in a struggle with the burglar.

The way in which Annie and Hugh each knows the direction of the other is a supernatural talent. But apart from that and that fact of a dead man walking, everything else in the novel is matter-of-factly realistic. The scenery of both Jersey and Cape Wrath is sensitively and atmospherically described and is essential to the success of the story. The characters of Annie and Hugh are very believable: two vulnerable young people who are perfectly suited to each other and find it quite natural to shun the rest of the world. A peculiarity of the book is that Hugh never speaks in dialogue; all his words are given in reported speech except for the one brief sentence to Annie: "I will always love you." It is a sentence which she says back to him at the very end, when they are together in the rising tide in St. Ouen's Bay. The title comes from two lines by the poet Ross Guyot: "Neither the sea nor the sand will kill their love / Nor the wind take it in envy from them."

For a first novel this is competent and remarkably accomplished. If there are problems they are mainly to do with plot and point of view. The first two thirds of the book are original, seamless and gripping. But Annie's retreat in a kind of zombie state, the creation of several new characters, the seven-month hiatus and the coincidence of burglar and anniversary all conspire to drive a wedge between the lovers and the reader. The last third is fitting, though the rather drawn-out finale is perhaps too much of an easy solution. While Honeycombe's later novel *Dragon under the Hill* is a dark fantasy about a revenant Viking chief, it is a pity that he has not written more outright horror in the vein of his first.

—Chris Morgan

HOOD, Robert (Maxwell)

Nationality: Australian. **Born:** Parramatta, New South Wales, 24 July 1951. **Education:** Rydalmere Primary School, NSW; Collaroy Plateau Primary School, NSW; Narrabeen Boys' High School, NSW; Macquarie University, 1970-77, Dip. Ed., B.A. (Honours) in English Literature. **Family:** Married 1) Margaret Curtis in 1979 (divorced 1985); married 2) Deborah Jean Westbury in 1987 (separated), one son. **Career:** Freelance writer, 1975-78; secondary-school teacher, New South Wales, 1978-84; radio comedy writer, Sydney 2SM, 1985; on-air comedy radio show, "Something Different for Sunday Breakfast," Wollongong 2-Double-0, 1985; journalist, *Liverpool Leader* (Cumberland Press), 1985-87; research assistant in Australian political and social history, 1987-91; various freelance editorial activities from 1988, including acting editor, *SCARP* magazine, 1989-90 and 1991; casual tutoring in School of Creative Arts, University of Wollongong, 1989-94; editorial cartoonist, *Liverpool Leader*, 1987-96; publication officer, Economics Department, University of Wollongong, from 1991. **Awards:** *Canberra Times* National Short Story Competition winner, 1975; Australian Golden Dagger Award, 1988. **Address:** PO Box 271, Thirroul, NSW 2515, Australia. **Online Address:** robert_hood@uow.edu.au.

Horror, Ghost and Gothic Publications

Short Stories

Day-dreaming on Company Time. Wollongong, Five Islands Press, 1988.

Novels for Children, with Bill Condon (series: The Creepers in all titles)

Ghoul Man. Sydney, Hodder Headline, 1996.
Freak Out! Sydney, Hodder Headline, 1996.
Loco-Zombies. Sydney, Hodder Headline, 1996.
Slime Zone. Sydney, Hodder Headline, 1996.
Bone Screamers. Sydney, Hodder Headline, 1996.
Rat Heads. Sydney, Hodder Headline, 1997.
Brain Sucker. Sydney, Hodder Headline, 1997.
Humungoid. Sydney, Hodder Headline, 1997.
Feeding Frenzy. Sydney, Hodder Headline, 1997.

Plays

On Getting to the Heart of the Monster, or the Reviewer's Revenge (produced 1983).
The Fantastic Failures. In *Enjoying English: Book 1*, edited by R. K. Sadler, T. A. S. Hayllar and C. J. Powell, Melbourne, Melbourne, Macmillan, 1989.
The Mummy's Purse. In *Enjoying English: Book 3*, edited by R. K. Sadler, T. A. S. Hayllar and C. J. Powell, Melbourne, Macmillan, 1991.

Other

Editor, with Stuart Coupe and Julie Ogden. *Crosstown Traffic.* Wollongong, Five Islands Press, 1996.
Editor, with Bill Congreve. *Bonescribes: Year's Best Australian Horror 1995.* Sydney, MirrorDanse Press, 1996.

Other Publications

Novel for Children

Bad Boy Bunyip Goes Nuts. Sydney, Ferrero, 1995.

Plays

Firebird (produced, 1983).
Still in the Cold World (produced, 1985).

Roads, Rates and Rubbish, with Bill Condon (produced, 1988).
The Red Terror, with Bill Condon (produced, 1989).
It's Not Easy Saving the World, You Know! In *Enjoying English, Book 2*, edited by R. K. Sadler, T. A. S. Hayllar and C. J. Powell, Melbourne, Macmillan, 1990.

Other

Lessons in English, with Ray Capner. Sydney, Science Press, 1986.
Issues in Contemporary English. Melbourne, Macmillan, 1989.

Editor, with Raymond Markey. *Proceedings of the Seminar on Industrial Democracy and Employee Participation at Port Kembla.* Wollongong, CWALMS, 1988.

*

Theatrical Activities:
Manager, 1983-87, and director, 1983-88, Nexus Theatre.

*   *   *

Robert Hood is recognized primarily as a writer of well-crafted horror short stories, although his short fiction often explores the related genres of crime, science fiction and fantasy. In recent years, however, he has co-authored (with Bill Condon) a series of juvenile horror novels. Unfortunately, most of Hood's short stories are uncollected, and some are available only in their original magazine and anthology sources.

Hood's only collection to date, *Day-dreaming on Company Time*, is a collection of mixed-genre stories, though predominantly horror and fantasy. It was nominated for an award for Best Collection by a Single Author at the 1990 Readercon in Massachusetts. "Orientation" (which won the *Canberra Times* short-story competition in 1975) was written in response to Hood's initial exposure to high-school teaching; it is an exercise in surreal "reductionism"—a new teacher reduced to being "part of the machine" by the school system's unnatural atmosphere and the unseen forces that structure it. "Dead End," a crime story, won the inaugural 1988 Australian Golden Dagger Award and is certainly his most reprinted short story. Curiously, although it is definitely a crime tale, it has a zombie in it, albeit briefly! "Last Remains" is a metaphysical story that follows the main character's journey (through supernatural attack by moths) to the realization that something has died; it is Hood's own favourite piece from the collection and one he believes is both personal and universal. The title story, "Day-dreaming on Company Time," was almost made into a movie (although the book's blurb says it was made); the money actually fell through before the film eventuated. Overall, there is a theme running through the collection, a common thread that informs Hood's writing as a whole: exploring the spiritual nexus between the objective and the subjective world, as encapsulated in the quotations from William Blake appearing at the beginning of the volume. Blake has been a major influence on Hood's perception of things, both metaphysically and artistically, and Blake's work was the subject of Hood's postgraduate research study.

Of Hood's other stories, the following are of particular interest as horror: "Juggernaut" (1988) tells of a writer overwhelmed by his own creation; "Necropolis" (1986) is a ghost story about post-nuclear survival (one live person in a city of ghosts); "An Old Man and His Dog" (1987) belongs here because of its Gothic atmosphere—in it an unsympathetic nurse is dragged into the wilderness of extreme old age; "An Apocalyptic Horse" (1989) is about a man who comes upon the fourth horseman of the Apocalypse and then becomes him; "The Calling" (1988) concerns a repressed individual and his inability to escape from his background; "Grandma and the Girls" (1989) is a ghost story about obsessive family history; "Peripheral Movement in the Leaves Under an Orange Tree" (1989) is a story about haunted leaf-litter; "You're a Sick Man, Mr. Antwhistle" (1990) concerns a strange man at a poetry reading who has the power to affect those around him; "Dreams of Death" (1990) is a private-eye story about nightmares, murder, despair and immortality; "The Slimelight, and How to Step into It" (1991) is a humorous horror romance about an extra-dimensional blob that wants to be a great Shakespearean actor; "Nasty Little Habits" (1991) is about a young son with very bad personal habits and how he drives his mother to manslaughter—though the bad habits do not subsequently go away; "Groundswell" (1991), in a science-fictional setting, presents a policeman who tracks a murderer through a murdered landscape to a special place where life is being renewed; in "Separating Lenore" (1991) the main character marries a supernatural being—and finds he does not like it.

"The Backroom Boys" (1991), "Voyeur Night" (1993), "Dem Bones" (1992), and "A Place for the Dead" (1994) are all zombie stories, the latter exploring some of the consequences of legal and familial responsibility. Hood is clearly fond of zombie stories and explores the sub-genre from time to time. "Openings" (1993) is about corporate and supernatural opportunism; "Inchoate" (1992) is a surrealistic anecdote inspired by a series of paintings; "Mamandis Dreaming" (1993) is a love story involving the inhabitants of a devastated outback, and explores the nature of monstrosity; "Rough Trade" (1994) concerns role reversal between an embittered sculptor and his gargoyle; "Autopsy" (1994) is an outrageously gruesome tale of a psychopath and his messy inner-body search for the essence of life; "Instruments for the Removal of Body Parts" (1994) is about a psychopathic surgeon who finds a zombie to use in his experiments; "Rotting Eggplant on the Bottom Shelf of a Fridge" (1994) is a bizarre story about sympathetic energy-transfer, as a rotting eggplant becomes responsible for the destruction of Sydney; "Blurred Lines" (1994) concerns a man whose hearing sharpens as he goes blind, until he can "hear" beyond the world—it was inspired by the rainforest of the Illawarra escarpment; "Peeking" (1995) is a morality tale about voyeurism; "The Black Lake's Fatal Flood" (1995) is about dripping water that is inhabited by some very nasty creatures; "A Quickening in Stone" (1996) is an sf/horror story about new forms of artificial life, and the ethical and practical problems they create for a policeman investigating murder.

Hood's crime stories, for which he has something of a reputation, often veer toward the genre's boundary with the horror genre, and frequently have a dark violence, a Gothic atmosphere or an awareness of perceptual instability that often characterizes his horror work. "Sandcrawlers" (1993) is an horrific story based on the real-life murders of two young girls on Wanda Beach in 1976. The murder details were gruesome, and Hood focuses on the horror of that moment for an involuntary (and fictitious) witness. "Dead in the Glamour of Moonlight" (1995) takes his crime fiction explicitly into the horror field—not because the depicted murder is nasty (which it is), but because of the sensibility that informs the story and its ambiguous air of supernatural intent. Many of Hood's most effective stories refuse to see the supernatural as either an objec-

tive or a subjective experience: the line blurs. The possibility remains that it is both, or possibly that there is no real distinction.

The "Creepers" series of children's horror novels, written with children's author Bill Condon, push at the edge of what many might feel is acceptable for children. Yet the books have been greeted warmly by librarians, teachers and parents, as well as their intended audience. The books are gruesome and extravagant in terms of muck, mire, bodily dismemberment, blood, monstrousness and general weirdness. They work—and are generally acceptable—because they are funny, relentlessly action-packed, and exist within a fantastic context; there are no child-molesters or serial killers—this is the horror of ghosts, zombies, alien slime-beings, skeletal pirates, mutant street-kids, giant maggots, Godzilla-type monsters and brain-sucking blobs. Very much horror as a playground for fear—fear explored in a "safe" context. Yet, like all good horror, the books create metaphors for mortality and insecurity.

—Steven Paulsen and Sean McMullen

HOUSMAN, Clemence

Nationality: British. **Born:** Worcestershire, 1861; sister of the poet Alfred Edward Housman and the writer Laurence Housman. **Education:** Studied art in London. **Family:** None; lived with her brother Laurence. **Career:** Illustrator and writer; active in the suffragette movement. **Died:** 1955.

HORROR, GHOST AND GOTHIC PUBLICATIONS

Novel

The Unknown Sea. London, n.p., 1898.

Short Story

The Were-Wolf. London, John Lane, 1896; New York, Arno Press, 1976.

OTHER PUBLICATIONS

Novel

The Life of Sir Aglovale de Galis. London, n.p., 1905; revised edition, 1954.

*

Critical Study: *Laurence Housman 1865-1959, Clemence Housman 1861-1955, Alfred Edward Housman 1859-1936* by I. G. Kenyur-Hodgkins, London, National Book League, 1975.

*   *   *

Clemence Housman was the younger sister of Alfred (who signed himself A. E. Housman), born 1859, and the elder sister of Laurence, born 1865. All three siblings published works that might be reckoned their most outstanding in 1896: A. E. issued the unrepentantly homoerotic *A Shropshire Lad*; Laurence published a fine collection of mordant Christian fantasies, *All Fellows: Seven Legends of Lower Redemption*; and Clemence's novelette *The Were-Wolf*—which had previously appeared in *Atalanta*—was issued in book form by *Yellow Book* publisher John Lane. The British Decadent Movement had been murdered in its cradle the year before, by the Marquess of Queensberry's successful persecution of Oscar Wilde, and the two brothers took care to salute its passing by sending complimentary copies of their books to the unfortunate Wilde. The versatile Laurence went on to make his name with literary works of a very different kind and the atheistic but conservative A. E. established himself as the leading classical scholar of his day, but the abortion of the careers that all three siblings might have built was marked and mourned by their separate productions of 1896.

The Were-Wolf is to some small extent a collaborative work, as Laurence's two earlier collections of fairy tales had been, by virtue of the fact that his illustrations were painstakingly engraved by his sister. It is not surprising, therefore, that the story exhibits strong affinities with Laurence's early fantasies; the principal difference is that while Laurence's tales were (in effect) all about morality, Clemence's is all about immorality. *The Were-Wolf* is a tale of two brothers beguiled and beset by an illusion, recounting their different responses to the mysterious *femme fatale* White Fell, whose appearance out of the night is preceded by dark omens. The sceptical older brother Sweyn, the first to encounter her, immediately falls completely under her spell, as does his infant cousin Rol—but when the devout Christian appears in her wake he has already deduced from her tracks in the snow that she must be a werewolf. Sweyn's refusal to believe his brother has tragic consequences. After kissing White Fell, Rol and the aged Trella both disappear, but Sweyn will not admit that they have fallen victim to a werewolf and continues to insist that Christian's protests against his liaison with White Fell are based in sexual jealousy. When Christian finds out that Sweyn has also received the fateful kiss he acts, pursuing her across the wintry landscape. Sweyn follows behind them, determined to kill his brother if White Fell is harmed—but when he finds them dead together, she in her wolf form, he realizes the awful truth: that Christian, as befits his name, has died "to save him from his sins."

What literary models Clemence Housman had in mind while composing this tale it is impossible to determine for sure, but its meticulously archaic prose is strongly reminiscent of the fantasies of William Morris and its masochistic moralism has something in common with Christina Rossetti's poem "Goblin Market." Although the illustrations in *The Were-Wolf* are conspicuously second-rate by comparison with those in Laurence's own books the whole set share a spirit of common enterprise with the activities of Morris's Kelmscott Press and J. M. Dent's Beardsley-illustrated *Morte d'Arthur*. The Housmans would, of course, have been fully aware that the saintly Christina Rossetti's rakehell brother Dante Gabriel was the long-time lover of William Morris's wife. (Life in Victorian literary families rarely ran smoothly.)

The Were-Wolf did not become the British classic of werewolf fiction in the way that *Dracula*—published a year later—became the classic of vampire fiction. It is too slight, but it is also too precious; it is not a mystery or a thriller, and an extended prose-poem cannot reasonably aspire to become a classic of popular literature. It is, however, an extremely fine work, and there is cause to regret that the author never did anything remotely like it again. Her marginally supernatural novel *The Unknown Sea* is also a

femme fatale story, about a seaman caught between the contrasting attractions of the village on the shore where his home and family are and the strange island which seems to hold more exotic promise—but he has no one to come to his aid, and must submit to his fate. Following its publication, Clemence Housman became increasingly involved in the suffragette movement and after the production of her *Morte d'Arthur*-based study of *The Life of Sir Aglovale de Galis* her literary production dwindled away into silence.

—Brian Stableford

HUGHES, Rhys (Henry)

Nationality: British. **Born:** Cardiff, 24 September 1966. **Education:** Porthcawl Comprehensive School; School of Maritime Studies, Cardiff, 1984-86; University of Wales, B.Eng. 1991. **Career:** Test engineer, Swansea, Wales; contributor to small-press magazines since 1992. **Address:** 133 Rhondda Street, Swansea, SA1 6EU, UK.

HORROR, GHOST AND GOTHIC PUBLICATIONS

Romance with Capsicum. Duffield, Yorkshire, Wyrd Press, 1995.
Worming the Harpy, and Other Bitter Pills. Horam, East Sussex, Tartarus Press, 1995.
Eyelidiad. Leicester, Tanjen, 1996.
Nowhere Near Milk Wood. Unreal Novellas, 1997.

*   *   *

One of the most prolific short-story writers currently living in Wales, Rhys Hughes has created a brand of absurdist fantasy which owes much to the excesses of High Gothic and the darkest satires of Edgar Allan Poe. Perhaps his work is too grandiose and conceited for popular taste, though he is aware of his faults and his finest efforts combine self-indulgence with self-depreciation. Unhappy with the horror and fantasy labels which are applied to his work, he prefers to designate himself a "Romanti-Cynic," his term to describe authors who relish fantastical fiction but maintain an ironic distance from it. Obsessed with symmetry and style, he can be pedantic and awkward, but on occasions he achieves a genuine originality. Inventive rather than imaginative, he is a virtuoso at forcing extreme ideas into elaborate plots, but lacks the skills to involve his readers in anything deeper than peripheral emotions. It is difficult to identify with his characters, who tend to exist simply as foils for dehumanized themes rather than as beings in their own right. Despite the multitude of improbably named participants in his books, he employs only one man and one woman, and both are perfunctory, impatient and rashly idealized aspects of the misanthropic author.

Educated as an electronic engineer, Hughes's earliest publications were chess problems and mathematical puzzles for newspapers. These started to appear from 1988, but it was not until 1992 that he sold his first short fiction. His enormous output from this time has mostly been confined to the small press, though he has also appeared in various anthologies. His initial collection, *Romance with Capsicum*, contains a broad selection of apprentice stories, only two of which are of anything other than slight interest. Both "Trombonhomie" and "The Urban Freckle" are concise spoofs of Magic Realism and betray an affection for Latin American literature. Indeed, his major influences are becoming less Anglophone: aesthetically and politically he considers himself a Pan-European author. Whether this is an affectation remains to be seen, but the thumbprints of continental writers on his work are unmistakable.

Much more ambitious, his second collection, *Worming the Harpy*, is a frenetic foray into postmodernism in which the author seems barely to pause for breath from beginning to end. Though the tales are all linked, this does not become apparent until the final paragraph of the last story, which attempts to tie up the loose ends. Set in Chaud-Mell, a fictional Alpine republic, the three core stories—"The Good-News Grimoire," "Clair de Lune" and "Grinding the Goblin"—are crammed with Gothic allusions, in-jokes and complex puns, lengthy passages consisting of nothing but references to other works. Other notable pieces, "A Carpet Seldom Found" and "Cat o' Nine Tales," display a sympathy rarely found in Hughes, mainly avoiding the slapstick violence which is another of his trademarks. His fictions might make good puppet-shows, a genre where his weaknesses—character, psychology and credibility—are less vital than his strengths—irony, allegory and the devolution of logic.

Worming the Harpy inaugurated a huge story-cycle which, with Ptolemaic care, Hughes has arranged to be composed of epicycles, each a complete unit in itself. The Chaud-Mell sequence forms one of the axes of the project, around which revolve dozens of other linked tales. With maximum artifice, every cycle has been designed as a closed loop and a Moebius structure has been planned for the overall series, which will be assembled from exactly one thousand stories. Hughes makes few apologies for his fetish with numbers, claiming its application to his prose aids his creativity. Mathematical frameworks of varying complexity are found throughout his *oeuvre*, an approach echoed by the logarithmic quality of his metaphors and similes, which seek to multiply meanings by extending and adding symbols in predetermined combinations. His absurdist sequels to the entire corpus of ghost-story writer M. R. James, for example, are often patterned exactly after the originals, with identical punctuation in the same places, ostensibly to imitate James's rhythms but more likely to satisfy Hughes's craving for order.

His love of machines and explanations guarantees that even his most grotesque work is never truly frightening or traumatic. By examining the workings of ghosts, vampires and assorted nightmares, he loses the eerie qualities inherent in dark fantasy. Yet the outrageousness of his humour and the convoluted twists of his plotting can be almost as disturbing as the more visceral shocks of traditional Gothic. Two of his story-cycles, the Darktree and Lladloh Wheels, show him oscillating between parody and a serious attempt to forge an essentially Welsh variety of Fabulism. His highwayman, Robin Darktree, and even more absurd bard, Tin Dylan, wander the blistered valleys and mountains, destroying clichés with a flintlock pistol or a wrong note. Lladloh is the rural twin of Chaud-Mell, linked by a subterranean tunnel, the antithesis of the archetypal Welsh village. A wider picture is gradually emerging, though with all the component texts of his cycles scattered in little-known magazines, the craved uniformity is proving elusive. A sample of Lladloh tales, however, can be found in an appropriately titled chapbook, *Nowhere Near Milk Wood*. Overlapping and modifying each other as they jostle to achieve stability, the cycles increasingly resemble Venn diagrams.

Throughout his career, Hughes's work has grown steadily longer, and from 1995 he started producing a sequence of novellas also connected to his story-cycles. The first of these, "The Herb-Garden of Earthly Delights," a retelling of the Caspar Hauser myth, was followed by "Eyelidiad," and a superior ghost comedy, "Rawhead and Bloody Bones." His most peculiar, and stunning, story to date is "Elusive Plato," a novella postulating a time-line where the great philosopher was a potter. Again, the allusions and puns come thick and fast, but they add to the theme and plot rather than distract from them. The compelling richness of the language and the implications of the central idea combine to earn this work a conspicuous place in the rather small sub-genre of philosophical horror tales. A cult writer, Hughes needs to take a serious look at his deficiencies if he is to achieve wider appreciation. However his subversion of the traditions of Welsh writing can be very refreshing.

—Will Johnstone

HUNT, (Isobel) Violet

Nationality: British. **Born:** Durham, 1866; daughter of the painter Alfred Hunt. **Family:** Unmarried companion to the writer Ford Madox Hueffer (and known for a time as "Mrs. Hueffer"). **Career:** Novelist, biographer and journalist. Founder, Women Writers' Suffrage League. **Died:** London, 16 January 1942.

HORROR, GHOST AND GOTHIC PUBLICATIONS

Short Stories

Tales of the Uneasy. London, Heinemann, 1911.
Tiger Skin. London, Heinemann, 1924.
More Tales of the Uneasy. London, Heinemann, 1925.

OTHER PUBLICATIONS

Novels

The Maiden's Progress. London, Osgood McIlvaine, and New York, Harper, 1894.
A Hard Woman. London, Chapman and Hall, and New York, Appleton, 1895.
Unkist, Unkind! London, Chapman and Hall, and New York, Harper, 1897.
The Human Interest. London, Methuen, and New York, Stone, 1899.
Sooner or Later: The Story of an Ingenious Ingenue. London, Chapman and Hall, 1904.
The Workaday Woman. London, Werner Laurie, 1906.
White Rose of Weary Leaf. London, Heinemann, and New York, Brentano, 1908.
The Doll: A Happy Story. London, Stanley Paul, 1911.
The Governess, completion of a novel by Mrs. Alfred Hunt. London, Chatto and Windus, 1912.
The Celebrity's Daughter. London, Stanley Paul, 1913; New York, Brentano, 1914.

The House of Many Mirrors. London, Stanley Paul, and New York, Brentano, 1915.
The Last Ditch. London, Stanley Paul, 1918.

Short Stories

The Way of Marriage. London, Chapman and Hall, 1896.
Affairs of the Heart. London, Freemantle, 1900.
Zeppelin Nights, with Ford Madox Hueffer. London, New York, 1916.

Other

The Celebrity at Home. London, Chapman and Hall, 1904.
The Cat. London, Black, 1905; as *The Life Story of a Cat*, London, Black, 1910.
The Wife of Altamont. London, Heinemann, and New York, Brentano, 1910.
The Desirable Alien at Home in Germany, with Ford Madox Hueffer. London, Chatto and Windus, 1913.
Their Lives. London, Stanley Paul, and New York, Brentano, 1916.
The Flurried Years (autobiography). London, Hurst and Blackett, 1926; as *I Have This to Say: the Story of My Flurried Years*, New York, Boni and Liveright, 1926.
The Wife of Rossetti, Her Life and Death. London, John Lane, and New York, Dutton, 1932.

*   *   *

Violet Hunt was a prolific writer and biographer but only produced enough ghost stories to fill two volumes, and many of these were written at editorial request. She came from a literary and artistic background. Her mother was the novelist Averil Beaumont and her father, Alfred Hunt, was a noted watercolour artist who was associated with the Pre-Raphaelites. Violet was originally groomed to be an artist but by the age of 28 was firmly entrenched in the literary world. She was a popular society hostess and moved amongst senior literary circles. A devout feminist and supporter of the women's suffrage, she was as a key figure in the New Woman movement, and was open about her moral and sexual attitudes. She lived as the consort of Ford Madox Hueffer when his wife refused a divorce, and regarded herself as his wife, though they later became estranged. She was a friend of Joseph Conrad, D. H. Lawrence, H. G. Wells and William Somerset Maugham, all of whom influenced her fiction, though she modelled herself mostly on Henry James—in which respect it is interesting to compare her fiction with Edith Wharton's. None of her novels can be classified as horror or gothic; they are all progressive tales exploring the role of women and their influence in society. Her radicalism is equally evident in her ghost stories, where the supernatural is a vehicle to explore personal relationships and attitudes.

The first of these was "The Story of a Ghost" (*Chapman's Magazine*, 1895), later reprinted as "The Prayer." A wife is distraught at the death of her husband and prays for his return. He comes back to life but he is a soulless zombie with no will to live and resorts to drugs. After several years the wife repents of her prayer and murders him. The story offers no moral judgment but leaves the reader only too clear that the greater sin was to claim another's life not his death.

Hunt first met Ford Madox Hueffer via a ghost story, "The Coach" (*English Review*, 1909). H. G. Wells had suggested Hunt try Hueffer's new *English Review* as a market for her short fiction, and Hueffer selected "The Coach" from a batch of stories she sent him. The story is fairly traditional in content. The occupants of the death-coach discuss their rather macabre lives and the gruesome ways in which they met their deaths. Hunt uses the story as a vehicle to satirize society and at that level it works very effectively.

The concept of what constitutes sin and how society defines it and its punishment was a theme common throughout Hunt's work, not just her ghost stories, or "tales of the uneasy" as she preferred to call them. Here, however, through the use of the supernatural, which she used sparingly and seldom overtly, she was able to bring greater potency to her message. This is no more evident than in a trio of stories. Firstly "The Barometer": this tells of two playful children who live in a rather overbearing religious home in Yorkshire. They look for companionship but instead receive stern rebuke. They start to fear the Lord in a physical and very tangible way so that when they hear tales from the Bible of the Lord's retribution they become terrified at an approaching thunderstorm. They are told not to be silly and are sent to bed, but that night they are both killed by a lightning strike. Hunt is questioning why innocents should suffer, and who had committed a crime. In "The Telegram" Alice, who has thought nothing of flirting with men and then casting them aside, becomes aware of her increasing age and decides to marry one of those she had previously rejected. After an evening together Everard agrees to marry her and it is only later that Alice discovers Everard was already dead. In a twist on the usual spiritual tryst theme, Hunt scores a point against her own sex by emphasizing the danger of playing with emotions and allowing the dead their own revenge. Finally there is "The Corsican Sisters," a novella which was one of Hunt's most popular stories. It is a variant on the theme of *The Corsican Brothers* (1844) by Alexandre Dumas, which deals with twin brothers with a psychic bond. Hunt's story is far more complicated. A family of sisters grows up in society and we explore their relationship with Cecil, who marries Lelis, one of the sisters. In strange ways these relationships seem to continue, on a spiritual level, none of it clearly defined, but all of it affecting the lives of the individuals. Cecil and Lelis honeymoon in Corsica, where the sisters had previously holidayed. During the honeymoon Lelis is killed. The immediate interpretation is that Cecil was killed by a Corsican bandit, and the story can be read on a non-fantastic level, but the underlying mood is that the continuing relationship between the sisters both before and after death had engineered fate to bring about Cecil's death and Lelis's madness. The whole story hinges on fate and revenge.

An earlier story, "The Operation," reads like a dry run for "The Corsican Sisters." It explores the relationship between two women and a man, though not quite the classic *ménage à trois*. In this instance one woman willingly hands the man over to the other, though both women have portents of death and it seems as if possession of the man is itself the passport to either life or death.

Only one of Hunt's tales of the uneasy appeared as a separate book: *Tiger Skin*. It's more a character study than a story of the supernatural. The central woman is obsessed with giving birth to the perfect child and takes this passion to extreme lengths. She believes that the tiger is the most perfect of creatures and that she must therefore imbue herself (and thereby her offspring) with the same animal vibrancy. The story follows her spiritual metamorphosis.

In these stories and most others in the two collections Hunt challenged orthodox opinion and explored other perspectives on morals and manners. In most cases she reminded people that there are other perceptions of right and wrong and those powers above and beyond humankind may not have the same views as ours.

—Mike Ashley

HUTSON, Shaun

Pseudonyms: Samuel P. Bishop; Nick Blake; Mike Dickinson; Clive Harold; Wolf Kruger; Robert Neville; Stefan Rostov; Frank Taylor. **Nationality:** British. **Born:** 1958. **Education:** "Invited to leave." **Family:** Married Belinda Hutson; one daughter. **Career:** Worked in a cinema and held various other short-term jobs before becoming a full-time writer. **Address:** c/o Little, Brown and Company (UK), Brettenham House, Lancaster Place, London WC2E 7EN, England. Lives in Bedfordshire.

Horror, Ghost and Gothic Publications

Novels (series: Sean Doyle; Slugs)

The Skull. London, Hamlyn, 1982; New York, Leisure, 1989.
Slugs. London, Star, 1982; New York, Leisure, 1987.
Spawn. London, W. H. Allen, 1983; New York, Leisure, 1988.
Erebus. London, Star, 1984; New York, Leisure, 1988.
Shadows. London, W. H. Allen, 1985; New York, Leisure, 1990.
Breeding Ground (Slugs). London, W. H. Allen, 1985; New York, Leisure, 1987.
Relics. London, W. H. Allen, 1986.
Deathday. London, Star, 1987; as Robert Neville, New York, Leisure, 1989.
Victims. London, W. H. Allen, 1987.
Assassin. London, W. H. Allen, 1988.
Nemesis. London, W. H. Allen, 1989.
Renegades (Doyle). London, Macdonald, 1991.
Captives. London, Macdonald, 1991.
Heathen. London, Little Brown, 1992.
Deadhead. London, Little Brown, 1993.
White Ghost (Doyle). London, Little Brown, 1994.
Lucy's Child. London, Little Brown, 1995.
Stolen Angels. London, Little Brown, 1996.
Knife Edge. London, Little Brown, 1997.

Other

Horror Film Quiz Book. London, Sphere, 1991.

Other Publications

Novels

The Uninvited (as Clive Harold). London, W. H. Allen, 1979.
Sledgehammer. London, Hale, 1982; as Wolf Kruger, London, W. H. Allen, 1983.
Convoy of Steel. London, Hale, 1982; as Wolf Kruger, London, W. H. Allen, 1984.
Kessler's Raid. London, Hale, 1982; as Wolf Kruger, London, Star, 1984.
Blood and Honour. London, Hale, 1982; as Wolf Kruger, London, W. H. Allen, 1983.
Sabres in the Snow. London, Hale, 1983; as Stefan Rostov, London, W. H. Allen, 1985.
Men of Blood. London, Hale, 1984; as Wolf Kruger, London, W. H. Allen, 1985.
Chainsaw Massacre (as Nick Blake). London, Star, 1984.
The Terminator (novelization of screenplay). London, W. H. Allen, 1984.
The Uninvited II: The Visitation (as Frank Taylor). London, W. H. Allen, 1984.
No Survivors. London, Hale, 1985.
The Uninvited III: The Abduction (as Frank Taylor). London, W. H. Allen, 1985.
Track (as Samuel P. Bishop). New York, Covered Wagon, 1986.
Partners in Death (as Samuel P. Bishop). New York, Covered Wagon, 1986.
Taken by Force. London, Hale, 1987.
Apache Gold (as Samuel P. Bishop). New York, Covered Wagon, 1988.
Swords of Vengeance. London, W. H. Allen, 1988.

Fiction for Children as Mike Dickinson

My Dad Doesn't Even Notice. London, Deutsch, 1982.
My Brother's Silly. London, Deutsch, 1983.
The Rambling Rat. London, Deutsch, 1985.
Smudge. London, Deutsch, 1987.

*

Film Adaptation: *Slugs: The Movie*, 1988.

*   *   *

In the late 1980s, the horror writer Shaun Hutson commented that Frederick Forsyth's cool and logical explanation of how to smuggle a bomb into England (and by extrapolation, we can take the statement to include any country) was more frightening than anything he personally had written up to that time. Perhaps this assessment today would be different, now that Hutson has all but eschewed the style of writing employed in his gross-out early books and has developed a style that might be a nod of praise to Forsyth himself, and which at any rate is less dependent on supernatural forces or maniacal flesh-eating insects. There is no doubt that Hutson's work has gone from strength to strength since the early 1980s, when he first was published. Hutson started to write after reading a novel that was so badly done that he knew he would be able to do better (the tome in question, alas, goes unmentioned). *The Skull* was the result. This novel is now a rarity, and does not appear on his "by the same author" page—Hutson has more or less disowned it—but his second novel, *Slugs*, was a masterpiece of bad taste and good timing. Even compared with James Herbert's *The Rats* (1975) and Guy N. Smith's *Night of the Crabs* (1976), *Slugs* upped the ante with regards to implausibility.

The concept—that of the eponymous insects developing a taste for human blood after long periods of time in a deserted cellar—

was suggested to Hutson by a friend. Hutson spends a month or two preparing his books, right down to a cast list complete with distinguishing features (blue eyes, brown hair), and having planned *Slugs*, he started and finished it in 25 days, typing his customary 4,500 words per day. His career was off to a good start. It so happened that a recidivous nostalgia trip for the 1970s version of puke-up nasties (as above) was in favour, and Hutson was content to contribute further. The sequel, *Breeding Ground*, came along three years later. Hutson has referred to the book as a black comedy; written in 18 days, it is a riotous romp, the insects having grown more confident as well as now being the passers-on of a brain-cell-affecting virus. This is a plot in which the bad things cannot possibly get any worse.

Spawn was a strong development on from *Slugs*. The earlier book introduced the reader to Hutson's graphic over-the-top depiction of violence, as well as showing that he was no shrinking violet when it came to writing about sex either; the scenes that messily mix the two are intended to be tongue-in-cheek, we assume—there is, for example, the cruel bathos of an oral sex scene interrupted when the character Clive has his feet bitten into. *Spawn*'s tone is darker. Here we enter the realm of mental illness in the person of Harold Pierce, a maladjusted old boy who manages to secure work in the incinerating room of a hospital. It is his unenviable task to burn the aborted foetuses of women who have had terminations. This he does until they start to communicate with him telepathically. This premise shows that even early on in his career, Hutson was willing to tackle any subject matter; the scenes with the foetuses on Harold's bed, "talking" to him and demanding food and obedience, are ugly and extremely powerful. Hutson was already pushing back boundaries. This story of Harold and his betrayal by his own mind, is woven into a second plot regarding an escaped killer and the police investigation thereof. The way the stories knit together, including brief snapshots of potential killer-fodder, is skilful; and *Spawn* is a grim, exhilarating read. *Spawn* is also the first of Hutson's novels to explore the notion of time passing and of something coming to horrific fruition now that was seeded in the past.

Hutson's opinion of the genre in which he was primarily working started to change by the time he was working on *Relics*. By this point he had already novelized *The Terminator* (in ten days) and had started various pseudonymous projects, highlighting the horrific brutalities of World War II as Wolf Kruger (introducing man's man Sergeant Rolf Kessler), and had started his Track westerns as Samuel P. Bishop. He had also written his Nick Blake *Chainsaw Terror* novel, suggested to him by his publisher after an attempt to secure the rights to novelize *The Texas Chainsaw Massacre* fell through; Hutson's brief was to write a trio of books about a chainsaw-wielding nutcase (*Chainsaw Bloodbath* and *Chainsaw Slaughter* were to have followed, but as it was, the first was heavily edited and the other two have not emerged). In a later interview Hutson reflected on this period of his career, saying that there is "only so much you can do with an ancient curse, people going apeshit after eating contaminated meat, or an age-old monster that reappears after thousands of years to wreak havoc on the people who've inadvertently brought it back to life."

Along came *Victims*. Still one of his strongest performances, the book is a *tour de force* which keeps the supernatural element to a minimum and includes some of Hutson's best set pieces. Hutson works on the recognized idea of some people being born victims; it is partly their provocative behaviour that sparks violent impulses in killers. When Frank, a special-effects make-up man

(whose replications of human beings is disturbingly accurate) has his eye damaged in a special-effects explosion, the replacement eye is that of a deceased murderer; Frank is now able to tell a victim-to-be in a crowd, and can assist (or not) the police with this information and this skill. Most of the characters are the victims of some form of psychological distress, of varying degrees; and the mystery throughout is, whose story is being told in italics, in flashbacks? Who did the child become who was interested in death from an early age?

Assassin is a horror-gangster-thriller novel that was inspired by the film *The Long Good Friday* and by the fun Hutson had while writing the car-chases and gunfights in *The Terminator*. Again, the supernatural element is held back; here the horror of physical agony is the prevalent force. The concession to the supernatural is the resuscitation of dead gangsters who, after spending time in concrete pillars, need new faces every now and then. Gang warfare is rife; the assassin of the title is hired to bump off some of a ganglord's arch enemies. This hitman puts on a Walkman and plays heavy metal music while using his machine-gun . . . Where *Assassin* mixes horror and thriller, *Renegades* mixes alchemy and terrorism in a plot concerning a millionaire drugs-dealer, gun-runner and all-round bad egg, and his wife who enjoys masturbating to road accidents (in a doff of the hat to J. G. Ballard's *Crash*). This couple want immortality, and having learned that in the past the child-murdering Gilles de Rais did too, they decide they must own the mysterious stained-glass window which has been unearthed in the desecrated church in Brittany where de Rais performed his evil acts.

Recent years have seen Hutson moving further and further away from the supernatural and concentrating on horror-thrillers. *White Ghost* is an exciting and fast-paced tale of Triad gangs, the IRA, and Sean Doyle, a counter-terrorism maverick who reappears in Hutson's latest, *Knife Edge*. Oddly enough, one recent attempt to mingle the supernatural with a straightforward thriller, *Lucy's Child*, does not work as well as many of Hutson's books, since the supernatural element appears rather forced, almost like an afterthought.

At one time Shaun Hutson was Britain's youngest writer of bestselling horror fiction; and while this is no longer true, he is certainly one of the most popular to this day. Prolific and modest, Hutson writes books for his fans and always remembers to thank them in his acknowledgements. He does not have pretensions about his books and does not bother to defend them in interviews when he is attacked. His standard response is to say that at least he is making a living out of writing. Indeed, his energy is remarkable, and by dint of the fact that he has never written a complete dud, it is perfectly acceptable to infer that Hutson is a man with his finger on the pulse of modern horror fiction publishing—much more so than his casual manner might lead somebody to expect.

—David Mathew

HYDE, Christopher

Pseudonym: Nicholas Chase. **Nationality:** Canadian. **Born:** Ottawa, 1949; brother of the novelist Anthony Hyde. **Family:** Married, two children. **Career:** Researcher, story-editor and television interviewer, Canadian Broadcasting Corporation.

HORROR, GHOST AND GOTHIC PUBLICATIONS

Novels

The Wave. New York, Doubleday, 1979; London, Hodder and Stoughton, 1980.
The Icarus Seal. Toronto, McClelland and Stewart, 1982; London, Hodder and Stoughton, 1983.
Styx. Chicago, Playboy Press, and London, Severn House, 1982.
The Tenth Crusade. Boston, Massachusetts, Houghton Mifflin, 1983; London, Hodder and Stoughton, 1984.
Maxwell's Train. New York, Villard, and London, Hutchinson, 1985.
Jericho Falls. New York, Avon, 1986; London, Simon and Schuster, 1988.
Whisperland. London, Hutchinson, 1987.
Crestwood Heights. New York, Avon, 1988; London, Simon and Schuster, 1989.
Egypt Green. New York and London, Simon and Schuster, 1989.
White Lies. London, Simon and Schuster, 1990.
Black Dragon. London, Headline, 1992.

OTHER PUBLICATIONS

Novel

Locksley (with Anthony Hyde, as Nicholas Chase). London, Heinemann, 1983.

*   *   *

Exploring the Wellsian hinterland of scientific extrapolation, the novels of Christopher Hyde make use of up-to-date technology and theories, and imagine black dead-ends for them to run towards. Hyde's long involvement with the media as a TV interviewer covering stories about technology and the environment stored up plenty of interesting plotlines, and his work has been accurately described as techno-horror: we see the shape (perhaps) of things to come. *The Wave*, his first novel, set this credo in stone with a factually-accurate story about badly-planned dams and the terrifying possibilities of nuclear power stations; there are some decidedly Green and some decidedly anti-Green feelings, some conspiracy, and the resulting sensation that Hyde has put his finger on a modern catastrophe in the making. Inducing this sensation is one of Hyde's strengths.

Crestwood Heights continues the paranoid dream of a masterminded conspiracy involving lunatic technological aspirations. Chosen for an eco-experiment, the eponymous small community (its somewhat ironic slogan being "The Future is Now") obliges its inhabitants to install into their houses, or incorporate into their lifestyles, hi-tech inventions which will control the environment and their existences. Into this village of the damned, this variation on John Wyndham's Midwich, comes Kelly Rhine, who has inherited a house there. Not only does she find the place unsettlingly ordered, she also discovers that people before her arrival mysteriously and unnecessarily died (as it turns out) for the financial gratification of the bigwigs behind the project.

In *Egypt Green* the pill to swallow is much larger. The conspiracy is a collaborative effort between the Earth's governments who decide to disregard their economic, military and social dis-

agreements in order to solve the problem of the world's famine. The "what-if?" scenario is as follows: what if the world's brightest children could be kidnapped and kept safe from harm in protectively sterile environments? And then what if a deadly plague could be released which would kill vast numbers of citizens in the Third World? And finally, what if once the disease had gone away, the bright children could be released for the purposes of building a new world . . .? This, at any rate, is the plan. The dubious rationale proffered is that by the time the bright children are released, diseases would have killed similar numbers of people anyway before science starts to comprehend them. A character asks: "since when was the US government in the business of stealing kids and making human ant colonies?" It is, of course, a valid point; Hyde's plots are occasionally far-fetched; but then, viewed dispassionately, so is the progress of science. Sensing readership incredulity, Hyde provides an afterword explaining that a survey of intelligent university students really was made in the 1960s, and also adamantly protesting that chemical weapons in great quantities are stored (or at least were at the time of writing) in America, France, Germany, Canada, Italy, and Russia. If Christopher Hyde often balances between the paranoid and the passionate, at least he also offers a thrill-a-minute ride.

When Hyde is not predicting the future of current scientific applications, the other side of his writing is what might be called the urban thriller in which he predicts alternatives to current social applications. For example, in *Black Dragon*, Hyde takes on the task of chronicling the drug wars of Triad gangs. His research, as ever, shines light on matters that the ordinary reader might otherwise have no reason to learn; to an extent Christopher Hyde is like a religious man in his pulpit, insisting on and gospelizing what alarming facts he unearths. In the afterword this time is the following: "Information contained within *Black Dragon* concerning the complicity of various government agencies in the trafficking of narcotics, particularly heroin, is accurate." Hyde leaves nothing to chance; he wants the reader to know what he knows.

White Lies is an Oval Office horror story which shows that Hyde can deal with political intrigue among politicians as effectively as he can when it is politicians manipulating the common man. "Romulus" is a secret codeword which was last used during the Second World War, when President Roosevelt was dying. The Romulus plan related then to an idea of assassinating Roosevelt, and now, decades on, the word is being whispered again—this time in connection with the fictitious President Tucker, the youngest man to hold office in the United States since John F. Kennedy. When Tucker is diagnosed as having the early signs of senile dementia and is reported to have only six months to live, the Romulus committee is commissioned to bring a more abrupt end to his term than Tucker might have imagined. After the diagnosing doctor is silenced, the Deputy Director of Operations at the CIA is called upon to find somebody to do the dirty deed. *White Lies* poses the question: how safe are the world leaders if somebody really wants them dead? And (as ever with Hyde) who exactly can you trust?

Whether they are techno-horror or tense political thrillers with horror undertones, Christopher Hyde's novels are examples of surveillance on the machinations of high authority; in his books we see the grubby preoccupations of the power-hungry, power-starved and just plain powerful. Regarding the machiavellian schemes is sometimes an ugly, lowering experience, but there is always enough hope to go around, both for the reader and for the main protagonist; battling, on occasion, steep odds leaves the heroes drained and scarred, but filled with the moral rectitude to fight another day.

—David Mathew

J

JACKSON, Shirley (Hardie)

Nationality: American. **Born:** San Francisco, California, 14 December 1916. **Education:** Burlingame High School, California; Brighton High School, Rochester, New York; University of Rochester, 1934-36; Syracuse University, New York, 1937-40, B.A. 1940. **Family:** Married the writer Stanley Edgar Hyman in 1940; two sons and two daughters. **Career:** Lived in North Bennington, Vermont, after 1945. **Awards:** Mystery Writers of America Edgar Allan Poe Award, 1961; Syracuse University Arents Medal, 1965. **Died:** 8 August 1965.

HORROR, GHOST AND GOTHIC PUBLICATIONS

Novels

The Sundial. New York, Farrar Straus, and London, Joseph, 1958.
The Haunting of Hill House. New York, Viking Press, 1959; London, Joseph, 1960.
We Have Always Lived in the Castle. New York, Viking Press, 1962; London, Joseph, 1963.
The Masterpieces of Shirley Jackson (omnibus; includes *The Lottery, The Haunting of Hill House, We Have Always Lived in the Castle*). London, Raven, 1996.

Short Stories

The Lottery; or, The Adventures of James Harris. New York, Farrar Straus, 1949; London, Gollancz, 1950.
The Magic of Shirley Jackson, edited by Stanley Edgar Hyman. New York, Farrar Straus, 1966.
Just an Ordinary Day, edited by Laurence Jackson Hyman and Sarah Hyman Stewart. New York, Bantam, 1996.

Play

The Lottery, from her own story, in *Best Television Plays 1950-1951,* edited by William I. Kauffman. New York, Merlin Press, 1952.

OTHER PUBLICATIONS

Novels

The Road through the Wall. New York, Farrar Straus, 1948; as *The Other Side of the Street,* New York, Pyramid, 1956.
Hangsaman. New York, Farrar Straus, and London, Gollancz, 1951.
The Bird's Nest. New York, Farrar Straus, 1954; as *Lizzie,* London, Joseph, 1957.

Play

The Bad Children: A Play in One Act for Bad Children. Chicago, Dramatic Publishing Company, 1959.

Other

Life among the Savages. New York, Farrar Straus, 1953; London, Joseph, 1954.
The Witchcraft of Salem Village (for children). New York, Random House, 1956.
Raising Demons. New York, Farrar Straus, and London, Joseph, 1957.
Special Delivery: A Useful Book for Brand-New Mothers. Boston, Little Brown, 1960; as *And Baby Makes Three,* New York, Grossett and Dunlap, 1960.
9 Magic Wishes (for children). New York, Crowell Collier, 1963.
Famous Sally (for children). New York, Harlin Quist, 1966.
Come Along with Me: Part of a Novel, Sixteen Stories, and Three Lectures, edited by Stanley Edgar Hyman. New York, Viking Press, 1968.

*

Critical Studies: *Shirley Jackson* by Lenemaja Friedman, Boston, Twayne, 1975; *Private Demons: The Life of Shirley Jackson* by Judy Oppenheiner, New York, Putnam, 1988; *Shirley Jackson: A Study of the Short Fiction* by Joan Wylie Hall, 1993.

*   *   *

Shirley Jackson is one of those "mainstream" authors whose work lies on the very borderline of the horrific; but unlike other such writers—Henry James, Edith Wharton, Thomas Pynchon—nearly all Jackson's novels and short stories are on this borderline, to the point that she becomes, almost in spite of herself, one of the leading figures in horror fiction subsequent to Lovecraft.

It is not paradoxical to begin examining Jackson's fictional work by means of her two major non-fiction books, *Life among the Savages* and *Raising Demons.* These volumes delightfully recount the various adventures experienced by herself and her husband, Stanley Edgar Hyman, as they raised their four children; both books are compilations of articles published separately in women's magazines of the 1950s and very skilfully revised into an episodic but naturally flowing narrative. Although Jackson appears to pay lip service to the conventions of middle-class life in the 1950s, the vibrancy of her writing in these books, the flawlessly exact capturing of her children's idiosyncrasies, and above all Jackson's complete lack of sentimentality make these narratives pungent and vivid even today.

While it would be false to say that these two volumes present a picture of unadulterated happiness, it is nevertheless the case that they are designed to portray a family that is mutually loving and well integrated into the life of its community. It is exactly these scenarios that are repeatedly subverted in Jackson's horror fiction.

Her most celebrated tale, "The Lottery" (1948), which received a shower of abuse when it was published in the *New Yorker,* presents just such a subversion. Jackson herself thought that this tale—involving a lottery in a small town, the "winner" of which will be stoned to death to ensure a bountiful harvest—was about race prejudice (something she herself experienced by her marriage to a Jew); but the fundamental *randomness* of the lottery seems designed to suggest how the surface harmony of bourgeois life can suddenly and irrationally turn to violence and death. A stray remark in her mainstream novel *Hangsaman* may get to the heart of this tale: "Another instance . . . of ritual gone to seed." The ritual of sacrificing a human being for the sake of crops is a mindless holdover from primitive times, and the true horror of the tale is the possibility that such a thing might actually occur in our purportedly civilized age.

The fundamental theme in Jackson's work is isolation—either an individual within a family or a family within a community. The principal effect of isolation is, of course, loneliness, and Jackson presents some of the most searing instances of loneliness in all literature. "The Daemon Lover" tells of an apparently neurotic young woman who thinks she is going to be married, but finds that her fiancée does not show up at her apartment at the appointed time; she canvases the city looking for him, and a variety of random individuals claim that they have seen him and point her in various directions. Are these people merely trying to get rid of her, or are they somehow conspiring sadistically to drive her mad? Did her lover in fact ever exist outside of her own imagination? The answers to these questions are never revealed. The harrowing isolation of an elderly couple is conveyed in "The Summer People": the couple have decided to stay in their vacation cottage beyond Labor Day, even though they have been informed by the native residents that no one stays there after Labor Day; the couple find that the natives' friendliness turns to indifference and then to outright hostility as they simply fail to provide the food, fuel and other necessities the couple need to survive.

The Haunting of Hill House is at once Jackson's most powerful exploration of individual loneliness and her greatest work of horror fiction. Eleanor Vance is one of four individuals who is asked to come to Hill House in order to investigate the possibility of paranormal phenomena there. It rapidly becomes clear that Eleanor—who herself admits, "I am always afraid of being alone"—has led a wretched, meaningless life up to this point, and that her loneliness and weakness of will make her unusually susceptible to the influences at the house. In effect, the house subsumes her (the doctor who summoned the group has noted: "Hill House has a reputation for insistent hospitality; it seemingly dislikes letting its guests get away"): she identifies herself with the house and its previous occupants, and the supernatural manifestations—not all of which, it must be admitted, are presented plausibly or are successfully integrated within the narrative framework—make it clear that she will not be allowed to leave. She attempts to drive away, but the car crashes into a tree and she dies. *The Haunting of Hill House* is the classic "haunted house" novel of its age, and perhaps of any age.

Jackson's last novel, *We Have Always Lived in the Castle*, can be considered a horror story only incidentally. It is her most violent portrayal of familial isolation, as the Blackwood family has been ostracized because of the suspicious murders that occurred years before; eventually the local residents ransack and partially burn the Blackwood house, but the two sisters who have lived there obstinately refuse to leave and attempt to carry on in their accustomed dignity as if nothing had happened. An earlier novel, *The Sundial*, one of the most bizarre works in Jackson's *oeuvre*, seems to have been a prelude to this work: the Halloran family becomes convinced that the rest of the world is going to end, and the narrative tone suggests that this belief might in fact be correct; the novel is occupied with the family's preparations to con-

tinue life after the rest of humanity has ceased to exist. Both these novels, as well as a number of short stories—especially the celebrated "One Ordinary Day, with Peanuts" (1955)—display the misanthropy that is a central element of Jackson's work, and one which she conveys with consummate skill.

It should be clear that many of Jackson's works tread the boundary between the natural and the supernatural; indeed, aside from *The Haunting of Hill House* and a few short stories, the supernatural can never be said to be clearly present in any of her works. One tale that introduces the supernatural in the subtlest way is "The Lovely Night" (later retitled "A Visit"), in which it gradually becomes evident that a young woman visiting a friend's family is trapped there by being insidiously incorporated into a tapestry woven by her friend's mother. In other tales it is impossible to know whether the supernatural has come into play or whether we are dealing with an aberrant psychological state.

All Jackson's work—with the exception, perhaps, of *The Bird's Nest*, a clumsy novel about multiple personality—is subtle, powerful and flawlessly written; it reveals Jackson's keen insight into human personality and human society and her cynical, even jaundiced view of the world and its occupants. She has left a legacy of complex, richly textured horror writing that requires little or no bloodletting for its haunting effectiveness.

—S. T. Joshi

JACOBI, Carl (Richard)

Nationality: American. **Born:** Minneapolis, Minnesota, 10 July 1908. **Education:** University of Minnesota, B.A. 1931. **Career:** Reporter, *Minneapolis Star*; editor, *Midwest Media*; also worked in publicity. **Died:** 25 August 1997.

<small>HORROR, GHOST AND GOTHIC PUBLICATIONS</small>

Short Stories

Revelations in Black. Sauk City, Wisconsin, Arkham House, 1947; abridged as *The Tomb from Beyond*, London, Panther, 1977.
Portraits in Moonlight. Sauk City, Wisconsin, Arkham House, 1964.
Disclosures in Scarlet. Sauk City, Wisconsin, Arkham House, 1972.
East of Samarinda. Bowling Green, Ohio, Bowling Green State University Popular Press, 1989.
Smoke of the Snake, edited by R. Dixon Smith. Minneapolis, Minnesota, Fedogan and Bremer, 1994.

*   *   *

There is no more eloquent testimony to the durability of the basic weird tale than the fiction of Carl Jacobi. Jacobi's reputation is based almost entirely on his simple treatment of supernatural themes in stories that run no more than several thousand words. His style has evolved little since his first published tale appeared in 1932, yet his five collections are filled with the kind of timeless stories that are the backbone of the genre.

Like many weird-fiction writers of his generation, Jacobi broke into print in the pages of *Weird Tales*. "Mive," his debut, is a dark fantasy built on the weird visions induced by the narrator's contact with the flora and fauna of an unexplored swamp. Virtually plotless, the story showed Jacobi to be a competent scene-setter capable of building a mood of eerie menace from straightforward description. The story merits comparison to "Moss Island," published at approximately the same time. This tale, too, is largely a mood piece concerned with a fog-shrouded island whose vegetation comes hideously to life, yet it appeared in the pages of the science-fiction magazine *Wonder Stories*. Jacobi was able to work the fundamental themes of his writing into the subjects of science fiction, weird menace, mystery and adventure fiction as well as horror stories. His adaptability suggests that he could have made a competent pulpsmith, grinding out copy for a variety of markets. Instead, he wrote fiction mostly for pleasure, as a sideline to his career as an editor and journalist. This explains to some extent the limited size and scope of his stories, but also why most of his work is superior to that of colleagues whom he competed with in the back pages of magazines.

Jacobi's best-known story, "Revelations in Black," sets the pattern for most of his work. It concerns a man who chances upon a book in an antique store that leads him unsuspectingly to the lair of a female vampire. Jacobi's protagonists are almost always solitary men with ordinary appetites. "I am not one of those adventurous souls who revel in the unusual," confesses the narrator of "Mive." Jason Carnaby, the protagonist of "Carnaby's Fish," is the stereotypical Jacobi character: "a man of medium height, medium features, and medium habits." These characters are catapulted out of their predictable routines usually through contact with a magic talisman: a family heirloom in "The Coach on the Ring," a vintage walking stick in "The Cane," a mysterious deck of playing cards in "The King and the Knave," historical firearms in "The Spectral Pistol," a vintage camera in "The Spanish Camera." The supernaturally-endowed objects usually come into their possession accidentally, as a consequence of their collecting habits or as bequests from deceased relatives. Occasionally, as in "The Corbie Door" or "The Face in the Wind," they are inherited family properties. Invariably, these possessions are imbued with the personalities of their previous owners or a dark history that attempts to reassert itself. Often, as in "A Pair of Swords," in which a man witnesses the re-enactment of a duel fought centuries before with weapons preserved in a museum, the protagonists are passive witnesses to the supernatural. Sometimes, though, they are actively possessed by the spirits that haunt these items, as in "The Cocomacaque," in which a souvenir club that comes into a man's possession drives him to commit a murder similar to one committed with it years before.

The most pernicious aspect of the supernatural in Jacobi's tales is its irresistibility. "Something seemed to take hold of me," says a painter inspired by a monstrous influence from the past in "The Face in the Wind"—"I felt as if a will other than my own were controlling my thoughts." In "Revelations in Black," the narrator's near fatal dalliance with the vampire begins with "an indefinable urge to leave my apartment and walk the darkened streets." Jacobi describes his characters' gradual involvement with the terrors that unfold as an insidious seduction that breaks down will power and leads to ungovernable obsession. An undercurrent of sexual anxiety runs through a number of his stories. "Revelations in Black," "The Face in the Wind" and "Carnaby's Fish" comprise a triptych in which male bachelors are threatened by female embodiments of horror: a vampire, a harpie, and a lorelei respectively. Unfaithful wives are responsible for the horrors in "The King and

the Knave" and "Incident at the Galloping Horse," and a nagging mate for those in "The Lorenzo Watch." Jacobi's stories are not misogynistic, but rather filled with male characters for whom romantic male-female relationships represent a personal vulnerability. Sometimes his women are themselves victims, avenged from beyond the grave in "Sagasta's Last" and "The Digging at Pistol Key," and protagonists the equal of their male counterparts in "The Spanish Camera."

Several of Jacobi's best stories do not fit this template. "Matthew South and Company" is deceptive tale of paranoia and illusion concerning a man whose many aliases appear to take on physical form. "The Tomb from Beyond" is a blend of science fiction and horror concerning a mausoleum that houses a gateway to another dimension. "The Unpleasantness at Carver House" is a nasty study of psychopathology employing an unreliable narrator with a perfect poker face. "The Aquarium" and "The Corbie Door" both skirt the fringe of the Cthulhu Mythos derived from H. P. Lovecraft's fiction. Indeed, Jacobi seems to have taken several tips from Lovecraft, inventing Richard Verstegan's *Restitution of Decayed Intelligence*, a mythic tome as ubiquitous as the *Necronomicon* in "The Face in the Wind," "The Corbie Door," "Offspring" and "The Random Quantity," and the equally imaginary town of Rentharp, from which characters in "Moss Island" and other stories hale. The majority of his supernatural stories are set in everytown America or rural England, but a handful are set in Borneo ("The Kite," "Smoke of the Snake") or the West Indies ("Portrait in Moonlight," "The Digging at Pistol Key," "Incident at the Galloping Horse") and draw on native superstitions and folklore for their atmosphere. Such flourishes give Jacobi's work a variety on the surface that effectively conceals its ordinary, if solid, architecture.

—Stefan Dziemianowicz

JACOBS, W(illiam) W(ymark)

Nationality: British. **Born:** Wapping, London, 8 September 1863. **Education:** Private. **Family:** Married Agnes Eleanor Williams in 1900; two sons and three daughters. **Career:** Clerk, Savings Bank Department, Civil Service, London, 1883-99; contributor of short stories to the *Idler*, *To-day*, the *Strand Magazine* and other publications; freelance writer. **Died:** 1 September 1943.

HORROR, GHOST AND GOTHIC PUBLICATIONS

Short Stories

The Lady of the Barge and Other Stories. London, Harper, and New York, Dodd Mead, 1902.
Night Watches. London, Hodder and Stoughton, 1914.
Sea Whispers. London, Hodder and Stoughton, 1926.
The Monkey's Paw and Other Stories. Stroud, Gloucestershire, Alan Sutton, 1994.

Plays (all adapted from his short stories)

The Ghost of Jerry Bundler, with Charles Rock (produced London, 1899). London, French, 1908.

The Monkey's Paw, with Louis N. Parker (produced London, 1903). London, French, 1910.
In the Library, with Herbert C. Sargent (produced London, 1913). London, French, 1912.

OTHER PUBLICATIONS

Novels

The Skipper's Wooing, and The Brown Man's Servant. London, Pearson, 1897.
A Master of Craft. New York, Stokes, and London, Methuen, 1900.
At Sunwich Port. London, Newnes, 1902.
Dialstone Lane. London, Newnes, 1904.
Salthaven. London, Methuen, 1908.
The Castaways. London, Hodder and Stoughton, 1916.

Short Stories

Many Cargoes. London, Lawrence and Bullen, 1896.
Sea Urchins. London, Lawrence and Bullen, 1898; as *More Cargoes*, New York, Stokes, 1898.
Light Freights. New York, Dodd Mead, and London, Methuen, 1901.
Odd Craft. New York, Scribner, and London, Newnes, 1903.
Captains All. London, Hodder and Stoughton, 1905.
Short Cruises. London, Hurst and Blackett, 1907.
Sailors' Knots. London, Methuen, 1909.
Ship's Company. London, Hodder and Stoughton, 1911.
Deep Waters. London, Hodder and Stoughton, 1919.
Fifteen Stories. London, Methuen, 1926.
Snug Harbour: Collected Stories. New York, Scribner, 1931; as *The Night-Watchman and Other Longshoremen.* London, Hodder and Stoughton, 1932.
Cruises and Cargoes (omnibus). London, Methuen, 1934.
Selected Short Stories, edited by Denys Kilham Roberts. London, Penguin, 1959; as *The Monkey's Paw and Other Stories*, Penguin, 1962.
W. W. Jacobs' Uncollected Cargoes. Lancaster, Pennsylvania, Hazelwood Press, 1996.

Plays (all adapted from his short stories)

The Grey Parrot, with Charles Rock (produced London, 1899). London, French, 1908.
Beauty and the Barge, with Louis N. Parker (produced London, 1904). London, French, 1910.
The Temptation of Samuel Burge, with Frederick Fenn (produced London, 1905).
The Boatswain's Mate, with Herbert C. Sargent (produced London, 1907). London, French, 1907.
The Changeling (produced London, 1908). London, French, 1908.
Admiral Peters, with Horace Mills (produced London, 1909). London, French, 1909.
A Love Passage, with P. E. Hubbard (produced London, 1913). London, French, 1913.
Keeping Up Appearances (produced London, 1915). London, French, 1919.
The Castaway, with Herbert C. Sargent. London, French, 1924.
Establishing Relations. London, French, 1925.

The Warming Pan. London, French, 1929.
A Distant Relative. London, French, 1930.
Master Mariners. London, French, 1930.
Matrimonial Openings. London, French, 1931.
Dixon's Return. London, French, 1932.
Double Dealing. London, French, 1935.
Six Collected One-Act Plays. London, French, 1937.

*

Film Adaptations (selection): *The Monkey's Paw*, from the short story, 1915, 1923, 1933; *Footsteps in the Fog*, from the short story "The Interruption," 1955.

* * *

In the weird fiction line there was a good deal more to William Wymark Jacobs than "The Monkey's Paw," undeniably chilling though that celebrated horror story is—as well as much reprinted: nearly 70 times in ghost-story and strange-tale anthologies alone, over the past 80-odd years, according to Ashley and Contento's *Supernatural Index*. There were also many film and television versions. Nevertheless there were other stories, other themes, other modes. Jacobs, as a creative plotter, pondered murder, blackmail, full-blown tragedy as well as full-blown farce, which is for what, for most of his life, he was especially renowned. Indeed, in the humorous field he not only defined an area of popular fiction—the comic seafaring tale—he created a genre.

In the main, his world was the world of London wharves and docks and waterside parishes (though his characters were more often to be found in the local taverns than in church), running down the Thames into the Essex marshes. He told of simple sailormen, and lightermen, and Thames Bargees, and captains of humble barques, and first mates, cabin boys, able seamen and cooks aboard luggers, colliers, barquentines, brigs, and fore-and-aft-rigged clippers. On the whole his heroes were jovial rascals, agreeable rogues, artful dodgers who were never, in fact, quite as clever as they cracked themselves up to be, as a consequence continually floored by the rug-pulling tricks of Fate, or well-aimed pieces of heavy domestic equipment wielded by wives who were sharp and, in their modes of thought and behaviour, distressingly to the point (Jacobs's own wife, Agnes Eleanor, 20 years younger, was hoydenish and spirited, a "new woman" suffragette who heaved bricks through Downing Street windows and wrote intemperate letters to the papers, much to Jacobs's anguish).

From the 1890s through to the Second World War Jacobs's short-story collections (though he wrote them, novels were not truly his *forte*) sold in their scores of thousands. Their influence, during that period, was profound (Edgar Wallace was not the only writer who transferred the Jacobs milieu of dockside taverns and tiny cabins stuffed with comic grumblers onto dry land, in Wallace's case to army barracks for his "Smithy" soldier stories and sketches, then refined the process of telling the tale until it was identifiably his own). He had a sharp eye for his fellow humans' idiosyncrasies and delinquencies; an even sharper ear for their colloquies. He was a master of understatement, quiet pugnacity, and the ironic nudge in the ribs.

If he had a fault it was that the Jacobs of 1899, say, was almost identical to the Jacobs of 1929. Not much changed in his comic continuum. Not much progressed. Nothing developed. His chief tale-teller, the night-watchman (memorably personated by the Cockney character actor Wally Patch in a series of television playlets in the early 1950s) related roughly the same sharp comic parables in the early 1900s as 20 or more years later.

By rights, when in weird or macabre mode, Jacobs ought to have written tales like "Man Overboard!" (F. Marion Crawford), "The Haunted 'Jarvee'" (William Hope Hodgson) or "While the Passengers Slept" (Edgar Wallace), all three more or less classics of high-seas horror. Yet he didn't; he stayed stubbornly inland. Approximately. Not only that: the sea and sailormen are almost entirely excluded from Jacobs's macabre, as opposed to comic, universe. Arguably, this was a deliberate move on Jacobs's part, for even when he is presented with an opportunity for including a tar, simply in a minor role, he usually declines—the bearer to the unfortunate Whites of "the monkey's paw," for instance, is not some old salt who's roamed the world and picked up the dreadful talisman in some quayside game of chance, but an ex-sergeant-major, 21 years in the Indian Army.

"The Monkey's Paw" itself is a highly moral tale. If you interfere in what is not natural there is always a price to pay. The Whites wish for money and they duly get it—but at the cost of their only son's life. The White's wish for their son to be alive again, and this is granted—but the being that knocks so softly on their door at midnight may be alive, but it has also just emerged from the grave. In other words, you can't beat the devil.

Nor can you make fun of him, or by extension the supernatural in general. In "The Toll House" (Sailors' Knots), Meagle crashes the knocker on the door of the eponymous dwelling demanding to be let in, then later jangles the servants' bell as a joke. This is impudence, and he pays for it—rushing hither and thither in the hurtling blackness, pursued and hounded to his doom. "The Toll House" is surely one of the very finest examples of the "house with something wrong" plot in the entirety of weird literature (and a tale that must have made a profound impression upon H. Russell Wakefield, whose "Blind Man's Buff" and "The Frontier Guards" both utilize much the same artistic template).

The superb "Jerry Bundler" (Light Freights) is a ghost story, yet perhaps not a ghost story—at any rate a snook is cocked at the supernatural by the egregious practical joker Hirst, and a grim price is paid in the end. Payment is made in "The Well" (The Lady of the Barge), too, but there is no whimsy or high jinks here, simply a terrible revenge. Twenty years later Jacobs refined the plot of "The Well" (the corpse that won't lie quiet) and updated it for the superlative "His Brother's Keeper" (Sea Whispers), a tale of surpassing wired-out tension mixed in with a good deal of gallows' humour.

One of Jacobs's outstanding gifts was an ability to take the simplest, least threatening of situations and imbue it with horror and tension to the point where it becomes something quite other. A man strolling into an inn on a chill October afternoon and warming himself before the coffee-room fire in "Captain Rogers" (The Lady of the Barge) is in fact a blackmailer and luster after the landlord's young daughter. But the landlord himself is no paragon: indeed, an erstwhile buccaneer with blood on his hands and a price (of a hundred guineas) on his head still. Given this promising beginning Jacobs proceeds to screw up the tension until a violent (and utterly amoral) denouement that is not for the faint-hearted. Similarly "In the Library" (The Lady of the Barge) starts in classic "comfort-style"—"The fire had burnt low in the library . . ."—but soon becomes an essay in hatred, violence and murder.

These two stories are not precisely weird, per se; nor are "The Interruption" (Sea Whispers), in which a murderer finds himself

in craven thraldom to his cook, who knows his secret, or "The Brown Man's Servant" (The Skipper's Wooing), a brilliant 12,000-word novelette with a devastating punchline, which may, or may not, have a paranormal explanation of its odd events (can the "brown man" really call up the devil to destroy his enemies, or is it all hocus-pocus?). Yet all four, and others in the Jacobs oeuvre, are incontestably macabre in tone, in mood, in atmosphere.

Once upon a time the comic tales of W. W. Jacobs were praised by all and read by (nearly) all. His technique was justly admired. Certain critics put him on a higher pedestal than Wodehouse. J. B. Priestley and Reginald Pound were noted, and fierce, Jacobs champions—Pound especially, who thought that close adherence to the creator of Jeeves indicated a certain "extended immaturity."

If the case then—rather more than a generation ago—it is by no means the case now, when the critic Everett Bleiler can dismiss Jacobs's tales as "maudlin and trivial." There is doubtless and argument to be made out for both points of view. What is not at all in doubt, however, is Jacobs's genius at creating tales of the uneasy—indeed, tales of outright horror. For some unfathomable reason, no one has ever thought to publish a full collection of these perfect little gems of the macabre.

—Jack Adrian

JAMES, G(eorge) P(ayne) R(ainsforth)

Pseudonym: Bernard Marsh. **Nationality:** British. **Born:** London, 9 August 1799. **Family:** Married in 1828. **Career:** Writer, 1827-1860; Historiographer Royal to William IV; diplomat, 1850-1860. **Died:** 9 May 1860.

HORROR, GHOST AND GOTHIC PUBLICATIONS

Novels

The String of Pearls. London, Richard Bentley, 1832.
The Castle of Ehrenstein: Its Lords Spiritual and Temporal, Its Inhabitants Earthly and Unearthly. London, Smith Elder, and New York, Harper, 1847.
The Last of the Fairies. London, Parry, 1847; New York, Harper, 1848.

Plays

Camaralzaman: A Fairy Drama. London, Ollier, 1848.

OTHER PUBLICATIONS

Novels

Adra; or, The Peruvians. London, Colburn, 1829.
Richelieu: A Tale of France. London, Colburn, and New York, Harper, 1829.
Darnley, or The Field of the Cloth of Gold. London, Colburn and Bentley, and New York, Harper, 1830.
De l'Orme; or Le Comte de Soissons. London, Colburn and Bentley, and New York, Harper, 1830.

Philip Augustus; or, The Brothers in Arms. London, Colburn and Bentley, and New York, Harper, 1831.

Henry Masterton, or The Adventures of a Young Cavalier. London, Colburn and Bentley, 1832.

Mary of Burgundy; or, The Revolt of Ghent. London, Longman, and New York, Harper, 1833.

Delaware; or, The Ruined Family. London, Whittaker, and Philadelphia, Carey Lea and Blanchard, 1833; as *Thirty Years Since; or, The Ruined Family*, New York, Harper, 1848.

The Life and Adventures of John Marston Hall; or, Little Ball of Fire. London, Longman, and New York, Harper, 1834.

The Gipsy: A Tale. London, Longman, and New York, Harper, 1835.

My Aunt Pontypool. London, Saunders and Otley, 1835; Philadelphia, Carey and Hart, 1836.

The Desultory Man. London, Saunders and Otley, and New York, Harper, 1836.

One in a Thousand; or, The Days of Henry Quatre. London, Longman, 1835; New York, Harper, 1836.

A History of the Life of Edward the Black Prince. London, Longman, 1836; New York, Harper, 1837.

Attila: A Romance. London, Longman, and New York, Harper, 1837.

The Robber: A Tale. London, Longman, and New York, Harper, 1838.

A Gentleman of the Old School. London, Longman, and New York, Harper, 1839.

The Huguenot: A Tale of the French Protestants. London, Longman, and New York, Harper, 1839.

Henry of Guise; or, The States of Blois. London, Longman, and New York, Harper, 1839.

Charles Tyrrell; or, The Bitter Blood. London, Bentley, and New York, Harper, 1839.

The King's Highway. London, Longman, and New York, Harper, 1840.

The Man-at-Arms. London, Bentley, 1840.

Corse de Leon; or, The Brigand. London, Longman, and New York, Harper, 1841.

The Ancient Regime: A Tale. London, Longman, and New York, Harper, 1841; as *Castelnau; or, The Ancient Regime*, London, Simms and McIntyre, 1850.

The Jacquerie. London, Longman, 1841; New York, Harper, 1842.

A History of the Life of Richard Coeur-de-Lion. London, Saunders and Otley, and New York, Langley, 1842.

Morley Ernstein; or, The Tenants of the Heart. London, Saunders and Otley, and New York, Harper, 1842.

The False Heir. London, Bentley, and New York, Harper, 1843.

Forest Days: A Romance of Old Times. London, Saunders and Otley, and New York, Harper, 1843; as *Forest Days, or Robin Hood*, London and New York, Routledge, 1866.

The Commissioner; or, De Lunatico Enquirendo, published anonymously. Dublin, William Curry, 1843; as *The Commissioner, or Travels of a Gentleman*, Dublin, Curry, 1846.

Agincourt. London, Bentley, and New York, Harper, 1844.

Arabella Stuart. London, Bentley, and New York, Harper, 1844.

Rose d'Albret; or, Troublous Times. London, Bentley, and New York, Harper, 1844.

Arrah Neil; or, Times of Old. London, Smith Elder, and New York, Winchester, 1845.

The Smuggler. London, Smith Elder, and New York, Harper, 1845.

Heidelberg. London, Smith Elder, and New York, Harper, 1846.

The Stepmother. London, Smith Elder, and New York, Harper, 1846.

The Convict: A Tale. London, Smith Elder, 1847; as *The Convict; or, The Hypocrite Unmasked*, New York, Harper, 1847.

Russell: A Tale of the Reign of Charles II. London, Smith Elder, and New York, Harper, 1847.

Margaret Graham; or, The Reverses of Fortune. New York, Harper, 1847; as *Margaret Graham: A Tale Founded on Facts*, London, Parry, 1848.

Beauchamp; or, The Error. New York, Harper, 1847; London, Smith Elder, 1848.

A Whim and Its Consequences. London, Smith Elder, 1847; New York, Harper, 1848.

Sir Theodore Broughton; or, Laurel Water. London, Smith Elder, and New York, Harper, 1848.

Gowrie. London, Simpkin Marshall, 1848.

The Fight of the Fiddlers: A Serio-Comic Verity. London, Bogue, 1849.

The Woodman: A Romance of the Time of Richard III. London, Newby, and New York, Harper, 1849.

The Forgery; or, Best Intentions. London, Newby, and New York, Harper, 1850.

The Old Oak Chest. London, Newby, and New York, Harper, 1850.

Henry Smeaton. New York, Harper, 1850; London, Newby, 1851.

The Fate: A Tale of Stirring Times. London, Newby, and New York, Harper, 1851.

Pequinillo. London, Newby, and New York, Harper, 1852.

Revenge. London, Newby, 1852.

Adrian; or, The Clouds of the Mind, with Maunsell B. Field. New York, Appleton, 1852.

A Life of Vicissitudes: A Story of Revolutionary Times. New York, Harper, 1852; as *The Vicissitudes of Life*, London, Newby, 1853.

Agnes Sorel. London, Newby, and New York, Harper, 1853.

Ticonderoga. London, Newby, 1854; as *Ticonderoga; or, The Black Eagle*, New York, Harper, 1854.

The Old Dominion. London, Newby, and New York, Harper, 1856.

Leonora d'Orco. London, Newby, 1857; New York, Routledge, 1858.

Lord Montague's Page. London, Newby, and Philadelphia, Childs and Peterson, 1858.

The Cavalier (as Bernard Marsh). Philadelphia, Peterson, 1859; London, Bentley, 1864.

The Man in Black. Philadelphia, Peterson, 1860.

Short Stories

A Book of the Passions. London, Longman, and Philadelphia, Lea and Blanchard, 1839.

Eva St. Clair and Other Collected Tales. London, Longman, 1843.

John Jones's Tales for Little John Joneses (for children). London, Cradock, 1849.

Dark Scenes of History. London, Newby, 1849; New York, Harper, 1850.

Prince Life: A Story for My Boy by an Old Author (for children). New York, Dickerson, and London, Newby, 1856.

Play

Blanche of Navarre. New York, Harper, 1838; London, Longman, 1839.

Poetry

The Ruined City. London, Colburn, 1829.

Other

The History of Chivalry. London, Colburn and Bentley, 1830; New York, Harper, 1831.
The History of Charlemagne. London, Longman, 1832; New York, Harper, 1833.
Lives of the Most Eminent Foreign Statesmen, with Eyre Evans Crowe. London, Longman, 5 vols., 1833-38.
Memoirs of Great Commanders. London, Routledge, and Philadelphia, Carey and Hart, 1835.
On the Educational Institutions of Germany. London, Saunders and Otley, 1835.
Lives of Cardinal de Retz, John Baptiste Colbert, John de Witt and the Marquis de Louvois. Philadelphia, Carey Lea and Blanchard, 1837.
Memoirs of Celebrated Women. London, Bentley, 1837; Philadelphia, Carey and Hart, 1839.
The Life and Times of Louis the Fourteenth. London, Bentley, 1838.
A Brief History of the United States Boundary Question. London, Saunders and Otley, 1839.
Some Remarks on the Corn Laws. London, Ollivier, 1841.
The Life of Henry the Fourth, King of France and Navarre. London, Boone, and New York, Harper, 1847.

Editor, *Letters Illustrative of the Reign of William III from 1696 to 1708.* London, Colburn, 1841.
Editor, *Rizzio; or, Scenes in Europe during the Sixteenth Century,* by W. H. Ireland. London, Newby, 1849.

*

Critical Studies: *The Solitary Horseman; or, The Life and Adventures of G. P. R. James* by S. M. Ellis, London, Cayme Press, 1927; "Gothic, History and the Middle Classes" in *The Literature of Terror* by David Punter, London, Longman, 1980.

*   *   *

The most productive of the late Georgian and early Victorian historical novelists, G. P. R. James came from a middle-class family (his father was a physician) and his elegance and manners enabled him to move in higher circles, ending his days as a respected diplomat. In his youth he met Byron and led something of a Byronic existence, with a passion for duels, until he settled down to write after 1827. He was encouraged in his early work by Washington Irving, himself a devotee of gothic fiction, but James avoided the standard gothic frame, choosing instead as his model the works of Sir Walter Scott, who praised his early novel *Richelieu.* James lacked the craftsmanship and creativity of Scott, pandering rather to an undiscriminating readership who enjoyed his novels of action, romance and adventure. His writing became formulaic and he soon earned the nickname "the solitary horseman," because one such character usually appears near the start of his novels. At his best James is comparable to Alexandre Dumas or Bulwer Lytton. Generally, though, his works responded to public whim rather than establishing any trend, but within his abilities he could create atmospheric scenes, rousing action and chivalric romance. Despite

his speed of composition, with all its inevitable lapses, James was a good historian and for a period in the 1830s was Historiographer Royal to William IV.

At the height of his fame his name was a byword for the action-packed historical adventure, but little of his work has dated well and most has long been out of print. Some of his early historical novels are described as "Radcliffean," though this is more as a result of the atmosphere of brooding menace that James created rather than a direct gothic influence. When Charlotte Bronte's *Jane Eyre* first appeared under the pseudonym Currer Bell a few critics believed this to be the work of James because of the similarity of atmosphere. An example from his own output is the popular *De l'Orme,* about the revolt of the Catalans from Philip of Spain in the early 17th century. The core of the adventure deals with the fortunes and misfortunes of a group of Pyrenean smugglers, but there is considerable atmosphere in the local castle run by its demonic count.

James's primary work of gothic fiction was *The Castle of Ehrenstein,* written quite late in his career when he was broadening the scope of his books. The novel revolves around the love between young Ferdinand of Altenburg and Adelaide, whose father has usurped the position of Count of Ehrenstein during his brother's absence in the Crusades. The Castle is replete with every form of gothic spectral manifestation, James laying it on far more thickly than Walpole or Radcliffe who were his inspirations. It transpires that all of these hauntings have a natural explanation. They were caused by Adelaide's uncle, the legitimate Count, who has returned from the Crusades and seeks to terrify his brother into submission. The whole book is contrived and rather tired in its theatrical gothic conventions, but is saved by James's gusto and ability to create tension and atmosphere. It bears some comparison with a few of his other historical novels which focused on an atmosphere of dread and foreboding rather than on historical action and adventure, such as *The Gipsy, The Ancient Regime, The Convict, Rose d'Albret* or *The Fate,* though none of these would normally be classified as gothic. His series of short studies, *Dark Scenes of History,* did resort more to atmospheric recreations of dark deeds, all the more frightening for being based on real incidents.

James's only other published work involving the fantastic was his piece of juvenilia, *The String of Pearls,* not to be confused with the novel of the same title by Thomas Peckett Prest. This was a compendium of tales written by James when he was in his late teens and brought into print as he found fame. They are mostly oriental fantasies, inspired by *The Arabian Nights,* demonstrating that James was able to imitate any popular fiction of the day. Most of the stories are passable, allowing for their immaturity, and are not unlike H. P. Lovecraft's similar stories of this period. They are more fantastic adventure than supernatural horror, almost every story involving a transformation to test the love or moral rectitude of others. The best is "The Building of Bagdat," about the caliph Almansur who, with the help of a young artist Ahnaf, is transforming Baghdad into a city of wonders. The two, however, disagree, and Almansur pursues Ahnaf into the desert. There, by means of magic, Ahnaf escapes, causing an earthquake which strands the caliph in the desert where must undergo a series of perils to return to Baghdad. It is an exciting story with much imagination. James's juvenile exuberance gives the stories a zest and bounce lacking from other works of the period. Later in his career James produced a few children's fantasies for his family, including *The Last of the Fairies* and a fairy play,

Camaralzaman, which conveys some of the spirit of his Arabian tales.

The only other book of James's in the realm of the fantastic was *The Commissioner; or, De Lunatico Enquirendo,* a fanciful trip of a lunarian to Earth which James uses to satirize the current political situation. It was published anonymously and without the draw of James's name it was a commercial failure. James never tried another political satire.

James's other 90 or so books blur into a haze of similarity. He liked to think he was writing popular history rather than fiction, so his books were intended as much to be educational as entertaining. He maintained a remarkable output for over 30 years, and even though his new books in the 1850s failed to sell in such huge numbers, he was still much fêted as a celebrity and his early popular works were never out of print. The best of them might still be enjoyed today.

—Mike Ashley

JAMES, Henry

Nationality: American; became British citizen, 1915. **Born:** New York City, 15 April 1843; brother of the philosopher William James. **Education:** Richard Pulling Jenks School, New York; travelled with his family in Europe from an early age: studied with tutors in Geneva, London, Paris and Boulogne, 1855-58, Geneva, 1859, and Bonn, 1860; lived with his family in Newport, Rhode Island, 1860-62; attended Harvard Law School, Cambridge, Massachusetts, 1862-63. **Career:** Lived with his family in Cambridge and wrote for *Nation* and *Atlantic Monthly,* 1866-69; toured Europe, 1869-70; returned to Cambridge, 1870-72; art critic, *Atlantic Monthly,* 1871-72; lived in Europe, 1872-74, Cambridge, 1875, and Paris, 1875-76; writer for New York *Tribune,* Paris, 1875-76; moved to London, 1876, and lived in England for the rest of his life; settled in Rye, Sussex, 1896; travelled throughout the U.S., 1904-05. **Awards:** L.H.D.: Harvard University, 1911; Oxford University, 1912. Order of Merit, 1916. **Died:** 28 February 1916.

HORROR, GHOST AND GOTHIC PUBLICATIONS

Novels

The Two Magics: The Turn of the Screw, Covering End. London, Heinemann, and New York, Macmillan, 1898.
The Sacred Fount. New York, Scribners, and London, Methuen, 1901.
The Sense of the Past, edited by Percy Lubbock. London, Collins, and New York, Scribners, 1917.

Short Stories

A Passionate Pilgrim and Other Tales. Boston, Osgood, 1875.
The Lesson of the Master and Other Stories. London and New York, Macmillan, 1892.
The Real Thing and Other Tales. New York, Macmillan, and London, Macmillan, 1893.
The Private Life, The Wheel of Time, Lord Beaupré, The Visits, Collaboration, Owen Wingrave. London, Osgood McIlvaine, 1893.

The Wheel of Time. New York, Harper, 1893.
Terminations and Other Stories. London, Heinemann, and New York, Harper, 1895.
Embarrassments: The Figure in the Carpet, Glasses, The Next Time, The Way It Came. London, Heinemann, and New York, Macmillan, 1896.
The Soft Side. London, Methuen, and New York, Macmillan, 1900.
Travelling Companions, edited by Albert Mordell. New York, Boni & Liveright, 1919.
The Ghostly Tales of Henry James, edited by Leon Edel. New Brunswick, New Jersey, Rutgers University Press, 1948; as *Stories of the Supernatural,* New York, Taplinger, 1970.
The Turn of the Screw and Other Short Novels. New York, Signet, 1962.
The Turn of the Screw and Other Stories, edited by S. Gorley Putt. London, Penguin, 1969.
The Turn of the Screw and Other Stories, edited by T. J. Lustig. Oxford, Oxford University Press, 1992.

OTHER PUBLICATIONS

Novels

Roderick Hudson. Boston, Osgood, 1876; revised edition, 3 vols., London, Macmillan, 1879; 1 vol., Boston and New York, Houghton, Mifflin, 1882.
The American. Boston, Osgood, and London, Ward, Lock, 1877.
Watch and Ward. Boston, Houghton, Osgood, 1878.
The Europeans: A Sketch. 2 vols., London, Macmillan, 1878; 1 vol., Boston, Houghton, Osgood, 1879.
An International Episode. New York, Harper, 1879.
Confidence. 2 vols., London, Chatto and Windus, 1880; 1 vol., Boston, Houghton, Osgood, 1880.
Washington Square. New York, Harper, 1881.
The Portrait of a Lady. 3 vols., London, Macmillan, 1881; 1 vol. Boston and New York, Houghton, Mifflin, 1882.
The Bostonians. 3 vols., London, Macmillan, 1886; 1 vol., London and New York, Macmillan, 1886.
The Princess Casamassima. 3 vols., London, Macmillan, 1886; 1 vol., New York, Macmillan, 1886.
The Reverberator. 2 vols., London, Macmillan, 1888; 1 vol., New York, Macmillan, 1888.
The Tragic Muse. 2 vols., Boston and New York, Houghton, Mifflin, 1890; 3 vols., London, Macmillan, 1890.
The Other House. 2 vols., London, Heinemann, 1896; 1 vol., New York and London, Macmillan, 1896.
The Spoils of Poynton. London, Heinemann, 1897; Boston and New York, Houghton, Mifflin, 1897.
What Maisie Knew. London, Heinemann, 1897; Chicago and New York, Stone, 1897.
In the Cage. London, Duckworth, 1898; Chicago and New York, Stone, 1898.
The Awkward Age. London, Heinemann, 1899; New York and London, Harper, 1899.
The Wings of the Dove. 2 vols., New York, Scribners, 1902; 1 vol., Westminster, Constable, 1902.
The Ambassadors. London, Methuen, and New York, Harper, 1903.
The Golden Bowl. New York, Scribners, 1904; London, Methuen, 1905.

The Finer Grain. New York, Scribners, and London, Methuen, 1910.

The Outcry. London, Methuen, and New York, Scribners, 1911.

The Ivory Tower, edited by Percy Lubbock. London, Collins, 1917; New York,: Scribners, 1917.

Gabrielle de Bergerac, edited by Albert Mordell. New York, Boni and Liveright, 1918.

Short Stories

Daisy Miller: A Study. New York, Harper, 1878.

The Madonna of the Future and Other Tales. London, Macmillan, 1879.

A Bundle of Letters. Boston, Loring, 1880.

The Diary of a Man of Fifty, and A Bundle of Letters. New York, Harper, 1880.

Novels and Tales. 14 vols., London, Macmillan, 1883.

The Siege of London, The Pension Beaurepas, and The Point of View. Boston, Osgood, 1883.

Tales of Three Cities. Boston, Osgood, and London, Macmillan, 1884.

The Author of Beltraffio, Pandora, Georgina's Reasons, The Path of Duty, Four Meetings. Boston, Osgood, 1885.

Stories Revived. London, Macmillan, 1885.

The Aspern Papers, Louisa Pallant, The Modern Warning. 2 vols., London, Macmillan, 1888; 1 vol., New York, Macmillan, 1888.

A London Life, The Patagonia, The Liar, Mrs. Temperly. 2 vols., London, Macmillan, 1889; 1 vol., New York, Macmillan, 1889.

The Better Sort. London, Methuen, and New York, Scribners, 1903.

The Novels and Tales of Henry James (New York Edition), revised by James. New York, Scribner, 26 vols., 1907-17.

A Landscape Painter, edited by Albert Mordell. New York, Scott and Seltzer, 1919.

Master Eustace. New York, Seltzer, 1920.

Novels and Stories, edited by Percy Lubbock. 35 vols., London, Macmillan, 1921-23.

Eight Uncollected Tales, edited by Edna Kenton. New Brunswick, New Jersey, Rutgers University Press, 1950.

Complete Tales, edited by Leon Edel. 12 vols., London, Hart-Davis; and Philadelphia and New York, Lippincott, 1962-64.

Plays

Daisy Miller, from his own story. Boston, Osgood, 1883.

The American, from his own novel (produced 1891). London, Heinemann, 1891.

Guy Domville (produced 1895). N.p., 1894.

Theatricals (includes *Tenants, Disengaged*) (produced 1909). London, Osgood, McIlvaine, and New York, Harper, 1894.

Theatricals: Second Series (includes *The Album, The Reprobate*) (produced 1919). London, Osgood, McIlvaine, and New York, Harper, 1895.

The High Bid (produced 1908). In *Complete Plays,* 1949.

The Saloon (produced 1911). In *Complete Plays,* 1949.

The Outcry (produced 1917). In *Complete Plays,* 1949.

Complete Plays, edited by Leon Edel. Philadelphia and New York, Lippincott, 1949; London, Hart-Davis, 1949.

Other

Transatlantic Sketches. Boston, Osgood, 1875.

French Poets and Novelists. London, Macmillan, 1878.

Hawthorne. London, Macmillan, 1879; New York, Harper, 1880.

Portraits of Places. London, Macmillan, 1883; Boston, Osgood, 1884.

Notes on a Collection of Drawings by George du Maurier. N.p., 1884.

A Little Tour in France. Boston, Osgood, 1884; revised edition, Boston and New York, Houghton, Mifflin, and London, Heinemann, 1900.

The Art of Fiction, with Walter Besant. Boston, Cupples, Upham, 1885.

Partial Portraits. London and New York, Macmillan, 1888.

Picture and Text. New York, Harper, 1893.

Essays in London and Elsewhere. London, Osgood, McIlvaine, and New York, Harper, 1893.

William Wetmore Story and His Friends. 2 vols., Edinburgh and London, Blackwood, 1903, and Boston, Houghton, Mifflin, 1903.

The Question of Our Speech, The Lesson of Balzac: Two Lectures. Boston and New York, Houghton, Mifflin, 1905.

English Hours. London, Heinemann, 1905; Boston and New York, Houghton, Mifflin, 1905.

The American Scene. London, Chapman and Hall, 1907; New York and London, Harper, 1907.

View and Reviews. Boston, Ball, 1908.

Italian Hours. London, Heinemann, 1909; Boston and New York, Houghton Mifflin, 1909.

A Small Boy and Others. New York, Scribners, and London, Macmillan, 1913.

Notes of a Son and Brother. New York, Scribners, and London, Macmillan, 1914.

The Middle Years, edited by Percy Lubbock. London, Collins, and New York, Scribners, 1917.

Notes on Novelists and Some Other Notes. London, Dent, and New York, Scribners, 1914.

Within the Rim and Other Essays 1914-1915. London, Collins, 1918.

Letters, edited by Percy Lubbock. 2 vols., New York, Octagon, 1920.

Notes and Reviews. Cambridge, Massachusetts, Dunster House, 1921.

Three Letters to Joseph Conrad, edited by Gerard Jean-Aubry. N.p., 1926.

Letters to Walter Berry. N.p., 1928.

Letters to A. C. Benson and Auguste Monod, edited by E. F. Benson. N.p., 1930.

Theatre and Friendship: Some James Letters, edited by Elizabeth Robins. N.p., 1932.

The Art of the Novel: Critical Prefaces, edited by R. P. Blackmur. New York and London, Scribners, 1934.

Notebooks, edited by F. O. Matthiessen and Kenneth B. Murdock. New York, Oxford University Press.

The Art of Fiction and Other Essays, edited by Morris Roberts. New York, Oxford University Press, 1948.

Henry James and Robert Louis Stevenson: A Record of Friendship and Criticism, edited by Janet Adam Smith. N.p., 1948.

The Scenic Art: Notes on Acting and the Drama 1872-1901, edited by Allan Wade. New Brunswick, New Jersey, Rutgers University Press, 1948; London, Hart-Davis, 1949.

Daumier, Caricaturist. N.p., 1954.

The American Essays, edited by Leon Edel. New York, Vintage, 1956.

The Future of the Novel: Essays on the Art of the Novel, edited by Leon Edel. New York, Vintage, 1956.

The Painter's Eye: Notes and Essays on the Pictorial Arts, edited by John L. Sweeney. London, Hart-Davis, and Cambridge, Massachusetts, Harvard University Press, 1956.

Parisian Sketches: Letters to the New York Tribune 1875-1876, edited by Leon Edel and Ilse Dusoir Lind. New York University Press, 1957.

Literary Reviews and Essays on American, English, and French Literature, edited by Albert Mordell. Boston, Twayne, 1957.

Henry James and H. G. Wells: A Record of Their Friendship, Their Debate on the Art of Fiction, and Their Quarrel, edited by Leon Edel and Gordon N. Ray. Westport, Connecticut, Greenwood Press, 1958.

The Art of Travel: Scenes and Journeys in America, England, France, and Italy, edited by Morton Dauwen Zabel. Freeport, New York, Books for Libraries, 1958.

French Writers and American Women: Essays, edited by Peter Buitenhuis. Branford, Connecticut, Compass, 1960.

Selected Literary Criticism, edited by Morris Shapiro. Westport, Connecticut, Greenwood Press, 1963.

Henry James and John Hay: The Record of a Friendship, edited by George Monteiro. N.p., 1965.

Switzerland in the Life and Work of James: The Clare Benedict Collection of Letters from James, edited by Jörg Hasler. N.p., 1966.

Letters, edited by Leon Edel. 4 vols., Cambridge, Massachusetts, Harvard University Press, 1974-84; *Selected Letters,* Cambridge, Massachusetts, Harvard University Press, 1987.

Literary Criticism (Library of America), edited by Leon Edel. 2 vols., N.p., 1984.

The Art of Criticism: James on the Theory and Practice of Fiction, edited by William Veeder and Susan M. Griffin. Chicago, University of Chicago Press, 1986.

The Complete Notebooks, edited by Leon Edel and Lyall H. Powers. New York, Oxford University Press, 1986.

The Critical Muse: Selected Literary Criticism, edited by Roger Gard. London, Penguin, and New York, Viking Penguin, 1987.

Selected Letters to Edmund Gosse 1882-1915: A Literary Friendship, edited by Rayburn S. Moore. Baton Rouge, Louisiana State University, 1988.

Letters 1900-1915, with Edith Wharton, edited by Lyall H. Powers. New York, Scribners, 1990.

Translator, *Port Tarascon,* by Alphonse Daudet. N.p., 1891.

*

Film Adaptations: *Berkeley Square,* 1933, *The House in the Square (I'll Never Forget You),* 1951, both from the novel *The Sense of the Past; The Lost Moment,* 1947, *Aspern,* 1983, both from the short novel *The Aspern Papers; The Heiress,* 1949, from the novel *Washington Square; The Innocents,* 1961, *The Nightcomers,* 1972, *The Turn of the Screw,* 1974 (television miniseries), all from the short novel *The Turn of the Screw; The Ambassadors,* 1965 (television serial); *The Portrait of a Lady,* 1968 (television serial), 1996; *What Maisie Knew,* 1968 (television serial), 1975; *The Spoils of Poynton,* 1970 (television serial); *The Golden Bowl,* 1972 (television serial); *Daisy Miller,* 1974; *The Europeans,* 1979; *The Bostonians,* 1984.

Bibliography: *A Bibliography of Henry James* by Leon Edel and Dan H. Laurence, 1957, revised edition, 1961, 1982, New York, Clarendon Press; *Henry James: A Bibliography of Secondary Works* by Beatrice Ricks, Metuchen, New Jersey, Scarecrow Press, 1975; *Henry James 1917-1959: A Reference Guide* by Kristin Pruitt McColgan, Boston, G. K. Hall, 1979; *Henry James 1960-1974: A Reference Guide* by Dorothy M. Scura, Boston, G. K. Hall, 1979; *Henry James 1866-1916: A Reference Guide* by Linda J. Taylor, Boston, G. K. Hall, 1982; *Henry James: A Bibliography of Criticism 1975-1981* by John Budd, Westport, Connecticut, Greenwood Press, 1983; *An Annotated Critical Bibliography of Henry James* by Nicola Bradbury, New York, St. Martin's Press, 1987; *Henry James 1975-1987: A Reference Guide* by Judith E. Funston, Boston, G. K. Hall, 1991.

Critical Studies (selection): *The Expense of Vision: Essays on the Craft of Henry James* by Laurence B. Holland, Baltimore, Johns Hopkins University Press, 1964; *Henry James: The Critical Heritage* edited by Roger Gard, London, Routledge, and New York, Kegan Paul, 1968; *Henry James: The Writer and His Work,* by Tony Tanner, Amherst, University of Massachusetts Press, 1985; *The Novels of Henry James: A Study of Culture and Consciousness* by Brian Lee, New York, St. Martin's Press, 1978; *Studies in Henry James* by R. P. Blackmur, edited by Veronica A. Makowsky, New York, New Directions, 1983; *The Phenomenology of Henry James* by Paul Armstrong, Chapel Hill, University of North Carolina Press, 1983; *Henry James: Fiction as History,* London, Vision, and Totowa, New Jersey, Barnes and Noble, 1984, and *Henry James and the Past,* New York, St. Martin's Press, 1990, both edited by Ian F. A. Bell; *Critical Essays on Henry James* edited by James W. Gargano, 2 vols., Boston, G. K. Hall, 1987; *A Ring of Conspirators: Henry James and His Literary Circle 1895-1915* by Miranda Seymour, Boston, Houghton Mifflin, 1988; *Henry James: A Study of the Short Fiction* by Richard A. Hocks, Boston, Twayne, 1991; *Henry James: The Imagination of Genius* (biography) by Fred Kaplan, New York, Morrow, 1992.

*   *   *

In the field of the ghost story, *The Turn of the Screw* (definable as either a long novella or a short novel) is perhaps the masterpiece; certainly it is the most popular and best-known of Henry James's tales. Besides being adapted for film and television, it provided the basis for the opera by Benjamin Britten.

The Turn of the Screw is introduced in the traditional context of a house-party at which ghost stories are being told. One of the guests produces the copy of a manuscript which he explains was written by a woman now dead. The first-person narration which follows is by this nameless woman who had gone to be governess to two parentless children in an English country house. There she sees two ghosts—one of a handsome yet dangerous-looking man, the other of a sad and beautiful woman—and identifies them as Peter Quint, formerly a manservant in the house before his death in a drunken accident, and Miss Jessel, the children's previous governess who had died, after leaving her post, in some unspecified yet sinister way. She realizes that the ghosts intend to corrupt and destroy the children, and becomes determined to save the children, at whatever cost. At the end, the little girl, Flora, is sent away in the care of the housekeeper, and Miles dies, apparently of fright, in the governess' arms as she shields him from the leering face of Peter Quint at the window. Perhaps, as she believes, she has saved his soul, but his body is dead.

While *The Turn of the Screw* can be enjoyed as one of the best ghost stories ever written, it is not entirely clear how James intended his ghosts to be taken. This is a genuinely creepy, terrifying tale, suspenseful and well-paced, but it is also beautifully ambiguous. Only the governess sees the ghosts, and everything we "know" about them is filtered through her observations, fears and feelings. She interprets the children's possibly innocent speech and actions to mean that they are hiding the fact that they are in contact with the ghosts, but there is no external evidence for this, and the housekeeper, Mrs. Grose, can see nothing when the governess points out the ghosts to her. The governess is not an unreliable narrator in the sense that she lies or misleads; she tells the truth as she sees it, quite simply. Rather than a tale of the supernatural, *The Turn of the Screw* may be instead a devastatingly believable portrait of a mind under strain: a sexually repressed woman haunted by hysterical delusions, and destroying the children in the belief that she is saving their souls. On either reading, whether the haunting is supernatural or psychological, the atmosphere of evil is palpably real, and the story is terrifying, well deserving of its status as a classic.

James's theory about ghost stories (which he considered fairy tales for adults) was that the more ambiguous the tale of the supernatural, the more powerful its effect on the reader. "So long as the events are veiled the imagination will run riot and depict all sorts of horrors, but as soon as the veil is lifted, all mystery disappears," he wrote. "Only make the reader's general vision of evil intense enough . . . and his own experience, his own imagination . . . will supply him quite sufficiently with all the particulars."

Throughout his long career James had an abiding interest in the supernatural, but nothing else he wrote ever struck such a powerful chord with the public as *The Turn of the Screw*. His early stories, including "The Romance of Certain Old Clothes," "The Last of the Valerii" and "The Ghostly Rental" are conventional ghost stories, traditional in form: the supernatural element is unambiguous. Later, he moved away from the more conventional idea of hauntings to explore the psychological meaning more deeply, dealing with what he described as the "quasi-supernatural" in such tales as "The Altar of the Dead" in which a man becomes obsessed with remembering his dead friends; "The Friends of the Friends," in which a woman breaks off her engagement because of her conviction that her fiancé has been visited by the ghost of her dead friend—the woman he "should" have loved if he had met her in life (both of them shared the experience of having seen a ghost before); "The Real Right Thing" in which a respectful biographer is warned off by the spirit of his subject; and even, perhaps, "The Beast in the Jungle," not a ghost story in any traditional sense (there is no ghost), but which James apparently regarded as a portrait of the haunted state, as he himself grouped it with his other supernatural tales.

James's short novel *The Sacred Fount*, which most readers have found bafflingly obscure—Edmund Wilson, who suggested it is a sort of companion piece to *The Turn of the Screw* called it "not merely mystifying but maddening"—makes more sense if it is understood as being a horror story about psychic vampirism, a more subtle, sophisticated—and ambiguous—version of one of his earliest stories, "De Grey: A Romance." In the early story, a family curse means that any woman who loves a man of the De Grey family will die; the young heroine of the story manages to resist this fate, only to discover that while she is growing stronger through her love, her lover is "dying of her." In *The Sacred Fount* a young man is being drained of his youth by an older wife, who grows visibly younger as he grows older, and another, formerly clever, woman grows dull as her lover begins to shine.

Near the end of his life James embarked on what was meant to be a full-length novel of the supernatural, *The Sense of the Past*, about a young American who inherits a house in England and, on entering it, walks into the past. There, his fear of being trapped in the past makes him an object of terror to the people he meets—to his ancestors, he is the ghost. That novel was never finished (although it inspired the successful stage play and film *Berkeley Square*), but after James returned for a visit to America after more than 20 years of living abroad, he drew upon what he felt was the central idea of *The Sense of the Past* to write his final ghost story, "The Jolly Corner." This, the most autobiographical of his supernatural tales, concerns an expatriate who returns to America and has a frightening encounter with his other self—the person he would have been if he had never left.

—Lisa Tuttle

JAMES, M(ontague) R(hodes)

Nationality: British. **Born:** Goodnestone Parsonage, Goodnestone, Kent, 1 August 1862. **Education:** Eton School; King's College, Cambridge. **Family:** None. **Career:** Director of Fitzwilliam Museum, Cambridge, 1893-1908; Provost, King's College, 1905-18; also Vice-Chancellor, Cambridge University, 1913-15; Provost, Eton, 1918-36. **Awards:** Various honorary degrees; Bibliographical Society Gold Medal, 1929; Order of Merit, 1930. **Died:** 12 June 1936.

HORROR, GHOST AND GOTHIC PUBLICATIONS

Novel

The Five Jars (for children). London, Edward Arnold, 1922; New York, Arno Press, 1976.

Short Stories

Ghost Stories of an Antiquary. London, Edward Arnold, 1904; New York, Longmans Green, 1905.
More Ghost Stories of an Antiquary. London, Edward Arnold, and New York, Longmans Green, 1911.
A Thin Ghost, and Others. London, Edward Arnold, 1919; New York, Longmans Green, 1920.
A Warning to the Curious, and Other Ghost Stories. London, Edward Arnold, and New York, Longmans Green, 1925.
Wailing Well. Stanford Dingley, Berkshire, Mill House Press, 1928.
The Collected Ghost Stories of M. R. James. London, Edward Arnold, and New York, Longmans Green, 1931; as *The Penguin Complete Ghost Stories of M. R. James*, London, Penguin, 1984.
Thirteen Ghost Stories. Hamburg, Albatross, 1935.
Best Ghost Stories of M. R. James. Cleveland, World, 1944.
Ghost Stories of M. R. James, edited by Nigel Kneale. London, Folio Society, 1973.

Ghost Stories of an Antiquary and More Ghost Stories (omnibus). London, Penguin, 1974.

Book of the Supernatural, edited by Peter Haining. London, Foulsham, 1979; as *The Book of Ghost Stories*, New York, Stein and Day, 1979.

The Illustrated Ghost Stories of M. R. James, edited by Michael Cox. Oxford, Oxford University Press, 1986.

Casting the Runes, and Other Ghost Stories, edited by Michael Cox. Oxford, World's Classics, 1987.

A Warning to the Curious: The Ghost Stories of M. R. James, edited by Ruth Rendell. London, Hutchinson, 1987.

Editor, "Twelve Mediaeval Ghost Stories" (in Latin, from old MSS), *English Historical Review*, July 1922; translated in *The Man-Wolf and Other Horrors*, edited by Hugh Lamb, London, Allen, 1978.

Editor, *Madam Crowl's Ghost, and Other Tales of Mystery*, by Joseph Sheridan Le Fanu. London, Bell, 1923.

OTHER PUBLICATIONS

Other

Old Testament Legends. London, Longmans, 1913.

The Wanderings and Homes of Manuscripts. London, Society for the Propagation of Christian Knowledge, 1919.

List of Manuscripts Formerly Owned by Dr. John Dee. Oxford, Oxford University Press-Bibliographical Society, 1921.

Abbeys. N.p., Great Western Railway, 1925.

Eton and King's: Recollections, Mostly Trivial, 1875-1925. London, Williams and Norgate, 1926.

Suffolk and Norfolk. London, Dent, 1930.

Letters to a Friend. London, Edward Arnold, 1956.

Some Remarks on Ghost Stories. Edinburgh, Tragara Press, 1985.

Editor and translator, *The Apocryphal New Testament*. N.p., 1924.

*

Media Adaptations: Film—*Night of the Demon* (1957), from his story "Casting the Runes." Television—"Room 13," "Lost Hearts," "The Tractate Middoth," all in *Mystery and Imagination* series, 1966-68; *Whistle and I'll Come to You*, 1968, from his story "Oh, Whistle, and I'll Come to You, My Lad"; "The Stalls of Barchester Cathedral," 1971, "A Warning To the Curious," 1972, "Lost Hearts," 1973, "The Treasure of Abbot Thomas," 1974, "The Ash Tree," 1975, all in *A Ghost Story for Christmas* series.

Critical Studies: *A Memoir of Montague Rhodes James* by S. G. Lubbock, Cambridge, Cambridge University Press, 1939; *Montague Rhodes James* by Richard William Pfaff, London, Scholar Press, 1980; *M. R. James: An Informal Portrait* by Michael Cox, Oxford, Oxford University Press, 1983.

*   *   *

Montague Rhodes James enjoyed an immaculately successful academic career as an expert on classical languages, palaeography and medieval and Biblical (especially Apocalyptic) legend. Meanwhile, out of his extensive, eccentric knowledge of dusty manu-scripts and scholarly byways, James produced the 20th century's most influential canon of ghost stories.

The secret of James's special charm can be dissected into a number of elements. His donnishness and erudition are always present, giving an air of genuine authority to the old manuscripts and cryptic fragments which so often lure his victims to their fates. Thus, although the eponymous relic in "Canon Alberic's Scrapbook" (*Ghost Stories of an Antiquary*) contains only one picture of sinister importance, the extensive, scholarly account of its other rarities lends conviction. "The Treasure of Abbot Thomas" boldly opens with a solid chunk of Latin—whose translation seems added almost as an afterthought—and entangles us in the intellectual thrill of solving the Abbot's stained-glass cryptogram.

There is more than mere erudition in James's control of tone and diction. Only a few patronizing renditions of the speech of the contemporary "lower orders" have slightly dated. A memorable passage of "The Ash-Tree" is written word-perfect in the manner of the late 17th century, enhancing its account of dire portents from Biblical sortilege. "The Stalls of Barchester Cathedral" (*More Ghost Stories . . .*) begins with a pastiche obituary which, with just perceptible irony, pretends to extol a cleric of minimal distinction. The dark, wet revenant of "Martin's Close" peeps at us through the cracks of a 1684 trial transcript with Judge Jeffreys presiding. A cod sermon of similar vintage, about the perils of the world's labyrinth, deepens the shadows of the garden maze in "Mr. Humphreys and his Inheritance." One notable *tour de force* of pretended artlessness is the extreme and unnerving simplicity of a Swedish rustic's narration in "Count Magnus" (*Ghost Stories . . .*), culminating not so much in the frightfulness of "his face was not there, because the flesh of it was sucked away off the bones" as in the reactions of those who must bury this shockingly disfigured corpse.

Such narratives within narratives are characteristic of the author's cunning indirection. Through third-party reports, perceptual uncertainty, hinted conjecture, MS fragments and *oratio obliqua*, James carefully distances his horrors as things seen in a glass, darkly. Perhaps the most remote of all—yet still alarming—is "The Mezzotint," where the murky picture of the title changes to hint, step by step, at the stealing of a child by a dead something in the previous century. Often the central apparition comes and goes in a flash, like the disquieting glimpse of a pink, masklike, sweating face amid the foliage in "The Rose Garden" (*More Ghost Stories...*). Sometimes it may be felt rather than seen, as in "Casting the Runes," where the rune-cursed man reaches under his pillow for a matchbox and touches "a mouth, with teeth, and with hair about it, and, he declares, not the mouth of a human being." Almost always, James is adept at minimal descriptions of unpleasantness: a bare phrase or two that evokes more and worse than is said. The technique echoes the guilt-ridden Cardinal's premonitions in John Webster's *The Duchess of Malfi*: "When I look into the fishponds in my garden, / Methinks I see a thing arm'd with a rake, / That seems to strike at me."

Perhaps James's greatest strength is inventiveness, an ability to unveil the unexpected horror in the unexpected place—like that bestial mouth underneath the pillow. Even the acclaimed critic Edmund Wilson, whose essay "A Treatise on Tales of Horror" (1944) is generally dismissive, credits James with "some really fiendish flashes of fancy." Best known is the spirit called by the whistle in "Oh, Whistle, and I'll Come to You, My Lad" (*Ghost Stories . . .*), which after disturbing pursuits across an empty seafront eventually animates the hapless summoner's bedsheets and presents "a horrible, an intensely horrible, face *of crumpled linen.*" Others include the bulging, musty "treasure bag" of "The Treasure of Abbot Thomas," which suddenly puts its arms around a looter's neck; the nightmare burnt creature which crawls with wasplike writhings from a black hole in a sheet of paper, in "Mr. Humphreys and His Inheritance"; the pink hand groping feebly from amid ordinary linen in a drawer at "The Residence in Whitminster" (*A Thin Ghost*); the faceless creature made all of hair in "The Diary of Mr. Poÿnter"—an echo of "Oh, Whistle . . ." which seems almost self-parodic; and the binoculars of "A View from a Hill" (*A Warning to the Curious*), which see into the past because filled with an unholy fluid distilled from dead men's bones.

Meticulous scenic descriptions add to the effect, notably (as commended by John Betjeman) those of East Anglia and the West Country. The Preface to *The Collected Ghost Stories* identifies several inspirational locales—for example, the Burnstow of "Oh, Whistle . . ." is Felixstowe.

James's own view of supernatural beings was unrepentantly traditional: "On the whole, then, I say you must have horror and also malevolence." ("Ghosts—Treat Them Gently!"; *Evening News*, 1931) He also added "reticence," his own term for the grisly understatement already discussed. Indeed his hauntings are always malign—although occasionally the lead character is not the object of ill-will and is incidentally helped. Young Simon is saved from human sacrifice in "Lost Hearts" (*Ghost Stories . . .*) by the vengeful shades of the would-be magus's previous victims; the revenant with cobwebbed eye-sockets in "The Tractate Middoth" (*More Ghost Stories . . .*) is concerned only with the malefactor who means to destroy this dead man's secret will. But in "The Mezzotint" and the thematically similar "The Haunted Doll's House" (*A Warning to the Curious*) the essential *frisson* is that innocent children pay an unfair penalty for the sins of the fathers.

The typical Jamesian spectre is not only malign but distinctly physical—though it may be "light and weak," like the pursuing avenger in the title piece of *A Warning to the Curious*, which to those not in the know seems merely an old dark overcoat left on the ground. Generally only a few horrid details loom to haunt the reader's dreams: teeth, claws, cerements, matted hair, a face which may be fleshless, an insectile or spider-like limb.

Although James was far from being a formula writer, he relied heavily on those "flashes of fiendish fancy" and seems to have found them increasingly hard to come by . . . as suggested in the good-humoured "Stories I Have Tried to Write" (*Collected Ghost Stories...*), with its list of abortive fancies. An interesting alternative approach is seen in "Wailing Well," written—like so many previous tales—to be read aloud. The intended audience was a Boy Scout troop: the story's rather conventional skeletal horrors are complemented by the farcical account of a singularly appalling Scout who more or less deserves his sticky end.

A younger audience is likewise addressed in *The Five Jars*, a whimsical fairy tale whose first-person narrator has James's own persona. A talking stream leads him to a magic plant which confers the power of seeing underground (". . . surprising, too, in how many places there lie, unsuspected, bones of men") and thus finding the Five Jars. These contain unguents which further extend the senses into animal and Faerie realms normally hidden from dull human perception. Sinister forces, first seen as pillars of mist with red eyes, covet the jars and make various attempts on them, but James, seemingly more concerned to avoid distress to children than Lewis Carroll ever was, downplays the tension almost to the point of inconsequentiality. The book has a gentle charm.

M. R. James continues to be read, and to be influential—as may be seen from Rosemary Pardoe's useful *The James Gang: A Bibliography of Writers in the M. R. James Tradition* (1991). Writers treated in the present volume who are to some extent part of the "gang" include E. F. Benson (a friend), Ramsey Campbell, John Gordon (in particular for *The House on the Brink*) and H. Russell Wakefield.

—David Langford

JAMES, Peter

Nationality: British. **Born:** Brighton, Sussex, 1948. **Education:** Charterhouse School. **Family:** Married Georgina James. **Career:** Worked in television and film production, in Canada; freelance novelist in Britain since the 1980s. **Address:** c/o Orion Publishing, Orion House, 5 Upper St. Martin's Lane, London WC2H 9EA, England. Lives in Clayton, near Brighton, East Sussex, England.

HORROR, GHOST AND GOTHIC PUBLICATIONS

Novels

Possession. London, Gollancz, and New York, Doubleday, 1988.
Dreamer. London, Gollancz, 1989; New York, St. Martin's Press, 1990.
Sweet Heart. London, Gollancz, 1990; New York, St. Martin's Press, 1991.
Twilight. London, Gollancz, 1991; New York, St. Martin's Press, 1992.
Prophecy. London, Gollancz, 1992; New York, St. Martin's Press, 1994.
Host. London, Gollancz, 1993; New York, Villard, 1995.
Alchemist. London, Gollancz, 1996.
The Truth. London, Orion, 1997.

OTHER PUBLICATIONS

Novels

Dead Letter Drop. London, W. H. Allen, 1981.
Atom Bomb Angel. London, W. H. Allen, 1982.
Billionaire. London, W. H. Allen, 1983.
Travelling Man (novelization of television script). London, Star, 1984.
Biggles: The Untold Story (novelization of screenplay). London, Star, 1986.
Getting Wired!: A TechnoTerrors Story (for children). London, Gollancz, 1996.

*

Film Adaptation: *Prophecy* (television movie), 1995.

Theatrical Activities:
Producer: **Films**—*Children Shouldn't Play with Dead Things,*

1972; *Dead of Night* (*Deathdream*), 1972; *Blue Blood*, 1973; *Sunday in the Country*, 1975.

* * *

Peter James worked in Canada for some years, writing for TV and producing cult horror films before returning to Britain to become a novelist. Only after three thrillers did he turn to horror fiction. For each of his first seven supernatural horror novels, he has most thoroughly researched some aspect of the supernatural (or occult fringe), together with any institution or profession that he needs to include. (His acknowledgments lists are lengthy, sometimes spilling over onto a second page.) His characters are generally well-off professionals; his settings are in London or southern England. The result is that he has written fast-moving thriller-type horror with a surface slickness. It has sold well in Britain, the United States and (in translation) many other countries.

The supernatural subject in *Possession* is communication with the dead. The psychic experiences of a mother after her son's death in a car crash lead her to approach mediums in ever more desperate attempts to understand him and to discover what she feels he wants to tell her before he can rest in peace.

The psychology of dreams and precognitive dreaming feature in *Dreamer*. A London-based TV writer called Sam is the dreamer in question. She is in her early 30s, upset at her inability to have more children and struggling to save her marriage to Richard, a high-powered financial advisor. The dreams which are upsetting her hark back to the time when she was aged seven and was nearly killed by the teenage handicapped son of neighbours. This boy, called Slider, with mental problems, a false eye and a deformed hand, was interrupted by Sam just after he had raped and murdered another teenager. Sam was lucky to survive Slider's attack, during which Slider was killed in a fall. Now Sam is having terrifying dreams, some of which involve Slider in the past, and others about an air-crash in the future. This is an exciting tale of revenge, even allowing for its problems of plot coherence.

Sweet Heart is a haunted-house novel, engaging and entertaining despite the clichés. The house is Elmwood Mill, an old dilapidated property in rural Sussex, obviously haunted to the reader but not to the characters, who seem determined to ignore what they see and hear. It was previously owned by a mad female recluse, who died there. The young people who move in, lawyer Tom and his wife Charley, have a fragile marriage and are trying to start a baby. Charley, with psychological problems before the haunting starts, is undergoing hypnotic regression therapy and getting strange, frightening results. She has a best friend called Laura, whose plot function is to lure Tom away for a brief affair so that the author can have Charley on her own in the house. The minor characters are mostly neighbours—some awful yuppies and others, with long memories, who will not speak to Charlie because she resembles somebody who used to live there. The exception, living conveniently close up the lane, is Hugh, a handsome, dependable and single man with some interest in the supernatural who is at hand to comfort Charley in her time of need. Many of the circumstances are too familiar, but the pace never slackens and the small details of character and setting are well chosen.

Twilight is almost a medical thriller, reminiscent of Robin Cook's filmed bestseller *Coma*. It features Near-Death and Out-of-Body Experiences, with an emotionless surgeon, Harvey Swire, researching these things (unofficially, by betraying his medical ethics). He, in his turn, is being investigated by Kate Hemingway, who be-

trays any ethics that journalists might have. Some of the job details (surgeon and journalist) are first-rate, though the characters themselves are most unappealing. There are plenty of supernatural manifestations: meetings with the dead, noises from a newly buried coffin, and so on. At one point Kate breaks into a mortuary and is forced to hide on top of a body. Except that it fails to engage the emotions, this is another slick and readable novel.

Featured in *Prophecy* are coincidence, psychometry, the predictions of an ouija board and the channelling of spirits of the dead. The novel formed the basis of a moderately successful television movie.

An interesting aspect of *Host* is that it was issued (more than a year after its hardcover first edition) on two floppy discs, claimed as the world's first electronic novel. Its subject matter is cryonics and artificial intelligence, and its contention is that immortality is almost within mankind's grasp. Its protagonist, Dr. Joe Messenger, is a computer scientist who supports cryonics. He becomes influenced by Juliet Spring, a neuroscientist who has managed to programme a computer with a complete human consciousness, but who dies suddenly. Then Joe's super-computer displays its intelligence and demands the impossible from him, while gruesome events happen around him. Although set in the present, this novel operates in the territory of near-future science fiction.

Alchemist seems to be about the unscrupulous practices of a multinational pharmaceuticals corporation. Bendix Schere seems to monitor and partly control the habits and whereabouts of its employees, murdering some of them for disloyalty. It carries out trials of new drugs without informing the human guinea pigs. Montana Bannerman and her father join Bendix Schere when their own small pharmaceuticals company is taken over. At the same time, Conor Molloy, an American patents lawyer, also joins. Various odd circumstances alert Monty and Conor to the possibility that Bendix Schere is implicated in world-wide evil-doing, and they begin to investigate. Gradually a black-magic sub-plot emerges and is integrated with the rest (and with a romantic sub-plot). Once again, there are plot clichés, coincidences and telegraphed surprises. This is James's biggest novel (their size gradually increases over the years) though not his best. It is fast but unconvincing.

Peter James's only published story is "Propellor" in *Dark Voices 4*, in which a woman's precognitive dream comes true, though not in the way she expects.

—Chris Morgan

JETER, K(evin) W(ayne)

Pseudonym: Dr. Adder. **Nationality:** American. **Born:** Los Angeles, California, 1950. **Education:** California State University, Fullerton; B.A. in sociology. **Family:** Married Geri Jeter. **Agent:** Russ Galen, Scovil-Chichak-Galen Literary Agency, 381 Park Avenue South, Suite 1112, New York, NY 10016, USA. **Lives in Oregon.**

HORROR, GHOST AND GOTHIC PUBLICATIONS

Novels

Soul Eater. New York, Tor, 1983; London, Kinnell, 1989.

Dark Seeker. New York, Tor, 1987; London, Pan Books, 1991.
Mantis. New York, Tor, 1987; London, Pan Books, 1992.
In the Land of the Dead. New York, New American Library, and Bath, England, Morrigan, 1989.
The Night Man. New York, New American Library, 1990; London, Pan Books, 1991.
Wolf Flow. New York, St. Martin's Press, 1992.

OTHER PUBLICATIONS

Novels

Seeklight. Don Mills, Ontario, Laser, 1975.
The Dreamfields. Toronto, Laser, 1976.
Morlock Night (sequel to *The Time Machine* by H. G. Wells). New York, DAW, 1979; London, Grafton, 1989.
Dr. Adder. New York, Bluejay, 1984; London, Grafton, 1987.
The Glass Hammer. New York, Bluejay, 1985; London, Grafton, 1987.
Infernal Devices: A Mad Victorian Fantasy. New York, St. Martin's Press, 1987; London, Grafton, 1988.
Death's Arms. New York, St. Martin's Press, 1987; Bath, England, Morrigan, 1989; as *Death Arms,* London, Grafton, and New York, St. Martin's Press, 1989.
Farewell Horizontal. New York, St. Martin's Press, 1989; London, Grafton, 1990.
Alligator Alley (as Dr. Adder), with Ferret writing as Mink Mole. Scotforth, Lancashire, Morrigan Publications, 1989.
Madlands. New York, St. Martin's Press, 1991.
Bloodletter. New York and London, Pocket Books, 1993.
Dark Horizon. New York and London, Pocket Books, 1993.
Blade Runner 2: The Edge of Human. New York, Bantam, and London, Orion, 1995.
Warped. New York and London, Pocket Books, 1995.
Blade Runner 3: Replicant Night. New York, Bantam, and London, Orion, 1996.

Graphic Novel

Mister E, with John K. Snyder III and Jay Geldhof. New York, DC Comics, 4 vols., 1991.

* * *

It is perhaps surprising that there is so little crossover between science fiction and horror writers. Possibly this is because the former are so firmly rooted in a tradition that says everything is knowable if not known, while the latter explore the possibility that there is more to existence than we can ever know, and certainly more than science can describe. K. W. Jeter is one of those rare writers who has had a successful career in both genres. He has written a considerable amount of excellent science fiction, including two sequels to the film *Blade Runner,* as well as a number of well-received horror novels.

Soul Eater is an effective if superficially formulaic story of the child as monster. Dee seems a perfectly ordinary little girl until an evil spirit takes control of her mother's body and uses her as a bridge to influence her daughter as well. The story focuses primarily on the relationship between Dee and her father, who recognizes the supernatural power at work even if he doesn't understand it, and who desperately attempts to save his daughter from

her own mother. A particularly vivid climax helps turn what could have been just another pedestrian novel into a very effective horror debut.

A series of experiments with a powerful hallucinative drug is the basis of *Dark Seeker.* During one session, a group of students merge into a single group consciousness, but rather than being a pleasant, revelatory experience, it's the beginning of a nightmare that will pursue them for the rest of their lives. Melded together, they are exposed to all of the bad aspects of the human psyche, an exposure that leads to death and insanity. The experiments are immediately brought to a close, but the participants must take drugs periodically thereafter to suppress the lingering effects of that initial experience.

Mike Tyler is pursued by at least one of his fellow experimenters, a man called Slide who has surrendered his individuality to what he sees as a greater whole. And he wants Mike Tyler to rejoin the circle and, even more importantly, Mike Tyler's son, who may have been conceived while his parents were part of the group mind. Jeter plays the reader skilfully, with a plot that seems to be headed toward a specific, discernible climax, but which changes direction in the final pages to catch us with our guard down.

Mantis is just as unpredictable as its predecessors. The title refers to the character Rae, a predatory woman whose obsession with Michael dominates every other emotion. But is it her obsession, or is there another presence lurking inside, an entity that can occupy more than one body at a time, and whose value system might therefore be different than that of a human? A strange and almost indescribable plot, occasionally difficult to follow, but with a payoff worth the effort.

In the Land of the Dead is easily the best of Jeter's horror novels, and the most restrained. The setting is California, farm country during the Great Depression. The protagonist is a petty criminal named Cooper who has been hired as a bookkeeper for a rapacious businessman who uses his employees' past crimes as a weapon to force them to work long hours for substandard wages. Cooper also meets a young woman who has the power to animate the dead. Although she's the one possessing the supernatural power, it's their mutual employer, Vandervelde, who is the true monster of the story. Jeter conveys an image of hopelessness and despair that encompasses all of the characters, until Cooper finds the will to act against his oppressor.

The Night Man presents the world seen through the eyes of Steven, a shy young introvert whose mother is an alcoholic and whose sister is a tramp. Teased and tormented by peers and adults alike, Steven retreats into a fantasy world, creating the Night Man, a fearsome creature who can push back at the rest of the world. But Steven's imagination proves to be powerful enough to change reality and the Night Man becomes real, a sinister figure who prowls the streets in his phantom car, exacting exaggerated revenge until Steven realizes that he has unleashed a monster.

Two short stories are worth noting as well. "Rise Up and Walk" is set within the world created by George Romero's film, *Night of the Living Dead.* As the world dissolves into chaos with the dead rising and attacking the living, a monomaniacal inmate at an insane asylum has his religious fervour reinforced when he seems to be able to raise the dead. "Blue on One End, Yellow on the Other" is more introspective, a mentally disturbed man cycling down to ineffectiveness as he struggles with conflicting impulses about taking his medication.

Jeter's success with his science fiction seems to have placed his career as a horror writer on hold, and his work in that genre is sufficiently out of the ordinary that he never attracted the main-stream readership that might have encouraged further work along those lines. His existing work is however a significant component of the horror fiction of the 1980s.

—Don D'Ammassa

JOYCE, Graham (William)

Nationality: British. **Born:** Warwickshire, 22 October 1954. **Education:** Bishop Lonsdale College of Education, B.Ed. 1978; Leicester University, M.A. 1981. **Family:** Married Suzanne Johnsen in 1988; one daughter. **Career:** Teacher, 1980-81; development officer, National Association of Youth Clubs, 1981-88; freelance writer since 1988; part-time tutor of creative writing, Nottingham Trent University, since 1995. **Awards:** British Fantasy award for novel, 1993, 1996. **Agent:** Luigi Bonomi, Sheil Land Associates Ltd., 43 Doughty Street, London WC1N 2LF, England. Lives in Leicester.

HORROR, GHOST AND GOTHIC PUBLICATIONS

Novels

Dreamside. London, Pan, 1991.
Dark Sister. London, Headline, 1992.
House of Lost Dreams. London, Headline, 1993.
Requiem. London, Creed, 1995; New York, St. Martin's Press, 1996.
The Tooth Fairy. London, Signet, 1996.

OTHER PUBLICATIONS

Novel

Spiderbite (for children). London, Orion, 1997.

*

Graham Joyce comments:

I figure it's one of my jobs as a writer to raise questions about *genre* so when people puzzle about which genre I'm working in I feel as if I'm doing at least something right. And that's not just to confuse; it's more an occasional impatience with some of the conventions of genre. For example, I'm rather more interested in looking at the person seeing a ghost than in the ghost itself. At the end of it, narrative and character become the same thing, or should do, and I wouldn't want to subordinate one to the other in the way that genre writing, on the one hand, and literary fiction on the other, often do.

The books are consciously different from each other. Otherwise it would be like serving up the same dish every time you had friends over for dinner. That's another reason for writing at the edge of horror, fantasy, sf, etc, and though there is a trajectory to the novels I like to surprise myself by what emerges.

*   *   *

One effect of the commercial codification of the horror genre has been the increasing rarity of fiction which explores the metaphorical nature of supernatural themes. The genre's conventions dictate that a literally interpreted supernatural threat must be portrayed as disrupting an unquestioned "normal" reality. The work of Graham Joyce offers a compelling alternative to this outlook. Joyce's novels are profoundly supernatural in theme; but they use supernatural elements in the context of an exploration of human psychology, identity and belief. They could be described as metaphysical thrillers; but this does not convey their sensitive humanism or their poetic tone. Their essential darkness is not imposed by "horror" events, but is conveyed through the sense of dealing with matters of life and death.

Dreamside, Joyce's first novel, is about lucid dreaming: a dreamer's awareness of the dream state enabling him/her to direct events. A group of four students involved in a psychology experiment develop the ability to "meet" in their dreams, at a location which corresponds to an actual lake. After one of the group is raped and impregnated by another on "dreamside," the group breaks up. Ten years later, nightmares and violent "waking dreams" force the group back together to resolve this trauma, whose effects are destroying the lives of two of them. They find the real lake polluted and the "dreamside" one frozen over. In a crucial revelation, they see themselves trapped under the ice. *Dreamside* is an uneven, rather wordy novel, with too much dialogue; but its linking of supernatural elements to character emotions is both original and powerfully intense. The inner lives of the characters are lit up with a hallucinatory brightness. The portrayal of Brad, a guilt-corroded alcoholic, foreshadows many of the troubled men in Joyce's later work.

Dark Sister is a calmer, more conventionally structured novel; but its underlying sensibility is fiercely subversive. It's about the sexual politics and intrinsic spirituality of witchcraft. A family moves into an old house where Maggie, the wife, finds the concealed diary of a woman called Bella, who practised magic. Inspired by the diary, Maggie rebels against her husband's dictatorial authority; as her marriage deteriorates, she is haunted by images of a vicious old woman. She comes to see Bella's spirit as her mentor or "dark sister"; but behind Bella is the looming, malign presence of another woman. Maggie's husband, an archaeologist, finds evidence that a "witch" was horrifically mutilated, tortured and buried alive nearby. With help from a local herbalist, Maggie reaches back through time to release the trapped pain of Bella's "dark sister."

Dark Sister inverts the rhetoric of most "black magic" novels, attacking the violence and misogyny of Christian culture. Joyce looks to witchcraft as a positive expression of female sexuality and identity, the means by which Maggie discovers "her own, inner voice." Less a feminist novel than a humanist one, *Dark Sister* is really concerned with identifying spirituality outside the boundaries of the Judaeo-Christian tradition: in the realms of human instinct and its natural analogue, the wilderness. It's tempting to regard D. H. Lawrence as Graham Joyce's "dark brother."

The themes of sexuality and religious faith recur in Joyce's next two novels. *House of Lost Dreams* interprets the Orpheus myth as a statement about people's inability to deal with the power and intensity of their own dreams—that is, of their own true natures. There are few overtly supernatural events; rather, Joyce implies that the whole story has an occult substructure. An English couple undertake an extended stay on a small Greek island, where they experience troubled sleep and disturbing visions. It seems that the island is somehow an oracle which speaks through people. Through a visit from two shallow, manipulative English friends, the wife learns that the husband has had an affair. This precipitates a crisis in their relationship which is only resolved when the husband is led into the mountains by a local shepherd, who helps him to confront his own destructive nature (in the form of a violent angel) and tells him the island's ugly and tragic secret: that the house where the couple are staying was occupied by the foreign mistress of a local man, and that she was murdered by the local women out of jealousy. This fine, perceptive but by no means scary novel brings Joyce's recurrent obsessions to a fragile and guardedly optimistic resolution.

It is perhaps not surprising that Joyce's next novel, *Requiem*, examines the same issues in a darker and more explicit vein. It's set in Jerusalem, in the early stages of the (now largely destroyed) Middle East peace negotiations. After the death of his wife, an English schoolteacher (Tom) travels to Jerusalem to try to recover his mental balance and his Christian faith. What he finds is not only a theme park, full of spurious relics, but a war zone. Tom is haunted by a black-veiled apparition who gives him a scroll; he becomes passionately involved with a Jewish woman whose friend, an Arab scholar, translates the scroll. It contains evidence that early translators of the New Testament falsified the life of Jesus in order to pursue a misogynistic and anti-Semitic agenda. Tom has falsified his own life out of guilt, confessing to an affair (with a schoolgirl) which happened only in his fantasies, and planting false accusations against himself in the school. The story cul-

minates in gunfire and tragedy on the streets. Finally, Tom sees what has been implicit throughout: that the lies and divisions of Jerusalem represent those of the human heart. This magnificent, intensely disturbing novel focuses the emotional and religious conflicts which underlie Joyce's first three novels. Its refusal to offer any reassuring solution reflects the maturity of Joyce's outlook.

The Tooth Fairy is, on the face of it, a departure: a novel about childhood and adolescence in rural Warwickshire. But the protagonist's recurrent encounters with an amoral guardian spectre, the Tooth Fairy, give the story its underlying dialectic: the contradictions of sexuality and identity in the developing male psyche. As Sam's life develops through traumas, friendship, love and violence, the Tooth Fairy comes to represent the destructive obsessions which tear many lives apart; yet his struggle against the Tooth Fairy is also a process of learning to accept his own nature, and to balance his needs with those of the people around him. (Two of Joyce's short stories, "Under the Pylon" and "Last Rising Sun" [both 1992] sensitively depict the tensions and dangers of adolescence.) *The Tooth Fairy* contains some astonishing lyrical passages describing Sam's hallucinatory/supernatural encounters, as well as some chilling reminders of the grimmer aspects of real life. Along with *Requiem*, it confirms Joyce's status as a major figure on the literary side of the supernatural horror genre: one whose treatment of supernatural themes offers valuable insights into the human condition.

—Joel Lane

K

KALOGRIDIS, Jeanne (M.)

Pseudonym: J. M. Dillard. **Nationality:** American. **Born:** 1954.
Career: Teacher of English as a second language, American University, Washington, D.C.; freelance writer since the late 1980s.
Address: c/o Pocket Books, 1230 Avenue of the Americas, New York, NY 10020, USA.

HORROR, GHOST AND GOTHIC PUBLICATIONS

Novels (series: Diaries of the Family Dracul)

Specters (as J. M. Dillard). New York, Dell, 1991.
Covenant with the Vampire (Dracul). New York, Delacorte, and London, Headline, 1994.
Children of the Vampire (Dracul). New York, Delacorte, and London, Headline, 1995.
Lord of the Vampires (Dracul). London, Headline, and New York, Delacorte, 1996.

OTHER PUBLICATIONS

Novels as J. M. Dillard

Mindshadow. New York, Pocket, 1986; London, Titan, 1990.
Demons. New York, Pocket, 1986; London, Titan, 1991.
Bloodthirst. New York, Pocket, 1987; London, Titan, 1987.
War of the Worlds: The Resurrection (novelization of television script). New York, Pocket, and London, Titan, 1988.
Star Trek V: The Final Frontier (novelization of screenplay). New York, Pocket, and London, Grafton, 1989.
The Lost Years. New York, Pocket, 1989; London, Pan, 1990.
Star Trek VI: The Undiscovered Country (novelization of screenplay). New York and London, Pocket, 1992.
Emissary. New York and London, Pocket, 1993.
The Fugitive (novelization of screenplay). New York, Dell, and London, Signet, 1993.
Star Trek: Generations (novelization of screenplay). New York and London, Pocket, 1994.
Recovery. New York and London, Pocket, 1995.
Possession, with Kathleen O'Malley. New York and London, Pocket, 1996.
Star Trek: First Contact (novelization of screenplay). New York and London, Pocket, 1996.

Other

Star Trek: "Where No One Has Gone Before": A History in Pictures (as J. M. Dillard). New York and London, Pocket, 1994.

* * *

Although better known as J. M. Dillard for her *Star Trek* TV-series spinoff novels (into one of which, *Bloodthirst*, she introduced a vampire) and for her movie novelizations, Jeanne Kalogridis has chosen to publish a horror trilogy under her real name. These three books follow the fortunes of the Tsepesh family in the years leading up and including the events recounted in Bram Stoker's *Dracula*. She has kept close to the format of the latter, recounting the story as first-person entries in journals kept by the principal characters. She has also managed to capture much of Stoker's style but without the floridness of description prevalent at the time he was writing.

Covenant with the Vampire begins in 1845 as Arkady Tsepesh journeys back to his native Transylvania accompanied by his pregnant wife, Mary. Summoned by the imminent death of his father he arrives in time for the funeral. Expecting to take over the management of the Tsepesh estates on behalf of his elderly and reclusive Uncle Vlad, he quickly finds aspects he had not bargained for. Until now he has been sheltered from the knowledge of the true nature of his uncle (but which anyone even vaguely familiar with the original *Dracula* will have guessed) but gradually as he discovers first that his father's body has been mutilated and then a cache of severed heads in the woods, he is enlightened. It seems strange that he hadn't noticed anything peculiar during his upbringing—he left home as a young man to study in England. Perhaps it is a case of not noticing things which are familiar, since it is Mary who seems to be the more observant.

The covenant with the vampire, we discover, is that as long as Arkady and the local villagers do as Vlad requires neither Arkady's family or the villagers will be preyed upon by the vampire. They will supply him with strangers, then behead them to ensure no more vampires are created. Vlad, however, breaks the covenant by turning Arkady's crippled sister, Zsuzsanna, into a vampire. This gives Arkady the strength to break free and, as the first volume closes, his new-born son is being smuggled away by a potential victim while Mary and Arkady flee in the opposite direction to draw Vlad from the scent.

Covenant with the Vampire adds very little to the vampire myth, drawing heavily on Stoker's *Dracula* for much of its material. The second volume, *Children of the Vampire*, provides much greater scope for the author's imagination. The doctor who took Arkady's son to safety was Jan van Helsing who then married Mary and raised her son, and the waif they adopted, as his own children. Twenty-six years after the events of the first volume Jan dies and Arkady re-enters Mary's life. After his death at her hands, Vlad had transformed him into a vampire and he has spent his time keeping Vlad's agents from finding Mary and her son. Now they are too close and the family are in danger. The events that follow change Abraham van Helsing from dedicated physician to dedicated vampire-hunter, the role which Stoker assigned him. The difference is that Stoker's van Helsing seems to have only a superficial knowledge of vampires until he is called to treat Lucy Westenra, whereas Kalogridis's van Helsing is an accomplished and dedicated hunter. He is also a lot younger and Vlad has already been talking of relocating to England for a quarter of a century—and it is surprising he hasn't since the village beneath the castle has been deserted for a long time and it must be increasingly difficult to obtain sustenance.

The third volume, *Lord of the Vampires*, completes the series and provides a different slant to the events related in Stoker's novel. It begins with a reprise of the events that lead to Dracula becoming a vampire in the 15th century, then shifts rapidly to 1893. In the intervening 20 years van Helsing has killed a lot of vampires and weakened Dracula almost to the point where van Helsing could safely enter his lair and kill him. Before he can do this Dracula calls on an old friend, another immortal but not a blood-drinker. Elisabeth Bathory is an historical figure renowned for torturing and killing young women in the belief that by bathing in their blood she would remain forever young. In this novel she has achieved immortality and is able to strengthen Dracula enough so that he can complete his ambitions to relocate to London. Naturally, Elisabeth has a hidden agenda of her own and takes Zsuzsanna, Arkady Tsepesh's sister (and van Helsing's aunt) as her lover. She teaches Zsuzsanna that a number of the traits that identify a vampire, such as invisibility in mirrors, fear of sunlight, garlic and crucifixes, are true for Dracula only because his superstitious mind believes in them. They don't apply to Zsuzanna, so we find these two immortals venturing out in the daytime.

Kalogridis has tried to merge Stoker's novel with her own ideas by choosing extracts from different diaries; thus we discover what really happened to Jonathan Harker in Dracula's castle from the viewpoint of Zsuzsanna Tsepesh. In London we are privy to van Helsing's diary and discover a good deal of subterfuge—he was a guest of Dr. Seward in the asylum, along with his mad wife, at times when other characters believed him to be in Amsterdam, and his English, and knowledge of vampires, is far better than the diaries Stoker showed us led us to believe. Similarly, Dr. Seward, who in the original loved and lost Lucy Westenra, keeps two diaries, one that Stoker revealed in his novel, and a second which told the true sequence of events. While these strategies are important to make this novel fit seamlessly with the original it is bound to annoy purists who feel that classics should not be tampered with. This version does offer a different slant on the original but changes the focus of the original intention. Placed side by side, both show how attitudes have changed between the societies in which each has been written, and historically they make an interesting comparison.

—Pauline Morgan

KAY, Susan

Nationality: British. **Born:** 1953. **Family:** Married, with children. **Career:** Primary-school teacher; novelist. **Awards:** Georgette Heyer Historical Novel prize, 1986; Betty Trask award for novel, 1986; Boots/Romantic Novelists' Association award for novel, 1991. Lives in Cheshire.

HORROR, GHOST AND GOTHIC PUBLICATIONS

Novel

Phantom. London, Doubleday, 1990; New York, Delacorte, 1991.

OTHER PUBLICATIONS

Novel

Legacy. London, Random House, 1985; New York, Crown, 1986.

*   *   *

There have been many versions of *The Phantom of the Opera* since Gaston Leroux's novel of 1910 (1911 in its English translation). Leroux tried to persuade his readers that his story of a half-demented but very musical grotesque living as a "ghost" in the basements of the Paris Opera House was true. In fact only the building is real. The story has almost passed into folklore, outstripping any memory of Leroux himself and relying mostly on at least twelve films and a very successful stage musical for its enduring popularity.

What Susan Kay has tried to do is to take the Leroux story and extend it to cover the complete life of Erik, the Phantom, instead of only his last few months. The result is a big book (over 500 pages) and more than 65 years of events. But there are few surprises; given the character of Erik at the end of his life, his childhood, youth and earlier exploits are slightly more clichéd than one would hope but otherwise as expected. Kay has followed the Leroux line in steering clear of the supernatural; the horror here is physical and psychological.

Erik is born in 1831, in a small French village. His architect father has just been killed in a building-site accident. Everybody at Erik's birth is horrified by his facial deformity, including "sunken, mismatched eyes and grossly malformed lips, a horrible gaping hole where the nose should have been." His mother, Madeleine, is revolted by the sight of him, the midwife expects him to die, the maidservant leaves the house at once, and only the village priest has compassion.

Madeleine sews a face mask, and Erik wears a mask for most of the rest of his life. She does as little as possible for him, will not touch him or show him any affection, never takes him out of the house. He becomes a precocious child, a musical and architectural genius, but very disruptive. When he is nine he runs away, is captured by gypsies and put on show as a freak; they travel widely in France and Spain. From the gypsies he learns how to pick pockets and how to heal most ailments with infusions of herbs, but he hates being caged. At the age of twelve, faced with rape at the hands of his "owner," Javert, he kills him.

The next year he turns up in Rome and is lucky to be taken on as a sort of apprentice by Giovanni, an ageing master stonemason. He learns to do excellent work, earning Giovanni's trust and forming a bond with the man. This is the closest he ever comes to finding a family, for Giovanni is grooming Erik to take over his business. But Giovanni's daughter Luciana, an unstable girl usually cared for by nuns, comes home and falls in love with Erik. She demands that he should remove his mask, and when he does she is so shocked that she falls to her death. Erik moves on.

By the age of 19 he is making a good living as a magician (another of his early talents) in Russia. An offer of great wealth persuades him to travel to Persia to act as the entertainer to the Shah and his court. He forms a friendship with Nadir, the country's chief of police, who has been sent to fetch him, and he is delighted to be allowed to design and control the building of a new winter palace for the Shah.

After four years in Persia and another three wandering Europe, Erik is a rich man of 25—eccentric, twisted and lonely, having never known the love of a woman. He settles in Paris and is quickly drawn into the building of a new opera house. He makes himself known to the architect, Charles Garnier, who is happy to have Erik's artistic and financial help with the project. During the building, Erik makes himself a secret apartment in the sub-basement, a suite of sumptuously furnished rooms which can be reached only by boating across a subterranean lake. One of the rooms is a mirrored "torture chamber" which it is impossible to escape from without Erik's assistance. In addition, he constructs a warren of secret passages to enable himself to move about the inside of the opera house without being seen, for his mask always attracts attention and he prefers to keep away from public sight. In 1875, after nine years of construction and a war with Prussia, the Paris Opera House is opened. Erik lives quietly on the proceeds of blackmail, occasionally making his presence known to keep up the pretence of a ghost. The non-supernatural but gothic atmosphere of the opera house is one of the best aspects of the novel.

Only in 1881, when he is 50 and already suffering from (presumably) angina, does Erik first see and fall in love with Christine Daae, who closely resembles his mother and whose voice is potentially perfect. He spies on her through one-way mirrors, gives her much voice-coaching as an unseen "Angel of Music" and arranges for others to fall ill so that she gets the opportunity to display her talent in leading rôles. Christine reciprocates Erik's feelings of love—even when she meets him face to face, though he is too cynical to believe in this all the time. A problem is that Christine also loves her childhood sweetheart, Raoul, the Vicomte de Chagny. There is much vacillating all round, with promises made and broken, before Erik dies and Christine marries Raoul. But, as a tailpiece to the story makes clear, Raoul and Christine's son Charles is actually Erik's child.

The story is narrated, in turn, by Erik, Christine, Raoul, Madeleine, Giovanni and Nadir, but the characters remain shallow. Kay has researched her period and her countries, yet one still feels disappointed at a lack of interesting detail. Perhaps it is Erik's failure to interact with other characters for so much of his life that has removed a certain spark from the book. While the terrible nature of Erik's disfigurement is always present, while his behaviour is often unpleasant, and while his spying is sinister, this is not really a novel to be read for it its horror content. Nevertheless, it won an award as the best romantic novel of its year, and no doubt is capable of giving pleasure to many readers.

—Chris Morgan

KAYE, Marvin (Nathan)

Nationality: American. **Born:** Philadelphia, 1938. **Education:** Pennsylvania State University, B.A. in Liberal Arts, 1960, M.A. in Theatre and English Literature, 1962. **Career:** Adjunct Professor of Creative Writing, New York University, 21 years; Artistic Director, The Open Book (a New York theatre company), 21 years; senior editor, Harcourt, Brace, Jovanovich, 5 years. **Address:** c/o St. Martin's Press, 175 Fifth Avenue, New York, NY 10010, USA.

HORROR, GHOST AND GOTHIC PUBLICATIONS

Novels (series: Aubrey House)

A Cold Blue Light, with Parke Godwin (Aubrey House). New York, Berkley, 1983.
Ghosts of Night and Morning (Aubrey House). New York, Berkley, 1987.
Fantastique. New York, St. Martin's Press, 1992.

Short Stories

The Possession of Immanuel Wolf and Other Improbable Tales. New York, Doubleday, 1981.

Other

Editor, with Brother Theodore, *Brother Theodore's Chamber of Horrors.* New York, Pinnacle, 1975.
Editor, *Fiends and Creatures.* New York, Popular Library, 1975.
Editor, with Saralee Kaye, *Ghosts: A Treasury of Chilling Tales Old and New.* New York, Nelson Doubleday, 1981.
Editor, with Saralee Kaye, *Masterpieces of Terror and the Supernatural: A Treasury of Spellbinding Tales Old & New.* New York, Doubleday, 1985.
Editor, with Saralee Kaye. *Devils & Demons: A Treasury of Fiendish Tales Old & New.* New York, Doubleday, 1987.
Editor, with Saralee Kaye, *Weird Tales: The Magazine That Never Dies.* New York, Doubleday, 1988.
Editor, *Witches & Warlocks: Tales of Black Magic, Old & New.* New York, Guild America, 1990; as *The Penguin Book of Witches and Warlocks*, New York, Penguin, 1991.
Editor, *13 Plays of Ghosts and the Supernatural.* New York, Doubleday Book and Music Clubs, 1990.
Editor, with Saralee Kaye, *Haunted America: Star-Spangled Supernatural Stories.* New York, Guild America, 1991.
Editor, *Lovers and Other Monsters.* New York, Guild America, 1992.
Editor, *Sweet Revenge: 10 Plays of Bloody Murder.* New York, The Fireside Theatre, 1992.
Editor, *Masterpieces of Terror and the Unknown.* New York, Guild America, 1993.
Editor, *Angels of Darkness.* New York, Guild America, 1995.
Editor, *Resurrected Holmes.* New York, St. Martin's Press, 1996.
Editor, *Don't Open This Book!* New York, Doubleday Direct, 1997.
Editor, with John Betancourt. *The Best of Weird Tales, 1923 (The First Year).* Berkeley Heights, New Jersey, Bleak House, 1997.

OTHER PUBLICATIONS

Novels

A Lively Game of Death. New York, Saturday Review, 1972; London, Barker, 1974.
The Grand Ole Opry Murders. New York, Saturday Review, 1974.
Bullets for Macbeth. New York, Saturday Review, 1976; London, Hale, 1978.
The Laurel and Hardy Murders. New York, Dutton, 1977; London, Curley, 1978.
My Son, the Druggist. New York, Doubleday, 1977.
The Masters of Solitude, with Parke Godwin. New York, Doubleday, 1978.
My Brother, the Druggist. New York, Doubleday, 1979.
The Incredible Umbrella. New York, Doubleday, 1979.
The Amorous Umbrella. New York, Doubleday, 1981.
The Soap Opera Slaughters. New York, Doubleday, 1982.
Wintermind, with Parke Godwin. New York, Doubleday, 1982.

*

Critical Study: "Marvin Kaye: Ghosts, Anthologies, *Fantastique*, and a Calendar of Petite Murders" by Darrell Schweitzer, *Science Fiction Chronicle*, Vol. 14, No. 1. (November 1992).

*   *   *

Marvin Kaye's horror fiction represents only a small part of a richly varied career. He has published numerous mystery novels (*Bullets for Macbeth*, etc.), some science fiction (*The Masters of Solitude* and *Wintermind*, both with Parke Godwin), and a larger body of satirical and humorous fiction, most notably the novels *The Incredible Umbrella* and its sequel *The Amorous Umbrella* which are among the best modern continuations of the *Unknown Worlds* tradition of wacky, rationalistic fantasy typified by de Camp and Pratt's *The Incomplete Enchanter*. He has also written books on magic, edited two fat anthologies of Sherlockiana, plus the definitive edition of *Dracula*. He has written, acted in, and directed plays (also singing in *The Hoboken Chicken Emergency*, a comic operetta based on a book by Daniel Pinkwater). He has also done some film work.

The first of Kaye's two Aubrey House novels, *A Cold Blue Light*, a collaboration with Parke Godwin, is a lyrical haunted-house story in the tradition of Shirley Jackson's *The Haunting of Hill House*. Professional investigators intrude into a thoroughly haunted manse. Each of the investigators has his or her own secrets and hidden agendas. So does the house. The results are considerably bloodier than, at least, the investigators were expecting. In the sequel, *Ghosts of Night and Morning*, the sole survivor of the original party is finagled back to the scene by his publisher, who hopes this will inspire a suitable ending to the book the fellow is writing about the first disastrous venture. Murders follow, as another cast of characters gropes to achieve new and old agendas, and the secrets of Aubrey House are unearthed, along with at least a hypothesis explaining the unnatural phenomenon of the "cold blue light," which is supposedly the source of all the trouble. But Kaye, without his collaborator Godwin, is more inclined toward clever plot twists and atmospherics. The tone is different from the first book. *Ghosts of Night and Morning* seems almost, at times, to be a particularly convoluted mystery novel. It has less awe and wonder, but, certainly, plenty of suspense. Indeed, the last few chapters offer a veritable avalanche of Hitchcockian developments: lost letters, hidden tunnels, missing relatives, identity switches, and virtually everybody turning out to be other than they seem. The supernatural element is downplayed. While it may not be the author's intention, it is possible to interpret the "ghostly" elements in purely psychological terms.

Indeed, this borderline between the supernatural and the rationally-explicable is precisely the region the Aubrey House novels most fruitfully explore. They are latter-day continuations of the Carnacki or John Silence school of psychic-investigation story, making use of the terminology and lore of contemporary psychical research, but without anything which could possibly be accused of being New Age credulity. In one sense, these books are almost science fiction: disciplined speculations into fringe science. In addition to making much use of the concept of a haunted house as a psychic "battery" (which retains the emotional residue, but not necessarily intelligence of its former inhabitants), both books feature scenes of out-of-body travel. Kaye seems to be well up on contemporary research on the subject. (For an enlightening

glimpse of Kaye's own attitudes and beliefs regarding such matters, see his essay "Ralph" in *The Possession of Immanuel Wolf*.)

Out-of-body experiences figure largely in Kaye's most ambitious novel, *Fantastique*, which is based on his extensive theatre career and on Hector Berlioz's *Symphonie Fantastique*, in which the composer imagines that he has murdered his beloved and gone to Hell. Musical parallels permeate the book and dictate much of its structure. There are, indeed, vast layers of meaning in *Fantastique* which are likely to be opaque to the musically illiterate. Kaye describes the symphonic nature of the book in considerable detail in his 1992 interview in *Science Fiction Chronicle*. Fortunately, he is a sufficiently capable novelist to keep the book working on many levels at once, so even the musically illiterate will find *Fantastique* worth reading. The protagonist is an *enfant terrible* theatre director, who marries a superstar actress, becomes involved, very destructively with someone else, and begins to experience increasingly frightening out-of-body journeys at the same time. A descent into Hell and madness follows, and the hero tries to rescue his *belle dame sans merci* from her own, possibly terminal out-of-body wanderings, with echoes of Dante and techniques reminiscent of Alfred Bester. The result is a vivid, explosive, demanding novel, quite unlike anything else published in the horror field at the time. It is a genuine original, not part of a predictable demographic curve.

Kaye's short fiction tends to be whimsical rather than horrific. The title novella of his one collection, a collaboration with performer Brother Theodore (whom Kaye describes as a "macabre monologist") is about an elderly Jew possessed by the *dybbuk* of Hitler, which is certainly a horrific situation, but it seems rushed and is far less impressive than any of the novels.

Kaye's anthologies are thoroughly research compilations of new and old ghostly and horrific material, very solidly done. They could serve to educate a whole generation readers into the possibilities of the field, rather as Fraser and Wise (of *Great Tales of Terror and the Supernatural* fame) and August Derleth did in decades gone by.

—Darrell Schweitzer

KELLEHER, Victor (Michael Kitchener)

Pseudonym: Veronica Hart. **Nationality:** British. **Born:** London, 19 July 1939. **Education:** University of Natal, Pietermaritzburg, B.A. in English 1962; University of St. Andrews, Fife, Dip. Ed. 1963; University of the Witwatersrand, Johannesburg, B.A. (honours) 1969; University of South Africa, Pretoria, M.A. 1970, D.Litt. et Phil. 1973. **Family:** Married Alison Lyle in 1962; one son and one daughter. **Career:** Junior lecturer in English, University of the Witwatersrand, 1969; lecturer, then senior lecturer, in English, University of South Africa, 1970-73; lecturer in English, Massey University, Palmerston North, New Zealand, 1973-76; senior lecturer, 1976-84, and associate professor of English, 1984-87, University of New England, Armidale, New South Wales. **Awards:** Patricia Hackett prize, for short story, 1978; Australia Council fellowship, 1982, 1989; Australian Children's Book of the Year award, 1983, 1987; Australian Science Fiction Achievement award, 1984; Australian Peace prize, 1989. **Address:** 149 Wigram Road, Glebe, New South Wales 2037, Australia.

HORROR, GHOST AND GOTHIC PUBLICATIONS

Novels

The Green Piper. Melbourne, Viking Kestrel, 1984; London, Viking Kestrel, 1985.

Baily's Bones. Melbourne, Viking Kestrel, 1988; New York, Dial Press, 1989.

Del-Del. London, MacRae, 1991; New York, Walker, 1992.

Double God (as Veronica Hart). Port Melbourne, Mandarin/Reed, 1994.

The House That Jack Built (as Veronica Hart). Port Melbourne, Mandarin/Reed, 1994.

Storyman. Sydney, Random House, 1996.

OTHER PUBLICATIONS

Novels

Voices from the River. London, Heinemann, 1979.

The Beast of Heaven. St. Lucia, University of Queensland Press, 1984.

Em's Story. St. Lucia, University of Queensland Press, 1988.

Wintering. St. Lucia, University of Queensland Press, 1990.

Novels for Children

Forbidden Paths of Thual, illustrated by Antony Maitland. London, Kestrel, 1979.

The Hunting of Shadroth. London, Kestrel, 1981.

Master of the Grove. London, Kestrel, 1982.

Papio. London, Kestrel, 1984.

Taronga. Melbourne, Viking Kestrel, 1986; London, Hamish Hamilton, 1987.

The Makers. Melbourne, Viking Kestrel, 1987.

The Red King. Melbourne, Viking Kestrel, 1989; New York, Dial Press, 1990.

Brother Night. London, MacRae, 1990; New York, Walker, 1991.

To the Dark Tower. Sydney, Random House, and London, MacRae, 1992.

Parkland. Melbourne, Viking, 1994; London, Viking, 1995.

The Beast of Heaven (young-adult version). St. Lucia, University of Queensland Press, 1995.

Earthsong. Melbourne, Viking, 1995.

Fire Dancer. Melbourne, Viking, 1996.

Short Stories

Africa and After. Brisbane, University of Queensland Press, 1983; as *The Traveller*, 1987.

*　　*　　*

Victor Kelleher is difficult to categorize as a writer. He writes both for children and adults and moves between genre and mainstream fiction. His young adult novels are mainly genre fiction, ranging across high fantasy, contemporary fantasy, science fiction, horror/terror, dark fantasy, and fable. Until recently his adult work has been mainly mainstream literary fiction, but he has lately begun to explore horror in adult novels under a pseudonym and is now beginning to publish this work under his own name. In fact, Kelleher has never shied away from horror and terror, and there have been elements of it in his work since his early young-adult fantasy novels.

This is most strongly evident in his second children's book, *The Hunting of Shadroth*, which is a quest-style fantasy set in an imaginary prehistoric land, where a monster known to the people as "Shadroth" terrorises the hunter-gather tribe and kills its victims by freezing them. Ultimately, the monster is defeated but the book maintains a high level of fear and tension and can easily be read as horror. A number of Kelleher's other fantasies such as *The Forbidden Paths of Thual* (winner of the 1982 West Australian Young Readers' Book Award) and *Master of the Grove* (winner of the 1983 Australian Children's Book of the Year), which both have a medieval feel, also have threads of horror running through them.

Kelleher's young-adult book, *The Green Piper*, was his first full horror novel. In fact it was the first-ever Australian children's horror novel, although it was not marketed as such. It is a mysterious, menacing book loosely based on a contemporary "Pied Piper" theme. An inexplicable flash of light in the night sky heralds the arrival of a stranger, and a soft, haunting melody is heard drifting through the woodland. At first birds and animals are attracted to the music, but then it starts to affect people too, and a sinister and bewildering tale unfolds. It is a well told, gripping book with strong characters.

After *The Green Piper* Kelleher wrote two straight science-fiction books with few, if any, horror elements. But *Baily's Bones*, which followed, is an effective ghost/horror novel, a frightening contemporary story of possession with links to Australia's aboriginal and convict past, a past full of violence and death. A family discovers some old bones in a gully on their farm which turn out to be the remains of a crazed old convict. Following this, the youngest of the children becomes possessed and the horrors of the past are unleashed on an unsuspecting community. *Baily's Bones* was the first work of children's horror to come close to winning a major Australian literary prize when it became the joint runner-up for the South Australian Festival Award.

Kelleher returned to high fantasy with *The Red King* and *Brother Night* which were both short-listed for the Children's Book of the Year. Both contain small elements of horror. *Del-Del*, which followed, is Kelleher's third horror novel and was short-listed for both the Carnegie Medal and the Australian Children's Book of Year Award for Older Readers. *Del-Del* is a kind of mystery/suspense, terror/horror novel. Kelleher describes it as a novel which "employs psychological terror and also plays with a deep sense of mystery." It is a tale of possession about a young boy who becomes inhabited by a an evil murderous spirit called Del-Del, a theme which Kelleher previously explored in *Baily's Bones*. Del-Del is, however, more a taut psychological thriller than a supernatural horror novel, and foreshadows Kelleher's later adult horror work.

Under the pseudonym "Veronica Hart," Kelleher published *Double God*, a suspenseful terror/horror novel which marked a new turn in his writing for adults. *Double God* is a psychological horror novel relying on strong narrative drive and a heightened sense of suspense. It was marketed as a thriller "in the tradition of Mary Higgins Clark" although there is little in common here with Clark. The horror begins when a 15-year-old girl retreats inside her mind after an incident with a dog while she was babysitting a young child. The girl goes to the country with her family, but the house they purchase has a dark legacy of its own. The story is well-plotted, with plenty of twists culminating in an unexpected terrifying climax.

The second Kelleher "Hart" novel, *The House That Jack Built*, is similar in style to *Double God*, driven once again by Kelleher's sheer story-telling ability. A séance at a drunken party apparently draws the ghost of Jack the Ripper from his grave and a woman and her teenage daughter find themselves in the middle of a series of brutal murders. The third novel in the sequence, *Storyman*, a crime novel, this time published under Kelleher's own name, is about a serial killer whose crimes are based on popular nursery stories. Here the horror element is maintained entirely through psychological suspense without any form of supernatural intervention. These books are consciously more commercial than any of Kelleher's other adult work. They are slick and fast-paced, building their tension with a strong whodunnit element combined with suspense and mounting terror. For the most part these are psychological horror books, even though some contain supernatural elements, drawing the reader in by their deep sense of mystery.

Kelleher is one of Australia's finest fantasists. He writes strong, original, accessible prose which works on multiple levels. On the surface his stories are compelling and adventurous, but at the same time many have deeper levels of meaning, examining the human condition and human relationships, showing great respect for animals and environment. His horror tends to explore fear and terror, utilizing science fiction, fantasy and crime to maintain suspense and mystery. Although much of this work is published for young adults, it can be read and enjoyed by teenagers and adults alike.

—Steven Paulsen and Sean McMullen

KELLER, David H(enry)

Pseudonym: Henry Cecil. **Nationality:** American. **Born:** Philadelphia, Pennsylvania, 23 December 1880. **Education:** University of Philadelphia Medical School. **Military Service:** Served as a physician working in shell-shock during World War I; medical professor on the faculty of the Army Chaplain's School at Harvard University, Cambridge, Massachusetts, during World War II. **Family:** Married in 1903. **Career:** Physician, specializing in psychoanalysis; junior physician, Illinois Mental Institute, after 1915, and worked in other hospitals in Louisiana, Tennessee, and Pennsylvania; editor, *Sexology* and *Your Body* in the 1930s. **Died:** 13 July 1966.

HORROR, GHOST AND GOTHIC PUBLICATIONS

Novels

The Solitary Hunters, and The Abyss: Two Fantastic Novels. Philadelphia, New Era, 1948.

Short Stories

The Thing in the Cellar. Millheim, Pennsylvania, Bizarre Series, 1940.
Life Everlasting, and Other Tales of Science, Fantasy, and Horror, edited by Sam Moskowitz and Will Sykora. Newark, New Jersey, Avalon, 1947.

Tales from Underwood. Sauk City, Wisconsin, Arkham House, 1952.
The Folsom Flint, and Other Curious Tales. Sauk City, Wisconsin, Arkham House, 1969.
The Last Magician: Nine Stories from Weird Tales, edited by Patrick H. Adkins. New Orleans, P.D.A. Enterprises, 1978.

OTHER PUBLICATIONS

Novels

The Sign of the Burning Hart: A Tale of Arcadia. St. Lo, France, Imprimerie de la Manche, 1938; Hollywood, National Fantasy Fan Federation, 1948.
The Devil and the Doctor. New York, Simon and Schuster, 1940.
The Eternal Conflict. Philadelphia, Prime Press, 1949.
The Homunculus. Philadelphia, Prime Press, 1949.
The Lady Decides. Philadelphia, Prime Press, 1950.
The Human Termites: A 1929 Science Fiction Extravaganza. New Orleans, P.D.A. Enterprises, 1979.

Short Stories

The Thought Projector. New York, Stellar, 1929.
Wolf Hollow Bubbles. Jamaica, New York, Arra Printers, 1934(?).
Men of Avalon. Everett, Pennsylvania, Fantasy, 1935(?).
The Waters of Lethe. Great Barrington, Massachusetts, Kirby, 1937.
The Television Detective. Los Angeles, Los Angeles Science Fiction League, 1938.
The Final War. Portland, Oregon, Perri Press, 1949.
A Figment of a Dream. Baltimore, Mirage Press, 1962.

Poetry

Songs of a Spanish Lover (as Henry Cecil). Alexandria, Louisiana, Wall Printing Co., 1924.

Other

The Kellers of Hamilton Township: A Study in Democracy. Alexandria, Louisiana, Wall Printing Co., 1922.
The Sexual Education Series. New York, Popular Book Corporation, 10 vols., 1928.
Know Yourself! Life and Sex Facts of Man, Woman, and Child. New York, Popular Book Corporation, 1930.
Portfolio of Anatomical Manikins. New York, Sparacio, 1932.
Picture Stories of the Sex Life of Man and Woman: 317 Simple Instructions Explaining How Sex Functions in Human Beings. New York, Popular Medicine, 1941.

*   *   *

David H. Keller's literary work extends across the whole spectrum of imaginative fiction. He achieved his greatest popularity as an early recruit to Hugo Gernsback's science-fiction pulps, and it was small presses associated with the science-fiction field which issued most of his books, but it is arguable that his most interesting work falls into the neighbouring genres of fantasy and weird fiction. As a writer of horror fiction he made significant use of his training in psychiatric medicine; his most powerful stories are those which describe in relatively matter-of-fact terms the affliction of hapless individuals by delusions of various kinds—delusions whose cruelty can sometimes only be accurately measured by uninvolved observers.

Eight tales of this kind are gathered under the subheading "The Psychiatrist" in Keller's best collection, *Tales from Underwood*. They include the harrowing *conte cruel* "A Piece of Linoleum," whose fussy female narrator cannot understand how she drove her husband to suicide; the terrible delusory fantasy "The Dead Woman," in which a man becomes erroneously convinced that his wife is dead; and an oft-replicated tale of an imaginary monster whose non-existence is no barrier to lethal effect, "The Thing in the Cellar." The science-fiction section of the same collection includes "The Worm," a story as readily submissible to Freudian interpretation as the author's painstakingly elaborate dream-fantasy *The Eternal Conflict*, which also exhibits his enduring fascination with gargantuan creepy-crawlies. Several garish science-fiction stories about monstrous insects—including the melodramatic novels *The Human Termites* and *The Solitary Hunters*—might be reckoned among the most horrific things he ever wrote were they not so ham-fisted in their execution.

Although Keller did write several notable non-horrific fantasies all the stories in *Tales from Underwood* which are placed under the rubric of "The Fantaisiste" are disturbing weird tales. The most effective of them are rooted in sexual fantasy, notable among them the sado-masochistic tale of "The Bridle" and a deceptively delicate account of a dissatisfied wife wooed by Pan, "The Golden Bough." The horror stories in *Life Everlasting*—which was assembled later, although it reached print sooner because *Tales of Underwood*'s prospective publisher, Arkham House, ran into difficulties—are much less effective than those in the more substantial collection, although the psychoanalytic allegories "Heredity" and "The Face in the Mirror" are interesting in spite of their relative orthodoxy.

The second story in *The Solitary Hunters, and The Abyss*, which was original to that volume, would probably have been considered too indecent for magazine publication at the time of its composition by virtue of its assumptions about the motivational wellsprings of human nature. The lever of the plot is a chewing-gum laced with a powerful drug which releases its users from all the inhibitions of everyday social life. The gum is released in New York by its experimentally-inclined developer in order to demonstrate the fragility of civilized mores. The resulting slide into gaudily violent and sexually-uninhibited savagery owes something to Jung's account of the archetypes of the collective unconscious, although is primary inspiration derives from Freud's later works—especially *Civilization and its Discontents* and *Totem and Taboo*. The "result" of the thought-experiment, as summarized by its instigator, imply that an understanding of such historical phenomena as Fascism and war cannot be achieved without an understanding of the unconscious—but the summary also strikes a surprisingly querulous note in suggesting that the delving has, in fact, gone deeper than was altogether wise. "The Abyss" remains the most striking and most intriguing of all Keller's works, although it is as much a commentary on the substance and underlying psychology of horror fiction as a horror story *per se*.

Keller was always half-hearted in his attempts to publish his writings commercially, perhaps because of disappointments associated with Simon & Schuster's apparent withdrawal, in the face of criticism, of his bold exercise in literary Satanism *The Devil and the Doctor*. When Hugo Gernsback moved out of pulp fiction into the field of popular sexology Keller went with him, and virtually ceased to function as a professional fiction writer. Occasional works which were not produced with the pulps in mind often languished in manuscript or appeared in obscure amateur publications. Although *The Folsom Flint* had to reprint "The Thing in the Cellar," "The Dead Woman" and "A Piece of Linoleum" in order to compensate for the evident fact that it was raking through the dregs of Keller's production it does contain some interesting materials from amateur sources. These include the title story, about a skull given the means to talk, and the striking Freudian allegory "The Golden Key"

Oddly enough, however, when *The Folsom Flint* appeared numerous unreprinted Keller stories were still to be found in the pages of *Weird Tales*; nine of these were subsequently gathered into the slim collection *The Last Magician*. They are more orthodoxly melodramatic than Keller's better-known tales, but they do include one thoroughly typical *conte cruel*, "Bindings Deluxe," and two fabulously graphic exaggerations of sexual anxiety: "The Damsel and the Cat" and "The Little Husbands." Still unreprinted in book form *en masse*—although one or two have been anthologized—is a series of grotesque quasi-folkloristic stories set in Cornwall. Keller presumably hoped to gather them into a collection when the opportunity presented itself, but it never did.

Keller's prose style is calculatedly naive, and seems to some readers to be unbearably crude, but when it is well-suited to his material—as it is in the best of his *contes cruels* and the most vivid of his Freudian allegories—it is capable of formulating works that are fascinating as well as highly idiosyncratic. His was always a distinctive narrative voice, and he deserves some credit for his determination to explore—albeit tentatively—ideative avenues in whose murky shade others were reluctant to tread. The worst examples of his pulp hackwork are very bad indeed but his best and most heartfelt tales can still generate an authentic frisson by virtue of the palpable honesty of their conviction that the surfaces of human behaviour conceal dark and libidinous depths.

—Brian Stableford

KENNETT, Rick

Nationality: Australian. **Born:** Melbourne, Australia, 11 January 1956. **Education:** Kensington Primary School, Melbourne, 1962-67; Essendon Technical School, Melbourne, 1968; Williamstown Technical School, Melbourne, 1968-71. **Career:** Apprentice fitter and turner, 1972-75; motor-cycle courier, from 1976; contributor of short stories to horror, fantasy and science-fiction magazines and anthologies from 1979; editorial assistant, *Australian SF Writers News*, Melbourne, 1992-94. **Address:** PO Box 118, Pascoe Vale South, 3044, Australia.

HORROR, GHOST AND GOTHIC PUBLICATIONS

Novel

Abracadabra. Canada, Ghost Story Society, 1997.

Short Stories

The Reluctant Ghost-Hunter. Chester, Cheshire, Haunted Library, 1991.

472 Cheyne Walk: Carnacki: The Untold Stories, with A. F. Kidd. Liverpool, England, Ghost Story Society, 1992.

Other Publications

Novel

A Warrior's Star. Melbourne, Alternative Production Company, 1982.

*   *   *

Rick Kennett is primarily recognized as ghost-story writer, although his early work was science fiction, and he still returns to the form occasionally. The influences of M. R. James and William Hope Hodgson are evident in his work, which has been widely published in various magazines and anthologies in Australia and the UK. He is perhaps best known for his "Ernie Pine" stories, tales of a motorbike-riding "reluctant ghost-hunter," but Kennett has also authored a number of William Hope Hodgson "Carnacki" pastiches, and numerous stand-alone short stories.

Kennett's interest in the works of William Hope Hodgson led to the publication of *472 Cheyne Walk* (co-authored with English writer A. F. "Chico" Kidd), a booklet of "Carnacki the Ghost-Finder" stories published by the Ghost Story Society. Kennett's contribution to the collection are: "The Silent Garden" in which Carnacki is asked by a prominent botanist to investigate the peculiar silence haunting his garden of rare flowers; "The Steeple Monster" (with Chico Kidd) where Carnacki investigates the bell-tower of a rural church after the new steeple-keeper inexplicable vanishes. In these stories Kennett successfully captures the feel of Hodgson's original stories, both in the characterization and plot-style.

In a sense, Kennett's Ernie Pine character is also derivative of his interest in Carnacki, as both are ghost-hunters. The similarity ends there, however, because unlike Carnacki, Pine is a very Australian smart-alec while a reluctant ghost hunter. These stories have thus far been published separately, although three of the tales were published in a booklet, *The Reluctant Ghost-Hunter* (1991), by Rosemary Pardoe's Haunted Library. The Ernie Pine sequence consists of the following tales. In "The Roads of Donnington" (1984) Pine is asked to investigate a phantom motorcyclist haunting a country town, only to find himself on the very bike the dead man rides. In "Alley Ghost" (1988) children ask Pine to "kill" the frog-eyed ghost haunting their back yard. In "Strange Fruit" (1989) Ernie holds an all-night vigil in a second-hand bookshop haunted by poltergeist activity. In "The Impromptu Seance" (1991) Pine finds traces of amateur magic in a launderette which has invited something dangerous into one of the washing machines. In "Time in a Rice Bowl" Pine's niece has turned into an ancient Chinaman and disappeared into the ghost of a house long since demolished. In "Dead Air" (1992) while working at a public radio station Pine comes up against an evil magician intent on bringing inter-dimensional monsters through a portal in the space occupied by the station. In "The Outsider" (1992) while on a motor-cycle tour of England Pine has a collision with the Earl of Woolsthorpe's Rolls Royce and finds himself investigating an ancient haunting. This last story was reprinted by Karl Edward Wagner in his *Year's Best Horror* anthology series.

In "The Seas of Castle Hill Road" (1992) while staying with a friend in Queensland Ernie Pine hears the sound of sea surging through the windows at night even though he is 40 kilometres from the coast. "Big Magic" (1994) is actually an extract from Kennett's Ernie Pine novel, *Abracadabra*, where Pine breaks into an antique shop with the best intentions, but finds himself in the shop as it was in 1914. The strength of the Ernie Pine stories is the Pine character himself, and more than one critic has suggested Ernie Pine is Rick Kennett—who is a long-time motorcycle rider. At the same time the stories show originality of plot, and though they are often chilling, they maintain a fun sense of humour.

The novel featuring Ernie Pine, *Abracadabra*, tells of an enchanted remnant from World War I, and its protective spells which are being activated by contact with the dead in modern Australia. There are some spine-tingling scenes, especially where a giant spectral hand is spidering down the road at night after Ernie and his bike. Also fascinating is when he and his friends are attacked by sharks in their living room. *Abracadabra* is a supernatural horror novel, without splatter or gore, and relying instead on atmosphere and the quiet chills of the unknown. Nevertheless, it moves at a compelling pace. There is a risk, however, that readers who are unfamiliar with the Ernie Pine character will not get as much from this book as readers who have already read the short stories.

On occasion Kennett stretches genre boundaries with interesting and often successful results. "The Battle of Leila the Dog," "Kindred Spirits" and "On Sherman's Planet" are all science-fiction stories on the one hand and ghost stories on the other. Other Kennett horror stories of note are: "Isle of the Dancing Dead" (1991), an ingenious but sad ghost story in which a young grave-digger tries to disprove a legendary curse. "Log Recording Found in a Dead Man's Gut" (1991) is a frightening tale of gremlins in space. "The Wilcroft Inheritance (1997), written with Paul Collins, is a Gothic ghost story.

Kennett's ghost and horror stories have yet to be collected in a single authoritative volume, but are worth hunting up in anthologies such as *The Fontana Books of Great Ghost Stories*, *After Midnight Stories*, *Terror Australis*, *Strange Fruit* and *Gothic Ghosts*. His style is readable and his plots are original, and Kennett is really the only Australian writer to have produced a substantial body of work in the ghost-story field.

—Steven Paulsen and Sean McMullen

KERRUISH, Jessie Douglas

Nationality: British. **Born:** Near Hartlepool, County Durham, 1884. **Career:** Contributor to various British pulp magazines from the 1900s, and to anthology series of the 1930s. Suffered chronic ill-health in later life. **Awards:** Hodder and Stoughton First Novel prize, 1917. **Died:** 1949.

Horror, Ghost and Gothic Publications

Novel

The Undying Monster: A Tale of the Fifth Dimension. London, Heath Cranton, 1922; New York, Macmillan, 1936.

OTHER PUBLICATIONS

Novels

Miss Haroun al-Raschid. London, Hodder and Stoughton, 1917.
The Girl from Kurdistan. London, Hodder and Stoughton, 1918.

Short Stories

The Raksha Rajah; or, The King of the Ogres (for children). London, n.p., n.d. (1911?).
Babylonian Nights' Entertainments: A Selection of Narratives from the Text of Certain Undiscovered Cuneiform Tablets. London, Archer, 1934.

*

Film Adaptation: *The Undying Monster,* 1943.

* * *

There is, surely, no more lowering an example of "what-might-have-been" in the field of supernatural and weird literature than the case of Jessie Douglas Kerruish, who created an authentic, undisputed, and much-lauded (even, unusually in this genre, at the time of first publication) masterpiece of the macabre, yet who ended her career in pain, near-blindness and almost total obscurity.

The tragic irony is that photographs of Kerruish in her 20s, when she had just begun writing, show an eupeptic and determined young woman with an engaging seriousness of mien (a younger version of the Bluestocking novelist Beatrice Harraden, even down to her wire-rimmed spectacles), who looks as though the literary world—and perhaps not just the literary world—is about to roll on its back and kick its legs in the air in front of her.

Kerruish's *oeuvre* is by no means fixed and immutable. She seems to have been fairly productive just prior to the Great War, certainly in the matter of short stories, although her main market was one that, due to an accident of history (the *Luftwaffe* fire-bombs that, in 1941, destroyed quantities of periodicals held by the British Museum) will probably now never be exhaustively researched. The earliest work noted so far is a short children's fantasy, "Lancelot James and the Dragon," which appeared in the *Novel Magazine* in 1907. This imaginative re-creation of the "old woman who swallowed a fly" theme is skillfully handled, implying an already professional status at the age of only 23. It may well be that, like a good many young and aspiring novelists at a time when there was a positive glut of markets, Kerruish was an old, or at any rate old-ish, hand at periodical publication. Only two years before, the *Novel* had undergone a complete editorial makeover, becoming, in its present form, a multi-story magazine aimed at a general audience; prior to 1905, however, it had been *The Lady's Magazine,* with a preponderance of good first- and second-line women writers (Rosalie Neish and Nellie Blissett; Alice Williamson, Anna Katherine Green and Mary E. Wilkins from America; the prolific L. G. Moberly); Kerruish may well have cut her literary teeth in its columns.

Whatever the case, a year or so into the second decade of the century, she fell under the energizing influence of Isabel Thorne who, though working for one of the less grand Fleet Street outfits, Shurey's Publications, may be considered to be one of the superlative short-fiction editors of the first 30-odd years of this century. The periodicals under her control—mainly the *Weekly Tale-Teller* and the legendary (because virtually its entire run vanished in the *Luftwaffe* firestorms) *Yes or No,* but such lilac-atmosphered trifles as *Smart Fiction* and *Dainty Novels,* not to mention *Sketchy Bits,* as well—flourished mightily in the decade before the Great War. Thorne was a hugely skilled, hands-on editor who knew precisely what she wanted and precisely what her section of the market wanted; she was especially adroit at cajoling rising stars and interesting eccentrics away from the big publishers every now and then, at no huge expense—Sax Rohmer, Rafael Sabatini, Jack London, Guy Thorne, Louis Tracy and M. P. Shiel all adorned her columns. Her triumph was Edgar Wallace. She recognized before all other Fleet Street editors that Wallace's real genius lay not in journalism but in characterful fiction: it is arguable that had it not been for Isabel Thorne, Wallace might never have created his immensely popular, and influential, "Sanders of the River" series (the stories in the initial four volumes of which first saw life in the *Weekly Tale-Teller*).

It is clear that Kerruish wrote busily for Thorne. Those stories that are extant—mainly her *Weekly Tale-Teller* appearances—exhibit all the accomplishments of the practiced writer: a fine sense of place, and pace, a knack for speakable dialogue and, above all, sure-footed and skilful plotting. By 1915 she was writing for Thorne not only excellent 20,000-word novellas of both contemporary and historical adventure but, in "Babylonian Nights' Entertainments," a series (collected in book form in 1934, as her final published work) of Arabian semi-fantasies launched with a humorous twist (unlike the Sultana Scheherezade, who told tales to keep her homicidal husband awake, the storytellers in Kerruish's series are trying to put Nebuchadnezzar to sleep, since the Lord of the Four Quarters of the World has a terrible case of insomnia).

One of the genres for which Thorne had a distinct, indeed greedy, appetite was the supernatural, fed to a greater or lesser extent by most of her regular authors (including Wallace, who even penned a couple of Sanders weirds). Kerruish wrote one or two light or humorous fantasies, including "Morad and the Magic Mirror" (*Weekly Tale-Teller,* 18 September 1915), which involves, almost parenthetically, a sorcerer and a form of "skrying mirror" whose message is misinterpreted. The one authentic horror story, however, which seems to have survived from this period is "The Swaying Vision" (*Weekly Tale-Teller,* 16 January 1915), a quite superb tale which features a psychic detective, cannibalism, a spar taken from the raft of the frigate *Medusa,* and scenes of genuine grue.

It may perhaps be thought that this is a unique tale, standing in splendid isolation—save that all of Kerruish's work at this time has much the same descriptive power and superior quality of plotting and writing. Indeed, such is the mastery of form manifested in the tale that it can hardly be the case that "The Swaying Vision" is merely an impressive "one-off." Locating more of the same, however, has proved a problem (one can only wryly conjecture at the kind of material she almost certainly turned out for *Yes or No*).

Kerruish was now ready to master another form, that of the novel. She did this triumphantly, winning the Hodder & Stoughton "First Novel" £1,000-pound prize with *Miss Haroun al-Raschid,* quickly following it with *The Girl from Kurdistan.* Both are absorbing and pacey romantic adventure yarns set mainly in the Near and Middle East, and there seems every likelihood that Kerruish herself visited the region at some stage—perhaps lived there for a while—possibly around 1910. Her descriptions of the area in both novels and short stories—flora, fauna; princes, merchants, beggars, thieves; bustling *souks* and caravanserais; archaeological digs—and the often intimate background detail, do not at all read like midnight muggings-up from selected travel books or judicious swipings from Wallace Budge.

Her next novel, notoriously, ran a multi-rejection gauntlet before final acceptance and publication in 1922. It is easy to see why, and doubtless those library subscribers who had read her first two novels were baffled by it. No light adventure this. Yet there is no doubt *The Undying Monster* is Kerruish's masterpiece. Into it she threw just about the full complement of E. F. Bleiler's celebrated *Checklist* categories, from Anthropology through to Wizardry, including, on the way: hypnotic suggestion; psychic regression; ancestral memory; race memory; hereditary curses; a "Hand of Glory"; Norse legends; runes; the Twilight of the Gods; pagan rituals; an occult sleuth; mental aberration; the Fourth (and Fifth, and Sixth) Dimension; religious fantasy; personality collapse; possession. Not to mention the nub of the matter: lycanthropy.

And even that inventory of some of the chief ingredients hardly does justice to the dazzling, ravelled plot—or the fact that one of the most triumphant features of the novel is not actually supernatural at all. Part of the plot-line hinges on the search for a crucial missing word on an ancient stone tablet, which can only be six letters from a seemingly impossible choice. The gist of the problem is solved by the psychic detective—the refreshingly feisty Luna Bartendale—in a riveting feat of ratiocination.

Contrary to later legend, the book was by no means a disaster. It was reprinted twice in its month of publication (March 1922) and received a good press, including a wildly enthusiastic review from one of the foremost (and formidable) critics of the day, Edward Shanks: two out of three columns in his influential weekly page in *The Queen*. "Pretty nearly the best thing . . . in this sort since . . . *Dracula*," he applauded; "a genuine power of invention."

That is Kerruish's ultimate triumph: a formidable and teeming imagination coupled with an ability to make what lesser writers would balk at (or, if they tried it, fluff) into a strong narrative that is, if not precisely real-life, at least authentic-feeling and, above all, entirely engrossing. She is a terrific read.

She also, for the time, exhibited a curiously un-feminine sense of narrative drive—at times *The Undying Monster* scorches along—and a tone which, when necessary, is remarkably hard-edged, even tough. This was certainly useful in the early part of her career when she hid her sex behind the wholly uninformative "J. D. Kerruish," as well as the rather less scrupulous "J. Douglas Kerruish," the latter more often than not used for adventure yarns such as the gripping, pursuit-driven novella "The Los Oasis" (*Weekly Tale-Teller*, 14 August 1915) which, despite its suggestive title, was a non-fantasy, though certainly none the worse for that.

Yet after *The Undying Monster*, tragically, Kerruish declined, in large part due to a cruel disability (as reported by her agent Christine Campbell Thomson): fierce and debilitating migraines. There was perhaps a handful of late, and more or less trifling, stories, some written for the *Not at Night* series of anthologies. In "The Seven-Locked Room" (*Keep on the Light*, 1933) what is said to be a ghastly secret merely (the word is used advisedly) turns out to be the "San Grael" (the silver cup of Christ hidden for centuries in a West Country mansion). "The Gold of Hermodiké" (*Nightmare by Daylight*, 1936) has a certain grim fatality about it—ra-

pacious archaeologist doomed by 3,000-year-old revenge—but little tension. The fiddler in "The Wonderful Tune" (*At Dead of Night*, 1931) plays an accursed piece of music and summons up what you might expect.

Two stories stand out from this period. "Country House Fire" (*Tales of Murder and Mystery*, circa 1945) is a non-fantasy but demonstrates that even at this very late stage Kerruish could still produce an offbeat plot (arsonists utilize quantities of *ghee*—clarified butter—to slow-burn a Sussex manor house, for the purpose of *suttee*). In "The Badger" (*20-Story Magazine*, April 1932) the sexual tension, and imagery—on a hot, thundery night, frustrated English schoolmaster's wife in back-country part of Japan is attracted to young helper, then assailed by metamorphosing demon—lend to the story a by no means low-key erotic undertow that in the end begs all kinds of interesting questions about Jessie Douglas Kerruish.

—Jack Adrian

KERSH, Gerald

Nationality: British; naturalized U.S. citizen, 1959. **Born:** Teddington-on-Thames, Middlesex, 6 August 1911. **Education:** Regent Street Polytechnic, London. **Military Service:** Served in the Coldstream Guards, 1940-41; transferred to special duties, 1942; scriptwriter, Army Film Unit, 1943; specialist in the Films Division, Ministry of Information, 1943-44; accredited to SHAEF, 1944. **Family:** Married 1) Alice Thompson Rostron in 1938 (marriage dissolved 1943); 2) Claire Alyne Pacaud in 1943 (marriage dissolved 1955); 3) Florence Sochis in 1955. **Career:** Worked as a baker, nightclub bouncer, fish-and-chips cook, and wrestler in the 1930s; chief feature writer (as Piers England), 1941-45, and war correspondent, 1943, *The People,* London; settled in the U.S. after World War II. **Awards:** Mystery Writers of America Edgar Allan Poe Award, 1957. **Died:** 5 November 1968.

HORROR, GHOST AND GOTHIC PUBLICATIONS

Short Stories

I Got References (stories and autobiographical sketches). London, Joseph, 1939.
Selected Stories. London, Staples Press, 1943; abridged as *The Battle of the Singing Men*, London, Everybody's Books, 1944.
The Horrible Dummy and Other Stories. London, Heinemann, 1944.
Neither Man nor Dog: Short Stories. London, Heinemann, 1946.
Sad Road to the Sea: A Collection of Stories. London, Heinemann, 1947.
The Brighton Monster and Others. London, Heinemann, 1953.
Guttersnipe: Little Novels. London, Heinemann, 1954.
Men without Bones and Other Stories. London, Heinemann, 1955; revised edition, New York, Paperback Library, 1962.
On an Odd Note. New York, Ballantine, 1958.
The Ugly Face of Love and Other Stories. London, Heinemann, 1960.
The Best of Gerald Kersh, edited by Simon Raven. London, Heinemann, 1960.
The Terribly Wild Flowers: Nine Stories. London, Heinemann, 1962.

More Than Once Upon a Time: Stories. London, Heinemann, 1964.
The Hospitality of Miss Tolliver and Other Stories. London, Heinemann, 1965.
Nightshade and Damnations, edited by Harlan Ellison. New York, Fawcett, 1968; London, Coronet, 1969.

OTHER PUBLICATIONS

Novels

Jews Without Jehovah. London, Wishart, 1934.
Men Are So Ardent. London, Wishart, 1935; New York, Morrow, 1936.
Night and the City. London, Joseph, 1938; New York, Simon and Schuster, 1946.
They Die with Their Boots Clean. London, Heinemann, 1941; in *Sergeant Nelson of the Guards*, 1945.
The Nine Lives of Bill Nelson. London, Heinemann, 1942; in *Sergeant Nelson of the Guards*, 1945.
The Dead Look On. London, Heinemann, and New York, Reynal, 1943.
Brain and Ten Fingers. London, Heinemann, 1943.
Faces in a Dusty Picture. London, Heinemann, 1944; New York, McGraw Hill, 1945.
An Ape, a Dog, and a Serpent. London, Heinemann, 1945.
Sergeant Nelson of the Guards. Philadelphia, Winston, 1945.
The Weak and the Strong. London, Heinemann, 1945; New York, Simon and Schuster, 1946.
Prelude to a Certain Midnight. New York, Doubleday, and London, Heinemann, 1947.
The Song of the Flea. New York, Doubleday, and London, Heinemann, 1948.
The Thousand Deaths of Mr. Small. New York, Doubleday, 1950; London, Heinemann, 1951.
The Great Wash. London, Heinemann, 1953; as *The Secret Masters*, New York, Ballantine, 1953.
Fowlers End. New York, Simon and Schuster, 1957; London, Heinemann, 1958.
The Implacable Hunter. London, Heinemann, 1961.
A Long Cool Day in Hell. London, Heinemann, 1965.
The Angel and the Cuckoo. New York, New American Library, 1966; London, Heinemann, 1967.
Brock. London, Heinemann, 1969.

Short Stories

Clock Without Hands. London, Heinemann, 1949.
The Brazen Bull. London, Heinemann, 1952.

Plays

Screenplays: *Nine Men*, with Harry Watt, 1943; *The True Glory* (documentary), with others, 1945.

Other

Clean, Bright, and Slightly Oiled (wartime memoirs). London, Heinemann, 1946.

*

Film Adaptations: *Dead of Night*, 1945, from the short story "The Extraordinarily Horrible Dummy"; *Night and the City*, 1950, 1992, from the novel.

*   *   *

Gerald Kersh was a once very popular literary all-rounder who brought a fantastic imagination and streetwise gusto to a wide range of genres. None of his novels can entirely be classified as horror—even *The Implacable Hunter*, colourfully retelling the story of St. Paul, keeps its distance from the supernatural. But chilling, grisly and macabre touches abound. Examples include an almost unbearable evocation of the Lidice atrocities in *The Dead Look On*, the shuddering moment in that grim *noir* detection *Prelude to a Certain Midnight* when a "fat grey insect" runs from the murdered child's ear, and the comic-horrific account of a VD cautionary movie in the deeply sleazy *Fowlers End* (perhaps his masterpiece). *The Weak and the Strong*, dealing with an ill-assorted group of people trapped underground, has a claustrophobic *Huis Clos* intensity which verges on the surreal.

Although he was a rather less polished writer, Kersh's audacity, versatility and vigorous handling of low-life dialogue can be compared with that of Kipling; and as with Kipling, his supernatural and horror stories are widely scattered throughout numerous collections. Of these, *On an Odd Note* and *Nightshade and Damnations* are reprint selections which concentrate on fantastic material, as to some extent does *The Best of Gerald Kersh*.

His first collection *I Got References* includes such disturbing pieces as "The Horrible House with the Secret Pipes," a creepy "true life apparition" fragment; "The Devil that Troubled the Chessboard," where the demon that afflicts an ageing and obsessive chess-player proves to emanate from his own mind; and "Comrade Death," a story of the arms trade which escalates into grotesque nightmare as Death escapes like a genie from the bottle. Another early story, the 1939 "The Extraordinarily Horrible Dummy" (in *Selected Stories* and *The Horrible Dummy*) establishes the now classic horror theme of a ventriloquist's dummy whose malign personality—or apparent personality—comes to dominate its owner. This thread of the fantastic and horrific continues through many collections to the last which Kersh himself assembled, *The Hospitality of Miss Tolliver*—whose title piece features, uniquely for Kersh, some merely conventional denizens of horror: an elderly vampire and a child whose Halloween "trick or treat" ghoul mask is not a mask. . . .

Ghosts and the afterlife appear in such tales as "In a Room Without Walls" (*Neither Man nor Dog*), where a womanizing stage star's eternal punishment consists of giving eternal joy to one of his casual pick-ups; "The Scene of the Crime" (*Sad Road to the Sea*), which is also a murder mystery; "Carnival on the Downs (*Men Without Bones*), a double-punch story with more ghosts than might be expected; "Terraces" (*The Ugly Face of Love*) with its glimpse of a tawdry, poisoned Paradise; and "No Matter How You Slice It" (*More Than Once Upon a Time*), a homage to Kipling's "On the Gate" which shows angels bending the Law to get sinners into Heaven.

Other supernatural themes abound, like the identity exchange in "Fantasy of a Hunted Man" (*Neither Man nor Dog*) and the partial identity transfer from gangster to child *via* an eye transplant in "The Eye" (*The Ugly Face of Love*). Ghastly premonitions or prophetic dreams—with varied twists—feature in "The White Flash" (*The Horrible Dummy*), "Doctor Ox Will Die at Midnight" or "The Earwig" (*Neither Man nor Dog*), "A Vision of a Lost Child" (*Sad Road to the Sea*), and "The White-Washed Room" (*Men Without Bones*). "Prophet Without Honour" (*The Ugly Face of Love*) sees Nostradamus-like prophecies emerging from a newspaperman's sabotaged typewriter.

Though never Lovecraftian in his vigorous style, Kersh enjoyed H. P. Lovecraft's trick of dressing science-fictional rationales in the trappings of horror. The eerie Little Folk in "Voices in the Dust of Annan" (*Sad Road to the Sea*) are pitifully debased descendants of World War III shelter-dwellers; "The Oracle of the Fish" (*The Terribly Wild Flowers*) uses a closely similar theme of debasement, made magical by a Celtic talking fish. Boneless horrors in "Men Without Bones" (*Men Without Bones*) prove to be Earth's native humans, for we ourselves are colonizing Martians. In *The Brighton Monster*'s title story, the monstrous and pitiable "sea creature" described by a 1745 diarist emerges as a tattooed Japanese wrestler blown back through time from 1945 Hiroshima, and dying of radiation sickness. The black comedy of "Whatever Happened to Corporal Cuckoo?" is that the priceless elixir of immortality has been bestowed on an unimprovable grunt soldier who now carries the frightful scars of every major battle since Turin in 1537. An infection of evil crosses from the animal to the vegetable kingdom, and back again, in the title piece of *The Terribly Wild Flowers*.

Other grotesque and Gothic narrations include "The Queen of Pig Island" (*The Brighton Monster*), with lust and murder amid a party of marooned circus freaks; "The Crewel Needle" (*Guttersnipe*), whose evil child adapts a parlour-science trick into a chilling murder method; "The King Who Collected Clocks," in which a marvellous clockwork automaton replaces dead King Nicolas until the machinery meets with a bizarre accident; "The Sympathetic Souse" (*Men Without Bones*), a sick joke about Siamese twins, one of whom drinks the other to death; "The Shady Life of Annibal" (*The Ugly Face of Love*), where the imaginary child Annibal overshadows the life of a couple who invented him as comforting fiction; "The Oxoxoco Bottle," featuring the last MS of Ambrose Bierce—famously lost in Mexico—who finds himself among cannibals; "The Wrong Side of Things" (*The Terribly Wild Flowers*), where a cask-of-Amontillado crime is fatally bungled; and "A Lucky Day for the Boar" (*More Than Once Upon a Time*), a genuinely frightening account of a cruel and imaginative brainwashing that uses neither torture nor electronics. This last item pastiches Poe, and is presented as an unknown story by him. Further, more marginal stories play with other noted historical figures, including Christ and his disciples, Shakespeare, Leonardo da Vinci (several times) and Hitler.

Gerald Kersh was a born writer, compulsively readable; one hopes that he will again be rediscovered and emerge from his present obscurity.

—David Langford

KETCHUM, Jack

Pseudonym for Dallas William Mayr. **Nationality:** American. **Born:** 1946. **Career:** Actor, teacher, literary agent, author. **Awards:** Horror Writers of America Bram Stoker award for short story, 1995.

HORROR, GHOST AND GOTHIC PUBLICATIONS

Novels

Off Season. New York, Ballantine, 1980.
Hide and Seek. New York, Ballantine, 1984.
Cover. New York, Warner, 1987.
The Girl Next Door. New York, Warner, 1989.
She Wakes. New York, Berkley, 1989.
Offspring. New York, Diamond, 1991.
Joyride. New York, Berkley, 1994; as *Road Kill*, London, Headline, 1994.
Stranglehold. New York, Berkley, 1995; as *Only Child*, London, Headline, 1995.
Red. London, Headline, 1995.

*   *   *

Jack Ketchum is the pseudonym of New York-based writer Dallas Mayr. Before his debut in the horror field with his first novel, *Off Season*, he worked as an actor, teacher and literary agent. He has nine books to his credit, many of them translated and published in Russia, Italy, Japan and France. Although known for his novels, he has published over 75 short stories and articles, with his story "The Box" (*Cemetery Dance*, Spring 1994) receiving the Bram Stoker Award and reprinted in *The Year's Best Fantasy and Horror* (St. Martin's Press, 1995).

Ketchum bases much of his fiction on true-life crimes and events, and he uses these situations to closely examine the human condition. Three common themes run through his novels: an exploration of the boundaries of human behaviour when the normal rules of civilization no longer apply, the role of love as a motivating force (as strong as the struggle for survival) and a justice system that fails those it should protect.

Off Season became an instant cult classic and has often been referred to as the ultimate horror novel. *The Philadelphia Inquirer* correctly called the book "*Lord of the Flies* by way of Sam Peckinpah." William Golding's *Lord of the Flies* deals with the need for human beings to become socialized in order to live peacefully together—demonstrating this by showing the breakdown of society when a group of shipwrecked adolescent boys "go native." *Off Season* introduces the reader to a second-generation family of cannibals who originally came from an early-1900s settlement cut off by storms. In a sense, then, *Off Season* extrapolates the further breakdown of societal bonds that would have occurred in *Lord of the Flies* had the boys not been rescued from their predicament. The book serves as a foundation, or a blueprint, for Ketchum's other works, which are often as concerned with the aftermath of the breakdown as with the process of barbarism itself. It also features a setting, Dead River, Maine, that Ketchum would return to in *Offspring* (the sequel to *Off Season*) and his second novel, *Hide and Seek*.

Whereas *Off Season* covered a 24-hour period in excruciating detail, *Hide and Seek* covers an entire season. The novel follows the lives of four young-adult characters: three wealthy, spoiled college students stuck in Dead River for the summer, and one local boy, Dan Thomas, who is included in their (mis)adventures. Written in first person, from Thomas's eyes, the book relates how Thomas came to meet up with Steve, Kimberly and Casey and how he fell in love with Casey. Unlike *Off Season*, this novel quietly and slowly builds up to its terrifying end. Again Ketchum explores the theme of what people do when the rules of social conduct are relaxed, as Casey takes risk after risk—stealing groceries and cars, vandalizing property and finally playing a dangerous game of hide and seek in the local haunted house. But this book is not about the haunted house, or even about what they find there. Instead, it delves into why Casey takes these chances and why Thomas follows her blindly into certain disaster. In this sense, much of Ketchum's work could be considered mainstream, character-driven fiction, in the same way that Thomas Harris's books are mainstream. Except for *She Wakes*, his only supernatural novel (set in Greece), all Ketchum's novels are vividly realistic.

This mainstream influence is more evident in his novel *Cover*. Once again, Ketchum creates very complex characters. Moravian is a Vietnam veteran who has suffered greatly from his war experience, but nevertheless has a seldom-seen softer side. Ketchum first introduces us to this battle-scarred survivor in his relationship with his wife and son; tender moments that contrast with later moments of ferocity towards his victims.

Cover has a depth lacking from the earlier novels because Moravian's character is more complex and more fully developed than that of the cannibal tribe in *Off Season*, whose motivations were purely instinctual, or *Hide and Seek*, whose characters are driven by their own personal demons. The victims in *Cover* are six urban dwellers who go camping to escape the fast pace of the city, unaware of the terrors that await them. They become Moravian's prey as his paranoia gets the better of him and he sees everyone as an enemy. The recurring theme of civilization versus barbarism appears here again, but meshed to a detailed examination of Moravian's descent into madness, and a textbook examination of how the other six characters react in their attempt to survive.

The Girl Next Door takes the theme of understanding human behaviour straight to and over the edge. By far the most difficult of his books to read, the novel tells the story of David, a twelve-year-old boy. Similar to *Hide and Seek* in structure, the story is told from David's point of view as a grownup looking back on events in the past. As in *Hide and Seek*, the theme of first love is revisited, but instead of a young adult being drawn into his lover's psychosis, a young boy witnesses first-hand the torture and eventual death of Meg Loughlin, the girl he has come to love.

The novel's horror does not lie merely in the graphic descriptions of Meg's torture, but in how David can live with himself afterwards, knowing he could have done something to save her, if he had not been paralysed by his morbid fascination. Just as Dan Thomas in *Hide and Seek* must come to terms with Casey's death, David must live with his guilt and the part he played in Meg's death.

Because in *The Girl Next Door* the breakdown in society is internal, it differs from *Off Season* and *Offspring*. Even in *Cover* the reader can more easily dismiss Lee's behaviour because of the cruelties of war. But the people responsible for the vile acts in *The Girl Next Door* have not been separated from society and civilization, or suffered a traumatic event. This is probably the most terrifying of Ketchum's novels because it addresses the sick desire of all human beings to be voyeurs into the pain and suffering of others.

The reader is also introduced to the strength of love in this book, a theme that prevails in most of Ketchum's novels, but becomes more prevalent and takes in increasingly diverse guises in his later works: parental love in *Offspring* and *Stranglehold*, romantic love

in *Joyride*, and the underlying love relationship between an old man and his dog in *Red*. These expansions of his examination of love, which he only hinted at in his earlier works (indeed, *She Wakes* is driven by the force of lust, which is often mistaken for love) have allowed Ketchum to grow as a writer while retaining his original themes and concerns.

In addition, these later books begin to explore permutations of how the justice system can fail its citizens. In *Joyride*, just as in *Stranglehold*, an abused woman, whom the law is unable to protect from her vicious ex-husband (this type of character crops up too many times in Ketchum's novels and tends to be stereotypical), must take the law into her own hands. In *Red*, the old man's dog is coldly killed while he watches helplessly, and when the legal system cannot satisfy him he seeks justice in his own way.

Ketchum has made a major contribution to the field of psychological horror by virtue of his sparse, tight prose, his well-rounded characters and his unflinching gaze into the depths of human depravity. Like the crime novelist Andrew Vachss, Ketchum is at heart a moralist, and his excesses are in the services of morality.

—Ann Kennedy

KILPATRICK, Nancy

Pseudonym: Amarantha Knight. **Nationality:** Canadian. **Born:** Philadelphia, Pennsylvania, 1946. Lives in Montreal, Canada. **Awards:** Arthur Ellis award for short story, 1993; Standing Stone short story contest winner; has received five Ontario Arts Council publishers' grants.

HORROR, GHOST AND GOTHIC PUBLICATIONS

Novels

As One Dead, with Don Bassingthwaite. Clarkston, Georgia, White Wolf, 1993.
Near Death. New York, Pocket, 1994.
Child of the Night. London, Raven, 1996.

Novels as Amarantha Knight (series: The Darker Passions, all books)

Dracula. New York, Masquerade, 1993.
Dr. Jekyll and Mr. Hyde. New York, Masquerade, 1995.
Frankenstein. New York, Masquerade, 1995.
The Fall of the House of Usher. New York, Masquerade, 1995.
The Portrait of Dorian Gray. New York, Masquerade, 1996.

Short Stories

Sex and the Single Vampire. Leesburg, Virginia, Tal Publications, 1994.
The Amarantha Knight Reader (as Amarantha Knight). New York, Masquerade, 1996.

Editor (as Amarantha Knight), *Love Bites*. New York, Masquerade, 1994.

Editor (as Amarantha Knight), *Flesh Fantastic*. New York, Masquerade, 1995.

Editor (as Amarantha Knight), *Sex Macabre*. New York, Masquerade, 1996.

Editor (as Amarantha Knight), *Seductive Spectres*. New York, Masquerade, 1996.

*   *   *

Nancy Kilpatrick is a prolific writer of horror and erotic-horror short stories and novels, publishing the erotica under a pseudonym. Critics have frequently compared the Canadian writer Kilpatrick to America's Ann Rice: Kilpatrick's major works have been her vampire novels and short stories, and like Rice, who penned fairy-tale erotica under a pseudonym (A. N. Roquelaure), Kilpatrick has taken classic horror plots and settings and used them to frame stories of erotica.

Kilpatrick's best novels are clearly *Near Death* and the prequel that followed it, *Child of the Night*. These stories feature a vampire world in which the vampires have most of the usual traits: an intolerance of the sun, superhuman strength, a thirst for blood, and a general dislike for other vampires. However, Kilpatrick's vampires have sex with mortals, and sometimes turn their lovers into vampires as well, taking them on as monogamous life-mates or, perhaps, death-mates. This aspect of her work is doubly important due to the romantic story elements, particularly in *Near Death*. The novel tells the story of a tragic young woman, a heroin addict, sent off unaware to kill a vampire. This only results in her capture, which then turns to a hunt for those who sent her. Kilpatrick's vampires are generally sympathetic characters, so the young woman's relationship with her former target results in her recovery from addiction, a relationship with him, as well as her own vampiric change. The central figures of this as-yet incomplete trilogy (*Reborn* currently awaits publication) are the vampires Andre, David and Karl. Although co-operation among vampires is a rarity in their world, these three share a special bond, having developed a sort of truce, an uneasy friendship, and a method of working together toward mutually beneficial goals (*Child of the Night*). The three vampires mesh together quite well, a thematic triumvirate. Andre, the French vampire, represents the body; David, the English vampire, represents the soul; and Karl, the German vampire, represents the mind. In their collective world, they also display a rarity in vampire fiction, a half-breed son, who is half-human and half-vampire, as well as half-Anglo and half-Franco. *Near Death* takes a contemporary view of these three, and their families and lovers, while *Child of the Night* chronicles the beginning of their unique relationship. In *Near Death*, the theme of transformation controls the narrative. All of it builds up to the protagonist's transformation from mortal to vampire, which is not achieved until the climax of the story. The theme is repeated often: transformation from addict to recovering drug-user, from street punk to wise man, from sequestered to social. David, the main vampire in the story, undergoes an almost human transformation, from his chosen loneliness, to his return to the modern world.

A collaborative novel with writer Don Bassingthwaite, *As One Dead*, is based on the White Wolf company's story-telling game, *Vampire: The Masquerade*. Written within the world set out by the game, Kilpatrick and Bassingthwaite tell a story of two vampire sects, the Sabbat and the Camarilla, and their master/slave relationship in the city of Toronto. A half-breed vampire named Bianka attempts to upset the balance between the sects, trying to assist in freeing the Camarilla from the Sabbat's rule. This game story is lush with the scenery of the modern post-punk Gothic aesthetic, including industrial music bars full of heavy Goth vampire wannabes.

As Amarantha Knight, Kilpatrick has taken classic horror tales and put them in an erotic setting, drawing heavily on the Gothic attraction to sadomasochism and bondage & domination. These books explore the extremes of these and other sexual diversions. Given the immortal and supernatural nature of most of the basic players, the extremes in these books go well beyond human endurance. The series, "The Darker Passions" from Masquerade Books, includes Kilpatrick's erotic takes on *Dracula, Frankenstein, Dr. Jekyll and Mr. Hyde, The Fall of the House of Usher* and *The Portrait of Dorian Gray*. Also to be included in the series are *Carmilla* and *The Werewolf of Paris*. *The Aramantha Knight Reader* contains excerpts from four of these novels. In addition to these novels, Kilpatrick also edits erotic-horror anthologies under the Knight name, with titles including *Love Bites, Flesh Fantastic, Sex Macabre, Seductive Spectres* and the upcoming *Demon Sex*.

A few stories from Kilpatrick's broad range of short-story output stand out as highlights. "Memories of *el dia de los Muertos*," which first appeared in *Dead of Night* magazine, captures the spirit of the Mexican Day of the Dead, in an effectively atmospheric encounter with one of the dead. "Metal Fatigue," from *Bizarre Sex and Other Crimes of Passion*, is a quirky story with a unique protagonist, caught in a delusional dream of alien sex which parallels his dead-end job. "Farm Wife," a Bram Stoker award finalist, from *Northern Frights 1*, tells the story of a bizarre and independent woman who, Kilpatrick says, "reminded me a bit of my great-grandmother." The story "Heartbeat," which appears in the Barnes and Noble anthology *100 Wicked Little Witches*, is also a moody, ethereal piece, looking at the world through the eyes of split ethnicity, and the wonder it brings this particular character. "Mantrap" won the 1994 Arthur Ellis award for Best Canadian Mystery, showing Kilpatrick's talents outside the genre, in a short, sweet whodunit based in a museum of natural history. VampErotica comics adapted her story "Dead Shot" for issues #5 and #6, as well as "Theater of Cruelty" and "Metadrama" for issue #13. With almost 100 short-fiction titles to her credit, and more scheduled, Nancy Kilpatrick/Amarantha Knight is showing up almost everywhere in horror, and should be around for some time to come.

—Tom Winstead

KING, Stephen (Edwin)

Pseudonym: Richard Bachman. **Nationality:** American. **Born:** Portland, Maine, 21 September 1947. **Education:** University of Maine at Orono, B.Sc. 1970. **Family:** Married Tabitha Jane Spruce in 1971; one daughter and two sons. **Career:** Worked as a janitor, a labourer in an industrial laundry, and in a knitting mill; English teacher, Hampden Academy, Hampden, Maine, 1971-73; full-time writer from 1973. Writer in residence, University of Maine, Orono, 1978-79. Owner, Philtrum Press, a publishing house, and WZON-AM, a rock-and-roll radio station, both in Bangor, Maine. Guest of Honor, Fifth World Fantasy Convention, 1979. **Awards:** Alumni Career award, University of Maine,

1980; World Fantasy award, 1980, for contributions to the field, 1982, for short story, and 1994, for short story; special British Fantasy Society award for outstanding contribution to the genre, 1982; Hugo award, World Science Fiction Convention, 1982, for nonfiction; named *Us* Magazine Best Fiction Writer of the Year, 1982; Locus award for best collection, Locus Publications, 1986; Horror Writers of America Bram Stoker award for novel, 1988, for collection, 1990, and for novella, 1996; O. Henry award for short story, 1994. **Agent:** Arthur Greene, 101 Park Avenue, New York, NY 10178. **Address:** P.O. Box 1186, Bangor, ME 04001, USA.

HORROR, GHOST AND GOTHIC PUBLICATIONS

Novels (series: The Dark Tower)

Carrie. New York, Doubleday, and London, New English Library, 1974.

'Salem's Lot. New York, Doubleday, 1975; London, New English Library, 1976.

The Shining. New York, Doubleday, and London, New English Library, 1977.

The Stand. New York, Doubleday, 1978; London, New English Library, 1979; restored edition, with illustrations by Berni Wrightson, New York, Doubleday, and London, Hodder and Stoughton, 1990.

The Dead Zone. New York, Viking, and London, Macdonald and Jane's, 1979.

Firestarter. Huntington Woods, Michigan, Phantasia Press, and London, Futura, 1980.

Cujo. New York, Viking, 1981; London, Macdonald, 1982.

The Shining, 'Salem's Lot, Night Shift, Carrie (omnibus). London, Octopus Books, 1981.

The Dark Tower: The Gunslinger, illustrated by Michael Whelan. West Kingston, Rhode Island, Donald M. Grant, 1982; as *The Gunslinger,* New York, New American Library, 1988; London, Sphere, 1989.

Christine. West Kingston, Rhode Island, Donald M. Grant, and London, Hodder and Stoughton, 1983.

Cycle of the Werewolf, illustrated by Berni Wrightson. Westland, Michigan, Land of Enchantment, 1983; London, New English Library, 1985.

Pet Sematary. New York, Doubleday, and London, Hodder and Stoughton, 1983.

The Eyes of the Dragon (for young adults), illustrated by Kenneth R. Linkhauser. Bangor, Maine, Philtrum Press, 1984; new edition, illustrated by David Palladini, New York, Viking, 1987; London, Macdonald, 1988.

The Talisman, with Peter Straub. New York, Viking Press/Putnam, and London, Viking, 1984.

Silver Bullet (omnibus; includes *Cycle of the Werewolf* and *Silver Bullet* [screenplay]). New York, New American Library, 1985.

The Bachman Books: Four Early Novels (omnibus; includes *Rage, The Long Walk, Roadwork, The Running Man*). New York, New American Library, 1985; London, Hodder and Stoughton, 1986.

It. London, Hodder and Stoughton, and New York, 1986.

Misery. New York, Viking, and London, Hodder and Stoughton, 1987.

The Dark Tower II: The Drawing of Three, illustrated by Phil Hale. West Kingston, Rhode Island, Donald M. Grant, 1987; London, Sphere, 1989.

The Tommyknockers. New York, Putnam, 1987; London, Hodder and Stoughton, 1988.

The Dark Half. New York, Viking, 1989; London, Hodder and Stoughton, 1990.

The Dark Tower III: The Waste Lands, illustrated by Ned Dameron. Hampton Falls, New Hampshire, Grant, 1991.

Needful Things. New York, Viking, 1991; London, Hodder and Stoughton, 1992.

Gerald's Game. New York, Viking, and London, Hodder and Stoughton, 1992.

Dolores Claiborne. New York, Viking, and London, Hodder and Stoughton, 1993.

Insomnia. Shingletown, California, Ziesing, and London, Hodder and Stoughton, 1994.

Rose Madder. New York, Viking, and London, Hodder and Stoughton, 1995.

The Green Mile (in six parts: *The Two Dead Girls, The Mouse on the Mile, Coffey's Hands, The Bad Death of Eduard Delacroix, Night Journey* and *Coffey on the Mile*). New York, Signet, and London, Penguin, 1996.

Desperation. New York, Viking, and London, Hodder and Stoughton, 1996.

Novels as Richard Bachman

Rage. New York, Signet, 1977.

The Long Walk. New York, Signet, 1979.

Roadwork: A Novel of the First Energy Crisis. New York, Signet, 1981.

The Running Man. New York, Signet, 1982; London, New English Library, 1988.

Thinner. New York, New American Library, 1984; London, New English Library, 1987.

The Regulators. New York, Dutton, and London, Hodder and Stoughton, 1996.

Short Stories

Night Shift. New York, Doubleday, and London, New English Library, 1978.

Different Seasons. New York, Viking, and London, Futura, 1982.

The Plant. Bangor, Maine, Philtrum Press, Part I, 1982; Part II, 1983; Part III, 1985.

The Breathing Method. Bath, Avon, England, Chivers Press, 1984.

Rita Hayworth and Shawshank Redemption: A Story from "Different Seasons." Thorndike, Maine, Thorndike Press, 1983.

Skeleton Crew. New York, Putnam, and London, Macdonald, 1985; as *Stephen King's Skeleton Crew,* illustrated by J. K. Potter, Santa Cruz, California, Scream/Press, 1985.

Dolan's Cadillac. Northridge, California, Lord John Press, 1989.

My Pretty Pony, illustrated by Barbara Kruger. New York, Library Fellows of the Whitney Museum, 1989.

Four Past Midnight. New York, Viking, and London, Hodder and Stoughton, 1990.

Nightmares and Dreamscapes. New York, Viking, and London, Hodder and Stoughton, 1993.

Plays

Screenplays: *Creepshow,* 1982, from the short stories "Father's Day," "Weeds," "The Crate" and "They're Creeping Up on You"; *Cat's Eye,* 1984, from the short stories "Quitters, Inc.,"

"The Ledge" and "The General"; *Silver Bullet*, 1985, from the novel *Cycle of the Werewolf*; *Maximum Overdrive*, 1986, from the short stories "The Mangler," "Trucks" and "The Lawnmower Man"; *Pet Sematary*, 1989; *Stephen King's Sleepwalkers*, 1992.

Television Plays: *Sorry, Right Number* (episode of *Tales from the Dark Side* series), 1987; *Stephen King's Golden Years*, 1991; *Stephen King's The Stand*, 1994.

Other

Stephen King's Creepshow: A George A. Romero Film (comic-strip adaptations), illustrated by Berni Wrightson and Michele Wrightson. New York, New American Library, 1982.

<small>OTHER PUBLICATIONS</small>

Poetry

Another Quarter Mile: Poetry. Pittsburgh, Pennsylvania, Dorrance, 1979.

Other

Stephen King's Danse Macabre. New York, Everest House, 1981; London, Futura, 1982.
Black Magic and Music: A Novelist's Perspective on Bangor. Bangor, Maine, Bangor Historical Society, 1983.
Stephen King's Year of Fear 1986 Calendar. New York, New American Library, 1985.
Nightmares in the Sky: Gargoyles and Grotesques, photographs by f.Stop FitzGerald. New York and London, Viking, 1988.

*

Film Adaptations: *Carrie*, 1976; *'Salem's Lot* (television miniseries), 1979; *The Shining*, 1980; *Creepshow*, 1982, from the short stories "Father's Day," "Weeds," "The Crate" and "They're Creeping Up on You"; *Christine*, 1983; *Cujo*, 1983; *The Dead Zone*, 1983; *Children of the Corn*, 1984; *Firestarter*, 1984; *Cat's Eye*, 1984, from the short stories "Quitters, Inc.," "The Ledge" and "The General"; *Silver Bullet*, 1985, from the novel *Cycle of the Werewolf*; *Maximum Overdrive*, 1986, from the short stories "The Mangler," "Trucks" and "The Lawnmower Man"; *Stand by Me*, 1986, from the novella "The Body"; *Creepshow 2*, 1987; *The Running Man*, 1987; *Pet Sematary*, 1989; "The Cat from Hell," segment of *Tales from the Darkside: The Movie*, 1990; *Stephen King's Graveyard Shift*, 1990; *Misery*, 1990; *It* (television miniseries), 1990; *Stephen King's "Sometimes They Come Back"* (television movie), 1991; *Stephen King's Golden Years* (television mini-series), 1991; *The Dark Half*, 1992; *Stephen King's Sleepwalkers*, 1992; *The Tommyknockers* (television mini-series), 1993; *Needful Things*, 1993; *The Lawnmower Man*, 1993; *The Shawshank Redemption*, 1994; *Stephen King's The Stand* (television mini-series), 1994; *Dolores Claiborne*, 1995; *The Langoliers* (television movie), 1995; *Stephen King's Thinner*, 1996; *Stephen King's The Shining* (television movie), 1997.

Biography: Entry in *Dictionary of Literary Biography Yearbook:*
1980, Detroit, Gale, 1981; essay in *Authors and Artists for Young Adults,* Volume 1, Detroit, Gale, 1989.

Bibliography: *The Annotated Guide to Stephen King: A Primary and Secondary Bibliography of the Works of America's Premier Horror Writer* by Michael R. Collings, Mercer Island, Washington, Starmont House, 1986; new edition, as *The Work of Stephen King: An Annotated Bibliography and Guide*, San Bernardino, Borgo Press, 1996.

Critical Studies (selection): *The Novels of Stephen King: Teacher's Manual* by Edward J. Zagorski, New York, New American Library, 1981; *Fear Itself: The Horror Fiction of Stephen King* edited by Tim Underwood and Chuck Miller, San Francisco, California, and Columbia, Pennsylvania, Underwood-Miller, 1982; *Stephen King* by Douglas E. Winter, Mercer Island, Washington, Starmont House, 1982; *Stephen King: The Art of Darkness* by Douglas E. Winter, New York, New American Library, 1984; *Discovering Stephen King* edited by Darrell Schweitzer, Mercer Island, Washington, Starmont House, 1985; *The Many Facets of Stephen King* by Michael R. Collings, Mercer Island, Washington, Starmont House, 1985; *The Shorter Works of Stephen King* by Michael R. Collings and David Engebretson, Mercer Island, Washington, Starmont House, 1985; *Stephen King as Richard Bachman* by Michael R. Collings, Mercer Island, Washington, Starmont House, 1985; *Kingdom of Fear: The World of Stephen King* edited by Tim Underwood and Chuck Miller, San Francisco and Columbia, Underwood-Miller, 1986; *The Films of Stephen King* by Michael R. Collings, Mercer Island, Washington, Starmont House, 1986; *Stephen King: At the Movies* by Jessie Horsting, New York, Signet/Starlog, 1986; *The Stephen King Phenomenon* by Michael R. Collings, Mercer Island, Washington, Starmont House, 1987; *Stephen King Goes to Hollywood: A Lavishly Illustrated Guide to All the Films Based on Stephen King's Fiction* by Jeff Connor, New York, New American Library, 1987; *The Gothic World of Stephen King: Landscape of Nightmares* edited by Gary Hoppenstand and Ray B. Browne, Bowling Green, Ohio, Bowling Green State University Popular Press, 1987; *Stephen King: The First Decade, "Carrie" to "Pet Sematary"* by Joseph Reino, Boston, Twayne, 1988; *Landscape of Fear: Stephen King's American Gothic* by Tony Magistrale, Bowling Green, Ohio, Bowling Green State University Popular Press, 1988; *Bare Bones: Conversations on Terror with Stephen King* edited by Tim Underwood and Chuck Miller, Los Angeles and Columbia, Underwood-Miller, 1988; *Reign of Fear: Fiction and Film of Stephen King* edited by Don Herron, Los Angeles and Columbia, Underwood-Miller, 1988; *The Unseen King* by Tyson Blue, Mercer Island, Washington, Starmont House, 1989; *Feast of Fear: Conversations with Stephen King* edited by Tim Underwood and Chuck Miller, Novato, California, and Lancaster, Pennsylvania, Underwood-Miller, 1989; *The Stephen King Companion* edited by George Beahm, Kansas City, Missouri, Andrews and McMeel, 1989; *The Moral Voyages of Stephen King* by Anthony Magistrale, Mercer Island, Washington, Starmont House, 1989; *Stephen King and Clive Barker: The Illustrated Masters of the Macabre* by James Van Hise, Las Vegas, Pioneer Books, 1990; *Stephen King: Man and Artist* by Carroll F. Terrell, Orono, Maine, Northern Lights Publishing Company, 1990; *"The Shining" Reader* edited by Anthony Magistrale, Mercer Island, Washington, Starmont House, 1991; *The Complete Stephen King Encyclopedia: The Definitive Guide to the Works of America's Master of Horror* by Stephen J. Spignesi, Chicago, Contemporary Books, 1991; *The Stephen King Story* by George Beahm, Kansas City, Andrews and McMeel, 1991; *The Dark Descent: Essays Defining Stephen King's Horrorscape* edited by Tony Magistrale, New York, Greenwood Press, 1992; *Stephen King: The Second Decade—"Danse Macabre" to "The Dark Half"* by Tony Magistrale, New York, Twayne, 1992; *Stephen King and Clive Barker: Masters of the Macabre II* by James Van Hise, Las Vegas, Pioneer Books, 1992; *A Casebook on "The Stand"* edited by Tony Magistrale, Mercer Island, Washington, Starmont House, 1992; *The Films of Stephen King* by Ann Lloyd, London, Brown, and New York, St. Martin's Press, 1993; *Stephen King's America* by Jonathan P. Davis, Bowling Green, Ohio, Bowling Green State University Popular Press, 1994; *Stephen King* by Amy Keyishian and Marjorie Keyishian, New York Chelsea House, 1995; *Writing Horror and the Body: The Fiction of Stephen King, Clive Barker, and Anne Rice* by Linda Badley, Westport, Connecticut, Greenwood Press, 1996; *Stephen King: A Critical Companion* by Sharon A. Russell, Westport, Connecticut, Greenwood Press, 1996.

Theatrical Activities:
Director: **Film**—*Maximum Overdrive*, 1986. Actor: Has made cameo appearances in numerous films including *Knightriders*, as Steven King, 1980; *Creepshow*, 1982; *Maximum Overdrive*, 1986; *Creepshow II*, 1987; *Land of Confusion* (Genesis music video), 1988; *Pet Sematary*, 1989; *Stephen King's Sleepwalkers*, 1992; *The Stand*, 1994; and *The Langoliers*, 1995. Also appeared in American Express credit-card television commercial, 1984; as a "Guest VJ" on cable network TV, 27 June 1986; and on a videocassette, *Stephen King at the Pavillon*, 1987, featuring a 1986 King speech.

*   *   *

Ongoing debates about the literary value of Stephen King's works, while often spirited, are essentially irrelevant; by means of his enormous energy and visibility, King has already earned himself a permanent place in the history of literature, no matter what his contemporaries say about him. At the very least, he will enjoy the status of a latter-day Anthony Trollope, an author respected for his popularity and social commentary and the centre of periodic revival campaigns. More likely, he will be enshrined as the Charles Dickens of the late 20th century, the writer who perfectly reflected, encapsulated and expressed the characteristic concerns of his era. We have learned to understand the world we live in, and we are horrified.

King has enjoyed such spectacular success in part because he was the first, and best, writer to recognize that the tropes and conventions of horror fiction provided the ideal vehicle to convey the experience of life in postwar America—and, by extension, of growing up in all modern societies strongly influenced by America. Indeed, his major works can be fruitfully organized as a decade-by-decade indictment of growing up as part of the baby-boom generation. He emphasizes those people who are traditionally marginalized by society—the young, the old, women, the socially maladroit—but since almost all people have, at some point, identified themselves as "Losers," that helps to make King's fiction so widely appealing. Thus, to begin by examining the agonies of childhood in the 1950s—the time falsely presented as an interval of blissful innocence in orgies of nostalgia like *Happy Days* and *Grease*—consider *It* and its alienated pre-teens enduring a torturous existence of parental neglect and abuse, lurking predators, vengeful bullies, and fears of atomic annihilation. For a look at

the torments of adolescence in the 1960s and 1970s, *Carrie* provides a good preliminary sketch, but *Christine* covers much the same territory in more chilling detail. For insight into the various pains of adulthood in the 1980s and 1990s, *Needful Things* offers a helpful compendium of unhappy men and women vainly hoping that some wished-for artefact will fill the gaping holes in their lives, while novels like *The Shining*, *Thinner*, *Misery* and *Rose Madder* provide some striking case studies. And, for a look ahead to the horrors of old age, *Insomnia* epitomizes all the loneliness, pain, helplessness and condescension older Americans can look forward to. Amidst all the sharply rendered and all-too-real problems his protagonists encounter, all the cruelties and frustrations of their everyday lives, King's supernatural menaces and alien monsters, while persuasively and gruesomely disturbing, sometimes seem like the least of his characters' problems.

Yet many writers can depict real and imaginary horrors; the other reason for King's success is that, despite all the travails of contemporary life that he so tellingly delineates, his characters refuse to abandon hope. While his early novels may seem like cautionary tales, in which tormented people fall victim to supernatural forces, King increasingly focuses on those who painstakingly and triumphantly resist the encroachment of evil. Even in a world which increasingly drives people to isolation, cynicism and despair, King insists, it remains possible for individuals to forge bonds of love and friendship, to discover unexpected resources in themselves and in others around them, and to conquer the malevolent powers that would suppress or destroy them. So baldly stated, this message might sound cloying and simplistic; yet King avoids these pitfalls because he fully recognizes and conveys that such triumphs are far from easy. His protagonists must engage in long and difficult struggles, passing through several stages and even rites of passage, in order to overcome their opponents. King's longest, and arguably most successful, novels like *It* and *Insomnia* therefore move away from the quick final reversal of horror fiction to achieve the grandeur and stately pace of heroic fantasy—which may be why these longer novels sometimes disconcert readers who are conditioned by other horror fiction to expect a rapid succession of frightening moments culminating in a snappy surprise ending. However, King asserts, horror doesn't work that way, and horror cannot be confronted and overcome so neatly; instead, people first must bond, must educate themselves, and must work hard and purposefully in order to earn their victories.

Since modern life is instead so often characterized by isolation, ignorance and purposelessness, it becomes possible to completely reverse the standard summation of King, which is that his novels are popular because they blend imaginative horrors with realistic portrayals of everyday life. Yet King's horrors are generally linked so effectively to the characters' mundane problems that they can almost be viewed as metaphors for those problems, while the close relationships his characters forge and their earnest and dedicated struggles can seem less than plausible in contemporary society. In other words, by this argument, King brilliantly combines realistic horrors with inspirational, but utterly fantastic, personal responses to those horrors.

If the foregoing seems an incomplete reading of King based on a selective trawling of his works, that in part illustrates another dimension of King's talents: his clear determination to be unpredictable, to avoid falling into patterns. His career reveals a consistent policy of noticing critical expectations regarding his fiction and deliberately setting out to confound those expectations. Noted for his frequent choice of younger protagonists, King has since

1985 focused primarily on adults. Praised for the fidelity of his depiction of small-town American life, King has experimented with urban settings and has even returned with renewed enthusiasm to the surrealistic future wilderness introduced in *The Dark Tower: The Gunslinger*. Criticized for neglecting his female protagonists, King has laboured successfully to provide fully-realized women characters in his recent fiction. The 1996 appearance of *The Green Mile* in six instalments, some published before the work was completed, further attests to a continuing urge to keep himself fresh, to keep reinventing himself, which augurs well for his future fiction even as it threatens to keep making all of his commentators look silly. As Algis Budrys noted, King "is the first writer, ever, to have truly baffled the critics."

If there is a dark side to King's maturation as a writer, it lies in a burgeoning tendency to self-referentiality; virtually all of his recent novels include a reference to one or more previous King works. Thus, the monster of *It* is briefly glimpsed in *The Tommyknockers*, *Needful Things* alludes to the story of *Cujo* and other Castle Rock novels, *Insomnia* employs the character of Mike Hanlon from *It* and offers a penultimate scene featuring Roland from the *Dark Tower* series, *Rose Madder* mentions a picture of Susan Day, the feminist crusader from *Insomnia*, and a character from *Rose Madder*, Cynthia King, figures in both *Desperation* and *The Regulators*. That recent pair of closely-linked novels raises further concerns, although they constitute a remarkable *tour de force*, as King takes the same premise—an ancient evil spirit unearthed in a Nevada mine—to create two wildly different stories: *Desperation*, the relentlessly grim story of a murderous spirit inhabiting the bodies of adults in a remote town, opposed by a virtuous child, and *The Regulators*, the wickedly comic story of a murderous spirit inhabiting the body of a child in a familiar suburb, opposed by virtuous adults. Despite their effectiveness, their use of many common characters, subtly or significant altered, generates the atmosphere of a literary game to an extent never before seen in King's fiction. *It* includes some barbs aimed at creative-writing teachers who value themes and allusions more than stories; it would be ironic if King himself, the premiere storyteller of his generation, succumbed to the same delusion.

There are many other things that can be said, and need to be said, about King's amazing talents and accomplishments, as are amply demonstrated by the vast and rich critical literature that has emerged in response to King. While purists and taxonomists might reasonably move some of his works into the categories of science fiction (e.g., *The Running Man* and *The Tommyknockers*), fantasy (e.g., *The Eyes of the Dragon* and *The Dark Tower* novels), or mainstream fiction (e.g., *Misery* and *Dolores Claiborne*), there reverberates throughout King's fiction an interest in examining individuals under extreme stress that connects virtually all of his fiction, at least tangentially, to the genre of horror. His novels are richly textured with multitudinous references to literature, films, television, rock music and popular culture that may not be fully appreciated until annotated editions of his works are produced; one excellent example occurs in *Desperation*, when Mary Jackson recognizes a quotation from Edward Albee's *Who's Afraid of Virginia Woolf?* and exclaims, "We're not *all* bozos on this bus," alluding to an old Firesign Theater comedy album and moving immediately from high culture to low culture. Because of this texture, and because of King's attentiveness to detailed development, his stories are often ineffective when stripped down to pure plot and adapted as films. (Oddly, considering King's reputation for imaginative horror, his stories which lack supernatural elements,

inviting more of a focus on character and context, have generated the best King films—*Stand by Me*, *Misery* and *The Shawshank Redemption*).

Since he has written so many excellent novels, it is regretfully easy to ignore his short fiction, though stories like "The Body: Fall from Innocence" (in *Different Seasons* and the basis of the film *Stand by Me*), "Gramma" (in *Skeleton Crew*), and "The Man in the Black Suit" (*The New Yorker*, 31 October 1994) are among his finest achievements. King can be an enormously *funny* writer, and almost every one of his novels has at least one moment to make readers laugh out loud. (Recall, for example, the scene in *The Tommyknockers* when the policemen shoot down the attacking, alien-altered Coke machine, then babble hysterically about their shameful violation of the Coke machine's civil rights.) When one considers all of his strong points, the common criticisms of King can seem frivolous and not without precedent: that he can be long-winded (like Dickens), that he derives ideas from other writers (like William Shakespeare), that he is obsessed with violence and morbidity (like Edgar Allan Poe), and so on.

Yet balanced against all criticisms of King must be placed one inarguable fact: while there were many precedents for the stories that King told (as he generously acknowledged in his *Danse Macabre*), Stephen King single-handedly created the modern genre of horror fiction, which suggests a comparison to another literary giant, J. R. R. Tolkien, who single-handedly created the modern genre of fantasy. By adapting the approach of horror to contemporary topics and issues, King showed readers that horror could be interesting, showed other writers that horror could be intellectually stimulating, and showed publishers that horror could be profitable. King is the reason why modern bookstores now commonly feature a section of horror literature, why there exists an organization called the Horror Writers of America, and why a book called the *St. James Guide to Horror, Ghost and Gothic Writers* is being published. Who could possibly maintain that such monumental accomplishments could stem from a second-rate writer? Still, any admirer of King should not attempt to suppress criticism of King, but rather should encourage it; scathing critiques will certainly do no harm, as already noted, and might even provide King with an interesting challenge for a future story. He is a writer forever in need of new worlds to conquer, and thus an appropriate spokesperson for his generation and the ideal leading figure of a literary genre.

—Gary Westfahl

KIRK, Russell (Amos)

Nationality: American. **Born:** Plymouth, Michigan, 19 October 1918. **Education:** Plymouth High School, graduated 1936; Michigan State University, East Lansing, B.A. 1940; Duke University, Durham, North Carolina, M.A. 1941; St. Andrews University, Scotland, D.Litt. 1952. **Military Service:** Served in the U.S. army, 1942-46: staff sergeant. **Family:** Married Annette Yvonne Cecile Courtemanche in 1964; four daughters. **Career:** Assistant professor of history, Michigan State University, 1946-53; Daly Lecturer, University of Detroit, 1954; Research Professor of Politics, C. W. Post College, Long Island University, Greenvale, New York, 1957-61; member of the Politics Faculty, New School for Social Research, New York, 1959-61; also visiting professor at several universities. Columnist ("From the Academy"), *National Review*, New York, 1955-80, and for *Los Angeles Times* syndicate, 1962-75. From 1960 editor, *University Bookman*. **Awards:** American Council of Learned Societies Senior fellowship, 1950; Guggenheim fellowship, 1956; Ann Radcliffe award, 1966; Christopher award, for non-fiction, 1972; World Fantasy award, 1977; Ingersoll award, 1985. Honorary doctorates: Boston College; St. John's University; Park College, Kansas City; Loyola College, Baltimore; LeMoyne College, Syracuse, New York; Gannon College, Erie, Pennsylvania; Niagara University, New York; Olivet College, Michigan; Albion College, Michigan; Central Michigan University, Mount Pleasant. **Died:** 29 April 1994.

Horror, Ghost and Gothic Publications

Novels

Old House of Fear. New York, Fleet, 1961; London, Gollancz, 1962.
A Creature of the Twilight: His Memorials. New York, Fleet, 1966.
Lord of the Hollow Dark. New York, St. Martin's Press, 1979; revised edition, 1989.

Short Stories

The Surly, Sullen Bell: Ten Stories and Sketches. New York, Fleet, 1962; as *Lost Lake*, New York, Paperback Library, 1966.
The Princess of All Lands. Sauk City, Wisconsin, Arkham House, 1979.
Watchers at the Strait Gate. Sauk City, Wisconsin, Arkham House, 1984.

Other

Editor, *The Scallion Stone*, by Basil A. Smith. Chapel Hill, North Carolina, Whispers Press, 1980.

Other Publications

Other

Randolph of Roanoke: A Study in Conservative Thought. Chicago, University of Chicago Press, 1951; as *John Randolph of Roanoke*, Chicago, Regnery, 1964.
The Conservative Mind from Burke to Santayana. Chicago, Regnery, 1953; London, Faber, 1954; revised editions, Regnery, 1964, 1972.
St. Andrews. London, Batsford, 1954.
A Program for Conservatives. Chicago, Regnery, 1954; revised edition, 1962.
Academic Freedom: An Essay in Definition. Chicago, Regnery, 1955.
Beyond the Dreams of Avarice: Essays of a Social Critic. Chicago, Regnery, 1956.
The Intelligent Woman's Guide to Conservatism. New York, Devin Adair, 1957.
The American Cause. Chicago, Regnery, 1957.
Confessions of a Bohemian Tory: Episodes and Reflections of a Vagrant Career. New York, Fleet, 1963.

The Intemperate Professor and Other Cultural Splenetics. Baton Rouge, Louisiana State University Press, 1965; revised edition, Peru, Illinois, Sugden, 1988.
Edmund Burke: A Genius Reconsidered. New Rochelle, New York, Arlington House, 1967; revised edition, Peru, Illinois, Sugden, 1988.
The Political Principles of Robert A. Taft, with James McClellan. New York, Fleet, 1967.
Enemies of the Permanent Things: Observations of Abnormality in Literature and Politics. New Rochelle, New York, Arlington House, 1969; revised edition, Peru, Illinois, Sugden, 1988.
Eliot and His Age: T. S. Eliot's Moral Imagination in the Twentieth Century. New York, Random House, 1971; revised edition, Peru, Illinois, Sugden, 1988.
The Roots of American Order. La Salle, Illinois, Open Court, 1974.
Decadence and Renewal in the Higher Learning: An Episodic History of American University and College Since 1953. South Bend, Indiana, Regnery, 1978.
Reclaiming a Patrimony (lectures). Washington, D.C., Heritage Foundation, 1982.
Irving Babbitt 1865-1933: Literature and the American College (lecture). Washington, D.C., National Humanity Institute, 1986.
The Wise Men Know What Wicked Things are Written on the Sky (essays). Chicago, Regnery, 1987.
The Conservative Cause (lecture). Washington, D.C., Heritage Foundation, 1987.

Editor, *The Portable Conservative Reader.* New York, Viking Press, and London, Penguin, 1982.
Editor, *The Assault on Religion.* Lanham, Maryland, University Press of America, 1986.

*

Bibliography: *Russell Kirk: A Bibliography* by Charles Brown, Mount Pleasant, Michigan, Clarke Historical Library, 1981.

Manuscript Collection: Clarke Historical Library, Central Michigan University, Mount Pleasant.

*   *   *

The late Russell Kirk would never have been easily mistaken for a postmodern auteur of frights like, say, Clive Barker. Conservative in both his moral code and his politics, more inclined toward traditional modes of horror (the Gothic, the Baroque) than to splatterpunk, happily maintaining a reticent profile in the small town of his birth, Kirk seems from one angle a figure from another age: a genteel, albeit talented dilettante of horror writing, resembling his hero, M. R. James.

Yet considered from a different slant, Kirk is amazingly influential, extroverted and contemporary. Establishing his lifelong cosmopolitanism in his early thirties, he received his doctorate from St. Andrews University in Scotland. With the publication of *The Conservative Mind*, he became an early spokesman and father-figure in the modern conservative movement in the United States. Soon followed a syndicated newspaper column read by millions, and an extensive programme of live lectures and various visiting professorships. His conversion to Roman Catholicism in 1964 signalled his enthusiastic activism in another sphere of contention and faith. To this day, Kirk's work in the socio-political realm is kept alive on such an ultramodern outlet as the worldwide web.

The writing of horror, then, was always a sideline for the polemically prolific Kirk. Yet one senses that it was an absolutely vital avocation, a means for him to express all those deeply personal sentiments, certain and uncertain, all those flashes of insight, those hopes and dreads, which could not otherwise take shape in his sober non-fiction works. (Kirk was a great believer in what he called "the illative sense—everything suddenly falling into place . . ., fitting together like parts of a puzzle, some obscure catalyst of the brain ingeniously combining fragmentary perceptions into a whole.") In fact, after all the tides of politics have perhaps in the future stranded Kirk's ideological boats, his determinedly non-dogmatic fiction will remain afloat.

In "A Cautionary Note on the Ghostly Tale" (an essay first published in *The Surly Sullen Bell* and later revised for *Watchers at the Strait Gate*), Kirk is plain-spoken about his authorial role-models and the effects he was aiming for in his fiction. Harking back to the earliest Gothic writers (Ann Radcliffe, Horace Walpole), then encompassing the classic Victorians and Edwardians (Le Fanu, MacDonald, M. R. and Henry James, Chesterton), Kirk terminated his list of influences with C. S. Lewis and Charles Williams. One does not picture him reading many of his own contemporaries, nor of worrying about their competition. As for achieving his desired effect:

> The political ferocity of our age is sufficiently dismaying: men of letters need not conjure up horrors worse than those suffered during the past decade by the Cambodian and Ugandans, Afghans and Ethiopians.

> What I have attempted, rather, are experiments in the moral imagination. Readers will encounter elements of parable and fable . . . some clear premise about the character of human existence . . . a healthy concept of the character of evil. . . .

That these "experiments in the moral imagination" need not always include the supernatural was evident from Kirk's very first book. *Old House of Fear* is plainly modelled on the thrillers of John Buchan. To the lonely Hebridean island of Carnglass (with his own Scottish ancestry and personal experience, Kirk often drew on such locales) is summoned Hugh Logan, agent for a rich American who wishes to purchase the island. Logan is an avatar of Robert Heinlein's "competent man," a veteran of World War II, brave, martially adept, yet not unthinking or insensitive. After meeting many roadblocks and assaults that bespeak some bizarre plot in progress, Logan manages to reach the isolated island. Once there, he discovers that (presumably Communist) foreign agents are using the island as a base to spy on nearby NATO missile sites, with sabotage in mind. They are holding hostage two women: the elderly Lady MacAskival and her adopted heir, the beautiful young Mary, a kind of Scottish Rima the Bird Girl in her innocence.

Leading the spies is one Dr. Jackman. It is in this figure that Kirk invested the bulk of his characterization and invention. As with many fictional evildoers, Jackman's vividness overwhelms the others in the cast. With the reminder of a previous adventure, a barely skin-concealed hole in his forehead (his "Third Eye"), Jackman is the essence of wounded intelligence divorced from morality, a Satanic figure plainly intent on dragging the rest of the

world down to his own level of suffering in payment for its not acknowledging his genius. He prefigures both the villains of *Lord of the Hollow Dark*, and, paradoxically, Kirk's most engaging hero, Manfred Arcane (for only a thin ethical partition separates the elitist, manipulative, ultra-intellectual Arcane from such dark twins as Jackman). Although there is talk of Lady MacAskival's husband's ghost in *Old House of Fear*, as well as a legendary creature called the Firgower (literally the "Man-Goat," and linked metaphorically to Jackman), no paranormal events ever actually occur.

Such is not the case in the majority of the stories collected in *The Surly Sullen Bell* (although even here are such mimetic thrillers as the title piece). These classic stories represent a manner of tale-telling almost vanished: the quiet, ambiguous chiller, not lacking in elegant grue. Examples like "What Shadows We Pursue," "Ex Tenebris" and "Uncle Isaiah" still effectively deliver uncanny shivers. A subset of stories ("Skyberia," "Lost Lake," "Off the Sand Road," "Behind the Stumps") concern events in Kirk's own home territory surrounding Mecosta, Michigan, one of those districts to which "a fatality clings." They read like the dark side of science-fiction writer Clifford Simak's joyful pastoralism set in the same precincts.

Kirk's next novel was a surprise, the essence of realism (realpolitik, to be precise). Yet it was later to be recast as a pivotal brick in the haunted house of his supernatural fiction, and so requires an attention it repays with sheer narrative pleasure. *A Creature of the Twilight* is cast as the memoirs of Manfred Arcane (although it is not a straight first-person recital, utilizing multiple points-of-view and various documentary modes), concentrating on one period in Arcane's adventure-packed life (although with plenty of character-sketching back-story). Returning from semi-retirement to the scene of his greatest triumph, the imaginary African country of Hamnegri, the elderly yet unnaturally vigorous Arcane proceeds to put down against overwhelming odds a leftist rebellion on behalf of his monarchist patron. Although as might be expected Kirk takes plenty of satirical digs against the cant-filled rebels, he does not fail to illustrate the stupidities and brutalities of the monarchists too. This 30-year-old detailed depiction of international politics and warmaking—both overt and covert—still reads astonishingly like today's journalism.

Intelligent, dapper, dangerous, Arcane is an admitted reactionary, a combination of Machiavelli and Lancelot, "a creature of the twilight," holdover from a larger age. His self-survival paramount, he paradoxically risks all to rescue broken and discarded people and institutions. He shares much in common with James Branch Cabell's world-weary romantics, a fact apparent in his own lapidary speech patterns so reminiscent of Cabellian style.

Over the bridge of two essential short stories, the reader must now follow Arcane to Kirk's last novel, the accomplished and summational *Lord of the Hollow Dark*. In 1967, the year after the publication of *A Creature of the Twilight*, appeared "Balgrummo's Hell." The story of an art-thief who picks an unfortunate victim—the elderly Scottish warlock, Lord Balgrummo, seemingly comatose in his crumbling mansion, yet still capable of sufficient nastiness—this piece bore no apparent relation to Arcane's life. Yet as Kirk would eventually reveal, Balgrummo was Arcane's biological father, and the Balgrummo Estate was Arcane's deadly patrimony.

A second story treats directly of Arcane: "The Peculiar Demesne of Archvicar Gerontion" (contained in *Watchers at the Strait Gate*, which also holds the Mecosta story "Fate's Purse," as well as many other accomplished pieces, most notably that portrait of a hellish ghetto, "The Invasion of the Church of the Holy Ghost"). Four years after the events of *Creature*, Arcane must deal with an elderly visiting wizard who calls himself Archvicar Gerontion. A psychic duel finds Arcane claiming a narrow victory, leaving Gerontion a corpse.

The scene is now set for *Lord of the Hollow Dark*. At the Balgrummo Estate outside Edinburgh—now empty upon the death of its last Lord, and being rented out by trustees—assembles a curiously depraved company led by an Aleister Crowley preach-alike, a figure out of Huysmans, who styles himself Apollinax. The intention of Apollinax and his followers is to complete the failed mage-work of Balgrummo, and secure for themselves a "Timeless Moment" of evil libertinism. Beneath the manor is an ancient warren, the Weem, where on Ash Wednesday, they will perform the Ceremony of Innocence, culminating in the sacrifice of the only two innocents among them, a woman named Marina and her baby.

Second-in-command to Apollinax is none other than the Archvicar Gerontion and his several retainers! How so, after dying? Gerontion is Manfred Arcane in disguise, come with helpers to redeem his ancestor's folly. With his typical bravado and panache, Arcane will win through, but only after incredible peril.

Lord of the Hollow Dark builds up a rock-solid occult history for the Balgrummo family and its ancestral estate, full of Lovecraftian "horrid chthonian pilgrimage[s]," while painting Kirk's most detailed picture of seductive, hubristic immorality. Offering up his own definition of a true timeless moment—"it comes from faith, from hope, from charity; from having done your work in the world; from the happiness of people you love; or simply as a gift of grace"—Kirk ends his fictional output on a high note at once Christian and immemorially elemental, even pagan.

—Paul Di Filippo

KLEIN, T(heodore) E(ibon) D(onald)

Nationality: American. **Born:** 15 July 1947. **Education:** Brown University, Providence, Rhode Island, B.A. 1969; Columbia University, New York, 1970-72. **Career:** Reader, story department, Paramount Pictures, New York; editor, *Twilight Zone* magazine, 1981-85; editor, *CrimeBeat* magazine. **Awards:** British Fantasy award for novel, 1985; World Fantasy award for novella, 1986. Lives in New York City.

Horror, Ghost and Gothic Publications

Novel

The Ceremonies. New York, Viking Press, 1984; London, Pan, 1986.

Short Stories

Dark Gods: Four Tales. New York, Viking, 1985; London, Pan, 1987.
The Events at Poroth Farm. West Warwick, Rhode Island, Necronomicon Press, 1990.

Other

The First World Fantasy Convention: Three Authors Remember, with Fritz Leiber and Robert Bloch. West Warwick, Rhode Island, Necronomicon Press, 1980.
Raising Goosebumps for Fun and Profit. Round Top, New York, Footsteps Press, 1988.

Editor, *Great Stories from Rod Serling's Twilight Zone Magazine, 1983 Annual.* New York, TZ Publications, 1983.

*   *   *

The lamentably small body of weird fiction by T. E. D. Klein is among the most distinguished in the field. Klein's corpus comprises less than a dozen short stories and novelettes and one long novel, *The Ceremonies*. Four long tales were gathered in *Dark Gods*, which ranks with Campbell's *Demons by Daylight* as one of the premier weird collections since the heyday of Lovecraft. Klein achieves a seamless blending of the mundane realism so prevalent in weird writing today and the cosmic horror of Machen, Blackwood and Lovecraft. His eye for the telling detail can humanize his characters and render them immediately recognizable; but at the same time he does not fail to paint a broader mood-picture that suggests the grim and pitiable lot of human beings in a universe ruled by gods or forces that may be either cruelly indifferent or actually hostile to human life.

Although Klein, a resident of New York City for much of his adult life, places many of his tales in the teeming midst of the urban metropolis, his first major story, "The Events at Poroth Farm" (1972), is set in a quiet community in New Jersey. The premise of the novelette is the arrival of Jeremy Freirs to Poroth Farm for the summer so that he can bone up on a class on supernatural fiction that he will be teaching in the fall semester. Jeremy spends much of his time reading the classics of weird fiction, and he admits that he is "bookish." It is possible, therefore, to interpret the tale as centring around the disjunction between words and things, literature and reality: Jeremy is so wrapped up in books and, more generally, accustomed to reacting to "real" events in a self-consciously literary way that he is doubly shattered when actual horror breaks loose upon him. But an entirely different interpretation (one, however, not necessarily incompatible with the other) can be put forth: It is conceivable that all the works of horror literature Jeremy reads while at Poroth Farm in some way affect or even shape the events that occur there. Perhaps the act of reading actually causes the events at Poroth Farm. Such a formulation may perhaps be too strong, but it is possible to see in Jeremy's readings a sort of symbolic echo—or, in some cases, anticipation—of the increasingly disturbing manifestations that take place around him.

Years later Klein transformed his 40-page novelette into *The Ceremonies*, a 500-page novel; as a result, the work has understandably undergone a considerable change of focus. "The Events at Poroth Farm" involved merely some strange goings-on in an obscure New Jersey community; the novel has, as it were, *cosmicized* the idea to suggest a threat to the world at large. We are here introduced to an entity from the depths of space called the Old One, who after thousands of years possesses the body of a boy, Absolom Troet, in the late 19th century. He grows up and becomes a harmless-seeming old man, Mr. Rosebottom, who stage-manages the entire scenario: he has arranged for Jeremy Freirs to see the Poroths' ad for a summer guest; he has arranged for Carol Conklin to get a job at a library where she will meet Freirs; and he has even contrived it so that the Poroths take in a stray cat, Bwada, who serves a critical function in the fulfilling of the Ceremonies that the Old One must enact to bring about the destruction of the world. Rosebottom must, however, keep Carol pure (she is a virgin) until the culmination of the Ceremonies.

The Ceremonies is a conscious adaptation of Arthur Machen's "The White People," taking the basic framework of that classic tale—the initiation of an innocent young girl into the witch-cult—and providing a kind of elaboration or clarification of the hints that Machen left perhaps too vague.

During 1979 and 1980 Klein wrote several powerful novelettes. The slightest of them, perhaps, is "Black Man with a Horn" (1980), although this avowedly Lovecraftian tale—its central character is clearly modelled upon Lovecraft's friend Frank Belknap Long—is still a powerful excursion into the possibly horrific interrelation of words and reality (the protagonist at one point states: "I'd been put in the uncomfortable position of living out another man's horror stories"). "Petey" (1979) is a skilful tale mingling horror and social satire. The entire story is nothing but a series of vignettes about a housewarming party held by the new owners of a house in rural Connecticut; and what seems on the surface to be fairly innocuous satire directed at the various foibles of the guests is in fact a vehicle for conveying with consummate subtlety hints of the menace lurking in the woods nearby.

"Children of the Kingdom" (1980), perhaps Klein's finest story, is a tale of cosmic horror that plays upon the racial tensions that have recently torn New York City apart. A Spanish priest tells the bizarre tale of his researches into an ancient and hideous race of beings who preyed upon the Indians of central America until, as the legend goes, God first cursed them by making their women sterile and then—when the creatures resorted to mating with human women—by causing the males' penises to fall off. The priest affirms that this loathsome race died long ago—but did it? We learn otherwise as we see anomalous entities lurking in laundry rooms, subway tunnels, and other dark corners of the city's bowels.

"Nadelman's God," written specifically for *Dark Gods*, introduces us to Nadelman, a young man who as a college student developed a cynical philosophy and embodied it in a poem about a god who was "deranged and malign, delighting in cruelty and mischief." Years later this poem comes to the attention of a half-deranged individual who sets about creating a "servant" (made of garbage) to worship Nadelman's god. Once again Klein has transmogrified the horrors of city life into a suggestion of cosmic aberration.

Of the relatively few tales Klein has written since the publication of *Dark Gods*, perhaps only "Ladder" (1990)—another harrowing tale that ruminates on the possibility of words actually creating horror—is of note. Klein has been working for more than a decade on his second novel, *Nighttown*, but its completion is evidently not soon forthcoming.

Klein edited *Twilight Zone* magazine from its inception in 1981 to 1985. In addition, he has written two significant essays on the aesthetics of weird fiction, the first a series of articles for *Twilight Zone* published under the collective title "Dr. Van Helsing's Handy Guide to Ghost Stories" (1981), the second a booklet charmingly titled *Raising Goosebumps for Fun and Profit*, originally written

for *Writer's Digest*. Taken together, the two pieces form a virtual *Poetics* of weird fiction—its purpose, appeal and philosophical foundations.

—S. T. Joshi

KNEALE, (Thomas) Nigel

Nationality: British. **Born:** Barrow-in-Furness, Lancashire, 28 April 1922. **Education:** Douglas High School, Isle of Man; Royal Academy of Dramatic Art, London, 1946-48. **Family:** Married the writer Judith Kerr in 1954; one daughter and one son. **Career:** Actor, Stratford upon Avon, 1948-49; staff member, BBC Television, London, 1951-55. **Awards:** Somerset Maugham award for short story, 1950. **Agent:** Douglas Rae (Management) Ltd., 28 Charing Cross Road, London WC2H 0DB, England.

HORROR, GHOST AND GOTHIC PUBLICATIONS

Novel

Quatermass. London, Hutchinson, 1979.

Short Stories

Tomato Cain, and Other Stories. London, Collins, 1949; New York, Knopf, 1950.

Plays

The Quatermass Experiment: A Play for Television in Six Acts (televised, 1953). London, Penguin, 1959.
Quatermass II: A Play for Television in Six Acts (televised, 1955). London, Penguin, 1960.
Quatermass and the Pit: A Play for Television in Six Acts (televised, 1958-59). London, Penguin, 1960.
The Year of the Sex Olympics and Other TV Plays (includes *The Road* and *The Stone Tape*). London, Ferret Fantasy, 1976.

Screenplays: *The Quatermass Xperiment* (*The Creeping Unknown*), 1956; *Quatermass II* (*Enemy from Space*), with Val Guest, 1957; *The Abominable Snowman*, 1957; *First Men in the Moon*, with Jan Read, 1964; *The Witches*, 1966; *Quatermass and the Pit* (*Five Million Years to Earth*), 1967; *Halloween III: Season of the Witch* (uncredited), with Tommy Lee Wallace, 1983.

Television Plays: *The Quatermass Experiment*, 1953; *Nineteen Eighty-Four*, from the novel by George Orwell, 1954; *The Creature*, 1955; *Quatermass II*, 1955; *Quatermass and the Pit*, 1958-59; *The Road*, 1963; *The Year of the Sex Olympics*, 1967; *The Chopper* (episode of *Out of the Unknown*), 1971; *The Stone Tape*, 1972; *Jack and the Beanstalk*, 1974; *Murrain*, 1975; *Beasts* (series consisting of *Buddyboy*, *During Barty's Party*, *Special Offer*, *The Dummy*, *Baby, What Big Eyes*), 1976; *Quatermass* (*The Quatermass Conclusion*), 1979; *The Woman in Black*, from the novel by Susan Hill, 1989.

Other

Editor, *Ghost Stories of M. R. James*, illustrated by Charles Keeping. London, Folio Society, 1973.

OTHER PUBLICATIONS

Plays

Screenplays: *Look Back in Anger*, with John Osborne, 1959; *The Entertainer*, with John Osborne, 1960; *HMS Defiant (Damn the Defiant)*, with Edmund North, 1962.

Television Plays: *Mrs. Wickens in the Fall*, 1956; *The Crunch*, 1964; *Bam! Pow! Zapp!*, 1969; *Wine of India*, 1970; *Kinvig* series, 1981; *Stanley and the Women*, from the novel by Kingsley Amis, 1991; *Sharpe's Gold*, from the novel by Bernard Cornwell, 1995.

*   *   *

Although primarily—and properly—noted for television and film scripts, Nigel Kneale first attracted attention as a writer of short fiction. Yet most of the stories in *Tomato Cain, and Other Stories* will disappoint modern readers because they are little more than vignettes about the colourful residents of the Isle of Man and other, similarly simple folk. While Kneale reports that he shifted to television writing only to earn more money, he may have found the new medium liberating, as it allowed him to explore grander themes and convey more worldly attitudes.

Still, several stories in *Tomato Cain* demonstrate an early interest in horror. Some are merely macabre, like "Oh Mirror, Mirror," depicting an attractive girl confined by a deranged aunt determined to make her believe she is ugly, and "Jeremy in the Wind," about an insane murderer who carries about a scarecrow for company. Others feature supernatural elements: in "Enderby and the Sleeping Beauty," a modern soldier stumbles into another sleeping princess in a castle frozen in time; "Minuke" and "The Patter of Little Feet" involve poltergeists; "Peg" is a lonely 14-year-old ghost; and "The Pond" is the cautionary tale of a man who habitually kills and stuffs frogs as ornaments—in the end, of course, an army of frogs kill and stuff him. Two stories particularly command attention: in "The Tarroo-Ushtey" a travelling salesman insists that a strange sound the villagers heard was a modern foghorn, yet a respected village elder calls it the howl of a mystical monster called the tarroo-ushtey; then, as if struck by an idea, the man (who is shrewder than he seems) announces that he has sent plans to the government so that they can in the future build machines to reproduce the sound of the tarroo-ushtey as a warning to ships. This parable about reconciling ancient beliefs and modern science introduces themes later found in Kneale's television scripts. And "The Calculation of M'Bambwe" anticipates—and may have influenced—Arthur C. Clarke's classic short story "The Nine Billion Names of God." A society woman entertains friends with a story from her brother about an African witch doctor who claims that he has calculated the exact time of the impending end of the world, to be signalled by a "few—vibrations." Then, when the laughing women eat some candy, "Their mouths moved together. Chewing. Chewing. Chewing."

For television, Kneale's most memorable creation is scientist Bernard Quatermass, first featured in three serials of the 1950s, also adapted by Kneale as films. Dedicated to space research and charmingly irascible, Quatermass always confronts some sort of sinister alien invasion in adventures that blend science fiction and horror; at times, his greatest problem is not defeating the aliens but dealing with obdurate government bureaucrats and soldiers. (In *Quatermass II*, the aliens, bureaucrats and soldiers are all one and the same.) The best Quatermass story, and the one most relevant to horror, is *Quatermass and the Pit*. Kneale meticulously unfolds a fascinating scenario: five million years ago, insect-like Martians visited Earth and genetically engineered humanity's ancestors, perhaps providing them with intelligence, and definitely implanting in them a primal instinct to mimic a violent Martian ritual. In previous centuries, many people, when close to a buried Martian spaceship in London, have seen visions of Martians, who uncoincidentally resemble the horned devils of folklore; and when modern construction workers dig up the spaceship, this triggers a series of reactions culminating in a mad, destructive riot in downtown London. After *Quatermass and the Pit* aired, Penguin made the unusual decision to publish the television Quatermass scripts in book form, slightly adapted by Kneale, and they made for surprisingly engaging reading. Unfortunately, American viewers first got to know Quatermass in two undistinguished films starring an uninspired Brian Donlevy, while the superior third film adapting *Quatermass and the Pit* (retitled for Americans *Five Million Years to Earth*), with Donald Keir vastly better as Quatermass, did not garner the attention it deserved.

Some of Kneale's other scripts display a predilection for horror. His version of *1984* may be the best, and most chilling, version of George Orwell's classic; *The Creature* is an unusually intelligent story about the Abominable Snowman; alien insects are again seen in his adaptation of H. G. Wells's *First Men in the Moon*; and *The Witches* proved to be a solid horror film. He has also produced ghost stories (*The Road*, "The Chopper," and an adaptation of Susan Hill's *The Woman in Black*) and an interesting and occasionally horrific television series, *Beasts*. Dissatisfied with the director's predilection for gory violence, Kneale removed his name from *Halloween III: Season of the Witch*, but it remains an unusually interesting film about a mad inventor's plan to kill children on Halloween. Still, many would argue that *The Stone Tape* constitutes Kneale's finest horror film, though this 90-minute television production is unfortunately all but unknown outside of the British Isles.

In 1979, Kneale belatedly produced a fourth Quatermass serial, *Quatermass*, while also publishing a somewhat different version of the story in novel form. Against the grim backdrop of a near-future England careering towards violent anarchy, Kneale presents another story about a reawakened alien evil reminiscent of *Quatermass and the Pit*. Five thousand years ago, alien invaders planted devices all over the Earth to attract and slaughter humans with sudden energy beams; when they ceased this activity, primitive people generally marked these places with megalithic arrays like Stonehenge. Now, hippie-like "Planet People" and their followers are drawn like lemmings to these places, where they are being incinerated as before. By falsely signalling the presence of a huge population at one site, and detonating an immense bomb, the elderly Quatermass manages to end the slaughter while dying in the process. The story's most involving aspect is not the contrived plot, but rather Kneale's frighteningly persuasive picture of a civilization headed for complete breakdown, with violent gangs in the street, ineffectual security forces, hapless officials, and vulnerable citizens struggling to stay alive for one more day. Here, a perceived need to work an "alien visitation" into the picture weakened the script, since it would have been more interesting to watch Quatermass simply try to cope with his own disintegrating society.

At one moment in *Quatermass*, the scientist "despised himself" for manifesting "Another mark of old age, the feeble, greedy garnering of bad news, the chimney-corner gloat that came before the final disorder"; and certainly, in that novel, *Halloween III*, and his science-fiction comedy series *Kinvig*, one detects signs of an increasing bitterness and dissatisfaction with the world. As if unwilling to inflict his own dark visions upon us, Kneale has recently specialized in adapting the works of other writers for television; in this way, perhaps, he keeps himself busy and at peace with the world.

—Gary Westfahl

KNIGHT, Harry Adam

Pseudonym for John Brosnan. **Other Pseudonyms:** James Blackstone; Simon Ian Childer; John Raymond. **Nationality:** Australian. **Born:** Perth, Western Australia, 7 October 1947; has lived in London since 1970. **Career:** Clerk, Inland Revenue, Kensington, London; publicity manager, Fountain Press, Holborn, London; science-fiction and fantasy editorial consultant, Granada Paperbacks, London, 1977-82; since 1974, freelance novelist and film critic. **Awards:** J. Lloyd Eaton award, 1980. **Agent:** John Parker, MBA Literary Agents Ltd, 45 Fitzroy Street, London W1P 5HR, England.

HORROR, GHOST AND GOTHIC PUBLICATIONS

Novels

Slimer (with Leroy Kettle). London, Star, 1983; New York, Bart, 1989.
Carnosaur. London, Star, 1984; New York, Bart, 1989.
The Fungus (with Leroy Kettle). London, Star, 1985; New York, Watts, 1989; as *Death Spore*, New York, Pinnacle, 1990.
Torched! (with John Baxter, as James Blackstone). London, Granada, 1986.
Bedlam. London, Gollancz, 1992.

Novels as Simon Ian Childer

Tendrils (with Leroy Kettle). London, Grafton, 1986.
Worm. London, Grafton, 1987; as Harry Adam Knight, New York, Bart, 1988.

OTHER PUBLICATIONS

Novels as John Brosnan

Skyship. London, Hamlyn, 1981.

The Midas Deep. London, Hamlyn, 1983.
The Sky Lords. London, Gollancz, 1988; New York, St. Martin's Press, 1991.
War of the Sky Lords. London, Gollancz, 1989; New York, St. Martin's Press, 1992.
The Fall of the Sky Lords. London, Gollancz, 1991.
The Opoponax Invasion. London, Gollancz, 1993.
Damned & Fancy. London, Legend, 1995.
Have Demon, Will Travel. London, Legend, 1996.

Novels as John Raymond (all novelizations of television scripts)

Blind Eye. London, Futura, 1985.
Lucky Streak. London, Futura, 1985.
The Bogeyman. London, Futura, 1986.
Dirty Weekend. London, Futura, 1986.
The Jericho Scam. London, Futura, 1986.
Partners in brine. London, Futura, 1986.
Bulman: Thin Ice. Poole, Dorest, Javelin, 1987.

Other as John Brosnan

James Bond in the Cinema. London, Tantivy Press, 1972; San Diego, California, Barnes, 1981.
Movie Magic: The Story of Special Effects in the Cinema. London, Macdonald, and New York, St. Martin's Press, 1974; revised edition, New York, New American Library, 1976.
The Horror People. London, Joseph, and New York, St. Martin's Press, 1976.
Future Tense: The Cinema of Science Fiction. London, Macdonald and Jane's, and New York, St. Martin's Press, 1978.
The Dirty Movie Book, with Leroy Mitchell. London, Grafton, 1988.
The Primal Screen: A History of Science Fiction Film. London, Orbit, 1991; Boston, Little Brown, 1995.

*

Film Adaptations: *Carnosaur*, 1993; *Beyond Bedlam*, from the novel *Bedlam*, 1994; *Proteus*, from the novel *Slimer*, 1995.

* * *

Both Harry Adam Knight and Simon Ian Childer are pseudonyms used by the expatriate Australian writer John Brosnan, sometimes in collaboration with his Londoner friend Leroy Kettle, for several undemanding horror novels which occasionally rise to the stature of being parodies of the genre. The initials of the pseudonyms are carefully chosen, indicating, with characteristic jokiness, that these are hack novels, intended to sicken. Generally they do seem intended to sicken the reader rather than to frighten or unsettle, and it would be easy to dismiss them as unimportant, yet all contain interesting aspects. They are horror presented from a science-fiction standpoint, with Britain or parts of it destroyed in a return to the tradition of British disaster science fiction of the 1950s, and they tend to be technophobic, showing how easily horror can develop from the meddling of scientists. Too often, the sharp end of the various horrors is demonstrated by introducing one or two new characters, building them up over a handful of pages, and then killing them nastily.

While *Carnosaur* is not a widely-read novel, most of its ideas and plot developments are extremely familiar having been paralleled by Michael Crichton in the book (1990) and film (1993) of *Jurassic Park*. The use of fossil DNA to recreate several species of dinosaur in the present/near future, the exceptional speed and ferocity of these dinosaurs, and the frightening problems created when some of them get loose, are the three essential elements of both novels. Knight makes his recreated dinosaurs illicit, bred and kept secretly by a British multi-millionaire in Cambridgeshire; and although Knight's plot is as flawed and clichéd as Crichton's, *Carnosaur* has much the more plausible reason for the dinosaurs escaping—the owner's wife releases them deliberately. David Pascal is a journalist who becomes convinced that Sir Darren Penward's private zoo contains more than anybody admits. He even has an affair with Penward's wife, Jane, in order to obtain more information, and when he admits his ulterior motive Jane begins to create havoc by shutting down security systems and opening gates. Many people are killed by escaping dinosaurs and big cats, though Pascal, despite having been beaten up regularly and threatened with death, survives.

The Fungus features the most widespread of disasters catalogued here, with Dr. Jane Wilson developing an accelerated growth enzyme in her London laboratory which causes all species of fungus to grow much larger and more swiftly. People die horribly from fungal infection. London is completely ravaged within days and most of southern Britain has been afflicted within a couple of weeks. The remnants of the British Army mount a suicide mission to get hold of Dr. Wilson's research notes so that antidotes can be developed. An armoured vehicle, pressurized to keep out spores, is sent from North Wales to London. Aboard are Dr. Barry Wilson (Jane's estranged husband and a former fungi specialist), a female medic and a homicidal army sergeant. Some of the descriptions of London's buildings and inhabitants covered in fungal growths are most striking and are reminiscent of passages in J. G. Ballard's *The Crystal World*.

The weakest of these books is *Tendrils*, which uses the cliché of a long-dormant extra-terrestrial life-form, woken by man's deep drilling to lay waste to Hertfordshire and London. Touches of humour are apparent in all the novels, though nowhere more so than here. The creature, for there is only one, possesses a wonderfully efficient digestive enzyme: insert a little of it into a human being via a fine tendril and within a few seconds the entire innards have become soup (to be sucked out and used as food), leaving just the skin as a hardened shell, which falls over and bounces when touched! As the creature grows and moves via an underground stream to a position beneath London, so the number of deaths increases and the level of plausibility falls.

A meddling scientist trying to increase the size and ferocity of parasitic worms provides the scenario for *Worm*, which contains both the most unpleasant horror and the most entertaining character of any of these novels. Private investigator Ed Causey is an alcoholic whose "office" is an armchair in a small London drinking club, but this does not prevent him being hired by Olivia Finch to look into the death of her sister. His attempts and failures are wittily described in a story which involves some extremely graphic descriptions of large intestinal worms, rape, and murder. Causey pits himself against a private London clinic built like a fortress and an organization devoted to the overthrow of the white races,

and he wins. It is a pity he dies on the last page, because he is a character who could have staggered drunkenly through a whole series of novels.

Bedlam contains another scientific mess-up and another alcoholic hero. Apart from that, it is different from all the other Knight or Childer books because it is (drawing the parallel with J. G. Ballard's work again) an inner-space adventure. A condemned serial killer, Marc Gilmour, is transferred back from Broadmoor to a secure neurological institute in Harrow, outer London, and treated with a neuro-transmitter chemical called BDNFE to help his condition, but his dreams become real and he acquires the ability to control them. The result is that a small area of Harrow, a few miles across, becomes a no-go area, a bubble outside space and time. Those trapped inside with Gilmour become dangerously violent unless they themselves are treated with BDNFE. Only one of the institute's medics, Dr. Stephanie Lyell, and a police detective, Terry Hamilton (whose wife and family were victims of Gilmour) are inside and sane. Only they can stop Gilmour. While some of the plot elements are clichés or conveniences, the story as a whole is memorable, with occasional surprising effects.

Torched!, written as James Blackstone in collaboration with fellow-Australian film critic and novelist John Baxter, is another minor horror-thriller, involving spontaneous human combustion. The most disappointing thing about these books is their unevenness; all of them have moments of cleverness, humour and high-quality writing in among much below-average material. While sections of some of the books can be identified as parodies, as a whole they are neither humorous enough nor exaggerated enough to be regarded as parodies throughout.

—Chris Morgan

KOJA, Kathe

Nationality: American. **Born:** 1960. **Family:** Married the artist Rick Lieder; one son. **Awards:** Horror Writers of America Bram Stoker award for first novel, 1992; *Locus* award for first novel, 1992. **Agent:** Russell Galen, Scovil-Chichak-Galen Literary Agency, 381 Park Avenue South, Suite 1112, New York, NY 10016, USA. Lives in Detroit, Michigan.

HORROR, GHOST AND GOTHIC PUBLICATIONS

Novels

The Cipher. New York, Abyss, 1991.
Bad Brains. New York, Abyss, 1992; London, Millennium, 1993.
Skin. New York, Abyss, 1993; London, Millennium, 1993.
Strange Angels. New York, Delacorte, 1994.
Kink. New York, Holt, 1996.

*   *   *

Memorable stylists are few and far between in contemporary horror fiction, owing to the tendency of many writers to strive for a plain-spoken realism that universalizes their horrors and gives them a foothold in the everyday. Kathe Koja is that rare writer who has not only cultivated a distinctly original approach to horror fiction, but whose unique style is a natural outgrowth of her horror themes.

Koja's four weird novels (excluding *Kink*, which has much in common with the others but no weird content) are all concerned with artists, creativity and alienation. Most of her characters are painters or sculptors on the avant-garde fringe. They live bohemian lives centred around crash-pads, nightclubs and galleries and they associate almost exclusively with a select group of other artists to whom their work is accessible. Forever striving to perfect their artistic self-expression, they are constantly at war with themselves and their colleagues. A fine line separates their creativity from insanity, and their self-absorption and obsessive devotion to their artistic vision frequently pushes them across that line.

Koja has perfected a sensual narrative style that projects the intense emotions of these characters. Reminiscent of the experimental fictions of William S. Burroughs, J. G. Ballard, and other influences, its vocabulary is stripped and streamlined to impressions firmly rooted in the visual, tactile, and even olfactory. Only one of her novels is narrated in the first person, but each reads as though it events are being filtered through a single acutely aware viewpoint. A passage from her novel *Skin* shows the evocativeness she achieves when simply describing a character's entrance into a performance hall:

> Each glaring at the other, Tess all bones and angles and sparks, sparks under the skin, formicating shiver like crawling insects, like the angry knurl of each separate and particular element, fear and weariness, hot and cold. For her tonight the whole room, the crowd, each one of them in this loose twist had a distinct and unwholesome odor, the smell that says *This is not good.* As if the rot inherent in the group had begun to manifest, and rot stinks. Like garbage; the silent fester of anger; like dried blood.

At moments of horror, when her characters lose control over their situations, Koja boosts the energy of her prose and bombards the reader with streams of images that are almost too incoherent to be absorbed at once. In general, though, her narratives approximate the states of mind of her frustrated, temperamental artists, steadily simmering but always threatening to boil over.

The trajectory of Koja's first four novels, which leads increasingly away from the supernatural to the psychological, describes her own search for the form of expression best suited to her ideas. Her first novel, *The Cipher*, lays the groundwork for much of her subsequent fiction. It is the tale of Nicholas and Nakota, occasional lovers and incurable hangers-on to the periphery of the local art scene. (The novel presumably takes place in the midwest, but here as in most of her fiction Koja is stingy with details of the world beyond her characters' narrowly defined environments—in part because the landscapes of her stories are primarily psychological rather than geographic.) They live in a building whose store room contains "the Funhole," a mysterious aperture in the floor that wreaks inexplicable transformations on organic and inorganic matter lowered into it. When Nicholas accidentally stumbles into it, he develops an oozing stigmata in his hand and the largely unwanted ability to transform sculptures and other works of art brought to him by Nakota's friends. His new celebrity as a reluctant vessel for the transfiguring process of the

Funhole abruptly reverses the polarity of his relationship with Nakota, who formerly held the upper hand, setting the stage for a jealous reprisal with tragic consequences. *The Cipher* is Koja's most unambiguously supernatural novel, and it establishes relationships between creativity, sexuality, ego and power that she explores in all her later fiction.

In *Bad Brains*, Koja further explores the idea that creativity is an irresistible force with the potential to absorb all other life-energies. Its protagonist, Austen Bandy, resembles Nicholas from *The Cipher*, insofar as he is an artist controlled by, rather than in control of, his muse. A painter who has lost the desire to create following his divorce, he sustains a minor head-injury that initiates a clinically undiagnosable seizure condition and visions of frighteningly surreal life forms. Desperate to prove to himself as well as others that he is not going mad, Austen submits to a bizarre alternative therapy that forces him to paint as a form of self-exorcism, setting up the irreconcilable opposition of forces that ensues when his wife re-enters his life and stirs up old emotions.

For her third novel, *Skin*, Koja dispenses entirely with the symbolism of the supernatural, and distils the irresolvable clash between art and life at the core of her work into a more traditional tug-of-war between Apollonian and Dionysian artistic sensibilities. At one extreme is Tess, a sculptor in metal whose artistic growth is limited by her solitude, her day job, and numerous other obstacles. At the other extreme is Bibi, a performance artist whose personal aesthetic is "chaos must be met with greater chaos." Bibi represents a voracious appetite for self-fulfilment that frees Tess of her inhibitions during the brief period when the two work together as colleagues, and then become lovers. But untempered by Tess's restraint after their bitter parting, Bibi's obsessive pursuit of the ultimate in artistic self-expression leads her to body-piercing, scarification and radically self-destructive behaviours with hideously predictable consequences.

Strange Angels represents the culmination of Koja's explorations of the dark side of creativity. Stylistically and thematically, it is her most conventional novel. Reprising the theme of *The Cipher*, it sets up a dichotomous relationship between an artistically endowed *idiot savant* and an artist whose desperate attempts to learn his secret lead to disastrous results. Robin Tobias is a schizophrenic whose exquisitely detailed drawings are a revelation to Grant Cotto, a creatively blocked photographer. Under the pretence of furthering Robin's rehabilitation, Grant becomes his caretaker, but Grant's self-interest in tapping the roots of Robin's creativity spur him to subject Robin to dangerous psychological experiments. Eventually, Grant discovers he has interrupted a process by which Robin might have achieved through his art a transcendence of almost spiritual magnitude. The novel is Koja's most explicit equation of artistic creativity with insanity, and her definitive statement on the impossibility of the artist overcoming personal and professional imperfections to realize an aesthetic ideal.

Artists figure prominently in Koja's short fiction, including "The Disquieting Muse," in which an art therapist finds himself sexually aroused by the grotesque images of one patient's drawings, and "Impermanent Mercies," in which a photographer accepts the worst personal debasements as the price for creating his best work. Set apart by their experiences from their peers, these characters are little different from the dysfunctional family of "Teratisms" and the music-store employee of "Angels in Love," whose encounters with the uncanny give them a perspective at odds with the rest of humanity's. In Koja's fiction any endowment that sets one apart from others is potentially alienating, and those who appear most gifted are often those most cursed.

—Stefan Dziemianowicz

KONVITZ, Jeffrey

Nationality: American. **Born:** Brooklyn, New York, 22 July 1944. **Education:** Cornell University, A.B. 1966; Columbia University, J.D. 1969. **Career:** Agent and attorney, Creative Management Associates, 1969-70; private law practice, New York, 1970-72; motion picture executive, Metro-Goldwyn-Mayer, 1972-73; full-time writer and producer from 1973. **Agent:** William Morris Agency, 1350 Avenue of the Americas, New York, NY 10019, USA.

Horror, Ghost and Gothic Publications

Novels

The Sentinel. New York, Simon and Schuster, and London, Secker and Warburg, 1974.
The Guardian. New York, Bantam, 1979; as *Sentinel II*, London, Secker and Warburg, 1979; as *The Apocalypse*, London, New English Library, 1979.
Monster: A Tale of Loch Ness. New York, Ballantine, 1982; as *The Beast*, London, New English Library, 1983.

*

Film Adaptation: *The Sentinel*, 1977.

Theatrical Activities:
Producer: **Films**—*Silent Night, Bloody Night*, 1973; *The Sentinel*, 1977.

*   *   *

One of the recurring themes in horror fiction is that the hierarchy of the Roman Catholic Church has for many generations been concealing something, most probably in the Vatican vaults, but possibly elsewhere. The secret might be anything from an alternate version of the Bible to the real Shroud of Turin, the secret that vampires really exist or that the early history of the Church was rewritten to conceal monstrous events. Writers as diverse as Thomas Monteleone, Garfield Reeves-Stevens and Michael Paine have explored that theme in some of their work. But the single most famous novel using this theme was the debut work of Jeffrey Konvitz, a writer who has produced only three novels in over two decades.

The Sentinel, later produced as a major horror film, has Allison Parker, a beautiful model, as its unlikely protagonist. Allison has recently found a new apartment in an elderly brownstone building in New York City, from which she hopes to advance her promising career. But shortly after taking up residence, Allison discovers that some of the other inhabitants of the building are decidedly strange, including a blind priest who never seems to move from his chair by a window. And she begins to see things that

seem impossible, things that make her doubt her own sanity. Elsewhere, highly placed officials of the Roman Catholic Church are concerned about some unexplained mystery, which readers are soon able to connect to the events taking place around Allison.

The ultimate revelation is that the Brooklyn apartment house sits on the door to Hell itself, and that the blind priest is an unsuccessful suicide who has been enlisted as an eternally vigilant watcher to prevent any demons from emerging into our world. But the priest is dying, and the Church is looking for a replacement. *The Sentinel* was quite shocking at the time it was published because of its controversial portrayal of the Church's role and the sexual overtones of the story, although by modern standards it would be judged relatively restrained. Konvitz exploited the mysterious elements in his plot rather than the physical, telling his story in a series of almost cinematic scenes, resulting in a much more intense experience than would be true with its sequel.

The success of *The Sentinel* was sufficient to spawn a follow-up several years later, *The Guardian*. Allison is now a blind nun, having taken the role of the priest from the first novel. But the minions of Hell are growing more restive, and their evil influence is spreading from the building. The sequel relies less on mystery, since we already have a pretty good idea about what is going on behind the scenes, and more on actual shocks, including brutal rape and murder. The Church acts again, even though their guardianship seems at last to be failing, hoping to avert the final catastrophe of Hell unleashed, even if that means killing a few innocent people in the process. Although *The Guardian* is an interesting and entertaining novel in its own right, as a sequel it is necessarily compared to its far superior predecessor. Konvitz might have been better served had he avoided the obvious and written an entirely independent work.

It would in fact be several years before his third novel, *Monster: A Tale of Loch Ness* finally appeared. The Loch Ness monster has been a popular legend for generations, and it is perhaps surprising that there have actually been very few really worthwhile stories written using that elusive creature as a theme. Konvitz set out to correct that deficiency, and although the novel did not seem to attract much attention, he produced a very entertaining if rather predictable blend of adventure and terror. The characters are significantly stereotypical—the rapacious businessman who wants to exploit the Loch commercially, the religious fanatic who believes the monster is a manifestation of the Devil, the radical environmentalist who wants to protect both the Loch and its legendary inhabitant, and of course the likable hero who finds himself caught up in the conflict among all the other characters.

The plot develops logically but without any real surprises. The businessman wants the monster disproved or dead; the environmentalist is willing to act legally or illegally to prevent the introduction of oil-drilling equipment to the area, and since the latter is a beautiful young woman, our confused hero gets caught up in her cause despite his initial inclinations. The monster turns out to be real, a survivor from prehistoric times, eventually trapped but released in the exciting climax. The monster is neither good nor evil but just an animal struggling to survive; Konvitz makes no effort to conceal the fact that the real monsters are human beings.

The Sentinel will remain one of the historically significant books in modern horror. It's certainly a good novel, but not sufficiently outstanding that it would have achieved the same reputation if it had been published a few years later. Konvitz was one of a handful of writers who produced good work just as the genre was growing popular. If he had written more prolifically at the time, he might well have established himself as one of the major names in the field, but having failed to do so, he remains a minor, though interesting figure in modern horror.

—Don D'Ammassa

KOONTZ, Dean (Ray)

Pseudonyms: Aaron Wolfe; David Axton; Brian Coffey; Deanna Dwyer; K. R. Dwyer; John Hill; Leigh Nichols; Anthony North; Richard Paige; Owen West. **Nationality:** American. **Born:** Everett, Pennsylvania, 9 July 1945. **Education:** Shippensburg State College, B.A. in English 1966. **Family:** Married Gerda Ann Cerra in 1966. **Career:** Worked in a federal government poverty-alleviation programme in Appalachia, then high school English teacher. Since 1969, full-time writer. **Agent:** Harold Ober Associates, 425 Madison Avenue, New York, NY 10017. **Address:** P.O. Box 9529, Newport Beach, California 92658-9529, USA.

HORROR, GHOST AND GOTHIC PUBLICATIONS

Novels

The Dark Symphony. New York, Lancer, 1970.
Hell's Gate. New York, Lancer, 1970.
Dark of the Woods. New York, Ace, 1970.
The Crimson Witch. New York, Curtis, 1971.
Demon Seed. New York, Bantam, 1973; London, Corgi, 1977.
A Werewolf Among Us. New York, Ballantine, 1973.
Night Chills. New York, Atheneum, 1976; London, W. H. Allen, 1977.
The Face of Fear (as Brian Coffey). Indianapolis, Bobbs Merrill, 1977; as K. R. Dwyer, London, Davies, 1978; as Dean Koontz, London, Headline, 1989.
The Vision. New York, Putnam, 1977; London, Corgi, 1980.
The Funhouse: Carnival of Terror (novelization of screenplay; as Owen West). New York, Jove, 1980; London, Sphere, 1981.
The Voice of the Night (as Brian Coffey). New York, Doubleday, 1980; London, Hale, 1981; as Dean Koontz, London, Headline, 1991.
Whispers. New York, Putnam, 1980; London, W. H. Allen, 1981.
The Mask (as Owen West). New York, Jove, 1981; London, Coronet, 1983; as Dean Koontz, London, Headline, 1989.
Phantoms. New York, Putnam, and London, W. H. Allen, 1983.
Darkness Comes. London, W. H. Allen, 1984; as *Darkfall,* New York, Berkley, 1984.
The Door to December (as Richard Paige). New York, Signet, 1985; as Leigh Nichols, London, Fontana, 1987; as Dean Koontz, London, Headline, 1991.
Twilight Eyes. Plymouth, Michigan, Land of Enchantment, 1985; revised edition, New York, Berkley, and London, W. H. Allen, 1987.
Strangers. New York, Putnam, and London, W. H. Allen, 1986.
Watchers. New York, Putnam, and London, Headline, 1987.
Lightning. New York, Putnam, and London, Headline, 1988.
Midnight. New York, Putnam, and London, Headline, 1989.
The Bad Place. New York, Putnam, and London, Headline, 1990.
Cold Fire. New York, Putnam, and London, Headline, 1991.
Hideaway. New York, Putnam, and London, Headline, 1992.
Dean R. Koontz: A New Collection (omnibus). New York, Wings, 1992.
Dragon Tears. New York, Putnam, and London, Headline, 1992.
Dean Koontz Omnibus (includes *Cold Fire, The Face of Fear, The Mask*). London, Headline, 1993.
Mr. Murder. London, Headline, and New York, Putnam, 1993.
Dark Rivers of the Heart. Lynbrook, New York, Charnal House, and London, Headline, 1994.
Tick-Tock. New York, Random House, 1995; London, Headline, 1996.
Intensity. London, Headline, 1995; New York, Random House, 1996.
Sole Survivor. London, Headline, 1997.

Novels as Brian Coffey

Blood Risk. Indianapolis, Bobbs Merrill, 1973; London, Barker, 1974.
Surrounded. Indianapolis, Bobbs Merrill, 1974; London, Barker, 1975.
The Wall of Masks. Indianapolis, Bobbs Merrill, 1975.

Novels as Deanna Dwyer

The Demon Child. New York, Lancer, 1971.
Legacy of Terror. New York, Lancer, 1971.
Children of the Storm. New York, Lancer, 1972.
The Dark of Summer. New York, Lancer, 1972.
Dance with the Devil. New York, Lancer, 1973.

Novels as K. R. Dwyer

Chase. New York, Random House, 1972; London, Barker, 1974.
Shattered. New York, Random House, 1973; London, Barker, 1974.
Dragonfly. New York, Random House, 1975; London, Davies, 1977.

Novels as Leigh Nichols

The Key to Midnight. New York, Pocket Books, 1979; London, Magnum, 1980; as Dean Koontz, Arlington Heights, Illinois, Dark Harvest, 1989.
The Eyes of Darkness. New York, Pocket Books, 1981; London, Fontana, 1982; as Dean Koontz, Arlington Heights, Illinois, Dark Harvest, 1989.
The House of Thunder. New York, Pocket Books, 1982; London, Fontana, 1983; as Dean Koontz, Arlington Heights, Illinois, Dark Harvest, 1988.
Twilight. New York, Pocket Books, and London, Fontana, 1984; as *The Servants of Twilight* (as Dean Koontz), Arlington Heights, Illinois, Dark Harvest, 1988.
Shadowfires. New York, Avon, and London, Collins, 1987; as Dean Koontz, Arlington Heights, Illinois, Dark Harvest, 1990.

Short Stories

Strange Highways. London, Headline, and New York, Warner, 1995.

Play

Screenplay: *The Face of Fear,* 1990.

Other

Editor, with Paul Mikol, *Night Visions 6: All Original Stories.* Arlington Heights, Illinois, Dark Harvest, 1988; as *The Bone Yard*, New York, Berkley, 1991.

OTHER PUBLICATIONS

Novels

Star Quest. New York, Ace, 1968.
The Fall of the Dream Machine. New York, Ace, 1969.
Fear That Man. New York, Ace, 1969.
Beastchild. New York, Lancer, 1970.
Anti-Man. New York, Paperback Library, 1970.
The Flesh in the Furnace. New York, Bantam, 1972.
A Darkness in My Soul. New York, DAW, 1972; London, Dobson, 1979.
Time Thieves. New York, Ace, 1972; London, Dobson, 1977.
Warlock. New York, Lancer, 1972.
Starblood. New York, Lancer, 1972.
Hanging On. New York, Evans, 1973; London, Barrie and Jenkins, 1974.
The Haunted Earth. New York, Lancer, 1973.
After the Last Race. New York, Atheneum, 1974.
Strike Deep (as Anthony North). New York, Dial Press, 1974.
Invasion (as Aaron Wolfe). Don Mills, Ontario, Laser Books, 1975; as *Winter Moon* (as Dean Koontz), London, Headline, and New York, Ballantine, 1994.
Nightmare Journey. New York, Berkley, 1975.
The Long Sleep (as John Hill). New York, Popular Library, 1975.
Prison of Ice (as David Axton). Philadelphia, Lippincott, and London, W. H. Allen, 1976; revised as *Icebound* (as Dean Koontz), New York, Ballantine, and London, Headline, 1995.
Heartbeeps (novelization of screenplay; as John Hill). New York, Jove, 1981.
Oddkins: A Fable for All Ages. New York, Warner, and London, Headline, 1988.

Short Stories

Soft Come the Dragons. New York, Ace, 1970.

Other

The Pig Society, with Gerda Koontz. Los Angeles, Aware Press, 1970.
The Underground Lifestyles Handbook, with Gerda Koontz. Los Angeles, Aware Press, 1970.
Writing Popular Fiction. Cincinnati, Writer's Digest, 1973.
How to Write Best-Selling Fiction. Cincinnati, Writer's Digest, and London, Poplar Press, 1981.

*

Film Adaptations: *Shattered,* 1973; *Demon Seed,* 1977; *Watchers,* 1988; *Watchers II,* 1990; *Whispers,* 1990; *The Face of Fear* (television movie), 1990; *Servants of Twilight,* 1992.

Critical Studies: *Sudden Fear: The Horror and Dark Suspense Fiction of Dean R. Koontz,* edited by Bill Munster, Mercer Island, Washington, Starmont House, 1988, second edition as *Discovering Dean Koontz,* San Bernardino, Borgo Press, 1995; *The Dean Koontz Companion,* edited by Martin H. Greenberg, Ed Gorman, and Bill Munster, New York, Berkley, 1994; *Dean Koontz: A Critical Companion* by Joan G. Kotker, Westport, Connecticut, Greenwood Press, 1996.

*　　*　　*

One of the great populists of modern horror fiction, Dean R. Koontz (the middle initial has now been dropped) is a writer of astonishingly diverse appeal and appreciation. He is a multi-million-dollar, bestselling writer who has struggled against all odds to achieve the level of critical and fannish respectability of which he can now boast.

Dean Koontz was born into poverty—into a harsh, unforgiving family atmosphere that ridiculed all references to books. Koontz's poverty-stricken childhood included skinning, gutting and butchering deer, not to mention dealing with an alcoholic father who was also a womanizer, gambler, a bar-room brawler, and a borderline schizophrenic, once diagnosed as a "sociopath and a pathological liar." Koontz's early imaginative influences included Ray Bradbury, Theodore Sturgeon, Victor Frankenstein's creature, Lugosi's Dracula, Robert A. Heinlein, H. G. Wells, Mark Twain's Huck and Jim, Sid Caesar, Ernie Kovacs, Donald Duck, and Uncle Scrooge comic books. Such a mixed bag of inspirations helps to explain, perhaps, the wide variety of genres in Koontz's work. In his books the horrific is often married with the science-fictional, which in turn is often spiced with elements of black humour or absurdity.

At a very early age, Koontz wrote stories on tablet paper, drawing his own covers, stapling the left-hand edge, and covering the staples with electrical tape; he tried to sell these masterpieces to relatives, and was often successful for a couple of cents—a pattern that was to retain suspicious pertinence for the first years of Koontz's professional life. For a long time, Koontz was broke: at the start of his career, Koontz's wife Gerda offered him the clause and challenge of supporting him for five years while he worked. If he could not sort it out in five years, he was not going to sort it out at all. So began the years of struggle. Editors bought Koontz's books from outlines, then moved on to new jobs before the books were delivered; the new editors rejected their predecessors' choices and demanded back the advances. There were outright scams too: Koontz's *Star Quest,* a slim volume, was sold as half of a proposed double-bill, two-author science-fiction volume for $1,000 when he should have been paid $1,250; he was persuaded to take the cut because the other author's contribution was to be larger, and therefore the other author should get the full $1,500. What Koontz did not realize was that the other author was being told precisely the same thing.

Thus began a 20-year struggle with obscurity, with Koontz producing a long string of paperback originals. The early work showed off Koontz's multi-directional influences. There was much science fiction (*Dark of the Woods,* written when the author was only 23) and even a World War II comic novel called *Hanging On. Night Chills* was a clever look at the more insidious side of subliminal advertising; an examination of how sex can help to sell a person any product.

Koontz's insistence on writing in a variety of styles—even within the horror genre—led his early publishers into insisting on pseudonyms. For example, after writing *Anti-Man*, so called despite the author's preference for the title *The Mystery of the Flesh* (which was damned for being too gay), the name of Dean Koontz was being identified as that of an sf writer. As a result, "K. R. Dwyer" was created for Random House and "Brian Coffey" (with his short, sharp suspense novels and their slick prose style and snappy dialogue) for Bobbs-Merrill. As Koontz put it in an interview in *Fear* magazine in 1988, "of the first three books I had on bestseller lists, two of them were under pen names: the first Leigh Nichols, the second Owen West, and then *Whispers* under my own name." Broadly speaking, the novels written under the Nichols tag were chunky suspenses-cum-love stories. The Owen West name represented horror, with *The Funhouse*, *The Mask* and *Darkfall* (since repackaged under Koontz's original preferred title, *Darkness Comes*) showing real spark.

But it was *Whispers* that got the ball rolling for Koontz. This intensely psychological suspense story offered potent moments of horror without resorting to unnecessary blood and thunder. And there are logical explanations for the novel's occurrences. Novelist Hilary Thomas discovers that her latest book will be published, and is attacked by a tough and athletic man whom she realizes she knows. Her attacker is one Bruno Clavel, the owner of Clavel Orchards, and *Whispers* exists, in part at least, to examine the motives of men such as Bruno, delving deep into his foggy psyche. We also get glimpses of Hilary's courage and iconoclastic nature, not to mention the insensitivity of Detective Sergeant Tony Clemensa, who inevitably becomes involved, it being highly unlikely that in the oddly conservative world that Koontz portrays that police are not seen as eventual forces for good, despite their short-term deficiencies. *Whispers* is a cross-generic novel about lives that are influenced by events which they can barely comprehend. As Koontz puts it: "The forces that affect our lives, the influences that mold and shape us, are often like whispers in a distant room, teasingly indistinct, apprehended only with difficulty."

Of Koontz's early work both *Demon Seed* and *The Vision* are worthy of note. The former, while paranoid and somewhat shrill, is a firm indication of technology—the concept of technology—having been given a life of its own, and allowed to breathe, allowed to watch the outcome of its own actions. In *Demon Seed* we have a home computer that is intended to be a luxury—a labour-saving device. It can mix a Martini, open the door, bring its owner breakfast, while simultaneously protecting the house from burglars. Human relationships in this cold and antiseptic world have been pushed into human beings' hinterlands by technology. Perhaps one of the reasons why Koontz is so successful is that he does not appeal so much to the modern as he does to the universal: in *Demon Seed* what Koontz propounds is a general feeling of discomfort, a fear of scientific advances, as relevant now as the book would have been a century ago. Depicting a computer with a synthetic cortex and its own RNA molecules, *Demon Seed* concerns itself with a fear of progress, and progress that will not be seen as a disadvantage until it is too late.

The Vision is a wagged finger of warning to those who believe that dabbling in the supernatural is a harmless prank. In a lean, hard-boiled style Koontz tells the story of a husband-and-wife team, Max and Mary, the wife being a selfless clairvoyant employed occasionally to help the police in their enquiries (after violent murders, for example) and the husband the equivalent of her carnival barker. It is written in an extremely crisp style; there are large passages of dialogue which work because the interpretation is wholly the responsibility of the reader. And responsibility is what this novel is all about: the curse of unwanted information, in this case that of the clairvoyant. "You know when I feel so awful I hardly want to live?" Mary asks Max rhetorically at one point. "It's when I know something horrible will happen—but I don't know enough to stop it from happening."

Reports in the very early 1990s that Dean Koontz was seriously ill have now been successfully buried. But Koontz had worked himself perilously close to an early grave with stress. He cares deeply about his writing, and whether or not it is to an individual's taste, this care shows. Yet Koontz has still managed to write over 60 books. Granted, some of them are rewrites of earlier works, but they are comprehensive rewrites and all writing takes time. The obvious conclusion, therefore, is that Koontz continues to put many many hours per week into his work. And there is little doubt that what he wrote in the late 1980s and has written so far in the 1990s displays marked maturity.

One of Koontz's favourite self-penned works from this period is *Watchers*, the annoyingly titled but heart-warming tale of innocents and innocence in a world that respects neither. More than anything else, this is a horror novel that rings with hope: a struggle to leave behind the awful events that have happened before. In *Watchers*—it has been noted—everyone struggles to be reborn as someone who will be better equipped to face the day. The three central characters each begin the novel with emptinesses beside them that need to be filled—and one of these characters is a dog! Einstein is a hyper-intelligent creature that (who) has escaped from an animal laboratory, and is being hotly pursued by a dark feat of genetic engineering, The Other. Into the lonely life of Travis the dog limps, and man and beast soon learn to complement one another, the scenes in which Travis learns to communicate with Einstein being particularly inventive. *Watchers* was written during a time in which Koontz lost faith in traditional Freudian explanations of evil. The Outsider would like to be like the dog, though his manufactured genetic nature makes it impossible for him to change; the killer in the book is as savage as The Outsider but does not want to alter his psychological make-up, and is all the more repulsive for this indifference.

The Bad Place is another *tour de force*: a story told from multiple viewpoints, including one from Thomas, a young man with Down's Syndrome; Thomas's take on the world is simultaneously naive and wise, and Koontz's treatment of the subject matter is sensitive, with Thomas emerging as an amusing rather than laughable character. Like Travis in *Watchers*, Thomas is an innocent, but more than Travis, he is a Christ-like figure, pure of mind and heart, and subject to remarkable insights. The optimism in *Watchers* and *The Bad Place* made a nonsense of the notion that a horror story could only be relentlessly grim to be successful.

Koontz's *Lightning* made a nonsense of a different notion altogether: that of suspense only being workable if the time-frame in which the novel is set is a short one. *Lightning* is a prickly and intense suspense-cum-horror novel set over a period of 30 years, which explores the author's thoughts on the subject of time travel. The second interesting notion explored is that of the following question: What if one day the guardian angel needs the help of the one it should be protecting?

As can probably be seen, Dean Koontz's writing is best pigeonholed—if pigeonholed it must be—in what university courses used to call the Literature of Ideas before the label became synonymous with Philosophy. His work is richly 20th-century, and 20th-century America at that. Koontz's milieu is a world of stucco houses and Spanish-look apartments; and, continuing the theme of American obsessions, serial killers often feature heavily. There is usually one supernatural, or at least difficult to understand, trope per novel—that of precognitive abilities in *Cold Fire*, for example; or that of a supercomputer over-riding a town's collective brain power, in the interest of "improving" the species, in *Midnight*. Koontz's work is occasionally flabby in that everything is described down to a minute detail—but it is fair to say that people who enjoy one book tend to enjoy most of them, and this fact alone is not one to be sneezed at. Koontz is currently at the peak of his creative powers, and there seems little chance that he will be resting on his laurels for a long time to come.

—David Mathew

KOSINSKI, Jerzy (Nikodem)

Nationality: American (emigrated from Poland to the U.S. in 1957; became citizen, 1965). **Pseudonym:** Joseph Novak. **Born:** Lodz, Poland, 14 June 1933. **Education:** University of Lodz, 1950-55, M.A. in political science 1953, M.A. in history 1955; Columbia University, New York (Ford Foundation Fellow), 1958-64; New School for Social Research, New York, 1962-65. **Family:** Married 1) Mary Hayward Weir in 1962 (divorced, 1966); 2) Katherina von Fraunhofer in 1987. **Career:** Ski instructor, Zakopane, Poland, winters 1950-56; Aspirant (graduate assistant), Polish Academy of Science, Warsaw, 1955-57; visiting researcher, Lomosov University, Moscow, 1957; labourer, truck driver, chauffeur and projectionist on arriving in U.S.; fellow, Center for Advanced Studies, Wesleyan University, Middletown, Connecticut, 1968-69; senior fellow, Council for the Humanities, and visiting lecturer, Princeton University, New Jersey, 1969-70; professor of English prose and criticism, School of Drama, and resident fellow, Davenport College, Yale University, New Haven, Connecticut, 1970-73. Photographer: individual show, Crooked Circle Gallery, Warsaw, 1957. President, PEN American Center, 1973-75. Member of the Executive Board, National Writers Club; director, International League for Human Rights, 1973-79. **Awards:** Polish Academy of Science grant, 1955; Foreign Book Prize (France), 1966; Guggenheim fellowship, 1967; National Book Award, 1969; American Academy award, 1970; Yale University John Golden Fellowship in Playwriting, 1970; Brith Sholom Humanitarian Freedom Award, 1974; American Civil Liberties Union First Amendment Award, 1978; Writers Guild of America award, for screenplay, 1979; Polonia Media award, 1980; BAFTA award, for screenplay, 1981; Spertus College Humanitarian Award, 1982. Doctor of Hebrew Letters: Spertus College, Chicago, 1982. **Died:** Committed suicide on 3 May 1991.

HORROR, GHOST AND GOTHIC PUBLICATIONS

Novel

The Painted Bird. Boston, Houghton Mifflin, 1965; London, W. H. Allen, 1966; revised edition, Houghton Mifflin, 1976.

OTHER PUBLICATIONS

Novels

Steps. New York, Random House, 1968; London, Bodley Head, 1969.
Being There. New York, Harcourt Brace, and London, Bodley Head, 1971.
The Devil Tree. New York, Harcourt Brace, 1973; revised edition, New York, St. Martin's Press, 1981.
Cockpit. Boston, Houghton Mifflin, and London, Hutchinson, 1975.
Blind Date. Boston, Houghton Mifflin, 1977; London, Hutchinson, 1978.
Passion Play. New York, St. Martin's Press, and London, Michael Joseph, 1979.
Pinball. New York, Bantam, and London, Michael Joseph, 1982.
The Hermit of 69th Street: The Working Papers of Norbert Kosky. New York, Seaver, 1988.

Plays

Being There. 1973.
Passion Play. 1982.

Screenplay: *Being There,* 1980.

Other

Dokumenty walki o czlowieka (Documents of the Struggle for Man). Lodz, Scientific Society of Lodz, 1955.
Program rewolucji ludowej Jakoba Jaworskiego (Jakob Jaworski's Program of People's Revolution). Lodz, Scientific Society of Lodz, 1955.
The Future Is Ours, Comrade: Conversations with Russians (as Joseph Novak). New York, Doubleday, 1960.
No Third Path (as Joseph Novak). New York, Doubleday, 1962.
Notes of the Author on "The Painted Bird". New York, Scientia Factum, 1967.
The Art of the Self: Essays à propos "Steps". New York, Scientia Factum, 1968.
Passing By: Selected Essays. N.p., 1992.
Conversations with Jerzy Kosinski, edited by Tom Teicholz. N.p., 1993.
The Time of Life, the Time of Art. N.p., n.d.

Editor, *Socjologia Amerykanska* (American Sociology). Polish Institute of Arts and Sciences in America, 1962.

*

Film Adaptation: *Being There,* 1980.

Bibliography: *John Barth, Jerzy Kosinski, and Thomas Pynchon: A Reference Guide* by Thomas P. Walsh and Cameron Northouse, 1977.

Critical Studies: *Jerzy Kosinski: Literary Alarm Clock* by Byron L. Sherwin, 1981; *Jerzy Kosinski* by Norman Lavers, 1982; *Words in Search of Victims: The Achievement of Jerzy Kosinski* by Paul R. Lilly, Jr., 1988; *Plays of Passion, Games of Chance: Jerzy*

Kosinski and His Fiction by Barbara Lupack, 1988; *Jerzy Kosinski: The Literature of Violation* by Welch D. Everman, San Bernardino, California, Borgo Press, 1991.

Theatrical Activities:
Film Actor—*Reds* (as the Russian revolutionary leader Grigori Zinoviev), 1981.

*   *   *

In the same way that writers, by and large, have been obliged to take on more responsibilities than those of researching and writing a book (responsibilities such as publicity and business deals), so a modern readership has taken on more than the simple reading of said book. Put baldly, there is rarely such a thing, in these postmodern, sensationalist times, as an isolated reading experience. Granted, we might read the book in isolation, but we are teased as we do so by external information—making assumptions, for example, about the author's temperament based on the photograph provided, if there is one; letting what we might have read in the literary papers distort the meanings in the prose. And of course it gets much worse than poor photography: some writers are now better known for the scandals from which they emerged (or in which they were finished) than for the writing they produced. Christopher Marlowe not only wrote *Doctor Faustus*, he was also murdered in a tavern brawl for allegedly being a spy. Oscar Wilde was a brilliant wit and playwright, but is equally well-remembered for his decadent lifestyle and homosexual proclivities. Dylan Thomas drank himself to death in New York. It is not the case that the work is irrelevant; it is more the case that with the modern readership demanding more and more personal information, a writer is in danger of losing the right to informed literary criticism. The extreme case might be the fact that considerably more people know about the death sentence on the head of Salman Rushdie than have ever read a single word of his prose. And then there was the ludicrous fuss made in the British press about Martin Amis spending a fortune to have his teeth fixed.

Jerzy Kosinski, in many respects, sacrificed his claim for sober criticism the moment he killed himself in 1991. From that point on it would be (and indeed, has been) impossible to regard his work without contemplating the dark shadow hanging over the *oeuvre*. Not only that, but since his suicide it has emerged that Kosinski was something of a self-mythologizer; he invented certain parts of his life, and *The Painted Bird* (for example) is not so autobiographical as once we thought it was. This fictionalization of the self is another factor that one has little choice but to bear in mind when considering the man's work. It is a body of work haunted by intention; there is a vein of sadness running throughout, not least in the themes of alienation and of being lost in strange places, which Kosinski himself, as a Polish man having moved to America, might well have experienced—he certainly seemed both horrified and appeased by America. In the sense that his books are very dark parables, it might even be arguable that they represent, vaguely, suicide notes. In legal jargon, Kosinski's books might be accessories before and after the fact.

The Painted Bird is the closest Kosinski came to writing a horror story *per se*. This is a wartime quest story from the heartbreaking point of view of a young Polish boy who has been separated from his parents in order to protect him from the Nazis. This act of protection, however, is one of the worst things that could happen to the boy because he is unable to find warmth or affection in the households of the dysfunctional Polish families and strange *personae* that he encounters as he wanders from village to village. The way the boy is flogged, beaten and generally mistreated tells us a lot about the worthless person in times of war. For this is the peasants' contribution to the country's struggles: to beat up a child. The boy is an innocent abroad in a land diminished by brutality, except that there is little reference made to war in the first third of the book, even in the form of the child reporting the peasants' conversations. It is almost as though the war does not affect their torpid existences, where the only pleasures to be had otherwise are in the shots of vodka that are knocked back, and in the forcible sex with peasant girls that is executed (for peasant life in *The Painted Bird* is almost certainly a male life, with notable exceptions: a character known as Stupid Ludmila strikes an odd blow for feminism in that she has sex with men on her own terms—but then, she is also clearly insane).

The boy, with his dark hair and complexion, is mistaken for a Jew and a gypsy and is despised; for even as the country is being decimated by the Germans, there is another force to be feared—the Gypsies. Paradoxically, however, he represents one of the most exciting things to happen to most of the villages he visits for some time; yet like Odysseus, the boy is simply trying to find his way home, or to a place that he might regard as such. In many ways, he is literally the Wandering Jew, limping from village to village with his "comet"—a small type of oven which at one point he eulogizes at great length as it has become a life-saver. Fighting prejudices and superstitions becomes a daily reality. The words "ghost" and "demon" are bandied about, not only because *The Painted Bird* is from the point of view of a boy who still believes in such things, but because in the land of the peasants these beliefs still remain. "The carpenter and his wife were convinced that my black hair would attract lightning to their farm." One time, the boy is buried up to his neck in the ground so that a common cold might be cured, and is attacked by hungry and curious birds. In the employ of Garbos, a sadistic farmer with "a dead, unsmiling face and half-open mouth," the boy is dangled from the ceiling by hooks and leather straps, and beneath him a snarling guard dog called Judas is placed; and this becomes an everyday occurrence. Unfortunately, it would be possible for the boy simply to stand still and attract trouble, and this, perhaps, is the point: that he is a victim, and therefore he must be victimized as much as possible.

Not only does the boy have acts of carnality and brutality thrust upon him, he is also witness to others: from the (relatively) tame example of the farmer who puts down a horse, to the extreme case of a miller who scoops out the eyes of a ploughboy because he doubts his wife's fidelity. Elsewhere, two soldiers rape a woman while all three are on horseback.

We know that the only logical conclusion is that this is a boy who will grow up to perpetrate violence himself. Any child who can say, "I was certain that the soldier had orders to shoot me, pour the gasoline over my body and burn it . . . I had seen this happen many times," is not destined for a stable adult existence. At first, rather generously, the boy tries to find ulterior motives for the adults' general nastiness—motives that take the blame away from those who are perpetrating the violence: "My next guess was that the gate in the fence leading to the clover field had something to do with it. Three times after I went through that gate Garbos called me to him and slapped me when I approached him. I concluded that some hostile spirit was crossing my path at the gate and inciting Garbos against me. . . ."

Very soon, though, the boy is showing little emotion when he is forcing a character into a pit that is swarming with hungry rats, or when he blows up another character's barns (and whoever else might be in the vicinity). He has of course been changed forever—and much earlier than the reader might have expected. On one farm, the farmer's daughter invites the boy to bring her to orgasm with his mouth. It is this and other similar acts of intimacy that bring on the boy's temporarily optimistic state of mind. "I forgot my fate of a Gypsy mute destined for fire. I ceased to be a goblin jeered at by herders, casting spells on children and animals. In my dreams I turned into a tall, handsome man, fair-skinned, blue-eyed, with hair like pale autumn leaves. I became a German officer in a tight, black uniform." But before long, the novel has returned to the bleaker subject matter.

The Painted Bird gets grimmer and grimmer, of course. Such a story about the Second World War can do nothing else. The novel is 250 pages of virtually unrelieved gloom. Soon "innumerable scraps of paper, notebooks, calendars, family photographs, printed personal documents, old passports, and diaries" from those who have been bundled into death trains are being collected; and humour (what there is of it) is becoming sicker. A man nicknamed Rainbow rapes a Jewess who has been found by railroad tracks, surmised to have fallen through a gap in the floor of a death-train's carriage; after the act of sex he is unable to withdraw. There is almost a fairy-tale ambience, making the reader think that the story has been translated from a language such as Chinese, for example, rather than something much closer to home. For although the book is set in a specific past, it reads in a chillingly detached fashion, like a post-apocalyptic fable, a warning, a hint. There is no connection to the world outside the villages through which the boy wanders apart from the link of violence; it is the string that ties him from one place to the next. The reason it qualifies as a horror story is because of its sheer relentlessness—or rather, the relentlessness of the vicious acts that it catalogues; there is a cumulative effect—*The Painted Bird* builds like a horror novel of the supernatural, where once the forces have been released it is hard to get the damned things back underground.

Possibly more famous than *The Painted Bird* is *Being There*, the success of which was helped by the Kosinski-penned movie starring Peter Sellars with its award-winning script. *Being There* is far more charming than *The Painted Bird*, but is dependent on a grim opening premise. A man who has lived all his life in the house of a benefactor, having done nothing—absolutely nothing—apart from watch TV and tend the garden, is suddenly thrust into the real world when the benefactor dies. Chance, like the boy in *The Painted Bird*, is an innocent, with no idea as to why such things have to happen. Chance has never earned a penny in his life and is present on no government record; his only rewards for looking after the master's plants have been his regular meals, brought to him in his room. The reason why *Being There* cannot qualify as a horror novel, but is instead a blackly humorous fable, is that Chance's adventures (as his name might suggest) are diametrically opposed to the extremely bad fortune that befalls the boy. Like novelist Winston Groom's later creation, Forrest Gump, Chance is something of an *idiot savant*, who strolls into pocket after pocket of good luck, where his freshness of opinion is considered wise and wonderful. Like another character, Bruce Gold in Joseph Heller's *Good as Gold*, Chance rebounds quickly into government. Every one of Chance's opinions and reactions has been formed by years of subliminal absorption of the wisdom of soap stars and game-show hosts.

Jerzy Kosinski (like Vladimir Nabokov, to name but one) was able to discuss America from the point of view of a visitor, although he made it his home as early as 1957, becoming a citizen eight years later. In the light of the suicide (if light is the right word), we can probably read far too much into portions of the work that take on the USA. In *Pinball*, Domostroy (note, another alien) is obliged to take his car battery to be charged. While he is waiting he goes through his morning's mail: "A letter from the National Vasectomy Club asked in large print, 'Had a Vasectomy?' and then suggested, 'Now Encourage Others!' . . . Domostroy stopped to think . . . If in search of external identity he should decide to define himself as an American Vasectomite, where would he feel confident wearing the National Vasectomy Club lapel pin or the tie tack? To cocktails? To dinner with a date? To church?"

Although we might try to resist the impulse, we will regard Kosinski's *oeuvre* with this same mixture of amusement, disgust, indignation and horror in mind.

—David Mathew

L

LAING, Alexander (Kinnan)

Nationality: American. **Born:** Great Neck, Long Island, New York, 7 August 1903. **Education:** Dartmouth College, Vermont, 1921-25 (left before taking degree), B.A. 1933, A.M. 1947. **Family:** Married 1) Isabel Lattimore Frost in 1930 (divorced); 2) Dilys Bennet in 1936 (died 1960), one son; 3) Veronica Ruzicka in 1961. **Career:** Technical journalist and editor, interrupted by periods as a seaman; technical editor, *Radio News*, 1925-26; editor, *Power Specialist*, 1927-28; tutorial adviser in English, Dartmouth College, from 1930; travelled around the world, 1934-35; assistant librarian, Dartmouth College, 1937-50; Professor of Belles Lettres, Dartmouth College, from 1952; poet, novelist and non-fiction writer. **Awards:** Guggenheim Fellowship for Creative Writing Abroad, 1934. **Died:** 1976.

Horror, Ghost and Gothic Publications

Novels

The Cadaver of Gideon Wyck, by a Medical Student. New York, Farrar and Rinehart, and London, Butterworth, 1934.
The Motives of Nicholas Holtz, Being the Weird Tale of the Ironville Virus, with Thomas Painter. New York, Farrar and Rinehart, 1936; as *The Glass Centipede*, London, Thornton Butterworth, 1936.

Other

Editor, *The Haunted Omnibus.* New York, Farrar and Rinehart, and London, Cassell, 1937; abridged edition, as *Great Ghost Stories of the World*, New York, Blue Ribbon, 1941.

Other Publications

Novels

End of Roaming. N.p., 1930.
Dr. Scarlett: A Narrative of His Mysterious Behavior in the East. New York, Farrar and Rinehart, 1936; London, Rich and Cowan, 1937.
The Methods of Dr. Scarlett. New York, Farrar and Rinehart, 1937; London, Cassell, 1938.
Jonathan Eagle. New York, Duell Sloan and Pearce, 1955.
Matthew Early. New York, Duell Sloan and Pearce, 1957.

Poetry

Hanover Poems, with R. A. Lattimore. New York, Vinal, 1927.
Fool's Errand. New York, Doubleday Doran, 1928.
The Flowering Thorn. N.p., 1933.
The Sea Witch. New York, Farrar and Rinehart, and London, Thornton Butterworth, 1933.
Brant Point. Hanover, New Hampshire, University Press of New England, 1975.

Other

Wine and Physic: A Poem and Six Essays on the Fate of Our Language. New York, Farrar and Rinehart, 1934.
Sailing In (for children). N.p., 1937.
Way for America. New York, Duell Sloan and Pearce, 1943.
Clipper Ship Men. New York, Duell Sloan and Pearce, 1944.
American Sail: A Pictorial History, with R. A. Lattimore. New York, Dutton, 1961.
Clipper Ships and Their Makers. New York, Putnam, 1966.
American Ships. New York, American Heritage, 1971.
The American Heritage History of Seafaring America. New York, American Heritage, 1974.

Editor, *The Life and Adventures of John Nicol, Mariner.* N.p., 1936.

*   *   *

Alexander Laing's earliest literary works were poems and mildly effete naturalistic novels, but during his most sustained burst of literary activity in the 1930s he produced an interesting quartet of thrillers, and also compiled one of the most wide-ranging eclectic anthologies of fantastic fiction in *The Haunted Omnibus*. These experiments in genre fiction were presumably less rewarding than he had hoped; it was the commercial success of his epic *The Sea Witch* that he chose to follow up, most of his later literary efforts being non-fiction works about the sea and sailing.

Laing's thrillers are distinguished by considerable vigour and experimental enterprise, and he would doubtless have been able to produce interesting work had he not chosen to abandon the field of popular fiction. His novels fall into two pairs, the second consisting of baroque adventure stories starring the enterprising Dr. Scarlett, while the first consists of two medical mystery stories solidly based in biological possibility. The second, *The Motives of Nicholas Holtz*—which is accredited in the byline as a collaboration with Thomas Painter—is a moderately hardboiled thriller in which an artificially created virus escapes from captivity with deadly consequences; it is not without horrific moments but does not really warrant consideration as a horror story. The first, however, is one of the few books published in the 1930s to have been considered so unduly repulsive that all its subsequent editions have been abridged.

The Cadaver of Gideon Wyck is a murder mystery whose unravelling involves much research into the medical discipline of teratology: the study of human monsters and mutations. The story is unusually conscientious in reporting the author's researches in this field, and unusually ingenious in integrating their produce into the plot. Laing poses, in fact, as the editor of the text, in which capacity he adds occasional footnotes, including one which specifies the narrow definition of the word "monster" employed in the story. (He also credits Thomas Painter and Gertrude McClure as equal sharers in "preparing the book for the printers" and as verifiers of the technical references, although it is not clear whether they ought, in consequence, to be recognized as co-authors of the work).

If the key to the mystery laid out in *The Cadaver of Gideon Wyck* were simply a matter of identifying the culprit it would not be a particularly interesting book, but the question of who killed whom and how is always subservient to the question of why, and to the curiously elusive question of exactly what kind of crime it was. The monstrousness of Gideon Wyck has, in the end, far less to do with conventional deformity than with the nature of his scientific speculations and endeavours. Some of the notions deployed in the course of this revelation might be reckoned supernatural, but it is not obvious that the author intended them to be seen in that light and his character's rigorously experimental approach to the phenomena places them squarely within the framework of scientific enquiry.

Although it is most certainly not a Frankensteinian fable, *The Cadaver of Gideon Wyck* is a conscientiously modern attempt to address some of the issues raised by Mary Shelley's classic regarding the nature of life, heredity and monstrousness. The figure depicted in Lynd Ward's excellent frontispiece to the 1934 edition could easily pass for Victor Frankenstein, complete with symbolic lightning (and Ward was later to produce an illustrated edition of *Frankenstein*). The work he put into *The Haunted Omnibus* demonstrates that Laing was very well acquainted with the tradition of horror fiction, and that he could trace it back far beyond the 19th century to all manner of folkloristic and early literary sources. It is a shame that he did not see fit to produce more work of that kind himself.

—Brian Stableford

LAMSLEY, Terry

Nationality: British. **Born:** 1941. **Awards:** World Fantasy award for novella, 1994; International Horror Critics' Guild award for collection, 1997. Lives in Buxton, Derbyshire.

HORROR, GHOST AND GOTHIC PUBLICATIONS

Short Stories

Under the Crust: Supernatural Tales of Buxton, photographs by Michael Patey-Ford. Buxton, Derbyshire, Wendigo, 1993; new edition, Chester, Cheshire, Ash-Tree Press, 1997.
Conference with the Dead. Chester, Cheshire, Ash-Tree Press, 1996.

*   *   *

Terry Lamsley's early childhood was spent around Maidstone, Kent, and his teens in the North of England. In 1978 he moved to Buxton. Convinced that the atmosphere of the town deserved celebrating in ghost stories, between December 1991 and July 1992 he wrote a group of them, as a response to the decaying of the centre of the town. They were collected as *Under the Crust: Supernatural Tales of Buxton*, which Lamsley published in collaboration with photographer and book designer Michael Patey-Ford under an imprint, Wendigo, invented for the occasion.

The book is a major debut in the field. The first story, "Two Returns," displays Lamsley's talent for spectral imagery in its opening scene. As a figure glimpsed at the far end of a dark sta-

tion platform vanishes into what might be a doorway "his arms and legs appeared to fold into him, like blades returning to the handles of a knife." While the economy of effect is reminiscent of M. R. James, the apparition is admirably original. Manifestations of it pursue a retired schoolteacher home, drawn by research he conducted into the history of his house. In "Living Waters" Druidic survivors that Christian practices have imperfectly subsumed take shape in the spa water and begin to overrun the town in forms a lesser writer would have rendered unintentionally comic, but Lamsley's imagination doesn't falter. These tales have the traditional ghost story's sense of an ignored past, but in "Killjoy" there's no hint of it. Doz, a solvent-sniffing teenage schoolboy with a fondness for violent (though pointedly not horror) videos is dogged by a progressively incomplete tramp, who begins by having a silhouette that changes "in small ways" but who soon does without eyes. While the reader may make a guess at the tramp's identity, it isn't as simple as it seems.

"Something Worse" studies a family, the Saltrees, who become obsessed with life after death. The accent on psychological detail, and the restriction of supernatural effects to a very few subtle manifestations, recall Walter de la Mare and his successor Robert Aickman. "Tabitha after Life" is a darkly comic tale in which a spectral spinster offended by the class of the other ghosts haunting Buxton becomes involved with somebody not quite as dead. "Under the Crust" turns the Peak District landscape around Dove Holes, in particular a rubbish tip, into a vision of hell more closely related to surrealism than medievalism. The story gained the 1994 World Fantasy award for best novella.

If *Under the Crust* gives the impression of having been designed to demonstrate Lamsley's skills in the various modes of English supernatural fiction up to the present, his second book, *Conference with the Dead*, has even greater range. "Walking the Dog" would once have been called science fantasy, presenting as it does the symbiotic relationships between a voracious alien being and the various unfortunates employed to feed it. "Blade and Bone" sends the luckless Ogden Minter on the sort of antiquarian quest M. R. James's protagonists pursued. There's an admirably unnerving touch when on learning that Minter has been talking to a character who we gather at this point was spectral, the manageress of a cafe doesn't recoil but laughs uproariously. Minter's enquiries attract a revenant from the days when trespassers were tortured, and the story ends on a grisly turn of phrase.

"The Break," set in a seaside resort overrun with confused old people, communicates with exceptional power the nightmarishness of which childhood can seem to consist. "Running in the Family" is also concerned with childhood and its perceptions of an alien world gradually revealed, as the young narrator learns that her father is not a Russian and her mother is not her mother, and becomes psychologically involved with a ghost that can't stop running. "Someone to Dump On" triumphantly revives a classic trope of the genre, the ghost that goes unrecognized as one until it's too late. "Screens" might be discussed as an example of the kind of ghost story that uses everyday objects as its props, but is more bizarre than that: a murderer returns through the medium of a blurry video that hints at where he went just before his death—not, we are led to believe, on an ordinary holiday, given the companions he brings back with him. The perverse sexual undercurrent of this tale is clearer in "The Toddler," where the results of an episode of 16th-century licentiousness manifest themselves today, in prose as reticent as it is suggestive. In "The Outer Darkness" the obsession of two men with the woman they both loved when she was alive leads them to follow her into an afterlife as skewed as at first sight it looks banal. "Inheritance" offers two explanations for itself, neither of them reassuring: first paranoid schizophrenia and then the supernatural. In "The Extension" the son of two killers returns to their home, only to discover that they were involved in more than murder and the past has the power to reclaim him.

In his two books to date Lamsley has established himself as an inheritor of all the qualities of classic English supernatural horror fiction: wit, detachment, an economy of effect bordering on the poetic, a seemingly effortless originality. As a result, in 1997 *Conference for the Dead* received an award for best collection from the International Horror Critics' Guild.

—Ramsey Campbell

LANE, Joel

Nationality: British. **Born:** Exeter, Devon, 1963. **Career:** Journalist, poet and short-story writer; works in educational publishing. **Awards:** Eric Gregory award for poetry, 1993. Lives in Birmingham, England.

HORROR, GHOST AND GOTHIC PUBLICATIONS

Short Stories

The Earth Wire and Other Stories. London, Egerton Press, 1994.

OTHER PUBLICATIONS

Poetry

Private Cities, with Robin Lindsay Wilson and Tony Lucas. Exeter, Devon, Stride, 1993.

*

Joel Lane comments:

The Earth Wire represents my best work over a ten-year period. I'm fascinated by the power of supernatural imagery as metaphor, and its ability to evoke a dreamlike state of awareness where the boundary between internal and external reality is blurred. In my stories, I've tried to make some kind of composite statement about aspects of life in an English city: families and communities; love and desire; violence and exploitation. I've tried to find supernatural metaphors for the things that concern me most strongly in real life.

*   *   *

Lane is a young poet and journalist with just over 50 short stories published. His work has the subtlety of Robert Aickman, the copious subtext of M. John Harrison and the strong regional atmosphere of Ramsey Campbell's early Liverpool stories, and all of these have influenced him. Yet Lane's is an original voice, operating in horror's penumbra, where it overlaps with literary

fiction and the so-called "slipstream." Most of his stories build up gradually towards strong (but unexplained) supernatural climaxes.

He is noted for setting most of his stories in urban Birmingham, England's second city, describing its areas by name and frequently including details from life. In particular he concentrates his attention upon older working-class districts, where students or the poor live in large, shabby houses split into apartments. He writes about poverty and illness, deals in detail with the gay subculture, rails against political injustice, shows derelict factories and disused canals, sets many of his scenes after dark, all in attractive prose full of metaphor and simile.

Some of Lane's most powerful stories are near-future dystopias. With a deliberate avoidance of explanations and causes (which one can only get away with in short stories, not at novel length, and which make his stories all the more horrific) he paints brief, disturbing pictures of society breaking down. In "The Earth Wire" there have been "disturbances"—the protagonist's family home has been burned out and he cannot trace his parents—while in "The Clearing," sinister groups of grey-uniformed men are commandeering food, electrical equipment, anything scarce or useful. The threat is slightly more specific in "Thicker than Water," where groups of homeless people are supposedly being moved around the country, rehoused by the government, but Paul, a journalist on a local newspaper, finds that one such group has been shot and dumped into a canal, presumably by some of the many "young army recruits" in the area. He is told by his editor not to worry, that it is an isolated incident and is, anyway, for the public good. But Paul continues to investigate, returns to the canal site, gets caught up and killed in a hooked trap and then, posthumously, meets the canal people, becoming one of them. The theme of linking up with others, of finding your own kind in a frightening world, runs through many of Lane's stories and is particularly noticeable in these three.

In another striking futuristic piece, "An Angry Voice," he uses a Pied Piper figure, who is able to bring back birds or even humans from the dead with a few notes from his pipe, yet this is no Christ figure but an embittered character, presumably dead, determined to teach humanity (in the shape of the young protagonist) a lesson and to take his revenge upon society. Lane's more recent dystopian tale, "The Pain Barrier" (*Little Deaths*, edited by Ellen Datlow, 1994), shows, among other things, the growing gap between the legitimate and black market sections of the economy.

If his futures are dystopian, his views of the present are generally no less pessimistic, being bleak and hopeless. In perhaps his best-known story, "The Foggy, Foggy Dew," he portrays a group of manual workers cleaning up a disused and very dusty factory. The dust follows at least one of the young workers home, clogging up his house and his life. The dust directly represents all industrial illness, though specifically, from the song which provides the title, it refers to tuberculosis. In a wider sense the dust is a metaphor for apathy and silence.

"And Some Are Missing" is perhaps the quintessential Lane story. It describes the helpless—victims of mugging or drunkenness—being set upon by some kind of vampire. All the scenes occur by night; the relationships here are gay; the Birmingham setting is sharp though unobtrusive. But the text makes it reasonably clear that no supernatural figure is at work; this is a projection, perhaps by the narrator, of the cold and exploitative nature of society itself: if we see people who need help we pass by on the other side. As Lane says, "The opposite of love is indifference." And although the story's narrator helps a little to scare away the "vampire," one can be sure that it will return. A similar point is being made in "Other than the Fair," in which three young people go along one evening to a local fair and enjoy themselves with the sanitized "danger" which the rides offer. But on an adjacent site is an alternative fair where everything is a risk and people get hurt. It is a metaphor for real life, as opposed to the protected (though seemingly exciting) state of childhood.

The breadth of Lane's subject matter is considerable. "In the Brightness of My Day" takes the science-fictional idea of alien entities gathering information about humanity and twists it into a deformed man sitting in a dark apartment, sending out youths to experience life and feeding on their sensations. "Common Land" is about the failure of communes and the production of ectoplasm. "Take Me When You Go" (*The Third Alternative* #1, 1994) shows how growing up can be a process of losing vision. "Real Drowners" (*Cold Cuts II*, 1994) is concerned with alcoholism and surviving traumatic experiences. An example of Lane's distaste for the business of politics is "Power Cut" (*Skeleton Crew*, 1991), in which a right-wing politician's sins find him out.

Where Lane departs from Birmingham and uses other parts of Britain as settings, his descriptions are no less poetic. In "Wave Scars" it is the Welsh port of Fishguard, in a tale of recurring personal ghosts. In "Real Drowners" it is Cornwall, and in "Playing Dead" it is a hotel in a small town in the north of England, where the protagonist picks up a woman, sleeps with her and is forced to reenact her suicide attempts.

Other recent stories of note include "Like Shattered Stone" (*The Science of Sadness*, edited by Chris Kenworthy, 1994), "Every Scrapbook Stuck with Glue" (*Ambit* #137, 1994), "The Outside World" (*The Urbanite* #6, 1995), "Contract Bridge" (*The Urbanite* #7, 1996), "Scratch" (*Twists of the Tale*, edited by Ellen Datlow, 1996) and "Your European Son" (*The Mammoth Book of Dracula* edited by Stephen Jones, 1997). Most of Lane's stories have first been published in the little magazines or small-press anthologies, but it is a mark of his quality that he appeared five times in Karl Edward Wagner's now-defunct *Year's Best Horror* series and has so far had three stories in the ongoing *Best New Horror* volumes edited by Stephen Jones (sometimes with Ramsey Campbell).

—Chris Morgan

LANSDALE, Joe R(ichard Harold)

Pseudonym: Ray Slater. **Nationality:** American. **Born:** Gladewater, Texas, 28 October 1951. **Education:** Tyler Junior College for one year; University of Texas, Austin; Stephen F. Austin State University, Nacogdoches, Texas for two years. **Family:** Married 1) Cassie Ellis in 1970 (divorced 1972); 2) Karen Ann Morton in 1973, one son and one daughter. **Career:** Has had a variety of jobs including factory worker, ditch digger, carpenter's and plumber's helper, farmer, and custodial supervisor; since 1981, full-time writer. **Awards:** Bram Stoker award, for short story 1988, 1989, for novella, 1992, for other media, 1993; British Fantasy award, 1989; American Mystery award, 1989. **Member:** Horror Writers of America (vice president, 1987-88). **Agent:** Jimmy Vines Literary Agency, 409 East 6th St. #4, New York, NY 10009-6347. **Address:** P.O. Box 630903, Nacogdoches, TX 75963-0903, USA.

HORROR, GHOST AND GOTHIC PUBLICATIONS

Novels

Dead in the West. New York, Space and Time, 1986; revised edition, London, Kinnell, 1990.
The Magic Wagon. New York, Doubleday, 1986.
The Nightrunners. Arlington Heights, Illinois, Dark Harvest, 1987.
The Drive-In: A "B"-Movie with Blood and Popcorn, Made in Texas. New York, Bantam, 1988; London, Kinnell, 1990.
The Drive-In 2: Not Just One of Them Sequels. New York, Bantam, and London, Kinnell, 1990.
Batman: Captured by the Engines. New York, Warner, 1991.
Batman: Terror on the High Skies (for children). Boston, Little Brown, 1992; London, Fantail, 1993.
Drive-By, with Andrew H. Vachss and Gary Gianni. Holyoke, Massachusetts, Crossroads Press, 1993.

Short Stories

By Bizarre Hands. Shingletown, California, Ziesing, 1989; London, New English Library, 1992.
Stories by Mama Lansdale's Youngest Boy. Eugene, Oregon, Pulphouse, 1991; expanded as *Bestsellers Guaranteed,* New York, Ace, 1993.
On the Far Side of the Cadillac Desert with the Dead Folks. Arvada, Colorado, Roadkill Press, 1991.
The Steel Valentine. Eugene, Oregon, Pulphouse, 1991.
Steppin' Out, Summer '68. Arvada, Colorado, Roadkill Press, 1992.
Tight Little Stitches on a Dead Man's Back. Eugene, Oregon, Pulphouse, 1992.
Writer of the Purple Rage. Baltimore, CD Publications, 1994.
Electric Gumbo. Quality Paperback Book Club, 1994.
A Fistful of Stories. Baltimore, CD Publications, 1997.

Graphic Novel

Jonah Hex: Two Gun Mojo. New York, DC/Vertigo, 1993.

Other

Editor, *Razored Saddles,* with Pat LoBrutto. Arlington Heights, Illinois, Dark Harvest, 1989.
Editor, *Dark at Heart: All New Tales of Dark Suspense,* with Karen Lansdale. Arlington Heights, Illinois, Dark Harvest, 1992.
Editor, *Weird Business,* with Richard Klaw. Mojo Press, 1995.

OTHER PUBLICATIONS

Novels

Act of Love. New York, Zebra, 1981; London, Kinnell, 1989.
Texas Night Riders (as Ray Slater). New York, Leisure, 1983; Bath, Chivers, 1990.
Cold in July. New York, Bantam, 1989.
Savage Season. Shingletown, California, Ziesing, 1990; London, New English Library, 1992.
Mucho Mojo. New York, Mysterious Press, 1994; London, Gollancz, 1995.
The Two-Bear Mambo. New York, Mysterious Press, 1995; London, Indigo, 1996.

Tarzan: The Lost Adventure, with Edgar Rice Burroughs. Dark Horse Publications, 1996.

Other

Atomic Chili: The Illustrated Joe R. Lansdale (comic-strip adaptations). Austin, Texas, Mojo Press, 1996.

Editor, *Best of the West* (short story anthology). New York, Doubleday, 1986.
Editor, *The New Frontier: The Best of Today's Western Fiction.* Garden City, New York, Doubleday, 1989.
Editor, *The West That Was,* with Thomas W. Knowles. New York, Wings Books, 1993.
Editor, *Wild West Show!*, with Thomas W. Knowles. New York, Wings Books, 1994.

*

Manuscript Collection: Southwest Texas State University, San Marcos, Texas.

* * *

Joe R. Lansdale is very much of a cross-genre writer. Other than one early western novel (*Texas Night Riders*, bylined Ray Slater) and perhaps his completion of an Edgar Rice Burroughs novel-fragment (*Tarzan: The Lost Adventure*), everything Lansdale has written is of interest to horror readers and forms a coherent body of work, whether it has fantastic content or not. This is not a writer who is limited to the ghost story (though he has written his share of supernatural fictions) or Cthulhu Mythos (though the zombie-fighting doctor in *Dead in the West* has the inevitable *Necronomicon* on his shelf), or the strictures of detective fiction, though, for publishing purposes, several of his novels fall into the "crime fiction" category.

The Horror Writers of America saw fit to give Lansdale an award for "The Night They Missed the Horror Show," as best horror story of the year. It's about two moronic, racist Texas teenagers who don't want to go see *Night of the Living Dead* because it has a black man as the hero. Instead, they can find no better amusement than to drag a roadkilled dog around by a chain attached to a car bumper. The fun pales when they encounter a mob about to murder a black boy from their school, whom they rescue, not so much to save a life, but because he's valuable on the football team.

They escape the original situation, only to fall into the hands of two homicidal degenerates, who kill the black boy on general principles, but then are so appalled at the mistreatment of the dog's carcass, that they kill the white boys too. One meets his end with a dog-collar around his neck, chained to the bumper of the car as it is pushed off a bridge. Is this a horror story? It's certainly grim enough. "Most of the things in that story either happened, or they were apocryphal stories that I'd heard when I was growing up," Lansdale has commented in an interview. "They didn't all happen to those people in one night, but a friend of mine is actually the guy who dragged the dog around. He wasn't a bad guy . . . just drunk and stupid that night. These two guys who were the villains, Vinnie, and Pork, I knew those guys . . . they were real and did things very similar. So that's realistic."

A sense of twisted realism is a leading characteristic of Lansdale's fiction, as is an intensely vulgar idiom and a tendency to pile outrageous and absurd situations on top of one another to such a degree that, in the hands of a lesser writer, the result would have to be either parody, or trash. But Lansdale's fiction is redeemed, first, by an authentic regional voice, which captures the ways and mores (and seamy underside) of rural Texas life as no outsider ever could. Then there is a strong, uninhibited sense of macabre humour, which marks Lansdale as the *funniest* horror writer since Robert Bloch (whose influence Lansdale acknowledges). But he is also effectively satirical, enormously inventive, and genuinely grim when he chooses. If Mark Twain, Ambrose Bierce, and the Marx Brothers had collaborated on a horror story, the result might have resembled Lansdale's "Steppin' Out, Summer '68," in which three Texas boys' night's adventure begins with an attempt to find a prostitute, and ends with one of the three hit by a truck and swallowed by an alligator; proceedings along the way would have been grotesque slapstick if they weren't so lethal. The fan who commented about a Lansdale story, "I didn't know whether to laugh or throw up" meant that as high praise indeed.

Lansdale's overtly fantastic short fiction can range from the quietly eerie "Fish Night" to "On the Far Side of the Cadillac Desert with the Dead Folks," which is set in the universe of George Romero's *Night of the Living Dead* and manages to make the living humans more monstrous than the flesh-eating zombies. Then there is "Bubba Ho-Tep," in which an aged Elvis Presley and a crazed black man who thinks he is John F. Kennedy (having survived the assassination, his brain now stored in a jar) defeat a soul-sucking mummy that threatens their retirement home.

This same genius for the preposterous carries Lansdale through several of his novels. *Dead in the West* is a deliberate homage to pulp fiction and B-movies. It is a zombie-filled slaughterfest, set in the imaginary town of Mud Creek, Texas. The two *Drive-In* books involve teenagers attending a gigantic horror-movie marathon, which is taken over by extra-terrestrials, who produce ghouls, dinosaurs, etc., and massacre most of the audience. In *Batman: Captured by the Engines*, the Caped Crusader battles Native American shape-changers who transform themselves, not into animals as might be expected, but into cars and motorcycles. This book also features the God of the Razor, a memorable demon encountered in earlier short fiction and in the novel, *The Nightrunners*.

The Magic Wagon is much quieter and more subtle, a splendid evocation of rural Texas in the early 20th century, told in a charming, completely authentic voice. The story concerns a travelling medicine show and freakish characters who may or may not have supernatural powers. The other novels, from *Act of Love* to the recent *Mucho Mojo* and its sequel *The Two-Bear Mambo* are crime stories; most of the latest titles feature Hap Collins and Leonard Pine, an unlikely pair of investigators (particularly for back-country Texas), one white and straight, the other black and gay.

At this point, Lansdale might be seen as having departed from the horror field altogether, but his mystery novels are of a piece with his earlier horror fiction, displaying the same panache and inner darkness.

—Darrell Schweitzer

LASKI, Marghanita

Nationality: British. **Born:** London, 24 October 1915; granddaughter of the Chief Rabbi of England; niece of the writer and political scientist Harold Laski. **Education:** St. Paul's School, London; Somerville College, Oxford University, B.A. in philology. **Family:** Married the publisher John Howard in 1937; two children. **Career:** Worked briefly as a nurse and in intelligence during World War II; journalist, critic and novelist; prolific contributor to the *Oxford English Dictionary*; occasional broadcaster; active in the Campaign for Nuclear Disarmament, 1950s. Chairman, Literature Panel, Arts Council of Great Britain, mid-1980s. **Died:** 6 February 1988.

HORROR, GHOST AND GOTHIC PUBLICATIONS

Novel

The Victorian Chaise Longue. London, Cresset Press, 1953; Boston, Houghton Mifflin, 1954.

Short Story

The Tower. Tacoma, Washington, Lanthorne Press, 1974.

OTHER PUBLICATIONS

Novels

Love on the Super-Tax. London, Cresset Press, 1944.
To Bed with Grand Music. London, Cresset Press, 1946.
Tory Heaven; or, Thunder on the Right. London, Cresset Press, 1948; as *Toasted English*, n.p.
Little Boy Lost. London, Cresset Press, 1949.
The Village. London, Cresset Press, 1952.

Plays

The Offshore Island (produced 1954). London, Cresset Press, 1959.

Television Play: *The Offshore Island*, 1959.

Other

Mrs. Ewing, Mrs. Molesworth and Mrs. Hodgson Burnett. London, Barker, 1950.
Apologies. London, Harvill Press, 1956.
Ecstasy: A Study of Some Secular and Religious Experiences. London, Cresset Press, 1961.
Jane Austen and Her World. London, Thames and Hudson, 1969.
Everyday Ecstasy. London, n.p., 1980.

Editor, *The Patchwork Book: A Pilot Omnibus for Children.* London, n.p., 1946.

*   *   *

Despite having been written more than forty years ago and being very genteel in its approach, *The Victorian Chaise Longue* is a chilling novel. It is a timeslip story, familiar in science fiction, wherein a character inadvertently shifts backwards or forwards in time and becomes a stranger in a strange land. Richard Matheson's *Bid Time Return* is one of the best known examples.

In Laski's short novel the accent is not upon the discovery of the age travelled to, not a romance or an adventure; it concentrates on gradual revelations which mount up to create an impres-

sive spider's web of horror. The protagonist is Mrs. Melanie Langdon, living happily in 1953. She has been married two years to Guy and has a seven-month-old baby son. Because Guy is a rising young barrister, they are comfortably off in a newly fashionable part of inner London. The only problem is that Melanie has been suffering from tuberculosis, though this is responding well to treatment. Still weak, she is being allowed to move from her bedroom into the drawing room. There she sits and lies upon a Victorian chaise longue which she bought on impulse the very day her TB was diagnosed.

As a piece of furniture it is far from elegant: "It was ugly and clumsy and extraordinary, nearly seven feet long and proportionately wide. The head and foot ends of the seat curled round a little as though to meet each other, raising, above the elaborately carved legs and frame, a superstructure of wine-red crimson felt. At the right-hand end a curved padded support rolled backwards on curlicues of carving and a carved framework supported padding to halfway down the back. Its Regency ancestor had probably been delicate and enchanting; this descendant was gross."

She falls asleep on this and wakes up in a nightmare. She is still a young woman weak from illness, and still lying on the same chaise longue, but all else has changed. Gradually her situation and environment are revealed: she has somehow moved back in time to 1864, and she lives with Adelaide, her elder sister. Clearly she is being treated badly, almost as if she were mentally deficient, even though servants look after her. She is referred to as Milly, close enough to her own name to wonder if some of the people in that age know who she really is.

All Melanie wants to do is to return to her own time, to her husband and child—to be happy. But she only seems to cause trouble for herself when she mentions Guy's name. Clearly Adelaide believes that "Milly" is in possession of a secret to which Melanie has no answer. Fairly quickly Melanie realizes that she must co-operate and try to understand the complexities of relationships and life with servants. The small details of mid-Victorian England are very convincingly portrayed.

In a brief but tense novel, Melanie tries to talk to the clergyman, Mr. Endworthy, who has known Milly almost all her life. It is difficult for her to speak to him without Adelaide being present, and when an opportunity comes she tries to explain exactly who she is—that in reality only she is still alive, and all those living in 1864 are dead. Mr. Endworthy asks about her soul and whether she repents of her sins. He kneels down and prays for her, but the reader is made to feel that he fears for her sanity.

Then there is Mr. Charters, a young man who seems to be a friend of the family, yet who obviously has or wishes to have some special relationship with Milly. He even calls her "Melly," which Guy has done. There is also the doctor, who chides Milly for not confiding in him. She tries to tell him how she should be treated for the TB from which, it becomes obvious, she is very ill. As the story nears its climax, Milly's fondness for alcohol, perhaps only to help with the pain, is clear. And, when she undresses herself to see whose body she has—Melanie's or Milly's—she discovers that this young spinster has a mother's breasts. So Milly's dark secret is that she has had an affair, presumably with Mr. Charters, and has given birth.

She confronts Adelaide with this, demanding to know where the baby is. But she—Melanie in Milly's body—dies, unable to return to the time she came from, never knowing what happened to Melanie's own body or to Milly's persona. This is a chilling finale, all the more impressive for being understated.

Laski's style is light and almost frivolous, to fit in with Melanie's character. Part of the time the narrative is dreamlike, reflecting the situation and Melanie's state of mind. There is no attempt to rationalize what has happened; the cause matters little beside the tragedy of the fact. Of course, Laski is drawing a parallel between the lot of the middle-class Englishwoman at the time of writing and a century earlier. Melanie comes to see this parallel: "I think we did the same things," she thinks to herself near the end. "We loved a man and we flirted and we took little drinks, but when I did those things there was nothing wrong, and for you it was a terrible punishable sin."

Although Laski's earlier novel *Little Boy Lost* is not genre horror, it includes some elements of the horrific. It describes a father's search for his young son, who has disappeared in Paris during World War II. His wife, the boy's father, has been tortured and killed by the Gestapo, and some references to torture methods are made. The war-devastated small town, where the father goes to try and identify his son at an orphanage in 1945, is very grim. And the final irony of the father deciding, after several meetings, that the boy is not his son—and being wrong in this—provides a nasty twist.

At least one of Laski's short stories is a subtle horror piece. "The Tower," which first appeared in Cynthia Asquith's *The Third Ghost Book* (1956), and later as a very slim volume, tells of an English wife sightseeing alone in Italy and being caught, perhaps, in a web of black magic spun four centuries earlier.

—Chris Morgan

LAWRENCE, Margery (H.)

Nationality: British. **Born:** Wolverhampton, Staffordshire, 8 August 1889. **Education:** Attended art schools in Birmingham, London and Paris. **Family:** Married Arthur Edward Towle (died 1948). **Died:** 13 November 1969.

HORROR, GHOST AND GOTHIC PUBLICATIONS

Novels

The Madonna of Seven Moons. London, Hurst and Blackett, 1931; Indianapolis, Bobbs Merrill, 1933.
The Rent in the Veil. London, Hale, 1951.
Bride of Darkness. London, Hale, 1967; New York, Ace, 1969.
A Residence Afresh. London, Hale, 1969.

Short Stories

Nights of the Round Table: A Book of Strange Tales. London, Hutchinson, 1926.
The Terraces of Night, Being Further Chronicles of the Club of the Round Table. London, Hurst and Blackett, 1932.
The Floating Café and Other Stories. London, Jarrolds, 1936.
Number Seven Queer Street. London, Hale, 1945; abridged edition, Sauk City, Wisconsin, Mycroft and Moran, 1969.
Master of Shadows. London, Hale, 1959.

OTHER PUBLICATIONS

Novels

Red Heels. London, Hutchinson, 1924.
Fine Feathers. New York, Curtiss, 1928.
Bohemian Glass. London, Hurst and Blackett, 1928.
Drums of Youth. London, Hurst and Blackett, 1929.
Silken Sarah. London, Hurst and Blackett, 1932.
Madame Holle. London, Jarrolds, 1934.
The Crooked Smile. London, Jarrolds, 1935.
Overture to Life. London, Jarrolds, 1937.
The Bridge of Wonder. London, Hale, 1939.
Step Light, Lady. London, Hale, 1942.
The Gilded Jar. London, Hale, 1948.
Emma of Alkistan. London, Hale, 1953.
Evil Harvest. London, Hale, 1954.
Daughter of the Nile. London, Hale, 1956.
Spanish Interlude. London, Hale, 1959.
The Gate of Yesterday. London, Hale, 1960.
Skivvy. London, Hale, 1961.
Green Amber. London, Hale, 1962.
The Unforgetting Heart. London, Hale, 1963.
Dead End. London, Hale, 1964.
The Yellow Triangle. London, Hale, 1965.
The Tomorrow of Yesterday. London, Hale, 1966.
The Green Bough. London, Hale, 1968.
Over My Shoulder. London, Hale, 1968.
Autumn Rose. London, Hale, 1971.

Short Stories

Miss Brandt: Adventuress. London, Hutchinson, 1923.
Snapdragon. London, Hurst and Blackett, 1931.
Strange Caravan. London, Hale, 1941.
Cardboard Castle. London, Hale, 1951.

Poetry

Songs of Childhood and Other Verses. London, Grant Richards, 1913.
Fourteen to Forty-Eight: A Diary in Verse. London, Hale, 1950.

Other

Ferry Over Jordan. London, Hale, 1944.
What Is This Spiritualism? London, Spiritualist Press, 1946.

*

Film Adaptations: *Das Spielzeug von Paris*, from the novel *Red Heels*, 1925; *The Madonna of Seven Moons*, 1944.

*   *   *

Margery Lawrence had a long literary career during which she worked in several different genres; she published poetry in her teens and dabbled in book illustration before publishing her first novel in 1925. Some of her numerous romances and adventure stories stray into the borders of supernatural fiction by virtue of her pseudo-scholarly interest in occult matters and her belief in spiritualism—a faith whose associated doctrines provide the inspiration for her more full-blooded ventures into fantasy. The most extravagant of these is *The Tomorrow of Yesterday*, in which Martian colonists found the great civilization of Atlantis. The timeslip romance *The Rent in the Veil* and the afterlife fantasy *A Residence Afresh* are more orthodox as well as more restrained. None of her novels, however, really warrants consideration as a true horror story. Although *Bride of Darkness*, about a man married to a witch, is keenly concerned with matters conventionally associated with horror fiction it is in essence a conventional romance. *The Madonna of the Seven Moons* is a "case-study" in split personality (backed up by an afterword summarizing actual case-studies) but the heroine's confusion never reaches a horrific pitch. It is Lawrence's short fiction which entitles her to a place of some significance within the horror genre.

Nights of the Round Table is a quintessential collection of club stories, whose introduction claims that they were actual anecdotes told to "Laurie" by the original models of the "Charming Men" here identified by pseudonyms. The book lays out with remarkable comprehensiveness a full set of the most commonly used motifs in English supernatural fiction, kicking off with "The Occultist's Story: Vlasto's Doll," a tale of a stage-magician and his principal prop which could serve as a prototype for many subsequent accounts of ventriloquists and overactive dummies. "The Poet's Story: Robin's Rath" features Robin Goodfellow as the mercurial haunter of a patch of woodland. In "The Hypnotist's Story: The Woozle" a child's bogey-man briefly becomes real. "The Golfer's Story: The Fifteenth Green" is exactly what the title might lead the connoisseur to expect, as is "The Priest's Story: How Pan Came to Little Ingleton." "The Soldier's Story: Death Valley" is a tale of African mystery, while "The Egyptologist's Story: The Curse of the Stillborn" shows admirable restraint in substituting a golden burial-mask for the usual bandage-clad mummy. The remaining stories are similarly familiar generic tales of revenants and accursed objects, concluding with "The Engineer's Story: The Haunted Saucepan."

Precedents exist for all the tales in *Nights of the Round Table*, but they still constitute a remarkable compendium, exhibiting considerable sensitivity to the methods and concerns which were to remain central to the tradition of the English supernatural short story long after 1926. They are less polished than the works of M. R. James, but they have an admirable liveliness. Unfortunately, although she repeated the recipe several times over, including one perfectly straightforward reprise in *The Terraces of Night*, Lawrence never produced anything quite as impressive again. *The Terraces of Night* and *The Floating Café* are as readable but they are noticeably less wide-ranging, and thus are nowhere near as definitive as the original collection. In the former volume "The Crystal Snuff-Box (The Antiquarian's Tale)" and "The Shrine at the Cross Roads (The American Girl's Tale)" are engaging tales of witchcraft while "The Portrait of Comtesse X (The Concierge's Tale)" is a suitably stirring exercise in supernatural *crime passionel*. The title story of the latter volume is an intriguingly unusual account of a nasty mermaid, and "John Challoner's Wife" musters a fair measure of intensity. All the tales in the two volumes have an air of repetition about them, however, and are not improved by the author's attempts to display lower-class accents in several items in the latter collection. It was not until Lawrence began to move decisively in a new direction, in *Number Seven, Queer Street*, that her work recovered some of its vigour.

The stories in the three earlier collections are clearly the work of a sceptic who is prepared to use any arbitrary device for the sake of a thrill, but those in *Number Seven, Queer Street* are the work of someone who has begun to formulate a generalized occult theory capable of commanding at least tentative belief. The hero of the tales is Miles Pennoyer, an investigator of strange phenomena working solidly within the tradition of Algernon Blackwood's John Silence and Dion Fortune's Dr. Taverner (both of which influences are dutifully acknowledged in the foreword). The narrative style is far more earnest—and far more verbose—than that deployed in *Nights of the Round Table*. The substance of one story—"No. 5. The Case of the Moonchild"—is obviously borrowed from Aleister Crowley. Another, "No. 7. The Case of the Leannabh Sidhe," is a vulgarization of motifs treated much more effectively by Arthur Machen, infected (perhaps inappropriately) by an anarchically humorous spirit whose ironic sensibility the author could never entirely suppress, no matter how hard she tried. These two stories are novellas, as are "No. 4. The Case of the White Snake," whose phallic symbolism is carefully sanitized, and "No. 6. The Case of the Young Man with the Scar," which makes a half-hearted attempt to capture the essence of Amerindian religion and mythology. (The Mycroft & Moran edition omits stories nos. 6 and 7.) The four stories making up the second Robert Hale collection of Pennoyer tales, *Master of Shadows*—"Saloozy," "Circus Child," "The Woman on the Stairs" and "The Twisted Christ"—are as conscientiously long-winded as their predecessors but not as versatile.

Pennoyer's ostensible purpose in pursing all his cases is, of course, to put an end to the supernatural disturbances by healing the experiential wounds they symbolize—sometimes, but not always, instituting a formal exorcism. The underlying rhetoric of the two collections, viewed as a whole, however, is a syncretic unification of all individual myth-systems into a single Spiritual Truth concerning the relationships of the dead and the living. Lawrence's version of that Truth is as muddled as everyone else's, possessed of less élan than Jack Mann's and less metaphysical depth than Blackwood's, but it is nevertheless engaging. However sentimental she became, and however bogged down her flights of the imagination were by soggy credulity, something of the youthful spirit of "Laurie" always remained within the redoubtable Mrs. Towle. It is unfortunate that so many of her works are exceedingly difficult to find, and an eclectic collection of her best supernatural short stories—which could dip into *Strange Caravan* and *Cardboard Castle* as well as the collections exclusively made up of "strange tales"—is long overdue.

—Brian Stableford

LAWS, Stephen

Nationality: British. **Born:** Newcastle upon Tyne, 13 July 1952. **Education:** Manor Park Technical School, 1963-68. **Family:** Married Melanie Jane Laws in 1992; two daughters, one son. **Career:** Worked in local government; since 1992, full-time writer. **Awards:** *Sunday Sun* (Newcastle) award for best short story 1981; BBC/Rediffusion award for best short story 1983; Children of the Night award, Count Dracula Society, 1993. **Agent:** Antony Harwood, Aitken, Stone and Wylie Ltd., 29 Fernshaw Road, London SW10 0TG, England.

Novels

Ghost Train. London, Souvenir Press, 1985; New York, Beaufort, 1986.
Spectre. London, Souvenir Press, and New York, Tor, 1986.
The Wyrm. London, Souvenir Press, 1987.
The Frighteners. London, Souvenir Press, 1990.
Darkfall. London, Hodder and Stoughton, 1992.
Gideon. London, Hodder and Stoughton, 1993.
Macabre. London, Hodder and Stoughton, 1994.
Daemonic. London, Hodder and Stoughton, 1995.
Somewhere South of Midnight. London, Hodder and Stoughton, 1996.

Short Stories

Voyages Into Darkness, with Mark Morris. N.p., Bump in the Night Books, 1993.
Annabelle Says, with Simon Clark. N.p., British Fantasy Society, 1995.

*   *   *

The literary land tilled by Stephen Laws is the more traditional side of the horror genre and, despite the fact that there are many other hands ploughing the same furrow, he is remarkably successful. Even in horror and dark fantasy fiction, it seems, quality will out.

Laws published his first novel, the macabre *Ghost Train*, to excellent reviews and the dubious honour of having the posters advertising the paperback edition of the book removed by British Rail from its mainline stations. He had set out to write a modern ghost story and had succeeded, breathing new life into a genre already jaded by innumerable attempts on the parts of less talented practitioners at repeating and even exceeding the excesses of William Blatty's *The Exorcist* a decade earlier.

Early comparisons with Stephen King were well-judged, particularly when it came to the follow-up, *Spectre*. Here, a group of college friends who have lost touch with each other find that someone or something is killing them off one by one. The focal point of the story is a group photograph depicting them all, with the appropriate image disappearing as a murder is committed. The survivors must first track each other down and then try to discover the nature of the threat.

Like King, Laws concentrates his attention on the minutiae of everyday life, substituting the Newcastle suburb of Byker for the beleaguered Maine, New England, township of Castle Rock, and featuring a real-life cinema that made a great impression on Laws when he was a child. In fact, the book contained what was to become something of a Laws trademark in its numerous nods towards the movies.

With his third novel, *The Wyrm*, Laws set out to create his own version of the glorious black-and-white B-feature movie monsters. Basing the story on the local legend of the Lambton Worm, Laws created Shillingham, an archetypal fog-shrouded Borders village, and had workmen unleash a monstrous evil which had been imprisoned below the ground beneath an old gibbet. The plot may sound hackneyed in this bald description, but *The Wyrm* remains a breath of fresh air when compared to much traditional horror fiction.

Now on a roll, Laws flexed his creative muscles and embarked on a story which not only involved criminal activities but also a right-wing government programme aimed at eradicating anti-social tendencies from prisoners. The result, *The Frighteners*, had more going for it in terms of ambition than it did in execution and, with the introduction of the almost obligatory supernatural psychopath, the whole thing proved to be less than the sum of its parts.

Darkfall, however, had Laws back on form with a vengeance. The occupants of a Newcastle office block vanish in the middle of a Christmas Eve party after the building is struck by lightning from a darkfall storm, a deadly form of electrical turbulence which affects both inert matter and living tissue. The result is that the hapless party goers are absorbed into the fabric of the building where they remain trapped alive. When they return, they are changed—gruesome amalgams of construction materials and flesh. The book is a powerhouse of action, with the office block serving as a refreshing take on that staple of horror fiction, the community isolated from civilization, and allowing for a nerve-wracking series of set-pieces.

Laws has gone on to produce four more novels, culminating with *Somewhere South of Midnight*, but it is perhaps *Gideon* which best secures his position at the vanguard of the British side of the genre. Essentially a vampire novel, *Gideon* is actually much more—not least in terms of its execution. Laws steers clear of the stereotyped cape-clad bloodsuckers and opts for a more conventional antagonist, whose story begins with his murder in a parking lot at the hands of three women.

From there, Laws painstakingly fills in the background—where we learn, slowly, of just what this man had done to warrant such treatment—before embarking on the long chase and a fraught conclusion. As the story's events catch up with the killing scene depicted in the first few pages, we realize that disposing of Gideon is not going to be as easy as the women think . . . and, sure enough, he poses a far greater threat to them dead than he did when he was "alive." Again, the set-pieces are where Laws scores most effectively. Some of the scenes—particularly a section where one of the characters is trapped in the town library, in broad daylight, by a pack of deranged dogs—are reminiscent of Hitchcock's approach to movie-making, most notably the latter's somewhat audacious adaptation of Daphne du Maurier's short story "The Birds."

But then this is what Laws does best: he works as though he's writing a screenplay, with every piece of scenery intact and in place, and every character behaving in accordance with the personality he has carefully constructed for them, breaking his literary viewpoints like camera angles to promote speed with dizzying effect.

—Peter Crowther

LAYMON, Richard (Carl)

Pseudonyms: Richard Kelly; Carl Laymon; Lee Davis Willoughby. **Nationality:** American. **Born:** Chicago, 14 January 1947. **Education:** Willamette University, Oregon, BA in English Literature; Loyola University, Los Angeles, MA. **Family:** Married Ann Laymon in 1976; one daughter. **Career:** Has worked as a schoolteacher, librarian, magazine editor and legal report-writer; now a full-time novelist. **Address:** c/o Hodder Headline PLC, 338 Euston Road, London NW1 3BH, England.

HORROR, GHOST AND GOTHIC PUBLICATIONS

Novels

The Cellar. New York, Warner, 1980; London, New English Library, 1981.
Your Secret Admirer (as Carl Laymon). New York, Scholastic, 1980.
The Woods Are Dark. New York, Warner, 1981; London, New English Library, 1983; revised edition, London, Headline, 1991.
Out Are the Lights. New York, Warner, and London, New English Library, 1982.
Nightmare Lake (as Carl Laymon). New York, Dell, 1983.
Night Show. London, New English Library, 1984.
Beware! London, New English Library, 1985; New York, Paperjacks, 1987.
Allhallows Eve. London, New English Library, 1985.
The Beast House. London, New English Library, 1986.
Tread Softly (as Richard Kelly). London, W. H. Allen, 1987; as *Dark Mountain* by Richard Laymon, London, Headline, 1992.
Midnight's Lair (as Richard Kelly). London, W. H. Allen, 1988; as Richard Laymon, London, Headline, 1992.
Flesh. London, W. H. Allen, 1988.
Resurrection Dreams. London, W. H. Allen, 1988.
Funland. London, W. H. Allen, 1989.
The Stake. London, Headline, 1990.
One Rainy Night. London, Headline, 1991.
Darkness, Tell Us. London, Headline, 1991.
Blood Games. London, Headline, 1992.
Savage. London, Headline, 1993.
Alarums. London, Headline, 1993.
Endless Night. London, Headline, 1993.
In the Dark. London, Headline, 1994.
Quake. London, Headline, 1995.
Island. London, Headline, 1995.
Body Rides. London, Headline, 1996.
Bite. London, Headline, 1996.

Short Stories

Out Are the Lights and Other Tales. London, Headline, 1993.
A Good, Secret Place. N.p., Deadline Press, 1993.
Fiends. London, Headline, 1997.

OTHER PUBLICATIONS

Novel

The Lawmen (as Lee Davis Willoughby). New York, Dell, 1983.

*   *   *

Richard Laymon's brand of horror has been at times controversial, primarily because of his willingness to take violence and sex, sometimes simultaneously, in directions and to extremes which frighten off other writers. His novels often portray humans at their very worst—vengeful, irrational, insane, consumed by lust—and the dangers they face are often violent, gruesome, even disgusting. Oddly, although he continues to live in the United States and to set most of his fiction there, Laymon is more published in Britain than in his homeland: perhaps British readers have stronger tastes.

The Cellar rests under a sprawling house, a tourist trap luring people to visit the site of a ghastly crime. A woman and her daughter are on the run from her abusive husband when she stops there on impulse. Unfortunately she and her daughter are just in time to become the next set of victims, preyed upon by humanoid creatures living beneath the ground who emerge to kill any men and sexually enslave any women they can find. The abusive husband turns up as well, to meet a satisfyingly gruesome fate. The sequel, *The Beast House*, is set some years later, when the house has been turned into a bizarre museum dedicated to the supposed legend of the creatures. But they're not imaginary, and they make another series of raids above, this time with a happier ending for the human characters. Both novels are clumsy at times, but Laymon's skill at creating genuinely intense situations was already evident.

The Woods Are Dark is a minor work in which an alien creature is stranded in a remote part of California, served by the local population which has succumbed to its mental control. There are some good scenes late in the book, but for the most part it fails to maintain any real suspense. The same is true for *Out Are the Lights*, an implausible story about a movie-maker who really kills the people who die in the stories. *Nightmare Lake*, aimed at younger readers, is a fairly good though predictable vampire story. Two teens disturb an ancient skeleton and inadvertently allow the vampire to resume human form, but of course no one believes what's happening until it's too late.

Beware! marked a turning point in Laymon's career, the first of a steady string of noteworthy novels. Lacey Allen discovers that the customers at a local market have been massacred, their bodies literally torn apart by an invisible creature. She escapes, but the unseen killer pursues, claiming fresh victims until the man responsible for unleashing the force is killed. *Flesh*, a blend of science fiction and horror, is one of the best of Laymon's novels. A single alien parasite lands on Earth, a creature that invades human bodies and uses them as its host. Even worse, it feeds on the psychic energy generated by fear and pain, so it drives its hosts to kill and maim others. The authorities are perplexed by the sudden wave of apparent insanity and murder, until the protagonist detects the pattern and realizes that a single entity is responsible.

Tread Softly demonstrates why it's foolish to aggravate a witch unnecessarily. A group of campers become embroiled in a violent argument with an elderly woman and her son, during the course of which the son is killed. The campers return to their ordinary lives, but then begin to die one by one, each the victim of a strange accident, until the survivors realize that this isn't just coincidence, that they have been cursed. Their only chance to remain alive is to track her down before she completes her revenge. *Resurrection Dreams* is a decidedly bizarre take on the Frankenstein theme. Melvin is the school misfit, mentally deranged, but with the ability to tap into the power of black magic. When he becomes infatuated with a beautiful girl, he begins murdering people and reanimating their bodies, sometimes physically rebuilding them, as part of his plan to impress her. A young doctor arrives in town just as the grotesque activities reach the point where they can no longer be concealed, and the girl is instrumental in Melvin's eventual destruction. It's a powerful, often repulsive novel involving sexual obsession and the quest for power. Laymon bludgeons the reader with shock after shock rather than slowly building suspense, revealing one grotesquerie after another.

There's nothing supernatural in *Midnight's Lair*, but that doesn't make it any less effective. A power failure strands a group of tourists in an underground cave system. In their attempts to find an alternate exit, they stumble across a small tribe of humans who have been living in the darkness for generations, and who view the newcomers as an interesting new food source. The struggle in the darkness is convincingly claustrophobic, and the troglodytic cannibals, reminiscent of the creatures from the *Beast House* series, are convincingly nasty.

Funland is relatively disappointing. The opening chapters are interesting, chronicling the escalating warfare between a pack of juvenile delinquents and the homeless community of a small town. Much of the action takes place in the shadow of Funland Amusement Park, and Laymon builds the suspense skilfully during the first few exchanges. The climactic battle is unconvincing, complicated by the manifestation of a genuine monster on the midway.

The Stake, on the other hand, is one of Laymon's best. It's a vampire novel, even though the vampire doesn't appear until the book is almost done. Two families stop in a ghost town and discover the remains of a body concealed in one of the abandoned buildings. They leave it there but fail to report it to the authorities, afraid they will get into trouble for breaking into the property. The husbands return later on impulse and steal the body after the protagonist becomes obsessed with knowing what happened to her. He subsequently turns detective, and unearths evidence that she may have been one of several victims of a madman who thought he was killing vampires.

. The vampire killer is around as well, and he's not happy about the possibility that one of his victories might be reversed. He also knows where the protagonist and his family live and he's coming to visit. Laymon does an excellent job of portraying an ordinary family caught up in extraordinary events, and delivers one of his best efforts. Since the appearance of *The Stake*, Laymon has been prolific (and, apparently, successful) on behalf of his new British publishers, Headline, who have done much to promote him. Among the more interesting books he has written for them is *Savage*, a Jack-the-Ripper western horror novel.

An occasional short-story writer, Laymon's best work at that length includes "Bad News," "Good Vibrations" and "The Champion." His recent book *Quake* is a disaster novel rather than horror fiction, but his grounding in the supernatural horror genre is obvious in the way he portrays the aftermath.

—Don D'Ammassa

LEE, Vernon

Pseudonym of Violet Paget. **Nationality:** British. **Born:** Boulogne, France, 14 October 1856. **Education:** Extensive but informal, during continual travels throughout Europe. **Career:** Art historian, critic, essayist, travel writer and occasional novelist and short-story writer. Lived much of her life in Italy, visiting England on occasion. **Died:** 13 February 1935.

HORROR, GHOST AND GOTHIC PUBLICATIONS

Short Stories

A Phantom Lover: A Fantastic Story. Edinburgh, Blackwood, 1886.
Hauntings: Fantastic Stories. London, Heinemann, 1890.

Pope Jacynth and Other Fantastic Tales. London, John Lane, 1907.
For Maurice: Five Unlikely Tales. London, John Lane, 1927.
The Snake Lady and Other Stories, edited by Horace Gregory. New York, Grove Press, 1954.
Supernatural Tales: Excursions into Fantasy. London, Peter Owen, 1955; as *The Virgin of the Seven Daggers*, London, Corgi, 1962.
Pope Jacynth and More Supernatural Tales. London, Peter Owen, 1956; as *Ravenna and Her Ghosts*, London, Corgi, 1962.

OTHER PUBLICATIONS

Novels

Ottilia: An Eighteenth-Century Idyll. London, Unwin, 1883.
Miss Brown. Edinburgh, Blackwood, 1884.
Ariadne in Mantua: A Romance in Five Acts. Oxford, Blackwell, 1903.
Penelope Brandling: A Tale of the Welsh Coast. London, Unwin, 1903.
Louis Norbert: A Two-Fold Romance. London, Lane, 1914.

Short Stories

Vanitas: Polite Stories. London, Heinemann, 1892.
Au Pays de Vénus. N.p., 1894.
Sister Benvenuta and the Christ-Child: An Eighteenth-Century Legend. London, Grant Richards, 1906.
The Ballet of the Nations: A Present-Day Morality. London, Chatto and Windus, and New York, Putnam, 1915.

Other

Studies of the Eighteenth Century in Italy. London, Satchell, 1880.
Belcaro: Being Essays on Sundry Aesthetical Questions. London, Satchell, 1883.
The Prince of the Hundred Soups. London, Unwin, 1883.
Euphorion: Being Studies of the Antique and the Medieval in the Renaissance. London, Unwin, 1884.
The Countess of Albany. London, Allen 1884.
Baldwin: Being Dialogues on Views and Aspirations. London, Unwin, 1886.
Juvenilia: Being a Second Series of Essays on Sundry Aesthetical Questions. London, Unwin, 1887.
Althea: A Second Book of Dialogues on Aspirations and Duties. London, Osgood McIlvanie, 1894.
Renaissance Fancies and Studies: Being a Sequel to Euphorion. London, Smith Elder, 1895.
Limbo and Other Essays. London, Grant Richards, 1897.
Genius Loci: Notes on Places. London, Grant Richards, 1899.
Hortus Vitae: Essays on the Gardening of Life. London, Lane, 1904.
The Enchanted Woods and Other Essays. London, Lane, 1905.
The Spirit of Rome: Leaves from a Diary. London, Lane, 1906.
The Sentimental Traveller: Notes on Places. London, Lane, 1908.
Gospels of Anarchy, and Other Contemporary Studies. London, Unwin, 1908.
Laurus Nobilis: Chapters on Art and Life. London, Lane, 1909.
Vital Lies: Studies of Some Varieties of Recent Obscurantism. London, Lane, 1912.
Beauty and Ugliness, and Other Studies in Psychological Aesthetics, with C. Anstruther-Thomson. London, Lane, 1912.

The Beautiful: An Introduction to Psychological Aesthetics. Cambridge University Press, 1913.

The Tower of Mirrors, and Other Essays on the Spirit of Places. London, Lane, 1914.

Satan the Waster: A Philosophical War Trilogy. London, Lane, 1920.

The Handling of Words, and Other Studies in Literary Psychology. London, Lane, 1923.

The Golden Keys, and Other Essays on the Genius Loci. London, Lane, 1925.

Proteus, or The Future of Intelligence. London, Kegan Paul Trench Trubner, 1925.

The Poet's Eye. London, Hogarth Press, 1926.

A Vernon Lee Anthology, edited by Irene Cooper Willis. London, Lane, 1929.

Music and Its Lovers. London, Allen and Unwin, 1932.

Letters, edited by Irene Cooper Willis. London, privately printed, 1937.

Editor, *Tuscan Fairy Tales.* London, Satchell, 1880.

Editor, *Art and Man*, by C. Anstruther-Thomson. London, Lane, 1924.

*

Critical Study: *Vernon Lee: Violet Paget 1856-1935* by Peter Gunn, Oxford, Oxford University Press, 1964.

*   *   *

Vernon Lee was one of the pioneers of the British Aesthetic Movement; she was an ardent supporter of Walter Pater's aesthetic theories and she produced *Studies of the Eighteenth Century in Italy* in her early 20s. Although she never formally "came out" as a lesbian the fact that she spent most of her life as an expatriate had at least a little to do with the fact that she was considered a danger to other people's daughters. Like many other writers whose sexuality was unorthodox or ambiguous she was able to insert into her literary accounts of sexual passion a mock-objectivity which insisted on construing erotic attraction as a fever both dangerous and overheated, and evaluated its works with a cutting sarcasm that was as cynical as it was clinical.

In the novella first issued as *A Phantom Lover* and then reprinted in *Hauntings* under the more familiar title "Oke of Okehurst," the careful narrative manner subjects the fever of attraction to a heavy repression, which helps to provide the text with a remarkable tautness. The not-altogether-reliable narrator is a painter commissioned to produce a portrait of the lovely Mrs. Oke, who is then forced to witness the tragic unwinding of a family curse rooted in ancestral adultery. Two of the other stories in *Hauntings*, "Amour Dure" and "Dionea," gradually release the repression exerted by their quasi-academic style to allow gaudier displays of seductive power, although the contemplative eye of the author never loses its coolness. "Amour Dure" offers a less orthodox but more intense development of the *femme fatale* motif than "Dionea," and is entitled to classic status on that account. Like Honoré de Balzac's "Sarrasine," "A Wicked Voice" is not quite a *femme fatale* story, because its alluring phantom is a castrato male rather than a female; the story is, in consequence, slightly calmer than its three companions, aspiring—though not without a certain telling ambiguity—to a higher degree of aesthetic purity.

The four stories making up *Hauntings* are all excellent, and Lee presumably considered them definitive of her achievements in supernatural fiction, or she would surely have added in other previously published items that she let languish for many years thereafter. It is certainly one of the landmark collections of British supernatural fiction. The longest story in *Pope Jacynth* is "Prince Alberic and the Snake Lady," which originally appeared in John Lane's *Yellow Book*. As befits a conscientiously Decadent sexual fantasy it is much more heavily ironic than Lee's earlier *femme fatale* stories. As in the classic works by Keats and Gautier which are loosely based on the same anecdote from Philostratus's *Life of Apollonius of Tyana*—"Lamia" and "Clarimonde"—the reality principle intrudes upon the young Alberic's dream of making an honest woman of the lamia in the form of a spoilsport elder, and Lee carries forward the dynamic instituted by the earlier tales in representing this as a blatant tragedy. The other supernatural tales in the volume are decorative fantasies in the exquisite manner of Richard Garnett's *The Twilight of the Gods*. Viewed as a whole, this second collection of Lee's supernatural tales is far lighter in tone than its predecessor, but its slightly submerged cynicism and strong sense of irony licence its assimilation to the tradition of *contes cruels*.

For Maurice (the dedicatee in question was Maurice Baring) belatedly assembled five more fanciful tales, including the novella "Winthrop's Adventure" (1881), which had served as a prototype for "A Wicked Voice." "The Virgin of the Seven Daggers" (1889) is the most unrepentantly feverish of all Lee's sexual fantasies, setting Don Juan in place of Don Quixote in a marvellously overblown mock-chivalric romance. "Marsyas in Flanders" (1900) is a fantasy in the manner of Anatole France, about a pagan idol mistaken for a Christian image, whose true nature cannot be entirely suppressed by adoption and attempted assimilation. "The Gods and Ritter Tanhauser" (1913) is the longest and funniest of all Lee's homages to Richard Garnett, while "The Doll" is a slight anecdote in much the same vein. As in *Pope Jacynth* the dominant tone is flirtatious rather than horrific, but an element of callousness is still present even in the lightest of the tales.

The reissuing of Lee's supernatural fiction in the 1950s by the Grove Press in America and Peter Owen in Britain gave her work a new lease of life and helped to establish her as a regular presence in anthologies of supernatural fiction. The remixed collections recovered a number of additional items which had previously appeared in collections of essays and are mostly on the borderline between fiction and non-fiction. The one which most warrants consideration as a horror story is "The Legend of Madame Krasinska," a fine tale of ineptly repressed sexuality which is as sly as it is subtle. "Ravenna and Her Ghosts" is not ineffective but remains, in essence, a travelogue. One semi-story in the Grove Press volume that does not appear in either of the Peter Owen collections is "A Seeker of Pagan Perfection," which had earlier appeared in *Renaissance Fancies and Studies* as "Pictor Sacrilegus."

Lee never saw her supernatural stories as central elements of her literary endeavour. She never deigned to write anything of that kind as feverish—or as painstakingly extended—as her half-brother Eugene Lee-Hamilton's magnificently lurid historical novel *The Lord of the Dark Red Star* (1903). In spite of her tendency to suffer nervous breakdowns she was always more controlled than that, and although her disappointingly verbose novel *Louis Norbert* has a few quasi-Gothic touches it flatly refuses to become a horror story. It was, of course, the tense antagonistic combination of fever and control which gave her best work its considerable power and its unique flavour.

—Brian Stableford

LEECH, Ben

Pseudonym of Stephen Bowkett. **Nationality:** British. **Born:** South Wales, 1953. **Career:** English teacher, Leicestershire; freelance writer, mainly of children's books. **Address:** c/o Pan Books, Macmillan Publishers Ltd., 25 Eccleston Place, London SW1W 9NF, England. Lives in Market Harborough, Leicestershire.

HORROR, GHOST AND GOTHIC PUBLICATIONS

Novels

The Community. London, Pan, 1993.
The Bidden. London, Pan, 1994.
A Rare Breed. London, Pan, 1996.

OTHER PUBLICATIONS

Novels as Stephen Bowkett

Spellbinder. London, Gollancz, 1985.
Gameplayers. London, Gollancz, 1986.
Dualists. London, Gollancz, 1987.
Frontiersville High. London, Gollancz, 1990.
Panic Station. London, Henderson, 1996.
Dinosaur Day. London, Heinemann, 1996.
For the Moon There is a Cloud. London, Collins, 1996.
The World's Smallest Werewolf. London, Macdonald, 1996.
Dreamcastle. London, Orion, 1997.

Short Stories

Catch and Other Stories. London, Gollancz, 1987.

Other

Meditations for Bus People: How to Stop Worrying and Stay Calm. London, Thorsons, 1996.

* * *

Ben Leech is the pseudonym of Stephen Bowkett, who has published many books under his real name—including a number of fantasy, science-fiction and supernatural novels aimed at children and teenagers. As Ben Leech, he has written three adult novels which blend science fiction with supernatural horror. Strongly indebted to the pulp tradition, Leech's novels contain echoes of 1950s B-movies, *Quatermass*, H. P. Lovecraft and Quentin Tarantino. They also contain a strong thread of social commentary and a sensitive eroticism. Like the best pulp writers, Leech varies his pace and tone in order to create memorable set-pieces. While his three novels are uneven and melodramatic, they all display careful narrative crafting and moments of genuine literary flair.

The Community, Leech's debut novel, is probably his best. Set against a background of small-town poverty and deprivation, it describes the coming together of a secret family or "kin" of human appearance but inhuman nature. The Kin are able to imitate any living form: they harness the "morphogenetic fields" of terrestrial life to develop their own bodies, but have a common memory and identity. As their nucleus is shifting from one obscure rural town to another, a psychotic Kin-human hybrid is systematically hunting them down. Leech invests this hackneyed storyline with genuine passion and intensity in a number of ways. The depressed atmosphere of the town and its inhabitants is powerfully conveyed, establishing a link between the violent energy of the Kin and the frustrated needs of the human characters. This link is also made at the level of imagination and sexual desire: the need for an "ecstasy" of direct contact with nature. Leech's descriptions of the forms taken by the Kin recall Arthur Machen's "The Great God Pan." There's also a chilling description of the blank facsimile of a village inhabited only by dying Kin. Among the more obvious B-movie trappings is a classic bit of gallows humour involving a brain in a jar. Leech's background in juvenile fiction shows through in his excessive use of exclamation marks and ellipses; but his restless visual imagination and sympathetic identification with the monstrous make *The Community* worthwhile at an adult level.

Leech's second novel, *The Bidden*, is a colder, more cynical retread of his first. This time, Leech draws inspiration from gangster films, including *Reservoir Dogs*; the hard-bitten attitude of his characters hints at a pessimistic subtext, a negative view of humanity. The plot concerns a race of parasitic creatures who form themselves into replicas of human faces, and can live either attached to human hosts or independently. Smuggled into Britain with some Cretan artifacts, they are the ancient reality behind the Gorgon myth. Leech grafts the infestation onto a particularly selfish, duplicitous cross-section of humanity, implying that the Gorgon-creatures represent the unacceptable face of capitalism. However, this political subtext doesn't save *The Bidden* from being a contrived and predictable novel. It's redeemed by a couple of breathtaking set-pieces, including one in which a detective goes down into the cellar of a house to find the walls crawling with faces.

Two of Leech's short stories reflect his radical sensibility. In "Rare Breed" (*Peeping Tom* 15, 1994) two young people with bizarre supernatural abilities are drawn into an unnecessary and destructive conflict with the police. In "The Gift" (*Cold Cuts II* edited by Paul Lewis and Steve Lockley, 1994), a more openly allegorical piece, a boy with the ability to make wishes come true is murdered by a clergyman. To Leech, clearly, the supernatural is not a metaphor for "evil" but for human vitality: the creative potential stifled by social norms.

A Rare Breed, Leech's third novel, is a heady mix of political satire and metaphysics. It concerns a tycoon, Reece, whose empire of genetic science generates a "hologenic" drug which enables people to change shape. It turns out that Reece's success is based on a Faustian pact with demonic forces, and that the new drug enables demons to be incarnated through human flesh. Resistance to the new order arises in the form of a group of hologen-affected idealists—dropouts, a journalist, a policewoman and others—who use their new powers to combat Reece's empire of evil. Since both sides have arbitrary powers and access to ill-defined metaphysical resources, the novel inevitably declines into a farfetched and protracted battle scene. Somewhat unexpectedly, humanity loses.

Despite its unconvincing storyline, *A Rare Breed* has much to recommend it: sharp, intelligent dialogue; strong female characters who function independently of men; a compelling set-piece involving a community of derelicts around a comatose mutant god; and above all, a bitter kiss-off ending in which Reece gets his "reward" from his demonic masters. In two pages of brilliance, Leech shows that he is capable of far more than pulpish melodramas with a left-wing slant. Whether he can focus his imaginative gaze consistently enough to become an important figure in the supernatural horror genre, only time will tell.

—Joel Lane

LE FANU, J(oseph) Sheridan

Nationality: Irish. **Born:** Dublin, 28 August 1814. **Education:** Trinity College, University of Dublin, graduated with honours 1837; Dublin Inns of Court. **Family:** Married Susanna Bennett in 1843 (died 1858); four children. **Career:** Owner and editor, *Dublin University Magazine*, 1861-69; called to the Irish Bar in 1839, though never practised; part-owner, the *Statesman*, 1840-46, the *Warder*, 1840-70; part-owner and editor, *Dublin Evening Mail*, from 1861. **Died:** 7 February 1873.

Horror, Ghost and Gothic Publications

Novel

Uncle Silas: A Tale of Bartram-Haugh. London, Bentley, 1864; New York, Harper, 1865; as *No Escape*, Waterford, Carthage Press, 1942.

Short Stories

Ghost Stories and Tales of Mystery (anonymous). Dublin, McGlashan, and London, Orr, 1851.
The Chronicles of Golden Friars. London, Bentley, 1871; New York, Arno Press, 1977.
In a Glass Darkly. London, Bentley, 1872; New York, Arno Press, 1977.
The Purcell Papers. London, Bentley, 1880; New York, AMS Press, 1975.
The Watcher and Other Weird Stories. London, Downey, 1894.
A Chronicle of Golden Friars and Other Stories. London, Downey, 1896.
Madam Crowl's Ghost and Other Tales of Mystery, edited by M. R. James. London, Bell, 1923; New York, Books for Libraries Press, 1971.
Green Tea and Other Ghost Stories, edited by August Derleth. Sauk City, Arkham House, 1945.
Sheridan Le Fanu: The Diabolic Genius. New York, Juniper Press, 1959.
Best Ghost Stories of J. S. Le Fanu, edited by E. F. Bleiler. New York, Dover, 1964.
The Vampire Lovers and Other Stories. London, Fontana, 1970.
The Best Horror Stories. London, Sphere, 1970.
Irish Ghost Stories of Sheridan Le Fanu. Dublin, Mercier Press, 1973.

Ghost Stories and Mysteries, edited by E. F. Bleiler. New York, Dover, 1975.
The Hours After Midnight, edited by Leslie Frewin. London, Frewin, 1975.
The Purcell Papers, edited by August Derleth. Sauk City, Arkham House, 1975.
Borrhomeo the Astrologer. Edinburgh, Tragara Press, 1985.
The Illustrated J. S. Le Fanu: Ghost Stories and Mysteries by a Master Victorian Storyteller, edited by Michael Cox. Wellingborough, Northamptonshire, Equation, and New York, Sterling, 1988.
Ghost and Horror Stories. London, Tynron Press, 1990.
Carmilla and Other Classic Tales of Mystery, edited by Leonard Wolf. New York, Signet, 1996.

Other Publications

Novels

The Cock and Anchor: Being a Chronicle of Old Dublin City (anonymous). Dublin, William Curry, and London, Longmans, 1845; New York, Colyer, 1848; revised as *Morley Court,* London, Chapman, 1873.
The Fortunes of Colonel Torlogh O'Brien. Dublin, James McGlashan, 1847; New York, W.H. Colyer, 1847.
The House by the Church-Yard. London, Tinsley, 1863; New York, Carleton, 1866.
Wylder's Hand. London, Bentley, 1864; New York, Carleton, 1865.
Guy Deverell. London, Bentley, 1865; New York, Harper, 1866.
All in the Dark. London, Bentley, and New York, Harper, 1866.
The Tenants of Malory. London, Tinsley, and New York, Harper, 1867.
A Lost Name. London, Bentley, and New York, Harper, 1868.
Haunted Lives. London, Tinsley, 1868; New York, Arno Press, 1977.
The Wyvern Mystery. London, Tinsley, 1869; New York, Arno Press, 1977.
Checkmate. London, Hurst and Blackett, and Philadelphia, Evans and Stoddart, 1871.
The Rose and the Key. London, Chapman and Hall, 1871; New York, Arno Press, 1977.
Willing to Die. London, Hurst and Blackett, 1873; New York, Arno Press, 1977.
The Evil Guest. London, Downey, 1895; New York, Arno Press, 1977.

Poetry

The Beautiful Poem of Shamus O'Brien. London, Heywood, 1867; as *Shamus O'Brien*, New York, Amsterdam News Company, 1871.
The Poems of Joseph Sheridan Le Fanu, edited by A. P. Graves. London, Downey, 1896; New York, AMS Press, 1975.

Other

The Prelude. Dublin, Herbert, 1865.

*

Film Adaptations: *Vampyr*, 1931, *Et Mourir de Plaisir*, 1961, *The Vampire Lovers*, 1970, *La Novia Ensangrentada*, 1972, all from the novella "Carmilla" (in *In a Glass Darkly*); *Uncle Silas* (also released as *The Inheritance*), 1947, 1968 (television serial).

Manuscript Collection: National Library of Ireland (microfilm); Trinity College, Dublin.

Bibliography: *J. Sheridan Le Fanu: A Bio-Bibliography* by Gary William Crawford, Westport, Greenwood Press, 1995.

Critical Studies: *Wilkie Collins, Le Fanu and Others* by S. M. Ellis, London, Constable, 1931; *Sheridan Le Fanu* by Nelson Browne, London, Morrison and Gibb, 1951; *Joseph Sheridan Le Fanu* by Michael H. Begnal, Lewisburg, Bucknell, Bucknell University Press, 1971; *Sheridan Le Fanu and Victorian England* by W. J. McCormack, Oxford, Clarendon Press, 1980; *Sheridan Le Fanu* by Ivan Melada, Boston, Twayne, 1987.

*   *   *

Joseph Sheridan Le Fanu is regarded by many as the leading writer of supernatural fiction in the Victorian era and the father of the modern ghost story. Yet for many years his works were all but forgotten and though he undergoes bouts of rediscovery even now his reputation is not as wide as, say, that of Mary Shelley or Bram Stoker, other progenitors of horror fiction. Most people would be hard-pressed to name even one of Le Fanu's stories, although some may recall the much reprinted "Green Tea" or "Carmilla." Yet Le Fanu's reputation rests firmly on his fiction and on its influence upon others. It was Le Fanu who dragged the ghost story out from the gothic dungeons in which it had become hideously chained and breathed life into it, gradually shifting it to the more unsettling psychological ghost story. Le Fanu, more than any of his contemporaries, demonstrated the potential of the ghost story beyond its traditional roots and bridged the gap between the gothic fiction of the early 19th century and the modern ghost story of the 20th century.

Le Fanu was not unduly influenced by the gothic tradition. In his youth he spent much of his time in the old suburbs of Dublin, such as the village of Chapelizod, and loved to hear the local folk tales, many of which he adapted for his stories. These were the sources for his earliest tales such as "The Ghost and the Bonesetter" (*Dublin University Magazine*, 1838), his first known story, and most of the others that made up the collection *The Purcell Papers*. There are, though, two early stories worthy of further consideration. The best is "A Strange Event in the Life of Schalken the Painter" (*Dublin University Magazine*, 1839). Set in the 17th century during the apprenticeship of the Dutch painter Godfried Schalken to Gerard Douw, it interprets one of Schalken's paintings. Douw's niece, Rose, is married to the hideous Wilken Vaderhausen, but the girl soon returns to her uncle in mortal fear. Left alone for a brief moment the girl vanishes after one long and agonizing scream. Some years later Schalken is investigating a church in Rotterdam where he encounters a ghostly female who leads him into the church's vaults where he sees the dead-alive corpse of Vanderhausen. The second story is "The Fortunes of Sir Robert Ardagh" (*Dublin University Magazine*, 1838) about the bond between Ardagh and the devil. Although a weak story and clearly derivative of the Faust legend and Charles Maturin's *Melmoth the Wanderer*, it is an interesting example of how Le Fanu

would regularly return to a theme, remoulding and experimenting. This story would evolve into "Sir Dominick's Bargain" (*All the Year Round*, 1872) where Le Fanu introduced a clever twist in Sir Dominick believing his soul is safe when the day of reckoning passes, but he'd forgotten to account for the leap year.

Le Fanu also used the pact-with-the-devil motif in "The Haunted Baronet" (*Belgravia*, 1870), a novel-length work incorporated in *The Chronicles of Golden Friars*. Unlike the shorter stories this is a powerfully sinister tale of supernatural revenge between two rivals families, the Feltrams and the Mardykes. The Feltrams have been dispossessed and are now subservient to the Mardykes. Feltram is believed to have committed suicide in a notorious haunted lake, but he returns with supernatural power and turns the screws on Mardyke who finds he has entered a pact with the Devil and must meet its terms. The scenes around the haunted lake and the surrounding forest are amongst the most evocative in all of Le Fanu's writings.

These works show that Le Fanu would use gothic motifs but would not let them dominate his work. He preferred to use them as background and sought to develop character and everyday incident to dictate his story. This was part of the new sensation fiction emerging from the pens of Wilkie Collins, Bulwer Lytton and Charles Dickens, to whose work Le Fanu's is comparable. In fact for a period Le Fanu moved away from the supernatural story, producing two historical adventures set in Ireland's turbulent past—*The Cock and Anchor* and *The Fortunes of Colonel Torlogh O'Brien*—but the reception of these books was mild. So Le Fanu returned to supernatural fiction and his next book became one of the cornerstones of the genre: *Ghost Stories and Tales of Mystery*. The book contained only four stories. Two of them, "The Murdered Cousin," which would later evolve into *Uncle Silas*, and "The Evil Guest," later revised as *A Lost Name*, were non-supernatural but were heightened tales of mystery. The third was a revised version of "Schalken the Painter," whilst the fourth was "The Watcher." Later revised as "The Familiar," this is one of Le Fanu's best stories. It relates the fate of retired naval officer, Captain Barton, who firmly disbelieves in anything preternatural. However he soon finds himself being followed by the sound of footsteps and has fleeting visions of the Watcher with a face of "menace and malignity." Barton eventually finds himself, trapped in a room with his nemesis now in the form of an owl. Thereafter the reader is left to consider whether Barton is genuinely haunted by the spirit of a fellow sailor whose death he caused years before, or whether the guilt is driving him mad.

Le Fanu liked this reader-dilemma and began to explore it further. He used it in "An Account of Some Strange Disturbances in Aungier Street" (*Dublin University Magazine*, 1853), which was revised to less effect as "Mr. Justice Harbottle" (*Belgravia*, 1872), where the reader is left to decide whether a series of bizarre deaths are caused by supernatural means or as the result of a fit, drunkenness or accident. He returned to it to great effect in "Green Tea" (*All the Year Round*, 1869) which became the lead story in his second cornerstone volume, *In a Glass Darkly*. It concerns the unfortunate Reverend Jennings who, like Le Fanu, had become addicted to green tea. He finds himself haunted by the image of a small black monkey with red eyes and a manner of "unfathomable malignity." The monkey is visible to him alone, and though it departs for weeks at a time it always returns. Its continued presence eventually drives the Reverend to madness and suicide. The reader is left totally perplexed as to whether Jennings's experience is as the result of a supernatural agency or mental degradation. Le Fanu heightens this uncertainty in the book version of the story by having it introduced by Dr. Martin Hesselius, the forerunner of the psychic detective figure that crops up in the work of so many later writers, who has collected a number of unusual cases in which he is interested.

The stories in *In a Glass Darkly* reflected Le Fanu's interest in the mystical doctrine of the Swedish philosopher Emanuel Swedenborg who proposed that the human world was an outgrowth of the spiritual world, which was itself an outgrowth of a mental world. Contact might be made between these worlds by re-attuning the mind. These theories suited Le Fanu's purpose extremely well, allowing his ghost stories to have a third possible interpretation of religious experience.

In addition to the revised stories "The Familiar" and "Mr. Justice Harbottle", *In a Glass Darkly* also contained Le Fanu's classic vampire story "Carmilla" (*The Dark Blue*, 1871-2), and the excellent mystery story "The Room at the Dragon Volant" (*London Society*, 1872). "Carmilla" is arguably the definitive vampire story, as it contains all of the necessary elements without the Byronic sensationalism of *Varney the Vampire* which also pervaded *Dracula*. It is portrayed more as a love story, and the overtones of lesbianism would have shocked Victorian society more had it not been for the calm and placid way in which Le Fanu introduced these elements. "Carmilla" showed Le Fanu as the master of the supernatural short story.

Le Fanu had written other ghost stories over the years, a number of which were rediscovered by M. R. James who assembled them into the volume *Madam Crowl's Ghost*. Many of these stories are attractive but slight pieces by Le Fanu based on Irish folklore and legend, but amongst them is "Squire Toby's Will" (*Temple Bar*, 1868). Two brothers argue over their inheritance but the ghost of the squire visits them in the form of dreams and even as a bulldog in order to resolve the dispute. Le Fanu also included a self-contained story in his novel *The House by the Churchyard*. This is the variously titled "Ghost Stories of the Tiled House" or "The Narrative of the Ghost of a Hand" and was the first of that subgenre of stories about a ghostly disembodied hand. Le Fanu was able to imbue it with a presence and malevolence that caused one of his devotees, S. M. Ellis, to call it (in 1931) "the most terrifying ghost story in the language."

Despite its title, *The House by the Churchyard* is not a supernatural or even a horror novel. None of Le Fanu's separately published novels ventured into the realms of the weird, though many of them had heightened atmospheres of dread and foreboding. In some ways Le Fanu channeled the gothic influence into these novels rather than his short fiction, but tempered it to reflect the public mood for sensation novels and the neo-gothic romances of the Brontës. Le Fanu's classic was *Uncle Silas*, about a murderous and vengeful old man who lives in a remote Derbyshire house and who seeks to gain the inheritance of his niece, Maud, who becomes his ward. The mounting terror that surrounds Maud as she fights for her survival is a model of Victorian suspense. Most of Le Fanu's other novels involve murder and suspense but none have the charged atmosphere of *Uncle Silas*.

With Le Fanu we find a writer exploring and experimenting with fictional devices. Whilst he followed trends to a degree, he also set them, revising his stories as necessary to see what worked best given a certain development in fiction. It was Le Fanu who created the psychological ghost story and you can see the process working through a period of over 30 years until with the collection *In a Glass Darkly* he was able to present the refined and polished article which served as a model for generations to come.

—Mike Ashley

LEIBER, Fritz (Reuter, Jr.)

Nationality: American. **Born:** Chicago, Illinois, 24 December 1910. **Education:** University of Chicago, Ph.B. 1932; Episcopal General Theological Seminary, Washington, D.C. **Family:** Married 1) Jonquil Stephens in 1936 (died 1969), one son (the writer Justin Leiber); 2) Margo Skinner in 1991. **Career:** Episcopal minister at two churches in New Jersey, 1932-33; actor, 1934-36; editor, Consolidated Book Publishers, Chicago, 1937-41; instructor in speech and drama, Occidental College, Los Angeles, 1941-42; precision inspector, Douglas Aircraft, Santa Monica, California, 1942-44; associate editor, *Science Digest,* Chicago, 1944-56. Lecturer, Clarion State College, Pennsylvania, summers 1968-70. **Awards:** Hugo award, 1958, 1965, 1968, 1970, 1971, 1976; Nebula award, 1967, 1970, 1975, and Grand Master Nebula award, 1981; Ann Radcliffe award, 1970; Gandalf award, 1975; Derleth award, 1976; World Fantasy award, 1976, 1978; Locus award, 1985; Bram Stoker Lifetime Achievement award, 1988. Guest of Honour, World Science Fiction Convention, 1951, 1979. **Died:** 5 September 1992.

HORROR, GHOST AND GOTHIC PUBLICATIONS

Novels

Conjure Wife. New York, Twayne, 1953; London, Penguin, 1969.
The Sinful Ones. New York, Universal, 1953; revised edition, New York, Pocket, 1980.
Our Lady of Darkness. New York, Berkley, 1977; London, Millington, 1978.
The Dealings of Daniel Kesserich: A Study of the Mass-Insanity at Smithville, illustrated by Jason van Hollander. New York, Tor, 1997.

Short Stories

Night's Black Agents. Sauk City, Wisconsin, Arkham House, 1947; London, Spearman, 1975.
Shadows with Eyes. New York, Ballantine, 1962.
The Secret Songs. London, Hart Davis, 1968.
Night Monsters. New York, Ace, 1969; revised edition, London, Gollancz, 1974.
You're All Alone. New York, Ace, 1972.
Heroes and Horrors, edited by Stuart David Schiff. Browns Mills, New Jersey, Whispers Press, 1978.
The Ghost Light (includes autobiographical essay). New York, Berkley, 1984.

OTHER PUBLICATIONS

Novels

Gather, Darkness! New York, Pellegrini and Cudahy, 1950; London, New English Library, 1966.

The Green Millennium. New York, Abelard Press, 1953; London Abelard Schuman, 1959.

Destiny Times Three. New York, Galaxy, 1957.

The Big Time. New York, Ace, 1961; London, New English Library, 1965.

The Silver Eggheads. New York, Ballantine, 1962; London, New English Library, 1966.

The Wanderer. New York, Ballantine, 1964; London, Dobson, 1967.

Tarzan and the Valley of Gold (novelization of screenplay). New York, Ballantine, 1966.

The Swords of Lankhmar. New York, Ace, 1968; London, Hart Davis, 1969.

A Specter is Haunting Texas. New York, Walker, and London, Gollancz, 1969.

Rime Isle (novella). Chapel Hill, North Carolina, Whispers Press, 1977.

Ship of Shadows (novella), published with *No Truce With Kings,* by Poul Anderson. New York, Tor, 1989.

Ill Met in Lankhmar (novella), published with *The Fair in Emain Macha* by Charles de Lint. New York, Tor, 1990.

Short Stories

Two Sought Adventure. New York, Gnome Press, 1957; revised and expanded as *Swords Against Death,* New York, Ace, 1970; London, New English Library, 1972.

The Mind Spider and Other Stories. New York, Ace, 1961.

A Pail of Air. New York, Ballantine, 1964.

Ships to the Stars. New York, Ace, 1964.

The Night of the Wolf. New York, Ballantine, 1966; London, Sphere, 1976.

Swords Against Wizardry. New York, Ace, 1968; London, Prior, 1977.

Swords in the Mist. New York, Ace, 1968; London, Prior, 1977.

Swords and Deviltry. New York, Ace, 1970; London, New English Library, 1971.

The Best of Fritz Leiber, edited by Angus Wells. London, Sphere, and New York, Doubleday, 1974.

The Book of Fritz Leiber. New York, DAW, 1974.

The Second Book of Fritz Leiber. New York, DAW, 1975.

The Worlds of Fritz Leiber. New York, Ace, 1976.

Swords and Ice Magic. New York, Ace, and London, Prior, 1977.

Bazaar of the Bizarre. West Kingston, Rhode Island, Grant, 1978.

The Change War. Boston, Gregg Press, 1978; revised edition, as *Changewar,* New York, Ace, 1983.

Ship of Shadows. London, Gollancz, 1979.

The Mystery of the Japanese Clock. Santa Monica, California, Montgolfier Press, 1982.

Riches and Power: A Story for Children. New Castle, Virginia, Cheap Street, 1982.

In the Beginning. New Castle, Virginia, Cheap Street, 1983.

Quicks Around the Zodiac: A Farce. New Castle, Virginia, Cheap Street, 1983.

The Knight and Knave of Swords. New York, Morrow, 1988; London, Grafton, 1990.

The Three of Swords (omnibus; includes *Swords and Deviltry, Swords Against Death, Swords in the Mist*). New York, Nelson Doubleday, 1989.

The Leiber Chronicles: Fifty Years of Fritz Leiber, edited by Martin H. Greenberg. Arlington Heights, Illinois, Dark Harvest Press, 1990.

Swords' Masters (omnibus; includes *Swords Against Wizardry, Swords of Lankhmar, Swords and Ice Magic*). New York, Guild America, 1990.

Poetry

The Demons of the Upper Air. Glendale, California, Squires, 1969.
Sonnets to Jonquil and All. Glendale, California, Squires, 1978.

Other

Fafhrd & Me, edited by John Gregory Betancourt. Newark, New Jersey, Wildside Press, 1990.

Editor, with Stuart David Schiff, *The World Fantasy Awards 2.* New York, Doubleday, 1980.

*

Bibliography: *Fritz Leiber: A Bibliography 1934-1979* by Chris Morgan, Birmingham, England, Morgenstern, 1979; *Fritz Leiber: Sardonic Swordsman—A Working Bibliography, 2nd ed.* by Phil Stephensen-Payne and Gordon Benson, Jr., Leeds, West Yorkshire, Galactic Central Publications, 1990.

Critical Studies: "Fritz Leiber Issue" of *Fantasy and Science Fiction* (New York), July 1969; *Fritz Leiber* by Jeff Frane, San Bernardino, California, Borgo Press, 1980; *Fritz Leiber* by Tom Staicar, New York, Ungar, 1983; *Witches of the Mind: A Critical Study of Fritz Leiber* by Bruce Byfield, West Warwick, Rhode Island, Necronomicon Press, 1991.

*   *   *

When a character in Fritz Leiber's short story "The Automatic Pistol" remarks "Times change and styles change," he could just as well be describing the foundation of Leiber's aesthetic for the weird tale. Perhaps no other writer of horror fiction devoted as much of his career as Leiber did to refurbishing traditional supernatural horrors for a new life in modern times. Although his horror stories constitute only a fraction of his total output as a writer of fantasy and science fiction, they form a solid bridge between the classic and contemporary weird tale and are among the most important written in the 20th century.

Leiber's approach to horror was influenced by his correspondence with H. P. Lovecraft and his interest in *Unknown Worlds,* a pulp magazine that specialized in fantasy with a logical modern spin. Both impressed upon Leiber the inadequacy of traditional ghosts, vampires, witches and werewolves—all holdovers from the Gothic era of a century-and-a-half before—for frightening people for whom the theory of relativity and World War I were part of the cultural mind-set. Leiber articulated the problem himself in his short story, "The Hound": "We begin by denying all the old haunts and superstitions. Why shouldn't we? They belong to the era of cottage and castle. They can't take root in the new environment. Science goes materialistic, proving that there isn't anything in the universe except tiny bundles of energy." Nevertheless, the same impulse that drove cathedral builders in the middle ages to imagine "grey shapes gliding around at night to talk with the gargoyles" persists in the men who build skyscrapers and factories. "Fear is accumulating. Horror is accumulating. A new kind of awe of the mysteries of the universe is accumulating. A psychological environment is forming along with the physical one . . . our culture suddenly spawns a horde of demons. And like germs, they have a peculiar affinity for our culture. They're unique. They fit in. You wouldn't find the same kind any other time or place."

In his early horror stories, published mostly in *Weird Tales* and *Unknown Worlds*, Leiber simply adapted the horrors of the past to the present. Comparing witch familiars to "stooges sent out by the Big Boy to watch over his chosen" in "The Automatic Pistol," he made it seem perfectly logical that a gangster's gun could be the latter-day equivalent of a demonic protector. In "The Hound," the city's "endlessly varying howls and growls of traffic and industry—sounds at once animal and mechanical" become the voice of the modern werewolf. The vampire in "The Girl with the Hungry Eyes" is an advertising image that feeds not on blood but on the hopes and fears of the consumer culture. "Smoke Ghost" features a spectre of soot and grime whose features are "A smoky composite face with the hungry anxiety of the unemployed, the neurotic restlessness of the person without purpose, the jerky tension of the high-pressure metropolitan worker, the uneasy resentment of the striker, the callous opportunism of the scab, the aggressive whine of the panhandler, the inhibited terror of the bombed civilian, and a thousand other twisted emotional patterns."

Leiber made his horrors believable by making them seem natural outgrowths of their environment. His first novel, *Conjure Wife*, remains one of the finest examples of his craft. Set at Hempnell College, a fictional school indistinguishable from many other small colleges, it proposes that all women are witches who secretly practice magic to further their husbands' careers. When Norman Saylor, a professor of sociology and sceptic by nature, forces his wife, Tansy, to destroy the magic charms that she fashions to protect him, his life begins to fall apart. Petty personal and professional annoyances escalate into major problems, and under their stress he begins seeing illusions that a less enlightened person might attribute to supernatural agents. Ultimately, he reestablishes the balance of his life through a system of logic that allows him to integrate a belief in witchcraft with the rationality of science. By weaving threads of the supernatural into the fabric of daily life so invisibly that even non-believers would be hard-pressed to refute them, Leiber created a model that influenced the entire generation of dark fantasists who followed him.

Leiber's career as a science-fiction writer dovetails with his career as a fantasy writer, so it comes as no surprise that much of his weird fiction is laced with scientific elements. "Mr. Bauer and the Atoms" concerns the consequences of a man's discovery that the atoms of his body contain the nuclear potential of an atom bomb. "Alice and the Allergy" and "In the X-Ray" both feature physicians too blinded by their faith in medical science to accept the supernatural as a cause for their patients' illnesses, while "Spider Mansion" and "The Dead Man" are about medical experiments horribly undone by the subliminal psychological problems of their protagonists. In the posthumously-published but early-written short novel *The Dealings of Daniel Kesserich*, a succession of horrors that includes apparent supernatural materializations, premature burial, graverobbing and mass hysteria eventually are explained as the outcome of time-travellers attempting to change the past.

Much of Leiber's fiction is dominated by a cosmic viewpoint in which these intersections of the scientific and the supernatural are not inconsistent, but rather suggest a universal order that transcends ordinary human frames of reference. In "The Dreams of Albert Moreland" and "Midnight by the Morphy Watch," men discover that they are merely pawns in a game of chess being played on a cosmic scale. *The Sinful Ones*, an expansion of his short novel "You Are All Alone," extends this idea further into the realm of existential terror. Its protagonist is "awakened" one day from the ordinary routine of his life to discover that, "the universe was a machine. The people in it, save for a very few, were mindless mechanisms, clockwork things of flesh and bone." Flitting among unawakened automatons oblivious to his independent existence, he discovers that individuality is not only unrecognized within the system, but potentially fatal if indulged too conspicuously.

Published in 1953, *The Sinful Ones* turned the social conformity that defined postwar American culture into the stuff of nightmares. It showed Leiber to be not just a skilful modernizer of classic horrors, but a writer whose spooks were inextricably bound up with the spirit of the age. In many of his stories the horrors are unique products of their time and place. In "The Man Who Made Friends with Electricity" and "The Black Gondolier," the ubiquitousness and significance of energy-sources to industrial civilization leads to the speculation that electricity and oil, respectively, are sentient life forms that manipulate the course of human affairs. His World Fantasy award-winning novel, *Our Lady of Darkness*, is the culmination of his earlier urban horror stories and a direct response to his reflection in a 1962 fantasy, "A Bit of the Dark World," that the modern city is an unimaginative "human stamping ground, where we've policemen to guard us, and psychiatrists to monitor our minds and neighbors to jabber at us and where our ears are so full of the mass media that it's practically impossible to think or sense or feel anything deeply, anything that's beyond humanity." The hero of this tale discovers, instead, that "modern cities were the world's supreme mysteries, and skyscrapers their secular cathedrals," when he finds contemporary San Francisco a magnet for *paramentals*, or supernatural beings drawn to cityscapes much the same way that the demons and devils of mythology were attracted to medieval towns.

It is easy to be awed by the inventiveness of Leiber's weird tales and take for granted the human dimension that make their horrors effective. Leiber, perhaps more than any other fantasy writer of his generation, understood the psychology of fear and its relationship to emotional vulnerability. In story after story, his characters reveal anxieties that are the gateways to the supernatural dimension: job dissatisfaction in "The Belsen Express," troubled child-parent relationships in "The Terror from the Depths," loneliness in "The Button Molder." With a candour uncommon for writers of his generation, Leiber openly acknowledged sexuality as one of the weak points in human emotional armour. Love and passion are common catalysts for the horrors that overtake his male protagonists, and women serve as embodiments of death that both attract and repel them in "I'm Looking for Jeff," "Midnight in the Mirror World" and "Horrible Imaginings." No matter how much imagination he invested in his horrors, Leiber never failed to convey that their inhumanity could only be defined in terms of the fundamental humanity of his characters.

—Stefan Dziemianowicz

LEVEN, Jeremy

Nationality: American. **Born:** South Bend, Indiana, 16 August 1941. **Education:** St. John's College, Annapolis, Maryland, B.A. 1965; Harvard University, M.Ed, 1973; Yale University, University of Connecticut, doctoral studies 1977—. **Family:** Married

Roberta Danza in 1980; one daughter and one son (from a previous marriage). **Career:** Director and producer, WBZ-TV, Boston, 1965-66; English teacher at public schools in Medford, Massachusetts, 1967; founder, director, and writer, Proposition (theatre group), Cambridge, Massachusetts, 1968-70; research associate, Harvard University, Cambridge, 1968-69; director of education research and development, Cambridge Model Cities Program, Cambridge, 1969-70; assistant professor of psychology, Newton College, Newton, Massachusetts, 1971-72; clinical director, Cambridge Psychological Associates, Cambridge, 1972-74; principal psychologist, 1974-75, mental health center director, 1975-76, associate area director for children's and drug programs, 1976-77, Massachusetts Department of Mental Health, Northampton; writer and clinical psychologist, 1977—. **Agent:** Elaine Markson Literary Agency, Inc., 44 Greenwich Ave., New York, NY 10011; (films) Alain Bernheim, c/o Lorimar Productions, MGM Studios, Gable Bldg., West Washington Blvd., Culver City, California 90230. **Address:** 105 Woodside Ter., New Haven, Connecticut 06515, USA.

HORROR, GHOST AND GOTHIC PUBLICATIONS

Novels

Creator. New York, Coward McCann, 1980.
Satan: His Psychotherapy and Cure by the Unfortunate Dr. Kassler, J.S.P.S. New York, Knopf, 1982.

Plays

Screenplays: *Creator*, 1985; *Don Juan DeMarco*, 1995.

*

Film Adaptation: *Creator*, 1985.

Theatrical Activities:
Director: **Film**—*Don Juan DeMarco*, 1995.

*　　*　　*

Jeremy Leven's first novel, *Creator*, tells the story of the quasi-Frankensteinian scientist Harry Wolper, who is attempting to create life in the hope of cloning his much-beloved but long-dead wife. Harry's scientific quest is, however, run in parallel with a literary quest which seeks to make more conventional sense of the history of one Boris Lafkin, who has also lost his wife to an outrageous stroke of ill-fortune. In the end, a sudden flip of perspective makes Lafkin the creator by establishing his story as "real" and Wolpert's as the fiction-within-the-fiction. This move deliberately demolishes the novel's already tenuous affiliation to the Gothic tradition, setting it instead firmly and explicitly within the rich tradition of Jewish-American only-slightly-magical realism.

It is conceivable that Leven eventually came to regret that abrupt shift away from fantasy, perhaps even to think of it as an act of cowardice. His script for the film *Don Juan DeMarco*, which he also directed, is certainly much more sympathetic to the healing and life-enhancing potential of fantasy, although it remains stubbornly committed to the dutiful recognition that fantasy is, after all, the stuff of dreams, delusions and creative play. In much the

same fashion, Leven's second novel—which certainly warrants consideration as a neo-Gothic horror story—never loses sight of the fact that Satan is a figment of the human imagination: a fiction whose purpose is to dramatize the problem of evil, and hopefully to assist in paving the way for that problem's elaborate contemplation and tentative solution.

As the extended title indicates, the hero of *Satan* is Dr. Kassler, a Jewish-American psychotherapist who bears all the burdens of guilt and anguish characteristic of his culture and his profession. His personal life is a guilt-ridden mess and his professional life is cursed by a quixotic determination to oppose the contemporary trends in psychotherapeutic practice which favour treatment by heavy medicine. The boundaries separating the personal and the professional are comprehensively breached when he takes a number of patients into his home in the hope of saving them from the deadening courses of treatment proposed by his superior. As in *Creator*, however, this tragicomic account of "real" endeavour runs parallel to a "fictitious" sequence of events in which he is recruited by Satan—manifest by mysterious means as the intelligence of a Quintessential Entropy Device—to serve as his psychotherapist.

As might be expected in a Jewish novel, the Satan who figures in it is not the Satan of the New Testament, who is evil incarnate, but the fugitive Satan of the Old Testament, personalized only in the Book of Job as the valuable Adversary whose task is to challenge God with scepticism. This Satan is deeply disappointed, and not a little confused, by the irreparable damage done to his image by the Catholic Church. He is in need of wise counsel and sound explanation, and he thinks that Kassler is the man to provide it—although Kassler cannot imagine why. It is Satan, not Kassler, who provides the text's account of his therapeutic sessions, occasionally addressing the reader directly in order to explain what he is about. It is also Satan who eventually has the last word within the text, passing judgment not merely on Kassler but on the whole human world . . . and of course, the reader.

The great tradition of "literary Satanism"—which sprang from Blake's observation that Milton was "of the Devil's party without knowing it" and was further elaborated in Shelley's *Defence of Poetry*—has produced a long series of careful reappraisals of Satan's role in the scheme of things. Every item in the series has attempted to cast new light of the problem of evil by challenging the assumptions built into our notion of good. Leven's is one of the finest modern additions to the tradition, and one of the most elaborate and intellectually conscientious of all modern *contes philosophiques*. It would be unduly churlish to regret the fact that the author continued to maintain footholds in clinical practice and education alongside his literary work, or that he eventually contrived to move on from the theatre and TV to import a much-needed dose of intelligence and sensitivity into Hollywood, but one can hardly help thinking it a pity that such a very fine and imaginative writer has not found time to write more novels.

—Brian Stableford

LEVIN, Ira

Nationality: American. **Born:** New York, 27 August 1929. **Education:** Drake University, Des Moines, Iowa, 1946-48; New York University; 1948-50, A.B. 1950. **Military Service:** Served in the U.S. Army Signal Corps, 1953-55. **Family:** Married 1) Gabrielle

Aronsohn in 1960 (divorced 1968), three sons; 2) Phyllis Finkel in 1979 (divorced 1982). **Awards:** Mystery Writers of America Edgar Allan Poe award, 1954, and Special Award, 1980. **Agent:** Harold Ober Associates, 425 Madison Avenue, New York, NY 10017, USA.

Horror, Ghost and Gothic Publications

Novels

Rosemary's Baby. New York, Random House, and London, Joseph, 1967.
The Stepford Wives. New York, Random House, and London, Joseph, 1972.
The Boys from Brazil. New York, Random House, and London, Joseph, 1976.
Sliver. New York, Bantam, and London, Joseph, 1991.

Other Publications

Novels

A Kiss Before Dying. New York, Simon and Schuster, 1953; London, Joseph, 1954.
This Perfect Day. New York, Random House, and London, Joseph, 1970.

Plays

No Time for Sergeants, adaptation of the novel by Mac Hyman (produced New York, 1955; London, 1956). New York, Random House, 1956.
Interlock (produced New York, 1958). New York, Dramatists Play Service, 1958.
Critic's Choice (produced New York, 1960; London, 1961). New York, Random House, 1961; London, Evans, 1963.
General Seeger (produced New York, 1962). New York, Dramatists Play Service, 1962.
Drat! That Cat!, music by Milton Schafer (produced New York, 1965).
Dr. Cook's Garden (also director: produced New York, 1967). New York, Dramatists Play Service, 1968.
Veronica's Room (produced New York, 1973; Watford, Hertfordshire, 1982). New York, Random House, 1974; London, Joseph, 1975.
Deathtrap (produced New York and London, 1978). New York, Random House, 1979; London, French, 1980.
Break a Leg (produced New York, 1979). New York, French, 1981.
Cantorial (produced Stamford, Connecticut, 1984; New York, 1989). New York and London, French, 1990.

*

Film Adaptations: *A Kiss Before Dying,* 1956, 1991, from the novel; *Rosemary's Baby,* 1968, from the novel; *The Stepford Wives,* 1975, from the novel; *The Boys from Brazil,* 1978, from the novel; *Deathtrap,* 1982, from the play; *Sliver,* 1993, from the novel.

Critical Study: *Ira Levin* by Douglas Fowler, Mercer Island, Washington, Starmont, 1988.

Theatrical Activities:
Director: **Play**—*Dr. Cook's Garden,* New York, 1967.

*   *   *

There are some novelists who can be thought of as "filmic" in that virtually nothing they write does not make it to the screen. The most obvious example is Stephen King: many movies have been based on his novels and even on his short stories. William Goldman is another, although in his case there is a chicken-and-egg dilemma: he could be more rightly regarded as a screenwriter who also produces excellent novels. Of all such novelists, however, Ira Levin is perhaps the most "filmic," but this tends to go little noticed because his output has been so sparse over the years: only one of his books, *This Perfect Day*—a gloomy view of a future in which everything has been made perfect so human beings have, in essence, lost the experience of *true* pleasure—has not been filmed. *A Kiss Before Dying* has been filmed twice (1956 and 1991); *Rosemary's Baby* has been not only filmed but, for television, sequelled by the poor *Look What's Happened to Rosemary's Baby* (1973); *The Stepford Wives* made its screen debut in 1974 and was followed by *Revenge of the Stepford Wives* (1980) and *The Stepford Children* (1987), the latter two being for television; *The Boys from Brazil* was filmed in 1978 (it comes as something of a surprise that there was no television follow-up called *The Girls from Brazil*); and *Sliver* was filmed in 1993.

A Kiss Before Dying is the paradigmatic psychological thriller. A youthful and winsome psychopath, believing that all his ills are to be blamed on the poverty of his family, determines to marry money. He cold-bloodedly woos and wins the daughter of a wealthy family but, before they can be wed, she begins to cotton on that there is something very wrong with the set-up and indeed that dark secrets lurk in her past. He therefore murders her, and gets away with it: the death is believed to be either accident or suicide. But she had a sister, and in a short while he is insinuating himself into the latter's emotions instead.

The book is immensely effective not just because of Levin's undoubted skill in the use of language but also because of a novelistic craft that, at the very least, borders on artistry. Where others might have turned the overall plot into a whodunnit, he instead lets the reader see what is going on: there is no detective mystery to solve except the one in the reader's mind, the question of whether or not the second sister will be able to save herself. Since Levin is good at characterization and our sympathies are with her, the matter of her dying or not dying becomes knuckle-whitening in the later stages of the book. Levin was certainly not the first to use the psychological chiller in this way, and the style has become popular today (some of Ruth Rendell's/Barbara Vine's work has resonances), but it is hard to find a better model of the genre.

Rosemary's Baby is a different kettle of fish: it is a full-fledged novel of the occult . . . or perhaps it is not, for we are left at its end to wonder if the entirety of its events might not be the result of the constant misperceptions of a woman who is either neurotic or descending into a nervous breakdown. Young Guy and Rosemary Woodhouse move into a New York apartment and are befriended by their elderly neighbours, the Castevets, who live in an adjacent apartment. The Castevets seem somewhat eccentric, talking a deal about magic, but then elderly people often are: the Woodhouses are unconcerned. Rosemary becomes pregnant, but assumes this is through Guy, her husband. Then she recalls a half-vision, half-dream in which she was made by the Castevets, Guy and others to copulate with the Devil. What is her baby going to *be?*

The Stepford Wives, a much lighter novel—barely more than a novella, in fact—is a well handled satire of the attitudes of US males towards their females. In the small New England town of Stepford the members of the enigmatic "Men's Association" have discovered, thanks to the efforts of an ex-Disneyland engineer, how to replace their living wives with android versions who are always perfectly obedient and subservient, both in bed and out of it. New arrival Joanna discovers much of this but, before she can make anything public, is, at the request of her husband, herself destroyed and replaced. The improbability of the plot is obvious, but the book is effective. Although its stereotyping of small-town males and females could be regarded as sexistly offensive, especially since, after the appearance of the movie version, to describe someone as a Stepford Wife was to use a term of exceptionally cruel sexist abuse. The book shares the overt theme with *Rosemary's Baby* of a woman being disgustingly betrayed by her husband; there is, in both novels, an unpleasing sense that the women deserved to be betrayed. This disturbing (apparent) misogyny recurs occasionally in Levin's work, although it is possible to argue in these two cases that his purpose is the opposite of sexist. (The movie of the novel was scripted by William Goldman.)

Again there was a long gap before Levin's next novel, *The Boys from Brazil*. As with *The Stepford Wives*, this horror-techno-fantasy can be read as science fiction, but the "scientific" element of the plot is again ludicrous. Somewhere in the South American jungle the vile Nazi Dr. Joseph Mengele is manufacturing clones of cells from Der Fuehrer's body so that they can be implanted into suitable women. The impregnated women have to be carefully selected: their husbands must be suitably elderly and, so that nurture plays as much a part as nature in the development of the new Hitler, die while the child is still young. This latter proviso necessitates an international hit squad to rush around bumping off the surrogate fathers. This is material born from pulp fiction—a *Nick Carter* novel, perhaps—and yet the tale is so well told that it is only later that one starts to think about its risibilities.

There was a vast delay before the appearance of *Sliver*, which is Levin's weakest novel. This is another techno-fantasy. A young woman moves into a luxury apartment in the tower block that is the Sliver of the title. Little does she know it but the owner of the building is a voyeur who has rigged every apartment with hidden cameras so that he can watch the secret lives (primarily sex lives) of his tenants. When she discovers this she is at first horrified, but then finds herself drawn into the fascination of the observation and into an affair with him that is displayed with an eroticism that is not modest. In due course, however, she deduces that he has already murdered others who discovered his voyeurism.

In *The Encyclopedia of Science Fiction* (1993) John Clute observes that Levin "applies to [science-fiction] themes meticulous style and plotting, along with a certain fascination with the multitude of ways in which women can be violated." Whether any of Levin's work, aside from *This Perfect Day*, is science fiction is a moot point, but Clute is right to refer to the fact that the frequent resort to the violation of women is disconcerting. It is likely that

he is trying to convey an anti-bullying-male message, but sometimes that message is muddled.

—John Grant

LEWIS, D(esmond) Francis

Nationality: British. **Born:** Essex, 18 January 1948. **Education:** Colchester Royal Grammar School, Essex, 1959-66; Lancaster University, 1966-69, B.A. in English. **Family:** Married in 1970; one son and one daughter. **Career:** Principal Pension Trust Secretary, Legal and General Assurance Society Ltd, 1970-92; prolific contributor of short stories to small-press magazines and anthologies. **Address:** 113 Dulwich Rd., Holland-on-Sea, Essex CO15 5LU, England.

HORROR, GHOST AND GOTHIC PUBLICATIONS

Short Stories

The Best of D. F. Lewis. Leesburg, Virginia, TAL Publications, 1993.
The Weirdmonger's Tales. Driffield, Yorkshire, Wyrd Press, 1994.

*   *   *

D. F. Lewis is a leading figure in contemporary "small-press" horror fiction, with a reputation that is expanding into the professional field. Since 1987, he has published nearly a thousand short stories—most of them very short in length. Lewis's fiction offers a highly idiosyncratic, surreal interpretation of the classic themes of supernatural and Gothic fiction: ghosts, insanity, blighted heredity, alienation, deformity, occult knowledge. His characteristic approach is to make the abnormal seem familiar and the familiar seem abnormal. Thus most of his stories are rooted in the everyday: the landscapes, lives and vernacular language of the Thames estuary and thereabouts. But the details don't quite fit in a normal picture; somehow, they add up to a different reality which the use of supernatural imagery helps to codify and resolve. The typical "Lewis twist" relates the supernatural element back to the mundane starting point, making a new sense of the latter.

In their condensed form and surprising reversals of logic, Lewis' stories can resemble those of John Collier—though Lewis is quicker to leave the familiar behind. Collier's "Are You Too Late or Was I Too Early?" has something of Lewis's restless, dislocated energy. In his obsession with monstrosity and corrupt heredity, Lewis sometimes recalls the early Lovecraft—his brilliant story "Blasphemy Fitzworth" was described by the editors of *Dark Dreams* magazine as "a cross between H. P. Lovecraft and Charles Dickens." In contemporary horror fiction, Lewis seems most closely allied to Thomas Ligotti; but whereas Ligotti is primarily concerned with philosophical issues, Lewis's concerns have to do with the body and human emotions. Two major thematic strands run through his fiction: childhood and the family on the one hand; sex, disease and deformity on the other. This dual emphasis allows Lewis to run a gamut of styles, from sensitive ghost stories to feverish quasi-erotic nightmares.

The prolific nature of Lewis' output has, inevitably, provoked the criticism that his work is dilute and repetitive. For a while, it seemed that a D. F. Lewis story was the small-press equivalent of an ISBN. However, it is undeniable that the best of his work is both varied and original. His stories have repeatedly appeared in professional horror anthologies, and in literary magazines. Thomas Ligotti has praised Lewis's "expertly controlled and sardonic vision," while novelist Graham Joyce has commented: "D. F. Lewis . . . is a national treasure. He writes in a genre of one." The problem for the reader, perhaps, is to sift out the best of Lewis from his vast output, in the absence of a full-length collection.

At least the TAL Publications booklet *The Best of D. F. Lewis* offers a sound introduction to the early Lewis. There is some breathtaking work on display here. "Dognahnyi" is a grim speculative portrayal of a society gripped by cancer and disfigurement: "the imminent war between life and death and that insidious state that is not really either." In "Pogrom Panjandrum," an adult is destroyed by childhood memories that have warped into fascistic terror. "Beyond the Park" is a Robert Aickman-esque fable in which a doll's house becomes the catalyst for a family's shared erotic discovery. In "Blasphemy Fitzworth," a pragmatic individual's adaptation to nightmarish changes suggests that nothing is too horrific to become the source of someone's livelihood. "Look Don't Touch" is a moving account of the desolate loneliness of a borderline schizophrenic. Best of all, "Entries" shows an alienated child coming to terms with his parents' unhappy marriage and the threat of a distorted natural world. The last entry in his diary is: "All creatures great and small really DO love each other, but they're probably estranged." Which is a fairly accurate summary of Lewis's worldview.

A second *Best of . . .* booklet, covering Lewis's more recent work, is forthcoming. Meanwhile, the Wyrd Press booklet *The Weirdmonger's Tales* presents ten previously unpublished D. F. Lewis stories. These are somewhat abstract, playing on ideas about narrative and storytelling in a way reminiscent of such Ramsey Campbell stories as "Beyond Words." The closing story, "Prattling Stones," uses a change in the narrative voice to show an author being stripped of *authority*. "Numbskull," a lengthy monologue, draws the reader into the solipsistic world of dolls in a doll's house. "A Long Tail" is a remarkably bitter portrayal of emotional manipulation among teenagers. Some of the other stories are frankly baffling.

From many notable uncollected Lewis stories, a few can be listed here. "Splints" (*Touch Wood* edited by Peter Crowther, 1993) is a beautifully focused account of self-mutilation driven by superstition; it ends with the image of a severed finger touching a wooden floor. "The Walking Mat" (*Sugar Sleep* edited by Chris Kenworthy, 1993) is a love story set in a hotel which is partly submerged below the sea; the image of fish visible through a bedroom window gives a voyeuristic intensity to the symbolism of tidal change and permanence. "Kites and Kisses" (*Peeping Tom* 22, 1996) shows the logic of childhood imagination breaking down into paranoia. "Sponge and China Tea" (*Dagon* 26, 1989) blends the disparate themes of bereavement and sexual fetishism, with a startling resolution. "Clad Bone" (*Darklands 2* edited by Nicholas Royle) is a stark erotic nightmare about a touch that reshapes the skin. "Welsh Pepper" (*Vandeloecht's Fiction Magazine*, Spring 1992) is a beautifully structured story about adolescent trauma and the relationship between past and present. Less seriously, "Watch the Whiskers Sprout" (*Cthulhu's Heirs* edited by Thomas Stratman, 1994) reconstructs "Blasphemy Fitzworth" through the lens of an alternative cosmology where Lovecraft and Dickens are related through a dynasty of cat's-meat merchants. "The Ice Monster" (*Night Dreams* 5, 1996) is an ambitious story told from the viewpoint of a supernatural entity whose nature changes over the years, fluctuating between humanity and ice.

The overall development of D. F. Lewis's work over the last decade has been towards greater length and continuity: from the stinging, angry brevity of the early work towards a more discursive, structured approach which recalls the metaphysical ghost stories of Robert Aickman. Lewis's work is as remarkable for its intensity, poetic flair and bitter passion as for its protean scope and variety. Whether his prolific output has served, in the long term, to spread his reputation or to dilute it remains to be seen. But for now, his status is unassailable—both as a figurehead of horror fiction's *avant-garde* and as a dedicated excavator of its traditions.

—Joel Lane

LEWIS, M(atthew) G(regory)

Nationality: British. **Born:** London, 9 July 1775. **Education:** Dr. Fountaine's school; Westminster School; Christ Church, Oxford University. **Career:** Attaché to British Embassy, the Hague, 1794-96; Member of Parliament, 1796-1802. **Died:** 10 May 1818.

HORROR, GHOST AND GOTHIC PUBLICATIONS

Novels

The Monk: A Romance. London, Bell, 1796; revised as *Ambrosio; or, The Monk*, London, Bell, 1798, and Philadelphia, Cobbett, 1798.

Short Stories

Romantic Tales. London, Longman, 1808; New York, Ward, 1809.
Raymond and Agnes; or, The Bleeding Nun (extract from *The Monk*). N.p., 1820.

Plays

The Castle Spectre. London, Bell, 1798, and Boston, n.p., 1798; novelized as *The Castle Spectre; or, Family Horrors* by Sarah Wilkinson, London, Hughes, 1807.
Adelmorn, the Outlaw. London, Bell, 1801; Philadelphia, Rawle and Byrne, 1802.
The Wood Daemon; or, The Clock has Struck. London, Scales, 1807; Boston, True, 1808; revised as an opera, *One o'Clock! or, The Knight and the Wood Daemon*, London, Lowndes and Hobbs, 1811; New York, Longworth, 1813.
Zoroaster (unpublished, written 1811).

Poetry

Tales of Wonder, with others. London, Bell, 2 vols., 1801; New York, Samuel Campbell, 1801.
Poems. London, Hatchard, 1812.
The Isle of Devils. Kingston, Jamaica, privately printed, 1827.

OTHER PUBLICATIONS

Novels

Village Virtues: A Dramatic Satire. London, Bell, 1796.
The Bravo of Venice, freely translated from *Abllino, der grosse Bandit* by Heinrich Zschokke. London, Hughes, 1804; adapted for the stage by Lewis as *Rugantino; or The Bravo of Venice*, London, Hughes, 1805.

Plays

The Minister: A Tragedy, freely translated from *Kabale und Liebe* by Friedrich von Schiller. London, Bell, 1797; as *The Harper's Daughter; or, Love and Ambition*, London, Bell, 1803; Philadelphia, Carey, 1813.
The Twins; or, Is it He or His Brother (performed London, 1799).
The East Indian. London, Bell, 1800; as *Rivers; or, The East Indian*, Dublin, 1800; adapted as opera, *Rich and Poor* (performed London, 1812).
Alfonso, King of Castile. London, Bell, 1801.
Adelgitha; or, The Fruits of a Single Error. London, Hughes, 1806; New York, Longworth, 1808.
Venoni; or, The Novice of St. Mark's. London, Longman, 1809, and New York, Longworth, 1809.
Timour the Tartar. London, Lowndes and Hobbs, 1811; Boston, Buckingham, 1812.

Poetry

The Love of Gain. London, Bell, 1799.

Other

The Journal of a West Indian Proprietor. London, Murray, 1834; New York, Negro Universities Press, 1969.

Translator, *Rolla; or, The Peruvian Hero* by August von Kotzebue. London, Bell, 1799.
Translator, *Feudal Tyrants; or, The Counts of Carlsheim and Sargans* by Christiane Naubert. London, Hughes, 1806.

*

Critical Studies: *The Life and Correspondence of M. G. Lewis* by Mrs. Cornwall Baron-Wilson (published anonymously), London, Colburn, 1839; *The Gothic Quest* by Montague Summers, London, Fortune Press, 1938; *A Life of Matthew G. Lewis* by Louis F. Pecke, Cambridge, Massachusetts, Harvard University Press, 1961.

*   *   *

M. G. Lewis wrote what became the most notorious of all Gothic novels, *The Monk*. The story concerns Ambrosio, a monk who is regarded by many as pious and exemplary but who is really a lecher. Satan tempts Ambrosio further, through the lure of a young novice, Matilda, who beguiles Ambrosio and through the use of magic leads him further into sin. Before long Ambrosio has become a rapist and a murderer, and at the end the Devil claims him. The novel was an instant success and quickly earned a repu-

tation as being salacious and semi-pornographic. Lewis later admitted to his youthful impropriety and toned the book down for a subsequent edition, as *Ambrosio, or The Monk*. The novel so earned Lewis's reputation that he became known as "Monk" Lewis. Although it was inspired by Lewis's delight in Walpole's *Castle of Otranto* and Radcliffe's *Mysteries of Udolpho* it is not directly imitative of these, which is perhaps what makes *The Monk* more alive and refreshing than most traditional Gothic novels. In fact Lewis had originally attempted to write a novel in direct imitation of these two books but could not complete it. He was perhaps better encouraged by his visit to Weimar in 1792 to learn German, where he met many of the German *literati*, including Goethe, and was inspired by their direct approach to fiction. Lewis's *The Monk* probably owes much to *Faust*, which was still shaping in Goethe's thoughts during this period.

There is a secondary story embedded in *The Monk* which sometimes has been published separately as *Raymond and Agnes; or, The Bleeding Nun*. Raymond is a young nobleman who is in love with Agnes, who has been sent to a convent. With the permission of the Pope, Raymond leads an army into the convent and rescues Agnes from the vicious nuns. Featured in this story is the ghostly episode of "The Bleeding Nun," based on German folklore, where Agnes disguises herself as the ghostly Bleeding Nun but Raymond encounters the real ghost.

The novel does have its flaws. It was written in youthful exuberance and Lewis does not tie together all of the loose threads, leaving some episodes incomplete or of rather dubious outcome. But its pace and vibrancy more than compensate for this, and the novel can still be enjoyed today when many of its companion-pieces are forgotten. It was the inspiration of many other novels, the best known being Charles Maturin's *Melmoth the Wanderer*. Others include *The New Monk* (1798) by the unidentified "R.S.", *Zofloya; or, The Moor* (1806) by Charlotte Dacre, *The Demon of Sicily* (1807) by Edward Montague, and that ultimate in gothic imitation, *The Monk of Udolpho* (1807) by Horsley Curties. It also echoed down the years to inspire the penny dreadfuls of the next generation with such works as *The Black Monk* by J. M. Rymer.

Lewis was himself inspired by its success and returned to an earlier unfinished gothic novel and recast it as a play, *The Castle Spectre*, first performed at Drury Lane in December 1797. The story-line is pure gothic. Osmond has usurped Castle Conway from his brother, Reginald, whom he believes to have been murdered but is in fact imprisoned secretly elsewhere in the castle under the guardianship of Kenric, the castellan. Kenric has also saved Reginald's daughter, Angela, but had been unable to save Reginald's wife who was murdered and becomes the spectre of the castle. Osmond seeks to seduce Angela but she is saved at the last moment by her suitor, Earl Percy, and by the intervention of her mother's ghost who puts in a *deus-* (or *spiritus-*) *ex-machina* appearance.

Although *The Monk* remained ever-popular, Lewis was probably more renowned in his day as a playwright, and although as archetypal melodramas his plays lack any finesse, they delighted in gothic atmosphere and helped progress special effects on the stage into a new era. Lewis's plays were the Georgian equivalents of the B-movie horror films of the early 1960s. He continued to write his own plays or adapt stories by others. Whilst all of these may be classified as "gothic" in the broadest definition, most of them were historical tragedies and only a few were genuine horror-gothic, with or without supernatural intervention. The best of these was *Adelmorn, the Outlaw*, written in 1795 but not performed until May 1801, again at Drury Lane. Adelmorn has been falsely accused of the murder of Count Roderic and is condemned to death. He escapes but is later captured and it is only as he steps up to the gallows that the ghost of Roderic intercedes and forces the real murderer to confess. According to Montague Summers the original staging of the play included three appearances of the ghost but this was seen as excessive and in later performances a solitary appearance was saved for the climax. Lewis's most ambitious and atmospheric play was *The Wood Daemon*, first performed in April 1807. Hardyknute, Count of Holstein, has been granted eternal youth and power over women by the wood demon, but in return he has to sacrifice a human victim once each year. When Hardyknute fails to provide his victim he is carried off by demons to his fate in the Necromantic Cavern. As a story, the play is basic but it was written for the most spectacular and dramatic stage effects which made it extremely popular.

Lewis's interest in gothic fiction and drama led him to work with Walter Scott in collecting together examples of the genre in poetry. The planned volume, *Tales of Terror*, containing narrative verse, never emerged and Scott later issued his own *An Apology for Tales of Terror* in 1799. However, by 1801 Lewis had produced *Tales of Wonder*. This is a two-volume anthology of which the second volume was a miscellany of reprints. The first volume, however, contained original poems by Lewis, Scott and others, including Lewis's "Alonzo the Brave" and "The Erl-King's Daughter," and was a significant influence on the emerging Romantic movement. Its many imitations, including a volume called *Tales of Terror* which is often erroneously attributed to Lewis but which was really a spoof, testify to its impact.

Lewis also produced a volume of shorter works, *Romantic Tales*, which was a mixture of ballads, tales and adaptations from the continent. "Mistrust; or, Blanche and Osbright" is the most gothic of these. Lewis freely adapted it from the drama *Die Familie Schroffenstein* (1803) by Heinrich von Kleist, which was itself a reworking of the Romeo and Juliet theme. In Lewis's version the tragedy is heightened in the emphasis of hatred and the fatal consequences between the two rival families. Lewis also produced two oriental tales for the book. "The Four Facardins" is a translation and completion of Anthony Hamilton's unfinished fairy tale, whilst "Amorassan; or, the Spirit of the Frozen Ocean" is freely adapted from Friedrich Klinger's *Der Faust der Morgenländer*. Both of these stories show Lewis's adaptability, as Hamilton's tale is given a light-hearted ebullience, whilst "Amorassan" captures something of the complex morality of *The Arabian Nights*. "The Anaconda," a grotesque East-Indian terror tale, is also apparently based on a German source but this has not been traced and may be almost wholly original with Lewis.

Although the content of Lewis's works may suggest a profligate and irreverent individual, he was in fact a generous and kind-hearted man who might be criticized for being too eager a social-climber, but who was also a supporter of those less fortunate than he. He was a vehement opposer of asylums and other institutions for the insane as they existed in his day, and one of his most effective stage monologues, "The Captive," which depicted the fate of a prisoner on the edge of madness in a dungeon, caused hysteria and fainting among part of the audience at its only delivery at Covent Garden in March 1803. Lewis was also an ardent supporter of the anti-slavery movement, and was generous to his own slaves on his estates in the West Indies, promising them freedom upon his death. His works were therefore not the product of a

warped mind, as some of his contemporaries alleged, but the writings of an intelligent and sympathetic man with an active imagination and a keen interest in the new and emerging field of the gothic romance. He, more than any other of his day, popularized the genre.

Lewis's death is perhaps symbolic of his life and work. He died at sea of yellow fever. Anxious to avoid contagion, the captain rapidly arranged for Lewis's burial at sea. Unfortunately the weights intended to sink the coffin broke loose, the wind lifted the shroud, and the coffin floated away into the distant misty waters.

—Mike Ashley

LIGOTTI, Thomas

Nationality: American. **Born:** Detroit, Michigan, 1953. **Career:** Contributor to small-press magazines, such as *Nyctalops, Fantasy Tales, Eldritch Tales* and *Dark Horizons*, from 1981. **Awards:** Horror Writers of America Bram Stoker award for novella, and for collection, both 1997; British Fantasy award for collection, 1997. **Address:** c/o Carroll and Graf Publishers, Inc., 260 Fifth Ave., New York, NY 10001, USA.

HORROR, GHOST AND GOTHIC PUBLICATIONS

Short Stories

Songs of a Dead Dreamer. Albuquerque, New Mexico, Silver Scarab Press, 1986; expanded edition, London, Robinson, 1989; New York, Carroll and Graf, 1990.
Grimscribe: His Lives and Works. New York, Carroll and Graf, and London, Robinson, 1991.
Noctuary. London, Robinson, and New York, Carroll and Graf, 1994.
The Agonizing Resurrection of Victor Frankenstein & Other Gothic Tales. Eugene, Oregon, Silver Salamander Press, 1994.
The Nightmare Factory. London, Raven, and New York, Carroll and Graf, 1996.

*

Critical Studies: *Dagon* 22-23, September-December 1988; small-press magazine, London; *Contemporary Literary Criticism*, Detroit, Gale, 1987; *Short Story Criticism*, Detroit, Gale, 1994; *Contemporary Authors*, Vol. 123, Detroit, Gale, 1988; *Contemporary Authors*, New Revision Series, Vol. 49, Detroit, Gale, 1995.

*   *   *

The school of American horror fiction which crystallized out around the central figure of H. P. Lovecraft—as much by virtue of his indefatigable letter-writing as his insistent theorizing—was never fully professionalized; even its long-time association with the pulp magazine *Weird Tales* was weakened by the uncertainty and unsteadiness of the various editors' sympathies. August Derleth's small press Arkham House provided a more secure anchorage through the 1950s and 1960s, but after Derleth died the torch was taken up by even smaller presses whose products were conspicuously amateurish. Such enterprises still remain, however, the only available practice-ground for writers whose interest in the horrific and the Gothic is rooted in the calculatedly artificial and conscientiously ornate kind of prose style which Theophile Gautier—referring to works produced by Charles Baudelaire under the influence of Edgar Allan Poe—called "decadent." Lovecraft's friend and associate Clark Ashton Smith was by far the finest American writer in this exotic vein while he was active in the 1930s, and was unrivalled thereafter until the emergence in the 1980s of Thomas Ligotti.

Ligotti's first story, "The Chymist," appeared in *Nyctalops* in 1981. After Harry O. Morris's Silver Scarab Press had reprinted the cream of his production in a 300-copy edition of *Songs of a Dead Dreamer* much of the remainder was assembled in Robert M. Price's *Crypt of Cthulhu* 68 (Hallowmass 1989). By then, Carl Ford's *Dagon* 22-23 (September-December 1988) had already offered a volume of critical essays on Ligotti's work, including an interview, a bibliography and a handful of new works. The bibliography revealed that the first item for which Ligotti was paid at a commercial rate was probably his 22nd, "Masquerade for a Dead Sword," which appeared in Jessica Amanda Salmonson's anthology *Heroic Visions II* (1986). Ligotti's was for many years a pure labour of love which was not ashamed to flourish in near darkness—and if there is any one theme binding his work together, it is that: the notion that on the edge of illimitable darkness, endeavour proceeds, exhibiting in its creativity a particular kind of heroism, a peculiar kind of beauty and a problematic kind of love.

The expanded trade edition of *Songs of a Dead Dreamer* is still the definitive Ligotti collection. It establishes his Lovecraftian world-view, which takes as given that everyday life is only sustainable by those who refuse to cultivate an awareness of the awesome magnitude and utter unfriendliness of the universe in which we live. It also establishes his unusually catholic approach to the exploration of this world-view. A few of his characters, including the dead Dr. Locrian in "Dr. Locrian's Asylum" and the protagonists of "The Journal of J. P. Drapeau" and "Vastarien," are scholars in the classic Lovecraftian mode, who unwisely pursue their researches to the only possible conclusion. Ligotti prefers, however, to use protagonists unwillingly drawn across a borderland whose threat they appreciate even though they cannot measure it. The psychiatrist in "The Frolic," the author in "Alice's Last Adventure" and the half-human artist in "The Lost Art of Twilight" all belong to this category. The strangest of the author's products are, however, those which deal with casts of characters who have already crossed those borderlands and have made what efforts they can to adapt themselves to a world of terrible strangeness and intrinsic hostility. It is in these stories that Ligotti penetrates to the heart of the Decadent sensibility—and where Clark Ashton Smith once discovered an incredibly gorgeous exoticism Ligotti discovers a marvellously disturbing surreality. "Masquerade of a Dead Sword," "Dr. Voke and Mr. Veech" and "The Sect of the Idiot" displace the reader into realms whose eeriness is entirely new.

Grimscribe contains a few pre-1989 items which failed to make it into the trade edition of *Songs of a Dead Dreamer* but mostly consists of newer works. It opens with the excellent novella "The Last Feast of Harlequin," in which an anthropologist pursuing his research into "clown figures" visits the small town of Mirocaw to witness its annual Fool's Feast and finds it odder than he could ever have imagined. "The Dreaming in Nortown" and "The Mystics of Muelenberg" are similar in kind, the three stories taken together developing a nexus of bizarre urban locations whose inhabitants are drawn *en masse* into improbable modes of existence—a nexus further extended by the longest and most impressive story in *Noctuary*, "The Tsalal." The calmest and most detailed exposition of the sensibility underlying these stories is to be found in "In the Shadow of Another World," while the seductive power extending from beyond the borderlands is further surrealized in "The Night School" and "The Glamour." This mission is further extended in the first two parts of *Noctuary*, in such tales as "The Medusa" and "Mrs. Rinaldi's Angel."

The third part of *Noctuary* consists of prose poems which are, as might be expected given the general tenor of Ligotti's work, darker in tone and more surreal than those of Baudelaire or Clark Ashton Smith. The sarcastic wit typical of many of Baudelaire's expositions of the Spleen de Paris is, however, echoed in the glosses on classic literary works collected in *The Agonizing Resurrection of Victor Frankenstein & Other Gothic Tales*, a collection opened by "One Thousand Painful Variations Performed Upon Diverse Creatures Undergoing the Treatment of Dr. Moreau, Humanist" (1986), on which foundation the inspiration of the whole collection might have been based. All the expectable characters are gathered in its pages—Dr. Jekyll, Dracula, the Phantom of the Opera, etc—and there are special sections devoted to the imaginative offspring of Poe and Lovecraft. Six of Ligotti's post-*Noctuary* short stories were added to an omnibus edition of items from *Songs of a Dead Dreamer* and *Grimscribe* released as *The Nightmare Factory*.

Although Ligotti has now broken out of the amateur realm of small-press publications to receive his due acclaim as one of the most impressive stylists working within the fields of imaginative literature he remains a stubbornly uncommercial writer. The kinds of work that he does cannot be extended to novel length; were he to begin writing novels he would have to change his whole approach to writing. Ligotti's work to date is set against every trend of commercial publication, and must be reckoned all the more precious because of it. His is a unique voice, which speaks with a profound elegance—and a precious seriousness—of matters which few other literary voices have ever touched. An interest in decadent style is, virtually by definition, old-fashioned, but Ligotti is old-fashioned in the very best sense of the term and there is nothing dated about his work, which is unmistakably contemporary. He is, in fact, the only writer who has succeeded in bringing the ambitions of the Lovecraft school up to date.

—Brian Stableford

LINDSEY, David L(ance)

Nationality: American. **Born:** Kingsville, Texas, 6 November 1944. **Education:** North Texas State University, Denton, B.A. 1969. **Family:** Married Joyce Grace in 1965; one son and one daughter. **Career:** Book editor for various regional publishers, 1970-80; founder, Heidelberg Publishers, 1972-76. **Address:** c/o Doubleday, 1540 Broadway, New York, New York 10103, USA. Lives in Austin, Texas.

HORROR, GHOST AND GOTHIC PUBLICATIONS

Novels (series: Stuart Haydon)

A Cold Mind (Haydon). New York, Harper and Row, 1983; London, Arlington, 1984.

Heat from Another Sun (Haydon). New York, Harper and Row, 1984; London, Arlington, 1985.

Spiral (Haydon). New York, Atheneum, 1986; London, Arlington, 1987.

In the Lake of the Moon (Haydon). New York, Atheneum, 1988; London, Corgi, 1989.

Mercy. New York, Doubleday, 1990; London, Futura, 1991.

Body of Truth (Haydon). New York, Doubleday, and London, Little Brown, 1992.

An Absence of Light. New York, Doubleday, and London, Little Brown, 1994.

Requiem for a Glass Heart. New York, Doubleday, and London, Little Brown, 1996.

OTHER PUBLICATIONS

Novel

Black Gold, Red Death. New York, Gold Medal, 1983; London, Warner, 1994.

* * *

Given that sub-genres are by definition attempts to isolate and even ghettoize a certain theme of writing previously prevalent in the genre from which they spring, it should be easy to define the term "psychological thriller." But it is not. The psychological thriller—the ground into which David Lindsey's novels fall—is in fact something of a misnomer: not so much the child of the thriller as the mutant spawned of thriller and horror. But, to confuse matters further, not the sort of mutant born of a coupling between thriller and supernatural horror—a hybrid exemplified, perhaps, by William Hjortsberg's *Falling Angel* or Stephen Gallagher's *Valley of Lights*—but the offspring of real-life horror, or, if it is not too coy a term, *everyday* horror. Often in the psychological thriller, a police officer examines the motivation and clues left by a particularly cunning serial killer. The horror part—if it can be boiled down this far—is the killer's half; the thriller part, as the detective pieces together the puzzle, is the police-procedural half.

Which introduces David L. Lindsey. Thomas Harris brought to the attention of the world the intelligent psychopath, as personified by Dr. Hannibal Lecter in *The Silence of the Lambs* and (fleetingly) *Red Dragon.* David Lindsey's psychopath in *Mercy* is a different kind altogether. "Mercy" is the escape-word used by some of this novel's characters while playing kinky sado-masochistic sex-games; and *Mercy* is a novel that deals with the themes of lesbianism, sado-masochism and, of course, cold, cruel murder. Two wealthy women have been killed during S&M congress—one a spunky career woman, the other a seemingly happy housewife whose husband is blissfully ignorant of his spouse's alternative proclivities. The victims lived near each other, had been in the same social background, in their 30s, and blonde. The murders are strongly sexually related. Sexual organs have been mutilated or removed, as have—bafflingly at first—the victims' eyelids; there are numerous bite marks on both bodies. Enter Detective Carmen Palmer, who has a penchant for solving sex-crimes: "Nor would she forget the eerie intuition she had when she entered the presence of these victims for the first time, as if the mind that produced the horror had lingered behind with the corpse to await its final pleasure: observing the reasonable mind's revulsion at its

crime." Detective Palmer soon uncovers an underworld of successful, good-looking lesbian and bisexual women, the discovery of which goes against her own preconceived ideas.

In an updating of the Dracula myth, Palmer going after the blood-sucking sex-fiend is akin to Van Helsing's pursuit of the Prince of Darkness. Indeed, the psychological battle of wills between the detective and the violent murderer is like the old supernatural Good versus Evil. Furthermore, the shadows of SS Gestapo techniques hang disturbingly over portions of the book. And there is another suitable comparison: that of Robert Louis Stevenson's *Dr. Jekyll and Mr. Hyde* (1886), with its characters obliged to accept painful truths about the doctor. This is also true of the patients of Dr. Broussard in *Mercy*—Broussard with his sex fixation and his finally-revealed dark secret (there is also the blackly humorous touch of his hardly believing a word his patients tell him). Sander Grant, an FBI criminal-personality profiler, joins the investigation and conducts a psychological profile of the killer which reveals the sex-criminal to be as much a victim as the women whose eyelids and nipples have been removed. Grant and Palmer are at first wary of each other, then learn to complement each other's skills; and they end up learning as much about each other as they do about the killer they are trying to catch.

Accompanying Palmer, the reader takes glimpses into a perverted yet cautious mind. No blood is left at a scene of crime; a corpse is cleaned, laid on her back, and the temperature is lowered for the purpose of preservation. Like art spectators, Carmen Palmer and the team arrive at the gallery of atrocities to judge, to score points, to interpret the artist at work. Palmer confronts the full horror not of sexual choices that might be contrary to her own (which is fair enough), but of someone trying to hide these truths—which are nobody else's business—and then being harmed. Palmer feels the disgust and horror not of choice, but of victim gullibility.

Clearly *Mercy* is a novel about sex and modern sexual attitudes. Sex crimes are implied to be worse than ordinary murders, whereas sado-masochistic sex crimes are one subset further down even than that. From the psychiatrist doctor who observes his patients' legs during therapy and is having an affair with one of them, to Cushing, the bullying colleague of Palmer's who drinks from a *Playboy* mug, to the fashion magazines on the coffee table of the first victim's close friend, not showing pornography but plenty of nudity, *Mercy* makes the reader a voyeur at a roadside accident or a peepshow; it is horrific in the sense that we do not want to turn away and is horror in that it teaches us ugly things about our reading tastes and voyeuristic expectations.

An Absence of Light is up-to-date in a different way, relying as it does on the use of computers, of drug cartels, of regimental power, the selling of investigation information, stolen guns and a smattering of under-aged sex. Good psychological thrillers in general also examine the motives and mental profiles of the investigators, while under the guise of doing so for the criminals. In *An Absence of Light*, Marcus Graver's investigations reveal as much about himself as they do about the man who has unexpectedly and inexplicably committed suicide. At one point Graver knows that Burtell, a corrupted colleague, is lying to him; not so much furious, Graver is more impressed by the subterfuge that allows Burtell to have a sub-text to the lie—the assumption that not everything is done by the book, and that Graver knows it. Also, Burtell misses his last opportunity to get out of the lie after Graver gives him the chance to do so. Graver is lying to Burtell by pretending to believe the lie that Burtell is giving him. At the same time Burtell is lying to cover up something even more sinister. An absence of light indeed: and this is in Graver's own office, with his own staff. Furthermore, Lara, Graver's secretary, understands Graver better than he understands himself. It is a shame that the *Oxford English Dictionary*'s definition of horror as a "ruffling of a surface" is now obsolete, because it is an apt definition here.

Apart from the short epilogue, the novel's action takes place over five days—and *An Absence of Light* is well over 600 pages long. This alone should give a fair indication of the breadth and richness of detail that is included in the story. This is a police investigation with a loud ring of truth; details are not omitted, not even for the sake of brisker reading. Every lead is explored to the fullest; every interrogation and disappearance examined from every angle. Which could also be said for every goodnight kiss and breakfast, and by this no flippancy is intended. *An Absence of Light* is a stab at the all-encompassing police-procedure novel, and we see Graver's life whole: how he works, what he eats, and most importantly, how he thinks: "His career had been devoted to shedding light on a subject of mystery. . . . He had had the right objective all those years, but had employed the wrong technique in trying to achieve it . . . he was arriving too late in the sequence of events. Perhaps he should have been trying to understand, instead, the character of darkness itself, and what it was that happened when men's desires were shaped and formed in an absence of light."

David Lindsey's strongest work has been spoken of above, but his strongest theme is one which runs through his *oeuvre*. *In the Lake of the Moon*, for example, has homicide detective Stuart Haydon (reappearing after earlier novels) receiving six mysterious photographs: two of his late father, three of beautiful woman, all five of them taken 50 years ago. The sixth is of Haydon himself, taken a few days earlier, with a felt-tip pen addition to show the trajectory of a bullet into his right eye and the exit wound as it leaves his skull. Haydon goes to Mexico City, and enters an unexpected and dangerous stratum of his father's past. In *Body of Truth* a wealthy daughter of a Houston businessman goes missing in Guatemala, and six weeks later Stuart Haydon receives a phone call from Guatemala City to say that she is still alive but is in danger. True, Haydon is a common factor in these novels, as is the exotic location; the most notable fact about Lindsey's work as a whole, however, is that nobody can be trusted and nothing is ever as it seems. And it is never over. Lindsey's novels are studies in disillusionment; structures of solid rock which nobody can see at first are sinking into the unsubstantial dirt on which they were built. Lindsey shows a world tainted by greed and cynical motives, be they political or sexual. He is an extremely powerful writer; a commentator whose voice is formal and guide-like, but which is prone on occasion to unexpected squeals of paranoia.

—David Mathew

LITTLE, Bentley

Pseudonym: Phillip Emmons. **Nationality:** American. **Born:** Arizona, 1960. **Education:** California State University, Fullerton, BA in communications, MA in English. **Career:** From the age of 16 worked through his summers as a reporter for a weekly small-town newspaper; news editor for his university newspaper; turned to fiction writing after several years of journalism; now a full-time writer. **Awards:** Horror Writers of America Bram Stoker award for best first novel, 1991. Lives in Fullerton, California.

HORROR, GHOST AND GOTHIC PUBLICATIONS

Novels

The Revelation. New York, St. Martin's Press, 1989; London, Headline, 1993.
The Mailman. New York, Onyx, 1991; London, Headline, 1994.
Death Instinct (as Phillip Emmons). New York, Signet, 1992; as *Evil Deeds* (as Bentley Little), London, Headline, 1994.
The Summoning. New York, Zebra, and London, Headline, 1993.
The Night School. London, Headline, 1994; as *University*, New York, Signet, 1995.
Dark Dominion. London, Headline, 1995; as *Dominion*, New York, Signet, 1996.
The Store. London, Headline, 1996.
Houses. London, Headline, 1997.

*   *   *

The title essay in Martin Amis's collection of non-fiction pieces, *The Moronic Inferno* (1986), contains the following: "British critics tend to regard the American predilection for Big Novels as a vulgar neurosis—like the American predilection for big cars or big hamburgers. Oh God, we think: here comes another sweating, free-dreaming maniac with another thousand-pager; here comes another Big Mac." British critics of horror fiction are probably not so jaded; but the fact remains that in this genre too Americans do tend to write long novels. Why should this be? Amis narrows it down to this: "American novels are big all right, but partly because America is big too." And so, by extrapolation, are its horrors. Not simply the buzzwords (or buzzplaces) that most people know: the take-your-chance streets of the Bronx, or of East St. Louis. Here we speak of the hidden, of subterrenes; which is something that American authors seem particularly adept at describing. In American non-city life (it seems) there is a lot of space in which awful truths can be hidden; in American horror novels the same principle applies. The reader inhabits a fictional atmosphere of taut strings and fraying consciousnesses. This, in every sense, is the Restless Calm: and this is the area that Bentley Little chronicles.

Gary Brandner, author of *The Howling*, described Little's first novel, *The Revelation*, as a depiction of "a corner of hell." The religious connotations are apt, as might be gathered from the book's title. *The Revelation* reveals Little's fascination and love affair with the American state of Arizona. From an outsider's point of view, this is already good news; Arizona—the Grand Canyon—the desert—sun—small communities—oblivion: such might be a typical thought train on hearing mention of the grand old empty state. Most importantly of all, Arizona hosts many remote communities, untouched by the influences of the most up-to-date technology and unreachable quickly in times of emergency. A perfect end-of-the-world scene waiting to happen: Hell on Earth.

In Randall, Arizona, an old woman becomes pregnant—inexplicably. Having taken into our subconsciousness the book's title (not to mention the back-flap photo, which is a bad thing to do, but we all do it: the picture showing an oddly-angled Bentley Little in smart off-duty-reverend clothes and bolo tie, posing menacingly in front of a Little House on the Prairie-style church), the first thing we think of is: Virgin Birth. Already the possibilities are endless. A Grand Guignol epic in the style of Nick Cave's *And the Ass Saw the Angel* (1989), maybe? But there is considerably more to come. The town's beloved minister disappears in mysterious circumstances, his "Dear John" letters nothing more than filthy language scrawled in blood in the church and in his home. Farmers' goats die, swiftly followed by their human owners. The town begins to seem like a rotting carcass, already being circled by vultures.

Then a preacher with unusual eyes arrives; he has come to find three men who will help him fight in the upcoming battle. As with Little's later novel, *The Mailman*, *The Revelation* looks at the effects of unexpected knowledge: that is, the effects of someone knowing something that you had thought had not been for public consumption. For example, "You look an awful lot like your great-grandfather," the eerie Brother Elias tells one character, much to the latter's chagrin. "How do you know my great-grandfather's name? And how do you know he was a sheriff?" Jim asks. "He was with me last time," is the answer. Obviously, forces as old as the sun have converged on Randall, Arizona: "'There will be fires,' Brother Elias continued, his voice chanting in a monotonic cadence. 'And the lightning will turn red, signifying the coming of the adversary.' There will be flies. There will be earthquakes . . . .'"

The Mailman is possibly Bentley Little's *tour de force* to date. Again, in a small community, a form of hell breaks out—but it is a very strange version indeed. Showing the flip-side of *The Revelation*'s overtly supernatural and *faux*-religious horrors, *The Mailman* is squarely built on a foundation of paranoia. What would happen if the mailman—a figure you trust to bring you the morning's missives—was corrupt? Not simply to the extent of tearing open envelopes in order to cash cheques intended for birthday money, or to steal erotic magazines in their brown paper covers, but actually corrupt? What if you couldn't trust him at all? What if he stopped delivering your bills so that your supplies and services—your electricity, your gas—were cut off? What if he delivered your well-meant love letter to a different recipient entirely?

These postal indiscretions are only the beginning of John Smith's satanic reign over the town. Inch by inch he manages to make the townspeople drift from a happy-go-lucky *joie de vivre*, to a sense of mutual suspicion, to outright hatred. After all, a town is a body, a living vessel, kept strong by the information that flows around its frame like blood through veins and arteries. Cut an artery and there is a spurt. But the mailman also manages to clog the town's arteries; and almost brings the town to its knees in that way alone.

But why is he doing it? Bentley Little makes us doubt the services that we believe we can trust. The occasional postcard from abroad going astray can be attributed to human error, but when a town is easing itself into a state of universal misery and "Directly or indirectly, everything [is] connected to the mail," there are problems no simple employee disciplinary tribunal is going to sort out. Tritia, the heroine of the novel, soon starts to bury her mail rather than read what the mailman (by now) has concocted; thereby she denies the postman the consummation of his invasive act. Her friend, Irene, has received her long-dead husband's toe through the mail in a box; it is the first body part of many.

"What was this malaise that had so gripped the community?" Bentley Little asks. "What forced them to stay here, against common sense, against what must surely be natural instinct?" Good questions. Pride, perhaps? It is hard to say. What is clear, however, is that Little handles insecurity very well. A friend of Tritia's husband, called Hobie, is reasonably worried that his brother will come to pay a visit, even though he was killed in Vietnam. Later, the same Hobie is set up as being a brutal sex-offender and killer

of a young girl. A confrontation with the mailman is surely in order. But after John Smith has been addressed in the mail sorting depot, the accusers "walked out of the hot dark building and into the fresh outside air. Behind them, from somewhere deep within the post office, they heard the mailman laugh." The mailman, in his own private hell.

Later in the novel, it becomes clear that our theories about the effectiveness of Arizona as an horrific locale (even if we have never seen the movie *Tremors*) are on the mark. The small town is an incubator for the forces of evil. The mailman has stopped paying the gas station's bills, and no gas will be delivered until they settle up their debts. This of course means that nobody can get very far from the scene of the crimes, even with a full tank. The scene is set for a form of fiery apocalypse.

That Bentley Little has been praised liberally by writers as non-diverse as Richard Laymon, Stephen King and Gary Brandner (by generic horror writers, in other words) gives the reader two matters to think about. The first is that there should be no doubt as to what is in store (or even in Store) with a Bentley Little novel: his writing is one-hundred per cent horror, and he is clearly at ease with this. And the second is that he offers additions to the small-town-under-threat canon that the aforementioned trio have contributed to in the past. Bentley Little is well on his way to achieving—perhaps surpassing—their critical stature.

—David Mathew

LONG, Frank Belknap

Pseudonym: Lyda Belknap Long. **Nationality:** American. **Born:** New York City, 27 April 1903. **Education:** New York public schools; New York University School of Journalism, 1920-21. **Family:** Married Lyda Arco in 1960. **Career:** Writer for *Captain Marvel, Green Lantern, Congo Bill,* and *Planet Comics* in the 1940s; uncredited associate editor, *The Saint Mystery Magazine* and *Fantastic Universe* in the 1950s; associate editor, *Satellite Science Fiction,* 1959, *Short Stories,* 1959-60, and *Mike Shayne Mystery Magazine* until 1966. **Awards:** First Fandom Hall of Fame award, 1977; 4th World Fantasy Convention Life Achievement award, 1978; Bram Stoker Life Achievement award, 1988. **Died:** 9 January 1994.

HORROR, GHOST AND GOTHIC PUBLICATIONS

Novels

The Horror Expert. New York, Belmont, 1961.
The Horror from the Hills. Sauk City, Wisconsin, Arkham House, 1963.
So Dark a Heritage. New York, Lancer, 1966.
The Night of the Wolf. New York, Popular Library, 1972.
Rehearsal Night. Boston, Cat's God, 1981.

Novels as Lyda Belknap Long

To the Dark Tower. New York, Lancer, 1969.
Fire of the Witches. New York, Popular Library, 1971.
The Shape of Fear. New York, Beagle, 1971.

The Witch Tree. New York, Lancer, 1971.
House of the Deadly Nightshade. New York, Beagle, 1972.
Legacy of Evil. New York, Beagle, 1973.
Crucible of Evil. New York, Avon, 1974.
The Lemoyne Heritage. New York, Zebra, 1977.

Short Stories

The Hounds of Tindalos. Sauk City, Wisconsin, Arkham House, 1946;
abridged edition, London, Museum Press, 1950; in 2 vols. as *The Hounds of Tindalos* and *The Dark Beasts and Eight Other Stories from The Hounds of Tindalos,* New York, Belmont, 1963-64; as *The Black Druid, and Other Stories,* London, Panther, 1975.
The Challenge from Beyond, with others. N.p., William H. Evans, 1954; as *The Illustrated Challenge from Beyond,* West Warwick, Rhode Island, Necronomicon Press, 1978.
The Rim of the Unknown. Sauk City, Wisconsin, Arkham House, 1972.
The Early Long. Garden City, New York, Doubleday, 1975; London, Hale, 1977.
When Chaugnar Wakes. Warren, Ohio, Fantome Press, 1978.
Night Fear, edited by Roy Torgeson. New York, Zebra, 1979.

Other Publications

Novels

Space Station No. 1. New York, Ace, 1957.
Woman from Another Planet. New York, Chariot, 1960.
The Mating Center. New York, Chariot, 1961.
Mars Is My Destination: A Science-Fiction Adventure. New York, Pyramid, 1962.
It Was the Day of the Robot. New York, Belmont, 1963; London, Dobson, 1964.
Three Steps Spaceward. New York, Avalon, 1963.
The Martian Visitors. New York, Avalon, 1964.
Mission to a Star. New York, Avalon, 1964.
This Strange Tomorrow. New York, Belmont, and London, Digit, 1966.
Lest Earth Be Conquered. New York, Belmont, 1966; as *The Androids,* New York, Tower, 1969.
Journey into Darkness. New York, Belmont, 1967.
. . . and Others Shall Be Born. New York, Belmont, 1968.
The Three Faces of Time. New York, Tower, 1969.
Monster from Out of Time. New York, Popular Library, 1970; London, Hale, 1971.
Survival World. New York, Lancer, 1971.

Short Stories

John Carstairs, Space Detective. New York, Fell, 1949; London, Cherry Tree, 1951.

Play

Television Play: *A Guest in the House,* 1950.

Poetry

A Man from Genoa and Other Poems. Athol, Massachusetts, Cook, 1926.

The Goblin Tower. Cassia, Florida, Dragon-Fly Press, 1935.
On Reading Arthur Machen: A Sonnet. Pengrove, California Dog and Duck Press, 1949.
In Mayan Splendor. Sauk City, Wisconsin, Arkham House, 1977.

Other

Howard Phillips Lovecraft: Dreamer on the Nightside. Sauk City, Wisconsin, Arkham House, 1975.
Autobiographical Memoir. West Warwick, Rhode Island, Necronomicon Press, 1985.

*

Manuscript Collection: Lovecraft Collection, Brown University, Providence, Rhode Island.

*   *   *

Of all the pulp weird-fiction writers who laboured in H. P. Lovecraft's shadow, Frank Belknap Long was the one least able to break free of it. A protegé and eventual biographer of Lovecraft, Long was regarded for much of his literary career as a footnote to Lovecraft and the weird-fiction tradition he established, even though Long's Lovecraftian tales comprise only a small percentage of his total weird-fiction output and his weird fiction is dwarfed by the bulk of his mystery and science fiction.

Long was still a teenager when he came to Lovecraft's attention through his writings for the amateur press, among them "The Eye Above of the Mantel" and "In the Tomb of Semenses," two accomplished Poe-esque fantasies whose imagery also revealed his burgeoning talents as a poet. Lovecraft introduced Long's work to Farnsworth Wright, the newly-appointed editor of *Weird Tales,* who praised Long effusively in the November 1924 issue and compared his writing to that of Kipling and Daudet. "The Desert Lich," which appeared in that issue, was actually a slight adventure tale set in caverns beneath the sands of the Far East, but it established Long as an artful storyteller who could bring exotic locales and their people to life. Long would explore other colourful settings in his early *Weird Tales* fiction, including Africa in "The Red Fetish," revolutionary Haiti in "You Can't Kill a Ghost," Arabia in "The Were-Snake," and medieval France in "Men Who Walk Upon the Air," usually from the perspective of a jaded observer who takes their marvels for granted. This pose of world-weariness was rooted in the same romantic sensibility Long was cultivating in his verse. Most of his poems from this period, collected in *A Man from Genoa and Other Poems* and *The Goblin Tower,* are imbued with a longing for past splendours and a dissatisfaction with the uninspired present.

Long earned the cover of the December 1924 issue with his second story, "Death Waters," a revenge tale with a mild supernatural element reminiscent of Irvin S. Cobb's "Fishhead." The first of several stories in which he used horrors of the sea to evoke a sense of otherworldliness, it was followed by "The Ocean Leech," "The Sea Thing," "The Horror in the Hold," and his oft-reprinted "Second Night Out" (published as "The Black, Dead Thing"), a reworking of F. Marion Crawford's "The Upper Berth" in which a traveller is stalked by a monster that visits his cruise ship the second night out of each voyage. Another of Long's favourite horror themes, the incarnation of mythological beings in contemporary settings, allowed him to show off his knowledge of classics and literature. "The Were-Snake" features a modern avatar of the goddess Ishtar, and "A Visitor from Egypt" a mummy possessed by the god Osiris on the loose in New England. In "The Black Druid," a man who mistakenly dons an ancient ceremonial cloak slowly transforms into its Druidic owner. Long's fondness for this type of story ultimately served him well in the pages of *Unknown*, which published a number of his better works in this vein, among them "Fisherman's Luck," about a sportsman who discovers that his fishing rod has been exchanged for the magic staff of Hermes, and "Step into My Garden," in which a man discovers the Garden of Proserpine has overrun his backyard. Like most of Long's supernatural fiction, these tales are less interesting for what they tell than how they are told. Long's plotting was fairly routine, but his narrative style effectively blended the philosophically lofty and the physically gruesome. Within mere paragraphs of a single story such as "The Brain Eaters," for example, he could evoke horror obliquely through allusions to "an alien and utterly incomprehensible world which makes the fears and agonies of common life seem curiously impersonal and remote," and then directly with the image of monsters who "wrap themselves tightly about human heads, and suck out the contents of the cranium through the eyes and nostrils."

Given his predilection for stories of the otherworldly and the mythological, it is not surprising that Long was attracted to Lovecraft's tales of extradimensional monsters who have been assimilated into occult lore and legend. Long's casual mention of Abdul Alhazred, author of Lovecraft's infamous forbidden book the *Necronomicon*, in his 1925 story "The Were-Snake," was the first mention of a Lovecraft creation in a story not Lovecraft's own. In 1928, Long produced "The Space Eaters," the first contribution to what has since become known as the Cthulhu Mythos, an informal sub-genre of horror stories by different writers set in Lovecraft's universe. The tale, which features fictional representations of Lovecraft and Long as "Frank" and "Howard," is an attempt to embody Howard's aesthetic for "the horror that transcends everything" in a race of extraterrestrial beings who prey upon human brains. Long followed this with the loosely connected diptych "The Hounds of Tindalos" and "The Horror from the Hills," the latter of which contains a paraphrase of a lengthy dream sequence from one of Lovecraft's letters to Long. Lovecraft honoured both stories by later incorporating their monsters into the pantheon of extradimensional terrors that dominates his own fiction. Although these stories were not as successful as Lovecraft's at grounding their horrors in the modern scientific understanding of the universe, they show Long to have been more in tune with Lovecraft's notion of cosmic horror than possibly any other writer who contributed to the Mythos. Nearly all of Long's stories from this period show the impact of Lovecraft in their fusion of horror and science fiction, in particular "In the Lair of the Space Monsters," "The Brain Eaters," and "The Malignant Invaders," all of which are set at nexes where the normal world intersects with that of creatures from a different space-time continuum.

By the mid-1930s, most of Long's weird fiction was behind him, save for the handful of stories he contributed to *Unknown*. These tales, which showcase the wit and humour that occasionally leaven his work for *Weird Tales*, represent some of his strongest fantasy writing. He was one of the few *Weird Tales* writers to find a home in its pages or to adapt comfortably to the science-fiction market during the war years. Even his contributions to *Weird Tales* in the 1940s and '50s were science fiction, with

one exception. "The Peeper," published in 1944, is the tale of a cynical newspaper columnist haunted by memories of the past when he was a young fantasy writer of great promise. It is impossible to read this fantasy of youthful dreams foundering against adult realities as not a little autobiographical.

—Stefan Dziemianowicz

LORY, Robert (Edward)

Pseudonym: Paul Edwards. **Nationality:** American. **Born:** Troy, New York, 29 December 1936. **Education:** Harpur College, Binghamton, New York, B.A., 1961. **Family:** Married Barbara Banner in 1968; four children. **Career:** Worked in public relations from 1963.

HORROR, GHOST AND GOTHIC PUBLICATIONS

Novels (series: Dracula; Horrorscope)

Dracula Returns! New York, Pinnacle, and London, New English Library, 1973.
The Hand of Dracula. New York, Pinnacle, and London, New English Library, 1973.
Dracula's Brother. New York, Pinnacle, 1973; London, New English Library, 1974.
Dracula's Gold. New York, Pinnacle, 1973; London, New English Library, 1975.
The Witching of Dracula. New York, Pinnacle, 1974.
Drums of Dracula. New York, Pinnacle, 1974; London, New English Library, 1976.
Dracula's Lost World. New York, Pinnacle, 1974.
The Green Flames of Aries (Horrorscope). New York, Pinnacle, 1974.
The Revenge of Taurus (Horrorscope). New York, Pinnacle, 1974.
The Curse of Leo (Horrorscope). New York, Pinnacle, 1974.
Gemini Smile, Gemini Kill (Horrorscope). New York, Pinnacle, 1975.
Dracula's Disciple. New York, Pinnacle, 1975.
Challenge to Dracula. New York, Pinnacle, 1975.

Short Stories

More Tales of the Frightened. New York, Pyramid, 1975.

OTHER PUBLICATIONS

Novels

The Eyes of Bolsk. New York, Ace, 1969.
Master of the Etrax. New York, Dell, 1970.
Masters of the Lamp. New York, Ace, 1970.
The Veiled World. New York, Ace, 1972.
The Fist of Fatima (as Paul Edwards). New York, Pyramid, 1973; London, Mews, 1976.
The Laughing Death (as Paul Edwards). New York, Pyramid, 1973; London, Mews, 1976.

The Glyphs of Gold (as Paul Edwards). New York, Pyramid, 1974.
The Death Devils (as Paul Edwards). New York, Pyramid, 1974.
The Holocaust Action (as Paul Edwards). New York, Pyramid, 1974.
Identity Seven. New York, DAW, 1974.
The Thirteen Bracelets. New York, Ace, 1974.

Short Stories

A Harvest of Hoodwinks. New York, Ace, 1970.

* * *

For a little more than a decade, Robert Lory was a prolific author of science-fiction, fantasy and horror novels and short fiction. His first story, "Rundown" (*If*, 1963), was science fiction, but his second story, "Appointment at Ten o'Clock" (*Fantasy & Science Fiction*, 1964) was an amusing fantasy in which the afterlife becomes overcrowded. Over the next few years, Lory developed a talent for short, light-hearted, usually clever stories that were subsequently collected under the appropriate title of *A Harvest of Hoodwinks.* These stories, however, gave no indication of the outburst that was to come when, starting in 1969, Lory began to produce a series of action-oriented science-fiction and science-fantasy novels. The early novels were derivative of the works of Henry Kuttner and Jack Vance, interplanetary adventures with a touch of the exotic. Then, starting in 1973, Lory began two series which are of more relevance to this volume. Both series were packaged by the Canadian agent Lyle Kenyon Engel, who developed the concept with the publisher and author, but it was Lory who then took the series forward.

He is perhaps best remembered for his nine-volume Dracula series. Lory was, in fact, the first author to return to the Dracula legend created by Bram Stoker and resurrect it for a novel series, as distinct from (at that time) the occasional one-off pastiche. In the first novel, *Dracula Returns!*, Dr. Harmon finds the vampire Count's tomb in Romania. Although Dracula is still perfectly well preserved, the stake remains driven through his heart. Harmon has perfected a device with a sliver of wood that he can drive electronically into Dracula's heart at the switch of a button. Although he removes the main stake, he implants this device and, when Dracula recovers, Harmon demonstrates that he has control of life and death over the Count. The main twist of the series is that Harmon then uses Dracula in his fight against evil. This makes Dracula a representative of good; and it makes the series as a whole a precursor of later novels, such as those by Fred Saberhagen, which explored the benign side of Dracula in more detail. Lory's Dracula developed only gradually as the series progressed. He was, to a large extent, merely a pawn in the hands of Harmon, little able to exercise his own control, and Lory endeavoured to make him into a super-hero, like many of the pulp and comic-book heroes who were emerging into paperback at that time. In this respect the series is little more than pulp hackwork, but Lory's abilities to create interesting and sometimes amusing moments developed the stories above the hack level.

The Horrorscope series, consisting of four novels beginning with *The Green Flames of Aries*, is of less note, but achieved a proficient level of pulpish entertainment in its use of astrological icons to explore fate and destiny. Like his contributions, writing as "Paul Edwards," to the pseudonymous John Eagle series (about a highly trained agent equipped like James Bond but with the native skills

of an American Indian), the Horrorscope books were in the contemporary vogue for fast-paced action thrillers along the line of the *Man From U.N.C.L.E.* series, but involving elements of the supernatural. They were far less successful than his Dracula books and the series was dropped after only four volumes.

Lory could have developed into a capable writer, as his early work showed promise, but he fell into the trap of producing formulaic books for a non-discriminating market, and within a few years had fallen by the wayside, returning to his work as a public relations officer.

—Mike Ashley

LOVECRAFT, H(oward) P(hillips)

Nationality: American. **Born:** Providence, Rhode Island, 20 August 1890. **Education:** Tutored at home, at a local elementary school and at Hope Street High School, Providence, 1904-05, 1907-08. **Family:** Married Sonia Greene in 1924 (divorced 1929). **Career:** Freelance writer from 1908, working as a ghost writer and, after 1918, a revisionist; astronomy columnist, *Providence Evening News*, 1914-18; active in the amateur journalism movement from 1914; published *The Conservative*, 1915-19, 1923, and president of the United Amateur Press Association, 1917-18, 1923; regular contributor to *Weird Tales* after 1923. **Died:** 15 March 1937.

HORROR, GHOST AND GOTHIC PUBLICATIONS

Novels

The Case of Charles Dexter Ward. London, Gollancz, 1951; New York, Belmont, 1965.
The Dream-Quest of Unknown Kadath. Buffalo, Shroud, 1955.
At the Mountains of Madness. West Kingston, Rhode Island, Grant, 1990.

Novel with August Derleth (largely by Derleth)

The Lurker at the Threshold. Sauk City, Wisconsin, Arkham House, 1945; London, Gollancz, 1948.

Short Stories

The Shunned House. Athol, Massachusetts, Recluse Press, 1928.
The Battle That Ended the Century (Ms. Found in a Time Machine). De Land, Florida, Barlow, 1934.
The Cats of Ulthar. Cassia, Florida, Dragonfly Press, 1935.
The Shadow over Innsmouth. Everett, Pennsylvania, Visionary Press, 1936.
The Outsider and Others, edited by August Derleth and Donald Wandrei. Sauk City, Wisconsin, Arkham House, 1939; abridged as *The Dunwich Horror*, New York, Bart House, 1945.
Beyond the Wall of Sleep, edited by August Derleth and Donald Wandrei. Sauk City, Wisconsin, Arkham House, 1943.
Marginalia, edited by August Derleth and Donald Wandrei. Sauk City, Wisconsin, Arkham House, 1944.
The Weird Shadow over Innsmouth and Other Stories of the Supernatural. New York, Bart House, 1944.

Best Supernatural Stories of H. P. Lovecraft, edited by August Derleth. Cleveland, World, 1945; expanded as *The Dunwich Horror and Others,* Sauk City, Wisconsin, Arkham House, 1963; abridged as *The Colour Out of Space and Others,* New York, Lancer, 1964; original version as *The Best of H. P. Lovecraft: Bloodcurdling Tales of Horror and the Macabre,* New York, Ballantine, 1982.

The Lurking Fear and Other Stories. New York, Avon, 1947; as *Cry Horror!,* 1958; revised edition, London, Panther, 1964; further revised, New York, Beagle, 1971.

Something about Cats and Other Pieces, edited by August Derleth. Sauk City, Wisconsin, Arkham House, 1949.

The Haunter of the Dark and Other Tales of Horror. London, Gollancz, 1951.

Dreams and Fancies. Sauk City, Wisconsin, Arkham House, 1962.

At the Mountains of Madness and Other Novels. Sauk City, Wisconsin, Arkham House, 1964; London, Gollancz, 1966.

Dagon and Other Macabre Tales, edited by August Derleth. Sauk City, Wisconsin, Arkham House, 1965; London, Gollancz, 1967; abridged as *The Tomb and Other Tales,* London, Panther, 1969; New York, Ballantine, 1973.

3 Tales of Horror. Sauk City, Wisconsin, Arkham House, 1967.

The Shadow Out of Time and Other Tales of Horror, with August Derleth. London, Gollancz, 1968; abridged edition, as *The Shuttered Room and Other Tales of Horror,* London, Panther, 1970.

Ex Oblivione. Glendale, California, Squires, 1969.

Memory. Glendale, California, Squires, 1969.

The Horror in the Museum and Other Revisions, with others; edited by August Derleth. Sauk City, Wisconsin, Arkham House, 1970; abridged edition, New York, Beagle, 1971; as *The Horror in the Burying Ground and Other Tales,* London, Panther, 1975.

Nyarlathotep. Glendale, California, Squires, 1970.

What the Moon Brings. Glendale, California, Squires, 1970.

The Shadow over Innsmouth and Other Stories of Horror. New York, Scholastic, 1971.

The Doom That Came to Sarnath, edited by Lin Carter. New York, Ballantine, 1971.

Herbert West, the Reanimator. West Warwick, Rhode Island, Necronomicon Press, 1977.

The Statement of Randolph Carter. N.p., The Strange Company, 1976.

Collapsing Cosmoses, with Robert H. Barlow. West Warwick, Rhode Island, Necronomicon Press, 1977.

H. P. Lovecraft in the "Eyrie," edited by S. T. Joshi and Marc A. Michaud. West Warwick, Rhode Island, Necronomicon Press, 1979.

The Night Ocean, with Robert H. Barlow. West Warwick, Rhode Island, Necronomicon Press, 1982.

Four Prose Poems. West Warwick, Rhode Island, Necronomicon Press, 1987; 2nd edition, 1990.

Re-Animator: Tales of Herbert West, edited by Steven Philip Jones. Westlake, California, Malibu, 1991.

Crawling Chaos: Selected Works, 1920-1935, edited by James Havoc. London, Creation Press, 1992.

The Dream Cycle of H. P. Lovecraft: Dreams of Terror and Death. New York, Del Rey, 1995.

The Transition of H. P. Lovecraft: The Road to Madness. New York, Del Rey, 1996.

Short Stories with August Derleth (largely by Derleth)

The Survivor and Others. Sauk City, Wisconsin, Arkham House, 1957.

The Shuttered Room and Other Pieces, with others, edited by August Derleth. Sauk City, Wisconsin, Arkham House, 1959.

The Dark Brotherhood and Other Pieces, with others, edited by August Derleth. Sauk City, Wisconsin, Arkham House, 1966.

The Shuttered Room and Other Tales of Terror. New York, Beagle, 1971.

The Watchers Out of Time and Others. Sauk City, Wisconsin, Arkham House, 1974.

OTHER PUBLICATIONS

Poetry

The Crime of Crimes. Llandudno, Wales, Harris, 1915.

A Sonnet. N.p., Shepherd and Wollheim, 1936.

H.P.L. Belleville, New Jersey, Stickney, 1937.

Fungi from Yuggoth. Salem, Oregon, Evans, 1943; expanded edition, West Warwick, Rhode Island, Necronomicon Press, 1977.

Collected Poems. Sauk City, Wisconsin, Arkham House, 1963; abridged edition, as *Fungi from Yuggoth and Other Poems,* New York, Ballantine, 1971.

Medusa: A Portrait. New York, Oliphant Press, 1975.

A Winter Wish, edited by Tom Collins. Chapel Hill, North Carolina, Whispers Press, 1977.

Antarktos. Warren, Ohio, Fantome Press, 1977.

H. P. Lovecraft Christmas Book, edited by Susan Michaud. West Warwick, Rhode Island, Necronomicon Press, 1984; revised edition, 1991.

The Fantastic Poetry, edited by S. T. Joshi. West Warwick, Rhode Island, Necronomicon Press, 1990.

Other

United Amateur Press Association: Exponent of Amateur Journalism. N.p., United Amateur Press Association, 1916(?).

Looking Backward. Haverhill, Massachusetts, C.W. Smith, 1920(?).

The Materialist Today. North Montpelier, Vermont(?), n.p., 1926.

Further Criticism of Poetry. Louisville, Fetter, 1932.

Charleston. Privately printed, 1936.

Some Current Motives and Practices. DeLand, Florida, Barlow, 1936(?).

A History of the Necronomicon. Oakman, Alabama, Rebel Press, 1938.

The Notes and Commonplace Book Employed by the Late H. P. Lovecraft, edited by R. H. Barlow. Lakeport, California, Futile Press, 1938.

Supernatural Horror in Literature. New York, Abramson, 1945; revised edition, Arlington, Virginia, Carrollton-Clark, 1974.

The Lovecraft Collector's Library, edited by George T. Wetzel. Tonowanda, New York, SSR, 5 vols., 1952-55.

Autobiography: Some Notes on a Nonentity. Sauk City, Wisconsin, Arkham House, and London, Villiers, 1963.

Selected Letters 1911-1937, edited by August Derleth, James Turner and Donald Wandrei. Sauk City, Wisconsin, Arkham House, 5 vols., 1965-76.

Hail, Klarkash-Ton! Being Nine Missives Inscribed upon Postcards by H. P. Lovecraft to Clark Ashton Smith. Glendale, California, Squires, 1971.

Ec'h-Pi-El Speaks. Saddle River, New Jersey, Gerry de la Ree, 1972.

The Occult Lovecraft. Saddle River, New Jersey, Gerry de la Ree, 1975.

Lovecraft at Last (correspondence with Willis Conover). Arlington, Virginia, Carrollton Clark, 1975.

To Quebec and the Stars, edited by L. Sprague de Camp. West Kingston, Rhode Island, Grant, 1976.

Writings in The United Amateur 1915-1925, edited by Marc A. Michaud. West Warwick, Rhode Island, Necronomicon Press, 1976.

First Writings: Pawtuxet Valley Gleaner 1906, edited by Marc A. Michaud. West Warwick, Rhode Island, Necronomicon Press, 1976.

The Conservative: Complete 1915-1923, edited by Marc A. Michaud. West Warwick, Rhode Island, Necronomicon Press, 1977.

Memoirs of an Inconsequential Scribbler. West Warwick, Rhode Island, Necronomicon Press, 1977.

Writings in The Tryout, edited by Marc A. Michaud. West Warwick, Rhode Island, Necronomicon Press, 1977.

The Californian 1934-1938. West Warwick, Rhode Island, Necronomicon Press, 1977.

Uncollected Poetry and Prose, edited by S. T. Joshi and Marc A. Michaud. West Warwick, Rhode Island, Necronomicon Press, 2 vols., 1978-80.

Science versus Charlatanry: Essays on Astrology, with J. F. Hartmann, edited by S. T. Joshi and Scott Connors. N.p., The Strange Company, 1979.

H. P. Lovecraft's Waste Paper: A Facsimile and Transcript of the Original Draft. Providence, Rhode Island, Brown University, 1979.

Juvenilia 1895-1905, edited by S. T. Joshi. West Warwick, Rhode Island, Necronomicon Press, 1984.

H. P. Lovecraft: Uncollected Letters. West Warwick, Rhode Island, Necronomicon Press, 1986.

H. P. Lovecraft: Commonplace Book, edited by David E. Schultz. West Warwick, Rhode Island, Necronomicon Press, 2 vols., 1987.

European Glimpses, with Sonia H. Greene. West Warwick, Rhode Island, Necronomicon Press, 1988.

H. P. Lovecraft: The Conservative (essays), edited by S. T. Joshi. West Warwick, Rhode Island, Necronomicon Press, 1990.

The Vivisector (essays). West Warwick, Rhode Island, Necronomicon Press, 1990.

H. P. Lovecraft: Letters to Henry Kuttner, edited by David E. Schultz and S. T. Joshi. West Warwick, Rhode Island, Necronomicon Press, 1990.

H. P. Lovecraft: Letters to Richard Searight, edited by David E. Schultz, S. T. Joshi, and Franklyn Searight. West Warwick, Rhode Island, Necronomicon Press, 1992.

H. P. Lovecraft: Letters to Robert Bloch, edited by David E. Schultz and S. T. Joshi. West Warwick, Rhode Island, Necronomicon Press, 1993.

Miscellaneous Writings, edited by S. T. Joshi. Sauk City, Wisconsin, Arkham House, 1995.

Editor, *The Poetical Works of Jonathan E. Hoag.* Privately printed, 1923.

Editor, *White Fire,* by John Ravenor Bullen. Athol, Massachusetts, Recluse Press, 1927.

Editor, *Thoughts and Pictures,* by Eugene B. Kuntz. Haverhill, Massachusetts, Lovecraft and Smith, 1932.

*

Film Adaptations: *The Haunted Palace,* 1963, *The Resurrected,* 1991, both from the novel *The Case of Charles Dexter Ward; Monster of Terror (Die, Monster, Die!),* 1965, *The Curse,* 1987, both from the story "The Colour Out of Space"; *The Dunwich Horror,* 1970; *Re-Animator,* 1985, from the story "Herbert West—Reanimator"; *From Beyond,* 1986; *The Unnameable,* 1988; *Beyond the Wall of Sleep (Necronomicon),* 1993.

Bibliography: *The New H. P. Lovecraft Bibliography* by Jack L. Chalker, Baltimore, Anthem Press, 1962, revised edition, with Mark Owings, as *The Revised H. P. Lovecraft Bibliography,* Baltimore, Mirage Press, 1973; *A Catalog of Lovecraftiana* by Mark Owings and Irving Binkin, Baltimore, Mirage Press, 1975; *H. P. Lovecraft: An Annotated Bibliography* by S. T. Joshi, Kent, Ohio, Kent State University Press, 1981; *Howard Phillips Lovecraft: The Books, Addenda and Auxiliary* by Joseph Bell, Toronto, Soft Press, 1983.

Manuscript Collection: Brown University, Providence, Rhode Island.

Critical Studies (selection): *In Memoriam Howard Phillips Lovecraft: Recollections, Appreciations, Estimates* edited by W. Paul Cook, privately printed, 1941; *H. P.L.: A Memoir,* New York, Abramson, 1945, and *Some Notes on H. P. Lovecraft,* Sauk City, Wisconsin, Arkham House, 1959, both by August Derleth; *Rhode Island on Lovecraft* edited by Donald M. Grant and Thomas P. Hadley, Providence, Rhode Island, Grant Hadley, 1945; "H. P. Lovecraft Issue" of *Fresco* (Detroit), Spring 1958; *Lovecraft: A Look Behind the Cthulhu Mythos* by Lin Carter, New York, Ballantine, 1972, London, Panther, 1975; *Lovecraft: A Biography* by L. Sprague de Camp, New York, Doubleday, 1975, London, New English Library, 1976; *Howard Phillips Lovecraft: Dreamer on the Nightside* by Frank Belknap Long, Sauk City, Wisconsin, Arkham House, 1975; *Essays Lovecraftian* edited by Darrell Schweitzer, Baltimore, T-K Graphics, 1976, and *The Dream Quest of H. P. Lovecraft* by Schweitzer, San Bernardino, California, Borgo Press, 1978; *The H. P. Lovecraft Companion* by Philip A. Schreffler, Westport, Connecticut, Greenwood Press, 1977; *The Major Works of H. P. Lovecraft* by John Taylor Gatto, New York, Monarch Press, 1977; *The Roots of Horror in the Fiction of H. P. Lovecraft* by Barton Levi St. Armand, Elizabethtown, New York, Dragon Press, 1977; *H. P. Lovecraft* by S. T. Joshi, Mercer Island, Washington, Starmont House, 1982; *H. P. Lovecraft: A Critical Study* by Donald R. Burleson, Westport, Connecticut, Greenwood Press, 1983; *Lovecraft: A Study in the Fantastic* by Maurice Lévy, translated by S. T. Joshi, Detroit, Wayne State University Press, 1988; *Lovecraft: A Life* by S. T. Joshi, West Warwick, Rhode Island, Necronomicon Press, 1996.

*   *   *

H. P. Lovecraft is the most significant American writer of weird fiction subsequent to Edgar Allan Poe. Although he himself died in poverty, his work has attained a popular and (more recently) critical success he could scarcely have imagined.

First, a bibliographical note: Lovecraft wrote just three works which are lengthy enough to be called "novels." All three made their first book appearances in Lovecraft's posthumous collections of the 1940s, but have been republished since in slim single volumes as detailed in the bibliography above. A fourth "novel," *The Lurker at the Threshold*, is almost entirely the work of August Derleth and does not properly belong to Lovecraft's bibliography; similarly, there are several posthumous "collections" by Derleth which contain very little by Lovecraft despite his name appearing on title page and cover. In the paragraphs that follow all dates given for Lovecraft's genuine stories are those of composition, not publication.

Lovecraft's life, work and thought are intimately connected, and each must be understood before the totality of his achievement can be gauged. Growing up as a fringe member of the conservative New England aristocracy, just at the time when enormous political, social and cultural changes would overwhelm the United States and the world, Lovecraft spent the whole of his life adjusting to new literary trends, revolutionary findings in science and new social realities; in some ways he adjusted remarkably well, in others he lagged lamentably behind.

Lovecraft's mature fiction commences with "The Tomb" (1917), and in his early career he struggled to assimilate the many literary influences he encountered: Edgar Allan Poe, whom he read as early as the age of eight; Ambrose Bierce and Lord Dunsany, both of whom he discovered in 1919 (the latter author inspired him to write several tales of pure fantasy, culminating with the short novel *The Dream-Quest of Unknown Kadath* [1926-27]); Arthur Machen in 1923; Algernon Blackwood and M. R. James in 1924. In the end Lovecraft did assimilate these varied influences, although in his early years he wrote many blatant imitations of his mentors.

The early phase of Lovecraft's writing ends with "Cool Air" (1926). Discounting the Dunsany imitations, these early tales are marked by a concentration on relatively conventional macabre scenarios: fascination with death and tombs ("The Tomb," "The Statement of Randolph Carter," "The Outsider"), the haunted house ("The Rats in the Walls," "The Shunned House"), the mad scientist ("From Beyond," "Cool Air"). If Lovecraft had written nothing more than these tales, he would be remembered as little more than a minor competent craftsman in the field.

And yet, by 1921 Lovecraft had already forged the central tenets of his philosophical thought, but had yet to learn how to incorporate them into his fiction. Having discarded religion at an early age and declaring himself a mechanistic materialist who rejected all forms of mysticism and idealism, Lovecraft evolved the notion of "cosmicism." This stance, which emphasizes the spatial and temporal vastness of the universe and the consequent insignificance of all human affairs, is not especially original as a philosophical conception—Lovecraft derived it from an early interest in astronomy as well as from the Greek atomists, Epicurus, Lucretius, and Nietzsche—but his distinctiveness comes in embodying it powerfully in fiction.

But cosmicism is not expressed in much of the fiction prior to 1926. Many of the early tales are certainly enjoyable and powerful—"The Rats in the Walls" is not merely a flawless Poe imitation (much more successful than the famous but excessively derivative "The Outsider") but a model of concision and cumulative suspense—although some of them ("Herbert West—Reanimator," "The Hound") have not been recognized to be the intentionally lurid and bombastic self-parodies that they are.

It was only after Lovecraft returned in April 1926 to his native Providence, after two miserable years spent in New York in an unsuccessful marriage, that he and his work truly flowered. Having settled into a congenial if very impecunious existence with two aunts, at the centre of a complex network of epistolary ties to other writers (notably August Derleth, Donald Wandrei, Robert E. Howard, Henry S. Whitehead and Robert Bloch), secure enough in his beloved hometown to take ambitious antiquarian explorations as far north as Quebec and as far south as Key West, Lovecraft became the "gentleman from Providence" of a partially self-fostered legend.

His return to New England also spelled an important change in his aesthetics. Around 1920 Lovecraft had become enamoured of what he called "Decadence"—which really meant the languid and sophisticated "art for art's sake" attitude initially found in Poe's critical work and taken up by Oscar Wilde, Walter Pater and others. But his return to Providence made him realize the importance of his New England heritage both to his own psychological well-being and to the strength of his work.

The result is a series of tales and novelettes which, although relatively small in number, gives Lovecraft the reputation he deserves as a watershed in the history of weird fiction. What we find in these later tales is an enormously rich, complex evocation of New England topography, history and society ("The Colour Out of Space," *The Case of Charles Dexter Ward* [1927], "The Dunwich Horror, "The Whisperer in Darkness" [1930], "The Shadow over Innsmouth" [1931], "The Dreams in the Witch House" [1932], "The Thing on the Doorstep" [1933], "The Haunter of the Dark" [1935]), combined—not paradoxically—with a spectacular cosmicism that results in a wholly unique fusion of horror and science fiction ("The Call of Cthulhu" [1926], *At the Mountains of Madness* [1931], "The Shadow out of Time" [1934-35]).

The depth and richness of Lovecraft's later work are difficult to characterize, but it can be said to represent a fusion of extremely skilful narrative pacing, powerful philosophical conceptions embodied in imaginatively stimulating but highly plausible scenarios, and a prose style that unites scientific precision with a sort of incantatory prose-poetry.

Many of these tales utilize a pseudo-mythological framework that has now been termed (although it was never so termed by Lovecraft) the "Cthulhu Mythos." Much recent scholarship has been concerned with whether this term—and the demarcation of those stories that incorporate this myth-cycle—is of genuine value in the understanding of Lovecraft's work. He himself was convinced that *all* his fictional output embodied his fundamental philosophical principles, notably cosmicism; as he wrote in a letter of 1927: "Now all my tales are based on the fundamental premise that common human laws and interests and emotions have no validity or significance in the vast cosmos-at-large. . . . To achieve the essence of real externality, whether of time or space or dimension, one must forget that such things as organic life, good and evil, love and hate, and all such local attributes of a negligible and temporary race called mankind, have any existence at all." Perhaps the most that can be said is that the "Cthulhu Mythos" is largely a series of props or plot devices—involving such things as an entire mythical New England topography (Arkham, Dunwich, Innsmouth, Kingsport), mythical books of occult lore (chiefly the *Necronomicon* of Abdul Alhazred, along with a library full of other tomes invented by Lovecraft and his colleagues), and, most distinctively, the creation of vast "gods" or entities who appear to rule the cosmos (Azathoth, Nyarlathotep, Yog-Sothoth, Cthulhu)—that structures much of Lovecraft's later work. Its precise significance has, however, perhaps not been properly grasped: its true function is in allowing Lovecraft to express most potently and concentratedly his overriding philosophical concerns. In this sense, the "Cthulhu Mythos" becomes (in David E. Schultz's felicitous term) an *anti-mythology*: in contrast to conventional religions or mythologies that place humanity at the moral centre of the universe and as the creation of a beneficent and divine cosmic order, Lovecraft's tales brutally reduce us to a position of utter inconsequence in the cosmic scheme of things, the hapless victims of vast and incomprehensible forces to whom we are as nothing. It is not surprising that this bleak message has been misinterpreted even by some of Lovecraft's most ardent supporters—notably August Derleth, who fostered a largely erroneous view of the "Cthulhu Mythos" as somehow in consonance with Christian mythology.

Another body of Lovecraft's work that deserves some consideration is a group of tales referred to as "revisions" (really stories ghost-written for would-be writers, usually on the slimmest of plot-germs). These tales are on the whole inferior to Lovecraft's original work, but some of them—"The Mound," "Out of the Aeons," "The Night Ocean"—are important adjuncts to his own fiction. Many of them are, however, inferior even to the general level of pulp fiction published in *Weird Tales*, where most of Lovecraft's original work appeared.

—S. T. Joshi

LOVEGROVE, James (Matthew Henry)

Nationality: British. **Born:** Lewes, East Sussex, 24 December 1965. **Education:** Radley College, Oxfordshire; St. Catherine's College, Oxford University, M.A. in English Literature. **Agent:** Antony Harwood, Aitken, Stone and Wylie Ltd., 29 Fernshaw Road, London SW10 0TG, England.

HORROR, GHOST AND GOTHIC PUBLICATIONS

Novels

The Hope. London, Macmillan, 1990; Clarkston, Georgia, White Wolf, 1996.
Escardy Gap, with Peter Crowther. New York, Tor, 1996.

* * *

The Hope, James Lovegrove's single solo book-publication to date, rather stretches the definition of a novel, as it has no continuity of action and very little of character. It is written as a series of episodes, each with its own viewpoint; although some viewpoints achieve walk-on parts when the focus drifts elsewhere, and some central episodes may take on the character of gossip or background information later, the book studiously eschews any defining structure. Against that, there is obvious unity of place and of *genius loci*, and a progression imposed by the sequence of protagonists—for each is crazier, and leads the reader into realms of deeper horror, than the last.

The setting is the gigantic ship of the title, five miles long, two miles wide, one mile high. Launched some three decades previously for reasons long forgotten (if ever known) and now beyond speculation, the only home of an entire generation that has never trodden dry land, it recalls the *Titanic* in its layout, technology and class-structure. In mood it recalls the most angst-ridden passages of Brian Aldiss's *Non-Stop*, for its voyage is endless and purposeless, its construction a grandiose act of folly which beggared the billionaire philanthropist whose hubris sponsored it, and who hanged himself as it set sail for the first and only time. Despite its size, the atmosphere of *Hope* is claustrophobic at all points; whoever you are, most of the ship consists of places where you cannot or fear to venture.

Over the decades the ship's conceptual flaws and general unviability as an arcology have become ever more apparent to its inhabitants. The only doctor has killed himself, leaving the health of a million people in the hands of a half-trained apprentice; the only priest is a deranged pervert; the captain is purely a social functionary, with neither navigational skills nor concern for the people in his charge; law is non-existent, and order local at best, so that when the head chef poisons 23 first-class passengers and a waiter (accidentally, as it happens) no attempt is made to apprehend him for questioning once he flees to the lower decks. Conversely, when a girl scratches out the eyes of her gangster boyfriend, no one seeks vengeance against her once she is afforded sanctuary in First Class.

Even among the highest social category, those First Class passengers who boarded the ship as adults or teenagers, there is a *fin de siècle* atmosphere, brilliantly evoked as Lovegrove describes a dance in one of the saloons. Beneath the crystal chandelier old men and women pace the 30-years practised measures of the waltz and quickstep. Their patrician stoicism quells the pain of their arthritic joints, but the white ties of the gentlemen have been washed too often; the silk dresses of the ladies are threadbare, and no longer fit bodies grown gaunt; and there are no young people.

The Hope is less an allegory than a prolonged exploration of the concept of non-renewal, its spiritual aspect being aptly if obviously counterpointed against the universal inadequacy of recycling systems. The only fresh foods aboard are fish gathered from the sea and fruit and vegetables grown in the ship's own greenhouses; all else is canned, without resemblance to anything which might once have lived, and its complement are no better. They regard each other as rubbish and better dead, a view based not on commonplace racial or class-based animosities, but the simple observation that there are for too many of them, with far too little room.

While *The Hope* works well as an exercise in mood writing, it is less effective as allegory, for three reasons. The first is that Lovegrove never presents any rationale, however far-fetched, for its construction and launching. The occasional vague references to an ultimate destination across the "never-ending ocean" vitiate the atmosphere, because although the voyage has already gone on far too long, that is the one aspect of which no one ever complains. The second is that although various forms of economic activity, many of them sordid, criminal or both, are referred to and sometimes described, nothing seems to keep the economy afloat. Items are scavenged or stolen, sometimes for barter but mainly for cash—and there is no obvious reason why, in such a fragmented society, the value of such an abstraction as money should be so uniformly acknowledged. Finally, the most important viewpoint of all is never presented: we are never shown the view through the captain's eyes—perhaps inevitably. For if the captain has no answers, then there can be none, which would present a resolution of sorts; but *The Hope* is not about answers, only about the unanswerable.

Escardy Gap, Lovegrove's very different horror novel in collaboration with Peter Crowther, is considered under Crowther's entry. This is purely for convenience, and not because Crowther, although senior in years, is to be regarded as the "primary" writer of that book. Lovegrove also has a few published short stories to his name, some of them science fiction rather than horror, weird or gothic.

—Chris Gilmore

LUCAS, Tim(othy)

Nationality: American. **Born:** Cincinnati, Ohio, 1956. **Family:** Married Donna Goldschmidt in 1974. **Career:** Journalist; editor, *Video Watchdog* magazine. Lives in Ohio.

HORROR, GHOST AND GOTHIC PUBLICATIONS

Novel

Throat Sprockets. New York, Dell, 1994; London, Fourth Estate, 1995.

Graphic Novels

"Throat Sprockets," illustrated by Mike Hoffman, in *Taboo* #1, 1987.
"Sweet Nothings," illustrated by Simonida Perica, in *Taboo* #2, 1988.
"Transylvania Mon Amour," illustrated by Mike Hoffman, in *Taboo* #3, 1989.
"Blue Angel," illustrated by Stephen Blue, in *Taboo* #4, 1990.
"The Disaster Area," illustrated by David Lloyd, in *Taboo* #8, 1994.

OTHER PUBLICATIONS

Other

Your Movie Guide to Horror/Science Fiction & Fantasy/Mystery & Suspense/Movie Classics on Tape and Disc (4 vols. of 12-vol. series). New York, Signet, 1985.
The Video Watchdog Book. New York, Video Watchdog, 1992.

*   *   *

With one published novel, *Throat Sprockets*, to his credit, Tim Lucas is an author with real potential. As the editor of the *Video Watchdog*, Lucas has drawn on his extensive knowledge of film and pop culture to construct a disturbing, haunting world of a man taken over by a film and its fetish. It is apparent from the book's unobtrusive lecturing on film and its place and effect on society that the author has expertise in his chosen subject matter. Lucas's *Watchdog* experience allows him to accomplish the almost impossible feat of bringing an imaginary film to life on the page.

Critical to *Throat Sprockets*' success is Lucas's ability to portray the power of film, almost as a narcotic, which can change, if not ruin, a person's entire outlook on life. Secondly, he shows, with good use of detail, the power of the fetish, which, in this case, as in the film described in the novel, focuses on the erotic aspects of the female throat. With this fetish, the internal change undergone by the first-person narrator, and a vampiric twist, Lucas paints a world at odds with its inhabitants, and a doomed man in a doomed society.

Although many of Lucas's contemporaries lapse into pornography when writing erotica, Lucas has managed to use that very vehicle to comment not only on horror, but on pornography as well. "Sprocketing," as described in the book, is the inverse of the splatter-gore vampiric conceit that it draws on, an act of gentle submission both augmenting and replacing sexual intercourse, and ultimately replacing the original obsession with the film itself. The setup is ironic and well concealed in the telling. A happily married man seeks his own fulfilment from film in the shabby downtown porn theatre near his office. He is drawn not to the sexual nature of the films, he tells himself, but by the promise of escape from the vanilla plainness of big-budget Hollywood releases. Without warning, the film *Throat Sprockets* plays at his local theatre, and he is hooked. Like a junkie gone on his first time needling heroin, he will never be the same. The film is crude and strangely erotic, and it is spliced over critical points, which only serves to further entice him. His spiral begins. In inverse proportions, his personal and professional life begin to dive and soar, respectively. His fetish undermines and destroys his long-term relationship with his wife, and he is left alone. At his work at an advertising agency, his stock begins to rise, each campaign under his charge uniquely energized by his newfound "insights," and each product married to the periphery of his newfound fetish.

Here Lucas successfully comments on consumerism and obsession, following the career almost as closely as the fetish. After a particularly horrifying attempt to fulfil his part in *Throat Sprockets*' play, the advertising man finally meets his match in a young woman named Emma, who has also seen and been affected by the film. This allows for the enactment of his darkest desires, and ultimately sets him apart from the power of the film, at least temporarily. But the cost of the obsession, the totality of it, slowly and permanently drains the life from the man, taking him beyond the limits of reason, to a bleak, disturbing conclusion.

Throat Sprockets shows signs of straining under the weight of its own detail in a few places, but is surprisingly deft and atmospheric for a first novel. Lucas also has one as-yet unpublished novel, *The Only Criminal*, and another currently in the works, provisionally called *Scars and Stripes*. These novels, taken as a group with *Throat Sprockets*, are transformational tales, each brought on by an unnatural catalyst—for example, the film in *Throat Sprockets*. An element of absence draws the characters forward. In *Throat Sprockets*, the protagonist asks, "Who did this to me?" The reader is taken on the same quest, to answer that question. Lucas's goal, then, is to seduce his readers into believing that they have also seen the movie, that they have also succumbed to the obsession. In this, a nigh-impossible thing to achieve, he has done remarkably well. Lucas credits this "Godot" principle as influenced by his father, who passed away shortly before he was born, leaving this theme of absence as a primary influence on his son's life and his fiction.

—Tom Winstead

LUMLEY, Brian

Nationality: British. **Born:** Horden, Durham, 2 December 1937. **Family:** Married Dorothy Houghton. **Military Service:** Served in the British Army, in Germany and Cyprus; career soldier. **Career:** Began selling stories and novels while still in the army; became a full-time author on discharge. **Awards:** British Fantasy award for short story, 1989. **Address:** c/o Hodder Headline, 338 Euston Road, London NW1 3BH, England.

HORROR, GHOST AND GOTHIC PUBLICATIONS

Novels (series: Dreamlands; Necroscope; Primal Land; Psychomech; Titus Crow; Vampire World)

Beneath the Moors. Sauk City, Wisconsin, Arkham House, 1974.
The Burrowers Beneath (Titus Crow). New York, DAW, 1974.
The Transition of Titus Crow. New York, DAW, 1975; revised edition, London, Grafton, 1991.
The Clock of Dreams (Titus Crow). New York, Jove, 1978.
Spawn of the Winds (Titus Crow). New York, Jove, 1978; London, Grafton, 1992.
In the Moons of Borea (Titus Crow). New York, Jove, 1979; London, Grafton, 1993.
Khai of Ancient Khem. New York, Berkley, 1981; London, Grafton, 1990.
Psychomech. London, Panther, 1984.
Psychosphere (Psychomech). London, Panther, 1984.
Psychamok! (Psychomech). London, Panther, 1985.
Hero of Dreams (Dreamlands). Buffalo, New York, Ganley, 1986; London, Headline, 1989.
Necroscope. London, Granada, 1986; New York, Tor, 1988.
Ship of Dreams (Dreamlands). Buffalo, New York, Ganley, 1986; London, Headline, 1989.
Demogorgon. London, Grafton, 1987; New York, Tor, 1992.
Mad Moon of Dreams (Dreamlands). Buffalo, New York, Ganley, 1987; London, Headline, 1990.
Necroscope II: Wamphyri! London, Grafton, 1988; as *Necroscope II: Vamphyri!*, New York, Tor, 1989.
Elysia: The Coming of Cthulhu! (Dreamlands; Primal Land; Titus Crow). Buffalo, New York, Ganley, 1989; London, Grafton, 1993.
Necroscope III: The Source. London, Grafton, and New York, Tor, 1989.
The House of Doors. New York, Tor, 1990.
Necroscope IV: Deadspeak. London, Grafton, and New York, Tor, 1990.
Necroscope V: Deadspawn. London, Grafton, and New York, Tor, 1991.
Blood Brothers (Vampire World). London, Roc, and New York, Tor, 1992.
The Last Aerie (Vampire World). London, Roc, and New York, Tor, 1993.
Bloodwars (Vampire World). London, Roc, and New York, Tor, 1994.
Necroscope: The Lost Years. London, Hodder and Stoughton, and New York, Tor, 1995.
Necroscope: The Lost Years, Volume II. London, Hodder and Stoughton, 1996; as *Necroscope: Resurgence*, New York, Tor, 1996.

Titus Crow (omnibus; includes *The Burrowers Beneath, The Transition of Titus Crow*). New York, Tor, 1996.
Brian Lumley's Mythos Omnibus (includes *The Burrowers Beneath, The Transition of Titus Crow, The Clock of Dreams*). London, HarperCollins, 1997.
Brian Lumley's Mythos Omnibus, Volume II (includes *Spawn of the Winds, In the Moons of Borea, Elysia*). London, HarperCollins, 1997.
Titus Crow, Volume Two (omnibus; includes *The Clock of Dreams, Spawn of the Winds*). New York, Tor, 1997.

Short Stories

The Caller of the Black. Sauk City, Wisconsin, Arkham House, 1971.
The Horror at Oakdeene and Others. Sauk City, Wisconsin, Arkham House, 1977.
The House of Cthulhu, and Other Tales of the Primal Land. Buffalo, New York, Weirdbook Press, 1984; revised as *House of Cthulhu: Tales of the Primal Land, Volume One.* London, Headline, 1991.
The Compleat Crow (Titus Crow). Buffalo, New York, Ganley, 1987.
Synchronicity, or Something. England, Dagon Press, 1988.
Iced on Aran & Other Dream Quests (Dreamlands). London, Headline, 1990.
The Compleat Khash, Volume One: Never a Backward Glance (Primal Land). Buffalo, New York, Ganley, 1991.
Tarra Khash: Hrossak! Tales of the Primal Land, Volume Two. London, Headline, 1991.
Sorcery in Shad: Tales of the Primal Land, Volume Three. Headline, London, 1991.
The Last Rite. N.p., 1992.
Fruiting Bodies and Other Fungi. London, Roc, 1993; New York, Tor, 1996.
Return of the Deep Ones, and Other Mythos Tales. London, Roc, 1994.
Dagon's Bell and Other Discords. London, New English Library, 1994.
The Second Wish, and Other Exhalations. London, New English Library, 1995.

Poetry

Ghoul Warning and Other Omens. N.p., 1982.

*

Bibliography: *Brian Lumley: A New Bibliography* by Leigh Blackmore, Penrith, New South Wales, Australia, Dark Press, 1984.

*   *   *

Brian Lumley is universally regarded as a horror writer, and is marketed as one, but he admits to many influences in his extensive body of work which come as much from science fiction or adventure fantasy. However, few would deny that the clearest influence on Lumley's work is H. P. Lovecraft, to whose memory the novel *The Transformation of Titus Crow* is dedicated. Lumley first read Lovecraft as a teenager, and contacted August Derleth at the specialist press Arkham House. It seems it was Derleth who suggested that he try his hand at fiction writing. (Though according to the interview in the "Lumley Special" issue of *Weird Tales* [Winter 1989], he had previously tried his hand at humorous science-fiction stories: ". . . luckily none of them have survived.")

Lumley is indeed noteworthy for the number of different elements and sub-genres featured in his work. Reviewer Steve Jones once remarked that one of Lumley's works included everything but the kitchen sink; Lumley made sure to include a kitchen sink in his next novel, *Elysia: The Coming of Cthulhu!*.

Lumley did not start writing full-time until he was fairly well established. Having done an apprenticeship apparently to please his parents, he joined the British army and for two decades he was a forces professional with a sideline career as a writer. This gave him the freedom to write more or less what he pleased. His first published work was via U.S. small presses like Arkham House, and little appeared in Britain. His breakthrough novel was *The Burrowers Beneath*.

Burrowers has a very explicit Lovecraftian influence, though Lumley makes it clear that he does not attempt to pastiche Lovecraft's style. What he does incorporate very explicitly is undisguised elements from the Cthulhu Mythos. Great Cthulhu himself makes a brief telepathic intervention without actually leaving sunken R'lyeh. However, the main focus is on races of ancient horrors added by Lumley himself. The Burrowers are followers and descendants of a being called Shudde-M'ell who has been imprisoned by the benign Elder Gods beneath a lost city in Africa. The Great Old Ones are contained and imprisoned by assorted devices which usually take the physical form of Star Stones. In the back-story to *Burrowers*, African witch doctors have been privatizing the star stones to exploit their powers for their own ends, enabling Shudde-M'ell to escape and establish colony burrows under, among other places, Britain.

In this version of the Mythos, the Great Old Ones are essentially physical rather than supernatural beings, and can be combatted and even destroyed by physical means. The Burrowers breed, rather slowly, by laying eggs: they are protective of their eggs and young which can sometimes be used to trap them.

One difference from Lovecraft which rapidly becomes apparent is that while in the original stories the human investigators have few powers, are motivated by dangerous obsessions, and usually come to a bad end, in Lumley's variations the investigators are associated with a worldwide organization based at Miskatonic University which includes many expert monster-hunters: indeed after a while the process of locating and destroying Great Old Ones seems to become so routine as to be almost industrialized.

At the end of *Burrowers*, the two principal investigators, de Marigny and the Van Helsing-like Titus Crow, are trapped in Crow's house by minions of the wind-demon Ithaqua. Luckily, Crow possesses a mysterious grandfather clock which he has guessed is a time machine but has never dared to use. The two escape and a series of adventures starts, which spread in time, space, and influence. A subsidiary hero, Hank Silberhutte, travels to a planet, Borea, where he becomes chief of a tribe of Indians and Eskimos also originating on Earth, and marries Ithaqua's human daughter Armandra, a scenario which to my mind owes as much to E. R. Burroughs as to H. P. Lovecraft.

More, and more modern, influences appear in Lumley's massive Necroscope series. The title is an eponym for the hero, Harry Keogh, who has the ability to read the minds of the dead and speak to them. He is recruited by a paranormal branch of British intelligence, and becomes involved in battles with other intelligence agencies, as well as the conventional horror staple of tribes of vampires, originally exiles from an alien world, who have been fighting each other and everyone else for centuries. Later Keogh acquires other powers, such as teleportation: less conveniently, his mind is transferred to the body of a "total stranger," Alec Kyle. His wife takes objection to this innovation, and disappears so completely with their son that even his Necroscope powers do not enable Harry/Alec to find her. Instead, he falls under the influence of a woman called Bonnie Jean Mirlu, who appears to be a young Edinburgh bartender but is in fact a 200-year-old werewolf, servant of a werewolf-vampire who is waiting to be reanimated in order to continue a feud with other ancient vampires. Bonnie Jean's mission is to turn the Necroscope over to her Master, Radu, for him to possess, but she is in love with Harry.

Lumley is a writer whose horror is noted for its page-turning excitement, but also for its humour. In the story "The Disapproval of Jeremy Cleave," in the *Weird Tales* special issue, the eponymous character, having lost an eye and a leg on expeditions "up rivers," but having acquired knowledge of Juju, has just been murdered by his best friend, who has been sleeping with Cleave's beautiful but dim and neurotic young wife. Every time the couple try to consummate their guilty affair, they find Cleave's glass eye watching them. The opening is amusing, but the conclusion is pure horror, pure Lumley.

—Peter T. Garratt

M

MACARDLE, Dorothy

Nationality: Irish. **Born:** Dorothea Marguerita Callan Macardle, in Dundalk, County Louth, 10 March 1889. **Education:** Alexandra School for Girls, Dublin; Alexandra College, Dublin, B.A. in English 1912, teaching diploma 1914. **Career:** Taught at Alexandra College, 1914-22; active in the Irish nationalist movement; jailed, 1922-23; became a journalist; theatre critic, *Irish Press*; correspondent at the League of Nations, Geneva, 1938; after World War II worked with displaced and refugee children; lecturer and broadcaster. **Died:** 23 December 1958.

Horror, Ghost and Gothic Publications

Novels

Uneasy Freehold. London, Peter Davies, 1941; as *The Uninvited*, New York, Doubleday Doran, 1942.
Fantastic Summer. London, Peter Davies, 1946; as *The Unforeseen*, New York, Doubleday, 1946.
Dark Enchantment. London, Peter Davies, and New York, Doubleday, 1953.

Other Publications

Novels

The Seed Was Kind. London, Peter Davies, 1944.

Short Stories

Earth-Bound: Nine Stories of Ireland. Worcester, Massachusetts, Harrigan Press, 1924.

Plays

Asthara (produced Dublin, 1918).
Atonement (produced Dublin, 1918).
Ann Kavanagh (produced Dublin, 1922). New York, French, 1937.
The Old Man (produced Dublin, 1925).
Witch's Brew. London, Deane, 1931.
The Children's Guest (for children). Oxford, Oxford University Press, 1940.
The Loving Cup (for children). London, Nelson, 1943.

Other

Tragedies of Kerry 1922-1923. Dublin, Emton Press, 1924.
The Irish Republic: A Documented Chronicle of the Anglo-Irish Conflict and the Partitioning of Ireland, with a Detailed Account of the Period 1916-1923. London, Gollancz, 1937; New York, Farrar Straus, 1965.
Without Fanfares: Some Reflections on the Republic of Eire. Dublin, Gill, 1946.

Children of Europe: A Study of the Children of Liberated Countries. . . . London, Gollancz, 1949; Boston, Beacon Press, 1951.
Shakespeare: Man and Boy, edited by George Bott. London, Faber, 1961.

*

Film Adaptation: *The Uninvited*, 1944.

Critical Study: "A Reflection of Ghosts" by Peter Tremayne, in *Gaslight & Ghosts* edited by Stephen Jones and Jo Fletcher, London, Robinson, 1988.

*   *   *

Dorothy Macardle made her name as a political activist, playwright (including work for the prestigious Abbey Theatre) and historian before branching out into fiction. The British edition of her novel *Uneasy Freehold* was handicapped by the fact that the United Kingdom was at war, but America was not yet involved and as *The Uninvited* it was a big hit there; the Literary Guild helped to boost it to best-seller status and Paramount filmed it—with Ray Milland in the lead—in 1944. Unfortunately, the author was unable to repeat the coup; she followed up with a very different novel in *The Seed Was Kind*, and her partial reversion to type in *Fantastic Summer* could not recover the lost ground, in spite of being carefully retitled *The Unforeseen* for American publication. *Dark Enchantment* subsequently escaped almost unnoticed.

The Uninvited is what American paperback publishers of a later period would call a "Gothic romance": a love story in which the play of the characters' emotions is melodramatically heightened by anxiety and unease. It differs in two important respects, however, from the formula which was eventually refined by paperback editors: the phenomena which generate unease are forthrightly supernatural and (more significantly, in terms of narrative strategy) the story is told from the viewpoint of the male protagonist.

The hero of *The Uninvited* is a playwright in search of peaceful rural isolation, who buys a house in Devon that seems to suit his needs perfectly—until it turns out to be haunted. The grand-daughter of the former owner remains under the spell of the haunting, continually drawn back to the house and increasingly disturbed by its combative apparitions. The hero and his sister soon discover that the former lady of the house and an artist's model employed by her husband both died there, but it takes much longer to figure out the logic of the haunting (although alert readers are likely to be a long way ahead of the inept and inexperienced psychic detectives).

The success of *The Uninvited* was rather surprising, given that ghost stories had not previously been regarded as having best-selling potential, but the unashamedly excessive sentimentality of the story helped establish a cinematic tradition that was to be carried forward by such movies as *The Ghost and Mrs. Muir* (1947) and *Portrait of Jennie* (1949). It also helped to launch a number of partly imitative novels, including Philip Wylie's *Night Unto Night* (1944), whose attempts to add psychological depth to a similar plot are grotesquely uncomfortable.

The failure of Macardle's second supernatural romance to recapitulate the success of *The Uninvited* probably had much to do with the fact that its invocation of extrasensory perception was not nearly as effective a heightening-device as a full-blooded haunting. There is no significant element of horror in *The Unforeseen*, and hence no authentic unease. The author seems to have repented of this omission, and made what effort she could to remedy it in *Dark Enchantment*, but there is a curious awkwardness about the devices deployed there which prevent the story acquiring any substantial narrative drive.

Dark Enchantment is mostly told from the viewpoint of its female protagonist, a shy young Englishwoman whose life has been severely disrupted by her parents' divorce. She is forced by the threat of poverty to accept a menial job at a tiny guest-house in the mountain village of St. Jacques in the south of France. While being inexpertly courted by the only Englishman around—a research botanist—she becomes involved in a steadily escalating "war" between the people of the village and a gypsy woman named Turka, who is generally believed to be a witch.

In a sense, the most interesting aspect of *Dark Enchantment*—although it certainly does not work to the story's advantage—is the fact that the author clearly could not make up her mind where she stood on the question of Turka's guilt. The early chapters imply that what is to come will be a frank condemnation of the kinds of superstition which have preserved the habit of witch-hunting into the present day, but after a great deal of prevarication proof is eventually provided that the much-maligned Turka really is evil, although not materially aided by the devil (such supernatural power as she has is a telepathic power which even she does not fully understand). Perhaps Macardle favoured this conclusion because it imported a measure of healthy melodrama into the closing phases of a rather weak-kneed story, but she must have known that it amounted to a shabby betrayal of the high ideals with which the narrative set out. Even at the end she keeps on reminding her readers (and, presumably, herself) that Turka had been a heroine of the resistance, and had been ill-used by the man who is eventually driven to shoot her by her niggling harassment of the wife he married in her stead.

However successful the first of them was, Macardle's novels are trivial achievements by comparison with her massive history of *The Irish Republic*; even as entertainments written primarily for self-amusement they cannot stand comparison with the works of such dabblers as John Buchan (who was, of course, situated at the far end of the political spectrum). They are, however, the work of an intelligent and thoughtful writer who cannot entirely prevent her intelligence showing through and cannot entirely set aside the habit of thinking; the novels would be even less interesting had they reduced themselves entirely to formulaic exercises in genre. *The Uninvited* now seems to be a very dated book, and the movie made from it seems equally naive, but it was a landmark of sorts in its day. *Dark Enchantment* probably provides a better map of the psychology of unease than its untidily knotted plot intends.

—Brian Stableford

MACHEN, Arthur (Llewellyn)

Nationality: British. **Born:** Arthur Llewellyn Jones, in Caerleon-on-Usk, Wales, 3 March 1863; adopted his mother's maiden name, Machen, in childhood. **Education:** Hereford Cathedral School, 1874-80. **Family:** Married twice; one son and one daughter. **Career:** Writer from 1880; clerk for a publisher in London, 1883; actor with the Benson Shakespearian Repertory Company from 1901; toured with the company until 1909; regular contributor to the *Evening News*, London, from 1912. Granted Civil List pension, 1933. **Died:** 30 March 1947.

HORROR, GHOST AND GOTHIC PUBLICATIONS

Novels

The Hill of Dreams. London, Grant Richards, 1907; New York, Knopf, 1923.
The Terror: A Fantasy. London, Duckworth, 1917; New York, Norton, 1965.
The Secret Glory. London, Secker, and New York, Knopf, 1922.
The Green Round. London, Benn, 1933; Sauk City, Wisconsin, Arkham House, 1968.

Short Stories

The Great God Pan and The Inmost Light. London, John Lane, and Boston, Roberts, 1894.
The Three Impostors; or, The Transmutations. London, John Lane, and Boston, Roberts, 1895; as *Black Crusade*, London, Corgi, 1966.
The House of Souls. London, Grant Richards, 1906; New York, Knopf, 1922; in 2 vols. as *The Novel of the Black Seal and Other Stories* and *The Novel of the White Powder and Other Stories*, London, Corgi, 1965.
The Angel of Mons: The Bowmen and Other Legends of the War. London, Simpkin Marshall, and New York, Putnam, 1915.
The Great Return. London, Faith Press, 1915.
The Shining Pyramid. Chicago, Covici McGee, 1923; with differing contents, London, Secker, 1925.
Ornaments in Jade. New York, Knopf, 1924.
The Children of the Pool and Other Stories. London, Hutchinson, 1936; New York, Arno Press, 1976.
The Cosy Room and Other Stories. London, Rich and Cowan, 1936; New York, Arno Press, 1976.
Holy Terrors. London, Penguin, 1946.
Tales of Horror and the Supernatural, edited by Philip Van Doren Stern. New York, Knopf, 1948; London, Richards Press, 1949.
The Strange World of Arthur Machen. New York, Juniper Press, 1960.

OTHER PUBLICATIONS

Novel

The Chronicle of Clememdy. London, privately printed, 1888; New York, Knopf, 1926.

Poetry

Eleusinia. Hereford, Wales, Joseph Jones, 1881; West Warwick, Rhode Island, Necronomicon Press, 1988.

Other

The Anatomy of Tobacco; or, Smoking Methodised, Divided, and Considered After a New Fashion. London, Redway, 1884; New York, Knopf, 1926.

A Chapter from the Book Called The Ingenious Gentleman Don Quijote de la Mancha, Which by Some Mischance Has Not Till Now Been Printed. London, Redway, 1887.

Thesaurus Incantatus: The Enchanted Treasure; or, The Spagyric Quest of Beroaldus Cosmopolita. London, Marvell, 1888.

Hieroglyphics: A Note Upon Ecstasy in Literature. London, Grant Richards, 1902; New York, Mitchell Kennerley, 1913.

The House of the Hidden Light, with A. E. Waite. London, privately printed, 1904.

Dr. Stiggins: His Views and Principles. London, Griffiths, 1906; New York, Knopf, 1925.

"Parsifal": The Story of the Holy Grail. London, General Cinematograph Agencies, 1913(?).

War and the Christian Faith. London, Skeffington, 1918.

The Pantomime of the Year. London, privately printed, 1921.

Far Off Things (autobiography). London, Secker, and New York, Knopf, 1922.

The Grand Trouvaille: A Legend of Pentonville. London, First Edition Bookshop, 1923.

Things Near and Far (autobiography). London, Secker, and New York, Knopf, 1923.

Works (Caerleon Edition). London, Secker, 9 vols., 1923.

The Collector's Craft. London, First Edition Bookshop, 1924.

The London Adventure; or, The Art of Wandering (autobiography). London, Secker, 1924; New York, Knopf, 1925.

Strange Roads and With the Gods in Spring. London, Classic Press, 1924.

Dog and Duck. London, Cape, and New York, Knopf, 1924.

The Glorious Mystery, edited by Vincent Starrett. Chicago, Covici McGee, 1924.

Precious Balms. London, Spurr and Swift, 1924.

A Preface to "Casanova's Escape from the Leads." London, Casanova Society, 1925.

The Canning Wonder. London, Chatto and Windus, 1925; New York, Knopf, 1926.

Dreads and Drolls. London, Secker, 1926; New York, Knopf, 1927.

Notes & Queries. London, Spurr and Swift, 1926.

A Souvenir of Cadby Hall. London, Lyons, 1927.

Parish of Amersham. Amersham, Buckinghamshire, Mason, 1930.

Tom O'Bedlam and His Song. Westport, Connecticut, Apellicon Press, 1930.

Beneath the Barley: A Note on the Origins of "Eleusinia." London, privately printed, 1931; West Warwick, Rhode Island, Necronomicon Press, 1988.

In the 'Eighties. Amersham, Buckinghamshire, privately printed, 1931.

An Introduction to John Gawsworth's "Above the River." Amersham, Buckinghamshire, privately printed, 1931.

A Few Letters. Cleveland, Rowfant Club, 1932.

The Glitter of the Brook. Dalton, Georgia, Postprandial Press, 1932.

Autobiography (omnibus; includes *Far Off Things*, *Things Near and Far*). London, Richards Press, 1951.

Bridles and Spurs. Cleveland, Rowfant Club, 1951.

Guinevere and Lancelot and Others, edited by Cuyler W. Brooks, Jr., and Michael Shoemaker. Newport News, Virginia, Purple Mouth Press, 1987.

Selected Letters, edited by Mark Valentine and Roger Dobson. London, Thorsons, 1988.

Translator, *The Heptameron*, by Marguerite of Navarre. London, privately printed, 1886; New York, Dutton, 1905.

Translator, *Fantastic Tales or the Way to Attain*, by Beroalde de Verville. London, privately printed, 1890; New York, Boni and Liveright, 1923.

Translator, *The Memoirs of Jacques Casanova.* London, privately printed, 12 vols., 1894; New York, Knopf, 2 vols., 1929.

Translator, *Remarks Upon Hermodactylus*, by Lady Hester Lucy Stanhope. London, privately printed, 1933.

*

Bibliography: *A Bibliography of Arthur Machen* by Adrian Goldstone and Wesley Sweetser, Austin, University of Texas Press, 1965.

Critical Studies: *Arthur Machen: Weaver of Fantasy* by William Francis Gekle, Millbrook, New York, Round Table Press, 1949; *Arthur Machen: A Short Account of His Life and Works* by Aidan Reynolds and William Charlton, London, Richards Press, 1963; *Arthur Machen* by Wesley D. Sweetser, Boston, Twayne, 1964; *Arthur Machen: Apostle of Wonder* edited by Mark Valentine and Roger Dobson, Oxford, Caermaen, 1985; *Arthur Machen* by Mark Valentine, Bridgend, Mid-Glamorgan, Seren, 1995.

*   *   *

Arthur Machen was an extraordinarily prolific writer whose efforts ranged from journalism and translation to various esoteric fields, including academic occultism. His literary career was a thing of fits and starts, his books never bringing him sufficient income to save him from hackwork and other odd jobs (including, for a while, acting). He was one of the great eccentrics of English letters, and the uniquely vivid horror stories which he wrote in the "yellow nineties" became the definitive British works of their period, parallel to—but far more prolific than—the American works of Ambrose Bierce and Robert W. Chambers. As with many other writers of the period, however, Machen's work became steadily more pedestrian as the tide of literary fashionability turned decisively against stylistic flamboyance and outré

subject-matter. Although he never managed to adapt his work to the new regime his continuation of the lost tradition inevitably became ever more dispirited and anaemic.

The novella "The Great God Pan," originally published in 1890, became the archetypal Decadent horror story. A scientist operates on the brain of a young woman in order to deactivate the sensory and intellectual censors which prevent the human mind from confrontation with the ultimate reality, symbolized by Pan (the god of Nature, whose name can also be interpreted as "all-encompassing"). Nine months thereafter the woman gives birth to a child, and promptly dies—but the child is the offspring of Pan and she becomes a *femme fatale* before dissolving into filthy ooze. Although somewhat influenced by *The Strange Case of Dr. Jekyll and Mr. Hyde* the story is highly original, and after achieving a modest *succès de scandale* it was to prove highly influential. Ideas inherent in it are ancestral to the ideative underpinnings of much modern horror fiction, including those of the Lovecraftian school, as well as more optimistic exercises in speculative metaphysics like those developed by David Lindsay. "The Inmost Light" is a far less successful reprise involving the extraction of a soul and its embodiment in a gemstone.

Robert Louis Stevenson's influence on Machen is more blatantly displayed in *The Three Impostors*, a horrific variant of *The New Arabian Nights*. Its narrative frame is rather dull, but the whole is redeemed by two particularly spectacular inclusions. The "Novel of the Black Seal" substitutes fairies for Pan as hidden but still-active agents of a protean reality against which human form and intelligence need defences. The "Novel of the White Powder" repeats the theme yet again, this time featuring a drug which duplicates the transformative agent employed by witches in their Sabbats. Illustrations by Beardsley confirmed Machen's affiliation to the Decadent Movement—an affiliation which proved somewhat deleterious to his prospects after the Oscar Wilde trials. Although he was able to publish such neat horror stories as "Witchcraft" and "The Ceremony" (both 1897) in periodicals 11 years was to pass before he published another book of that kind, when Grant Richards reissued the contents of the two John Lane volumes along with some extra materials in the gaudily-decorated *The House of Souls*.

The version of Machen's mythos sketched out in the "Novel of the Black Seal" is much extended in the text-within-a-text that forms the bulk of "The White People" (originally published in 1899). This takes the form of a diary written by an adolescent girl who is gradually initiated into awareness and knowledge of the malign reality which underlies fairy lore. The frame story seems to be a makeshift device employed to pass off an aborted novel as a short story—perhaps because Machen had accepted by 1899 that the marketplace had been sealed tight against Decadent fiction—but the piece remains a rough-hewn masterpiece, plausibly nominated by Everett Bleiler as the finest supernatural story of all time. "The Red Hand" employs the same mythos to far less effect—as does "The Shining Pyramid," which was not included in *The House of Souls* although it had been written in the mid-1890s.

Like "A Fragment of Life" in *The House of Souls*, but in a far more robust and resolute manner, *The Hill of Dreams* transmutes Machen's own experiences into fantasy. The novel explains how a highly imaginative but unsuccessful Welsh writer employs occult wisdom to cultivate visionary experiences of a glorious Other World recalling the period of Roman occupation. When he moves from Caerleon to London, his visions undergo a parallel transformation, the quiet splendour of rural civilization giving way to an urban bacchanal of Decadence by which his fragile spirit is soon consumed. That glorious but dangerous Other World continually broke through the veil of imperception in Machen's later fiction, despite the fact that the horrific sublimity of "The Great God Pan" and "The White People" was markedly toned down, often serving the cause of moral rearmament rather than destruction.

Although Machen had experimented with a more positive approach to the Ultimate Reality as early as 1897, when he published "The Holy Things," it was "The Bowmen"—in which St. George brings a corps of phantom bowmen to cover the allied retreat at the Battle of Mons—that encouraged him further. The brief tale discovered an avid public need, whose force far outweighed the hostility that had greeted his early experiments in horror. Machen took the lesson to heart, beginning in "The Great Return" the development of a new dualism in which the panic quality of the ultimate reality was opposed by the ameliorating force of the Holy Grail. This optimistic metaphysical system was

more fully explored in *The Secret Glory*, and after the publication of that novel Machen never wrote another wholehearted horror story; his one concerted attempt to do so, in *The Green Round*, proved disastrously anodyne.

Machen's experience as a journalist had a dramatic calming effect on his prose style, whose new modesty was exhibited in his short novel *The Terror*. This story features a revolt of Nature so inept and so ridiculous that it is hardly surprising that the Great God Pan would have nothing to do with it. Machen's new fairy mythos was not entirely set aside during the war years but "Out of the Earth"—in which the slaughter in the trenches is cause for celebration among the little people—is a distinctly half-hearted work. The little people were to inflict similarly malicious visitations upon others, most notably upon the luckless heroes of "The Children of the Pool" and *The Green Round*, but they never did so with any real flair or élan, always remaining mere shadows of their magnificently malign counterparts in "The White People." By the time he wrote "Opening the Door," one of the more recent stories reprinted in *The Cosy Room*, Machen's fairies were little different from anyone else's; the only late story in the book of any real interest, "N," develops a very different account of ultimate reality based in the occult metaphysics of Jacob Boehme.

Had Machen suffered the fate of his alter ego in *The Hill of Dreams* the world would have lamented the loss of the work he had not time to produce. Alas, although he had the time, he still did not produce it; he slowly faded away into ignominious inconsequentiality. In the ten years between 1890 and 1899, however, he changed the face of British supernatural fiction, blasting away both the genteel narrative conventions and the ideological foundations of the Victorian ghost story. He was the first British writer of authentically modern horror stories, and his best works must still be reckoned among the finest products of the genre.

—Brian Stableford

MAGINN, Simon

Nationality: British. **Born:** Wallasey, Merseyside, 1961. **Education:** University of Sussex. **Address:** c/o Corgi Books, Transworld Publishers, 61-63 Uxbridge Rd., London W5 5SA, England. Lives in Hove, East Sussex.

HORROR, GHOST AND GOTHIC PUBLICATIONS

Novels

Sheep. London, Corgi, 1994; Atlanta, Georgia, White Wolf, 1996.
Virgins and Martyrs. London, Corgi, 1995; Atlanta, Georgia, White Wolf, 1996.
A Sickness of the Soul. London, Corgi, 1995.
Methods of Confinement. London, Black Swan, 1996.

*   *   *

Simon Maginn is a very subtle writer, always original and unsettling in his subject matter and treatment. He is the most talented of the younger British horror writers, and he has the potential to become the best of them all. Already his work may be compared to the recent novels of Ramsey Campbell and to the early writings of Ian McEwan. Maginn's trademark is bleakness; he deals realistically with disturbed or disintegrating characters at the edge of madness, for whom there will be no happy ending.

Sheep is a startlingly assured debut novel. It begins with horror clichés—a young couple with a son who has visions move from London to an old haunted farmhouse in Wales—but these are soon left behind as the characters and literary qualities develop. James is a builder, a taciturn man who is persuaded to renovate the farmhouse for a rich relative; his wife Adèle is a successful painter; their seven-year-old son shows signs of knowing too much, of sensing things about the farmhouse before they arrive. The relationships and tensions between them are very believable. All around the farmhouse are flocks of grazing sheep. Adèle begins to introduce them into her paintings as she gradually succumbs to a breakdown. They have a strange, rather sinister neighbour, Lewyn, who is haunted by sheep and who knows about the farmhouse's terrible history. Maginn makes clever use of the sheep as a plot device and in various metaphorical and allegorical ways.

Virgins and Martyrs is one of the most magnificently bleak horror novels ever written. Its slight touches of wit and humour only serve to reinforce the mood of hopelessness rather than relieving it. Nor is there much action to the plot. Daniel, a post-graduate student, is writing a dissertation on medieval history and is living on the top floor of a shared house near Brighton, owned by a mysterious skinhead. Daniel's room was formerly occupied by an anorexic young woman whose spirit is affecting him, helping him to starve himself. The story is about Daniel's gradual disintegration, though it also entails his discovery of what happened to Wendy, his predecessor, and much astonishingly unpleasant detail about the putrefaction of corpses and the behaviour of medieval martyrs.

It is a testament to Maginn's qualities as a writer that he makes such a static and unpromising subject into a surprising and entertaining novel. Daniel's thought processes are always fascinating, and a plethora of small, telling details make the whole thing wonderfully plausible. There are occasional scenes featuring a police inspector who is searching for the owner of an arm washed up on Brighton's beach, and there is a marvellous *grand guignol* finale on Brighton Pier.

After the relative conventionality of the first two novels, *A Sickness of the Soul* is disconcerting to read and, at first sight, deceptively lightweight. The story it tells is of an investigative journalist called Robert who wants to write an exposé of the Sons of the New Bethlehem, a group of bikers whose enormously charismatic leader, Teacher, is apparently healing people's behavioural problems in person and via a phone-in radio show. Although Robert approaches them as an ordinary seeker after help, he is incarcerated by some of the bikers and held incommunicado for weeks at an isolated motel in the English Midlands. The biker characters are at once too believable and too exaggeratedly gross to be funny. Eventually, without having a satisfactory talk with Teacher, Robert escapes. But after his pregnant partner Fiona leaves him, he goes back to get his story, is recaptured and is hideously maimed in an attempt by the Sons to solve his problem. This is set in contemporary England.

More fascinating and upsetting is the manner in which the story is told, for Robert is narrating and everything is subjective. The intimidation and degradation he suffers during his periods of im-

prisonment have an effect upon his mind, bringing on a near-nervous breakdown and perhaps leading to delusions. Or perhaps Robert really does experience (and has always experienced) occasional cryptic premonitions of death and injury. He seems to see a screwdriver before one of his captors, Len, who is helping Robert to escape, hammers a screwdriver into his own ear and then hangs himself, and a syringe before another takes a deliberate overdose. After his escape, Robert has become alienated from Fiona; he has changed and their rapport has gone; she believes that he is dangerous to live with. And after the Sons have drilled into Robert's brain to stop him seeing premonitory symbols, he is actually a happier person. This is what is so disconcerting: it is never clear who is right and who is wrong. Perhaps Robert, who begins the book as a reluctant hero, has been deluding himself throughout, and his sickness of soul has been cured by Teacher and the Sons.

While *Methods of Confinement* tells a very different story, it deals largely with an admitted lunatic—no doubts here. Declan is a personable young Irishman with a personality disorder who manages to attach himself to a young married couple, Luke and Anna. The way in which Declan can be both charming and uncomfortable to be with is brilliantly portrayed. The facts are that Declan gradually makes more of a nuisance of himself (mostly due to his need for more medication). The couple drop him and then, feeling guilty, try to help him again. He has sex with Anna (who is more sympathetic to him) and stabs Luke to death.

But, once again, Maginn's novel is much deeper and more subtle than the bald facts of the plot might suggest. He is showing how badly the mentally unstable are treated in Britain today, making the point that Declan had been far happier in an institution and that he feels more confined out in the community. And the book makes it clear that Declan may be unstable but is not without intelligence and talents. He is a fine mimic and actor and has clearly been watching Luke and learning to imitate him. Except that Luke's behaviour gradually becomes more unreliable; he drinks too much, smokes dope, takes unnecessary time off work and is obsessed with a fantasy world he is writing about. (So, as Declan becomes more like Luke, and Luke grows more unstable, who is the madman?) Even if some scenes are intended as black comedy, they are too plausible to be regarded as humour; black satire is closer to the truth. The clever title also refers to Anna's desperate wish to have a child; she is infertile and IVF treatments have been unsuccessful. At the end, after Declan has murdered Luke, Anna destroys the evidence and, calling Declan her brother, controls him as one would a child.

Maginn is not a flashy writer of commercial horror like Clive Barker, but his work is full of exquisite qualities and deserves rereading for its layers of meaning. He may come to be regarded as one of the best in the field.

—Chris Morgan

MARSH, Richard

Pseudonym for Richard Bernard Heldmann. **Nationality:** British. **Born:** 1867. **Education:** Eton School; Oxford University. **Career:** Contributor to boys' magazines from the age of 12; later a professional novelist. **Died:** 9 August 1915.

HORROR, GHOST AND GOTHIC PUBLICATIONS

Novels

The Beetle: A Mystery. London, Skeffington, 1897; New York(?),
Mansfield, 1898; as *The Mystery of the Beetle; or, The House
With the Open Window*, Cleveland, Ohio, Westlake, 1912.
Tom Ossington's Ghost. London, Bowden, 1898.

Short Stories

Marvels and Mysteries. London, Methuen, 1900.
The Seen and the Unseen. London, Methuen, 1900.
Both Sides of the Veil. London, Methuen, 1902.

OTHER PUBLICATIONS

Novels

The Devil's Diamond. London, Henry, 1893; as *The Ape and the Dia-
mond; or, A Brother's Legacy*, New York, Street and Smith, 1928.
The Mahatma's Pupil. London, Henry, 1893.
Mrs. Musgrave—and Her Husband. London(?), Pioneer, 1894;
New York, Appleton, 1895.
The Strange Wooing of Mary Bowler. London, Pearson, 1895; as
A Strange Wooing, New York, Street and Smith, 1929.
The Crime and the Criminal. London, Ward, 1897.
The Mystery of Philip Bennion's Death. London, Ward, 1897.
The Datchett Diamonds. London, Ward, 1898.
The House of Mystery. London, White, 1898.
In Full Cry. London, White, 1899; New York, Street and Smith,
1928.
Ada Vernham, Actress. London, Long, and New York, Page, 1900.
The Chase of the Ruby. London, Skeffington, 1900.
The Goddess: A Demon. London, White, 1900.
A Hero of Romance. London, Ward, 1900.
A Second Coming. London, Bodley Head, 1900.
The Joss: A Reversion. London, White, 1901.
Between the Dark and the Daylight. London, Long, 1902.
The Twickenham Peerage. London, Methuen, 1902; as *A Case of
Identity*, New York, Street and Smith, n.d.
The Death Whistle. London, Treherne, 1903; as *The Whistle of
Fate*, New York, Street and Smith, 1906.
The Magnetic Girl. N.p., 1903.
A Metamorphosis. London, Methuen, 1903.
A Duel. London, Methuen, 1904; as *Cuthbert Grahame's Will*, Lon-
don, Pearson, 1930.
Miss Arnott's Marriage. London, Long, 1904.
The Marquis of Putney. London, Methuen, 1905.
The Garden of Mystery. London, Long, 1906.
In the Service of Love. London, Methuen, 1906.
The Girl and the Miracle. London, Methuen, 1907.
The Romance of a Maid of Honour. London, Long, 1907.
The Coward Behind the Curtain. London, Methuen, 1908.
The Surprising Husband. London, Methuen, 1908.
The Interrupted Kiss. London, Cassell, 1909.
A Royal Indiscretion. London, Methuen, 1909.
Live Men's Shoes. London, Methuen, 1910.
The Lovely Mrs. Blake. London, Cassell, 1910.
A Spoiler of Men. London, Chatto and Windus, 1911.

Twin Sisters. London, Cassell, 1911.
Violet Forster's Love. London, Cassell, 1912.
Justice—Suspended. London, Chatto and Windus, 1913.
A Master of Deception. London, Cassell, 1913.
Margot—and Her Judges. London, Chatto and Windus, 1914.
Molly's Husband. London, Cassell, 1914.
The Woman in the Car. London, Unwin, 1914.
The Flying Girl. London, Ward, 1915.
His Love or His Life. London, Chatto and Windus, 1915.
Love in Fetters. London, Cassell, 1915.
A Man with Nine Lives. London, Ward, 1915.
Coming of Age. London, Long, 1916.
The Great Temptation. London, Unwin, and New York, New York,
Brentano's, 1916.
The Deacon's Daughter. London, Long, 1917.
On the Jury. London, Methuen, 1918.
Outwitted. London, Long, 1919.
Apron-Strings. London, Long, 1920.

Short Stories

Curios: Some Strange Adventures of Two Bachelors. London,
Long, 1898.
Frivolities. London, Bowden, 1899; as *The Purse Which Was
Found and Other Stories*, London, Pearson, 1918.
The Woman With One Hand, and Mr. Ely's Engagement. London,
Bowden, 1899.
An Aristocratic Detective. London, Bell, 1900.
Amusement Only. London, Hurst, 1901.
The Adventures of Augustus Short. London, Treherne, 1902.
Garnered. London, Methuen, 1904.
The Girl in the Blue Dress. London, Long, 1909.
The Drama of the Telephone and Other Tales. London, Long,
1911.
Judith Lee: Some Pages from Her Life. London, Methuen, 1912.
If It Please You. London, Methuen, 1913.
The Adventures of Judith Lee. London, Methuen, 1916.

*   *   *

If, as is widely rumoured, Richard Marsh wrote *The Beetle* as a
result of a bet with Bram Stoker—who allegedly produced
Dracula for his part—he was evidently cheated. We now know
that Stoker had been at work on *Dracula* for some years before
any such bet could have been struck, and must therefore have got
off to a flying start when the deadline was decided. On the other
hand, Marsh probably had the last laugh, for his slapdash melodrama followed its rival into the bestseller lists and must have
delivered a far grater reward relative to the time devoted to its
composition. Like most of Marsh's novels it gives the impression
of having been written in a tearing hurry, and the fact that it never
comes remotely close to making sense strongly implies that its
bizarre plot was made up as the author went along. Oddly enough,
Marsh made no real attempt to follow it up with other work of
the same kind; although he continued to reel off romances and
crime stories in great abundance very few of them involve any
unrationalized supernatural phenomena and none attains anything
like the glorious absurdity of *The Beetle.*

The eponymous villain of *The Beetle* belongs to an obscure religious sect given to offering human sacrifices to Isis, whose members are rewarded by magical powers. Whether the person in ques-

tion is ever actually transformed into a giant beetle or not remains stubbornly unclear, but the menacing apparition provides the key moments in an otherwise undistinguished plot. The diplomat Paul Lessingham, who once had a run-in with the Beetle in Egypt, enlists the aid of a research chemist specializing in poison gases when his fianceé is kidnapped, but the technology which finally—and somewhat arbitrarily—puts paid to the monster is a steam locomotive. The runaway success of the novel must have surprised everyone, and it is conceivable that such evident imitations as Guy Boothby's *Pharos, the Egyptian* were deliberately designed to make no sense whatsoever in the hope of capturing some of its perverse and elusive magic.

The most wholeheartedly supernatural of Marsh's subsequent melodramas, *Tom Ossington's Ghost*, is unfortunately mediocre. The author's off-hand attempt to recomplicate a standardized Victorian ghost story betrays his inability to take such motifs seriously; the ghost is very active but hardly raises a flicker of fear before benignly pointing the way to a concealed fortune. *The House of Mystery* features a neo-Gothic villain in Mr. Lazarus but he has none of the weird charm of the Beetle and the novel is a thriller rather than a horror story. *The Goddess: A Demon* is nothing of the sort; it is actually a puppet which plays a key role in an implausible murder mystery but fails woefully to convince the reader that it is as sinister as the author and his characters allege. *The Strange Wooing of Mary Bowler* involves somnambulism, but the story remains a stubbornly dull romance. Marsh evidently felt that the appropriate literary medium for the use of fantastic motifs was slapstick comedy of the kind popularized by F. Anstey; he wrote three such works of no particular distinction, of which the most bizarrely extravagant is *The Devil's Diamond*.

Marsh's short stories usually avoid the pitfalls of his inability to produce a sensibly structured plot, but they still suffer from the half-heartedness which overtook him every time he tried to suspend his disbelief in the supernatural. The only supernatural story in *Curios*, "The Adventure of Lady Wishaw's Hand," is interesting as an early example of the motif deployed to far better effect in W. F. Harvey's "The Beast with Five Fingers." The best of the tales in *The Seen and the Unseen* is "The Violin," in which the eponymous musical instrument reveals the secret of its former owner's demise, but "A Psychological Experiment" is more convincing by virtue of its ambiguity. *Both Sides of the Veil* is a better collection, including several items which possess a dash of originality, but most of its supernatural stores are ironic fantasies; the best of them is "A Knight of the Road," which has a horrific element by virtue of the Devil's presence, but a "A Set of Chessmen" is a neater weird tale. The only weird tale in *If It Please You* is the novella "The Touchstone of Fortune," a rather unconvincing but not uninteresting mystery involving a modest version of the philosopher's stone.

The commercial success of *The Beetle* still remains the most mysterious thing about the novel; it evidently touched some chord in the late Victorian audience akin to that touched by the many near-contemporary romances of revivified mummies and that resonantly struck by *Dracula*. Perhaps it was simply the nearest thing to hand when readers who had loved *Dracula* went looking for something similar, but, for whatever reason it did become a significant item in the history of weird fiction, helping to initiate a brief vogue which secured publication for several other (and mostly better) works.

—Brian Stableford

MARTIN, David (Lozell)

Nationality: American. **Born:** Granite City, Illinois, 13 March 1946. **Education:** University of Illinois, B.Sc. 1969. **Military Service:** Served in the U.S. Air Force, 1969. **Family:** Married 1) Gretchen Bayon, 1968 (divorced 1987), two sons; 2) Arabel Allfrey, 1988. **Career:** Managing editor, *American School Board Journal*, Evanston, Illinois, 1971-76; managing editor, *Learning*, Palo Alto, California, 1976-78; editor and assistant publisher, *American School Board Journal* and *Executive Educator*, Washington D.C., 1978-82; vice-president, Association of Governing Boards of Universities and Colleges, Washington, D.C., beginning 1984; currently writing and farming full-time. **Agent:** Robert Datilla, Phoenix Literary Agency, 315 South F. St., Livingston, Montana 59047. **Address:** Blue Goose Farm, H.C. 73, Box 9, Alderson, West Virginia, 24910, USA.

HORROR, GHOST AND GOTHIC PUBLICATIONS

Novels

Tethered. New York, Holt, Rinehart and Winston, 1979.
The Crying Heart Tattoo. New York, Holt, Rinehart and Winston, 1982.
Final Harbor. New York, Holt, Rinehart and Winston, 1984.
The Beginning of Sorrows. New York, Weidenfeld and Nicolson, 1987.
Lie to Me. New York, Random House, 1990; London, Headline, 1991.
Bring Me Children. New York, Random House, and London, Headline, 1992.
Love Me to Death. New York, Random House, 1993; London, Headline, 1994; as *Tap, Tap*, New York, Random House, 1994.
Cul-de-sac. New York, Villard, 1997.

*   *   *

David Martin's novels are unsettling explorations into the minds of ontologically insecure individuals. While all of Martin's work is energetic, frightening and partly dependent on lashings of the neo-gothic bizarre, his strongest novels (the most convincing and most chilling) are, interestingly, those with the word "Me" in the title: to date, *Lie to Me*, *Bring Me Children* and *Love Me to Death*. With these titles and their direct imperatives (and, paradoxically, the imagined notes of pleading) there is the notion that one will confront a selfish, brattish personality before too long: someone who will demand of the other characters (and quite possibly, of the reader too) his own way. Before the books have even been opened, implicit in the titles is the idea that we are about to enter new and confusing personalities.

Love Me to Death has a serial killer who is also an adroit vocal impersonator with a fondness for traditional rock'n'roll and for an ugly ventriloquist's dummy called Dondo (in which the spirit of his dead brother might or might not live on). This killer believes himself to be a vampire; certainly the blood-sucking of his victims is one of his preoccupations. At first it seems that all the killer, Peter Tummerlier, wants is to take his revenge on the rich couple whom Peter believes drove a friend's charter-company-owning father to suicide years earlier. Martin depicts an unpleasant Philip Burton without resorting to hyperbole—to shade the character to just such an extent that Peter's murder of him seems motivated solely by righteousness. But the killing does not stop here. One terrifying scene is the next, in which Peter climbs into bed with Burton's wife and initiates foreplay in the dark while her back is to him. The vignette teeter-totters between a hope that she will acknowledge the differences between the intruder's ministrations and her husband's, and a fear for her safety when she does. What finally gives the game away is when Diane reciprocates the attention.

Lie to Me opens in the first person with a voyeur spying on a family house whilst holding a dead hitchhiker's severed hand and being eaten alive by forest bugs. This spy's initial namelessness adds to his eeriness and to the reader's misunderstanding. From the first page we are trying to pick up clues. The long opening chapter provides the reader with the full intimidation of the viewpoint character's madness and neuroses; it also highlights his optimism, forgetfulness and determination to "get what is his." Although it is a shocking opening chapter, Martin's skill is in not showing everything too quickly. The reader knows that he is carrying around a hand and that he has staked out the house; but does not know how he obtained the hand, nor precisely whose hand it is. *Lie to Me* is a horror novel built on insecurity rather than on the splashes of grue and gore that appear intermittently.

The novel's blurb mentions Thomas Harris's *The Silence of the Lambs*, but at best this is a strained comparison. Where Hannibal Lecter was vicious and clever, *Lie to Me*'s Philip is only trying to claim back one hundred dollars for every week of every year since his father abandoned him and his sister. The killer in *Lie to Me* is not a blood-crazed intellectual like Dr. Lecter, nor a psychopathic smartarse like the movies' Freddy Krueger. Philip, half the time, is simply stumbling around, constantly self-pitying. He cannot see why everything he does turns bad.

Not that Martin's killers are the only characters to receive in-depth authorial psychoanalysis. Martin touches on and off the concept of what might be called victimology. Tied-up and frightened by *Love Me to Death*'s protagonist, a character called Lois experiences one law of victimology: her thoughts reach beyond brutality-anticipation to a time when she will be able to tell the other members of the victim-support group that she already attends how bad this new experience was; up to now she has always felt her previous trauma paltry compared with the problems of the other women in attendance. ("Can you be a victim of not being sufficiently victimized? Is that a category Lois could pioneer?") Elsewhere, the condition of vampirism is given a fresh explanation, the upshot of which is that it may as well exist for the people who find themselves the victims of killers who believe they are vampires.

David Martin uses several techniques to create his atmosphere. In *Lie to Me*, for example, the chapters alternate between the present tense and a past-tense first-person narrative. The former is mainly told from Philip's point of view and represents the reader's step closer to the evil forces; we breathe the same air as the killer, and the latter is told from the point of view of Teddy Camel, a burnt-out cop in his fifties, pushing bits of paper around until such time as he can retire with full benefits. Camel, oddly enough, is also a victim—the chronic drinking problem being one symptom of the condition—but Martin makes an engaging, endearing, even intellectually involving, character out of what at first seem like fairly ordinary cop cliches. Years earlier Camel's family broke up and now he drinks to stop himself thinking about how

things might have been different. Camel also has the unusual talent (or curse) of telling when somebody—anybody—is lying to him: not *suspecting* that someone is lying to him, but *knowing* it beyond a shadow of a doubt. Furthermore, Camel's wilful suspension of memory (by over-drinking) is a neat effect in that we do not need to believe that what he tells us is the complete truth. A full-length narrative where the first-person character is lying throughout might be difficult to maintain; but a novel where the character cannot remember everything? Possibly.

By alternating chapter styles, there is the impression from the beginning that somehow Camel and Philip are linked, and even a suspicion that the policeman might have been involved in the sex murders—a guess given added weight by Camel's disgust at his daughter's sexuality and by his wife's desertion. What is more, the switches of patterns, registers and tones in David Martin's novels are themselves reminiscent of mental insecurity; his books are themselves schizophrenic creatures, possibly mental asylum patients.

Lie to Me has the feel of Roman Polanski's movie *Chinatown*, or Alan Parker's *Angel Heart*. Indeed, the film comparison is important. As with his other novels, *Lie to Me* works on one level by the sheer briskness of its prose. There is not a stodgy sentence or a wasted word in its 400 pages. It is an extremely visual book. The images come and go quickly, building in the reader's mind a collage of snapshots that run together like a slightly jerky film. There is also the strong influence of the gothic on Martin's work. As well as paranoia and the reasonable rationalizing of evil forces (both gothic traits), there are often scenes of the persecution of women in isolated locales and sex is sometimes seen as a corrupting force. As inescapable as the castle on the hill is Martin's sense of a past that is always reaching out to claim those who believe they have lived through it. Martin's line in gothic grisliness is also fine: one particularly striking image is that of the naked boy perched on a toilet seat with a decomposing severed hand clutching his penis. In the novels of David Martin, children (but adults too) have their innocences shattered, and memories filter in to affect their lives with the force of inescapable dreams.

—David Mathew

MARTIN, George R(aymond) R(ichard)

Nationality: American. **Born:** Bayonne, New Jersey, 20 September 1948. **Education:** Medill School of Journalism, Northwestern University, Evanston, Illinois, B.S. (summa cum laude) 1970, M.S. 1971. **Military Service:** Conscientious objector; did alternative service with VISTA, 1972-74. **Family:** Married Gale Burnick in 1975 (divorced 1979). **Career:** Served with the Cook County Legal Assistance Foundation, for Vista, Chicago, 1972-74. Chess tournament director, Continental Chess Association, Mount Vernon, New York, 1973-75; journalism instructor, Clarke College, Dubuque, Iowa, 1976-79. Since 1979, freelance writer. **Awards:** Hugo award, 1975, 1980 (2 awards); Bread Loaf Writers Conference Fellowship, 1977; Nebula award, 1979, 1985; *Locus* award, 1981, 1982 (twice), 1984; Bram Stoker award, 1987; World Fantasy award, 1988. **Member:** Science Fiction Writers of America; Writers' Guild of America, West. **Agent:** Pimlico Literary Agency, 155 East 77th Street, Suite 1A, New York, NY 10021, USA. **Address:** 102 San Salvador, Santa Fe, NM 87501, USA.

HORROR, GHOST AND GOTHIC PUBLICATIONS

Novels

Fevre Dream. New York, Poseidon Press, 1982; London, Gollancz, 1983.
The Armageddon Rag. New York, Poseidon Press, 1983; London, New English Library, 1984.

Short Stories

Portraits of His Children. Arlington Heights, Illinois, Dark Harvest, 1987.

OTHER PUBLICATIONS

Novels

Dying of the Light. New York, Simon and Schuster, 1977; London, Gollancz, 1978.
Windhaven, with Lisa Tuttle. New York, Timescape, 1981; London, New English Library, 1982.
A Game of Thrones. London, Voyager, and New York, Bantam, 1996.

Short Stories

A Song for Lya and Other Stories. New York, Avon, 1976; London, Coronet, 1978.
Songs of Stars and Shadows. New York, Pocket Books, 1977.
The Sandkings. New York, Timescape, 1981; London, Futura, 1983.
Songs the Dead Men Sing. Niles, Illinois, Dark Harvest, 1983; London, Gollancz, 1985.
Nightflyers. New York, Bluejay, 1985.
Tuf Voyaging. New York, Baen, 1986; London, Gollancz, 1987.
The Pear-Shaped Man. Eugene, Oregon, Pulphouse, 1991.

Plays

Television Plays: 5 episodes in the *Twilight Zone* series, 1986; 13 episodes in the *Beauty and the Beast* series, 1987-90.

Other

Sandkings, with Pat Broderick, Neal McPheeters, and Doug Moench (graphic novel adapted from author's story of the same name). New York, DC Graphics, 1987.

Editor, *New Voices in Science Fiction: Stories by Campbell Award Nominees.* New York, Macmillan, 1977; as *New Voices I[-IV]: Spellbinding Original Stories by the Next Generation of Science Fiction Greats: The Campbell Award Nominees,* New York, Harcourt Brace, 2 vols., 1978-79; New York, Berkley, 2 vols., 1980-81.
Editor, with Isaac Asimov and Martin H. Greenberg, *The Science Fiction Weight-Loss Book.* New York, Crown, 1983.
Editor, *The John W. Campbell Awards, Volume 5.* New York, Bluejay, 1984.
Editor, with Paul Mikol, *Night Visions 3.* Niles, Illinois, Dark Harvest, 1986; as *Night Visions: All Original Stories,* London, Century, 1987; as *Night Visions: The Hellbound Heart,* New York, Berkley, 1988.

Editor, *Wild Cards: A Mosaic Novel.* New York, Bantam, 1986; London, Titan, 1988-91.
Editor, *Aces High.* New York, Bantam, 1987; London, Titan, 1988.
Editor, *Jokers Wild: A Wild Cards Mosaic Novel.* New York, Bantam, 1987; London, Titan, 1988.
Editor, *Aces Abroad: A Wild Cards Mosaic Novel.* New York, Bantam, 1988; London, Titan, 1989.
Editor, *Down and Dirty: A Wild Cards Mosaic Novel.* New York, Bantam, 1988; London, Titan, 1989.
Editor, with Melinda M. Snodgrass, *Ace in the Hole: A Wild Cards Mosaic Novel.* New York, Bantam, 1990; London, Titan, 1991.
Editor, with Melinda M. Snodgrass, *Dead Man's Hand: A Wild Card Novel,* by John J. Miller. New York, Bantam, 1990; London, Titan, 1991.
Editor, with Melinda M. Snodgrass, *One-Eyed Jacks: A Wild Cards Mosaic Novel.* New York, Bantam, 1991.
Editor, with Melinda M. Snodgrass, *Jokertown Shuffle: A Wild Cards Mosaic Novel.* New York, Bantam, 1991.
Editor, with Melinda M. Snodgrass, *Double Solitaire: A Wild Cards Mosaic Novel.* New York, Bantam, 1992.
Editor, with Melinda M. Snodgrass, *Dealer's Choice: A Wild Cards Mosaic Novel.* New York, Bantam, 1992.
Editor, with Melinda M. Snodgrass, *Card Sharks: A Wild Cards Mosaic Novel.* Riverdale, New York, Baen, 1993.
Editor, with Melinda M. Snodgrass, *Marked Cards: A Wild Cards Mosaic Novel.* Riverdale, New York, Baen, 1994.

*   *   *

George R. R. Martin has had a sufficient number of writing careers to satisfy an entire room full of authors. He has produced award-winning science fiction, edited the popular *Wild Cards* shared-universe anthology series, authored screenplays, and most recently produced the first volume of an impressive new fantasy series. Martin has also written horror fiction, and in fact *The Armageddon Rag* is both Martin's best single work and one of the most interesting and insightful examinations of what happened to the optimism and enthusiasm of the generation that attended college in the late 1960s.

The protagonist of *The Armageddon Rag* is Sandy Blair, a semi-successful novelist who once co-founded a counter culture magazine that later fired him. Suddenly his life is turned on end when his ex-partner calls and talks him into doing an article about the murder of a well-hated rock music promoter. Blair stops work on his latest novel despite complaints from his agent and the woman he lives with in order to travel to a remote town in Maine. There he discovers that the murdered man was killed in a bizarre ritual involving the music of a legendary rock group, the Nazgul, who broke up when their lead singer was assassinated during an open air concert.

Blair becomes obsessed with the case, tracing connections to Edan Morse, a wealthy man who allegedly was the secret identity of an ultra-violent revolutionary during the 1970s. Morse is also interested in reuniting the Nazgul. With the promoter dead, there is no legal barrier, and a disastrous case of arson helps force the three surviving members back together. Then Morse reveals his surprise, a young man who is a literal double for the dead singer, although his musical talents are significantly less impressive. Blair has reservations. The times have changed, the surviving musicians have lost their edge, and the impersonator lacks the charisma of the man he is replacing. Even worse, he suspects that

Edan Morse is responsible for murder and arson, and knows that the man believes the reunion will bring to life an occult force that will restore the rebellious passions of his youth.

Martin carries this all off brilliantly. Through Blair's reactions, we grow to understand the evolution of the counterculture. The novel is filled with fascinating characters, nostalgic recollections of forgotten innocence, and even a sense of outrage that the world remains so unchanged despite all the effort that was expended to change it. It's also a powerful story of supernatural suspense, all the more so because most of the violence takes place offstage, with some great plot twists in the last few chapters. Martin uses anticipation to keep the reader on edge throughout the entire novel.

Martin was also one of the first to rationalize the vampire legend, in a novel set on the Mississippi River in the 19th century. In *Fevre Dream* vampires are not supernatural. They have remarkable recuperative powers and cannot remain long in the daylight, but they have no fear of garlic, holy water, crosses and mirrors, and they cannot change shape or convert their victims into others of their kind. Vampires are in fact another race that evolved on earth, natural predators with a low birth-rate and no culture of their own, only what they have stolen from humans, whom they consider cattle.

Joshua York is a different breed. He has developed a blend of blood and wine which satisfies the bloodlust of his kind and allows them to survive without killing human prey. He is also a bloodmaster, whose will is strong enough to influence others to follow his way rather than indulging their natural instincts. Through the use of both, he hopes to eventually forge a peace between the two species. To establish a mobile base of operations, he buys half interest in a new riverboat and moves aboard with those followers he has drawn to his side.

But Damian Julian is a rival bloodmaster with other ideas. He has no intention of giving up the old ways, uses his mesmeric power to compel his followers not just to kill, but to engage in cruel and unnecessary atrocities. When York invites him to the Mississippi steamship, *Fevre Dream*, the ensuing battle of wills nearly destroys them both, and brings disaster to the humans caught in the battle. Martin creates a wonderfully realistic world, and the battle between York and Julian, seen primarily through the eyes of a riverboat captain named Abner Marsh, is masterfully done. This is without question one of the greatest vampire novels of all time.

Martin's other horror fiction is all at shorter length, and even his science fiction occasionally nods in that direction. A legendary beast is hunted across a mist-covered planet in "With Morning Comes Mistfall," and tiny, insectlike creatures escape their imprisonment in "The Sandkings." In "Meat Man" dead human bodies are revivified as remotely controlled tools, a bizarre sort of rationalized zombie story. Other tales are more specifically horror. "Remembering Melody" is a smooth, understated ghost story that leads the reader toward one conclusion, then provides a shocking twist ending. "The Monkey Treatment" involves an obese man who is saddled with an invisible monkey that lives on his back and eats all the food within reach before he can get it to his mouth. "The Skin Trade," a short novel, is one of the rare successful werewolf stories. The best of Martin's supernatural fiction, including the excellent title story, were collected as *Portraits of His Children*.

Although not specifically a horror writer, Martin's reputation in the field has been firmly established by *The Armageddon Rag*, which attracted favourable attention from non-genre critics as well,

and *Fevre Dream*, both of which have become benchmarks against which newer works are compared. His versatility and gift for strongly delineated characters and fascinating plots are strong assets he brings to every genre in which he works.

—Don D'Ammassa

MASSIE, Elizabeth

Nationality: American. **Born:** Waynesboro, Virginia, 6 September 1953. **Career:** Contributor of short stories to various magazines and anthologies from 1984. **Awards:** Horror Writers of America Bram Stoker award for short story, 1991, and for novel, 1993. Lives in Virginia.

HORROR, GHOST AND GOTHIC PUBLICATIONS

Novels

Sineater. London, Pan, 1992; New York, Carroll and Graf, 1994.
American Chills: Ghost Harbor (for children). N.p., nd.

Short Stories

Stephen. Leesburg, Virginia, TAL Publications, 1992.
The Selected Works of Elizabeth Massie: Southern Discomfort. Concord, California, Dark Regions Press, 1993.
Shadow Dreams. Seattle, Washington, Silver Salamander Press, 1996.

*   *   *

Elizabeth Massie's work places itself at the far end of the horror spectrum from such classic writers as H. P. Lovecraft or M. R. James. Her fiction is never cosmic and seldom ghostly. It does not expand outward from life, but closes in, smothering its characters in very restrictive, horrible situations, so that they all seem, like the prisoner in "Shadow of the Valley," buried alive in a lightless, inescapable cell. Supernatural or fantastic content rarely occurs, and is even more rarely used to good effect. Massie's true talents are those of a realist, who deliberately reaches for the most extreme (albeit not literally impossible) situations in which to entrap her protagonists.

Most impressive is the novel *Sineater*, which, after a somewhat sluggish start, is a grimly effective look at the dark side of primitive Christianity in rural America. The "sineater" of the title is a man whose function is to eat symbolic food laid out on a corpse, thus taking away the deceased's sins and allowing the departed soul to enter into Heaven. But since he is filled with other people's sins, the sin-eater, a human scapegoat, is shunned by all. To look on his face is to know madness and death. This makes things particularly difficult for his family, should the sineater be married and have children. His wife may only encounter him in the dark. His children must never see him. The family, too, is shunned by the neighbours.

When bizarre signs begin to appear in a remote town in the mountains of Virginia, the people begin to believe that the sineater has gone mad and must be destroyed. This is God's punishment for the offence of allowing Joel, the sineater's youngest son, to go to school, as the laws of the United States require. Fanatical cultists take to the woods, scar themselves with magical talismans carved into their flesh, and await the Second Coming. It is up to the virtually friendless Joel, as the signs escalate into animal mutilations and several murders, to find out who is really responsible for the outrages, and to confront his father and come to terms with his own heritage. While it would seem easy enough to say that all Joel's family needs to do is forget about sin-eating, turn secular humanist, and move to civilization, the answers are not so easy. The social microcosm which had produced them will not let them go. They cannot toss aside the values hammered into them for generations.

While one could argue that, in form, this is a mystery novel, if we accept Douglas Winter's argument that horror is a mood, not a genre, then *Sineater* is a masterful piece of horror, the grimly hopeless mood resulting not from any supernatural agency, but from the unshakable delusions of the human mind.

Massie's shorter fiction, unfortunately, is nowhere near as impressive. Despite a ludicrously hyperbolic introduction by Gary Braunbeck to her second collection, placing it on the same shelf with Borges's *Labyrinths* and Carson McCullers's *The Ballad of the Sad Cafe and Other Stories*, and suggesting that anyone who isn't stirred to the innermost depths of their soul by the contents of this book is inadequate as a human being, the best that can be said of the actual stories is that a couple of them are almost good, particularly "Snow Day" (static, hopeless picture of an abused child's home life), and "Meat," which lurches rather clumsily in the direction of the sort of macabre humour John Collier wrote and Alfred Hitchcock brought to the TV screen so much more elegantly.

Massie's short fiction skims over moral surfaces. It can certainly be called unflinching, but it also lacks depth or insight. Imagination expresses itself mostly in the number of truly disgusting details she can cram in. Typical situations include the derelict bag-lady in "I am Not My Smell," dying of a gangrenous foot injury, who not very plausibly finds triumph and transcendence by causing a stray dog to eat her—so that she will live on in the dog, presumably, though the dog's prospects don't look very bright either. "Sanctuary of the Shrinking Soul" is an ungainly story, much inferior to similar work by, say, Shirley Jackson, which does, however, effectively depict a descent into madness at the end. In the previously mentioned "Meat," a detective becomes involved when an eccentric woman complains about a rotten-meat smell coming from the basement of an apartment building. The ending is not all that surprising, hopefully intended to be funny, as romance leads the detective to murder the complainer and bury her in the same basement—only he does a better job, so no odours escape, since this is an old family tradition, and the basement is actually quite filled with corpses already. He expresses his love for his sweetheart (a murderess, whose poorly-concealed victim was the source of the smell) by showing her how to do these things right. In "Shadow of the Valley," a sadistic prison guard bullies his hopeless girlfriend into having sex with a mutilated prisoner who has been kept in darkness and solitary confinement for the last two years. Grim justice results, as one might expect from an X-rated *Tales from the Crypt* episode.

The Stoker-winning "Stephen" is considerably stronger, but showing the same hopelessness without any particular gain or insight. This time a nurse falls in love with (and has sex with) a multiple amputee who is little more than a disembodied head. The story effectively describes her inability to draw away from this truly perverse longing. The technology which keeps the title character alive arguably pushes the story into the science-fiction category.

One other instance of the fantastic in Massie's short work is "That Old Timer Rock and Roll" (in *Southern Discomfort*), about an obnoxious, uncaring jerk who works as a night-watchman at a particularly decrepit nursing home. He'd rather be in a rock band than doing this. Eventually he manages to conjure up the God of Rock and Roll, which immediately destroys him, and good riddance. This and other short stories which fade from the mind almost as fast as one reads them, seem like routine slush-pile material, and have mostly been published in small-press magazines which may not have the highest standards.

But the quality of *Sineater* and a very few other items suggests that if Massie can only break free of the greenhouse garden of Small-Press Horror Fandom, she may have an impressive career in front of her yet.

—Darrell Schweitzer

MASTERTON, Graham

Pseudonyms: Thomas Luke; Anton Rimart. **Nationality:** British. **Born:** Edinburgh, 1946. **Family:** Married Wiescka Masterton; three sons. **Career:** Journalist; editor, *Mayfair* and *Penthouse* magazines, London; freelance writer since the 1970s. **Address:** c/o William Heinemann Ltd., Michelin House, 81 Fulham Rd., London SW3 6RB, England. Lives in Epsom, Surrey.

HORROR, GHOST AND GOTHIC PUBLICATIONS

Novels (series: Manitou; Night Warriors; Rook)

The Manitou. London, Spearman, 1975.
Plague. London, Star, 1977.
The Djinn. New York, Pinnacle, 1977; London, W. H. Allen, 1982.
Charnel House. Los Angeles, Pinnacle, 1978; London, W. H. Allen, 1979.
The Devils of D-Day. Los Angeles, Pinnacle, 1978.
The Sphinx. Los Angeles, Pinnacle, 1978.
Revenge of the Manitou. Los Angeles, Pinnacle, 1979; London, Piatkus, 1984.
The Sweetman Curve. New York, Ace, 1979.
The Hell Candidate (as Thomas Luke). New York, Pocket, 1980; as by Graham Masterton, London, Severn House, 1985.
Phobia (as Thomas Luke; novelization of screenplay). New York, Pocket, 1980.
The Wells of Hell. New York, Pocket, 1980; London, Sphere, 1981.
Famine. London, Sphere, and New York, Ace, 1981.
The Heirloom. London, Sphere, 1981; as Thomas Luke, New York, Pocket, 1982.
Ikon. London, Star, 1983; New York, Tor, 1984.
Tengu. New York, Tor, 1983; London, W. H. Allen, 1984.
The Pariah. London, Star, 1983.
Condor (as Thomas Luke). London, Star, 1984; as by Graham Masterton, New York, Tor, 1985.

Family Portrait. London, Arrow, 1985; as *Picture of Evil*, New
   York, Tor, 1985.
Sacrifice. London, W. H. Allen, 1985; New York, Tor, 1986.
Death Trance. New York Tor, 1986; Sutton, Surrey, Severn House,
   1987.
Night Warriors. London, Sphere, 1986.
Death Dream (Night Warriors). New York, Tor, 1988; Sutton, Sur-
   rey, Severn House, 1989.
Feast. New York, Pinnacle, 1988.
The Mirror. New York, Tor, and Sutton, Surrey, Severn House, 1988.
Ritual. London, Severn House, 1988.
Walkers. New York, Tor, 1989; Sutton, Surrey, Severn House, 1990.
The Burning. New York, Tor, 1991; as *The Hymn*, London,
   Macdonald, 1991.
Night Plague (Night Warriors). New York, Tor, and Sutton, Sur-
   rey, Severn House, 1991.
Black Angel. Sutton, Surrey, Severn House, 1991.
Burial (Manitou). London, Heinemann, 1992; New York, Tor,
   1994.
Master of Lies. New York, Tor, 1992.
Prey. Sutton, Surrey, Severn House, 1992.
The Sleepless. London, Heinemann, 1993.
Flesh and Blood. London, Heinemann, 1994.
Spirit. London, Heinemann, 1995.
The House That Jack Built. London, Heinemann, and New York,
   Carroll and Graf, 1996.
Rook. Sutton, Surrey, Severn House, 1996.
Tooth and Claw (Rook). Sutton, Surrey, Severn House, 1997.
The Chosen Child. London, Heinemann, 1997.

Short Stories

Hurry Monster. Round Top, New York, Footsteps Press, 1988.
Fortnight of Fear. Sutton, Surrey, Severn House, 1994.
Flights of Fear. Sutton, Surrey, Severn House, 1995.
Faces of Fear. Sutton, Surrey, Severn House, 1996.

Other

Editor, *Scare Care.* New York, Tor, 1989; London, Grafton, 1991.

OTHER PUBLICATIONS

Novels

Inserts (as Anton Rimart; novelization of screenplay). London,
   Star, 1976.
Solitaire. N.p., 1982.
Maiden Voyage. N.p., 1984.
Lords of the Air. London, Hamish Hamilton, 1988.

Other

How to Drive Your Man Wild in Bed. N.p., 1975.

*

Film Adaptation: *The Manitou*, 1976.

*   *   *

Graham Masterton had previously written sex manuals and
competent but undistinguished fiction before he made an impact
with his impressive horror debut, *The Manitou*, in 1975. The story
becomes intensely suspenseful right from the outset; in the opening chapter we learn that a young woman has a strange tumour
that grows perceptibly overnight. Eventually the anomaly resolves
itself as an ancient American Indian sorcerer who has returned to
fleshly form in this fashion. The subsequent magical duel never
allows the reader a moment to catch breath, each confrontation
building on the previous ones. Masterton recapitulated the story
in *Revenge of the Manitou* a few years later, equally filled with
chills and danger, but even though the evil spirit has returned with
allies this time, the novel never rose to the level of its predecessor.
He was more successful with a third in the series, *Burial*, in which
the disembodied magician allies himself with voodoo magic and
literally begins to draw entire buildings into the realm of the dead.

Masterton's early popularity gave rise to a series of short,
graphic horror novels. *The Djinn* features a malevolent genie whose
release in the modern world foreshadows horrible deaths for several of the main characters. *The Sphinx* apparently drew inspiration from the *Cat People* movies, with a beautiful, young, and not
quite human woman romantically involved with a career diplomat
who discovers his lover has some unusual recreational interests.
Neither of these were entirely successful, but the following two
thrillers, *Charnel House* and *The Devils of D-Day* were both much
more effective. The former invokes another malevolent Indian
spirit, this one with less ambitious plans but just as frightening
manifestations. The latter is a haunted-house story with a twist—
the house is a salvaged World War II tank that is home to uneasy,
and bloodthirsty spirits.

In the early 1980s, Masterton used the pseudonym Thomas
Luke for several novels, only one of which was particularly noteworthy. *Phobia* is a competent novelization of a minor suspense
film. *The Heirloom* refers to an ornate chair bought by a collector
who is unaware that it is the seat of Satan himself, and the means
by which ultimate evil might gain access to the world. Much more
effective is *The Hell Candidate*, in which a Presidential candidate
who seems destined to lose strikes a deal with the powers of evil
and becomes the favourite for election. But what will his victory
cost the world?

The Wells of Hell is a story of the "bad place." An evil force
living within the ground itself begins claiming victims from the
populace of a small town. Although reasonably suspenseful, it
lacks the impact of most of Masterton's other novels. His next,
Tengu, was much more original. The title refers to a variety of
Japanese demon, one of which has been recruited by international
terrorists in a plot to undermine the stability of the US government. The mixture of supernatural horror and spies ought not to
have worked, but Masterton rose to the occasion and produced
one of his most effective and interesting works. He returned to
more familiar but less original ground with *The Pariah*, wherein
the action centres around vengeful spirits unleashed when an elderly ship is raised from its watery grave.

Picture of Evil is one of Masterton's best works. The Gray family are the "real" people from whom Oscar Wilde drew inspiration for *The Portrait of Dorian Gray*. The family exists by draining the life-force from various victims, continuing into the present
day. Their secret immortality comes to an end when a particularly resourceful man discovers the truth and vows vengeance.
There is a particularly effective sequence in which a chase scene
is conducted through the landscapes of several paintings. *Death*

Trance explores astral projection. The protagonist's family has been murdered and, desperate to understand what has happened, he resorts to a mystic to communicate with them, eventually projecting himself into the land of the dead. The dreamscapes are unique and interesting, although the story itself is relatively minor.

Masterton apparently enjoyed the device used in *Death Trance* because he used elements of it in his *Night Warriors* trilogy, consisting of *Night Warriors*, *Death Dream* and *Night Plague*. The Night Warriors are apparently ordinary people who discover that they are reincarnations of ancient occult warriors who battled demons in a dream world beyond ordinary human senses. They discover their destiny and overcome a series of attacks during the course of the three volumes. Some of the most effective scenes are those in which the occult world infiltrates our reality, but the real value of the trilogy is the exotic, and often terrifying dreamscapes Masterton creates as settings for the battles.

Feast is one of Masterton's strangest concepts. A restaurant reviewer discovers that his son has been seduced by a cult that practices self-cannibalism. He attempts to rescue the boy, and in the process learns that the cultists have opened a channel to both heaven and hell. *The Mirror* is much more conventional. A child actor who died young still exists inside a magical mirror, and he can return to the world of the living if he finds someone to take his place. A few effective scenes, but this was one of Masterton's weakest efforts. There's a good setup in *Walkers*, an abandoned asylum that closed when all of its inmates magically vanished one night. A businessman hoping to develop the property discovers that they have somehow moved to a dimension inside the building's walls, and that they can escape if they can kill enough visitors to the property.

There's another weird cult in *The Burning*, this one having discovered the road to immortality lies through self-immolation; an occasionally interesting variation of *Feast*, but lacking the tight plotting of that book. The Fog City Killer is a serial murderer in *Master of Lies*, but he's also a cult member, seeking immortality through the sacrifice of others. Masterton broke out of this pattern with *The House That Jack Built*, a conventional but highly effective haunted-house story. A successful lawyer and his wife are visiting the country during his recovery from a brutal mugging when he becomes fascinated by a crumbling mansion. To his wife's horror, he abandons his practice and sinks all of their money into purchasing and restoring the building, even though it has an unpleasant history, and despite a tragic death that takes place on the property while they are in the process of buying it. Possession, ghostly warnings, poltergeist activity, and insanity all figure prominently.

Masterton's other thrillers often incorporate elements of horror, most notably *Plague*, in which a deadly disease threatens the entire world. He edited the highly regarded anthology *Scare Care*, and has written a number of fine short stories, including "Absence of the Beast," "The Root of All Evil," "Hungry Moon" and "Beijing Craps."

—Don D'Ammassa

MATHESON, Richard (Burton)

Pseudonym: Logan Swanson. **Nationality:** American. **Born:** Allendale, New Jersey, 20 February 1926. **Education:** University of Missouri, Columbia, B.A. in journalism 1949. **Military Service:** Served in the 87th Division of the United States Army during World War II. **Family:** Married Ruth Ann Woodson in 1952; two daughters and two sons (the screenwriters Richard Christian Matheson and Chris Matheson). **Career:** Freelance writer. **Awards:** Hugo award, for screenplay, 1958; Writers Guild of America award, for television writing, 1960, 1974; World Fantasy award, 1976, 1990, and Life Achievement award, 1984. Guest of Honour, 16th World Science Fiction Convention, 1958; Bram Stoker award, 1990. **Agent:** Don Congdon Associates, 156 Fifth Avenue, Suite 625, New York, NY 10010, USA. **Address:** P.O. Box 81, Woodland Hills, California 91365, USA.

HORROR, GHOST AND GOTHIC PUBLICATIONS

Novels

I Am Legend. New York, Fawcett, 1954; London, Corgi, 1956; as *The Omega Man: I Am Legend*, New York, Berkley, 1971.
The Shrinking Man. New York, Fawcett, and London, Muller, 1956; as *The Incredible Shrinking Man*, London, Sphere, 1988.
A Stir of Echoes. Philadelphia, Lippincott, and London, Cassell, 1958.
Hell House. New York, Viking Press, 1971; London, Corgi, 1973.
Bid Time Return. New York, Viking Press, 1975; London, Sphere, 1977; as *Somewhere in Time*, New York, Ballantine, 1980.
What Dreams May Come: A Novel. New York, Putnam, 1978; London, Joseph, 1979.
Earthbound (as Logan Swanson). New York, Playboy, 1982; restored edition (as Richard Matheson), London, Robinson, 1989; New York, Tor, 1994.
Through Channels. Roundtop, New York, Footsteps Press, 1989.
Somewhere in Time: What Dreams May Come: Two Novels of Love and Fantasy. Los Angeles, Dream/Press, 1991.
7 Steps to Midnight. New York, Forge, 1993.
Now You See It. . . . New York, Tor, 1995.

Short Stories

Born of Man and Woman: Tales of Science Fiction and Fantasy. Philadelphia, Chamberlain Press, 1954; abridged edition, London, Reinhardt, 1956; abridged edition, as *Third from the Sun*, New York, Bantam, 1955.
The Shores of Space. New York, Bantam, 1957; London, Corgi, 1958.
Shock! New York, Dell, 1961; London, Corgi, 1962; as *Shock 1: Thirteen Tales to Thrill and Terrify*, New York, Berkley, 1979.
Shock II. New York, Dell, 1964; London, Corgi, 1965.
Shock III. New York, Dell, 1966; London, Corgi, 1967.
Shock Waves. New York, Dell, 1970.
Shock 4. London, Sphere, 1980.
Richard Matheson: Collected Stories. Los Angeles, Scream/Press, 1989.

Plays

Screenplays: *The Incredible Shrinking Man*, 1957; *The House of Usher (The Fall of the House of Usher)*, 1960; *The Pit and the Pendulum*, 1961; *Tales of Terror*, 1962; *Burn, Witch, Burn (Night of the Eagle)*, with Charles Beaumont and George Baxt, 1962;

The Raven, 1963; *The Comedy of Terrors*, 1964; *The Last Man on Earth* (pseudonymous co-writer), 1964; *Die! Die! My Darling! (Fanatic)*, 1965; *The Devil Rides Out (The Devil's Bride)*, 1968; *De Sade*, 1969; *The Legend of Hell House*, 1973; *Dracula*, 1974; *Somewhere in Time*, 1980; *Twilight Zone: The Movie*, with others, 1983; *Jaws 3-D*, with Carl Gottlieb and Guerdon Trueblood, 1983.

Television Plays: *And When the Sky Was Opened, Third from the Sun, The Last Flight, A World of Difference, A World of His Own, Nick of Time, The Invaders, Once upon a Time, Little Girl Lost, Young Man's Fancy, Steel, Nightmare at 20,000 Feet, Night Call,* and *Spur of the Moment* (all in *The Twilight Zone* series), 1959-63; *The Return of Andrew Bentley* (*Thriller* series), 1961; *Duel*, 1971; *The Night Stalker*, 1971; *The Night Strangler*, 1972; *Dying Room Only,* 1973; *The Stranger Within*, 1974; *Dracula*, 1974; *Scream of the Wolf,* 1974; *The Morning After,* 1974; *Amelia* (in *Trilogy of Terror*), 1975; *Dead of Night*, 1977; *The Strange Possession of Mrs. Oliver*, 1977; and scripts for *Alfred Hitchcock Hour, Night Gallery, Ghost Story*, the new *Twilight Zone, Amazing Stories* and the new *Outer Limits* series.

Other

Editor, with Martin H. Greenberg and Charles G. Waugh, *The Twilight Zone: The Original Stories*. New York, Avon, 1985.

OTHER PUBLICATIONS

Novels

Someone Is Bleeding. New York, Lion, 1953.
Fury on Sunday. New York, Lion, 1953.
Ride the Nightmare. New York, Ballantine, 1959; London, Consul, 1961.
The Beardless Warriors: A Novel. Boston, Little, Brown, 1960; London, Heinemann, 1961.
Journal of the Gun Years: Being Choice Selections from the Authentic Never-Before-Printed Diary of the Famous Gunfighter-Lawman Clay Halser! Whose Deeds of Daring Made His Name a By-Word of Terror in the Southwest between the Years of 1866 and 1878. New York, Evans, 1991.
The Gun Fight. New York, Evans, 1993.
Shadow on the Sun. New York, Evans, 1994.
The Memoirs of Wild Bill Hickock. New York, Jove, 1995.

Short Stories

By the Gun: Six from Richard Matheson. New York, Evans, 1993.

Plays

Screenplays: *The Beat Generation (This Rebel Age)*, with Lewis Meltzer, 1959; *Master of the World*, 1961; *The Young Warriors*, 1967; *Loose Cannons*, with Richard Christian Matheson, 1990.

Television Plays: *Yawkey* (*Lawman* series), 1959; *The Enemy Within (Star Trek* series), 1966; *The Martian Chronicles*, from the novel by Ray Bradbury, 1979; *The Dreamer of Oz*, 1990; and scripts for *Chrysler Playhouse, The Girl from U.N.C.L.E.,*

Have Gun—Will Travel, Wanted Dead or Alive, The D.A.'s Man, Cheyenne, Bourbon Street Beat, Philip Marlowe, Buckskin, Markham, and *Richard Diamond* series.

Other

The Path: Metaphysics for the 90s. Santa Barbara, Capra Press, 1993.

*

Film Adaptations: *The Incredible Shrinking Man*, 1957, from the novel *The Shrinking Man*; *The Last Man on Earth*, 1964, *The Omega Man*, 1971, both from the novel *I Am Legend*; *The Young Warriors*, 1967, from the novel *The Beardless Warriors*; *Duel*, 1971, from the short story; *The Legend of Hell House*, 1973, from the novel *Hell House*; *Somewhere in Time*, 1980; *Twilight Zone: The Movie*, 1983, partly from the short story "Nightmare at 20,000 Feet."

Critical Study: *Richard Matheson—He is Legend: An Illustrated Bio-Bibliography* by Mark Rathbun and Graeme Flanagan, Chico, California, Rathbun, 1984.

*   *   *

To read the fiction of Richard Matheson is to enter a world in which the ordinary unexpectedly shows its dark side and the familiar objects of daily life suddenly develop teeth and claws. More than any other writer, Matheson set the tone for dark fantasy fiction in the postwar era, turning his hybrids of horror, suspense and science fiction into paranoid explorations of the everyday world and its hidden horrors. In *Supernatural Fiction Writers*, Keith Nielson credits Matheson as the writer who "moved the horrific from the ornate, bizarre, and self-consciously 'mythic' world of H. P. Lovecraft and the *Weird Tales* tradition to the everyday world of ordinary people." More to the point, Matheson showed how virtually anything, no matter how unremarkable, could become a source of menace if viewed from the right frame of reference.

In the introduction to his *Collected Stories*, Matheson sums up this paranoid world-view in a leitmotif that recurs throughout his fiction: "The individual isolated in a threatening world, attempting to survive." His first horror novel, *I Am Legend*, is his most dynamic example of this motif, although in some respects it not Matheson's most typical story. *I Am Legend* is set in a world where the everyday order has been turned inside out. A virus has transformed everyone but the narrator, Robert Neville, into a vampire. Neville spends his nights defending his home against vampire armies and his days tracking them to their lairs and killing them. The novel has been praised for its scientific explanation of vampirism and its oppressive atmosphere of claustrophobia (ultimately, a major inspiration for George Romero's cult film *Night of the Living Dead*). Its greatest achievement, however, is its extrapolation of Neville's predicament into an inversion of the traditional vampire-victim relationship. In a world where vampires rule, Neville is the abomination, and in their eyes a frightening "invisible specter who had left for evidence of his existence the bloodless bodies of their loved ones."

Matheson devotes considerable imagination to making the worlds of his more ordinary protagonists seem as hostile as

Neville's. The hero of *7 Steps to Midnight* finds himself caught in an inescapable web of intrigue spun from the plots of popular genre novels. The narrator of *Now You See It. . .* is paralysed by a stroke that leaves him physically incapable of stopping a murder committed before his eyes. By contrast, the things that pose a threat in these worlds are often very banal. In *The Shrinking Man*, Scott Carey discovers that his irreversible shrinking at the rate of one-seventh of an inch per day is slowly transforming the world he has known all his adult life into a Darwinian proving ground. Simple clutter in his basement becomes insurmountable and potentially fatal obstacles: an oil burner looms like "a silent steel tower," a garden hose appears like "a coiled red serpent," and a high stairway step proves an Everest that he cannot scale to attain the comfortable environment of the house above. Carey spends most of the novel struggling to avoid a common garden-spider that bulks more monstrously every day. However, his predicament is no different from that of other Matheson protagonists who are shocked to find that their secure feelings about their world have all been based on a trick of perspective.

In his short fiction, Matheson endows some of the simplest objects with malevolent potential. Household appliances become a conduit for a man's self-destructive rage in "Mad House." In "Through Channels" and "Little Girl Lost," respectively, a plain television set and the crawlspace beneath a couch serve as portals to alien dimensions. A telephone terrorizes an elderly woman with a dead man's voice in "Long Distance Call" and a child's toy is revealed to be an sentient monster in "The Doll That Does Everything." Once Matheson reveals that the airplane in "Nightmare at 20,000 Feet" is ridden by a gremlin and that the truck in "Duel" is waging mortal combat with the hero's car, these common vehicles become symbols for the inescapable horrors of a cold, mechanically-driven universe. Even basic human relationships are prone to show a sinister side in Matheson's fiction. His suspense novels *Someone is Bleeding* and *Ride the Nightmare* both feature characters disoriented by the discovery of what loved ones have hidden that totally changes their identities.

In other stories, he repeatedly undermines the traditional foundations of domestic harmony and the nuclear family. "First Anniversary" features a man who discovers that his wife is a hideous creature who has maintained a facade of beauty for the duration of their marriage. "Trespass" (a.k.a. "Mother by Protest") presents the peculiar cravings of a pregnant woman as signs than an alien being has taken over her womb. "Born of Man and Woman" exaggerates a loveless parent-child relationship into a tale of mutant birth.

The key to Matheson's fiction and its unsettling effect is his style, which is as plain and simple as the ordinary objects he imbues with malice. His prose is straightforward, and devoid of the portentous descriptions many horror writers use to create atmosphere. The almost clinical quality of his writing actually adds gravity to his horrors by giving them a solid and seemingly irrefutable basis in reality, no matter how outlandish they seem at first. "Legion of Plotters," for example, is a simple catalogue of the minor annoyances a man endures during his daily commute to his job. Each described by itself seems utterly inconsequential, but when considered as components of a larger pattern, it is possible to see them (as he does) as signs of a conspiracy to drive him mad.

Several of Matheson's better-known stories are frank explorations of paranormal phenomena. *A Stir of Echoes* features a suburban everyman who discovers latent psychic talents that alien-

ate him from family and friends, once he is privy to their private—and in some cases darkly secret—thoughts. *Hell House*, a homage to Shirley Jackson's *The Haunting of Hill House*, chronicles the fate of a team of parapsychological investigators who test out different theories of psychic phenomena in their efforts to exorcize the ghosts of a dangerously haunted house. *Earthbound* concerns the disembodied spirit of a *femme fatale* who seduces men with a body made from the ectoplasm she steals during sexual encounters with them. Although these stories feature fairly conventional supernatural horrors, they can be seen as the inevitable culmination of Matheson's more unconventional horror stories which, after all, suggest a world of mystery and terror that lies just beyond the familiar boundaries of existence.

—Stefan Dziemianowicz

MATHESON, Richard Christian

Nationality: American. **Born:** Santa Monica, California, 14 October 1953; son of the writer Richard Matheson (q.v.). **Education:** University of Southern California. **Career:** Advertising copywriter; drummer in a rock band; screenwriter; television producer; contributor of short stories to *Penthouse, Omni, Twilight Zone* and other magazines and anthologies. Not to be confused with his similarly named younger brother, Chris Matheson (born 1958; co-screenwriter of the movie *Bill & Ted's Bogus Journey*, 1991.) **Address:** c/o Bantam Books, Bantam Doubleday Dell Publishing Group, Inc., 1540 Broadway, New York, NY 10036, USA.

HORROR, GHOST AND GOTHIC PUBLICATIONS

Novels

Created By. New York, Bantam, 1993; London, Macmillan, 1994.

Short Stories

Holiday. Round Top, New York, Footsteps Press, 1988.
Scars, and Other Distinguishing Marks. Los Angeles, Scream Press, 1987; expanded edition, New York, Tor, 1988.

OTHER PUBLICATIONS

Plays

Screenplays: *Three O'Clock High*, 1987; *Loose Cannons*, with Richard Matheson Senior, 1990; *Full Eclipse*, 1994.

Television Plays: Over 500 episodes of various series, including *The Incredible Hulk, Three's Company, Knightrider, Stir Crazy, Hill Street Blues, Magnum, Amazing Stories, Tales from the Crypt* and *Wiseguy*.

* * *

Richard Christian Matheson achieved recognition as a horror writer in the late 1980s, at approximately the same time that the controversy over Splatterpunk divided the horror community into two camps: proponents of suggestive dark fantasy, and champions of graphic treatments of violence and bloodshed. Although Matheson's stories were embraced by members of the latter group, his fiction shows how inadequately such pigeonholing accommodates the work of any one author. A screenwriter by profession, his writing has a strong "visual" style that reflects the cinematic influences considered a hallmark of Splatterpunk. However, an equally strong (and oft-acknowledged) influence is the writing of his father, Richard Matheson, which is renowned for its restraint and subtlety.

Indeed, Matheson's first published story, "Graduation" (1977) reads very much like one of his father's works. Presented as a series of letters from a first-year college student to his parents, it captures the loneliness and insecurity of a young man acclimating to a unfamiliar environment full of new people and new ideas. When reports of classmate deaths begin creeping into his correspondence, one has to read between the lines to divine that he is the murderer, lashing out against anyone who threatens his fragile psyche. This oblique approach to horror characterizes much of Matheson's writing, including (not surprisingly) his collaboration with his father, "Where There's a Will," a tale told from the viewpoint of a prematurely buried man that deftly misdirects the reader's attention from the real horror until its shock ending. In some of his most effective stories, the horrors happen entirely offstage: "Timed Exposure" ends with a sheet of photographs taken at a carnival novelty booth foreshadowing the grisly fate of a girl enjoying a one-night stand, and "Mobius" with the revelation that an apparent interrogation of a serial killer has actually been a deviously staged brainwashing.

Stories that Matheson wrote between 1980 and 1987, the majority of which were collected in *Scars, and Other Distinguishing Marks*, established his reputation as one of the most distinctive writers of the post-Stephen King generation. Most are concise exercises of no more than several thousand words that vividly capture a mood or conclude with a sharp twist to a simple plot. Their narratives are spare and streamlined, sometimes to the point of starkness: "Vampire," the story of a creature that feeds on the psychic residue left at car-accident scenes, is related in 187 one-word sentences of almost total sensory impression. Some take the form of letters, interview excerpts and diary extracts. Most feature descriptive passages whose staccato, hard-boiled style sets the scene like directions in a movie script. A character in "Hell" who sits on a bluff overlooking Hollywood sees the city "spread before her, eating electricity, hibachi-bright." "Commuters" opens with the following impression: "Morning traffic snailed along the freeway, taillights pulsing splinters on rainy lanes." Against backdrops reduced to such compressed images, the horrors stand out in sharp relief.

Although non-traditional, Matheson's stories are built around themes appropriate for their modern characters and contemporary settings. In some, the horrors manifest as exaggerated externalizations of a character's state of mind. "Third Wind" tells of a competitive and obsessively driven businessman who discovers that his legs refuse to stop running during his daily workout. "Dead End" features a couple whose crumbling relationship is mirrored in their entrapment on an endlessly circling roadway with no exit. The lovers who end their relationship in "Break-Up" transform physically into total strangers. Most of Matheson's stories have West Coast settings and several reflect concerns specific to the cultures of Los Angeles and Hollywood. "Cancelled,"

"Sentences" and "Sirens" all feature characters who find the reality of their lives intersecting with the hyperreality of film. "Commuters" uses a massive traffic jam on the Los Angeles freeway system to symbolize the futility and inescapableness of life's daily grind. In "Hell," random acts of senseless violence brought on by the suffocating heat of a Los Angeles summer conjure a Dante-esque vision of the underworld.

Few of Matheson's stories are explicitly violent, but many evoke a culture of violence through the actions of characters whose sensitivities have been blunted by their daily exposure to life's atrocities. "Guys on the road. They see it all. They lose interest. They need something new," says a character in "Groupies" who commits a murder to thrill a jaded rock band. Some characters seek to relieve their *ennui* by extreme means, like the psychotherapist in "Mr. Right" who is eager to date a psychopath who mixes cruel physical abuse with sexual ecstasy, and the narrator of "Region of the Flesh," who doesn't leave his bed once he discovers that his dreams of the murder that left stains on its mattress have him "starting to feel for the first time." For others, fulfilment can only be achieved through self-destruction: "Menage" features a woman who kills her male lover so she can have the knife they use to please each other sexually all to herself; in "Mutilator," a man who believes that everyone hurts him finds self-mutilation a substitute for interacting with others because "In a world filled with cruelty and misery I'm never alone"; the point-of-view character in "The Edge" becomes so dependent on physical violence for feeling that he savours the airplane crash about to take his life.

For many of Matheson's characters, like the narrator of "Region of the Flesh," "Violence . . . is just another form of emotion. Of expression." Matheson's fullest exploration of this attitude and the personal and social circumstances that give rise to it can found in his novel *Created By*. Both an insightful examination of the psychological roots of creativity and a critique of how Hollywood shapes cultural values, it is the story of screenwriter Alan White, who finds a hit formula for television with "The Mercenary," an over-the-top adventure series that violates every censorship taboo. Unknown to everyone involved with the show—initially including its creator—Alan has channelled subliminal feelings of rage at his family, job and viewing audience into A. E. Barek, the cold-blooded amoral hero of the series. When Alan's creative spark ignites Hollywood's exploitative irresponsibility and the needs of viewers desensitized by the nightly barrage of television, the result is Barek's incarnation as a flesh-and-blood monster who acts upon Alan's subconscious wishes and thwarts all efforts to suppress him. The novel is a touchstone for many of the themes and ideas Matheson grapples with in his short fiction, and in its cynical estimation that "Hate is what people love," it articulates a grimmer horror than even the most viscerally written Splatterpunk fiction.

—Stefan Dziemianowicz

MATURIN, Charles R(obert)

Pseudonym: Dennis Jasper Murphy. **Nationality:** Irish. **Born:** Dublin, 1782. **Education:** Trinity College, Dublin. **Family:** Married Henrietta Kingsbury. **Career:** Ordained at 21, became curate of St. Peter's, Dublin, from 1806 until his death; began writing in order to supplement small income. **Died:** 30 October 1824.

HORROR, GHOST AND GOTHIC PUBLICATIONS

Novels

The Fatal Revenge; or, The Family of Montorio (as Dennis Jasper Murphy). London, Longman Hurst, 1807.
The Wild Irish Boy. London, Longman Hurst, 1808.
The Milesian Chief. London, Colburn, 1812.
Melmoth the Wanderer: A Tale. London, Hurst and Robinson, 4 vols., 1820.
The Albigenses: A Romance. London, Hurst and Robinson, 1824.

Plays

Bertram; or, The Castle of Saint Aldobrand. London, Murray, 1816.

*

Critical Study: *Charles Robert Maturin: His Life and Works* by Niilo Idman, Helsinki, Helsingfors, 1923.

*   *   *

Charles R. Maturin's best-known novel, *Melmoth the Wanderer*, is a *tour de force*, one of the greatest examples of Gothic horror. For a start, the novel is large and complex, consisting of five cleverly interlinked tales in addition to an extensive framing device, covering different historical periods between the 1660s and 1816. But breadth and complexity are easily achieved through persistence; what Maturin possessed was an outstanding ability to create atmosphere in just a few sentences and to demonstrate the traits of character in a handful of words. That he was a highly educated and well-read author is evident throughout; if anything, he shows off his scholarship through the use of an excess of literary allusions, both at the heads of chapters and in the text.

As soon as *Melmoth the Wanderer* appeared, a host of literary luminaries of the day heaped praise upon it, including Scott, Byron and Goethe, while Balzac was moved to write a sequel (*Melmoth Reconciled*, 1835). And later authors from Baudelaire to Wilde (who not only borrowed and built upon the idea of the Wanderer's portrait in *The Picture of Dorian Gray*, but also used "Sebastian Melmoth" as a pseudonym towards the end of his life) and Thackeray to Lovecraft acknowledged its influence upon them. The novel was quickly adapted into a stage play, despite being far too complex in its plot for such treatment.

It is an early deal-with-the-devil story. John Melmoth, who becomes the Wanderer, has retained his youthful appearance for 150 years. All that time he has been trying to persuade some other person to take on his pact—which would save Melmoth from the eventual torments of hell. A portrait of Melmoth (dated 1646) hangs in a small room of the family's County Wicklow estate. At the "present day" of 1816 the estate and its house are run down, but the portrait shows a young John Melmoth. As the old and dying owner, a terrible miser, tells his nephew (also called John Melmoth), the man in the portrait is still alive.

The uncle dies and the nephew inherits, along with the estate, a mouldering manuscript which tells an early episode in Melmoth's wanderings ("John Stanton's Story"), concerning Stanton's obsession to expose and destroy Melmoth, and the way that he is confined in an asylum and offered one terrible escape route by Melmoth, which he refuses. Then, coincidentally, a bad storm wrecks a ship on the coast, and the young John Melmoth is joined at the house by Alonzo Moncada, a Spaniard who has been tempted by the Wanderer, and who tells his own story ("Tale of the Spaniard") and others.

In the "Tale of the Spaniard," Moncada describes his experiences in the clutches of the Inquisition, and how he has not sunk low enough to accept the unspecified offer made to him by the Wanderer. "Tale of the Indians" shows Melmoth trying to corrupt an innocent young woman raised alone by nature upon a small island just off Calcutta in India. "The Tale of Guzman's Family" concerns the Walbergs and their poverty, and "The Lovers' Tale" is about Elinor Mortimer's problems; these are shorter and less arresting for bringing little that is new to the book as a whole. The Wanderer's part in all these stories varies from large to small, yet he is always present as an horrific figure, trying all the time to widen the power of evil in the world.

Each tale is a brief Gothic novel, varying in style and atmosphere, yet closely connected with the others in theme. Family problems and monetary problems go hand-in-hand through all five and the framing device. But they were inherent in Maturin's own life, too. And in each tale is an acceptance of the unpleasantness of fate, which is crystallized by individuals who consider and then reject the Wanderer's offer to them. At the end of *Melmoth the Wanderer*, the eponym puts in an appearance, back at the house in Wicklow, though only for long enough to be claimed by the devil in a magnificent final scene.

While the novel is longer and more digressive than a 20th-century reader would normally welcome, its best passages are breathtaking and it evokes a series of strong emotions. Many of its ingredients, now regarded as the most base of clichés, were fresh in 1820, and it is only the too-frequent borrowing of them by later writers which has debased their coinage.

Maturin's other Gothic novels are less exceptional. *The Fatal Revenge* is an over-complex sub-Radcliffe piece set in the 17th century and full of murders and tortures by the Inquisition. It is spoilt by an excess of incredible twists. *The Wild Irish Boy* is more about Irish nationalism than anything else, being at least partly written as propaganda. Maturin took this same theme in *The Milesian Chief*, but made a more entertaining story out of it; it is a Gothic romance full of strong Irish emotions and was praised by Scott, who borrowed from it for *The Bride of Lammermoor*. The final Gothic novel of Maturin's, published in the year of his death, was *The Albigenses*, which deals with the persecution and massacre of a religious sect in the early 13th century. It was an influential novel, in that it helped to popularize historical novels which used real events and people, rather than romanticizing a past era as so many Gothic novels had done.

Maturin's one surviving short story, "Leixlip Castle," is occasionally anthologized. It is a rather rambling supernatural piece about the fates of the three daughters of a baronet, who rents Leixlip Castle. Although Maturin wrote several plays, only *Bertram* achieved any great success. This was one of the finest of Gothic plays, much praised and highly popular at the time though now forgotten.

—Chris Morgan

McCAMMON, Robert R(ick)

Nationality: American. **Born:** 1952. **Family:** Married. **Career:** Full-time writer since his mid-20s; founder, Horror Writers of America association. **Awards:** Horror Writers of America Bram Stoker award for novel, 1988, 1991 and 1992. **Address:** c/o Pocket Books, 1230 Avenue of the Americas, New York, NY 10020, USA. Lives in Birmingham, Alabama.

HORROR, GHOST AND GOTHIC PUBLICATIONS

Novels

Baal. New York, Avon, 1978; London, Sphere, 1979.
Bethany's Sin. New York, Avon, and London, Sphere, 1980.
The Night Boat. New York, Avon, 1980; London, Kinnell, 1990.
They Thirst. New York, Avon, 1981; London, Kinnell, 1990.
Mystery Walk. New York, Holt Rinehart and Winston, 1983; London, Pan, 1985.
Usher's Passing. New York, Holt Rinehart and Winston, 1984; London, Pan, 1986.
Swan Song. New York, Pocket, 1987; London, Sphere, 1988.
Stinger. New York, Pocket, and London, Kinnell, 1988.
The Wolf's Hour. New York, Pocket, and London, Grafton, 1989.
Mine. New York, Pocket, 1990; London, Grafton, 1991.
Boy's Life. New York, Pocket, 1991; London, Michael Joseph, 1992.
Gone South. New York, Pocket, 1992; London, Michael Joseph, 1993.

Short Stories

Blue World and Other Stories. London, Grafton, 1989; New York, Pocket, 1990.

Other

Editor, with Paul Mikol, *Night Visions 8: All Original Stories.* Arlington Heights, Illinois, Dark Harvest, 1990.
Editor, *The Horror Writers of America Present: Under the Fang.* New York, Pocket, 1991.

*   *   *

In the 1980s, Robert R. McCammon was one of the few writers outside the charmed circle that included Stephen King, Peter Straub, Dean Koontz and Anne Rice to achieve the status of a bestselling horror writer. By the 1990s, little of his writing was categorizable as horror fiction. Despite this apparent shift in focus, McCammon's work is notable for its ambitious themes and the consistency of its humanist concerns which transcend the boundaries of any one genre.

McCammon's earliest novels are entertaining variations on trademark horror themes of the 1970s and '80s. *Baal* is a tale of the anti-Christ, in which the Satanic offspring of a rape becomes the mystical figurehead for fanatical terrorist groups who threaten the world order. In *The Night Boat,* the ghost crew of a Nazi U-boat menaces the Caribbean island it was sunk off decades before. *Bethany's Sin* takes a page from Thomas Tryon's *Harvest Home*

in its account of an ancient matriarchal society devoted to ritual sacrifice that has taken root in a rural Pennsylvania town. *They Thirst* is the tale of a megalomaniacal vampire king who schemes to turn the eight million inhabitants of Los Angeles into his personal army of the undead. These novels stand apart from scores of thematically similar genre efforts through McCammon's portrayal of psychologically complex characters as the linchpins of their plots.

In *Baal,* theology professor James Virga must overcome the crisis of faith brought on by his confrontation with a concrete embodiment of pure evil before he can play his pivotal heroic role. Evan Reid, the protagonist of *Bethany's Sin,* is a guilt-ridden survivor of the Vietnam War who uses his battle with the evil overrunning his town to master his personal demons as well. Their traditional horror scenarios notwithstanding, these novels, like all of McCammon's stories, are notable for their restraint. The supernatural, when it is introduced, serves primarily as a mirror that reflects the struggles of the soul to which the human characters are vulnerable. An exception is *They Thirst,* a tour-de-force of modern vampire fiction whose large cast of characters and clever rendering of a contemporary urban setting as a classic Gothic landscape show McCammon's skill at evoking horrors on an epic scale.

Elements from McCammon's early novels resurface in the books that are considered his landmark contributions to horror fiction. An idea that he first addresses in *Baal*—"There is a completeness in the combination of good and evil . . . Without one the other could not exist"—describes the ambiguous moral landscape from which the horrors of these novels arise. In *Mystery Walk,* the contentious relationship between good and evil is distilled into the personalities of a pair of psychically endowed young men: Billy Creekmore, who is sensitive to the spirits of the dead, and Wayne Falconer, who works as an evangelistic faith healer. Neither is entirely comfortable with his talents—Billy brings misery as well as hope to those whose lives he touches, and Wayne's work is tainted with his personal ambitions—and matters are complicated further when it is discovered that their powers, which seem diametrically opposed, actually share a common origin.

The ambiguity of evil and its development as a distortion of goodness is a theme McCammon revisits through the characters of many of his stories: the fascistic Roland Croninger and the benevolent Sue Wanda, each of whom represents a different evolutionary path for childhood innocence in the post-apocalyptic world of *Swan Song;* Michael Gallatin, a werewolf who fights for the Allied cause in World War II, in *The Wolf's Hour;* Mary Terrill, a.k.a. "Mary Terror," a 1960s radical whose fanatical devotion to her ideals pushes her into bomb-making and kidnapping in *Mine.* The theme receives its fullest treatment in *Usher's Passing,* McCammon's brilliant retooling of the classic southern Gothic as a contemporary morality tale. Working from the premise that Poe's classic "Fall of the House of Usher" was an oblique and fanciful history of a real family, McCammon gives the "true" account of the Ushers, a southern clan that has made its fortune as arms-manufacturers. Rix Usher, the pacifistic black sheep of the family, hopes to put an end to its legacy when he returns home for his father's death and the inevitable passing of responsibility for the family business to one of the heirs. However, Rix is mortified to discover that every evil he has associated with his family— from the monsters that prowl the Usher estate and have given rise to a rich and morbid family folklore, to the purpose of the weapons themselves—has a potential benefit that he cannot dismiss unequivocally any more than any of his ancestors could.

Although McCammon's fiction has a refreshing moral complexity that distinguishes it from many more facile delineations of good and evil in horror fiction, the key to its popular appeal is his optimism. His characters always find the hope they need to extricate themselves from the moral quagmires at the heart of his stories. Indeed, the word "hope" recurs like a protective mantra throughout his fiction. In *They Thirst*, one woman counsels another who refuses to believe that her husband is dead to "hope . . . And don't ever stop because once that's gone, you might as well sit down right here and never move again." In *Swan Song*, a woman struggling to understand why she and a handful of other survivors were spared from the nuclear holocaust that took the lives of hundreds of millions of others says, "I don't know if God has an eye on me or not . . . But I hope He does. I hope I'm important enough—that we're all important enough."

Swan Song is McCammon's ultimate expression of the hope that makes us human and empowers us to triumph over adversity. Set in a post-apocalyptic future, it follows the lives of diverse groups of individuals who set about re-establishing the foundations of civilization. Its heroes and heroines (like its villains and villainesses) are ordinary people that include a reformed derelict, a former small-time wrestler, an orphaned child, and scores of others working together to ensure a greater good that will outlast their individual lives. This faith in the inherent decency of humanity extends to the plots of McCammon's short fiction as well. In "Nightcrawlers," a Vietnam veteran who is able to dream his nightmares about the war into reality saves a diner full of strangers by sacrificing his life to the ghost regiment that hunts him. In "Night Calls the Green Falcon," an aging movie star is able to assume the persona of the superhero he once played thanks to the faith of those he meets in his sincerity. The hero of "Blue World" is a priest who rescues and reforms a pornography starlet by appealing to her sense of self-respect and dignity. Even the protagonist of "I Scream Man," who denies his family's death, demonstrates a refusal to capitulate to the hopelessness of his world.

The horror content of McCammon's fiction began to diminish in 1989. *The Wolf's Hour*, published that year, features a werewolf hero whose lycanthropy is almost incidental to his exploits in the Second World War. *Mine* and *Gone South* are non-supernatural suspense stories, and *Boy's Life* is a fictional autobiographical memoir seasoned with fanciful moments in which the ordinary and the fantastic intersect. Despite their apparent deviation from McCammon's tales of horror, these books share many elements with their predecessors. *The Wolf's Hour* casts Nazis as evil incarnate, much as *The Night Boat* and *Swan Song* do. *Mine*, whose villainess is an unregenerate radical from the 1960s, echoes *Bethany's Sin* and *Usher's Passing*, in its exploration of the evils and ideals of the Vietnam War era. *Gone South*, which is centerd around a manhunt in the Louisiana bayous, features a cast of grotesques as memorable and as representative of humanity as the scarred survivors of nuclear armageddon in *Swan Song*. The small-town setting of *Boy's Life* evokes the middle-American values that bind together the citizens of the small southwestern town under siege by an extraterrestrial invader Stinger. The correspondences between McCammon's horror and non-horror stories ultimately reveal him to be a writer concerned with human experience, for whom horror is a powerful—but by no means the sole—idiom of expression.

—Stefan Dziemianowicz

McDOWELL, Michael (M.)

Pseudonyms: Nathan Aldyne; Axel Young. **Nationality:** American. **Born:** Enterprise, Alabama, 1 June 1950. **Education:** Harvard University, 1968-71; Brandeis University, Ph.D. in English, 1978. **Career:** Teaching, secretarial work; freelance novelist, theatre critic and screenwriter. Lives in Medford, Massachusetts.

<small>HORROR, GHOST AND GOTHIC PUBLICATIONS</small>

Novels (series: Blackwater)

The Amulet. New York, Avon, 1979; London, Fontana, 1982.
Cold Moon Over Babylon. New York, Avon, 1980; London, Fontana, 1982(?).
The Elementals. New York, Avon, 1981; London, Fontana, 1983.
Blood Rubies (with Dennis Schuetz, as Axel Young). New York, Avon, 1982.
Katie. New York, Avon, 1982.
The Flood (Blackwater). New York, Avon, 1983; London, Corgi, 1985.
The Levee (Blackwater). New York, Avon, 1983; London, Corgi, 1985.
The House (Blackwater). New York, Avon, 1983; London, Corgi, 1985.
The War (Blackwater). New York, Avon, 1983; London, Corgi, 1985.
The Fortune (Blackwater). New York, Avon, 1983; London, Corgi, 1986.
Rain (Blackwater). New York, Avon, 1983; London, Corgi, 1986.
Wicked Stepmother, with Dennis Schuetz (as Axel Young). New York, Avon, 1983.
Toplin. Santa Cruz, California, Scream Press, 1985.

Plays

Television Plays: Various episodes of *Tales from the Darkside*, 1984-86, and *Amazing Stories*, 1986-87.

Screenplays: *Beetlejuice*, 1988; *High Spirits*, 1988; *Tales from the Darkside: The Movie*, 1990; *The Nightmare Before Christmas*, 1993; *Thinner*, 1996.

<small>OTHER PUBLICATIONS</small>

Novels

Gilded Needles. New York, Avon, 1980.
Vermilion, with Dennis Schuetz (as Nathan Aldyne). New York, Avon, 1980.
Cobalt, with Dennis Schuetz (as Nathan Aldyne). New York, St. Martin's Press, 1982.
Slate, with Dennis Schuetz (as Nathan Aldyne). New York, Villard, 1984.
Jack and Susan in 1953. New York, Ballantine, 1985.
Canary, with Dennis Schuetz (as Nathan Aldyne). New York, Villard (?), 1986.

Jack and Susan in 1913. New York, Ballantine, 1986.
Jack and Susan in 1933. New York, Ballantine, 1987.

*   *   *

When Stephen King's novels began achieving bestseller status with relentless regularity, his success attracted numerous other writers to a genre that had never enjoyed much popularity in the United States, although it had a respected tradition throughout Europe. One of the young writers who entered the field in the late 1970s was Michael McDowell, a man with unusually strong talents for developing characters and atmosphere, and one of the few who moved from imitation to experimentation remarkably quickly. Although he would abandon the horror genre within a few years to write murder mysteries, historical adventures and screenplays instead, his brief sojourn in horror produced a remarkably satisfying body of work.

McDowell's first horror novel, *The Amulet*, was entertaining although not nearly as effective as those which would follow. The amulet of the title is a magical object whose presence in a small southern town changes the lives of those whom it touches. It's a beautiful item, but everyone who assumes ownership loses his or her life, or future, or family, or experiences some other tragedy. As the amulet moves from one citizen to another, the town is racked by a series of shocks, until the protagonist begins to suspect the nature of the link connecting them all. The novel is straightforward and predictable, memorable chiefly because of the strong characterization of Sarah Howell, the woman who discovers the truth.

McDowell was far more effective in *Cold Moon Over Babylon*, although once again the actual plot is a familiar one. Margaret Larkin was murdered and her body tossed into a river, but her spirit has remained on Earth. During the hours of darkness, it rises to pursue the man who killed her, in a series of progressively more frightening sequences, while he in turn is systematically murdering the rest of the Larkin family. Although much of modern horror fiction used small towns as settings, McDowell's communities seem far more authentic, and his evocation of rural mind-sets and power struggles in the midst of other worldly intervention gives his stories a fine balance between reality and unreality. *Cold Moon* is one of the best ghost stories ever written at novel length.

The Elementals was the most ambitious of McDowell's supernatural horror novels. This time the focus is on a ruined house sitting on a sand bar, a house long cursed with a bad reputation. On the surface, what follows is just another haunted house variation, but the spirits that live in the structure are not ghosts of the departed, but rather physical manifestations of primordial forces, or elementals. The arrival of a varied cast of visitors sets off a series of increasingly frightening events, made even more compelling by McDowell's gift for creating realistic, if not always likeable, characters and portraying their reactions to each other as well as the disembodied forces that threaten their lives.

Katie is one of two novels McDowell produced that examine the nature of sanity and reality. Katie is a struggling young woman, attractive and intelligent, but also a serial killer. Her parents know that she's murdering people, but since her activities turn a profit, they are disinclined to do anything about it. And Katie is very difficult to catch because she experiences flashes of clairvoyance whenever she is in danger. An interesting but not entirely successful blend of horror and dark humour. McDowell explored the world of madness much more effectively in *Toplin*, perhaps the best novel ever written from the point of view of a schizophrenic. Toplin's world is filled with hideous monsters and inexplicable events, all manufactured within his own mind, and McDowell's examination of how Toplin manages to interact with the his environment despite his delusions is thoroughly fascinating, easily his best single work.

Stephen King's six-part novel, *The Green Mile*, was foreshadowed by McDowell's Blackwater series. Although the six individual volumes are long enough to constitute individual novels, they really don't stand well on their own and are, rather, instalments of a southern family saga with supernatural overtones. The opening volume, *The Flood*, establishes the Caskey family, a southern institution in their own right, decaying but defiant. And there's a secret in their past, a hint of the supernatural that has something to do with the nearby river. Elinor Dammert is an outsider who marries into the family and becomes involved in an occult power struggle that continues in the second volume, *The Levee*, following the birth of her first child. With the coming of the Great Depression, Elinor and the matriarch of the Caskeys strike an uneasy truce in order to maintain the family's status and property, and outsiders who seek their fortunes at the expense of the Caskeys often end up dead, and occasionally dismembered. The story is chronicled through the first world war in *The War*, the aftermath in *The Fortune*, and concludes in *Rain*, wherein the bill comes due for all the supernatural protection the Caskeys have enjoyed throughout the years. Although very low-key and decidedly non-graphic, the six-volume novel is particularly effective in creating and sustaining a brooding, unsettling mood, and the tension between the outsider and the Caskey matriarch is superbly handled.

McDowell wrote only a handful of short stories before leaving the horror field, but of those several are excellent, including "Halloween Candy," "Inside the Closet," "In the Cards," and "Odds." Some of his television work involved horror tales, but McDowell has largely abandoned the genre since the mid-1980s and seems unlikely to resume his career. His published horror fiction grew steadily more sophisticated and original, but he left the field before he had established himself as one of its major names. The Blackwater books and *Cold Moon Over Babylon* may well be the only works that will be remembered.

—Don D'Ammassa

McEWAN, Ian (Russell)

Nationality: British. **Born:** Aldershot, Hampshire, 21 June 1948. **Education:** Woolverstone Hall School; University of Sussex, Brighton, B.A. (honours) in English 1970; University of East Anglia, Norwich, M.A. in English 1971. **Family:** Married Penny Allen in 1982 (divorced 1995); two stepdaughters and two sons. **Awards:** Somerset Maugham award, 1976; *Evening Standard* award, for screenplay, 1983. D.Litt.: University of Sussex, 1989; University of East Anglia, 1993. Fellow, Royal Society of Literature, 1984. **Address:** c/o Jonathan Cape Ltd., 20 Vauxhall Bridge Road, London SW1V 2SA, England. Lives in Oxford.

HORROR, GHOST AND GOTHIC PUBLICATIONS

Novels

The Cement Garden. London, Cape, and New York, Simon and Schuster, 1978.

The Comfort of Strangers. London, Cape, and New York, Simon and Schuster, 1981.
The Child in Time. London, Cape, and Boston, Houghton Mifflin, 1987.
The Innocent. London, Cape, and New York, Doubleday, 1990.
Black Dogs. London, Cape, and New York, Doubleday, 1992.

Short Stories

First Love, Last Rites. New York, Random House, and London, Cape, 1975.
In Between the Sheets. London, Cape, 1978; New York, Simon and Schuster, 1979.

OTHER PUBLICATIONS

Plays

The Imitation Game: Three Plays for Television (includes *Solid Geometry* and *Jack Flea's Birthday Celebration*). London, Cape, 1981; Boston, Houghton Mifflin, 1982.
Or Shall We Die? (oratorio), music by Michael Berkeley (produced London, 1983; New York, 1985). London, Cape, 1983.
The Ploughman's Lunch (screenplay). London, Methuen, 1985.
Soursweet (screenplay). London, Faber, 1988.
A Move Abroad: Or Shall We Die? and *The Ploughman's Lunch.* London, Pan, 1989.

Screenplays: *The Ploughman's Lunch,* 1983; *Soursweet,* 1989; *The Good Son,* 1994.

Radio Play: *Conversation with a Cupboardman,* 1975.

Television Plays and Films: *Jack Flea's Birthday Celebration,* 1976; *The Imitation Game,* 1980; *The Last Day of Summer,* from his own short story, 1983.

Other (for children)

Rose Blanche. London, Cape, 1985.
The Daydreamer. London, Cape, and New York, HarperCollins, 1994.

*

Critical Studies: "*The Cement Garden* d'Ian McEwan" by Max Duperray, in *Études Anglaises* (Paris), vol. 35, no. 4, 1982; "McEwan/Barthes" by David Sampson, in *Southern Review* (Adelaide), March 1984.

*   *   *

"Postmodern macabre" might be the best shorthand description of dramatist, novelist and short-story writer Ian McEwan's powerfully disturbing cinematic prose. Graceful, restrained, yet capable of visceral shocks and unflinching brutality (as well as the driest humour), McEwan's books chart the snares, pits and deadfalls of our contemporary psycho-terrain, venturing perhaps a little into the past (*The Innocent*) and a little into the future (*The Child in Time*) for variety's sake and in pursuit of differing aesthetic goals. Unaffiliated with "horror" as an exercise in genre publishing, McEwan has secured a much wider reputation as one of modern fiction's brightest lights.

Intimations of McEwan's forceful abilities to astound and frighten arrived with *First Love, Last Rites* (the yoking of sex and mortality in the title signalled a major continuing theme in his work). Comprised of stories written circa 1972-75, these fictions were among the first to hint at a generational shift in the writing of horror, a passing of the torch from older to younger writers, McEwan himself being only 20-something at the time. New narrative modes, fresh concerns and updated bogeymen would now prevail. Without McEwan's trail-blazing efforts, no such a writer as Clive Barker, for instance, would have been possible.

Incest—a phenomenon that will partially propel McEwan's first novel—crops up in "Homemade." "Solid Geometry," one of McEwan's rare genre appearances, having appeared in *Amazing Stories* magazine, features a kind of steampunkish, *Flatland* ambience of mathematical terror. "Butterflies" is the first-person narrative of a child molester, evoking some of the same readerly pity that will be found in *The Child in Time*.

Hard on the heels of this accomplished first book came *The Cement Garden.* Employing the rich template used by Shirley Jackson in *We Have Always Lived in the Castle* (1962) of a family in morbid isolation, as well as ringing changes on Poe's "The Fall of the House of Usher" (1839), *Cement Garden* tells the story of four children: Jack, Tom, Sue and Julie. Upon the death of their mother, already a widow, the children conspire to bury her in the cellar and maintain a facade of life as usual. Adolescent Julie and Jack (the narrator) at first manage to keep up appearances, but undercurrents of apathy, *ennui* and burgeoning sexuality soon lead to disaster.

The Cement Garden proves that the lessons of Golding's *Lord of the Flies* (1954) apply equally well in the midst of civilization as on a deserted island. In retrospect, the book foreshadows the sociological trend of child abandonment and mistreatment that would come to dominate headlines and fiction over the next two decades, as well as functioning as a parable of England's general decay. (The quintessential Britishness of McEwan's work makes his rare fictional forays abroad stand out.)

In Between the Sheets, another story collection, appeared the same year as McEwan's first novel, and it seemed he would continue to alternate working at both short and longer lengths. But this collection was to be his final one to date, as he concentrated on novels and screenplays. The loss to readers is real.

"Pornography" is a reflection on obsessional abuse of both self and others, with consequent gory payback (and perhaps can be read as McEwan inflicting a jokey punishment on himself for the same obsessional attitude, before his critics can do it themselves!). "Two Fragments: March 199—" is a tentative stab at evoking the atmosphere of totalitarian squalor to be found in *The Child in Time*. "Dead as They Come" conflates sex and murder once more. The standout story, for its wry humour, is "Psychopolis," whose British narrator finds himself losing his grip on the stage-set of Los Angeles, where mindgames proliferate.

The Comfort of Strangers is McEwan's second novel, and possibly his slightest, although it does not fail to deliver what was promised. Highly reminiscent of Nicolas Roeg's 1973 film, *Don't Look Now*, as well as the early stylish thrillers of Roman Polanski, *Comfort* is the story of Colin and Mary, an unmarried couple vacationing in Venice, Italy (not the Venice, California, of "Psychopolis"). Befriended by locals Robert and Caroline, the two tourists are sucked into the pathologies of the latter pair, heading blithely to their doom. A Jamesian seduction of "innocent" non-Continentals, this book will be echoed by McEwan's fourth novel.

Technically science fiction, *The Child in Time* is set in an utterly Thatcherized future England of licensed beggars and other civilized atrocities. Married couple Stephen and Julie Lewis, with daughter Kate, are typical citizens, Stephen working for the government and hence somewhat complicit in his shabby country's fate. One day Kate is kidnapped during a moment of parental inattention. This fateful incident—the source of whatever not inconsequential horror there is in this book—shatters all futures, driving the characters to painful realizations. Employing the quasi-metaphysical theories of physicist David Bohm, McEwan eventually provides Stephen with a time-travel incident back to his own parents' courtship as a purgative that makes redemption possible.

The horror in *The Innocent* is twofold: the apocalyptic insanity of the Cold War at its height (the book's setting is divided Berlin circa 1955) and the complicitous shock of individual murder upon an uncalloused soul. Taken together, these two forces compound the terror that overtakes "the innocent," Leonard Marnham, young electronics technician abroad. Finding himself caught up both in espionage and a dangerous love affair with a local woman named Maria Eckdorf, Marnham eventually must face the darkest parts of himself, with only "some general notion of decency" to guide him. Typical of McEwan's resolute gaze on the worst life has to offer is the protracted, stomach-wrenching scene wherein Marnham must dismember his victim and dispose of the packaged remains. With flavours of James M. Cain and James Bond, *The Innocent* neatly fuses the personal and the political.

Black Dogs, the latest of McEwan's ever-shifting explorations into what truly horrifies, reminds this reader somewhat of Brian Aldiss's "Squire Quartet": an investigation into sustainable philosophical bases for conducting one's life in the late-20th century, not ignoring the mystical. Bernard and June Tremaine are visited by the titular animals, a kind of avatar of Churchillian melancholy and Dunsanian embodied lusts. Meeting on "[a] path, which belonged to any creature that could walk it," June and the devil dogs undergo a confrontation revelatory of life's implicit unfairness, an unfairness mediated only by "the human heart, the spirit, the soul, consciousness itself."

With his propensity for gripping first-person narratives and tight prose, and his willingness to examine both the best and worst in human nature, McEwan is a mask-wearing shaman guiding his readers on the blackest of night-sea journeys.

—Paul Di Filippo

McGRATH, Patrick

Nationality: British. **Born:** London, 1950. **Education:** Beaumont College; University of London, B.A. in English. **Career:** Orderly, Ontario State Mental Hospital, Oakridge, from 1971, then a teacher in Vancouver, Canada; contributor to various magazines and newspapers. Has lived in New York City since 1981. **Agent:** Jane Gregory Agency, Riverside Studios, Crisp Road, London NW6 9RL, England.

HORROR, GHOST AND GOTHIC PUBLICATIONS

Novels

The Grotesque. London, Viking, and New York, Poseidon Press, 1989.
Spider. New York, Poseidon Press, 1990; London, Viking, 1991.
Dr. Haggard's Disease. London, Viking, and New York, Poseidon Press, 1993.
Asylum. London, Viking, 1996.

Short Stories

Blood and Water and Other Tales. New York, Poseidon Press, 1988; London, Penguin, 1989.
The Angel and Other Stories (three stories from *Blood and Water*). London, Penguin, 1995.

Play

Screenplay: *The Grotesque*, 1995.

Other

Editor, with Bradford Morrow, *The New Gothic: A Collection of Contemporary Gothic Fiction*. New York, Random House, 1991; as *The Picador Book of the New Gothic*, London, Picador, 1992.

*

Film Adaptation: *The Grotesque*, 1995.

*   *   *

Way out on the fringe of genre horror, Patrick McGrath is writing bizarre tales about grotesque characters set in England some decades ago. The most striking aspect of his novels is the clever way in which he holds back information from the reader. These are dark psychological studies, often involving obsessions and mental hospitals.

The most grotesque and gothic of his four novels is, suitably enough, *The Grotesque*, which is also a black comedy and comes close to being a farce that parodies the gothic. It is set in 1949-50 at Crook Manor in Berkshire and is narrated by Sir Hugo Coal. He comes across from the start as an opinionated tyrant who is rude to most people and terrorizes his wife, his marriageable daughter Cleo and his daughter's prospective husband Sidney Giblet. He has a poor opinion of the newly-appointed butler, Fledge.

Initially he seems to be a figure of fun, obsessive about dinosaur fossils, at loggerheads with the Secretary of the Royal Society (to whom he is desperate to give a lecture on his own great dinosaur theory), inhabiting a crumbling ruin of a house and friendly only with George Lecky, who runs a pig farm on land rented from Sir Hugo. Only gradually does the reader come to realize that, at the time from which he is narrating, Sir Hugo is paralysed with a stroke and regarded as no more than a vegetable by all except his daughter; there is nobody to hear or be affected by his narration, yet from his position of immobility in a wheelchair he can see and hear much of what occurs in the house. And one comes to have great sympathy for him.

The nine months he describes mark the downfall of Crook Manor in many respects, from the disappearance of Sidney one night in October to the hanging of George Lecky for his murder the following May. The butler, whom Sir Hugo suspects of Sidney's murder, seems to be having an affair with Sir Hugo's wife Harriet, and he has dispensed with his butler's uniform to wear tweeds: the servant has become the master. The erudite narration (which is too subjective for the reader ever to discover the truth behind the mysteries at the Manor) and the search for a happy ending (it never comes) help to counterbalance the silly names of people and places.

With *Spider*, McGrath has performed a similarly clever trick of gradually revealing layers of truth concerning another narrator, this time a man of humble origins. Spider is a family nickname for Dennis Clegg, son of a plumber in London's East End. The father drinks too much and probably murders Spider's mother, burying her on his allotment garden. A plump prostitute is installed in the family home, and eventually young Spider is locked away in an asylum for his mother's murder. That happens in the 1930s. When he is released in the 1950s he is an odd, secretive individual, paranoid, scarcely able to cope with life and easily upset. It is his journal of his years at home and in the asylum which, together with his flawed memories, makes up the novel. And it is partly the psychology of this odd, inadequate person which provides the horror. Clearly he is subject to delusions, and one can only be sad at the waste of his life.

Dr. Haggard's Disease might almost be dismissed as a love story with an unhappy ending, except that the unhappiness is so consuming in its effects and the eventual outcome is so bizarre. It is set in London and on the south coast of England just before and during World War II. The eponymous doctor is a junior surgeon at a major London hospital who has an affair with Fanny, the wife of the hospital's senior pathologist. They are happy with elicit meetings for a few months, once making love late at night in the vast marble lobby of the hospital itself. But the strain of secrecy becomes too much for Fanny, and she ends their relationship. Moreover, her husband, finding out, knocks Haggard down a flight of steps at the hospital, so that he breaks his hip.

Haggard is forever changed. He never manages to stop loving Fanny; and the metal pin in his hip, which he anthropomorphizes as "Spike," leaves him walking with a stick and in permanent pain. He injects himself with morphine to kill the pain and becomes addicted. But he manages to move to a small town on the south coast, not too far from Brighton, where he buys the practice and house of a doctor who is retiring. There, at the beginning of the war, he tells some of this story to James, the barely adult son of Fanny and her husband, who is a young Spitfire pilot. (Fanny is, by this time, only two years after their affair, dead from a kidney ailment.) It is this friendship which revives Haggard's zest for life. But when Haggard treats James for a minor combat wound he notices that James looks more feminine than he should: it seems that his endocrine balance may have been disturbed by the stress of flying in the Battle of Britain. James suspects Haggard's motives, thinking that his genitals are being examined with homosexual intent. (And it may be that there is an element of this in Haggard's feeling for the attractive young man who looks so much like Fanny.) So Dr. Haggard's disease of unrequited love is cured by James, but his dream of James's condition being named Dr. Haggard's disease never works out, because James dies when his damaged aircraft crash-lands on the airfield, and Haggard, holding the body, dies when its fuel tanks explode.

Similarly tragic and concerned with sexual obsession is *Asylum*, set partly at a fictionalized Broadmoor Hospital. Stella, the wife of Max Raphael, the institution's deputy superintendent, has an affair with Edgar Stark, a patient who has murdered his wife. After Stark escapes, due partly to Stella's unwitting help, he has the audacity to phone her; they meet in London and later she lives with him there. He is a sculptor, sometimes insanely jealous, and she runs away from him in fear of her life. She goes back to her husband, but distrust and bad publicity force them to leave; Max Raphael gets a worse job at an asylum in Wales. Husband and wife become alienated and after their young son drowns without Stella trying to save him she is institutionalized at the fictional Broadmoor.

The story is set in 1959-60 and is narrated by Dr. Peter Cleve, the new medical superintendent of the hospital, who personally treats Stella. His incisive clinical detail makes a sharp contrast to the obsession of Stella's love for Stark. Although Cleve does his best for her, and even plans to marry her upon her release, nothing can change her desire for Stark, and she commits suicide.

McGrath's collection *Blood and Water and Other Tales* was his first book, very well received, and hailed as "postmodern-gothic." Its contents are very varied and often more gruesome than anything in the novels. Featured in "The Angel," for example, is an elderly man, actually an angel, whose body is decomposing but who cannot die.

—Chris Morgan

McKENNEY, Kenneth

Nationality: Fiji Islander. **Born:** Suva, Fiji, 4 April 1929. **Education:** University of Auckland, B.Sc. 1952. **Family:** Married Pamela Webster, 1952 (divorced); married Virginia Susan Whalley, 20 October 1972; one daughter. **Career:** Geologist in northwest Queensland, Australia, 1954-55, and gold mines in Fiji, 1955-56; advertising copywriter in Auckland, New Zealand, 1957-58; Ponsonby Post (newspaper), Auckland, founder, editor, copywriter, 1960; writer and producer of television commercials in Australia, 1962-65; Young & Rubicam, London, England, television producer in Europe, Mexico, and Japan, 1967-77; director of television commercials in Mexico, 1977. **Agent:** International Creative Management, 40 West 57th St., New York, NY 10019, USA.

HORROR, GHOST AND GOTHIC PUBLICATIONS

Novels (series: Moonchild)

The Plants. New York, Putnam, 1976.
The Moonchild. New York, Simon and Schuster, 1978.
The Fire Cloud. New York, Simon and Schuster, 1979; London, Macdonald, 1980.
The Changeling (Moonchild). New York, Avon, 1985.
The Offspring (Moonchild). New York, Ballantine, 1990.

OTHER PUBLICATIONS

Novel

The Terminator. New York, Franklin Watts, 1972.

* * *

As with any other genre, it is sometimes difficult to pin down just exactly what the term "horror fiction" means. Stephen King's *The Tommyknockers* uses a classic science-fiction plot device, for example, but few would argue that it isn't horror. Thomas Harris employs no supernatural or occult forces in *The Silence of the Lambs*, but that novel won the Bram Stoker award. Yvonne Navarro's *Final Impact* and Richard Laymon's *Quake* are about the aftermath of a major disaster and the way some of the survivors prey upon one another, but these also are horror novels of a sort. Kenneth McKenney has drawn on elements of horror found in each of these at one time or another as well as in the more familiar supernatural realm.

His first novel, *The Plants*, was one of a wave of books that appeared with the general theme of nature gone wild. England is blessed with a warm, rainy summer that is ideal for plantlife. In one small village, an oversized squash that seems to have grown overnight is the focal point for mounting tension between its owner, who initially enjoys his sudden notoriety, and a neighbour who insists that the plant is unnatural and dangerous. In due course, plants begin to actively attack people they don't like, tearing them apart with thorns or strangling them. There's a lot of subsequent pseudoscience about plants having created animals to provide them with carbon dioxide and finally being bestirred to take back control of the Earth, a weak rationalization best ignored. The incidents escalate and the villagers begin to panic, believing that the devil walks among them, but a young girl has learned to communicate with the plants and she eventually provides the key to working out an understanding with them. The implausible plot detracts considerably from what might otherwise have been a powerful story, as McKenney does an excellent job of creating individual scenes, and his characterization is well above average.

The Fire Cloud is a disaster novel set in Mexico. A dormant volcano near Mexico City rouses from its slumber to devastate the surrounding countryside. Although the novel is mostly about surviving the aftermath, there are distinct horror elements to be found within it. A young woman is desperately searching for her daughter, who has been kidnapped by a mysterious Aztec cult who plan to sacrifice the girl to placate the angry volcano god. There's also a scientist who believes he has discovered the key to predicting and even controlling eruptions, but whose knowledge may actually cause more trouble than it prevents. *The Fire Cloud* is a nicely paced thriller with only minor interest to horror readers.

McKenney's major contribution to the horror field is the trilogy consisting of *The Moonchild*, *The Changeling* and *The Offspring*. The Blackstone family is vacationing in Europe when young Simon is struck down by a mysterious illness which eventually kills him, though *rigor mortis* never sets in. At the wake, when his governess remains alone with the body, young Simon Blackstone's corpse becomes reanimated long enough to strangle her. The couple encounter an enigmatic old woman the following day who informs them their son has become a moonchild, his soul lost forever, unless they act to bring him eternal peace. The only way to achieve that is to bury him on the spot where he was born. Although initially sceptical, the Blackstones are forced to accept what they have been told when they see that their son's body has begun to change into that of a demon, and later when he claims another victim. Their voyage back to England is not uneventful, unfortunately, but they persevere in time to inter the boy's body as they have been directed. Well plotted and occasionally very eerie, but flawed by a great deal of very stilted dialogue.

The two sequels were less successful. Although his soul was supposed to have been allowed to ascend to heaven, it turns out that wasn't the case. When a labourer inadvertently opens Simon's casket, he is killed and Simon immediately matures into a handsome young man. This time he's able to function in daylight without being compelled to kill everyone in sight, but he still has a problem when the moon is out. It causes him to have violent seizures and a tendency to slaughter his companions. The dialogue is much improved in both *The Changeling* and *The Offspring*, but the mystery of Simon's continued existence makes progressively less sense.

McKenney is at his best capable of creating interesting scenes and images, and his characters are frequently a cut above the average found in similar novels. His prose style is transparent and usually smooth, although *The Moonchild* sometimes feels like a rough draft that never received its final polish. The Moonchild series is his major contribution to the horror field, but it is not a memorable enough work to mark him as having any lasting influence in the genre.

—Don D'Ammassa

McNALLY, Clare

Nationality: American. **Address:** c/o Tor Books, Tom Doherty Associates, Inc., 175 Fifth Avenue, 14th Floor, New York, NY 10010, USA.

Nationality: American. **Address:** c/o Tor Books, Tom Doherty Associates, Inc., 175 Fifth Avenue, 14th Floor, New York, NY 10010, USA.

HORROR, GHOST AND GOTHIC PUBLICATIONS

Novels

Ghost House. New York, Bantam, 1979; London, Corgi, 1980.
Ghost House Revenge. New York, Bantam, and London, Corgi, 1981.
Ghost Light. New York, Bantam, and London, Corgi, 1982.
What About the Baby? New York, Bantam, 1983; London, Corgi, 1990.
Somebody Come and Play. New York, Tor, and London, Corgi, 1987.
Addison House. New York, Avon, 1988.
Come Down into Darkness. London, Corgi, 1989.
Hear the Children Calling . . . . New York, Onyx, and Sutton, Surrey, Severn House, 1990.
Cries of the Children. New York, Onyx, 1992.
There He Keeps Them Very Well. New York, Tor, 1994; as *The Evil That Christy Knows*, Sutton, Surrey, Severn House, 1995.
Stage Fright. New York, Tor, 1995.
Goodnight, Sweet Angel. New York, Tor, 1996.

*   *   *

Ghost stories have always been more popular in Europe than America, perhaps because there are no ancient castles in the western hemisphere, no buildings with long and half-forgotten histories of dark deeds and old pain. Most American novels of hauntings are very untraditional, as for example Peter Straub's *Ghost Story*, Richard Matheson's *Hell House*, or Stephen King's *The Shining*. But there have been exceptions, among which Clare McNally's early novels are definitely to be included.

Ghost House was almost certainly inspired by the "Amityville" books, which initially pretended to be factual. The Van Buren family moves into their new home on Long Island, expecting to have some problems adjusting to their new environment, but never expecting that their house itself would be their greatest challenge. The evidence of a haunting escalates rapidly from mildly spooky pranks to outright possession of the bodies of the living. Although the Van Burens believe at the end of that novel that their home has been cleansed of the evil spirits, they find out differently in *Ghost House Revenge*. There's a new spirit, even nastier than what went before, but even though the manifestations come faster and with greater impact, the sequel fails to build suspense as well as its predecessor.

Ghost Light is reminiscent of Frank De Felitta's *Audrey Rose*. A young girl who was killed in a terrible fire in a theatre returns in spirit form to haunt the scene of her death. With a disturbing childlike brutality, she begins to kill people in what appear to be accidents, gradually building toward the inevitable climactic confrontation with the reincarnation of her long-dead father. *What About the Baby?* breaks the pattern of the early novels slightly, although like virtually all of McNally's work, the focus is on children. In the early 19th century, a woman with occult powers discovers that her infant son has been murdered. She uses her magic to reach into the present, where she inflicts terrible visions upon a pregnant teenager. Her plan to steal the child at birth goes awry however when the new mother enlists the aid of friends who can counter her dark magic.

Nicole is a mysterious young child in *Somebody Come and Play*, one whom no adult ever sees. She lures a group of youngsters to an abandoned building and initiates them into a new game, a game that kills one and injures another. Nicole is a vengeful ghost, awakened from her long sleep by the presence of children in her original home. *Somebody Come and Play* was a major leap forward for McNally, the first of her ghost stories to generate its greatest impact with subtlety. Nicole is a far more convincing menace than the more overtly evil spirits that preceded her. McNally's growing confidence in her ability to create characters is evident as well in *Addison House*, a fairly traditional haunted-house story that derives added impact from the way the ghostly characters intermingle with the live ones, so that neither they, nor sometimes the reader, can distinguish between the living and the dead. Once again, the children are a major focus of attention, but this time the adults are more than the simple sketches in her earlier novels.

Hear the Children Calling . . . abandoned ghosts entirely. The LaMane Center is supposedly dedicated to helping children, but the staff are actually involved in a secret research project designed to enhance the mental abilities of those under their care through illegal experimentation. The villains this time are human, and the novel is more of a detective story than horror. McNally's next effort was a variation of this theme. *Cries of the Children . . .* features three abandoned youngsters with psychic powers. Although they are adopted, someone later kidnaps them and the adoptive parents set out on a far-ranging quest to rescue them from an evil power that plans to use the children as expendable tools in a quest for political power. Both of these novels play with extrasensory abilities and hints of the occult, but their tone is decidedly more that of a contemporary thriller.

Stage Fright resembles *Ghost Light* but with noticeable improvements. Hayley was stalked for years by an insane playwright who committed several murders before committing suicide. Following his death, she makes a new life for herself with a small theatre group, but before long a series of mysterious accidents reminds her of his final admonition that she wait for the playwright to return. As the angry spirit strikes at those around her, Hayley ultimately draws on her own unsuspected occult powers to destroy her tormentor before he kills everyone she loves. *Stage Fright* is McNally's strongest, most sustained novel.

Good Night, Sweet Angel is another ghost story, but this one with a new twist. Emily is a young child whose father died while trying to kill his entire family. She and her mother survived, but her father's angry spirit has remained tied to the world of the living and is waiting for an opportunity to complete the task at which he previously failed. Emily is defended not only by her mother but by the ghost of Tara, a long-dead child, who seems to be able to neutralize the man's efforts. But Tara isn't as selfless as she appears; she is unhappy about the life she never had and plans to possess Emily's body for her own use. It is smoothly written and nicely plotted, but less suspenseful than *Stage Fright*.

McNally's novels of children in jeopardy have been so successful that there's little incentive for her to experiment. Her occasional variations, *Stage Fright* and *Addison House*, indicate that she can write well outside of that pattern, creating interesting adult characters as well as children. Although well known for her ghost stories, she has attracted little attention from horror fans in general because of her specialization.

—Don D'Ammassa

METCALFE, John

Nationality: British. **Born:** Heacham, Norfolk, 1891. **Education:** St. Felix College, Felixstowe, Suffolk; Nelson's School, North Walsham, Norfolk; University of London, B.A. in philosophy 1913. **Military Service:** Served in the Royal Air Force in both World Wars. **Family:** Married the novelist Evelyn Scott in 1930. **Career:** Teacher, Highgate School, London; emigrated to the United States, 1928, but travelled much thereafter; freelance writer. **Died:** 31 July 1965.

HORROR, GHOST AND GOTHIC PUBLICATIONS

Novels

The Feasting Dead. Sauk City, Wisconsin, Arkham House, 1954.
My Cousin Geoffrey. London, Macdonald, 1956.

Short Stories

The Smoking Leg and Other Stories. London, Jarrolds, 1925; New York, Doubleday, 1926.
Judas and Other Stories. London, Constable, 1931.
Brenner's Boy. London, White Owl Press, 1932.

OTHER PUBLICATIONS

Novels

Spring Darkness. London, Constable, 1928; as *Mrs. Condover*, n.p., n.d.

Arm's-Length. London, Constable, and New York, Scribner, 1930.
Foster-Girl. N.p., 1935; as *Sally*, n.p., n.d.
All Friends Are Strangers. N.p., 1948.

*   *   *

John Metcalfe's contribution to the genre of weird fiction was by no means prolific but it includes a number of stories which are highly distinctive, aided in their metaphysical adventurousness by his academic training in philosophy. The manifestations of the supernatural in his stories are rarely overtly menacing but their sheer peculiarity is such that they build up a unique sense of unease.

In the title story of *The Smoking Leg* a surgeon implants a magical gem and a powerful amulet in the leg of a seaman in order that they may be safely smuggled into England. Although the amulet is supposed to cancel out the effects of the gem the energy of their antagonism becomes manifest—and their removal does not proceed smoothly. An equally powerful but similarly uncontrollable gem is featured in "Nightmare Jack." "The Double Admiral" is an excellent enigmatic tale of doppelgängers and an illusory island. "The Grey House" is a similarly studied metaphysical fantasy whose tentative theme is carried to a much further extreme in the oft-reprinted and highly atmospheric "The Bad Lands." The non-supernatural tales in the collection are equally quirky, several of them involving fearful dreams, obsessions and deliriums. "Paper Windmills" is an excellent account of a boy's anxieties running out of control; "The Tunnel" and "The Flying Tower" are neat *contes cruels.*

The fantastic stories in *Judas and Other Stories* continue the author's painstaking development of his own subtle species of weird tale. The most interesting and effective are "Mortmain," in which a honeymoon cruise is dogged by a ghostly barge and sinister moths, and "Mr. Meldrum's Mania," about a man who believes that his transformation into a god is beset by problems of adaptation. "Time Fuse" is an ironic reflection of the assumption that faith may enable ordinary people to perform little miracles, and "Face of Bassett" is an equally trivial tale of a delusory apparition. "No Sin," which follows the example of "Mortmain" and "Face of Bassett" in allowing the dead to intrude upon the new romances of their one-time partners, is an effective *conte cruel.* Although separately published, *Brenner's Boy* is a short story closely akin to those in *Judas and Other Stories*, in which the horrid behaviour of a child who turns out to be a ghost stirs up murky resonances within the relationship of the couple with whom he comes to stay.

During the next 20 years Metcalfe painstakingly assembled enough material to make another collection, which he attempted to publish with the novella *The Feasting Dead* as a title-piece, but he could not place it. August Derleth's Arkham House issued the novella as a separate item and Derleth then used four more of the stories in various anthologies issued between 1962 and 1971. Like *Brenner's Boy, The Feasting Dead* involves the son of a military man whose behaviour becomes puzzlingly troublesome; in this instance the change is correlated with the boy's association with a French servant he first encounters on an exchange visit to Auvergne. When the boy's father investigates the background on his unwelcome guest he finds that the man is supposedly dead, and concludes that he is now *un épouvantail.* The French word in question usually refers to a scarecrow, but here is used in a more general sense as "bogeyman"—although the monster does indeed contrive his final return in the guise of a scarecrow. Although *l'épouvantail* is not a vampire in any explicit sense his attachment to the child ultimately proves fatal, his soul having provided the "feast" referred to in the title.

Derleth reprinted *The Feasting Dead* in an anthology which he did for the British Souvenir Press in 1963, *When Evil Wakes*; that presumably reached a wider audience than the Arkham House edition, but the story remains little-known, although it is one of the most elegantly constructed literary accounts of "psychic vampirism." Metcalfe re-employed the motif in a more acceptably metaphorical fashion in his final novel, *My Cousin Geoffrey*, an intense psychological study of hero-worship and rivalry, but the diplomatic hesitancy with which he develops the theme does not work to its advantage. The four stories which Derleth included—two of them posthumously—in Arkham House anthologies are mostly lighter in tone. "The Firing-Chamber" is a *conte cruel* involving an unlikely coincidence, while "The Renegade" and "Not There" have more comedy in them than horror. On the other hand, "Beyondaril," in *Dark Things* (1971), is one of Metcalfe's finest tales of mental breakdown and sinister obsession.

Metcalfe's literary career, like that of his American wife Evelyn Scott, suffered a marked decline after some initial success; they ended their lives in desolate poverty. Metcalfe obtained slightly more critical acclaim for his naturalistic work than for his weird tales but all his work is now virtually forgotten. He fell between two stools, in that he retained the melodramatic motifs of popular horror fiction while subjecting them to unusually subtle development, thus failing to entertain the popular genre audience while never achieving the respectability claimed by such near-surreal writers of supernatural fiction as Walter de la Mare. The example he set was, however, of some relevance to the work of such later writers as L. P. Hartley and Robert Aickman, who might be seen as further developers of his idiosyncratic method. The neglect into which Metcalfe's work has fallen is very unfortunate; an excellent eclectic collection could be compiled by combining *The Feasting Dead* with the cream of his short fiction, and it is high time that some such project was attempted.

—Brian Stableford

MIDDLETON, Richard B(arham)

Nationality: British. **Born:** Staines, Middlesex, 28 October 1882. **Education:** University of London. **Career:** Clerk; magazine editor; poet and short-story writer. **Died:** 1 December 1911.

HORROR, GHOST AND GOTHIC PUBLICATIONS

Short Stories

The Ghost Ship, and Other Stories. London, Fisher Unwin, and New York, Michael Kennerley, 1912.

OTHER PUBLICATIONS

Short Stories

The Pantomime Man, edited by John Gawsworth. London, Rich and Cowan, 1932.

Play

The District Visitor. Baltimore, Remington, 1924.

Poetry

Poems and Songs, First Series. London, Fisher Unwin, and New York, Michael Kennerley, 1912.
Poems and Songs, Second Series. London, Fisher Unwin, and New York, Michael Kennerley, 1912.

Other

The Day Before Yesterday. London, Fisher Unwin, and New York, Michael Kennerley, 1912.
Monologues. London, Fisher Unwin, and New York, Michael Kennerley, 1912.
Richard Middleton's Letters to Henry Savage. London, Mandrake Press, 1929.

*

Critical Studies: *Richard Middleton: The Man and His Work* by Henry Savage, London, Cecil Palmer, 1922; "Two Suicides" in *Buried Caesars* by Vincent Starrett, New York, Covici-Mcgee, 1923; "A Poet's Death: Richard Middleton" by Stephen Wayne Foster in *The Romantist* #4-5, 1980-81; "Richard Middleton: Beauty, Sadness and Terror" by Darrell Schweitzer in *Discovering Classic Horror Fiction I* edited by Schweitzer, Mercer Island, Washington, Starmont House, 1992.

*   *   *

Richard Middleton is one of those tragic figures with which writing and the arts are too often presented. A manic depressive who believed he would never achieve success, he killed himself on the eve of potential greatness. His books were all published posthumously. A gifted poet with tender vision, Middleton brought much of that grace to his short stories. The best of these, most of them ghost stories or mystical evocations, can be found in a single volume, *The Ghost Ship.* The original binding bears Middleton's signature only on the cover, no title, and the frontispiece presents us with the forlorn visage of Middleton. These two aspects give a sad, almost despairing feel to the book which is balanced by Arthur Machen's effusive introduction which reminds us what a gifted talent had been lost.

It is all the more surprising, therefore, that the volume opens with a humorous story, "The Ghost Ship" (*The Century*, 1912), one of the few successful humorous ghost stories and held in high regard by many. A ghostly pirate ship is blown by a storm inland onto a turnip field, which decidedly upsets the farmer. The rowdy crew disturbs the villagers and the ship is something of a nuisance. It is eventually blown away in another gale, taking with it many of the village ghosts plus one "daft lad" who couldn't wait till he was dead. The story works because of its reflection upon human nature—it would work even if it hadn't been a ghost story. Middleton simply uses the spectral ship and its ghostly crew to add further moments of humour. The way the dead play tricks upon the living and the fact that only the village simpleton returns suggest Middleton was also playing his own game with "The Pied Piper of Hamelin."

"On the Brighton Road" is another classic which reflects the melancholy of the author. A tramp encounters another on the road and it is only as the story progresses that we discover that the tramp is a ghost soon to be joined by the ghost of the boy, and that the road is their eternal afterlife from which they cannot escape. The mood of being trapped pervades many of the stories and draws us in to Middleton's own tortured agonies. Even the non-fantastic stories in the collection become almost suffocatingly oppressive, although all are beautifully written from a poet's perspective. Many of the stories are painfully autobiographical. In "Fate and the Artist" we endure the feelings of George, to whom street railings "keep all London in a cage" and who yearns to be free. He tells escapist stories to children and though they enjoy them they do not believe them. When imagination dies, so does George. In "A Drama of Youth" (*English Review*, 1911) a child so hates his time at school that he encourages his own illness in order to escape. In Middleton's stories escapism never succeeds, or if it does, it is only illusory.

Two of the most beautiful stories in the book are also the most tragic. In "Children of the Moon," two children seek magic and enchantment by moonlight and their imagination conjures up wondrous visions, which they are able to share only with a lunatic. "The Bird in the Garden" (*The Academy*, 1911) reveals the perceptions of a little boy whose imagination escapes the sordid reality of life to a garden of beauty where he waits expectantly for a magical bird. As he grows older the real world fights to control him and at the end the boy summons the bird which is "the end of everything."

These stories are Middleton's best and include some of the most magical writing in all fantastic literature. Others, previously unpublished, were salvaged by John Gawsworth who incorporated them in his anthologies and collected others in a second volume, *The Pantomime Man.* Most of these stories are non-fantastic and far from Gothic though a few, like "The Murderer" (*New Tales of Horror*, 1934), "Murray's Child" and "Eccentric Lady Tullswater" (both in *Crimes, Creeps and Thrills*, 1936), are further explorations of Middleton's perception of madness.

The death of Middleton was a tragedy, but it is only the tortured muse of a suicide like Middleton that can infuse so much vision and magic into fiction. Middleton's stories were his escape from reality, but the tragedy is that he never knew it.

—Mike Ashley

MILLER, Rex

Nationality: American. **Born:** 1929. **Career:** Radio disc jockey; initiated a successful James Bond satire on the radio which became an internationally syndicated series; mail-order entrepreneur; novelist and short-story writer. Lives in Missouri.

HORROR, GHOST AND GOTHIC PUBLICATIONS

Novels (series: Chaingang in all titles)

Slob. New York, Signet, 1987; London, Pan, 1988.
Frenzy. New York, Onyx, 1988; London, Pan, 1989.

Stone Shadow. New York, Onyx, 1989.
Profane Men. New York, Onyx, 1989.
Iceman. New York, Onyx, 1990.
Slice. New York, Onyx, 1990.
Chaingang. New York, Pocket, 1992.
Savant. New York, Pocket, 1994.
Butcher. New York, Pocket, 1994.

* * *

"And the scary thing is they all seem to have it now . . . Even the dumbest baby raper has learned the verbal tap dance, the combative vocal retroflex, the conversational tennis match . . ." These are the words of Rex Miller, in one of the frequent asides that aim to discuss the state of the world from Miller's Missouri safehouse—from behind the walls of his thick-skinned fiction. Something more evil than the average reader could imagine has arrived; and here comes Rex Miller to tell everybody all about it. But just think about that comparative for a moment: more evil than the average reader could imagine. When discussing Rex Miller there is nothing to be gained by exaggerating; Miller has already done all of the exaggerating for us. What he presents is a vision of cruelty and moral obsolescence, filtered through or exacerbated by the primitively nasty, self-lovingly preservatory imagination of one Daniel Bunkowski—also known as Chaingang—a serial killer, once abused by his parents and mind-controlled while in the killing fields of Vietnam. And Chaingang knows the "verbal tap dance," even if he chooses not to employ it most of the time. Raw force, for Bunkowski, is often the ticket.

Chaingang is Miller's finest and most frightening creation: a 500-pound mountain of blubber and nervous, vicious energy; a man of whom it is rumoured that for every pound of his body weight he has killed one person. The character of Chaingang was created for Miller's first novel, a tale of the Vietnam War called *Profane Men*, written in 1986 but not published until several years later. Rex Miller had wanted to write the book since 1971, but had had little success in its progression. Then Harlan Ellison introduced Miller to the agent Richard Curtis, who believed in the book but was wary because of the glut of other Vietnam novels already on the market. It was Curtis who suggested the composition of a novel solely about the lead character.

The revolting, powerful, unbelievable *Slob* was soon in embryo. Partly because of Miller's reclusive public figure, early audiences believed that Miller was Stephen King. It did not matter that King himself went on record with praise for the book: "Almost too crudely terrifying to be read . . . But it is too compelling to be put down," he said. The magazine *Publishers Weekly* wrote: "Fans for whom Stephen King doesn't write fast enough . . . should have a ripping good time." In fact, much more so than Stephen King, Rex Miller writes like Joe R. Lansdale, though Miller eschews the genre-hopping tendencies of Lansdale. Miller is horror, raw and simple: no punches are pulled in his work. While reading, the word "raw" springs to mind almost constantly. This fiction is like barely-cooked steak: still bleeding, but enormously rich and nourishing *in potentia*. His radio background has landed Miller in good stead; like the disc jockey he once was, Miller uses language that is both sassy and self-congratulatory; it is an electrifying mixture of hipster be-bop and true-crime murder factsheet. His fiction in many ways harks back to the 1970s, but is written with

the eye of experience. In Miller the reader finds a cocktail of the hardboiled style of Jim Thompson and the slangy quips of a modern-day Raymond Chandler.

Though Chaingang is slightly different in every book, the strength of his character is such that one can tune into the saga at any point and get an immediate impression of Chaingang's physical, mental and—above all—psychological vastness. From the high-profile violence in *Slob* and *Frenzy*, Chaingang emerged in *Slice* as badly disfigured, determined to terminate the only man who knows his *modus operandi*.

Most audiences with fondnesses for most genres welcome changes—albeit in small amounts at a time. For quite a while there has been an expectation in the horror genre that a villain will arrive who is not unduly motivated by sex, or perhaps has normal sexual relationships. Chaingang is not such a villain; he is crudely and diffidently charged with regard to his sex drive. His libidinous notions involve rape, torture and heart surgery. As a comment on what the Vietnam War did to some of its soldiers, this is a damning indictment indeed.

One gets the impression that the real Rex Miller is writing in the Chaingang novels—without the bracing distance of an imagined tale-teller. Miller knew all about the 1960s and 'Nam, and here he is—in *Slob*, *Chaingang*, *Slice*, *Savant*, among others—to comment on it, as though his imagination for murder (one must assume that Miller believes it to be a negative impulse) was formed in the same way that Chaingang's positive response was spawned. "Serial murders had seemed to spring out of the sixties like some kind of wartime anomaly or mutation caused by the poisonous karma of the Vietnam era." In all of the Chaingang novels, the Vietnam dream sequences feed the present fury, and the present fury feeds the Vietnam dream sequences: a circle of hatred and self-hatred.

Chaingang opens with some very specific feeding instructions for the man who is habitually called the beast. Bunkowski has been captured, and is now in maximum security. This novel is about control: financial and psychological.. An experiment is hatched to see if Chaingang can be controlled by those who are imprisoning him, using an implant in the killer's brain and radiophonic emissions to monitor Chaingang's behaviour. But in Miller's postmodern, sarcastic world, it is deemed fair play for Chaingang to kill killers, the rationale being that the beast wants to kill someone and that the killers would only hurt the innocent if they had a chance to do so. Thus, Chaingang becomes a commentary not only on the effects of war, but on the effects of violence being injected into the torpid lives of some ambitiously-challenged Americans. Like David Lynch's movie *Blue Velvet* the novel examines suburban America; it does not particularly highlight sudden acts of weirdness and corruption; rather, *Chaingang* highlights the rich tangy flavours of small-town America, Miller using a good ear for dialogue to make his characters speak in a convincing mix of slang and jokey banter.

Rex Miller does not write slasher novels; not novels in which characters are set up in a couple of paragraphs only to be cut down viciously—in great gory detail—in a further ten. Miller writes about people into whose lives Chaingang stumbles. In an exploitative slash-and-hack novel, a character destined to be killed in a page or two has no other purpose. In Miller's novels, the other characters have an existence completely distinct from that of corpse-to-be. Indeed, the characters in *Chaingang* have problems of their own long before Chaingang comes to town. Mary's hotshot real-estate husband has gone missing; her ex-boyfriend

Royce is trying to cope with serious debts and a raging cocaine habit. Business deals are souring; relationships are fraying . . . .

One ends up feeling almost sympathetic for Chaingang, although he is repulsive. Not only is Chaingang unable at times to separate the past from the present (the past, in the main, being wartime; Chaingang being haunted by murders he committed in the line of battle), the reader also learns from the paranoid, quick-thinking sentences of his dreamy flashbacks that not even when fighting in Vietnam did he have any sense of camaraderie. When Chaingang becomes detached from his troop he is pleased to be able to kill by himself, describing the presence of his fellow soldiers as a "cloying, maddening proximity." In fact, the most effective sequences in Miller's work are those in which Chaingang, using chilling, robotic thought processes, mingles the past and the present, when the reader senses his dislocation. In the eponymous novel one gets a peek into a mind befuddled by pacifying drugs, while simultaneously sensing the power that is being held in check. The horror of Chaingang is not so much what he does, or has done, but what he might do, given the opportunity.

Miller's novels take place in the moments between dread and loss; between anticipation and the sense that one cannot go on. Real life, as such, does not occur; while the characters are not exactly lining up to be slaughtered, nor do we see their lives—professional, marital—examined in detail. This is not Rex Miller's style. What is unusual, perhaps, is that we see the characters and the characters' friends and families after a great wrong has been done. As the errant puppy has its nose pushed into its own faeces to teach it a lesson, so we are forced to regard the after-effects of brutal crime: the implication not being that Miller believes us all to be conspiratorially guilty of the depicted violences, but that we as human beings share the burdens of past wars that led to creatures like Chaingang, whether we like these burdens or not. The reader is not meant to feel sorry exactly; but the reader is meant to understand Miller's point of view.

—David Mathew

MILLHISER, Marlys (Joy)

Nationality: American. **Born:** Marlys Enabnit, in Charles City, Iowa, 27 May 1938. **Education:** University of Iowa, Iowa City, 1956-60, B.A. in history 1960; University of Colorado, Boulder, 1961-63, M.A. in history 1963. **Family:** Married David Millhiser in 1960; one son and one daughter. **Career:** History teacher, Boulder Valley schools, Lafayette, Colorado, 1963-65; freelance writer from 1972.

HORROR, GHOST AND GOTHIC PUBLICATIONS

Novels

Nella Waits. New York, Putnam, 1974.
The Mirror. New York, Putnam, 1978.
Nightmare Country. New York, Putnam, 1981.
The Threshold. New York, Putnam, 1984.
Murder at Moot Point. New York, Doubleday, 1992.
Death of the Office Witch. New York, Penzler, 1993.

OTHER PUBLICATIONS

Novels

Michael's Wife. New York, Putnam, 1972.
Willing Hostage. New York, Putnam, 1976.

* * *

Marlys Millhiser, best known as a gothic suspense writer, is now an author of psychic detective mysteries. Her most popular gothics are *The Mirror* and *The Threshold*. Millhiser's writing style in her gothics has produced works above the usual romance level, resulting in books popular with readers of supernatural romance, who refer to her titles as "weird." Proof of her skill and reputation is the fact that throughout the 1970s and 1980s her books were never published as paperback originals and always came out first in hardcover.

The Mirror was marketed as a horror title in its paperback edition. The typical black cover is highlighted with a terrified woman reflected in the ornate mirror of the title, and the cover blurb declares, "On the eve of their weddings, two women are caught in a nightmare of supernatural horror . . ." The book, however, is not a horror story but a superior gothic romance involving a time-slip and a body switch. Shay Baker, the contemporary heroine living in Boulder, Colorado, is intrigued but somewhat repulsed by the old mirror that has been in her family for generations. On her wedding eve, the mirror transports her back in time and Shay finds herself inhabiting the body of her own grandmother, Brandy McCabe, who is also about to be married. Both women are frightened and appalled and both try to return to their own bodies and time by pleading with the obviously evil mirror. Although there are occasional partial slips and visions of their original bodies and times, both are condemned to live out their lives in their new existence. Shay finds herself thrust into an arranged marriage and life. As Brandy, she was considered daft by her family because she spoke of the visions of the future she had seen in the mirror, and her knowledge of what will happen to the family and the world in general is finally put down to the gift of second sight. Brandy must adapt to a new and confusing world with nothing but her past glimpses of the future in the mirror to guide her and a diary Shay has written in her new life to help her young and confused grandmother. Brandy's wedding is postponed because of the death of her grandmother (the original Brandy/Shay) at the same second the body switch occurs. Brandy gives birth to twins fathered by her fiance, and it appears by book's end that they will probably marry. For the most part, the novel is well constructed with loose ends carefully tied up. The only detail that nags at the reader is any explanation of why the two women have been switched. The mirror is clearly evil and its other victims have died of shock or suicide. There is really no rational (or even supernatural) explanation for why the mirror handled Brandy and Shay in this particular way other than an electrical storm that happened simultaneously in both time periods. Certainly, it creates an intriguing idea for the novel's plot.

The writing is well done without the overblown excesses usually associated with the gothic genre. The characters, especially the women, are well drawn, especially that of the pivotal character of Rachael, Brandy's daughter and Shay's mother. The historical details ring true, and the depiction of Brandy's bewilderment over today's society even provides a few sly bits of humour, such as the description of a fern bar and the Phil Donahue show on television. Particularly well done is the subplot full of growing tension over whether or not one individual's persona can exist in the same time with itself, albeit at different ages.

Between her two best-known books, Millhiser published *Nightmare Country*, a tale of dreams and suspense in the mining country of the Rocky Mountains where a divorced schoolteacher finds mystery and romance. This novel has a stronger romance theme, and seems reminiscent of Millhiser's earlier adventure suspense title, *Willing Hostage*. The landscape itself becomes a prominent presence in *Nightmare Country* and *Willing Hostage*.

Millhiser's other popular time-slip novel, *The Threshold*, is also set in the Colorado mining country. Here the time accidents involve clear visions into other times, as well as time travel. Aletha, the 20th-century protagonist, sees tears, or windows, into the past which show Callie, a girl and sometimes woman, from the early days of the century. Callie also sees Althea in the future through their mutual time window. Others can also see through the tear, such as Aletha's romantic interest, Cree. Objects can cross over through the time-slip, and Aletha's sketchbook of scenes showing the ghost town causes considerable puzzlement by the original inhabitants of the mining community.

Callie even throws her beloved cat, Charles, to Aletha through the time hole in order to save the animal's life. Aletha is intrigued by Callie, particularly after discovering her grave in the cemetery marked only with the first name, "Callie." Aletha investigates further, and slowly discovers the story of the haunting figure from the past. As the story progresses, Aletha discovers that the time warps do not happen in sequence since Callie can be any age in the encounters, and sometimes Callie isn't even present. In her own time, Aletha is involved with danger involving drug smuggling, but she still becomes obsessed with Callie.

Nella Waits is a spooky, moody story set in bleak rural Iowa country. The heroine, Lynette, has returned to the old family farm for her father's funeral. She is attracted to Jay Van Fleet, but discovers that it will not be easy to get him away from his dead mother, Nella, who loves her son obsessively and incestuously. Certainly, Nella is not about the tolerate any other woman in her son's life. Millhiser creates a feeling of doom and foreboding, using motifs of heat, dust and old farm houses effectively, somewhat reminiscent of the supernatural works of Thomas Tryon.

Millhiser uses the supernatural more effectively in her romances since it seems to work naturally into the plot than in her current writing of psychic mysteries. The heroine of *Murder at Moot Point* and *Death of the Office Witch*, Charlie Greene is a literary agent who finds herself mixed up in crimes for which her psychic experiences provide clues for the mysteries' solutions. The mysteries are written in a sprightly style with tongue-in-cheek touches of humour, such as Charlie accidentally using bathroom deodorizer spray on her hair. When asked later what her perfume is, she replies, "Eau de Potty". Millhiser was no doubt influenced by earlier women mystery writers, such as Charlotte MacLeod, who produce screwball mysteries. The first book, *Murder at Moot Point*, takes place at a New Age compound in Oregon where Charlie must clear herself of suspicion of murder. The action of *Death of the Office Witch* takes place in Beverly Hills with much "in" gossip about the movie and television industry. Although the action is fast-paced, there are unbelievable details, such as the way Charlie is treated by a member of the Los Angeles Police Department. He gives her incredible license so he can discover how psychic Charlie really is. Charlie's romances tend to be a bit brittle, and her rela-

tionship with her difficult teenage daughter, Libby, becomes irritating with the daughter coming across as a conniving and manipulative adolescent with few, if any, redeeming characteristics.

It seems a bit ironic that Millhiser has turned her considerable talent for creating supernatural romance to less convincing psychic mysteries at a time when romance readers are rediscovering the joys of gothics. Still, Millhiser is able to produce good supernatural stories in both genres.

—Cosette Kies

MOLESWORTH, Mary L(ouisa)

Pseudonym: Ennis Graham. **Nationality:** British. **Born:** Mary Stewart, in Rotterdam, 29 May 1839. **Education:** Private, at home and in Switzerland. **Married:** Major Richard Molesworth in 1861 (separated 1879; died 1900); seven children. **Career:** Writer, 1869-1921. **Died:** 20 July 1921.

HORROR, GHOST AND GOTHIC PUBLICATIONS

Short Stories

Four Ghost Stories. London, Macmillan, 1888.
Uncanny Tales. London, Hutchinson, and New York, Longmans Green, 1896.
The Wrong Envelope, and Other Stories. London, Macmillan, 1906.

OTHER PUBLICATIONS

Novels

Lover and Husband (as Ennis Graham). London, Skeet, 1870.
She Was Young and He Was Old (as Ennis Graham). London, Tinsley, 1872.
Not Without Thorns (as Ennis Graham). London, Tinsley, 1873; Boston, Osgood, 1873.
Cicely (as Ennis Graham). London, Tinsley, 1874.
Hathercourt Rectory. London, Chatto and Windus, 1878; as *Hathercourt*, New York, Munro, 1878.
Miss Bouverie. London, Hurst and Blackett, 1880.
A Charge Fulfilled. London, Society for Promoting Christian Knowledge, 1886.
Marrying and Giving in Marriage. London, Longmans Green, 1887; New York, Hurst, n.d.
The Abbey by the Sea. London, Society for Promoting Christian Knowledge, 1887.
Neighbours. London, Hatchards, 1889; New York, Whittaker, 1890.
The Laurel Walk. London, Isbister, and Philadelphia, Biddle, 1898.
The Grim House. London, Nisbet, 1899; New York, Whittaker, 1900.

Novels for Children

Carrots—Just a Little Boy (as Ennis Graham). London, Macmillan, 1876; (as Mrs. Molesworth) New York, Burt, 1890.

The Cuckoo Clock (as Ennis Graham). London, Macmillan, 1877; (as Mrs. Molesworth) New York, Caldwell, 1877.

Grandmother Dear. London, Macmillan, 1878; New York, Burt, n.d.

The Tapestry Room. London, Macmillan, and New York, Burt, 1879.

A Christmas Child. London, Macmillan, 1880.

Hermy. London and New York, Routledge, 1881.

The Adventures of Herr Baby. London, Macmillan, 1881; New York, Macmillan, 1886.

Hoodie. London and New York, Routledge, 1882.

Rosy. London, Macmillan, 1882; New York, Macmillan, 1896.

The Boys and I. London and New York, Routledge, 1883.

Two Little Waifs. London, Macmillan, 1883; New York, Macmillan, 1890.

Christmas-Tree Land. London, Macmillan, 1884; as *Christmas-Tree Land and A Christmas Posy*, New York, Macmillan, 1893.

Lettice. London, Society for Promoting Christian Knowledge, and New York, Young, 1884.

The Little Old Portrait. London, Society for Promoting Christian Knowledge, 1884; as *Edme: A Tale of the French Revolution*, London, Macmillan, 1916.

Us: An Old-Fashioned Story. London, Macmillan, and New York, Harper, 1885.

Silverthorns. London, Hatchards, 1886; New York, Dutton, 1900(?).

Four Winds Farm. London, Macmillan, 1887.

The Palace in the Garden. London, Hatchards, and New York, Whittaker, 1887.

Little Miss Peggy. London, Macmillan, and New York, Burt, 1887.

The Third Miss St. Quentin. London, Hatchards, and New York, Whittaker, 1888.

The Old Pincushion. London, Griffith Farran Okeden and Welsh, 1889; New York, Dutton, 1890.

The Rectory Children. London, Macmillan, 1889.

Little Mother Bunch. London, Cassell, 1890

The Children of the Castle. London, Macmillan, 1890

The Red Grange. London, Methuen, and New York, Whittaker, 1891.

Nurse Heatherdale's Story. London, Macmillan, 1891; as *Nurse Heatherdale's Story and Little Miss Piggy*, New York, Macmillan, 1893.

Sweet Content. London, Griffith Farran Okeden and Welsh, and New York, Dutton, 1891.

Farthings. London, Wells Gardner Darton, and New York, Young, 1892.

Robin Redbreast. London, Chambers, and New York, Burt, 1892.

The Girls and I. London, Macmillan, 1892; Chicago, Donahue, 1900.

Leona. London, Cassell, 1892.

Imogen, or Only Eighteen. London, Chambers, and New York, Whittaker, 1892.

The Next Door House. London, Chambers, and New York, Cassell, 1893.

Mary. London and New York, Macmillan, 1893.

Blanche. London, Chambers, 1894.

My New Home. London, Macmillan, 1894; New York, Macmillan, 1898.

Olivia. London, Chambers, and Philadelphia, Lippincott, 1895.

Sheila's Mystery. London, Macmillan, 1895.

The Carved Lions. London, Macmillan, 1895.

White Turrets. London, Chambers, and New York, Whittaker, 1895.

The Oriel Window. London and New York, Macmillan, 1896.

Phillipa. London, Chambers, and Philadelphia, Lippincott, 1896.

Meg Langholme, or The Day After Tomorrow. London, Chambers, and Philadelphia, Lippincott, 1897.

Miss Mouse and Her Boys. London and New York, Macmillan, 1897.

Greyling Towers. London, Chambers, 1898.

The Magic Nuts. London, Macmillan, 1898; Philadelphia, Altemus, 1899.

This and That. London, Macmillan, 1899.

The Three Witches. London, Chambers, 1900.

The House That Grew. London, Macmillan, 1900.

The Wood Pigeons and Mary. London and New York, Macmillan, 1901.

Peterkin. London, Macmillan, 1902.

The Ruby Ring. London, Macmillan, 1904.

Jasper. London, Macmillan, 1906

The Little Guest. London, Macmillan, 1907.

The February Boys. London, Chambers, and New York, Dutton, 1909.

The Story of a Year. London, Macmillan, 1910.

Short Stories

That Girl in Black, and Bronzie. London, Chatto and Windus, and New York, Lovell, 1889.

The Story of a Spring Morning. New York and London, Longmans Green, 1890.

Short Stories for Children

Tell Me a Story (as Ennis Graham). London, Macmillan, 1875; New York, Macmillan, 1893.

Summer Stories for Boys and Girls. London, Macmillan, 1882.

Five Minute Stories. London, Society for Promoting Christian Knowledge, 1888.

A Christmas Posy. London, Macmillan, 1888; as *Christmas-Tree Land and A Christmas Posy*, New York, Macmillan, 1893.

Great Uncle Hoot Toot. London, Society for Promoting Christian Knowledge, 1889.

A House to Let. London, Society for Promoting Christian Knowledge, and New York, Young, 1889.

Nesta; or, Fragments of a Little Life. London, Chambers, 1889.

The Green Casket, and Other Stories. London, Chambers, 1890.

Family Troubles. London, Society for Promoting Christian Knowledge, and New York, Young, 1890.

Twelve Tiny Tales. London, Society for Promoting Christian Knowledge, and New York, Young, 1890

The Bewitched Lamp. London, Chambers, 1891.

The Lucky Ducks, and Other Stories. London, Society for Promoting Christian Knowledge, and New York, Young, 1891.

An Enchanted Garden. London, Fisher Unwin, and New York, Cassell, 1892.

The Man With the Pan Pipes. London, Society for Promoting Christian Knowledge, and New York, Young, 1892.

Studies and Stories. London, Innes, 1893.

Thirteen Little Black Pigs. London, Society for Promoting Christian Knowledge, 1893; New York, Burt, 1901.

Opposite Neighbours. London, Society for Promoting Christian Knowledge, 1895.

Friendly Joey, and Other Stories. London, Society for Promoting Christian Knowledge, 1896.
The Children's Hour. London, Nelson, 1899.
The Blue Baby, and Other Stories. London, Fisher Unwin, 1901.
My Pretty, and Her Little Brother Too. London, Chambers, and New York, Dutton, 1901.
The Bolted Door, and Other Stories. London, Chambers, 1906.
Fairies—of Sorts. London, Macmillan, 1908.
Fairies Afield. London, Macmillan, 1911.
Stories by Mrs. Molesworth, edited by Sidney Baldwin. New York, Duffield, 1922.
Fairy Stories, edited by Richard Lancelyn Green. London, Harvill Press, 1957; New York, Roy, 1958.

Other

French Life in Letters (in French). London, Macmillan, 1889.
Stories of the Saints for Children. London and New York, Longmans Green, 1892.
Stories for Children in Illustration of The Lord's Prayer. London, Gardner Darton, 1897.

*

Critical Studies: *Mrs. Ewing, Mrs. Molesworth and Mrs. Hodgson Burnett* by Marghanita Laski, 1950; *Mrs. Molesworth* by Roger Lancelyn Green, 1961.

*   *   *

Mary Molesworth has been mostly forgotten by the wider literary world, and certainly her adult novels scarcely survived her own day, but she has carved a niche for her children's novels and for her dozen or so ghost stories. She was an immensely prolific writer, and when she found her proclivity for children's fiction met with financial success she ploughed that furrow relentlessly, only occasionally surfacing for a gulp of fresh air in the adult world. Many have criticized her works for young children because of her frequent use of baby talk, and that is one of the main reasons why her books rapidly dropped out of favour in the twentieth century, but she had her admirers, not least the poet Algernon Swinburne, with a later critic, Roger Lancelyn Green, rating her best books as among the very best works for children of the nineteenth century.

None of her books for children are horror or gothic, but a few are fantastic, and though fantasy and fairy tales are outside the scope of this volume it is worth covering some of these titles briefly because they do cast a light on her few genuine ghost stories. The first of note was *The Cuckoo Clock*, where Griselda is a lonely little girl who lives with two elderly aunts and who finds escape through the magic bird in a cuckoo clock in the room where she takes her lessons. The bird takes Griselda on a series of magical adventures until at last she finds a young boy companion with whom she stays. At the start of the novel Molesworth creates a wonderful atmosphere of alienation. The house is not in itself alien—it's a beautiful old house with a lovely garden, and the aunts and their butler try to be friendly. But Griselda is not used to such a life and everything feels strange, especially the cuckoo clock. She becomes convinced that the cuckoo is spying on her, mocking her, and in her fury she throws a book at the clock which, for the first time in 50 years, stops working. At that point the aunts be-

come convinced it is an omen and that their appointed time has come. Griselda becomes almost frantic in her desire to repair the clock and make friends with the cuckoo. This episode contains some of Mrs. Molesworth's best writing, as the girl's fear becomes almost tangible as she worries about what she might have done, so that the relief is great when, in the still of the night, the cuckoo appears.

The plot of *The Tapestry Room* is similar. Two young cousins, Jeanne and Hugh, live in an old French chateau, and Hugh becomes entranced by a huge tapestry depicting a castle and adjoining lands. Hugh becomes acquainted with a number of Jeanne's animal friends, especially Dudu, an old raven, and Dudu takes Hugh and Jeanne into the world of the tapestry where they have a number of adventures.

The third novel of a similar tone is *The Carved Lions*, which Roger Lancelyn Green called "a jewel without a flaw." This novel is a real plea from the heart for escape from the harsh reality of life to the surroundings of friends. Geraldine is unhappy at school and runs away. She stops by an antique shop where she and her brother have long been fascinated by two carved lions which stand outside. Exhausted she falls asleep and dreams that the lions take her and her brother to her parents in South America. When she wakes she finds that her wishes have come true and that she need not go back to her old school but will be cared for by friends.

The theme of all these stories is one of wish-fulfilment and an escape from mundane reality, a theme common in children's fiction but one exploited overtly by Mrs. Molesworth and which she handed on to a superior successor in Edith Nesbit. She also treated children as having a great imagination and perception of the odd so that they are more open to the supernatural.

She used these factors to good effect in her ghost stories. "The Shadow in the Moonlight" in *Uncanny Tales* is the best of them. It opens like one of her children's adventures. A family, with several young children, move into an old castle by the sea for a period of recuperation. In case the castle is draughty the mother buys an old tapestry in a second-hand store to serve as curtains. Soon after they've moved in the youngest child shows a fear of passing through the gallery. When questioned he shows his brothers and sisters a shadow that gropes its way round the gallery. It transpires that it is not the gallery but the tapestry that is haunted and when the tapestry was restored to the old castle the ghostly residuum was revived. Efforts to discover the original hanging place of the tapestry reveal hidden treasure. The ghostly scenes are effectively handled but not so strongly that the story would not still be suitable for older children.

In "Unexplained" (*Macmillan*, 1885) a woman and her two children are on holiday in Germany. They find an unusual cup, and this opens up a psychic link between the daughter of the family and a young Englishman who had been killed by lightning in that area a few years earlier. The story is never fully resolved, hence the title, but by handling it so, Molesworth heightens the difference in perception and attitude between the mother and her daughter. Children are again the witnesses of a ghost in "Old Gervais" from *Studies and Stories*. An old lady remembers an episode from her childhood in France when staying with her godmother's grandchildren. They befriend an old mason, Gervais, who is repairing stonework in a cellar. Gervais dies but because the cellar was unsafe his ghost completes the work. In a chilling scene at the end of the story one of the granddaughters, Virginie, has a conversation with the ghost that no one else can hear.

"At the Dip of the Road" also tells of a ghost trying to complete a task. It appears as a man seen running only at a certain stretch of road. It transpires this is the ghost of a servant who died before he could convey a message to his master. Others of her stories have ghosts appearing just at the point of death as in "The Story of the Rippling Train" (*Longmans Green,* 1887), "A Strange Messenger" from *The Wrong Envelope,* and "Lady Farquhar's Old Lady" (*Tinsley,* 1873). The last purports to be based on a true ghost story and may have been the earliest written by Mrs. Molesworth.

Her work must have had some effect upon her son Bevil, who died tragically in 1899 in Patagonia where he was a rancher, aged only 27, for he too wrote a ghost story, "A Ghost of the Pampas," which she included in her collection *The Wrong Envelope.* It's a rather trivial story of Darcy whose friend is killed by a bull but whose spirit returns to help Darcy when in trouble. No doubt the story represented a catharsis for Mrs. Molesworth, as it is a celebration of life. Had Mrs. Molesworth chosen she could no doubt have established a stronger reputation as a writer of ghost stories, but instead these seemed to be occasional excursions from her main work.

—Mike Ashley

MONAHAN, Brent (Jeffrey)

Nationality: American. **Born:** 1948. **Address:** c/o St. Martin's Press, 175 Fifth Avenue, New York, NY 10010, USA. Lives in Pennsylvania.

HORROR, GHOST AND GOTHIC PUBLICATIONS

Novels

DeathBite, with Michael Maryk. Kansas City, Andrews and McMeel, 1979.
Satan's Serenade. New York, Pocket, 1989.
The Uprising. New York, Pocket, 1992; London, New English Library, 1996.
The Book of Common Dread. New York, St. Martin's Press, 1993; London, New English Library, 1995.
The Blood of the Covenant. New York, St. Martin's Press, 1995; London, New English Library, 1996.
The Bell Witch. New York, St. Martin's Press, 1997.

*   *   *

Brent Monahan's witty, literate horror novel *Satan's Serenade* is an interesting though predictable tale of ghostly possession. Jack Horn is an opera singer who has lately begun to realize that his career is effectively over, that he lacks the talent to advance from the anonymous ranks to a position where he can command a personal following. All of that changes when he meets Belinda Fausse, a well known opera star with whom he falls in love. Belinda is a talented teacher as well, and she helps him develop the skills required to distinguish himself.

All of this appears to have come to an end when Belinda is killed in an air crash over the ocean. Jack is despondent at first, but then he begins to sense her presence at night, smells her perfume in the air, and eventually she manifests herself, taking possession of his body so that she can sing once more. As he struggles to regain control of his own life, Jack is horrified to discover that his friends are being killed, apparently at the instigation of a jealous spirit who doesn't want to share him with anyone. A straightforward suspense story that holds its audience breathless waiting to see which personality will prevail.

Monahan followed this with *The Uprising.* An expert on Celtic history travels to Ireland in order to combine research and vacation exploring the land of his ancestors. To his utter horror, he discovers that several women who died long ago have returned to life, and that they plan to use human sacrifices to restore others from their tribe to the world, in retribution for a great evil committed against them in the far past. The scientist and an eccentric old woman filled with Irish lore team up to prevent the cataclysm from taking place, mixing Irish legends and history with modern horror motifs. A workmanlike novel with some good scenes, but most of its devices were already overly familiar when it was published.

That wasn't true of *The Book of Common Dread,* Monahan's next and best book to date. Vampire novels had already begun to flood the market, including many with the undead as heroes rather than villains. Monahan's creation of Vincent DeVilbiss ignored both stereotypes and broke new ground. DeVilbiss is a vampire, committed to evil, but he is uneasy about some of the things he is forced to do by his master, who is not another vampire but actually a minion of Satan himself. His latest assignment is to help retard the progress of the human race by destroying an ancient scroll, which is currently at Princeton University waiting to be translated. Opposed to him is the local curator and rare book collector, who has fallen in love with the woman DeVilbiss plans to use as his agent. Their shadowy battle for possession of the scroll is cleverly plotted and skilfully narrated, and DeVilbiss himself, despite his evil nature, comes across as a flawed rather than monstrous character. He is in fact charming at times and even subscribes to an informal code of honour. *The Book of Common Dread* is highly successful, in large part because Monahan has managed to make his characters and situations feel authentic despite their fantastic nature.

Monahan capitalized on his success with a sequel, *The Blood of the Covenant.* DeVilbiss has been destroyed and his master thwarted, but the scrolls haven't been translated yet. The curator and his lover are on the run now, pursued by the police who suspect them of theft, as well as another vampire agent of Hell, this time an ancient creature who once served as tutor to Vlad Tepes. The book is largely a protracted series of chase scenes, more adventure than horror. The strong characterization and skilful pacing are a match for its predecessor, but the sequel's villain is considerably less interesting. The novel suffers only by comparison to Monahan's other work; alone it still towers above the flood of derivative vampire novels flooding the bookstores.

The Bell Witch is a decided change of pace. Apparently based at least in part on an actual reported poltergeist case, the story is set in late 19th-century America. The rivalry between two families gets ugly when a woman threatens her enemies with what could be construed as a curse. Shortly thereafter, poltergeist phenomena began to plague the Bell family, playful at first, becoming increasingly frequent and violent, eventually resulting in a death. Initially only the Bell family are witnesses, but eventually friends and neighbours begin to experience the poltergeist as well. Monahan's fictionalized version remains objective and non-judgmental, although most of the activity could clearly be explained as mass hysteria and the power of suggestion. An interesting book, but one that lacks power as a novel because of its narrative style, which is almost journalistic throughout.

Monahan's short story, "Shedding Light on the Black Forest," is a clever rendition of the story of Hansel and Gretel. An elderly woman with a fondness for baking elaborate pastries runs a school for obstreperous youths. She meets her match when a brother and sister arrive from Germany and plot her destruction by convincing the rest of the students that she's a witch and ultimately by pushing her into an oven. Although he is not a prolific writer, Monahan's strongly drawn characters, literate prose style, and clever plotting have already secured for him a following. The variety of themes he has already embraced promises an unpredictable but fascinating career to come.

—Don D'Ammassa

MONTELEONE, Thomas F(rancis)

Nationality: American. **Born:** Baltimore, Maryland, 14 April 1946. **Education:** University of Maryland, College Park, B.S. in Psychology 1968, M.A. in English 1973. **Family:** Married 1) Natalie Monteleone in 1969 (divorced 1979), one son; 2) Linda Smith in 1981, one son. **Career:** Psychotherapist, C. T. Perkins Hospital, Jessup, Maryland, 1969-78. Secretary, Science Fiction Writers of America, 1976-78. **Awards:** Gabriel award, for television play, 1984; International Television and Film award, 1984; Maryland State Arts Council award, 1991; Horror Writers of America Bram Stoker award, 1993. **Agent:** Howard Morhaim Literary Agency, 175 Fifth Avenue, New York, NY 10010, USA. **Address:** P.O. Box 5788, Baltimore, MD 21208, USA.

HORROR, GHOST AND GOTHIC PUBLICATIONS

Novels

Night Things. New York, Fawcett, 1980.
Night-Train. New York, Pocket Books, 1984; London, Arrow, 1987.
Lyrica: A Novel of Horror and Desire. New York, Berkley, 1987.
The Magnificent Gallery. New York, Tor, 1987.
The Crooked House, with John de Chancie. New York, Tor, 1987.
Fantasma. New York, Tor, 1989.
The Blood of the Lamb. New York, Tor, 1992; London, Orion, 1993.
The Resurrectionist. New York, Tor, 1995.
The Night of Broken Souls. New York, Tor, 1997.

Other

Editor, *Borderlands [1]-6: An Anthology of Imaginative Fiction.* Baltimore, Maclay, 1990-94.

OTHER PUBLICATIONS

Novels

Seeds of Change. Don Mills, Ontario, Laser, 1975.

The Time Connection. New York, Popular Library, 1976; London, Hale, 1979.
The Time-Swept City. New York, Popular Library, 1977.
The Secret Sea. New York, Popular Library, 1979; London, Hale, 1981.
Guardian. Garden City, New York, Doubleday, 1980.
Ozymandias. Garden City, New York, Doubleday, 1981.
Day of the Dragonstar, with David F. Bischoff. New York, Berkley, 1983.
Night of the Dragonstar, with David F. Bischoff. New York, Berkley, 1985.
Dragonstar Destiny, with David F. Bischoff. New York, Ace, 1989.

Short Stories

Dark Stars and Other Illuminations. Garden City, New York, Doubleday, 1981.

Plays

U.F.O.!, with Grant Carrington (produced Ashton, Maryland, 1977).
Mister Magister (produced Silver Spring, Maryland, 1978). Included in *Dark Stars and Other Illuminations,* 1981.

Screenplays: *Sun-Treader,* 1983; *Three, Two, One: Countdown to Love,* 1984; *The Nowhere Man,* 1985.

Television Plays: *Mister Magister,* 1983; *Spare the Child,* 1983.

Other

Editor, *The Arts and Beyond: Visions of Man's Aesthetic Future.* Garden City, New York, Doubleday, 1977.
Editor, *Random Access Messages of the Computer Age.* Hasbrouck Heights, New Jersey, Hayden, 1984; as *Microworlds,* London, Hamlyn, 1985.

*

Manuscript Collection: University of Maryland, Baltimore.

*   *   *

Thomas F. Monteleone started his writing career in science fiction, publishing a number of entertaining and increasingly interesting adventure stories of which the best is *The Time-Swept City.* At the beginning of the 1980s, however, his career changed direction, starting with the publication of *Night Things,* and he has been far more successful in the horror genre, as writer, editor and publisher.

Night Things broke no new ground in terms of plot. A small southwestern town is the setting for a series of escalating attacks by small furry creatures, not dangerous as individuals, but overwhelming when they attack in large numbers. And there are lots of them out there. An uncomplicated, uncluttered plot and a talent for creating genuinely suspenseful scenes marked *Night Things* as a promising new direction for this author, a promise reflected in his next, *Night-Train*. An entire subway train mysteriously disappeared in the tunnels below New York City during the 1930s, and now two investigators have decided to enter the abandoned warren of tunnels to see if they can discover its fate 50 years later. But rather than lay the mystery to rest, they are involved in the reawakening of an evil force that has bided its time, and now seeks fresh victims from among the daily commuters. Filled with claustrophobic terror, it is neatly tied up in a well handled climax.

Lyrica is a variation of the succubus, a woman who drains the souls from the men she lures into her arms by creating a shell of sexuality. Although Monteleone does a good job of mixing eroticism and horror, the novel seems too long for its premise, and rapidly loses momentum during the concluding chapters. There's a travelling carnival in *The Magnificent Gallery*, which bears some resemblance to Ray Bradbury's *Something Wicked This Way Comes*. Some of the exhibits in the carnival seem to be warning customers of their fate, but it isn't long before some begin to suspect that rather than just warning the victims, it is also choosing them. The Dark Man is an obvious nod to Bradbury's Mr. Dark, but Monteleone has created a different kind of terror in his novel, which generates its terrors in more subtle fashion than in his earlier novels.

Crooked House, written in collaboration with John de Chancie, is a decidedly modern version of the traditional haunted-house story. Pikadon seems to have been designed by a madman; doors open to reveal walls, stairways lead nowhere. But there are strange beings living in its many rooms and corridors, some of whom may not be alive at all. *Crooked House* is, strangely enough, an indictment of nuclear weapons, among other things, and although its message isn't always clear, and its plot sometimes stumbles, it is filled with bizarre and unsettling scenes. Organized crime finds a new enemy in *Fantasma*, when the leader of one gang enlists the help of a genuine witch to resolve a power struggle. The struggle between Mafia killers and an actual demon is amusing and entertaining, but the shortage of sympathetic characters prevents the story from ever developing any serious element of suspense.

Monteleone proved himself a far superior writer with *The Blood of the Lamb*, for which he won a Bram Stoker award from the Horror Writers Association. As the millennium approaches, a popular Brooklyn priest discovers that he has suddenly developed miraculous powers, that he can heal the sick and even raise the dead. But while his parishioners rejoice and talk of the Second Coming, the priest doubts the wisdom of using his power, and the Church questions from where they are derived. The combination of Church politics, theological disputation, the protagonist's mental state, the growing chaos outside, and the underlying uncertainty about the nature of his powers all combine into a riveting, suspenseful story that is easily one of the major horror novels of the last two decades.

The Resurrectionist makes use of a similar theme. A charismatic Presidential candidate survives a terrible plane crash and discovers in the aftermath that he can bring the dead back to life. No one believes what has happened initially, but eventually the word gets out, and suddenly Flanagan's political career seems ended because of the controversy. Even more serious for his future is the desire by certain elements within the government, and the military, to make use of him for their own purposes. *The Resurrectionist* is nearly as good as *The Blood of the Lamb*, particularly the early chapters during which Flanagan reluctantly accepts the existence of his newfound power. *The Night of Broken Souls* also explores a wider world than the focused nature of most horror fiction. Vari-

ous people are experiencing incredibly vivid dreams of former lives when they were interned in concentration camps by the Nazis. A psychologist is trying to discover the cause of this new ailment when he stumbles across repeated references to a Jewish turncoat who aided the Nazis, eventually discovering that the latter has possessed the body of a CIA killer and is systematically killing his patients. The novel is a nicely paced contemporary thriller, although considerably less atmospheric than in the novels that preceded it.

Monteleone is also editor of the highly regarded *Borderlands* anthology series, and publisher of Borderlands Press, which specializes in high-quality, limited hardcover editions of notable horror novels and collections. He is as well the author of a large number of highly regarded short stories, of which the best is probably "Looking for Mr. Flip." Other outstanding stories include "Time Enough to Sleep," "Roadside Scalpel," "Identity Crisis," "The Night is Freezing Fast" and "Spare the Child." Monteleone has developed dramatically as a writer during the past decade and is likely to emerge as one of the major voices in horror fiction in the years to come.

—Don D'Ammassa

MORLAN, A(rlette) R(enée)

Nationality: American. **Born:** Chicago, 3 January 1958. Lives in Ladysmith, Wisconsin.

HORROR, GHOST AND GOTHIC PUBLICATIONS

Novels

The Amulet. New York, Bantam, 1991.
Dark Journey. New York, Bantam, 1991.

Short Stories

The Cat with the Tulip Face. Eugene, Oregon, Pulphouse, 1991.

* * *

The chronic instability of horror publishing in the USA has spoiled and frustrated several promising careers, but it seems particularly perverse that a writer as accomplished as A. R. Morlan should have suffered active ill-treatment as well as neglect. Her career was launched, as so many careers in horror fiction were, during the explosion of small-press magazines which took advantage of the new technologies of desktop production in the mid-1980s, but her seemingly inevitable break from that milieu was stifled and ultimately strangled by editorial folly.

Many of the early stories which Morlan sold to *Night Cry*—including the novelette "Four Days Before the Snow" (1985), the brief but highly effective "Scrap When Empty" (1985), "The Holiday House" (1986), "Garbage Day in Ewerton" and the brilliant tale of childhood cruelty "Simon Says" (1986)—were set in Ewerton, an imaginary small town in Wisconsin, not unlike the town of Ladysmith where Morlan went to school and still lives. Although each story has its own cast of characters, whose particular failings provide the narrative hooks on which the stories are suspended, they share a sense of the peculiar claustrophobia of life in a small town where almost everyone is related by blood or marriage. Ewerton is a place where the near-total lack of privacy puts a terrible pressure on those secrets which people want and need to keep, but in a rather paradoxical manner its inhabitants also collude with the maintenance of the darkest of those secrets. Encouraged by an editor at Bantam who saw the potential in such a project, Morlan began work on a novel set in Ewerton, which grew by degrees into *Dark Journey*.

After rewriting *Dark Journey* several times at the request of the editor and her agent, Morlan was then told that the publisher was reluctant to launch such a big novel without preparation. She was requested to write another, shorter, Ewerton novel which might serve as an easier introduction to the mass market. This was to be based on a device employed in "Night Skirt" (1987)—except that Bantam insisted that the magical object be changed into an item of jewellery because the "art department can't do a cover based on a *night skirt*." Not surprisingly, the item of jewellery is the least convincing item in the rather hastily-contrived *The Amulet*, but the novel does capture the evil spirit of Ewerton with almost painful intensity. The catalogue of murders which supplies the plot is handled efficiently enough, but the horror associated with the everyday life of the luckless heroine is far more intense and highly distinctive. The novel amply confirmed the promise of Morlan's short fiction and demonstrated that—unlike many other writers of finely-crafted short stories—she could extend the sensibility of her work into a sustained narrative crescendo.

Editorial interference with *Dark Journey* continued even after submission; substantial cuts were made in the text—a pointless parsimony, given that the book remained very long—and the evidence provided by "Dark Journey—The Lost Prologue," which appeared in *Eldritch Tales* 28 (1993) suggests that the excisions certainly did not work to its advantage. Even as it stands, however, *Dark Journey* is a remarkable novel, a little less intense than *The Amulet* but more rounded and more confidently measured. It is the story of how the lives of two Ewerton inhabitants, Palmer Winston and Palmer Nemmitz, were blighted by their brief encounters with one of the town's least-favoured children, and how that ruination was a legacy of the town's own sickness. The later phases of the plot reveal an alternative Ewerton to which privileged members of the real town's populace may go, preserving their own dire legacies even after death so that the occasional living visitor might witness the judgment to which their secrets have brought them.

Although it has obvious links with the tradition of "carnival horror" whose backbone is Charles Finney's *The Circus of Dr. Lao*, Tod Browning's *Freaks* and Ray Bradbury's *Something Wicked This Way Comes*, and certain affinities with the small-town horror novels of Stephen King, there is no other book quite like *Dark Journey*. Unfortunately the uniqueness of a *tour de force* is not much help to a publisher's marketing department, which is bound to favour consistency of product and of sales. Although Morlan circulated an outline for a third Ewerton novel, based on the *Eldritch Tales* serial "When the Bad Thing Comes" (1990-91), she has not published another horror novel since 1991. Her only other "book" within the field, *The Cat with a Tulip Face*—a brief "prequel" to *The Amulet*—was also issued in 1991.

The dark fantasies set in Ewerton inevitably loom large within Morlan's oeuvre but she is a versatile writer. Her short work ranges from the zestful black comedy of the highly atypical Ewerton story "Does it Ploop?" (1986) and "Just Another Bedtime Story" (1987) to the earnest surreal fantasy of "In the Great Milk White Eye of God" (1989). She has also written some excellent *contes cruels*, including the stylized prose poem "What the Janitor Found" (1987). Most of her work is conscientiously unsentimental, refusing the homely palliatives which Stephen King is careful to balance against the external horrors of his small-town tales, but she is certainly not without charity and her sense of beauty is often acute. "With Cockles and Mussels Alive, Alive-O" (1992) provides its outsiders with a small compensatory miracle but is careful not to overstate its utility, while ". . . and the Horses Hiss at Midnight" (1994) and "Warmer" (1996) are unusually soulful contributions to the anthologies of erotic horror stories in which they appear.

It is dangerous to speculate as to the precise extent to which an author's work has been affected by her life, but Morlan advertises the harrowing "Hunger" in *Night Terrors 3* (1997) as "90% autobiographical" and this may provide interested readers with extra insight into the extraordinarily painful family relationships described in *The Amulet*. Whatever its sources, however, almost all Morlan's fiction is genuinely discomfiting in a fashion that many horror writers attempt but few achieve. A collection of her best short fiction is long overdue.

—Brian Stableford

MORRELL, David (Bernard)

Nationality: American. **Born:** Kitchener, Ontario, Canada, 24 April 1943; moved to the United States in 1966. **Education:** St. Jerome's College, Waterloo, Ontario, B.A. 1966; Pennsylvania State University, M.A. 1967, Ph.D in English literature 1970. **Family:** Married Donna Maziarz 10 October 1965; two children, Sarie and Matthew (died). **Career:** Professor of American Literature, University of Iowa, 1970-86; freelance writer since 1986. **Awards:** Distinguished Recognition award, Friends of American Writers, 1972; best novella awards, Horror Writers of America, 1989, 1991. **Member:** Horror Writers of America, Mystery Writers of America, Writers Guild of America. **Agent:** Henry Morrison, P.O. Box 235, Bedford Hills, New York 10507. **Address:** c/o Warner Books, Inc., 1271 Avenue of the Americas, New York, New York 10020, USA. Lives in Santa Fe, New Mexico.

HORROR, GHOST AND GOTHIC PUBLICATIONS

Novels

Testament. New York, Evans, 1975; London, Chatto and Windus, 1976.
The Totem. New York, Evans, 1979; London, Pan, 1981; revised edition, as *The Totem (Complete and Unaltered)*, n.p., 1991.

Short Story

The Hundred-Year Christmas. West Kingston, Rhode Island, Grant, 1983.

OTHER PUBLICATIONS

Novels

First Blood. New York, Evans, and London, Barrie and Jenkins, 1972.

Last Reveille. New York, Evans, 1977.

Blood Oath. New York, St. Martin's Press, 1982; London, Pan, 1983.

The Brotherhood of the Rose. New York, St. Martin's Press, 1984; London, New English Library, 1985.

The Fraternity of the Stone. New York, St. Martin's Press, 1985; London, New English Library, 1986.

Rambo: First Blood Part II (novelization of screenplay). New York, Jove, and London, Arrow, 1985

The League of Night and Fog. New York, St. Martin's Press, and London, New English Library, 1987.

Fireflies. New York, Dutton, 1988.

Rambo III (novelization of screenplay). New York, Berkley, and London, New English Library, 1988.

The Fifth Profession. New York, Warner, and London, Headline, 1990.

The Covenant of the Flame. New York, Warner, and London, Headline, 1991.

Assumed Identity. New York, Warner, 1993.

Other

John Barth: An Introduction. University Park, Pennsylvania State University Press, 1976.

*

Media Adaptations: *First Blood* (film) 1982; *Rambo: First Blood, Part II,* 1985, and *Rambo III,* 1988 (films based on characters created by Morrell); *The Brotherhood of the Rose* (television miniseries), 1989.

*   *   *

To the public at large, David Morrell will always be remembered for his debut novel, *First Blood,* and for Rambo, the survivalist character who has since become an icon of popular culture. Morrell's fans probably know him best for the many fine novels of suspense that have followed, most notably *The Brotherhood of the Rose* and *Assumed Identity.* But he has done some of his best work in the horror genre, a genre that seems so very different from the one Morrell has thrived in—and yet one that's uniquely suited to his talents.

Many have called Morrell's second novel, *Testament,* a horror story, and while it confronts the ultimate horror of a man losing his family, Morrell's fourth novel, *The Totem,* is where his affection for traditional horror really shines through. A variation on the zombie/vampire theme, *The Totem* incorporates all the traditions of this type of tale, yet brings something fresh and exciting to the mix.

Although Morrell has since given us an uncut version of *The Totem,* there is something very satisfying—and very primal—about the stripped-down, breakneck novel as it originally appeared. The setting is Potter's Grove, Wyoming. Chief Nathan Slaughter heads

up the local police force, and when he walks into a bar to calm down a jealous husband with a gun, we immediately know two things about him: he takes the job of upholding the law very seriously, and he's not afraid to use violence to do it. Slaughter is a former Detroit policeman who's seen and done too much; like Rambo, he is a prototype for many of the Morrell characters who will follow in his wake, men submerged in violence but searching for peace.

After the close call in the bar, Slaughter is called to the scene of an apparent hit-and-run accident. But when the dead man wakes up and walks out of the morgue, the wave of terror is kicked into motion. Slaughter soon finds that he's got more to deal with a missing corpse—there are assaults, reports of a prowler, and ultimately another dead man. For Slaughter, Potter's Grove is quickly becoming more and more like the city he left behind.

Even as Slaughter tries to hold the town together, Gordon Dunlap arrives, a burned-out reporter who is compelled to return to the place where he'd last enjoyed success. Dunlap made a name for himself by covering the sensational story of a cult leader named Quiller who led his followers into the wilderness surrounding Potter's Grove. Some of the cult members died in the winter cold, and the others simply disappeared. But the cult is old news, and so is Gordon Dunlap, until he meets up with his old friend from Detroit, Nathan Slaughter.

As the attacks—by humans and by animals—continue to escalate, Slaughter is forced to put his reputation and his life on the line. He enlists Dunlap to chronicle his story, and the two become strangely dependent on each other as they fight this menace and discover the hidden secret of the cult.

While *The Totem* is Morrell's only unabashed horror novel, he has produced a lot of horror as a short-story writer. He was a regular contributor to Charles Grant's *Shadows* series of anthologies, but perhaps the best example of his versatility is shown in the volume *Night Visions 2* (also edited by Grant). Although this anthology appeared a year after his bestseller *The Brotherhood of the Rose,* a book which became the springboard for his career as a major suspense writer, *Night Visions* shows us the other side of Morrell: a writer who doesn't need to rely on hi-tech weaponry or high-voltage chase scenes to make the reader's heart skip a beat; a writer, ultimately, whose greatest gift is for creating characters we believe in.

The three stories in *Night Visions 2* are all narrated in the first person, and this is one of the most telling differences between Morrell's suspense novels and his horror stories. They have the flavour of being more intimate, and even though they may be less realistic than his tales of espionage, they are in many ways more real. Although Morrell has a flair for bringing humanity to his array of fictional assassins and agents, he is equally skilled at painting portraits of more ordinary people, in this case a paperboy, a high-school football player, and a Hollywood screenwriter.

In "Black and White and Red All Over" the main character is a young boy whose life revolves around his paper route. But this young man will be forced to grow up quickly when a stalker begins kidnapping paperboys. The story paints an almost Bradbury-esque image of the small town of Crowell, where simple pleasures are almost always best. Narrated in a child's easy-going tone, the story might creak from nostalgia but doesn't; instead, you feel the harsh chill of the winter mornings and the boy's fear as he faces an unknown menace.

Ultimately, though, the danger is never too close-at-hand, even when more paperboys begin to vanish and our hero is forced to consider giving up the job he loves. His confrontation with the kidnapper is inevitable, and the fact that he is telling us the story at all suggests that he won't be severely injured, physically or mentally. "Black and White and Red All Over," like the old childhood riddle that inspired its title, is comfortable and familiar. Morrell's careful rationing of details creates a kind of gentle suspense, and the narrator's voice itself is so compelling that Morrell creates a different kind of page-turner.

In "Mumbo Jumbo" Morrell forsakes Bradbury for what was once Stephen King territory, only instead of chronicling the plight of high school's outsiders, Morrell takes us inside the football team's locker room . . . and shows us the price of wanting to win at any cost.

Danny, the narrator, and his best friend Joey are high-school students with little direction or sense of ambition. When Joey decides he wants to go out for the football team, he does it with Danny's reluctant participation. The teenagers—overweight and out of shape—know it won't be easy, and indeed it isn't. Coach Hayes, the football team's taskmaster, puts them through a gruelling training period. When they make the cut, they're thrilled. But Danny and Joey soon realize that the key to the football team's success is not just Coach Hayes's belief in hard work; it's a statue called Mumbo Jumbo. Although Danny passes it off as a good-luck charm, he soon realizes that the statue does more than provide luck: it gives the players almost supernatural skills on the field.

Soon, the team is winning and Danny is dating one of the prettiest girls in school—it's the kind of high-school life that every teenager dreams about. But the players' reliance on Mumbo Jumbo makes Danny uneasy, and when the statue becomes the focus of a school controversy, Danny discovers its true nature. While Danny fears the statue, his friend Joey is ultimately willing to embrace its power if it will guarantee his success. The ending offers neither a simple moral nor an easy answer: both Danny and Joey must sacrifice for their choices, and neither seems completely satisfied with what they achieve.

"Dead Image" is Morrell's take on Hollywood, the town that made Rambo a household name. While Morrell doesn't simply sound off against the movie business, he maintains a healthy scepticism about the film-making process. The narrator is David Sloane, a screenwriter who's unhappy with the clumsy handling of his last script. Determined to make a film his way, he engineers a plan to get his first directing job. But the key to his success is landing a talented newcomer named Wes Crane, a young actor who reminds everyone of the late star James Deacon.

Morrell has obviously cast James Deacon as a fictional James Dean, and just as clearly Wes Crane is more than a dead ringer for Deacon. Although Morrell tries to raise the question of whether Crane is simply an obsessed fan, any seasoned horror fan knows better. What "Dead Image" lacks in surprises most of the way it makes up for with a stunning development late in the story, when Sloane tries to save Crane from an untimely death. He does, but with tragic results. Despite its crude comic punchline—that Deacon's final role is as a zombie in a horror movie—the image of a decomposing Deacon lingers in the mind, as does the questions the story raises about fate and the nature of stardom.

Though Morrell seems more firmly entrenched than ever in the suspense genre, an examination of his horror stories will only enhance appreciation of his other work. Besides, Morrell hasn't forsaken horror fiction entirely. His offering in the latest Douglas Winter anthology is a reminder that David Morrell is a writer with

many faces—and he still keeps his Halloween mask around for special occasions.

—Adam Meyer

MORRIS, Mark

Nationality: British. **Born:** Bolsover, Derbyshire, 1963. **Family:** Married the artist Nel Whatmore; one son, one daughter. **Career:** Contributor to various anthologies and magazines; full-time writer from 1988. **Address:** c/o Piatkus Books, 5 Windmill St., London W1P 1HF, England. Lives in Boston Spa, West Yorkshire.

HORROR, GHOST AND GOTHIC PUBLICATIONS

Novels

Toady. London, Piatkus, 1989; revised as *The Horror Club*, New York, Bantam, 1991.
Stitch. London, Piatkus, 1991; New York, Dell, 1992.
The Immaculate. London, Piatkus, 1992; Atlanta, Georgia, White Wolf, 1996.
The Secret of Anatomy. London, Piatkus, 1994.
Mr. Bad Face. London, Piatkus, 1996.
Longbarrow. London, Piatkus, 1997.

Short Stories

Birthday. N.p., British Fantasy Society, 1992.
Voyages Into Darkness, with Stephen Laws. N.p., Bump In the Night Books, 1992.
Close to the Bone. London, Piatkus Books, 1995.

OTHER PUBLICATIONS

Novel

The Bodysnatchers. London, BBC Books, 1997.

*   *   *

Mark Morris is the author of five horror novels (with a sixth, *Longbarrow*, out in 1997, too late for consideration in this essay). His work belongs to the humanistic strand of horror fiction that includes the stories of Richard Matheson and Stephen King, using supernatural themes to explore issues of human responsibility. Morris's key strength is his depth of characterization. The theme of masculinity runs through all of his work, arising in a variety of contexts: fathers, sons, husbands, teenagers, thugs. Morris recurrently uses bullying as an archetypal scenario: the roles of aggressor and (male) victim serving to establish adult patterns of aggression and passivity. As supernatural fiction, Morris's work was initially limited by the sheer normality of his characters; but his novels have shown a growing awareness of the moral complexity of the individual and the implication of human character in the emergence of "evil." This awareness is handled optimistically in *The Immaculate* and more darkly in "The Chisellers' Reunion" and *Mr. Bad Face.*

Morris's first book, *Toady*, is a long horror novel set in a Northern English coastal town. Four teenage boys hold a seance and let in a "creature" which wreaks gradual havoc. The influence of Peter Straub shows in the carefully detailed background and its slow infiltration by supernatural elements. The abundance of weird effects is explained as the "creature" playing games with its victims (well, it's a good excuse). Unable to defeat the creature, three of the boys are drawn into its world, where they encounter archetypal figures of authority and cruelty; in the process, they realize the limits of the creature's power. This step into metaphysical fantasy, though well-justified, is executed in a sketchy way reminiscent of the TV series *Doctor Who*; and overall, the storyline is somewhat bland. But Morris's sensitive characterization and authentic sense of place are evidence of real ability.

Stitch has a similar premise: a capricious demon twisting reality in a localized setting. But this time, the "evil" is disseminated via an authoritarian cult, and its malignancy is unequivocal. Set in a university, *Stitch* explores both the romantic and the visceral aspects of sexual discovery. The latter are developed in a number of grotesque and implicitly anti-erotic scenes of "transformation." Angry and idealistic, *Stitch* blazes along to a pulpish conclusion in which the demon—visible as a male body composed of trapped souls—is defeated by the reciprocal "white magic" of a female student. At the core of the book is a powerful sequence about the sexual abuse of a young boy, and his subsequent breakdown and appalling self-injury. This realistic scenario establishes an archetype of trauma which motivates the rest of the novel.

The theme of childhood trauma dominates *The Immaculate*, a shorter and quieter novel about coming to terms with the past. Jack Stone, a successful writer, has moved to London from the small town where he grew up. A new girlfriend, Gail, encourages him to talk about a childhood in which he was victimized both by his alcoholic father (who blamed him for his mother's death in childbirth) and by a local bully. After his father's death, Jack returns to his home town, where he discovers evidence of his father's hidden sensitivity and paternal love. But the bully has grown still worse, poisoned by resentment. In a spectral finale, Jack learns that Gail is the ghost of his stillborn twin sister. (Ironically, one of Jack's key traumatic memories is of being forced to eat a bird foetus.) In both style and theme, *The Immaculate* shows Morris coming of age as a writer. His exploration of damaged masculinity is fluent and illuminating. The title's image of purity—the unborn or completed soul—balances the novel's images of violence and loss.

The Secret of Anatomy, then, is a slightly uncomfortable return to the "epic" form. This time, "evil" is represented by a secret society with totalizing ambitions. Like Ramsey Campbell's *The Parasite*, this novel identifies metaphysical evil with fascism: the worship of power. "Good" is represented by a splinter group who struggle to hold back the organization. Both sides possess a range of supernatural gifts. This is essentially a politicized version of *Stitch*, with an even stronger sense of human vulnerability. The key scenes are not intrinsically supernatural: a massacre in a restaurant, where one man uses his girlfriend as a shield; a vicious attempted gang-rape in a department store. There's one very fine short chapter about the spread of atrocity in a single day. But the finale is weak: a stereotyped "battle of the giants" in a derelict cinema. *The Secret of Anatomy* somehow has too much *gravitas* for its own plot: it's as if Morris knows he has outgrown this kind of book, but can only address his deeper concerns by annotating the pulpish storyline.

Close to the Bone, a collection of short stories (incorporating material from the 1992 small-press collection *Voyages Into Darkness*), reflects the diversity of Morris's approaches to the horror genre. There are paranoid science-fiction episodes, dark psychological stories, grotesque erotic nightmares, and more. "Warts and All" is a horrific update of the Book of Job; "Down to Earth" is a violent fable in which a garden leads a suburban couple to discover their sexual and mortal nature. "The Other One" is a quietly terrifying study of a divided identity: a man hiding in a flat, made aware of a murderous "other" who may be himself in a fugue state. In "The Chisellers' Reunion," four young men are forced to relive an incident from their adolescence: the accidental killing of a manipulative liar. His ghost attacks their families, making the four hold annual "reunions" in which he kills them one by one. Morris implicitly links the Northern slang term "chiseller" to the idea of a past written in stone.

This last story is closely connected to *Mr. Bad Face*, a bitterly downbeat psychological thriller with echoes of *Psycho*. Four adolescents have killed a disfigured war hero in a prank that went wrong. Twenty years later, they and their families are subjected to violent attacks by an apparently supernatural creature. It turns out that one of them is victimizing the other three. The maniac, a former victim of bullying, has been driven over the edge by the death of his possessive mother. The careful structuring and intense, evocative prose of *Mr. Bad Face* make it Morris's most accomplished and significant novel yet. The twist whereby one strand (the only clearly supernatural part) of the novel turns out to be a delusional fiction is both an ingenious plot device and a thought-provoking comment on the unreliability of narrative. By examining the psychological roots of his own supernaturalism, Morris has achieved a full integration of his flair for horrific imagery and his realistic awareness of emotional issues.

—Joel Lane

MORROW, W(illiam) C(hambers)

Nationality: American. **Born:** Alabama, 1853. **Career:** Journalist in San Francisco. **Died:** 3 April 1923.

HORROR, GHOST AND GOTHIC PUBLICATIONS

Short Stories

The Ape, the Idiot and Other People. Philadelphia, Lippincott, 1897; London, Grant Richards, 1898.

OTHER PUBLICATIONS

Novels

Blood-Money. N.p., Walker, 1882.
A Man: His Mark. Philadelphia, Lippincott, and London, Grant Richards, 1900.
Lentala of the South-Seas: The Romantic Tale of a Lost Colony. New York, Stokes, 1908.

Other

Bohemian Paris of To-day. N.p., 1900.

*

Critical Study: *Science Fiction in Old San Francisco: History of the Movement from 1854 to 1890* by Sam Moskowitz, West Kingston, Rhode Island, Grant, 1980.

* * *

W. C. Morrow was one of the West Coast Bohemians who were as close as America ever came to a Decadent Movement. He was, in fact, the man who emphasized their cultural and ideological links with the French Decadent writers and helped secure the more diplomatic alternative label in his non-fictional account of *Bohemian Paris of To-day* in 1900. By then, he had already imported the French *conte cruel* in spectacular fashion in his collection of 14 stories *The Ape, the Idiot and Other People.* His later novel, *Lentala of the South-Seas,* was similarly influenced by French Orientalism, perhaps especially by the works of "Pierre Loti," but has no relevance to the horror genre.

Sam Moskowitz's researches into imaginative fiction published in West Coast periodicals in the late 19th century, as reported in his *History of the Movement from 1854 to 1890,* have revealed that Morrow's earliest literary works appeared in *The Argonaut* in 1879-80. "Punishing a 'Shacker'; An Episode of Southern Life" is a tale of violent punishment inflicted by negro labourers on an idler. "Awful Shadows" is a tale of child-murder and lynch law. "Among the Moonshiners" and "A Sombre Incident of the Civil War" are further tales of rough and bloody justice, but "A Night in New Orleans" is a subtler horror story of a female tightrope-walker who suffers a fall when the torches illuminating her act are doused. "After the Hanging" is a more sophisticated *conte cruel* in which the victim is an unwise volunteer. One tale from this early phase preserved in *The Ape, the Idiot and Other People* is "The Man from Georgia," reprinted under the title "A Hero of the Plague."

Moskowitz tracks Morrow's subsequent development as a prolific writer of short stories for *The Californian* (later the *Overland Monthly*), lamenting the sentimentality which crept into his work there, presumably in response to editorial instruction. After the failure of his first novel, *Blood-Money*—which includes a gruesome self-amputation scene—Morrow apparently diverted his efforts to journalism but resumed writing *contes cruels* for William Randolph Hearst's *San Francisco Examiner* in 1887, beginning to cultivate more bizarre notions in "A Gloomy Shadow." It was, however, *The Argonaut* which published "A Peculiar Case of Surgery" (1889), in which a doctor decides that a stabbed man might live if only the weapon is never withdrawn or its position disturbed. A revised version of the story appears in *The Ape, the Idiot and Other People* as "The Permanent Stiletto." *The Argonaut* also published the even more exotic and far more horrific "The Rajah's Nemesis" (1889), in which a severely maimed victim of torture contrives a near-miraculous escape in order to revenge himself upon his tormentor. Reprinted as "His Unconquerable Enemy," this story set the baroque tone for the most excessive items in the collection.

"The Inmate of the Dungeon" is a less melodramatic but more ironic revenge-fantasy; it displays the same combination of bi-

zarre unlikelihood and ghoulish excess as "His Unconquerable Enemy." Continuing in the same vein, "An Original Revenge" requires the would-be avenger to kill himself while "An Uncommon View of It" involves an even more convoluted logical assessment of the possibilities of retribution. "A Game of Honour" and "A Story Told by the Sea" are accounts of strange but exacting justice in much the same reckless spirit as the revenge-fantasies, while "Treacherous Velasco" is a more sentimental account of betrayal and arduous reparation.

"The Monster-Maker" (originally published as "The Surgeon's Experiment") describes an experiment to ascertain whether a man can be kept alive in the absence of a brain; it succeeds, but with the inevitable Frankensteinian consequence. Closer in spirit to the ironic Grand Guignol *contes* of Maurice Level are "The Resurrection of Little Wang Tai," a tale of premature burial, and "Over an Absinthe Bottle," in which a desperate gambler wins a fortune that he cannot spend—perhaps posthumously, although the tale is unclear as to the exact moment of his death. "Two Singular Men" is a tale of carnival freaks, unapologetically relayed in the worst possible taste, while "The Faithful Amulet" is a gleefully violent black comedy of remarkable coincidences.

Read individually, Morrow's tales are startling; read as a series they have a collective effect which is unequalled by any other volume. *The Ape, the Idiot and Other People* is a remarkable concatenation of violent images: a gallery of Sadisms which is, in sum, so surreal as to be almost sublime. Although it has obvious affinities with the work of Villiers de l'Isle Adam in France and that of Ambrose Bierce within Morrow's local literary community, there is no other book quite like it. Although Morrow's name has been preserved because his stories continue to be reprinted in anthologies it is a great pity that the collection has never been reprinted as a whole and that no effort has been made to follow up Sam Moskowitz's discovery of a rich trove of unreprinted materials. Had Morrow made more frequent use of supernatural motifs he would undoubtedly have attracted the attention of one of the specialist presses, but his relative neglect testifies to the unfortunate marginalization of the *conte cruel* within the horror genre.

—Brian Stableford

MUNBY, A(lan) N(oel) L(atimer)

Nationality: British. **Born:** London, 25 December 1913. **Education:** Clifton College, Bristol; King's College, Cambridge. **Family:** Married 1) Joan Munby; 2) Sheila Crowther-Smith. **Career:** Bookdealer and antiquarian, 1935-39; prisoner-of-war, 1940-1945; librarian, King's College, Cambridge, 1947-74; Lyell Reader in Bibliography at Oxford, 1962-63; Sandars Reader at Cambridge, 1969-70. **Died:** 26 December 1974.

HORROR, GHOST AND GOTHIC PUBLICATIONS

Short Stories

The Alabaster Hand, and Other Ghost Stories. London, Dobson, 1949.

OTHER PUBLICATIONS

Other

Phillipps Studies. Cambridge, University Press, 5 vols., 1951-60; reissued in 2 vols., London, Sotheby Parke-Bernet, 1971.
Floreat Bibliomania. Cambridge, Rampant Lions Press, 1953.
Cambridge College Libraries. Cambridge, Heffer, 1960.
The Cult of the Autograph Letter in England. London, Athlone Press, 1962.
The Library of English Men of Letters. London, Library Association, 1964.
Macauley's Library. Glasgow, Jackson, 1966.
Portrait of an Obsession: the Life of Sir Thomas Phillipps, the World's Greatest Book Collector, edited by Nicolas Barker. London, Constable, 1967; New York, Putnam, 1967.
The History and Bibliography of Science in England: The First Phase, 1833-1845. Berkeley, University of California, 1968.
The Earl and the Thief: Lord Ashburnham and Count Libri. Cambridge, Massachusetts, Houghton Library, 1969.
The Flow of Books and Manuscripts. Los Angeles, University of California Clark Memorial Library, 1969.
Connoisseurs and Medieval Miniatures, 1750-1850. Oxford, Clarendon Press, 1972.
Book Collecting in the 1930s. Brighton, Appleton, 1973; as *Book Collecting in Britain in the 1930s,* Nevada City, California, Berliner, 1973.
Book-collectors: Preservers of the Humanities. Orange, California, Rasmussen Press, 1976.
Essays and Papers, edited by Nicholas Barker. London, Scholar Press, 1977.

Editor, with Lenore Coral, *British Book Sale Catalogues, 1676-1800: A Union List.* London, Mansell, 1975.

*   *   *

A. N. L. Munby, known as Tim to his acquaintances, wrote only one collection of ghost stories, and he might not have written those had he not spent most of the war as a prisoner at Eichstätt, yet he can truly claim to be one of the few who genuinely inherited the mantle of M. R. James. Like James, Munby was a devoted bibliophile who wrote and lectured copiously about books, libraries and book collecting. Books are sometimes the key to supernatural events in his stories. "Herodes Redivivus" is the title of a 16th-century volume that reminds the narrator of the experiences he had as a near-victim of the murderer who once owned it and who claimed descent from Giles de Retz; "The Tregannet Book of Hours" reveals a 15th-century mystery of a landowner haunted by the corpse of a neighbour he had killed; "Number Seventy-Nine" refers to a manuscript of magical rites which is destroyed before it goes on sale because the dealer's assistant had been tempted to raise the dead. Perhaps because of their comparative self-indulgence these stories are the weakest of Munby's if you are looking for genuine frights.

The strongest are those where Munby ploughs James's own territory and looks for ghosts trapped by the living. "The Tudor Chimney" is one such. An old walled-up fireplace is re-opened during the renovation of a house. A horrible smell as of old fat and grease presages the release of the foul ghost of a vicious squire who had been burned to death. "The White Sack" is reminiscent

of James's "Oh, Whistle, and I'll Come to You, My Lad." The narrator on a walking holiday in Skye finds himself being chased by a mist-like wraith which eventually wraps itself round his face like wet paper. "The Inscription" is revealed when an old grave is uncovered, releasing the guardian of the tomb who pursues the desecrator. In "The Alabaster Hand" Munby succeeds in mixing a healthy blend of the antiquarian ghost story with a sense of humour, something more prevalent in James's work than most remember. The story concerns a church stall haunted by the ghost of a pre-Reformation clergyman who seems to seek his revenge upon Anglican ministers.

Like any stories imitative of M. R. James's work, they may seem derivative and lacking in originality. It requires skill to achieve the same *frisson* and few succeed like James. Munby gets it right more often than not. His only weakness seems to be in creating a sufficiently malevolent ghost and bringing the story to a natural denouement. His weakest tales read rather like incidents, but his best, like James's, have a tangible atmosphere of threat and are amongst the best of all antiquarian ghost stories.

—Mike Ashley

MUNN, H(arold) Warner

Nationality: American. **Born:** Athol, Massachusetts, 5 November 1903. **Family:** Married Malvena Ruth Beaudoin in 1930 (died 1972); four sons. **Career:** Full-time writer, 1925-1930; afterwards held various jobs, ending as office manager of a heating company; retired 1968. **Died:** 10 January 1981.

HORROR, GHOST AND GOTHIC PUBLICATIONS

Short Stories

The Werewolf of Ponkert. Providence, Rhode Island, Grandon, 1958.
Tales of the Werewolf Clan, Volume 1: In the Tomb of the Bishop. West Kingston, Rhode Island, Grant, 1979.
Tales of the Werewolf Clan, Volume 2: The Master Goes Home. West Kingston, Rhode Island, Grant, 1979.

OTHER PUBLICATIONS

Novels

King of the World's Edge. New York, Ace, 1966.
The Ship from Atlantis. New York, Ace, 1967.
Merlin's Ring. New York, Ballantine, 1974; London, Futura, 1977.
Merlin's Godson (omnibus; includes *King of the World's Edge, The Ship from Atlantis*). New York, Ballantine, 1976.
The Lost Legion. New York, Doubleday, 1980.

Short Stories

The Affair of the Cuckolded Warlock. Tacoma, Washington, Lanthorne Press, 1975.
What Dreams May Come. Tacoma, Washington, Swan Press, 1978.

In the Hulks. Tacoma, Washington, Swan Press, 1979.
The Transient. Tacoma, Washington, Swan Press, 1979.
The Baby Dryad. Tacoma, Washington, Folly Press, 1980.

Poetry

Christmas Comes to the Little Horse. Tacoma, Washington, privately printed, 1974.
Twenty-Five Poems. Tacoma, Washington, Folly Press, 1975.
The Banner of Joan. West Kingston, Rhode Island, Grant, 1975.
To All Amis. Tacoma, Washington, privately printed, 1976.
Season Greetings With Spooky Stuff. Tacoma, Washington, privately printed, 1976.
There Was a Man. Tacoma, Washington, privately printed, 1977.
The Pioneers. Tacoma, Washington, Swan Press, 1977.
In Regard to the Opening of Doors. Tacoma, Washington, Swan Press, 1979.
Dawn Woman. Tacoma, Washington, Swan Press, 1979.
Fairy Gold. Tacoma, Washington, Swan Press, 1979.
Of Life and Love and Loneliness. Tacoma, Washington, privately printed, 1979.
The Book of Munn; or, A Recipe for Roast Camel. Tacoma, Washington, privately printed, 1979.

*

Critical Studies: *Presenting Moonshine,* Tacoma, Washington, privately printed, 1975; "Warlock of Tacoma: An Appreciation" by Jessica Amanda Salmonson, *The Chicago Fantasy Newsletter,* February-May 1981; "H. Warner Munn: A Bibliography" by Mike Ashley, *Kadath,* July 1981.

*   *   *

Were an author's reputation based exclusively on the genre to which he contributed most of his fiction, then H. Warner Munn would be remembered today as an historical fantasist whose four novels include the World Fantasy award-nominated *Merlin's Ring.* That he is still best known as the author of "The Werewolf of Ponkert," his first professional fiction sale, says a great deal about his skills as a horror writer.

Munn wrote "The Werewolf of Ponkert" in 1925, in response to a letter published in *Weird Tales* in which H. P. Lovecraft proposed that someone write a werewolf story narrated from the werewolf's point of view. At the time, the body of werewolf fiction was relatively small and there was no classic novel that codified werewolf lore the way *Dracula* had standardized the mythology of the vampire. Nevertheless, Munn's tale was immediately recognized as an original contribution to the werewolf canon, particularly in its sympathetic portrayal of a supernatural monster as a victim of circumstance. Set in 14th-century Hungary, it is the account of Wladislaw Brenryk, a kind and gentle man who is chased down one night by a pack of wolves. The wolves prove to be men enslaved by the Master, an inhuman being who combines aspects of the vampire and werewolf and leads the pack on their nightly rampages. Brenryk has killed one of the pack and is forced to take his place under the penalty of death. Sickened over time by the slaughters he perpetrates, including those of his wife and daughter, he confesses to local authorities and helps set a trap for the wolf pack. All are slain except the Master, who escapes.

In a final poignant note, it is revealed that Brenryk's account was written in a book made from his own skin, which was flayed from him before his execution.

Munn's story showed a literary sensibility uncommon for the pulp magazines. Brenryk's descriptions of his physical transformation and kills are powerful without being physically gruesome, and the pangs of conscience he expresses are conveyed with a genuine sense of tragedy. The story was instantly popular with *Weird Tales* readers, and like many popular stories in the magazine spawned sequels. Thereby hangs the tale of Munn's weird-fiction legacy, and one of the most interesting sagas to be published in the weird-fiction pulps.

In 1927, Munn published "The Return of the Master," a continuation of the frame narrative of "The Werewolf of Ponkert." The original story was actually a tale within a tale, in which Munn's fictionalized self, Monsieur M—, stumbles upon Brenryk's book in a contemporary French inn. Munn brought back Monsieur M— for a personal confrontation with the Master, some 600 years after the action of the first story. In one scene, the Master proves completely invulnerable to a Christian exorcism, and Munn teases the reader with the speculation that he represents a power "so anciently evil, so horribly unnatural, that only other magic as ancient as itself could prevail against it."

Although the Master was vanquished at the end of the tale, his story was far from over. "The Werewolf's Daughter," published the following year, picked up immediately after the events of "The Werewolf of Ponkert." Ostensibly the story of Brenryk's daughter Ivga (whom, it is revealed, was miraculously saved from the wolf pack) and her persecution by the townsfolk of Ponkert, it began a much larger scheme that Munn had developed for the series. To escape "the martyrdom of the innocent," Ivga promises one descendant from each future generation of the Brenryks to the Master. In his subsequent "Tales of the Werewolf Clan," Munn followed the Brenryk family down through the centuries, relating their struggle with the Master against well-researched backdrops that included the St. Bartholomew's Day Massacre, the Thirty Years War, the Salem Witch Trials and other historical monuments to prejudice and intolerance.

Although the Master appears in each one to torment the Brenryk progeny with Mephistophelean bargains, there is very little supernatural content to the stories. Rather, Munn lets history itself supply the horrors, making it out to be a succession of inhuman atrocities touched off by the Master's cruel games with his victims. The vast scope of the series was unique in the weird-fiction pulps, and the stories remain among the most original variants on the werewolf theme ever attempted. Munn expanded the saga yet again between 1977 and 1979, with additional tales that finally revealed the Master to be a god who loathes humanity because he was imprisoned in the body of human being by a Babylonian witch thousands of years before.

The achievement of Munn's werewolf saga has overshadowed his other distinguished horror stories. "City of the Spiders," a cautionary tale related much in the style of H. G. Wells's "Empire of the Ants," is the narrative of an explorer who chances upon a city of giant spiders and proof that they once ruled the earth. Both "The Chain" and "The Wheel" show the influence of Poe's fiction, particularly "The Pit and the Pendulum," in their accounts of men who endure tortures on ingenious mechanisms designed by vengeful madmen. Munn was equally skilled at writing sentimental supernatural stories like "A Sprig of Rosemary," about a love from beyond the grave, and grimmer efforts like "What

Dreams May Come," in which a woman who sees the future commits suicide to prevent the misery she will cause.

Munn's contributions to the small-press magazines in the 1970s are also noteworthy, especially his trilogy of novellas featuring biologist and antiquarian Hugh Lamont. "The Merlin Stone," "The Stairway in the Sea" and "Wanderers of the Waters" all describe Lamont's investigations into underground and undersea races that have emerged in the modern world. Rich with the historical detail that make his werewolf saga so memorable, they are also homages to the supernatural fiction of Robert E. Howard and H. P. Lovecraft, and thus bring his career as a fantasist full circle.

—Stefan Dziemianowicz

NAVARRO, Yvonne

Nationality: American. **Born:** Chicago, 1957. **Career:** Writer of short stories for magazines and anthologies from 1984. **Address:** c/o Bantam Books, 1540 Broadway, New York, NY 10036, USA.

HORROR, GHOST AND GOTHIC PUBLICATIONS

Novels

Afterage. New York, Bantam, 1993.
Species (novelization of screenplay). New York and London, Bantam, 1995.
Deadrush. New York, Bantam, 1995.
Aliens: Music of the Spears. New York, Bantam, 1996; London, Millennium, 1997.
Final Impact. New York, Bantam, 1997.

* * *

As horror fiction continued its decline in popularity in the US through the early 1990s, it became increasingly difficult for new writers to enter that genre. Only those with unusually strong talents and fresh ideas had any real chance of success. One of these was Yvonne Navarro, whose high-powered short stories had been appearing in the small press with some regularity, but who did not attract major attention until the publication of her first novel, *Afterage.*

Afterage took advantage of the continuing popularity of vampires but avoided traditional treatments in favour of a much more ambitious approach. The vampires have taken over the world, a logical result of their ability to convert their victims that has figured in fiction previously, most notably in Richard Matheson's *I Am Legend* and the Horror Writers Association anthology, *Under the Fang.* As the supply of ordinary humans dwindles, the growing vampire population is faced with a crisis. If all of their prey are killed, their species will soon follow. Their solution is to begin capturing the surviving humans and imprison them in anticipation of forced breeding programmes. In essence, the human race has become livestock.

Just when all seems lost, a strange thing happens. A vampire attacks one of the few humans not yet captured and dies himself, poisoned by her blood. A brilliant doctor realizes the potential of the situation and sets out to manufacture a plague that will sweep through the vampire population and end their menace forever. This blend of horror and global disaster novel is extremely well handled, and in fact most of Navarro's subsequent work borrows heavily from science fiction as a source of its horrific elements.

Her second title was a novelization of the film *Species.* An apparently human child is grown from genetically altered material created through the instructions of a communication from outer space. But the result is not human at all, but rather a shape-changing creature who is genetically programmed to create more of her kind and eventually supplant the human race. The superficial similarity to *Afterage* may have been part of the reason Navarro chose to turn this screenplay into a novel. She also wrote the novel version of one of the ongoing *Aliens* graphic adventure stories, *Music of the Spears.* The human race has become inextricably involved with the alien species by now, and a substance from their bodies has become a highly addictive drug on Earth. Against this background we follow the efforts of a brilliant but twisted musician whose crowning achievement is designed to be a symphony that incorporates the shrill cries of an angry alien into its structure. To do so, he illegally smuggles one of the creatures onto the planet and keeps it in captivity, periodically feeding it a human sacrifice while the sound recorders are active. Unsurprisingly, the villain underestimates his prisoner and pays the ultimate price.

Navarro returned to original work with *Deadrush.* Once again, the world is menaced by a contagious evil. An evangelist whose religion seems more born of hate than love discovers that he has the power to raise the recently dead. That's unsettling enough on the face of it, but each of his resurrectees shares the same power, and there's a rush of feeling that accompanies the act that is clearly addictive. It's so addictive, in fact, that the resurrected begin killing people in order to bring them back to life. *Deadrush* is an immensely powerful novel and has helped to establish Navarro firmly as one of the major horror writers of the 1990s.

Final Impact moved more directly into the preserves of science fiction, although there are still hints of the supernatural. The Earth is about to be struck by an interplanetary object with such force that civilization is unlikely to survive. A handful of people have received prescient warning of the disaster, but there is little they can do in advance to prepare. The reader is also introduced to several other characters with unusual powers—telekinesis, healing—and told that they are in some fashion fated to act together to preserve themselves in the aftermath of the cataclysm. Most of what follows is standard post-disaster fare, well told but breaking no new ground. Navarro's characters are as well drawn as ever, and the story is certainly gripping, but the psychic abilities of several of the characters never seem to mesh with the rest of the story. They seem almost an afterthought.

Navarro's better short stories include a nasty but lonely witch in "This House," a man who steals the life-force from women in "The Best Years of My Life," and a woman whose need to be needed causes her to affect the life and health of people around her in "Folds of the Faithful." In "For Love of Mother" we discover that superstitions might be grounded in reality, and in "I Know What to Do" a man discovers a super-powerful cockroach living in his new home, eventually captures it and mails it off to his ex-wife. Other stories of note include "Memories" and "Zachary's Glass Shoppe." Navarro's proven talents and the continuing popularity of her novels is a strong indicator that she will retain her prominence as a horror writer, and her willingness to incorporate plot elements from outside that genre is likely to attract additional readers as well.

—Don D'Ammassa

NEIDERMAN, Andrew

Pseudonym: V. C. Andrews. **Nationality:** American. **Born:** 1940.

HORROR, GHOST AND GOTHIC PUBLICATIONS

Novels

Pin. New York, Pocket, 1981; London, Arrow, 1982.
Brainchild. New York, Pocket, 1981; London, Arrow, 1983.
Someone's Watching. New York, Pocket, 1983; London, Arrow, 1984.
Tender, Loving Care. New York, Pocket, 1984; London, Arrow, 1985.
Imp. New York, Pocket, and London, Severn House, 1985.
Child's Play. New York, Zebra, 1985.
Night Howl. New York, Pocket, 1986; London, Severn House, 1987.
Love Child. New York, Tor, 1986.
Teacher's Pet. New York, Zebra, 1986.
Sight Unseen. New York, Zebra, 1987.
Playmates. New York, Berkley, 1987; London, Arrow, 1988.
Reflection. London, Worldwide, 1987.
Surrogate Child. New York, Berkley, 1988; London, Legend, 1989.
Perfect Little Angels. New York, Berkley, 1989; London, Severn House, 1990.
The Devil's Advocate. New York, Pocket, and London, Legend, 1990.
Bloodchild. New York, Berkley, 1990.
The Immortals. New York, Pocket, 1991.
Sister, Sister. New York, Berkley, and London, Legend, 1992.
The Need. New York, Putnam, 1992.
After Life. New York, Berkley, 1993.
The Solomon Organization. New York, Putnam, 1993.
Duplicates. New York, Berkley, 1994.

Novels as V. C. Andrews

Garden of Shadows, with V. C. Andrews. New York, Pocket, and London, Collins, 1987.
Fallen Hearts. New York, Pocket, and London, Collins, 1988.
Gates of Paradise. New York, Pocket, and London, Collins, 1989.
Web of Dreams. New York, Pocket, and London, Collins, 1990.
Dawn. New York, Pocket, 1990; London, Simon and Schuster, 1991.
Ruby. New York, Pocket, 1991; London, Simon and Schuster, 1994.
Secrets of the Morning. New York, Pocket, and London, Simon and Schuster, 1991.
Twilight's Child. New York, Pocket, and London, Simon and Schuster, 1992.
Midnight Whispers. New York, Pocket, 1992; London, Simon and Schuster, 1993.
Darkest Hour. New York, Pocket, 1993; London, Simon and Schuster, 1994.
Pearl in the Mist. New York, Pocket, and London, Simon and Schuster, 1994.
All That Glitters. New York, Pocket, and London, Simon and Schuster, 1995.
Hidden Jewel. New York, Pocket, 1995; London, Simon and Schuster, 1996.
Tarnished Gold. New York, Pocket, and London, Simon and Schuster, 1996.
Melody. New York, Pocket, 1996; London, Simon and Schuster, 1997.

*

Film Adaptation: *Pin,* 1988.

*   *   *

Andrew Neiderman's first novel, *Pin,* though not his best, is in many ways his most interesting. Two children with obsessive compulsive parents lead an unhappy childhood until their father hits upon a diversion. He creates the imaginary person, Pin, who can answer their questions and see to their needs while their parents are occupied elsewhere. Everything seems fine until the parents die, and the children go on, with Pin to guide them. A very fine concept with understated horror that even translated reasonably well into a low-budget film some time later. Unfortunately, though Neiderman's writing skills would improve with subsequent books, he became much more derivative as his career progressed, and has to date produced very few actively interesting stories.

Brainchild was the first of several "evil children" novels which Neiderman would write. Lois is a self-centred genius, fascinated with behavioural science, obsessed with the desire to control the will of her experimental subjects. But when her father and mother both become ill, there's no one to watch her, and no one to discover that she has developed the ability to manipulate human beings as well as animals. Another weak woman mothers a monstrous child in *Imp,* in this case banishing him to live in the secret tunnels beneath their house. But Imp has a tendency to explore and cause hellish trouble for those he stumbles across.

Somewhat more interesting is *Love Child.* Carol is something more than human. In her genetic structure is the impulse to hunt, to commit violent acts, and life as a teenager provides ample opportunities to answer the call of blood. But Carol falls in love as well, and the human and non-human sides of her nature find themselves at war in this variation of the werewolf theme. *Night Howl* is reminiscent of Dean Koontz's *Watchers.* A scientific experiment results in killer dogs with unusual strength and intelligence, and one of them is loose and bringing down human prey in a nearby community. The power to alter the minds of others against their own inclinations is central to *Teacher's Pet,* this time involving an evil school-teacher who turns his pupils into instruments of his will.

There's another demon child in *Sight Unseen,* this one a young boy who possesses both telepathy and clairvoyance. As he matures, the boy begins to use his power to alter the lives of his neighbours, until finally one of them realizes the truth and confronts the young man. Similarly, in *Surrogate Child* grief-stricken parents adopt a boy when their own son dies, but the newcomer acts very strangely at times, as though he wished to conceal some dangerous secret that might give them second thoughts about allowing him into their lives. *Perfect Little Angels* is a reprise of many of Neiderman's recurring themes. Another scientific experiment has gone wrong, yet another experiment in mind-control, and the teenagers in a small town have been turned into pre-programmed monsters whose good behaviour masks a seething inner rage.

Neiderman weds the demon child to the vampire story in *Bloodchild.* The Hamiltons adopt a baby to fill a void in their lives, but the child is more inclined to drink blood than milk, and the Hamiltons quickly discover that where there's one vampire, there soon will be more. Neiderman's second vampire novel, *Need,* is far and away his best work, and certainly the most original in concept. A brother and sister share the same body, and the brother has a taste for human blood. When the sister side of their personality discovers that her alter ego has murdered the man she loves, she vows to destroy him forever, and the duel of wills that ensues is the best writing Neiderman has yet produced.

The Devil's Advocate is a supernatural John Grisham novel. The protagonist is flattered when he is asked to join a prominent law firm, but confused when he discovers that sometimes cases for the defence are prepared even before the crimes are committed. Ultimately he must decide whether or not to sell his soul, quite literally, in order to guarantee himself a prosperous future. *The Immortals* is very similar in structure. In this case the central character is employed by a prominent cosmetics firm, a development that pleases both him and his wife. Unfortunately, she discovers that the spouses of managers at the firm have a tendency to die young, and mysteriously, and that the secret of prolonged life requires the sacrifice of a loved one.

Sister, Sister reverted to the demon child theme. In this case, the children are Siamese twins whose ability to share thoughts gives them the power to influence those of others. Their new tutor discovers the truth, and must decide whether or not to destroy them, if she can. An unhappy man unwisely contacts a secret society in *The Solomon Organization* and realizes he has risked the lives of everyone he loves. In *After Life*, a blind woman hears mysterious voices that tell her of the torments of the dead, an unusual and better than average story of zombies, possession, and communication with the dead.

Perhaps because of his frequent use of children as main characters, Neiderman was chosen as the ghost-writer for the last several "V. C. Andrews" novels which, while not supernatural, often contain horror themes and concepts. He has written other non-supernatural suspense under his own name, most notably *Playmates* and *Child's Play*, both involving evil children. When he steps outside of his recurring themes, Neiderman occasionally produces notable work, but for the most part his novels tend to fade quickly from the reader's memory.

—Don D'Ammassa

NESBIT, E(dith)

Pseudonyms: E. Bland; Fabian Bland. **Nationality:** British. **Born:** London, 15 August 1858. **Education:** Attended an Ursuline convent in Dinan, France, 1869, and schools in Germany and Brighton. **Family:** Married 1) the writer Hubert Bland in 1880 (died 1914), two sons, one daughter, one adopted daughter, and one adopted son; 2) Thomas Terry Tucker in 1917. **Career:** Journalist, elocutionist, greeting-cards decorator; poetry critic, *Athenaeum* magazine, London, 1890s; co-editor, *Neolith* magazine, London, 1907-08; general editor, Children's Bookcase series, Oxford University Press and Hodder and Stoughton, 1908-11. Founding member, 1884, and member of the Pamphlet Committee, Fabian Society. **Awards:** Granted a Civil List pension, 1915. **Died:** 4 May 1924.

HORROR, GHOST AND GOTHIC PUBLICATIONS

Novels

Salome and the Head: A Modern Melodrama. London, Alston Rivers, 1909; as *The House with No Address*, New York, Doubleday, 1909.
Dormant. London, Methuen, 1911; as *Rose Royal*, New York, Dodd Mead, 1912.

Short Stories

Grim Tales. London, Innes, 1893.
Fear. London, Stanley Paul, 1910.

Tales of Terror, edited by Hugh Lamb. London, Methuen, 1983.
In the Dark: Tales of Terror, edited by Hugh Lamb. Wellingborough, Northamptonshire, Thorsons, 1988.

OTHER PUBLICATIONS

Novels

The Prophet's Mantle (as Fabian Bland, with Hubert Bland). London, Drane, 1885; Chicago, Belford Clarke, 1889.
The Secret of the Kyriels. London, Hurst and Blackett, and Philadelphia, Lippincott, 1899.
The Red House. London, Methuen, and New York, Harper, 1902.
The Incomplete Amorist. London, Constable, and New York, Doubleday, 1906.
Daphne in Fitzroy Street. London, George Allen, and New York, Doubleday, 1909.
The Incredible Honeymoon. New York, Harper, 1916; London, Hutchinson, 1921.
The Lark. London, Hutchinson, 1922.

Novels for Children

The Story of the Treasure Seekers, Being the Adventures of the Bastable Children in Search of a Fortune, illustrated by Gordon Browne and Lewis Baumer. London, Unwin, and New York, Stokes, 1899.
The Wouldbegoods, Being the Further Adventures of the Treasure Seekers, illustrated by Arthur H. Buckland and John Hassell. London, Unwin, 1901; New York, Harper, 1902.
Five Children and It, illustrated by H. R. Millar. London, Unwin, 1902; New York, Dodd Mead, 1905.
The New Treasure Seekers, illustrated by Gordon Browne and Lewis Baumer. London, Unwin, and New York, Stokes, 1904.
The Phoenix and the Carpet, illustrated by H. R. Millar. London, Newnes, and New York, Macmillan, 1904.
The Railway Children, illustrated by C. E. Brock. London, Wells Gardner, and New York, Macmillan, 1906.
The Story of the Amulet, illustrated by H. R. Millar. London, Unwin, 1906; New York, Dutton, 1907.
The Enchanted Castle, illustrated by H. R. Millar. London, Unwin, 1907; New York, Harper, 1908.
The House of Arden, illustrated by H. R. Millar. London, Unwin, 1908; New York, Dutton, 1909.
Harding's Luck, illustrated by H. R. Millar. London, Hodder and Stoughton, 1909; New York, Stokes, 1910.
The Magic City, illustrated by H. R. Millar. London, Macmillan, 1910; New York, Coward McCann, 1958.
The Wonderful Garden; or The Three C's, illustrated by H. R. Millar. London, Macmillan, 1911; New York, Coward McCann, 1935.
The Magic World, illustrated by H. R. Millar and Spencer Pryse. London and New York, Macmillan, 1912.
Wet Magic, illustrated by H. R. Millar. London, Laurie, 1913; New York, Coward McCann, 1937.

Short Stories

Something Wrong. London, Innes, 1893.
The Butler in Bohemia, with Oswald Barron. London, Drane, 1894.

In Homespun. London, Lane, and Boston, Roberts, 1896.

The Book of Dragons, illustrated by H. R. Millar. London and New York, Harper, 1900.

Nine Unlikely Tales for Children, illustrated by H. R. Millar and Claude Shepperson. London, Unwin, and New York, Dutton, 1901.

Thirteen Ways Home. London, Treherne, 1901.

The Literary Sense. London, Methuen, and New York, Macmillan, 1903.

Man and Maid. London, Unwin, 1906.

These Little Ones. London, George Allen, 1909.

To the Adventurous. London, Hutchinson, 1923.

Fairy Stories, edited by Naomi Lewis, illustrated by Brian Robb. London, Benn, 1977.

Fiction for Children

Listen Long and Listen Well, with others. London, Tuck, 1893.

Sunny Tales for Snowy Days, with others. London, Tuck, 1893.

Told by Sunbeams and Me, with others. London, Tuck, 1893.

Fur and Feathers: Tales for All Weathers, with others. London, Tuck, 1894.

Lads and Lassies, with others. London, Tuck, 1894.

Tales That Are True, for Brown Eyes and Blue, with others, edited by Edric Vredenburg, illustrated by M. Goodman. London, Tuck, 1894.

Tales to Delight from Morning till Night, with others, edited by Edric Vredenburg, illustrated by M. Goodman. London, Tuck, 1894.

Hours in Many Lands: Stories and Poems, with others, edited by Edric Vredenburg, illustrated by Frances Brundage. London, Tuck, 1894.

Doggy Tales, illustrated by Lucy Kemp-Welch. London, Ward, 1895.

Pussy Tales, illustrated by Lucy Kemp-Welch. London, Ward, 1895.

Tales of the Clock, illustrated by Helen Jackson. London, Tuck, 1895.

Dulcie's Lantern and Other Stories, with Theo Gift and Mrs. Worthington Bliss. London, Griffith Farran, 1895.

Treasures from Storyland, with others. London, Tuck, 1895.

Tales Told in Twilight: A Volume of Very Short Stories. London, Nister, 1897.

Dog Tales, and Other Tales, with A. Guest and Emily R. Watson, edited by Edric Vredenburg, illustrated by R. K. Mounsey. London, Tuck, 1898.

Pussy and Doggy Tales, illustrated by Lucy Kemp-Welch. London, Dent, 1899; New York, Dutton, 1900.

The Revolt of the Toys and What Comes of Quarrelling, illustrated by Ambrose Dudley. London, Nister, and New York, Dutton, 1902.

Playtime Stories. London, Tuck, 1903.

The Rainbow Queen and Other Stories. London, Tuck, 1903.

The Story of the Five Rebellious Dolls. London, Nister, 1904.

Cat Tales, with Rosamund Bland, illustrated by Isabel Watkin. London, Nister, and New York, Dutton, 1904.

Pug Peter: King of Mouseland, Marquis of Barkshire, D.O.G., P.C. 1906, Knight of the Order of the Gold Dog Collar, Author of Doggerel Lays and Days, illustrated by Harry Rountree. Leeds, Alf Cooke, 1905.

Oswald Bastable and Others, illustrated by C. E. Brock and H. R. Millar. London, Wells Gardner, 1905; New York, Coward McCann, 1960.

Our New Story Book, with others, illustrated by Elsie Wood and Louis Wain. London, Nister, and New York, Dutton, 1913.

The New World Literary Series, Book Two, edited by Henry Cecil Wyld. London, Collins, 1921.

Five of Us—And Madeline, edited by Mrs. Clifford Sharp, illustrated by Nora S. Unwin. London, Unwin, 1925; New York, Adelphi, 1926.

Plays

Cinderella (produced London, 1892). London, Sidgwick and Jackson, 1909.

A Family Novelette, with Oswald Barron (produced London, 1894).

The King's Highway (produced London, 1905).

The Philandrist; or, The Lady Fortune-Teller, with Dorothea Deakin (produced London, 1905).

The Magician's Heart (produced London, 1907).

Unexceptionable References (produced London, 1912).

Poetry

Lays and Legends. London and New York, Longman, 2 vols., 1886-92.

The Lily and the Cross. London, Griffith Farran, and New York, Dutton, 1887.

The Star of Bethlehem. London, Nister, 1887.

Leaves of Life. London and New York, Longman, 1888.

The Better Part and Other Poems. London, Drane, 1888.

Easter-Tide: Poems, with Caris Brooke. London, Drane, and New York, Dutton, 1888.

The Time of Roses, with Caris Brooke and others. London, Drane, 1888.

By Land and Sea. London, Drane, 1888.

Landscape and Song. London, Drane, and New York, Dutton, 1888.

The Message of the Dove: An Easter Poem. London, Drane, and New York, Dutton, 1888.

The Lilies Round the Cross: An Easter Memorial, with Helen J. Wood. London, Nister, and New York, Dutton, 1889.

Corals and Sea Songs. London, Nister, 1889.

Life's Sunny Side, with others. London, Nister, 1890.

Sweet Lavender. London, Nister, 1892.

Flowers I Bring and Songs I Sing (as E. Bland), with H. M. Burnside and A. Scanes. London, Tuck, 1893.

Holly and Mistletoe: A Book of Christmas Verse, with Norman Gale and Richard Le Gallienne. London, Ward, 1895.

A Pomander of Verse. London, Lane, and Chicago, McClurg, 1895.

Rose Leaves. London, Nister, 1895.

Songs of Love and Empire. London, Constable, 1898.

The Rainbow and the Rose. London and New York, Longman, 1905.

Ballads and Lyrics of Socialism 1883-1908. London, Fabian Society, 1908.

Jesus in London: A Poem. London, Fifield, 1908.

Ballads and Verses of the Spiritual Life. London, Elkin Mathews, 1911.

Garden Poems. London, Collins, 1912.

Many Voices. London, Hutchinson, 1922.

Poetry for Children

Songs of Two Seasons, illustrated by J. MacIntyre. London, Tuck, 1890.
The Voyage of Columbus, 1492: The Discovery of America, illustrated by Will and Frances Brundage. London, Tuck, 1892.
Our Friends and All about Them. London, Tuck, 1893.
As Happy as a King, illustrated by S. Rosamund Praeger. London, Ward, 1896.
Dinna Forget, with G. C. Bingham. London, Nister, 1897; New York, Dutton, 1898.
To Wish You Every Joy. London, Tuck, 1901.

Other

Wings and the Child; or, The Building of Magic Cities. London, Hodder and Stoughton, and New York, Doran, 1913.

Editor, *Battle Songs.* London, Max Goschen, 1914.
Editor, *Essays,* by Hubert Bland. London, Max Goschen, 1914.

Other for Children

The Children's Shakespeare, edited by Edric Vredenburg, illustrated by Frances Brundage. London, Tuck, 1897; Philadelphia, Altemus, 1900.
Royal Children of English History, illustrated by Frances Brundage. London, Tuck, 1897.
Twenty Beautiful Stories from Shakespeare: A Home Study Course, edited by E. T. Roe, illustrated by Max Bihn. Chicago, Hertel and Jenkins, 1907.
The Old Nursery Stories, illustrated by W. H. Margetson. London, Oxford University Press-Hodder and Stoughton, 1908.
My Sea-Side Book, with George Manville Fenn. London, Nister, and New York, Dutton, 1911.
Children's Stories from Shakespeare, with *When Shakespeare Was a Boy,* by F. J. Furnivall. Philadelphia, McKay, 1912.
Children's Stories from English History, with Doris Ashley, edited by Edric Vredenburg, illustrated by John H. Bacon and Howard Davie. London, Tuck, 1914.
Long Ago When I Was Young, illustrated by Edward Ardizzone. London, Whiting and Wheaton, and New York, Watts, 1966.

Editor, with Robert Ellice Mack, *Spring [Summer, Autumn, Winter] Songs and Sketches.* London, Griffith Farran, and New York, Dutton, 4 vols., 1886.
Editor, with Robert Ellice Mack, *Eventide Songs and Sketches.* London, Griffith Farran, 1887; as *Night Songs and Sketches,* New York, Dutton, 1887.
Editor, with Robert Ellice Mack, *Morning Songs and Sketches.* London, Griffith Farran, 1887; as *Noon Songs and Sketches,* New York, Dutton, 1887.
Editor, with Robert Ellice Mack, *Lilies and Heartsease: Songs and Sketches.* New York, Dutton, 1888(?).
Editor, *The Girl's Own Birthday Book.* London, Drane, 1894.
Editor, *Poet's Whispers: A Birthday Book.* London, Drane, 1895.
Editor, *A Book of Dogs, Being a Discourse on Them, with Many Tales and Wonders,* illustrated by Winifred Austin. London, Dent, and New York, Dutton, 1898.
Editor, *Winter-Snow,* illustrated by H. Bellingham Smith. New York, Dutton, 1898(?).

*

Film Adaptations: *Five Children and It,* 1951, 1991 (television serials); *The Railway Children,* 1951 (television serial), 1968 (television serial), 1970; *The Story of the Treasure Seekers,* 1953, 1961, 1982 (television serials); *The Phoenix and the Carpet,* 1976 (television serial); *The Enchanted Castle,* 1979 (television serial); *The Return of the Psammead,* 1993 (television serial), from the novel *The Story of the Amulet.*

Critical Studies: *E. Nesbit: A Biography* by Doris Langley Moore, London, Benn, 1933, revised edition, Philadelphia, Chilton, 1966, Benn, 1967; *Magic and the Magician: E. Nesbit and Her Children's Books* by Noel Streatfeild, London, Benn, and New York, Abelard Schuman, 1958; *E. Nesbit* by Anthea Bell, London, Bodley Head, 1960, New York, Walck, 1964; *A Woman of Passion: The Life of E. Nesbit* by Julia Briggs, London, Hutchinson, 1987.

*   *   *

Edith Nesbit achieved lasting celebrity as a writer of children's books after the success of *The Treasure Seekers* in 1899. Several of her books of that kind have remained in print until the present day. In the early part of her career, however, she was also a prolific contributor to a wide range of popular periodicals, and a significant minority of her contributions were horror stories. By 1893 there were enough of these to fill a slim volume of *Grim Tales.*

The stories in *Grim Tales* are conventional Victorian ghost stories, typical of the commercial fiction of the day—except, perhaps, for the intensity of their preoccupation with erotic matters. In "The Ebony Frame" a *femme fatale* reaches across time with the aid of a magical portrait. The protagonist of "John Charrington's Wedding" swears that nothing—not even death—will prevent him marrying, while the central character of "Uncle Abraham's Romance" has an opposite problem. "From the Dead" is a more complicated tale of a dead wife who has too weak a claim on her husband's affections to become a revenant. The female protagonist of "The Mass for the Dead" hears the phantom service in question being offered for the man she does not want to marry. The only innocent love-match in the book is that featured in "Man-Size in Marble," but it is casually put asunder by supernaturally animated figures strayed from a sinister church on Halloween.

Five of these tales were reprinted in *Fear* alongside six more recent items and one other reprinted from another A. D. Innes collection, *Something Wrong.* The story from *Something Wrong,* "Hurst of Hurstcote," is another tale of a dead wife whose magical reanimation goes awry. The additional items are more frankly melodramatic, and make significant attempts to be more modern in their themes and outlook. "The Three Drugs" is a tale of a mad doctor who kidnaps victims for experimental purposes. "The Violet Car" is an early tale of a ghostly automobile. "In the Dark" is concerned with a "hallucination of touch" which turns out to be solid after all, while "The Head" similarly deals with a supposed fake that is horribly real. "The Five Senses"—perhaps the best of all Nesbit's horror stories—offers a much more sensitive development of the theme of "The Three Drugs" in her favourite context of a wrecked romance. Hugh Lamb's retrospective collection *In the Dark* reprints the entire contents of *Fear* but adds two further items, one being an unreprinted story from *Grim Tales* and the other a late story about a man-eating creeper, "The Pavilion."

Nesbit re-used the central motif of "The Head" much more effectively in the key episode in her curiously bitter melodrama *Salome and the Head*. The novel also has echoes of George du Maurier's *Trilby* in its account of a talented dancer attempting to win free of her Svengali-esque husband, and although it is not really a horror story when viewed as a whole the passage in which the dancer realizes that she has been given a real severed head in order to play the part of Salome to the hilt is highly effective. *Dormant* is a more conventional neo-Gothic novel whose hero discovers that in searching for the elixir of life he has been following in the family tradition. A *femme fatale* from another era brings him, apparently, to the very brink of success—but also to the threshold of disaster.

Nesbit's novels for adult readers are possessed of an awkward stylistic uncertainty, as if she could never quite settle on an appropriate tone of voice. *Salome and the Head* is inappropriately flippant, *Dormant* too conscientiously dull, and although both have their moments neither can be reckoned successful. She was, of course, reluctant to introduce horrific ideas into her children's books, although *The Enchanted Castle* was criticized at the time for being too frightening, especially in the passage where the Ugly-Wuglies are brought to life. Her shorter fiction was mostly hackwork, and her attempts to drag the Victorian ghost story into the 20th century were half-hearted as well as ham-fisted, but her best stories do have a significant depth of feeling—borrowed, one presumes, from the emotional hardships inflicted on her by her husband Hubert Bland and his live-in mistress. One of the very few opportunities a Victorian wife had to air the hard-won conclusion that love and marriage went together like a runaway horse and a broken-wheeled carriage was to write horror stories in which weddings and wives were continually linked to death and damnation.

—Brian Stableford

NEWMAN, Kim (James)

Pseudonym: Jack Yeovil. **Nationality:** British. **Born:** Bridgwater, Somerset, 31 July 1959. **Education:** Dr. Morgan's Grammar School, Bridgwater, 1970-75; Bridgwater College, 1975-77; University of Sussex, Brighton, 1977-80, B.A. in English. **Career:** Stage performer, film critic, broadcaster and writer; contributor, *Monthly Film Bulletin, Interzone, Empire, Sight and Sound* and many other magazines. **Awards:** Horror Writers of America Bram Stoker award for non-fiction, 1989; British Science Fiction Association award for short story, 1991; Dracula Society Children of the Night award for novel, 1993; Lord Ruthven Assembly fiction award, 1994; International Horror Critics' Guild award, 1995. **Agent:** Antony Harwood, Aitken, Stone and Wylie Ltd., 29 Fernshaw Road, London SW10 0TG, England.

HORROR, GHOST AND GOTHIC PUBLICATIONS

Novels (series: Anno Dracula)

The Night Major. London, Simon and Schuster, 1989; New York, Carroll and Graf, 1991.
Bad Dreams. London, Simon and Schuster, 1990; New York, Carroll and Graf, 1991.

Jago. London, Simon and Schuster, 1991; New York, Carroll and Graf, 1993.
Anno Dracula. London, Simon and Schuster, 1992; New York, Carroll and Graf, 1993.
Orgy of the Blood Parasites (as Jack Yeovil). London, Pocket, 1994.
The Quorum. London, Simon and Schuster, and New York, Carroll and Graf, 1994.
The Bloody Red Baron (Anno Dracula). New York, Carroll and Graf, 1995; London, Simon and Schuster, 1996.

Short Stories

The Original Dr. Shade and Other Stories. London, Pocket, 1994.
Famous Monsters. London, Pocket, 1995.

OTHER PUBLICATIONS

Novels as Jack Yeovil

Drachenfels. Brighton, East Sussex, Games Workshop, 1989.
Demon Download. Brighton, East Sussex, Games Workshop, 1990.
Krokodil Tears. Brighton, East Sussex, Games Workshop, 1991.
Beasts in Velvet. Brighton, East Sussex, Games Workshop, 1991.
Comeback Tour: The Sky Belongs to the Stars. Brighton, East Sussex, Games Workshop, 1991.
Genevieve Undead. London, Boxtree, 1993.
Route 666. London, Boxtree, 1994.

Plays

Another England (produced, Bridgwater, Somerset, 1980).
My One Little Murder Can't Do Any Harm (produced, Bridgwater, 1981).
The Gold-Diggers of 1981 (produced, Bridgwater, 1981).
Deep South (produced, Bridgwater, 1981).
The Roaring Eighties (produced, Bridgwater, 1982).
Rock Rock Rock Rock Rock, with Eugene Byrne, Neil Gaiman and Brian Smedley (produced, Bridgwater, 1987).

Other

Nightmare Movies. London and New York, Proteus, 1984; revised edition, London, Bloomsbury, and New York, Harmony, 1989.
Wild West Movies. London, Bloomsbury, 1990.

Editor, with Neil Gaiman, *Ghastly Beyond Belief.* London, Arrow, 1985.
Editor, with Stephen Jones, *Horror: 100 Best Books.* London, Xanadu, 1988; New York, Carroll & Graf, 1989; revised edition, London, New English Library, 1992.
Editor, with Paul J. McAuley, *In Dreams.* London, Gollancz, 1992.
Editor, *The BFI Companion to Horror.* London, Cassell, 1996.

*   *   *

While biographical sources unanimously report that Kim Newman is a native and lifelong resident of Great Britain, the American Library of Congress peculiarly classifies him as an American author. Given Newman's long-standing fascination with alternate realities, and solipsistic creations of personal realities, one inevitably devises imaginative reasons for this error: perhaps a Library of Congress employee briefly entered a parallel world in which Newman is an American (and no doubt wrote a novel about Count Dracula becoming President of the United States); or perhaps Newman, at one point longing for wider recognition, wished so hard to be an American that, for a short but strategic length of time, he made the wish come true.

A more prosaic, and more likely, explanation is that someone read his first novel, *The Night Major*, and concluded that any author so knowledgeable about American film actors simply had to be an American. Certainly, for readers who share that knowledge, the novel is an especially fascinating feast. Its premise is that a despised 21st-century criminal named Truro Daine, rendered permanently inactive while connected to the world-controlling computer Yggdrasil, somehow gains the power to construct his own virtual-reality world within the computer, modelled on American movies of the 1940s and 1950s, and threatens to take over the entire system. Two Dreamers—people who create dreams that are then mass-produced and marketed to the general public—are sent into this world to find and destroy Daine. The joy of this engaging but inconsequential story is encountering so many familiar stars, like Edward G. Robinson, John Carradine, Peter Lorre, Gloria Grahame and Mickey Rooney, playing characteristic roles in Daine's surrealistic black-and-white city; even an apparent casting mistake—Ralph Bellamy rarely if ever played a policeman—turns out to be a vital clue, since it is finally revealed that Bellamy is really Daine in disguise.

While both are enjoyable, neither *The Night Major* nor Newman's next novel *Bad Dreams*, in which a "psychic vampire" with strange mental powers threatens a London woman, could be described as ambitious. The massive *Jago*, however, attempted nothing less than a vision of apocalypse set in the English countryside. In a small town noted for earlier sightings of an angelic Burning Man, Anthony William Jago, the charismatic leader of a small cult, sponsors an annual, and usually uneventful, rock festival. Then, one year, Jago's transcendent psychic talents essentially engender a breakdown in consensus reality, as various characters experience inexplicable events, like an attack by Martian war machines and the transformation of a farmer into a plant-like Green Man. Then, just as all hell literally seems to be breaking loose, the assassination of Jago restores everything to normality, leaving thousands of dead bodies and uninformed outcries about young people using dangerous drugs. While consistently lively and colourful, *Jago* ultimately fails to convey the deeper, resonating horror of genuine apocalypse—which is not a particularly harsh criticism, since this is something only a few writers have managed to do.

Jago may have been designed to be Newman's masterpiece, but *Anno Dracula* actually earned that status. An outrageous account of what would have happened if the Count Dracula of Bram Stoker's novel had emerged victorious, *Anno Dracula* painstakingly constructs a Victorian England in which vampires are known and respected citizens; indeed, Dracula has married Queen Victoria and has become the virtual ruler of the nation. Stoker's Dr. Seward, still an opponent of Dracula, becomes this world's Jack the Ripper by attacking and disembowelling several vampire prostitutes, causing national outrage; a concerned human being—a "warm"—and a sympathetic lady vampire join forces to track down the killer but ultimately confront Dracula himself, and provide Victoria with a silver scalpel so she can kill herself and thus rid the country of her husband's evil influence. In addition to its fascinating

and singular alternate history, *Anno Dracula*, like *The Night Major*, is enjoyable because it features many familiar faces—here, an abundance of real and fictional characters from late Victorian England like Oscar Wilde, Mycroft Holmes, Dr. Jekyll, Algernon Swinburne, Varney the Vampire, and innumerable others. Indeed, the only frustrating thing about the novel is that so many potentially interesting characters are only mentioned in conversation or hurried offstage—for example, a brief conversation between Dr. Jekyll and Dr. Moreau about the essential nature of humanity might have been profitably sustained.

As one answer to such demands, perhaps, Newman soon produced a direct sequel to the novel, *The Bloody Red Baron*, where Dracula, after being exiled from England, gradually took control of Germany and became Britain's major opponent in World War I. The most interesting character is the resurrected vampire Edgar Allan Poe, now living in Europe, who has a series of intriguing encounters with characters like Franz Kafka, Dracula and Baron von Richthofen, who here has become a vampire as well. Again, there are many other striking cameo appearances—Moreau returns, now in the company of H. P. Lovecraft's Herbert West, and Winston Churchill is strikingly seen as an alcoholic vampire, sucking the blood of a wine-soaked rabbit—but, like most sequels, *The Bloody Red Baron* is less memorable than its predecessor.

Along with another horror novel under his own name, *The Quorum*, Newman has published many worthwhile horror stories, ranging from atmospheric vignettes like "The Pale Spirit People" (*Interzone* no. 79, January 1994), a Native American ghost story, to riotous satires like "Slow News Day" (*Interzone* no. 90, December 1994), an alternate history where Prime Minister John Major participates in a ceremony commemorating the 50th anniversary of a D-Day when Germany successfully invaded Britain ("we are celebrating not a British defeat but a British victory," he dully intones, "a victory over that part of ourselves which was inefficient, was heartless, was impure, was ignoble"—but "even he didn't listen to the rest of what he said"). It is unfortunate that Newman's story collections have not yet been published in America.

In addition, writing as Jack Yeovil (a name he cutely works into all his novels), he has written a tongue-in-cheek horror "nasty," *Orgy of the Blood Parasites* (in a similar vein as the books of his London-based friend Harry Adam Knight), plus several surprisingly successful fantasy and science-fiction novels for a games company. This last group of witty novels has some horrific elements, notably the recurring character of vampire Genevieve Dieudonné (who also figures in *Anno Dracula*). When one also notes that he has edited books and has written several plays, numerous reviews and a noteworthy critical book—the crisp and insightful *Nightmare Movies*—it becomes apparent that, to maintain such an output, the British Newman somehow must be obtaining and publishing manuscripts written by his alternate-world American counterpart.

—Gary Westfahl

NISBET, Hume

Nationality: British. **Born:** Stirling, Scotland, 8 August 1849; emigrated to Australia in 1865, returning to Britain in 1872. **Education:** Private. **Career:** Art master, Watt College and Old School of Arts, Edinburgh, 1873-85; publisher's representative in Australia and New Guinea, 1886; artist and novelist. **Died:** 1921.

HORROR, GHOST AND GOTHIC PUBLICATIONS

Novels

The "Jolly Roger": A Story of Sea Heroes and Pirates. London, Digby Long, 1893.
Valdmer the Viking: A Romance of the Eleventh Century by Sea and Land. London, Hutchinson, 1893.
The Great Secret: A Tale of To-morrow. London, White, 1895.

Short Stories

The Haunted Station and Other Stories. London, White, 1894.
Stories Weird and Wonderful. London, White, 1900.

OTHER PUBLICATIONS

Novels

Doctor Bernard St. Vincent. London, Ward, 1889.
Ashes: A Tale of Two Spheres. N.p., Author's Cooperative, 1890; as Wasted Fires, London, Methuen, 1902.
"Bail Up!" London, Chatto, 1890.
The Black Drop. London, Trischler, 1891.
The Divers. London, Black, 1892.
The Queen's Desire. London, White, 1893.
A Bush Girl's Romance. N.p., 1894.
Her Loving Slave. London, Digby Long, 1894.
A Singular Crime. London, White, 1894.
My Love Noel. London, White, 1896.
The Rebel Chief. London, White, 1896.
Hunting for Gold; or, Adventures in the Klondyke. London, White, 1897.
The Swampers. London, White, 1897.
A Sweet Sinner. London, White, 1897.
For Liberty. London, White, 1898.
Paths of the Dead. London, Long, 1899.
In Sheep's Clothing. London, White, 1900.
The Revenge of Valerie. London, White, 1900.
The Empire Builders: A Romance of Adventure and War in South Africa. London, White, 1900.
Children of Hermes. London, Hurst, 1901.
A Crafty Foe. London, White, 1901.
A Losing Game. London, White, 1901.
A Dream of Freedom. London, White, 1902.
A Desert Bride. London, White, 1904.
A Colonial King. London, White, 1905.

Other

Life and Nature Studies. N.p., 1915.

*   *   *

Hume Nisbet was a Scottish-born author and artist who spent much of his early life in Australia. Art seems to have been his primary vocation, and most of his fiction was produced as commercial hackwork. The illustrations which he did for *Valdmer the Viking* and the frontispiece he contributed to *The "Jolly Roger"* are by no means inspiring, and it is not entirely surprising that he could not build a reputation as a painter or a career as an illustrator. Most of his novels are slapdash tales of adventure, usually involving sea voyages. His early fiction employed many fantasy elements but these were almost entirely purged from his later work.

The preface of *The "Jolly Roger"* is dated 1891, so it definitely predates *Valdmer the Viking*, whose preface is dated 1893. The story is set in the early years of the 17th century and features William Shakespeare in a minor role. The first part of the story, which may have been written even earlier as an independent novelette, deals with the arrival and departure of a "ghostly carrack" in the tiny Channel port of Witestaple. The ship has been summoned by the necromancer Sir John Fenton and his female "familiar" Penelope, who performs for him the same functions that Edward Kelley performed for his model, John Dee. It is this *femme fatale* who has the real magical powers, and also the secret of the fountain of youth, for which the carrack sets sail in the nick of time when the local populace rise up against their resident black magician. The second part of the book is narrated by a young mate who is fascinated by Penelope and by the younger-seeming Quassatta who eventually emerges from the fountain of youth to take her place. Unfortunately, once this miracle is achieved the author—who was obviously making up the plot as he went along—runs out of inspiration, and the remainder of the volume is a tedious account of common-or-garden piracies only slightly enlivened by an unexpected twist in the tail. The title must have been imposed by the publisher, because the text takes great pains to point out that the carrack's flag is *not* the traditional jolly roger.

Valdmer the Viking reverses the pattern of the earlier volume, beginning with a lengthy account of ordinary Viking adventures, then using a transatlantic voyage to take the story into very different literary territory. Having established friendly relations with the local native Americans, Valdmer and his brother encounter civilized travellers from the mysterious land of Tule, who take the Vikings to their warm homeland beyond the Arctic ice. Valdmer has been recruited in order to import a little hybrid vigour into a marriage with the queen of Tule, but he is beset by dreams of former incarnations and of a long-lost lover held in suspended animation by the "earth current" which lights and heats the Tulan city. Alas, his attempt to reach her precipitates a large-scale disaster. Clearly inspired by the work of H. Rider Haggard, the book almost certainly combined its influence with Edwin Lester Arnold's *Phra the Phoenician* to prompt George Griffith to produce *Valdar the Oft-Born* and may also have been read by William Hope Hodgson, who invoked a similar "earth current" in *The Night Land*.

The Great Secret follows Haggard's unfortunate example in moving towards serious occult romance based in contemporary theories of spiritualism and reincarnation, with the same result. Devoid of romantic adventures, the book lacks energy—and the chapters in which survivors of anarchist sabotage at sea are lectured at great length by the earnest spirits which come to their aid are dull as well as preposterous. It may be that the book's cold reception was responsible for Nisbet's resolution to stick to light-weight work in future. Novels such as *Paths of the Dead* and *The Revenge of Valerie* retain an interest in the occult but relegate it to the margins of the work, while *The Empire Builders* is a lost-race story far less vigorous and engaging than *Valdmer the Viking*.

Nisbet claimed that the stories in *The Haunted Station* were based on real experiences and illustrated the actual contemporary workings of malign forces—but only a true Victorian could have made that ingenuous pronouncement about a collection with so many *femmes fatales* in it. As with so many credulous ghost stories, the tales are mostly ill-formulated, although they do contain some effective descriptions of terrified states of mind. The title story, set in the Australian outback, is perhaps the best, although "Delphine," "Marie St. Pierre" and the London-set "The Phantom Model" have an intriguing hint of fashionable decadence about them, and "The Demon Spell" is a notable early account of a supernaturally-afflicted serial killer. The five weird tales in *Stories Weird and Wonderful* are more obviously commercial, striving without much success for sensational effect; "A Cup of Samos" is the only one which takes itself even half-seriously. "The Vampire Maid" was obviously inspired by the success of *Dracula*, although the vampiric spirit released by "The Old Portrait" once its imprisoning overcoat has been removed by a restorer is a more interesting predator.

Nisbet was never more than a pale shadow of Rider Haggard and never had the kind of entrée into the secluded world of Victorian high society séances that added interest to the work of Mrs. Campbell Praed. Mrs. Praed was better at writing about Australia than Nisbet was, and Clark Russell had a far more secure grasp of nautical romance. If Nisbet had only given more thought and attention to their fantastic elements, The *"Jolly Roger"* and *Valdmer the Viking* might have been far more interesting, at least to modern critics, but he found it more profitable to specialize in the production of books that were far less imaginatively adventurous—and he was certainly not alone in that.

—Brian Stableford

NYE, Robert

Nationality: British. **Born:** London, 15 March 1939. **Education:** Dormans Land, Sussex; Hamlet Court, Westcliff, Essex; Southend High School, Essex. **Family:** Married 1) Judith Pratt in 1959 (divorced 1967), three sons; 2) Aileen Campbell in 1968, one daughter, one stepdaughter, and one stepson. **Career:** Since 1961 freelance writer; since 1967 poetry editor, *The Scotsman*; since 1971 poetry critic, *The Times*. Writer-in-residence, University of Edinburgh, 1976-77. **Awards:** Eric Gregory award, 1963; Scottish Arts Council bursary, 1970, 1973, and publication award, 1970, 1976; James Kennaway Memorial award, 1970; *Guardian* Fiction prize, 1976; Hawthornden prize, 1977. Fellow, Royal Society of Literature, 1977; Society of Authors travel scholarship, 1991. **Agent:** Sheil Land Associates, 43 Doughty Street, London WC1N 2LF, England; or, Wallace, Aitken, and Sheil Inc., 118 East 61st Street, New York, NY 10021, USA. **Address:** 2 Westbury Crescent, Wilton, Cork, Ireland.

HORROR, GHOST AND GOTHIC PUBLICATIONS

Novels

Faust. London, Hamish Hamilton, 1980; New York, Putnam, 1981.
The Life and Death of My Lord Gilles de Rais. London, Hamish Hamilton, 1990.

OTHER PUBLICATIONS

Novels

Doubtfire. London, Calder and Boyars, and New York, Hill and Wang, 1968.
Falstaff. London, Hamish Hamilton, and Boston, Little Brown, 1976.
Merlin. London, Hamish Hamilton, 1978; New York, Putnam, 1979.
The Voyage of the Destiny. London, Hamish Hamilton, and New York, Putnam, 1982.
The Memoirs of Lord Byron. London, Hamish Hamilton, 1989.
Mrs. Shakespeare: The Complete Works. London, Sinclair Stevenson, 1993.

Short Stories

Tales I Told My Mother. London, Calder and Boyars, 1969; New York, Hill and Wang, 1970.
Penguin Modern Stories 6, with others. London, Penguin, 1970.
The Facts of Life and Other Fictions. London, Hamish Hamilton, 1983.

Plays

Sawney Bean, with Bill Watson (produced Edinburgh, 1969; London, 1972; New York, 1982). London, Calder and Boyars, 1970.
Sisters (broadcast 1969; produced Edinburgh, 1973). Included in *Penthesilea, Fugue, and Sisters,* 1975.
Penthesilea, adaptation of the play by Heinrich von Kleist (broadcast 1971; produced London, 1983). Included in *Penthesilea, Fugue, and Sisters,* 1975.
The Seven Deadly Sins: A Mask, music by James Douglas (produced Stirling, 1973; Edinburgh, 1974). Rushden, Northamptonshire, Omphalos Press, 1974.
Mr. Poe (produced Edinburgh and London, 1974).
Penthesilea, Fugue, and Sisters. London, Calder and Boyars, 1975.

Radio Plays: *Sisters,* 1969; *A Bloody Stupit Hole,* 1970; *Reynolds, Reynolds,* 1971; *Penthesilea,* 1971; *The Devil's Jig,* with Humphrey Searle, from a work by Thomas Mann, 1980.

Poetry

Juvenilia 1. Northwood, Middlesex, Scorpion Press, 1961.
Juvenilia 2. Lowestoft, Suffolk, Scorpion Press, 1963.
Darker Ends. London, Calder and Boyars, and New York, Hill and Wang, 1969.
Agnus Dei. Rushden, Northamptonshire, Sceptre Press, 1973.
Two Prayers. Richmond, Surrey, Keepsake Press, 1974.
Five Dreams. Rushden, Northamptonshire, Sceptre Press, 1974.
Divisions on a Ground. Manchester, Carcanet, 1976.
A Collection of Poems 1955-1988. London, Hamish Hamilton, 1990.

Other

Taliesin. London, Faber, 1966; New York, Hill and Wang, 1967.
March Has Horse's Ears. London, Faber, 1966; New York, Hill and Wang, 1967.

Bee Hunter: Adventures of Beowulf. London, Faber, 1968; as *Beowulf: A New Telling,* New York, Hill and Wang, 1968; as *Beowulf, The Bee Hunter,* Faber, 1972.

Wishing Gold. London, Macmillan, 1970; New York, Hill and Wang, 1971.

Poor Pumpkin. London, Macmillan, 1971; as *The Mathematical Princess and Other Stories,* New York, Hill and Wang, 1972.

Cricket: Three Stories. Indianapolis, Bobbs Merrill, 1975; as *Once upon Three Times,* London, Benn, 1978.

Out of the World and Back Again. London, Collins, 1977; as *Out of This World and Back Again,* Indianapolis, Bobbs Merrill, 1978.

The Bird of the Golden Land. London, Hamish Hamilton, 1980.

Harry Pay the Pirate. London, Hamish Hamilton, 1981.

Three Tales (includes *Beowulf, Wishing Gold, Taliesin*). London, Hamish Hamilton, 1983.

Editor, *A Choice of Sir Walter Ralegh's Verse.* London, Faber, 1972.

Editor, *William Barnes: A Selection of His Poems.* Oxford, Carcanet, 1972.

Editor, *A Choice of Swinburne's Verse.* London, Faber, 1973.

Editor, *The Faber Book of Sonnets.* London, Faber, 1976; as *A Book of Sonnets,* New York, Oxford University Press, 1976.

Editor, *The English Sermon 1750-1850.* Cheadle, Cheshire, Carcanet, 1976.

Editor, *PEN New Poetry.* London, Quartet, 1986.

Editor, with Elizabeth Friedmann and Alan J. Clark. *First Awakenings: The Early Poems of Laura Riding.* Manchester, Carcanet, and New York, Persea Press, 1992.

Editor, *A Selection of the Poems of Laura Riding.* Manchester, Carcanet, 1994.

*

Manuscript Collections: University of Edinburgh; University of Texas, Austin; Colgate University, Hamilton, New York; National Library of Scotland, Edinburgh.

*   *   *

Robert Nye is a fine literary writer who regards himself principally as a poet yet is much better known as the author of several outstanding biographical novels. Both real and fictional characters are dealt with in these, but they fall easily into two categories according to the style of writing. Some, particularly *Falstaff, Merlin* and *Faust,* are presented in a flashy postmodern style, intended to be outrageous and eye-catching, and involving many single-line paragraphs, very brief chapters and lists, among other devices. Other novels, including those about Gilles de Rais and Sir Walter Raleigh, are far more staid and conventional in their approach.

Both *Merlin* and *Faust* include (amongst their fantasy, bawdy details and pyrotechnics) some elements of horror. Apart from being the offspring of the devil, Merlin is narrating his story from an eternal prison. Faust, for his part, is shown during the last 40 days of his life, before the devil collects his bargained-for soul. Nye has also written plays, such as *Sawney Bean* and *Mr. Poe,* which touch on horrific themes.

But it is *The Life and Death of My Lord Gilles de Rais* which contains most of the horror in Nye's work. Gilles de Rais, 1404-1440, nick-named Bluebeard, was a Marshal of France, a nobleman who in his younger days fought bravely and successfully alongside Joan of Arc to expel the English army from his country.

In his later years he became obsessed with the raising of demons and paedophile sex, for which crimes he was tried and executed.

Nye's novel is narrated by Eustache Blanchet, a personal cleric of de Rais, who was with his master for less than three years. It was Blanchet who was sent to Florence to find and return with an alchemist, for not only was Florence the home of the best alchemists, but alchemy was not a sin, while black magic and the raising of demons most certainly were. So Blanchet brings back Francesco Prelati—who describes himself as an alchemist, a man of science, but is also a magician. (Nye's grasp of the indivisibility of science and magic in the 15th century is precise and revealing.)

Because Blanchet was not privy to de Rais's secret life and did not partake in any magical ceremonies or perverted orgies, such events are not dramatized in the book. Yet there are hints and rumours. It is suggested that de Rais will not go to confession because he has behaviour to confess which is too terrible to be spoken. Certainly de Rais is wild, the leader of a small group of drunken noblemen; he defies the laws of France, supposing himself above them. Blanchet hears stories of de Rais being feared as a magician and child-murderer. And this is shocking to Blanchet and to the reader. Blanchet tries to leave de Rais's service but is called back, fetched by de Rais's men.

Rumours pile up; de Rais has his confession heard, but only by a dying priest, not by Blanchet; de Rais acts sacrilegiously over the relatively small matter of possession of one of his several castles, which he had sold, the quarrel ending with him having a priest beaten and imprisoned. For this last misdemeanour he is put on trial.

By the time the trial begins, however, things are much more serious—de Rais is to be tried on 49 indictments including satanism, other heresies, unnatural vice, sacrilege and the violation of ecclesiastical privilege. The charges are laughed off by de Rais, who says he will answer them all and defend himself. He does not recognize the court's right to try him in any case.

The witness statements are both powerful and pitiful. They are given by peasants and artisans whose children have been taken to one of de Rais's castles on a pretext—usually to become a servant—and who have never returned. A priest speaks of the young Gilles as a boy who enjoyed inflicting pain, as a youth who was married at 16 by his grandfather's arrangement but never cared for the company of women, as a young man caught in bed with a page boy. Then the procurers of young boys and girls (preferably aged eight to twelve) for de Rais give damning evidence. It is claimed that de Rais and his cronies would use live, dying and freshly dead children for sexual gratification. More than 140 children are said to have been abused and killed, many of them killed by de Rais himself.

During this evidence de Rais is calm and contemptuous. Only when faced with excommunication does he become concerned. He agrees to recognize the court and, eventually, he makes a full confession to all the crimes, is condemned and executed by hanging and burning.

The tone of the novel is always restrained, and the horrors are understated, so as to make it a less harrowing read than it might have been. Much of the detail was taken by Nye from trial records, though this in no way detracts from the author's skill in presenting a believable and very moving account of the last years of one of the world's greatest mass-murderers.

—Chris Morgan

O

OATES, Joyce Carol

Pseudonym: Rosamond Smith. **Nationality:** American. **Born:** Millersport, New York, 16 June 1938. **Education:** Syracuse University, New York, 1956-60, B.A. in English 1960 (Phi Beta Kappa); University of Wisconsin, Madison, M.A. in English 1961; Rice University, Houston, 1961. **Family:** Married Raymond J. Smith in 1961. **Career:** Instructor, 1961-65, and assistant professor of English, 1965-67, University of Detroit; member of the department of English, University of Windsor, Ontario, 1967-78. Since 1978, writer-in-residence, and currently Roger S. Berlind Distinguished Professor, Princeton University, New Jersey. Since 1974, publisher, with Raymond J. Smith, *Ontario Review*, Windsor, later Princeton. **Awards:** National Endowment for the Arts grant, 1966, 1968; Guggenheim fellowship, 1967; O. Henry award, 1967, 1973, and Special Award for Continuing Achievement, 1970, 1986; Rosenthal award, 1968; National Book award, 1970; Rea award, for short story, 1990; Bobst Lifetime Achievement award, 1990; Heideman award, 1990, for one-act play; Horror Writers of America Bram Stoker award for lifetime achievement, 1994, and for best novel, 1996; Walt Whitman award, 1995. **Member:** American Academy, 1978. **Agent:** John Hawkins and Associates, 71 West 23rd Street, Suite 1600, New York, NY 10010, USA. **Address:** 185 Nassau Street, Princeton, NJ 08540, USA.

HORROR, GHOST AND GOTHIC PUBLICATIONS

Novels

Wonderland. New York, Vanguard Press, 1971; London, Gollancz, 1972.
Son of the Morning. New York, Vanguard Press, 1978; London, Gollancz, 1979.
Bellefleur. New York, Dutton, 1980; London, Cape, 1981.
A Bloodsmoor Romance. New York, Dutton, 1982; London, Cape, 1983.
Mysteries of Winterthurn. New York, Dutton, and London, Cape, 1984.
Black Water. New York, Dutton, 1992.
Zombie. New York, Dutton, 1995.
First Love: A Gothic Tale. New York, Dutton, 1996.

Novels as Rosamond Smith

Lives of the Twins. New York, Simon and Schuster, 1987; as *Kindred Passions*, London, Collins, 1988.
Soul-Mate. New York, Dutton, 1989.
Nemesis. New York, Dutton, 1990.
Snake Eyes. New York, Dutton, 1992.
You Can't Catch Me. New York, Dutton, 1995.
Double Delight. New York, Dutton, 1997.

Short Stories

The Hungry Ghosts: Seven Allusive Comedies. Los Angeles, Black Sparrow Press, 1974; Solihull, Warwickshire, Aquila, 1975.

Night-Side. New York, Vanguard Press, 1977; London, Gollancz, 1979.
Haunted: Tales of the Grotesque. New York, Dutton, 1994.
Demon and Other Tales. West Warwick, Rhode Island, Necronomicon Press, 1996.

Other

Editor, *American Gothic Tales.* New York, Penguin, 1996.
Editor, *The Best of H. P. Lovecraft.* Hopewell, New Jersey, Ecco Press, 1997.

OTHER PUBLICATIONS

Novels

With Shuddering Fall. New York, Vanguard Press, 1964; London, Cape, 1965.
A Garden of Earthly Delights. New York, Vanguard Press, 1967; London, Gollancz, 1970.
Expensive People. New York, Vanguard Press, 1968; London, Gollancz, 1969.
Them. New York, Vanguard Press, 1969; London, Gollancz, 1971.
Do with Me What You Will. New York, Vanguard Press, 1973; London, Gollancz, 1974.
The Assassins: A Book of Hours. New York, Vanguard Press, 1975.
Childwold. New York, Vanguard Press, 1976; London, Gollancz, 1977.
Cybele. Santa Barbara, California, Black Sparrow Press, 1979.
Unholy Loves. New York, Vanguard Press, 1979; London, Gollancz, 1980.
Angel of Light. New York, Dutton, and London, Cape, 1981.
Solstice. New York, Dutton, and London, Cape, 1985.
Marya: A Life. New York, Dutton, 1986; London, Cape, 1987.
You Must Remember This. New York, Dutton, 1987; London, Macmillan, 1988.
American Appetites. New York, Dutton, and London, Macmillan, 1989.
Because It Is Bitter, and Because It Is My Heart. New York, Dutton, 1990; London, Macmillan, 1991.
I Lock My Door Upon Myself. New York, Ecco Press, 1990.
The Rise of Life on Earth. New York, New Directions, 1991.
Foxfire: Confessions of a Girl-Gang. New York, Dutton, 1993.
What I Lived For. New York, Dutton, 1994.
We Were the Mulvaneys. New York, Dutton, 1996.
Man Crazy. New York, Dutton, 1997.

Short Stories

By the North Gate. New York, Vanguard Press, 1963.
Upon the Sweeping Flood and Other Stories. New York, Vanguard Press, 1966; London, Gollancz, 1973.
The Wheel of Love and Other Stories. New York, Vanguard Press, 1970; London, Gollancz, 1971.
Cupid and Psyche. New York, Albondocani Press, 1970.

Marriages and Infidelities. New York, Vanguard Press, 1972; London, Gollancz, 1974.

A Posthumous Sketch. Los Angeles, Black Sparrow Press, 1973.

The Girl. Cambridge, Massachusetts, Pomegranate Press, 1974.

Plagiarized Material (as Fernandes/Oates). Los Angeles, Black Sparrow Press, 1974.

The Goddess and Other Women. New York, Vanguard Press, 1974; London, Gollancz, 1975.

Where Are You Going, Where Have You Been? Stories of Young America. Greenwich, Connecticut, Fawcett, 1974.

The Seduction and Other Stories. Los Angeles, Black Sparrow Press, 1975.

The Poisoned Kiss and Other Stories from the Portuguese (as Fernandes/Oates). New York, Vanguard Press, 1975; London, Gollancz, 1976.

The Triumph of the Spider Monkey. Santa Barbara, California, Black Sparrow Press, 1976.

The Blessing. Santa Barbara, California, Black Sparrow Press, 1976.

Crossing the Border. New York, Vanguard Press, 1976; London, Gollancz, 1978.

Daisy. Santa Barbara, California, Black Sparrow Press, 1977.

A Sentimental Education. Los Angeles, Sylvester and Orphanos, 1978.

The Step-Father. Northridge, California, Lord John Press, 1978.

All the Good People I've Left Behind. Santa Barbara, California, Black Sparrow Press, 1979.

The Lamb of Abyssalia. Cambridge, Massachusetts, Pomegranate Press, 1979.

A Middle-Class Education. New York, Albondocani Press, 1980.

A Sentimental Education (collection). New York, Dutton, 1980; London, Cape, 1981.

Funland. Concord, New Hampshire, Ewert, 1983.

Last Days. New York, Dutton, 1984; London, Cape, 1985.

Wild Saturday and Other Stories. London, Dent, 1984.

Wild Nights. Athens, Ohio, Croissant, 1985.

Raven's Wing. New York, Dutton, 1986; London, Cape, 1987.

The Assignation. New York, Ecco Press, 1988.

Heat and Other Stories. New York, Dutton, 1991.

Where Is Here? Hopewell, New Jersey, Ecco Press, 1992.

Will You Always Love Me? and Other Stories. New York, Dutton, 1996.

Where Are You Going, Where Have You Been?: Selected Early Stories. Princeton, New Jersey, Ontario Review Press, 1993.

Plays

The Sweet Enemy (produced New York, 1965).

Sunday Dinner (produced New York, 1970).

Ontological Proof of My Existence, music by George Prideaux (produced New York, 1972). Included in *Three Plays,* 1980.

Miracle Play (produced New York, 1973). Los Angeles, Black Sparrow Press, 1974.

Daisy (produced New York, 1980).

Three Plays (includes *Ontological Proof of My Existence, Miracle Play, The Triumph of the Spider Monkey*). Windsor, Ontario Review Press, 1980.

The Triumph of the Spider Monkey, from her own story (produced Los Angeles, 1985). Included in *Three Plays,* 1980.

Presque Isle, music by Paul Shapiro (produced New York, 1982).

Lechery, in *Faustus in Hell* (produced Princeton, New Jersey, 1985).

In Darkest America (*Tone Clusters* and *The Eclipse*) (produced Louisville, Kentucky, 1990; *The Eclipse* produced New York, 1990).

American Holiday (produced Los Angeles, 1990).

I Stand Before You Naked (produced New York, 1991).

How Do You Like Your Meat? (produced New Haven, Connecticut, 1991).

Twelve Plays. New York, Dutton, 1991.

Black (produced Williamstown, 1992).

The Secret Mirror (produced Philadelphia, 1992).

The Perfectionist (produced Princeton, New Jersey, 1993). In *The Perfectionist and Other Plays,* 1995.

The Truth-Teller (produced New York, 1995).

Here She Is! (produced Philadelphia, 1995).

The Perfectionist and Other Plays. Hopewell, New Jersey, Ecco, 1995.

Poetry

Women in Love and Other Poems. New York, Albondocani Press, 1968.

Anonymous Sins and Other Poems. Baton Rouge, Louisiana State University Press, 1969.

Love and Its Derangements. Baton Rouge, Louisiana State University Press, 1970.

Woman Is the Death of the Soul. Toronto, Coach House Press, 1970.

In Case of Accidental Death. Cambridge, Massachusetts, Pomegranate Press, 1972.

Wooded Forms. New York, Albondocani Press, 1972.

Angel Fire. Baton Rouge, Louisiana State University Press, 1973.

Dreaming America and Other Poems. New York, Aloe Editions, 1973.

The Fabulous Beasts. Baton Rouge, Louisiana State University Press, 1975.

Public Outcry. Pittsburgh, Slow Loris Press, 1976.

Season of Peril. Santa Barbara, California, Black Sparrow Press, 1977.

Abandoned Airfield 1977. Northridge, California, Lord John Press, 1977.

Snowfall. Northridge, California, Lord John Press, 1978.

Women Whose Lives Are Food, Men Whose Lives Are Money. Baton Rouge, Louisiana State University Press, 1978.

The Stone Orchard. Northridge, California, Lord John Press, 1980.

Celestial Timepiece. Dallas, Pressworks, 1980.

Nightless Nights: Nine Poems. Concord, New Hampshire, Ewert, 1981.

Invisible Woman: New and Selected Poems 1970-1982. Princeton, New Jersey, Ontario Review Press, 1982.

Luxury of Sin. Northridge, California, Lord John Press, 1984.

The Time Traveller: Poems 1983-1989. New York, Dutton, 1989.

Tenderness. Princeton, New Jersey, Ontario Review Press, 1996.

Other

The Edge of Impossibility: Tragic Forms in Literature. New York, Vanguard Press, 1972; London, Gollancz, 1976.

The Hostile Sun: The Poetry of D. H. Lawrence. Los Angeles, Black Sparrow Press, 1973; Solihull, Warwickshire, Aquila, 1975.

New Heaven, New Earth: The Visionary Experience in Literature. New York, Vanguard Press, 1974; London, Gollancz, 1976.

The Stone Orchard. Northridge, California, Lord John Press, 1980.
Contraries: Essays. New York, Oxford University Press, 1981.
The Profane Art: Essays and Reviews. New York, Dutton, 1983.
Funland. Concord, New Hampshire, Ewert, 1983.
On Boxing, photographs by John Ranard. New York, Doubleday, and London, Bloomsbury, 1987; expanded edition, Hopewell, New Jersey, Ecco Press, 1994.
(Woman) Writer: Occasions and Opportunities. New York, Dutton, 1988.
Conversations with Joyce Carol Oates, edited by Lee Milazzo. Jackson, University Press of Mississippi, 1989.
George Bellows: American Artist. Hopewell, New Jersey, Ecco Press, 1995.

Editor, *Scenes from American Life: Contemporary Short Fiction.* New York, Vanguard Press, 1973.
Editor, with Shannon Ravenel, *The Best American Short Stories 1979.* Boston, Houghton Mifflin, 1979.
Editor, *Night Walks: A Bedside Companion.* Princeton, New Jersey, Ontario Review Press, 1982.
Editor *First Person Singular: Writers on Their Craft.* Princeton, New Jersey, Ontario Review Press, 1983.
Editor, with Boyd Litzinger, *Story: Fictions Past and Present.* Lexington, Massachusetts, Heath, 1985.
Editor, with Daniel Halpern, *Reading the Fights* (on boxing). New York, Holt, 1988.
Editor, *The Best American Essays 1991.* Boston, Ticknor and Fields, 1991.
Editor, *The Oxford Book of American Short Stories.* New York, Oxford University Press, 1992.
Editor, with Daniel Halpern. *The Sophisticated Cat: A Gathering of Stories, Poems and Miscellaneous Writings About Cats.* New York, Dutton, 1992.
Editor, *The Essential Dickinson.* Hopewell, New Jersey, Ecco Press, 1996.
Editor, *Telling Stories: An Anthology for Writers.* New York, Norton, 1997.

*

Film Adaptations: *Smooth Talk,* 1985, from the short story "Where Are You Going, Where Have You Been?"; *Lies of the Twins,* 1991 (TV movie); *Foxfire,* 1996.

Bibliography: *Joyce Carol Oates: An Annotated Bibliography* by Francine Lercangée, New York, Garland, 1986.

Manuscript Collection: Syracuse University, New York.

Critical Studies: *The Tragic Vision of Joyce Carol Oates* by Mary Kathryn Grant, Durham, North Carolina, Duke University Press, 1978; *Joyce Carol Oates* by Joanne V. Creighton, Boston, Twayne, 1979; *Critical Essays on Joyce Carol Oates* edited by Linda W. Wagner, Boston, Hall, 1979; *Dreaming America: Obsession and Transcendence in the Fiction of Joyce Carol Oates* by G. F. Waller, Baton Rouge, Louisiana State University Press, 1979; *Joyce Carol Oates* by Ellen G. Friedman, New York, Ungar, 1980; *Joyce Carol Oates's Short Stories: Between Tradition and Innovation* by Katherine Bastian, Bern, Switzerland, Lang, 1983; *The Image of the Intellectual in the Short Stories of Joyce Carol Oates* by Hermann Severin, New York, Lang, 1986; *Joyce Carol Oates: Artist in Residence* by Eileen Teper Bender, Bloomington, Indiana University Press, 1987; *Understanding Joyce Carol Oates* by Greg Johnson, Columbia, University of South Carolina Press, 1987.

*   *   *

If horror resides in the tone of a work rather than specific content, there is a case for virtually all of Joyce Carol Oates's work to be so classified. Certainly there is a thick vein of darkness throughout. Her work displays a highly literary sensibility (derived in part from the "Southern Gothic" of such writers as William Faulkner and Flannery O'Connor and in part from contemporary mainstream—she is particularly fond of using the present tense, for example) and at the same time is always intense, often violent, turbulent and sometimes—deceptively—seeming barely in the author's control. (*Bellefleur,* at nearly 300,000 words probably her longest novel, is a particular case in point. Compare its opening sentence with that of Isabel Allende's *The House of the Spirits:* both are a page long, but Oates's prose has the qualities described above—by contrast Allende's seems the epitome of authorial control.) Redemptive endings, like that of *What I Lived For,* are rare and hard-won, our reward for following the collapse of the life of the protagonist, successful businessman Jerome "Corky" Corcoran, over one long Memorial Day weekend and 600 pages. (It should be noted in passing that Oates is extremely good at writing about men—Corky is thoroughly convincing. The story "Golden Gloves," collected in *Raven's Wing,* about an ex-boxer's experience of impending fatherhood, is another fine example, particularly when one considers that Oates herself is childless.)

Oates is a remarkably prolific writer. Certainly there are less successful works in her bibliography: *Expensive People,* about a son's plot to assassinate his mother, is a heavy-handed attempt at black comedy (humour is definitely not Oates's forte); *Childwold* contains powerful passages but is incoherent. Some novels are routine by her standards, strong writing that somehow falls flat, fails to connect: *Angel of Light* and *Cybele* particularly come to mind. Many of her early novels and stories feature seemingly arbitrary violent conclusions which do not arise naturally from the preceding events.

Her range of character and subject matter is wide: from campus drama (*Unholy Loves, American Appetites,* the latter also a courtroom drama) to Victorian genre pastiche (*Bellefleur, A Bloodsmoor Romance, Mysteries of Winterthurn*), from stories of transgressive desire (interracial in *Because it is Bitter, and Because it is My Heart* and *I Lock My Door Upon Myself,* incestuous in *You Must Remember This* and the title novella of *A Sentimental Education*) to semi-autobiography (*Marya: A Life,* one of her best). Those published under the pseudonym Rosamond Smith (a name derived from that of her husband, Raymond Smith), are psychological suspense thrillers.

If one defines horror as a genre using certain themes and tropes, Oates is undoubtedly a writer who uses some of them in her work. Though published as a mainstream writer, she is certainly no stranger to horror, with publications in genre magazines such as *Omni* and *Twilight Zone* and anthologies including *Metahorror* (edited by Dennis Etchison, 1992) and *Skin of the Soul* (edited by Lisa Tuttle, 1990). Supernatural events are rare, though *Night-Side* and *Haunted* collect some exceptions to this rule. *Son of the Morning,* a fever-dream of a novel and one of her best, features an evangelical preacher who is granted seven visions, each more terrifying than the last, notably a memorable scene where, on live TV, he takes literally the edict "If thine eye offends thee, pluck it out." The horror in Oates's work derives more from people's behaviour and states of mind. Bizarre events do occur, but they are of a kind that may be unusual but is not impossible.

Bellefleur, a seven-generation anti-chronological family saga, is a case in point. Germaine, the central character, absorbs a male twin in the womb; all that remains of him are his genitals, growing from her chest. Even in *Foxfire*, a 1950s-set account of life in a girl gang (filmed in 1996), there is a disturbing, almost extraneous episode where two of the gang members witness the sexual exploitation of a retarded dwarf woman. *Wonderland* depicts a cycle of horror in one life: Jesse, the protagonist, is the only one to escape the massacre of his family by his father, who then kills himself. Taken in as an orphan by a doctor, Jesse becomes a distinguished brain surgeon himself (via some harrowingly-described hospital scenes). He marries unsuccessfully and has an affair, and alienates his daughter. The near-victim of infanticide by his father has become a dysfunctional father himself.

"Martyrdom" (collected in *Haunted*; originally published in *Metahorror*) juxtaposes an abused woman and a laboratory rat, who meet in an ending probably inspired by Bret Easton Ellis's *American Psycho*. "In the Warehouse" (in *The Goddess and Other Women*) begins as a memoir of teenage-girlhood friendship and ends as something else: the narrator murders her stifling "friend" with impunity. In the book-length novella *Black Water*, a woman drives into a river during a storm. We flash back over her recent life and how she came to be driving at this time and to this place, while she drowns.

Zombie, for which Oates won the Stoker Award (her second, after one in 1994 for continuing achievement), is something of a departure. Told in a first-person narrative (unusual for Oates) in which some literary flourishes sit occasionally awkwardly, it is the story of Quentin P—, a sexual psychopath (preying on young men) whose life's project is to make the zombie of the title. He disassociates himself from his victims by giving them nicknames (Bunnygloves, Raisineyes, Squirrel) and sometimes referring to himself in third person. The text is interspersed with some of Quentin's crude drawings. His attempts are foiled by ineptitude, but Quentin is almost comical in his persistence; the novel's achievement is that we recognize the human in him, although what he does is aberrant. At the end of this short novel, he has his eyes on another potential zombie—life goes on.

Oates at her finest is a living refutation of the belief that a prolific output and high literary quality are incompatible. Her bibliography is prodigious, her quality-rate high, and both are still continuing.

—Gary Couzens

O'DONNELL, Elliott

Nationality: Irish. **Born:** Near Bristol, England, 27 February 1872. **Education:** Dublin University. **Family:** Married Ada Bullivant Williams in 1905 (died 1937). **Career:** Various jobs including rancher, policeman, journalist, actor and schoolteacher, before becoming a full-time writer, researcher and lecturer on psychic research, 1907. **Died:** 8 May 1965.

HORROR, GHOST AND GOTHIC PUBLICATIONS

Novels

For Satan's Sake. London, Greening, 1904.
The Unknown Depths. London, Greening, 1905.
The Sorcery Club. London, Rider, 1912.
The Haunted Man. London, Heath Cranton, 1917.
The Devil in the Pulpit. London, Denis Archer, 1932.
The Dead Riders. London, Rider, 1952.

Short Stories

Dread of Night. Dublin, Pillar Publishing, 1945.
Caravan of Crime. Dublin, Grafton, 1946.
Hell Ships of Many Waters. Dublin, Grafton, 1946.
Haunted and Hunted. Dublin, Grafton, 1946.

Other

Bona Fide Adventures With Ghosts. Clifton, Baker, 1908.
Some Haunted Houses of England and Wales. London, Eveleigh Nash, 1908.
Haunted Houses of London. London, Eveleigh Nash, 1909.
Ghostly Phenomena. London, Werner Laurie, 1910.
Byways of Ghostland. London, Rider, 1911.
Scottish Ghost Stories. London, Kegan Paul, 1911.
Werwolves. London, Methuen, 1912.
Animal Ghosts. London, Rider, 1913.
Haunted Highways and Byways. London, Eveleigh Nash, 1914.
Twenty Years' Experience as a Ghost Hunter. London, Heath Cranton, 1916.
Haunted Places of England. London, Sands, 1919.
The Banshee. London, Sands, 1920.
More Haunted Houses of London. London, Eveleigh Nash, 1920.
Ghosts Helpful and Harmful. London, Rider, 1924.
Ghostland. London, Cecil Palmer, 1925.
Confessions of a Ghost Hunter. London, Thornton Butterworth, 1928.
Rooms of Mystery. London, Philip Allan, 1931.
Ghosts of London. London, Philip Allan, 1932.
Family Ghosts. London, Philip Allan, 1933.
Spookerisms. London, Universal, 1936.
Haunted Churches. London, Quality Press, 1939.
Haunted Britain. London, Rider, 1948.
Ghosts with a Purpose. London, Rider, 1951.
Dangerous Ghosts. London, Rider, 1954.
Haunted People. London, Rider, 1955.
Phantoms of the Night. London, Rider, 1956.
Haunted Waters. London, Rider, 1957.
Trees of Ghostly Dread. London, Rider, 1958; as *Shadows of Evil*, London, Digit, 1963.
The Screaming Skulls. London, Foulsham, 1964.
The Midnight Hearse. London, Foulsham, 1965.
Elliott O'Donnell's Casebook of Ghosts, edited by Harry Ludlam. London, Foulsham, 1969.
The Hag of the Dribble, edited by Harry Ludlam. London, Robert Hale, 1971.
Elliott O'Donnell's Ghost Hunters, edited by Harry Ludlam. London, Foulsham, 1971.
Elliott O'Donnell's Great Ghost Stories. London, Foulsham, 1983.
Editor, *Ghosts: Stories of the Supernatural*. London, Foulsham 1959.

OTHER PUBLICATIONS

Novels

Jennie Barlowe, Adventuress. London, Greening, 1906.
Dinevah the Beautiful. London, Greening, 1907.
Murder at Hide and Seek. London, Eldon Press, 1945.

Other

The Meaning of Dreams. London, Eveleigh Nash, 1911.
The Irish Abroad. London, Pitman, 1915.
The Menace of Spiritualism. London, Werner Laurie, 1919.
Spiritualism Explained. London, Pearson, 1920.
Strange Sea Mysteries. London, Bodley Head, 1926.
Strange Disappearances. London, Bodley Head, 1927.
Famous Curses. London, Skeffington, 1929.
Fatal Kisses. London, John Hamilton, 1929.
Great Thames Mysteries. London, Selwyn and Blount, 1930.
Women Bluebeards. London, Stanley Paul, 1931.
Strange Cults and Secret Societies of Modern London. London, Philip Allan, 1934.

Editor, *Mrs. E. M. Ward's Reminiscences.* London, Pitman, 1911.
Editor, *The Trial of Kate Webster.* London, Hodge, 1925.

*   *   *

Elliott O'Donnell liked to be known as a ghosthunter though today he'd be called a psychic researcher. He investigated strange cases for over 60 years and most of his books are accounts of strange phenomena. In many cases he would retell these narratives in story-form, so it is not always easy to distinguish his fiction from his non-fiction. He was a prolific contributor to the popular magazines from the start of the century and many of his short stories were not collected in book form, although some have appeared in anthologies. His earliest writings are lost among obscure newspapers for which he produced regular fodder, but by 1904 he had emerged as a writer of fiction with his novel *For Satan's Sake.* This is a rather absurd story that has not dated well but which seems to have pandered to the dying though still popular vogue for the spiritualistic works of Marie Corelli. Penruddock, a suicide, enters the service of Satan and tempts humans to evil ways, especially murder. It is only through the intervention of a good spirit, his former girlfriend, that Penruddock's soul is saved and he enters heaven. It's unlike any of O'Donnell's later works and was almost certainly written to order.

Much the same may be said of his second novel, *The Unknown Depths,* full of African black magic and adventure, which at least had an air of realism about it even if it was imitation Rider Haggard. Two similar but non-fantastic adventures followed before O'Donnell produced one of his better novels, *The Sorcery Club.* Following the discovery of black magic documents dating from Atlantis, Hamar and his two friends form a bond by which they can advance through the levels of sorcery provided they remain together. When Hamar tries to use his powers to seduce a woman, her friends are able to break the pact. O'Donnell was not a student of the occult, though he almost certainly was acquainted with those who were, including Lewis Spence and probably Arthur Machen, with whom he was a fellow provider of copy for the London papers, so the detail utilized in his novel is at best sec-

ond-hand. But the book is fun—if one excuses O'Donnell's poor writing—and more realistic than his earlier novels.

Although only one other novel was published during this period, the extremely rare *The Haunted Man,* it is entirely probable that O'Donnell's final two novels of the supernatural were also written at this time, since they convey the same mood and content and may have only been revised when a suitable publisher was found. Although *The Dead Riders* did not appear until 1952 it reads just like O'Donnell's early fantastic adventures. It is full of excellent ideas and imagery but poorly written. Blake is a soldier of fortune who becomes lost in the Gobi Desert and encounters the Lovonans, skilled black magicians who are searching for the tomb of Genghis Khan. The Lovonans can summon the Dead Riders, an army of ghosts who are in the power of a long-dead Lovonan magician, Shadna Rana. Blake faces many perils before he escapes, but still has to outwit the Dead Riders. The book would work well if adapted by a skilled writer for an Indiana Jones movie, but in O'Donnell's hands it is episodic and weak.

O'Donnell's skills were much greater in the short form when he stuck to reporting his own investigations. He had a pleasing, light narrative effect which brought his ghostly explorations vividly into the mind's eye. His short fiction is just the same. There is seldom much plot, merely the reporting of a strange occurrence. Some of these could be quite atmospheric, especially "The Cupboard of Dread" (*Quakes,* 1933) in which a cupboard is haunted by the spirit of a suicide which enables clothing to take human form, and "The Mystery of Beechcroft Farm" (*Terrors,* 1933) where relatives seek their aunt and find only her headless spirit. O'Donnell also created a fictionalized form of himself in the shape of ghosthunter Damon Vane, starting with "The Seventh Stair" (*Novel Magazine,* 1922). None of these better stories have been collected, and those in *Dread of Night* and his other wartime paperbacks consist of rather too matter-of-fact reportage. O'Donnell is an author one can appreciate for his ideas and his experiences, and only secondarily as a writer.

—Mike Ashley

OLIPHANT, Mrs. (Margaret)

Nationality: British. **Born:** Margaret Wilson, at Wallyford, near Edinburgh, 4 April 1828. **Family:** Married Francis William Oliphant in 1852 (died 1859); six children (all died). **Career:** Published novelist at 21; moved to London on her marriage, and suffered a tragic family life; cared for three of her brother's children after his wife's death (following the deaths of her own husband and several children); settled in Windsor, and produced fiction and non-fiction copiously in order to support the household. **Awards:** Civil List pension, 1868. Reputed to be Queen Victoria's favourite novelist. **Died:** 25 June 1897.

HORROR, GHOST AND GOTHIC PUBLICATIONS

Novels

A Beleaguered City: Being a Narrative of Certain Recent Events in the City of Semur. New York, Munro, 1879; revised edition, London, Macmillan, 1880.

The Wizard's Son. New York, Lovell, 1883; London, 3 vols., 1884.

Old Lady Mary: A Story of the Seen and Unseen. Boston, Roberts, 1884.

"Dies Irae": The Story of a Spirit in Prison. Edinburgh and London, Blackwood, 1895.

Short Stories

The Lady's Walk: A Story of the Seen and Unseen. New York, Munro, 1883; revised edition, London, Methuen, 1897.

A Little Pilgrim in the Unseen. London, Macmillan, 1882.

The Open Door, and The Portrait: Two Stories of the Seen and Unseen. Boston, Roberts, 1885.

Two Stories of the Seen and Unseen: The Open Door; Old Lady Mary. Edinburgh and London, Blackwood, 1885.

The Land of Darkness; Along with Some Further Chapters in the Experiences of the Little Pilgrim. London, Macmillan, 1888.

Stories of the Seen and Unseen. Boston, Roberts, 1889; with differing contents, Edinburgh, Blackwood, 1902.

Selected Short Stories of the Supernatural, edited by Margaret K. Gray. Edinburgh, Scottish Academic Press, 1985.

A Beleaguered City and Other Stories, edited by Merryn William. Oxford and New York, Oxford University Press, 1988.

OTHER PUBLICATIONS

Novels

Passages in the Life of Mrs. Margaret Maitland of Sunnyside. 3 vols., London, Colburn, 1849; 1 vol., New York, Appleton, 1851.

Caleb Field: A Tale of the Puritans. London, Colburn, and New York, Harper, 1851.

Merkland: A Story of Scottish Life. 3 vols., London, Colburn, 1851; as *Merkland, or Self-Sacrifice,* 1 vol., New York, Stringer and Townsend, 1854.

Memoirs and Resolutions of Adam Graeme of Mossgray. 3 vols., London, Colburn, 1852; 1 vol., New York, Munro, 1885.

Katie Stewart: A True Story. New York, Harper, 1852; Edinburgh and London, Blackwood, 1853.

Harry Muir: A Story of Scottish Life. 3 vols., London, Hurst and Blackett, 1853; 1 vol., New York, Appleton, 1853.

The Quiet Heart: A Story. Edinburgh and London, Blackwood, and New York, Harper, 1854.

Magdalen Hepburn: A Story of the Scottish Reformation. 3 vols., London, Hurst and Blackett, 1854; 1 vol., New York, Riker, Thorne, 1854.

Lilliesleaf: Being a Concluding Series of Passages in the Life of Mrs. Margaret Maitland. (anonymously) 3 vols., London, Hurst and Blackett, 1855; 1 vol., Boston, Burnham, 1862.

Zaidee: A Romance. 3 vols., Edinburgh and London, Blackwood, 1856; 1 vol., Boston, Jewett, 1856.

The Athelings; or, The Three Gifts. 3 vols., Edinburgh and London, Blackwood, 1857; 1 vol., New York, Harper, 1857.

Sundays. London, Nisbett, 1858.

The Laird of Norlaw: A Scottish Story. (anonymously) 3 vols., London, Hurst and Blackett, 1858; 1 vol., New York, Harper, 1859.

Orphans: A Chapter in Life. London, Hurst and Blackett, 1858; New York, Munro, 1880.

Agnes Hopetown's Schools and Holidays. London, Macmillan, and Boston, Gould and Lincoln, 1859.

Lucy Crofton. (anonymously) London, Hurst and Blackett, and New York, Harper, 1860.

The House on the Moor. (anonymously) 3 vols., London, Hurst and Blackett, 1861; 1 vol., New York, Harper, 1861.

The Last of the Mortimers: A Story in Two Voices. (anonymously) 3 vols., London, Hurst and Blackett, 1862; 1 vol., New York, Harper, 1862.

The Chronicles of Carlingford, contains "The Rector," "The Executor," and "The Doctor's Family." Boston, Littell, 1862(?); republished, without "The Executor," as *The Rector; and the Doctor's Family* (anonymously), 3 vols., Edinburgh and London, Blackwood, 1863.

Salem Chapel. (anonymously) 2 vols., Edinburgh and London, Blackwood, 1863.

Heart and Cross. London, Hurst and Blackett, and New York, Gregory, 1863.

The Perpetual Curate. (anonymously) 3 vols., Edinburgh and London, Blackwood, 1864; 1 vol., New York, Harper, 1865.

A Son of the Soil. 1 vol., New York, Harper, 1865; 2 vols., London, Macmillan, 1866.

Agnes. 3 vols., Edinburgh and London, Blackwood, 1866; 1 vol., New York, Harper, 1866.

Madonna Mary. 1 vol., New York, Harper, 1866; 3 vols., London, Hurst and Blackett, 1867.

Miss Marjoribanks. (anonymously) 3 vols., Edinburgh and London, Blackwood, 1866; 1 vol., Boston, Littell and Gay, 1866.

The Brownlows. 3 vols., Edinburgh and London, 1868; 1 vol., New York, Harper, 1868.

The Minister's Wife. 3 vols., London, Hurst and Blackett, 1869; 1 vol., New York, Harper, 1869.

John: A Love Story. 2 vols., Edinburgh and London, Blackwood, 1870; 1 vol., New York, Harper, 1870.

The Three Brothers. 3 vols., London, Hurst and Blackett, 1870; 1 vol., New York, Appleton, 1870.

Squire Arden. 3 vols., London, Hurst and Blackett, 1871; 1 vol., New York, Harper, 1874.

At His Gates. 3 vols., London, Hurst and Blackett, 1872; 1 vol., New York, Scribners, Armstrong, 1873

Ombra. 3 vols., London, Hurst and Blackett, 1872; 1 vol., New York, Harper, 1872.

Innocent: A Tale of Modern Life. 3 vols., London, Low, Marston, Low and Searle, 1873; 1 vol., New York, Harper, 1873.

May. 3 vols., London, Hurst and Blackett, 1873; 1 vol., New York, Scribners, Armstrong, 1873.

A Rose in June. Boston, Osgood, 1874; 2 vols., London, Hurst and Blackett, 1874.

For Love and Life. 3 vols., London, Hurst and Blackett, 1874; 1 vol., New York, Munro, 1879.

Whiteladies. 3 vols., London, Tinsley, 1874; 1 vol., New York, Holt, 1875.

The Story of Valentine and His Brothers. 3 vols., Edinburgh and London, Blackwood, 1875; 1 vol., New York, Harper, 1875.

Phoebe Junior: A Last Chronicle of Carlingford. London, Hurst and Blackett, 3 vols., 1876.

The Curate in Charge. 2 vols., London, Macmillan, 1876; 1 vol., New York, Harper, 1876.

Carità. 3 vols., London, Smith, Elder, 1877; 1 vol., New York, Harper, 1877.

Mrs. Arthur. 3 vols., London, Hurst and Blackett, 1877; 1 vol., New York, Harper, 1877.

Young Musgrave. 3 vols., London, Macmillan, 1877; 1 vol., New York, Harper, 1878.

The Primrose Path: A Chapter in the Annals of the Kingdom of Fife. 3 vols., London, Hurst and Blackett, 1878; 1 vol., New York, Harper, 1878.

Within the Precincts. 3 vols., London, Smith, Elder, 1879; 1 vol., New York, Harper, 1879.

The Greatest Heiress in England. 3 vols., London, Hurst and Blackett, 1879; New York, Harper 1880.

He That Will Not When He May. 3 vols., London, Macmillan, 1880; 1 vol., New York, Harper, 1880.

Harry Joscelyn. 3 vols., London, Hurst and Blackett, 1881; 1 vol., New York, Harper, 1881.

In Trust: The Story of a Lady and Her Lover. New York, Munro, 1881; 3 vols., London, Longmans, Green, 1882.

Hester: A Story of Contemporary Life. 3 vols., London, Macmillan, 1883; 1 vol., New York, Macmillan, 1882.

It Was a Lover and His Lass. 3 vols., London, Hurst and Blackett, 1883; 1 vol., New York, Harper,1883.

The Ladies Lindores. 3 vols., Edinburgh and London, Blackwood, 1883; 1 vol., New York, Harper, 1883.

Sir Tom. New York, Harper, 1883; 3 vols., London, Macmillan, 1884.

Madam. New York, Harper, 1884; 3 vols., London, Longmans, Green, 1885.

Oliver's Bride: A New Novel. New York, Munro, 1885; revised and enlarged as *Oliver's Bride: A True Story,* London, Ward and Downey, 1886.

A Country Gentleman and His Family. 3 vols., London, Macmillan, 1886; 1 vol., New York, Macmillan, 1886.

Effie Ogilvie: The Story of a Young Life. 2 vols., Glasgow, Maclehose, 1886; 1 vol., New York, Harper, 1886.

A House Divided against Itself. 3 vols., Edinburgh and London, Blackwood, 1886; 1 vol., New York, Harper, 1886.

A Poor Gentleman. New York, Munro, 1886; 3 vols., London, Hurst and Blackett, 1889.

The Son of His Father. New York, Harper, 1886; 3 vols., London, Hurst and Blackett, 1887.

Cousin Mary. London, Partidge, 1888.

Joyce. 3 vols., London, Macmillan, 1888; 1 vol., New York, Harper, 1888.

The Second Son, with Thomas Bailey Aldrich. 3 vols., London, Macmillan, 1888; 1 vol., Boston and New York, Houghton, Mifflin, 1888.

Lady Car: The Sequel of a Life. London, Longmans, Green, 1889; New York, Harper, 1889.

Kirsteen: A Story of a Scottish Family Seventy Years Ago. 3 vols., London, Macmillan, 1890; 1 vol., New York, Harper, 1890.

Sons and Daughters. Edinburgh and London, Blackwood, 1890.

The Mystery of Mrs. Blencarrow. London, Blackett, 1890; Chicago, Donohue, Henneberry, 1894.

Janet. 3 vols., London, Hurst and Blackett, 1891; as *The Story of a Governess,* New York, Fenno, 1895.

The Heir Presumptive and the Heir Apparent. New York, Lovell, 1891; 3 vols., London, Macmillan, 1892.

The Marriage of Elinor. New York, US Book, 1891; 3 vols., London, Macmillan, 1892.

The Railwayman and His Children. 3 vols., London, Macmillan, 1891; 1 vol., New York, Lovell, 1891.

Diana Trelawney: The History of a Great Mistake. 2 vols., Edinburgh and London, Blackwood, 1892; as *Diana: The History of a Great Mistake,* New York and Chicago, US Book, 1892.

The Cuckoo in the Nest. 3 vols., London, Hutchinson, 1892; 1 vol., New York and Chicago, US Book, 1892.

Lady William. 3 vols., London, Macmillan, 1893; 1 vol., New York, Macmillan, 1893.

The Sorceress. 3 vols., London, White, 1893; 1 vol., New York, Taylor, 1893.

A House in Bloomsbury. 2 vols., London, Hutchinson, 1894; 1 vol., New York, Dodd, Mead, 1894.

Who Was Lost and Is Found. Edinburgh and London, Blackwood, 1894; New York, Harper, 1895.

Sir Robert's Fortune: The Story of a Scotch Moor. New York, Harper, 1894; London, Methuen, 1895.

Two Strangers. London, Unwin, 1894; New York, Harper, 1895.

Old Mr. Tredgold: A Story of Two Sisters. New York, Longmans, 1895; as *Old Mr. Tredgold,* London, Longmans, 1896.

The Unjust Steward; or, The Minister's Debt. London and Edinburgh, Chambers, and Philadelphia, Lippincott, 1896.

Short Stories

Neighbours on the Green: A Collection of Stories. London and New York, Macmillan, 1889.

Grove Road, Hampstead. New York, Munro, 1889; enlarged as *The Two Marys and Grove Road, Hampstead: Tales.* London, Methuen, 1896.

The Ways of Life: Two Stories. London, Smith, Elder, and New York, Putnam, 1897.

A Widow's Tale, and Other Stories. Edinburgh and London, Blackwood, 1898; New York, Fenno, 1898.

That Little Cutty, and Two Other Stories. London and New York, Macmillan, 1898.

Other

The Days of My Life: An Autobiography. 3 vols., London, Hurst and Blackett, 1857; 1 vol., New York, Harper, 1857.

The Life of Edward Irving, Minister of the National Scotch Church. 2 vols., London, Hurst and Blackett, 1862; 1 vol., New York, Harper, 1862.

Francis of Assisi. London, Macmillan, 1868; New York, Macmillan, 1888.

Historical Sketches of the Reign of George II. 2 vols., Edinburgh and London, Blackwood, 1869; 1 vol., Boston, Littell and Gay, 1869.

Memoir of Count de Montalembert: A Chapter of Recent French History. 2 vols., Edinburgh and London, Blackwood, 1872.

Dress. London, Macmillan, 1876; Philadelphia, Porter and Coates, 1879.

The Makers of Florence: Dante, Giotto, Savonarola and Their City. London, Macmillan, 1876; New York, Macmillan, 1878.

Dante. Edinburgh and London, Blackwood, and Philadelphia, Lippincott, 1877.

Molière, with F. Tarver. Edinburgh and London, Blackwood, and Philadelphia, Lippincott, 1879.

Cervantes. Edinburgh and London, Blackwood, 1880; Philadelphia, Lippincott, 1881.

The Literary History of England in the End of the Eighteenth and Beginning of the Nineteenth Century. 3 vols., London, Macmillan, 1882; 1 vol., New York, Macmillan, 1882.

Sheridan. London, Macmillan, and New York, Harper, 1883.

The Makers of Venice: Doges, Conquerors, Painters and Men of Letters. London and New York, Macmillan, 1887.

A Memoir of the Life of John Tulloch. Edinburgh and London, Blackwood, 1888.

Royal Edinburgh: Her Saints, Kings, Prophets, and Poets. London, Macmillan, and New York, Mershon, 1890.

Jerusalem: Its History and Hope. London, and New York, Macmillan, 1891.

A Memoir of the Life of Laurence Oliphant, and of Alice Oliphant, His Wife. 2 vols., Edinburgh and London, Blackwood, and New York, Harper, 1891.

The Victorian Age of English Literature, with F. R. Oliphant. 2 vols., London, Percival, and New York, Dodd, Mead, 1892.

Thomas Chalmers, Preacher, Philosopher and Statesman. London, Methuen; and Boston and New York, Houghton, Mifflin, 1893.

Historical Sketches of the Reign of Queen Anne. New York, Century, 1894.

A Child's History of Scotland. London, Unwin, 1895.

The Makers of Modern Rome. London and New York, Macmillan, 1895.

Jeanne d'Arc: Her Life and Death. London and New York, Putnam, 1896.

Annals of a Publishing House: William Blackwood and His Sons. 2 vols., Edinburgh and London, Blackwood, 1897; 3 vols., New York, Scribners, 1897-98.

The Autobiography and Letters of Mrs. Oliphant, edited by A. L. Coghill. Edinburgh and London, Blackwood, and New York, Dodd, Mead, 1899.

Queen Victoria: A Personal Sketch. London, Cassell, 1901.

Translator, *The Monks of the West from St. Benedict to St. Bernard*, by Count de Montalembert. 7 vols., 1861-79.

*

Critical Studies: *The Equivocal Virtue: Mrs. Oliphant and the Victorian Literary Market Place* by Vineta Colby and Robert A. Colby, New York, Archon, 1966; *Margaret Oliphant: A Critical Biography* by Merryn Williams, London, Macmillan, 1978; "Queen of Popular Fiction: Mrs. Oliphant and the Chronicles of Carlingford" by R. C. Terry, in *Victorian Popular Fiction, 1860-80*, London, Macmillan Press, and Atlantic Highlands, New Jersey, Humanities Press, 1983.

*   *   *

Mrs. Oliphant was an extraordinarily prolific novelist, almost all of whose produce is now forgotten. A few of her domestic dramas, especially those which preserve images of ways of rural life that were dissolving under the onslaught of industrialization, are not without interest to the modern reader, but her contemporary reputation—such as it is—rests on her "stories of the seen and unseen." To some extent, these too are interesting merely as honest accounts of the Victorian world-view, still darkly threatened at the margins by anxieties as to whether the dead were sufficiently honoured by the living, and still feebly supported at the core by the notion that virtue would obtain its due reward in Heaven; Mrs. Oliphant's developments of these ideas are, however, intriguingly idiosyncratic as well as unusually elaborate.

She wrote so much because she had to, having been widowed at 31 with her husband's debts to pay, two boys under six and a third child on the way. Alas, it was all to no avail—or so it came to seem to her. Her children all died before she did, both her sons perishing in the late 1880s having thoroughly disappointed all her

hopes and expectations; a nephew whose expenses she also took on went the same way. It is hardly surprising that her tales in which family life is disturbed by enigmatic hauntings are written with such keen intensity and such infinitely extended weariness.

Although Margaret Gray's list of Mrs. Oliphant's supernatural tales begins with a borderline item from 1857, the author's first ghost story of any real interest was "The Secret Chamber" (1876), whose plot she was to expand very elaborately in the unremittingly tedious *The Wizard's Son*, her one attempt to accommodate the ghost story to her usual three-decker format. "The Secret Chamber" was followed by the remarkable extended *conte philosophique*, *A Beleaguered City*, which first appeared in the Christmas supplement of the *New Quarterly Magazine* in 1878. The title echoes that of Longfellow's poem "The Beleaguered City," in which Prague is briefly besieged by a phantom army, but the inhabitants of Mrs. Oliphant's French city of Semur are actually driven from their homes by their dead ancestors, who arrive *en masse* to demand redress for their neglect. The success of the American edition, which was published in advance of the revised and augmented British book version, created a demand which resulted in the magazine versions of some of Mrs. Oliphant's subsequent tales being swiftly reprinted in America in advance of the revised versions she produced for British book publication, thus adding to the bibliographical confusion caused by the enormousness of her output.

The first story which Mrs. Oliphant subtitled "a story of the seen and unseen" was "Earthbound" (1880), although she quickly attached the label to the Macmillan edition of *A Beleaguered City*. "Earthbound" was another Christmas-supplement story, in which a young man encounters a spirit whose refusal to pass on to the ethereal regions set aside for the afterlife is a kind of self-inflicted punishment. During the next seven years Mrs. Oliphant became a regular contributor of tales to the Christmas supplements of various magazines—all of which were, of course, published in December although the issues were invariably dated January of the following year, thus making a further contribution to the bibliographical muddle.

"The Open Door," "Old Lady Mary" and "The Portrait" were written for *Blackwood's* supplements for Christmas in 1881, 1883 and 1885, while "The Lady's Walk" appeared in *Longman's* in 1882. "The Lady's Walk" is an elaboration of the theme of "Earthbound" and the new tale was to be further elaborated for British book publication. The earthbound spirit of "The Open Door" is a prodigal son whose return is unfortunately belated. The spirit of "Old Lady Mary" returns from the Great Beyond in order to undo some mischief she wrought in her dotage, but finds it difficult to communicate her good intentions. "The Portrait" is a more optimistic version of a similar plot, in which the female revenant's redemptive ambitions eventually bear healthy fruit.

When she wrote "Old Lady Mary" Mrs. Oliphant had recently set forth to map the regions of that Great Beyond as assiduously as the great Victorian explorers had mapped the dark continent of Africa. This mission, begun in "A Little Pilgrim in the Unseen" (1882), was to run parallel to her tales of the earthbound and earth-returned. "A Little Pilgrim in the Unseen" is not a horror story, but those elements of the series which deal with the infernal regions may be considered as such, and are certainly more effective in literary terms than their paradisal equivalents. "The Land of Darkness" (1887) is a fine vision of the outer circles of a quintessentially Victorian Hell, better than "On the Dark Mountains" (1888), which followed rapidly upon its heels.

There was a brief hiatus in the flow of Mrs. Oliphant's supernatural fictions after 1888; nearly five years passed before she produced the rather trivial "A Visitor and His Opinions." For *Blackwood's* Christmas number in 1895, however, she produced "The Library Window," which is perhaps the best of all her ghost stories. Its narrator is a young woman who returns to a house in her native Scotland, where a non-existent window offers her a fugitive glimpse of a man she wrongly assumes to be her dead father. Fuelled by nostalgia as well as moral conviction, it may be the most revealing of all the author's supernatural stories. Having made a new beginning she then returned to her explorations of the afterlife, but the long-drawn-out "Dies Irae" is markedly less effective than "The Land of Darkness." The unreprinted "The Land of Suspense," which was in the Christmas issue of *Blackwood's* after the one which featured "The Library Window," is also less vivid than its earlier models, but perhaps more disturbing by virtue of its intimacy; the protagonist is very obviously modelled on the author's older son.

It is Mrs. Oliphant's shorter ghost stories which are best-known today, but that is mainly because the others are too long to be conveniently included in anthologies. Margaret Gray's collection omits the most oft-reprinted ("The Open Door") and only includes one novella ("Old Lady Mary") but still only has room for six items. A comprehensive collection would be massively large, unless it could be divided into three or four volumes. Even so, such a project would have the virtue of bringing together a fascinating body of work—an *oeuvre* which is certainly the most sustained and adventurous extrapolation of the definitive ideologies of Victorian supernatural fiction.

—Brian Stableford

ONIONS, (George) Oliver

Nationality: British. **Born:** George Oliver, in Bradford, Yorkshire, 1873; adopted the surname Onions (previously used as a pseudonym) in 1918. **Education:** National Art Training School (now Royal College of Art), London, 1894-97. **Family:** Married the novelist Berta Ruck in 1909; two sons. **Career:** Editor, *Le Quartier Latin*, Paris, 1897; had various jobs, including book illustrator, poster designer, draughtsman, and war artist during the Boer War. **Awards:** James Tait Black Memorial prize, 1947. **Died:** 9 April 1961.

HORROR, GHOST AND GOTHIC PUBLICATIONS

Novels

The Tower of Oblivion. London, Hodder and Stoughton, and New York, Macmillan, 1921.
A Certain Man. London, Heinemann, 1931.
The Hand of Kornelius Voyt. London, Hamish Hamilton, 1939.

Short Stories

Widdershins. London, Secker, 1911.
Ghosts in Daylight. London, Chapman and Hall, 1924.
The Painted Face. London, Heinemann, 1929.

The Collected Ghost Stories of Oliver Onions. London, Nicholson and Watson, 1935; New York, Dover, 1971.

OTHER PUBLICATIONS

Novels

The Compleat Bachelor. London, Murray, 1900; New York, Stokes, 1901.
The Odd-Job Man. London, Murray, 1903.
The Drakestone. London, Hurst and Blackett, 1906.
Pedlar's Pack. London, Nash, 1908.
Little Devil Doubt. London, Murray, 1909.
The Exception. London, Methuen, 1910; New York, Lane, 1911.
Good Boy Seldom: A Romance of Advertisement. London, Methuen, 1911.
In Accordance with the Evidence. London, Secker, 1912; New York, Doran, 1913.
The Debit Account. London, Secker, 1912; New York, Doran, 1913.
The Story of Louie. London, Secker, 1913; New York, Doran, 1914.
The Two Kisses: The Tale of a Very Modern Courtship. London, Methuen, and New York, Doran, 1913.
A Crooked Mile. London, Methuen, and New York, Doran, 1914.
Gray Youth: The Story of a Very Modern Courtship and a Very Modern Marriage (omnibus; includes *The Two Kisses, A Crooked Mile*). New York, Doran, 1914.
Mushroom Town. London, Hodder and Stoughton, and New York, Doran, 1914.
The New Moon: A Romance of Reconstruction. London, Hodder and Stoughton, 1918.
A Case in Camera. Bristol, Arrowsmith, 1920; New York, Macmillan, 1921.
Peace in Our Time. London, Chapman and Hall, 1923.
The Spite of Heaven. London, Chapman and Hall, 1925; New York, Doran, 1926.
Whom God Hath Sundered (omnibus; includes *In Accordance with the Evidence, The Debit Account, The Story of Louie*). London, Secker, 1925; New York, Doran, 1926.
Cut Flowers. London, Chapman and Hall, 1927.
The Open Secret. London, Heinemann, and Boston, Houghton Mifflin, 1930.
Catalan Circus. London, Nicholson and Watson, 1934.
Cockcrow; or, Anybody's England. London, Hamish Hamilton, 1940.
The Blood Eagle. London, Staples Press, 1941.
The Story of Ragged Robyn. London, Joseph, 1945.
Poor Man's Tapestry. London, Joseph, 1946.
Arras of Youth. London, Joseph, 1949.
A Penny for the Harp. London, Joseph, 1952.
A Shilling to Spend. London, Joseph, 1965.

Short Stories

Tales from a Far Riding. London, Murray, 1902.
Buck o' the Moon and Other Stories. London, Hurst and Blackett, 1906.
Admiral Eddy and Other Tales. London, Murray, 1907.
Draw in Your Stool. London, Mills and Boon, 1909.
The Italian Chest and Other Stories. London, Secker, 1939.
Bells Rung Backwards. London, Staples Press, 1953.

*   *   *

Oliver Onions took up the tradition of ghost-story writing that had been carried forward from Victorian times into the Edwardian era by such writers as M. R. James, and accomplished more than any other writer in extending that tradition through one more generation. He might have got more credit for his endeavours in that vein had it not been for the fact that his one acknowledged masterpiece was the first ghost story he set before the public; all his subsequent works, however good they were, seemed a little weak by comparison.

That masterpiece, which vies with only a handful of others for the title of the best ghost story ever written, was "The Beckoning Fair One," which leads off the collection *Widdershins*. Its protagonist is a young writer named Oleron, who is struggling to complete a novel. The story and its heroine have the full approval of Oleron's girlfriend Elsie, but when he moves into new rooms he falls under the sway of a jealous ghost whose subtle manifestations are associated with the soft sound of long hair being combed and the melody of the folk-song which provides the story's title. The phantom *femme fatale* alienates him from his work and from Elsie, and brings him to the brink of that death by self-neglect which traditionally befalls all who hear the sirens' song. The story was apparently inspired by the sound of the author's newly acquired wife—the romantic novelist Berta Ruck—combing her hair soon after they had moved into a flat in a gloomy Georgian mansion. He never managed to reproduce so intimately personal a sense of threat, perhaps because he was never again subject to quite the same combination of personal apprehensions and anxieties.

Several other stories in *Widdershins* also deal with exotic problems of creativity. The hack writer in "Hic Jacet" is supernaturally inhibited in his attempt to write the biography of an artist who refused to prostitute his talents. The sculptor in "Benlian" dotes on his favourite work like an overfond parent, and spoils the "child" in consequence. The dilettante engineer in "Rooum" is dogged by a mysterious Runner who embodies his anxieties about the solidity and reliability of matter. The Renaissance shipwright in "Phantas" bridges time with his dream of maritime perfection. "The Accident" and "The Cigarette Case" are also deft timeslip stories, while "Io"—retitled "The Lost Thyrsus" in the *Collected Ghost Stories*—looks at creativity from the other side in an ironic tale of a woman elevated to insane ecstasy by immersion in the poetry of Keats. One trivial tale of a ghost-child, "The Rocker," was omitted from later editions.

The first of Onions's three fantastic novels, *The Tower of Oblivion*, never actually becomes a horror story although it continually gives the impression that it might. It is an odd account of the reversed life of Derwent Rose, who begins to grow young at the age 45, slipping back by erratic degrees to the physical and mental age of 16. The novel attempts to weigh his gains and losses with unusually scrupulous accuracy. It is interesting that Berta Ruck's only fantasy, *The Immortal Girl*—which was published four years later—applies a very different accounting process to the rejuvenation of its heroine.

Two of the four supernatural stories in *Ghosts in Daylight*, "The Ascending Dream" and "The Dear Dryad," carry forward Onions's fascination with time, each displaying the extension of different aspects of human aspiration across three eras. The novella "The Real People" carries forward his fascination with problems of creativity in a tale of characters who come to life. "The Woman in the Way" is a pseudo-scholarly study of a textbook haunting. Time is bent in a more substantial and more intriguing fashion in the title novella of *The Painted Face*, another story of a siren from

the past, this time told from the point of view of the woman who is host to the renegade spirit. "The Rosewood Door" is a similar tale of love blighted by possession, again told from he female viewpoint although it is the male partner who is taken over by the time-displaced spirit. "The Master of the House" is a more sensational piece which never musters any real conviction.

The *Collected Ghost Stories* includes all the above-mentioned items except "The Rocker" and "The Dear Dryad" and adds four new items. "John Gladwyn Says . . ." is a curious item in which Death, here incarnate as a motor car, misses its first appointment with the protagonist and thus permits him visionary glimpses of the world beyond; "The Out Sister" is an ordinary tale of a ghostly nun; "The Rope in the Rafters" is another tale of a malevolent timeslipped spirit; "Resurrection in Bronze" is another tale of obsessive creativity. Two uncollected fantasies dating from the early 1920s—"The Ether Hogs" and "The Mortal"—are comedies.

Onions's second fantastic novel, *A Certain Man*, is an extended fable, as was the one he left incomplete at his death, but *The Hand of Kornelius Voyt* is a neo-Gothic novel somewhat reminiscent of J. Sheridan Le Fanu's *Uncle Silas*. Here, though, the orphan delivered into the custody of a sinister guardian is a boy, and the mysticism in which his guardian seeks to embroil him is a unique theory of Onions's own. The deaf-mute Voyt has compensated for his disabilities by developing powers of perception and imposition, and he causes his young ward to achieve a remarkable premature maturity which is a reversal of Derwent Rose's predicament; his disturbed attitude to sex is a confusion of fascination and disgust which echoes that of the middle-aged narrator of *The Tower of Oblivion*.

Almost all Onions's fantasies embody a seemingly serious interest in the offbeat kinds of "time theories" which became very fashionable after the publication of J. W. Dunne's *An Experiment with Time* in 1927. Such theories had previously affected the work of several other writers of weird tales, including Rudyard Kipling, but none so extensively as Onions. His best tales are accounts of supernatural seduction by agents displaced from their own eras; he achieved his greatest intensity in those versions which involve actual sirens but he also paid some heed to the fantasy figures of female romantic fantasy—the Cavalier in "The Rosewood Door," for example—and to figures of a more enigmatic kind, like the strangely pathetic Kornelius Voyt. It is significant that such agents are at their most menacing in Onions's work when they threaten artistic productivity as well as—or perhaps rather than—life itself. There is a sense in which the past is always loomingly present in the minds of writers, even if they are not engaged in writing historical fiction (as Onions sometimes was); it is not surprising that the most sensitive of the breed not only feel but fear its pressure, although few have transcribed the feel or the fear as brilliantly as Onions did in "The Beckoning Fair One."

—Brian Stableford

O'SULLIVAN, Vincent

Nationality: American. **Born:** New York City, 27 November 1868. **Education:** Attended schools in New York, at Exeter College, Oxford, England, and in France. **Career:** Adjutant professor of English and American Literature, University of Rennes, France, 1918-19; lived in France for the remainder of his life and wrote much poetry and journalism in French. **Died:** 1940.

HORROR, GHOST AND GOTHIC PUBLICATIONS

Short Stories

A Book of Bargains. London, Leonard Smithers, 1896.
A Dissertation Upon Second Fiddles. London, G. Richards, 1902.
Human Affairs. London, David Nutt, 1907.
The Next Room. Edinburgh, Tragara Press, 1988.
Master of the Fallen Years. Edinburgh, Tragara Press, 1990.
Master of Fallen Years: Complete Supernatural Stories of Vincent O'Sullivan, edited by Jessica Amanda Salmonson. London, Ghost Story Press, 1995.

OTHER PUBLICATIONS

Novel

The Good Girl. London, Constable, 1912; Boston, Small, Maynard, 1917.

Short Stories

The Green Window. London, Leonard Smithers, 1899.
Sentiment, and Other Stories. London, Duckworth, 1913; Boston, Small, Maynard, 1917.

Poetry

Poems. London, E. Mathews, 1896.
The Houses of Sin. London, L. Smithers, 1897.

Plays

The Hartley Family. N.p., n.d.
The Lighthouse. N.p., n.d.

Other

Aspects of Wilde. London, Constable, and New York, Holt, 1936.

*   *   *

In the prefatory essay of her definitive collection of Vincent O'Sullivan's supernatural stories Jessica Amanda Salmonson introduces her subject by quoting his observation that "the Romantic point of view was that the poet is vowed to disaster." O'Sullivan's career was launched in the 1890s, long after Romanticism had passed its sell-by date and spoiled, but the rotting of Romanticism into Decadence only served to set the seal on his commitment to disaster.

With masterful ill-timing, the expatriate O'Sullivan remained idle during the brief heyday of the English Decadent Movement, preserving his best endeavours until the trials of Oscar Wilde had laid waste to the entire project—at which point the only publisher in London who was willing to risk the opprobrium of being associated with such work was the only one whose reputation was so badly tarnished that he could not avoid it: Leonard Smithers. At that time, O'Sullivan was still rich and could do what he liked, but when his inheritance ran out eight or nine years after the end of the century he found himself quite alone; the men he had appointed his artistic peers—Aubrey Beardsley, Oscar Wilde, Ernest Dowson and John Davidson—were dead, save only for Arthur Symons, who had turned Symbolist and moralist for appearances sake.

O'Sullivan's early stories and poems mostly appeared in *The Senate*, a monthly "review of progressive thought." The posthumous fantasy "Revenge of the Soul," reprinted as "When I was Dead," appeared there in 1895, as did "The Monkey and Basil Holderness," a bizarre tale in which a debauched socialite besotted with a prostitute gradually exchanges both physical and mental attributes with his simian companion. O'Sullivan did not reprint the latter story in any of his collections, perhaps considering it too garish, and he saved the relentlessly morbid but far more poetic "Will" for his rather lapidary second collection, *The Green Window*. His first, *A Book of Bargains*, is ostentatiously Poe-esque, mostly consisting of colourful tales of exotic crime; those which extend to supernatural revenge—or at least supernatural extension—are "My Enemy and Myself" and "The Business of Madame Jahn." The latter story is a garish celebration of the processes of decay, as not-quite-embodied by the serial appearances of a revenant woman. Another tale of decay from the same collection is "The Bargain of Rupert Orange," in which a young man gifted with five years of wealth and happiness by a tacit diabolical pact finds the burden of his remaining life hard to bear. So it was with O'Sullivan himself, who simply could not contrive his own death no matter how hard he tried—although he never did attempt to emulate Davidson by throwing himself off a cliff.

While his money lasted O'Sullivan found it possible to write what is perhaps his finest story, the novella "Verschoyle's House," which appeared in his otherwise non-supernatural collection *Human Affairs*, in 1907. Set at the time of the English Civil War, it is a striking tale of confused loyalties and confused personalities, which replaces the crises of decadent aristocracy which fascinated Poe in an actual historical context, adding an extra dimension to the process by which a landowner's heritage is reclaimed by time and the land to which his family laid fervent claim.

Once the 19th century was dead and conclusively buried—the interment proper took place in the fields of Flanders in 1914—O'Sullivan tried to move with the times. He returned to his native America for a brief while, during which time he published "The Burned House" (1916), the much-anthologized and uncharacteristically sentimental ghost story "The Interval" (1917) and the *conte cruel* "The Abigail Sheriff Memorial" (1917). Once the Great War was over O'Sullivan returned to Europe and took up residence in Paris, the spiritual home of all true Decadents. He continued to find markets in America, publishing "Master of Fallen Years" (1921) in H. L. Mencken's *The Smart Set*. This London-set tale of a man misfortunately afflicted in his sleep was named by the author as one of his personal favourites—as was "They," a delicate account of spiritual leeching—but the judgment was made late in life, by which time he had come to think of his early tales as "burlesques." His last consistent market was the *Dublin Magazine*, for which he continued the work in literary criticism that had gradually taken over the greater part of his effort, but the stories reprinted therefrom in Salmonson's collection are distinctly weak by comparison with the remainder.

O'Sullivan was by no means the only Decadent writer who only wrote enough supernatural stories to fill a single volume, nor was he the only one who was long dead before anyone found it practical to put such a book together. In this respect he requires to be compared with such similar figures as Count Stenbock and Murray Gilchrist, but he retained far more bizarrerie in his later works than Gilchrist did, and he was always a more robust litterateur than Stenbock. Had he only made a novel out of "Verschoyle's House"—which he might easily have done had he cared to—he might be far better known and more widely appreciated than he is. He does, however, have a fitting monument in *Master of Fallen Years: Complete Supernatural Stories of Vincent O'Sullivan*, which represents the fruit of unusually painstaking bibliographical labour and allows O'Sullivan's highly individual contribution to the tradition of Poe-esque fiction to be measured with pinpoint accuracy; it a fine book which every serious scholar of the genre ought to possess. After her own prefatory essay Salmonson reprints a brief essay by O'Sullivan "On the Kind of Fiction Called Morbid," which plaintively observes that among writers "the man who would always be introducing the thin presence of Death is, without doubt, the most reviled." He did, he was, and he was right to complain.

—Brian Stableford

P-Q

PALMER, Jessica

Nationality: American. **Born:** Chicago, 5 June 1953. **Education:** Mary Mount College, Salina, Kansas, degree in practical nursing, 1975; degree in alcoholism counselling, 1978. **Family:** Married in 1979 (husband died 1985). **Career:** Psychiatric nurse, Salina, Kansas; scriptwriter, 12-part television series on alcoholism, Alcohol Foundation of Central Kansas and Public Broadcasting Service, c. 1978; technical writer, oil-well services company (writer of many unsigned textbooks on radiation and explosives); moved to London, England, 1988; freelance novelist; editorial director, Publishing Initiatives, Beckenham, Kent, from 1997. **Agent:** Serafina Clarke, 98 Tunis Rd., London W12 7EY, England.

HORROR, GHOST AND GOTHIC PUBLICATIONS

Novels

Dark Lullaby. New York, Pocket, 1991.
Cradlesong. New York, Pocket, 1993.
Shadow Dance. New York, Pocket, 1994.
Sweet William. New York, Pocket, 1995.

OTHER PUBLICATIONS

Novels

Healer's Quest. London, Point Fantasy, 1993.
Fire Wars. London, Point Fantasy, 1994.
Random Factor. London, Point SF, 1994.
Return of the Wizard. London, Point Fantasy, 1995.
Human Factor. London, Point SF, 1996.

*   *   *

Jessica Palmer writes for children and adolescents as well as adults, and most of her horror is about families and children. Her work includes realistic as well as supernatural horrors: indeed the epigraph to her 1991 novel *Dark Lullaby* reads: "Every child has the right to protection and . . . to a life free from violence, exploitation, and abuse," a quote from the 1989 United Nations Convention on the rights of children.

In the novel, a seriously dysfunctional family has just moved to a new home. It is nearly Christmas, and they can't find the decorations. Indeed, they wonder if Christmas will be worth celebrating at all that year. Elliot Graves is a failed musician working as a teacher. He blames his near-alcoholic wife Jane for a fire which destroyed their previous home and took the life of 11-year-old Shelley, their oldest daughter. Jane resents that blame, because although she can't stop drinking, she at least doesn't smoke. Elliot is plagued by nightmares that merge the fire and other horrifying aspects of his life, such as the ulcer that killed his conformist father and which he fears he will inherit. Something gnaws his innards, and snakes explode from his navel. Firemen rescue his relatives one by one, even his bedridden mother-in-law, but they do not get to Shelley. Worst of all, before he wakes he realizes that in this dream the fire is in his new house, not in the old.

While her parents quarrel over the unpacking, and drunken violence eventually results, nine-year-old Sara sits upstairs, alone and terrified. She does not allow herself to cry, because she understandably doesn't want to attract their attention. She is disillusioned with all her surviving relatives, even her grandmother. "Nana" is bedridden by a stroke, still aware of her surroundings and the situation the family is in, and increasingly frustrated by her inability to do anything to put it right.

What Sara wants more than anything is for Shelley to return. Shelley was older and the leader . . . though recently she had taken to preening herself in front of the mirror to the accompaniment of Michael Jackson records. Sara wishes Shelley were there . . . but maybe Shelley is closer than she thinks.

Palmer's second novel, *Cradlesong*, gives us a slightly happier family in a more conventional house of horrors. The non-supernatural element is not absent: in one of the most effective scenes, two very young brothers, new to the neighbourhood, are set on by a large gang of local bullies old enough to ride bicycles.

At least the family is happy until they make the inevitable mistake of buying a big, creepy house which is cheap just because people don't want to live in a place where murders have occurred and a whole family was once wiped out. Even the person who sells it to them has the decency to warn them that too many deaths have happened there for it to be a happy place to live. We, of course, know this, as in the prologue we have already seen a child lured to his death in the house by a ghost. Tom Erwin, who (rather self-referentially) is himself a horror writer, has only just moved his pregnant wife Allison and their two sons into the underpriced death-trap when disasters begin. Allison falls down the steps and winds up in the hospital emergency room. Only when he has been sent home to look after the children while his wife hovers on the brink of life and death does Tom sit down to read the history of the house in macabre press cuttings.

Palmer's more recent novel, *Sweet William*, has a theme of possession, of evil and innocence. A four-year-old boy has something very strange and worrying about him, but his immediate family find it hard to persuade anyone to believe them.

There is a wider variety of approaches to horror in Palmer's few short stories. "Full Moon Rising" is essentially a dark crime item, and appeared in a *London Noir* anthology edited by Maxim Jakubowski. "What the Dickens" (*Substance*, Spring 1995) adds a touch of humour: Charles Dickens finds himself trapped in time and is confronted with a demonic editor who wants to make changes to "A Christmas Carol": these proposals reflect a future sadly and familiarly less comforting than that manipulated by the ghosts, but recognizable to all too many writers.

Even more autobiographical is her story "Ortygia" in *Interzone* 88, October 1994 (a special issue edited by Paul Brazier). This was published among a number of non-fiction pieces by various hands all concerning a real-life house in Harrow, London (built originally for a Classics teacher), where a number of writers and actors lived in a strange, timeless atmosphere dominated by Eve, the near-centenarian owner. In a sense the whole mini-collection is an elegy to this lady: she symbolizes a way of life which, though not very tolerant, was gracious and gentle. Jessica Palmer's story fictionalizes the relationship between Eve in her last years and Jessica herself, the most recent arrival.

A house can be many things. No one now knows much about the early and middle years of Ortygia House, but by Jessica's time it seems to have been a dilapidated, ambiguous oasis in which contrasting and not-quite-conflicting traditions of culture were surrounded by insensitive developments. Houses are a central theme in Jessica Palmer's work: a house is supposed to be a home, but home can be treacherous, home is where the greatest horrors may lurk.

—Peter T. Garratt

PARKINSON, T(erry) L(ee)

Nationality: American. **Born:** Ohio, 1949. **Career:** Contributor of short stories to various anthologies and magazines including *Predators, Full Spectrum, Fantasy & Science Fiction, Semiotexte SF, I Shudder at Your Touch, After Midnight,* and three volumes of Charles Grant's *Shadows* series. **Died:** 7 January 1993.

HORROR, GHOST AND GOTHIC PUBLICATIONS

Novel

The Man Upstairs. New York, Dutton, 1991.

*   *   *

Before his untimely death from AIDS in 1993 at the age of 43, T. L. Parkinson published a fistful of unusual short stories and a novel that stands as a minor masterpiece of latter-day dark American surrealism.

In much of his writing the characters are noticeably removed from their lives. As they pass from one event to another, the only existing links between them Parkinson renders so slyly yet so tellingly that the characters' emotional isolation comes to suggest personality disintegration. Often they breathe, move and think in dreamlike states, making micro-transitions from fantasy to reality and back again quickly and/or subtly enough to let the reader know definitively the extent of their (often self-induced) confusion. The links between their lives' events, though tentative, are nevertheless resonant and evoke the dread of the absolute uncertainty of identity.

In "Sleep" the main character, Marcia, suffers from narcolepsy. The story is developed in a fragmented style that intermixes dream, waking and the juncture between sleep and wakefulness so closely as to be barely distinguishable. The effect is to portray Marcia as overwhelmed by experience, whether awake, dreaming, or not-quite-asleep. Ultimately she is hospitalized, but there is no end in sight of her condition. In "The Blue Man" Curtis, lost to himself—shown, among other things, by the self-imposed assumption of his identity by inanimate objects ("He falls into the waiting imprint of himself in his favorite armchair")—continues to see a ghost (or more accurately, parts of a blue man) grown directly from his isolated life, starting at the age of seven. Near the end of the story it is night, and Curtis finally encounters the blue man in his entirety, whose eyes "express the fulfilled longing of half a

life." Curtis loses himself even further right outside his house; he has slowly but surely been transformed into his own ghost.

It is the skilful alternation of the main characters' internal and external lives, the juxtaposition of his/her memories and current encounters that gives Parkinson's work its depth. This is significantly enhanced by his language, which is sparse and cutting, yet also metaphoric, elliptical. Startling images emerge and fade as quickly as they come: "the seasons seemed to have merged together into a sort of blurry, heavy mass. She felt it on her shoulders, in her throat, pressing on her mind like a big, soft hand"; "But the black of her eyelids are him and she opens her eyes, falling into the kitchen"; "He had fallen from her inner eye."

Parkinson often tells of those who are insecure to begin with and who, in the course of the story, confront the very experiences, always internalized, that do most to damage their already weak psyches. One of the most powerful negative events that can crack the mind is sexual violence, a common theme in Parkinson's writing. For him there is little if any respite in physical intimacy from life's constant barrage. Whatever physical closeness there is usually engenders greater distress. In "Mistaken Identity" Francine is raped, yet remembering with great longing the much gentler ministrations of her long-divorced ex-husband, awaits the second coming of her assailant with nervous anticipation. The rapist has killed three of his other victims; having survived with bruised arms, Francine convinces herself he means her no harm. When at last he comes to her again, the brutality of his attack convinces her of his apathetic rage. Left with a "streaming body," she calls her neighbour.

Similarly, in "The Tiger Returns to the Mountain" the Tiger Man, a feral rapist, terrorizes the area that includes Molly's neighbourhood. But remembering Carl, her virile, drug-dealing ex-lover, Molly visualizes the Tiger Man's visit with perverse fascination. His arrival occasions in her a mixture of fear and tentative desire that evolves into a lust-revulsion, culminating in both copulation and the animal man's death from Molly's surprise attack. But her encounters have not ended; in fact, after a subsequent accidental rendezvous with an impostor Tiger Man whom she also dispatches, a plunge into surrounding woods brings her to a third man, unnamed and by implication, threatening. Molly's strongest longings cannot help but result in a never-ending sequence of sexually rewarding yet obviously dangerous meetings. And in "The Sex Club" the narrator, given a ticket to the eponymous establishment by a dying man he tried to save from a colliding car, goes to the place where he finds a number of rooms enclosing various bizarre homoerotic, sometimes violent scenarios, enacted by one or more men. Moving through them with the flat emotional superficiality of blind lust, he leaves and meets the first man, supposedly dead from a car accident. In actuality, the accident was staged to make more intense the next voyeur's interest. Though the narrator does not seem to suffer any collapse of identity, his inability to experience emotional depth of any kind brands him none too vaguely as the shell of a human being, someone whose empty heart confines him to permanent isolation.

But it is in *The Man Upstairs*, Parkinson's novel, that the themes of brutal sexuality and disintegration of personality most dramatically collide, with telling results. The narrator, Michael West, divorced, lives in a San Francisco apartment building. When the quarrelsome couple above him moves out, they are replaced by Dr. Paul Marks, a wealthy plastic surgeon. Within a short time, West realizes his upstairs neighbour is enjoying the favours of several women—some from the building, some not. But more is going on than sex alone; West hears other sounds indicating rough play. Driven to discover Marks's activities, West repeatedly hauls himself up to the surgeon's balcony where he typically finds his neighbour engaged in brutal sex. The man's enormous penis excites and disturbs West, who eventually finds himself in Marks's apartment alone with the other man. And then it is that West lets himself be penetrated by the surgeon, who seems to take pleasure only in his conquest of his downstairs neighbour.

West is initially portrayed as insecure; the author's tell-tale subtle indicators make known his narrator's weakness. But following his sexual encounter with Marks, West begins to see another self of his in the mirror, or in the building's swimming pool. West's dog is murdered, as are another neighbour's young son and a female neighbour West and Marks both have had sex with. Evidence seems to indicate Marks is the likely murderer, but when Marks himself is killed, having been stabbed with West's large knife, it's not clear who the murderer really is. The conclusion of the novel finds West's mirror-self assuming West's identity, with the distinct implication that not only has his individuality fragmented, but, more insidiously, that because of psychic decay, some nameless evil entity has been transferred from Marks to West.

Were Terry Parkinson still alive, it's more than likely that his finely honed, dark-edged writing would find a growing audience. His death cut short a voice notable for its incisive view of the mortality all of us know, that makes us reach for what lives just over the edge of outwardly accepted life. He knew what happens when we fall into ourselves.

—Lawrence Greenberg

PARTRIDGE, Norman

Nationality: American. **Born:** 1958. **Career:** Has worked in a library and in a steel mill; contributor to many small-press magazines and anthologies. **Awards:** Horror Writers of America Bram Stoker Award for collection, 1993. Lives in Lafayette, California.

HORROR, GHOST AND GOTHIC PUBLICATIONS

Novel

Slipping into Darkness. Baltimore, Maryland, CD Publications, 1994.
Saquaro Riptide. Berkley, 1997.
Ten Ounce Siesta. Berkley, 1998.

Short Stories

Mr. Fox and Other Feral Tales. Arvada, Colorado, Roadkill Press, 1992.
The Bars on Satan's Jailhouse. Arvada, Colorado, Roadkill Press, 1995.
Bad Intentions. Subterranean Press, 1996.

Graphic Novel

Gorilla Gunslinger: The Good, the Bad . . . and the Gorilla, with Marc Erickson. N.p., n.d.

Other

Editor, with Martin H. Greenberg. *It Came from the Drive-In.* New York, DAW, 1996.

* * *

Norman Partridge is one of those rare writers who can take the physical world, distort it through a literary lens of their own contriving, and present it to his readers so convincingly that the most absurd events seem plausible. His settings frequently suggest black-and-white movies of years past, but with darker themes, and much of his horror fiction avoids supernatural or other fantastic content. When something supernatural *is* taking place, it rarely takes a conventional form. In "The Bars on Satan's Jailhouse," for example, one of the major characters is half-coyote and the entire atmosphere is a kind of dreamlike version of our world, a knack that was apparent from Partridge's very early stories like "Guignoir," where a second-rate carnival type takes the wheel of a car once owned by a depraved and insane serial killer. In fact in many cases, such as "Mr. Fox," it isn't even clear on a purely narrative level what is happening; more is implied by tone and implication than is actually revealed.

Although most of his stories are style-intensive, Partridge writes more straightforward narrative as well, often drawing inspiration from the horror films of the 1950s, but elevating their devices and images to a new level. In "The Baddest Son of a Bitch in the House," for example, a very full-of-himself criminal discovers that he's a relative amateur compared to supernatural evil. Partridge can take all-too-familiar plot devices—like the cult of satanists in "Black Leather Kites"—and transform them into new creations filled with vivid imagery. Even when his settings are clearly a kind of alternate America, as for example his recurring imaginary town of Fiddler, California, in "Save the Last Dance for Me," they retain a sense of reality that prevents the reader from feeling a safe sense of distance. "Styx" is a ghost story, but Partridge twists the cliches of that form completely around.

Partridge's horrors are generally subtle ones. A lifeguard in "Vessels" is haunted by a failure from his past when confronted with the possibility that he is witnessing another drowning in a dangerous quarry. A small-town sheriff in "Johnny Halloween" reveals a dark secret from his youth and kills a man to keep it from surfacing. But in other cases they're visceral and effective. Zombies walk the earth, for example, in "In Beauty, Like the Night," but while Partridge is clearly nodding to George Romero's films he imbues his story with a thoughtful intensity that raises it above the level of a simple homage. There's a costume party to which everyone is supposed to come as a deceased star in "Dead Celebs," but there's a darker secret in the cupboard upstairs. An unscrupulous man invades the privacy of a house where a prominent writer died in "Bad Intentions," and gets caught up in the madness surrounding his family. A woman burns her violent, enraged husband to death in his car in "Tyrannosaurus," unaware that her son is trapped in the trunk.

One of his most chillingly effective stories is "Wrong Side of the Road," wherein a disabled veteran sets off on a ghoulish visit to the graves of his fellows who died, seeking parts of his own personality which he has somehow left with them. A demonic gunfighter with boots made of living bats fights to retrieve his stolen hand from an ambitious witch and her outlaw assistants in "Dead Man's Hand." "Apotopaics" is an unconventional handling of an otherwise very familiar vampire story. Vampires are featured again in "Undead Origami" and "Do Not Hasten to Bid Me Adieu," werewolves in "The Pack," and the Frankenstein story in "The Man with Barbed Wire Fists," but in each case Partridge creates his own unique visions.

"'59 Frankenstein," which Partridge wrote for the anthology he edited, *It Came from the Drive-In*, provides what might have happened had someone done a crossover between teen-rebel movies and Universal Studios' horror. Hot rods, teens and dark magic mix in "She's My Witch," when an unpopular girl who believes in the supernatural raises a murdered boy from his grave to be her boyfriend. Other stories worth noting include "Eighty-Eight Sins," "The Cut Man," "Candy Bars for Elvis," "Cosmos," "How Naethen Learned to See," "Harvest," "Spyder" and "Those Kids Again." Partridge is a conscious stylist whose use of the supernatural is almost incidental much of the time, because the darker horrors are entirely plausible. Although his first novel, *Slippin' into Darkness*, was well received, it is as a writer of short stories that he is most likely to be remembered because his style seems best suited for short, penetrating insights into the human, and inhuman, condition.

—Don D'Ammassa

PICCIRILLI, Tom

Nationality: American. **Born:** Thomas Edward Piccirilli, in New York, 27 May 1965. **Education:** Suffolk Community College, A.A. 1985; Hofstra University, B.A. 1987. **Career:** Publisher's reader, Baen Books, New York; co-editor, *Pirate Writings* magazine; fiction editor, *Epitaph* and *Space & Time* magazines; book reviewer, *Mystery News*, *Horror* magazine, *New York Review of Science Fiction* and Barnes & Noble website. **Awards:** *Deathrealm* award for collection, 1995. **Address:** 1529 Baldwin Boulevard, Bay Shore, NY 11706, USA.

HORROR, GHOST AND GOTHIC PUBLICATIONS

Novels

Dark Father. New York, Pocket, 1990.
Shards. Aurora, Colorado, Write Way, 1996.
Hexes. Forthcoming.

Short Stories

Pentacle. Brightwaters, New York, Pirate Writings, 1995.
The Hanging Man & Other Strange Suspensions. Greenfield, Massachusetts, Wilder, 1996.
Inside the Works, with Edward Lee and Gerard Houarner. Orlando, Florida, Necro, 1997.
The Dog Syndrome & Other Sick Puppies. Marietta, Georgia, Dark Dixie, 1997.

OTHER PUBLICATIONS

Novel

The Dead Past. Aurora, Colorado, Write Way, 1997.

*

Tom Piccirilli comments:

Dark fiction, whether you're dealing with demons out of mythology or ones of the mind, has a common ground. Some people like tales that are fundamentally based in reality while others enjoy fantastical works. The two avenues aren't so much opposite ends of each other as they are different routes to the same sense of terror. That's what the end product should be. Nightmare is nightmare, so long as you can impress action and fear on the reader. Wit is always important. Nothing underscores an honest emotion as much as wit. Whether you're writing a love scene or raising the devil, a sense of humor can contrast the situation and bring it further to life. Besides, people like to laugh, especially at tense moments.

I don't believe lovers of horror fiction will ever be anesthetized to works that do more than splash viscera or nail body-parts to the ceiling. Don't misunderstand me: there's a place for all avenues of profane, blood-flecked shadows and vulgarity in the industry, so long as it is evocative as well as provocative. A well-told story that provides chills and leaves the reader with a genuine sense of the eerie or horrifying will always be sought after by someone. It's human nature to pursue thrills, to step as close to the edge as possible without going over. The most disturbing fiction centers on the mind, and how it does or doesn't function when you're alone at night. Failure, I think, is the greatest horror of all, and that's ultimately what I write about.

*   *   *

As a writer, as an editor, and as a reviewer, Tom Piccirilli has become one of the major forces in small-press horror fiction. His novel *Hexes* is due out soon from a major publisher, and it will likely show the larger public what the small-press audience already knows: that Tom Piccirilli is a serious talent. Few writers have a broader knowledge or love of the horror genre, and almost none have done as much to test—and ultimately expand—its boundaries.

Dark Father, Piccirilli's first novel, is a sprawling book which takes on nothing less than the nature of good and evil—not to mention the destruction of an entire town in the process. If the novel sometimes fails in its execution, it is never for lack of trying, and as Piccirilli has since shown, it was only a matter of time before his talent caught up to his ambition.

At the centre of *Dark Father* are the characters Samuel and Daniel, twins and orphans who share a sprawling mansion in the quaint town of Gallows. Their mother has died and they've never known their father, although it quickly becomes apparent that a macabre family reunion is just part of what Dad has in mind.

The brothers are immediately cast as polar opposites, with Samuel as the wild and dangerous one and Daniel as the level-headed one. Daniel knows he must watch out for Samuel's welfare (it was his mother's dying wish), but as Samuel gets involved with demonic forces, Daniel finds that there's little he can do. Besides, Daniel has distractions of his own, namely the beautiful hitchhiker, Laurie.

Intercut with the brothers' story are the supernatural experiences of various townspeople as the devil wreaks havoc on Gallows. Although Piccirilli paints a broad and colourful canvas, he has trouble giving clear definition to some of his many characters. A few scenes, however, show how skilful Piccirilli can be. In one, a couple faces the difficult task of telling their son that his beloved dog Ace has died. Adding to their dilemma is the disappearance of Ace's body. Finally, the father decides that he can't deceive his son any longer, but when he tells him about the dog's death, the boy replies, "But I gave Ace a bath this morning." The combination of the parent's dilemma, and the chilling punchline, make the scene eerily effective.

The strongest aspect of the novel is the developing relationship between Daniel and Laurie. Although their immediate attraction is believable, their instant conviction that they are meant for each other seems more literary invention than genuine emotion. But the exchanges between the young couple, and their struggle to find an identity for themselves, feel all too real. In the end, however, the bond of love forged between Daniel and Laurie can't overpower the blood ties that exist between him and Samuel. In *Dark Father*, Piccirilli's attempts to take on religion, morality, and the afterlife are either too heavy-handed or else too obtuse. Five years later, however, he explores many of the same issues with a more subtle approach and the ideal vehicle: the Self series.

The volume entitled *Pentacle* forms the backbone of the Self series, collecting the first five tales which chronicle a nameless necromancer and his demon familiar Self. In the opening story, "Neverdead," the necromancer and Self find themselves behind bars. They must not only escape from jail, but they've got to defeat the demon which is worshipped by the local townspeople. They accomplish their mission, of course, and do it with wit and cleverness to spare.

In "Bury St. Edmonds," the duo follow a bus full of dead children into the town of Walkerwood, Oregon. As they try to figure out what's going on, they rent a room from a family whose members aren't what they seem. Soon the necromancer and Self are facing off against a centuries-old witch, and it seems their only chance to survive is to kill an innocent woman. Self argues for survival at any cost, but the necromancer is desperate to save himself and the woman. He does, but the tension between him and his familiar continues to grow.

In "Maleficia," the supernatural adventurers find themselves in New York City. Or, to be more precise, in the area known as Hell's Kitchen. Here they must determine whether the evil that surrounds them is garden-variety New York darkness or something more sinister. In "Paindance," the necromancer travels into the world of Native American legends.

In "Eyebiting and Other Displays of Affection," the collection's final story, Piccirilli really flexes his writing muscle, giving us a chilling confrontation between darkness and light. The necromancer and Self arrive in the town of Summerfell, where they face Matthew Hopkins, England's 17th-century witchfinder general. Hopkins has turned the local mental hospital into a modern-day witch-prison where he acts as judge, jury and executioner. The necromancer defeats Hopkins, but it takes everything he has. Brought to the brink of death, he knows that Self is the only one who can save him. Suddenly, however, he realizes that their rela-

tionship has changed: he can no longer define who is the master and who is the servant, just as it's impossible to pinpoint which of them is good and which is evil.

The stories in *Pentacle* are both lyrical and lean. Here Piccirilli perfects his unique blend of horror and suspense. His monsters are as fearsome as anything devised by H. P. Lovecraft, but his fast pacing and sharp dialogue call to mind James Cain or Jim Thompson. So much horror fiction now deals with the horrific invading the ordinary, but Piccirilli shows us a different world. Here the ordinary is a thin facade; he peels it away, revealing the darkness that lies beneath.

Tom Piccirilli proves equally adept at depicting the harsh realities of life with only the faintest hint of the unknown. In his novel *Shards* he tips the balance away from the supernatural and towards the psychological, telling the story of writer Nathaniel Follows and his ill-fated love affair with the beautiful Susan Hartford. When Follows breaks up with his girlfriend, he goes to the end of Long Island—and seemingly, the end of the world—to look for answers. Instead, he finds Susan, a woman even more tortured than he is.

After a night of masochistic sex, Susan invites him to a birthday party at her lavish mansion. Then, apparently only opening a window, she promptly jumps to her death—thus opening the window onto a mystery that Follows feels compelled to solve. Although the convention of a mystery writer working on a real-life case isn't new, Follows is more than just another amateur private eye. He must deal with his own buried past even as he tries to uncover Susan's. The path of discovery is littered with realistic evils—pornography, drug abuse and murder—but Follows's journey is underlaid with a sense of dark mysticism. At times, his rage is described as an almost palpable presence that calls to mind the Self character; the ghosts that haunt him are only the aftereffects of violence and pain, but they too are almost physical manifestations. One feels that the world Follows inhabits is no different than the one in which the necromancer and Self operate; all these character's lives are filled with equal parts good and evil, and nowhere are these forces more powerful than inside themselves.

—Adam Meyer

PIKE, Christopher

Pseudonym of Kevin Christopher McFadden. **Nationality:** American. **Born:** 1961(?). **Career:** Worked as a computer programmer and house-painter, and in a factory; latterly a writer of novels for both young and adult readers. **Agent:** Joe Rinaldi, St. Martin's Press Publicity Department, 175 Fifth Avenue, New York, NY 10010, USA. Lives in Los Angeles.

HORROR, GHOST AND GOTHIC PUBLICATIONS

Novels

The Season of Passage. New York, Tor, 1992; London, New English Library, 1994.
The Listeners. New York, Tor, and London, New English Library, 1994.

The Cold One. New York, Tor, and London, New English Library, 1995.

Novels for Young Adults (series: Chain Letter; Final Friends; The Last Vampire; Remember Me; Spooksville)

Slumber Party. New York, Scholastic, 1985; London, Hodder and Stoughton, 1990.
Chain Letter. New York, Avon, 1986; London, Hodder and Stoughton, 1989.
Getting Even. London, Hippo, 1986.
Weekend. New York, Scholastic, 1986; London, Hodder and Stoughton, 1990.
Thrills, Chills, and Nightmares. New York, Scholastic, 1987.
Last Act. New York, Archway, 1988; London, Hodder and Stoughton, 1989.
Spellbound. New York, Archway, 1988; London, Hodder and Stoughton, 1989.
The Party (Final Friends). New York, Archway, 1989; London, Hodder and Stoughton, 1991.
The Dance (Final Friends). New York, Archway, 1989; London, Hodder and Stoughton, 1991.
The Graduation (Final Friends). New York, Archway, 1989; London, Hodder and Stoughton, 1991.
Gimme a Kiss. New York, Archway, 1989; London, Hodder and Stoughton, 1991.
Remember Me. New York, Archway, 1989; London, Hodder and Stoughton, 1990.
Scavenger Hunt. New York, Archway, 1989; London, Hodder and Stoughton, 1991.
Fall Into Darkness. New York, Archway, 1990; London, Hodder and Stoughton, 1991.
See You Later. New York, Archway, 1990; London, Hodder and Stoughton, 1992.
Witch. New York, Archway, 1990; London, Hodder and Stoughton, 1992.
Bury Me Deep. New York, Archway, 1991; London, Hodder and Stoughton, 1993.
Die Softly. New York, Archway, 1991; London, Hodder and Stoughton, 1993.
Whisper of Death. New York, Archway, 1991; London, Hodder and Stoughton, 1993.
Chain Letter 2: The Ancient Evil. New York, Archway, and London, Hodder and Stoughton, 1992.
Master of Murder. New York, Archway, 1992; London, Hodder and Stoughton, 1993.
Monster. New York, Archway, 1992; London, Hodder and Stoughton.
Road to Nowhere. New York, Archway, and London, Hodder and Stoughton, 1993.
The Eternal Enemy. New York, Archway, and London, Hodder and Stoughton, 1993.
The Immortal. New York, Archway, and London, Hodder and Stoughton, 1993.
Chained Together. London, Hodder and Stoughton, 1994.
The Last Vampire. New York, Archway, and London, Hodder and Stoughton, 1994.
The Last Vampire 2: Black Blood. New York, Archway, 1994; London, Hodder and Stoughton, 1995.
The Midnight Club. London, Hodder and Stoughton, 1994.
Remember Me 2: The Return. New York, Archway, 1994; London, Hodder and Stoughton, 1995.

The Wicked Heart. London, Hodder and Stoughton, 1994.
The Last Vampire. 3: Red Dice. New York, Archway, and London, Hodder and Stoughton, 1995.
The Lost Mind. New York, Archway, 1995; London, Hodder and Stoughton, 1996.
Remember Me 3: The Last Story. New York, Archway, and London, Hodder and Stoughton, 1995.
The Visitor. New York, Archway, 1995; London, Hodder and Stoughton, 1996.
The Haunted Cave (Spooksville). London, Hodder and Stoughton, 1995.
Aliens in the Sky (Spooksville). London, Hodder and Stoughton, 1996.
Cold People (Spooksville). London, Hodder and Stoughton, 1996.
The Dark Corner (Spooksville). London, Hodder Headline, 1996.
The Deadly Past (Spooksville). London, Hodder and Stoughton, 1996.
The Hidden Beast (Spooksville). London, Hodder and Stoughton, 1996.
The Howling Ghost (Spooksville). London, Hodder and Stoughton, 1996.
The Secret Path (Spooksville). London, Hodder and Stoughton, 1996.
The Wicked Cat (Spooksville). London, Hodder and Stoughton, 1996.
The Wishing Stone (Spooksville). London, Hodder and Stoughton, 1996.
The Witch's Revenge (Spooksville). New York, Archway, 1995; London, Hodder and Stoughton, 1996.
The Last Vampire 4: Phantom. London, Hodder and Stoughton, 1996.
The Little People. London, Hodder and Stoughton, 1996.
Alien Invasion. London, Hodder and Stoughton, 1997.
Time Terror. London, Hodder and Stoughton, 1997.

OTHER PUBLICATIONS

Novels

The Tachyon Web. New York, Bantam, 1986.
Sati. New York, St. Martin's Press, 1990; London, Hodder and Stoughton, 1993.
The Starlight Crystal. New York, Archway, 1996.

*   *   *

"I don't think of myself as writing specifically a young-adult book; I try to write just a good book that has young adult characters."

So said Christopher Pike in an interview in *Fear* magazine in 1989. Although it seems like a simple and innocent statement to make, it perhaps goes some way to explaining the phenomenal success that Pike has had as a writer of horror fiction for children and teenagers. The key word is *respect*: Pike respects the young adults who read his books, and it shows. This has reaped the obvious rewards: the sheer volume of space alone that is needed to list completely all of Pike's novels tells the tale of an extremely prolific author; and it is highly likely that he is currently one of the most successful writers for young adults still working. Often the packaging on the novel will have simply the word PIKE on the spine, cover and title page in very big letters, like a logo. This writer is now so popular that not even the acknowledgement of the forename is always deemed necessary. Christopher Pike often has his own section in the children's libraries.

Christopher Pike writes novels in which children and teenagers are the stars, but one of the secrets to his success is that he does not water down his material for his younger audience. Naturally, he does not write graphic scenes of violence and sex, or he would not be published in the way that he is. But violence and sex figure. Pike proposes a sort of alternative world (or a set of alternative worlds, his books having many different slants on modern-day teenaged life) in which children are the adults; as such they must be expected to understand the ways of the world—and violence and sex are ingredients. Pike explores the feelings, secrets and morals of young adults who are suddenly forced to do a lot of growing up very quickly. "I think one of the difficulties with the young adult market is—and this may sound arrogant and I don't mean it to—that most of the books are dumb," Pike went on to say in the same *Fear* interview. "They don't treat teenagers as if they are intelligent."

None of which is to say that adults cannot enjoy the books too. Children's books in general are more tightly plotted than their adult equivalents, their sense of pace often better, with their authors less likely to try to splash their opinions and philosophies willy-nilly on the page. Pike delivers tight, informed prose, and the messages are there only if we want to read them into the work. In the *Last Vampire* series, for example, Pike has clearly identified a source of teenaged angst; and in turning the tale to the supernatural he makes a creation all of his own. One of the principle themes of the *Last Vampire* series is loneliness; perhaps iconoclasm. A lonely female vampire, adrift in contemporary America: we see a hostile and unforgiving world through her eyes, even though (in truth) she has had plenty of time to get used to it: she is much, much older than her outward appearance would have her victims and enemies believe.

Alisa is the vampire's name. Showing freely to the younger audience the principles of sexual equality (or of what has become known as Girl Power), it is Alisa who seduces a religious teacher-figure and not the other way around; he resists at first, but to no end. With this Pike plays off against stereotypical teenage girl fantasies of the attractive teacher paying more than is customary attention—he takes the idea to its logical metaphorical conclusion. The fact that here the seducee is a religious type is important in that it shows off Alisa's winning way with anybody. Pike writes of adolescent yearning and first sexual encounters in a way that eschews smut but leaves the reader in no doubt. In *The Visitor* a girl misses her dead boyfriend so much that she is prepared to take part in a group session with an ouija board; what follows is not even close to what she had in mind. Yet after these infrequent nudges and winks to hint at teenaged sex, there are stern warnings, as might be expected. In one concise sentence in *The Last Vampire 3: Red Dice* Pike phrases it perfectly when he writes: "Mother Nature gives each age its own special horror."

Christopher Pike seems to enjoy the occasional name-check of one of his sources or inspirations. A reference to the *Aliens* movies makes a contact point with teenage popular culture; for the reader it is a reality-check, a buzzword; it gives the story a place in time. Pike even confesses to choosing his pseudonymous surname after the first captain of the *Starship Enterprise* (his pseudonymous forename Christopher simply being his real middle name).

In the third of the *Last Vampire* novels comes one of the more

blatant acknowledgments, albeit in the form of a play for sympathy: "One of the saddest stories told in modern literature . . . is Mary Shelley's *Frankenstein*. Because in a sense I am that monster. . . the primeval fear, something dead come to life . . . something that refuses to die." But is Alisa evil? She is certainly given to spells of tragic introspection ("The endless slaughter weighs heavily on me," Alisa sighs), and she cannot be without the occasional drop of blood: but do these things, in the eyes of the book, make her evil? In the way in which she is constantly pursued we encounter the theme of false persecution—a clear analogy for any sort of unfair treatment that any number of young adults believe themselves to be unwitting players in; a classic example of this might be simple playground bullying. Vampires are different, not bad; not everyone is made the same or looks the same, the message runs, but that does not make them unpleasant people. In *The Wicked Heart* Pike even goes as far as to rake up some sympathy for a high-school senior who is also a part-time serial killer. Having murdered three women, he has several more lined up. But it is not his fault: he is being compelled to do it by the secret of the Wicked Heart. (Quite what messages might be read into such a scenario would make for a very interesting discussion.)

The Last Vampire 4: Phantom has Alisa waking up thinking of her old ancient self, Sita, only to find that she has actually become human. A wound she receives does not immediately heal; her tears "are salty and clear, not dark and bloody." Despite the odds stacked against you, situations can be altered. Alisa weighs up her sense of loneliness and her need to trust somebody again, with the fear of being betrayed once more. This novel affirms the elasticity of the human spirit. There is a loud cheer to be heard when Alisa, a human now, is confronted by two drunken good old boys who decide to show her what a good time is made of. Unflinchingly the militant feminist Alisa comments that vampire or no, she is "still a master of martial arts. . . . Yet, I usually do not kill when I have the upper hand. I do not kill for pleasure. But I know these two will harm others in the future, and therefore it is better that they die now."

The Last Vampire 4 sees the love of Alisa's life return, also no longer a vampire; together, like two reformed drug addicts or alcoholics, they have emerged from their respective fugue states and are ready, finally, to settle down together to have a child. Alisa is content with an average house, a second-hand car, and local, regular grocery shopping. In fact, more than content: "I have lived five thousand years to do all these things," she remarks.

Christopher Pike once said, "I don't think I'm a great writer, but I think I've become a good storyteller. I'm a sucker for a good story myself. I love science fiction, particularly if it's a good story, I love horror, I can get into a good love story. . . ." Such a diverse appreciation of the genres can only be healthy for a writer, not least when all of them appear variously in that author's work. More important, perhaps, is that a respectable pride in one's work without a sense of big-headedness will, with luck, keep Christopher Pike striving harder and harder to please his readership, instead of getting lazy with his success.

—David Mathew

POE, Edgar Allan

Nationality: American. **Born:** Boston, Massachusetts, 19 January 1809. **Education:** Attended private schools, 1815-20; University of Virginia, 1826, dismissed, 1826; West Point, 1829-30, dismissed, 1830. **Military Service:** U.S. Army (enlisted under assumed name and age), 1827-29; sergeant-major. **Family:** Married Virginia Clemm (died 1847). **Career:** Editor, *Southern Literary Messenger,* Richmond, Virginia, 1835-37; assistant editor, *Burton's Gentleman's Magazine,* 1839-40; founded *The Penn,* 1840; editor, *Graham's Magazine,* 1842-43; purchased *Broadway Journal,* 1845; cancelled lecture tour due to nervous breakdown, 1849. **Died:** 7 October 1849.

HORROR, GHOST AND GOTHIC PUBLICATIONS

Novel

The Narrative of Arthur Gordon Pym of Nantucket. New York, Harper, 1838; as *Arthur Gordon Pym; or, Shipwreck, Mutiny, and Famine,* London, Cunningham, 1841; as *The Wonderful Adventures of Arthur Gordon Pym,* London, Kent, 1861.

Short Stories

Tales of the Grotesque and Arabesque. Philadelphia, Pennsylvania, Lea and Blanchard, 2 vols., 1840.
The Prose Romances of Edgar A. Poe, No. 1, Containing the Murders in the Rue Morgue, and The Man That Was Used Up. Philadelphia, Graham, 1843.
Tales by Edgar A. Poe. New York and London, Wiley and Putnam, 1845.
The Works of the Late Edgar Allan Poe, with A Memoir by Rufus Wilmot Griswold and Notices of His Life and Genius by N. P. Willis and J. R. Lowell, edited by Rufus Wilmot Griswold. New York, Redfield, 4 vols., 1850-56.
The Complete Tales and Poems of Edgar Allan Poe. New York, Modern Library, 1938.
The Short Fiction of Edgar Allan Poe: An Annotated Edition, edited by Stuart Levine and Susan Levine. Indianapolis, Indiana, Bobbs Merrill, 1976.

(Note: Although several hundred different collections of Poe's poetry and prose have been published, all are variations of the earliest volumes published during his lifetime. All of these works are collected into the 1938 omnibus listed above.)

*

Film Adaptations (selection): *The Fall of the House of Usher,* 1928, 1949, 1960, 1982 (TV movie), 1988; *The Murders in the Rue Morgue,* 1932, 1954, 1971, 1986 (TV movie); *The Pit and the Pendulum,* 1961; *The Premature Burial,* 1963; *The Masque of the Red Death,* 1964; *The Tomb of Ligeia,* 1964.

Bibliography: *Edgar Allan Poe: A Bibliography of Criticism 1827-1967* by J. Lasley Dameron and Irby B. Cauthen, Jr., Charlottesville, University Press of Virginia, 1974; *Edgar Allan Poe: An Annotated Bibliography of Books and Articles in English, 1827-1973* by Esther K. Hyneman, Boston, Hall, 1974.

Manuscript Collections: University of Texas; Pierpont Morgan Library, New York; Free Library of Philadelphia; Henry E. Huntington Library and Art Gallery, San Marino, California; Indiana University; New York Public Library; University of Virginia; Enoch

Pratt Free Library, Baltimore; Poe Foundation, Richmond; Boston Public Library; Library of Congress; Columbia University Libraries; Duke University Library; Yale University.

Critical Studies (selection): *Edgar Allan Poe: The Man Behind the Legend* by Edward Wagenknecht, New York, Oxford University Press, 1963; *Poe the Detective: The Curious Circumstances Behind "The Mystery of Marie Roget"* by John Walsh, New Brunswick, New Jersey, Rutgers University Press, 1968; *Poe Poe Poe Poe Poe* by Daniel Hoffman, 1973; *The Edgar Allan Poe Scrapbook* edited by Peter Haining, New York, Schocken, 1977; *The Extraordinary Mr. Poe* by Wolf Mankowitz, London, Weidenfeld and Nicolson, 1978; *The Tell-Tale Heart: The Life and Works of Edgar Allan Poe* by Julian Symons, New York, Harper, and London, Faber, 1978; *The Rationale of Deception in Poe* by David Ketterer, Baton Rouge, Louisiana State University Press, 1979; *The Sign of Three: Dupin, Holmes, Pierce* edited by Umberto Eco and Thomas A. Sebeok, Indiana University Press, 1984; *Critical Essays on Edgar Allan Poe* edited by Eric Carlson, Boston, Hall, 1987; *Edgar Allan Poe: Mournful and Never-Ending Remembrance* by Kenneth Silverman, London, HarperCollins, 1991; *Edgar Allan Poe: His Life and Legacy* by Jeffrey Meyers, London, John Murray, 1992.

*   *   *

Edgar Allan Poe was less prolific and less popular in his native land than his contemporary Nathaniel Hawthorne, in company with whom he laid the groundwork for American supernatural fiction. He was, however, much more versatile than Hawthorne and markedly more adventurous; although the externalization of conscience played a major part in his works his imagination was never anchored by narrowly Puritan concerns and its roaming allowed him to explore and extend the stylistic and thematic boundaries of the genre with a flamboyance that has never been surpassed. Although Poe has always been regarded with a certain critical disdain in America and England, his reputation has been much higher in France. The translations of his works by Charles Baudelaire became key exemplars for all late-19th century French writers of supernatural fiction, but his influence in America was relatively slight until French-influenced writers like Ambrose Bierce and Robert W. Chambers took up the torch and handed it on to writers of the Lovecraft school.

Poe's only novel—whose text breaks off abruptly, although critical opinion is divided as to whether it is incomplete—employs a marine odyssey aboard whaling and sealing ships as a bleak allegory of human endeavour, much as Mary Shelley had done in the frame-narrative of *Frankenstein* and Herman Melville was later to do in *Moby-Dick.* After a due ration of storm and stress, thirst and cannibalism, however, the luckless Pym passes beyond the known hazards of Antarctic exploration, visiting the exotic island of Tsalal before proceeding towards a polar rendezvous with an enigmatic white-shrouded giant. The significance of this climax has been much debated, some commentators linking it to John Cleve Symmes' theory that the earth is hollow and that openings to the interior layers are to be found at the poles. Jules Verne's continuation of the story, usually known in translation as *The Sphinx of the Ice-Fields,* provides a science-fictional "explanation" but Poe would probably have liked H. P. Lovecraft's *At the Mountains of Madness* far better, and would surely have loved Rudy Rucker's "substitute text" *The Hollow Earth.*

Poe's best short pieces were first collected (with only a few first-rate exceptions) in *Tales of the Grotesque and Arabesque*; they were subsequently reissued in countless selections and editions of his *Collected Works*. Several of them feature the descendants of aristocratic families who have become prone to various kinds of physical and mental enfeeblement by virtue of some kind of gradual hereditary degeneration. This image of the Decadent Aristocrat, the antiquity of whose noble ancestry is embodied in the stigmata of "neurasthenia"—the kind of madness which was, according to proto-psychologists like Lombroso, closely akin to and often inextricably blended with artistic genius—was to become a key figure in Decadent prose, taking the place of the Gothic villain in tales which dramatized the sublime hostility of existence itself rather than the evil of mere men.

Such individuals can be found in Poe's first-published story, "Metzengerstein" (1832), as well as his three lyrically bizarre *femme fatale* stories, "Berenice," "Morella" and "Ligeia," the far more nostalgic "Eleanora," and the most vividly exaggerated of all his tales, "The Fall of the House of Usher" (1839) and "The Masque of the Red Death" (1842). The last-named is an extended poem in prose which can also be placed in a set with the more abstract pieces "Shadow—a Parable" and "Silence—a Fable" and such verse works as "The Conqueror Worm" and "The Haunted Palace." Poe's characterization of the Decadent Aristocrat had an element of aspiration in it, most clearly expressed in the early pages of "The Murders in the Rue Morgue"; the exotic lifestyle adopted by C. Auguste Dupin was to be the parent of many subsequent literary blueprints—including those set out in Joris-Karl Huysmans' *A rebours* and M. P. Shiel's *Prince Zaleski*—as well as a few actual adventures in lifestyle fantasy.

A second group of Poe's tales includes those which feature, in graphically obsessive fashion, ominous or vengeful symbols of guilty conscience. These include "The Black Cat," "The Tell-Tale Heart" and the most effective of all doppelgänger stories, "William Wilson." The poem "The Raven" belongs to this group as well as the first, and the *contes cruels* "Hop-Frog," "The Pit and the Pendulum" and "The Cask of Amontillado" are dramas of ingenious and excessive punishment which are linked to the group by virtue of their paranoid intensity.

Much of the remainder of Poe's supernatural fiction is humorous, although the comedy is edged with blackness in such tales as "The Devil in the Belfry," "The Duc de l'Omelette," "Bon-Bon" and "Never Bet the Devil Your Head," all of which employ the Devil as an ironic figure of fun. There is, however, one further small subset of fantasies which is of considerable relevance to the subsequent evolution of horror fiction. This consists of visionary tales in quasi-scientific guise; its most famous inclusion is "The Facts in the Case of M. Valdemar," in which a mesmerized man is preserved from the decay which is supposed to follow death until released from his "trance," but "Mesmeric Revelation" is even more adventurous. The timeslip story "A Tale of the Ragged Mountains" also belongs to this group.

Poe's fiction takes it for granted that such traditional figures of menace as the Devil have been rendered impotent by the triumph of the rationalistic world-view of the Enlightenment, and that the apparatus of conventional superstition—ghosts, curses, vampires and so on—has been rendered irrelevant. (It is hardly surprising that these assumptions struck a more resounding chord in France, the home of the Encyclopedists and the philosophers of progress, than they did in America.) For Poe, horror could have only two sources: paranoia rooted in personal psychology, and the rapt contemplation of a cosmos so vast that it reduced all human endeavours to annihilating insignificance. The cosmos was, however, a source of wonder and inspiration as well as horror, as Poe set out to demonstrate in his visionary essay "Eureka!", which concluded by restoring an element of comfort to the supposed message of scientific enlightenment.

Death and the Conqueror Worm retained their domination over the empires of man, unameliorated by any plausible hope of salvation, but the worst horrors of all were, for Poe, those which brought damnation before death; his was essentially a psychosomatic theory of Hell. A damnation which men must visit upon themselves (and it is, in Poe, always men who visit damnation upon themselves, often employing visions and memories of women for the purposes of torment) is frankly perverse, and it was not only in "The Imp of the Perverse" that Poe freely acknowledged the essential perversity of his outlook. The development of that particular kind of ironic perversity has been the central quest of sophisticated horror fiction ever since Poe laid down its most significant precedents, and will probably continue to be for some time to come.

—Brian Stableford

POLIDORI, John (William)

Nationality: British. **Born:** London, 7 September 1795. **Education:** Edinburgh University, M.D. 1815 (wrote thesis on nightmares and somnambulism). **Career:** Physician to the poet Lord Byron, 1816; medical practitioner in Norwich, 1817. Suffered brain damage in a carriage accident. **Died:** August 1821 (possible suicide).

HORROR, GHOST AND GOTHIC PUBLICATIONS

Novel

Ernestus Berchtold; or, The Modern Oedipus. London, Longman Hurst, 1819.

Short Story

The Vampyre: A Tale. London, Sherwood Neely and Jones, 1819.

* * *

The short-lived John Polidori owes his fame to the accident of fate which placed him in the Villa Diodati in June 1816, in the company of Lord Byron, Mary Shelley, Mary Godwin and Claire Clairmont. Byron was already sick of him and he had retreated into a sulk, but he was there when they spent a rainy evening reading from *Fantasmagoriana* (a French translation of some German tales of terror) and improvising similar tales for themselves. He was party to the pact whereby they all agreed to write horror stories of their own, and—like Godwin—eventually followed through where Byron and Mary Shelley both failed. Polidori's first effort seems to have been abandoned, but he stuck to the task. He took inspiration from the fragment which Byron produced, based in the Greek folklore of vampirism, to write a tale of his own on the same theme, into which he poured all his bitter resentment against the man who had rejected him.

It is not clear whether Polidori intended to publish the tale at all, but one way or another it found its way to England and was published anonymously in the April 1819 issue of the *New Monthly Magazine*. In the absence of copyright protection it was widely pirated, many of the editions representing it as the work of Lord Byron—who, not unnaturally, deeply resented the implication that he could have penned such a deeply unflattering caricature of himself. It was the mis-attribution rather than any innate merit that guaranteed the tale wide circulation, and Byron's attempts to combat it—which went so far as to cause facsimiles of a handwritten letter of denial to be tipped into an edition of his collected works—only served to add further publicity to the scandal. Nor can Polidori have been pleased with the controversy, which directed public attention away from *Ernestus Berchtold*, whose subtitle implies that he was by that time more interested in following up Mary Shelley's "Modern Prometheus" than in paying back his one-time employer.

The idea of damning Byron by caricature was not Polidori's own; he had taken his inspiration from Lady Caroline Lamb's *Glenarvon*, even going so far as to borrow the protagonist's name, Lord Ruthven, from that book. *The Vampyre* tells the tale of a sensitive young man named Aubrey who is initially impressed by the charismatic Ruthven and gladly sets out to tour Europe with him, but becomes disillusioned with the older man's dissolute ways and breaks off the tour. He falls in love with a Greek girl but she is killed by a vampire and his delirious dreams associate the event with Ruthven. When Ruthven reappears, however, he consoles and reassures the grief-stricken Aubrey, and when he is wounded—apparently mortally—he makes Aubrey swear not to speak any ill of him for a year and a day. On returning home, Aubrey is astonished to find that his sister is engaged to be married to Ruthven, who now appears perfectly well, and the pressure of his inconvenient oath proves intolerable. It prevents him from revealing even to save his sister the dread secret of which he is now convinced—that she is destined to "glut the thirst of a VAMPYRE!"—and he dies of frustration.

The Vampyre is of negligible literary value in itself, but its influence has proved enormous. It was even more popular in France than in England, and the popularization of its central motif by Charles Nodier launched a tradition of highly erotic vampire tales that reached its apogee in Théophile Gautier's "La morte amoureuse," usually known in translation as "Clarimonde." The parallel English tradition was confined for some while to the stage and the lowest strata of the literary marketplace, but when the male vampire burst forth to new prominence in Bram Stoker's *Dracula* he retained many of the Byronic attributes grafted on to him by Polidori—attributes which eventually became key elements in the vampire's rehabilitation by the revisionist fantasies of the 1970s. Nor was the influence of Lord Ruthven confined entirely to vampire tales, for his Byronic attributes infected the many later specimens of the species of Gothic villains.

The eponymous hero of *Ernestus Berchtold* owes his surname to the priest who raises him, along with his twin sister Julia, after the death of their unidentified mother. When the priest dies Ernestus and Julia are taken in by Filberto Dori, whose son Olivieri has served in the army alongside Ernestus. Dori has made a Faustian bargain, whereby the money provided by his familiar must be paid for in pain, grief and loss. The implicit results of this bargain are that Olivieri seduces Julia—who subsequently dies in childbirth—before being arrested as a robber, while the luckless Ernestus's marriage to Olivieri's sister Louisa is ruined by the final revelation that the mother of the twins was Dori's lost wife. (The parallel with Oedipus is not pronounced, and Ernestus dos not feel any necessity to pluck out his eyes—although that would certainly have livened up the novel's excessively sanctimonious climax.)

Publication of *Ernestus Berchtold* failed to relieve the experiential and financial pressures which drove Polidori to likely suicide, but it is slightly surprising that the author's renewed celebrity has not caused it to be reprinted. The circumstances of *The Vampyre*'s production have now acquired a mythical status of their own, largely due to the awesome success of Mary Shelley's *Frankenstein*, although Polidori's problematic role within the myth has not worked to his advantage. The most striking of the modern works in which Polidori figures as a character are Ken Russell's movie *Gothic* (1986) and Tom Holland's novel *The Vampyre: Being the True Pilgrimage of George Gordon, Sixth Lord Byron* (1994), both of which show him in an exceedingly unflattering light. Any attempted redemption of his reputation would probably be too late.

—Brian Stableford

POPESCU, Petru (Demetru)

Nationality: American. **Born:** Romania, 1946(?). **Career:** Novelist and screenwriter, initially in his native Romania, and later in the United States; defected to the west in the mid-1970s (tried for treason *in absentia* by the Ceaucescu regime); has worked in Hollywood, and as a journalist around the world. **Address:** c/o William Morrow and Company, Inc., 1350 Avenue of the Americas, New York, NY 10019, USA.

HORROR, GHOST AND GOTHIC PUBLICATIONS

Novels

The Last Wave (novelization of screenplay). Sydney, Angus and Robertson, 1977; London, Arrow, 1978.
In Hot Blood. New York, Ballantine Fawcett, 1989.
Almost Adam. New York, Morrow, 1996.

Play

Screenplay: *The Last Wave*, with Peter Weir and Tony Morphett, 1977.

OTHER PUBLICATIONS

Novel

Before and After Edith. London, Quartet, 1978.

Other

Amazon Beaming. N.p., 1991(?).

*   *   *

The Last Wave is the novelization of a screenplay. Hence it is more filmic and rather less coherent than most novels tend to be. Popescu, who was one of the authors of the screenplay, seems inexperienced as a novelist, and the result is a patchily told story, uneven and in places unconvincing.

The story is set in Sydney, Australia, in about the present day, marginally in the future of the time when it was originally written. And at its heart is Aboriginal magic. This is unusual, sometimes very powerful, and is responsible for creating all the horror in the book. It is all the more striking because nearly all of it takes place not out in the bush, but in the streets and houses of a sophisticated city, whose inhabitants, by and large, do not believe in such things.

A young half-caste Aboriginal living in Sydney, Billy Corman, sneaks down into tribal caves immediately adjacent to railway tunnels and Sydney beach. He steals four carved stones which are important Aboriginal relics and whose images of dots and dashes indicate (among other things) the coming of a mighty flood. He has great expectations from the stones, though whether he hopes to sell them for money or to gain power from their possession is never made clear. He is found in a bar by five other young Aboriginals, who chase him outside. There, beside a building site, he sees an elderly white-haired Aboriginal point a finger at him, and he dies. This old man is Charlie, a tribal elder, the guardian of the caves. The police believe that Billy has been held down in a puddle and drowned by the other five, but the youths will say nothing except that they did not kill Billy.

David Burgess, a young solicitor, is persuaded to act for the five accused. He has no experience of Aboriginal affairs, but reads up on the subject, discovering that tribal law has sometimes led to uninitiated natives being killed for trespassing on secret tribal ceremonies or selling off sacred objects. The power of killing by magic is possessed by the guardians of sacred sites. Burgess gradually comes to believe that the five young men had nothing to do with Billy's death, and that Billy was killed for stealing the stones.

Around and between these mundane events is another strand of the story. Freak weather hits Sydney and other parts of Australia, with unseasonable heavy rain and hailstones. Burgess begins to have strange dreams involving a tidal wave and a great flood carrying away the bodies of people he knows. And, most supernatural of all, Chris Lee, one of the five accused, appears one night in Burgess's study. Chris is naked and holds out one of the carved stones found on Billy; then he disappears; and this occurs before Burgess has met Chris. Because Burgess is fascinated and a little scared by what is happening, and because Chris seems to be the most articulate of the group, he invites him over for an evening meal. When Chris arrives he has Charlie with him. In this way, Burgess becomes aware of Charlie's existence and is sure that Charlie has magical abilities.

From his dreams, his reading and his conversations with the five accused, Burgess realizes that they must not be convicted, because prison life will kill them. He takes over the job of defending them in court, although he is not a trained barrister, believing that his knowledge of their culture and of the truth behind Billy's death can be put across to the court. Even though Chris has no confidence in this approach, he suggests that Burgess is Mulkurul, the mythic archetypal protector of sacred sites, who possesses special powers and only appears at times of need.

There are tense courtroom scenes in which Burgess seems to be doing well, cross-examining witnesses and fighting off the prosecution. But he loses. The five are all found guilty of murder or manslaughter and given long prison sentences. In a melodramatic finale, Chris escapes from custody (with a bullet wound in his leg) and guides Burgess to the sacred caves before dying. There, Charlie welcomes Burgess as Mulkurul, but Burgess denies it and climbs back up to the beach in time to see the great wave "hundreds of feet high" sweep in to destroy the city.

The book is a curious blend of fantasy, horror and science fiction, as well as a novel which tries to make serious points about the situation of Aboriginals in Australia today. There is insufficient atmosphere to make the sudden appearances and disappearances horrific. And although the possibility of instant death from Charlie's abilities is often present, not enough is made of it for it be considered a threat. The best and most horrifying parts of the story are the dreams. Several times they seem real before achieving the surrealist nature of all dreams. And, in a world where most novels (especially those with handsome heroes) end happily, it comes as a pleasantly horrific change to encounter a truly downbeat ending.

Popescu's next horror novel, after a long gap, is *In Hot Blood*, which is concerned with vampires in and around New Orleans. It is also a romance and is far longer than it should be. The Lecouveurs are an old, aristocratic family of vampires, originally from Wallachia, who possess the ability to travel through time and are not as terminally bothered by sunlight as some of their literary predecessors. Unfortunately, Popescu concentrates on a less than convincing romantic triangle involving members of the family and does relatively little with his vampiric elements.

Equally over-long is *Almost Adam*, in which Popescu tries very hard to convince the reader that a species of pre-humans, Australopithecines, has survived unnoticed in a remote area of Kenya for more than a million years, into the present day. There are thriller aspects to the novel, though the amount of actual horror is fairly marginal.

—Chris Morgan

PRAED, Mrs. Campbell

Nationality: Australian. **Born:** Rosa Caroline Murray-Prior, in Bromelton, Queensland, 27 March 1851; daughter of a local politician. **Family:** Married Campbell Mackworth Praed in 1872 (died 1901); two sons and one daughter. **Career:** Moved to London with her family in 1876, and became a novelist and writer on Australian subjects; met the Irish writer and Member of Parliament Justin McCarthy in 1882, and collaborated with him on three novels, mainly on political themes; in later life lived with the spiritual medium Nancy Harward, who was the subject of her book *Nyria*. **Died:** 10 April 1935.

HORROR, GHOST AND GOTHIC PUBLICATIONS

Novels

Affinities: A Romance of To-day. London, Bentley, 2 vols., 1885.
The Brother of the Shadow: A Mystery of To-day. London, Routledge, 1886.
The Soul of Countess Adrian: A Romance. London, Trischler, 1891.

"As a Watch in the Night": A Drama of Waking and Dreaming in Five Acts. London, Chatto and Windus, 1901.
The Insane Root: A Romance of a Strange Country. London, Unwin, 1902.
The Body of His Desire: A Romance of the Soul. London, Cassell, 1912.
The Mystery Woman. London, Cassell, 1913.

OTHER PUBLICATIONS

Novels

An Australian Heroine. London, Chapman and Hall, 1880.
Policy and Passion. London, Chapman and Hall, 1881.
Nadine: The Study of a Woman. London, Chapman and Hall, 1882.
Zéro. London, Chapman and Hall, 1884.
The Head Station. London, Chapman and Hall, 1885.
The Right Honourable: A Romance of Society and Politics, with Justin McCarthy. London, Chatto and Windus, 1886.
The Bond of Wedlock. London, F.V. White, 1887.
The Ladies' Gallery, with Justin McCarthy. London, Bentley, and New York, Appleton, 1888.
The Rebel Rose, with Justin McCarthy. New York, Harper, 1888; as *The Rival Princess*, London, F.V. White, and New York, Lovell, 1890.
The Romance of a Station. London, Trischler, 1889.
December Roses. N.p., 1893.
Outlaw and Lawmaker. London, Chatto and Windus, 1893; New York, Appleton, 1894.
Christina Chard. London, Chatto and Windus, 1894.
Mrs. Tregaskiss. London, Chatto and Windus, 1895.
Nulma. London, Chatto and Windus, 1897.
The Scourge-Stick. London, Heinemann, 1898.
Fugitive Anne: A Romance of the Unexplored Bush. London, Long, 1902.
The Maid of the River. London, Long, 1905.
By Their Fruits. London, Cassell, 1908.
Lady Bridget in the Never-Never Land. London, Hutchison, 1915.

Other

Australian Life: Black and White. London, Chapman and Hall, 1885.
My Australian Girlhood. London, Unwin, 1902.
Nyria. London, Unwin, 1904; revised as *The Soul of Nyria*, London, Rider, 1931.

Editor, *Our Book of Memories: Letters of Justin McCarthy to Mrs. Campbell Praed.* London, Chatto and Windus, 1912.

*   *   *

Mrs. Praed came to England when she married in the 1870s. She was a prolific novelist, many of her early works being romances set in her native Australia. Once in England, however, she became a keen observer and chronicler of the London society into which she had been introduced, which she viewed with a certain degree of detachment. In particular, she developed a strong and credulous interest in the fashionable occultism of the day, which she soon began to incorporate into her novels. As is often the case with credulous occultists, Mrs. Praed failed to exploit the literary and melodramatic potential of supernatural apparatus and occult themes to any great effect, but she offers the modern reader a useful insight into the social context of late Victorian occultism and the brief infatuation of the upper classes with Theosophy, spiritualism, Eastern mysticism and reincarnation.

Nadine was the first of Mrs. Praed's novels to include a good deal of talk of paranormal phenomena and their possible explanation, but the apparitions included in the narrative are peripheral to the plot and the reader is free to interpret them as delusions. Her first wholehearted supernatural novel was *Affinities*, an account of the psychic domination of a vulnerable young woman by a decadent poet named Esme Colquhoun, who has learned black magic during a tour of America. Colquhoun is presumably based on Oscar Wilde (later to be parodied as Esme Amarinth in Robert Hichens's *The Green Carnation*), who had yet to hit his stride as a dramatist in 1885 and was some years short of his greatest fame. *Affinities* also features a female occultist modelled on Madame Blavatsky, whose ideas provided the basis for the much shorter but far more sensational *The Brother of the Shadow*. In the latter novel Lemuel Lloyd, a physician who specializes in the treatment of neurasthenic distress while dabbling in the occult, falls in love with the wife of a friend whose talents as a medium have attracted his attention. She makes contact with the spirit of an Egyptian black magician, who urges Lloyd to pursue his *amour*, but his attempt to use elemental spirits to murder her husband goes awry. The Riviera setting enables the plot to remain free from the drawing-room gossip which clutters most of Mrs. Praed's work, and the story is more readable in consequence.

The Soul of Countess Adrian and *The Insane Root* are both tales of personality-displacement. In the former novel Countess Adrian is an occultist *femme fatale* who has difficulty luring the hero away from a younger rival while she is still alive but enjoys greater success after her death, when her spirit possesses the girl. Evil is not allowed to triumph, although it requires a blatant *deus ex machina* to prevent it, the evil spirit being driven out by the altruistic Masters of the White Brotherhood. *The Insane Root* is more interesting, by virtue of its intriguingly confused morality. A magical mandrake allows the well-intentioned Dr. Marillier to displace the personality of an undeniably unworthy rival and marry the lovely ward of a diplomat from the Near East—but the disembodied spirit refuses to go quietly, and eventually succeeds in wrecking the marriage. *The Scourge-Stick* is a melodrama in much the same vein, incorporating a few "glimpses of the Other Side," but is more thriller than horror story.

"As a Watch in the Night" is another Theosophical romance, much more studied than *The Soul of Countess Adrian*. The heroine, an artist, continually dreams of a previous incarnation in the days of the Roman Empire. She learns from a guru who has allegedly been her guide throughout the ages that she is carrying some bad karma which must be paid off by virtuous self-sacrifice. Unfortunately for the plot, this mission is buried and almost lost in a dense tangle of social and romantic trivia. The story is only marginally relevant to the horror genre, and obviously drew upon the same sources of inspiration as the allegedly non-fictional "case-study" of a reincarnation, *Nyria*.

The Body of His Desire seems to have been an attempt by the aging Mrs. Praed to recover something of the narrative vigour of her early occult romances; it involves the temptation of an Anglican clergyman by a supernatural *femme fatale* and his recruitment of an occultist to help in her exorcism. The conclusion, in which the wayward spirit is converted to Christianity, is monumentally silly. *The Mystery Woman*, which begins on the first day of the new century, features an earthly *femme fatale* in the psychically talented Althea Stanmount, who turns out to harbour occult memories of the oracle at Delphi. Those prophetic powers, brought to fruition by a male mentor, come in handy in political as well as personal terms, helping to lift the ominous clouds of disaster gathering over Europe. Mrs. Praed's unfortunate lack of prophetic acumen in this particular respect was made painfully evident only a year later.

All Mrs. Praed's work suffers from the fact that she had too many irons in the fire. The occult, the personal and the political are all confusedly heaped together and the courses steered by her stories are hectically erratic. She was presumably one of those writers who make up their plots as they go along, and she was never reluctant to drop in any topic of interest which cropped up along the way, however irrelevant it might be. Unfortunately, the matters which happened to interest her could not be as uniformly interesting to the readers of her books, and it is probable that almost everyone could find something in them to annoy him (or, more likely, her). She was, however, capable of writing individual scenes with considerable verve and some effect, and her work does contain and communicate brief flashes of supernatural menace.

—Brian Stableford

PREST, Thomas Peckett

Pseudonym: Bos. **Nationality:** British. **Born:** 1810. **Career:** Prolific editor and writer of serials and part-works for Edward Lloyd and other publishers of cheap literature; also a song composer. **Died:** 5 June 1859.

HORROR, GHOST AND GOTHIC PUBLICATIONS

Novels (first published as serials or part-works)

The Maniac Father; or, The Victim of Seduction. London, Lloyd, 1842.
The Death Grasp; or, A Father's Curse. London, Lloyd, 1842.
The Skeleton Clutch; or, The Goblet of Gore. London, Lloyd, 1842.
Ranger of the Tomb; or, The Gipsy's Prophecy. London, Lloyd, 1845.
The Lone Cottage; or, Who's the Stranger? London, Lloyd, 1845.
The Death Ship; or, The Pirate's Bride and the Maniac of the Deep. London, Lloyd, 1846.
The Apparition. London, Lloyd, 1846. (Also attributed to James Malcolm Rymer.)
The Rivals; or, The Spectre at the Hall. London, Lloyd, 1847.
The String of Pearls; or, The Sailor's Gift, with George Macfarren. London, Lloyd, 1846-48; revised (probably by George Augustus Sala) as *Sweeney Todd, The Demon Barber of Fleet Street*, London, Charles Fox, 1878.
Angelina; or, The Mystery of St. Mark's Abbey. London, Lloyd, 1849.
Almira's Curse; or, The Black Tower of Bransdorf. London, Lloyd, 1849.
Sawney Bean, the Man-Eater of Midlothian. London, Lloyd, 1851.

Jonathan Bradford; or, The Murder at the Road-Side Inn. London, Lloyd, 1851.
Schamyl; or, The Wild Woman of Circassia. London, Henry Lea, 1856.

Other

Editor, *The Calendar of Horrors.* London, Lloyd, 1835-36.
Editor, *The Magazine of Curiosity and Wonder.* London, Lloyd, 1835-36.
Editor, *Tales of Enchantment; or, The Book of Fairies.* London, Lloyd, 1836.

OTHER PUBLICATIONS

Novels (first published as serials or part-works)

The Sketch-Book (as Bos). London, Lloyd, 1836
Nicholas Nicklebury (as Bos). London, Lloyd, 1838.
The Posthumous Notes of the Pickwickian Club; or, The Penny Pickwick (as Bos). London, Lloyd, 1838-39.
The Life and Adventures of Oliver Twiss, the Workhouse Boy (as Bos). London, Lloyd, 1839.
Ela the Outcast; or, The Gipsy of Rosemary Dell. London, Lloyd, 1839.
Gallant Tom; or, the Perils of a Sailor Ashore and Afloat. London, Lloyd, 1840.
Jack Junk; or, the Tar for All Weathers. London, Lloyd, 1840.
Mary Clifford; or, the Foundling Apprentice Girl. London, Lloyd, 1841.
Emily Fitzormond; or, The Deserted One. London, Lloyd, 1841.
The Hebrew Maiden; or, The Lost Diamond. A Tale of Chivalry. London, Lloyd, 1841.
Fatherless Fanny; or, The Mysterious Orphan. London, Lloyd, 1841.
Ernestine De Lacy; or, The Robber's Foundling. London, Lloyd, 1842.
Emily Percy. London, Lloyd, 1842.
May Grayson; or, Love and Treachery. London, Lloyd, 1842.
Kathleen; or, The Secret Marriage. London, Lloyd, 1842.
Gertrude of the Rock. London, Lloyd, 1842.
Susan Hoply; or, The Trials and Vicissitudes of a Servant Girl. London, Lloyd, 1842.
The Highland Watch-Tower, or The Sons of Glenalvon. London, Lloyd, 1842.
Phoebe, or the Miller's Maid. London, Lloyd, 1842.
Ben Bolt. London, George Pierce, 1842(?).
The Wife's Dream; or, A Profligate's Lesson. London, Lloyd, 1843(?).
Crime; or, The Gamester's Daughter. London, Lloyd, 1843(?).
Geraldine; or, The Secret Assassins of the Old Stone Cross. London, Lloyd, 1844.
Gilbert Copley. London, Lloyd, 1844.
Paul Clifford. London, Lloyd, 1844.
Theresa; or, The Orphan of Geneva. London, Lloyd, 1844.
Martha Willis; or, The Maid, the Profligate, and the Felon. London, Lloyd, 1844.
The Smuggler King; or, The Foundling of the Wreck. London, Lloyd, 1844.
Mariette; or, The Forger's Wife and the Child of Destiny. London, Lloyd, 1844-45.
Marianne, the Child of Charity. London, Lloyd, 1844.

Luke Somerton, or the English Renegade (novelization of a play by George Soane). London, Lloyd, 1845.

The Old House at West Street; or, London in the Last Century. London, Lloyd, 1846.

Jonathan Bradford; or, The Murder at the Roadside Inn. London, Lloyd, 1846.

Adventures by Night. London, Lloyd, 1846.

The Convict. London, Lloyd, 1846.

The Gipsy Boy: A Romance of the Woods and the Wilds. London, Lloyd, 1847.

Helen Porter; or, a Wife's Tragedy and a Sister's Trials. London, Lloyd, 1847.

The Divorce; or, The Mystery of the Wreck. London, Lloyd, 1847.

Newgate. London, Lloyd, 1847.

The Miller's Maid. London, Lloyd, 1847.

Blanche; or, The Mystery of the Doomed House. London, Lloyd, 1847.

The Love Child. London, Lloyd, 1847.

Blanche Langdale, the Outlaw's Bride. London, Lloyd, 1847.

Royal Twins; or, The Sisters of Mercy. London, Lloyd, 1848.

Ethelinde; or, The Fatal Vow. London, Lloyd, 1848.

The Child of Two Fathers; or, The Mysteries of the Days of Old. London, Lloyd, 1848.

Rosalie; or, The Vagrant's Daughter. London, Lloyd, 1848.

Pedlar's Acre; or, The Murderess of Seven Husbands. London, Lloyd, 1848.

Agnes the Unknown; or, The Beggar's Secret. London, Lloyd, 1849.

Love and Mystery; or, Married and Single. London, Lloyd, 1849.

Retribution; or, The Murder at the Old Dyke. London, Lloyd, 1849.

My Poll and My Partner Joe. London, Lloyd, 1849(?).

The Miser of Shoreditch; or, The Curse of Avarice. London, Lloyd, 1849.

Widow Mortimer; or, The Marriage in the Dark. London, Lloyd, 1850.

Ben Bolt, or, the Pents of a Sailor. London, Lloyd, 1850.

Mazeppa; or, The Wild Horse of the Ukraine. London, Lloyd, 1850.

The Blighted Heart; or, The Murder in the Old Priory Ruins. London, Lloyd, 1851.

Richard Parker; or, The Mutiny at the Nore. London, Lloyd, 1851.

The Bridal Ring; or, the Maiden's Sacrifice. London, Lloyd, 1851.

Blanche Heriot; or, The Chertsey Curfew (novelization of a play Albert Smith). London, Lloyd, 1851.

Evelina. London, Lloyd, 1851.

The Brigand; or, The Mountain Chief. London, Lloyd, 1851.

The Miller and His Men; or, The Secret Robbers of Bohemia (novelization of a play by Isaac Pocock). London, Lloyd, 1852.

The Robber's Wife. London, Lloyd, 1852.

The Harvest Home. London, Lloyd, 1852.

Vice and Its Victim; or, Phoebe, the Peasant's Daughter. London, Henry Lea, 1854.

Grace Walton, or the Wanderers of the Heath. London, Henry Lea, 1855.

Short Stories

Tales of the Drama. London, Lloyd, 1837.

Other

Editor, *The Penny Play Book.* London, Lloyd, 1836.
Editor, *The Horrors of War.* London, Lloyd, 1836.

*

Critical Studies: "The Demon Barber" in *Boys Will Be Boys* by E. S. Turner, London, Michael Joseph, 1948, revised 1975; *Fiction for the Working Man* by Louis James, London, Oxford University Press, 1963.

*   *   *

Prest was one of the more prolific writers of penny dreadfuls for the London publisher Edward Lloyd. A battery of writers churned out weekly stories and serials pandering to the latest scandal or news story. Many of the serials were subsequently bound into book form. Since almost all of these were published anonymously, other than by identifying the author as the writer of a previously popular serial, it is unlikely that Prest's total output will ever be known. The position is further complicated by the confusion between his work and that of James Malcolm Rymer. Many serials now attributed to Rymer were once believed to be the work of Prest, including the notorious *Varney the Vampire*. Most scholars now seem to accept that Rymer was the author, although it is entirely possible that Prest contributed some of the weekly episodes, since the book is uneven. Though the reattribution of *Varney* might weaken Prest's reputation, he was so prolific that it doesn't dent it much. He is still recognized as the author of the most notorious of all the penny dreadfuls, *The String of Pearls*, which gave us the legend of Sweeney Todd, the Demon Barber.

The story was not original with Prest. It had apparently been started by another of Lloyd's regular hacks, George Macfarren, but he had to stop writing because of cataracts. Prest took over and made the serial his own. The story is allegedly based on a real barber whose shop was in Fleet Street and who murdered a number of people. This narrative became linked with that of a real crime in Paris in 1800 where a man was convicted of cutting up his murder victims and serving them in meat pies. Prest is to be admired for his ability to continue the story through more than 90 weekly episodes. The story initially explores the set-up at Todd's shop and how he disposes of his victims through a trapdoor into the basement where they are killed and made into meat pies by Mrs. Lovett, who owns the pie-shop behind Todd's. Todd has a boy assistant, Tobias, who is not part of the set-up and who gets sent on various errands each time a victim is selected. Needless to say Todd can only maintain this pretence for so long and when Tobias becomes suspicious he is despatched to the nearest mental asylum. However suspicions do begin to grow in various other quarters, especially the neighbouring church in whose vaults the remains of the victims are buried. Investigations by the church, the police, by another innocent assistant who helps make the meat pies, and by a new applicant for the post of Todd's assistant, eventually uncover the facts, and Todd goes to prison. When the serial was running there was an outcry from the authorities who maintained it was encouraging the working-class to become cannibals. Like most such objections it only increased interest in the story.

Prest was an able writer with a vivid imagination and though he was no literary master his writing was of an acceptable standard. He had served his writing apprenticeship by producing near-plagiarisms of Dickens's most popular books under the pseudonym of "Bos." These included such original titles as *Oliver Twiss* and *Nicholas Nicklebury*. (It is believed that the "Bos" plagiarisms were collaborative efforts between Prest and William Bayle Bernard and Morris Barnett; it is uncertain just how much Prest contributed to them.) Prest also had a firm grounding in gothic fiction. His earliest work for Lloyd had been in the production of a series of magazines which reprinted gothic fiction from the continent, or plagiarized anything readily available in England. The most notorious was *The Calendar of Horrors* where Prest freely adapted German stories to emphasize their most lurid and gruesome aspects. By the time Prest began writing his own stories he knew what the public liked best. More than any of his colleagues Prest concentrated on the most grotesque and terrifying aspects of life.

It was the success of one of these novels, *Ela the Outcast*, that encouraged Lloyd to issue original stories rather than reprints or plagiarisms. *Ela* is not a true gothic story, though it has all the elements of a blood-and-thunder sensational adventure and set the vogue for the penny dreadfuls. Its story-line became typical of most of Prest's work. Ela, the daughter of an aristocrat is seduced and abandoned by another nobleman, Wallingford, and becomes an outcast, surviving in the woods with the gypsies. She curses Wallingford, and though she later becomes reconciled to him her curse still takes effect. The book became a bestseller, causing Prest to churn out endless repetitions about foundling children, few showing much originality. The most gothic of these was *Almira's Curse* with its delightfully brooding Black Tower of Bransdorf.

Prest's background of plagiarism allowed him to rapidly adopt and adapt any popular work. With *The Maniac Father* he rewrote *Father and Daughter* (1801) by Amelia Opie, the story of a father who goes insane because of his daughter's loose conduct. This gave rise to another series of imitations. Of more interest was *The Death Grasp*, a psychological horror story with supernatural undertones. Adolphe de Fronville murders Eugene de Bonison and ever after is plagued by the dying man's curse. Throughout a life of murder and debauchery Fronville feels the cold, clammy grasp of Bonison's hand gripping his heart. The popularity of this work caused Prest to repeat it with *The Skeleton Clutch*, and this drove him further into the world of the feigned supernatural with *The Death Ship* and *The Rivals*, both stories of hauntings arising from frayed nerves and bad consciences. Finally the success of *The String of Pearls* made Prest seek out an equally nasty specimen of humankind and write the life of Sawney Bean the Scottish cannibal.

Had Prest lived in the early 20th century he would have been a prolific contributor to the pulp magazines, and had he lived at the end of the 20th century he would doubtless have written endless plot-lines for television soap operas. He was the ideal channel for popular fiction, responding instantly to the public's taste for gore and sensationalism, but he scarcely ever had an original idea of his own.

—Mike Ashley

PRICHARD, K. & Hesketh

Pseudonyms: E. & H. Heron.

PRICHARD, K(atherine O'Brien)
Nationality: British. **Born:** Katherine O'Brien Ryall, 1851; daughter of an army general. **Family:** Married Hesketh Prichard at Peshawar, India (died 1876, six weeks before his son and namesake Hesketh was born). **Career:** Journeyed to England with her

young son, 1877, and later spent much time travelling in his company and writing in collaboration with him. **Died:** 1935.

PRICHARD, Hesketh (Vernon Hesketh)
Nationality: British. **Born:** Jhansi, India, 17 November 1876. **Education:** Fettes School, Edinburgh, 1887-94; studied law but did not practise. **Family:** Married Lady Elizabeth Grimston in 1908; one son and one daughter. **Military Service:** Served in the British Army during World War I: Major. **Career:** Traveller, explorer, big-game hunter, sportsman, writer, soldier, and reputed real-life model for fictional heroes such as E. W. Hornung's "Raffles." Fellow, Royal Geographical Society. **Awards:** Distinguished Service Order; Military Cross. **Died:** 14 June 1922.

HORROR, GHOST AND GOTHIC PUBLICATIONS

Short Stories

Ghosts, Being the Experiences of Flaxman Low. London, Pearson, 1899; in 2 vols. as *Ghost Stories* and *More Ghost Stories*, as by E. & H. Heron, London, Pearson, 1917.

OTHER PUBLICATIONS

Novels

Tammers' Duel, as E. & H. Heron. London, n.p, 1898.
A Modern Mercenary. London, Smith Elder, and New York, Doubleday, 1899.
Karadac, Count of Gersay. London, Constable, and New York, Stokes, 1901.
Don Q's Love Story. London, Greening, 1909; New York, Grosset and Dunlap, 1925.
The Cahusac Mystery. London, Heinemann, and New York(?), Sturgis, 1912.

Short Stories

Roving Hearts. London, Smith Elder, 1903.
The Chronicles of Don Q. London, Chapman and Hall, and Philadelphia, Lippincott, 1904.
The New Chronicles of Don Q. London, Unwin, 1906; as *Don Q in the Sierra*, Philadelphia, Lippincott, 1906.
November Joe, the Detective of the Woods (by Hesketh Prichard). London, Hodder and Stoughton, and Boston, Houghton Mifflin, 1913.

*

Film Adaptation: *Don Q, Son of Zorro*, 1925.

*   *   *

There are two unique circumstances concerning the ghost stories published as by "K. & Hesketh Prichard." One is that the authors' names conceal a mother-and-son writing partnership; Kate Prichard and her son Hesketh (a real-life hero who once was described as "a golden-haired, grey-eyed giant of six feet four inches") apparently wrote all their ghostly tales together. And when the stories first appeared, in *Pearson's Magazine* from January 1898, they were presented as true accounts of haunted places, even accompanied by photographs.

Unjustly neglected today, these are vivid stories featuring dangerous ghosts. For the period, there are extremely horrific scenes; there is plenty of action; people die nastily. And there is always a mystery to be solved by application of the scientific method and logical deduction.

All twelve of the tales are "solved" by Flaxman Low, a trained psychologist who is clearly based on Sherlock Holmes (though Hugh Lamb, in *Victorian Nightmares*, says he is "reputed to be a thinly disguised portrait of one of the leading scientists of the Victorian era"). He acts as an amateur psychic detective, visiting the scenes of hauntings and quickly working out the explanations behind baffling occurrences. Nor is he just a theorist, for in several cases he is willing to use physical force in attempts to restrain supernatural beings and is almost killed by them. In "The Story of Yand Manor House," Low comes close to being stifled by a much-expanded ghost with some physical presence. Stifling or smothering nearly gets him again in "The Story of the Spaniards, Hammersmith," when only brute strength and "a lucky twist" enable him to get out from underneath the murderous ghost of a leper. In "The Story of the Grey House," Low is partly strangled by a large climbing plant with homicidal tendencies. And in "The Story of Baelbrow" he is forced to use a pistol to shoot off part of the foot of his supernatural assailant.

Low's character is not much developed in the series. Certainly he is less distinctive in his habits and opinions than Sherlock Holmes, but he is an early example of the psychic detective, antedating Algernon Blackwood's John Silence and William Hope Hodgson's Carnacki.

All the stories are spare and pacey, covering a lot of ground in a dozen pages or so. Descriptions of place and person are brief and to the point, rather than lingeringly atmospheric, yet the images are sharp and memorable. The intention is to entertain the reader with something novel. Hence the characterization is perfunctory and the dialogue is loaded with information and crackles with dated clichés. Two examples: "This is almost beyond belief." "It has beaten even you, Low! . . . There is something much more terrible and tangible than a ghost in this cursed house!" It is, in fact, a journalistic approach to story writing.

The plots of each story generally follow the Prichards' own formula: people are found dead in a particular location, Flaxman Low is asked to investigate (being quickly filled in on the circumstances by the house owner or tenant), Low and his host and a male friend are menaced by the supernatural agency and, on the last page, Low advances a theory (based firmly on science) as to what is causing the problem and how it can be overcome. Obviously, a more flexible approach to plotting and more words would have resulted in a larger and more intriguing range of stories.

The ideas are often ingenious. One of the most fantastic occurs in "The Story of Baelbrow," in which an ancient Egyptian mummy, kept in a house built above a British barrow (or burial mound) is animated by an elemental spirit. The mummy periodically comes to life and sustains itself through vampirism, sucking the blood of those living in the house. It kills a maid and causes anaemia in the daughter of the house. The solution is to smash up the mummy and burn its pieces.

Another exceptional idea, described in "The Story of Konnor Old House," is based around sightings of a phenomenon known as the Shining Man. The culprit is an exotic phosphorescent fun-

gus which is also poisonous, taking over a human body and maddening the mind. There is also a slight suggestion of a supernatural agency at work, though this may be subjective, due to the fungus's effect upon the brain. In "The Story of the Moor Road," the location is not a house but a stretch of haunted road. It is briefly inhabited by an Elemental Earth Spirit, a kind of superman figure which jumps down a 30-foot drop without injury, runs faster than a bicycle pedalled by an athlete, and bends the barrels of a shotgun as if they were paper. It has been released from some kind of imprisonment by a local earthquake and has been feeding through psychic vampirism; when its remote host dies it loses power suddenly—but the elemental is not actually destroyed and is believed still to be wandering around the country, doing terrible damage to human beings.

The Prichards produced at least one other horror story, outside the Flaxman Low series. This is "The Fever Queen," concerning a disturbed young painter named Sidney Broderick who disappears, leaving a single masterpiece behind him and is tracked down in a tropical forest.

The mother-and-son team travelled widely abroad in the earliest years of the 20th century. Resulting from their travels was a series of stories (consisting of adventure fiction rather than horror) and articles which appeared in *Pearson's Magazine*, *Cornhill Magazine* and the *Daily Express*.

—Chris Morgan

PRITCHARD, John

Nationality: British. **Born:** Wales, 1964. **Career:** Has worked in administrative capacities in various British hospitals. **Address:** c/o HarperCollins Publishers, 77-85 Fulham Palace Road, London W6 8JB, England.

HORROR, GHOST AND GOTHIC PUBLICATIONS

Novels (series: Sister Rachel Young and Razoxane in all titles)

Night Sisters. London, HarperCollins, 1993.
Angels of Mourning. London, HarperCollins, 1995.
The Witching Hour. London, Voyager, 1997.

*   *   *

A standard piece of advice for new writers is "write about what you know," and John Pritchard did so, producing a splendid debut novel, *Night Sisters*. He knows about present-day English hospitals and he sets a compulsively believable and truly frightening piece of work in a large hospital in the English Midlands, particularly in its accident and emergency department.

In fact the ingredients are fairly standard: an ancient menace which can maim and kill in particularly nasty ways and which no locks or security systems will guard against; a battle between good and evil with no quarter given; a combination of psychological, physical and supernatural horror, with a lot of action and a high body count; a vulnerable protagonist who is isolated and forced to act against her will. But Pritchard combines his ingredients well, finding new twists and keeping up the suspense. Right from the first chapter, in which he tells the tale of a nurse strangled by a patient who has been declared dead, the reader is hooked.

Rachel Young is a night-shift Ward Sister. Gradually she realizes that she is at the centre of an increasing number of bizarre and mostly very bloody killings which are being perpetrated inside and outside the hospital. She hears whispers about the Clinicians and eventually discovers that these are a small group of 17th-century doctors who have survived down the ages, killing for reasons of medical research. Normally they dress like vagrants, yet they possess great powers of sorcery and can appear and disappear at will. Their trademark is to dissect their victim, quickly and scientifically, into a pile of separate organs, or perhaps just to remove part of the brain without killing. As the book begins, only five of them survive, led by Melphalan, though they have threatened or bribed others to help them.

If the Clinicians represent absolute evil, then a lesser evil (certainly not good) is represented by Carol McCain, usually known as Razoxane. She appears to be a slim young woman, who wears dark glasses and also dresses like a vagrant, though she has memories far older than the Clinicians. Having once tried to join them, but having been rejected, she now does her best to destroy them—which can only be done by cutting up their bodies and burning the parts. The force of good is represented by Rachel herself, whose faith in Christianity keeps the Clinicians at bay several times.

So while the Clinicians use derelict houses or closed-down operating theatres for their bloody experiments, Razoxane pursues them, always trying to catch one Clinician alone and kill him. And while the Clinicians do their best to persuade Rachel to help them, Razoxane protects her from them. The leitmotif of the novel is somebody stepping unexpectedly out of the shadows, brandishing a knife and being perfectly willing to kill anyone who gets in their way. The Clinicians kill Rachel's flatmate and the flatmate's boyfriend; they threaten Rachel with excruciating pain. When she develops appendicitis, she feels safe as a patient at her own hospital, but the surgeon for her operation is a locum, Dr. Alan—actually Melphelan. Razoxane succeeds in killing four of the Clinicians, but Melphalan survives and it is Rachel, the champion of non-violence, who is forced to kill him, by pouring acetone into his body and lighting it, so that he burns to death from within.

The night-time hospital settings are wonderfully atmospheric, made all the more believable by the fact that staff is not sharply differentiated but tend to blur together. Rachel and Razoxane are both fascinating characters, bound together in their aims and representing two sides of the same coin—the good and evil sisters, perhaps. Only very occasionally does the action slow as too much is explained.

By contrast, *Angels of Mourning*, a sequel, fails to work as well because Pritchard is trying too hard. Very little of it is set in a hospital (even though Rachel is now, three years on, working in Intensive Care in a central London hospital), which is a shame. And it is too slow, with nothing much happening in the first 60 pages except for the reappearance, from the dead, of Razoxane. The excess of ingredients causes confusion, and the over-long final scenes are too deliberate and too exaggerated. Many plot elements are coincidental or contrived, and quite a few of these are repeated from the previous novel. Nevertheless, Pritchard achieves occasional good effects, particularly from the use of deserted Underground stations and derelict buildings.

Rachel is now living with a policeman boyfriend called Nick. Razoxane asks for her help, but this entails helping the IRA, whom Razoxane is using for her own ends. The supernatural theme, of trying to release and then destroy demon creatures who have coalesced from the ghosts of Britons massacred by Queen Boadicea's forces 1900 years before, seems weak and unconvincing. By contrast, the physical horror of small groups of ruthless armed mercenaries roaming around inner London, dressed as police and prepared to torture and kill, is very disturbing.

Once again, the uneasy partnership of Rachel and Razoxane is striking and well sustained. For too long women have been regarded as no more than victims in horror fiction, so it is refreshing to find two such strong female characters together, one a truly caring person who is forced to compromise her principles to protect those she cares for, and the other a psychotic killer with scarcely any morals.

At his best, Pritchard is an inspired writer of genre horror. It will be a shame if he cannot produce more hospital-based novels of the high calibre of *Night Sisters*.

—Chris Morgan

PTACEK, Kathryn (Anne)

Pseudonyms: Kathryn Atwood; Kathryn Grant; Kathleen Maxwell, Anne Mayfield; Les Simons. **Nationality:** American. **Born:** 1952. **Family:** Married to the novelist Charles L. Grant (q.v.). **Career:** Contributor of short stories to numerous magazines and anthologies; in addition to the books listed below, has written a number of romantic novels under the names Kathleen Maxwell and Anne Mayfield; editor and publisher, *The Gila Queen's Guide to Markets*. **Address:** P.O. Box 97, Newton, NJ 07860, USA.

HORROR, GHOST AND GOTHIC PUBLICATIONS

Novels

Gila! (as Les Simons). New York, Signet, 1981.
Shadoweyes. New York, Tor, 1984; as *Shadow-Eyes*, London, Arrow, 1986.
Blood Autumn. New York, Tor, 1985.
Kachina. New York, Tor, 1986.
In Silence Sealed. New York, Tor, 1988.
Ghost Dance. New York, Tor, 1990.
The Hunted. New York, Walker, 1993.

Other

Editor, *Women of Darkness*. New York, Tor, 1988.
Editor, *Women of Darkness II*. New York, Tor, 1990.

OTHER PUBLICATIONS

Novels as Kathryn Atwood

Satan's Angel. New York, Jove, 1981.
Renegade's Lady. New York, Jove, 1982.
The Lawless Heart. New York, Jove, 1984.
My Lady Rogue. New York, Jove, 1986.

Novels as Kathryn Grant

The Pwhoenix Bells. New York, Ace, 1987.
The Black Jade Road. New York, Ace, 1989.
The Willow Garden. New York, Ace, 1989.

Other

Editor, *Women of the West.* New York, n.p., 1990.

*   *   *

The resurgent popularity of modern horror which started with Stephen King, Ira Levin and William Peter Blatty was largely at the hands of male writers until the middle of the 1980s when a number of outstanding women entered the field including Anne Rice, Kathe Koja, Nancy Holder and Chelsea Quinn Yarbro. One of the most important of these was Kathryn Ptacek, who proved herself equally adept at both book and short-story length. Ptacek's debut novel *Gila!*, written as Les Simons, did not accurately predict the direction her career would take. It is essentially a pastiche of 1950s style overgrown-animal movies, in this case a gila monster mutated by nuclear radiation into a gigantic, man-eating creature. It's fun to read but nothing on which to base a career.

All of that changed with *Shadoweyes*, another monster story of sorts but this one entirely original. This time the menace is very small, tiny creatures with razor-sharp teeth that emerge from their cavern in New Mexico in such enormous numbers that they can overcome victims like land-dwelling piranhas. After their initial successes, the creatures begin to strike within the city limits of Albuquerque, a situation which the authorities seem determined to ignore until a news reporter and an Apache take things into their own hands and use an old tribal secret to end the threat. Ptacek creates suspense deftly, unnerves rather than shocks, and most importantly develops her two protagonists as credible individuals whose plight matters to the reader.

Blood Autumn is an historical horror novel in which events begin in India in 1857 that will reverberate in Georgia, USA, 30 years later. A mysterious woman seduces a British officer against the backdrop of a strange fever that strikes only children. August Parrish is a lamia, an ageless creature that survives by drawing the life-force from children and by seducing men to their destruction. Now she's set her eyes on a priest who is wavering in his faith. Once again Ptacek draws upon the horror of situation rather than of action, and the result, though subtle, is effective.

In *Kachina* the wife of an anthropologist accompanies her husband to New Mexico in 1880 and experiences a series of unsettling dreams in which native American spirits appear to her. Eventually she is overcome, convinced that she is a reincarnation of a primitive goddess who will lead the tribe to the restoration of its tribal lands. In the process, she kills her husband and anyone else who appears to be an obstacle. Her gradual descent into obsession and murder is skilfully done so that the reader feels sympathy for her plight even while recoiling from the acts she commits.

In *Silence Sealed* is also an historical novel, and once again draws upon the legend of the lamia. Byron, Keats and Shelley all died young, but perhaps there was a reason for that: Ptacek suggests that they were caught up by two lamia, or succubi, one of whom is named August, although there's no direct connection to *Blood*

Autumn. This is the most restrained and thoughtful of Ptacek's horror novels. *Ghost Dance*, by contrast, is a contemporary thriller with a rapidly paced plot and a great deal of action. The protagonist of *Shadoweyes* is back, this time trying to uncover the secret of a series of murders taking place in various locations across the country. In each case, a single feather is discovered at the murder scene. Although the authorities believe that a gang of mundane killers is responsible, our hero recognizes the feather as indicating that ancient tribal magic is at work. But the Ghost Dancers have unleashed a power that not even they can control, a power that could devastate the entire modern world.

Ptacek's next horror novel was marketed as straight suspense. *The Hunted* concerns Jessie, a young girl struggling to deal with a stepfather she doesn't love and a mother who has become an alcoholic. After what should have been a routine visit to a new doctor, Jessie falls prey to fits of inexplicable terror and at times speaks in a foreign language. A neighbour becomes concerned with the girl's plight and eventually discovers that she is the reincarnation of a victim of the Nazi concentration camps, her former identity awakened by recognition that the doctor she visited is actually a war criminal hiding behind a new identity. This is a much more restrained work than Ptacek's previous efforts, and with minimal horror content, but still notable for its strong characterizations and finely crafted suspense.

Ptacek is also a prolific short-story writer. A woman discovers she has vampires for neighbours in "Moving Day (Night?)," witches ply their trade in "Poppet," "Neighbours" and "Reunion," usually with the reader's blessing, punishing the inconsiderate and unkind for their transgressions. The protagonist of *Shadoweyes* confronts another witch in a nearly abandoned airport in "Bruja." The protagonist of "Dead Possums" learns too late the penalty for casual cruelty to animals.

Many of Ptacek's short stories deal with the problems an individual has coping with everyday situations. One of her best tales, for example, is "Driven," wherein a woman's life is unsettled by the loss of her husband and her job, along with a number of petty annoyances, to the point where her personality alters to that of a predator. "Each Night, Each Year" is a quietly understated ghost story in which the ghost is a product of the protagonist's guilt. A promiscuous woman finds an unorthodox and chilling cure in "Hunger" and a housewife becomes obsessed with removing body hair in "Hair." Other stories of interest include "Three, Four, Shut the Door" and "Pleasure Domes." Ptacek also edited the highly regarded horror anthologies *Women of Darkness* and *Women of Darkness II.*

—Don D'Ammassa

QUILLER-COUCH, (Sir) Arthur (Thomas)

Pseudonym: Q. **Nationality:** British. **Born:** Bodmin, Cornwall, 21 November 1863. **Education:** Newton Abbot College, Devon; Clifton College, Bristol; Trinity College, Cambridge University. **Family:** Married Louisa Amelia Hicks in 1889. **Career:** Freelance writer from 1887; contributor to *The Speaker* and other publications; King Edward VII Professor of English, Cambridge University, from 1912. Created a Knight Batchelor, 1910. Lived for much of his life in Fowey, Cornwall. **Died:** 12 May 1944.

HORROR, GHOST AND GOTHIC PUBLICATIONS

Novel

Castle d'Or, completed by Daphne du Maurier. London, Dent, and New York, Doubleday, 1962.

Short Stories as Q

Noughts and Crosses. London, Cassell, 1891.
"I Saw Three Ships" and Other Winter's Tales. London, Cassell, 1892.
Wandering Heath: Stories, Studies and Sketches. London, Cassell, 1895.
Old Fires and Profitable Ghosts: A Book of Stories. London, Cassell, 1900.
The Laird's Luck and Other Fireside Tales. London, Cassell, 1901.
The White Wolf and Other Fireside Tales. London, Methuen, 1902.
Two Sides of the Face: Midwinter Tales. Bristol, Arrowsmith, 1903.
Q's Mystery Stories. London, Dent, 1937.

OTHER PUBLICATIONS

Novels as Q

Dead Man's Rock. London, Cassell, 1887.
The Astonishing History of Troy Town. London, Cassell, 1888.
The Splendid Spur. London, Cassell, 1889.
The Blue Pavilions. London, Cassell, 1891.
Ia. London, Cassell, 1896.
St. Ives, Being the Adventures of a French Prisoner in England, with Robert Louis Stevenson. New York, Scribner, 1897; London, Heinemann, 1898.
The Ship of Stars. London, Cassell, 1899.
The Westcotes. Bristol, Arrowsmith, 1902.
The Adventures of Harry Revel. London, Cassell, 1903.
Hetty Wesley. London, Harper, 1903.
Fort Amity. London, Murray, 1904.
Shining Ferry. London, Hodder and Stoughton, 1905.
Sir John Constantine. London, Smith Elder, 1906.
The Mayor of Troy. London, Methuen, 1906.
Poison Island. London, Dent, 1907.
Major Vigoureux. London, Methuen, 1907.
True Tilda. Bristol, Arrowsmith, 1909.
Lady Good-for-Nothing. London, Nelson, 1910.
Brother Copas. Bristol, Arrowsmith, 1911.
Hocken and Hunken: A Tale of Troy. Edinburgh, Blackwood, 1912.
Nicky-Nan, Reservist. Edinburgh, Blackwood, 1915.
Foe-Farrell. London, Collins, 1918.
Tales and Romances (Duchy edition). London, Dent, 30 vols., 1928.

Short Stories as Q

The Delectable Duchy. London, Cassell, 1893.
Historical Tales from Shakespeare. London, Arnold, 1899.
Shakespeare's Christmas and Other Stories. London, Smith Elder, 1905.
Merry Garden and Other Stories. London, Methuen, 1907.

Corporal Sam and Other Stories. London, Smith Elder, 1910.
The Roll Call of Honour. London, Nelson, 1912.
My Best Book. Privately printed, 1912.
News from the Duchy. Bristol, Arrowsmith, 1913.
Mortallone and Aunt Trinidad: Tales of the Spanish Main. Bristol, Arrowsmith, 1917.
Q's Shorter Stories. London, Dent, 1944.

Poetry

Athens: A Poem. Bodmin, Liddell, 1891.
Green Bays: Verses and Parodies. London, Methuen, 1893; expanded edition, Oxford University Press, 1930.
Poems and Ballads. London, Methuen, 1896.
A Fowey Garland. London, Cassell, 1899.
The Vigil of Venus and Other Poems. London, Methuen, 1912.
Poetry. N.p., Fellowship Books, 1914.
Poems. Oxford, Oxford University Press, 1929.

Other

The Warwickshire Avon. London, Osgood McIlvaine, 1892.
Adventures in Criticism. London, Cassell, 1896.
From a Cornish Window. Bristol, Arrowsmith, 1906.
On the Art of Writing. Cambridge, Cambridge University Press, 1916.
Studies in Literature: First Series. Cambridge, Cambridge University Press, 1918.
On the Art of Reading. Cambridge, Cambridge University Press, 1920.
Studies in Literature: Second Series. Cambridge, Cambridge University Press, 1922.
Charles Dickens and Other Victorians. Cambridge, Cambridge University Press, 1925.
Studies in Literature: Third Series. Cambridge, Cambridge University Press, 1929.
The Poet as Citizen, and Other Papers. Cambridge, Cambridge University Press, 1934.
Cambridge Lectures. London, Dent, 1943.
Memories and Opinions: An Unfinished Autobiography. Cambridge, Cambridge University Press, 1944.

Editor, *The Golden Pomp: A Procession of English Lyrics from Surrey to Shirley.* London, Methuen, 1895.
Editor, *Fairy Tales Far and Near.* London, Cassell, 1895.
Editor, *English Sonnets.* London, Chapman and Hall, 1897; expanded edition, 1935.
Editor, *The Cornish Magazine.* Truro, Cornwall, Pollard, 2 vols., 1899.
Editor, *The Oxford Book of English Verse, 1250-1900.* Oxford, Oxford University Press, 1900; expanded edition, as *The Oxford Book of English Verse, 1250-1918,* 1939.
Editor, *The Pilgrim's Way: A Little Scrip of Good Counsel for Travellers.* London, Seeley, 1906.
Editor, *The Oxford Book of Ballads.* Oxford, Oxford University Press, 1910.
Editor, *The Sleeping Beauty and Other Fairy Tales, Retold from the French.* London, Hodder and Stoughton, 1910.
Editor, *The Oxford Book of Victorian Verse.* Oxford, Oxford University Press, 1912.
Editor, *In Powder and Crinoline: Old Fairy Tales Retold.* London, Hodder and Stoughton, 1913.
Editor, *The Cambridge Shorter Bible.* Cambridge, Cambridge University Press, n.d.

Editor, *The Oxford Book of English Prose*. Oxford, Oxford University Press, 1925.

Editor, *Pages of English Prose, 1390-1930*. Oxford, Oxford University Press, 1930.

Editor, *Felicities of Thomas Traherne*. N.p., Dobell, 1934.

*

Film Adaptations: *St. Ives*, 1955, 1960, 1967 (all television serials); *The Splendid Spur* (television serial), 1960.

Critical Study: "Sir Arthur Quiller-Couch" by Charlotte Weychan, in *Book and Magazine Collector* (London), no. 99, June 1992.

*   *   *

Almost forgotten today (except by lovers of the play and film *84 Charing Cross Road*, in which his name and example are inspirational to the heroine), Quiller-Couch was an important writer of novels, stories, poetry and criticism in his time. He was also a noted academic (a professor of English at Cambridge University from 1912 until his death) and an editor of popular anthologies of poetry and prose from which at least two generations of British schoolchildren were taught. His surname was originally Couch; he began to use the hyphen only in his 20s. For his novels he always used the pseudonym Q. He was knighted in 1910, though for political services rather than for his writing.

Above all else, perhaps, Quiller-Couch was a Cornishman, who was born and died in that far southwestern county of England. Much of his writing, in all forms, was set in Cornwall. In particular, he is associated with the small coastal town of Fowey, of which he was mayor during the 1930s and which he immortalized in his lighthearted series of Troy Town novels and stories. (Fowey also became the home of another famous writer, Daphne du Maurier, and later she was to complete Quiller-Couch's unfinished novel *Castle d'Or*, a supernaturally tinged love story in which a 19th-century Cornish couple re-enact the tale of Tristan and Iseult. Many decades earlier "Q" had performed a similar service for the late Robert Louis Stevenson, when he completed the latter's fragmentary adventure novel *St. Ives*—subsequently much adapted for British television.)

A relatively small proportion of Quiller-Couch's fiction is of ghost and horror interest, and these stories have never been collected in a single volume. Yet his contribution to the genre is of more significance than its slimness would suggest, for he demonstrated that rugged Cornwall is an excellent setting for ghostly stories, and he wrote what must be the perfect quiet ghost story, "A Pair of Hands." Sub-titled "An Old Maid's Ghost Story," "A Pair of Hands" is narrated by the elderly Miss Emily Le Petyt, telling of the three years she spent living in a rented cottage called Tresillack in a secluded spot on the south coast of Cornwall. In his full description, Quiller-Couch makes it sound idyllic, being picturesque, covered in summer blossom and within easy walking distance of the beach. The narrator gets on well with the resident housekeeper, a widow named Mrs. Carkeek, yet she is surprised at how this woman manages to keep the cottage so clean and tidy all the time. The answer is that most of the work is performed by a ghost which manifests itself as a pair of child's hands. After the narrator has seen the ghost, though not been upset by it, Mrs. Carkeek explains that it is the ghost of Margaret, the squire's daugh-

ter, who died of diphtheria 20 years earlier. The only horror elements in the story are derived, ironically, not from the ghost but from the tales the housekeeper tells of previous tenants—drinking and beating their children.

"The Seventh Man" is a wonderfully claustrophobic ghost story set within the Arctic Circle. The crew of a wrecked ship have built themselves a small one-roomed hut on the ice and are trying to survive the Arctic winter. One of their number has died, but the other six are determined to sit it out until the sun rises again and the whaling fleet comes to save them in the summer. From outside they hear the unsettling sounds of bears, foxes, or perhaps ghosts. One of them (a Cornishman) goes outside with a gun to frighten off the animals; he seems to see human footprints and smears of blood—perhaps their dead comrade walking back from his grave. Later, inside the hut, there seem to be seven of them, yet somehow the extra man (not identifiable) improves the atmosphere, and they survive. Both this story and "A Pair of Hands" have been frequently anthologized.

Quiller-Couch was particularly adept at historical settings. Along with others of his stories, "The Roll-Call of the Reef" is set during the Napoleonic War, though its frame is about 50 or 60 years later, and it is likely that the story might have been based on a tale heard by Quiller-Couch as a boy. It deals with shipwrecks (frequent off the Cornish coast during bad winter storms) and their survivors. A cavalry trumpeter and a Marines drummer-boy are both saved one night when their ships are separately wrecked fairly close to each other. Both are injured, the trumpeter mentally, yet they strike up a friendship and sometimes venture out by boat to salute their dead comrades with trumpet and drum. The drummer-boy recovers fully and reports back for duty, but he returns to see his friend as a ghost on the day he is killed (in action in France), and the trumpeter also dies that day.

"My Grandfather, Hendry Watty" is a comic ghost story, explaining how the narrator's grandfather was, due to a ghostly summons, not the man he might have been. Or this might all have been founded on a dream, for Quiller-Couch wrote several dream-fantasies that might or might not be ghost stories. "Widdershins" and "Oceanus" are examples of this.

"The Room of Mirrors" is a peculiar piece which must be mentioned here. The narrator, Reg Travers, follows Gervase, his rival for the love of Elaine. They walk across central London by night, with Reg intending to shoot Gervase. One of them is shot dead, but his identity is in doubt. Or they might both be dead, because neither can survive without the other as an adversary. "The Lady of the Ship" is a 16th-century story of shipwreck and alleged witchcraft, set in Cornwall. "The Mystery of Joseph Laquedem" concerns the reincarnation of a pair of lovers. And there are several other stories containing elements of horror or fantasy amongst the author's work.

Quiller-Couch was a clever and allusive writer, sometimes allowing his quotations from Latin and Greek to get in the way of his story. Yet he was capable of producing excellent fiction for popular consumption in several genres.

—Chris Morgan

QUINN, Seabury (Grandin)

Nationality: American. **Born:** Washington, D.C., 1 January 1889. **Education:** National University, Washington, L.D. 1910. **Career:**

Lawyer; editor of trade newspapers; teacher of medical jurisprudence; government lawyer during World War II; contributed some 500 stories to pulp magazines. **Died:** 24 December 1969.

HORROR, GHOST AND GOTHIC PUBLICATIONS

Novels (series: Jules de Grandin)

Roads. Sauk City, Wisconsin, Arkham House, 1948.
The Devil's Bride (Jules de Grandin). New York, Popular Library, 1976.
Alien Flesh. Philadelphia, Oswald Train, 1977.

Short Stories

The Phantom Fighter: The Memoirs of Jules de Grandin. Sauk City, Wisconsin, Mycroft and Moran, 1966.
Is the Devil a Gentleman? Baltimore, Mirage, 1970.
The Adventures of Jules de Grandin. New York, Popular Library, 1976.
The Casebook of Jules de Grandin. New York, Popular Library, 1976.
The Skeleton Closet of Jules de Grandin. New York, Popular Library, 1976.
The Hellfire Files of Jules de Grandin. New York, Popular Library, 1976.
The Horror Chambers of Jules de Grandin. New York, Popular Library, 1977.

*   *   *

Seabury Quinn is often quoted as the paradigm example of the run-of-the-mill *Weird Tales* writer: a fluent hack of archetypal mediocrity. The chief exhibit entered in evidence to support this verdict is his long-running series of occult detective stories starring Jules de Grandin—who was not so much a conspicuously down-market C. Auguste Dupin as a slightly dandified Hercule Poirot—and his trusty henchman Dr. Trowbridge, who hailed from New Jersey. Arkham House, the specialist press set up to carry forward the interrupted cause of the *Weird Tales* school of horror fiction, did not ignore him entirely but pointedly elected to reprint the highly atypical and conspicuously unhorrific Christmas fantasy *Roads* instead of his darker material. It was not until 1966 that Arkham's companion press Mycroft & Moran deigned to issue a collection of de Grandin stories, and Quinn's other work was abandoned to the care of less prestigious small presses. *Alien Flesh*, his only authentic novel—*The Devil's Bride* is a lumpen portmanteau of ill-matched de Grandin cases—was not published until eight years after his death. This dubious literary reputation is fitted with ironic perfection to the highly unusual nature of Quinn's day jobs, which included the editing of a trade journal for undertakers and legal practice in the field of mortuary law.

The de Grandin series is indeed rather undistinguished, and it is obvious that the author did not expect it to last nearly as long as it did. He was perfectly prepared to keep turning out the stories as long as they remained popular, but the strain on his imagination clearly showed as he doggedly worked his way through the entire gamut of available supernatural adversaries. Had he known in advance that he would have to find more than 90 plots he might have attempted to sketch out some unifying metaphysical scheme which could be gradually revealed by the encounters, but as things were found himself adding items piecemeal, with an increasing des-

peration that multiplied ghosts, vampires, werewolves, zombies and—most prolifically of all—mad scientists with wild abandon. He did his research piecemeal, and usually very sketchily; de Grandin's supposedly encyclopedic wisdom in respect of occult matters often demonstrated awkward limitations and was increasingly wont to elaborate greatly on—or even flatly to contradict—its earlier manifestations.

The most intriguing de Grandin tales are those which involve ambivalent *femmes fatales*; these include "Restless Souls" and "The Silver Countess," both in *The Phantom-Fighter* (the latter also in *The Casebook*), "The Devil-People" in *The Hellfire Files* and "Daughter of the Moonlight" in *The Skeleton Closet*. *The Devil's Bride*, originally serialized in 1932, features an innocent who is snatched by Yezidees intent on making her their high priest, but that plot-element is sidelined by a world-wide conspiracy reminiscent of that featured in Sax Rohmer's Fu Manchu novels—although Robert W. Chambers's *The Slayer of Souls* is likely to have been a more immediate inspiration. The later stories are usually more lacklustre than the earlier ones, and most of the memorable ones were written in the 1920s. "The Tenants of Broussac" (in *The Adventures*), "The Chapel of Mystic Horror" (in *The Casebook*) and "The Gods of East and West" (in *The Horror Chambers*) are all rather silly and show little artistic conscience in their manipulation of blatant *deus ex machina* resolutions, but they have a certain lurid charm.

The most oft-reprinted of Quinn's other stories is one of his earliest, the solidly conventional werewolf story "The Phantom Farmhouse" (1923). This is, however, unaccountably omitted from the eclectic collection *Is the Devil a Gentleman?* The best stories here are all ironically perverted love stories, ranging from the conventional *femme fatale* story "Glamour" through the engaging historical fantasy "The Globe of Memories" and the sentimentalized tales of lycanthropy "Uncanonized" and "The Gentle Werewolf" to the gauchely effective title story and "The Masked Ball." The last two examples might be considered Quinn's most interesting short stories on account of their concerted attempts to confuse, if not outrightly to challenge, the customary moral and aesthetic standards which were so casually taken for granted in the de Grandin stories.

Such tentative examples as these, however, could not have prepared Quinn's readers for the extraordinarily elaborate erotic fantasy laid out in *Alien Flesh*. The novel describes the adventures of a young male archaeologist who must submit to metamorphosis into a lovely Circassian slave-girl. Her eventual escape from the harem into which she is co-opted is the prelude to a long career as a *femme fatale*, whose climax arrives when she journeys to America and falls in love with an old friend. Stylistically speaking, the novel is a far cry from Gautier's *Mademoiselle de Maupin* or Pierre Louys's *The Adventures of King Pausole*, but in its own dilettante fashion it is a bold and striking celebration of sexual confusion.

The abandonment of Popular Library's series of de Grandin collections with the series only half-reprinted hardly qualifies as a tragedy, although one is always aware of an awkward aesthetic gap when such projects remain incomplete. It is probable that Quinn is now fated to suffer terminal neglect even within the twilit dimension of the speciality presses, but he did contrive to overcome his limitations in a reasonable number of interesting short stories as well as in *Alien Flesh* and it would be a pity if his work were to disappear from memory entirely.

—Brian Stableford

R

RADCLIFFE, Ann

Nationality: British. **Born:** Ann Ward, in London, 9 July 1764.
Education: Private. **Family:** Married William Radcliffe in 1787.
Career: Rapidly became the most successful novelist of her day,
but lived quietly, undertaking no travel abroad and writing very
little after 1797. **Died:** 7 February 1823.

HORROR, GHOST AND GOTHIC PUBLICATIONS

Novels

The Castles of Athlin and Dunbayne: A Highland Story. London,
    Hookham, 1789; Philadelphia, Bradford, 1796.
A Sicilian Romance. London, Hookham and Carpenter, 2 vols.,
    1790; Philadelphia, Rice, 1795.
*The Romance of the Forest, Interspersed with Some Pieces of Po-
    etry.* London, Hookham and Carpenter, 3 vols., 1791; Boston,
    Etheridge, 1795.
*The Mysteries of Udolpho: A Romance Interspersed with Some
    Pieces of Poetry.* London, Robinson, 4 vols., 1794; Boston,
    White and Spotswood, 3 vols., 1795.
The Italian; or, The Confessional of the Black Penitents. London,
    Cadell and Davies, 3 vols., and New York, Magill, 2 vols., 1797.
*Gaston de Blondeville; and St. Alban's Abbey, with Some Poetical
    Pieces.* London, Colburn, 4 vols., 1826.

OTHER PUBLICATIONS

Poetry

The Poems of Mrs. Ann Radcliffe. London, Smith, 1816.
The Poetical Works of Ann Radcliffe. London, Colburn and Bentley,
    2 vols., 1834.

Other

*A Journey Made in the Summer of 1794 Through Holland and the
    Western Frontiers of Germany.* London, Robinson, 1795.

* * *

Mrs. Radcliffe was the most popular of the early Gothic writers. *The Mysteries of Udolpho* was read by just about everybody
who read novels at all in the last few years of the 18th century or
the first half of the 19th, and its author's influence upon the Gothic
tradition both at the time and since has been immense. When Jane
Austen was looking for a typical Gothic novel to satirize in
Northanger Abbey (1818), she found that *The Mysteries of
Udolpho* was still the best known and most widely read of them
all.

What Radcliffe brought to the Gothic was poetry. In all her
novels she has lush descriptions of landscape, mostly French and
Italian, which seemed more romantic than her native England; and
this is not merely background but affects the moods of her characters and comes almost to dominate characters and plot. More
obviously, she inserts her own verse into some of the novels,
achieving a softer and more picturesque result than any of the
other major Gothic authors. It is ironic that these landscapes came
not from her own travels but from the works of contemporary
travel writers and painters. Nor are they always true to life; she
places palm trees on French hill-tops in one scene.

The Mysteries of Udolpho is set in Gascony (France) and the
Apennines (Italy) in the late 16th century. It is a *bildungsroman*
(or novel of development), following the fortunes of Emily St.
Aubert as she grows up, loses first her father then her mother,
meets (while travelling with her father) the man she is eventually
to marry, is made a ward of her aunt Madame Cheron, is carried
off to the sinister Castle Udolpho by the villainous Montoni (her
aunt's husband), suffers the many terrors and discomforts of
Udolpho, escapes, is reunited with Valancourt (her rather insipid
loved one), and at last is happily married.

There are some complications of plot, though fewer than one
might suspect in a very lengthy novel. But many mysteries are
set up at intervals, only to be explained hundreds of pages later.
Characterization is not deep, so that Emily is a moral young
woman who is a prototype for later Gothic heroines: she faints at
the slightest suggestion of horror or the supernatural. On the other
hand, Montoni is the archetypal villain, with no redeeming features, except for being more entertaining than most of the other
characters. As in most of Radcliffe's novels, there are no actual
supernatural circumstances; in the end all is explained by natural
means. Yet this does little to spoil the impact of Radcliffe's atmospheric effects. Emily is made to believe in ghosts at Udolpho
Castle, and that is enough.

In the wake of *The Mysteries of Udolpho*, Radcliffe was a household name among the reading classes. Her next novel took three
years to come but did not disappoint. *The Italian* is a more pacey,
more suspenseful and more horrifying tale, very much in company (and competition) with M. G. Lewis's *The Monk*, published
the previous year (1796).

Set in 17th-century Italy, *The Italian* is Radcliffe's most complex work. In it, the beautiful heroine Ellena is in love with the
handsome though rather naive young hero Vincentio di Vivaldi,
and he returns her love. But their romance is continually thwarted
by the Italian of the title, who is an evil monk, Schedoni. He persuades Vivaldi's mother to prevent the marriage, and he arranges
for Ellena to be confined in the convent of San Stefano, where she
is threatened and tortured by some very nasty nuns who try to
force her to join their order. At the same time there is an attempt
to persuade Vivaldi that he must leave Ellena to her destiny in the
convent. Vivaldi does persist, though, rescuing her with a little
help from the one kindly nun in the whole order, and arranging a
wedding ceremony. This is interrupted by Schedoni's agents, who
see to it that Ellena is imprisoned in a forbidding mansion while
Vivaldi is handed over to the Inquisition. Schedoni almost murders Ellena, pausing only when it is revealed to him that he may
be her long-lost father. In fact he is Ellena's uncle. All kinds of
less-than-credible revelations of identity occur in the final chapters, though happiness is achieved for Ellena and Vivaldi.

Overall, *The Italian* is a cleverly plotted novel building to a powerful ending. Schedoni is its most interesting character. The

"haunted" castle backdrop of *The Mysteries of Udolpho* was replaced by the equally Gothic backdrop of a religious institution and the dreaded inquisition. There are many sub-plots and additional, even irrelevant, tales in the book.

Radcliffe's three earlier Gothic novels were less memorable, with their main plots blurred and diluted by excessive complications, though in her own lifetime *The Romance of the Forest* was highly regarded. It is an overplotted piece full of what were, even then, Gothic clichés: a beautiful young woman being protected, an abbey used by a highwayman as a base, a nightmare featuring a message, a secret chamber, terrible family revelations, injustices and romantic misunderstandings. It was given Radcliffe's original touches only through the periodic insertion of her own poems.

The brief *Castles of Athlin and Dunbayne* is a complicated revenge story set in late-medieval Scotland, with a plot best forgotten and notable only for its attractive Scottish landscapes and atmospheric castles. *A Sicilian Romance* is, again, standard Gothic, with a 16th-century Sicilian marquis marrying a second wife while his first is incarcerated in a wonderfully described castle (more practice for Udolpho). It must be noted that Mary-Anne Radcliffe, author of *Manfroné; or, The One-Handed Monk* (1809) is a different person, though she has often been confused with Ann Radcliffe.

—Chris Morgan

RAUCHER, Herman

Nationality: American. **Born:** New York City, 13 April 1928. **Education:** New York University, B.S. 1949. **Family:** Married Mary Kathryn Martinet in 1960; two daughters. **Career:** Advertising copywriter, Twentieth Century Fox, 1950-54, Walt Disney, 1954-55, Calkins and Holden, New York, 1956-57; vice-president, Reach McCluton, New York, 1957-63, Maxon, New York, 1963-64, Gardner, New York, 1964-65; consultant, Benton and Bowles, New York, 1965-67; television writer; freelance novelist and screenwriter from 1967. **Agent:** William Morris Agency, Los Angeles, California, USA.

HORROR, GHOST AND GOTHIC PUBLICATIONS

Novel

Maynard's House. New York, Putnam, 1980; London, Michael Joseph, 1981.

OTHER PUBLICATIONS

Novels

Watermelon Man (novelization of screenplay). New York, Ace, 1970.
Summer of '42. New York, Putnam, 1971; London, W. H. Allen, 1971.
A Glimpse of Tiger. New York, Putnam, 1971; London, W. H. Allen, 1972.
Ode to Billy Joe. New York, Dell, and London, Star, 1976.
There Should Have Been Castles. New York, Delacorte, 1978; London, Macmillan, 1979.

Plays

Harold. N.p., n.d.

Screenplays: *Sweet November*, 1968; *Can Hieronymus Merkin Ever Forget Mercy Humpe and Find True Happiness?*, 1969; *Watermelon Man*, 1970; *Summer of '42*, 1971; *Class of '44*, 1973; *A Glimpse of Tiger*; *Ode to Billy Joe*, 1976.

*   *   *

Raucher moved from an advertising career, via television scriptwriting, to become a successful writer of screenplays for Hollywood and of the novels which accompanied them. His most notable novel is *Summer of '42*, which sold over three million copies and was also a success as a film.

In his first novel, *Watermelon Man*, there is a moment of horror early on when the protagonist, Jeff Gerber, a white racial bigot, discovers that he has become a black man overnight. But the book is a humorous satire on race rather than horror. *Maynard's House* is Raucher's only real horror fiction, a subtle piece which remains enigmatic throughout.

Maynard's House is like Stephen King crossed with Henry David Thoreau: a slow and restrained novel set in rural Maine in the middle of winter, which concentrates on the problems of nature and self-sufficiency. The book begins (and, indeed, ends) with Austin Fletcher, a young man just discharged from the US army, travelling by train through a winter landscape to take possession of a house. He is a Vietnam veteran (for this is the winter of 1972-73) and the house has been willed to him by his army buddy, Maynard Whittier, recently killed in Vietnam.

What Austin does not realize, for he is a city boy from Cincinnati, is that Maynard's house is almost unreachable during Maine's harsh and extended winter. The train goes, with difficulty, as far as the small town of Belden, some 70 miles north of Bangor, from where Austin gets a lift from the stationmaster, postmaster and general factotum, Jack Meeker, in a four-wheel-drive Jeep. The snow is thigh-deep and snowshoes are necessary for the mile-or-so trek up from the road to the house (and even for the 50-yard walk to the outside toilet). The house is wooden, lacking a telephone or electricity, heated by a small wood-burning stove and lit by kerosene lamps. It is well supplied with tins and preserves and other foodstuffs. It is also rumoured to have been the abode of a witch in earlier times, and there is a "witch's tree" (from which a witch was hanged) close by.

Left to himself, with no neighbours for miles, Austin gradually discovers how the systems of the house operate. He reads Maynard's notes and his books (including Thoreau's *Walden*), meets some of the local animals, and learns about the Minnawickies, which are meant to be small elves or goblins with an odd sense of humour. He even sees the Minnawickies, colourful little creatures who throw snowballs at him and scamper away, leaving words written in the snow. At night there are small disturbing sounds, including that of the rocking chair moving by itself. On the wall is a plank with carved messages from previous inhabitants of the house, most of whom suffered bad luck or were otherwise unwilling to stay there for long.

Some excitement is provided by a deer which enters his house while he is visiting the outhouse, and by an injured bear which nearly kills him. He meets an elderly hunter named Benson (responsible for the injured bear), who helps himself to food from the house, and he is kept supplied with a few necessary provisions by Meeker, who leaves food-parcels and messages in his mailbox by the road. All the time, Austin is coping with the feeling that the house may be haunted or bewitched.

At last, he manages to catch the Minnawickies, who seem to be two children, a boy of 11 and a girl of perhaps 16. Over a period of weeks he falls in love with the girl, Ara, who is strange and cheeky. She explains that she and her brother live eight miles away and sled across to his house occasionally, but he is not convinced that this is the truth.

Gradually the atmosphere of the place gets to Austin. A number of small impossibilities occur, such as the stove giving out cold rather than heat . . . unless he is imagining them. Ara tells him that Jack Meeker is dead, and Benson the hunter, too, but Austin does not believe her. He keeps on having conversations with Maynard, in his sleep to begin with but later on while he is awake. Austin manages to kiss Ara, but he slowly becomes convinced that he is a fool to stay in the house, and he prepares to leave. And one night, just as he is leaving, Ara comes on her own and shares his bed . . . unless he is imagining the whole experience. Days later she seems to deny that it happened.

Towards the end, Austin is imagining that he is under attack, perhaps by spectres gathering around the house or perhaps by the Vietcong. He fires the rifles left by Maynard, and he may even have managed to set fire to the house—though it is rumoured that, as a witch's house, it cannot be burnt to the ground. He gets down into the root cellar to avoid being burnt to death, and he believes that he crawls a considerable distance, following the stream, meeting the witch and possibly all the house's previous inhabitants.

But he wakes up in the root cellar to find the house intact. Everything is fine except that he is now Maynard and the date is two years earlier, January 1971, and Meeker has arrived to give him a lift on his journey to join the army. The last chapter mirrors the first except for small changes—Austin meets Ara and her brother at Belden railway station—so the cycle may not happen again.

Raucher has made this almost into a literary novel, with fine descriptions of place and much space devoted to the dialect and odd, dry sense of humour of the inhabitants of rural Maine. There is a great deal of zany light banter in the early pages. Heavy descriptive passages are alternated with several pages of brief, punchy dialogue. And gradually everything becomes darker as Austin's mood is affected by isolation and the atmosphere of the house. Although told in the third person, this is a very subjective novel. It may be that Austin is being haunted by ghosts and a witch, or it may be that he is being driven mad by memories and by the loneliness, so that he imagines the supernatural events. But could it be that it is the influence of the witch that is driving him mad? And could Ara possibly be the witch reincarnated? All these are possibilities, and Raucher leaves the reader to make up his own mind.

—Chris Morgan

REEVES-STEVENS, (Francis) Garfield

Nationality: Canadian. **Born:** 1953. **Family:** Married Judith Reeves-Stevens. **Career:** Writer of primary science textbooks and educational computer software, Toronto; freelance writer. **Address:** c/o Pocket Books, 1230 Avenue of the Americas, New York, NY 10020, USA. Lives in Beverly Hills, California.

HORROR, GHOST AND GOTHIC PUBLICATIONS

Novels

Bloodshift. Toronto, Virgo Press, 1981; New York, Popular Library, 1990; London, Pan, 1993.
Dreamland. Toronto, McClelland-Bantam, 1985; New York, Warner, 1991.
Children of the Shroud. Toronto, Doubleday Canada, 1987; New York, Popular Library, 1990.
Nighteyes. New York, Doubleday, 1989.
Dark Matter. New York, Doubleday, 1990; London, Pan, 1992.

OTHER PUBLICATIONS

Novels with Judith Reeves-Stevens

Star Trek: Memory Prime. New York, Pocket, and London, Titan, 1988.
The Chronicles of Galen Sword, Book 1: Shifter. New York, Roc, 1990; London, Roc, 1991.
Star Trek: Prime Directive. New York, Pocket, 1990; London, Simon and Schuster, 1991.
The Chronicles of Galen Sword, Book 2: Nightfeeder. New York, Roc, 1991.
Alien Nation 1: The Day of Descent. New York, Pocket, 1993.
Star Trek: Federation. New York and London, Pocket, 1994.
Star Trek: The Ashes of Eden, with William Shatner. New York and London, Pocket, 1995.
Star Trek: The Return, with William Shatner. New York and London, Pocket, 1996.
Star Trek: Avenger, with William Shatner. New York and London, Pocket, 1997.

Other with Judith Reeves-Stevens

The Making of Star Trek: Deep Space 9. New York and London, Pocket, 1994.
The Art of Star Trek. New York and London, Pocket, 1995.
Star Trek Phase II: The Lost Series. New York and London, Pocket, 1997.

*

Film Adaptation: *Phoenix: The Final Cure,* from his novel *Bloodshift,* 1988.

*   *   *

In deference to the wishes and obsessions of the megalomaniacal lead character in Garfield Reeves-Stevens's science-fiction horror novel, *Dark Matter,* we should begin at the beginning. But the phrase, as familiar as it seems, has unusual connotations when applied to the solo horror work of Garfield Reeves-Stevens.

Anthony Cross, a Nobel Prize-winning brain surgeon (and lothario) is obsessed with the notion of understanding the Beginning: he feels the "secret closing in on him . . . [of the] final ultimate knowledge of the Beginning." And elsewhere it is written that there "were no absolutes in science. But [Cross] had surpassed science. What he saw was no longer a description. It was nature herself." Anthony Cross is fascinated by the notion of singularity, of being able to see over the fences, and gaze upon space, time, gravity, existence and the universe itself as one single particle. True knowledge being a dangerous thing, it is nevertheless (or therefore) what Cross longs for singularly. The Beginning does not refer simply to the beginning of time: it means more than that—a state of mind and body; a dreaming visionary moment of pure understanding; what William Burroughs once described (in miniature) as the Naked Lunch: "a frozen moment when everyone sees what is on the end of every fork."

Taking the vision in one hungry stare, then, we examine the work of Garfield Reeves-Stevens. Judging from the eclecticism of his genre options and the catholicism of his sources, one might argue that Reeves-Stevens would hold Cross's obsessions in some favour. It is apparent that Reeves-Stevens enjoys the encapsulation of The Moment; trying to see, be and write about everything at once. Writing about Reeves-Stevens's first horror novel, *Bloodshift*, the American novelist Chelsea Quinn Yarbro stated that the book mixed the "best elements of Robert Ludlum and Anne Rice," and went on: "It is a fast-moving international adventure with a rational horror element served up with corkscrew plot twists and an unexpected ending . . . something different and exciting in revisionist horror."

"Revisionist horror" is a good way of putting it. Horror is either the fiction that concentrates on random occurrences that lead to the formation of bad energy; or it is the intertwining of existing streams of bad energy. The third possibility, most intriguing of all, is that horror is concerned with energies that are only made to seem bad on their eventual connection. The last most aptly describes the horror work of Mr. Reeves-Stevens—remarkably deep and complex novels of a mix-and-match sensibility. What (to be fair) some regard as a sort of try-your-luck serendipitous gamble of fictional choices, is to others breathtakingly audacious, as evidenced by the clutch of excellent reviews that *Bloodshift* and *Dark Matter* received. The former uses an unlikely plot formulation, as follows: a set of crossbow-wielding Jesuits battle a set of superhuman assassins for a coffin in which an important member of the Undead is being kept. Meanwhile, in Washington, D.C., a terrible experiment known as the Nevada Project tries to hide the truth behind its deadly viral research. A New York cult plots to kill one of its own members in order to stop that member from revealing a grave secret. And our hero, Granger Helman, an ex-Mob hitman, is teased out of retirement in order to assassinate a vampire named Adrienne St. Clair, whom he subsequently falls in love with.

Crowded? Undoubtedly. And yet it works. Reeves-Stevens uses certain horror tropes, of course, yet there is much in his work that is original. As is often the case with horror fiction, in Reeves-Stevens's novels there is always a predetermined winner, and the loser is someone who will have to adjust his way of thinking at least twice: once, to come to terms with what is going on (to believe it all), and twice, to find a solution. (Possibly three times, if a mental journey back to the way things were before is undertaken). It is likely that some of the research that Garfield Reeves-Stevens did with his wife for some of their co-authored projects (the Star Trek tie-ins, for example) gave the author a feel for movies and for movie-plotting; certainly *Bloodshift* is composed like a movie—even to the degree of many chapters having a few para-

graphs and then the place and date of the scene in italics, like subtitles on the screen. This technique gives the reader a set of focuses, as the reader would have as a film-viewer, film being a medium in which stasis is more or less held in general disdain.

In the swirl of *Bloodshift*'s plots, there is an involved secret history of Jesuit factions. The Jesuits: the Society of Jesus, taught to kill if need be in the name of God. Formed 400 years ago, the Jesuits were denigrated by the Spanish Inquisition who thought that they would become too powerful. Indeed, the Jesuits studied and got involved in politics, creating wars through the combined techniques of "lying, manipulation, and assassination." *Bloodshift* highlights the insidiousness of this hierarchical system, where Jesuits swear allegiance to other Jesuits and not to the church; and where, in the throes of doing something sinful, a Jesuit checks with another Jesuit for a moral thumbs-up.

It quickly becomes clear that in a smaller, less ambitious way, Reeves-Stevens has written a book in the vein of Anthony Burgess's *Earthly Powers*: a study of sin in (by and large) the 20th century. Reeves-Stevens shows us a different angle, but all the same, it is sin growing up in public. As Major Weston points out: "This is not a little group of monks we're dealing with. These are fanatics of the worst sort: brilliant, and able to justify any means to accomplish their ends."

Adrienne St. Clair, the beautiful vampire whose would-be exterminator develops a crush on her, can stop the End Days. In the cowboy-shoot-'em-up finale, with the Jesuits having followed the killer and Adrienne to the Conclave (a sort of sally-port for vampires, supposedly), a scene develops that resembles the cinematic hybridization of *From Dusk Till Dawn* and *The Name of the Rose*.

Dark Matter shares *Bloodshift*'s plethora of international settings, and as with the previous novel (and with thriller movies) opens with a bang, a scene of twitchy unpleasantness: "'Let me explain it to you again,' the teacher said, gently sliding the scalpel across the forehead of the student so the first blood of her understanding welled up in a sudden crimson thread. The teacher smiled. It was going to be a good lesson."

Dark Matter was incorrectly published as science fiction, for despite its opening—the neurosurgery, the Einsteinian scientific theories—and despite the pulsing generators, laboratories, artificial-gravity belts, and sf props and tools—this is a novel about a man with his heart set on the Void. It is science-fictional in places of course, but the overall effect seems to lean towards horror—there is the mystical connection with the ethereal that is decidedly M. R. Jamesian in tone, and there is the Lovecraftian sense of awe in finally coming to terms with What is Beyond. Charis Neale (having earned not one but two doctorates) bemoans the fact at the start that she is still a laboratory assistant; by the end, truth be told, her luck has taken a turn for the worse, and she has turned into Anthony Cross's crime janitor, the clearer-up of his various scientific excesses.

Reeves-Stevens proposes a shift of moral perceptions when one is in the grip of genuine greatness. In Cross's defence, Charis Neale says to Duvall, a female detective on the trail: "He's a genius. In physics, and in manipulating people. I think we're all as predictable as billiard balls to him. But he's probably the greatest mind we've ever known, so isn't that worth the greatest sacrifice?" Duvall replies, "He's insane." Neale: "He created artificial gravity. He built a quantum field generator." Duvall: "He's killed more than 20 people." The punchline is Neale's last word: "Acceptable losses, our government says."

And all the while, in this and other of Reeves-Stevens's books, black holes, both literal, emotional and figurative yawn wider. His characters are often trying to go back to a point long ago—to touch forbidden fruit, perhaps; or to rid the world of a terrible scourge. The question often posed is this: What price a return to the Beginning?

—David Mathew

REYNOLDS, G(eorge) W(illiam) M(acarthur)

Nationality: British. **Born:** Sandwich, Kent, 23 July 1814. **Education**: Royal Military College, Sandhurst, 1828-30; received a legacy which enabled him to travel widely, particularly in France, during the 1830s. **Family:** Married Susannah Frances Reynolds, circa 1844. **Career:** Journalist and publisher, London; editor, *London Journal, Reynolds's Miscellany* and *Reynolds's Weekly*. **Died:** 17 June 1879.

HORROR, GHOST AND GOTHIC PUBLICATIONS

Novels (first published as serials or part-works)

Faust: A Romance of the Secret Tribunals. London, *London Journal*, 1845-46, and Vickers, 1847.
Wagner, the Wehr-Wolf: A Romance. London, *Reynolds's Miscellany*, 1846-47, and Dicks, 1857.
The Necromancer: A Romance. London, *Reynolds's Miscellany*, 1851-52.

OTHER PUBLICATIONS

Novels (first published as serials or part-works)

The Youthful Impostor. 3 vols., London and Paris, n.p., 1835; 2 vols., Philadelphia, Carey and Hart, 1836.
Pickwick Abroad; or, The Tour in France. Philadelphia, Carey and Hart, 1838; London, Tegg, 1839.
Grace Darling. London, Henderson, 1839.
The Mysteries of London. 4 vols., London, Vickers, 1844-46.
The Coral Island. N.p., 1848.
The Pixy. N.p., 1848.
The Mysteries of the Court of London. 8 vols., London, Dicks, 1849-56.
Pope Joan. N.p., 1851.
Agnes. 2 vols., London, Dicks, 1852; as *Agnes Evelyn,* New York, Long, 1860.
The Soldier's Wife. N.p., 1853.
Rosa Lambert. N.p., 1854.
The Loves of the Harem. London, Dicks, 1855; New York, Long, 1880.
Ellen Percy. 2 vols., London, Dicks, 1856; 1 vol., New York, 1885.

*

Critical Studies: *Fiction for the Working Man* by Louis James, London, Oxford University Press, 1963; introduction by E. F. Bleiler to *Wagner, the Wehr-Wolf*, New York, Dover, 1975.

*   *   *

Although he is almost completely forgotten today, G. W. M. Reynolds was the most popular English author of his time. His first great bestseller, *The Mysteries of London*, sold over a million copies at a time when relatively few people could read. He was an extraordinarily prolific writer, producing perhaps 35 or 40 million words of fiction over the ten years or so which followed that breakthrough novel.

Reynolds's high productivity both helped to make his name at the time and has been responsible for his neglect in recent decades. Like many other popular authors of the mid-Victorian era, he wrote highly sensational adventure-romance fiction which appeared in parts in weekly story papers. It suited the public mood, being a faster-moving and more emotionally intense variant on the familiar Gothic style, but by the standards of today it is purple prose, full of hyperbole and sentimentality, its plots held together by coincidence and contrivance, and with many plot elements borrowed from earlier and better writers.

Wagner, the Wehr-Wolf is an important contribution to that subgenre of horror, since it is the first werewolf novel written in English, being predated by only a few stories, some translated from the German. The werewolf elements are small but significant in a long novel which dwells much upon romantic dalliances, swift reversals of personal fortune, murders, kidnapping, great revelations, real skeletons in the cupboard and frequent changes of scene (the Black Forest, Florence, Constantinople, islands and ships in the Mediterranean, and so on). The plot (as in all of Reynolds's novels) is too convoluted to be précised briefly. It is set in the early years of the sixteenth century.

A werewolf is created in the Prologue, when the Devil (presumably) approaches a very elderly German shepherd, Fernand Wagner, and strikes a bargain with him: in exchange for renewed youth and great riches, Wagner must become the Devil's companion and wander the world with him for 18 months, and he must forever after live as a wolf between sunset and sunrise on the last night of each month, preying upon the human race. As the alternative seems to be an early death, Wagner is quick to agree. He does come into riches (and also manages to become both educated and sophisticated). His lycanthropic tendencies generally cause him few problems until he falls in love with the beautiful Nisida, daughter of the late Count of Riverola. She wonders why he is absent from her (or, indeed, rushes away from her) at a certain time of the month.

This transformation scene from Chapter XII gives a hint of Reynolds's style: "But, lo! what awful change is taking place in the form of that doomed being? His handsome countenance elongates into one of savage and brute-like shape;—the rich garment which he wears becomes a rough, shaggy, and wiry skin;—his body loses its human contours—his arms and limbs take another form; and, with a frantic howl of misery, to which the woods give horribly faithful reverberations, and with a rush like a hurling wind, the wretch starts wildly away—no longer a man, but a monstrous wolf!" The author is often vivid to the point of hysteria.

The novel remains sensational and complicated to the end—which is not a happy one. Both Wagner and Nisida die in the closing chapters. Reynolds's narrative method, here as elsewhere, is to give the reader a great deal of information about each character, but always to withhold some vital facts of plots, liaisons or trickery to be brought out like a rabbit from a hat at a much later stage. He also conceals many events from most of his characters, and it is their misunderstandings of the true situation which give rise to much of the character interaction.

Both *Faust* and *The Necromancer* are also set in the early sixteenth century. The former is a variant on the legend, with Wilhelm Faust (who is in prison in Germany) selling his soul in exchange for just 24 years of powerful living and the sacrifice of his first child. He reneges and is tossed into the volcano of Vesuvius. *The Necromancer* features yet another deal with the Devil: this time it is Lionel Danvers, an English peer, who has sold his soul and has bargained well to obtain a century and a half of life, in addition to the power of being impervious to swords or pistols. Indeed, he will be able to win his soul back from the Devil if he can find six virgins willing to love him more than their own souls, who can be sacrificed in his place. So far he has found five and has their names inscribed upon a wall of his castle. He tries hard to add the beautiful Musidora to the list, but fails. At the end he suddenly loses "the exquisite beauty of his youthful appearance," becoming a withered old man in seconds. The lights go out, there is a sound of great wings and Danvers is carried away screaming.

Many of Reynolds's novels include horrific passages, both supernatural and otherwise, yet it would be wrong to call him a writer of horror. He was a popular entertainer who threw any aspects of reality or fantasy into his fiction if he thought they would improve the mixture. As may be judged from the three novels which are most concerned with horror, he tended to re-use plot-devices. His strengths were his ability to produce vivid prose at a phenomenal rate and to hold, in his mind, all the fine details of his extremely complicated plots, since he had no time for more than a first draft and was always writing journalism in-between chapters of his novels. It is interesting to note how he used his novels to disseminate his own views of social and political issues. He was often scathing about the way in which the rich misused their privileged positions, and he was an early advocate of equal rights for women.

Perhaps if Reynolds could have slowed down, written more carefully and less sensationally, he would have been, if not a rival of Dickens, for he lacked Dickens' originality, at least more highly regarded than he is today.

—Chris Morgan

RHODES, Daniel

Pseudonym for Neil McMahon. **Nationality:** American. Lives in Missoula, Montana.

HORROR, GHOST AND GOTHIC PUBLICATIONS

Novels

Next, After Lucifer. New York, St. Martin's Press, and London, New English Library, 1988.
Adversary. New York, Tor, and London, New English Library, 1989.

Kiss of Death. New York, St. Martin's Press, and London, New English Library, 1990.

*   *   *

The recurring theme in the three horror novels by Daniel Rhodes is that evil can and does corrupt the innocent, that even people motivated toward good ends can be seduced into committing evil acts either against their will or without their conscious knowledge. His powerful first novel, *Next, After Lucifer* (dedicated to the memory of M. R. James), consists of a relentless, inevitable descent into evil by its protagonist, John McTell, a professional historian who allows his curiosity to overwhelm his wariness.

McTell is a complex character driven throughout his life by impulses and desires he does not understand. Thwarted in love, bored by his studies, he changes careers in midstream and becomes a well-respected historian, only to become bored by that in turn. Although he does eventually marry a woman he truly loves, there are flaws in that relationship as well which the evil force he is about to encounter will exploit to their fullest. At the same time, he is puzzled by a sense that he is waiting for something to happen in his life. While conducting research in France, McTell learns the legend of Guilhem Suloy, the leader of an order of the Knights Templar who was burned at the stake when the Knights were disbanded, and whose memory still frightens the local villagers even though he has been dead for seven centuries. McTell also learns that Suloy's burial place has never been found, nor has the grimoire that was supposedly the source of his power to command spirits, resurrect the dead and call upon a demonic beast to do his bidding.

While this portion of the story is being revealed, a series of disturbing events unsettles McTell, his wife, and some of the villagers. He sees the apparition of a young woman rising from the water, his wife Linden feels compelled to approach the small pool by a presence she cannot identify, and others see the figure of a man in the distance, sometimes carrying a sword. Alysse, a young local girl, is similarly troubled, feeling as though unseen eyes are watching her every action. And she and McTell feel drawn to one another by a force that isn't exactly sexual, although that element is there as well. Elsewhere in the village people hallucinate or have uneasy dreams, and everyone seems unusually irritable.

This deterioration accelerates when McTell discovers the grimoire, apparently at the direction of the lingering spirit of Suloy. He begins to translate the manuscript but discovers that fresh words appear in the original when he isn't looking. A strange mark appears on his hand, as though it had been held to a fire, and a formerly friendly dog bolts from his presence and is later found mutilated beyond recognition. Ultimately others in the village realize what's happening, but not before McTell is driven to murder his wife, seduce Alysse, and become the involuntary host to the spirit of the evil Knight Templar.

Rhodes constructed this novel masterfully. It is rich in historical detail and each scene helps advance the plot. The demonic Knight Templar is a powerful personality who dominates the book, even though he is never actually on stage. McTell's slow descent into obsession, then outright possession, is beautifully told, and the series of odd events external to his inner conflict are suspenseful and chilling. Rhodes's prose is rich and full of detail, his characters are people we care about, and the plot proceeds so logically that it is possible to believe real even the most impossible events.

Adversary is a direct sequel to *Next, After Lucifer*, and shares many of its assets, though it suffers from one major drawback.

McTell, his personality now completely supplanted, returns to the United States where he assumes the identity of Guy-Luc Valcourt, a wealthy if somewhat idiosyncratic European. Valcourt begins to recruit followers from among the young, seeking a handful of people whom he can introduce to his arcane practice. It would be easy enough to find willing volunteers if he was straightforward, but for his purposes he must corrupt the innocent, find people who will join him believing that they are searching for knowledge and power in order to do good in the world, gradually allowing the power to corrupt them. He has also arranged to have Alysse's body brought from France so that he can resurrect it as well.

His plans almost succeed, failing for two reasons. Two of his acolytes realize that the Adversary whom their leader worships is actually the devil and that they are endangering their souls. At the same time, his old enemies from France are aware of his continued existence and eventually trace his present whereabouts, crossing the ocean to try once more to return him to eternal imprisonment. The story ends with the ultimate issues unresolved, a disappointing ending to an uneven book. The difficulty with *Adversary* is that we see too much of Valcourt this time. Ultimately he becomes just another evil man with occult powers, not the insidious, unnerving force that he represented in *Next, After Lucifer*. Rhodes writes well enough to make this a worthwhile, occasionally gripping adventure, but there's very little suspense.

Rhodes's third novel, *Kiss of Death*, is also something of a letdown. A woman who is heir to a number of occult powers forsakes them in order to pursue her love for an ordinary mortal. Unfortunately, there are other forces involved who aren't happy with her decision, and who endanger the life of the man she loves. Once again, Rhodes's superior prose and strong characterization provide memorable moments, but the pace of the novel is uneven and there's little of the subtle menace that made his first book so impressive.

—Don D'Ammassa

RICE, Anne

Pseudonyms: Anne Rampling; A. N. Roquelaure. **Nationality:** American. **Born:** Howard Allen O'Brien, New Orleans, Louisiana, 4 October 1941; name changed to Anne in 1947. **Education:** Texas Women's University, Denton, Texas, 1959-60; San Francisco State College (now University), California, B.A. 1964, M.A. 1971; graduate study at University of California, Berkeley, 1969-70. **Family:** Married Stan Rice in 1961; one daughter (deceased), and one son. **Career:** Has held a variety of jobs, including waitress, cook, theatre usherette and insurance claims examiner; latterly a full-time writer. **Awards:** Joseph Henry Jackson award honourable mention, 1970. **Address:** 1239 First St., New Orleans, Louisiana 70130, USA.

HORROR, GHOST AND GOTHIC PUBLICATIONS

Novels (series: Mayfair Witches; Vampire Chronicles)

Interview with the Vampire. New York, Knopf, and London, Raven, 1976.

The Vampire Lestat. New York, Ballantine, and London, Macdonald, 1985.
The Queen of the Damned (Vampire). New York, Knopf, 1988; London, Macdonald, 1989.
The Mummy; or, Ramses the Damned. New York, Ballantine, and London, Chatto and Windus, 1989.
The Witching Hour (Witches). New York, Knopf, 1990; London, Chatto and Windus, 1991.
The Tale of the Body Thief (Vampire). New York, Knopf, and London, Chatto and Windus, 1992.
Lasher (Witches). New York, Knopf, and London, Chatto and Windus, 1993.
Taltos: Lives of the Mayfair Witches. New York, Knopf, and London, Chatto and Windus, 1994.
Memnoch the Devil (Vampire). New York, Random House, and London, Chatto and Windus, 1995.
The Servant of the Bones. New York, Knopf, and London, Chatto and Windus, 1996.

OTHER PUBLICATIONS

Novels

The Feast of All Saints. New York, Simon and Schuster, 1980; London, Penguin, 1982.
Cry to Heaven. New York, Knopf, 1982; London, Chatto and Windus, 1990.
Exit to Eden (as Anne Rampling). New York, Arbor House, and London, Futura, 1985.
Belinda (as Anne Rampling). New York, Arbor House, 1986; London, Macdonald, 1987.

Novels as A. N. Roquelaure

The Claiming of Sleeping Beauty. New York, Dutton, and London, Macdonald, 1983.
Beauty's Punishment. New York, Dutton, 1984.
Beauty's Release. New York, Dutton, 1985; London, Warner, 1994.
The Sleeping Beauty Novels (omnibus). New York, New American Library/Dutton, 1991.

*

Film Adaptations: *Interview with the Vampire*, 1994; *Exit to Eden*, 1994.

Critical Studies: *Prism of the Night: A Biography of Anne Rice*, New York, Dutton, 1991, *The Vampire Companion*, New York, Ballantine, 1993, and *The Witches Companion*, New York, Ballantine, 1994, all by Katherine M. Ramsland; *Anne Rice* by Bette B. Roberts, New York, Twayne, and Oxford, Maxwell Macmillan, 1994; *Writing Horror and the Body: The Fiction of Stephen King, Clive Barker, and Anne Rice* by Linda Badley, Westport, Connecticut, Greenwood Press, 1996; *Anne Rice: A Critical Companion* by Jennifer Smith, Westport, Connecticut, Greenwood Press, 1996.

* * *

When *Interview with the Vampire* appeared vampire fiction was in the doldrums; for decades very little had been produced, and the field seemed too narrow to be taken seriously—there was *Dracula* plus associated hangers-on. Since the extraordinary international success of that book there has been an outpouring of imitators and would-be rivals (predictably); but more significantly, most of them have written about vampirism from the inside, like Rice. *Interview with the Vampire* is only the second seminal vampire book.

In construction it harks back to the earliest modern novels, being a pseudo-autobiography, allegedly dictated to a young man who seeks out the vampire Louis, by birth an 18th-century planter from French Louisiana. The young man's motives are mixed; he wants the story, but he also wants to become a vampire himself. As the book ends he is seeking out the vampire Lestat, the vampire who "turned" Louis so long ago, and who is still alive but in a state of terminal degradation.

It's a haunting tale and richly atmospheric, with many well-made set-piece scenes, but its chief strength lies in the pathos of Louis's dogged but doomed endeavours to retain as much as he can of his human essence (and especially human moral values), while sinking ever deeper into a way of life that is ineluctably unnatural and profoundly wicked. Even so, aspects of the story require a more radical suspension of disbelief than is altogether desirable. Louis, Lestat and Claudia, a little girl whom Lestat turns at Louis's instance, set up a coven (not a menage—there's no sex among vampires) which endures for 50 years in New Orleans, while all three feed liberally. Even in so large and louche a seaport, one wonders how the authorities manage to miss such a steady and remorseless depletion of the population. Moreover, Lestat himself seems to have no antecedents and to know no other vampires, who don't come on the scene until the three meet a coven in Paris.

But the principal virtue of the book lies in the emotional bond between the aristocratic, conscience-ridden Louis, their "daughter" Claudia, who grows into a vampire sophisticate of what should be middle age while remaining a little girl to outward appearances, and the cruel, vulgarly materialist Lestat—a strength that Rice regrettably throws away in her next novel, *The Vampire Lestat*. It's legitimate to present Lestat's rival viewpoint, but in order to make him sympathetic enough to sustain interest, Louis has to be presented as a seriously unreliable witness, which falsifies the spirit of the earlier and better book while resolving none of its problems.

As the chronicles proceed the tone becomes increasingly sentimental, reading at times like a series of homosexual love stories with the sex left out. They also become preoccupied with the theology of damnation, and not only *vis-à-vis* vampires. *The Tale of the Body Thief* considers the status of a nun who has lost her belief in God but remains passionately devoted to good works, while in *Memnoch the Devil* Satan appears as a major character who presents his apologia in terms explicitly derived from the Book of Job.

None of this appears to be accidental; indeed, turning to Rice's other major series it becomes apparent that she is constructing an entire theologically coherent universe with its own metaphysics. The key element is the Talamasca Order, a centuries-old band of scholars and illuminati with obvious similarities to the Rosicrucians and the A∴A∴ (at least, as projected by themselves). Their ultimate purpose is ill-defined but meanwhile they are keeping track of both the vampires and the Mayfair Witches in so far as they can.

The stories of the Mayfair Witches exhibit a similar self-indulgence; like the vampires, with their great inherited wealth, voracious sexuality, beauty and (in many cases) intellectual brilliance, they are drawn a little too large to be taken entirely seriously, the more so because the lady most burdened with all those attributes in each generation gets to wear the accursed family emerald. They are also burdened with unique problems on an heroic scale. The "Lasher" of the second title is a male demon who has become attached to the family, and whose penchant for incest is even stronger than their own; having been incarnated as the child of one member, he immediately grows to full size, abducts his mother, and proceeds to ravish her with the explicit intention of fathering a monstrous offspring upon her. The parallel with the relationship between Satan, Sin and Death described in Milton's *Paradise Lost* carries on Rice's theme of damnation, but Rice adds a dimension: unlike that explicit trio, Lasher is monstrously hypocritical. Her symbol of his character is the bed to which he has lashed and on which he has coupled with his mother, stiff with urine and faeces but overlain with a clean sheet and garnished with cut flowers.

The theme of damnation continues in *The Mummy; or, Ramses the Damned*, a free-standing novel which also features an immortal individual of enormous intelligence, personal force and sexual appetite. Unlike the witches and vampires he is indestructible as well, being restrained only by a highly malleable conscience and a vestigial sense of duty towards the people whose king he once was. The book describes in vivid detail the havoc he causes among a coterie of English aristocrats c. 1914, not least by discovering the mummy of Cleopatra and bringing it to a life no less passionate and even less constrained by moral considerations than his own.

At her best Anne Rice is too good a writer to ignore. None of her books lacks descriptive passages of considerable power, but she cannot be said to have fulfilled her first promise. None of her later characters has a depth to equal Louis, and the uses to which they put the huge advantages they acquire or are given seem ever more trivial. Though they lay extravagant claim to sundry emotional attachments, their principal emotion is invariably a self-regard bordering on the solipsistic. Moreover, most of her books show signs of haste in construction, research or both, which can vitiate the originality of her approach. In *Lasher*, for instance, we find the Tudors ruling Scotland, and in *The Mummy* the blonde Cleopatra appears as a brunette; moreover, when her indestructible body cannot be found after a car crash, allegedly intelligent people who know her secret assume that it has been totally consumed in the resulting fire. They're wrong, of course—but how could they be so wrong? Anne Rice's enormous popular success cannot be denied, but the overall impression given by her work is of a gorgeous façade masking incoherence.

—Chris Gilmore

RICKMAN, Phil(ip)

Nationality: British. **Born:** Lancashire, England. **Family:** Married Carol Rickman. **Career:** Reporter for the British Broadcasting Corporation; radio presenter for *And Now Read On*, Radio Wales and Radio 5; freelance writer. **Awards:** Named Wales TV

Reporter of the Year, 1986, and Welsh Current Affairs Reporter of the Year, 1987. Lives in Hereford, on the English-Welsh border.

HORROR, GHOST AND GOTHIC PUBLICATIONS

Novels

Candlenight. London, Duckworth, 1991.
Crybbe. London, Macmillan, 1993; as *Curfew,* New York, n.p., 1993.
The Man in the Moss. London, Macmillan, 1994.
December. London, Macmillan, 1994; New York, Berkley, 1996.
The Chalice. London, Macmillan, 1997.

OTHER PUBLICATIONS

Other

Mysterious Lancashire. Skipton, North Yorkshire, Dalesman, n.d.
Mysterious Derbyshire. Skipton, North Yorkshire, Dalesman, n.d.
Mysterious Cheshire. Skipton, North Yorkshire, Dalesman, 1980.

* * *

Phil Rickman made his first fictional appearance in 1991 and immediately became a name to watch in the supernatural horror genre. Years of journalistic training and experience had secured him an unusual and breezy writing style as well as equipped him with the talent and will to investigate real-life situations and historical facts, then to build on them for his fictional requirements. For example, his first novel, *Candlenight,* was partly inspired by his own radio documentary *Aliens,* which won him the award of Wales Current Affairs Reporter of the Year in 1987. *Candlenight* explores the current social and political situation that exists between England and Wales; in other words, Rickman chose a conflict within the British Isles that is often ignored or sidelined when compared to the tensions in Northern Ireland, but which is obviously as valid a contender for serious discussion and as important to those involved. The themes of invasion and unwanted presences run through Rickman's work (right up to the New Age Travellers swarming upon Glastonbury in the most recent novel, *The Chalice*), and one of *Candlenight*'s premises is of a multitude of English people moving to the rural backwaters of Wales.

This by itself does not qualify the book as a horror novel; but in this and his subsequent work, having established his factual foundations, Rickman starts to look at local folklore, and slowly to release the horrors—such as why so many English people are being drawn to a particular Welsh village and its environs. As with Ramsey Campbell's *The Long Lost, Candlenight* opens with subtly hinted-at static charges between the English and the Welsh, only to move quickly to a scene which displays Rickman's skill for creating a convincingly menacing atmosphere. Thomas Ingley is in his bed at the inn having emerged from a church where he wanted to sketch a knight's effigy, and he's hallucinating. High on painkilling drugs, and sick, Ingley cannot escape the scenes at the church and the question is, has he made it back to the inn at all, or does he only believe he has? Using dislocated sentences and phrases, Rickman builds the picture of an extremely troubled mind; Ingley attempts to separate the here and now from the there and

then. "Creaking of the bed. Wooden bed. Wooden bellstage, moulded doorway eighteenth century, heptagonal front, perpendicular tower . . . black on purple . . . falling . . . Oh God in heaven, I don't know where I am . . ."

Rickman deals with such hallucinatory scenes and schizophrenic mood pieces adroitly. A character in *The Man in the Moss* wakes up from a pornographic dream-trance to find himself painfully having sex with a wall of stone. In *December,* Dave, an Angel of Death, is regarding his own appearance when his mirror describes him (in a nervously comic scene) as "a useless twat . . . physically wasted, emotionally stunted, spiritually sterile . . ."

Crybbe and *December* are more ambitious novels in almost every respect, the latter using as one of its factual bases the massacre at Abergavenny Castle in 1175, and dealing with the concept of auras and psychic abilities. However, one of the strengths of *Candlenight* is precisely its concentrated feel. It is almost the horror equivalent of a locked-room murder mystery: a small set on which everything is possible. Both the character Claire and the village of Y Croes (where the bulk of the novel's action takes place) start attracting tragedy. Why? "Is it isolation? In-breeding? Perhaps it's something endemic to the whole area." Posed near the end of *Candlenight,* it is a query repeated tacitly throughout the body of Rickman's work. In *Candlenight* the village has the feel of a living entity, a place that is breathing. This supposition is given extra validity by Bethan's admission that before returning to the village to be the school's head-teacher, she had been in the early stages of pregnancy and had had a termination in Swansea: but it had not been her deceased husband's child; it had been Y Croes's child—the village's child. This moves the novel on to the notions of virgin births and ethereal dream lovers—and even fairy tales, in that she was dreaming of Tylwyth Teg, the beautiful fairy folk, when she woke in the open air with no memory of what had happened, only post-coital residue to alarm her.

Y Croes is a village out of time; a place that incorporates radical pro-Welsh politics, pre-Christian religion, and "accepts all the eerie psychic things . . . as part of life's fabric . . . rural west Wales is riddled with superstition, but here it's a way of life." It also exudes an atmosphere that makes the English people who are seduced into going there lose the will to live or fail at what they most want to achieve, like one character failing to learn Welsh; like other characters developing tumours and heart problems. The village is a confidence trickster, convincing unwary visitors that (for example) the weather is not cold—even though there is the tell-tale presence of snow on the ground. One character, about to have sex with his girlfriend in the open air, almost sees through the village's deceptions. "He . . . saw the sweat freezing rapidly on her grinning face, the skin of her exposed body blue and mottled. And he thought, it isn't warm at all, it just seems warm to us . . . And then the moment passed, and nothing was clear any more."

Nowhere is Rickman's talent for making the innocuous and familiar pulse with hidden life better identified than in *The Man in the Moss.* This is mainly set in and around a small village—Bridelow—in the Pennine region, where a fossilized man has been exhumed from a vast area of peat. The novel is written in small fragments which dart between characters, time frames, states of mind—but rarely place. The peat and moss, arguably, are the stars of the show. Indeed the novel could be seen as being from the point of view of the man in the moss as he uses his telepathic powers to tune in and out of the lives he is effecting and/or wrecking: Ma Wagstaff's arthritis medicine no longer works on the Rector; Roger Hall cannot at first get an erection with his mistress,

Chrissie, and seems always to have the fossil-man on his mind (this changes soon enough, however, particularly after Chrissie has an arguably amorous encounter with the man in the moss on his slab.)

With its fast pacing, *The Man in the Moss* resembles nothing more than a vast and hugely entertaining supernatural, or parapsychological, soap opera; a sort of Northern English version of *Twin Peaks*, with far-reaching elements of the bizarre at a premium. There is easily a season's worth of entertainment. *The Man in the Moss* is packed and crammed with stories that feed into the central vein of action. The filigrees weave and intermingle, and occasionally knot together. It is fair to say that not every small section at first seems worthy of inclusion. Only as the novel progresses does it become apparent that even the half page of noted conversation back in (say) chapter two had a relevance. This is to Rickman's credit. The instances of the macabre are finely tuned (e.g. antlers falling off the wall to spear a woman's coiffure) and every act of brutality or mysticism is timed and paced, given power because of the sections which threaded their way through the other subplots to lead to the denouement. The flashing between scenes also gives the idea of events passing simultaneously, and of the inevitable interconnectedness of the tales. This is a novel not of one fight of Good against Evil, but of several, ongoing.

Examining furthermore the compulsion of narrative, *The Man in the Moss* extrapolates and offers alternative possibilities to the guidebook that Rickman cites as an essential research tool and which he quotes throughout—Dawber's *Book of Bridelow*. Where this book offers information to visitors about religion and the Bridelow Moss, Dawber's *Secret Book of Bridelow* offers chapters on the excavation of the mound on which St. Bride's church is built and on the production of beer using runes—altogether darker subjects in connection with the village. Ernie Dawber, the author of both guides, is a character in the novel, and what he writes is both for information and as a warning.

Since his first appearance, there has been no shortage of writers and critics willing to praise Rickman's work. A blurb from Stephen King (for *December*: "Remarkable . . . Something new and creepy") one might almost expect; but quite outside the horror field, such writers as Jilly Cooper and Joanna Trollope were quoted for *Crybbe*, and Ruth Rendell had nice things to say about *Candlenight*. It is interesting to note that both Trollope and Rendell offered, along with their praise, preemptive strike clauses concerning their respective views on the horror field in general. Trollope wrote, "I don't like horror novels, but I loved this one. I believed in the characters and relished the wit." And Rendell wrote, "The supernatural thriller has never been a favourite genre of mine, but *Candlenight* was exciting enough to overcome my prejudices."

This seems important: not only do two writers famous in their own fields sweep together the entire output from the horror genre and then trash it, but both of them go on to say how Rickman transcended their expectations. It might be construed, then, that Rickman was seen by them as something other than horror: something under the auspices of horror, but classier, more palatable. Anyone who reads horror regularly knows that there is no longer any such thing as an "ordinary" horror novel, and that the summer-camp-murder-of-the-innocents type of exploitative nonsense, or the senselessly-malicious ghost tale are both more or less of the past; but the point about Rickman is nevertheless valid. His structures are as vast and impressive as the architectural achievements (abbeys, churches) around which his plots revolve; and his

grip on story and characterization is very strong. He is a genuinely exciting writer, and one of the most important additions to the field to have emerged so far in the 1990s.

—David Mathew

RIDDELL, Mrs. J. H.

Pseudonyms: R. V. Sparling, Rainey Hawthorne, F. G. Trafford. **Nationality:** Irish. **Born:** Charlotte Elizabeth Lawson Cowan, in Carrickfergus, 30 September 1832. **Family:** Married Joseph Hadley Riddell in 1857 (died 1880). **Career:** Writer, 1856-1902. **Died:** 24 September 1906.

HORROR, GHOST AND GOTHIC PUBLICATIONS

Novels

Fairy Water: A Christmas Story. London, Routledge, 1873; as *The Haunted House at Latchford* in *Three Supernatural Novels of the Victorian Period* edited by E. F. Bleiler, New York, Dover, 1975.
The Uninhabited House. London, Routledge, 1875; in *Five Victorian Ghost Novels* edited by E. F. Bleiler, New York, Dover, 1971.
The Haunted River. London, Routledge, 1877.
The Disappearance of Mr. Jeremiah Redworth. London, Routledge, 1878.
The Nun's Curse. London, Ward and Downey, and New York, Lovell, 1888.

Short Stories

Weird Stories. London, Hogg, 1882.
The Collected Ghost Stories of Mrs. J. H. Riddell, edited by E. F. Bleiler. New York, Dover, 1977.

OTHER PUBLICATIONS

Novels

Zuriel's Grandchild (as R. V. Sparling). London, Newby, 1856; as *Joy after Sorrow* (as Mrs. J. H. Riddell), London, Warne, 1873.
The Ruling Passion (as Rainey Hawthorne). London, Bentley, 1857.
The Rich Husband (as Rainey Hawthorne). London, Skeet, 1858.
The Moors and the Fens (as F. G. Trafford). London, Smith Elder, 1858.
Too Much Alone (as F. G. Trafford). London, Skeet, 1860.
City and Suburb (as F. G. Trafford). London, Skeet, 1861.
The World in the Church (as F. G. Trafford). London, Skeet, 1862.
George Geith of Fen Court (as F. G. Trafford). London, Tinsley, 1864; New York, Felt, 1865.
Maxwell Drewitt (as F. G. Trafford). London, Tinsley, 1865; New York, Garland, 1879.
Phemie Keller (as F. G. Trafford). London, Tinsley, and New York, Harper, 1866.
The Race for Wealth. London, Tinsley, and New York, Harper, 1866.
Far above Rubies. London, Tinsley, 1867.
My First Love. London, F. Enos Arnold, 1869.

Austin Friars. London, Tinsley, 1870.

Long Ago. London, F. Enos Arnold, 1870.

A Life's Assize. London, Tinsley, and New York, Harper, 1871.

The Earl's Promise. London, Tinsley, 1873; New York, Scribner Welford and Armstrong, 1880(?).

Home, Sweet Home. London, Tinsley, 1873.

Mortomley's Estate. London, Tinsley, 1874.

Above Suspicion. London, Tinsley, 1876.

Her Mother's Darling. London, Tinsley, 1877.

The Mystery in Palace Gardens. London, Bentley, 1880.

Alaric Spenceley; or, A High Ideal. London, Skeet, 1881.

The Senior Partner. London, Bentley, 1881.

Daisies and Buttercups. London, Bentley, 1882.

A Struggle for Fame. London, Bentley, 1883.

Susan Drummond. London, Bentley, 1884; New York, Munro, 1884(?).

Berna Boyle: A Love Story of the County Down. London, Bentley, 1884; New York, Macmillan, 1900.

Mitre Court: A Tale of the Great City. London, Bentley, 1885.

For Dick's Sake. London, Society for Promoting Christian Knowledge, 1886.

Miss Gascoyne. London, Ward and Downey, and New York, Munro, 1887.

The Government Official, with Arthur H. Norway (published anonymously). London, Bentley, 1887.

The Head of the Firm. London, Heinemann, 1892.

The Rusty Sword; or, Thereby Hangs a Tale. London, Society for Promoting Christian Knowledge, 1893.

A Silent Tragedy. London, White, 1893.

A Rich Man's Daughter. London, White, 1895(?); New York, American Book Company, 1897.

Did He Deserve It? London, Downey, 1897.

The Footfall of Fate. London, White, 1900.

Poor Fellow! London, White, 1902.

Short Stories

Frank Sinclair's Wife and Other Stories. London, Tinsley, 1874.

The Prince of Wales's Garden Party and Other Stories. London, Chatto and Windus, 1882.

Idle Tales. London, Ward and Downey, 1888.

Princess Sunshine and Other Stories. London, Ward and Downey, 1889; New York, Lovell, 1890.

The Banshee's Warning and Other Tales. London, Remington, 1894.

Handsome Phil and Other Stories. London, White, 1899.

Other

Editor, *How to Spend a Month in Ireland,* by Sir Cusack P. Roney. London, Chatto and Windus, 1872.

A Mad Tour; or, A Journey Undertaken in an Insane Moment through Central Europe on Foot, with Arthur H. Norway. London, Bentley, 1891.

*

Critical Study: "Mrs. Riddell, Mid-Victorian Ghosts, and Christmas Annuals" by E. F. Bleiler, in *The Collected Ghost Stories,* New York, Dover, 1977.

*   *   *

Mrs. Riddell, who was born Charlotte Cowan, is regarded by many as the leading Victorian woman writer of supernatural fiction. In an era that produced the likes of Mrs. Oliphant, Mrs. Molesworth, Rhoda Broughton, Mary Braddon and Amelia Edwards, this is a claim that needs defending, but there is no denying that she was a craftswoman who developed good characters who are affected convincingly by the circumstances around them. Charlotte Riddell did not use the supernatural for its own sake. She used it to explore relationships between people and, more particularly, how individuals wrestled with their own lives and inner beliefs. What she did not do was introduce any original thinking in relation to the supernatural itself. Her stories are essentially hauntings, though her creation of certain scenes, such as the ghost approaching from across a field in "Nut Bush Farm," are very effectively handled. Mrs. Riddell was essentially a realist. Most of her books revolved around city life and the business world and she knew the cut and thrust of commerce. She thus had a no-nonsense approach to the supernatural, making it all the more powerful when she used it.

Much of her early work appeared anonymously, and some pseudonymously, so it is possible that other ghost stories by her exist. Nevertheless E. F. Bleiler has done us all a good service in rescuing most of her known material, reprinting two of her novel-length works in his anthologies and the shorter works in her *Collected Ghost Stories.*

The core of Mrs. Riddell's weird fiction reworks the theme of the haunted house and supernatural revenge or retribution. She did not seek to ring the changes to any great extent on this theme: she simply did it better than most. For instance, two of her best stories deal with the discovery of past child abuse. In "Walnut-Tree House" Stainton inherits an old family house which is falling into disrepair. The previous owner had died insane, and the house had long remained empty as all successive tenants have been driven out by the ghost of a young boy. Stainton investigates the haunting and learns of a dreadful treatment imparted upon the boy and his sister. When the children were separated the boy continued to look for her and, after he pined away, his spirit continued the search. In "A Terrible Vengeance" Murray finds himself followed by the wet footprints of the child he has murdered and the guilt eventually drives him to depression and death.

Ghosts of murder victims appear frequently in Mrs. Riddell's fiction, either seeking help or revenge. "The Open Door" is an especially fine example wherein the clerk at an estate agency seeks to rationalize the mystery behind a door that refuses to be closed at Ladlow Hall. In "The Old House at Vauxhall Walk" the deserted house is haunted by both the murder victim and her murderers, still looking for her riches. Mrs. Riddell often makes the connection between ghosts and their early treasures, clearly making the point that striving for riches in this world is of no help in the next. This is the underlying theme of her supernatural novels, particularly *Fairy Water* and *The Uninhabited House.* The same is true of *The Nun's Curse,* for though no hauntings occur a family is cursed down the generations for an ancestor's murder of the nuns in an abbey.

Mrs. Riddell's ghosts usually invoke sympathy and are rarely malevolent, but in "Old Mrs. Jones" she created a wonderfully nasty ghost. It transpires Mrs. Jones had been murdered by her husband who promptly disappeared and set up in a new life. Mrs. Jones seeks revenge on any who get near her spirit whilst also trying to find her murderer.

A few of Mrs. Riddell's supernatural stories are not about ghosts. It is tempting to compare these with some of Sheridan Le Fanu's work, partly because both were Irish and drew upon their local folklore. Also Mrs. Riddell treated these stories in a similar fashion to Le Fanu. "Hertford O'Donnell's Warning," also known as "The Banshee," uses the wailing of the banshee to betray O'Donnell's sexual indiscretion. "Conn Kilrea" also receives a death portent which causes him to reform. In "The Last of Squire Ennismore" the wicked squire falls one last time to temptation and is taken by the devil. "Sandy the Tinker," set in Scotland rather than Ireland, looks at the hypocrisy of the church where a clergyman seeks to save his own soul by betraying that of an innocent tinker to the Devil.

Readers used to Victorian ghost stories will find little that is new in Mrs. Riddell's work, but they will find a skilled writer who used the theme of supernatural vengeance to good advantage and produced some of the best work of her age.

—Mike Ashley

ROBBINS, Tod

Nationality: American. **Born:** Clarence Aaron Robbins, in Brooklyn, New York, 1888. **Family:** Married six times. **Career:** Travelled widely, and settled on the French Riviera; imprisoned by the Germans during World War II. **Died:** 10 May 1949.

Horror, Ghost and Gothic Publications

Novels

Mysterious Martin. New York, Ogilvie, 1912.
The Unholy Three. London and New York, John Lane, 1917; as
    The Three Freaks, London, Philip Allan, 1934.
The Master of Murder. London, Philip Allan, 1933.

Short Stories

Silent, White and Beautiful, and Other Stories. New York, Boni
    and Liveright, 1920.
Who Wants a Green Bottle? and Other Uneasy Tales. London,
    Philip Allan, 1926.

Other Publications

Novels

In the Shadow. N.p., 1929.
Close Their Eyes Tenderly. N.p., 1940(?).

*

Film Adaptations: *The Unholy Three,* 1925, 1930; *Freaks,* 1932, from the short story "Spurs."

*   *   *

Tod Robbins is virtually forgotten as a writer, although he provided the basis for two films which still command some attention. Lon Chaney liked the 1925 silent version of *The Unholy Three* well enough to remake it as his only talkie in 1930, but it was Tod Browning's *Freaks* that became a landmark in cinema history. It was severely cut in the USA and banned in Britain for 30 years, not because it is uniquely horrible—even before bits began disappearing from the completed movie the script had carefully censored the nastiest element of Robbins's *conte cruel* "Spurs"—but because it seemed so blithely exploitative of the mentally and physically handicapped individuals who took part in it. Because the three circus performers who turn to crime in *The Unholy Three* were played by professional actors it did not seem that the cynical exhibitionism of the carnival freak show were simply being translocated on to the screen—although the retitling of the novel as *The Three Freaks* after the second movie was made does show a certain lack of sensitivity. (The original title of the novel, when it appeared in 1917 as a serial in the pulp magazine *All-Story Weekly,* was "The Terrible Three.")

The morbidity of the kinds of voyeurism which draw gawkers to freak shows and make gruesome murders headline news is Robbins's primary subject-matter. *Mysterious Martin* is an early novel about a serial killer drawn to that activity because he feels a deep and compelling need to know how it feels to commit murder; the interface of psychology and morality was evidently a matter of some fascination to Robbins. The two books issued by Ogilvie—the other being a collection of poems—seem to have been attempts by Robbins to launch a career as an offbeat but upmarket litterateur, but his subsequent work was mostly published in the pulp magazines.

The Master of Murder, which originally appeared in *Silent, White and Beautiful, and Other Stories* as "For Art's Sake," is a calculatedly melodramatic account of a writer of murder mysteries whose work is so fascinating that it inspires readers to go forth and do likewise. The choice of such themes may have been an eccentric form of self-analysis; when Robbins tried once again to rise above the sensationalism of pulp fiction and to write a serious literary novel in *In the Shadow*—which he wrote when his brief pulp career was in he past—he took as its subject-matter the various effects of a death on the close kin of the deceased, and each chapter is a minutely dissected study in the anatomy of grief. The far more garish "Spurs" is a nightmarishly sadistic revenge fantasy, which is all the more discomfiting for bringing the reflexive repugnance which many people feel towards the mentally and physically handicapped into sharp focus. "Silent, White and Beautiful" is another tale of murder for art's sake, using the oft-repeated motif of a corpse hidden within an uncommonly lifelike statue.

The most effective of the tales assembled with "Spurs" in *Who Wants a Green Bottle?* is "Toys" (originally published in 1921 as "Toys of Fate"), an allegory in which a shopkeeper sells a model of his village to Mr. Fate, who begins to play with it in the casually destructive way that children often exhibit. The two other stories reprinted along with "Silent, White and Beautiful" from the Boni & Liveright collection, "Who Wants a Green Bottle?" and "Wild Wullie the Waster" are bizarre fantasies based in Scottish folklore; the protagonist of the former is taken on a tour of Hell by the minuscule soul of his miserly uncle, while the game-playing ghosts in the latter explain how they were brought to the tedious business of haunting. Two tales based in Irish folklore, "A Bit of a Banshee" and "A Son of Shaemas O'Shea," are comedies with only a slight edge of malice, but the humour in the thoroughly English "Cockcrow Inn," about the ghost of a rakehell pirate who exacts his revenge upon the hangman, is much blacker. The ever-economical Philip Allan reprinted most of the stories from *Who Wants a Green Bottle?* in various volumes of his *Creeps* series of anthologies (1932-6); he also reprinted the novella "The Whimpus" (1919)—a somewhat tongue-in-cheek sea story about a nasty siren which is "half-fish, half-vampire"—in *Nightmares* (1933) and the murder story "The Confession" in *Thrills* (1935).

Robbins's work for the Munsey pulps—almost all of which was produced in a period of intense activity between 1917 and 1921—enjoyed a brief renewal of popularity in the 1940s when many of his tales appeared in the reprint magazines *Famous Fantastic Mysteries* and *Fantastic Novels*. These included "The Living Portrait," a doppelgänger story presumably inspired by *The Picture of Dorian Gray*, in which an animate picture becomes the repository and agent of a man's murderous impulses. Several other fantasies and crime stories published during that spectacular burst of productivity have never been reprinted at all.

Robbins was one of the most stylish and imaginative writers who worked for the pulp magazines as they approached their heyday. Although he does not seem to have considered his work in that vein to have been worthy of continuation it does demonstrate a certain dramatic flair that is sadly subdued in what he evidently considered to be his more ambitious literary endeavours. An eclectic collection of his best work is long overdue.

—Brian Stableford

RODGERS, Alan (Paul)

Nationality: American. **Born:** Montclair, New Jersey, 11 August 1959. **Family:** Married the writer Amy Stout; three children. **Career:** Editor, *Night Cry* magazine, 1984-87; assistant editor, *Rod Serling's The Twilight Zone* magazine during the same period. **Awards:** Horror Writers of America Bram Stoker Award for novelette, 1988.

HORROR, GHOST AND GOTHIC PUBLICATIONS

Novels

Blood of the Children. New York, Bantam, 1990; London, Bantam, 1990.
Fire. New York, Bantam, 1990.
Night. New York, Bantam, 1991.
Pandora. New York, Bantam, 1994; London, Millennium, 1995.
Bone Music. Stamford, Connecticut, Longmeadow, 1995.

Short Stories

New Life for the Dead. Newark, New Jersey, Wildside Press, 1991.

*   *   *

Alan Rodgers is fondly remembered by both writers and readers as the exceptionally able editor of *Night Cry*, the digest com-

panion to *Rod Serling's The Twilight Zone Magazine*, which began as a reprint vehicle for stories from that magazine, but soon switched to original fiction of a darker and somewhat more violent cast than the typical *Twilight Zone* story. Within just a couple of issues, *Night Cry* was the premier professional horror magazine of the 1980s, publishing substantial stories by Dean Koontz, Robert Bloch, Ramsey Campbell, Lucius Shepard and many others. Unfortunately the publisher failed adequately to back *Night Cry*, and it soon failed, despite the high quality of its content.

Rodgers's advent as a fiction writer was sufficiently spectacular that it must have tempted struggling wannabes to leap off tall buildings. The first story he ever *wrote*, "The Boy Who Came Back from the Dead," not only achieved publication in the landmark anthology *Masques* (edited by J. N. Williamson), but won a Bram Stoker Award the first year there were Bram Stoker Awards, and then went on to garner a World Fantasy Award nomination.

It *was* an outstanding story, demonstrating at once Rodgers's great strength, aside from a lucid and often lyrical style: an unflinching ability to stay with a horrible or uncomfortable situation, without convenient ellipses, fadeouts, or other evasions. The boy of the title, age eight, did unquestionably die. There was a funeral. He was buried. Now, incomprehensibly, he is back, not a ghost or a vampire or a zombie, but a live boy again, who cannot escape the fact he was dead. He tries to return to family life and to school, and the story develops a very powerful sense of the helplessness and alienation inherent in the situation. The actual ending, which tries to explain the phenomenon as the work of extraterrestrials, is disappointing, but this is one of those stories which is virtually impossible to conclude properly, and which leaves the writer desperately trying to reach *any* conclusion in order to allow the superlative beginning to get into print.

Another early story, "Emma," deals with similar turmoil and torment as a grieving mother reanimates her dead child by means of Santeria magic and tries to go on loving the slowly rotting zombie that results. "Frankenstein Goes Home" explores similar themes, as a creature stitched together from corpses and containing the fragmentary memories of a dozen individuals tries to reclaim its former life. The result is confusion and the painful assumption of a new identity.

Rodgers's novels are characterized by similarly wrenching emotional situations, and also, sometimes, by an inventiveness which threatens to overwhelm all else. *Night* and *Fire* both feature epic apocalypses. In the latter a virus causes dead things, from human corpses all the way back to dinosaurs, to come back to life. Bizarre and terrifying situations are piled upon one another in a truly extravagant fashion. *Pandora* is borderline science fiction, involving UFOs and the Roswell incident, which is now permanently embedded in American folklore. *Blood of the Children* is a truly extreme novel about childhood cruelty, with supernatural elements. It is characterized by some of the goriest scenes in any horror novel with a claim to serious merit. *Bone Music* is another epic, very vaguely reminiscent of King and Straub's *The Talisman*, involving Blues music, Hoodoo, and a quest into Hell to repair the Eye of the World and prevent Judgment Day. Like "Emma's Daughter," *Bone Music* makes effective use of American urban Hispanic culture, an element not previously featured in much horror fiction. It also features real Blues and Jazz musicians, and excellent local colour (Spanish Harlem, New Orleans, etc.). This novel has been widely praised and was nominated for a Stoker Award, but is also, unfortunately, out of print without having ever had a paperback printing. It may well become a cult classic.

With the near total collapse of the horror category in American publishing in the mid-1990s, Rodgers's career seems to be on hold. He will certainly be one of the leaders when the horror field comes back from the dead.

—Darrell Schweitzer

ROHMER, Sax

Pseudonym for Arthur Henry Sarsfield Ward; adopted name Sarsfield at the age of 18; later used Sax Rohmer even in personal life. **Other Pseudonym:** Michael Furey. **Nationality:** British. **Born:** Birmingham, Warwickshire, 15 February 1883. **Family:** Married Rose Elizabeth Knox in 1909. **Career:** Journalist: covered the underworld in London's Limehouse; wrote songs and sketches for entertainers. Later lived in New York City. **Died:** 1 June 1959.

HORROR, GHOST AND GOTHIC PUBLICATIONS

Novels

The Brood of the Witch-Queen. London, Pearson, 1918; New York, Doubleday, 1924.
Grey Face. London, Cassell, and New York, Doubleday, 1924.
She Who Sleeps. New York, Doubleday, and London, Cassell, 1928.
The Day the World Ended. New York, Doubleday, and London, Cassell, 1930.
The Bat Flies Low. New York, Doubleday, and London, Cassell, 1935.

Short Stories

Tales of Secret Egypt. London, Methuen, 1918; New York, McBride, 1919.
The Dream-Detective. London, Jarrolds, 1920; New York, Doubleday, 1925.
The Haunting of Low Fennel. London, Pearson, 1920.
Tales of Chinatown. London, Cassell, and New York, Doubleday, 1922.
Tales of East and West. London, Cassell, 1932; with different contents, New York, Doubleday, 1933.
The Wrath of Fu Manchu and Other Stories. London, Stacey, 1973; New York, DAW, 1976.

OTHER PUBLICATIONS

Novels

The Mystery of Dr. Fu-Manchu. London, Methuen, 1913; as *The Insidious Dr. Fu-Manchu*, New York, McBride, 1913.
The Sins of Séverac Bablon. London, Cassell, 1914; New York, Bookfinger, 1967.
The Yellow Claw. London, Methuen, and New York, McBride, 1915.
10.30 Folkestone Express. London, Lloyds, n.d.

The Devil Doctor. London, Methuen, 1916; as *The Return of Dr. Fu-Manchu*, New York, McBride, 1916.
The Si-Fan Mysteries. London, Methuen, 1917; as *The Hand of Fu-Manchu*, New York, McBride, 1917.
The Orchard of Tears. London, Methuen, 1918; New York, Bookfinger, 1970.
The Quest of the Sacred Slipper. London, Pearson, and New York, Doubleday, 1919.
Dope. London, Cassell, and New York, McBride, 1919.
The Golden Scorpion. London, Methuen, 1919; New York, McBride, 1920.
The Green Eyes of Bâst. London, Cassell, and New York, McBride, 1920.
Bat-Wing. London, Cassell, and New York, Doubleday, 1921.
Fire-Tongue. London, Cassell, 1921; New York, Doubleday, 1922.
Yellow Shadows. London, Cassell, 1925; New York, Doubleday, 1926.
Moon of Madness. New York, Doubleday, and London, Cassell, 1927.
The Emperor of America. New York, Doubleday, and London, Cassell, 1929.
Daughter of Fu Manchu. New York, Doubleday, and London, Cassell, 1931.
Yu'an Hee See Laughs. New York, Doubleday, and London, Cassell, 1932.
The Mask of Fu Manchu. New York, Doubleday, 1932; London, Cassell, 1933.
Fu Manchu's Bride. New York, Doubleday, 1933; as *The Bride of Fu Manchu*, London, Cassell, 1933.
The Trail of Fu Manchu. New York, Doubleday, and London, Cassell, 1934.
President Fu Manchu. New York, Doubleday, and London, Cassell, 1936.
White Velvet. New York, Doubleday, and London, Cassell, 1936.
The Drums of Fu Manchu. New York, Doubleday, and London, Cassell, 1939.
The Island of Fu Manchu. New York, Doubleday, and London, Cassell, 1941.
Seven Sins. New York, McBride, 1943; London, Cassell, 1944.
Egyptian Nights. London, Hale, 1944; as *Bimbâshi Barûk of Egypt* (short stories version), New York, McBride, 1944.
Shadow of Fu Manchu. New York, Doubleday, 1948; London, Jenkins, 1949.
Hangover House. New York, Random House, 1949; London, Jenkins, 1950.
Nude in Mink. New York, Fawcett, 1950; as *Sins of Sumuru*, London, Jenkins, 1950; New York, Bookfinger, 1977.
Wulfheim (as Michael Furey). London, Jarrolds, 1950.
Sumuru. New York, Fawcett, 1951; as *Slaves of Sumuru*, London, Jenkins, 1952.
The Fire Goddess. New York, Fawcett, 1952; as *Virgin in Flames*, London, Jenkins, 1953.
The Moon Is Red. London, Jenkins, 1954.
Return of Sumuru. New York, Fawcett, 1954; as *Sand and Satin*, London, Jenkins, 1955.
Sinister Madonna. London, Jenkins, and New York, Fawcett, 1956.
Re-Enter Fu Manchu. New York, Fawcett, 1957; as *Re-Enter Dr. Fu Manchu*, London, Jenkins, 1957.
Emperor Fu Manchu. London, Jenkins, and New York, Fawcett, 1959.
The Fu-Manchu Omnibus, vol. 1. London, A and B, 1995.

Short Stories

The Exploits of Captain O'Hagan. London, Jarrolds, 1916; New York, Bookfinger, 1968.
Salute to Bazarada and Other Stories. London, Cassell, 1939; New York, Bookfinger, 1971.
The Secret of Holm Peel and Other Strange Stories. New York, Ace, 1970.

Plays

Round in 50, with Julian and Lauri Wylie, music by H. Finck and J. Tate (produced Cardiff and London, 1922).
The Eye of Siva (produced London, 1923).
Secret Egypt (produced London, 1928).
The Nightingale, with Michael Martin-Harvey, music by Kennedy Russell (produced London, 1947).

Other

Pause! (published anonymously). London, Greening, 1910.
The Romance of Sorcery. London, Methuen, 1914; New York, Dutton, 1915.

Ghostwriter: *Little Tich: A Book of Travels and Wanderings,* by Harry Relph, London, Greening, 1911.

*

Film Adaptations: *The Mysterious Dr. Fu Manchu,* 1929; *The Return of Dr. Fu Manchu,* 1930; *Daughter of the Dragon,* 1931; *The Mask of Fu Manchu,* 1932; *Drums of Fu Manchu* (serial), 1939; *The Adventures of Fu Manchu* (television series), 1955-56; *The Face of Fu Manchu,* 1965; *The Brides of Fu Manchu,* 1966; *Sumuru* (*The Million Eyes of Su-Muru*), 1967; *The Vengeance of Fu Manchu,* 1967; *The Blood of Fu Manchu,* 1968 (also known as *Kiss and Kill* and *Against All Odds;* released on video as *Kiss of Death*); *The Castle of Fu Manchu,* 1972; *The Fiendish Plot of Dr. Fu Manchu,* 1980.

Bibliography: *Sax Rohmer: A Bibliography* by Bradford M. Day, Denver, New York, Science Fact and Fantasy, 1963.

Critical Studies: *Master of Villainy,* by Cay Van Ash and Elizabeth Sax Rohmer, edited by R. E. Briney, Bowling Green, Ohio, Popular Press, 1972 (includes bibliography); *The Rohmer Review* irregular), edited by R. E. Briney, Salem, Massachusetts, Sax Rohmer Society.

*   *   *

For a good deal of his life—and certainly in the first decade or so of his career as one of the most successful concocters of popular fiction of the 20th century—Arthur Sarsfield Ward, far better known as Sax Rohmer, operated on two quite distinct levels. On the one hand he was an entertainer (though by no means pure, and not at all simple) with the brassiest of brass necks; a conscienceless manipulator of public trepidation; a shameless inflater of a peril that was no peril at all (the "Yellow Peril") into an absurd global conspiracy.

He had not even the excuse (if excuse is the word) of his predecessor in this shabby lie, M. P. Shiel, who was a vigorous racist, sometimes exhibiting a hatred and horror of Jews and the Far Eastern races. Rohmer's own racism was careless and casual, a mere symptom of his times. But he recognized other people's fears and loathings and tapped directly into them with his saga of the fiendish, and seemingly deathless, Dr. Fu Manchu, whose millions of minions were ever biding their time, awaiting the order to inundate and subjugate the Western white races, and particularly the British Isles. Even more particularly London, for at the heart of the Empire the teeming hordes of "heathen Chinee" swarmed like hyperactive rats around Limehouse Reach and Wapping Old Stairs, poised to flood the capital, turn its citizens into opium or cocaine addicts, and carry off the flower of British maidenhood to the stews of Shanghai.

This nonsense was believed more or less seriously by just about all classes, even though, as the sociologist Virginia Berridge has determined, the ethnic Chinese population of the Limehouse area—indeed, the whole of London's East End—in the period 1900 through to the Second World War ran to a few hundred at most, the majority of whom were engaged in respectable professions such as cooking and laundering (clothes, not money). As for narcotics, this was notably the province of "black" immigrants rather than "yellow" (the well-heeled Chinese restaurant-owner "Brilliant Chang" notwithstanding), most of the actual drugs coming from Germany, where cocaine production was virtually unregulated. And so far as white slavery went, it was to Buenos Aires that most of the young girls (dancers, usually, lured by spurious advertisements in *The Stage*) travelled.

Nevertheless, with Fu Manchu and his strange cohorts and even more bizarre "pets" (monstrous spiders, lizards, hamadryads, batrachians unknown to science, murderous *lepidopterae*, Venus flytraps capable of digesting a man) Rohmer accomplished what all writers of popular fiction yearn for but rarely achieve—the creation of a character who transcends mere popularity and becomes an entry in the dictionary.

In his latter days Rohmer may well have believed his own myths. His younger persona, however, operated on a quite different level, to an extent at war with his brasher self. On this level, Rohmer dabbled in the occult, and carried out research into the more esoteric religions, and otherwise, cults (although it is doubtful that he was ever actually a member of the Order of the Golden Dawn, as some have claimed). This Rohmer—the Rohmer of the years 1910 through to the early 1920s—created carefully as well as lazily (and at times he did exhibit an appalling carelessness: as when, in *The Si-Fan Mysteries*, the "secret that threatens the Empire," once articulated, is never actually explained, or even referred to again), and showed in his better fiction an enviable dramatic promise, never entirely fulfilled.

"The Cardinal's Stair" (*Tales of East and West*, but originally published in 1916) is typically Rohmerian in that while its premise is excellent (old house inhabited by beautiful mystic who has written a book of arcane lore), its effectuation is hopeless, the ghost at the end merely thrown in to strap up an increasingly unconvincing narrative (Rohmer later salvaged one of the story's motifs—the wonderful tome of lost mystical wisdom—utilizing it in a far more sophisticated way in *The Orchard of Tears*, perhaps the closest he ever came to writing a straight, untricksy novel, even though the weird element is strong).

Other macabre tales were handled more effectively. In "The Hand of the White Sheik" (rewritten as "The Hand of Mandarin Quong" for *Tales of Chinatown*), the brutal Adderley, abductor of a sheik's (or mandarin's) favourite wife, is pursued by the sheik's (or mandarin's) vengeful hand, severed at the wrist but still horribly deadly. Another dark nemesis is the eponymous animal in "The Cat" (*New Magazine*, March 1914), who saves the heroine from a crooked financier: however, the girl herself may be a reincarnation from ancient Egypt, and the cat can certainly "shape-change" into a priestess of Bubastis. In the very early "The Leopard Couch" (finally collected in *The Wrath of Fu Manchu*, but written in 1903) an inanimate object causes those receptive to its influence to experience the past. Other visions occur in "The Treasure of Taia" (*The Wrath of Fu Manchu*), in which the hero slips momentarily back to pharaonic Egypt, and the excellent "In the Valley of the Sorceress" (*Tales of Secret Egypt*), in which, bafflingly—and eerily—archaeologists are faced with the Sisyphean task of constantly reopening the shaft to the tomb of an ancient Egyptian witch, which keeps getting filled up to the top again at night.

Probably Rohmer's most elaborate macabre tale is the much-reprinted "Tchériapin" (*Tales of Chinatown*). Here black magic melded with modern science has prolonged the life of a notorious violinist as a miniature creature (a gruesome detail is that to be thus treated, all one's teeth must be extracted). In "The Master of Hollow Grange" (*The Haunting of Low Fennel*) another crazed scientist is determined to extract, in the most ghoulish manner possible, the vital glands from a young girl to prolong his own life (this, of course, is Rohmer's version of M. R. James's "Lost Hearts," just as "Torturer" from *Tales of East and West* is, to a certain extent, "The Pit and the Pendulum"). *The Dream-Detective* has an unusual premise: a psychic sleuth (virtually) has tuned his mind to reproduce from the atmosphere the last images seen by murder victims. This kind of plotline needs careful handling, however, and the resulting collection is a very mixed bag.

As with the short stories, so with the novels: some start triumphantly, but end abysmally. Initially *She Who Sleeps* bids fair to be one of the great supernatural novels of the 20th century—when it appears that an ancient Egyptian princess can be awoken from a mystic, millennia-long trance in her sarcophagus—then turns into an elaborate hoax, on both the characters in the story and on the frustrated reader. *The Day the World Ended* begins promisingly with voices from nowhere and giant vampire bats, then degenerates into a chaotic chase sequence for the final third of the book, after which a mere conspiracy to destroy the world by a mad scientist is exposed (the voices: radio-enhanced; the bats: simply men in powered flying-suits—ho-hum).

By comparison *Grey Face*, though somewhat incoherent at times, has some genuinely creepy moments and a powerful climax, reminiscent of Poe's "The Facts in the Case of M. Valdemar." Even so it has nowhere near the abiding sense of horror of Rohmer's masterpiece, *The Brood of the Witch-Queen*, an authentic weird novel which cleverly combines the excitement of the chase with the enticing allure of strange secrets revealed (pyramidologists in 1914 became extremely excited when the story was serialized, thinking that Rohmer, when he invented a secret second chamber in the pyramid at Meydum, was disclosing a truth lost for thousands of years). Very little that Rohmer wrote after the Great War can compare with certain of the novel's set-pieces, especially the scene in which the hero and his father are about to destroy the villain (Anthony Ferrara, a sorcerer of ancient Egypt reborn into the modern world, and now lying, Dracula-like, in a trance on his mother's sarcophagus absorbing its malign influence) when thousands of fat and hirsute tarantulas begin dropping from the shadowy ceiling . . . .

Rohmer's main problem was that in general he demonstrated no real involvement with his stories or the characters that thronged them. In some of his early work there is a sense that its creator cared about what he was writing, but very soon fame and fortune—and Dr. Fu Manchu—nudged such feelings aside. It was as though he were trapped in some particularly wearisome corner of Dante's Inferno, his punishment to crank out the same old stuff again and again and again.

—Jack Adrian

ROLT, L(ionel) T(homas) C(aswell)

Nationality: British. **Born:** Chester, Cheshire, 11 February 1910. **Education:** Cheltenham College. **Family:** Married 1) Angela Orred in 1939 (separated); 2) Sonia Smith in the 1950s; two sons. **Career:** Apprentice mechanical engineer, 1926-32; automobile fitter; garage owner; writer on transport and engineering topics from 1940; co-founder, with Robert Aickman (q.v.), Inland Waterways Association; general manager, Talyllyn Railway, Towyn, Merioneth, Wales; lecturer and broadcaster. **Member:** Science Museum Advisory Council, from 1964. **Died:** 9 May 1974.

HORROR, GHOST AND GOTHIC PUBLICATIONS

Short Stories

Sleep No More. London, Constable, 1948; expanded edition edited by Barbara and Christopher Roden, Penyffordd, Chester, Ash-Tree Press, 1996.
Two Ghost Stories. Chester, BC Enterprises, 1994.

OTHER PUBLICATIONS

Novels

High Horse Riderless. London, Allen and Unwin, 1947(?).
Winterstoke. London, Constable, 1954.

Other

Narrow Boat. London, Eyre and Spottiswoode, 1944.
Green and Silver. London, Allen and Unwin, 1949.
Worcestershire. London, Hale, 1949.
Horseless Carriage. London, Constable, 1950.
The Inland Waterways of England. London, Allen and Unwin, 1950.
The Thames from Mouth to Source. London, Batsford, 1951.
Lines of Character, with P. B. Whitehouse. London, Constable, 1952.
Railway Adventure. London, Constable, 1953.
The Clouded Mirror. London, Bodley Head, 1955.
Red for Danger. London, Bodley Head, 1955.
A Picture History of Motoring. London, Hulton Press, 1956.
Isambard Kingdom Brunel. London, Longman, 1957.
Motor Cars. London, Educational Supply Association, 1957.

Transport Treasures. London, British Transport Commission, 1957.

Holloways of Millbank: The First Seventy-Five Years. London, Neame, 1958.

Inland Waterways. London, Educational Supply Association, 1958.

Thomas Telford. London, Longman, 1958.

Look at Railways. London, Hamilton, 1959.

The Cornish Giant: The Story of Richard Trevithick. London, Lutterworth Press, 1960.

George and Robert Stephenson. London, Longman, 1960.

Mariners' Market: Burnyeat Ltd. London, Neame, 1961.

Great Engineers. London, Bell, 1962.

James Watt. London, Batsford, 1962.

Look at Canals. London, Hamilton, 1962.

The Dowty Story (Part 1). London, Neame, 1963.

Thomas Newcomen: The Prehistory of the Steam Engine. London, Macdonald, 1963.

A Hunslet Hundred. London, Macdonald, 1964.

Inside a Motor Car. London, Ian Allan, 1964.

Motoring History. London, Studio Vista, 1964.

Patrick Stirling's Locomotives. London, Hamilton, 1964.

Alec's Adventures in Railwayland. London, Ian Allan, 1964.

Tools for the Job: A Short History of Machine Tools. London, Batsford, 1965.

Talyllyn Century: The Talyllyn Railway 1865-1965. Newton Abbott, David and Charles, 1965.

The Aeronauts: A History of Ballooning 1783-1903. London, Longman, 1966.

Transport and Communications. London, Methuen, 1967.

The Mechanicals: Progress of a Profession. London, Heinemann, 1967.

Railway Engineering. London, Macmillan, 1968.

Navigable Waterways. London, Longman, 1969.

Waterloo Ironworks: A History of Taskers of Andover, 1809-1968. Newton Abbott, David and Charles, 1969.

The Potters' Field: A History of the South Devon Ball Clay Industry. Newton Abbott, David and Charles, 1969.

Victorian Engineering. London, Allen Lane, 1970.

From Sea to Sea: The Canal du Midi. London, Allen Lane, 1973.

Landscape with Machines (autobiography). London, Longman, 1971.

The Dowty Story (Part 2). London, Cooper, 1973.

Landscape with Canals (autobiography). London, Allen Lane, 1977.

Editor, *The Motor Car: An Exhibition Organised by L. T. C. Rolt.* London, National Book League, 1958.

*

Bibliography: *L. T. C. Rolt: A Bibliography* by Ian Rogerson and Gordon Maxim, Kidderminster, Baldwin, 1986.

*   *   *

L. T. C. Rolt, known informally as Tom, established himself as an authority on the products of the British Industrial Revolution. The majority of his writings, and the apogee of his enthusiasms, was on canals, railways and industrial history, plus the motor-car. He was co-founder of the Inland Waterways Association, and his first book, *Narrow Boat*, was an expression of a devotee's delight in travelling throughout England on its canals. This expertise and experience was something akin to that of M. R. James, but rather than related to that man's abbeys and old books, Rolt's enthusiasms were of the engineering age, but no less part of our history and landscape. When Rolt turned to ghost stories it was these areas of interest that he utilized, imbuing the industrial age with the antiquarian spirit, and finding something equally strange. If anything, because railways, canals, cars, are part of our everyday life and associated more with leisure and enjoyment than the death and decrepitude of churches and decaying old tombs, the association of them with the sinister and supernatural creates a greater shock. Rolt's ghost stories, of which there are only 14, are arguably the very best of those using a traditional approach but rooting them in our industrial landscape.

Rolt's ghost stories were collected as *Sleep No More* in 1948, though a few of these had been written as early as 1936-37. Two final stories were written just before his death and printed in anthologies by Hugh Lamb, and these were subsequently incorporated in the revised edition of *Sleep No More* which is now the definitive volume of Rolt's supernatural stories.

Rolt often uses remote settings for his stories, locations associated with holiday explorations or beauty spots, but nearly always where there had once been evidence of industrial development. These settings are usually in the West Country or the Welsh Marches. "The Mine" (*Mystery Stories*, 1942) is a good example. It is set amidst the abandoned lead-mining hills of Shropshire where the miners are opening up a new level. One of the miners goes missing and, a few weeks later, another incident puts the fear of God in the others and they close the level down. One of the miners is seen fleeing from the mine, having witnessed something sitting atop the miners' cage, something dirty white which has never seen the light of day, and which pursues him to his death.

"Bosworth Summit Pound" is one of his most atmospheric stories. It is set near a tunnel on the Great Central Canal in the heart of the English Midlands. One night the narrator, on his narrow boat, witnesses the retribution arising from a Victorian murder. The scene where the dead regains its vengeance upon the ghost of its murderer is a masterful piece of writing. "Cwm Garon" is, perhaps, the closest Rolt comes to Jamesian territory, though it is set in a lovely Welsh valley with only a hint of the antiquarian, but he also trespasses into the world of Arthur Machen by invoking the ancient "little people" who mete out their hatred on the professor who dares explore their world. Something of this same treatment is evident in Rolt's last story, "The House of Vengeance," where the experiences of the Victorian antiquary Francis Kilvert provide a clue to a modern haunting in a remote Herefordshire valley. "A Visitor at Ashcombe" may also be seen as Jamesian in content, primarily because it is set in an old Gloucestershire manor-house where the mirror in one of the rooms serves as a portal for ghosts of the past. More in keeping with Rolt's own territory are "The Garside Fell Disaster" and "Hawley Bank Foundry," where a railway tunnel and an abandoned iron foundry become the scenes for vengeful hauntings.

Rolt maintained he found it difficult to write fiction, though he was a devotee of the ghost-story field (discussed in his article "The Passing of the Ghost Story," *The Saturday Book*, 1956). It is almost certain that his own inhibition when it came to fiction caused him to concentrate on setting and atmosphere, and to cultivate an eye for detail. The result is a rich and very effective but sadly small sequence of some of the best short ghost stories of the mid-century. Rolt's work may not have been as influential as

James's, but parallels to his work may be seen in the ghost fiction of Fritz Leiber and Ramsey Campbell, the two best exponents of the industrialized territory that Rolt first explored.

—Mike Ashley

ROSS, Adrian

Pseudonym for Arthur Reed Ropes. **Nationality:** British. **Born:** 1859. **Career:** Academic historian, Cambridge University; later an opera librettist, song lyricist and producer of musical comedies. **Died:** 1933.

HORROR, GHOST AND GOTHIC PUBLICATIONS

Novel

The Hole of the Pit. London, Edward Arnold, 1914.

*   *   *

The Hole of the Pit is the work of a Cambridge don, who usually employed the pseudonym under which it was issued for his work as a lyricist. The novel differs sharply from his work in that vein, which was almost exclusively for musical comedies and light operettas; he worked on versions of *The Merry Widow* and *Lilac Time* as well as many others. Under his own name he edited books (in the original languages) by numerous French and German authors, including Prosper Mérimée, Jules Verne and Erckmann-Chatrian, and published two books on the period of the Seven Years' War (1756-63), but none of that work connects in any way to *The Hole of the Pit*. The only other novel he wrote was a collaboration with his wife which is also very different.

The dedication of *The Hole of the Pit* to M. R. James affirms its affiliation to the tradition of academic weird fiction which James instituted in the early years of the century but it bears little or no similarity to the studiously economical ghost stories set in the present which formed the backbone of that tradition. It takes the form of a historical romance set in the mid-17th century (nearly a hundred years before the time of Ropes's specialism), and is just long enough to be considered as a novel rather than a novella. It is, in sum, a marvellous and unaccountable anomaly: a literary mutant.

The story's narrator, Hubert Leyton, is unwillingly caught up in the side-effects of the English Civil War. He refuses a summons from his cousin, the Earl of Deeping, to join the Royalist cause, but also refuses to join Cromwell in spite of his puritan leanings. After the battle of Naseby, Deeping retreats with his mercenary troop—who are, in reality, no more than bandits—to Deeping Hold, a fortress surrounded by salt marshes, there becoming a predator upon the neighbouring estates. Leyton agrees to go to his cousin to intercede on behalf of those whose property is endangered, passing *en route* a region of the marsh called the Hole, where a monster is said to lurk that will one day bring doom upon Deeping Hold.

The earl is not pleased to see his cousin, who is forced into an intricate diplomatic game further confused by the schemes of the earl's new consort, the reputed sorceress Fiammetta Bardi. He finds one ally in a girl named Rosamund, but she is already under suspicion and under threat from the earl and his jealous lover. The earl's obduracy in the face of the pleas and threats of his puritan neighbours results in a sequence of murders which bring forth a prompt response from the Hole. Although the monster is never clearly seen—despite its possession of slimy "tendrils" it seems to be an animation of the stinking black ooze of the marsh rather than some worm-like dweller therein—it quickly progresses from assaults on individuals to the undermining of Deeping Hold itself. As the Earl's personal and political ambitions come apart the fortress disintegrates, the darkness of the Hole reclaiming by dissolution the solidity of the Hold.

The Hole of the Pit is a exceedingly rare book, but the text of the novel was made available to modern readers in Ramsey Campbell's anthology *Uncanny Banquet* (1992). Campbell likens it to the work of William Hope Hodgson, presumably because of its use of a marine monster, but Hodgson preferred to employ monsters whose fleshy reality was all too obvious. The inchoate "fiend" which emerges from the Hole of the Pit is a very different and much more elusive entity which is more akin to the dormant monstrosities of the Lovecraft school. The archaic prose of the narration has something in common with the artificial diction of Hodgson's *The Night Land*, but is more carefully and more delicately rendered. The only other work with which it has much in common, in both content and style, is Vincent O'Sullivan's ideologically similar Civil War romance "Verschoyle's House," which was published so obscurely that it is highly unlikely that Ropes had the opportunity to read it.

However mysterious its inspiration, *The Hole of the Pit* is a fine work which fully deserves its reinstatement, courtesy of Ramsey Campbell, as a minor classic of the genre. Perhaps Ropes would have followed it up with other works had not World War I arrived to make such petty antique horrors as the Hole seem tame and obsolete.

—Brian Stableford

ROSS, Marilyn

Pseudonym of William Edward Daniel Ross. **Other Pseudonyms:** Leslie Ames; Rose Dana; Ruth Dorset; Ann Gilmer; Diane Randall; Ellen Randolph; Dan Roberts; Clarissa Ross; Dan Ross; Dana Ross; Jane Rossiter; Rose Williams. **Nationality:** Canadian. **Born:** Saint John, New Brunswick, 16 November 1912. **Education:** Various schools in New Brunswick; Provincetown Theatre School, New York, 1934; University of Chicago, Illinois; University of Oklahoma, Norman; Columbia University, New York; University of Michigan, Ann Arbor. **Military Service:** Served in the British Entertainment Services during World War II. **Family:** Married 1) Charlotte Edith MacCormack (died 1958); 2) Marilyn Ann Clark in 1960. **Career:** Worked as a travelling actor and actor/manager with own touring company, 1930-48; film distributor, for own company, for Paramount, and for Monogram Films, 1948-57; full-time writer since 1957. **Awards:** Dominion Drama Festival Prize, 1934; Queen Elizabeth Silver Jubilee Medal, 1978; Honorary Doctorate of Letters, University of New Brunswick, 1988. **Agent:** Martha Millard, 204 Park Avenue, Madison, NJ 07940, USA.

HORROR, GHOST AND GOTHIC PUBLICATIONS

Novels (series: Barnabas Collins/Dark Shadows; Birthstone; Fog Island)

The Fog and the Stars (as Ann Gilmer). New York, Avalon, 1963.
The Castle on the Hill (as Ellen Randolph). New York, Avalon, 1964.
Beware My Love! New York, Paperback Library, 1965.
The Locked Corridor. New York, Paperback Library, 1965.
Winds of Change (as Ann Gilmer). New York, Bouregy, 1965.
Bride of Donnybrook (as Leslie Ames). New York, Arcadia House, 1966.
Dark Shadows. New York, Paperback Library, 1966.
The Hidden Chapel (as Leslie Ames). New York, Arcadia House, 1967.
The Mystery of Fury Castle. New York, Warner, 1967.
Victoria Winters (Dark Shadows). New York, Paperback Library, 1967.
Strangers at Collins House. New York, Paperback Library, 1967.
The Mystery of Collinwood (Dark Shadows). New York, Paperback Library, 1968.
The Curse of Collinwood (Dark Shadows). New York, Paperback Library, 1968.
Barnabas Collins. New York, Paperback Library, 1968.
The Secret of Barnabas Collins. New York, Paperback Library, 1969.
The Demon of Barnabas Collins. New York, Paperback Library, 1969.
The Foe of Barnabas Collins. New York, Paperback Library, 1969.
The Phantom and Barnabas Collins. New York, Paperback Library, 1969.
Barnabas Collins versus the Warlock. New York, Paperback Library, 1969.
The Peril of Barnabas Collins. New York, Paperback Library, 1969.
Barnabas Collins and the Mysterious Ghost. New York, Paperback Library, 1970.
Barnabas Collins and Quentin's Demon. New York, Paperback Library, 1970.
Barnabas Collins and the Gypsy Witch. New York, Paperback Library, 1970.
Barnabas Collins and the Mummy's Curse. New York, Paperback Library, 1970.
Barnabas, Quentin, and the Avenging Ghost. New York, Paperback Library, 1970.
Barnabas, Quentin, and the Nightmare Assassin. New York, Paperback Library, 1970.
Barnabas, Quentin, and the Crystal Coffin. New York, Paperback Library, 1970.
Barnabas, Quentin, and the Witch's Curse. New York, Paperback Library, 1970.
Barnabas, Quentin, and the Haunted Cave. New York, Paperback Library, 1970.
Barnabas, Quentin, and the Frightened Bride. New York, Paperback Library, 1970.
House of Dark Shadows (novelization of screenplay). New York, Paperback Library, 1970.
Barnabas, Quentin, and the Scorpio Curse. New York, Paperback Library, 1970.
Barnabas, Quentin, and the Serpent. New York, Paperback Library, 1970.
Barnabas, Quentin, and the Magic Potion. New York, Paperback Library, 1971.
Barnabas, Quentin, and the Body Snatchers. New York, Paperback Library, 1971.
Barnabas, Quentin, and Dr. Jekyll's Son. New York, Paperback Library, 1971.
Barnabas, Quentin, and the Grave Robbers. New York, Paperback Library, 1971.
Barnabas, Quentin, and the Sea Ghost. New York, Paperback Library, 1971.
Barnabas, Quentin, and the Mad Magician. New York, Paperback Library, 1971.
Barnabas, Quentin, and the Hidden Tomb. New York, Paperback Library, 1971.
Phantom of Fog Island. New York, Warner, 1971.
Barnabas, Quentin, and the Vampire Beauty. New York, Paperback Library, 1972.
Dark Stars over Seacrest. New York, Paperback Library, 1972.
The Long Night of Fear. New York, Warner, 1972.
Mistress of Moorwood Manor. New York, Warner, 1972.
Night of the Phantom. New York, Warner, 1972.
Phantom of the Swamp. New York, Paperback Library, 1972.
The Sinister Garden. New York, Warner, 1972.
Witch of Bralhaven. New York, Warner, 1972.
Behind the Purple Veil. New York, Warner, 1973.
Don't Look Behind You. New York, Warner, 1973.
Face in the Shadows. New York, Warner, 1973.
House of Ghosts. New York, Warner, 1973.
Marta. New York, Warner, 1973.
Step into Terror. New York, Warner, 1973.
The Vampire Contessa, from the Journal of Jeremy Quentin. New York, Pinnacle, 1974.
Witch's Cove. New York, Warner, 1974.
A Garden of Ghosts. New York, Popular Library, 1974.
Loch Sinister. New York, Popular Library, 1974.
Cameron Castle. New York, Warner, 1975.
Dark Towers of Fog Island. New York, Popular Library, 1975.
Ghost Ship of Fog Island. New York, Popular Library, 1975.
Fog Island Secret. New York, Popular Library, 1975.
The Ghost and the Garnet (Birthstone). New York, Beagle, 1975.
The Amethyst of Tears (Birthstone). New York, Beagle, 1975.
Shadow over Emerald Castle (Birthstone). New York, Ballantine, 1975.
Phantom of the 13th Floor. New York, Popular Library, 1975.
Ravenhurst. New York, Popular Library, 1975.
Satan's Island. New York, Warner, 1975.
Brides of Saturn. New York, Berkley, 1976.
The Widow of Westwood. New York, Popular Library, 1976.
The Curse of Black Charlie. New York, Popular Library, 1976.
Haiti Circle. New York, Popular Library, 1976.
Phantom Wedding. New York, Popular Library, 1976.
Shadow over Denby. New York, Popular Library, 1976.
Stewards of Stormhaven: Cellars of the Dead. New York, Popular Library, 1976.
Waiting in the Shadows. New York, Popular Library, 1976.
Cauldron of Evil. New York, Popular Library, 1977.
Death's Dark Music. New York, Popular Library, 1977.
Mask of Evil. New York, Popular Library, 1977.
Phantom of the Snow. New York, Popular Library, 1977.
This Evil Village. New York, Popular Library, 1977.
Delta Flame. New York, Popular Library, 1978.
Rothby. New York, Popular Library, 1978.
Horror of Fog Island. New York, Popular Library, 1978.
The Twice Dead. New York, Fawcett, 1978.

Novels as Clarissa Ross (series: Dark Harbor)

Durrell Towers. New York, Pyramid, 1965.

Mistress of Ravenswood. New York, Arcadia House, 1966.
The Secret of Mallet Castle. New York, Arcadia House, 1966.
Fogbound. New York, Arcadia House, 1967.
Face in the Pond. New York, Avon, 1968.
Gemini in Darkness. New York, Lancer, 1969.
Secret of the Pale Lover. New York, Magnum, 1969.
Beware of the Kindly Stranger. New York, Lancer, 1970.
The Corridors of Fear. New York, Avon, 1971.
Glimpse into Terror. New York, Magnum, 1971.
The Ghosts of Grantmeer. New York, Avon, 1972.
The Spectral Mist. New York, Magnum, 1972.
Phantom of Glencourt. New York, Magnum, 1972.
Whispers in the Night. New York, Bantam, 1972.
China Shadow. New York, Avon, 1974.
Drifthaven. New York, Avon, 1974.
Ghost of Dark Harbor. New York, Avon, 1974.
A Hearse for Dark Harbor. New York, Avon, 1974.
Mists of Dark Harbor. New York, Avon, 1974.
Dark Harbor Haunting. New York, Avon, 1975.
Evil of Dark Harbor. New York, Avon, 1975.
Terror at Dark Harbor. New York, Avon, 1975.
Satan Whispers. New York, Leisure, 1981.
Summer of the Shaman. New York, Warner, 1982.

Novels as Dan Ross or W. E. D. Ross

The Castle on the Cliff. New York, Bouregy, 1967.
The Ghost of Oaklands. New York, Arcadia House, 1967.
The Third Specter. New York, Arcadia House, 1967.
Behind Locked Shutters. New York, Arcadia House, 1968.
Dark of the Moon. New York, Arcadia House, 1968.
Dark Villa of Capri. New York, Arcadia House, 1968.
The Twilight Web. New York, Arcadia House, 1968.
Christopher's Mansion. New York, Bouregy, 1969.
The Whispering Gallery. New York, Lenox Hill, 1970.
The Music Room. New York, Dell, 1971.
The Yesteryear Phantom. New York, Lenox Hill, 1971.
The Haunting of Clifton Court. New York, Popular Library, 1972.
House on Mount Vernon Street. New York, Avon, 1974.
Nightmare Abbey. New York, Berkley, 1975.
Witch of Goblin's Acres. New York, Belmont, 1975.
Dark Is My Shadow. New York, Manor, 1976.
Phantom of Edgewater Hall. New York, Arcadia House, 1980.
The Ghostly Jewels. New York, Arcadia House, 1983.

Novels as Dana Ross

Demon of Darkness. New York, Popular Library, 1975.
Lodge Sinister. New York, Popular Library, 1975.
This Shrouded Night. New York, Popular Library, 1975.
The Raven and the Phantom. New York, Popular Library, 1976.

OTHER PUBLICATIONS

Novels as W. E. D. Ross

Summer Season. N.p., 1962.
Alice in Love. New York, Popular Library, 1965.
Journey to Love. New York, Bouregy, 1967.
Love Must Not Waver. London, Hale, 1967.

Winslow's Daughter. New York, Bouregy, 1967.
Our Share of Love. London, Hale, 1967.
Let Your Heart Answer. New York, Bouregy, 1968.
Luxury Liner Nurse. London, Hale, 1969.
The Need to Love. New York, Avalon, 1969.
Sable in the Rain. New York, Lenox Hill, 1970.
The Web of Love. London, Hale, 1970.
An Act of Love. New York, Bouregy, 1970.
Magic Valley. London, Hale, 1970.
The Man I Love. London, Hale, 1970.
Beauty Doctor's Nurse. New York, Lenox Hill, 1971.
King of Romance. London, Hale, 1971.
The Room without a Key. New York, Lenox Hill, 1971.
Wind over the Citadel. New York, Lenox Hill, 1971.
Rothhaven. New York, Avalon, 1972.
Mansion on the Moors. New York, Dell, 1974.
An End of Summer. London, Hale, 1974.
Surgeon's Nurse. London, Hale, 1975.
Our Louisburg Square. New York, Belmont, 1975.
Summer's End. New York, Fawcett, 1976.
House on Lime Street. New York, Bouregy, 1976.
Pattern of Love. New York, Bouregy, 1977.
Shadows over Garden. New York, Belmont, 1978.
Return to Barton. New York, Avalon, 1978.
Queen's Stairway. New York, Arcadia House, 1978.
The Dark Lane. New York, Arcadia House, 1979.
Magic of Love. New York, Arcadia House, 1980.
Nurse Ann's Secret. New York, Arcadia House, 1980.
Onstage for Love. New York, Arcadia House, 1981.
Nurse Grace's Dilemma. New York, Arcadia House, 1982.
This Uncertain Love. New York, Arcadia House, 1982.
Flight to Romance. New York, Arcadia House, 1983.
Rehearsal for Love. New York, Arcadia House, 1984.
A Love Discovered. New York, Arcadia House, 1984.
Nurse Janice's Dream. New York, Arcadia House, 1984.

Novels as Leslie Ames

The Hungry Sea. New York, Arcadia House, 1967.
The Hill of Ashes. New York, Arcadia House, 1968.
King's Castle. New York, Lenox Hill, 1970.

Novels as Rose Dana

Citadel of Love. New York, Arcadia House, 1965.
Down East Nurse. New York, Arcadia House, 1967.
Nurse in Jeopardy. New York, Arcadia House, 1967.
Labrador Nurse. New York, Arcadia House, 1968.
Network Nurse. New York, Arcadia House, 1968.
Whitebridge Nurse. New York, Arcadia House, 1968.
Department Store Nurse. New York, Lenox Hill, 1970.

Novels as Ruth Dorset

Front Office Nurse. New York, Arcadia House, 1965.
Hotel Nurse. New York, Arcadia House, 1967.
Nurse in Waiting. New York, Arcadia House, 1967.

Novels as Ann Gilmer

Travelling with Sara. New York, Bouregy, 1965.

Private Nurse. New York, Bouregy, 1969.
Nurse on Emergency. New York, Bouregy, 1970.
Skyscraper Nurse. New York, Bouregy, 1976.
Nurse at Breakwater Hotel. New York, Arcadia House, 1982.

Novels as Diane Randall

The Secret of Graytowers. New York, Bouregy, 1968.
A Shadow on Capricorn. New York, Bouregy, 1970.
Psychiatric Nurse. New York, Bouregy, 1971.
Jennifer by Moonlight. New York, Bantam, 1973.
Love Is a Riddle. New York, Bouregy, 1975.
Midhaven. New York, Bouregy, 1975.
Temple of Darkness. New York, Ballantine, 1976.
Pleasure's Daughter. New York, Popular Library, 1978.
Love in the Sun. New York, Avalon, 1978.

Novels as Ellen Randolph

Personal Secretary. New York, Avalon, 1963.
Nurse Martha's Wish. New York, Arcadia House, 1983.

Novels as Dan Roberts

The Wells Fargo Brand. New York, Arcadia House, 1964.
The Cheyenne Kid. New York, Arcadia House, 1965.
Durez City Bonanza. New York, Arcadia House, 1965.
Outlaw's Gold. New York, Arcadia House, 1965.
Stage to Link City. New York, Arcadia House, 1966.
Wyoming Range War. New York, Arcadia House, 1966.
Vengeance Rider. New York, Arcadia House, 1966.
Yuma Brand. New York, Arcadia House, 1967.
Lawman of Blue Rock. New York, Arcadia House, 1967.
The Dawn Riders. New York, Arcadia House, 1968.
Vengeance Spur. New York, Arcadia House, 1968.
Incident at Haddon City. New York, Arcadia House, 1968.
Wyoming Showdown. New York, Arcadia House, 1969.
The Sheriff of Mad River. New York, Arcadia House, 1970.

Novels as Clarissa Ross

Jade Princess. New York, Pyramid, 1977.
Moscow Mists. New York, Avon, 1977.
A Scandalous Affair. New York, Belmont, 1978.
Kashmiri Passions. New York, Warner, 1978.
Istanbul Nights. New York, Jove, 1978.
Flame of Love. New York, Belmont, 1978.
Wine of Passion. New York, Belmont, 1978.
Casablanca Intrigue. New York, Warner, 1979.
So Perilous My Love. New York, Leisure Press, 1979.
Eternal Desire. New York, Jove, 1979.
Fan the Wanton Flame. New York, Pocket, 1980.
Only Make Believe. New York, Leisure Press, 1980.
Masquerade. New York, Pocket, 1980.
Venetian Affair. New York, Jove, 1980.
Beloved Scoundrel. New York, Belmont, 1980.
Fortune's Mistress. New York, Popular Library, 1981.
The Dancing Years. New York, Pinnacle, 1982.

Novels as Dan Ross

Nurse in Crisis. New York, Avalon, 1971.

Nurse in Love. New York, Avalon, 1972.
Moscow Maze. New York, Dorchester, 1983.

Novels as Marilyn Ross

Beloved Adversary. New York, Popular Library, 1981.
Forbidden Flame. New York, Popular Library, 1982.

Novels as Jane Rossiter

Backstage Nurse. New York, Avalon, 1963.
Love Is Forever. New York, Avalon, 1963.
Summer Star. New York, Avalon, 1964.

Novels as Rose Williams

Five Nurses. New York, Arcadia House, 1964.
Nurse in Doubt. New York, Arcadia House, 1965.
Nurse Diane. New York, Arcadia House, 1966.
Nurse in Spain. London, Hale, 1967.
Nurse in Nassau. New York, Arcadia House, 1967.
Airport Nurse. New York, Arcadia House, 1968.

Plays

Murder Game (as Dan Ross). New York, Playwrights Press, 1982.
This Frightened Lady (as Dan Ross). New York, Marginal, 1984.

*

Critical Study: "Dan Ross Is a Busy Man" by Hilary MacLeod, *Canadian Author and Bookman*, February 1986.

* * *

Dan Ross is one of Canada's most prolific authors. Under some 21 pseudonyms, including his wife's name, Marilyn Ross, he has produced over 345 novels and allegedly some 600 short stories. The majority of these books fall into four categories: westerns, historical family sagas, romances and mysteries. He began writing short mystery fiction for the digest magazines in the mid-1950s, and sold his first book, *Summer Season*, in 1962. Frequently his romance and mystery fiction would cross over into the popular gothic romance field, but few of these included genuine moments of horror and even fewer involved the supernatural. As in all gothic romances, Ross places a vulnerable young girl into a bizarre and lonely situation where she undergoes many threats and terrors until finally being rescued. When, at his peak, Ross was producing a novel every one or two weeks, he stuck closely to this formula, occasionally sprinkling his stories with a slightly heavier dose of the bizarre. Few of his books are worth reading, despite sales in the millions, and his reputation has only risen above the mediocre because of the popularity of the *Dark Shadows* television series, for which Ross wrote 34 novels (one of which was unpublished).

Ross's Dark Shadows books were not strictly novelizations of the scripts of the television series, which ran for over 1,200 half-hour episodes between 1966 and 1971. Ross had a free hand to write his own adventures based on the key characters. The series began in the traditional Ross form. Victoria Winters comes to stay at the Collins House to act as governess for the children of Elizabeth Collins. Victoria is an orphan with an unknown past. Although the series had several supernatural elements it was mostly a gothic mystery story until, from April 1967, the television series introduced a new character in the form of the vampire Barnabas Collins. Ross followed the television story-line to a large degree, but brought rather more flair than was usual to his own novelization, *Barnabas Collins*, in 1968, probably the best book of the series. Following the TV series, Ross later introduced Barnabas's cousin, Quentin Collins, a werewolf, and the later novels in the series feature Barnabas and Quentin undergoing various adventures.

All of the books are routine, all of the characters are flat, all of the plotting is formulaic. Their high sales were achieved only because of the popularity of the television series, and in particular the character of Barnabas Collins as played by Canadian actor Jonathan Frid, whose face adorned all the later books in the series. Ross failed to take advantage of the potential implicit within the series notion of an underworld of supernatural creatures, and merely took the characters through their predictable paces in each book. He therefore failed to capitalize on a sub-genre which was later used to considerable acclaim by Chelsea Quinn Yarbro and Anne Rice.

Ross tried to repeat the Dark Shadows success with a series set on a fogbound island off the Maine coast at Dark Harbor, though the supernatural elements were minimal and the plotting was repetitive and uninspired. Ross loved to set his stories in fogbound, remote locales, always with the same naive heroine who would blunder into absurd situations. As if the Dark Harbor series were not enough, he wrote another almost identical series set on Fog Island! A one-off novel, *The Vampire Contessa*, reworked all the Dark Shadows elements, this time with a female vampire, the Contessa Maria, who menaces the innocent young virgin, Adele, who is saved by the Byronic character of Jeremy Quentain.

His other non-series books are just as predictable. In a few the supernatural is proved to be false, whilst in others it remains a real possibility within the narrative. Frequently the supernatural is feigned in an attempt to drive the heroine mad, as in *Mistress of Ravenswood* or *The Haunting of Clifton Court*. Ross's favourite supernatural devices (vampires and werewolves aside) were either spiritualism (frequently false), as in *The Mystery of Fury Castle* and *Out of the Fog*, where the heroine finds, in a remote mansion or castle, a relative who is a spiritualist, whose tampering with the unknown has long-term consequences; or the workings of fate, which he utilized in the Birthstone Gothic series of books (mostly written by other writers) where the hapless heroines find their fortunes dictated by the recklessness of destiny.

Although Ross's work has been the subject of doctoral theses and he was even honoured with a doctorate, his work is trite and derivative, and seldom rises above the level of pulp mediocrity.

—Mike Ashley

ROSZAK, Theodore

Nationality: American. **Born:** Chicago, 1933. **Education:** University of California, Los Angeles; Princeton University. **Family:** Married Betty Roszak in 1957; one daughter. **Career:** Has lived in New York, Los Angeles, Berkeley and London (where he edited the pacifist weekly *Peace News*, 1960s); teaches history at California State University, Hayward; director, Ecopsychology Institute. **Awards:** James Tiptree, Jr. award, 1996. **Agent:** International Creative Management, 40 West 57th Street, New York, NY 10019, USA. **Address:** 790 Cragmont Avenue, Berkeley, CA 94708, USA.

HORROR, GHOST AND GOTHIC PUBLICATIONS

Novels

Bugs. New York, Doubleday, 1981.
Dreamwatcher. New York, Doubleday, and London, Blond, 1985.
Flicker. New York, Simon and Schuster, 1991; London, Bantam, 1992.
The Memoirs of Elizabeth Frankenstein. New York, Random House, 1995.

OTHER PUBLICATIONS

Novel

Pontifex: A Revolutionary Entertainment for the Mind's Eye Theater. New York, Doubleday, and London, Faber, 1974.

Other

The Making of a Counterculture: Reflections on the Technocratic Society and Its Youthful Opposition. New York, and London, Faber, Doubleday, 1969.
Where the Wasteland Ends: Politics and Transcendence in Post-Industrial Society. New York, Doubleday, and London, Faber, 1972.
Unfinished Animal: The Aquarian Frontier and the Evolution of Consciousness. New York, Harper and Row, 1975.
Person/Planet: The Creative Disintegration of Industrial Society. New York, Doubleday, 1978.
The Cult of Information. New York, Pantheon, 1986.
The Voice of the Earth. New York, Simon and Schuster, 1992.

Editor, *The Dissenting Academy.* New York, Pantheon, 1967.
Editor, with Betty Roszak, *Masculine/Feminine: Readings in Sexual Mythology and the Liberation of Women.* New York, Harper Torchbooks, 1969.
Editor, *Sources.* New York, Harper Colophon, 1972.
Editor, with Mary Gomes and Allen Kanner. *Ecopsychology: Restoring the Earth, Healing the Mind.* California, Sierra Club, 1995.

*

Theodore Roszak comments:
Despite what you find in my bibliography, I am not a nonfiction writer who turned to fiction, but a novelist who got diverted into nonfiction when I could not get my novels published. My first few nonfiction efforts were so successful that I continued to pick up contracts, and so took the course of least resistance. As a cultural critic I developed a reputation as a leading spokesman for anti-science, and as a Neo-Luddite crusader. *Pontifex* was my first fiction to reach print, a literary drama about the 1960s. In the 1980s I got two Gothic science-fiction thrillers published: *Bugs*

(now being scripted for the screen) and *Dreamwatcher*. I think of these as trial runs for more serious work. They were successful enough to get me the contract for *Flicker*, which emerged from a lecture I once heard on film restoration at the Pacific Film Archives in Berkeley.

All my writing has to do with the demonic element in modern science and technology; *Flicker* is an example of that applied to the cinema. Having suffered through the great Balance of Terror years, I came to feel there is more than a bit of the diabolical haunting our supposedly rational culture, an evil so persistent that (as Angelotti says in *Flicker*) it is as if . . . as if the evil were deliberately scripted. If I had to locate where that evil resides most consequentially today, I would say in the nihilistic culture of the young, as embodied by Simon Dunkle in *Flicker*, and in those who confabulate with dark extremes for trivial motives. Recently, Quentin Tarantino appeared in a television interview sporting a tee-shirt that was emblazoned "Armies of the Night." Straight out of *Flicker*.

I think of my magnum opus as being *The Memoirs of Elizabeth Frankenstein*; I have been at work on that for over 25 years, re-telling the Mary Shelley original from the bride's viewpoint. *Memoirs* is the feminist *Frankenstein*, and in that capacity won the 1996 James Tiptree Prize for literature that extends our understanding of gender. My notion is that the original tale hides an alchemical subtext that prefigures the rape of the earth at the hands of Frankensteinian science. All my writing is a variation on themes sounded by William Blake, Lewis Mumford and Mary Shelley. It is meant to be a prophetical warning against the hubris of modern science. If we survive, it will be a miracle.

* * *

None of Theodore Roszak's novels can be regarded as minor works: they all have an agenda underpinning the fiction. *Pontifex* is a philosophical literary playground, a novel written in the form of a stage-script, complete with songs. (It has been listed elsewhere as a play, but this is wrong.) Even from the first Roszak was, in his fiction, unafraid of straddling genre boundaries. The setting is pleasantly vague: in a city somewhere and sometime there is a People's Park, and it is here that the action takes place. Various characters drawn from various areas of human concern, both realistic and mythical, evolve for themselves the notion of the anti-scientific philosophy which earlier, in his nonfiction, Roszak had dubbed the Counter Culture. *Pontifex* is by turns profound and funny; its more macabre elements are tempered by the fact that we know, through the book's format, that these are players on a stage.

Bugs is—as might be expected of a first-published straightforward novel—the weakest; the bugs concerned are computer bugs, activated by a telepathic child to infiltrate large systems and thereafter emerge to devour their operators. *Dreamwatcher*, however, despite the superficial gaudiness of its plot, is a haunting and intellectually interesting work. The basic story is of a woman who can enter and affect other people's dreams. Initially she does this for essentially psychiatric reasons, working with children, but then a covert US agency attempts to take her over, with plans of its own; if she will not comply with their wishes she will be terminated with extreme prejudice. There are races and chases before all is sorted out and the baddies get their comeuppance, but the overall effect is deeper than the thrillerish plot: we are asked to question the nature of evil, and also our feelings about intrusion into the most intimate parts of our lives. In a way, this novel might also have been called *Bugs*, because the central character is an eavesdropper on others' privacy to an extent that no currently predictable technology could accomplish.

Flicker is one of the major imaginative fictions of the 1990s; it is probably also the best novel written about the cinema, and almost certainly cinema's best techno-fantasy. Again Roszak is concerned with the alteration of our minds, but now he approaches the ethical considerations using a fictional device that relies on an external influence rather than the telepathic invasion of *Dreamwatcher*. The "flicker" of the title is the moment between each frame of a movie when—although we cannot perceive it because the flicker passes by so quickly—the screen is momentarily devoid of information. But need it lack data? The conceit of this long novel is that a subliminal message—a sort of counter-movie—might be placed in the flickers.

The central character, Gates, is a *naïf*, and remains one throughout. Having found a job, a sexual education and a fair measure of scholastic pomposity in a minor art-house cinema, he becomes obsessed with the obscure director Max Castle, who decades before, after a less than glittering career, vanished in mysterious circumstances. The director's *film noir* movies have a somewhat unsavoury effect on their audiences, which gives them an emotional impact that goes way beyond their surface material. Gates is able to engineer a Max Castle revival, before he embarks on what is essentially a process of detection as he discovers that concealed in the flickers of Castle's movies are nightmare scenes designed to subvert Western society. As the book progresses, Gates discovers much more besides: Castle worked with Orson Welles (who appears as a character) on an abortive version of Joseph Conrad's *Heart of Darkness*; there is still extant what could very loosely be called a sort of neo-fascist band of Castle disciples who are preparing a new youthful-prodigy director to carry on his indoctrinary work; and that much else has been happening of which he was unaware, because his world-view has up until now been as two-dimensional as any image projected onto a screen. Roszak could very easily have opted for an easy, conventional ending to this novel, the happy ending where all is resolved, but he refuses to: although the conclusion is not executed entirely satisfactorily, it is still refreshing to discover a gothic techno-fantasy that bucks the system.

Furthermore, *Flicker* could be read as a metafiction, even though the fiction that it can be seen to be commenting on is screened rather than printed. A punning hint at this metafictional aspect may be the presence of Orson Welles who, while he did not film Kafka's *The Castle* (1926), did film that author's *The Trial* (1925), in 1962. The idea that the vivid, gory imagery of horror movies might inspire audiences to rush out and try the stunts in real life is a common one, although there is no real evidence to support it; this is not what Roszak is concerned about. Nor does he concentrate on the somewhat trite notion that screened nightmares might brutalize society in general. The notion that seems to underpin the book is that horror movies and other filmic hellishness might instead coax society into negativity, a distancing from reality and a sense of futility.

The Memoirs of Elizabeth Frankenstein is another major work: it adopts a feminist take on Mary Shelley's *Frankenstein* tale. Presented as the journal of Victor Frankenstein's cousin and later wife, it was sufficiently effective to bring Roszak the first James Tiptree, Jr., award ever to have been presented to a man. (The science-fiction author who wrote as James Tiptree, Jr. was in fact the psychologist Alice Sheldon [1915-1987]; the prize is accordingly given by a largely feminist committee to authors who have written works that have significantly distorted the perceived barricades between the sexes.) It is a work of some importance yet—at the time of writing—has failed to achieve publication outside the USA except in Germany.

Roszak is not a novelist whose works should be relegated to the category of "good for a long train journey." Although they are easy page-turners, always there is the bubbling excitement of ideas beneath the artifice of the tale. In this he is like Colin Wilson, although he is the more accomplished novelist. He has also the knack of creating a false reality that is somehow more real that the genuine one—he is pestered by people who are convinced that the historical background of *Flicker* is genuine, and that Max Castle was a real director (the book possesses a cod filmography of Castle's work)—and of drawing the reader into nexi of ideas which, whether one agrees with them or not, are hard to shake off.

—John Grant

ROUSSEAU, Victor

Pseudonym for Victor Rousseau Emanuel. **Other Pseudonym:** H. M. Egbert. **Nationality:** American. **Born:** London, 1879. **Career:** Lived in South Africa at the turn of the century; emigrated to the United States, and wrote for pulp magazines until 1941. **Died:** 5 April 1960.

HORROR, GHOST AND GOTHIC PUBLICATIONS

Novels

The Sea Demons (as H. M. Egbert). London, Long, 1924; as Victor Rousseau, Westport, Connecticut, Hyperion Press, 1976.
Draught of Eternity (as H. M. Egbert). London, Long, 1924.

OTHER PUBLICATIONS

Novels

Derwent's Horse. London, Methuen, 1901.
The Messiah of the Cylinder. Chicago, McClurg, and London, Curtis Brown, 1917; as *The Apostle of the Cylinder,* London, Hodder and Stoughton, 1918.
Wooden Spoil. New York, Doran, 1919; London, Hodder and Stoughton, 1923.
The Big Muskeg. Cincinnati, Stewart Kidd, 1921; London, Hodder and Stoughton, 1923.
The Lion's Jaw. London, Hodder and Stoughton, 1923.
The Home Trail. London, Hodder and Stoughton, 1924.
The Big Man of Bonne Chance. London, Hodder and Stoughton, 1925.
The Golden Horde. London, Hodder and Stoughton, 1926.
Red Twilight, World's End: Two Classic Novels from Argosy. Mercer Island, Washington, Starmont House, 1991.

Novels as H. M. Egbert

Jacqueline of Golden River. New York, Doubleday, 1920; London, Hodder and Stoughton, 1924.
My Lady of the Nile. London, Hodder and Stoughton, 1923.
The Big Malopo. London, Long, 1924.
Eric of the Strong Heart. London, Long, 1925.
Mrs. Aladdin. London, Long, 1925.
Salted Diamonds. London, Long, 1926.
Winding Trails. London, Long, 1927.

Novels as V. R. Emanuel

The Story of John Paul. London, Constable, 1923.
Middle Years. New York, Minton Balch, 1925.
The Selmans. New York, Dial Press, 1925.

Plays

Screenplays: *West of the Rainbow's End,* with Daisy Kent, 1926; *Wanderer of the West,* with Arthur Hoerl and W. Ray Johnston, 1927; *Prince of the Plains,* with Arthur Hoerl, 1927; *Lightnin' Shot,* with J. P. McGowan, 1928; *Trailin' Back,* with Arthur Hoerl and J. P. McGowan, 1928.

*   *   *

Victor Rousseau was the name V. R. Emanuel used for most of the fiction he contributed to the American pulp magazines. In Britain he used the pseudonym H. M. Egbert on several books, but the two of most relevance to the present article were both initially published as Victor Rousseau stories in *All-Story Weekly,* *The Sea Demons* in 1916 and *Draught of Eternity* as "Draft of Eternity" in 1918. The best-known book for which he retained that pseudonym was his most adventurous endeavour, *The Messiah of the Cylinder,* a political tract framed as a dystopian reply to H. G. Wells's *When the Sleeper Wakes.*

The theme of *The Sea Demons* may also have been suggested by Wells, in that the alien species depicted therein has a hive organization similar to that of the Selenites in *The First Men in the Moon* and a plot somewhat reminiscent of *The War of the Worlds.* Having exhausted the resources of their natural habitat a race of invisible humanoids launches an assault upon the land, employing an arsenal of chemical and biological weapons. The plot is feverishly melodramatic, and the invasion is eventually subverted by a *deus ex machina* considerably less plausible than the one Wells used to kill off his seemingly invulnerable Martians. The two-part novella which Rousseau contributed to the first two issues of *Astounding Stories of Super-Science* in 1930, "The Beetle Horde," may have been derived from the same models but is even less inventive.

Draught of Eternity is a more interesting novel. It deals with drug-induced time-travel, although it will be difficult for modern readers to take seriously the superstitious awe in which *Cannabis sativa* is held by the author and his characters. The hero is an assistant in a mental hospital who is injected with the drug by one of his colleagues, and finds himself adrift in time. Unlike the many characters in such fantasies who are allowed to experience past incarnations he is shunted into one of his selves as yet unborn, who must fight for survival in a future New York whose post-catastrophe inhabitants have been reduced to Medieval primitivism. The story is an entertaining inversion of conventional karmic romances, although the plot remains a standardized pulp melodrama.

One of the two lost-race stories which Emanuel published in book form under the Egbert pseudonym, *Eric of the Strong Heart*, involves an Arctic race of diminutive Trolls who have various magical powers and a heroine who must labour under a personality-warping spell cast by an evil witch, but these devices do not suffice to draw it into the margins of the horror genre. The earlier *My Lady of the Nile* is far more restrained in its inventions and it seems probable that *Eric of the Strong Heart* was written with the pulp market in mind, although it failed to find a home there. Yet another Egbert book, *Mrs. Aladdin*, is a light fantasy which borrows its facilitating device from *The Arabian Nights*.

Rousseau's earliest short pieces included "The Seal-Maiden," a sentimental weird tale of a conventional *femme fatale*. His later work for the Munsey pulps included an action-packed lost-race novel set in a Pellucidar-like world inside the earth, "The Eye of Balamok," and the highly melodramatic disaster story "World's End" (1933). His contributions to the genre pulps included the "surgeon of souls" series of occult detective stories, featuring Dr. Ivan Brodsky, which appeared in *Weird Tales* in 1926-27. He was quick to begin another with "The Blackest Magic of All" (1928) in the rival *Ghost Stories*, in which a research officer for the Society for the Investigation of Psychic Phenomena has to deal with an "apport medium" (one with telekinetic powers), but the magazine did not last long enough to permit its continuation, with the result that "A Cry from Beyond" (1932)—in which an exactly similar narrator follows up a more conventional seance—was displaced into *Strange Tales*. The narrators of the more melodramatic tale of possession, "When Dead Gods Wake" (1931), and "The Curse of Amen-Ra" (1932)—one of many stories of a beautiful female mummy who still has sufficient glamour to operate as a *femme fatale*—are different individuals but they function in much the same fashion. Rousseau's later work for *Weird Tales* included a five-part serial in a similar vein, "The Phantom Hand" (1932).

Rousseau's pulp work is not without merit, having occasional touches of originality and a certain melodramatic zest, but it is not really surprising that it has attracted so little attention in modern times. His weird fiction shows traces of a real interest in psychic phenomena, of which he conceivably might have made more, but his plots always lacked complexity and were usually tidied up with casual flourishes devoid of any real conviction. Although his career eventually extended from 1913 to 1941 he seems to have allowed his productivity to peter out tamely once his only brief period of success—which lasted little more than ten years—ended with the collapse of the Clayton magazine chain in 1930.

—Brian Stableford

ROYLE, Nicholas (John)

Nationality: British. **Born:** Sale, Cheshire, 20 March 1963. **Education:** Manchester Grammar School; London University. **Family:** Married. **Career:** Magazine sub-editor, *Reader's Digest*, London, and *Time Out*, London; freelance journalist, contributor to *The Guardian*, *Independent*, *Independent on Sunday*, *The Times*, *Time Out* and others, London. **Agent:** Mic Cheetham, 138 Buckingham Palace Road, London SW1W 9SA, England.

HORROR, GHOST AND GOTHIC PUBLICATIONS

Novels

Counterparts. Preston, Lancashire, Barrington, 1993; Clarkston, Georgia, White Wolf, 1996.
Saxophone Dreams. London, Penguin, 1996.
The Matter of the Heart. London, Abacus, 1997.

Short Stories

The Crucian Pit and Other Stories. Clarkston, Georgia, White Wolf, forthcoming.

Other

Editor, *Darklands*. London, Egerton Press, 1991.
Editor, *Darklands 2*. London, Egerton Press, 1992; revised edition, London, New English Library, 1994.

OTHER PUBLICATIONS

Other

Editor, *A Book of Two Halves*. London, Gollancz, 1996.
Editor, *The Tiger Garden: A Book of Writers' Dreams*. London, Serpent's Tail, 1996.
Editor, *The Time Out Book of New York Short Stories*. London, Penguin, 1997.

*

Nicholas Royle comments:

By publishing my novels and some of my short stories in the mainstream/general fiction market—which is how I have been published in the UK by Penguin and continue to be published by Abacus—I am not turning my nose up at the horror genre, which is where I found initial acceptance and have enjoyed a lot of support from editors such as Karl Edward Wagner, Stephen Jones, David Sutton, Ellen Datlow and Dennis Etchison. I always wanted to work in both areas and I want to continue to work in both areas; I like to think that a lot of my stuff can work just as well in horror as in the mainstream, assuming that the two audiences are equally receptive and broad-minded, which in the UK is true at least to some extent. The kind of horror story I've always preferred is the kind that sits just as easily in general fiction as in the genre. Or, indeed, just as *uneasily* in both. I'm thinking of writers such as William Sansom, Iain Sinclair, Alex Hamilton, Derek Marlowe and M. John Harrison.

* * *

As a writer of short horror fiction, Nicholas Royle has had a comparable significance in the 1990s to that of Ramsey Campbell in the early 1980s. His stories not only appear consistently in anthologies, but represent a distinctive and exceptional voice. Royle's fiction combines elements of supernatural and psychological horror, spun together through a polished and fluent style that makes complex ideas accessible. Much of Royle's writing has to do with the individual in a state of crisis: paranoia, split personality, guilt, superstition and the effect of traumatic experiences. In the characteristic Royle story, these psychological factors are driven by—or give rise to—anomalies in the "outside world," resulting in what might be described as a psychosis of reality. A complementary strand of Royle's writing identifies pathology within the social order: exploitation, propaganda, authoritarianism and mass dehumanization. These processes are also represented by supernatural analogues. Just because you're paranoid, it doesn't mean they're not after you.

Royle's collection *The Crucian Pit and Other Stories* (not actually out, but forecast for publication by White Wolf at the time this essay is written) combines some of his best and most challenging short stories with a number of slighter, more overtly horrific pieces. "Glory" is a subtle, tragic story about the occult power of guilt. In the surreal "Moving Out," the narrator's compulsion to play cruel tricks continues after his death. Both this story and "Irrelativity" feature a recurrent Royle motif: animated dummies. "Tracks" draws a paranoid narrator into an alternative reality where the laws of nature are those of anxiety. In "Night Shift Sister," the music industry is represented as a literal factory where spiral grooves are inscribed on human foreheads. "Red Christmas" and "Crispy Notes" are typical of Royle's minor vein: brief, cruel tales with a note of irony and irrationality. "The Crucian Pit" is possibly Royle's best story: a haunting narrative about loss and the limits of magic, revolving around the strangeness of a place where a young couple find and lose each other.

Among Royle's many uncollected stories, the overall standard is remarkably high. "Archway" (in *Dark Fantasies*, edited by Chris Morgan, 1989), an early story, uses the hallucinatory image of a triangular face to condense the threat of a run-down urban environment. Despite its horrific aspects, the story's real theme is human responsibility. "The Mainstream" (in *The Sun Rises Red*, edited by Chris Kenworthy, 1992) is a superb existential horror story in which the protagonist escapes from a grotesque, terrifying pursuit only to undergo death by normality. "Flying into Naples" (*Interzone*, November 1993) describes an archetypal landscape, given over to images of death and stillness. "The Nightingale" (in *Sugar Sleep*, edited by Chris Kenworthy, 1993) and "The Mad Woman" (in *The Science of Sadness*, edited by Chris Kenworthy, 1994) both deal with traumatic love affairs: the former uses elements of science fiction to show the "mad twisted song" of a nightingale corrupting both a computer file and a human heart; the latter powerfully conveys a sense of home becoming outside, a nervous humour exposing layers of guilt and despair. "The Comfort of Stranglers" (in *Dark Terrors 2*, edited by Stephen Jones and David Sutton, 1996), one of Royle's most evocative and pessimistic stories, explores the effect on a boy of having to pretend that his uncle's death by erotic asphyxia was suicide. "The Homecoming" (in *Shadows Over Innsmouth*, edited by Stephen Jones, 1994) reworks Lovecraftian themes in the context of Romania at the time of the fall of Ceaucescu. A traumatized woman believes that the dictator and his followers are still alive in the tunnels under Bucharest; is this paranoia, or influence through dreams (following indoctrination), or a warped reality? This brilliant, ambiguous story allows for a range of interpretations, none of them comforting.

From that story it's only a short step to Royle's two novels, both of which deal with the transformation of Eastern Europe in 1989. Of the two, *Counterparts* is closer to the supernatural horror genre. It's a grim, chilling novel about the isolation that results from damaged identity. The protagonist, Gargan, is a tightrope-walker of mixed race and dual nationality. While his obsession with walking on wires in public places represents an attempt at inte-

gration, his unconscious impulse towards self-division is expressed by his tendency to cut himself in his sleep. Another character, an actor called Adam Midwinter, appears to be Gargan's doppelganger; he seems to have a fragile sense of identity, bordering on schizophrenia. Pursued by terrible dreams and unwanted responsibilities, the two men travel across Europe and arrive in Berlin, where their narratives converge: one of them walks along the Wall just as it is being destroyed. Back in London, Gargan discovers that his lover has given birth to conjoined twins; later, Midwinter catches up with Gargan, kills him and becomes him. What might have been merely an ingenious Gothic pastiche is developed into a substantial novel by Royle's literary skill: his precise, visually acute style lends conviction to the strangest events, and maps out the geographic and historical dimensions of his theme with bitter insight.

Saxophone Dreams covers similar ground, but in a spirit of historical and personal optimism. It links bebop jazz, the surrealist paintings of Paul Delvaux, sexual love and the resurrection of the dead in a darkly toned celebration of the human spirit. Beginning with the massacre of protesters in Prague, the novel blends political atrocity and supernatural horror with lyrical fantasy. A group of jazz musicians come together from different European countries, moving through the landscapes of Delvaux paintings. The victims of Stalinist atrocities are resurrected as walking corpses with a desire for revenge and consumer goods. As the totalitarian regimes of Eastern Europe crumble, the dead return to their graves. A woman driven mad by isolation is drawn into the shared dream of the music and healed. As the jazz band play on in the night, Delvaux sits at his canvas and paints an uncertain future. By turns horrific, comic, tender and bleak, *Saxophone Dreams* blows a new tune into the saxophone of Gothic fiction: the music of shared trauma and collective renewal.

Royle's editing of two anthologies of new British horror fiction, *Darklands* and *Darklands 2*, reflects his vision of the genre as a platform for serious and challenging work. Royle's distinctive contribution to the horror genre, achieved primarily through his short stories, has been a systematic linking of the genre's themes to a personal view of the social and psychological realities of contemporary life—with the apparent aim of demonstrating that horror fiction is the ideal literature for an age of anxiety.

—Joel Lane

RUSSELL, Ray (Robert)

Nationality: American. **Born:** Chicago, 4 September 1924. **Education:** Chicago Conservatory of Music, 1947-48; Goodman Memorial Institute, 1949-51. **Family:** Married Ada Beth Szczepanski in 1950; one son and one daughter. **Career:** Associate editor, 1954-55, executive editor, 1955-60, and contributing editor, since 1968, *Playboy* magazine; screenwriter and novelist. **Member:** Writers' Guild of America, West.

HORROR, GHOST AND GOTHIC PUBLICATIONS

Novels

The Case Against Satan: A Melodramatic Novel. New York, Obolensky, 1962; London, Souvenir, 1963.

Incubus. New York, Morrow, 1976; London, Sphere, 1977.
Absolute Power. Baltimore, Maryland, Maclay, 1992.

Short Stories

Sardonicus and Other Stories. New York, Ballantine, 1961.
Unholy Trinity: Three Short Novels of Gothic Terror. New York,
  Bantam, 1967; London, Sphere, 1971.
Sagittarius. Chicago, Playboy Press, 1971.
Prince of Darkness. London, Sphere, 1971.
The Book of Hell. London, Sphere, 1980.
The Devil's Mirror. London, Sphere, 1980.
Haunted Castles: The Complete Gothic Tales of Ray Russell. Bal-
  timore, Maryland, Maclay, 1985.

Plays

Screenplays: *Mr. Sardonicus,* 1961; *The Premature Burial,* 1961;
  Zotz!, 1962; *The Man with the X-Ray Eyes,* 1963; *The Horror
  of It All,* 1964.

Other

Editor (anonymously), *The Playboy Book of Horror and the Su-
  pernatural.* Chicago, Playboy Press, 1967; London, Souvenir,
  1968.
Editor (anonymously), *Playboy's Stories of the Sinister & Strange.*
  Chicago, Playboy Press, 1969.
Editor (anonymously), *The Fiend.* Chicago, Playboy Press, 1971.
Editor (anonymously), *Last Train to Limbo.* Chicago, Playboy
  Press, 1971.
Editor (anonymously), *Weird Show.* Chicago, Playboy Press,
  1971.

OTHER PUBLICATIONS

Novels

The Colony. N.p., 1969; London, Sphere, 1971.
Princess Pamela. . . . Boston, Houghton Mifflin, 1979.
The Bishop's Daughter. N.p., n.d.

Poetry

The Night Found. Dream House, 1987.

Other

The Little Lexicon of Love. N.p., n.d.

Editor (anonymously), *The Playboy Book of Science Fiction and
  Fantasy.* Chicago, Playboy Press, 1966; London, Souvenir, 1967.
Editor (anonymously), *The Playboy Book of Crime and Suspense.*
  Chicago, Playboy Press, 1966.
Editor (anonymously), *The Dead Astronaut.* Chicago, Playboy
  Press, 1971.
Editor (anonymously), *From the "S" File.* Chicago, Playboy Press,
  1971.
Editor (anonymously), *The Fully Automated Love Life of Henry
  Keanridge.* Chicago, Playboy Press, 1971.

Editor (anonymously), *Masks.* Chicago, Playboy Press, 1971.
Editor (anonymously), *Transit of Earth.* Chicago, Playboy Press,
  1971.

*

Film Adaptations: *Mr. Sardonicus,* from his story "Sardonicus,"
1961.

*   *   *

Russell's writing career has been similar to that of the better-
known Richard Matheson. Both have written a lot of short stories and some novels, inside and outside the horror genre, and both
have worked with Hollywood film studios, having their own work
filmed and writing scripts from the original ideas of other writers.
One reason for Russell being less prolific than Matheson is that
Russell worked for many years for *Playboy* magazine in various
editorial posts.

The earliest of Russell's stories to be successful (and the one
for which he is still best known) is "Sardonicus," a gothic novelette which first appeared in *Playboy* in the late 1950s and was
filmed in 1961 as *Mr. Sardonicus.* Its setting is an undisclosed
year in the 19th century (which internal evidence suggests to be
in the 1880s). A prominent Harley Street physician, Sir Robert
Cargrave, is invited to Bohemia to stay with Maude, a former
acquaintance, and her husband, Mr. Sardonicus. Castle Sardonicus
has all the gothic trappings: an isolated edifice at the end of a
rutted mountain road, resembling a death's head when first seen
by moonlight, reached by horse-drawn coach; creaking gates allow entrance, while inside are dank stone blocks and many unused rooms. Sardonicus himself proves to suffering from *Risus
sardonicus,* a rare medical condition in which the mouth is permanently locked open in a smile, and he tries to blackmail Cargrave
into developing a new treatment by threatening harm to Maude.
The ending is clever and extremely unpleasant. The atmospheric
period setting, the simple but striking plot and the grotesque though
non-supernatural horror elements have all become Russell's trademarks.

His fiction works well at novelette length. "Sagittarius," with a
1960s frame but set mostly in 1909 among the prostitutes and
theatres of Paris, actually has scenes set inside Le Théatre du
Grand Guignol, and *grand guignol* is an apt term to describe many
of Russell's stories. The plot is a variation on Stevenson's *Dr.
Jekyll and Mr. Hyde.* Another successful novelette is
"Sanguinarius," a supposedly true story from the 17th century of
cruelty and perversion among members of a noble Hungarian family. A new wife, Elisabeth, only 15 years old, is gradually inducted
into orgies, torture and bathing in the blood of virgins. Her eventual punishment is to be walled up in a room in the castle where
she has lived until she starves to death.

Medieval torture is a favourite element of Russell's fiction. It
turns up in several of his short stories, including "Prince of Darkness" (also known as "The Cage") and "The Runaway Lovers" as
well as in the novel *Incubus.*

Many of Russell's other stories have contemporary settings.
They are slick Hollywood-type tales of sex, such as "The Bell"
and "Naked in Xanadu." One, "Domino," another novelette, is
set in a fictional Latin American republic, where the President has
just died and our narrator has been sent to pose as a newspaper
reporter.

The horror in nearly all of Russell's stories is non-supernatural, though it frequently seems to portray a "hell on Earth." In his novels it is definitely supernatural. *The Case Against Satan* is a highly regarded novel which tells of how a priest battles against Satan for control of a girl. It was published nine years before the much better known novel (later filmed) *The Exorcist* by William Peter Blatty. "Dorian Black" is a full-length screenplay which does not appear to have been filmed; it is a modern variation on Oscar Wilde's *The Picture of Dorian Gray*, though with a carved block of stone instead of a portrait.

Incubus is probably Russell's best horror novel, though it is less striking and original than some of his novelettes. It is set in Galen, a small rural town in California whose atmosphere is more like New England than the West Coast. Julian Trask, one of the few men in America able to function as a psychic investigator, arrives in Galen soon after the start of a series of horrific rapes in which most of the victims die from rupture. The form of the novel is a detective story, as the number of victims mounts and the list of possible suspects apparently diminishes, though not enough clues are given for the reader to work out the solution.

The explanation is that an incubus is at work. Desperate to impregnate a woman and so continue its own line, it forces itself upon local women of childbearing age at ever-decreasing intervals. Unfortunately, its penis is gigantic, the size of an arm. It possesses supernatural strength, speed and agility, and reverts to being just another member of the Galen community between attacks.

Despite close cooperation between the local sheriff, the local doctor and Trask, the number of victims mounts alarmingly. Trask has with him an ancient book of magic, which seems to work, though he does not use it in the hunt. Perhaps surprisingly, the sheriff never seems to consider delegating authority to state or national forces, nor is there an invasion by the media.

This novel contains the most highly developed examples of Russell's tendency towards writing pornography. The rape scenes are not particularly graphic, on the whole, but the first third of the book has its sections intercut with descriptions of the torture of a naked and attractive young woman with a thumbscrew and on the rack.

Russell's other novels include his best book *The Colony*, which is general fiction, and *Princess Pamela . . .*, an historical romance set in an alternate history. He is also known and respected as a poet. As an editor at *Playboy* he did much to promote science fiction, fantasy and horror by selecting a disproportionate number of stories from those genres for publication in the magazine. In particular, he encouraged and promoted the work of horror writer Charles Beaumont.

—Chris Morgan

RUSSELL, W(illiam) Clark

Pseudonyms: Eliza Rhyl Davies; Sydney Mostyn. **Nationality:** British. **Born:** New York, 24 February 1844; son of the British song-writer Henry Russell. **Education:** Private schools, in Britain. **Family:** Married; one son. **Career:** Merchant seaman, 1858-66; journalist, *Newcastle Daily Chronicle*, and later contributor to the *Daily Telegraph*, London, under the pseudonym "Seafarer"; prolific novelist and biographer; lived in Bath, Somerset, in his later years, and contributed to the *Boys' Own Paper* and other juvenile periodicals. **Died:** 8 November 1911.

HORROR, GHOST AND GOTHIC PUBLICATIONS

Novels

The Frozen Pirate. London, Sampson Low, 2 vols., 1887.
The Death Ship: A Strange Story. London, Hurst and Blackett, 3 vols., 1888; as *The Flying Dutchman; or, The Death Ship*, New York, Lovell, 1888.

Short Stories

The Phantom Death and Other Stories. London, Chatto and Windus, and New York, Stokes, 1895.

OTHER PUBLICATIONS

Novels

The Hunchback's Charge: A Romance. London, Sampson Low, 1867.
Is She a Wife? (as Sydney Mostyn). London, n.p., 1871.
Memoirs of Mrs. Letitia Boothby, Written by Herself. London, King, 1872.
Perplexity (as Sydney Mostyn). London, King, 1872.
The Surgeon's Secret (as Sydney Mostyn). London, Tinsley, 1872.
Kitty's Rival (as Sydney Mostyn). London, Tinsley, 1873.
Which Sister? (as Sydney Mostyn). London, Bentley, 1873.
As Innocent as a Baby. London, Bentley, 1874.
The Mystery of Ashleigh Manor (as Eliza Rhyl Davies). London, Bentley, 1874.
A Dark Secret (as Eliza Rhyl Davies). London, Bentley, 1875.
Jilted! or, My Uncle's Scheme. London, Sampson Low, 1875.
John Holdsworth, Chief Mate. London, Sampson Low, 1875.
Captain Fanny. London, Bentley, 1876.
Is He the Man? London, Tinsley, 1876; as *The Copsford Mystery; or, Is He the Man?* New York, New Amsterdam, 1896.
The Wreck of the Grosvenor. London, Sampson Low, 1877.
Auld Lang Syne. London, Sampson Low, 1878.
The Little Loo (as Sydney Mostyn). London, Tinsley, 1878.
A Sailor's Sweetheart: An Account of the Wreck of the Sailing Ship "Waldershare." London, Sampson Low, 1880.
An Ocean Free-Lance: From a Privateersman's Log, 1812. London, Bentley, 1881.
The "Lady Maud": Schooner Yacht. London, Sampson Low, 1882.
My Watch Below . . . by a Seafarer. London, Sampson Low, 1882.
A Sea Queen. London, Sampson Low, 1883.
Jack's Courtship: A Sailor's Yarn of Love and Shipwreck. London, Sampson Low, 1884.
In the Middle Watch. London, Chatto and Windus, and New York, Harper, 1885.
A Strange Voyage. London, Sampson Low, 1885.
The Golden Hope: A Romance of the Deep. London, Hurst and Blackett, 1887.
Marooned. London, Macmillan, 1889.
An Ocean Tragedy. New York, Harper, 1889; London, Chatto and Windus, 1890.

A Marriage at Sea. New York, U.S. Book Co., 1890; London, Methuen, 1891.

My Shipmate Louise: The Romance of a Wreck. London, Chatto and Windus, 1890.

Master Rockafellar's Voyage. London, Methuen, 1891.

My Danish Sweetheart. London, Methuen, 1891.

The Tragedy of Ida Noble. New York, Appleton, 1891; London, Hutchinson, 1893.

Alone on a Wide, Wide Sea. London, Chatto and Windus, and New York, Taylor, 1892.

Mrs. Dines' Jewels: A Mid-Atlantic Romance. London, Sampson Low, 1892.

A Strange Elopement. London, Macmillan, 1892.

The Convict Ship. New York, Cassell, 1893; London, Chatto and Windus, 1895.

The Emigrant Ship. London, Sampson Low, 1893.

List! Ye Landsmen: A Romance. London, Cassell, 1893.

A Memorable Swim. London, Chapman and Hall, 1893.

The Good Ship "Mohock." London, Chatto and Windus, 1894.

Heart of Oak: A Three-Stranded Yarn. London, Chatto and Windus, 1895; as *A Three-Stranded Yarn: The Wreck of the Lady Emma,* Chicago, Weeks, 1895.

The Tale of the Ten: A Salt-Water Romance. London, Chatto and Windus, 1896.

What Cheer! London, Cassell, 1896.

The Last Entry. London, Chatto and Windus, 1897.

A Noble Haul. London, Unwin, 1897.

A Tale of Two Tunnels: A Romance of the Western Waters. London, Chapman and Hall, 1897; as *Captain Jackman; or, A Tale of Two Tunnels.* New York, Buckles, 1899.

The Two Captains. New York, Dodd Mead, and London, Sampson Low, 1897.

The Wreck of the Corsaire. Chicago, Sergel, 1897(?).

Romance of a Midshipman. London, Unwin, 1898.

Rose Island: The Strange Story of a Love Adventure at Sea. Chicago, Stone, 1899; London, Arnold, 1900.

A Voyage at Anchor. London, White, 1899.

The Pretty Polly: A Voyage of Incident. London, Chatto and Windus, 1900; as *The Cruise of the Pretty Polly,* Philadelphia, Lippincott, 1901.

The Ship's Adventure. London, Constable, 1901; as *The Mate of the Good Ship York; or, The Ship's Adventure,* Boston, Page, 1902.

The Captain's Wife. Boston, Page, 1903.

Overdue. London, Chatto and Windus, 1903.

Abandoned. London, Methuen, 1904.

Wrong Side Out. London, Chatto and Windus, 1904.

His Island Princess. London, Methuen, 1905.

The Yarn of Old Harbour Town. London, Unwin, 1905.

Short Stories

The Deceased Wife's Sister, and My Beautiful Neighbour. London, Bentley, 1874.

Round the Galley Fire. London, Chatto and Windus, 1883.

On the Fo'k'sle Head. London, Chatto and Windus, 1884.

A Book for the Hammock. London, Chatto and Windus, 1887.

The Mystery of "The Ocean Star": A Collection of Maritime Sketches. London, Chatto and Windus, 1888.

The Romance of Jenny Harlowe, and Sketches of Maritime Life. London, Chatto and Windus, 1889.

Miss Parson's Adventure, with others. London, Chapman and Hall, 1893.

The Honour of the Flag, and Other Stories. London, Unwin, 1896.

An Atlantic Tragedy and Other Stories. Philadelphia, Biddle, 1899; London, Digby Long, 1905.

Poetry

The Turnpike Sailor; or, Rhymes on the Road. London, Skeffington, 1907.

The Father of the Sea and Other Legends of the Deep. London, Sampson Low, 1911.

Other

The Book of Authors: A Collection of Criticisms. London, Warne, 1871.

Representative Actors: A Collection of Criticisms. London, Warne, 1872.

The Book of Table-Talk: Selections from the Conversations of Poets, Philosophers, Statesmen, Divines. London, Routledge, 1874.

Sailors' Language: A Collection of Sea-Terms and Their Definitions. London, Sampson Low, 1883.

English Channel Ports and the Estate of the East and West India Dock Co. London, Sampson Low, 1884.

A Forecastle View of the Shipping Commission. London, Sampson Low, 1885.

A Voyage to the Cape. London, Chatto and Windus, 1886.

Betwixt the Forelands. London, Sampson Low, 1889.

William Dampier. London, Macmillan, 1889.

The Ship: Her Story. London, Chatto and Windus, 1889.

Horatio Nelson and the Naval Supremacy of England, with W. H. Jacques. London, Putnam, 1890.

Collingwood. London, Methuen, 1891.

The British Seas: Picturesque Notes, with others. London, Seeley, 1892.

Pictures from the Life of Nelson. London, Bowden, 1897.

The Life of Nelson in a Series of Episodes. London, Christian Knowledge Society, 1905.

*　　*　　*

W. Clark Russell was a former merchant seaman who achieved considerable celebrity with an early novel, *The Wreck of the Grosvenor,* but was never able fully to repeat that success. While his striving for effect remained desperate he produced two novels which strayed over the border into fantasy, although he remained so parsimonious as to allow only a single fantastic idea into each book.

The hero of *The Frozen Pirate* is the sole survivor of a ship sunk by a storm off Cape Horn. The current carries his small boat into Antarctic waters, where he finds an old vessel embedded in an ice-floe. He is lucky enough to find supplies preserved by refrigeration and loot left over from the vessel's career as a pirate. The quick-frozen bodies of the crewmen are still present and he decides to remove their disturbing presence by throwing them overboard, but one awkward specimen cannot be removed from below decks without first thawing it out. When he builds a fire, however, the man revives. The pirate refuses to believe that he has been in suspended animation for half a century and his presence quickly becomes threatening, but his revivification is short-lived and he swiftly falls prey to an accelerated aging process. Although the pirate is not a pleasant soul the novel is only on the margin of the horror genre.

In terms of Gothic content, *The Death Ship* is much the more interesting of Russell's fantasies. After Captain Marryat's *The Phantom Ship* (1839)—which presumably provided Russell with the inspiration—it is the most significant literary development of the motif of the Flying Dutchman. The protagonist of the story has the misfortune to be washed overboard after the legendary phantom ship is sighted, and his terrified shipmates make no attempt to save him. On being taken aboard the accursed vessel he finds that Captain Vanderdecken, like the frozen pirate of the earlier novel, is quite incapable of believing that he has been lost for 150 years. Also aboard the ship is a young Englishwoman, with whom the hero naturally falls in love, but it is not easy to contrive an escape—and when they finally do so, Vanderdecken's evil influence reaches after them to dash their plans.

Russell's publishers never quite made up their minds as to how he ought to be marketed, and he ended up on the fringe of the "boys' book" market, although there was far too little blood and thunder in his plots to allow him to compete with Robert Louis Stevenson, or even Jules Verne. His accounts of life at sea are a trifle too realistic in their tediousness even when they are combined with fantastic motifs, and he might have done better to allow his imagination to run riot rather than imposing such careful restrictions on his use of such motifs. *The Death Ship* attempts to be creepy, but the author provides so little active menace to support the hero's paranoid anxieties that it almost begins to seem as if his troubles are self-inflicted. Russell could not bring himself to conclude that the seemingly haunted vessel in his short story "A Bewitched Ship" really was afflicted by ghosts, although the substitution of a mischievous ventriloquist is far more likely to annoy readers than to satisfy them.

Russell does warrant some consideration as a British pioneer of the tradition of sea horror stories, but he was not the man to carry it forward. That role was left to William Hope Hodgson, whose efforts in the literary line were much more successful—and who also followed Russell's example in fighting with some fervour for better working conditions for Britain's seamen.

—Brian Stableford

RUSSO, John (A.)

Nationality: American. **Born:** 1939. **Family:** Married; one daughter. **Career:** Worked as a maker of advertising films, Latent Image, Pittsburgh, Pennsylvania, 1960s; screenwriter, director, producer and novelist, working mainly in the area of low-budget horror films and their novel tie-ins, since 1968. Lives in Pittsburgh.

HORROR, GHOST AND GOTHIC PUBLICATIONS

Novels (series: Living Dead)

Night of the Living Dead (novelization of screenplay). New York, Warner, 1974.
Return of the Living Dead. New York, Dale, 1978.

The Majorettes. New York, Pocket, 1979.
Midnight. New York, Pocket, 1980.
Black Cat: A Novel of Terror. New York, Pocket, 1982.
Bloodsisters. New York, Pocket, 1982.
The Awakening. New York, Pocket, 1983.
Day Care. New York, Pocket, 1985.
Return of the Living Dead (novelization of screenplay based on his original novel). London, Arrow, 1985.
Inhuman. New York, Pocket, 1986.
Voodoo Dawn. Pittsburgh, Pennsylvania, Imagine, 1987.
Day of the Dead (novelization of screenplay), with George A. Romero. New York, Simon and Schuster, 1988.
Living Things. New York, Popular Library, 1988.

Plays

Screenplays: *Night of the Living Dead*, with George A. Romero, 1968; *The Booby Hatch*, 1975; *Midnight*, 1980; *Bloodsisters*, 1982; *Return of the Living Dead*, with Dan O'Bannon, 1983; *Day Care*, 1985; *One by One*, from the novel *The Majorettes*, 1986; *Heartstopper*, from the novel *The Awakening*, 1989; *Voodoo Dawn*, 1990.

Other

The Complete Night of the Living Dead Filmbook. Pittsburgh, Pennsylvania, Imagine, 1985.
Making Movies. N.p., 1989.
Scare Tactics: The Art, Craft and Trade Secrets of Writing, Producing, and Directing Chillers and Thrillers. N.p., 1992.

*

Film Adaptations: *Midnight*, 1980; *Bloodsisters*, 1982; *Return of the Living Dead*, 1983; *Day Care*, 1985; *One by One*, from the novel *The Majorettes*, 1986; *Heartstopper*, from the novel *The Awakening*, 1989; *Voodoo Dawn*, 1990.

Theatrical Activities:
Director: **Films**—*The Booby Hatch*, 1975; *Midnight*, 1980; *Heartstopper*, 1989; *Midnight 2: Sex, Death and Videotape*, 1993. Producer: **Films**—*The Booby Hatch*, 1975; *One by One*, 1986; *Night of the Living Dead* (remake), 1990.

*   *   *

John Russo was co-author with George Romero of the original screenplay for the classic horror film, *Night of the Living Dead*, and he has been closely linked to the film industry ever since. His novels all demonstrate his media connections, and most appear almost to have been written specifically to feel like a motion picture. His first published novel was the novelization of the Romero film, complete with stills from the movie. The story itself is straightforward and not particularly sensible. For some inexplicable reason, the dead have begun to rise from their graves, seeking to kill the living, and each of their victims rises in turn, vampire-like, unless the actual brain is destroyed. In a motion picture, it's easy to overlook the logical problems with the plot, because there isn't time to sit and think about the inconsistencies, but as a novel there are too many holes for it to be entirely effective, although some of the individual scenes remain chilling, and there is an undeniable power in the relentless siege of the farmhouse.

After splitting with Romero, Russo teamed up with Russell Streiner and Ricci Valentine to create the story-line for *Return of the Living Dead*. The film and Russo's subsequent novel of the same title have little in common, except that both are essentially sequels to the original film. In the screen version, humour is mixed with the horror as the living are besieged in a funeral home. The book more accurately conveys the tone of the original movie, and the walking dead are anything but humorous. *Return of the Living Dead* is actually more effective than the earlier novelization, although it too suffers from a plot that doesn't bear too close examination.

Midnight features four siblings obsessed with the occult. They have been told that they are descended from a man who had the power to summon demons and control the minds of other human beings, and they appear to have inherited some of those same powers. As the four children grow, their victims change from small animals to other children, even adults, and with each success, they become more ambitious and bloodthirsty. The book is a bizarre carnival of slaughter that begins to lose its effectiveness partway through because of the repetition, and the shallowness of the few sympathetic characters. *Black Cat* was much more effective. The soul of an evil witch-doctor has been reincarnated in a black panther worshipped by a secretive cult in the American southwest. An innocent family stumbles across the cult, and discovers that they have been signed up to be the next set of victims for the witch-doctor's bloodlust. Russo does a good job this time of blending primitive horror with a recognizable, contemporary setting, and the tension between the two elements helps create an interesting story.

Russo's *The Awakening* is much more conventional horror fiction. A 17th-century vampire, dormant for 200 years, rises to new activity in the modern world. Initially he finds it surprisingly easy to adapt to his new surroundings, but a trail of drained bodies attracts the attention of the police, and the vampire eventually decides that he must have an ally if he is to survive, preferably a willing one. Russo plays with the vampire mythos a bit; there's even a pseudo-rational explanation of their existence. They are not invulnerable to bullets, for example, although they can essentially regenerate almost any damaged parts. The story works well for the most part, although the vampire never seems particularly dangerous or efficient, certainly not the fearsome predator that we expect him to be.

Russo returned to a variation of the Living Dead zombies with *Inhuman*. A dozen people retreat to a remote area as part of their group counselling plan, but they find anything but peace waiting for them. A plane-load of terrorists crashes in the area, but before their "death," the terrorists were transformed by a misguided government attack into irrational, only marginally human creatures who immediately begin hunting down and killing the normal people in the area. The story develops predictably from there, with personal problems forgotten as the protagonists attempt to stay alive. There's another variety of zombie in *Living Things*, this time the more conventional shambling servants conjured up by a voodoo sorcerer. The villain has a grand plan this time. His growing army of the undead is pitted against the forces of the Mafia in an attempt to seize control of organized crime activities in Florida. As the two forces battle, an ex-police officer and an anthropologist team up to discover the source of the sorcerer's power and put

him out of business. This is one of Russo's better efforts, pitting natural versus supernatural evil.

He used conventional voodoo again in *Voodoo Dawn*, sequel to *Living Things*. The dead body of Chango, the sorcerer, is pulled from the ocean and buried along with his followers in a mass grave. Shortly after the interment, something begins claiming victims in the area, dismembering bodies and stealing portions thereof. Eventually we learn that Chango's spirit survives, and that he is essentially raising his own body as a zombie in order to return to life. Far superior to its predecessor, this is the most atmospheric and frightening of Russo's novels, the effect of which carried over well into the movie version.

Russo will undoubtedly be remembered chiefly because of his involvement with the Living Dead films, even though his better work as a writer came much later in his career. He has also written non-supernatural thrillers with horror elements, most notably *Bloodsisters* and *The Majorettes*, the latter of which was made into a mediocre slasher film, and *The Complete Night of the Living Dead Filmbook*.

—Don D'Ammassa

RYAN, Alan

Nationality: American. **Born:** New York City, 17 May 1943. **Education:** Regis High School; Fordham University, B.A. 1965; attended University of California, Los Angeles, 1965-67. **Career:** English teacher at a Catholic high school, New York, 1967-76; worked briefly in off-Broadway theatre, 1976; freelance writer from 1977; book reviewer, *New York Times*, *Washington Post* and other publications; part-time reader for various publishers and a literary agency, New York. **Member:** National Book Critics Circle. **Awards:** World Fantasy award for short story, 1985.

HORROR, GHOST AND GOTHIC PUBLICATIONS

Novels

Panther! New York, n.p., 1981.
The Kill. New York, Tor, 1982.
Dead White. New York, Tor, 1983.
Cast a Cold Eye. Niles, Illinois, Dark Harvest, 1984; London, Weidenfeld and Nicolson, 1985.

Short Stories

Quadriphobia. New York, Doubleday, 1986.
The Bones Wizard and Other Stories. New York, Doubleday, 1988.

Other

Editor, *Perpetual Light.* New York, Warner, 1982.
Editor, *Night Visions 1: All Original Stories.* Niles, Illinois, Dark Harvest, 1984; as *Night Visions: In the Blood*, New York, Berkley, 1988.
Editor, *Halloween Horrors.* New York, Doubleday, 1986.
Editor, *Vampires: Two Centuries of Great Vampire Stories.* New York, Doubleday, 1987; as *The Penguin Book of Vampire Stories*, New York and London, Penguin, 1988.

Editor, *Haunting Women.* New York, Avon, 1988.

*

Critical Study: "Alan Ryan" in *Faces of Fear: Encounters with the Creators of Modern Horror* by Douglas E. Winter, New York, Berkley, and London, Pan, 1990.

*   *   *

In his short story "I Shall Not Leave England Now," Alan Ryan refers to dark fantasy fiction as "those tales that explore the darker regions of the mind, the monsters of the night, the blackest passions that inhabit the human soul, stories that use as their ruling metaphor an overwhelming image of evil." While this definition accurately describes the subtle type of weird tale that Ryan and other writers championed in the early 1980s as an alternative to the traditionally blunter horror story, it neither encompasses all of his fiction nor the creative arc that eventually led him away from the horror/dark fantasy field.

Like Dennis Etchison, Charles L. Grant, Thomas Monteleone and other leading dark fantasists of his generation, Ryan began writing fiction at a time when there was no formal "horror" market. His earliest sales include fantasy stories tricked out with otherworldly trappings to sell to anthologies of speculative fiction in the 1970s, and the novel, *Panther!* a non-supernatural suspense story about a crazed film producer who releases 20 live panthers on the streets of New York City to promote his floundering adventure movie. Although there is little evidence in these stories of the careful craftsmanship and strong characterization for which his fiction would become known, *Panther!* introduces a theme that Ryan would return to in some of his best work: the primal horrors from which modern life insulates us.

Indeed, this is the subject of his first major work of dark fantasy, *The Kill.* The novel is set in Deacon's Kill, a small town in upstate New York that Ryan developed over a handful of stories into one of the more memorable settings for dark fantasy in the 1980s. "The Kill," as it is known to the locals, is a secluded village set at the base of the Adirondack Mountains. Although settled more than century before, it is surrounded by a wilderness with roots still firmly sunk in the region's primeval past. Manhattanites Megan Todd and Jack Casey expect a bucolic paradise when they move to the Kill to escape the rat-race of New York City, but quickly discover that the woods are home to a savage monster that incarnates the countryside's prehistoric past. Ryan builds a powerful mood of dread through atmospheric descriptions of the woods that invest its every leaf and blade of grass with the feeling of malignancy. Playing upon the average city-dweller's apprehensions of the unfamiliar and unpredictable natural world, Ryan's offers his monster and the ominous landscape it inhabits as proof that "The hills . . . would permit themselves to be tamed, but they would forever hold back—impenetrable—some secrets in reserve. Fields could be cleared and sown, towns built, human lives conducted well or ill, but the hills would remain ever and always silent, private, primitive." Much as he did in *Panther!* Ryan juxtaposes the pre-civilized past with the modern urban jungle to evoke horrors on a scale too vast and incomprehensible for even the most hardened contemporary human beings to fathom.

Different primeval horrors serve as "the overwhelming image of evil" for Ryan's other dark fantasies set in Deacon's Kill. "Onawa" features a vampiric being whose bloodline predates the Native American tribes who first settled the land. "Death to the Easter Bunny" reveals the Easter Bunny to be an ancient monster that has fooled adults for eons into believing it a harmless creature of fairy tales. These stories create an image of Deacon's Kill not unlike that of H. P. Lovecraft's Arkham, the legend-haunted New England town with one foot planted in an incalculably ancient past. In other stories, though, the Kill seems cut from the same cloth as Stephen King's Castle Rock, Maine, and Charles L. Grant's Oxrun Station, Connecticut, insular communities in which horrors evolve from the rhythm and rituals of daily life. In "Halloween House," intruders in a cursed house on the town's outskirts succumb to a fate appropriate for a Halloween evening. In the novel *Dead White*, a snowstorm cuts the Kill off from contact with the outside world, crystallizing the many social tensions that underlie the town's calm facade and setting it up for the re-enactment of a horrible tragedy that occurred a century before.

Ryan's third and apparently last dark fantasy novel, *Cast a Cold Eye*, both extends and deviates noticeably from his approach to the supernatural in the Deacon's Kill stories. Like them, it features horrors from the past that encroach upon the present. These horrors, however, prove to have a positive value that calls into question "the overwhelming image of evil" that is Ryan's defining criteria for dark fantasy. The story concerns American writer Jack Quinlan, who moves temporarily to Ireland to research the potato famine of 1847 as background for his forthcoming novel. Jack's slow assimilation into the insular society of the small town of Doolin is complicated by his horrifying visions of emaciated and dying people around the countryside. What he takes at first to be a spectral threat to his person and sanity he gradually discovers is the inescapable legacy of his Irish heritage demanding to be acknowledged and remembered before his assimilation can be complete. Although he employs the framework of a dark fantasy story, Ryan constructs the novel as one of intersecting personal and cultural identities, in which the ghostly approaches the spiritual.

The transition from the horrific to the mystical in Ryan's dark fantasy novels mirrors a similar change of direction in the short stories he wrote between 1979 and 1988, particularly those set in Ireland. His 1982 story, "The Rose of Knock," is a traditional tale of supernatural vengeance that follows the desecration of a religious shrine in a rural Irish town. The is no supernatural element in his World Fantasy Award-winning 1984 story "The Bones Wizard," but this haunting tale of a young musician who makes the ultimate sacrifice for his art evokes the same mood of personal darkness that characterizes effective dark fantasy fiction. "Bundoran, Co. Donegal," published the same year, is a *jeu d'esprit* in the tradition of Ray Bradbury's tales of Dublin whose magical attributes never penetrate deeper than the superstitions of simply country folk.

Ryan's other short stories are built upon more traditional horror themes. "Tell Mommy What Happened," "Baby's Blood" and "A Visit to Brighton" all feature imperilled children. In addition to "Onawa," he has written three other vampire stories: "I Shall Not Leave England Now," an homage to Dracula; "Kiss the Vampire Goodbye," a hybrid of the horror and detective story; and "Following the Way," one of the cleverest stories to superimpose the iconography of Catholicism upon vampire lore. Several of his best short fictions feature characters teetering on the brink of madness. "Sheets" is concerned with a disgruntled department-store employee driven insane by the patterns on the linens he sells, and "Sand" with a woman compelled to test her perception that everyone but her family bleeds red sand when wounded. Like the mad, characters in the grip of religious faith lose the ability to distinguish between delusion and reality in "Babies from Heaven," in which a barren woman believes the daily shower of infants she sees outside her window is a gift from God, and "Pieta," whose devout heroine interacts with the figures in Michelangelo's sculpture as though they were alive.

Ryan has written no new dark fantasy fiction since the publication of his collection *The Bones Wizard* in 1988. His withdrawal from the horror/dark fantasy market was prefigured as early as 1986 in *Quadriphobia*, a collection of four novellas that share characters and ideas but span a spectrum of genres ranging from supernatural horror to the gothic romance, the western and the adventure tale. These stories, like Ryan's compact but distinguished body of dark fantasy, support the argument that ultimately dark fantasy, like any literature, aspires to transcend the limits of genre.

—Stefan Dziemianowicz

RYAN, R(achel) R.

Nationality: British. **Career:** No biographical information available, despite the best efforts of several researchers in the horror-fiction field.

Horror, Ghost and Gothic Publications

Novels

The Right to Kill. London, Jenkins, 1936.
Death of a Sadist. London, Jenkins, 1937.
Devil's Shelter. London, Jenkins, 1937.
Freak Museum. London, Jenkins, 1938.
The Subjugated Beast. London, Jenkins, 1939.
Echo of a Curse. London, Jenkins, 1939.
No Escape. London, Jenkins, 1940.

* * *

R. R. Ryan (dates of birth and death unknown), the author of seven novels published in Britain by Herbert Jenkins in the later 1930s, is an enigma. The British Library ascribes the authorship to Rachel R. Ryan, but in contemporary advertising the author is referred to as male. The prose style seems feminine, and on the whole the female characters are drawn with more conviction than the male. The books were championed by the late Karl Edward Wagner. Given their extreme rarity, it is worth rescuing them from legend by an appraisal.

The Right to Kill appears to have been a study of the psychology of a crime. "Should women, in certain circumstances, defy the law?" the advertising asks. It is the scarcest of her books. *Death of a Sadist* shows similar concerns and a real sense of evil. Trevor Garron, an introverted bank clerk, filches 200 pounds from the accounts, only to fall foul of Selwyn Maine, his manager. (The manager's first name may be intended to recall George Selwyn, the famed 18th-century sadistic voyeur, or perhaps Selwyn & Blount, publishers of the *Not at Night* anthologies.) Maine is the sadist of the title, who takes advantage of Garron and of a defaulter tenant, Edna Ferrar. Garron ultimately kills him, but Edna

is convicted for the murder. Ryan's writing is strongest in conveying, reticently but oppressively, the psychological sufferings of the victims. The ending is unexpectedly bleak. Despite some concessions to library-fiction sentimentalism and romance, the book makes clear Ryan's intention to be relentless and disturbing.

Devil's Shelter is an early modern Gothic, written when the paraphernalia of the old dark house could be expected still to work. Divina Mason, an actress, sets out to drive from London to Newcastle but breaks down on the Yorkshire moors. The mansion in which she takes refuge during a thunderstorm proves to be an asylum, and worse. The butler who admits her says, "Excuse me, I am dumb." A dog howling as it is beaten is in fact a man. Patients are mutilated to subdue them. If the institutionalized sadism may seem to prefigure world events, the book (hardly uniquely in the popular fiction of the day) also expresses casual anti-Semitism. Midway the novel becomes more of a thriller, with a gun concealed by a portrait above a dinner-table, and produces a sane hero to help Divina escape; but it's the nightmarish first half, and scattered such episodes in the second, that stay in the mind.

Freak Museum is located in central London. Bridget O'Malley, impregnated by a boyfriend who then dies, is lured by the Mary Magdalen Guild to their nursing home in Climax Street, a hospital which turns out to serve the adjoining museum. Her baby either dies or is surgically deformed, and she is incarcerated in the museum, where she encounters various grotesques and is exhibited under hypnosis as one of them. An artist, Passport, eventually sees her plight and attempts to rescue her but is trapped himself. Like *Death of a Sadist*, this book keeps a minor character in reserve as a *deus ex machina*, but here the child who performs this function simply causes further deaths. While it seeks to horrify the book is ruthlessly effective; its later attempts to humanize some of the inmates slacken the momentum (though an encounter in which Passport discusses literature with the Elephant Woman is almost matter-of-fact enough for surrealism). The underlying notion that the owners of the museum have trapped the protagonists so as to use them to politically extremist ends is murkily expressed, but seems to be dear to the author.

The Subjugated Beast—"frankly a thriller," the half-title announces—begins with a short history of the Rock family, generations of which committed murder and even cannibalism. The tale is narrated by Kyrle Rock, last child of the line, who will inherit on condition that she lives with her uncle Paul, a researcher into abnormal psychology, and his mysteriously disturbed wife. The book artfully sustains the uncertainty of how the Rock history is to invade the present, and a mood of mounting horror.

Echo of a Curse is Ryan's most ambitious book, which attempts to combine social realism and the melodramatically supernatural. Mary Rodney marries a war hero, Vincent Border, only to discover he is a drunken sadist. He also claims kinship with a lycanthropic exhibit in a travelling fair. At the height of a domestic struggle, Mary curses her unborn child. Twins are born, one displaying traits of the monstrous side of the family. A normal child is substituted for the monster, which returns as an adult to wreak revenge, but Vincent, drawing on powers he derives from a rite known as the Black Commune, attempts to overcome it. While the book has powerful scenes, some of its fantastic elements lack conviction—not least THE INEXPLICABLE, the sideshow monster, always referred to in capitals.

No Escape is Ryan's most coherent novel. The narrator, Gerald Day, meets a young woman, Adela Beevers, on holiday and marries her, only to discover that she is so "narrow and terribly tight" that the marriage goes unconsummated. She also suffers from gastritis and self-pity, both chronic, and such are her demands on him that he becomes unable to move out of earshot. He spends much of the book planning to murder her, and eventually gives in to the compulsion, but his guilt proves more insistent than her need for him. If the book ultimately turns romantic, this sharpens rather than compromises the portrait of obsession maintained almost until the last page. As a story of everyday horror it is often oppressively convincing.

Most of Ryan's novels exhibit signs of haste. There are passages of real power, and a talent for horrific suspense, but these are sometimes weakened by tendencies to overwriting, some of it sentimental. Nevertheless for several years, and apparently to little or no critical notice, R. R. Ryan was one of the earliest 20th-century British novelists to specialize in the horrific, and as such should be noted.

—Ramsey Campbell

RYMER, James Malcolm

Pseudonyms: M. J. Errym; M. J. Merry. **Nationality:** British. **Born:** Scotland, 1804 or 1814. **Career:** Civil engineer, 1838-42; prolific writer and editor for Edward Lloyd and other publishers of cheap literature, 1842-64. **Died:** 1884.

HORROR, GHOST AND GOTHIC PUBLICATIONS

Novels (first published as serials or part-works)

The Black Monk; or, The Secret of the Grey Turret. London, Lloyd, 1844.
Manuscripts from the Diary of a Physician. London, Lloyd, 1844.
Varney the Vampire; or, The Feast of Blood. London, Lloyd, 1845-47.
The Apparition. London, Lloyd, 1846. (Also attributed to Thomas Peckett Prest.)

OTHER PUBLICATIONS

Novels (first published as serials or part-works)

Ada the Betrayed; or, The Murder at the Old Smithy. London, Lloyd, 1842.
Adeline; or, The Grave of the Forsaken. London, Lloyd, 1842.
Grace Rivers; or, The Merchant's Daughter. London, Lloyd, 1843.
Jane Brightwell. London, Lloyd, 1844.
The White Slave. London, Lloyd, 1844.
Woman's Life; or, The Trials of the Heart. London, Lloyd, 1844-45.
Don Caesar de Bazan. London, Lloyd, 1845.
Gold; or, The Strangers of the Wreck. London, Lloyd, 1845.
Family Secrets. London, Lloyd, 1846.
The First False Step; or, The Path of Crime. London, Lloyd, 1846.
The Black Mantle; or, The Murder at the Old Ferry. London, Lloyd, 1851.
The Night Adventurer. London, Lloyd, 1846.

Jane Shore. London, Lloyd, 1846.
The Oath; or, the Buried Treasure. London, Lloyd, 1846.
Lady in Black. London, Lloyd, 1847.
Love Child. London, Lloyd, 1847.
Retribution; or, Murder at the Old Dyke. London, Lloyd, 1847.
Miranda; or, The Heiress of the Grange. London, Lloyd, 1848; as *Rankley Grange*, London, Bennet, 1891.
Jessie Arnold; or, Murder at the Old Well. London, Lloyd, 1852.
The Unspeakable. London, Clarke, 1855.
The Wreckers of the Channel. London, Lloyd, 1855(?).
Edith the Captive; or, The Robbers of Epping Forest. London, Lloyd, 1860.
Edith Heron; or, The Earl and the Countess. London, Lloyd, 1860.
The Young Shipwright. London, Lloyd, 1860.
The Treasures of St. Mark: A Tale of Venice. London, Lloyd, 1860.
The Dark Woman; or, Plot and Passion. London, Lloyd, 1860.
The Shadow; or, The Wife's Devotion. London, Lloyd, 1860-61.
Love the Leveller; or, Fenella's Fortunes. London, Lloyd, 1861.
Secret Service: A Tale of the Sea. London, Lloyd, 1861.
Nightshade; or, Claude Duval the Dashing Highwayman. London, Lloyd, 1864.
The Dark Woman; or, the Days of Sixteen String Jack. London, Lloyd, 1864.
Kate Chudleigh; or, The Duchess of Kingston. London, John Dicks, 1864.
George Barrington; or Life in London a Hundred Years Ago. London, John Dicks, 1865.

*

Critical Studies: *Fiction for the Working Man* by Louis James, London, Oxford University Press, 1963; introduction by E. F. Bleiler to *Varney the Vampire*, New York, Dover, 1972.

*   *   *

Despite much research over the last 30 or 40 years an aura of mystery still hangs over James Rymer and his works. He was Scottish and had been a civil and mechanical engineer before he turned to writing around the year 1842. He was one of a handful of prolific writers who produced weekly chapbooks for the publisher Edward Lloyd of Salisbury Square in London. These sold for a penny and frequently covered such gruesome material that they became known as "penny dreadfuls." They were almost always published anonymously, though the author might be identified as "the author of" a previous popular work. Only by such attribution can Rymer's bibliography be pieced together, although the researcher Louis James acquired the scrapbooks of Rymer which allowed a reasonable assessment of his work. Even then, ascribing authorship without question was still difficult since various authors might have contributed to the same work in order to meet deadlines. This is almost certainly the reason why there is so much confusion between ascribing works to Rymer and his fellow hack Thomas Prest. On occasions they probably worked on serials together. It now seems almost certain that Rymer was the primary author of one of the more notorious penny dreadfuls of the period, *Varney the Vampire*, and it is on that, rather than his 40 or more other ascribed novels that his reputation rests.

Varney was the first vampire novel in the English language, and seems to have been inspired by a recent reprinting of John Polidori's Byronic "The Vampyre" (originally published in 1819) in *The Romancist's and Novelist's Library* in 1840. It stands as a landmark (albeit not a very literary one) between Polidori's story and Bram Stoker's *Dracula*. Rymer probably did not intend the story to run for as long as it did, but its evident popularity caused him (and probably his fellow writers) to string it out for 109 weekly parts so that the final serial when published in book form in 1847 ran to 868 pages. *Varney* has a similar Byronic hero, Sir Francis Varney, the new owner of Ratford Abbey, who chooses as his first victim Flora Bannerworth. Much of the first part of the story revolves about Varney's relationship with the Bannerworth family before eventually a mob drives Varney away; he spends much of the rest of the novel trying to survive until eventually he ends it all by hurling himself into the crater of Mount Vesuvius. Before his end Varney reveals his story. He is over 200 years old and became accursed as a vampire when he inadvertently killed his son in a fit of temper. Most of the writing and plotting of *Varney* is basic and puerile, not that it was ever written as anything other than a hack work. However with the popularity of the story Rymer began to develop the character of Varney until readers started to become sympathetic toward him. It is as much this, and Varney's tragic existence, that made *Varney* so memorable for its day. Readers loved the doomed villain-hero, and exactly that same love-hate feeling has passed on to the character of Dracula.

Rymer's other main work of gothic fiction, also sometimes attributed to Prest, was *The Black Monk*. Clearly inspired by Scott's *Ivanhoe*, with a nod to M. G. Lewis's *The Monk*, the novel is set in the time of King Richard the Lionheart, though Rymer cares little for historical accuracy. We are presented with the sinister, mesmeric character of Morgatini, the Black Monk, who lives in the Grey Tower and carries out his vile crimes with almost supernatural powers. His grand scheme is part of a conspiracy to overthrow King Richard in favour of John. Much of the action takes place through the Brandon family and their associates who are supported by the equally enigmatic Wizard of the Red Cave. At half the length of *Varney the Vampire*, *The Black Monk* has more action but less appeal. It has much in common with some modern horror films where the enjoyment relies more on the special effects than the characters. Rymer chose to dazzle his readers with the displays of power between the Black Monk and the Wizard of the Red Cave alongside much heroic action, but all this is padding within a plot that is otherwise superficial and peopled by characters who are cardboard.

Rymer was better when he moved away from the fantastic. As he showed in *Varney*, the story-line improves when he develops a more sympathetic character for the villain, and Rymer's best works are his social novels which echoed Dickens, such as *Ada the Betrayed* and *Grace Rivers*, stories that sought to feed on the sentimental emotions rather than on fear. Nevertheless, Rymer knew his readership, since he was deliberately writing down to them. His early efforts to produce a middle-class story-paper had failed and Rymer converted his contempt for working-class fiction into material gain. He was more financially successful than most of his fellow hack writers in that he succeeded in retiring and living out a long life in relative comfort.

—Mike Ashley

S

SABERHAGEN, Fred (Thomas)

Nationality: American. **Born:** Chicago, Illinois, 18 May 1930. **Education:** Wright Junior College, Chicago, 1956-57. **Military Service:** United States Air Force, 1951-55. **Family:** Married Joan Dorothy Spicci in 1968; one daughter and two sons. **Career:** Electronics technician, Motorola Inc., Chicago, 1956-62; freelance writer, 1962-67, and since 1973; assistant editor, *Encyclopaedia Britannica*, 1967-73. **Agent:** Eleanor Wood, Spectrum Literary Agency, 111 Eighth Avenue, Suite 1502, New York, NY 10011, USA.

HORROR, GHOST AND GOTHIC PUBLICATIONS

Novels (series: Dracula)

The Dracula Tape. New York, Warner, 1975.
The Holmes-Dracula File. New York, Ace, 1978.
An Old Friend of the Family (Dracula). New York, Ace, 1979.
Thorn (Dracula). New York, Ace, 1980.
Dominion (Dracula). New York, Tor, 1982.
The Frankenstein Papers. New York, Baen, 1986.
The Black Throne, with Roger Zelazny. New York, Baen, 1990.
A Matter of Taste (Dracula). New York, Tor, 1990.
Bram Stoker's Dracula, with James V. Hart (novelization of screenplay). New York, Signet, and London, Pan, 1992.
A Question of Time (Dracula). New York, Tor, 1992.
Seance for a Vampire (Dracula). New York, Tor, 1994.
Dancing Bears. New York, Tor, 1995.
A Sharpness on the Neck (Dracula). New York, Tor, 1996.

OTHER PUBLICATIONS

Novels

The Golden People. New York, Ace, 1964.
The Water of Thought. New York, Ace, 1965; complete edition, Los Angeles, Pinnacle, 1981.
The Broken Lands. New York, Ace, 1968.
Brother Assassin. New York, Ballantine, 1969; as *Brother Berserker*, London, Macdonald, 1969.
The Black Mountains. New York, Ace, 1971.
Changeling Earth. New York, DAW, 1973; as *Ardneh's World*, New York, Baen, 1988.
Berserker's Planet. New York, DAW, and London, Futura, 1975.
Specimens. New York, Popular Library, 1976.
The Veils of Azlaroc. New York, Ace, 1978.
The Empire of the East (omnibus; includes *The Broken Lands, The Black Mountains, Changeling Earth*). New York, Ace, 1979; London, Macdonald, 1984.
Love Conquers All. New York, Ace, 1979.
The Mask of the Sun. New York, Ace, 1979.
Berserker Man. New York, Ace, 1979; London, Gollancz, 1988.
Coils, with Roger Zelazny. New York, Tor, 1980; London, Penguin, 1984.

Octagon. New York, Ace, 1981; London, Sinclair Browne, 1984.
A Century of Progress. New York, Tor, 1983.
The Berserker Throne. New York, Simon and Schuster, 1985.
Berserker Blue Death. New York, Tor, 1985; London, Gollancz, 1990.
The First Book of Swords. New York, Tor, 1983; London, Futura, 1985.
The Second Book of Swords. New York, Tor, 1983; London, Futura, 1985.
The Third Book of Swords. New York, Tor, 1984; London, Futura, 1986.
The Complete Book of Swords (omnibus; includes *The First Book of Swords, The Second Book of Swords, The Third Book of Swords*). New York, Nelson Doubleday, 1985.
The First Book of Lost Swords: Woundhealer's Story. New York, Tor, 1986; London, Orbit, 1988.
Pyramids. New York, Baen, 1987.
The Berserker Attack. New York, Waldenbooks, 1987.
The Second Book of Lost Swords: Sightblinder's Story. New York, Tor, 1987; London, Orbit, 1989.
After the Fact. New York, Baen, 1988.
The Third Book of Lost Swords: Stonecutter's Story. New York, Tor, 1988; London, Orbit, 1989.
The White Bull. New York, Baen, 1988.
The Lost Swords: The First Triad (omnibus; includes *The First Book of Lost Swords, The Second Book of Lost Swords, The Third Book of Lost Swords*). New York, Nelson Doubleday, 1988.
The Fourth Book of Lost Swords: Farslayer's Story. New York, Tor, 1989; London, Orbit, 1991.
The Fifth Book of Lost Swords: Coinspinner's Story. New York, Tor, 1989.
The Sixth Book of Lost Swords: Mindsword's Story. New York, Tor, 1990.
The Lost Swords: The Second Triad (omnibus; includes *The Fourth Book of Lost Swords, The Fifth Book of Lost Swords, The Sixth Book of Lost Swords*). New York, Guild America, 1991.
The Seventh Book of Lost Swords: Wayfinder's Story. New York, Tor, 1992.
Berserker Kill. New York, Tor, 1993.
The Last Book of Swords: Shieldbreaker's Story. New York, Tor, 1994.
Merlin's Bones. New York, Tor, 1995.
Berserker Fury. New York, Tor, 1997.

Short Stories

Berserker. New York, Ballantine, 1967; London, Penguin, 1970.
The Book of Saberhagen. New York, DAW, 1975.
The Ultimate Enemy. New York, Ace, 1979; London, Gollancz, 1990.
The Berserker Wars. New York, Tor, 1981.
Earth Descended. New York, Tor, 1982.
Saberhagen: My Best. New York, Baen, 1987.
Berserker Lies. New York, Tor, 1991.

Other

Editor, *A Spadeful of Spacetime.* New York, Ace, 1981.
Editor, with Joan Saberhagen, *Pawn to Infinity.* New York, Ace, 1982.

Editor, with Martin H. Greenberg, *Machines that Kill*. New York, Ace, 1984.

Editor, *Berserker Base*. New York, Tor, 1985; London, Gollancz, 1990.

Editor, *An Armory of Swords*. New York, Tor, 1995.

*

Bibliography: *Fred Saberhagen, Berserker Man: A Working Bibliography* by Phil Stephensen-Payne, Leeds, West Yorkshire, Galactic Central Publications, 1991.

*   *   *

Fred Saberhagen launched his writing career with space operas describing mankind's encounters with the Berserkers: alien fighting-machines left over from some long-ended war, still carrying out their programme to exterminate all living things—a science-fictional version of the all-purpose agents of evil which are a staple of horror fiction, demons in robotic form. His subsequent work has ranged across the entire spectrum of fantastic genre fiction but has always tended to blur the boundaries between them, transplanting and reconfiguring their basic materials. Although most of the Berserker stories are straightforward action/adventure tales, lightly spiced with eccentric inspirations and references, the best of them do try to get to grips with philosophical problems; *Brother Berserker* and "The Bad Machines" (1996) are among the most analytically-inclined.

From the very beginning of his career Saberhagen was prone to base his plots on stories borrowed from mythology and imaginative literature. He often used supplementary characters from history and fiction, usually placing them in odd juxtapositions. He twice paid homage to Edgar Allan Poe, in the Berserker story "Masque of the Red Shift" (1965) and a novel co-authored with Roger Zelazny, *The Black Throne*. His method of looking at traditional materials with a modern eye, reinterpreting apparent magic in terms of the science-fictional vocabulary of ideas, achieved its greatest coup in *The Dracula Tape*, in which the events mapped out in Bram Stoker's classic novels are tracked from the viewpoint of the Count himself, who gives a very different account of them. Dracula explains the errors and misjudgments which arose from Jonathan Harker's paranoia, and the tragic deaths which occurred because of Professor van Helsing's insistence on performing blood transfusions without matching the blood-types of donor and recipient. The arch-vampire's own motives and actions are, in his own account, both benevolent and heroic. Published a year before the English translation of Pierre Kast's *The Vampires of Alfama* and Anne Rice's *Interview with the Vampire*, *The Dracula Tape* stands at the head of that rich modern tradition of revisionist vampire stories in which the Count and his kin are remodelled as Byronic outsiders battling with contemptuous dignity against the intellectual and imaginative cowardice embodied in human superstition and bigotry.

Saberhagen presumably did not intend to write a sequel when he published *The Dracula Tape*, but the success of such endeavours as Chelsea Quinn Yarbro's Comte St. Germain series must have made the temptation irresistible. *The Holmes-Dracula File* makes much of the odd similarities between Stoker's description of his ultimate villain and Conan Doyle's description of his ultimate hero, and allows the two to join forces against the menace posed by the giant rat of Sumatra. Although he was not loath to refer back to the Count's long and colourful history and to romantic liaisons which span the centuries—as he did at some length in *Thorn* and *A Matter of Taste*—Saberhagen could not compete with Chelsea Quinn Yarbro in the detailed evocation of past ages and he wisely decided to concentrate greater effort on more recent times. He draws heavily upon the distinctive spirit of American crime fiction in *An Old Friend of the Family* and most of the subsequent volumes in the series, although he stops short of the kind of hard-boiled pastiche practised by P. N. Elrod.

Saberhagen seems to have decided that the name of Dracula was something of an embarrassment and all-but-abandoned its explicit use for a while. He eventually decided, after some procrastination, that although his hero was fully entitled to recall previous eras when he was known by that name he should employ the pseudonym Matthew Maule for the purposes of his long residence in modern Chicago. That residence often brings him into conflict with vampires of a far less noble disposition and forces him into a slightly-uneasy alliance with the detectives of the city's homicide squad.

Although the dry humour of *The Dracula Tape* and the flamboyance of *The Holmes-Dracula File* were displaced in later volumes by melodrama of a more earnest stripe, the series retains a certain cynical stylishness which is both effective and appealing. All Saberhagen's series are uneven, but his vampire sequence holds its quality far better than his various sword-and-sorcery series, and better than all but the highest peaks of the Berserker series.

Saberhagen tried to repeat the triumph of *The Dracula Tape* in *The Frankenstein Papers*, which attempted to produce an alternative reading of Mary Shelley's classic. Unfortunately, the challenge of producing a rationalized account of the monster—in his own words, of course—required the substitution of an alien being for the patchwork of dead human flesh. The substitution in question takes place under highly implausible circumstances and the story never really recovers from the crudity of the narrative move. *Pyramids* is a more successful hybridization of horror and sf themes, although it falls far more decisively on the science fiction side of the line and takes its inspiration from a less notable set of originals. The section of *The Berserker Throne* that had previously appeared as "Some Events in the Templar Radiant" draws upon a more prestigious source (Marlowe's *Doctor Faustus*) but its horrific element is almost eradicated in the process of genre-translation. A much more robust fusion of genres is to be found in the intriguing historical fantasy *Dancing Bears*, set in pre-Revolutionary Russia. The novel has a significant and powerful horror element by virtue of its evocation of a werebear, whose depredations become symbolic of the subsequent fate of the post-Revolutionary USSR.

Saberhagen's work is slick commercial fiction produced at the steady pace required of a modern professional. It is unashamedly melodramatic and unrepentantly formulaic, but it is consistently enlivened by his propensity for odd juxtapositions and reinterpretations and frequently elevated by an intelligent interest in the woeful effects of bigotry and mechanisms of historical causation. His work is always readable, and some of it contains enough food for thought to remain memorable.

—Brian Stableford

SACKETT, Jeffrey

Nationality: American. **Born:** 1949. **Address:** c/o Bantam Books, 1540 Broadway, New York, New York 10036, USA.

HORROR, GHOST AND GOTHIC PUBLICATIONS

Novels

Stolen Souls. New York, Bantam, 1987.
Candlemas Eve. New York, Bantam, 1988.
Blood of the Impaler. New York, Bantam, 1989.
Mark of the Werewolf. New York, Bantam, 1990.
The Demon. New York, Bantam, 1991.

*   *   *

During its high point of popularity in the 1980s, the horror genre was at once exciting because of the influx of new writers, and discouraging because the explosion of titles resulted in the publication of countless derivative works. In some instances, as with Michael McDowell and Robert McCammon, imitation quickly gave way to originality, but many other newcomers to the field were content to reprise old themes without adding anything new or interesting. Jeffrey Sackett's early novels were not particularly original, although his prose style and plot structure were entertaining, but there was steady improvement from one volume to the next and the last, *The Demon*, provided clear evidence that he was potentially a much larger figure in the genre. Unfortunately, that was his last published novel, his career apparently derailed by the general decline of horror fiction in the early 1990s as well as the seriously awful packaging that Bantam provided for his books.

Stolen Souls was the first of four novels to make use of standard horror-movie monsters, in this case the mummy. A museum in upstate New York acquires seven Egyptian caskets, apparently a great archaeological coup, but actually the opening scene in a terrifying drama. A secretive cult of Egyptians not only resents the "theft" of the sacred objects, but also intends to recover them and use a magical ritual to re-animate the mummies and set them free. In order for each of the dead to be revived, one of the living residents of the small town must be sacrificed. Sackett could almost have borrowed the individual scenes from various horror films, and the melodrama is turgid and predictable. There are occasional moments of genuine suspense, particularly when the final ceremony is under way, but ultimately the story remains trite and forgettable.

Candlemas Eve showed some improvement. This time witchcraft, ancient curses, and the revivified dead are the themes. Simon Proctor is an out-of-work musician who grows despondent when it appears that his career is effectively over. Then two very attractive women enter his life, and under their guidance his career recovers, in fact takes off dramatically. Proctor knows that he should be very happy, but that ends when he discovers the truth about his new friends. They are both witches, and both hold long grudges against people who offended them in their previous incarnations. The first half of the novel moves quite well, but oddly enough it falters at the point where the plot ought to be picking up speed. Even the fast-paced, violent ending seems to plod at times.

Sackett's best novel technically is *Blood of the Impaler*, an indirect sequel to Bram Stoker's *Dracula*. The protagonist traces his family history and discovers that he is a descendant of one Jonathan Harker, apparently a real person upon whose experiences Bram Stoker based his story. Since he has long suffered from an aversion to sunlight, Malcolm Harker wonders how much truth there really is in the old story, and to that end he tracks down the grave of Lucy Westenra. Sure enough, she has been staked in traditional vampire fashion, so Malcolm removes the stake and uses his own blood to bring Westenra back to unlife. Shortly afterward, he discovers that he has been manipulated in all this in order to bring about the revival of her master, Dracula himself. Sackett does an excellent job of managing the slow building of tension, primarily by keeping Dracula offstage for most of the book and by concentrating on Malcolm, whose character is strongly developed. There's more suspense in *Blood of the Impaler* than either of its predecessors, a tighter and more original plot, and the prose flows easily and seems less forced.

Sackett switched to werewolves for his fourth novel, *Mark of the Werewolf*. This time he twists the usual plot-line even further. An immortal, nearly invincible werewolf has decided that it is time for eternal rest, if he can only find a way to destroy himself. At the same time he discovers that a group of right-wing militarists has learned of his existence, and seeks to channel his supernatural power for their own purposes, creating an army of unstoppable terrorists subject to their will. The juxtaposition of two very different evils works well, although the atmosphere is much more that of a straightforward adventure novel than a tale of horror. Sackett was clearly flexing his literary muscles at this point, however, making use of standard themes but finding new ways to use them rather than contenting himself with yet another rehash of the latest monster movie.

Sackett's fifth, and so far last horror novel was *The Demon*. It is also his best. Vernon Sweet is an ex-sideshow geek, the man who bit off the heads of live chickens in front of an audience. Sweet is a particularly ugly man, known in the business as "Grogo the Goblin." He retires to a small town where, with his companion, he is ostracized by the outside community which considers him a freak. When a series of murders occurs in the community, suspicion turns his way, and ultimately a lynch mob attacks Sweet's residence, even though he is not the killer. Unfortunately for the would be lynchers, however, Sweet's body and personality are actually a shell disguising a demonic spirit that has been carefully restrained for decades, and which now erupts with devastating consequences. This is far and away Sackett's most original, powerful and suspenseful novel. As a whole, Sackett's work was competent, entertaining, and occasionally exceptional, but does not to date include any single work that is likely to retain any significant popularity.

—Don D'Ammassa

ST. CLAIR, David

Nationality: American. **Born:** 1932. **Career:** Writer of bestselling works of the "non-fiction" occult.

HORROR, GHOST AND GOTHIC PUBLICATIONS

Novel

Bloodline. London, Corgi, 1989.

"Non-Fiction" Novels

Watseka: America's Most Extraordinary Case of Possession and Exorcism. Chicago, Playboy Press, 1977; as *Child Possessed*, London, Corgi, 1979.
Mine to Kill. London, Corgi, 1985.
The Devil Rocked Her Cradle. London, Corgi, 1987.
Say You Love Satan. London, Corgi, 1987.

OTHER PUBLICATIONS

Other

Psychic Healers. New York, Doubleday, 1974; revised edition, New York, Bantam, 1979.
How Your Psychic Powers Can Make You Rich. New York, Bantam, 1975.

*   *   *

After *Psychic Healers'* hymn of praise to matters cerebral—to the harnessing power of the open mind—and the metaphysical show-and-tell session of *How Your Psychic Powers Can Make You Rich*, David St. Clair settled down to work on books less esoteric and more horrific. *Watseka* was the first; it was born in America, but for residence in the UK was obliged to change its name to *Child Possessed*. While the original title eponymized the northern American town in which much of the book's events take place, the rechristening is the better-named. The title *Watseka* puts too much weight—some might say blame—on the town, implying that its influence, or aura, caused the spiritual possessions which are the book's *raison d'etre*. But the book is not about a haunted town (although clearly things are not quite right either; as an analogy we might say that a patch of quicksand's surface is smooth, while its depths eddy and suck). This book concerns itself with the demonic or spiritual possession of children; the important things to note at this point are, this volume has since been reprinted over ten times, and the book is allegedly a work of non-fiction.

"This is a true story," runs the paperback's blurb. "The town is real. The people are real. The events are real. And what happened to Mary Roff and Lurancy Vennum was very real indeed." *Child Possessed* is a challenge to one's belief (either way) in spiritual reincarnation; in a small town in 1840s America, Mary Roff, an unassuming, ordinary baby girl, becomes prone to sudden and inexplicable fits, during which, at first, she goes stiff as a board and is kept (by an unnamed power) in a state of paralysis, or stasis. "She didn't move, she didn't wet herself, she didn't eat." The implication is that control of her body has been given to another—to a force. "It was like having a dead baby in their bedroom, a dead baby that for some reason couldn't be buried yet." After the first such seizure, the first thing Mary does is suckle at her mother's breast; instincts have returned, showing the occupancy to have been but a temporary one. But the occupancies become more frequent. One early response to the possibility of

what is going on is: "spirits are the work of the Devil, and Mary is a Christian child . . ." We see a society hemmed in by its expectations and by its notions of the conceivable; the horror on offer is that of having such small-minded preoccupations and bigotries shaken, when small-minded preoccupations and bigotries were all you ever wanted. Mary's "ailment" is quickly and quackily diagnosed as a "female complaint," the proposed solution to which is the "Electro-Chemical Bath" in a lunatic asylum. Frontier attitudes.

The first act of the incumbent Devil is to erase the name Mary, or try to. Where there is identity there is strength; there is the plausible return of the one who has been eradicated. Enter, literally though temporarily, Katrina Hogan, a 63-year-old German lady; and then a Jesuit priest who is discovered beating a nun about the backside because she has broken her vows. The spirit inside Mary refuses to listen to various implorations, like a childish brat with its hands over its ears. At the incunabular stages of the occupancy Mary knows things that at her age she could not possibly know, and Ann (Mary's mother) eventually suggests that the girl stay in the lunatic asylum a little while longer. When Mary is blamed for her mother's recent miscarriage, the cause in her favour is hardly helped. Reverend Dille suggests that Mary's intruder is a spirit who has not travelled far enough away, rather than a devil. Even so, the fact that the devil is used even in comparison highlights the religious beliefs that these people have, and their dependency on the caste systems of heaven and hell; the fact that the devil is recognized in Mary's (and later, Lurancy Vennum's) assorted rantings suggests that it is the Prince of Lies they fear all along—he's in the collective subconscious; in the realm of the possible. The comparatively ignorant folk in the 19th century were unable to dilute any horrors they faced; no knowledge was available which could be used to blame weird occurrences on logical explanations; there was no science.

In the tradition set by Truman Capote's *In Cold Blood* (1966), David St. Clair's *Child Possessed* is a non-fiction work both packaged and written as a novel. Capote called his own book a "non-fiction novel," and the label fits St. Clair too. Set in the times of the American Civil War, it is on the other hand a document detailing life during distant conflict, the authenticity of which we have little choice but to believe as the war murmurs on in the background. There is certainly plenty of earthiness to *Child Possessed*; St. Clair has written an historical record in more ways than one, his treatment of the status of recently freed black slaves being particularly poignant. But neither *Child Possessed* nor *Say You Love Satan*, *Mine to Kill* or *The Devil Rocked Her Cradle* are journalism *per se*: St. Clair states categorically what characters are thinking. Knives feel good in Mary's hand, for example; she stabs chairs and then draws her own blood, the demon inside wanting to know intimately the makeup of its shell, its home.

Viewed from a modern cultural standpoint, *Child Possessed* reads like a novel in the tradition of William Peter Blatty's *The Exorcist* or Frank de Felitta's *The Entity*. The chronological placement of St. Clair's early work should not go unmentioned. As strong as today's fondness is for non-fiction books about serial killers which reflects the fashion for fictional killers, in the 1970s the equivalent taste was for real-life macabre to mirror the tendency and climate for fictional para-religious manifestations. Life will mirror art will mirror life. People look to stories about murderers not only to race the detective but to gain insight into an alien and very cold mind. The fans of the horror genre in those days, possibly, had loftier ambitions, or were more welcoming to the possibility of the supernatural. Books on ghostvilles and haunted houses still sell, of course, as do tomes on other aspects of the paranormal—but not as well as they have in the past.

David St. Clair's lone foray into acknowledged fiction is a supernatural volume with links to much of his non-fiction work. As in the latter, St. Clair uses children to uncover our deepest fears: not only do children in his work disappear (even if their physical shells remain), there is to contend with the notion that not even the innocent are spared—that there is no protection. In *Bloodline* Lois Bruno's child Tony is kidnapped, seemingly for no reason whatsoever; when the body is found and the request comes to identify it, the reader might think (as does the grieving mother) that a chapter has come to an end, tragically. But then the child starts to appear to Lois in psychic visions; in these the boy pleads with her to save him from a form of imprisonment. Here the reader infers that three awful bells are ringing together at once: distantly there is the possibility (shared between mother and reader) that the boy is still alive; this leads to the reader's understanding that Lois would rather the boy were dead and remained categorically so, rather than in a sort of limbo; and third is that human beings are frightened of there being more possibilities than those on obvious display.

Because of the earlier books, the reader has been conditioned partly into believing in St. Clair's words; to his credit, *Bloodline* reads no less plausibly for being fiction than the non-fiction works. As before, there is in the back of the reader's mind the gentle ring of sensationalism, St. Clair finding it difficult to use kid gloves on occasion with his material; but there is nothing overdone about the painting which is delivered to Lois's house, depicting an old country scene and including the figure of a mysterious old man; nor is there about Lois's desire to find her son and go to Scotland where, finally, she will confront a bloodline of which she was blissfully unaware. St. Clair's stories might seem somewhat far-fetched, but over the long haul he makes the reader *want* to believe, which requires a great deal of manipulative skill.

—David Mathew

SAKI

Pseudonym for Hector Hugh Munro. **Nationality:** British. **Born:** Akyab, Burma, 18 December 1870. **Education:** Private school in Exmouth, Devon, 1882-85; Bedford Grammar School, 1885-87. **Military Service:** King Edward's Horse, 1914; 22nd Royal Fusiliers, 1914-16; killed in action. **Career:** Military police, Burma, 1893-94 (invalided home); full-time writer, London, from 1900; political satirist for *Westminster Gazette*; correspondent for *Morning Post*, London, in Poland, Russia and Paris, 1902-08; parliamentary commentary writer for *Outlook*, 1914. **Died:** 14 November 1916.

HORROR, GHOST AND GOTHIC PUBLICATIONS

Short Stories

Reginald in Russia. London, Methuen, 1910.
The Chronicles of Clovis. London, John Lane, 1911.
Beasts and Super-Beasts. London, John Lane, 1914.
The Toys of Peace and Other Papers (with "A Memoir of H. H. Munro" by Rothay Reynolds). London, Bodley Head, 1919.

Reginald and Reginald in Russia. London, Methuen, 1921.
The Square Egg and Other Sketches, with Three Plays (with memoir by Ethel M. Munro). London, Bodley Head, 1924.
The Short Stories of Saki. London, Bodley Head, 1930; New York, Viking Press, 1930(?).
76 Short Stories. London, Collins, n.d.
Short Stories, edited by John Letts. London, Folio Society, 1976.
The Secret Sin of Septimus Brope, and Other Stories. London, Penguin, 1995.

OTHER PUBLICATIONS

Novels

The Unbearable Bassington. London, John Lane, 1912.
When William Came. London, John Lane, 1913.
The Novels and Plays of Saki (omnibus). London, Bodley Head, 1933; New York, Viking Press, 1933(?).
The Bodley Head Saki (omnibus), edited by J. W. Lambert. London, Bodley Head, 1963.

Short Stories

Reginald. London, Methuen, 1904.
Saki: A Life of Hector Hugh Munro by A. J. Langguth (includes six uncollected stories). London, Hamilton, 1981.

Plays

The East Wing, in *Lucas' Annual*, 1914.
The Watched Pot, with Cyril Maude (produced 1924), in *The Square Egg*, 1924.
The Death Trap, and *Karl-Ludwig's Window*, in *The Square Egg*, 1924.
The Miracle-Merchant, in *One-Act Plays for Stage and Study 8*, edited by Alice Gerstenberg. 1934.

Other

The Rise of the Russian Empire. London, Grant Richards, 1900.
The Westminster Alice (satirical sketches). London, The Westminster Gazette, 1902.

*

Critical Studies: *The Satire of Saki* by G. J. Spears, 1963; *H. H. Munro (Saki)* by Charles H. Gillen, 1969; *Saki: A Life of Hector Hugh Munro* by A. J. Langguth, London, Hamilton, 1981.

*   *   *

The stories which Hector Hugh Munro wrote as "Saki" are often thought of in terms of cosy nostalgia for the pre-World War I scene, with leisured fops swapping post-Wildean epigrams in an era of general opulence. This is indeed an element of their charm; but the tales have endured because of their subversiveness as well as their genuine wit. Saki loved to unleash strange beasts and disquieting violence in those Edwardian drawing-rooms. Again and again there are darkly grotesque episodes where the epigrammatic glitter takes on the chill of ice.

Wolves and hyaenas were perhaps his favourite animals. "The She-Wolf" (*Beasts and Super-Beasts*) is mere fun, a hoax on a pretended magic-maker who is dismayed to find he has apparently turned the house-party's hostess into a real and tangible wolf. The tale within a tale of "The Story-Teller" (*Beasts and Super-Beasts*) sees an unpleasantly moralistic child consumed by a fearful wolf as punishment for excess virtue; with equal relish, a hyaena in the witty "Esmé" (*The Chronicles of Clovis*) devours an unfortunate gypsy baby, to the very slight lessening of two society ladies' aplomb. "The Wolves of Cernogratz" (*The Toys of Peace*) twists the old supernatural tradition of beasts that howl for the dead, when Cernogratz Castle's wolves decline to mourn deaths among the parvenu owners, but terrifyingly salute the passing of the impoverished governess who is the last von Cernogratz. In "The Interlopers" (*The Toys of Peace*), two old enemies trapped by circumstance end their feud and vow friendship hereafter; but the setting is the Carpathians and, cruelly, the "rescuing" figures prove to be wolves. The title character of "Gabriel-Ernest" (*Reginald in Russia*) is a troublingly beautiful 16-year-old waif who—as emerges too late to save another small child—is also a werewolf.

Other alarming creatures abound. The eponymous cat of "Tobermory" (*The Chronicles of Clovis*) learns to talk at a country house-party, and only fortuitous death prevents his revealing all the hideous scandals seen through the windows by night. Sickly Conrad in the brilliant *conte cruel* "Sredni Vashtar" (*The Chronicles of Clovis*) makes a god of his illicit pet ferret, which duly savages to death the malicious guardian who would take away all the boy's pleasures. A rogue stag in the dark "The Music on the Hill" (*The Chronicles of Clovis*) kills the woman who has unbelievingly desecrated an offering to Pan; at the death, we hear the god's laughter. "The Remoulding of Groby Lington" has a protagonist who is persistently influenced by the traits of his pets: a monkey proves particularly disastrous, until Lington settles into stagnation with a tortoise. The mischievous title character of "Laura" dies and at her own wish is reincarnated as an otter that wreaks havoc among unloved neighbours' hens and gardens: although the otter is hunted to a grisly death, Laura's cycle of reincarnation and petty revenge continues. A monstrous spectral hedgehog crawls by night in "The Hedgehog" (*The Toys of Peace*).

Saki's less beast-ridden tales of the supernatural still take an eccentric approach. A quintessential example is "The Soul of Laploshka" (*Reginald in Russia*), featuring the unfearsome but dreadfully unhappy ghost of a miser whose death has allowed the narrator to bilk him of two francs. The haunting will continue until this trifling sum is repaid—not given to the poor, for whom Laploshka has no sympathy, but somehow bestowed on the deserving rich. In "The Saint and the Goblin" (*Reginald in Russia*), a carved saint in a church proves to have his own share of folly and vanity—leading, after attempts to manipulate a mortal through visions, to a hilarious come-uppance. A dreadfully petty struggle between rustic witches dominates "The Peace of Mowsle Barton" (*The Chronicles of Clovis*), its peak of dismaying wrongness coming when several bespelled ducks lose buoyancy and pathetically, strugglingly drown. "Ministers of Grace" (*The Chronicles of Clovis*) sees all England's politicians replaced by lookalike angels from Heaven who, being genuinely well-meaning, soon cause national disaster. The creepily effective ghost-*frisson* of "The Open Window" (*Beasts and Super-Beasts*) is not so much deflated as capped by the revelation that the story which sends a man fleeing in terror is an improvisation by one of Saki's ruthless children: "Romance at short notice was her speciality." Slightly more con-

ventional premonitions of death are noted and duly fulfilled in "The Cobweb" (*Beasts and Super-Beasts*) and "The Seventh Pullet" (*Beasts and Super-Beasts*). "The Infernal Parliament" (*The Square Egg*) presents a comic Hell where all constituents are compelled to listen to all political speeches, and the torment in preparation for an unnamed playwright is to spend eternity reading a gigantic volume of indexed theatrical press-cuttings *with the letter S omitted*—presumably a dig at the egotistic George Bernard Shaw.

The author's grim wit also spices non-supernatural stories of grotesquerie and weirdness. The punchline of "The Reticence of Lady Ann" (*Reginald in Russia*) highlights the failure of a marriage as, following a one-sided quarrel with his silent wife, Lady Ann's husband exits without realizing she has been dead for two hours. "The Background" (*The Chronicles of Clovis*) relates the sadly comic life of a visitor to Italy who impulsively has a masterpiece tattooed on his back, and is trapped there by art-export regulations. A recurring theme of practical joking attains savage intensity in "The Unrest-Cure" (*The Chronicles of Clovis*), whose victim spends a night of terror believing that all the Jews in the neighbourhood are to be lured to his house and massacred, with a Bishop presiding over the slaughter. There are several casual killings: murder is lightly condoned in "The Blind Spot" (*Beasts and Super-Beasts*) because, Wodehouseianly, one doesn't wish to lose a fine cook to the gallows; the comic-sinister plot to gas a hated lap-dog in "Louis" (*The Toys of Peace*) might have been too much for British sensibilities, if not for the neat closing twist.

Saki continues to be read as a celebrated Edwardian wit, but his poisoned barbs are always waiting for the unwary.

—David Langford

SARBAN

Pseudonym for John William Wall. **Nationality:** British. **Born:** 1910. **Career:** Diplomat, 1933-66. **Died:** 11 April 1989.

HORROR, GHOST AND GOTHIC PUBLICATIONS

Novels

The Sound of His Horn. London, Davies, 1952; New York, Ballantine, 1960.
The Doll Maker. New York, Ballantine, 1960.
Ringstones. New York, Ballantine, 1961.

Short Stories

Ringstones and Other Curious Tales. London, Davies, and New York, Coward McCann, 1951.
The Doll Maker and Other Tales of the Uncanny. London, Davies, 1953.

*   *   *

John Wall was a career diplomat who was stationed in the Middle East for many years. It was there that he wrote the stories that fill the three volumes issued in 1951-53; the pseudonym he adopted is a Persian term for a functionary in a caravanserai. Sarban's entire literary output consists of only nine stories, but they include three very striking novellas, one of which was long enough to warrant separate publication as a short novel.

All save one of the stories in *Ringstones* are related second-hand. Three of the shorter pieces are anecdotes represented as tall tales told to the author by European "exiles" in the East. The most effective is "Capra," a heavily ironic erotic fantasy in which a wife's adulterous lust summons a satyr to a costume party, where her jealous husband—a keen hunter whose sporting interests have helped provide opportunities for his rival—takes a pot-shot at it. "The Khan" is a tale of more exotic adultery in which a young woman deserts her loutish husband to live for a while with a huge and none-too-gentle bear. "A Christmas Story" is trivial, but "Calmahain"—the odd one out in its refusal of a distancing frame—is an intriguing and delicately understated tale of two lonely evacuee children in World War II. They take refuge from their distress in building a miniature boat in which they hope to escape to Calmahain, the home of the little people—a project of which the little people seem to approve.

"Ringstones" is presented as a manuscript received by a male student from Daphne Hazel, a female friend he knew at school. It describes how Daphne was recruited by an antiquarian named Ravelin to serve as governess and language-teacher to three children of uncertain origin. The remote house where she executes these duties is named for a stone circle far older than the Roman remains which surround it. Ravelin suggests that a "racetrack" within a natural amphitheatre may have been a "fairy ring," and it gradually becomes clear to the reader that the children in Daphne's charge must belong to some vanished race whose memory has helped to generate fairy mythology. The oldest of the three, Nuaman, is a deceptively sinister figure whose intentions toward Daphne become manifest—if not entirely clear—when she discovers the chariot which she must pull around the racetrack under the fury of his whip. The manuscript ends with a declaration of her intention to escape, but the reader already knows that she will fail and is bound to be suspicious of the sincerity of her intention.

Because it deals with a hypothetical future which has arisen from an alternative history in which the Nazis were victorious in World War II *The Sound of His Horn* is usually considered to be a science-fiction novel, but it is framed as a nightmarish visionary fantasy and it is certainly horrific. At a country house-party an ex-prisoner-of-war named Querdilion tells the story of his escape into a wood where he is shocked into unconsciousness. He wakes in a quasi-Feudal future where human beings are hunted as prey across the baronies of the Reich. He is the captive of a Master Forester whose name is a slight variant of that attached in German legend to the leader of the Wild Hunt (a legend whose best-known literary extrapolation is in the novella by Erckmann-Chatrian known in English as "The Wild Huntsman").

Querdilion falls in love with a young woman who is classified as an "Aryan recalcitrant" and thus condemned to the same treatment as the members of the "inferior races," whose few remaining representatives are employed as serfs, many having been reduced by unspecified means almost to animal status. When the two of them are hunted, the woman sacrifices herself to increase Querdilion's chances of escape. Querdilion returns to the present, where he is soon recaptured. The frame-narrative offers the story as a cautionary fable protesting against the cruelty of hunting, but its internal symbolism is strikingly erotic, in a markedly fetishis-

tic fashion which further elaborates the sado-masochistic imagery of "Ringstones."

The two shorter stories in *The Doll Maker* are "A House of Call," a routine timeslip story, and "The Trespassers," a curious *femme fatale* story involving two schoolboys and girl who might be reckoned a female counterpart of Nuaman in "Ringstones." "The Doll Maker" is, however, the most neatly-rounded of all Sarban's supernatural stories, bringing the major themes tentatively broached in the earlier tales together in an elegantly understated fashion.

The protagonist of "The Doll Maker," Clare, strongly resembles Daphne Hazel. She is a frustrated 18-year-old girl trapped in a dreadful boarding school. She falls in love with Niall, the son of a female artist who lives in a nearby house. The ingeniously sadistic Niall is obsessed with carving human figurines out of magical wood. These can be brought to life—but only at the cost of stealing the vitality of their human models, who die of "infantile paralysis." When Clare discovers the fate for which she has been marked down by her treacherous and perhaps not-entirely-human lover—and discovers, furthermore, that her life might be forfeit even if she rebels in spirit, thus "spoiling" her miniature counterpart—she naturally becomes determined to find an alternative consummation for her dangerous liaison.

There is nothing else in the horror genre quite like the three novellas which make up the bulk of Sarban's literary production and it is a pity that they are nowadays very difficult to get hold of, even in the Ballantine paperback editions. Their calculatedly perverse eroticism may seem unusually subdued by comparison with more recent works but it was unusually flagrant in its day and the surreal quality used to mask it adds a unique cutting edge to its effect. When Wall was belatedly identified as the author of the three books and was asked to comment on his brief literary career he readily explained that he had stopped writing because he could no longer find the time when his diplomatic duties became heavier—but he never ventured to say why he had started in the first place, or why his work took the remarkable form that it did.

—Brian Stableford

SARRANTONIO, Al

Nationality: American. **Born:** Queens, New York, 1952. **Family:** Married; two sons. **Career:** Worked in book publishing, New York; contributor of short stories and reviews to many magazines, including *Heavy Metal, Twilight Zone, Isaac Asimov's Science Fiction Magazine, Night Cry* and *Mystery Scene*. Lives in Putnam Valley, New York.

HORROR, GHOST AND GOTHIC PUBLICATIONS

Novels

Totentanz. New York, Tor, 1985.
The Worms. New York, Doubleday, 1985.
Campbell Wood. New York, Doubleday, 1986.
The Boy with Penny Eyes. New York, Tor, 1987.
Cold Night. New York, Tor, 1989.
Moonbane. New York, Bantam, 1989.

October. New York, Bantam, 1990.
House Haunted. New York, Bantam, 1991.
Skeletons. New York, Bantam, 1992.

Other

Editor, with Martin H. Greenberg. *100 Hair-Raising Little Horror Stories.* New York, Barnes and Noble, 1993.

OTHER PUBLICATIONS

Novel

Five Worlds #1: Exile. New York, Roc, 1996.

* * *

Carnivals have been a frequent plot element in horror fiction, everything from Charles G. Finney's *The Circus of Dr. Lao* to Ray Bradbury's *Something Wicked This Way Comes.* Al Sarrantonio exploited this in his first horror novel, *Totentanz,* with considerable success despite its lack of originality. The carnival appears overnight, as if by magic, and the local townspeople seem completely taken in by Ash, the master of the show. But Reggie Carson, only 13, can see with clear eyes, and he knows that the carnival is an illusion and a trap, that there is terror rather than pleasure to be found in its tents, and that Ash himself is a monster from one of his darkest nightmares. Had Sarrantonio been the first to use this theme, he might have made a significant impression, because *Totentanz* is a powerful, controlled work, unusually so for a first novel. But comparisons with more skilled writers were inevitable and the novel was largely overlooked.

The Worms borrows from science fiction, a genre in which Sarrantonio also writes occasionally. In this case, the worms are terrifying creatures who have been imprisoned for centuries, but some of whom have broken free in the ground beneath a remote New England town. When humans come close enough, the worms can infest their bodies and eventually transform their hosts into a variety of bizarre creatures equipped with fangs, claws, wings and other appendages. The transformations aren't particularly plausible scientifically, but as horror fiction the story is an engaging "B" movie in print, with lots of death and destruction and a very fast-paced plot.

Campbell Wood is considerably more sedate, although only by comparison. The inhabitants of Campbell Wood have faerie blood in their veins, and they can use the trees of the forest as weapons. When outsiders stray within their borders, the inhabitants of the wood destroy them in horrible ways, hoping to discourage others, but their magic may ultimately not be able to match another occult power ranged against them and their reign of terror. *The Boy with Penny Eyes* is Sarrantonio's most restrained and successful horror novel. The boy of the title appears to be autistic, never shows joy or sorrow, never speaks, and the adults who shuffle him from one home to another despair of ever reaching him. But he isn't entirely unaware. His eyes are always moving, watching, searching for another child, the other half of his personality from whom he has been supernaturally severed.

Moonbane is an admitted homage to bad science-fiction and horror films. The appearance of an unprecedented meteorite display gives all too brief warning of the invasion of Earth by werewolf-like creatures from the moon. As they land and disperse among the population, they increase their numbers constantly because each of their victims is transformed into one of their kind. The hero has lost his family in the opening onslaught and now he must travel cross-country to a secret conclave of scientists who are trying desperately to find an effective weapon before the last of the human race is absorbed by the shape-changing creatures from another world. Unabashedly melodramatic and simply plotted, the novel is more of an exercise in nostalgia than a genuinely suspenseful work.

An inhuman creature lives parasitically in human bodies in *October.* When a college professor returns to his remote home town, he becomes involved with an elderly woman who knows the secret of the creature's existence and weaknesses but who has suppressed the knowledge so deeply that she can no longer remember it. *House Haunted* is not, as the title might suggest, a traditional haunted-house story. Instead it deals with a powerful occult creature from another universe who was once thwarted in her attempt to invade our reality, and who is about to try again. Her mental powers allow her to contact and influence several very disparate humans and she causes them to get together physically so that they can create a gateway through which she can enter. Fortunately, others in the story realize what's going on and prevent her from doing so. Both of these are competent, reasonably entertaining stories, but in both cases the villains aren't convincing enough to sustain the suspense.

The most interesting and in some ways the best-written of Sarrantonio's horror novels is *Skeletons,* which also contains a great deal of very dark humour. Through some unexplained device, all of the skeletons on Earth have been restored to life, and each of them is determined to pursue his or her former career. In Russia, the bones of Lenin and Marx are plotting against the government, and in the United States Abraham Lincoln is about to reassume the Presidency. Despite the obvious satire, the mood of the novel is distinctly that of horror, because the armies of the undead intend to supplant the living and wrest from them control of the Earth. The protagonists live among a group of refugees from the cities, desperately trying to survive in a world where dying companions immediately return to life as enemies. This one's a bizarre twist on the *Night of the Living Dead* films.

Sarrantonio is also a fairly prolific short-story writer. "Father Dear" is an impressive exploration of the diseased mind of a man whose father tormented him relentlessly throughout his childhood. There's another abusive father in "Under My Bed," but this one succumbs to a variant of the monster-in-my-closet ending. In "Wish" a young boy wishes that it could be Christmas always, and discovers to his horror that he has gotten what he asked for. A retarded man is terrified of household dirt in "Dust," and eventually with good reason. A group of mischievous boys plan Halloween tricks in "Bogy" but instead run into a malevolent creature that can change shapes and impersonate each of them. In "The Coat" a misogynist is urged to kill women by his jacket. In general, Sarrantonio's short fiction seems more controlled and thoughtful than his novels, which often rely so much on physical action that the characters never achieve any depth. At the same time *The Boy With Penny Eyes* and *Skeletons* in particular indicate that Sarrantonio possesses the skills to be a successful novelist when he sets his mind to it.

—Don D'Ammassa

SAUL, John (Woodruff, III)

Nationality: American. **Born:** Pasadena, California, 25 February, 1942. **Education:** Attended Antioch College, 1959-60; Cerritos College, 1960-61; Montana State University, 1961-62; San Francisco State College, 1963-65. **Career:** Various positions in the 1960s and 1970s, including archaeological worker in New Mexico, technical writer, magazine editor, car rental agent, and author of pseudonymous sex novels (pseudonyms and titles not disclosed); worked on administrative staff of Stonewall drug and alcohol rehabilitation centre, 1973; director of Tellurian Communities, 1976-78; director, Seattle Theatre Arts, from 1978; full-time writer since 1977. **Agent:** Jane Rotrosen, 318 East 51st Street, New York, NY 10022, USA. Lives in Seattle, Washington, and Maui, Hawaii.

HORROR, GHOST AND GOTHIC PUBLICATIONS

Novels (series: The Blackstone Chronicles)

Suffer the Children. New York, Dell, 1977; London, Hodder and Stoughton, 1978.
Punish the Sinners. New York, Dell, and London, Hodder and Stoughton, 1978.
Cry for the Strangers. New York, Dell, and London, Hodder and Stoughton, 1979.
Comes the Blind Fury. New York, Dell, and London, Hodder and Stoughton, 1980.
When the Wind Blows. New York, Dell, and London, Hodder and Stoughton, 1981.
The God Project. New York, Bantam, 1982; as *All Fall Down*, London, Bantam, 1991.
Nathaniel. New York, Bantam, 1984; London, Bantam, 1991.
Brain Child. New York, Bantam, 1985; London, Bantam, 1991.
Hellfire. New York and London, Bantam, 1986.
The Unwanted. New York and London, Bantam, 1987.
The Unloved. New York and London, Bantam, 1988.
Creature. New York and London, Bantam, 1989.
Sleepwalk. New York and London, Bantam, 1990.
Second Child. New York, Bantam, 1990; London, Bantam, 1991.
Darkness. New York and London, Bantam, 1991.
Shadows. New York and London, Bantam, 1993.
Guardian. New York, Bantam, 1993; London, Bantam Press, 1994.
The Homing. New York, Fawcett Columbine, and London, Bantam Press, 1994.
Black Lightning. New York, Fawcett Columbine, and London, Bantam Press, 1995.
An Eye for an Eye: The Doll (Blackstone). New York, Fawcett Crest, 1997.
Twist of Fate: The Locket (Blackstone). New York, Fawcett Crest, 1997.
Ashes to Ashes: The Dragon's Flame (Blackstone). New York, Fawcett Crest, 1997.
In the Shadow of Evil: The Handkerchief (Blackstone). New York, Fawcett Crest, 1997.
Day of Reckoning: The Stereoscope (Blackstone). New York, Fawcett Crest, 1997.
Asylum (Blackstone). New York, Fawcett Crest, 1997.
The Presence. New York, Fawcett Columbine, and London, Bantam Press, 1997.

*

Film Adaptation: *Cry for the Strangers* (television movie), 1982.

Critical Studies: "John Saul: 'Remember, It's Only a Story'" by Laura Kramer, *Twilight Zone*, November, 1981; "Interview: John Saul" by James Kisner, *Mystery Scene* 16, 1987; "John Saul" in *Dark Dreamers: Conversations with the Masters of Horror* by Stanley Winter, New York, Avon, 1990; *John Saul: A Critical Companion* by Paul Bail, Westport, Connecticut, Greenwood Press, 1996.

* * *

Since John Saul has so often been promoted or positioned as a sort of low-rent alternative to Stephen King (the evidentiary smoking gun being the appearance of Saul's dull six-part serial novel, *The Blackstone Chronicles*, exactly one year after King's ground-breaking six-part serial novel *The Green Mile*), comparisons between the two authors are almost inevitable. The problem, from the perspective of Saul's admirers, is that such comparisons invariably seem unflattering to Saul. King has demonstrated a talent for writing variegated stories in several genres; Saul has largely limited himself to a narrow range of conventional horror stories. King repeatedly creates complex, involving characters; Saul tends to rely on stock characters, each distinguished by a set of mannerisms. King's novels are characteristically enriched by innumerable references to literature, film, television, rock music and popular culture; Saul's novels entirely lack such resonances. King displays a generally unostentatious but clever prose style, enlivened by flashes of sly humour; Saul writes at best competently while always maintaining a stone face. And so on and so forth; no matter what aspects of writing one focuses on, there appear to be grounds for casting King as a brilliant innovator and Saul as a plodding camp follower.

Despite the elements of truth in these charges, however, judgments based on comparisons to Stephen King are fundamentally unfair—to all modern writers, perhaps, but especially to Saul, since this line of thought particularly serves to obscure Saul's genuine and substantive talents as a horror writer.

Consider the fact that, as most would concede, horror is fundamentally a conservative genre, repeatedly urging people to follow the old rituals, obey the time-honoured rules, and honour the ancient taboos, and devising horrific punishments for all those who dare to flout these strictures. It would only seem appropriate, then, for horror writers to ply their craft in a rigorously traditional fashion. And that is exactly what Saul is careful to do. His stories starkly manipulate the foundational elements of scary stories as they have existed since the dawn of humanity: first, you establish characters and say enough about them to make them sympathetic; then, you juxtapose them with some evil force of unknown nature and extent; you place them within easy reach of that force; and you thus can captivate members of your audience, who will fearfully wonder whether these characters will survive their encounters, will be destroyed, or will be recruited to function as additional pawns of that force. Do this once, and you have a horror story; do this again and again, and you have a horror novel.

Stated so baldly, this formula might seem easy to realize; but actually, in these complicated times, it demands a remarkable sense of purpose and integrity to present such scenarios clearly and sincerely. This is manifestly true in the case of Saul. Consider, for example, his comment to critic Paul Bail that, despite his early efforts to write comic novels, he deliberately avoids humour in his novels because "There's nothing that breaks terror as quickly as a good laugh." There is, then, a deliberate intent and conscious artistry in Saul's flat, monochromatic approach; for Saul, that is what traditional, undiluted horror is all about. And, as a result, Saul's novels always work, just as horror stories have always worked, and they work at a powerful visceral level even when one's rational mind is howling in protest. Engrossed in one of his better novels, *The Homing*, readers might seriously question the scientific logic of genetically engineered miniature bees that infest human beings and take control of their behaviour, and they might vehemently resent the shoddy plotting that leads not one but two characters to go by themselves without telling anybody to confront the story's villain and thus make themselves available for immediate capture. But it doesn't matter; they will still keep turning the pages, and they will still feel a tingle of excitement each time a character is threatened by the scientist or by his victims.

Overall, while recent novels tend to be better than earlier efforts, Saul's works are remarkably consistent in their structure, subject matter, and entertainment value; a reader who likes one of them will very probably like all of the others. The typical elements include vulnerable young people, an isolated small town, an adult outsider struggling to understand things, and some nascent or renascent evil that repeatedly threatens the protagonists. His earlier novels, like *Suffer the Children*, involved or bordered on the supernatural, but beginning with *The God Project*, Saul has more often focused on advanced scientific menaces; since he evidences little knowledge of or interest in science, Saul's approach to scientific horror has not been noticeably different. Many hailed *Black Lightning* as a striking departure because it featured the spirit of an executed serial killer who occupies the body of an urban architect to commit a new string of murders; but Saul's Seattle (one of his home towns) resembles the close-knit communities of his other novels, and the ensuing story followed the usual pattern of implacable menace stalking vulnerable victims (although, undeniably, its similarities to recent true cases may have added an extra set of chills to the proceedings). The only true innovation in Saul's fiction, the six-part *Blackstone* saga, is also his only disaster: lacking any familiarity with or feel for short fiction, Saul could not build up sufficient energy in each vignette, yet their separability ensured that the series lacked any cumulative impact as well. Like the characters in his novels, Saul thus learned the dangers of departing from a tried and true approach; and he has recently returned to his standard form with *The Presence*, another novel of scientific experimentation gone wrong, this time employing as a setting his other regular residence, Hawaii.

If there is a conspicuous weakness in Saul's novels, it is that the final explanations behind their frightening events are often incomplete, muddled or unsatisfying. In *Nathaniel*, for example, readers are asked to believe that a farmer, confronting his wife's newly born son and knowing he is not the child's father, would respond by taking the infant to the other man and telling him to take care of the child, and that the man would respond by deciding to raise the boy all by himself, in complete and utter secrecy, never letting anyone else know of his existence. Here, the idea that such a torturously treated child might somehow develop unspecified psychic powers is the most plausible aspect of the plot. And in *Asylum*, the final volume of *The Blackstone Chronicles*, the revelation that the town's newspaper editor has been unknowingly obeying the implanted dictates of a long-dead murderer leaves many aspects of the preceding volumes basically unexplained. But these problems are not critical: Saul promises to frighten his readers, and he always does; complaining that he does poorly with final resolutions is like saying that a thrill-packed roller coaster ride is no good because it happens to come to a jarring and unpleasant end.

In sum, if Stephen King has splendidly demonstrated that the horror novel can be updated and made achingly relevant to contemporary life, Saul has demonstrated that such retrofitting and streamlining was not necessary; the old-time religion of straightforward horror still serves modern readers, just as it has always served readers who enjoy the vicarious pleasure of observing people in deadly peril. And one might even heretically revise the standard comparisons: while King needlessly clutters his horror novels with clever asides, jazzy innovations and stylistic brilliancies, Saul methodically and respectfully provides horror in its purest and most unadulterated form. To validate Saul in other words, one might say this: you can explain the appeal of a talent like King in innumerable ways, but to explain the appeal of John Saul, a theory of horror fiction is absolutely essential. And in that sense, he is one of the most important writers discussed in this volume.

—Gary Westfahl

SAXON, Peter

Pseudonym of Wilfred Glassford McNeilly. **Other Pseudonyms** (mostly shared house names): W. Howard Baker; W. A. Ballinger; Wilfred Glassford; Errol Lecale; Desmond Reid. **Nationality:** British. **Born:** Renfrewshire, Scotland, 8 March 1921. **Military Service:** British Army, later Captain in Second Royal Lanciers, Indian Army, and Lieutenant Commander in Royal Indian Navy, 1940-46. **Family:** Married Margaret Ferguson Macdonald Miller in 1946; five sons. **Career:** Journalist, *Northern Whig*, Belfast, 1938-40; snake charmer with an Indian circus, 1946-47; journalist, *Belfast Newsletter*, and part-time author, 1947-52; full-time author from 1952 (with occasional forays into photography for the BBC and fishing). **Died:** 1983.

HORROR, GHOST AND GOTHIC PUBLICATIONS

Novels (series: The Guardians)

The Darkest Night. London, Mayflower, 1966; New York, Paperback Library, 1967.
Drums of the Dark Gods (as W. A. Ballinger). London, Mayflower, 1966; New York, Paperback Library, 1967.
The Torturer. London, Mayflower, 1966; New York, Paperback Library, 1967.
The Disoriented Man. London, Mayflower, 1966; as *Scream and Scream Again*, New York, Paperback Library, 1967.
Satan's Child. London, Mayflower, 1967.
Dark Ways to Death (Guardians). London, Howard Baker, 1968; New York, Berkley, 1969.
The Curse of Rathlaw (Guardians). New York, Lancer, and London, Howard Baker, 1968.
Through the Dark Curtain (Guardians). New York, Lancer, and London, Howard Baker, 1968.

The Killing Bone (Guardians). New York, Berkley, and London, Howard Baker, 1969.

The Haunting of Alan Mais (Guardians). New York, Berkley, and London, Howard Baker, 1969.

The Vampires of Finistère (Guardians). New York, Berkley, and London, Howard Baker, 1970.

Vampire's Moon. New York, Belmont, and Manchester, England, PBS, 1970.

Novels as Errol Lecale (series: The Specialist in all titles)

Tigerman of Terrahpur. London, New English Library, 1973.
Castledoom. London, New English Library, 1974.
The Severed Hand. London, New English Library, 1974.
The Death Box. London, New English Library, 1974.
Zombie. London, New English Library, 1975.
Blood of My Blood. London, New English Library, 1975.

OTHER PUBLICATIONS

Novels

Unfriendly Persuasion (as W. A. Ballinger). London, Consul, 1964.
The Break Out (as Wilfred McNeilly). London, Mayflower, 1965.
The Case of the Stag at Bay (as Wilfred McNeilly). London, Mayflower, 1965.
Death in the Top Twenty (as Wilfred McNeilly). London, Mayflower, 1965.
Vengeance Is Ours. London, Mayflower, 1965.
Wanted for Questioning (as Wilfred McNeilly). London, Mayflower, 1965.
The Case of the Muckrakers (as Wilfred McNeilly). London, Mayflower, 1966; New York, Macfadden, 1967.
Land of the Free (as Wilfred McNeilly). London, Mayflower, 1966.
No Way Out (novelization of television script; as Wilfred McNeilly). London, Consul, 1966.
This Spy Must Die. London, Mayflower, 1967.
Slave Brain. London, Mayflower, 1967.
Black Honey. London, Mayflower, 1968.
Corruption. London, Sphere, 1968.
The Unfeeling Sky. London, Corgi, 1968.
The Enemy Sky. London, Corgi, 1969.
The Warring Sky. London, Corgi, 1970.
The War Runners (as Wilfred McNeilly). London, New English Library, 1970.
Alpha-Omega (as Wilfred Glassford). London, New English Library, 1977.

*

Film Adaptation: *Scream and Scream Again* (*The Screamer*), 1969, from the novel *The Disoriented Man*.

* * *

Would the real Peter Saxon please stand up? It is, of course, a hopeless request. Although it is commonly accepted that the driving force behind "Peter Saxon" was editor and writer William Howard Baker (1925-1991)—whose own name sometimes was used as a pseudonym by Wilfred McNeilly—the picture is more complicated than that. Like the Jarndyce-and-Jarndyce legal battle in Charles Dickens's *Bleak House*, the sequence of events, contracts and rights is seriously tangled. W. Howard Baker was primarily an editor and publisher, while Wilfred McNeilly was the writer-for-hire of scores of novels under various guises. The British paperback publisher Mayflower Books first introduced Peter Saxon, but the novels carrying that byline were not always the work of McNeilly alone: Peter Saxon was in fact an entity consisting of several writers, among them Howard Baker, Rex Dolphin, Stephen Frances, Ross Richards and Martin Thomas. Although McNeilly claimed to be the most prolific of these writers, it is probable that some of the Peter Saxon titles had no input from him whatsoever.

Before first publishing as Peter Saxon in 1966, McNeilly was already a prolific author for the "Sexton Blake Library" story-paper and elsewhere. His first book, *Unfriendly Persuasion*, came out in 1964 under the name W. A. Ballinger. But without doubt McNeilly's most productive decade was 1966 to 1975; and into these years falls Peter Saxon (and "Errol Lecale," a pseudonym which does seem to have been used solely by McNeilly). As McNeilly once said, "A paragraph on paper beats the hell out of a chapter in the mind."

Dark Ways to Death was an example of that rarefied and specific form of horror, the tale of the occult. Not set on a South Sea Island or anywhere else as apparently exotic, however, the novel explores the voodoo practices that were (supposedly) taking place in London at the time. Dennis Wheatley was one of the book's champions, even going so far as to republish it as volume 32 of the Dennis Wheatley Library of the Occult. However, Wheatley's enthusiasm was not unqualified; in the introduction he wrote, "I have rarely read a novel the first chapter of which was more colourless, impersonal and lacking in inducement to continue." More generously, maybe, one might say that the novel starts with something of a slow burn. Hyperbolically, Wheatley goes on: "From chapter two Mr. Peter Saxon's story grips the reader and carries him into a positive orgy of excitement and violence." The heroes of the volume are the Guardians, a troop of psychic vigilantes dedicated to the stomping out of inner-city satanism. A shabby chemist's shop owned by Dr. Obadiah Duval—who, on the sly, is a Devil-worshipper and voodoo chief—is the front for an easy access to an abandoned Underground line, where rites and rituals messily take place. Duval can project a psychic mind-cuff on to the would-be worshippers, rooting them in place while the evil deeds are being done. Deeds such as cat-sacrifice and rape, executed in the name of the satanic behemoth, Dambalawedo.

Dennis Wheatley praises the novel for pre-addressing certain concerns of the 1970s. Indeed, this is a 1970s novel, though possibly not in the way that Wheatley meant. *Dark Ways to Death* is to be applauded for its treatment of interracial emotional relationships, something which at the time was rare in horror (and is still largely eschewed). To a certain extent the voodoo rites are metaphorical; this is unquestionably an inner-city novel, one that twangs with racial tensions, and the examination of Black Magic in an urban setting is one way of examining racial conflicts. Ethnicity was under-represented in 1960s horror—that is, a realistic, non-comical exploration of such was under-represented—and if the implied author Saxon had been accused, on occasion, of racist attitudes himself in the book, then his attitudes towards the landed gentry must also be held in disdain. The comical delineation of the upper classes is in the form of two attendees at the ceremony that the Guardians hope to abort: a silly rich-bitch Duchess and her drunken old fool of a husband. The truth seems to be that Saxon hoped to highlight the class structure of London (implying that of any major city) and the static charges inherent.

The Disoriented Man (also known as *Scream and Scream Again*) sees once more a preoccupation with race relations, though it is handled differently. A jogger in a London park stumbles and falls into unconsciousness; when he wakes up in a hospital bed he no longer has his legs. As *Dark Ways to Death* was to the sub-genre of Black Magic, so *The Disoriented Man* is to the sub-genre of speculative scientific horror, of the type initiated by Mary Shelley's *Frankenstein*. Aristocratic megalomaniacs in England and in a German-speaking country that is a simple substitution for Nazi Germany have formed the plan to create superbeings using the body parts of unwitting living donors, such as the jogger. One such creature escapes to attack and drink the blood of a woman in London. After a manhunt, the creature is destroyed by acid, its amoral nature thwarted by the very humans who had wanted it to be the perfect man.

Vampire's Moon is a Peter Saxon contribution to Gothic fiction. Here is an homage to the 18th century cloying atmospheres of Ann Radcliffe and Matthew Gregory Lewis; to novels in which the imbalance of power between men and women was described in terms of powerful men chasing beautiful women in tatty castles, or in forests with surprisingly human characteristics, the chase being for the purposes of the male's sexual gratification. Saxon's twist on the theme is that the man pursuing the woman is not a tall Italian but a Rumanian vampire prince who is helped to find victims by the peasants over whom he lords; and the woman is in fact two women—two American ladies on vacation—who categorically do not believe in vampires. There are dream sequences worthy of the nightmare in *Wuthering Heights*—of Roman torture sessions, charred flesh, bloody floggings . . .

The precise contributions by writers other than McNeilly to the Peter Saxon books may never be known, but having a quorum of writers helped give Saxon's work its diversity. Although Saxon's output was primarily horror, there were interesting developments in his short career, especially so when one considers the fact that a house name would be expected to work to something of a formula. The nippy, pulpish style of writing which occasionally blossoms into elegance is a common thread (another advantage, perhaps, of writers working in conjunction) but the subject matters covered were interestingly varied—and presumably reflected, in fairness, similar subject matters dealt with fashionably and successfully by other houses.

—David Mathew

SCHOW, David J.

Pseudonym: Stephen Grave. **Nationality:** American. **Born:** Marburg, West Germany, 13 July 1955; German orphan adopted by American parents. **Family:** Married Christa Faust in 1995. **Career:** Freelance writer since the late 1970s; screenwriter since the late 1980s; according to unconfirmed reports has written 17 novels, probably all crime thrillers, under the Stephen Grave pseudonym. **Awards:** *Twilight Zone* magazine Dimension award for short story, 1985; World Fantasy award for short story, 1987. **Agent:** Creative Artists Agency, 9830 Wilshire Boulevard, Beverly Hills, CA 90212, USA. Lives in Hollywood, California.

HORROR, GHOST AND GOTHIC PUBLICATIONS

Novels

The Kill Riff. New York, Tor, 1988; London, Macdonald, 1989.
The Shaft. London, Macdonald, 1990.

Short Stories

Seeing Red. New York, Tor, 1990.
Lost Angels. New York, New American Library, 1990.
Sedalia. Eugene, Oregon, Pulphouse, 1991.
Black Leather Required: Stories. Shingletown, California, Ziesing, 1994.

Plays

Screenplays: *A Nightmare on Elm Street, Part IV: The Dream Child* (uncredited), with Leslie Bohem, 1988; *Leatherface: Texas Chainsaw Massacre III*, 1989; *Critters 3: You Are What They Eat*, 1991; *Critters 4: Critters in Space*, with Joseph Lyle, 1992; *The Crow*, with John Shirley, 1994.

Television Plays: episodes of *Freddy's Nightmares* 1989, *Tales from the Crypt*, 1994, *The Outer Limits*, 1995, *Perversions of Science*, 1996, and *The Hunger*, 1997.

Other

The Outer Limits: The Official Companion, with Jeffrey Frentzen. New York, Ace, 1986.

Editor, *The Silver Scream.* Arlington Heights, Illinois, Dark Harvest, 1988.

*

Critical Study: "David J. Schow and Splatterpunk" by S. T. Joshi, *Studies in Weird Fiction* no. 13, Summer 1993.

Theatrical Activities:
Actor: **Television**—cameo appearance in *Stephen King's The Shining*, 1997.

OTHER PUBLICATIONS

Novels as Stephen Grave (novelizations of television scripts)

The Florida Burn. New York, Avon, 1985; London, Star, 1987.
The Vengeance Game. New York, Avon, 1985; London, Star, 1987.
The Razor's Edge. New York, Avon, 1986; London, Star, 1987.
China White. New York, Avon, 1986; London, Star, 1987.
Probing by Fire. New York, Avon, and London, Star, 1987.

* * *

While many horror writers have grown up in or moved to Los Angeles, the milieu of that city is perhaps most powerfully reflected in the works of David J. Schow. Manifestly drawing upon first-hand knowledge, he often writes cynically but sympathetically about the inhabitants of its many colourful subcultures—film executives, rock musicians, models, gang members—as well as ordinary Angelenos with more mundane occupations. In addition, Schow regularly projects a uniquely Californian philosophy, on the one hand aggressively proclaiming one's independence from roots and traditions while embracing everything alien, heterodox and repulsive, and on the other hand shyly revealing a sentimental longing for the old-fashioned morality and loving relationships of *Leave It to Beaver*. So it is that Richard Christian Matheson, writing about the author proclaimed the "Father of Splatterpunk" (a term Schow coined) and renowned for his shockingly explicit violence, would speak of Schow's "secret tenderness."

While there are these continuities through Schow's short fiction, his collections each bring out a different aspect of his singular talents. *Lost Angels* (which contains the introduction by Richard Christian Matheson referred to above), designed to have "thematic unity," displays his fascination with Los Angeles in some of his gentlest and most understated works; *Seeing Red* demonstrates his mastery of the conventional horror story; and *Black Leather Required* shows Schow taking risks and going to extremes in depictions of kinky sex and graphic violence.

Three of the five stories in *Lost Angels* seem especially striking. In "Red Light" a glamorous model, after expressing fears that repeatedly having her photograph taken is somehow draining her life away, mysteriously vanishes. In "Pamela's Get" a neglected young woman invents three imaginary companions and somehow makes them real; when she dies, one of them makes a desperate but unsuccessful attempt to stay alive. "Monster Movies" is the touching story of a young boy who makes a ritual out of watching Friday-night monster movies, his cruel stepmother who burns his monster magazines and forbids his television viewing, and the woman who, many years later, lovingly restages the ritual for the now-adult fan.

A fascination with horror movies also surfaces in some of the stories in *Seeing Red*. "One for the Horrors" is about a seedy movie theatre that inexplicably shows old movies with never-before-seen scenes. "Blood Rape of the Lust Ghouls" involves a reviewer of exploitation movies who murders his wife and tries to escape through a movie poster into a parallel world. "Coming Soon to a Theater Near You" depicts another decrepit movie house that is run by dead bodies animated by colonies of cockroaches. Insects taking over human bodies also figure in "The Woman's Version," while "Night Bloomer" describes an executive who takes a seed from a mysterious woman to grow a magical plant which kills a despised superior—but then learns that his body has become an incubator for thousands of deadly seeds. Other stories in the collection include "Bunny Didn't Tell Us," where inept graverobbers unearth and struggle with a zombie; "Pulpmeister," about the hero of a hack writer's series who comes to life and takes over the task of writing his novels; "Incident on a Rainy Night in Beverly Hills," which describes a Hollywood conspiracy to murder people as a way to boost ticket sales; and "Visitation," where a man attempts to defeat an anticipated outbreak of demonic energy in a Los Angeles hotel.

One standout story in *Black Leather Required* is the astonishing "Scoop Makes a Swifty," where Mikey, a small-time hoodlum known as "Scoop," finds himself tied back-to-back to a headless corpse and left floating in an underground sewer, struggling to turn around and gulp some air before inhaling another mouthful of turd-filled water. He finally comes ashore, fighting off rats gnaw-

ing at his body, to encounter a strange group of subterranean exiles who regard him as the messiah predicted by their singular religion, destined to be blessed by a monstrous alligator. When they turn on Scoop after he refuses to follow the script and kills the approaching creature, he wriggles into its body to escape in the guise of a monster; he finally reaches a ladder to the surface and "ascended back into the world of hurt." In summary, the story sounds like little more than an excuse for one gross-out after another; yet readers will find Scoop remarkably endearing in his stubborn determination to survive in the face of some of the worst indignities imaginable, and he oddly emerges as a truly heroic figure, a Ulysses for the 1990s.

Other stories in the *Black Leather* collection that combine repulsiveness and charm are "Jerry's Kids Meet Wormboy," best described as a colourful comic romp set in the universe of George Romero's *Night of the Living Dead*; "Life Partner," where a woman discovers that her man is a better companion—and better lover—after he dies; and "Pitt Night at the Lewistone Boneyard," about a lonely man who is visited by the rotting remains of several dead relatives. Two other noteworthy stories feature dinosaurs: "Sedalia," where dinosaurs begin to briefly materialize to rampage and defecate in modern cities, and "Kamikaze Butterflies," a wild take on Ray Bradbury's "A Sound of Thunder" where people return to the days of the dinosaurs deliberately determined to do as much damage as possible and thus completely alter history.

Schow's novels to date have attracted less attention than his stories. *The Kill Riff* is essentially a gripping suspense novel about Lucas Ellington, a Vietnam veteran (a frequent figure in Schow's fiction) who is unhinged by his daughter's accidental death during a rock concert and methodically sets out to murder all members of the group that performed that night. Its most horrific touch is a psychologist's theory that Lucas's personality type—the psychopath who is utterly obsessed by his own world view and single-mindedly determined to achieve his goals—may represent a successful and soon-to-be common adaptation to the pressures of modern life. His other novel, *The Shaft*, is an expanded version of a story of that name included in *Black Leather Required*; it features a criminal who accidentally causes a woman's death, flees to Chicago, and eventually falls into a loathsome quagmire at the bottom of a ventilation shaft.

In recent years, while continually promising to publish a third novel and a fourth collection, Schow has focused on film and television scripts, his most significant known accomplishment being his rewrite of John Shirley's screenplay for *The Crow*. Given the titles of some of the other films he has worked on, one must hope that he is merely engaged in extended research for his next Hollywood horror story.

—Gary Westfahl

SCOTT, Michael

Nationality: Irish. **Born:** 1959. **Career:** Bookshop manager; freelance writer. Not to be confused with "Michael Scot" (a joint pseudonym for fantasy novelists Michael Scott Rohan and Allan Scott). **Address:** c/o Warner Books, Little, Brown and Company (UK), Brettenham House, Lancaster Place, London WC2E 7EN, England. Lives near Dublin.

HORROR, GHOST AND GOTHIC PUBLICATIONS

Novels

Banshee. London, Mandarin, 1990.
Image. London, Sphere, 1991.
Reflection. London, Warner, 1992.
Imp. London, Warner, 1993.
The Hallows. London, Signet Creed, 1995.

Short Stories

Irish Ghosts and Hauntings. London, Warner, 1994.

OTHER PUBLICATIONS

Novels

A Bright Enchantment. N.p., 1985.
A Golden Dream. N.p., 1985.
A Silver Wish. N.p., 1985.
The Last of the Fianna (for children). London, Pied Piper, 1987.
Magician's Law. London, Sphere, 1987.
Demon's Law. London, Sphere, 1988.
Navigator: The Voyage of St. Brendan, with Gloria Gaghan. London, Methuen, 1988.
The Quest of the Sons. N.p., 1988.
Death's Law. London, Sphere, 1989.
Wind Lord. N.p., 1991.
Gemini Game. N.p., 1993.

Other

Irish Folk and Fairy Tales. London, Sphere, 1983.
Irish Folk and Fairy Tales Volume II. London, Sphere, 1983.
Irish Folk and Fairy Tales Volume 3. London, Sphere, 1984.
Irish Folk and Fairy Tales Omnibus. London, Sphere, 1989.

*   *   *

Michael Scott began his career with fantasy retellings of traditional tales from Ireland, both for adults and for teenagers. He has an interest in mythology which he uses in his horror fiction, all of which has a supernatural bias but also tends to the bloodthirsty and a high body-count. He puts his knowledge to good use in *Banshee*, his first published horror novel. Michael Cullen is a researcher into Irish folklore and visits Ireland from the United States to gather material for a book on the subject. His presence wakens a banshee that has haunted his family for centuries. Hungry, it systematically sets out to destroy and feed on his family and friends. The folklore side of the novel and the Irish settings are convincing, as Scott draws on his own experiences, however the logic of the plot does not always hang together and the writing is at times clumsy.

Image and its sequel, *Reflection*, give the impression that they were written before *Banshee* because the writing style is of a lower standard. They, and *Imp*, seem to be potboilers of the supernatural thriller variety with wildly swinging points of view. The centre-piece for *Image* and *Reflection* is a very large, ancient mirror which is picked up for a song by antique-dealer Jonathan Frazer.

Almost as soon as he gets it home to Kensington, London, horrific events start to occur in its neighbourhood. The man who begins its restoration dies in a bloody accident, splattering the mirror with gore. Other deaths follow. Frazer discovers that if he feeds the mirror with blood it will show him images. Those of the past centre round the Elizabethan astrologer, John Dee; those of the present show Frazer his wife's infidelities. In dreams he learns that the mirror is a crystal prison for the Gorgon, Euryale, who wants a new body—and only the purest virgin will do. These books are also detective thrillers for, as one might expect, when corpses start turning up, the police get involved.

The sequel tries to do too much. It is set two years after *Image*, just before the Millennium and during the most severe winter that has been seen for a very long time. Crime has rocketed, homeless people are dying in their thousands and the transport system is at the point of breaking down. Troops have been called in to try to keep things under control. This is all background. The story still revolves around the mirror. Frazer's daughter, Emmanuelle, survived the slaughter but is now confined to a wheelchair and is having difficulty in coming to terms with her predicament. Once a fervent party-goer, she is now depressed and overweight. After having lain in Frazer's locked library for two years the mirror again becomes the focus of attention. Janos Ujvary wants to buy it and Manny Frazer is drawn to the images she sees behind the glass. The trapped image of a beautiful woman promises to let her walk again if she feeds it blood. Meanwhile, a number of vagrants have been killed nastily, ripped open and bits of their bodies devoured. Inspector Margaret Haaren is set the task of finding the killer. She was the one who actually shot Jonathan Frazer two years previously just before he cut the throat of her niece as she lay naked on the mirror. Haaren and Manny Frazer are brought together again by the death of Manny's gardener/handyman. Also woven into this novel are scenes from the past involving Countess Elisabeth Bathory, who in the 16th century believed she could stay young for ever by bathing in the blood of young girls. The link is the mirror. In the past, Elizabeth's henchman stole the mirror from Dr. John Dee and now his descendant, Janos Ujvary, is trying to steal it from Manny. By trying to deal with all these themes, the development of character suffers.

Inspector Margaret Haaren is also involved in *Imp*. It is a year or so after the events of *Reflection*, and there have been a number of bizarre murders where signs of the zodiac have been etched onto the bodies of the mutilated corpses of women. The other significant thread here is in the form of the best-selling horror writer, Robert Hunter, who is having problems delivering his 13th book. The publisher, Image Press, sends its best freelance editor to help him meet his deadline. Not only does the manuscript give her nightmares but Katherine Norton, the editor, notices similarities between the murders and the descriptions of killings in this and Hunter's previous book.

These three novels feature demons which work through human agencies to kill, providing the opportunity for graphic and gory descriptions of sex and death. Often the killings have erotic associations—either the victims are having sex just before they die, or the murders arouse sexual feelings. In both, the main characters experience horror and sexual arousal in dreams which link them to the actual murders.

Whereas these novels are not particularly well written *The Hallows* is a distinct improvement. There are still a lot of gory deaths and sexual encounters, but the style is better. Like the other novels, this book uses techniques of dreams and historical flashback, and gives a mythological bias to the supernatural elements. The Fomor, a demon race from Irish legend, have been banished from Britain and the gateway to their world is sealed by 13 keys. These are the Hallows of Britain. Someone is collecting the Hallows, and activating them by bathing them in the blood of their butchered keepers. Greg Matthews becomes involved when one of the keepers is mugged and he comes to her rescue. His family are murdered and he finds himself on the run with one of the Hallows and the niece of its original keeper. Somehow he has to stop the gateway being opened and the demons being set loose to ravage the world.

The quality of Scott's horror fiction does not reflect his overall ability as a writer. His three adult fantasy novels—*Magician's Law*, *Demon's Law* and *Death's Law*—are of a much higher calibre, and his collections of *Irish Folk and Fairy Tales* make very enjoyable reading.

—Pauline Morgan

SCOTT, (Sir) Walter

Pseudonyms: Jedediah Cleishbotham; Laurence Templeton. **Nationality:** British. **Born:** Edinburgh, 15 August 1771. **Education:** Edinburgh High School, 1778-83; Edinburgh University, 1783-86; apprenticed to his father's legal firm, 1786. **Military Service:** Royal Edinburgh Light Dragoons: Quarter-Master. **Family:** Married Charlotte Charpentier in 1797 (died 1826); two sons and two daughters. **Career:** Called to the bar, 1792; Sheriff-Depute of Selkirkshire from 1799; Clerk to the Court of Session, Edinburgh, from 1806. Built house at Abbotsford, near Selkirk, 1812. Declined Poet Laureateship, 1813. Created a baronet, 1820. Suffered financial ruin due to the bankruptcy of the publisher Ballantyne, with whom he was a partner, 1826; spent remainder of his life working to pay off debts. **Died:** 21 September 1832.

HORROR, GHOST AND GOTHIC PUBLICATIONS

Novels

The Black Dwarf in *Tales of My Landlord* (as Jedediah Cleishbotham). Edinburgh, Blackwood, 1816; Philadelphia, Thomas, 1817.
The Bride of Lammermoor, in *Tales of My Landlord, Third Series* (as Jedediah Cleishbotham). Edinburgh, Constable, and Philadelphia, Thomas, 1819.
The Monastery. Edinburgh, Constable, 1820; 1 vol., Philadelphia, Carey, 1820.
The Abbot. Edinburgh, Constable, 1820; 1 vol., Philadelphia, Carey, 1820.

Short Stories

Chronicles of the Canongate: First Series. Edinburgh, Cadell, 1827; Philadelphia, Carey, 1828.
The Supernatural Stories of Sir Walter Scott, edited by Michael Hayes. London, Calder, 1977.

Poetry

An Apology for Tales of Terror. Privately printed, 1799.

OTHER PUBLICATIONS

Novels (first published anonymously, in 3-vol. format)

Waverley, or 'Tis Sixty Years Since. Edinburgh, Ballantyne, 1814; 1 vol., Boston, Wells, 1815.
Guy Mannering, or The Astrologer. Edinburgh, Ballantyne, 1815; 1 vol., Boston, West and Richardson, 1815.
The Antiquary. Edinburgh, Ballantyne, 1816; 2 vols., New York, Van Winkle and Wiley, 1816.
Old Mortality, in *Tales of My Landlord* (as Jedediah Cleishbotham). Edinburgh, Blackwood, 1816; 1 vol., Philadelphia, Thomas, 1817.
Rob Roy. Edinburgh, Constable, 1817; 2 vols., New York, Eastburn, 1818.
The Heart of Midlothian, in *Tales of My Landlord, Second Series* (as Jedediah Cleishbotham). Edinburgh, Constable, and Philadelphia, Carey, 1818.
A Legend of Montrose, in *Tales of My Landlord, Third Series* (as Jedediah Cleishbotham). Edinburgh, Constable, and New York, Wiley, 1819.
Ivanhoe (as Laurence Templeton). Edinburgh, Constable, 1819; 2 volumes, Philadelphia, Carey, 1819.
Kenilworth. Edinburgh, Constable, 1821; Philadelphia, Carey, 1821.
The Pirate. Edinburgh, Constable, 1821; 2 vols., Boston, Wells and Lilly, 1822.
The Fortunes of Nigel. Edinburgh, Constable, 1822; 2 volumes, New York, Longworth, 1822.
Peveril of the Peak. Edinburgh, Constable, 1822; Philadelphia, Carey and Lea, 1823.
Quentin Durward. Edinburgh, Constable, 1823; 1 vol., Philadelphia, Carey and Lea, 1823.
St. Ronan's Well. Edinburgh, Constable, 1823; Philadelphia, Carey and Lea, 1824.
Redgauntlet. Edinburgh, Constable, 1824; 2 vols., Philadelphia, Carey and Lea, 1824.
Tales of the Crusaders, contains *The Betrothed* and *The Talisman.* Edinburgh, Constable, 1825; 2 vols., Philadelphia, Carey and Lea, 1825.
Woodstock. Edinburgh, Constable, 1826; 2 vols., Philadelphia, Carey and Lea, 1826.
Chronicles of the Canongate, Second Series: St. Valentine's Day; or, The Fair Maid of Perth. Edinburgh, Cadell, 1827; Philadelphia, Carey and Lea, 1827.
Anne of Geierstein. Edinburgh, Cadell, 1829; 2 vols., Philadelphia, Carey and Lea, 1829.
Waverly Novels (Magnum Opus Edition, with author's notes and revisions). 48 vols., Edinburgh, Cadell, 1829-33.
Count Robert of Paris, in *Tales of My Landlord, Fourth and Last Series* (as Jedediah Cleishbotham). 4 vols., Edinburgh, Cadell, 1832; 3 vols., Philadelphia, Carey and Lea, 1832.
Castle Dangerous, in *Tales of My Landlord, Fourth and Last Series* (as Jedediah Cleishbotham). 4 vols., Edinburgh, Cadell, 1832; 3 vols., Philadelphia, Carey and Lea, 1832.
The Lay of the Last Minstrel. London, Longman, 1805; Philadelphia, Riley, 1806.
Ballads and Lyrical Pieces. London, Longman, 1806; Boston, Etheridge and Bliss, 1807.
Marmion: A Tale of Flodden Field. Edinburgh, Constable, and Philadelphia, Hopkins and Field, 1808.
The Lady of the Lake. Edinburgh, Ballantyne, and Boston, Wait, 1810.

The Vision of Don Roderick. Edinburgh, Ballantyne, and Boston, Wait, 1811.

Rokeby. Edinburgh, Ballantyne, and Baltimore, Cushing, 1813.

The Bridal of Trierman; or, The Vision of St. John. Edinburgh, Ballantyne, and Philadelphia, Thomas, 1813.

The Lord of the Isles. Edinburgh, Longman, and New York, Scott, 1815.

The Field of Waterloo. Edinburgh, Constable, and Boston, Wait, 1815.

Harold the Dauntless. Edinburgh, Longman, and New York, Eastburn, 1817.

The Poetical Works, edited by J. G. Lockhart. Edinburgh, Cadell, 1833-34.

Plays

Halidon Hill. London, Constable, and New York, Campbell, 1822.

Macduff's Cross. N.p., 1823.

The Doom of Devorgoil: A Melodrama, with *Auchindrane, or the Ayrshire Tragedy.* Edinburgh, Cadell, and New York, Harper, 1830.

Other

Border Antiquities of England and Scotland. London, Longman, 1814-17.

Description of the Regalia of Scotland. N.p., 1819.

Lives of the Novelists. Edinburgh, Ballantyne, 4 vols., 1821-24.

The Life of Napoleon Buonaparte. 9 vols., Edinburgh, Longman, Philadelphia, Carey and Lea, 1827.

The Tales of a Grandfather (for children). 3 vols., Edinburgh, Cadell, 1831; 2 vols., Philadelphia, Carey and Lea, 1831.

History of Scotland. 2 vols., London, Longman, 1830.

Essays on Ballad Poetry. N.p., 1830.

Letters on Demonology and Witchcraft. London, Murray, and New York, Harper, 1830.

The Miscellaneous Prose Works. 30 vols., edited by J. G. Lockhart. Edinburgh, Cadell, 1834-36.

The Journal of Sir Walter Scott. 2 vols., Edinburgh, Douglas, 1890.

The Letters of Sir Walter Scott, edited by Herbert Grierson. London, Constable, 12 vols., 1932-37.

On Novelists and Fiction, edited by Ioan Williams. London, Routledge, 1968.

Editor, *Minstrelsy of the Scottish Border.* 3 vols., London, Cadell, 1802-03; Philadelphia, Carey, 1813.

Editor, *The Works of Dryden.* 18 vols., London, Miller. 1808.

Editor, *The Works of Swift.* 19 vols., Edinburgh, Constable, 1814.

Translator, *The Chase, and William and Helen: Two Ballads*, by Bürger. Edinburgh, Manners and Miller, 1796.

Translator, *Götz von Berlichingen*, by Goethe. London, Bell, 1799.

*

Film Adaptations: *Ivanhoe*, 1913, 1952, 1970 (television serial), 1982 (television movie), 1997 (television serial); *Rob Roy*, 1954, 1961 (television serial), 1977 (television serial), 1995; *The Adventures of Quentin Durward*, 1955; *Kenilworth*, 1957 (television serial), 1968 (television serial); *Redgauntlet*, 1959 (television serial), 1970 (television serial); *The Heart of Midlothian*, 1966 (tele-

vision serial); *Woodstock*, 1973 (television serial); *The Fortunes of Nigel*, 1974 (television serial); *The Talisman*, 1980 (television serial).

Bibliography: *A Bibliography of the Waverley Novels* by G. Worthington, London, Constable, and New York, Smith, 1931; *A Bibliography of Sir Walter Scott: A Classified and Annotated List of Books and Articles Relating to His Life and Works* by J. C. Corson, London, Oliver and Boyd, 1943.

Critical Studies (selection): *Memoirs of the Life of Sir Walter Scott* by J. G. Lockhart, Edinburgh, Cadell, 7 vols., 1837-38; *Sir Walter Scott*, New York, Scribner, 1906, and *Sir Walter Scott and the Border Minstrelsy*, London, Longman, 1911, both by Andrew Lang; *Sir Walter Scott* by John Buchan, London, Cassell, and New York, Coward McCann, 1932; *Sir Walter Scott* by Ian Jack, London, Longman, 1958; *The Hero of the Waverley Novels* by Alexander Welsh, New Haven, Connecticut, Yale University Press, 1963; *Witchcraft and Demonology in Scott's Fiction* by Coleman O. Parsons, London, Oliver and Boyd, 1964; *The Achievement of Walter Scott* by A. O. J. Cockshut, London, Collins, 1969; *Walter Scott: Modern Judgements* edited by D. D. Devlin, London, Macmillan, 1969; *Sir Walter Scott* by Edgar Johnson, New York, Macmillan, 2 vols., 1970; *Walter Scott and the Historical Imagination* by David Brown, London, Routledge and Kegan Paul, 1979; *The Laird of Abbotsford: A View of Sir Walter Scott* by A. N. Wilson, Oxford, Oxford University Press, 1980.

*   *   *

It is difficult for us today to appreciate just how highly Sir Walter Scott was regarded during his lifetime. His early writing marked him out as the leading poet of his age; he was offered and turned down the poet laureateship. He turned to writing romantic historical novels and was responsible for establishing the form of the historical novel (as a genre) and for shaping romanticism in British art and literature. The frequent Scottish settings of his novels helped to improve the image of Scotland, making it a respectable and a romantic place again, after the problems following the 1745 rebellion.

Scott wrote relatively few short stories, yet has been credited (by the writer and critic V. S. Pritchett) with originating the form of the contemporary short story, and his notable horror story, "Wandering Willie's Tale," has been called "a perfect example of the short story" (in *The Concise Oxford Companion to English Literature*). Scott's adulation lasted for nearly a century after his death; today his work is mostly neglected.

Scott's connections with horror and Gothic were strong but sporadic. He was clearly influenced by the rash of Gothic novels which were available during his formative years, and also by the supernatural and fantastic legends of Scotland, upon which he was to draw heavily for his poetry and historical novels. Some of his earliest stories were taken by a magazine edited by M. G. Lewis (author of that very famous Gothic novel *The Monk*), and it is true that Lewis both influenced and encouraged the young Scott.

While none of Scott's historical novels is more than a fringe Gothic, he used Gothic or fantastic elements in several. *The Black Dwarf* has a protagonist who (rather like Frankenstein's monster from just two years later) is a grotesque with an inner sensitivity. *The Bride of Lammermoor* is full of Gothic symbols, from its threatening setting of Wolf's Craig tower, its gloomy and ill-fated characters (the young Master of Ravenswood, who falls in love with Lucy Ashton, beautiful daughter of a family with which his ancestors have long feuded), and its over-dramatic plot, involving tragic accidents (Ravenswood is consumed, horse and all, by quicksands), misunderstandings, madness and death. *The Monastery* and its sequel *The Abbot* are perhaps too deliberately Gothic and do not represent Scott at his best. The setting is a fictionalized Melrose Abbey at the time of Elizabeth I. Against a romantic plot with a happy ending, the Gothic clichés include the White Lady of Avenal, a kindly ghost who performs various miracles including restoring one character (Sir Piercie) to life.

Probably the best known of all Scott's horror pieces is a self-contained episode from *Redgauntlet*, an epistolary novel about a fictional return to England of the Young Pretender, and this episode is variously known as "Wandering Willie's Tale" or "A Night in the Grave." The narrator is speaking of his "gudesire" (grandfather), Steenie the piper, who borrows money for his rent and goes along to Redgauntlet Castle to pay it to Sir Robert Redgauntlet. Both Sir Robert and his pet ape, called Major Weir, are intimidating, devilish to look at. Steenie is sent to have a drink with the butler while Sir Robert counts the money and writes a receipt, but Sir Robert has a vividly described attack, perhaps connected with his chronic gout, and dies, so Steenie leaves without his receipt. By the time the new laird, Sir John Redgauntlet, has taken over, a few days later, the butler has also died and there is no sign of the money, so its payment is doubted. In a very atmospheric scene, Steenie is forced to visit Hell to get his receipt from Sir Robert. There, in a grim facsimile of Redgauntlet Castle, Steenie is brave enough to ask for his due and clever enough not to accept any food or drink. He gets out alive and Sir John accepts the receipt (even though it is dated after Sir Robert's death) and finds the money where Sir Robert has said it would be, hidden by the pet ape. The tale is told completely in Scots dialect, which brings across the personality of the narrator and adds power to the account, but makes it difficult for the non-Scottish reader to understand without a comprehensive glossary.

Most of Scott's other short stories are in *Chronicles of the Canongate*. "The Two Drovers" shows how a prediction of death by a spae-wife (seer or witch) comes true. A Scots cattle-drover named Robin Oig is driving a herd to England to sell them when an unfortunate midunderstanding over grazing rights puts him at odds with an English drover friend of his. They fight and Robin Oig is sufficiently upset by his treatment to fetch his knife (which he has been warned not to carry) and to stab his ex-friend to death. Robin Oig is tried and executed. Scott suggests that this is based on truth, and it seems a sufficiently unnecessary killing for that to be the case. "The Highland Widow" also contains a prediction made by second sight. A son is warned not to return home before rejoining his regiment. The trouble is that he is Scots and has enlisted in the British Army. His mother, desperate to prevent this, detains him and causes his death for desertion. Both of these stories are too slow and too full of unimportant detail.

Three other horror stories of note are "The Tapestried Chamber" and "The Tale of the Mysterious Mirror" (sometimes referred to as "My Aunt Margaret's Mirror" or just as "The Mirror") and "The Fortunes of Martin Waldeck." The first is a standard haunted-room piece: a successful army officer, now a general, discovers that an old school and college friend has just inherited his father's title and estate, and visits him. He is placed in a room not normally used and, despite being a fearless soldier, is much disturbed by an apparition during the night. In "The Tale of the Mysterious Mirror" a wife whose husband has gone off to fight in the Peninsular War uses the talents of an Italian magician to see what he is up to. In a large mirror like a television screen or like the mirror via which Nostradamus is supposed to have obtained all his prophecies, she sees her husband getting married bigamously to a young woman and engaging in a swordfight with her brother—both of which are later proved to have occurred. "The Fortunes of Martin Waldeck" is set in Germany. Martin is one of three poor, charcoal-burner brothers who accepts a gift of gold from a demon and, after having achieved great riches, is eventually brought low, disgraced and killed due to the effects of the gift.

—Chris Morgan

SELTZER, David

Nationality: American. **Born:** Highland Park, Illinois, 1940. **Education:** Northwestern University School for Film and Television. **Career:** Hollywood screenwriter and director.

HORROR, GHOST AND GOTHIC PUBLICATIONS

Novels

The Omen. New York, Signet, and London, Futura, 1976.
Prophecy. New York, Ballantine, and London, Granada, 1979.

Plays

Screenplays: *The Omen*, 1976; *Damien—Omen II*, 1978; *Prophecy*, 1979.

OTHER PUBLICATIONS

Plays

Screenplays: *The Hellstrom Chronicle*, 1971; *King, Queen, Knave*, 1972; *One Is a Lonely Number*, 1972; *The Other Side of the Mountain*, 1975; *Six Weeks*, 1982; *Table for Five*, 1983; *Lucas*, 1986 (also directed); *Punchline*, 1988 (also directed); *Bird on a Wire*, 1990.

*   *   *

A successful screenwriter, David Seltzer has converted two of his own original screenplays into novels. The first of these, *The Omen*, from the film directed by Richard Donner and starring Gregory Peck and Lee Remick, was a considerable bestseller. According to critic John Sutherland, in *Bestsellers: Popular Fiction of the 1970s* (1981), *The Omen* has some claim to being "the bestselling novelization of all time." Such was the success of *The Omen* in paperback that a string of sequels has appeared, both film-tied—*Damien—Omen II* (1978) and *Omen III: The Final Conflict* (1980)—and "original"—*Omen IV: Armageddon 2000* (1982) and *The Abomination: Omen V* (1985); these, however, were not written by Seltzer but (apart from the first, which was signed by one

Joseph Howard) by novelizer Gordon McGill (born 1943; also responsible for such horror-movie tie-ins as *Amityville 3-D* [1984]).

For a writer whose titles seem to proclaim their author's fondness and longing for the future, David Seltzer's novels seem peculiarly rooted in the present. More realistically, they seem rooted in the *then*—in the what-has-been. *The Omen* and *Prophecy* are products of their time, and in one sense are damned forever to be regarded as nothing more than the cinema tie-ins that they are. But this is unfair—especially when we consider the fact that Seltzer himself was at least partly responsible for the movies on which the novels in question were based. Although Seltzer cannot be argued to be the most inventive writer of his generation, he cannot be labelled as a copycat either, and his two horror novels deserve consideration.

His first, and best, was *The Omen*. Seltzer made full use of the religious angle that was fashionable at the time (we refer, of course, to novels such as *The Exorcist*) by beginning the book with a doom-laden Biblical quotation from the Book of Revelations. The verse tells the reader the number of the beast—666. It is perhaps a struggle to remember that Seltzer's success with *The Omen* is paradoxically the reason that some of its ideas now seem a little dated. *The Omen* refers to Demon Seed—to a child on earth who is of the devil. The notion of 666 is now slightly old-hat and the music in the film is completely familiar—but David Seltzer and the popularity of his projects made it this way for us.

Using a sort of playful journalese, Seltzer tried to carve his own niche in the genre, and in many ways achieved his aims. The book's prologue has the Pre-Millennially-Tense touch of the imminence of worlds colliding, of Armageddon looming. The demise of the Thorns' world starts, in comparison, quietly. Following the exhibitionistic self-hanging of Damien's first nanny—the nice nanny—comes the bad nanny, Mrs. Baylock. This forthright woman, who says what she likes and likes what she says, is not afraid to offer her opinions from the start. There is no period of testing the water with her new employers—but, with hindsight, this is the woman who is shortly to be in direct league with Satanic forces, so perhaps this is understandable. (One of Mrs. Baylock's more humorous pronouncements is that the size of a nanny's breasts is in direct correlation with her efficacy in her job: the bigger the better, with no mentioned theoretical upper limit.) Damien—ostensibly the child of an American diplomat and his soppy, broody wife—takes to Mrs. Baylock immediately (he is the only one to do so; the other staff are soon complaining that Mrs. Baylock is not playing by house rules), and Mrs. B. certainly enjoys the company of her young charge. In a very literal way, Mrs. Baylock is a sort of Devil's Advocate.

Damien goes on the rampage, but in a strange fashion. First, giving us reason to believe that the child wants nothing to do with anything religious, Damien throws a fit of complaint at his proposed christening and then at a Catholic wedding. Later, he attempts to kill his adoptive mother in possibly the most memorable scene in the book and certainly the most memorable scene in the film. Maniacally speeding his toy bike around the large house's upper storey, Damien knocks into the stool on which Mrs. Thorn is standing; she topples, and falls over the banister to the floor far below. (Lee Remick's facial expressions during this scene in the movie are superb.)

One of the key messages in *The Omen* would seem to be that people who pretend to be God must be punished. From the moment that Robert Thorn agrees to swap his still-born son in Rome for a newly born orphan, we know that he is on the road to damnation. That he agrees to the substitution for the sake of maintaining his wife's mental equilibrium is neither here nor there. He is punished—as are the priests who propose the deal. The only innocent in the situation is the child with the number of the beast on his scalp, and he is the one who is permitted to go on to wreak havoc. One of the more pitiable characters in the novel is Father Tassone—a priest, but also a midwife who was on duty the night that Damien was born. Tassone is one of the few people who knows that Damien was born not of a woman, but of a jackal. To atone for his sins, Father Tassone has taken it upon himself to inform Mr. Thorn that the child he has adopted is not of this earth. After Robert Thorn opens an exhibition in a poor area of Chelsea, London, Tassone warns Rob's wife that she is in danger. For his troubles Tassone is attacked by lightning; for this is a world in which the dark forces are comfortably in command. *The Omen* is, apart from anything else, a study of how evil comes into the world, and a look at demonic randomness. The following sentence would seem to sum up the credo neatly: "He who will not be saved by the Lamb will be torn by the Beast."

Prophecy is much more of an eco-novel, and something of a disappointment in comparison. As opposed to *The Omen*'s by-and-large Britishness, *Prophecy* is an American novel, concerning O.P.'s—or Original People, or Opies: Native American Indians in other words. The novel's concern with environmental matters is kick-started by the sudden disappearances of several Indians, who are destroyed by an unknown assailant. Meanwhile, the Masaquoddy Indians are angry because of disputes over land rights. Robert Vern, newly of the Environmental Protection Agency, is a healer brought into the plot to sort out a volatile rift involving these Native Americans and some unpleasant land developers. Vern, however, is soon embroiled in a different sort of plot altogether, a plot about first encounters. For there are more than merely human forces at work. In the forest there are alien creatures, and in the air and more pertinently, the water, the effects of pollution. At first vast salmon are spotted in the lake; maniacal raccoons go berserk; a ranger's cat gets nasty: very quickly it is obvious that the forest's wild things are trying to take over, or are at least behaving uncharacteristically. Among the Native Americans, it becomes known that there is a "growing rate of stillbirths and deformed children"; and the Indian heroine's grandfather, Hector M'Rai (to whom the book is dedicated) is suffering the following symptoms: "In the last six months his mind had gone dim and his hands had begun to tremble." But the creatures are the stars of this show, and are pitiable. There is something in the woods that emits "a quiet squeal" and is known to ruin what is nearby; something that "raised an arm that revealed a skinfold beneath it, with veins traced like tree branches, back lit by the moon."

The novel is by and large a warning: a Green advertisement of necessarily shocking tactics. This, Seltzer seems to be saying, is what might happen to our forests, our planet. It can be read as an allegory, perhaps, but it lacks the pace of *The Omen* and ultimately rubs the reader's nose a little too often in the facts of how badly the world and the American Indians are being treated. Undoubtedly there are neat touches: one of these is Robert Vern playing God by trying to use the creatures' presence in the forests as a negotiation point *against* the land being razed. Another is the darkly humorous drunkard's poem after he has seen something "big as a dragon."

The epilogue of *Prophecy* is a non-fiction justification of the novel that we have just finished: "The story you have read is based, in its ecological substance, on actual events . . . The failing health, both mental and physical, of the local Indian populations has been labeled drunkenness. The Indians protest that they do not use alcohol." There is very little space in which we might form our own conclusions. As far as this novel goes, there is Seltzer's opinion, and there is the wrong opinion.

David Seltzer is a writer who has earned his position as a horror writer of note on the strength, more or less, of *The Omen*. It is the one he will be remembered for. His other work is filled with neat touches and good description, but does not gel in the way that *The Omen* does. In *The Omen*, the picture of devilish isolation and iconoclasm that is Damien Thorn (where even the name now sounds evil) is a fine and chilling piece of work.

—David Mathew

SHARMAN, Nick

Pseudonym of Scott Gronmark. **Other Pseudonym:** A. G. Scott. **Nationality:** British. **Born:** 1952.

HORROR, GHOST AND GOTHIC PUBLICATIONS

Novels

The Cats. London, New English Library, 1977.
Childmare. London, Hamlyn, 1980; (as A. G. Scott) New York, Signet, 1981.
The Scourge. New York, Signet, and London, Hamlyn, 1980.
The Surrogate. New York, New American Library, 1980; London, New English Library, 1981.
Judgment Day. New York, Signet, 1982.
The Switch. London, New English Library, and New York, Signet, 1984.
You're Next! London, New English Library, 1986; as *Next!*, New York, Signet, 1986.
Steel Gods (as Scott Gronmark). London, Corgi, 1990.

*   *   *

In England in the 1970s, when the face of horror fiction was changing to something uglier than it had previously been—when the respectable garb of the aristocratic ghost story had been well and truly shed as an out-of-fashion garment and something far punkier was required—a sub-genre of horror was invented. What became known as "the Nasty" included work that was red-raw and extremely visceral; novels that pulled no punches when it came to the depiction of violence. The Nasty—cinematic or literary—succeeded by adhering to two unwritten rules. One, that human life was more or less expendable, apart from the hero, heroine, or group of the same that would somehow save the day; and two, that the horror in question was relentlessly cruel and insatiable in its tendencies. The literary Nasty made little use of rational plots, at least from the point of view of the source of the horror; indeed, the best novels of this sub-genre found their strengths and energies by exploiting the graphically violent potential of creatures and situations previously ignored by horror fiction. Thus, James Herbert showed us a country swarming with killer-rats (*The Rats*, 1975)—and Nick Sharman wrote *The Cats*.

Nick Sharman was just one of the writers included in the publishing explosion that became known as the Nasties. Whether or not the inclusion is fair is another matter. In principle and on first appearances, Sharman's novel seems to be virtually a carbon copy of Herbert's original. "In the tradition of *The Rats*," the book's front cover screams; and on the back, not doing the author any favours, is written: "They came in their thousands, crazed with bloodlust, searching for victims . . ." The word bloodlust is even printed in contrasting red type. There would seem to be nothing required from the prose apart from a retelling of Herbert's story, substituting the animals. But quickly it seems as though Sharman is too intelligent (or maybe too conscientious) to do only that.

From the quasi-scientific explanation of why the cats cease their natural solo-hunting expeditions around London and start hunting in packs like wild dogs, to the denouement involving sulphuric acid and fire, this is a novel built on realistic premises, even if the basic notion of groups of killer-cats marauding around the Big Smoke with the relentlessness of zombies is ludicrous. However, the novel opens up possibilities in the reader's mind: the initial premise accepted, you might at first think that if cats could be so controlled they might make for a good army; then, so might any animal with teeth and claws which is physically nimble: so might humans. "I discovered that the bacteria had caused a disease which alters the very structure of the brain cells, changes the very nature of the animals affected," the book's professor explains. (Presciently, this was nigh-on 20 years before BSE—or Mad Cow Disease—was to affect Britain's livestock in a similar fashion.) It is clear that in *The Cats*, despite the presence of a standard array of baddies, the real bad character is science itself. It is more of an overall novel than *The Rats*—not simply a case of vignettes building to make a whole, but individual stories stretching and intertwining for the length of the book.

The Cats has many surprising elements to it. Inasmuch as it refers to the IRA, to the Notting Hill Gate riots during the Carnival of 1976, to the Arab potentate and his family who were gunned down outside the Royal Lancaster Hotel in 1977, and to the scorching summer of 1976, *The Cats* is both a political novel and an historical record, of sorts. There is, in the way that the cats' virus spreads out, a clear analogy with many a plague story, including those of the Holy Book: as one character puts it, the situation is like "something out of the Bible . . . Like Sodom and Gomorrah." Operatic, apocalyptic images abound: "Cars and buses had been brought to a halt, swarming with cats with partially chewed limbs hanging from their mouths." Before long, the novel has become farcical, but not in a disparaging sense; if anything, as events get more and more out of hand, Sharman has a tighter and tighter grip on his material. Paratroopers stalk the streets with machine guns, blowing away felines at the drop of a hat. It is all like a very bad joke, and there are more bad jokes throughout—grim jokes, provoking at best nervous laughter. A druggie is eaten alive, and almost all the way through—but not quite all the way through—he believes himself to be tripping: "It was all experience. It was only when they had reached the upper part of his chest that he began to worry. The trip was turning bad and pain was beginning to filter through to his chemically numbed mind." Then there is Basil Barry, a radio announcer who is obliged to strangle a cat that has gone for his face and is then obliged to sit down to continue his broadcast.

Nick Sharman writes swift and breezy horror, and his best characters are often male; his storylines are not complicated but they each have the ring of originality. In his books no prisoners are taken; and Sharman tends to balk at the forced happy ending—the Hollywood ending. *The Cats'* conclusion sees the boy who started the problems in the first place running with a pack of the wild creatures; to this extent, Sharman's work is far from comforting or life-affirming; it is honest—and the good guy might win, but he pays some high prices along the way to the victory. At best in Sharman's novels, the glass ends half full instead of half empty: there is the perception of fully-fledged happiness being proximate.

Childmare continues the earnest tone of *The Cats.* Apart from the corny title, this is another hard-hitting, socially relevant British commentary/satire, this time dealing with inner-city youth and the way that boredom gives rise to rioting. Max Donnelly is a security officer at a tough London school, and as such is used to any amount of teenage bother; but when a strange illness attacks the pupils and makes them go insane, even Max has his work cut out for him. The children's symptoms are a tendency to go on blood-letting rampages of rape, torture and murder—so perhaps we can forgive the erstwhile hero his nervousness. The children become zombies. Even so, in one humorous aside (a precognition of political correctness if ever there was one!) a character comments: "We don't want the press making political capital out of this. Hit the kids by all means, but hit them softly." Such weaknesses are swiftly pounced upon. Children close in on an Oxford Street Underground platform, forcing commuters on to the lines in the tunnel; the fact that the train is late (this being England, we must remember, sharing as we do in Sharman's parochial gloom) serves to heighten the tension—what will happen to the people on the line? Will they fight the children, or stay where they are?

The reason for the children's sudden rampage is again of a quasi-scientific bent, and is a splendid piece of bathos as well as a comment on pollution. It is a two-step process: bad cream from cakes served at the children's school one lunchtime has sent the pupils into fevers; these fevers have released deposits of lead (gathered from years of breathing petroleum fumes in the inner city) from the children's skeletons—lead in fact being stored in the bones of many people who live in areas of high traffic build-up. The lead affects the children's brain cells: simple. Perhaps biologists would argue with the reasoning; or perhaps, if viewed at the end of the 20th century, *Childmare* is a forewarningly Green novel.

The denouement, involving bombers spraying the river with tetra-ethyl lead, is shocking and cruel. The children have developed serious yearnings for the effects of lead on their brains, and have taken to sniffing at car exhausts. Luring these zombified hopeless creatures to the water for the sole purpose of mass destruction by F-111s has a chilling air of authorial superiority and carelessness to it; but Sharman's attitude (once more) seems to be: this stuff isn't meant to be comforting.

Witness the later novels too. In *The Surrogate,* the prologue alone sees some unpleasant child-abuse, and then sees that same child, Frank, killing a rat in the cellar, which unleashes some strong emotions, not least of which is a sense of hatred for his father which accompanies Frank to adulthood. Now that he has arrived as an adult, somebody is preying on his son, Simon, and Frank believes it is a plot that his now-deceased father arranged with the help of Frank's radio colleague, Eddie. In *The Surrogate* we learn a good deal about human frailties, human obsessions. Frank is more than willing to sacrifice his existing friendship with Eddie in order to prevent any chance of there being a supernatural explanation for recent mis-happenings. It is tempting to imagine how different the novel might have been—how postmodernly tricky—

if the theme of friendship-erosion and mistrust had been taken to its logical conclusion; when, after finally believing that the supernatural exists Frank is poleaxed in the final chapter by the discovery that it was all his friend's doing all along.

But no, not here: Nick Sharman is an entertainer, true, but postmodernism does not feature in his game-plan: the supernatural explanation is the correct one; at least, in part. The dead grandfather has not quite relinquished his hold on the real world, and is back to fight for a meagre moral victory. To show that he can beat his own son and show that he will not be denied, even while beyond the grave, the old man wants Simon to be heir to the Tillson fortune, and Frank wants nothing of the sort. The dead guy chooses moments of vulnerability in which to torment the boy, i.e. when he is taking a bath. Tempers fray; trust is scotched. "You said he was dead," the boy accuses his father; "but he isn't. I saw him . . . Please tell him to go away, dad. I . . . I don't know what he wants." The answer is: Simon himself, and power over Frank. The former is kidnapped from the flat in which they live, and the "ransom" phone-call orders Frank to the old man's old home, to which Frank once vowed never to return. Like an episode of *Scooby Doo* crossed with a bedroom farce and an Agatha Christie tale—all liberally spiced with the sort of child-in-danger hormone-releasers of *The Amityville Horror* (among many others)—the end reveals a mixture of intelligent hoax and the occult. Everything is explained neatly, and by now—with the boy having been lost forever to the old man who will live in his young body—we begin to suspect that Nick Sharman is not overfond of kids.

Scott Gronmark's first novel as Scott Gronmark, as opposed to Sharman, is *Steel Gods,* a book described as being the work of a "chilling new talent." It is as though Nick Sharman has been Gronmark's well-served apprenticeship, and that Gronmark wants now to walk away from Sharman's dark and bloody shadow. *Steel Gods* certainly represents a maturing, but not a pacifying, and it is a good portent for more fine work to come. Interestingly enough, the novel is amply praised by none other than James Herbert, which brings Sharman's story neatly full circle, given that Herbert's tale of vicious rodents was Sharman's point of departure in the first place. *Steel Gods,* in a sense, is an impressive debut.

—David Mathew

SHELLEY, Mary (Wollstonecraft Godwin)

Nationality: British. **Born:** Somers Town, London, 30 August 1797. **Family:** Married Percy Bysshe Shelley in 1816 (died 1822); two sons and two daughters. **Career:** Lived in Dundee, 1812, 1813-14, then returned to London; eloped to Europe with Shelley, 1814; writer from 1816; after Shelley's death lived in Genoa with the Leigh Hunts, 1822-23, then returned to England; travelled in Germany, 1840-41, and Italy, 1842-43. **Died:** 1 February 1851.

HORROR, GHOST AND GOTHIC PUBLICATIONS

Novels

Frankenstein; or, The Modern Prometheus. London, Lackington Hughes, 3 vols., 1818; revised edition, London, Colburn and Bentley, 1831; edited by M. K. Joseph, London and New York,

Oxford University Press, 1969; original edition edited by James Rieger, Indianapolis, Bobbs-Merrill, 1974.

The Last Man. London, Colburn, 3 vols., 1826; Philadelphia, Carey, 1833; revised edition, edited by Hugh J. Luke, Lincoln, University of Nebraska Press, 1965.

Short Stories

The Mortal Immortal: The Complete Supernatural Short Fiction, edited by Jacob Weisman. San Francisco, Tachyon, 1996.

OTHER PUBLICATIONS

Novels

Valperga; or, The Life and Adventures of Castruccio, Prince of Lucca. London, Whittaker, 3 vols., 1823.

The Fortunes of Perkin Warbeck: A Romance. London, Colburn and Bentley, 3 vols., 1830; Philadelphia, Carey, 1834.

Lodore. New York, Wallis and Newell, and London, Bentley, 3 vols., 1835.

Falkner. London, Saunders and Otley, and New York, Harper, 3 vols., 1837.

Mathilda, edited by Elizabeth Nitchie. Chapel Hill, University of North Carolina Press, 1959.

Short Stories

Mary Shelley: Collected Tales and Stories, edited by Charles E. Robinson. Baltimore, Maryland, Johns Hopkins University Press, 1976.

Plays

Proserpine and Midas: Two Unfinished Mythological Dramas, edited by A. H. Koszul. London, Milford, 1922.

Poetry

The Choice: A Poem on Shelley's Death, edited by H. Buxton Forman. London, privately printed, 1876.

Other

History of a Six Weeks' Tour through a Part of France, Switzerland, Germany and Holland, with Percy Bysshe Shelley. London, Hookham and Ollier, 1817; abridged edition, as *Shelley's Visits to France, etc.,* edited by C. I. Elton, London, Bliss Sands, 1894.

Rambles in Germany and Italy in 1840, 1842, and 1843. London, Moxon, 2 vols., 1844.

Shelley and Mary: A Collection of Letters and Documents of a Biographical Character. London, privately printed, 3 vols., 1882.

Letters of Mary Wollstonecraft Shelley, Mostly Unpublished, edited by Henry H. Harper. Boston, Bibliophile Society, 1918.

My Best Mary: The Selected Letters of Mary Wollstonecraft Shelley, wedited by Muriel Spark and Derek Stanford. New York, Roy, and London, Wingate, 1953.

The Letters of Mary Wollstonecraft Shelley, edited by Betty T. Bennett. Baltimore, Maryland, Johns Hopkins University Press, 3 vols., 1980-88.

The Journals of Mary Shelley 1814-44, edited by Paula R. Feldman and Diana Scott-Kilvert. Oxford, Clarendon Press, and New York, Oxford University Press, 2 vols., 1987.

The Mary Shelley Reader (contains *Frankenstein, Mathilda,* tales and stories, essays and reviews, and letters), edited by Betty T. Bennett and Charles E. Robinson. New York, Oxford University Press, 1990.

Editor, *Posthumous Poems,* by Percy Bysshe Shelley. London, Hunt, 1824.

Editor, *The Poetical Works of Percy Bysshe Shelley.* London, Moxon, 4 vols., 1839.

Editor, *Essays, Letters from Abroad, Translations, and Fragments,* by Percy Bysshe Shelley. London, Moxon, and Philadelphia, Lea and Blanchard, 2 vols., 1840.

*

Film Adaptations (selection): *Frankenstein,* 1931; *The Bride of Frankenstein,* 1935; *Son of Frankenstein,* 1939; *The Curse of Frankenstein,* 1957; *Frankenstein: The True Story,* 1973 (TV movie); *Frankenstein,* 1973 (TV movie); *Frankenstein,* 1984 (TV movie); *Frankenstein—The Real Story,* 1992 (TV movie); *Mary Shelley's Frankenstein,* 1994.

Bibliography: *Mary Shelley: An Annotated Bibliography* by William H. Lyles, New York, Garland, 1975.

Critical Studies (selection): *Child of Light: A Reassessment of Mary Wollstonecraft Shelley* by Muriel Spark, Hadleigh, Essex, Tower Bridge, 1951, revised edition, as *Mary Shelley: A Biography,* New York, Dutton, 1987, London, Constable, 1988; *Mary Shelley: Author of Frankenstein* by Elizabeth Nitchie, New Brunswick, New Jersey, Rutgers University Press, 1953; *Mary Shelley* by Eileen Bigland, New York, Appleton Century, and London, Cassell, 1959; *Mary Shelley dans son oeuvre* by Jean de Palaccio, Paris, Klincksieck, 1969; *Mary Shelley* by William A. Walling, New York, Twayne, 1972; *Ariel Like a Harpy: Shelley, Mary, and Frankenstein* by Christopher Small, London, Gollancz, 1972, as *Mary Shelley's Frankenstein: Tracing the Myth,* Pittsburgh, University of Pittsburgh Press, 1973; *Shelley's Mary: A Life* by Margaret Leighton, New York, Farrar Straus, 1973; *Daughter of Earth and Water: A Biography of Mary Wollstonecraft Shelley* by Noel B. Gerson, New York, Morrow, 1973; *Mary Shelley's Monster: The Story of Frankenstein* by Martin Tropp, Boston, Houghton Mifflin, 1976; *Moon in Eclipse: A Life of Mary Shelley* by Jane Dunn, London, Weidenfeld and Nicolson, and New York, St. Martin's Press, 1978; *The Endurance of Frankenstein: Essays on Mary Shelley's Novel* edited by George Levine and U. C. Knoepflmacher, Berkeley, University of California Press, 1979; *Frankenstein's Creation: The Book, the Monster, and Human Reality* by David Ketterer, Victoria, British Columbia, University of Victoria Press, 1979; *The Lonely Muse: A Critical Biography of Mary Shelley* by Bonnie Rayford Neumann, Salzburg, Institut für Anglistik und Amerikanistïk, 1979.

The Influence of William Godwin on the Novels of Mary Shelley by Katherine Richardson Powers, New York, Arno Press, 1980; *The Frankenstein Catalog* by Donald F. Glut, Jefferson, North Carolina, McFarland, 1984; *Scientific Attitudes in Mary Shelley's Frankenstein* by S. H. Vasbinder, Ann Arbor, Michigan, U.M.I. Research Press, 1984; *Mary Shelley and Frankenstein: The Fate of Androgyny* by William Veeder, Chicago, University of Chicago Press, 1986; *The Monster in the Mirror: Gender and the Sentimental/Gothic Myth in Frankenstein* by Mary K. Patterson Thornburg, Ann Arbor, Michigan, U.M.I. Research Press, 1987; *Mary Shelley: Her Life, Her Fiction, Her Monsters* by Anne K. Mellor, New York and London, Routledge, 1988; *Mary Shelley: Romance and Reality* by Emily W. Sunstein, Boston, Little Brown, 1989; *The Godwins and the Shelleys: The Biography of a Family* by William St. Clair, New York, Norton, and London, Faber, 1989; *Approaches to Teaching Shelley's Frankenstein* edited by Stephen C. Behrendt, New York, M.L.A., 1990; *Hideous Progenies: Dramatizations of Frankenstein from Mary Shelley to the Present* by Steven Earl Forry, Philadelphia, University of Pennsylvania Press, 1990; *In Frankenstein's Shadow: Myth, Monstrosity, and Nineteenth-Century Writing* by Chris Baldick, Oxford, Clarendon Press, 1990; *Making Monstrous: Frankenstein, Criticism, Theory* by Fred Botting, New York, St. Martin's Press, 1991; *Frankenstein, Creation and Monstrosity* edited by Stephen Bann, London, Reakton Books, 1994; *Mary Shelley's Frankenstein: A Classic Tale of Terror Reborn on Film* by Kenneth Branagh, New York, Newmarket Press, 1994; *"My Hideous Progeny": Mary Shelley, William Godwin, and the Father-Daughter Relationship* by Katherine C. Hill-Miller, Newark, University of Delaware Press, 1995.

*   *   *

To appreciate the achievements of Mary Shelley, one must first separate her fiction from her biography. Thanks to a generation of intensive, and deserved, critical attention, almost everyone knows her story: after growing up without her mother—pioneering feminist Mary Wollstonecraft, who died after giving birth to her—the teenage Shelley was briefly swept into an exhilarating and talented circle of friends—future husband Percy Shelley, Lord Byron, John Polidori, and others—who inspired her to write her first and greatest novel, *Frankenstein*. Then life became an unending series of sad losses, as almost everyone near and dear to her passed away, including her half-sister Fanny, Percy Shelley's first wife, Polidori, Byron, Percy Shelley, and three of her four children who died at an early age. Thus, this "lonely muse," to use Bonnie Neumann's epithet, was impelled to focus her fiction on the theme of the horror of personal loss.

As it happens, this template fits reasonably well on to her horror fiction—the five stories in *The Mortal Immortal, Frankenstein* and *The Last Man*—though two stories contrive happy endings: in "Transformation," a young man's irresponsible behaviour cuts him off from his comfortable lifestyle, family heritage and friends, but a temporary exchange of bodies with a demon, who mends fences and achieves reconciliation while occupying his body, fortuitously restores him to his position; while in "The Dream," when her father is killed by a faction including her lover, a woman feels she has lost both her past family and future family until a dream in a chapel famous for prophetic dreams persuades her to embrace her tainted suitor. But "Roger Dodsworth: The Reanimated Englishman" and "Valerius: The Reanimated Roman" both feature people from a dead past unhappily brought into an alien present where everyone they cherished has vanished, which is also the fate of "The Mortal Immortal," a student accidentally made immortal by a potion mixed by Cornelius Agrippa who must watch in horror as his beloved wife ages and dies while he remains young to continue drifting through a world of strangers. As for the novels, while Frankenstein's creation gradually strips Fran-

kenstein of the people close to him, the monster is similarly haunted by the loss of his creator's affections, the rural family he observed and hoped to join, and his never-completed mate, so that both end up lonely wanderers in an Arctic wasteland. And in *The Last Man*, the theme of agonizing loss is writ most large, as Lionel Verney literally watches everyone in the world—including his family and friends—die from a virulent plague, leaving him as the only survivor. Noting the pattern, and adding comments from Shelley's letters and journal suggesting an intent to blend memories into her fiction, and the case for Shelley's fiction as disguised autobiography seems compelling.

Nevertheless, this approach to Shelley is ultimately condescending, if not downright sexist: while other great (male) writers of her age employed their intellects to wrestle with important issues, poor, lonely (female) Mary was pouring out her heart on the page. Readers should stop shedding tears for Shelley, and stop reading her works as personal laments. She lived in an age when many children died in infancy, when many people died while still relatively young; she may have exceeded the average number of experiences of this kind, but people of her time had no real reason to see her as a victim of unusual or excessive misfortune. Thus, while granting there are autobiographical resonances in her work, readers must discern the broader, and more significant, concerns permeating her fiction.

Romantic writers were in the first generation to mature with two new realizations: the idea that the past might represent an era entirely distinct from the present in its attitudes and behaviour, as shown by Edward Gibbon's pioneering *The Decline and Fall of the Roman Empire* (first volume 1776); and the parallel, less widespread idea that the future might someday develop into an era entirely distinct from the present, as variously depicted in Louis-Sebastien Mercier's *Memoirs of the Year 2500* (1772), Jane Loudon's *The Mummy!* (1827), and Shelley's *The Last Man*. This created the possibility of a new type of horror that might be termed temporal displacement, a strong psychic identification with a past era now supplanted by a strange new world. Well able to perceive that scientific and social progress was irrevocably changing her own world, then, Shelley could clearly envision the horror of watching not only one's friends, but one's entire world, dying and vanishing forever. This is manifestly the dreadful fate of Dodsworth, Valerius and "The Mortal Immortal." The tragedy of Frankenstein, in part, is that of people mentally trapped in the past: Frankenstein began as a student of medieval philosopher Cornelius Agrippa and habitually calls his monster a "daemon," as if ancient stereotypical images prevent him from seeing his creation as it really is. The monster too, schooled by *Paradise Lost* and *The Sorrows of Young Werther*, seems haunted by outdated romantic views of justice, as it believes that being rejected by the world entitles it to embark on a campaign of gratuitous slaughter. The contrast to both is provided by narrator Walton, a man attuned to the new scientific age, who views the Arctic not as an arena for pursuit and personal revenge but an exciting place to gain new knowledge. And some of the most poignant passages of *The Last Man* involve people being forced to abandon, or condemned by their refusal to abandon, their traditional lifestyles in the face of a brave new world of unending and indiscriminate death.

One may properly speak of Shelley as a horror writer since her first novel, *Frankenstein*, resulted from a contest among her friends to write a ghost story; if classified by generic intent, then, it is a horror novel. However, the novel has also been aggressively promoted as the first work of science fiction—not entirely without justice, since Shelley departs from Gothic patterns in two key respects. First, Frankenstein is a university-educated man, and his monster is manifestly created by scientific, not magical, means, though Frankenstein is purposely vague in describing his methodology. While he says that the idea came to him in a "charnel house" and later speaks of gathering "materials" for a second monster, there is no specific textual support for the common notion that he built his monster by stitching together parts of dead bodies; indeed, since the creature is repeatedly described as being eight feet tall, some other method of fabrication must have been involved. Second, and perhaps more significant, the dying Frankenstein refuses to repent for his boldness in challenging the status quo. At the end, he begins by offering the standard lesson, "Farewell, Walton! Seek happiness in tranquillity, and avoid ambition, even if it be only the apparently innocent one of distinguishing yourself in science and discoveries." But he immediately recants: "Yet why do I say this? I have myself been blasted in these hopes, yet another may succeed." In refusing to dissuade those who might follow in his footsteps, Frankenstein leaves behind the Gothic mentality and looks forward to the modern scientific mentality, where the pursuit of knowledge is sanctioned and supported even if some of its products are monstrous.

Undoubtedly *Frankenstein* represents Shelley's most enduring legacy, kept alive in the public imagination by scores of film adaptions (a few recent ones actually adhere to the novel). The concept of scientifically created life, and its potentially disastrous consequences, are endemic themes in science fiction and recurring concerns in modern life, where any discussion of artificially created life inevitably provokes a warning about possibly creating a "Frankenstein" (since the name of the creator is usually applied to his monster). Still, those who wish to celebrate Shelley as a master of scientific horror should not neglect *The Last Man*. Shelley fully realized that a new and deadly plague might develop at any time, and that with modern means of transportation, it could easily spread throughout the world; and having achieved that realization, she was willing to follow it through to its logical and bitter conclusion. Although the long first volume of *The Last Man*, about the intertwined lives of some English aristocrats in the future, is tedious and almost unreadable, the novel comes alive when the plague begins to kill; the word "horror" begins to appear repeatedly, and through a series of alternately chilling and poignant vignettes Shelley achieves, and surpasses, the horrific power of the predecessor she acknowledges, Daniel Defoe's *A Journal of the Plague Year* (1722). Further, in visualizing this natural end of the human race, she found no consolation in religion; indeed, the one religious leader who emerges in the dying days of humanity is depicted as a duplicitous charlatan. To argue that this bleak and plausible account of the future extinction of the human race represents Shelley's way to express her grief about the loss of her family and friends is indeed to trivialize what was undoubtedly, even more than *Frankenstein*, the most horrifying vision of its age.

—Gary Westfahl

SHEPARD, Lucius

Nationality: American. **Born:** 1947 (some sources say 1944). **Career:** Globe-trotter and free spirit; attended Clarion Writers'

Workshop, 1980; latterly, full-time writer. **Awards:** Clarion award, 1984; *Locus* award, 1985; John W. Campbell award, 1985; *Science Fiction Chronicle* award, 1985; Nebula award, 1986; World Fantasy award, 1988. **Address:** c/o Arkham House, Box 546, Sauk City, Wisconsin 53583, USA.

HORROR, GHOST AND GOTHIC PUBLICATIONS

Novels

Green Eyes. New York, Ace, 1984; London, Chatto and Windus, 1986.
Life During Wartime. New York, Bantam, 1987; London, Grafton, 1988.
Kalimantan. London, Legend, 1990; New York, St. Martin's Press, 1992.
The Golden: A Novel. Shingletown, California, Ziesing, and London, Millennium, 1993.

Short Stories

The Jaguar Hunter. Sauk City, Wisconsin, Arkham House, 1987; with revised contents, London, Paladin, 1988.
The Scalehunter's Beautiful Daughter. Willimantic, Connecticut, Ziesing, 1988.
The Father of Stones. Baltimore, Maryland, Washington Science Fiction Association, 1989.
The Ends of the Earth: 14 Stories. Sauk City, Wisconsin, Arkham House, 1991; London, Millennium, 1994.

OTHER PUBLICATIONS

Short Stories

Nantucket Slayrides: Three Short Novels, with Robert Frazier. Nantucket, Massachusetts, Eel Grass Press, 1989.
Sports & Music. N.p., 1994.

Graphic Novel

Vermillion. New York, DC Comics, monthly parts, 1996-97.

Poetry

Cantata of Death, Weakmind & Generation. N.p., 1967.

* * *

If at the core of all horror fiction lies the writer's perception and depiction of an inimical universe—a cosmos where injustice reigns, mankind is the plaything of larger, enigmatic forces, a desultory Imp of the Perverse is every hapless soul's unlucky Jiminy Cricket, and any victories are temporary and illusory—then all of Lucius Shepard's fiction, even that which is ostensibly science fiction or fantasy, is undeniably horrific. (Although to honour a semantic quibble favored by the author, who once had a character call horror fiction "at best . . . sensual pessimism," we might categorize Shepard's tales as "terror" rather than horror, Shepard defining terror as "the comprehension that everything we dread is simply a reminder of [our] insignificance, one we assign a supernatural valence in order to boost our morale.")

Shepard's brilliant, astonishingly unwavering corpus of novels, stories and mid-length works all inhabit and define a landscape where intersecting planes of paranormal existence (the warrior realm of Moselantja in *Green Eyes*; the drug-attained parallel universe in *Kalimantan*, to name only two) serve as psychic and corporeal battlegrounds for men and women who aspire to peace and love and mercy, without fully believing themselves deserving of these graces, or capable of creating them. Doomed in no small measure by their own expectations and experience (a cardinal motif in horror), drawn and quartered by opposing pulls of different realms (the rich U.S. versus the poor Mexico, for example, in "On the Border"), Shepard's characters seldom reach story's end with mates, minds or morals intact.

A brief, necessarily fragmentary biography of Shepard is required to fully appreciate his fiction, since unlike most genre writers he draws deeply on his *curriculum vitae*—demi-monde doings in exotic locales—to lend both verisimilitude and emotional depth to his writing.

Age 15 finds Shepard in New York City, "a runaway from a draggy Florida town looking for a better situation than I had at home" (from the author's endnotes to *Vermillion* number one). The "Lucius" character, narrator of the story "A Spanish Lesson," resumes the profile a couple of years forward, "That winter of 1964, when I was seventeen . . . I dropped out of college and sailed to Europe, landing in Belfast, hitchhiking across Britain, down through France and Spain, and winding up on the Costa del Sol . . . [I was] six foot three, one ninety . . . [had an] erratic temper, and [an] ability to consume enormous quantities of drugs." This "Lucius" winds up in Nepal, as his creator himself, based on the evidence of other stories, undoubtedly did sooner or later.

As years passed and Shepard tumbled around the globe, supporting himself both licitly and illicitly, he developed a fascination with those places best characterized as "the ends of the earth," a touchstone phrase for Shepard, and one he employs consistently starting with the very early story "Solitario's Eyes" and continuing right up to his book, *The Golden*. Like Thoreau in the Maine woods, Shepard finds these locales—from Borneo to the Caribbean, but most vitally, Latin America—to be places where essentials of evil and good, duty and desire can be examined and confronted without the obscuring smoke of civilization.

Shepard graduated from the Clarion Writers Workshop in 1980. Then in his mid-30s, circa 1983, after much heavy living, including a stint in a rock band (a generational attitude of despair and distrust embodied in the darker, Jaggerish stylings of much pop music is one note in Shepard's symphony), Shepard began to place remarkably—yet understandably—mature stories in science-fiction magazines and anthologies. (The sf community welcomed Shepard wholeheartedly, granting him several awards, and he remains one of the finest authors to emerge from the churning, supercharged, cyberpunk/humanist/Hard SF feedback loop of the 1980s. Shepard straddles the former two camps uneasily, and with some antipathy for all poseurs, "Why is it, I ask you, that every measly little wimp in the universe thinks he can put on a pair of mirrored sunglasses and instantly acquire magical hipness and cool ... ?" From "Shades.")

Working mostly at novella lengths, his strongest suit, Shepard soon produced an astonishing array of demonstrably classic stories. Assembled in two volumes, *The Jaguar Hunter* and *The Ends*

of the Earth, these stories from the first phase of Shepard's career achieve heights of romantic desolation and fantastical imagery, and point toward the novels to come. (Two more of these early stories—"Solitario's Eyes" and "The Arcevoalo"—are included with the short novel *Kalimantan*.)

In various glamorously seedy settings (not excluding the United States, specifically the island of Nantucket, where Shepard resided for a time), Shepard's patented wounded American male, his cynicism a sour coating over a wistful, literate centre, nurses his hurts, abuses himself and others, misunderstands the natives (or becomes too much like them), and perhaps experiences a brief moment of physical and spiritual love, before meeting his ultimate, usually degenerative (although sometimes transcendant) fate.

Despite this occasionally too apparent template, Shepard's stories seldom pall, for several reasons. First off is the sheer quality of his writing. Shepard is a consumate stylist, possessing a seemingly limitless ability to spin off sparkling original metaphors and concrete visualizations of the bizarre. With a rich vocabulary that enlists all of the reader's senses, he conjures mind-movies of surpassing vividness. Secondly, Shepard's imagination is as extensive as his experience. Able to spin endless variations on his basic plot scenario, Shepard always offers enough variety to keep readers intrigued.

This is not to say he never nods. Several stories reveal a superficiality of concept and an over-reliance on other fiction. "How the Wind Spoke at Madaket" is a Stephen King-style gore-fest. "The Ends of the Earth" opens with the most ponderous Lovecraftian paragraph HPL never wrote. "The Black Clay Boy" is Ray Bradbury sentimentality with a smuttier mouth. "Nomans Land" is L. Ron Hubbard's *Fear* (1957) fused with Fritz Leiber's *The Sinful Ones* (1952). And "Surrender" is full of Ellisonian stridency and stacked-deck politics. Additionally, while Shepard's female characters are always believable and layered, they seldom assume central importance. (An exception is Lisa in "The End of Life as We Know It.") But these few slumps disappear in the bright turbulent flood of Shepard's dedicated inventiveness.

A series of three linked stories from this period are "The Man Who Painted the Dragon Griaule"; "The Scalehunter's Beautiful Daughter"; and "The Father of Stones." Set in a steam-era neverland where the baleful presence of an enormous, somnolent, mile-long dragon dominates the land, these stories are important for several reasons. The first piece is perhaps Shepard's central and clearest statement on the traps of being an artist. The second is the only story of Shepard's to feature a woman at its centre. And the third, a kind of riff on Roman Polanski's film *Chinatown* (1974), hints at the fusion of mystery and horror which informs Shepard's most recent novel, *The Golden*.

Shepard's first novel, a *tour de force*, is, to make a relevant analogy with pop music, the literary equivalent of Credence Clearwater Revival's "Bad Moon Rising." A Southern gothic, swamp-sf extravagance, *Green Eyes* is the story of a secret quasi-governmental project to reanimate the dead with injections of special bacteria. The zombies that result are synthetic personalities, archetypes with pseudo-histories derived perhaps from mankind's collective unconscious, their emerald eyes burning with a fierce intelligence and psychic abilities. One such, Donnell Harrison, eventually escapes confinement with his nurse-turned-lover, Jocundra Verret, and their resulting escapades, culminating in a telekinetic firestorm, fully exemplify what Shepard therein terms "a kind of general sadness attaching to every human involvement." With echoes of *Frankenstein* (1818), Disch's *Camp Concentration* (1968), and the Roger Corman film *The Man with the X-Ray Eyes* (1963), Shepard's debut novel would be hard to top.

Yet his second novel, *Life During Wartime*, manages to up the ante considerably. (A projected novel, *The End of Life As We Know It*, has not appeared to date. Judging from a public reading, it appears to involve UFO cultists.) Arguably Shepard's best book, the novel was anticipated both by pre-publication of selected portions ("R & R" won a Nebula award) and by the appearance of allied stories such as "Salvador" and "Fire Zone Emerald" (the latter of which shares none of the characters and only portions of the action of the identically named chapter in the novel).

A Vietnam-style hi-tech war rages in Central America. Young soldier David Mingolla finds his personality deteriorating under the strain of combat. When he meets an enemy agent named Debora, who counsels desertion to Panama, he reaches a crisis point. So far, the book might remind readers of, say, John Shirley's *Eclipse* (1985), an exercise in futuristic *realpolitik*. But Shepard soon sends his narrative into much stranger, more surreal territory.

Both the U.S. and the enemy are using psychics as human weapons, and Mingolla is recruited into the Psicorps (a very Philip K. Dickian concept), whereupon he begins to unconver the real dimensions and motivations of the war, which turns out to be a struggle between two ancient decadent families. As a portrait of corruption and redemption, as a phantasmagoric allegory, the book has few parallels in modern genre literature. Also of note is that here we find one of the few successful love affairs in Shepard's *oeuvre*—although the fact that Mingolla and Debora end up as grim avenging angels bereft of many human pleasures removes any possible trace of easy sentimentality.

Following this pinnacle, Shepard became somewhat less prominent in the field. Impressive, adroit stories like "Bound for Glory" and its stylistically and thematically similar cousin, "Human History" (both of which twist standard Wild West motifs profitably) continued to appear, but to less notice and effect (simply because so much good exciting work had already jaded readers). By the time of the short novel *Kalimantan*, Shepard seemed to have played out a certain arc. *Kalimantan*, narrated at a spatio-temporal remove by an older protagonist who is not the central actor of the drama, seems wan and vitiated, compared to the Faustian exuberance of earlier works. Luckily, Shepard's latest projects seem designed to break new ground.

The Golden joins the welter of Anne Ricean vampire novels flooding the market, but retains its own integrity. Set exclusively in the Gormenghastian Castle Banat during the 1860s, the story follows the efforts of vampire-detective Michel Beheim to solve the murder of a specially bred woman whose blood has unique properties desired by the vampires. With its portrayal of power-mad immortals, more alien than supernatural, engaged in feuds and schemes more bloody and recondite than those found in Roger Zelazny's Amber books, and with its focus on the historical past, *The Golden* stakes out new territory for Shepard.

Even more so does Shepard's script for *Vermillion*, an ongoing story told in comic-book form. At some far future point, the entire universe has undergone an unexplained phase-change, devolving into an endless cityscape where the very laws of physics have changed, making for a Boschian experience. Still in the process of unfolding, *Vermillion* seems calculated to give more scope and different costumes to Shepard's obsessive themes.

Like Graham Greene, B. Traven or Malcolm Lowry, Lucius Shepard is an outsider at home nowhere and everywhere, one whose sad, wise gaze is turned not without compassion on every person he depicts—and on himself most unsparingly of all.

—Paul Di Filippo

SHIEL, M(atthew) P(hipps)

Pseudonym: Gordon Holmes. **Nationality:** British. **Born:** Montserrat Island, West Indies, 21 July 1865. **Education:** Harrison College, Barbados; King's College, London; St. Bartholomew's Hospital Medical School, London. **Family:** Married 1) Carolina Garcia Gomez in 1898 (died), two daughters; 2) Mrs. Gerald Jewson, c. 1918. **Career:** Taught mathematics at a school in Derbyshire for two years. Granted Civil List pension, 1938. **Died:** 14 February 1947.

HORROR, GHOST AND GOTHIC PUBLICATIONS

Novel

The Purple Cloud. London, Chatto and Windus, 1901; revised edition, London, Gollancz, 1929; New York, Vanguard Press, 1930.

Short Stories

Shapes in the Fire: Being a Mid-Winter Night's Entertainment in Two Parts and an Interlude. London, John Lane, and Boston, Roberts, 1896.
The Pale Ape and Other Pulses. London, Werner Laurie, 1911.
The Best Short Stories of M. P. Shiel, edited by John Gawsworth. London, Gollancz, 1948.
Xlucha and Others. Sauk City, Wisconsin, Arkham House, 1975.

OTHER PUBLICATIONS

Novels

The Rajah's Sapphire. London, Ward Lock, 1896.
The Yellow Danger. London, Richards, 1898; New York, Fenno, 1899.
Contraband of War. London, Richards, 1899; revised edition, London, Pearson, 1914; Ridgewood, New Jersey, Gregg Press, 1968.
Cold Steel. London, Richards, 1899; New York, Brentano's, 1900; revised edition, London, Gollancz, and New York, Vanguard Press, 1929.
The Man-Stealers. London, Hutchinson, and Philadelphia, Lippincott, 1900; revised edition, Hutchinson, 1927.
The Lord of the Sea. London, Richards, and New York, Stokes, 1901; revised edition, New York, Knopf, 1924; London, Gollancz, 1929.
The Weird o' It. London, Richards, 1902.
Unto the Third Generation. London, Chatto and Windus, 1903.
The Evil That Men Do. London, Ward Lock, 1904.
The Yellow Wave. London, Ward Lock, 1905.
The Lost Viol. New York, Clode, 1905; London, Ward Lock, 1908.
The Last Miracle. London, Laurie, 1906; revised edition, London, Gollancz, 1929.

The White Wedding. London, Laurie, 1908.

This Knot of Life. London, Everett, 1909.

The Isle of Lies. London, Laurie, 1909.

The Dragon. London, Richards, 1913; New York, Clode, 1914; revised as *The Yellow Peril*, London, Gollancz, 1929.

Children of the Wind. London, Laurie, 1923.

Dr. Krasinski's Secret. New York, Vanguard Press, 1929; London, Jarrolds, 1930.

The Black Box. New York, Vanguard Press, 1930; London, Richards, 1931.

Say Au R'Voir but Not Goodbye. London, Benn, 1933.

This Above All. New York, Vanguard Press, 1933; as *Above All Else*, London, Cole, 1943.

The Young Men are Coming! London, Allen and Unwin, and New York, Vanguard Press, 1937.

Novels as Gordon Holmes (with Louis Tracy)

The Late Tenant. New York, Clode, 1906; London, Cassell, 1907.

By Force of Circumstances. New York, Clode, 1909; London, Mills and Boon, 1910.

The House of Silence. New York, Clode, 1911; as *The Silent House*, London, Nash, 1911.

Short Stories

Prince Zaleski. London, John Lane, and Boston, Roberts, 1895.

How the Old Woman Got Home. London, Richards, 1927; New York, Vanguard Press, 1928.

Here Comes the Lady. London, Richards, 1928.

The Invisible Voices, with John Gawsworth. London, Richards, 1935; New York, Vanguard Press, 1936.

Prince Zaleski; and, Cummings King Monk. Sauk City, Wisconsin, Mycroft and Moran, 1977.

The Empress of the Earth, 1898; The Purple Cloud, 1901; "Some Short Stories": Offprints of the Original Editions. Cleveland, Ohio, Reynolds Morse Foundation, 1979.

The New King, Plus an Unpublished Dialog with Cummings King Monk Omitted from The Pale Ape of 1911. Cleveland, Ohio, Reynolds Morse Foundation, 1980.

Poetry

(Poems), edited by John Gawsworth. London, Richards, 1936.

Other

Science, Life, and Literature. London, Williams and Norgate, 1950.

Editor, *An American Emperor: The Story of the Fourth Empire of France*, by Louis Tracy. New York, Putnam, and London, Pearson, 1897.

Translator, *The Hungarian Revolution: An Eyewitness's Account*, by Charles Henry Schmitt. London, Workers' Socialist Federation, 1919.

*

Bibliography: *The Works of M. P. Shiel: A Study in Bibliography* by A. Reynolds Morse, Los Angeles, Fantasy, 1948, new edi-

tion, as *The Works of M. P. Shiel Updated*, Dayton, Ohio, Reynolds Morse Foundation/JDS Books, 1980.

Critical Study: *Shiel in Diverse Hands: A Collection of Essays* edited by A. Reynolds Morse, Cleveland, Ohio, Reynolds Morse Foundation, 1983.

*   *   *

M. P. Shiel's early work was heavily influenced by Edgar Allan Poe and the French writers who had carried forward Poe's mission and mannerisms. *Prince Zaleski* features a detective whose lifestyle and posturings are clearly based on C. Auguste Dupin, but are casually raised to the nth degree. *Shapes in the Fire*, similarly issued by Yellow Book publisher John Lane, performs the same function for Poe's other subjects, with an unparalleled flamboyance; alongside two *contes*, three *nouvelles* and a narrative poem it sets out a literary manifesto which is far more outspoken than Oscar Wilde's flirtatiously modest "The Decay of Lying."

"Xlucha" is one of three *femme fatale* stories featured in *Shapes in the Fire*. It takes the form of diary entries recording an encounter between the diarist and the "splendid harlot" Xlucha, returned from the grave in the guise of a Piccadilly whore. "Maria in the Rose-Bush" is also a *femme fatale* story of sorts, told from the viewpoint of a woman whose passion for art drives her devoted husband to his death. "Vaila" was later to be rewritten as "The House of Sounds" but lovers of Decadent prose cannot prefer the later, much sparer, version. The story is a more extreme version of "The Fall of the House of Usher" but its extremism is underlaid with philosophical analysis, offering in the plight of its doomed neurasthenic aristocrat an adamantine allegory in which the earth and the universe are "a Machine of Death, a baleful Vast" and a vision of Creation, in which supreme Omniscience is not an All-Seeing Eye but a marvellously acute aural sensitivity.

"Tulsah," the third *femme fatale* story in *Shapes in the Fire*, is the tale of a saintly Hindoo beguiled and damned by the eponymous lamia, but the climax of "Phorfor," which recalls the nostalgic mood of Poe's "Eleanora," substitutes an almost-conventional sentimentality for the raw nihilism of the earlier stories—thus marking the beginning of Shiel's movement away from Decadent sensibility. Of all the British writers briefly involved in the movement, however, Shiel was the one who clung hardest to Decadent style—or, at least, to the conviction that vivid ideas require vivid expression and that extravagant artifice is a perfectly legitimate end of literary artistry. He took readily enough to more commercial subjects in the serials he began to write for C. Arthur Pearson's popular periodicals, but he addressed them in his own manner, and he was able to produce one more full-blown Decadent fantasy—which deserves recognition as the ultimate Decadent fantasy novel—in *The Purple Cloud*, whose serial version appeared in the final year of the 19th century.

The Purple Cloud is a version of the Book of Job in which the population of the Earth is destroyed, save for one man. The sole survivor of the poisonous cloud, Adam Jefferson, serves 17 years as emperor of the empty Earth, assailed more sharply than any potentate of old by the classic Decadent afflictions of *impuissance*, *ennui* and spleen. He builds an exotic palace from the ruins of civilization, furnishing it as if it were a palace in a painting by Gustave Moreau, before being forced to move on to a new existential phase by the discovery of a female born as the world died and raised in ignorance of its plight. He is then beset by a fierce internal conflict between "white" and "black" impulses, which differ as to whether he should allow the innocent to become a new Eve.

The stories in *The Pale Ape* show Shiel's Decadent affiliation weakening considerably, the recasting of "Vaila" as "The House of Sounds" providing an accurate measuring-device of its reduced ambition. The collection's three *femme fatale* stories all involve vengeful revenants: "Huguenin's Wife" is a tale of transmutation which recalls the work of the Decadent artist Fernand Khnopff; "The Great King" murders his cataleptic wife but cannot replace her; "The Bride" is a brutal tale of a jilted fiancée whose death does not prevent her from intruding upon her lover's wedding night. "The Pale Ape" is a sarcastic fantasy about prenatal influence whose absurdities are presumably calculated, as are those of "The Tale of Henry and Rowena" in *Here Comes the Lady*. The most notable items in the latter collection are "The Primate of the Rose" and the magnificently grim "Dark Lot of One Saul," which seem to owe their inspiration respectively to Poe's "The Cask of Amontillado" and "A Descent into the Maelstrom." By far the best of Shiel's later short stories is "The Place of Pain," which sticks out like a sore thumb from the calculated triviality of *The Invisible Voices*; it is a brilliantly economical visionary fantasy which contains a bitter allegory not dissimilar to that displayed in "Vaila," but far less nihilistic. Oddly enough, the eclectic collection issued by Gollancz in 1948 is more heavily biased toward Decadent items than the Arkham House sampler of 1975.

Although many of Shiel's 20th-century novels are unashamedly melodramatic their imaginative thrust is invariably constructive; several are science fiction, and although they frequently deal with destructive future wars they are buoyed up by the kind of faith in the upward thrust of evolution that Adam Jeffson discovered—after a long and desperate struggle—at the end of *The Purple Cloud*. Shiel's only supernatural fantasy, *This Above All*, is a study in frustration but it never surrenders its underlying faith in progress. Even when an element of horror does infect Shiel's later works, therefore, its implications tend to be conclusively dispelled. Such an element is most obvious in *The Last Miracle* and *Dr. Krasinski's Secret*, both of whose plots involve the imprisonment and torture of innocents by neo-Gothic villains, but both villains turn out to be much more complicated than they seem, and to be possessed of ideals far nobler—or, at least, far more intellectually respectable—than those of actual Gothic villains.

Shiel never lost his taste for recording gruesome episodes, nor the deftness of touch which made them effective—the botched experiment in brain surgery in *The Young Men are Coming!* is a cardinal example—but their horror is always defused in his later work by their context. Within his new framework of ideas and ideals Shiel remained a master of exotic prose, and the legacy of his flirtation with Decadence made his mastery more spectacular than it would otherwise have been, but he never again came close to the unsurpassable literary bravado of *Shapes in the Fire* and *The Purple Cloud*.

—Brian Stableford

SHIRLEY, John (Patrick)

Nationality: American. **Born:** Houston, Texas, 10 February 1953. **Education:** High school education. **Family:** Married Alexandra Allinne in 1982 (separated); twin sons. **Career:** Has had various jobs including fruit picker, dancer, and office worker; regularly performs as lead singer with rock bands; short-story writer, novelist and screenwriter. **Agent:** Lori Perkins, 301 West 53rd Street, New York, NY 10019, USA. Lives in Los Angeles.

HORROR, GHOST AND GOTHIC PUBLICATIONS

Novels

City Come A-Walkin'. New York, Dell, 1980; revised edition, Asheville, North Carolina, Eyeball Books, 1996.
Cellars. New York, Avon, 1982; London, Sphere, 1983.
Dracula in Love. New York, Zebra, 1983.
In Darkness Waiting. New York, Onyx, 1988.
Wetbones: A Novel. Shingletown, California, Ziesing, 1991.

Short Stories

New Noir. Boulder, Colorado, Black Ice Books, 1993.
The Exploded Heart. Asheville, North Carolina, Eyeball Books, 1996.

OTHER PUBLICATIONS

Novels

Transmaniacon. New York, Zebra, 1979.
Three-Ring Psychus. New York, Zebra, 1980.
The Brigade. New York, Avon, 1982; London, Sphere, 1983.
A Song Called Youth:
    Eclipse. New York, Bluejay, 1985; London, Methuen, 1986.
    Eclipse Penumbra. New York, Popular Library, 1988.
    Eclipse Corona. New York, Popular Library, 1990.
Kamus of Kadizhar: The Black Hole of Carcosa: A Tale of the Darkworld Detective. New York, St. Martin's Press, 1988.
A Splendid Chaos: An Interplanetary Fantasy. New York, Watts, 1988; London, Mandarin, 1989.
Silicon Embrace. Shingletown, California, Ziesing, 1996.

Novels as D. B. Drumm (series: Traveler in all titles)

Kingdom Come. New York, Dell, 1984.
The Stalkers. New York, Dell, 1984.
To Kill a Shadow. New York, Dell, 1984.
Road War. New York, Dell, 1985.
Border War. New York, Dell, 1985.
Terminal Road. New York, Dell, 1986.

Plays

Screenplays: *Video Girl*, n.d.; *The Other Side of Evil*, n.d.; *The Crow*, 1994.

*　　*　　*

John Shirley has been called a writer without a genre, and has indeed straddled the grey boundaries between science fiction and horror for most of his career. In both fields, he has produced important and influential work, with his sf containing distinct horror elements, and his horror revealing distinct sf influences. All of his work, however, is distinctly his own.

Shirley has been credited with being the first "cyberpunk" science-fiction writer by those who should know: William Gibson and Bruce Sterling. Growing out of his punk-music inspired youth—which has carried over into his adulthood—Shirley has continuously translated his love of anarchic music into a love of words. Music permeates most of his work, both horror and science fiction.

At the beginning of his writing career, Shirley's genre-straddling met with mixed success. His first real acclaim came as a science-fiction writer, although the horror influences on his early work were clear. Shirley's work tended towards the dark, voidoid, techno-future from the very beginning. He credits a great deal of his bleak future-vision to his own street sense, adopted from living among, and as one, of San Francisco's street people for a long time in the late 1960s and early 1970s.

Shirley saw publication first in the science-fiction field, although he actually wrote the novel *Dracula in Love* in his late teens. This was one of the earliest vampire novels to explore explicit rather than implicit sexual themes, and has been credited as an influence by later writers such as Nancy Collins. (Shirley continues to contribute to many of the seemingly endless erotic-horror anthologies.) Although out of print for many years, *Dracula in Love* seems very clearly to have left its mark.

A graduate of and later a teacher in the Clarion workshops, Shirley credits the workshop as a saving grace in his life, both as a writer and a person. Not squeamish in talking and writing about his personal battles with drugs, alcohol and the real world, Shirley has often indicated that Clarion seemed to have focused his punk spirit. Works that he published shortly after attending the workshops display an improved, more polished, and harnessed prose, but his infusion of a profound life-interest in punk music, the occult, street life, and words still dominated the work. For example, an early story written at the workshop, "The Shadow of a Snowstorm," posits a world of government make-work, and a guild of hum-mannequins that take their assignations to horrifying extremes, achieving perfection of form through sexual humiliation and lobal mutilation.

In the 1980s, suffering from marginal sales and distribution, and embroiled in the ongoing debate over the boundaries implicit in science fiction (through his championing of the Science Fiction Underground), Shirley made a statement that he was "leaving sf." Although this has turned out not to be entirely the case, his most significant work in horror followed the statement. Four novels account for the bulk of Shirley's horror output, along with quite a few short stories.

City Come A-Walkin', generally classified as sf but easily read as horror, garnered a great deal of attention for Shirley. *City* precedes the concept of "the Net" in what became cyberpunk sf, telling the story of the collective overmind of the cities we live in. In *City Come A-Walkin'*, the collective consciousness of San Francisco manifests itself into a single being, as it, and cities everywhere, are threatened by computerization of money and communications. The idea is that this will lead inevitably, through decentralization, to the downfall of the cities. The gestalt consciousness of the city makes itself known to a long-time city-dweller and punk-music club-owner, Stuart Cole, who fights the corruption controlling the electronic money system. Even though sf elements set up the story, it is clearly a tale of spiritual existence, control and emanation.

Cellars is a fairly graphic pre-Splatterpunk story of a sort of demonic manifestation in the underworld of New York. A writer who is sceptical about the supernatural is called upon to assist the police in solving a rash of horrible cult mutilation murders. The writer's employer shows undue interest in the case, and though the writer quits his employ, continues to pay him handsomely to assist the police. In the company of a psychic woman he has been interviewing, and who quickly becomes his lover, they track down the secrets taking place beneath New York, the rebirth of the cult of Ahriman. Many of the themes in this book foreshadow a much more successful use in the novel *Wetbones*.

In Darkness Waiting also shows signs of Shirley's sf influences, in a fairly standard story of possession. Here, a young musician and his aunt come to help an ailing cousin, who turns out to be possessed via a genetic variation called Sub-B3. This, as explained by a local doctor, results in manifestation of a "pilot," which can physically appear in insect-like form. Both *Cellars* and *In Darkness Waiting* have downbeat and somewhat ambivalent endings, and neither represent Shirley at his best.

Wetbones, arguably the most successful of Shirley's horror novels, combines many of the spiritual and supernatural elements of *City* and *Cellars* in a modern-day work of explicit horror. Here Shirley mixes a fully-formed splatterpunk ethic with a semi-erotic element. Searching for the truth about his ex-wife's death, a man joins with a friend who is trying to find his little brother. Horrible mutilation-murders are cropping up all over L.A., and all roads lead to one man: a Hollywood figure who should be in his 80s, but appears to be much younger. Here, Shirley explores the mind of a serial killer, and the mind of a man set on immortality through the literal use of torture and mutilation, tapping into the pleasure and pain centres of the victims. *Wetbones* collects many of Shirley's ongoing themes—including sex, drugs, and rock and roll—in an LA splatter-fest. Here, the spirit forms called the Akishra manifest in a manner similar to the wormy spirit energies in *Cellars*, but, except for a disappointing ending, much more successfully.

Shirley's early short stories contain many elements that have become common scenery in recent horror, both film and prose. Early stories such as "What He Wanted," seemed to anticipate the "death metal" music scene, describing that music as "agony rock," and the stories themselves experimented with different kinds of spiritual transcendence through music, usually accompanied by death or extreme suffering. In "Tricentennial," his future is so bleak that two city blocks cannot be traversed without heavy weaponry and heavy loss. In these and other early works of short fiction, the horror lies in the reality of the future, a bleak, dangerous fascism or anarchy that makes death the preferred escape. A short-story collection, *The Exploded Heart*, was released in 1996 along with a new edition of *City Come A-Walkin'*. *The Exploded Heart* is Shirley's third collection of stories (after *Heatseeker* and *New Noir*, which are both very collectible, and difficult to find). He also continues to contribute to horror anthologies.

As of this writing, potentially of most interest to Shirley followers is the forthcoming collection of straight horror stories called *Black Butterflies: The Dark Side of the Dark Side*. This will include much of his recently-published short fiction: "Barbara," "Pearldoll," "War and Peace," "The Rubber Smile," "The Gunshot" and several others, as well as a few previously unpublished works—"Answering Machine," "The Exquisitely Bleeding Heads of Doktur Palmer Vreedeez" and "In the Cornelius Arms." This collection, when it becomes available, will nicely round out Shirley's available horror-genre output.

Shirley has long performed as a vocalist in the San Francisco and LA punk-rock scenes, with bands such as Sado Nation, and more recently with the Panther Moderns. Carrying his combination of music and horror to its logical conclusion, Shirley often recites whole short stories to music, as is the case in "Dominant Impulse" from the band's *Red Star* recording.

John Shirley currently lives in Los Angeles and, in addition to his novels and short stories, writes for film and television. He adapted *The Crow* to the screen, and lately has released *Silicon Embrace*, a science-fiction novel built around the Roswell alien-visitor mythos.

—Tom Winstead

SIDDONS, (Sybil) Anne Rivers

Nationality: American. **Born:** Atlanta, Georgia, 9 January 1936. **Education:** Auburn University, B.A.A., 1958; attended Atlanta School of Art, c. 1958. **Family:** Married Heyward L. Siddons in 1966; children: (stepsons) Lee, Kemble, Rick, David. **Career:** Worked in advertising with Retail Credit Co., c. 1959, Citizens & Southern National Bank, 1961-63, Burke-Dowling Adams, 1967-69, and Burton Campbell Advertising, 1969-74; full-time writer since 1974. Senior editor, *Atlanta* magazine. Member of governing board, Woodward Academy; member of publications board and arts and sciences honorary council, Auburn University, 1978-83. **Awards:** Alumna achievement award in arts and humanities, Auburn University, 1985. **Address:** 3767 Vermont Rd. N.E., Atlanta, Georgia 30319; and (summer) Haven Colony, Brooklin, Maine 04616, USA.

HORROR, GHOST AND GOTHIC PUBLICATIONS

Novel

The House Next Door. New York, Simon and Schuster, 1978.

OTHER PUBLICATIONS

Novels

Heartbreak Hotel. New York, Simon and Schuster, 1976.
Fox's Earth. New York, Simon and Schuster, 1980.
Homeplace. New York, Harper, 1987.
Peachtree Road. New York, Harper, 1988.
King's Oak. New York, HarperCollins, 1990.
Outer Banks. New York, HarperCollins, 1991.
Colony. New York, HarperCollins, 1992.
Hill Towns. New York, HarperCollins, 1993.
Downtown. New York, HarperCollins, 1994.
Fault Lines. New York, HarperCollins, 1995.

Other

John Chancellor Makes Me Cry. New York, Doubleday, 1975.

Go Straight on Peachtree. New York, Dolphin, 1978.

*

Film Adaptation: *Heart of Dixie*, 1989, from the novel *Heartbreak Hotel*.

*   *   *

The House Next Door is an apparent anomaly within the pattern of Anne Rivers Siddons's literary production: a calculated venture into genre fiction by a writer of literary fiction who never again descended from the upper strata of the marketplace. It is possible that she initially thought of the project as a relaxing one that would be less demanding than her "real" novels—and having found it to be anything but, never repeated the experiment.

It is not surprising that a book originating in this manner should have adopted a format deemed obsolete by many of the genre's contemporary practitioners. The haunted-house story reached its apogee in Victorian times and the last truly notable venture of that kind had been Shirley Jackson's *The Haunting of Hill House* nearly 20 years earlier—itself the product of a "mainstream" writer, albeit one far more consistently interested in the outré and the supernatural. Richard Matheson's *Hell House* (1971) had been a virtual pastiche of Jackson's novel. There is, however, nothing old-fashioned about *The House Next Door*; a substantial part of its merit derives from its casual dismissal of the fundamental assumption that haunted houses must be *old*, or at least constructed on hallowed ground. The reconstruction of the motif forced by this move makes the novel a far more adventurous and interesting work than the rash of schlocky haunted-house movies which came soon after, launched by *The Amityville Horror* (1979) and carried forward by *Poltergeist* (1982).

Stephen King was sufficiently impressed by *The House Next Door* to contact the author while researching his book on the horror tradition, *Danse Macabre* (1981). King quotes Siddons's observation that the haunted-house story has a special significance to women because "to a woman, her house is . . . kingdom, responsibility, comfort, total world." In the heyday of the Gothic novel the architectural projection of personality was a castle or a manse, not a product of individual consciousness but something born of long tradition, fortified by time and the burdens of inheritance. Even in Victorian and Edwardian ghost stories, which might be set in recently bought terraced houses or oft-traded apartments, a home was far more than the achievement of a single individual; it always carried the weight of its history. *The House Next Door* is, by contrast, a haunted-house story for a world in which women, despite the partial liberation of feminist ideals, are "home-makers" by definition and by default. The horrors which afflict Siddons's house are not left over from times past; they spring up from tensions of the moment—tensions generated within the troubled matrix of the ultra-contemporary nuclear family.

The story is told by Colquitt Kennedy, whose calm, contented and childless marriage is disturbed—although she is ruthless in repressing her awareness of the disturbance and never does acknowledge its everyday reality—by the advent of a young architect who designs a house erected on the long-vacant next door lot. She watches helplessly as the family for whom the house is built disintegrates, wrecked by misfortune and horrid revelation. The architect flees to Europe, but inevitably remains present in spirit while the second family to move into the house is similarly devastated. When their replacements are afflicted in their turn—mortally, this time—the Kennedys can stand no more, and Colquitt forces her husband to condemn the house publicly as a place of evil which must never be lived in again. Alas, the evil in question rebounds on them as they are mocked and pilloried by everyone concerned, until they feel that they have no alternative left but to destroy the house themselves, even though they are perfectly convinced that it will wreak a terrible and conclusive vengeance upon them.

Like most first-rate horror novels *The House Next Door* is profoundly ambiguous, and hence profoundly sceptical of everything it seems to take for granted. If the narrator's story is accepted at face value the house really is an active agent of evil, and it really did acquire that agency from the man who designed it, who is a hapless carrier of demonic force. In the narrator's view, it really was *the house* which once threw her into the architect's avid arms, nearly breaking up her own happy home although her fidelity to her husband is absolute. The reader must, however, wonder whether the house has not been set up to serve as a scapegoat for all the evil impulses which infect and eventually obliterate the solidly middle-class, utterly *nice* families who inhabit and surround it. For the reader, if not for Colquitt Kennedy, the thought must be entertainable that perhaps—if only *perhaps*—the family values of middle America are just as fragile, just as rotten and just as false as the family values of the 18th and 19th centuries. That, at least, appears to have been Anne Rivers Siddons's conviction two years earlier, when she wrote *Heartbreak Hotel*—and it was the conviction to which she returned when she continued in the 1980s to write novels whose method and purpose were to flay the skin of illusion from the moral pretensions of the American south.

"So basic is it," the author continued, in the interview quoted by Stephen King ("it" being, of course, the very idea of *the house*), "that the desecration of it, the corruption as it were, by something alien takes on a peculiar and bone-deep horror and disgust." As a summary of the logic of the haunted-house story this can hardly be faulted—but its meaning depends on what one means by "alien": whether it is something outside us that we try to defy, or something inside us that we try to deny.

—Brian Stableford

SILVA, David B.

Nationality: American. **Born:** 1950. **Career:** Editor and publisher of the semi-professional magazine *The Horror Show*, Phantasm Press, 1982-90; writer. **Awards:** Balrog award, for magazine, 1985; World Fantasy award, for magazine, 1988. Lives in Oak Run, California.

HORROR, GHOST AND GOTHIC PUBLICATIONS

Novels

Child of Darkness. New York, Leisure, 1986.
Come Thirteen. New York, Leisure, 1988.
The Presence. London, Headline, 1994.
The Disappeared. London, Headline, 1995.

Other

Editor, *The Best of the Horror Show: An Adventure in Terror.* Chicago, 2AM Publications, 1987.
Editor, with Paul F. Olson, *Post Mortem: New Tales of Ghostly Horror.* New York, St. Martin's Press, 1989; Sutton, Surrey, Severn House, 1991.
Editor, with Paul F. Olson, *Dead End—City Limits: An Anthology of Urban Fear.* New York, St. Martin's Press, 1991.
Editor, *The Definitive Best of the Horror Show.* Baltimore, Maryland, CD Publications, 1992.

*   *   *

The story that David B. Silva contributed to the *Post Mortem* anthology which he co-edited with Paul F. Olson is a typical example of his work in miniature. In the story, "Brothers," the main characters are male children (predictably enough), and Silva's best characters in his novels are often boys in the throes or on the brink of adolescence. In common with Silva's novels there is in the story a challenge to one's Gestalt perception of a given situation; what the reader experiences turns out to have been the incorrect interpretation of the facts, which is all well and good for any kind of fiction, but Silva is particularly adroit at the technique. And most importantly of all, "Brothers" is a good example of American Gothic, as are his finest novels, *The Presence* and *The Disappeared.*

In "Brothers" the twin boys are emotionally close most of the time, although Trey cannot understand Dane's fondness for thunderstorms. Mentally, then, they are in tune, but physically the boys do not resemble one another. Trey is sickly, another reason (beyond that of the frustration of not knowing all of Dane's thoughts) why he should disrespect his brother from time to time. For Dane is healthy. And one begins to suspect that Dane might represent the personification of Trey's wish fulfilment and big-brother infatuation, especially if one has read Thomas Tryon's novel *The Other* (1971), in which two brothers get into increasingly bizarre brotherly scrapes—one of the boys only to discover at the end that the other is a figment of his imagination. One suspects the same with "Brothers": is Mom ignoring the sickly Trey? Dane thinks so: "You aren't real to her. You died twelve years ago, in her womb, before you even had a chance to be introduced. Now you're like one of those envelopes with a window, the ones with the bill inside. All she has to do is look at you and she sees a debt she'll never be free of." (Apart from anything else, this short monologue displays Silva's skill at conveying the nuances and bile of convincingly brutal childish speech; to a certain extent every American horror writer who writes about children would like to compose something with the energy and wit of Mark Twain's *Huckleberry Finn* or J. D. Salinger's *The Catcher in the Rye*, and some do get close to the spirit.) Trey watches his brother get weirder and weirder and then hang himself from their favourite tree; in fact, Dane died at birth with the umbilical cord around his neck, and Trey's own Gestalt mis-interpretations have been indulged by one and all ever since.

To a certain extent the titles of *The Presence* and *The Disappeared* can be regarded as puns. The being in the former novel is not actually present a lot of the time, at least not physically, and one of the clues that it has been close to a victim is that the victim's face becomes partly transparent—so, if anything, one is talking about an *absence*. Or perhaps the presence refers to the father of

Sean and Darrell, known for spontaneous trucking expeditions, and long since expected home; he appears in shadowy form every now and then, one of the parasite's long-dead hosts. *The Disappeared* refers mainly to a boy who has just done precisely the opposite: having been missing for a great deal of time, angelic Gabe returns to the bosom of his family—but cannot remember where he has been.

Silva focuses on moments of great significance in people's lives; moments that might seem small to the adult reader until he steps back and sees them through a child's eyes. *The Presence* documents three friends' last summer together, with grim portentousness, as this becomes the case in more ways than one; for kicks they break through a basement window into the Haberstock Mill, where they think they see a man-sized shadow. One of the boys dies and his face becomes coated in the substance that causes skin transparency; one runs; one (Sean Turner) is nearly burnt to death when the place ignites. Miles away, the younger brother, Darrell knows that it is Sean in the fire but cannot say where the fire is, not even to emergency services when he is all but accused of starting it. But is it the boys' father who rescues Sean from the blaze? If so, what was he doing there?

Luckily for the boys, investigator Roy Price knows strange occurrences when he sees them; accepting that they exist, after all, is one of the principles of American Gothic fiction. There is a very poignant moment when Roy goes to see Sean in the hospital and finds Sean's mother already there. To Roy she says: "I never realized how thin his legs are. They're trying to hold them together with ointments and netting and . . ." An unfamiliar sample has been found in the fire's remains: "a previously unknown organic substance," possibly the "natural progression in the evolutionary process of an existing organism." Or, as Roy suggests, "a mutation, perhaps."

The Guest is living in Sean's subconscious; it has moved around a great deal, and Silva takes us on an illuminating historical tour. One thing perhaps one might not expect from a horror novel is such a well thought-out documentation of the confusion of the parasite; it cannot understand that it is possibly its own presence that makes the creatures it inhabits turn violent.

The Disappeared is altogether a more heart-wrenching affair, dealing as it does with an analogy for child-abuse that is original and cruel. Like the alien in the previous novel, the boy, Gabe, finds himself now in a world the rules of which he no longer comprehends. When told how long he has been away: "'Then I should be older,' Gabe argued." The horror is seeing a child swamped with new and terrifying information, not least of which is the treachery of his own imagination. When Gabe starts to get older very quickly, one understands that Silva is telling us about the nature of time itself: the relativity of it, and the power. Gabe is diagnosed as having Hutchinson-Gilford Syndrome, a degenerative disease which afflicts some children; in a humorous aside Silva states that Teri has heard of the condition via audience-participation talk shows.

The agency responsible for the stealing of children (Gabe is only one of many) and the wiping of their minds is also responsible for the theft of their very childhoods: this agency steals time away from its victims, needless to say for its own ends. This agency also wants Gabe back, which starts a chase and a bitter struggle for an unusual type of custody. All the while, Gabe is getting older. *The Disappeared* nods to the type of horror where bodily changes (and often unnatural ones) are soon a race against the clock before the body has given up—for example, Stephen King's *Thin-*

ner, or Richard Matheson's *The Shrinking Man*. The agency in pursuit is akin to that in Dean Koontz's *Watchers*, the two novels having much in common (and Koontz even being thanked by Silva).

"Death is the sleep of the soul," Silva writes near the end of the novel. "It is a necessity for your renewal, for your expansion. Do not cower in the shadows when death comes knocking. Greet it eye-to-eye with a hardy handshake and know that it comes like sleep in cycles." This is all well and good: but somehow one assumes that children will be exempt. But this turns out not to be the case. One of the saddest scenes in *The Disappeared* is when Gabe tries to comprehend his own illness, but cannot accept that he will get older without getting bigger ("Weird"); this alongside the mother's valiant attempt not to be upset in front of him. He asks if he will get wrinkles, false teeth and gray hair.

Silva's writing is of an America that seems peculiarly unfettered by big-city problems; this is because his focal viewpoints are those of children and teenagers (by and large), and their worlds have less in common with those of the adults that preside over them than they do, for example, with the invading alien entity that visits in *The Presence*. Silva's America is rural—more or less American Gothic in the sense of the Norman Rockwell painting alone: there are the abandoned mills and the tire-swings, the brooks and the mine-caves. The imaginations of small communities that believe themselves outside the legislation and undesirous of the assistance of the big cities; imaginations that are forced to think on larger scales very suddenly. Even the names are quintessentially American.

The American Gothic is a germiniparous horror framework: a soil-bed from which offspring grow via seeds that were previously planted. Many plants similar of leaf and stem shoot up, and it is good to think of the novels of David B. Silva as akin to young trees with strong roots.

—David Mathew

SIMMONS, Dan

Nationality: American. **Born:** Peoria, Illinois, 4 April 1948. **Education:** Wabash College, Indiana, B.A. in English; Washington University, St. Louis, M.A. **Family:** Married Karen Simmons; one daughter. **Career:** Elementary school-teacher of gifted children for many years; full-time writer since 1987. **Awards:** Fulbright scholarship, 1977; *Twilight Zone* Rod Serling Memorial award for short story, 1982; World Fantasy award for novel, 1985; Hugo award for novel, 1989; *Locus* award for novel, 1989, 1990 and 1991; British Science Fiction Association award for novel, 1990; British Fantasy Society August Derleth award for novel, 1990; Horror Writers of America Bram Stoker award for novel, 1990, and for collection, 1991. **Address:** c/o Bantam Books, 1540 Broadway, New York, NY 10036, USA. Lives in Colorado.

Horror, Ghost and Gothic Publications

Novels (series: Elm Haven)

Song of Kali. New York, Bluejay, 1985; London, Headline, 1987.

Carrion Comfort. New York, Warner, 1989; London, Headline, 1990.

Summer of Night (Elm Haven). New York, Putnam, and London, Headline, 1991.

Children of the Night (Elm Haven). New York, Putnam, and London, Headline, 1992.

The Hollow Man. New York, Bantam, and London, Headline, 1992.

Fires of Eden (Elm Haven). New York, Putnam, and London, Headline, 1994.

Short Stories

Banished Dreams. Arvada, Colorado, Roadkill Press, 1990.

Entropy's Bed at Midnight. Northridge, California, Lord John Press, 1990.

Prayers to Broken Stones: A Collection. Arlington Heights, Illinois, Dark Harvest, 1990; London, Headline, 1992.

Lovedeath: Five Tales of Love and Death. New York, Warner, and London, Headline, 1993.

OTHER PUBLICATIONS

Novels

Phases of Gravity. New York, Bantam, 1989; London, Headline, 1990.

Hyperion. New York, Doubleday, 1989; London, Headline, 1990.

The Fall of Hyperion. New York, Doubleday, 1990; London, Headline, 1991.

Hyperion Cantos (omnibus; includes *Hyperion, The Fall of Hyperion*). New York, Guild America, 1990.

Endymion. New York, Bantam, and London, Headline, 1996.

The Rise of Endymion. New York, Bantam, 1997.

Other

Going After the Rubber Chicken. Northridge, California, Lord John Press, 1991.

Summer Sketches. Northridge, California, Lord John Press, 1992.

*   *   *

Ever since Harlan Ellison raved about "The River Styx Runs Upstream" at a 1981 writers' workshop, everyone has agreed that Dan Simmons is a writer of remarkable talents. Yet this in itself does not ensure success as a horror writer. At least at times, horror fiction must be visceral and explicit, not allusive and subtle, and a writer primarily focused on displaying his own literary sophistication may enervate his story and alienate his readers. This is a problem that Simmons faced and, fortunately, eventually conquered.

Despite many effective moments, Simmons's first three horror novels—*Song of Kali, Carrion Comfort* and *Summer of Night*—all suffer from an apparent authorial imperative to overwhelm readers with his erudition. To visibly distinguish Simmons's work from less elevated predecessors, the narrator of *Song of Kali* notes his wife's lack of interest in "trashy Stephen King novels," while the sheriff of *Carrion Comfort* confesses that he likes to "indulge in some junk. Well-written junk, y'understand, but junk all the same" like "the scary stuff—Stephen King, Steve Rasnic Tem . . . those guys."

In *Carrion Comfort,* while translating a long conversation in German, Simmons slows things down by also reproducing every statement in the original German, possibly including a few in-jokes for his German-speaking readers. One precocious youngster in *Summer of Night* demonstrates his ability by reading the first paragraph of Charles Dickens's *David Copperfield.* In both *Song of Kali* and *Summer of Night,* Simmons's narrator dignifies a momentary indulgence in gore by likening the scene to the layered transparencies in *Compton's Pictured Encyclopedia.* And, as if uncomfortable with uneducated characters, Simmons implausibly makes the obligatory sheriff of *Carrion Comfort* a former history professor with a fondness for reading scholarly works, while the obligatory drunken father of *Summer of Night* implausibly is also a college-educated intellectual who gets in bar-room arguments about Karl Marx—while his obligatory slaughtered dog is named, for heaven's sake, Wittgenstein.

Beyond this irritating tendency to show off his knowledge, Simmons's literary ambitions more broadly weaken the impact of these early novels. For much of its length, *Song of Kali* is the atmospheric story of an American writer trying to track down a dead Indian poet, mysteriously resurrected by members of a cult worshipping the destructive goddess Kali, and now anxious to publish his new poems celebrating her imminent return to prominence. But, as if such things were childish, Simmons refuses to provide an exciting climax: after the narrator's baby daughter is kidnapped by the cult and later found dead, he numbly returns to America, fights back an impulse for bloody revenge, and offers some empty profundities about increasing violence in contemporary life. *Carrion Comfort,* after an effective opening sequence almost identical to the story of that name, slows down to an absolutely leaden pace in describing the feuds of ancient "mind vampires" who can effortlessly control other people, the vast and all-powerful conspiracy they direct, and the efforts of a Holocaust survivor and a few allies to track them down and destroy them. Here, the story is weighed down, not enriched, by an urge to carefully describe every setting, provide short biographies for every character, and follow every tangent moving away from the central narrative. And *Summer of Night,* following what is perhaps the dullest opening chapter in the history of horror, proceeds like a version of King's *It* as rewritten by a committee of creative-writing teachers, with all of the interesting quirkiness, violence and narrative complexity stripped away to solemnly relate how a group of misfit youths in Elm Haven, Illinois, band together to combat the re-emergence of an ancient evil force that kills children. Readers who can make it through the first 200 pages will eventually find an involving narrative with its own distinctive take on the experience of American adolescence, but like *Carrion Comfort,* it is a novel that would have been equally powerful at half the length.

In the 1990s, with a growing reputation and several awards for his novels, Simmons evolved beyond the need to impress his audience and produced three leaner, less pretentious, and more impressive horror novels. *Children of the Night,* the first of two novels featuring a now-adult character from *Summer of Night* (the other being *Fires of Eden*), builds an intriguing scientific explanation for vampirism into the story of a biologist who adopts a sick Romanian baby and takes him to her American laboratory, where she learns of his strange regenerative powers. When the child is kidnapped, she returns to Romania with a helpful priest to search for him and learns that he is none other than the son of the legendary Vlad Dracula, about to become a vampire and his father's successor in an elaborate ritual. In a thrilling conclusion—exactly the sort of ending that *Song of Kali* lacked—she rescues her baby from the ceremony while all the attending vampires are destroyed in an explosion.

The Hollow Man describes a man with the power to read other people's minds who, depressed after the death of his wife who uniquely shared his ability, embarks on an aimless cross-country odyssey while reflecting back on his scientific efforts to understand human consciousness. Having reached the conclusion that consciousness is a "standing wave" capable of moving from body to body, he briefly enters the mind of a dying autistic child, enjoys an idyllic interlude with his wife (whose consciousness, he learns, he has been carrying with him all along), and then kills himself so as to somewhere enjoy a happy existence with his wife and the child. And in *Fires of Eden*, a divorced housewife vacationing in Hawaii stumbles into mysterious goings-on involving a shady developer and resurgent Hawaiian gods; here, for the first time, Simmons displays a healthy sense of humour regarding his own work that augurs well for his future fiction.

Were it commercially viable to do so, Simmons could profitably concentrate on short fiction, having produced a number of excellent stories, including "The River Styx Runs Upstream" (in *Prayers to Broken Stones*), where a child must cope with the presence of his strangely resurrected mother, and "Entropy's Bed at Midnight" (in *Lovedeath*), where a man contemplates the role that accidents play in human life. And no discussion of Simmons's horror fiction should entirely neglect his science-fiction novels *Hyperion* and *The Fall of Hyperion*, since they essentially relate the story of a confrontation with a powerful monster called the Shrike, and the final revelation is that a universe apparently dominated by humans is actually about to be taken over by computer intelligences that inhabit the teleportation beams connecting innumerable inhabited worlds. In a real sense, then, *Hyperion* and *The Fall of Hyperion* together constitute Simmons's longest, and most successful, horror novel.

—Gary Westfahl

SINCLAIR, Iain (MacGregor)

Nationality: British. **Born:** Cardiff, Wales, 11 June 1943. **Education:** Cheltenham College, 1956-61; London School of Film Technique; Trinity College, Dublin; Courtauld Institute, London. **Career:** Documentary film-maker; various short-term jobs, including council grass-cutter, London; founder, Albion Village Press; second-hand book dealer since 1979; poet and novelist. **Address:** c/o Jonathan Cape, Random House, 20 Vauxhall Bridge Road, London SW1V 2SA, England. Lives in London.

Horror, Ghost and Gothic Publications

Novels

White Chappell, Scarlet Tracings. Uppingham, Rutland, Goldmark, 1987.
Downriver; or, the Vessels of Wrath: a Narrative in Twelve Tales. London, Paladin, 1991.
Radon Daughters: A Voyage, Between Art and Terror, from the Mound of Whitechapel to the Limestone Pavements of the Burren. London, Cape, 1994.

Other Publications

Plays

An Explanation, with Christopher Bamford (produced, Dublin, 1963).
Chords, with Christopher Bamford (produced, Dublin, 1964).

Poetry

Back Garden Poems. 1970.
The Kodak Mantra Diaries (Allen Ginsberg in London). 1971.
Muscat's Wurm. 1972.
The Birth Rug. 1973.
Lud Heat: A Book of the Dead Hamlets. 1975.
Brown Clouds. 1977.
The Penances. 1977.
Suicide Bridge. 1979.
Fluxions. 1983.
Flesh Eggs and Scalp Metal. 1983.
Autistic Poses. 1985.
Flesh Eggs and Scalp Metal: Selected Poems (1970-87). 1989.
Jack Elam's Other Eye. 1991.
Lud Heat and Suicide Bridge. 1995.

Other

The Shamanism of Intent: Some Flights of Redemption. Uppingham, Rutland, Goldmark Gallery, 1991.
Lights Out for the Territory. London, Cape, 1997.

* * *

Not everyone would immediately think of Iain Sinclair as a horror novelist, even though dark themes like the legacy of Jack the Ripper occur again and again throughout his work. He is widely respected as a poet, and his latest work, *Lights Out for the Territory*, is an entirely non-fictional account of his peregrinations round London, the city at the epicentre of most of his work. He describes such events as a flying visit by prime minister John Major, the funeral of gangster Ronnie Kray, a walk through an area dominated by the headquarters of MI6 and other departments of the secret state, and an effort to visit novelist Jeffrey Archer in his penthouse. These are described with great humour and vividness, though whether they are horrific presumably depends on the reader's view of the characters depicted or nearly visited.

Sinclair, however, does not object to his novels being classed with horror, a genre he enjoys (he has written afterwords to paperback reprints of William Hope Hodgson's novels). The novels are much darker than the poetry and non-fiction, though they share the vividness, attention to detail, and love of the eccentric and grotesque.

White Chappell, Scarlet Tracings, is the work most explicitly concerned with Jack the Ripper, the enigma at the heart of London's darkness. Perhaps typically, a good deal of the story is that of an eccentric group of modern book-dealers with bad stomachs. Sinclair does not spare his readers the more unpleasant details of the unhealthy lives of his characters: all the least pleasant features of diseased human life are here.

Interestingly, for a novel which is more or less in the "realist" camp, *White Chappell, Scarlet Tracings* involves as its Ripper the figure of Sir William Gull. At the time much older than most first-time murderers, Gull was Queen Victoria's physician (not her surgeon, as is popularly supposed). Until recently, he was known as the first doctor to identify Anorexia Nervosa as a condition, and notorious mainly as a supporter of live animal vivisection. Gull returned to an unlooked-for posthumous prominence when a surgeon to whom a relative had entrusted his diaries speculated that Gull knew who the Ripper was. The diaries were later destroyed. Few criminologists would give Gull himself page-room as a serious Ripper suspect, though he is much loved by conspiracy theorists, who like to place him at the heart of a complex web of operators in darkness. What Sinclair does is use this figure as an emblem of the establishment whose cruelty leaks and drips onto the street.

There are also echoes of the Ripper and hints that some characters overlap with Ripperological figures in the longer novel *Downriver*. This is another study of London, in fictional form, though it is clear, indeed explicit, that pre-*Lights Out*, a good deal of the author's personalized rambling-research had been incorporated and only lightly fictionalized. There is a terrific feel for the ancient mysteries of the vast city, for its little-known corners and the odd characters who inhabit them (though there one tends sometimes to wonder if Sinclair ever encounters an inhabitant who isn't an odd eccentric, and whether he would have the means or motive to describe such a rare conformist if he did meet one). Characteristically, the novel opens with a dealer in second-hand curiosities going to visit a supplier who runs a chaotic business in a totally derelict area. (Sinclair tends in his novels to navigate round the islands of prosperity and superficially polite behaviour which do exist in London, as if he is a Venetian gondolier determined never to set foot on land.) Later we get the development of a complex, multi-stranded plot, the elements of horror and mystery circling the disappearance of Edith Cadiz, a nurse who had at one time been a dancer, who interests the most frequent of the many viewpoint characters. However, the main theme of the novel is always London, and the strange things which have taken place there, or do, or may, or will take place.

Many of these themes reappear in Sinclair's later novel, *Radon Daughters*. Indeed, the central character, Todd Sileen, has already been encountered in *Downriver*. Todd is odd even by Sinclair's standards, his habit even sillier than poteen. The crippled protagonist, who lives amidst circumstances and companions even more repellant than usual, hands a loaded brown-paper envelope to a dubious contact in a more dubious bar. Todd is not scoring drugs or magazines wrapped in brown paper, but the chance to submit himself illicitly to doses of radiation in an ill-guarded local hospital!

The sometimes rambling nature of Sinclair's novels, and the repetitive preoccupations, should not distract the would-be reader from the power of his prose and poetry, or the detail of his observations.

—Peter T. Garratt

SINCLAIR, May

Pseudonyms: Julian Sinclair; M. A. St. C. Sinclair; Mary Sinclair. **Nationality:** British. **Born:** Mary Amelia St. Clair Sinclair, Rock Ferry, Higher Bebington, Cheshire, 24 August 1863. **Military Ser-**

vice: Red Cross Ambulance Corps, Belgium, 1914. **Education:** Privately, and at Cheltenham Ladies College, 1881-82. **Career:** From 1895, full-time writer; active in Women's Freedom League, and the Women Writers Suffrage League, 1908-10; worked with the Hoover Relief Commission. Lived in Devon, Sidmouth, and London. Settled in Bierton, near Aylesbury, Buckinghamshire, 1936. **Awards:** Fellow, Royal Society of Literature, 1916. **Died:** 14 November 1946.

HORROR, GHOST AND GOTHIC PUBLICATIONS

Short Stories

The Flaw in the Crystal. New York, Dutton, 1912.
Uncanny Stories (includes *The Flaw in the Crystal*). London, Hutchinson, and New York, Macmillan, 1923.
The Intercessor and Other Stories. London, Hutchinson, 1931; New York, Macmillan, 1931.

OTHER PUBLICATIONS

Novels

Audrey Craven. Edinburgh, Blackwood, 1897; New York, Holt, 1906.
Mr. and Mrs. Nevill Tyson. Edinburgh and London, Blackwood, 1898; as *The Tysons*, New York, Dodge, 1906.
The Divine Fire. London, Constable, and New York, Holt, 1904.
The Helpmate. London, Constable, and New York, Holt, 1907.
Kitty Tailleur. London, Constable, 1908; as *The Immortal Moment*, New York, Doubleday Page, 1908.
The Creators: A Comedy. London, Constable, and New York, Dutton, 1910.
The Combined Maze. London, Hutchinson, and New York, Harper, 1913.
The Return of the Prodigal. New York, Macmillan, 1914.
The Three Sisters. London, Hutchinson, and New York, Macmillan, 1914.
Tasker Jevons: The Real Story. London, Hutchinson, 1916; as *The Belfry*, New York, Macmillan, 1916.
The Tree of Heaven. London, Cassell, and New York, Macmillan, 1917.
Mary Olivier: A Life. London, Cassell, and New York, Macmillan, 1919.
The Romantic. London, Collins, and New York, Macmillan, 1920.
Mr. Waddington of Wyck. London, Cassell, and New York, Macmillan, 1921.
Life and Death of Harriett Frean. London, Collins, and New York, Macmillan, 1922.
Anne Severn and the Fieldings. London, Hutchinson, and New York, Macmillan, 1922.
A Cure of Souls. London, Hutchinson, 1923; New York, Macmillan, 1924.
Arnold Waterlow: A Life. London, Hutchinson, and New York, Macmillan, 1924.
The Rector of Wyck. London, Hutchinson, and New York, Macmillan, 1926.
Far End. London, Hutchinson, and New York, Macmillan, 1926.
The Allinghams. London, Hutchinson, and New York, Macmillan, 1927.

History of Anthony Waring. London, Hutchinson, and New York, Macmillan, 1927.

Short Stories

Two Sides of a Question (novellas). London, Constable, and New York, Holt, 1901.
The Judgement of Eve and Other Stories. London, and New York, Harper, 1907.
Fame. London, Hutchinson, 1929.
Tales Told by Simpson. London, Hutchinson, and New York, Macmillan, 1930.

Poetry

Nakiketas and Other Poems (as Julian Sinclair). London, Kegan Paul, 1886.
The Dark Night: A Novel in Verse. London, Cape, and New York, Macmillan, 1924.

Other

Essays in Verse. London, Kegan Paul, Trench, Trubner, 1891.
Feminism. London, The Women Writers' Suffrage League, 1912.
The Three Brontës (biography). London, Hutchinson, and Boston, Houghton Mifflin, 1912.
A Journal of Impressions of Belgium. London, Hutchinson, and New York, Macmillan, 1915.
America's Part in the War. New York, Commission for Relief in Belgium, 1915.
A Defence of Idealism. London, and New York, Macmillan, 1917.
The New Idealism. London, and New York, Macmillan, 1922.

Translator, *Outlines of Church History*, by Rudolf Sohm. London, Macmillan, 1895; Boston, Beacon Press, 1958.
Translator, *England's Danger, The Future of British Army Reform*, by Theodore von Sosnosky. London, Chapman and Hall, 1901.

*

Manuscript Collections: University of Pennsylvania Library.

Critical Studies: *Miss May Sinclair: Novelist*, by T. E. M. Boll. Rutherford, New Jersey, Fairleigh Dickinson University Press, 1973; *May Sinclair*, by H. Zegger. Boston, Hall, 1976.

* * *

May Sinclair was one of many female British novelists who dabbled in the production of supernatural short stories, although she did not take to it until the heyday of such fictions was passed. Like her Victorian predecessor Rhoda Broughton she was primarily concerned with using supernatural devices to explore the difficulties and seeming perversities of amatory psychology, and she did so with considerable dexterity.

Uncanny Stories is much the better of Sinclair's two supernatural collections, although the second is by no means negligible. Her most frequently anthologized story is "Where Their Fire Is Not Quenched," whose protagonist is delivered after death into an extraordinarily subtle Hell, where every turning leads her back to a room in which—following the death by drowning of her first

love—she had a desultory affair with a married man. The implication is that she should have done far more with her life and her affections. "The Token" is another posthumous fantasy in which a dead wife who thought that her husband was more devoted to a paperweight than to her is condemned to haunt their house until he proves otherwise. A more robust eroticism, unusually frank for its time, is featured in yet another tale of a ghost compounded out of the unresolved frustrations of a dead wife. "The Victim" is unusual in employing only male characters, although the murderous chauffeur who belatedly discovers the error of his assumptions plays a distinctly wifelike role.

The interesting novella *The Flaw in the Crystal*, which had been separately published in the United States before its inclusion in *Uncanny Stories*, is a delusional fantasy about a woman who believes that she can serve as a lens focusing a numinous healing Power—but she is eventually forced to conclude that her performance is flawed. This is the only one of Sinclair's supernatural tales which seems unduly long-winded, perhaps because of its inflation for individual publication.

"The Finding of the Absolute" is a curious non-horrific *conte philosophique* whose academically-inclined male protagonist is allowed entry to a special Heaven reserved for philosophers, where he has a productive meeting with Immanuel Kant. Another custom-designed paradise is featured in "Heaven," the longest item in *The Intercessor*, which recapitulates and extends the theme of the weakest item in the first collection, "If the Dead Knew." Here a son who was the apple of his mother's eye is given posthumous entry into her ideal world, but finds it very uncongenial. His prayers for release are answered by a young woman whose love he could not answer in life—but, as in so many instances of similar release played out in the material world, he finds that his new paradise is under threat of becoming just as stifling as the old.

The excellent title-story of the second collection is a more orthodox, and more conventionally horrific, tale in which the ghost of a child serves as a lever to betray the awful legacy of guilt and hatreds which a family has long kept hidden. "The Villa Desire" is also a straightforward shocker, in which a young woman who plans to marry against the advice of her friends spends the night in the villa where her fiance's previous wife died of fright. Inevitably, she finds out why that tragedy occurred. The remaining tales, "The Mahatma's Story" and "Jones's Karma," are sarcastic fantasies making half-hearted use of devices casually borrowed from fashionable Eastern mysticism.

Although May Sinclair allegedly became a devout spiritualist, with an intense interest in psychic phenomena, her supernatural stories do not suffer the weakening effect which credulity usually produces. She was a feminist too, but one might have difficulty deducing that from the evidence of the supernatural fables which contemplate the ironically merited fates of unfulfilled women and cosseted men. Her novels are by no means unsubtle but they are considerably more robust in their exploration of feminist ideas and their pursuit of ideals. Comparison of her various works suggests that she probably employed her weird tales for mental relaxation, taking the opportunity to desist from propagandistic analysis and indulge in sardonic contemplation of the ideologically recalcitrant world. If so, she never allowed relaxation to encourage sloppiness; her supernatural tales are written with uncommon delicacy and precision, and they are among the most effective examples of their fugitive kind.

—Brian Stableford

SINGER, Isaac Bashevis

Nationality: American (originally Polish: immigrated to the United States, 1935; became citizen, 1943). **Born:** Icek-Hersz Zynger in Leoncin, Poland, 14 July 1904. **Education:** Religious primary schools in Radzymin and, from 1908, Warsaw, and schools in Bilgorny, 1917-20; Tachkemoni Rabbinical Seminary, Warsaw, 1921-22. **Family:** Married Alma Haimann in 1940; one son from earlier marriage. **Career:** Proofreader and translator, *Literarishe Bleter,* Warsaw, 1923-33; associate editor, *Globus,* Warsaw, 1933-35; journalist, *Vorwärts* (*Jewish Daily Forward*) Yiddish newspaper, New York, from 1935. Founder, *Svivah* literary magazine. **Awards:** Louis Lamed prize, 1950, 1956; American Academy grant, 1959; Daroff Memorial award, 1963; Foreign Book prize (France), 1965; two National Endowment for the Arts grants, 1966; Bancarella prize (Italy), 1968; Brandeis University Creative Arts award, 1969; National Book award, 1970, and for fiction, 1974; Association of Jewish Libraries Sydney Taylor award, 1971; Nobel Prize for Literature, 1978; Kenneth Smilen Present Tense award, 1980. D.H.L.: Hebrew Union College, Los Angeles, 1963; D.Litt.: Colgate University, Hamilton, New York, 1972; D.Litt.: Texas Christian University, Fort Worth, 1972; Ph.D.: Hebrew University, Jerusalem, 1973; D.Litt.: Bard College, Annandale-on-Hudson, New York, 1974; Long Island University, Greenvale, New York, 1979. **Member:** American Academy, 1965; American Academy of Arts and Sciences, 1969; Jewish Academy of Arts and Sciences; Polish Institute of Arts and Sciences. **Died:** 24 July 1991.

HORROR, GHOST AND GOTHIC PUBLICATIONS

Novels

Satan in Goray, translated by Jacob Sloan. New York, Farrar Straus, 1955; London, Owen, 1958.
The Magician of Lublin, translated by Elaine Gottlieb and Joseph Singer. New York, Farrar Straus, 1960; London, Secker and Warburg, 1961.
The Penitent. New York, Farrar Straus, 1983; London, Cape, 1984.

Short Stories

Gimpel the Fool and Other Stories, translated by Saul Bellow and others. New York, Farrar Straus, 1957; London, Owen, 1958.
The Spinoza of Market Street and Other Stories, translated by Elaine Gottlieb and others. New York, Farrar Straus, 1961; London, Secker and Warburg, 1962.
Short Friday and Other Stories, translated by Ruth Whitman and others. New York, Farrar Straus, 1964; London, Secker and Warburg, 1967.
The Séance and Other Stories, translated by Ruth Whitman and others. New York, Farrar Straus, 1968; London, Cape, 1970.
A Friend of Kafka and Other Stories, translated by the author and others. New York, Farrar Straus, 1970; London, Cape, 1972.
A Crown of Feathers and Other Stories, translated by the author and others. New York, Farrar Straus, 1973; London, Cape, 1974.
Passions and Other Stories. New York, Farrar Straus, 1975; London, Cape, 1976.
Old Love. New York, Farrar Straus, 1979; London, Cape, 1980.
The Image and Other Stories. New York, Farrar Straus, 1985; London, Cape, 1986.

Gifts. Philadelphia, Jewish Publication Society, 1985.
The Death of Methuselah and Other Stories. New York, Farrar Straus, and London, Cape, 1988.

Fiction for Children (translated by the author and Elizabeth Shub)

Zlateh the Goat and Other Stories, illustrated by Maurice Sendak. New York, Harper, 1966; London, Longman, 1970.
Mazel and Shlimazel; or, The Milk of a Lioness, illustrated by Margot Zemach. New York, Farrar Straus, 1967; London, Cape, 1979.
The Fearsome Inn, illustrated by Nonny Hogrogian. New York, Scribner, 1967; London, Collins, 1970.
When Shlemiel Went to Warsaw and Other Stories, translated by Channah Kleinerman-Goldstein and others, illustrated by Margot Zemach. New York, Farrar Straus, 1968; London, Longman, 1974.
Joseph and Koza; or, The Sacrifice to the Vistula, illustrated by Symeon Shimin. New York, Farrar Straus, 1970; London, Hamish Hamilton, 1984.
Alone in the Wild Forest, illustrated by Margot Zemach. New York, Farrar Straus, 1971; Edinburgh, Canongate, 1980.
The Topsy-Turvy Emperor of China, illustrated by William Pène du Bois. New York, Harper, 1971.
The Fools of Chem and Their History, illustrated by Uri Shulevitz. New York, Farrar Straus, 1973.
A Tale of Three Wishes, illustrated by Irene Lieblich. New York, Farrar Straus, 1976.
Naftali the Storyteller and His Horse, Sus, and Other Stories, translated by the author and others, illustrated by Margot Zemach. New York, Farrar Straus, 1976; London, Oxford University Press, 1977.
The Power of Light: Eight Stories for Hanukkah, illustrated by Irene Lieblich. New York, Farrar Straus, 1980; London, Robson, 1983.
The Golem, illustrated by Uri Shulevitz. New York, Farrar Straus, 1982; London, Deutsch, 1983.
Stories for Children. New York, Farrar Straus, 1984.
Meshugah, translated by the author and Nili Wachtel. New York, Farrar Straus, 1994.
Shrewd Todie and Lyzer the Miser and Other Children's Stories, illustrated by Margot Zemach. Boston, Barefoot Books, 1994.

OTHER PUBLICATIONS

Novels

The Family Moskat, translated by A. H. Gross. New York, Knopf, 1950; London, Secker and Warburg, 1966.
The Slave, translated by the author and Cecil Hemley. New York, Farrar Straus, 1962; London, Secker and Warburg, 1963.
The Manor, translated by Elaine Gottlieb and Joseph Singer. New York, Farrar Straus, 1967; London, Secker and Warburg, 1968.
The Estate, translated by Joseph Singer, Elaine Gottlieb, and Elizabeth Shub. New York, Farrar Straus, 1969; London, Cape, 1970.
Enemies: A Love Story, translated by Aliza Shevrin and Elizabeth Shub. New York, Farrar Straus, and London, Cape, 1972.
Shosha, translated by Joseph Singer. New York, Farrar Straus, 1978; London, Cape, 1979.
Reaches of Heaven. New York, Farrar Straus, 1980; London, Faber, 1982.

King of the Fields. New York, Farrar Straus, 1988; London, Cape, 1989.
Scum, translated by Rosaline D. Schwartz. New York, Farrar Straus, and London, Cape, 1991.

Short Stories

Selected Short Stories, edited by Irving Howe. New York, Modern Library, 1966.
The Collected Stories. New York, Farrar Straus, and London, Cape, 1982.

Plays

The Mirror (produced New Haven, Connecticut, 1973).
Shlemiel the First (produced New Haven, Connecticut, 1974).
Yentl, The Yeshiva Boy, with Leah Napolin, adaptation of a story by Singer (produced New York, 1974). New York, French, 1979.
Teibele and Her Demon, with Eve Friedman (produced Minneapolis, 1978; New York, 1979). New York and London, French, 1984.
A Play for the Devil (based on his short story "The Unseen," produced in New York City at the Folksbiene Theatre, 1984).

Other

In My Father's Court (autobiography), translated by Channah Kleinerman-Goldstein and others. New York, Farrar Straus, 1966; London, Secker and Warburg, 1967.
An Isaac Bashevis Singer Reader. New York, Farrar Straus, 1971.
The Hasidim: Paintings, Drawings, and Etchings, with Ira Moskowitz. New York, Crown, 1973.
Love and Exile: The Early Years: A Memoir. New York, Doubleday, 1984; London, Cape, 1985.
A Little Boy in Search of God: Mysticism in a Personal Light, illustrated by Ira Moskowitz. New York, Doubleday, 1976.
A Young Man in Search of Love, translated by Joseph Singer. New York, Doubleday, 1978.
Lost in America, translated by Joseph Singer. New York, Doubleday, 1981.
Nobel Lecture. New York, Farrar Straus, and London, Cape, 1979.
Isaac Bashevis Singer on Literature and Life: An Interview, with Paul Rosenblatt and Gene Koppel. Tucson, University of Arizona Press, 1979.
The Meaning of Freedom. West Point, New York, United States Military Academy, 1981.
My Personal Conception of Religion. Lafayette, University of Southwestern Louisiana Press, 1982.
One Day of Happiness. New York, Red Ozier Press, 1982.
Conversations with Isaac Bashevis Singer, with Richard Burgin. New York, Doubleday, 1985.
The Safe Deposit and Other Stories about Grandparents, Old Lovers and Crazy Old Men ("Masterworks of Modern Jewish Writing" series), edited by Kerry M. Orlitzky. Princeton, New Jersey, Wiener, Markus, 1989.
The Certificate, translated by Leonard Wolf. New York, Farrar Straus, 1992.

Editor, with Elaine Gottlieb, *Prism 2.* New York, Twayne, 1965.

Translator, *Pan,* by Knut Hamsun. Vilna, Kletzkian, 1928.
Translator, *Di Vogler* (The Vagabonds), by Knut Hamsun. Vilna, Kletzkian, 1928.

Translator, *In Opgrunt Fun Tayve* (In Passion's Abyss), by Gabriele D'Annunzio. Warsaw, Goldfarb, 1929.
Translator, *Mete Trap* (Mette Trap), by Karin Michäelis. Warsaw, Goldfarb, 1929.
Translator, *Roman Rolan* (Romain Rolland), by Stefan Zweig. Warsaw, Bikher, 1929.
Translator, *Viktorya* (Victoria), by Knut Hamsun. Vilna, Kletzkian, 1929.
Translator, *Oyfn Mayrev-Front Keyn Nayes* (All Quiet on the Western Front), by Erich Maria Remarque. Vilna, Kletzkian, 1930.
Translator, *Der Tsoyberbarg* (The Magic Mountain), by Thomas Mann. Vilna, Kletzkian, 4 vols., 1930.
Translator, *Der Veg oyf Tsurik* (The Road Back), by Erich Maria Remarque. Vilna, Kletzkian, 1931.
Translator, *Araber: Folkstimlekhe Geshikhtn* (Arabs: Stories of the People), by Moshe Smilansky. Warsaw, Farn Folk, 1932.
Translator, *Fun Moskve biz Yerusholayim* (From Moscow to Jerusalem), by Leon S. Glaser. New York, Jankowitz, 1938.

Other for Children (translated by the author and Elizabeth Shub)

A Day of Pleasure: Stories of a Boy Growing Up in Warsaw (autobiographical), translated by Channah Kleinerman-Goldstein and others, photographs by Roman Vishniac. New York, Farrar Straus, 1969; London, MacRae, 1980.
Elijah the Slave: A Hebrew Legend Retold, illustrated by Antonio Frasconi. New York, Farrar Straus, 1970.
The Wicked City, illustrated by Leonard Everett Fisher. New York, Farrar Straus, 1972.
Why Noah Chose the Dove, illustrated by Eric Carle. New York, Farrar Straus, 1974.

*

Bibliography: by Bonnie Jean M. Christensen, in *Bulletin of Bibliography 26* (Boston), January-March, 1969; *A Bibliography of Isaac Bashevis Singer 1924-1949* by David Neal Miller, Bern, Switzerland and New York, Lang, 1983.

Manuscript Collection: Butler Library, Columbia University, New York.

Critical Studies (selection): *Isaac Bashevis Singer and the Eternal Past* by Irving Buchen, New York, New York University Press, 1968; *The Achievement of Isaac Bashevis Singer* edited by Marcia Allentuck, Carbondale, Southern Illinois University Press, 1969; *Critical Views of Isaac Bashevis Singer* edited by Irving Malin, New York, New York University Press, 1969, and *Isaac Bashevis Singer* by Malin, New York, Ungar, 1972; *Isaac Bashevis Singer* by Ben Siegel, Minneapolis, University of Minnesota Press, 1969; *Isaac Bashevis Singer and His Art* by Askel Schiotz, New York, Harper, 1970; *Isaac Bashevis Singer, The Magician of West 86th Street* by Paul Kresh, New York, Dial Press, 1979; *The Brothers Singer* by Clive Sinclair, London, Allison and Busby, 1983; *Fear of Fiction: Narrative Strategies in the Works of Isaac Bashevis Singer* by David Neal Miller, Albany, State University of New York Press, 1985, and *Recovering the Canon: Essays on Isaac Bashevis Singer* edited by Miller, Leiden, Brill, 1986; *From Exile to Redemption: The Fiction of Isaac Bashevis Singer* by Grace Farrell Lee, Carbondale, Southern Illinois University Press, 1987;

Understanding Isaac Bashevis Singer by Lawrence S. Friedman, Columbia, South Carolina University Press, 1988.

*   *   *

It is difficult to separate Singer's horror from the rest of his work, because the supernatural pervades his writing as it does the culture that he's writing about. He draws upon a rich mix of the *Talmud*, of storytelling, and of demons and golems lurking in the interstices of society, yet only a few of his works have been written with the supernatural elements dominant.

Singer's father and grandfather were both Hasidic rabbis and he was educated at the Warsaw Rabbinical Seminary. His mother had a somewhat rationalistic or even sceptical outlook, however, and had a strong influence on Singer's upbringing due to his father being away much of the time with his religious duties. This contrast and conflict between traditional religious belief and secular, rationalist thought pervades much of his writing. Satan is often the narrator in Singer's stories, but Satan might also be seen as an *alter ego* of Singer himself, standing apart from his society and religion and conducting experiments with human weakness.

Left to himself much of the time, the young Singer taught himself Polish and German to put a broader selection of literature within his reach, and went on to read the likes of Dostoevsky and Poe. When his grandfather died his mother dreamed that it had happened, and this demonstration of the supernatural by his otherwise rationalist mother affected Singer deeply. He began studies in the mystical Cabbala, and this eventually led to his first novel, *Satan in Goray*. In 1935 he moved to America, correctly judging that Hitler's vow to eliminate all European Jews was not just empty political rhetoric. Singer adjusted to the change of language and culture with some difficulty, and it was only in the 1940s that he made a serious return to writing.

Singer's horror generally features a combination of rich social and religious detail contrasted with the behaviour of his characters when breaches are made in their social fabric. *Satan in Goray* follows these themes, and in this book Singer weaves a rich and detailed tapestry of 17th-century Jewish and village life, and contrasts it against a story of possession and exorcism. In 1648 a Cossack horde attack and lays waste Goray, inflicting hideous atrocities on its people. Nearly two decades later the survivors have returned and the commerce and routines of the town are being restored. This is only a facade, however, as the credibility and authority of the traditional leaders has been severely undermined by the years of exile and the trauma of the Cossack slaughter. Into this unstable society comes Sabbatai Zevi, Singer's false Messiah. With their social and religious underpinnings disrupted, many in Goray are tempted into assorted desecrations, sexual excesses and flagrant violations of religious law. A crippled girl named Rechele undergoes demonic possession and begins to speak prophecy. Even the facade of normal village life begins to break down, as shopkeepers and artisans abandon their trades. The Messiah's sect battles the established religious authorities, children rebel against parents, and finally Rechele is impregnated by Satan. Reb Mordecai Joseph finally drives the demonic spirit out of her, but she sickens and dies within a few days. Although the horror, such as Rechele vomiting reptiles and pulling stones and worms out of suppurating ulcers, is quite unsettling, it is the solid characterization of the people conjured by Singer that gives his depictions of the horrific a very disturbing tinge of realism. Like *Lord of the Flies*, indeed like much of science fiction, *Satan in Goray* main-

tains that a great deal of what we see as personal identity extends no further down than the society in which we live.

Many of Singer's works were more Gothic than horrific, and a substantial part of his output was for children. *The Golem* could be described as a Gothic children's novel, and is one of Singer's better-known children's books. Set in Prague during the reign of Emperor Rudolph II, its religious and historical detail is almost at the level seen in *Satan in Goray*. The Jews of the city are accused of murdering a Christian girl to use her blood in Passover matzohs. The cabbalist Rabbi Leib constructs a golem, a clay giant, then animates it by inscribing a holy name on its forehead. It finds the girl alive and so destroys the case against the city's Jews, but Rabbi Leib is compelled to keep the golem animate for too long. As it becomes more self-aware it grows rebellious and destructive. Finally it commits the very human act of drinking to excess and Rabbi Leib erases the holy name from its forehead as it lies in a stupor. The theme of the humanizing of a human creation can be found in works ranging from *Frankenstein* to *Terminator 2*, except that clay golems are not experiments gone wrong but established cabbalistic "technology," a divine resource for times of trouble. The moral is a mirror image of that in *Satan in Goray*, for here we have a stable society confronting a being that is dangerous because it lacks socialization.

Singer's short fiction (he had over 150 stories published) is tight and often compelling, and as a result he gained an unusually large American following for someone who could be labelled both European and literary. There are demons, sprites, ghosts and other such supernatural elements in many of his stories, but they are primarily used as a foil for Singer's characters. Thus in "Henne Fire," Henne's blazing and ill-restrained temper (one wonders who might have been the model for her!) causes real fires, and eventually consumes Henne as well. Remove the fire theme and Henne is still there, unrestrained and self-destructive. "A Wedding in Brownsville" has a man meet his former lover at a wedding, yet he suddenly remembers that she is long dead. Has he died as well, was it all an unusually realistic dream, or has he brushed against some reality where she did not die?

Singer's American and Yiddish-American characters are vivid and familiar, yet they often move against a background legacy of Eastern European folklore, history and religion which gives them exotic appeal. In 1978 he won the Nobel Prize for Literature, the same year that his story "A Party in Miami Beach" appeared in *Playboy*! While his mainstream writing about mid-European Jewish life and his own family probably weighed more heavily with the Nobel committee than his horror, he nevertheless brought the same skills to bear in all his writing. As a consequence his horror is of a very high standard, both in terms of accessibility and content. It is worth noting that Singer wrote primarily in Yiddish, but also supervised the translation of his works into English and considered the results to be original works in their own right.

—Steven Paulsen and Sean McMullen

SIODMAK, Curt

Nationality: American. **Born:** Kurt Siodmak, Dresden, Germany, 10 August 1902; brother of the film director Robert Siodmak. **Education:** University of Zurich, Ph.D. 1927. **Family:** Married Henrietta De Perrot in 1931; one son. **Career:** Railroad engineer and factory worker; journalist in Berlin; screenwriter and film director: worked for Gaumont British, 1931-37, and in the United States after 1937. **Awards:** Bundespreis, for film, 1964. Lives in Three Rivers, California.

HORROR, GHOST AND GOTHIC PUBLICATIONS

Novels (series: Dr. Patrick Cory in all titles)

Donovan's Brain. New York, Knopf, 1943; London, Chapman and Hall, 1944.
Hauser's Memory. New York, Putnam, 1968; London, Jenkins, 1969.
Gabriel's Body. New York, Leisure, 1992.

Plays

Screenplays: *The Invisible Man Returns,* with Lester Cole and Joe May, 1940; *The Ape,* with Richard Carroll, 1940; *Black Friday,* with Eric Taylor, 1940; *The Wolf Man,* with Gordon Kann, 1940; *The Invisible Woman,* with others, 1941; *The Invisible Agent,* 1942; *I Walked with a Zombie,* with Ardel Wray and Inez Wallace, 1943; *Frankenstein Meets the Wolf Man,* 1943; *Son of Dracula,* with Eric Taylor, 1943; *House of Frankenstein,* with Edward T. Lowe, 1944; *The Climax,* with Lynn Starling, 1944; *The Beast with Five Fingers,* with Harold Goldman, 1947; *Bride of the Gorilla,* 1951; *The Magnetic Monster,* with Ivan Tors, 1953; *Creature with the Atom Brain,* 1955; *Curucu, Beast of the Amazon,* 1956; *Love Slaves of the Amazon,* 1957; *The Devil's Messenger,* 1962; *Sherlock Holmes and the Deadly Necklace,* 1962.

OTHER PUBLICATIONS

Novels

Schluss in Tonfilmatelier. Berlin, Scherl, 1930.
F.P.1. Antwortet Nicht. Berlin, Keils, 1931; translated by H. W. Farrell as *F.P.1. Does Not Reply,* Boston, Little, Brown, 1933; as *F.P.1 Fails to Reply,* London, Collins, 1933.
Stadt Hinter Hebeln: Roman. Salzburg, Berglund, 1931.
Die Madonna aus der Markusstrasse. Leipzig, Goldmann, 1932.
Rache im Ather. Leipzig, Goldmann, 1932.
Bis ans Ende der Welt. Leipzig, Goldmann, 1933.
Die Macht im Dunkeln. Zurich, Morgarten, 1937.
Whomsoever I Shall Kiss. New York, Crown, 1952.
Skyport. New York, Crown, 1959.
For Kings Only. New York, Crown, 1961.
The Third Ear. New York, Putnam, 1971.
City in the Sky. New York, Putnam, 1974; London, Barrie and Jenkins, 1975.

Plays

Screenplays: *Menschen am Sonntag (People on Sunday)* (documentary), with Billy Wilder, 1929; *Le Bal,* 1931; *Der Mann der Seinen Mörder Sucht (Looking for His Murderer),* 1931; *F.P.1 Antwortet Nicht,* 1933; *La Crise est Finie,* 1934; *Girls Will Be Boys,* with Clifford Grey and Roger Burford, 1934; *I Give*

My Heart, with others, 1935; *The Tunnel (Transatlantic Tunnel),* with L. DuGarde Peach and Clemence Dane, 1935; *It's a Bet,* with Frank Miller and L. DuGarde Peach, 1935; *Non-Stop New York,* with others, 1937; *Her Jungle Love,* with others, 1938; *Pacific Blackout,* with others, 1941; *Aloma of the South Seas,* with others, 1941; *Midnight Angel,* with others, 1941; *London Blackout Murders,* 1942; *The Mantrap,* 1943; *False Faces,* 1943; *The Purple "V,"* with Bertram Millhauser, 1943; *Frisco Sal,* with Gerald Geraghty, 1945; *Shady Lady,* with others, 1945; *The Return of Monte Cristo,* with others, 1946; *Berlin Express,* with Harold Medford, 1948; *Tarzan's Magic Fountain,* with Harry Chandler, 1949; *Four Days Leave,* with others, 1950; *Riders to the Stars,* 1954; *Earth vs. the Flying Saucers,* with George Worthing Yates and Raymond Marcus, 1956; *Lightship,* 1963; *Ski Fever,* with Robert Joseph, 1967.

Television Plays: *13 Demon Street* series, 1959 (Sweden).

*

Film Adaptations: *F.P.1. Antwortet Nicht,* 1932; *The Lady and the Monster,* 1943, *Donovan's Brain,* 1953, *Vengeance,* 1963, all from the novel *Donovan's Brain; Hauser's Memory* (TV movie), 1970.

Theatrical Activities:
Director: **Films**—*Bride of the Gorilla,* 1951; *The Magnetic Monster,* 1953; *Curucu, Beast of the Amazon,* 1956; *Love Slaves of the Amazon,* 1957; *Ski Fever,* 1967.

*

Curt Siodmak comments:
  "Every night I say 'Heil Hitler!' . . . because without the son of a bitch I wouldn't be in Three Rivers, California. I'd still be in Berlin! . . . Dozens of my pictures still run on television and I don't get a penny out of it. But the guys [who made the money] are all dead and I'm still alive! So who's winning?" (Quoted by Stephen Jones in *The Illustrated Werewolf Movie Guide,* London, Titan, 1996).

*   *   *

Siodmak's two principal horror novels, *Donovan's Brain* and *Hauser's Memory,* concern a Dr. Patrick Cory, a researcher in the biochemistry of the brain. The latter novel should be a sequel, yet it makes no reference to the events of the first novel, and Cory's character and private life are significantly different between the two. The one factor which does link the novels closely is that they have an almost identical plot premise: that one man's mind can, effectively, be taken over by another's. Neither novel contains more than slight horror elements, and yet the first formed the basis of a number of horror movies.

Donovan's Brain is set in the United States during the 1940s, when science was less well developed and all men wore hats. Cory is a reclusive "backyard" researcher in rural Arizona. He is obsessed with brain research and treats his wife, Janice, like an unpaid servant, never considering her feelings or touching her body; he is a young man almost devoid of emotion.

When a light aircraft crashes a few miles away, the local doctor is drunk and Cory goes to help the injured. One man is dying, but

Cory secretly removes the man's brain and succeeds in keeping it alive. He is helped by the local doctor, an elderly alcoholic named Schratt. The news breaks that the dead man was W. H. Donovan, a millionaire businessman who has made his money through a mail-order corporation. Cory drives to Phoenix to explain to the authorities how he tried to help Donovan (including amputating his shattered legs), but nothing is said about the brain cavity being empty except for cotton wool. Cory even meets Donovan's son and daughter, who thank him for his attempts and are anxious to know if their father said anything before he died. Nothing that made any sense, is Cory's reply.

The truth is that the brain remains alive in a glass bowl, connected to an encephalograph. When Cory taps on the glass, the brain reacts slightly, and he spends weeks trying to communicate by tapping in morse code. He tries to increase the brain's electrical output by overfeeding it. The brain grows larger and there seem to be positive results, as Cory finds his own left hand writing Donovan's signature.

Gradually the brain becomes able to control Cory's actions, with Cory just an observer. So Donovan/Cory draws money from secret bank accounts in Los Angeles, trying to right some of the wrongs Donovan has done in his life. In particular, he has Cory contact Sternli, his long-term secretary. One at a time, Cory takes up some of Donovan's habits, including smoking a particular brand of cigar and walking with a limp. Donovan's daughter notices this. She and Sternli tell Cory of Donovan's ruthlessness in business and lack of concern for people.

In a melodramatic climax, Schratt manages to kill the brain; it kills him, too. But Cory survives and is gratified that his experiment has been a success. He even gets back together with his wife at the end.

The plot is fast-paced, made to seem even more so by the diary format of Cory's narration, despite some events seeming too contrived. All the characters are odd, most seeming to lack emotions, though this is probably a result of Siodmak's failings as an author rather than a deliberate effect. Donovan as a person is monstrous and inhuman, so his controlling of Cory (also lacking in humanity) seems just and thus less horrifying than it might have been. There are problems of logic and scientific accuracy, though this has not affected the book's commercial success; it has been filmed three times.

The Dr. Cory of *Hauser's Memory* is a Nobel prizewinner, a senior researcher at a United States laboratory and one of the top experts on RNA. He is approached by a CIA agent who asks him to carry out a tricky RNA experiment. A German missile scientist working for the Russians has defected but has been shot during his escape and is in a coma, dying. This is the Hauser of the title. Cory's task is to transfer the man's RNA into another person and see if the vital information in the man's memory is also passed on. The setting is the late 1960s, when the Cold War was at its height.

Cory has been intending to inject himself with the RNA, but one of his assistants, Dr. Hillel Mondoro, injects himself first. The horror content of this novel, as with *Donovan's Brain*, stems from the way in which one man's personality can take over and control another's. Here, Hauser dies soon after the RNA is taken, but he lives on in Mondoro, sometimes controlling and sometimes not.

The rest of the plot (the bulk of the book) consists of Hauser/Mondoro flying to Europe and trying to repay those who have injured or helped him (a very similar motive to Donovan). He gets money out of Van Kungen, a Dane who betrayed him to the Na-

zis, and who collapses and dies from the shock. He tries to give the money to his estranged wife in Berlin, but she refuses it, as does his son who is living in East Berlin. Later he manages to kill the German general who had him castrated in 1944. But surrounding these events is the most ludicrous spy plot, with agents and double-agents revealing themselves every chapter or two in attempts to capture or free Hauser/Mondoro and also Cory, who has joined him in Europe. The CIA and Hauser's Russian bosses are also sporadically present.

The best parts of the novel are the atmospheric descriptions and small details of European cities, especially East Berlin and Prague; also, Mondoro's random mood-swings, depending upon whether Hauser is in charge or not. In places the story descends into farce, especially when the Czechs agree to release Mondoro but only if they can separate Hauser's knowledge first.

Gabriel's Body is a little-known second "sequel," written very late in the author's career, and is more of a medical thriller than a horror novel. *Donovan's Brain* apart, Siodmak's most notable contributions to the horror-and-gothic genre have been his many screenplays for Hollywood horror movies. Some of these were ultra-cheap productions, best forgotten, but among his more notable screenplays are *The Wolf Man*, which did much to establish Hollywood werewolf lore, the atmospheric *I Walked with a Zombie* and the memorable *The Beast with Five Fingers* (from W. F. Harvey's short story).

—Chris Morgan

SKAL, David J.

Nationality: American. **Born:** 1952. **Career:** Novelist and critic. Lives in New York City.

HORROR, GHOST AND GOTHIC PUBLICATIONS

Novels

Scavengers. New York, Pocket, 1980.
When We Were Good. New York, Pocket, 1981.
Antibodies. New York, Congdon and Weed, 1988.

Other

Hollywood Gothic: The Tangled Web of "Dracula" from Novel to Stage to Screen. New York, Norton, and London, Deutsch, 1990.
The Monster Show: A Cultural History of Horror. New York, Norton, 1992; London, Plexus, 1993.
Dark Carnival: The Secret World of Tod Browning, Hollywood's Master of the Macabre, with Elias Savada. N.p., 1995.
V is for Vampire: An A-Z Guide to Everything Undead. New York, Plume, and London, Robson, 1996.
Screams of Reason: Mad Science and Modern Culture. N.p., 1996.

Editor, *Dracula: The Ultimate Illustrated Edition of the World-Famous Vampire Play.* N.p., 1993.
Editor, with Nina Auerach. *Dracula,* by Bram Stoker. New York, Norton, 1997.

*   *   *

To date, the writing career of David J. Skal has been made up of two distinct halves: the early novels that were published when the author was in his 30s, and the later non-fiction tomes. In ambitiously microscopic detail the later books, especially *Hollywood Gothic* and *The Monster Show*, analyze the cinematic interpretations of various horror myths (that of Dracula being an obvious authorial favourite); *The Monster Show* and *Hollywood Gothic* reveal how stories such as *Dracula* have affected the shape and attitudes of the 20th century, while, at a more local level, affecting the lives of the actors and directors who have taken on the challenges inherent in re-evaluating familiar tales. If it is true that the novels display Skal's healthy knowledge and appreciation of the then-current science-fiction and horror genres, it is also the case that not until the non-fiction appears do we get a clear picture of quite how much this man knows about these same genres' histories.

The novels are *Scavengers*, *When We Were Good* and *Antibodies*, and are linked, it seems, in one way only: they are written in a style that seems fresh and resilient. The writing is also a little distant and cold—deliberately so, we might assume, given that the non-fiction is written with warmth and exuberance. Skal's novels are hybrids of science fiction and horror. Not so much the overlap into which falls the paranoid consciousness of a writer like Christopher Hyde, who points to the horrific possibilities of extrapolating today's scientific applications; more the presentation of paranoia that has been made famous by Philip K. Dick or William Gibson, among others. With Dick, with Gibson, and of course with Skal, the scientific possibilities are presented as realities; all that is left to discuss is the horror. In the same way that the ancient genre of the pastoral is really a comment on town-life and not on the haywains and shepherds it purports to be fascinated by, science fiction can be read as social commentary: current social commentary. It is work set in the future that looks, subtextually, at today. With a nod to the burgeoning cyberpunk movement of the 1980s, *Scavengers*, for example, is concerned with memory-transfer and *Antibodies* takes the phrase "artificial limb" into new territories.

Antibodies is part of a series headed "Isaac Asimov Presents . . ." and in an introduction Asimov appears in the same way that Alfred Hitchcock used to appear on our screens before the evening's half-hour mystery. Having mentioned both Pinocchio and the Tin Man, he asks: "would human beings be content to have their body supplemented or even replaced by mechanical analogs?"—and indeed this is the subject-matter of Skal's novel.

In her job working for a department store, Diandra has become dissatisfied and wishes to partake of the services of Marin County's Resurrection House. Then there is Leah, an obnoxious talk-show host, who drum-rolls her next guest thus: "But first, I'll introduce you to a man who has been called 'The Rod Serling of Psychotherapy' and who has brought to light a truly chilling twilight zone of mental disorder and who has stirred up a lot of people in the process." Ontological insecurity is of course one of the novel's horror themes. The robopaths (a.k.a the antibodies of the title) believe, post-surgery, that they are more like machines than humans—a syndrome that Julian Nagy, the executive director and founder of the Resurrection House, sees as a perfectly logical reaction to living in the novel's proposed technological society. (If this rationale is not enough to make the reader doubt Nagy's own peace of mind, there is also the evidence of Nagy's surreptitious beneath-the-table self-abuse session while he is on the TV show—orgasming on prime-time while Leah pretends not

to notice). Organ donation is propounded as the next evolutionary step for the human race. America is in the grip of a fever of wish-fulfilment; medical staffs have to become resistant to "the phenomenon of ghoulish groupies, offering themselves as high-tech guinea pigs." A former Cybernetic Temple member makes a deposition, as follows: "Born meat, die meat—that was the worst thing you could possibly say to another person." On the one hand, *Antibodies* can be read as a piece of entertainment, in the mould of the H. P. Lovecraft-inspired movie *Reanimator*; on the other hand, there are a host of inferences to be made—the novel is a critique of faddishness, of religion, and of course, of cosmetic surgery.

Then, in the 1990s, David Skal's large non-fiction projects, his labours of love, proudly arrived in a fanfare of praise. Arguably, an author reveals himself more frequently and more thoroughly in a book of non-fiction than in a work of fiction: reveals his prejudices, preferences, maybe even his bigotries. The simple fact that a non-fiction author has chosen to write an entire book on a subject suggests that he has a strong emotion—be it fascination, be it abhorrence—for the topic in question. Skal's passion, given this, is horror movies. It is an all-consuming passion too. The credits lists alone are encyclopedic, suggesting that a great deal of work went into the successful deliveries of these texts.

Hollywood Gothic opens with a scene from a production (any production) of *Dracula*, and then mentions the audience's participation in horror stories. The black-caped vampire is now an instantly recognized figure, for the movie-goer in general as potent a symbol as the silhouette of Batman's template against the sky, or more sinisterly, the Swastika. Skal's book describes how the vampire image has come to be so readily recognizable. Any interpretation of *Dracula* comes now with a sense of symbol identification, a built-in response that can be triggered in the audience; just as the viewer gets from the Coca Cola symbol the understanding of simple thirst-control, or from the Batman symbol the idea of safety tinted by fear, with the Dracula symbol the viewer has the impression of power that can only be retained by constant sustenance. We all know, therefore, that vampires can be destroyed, and how they can be destroyed; but the Dracula image was not always like this. Max Schreck as the vampire in *Nosferatu* appeared as a variety of human vermin, which came partly from Bram Stoker's original novel and partly from universal fears; the switch to the "elegant, evening-clothed *blutsaugers* who were to come" is provided in detail.

But Skal's skill as a non-fiction writer is akin to his skill as a writer of fiction: it is to inform without overburdening. If anything, the "tangled web of *Dracula* from novel to stage to screen" is such a rich and unpredictable narrative that it reads like a horror story in itself; Skal's non-fiction is like a novel, right down to the official Dracula casualty-list. Helen Chandler, for example, a New York stage performer in the 1920s, took to cocktails of booze and sleeping pills; by 1940 she was safely locked up in a sanitarium; in 1950 she burned her face, arms and upper body as a result of drinking and smoking, and in 1965 she died, a victim of her own and Dracula's success. There is a neat chronology of vampires at the end of the book for easy reference.

While ostensibly ranging wider than *Hollywood Gothic* for its material, *The Monster Show* still clearly has its heroes—or, more specifically, its anti-heroes. The book is subtitled "A Cultural History of Horror," which is in fact misleading. *The Monster Show* does not deal with literature, so perhaps "a cinematic history" might have been more appropriate. The book begins this century, with one of its key players: Diane Arbus, a photographer who captured some of the scenes in a real-life New York 42nd Street freak show, a woman who was always "striving for and achieving an unflinching catalog of images previously forbidden or deliberately overlooked . . . The deformed. The retarded. The sexually ambiguous. The dying and the dead." Arbus appealed to a notion of voyeurism, as indeed does Skal by remarking on her, and as indeed do we by reading Skal. It was Arbus's ambition to show "the things people wanted to look at, but had been taught they must not." She gained notoriety by photographing the ageing Mae West and her monkey, whose feces had been ground into the bedroom's white carpet. Diane Arbus understood that there are monsters everywhere, and understood what Skal's Chapter One calls "Tod Browning's America." What David Skal has done with this book is to examine the events that led to some of the more unpleasant/brilliant works of photography and cinema this century, and Browning receives many an honorary mention in the book.

Initially the horror story surrounding Tod Browning is one of creative repression. Clearly one of Skal's favourite *auteurs*, Tod Browning was the dypsomaniacal genius-weirdo behind such movies as *Freaks*, which used for its cast real-life "human oddities" (to quote Tom Waits, who used the film for inspiration for his song "Lucky Day (Overture)"). Browning wrote and directed a movie that was so ahead of its time that he was regarded with some disdain from that time on, well into his legendarily reclusive period. The movie is truly horrible and truly brilliant, as Skal is at pains to persuade; a movie which had to fight for its own existence. The "original negative, one legend had it, had been dumped unceremoniously into San Francisco bay." "Tod Browning's America" gives Browning sole charge of a slice of Amercian Pie that quite frankly others might have found too bitter or too cold. The biography of Browning is illuminating in itself: his obsession with carnivals, wild men, geeks (who were usually brain-damaged alcoholics, known to bite the heads off small creatures for the prize of a bottle of liquor), vaudeville, and carnival barkers. This section of the book is so strange that, as happened in *Hollywood Gothic*, it reads like fiction: it resembles Peter Carey's *The Unusual Life of Tristan Smith*, for example, or Angela Carter's *Nights at the Circus*.

The history of the 20th century has fallen into neat chapters for Skal, or so he makes it seem, to his credit. Tod Browning appears often, and the passages that deal with his alcoholic fall from grace and his blacklisting in Hollywood are particularly poignant, as are his failure with an adaptation of *Dracula*, which presumably is close to Skal's heart. It is interesting to note that in the conflicting reports of how much money Browning made, one figure had his salary at $150,000 in the late 1920s, twice what the President of the U.S. earned.

In the work of David J. Skal there is a great deal of humour and a great deal of sadness. "Drive-ins are a Ghoul's Best Friend" is one of the chapter titles in *The Monster Show*, for example. He is an excellent critic who comprehends the horror genre and knows its history in great detail. What he chooses to tackle next we can only guess at, but one thing is likely: that Skal will find angles and facts that even the most hardened fan had not known or considered before; and for this reason alone his books are important reflections on horror in the 20th century.

—David Mathew

SKIPP, John (M.), & Craig SPECTOR

Nationality: American. **Born:** Skipp: Milwaukee, Wisconsin, 1957; Spector: Richmond, Virginia, 16 July 1958. **Career:** Novelists and screenwriters, regularly working in collaboration from early in their careers until 1993.

HORROR, GHOST AND GOTHIC PUBLICATIONS

Novels

Fright Night (novelization of screenplay). New York, Tor, and London, Star, 1985.
The Light at the End. New York, Bantam, 1986.
The Cleanup. New York, Bantam, 1987.
The Scream. New York, Bantam, 1988.
Dead Lines. New York, Bantam, 1989.
The Bridge. New York, Bantam, 1991.
Animals. New York, Bantam, 1993.

Plays

Screenplays: *Class of 1999*, 1988, with others; *Nightmare on Elm Street 5: The Dream Child*, 1989, with others.

Other

Editors, *Book of the Dead.* New York, Bantam, 1989.
Editors, *Still Dead: Book of the Dead II.* New York, Bantam, 1992.

*   *   *

As modern horror fiction grew popular enough to command a large audience, it was natural that facets of the field take on distinct identities. Vampires quickly became a sub-genre of their own, psychological horror has blurred the distinction between itself and conventional thrillers and even incorporated some murder mysteries. Another group of writers chose a difference of style and method rather than subject matter. These writers, soon christened Splatterpunks, were determined to push to and beyond the limits of explicit gore and graphic violence, a trend that had already overwhelmed motion-picture horror. The writing team of John Skipp and Craig Spector was not only identified with this extreme movement but eventually became its most visible members, partly because most of their work fitted the description, but also because they vocally announced their conscious decision to exploit that portion of the reading public which craved this type of story.

Their first-published novel, *Fright Night*, was not a valid predictor of what was to come. It was the novelization of a better-than-average vampire movie, and it was a better-than-average novelization as well. But the struggle of a teenager to expose his neighbour as a vampire left little opportunity for the authors to improvise or to leave their distinct signature. *The Light at the End* was a very different case. Someone or something is murdering people in the Manhattan subway system, killing them brutally and horribly and without leaving any clues for the police. Although this is a vampire novel, with most of the traditional trappings of that form, Skipp and Spector take advantage of their unusual setting, the subway system, and several strongly developed characters to create a riveting thriller that feels like something new even when it isn't.

The Cleanup illustrates the point that absolute power corrupts absolutely. Billy Rowe is an unhappy, unsuccessful young man struggling to survive in the big city, whose life changes dramatically when he witnesses a murder. In the aftermath, he hears voices and sees creatures invisible to the rest of the world. The voices tell him he has the power to make a difference and he does, a one-man vigilante visiting terrible vengeance on muggers and other villains. But the exercise of power takes its toll on Billy, who becomes something less than human in the process. *The Scream* was even more intense and graphic. A demonic creature from Asia exerts influence in America, chiefly through a popular rock band. Perhaps more than anything else they wrote, *The Scream* illustrates why Skipp and Spector were called splatterpunks. Mutilated bodies, exploding heads, and similar carnage provide most of the impact of the novel. But it would be unfair to assume that this was meant to substitute for a strong story line. Although the novel's excesses are sometimes numbing rather than disturbing, the underlying plot is strong and suspenseful.

Dead Lines is labelled a novel, but it's actually a series of shorter pieces linked together by a frame story. The frame is that of a woman who rents a new apartment and finds several manuscripts left by a previous tenant, reportedly dead. As she reads them, she begins to feel influenced by the personality of their author. The frame is actually stronger than most of the subordinate pieces. With *The Bridge*, Skipp and Spector adopted a traditional science-fiction theme. An illegal toxic-waste disposal site brings together by chance a combination of substances that creates a new, mutated form of life. The new life form multiplies rapidly, spreading across the countryside in what might be the ultimate challenge to the human race because each of its parts is in communication with the Overmind of the whole. And once it has access to human intelligence, it can reason and plan.

Animals was the last novel by Skipp and Spector before they ended their partnership (but neither has subsequently produced a solo novel). The protagonist is on the rebound from a ruined love affair when he meets a mysterious and sexy woman who turns out to be a werewolf. That might not have been so bad except that she has a boyfriend, and he's a werewolf also, and jealous as well. The novel alternates between erotica and horror as we are introduced to a hidden culture which the authors have developed in great detail. It is one of the handful of good werewolf novels ever written, and in some ways the best of their books.

Skipp and Spector also edited two anthologies, *The Book of the Dead* and *Still Dead*, both set in the universe of George A. Romero's classic horror film, *The Night of the Living Dead*. They collaborated on several short pieces. "Meat Market" is about a particularly violent and unsettling sexual encounter. In "Gentlemen" a fairly considerate man is infected by something that seems to be a distillation of all those aspects of the macho image that are the most appalling. A prisoner inside his own body, the protagonist watches as the new personality systematically destroys the life of the woman he loves. Skipp collaborated with Marc Levinthal for "On a Big Night in Monster History," a very offbeat vampire tale. Other stories of note include "Not with a Whimper," "The Cool King," "Film at Eleven," "Go to Sleep" and "The Long Ride." It is unclear whether either Skipp or Spector will actively pursue a writing career separately now that they are no longer a team, and it is possible in any case that the vogue for their style of over-the-top graphic horror has passed.

—Don D'Ammassa

SLADE, Michael

Pseudonym for Jay Clarke and John Banks. **Nationality:** Canadian. **Career:** Criminal lawyers, turned novelists. Others who have contributed to books written under the joint pseudonym include Lee Clarke and Richard Covell. Clarke and Banks live in Vancouver.

HORROR, GHOST AND GOTHIC PUBLICATIONS

Novels

Headhunter. London, W. H. Allen, 1984; New York, Morrow, 1985.
Ghoul. New York, Morrow, 1987; London, New English Library, 1993.
Cut-Throat. New York, Signet, 1992; London, New English Library, 1993.
Ripper. New York, Signet, and London, Hodder and Stoughton, 1994.
Zombie. London, Hodder and Stoughton, 1996.

OTHER PUBLICATIONS

Novel

The Horses of Central Park. New York, Scholastic, 1992.

*   *   *

The borderline between horror and mystery novels and thrillers is often blurry, a distinction made even less consistent by marketing categories driven by the perception of changes in reading patterns. In recent years, a subset of suspense fiction has come to be associated with horror, primarily because of mood and technique rather than subject matter. Some of the most prominent writers to straddle this gap are Thomas Harris, William Goldman, Rex Miller and Michael Slade, all writers who use an atmosphere of horror to alter the detective story's mood from intellectual puzzle to emotional rollercoaster ride. Slade, unlike the other three, is not a single person but rather a collaborative effort by two Canadian lawyers whose *gestalt* is recognized as one of the most effective producers of over-the-top suspense.

Slade's debut novel was *Headhunter*. Robert DeClerq is a retired detective brought back to active duty when the Headhunter, a deranged serial killer, throws an entire city into near panic. The Headhunter concealed his early victims, but his pattern of activity has changed, and now he displays his decapitated trophies as publicly as possible. A nun is slaughtered and her head replaced with a pumpkin; another headless body is found crucified between two totem poles. Although most of the story is actually narrated as a very detailed police-procedural, the investigation is interspersed with flashbacks to the childhood of the killer, who was abused by both parents, and with glimpses of the Headhunter's current activities and delusions. The dark atmosphere is further emphasized by the suicidal urges of the man leading the investigation, whose family was murdered some years earlier, and the growing tensions among various of his subordinates. *Headhunter* is more successful as a mystery novel than as horror, but it's a superior work regardless of its label.

Ghoul is without question Slade's best work. This time the reader is presented with a flood of serial murderers. In London, the Vampire Killer kidnaps young girls and drains their blood, discarding the bodies into the Thames. Elsewhere in that same city Jack the Bomber is carrying on a one-man crusade against the gay community, and the Sewer Killer is using the city's extensive system of underground tunnels to move about and claim victims in bizarre ways borrowed from horror films. In Vancouver, Canada, a vicious professional killer vivisects and destroys the bodies of his victims.

The various killings and the desperate efforts of the police of two nations to bring the perpetrators to justice are wrapped around the story of a rich Rhode Island family subject to hereditary insanity and already the source of at least one unsuspected murder. The novel employs a variety of devices to conceal what's happening, including multiple impersonations, split personalities, and other twists and turns. What makes *Ghoul* of particular interest to horror readers is that the chief villain is such a profound fan of H. P. Lovecraft's fiction that he believes himself to be an inhuman ghoul, harbinger of the return of the Great Old Ones to our universe. Other horror themes include murder scenes borrowed from the film *The Birds* and elsewhere, a sequence in which one character is buried alive, the kidnapping and bizarre imprisonment of Siamese twins, and an extended discussion of the morality of horror in fiction and film. The climactic confrontation in the madman's repulsive private world is more horrifying than almost any scene involving supernatural creatures.

Cut-Throat is for the most part a much more conventional crime novel. Someone has murdered two judges, and various other characters are being systematically slaughtered by a gang of criminals from Hong Kong, all in preparation for the move of a major crime cartel from that city state to Canada. Slade unites the detectives from his first two novels as a team to track down the killers in a suspenseful novel that nods toward horror only in the last several chapters, when we learn that the cartel has developed an apparently genuine longevity drug by extracting a hormone from the brains of Abominable Snowmen.

Ripper, on the other hand, while still avoiding anything overtly supernatural, has several links to horror fiction. There's another serial killer at work, but this one seems to have borrowed his techniques from an obscure horror novel called *Jolly Roger*. The police try to track down the mysterious author, known only as Skull & Crossbones, but not even his publisher knows the true identity behind the pseudonym. Elsewhere, Skull and Crossbones are the nicknames of two professional killers, and one of the investigating officers has been lured to a remote mansion for what is supposed to be a playful charity weekend involving a staged murder. But Skull and Crossbones plan a more realistic experience, involving the death of everyone else on the island. One of the subplots involves the skull of a pre-hominid that disappeared during Custer's Last Stand. There are frequent references to the Tarot, some of the murders are designed to mimic the activities of Jack the Ripper, and there's a satanic cult involved which practises human sacrifice and the skinning of its victims, all devices common to the horror genre.

None of Michael Slade's novels were marketed as horror fiction, and there is nothing supernatural in any of them. They are, strictly speaking, detective stories. But if horror is a mood and technique rather than simply subject matter, then it is difficult to

imagine any author producing a more consistently and skilfully written series of horror novels. Slade's killers are invariably over-the-top, insane, perverse and highly dangerous. Even the murders that take place off-stage are designed to be blood-curdling, and the references to Lovecraft and other horror writers clearly indicate the authors' familiarity with their work.

—Don D'Ammassa

SLOANE, William M(illigan, III)

Pseudonym: William Milligan. **Nationality:** American. **Born:** Plymouth, Massachusetts, 15 August 1906. **Education:** Hill School, graduated, 1925; Princeton University, New Jersey, A.B. 1929 (Phi Beta Kappa). **Family:** Married Julie Hawkins in 1930; one son and two daughters. **Career:** Publisher: in play department, 1929-31, and editorial department, 1931, Longmans Green and Company; manager, Fitzgerald Publishing Company, 1932-37; associate editor, Farrar and Rinehart, 1937-38; manager of the trade department, 1939-46, and vice-president, 1944-46, Henry Holt and Company; president, William Sloane Associates, 1946-52; editorial director, Funk and Wagnalls Company and Wilfred Funk Inc., 1952-55; director, Rutgers University Press, 1955-74. Director, Council on Books in Wartime; chairman of the Editorial Committee, Armed Services Editions, 1943-44; staff member, Bread Loaf Writers Conference, 1946-72. President, Association of American University Presses, 1969-70. **Died:** 25 September 1974.

HORROR, GHOST AND GOTHIC PUBLICATIONS

Novels

To Walk the Night: A Novel. New York, Farrar and Rinehart, 1937; London, Barker, 1938; revised edition, New York, Dodd Mead, 1954.
The Edge of Running Water. New York, Farrar and Rinehart, 1939; London, Methuen, 1940; as *The Unquiet Corpse,* New York, Dell, 1956.
The Rim of Morning, Including The Edge of Running Water and To Walk the Night. New York, Dodd Mead, 1964.

Plays

Back Home: A Ghost Play in One Act. New York, Longman, 1931.
Runner in the Snow: A Play of the Supernatural in One Act, adaptation of the story "I Saw a Woman Turn into a Wolf" by W. B. Seabrook. Boston, Baker, 1931.

OTHER PUBLICATIONS

Plays

Digging Up the Dirt: A Comedy in Three Acts, adaptation of a play by Bert J. Norton. New York, Longman, 1931.
Crystal Clear: A Romance in One Act. New York, Longman, 1932.
Ballots for Bill: A Light-Hearted Comedy of Politics, with William Ellis Jones. New York, Fitzgerald, 1933.

The Silence of God: A Play for Christmas in One Act. Boston, Baker, 1933.

Art for Art's Sake. Boston, Baker, 1934.

The Invisible Clue (as William Milligan). New York, Fitzgerald, 1934.

Gold Stars for Glory. Boston, Baker, 1935.

Other

Editor, *Space, Space, Space: Stories about the Time When Men Will Be Adventuring to the Stars.* New York, Watts, 1953.

Editor, *Stories for Tomorrow: An Anthology of Modern Science Fiction.* New York, Funk and Wagnalls, 1954; London, Eyre and Spottiswoode, 1955.

*

Film Adaptation: *The Devil Commands*, 1942, from the novel *The Edge of Running Water.*

*   *   *

Although some of his early plays used supernatural motifs in a perfectly straightforward fashion, William Sloane's work gradually moved away from such imagery. *Runner in the Snow* is based on an account entitled "I Saw a Woman Turn into a Wolf" by the renowned traveller and collector of arcana William B. Seabrook, whose reportage evidently interested Sloane greatly, but his interest was that of the curious sceptic rather than the believer. Both of his mystery novels are carefully situated in the grey area where science fiction and supernatural fiction overlap, and the two anthologies which he was to edit in a later phase of his career were selections of science-fiction stories whose eclecticism testified to a strong personal interest in that genre. *To Walk the Night* is one of very few attempts made in the United States in the 1930s to employ science-fictional ideas in a literary novel—at a time when the genre was still (justly, alas) regarded as an unusually extravagant subspecies of pulp melodrama—but their combination with supernatural motifs with a mystery framework can by no means be dismissed as a marketing ploy; it is the very essence of the exercise.

The narrator of *To Walk the Night*, Berkeley Jones, is attempting to explain to the father of a close friend who has committed suicide exactly what happened in the months leading up to the tragedy. The heart of the mystery is Selena, the wife of the dead man, whose origin is left carefully unsettled. The title of the novel is taken from a reference in *Hamlet* to "a spirit doomed for an uncertain time to walk the night," and Selena certainly seems to have taken possession of someone else's body. She also seems to carry a curse of sorts, her first husband having perished in advance of Jones's friend, who was her second. Her name is suggestive of the moon, reputed in some mythological systems to be the abode of the dead—but both her husbands are physicists who have been working on a theory of time not unlike that popularized by J. W. Dunne, and it seems more likely to the similarly-inclined Jones that she is an alien of some kind, displaced from another dimension.

When she is finally confronted, Selena admits that she is indeed an emotionless superhuman being, and suggests—after the fashion of many an unmasked movie monster—that there is some

knowledge with which mere human beings cannot bear to live, but it is not at all clear that the admission is honest, or even that she knows what the truth is. The mystery remains a mystery, and the *femme fatale* preserves her tantalizing magic by retaining her sphinxian secret. The problem is that there are too many theories that fit the data, and that the data are unreliable in themselves.

In *The Edge of Running Water* Richard Sayles plays much the same role as Berkeley Jones. He is a physiological psychologist involved in research using electroencephalography, who is peremptorily summoned to the home of his former teacher, Julian Blair. Blair has been working in association with a spiritualist medium, Mrs. Walters, to perfect a device which can "tune in" to the electrical residues of souls, thus allowing the voices of the dead to be heard. Like Jones, Sayles has long nursed a suppressed passion for his friend's wife, but in this case the wife is dead and Sayles can transfer his infatuation to her sister Anne. Sayles and Anne try to persuade Blair to desist from his experiments, but his obsession is too fully developed; in the end he disappears into an avid black vortex whipped up by the machine.

As in the earlier novel Sloane is far to subtle to allow this standardized format simply to carry the customary moral that "there are things man was not meant to know." It is never established that Blair's machine really does what he thinks it does, nor is it clear whether the maelstrom of darkness that consumes him is the world of the dead or a doorway into another dimension. Like its predecessor, the novel is calculatedly unsettled and genuinely unsettling—although the movie version directed by Edward Dmytryk, *The Devil Commands*, had no hesitation in throwing the subtlety overboard.

Sloane had a very successful career as an editor, soon rising to such heights of responsibility within the various publishing organizations for which he worked that he had no more time to devote to his writing. This is regrettable, because his two novels have a particular complexity that is quite unique. Purist fans of the horror genre might consider them marginal, but their very marginality allows them to cultivate a special kind of unease: the unease which comes from the uncertainty of not being able to ascertain what kind of phenomena one is dealing with—and, in consequence, what kind of universe one is living in. Without knowing that, of course, one cannot know how one should set about the business of living a sensible and constructive life. Most writers who choose to deal with such questions are interested in settling them, one way or the other, thus licensing the decision to characterize oneself as a physicist, a psychologist, a medium or a contented lover. Sloane stands out by virtue of his realization that the essence of this aspect of existential angst is the absolute unsettlability of the question.

—Brian Stableford

SMITH, Clark Ashton

Nationality: American. **Born:** Long Valley, California, 13 January 1893. **Education:** Auburn, California; left school at 14 and largely self-educated. **Family:** Married Carolyn Jones Dorman in 1954. **Career:** Farmer and general labourer; poet, short-story writer (from 1910), artist and sculptor: regular contributor to *Weird Tales* in the early 1930s; ceased writing commercially in 1936. **Died:** 14 August 1961.

HORROR, GHOST AND GOTHIC PUBLICATIONS

Short Stories

The Double Shadow and Other Fantasies. Auburn, California, privately printed, 1933.
The White Sybil. Everett, Pennsylvania, Fantasy, 1935(?).
Out of Space and Time (includes verse). Sauk City, Wisconsin, Arkham House, 1942; London, Spearman, 1971.
Lost Worlds. Sauk City, Wisconsin, Arkham House, 1944; London, Spearman, 1971.
Genius Loci. Sauk City, Wisconsin, Arkham House, 1948; London, Spearman, 1972.
The Abominations of Yondo. Sauk City, Wisconsin, Arkham House, 1960; London, Spearman, 1972.
Tales of Science and Sorcery. Sauk City, Wisconsin, Arkham House, 1964; London, Panther, 1976.
Other Dimensions. Sauk City, Wisconsin, Arkham House, 1970; London, Panther, 2 vols., 1977.
Zothique, Hyperborea, Xiccarph, Poseidonis (selections), edited by Lin Carter. New York, Ballantine, 4 vols., 1970-73.
The Mortuary. Glendale, California, Squires, 1971.
Prince Alcouz and the Magician. Glendale, California, Squires, 1977.
The City of the Singing Flame, edited by Donald Sidney-Fryer. New York, Pocket, 1981.
The Last Incantation, edited by Donald Sidney-Fryer. New York, Pocket, 1982.
The Monster of the Prophecy, edited by Donald Sidney-Fryer. New York, Pocket, 1983.
Untold Tales. Bloomfield, New York, Cryptic, 1984.
The Unexpurgated Clark Ashton Smith, edited by Steve Behrends. West Warwick, Rhode Island, Necronomicon Press, 6 vols., 1987-88.
A Rendezvous in Averoigne: Best Fantastic Tales of Clark Ashton Smith. Sauk City, Wisconsin, Arkham House, 1988.
Strange Shadows: The Uncollected Fiction and Essays of Clark Ashton Smith, edited by Steve Behrends, Donald Sidney-Fryer, and Rah Hoffman. New York, and London, Greenwood, 1989.

Poetry

The Star-Treader and Other Poems. San Francisco, Robertson, 1912.
Odes and Sonnets. San Francisco, Book Club of California, 1918.
Ebony and Crystal: Poems in Verse and Prose. Privately printed, 1923.
Sandalwood. Privately printed, 1925.
Nero and Other Poems. Lakeport, California, Futile Press, 1937.
The Dark Chateau and Other Poems. Sauk City, Wisconsin, Arkham House, 1951.
Spells and Philtres. Sauk City, Wisconsin, Arkham House, 1958.
Poems in Prose. Sauk City, Wisconsin, Arkham House, 1964.
Fugitive Poems. Privately printed, 4 vols., 1974-75.
Nostalgia of the Unknown: The Complete Prose Poetry, edited by Marc and Susan Michaud. West Warwick, Rhode Island, Necronomicon Press, 1988.
The Hashish-Eater; or, The Apocalypse of Evil. West Warwick, Rhode Island, Necronomicon Press, 1989.

OTHER PUBLICATIONS

Short Stories

The Immortals of Mercury. New York, Stellar, 1932.

Other

Grotesques and Fantastiques (drawings), edited by Gerry de la Ree. Saddle River, New Jersey, de la Ree, 1973.
Planets and Dimensions: Collected Essays, edited by Charles K. Wolfe. Baltimore, Mirage Press, 1973.
Klarkash-ton and Monstro Ligriv, with Virgil Finlay (letters), edited by Gerry de la Ree. Saddle River, New Jersey, de la Ree, 1974.
The Black Book of Clark Ashton Smith, edited by Donald Sidney-Fryer and Rah Hoffman. Sauk City, Wisconsin, Arkham House, 1979.
Clark Ashton Smith: Letters to H. P. Lovecraft, edited by Steve Behrends. West Warwick, Rhode Island, Necronomicon Press, 1987.
The Devil's Notebook: Collected Epigrams and Pensées of Clark Ashton Smith, edited by Don Herron. Mercer Island, Washington, Starmont House, 1990.

*

Bibliography: *The Tales of Clark Ashton Smith: A Bibliography* by G. L. Cockcroft, Melling, New Zealand, Cockcroft, 1952; *Emperor of Dreams: A Clark Ashton Smith Bibliography* by Donald Sidney-Fryer and others, West Kingston, Rhode Island, Grant, 1978.

Critical Studies: *In Memoriam Clark Ashton Smith* edited by Jack L. Chalker, Baltimore, Anthem, 1963; *The Last of the Great Romantic Poets* by Donald Sidney-Fryer, Albuquerque, Silver Scarab Press, 1973; *The Fantastic Art of Clark Ashton Smith* by Dennis Rickard, Baltimore, Mirage Press, 1973; *Clark Ashton Smith* by Steve Behrends, Mercer Island, Washington, Starmont House, 1990.

*   *   *

Clark Ashton Smith was that rarity among contributors to the genre magazines of the early 20th century, a writer who wrote like no other and whose work is recognized for its unique style. Over the course of a fiction-writing career that realistically lasted little more than a decade, Smith wrote tales of horror, fantasy and science fiction in which he ignored most conventions by which those genres were defined.

A protégé of George Sterling, Smith was an accomplished poet with five years of verse submissions to *Weird Tales* under his belt before he turned, in 1928, to prose fiction and its higher rate of payment. His stories, like his poems, were outgrowths of the 19th-century decadent tradition, filled with evocative images of death and decay. Smith distinguished his stories from those of his pulp contemporaries through his talent for ornate, and often baroque descriptions that drew the reader into the sensuality of their worlds. He could render both the height of passion and the depth of disgust with equal vividness. In "The White Sybil," published in 1932, he describes the title character's seductive charms in the following manner: "Something there was in her speech of time and its mystery; something of that which lies forever beyond time; something of the grey shadow of doom that waits upon world and sun; something of love, that pursues an elusive, perishing fire; of death, the soil from which all flowers spring; of life, that is a mirage on the frozen void." Four paragraphs later, though, "she seemed to change in his arms as he clasped her—to become a frozen corpse that had lain for ages in a floe-built tomb—a leper-white mummy in whose frosted eyes he read the horror of the ultimate void."

Most of Smith's stories are fantasies set in elaborately imagined worlds ruled by sorcerers and populated with life-forms that defy traditional taxonomies for flora and fauna. Nearly all are laced with grotesque elements intended to create a mood of horror. His tales of Zothique, which comprise the largest of his story cycles, are set in a far future where civilization is sliding into decadent decline. "The Empire of the Necromancers" and "The Dark Eidolon" both feature characters who use the resurrected dead as servants. In "The Witchcraft of Ulua," a sorceress tortures a youth who spurned her amorous advances with nightmares of phantom lovers composed of rotting flesh and graveyard vermin. "The Isle of Torturers" is a spectacularly gruesome story of the physical and mental torments practised by a culture that has turned the infliction of pain into an art form, and the centrepiece of "The Garden of Adompha" is a garden in which human body parts are grafted onto plants.

Save for their setting in prehistoric polar wastes, the stories in Smith's Hyperborea cycle differ little in tone from those of the Zothique cycle. "The White Sybil" and "Ubbo-Sathla" feature scenes of horrifying physical transformation, and "The Tale of Satampra Zeiros" and "The Ice Demon" hideous monsters. Typical of Smith's writing, plot, and character development in these stories are of secondary importance to the invention of fantastic wonders.

The cycle of stories Smith set in the medieval French locale of Averoigne feature more traditional horrors: vampires in "A Rendezvous in Averoigne" and "The End of the Story," werewolves in "The Beast of Averoigne" and "The Enchantress of Sylaire," witches and warlocks in "Mother of Toads and "The Mandrakes," and a variant on Frankenstein's monster in "The Colossus of Ylourgne." The characters in these stories are also more recognizably human than their counterparts in Smith's fantasies, and the fears that make them human are frequently mirrored in the horrors they encounter. "The Beast of Averoigne" offers a poignant reflection on the limits of human understanding in its account of a monk trying to track down a werewolf, unaware that he himself is the monster. In "Mother of Toads," Smith crystallizes the sexual anxiety of his protagonist through a finale in which an army of toads sent by a reptilian-featured sorceress whose advances he rejected smothers him to death beneath their bodies. Hints of taboo sexuality vivify the horrors in several of the Averoigne stories, most notably "The End of the Story" and "The Enchantress of Sylaire," in which characters find themselves simultaneously repelled by and attracted to the sensual pleasures promised by supernatural beings.

The dangerous allure of the forbidden is an undercurrent that runs through many of Smith's non-series stories. "Genius Loci," one of his most powerful horror tales, tells of a man drawn irresistibly to a stagnant pond that absorbs the essence of anyone who lingers near it too long. The protagonists of these stories are often bored or frustrated with their lives and find the thrill of such potentially self-destructive impulses a pleasing antidote to the tedium of existence. In "The Gorgon" and "The Symposium of the Gorgon," Smith incarnates these impulses in the figure of Medusa. "I was terrified, appalled—and fascinated to the core of my being," says the narrator of the former, "for that which I saw was the ultimate death, the ultimate beauty."

In still other stories, forbidden pleasures manifest as memories of fulfilment in a previous life that tempt characters into transactions with terrible consequences. "In the background of my mind there has lurked a sentiment of formless, melancholy desire for some nameless beauty long perished out of time," observes the narrator of "The Chain of Aforgomon." "And, coincidentally, I have been haunted by an equally formless dread, and apprehension of some bygone but still imminent doom." Under the influence of a mind-expanding drug, he attempts to relive the past but suffers the same excruciating fate as his earlier incarnation.

Smith corresponded with H. P. Lovecraft, and contributed to the Cthulhu Mythos, the shared world of horror and fantasy stories that Lovecraft and his colleagues created in *Weird Tales* and other pulps. However, Smith's best-known mythos tale, "The Return of the Sorcerer," shows more the influence of Poe than Lovecraft, particularly "The Fall of the House of Usher." Poe's influence is also obvious in "The Second Interment," a variation on "The Premature Burial" in which Smith describes every agonizing moment of a man's burial alive and slow asphyxiation. Few writers could match Smith for imagining physical horrors, as he did in "The Seed from the Sepulchre," about a plant that takes root in living tissue and grows through flesh and bone, and "The Nameless Offspring," in which a prematurely buried woman gives birth to the progeny of a ghoul.

This predilection got Smith into trouble in the science-fiction pulps, where his depiction of other planets as charnel houses full of inescapable horrors clashed with the prevailing sensibility that the stars were a new frontier that was mankind's manifest destiny to conquer. His Mars stories "The Vaults of Yoh-Vombis" and "The Dweller in the Gulf" featured scenes of death and dismemberment so horrifying that they were drastically edited before publication.

In a letter he wrote to H. P. Lovecraft shortly after taking up fiction writing, Smith outlined a simple aesthetic for all his work: "My own standpoint is that there is absolutely no justification for literature unless it serves to release the imagination from the bounds of everyday life." His fidelity to this principle can be measured by enduring reader interest in his stories, which feature some of the most original and imaginative horrors in 20th-century weird fiction.

—Stefan Dziemianowicz

SMITH, Guy N(ewman)

Pseudonyms: Jonathan Guy; Gavin Newman; Guy Newman. **Nationality:** British. **Born:** Tamworth, Staffordshire, 21 November 1939; son of the historical novelist E(lizabeth) M. Weale. **Education:** St. Chads Cathedral School, Staffordshire. **Family:** Married Jean Smith; four children. **Career:** Worked in a bank from 1956; contributed short stories to *London Mystery Magazine* from 1972; also published articles on game-shooting and the countryside; freelance writer and farmer from 1974; owner, Blackhill Books (mail-order bookselling business). **Address:** The Wain House, Black Hill, Clunton, Craven Arms, Shropshire SY7 0JD, England.

HORROR, GHOST AND GOTHIC PUBLICATIONS

Novels (series: Crabs; Sabat; Werewolf)

Werewolf by Moonlight. London, New English Library, 1974.
The Sucking Pit. London, New English Library, 1975.

The Slime Beast. London, New English Library, 1975.
The Ghoul (novelization of screenplay). London, Sphere, 1976
Night of the Crabs. London, New English Library, 1976.
Bamboo Guerillas. London, New English Library, 1977.
Return of the Werewolf. London, New English Library, 1977.
Killer Crabs. London, New English Library, 1978.
Bats Out of Hell. London, New English Library, 1978.
Son of the Werewolf. London, New English Library, 1978.
The Origin of the Crabs. London, New English Library, 1979.
Locusts. London, Hamlyn, 1979.
Deathbell. London, Hamlyn, 1980.
Thirst. London, New English Library, 1980.
Satan's Snowdrop. London, Hamlyn, 1980.
Caracal. London, New English Library, 1980.
Doomflight. London, Hamlyn, 1981.
Manitou Doll. London, Hamlyn, 1981.
Wolfcurse. London, New English Library, 1981.
Crabs on the Rampage. London, New English Library, 1981.
Warhead. London, New English Library, 1981.
Entombed. London, Hamlyn, 1982.
The Graveyard Vultures (Sabat). London, New English Library, 1982.
The Blood Merchants (Sabat). London, New English Library, 1982.
The Pluto Pact. London, Hamlyn, 1982.
The Lurkers. London, Hamlyn, 1982.
Cannibal Cult (Sabat). London, New English Library, 1983.
The Druid Connection (Sabat). London, New English Library, 1983.
Blood Circuit. London, New English Library, 1983.
The Undead. London, New English Library, 1983.
Accursed. London, New English Library, 1983.
Crabs' Moon. London, New English Library, 1984.
The Walking Dead. London, New English Library, 1984.
Throwback. London, New English Library, 1985.
The Wood (as Guy Newman). London, New English Library, 1985; as Guy N. Smith, 1987.
The Neophyte. London, New English Library, 1986.
Abomination. London, Arrow, 1986.
Snakes. London, New English Library, 1986.
Cannibals. London, Arrow, 1986.
Alligators. London, Arrow, 1987.
Bloodshow. London, Arrow, 1987.
Thirst 2: The Plague. London, New English Library, 1987.
Deathbell 2: Demons. London, Arrow, 1987.
Crabs: The Human Sacrifice. London, New English Library, 1988.
The Island. London, Arrow, 1988.
Fiend. London, Sphere, 1988.
The Master. London, Arrow, 1988.
Mania. London, Sphere, 1989.
The Camp. London, Sphere, 1989.
The Festering. London, Arrow, 1989.
Carnivore. London, Arrow, 1990.
Phobia. London, Grafton, 1990.
The Resurrected. London, Grafton, 1991.
The Unseen. London, Sphere, 1990.
The Black Fedora. London, Sphere, 1991.
Bargain Bumper Treble: Bats Out of Hell, The Sucking Pit, The Slime Beast. London, New English Library, 1991.
Witch Spell. New York, Zebra, 1993.
The Knighton Vampires. London, Piatkus, 1993.
The Plague Chronicles. London, Piatkus, 1993.

The Hangman (as Gavin Newman). London, Piatkus, 1994.
The Dark One. New York, Zebra, 1995.
Dead End. New York, Zebra, 1996.
Water Rites. New York, Zebra, 1996.

OTHER PUBLICATIONS

Novels

Sleeping Beauty (novelization of screenplay). London, New English Library, 1975.
Snow White and the Seven Dwarfs (novelization of screenplay). London, New English Library, 1975.
Song of the South (novelization of screenplay). London, New English Library, 1975.
The Legend of Sleepy Hollow (novelization of screenplay). London, New English Library, 1976.
The Black Knights. London, Mews Books, 1977.
Hi-Jack. London, Mews Books, 1977.
The Pony Riders. New York, Pinnacle, 1997.

Fiction for Children (as Jonathan Guy)

Badger Island. London, Julia MacRae, 1993.
Rak: The Story of an Urban Fox. London, Julia MacRae, 1994.
Pyne: The Story of a Polecat. London, Julia MacRae, 1995.
Hawkwood. London, Julia MacRae, 1996.

Other

Gamekeeping and Shooting for Amateurs. Liss, Spur Publications, 1976; revised edition, Woodbridge, Boydell, 1989.
Tobacco Culture: A DIY Guide. Liss, Spur Publications, 1977.
Ferreting and Trapping for Amateur Gamekeepers. Liss, Spur Publications, 1978.
Hill Shooting and Upland Gamekeeping. Hindhead, Saiga, 1978.
Sporting and Working Dogs. Hindhead, Saiga, 1979.
Profitable Fish Keeping. Liss, Spur Publications, 1979.
Ratting and Rabbiting for Amateur Gamekeepers. Hindhead, Saiga, 1979; revised edition, Nimrod Book Services, 1985.
Animals of the Countryside. Hindhead, Saiga, 1980.
Moles and their Control. Liss, Spur Publications, 1980.
The Rough-Shooters' Handbook. Woodbridge, Boydell, 1986.
Practical Country Living. Woodbridge, Boydell, 1988.
Writing Horror Fiction. London, Black, 1996.

*

Bibliography: *An Illustrated Guide to the Guy N. Smith Books* by Sandra Sharp, Guy Smith Fan Club (Sheringham, West Street, Knighton, Powys LD7 1EN, Wales), n.d.

*   *   *

Applied to Guy N. Smith, the old adage of never judging a book by its cover becomes a nonsense. Rarely will a reader judge so accurately a book by its cover than when the cover in question belongs to one of the many horror titles penned by the prolific

Mr. Smith. In fact, his titles alone give away much of his attitude towards the genre in which he primarily works. *The Slime Beast*, *Cannibal Cult*, *The Graveyard Vultures*, *The Festering*, and of course the remarkably christened *The Sucking Pit*—a book which no less an authority than Stephen King blessed as "a novel whose title is my nominee for the all-time pulp horror classic." In King's analysis of the horror genre, *Danse Macabre*, it is suggested that Smith writes in the tradition of pulp horror which is associated with (inter alia) Robert E. Howard, Seabury Quinn, early Henry Kuttner, and James Herbert. What is more immediate than comparisons is that Smith has written, over the last two decades, some of the fastest-paced, in-your-face horror to see print. And to borrow a phrase from Nick Cave, the breath stinks of death and vanilla.

In 1973, years after Guy N. Smith had been cutting his teeth writing three stories a month for women's magazines, his agent heard that New English Library was looking to publish a werewolf novel. Responding with a speed that was to become a trademark, Smith wrote the synopsis one Sunday afternoon for a novel called *Werewolf by Moonlight*. It sold. And his horror has been selling well ever since, with his British publishers starting a print run with approximately 20,000 copies, much to the chagrin of the critics who have more or less shrugged off his work from the start. His worldwide sales now are close to four million.

Smith's novels are furious, violent romps: pulp horror of the sort that, in truth, has become rather unfashionable; it is worth noting, however, that when Smith made his early sales, his style was moulded to something of a trend, whether intentionally or no. James Herbert's first novel, *The Rats*, was published in 1974 to great success, and although Smith had been writing much earlier, Herbert's style became something to emulate by writer-wannabes. A fad was established for the type of horror novel where animals (albeit some that are pretty damned vicious in the first place) take umbrage at their lowly status and set about redressing the balance. Herbert's rats, Nick Sharman's cats . . . and Guy N. Smith's biggest sellers—his crabs.

After the supernatural splatterfest of *Werewolf by Moonlight* came *Night of the Crabs*—a novel which, partly due to some amazingly good timing in that long hot summer, sold initially 160,000 copies. While it has been commented that the sort of horror we might label "wildlife on the rampage" can be viewed allegorically, symbolically—be it a political subtext, or a psychosexual one—in Smith's case it is tempting to believe that he wanted to write a novel based on the ridiculous premise of crustaceans (big ones) escaping the sea only to kill people: as simple as that. He wrote the novel in one week, and five sequels have followed. The silly plots are what make these novels quintessential Guy N. Smith. Smith makes no attempt to instruct; he only chronicles. And the crab novels involve some of Smith's finest tongue-in-cheek humorous work. *Crabs' Moon*? *Crabs: The Human Sacrifice*? Again, the titles alone are indicative; if one were forced to foist upon these books underlying meanings, the latter possibility above would surely be more applicable than the former: a commentary, perhaps, on human beings' fundamental, Freudian, fear of sexuality, or more pertinently, fear of sexuality's diseases. *Killer Crabs*, perhaps, makes the joke the most explicit—apart from the immortal, and much quoted line, "He would sleep with her tonight, crabs or no crabs." *Night of the Crabs* was promoted as "A seafood cocktail for the strongest stomachs," and these are novels in which one should eschew the search for meaning or credibility, and have a laugh at the crabs' expense—even as, at the end of

Killer Crabs, a blaze has done its work to fend them off—for now.

Favouring the small-town or countryside plot (his beloved rural England, often in disguise) Smith's fondness for finding the gruesome in life has not diminished over the years. *Locusts* sees tropical insects arriving to devour towns such as Knighton, Ludlow and Clun; *The Neophyte* has telepathic killings, amulets, "Witch-Spawn," and a through-vein of frustrated, pawing sexuality. *The Slime Beast* uses the trope of the ill-fated archaeological dig, with the nice twist of the professor in charge not being immediately devoured or eviscerated by the creature, but planning to tame its power: "This beast was a robot except that it lived. . . . It needed a master." In *The Camp*, a drug called C-551 is released with the intention being the production of harmlessly peaceful hallucinations in those the drug affects; instead, unhealthy desires are made acceptable. *The Black Fedora* (as much a crime story, in truth, as a horror title) anticipates the Antichrist in a denser-than-usual plot involving a recreation of an historic Cromwellian battle and its possible befizzlement at the hands of a peace convoy. When the characterization begins to sharpen noticeably—with *Fiend*, *Mania* and *The Camp*, for example (Smith having the savvy to understand a waning market when he sees one)—by no means was the violence held in check. With reckless abandon rapes, crucifixions, torture scenes and the supernatural are still unleashed to this day.

Possibly, though, Stephen King's favourite, *The Sucking Pit*, is the best place to look at Guy N. Smith's work in microcosm. A slight volume, it has the unusual beginning of being from the point-of-view of a fox being chased. Then within the first three chapters alone the reader sees a pit sucking in some hunting dogs, some blood-drinking, and a severed penis.

Visiting her strange Uncle Tom, Jenny finds not only Tom dead but a book that had been his gypsy wife's possession, which contains gypsy secrets. Such as: "To become strong and powerful. Mix hedgehog and shrew's blood. Boil. Drink at the time of full moon. No clothing to be worn during the rite." With either sarcasm or breathless cheek, Guy records Jenny's verdict on the recipe thus: "Strangely, the idea did not revolt her." Even more strangely, Jenny follows the tip, blowing creatures away with Tom's gun. *The Transformation of Jenny* might have been another possible title of the book, had not the transformation occurred so quickly. This wishy-washy woman (the word "gentle" is used often when describing her) turns into a physically strong and sexually voracious "bitch"; she goes sharking for men and kills her first victim with a slash to his private parts.

The Sucking Pit can be read in one or both of two ways: as a straightforward sexist rant (not uncommon for its day), or as a critique of such books—a study of the inherent power of womanhood, with the woman getting on top. In the sense that the original horror gothic was concerned with the imbalance of power implicit in the relationships between men and women, *The Sucking Pit* can also be said to have gothic strains; but it is written in an unadorned style, with great leaps between paragraphs—an extremely packed style—and is pulpish in the sense that Jenny has no hesitation doing things she would not otherwise do. Her psychological motivation is minimal, such as when she takes her ill-fated first sips of gypsy potion, or when she gets excited by one character hacking up a tramp.

Guy N. Smith's short novels might suggest a readership of short attention-span, but a readership wanting his customary thrills would probably be more accurate. And if he sets himself up for ridicule, the joke ultimately is not on him. With his "waste-not-want-not" attitude to words and sentences, and—come to that—peoples' lives, his books sell extremely well.

—David Mathew

SMITH, Lady Eleanor (Furneaux)

Nationality: British. **Born:** Birkenhead, Cheshire, in 1902; daughter of the First Earl of Birkenhead. **Education:** Miss Douglas's School, London, and at a boarding school. **Career:** Publicist for the Great Carmo Circus; columnist, and film critic for London *Dispatch*, *Sphere*, and *Bystander*. **Died:** 20 October 1945.

HORROR, GHOST AND GOTHIC PUBLICATIONS

Novel

Lovers' Meeting. London, Hutchinson, and New York, Doubleday, 1940.

Short Stories

Satan's Circus and Other Stories. London, Gollancz, 1932; Indianapolis, Bobbs Merrill, 1934.

OTHER PUBLICATIONS

Novels

Red Wagon: A Study of the Tober. London, Gollancz, and Indianapolis, Bobbs Merrill, 1930.
Flamenco. London, Gollancz, and Indianapolis, Bobbs Merrill, 1931.
Ballerina. London, Gollancz, and Indianapolis, Bobbs Merrill, 1932.
Tzigane. London, Hutchinson, 1935; as *Romany*, Indianapolis, Bobbs Merrill, 1935.
Portrait of a Lady. London, Hutchinson, 1936; New York, Doubleday, 1937.
The Spanish House. London, Hutchinson, and New York, Doubleday, 1938.
The Man in Grey: A Regency Romance. London, Hutchinson, 1941; New York, Doubleday, 1942.
A Dark and Splendid Passion. New York, Ace, 1941.
Caravan. London, Hutchinson, and New York, Doubleday, 1943.
Magic Lantern. London, Hutchinson, 1944; New York, Doubleday, 1945.

Short Stories

Christmas Tree. London, Gollancz, and Indianapolis, Bobbs Merrill, 1933; as *Seven Trees*, Bobbs Merrill, 1935(?).

Other

Life's a Circus (autobiography). London, Longman, 1939; New York, Doubleday, 1940.

British Circus Life, edited by W. J. Turner. London, Harrap, 1948.
The Etiquette of Letter Writing. Hemel Hempstead, Hertfordshire, John Dickinson, 1950(?).

*

Film Adaptations: *Red Wagon*, 1935; *Men in Her Life*, 1941, from the novel *Ballerina*; *The Man in Grey*, 1943; *Caravan*, 1946.

Critical Study: *Lady Eleanor Smith: A Memoir* by Lord Birkenhead, London, Hutchinson, 1953.

*   *   *

Lady Eleanor Smith's minor position in the horror-and-gothic field is entirely of her own choosing, a matter of inclination rather than lack of ability. Her one collection, *Satan's Circus*, reveals her to be an always capable and often sophisticated writer, although only six of the eleven stories are fantasy or horror. Much of her work is about theatre, circus life and Gypsies (indeed, she claimed Romany descent and was a specialist in Gypsy lore), and these interests are readily apparent in *Satan's Circus*.

The title story (which ran in *Weird Tales* in 1931, Smith's sole appearance in a genre publication), is about a high-quality, much-respected circus which is nevertheless feared. The owners resort to blackmail to keep one performer in the company. When he is forced to substitute for the lion tamer (who deserted) and is killed, we discover that the owners are vampires, which, at this point, has probably surprised very few readers. Somewhat more innovative, but still predictable is "Mrs. Raeburn's Waxwork," wherein the custodian of a wax museum is visited by what may be the ghost of a murderess in the chamber of horrors.

"The Brothers" is a borderline fantasy, about a pair of circus acrobats, twins, whose completely obsessive relationship is threatened when one of them falls in love. When one threatens murder, the other realizes that he, in the same position, would do the same thing, out of the same jealousy. They are reconciled on the high wire, by what might be telepathy.

What makes Lady Eleanor Smith worth an entry in a reference book of horror writers is the final three stories in *Satan's Circus*. "Lyceum" is about a man followed home from the theatre by a mysterious and beautiful lady who claims to be first, a spy on a preposterous mission, then the ghost of a character from a once popular melodrama. She can have life again if only the man (a screenwriter) will adapt the old play into a modern screenplay. As he starts to do so, she vanishes, but then a newsboy is heard shouting that a man has been found strangled with a lady's glove in the theatre, which is exactly what happened in the melodrama. The screenwriter moves from scepticism to near-belief to a haunted confusion: did his beginning the screenplay bring these fictional characters into actual existence? The story twists reality wittily and eerily, and points in the direction of Philip K. Dick and (particularly) Jonathan Carroll's *The Land of Laughs*.

"Whittington's Cat" is another theatre story. This time the obsessed, neurotic protagonist is followed home by the spirit of a character from an English pantomime, a gigantic, half-human cat which, cat-like, takes over the man's apartment and completely dominates his life before attacking and nearly killing him. Afterwards, only a missing cat-costume is found in the apartment.

"Tamar" is about a Gypsy woman so thoroughly wicked that the Devil himself proposes marriage to her. But she has other ideas and poisons the Devil, thinking to get the best of him, but as she escapes she is followed by his shadow. These stories are well worth an anthologist's time, as are several of the non-fantastic ones, which reveal character deftly, manipulate ironic tension in surprising ways, and are sometimes (for their time) surprisingly frank on sexual matters.

Smith's one fantastic novel, *Lovers' Meeting*, is not horror, but a romantic time-travel story of the *Berkeley Square* or *Somewhere in Time* sort, if considerably lest saccharine than is typical for such things. The lovers cannot marry in the present, so, by means of magic, they do so in the past.

—Darrell Schweitzer

SMITH, Martin Cruz

Pseudonyms: Nick Carter; Jake Logan; Martin Quinn; Simon Quinn. **Nationality:** American. **Born:** Martin William Smith in Reading, Pennsylvania, 3 November 1942. **Education:** University of Pennsylvania, Philadelphia, B.A. 1964. **Family:** Married Emily Stanton Arnold in 1968; two daughters and one son. **Career:** Reporter, Philadelphia *Daily News,* 1965, and Magazine Management, 1966-69. **Awards:** Crime Writers Association Gold Dagger award, 1982. **Agent:** Knox Burger Associates, 391/2 Washington Square South, New York, NY, 10012. **Address:** 240 Cascade Drive, Mill Valley, CA 94941, USA.

HORROR, GHOST AND GOTHIC PUBLICATIONS

Novels

Nightwing. New York, Norton, and London, Deutsch, 1977.
Stallion Gate. London, Collins Harvill, and New York, Random House, 1986.

Other

Nightwing (photo-novel based on the film). Los Angeles, Fotonovel Publications, 1979.

OTHER PUBLICATIONS

Novels

The Indians Won (as Martin Smith). New York, Belmont Tower, 1970; London, Star, 1982.
Gypsy in Amber. New York, Putnam, 1971; London, Barker, 1975.
The Analog Bullet. New York, Belmont Tower, 1972; as Martin Cruz Smith, New York, Leisure, and London, W. H. Allen, 1982.
Canto for a Gypsy. New York, Putnam, 1972; London, Barker, 1975.
The Adventures of the Wilderness Family (as Martin Quinn; novelization of screenplay). New York, Ballantine, 1976; London, Arrow, 1977.
North to Dakota (as Jake Logan). Chicago, Playboy Press, 1976.
Ride for Revenge (as Jake Logan). Chicago, Playboy Press, 1977.

Gorky Park. New York, Random House, and London, Collins, 1981.
Polar Star. London, Collins, and New York, Random House, 1989.
Red Square. New York, Random House, 1992.
Rose. New York, Random House, 1996.

Novels as Nick Carter

The Inca Death Squad. New York, Award, 1972; London, Tandem, 1973.
Code Name: Werewolf. New York, Award, and London, Tandem, 1973.
The Devil's Dozen. New York, Award, 1973; London, Tandem, 1974.

Novels as Simon Quinn

His Eminence, Death. New York, Dell, 1974.
Nuplex Red. New York, Dell, 1974.
The Devil in Kansas. New York, Dell, 1974.
The Last Time I Saw Hell. New York, Dell, 1974.
The Midas Coffin. New York, Dell, 1975.
Last Rites for the Vulture. New York, Dell, 1975.
The Human Factor (novelization of screenplay). New York, Dell, and London, Futura, 1975.

Play

Screenplay: *Nightwing,* with Steve Shagan and Bud Shrake, 1981.

*

Film Adaptations: *Nightwing,* 1979; *Gorky Park,* 1983.

* * *

Of all the ghosts that haunt modern Americans, perhaps the most powerful are those of the North American Indian civilizations largely eradicated or marginalized by European immigrants. And clearly, if the genre of horror fiction indeed relies upon a dynamic of the past threatening to overpower the present, placing remnants of Indian culture in opposition to contemporary protagonists would seem an obvious strategy for American horror writers. Yet the sorts of accursed relics and ghosts of medicine men employed as props in routine horror fiction can be thuddingly unpersuasive, like plastic curios sold in tourist traps; a truly effective Native American horror story, arguably, could only stem from a genuine awareness of and sensitivity to Native American culture.

As someone who is one-half Pueblo Indian, and someone who has researched the Indians of the American Southwest, Martin Cruz Smith was well prepared to produce this kind of story, and his extraordinary *Nightwing* may be best appreciated as a significant prototype and example of this nascent sub-genre of Native American horror. Working on the Hopi reservation in Arizona, Deputy Youngman Duran visits Abner Tasupi, an old Hopi shaman, who tells him that, due to the ongoing encroachments of the white man, it is time to end the world for the fourth time as dictated by Hopi mythology; and he proceeds to prepare a series of magical symbols designed to bring about that event. Soon, he and other residents of the Navajo and Hopi reservations are being attacked and killed by vicious vampire bats carrying a deadly plague. Scientist Hayden Paine, hired by the Navajos to deal with the problem, tells Duran and his girl friend, social worker Anne Dillon, that this is a natural phenomenon—vampire bats migrating from Mexico to Arizona—but Duran has his doubts, especially after visiting with Abner during a drug-induced hallucination. Finally, after Paine fails to kill the bats with poison gas, Duran ignites a ring of ritual fires that burns them to death. A 1979 film version, with a screenplay by Smith and two collaborators, is remarkably faithful to the novel, though it enlarges the role of the dead Abner to heighten the story's supernatural aura.

It is hardly necessary to note that the murderous bats somehow unleashed by Abner symbolize a proud and venerable Indian tradition determined to destroy modern usurpers, while Abner's opposite in the novel is Walker Chee, the Navajo tribal chairman, who dresses and acts like the white men while attempting to extract money from them. Indeed, one subplot of the novel, Chee's efforts to suppress or minimize news of the plague to avoid killing a prospective deal with oil companies, recalls the parallel duplicity of the city fathers in Peter Benchley's *Jaws*, though Smith avoids demonizing Chee and allows him to argue in his own defence. Duran represents a struggle to achieve an intermediary position between the old and the new: he respects and is sympathetic to Abner's beliefs, and despises Chee, but he also abhors the violence instigated by Abner's unyielding hostility and longs to escape from the monotony and sterility of his reservation life. Still, the novel ends without establishing whether Duran, described by Anne as a "desert creature," will really be able to detach himself from his homeland.

While the contents of the novel can be readily related to Native American concerns, *Nightwing* may be more notable for its uniquely Native American style. On first reading, the novel may seem thin and underdeveloped, but readers should note that the reticence of the narrator carefully matches the reticence of Duran. (As a character in another Smith novel, *Stallion Gate*, observes, "Indian men . . . don't talk a lot . . . they're nonverbal.") However, while sometimes wishing that Duran would say more, one finally realizes that Duran says all that he has to say, just as the novel does; indeed, the novel's matter-of-fact tone and terse descriptions of vampire-bat attacks and dead bodies are more evocative than the histrionic rhetoric and gruesome details found in other horror novels.

Despite the success of *Nightwing*, Smith manifestly does not want to be viewed as either an "Indian writer" or a "horror writer." He has instead worked to demonstrate his versatility; thus, after several crime novels and westerns, Smith distinguished himself for three suspense novels set in Russia—*Gorky Park*, *Polar Star* and *Red Square*—and recently produced an historical novel, *Rose*, about women coal miners. Yet another one of his novels, *Stallion Gate*, might be viewed as a companion piece to *Nightwing*, in part because it represents his only return to a setting in the American Southwest and to a Native American protagonist. To be sure, it is essentially a fact-based account of the building of the first atomic bomb in New Mexico during World War II, featuring a fictional Indian soldier, Joe Pena, who is assigned to serve as J. Robert Oppenheimer's chauffeur and bodyguard. Pena recalls Youngman Duran in his problematic efforts to reconcile his Native American background and his modern proclivities—here, a fondness for boxing and playing jazz piano—and *Stallion Gate* also recalls *Nightwing* in its concise, epigrammatic style. More significantly, Smith shows that Pena's realistic experiences at Los Alamos were

not unlike those found in fictional horror stories: he must deal not only with a slightly demented superior officer, Captain Augustino, determined to prove that Oppenheimer is a Soviet spy, but also with his growing awareness of the mysterious dangers of radioactivity and of the impending explosion of a strange super-bomb. The novel ends abruptly with Pena trapped near ground zero on 16 July 1945, when the first atomic bomb is detonated. So, while Youngman Duran had to deal with an Indian shaman implausibly attempting to destroy the world with vampire bats, Joe Pena confronts a team of scientists calmly threatening to destroy the world with an explosion of unknown and unpredictable force. Should we exclude this chilling scenario from the genre of horror fiction simply because it actually happened?

—Gary Westfahl

SMITH, Michael Marshall

Nationality: British. **Born:** Knutsford, Cheshire, 1965; lived in the United States, South Africa and Australia as a child. **Education:** Cambridge University; degree in philosophy. **Career:** Comedy writer, BBC radio; freelance short-story writer and novelist. **Awards:** British Fantasy award, 1991, 1992, 1995, 1996. **Address:** c/o HarperCollins Publishers, 77-85 Fulham Palace Road, London W6 8JB, England. Lives in London.

HORROR, GHOST AND GOTHIC PUBLICATIONS

Novels

Only Forward. London, HarperCollins, 1994.
Spares. London, HarperCollins, 1996.

*   *   *

Michael Marshall Smith is the author of two remarkable cross-genre novels which blend elements of science fiction and supernatural horror, and of a number of brilliantly successful short horror stories. Smith's writing is fluent, evocative and rich in emotional shading. He reworks familiar themes—pictures that come to life, violent psychosis, the living dead—in ways that alter and intensify their meaning. The quiet beauty of his prose is matched by an unerring sense of structure. Devotees of Ray Bradbury and Theodore Sturgeon may find in Smith a kind of writing which they had thought didn't occur any more. Which is not to say that Smith's fiction is derivative: though overtly a traditionalist, Smith never seems to take on a theme unless he can colour it with his own brand of dark emotion.

"The Man Who Drew Cats" (*Dark Voices 2*, edited by Stephen Jones and David Sutton, 1990), Smith's first published story, was also the first he wrote. It's an immaculately crafted piece of small-town Americana (having spent his childhood in the USA and his adult life in Britain, Smith is equally able to write about both cultures): the story of a pavement artist who redeems his own bitter past by drawing a tiger which, in some mysterious way, destroys a wife-beating drunkard. The story's underlying point is signalled by the narrator's observation that "Love . . . comes from both sides of a man's character and the deeper it runs the darker the pools it draws from."

Smith's next story, "The Dark Land" (*Darklands,* edited by Nicholas Royle, 1991), is a frightening account of alienation: threatened by unstable shifts in his environment and his own perceptions, a man becomes trapped in his own house. Eventually, unable to leave or to prevent invasion, he escapes into a visionary landscape. Like Charlotte Perkins Gilman's "The Yellow Wallpaper," this story can be read either as an account of schizophrenia or as a kind of existential ghost story in which the outside world and the inner self become indistinguishable. It is Smith's most disturbing story: the purest expression of the vein of unease which runs through his work. By contrast, "Always" (*Darklands 2,* edited by Nicholas Royle, 1992) is a gentle story about love and bereavement: a man uses a subtle form of magic to help his daughter overcome her grief at her mother's death.

Smith's more recent stories maintain a similar level of intensity. "More Bitter Than Death" (*Dark Voices 3,* edited by Stephen Jones and David Sutton, 1993) and "More Tomorrow" (*Dark Terrors,* edited by Stephen Jones and David Sutton, 1995) are studies of obsessional psychosis with precise, resonant endings. "Later" (*The Mammoth Book of Zombies,* edited by Stephen Jones, 1993) and "To Receive Is Better" (*The Mammoth Book of Frankenstein,* edited by Stephen Jones, 1994) are short, hard-hitting takes on familiar themes—the living dead and the abuse of transplant surgery, respectively—that succeed by virtue of their sincerity and emotional insight. "The Owner" (*Touch Wood,* edited by Peter Crowther, 1993) and "The Fracture" (*Dark Voices 6,* edited by Stephen Jones and David Sutton, 1994) are jittery existentialist nightmares about urban life, rather in the vein of Nicholas Royle (some of whose characters Smith deliberately incorporates). "Hell Hath Enlarged Herself" (*Dark Terrors 2,* edited by Stephen Jones and David Sutton, 1996) pitches from near-future science fiction into a vividly evoked metaphysical underworld where technology has erased the boundary between the living and the dead. What these stories lack in thematic innovation, they make up for in evocative power, timing and literary texture.

One of Smith's finest short stories, "Not Waving" (*Twists of the Tale,* edited by Ellen Datlow, 1996), appeared in an anthology of "cat horror." It uses the image of a mysterious feline community to evoke a perfect but unattainable human love, the path to which is blocked through an emotional blackmail symbolized by the murder of a cat. Here, Smith displays the ability to capture extremes of transcendence and degradation within a single brief narrative.

Smith's first novel, *Only Forward,* is both a pastiche of his favourite genres and a highly personal psychological allegory. It starts in a future world where the protagonist, Stark, is trying to find a kidnapped man. The book develops as a fast-paced comic thriller with a pessimistic undertone—and then, halfway through, takes a metaphysical twist. Stark crosses a suddenly frozen sea into a country where the laws of nature are those of dreams: twisted memories, archetypes and symbols live on through endless re-enactments of past traumas and hopes. In this tortured landscape, Stark has to confront his own past in order to put right what is going wrong around him in the "real" world. The whole novel can be read as an allegory of mental breakdown, and the fierce logic of manic-depressive psychosis underlies its strongest passages.

In many respects, *Spares* is a darker and more disciplined retread of *Only Forward.* Its germ was the short story "To Receive Is Better," about a future society where human clones are farmed as resources for transplant surgery. The image of naked people stumbling through blue-lit tunnels underlies the dreamlike brutality of *Spares.* Its narrator, Jack Randall, is a drug addict and veteran of the (initially unexplained) Gap War who has been employed as a caretaker at a "spares" farm. Appalled by this dehumanizing industry, he educates a group of spares and helps them to escape. As he and the spares are pursued by vicious bounty hunters in a multi-layered city, elements of the past emerge: the horrific murder and dismemberment of Randall's wife and daughter; and beyond that, the episode of the Gap. Teasingly explained as having something to do with computers and with cats, the Gap is a metaphysical wasteland of "gaps": lost opportunities, failed communication, broken promises. It's a cold, blue-lit wilderness of forests, with villages inhabited by ghostly, violent people. Gradually, the novel works back to reveal its primary trauma: a hideous massacre of Gap children by soldiers from Randall's world. It becomes clear that the farming of spares—which started after the Gap War—has a second, secret purpose: it allows a group of psychotic Gap veterans to re-enact the massacre, using the farm tunnels as a private theme-park of atrocity.

Bleak and chilling despite its wealth of cute jokes about computers and cats, *Spares* deliberately echoes the history, literature and cinema of the Vietnam War. There are two likely reasons for this. Firstly, Smith may be implying that the memory of that war is so deeply embedded in the collective American psyche that its ghost will haunt future generations even a hundred years from now. Secondly, Smith may be making a bitter cultural joke: after all the films and novels that have portrayed Vietnam as a metaphysical Hell, he creates a metaphysical Hell and then makes it sound like Vietnam. Both of these interpretations would be appropriate for a writer as obsessed with cultural pastiche as he is with memory, conscience and the principles of human rights.

—Joel Lane

SOMTOW, S. P.

Pseudonym for Somtow Papinian Sucharitkul. **Nationality:** Thai. **Born:** Bangkok, Thailand, 30 December 1952; grew up in Europe. **Education:** Eton College; St. Catherine's College, Cambridge University, B.A., M.A. **Career:** Conductor and composer; director, Bangkok Opera Society, 1977-78, and Asian Composer's Conference-Festival, Bangkok, 1978; represented Thailand at Asian Composer's Conference-Festival, Kyoto, Japan, 1974, and at the International Music Council of UNESCO; founder and chairman, Thai Composers Association; secretary, Science Fiction Writers of America, 1980-81; has also worked for television, including script for cartoon series *Chip and Dale's Rescue Rangers.* **Awards:** John W. Campbell award for new writer, 1981; *Locus* award for first novel, 1982; Edmond Hamilton Memorial award for short story, 1982; Daedalus award for fantasy novel, 1986; Rocky award for novel, 1990; Homer award for novel, 1990; Rocky award for young-adult novel, 1993; Horror Guild award for short story, 1997. **Agent:** Adele Leone Agency, 52 Riverside Drive, Suite 6A, New York, NY 10024. **Address:** 16 Ancell Street, Alexandria, CA 22305, USA.

HORROR, GHOST AND GOTHIC PUBLICATIONS

Novels (series: Valentine; Riverrun)

Vampire Junction (Valentine). Norfolk, Virginia, Donning, 1984; revised edition, New York, Berkley, 1985; London, Macdonald, 1986.
The Fallen Country (as Somtow Sucharitkul; for young adults). New York, Bantam, 1986.
Forgetting Places (for young adults). New York, Tor, 1987.
Moon Dance: A Novel. New York, Tor, 1990; London, Gollancz, 1991.
Riverrun. New York, Avon, 1991; London, Orbit, 1994.
Forest of the Night (Riverrun). New York, AvoNova, 1992; as *Armorica*, London, Orbit, 1994.
Valentine. London, Gollancz, and New York, Tor, 1992.
Vanitas (Valentine). Canada, Transylvania Press, London, Gollancz, and New York, Tor, 1995.
Riverrun Trilogy (omnibus; includes *Riverrun, Armorica,* "Yestern"). San Francisco, White Wolf, 1996.
The Vampire's Beautiful Daughter (for young adults). New York, Atheneum, 1997.
Darker Angels. London, Gollancz, 1997.

Short Stories

Fire from the Wine-Dark Sea (as Somtow Sucharitkul). Norfolk, Virginia, Donning, 1983.
Fiddling for Waterbuffaloes. Eugene, Oregon, Pulphouse, 1992.
I Wake from a Dream of a Drowned Star City. Eugene, Oregon, Axolotl, 1992.
Nova: Short Fiction by S. P. Somtow, translated by Thaithow Sucharitkul. Bangkok, Vanlaya Press, 1994.
Chui Chai: Short Fiction by S. P. Somtow, translated by Thaithow Sucharitkul. Bangkok, Vanlaya Press, 1995.
The Pavilion of Frozen Women. London, Gollancz, 1995.

Play

Screenplay: *The Laughing Dead,* 1989.

OTHER PUBLICATIONS

Novels

V: The Alien Swordmaster. New York, Pinnacle, 1985; London, New English Library, 1987.
The Shattered Horse. New York, Tor, 1986; London, Headline, 1987.
V: Symphony of Terror. New York, Tor, 1988.
Aquila and the Iron Horse. New York, Ballantine, 1988.
Aquila and the Sphinx. New York, Ballantine, 1988.
The Wizard's Apprentice (for young adults). New York, Atheneum, 1993.
Jasmine Nights. London, Hamish Hamilton, 1994; New York, St. Martin's Press, 1995.

Novels as Somtow Sucharitkul

Starship and Haiku. New York, Pocket, 1981; as by S. P. Somtow, New York, Ballantine, 1988.

Light on the Sound. New York, Pocket, 1982; revised as *The Dawning Shadow: Light on the Sound,* New York, Bantam, 1986.
Mallworld. Norfolk, Virginia, Donning, 1982.
The Throne of Madness. New York, Timescape, 1983; revised as *The Dawning Shadow: The Throne of Madness,* New York, Bantam, 1986.
The Aquiliad. Norfolk, Virginia, Donning, 1983; revised as *The Aquiliad: Aquila in the New World* (as S. P. Somtow), New York, Ballantine, 1987.
Utopia Hunters. New York, Bantam, 1984.
The Darkling Wind. New York, Bantam, 1985.

*   *   *

S. P. Somtow makes himself a hard man to pin down. He lives alternately in Thailand and Los Angeles, California, equally comfortable with Eastern and Western cultures; he is regularly active as a composer, conductor, writer, and film-maker; he has successfully written in the genres of science fiction, fantasy, horror and mainstream fiction, also listing a work of non-fiction, a collection of essays, as forthcoming; and his novels display an increasing tendency to resist easy classification. Most strikingly, Somtow has apparently managed to achieve the maturity and sophistication of an adult while retaining the innocence and sensitivity of a child, so that his fiction for children can seem unusually adult and his fiction for adults can seem appealingly childlike.

This duality is most apparent in Somtow's first and most noteworthy horror novel, *Vampire Junction.* Protagonist Timmy Valentine has lived for nearly 2,000 years as a twelve-year-old vampire, first transformed during the Pompeii eruption, and has recently become an internationally famous rock singer and teen idol. Although still very much a child, and even a eunuch as well, Timmy nevertheless functions as the nexus of a dreamily decadent world of sex, violence and perversion, drawing everyone around him into his world even as a team of elderly comrades scheme to finally destroy him. This is a novel of and about excess, filled with showy rhetorical flourishes and lush descriptions of both the attractive and repulsive elements of Timmy's vampire lifestyle. It is astounding how triumphantly Somtow makes this murderous child into an appealing character, so that readers calmly excuse his latest victim, like his retainers who mechanically fall into the routine of cleaning up the blood and disposing of the body.

Overall, *Vampire Junction* was the sort of performance that is hard to repeat, though Somtow later attempted exactly that with *Valentine,* with a visibly contrived plot about Timmy, somehow trapped on his way to peaceful oblivion by a manipulative medium, trying to return to existence by trading bodies with a young actor named Angel Todd hired to play him in a film biography. After a slow start, this more restrained story improves towards the end, as the attempted film reconstruction of the first novel's apocalyptic ending inevitably turns into the real thing in a conclusion that successfully tops the original ending; however, like the final novel *Vanitas,* which follows Timmy after he has achieved mortal existence in Angel's body, *Valentine* is a novel with many impressive parts that nevertheless somehow does not manage to justify its own existence.

In a typical paradoxical gesture, Somtow followed the nearly pornographic *Vampire Junction* by moving into the field of young-adult fiction. In *The Fallen Country,* an abused teenager named Billy Binder begins travelling to a perpetually frigid land where he must lifelessly battle monsters and rescue princesses in a world of people who have been drained of all emotions. After making some friends with the help of a sympathetic school counsellor, Billy returns to the Fallen Country and, with their help, manages to defeat the Ringmaster controlling this evil world, whose representative on Earth is Billy's violent stepfather, by refusing to surrender to hate and thus breaking the unending cycle of abuse. While defensibly marketed as fantasy, this novel seems horrific in frankly confronting the theme of child abuse.

But no debates about classification arise in connection with Somtow's next and more impressive young-adult novel, *Forgetting Places*. When J. J. Madigan's older brother commits suicide, the Kansas teenager runs away from home to live in Los Angeles with his aunt, who works as a fraudulent medium, while he is guided by a series of computer messages from his dead brother suggesting that he is watching and advising his sibling from beyond. He meets Zombie McPherson, the disturbed younger sister of his favourite rock star, and through his efforts to prevent her from committing suicide, along with some timely advice from his aunt and her friend, the enigmatic "guru dude" Jack, he begins to come to terms with his brother's death and finally returns to Kansas, while his brother's messages, which fail to mention the unexpected Zombie, are revealed as a macabre series of pre-recorded messages his brother prepared before his suicide. Even though its apparently supernatural elements are explained away rationally, *Forgetting Places* remains a novel that deals with death, and the effects that the dead have on the living, in a uniquely provocative and moving fashion; not only Somtow's finest young-adult novel, it is also one of his finest novels.

With *Moon Dance*, another adult horror novel, Somtow's proclivity for mixing genres first came to the forefront. In this convoluted tale of a band of European werewolves who relocate to Dakota Territory in the 1880s, only to discover some Native American werewolves already in place, Somtow's protagonist is a werewolf with multiple personalities who vainly struggles to repress his murderous self and blend all of his personae into a harmonious whole. *Moon Dance* thus blends the horror novel, the western, the psychological thriller, and pornography—depictions of violent and kinky sex are even more depraved and graphic here than they were in *Vampire Junction*—and, with cameo appearances by figures like Sigmund Freud and Buffalo Bill Cody, there is even the aura of an historical novel. While one must be impressed by Somtow's imaginative audacity, there are perhaps good reasons why all of these genres have usually remained separate, and the jarring juxtapositions in the novel, such as depictions of the protagonist's multiple personalities arguing with each other followed by scenes of cowboys engaged in homosexual rape and murderous werewolves, are almost indescribably disturbing, unpleasantly so. Yet future generations of readers may be better prepared to deal with these cataclysmic generic shifts, so that *Moon Dance* may simply be a novel ahead of its time.

Somewhat more congruent, but still variegated, is Somtow's trilogy of novels beginning with *Riverrun*. Like the book whose first word it borrows as a title, James Joyce's *Finnegans Wake*, *Riverrun* strives to launch an all-encompassing saga absorbing all human experiences and literary motifs. Young Theo Etchison—the name no doubt a reference to Somtow's friend Dennis Etchison—is yanked out of our world into a parallel universe where, revealed to be one of the universe's rare "Truthsayers," he and his family members and friends are drawn into a cosmic reenactment of *King Lear*, with the two sons and one daughter of the deranged King Strang struggling with each other and with their

father to maintain the connectedness of the universe, as Strang is madly attempting to sever the connections between innumerable alternate worlds linked by the visualized and realized metaphor of a vast river. Certainly, the publishing classification of "Fantasy" seems appropriate here, yet there are also elements of science fiction: in the novel's discussions of alternate realities, drawing upon quantum mechanics, and in its vast cosmic visions reminiscent of Olaf Stapledon; and of horror as well, since the son that first summons Theo into this maelstrom is a vampire. The resulting mixture, while impressive in its grandeur and creativity, was evidently unsatisfying to readers who prefer their fantasy, science fiction and horror in more undiluted form, since the third novel in the resulting trilogy only appeared in an omnibus edition from a minor publisher.

One of the many charms of children is their determination to engage in disparate activities and pursue multiple goals, and Somtow should be admired for maintaining this drive for eclecticism in his adult years; but in a world where adults are usually content to fit into pre-set pigeonholes, Somtow's ceaseless drive to break down barriers, blend opposites and effect impossible combinations may be harmful to his popularity as a writer. Still, one must hope that he will never feel obliged to be conventional.

—Gary Westfahl

SPENCER, William Browning

Nationality: American. **Born:** 16 January 1946. **Career:** Freelance graphic artist and writer. **Address:** 3220 Duval Rd., No. 209, Austin, TX 78759. **Agent:** Max Gartenberg, 521 Fifth Ave., Suite 1700, New York, NY 10175, USA.

HORROR, GHOST AND GOTHIC PUBLICATIONS

Novels

Maybe I'll Call Anna. Sag Harbor, New York, Permanent Press, 1990.
Résumé with Monsters. Sag Harbor, New York, Permanent Press, 1995.
Zod Wallop. New York, St. Martin's Press, 1995.

Short Stories

The Return of Count Electric and Other Stories. Sag Harbor, New York, Permanent Press, 1993.

*   *   *

William Browning Spencer published his first novel, *Maybe I'll Call Anna*, in 1990. He has since published two more novels and a collection of short stories, all of which have received critical acclaim within the genre. Spencer's stories are linked by his strong, subtle voice, a highly literary style, and a handful of recurring themes, meshed to a sense of humour and the absurd often given voice by an unreliable or off-kilter protagonist.

Maybe I'll Call Anna introduces most of the themes found in Spencer's later works. Although structurally flawed, the book displays glimpses of Spencer's sense of humour, as well as his "trademarks": drowning, psychiatry (mostly failed), mental health (mostly subjective), writers (either bad writers or writers of children's books), and a man's obsession with a woman. Although not easily categorized as a horror novel, *Maybe I'll Call Anna* follows a young man, David Livingston, through his relationship with a beautiful, deeply disturbed woman. The relationship is destructive for both parties, even through the apparent death of the girl in a drowning accident, staged by her other lover, who happens to be her psychiatrist. When Anna turns up alive 13 years later, David finds that he must follow this obsession to the end, regardless of the personal consequences. David's scenes are told through his relatively stable point-of-view, but most of the scenes shown through other characters' points-of-view (including Anna, her psychiatrist, and her killer) are elevated to nearly gothic levels of deviant awareness. To the end, David's obsession with Anna never wanes, and this leaves his reliability, and his sanity, in question as well.

Spencer next published the short-story collection *The Return of Count Electric*. In the book's introduction, Spencer talks about the short form, how he came to it, and about his approach to fiction—specifically, that his stories are meant to be fun and coherent—as a reaction against the work he first encountered when he began writing fiction. Several of the stories are standouts, and almost all are quite funny. "The Wedding Photographer in Crisis" is built around a wedding photographer who only wants to do his job, meaning the wedding must go on, at any cost. The title story repeats the theme of insanity of a very personal flavour, where the narrator is, at the very least, unreliable, if not outright delusional. "Graven Images" is a deal-with-the-devil story, with a unique twist. "A Child's Christmas in Florida" is a chilling holiday story of classes and dementia, which was included in Gardner Dozois' *The Year's Best Science Fiction, Eleventh Annual Collection* (1994). "Looking Out For Eleanor" follows the obsession trail, and is another take on an "Anna"-like figure—an innocent, naive, and deadly woman with incredible sexual charm.

Résumé with Monsters introduces some of Spencer's wackiest characters in a modern-day Cthulhu Mythos story which manages to be hilarious and menacing at the same time. The protagonist, Philip Kenan, has followed his ex-girlfriend from the Washington, D.C., area to Austin, Texas, in an effort to win her back. Although Philip's obsession is worthy of "Anna," unlike in *Maybe I'll Call Anna* it is clear that Philip is somewhat unbalanced. As a beleaguered worker at Ralph's One Day Resumes, and a tortured and failed novelist, Philip is surrounded by common everyday items in the workplace that seem to be under the sway of Yog Sothoth and The Old Ones. Philip is also the author of a huge, nearly unpublishable novel, *The Despicable Quest*, which seems to have odd powers itself, which he blames for driving away his girlfriend in the first place. That background is revealed in the mid-section of the book, "The Doom at Micromeg." Seeking help from his $10-per-session psychiatrist, Lily, Philip is clearly a disturbed individual. Or is he? The uncertainty of the narrative creates a dramatic tension which makes the potentially cheesy premise workable. Publication of the first volume of *Quest* leads to a visit from a fan, Sissy, who turns into more than just a fan. The Lovecraftian horrors in *Résumé with Monsters* always seem to lurk just over Kenan's shoulder, and, for the most part, Spencer manages to balance the horrific and the absurd throughout.

In *Zod Wallop* he combines many of his concerns from previous books to create a novel more satisfying than its predecessors.

It is less mimetic than *Maybe I'll Call Anna*, funnier than *Résumé with Monsters*, a story that manages to entertain as well as keep the reader off balance. The title of Spencer's novel comes from the name of an imaginary children's book in the story, which actually turns out to have two versions. One is the classic fairy-tale version, yet to be written by Harry Gainsborough, the other is the original version written by Harry while he was in a mental hospital, shortly after the death of his daughter in a drowning accident. A former fellow patient, Raymond Storey, escapes the hospital with the help of several other friends inside, and their mission is to track down Harry. The original, evil *Zod Wallop* is the source of great power, and as the story unfolds, its players— a couple of mad psychiatrists, a domineering mother, and others— take on roles that parallel the cast of *Zod Wallop*. The culmination of the story—a chance for redemption, a chance for reversal, is nicely counterpointed in another of Spencer's short stories, "The Ocean and All Its Devices," which shows the darker side of the cost of this sort of trade. *Zod Wallop* manages this redemption by having Harry make the right choice, although not without temptation to do otherwise.

Spencer's other short work has received a great deal of attention. "The Death of the Novel" (in *Century 1*) was nominated for the 1996 Bram Stoker Award. "Downloading Midnight" (*Tomorrow*, December 1995) made *Locus* magazine's recommended-reading list. With such a promising beginning, in such a relatively short period of time, Spencer should be expected to become one of the brightest stars in the genre over the coming years.

—Tom Winstead

STABLEFORD, Brian (Michael)

Pseudonyms: Francis Amery; Brian Craig. **Nationality:** British. **Born:** Shipley, Yorkshire, 25 July 1948. **Education:** Manchester Grammar School; University of York, B.A. (honours) in biology 1969, D. Phil, in sociology 1979. **Family:** Married 1) Vivien Owen in 1973 (divorced 1985); one son and one daughter; 2) Roberta Jane Rennie (née Cragg) in 1987. **Career:** Lecturer in sociology, University of Reading, Berkshire, 1976-88; lecturer in humanities, University of West England, 1995 (one-year appointment). **Awards:** J. Lloyd Eaton award, 1987; Distinguished Scholarship award, 1987; Readercon Small Press award, 1992. **Agent:** Abner Stein Agency, 10 Roland Gardens, London SW7 3PH; Richard Curtis, 171 East 74th St., New York, NY 10021, USA. **Address:** 113 St. Peter's Road, Reading, Berkshire RG6 1PG, England. **Online Address:** bstableford@cix.co.uk.

HORROR, GHOST AND GOTHIC PUBLICATIONS

Novels (series: David Lydyard)

The Empire of Fear. London, Simon and Schuster, 1988; New York, Carroll and Graf, 1991.
The Werewolves of London (Lydyard). London, Simon and Schuster, 1990; Carroll and Graf, 1992.
The Angel of Pain (Lydyard). London, Simon and Schuster, 1991; New York, Carroll and Graf, 1993.
Young Blood. London, Simon and Schuster, 1992.

The Carnival of Destruction (Lydyard). London, Pocket, and New York, Carroll and Graf, 1993.

The Hunger and Ecstasy of Vampires. Shingletown, California, Ziesing, 1996.

Short Stories

Slumming in Voodooland. Eugene, Oregon, Pulphouse, 1991.

The Innsmouth Heritage. West Warwick, Rhode Island, Necronomicon Press, 1992.

Fables & Fantasies. West Warwick, Rhode Island, Necronomicon Press, 1996.

Other

Editor, *The Dedalus Book of Decadence (Moral Ruins).* Sawtry, Cambridgeshire, Dedalus, 1990; second edition, 1993.

Editor, *Tales of the Wandering Jew: A Collection of Contemporary and Classic Stories.* Sawtry, Cambridgeshire, Dedalus, 1991.

Editor, *The Dedalus Book of British Fantasy: The 19th Century.* Sawtry, Cambridgeshire, Dedalus, 1991.

Editor, *The Second Dedalus Book of Decadence: The Black Feast.* Sawtry, Cambridgeshire, Dedalus, 1992.

Editor, *The Dedalus Book of Femmes Fatales: A Collection of Contemporary and Classic Stories.* Sawtry, Cambridgeshire, Dedalus, 1992.

OTHER PUBLICATIONS

Novels

Cradle of the Sun. New York, Ace, and London, Sidgwick and Jackson, 1969.

The Blind Worm. New York, Ace, and London, Sidgwick and Jackson, 1970.

The Days of Glory. New York, Ace, and Manchester, Five Star, 1971.

In the Kingdom of the Beasts. New York, Ace, 1971; London, Quartet, 1974.

Day of Wrath. New York, Ace, 1971; London, Quartet, 1974.

To Challenge Chaos. New York, DAW, 1972.

The Halcyon Drift. New York, DAW, 1972; London, Dent, 1974.

Rhapsody in Black. New York, DAW, 1973; London, Dent, 1975.

Promised Land. New York, DAW, 1974; London, Dent, 1975.

The Paradise Game. New York, DAW, 1974; London, Dent, 1976.

The Fenris Device. New York, DAW, 1974; London, Pan, 1978.

Swan Song. New York, DAW, 1975; London, Pan, 1978.

Man in a Cage. New York, Day, 1975.

The Face of Heaven. London, Quartet, 1976; revised as *The Realms of Tartarus,* New York, DAW, 1977.

The Mind-Riders. New York, DAW, 1976; as *The Mind Riders,* London, Fontana, 1977.

The Florians. New York, DAW, 1976; London, Hamlyn, 1978.

Critical Threshold. New York, DAW, 1977; London, Hamlyn, 1979.

Wildeblood's Empire. New York, DAW, 1977; London, Hamlyn, 1979.

The City of the Sun. New York, DAW, 1978; London, Hamlyn, 1980.

The Last Days of the Edge of the World. London, Hutchinson, 1978; New York, Ace, 1985.

Balance of Power. New York, DAW, 1979; London, Hamlyn, 1984.

The Walking Shadow. London, Fontana, 1979; New York, Carroll and Graf, 1989.

The Paradox of the Sets. New York, DAW, 1979.

Optiman. New York, DAW, 1980; as *War Games,* London, Pan, 1981.

The Castaways of Tanagar. New York, DAW, 1981.

Journey to the Center. Garden City, New York, Doubleday, 1982; revised as *Journey to the Centre,* London, New English Library, 1989.

The Gates of Eden. New York, DAW, 1983; London, New English Library, 1990.

Invaders from the Centre. London, New England Library, 1990.

The Centre Cannot Hold. London, New England Library, 1990.

Firefly: A Novel of the Far Future. San Bernardino, California, Borgo Press, 1994.

Serpent's Blood: The First Book of Genesys. London, Legend, 1995.

Salamander's Fire: The Second Book of Genesys. Legend, 1996.

Chimera's Cradle. London, Legend 1997.

Novels as Brian Craig

Zaragoz. Brighton, East Sussex, Games Workshop, 1989.

Plague Daemon. Brighton, East Sussex, Games Workshop, 1990.

Storm Warriors. Brighton, East Sussex, Games Workshop, 1991.

Dark Future: Ghost Dancers. Brighton, East Sussex, Games Workshop, 1991.

Short Stories

Sexual Chemistry: Sardonic Tales of the Genetic Revolution. London, Simon and Schuster, 1991.

The Cosmic Perspective, Custer's Last Stand. Polk City, Iowa, Drumm, 1985.

Other

The Mysteries of Modern Science. London, Routledge, 1977; Totowa, New Jersey, Littlefield Adams, 1980.

A Clash of Symbols: The Triumph of James Blish. San Bernardino, California, Borgo Press, 1979.

Masters of Science Fiction: Essays on Six Science Fiction Authors. San Bernardino, California, Borgo Press, 1981; revised and expanded as *Outside the Human Aquarium: Masters of Science Fiction,* 1995.

The Science in Science Fiction, with Peter Nicholls and David Langford. London, Joseph, 1982; New York, Knopf, 1983.

Future Man: Brave New World or Genetic Nightmare? London, Granada, and New York, Crown, 1984.

The Third Millennium: A History of the World, A.D. 2000-3000, with David Langford. London, Sidgwick and Jackson, and New York, Knopf, 1985.

Scientific Romance in Britain, 1890-1950. London, Fourth Estate, and New York, St. Martin's Press, 1985.

The Sociology of Science Fiction. San Bernardino, California, Borgo Press, 1987.

The Way to Write Science Fiction. London, Elm Tree, 1989.

Algebraic Fantasies and Realistic Romances: More Masters of Science Fiction. San Bernardino, California, Borgo Press, 1995.

Opening Minds: Essays on Fantastic Literature. San Bernardino, California, Borgo Press, 1995.

Translator (as Francis Amery), *Monsieur de Phocas* by Jean Lorrain. Sawtry, Cambridgeshire, Dedalus, 1994.

*

Brian Stableford comments:

The element of horror in my work is mainly the result of scholarly fascination. I have been sufficiently interested in the works of several long-dead writers to want to play with their ideas and methods; the two most obvious examples are Edgar Allan Poe and Clark Ashton Smith. I have also been interested in the underlying assumptions of supernatural horror fiction; like H. P. Lovecraft I have tried to pose the question of what kind of universe we would have to be living in if the apparatus of horror fiction were actually capable of existence. *The Empire of Fear* was initially conceived as an attempt to reconstruct human history in such a way as to accommodate rationally conceived vampires; it seemed only natural to follow that project with another—the trilogy begun with *The Werewolves of London*—which would offer a physical and metaphysical reconstruction of the universe capable of accommodating *all* the standard motifs of horror fiction.

I have written numerous vampire stories since completing *The Empire of Fear*, extrapolating an enduring fascination. The underlying project of all these stories is a search for the best way to reconstruct the world in order to make more capacious room for the gaudy display of vampiric hunger and ecstasy.

All of this work is, of course, one contemplative step removed from the writing of pure horror stories. When I have done that, I have rarely been comfortable with the invocation of supernatural horrors, preferring to dabble in the marginal genre of the *conte cruel*. There is no supernatural element to such stories as "Heartbreaker," "The Devil's Men" and "The Riddle of the Sphinx," whose focus is upon the cruelties to which the human mind is sometimes inclined and the misfortunes to which the human heart is sometimes prey. My revenants are usually confined to the eyes of their beholders, and even when they are disturbingly incarnate— as, for instance, in "Behind the Wheel"—they are less horrific than the people who observe and provoke them. This reflects my conviction that horror is, in essence, an aesthetic rather than an emotional response; when I write horror stories I intend to appal or to amaze, not to instil fear.

*   *   *

Brian Stableford is a very erudite man and it shows in the plethora of works he has produced. He is also one of the few people who had a million words in print before he was 30. His first novel, *Cradle of the Sun*, was science fiction, as were many of those that followed. He is a highly respected critic and editor and although he cannot be regarded as a writer of popular fiction any more his recent novels display a great depth of understanding of human motivation.

The novels that are overtly horror are difficult to classify as they contain elements drawn from all areas of Stableford's expertise. The short story "The Man Who Loved the Vampire Lady" that originally appeared in *The Magazine of Fantasy and Science Fiction* in 1988 eventually became the first section of *The Empire of Fear*. The setting is an alternate 17th century in which the ruling classes of Europe are all vampires. A student of the period might consider that this makes little difference, with the exception of the survival of earlier historical characters. There is still an upper and an under class, the former viewing the latter as a convenience to satisfy their needs, the latter looking on the former with envy and a desire either to join or to overthrow the hierarchy. The aristocracy, as ever, has the power to reward favoured underlings, the greatest being the gift of immortality. The path of history has deviated little from that we are familiar with, as the position of the masses has remained unchanged providing a changing pool of ideas for the entertainment of the nobility and technological advance. As always a two-tier society will breed discontent and attempted revolution. Edmund Cordery is a mechanician, an inventor, at the Court of Prince Richard (the Lionheart). One of his more recent inventions is a microscope which is powerful enough to see individual cells. He is also a dissident, and his attempt to introduce plague into the vampire court leads to the exile of his son Noell. *The Empire of Fear* is Noell's story: driven from England's shores in the company of a priest, a pirate captain and the pirate's mistress, he ends up in a tenuous African colony. The section which follows is reminiscent of Rider Haggard as Noell and his companions trek across Africa to Adamawara, a huge crater which is the place of origin of all vampires. Here a hint of science fiction is introduced, suggesting that the source arrived with the meteor that caused the crater. To escape, Noell has to discover how vampires are made, as his companions would not survive the return journey as mortals. Basically, it is a sexually transmitted disease to which Noell appears stubbornly immune. The final section is set in a contemporary world in which vampirism is available to all but only after they have produced children.

Inevitably, Stableford's method of generating vampires will be compared to the spread of AIDS, but more important is the comparison between the African and European cultures in their approach to an identical situation. Whereas the Africans revere their vampires, considering them a source of wisdom—engendered by the fact that conversion is a privilege reserved for tribal elders— the Europeans show themselves to be wilful children, selfish and possessive of their immortality. It becomes inevitable that someone, like Noell Cordery, will discover how to give the secret to the masses. This destroys the class barriers in the same way that education changed a feudal society into the one we recognize today.

Young Blood also concerns vampires but looks inwards for the generation of the syndrome. Anne Charet is a very conventional, naive philosophy student. Her younger sister is a sexually experienced, rebellious "Goth," but it is Anne who draws a vampire out of the shadows. Anne gives him substance and he gives her erotic pleasure. She feeds him and he turns her into a vampire. In turn she feeds on her boyfriend Gil Molari, but she is attacked and hospitalized before she has a chance to explain that he, too, is now a vampire. As a result, he doesn't understand the hunger that assails him, leading to the death of a child when he loses control of it. For lack of any other explanation he ascribes the problem to an infection by one of the psychotropic viruses he is trying to develop. The first part of the novel is told in first person by Anne, the second by Gil. Both characters explore their own conceptions of events, starting from a different set of criteria. In the final section Anne has to confront the vampire within her own psyche in order to control it. Throughout, the idea of vampirism is used as a means of exploring the different mind-sets of philosopher and scientist.

The Hunger and Ecstasy of Vampires is both a homage to the philosophers and writers of the late 19th century and a pastiche of H. G. Wells's *The Time Machine*. The narrator is a vampire who is invited to attend a private gathering hosted by Professor Edward Copplestone. In the audience are such luminaries as Oscar Wilde and H. G. Wells. Copplestone relates an account of his travels to the future, using drugs rather than a mechanical device. In his version of the far future, the overlords are vampires, much to the delight of the narrator. The novella-length sequel to this, "The Black Blood of the Dead," has since been published in *Interzone*, as have many of Stableford's excellent stories.

In these books the vampire is not a vision designed to terrify but a vehicle allowing deeper issues to be discussed. The same is true of the trilogy which begins with *The Werewolves of London*. As it is set in 1872, Stableford has adopted a Victorian style of narrative in which the characters show a proclivity for philosophical debate. Between these passages is a story that drags the reader in: it begins in the Egyptian desert where David Lydyard is bitten by a snake and becomes possessed by a recently wakened god-like being which uses his eyes to evaluate the state of the world. One of his companions, Sir Edward Tallentyre, is attacked by a sphinx and saved by an estranged member of the pack of London werewolves. Back in England, Jacob Harkender, a self-styled sorcerer, has awoken another of the Creators and hopes to use the being while unaware that it is using him. The culmination is a confrontation between the two Creators, referred to by Lydyard as Bast and the Spider, and disaster is only averted by Tallentyre's powers of persuasion. He convinces them that they need to learn more about the world before they take action.

The story continues 20 years later with *The Angel of Pain*. The Creators have watched and learned through Lydyard's and Harkender's eyes. Both men have spent the time in almost constant pain, Lydyard from arthritis, Harkender from hideous burns. Two more characters enter the stage, Jason Sterling, who by biological experiments hopes to discover immortality, and a deformed prostitute known as Hecate. The latter is an agent of a third awoken Creator whose presence is upsetting the balance of mutual suspicion between the other two. A fourth Creator, Machalalel, who made the werewolves of London and the immortal man known as Adam Clay (his sleeping body has been disinterred by Sterling), may still be around but no one knows for sure. The story progresses by discourse, vision and activity, both real and surreal, but ultimately it is clear that the Creators are still unsure of each other. The humans they use to explore the world are largely irrelevant to them—little more than insects. A generation later (for the human characters; an eye-blink for the Creators), a culmination is reached in *The Carnival of Destruction*. This is now an alternative timeline of history: the Americans never entered into World War I and the Germans over-ran France, while England withdrew into isolation.

In all three of these books, the metaphysical interludes and discussions break up the narrative, rendering the story elusive to some readers. There is enjoyment and imaginative writing here but it has to be searched for. Stableford's approach is very different from that of his early works. He has never talked down to his reader, but now he applies layer upon layer of significant discourse so that only the most thoughtful of readers can hope to comprehend fully all of the ideas assembled within the text. His books are not designed to be skimmed or considered lightly, and for someone who is prepared to take the time to consider his themes there are rich rewards.

—Pauline Morgan

STALLMAN, Robert

Nationality: American. **Born:** 1930. **Family:** Married Pat Stallman; three children. **Military Service:** Served in the U.S. Army. **Career:** Assistant professor of English, Western Michigan University; left a book of literary criticism, *The Fearless Poetry Reader*, unpublished at his death. **Died:** 6 August 1980.

HORROR, GHOST AND GOTHIC PUBLICATIONS

Novels (series: The Book of the Beast in all titles)

The Orphan. New York, Pocket, 1980; London, Granada, 1981.
The Captive. New York, Timescape Pocket, 1981; London, Granada, 1982.
The Beast. New York, Timescape, 1982; as *The Book of the Beast*, London, Granada, 1982.

* * *

Robert Stallman's first and last published fiction is his trilogy of novels about a werewolf figure set mostly in the rural United States. The action occurs between 1934 and 1938. This is a fantasy approach to the shapechanger sub-genre, even with suggestions of science fiction, rather than straightforward horror fiction.

The beast emerges from a sort of egg in a swampy area of, perhaps, Michigan or one of the other north-central states (though an extraterrestrial origin is hinted at). It is a fur-covered animal with claws, cross between a big cat and a bear, which can run very fast on two or four legs and which grows over its first twelve months of life to become about twice as massive and muscular as a human being. It is a hunting animal and lives mostly on raw meat, though it is of human intelligence and possesses several special powers. Certainly its sensory powers are exceptional, particularly in the dark; in addition to good night-vision and excellent senses of smell and hearing (at least equal to those of a dog) it can picture the whereabouts of any relatively close moving creature through tiny changes in air pressure. It is male, though this is of no particular consequence until the third book, where it meets a female of its own species.

Its most specialized power is that it can shift into the form of a human being. Stallman makes this a fantasy or magical power, with no scientific rationale, because the human form chosen is of somebody recently dead (which the beast has not actually seen, but has chosen, perhaps almost arbitrarily, from the realm of the dead) and because the mass of the human can be much less than the beast's. For example, the beast first becomes Robert, a scrawny five- or six-year-old boy.

The reason for the use of this power of transformation is mostly one of survival: a small boy will be fed and cared for by humans, whilst an unknown species of bear might well be shot on sight or dissected for scientific research. But also the beast tries to learn about human society so that it can survive in the long term. A strange kind of autonomy exists between the Person (Stallman's term for the created host) and the beast. The Person is only dimly aware of its true nature, having its own distinct personality; normally it exists during the day but the beast, which is in control of the shifting process, takes over at night and goes hunting.

In this fashion, the first novel passes cleverly and entertainingly, with the beast existing as Robert until a contrived robbery occurs at the farmhouse where he is being cared for. The beast tries to help the family who have helped him, but his intervention in beast shape results in the farmer being shot dead. So the beast moves to a new area and becomes Charles, an early-teens boy. He goes to school for the first time and becomes a star pupil.

Stallman was a professor of English by profession, so it is not too surprising that his writing style, particularly in the first book, is strikingly attractive, even poetic. Descriptions of background and characters are vivid and sensuous, occasionally verging on the sensual. The period is convincingly portrayed and character development, particularly of the two boys in the first novel, is sensitive and credible. There is use made of Beauty-and-the-Beast symbolism; the contrast between the fragile innocence of Robert or even Charles and the cynical, murderous presence of the beast is subtly drawn.

In the second and third books the Person is an adult male, Barry Golden, who falls in love with a married woman, Renee, in Chicago. He takes her (and her six-year-old daughter, Mina) away from her drunken boor of a husband, Bill Hegel, and they live happily in New Mexico, where Barry works as a journalist. These aspects of the story are delightfully written, but melodramatic plot elements are grafted on, which diminish the overall quality and credibility.

In *The Captive*, Bill objects to Barry having an affair with Renee: he somehow manages to leave Barry in a stationary car on a railway line. The beast shifts and escapes death but is seriously injured and takes months (partly in captivity in a farmer's cage) to recover. And once Renee has divorced Bill and is living with Barry in New Mexico, Bill comes along and steals her and Mina away. It emerges that Bill is an enthusiastic member of an American Nazi group, whom Stallman portrays as evil and stupid to a ridiculous degree. By a stroke of contrivance, Mina has seen the beast (and been totally unafraid of it, demanding rides on its back) and can communicate with it by telepathy over long distances, so she is able to guide Barry/the beast to the remote Boy Scout camp where she and her mother are prisoners. The only interesting aspect of their rescue is that both Barry and the beast seem to appear at once, suggesting an independence not previously thought possible.

The third novel begins with the fascinating further development that there are other shapechangers around, which can assume a variety of animal shapes (coyote, snake, eagle) but not take human form or that of the beast. Otherwise it is an awkwardly structured book which brings in a female beast, astral projection and the life of the Navajo Indians. The two beasts mate in both human and beast shape, achieving the purpose of their existence, and they fly off together, leaving behind them two Persons who are no longer attached to their beasts in any way.

At their best these novels have the quality of writing and nostalgia of Ray Bradbury or Tom Reamy. It is possible that if Stallman had not died in mid-1980, in between the publication of the first and second volumes of the trilogy, a more polished version of the third volume might have been published. He was potentially a very fine writer.

—Chris Morgan

STENBOCK, (Count) (Stanislaus) Eric

Nationality: Estonian. **Born:** Cheltenham, Gloucestershire, 12 March 1859. **Education:** Oxford University. **Career:** Contribu-

tor to various magazines of the 1890s. Led a dissolute life, contracting cirrhosis of the liver. **Died:** 29 April 1895.

HORROR, GHOST AND GOTHIC PUBLICATIONS

Short Stories

Studies of Death: Romantic Tales. Edinburgh, David Nutt, 1894; expanded edition, London, Durtro Press, 1996.
The True Story of a Vampire. Edinburgh, Tragara Press, 1989.

Poetry

Love, Sleep and Dreams: A Volume of Verse. Privately printed, 1881.
Myrtle, Rue and Cypress: A Book of Poems, Songs and Sonnets. Privately printed, 1883.
The Shadow of Death: A Collection of Poems, Songs and Sonnets. Privately printed, 1893.

* * *

Even before the English Decadent Movement had the misfortune to collide with the last noxious gasp of Victorian bigotry, when Oscar Wilde was destroyed by the malice of the Marquess of Queensberry, the English were too stiff in the upper lip to produce *wholehearted* Decadents. The most flagrant of those to whom London played temporary host were all imported: Wilde from Ireland, Arthur Machen from Wales, M. P. Shiel from the Caribbean and Count Stanislaus Eric Stenbock from Estonia. In literary terms, Stenbock was the least of them, but he did his level best to make up for that in his lifestyle, which Arthur Symons—never a man for understatement—described as "bizarre, fantastic, feverish, eccentric, extravagant, morbid and perverse." Stenbock was judged by many onlookers to be the perfect personification of the excesses and affectations of the "yellow nineties," and his contribution to the scene was given legendary status by John Adlard's *Stenbock, Yeats and the Nineties.*

Before he contrived to destroy himself—which he did with a fervour unmatched by anyone except Arthur Rimbaud—Stenbock published three collections of poems and one of short stories, all of which he paid for himself. The first, *Love, Sleep and Dreams,* is reputed to have secured his expulsion from Oxford by means of its flagrant homoeroticism and thus ensured Stenbock's hallowed place in the canon of what is nowadays called "Uranian literature," as defined and delimited by Timothy d'Arch Smith's *Love in Earnest.* The second, *Myrtle, Rue and Cypress,* is profoundly melancholy and the third, *The Shadow of Death,* is relentlessly morbid. (The library reprint edition of *The Shadow of Death* issued by Garland in the late 1980s also includes *Studies of Death.*)

The original edition of *Studies of Death* contains seven stories, although it is unclear why it omitted Stenbock's best story—the exotic allegorical werewolf story "The Other Side," which was published in the Oxford periodical *The Spirit Lamp* in 1893. The Durtro edition remedies this omission, also adding two translations from Balzac which were made for an edition of the French writer's shorter works issued by the Walter Scott company. The best story in the original volume is the *conte cruel* "Viol d'Amor," one of several notable weird tales in which the tone of a violin is much improved when it is restrung with human gut instead of catgut. The pre-Stokerian "The True Story of a Vampire" is of some historical interest in its depiction of an urbane Eastern European vampire, while "The Egg of the Albatross" offers a blithely sarcastic gloss on Coleridge's "Rime of the Ancient Mariner." "Hylas" is a typically morbid tale of doomed Uranian obsession and "Narcissus" can be read as an atypically optimistic Uranian allegory, although it might conceivably have been intended as a straightforward comment on the relativism of aesthetic values. "The Death of a Vocation" is a straightforward romance and "The Worm of Luck" a Mériméesque tale of gypsy culture.

There is little in these tales to magnify, or even to reflect, Stenbock's reputation for excess. They are, in fact, rather delicately executed and if read in ignorance of the man's reputation would probably conjure up the image of a refined, melancholy and effete aesthete who had to reach deep within himself to find the hint of misanthropic malice displayed in "Viol d'Amor" and "The Other Side." Even in "The Other Side," the youthful Gabriel is eventually saved from the wiles of the temptress Lilith, although the wolfishness cannot be entirely purged from his no-longer-innocent soul. The similarly-named protagonist of "The Tale of a Vampire" is not so lucky, but that is only to be expected given the sex of his tempter. The inclusion of the two translations in the Durtro edition makes for an interesting contrast. Balzac's stories are not merely more virile but also more calculatedly blasphemous; of the two Stenbock seems by far the better Catholic, although that appearance may derive from the fact that of the two he was the only authentic aristocrat.

Although *Studies of Death* is likely to be of more interest to literary antiquarians than thrill-seeking readers the collection certainly has merits and "The Other Side" deserves consideration as one of the most heartfelt of the classic 19th-century werewolf stories. Had he only left the drink and drugs alone, Stenbock might have made a decent vocation of his writing.

—Brian Stableford

STEVENSON, Robert Louis (Balfour)

Nationality: British. **Born:** Edinburgh, 13 November 1850; son of a famous engineer and lighthouse-builder. **Education:** Edinburgh Academy; Edinburgh University, 1867-72; studied law in the office of Skene Edwards and Gordon, Edinburgh; called to the Scottish bar, 1875, but never practised. **Family:** Married Fanny Van de Grift Osbourne in 1880; two stepsons, including Lloyd Osbourne. **Career:** Contributor, *Cornhill Magazine*, London, 1876-82; novelist, poet, essayist and writer of travel books. Travelled widely in Europe, America and the South Sea islands, finally settling in Samoa in 1889. **Awards:** Silver medal, Royal Scottish Society of Arts, 1871, for a scientific essay on lighthouses. **Died:** 3 December 1894.

HORROR, GHOST AND GOTHIC PUBLICATIONS

Novels

Strange Case of Dr. Jekyll and Mr. Hyde. London, Longmans, Green, and New York, Scribners, 1886.

Short Stories

New Arabian Nights. New York, Holt, and London, Chatto and Windus, 1882.
The Merry Men and Other Tales and Fables. London, Chatto and Windus, and New York, Scribners, 1887.
Island Nights' Entertainments: Consisting of The Beach of Falesa, The Bottle Imp, The Isle of Voices. London, Cassell, and New York, Scribners, 1893.
The Body-Snatcher. New York, Merriam, 1895.
The Strange Case of Dr. Jekyll and Mr. Hyde, with Other Fables. London, Longmans, Green, and New York, Scribner, 1896.
Tales and Fantasies. London, Chatto and Windus, 1905.
Thrawn Janet; Markheim. Portland, Maine, Mosher Press, 1906.
Markheim. London, Holerth Library, 1925.
Dr. Jekyll and Mr. Hyde and Other Stories of the Supernatural. New York, Scholastic, 1963.
The Suicide Club, and Other Stories. Oxford, Pergamon Press, 1970.
The Supernatural Short Stories of Robert Louis Stevenson, edited by Michael Hayes. London, Calder, 1976.
The Strange Case of Dr. Jekyll and Mr. Hyde and Other Stories, edited by Jenni Calder. London, Penguin, 1979.
The Body Snatcher and Other Stories, edited by Jeffrey Meyers. New York, Signet, 1988.
Strange Case of Dr. Jekyll and Mr. Hyde and Other Stories, edited by Claire Harman. London, Everyman, 1992.

OTHER PUBLICATIONS

Novels

Treasure Island. London, Cassell, 1883; Boston, Roberts, 1884.
Prince Otto: A Romance. London, Chatto and Windus, 1885; Boston, Roberts, 1886.
Kidnapped. New York, Scribner, and London, Cassell, 1886.
The Black Arrow: A Tale of the Two Roses. New York, Scribner, and London, Cassell, 1888.
The Master of Ballantrae: A Winter's Tale. New York, Scribner, and London, Cassell, 1889.
The Wrong Box, with Lloyd Osbourne. New York, Scribner, and London, Longman, 1889.
The Wrecker, with Lloyd Osbourne. New York, Scribner, and London, Cassell, 1892.
David Balfour. New York, Scribner, 1893; as *Catriona: A Sequel to Kidnapped*, London, Cassell, 1893.
Weir of Hermiston: An Unfinished Romance. New York, Scribner, and London, Chatto and Windus, 1896.
St. Ives, Being the Adventures of a French Prisoner in England (completed by Arthur Quiller-Couch). New York, Scribner, 1897; London, Heinemann, 1898.

Short Stories

The Story of a Lie. Hayley and Jackson, 1882; as *The Story of a Lie and Other Tales*, Boston, Turner, 1904.
More New Arabian Nights: The Dynamiter, with Fanny Stevenson. New York, Holt, and London, Longmans, Green, 1885.
The Misadventures of John Nicholson: A Christmas Story. New York, Lovell, 1887.

Island Nights' Entertainments. New York, Scribner, and London, Cassell, 1893.

The Ebb-Tide: A Trio and a Quartette, with Lloyd Osbourne. Chicago and Cambridge, Stone and Kimball, and London, Heinemann, 1894.

The Waif Woman. London, Chatto and Windus, 1916.

Two Mediaeval Tales. New York, Limited Editions Club, 1929.

Tales and Essays, edited by G. B. Stern. London, Falcon, 1950.

Great Short Stories of Robert Louis Stevenson. New York, Pocket, 1951.

The Complete Short Stories, edited by Charles Neider. New York, Doubleday, 1969.

The Complete Shorter Fiction. London, Robinson, and New York, Carrol and Graf, 1991.

Plays

Three Plays (includes *Deacon Brodie, or The Double Life*, with W. E. Henley). London, Nutt, 1892.

Poetry

A Child's Garden of Verses. London, Longmans, Green, and New York, Scribners, 1885.

Underwoods. London, Chatto and Windus, and New York, Scribners, 1887.

Ballads. London, Chatto and Windus, and New York, Scribners, 1890.

Other

An Inland Voyage. London, Kegan Paul, 1878; Boston, Roberts, 1883.

Edinburgh: Picturesque Notes. London, Seeley, 1879; New York, Macmillan, 1889.

Travels with a Donkey in the Cevennes. London, Kegan Paul, and Boston, Roberts, 1879.

Virginibus Puerisque. London, Kegan Paul, and New York, Collier, 1881.

Familiar Studies of Men and Books. London, Chatto and Windus, 1882; New York, Dodd, Mead, 1887.

The Silverado Squatters. London, Chatto and Windus, 1883; New York, Munro, 1884.

Memories and Portraits. London, Chatto and Windus, and New York, Scribners, 1887.

Father Damien: An Open letter. London, Chatto and Windus, 1890; Portland, Maine, Mosher, 1897.

Across the Plains. London, Chatto and Windus, and New York, Scribners, 1892.

A Footnote to History. London, Cassell, and New York, Scribners, 1892.

Vailima Letters. London, Methuen, 1895.

In the South Seas. New York, Scribners, 1896; London, Chatto and Windus, 1900.

Travels and Essays. New York, Scribner, 1900.

Essays in the Art of Writing. London, Chatto and Windus, 1905.

The Letters of Robert Louis Stevenson, edited by Sidney Colvin. London, Methuen, 4 vols., 1911.

Selected Writings of Robert Louis Stevenson, edited by S. Commins. New York, Modern Library, 1947.

From Scotland to Silverado, edited by James D. Hart. Cambridge, Massachusetts, Harvard University Press, 1966.

*

Film Adaptations (selection): *Dr. Jekyll and Mr. Hyde*, 1908, 1909, 1911, 1913, 1920, 1931, 1941, *The Two Faces of Dr. Jekyll*, 1960, *The Strange Case of Dr. Jekyll and Mr. Hyde* (television movie), 1974, *Dr. Jekyll and Mr. Hyde* (television movie), 1981, *Jekyll & Hyde* (television movie), 1990, all from the short novel *Strange Case of Dr. Jekyll and Mr. Hyde*; *The Imp of the Bottle*, 1909, from the short story "The Bottle Imp"; *The Body Snatcher*, 1945, from the short story.

Critical Studies (selection): *Stevenson and the Art of Fiction* by David Daiches, Folcroft, Pennsylvania, Folcroft Library Editions, 1951; *Robert Louis Stevenson and the Fiction of Adventure* by Robert Kiely, Cambridge, Massachusetts, Harvard University Press, 1964; *Robert Louis Stevenson and Romantic Tradition* by Edwin M. Eigner, Princeton, New Jersey, Princeton Univeristy Press, 1966; *RLS: A Life Study* by Jenni Calder, London, Hamilton, 1980; *The Definitive Dr. Jekyll and Mr. Hyde Companion* by Harry M. Geduld, New York, 1983; *Robert Louis Stevenson* edited by Andrew Noble, London, Vision Press, 1983; *Robert Louis Stevenson: A Biography* by Frank McLynn, London, Hutchinson, 1993.

*   *   *

Like both the other classics of nineteenth-century horror fiction that were given spectacular new life in the twentieth century by cinematic adaptations, Robert Louis Stevenson's *Strange Case of Dr. Jekyll and Mr. Hyde* (versions published after his death usually add the prefatory "The" that he deliberately omitted) grew from a seed planted by a nightmare. The story grew much more rapidly than either *Frankenstein* or *Dracula*, however. Mary Shelley and Bram Stoker laboured for years to bring their works to completion but Stevenson is reputed to have produced his first draft virtually overnight, in a single feverish burst of creativity. But the job was not yet done; rumour has it that the draft so alarmed his wife Fanny that she persuaded him to burn it and start again, taking as much as a week to formulate a version fit to print. It is, therefore, a more carefully considered—and, one must suppose, more carefully censored—tale that has actually been handed down to us.

In the extant version of *Dr. Jekyll and Mr. Hyde* the raw stuff of nightmare has been thoroughly domesticated, converted by literary artifice into a strident moralistic parable, which dutifully informs us that within every good and noble soul there is an evil twin who would run riot if ever the chains of repression that keep him out of sight and out of mind were loosed. Given an inch, Mr. Hyde is more than capable of taking a mile; once Dr. Jekyll has admitted the existence of his darker half he is consumed by inexorable degrees. In the late Victorian era, when aspirant self-delusion regarding the angelic nature of man had recently reached its zenith, only to call forth the sceptical spectre of Darwinian descent, this was not only a compelling fable but a terribly plausible one. More even than *Frankenstein* or *Dracula*, which likewise set modern myths in place, *Dr. Jekyll and Mr. Hyde* established that the worst horrors are not those which sprang full-grown from the realms of nightmare but those which result from our desperate and incompletely successful attempts to pretend that nightmares are mere delusions, which can be made to vanish by a blink of the awakened eye.

With his friend W. E. Henley, Stevenson had earlier written the melodramatic play *Deacon Brodie, or The Double Life*, about a murderous masquerader hanged in 1788. He had also produced his own variant of the celebrated case of grave-robbers-turned-murderers Burke and Hare in "The Body-Snatcher." The latter was originally published in the *Pall Mall* Christmas supplement for 1883 (dated, according to the usual practice, January 1884). Stevenson was to retain his fascination with spectacular crimes and criminals, and being a Scotsman could hardly help but place their exploits within the dark framework of the uncompromising Calvinist conscience.

New Arabian Nights begins with the extraordinary chronicles of "The Suicide Club," an early prototype of the kind of psychological horror story which does not require a descent into madness to generate its effects. "The Pavilion on the Links" is no Gothic monstrosity, and the story in which it plays a part is conscientiously reduced from Gothic extravagance to what was to become the standardized form of the modern thriller, but it retains a measure of horrific effect. "The Sire de Maledroit's Door" is similarly subject to a restraint which refuses to let it end as starkly as the French *contes cruels* on which it is obviously modelled.

The title story of *The Merry Men* is a hallucinatory fantasy in which conscience works to brutal effect; part of it is written in Scottish dialect, as is the equally brutal tale of witchcraft "Thrawn Janet." The collection also includes "Markheim," whose guilt-stricken protagonist mistakes an angel for the Devil, and "Will o' the Mill," in which the private world of a selfish man is finally invaded by a not-altogether-hostile personification of Death. "Olalla" is a more convoluted moral fantasy whose saintly heroine suffers for the sins of her animalistic relatives and cannot accept the mundane redemption offered by a wounded soldier. *Island Nights' Entertainments* includes "The Bottle Imp," Stevenson's version of the oft-told tale of the ultimate poisoned chalice, here reworked for the people of Samoa—among whom he had taken up residence in the hope that the benign climate of the tropical islands would put less strain on his tuberculosis—and "The Isle of Voices," another moral fantasy adapted to a South Sea setting.

Stevenson was a fine writer, whose cavalier style was ideally suited to the production of suspenseful romances. As a writer of horror stories, however, he was always handicapped by a tendency to stop short of the maximum effect. The several Hollywood adaptations of *Dr. Jekyll and Mr. Hyde* were blessed with uncommonly fine performances by the leading actors—especially Fredric March and Spencer Tracy—but would in any case have been more effective than the novel on which they were based. They added in the vital element of sex, which Stevenson had carefully left out, and they avoided the awkward convolutions imposed by the original's documentary structure. *Strange Case of Dr. Jekyll and Mr. Hyde* is certainly a masterpiece of sorts, but it needed further work to release the archetypal horror story that was lurking, half-strangled, within it. Of all Stevenson's tales, "Thrawn Janet" is the only one which really lets the horror breathe—and cloaks it even then with near-impenetrable dialect. In the final analysis, his conscience—augmented by the influence of his strong-minded wife—was not so much his guide as his brake, and he never fully released its inhibitory pressure.

Stevenson's best-known work of horror has inspired several recent sequels by other hands, including *Dr. Jekyll and Mr. Holmes*

by Loren D. Estleman (1979), *Jekyll, Alias Hyde: A Variation* by Donald Thomas (1988), *The Jekyll Legacy* by Robert Bloch and Andre Norton (1990) and *Mary Reilly* by Valerie Martin (1990). At least one of these, the last-named, is a notable work in itself and has been filmed.

—Brian Stableford

STEWART, Fred Mustard

Nationality: American. **Born:** 17 September 1936. **Education:** Princeton University, New Jersey, A.B. **Military Service:** U.S. Coast Guard, 1955-58: Lieutenant. **Family:** Married Joan Richardson in 1968. **Career:** Freelance novelist.

HORROR, GHOST AND GOTHIC PUBLICATIONS

Novels

The Mephisto Waltz. New York, Coward McCann, and London, Michael Joseph, 1969.
Star Child. New York, Arbor House, 1974; London, W. H. Allen, 1975.

OTHER PUBLICATIONS

Novels

Lady Darlington. New York, Arbor House, 1971
The Mannings. New York, Arbor House, 1973
The Methuselah Enzyme. New York, Arbor House, 1970; London, Michael Joseph, 1971.
Six Weeks. New York, Arbor House, 1976.
A Rage Against Heaven. New York, Viking, 1978.
Century. New York, Morrow, 1981.
Ellis Island. New York, Morrow, 1983.
The Titan. New York, Simon and Schuster, 1985; London, Pan, 1985.
The Glitter and the Gold. New York, New American Library, 1989.
Pomp and Circumstance. New York, Dutton, 1991.
The Magnificent Savages. New York, Forge, 1996.
The Young Savages. New York, Forge, 1998.

*

Film Adaptations: *The Mephisto Waltz*, 1971; *Ellis Island* (television mini-series), 1984.

*   *   *

Both of Fred Mustard Stewart's horror novels feature female protagonists who are persecuted, threatened by their husbands (and others), made to believe that they are mentally ill, and finally pushed into criminal acts. Other than that they are remarkably different books: *The Mephisto Waltz* is a clever and reasonably subtle supernatural tale, while *Star Child* is less convincing and less well constructed, masquerading as a science-fiction B-movie.

To begin with, *The Mephisto Waltz* is a sparkling piece of writing which is totally credible and promises great things. Myles and Paula Clarkson are an intelligent but struggling young married couple in New York. He is a failed pianist who works as a freelance journalist; she helps to run a small boutique. But from the time Myles goes along to interview Duncan Ely, the ageing but world famous pianist, their lives are changed. Ely, who normally shuns interviews, is charming and friendly. He and his daughter Roxanne shower Myles and Paula with gifts, invite them to parties, introduce them to influential people, encourage Myles to practise the piano again, and give the boutique a boost through word of mouth.

Paula is suspicious. Why should the rich pianist and his beautiful daughter be so over-generous? Then it is revealed that Ely is dying of leukemia and has wanted to take his mind off it by helping somebody. He has been excited by Myles's musical talent and large pianist's hands. So Ely dies, leaving a Steinway grand piano and a large cash bequest to Myles and Paula. And Roxanne seems very happy with this arrangement.

But from the moment of Ely's death, Myles seems different. He gives up writing and spends his time practising the piano, he develops a sudden expertise in *haute cuisine* (Ely's main hobby), he makes love to Paula as if it is their first exciting time together and he wants the light on (which he has never done), he no longer sleeps on his right side, which he has always done. After much consideration of the evidence, Paula wonders about possession or transmigration of souls. She further suspects that Myles and Roxanne are having an affair, but Myles has explanations for everything, making Paula feel she is the one who is being disloyal.

From this point on the plot settles back into mediocrity and cliché. There are mysteries involving the death of Ely's first wife in Switzerland 20 years before—she had her throat torn out by a big dog, and Roxanne seemed a different person after it happened. And further plot twists involve men in black hats, a large black Labrador owned by Roxanne, and Roxanne's ex-husband. Paula and Myles's seven-year-old daughter Abby dies suddenly of meningitis, which isolates Paula. A dream suggests that Roxanne and Myles were to blame. Paula and her business partner Maggie launch another branch of the boutique, which is wildly successful, but Paula feels she is losing Myles. He begins a career as a pianist, to great critical approval.

Paula is made to feel that she is imagining things. Nobody will take any of her suspicions seriously, not even when Roxanne's ex-husband is killed while Paula is staying with him. But Paula breaks into Roxanne's house and obtains evidence of witchcraft. Despite a stroke and hospitalization, Paula is determined to be revenged. In a surprising and not wholly convincing final twist, she practises witchcraft on the witches: she kills herself but transfers her soul to Roxanne's body, so that she can get Myles back. Of course, it is really Ely and not Myles inside there, in the same way that it was Ely ex-wife's soul inside Roxanne's body.

Many aspects of the novel are finely written. The piano-playing details, the New York arty rich, and the boutique scenes are all fascinating and totally convincing. Some scenes are full of almost unbearable tension. The characters hold the reader's interest and although Paula's situation is familiar, one can have sympathy for her. Only her decision to beat the enemy at their own game, and her overwhelming success at the first attempt, strike a false note.

By comparison, *Star Child* strikes false notes from start to finish. The small Connecticut town of Shandy suffers a late August outbreak of murder and madness. Stewart tries hard to convince the reader that this is the result of dream indoctrination by two conflicting creatures who claim to be from the planet of another star but are in fact just humans from 80 years in the future. The science-fiction elements, presented as dreams, show a heavily polluted totalitarian future, with most people reduced to a kind of slavery; they fail to convince.

But even worse than this is the way in which the characters, mainly teachers from a local college, lecture each other interminably on various technical and moral subjects. One of the themes of the novel is that inside every person is the capacity to commit murder. The local psychiatrist Dr. Norton Akroyd has advanced this hypothesis in his bestselling book. Although the book is multi-plotted, Helen Bradford is the main viewpoint character; she teaches French at the college, while her husband Jack teaches English.

Helen experiences strange dreams, first from Star Child, who claims to be trying to help humanity, then from Raymond, who announces himself as a god and demands worship. Raymond's speciality is love-death: you make love to somebody and then you kill them, immediately afterwards. The uneven plot jerks its way through bad-taste murders and ever odder encounters which might be dreams until, at the end, Stewart suggests that the science-fiction sequences were all created through hypnotism by Dr. Akroyd, who has also been responsible for quite a few murders.

It is difficult to believe that the two novels, one sensitive and polished, the other awkward and gross, were written by the same person. Stewart's other books are for the most part historical blockbusters, but he has also written one science-fiction novel (a more genuine specimen of that genre than *Star Child*) which may also be of interest to horror readers: *The Methuselah Enzyme*.

—Chris Morgan

STINE, R(obert) L(awrence)

Pseudonyms: Eric Affabee, Zachary Blue, Jovial Bob Stine. **Nationality:** American. **Born:** Columbus, Ohio, 8 October 1943. **Education:** Ohio State University, B.A. 1965; New York University, 1966-67. **Family:** Married Jane Waldhorn in 1969; one son. **Career:** Substitute teacher and history teacher in Columbus, Ohio, 1965-66; writer for several New York magazines, including *Country & Western Magazine*, *Adventures in Horror*, and *Soft Drink Industry*, 1966-68; writer and associate editor, *Junior Scholastic* magazine, New York, 1969-71; writer and editor, *Bananas* magazine, 1972-83; writer and editor, *Maniac* magazine, 1984-85; freelance writer from 1982. Has also worked as Head Writer for *Eureka's Castle* television series on Nickelodeon and as Editorial Director of *Nickelodeon* magazine. **Awards:** American Library Association Children's Choice award, for several novels. **Address:** c/o Parachute Press, 156 Fifth Avenue, New York, NY 10010, USA.

HORROR, GHOST AND GOTHIC PUBLICATIONS

Novel

Superstitious. New York, Warner, 1995; London, HarperCollins, 1996.

Novels for Young Adults

Blind Date. New York, Scholastic, 1986.
Twisted. New York, Scholastic, 1987.
Broken Date. New York, Pocket, 1988.
The Baby-Sitter. New York, Scholastic, 1989.
Curtains. New York, Pocket, 1990.
The Boyfriend. New York, Scholastic, 1990.
Beach Party. New York, Scholastic, 1990.
The Snowman. New York, Scholastic, 1991.
The Girlfriend. New York, Scholastic, 1991.
The Baby-Sitter II. New York, Scholastic, 1991.
Beach House. New York, Scholastic, 1992.
Hit and Run. New York, Scholastic, 1992.
The Hitchhiker. New York, Scholastic, 1993.
The Baby-Sitter III. New York, Scholastic, 1993.
The Dead Girlfriend. New York, Scholastic, 1993.
Halloween Night. New York, Scholastic, 1993.
Call Waiting. New York, Scholastic, 1994.
Halloween Night II. New York, Scholastic, 1994.
I Saw You That Night! New York, Scholastic, 1994.
The Baby-Sitter IV. New York, Scholastic, 1995.

Fear Street series:

The New Girl. New York, Pocket, 1989.
The Surprise Party. New York, Pocket, 1990.
The Overnight. New York, Pocket, 1990.
Missing. New York, Pocket, 1990.
The Wrong Number. New York, Pocket, 1990.
The Sleepwalker. New York, Pocket, 1991.
Haunted. New York, Pocket, 1991.
Halloween Party. New York, Pocket, 1991.
The Stepsister. New York, Pocket, 1991.
Ski Weekend. New York, Pocket, 1991.
The Fire Game. New York, Pocket, 1991.
Lights Out. New York, Pocket, 1991.
The Secret Bedroom. New York, Pocket, 1991.
The Knife. New York, Pocket, 1992.
The Prom Queen. New York, Pocket, 1992.
First Date. New York, Pocket, 1992.
The Best Friend. New York, Pocket, 1992.
The Cheater. New York, Pocket, 1993.
Sunburn. New York, Pocket, 1993.
The New Boy. New York, Pocket, 1994.
The Dare. New York, Pocket, 1994.
Bad Dreams. New York, Pocket, 1994.
Double Date. New York, Pocket, 1994.
The Thrill Club. New York, Pocket, 1994.
One Evil Summer. New York, Pocket, 1994.
The Mind Reader. New York, Pocket, 1994.
Wrong Number II. New York, Pocket, 1995.
Truth or Dare. New York, Pocket, 1995.
Dead End. New York, Pocket, 1995.
Final Grade. New York, Pocket, 1995.
Switched. New York, Pocket, 1995.
College Weekend. New York, Pocket, 1995.
The Stepsister 2. New York, Pocket, 1995.
What Holly Heard. New York, Pocket, 1996.
The Face. New York, Pocket, 1996.
Secret Admirer. New York, Pocket, 1996.

The Perfect Date. New York, Pocket, 1996.
The Confession. New York, Pocket, 1996.
The Boy Next Door. New York, Pocket, 1996.
Night Games. New York, Pocket, 1996.
Runaway. New York, Pocket, 1997.
Killer's Kiss. New York, Pocket, 1997.
All-Night Party. New York, Pocket, 1997.
The Rich Girl. New York, Pocket, 1997.
Cat. New York, Pocket, 1997.
Detention. New York, Pocket, 1997.

Fear Street Super Chillers series:

Party Summer. New York, Pocket, 1991.
Silent Night. New York, Pocket, 1991.
Goodnight Kiss. New York, Pocket, 1992.
Broken Hearts. New York, Pocket, 1993.
Silent Night 2. New York, Pocket, 1993.
The Dead Lifeguard. New York, Pocket, 1994.
Bad Moonlight. New York, Pocket, 1994.
The New Year's Party. New York, Pocket, 1995.
Goodnight Kiss 2. New York, Pocket, 1996.
Silent Night 3. New York, Pocket, 1996.
Goodnight Kiss: Collector's Edition (omnibus; includes *Goodnight Kiss, Goodnight Kiss 2,* "The Vampire Club"). New York, Pocket, 1997.
High Tide. New York, Pocket, 1997.
Silent Night: Collector's Edition (omnibus; includes *Silent Night, Silent Night 2, Silent Night 3*). New York, Pocket, 1997.

Fear Street Cheerleaders series:

The First Evil. New York, Pocket, 1992.
The Second Evil. New York, Pocket, 1992.
The Third Evil. New York, Pocket, 1992.
The New Evil. New York, Pocket, 1994.

Fear Street Saga series:

The Betrayal. New York, Pocket, 1993.
The Secret. New York, Pocket, 1993.
The Burning. New York, Pocket, 1993.
Fear Street Saga: Collector's Edition (omnibus; includes *The Betrayal, The Secret, The Burning*). New York, Pocket, 1995.

99 Fear Street: The House of Evil series:

The First Horror. New York, Pocket, 1994.
The Second Horror. New York, Pocket, 1994.
The Third Horror. New York, Pocket, 1994.

Fear Street: The Cataluna Chronicles series:

The Evil Moon. New York, Pocket, 1995.
The Dark Street. New York, Pocket, 1995.
The Deadly Fire. New York, Pocket, 1995.

Fear Street: Fear Park series:

The First Scream. New York, Pocket, 1996.
The Loudest Scream. New York, Pocket, 1996.
The Last Scream. New York, Pocket, 1996.

Fear Street Sagas series:

A New Fear. New York, Pocket, 1996.
House of Whispers. New York, Pocket, 1996.

Fear Street: Fear Hall series:

Fear Hall: The Beginning. New York, Pocket, 1997.
Fear Hall: The Conclusion. New York, Pocket, 1997.

Novels for Children

Goosebumps series:

Welcome to Dead House. New York, Scholastic, 1992.
Stay Out of the Basement. New York, Scholastic, 1992.
Monster Blood. New York, Scholastic, 1992.
Say Cheese and Die. New York, Scholastic, 1992.
The Curse of the Mummy's Tomb. New York, Scholastic, 1993.
Let's Get Invisible! New York, Scholastic, 1993.
Night of the Living Dummy. New York, Scholastic, 1993.
The Girl Who Cried Monster. New York, Scholastic, 1993.
Welcome to Camp Nightmare. New York, Scholastic, 1993.
The Ghost Next Door. New York, Scholastic, 1993.
The Haunted Mask. New York, Scholastic, 1993.
Be Careful What You Wish For. New York, Scholastic, 1993.
Piano Lessons Can Be Murder. New York, Scholastic, 1993.
The Werewolf of Fever Swamp. New York, Scholastic, 1993.
You Can't Scare Me! New York, Scholastic, 1994.
One Day at Horrorland. New York, Scholastic, 1994.
Why I'm Afraid of Bees. New York, Scholastic, 1994.
Monster Blood II. New York, Scholastic, 1994.
Deep Trouble. New York, Scholastic, 1994.
The Scarecrow Walks at Midnight. New York, Scholastic, 1994.
Go Eat Worms! New York, Scholastic, 1994.
Ghost Beach. New York, Scholastic, 1994.
Return of the Mummy. New York, Scholastic, 1994.
Phantom of the Auditorium. New York, Scholastic, 1994.
Attack of the Mutant. New York, Scholastic, 1994.
My Hairiest Adventure. New York, Scholastic, 1994.
A Night in Terror Tower. New York, Scholastic, 1995.
The Cuckoo Clock of Doom. New York, Scholastic, 1995.
Monster Blood III. New York, Scholastic, 1995.
It Came from Beneath the Sink! New York, Scholastic, 1995.
Night of the Living Dummy II. New York, Scholastic, 1995.
The Barking Ghost. New York, Scholastic, 1995.
The Horror at Camp Jellyjam. New York, Scholastic, 1995.
Revenge of the Lawn Gnomes. New York, Scholastic, 1995.
A Shocker on Shock Street. New York, Scholastic, 1995.
The Haunted Mask II. New York, Scholastic, 1995.
The Headless Ghost. New York, Scholastic, 1995.
The Abominable Snowman of Pasadena. New York, Scholastic, 1995.
Goosebumps Monster Edition #1 (omnibus; includes *Welcome to Dead House, Stay Out of the Basement, Say Cheese and Die*). New York, Scholastic, 1995.
How I Got My Shrunken Head. New York, Scholastic, 1996.
Night of the Living Dummy III. New York, Scholastic, 1996.
Bad Hare Day. New York, Scholastic, 1996.
Egg Monsters from Mars. New York, Scholastic, 1996.
The Beast from the East. New York, Scholastic, 1996.

Say Cheese and Die—Again! New York, Scholastic, 1996.
Ghost Camp. New York, Scholastic, 1996.
How to Kill a Monster. New York, Scholastic, 1996.
Legend of the Lost Legend. New York, Scholastic, 1996.
Attack of the Jack-O'-Lanterns. New York, Scholastic, 1996.
Vampire Breath. New York, Scholastic, 1996.
Calling All Creeps. New York, Scholastic, 1996.
Goosebumps Monster Edition #2 (omnibus; includes *Night of the Living Dummy, Night of the Living Dummy II, Night of the Living Dummy III*). New York, Scholastic, 1996.
Goosebumps Night Light Edition (omnibus; includes *Welcome to Camp Nightmare, The Horror at Camp Jellyjam, Ghost Camp*). New York, Scholastic, 1996.
Beware, the Snowman. New York, Scholastic, 1997.
How I Learned to Fly. New York, Scholastic, 1997.
Chicken Chicken. New York, Scholastic, 1997.
Don't Go to Sleep! New York, Scholastic, 1997.
The Blob That Ate Everyone. New York, Scholastic, 1997.
The Curse of Camp Cold Lake. New York, Scholastic, 1997.
My Best Friend Is Invisible. New York, Scholastic, 1997.
Deep Trouble III. New York, Scholastic, 1997.
The Haunted School. New York, Scholastic, 1997.
Werewolf Skin. New York, Scholastic, 1997.
I Live in Your Basement! New York, Scholastic, 1997.
Goosebumps Monster Edition #3 (omnibus; includes *The Ghost Next Door, Ghost Beach, The Barking Ghost*). New York, Scholastic, 1997.

Give Yourself Goosebumps series:

Escape from the Carnival of Horrors. New York, Scholastic, 1995.
Tick Tock, You're Dead! New York, Scholastic, 1995.
Trapped in Bat Wing Hall. New York, Scholastic, 1995.
The Deadly Experiments of Dr. Eeek. New York, Scholastic, 1996.
Night in Werewolf Woods. New York, Scholastic, 1996.
Beware of the Purple Peanut Butter. New York, Scholastic, 1996.
Under the Magician's Spell. New York, Scholastic, 1996.
The Curse of the Creeping Coffin. New York, Scholastic, 1996.
The Knight in Screaming Armor. New York, Scholastic, 1996.
Diary of a Mad Mummy. New York, Scholastic, 1996.
Deep in the Jungle of Doom. New York, Scholastic, 1996.
Welcome to the Wicked Wax Museum. New York, Scholastic, 1996.
Scream of the Evil Grave. New York, Scholastic, 1997.
The Creepy Creations of Professor Shock. New York, Scholastic, 1997.
Please Don't Feed the Vampire! New York, Scholastic, 1997.
Secret Agent Grandma. New York, Scholastic, 1997.
Little Comic Shop of Horrors. New York, Scholastic, 1997.
Attack of the Beastly Baby-Sitter. New York, Scholastic, 1997.
Escape from Camp Run-for-Your-Life. New York, Scholastic, 1997.
Toy Terror: Batteries Included. New York, Scholastic, 1997.
The Twisted Tale of Tiki Island. New York, Scholastic, 1997.

Short Stories for Children

Tales to Give You Goosebumps: Ten Scary Stories. New York, Scholastic, 1994.
More Tales to Give You Goosebumps. New York, Scholastic, 1995.

Even More Tales to Give You Goosebumps. New York, Scholastic, 1995.

Still More Tales to Give You Goosebumps. New York, Scholastic, 1996.

More and More Tales to Give You Goosebumps. New York, Scholastic, 1997.

OTHER PUBLICATIONS

Novels for Children

The Time Raider. New York, Scholastic, 1982.
The Golden Sword of Dragonwalk. New York, Scholastic, 1983.
Horrors of the Haunted Museum. New York, Scholastic, 1984.
Indiana Jones and the Curse of Horror Island. New York, Ballantine, 1984.
Indiana Jones and the Giants of the Silver Tower. New York, Ballantine, 1984.
Indiana Jones and the Cult of the Mummy's Crypt. New York, Ballantine, 1984.
Instant Millionaire. New York, Scholastic, 1984.
Through the Forest of Twisted Dreams. New York, Avon, 1984.
The Badlands of Hark. New York, Scholastic, 1985.
The Invaders of Hark. New York, Scholastic, 1985.
Demons of the Deep. New York, Golden, 1985.
Challenge of the Wolf Knight. New York, Avon, 1985.
James Bond in Win, Place, or Die. New York, Ballantine, 1985.
Conquest of the Time Master. New York, Avon, 1985.
Cavern of the Phantoms. New York, Avon, 1986.
Operation Deadly Decoy. New York, Ballantine, 1986.
Mystery of the Impostor. New York, Ballantine, 1986.
Operation: Mindbender. New York, Ballantine, 1986.
Golden Girl and the Vanishing Unicorn. New York, Ballantine, 1986.
Indiana Jones and the Ape Slaves of Howling Island. New York, Ballantine, 1987.
Serpentor and the Mummy Warrior. New York, Ballantine, 1987.
Jungle Raid. New York, Ballantine, 1988.
Siege of Serpentor. New York, Ballantine, 1988.
How I Broke Up with Ernie. New York, Pocket, 1990.
Phone Calls. New York, Pocket, 1990.
Jerks-in-Training. New York, Scholastic, 1991.
Losers in Space. New York, Scholastic, 1991.
Bozos on Patrol. New York, Scholastic, 1992.
The Beast. New York, Pocket, 1994.
The Beast II. New York, Pocket, 1995.

Novels for Children as Eric Affabee

The Siege of the Dragonriders. New York, Avon, 1984.
G.I. Joe and the Everglades Swamp Terror. New York, Ballantine, 1986.
Attack on the King. New York, Avon, 1986.
Operation: Star Raider. New York, Ballantine, 1986.
The Dragon Queen's Revenge. New York, Avon, 1986.

Novels for Children as Zachary Blue

The Protectors #1: The Petrova Twist. New York, Scholastic, 1987.
The Jet Fighter Trap. New York, Scholastic, 1987.

Novels for Children as Jovial Bob Stine

Gnasty Gnomes. New York, Random House, 1981.
Don't Stand in the Soup. New York, Bantam, 1982.
Miami Mice. New York, Scholastic, 1986.
Pork & Beans: Play Date. New York, Scholastic, 1989.
The Amazing Adventures of Me, Myself, and I. New York, Bantam, 1991.
Son of Furry. New York, Bantam, 1991.

Novels for Children as Jovial Bob Stine (novelizations of screenplays)

Spaceballs: The Book. New York, Scholastic, 1987.
Big Top Pee Wee: The Movie Storybook. New York, Scholastic, 1988.
My Secret Identity: A Novelization. New York, Scholastic, 1989.
Ghostbusters II Storybook. New York, Scholastic, 1989.

Other

It Came from Ohio! My Life as a Writer, with Joe Arthur. New York, Scholastic, 1997.

Other for Children as Jovial Bob Stine

How to Be Funny: An Extremely Silly Guidebook. New York, Scholastic, 1978.
The Absurdly Funny Encyclopedia and Flyswatter. New York, Scholastic, 1978.
The Complete Book of Nerds. New York, Scholastic, 1979.
The Dynamite Do-It-Yourself Pen Pal Kit. New York, Scholastic, 1980.
Dynamite's Funny Book of the Sad Facts of Life. New York, Scholastic, 1980.
Going Out! Going Steady! Going Bananas! New York, Scholastic, 1980.
The Pigs' Book of World Records. New York, Random House, 1980.
The Sick of Being Sick Book, with Jane Stine. New York, Scholastic, 1980.
Bananas Looks at TV. New York, Scholastic, 1981.
The Beast Handbook. New York, Scholastic, 1981.
The Cool Kids' Guide to Summer Camp, with Jane Stine. New York, Scholastic, 1981.
Bored with Being Bored: How to Beat the Boredom Blahs, with Jane Stine. New York, Four Winds, 1982.
How to Wash a Duck, and How to Do Everything Else. New York, Scholastic, 1982.
Blips! The First Book of Video Game Funnies. New York, Scholastic, 1983.
Everything You Need to Survive: Brothers and Sisters, with Jane Stine. New York, Random House, 1983.
Everything You Need to Survive: First Dates, with Jane Stine. New York, Random House, 1983.
Everything You Need to Survive: Homework, with Jane Stine. New York, Random House, 1983.
Everything You Need to Survive: Money Problems, with Jane Stine. New York, Random House, 1983.
Jovial Bob's Computer Joke Book. New York, Scholastic, 1985.
101 Silly Monster Jokes. New York, Scholastic, 1986.

The Doggone Dog Joke Book. New York, Scholastic, 1986.
101 Wacky Kid Jokes. New York, Scholastic, 1988.
101 More Monster Jokes. New York, Scholastic, 1990.
101 School Cafeteria Jokes. New York, Scholastic, 1990.
101 Creepy Creature Jokes. New York, Scholastic, 1990.
101 Vacation Jokes. New York, Scholastic, 1990.

*

Media Adaptations: Television—*Goosebumps* series, 1995—.

Critical Study: *R. L. Stine* by Jill C. Wheeler, Edina, Minnesota, Abdo, 1996.

*   *   *

It is hard to say that R. L. Stine's astounding success is undeserved: he has always worked extremely hard, he has a manifest talent for telling scary stories, and he displays a genuine affinity with and concern for his youthful audience. Furthermore, while previous generations of teachers and librarians would have blanched at the notion of impressionable young minds reading about murderers, monsters and mad scientists, their modern counterparts, thrilled to see their charges reading anything at all, are freely accepting—if not exactly embracing—Stine as a prominent fixture in the field of juvenile and young-adult literature. While one might in this manner praise Stine for pleasing young readers and encouraging them to read, it remains to be seen whether Stine deserves, or might someday attain, the status of a major horror writer.

Certainly, Stine's irregular literary apprenticeship did not augur future greatness. As described in his affable "as-told-to" autobiography, *It Came from Ohio!*, Stine spent many years in New York City labouring in the uncharted netherworlds of American children's publishing, churning out innumerable magazine articles, formulaic books, and other items normally ignored by even the most dedicated bibliographers, such as coloring books and bubblegum cards. His sudden emergence as the author of popular horror novels for young adults, beginning with *Blind Date* in 1986, was therefore surprising. Stine endeavours to make it all seem like destiny, emphasizing his long-standing fascination with horror stories and movies, but the major focus of his own writing from childhood to the mid-1980s was actually humour—which is paradoxical, since his horror novels, whatever their other strengths, are rarely noteworthy for their humorous touches.

His novels for young adults—singletons like *Blind Date*, *The Baby-Sitter* and *The Snowman*, as well as innumerable items in various Fear Street series—are rather distinguished by their sense of earnestness and realism. As a former junior high-school teacher, Stine may best understand readers of that age: he seems to always pay full attention to the task of writing young-adult novels, his teenagers talk and act like real teenagers, his story lines are interesting and unpredictable, and the occasional instances of idiot plotting do not offend one's sensibilities because, in odd or stressful situations, actual adolescents might really act like idiots. The Fear Street novels, lately his only works for that audience, are linked by the setting of the town of Shadyside and its most notorious neighbourhood, a winding road known as Fear Street, with old dark houses near a cemetery and a shadowy forest. Here, teenagers facing a normal array of problems with school, parents, and

boyfriends and girlfriends must additionally cope with mysterious goings-on, typically featuring a number of murders or threatened murders. Most often, as in *The New Girl*, apparently supernatural events are finally explained rationally—the dead girl attending high school is actually an evil sister using her name—but other stories, like the three novels of the Catalana Chronicles, are genuinely fantastic—a race car is haunted by the homicidal spirit of a vengeful girl from colonial New England. Early novels in the series stressed the milieu of Fear Street and included characters introduced in other stories, but such connections are usually not as strong in later novels. Overall, while an increasing tendency to multi-part series and sequels suggests some slackening in creativity, the Fear Street novels are generally effective, despite the inevitable limitations in content and style imposed by mass-market young-adult fiction.

Stine's other major series, Goosebumps, is more difficult to admire, despite its great popularity. These short novels for children involve no recurring characters or settings, except in occasional sequels, and might be properly celebrated for their variegated and frequently imaginative redactions of the tropes of horror fiction. Still, only the earliest Goosebumps novels are wholly satisfying. For example, the first and most popular Goosebumps book, *Welcome to Dead House*, achieves some evocative power in its story of a town of zombies that must continually attract and murder new families in order to sustain its existence, and *Stay Out of the Basement!*, one of Stine's favourites, is a well-developed look at a family devastated by the father's obsessive experiments with plant life. But the quality of the Goosebumps novels has visibly declined, as if Stine decided that time and effort in this arena were not really necessary: sentences, paragraphs, and chapters have grown shorter and shorter; story lines, once mildly illogical, now often seem completely senseless; certain stock devices—irrationally evil bullies, bratty kid brothers or kid sisters—crop up again and again and again; and character development and description are so attenuated that the prose begins to resemble the lifeless drone of the semi-literate, plot-your-own-story books he once specialized in (a format he has recently returned to in the Give Yourself Goosebumps series, with devastatingly dismal results). Surely, even the most dedicated Goosebumps fan must find subpar efforts like *Monster Blood III* and *The Beast from the East* disappointing; and if recent reports of a catastrophic decline in Goosebumps sales prove accurate, Stine will have only himself to blame.

One might excuse Stine's lesser works by charitably theorizing that the obsessively intrusive editors governing mass-market juvenile literature—whose input Stine gratefully acknowledges in *It Came from Ohio!*—were driving him to mediocrity with their mind-numbing constraints; if so, then, a moment of liberation occurred in 1995, when he finally produced a horror novel for adults, *Superstitious*. Beginning the book with the first of several sex scenes, as if to clearly announce that he was no longer writing for children, Stine by some standards meets the challenge; the prose is competent, if unspectacular, and the story is lively and involving throughout. Still, unfortunate habits acquired in a lifetime of writing for children mar the novel. Tricks to end chapters with an artificial moment of suspense are borrowed, quite literally, from Goosebumps novels. (In *Say Cheese and Die!* Chapter 1 ends, "a dark form leapt up from the shadows of the tall weeds and attacked him!"—but it is only a dog; in *Superstitious* Chapter 10 ends, "the dark creature leapt out from behind the trees and grabbed roughly for her waist"—but it is only a dog.)

The plot is an idiot plot, hard to tolerate when it involves adults. Folklore professor Liam O'Connor engages in an idiotic scheme to release himself from an ancient curse. The idiotic police make no significant progress towards apprehending the one obvious suspect in a series of campus murders. And O'Connor's new wife Sara is an absolute idiot: even after her parents' cat is decapitated on the one night when Liam visits, and even after she receives four severed rabbit's feet on the day after Liam's pet rabbit dies, she refuses to believe that Liam had anything to do with the murders; and in the novel's last chapters, when the evidence is finally unavoidable, she insanely wanders around the campus until she encounters him, at times riding in a taxicab and sitting in a diner, without ever thinking about contacting the police or asking anyone around her for help. The last major problem is that a colourful conclusion suitable for children's fiction may be less palatable in adult fiction—here, the notion that Liam is the host body for an army of demons which emerge from his mouth to kill people whenever somebody violates an old superstition. It seems a rather silly ending for a novel that tried so hard to be mature.

Despite its flaws, *Superstitious* could conceivably be someday regarded as the pretty good start of a serious writing career; however, Stine to date has not chosen to write any other novels, either for youngsters or adults, that reflect any meaningful ambition. Instead of heeding the Muses, he has continued to serve Mammon, still writing one Goosebumps novel and one Fear Street novel every month, doing additional side projects like the Give Yourself Goosebumps books and the Tales to Give You Goosebumps stories, and allowing his name to be prominently displayed on several dozen books that he did not write, further diminishing his reputation. Perhaps he has simply become addicted to the adrenalin rush of nonstop writing and to the thrill of signing yet another lucrative contract. Stine thus may be living out the lesson of many horror stories: after you have been running on a treadmill for a while, it is hard to get off.

—Gary Westfahl

STOKER, Bram

Nationality: British. **Born:** Abraham Stoker in Clontarf, Dublin, 8 November, 1847. **Education:** Trinity College, Dublin; honours degree in pure mathematics. **Family:** Married Florence Balcombe in 1878; one son. **Career:** Civil servant, Dublin, 1870-77; theatre reviewer, *Dublin Mail*, and contributor of fiction to various magazines, 1870s; business manager to actor Henry Irving, Lyceum Theatre, London, 1878-1905. **Died:** 20 April 1912.

HORROR, GHOST AND GOTHIC PUBLICATIONS

Novels

Dracula. London, Constable, 1897; New York, Doubleday and McClure, 1899; abridged edition, Constable, 1900.
The Jewel of Seven Stars. London, Heinemann, 1903; New York, Harper, 1904.
The Lady of the Shroud. London, Heinemann, 1909; abridged edition, New York, Paperback Library, 1966.

The Lair of the White Worm. London, Rider, 1911; abridged as *The Garden of Evil*, New York, Paperback Library, 1966.

Short Stories

Under the Sunset. London, Sampson Low, 1881.
Dracula's Guest and Other Weird Stories. London, Routledge, 1914; New York, Hillman Curl, 1937.
The Bram Stoker Bedside Companion: Stories of Fantasy and Horror, edited by Charles Osborne. London, Gollancz, 1973.
Shades of Dracula: Bram Stoker's Uncollected Stories, edited by Peter Haining. London, Kimber, 1982.
The Dualitists. Edinburgh, Tragara Press, 1986.
Midnight Tales, edited by Peter Haining. London, Peter Owen, 1990.

OTHER PUBLICATIONS

Novels

The Snake's Pass. London, Sampson Low, 1890.
The Watter's Mou'. London, Constable, 1895.
The Shoulder of Shasta. London, Constable, 1895.
Miss Betty. London, Pearson, 1898.
The Mystery of the Sea. New York, Doubleday Page, and London, Heinemann, 1902.
The Man. London, Heinemann, 1905; abridged as *The Gates of Life*, New York, n.d.
Lady Athlyne. London, Heinemann, 1908.

Short Stories

Snowbound: The Record of a Theatrical Touring Party. New York, Collier, 1908.

Other

The Duties of Clerks of Petty Sessions in Ireland. Dublin, Falconer, 1879.
A Glimpse of America. London, Sampson Low, 1886.
Personal Reminiscences of Henry Irving. London, Heinemann, 2 vols., 1906.
Famous Impostors. London, Sidgwick and Jackson, 1910.

*

Film Adaptations (selection): *Nosferatu*, 1922, *Dracula*, 1931, 1958, 1973 (TV movie), *Count Dracula* (TV movie), 1977, *Dracula*, 1979, *Bram Stoker's Dracula*, 1992, all from the novel *Dracula*; *Dracula's Daughter*, 1936, *Brides of Dracula*, 1960, both suggested by the short story "Dracula's Guest"; *Blood from the Mummy's Tomb*, 1971, *The Awakening*, 1980, both from the novel *The Jewel of Seven Stars*; *The Lair of the White Worm*, 1988.

Bibliography: *Bram Stoker: A Bibliography of First Editions* by Richard Dalby, London, Dracula Press, 1983.

Critical Studies: *A Biography of Dracula: The Life Story of Bram Stoker* by Harry Ludlam, London, Foulsham, 1962; *A Dream of Dracula: In Search of the Living Dead* by Leonard Wolf, New

York, Popular Library, 1972; *In Search of Dracula* by Radu Florescu and Raymond T. McNally, New York, Warner, 1973; *The Man Who Wrote Dracula* by Daniel Farson, London, Michael Joseph, 1975; *The Dracula Scrapbook* edited by Peter Haining, London, New English Library, 1976; *Dracula, The Novel and the Legend: A Study of Bram Stoker's Gothic Masterpiece* by Clive Leatherdale, Wellingborough, Northamptonshire, Aquarian Press, 1985; *Dracula: The Vampire and the Critics* edited by Margaret L. Carter, Ann Arbor, Michigan, UMI Research Press, 1988; *Hollywood Gothic: The Tangled Web of "Dracula" from Novel to Stage to Screen* by David J. Skal, New York, Norton, and London, Deutsch, 1990; *Bram Stoker* by Barbara Belford, New York, Knopf, and London, Weidenfeld and Nicolson, 1996.

*   *   *

Bram Stoker's *Dracula* completed the set of three 19th-century horror stories which were to create modern myths in alliance with Hollywood. Like Mary Shelley's *Frankenstein* and Robert Louis Stevenson's *Strange Case of Dr. Jekyll and Mr. Hyde* it owed its origin to a nightmare, but it took Stoker many years of research and forethought to get himself to the point of beginning an actual draft. Even then he encountered difficulties, eventually dropping the opening sequence that was later published separately as "Dracula's Guest." What remains is untidy, although the presentation of the story as a patchwork of documents helps to sustain the pretence that the untidiness is merely superficial. In fact, it could hardly be more deep-seated; the novel is shot through with loose ends, unsettled questions, inept transitions and dramatic changes of emphasis. Such conundrums and confusions are part of the book's very essence. Had Dracula not been such a changeable and paradoxical character he could not have been half so fascinating; nor could he have been qualified to become the central monster of 20th-century folklore, celebrated as much by humour as by horror schlock, and as often redeemed—at least in recent times—as re-damned.

Stoker borrowed some of the inspiration for *Dracula* from John Polidori's "The Vampyre" and J. Sheridan Le Fanu's "Carmilla"—Stoker and Le Fanu were both graduates of Trinity College, Dublin—but when he went in search of an aristocratic model for the "king-vampire" of his nightmare he found a new one, as different from its predecessors as Carmilla Karnstein was from Lord Byron. This was the 15th-century Voivode Vlad Tepes, "the Impaler," who was also nicknamed Dragul ("Dragon" or "Devil"; Dracul in the Latinized version) but whose scribes often signed him Dragulya, meaning "son of Dragul," to distinguish him from his similarly-nicknamed father. In re-characterizing Dracula Stoker borrowed extensively but selectively from the rich Eastern European vampire folklore popularized by Dom Augustine Calmet. It was this carefully-processed research which produced the archetype of all modern literary vampires, determining their appearance, their abilities and their limitations (especially, of course, the fatal flaws which permit their destruction). Every modern vampire which violates this template does so consciously and deliberately; it cannot simply be ignored. No other novel of any kind has ever stamped out an image so firmly and so decisively.

Stoker's Dracula is supposed to be an incarnation of pure evil, but this role is confused even in the original text—a confusion which has paved the way for a vast range of calculated variations. In the dream which provided the seed from which the story grew

the "king-vampire" appeared only at the end, interrupting the female vampires who posed a more immediate threat to the dreamer—as they do, in the text, to Jonathan Harker. Harker therefore owes his life to the creature he subsequently determines to destroy. The main threat which Dracula subsequently poses is that of conferring extraordinary sexual attractiveness and a kind of immortality on the novel's two main female characters, Lucy and Mina. Stoker dutifully declared such a fate to be far worse than death, but he must have known that it had already been viewed in a more ambiguous light in works by John Keats, Théophile Gautier and others.

Like "Carmilla," *Dracula* is among the most strikingly erotic works published in Britain during the Victorian era, but if its conscientious representation of female "voluptuousness" and sexual appetite as a manifest disgrace is not consciously hypocritical it must surely be reckoned severely neurotic. Had such hypocrisies and neuroses died with Victoria Dracula would not have become so astonishingly promiscuous in his more recent seductions, but they did not—and all the heroic Draculas of the 20th-century *fin de siècle* have not yet succeeded in staking the unnaturally-beating hearts of those hypocrisies and neuroses, nor in reducing them to ashen dust with bright Enlightenment.

Stoker had always suffered the effects of a morbid imagination and had made earlier efforts to turn its produce to useful effect. His collection of allegorical fairy tales *Under the Sunset*—which does not seem to the modern eye to be very suitable for children—includes such dark pieces as "The Invisible Giant," about the ravages of plague, and "How 7 Went Mad." When *Dracula* became a runaway bestseller Stoker tried to follow it up with something similar but he had no idea how he had worked the trick and his attempts to copy it ranged from the feeble to the fatuous. There is an element of supernatural horror in the treasure-hunt story *The Mystery of the Sea*, but it remains fugitive and the story itself fizzles out. *The Jewel of Seven Stars* employs the then-fashionable motif of a revivifiable mummy of a lovely but accursed Egyptian queen, but the action comes to an abrupt conclusion just as the story proper seems to be about to begin. The original ending was, in fact, so brutally opaque that another (perhaps by another hand) was substituted in later editions, but the revamped version fails dismally to save the plot from cringing self-destruction. *The Lady of the Shroud* is an old-fashioned political Gothic in which vampirism plays a very peripheral (and probably illusory) role.

The Lair of the White Worm is one of the most spectacularly incoherent novels ever to reach print; the only excuse for its existence one can suggest is that it must have been based on another actual nightmare, which the aging and ailing Stoker had not time to gather into an organized plot. On the other hand, its lurid portrayal of the *femme fatale*'s doppelgänger as a great White Worm has offered intriguing fuel for thought to critics interested in sexual symbolism. The other short pieces collected in *Dracula's Guest* are not handicapped by Stoker's incapacity for organizing novel-length texts but they are mostly very weak. "The Judge's House" is a tolerable pastiche of Le Fanu and "The Secret of the Growing Gold" is effective even though the gold in question is only blonde hair, but the remainder are trivial. Attempts by Peter Haining and others to locate "lost" Stoker stories that had not been previously reprinted have produced nothing of any real interest.

At the end of the day, it seems as if the inspiration that led Bram Stoker to write *Dracula* was an unrepeatable accident of fate owing more to luck than judgment—but that should not detract from the credit due to its author. Nobody else ever wrote a book like *Dracula*, and it certainly has not been for want of trying.

—Brian Stableford

STOUT, Tim

Nationality: British. **Born:** 1946. **Family:** Married; one son and one daughter. **Career:** Editor, film magazine *Supernatural* (two issues, 1969); legal journalist. Lives in Leigh-on-Sea, Essex.

HORROR, GHOST AND GOTHIC PUBLICATIONS

Novel

The Raging. London, Grafton, 1987.

Short Stories

Hollow Laughter. London, Abelard, 1978.
The Doomsdeath Chronicles. London, Abelard, 1980.

*   *   *

During the mid-1970s Tim Stout was a contributor to a number of science-fiction and horror anthologies for younger readers. His "Christmas With Frankenstein" in *Space 4*, edited by Richard Davis, fused both genres in a comic tale of rampaging "monster" dolls. Following these anthologies there appeared two collections, *Hollow Laughter* and *The Doomsdeath Chronicles*, in which he was able to continue his vein of mordant humour.

His only novel, *The Raging*, concerns a statuette which inspires ferocious blood-lust in its possessors. When photographer Martin Chandler is passed the statue following a strange encounter with an axe-attacker in a ruined church, he tracks down the source of evil to the village of Maidenbury, whose population have been involved in outbreaks of violence for centuries. Chandler and psychologist-turned-probation officer Lee Valance find the secret of the "Maiden" in Celtic times: the goddess Draghera, the "Merry Maiden," the Mushroom Queen propitiated by blood sacrifice.

Although much of the story comes from the standard stock of horror tropes, from the shock opening to the cycle of violence through the ages, it is held together by Stout's effective mixture of physical and psychic horror and an understated dark wit. One scene, for instance, set in the office of the local newspaper, reveals the "Nutters List" of frequent callers: one suspects that there is an in-joke here. Elsewhere, Stout dramatically exploits the device of having his hero involved with a local Historical Re-enactment Society.

Although there is nothing specifically Lovecraftian about the novel, either in prose style or plotting, its focus upon locality, history, psychic threats from outside, and its mixture of science fiction and supernaturalism make it slightly reminiscent of some of Lovecraft's stories. More appropriately, these elements, standard fare in much horror fiction, are by no means exhausted and are carefully put together here. While *The Raging* is no landmark of the genre it is the kind of story that would make an extremely

entertaining movie, and it is somewhat to be regretted that no one in the film world seems to have noticed it.

—Andy Sawyer

STRACZYNSKI, J(oseph) Michael

Nationality: American. **Born:** Paterson, New Jersey, 17 July 1954. **Education:** Kankakee Community College, 1972-73; Richland College, 1973; Southwestern College, A.A. 1975; San Diego State University, B.A. 1978. **Family:** Married Kathryn May Drennan in 1983. **Career:** Instructor, Grossmont Junior College, 1978; editor in chief, *Racquetball News*, 1978; personal and academic counsellor, San Diego State University, 1978-79; special correspondent and reviewer, *Daily Californian*, 1978-79; instructor, San Diego State University, 1979; entertainment editor, theatre and film reviewer, KSDO-AM radio, San Diego, 1979-81; artistic director, resident writer, producer, director and facilitator, Airstage Radiodrama Productions, 1980-81; contributing editor and columnist, *Writer's Digest*, 1981-91; executive story consultant, story editor and writer, *Captain Power and the Soldiers of the Future*, 1986-87; story editor and writer, *The Real Ghostbusters* (animated), 1986-89; host, weekly programme "Hour 25," KPFK-FM radio, Los Angeles, 1987-92; story editor, *Twilight Zone*, 1987-88; executive story consultant, *Jake and the Fatman*, 1989-90; producer, *Murder, She Wrote*, 1991-92; producer, *Walker: Texas Ranger*, 1993; creator and producer, *Babylon 5*, from 1993. **Awards:** Hugo award for dramatic presentation, 1995; named one of the 50 "most influential thinkers-innovators who will shape our lives as we move into the 21st century" by *Newsweek* magazine, 1995.

HORROR, GHOST AND GOTHIC PUBLICATIONS

Novels

Demon Night. New York, Dutton, 1988; London, Sphere, 1989.
OtherSyde. New York, Dutton, 1990; London, Headline, 1991.

Short Stories

Tales from the New Twilight Zone. New York, Bantam, 1989.

Plays

Radio Plays: Episodes of *Alien Worlds* series, 1979-80.

Television Plays: 9 episodes of *He-Man and the Masters of the Universe* (animated), 1984; 9 episodes of *She-Ra, Princess of Power* (animated), 1985; 14 episodes of *Jayce and the Wheeled Warriors* (animated), 1986; 11 episodes of *Captain Power and the Soldiers of the Future*, 1986-87; 23 episodes of *The Real Ghostbusters* (animated), 1986-89; 12 episodes of *Twilight Zone*, 1986-88; 2 episodes of *Nightmare Classics*, 1989; 5 episodes of *Jake and the Fatman*, 1989-90; 7 episodes of *Murder, She Wrote*, 1991-92; 1 episode of *Walker, Texas Ranger*, 1993; 71 episodes of *Babylon 5*, 1993-97.

Other

The Complete Book of Scriptwriting: Television, Radio, Motion Pictures, the Stage Play. Cincinnati, Writer's Digest, 1982; revised edition (including a complete script from *Babylon 5*), Writer's Digest, 1996.

Comic-book scripts for *Star Trek, Teen Titans, Twilight Zone.*

*   *   *

While the various *Star Trek* series are generically related to fantasy, with the brave knights of Starfleet defending the noble Federation of Planets from evil invaders, *Babylon 5* is closer in spirit to horror—with a universe that is far more unsettled, and unsettling, lacking a benevolent overarching order, and with aliens who are far less familiar and friendly, including the menacing Shadows whose appearance evokes the sort of visceral fear that *Star Trek* rarely if ever traffics in. It is only appropriate, then, that J. Michael Straczynski—the man who created, produced and largely wrote *Babylon 5*—devoted his brief career as a prose fiction writer to the genre of horror.

First novels are seldom scintillating, and Straczynski's first novel, *Demon Night*, is too visibly influenced by Stephen King, right down to its use of a small town in Maine as its locale. Eric Matthews, suffering from recurring nightmares and fits of telekinetic destructiveness, returns to his home town, Dredmouth Point, to eventually learn that he has inherited psychic powers to guard against a sinister ancient spirit imprisoned in the dark and mysterious Indian Caves. When an archaeologist unwittingly releases the spirit, it begins to kill residents and turn them into murderous zombies that seek out new victims; while a priest bravely resists an army of the dead invading his church, Eric and a local policeman enter the Caves to confront the source of the evil. Though the novel is competently executed, Straczynski conveys little affinity for his characters or setting, and the resulting story inevitably seems mannered and unpersuasive.

During the time that he was completing *Demon Night*, Straczynski worked one year as a writer and story editor for a syndicated version of *The Twilight Zone*; and the scripts he crafted, recast as short stories in *Tales from the New Twilight Zone*, are far more satisfying. Better than any of the other writers who worked on various revivals of *The Twilight Zone*, Straczynski perfectly entered into and maintained the ambience of Rod Serling's original vision. For example, although Alan Brennert's "Her Pilgrim Soul" was an intriguing story, it would have seemed out of place in the first series. In contrast, Straczynski's "The Curious Case of Edgar Witherspoon," about an eccentric elderly man who must continually collect odd items for a machine that enigmatically keeps the world running smoothly, evokes the quirky sense of humour of the first series; "The Call," in which a lonely man receives a phone call from a statue that comes to life at night and ultimately joins her in becoming a statue, recalls the poignancy of the old *Twilight Zone*; "Acts of Terror," where a wife's suppressed anger at her violent and abusive husband brings to life a vicious Doberman who attacks the man and lets her escape, illustrates the belief in cosmic justice often advanced by the first series; and "The Mind of Simon Foster," about a future America where a desperate unemployed man must sell his memories to survive, is a characteristic *Twilight Zone* scenario of a nightmarish future. And yet, as Straczynski's introductions to the stories demonstrate,

these are not mere homages, but are also organic products of Straczynski's experiences and personal vision. Overall, it is regrettable that Straczynski's version of *The Twilight Zone* ended after one season.

Despite the success of those stories, however, Straczynski's second novel, *OtherSyde*, must be regarded as his crowning achievement in prose. Strange creatures from an undefined "OtherSyde," who can manifest themselves as anything from cockroaches and spiders to beautiful women, seek people in our world who can serve as channels for their destructive energies. When high-school student Chris Martino moves from New Jersey to Los Angeles (just as Straczynski did), he befriends an unpopular boy named Roger Obst, and the notes they give each other written in lemon-juice invisible ink begin to include messages from OtherSyde denizens. More attracted to them than Chris, Roger constructs a telegraph machine following their instructions to communicate with them better, moves away from his abusive father to an underground den, and is soon having his OtherSyde companions kill various enemies from high school, though their deaths are regarded by puzzled police officers as an unexplained series of teenage suicides. As suspicions grow and Roger's alienation increases, he finally unleashes a night of terror, as the OtherSyde causes a massive power blackout in Los Angeles, leading to rioting and looting, while creatures begin to systematically kill every student at Roger's high school. Chris and the police locate and kill Roger, stopping the slaughter, but the OtherSyde moves on to recruit a new messenger in Chicago.

From the very beginning, it is apparent here that Straczynski has chosen characters and settings far more suitable for his talents and interests, and the novel is authentic and evocative throughout because its horrors, unlike the stalking zombies of Dredmouth Point, are effectively linked to real-world horrors of modern life like bullying, child abuse and urban crime. Furthermore, its final scenes of a Los Angeles engulfed in darkness, flames and looters (in some ways eerily anticipating the riots following the 1992 Rodney King verdicts) constitute a genuinely frightening vision of a modern apocalypse.

OtherSyde includes a prediction of another sort regarding Straczynski's own future: Chris enjoys watching a series called *Babylon 5* which is "one of his favorite programs, the only decent science-fiction series on TV." And, after finishing his second novel, Straczynski devoted the 1990s to making that prediction come true, focusing his energies so much on the series that in 1996 and 1997, he apparently became the first person to write an entire season of scripts for a dramatic television series. Yet the end of *Babylon 5* will find Straczynski still a relatively young writer with many productive years in front of him; and while he will undoubtedly have many good options, he seems well prepared for a triumphant career as a horror writer, and might also profitably pay another visit to *The Twilight Zone*.

—Gary Westfahl

STRAUB, Peter (Francis)

Nationality: American. **Born:** Milwaukee, Wisconsin, 2 March 1943. **Education:** University of Wisconsin-Madison, B.A. 1965;

Columbia University, M.A. 1966; attended University College, Dublin, 1969-72. **Family:** Married Susan Bitker, 1966; one son, one daughter. **Career:** University School, Milwaukee, Wisconsin, English teacher, 1966-69; writer from 1969. **Awards:** British Fantasy award and August Derleth award, both 1983; World Fantasy award for best novel, 1989. **Member:** Writers Action Group. **Address:** P.O. Box 395, Greens Farms, CT 06436, USA.

HORROR, GHOST AND GOTHIC PUBLICATIONS

Novels

Julia. New York, Coward McCann, 1975; London, Cape, 1976; as *Full Circle*, London, Corgi, 1977.
If You Could See Me Now. New York, Coward McCann, and London, Cape, 1977.
Ghost Story. New York, Coward McCann, and London, Cape, 1979.
Shadowland. New York, Coward McCann, 1980; as *Shadow Land*, London, Collins, 1981.
Floating Dragon. San Francisco, and Columbia, Pennsylvania, Underwood Miller, 1982; London, Collins, 1983.
The Talisman, with Stephen King. New York and London, Viking, 1984.
Wild Animals: Three Novels (omnibus; includes *Julia, If You Could See Me Now, Under Venus*). New York, Viking, 1984.
Koko. New York, Dutton, and London, Viking, 1988.
Mystery. New York, Dutton, and London, Grafton, 1990.
The Throat. New York, Dutton, and London, HarperCollins, 1993.
The Hellfire Club. New York, Random House, and London, HarperCollins, 1996.

Short Stories

Blue Rose. San Francisco, and Columbia, Pennsylvania, Underwood Miller, 1985.
Mrs. God. Hampton Falls, New Hampshire, Grant, 1990.
Houses Without Doors. London, Grafton, 1990; New York, Dutton, 1991.

Other

Editor, *Peter Straub's Ghosts.* New York, Pocket, 1995.

OTHER PUBLICATIONS

Novels

Marriages. London, Deutsch, and New York, Coward McCann, 1973.
The General's Wife. West Kingston, Rhode Island, Grant, 1982.
Under Venus. New York, Berkley, 1985.

Poetry

Ishmael. London(?), Turret Books, 1972.
Open Air. Dublin(?), Irish University Press, 1972.
Leeson Park and Belsize Square: Poems 1970-1975. San Francisco, and Columbia, Pennsylvania, Underwood Miller, 1983.

Other

Editor, *20 Under 35.* London, Sceptre, 1988.

*

Film Adaptations: *Full Circle* (*The Haunting of Julia*), 1976, from the novel *Julia*; *Ghost Story*, 1981.

*   *   *

After writing a mediocre mainstream novel, *Marriages*, Peter Straub was encouraged by his agent to write something more marketable—a "gothic." The result was *Julia*, and thereafter Straub has kept up a steady stream of substantial if inconsistent works of horror and suspense. He achieved bestseller status with *Ghost Story*; but in recent years Straub has turned almost exclusively to writing large novels mixing mainstream concern with the development of character with complex mystery/suspense plots. Some of these works have considerable merit, but cannot be said to belong to the realm of horror.

The bulk of Straub's weird work is structured around a single conception: a force or personality occupying the bodies of various human beings (usually women) over successive generations, sometimes over the course of centuries. This premise is utilized in three of his first five horror novels, and a slight variant is used in a fourth.

Julia concerns a woman, Julia Lofting, whose daughter Kate died at the age of nine. Julia is shattered by the loss and eventually leaves her domineering husband Magnus, who she believes accidentally killed her child. We are initially led to think that Kate is haunting Julia, but later we learn the truth: Julia was the one who killed her daughter, not Magnus—she had been repressing the incident all along. *Julia* is a compact and effective work, skilful in its false suggestion of the supernatural and subtle in its portrayal of a neurotic personality.

In *If You Could See Me Now*, Alison Greening, a fetching young girl who entrances the young Miles Teagarden, tells him just prior to her death at the age of 14 that they should make a vow to meet in their hometown in Wisconsin in 20 years, even if they are dead. Miles does indeed return to his hometown (ostensibly to write his Ph.D. dissertation, but in reality because he feels a strange need to adhere to Alison's portentous adjuration) and he keenly feels the town's lingering resentment of him for his role in Alison's death, a sentiment now augmented by his sophisticated ways in contrast to their small-town ways. Miles becomes the chief suspect in the several murders of young women that has been occurring around the town, but he himself comes to believe that the spirit of Alison has returned and is causing the deaths, a view that proves all too correct.

The core of *Ghost Story* is already evident in *If You Could See Me Now*. In that novel three men were fascinated with Alison Greening as boys. The four old men of *Ghost Story* were similarly fascinated as youths with the actress Eva Galli, whom another member of their circle, Edward Wanderley, brought into their small New York town. We eventually learn that these five men actually killed the actress and then concealed her body so as not to endanger their careers and reputations. The last third or so of the novel is largely an adventure story in which the men, who are being systematically killed off by the spirit of the actress, pursue and attempt to kill her.

Ghost Story is transparently derived from Machen's "The Great God Pan," in which a group of individuals compare notes and find that the strange woman who, under different guises, has haunted their lives is the same person. Straub has explicitly acknowledged the influence in an interview. The novel is, however, richly textured in its description of the small town in upstate New York where it is set, and in its complex interweaving of different narratives and different time-sequences.

Floating Dragon continues the theme of an evil spirit possessing a succession of bodies. The entity in question occupies male bodies this time; but otherwise the novel is startlingly similar in conception to *Ghost Story*. As in that novel, we are treated to a variety of different narrative voices, as the various protagonists gradually come together in the small and wealthy suburban town of Hampstead, Connecticut, to confront the horror. This horror has been causing periodic disasters in the town since colonial times, and for some unexplained reason it seems stronger once every hundred years. Alas, we are in one of those periods now, and people die in great numbers before the protagonists unite to dispel the creature—apparently by singing happy songs. *Floating Dragon* is a serious letdown after the relative success of the three works discussed previously; aside from the novel's verbosity, there is a fundamental confusion in the supernatural premise, since we never know how the body- and century-hopping spirit is supposed to relate to a poison gas that, at the outset of the novel, is accidentally released from a chemical plant and causes a variety of bizarre ailments.

In *Shadowland* Straub is clearly trying to do something very different from his other works. We are here concerned with breaking or expanding the bounds of reality; and the mechanism for this process is sleight-of-hand—progressing from card tricks to more and more elaborate feats of prestidigitation until finally we are evidently to perceive the utter instability and superficiality of a world that purports to be governed by science and rationality. But the novel ends up numbing and stupefying the reader with its plethora of bizarre events; toward the end they simply lose force through sheer surfeit. Add to this a pretentious writing style and unsympathetic characters, and the result is that *Shadowland* must be classed a noble failure.

Analogous to *Shadowland* in stressing fantasy over horror is Straub's collaboration with Stephen King, *The Talisman*. The novel is a colossal failure, and seems largely to have been the result of a publishing gimmick—the teaming up of the two most popular horror writers of the period. One would like to think that King had more to do with this plodding and atrociously written story of a boy's quest across a fantasized United States in search of a cure for his mother's illness than Straub did.

Straub's only other contribution to weird fiction is the story collection *Houses Without Doors*, which contains two fine long stories. In "The Buffalo Hunter" Straub appears to imitate Ramsey Campbell in its depiction of a character's gradual deterioration from seeming normalcy to lunacy and death as he invents a fantasy life for himself as a ladies' man so that his parents will think him "normal." In "Mrs. God" (also published separately in a somewhat augmented form) Straub produces a fine pastiche of Robert Aickman featuring a pervasive atmosphere of weirdness found nowhere else in his work. The story's setting in an English country house, the inexplicable events, and the polished, erudite atmosphere all proclaim allegiance to the elusive and occasionally confusing Aickman.

Straub's remaining novels are of the mystery/suspense type, with *Koko*, *Mystery* and *The Throat* forming a loose trilogy in their interrelated characters. *The Throat* in particular is a brilliant and compulsively readable work, as is *The Hellfire Club*, although many events in the latter stretch the bounds of credulity. But they are not true horror novels.

—S. T. Joshi

STRIEBER, (Louis) Whitley

Pseudonym: Jonathan Barry. **Nationality:** American. **Born:** San Antonio, Texas, 13 June 1945. **Education:** University of Texas. **Career:** Worked in advertising, New York, during the 1970s; became a successful novelist; later gained some notoriety with his book *Communion*, in which he claimed to have been abducted by aliens in 1985 (a memory which had become apparent to him, when under hypnosis, in 1986). Lives in Texas.

Horror, Ghost and Gothic Publications

Novels

The Wolfen. New York, Morrow, 1978; London, Coronet, 1979.
The Hunger. New York, Morrow, 1981.
Black Magic. New York, Morrow, 1982; London, Severn House, 1987.
The Night Church. New York, Simon and Schuster, 1983; London, Severn House, 1986.
Catmagic (as Jonathan Barry and Whitley Strieber). New York, Tor, 1986; as Strieber alone, London, Grafton, 1987.
Majestic. New York, Putnam, 1989; revised edition, London, Macdonald, 1990.
Billy. New York, Putnam, and London, Macdonald, 1990.
The Wild. New York, Tor, and London, Macdonald, 1991.
Unholy Fire. New York, Tor, and London, Macdonald, 1992.
The Forbidden Zone. New York, Dutton, 1993; London, New English Library, 1994.

Other Publications

Novels

War Day, and the Journey Onward, with James Kunetka. New York, Holt Rinehart, 1984.
Wolf of Shadows. New York, Knopf, 1985; London, Hodder and Stoughton, 1986.
Nature's End: The Consequences of the Twentieth Century, with James Kunetka. New York, Warner, and London, Grafton, 1986.

Plays

Screenplay: *Communion*, 1989.

Other

Communion: A True Story. New York, Morrow, and London, Hutchinson, 1987.

Transformation: The Breakthrough. New York, Morrow, and London, Hutchinson, 1988.
Breakthrough: The Next Step. New York, HarperCollins, 1995.

*

Film Adaptations: *The Wolfen*, 1981; *The Hunger*, 1983; *Communion*, 1989.

* * *

Whitley Strieber's reputation as a major horror writer would have been safe had he never published anything in the genre after his first novel, *The Wolfen*. That amazingly effective debut novel turned the werewolf story completely on its head, because the wolves in this case weren't shape-changers but rather a species of intelligent creature that had co-existed with humans throughout our history. They so strongly resemble wolves that they were able to pass unnoticed, and they carefully chose their human prey from the fringes of civilization, people whose absence would not be noticed, primarily from among the homeless population. Their secret is in jeopardy, however, when two detectives learn too much, and the wolves set out to track them down and kill them. The juxtaposition of wolves and a major city, and Strieber's description of their tenacity, creates an almost unbearable narrative tension. Breathtakingly suspenseful throughout, *The Wolfen* was immediately recognized as a classic, and subsequently made into a surprisingly good movie.

Strieber followed up by providing a marvellous twist to the vampire story, *The Hunger*. Vampires are real in this instance, but their existence has its own punishment. Although they are immortal, male vampires eventually wither and become almost insubstantial shades, powerless to act. Female vampires, on the other hand, appear to maintain their vigour forever. The protagonist watches her current lover fade away and searches for a new companion when his despair makes him unmanageable. The erotic side of vampirism comes through clearly, and the eerie fate of the protagonist's consort almost makes the reader sympathetic. This novel was also turned into a film, although not as successfully as was the case with *The Wolfen*.

Black Magic was marketed as horror, but is essentially a hi-tech spy story, with a few creepy scenes, perhaps written as a change of pace. *The Night Church* returned to genuine horror, this time in the form of a mysterious cult which plans to breed a new strain of human being, one that would be predisposed to worship Satan and act in his service. The individual scenes in the novel are better than the sum of its parts, hampered by an uneven pacing that interferes with the story flow. The novel remains enjoyable, but lacks the adventurous inventiveness of Strieber's previous work.

Catmagic is a quieter, more controlled novel, dealing with modern-day witchcraft. Amanda Walker is an artist who discovers that she has the potential to become a powerful witch, and that occult forces in the city intend to use her as their tool in a magical ceremony. In order to preserve her life, and avert the threatened evil, Amanda has to learn the ways of magic and engage in an occult duel with her enemies. A tightly controlled, almost soft-spoken horror novel that avoids excessive melodrama and violence in favour of careful plotting and restrained narration.

Strieber returned to the werewolf theme, this time in a more traditional fashion, for *The Wild*. Bob Duke is troubled by dreams in which he believes himself to be a wolf and is even more upset when his body does physically begin to change. Altered into the semblance of a wolf, he loses himself in a major city where his family desperately searches both for him and for a way to reverse the transformation. Although the theme is a common one in horror fiction, the treatment is very untraditional and carefully avoids genre motifs, preferring instead to deal seriously with the man's plight, and by implication commenting upon our mental dissociation from the natural world.

Father John Rafferty, a troubled priest, is the protagonist of *Unholy Fire*. Rafferty has had doubts about his avocation, and has been further dismayed by the plight of one of his parishioners, a beautiful young woman who is subsequently brutally murdered and her body left in his church. After discovering that the woman secretly led a life of great depravity, Rafferty considers this a personal failing of his own and is compelled to investigate the circumstances of her death. He eventually uncovers the existence of a serial killer, a charming figure inhabited by a spirit who has escaped from Hell itself.

The Forbidden Zone is a story of the bad place, in this case a mound of soil in upstate New York. A series of bizarre apparitions, strange lights, gelatinous tentacles and armies of deadly insects plague the area until a small group grow convinced that something in the mound has caused a rift in reality, and that unless it is closed the evil may spread to encompass the entire world. A skilfully contrived variation with several particularly unsettling scenes, but the characters never really come to life and their fate is therefore not as emotionally involving for the reader.

Whitley Strieber's short fiction, which generally has a much more artificial and distanced viewpoint than his novels, includes a number of noteworthy tales including "Perverts," in which a hobo is seduced into performing sexually before a strange audience, "The Pool," an almost surreal vision of a man, his son, and a deadly swimming pool, and "Pain," in which a writer studying sado-masochism and prostitution is initiated into another level of reality by a woman he is interviewing. "The Nixon Mask" is a very odd piece about Richard Nixon awaiting trick-or-treaters at the White House, and becoming obsessed with a mask of his own face that he spots on one of the visitors. In "I Walk the Night" a hideously disfigured man takes to the streets and finds a home of sorts with a female impersonator. Each of these stories is deliberately written in a non-realistic style that is quite different from Strieber's prose at novel length, and the horrors come from within rather than without.

Whitley Strieber remains one of the major players in the horror genre, although his recent novels rely more on conventional storytelling skills than on the original concepts that made his first two so memorable. His science-fiction novel *Majestic*, which deals with secret alien visitations on Earth (and hence ties in with his two bestselling "non-fiction" books, *Communion* and *Transformation*), may also be of interest to horror readers.

—Don D'Ammassa

STURGEON, Theodore (Hamilton)

Pseudonyms: Frederick R. Ewing; Ellery Queen. **Nationality:** American. **Born:** Edward Hamilton Waldo in Staten Island, New York, 26 February 1918; name changed on adoption, 1929. **Edu-**

cation: Attended Overbrook High School, Philadelphia. **Family:** Married 1) Dorothy Fillingame in 1940, two daughters; 2) Mary Mair in 1949; 3) Marion Sturgeon in 1951, four children; 4) Wina Golden in 1969, one son; 5) Jayne Tannehill. **Career:** Salesman in early 1930s; seaman, 1935-38; hotel manager, West Indies, 1940-41; assistant chief steward for United States Army, 1941; bulldozer operator, Puerto Rico, 1942-43; advertising-copy editor, 1944; literary agent, 1946-47; circulation staff member, *Fortune* and *Time*, New York, 1948-49; story editor, *Tales of Tomorrow*, 1950; feature editor, 1961-64, and contributing editor, 1972-74, *If*, New York; television writer, 1966-75. Book reviewer, *Venture*, 1957-58, *Galaxy*, 1972-74, and *New York Times*, 1974-75; columnist, *National Review*, New York, 1961-73. **Awards:** *Argosy* prize, 1947; International Fantasy award, 1954; Nebula award, 1970; Hugo award, 1971. Guest of Honor, 20th World Science Fiction Convention, 1962; World Fantasy Convention Life Achievement award, 1985. **Died:** 8 May 1985.

HORROR, GHOST AND GOTHIC PUBLICATIONS

Novels

The Dreaming Jewels. New York, Greenberg, 1950; London, Nova, 1955; as *The Synthetic Man*, New York, Pyramid, 1957.
Some of Your Blood. New York, Ballantine, 1961; London, Sphere, 1967.

Short Stories

It. Philadelphia, Prime Press, 1948.
Without Sorcery: Thirteen Tales. Philadelphia, Prime Press, 1948; abridged as *Not without Sorcery*, New York, Ballantine, 1961.
E Pluribus Unicorn. New York, Abelard Press, 1953; London, Abelard Schuman, 1960.
Beyond. New York, Avon, 1960.
The Worlds of Theodore Sturgeon. New York, Ace, 1972.
Visions and Venturers. New York, Dell, 1978; London, Gollancz, 1979.
The Golden Helix. Garden City, New York, Doubleday, 1979.

OTHER PUBLICATIONS

Novels

More Than Human. New York, Farrar Straus, 1953; London, Gollancz, 1954.
I, Libertine, with Jean Shepherd (as Frederick R. Ewing). New York, Ballantine, 1956.
The King and Four Queens (novelization of screenplay). New York, Dell, 1956.
The Cosmic Rape. New York, Dell, 1958.
Venus Plus X. New York, Pyramid, 1960; London, Gollancz, 1969.
Voyage to the Bottom of the Sea (novelization of screenplay). New York, Pyramid, 1961.
The Player on the Other Side (as Ellery Queen). New York, Random House, 1963.
The Rare Breed (novelization screenplay). Greenwich, Connecticut, Fawcett, 1966.
Godbody. New York, Fine, 1986.

Short Stories

Caviar. New York, Ballantine, 1955; London, Sidgwick and Jackson, 1968.
A Way Home: Stories of Science Fiction and Fantasy. New York, Funk and Wagnalls, 1955; abridged as *Thunder and Roses: Stories of Science Fiction and Fantasy,* London, Joseph, 1957.
A Touch of Strange. Garden City, New York, Doubleday, 1958; London, Hamlyn, 1978.
Aliens 4. New York, Avon, 1959.
Sturgeon in Orbit. New York, Pyramid, 1964; London, Gollancz, 1970.
The Joyous Invasions. London, Gollancz, 1965.
Two Complete Novels: ... And My Fear Is Great; Baby Is Three. New York, Galaxy Magabook, 1965.
Starshine. New York, Pyramid, 1966; London, Gollancz, 1968.
Sturgeon Is Alive and Well.... New York, Putnam, 1971; expanded edition, as *To Here and the Easel*, London, Gollancz, 1973.
Sturgeon's West, with Don Ward. Garden City, New York, Doubleday, 1973.
Case and the Dreamer and Other Stories. Garden City, New York, Doubleday, 1974; London, Pan, 1974.
Maturity: Three Stories, edited by Scott Imes and Stuart W. Wells III. Minneapolis, Science Fiction Society, 1979.
The Stars Are the Styx. New York, Dell, 1979.
Slow Sculpture. New York, Pocket Books, 1982.
Alien Cargo. New York, Bluejay, 1984.
Pruzy's Pot. Eugene, Oregon, Hypatia Press, 1986.
A Touch of Sturgeon, edited by David Pringle. London, Simon and Schuster, 1987.
To Marry Medusa. New York, Baen, 1987.
The [Widget], the [Wadget], and Boff, bound with *The Ugly Little Boy* by Isaac Asimov. New York, Tor, 1989.
The Ultimate Egoist: The Complete Stories, Volume 1, edited by Paul Williams. Berkeley, California, North Atlantic Books, 1994.
Microcosmic God: The Complete Stories, Volume 2, edited by Paul Williams. Berkeley, California, North Atlantic Books, 1996.
Killdozer!: The Complete Stories, Volume 3, edited by Paul Williams. Berkeley, California, North Atlantic Books, 1996.

Plays

It Should Be Beautiful (produced Woodstock, New York, 1963).
Psychosis: Unclassified, adaptation of his novel *Some of Your Blood* (produced 1977).

Radio Plays: *Incident at Switchpath,* 1950; *The Stars Are the Styx,* 1953; *Mr. Costello, Hero,* 1956; *Saucer of Loneliness,* 1957; *The Girl Had Guts, The Skills of Xanadu,* and *Affair with a Green Monkey,* all 1960s; *More Than Human,* 1967.

Television Plays: *Mewhu's Jet* and *The Adaptive Ultimate,* from fiction by Stanley Weinbaum (*Beyond Tomorrow* series), *They Came to Bagdad,* from the novel by Agatha Christie (*Playhouse 90* series), *Ordeal in Space,* from story by Robert Heinlein, and *The Sound Machine,* from story by Roald Dahl (both *CBS Stage 14* series)—all 1950s; *Dead Dames Don't Dial (Schlitz Playhouse* series), 1959; *Shore Leave,* 1966, and *Amok Time,* 1967 (both *Star Trek* series); *Killdozer!,* with Ed MacKillop, from the story by Sturgeon, 1974; *The Pylon Express (Land of the Lost* series), 1975-76.

Other

Argyll: A Memoir. Glen Ellen, California, Sturgeon Project, 1993.

Comic Books: *Iron Munro* (2 issues), 1940; *How to Build Boats,* 1940; *It,* 1972; *Killdozer!,* 1974; *Microcosmic God,* 1976.

*

Bibliography: *Theodore Sturgeon: A Primary and Secondary Bibliography* by Lahna F. Diskin, Boston, Hall, 1980.

Critical Studies: *Theodore Sturgeon* by Lucy Menger, New York, Ungar, 1981; *Theodore Sturgeon* by Lahna F. Diskin, Mercer Island, Washington, Starmont House, 1981.

*   *   *

Theodore Sturgeon began writing for the pulp magazines in the late 1930s but his subsequent career was subject to several interruptions. He wrote little during the years when the United States was involved in World War II and his publications petered out again after 1960; except for one short burst of creativity in 1969-71 he never really recovered from the lifelong block that afflicted him thereafter. He attained his greatest celebrity as a science-fiction writer but much of his work in that genre has a horrific edge and he wrote a number of exceptionally fine supernatural horror stories. He began writing such tales for *Unknown,* to which he contributed the ultimate monster story "It" (1940), in which a little girl falls prey to an entity which is the very essence of nastiness.

"Shottle Bop" (1941) and "The Hag Seleen" (1942, in collaboration with James H. Beard) are more flippantly ironic stories more typical of *Unknown*'s produce, but it was the keen sensitivity of "It," combined with the frank and intimate characterization which he gradually developed, that made Sturgeon a particularly deft writers of *contes cruels.* His most effective horror story of the first phase of his career, "Bianca's Hands"—about a man whose sexual obsession with the lovely hands of an idiot girl leads inexorably to a strangulatory consummation—was considered too extreme for magazine publication in the United States and eventually appeared in the United Kingdom in 1947. The work of Sturgeon's second prolific period includes several harrowing studies of obsession, all written with great feeling although his attitude to particular obsessions ranges from lachrymose pity to adamantine despite.

The one story Sturgeon wrote during the war years, "Killdozer!" (1944), is about the possession of a giant bulldozer by a homicidal alien intelligence. He wrote several other tales of malign possession for *Weird Tales,* including "Cellmate" (1947), "The Professor's Teddy Bear" (1948) and "The Perfect Host" (1948), all of which feature human characters forced by numinous demonic prompters to commit acts of cruelty. "One Foot and the Grave" (1949) features a battle between two opposed possessors, which the author refuses to characterize as good and evil; it is implied that they might rather be seen as the opposed forces of human reason and unrestrained appetite. In the similar contest described in "Excalibur and the Atom" (1951) it is the destructive combatant which needs to be given freer rein, so that stultifying edifices of belief might be blasted apart.

Sturgeon's first novel, *The Dreaming Jewels,* features the monstrous misanthrope Pierre Montre, a neo-Gothic villain who runs a carnival in order to justify and support his search for the freak-ish mutations caused by mysterious alien crystals. The hero of the tale is a boy who must come to terms with his own freakishness before he can turn his crystal-donated powers to far better ends than Montre's. Sturgeon subsequently adopted the pseudoscientific jargon of "psi-powers" in order to present a series of similar battles in which individuals granted supernatural powers must learn to use them responsibly—an unravelling chain of inquiry which examined with minute care the question of how godlike powers might best be used. The most horrific tales in this sequence are those which castigate various kind of evident misuse. "Talent" (1953) is a gruesomely ironic account of a sadistic little boy who eventually falls victim to one of his own supernaturally-aided whims. "A Way of Thinking" (1953) is the story of a lateral thinker who finds his own way to take revenge on a voodoo doll.

These allegorical stories continued to gain in sophistication as Sturgeon's prolific period progressed. He continued to invent striking neo-Gothic villains, relatively straightforward studies in sadomasochism like "Mr. Costello, Hero" (1953) and "When You're Smiling" (1955) giving way to the complex account of wayward genius Heri Gonza in "The Comedian's Children" (1958). "The Graveyard Reader" (1958) is a beautifully sensitive story about a man who learns to "read" graves, thus to empathize with the dead. "Need" (1960) is also a story of a man gifted with extraordinary empathy, this time to the pain of the living; it is perhaps the most harrowing of all Sturgeon's works by virtue of its careful analysis of the intolerability of such a condition.

Some of Your Blood takes the form of a case-study in psychoanalysis, whose hero must figure out exactly why a young soldier seems to have gone mad. It soon becomes evident that he is a vampire, but the point of the story is to address the reflexive repugnance caused by the novel way he has discovered of coping with his condition: consuming the menstrual discharges of a helpful female friend. In the later, unfortunately largely unproductive, part of his career Sturgeon became increasingly concerned with attacking what he considered to be unreasoning and unreasonable taboos, although he never produced another tale quite as deftly effective as *Some of Your Blood.* Very few of the stories he wrote after 1960 are horror stories but he did produce one more nasty-minded *conte cruel* in "Vengeance Is" (1980), in which a man begs his wife to submit to the desires of two would-be rapists because he knows that she is carrying an unusually horrible venereal disease.

Sturgeon used horror to sharpen the cutting edges of his moral fables and the points of its exploratory probes. He was always enthusiastic to heighten his readers' responses to ways of thinking, feeling and behaving that he deplored and he was never reluctant to load the narrative dice with all manner of graphic devices. It was because cruelty and intolerance horrified him so intensely that he tried so hard to make their horrific aspects clear to others, and he never worried about overstepping the mark because he believed passionately that there never was a mark that did not cry out to be overstepped. He had such faith in the beneficent power of rational thought that he could not consent to have anything ruled "unthinkable." He wanted everything to be clearly seen, so that it might be accurately weighed in the scales of conscience—and that included all particular horrors as well as the phenomenon of horror itself. His work in this vein is valuable and instructive as well as powerful.

—Brian Stableford

SUSTER, Gerald

Nationality: British. **Born:** London, 1951. **Education:** University of Cambridge. **Address:** c/o New English Library, Hodder Headline plc, 338 Euston Rd., London NW1 3BH, UK.

Horror, Ghost and Gothic Publications

Novels

The Devil's Maze. London, Sphere, 1979.
The Elect. London, Sphere, 1980.
The Scar. London, Hamlyn, 1981.
The Offering. London, Hamlyn, 1982.
The Victim. London, n.p., n.d.
The Force. London, Panther, 1984.
The Block. London, Panther, 1984.
Striker. London, New English Library, 1984.
The God Game. London, New English Library, 1997.

Other Publications

Novel

The Handyman. London, Severn House, 1985.

Other

Hitler and the Age of Horus. N.p., 1983.
The Legacy of the Beast: The Life, Work and Influence of Aleister Crowley. London, W. H. Allen, 1988.
Champions of the Ring: The Lives and Times of Boxing's Heavyweight Heroes. London, Robson, 1992.
Lightning Strikes: The Lives and Times of Boxing's Lightweight Heroes. London, Robson, 1994.

*   *   *

Gerald Suster's earliest work of horror is a brief non-supernatural novel set in Victorian London, an homage to Arthur Machen's *The Three Impostors.* Like the latter, *The Devil's Maze* is arranged in "told tales" set within its parts, which may be read as separate stories, while all the characters are pretending to be somebody else. While Suster is eager to emphasize his connection with the Machen book, through a pointed epilogue, arch references to Machen's tale titles, "Adventure of the Gold Tiberius" and "History of the Young Man with Spectacles," and even by copying a character name, Dr. Lipsius, such an arrangement of a novel was not original to Machen. It was Robert Louis Stevenson who used (though did not, of course, originate) this form in "The Suicide Club" (1882) and even more exactly in *The Dynamiter* (1885), ten years before Machen's novel.

While Machen tends to wander excessively and never tries to fit the separate stories into the rest of the work, Suster slavishly follows his lead and ends up with a similarly rambling book which is somewhat less than a novel. Yet it is an unusual book, far less standard than Suster's later work, all of which has contemporary settings, supernatural causes, much bloodthirsty killing and a preoccupation with sex.

The first of these is *The Scar,* the familiar and far-fetched tale of a teenage student possessed by the devil. She seduces several of her fellow students, each of whom dies violently soon afterwards. Her familiar is a crow, and she makes use of this and of a would-be rapist to despatch her victims. Her mistake is to accuse her history teacher of attempted rape and not to kill him, since he is the one who realizes what she is and destroys her. It is best to draw a veil over the claim that she is descended from a 17th-century witch and he from the witchfinder Matthew Hopkins. The devil's stigma of a scar beneath her left breast gives the book its title.

The Offering is a routine contemporary novel combining the supernatural (ghosts and black magic) with the physical threat from a cut-throat razor. A young couple, Richard and Carol, rent a house (peculiarly called The Offering) in a tiny coastal village in Sussex. Strangenesses accumulate, involving ghosts in the attic, the meaning of a standing stone on an adjacent hill (why are people laying bunches flowers at the stone's base?), and the reticence of other residents to talk about what might be happening (or what might have happened). Richard discovers that Kevin Street, a briefly-famous punk-rock musician, lived at The Offering. The ghosts of him and a girlfriend still inhabit the attic. Various people who offer information die of sudden heart attacks, and it emerges that the village has been ruled for centuries by a self-perpetuating matriarchal clique, presently led by Mrs. Devereux, who inhabits the manor house. And the metaphorical castration of the village's men by their wives becomes, in the end, a physical reality for Richard. The book is too brief and overstuffed with stock characters; none of these is sympathetic and what might have been big scenes slip by in a page or two without sufficient atmosphere.

Some of the same ingredients (ghosts and black magic) and problems afflict *The Block,* which is an uninspiring genre-horror version of J. G. Ballard's fine novel *High-Rise* (1975, nine years before Suster's book). A very large block of apartments in St. John's Wood, London, with the unportentous name of Lavender Gardens, has been the scene of black magic in 1901 (before the block was constructed) and of hideous murders by Nazi supporters of two Jewish children in 1938. Now, in 1984, a couple of elderly devil-worshippers have woken up a terrible power of evil.

Suster briefly introduces a selection of characters—mainly well-to-do professionals—who live in some of the 240 apartments, with a supermarket, bar and sports facilities for their exclusive use. The main protagonist is Tom, a young and struggling barrister, who, with wife Veronica and son Colin, is just moving in, and the most significant of the antagonists is Percy Syme, an accountant who worships Adolph Hitler and loves to dress up in Nazi uniform. But about 40 characters are dealt with by name, with very little development of each. Then the evil begins to possess people, and inhabitants of the block die. There is a suicide, a couple of fatal accidents, a murder. Perfectly normal human beings are pushed over the edge into abnormal behaviour. Admittedly, Percy Syme is responsible for several atrocities himself, but events quickly spiral out of control. All the block's electrical power is consumed in calling up the evil power, which affects some inhabitants—turning them at once into murderous zombies—but not others, for no reason except that Suster has decided which are to be his "good guys." The last third of the book is a catalogue of atrocity—torture, murder and cannibalism—as hundreds of zombies armed mainly with knives or axes try to take over the whole block. The defenders, armed with a few guns which they just happened to have lying around, retreat to the roof. Hundreds of people die as Suster demonstrates that mindless atrocity quickly becomes boring for the reader, especially when the characters are little more than names and professions. When the block is dynamited on the last page one wishes that this had occurred a hundred pages earlier to save trees from unnecessary pulping.

In *The Force* Suster tells a more entertaining story and avoids some of his earlier problems, though there are still too many characters dealt with too shallowly—and none of them sympathetic. The setting is a London advertising agency, Savage & Markby, seen mostly from the viewpoint of a new graduate recruit, Robert Slade. The hypocrisy, cynicism and underhand practices of advertising (including sex between employees) are detailed at great length. For 200 pages the minutiae of the agency's work are paraded, with some unsettling elements but no sign of horror.

Only after that point, when murders are committed and it becomes clear that the agency's chairmen are deliberately trying to frustrate their own staff, is there a suggestion of supernatural powers. The answer is that John Savage is a psychic vampire, who "lives off the energy generated by frustrated human endeavour." This is why he watches his employees via a bank of TV screens (though nobody, not even the police, ever notices any cameras).

This is why he plays all kinds of tricks from practical jokes (an electric shock occasionally from pressing the lift button) to strange promotions and demotions, to forcing his employees to work on campaigns to which they have moral objections, to the ruining of potential troublemakers. After several deaths and the intervention of a ghost he is only brought down by the power of the ankh.

Striker is a little different, in that its main narrator (Ed Striker) possesses mental superpowers, enabling him to control, or at least to disorient, the minds of others. The story shows him discovering and developing his power, and eventually losing it when he battles and overcomes a young woman with similar powers. Although this is usually regarded as a science-fiction plot element, its horrific and sexual aspects are stressed.

Suster is an example of a writer who uses the genre as a commercial vehicle; he has no real commitment to it, and little evidence of anything original to say. However, his return to horror writing in 1997 with *The God Game* may prove this judgment wrong: the present essay has been written before the appearance of that new novel.

—Chris Morgan

T

TALBOT, Michael (Coleman)

Nationality: American. **Born:** 1953. **Career:** Contributor to the *Village Voice*, New York; novelist and writer of non-fiction about the paranormal. **Died:** 3 June 1992.

HORROR, GHOST AND GOTHIC PUBLICATIONS

Novels

The Delicate Dependency: A Novel of the Vampire Life. New York, Avon, 1982.
The Bog. New York, Morrow, 1986.
Night Things. New York, Morrow, 1988.

OTHER PUBLICATIONS

Other

Beyond the Quantum. New York, Macmillan, 1986.
Your Past Lives: A Reincarnation Handbook. New York, Harmony, 1987.
The Holographic Universe. New York, Harpercollins, 1991.
Mysticism and the New Physics. London, Arkana, 1992.

*   *   *

Michael Talbot's first novel begins, not quite auspiciously, with an allegedly late 19th-century British narrator who gives the address of his father's medical practice as "*on* Bond Street" rather than *in* it and then goes on to talk about "Victorian" manners, architecture, etc., when to such a person they would be "modern" or merely "English." The narrator also uses the term "surreal" decades before it was invented, and there are enough Americanisms strewn throughout to make the American reader suspect the British reader could spot a lot more of them.

But if the period narration is never completely convincing, the reader will still quickly realize that *The Delicate Dependency* is an intriguing, suspenseful, even sometimes eloquent vampire novel. It begins with the hero's vision of an "angel" in his father's garden. In adulthood, he meets the "angel" again, an exquisite, ageless Italian youth who was used by Leonardo da Vinci as the model for the angel in his painting *Madonna of the Rocks*. The boy is, of course, a vampire, but a more physical, less supernatural vampire than those of the Dracula variety. The hero, a doctor, is convinced that vampirism is a medical condition, a quasi-benevolent disease which may be studied and perhaps mastered.

But when the vampire disappears with the doctor's idiot-savant daughter, the doctor gives chase, and learns that vampirism is a lot more. The vampires, who are not of the Devil and do not have to kill their blood-sources, or even subsist on human blood at all, are actually illuminati, who have been manipulating mankind and now, at the end of the 19th century, are particularly interested in suppressing or stealing certain technical developments, for what seem ambiguous, or even sinister motives. The doctor's recent discovery of an influenza strain which could virtually depopulate the world has drawn the vampires' attention to him.

Ultimately the book becomes a fascinating meditation on history and immortality. It is Talbot's intriguing conclusion that a really intellectual vampire would have vast accumulations of books, artefacts, and the like. It would be utterly fascinating to rummage through their shelves. Indeed, by the time the novel is over we've met a vampire who possesses the entire contents of the lost Library of Alexandria. The real strength of *The Delicate Dependency* is in such rummagings, with its view of the vampiric mindset as distinctly different from that of regular humans, and its glimpse of the secret vampire society which may or may not form the nucleus for a species which will subjugate or even replace mankind.

Contrary to the current fashion, nobody gets a stake through the heart in *The Delicate Dependency*, nobody gets slowly bled to death through the neck, and there are no long, quasi-pornographic "erotic" sequences. In fact this is one of the *tidiest* vampire novels ever, which only makes it all the more resonant, as there is nothing to distract the reader's attention from the labyrinthine plot and the subtle implications of the subject matter.

Talbot's other two horror novels are of somewhat less interest, both family-unit-is-threatened books in the Stephen King mode. *The Bog* is set in a briefly sketched contemporary England, but fortunately most of the characters are American, so there are no obvious blunders of language. The hero is an archaeologist, who discovers several Bronze Age bodies preserved in a peat bog near a remote village. The villagers are weirdly hostile or just weird. The family dog disappears. There is a dreadful local legend. After a slow start, it emerges that that this is all the work of a shape-changing demon conjured up by a 4,000-year-old sorcerer of Middle Eastern origin. The book does not resonate nearly as well as *The Delicate Dependency*, if only because the Sumerian/Babylonian lore has nothing to do with the Celtic origins of the bog-bodies, or, for that matter, the setting. This immortal, too, has an intriguing library, some of it in cuneiform.

Night Things is, like *The Bog*, a competent enough thriller after a couple of slow chapters, but no more. This time a woman marries the man of her dreams, a famous pop star, and moves with him and her young son into an architecturally bizarre edifice of the sort familiar to readers of *The Haunting of Hill House* or *The Shining*, a place shaped by the eccentricities and passions of its builder, rather like the real-life Winchester Mystery House in San Diego, to which Talbot draws the obvious analogy. Of course the place is haunted, a kind of gateway to other planes of existence, through which pass various fallen angels and metaphysical beings, as described in an apocryphal, ancient text, *The Book of the Secrets of Enoch*. The plot devices are similar to those in *The Bog*: sinister legends and apparitions, transformations, people who turn out to be other than what they seem (and not necessarily human), magic-duels replete with fireballs flicked from fingertips, etc.

It is not fair to say that after a promising start Talbot settled into routine. His extremely early death (of leukemia) cut him off before his talents were fully developed.

—Darrell Schweitzer

TAYLOR, Bernard (Irvin)

Nationality: British. **Born:** Swindon, Wiltshire, 2 October 1936. **Education:** Studied art in Swindon, London and Birmingham. **Career:** Teacher, painter, actor, playwright and novelist. Lived in the United States, 1963-69. **Address:** c/o Hodder Headline plc, 338 Euston Road, London NW1 3BH, England.

HORROR, GHOST AND GOTHIC PUBLICATIONS

Novels

The Godsend. London, Souvenir Press, and New York, St. Martin's Press, 1976.
Sweetheart, Sweetheart. London, Souvenir Press, 1977; New York, St. Martin's Press, 1978.
The Reaping. London, Souvenir Press, and New York, St. Martin's Press, 1980.
The Moorstone Sickness. London, Piatkus, 1982; as *Moorstone*, New York, St. Martin's Press, 1988.
The Kindness of Strangers. New York, St. Martin's Press, 1985; London, Severn House, 1986.
Madeleine. London, Grafton, 1987; New York, Leisure, 1993.
Mother's Boys. London, Grafton, 1988.
Charmed Life. London, Grafton, 1991.
Evil Intent. London, Headline, 1994; New York, Leisure, 1996.

OTHER PUBLICATIONS

Other

Cruelly Murdered. London, Souvenir, 1979.
Perfect Murder, with Stephen Knight. London, Grafton, 1987.
Murder at the Priory, with Kate Clarke. Leicester, Ulverscroft, 1991.

*

Film Adaptation: *The Godsend*, 1980.

* * *

Bernard Taylor was one of the first writers to jump on the bandwagon built by Ira Levin's *Rosemary's Baby* and William Peter Blatty's *The Exorcist*. His first novel, *The Godsend*, draws inspiration from both. The Marlows already have four children but they decide to adopt a fifth, Bonnie, abandoned as a baby by an unknown mother. Unfortunately, Bonnie never quite fits in; she's quarrelsome, self-centred, and much too intelligent for her age. The Marlows are patient and attempt to moderate her behaviour, but their plans begin to fall apart when a series of accidents claims one after another of their natural children. Although *The Godsend* is clearly a reworked, and subsequently overworked horror plot, Taylor's demonically possessed child is effectively malevolent, and the reactions of her parents are well conceived and executed.

Sweetheart, Sweetheart is much more interesting. David and Colin are identical twins, close throughout their childhood, now separated by an ocean as Colin moves to England to be with his new wife. They seem to be adjusting to the separation until David experiences a feeling of foreboding so powerful that he eventually tells his fiancée he is travelling to England to visit his sibling. Arriving there he discovers that Colin and his wife have both been murdered by persons unknown. David eventually learns the truth, that Bronwen, a powerful ghost, is responsible for their deaths, and has chosen David's fiancée to be a victim as well. His desperate attempts to save her, while his friends are slaughtered one by one, are convincing and suspenseful, but Bronwen is a little too powerful to admit the possibility that he might succeed, and the inevitable downbeat ending, though predictable, is not emotionally satisfying.

The Reaping was considerably more original than its predecessors. Tom Rigby is commissioned to paint a portrait of a young woman living at Woolvercombe Mansion and reluctantly agrees to do so. Upon arriving he discovers a large household roiling with unexplained tensions, some of them sexual, some inexplicable. When the painting is completed, he is prevented from leaving by mysterious car trouble until after he has been seduced by his subject, and as he is departing he discovers that the portrait has been tossed in a corner and damaged. Obviously it was not his artistic talent that caused him to be brought to Woolvercombe. He subsequently learns that the woman with whom he made love was an actress hired to seduce him in order to collect some of his sperm, because the purpose of the entire enterprise was to breed the seventh son of a seventh son, whose sacrifice could extend the life of the sorceress operating behind the scenes. A nicely contrived mystery whose supernatural content only appears in the closing chapters.

The Moorstone Sickness was a variation of the same theme. The Grahams have decided that London is just too big, fast, and busy for them, so they move to the village of Moorstone for some respite. The ancient standing stone located in the village seems nothing more than a curiosity, and the clannishness of the locals seems perfectly understandable. What the Grahams don't realize is that the entire village is part of a cult that extends its lives by draining the life-force from newcomers and visitors, and that they've just become prime targets. Tightly written and well plotted, but even casual readers will suspect what's going on very early in the story, which makes the mysterious atmosphere considerably less effective.

Charmed Life has an interesting premise. The protagonist lives under a curse of good luck. No matter what happens, he will come to no harm, although that aura of protection doesn't extend to people around him. It's a mixed blessing in more than one way, he discovers, when an apparently dead woman reveals to him that he is a pawn in a struggle between superhuman forces of good and evil, possibly an expendable one. Despite the melodramatic plot, *Charmed Life* is an understated, entertainingly mysterious story.

There's considerably less restraint in *Evil Intent*. Jack Forrest and his family move to a small village to find a new life, but an unpleasant confrontation with one of their new neighbours sets off a chain of ghastly deaths. John Callow has long cherished his hatred of everyone else in the village, and now he has called upon supernatural forces to help him avenge every real and imagined slight he has ever experienced. *Evil Intent* is much more violent than Taylor's other novels, but it still avoids the graphic excesses other writers employ for shock value, and like *Charmed Life*, represents the best of Taylor's work.

Taylor has occasionally written short stories as well. "Out of Sorts" is an amusing werewolf story. The protagonist locks her husband in the attic during periods when he is "out of sorts," but a nosy neighbour pays an unexpected visit at the wrong time. A teacher newly moved to London becomes obsessed with the house where several murders were committed in "Forget-Me-Not." "Cera" relates the story of two close friends whose relationship ends when a beautiful woman chooses one over the other. Years later the rejected suitor agrees to visit and finds the couple transformed, she grossly overweight, he even smaller than ever. But more years pass before he realizes that they have a parasitic relationship similar to that of some primitive sea creatures. It's an extremely effective and unsettling story. In "Pat-a-Cake, Pat-a-Cake" an abused infant manages to kill his thoughtless mother by driving a dart into her jugular vein. Taylor's short fiction is particularly effective, and might well come to be regarded more highly than his novels.

—Don D'Ammassa

TAYLOR, Lucy

Nationality: American. **Born:** Richmond, Virginia, 30 November 1951. **Education:** University of Richmond, B.A. in art history and philosophy. **Career:** Non-fiction and travel writer for the Richmond *Times-Dispatch* and other publications, 1980-90; full-time fiction writer from 1991. **Awards:** Horror Writers of America Bram Stoker award for first novel, 1996; International Horror Critics award, 1996; *Deathrealm* award, 1996. Lives in Boulder, Colorado.

HORROR, GHOST AND GOTHIC PUBLICATIONS

Novel

The Safety of Unknown Cities. Eugene, Oregon, Darkside Press, 1995; London, Eros Plus, 1996.

Short Stories

Close to the Bone. Woodinville, Silver Salamander Press, 1993.
Unnatural Acts and Other Stories. New York, Masquerade, 1994.
The Flesh Artist. Woodinville, Silver Salamander Press, 1994.

*   *   *

In the horror genre today, no contemporary American woman writer is as highly regarded for her graphic erotic tales of terror as Lucy Taylor. A former ballroom-dance instructor, massage therapist and freelance writer, Taylor made her mark starting in the late 1980s exclusively with her short stories, of which she has published over 60 to date. In the best of them, she mixes pleasure and pain, sex and (the threat of) death closely and intensely enough to create in her characters beings who live to feel—or come to feel—the extremes of human experience. The ultimate results are complete emotional breakdown, or radical physical transformation, or perhaps some strange fusion of the two—or death, in some cases. Because her characters push themselves to these extremes, her stories have a powerful built-in momentum, frequently heightened by her exploration of the psychological basis for the bizarre

behaviour on display. Often caused by one or more severely dysfunctional parents, her characters' actions do make sense, even if dangerously skewed.

In "Blessed Be the Bound" a woman is sentenced to Binding, a futuristic punishment for certain crimes including premarital sex. Binding involves the dismemberment of one or more limbs and the subsequent fusing of the two guilty parties to each other where their limbs have been avulsed. But the woman's mother, insanely over-protective, takes advantage of her daughter's lover's terror at his punishment and convinces him, while imprisoned awaiting the Binding, to kill himself with a cyanide pill she gives him. The woman is also equally terrified and had told her mother to bring the pill so she herself could commit suicide. But there are no more pills and the daughter lives, ultimately Bound to her mother who is guilty of murder. The mother's over-protectiveness is thus permanently assured.

For Taylor, "erotic" is not the type of sensation necessarily confined to sexual activity. It is associated with sensory experience pushed well beyond the limits of the everyday, with the outright violence of feeling that erupts when desire is far more than obsessive. In most cases sexuality is the focal point of her characters' actions, but it can equally be a monstrous hunger for mastery of flesh, even if not sexual. In "The Family Underwater" a submerged family of four somehow immediately adapts to life in a house "full of water, like a toy house that you'd put in the bottom of an aquarium for the guppies to swim through." The father, a nasty drunk, eventually mutates into a shark after beginning the rape of his ten-year-old daughter, and swallows her whole.

Surrealism is a distinctive trademark of Taylor's writing, but traditional supernatural events typically are not. Taylor emphasizes how the frenzied lusts of outwardly normal-looking people can make them monsters. Black magic or the sprouting of fangs or claws is not necessary; horror arises from within. Damage is done without resorting to spells or mystical transformations.

In "Choke Hold" a teenager discovers that self-inflicted choking can induce autoerotic pleasure dramatically greater than sexual congress with any girl. A vision of a woman far more enticing than any in real life comes to him during his sessions; unfortunately, in trying to prolong his contact with her, he unintentionally hangs himself. In "Love in the Age of Ice," set in the near future, a man obsessed with his recently deceased wife, a porno star, has her cryogenically entombed immediately after death and subsequently reanimated. But no matter how much sex she engages in, and with whom, she is not "touched," a term she uses to denote the experience of total, soul-to-soul merging with the partner, available only in her transmuted form. Because of her husband's obsession, she is able to ultimately transform him to a newly undead being, the better to "touch" each other unendingly.

In "Hungry Skin" Mica inherits a mansion and its contents from her now-deceased father, dead by his own hand. The man, a famous sculptor, was known both for his sexual profligacy and his equally explicit sculptures. The mansion is full of them. One in particular, entitled "The Family Reunited," intrigues Mica. Is her father represented therein? She herself? Initially repulsed by what surrounds her, she is eventually drawn in by the complexities of the piece, however obscene, the details of which seem different from varying angles, at different times of day. The only way, she finally decides, to ascertain the true nature of the work is to see it from the inside—from a space she has discovered in its middle when viewing it from above. She climbs into its largest cavity and finds its perverseness strangely compelling. So much so that when she cannot extricate herself after repeated attempts, she stays within the sculpture, feeling the cold stone skin of the hungry pieces close in to feel her living warmth.

Taylor's joint themes of ravaging lust and parental derangement find their fulfilment in her novel, *The Safety of Unknown Cities*. The main character, Val Petrillo, is a woman forever unsatisfied with stability. Thus she moves from place to place, lover to lover, her sexual hunger always in need of new twists and variations. Her mother, an inmate in a mental hospital, has gouged out her eyes; it was she who gave rise to Val's wanderlust as a result of frequent episodes in which Val was both beaten and confined to a closet for minor transgressions. During her travels Val hears of a fabled City, notorious as a place of unbridled lust, no matter what its expression. Desperate to find what she is looking for, she meets Majeed, a Middle Eastern hermaphrodite, with whom she not only has varieties of unusual sex but from whom she also hears more about the City. Eventually both she and Majeed find their way there, but not before Breen, a former lover of Val's, finds her and vows to make her die a slow, tortured death for abandoning him. She was the only woman he ever loved who spurned his marriage proposal because of her obsessive need to move, to explore, to find what had not yet been found.

Breen is more than a jilted lover; he is a twisted murderer who follows Val and kills those she has sex with in creatively gruesome ways. Ultimately, Val, Breen, Majeed and the Turk, an enigmatic half-man, half-spirit—here Taylor takes some licence with her usual abstention from occult phenomena—converge in the City where Skinners, Deadenders and a whole host of strange beings interact in perverse and horrific ways with the main characters before the tale reaches its conclusion. The same green fire that took Val out of North Africa and into the City returns her to the real world where she buries her mother and is still tempted by the City's dubious charms.

Though Taylor seems influenced in this novel, more than anywhere else, by the writing of Clive Barker, she has a distinctive voice that blends the powerfully erotic and the intensely horrific— so much so, in fact, that the novel was lauded with three different awards. Her stories remind us that we have needs that must be met, and whether we choose to meet them in the ways her characters do or not, they will always be with us wherever we are.

—Lawrence Greenberg

TEM, Melanie

Nationality: American. **Family:** Married Steve Rasnic Tem (q.v.). **Awards:** Horror Writers of America Bram Stoker award for first novel, 1992. Lives in Denver, Colorado.

HORROR, GHOST AND GOTHIC PUBLICATIONS

Novels

Prodigal. New York, Dell, 1991.
Blood Moon. London, Women's Press, 1992.
The Wilding. New York, Dell, 1992.
Revenant. New York, Dell, and London, Headline, 1994.
Desmodus. London, Headline, and New York, Dell, 1995.

Making Love, with Nancy Holder. New York, Dell, 1993; London, Raven, 1995.
Tides. London, Headline, 1996.
Witchlight, with Nancy Holder. New York, Dell, 1996.

Short Stories

Daddy's Side. Arvada, Colorado, Roadkill Press, 1991.
Beautiful Strangers, with Steve Rasnic Tem. Arvada, Colorado, Roadkill Press, 1992.

*   *   *

Melanie Tem writes about damaged people. Although most of her novels have supernatural elements the chill comes from what people do to each other and themselves. She excels at understanding how apparently ordinary people think in times of crisis or under mental stress. Her first-written though second-published novel, *Blood Moon*, is typical. It involves the developing relationship between Breanne Novak and her newly adopted son, Greg. Greg is eleven and has been passed from foster-home to foster-home because no one can cope with him. He is an angry child and things happen around him—tires deflate, toys break, handles fall off buckets, crockery falls from shelves. Greg believes he is the cause and at times this frightens him; at other times he revels in his power. Breanne recognizes something of herself in him, which is why she is prepared to take him on. Her father, Andy, also sees Greg's anger as like his own. He has kept it carefully in check all his life and as a result seems incapable of sharing his emotions. When Andy has a stroke which impairs his ability to communicate, Greg knows it is his fault. Breanne struggles to reach Greg as a person and help him to come to accept that some people care about him and that not all adults lie.

Like *Blood Moon*, *Prodigal* deals with the relationships between children and adults. Twelve-year-old Lucy Ann Brill has much in common with Greg, as it is ambiguous whether the things that she perceives as real are actually products of a disturbed mind. Lucy is part of a large, caring family which nevertheless has problems. Her elder brother has been missing for two years but his ghost has been appearing to her before he is found dead. Then her elder sister also disappears and Lucy sees her ghost too. Perhaps Lucy creates them, or because she is the viewpoint character she wants to see them as a way of hanging on to the past. Is the family falling apart from within, or is there a malignant outside agency involved? To complicate the picture the family's social worker is not what you would expect. Jerry Johnston is a twisted person, but because of his job he is invited into a position of trust by the family. That is what is scary.

Revenant explores another aspect of the human condition, grief. In a series of set pieces we are introduced to characters from a wide variety of backgrounds. The thing they have in common is grief. Either a loved one has died, or their situation has changed so much that it is as if they had. None of these characters has come to terms with the changes; they desperately cling onto the past. Hannelore has kept her dead children alive by buying them presents and holding parties for them; Annie's guilt about her abortion manifests itself in dreams and an obsession with babies; Gabriel fantasizes about the mother who dumped him at birth; Elinor is unable to cope with the husband who has been destroyed by senile dementia. These and others are all drawn to the ghost town of Revenant. There they have the opportunity to confront their ghosts. Some make their peace with the past and walk back into life, others are destroyed, their grief feeding the entity that lies at the heart of the town. Tem writes sensitively and convincingly about motivations and she is not afraid to deal with uncomfortable issues. One of the characters drawn to Revenant is a paedophile grieving for the loss of the girl he regularly abused. She eventually found the strength to reject him but in his mind she always enjoyed their games. The horrific element is that, to him, he was doing nothing wrong.

In *Tides*, Tem again gets successfully into the minds of damaged people. She makes us feel the confusion in the mind of Alzheimer's-sufferer Marshall Emig, as he has periods of lucidity and episodes where the past overlays reality. He is a resident at the Tides nursing home of which his daughter, Rebecca, is the administrator. All the residents have either mental or physical disabilities. Rebecca cares about all of them, and you feel that given the freedom to do things the way she would like the environment would be such as to care adequately for all their needs. However, she is under pressure from the presence of her father and the need to run the home the way the boss thinks it should be run—for profit rather than the welfare of the residents. To complicate matters worse a ghost is manifesting itself. Rebecca has never heard of Faye, Marshall's first wife and her biological mother, but as Marshall's mind deteriorates Faye appears to try and reclaim the daughter she tried to drown. The residents sense Faye's increasing malevolence and she affects their behaviour. People die. Rebecca begins to drown in the tide of events. Again it is Tem's portrayal and understanding of dysfunctional people that gives the novel its strengths, with the supernatural elements acting as triggers rather than being central to the appreciation of the book.

The Wilding and *Desmodus* move away from the problems of ordinary people to embrace the traditional horror motifs of werewolves and vampires. Neither, though, takes a traditional line. The matriarchal werewolf clan of *The Wilding* lives in Denver, and consists of four generations. There are no male werewolves, boy children being disposed of soon after birth, but there are a lot of political maneuverings amongst the older generations in order to be the alpha female of the whole pack. Males in Tem's vampire clan in *Desmodus*, though allowed to survive, don't fare much better. None of them seem to have much going for them and they are totally dominated by the females of their society. They live in isolated communes in America, spending summers in the north and migrating south for the winters. In winter, the females hibernate in huge refrigerated trucks while the males have the freedom to enjoy themselves. *Desmodus* is narrated by Joel who, as this particular migration gets underway, begins to make discoveries about his people and why the males seem such a poor lot. In both novels the emphasis is on the alien societies hidden within America rather than the expected narratives the notions of werewolves and vampires normally conjure. The approaches are fresh and original.

Tem's collaborations with Nancy Holder have produced two sexually explicit and disturbing novels. *Making Love* studies the thin line between madness and sanity. Cameron is recognized as crazy with medical diagnostic labels but his sister, Charlotte, descends into obsession when Cameron creates a dream-lover for her. The heroine of *Witch-Light* also has a dream-lover but here the conflict is between good and evil.

Tem's short stories, as well as her novels are deeply rooted in relationships and the things that shape lives. In all her writing it is the understanding of how mental processes work that shines

through, so much so that the reader is given insight into how even the most deeply disturbed person is able to rationalize their actions. The most horrifying aspect of her work is the realization that these people are all around us.

—Pauline Morgan

TEM, Steve Rasnic

Nationality: American. **Born:** Pennington Gap, Virginia, 1950. **Education:** Colorado State University, M.A. in creative writing. **Family:** Married Melanie Tem (q.v.). **Career:** Contributor of hundreds of poems and short stories to small-press magazines and original anthologies. **Awards:** British Fantasy award for short story, 1988. Lives in Denver, Colorado.

HORROR, GHOST AND GOTHIC PUBLICATIONS

Novel

Excavation. New York, Avon, 1987.

Short Stories

Fairytales. Arvada, Colorado, Roadkill Press, 1990.
Absences: Charlie Goode's Ghosts. Hoole, Cheshire, Haunted Library, 1991.
Celestial Inventory. Polk City, Iowa, Drumm, 1991.
Beautiful Strangers, with Melanie Tem. Arvada, Colorado, Roadkill Press, 1992.
Decoded Mirrors: Three Tales After Lovecraft. West Warwick, Rhode Island, Necronomicon Press, 1992.

Other

One View: Creating Characters in Fantasy and Horror Fiction. Eugene, Oregon, Pulphouse, 1991.

Editor, *The Umbral Anthology of Science Fiction Poetry.* Denver, Colorado, Umbral, 1982.
Editor, *High Fantastic.* N.p., Ocean View Books, 1995.

*   *   *

Steve Rasnic Tem is not merely the most prolific short story writer working in modern horror, he is also one of its most skilled practitioners. Although Tem did publish a single novel, *Excavation*, his reputation is staked on the dozens of stories which began appearing in the late 1970s and continue to thrill audiences today. While Tem's work has appeared in virtually every genre magazine and many anthologies, one of the best places to find an overview of his work is in the first installment of the venerable *Night Visions* series (1984).

An introduction by editor Alan Ryan reveals that Tem was a poet only beginning to make a name for himself at the time, but Tem's offering of seven tales makes a solid foundation for his reputation as a master of short fiction. Even in these early tales, one of Tem's most prominent recurring characters begins to emerge: the loving husband and devoted father who is plagued by fears grounded in reality but which quickly spiral out of control.

"Punishment" plays on the same fear as Ray Bradbury's "The Small Assassin": what is really going on in the minds of babies? The narrator of this story tells us about his daughter Jennifer, and his struggle to keep her in line. But the source of his terror is not merely that his daughter is getting out of control, but that he somehow isn't qualified to raise a child. By the end of the story you might agree, but in this subtle tale of crime and punishment nothing is quite that clear cut.

In "Dark Shapes in the Road," Charlie's fear is that his children will be killed in a car accident. He tries to protect them from his estranged wife by stealing them away in the middle of the night. But making his getaway in a car is no way to go. First, Charlie's son dreams of dark shapes in the road, and in the end these beings are Charlie's undoing. But the story isn't about supernatural creatures, it's about the very real terrors of parenting and of fate, which like a car, is all too apt to spin out of control.

In "A Hundred Wicked Little Witches," from the anthology *100 Wicked Little Witch Stories* (1995), Tem shows another side of his story-telling prowess: a rarely-glimpsed sense of humour. Here the Tem protagonist is taken to the ludicrous extreme. Jack believes that every injustice or difficulty in his life is caused by witches. He blames them for his loneliness, for his desire, and for his problems with the opposite sex. When he meets what seems like the perfect woman, he runs away from her in a fit of seemingly paranoid terror . . . but the last laugh may be on us when Jack's paranoia shows some grounding in reality.

Tem's best story in this vein comes appropriately enough from what is arguably the best horror anthology of the 1980s, Dennis Etchison's *Cutting Edge* (1986). "Little Cruelties" begins with a story within the story, as Paul—a father and a husband—explains how ten years earlier, he left his son Joey's pet chicks out in the snow to die. They were sick, he explains, and he thought he was doing the right thing.

As Paul soon discovers, however, acting on your beliefs can sometimes have a price, and love is never without its small cruelties. Every day, Paul witnesses the petty thefts and the minor brutalities which occur in the city, and he believes that the accumulation of these is a cancer on his family. Although he tries to take care of them by moving them away, he doesn't go far enough, buying a Victorian house in a rundown suburb, where he thinks he can monitor the city's decay and yet still be untouched by it.

Through the arguments of Paul's wife and son, Tem gently shows us that his protagonist is not quite sane, and yet all of Paul's concerns are totally within reason, at least initially. But Paul has isolated himself and those he loves not only from the outside world but from common sense, and as his family begins to crumble, the degree of his own cruelties increases. He tells of throwing out Charlie's homework or shutting off the power so that the boy, who's afraid of the dark, will be forced to wander through a lightless house.

As the family disintegrates, so does their home, as dirt and bugs begin to accumulate and graffiti scars the walls. Paul's wife leaves him behind and ultimately so does his son, but Paul is convinced he sees the boy digging up the backyard, perhaps exposing the crimes his father has committed. If one were to describe the ultimate Steve Rasnic Tem tale, "Little Cruelties" would be it, for it is a story of contradictions, where the descriptions of horror are in themselves beauty, and though on the surface nothing much

seems to happen, what more could possibly happen than life and death?

"Little Cruelties," which appeared a year before *Excavation*, is a fitting lead-in to Tem's only novel. The story functions in many ways as a prototype for the book, but it also underscores many of the novel's shortcomings. In *Excavation*, archaeologist Reed Taylor had run away from home—and from his abusive father—years ago, and while he was gone, a flood washed over the town of Simpson's Creek, burying Reed's childhood home and his family with it. Now Reed is an archaeologist with a family of his own, living in Denver and trying to bond with his daughter and adopted son. But a phone call from his dead father summons Reed back to the town he left behind, and into a journey of his past that he had hoped he wouldn't take.

Reed's story is intercut with the stories of surviving residents of Simpson's Creek, such as Ben Taylor, Reed's uncle, and Hector Pierce, the only survivor of a mine cave-in. The individual stories of the townspeople continue to unfold as Reed embarks on what he considers a necessary project: excavating his old house. The metaphor is obvious as Reed quickly unearths more than just an old building, upsetting not just the balance between the past and the present but between man and nature. When the floodwaters ultimately return to Simpson's Creek, the reader is swept along in the tidal waves, but by then it's a case of too little too late.

Like Tem's best stories *Excavation* is elegant and thoughtful, but it is neither chilling nor compelling. Although Tem has incorporated many of the concerns that reverberate through his short fiction, he doesn't bring much that's new to the mix, and he doesn't say anything he hasn't already said more succinctly in work like "Small Cruelties" or "Punishment." In his short fiction, emotion alone drives the narrative, but a work of this length demands more plot than Tem provides. Besides, what he might have said in a sentence of a short story he tells us in a page of *Excavation*, even when it's clear that the sentence alone would have sufficed.

Perhaps Tem will produce a novel more worthy of his talent someday, but in the meantime, he continues to write and publish stories with a frequency that few authors can match. In length these tales may seem like a snack, an appetizer to hold us over until dinner time, but as long the chef is Steve Rasnic Tem, I don't care if they hold off on the main course all night long.

—Adam Meyer

TESSIER, Thomas

Nationality: American. **Born:** Connecticut, 1947. **Education:** University College, Dublin. **Career:** Publisher, Millington Books, London; contributor to *Vogue* magazine, London edition. **Address:** c/o Gollancz, The Cassell Group, Wellington House, 125 Strand, London WC2R 0BB, England. Lives in Connecticut.

HORROR, GHOST AND GOTHIC PUBLICATIONS

Novels

The Fates. London, Futura, 1978; New York, Berkley, 1986.
The Nightwalker. London, Macmillan, and New York, Atheneum, 1979.

Phantom. New York, Atheneum, 1982; London, Pan, 1983.
Shockwaves. London, Fontana, 1983.
Finishing Touches. New York, Atheneum, 1986; London, Grafton, 1987.
Rapture. New York, Atheneum, 1987; London, Futura, 1989.
Secret Strangers. London, Macdonald, 1990.
Fog Heart. London, Gollancz, 1997; New York, St. Martin's, 1998.

*

Film Adaptation: *Rapture*, n.d.

*   *   *

There is little in *The Fates* to suggest how good an author Tessier would become. It is a fairly standard tale of strange events occurring in a small American town. A cow is found torn apart, blue lights are seen, then a man is ripped apart, then a car, then a couple of people. Children and some of their parents believe that the blue fiery lights are the Virgin Mary, with a message. But when the blue radiance leads to the death of dozens, it seems more likely that, as one character suggests, a jinn might be to blame. This is a sort of demon, and it may be protesting about the way the area has been developed by humans. The events are competently put across, but there are two unusual aspects: one is that there is no happy ending; the blue radiance may have become inactive, but there is nothing to stop it killing again. And the other aspect is that no one character predominates; some 20 characters are built up a little and most are killed within the confines of a fairly brief novel.

The Nightwalker is set in London, and written while Tessier lived there. It is much more original and frightening, being an account of the descent into madness, murder and death of a young American, a Vietnam veteran, who is living in a room in central London. Bobby Ives has had two odd experiences, one in Vietnam when he was (by error) declared dead, and the other as a waking dream when it seemed that he lived in Guadeloupe and became a zombie.

He seems to be having strange pains in his hands. Can it be these that cause him, involuntarily perhaps, to push his girlfriend under a bus so that she dies? Or is he imagining it? But he really does attack a man who is jogging in Hyde Park, tearing out his throat. He consults a clairvoyant who is frightened by what she sees in him. For a while a teenage girl with punk hair lives with him; they have wild sex that becomes even wilder when another punk girl joins them. Ives, who seems to be becoming a werewolf, kills them both in an uncontrollable fit of rage. He kills two other women and only just escapes a police cordon around Hyde Park, seeking help from the clairvoyant. She understands and tries to control his behaviour, but he escapes from her and is killed by a silver knife.

Although told in the third person, *The Nightwalker* is very subjective, credibly describing the short step from eccentricity to mania. The reader's sympathy for Ives may be slight, yet the novel's overall effect is very powerful, with shocking scenes of brutality and murder. Writing an original and worthwhile werewolf story is difficult these days, yet Tessier succeeds very well.

With *Shockwaves* Tessier was trying to combine horror and romance for a particular publishing imprint. The result is a clichéd novel, relieved only by two unexpected scenes. Brooks Matthews is a middle-aged district attorney from Utah, highly regarded and tipped for political office. In a series of scenes which only a die-hard romantic would find at all believable, he meets Jackie, a student almost 30 years his junior, falls in love and marries her. Both of these characters are unbelievably earnest. Interspersed are scenes in which a young serial killer, "The Blade," finds and kills his victims.

When a young man is arrested and charged with the murders, Matthews prosecutes and gets a conviction (perhaps unjustly). Meanwhile, Jackie has become pregnant by a casual or dream lover who may be the man on trial, and who returns after the execution to kill her and his child in an unexpectedly downbeat ending.

Phantom shows Tessier at his subtle best. It is an outstanding example of the haunted-house tale, showing how a disturbing atmosphere can play on the mind of a nine-year-old boy. Ned and his parents have recently moved to the run-down coastal village of Lynnhaven on Chesapeake Bay, within commuting distance of Washington DC. There seem to be no other boys of his age around during this hot summer, so Ned spends his time talking to two old men, Peeler and Cloudy, who make a small living out of selling bait to fishermen. He also explores the dangerous and frightening spa building (long since abandoned to vegetation, spiders and ghosts) on a hill above the village. With very few characters and little action, Tessier tells a gripping story about a strong-minded and resourceful child.

Both *Finishing Touches* and *Secret Strangers* are non-supernatural. The former is meant to be shocking—the story of a young American medic in London, who is gradually drawn into the exploits of a cosmetic surgeon who keeps a number of quadruple amputees prisoner in his basement. This is a particularly raunchy novel, though the sex is often mixed up with violence and the whole thing becomes more tacky and aimless as it proceeds towards a non-conclusion. Its importance is to show how easily a respectable person can become a mass-murderer. *Secret Strangers*, on the other hand, is a dark thriller of the highest quality, cleverly plotted and with a greater range of characters than Tessier's other novels. It centres around Heidi Luckner, a teenager who becomes mixed up in a child sex ring through discovering some photos. She has to grow up quickly in order to stay alive. This is a brilliant exposé of middle-class urban America, showing the sleaze beneath the respectable facade. As Heidi moves easily from her own milieu into the world of theft, blackmail and murder she makes wrong decisions and is lucky to survive. The excitement builds steadily throughout the novel.

In *Fog Heart* the author is back with the supernatural, with the action shifting between the American East Coast and Europe. The story centres around two sisters in their early twenties: Oona, who is genuinely psychic and clairvoyant, able to communicate with the dead and pluck secrets from the living yet scarcely able to cope with life, and Roz, who is her business manager and carer. They are of Scottish extraction, living in Connecticut. Among their clients are Carrie, who keeps seeing her dead father but cannot understand his message, and Jan, whose baby died terribly ten years before. Carrie's husband is Oliver, an English businessman now domiciled in New York; he is a control freak who has affairs and enjoys strangling people. Jan's husband is Charley, a fake Irishman whose alcoholism is beginning to interfere with his college lecturing.

Over the course of several visits by the couples, in pairs and as a foursome, Oona extracts the answers to some of their problems.

But she also discovers Oliver's secrets—and he knows that she knows. Oliver desperately wants to possess Oona, and to strangle her; he has her investigated and discovers her murky past. For the most part, Oona's revelations are framed in language that is difficult to understand. Apart from the sad and terrifying events which form the plot, this is a novel about scepticism turning to belief and about very odd characters who are unable to love those who love them. It is a clever, though not always rewarding book, as subtle as *Phantom* though less exciting than *Secret Strangers*.

While Tessier has written relatively few stories, they have appeared in prestige anthologies such as Douglas Winter's *Prime Evil* and various *Year's Best* volumes. The excellent "Blanca" is set in the country of that name, where the slightest of infringement of the law can mean death—even for a visiting American. But his best short piece is the wild novella "The Dreams of Dr. Ladybank," in which a psychiatrist discovers a means of controlling two of his patients.

—Chris Morgan

THEROUX, Paul (Edward)

Nationality: American. **Born:** Medford, Massachusetts, 10 April 1941; brother of the writer Alexander Theroux. **Education:** Medford High School; University of Maine, Orono, 1959-60; University of Massachusetts, Amherst, B.A. in English 1963. **Family:** Married Anne Castle in 1967; two sons. **Career:** Lecturer, University of Urbino, Italy, 1963; Peace Corps lecturer, Soche Hill College, Limbe, Malawi, 1963-65; lecturer, Makerere University, Kampala, Uganda, 1965-68, and University of Singapore, 1968-71; writer-in-residence, University of Virginia, Charlottesville, 1972. **Awards:** *Playboy* award, 1971, 1977, 1979; American Academy award, 1977; Whitbread award, 1978; *Yorkshire Post* award, 1982; James Tait Black Memorial prize, 1982; Thomas Cook award, for travel book, 1989. D. Litt.: Tufts University, Medford, Massachusetts, 1980; Trinity College, Washington, D.C., 1980; University of Massachusetts, 1988. **Member:** Fellow, Royal Society of Literature, and Royal Geographical Society; American Academy, 1984. **Address:** c/o Hamish Hamilton Ltd., 27 Wright's Lane, London W8 5TZ, England.

HORROR, GHOST AND GOTHIC PUBLICATIONS

Novels

The Black House. London, Hamish Hamilton, and Boston, Houghton Mifflin, 1974.
Chicago Loop. London, Hamish Hamilton, 1990; New York, Random House, 1991.

Short Stories

The Consul's File. London, Hamish Hamilton, and Boston, Houghton Mifflin, 1977.
World's End and Other Stories. London, Hamish Hamilton, and Boston, Houghton Mifflin, 1980.

OTHER PUBLICATIONS

Novels

Waldo. Boston, Houghton Mifflin, 1967; London, Bodley Head, 1968.
Fong and the Indians. Boston, Houghton Mifflin, 1968; London, Hamish Hamilton, 1976.
Girls at Play. Boston, Houghton Mifflin, and London, Bodley Head, 1969.
Murder in Mount Holly. London, Ross, 1969.
Jungle Lovers. Boston, Houghton Mifflin, and London, Bodley Head, 1971.
Saint Jack. London, Bodley Head, and Boston, Houghton Mifflin, 1973.
The Family Arsenal. London, Hamish Hamilton, and Boston, Houghton Mifflin, 1976.
Picture Palace. London, Hamish Hamilton, and Boston, Houghton Mifflin, 1978.
The Mosquito Coast. London, Hamish Hamilton, 1981; Boston, Houghton Mifflin, 1982.
Doctor Slaughter. London, Hamish Hamilton, 1984.
Half Moon Street: Two Short Novels (includes *Doctor Slaughter* and *Doctor DeMarr*). Boston, Houghton Mifflin, 1984.
O-Zone. London, Hamish Hamilton, and New York, Putnam, 1986.
My Secret History. London, Hamish Hamilton, and New York, Putnam, 1989.
Doctor DeMarr. London, Hutchinson, 1990.
Millroy the Magician. London, Hamish Hamilton, 1993; New York, Random House, 1994.
My Other Life. London, Hamish Hamilton, and Boston, Houghton Mifflin, 1996.
Kowloon Tong. London, Hamish Hamilton, and Boston, Houghton Mifflin, 1997.

Short Stories

Sinning with Annie and Other Stories. Boston, Houghton Mifflin, 1972; London, Hamish Hamilton, 1975.
The London Embassy. London, Hamish Hamilton, 1982; Boston, Houghton Mifflin, 1983.
Collected Stories. New York, Viking, 1997.

Plays

The Autumn Dog (produced New York, 1981).
The White Man's Burden. London, Hamish Hamilton, 1987.

Screenplay: *Saint Jack,* with Peter Bogdanovich and Howard Sackler, 1979.

Television Play: *The London Embassy,* from his own story, 1987.

Other

V. S. Naipaul: An Introduction to His Work. London, Deutsch, and New York, Africana, 1972.
The Great Railway Bazaar: By Train Through Asia. London, Hamish Hamilton, and Boston, Houghton Mifflin, 1975.
A Christmas Card (for children). London, Hamish Hamilton, and Boston, Houghton Mifflin, 1978.

The Old Patagonian Express: By Train Through the Americas. London, Hamish Hamilton, and Boston, Houghton Mifflin, 1979.

London Snow (for children). Salisbury, Wiltshire, Russell, 1979; Boston, Houghton Mifflin, 1980.

Sailing Through China. Salisbury, Wiltshire, Russell, 1983; Boston, Houghton Mifflin, 1984.

The Kingdom by the Sea: A Journey Around the Coast of Great Britain. London, Hamish Hamilton, and Boston, Houghton Mifflin, 1983.

Sunrise with Seamonsters: Travels and Discoveries 1964-1984. London, Hamish Hamilton, and Boston, Houghton Mifflin, 1985.

The Imperial Way: Making Tracks from Peshawar to Chittagong, photographs by Steve McCurry. London, Hamish Hamilton, and Boston, Houghton Mifflin, 1985.

Patagonia Revisited, with Bruce Chatwin. Salisbury, Wiltshire, Russell, 1985; Boston, Houghton Mifflin, 1986.

The Shortest Day of the Year: A Christmas Fantasy. Leamington, Warwickshire, Sixth Chamber Press, 1986.

Riding the Iron Rooster: By Train Through China. London, Hamish Hamilton, and New York, Putnam, 1988.

Travelling the World. London, Sinclair Stevenson, 1990.

The Happy Isles of Oceania: Paddling the Pacific. London, Hamish Hamilton, and New York, Putnam, 1992.

The Pillars of Hercules: A Grand Tour of the Mediterranean. New York, Putnam, and London, Hamish Hamilton, 1995.

*

Film Adaptations: *Saint Jack*, 1974; *The Mosquito Coast*, 1985; *Half Moon Street*, 1986.

*   *   *

One of the more distinguished and prolific writers working today, Paul Theroux, for much of his career an American expatriate living in England, is also versatile enough to have authored short stories and a novel in the tradition of horror literature. Theroux's style is erudite, probing, revealing the nuances of his characters' innermost thoughts as though they were the most delicate of sense impressions. He can also describe the most gruesome details of a terrifying experience in such a way that the reader is simultaneously horrified and captivated—this because Theroux creates atmospheres based on his characters' mental and emotional revelations that are all-encompassing. In each of his tales of terror the author utilizes a foreign setting to underline both the strangeness of the events that befall his characters and their inability to cope with those events.

In "Dengue Fever" (collected in *The Consul's File*), set in Malaysia in the mid-1970s, a friend of the narrator contracts the eponymous illness at the height of which he hallucinates, seeing Vietcong and some of their victims—two toothless women in particular. Yet the narrator himself, later in the story, briefly sees the faces of two Chinese women at the same window as his friend, and he is completely healthy. Once his friend recovers, the narrator goes out to dinner with him at a local restaurant. And there on the wall closest to their table is a photograph of the same two women—two aunts of the restaurant's owner, killed by the Japanese during World War II. Neither man has seen this photograph before. The shock of the reappeared image triggers what seems to be a recurrence of the fever in the narrator's friend. The narrator is spared such a shock because initially he cannot definitively identify the two women in the photograph as those he saw in the window. When a feverish man sees a ghostly presence, there's no need to suspect any supernatural doings; he's obviously suffering from his condition. But the narrator's glimpse of what is ultimately revealed to be the same image, that of two real people mercilessly slaughtered, makes this a subtle ghost story and not easily forgettable.

"White Lies" (collected in *World's End and Other Stories*) is very likely the author's most horrific tale. In it, the narrator relates what befell his friend Jerry Benda when the two of them were in Africa for some while. There Jerry has developed a relationship with a native girl, Ameena, but is quickly attracted to a new European arrival, and lies to and almost cheats on the African soon after the story's outset. Subsequently, Ameena gives Jerry a present, a brightly-coloured shirt. Though he burns it, he has already handled it when unwrapping the gift. A few days later Jerry is afflicted with an enormous number of "tiny reddened patches, like fly bites, some already swollen into bumps." Regardless of treatment the condition worsens until his skin is "grotesquely inflamed." When the narrator squeezes one of Jerry's now larger boils, a small "white knob" protrudes. It is a live maggot, and there are close to 200 of them buried all over his body. Eventually the narrator burns them all out, and in spite of his horrible scars Jerry is understandably relieved—he's alive. The narrator, an entomologist, keeps the maggots for further study. They hatch into a species of fly "not in any book." Ameena is, by inference, a witch, but she is not seen again. Jerry, an inveterate liar, is likened to a fly that feeds on human credulity; the narrator forgets his supposed friend after the ordeal, quite content with his new invertebrate discovery.

While in his short stories Theroux's foreign settings dramatize his characters' unwanted surrender to unknown forces, in *The Black House*, a novel that neatly melds the psychological with the supernatural, there's a clever reversal of the foreign setting to achieve the same end. Albert and Emma Munday, having returned from Africa after a prolonged stay based on Albert's anthropological research, find a house in rural England far from their native London. There they settle in uneasily; their marriage has obviously weakened. Emma throws herself into housework, seeking to offset her marital frustration; Albert combines an attempt to understand the locals with a continuation of his academic pursuits. But his peculiar blend of ivory-tower snobbery and substantial knowledge of African village life ultimately has a negative effect on those he meets.

Only one person finds his company (more than) attractive—Caroline Summers, an enigmatic woman who appears, suddenly, at a New Year's Eve party to which the Mundays have been invited. Prior to her appearance the couple senses something unsettling about their residence, Bowood House, dubbed the Black House by the locals. It is as if there is a third presence with them; once, Emma is certain she's seen a woman staring out from one of their windows at the couple outside the house. And Emma automatically thinks, for no reason, that the house belongs to the woman. Albert is simultaneously haunted both by this unseen presence—which he does not speak of—and by the gnawing fear that his wife, voicing her apprehension, has already left him emotionally defenceless by revealing what haunts the two of them.

Though English, the Mundays are decidedly foreigners in their native land; they are habituated to African culture, African mores,

African natives. The England that was once long ago familiar has become unknown. The contrast of the two environments ultimately proves unmanageable for them—hence the theft of one of Albert's African ceremonial daggers, the departure of their domestic, the warning by the formerly generous resident who invited them to the party.

After Caroline is introduced, it becomes apparent, gradually, subtly, that she is the presence both Emma and Albert have felt in and around the house. At her New Year's Eve party arrival she speaks to several guests but whenever she appears after that, she is either alone with Albert or with Albert and Emma. No one else is present at these subsequent meetings. The powerful erotic attraction she and Albert share, and its repeated consummation, create both a more dramatic separation of Albert from his wife and a heightened realization that even more than Emma, what really haunts Albert is something he has not previously known but has always both feared and desired. Caroline knows things about the Black House that surprise both the Mundays; she tells Albert the Black House is hers; she leaves, suddenly, after each romantic tryst; she tells Albert he invented her.

The house is haunted, not by a ghost, but by the ghost of desire, the ghost of need, the ghost of the fear that connects us to and separates us from each other. The Mundays are too afraid to form a solid union between them, but too afraid as well to break what union they do have; too afraid to adapt to new surroundings, but too afraid as well to leave those surroundings. Caroline keeps them where they are because she needs them to exist, and because they need her to sustain their multiple fears. Theroux's narrative is certainly not a traditional ghost story, but it is a work that captures far more effectively why ghosts have always had their terrifying impact—because we cannot escape what exists within us, both past and present.

At least one other of Theroux's novels contains elements of the horrific and deserves some mention here. *Chicago Loop*'s sexually obsessed protagonist, Parker Jagoda, bites a woman to death, but is so filled with remorse after this event that he ultimately commits suicide. His massive guilt makes this a tragic drama more than a horror novel *per se*. Surprisingly, Theroux has also written a science-fiction novel (with horrific elements), *O-Zone*, but this generally was judged to be a failure.

—Lawrence Greenberg

THOMAS, D(onald) M(ichael)

Nationality: British. **Born:** Redruth, Cornwall, 27 January 1935. **Education:** Redruth Grammar School; University High School, Melbourne; New College, Oxford, B.A. (honours) in English 1958, M.A. 1961. **Military Service:** Served in the British Army (national service), 1953-54. **Family:** Divorced; two sons and two daughters. **Career:** Teacher, Teignmouth Grammar School, Devon, 1959-63; senior lecturer in English, Hereford College of Education, 1964-78. Visiting lecturer in English, Hamline University, St. Paul, Minnesota, 1967; creative writing teacher, American University, Washington, D.C., 1982. **Awards:** Richard Hillary Memorial prize, 1960; Cholmondeley award, 1978; *Guardian*-Gollancz Fantasy Novel prize, 1979; *Los Angeles Times* prize, 1981; Silver Pen award, 1982. **Address:** The Coach House, Rashleigh Vale, Cornwall TR1 1TJ, England.

HORROR, GHOST AND GOTHIC PUBLICATIONS

Novels

The Devil and the Floral Dance (for children). London, Robson, 1978.
The Flute-Player. London, Gollancz, and New York, Dutton, 1979.
The White Hotel. London, Gollancz, and New York, Viking Press, 1981.
Pictures at an Exhibition. London, Bloomsbury, and New York, Scribner, 1993.
Eating Pavlova. London, Bloomsbury, and New York, Carroll and Graf, 1994.

OTHER PUBLICATIONS

Novels

Birthstone. London, Gollancz, 1980; revised, London, Penguin, 1982.
Ararat. London, Gollancz, and New York, Viking Press, 1983.
Swallow. London, Gollancz, and New York, Viking Press, 1984.
Sphinx. London, Gollancz, 1986; New York, Viking Press, 1987.
Summit. London, Gollancz, 1987; New York, Viking Press, 1988.
Lying Together. London, Gollancz, and New York, Viking Press, 1990.
Flying in to Love. London, Bloomsbury, and New York, Scribner, 1992.

Plays

The White Hotel, adaptation of his own novel (produced Edinburgh, 1984).

Radio Plays: *You Will Hear Thunder,* 1981; *Boris Godunov,* from play by Pushkin, 1984.

Poetry

Personal and Possessive. London, Outposts, 1964.
Penguin Modern Poets 11, with D. M. Black and Peter Redgrove. London, Penguin, 1968.
Two Voices. London, Cape Goliard Press, and New York, Grossman, 1968.
The Lover's Horoscope: Kinetic Poem. Laramie, Wyoming, Purple Sage, 1970.
Logan Stone. London, Cape Goliard Press, and New York, Grossman, 1971.
The Shaft. Gillingham, Kent, Arc, 1973.
Lilith-Prints. Cardiff, Second Aeon, 1974.
Symphony in Moscow. Richmond, Surrey, Keepsake Press, 1974.
Love and Other Deaths. London, Elek, 1975.
The Rock. Knotting, Bedfordshire, Sceptre Press, 1975.
Orpheus in Hell. Knotting, Bedfordshire, Sceptre Press, 1977.
The Honeymoon Voyage. London, Secker and Warburg, 1978.
In the Fair Field. N.p., Five Seasons Press, 1978.
Protest: A Poem after a Medieval Armenian Poem by Frik. Privately printed, 1980.
Dreaming in Bronze. London, Secker and Warburg, 1981.
Selected Poems. London, Secker and Warburg, and New York, Viking Press, 1983.

News from the Front, with Sylvia Kantaris. Todmorden, Lancashire, Arc, 1983.

The Red River. N.p., Cornerhouse, 1989.

The Puberty Tree: New and Selected Poems. Newcastle upon Tyne, Bloodaxe, 1992.

Other

Memories and Hallucinations (memoir). London, Gollancz, and New York, Viking Press, 1988.

Editor, *The Granite Kingdom: Poems of Cornwall.* Truro, Cornwall, Barton, 1970.

Editor, *Poetry in Crosslight.* London, Longman, 1975.

Editor, *Songs from the Earth: Selected Poems of John Harris, Cornish Miner, 1820-84.* Padstow, Cornwall, Lodenek Press, 1977.

Translator, *Requiem, and Poem without a Hero,* by Anna Akhmatova. London, Elek, and Athens, Ohio University Press, 1976.

Translator, *Way of All the Earth,* by Anna Akhmatova. London, Secker and Warburg, and Athens, Ohio University Press, 1979.

Translator, *Invisible Threads,* by Evtushenko. New York, Macmillan, 1981.

Translator, *The Bronze Horseman and Other Poems,* by Pushkin. London, Secker and Warburg, and New York, Viking Press, 1982.

Translator, *A Dove in Santiago,* by Evtushenko. London, Secker and Warburg, 1982; New York, Viking Press, 1983.

Translator, *You Will Hear Thunder,* by Anna Akhmatova. London, Secker and Warburg, and Athens, Ohio University Press-Swallow Press, 1985.

Translator, *Boris Godunov,* by Pushkin. N.p., Sixth Chamber Press, 1985.

Translator, *Selected Poems,* by Anna Akhmatova. London, Penguin, 1989.

*   *   *

The novels of D. M. Thomas are haunted. Although his work cannot accurately be described as ghost stories, there are certainly ghosts, visions and visitations present. In *Eating Pavlova,* for example, there is the deathbed confession of Sigmund Freud, his mind occasionally far from clear, leaving the reader wondering if the mind can be trusted (one quarter of the novel passes before Freud laments that as yet he has not divulged any facts). In *Eating Pavlova* dreams are viewed as real, and reality is dreamlike. Elsewhere, spectres roam through the pages, very often as spectators to the course of events as much as the readers are, and often in the form of hallucinations or Nabokovian aberrancies of a character's memory. Neither haunted houses nor castles figure predominantly in Thomas's work; Thomas's technique is to surrealize the action so that only with some imaginative weeding, or some later explanation, do certain events become absolutely clear (and sometimes, not even then). His books are not about ghosts (not specifically); but mildly supernatural occurrences inform the writing and hang in the air like clouds, like portents. Or, in the case of *Pictures at an Exhibition,* like reminders—and not for the only time—of the Holocaust of World War II.

Thomas's first novel, the juvenile *Devil and the Floral Dance,* was followed by the fantastic and satirical *Flute-Player,* a novel which was marketed as generic fantasy even though the description does not apply. *The Flute-Player* concerns itself with the na-

ture of art and the problem of how art is meant to survive in a totalitarian regime. While the latter novel marked a huge development on the former, it did not sell much better.

Big sales, however, were to follow—with *The White Hotel,* a novel which was written out of some necessity. Near the end of the 1970s, the government in England was cutting the financing of education across the board. Schools were being obliged to economize, and Thomas, then Head of the English Department at the Hereford College of Education, lost his job. His severance pay was the equivalent of his yearly salary, which allowed Thomas to write *The White Hotel*—a novel in which he wished to explore his interest in Freudian teachings with an imaginative extrapolation that would include the thoughts of one of Freud's young patients. Thomas also wanted to write a radically erotic novel that would build to the horrific climax that had been inspired by his reading of Anatoli Kuznetsov's *Babi Yar,* a description of wartime massacres of Jews at Kiev in the Soviet Union. Not to mention a novel that was not, strictly speaking, a novel—in that it is not a linear narrative, nor even a circular or fragmented narrative; *The White Hotel* encompasses the epistolary form, poetry in heroic couplets, a pastiche of a Freudian case study, and a grim re-enactment of concentration-camp camaraderie, and even soldier-prisoner banter, which is redolent of Tadeusz Borowski's *This Way for the Gas, Ladies and Gentlemen* (1959).

Ambitiously enough, the White Hotel symbolizes life itself, and within the novel Freud's conflicting impulses of the life instinct and the death instinct figure prominently. Near the beginning of the book is the long erotic poem by "Frau Anna G" which goes into explicit detail about the sexual shenanigans she and Freud's son have indulged in. The poem is dreamlike, splintered, transitory; what is alarming is not the erotic candour, but this openness framed against backdrops of terrible scenes of death and destruction involving some of the other guests at the hotel. As the fictional Freud mentions in the book's case study, Frau Anna G's letters show "an extreme of libidinous phantasy combined with an extreme of morbidity." Other guests watch Frau Anna G's acts of lustful desperation in states of near catatonia and non-involvement, which statuesque lack of commitment only fans the flames higher. On occasion there is third-party participation, such as when a chef holds out a glass to catch the milk pouring from Frau Anna's breast, but usually a condition of existential *amour* predominates against, for example, the apocalyptic images of stars falling from the sky—the end of the world.

The novel was better received in America than in England; in his memoir, *Memories and Hallucinations,* Thomas comments that John Updike's view of the Americans having verbally hyped the book into an area of excellent sales might be true. Some British critics found the sex scenes to be overdone, and the complex structure—examining events from a multitude of different angles—was not always warmly welcomed. The biggest problem, however, that critics in general had was to do with the book's dark feel. From the memoir: "'Why are you obsessed with violence?' is a question I'm often asked. A holocaust in *The White Hotel,* and then another one! But that's the story of the twentieth century . . . I recognized that my work might not be without disturbing undertones; simply because I, like every one of my readers, was not without sin, not without shadows. This was in part what *The White Hotel* was about: that we were all involved in the evil, we could not pretend it was outside us."

As Martin Amis's *Time's Arrow* was also to achieve a decade later, *The White Hotel* throbs with the energy of an atrocity-in-waiting at the book's tail-end: in Thomas's case, it is the chilling account of Frau Anna G's execution in 1941 at Babi Yar, along with that of thousands of other Russian Jews. She has been able to see the future but has been unable to understand it: this has been her personal curse. Now her personal suffering becomes part of the Holocaust. The ghost in the air—the smoke of the concentration camp—gains substance and depth with every body burned.

—David Mathew

TIMPERLEY, Rosemary (Kenyon)

Pseudonym: Ruth Cameron. **Nationality:** British. **Born:** London, 20 March 1920. **Education:** Hornsby High School, London; King's College, London University, B.A. 1941. **Family:** Married James McInnes Cameron in 1952 (died 1968). **Career:** Technical-school teacher, Essex, 1941-49; staff writer, *Reveille*, 1950-59; freelance author from 1959. **Died:** 1988.

HORROR, GHOST AND GOTHIC PUBLICATIONS

Novels

The Haunted Garden. London, Hale, 1966.
Walk to San Michele. London, Hale, 1971.
The Long Black Dress. London, Hale, 1972.
Juliet. London, Hale, 1974.
The Stranger. London, Hale, 1976.
The Man with the Beard. London, Hale, 1977.
The Phantom Husband. London, Hale, 1977.
The Nameless One. London, Hale, 1978.
Miss X. London, Hale, 1979.
The House of Mad Children. London, Hale, 1980.

Short Stories

Child in the Dark. New York, Crowell, 1956; as *The Listening Child*, London, Barrie, 1956.

Other

Editor, *The Fifth Ghost Book.* London, Barrie and Rockliff, 1969.
Editor, *The Sixth Ghost Book.* London, Barrie and Jenkins, 1970.
Editor, *The Seventh Ghost Book.* London, Barrie and Jenkins, 1971.
Editor, *The Eighth Ghost Book.* London, Barrie and Jenkins, 1972.
Editor, *The Ninth Ghost Book.* London, Barrie and Jenkins, 1973.

OTHER PUBLICATIONS

Novels

A Dread of Burning. London, Barrie, 1956.
Web of Scandal. London, Barrie, 1957.
The Fairy Doll. London, Hale, 1959.
Dreamers in the Dark. London, Hale, 1960.
Shadow of a Woman. London, Hale, 1960.
The Velvet Smile. London, Hale, 1961.

Yesterday's Voices. London, Hale, 1961.
Across a Crowded Room. London, Hale, 1962.
Twilight Bar. London, Hale, 1962.
The Bitter Friendship. London, Hale, 1963.
Let Me Go. London, Hale, 1963.
Broken Circle. London, Gresham, 1964.
The Veiled Heart. London, Gresham, 1964.
Devil's Paradise. London, Hale, 1965.
Blind Alley. London, Hale, 1967.
The Cat Walk. London, Hale, 1969.
The Echo-Game. London, Hale, 1973.
Forgive Me. London, Hale, 1967.
Lights on the Hill. London, Hale, 1968.
The Passionate Marriage. London, Hale, 1972.
Rome with Mrs. Evening. London, Hale, 1970.
My Room in Rome. London, Hale, 1968.
The Suffering Tree. London, Hale, 1965.
They Met in Moscow. London, Hale, 1966.
The Tragedy Business. London, Hale, 1969.
Tunnel of Shadows. Hale, 1986.
The Washers-Up. London, Hale, 1968.
Doctor Z. London, Hale, 1969.
House of Secrets. London, Hale, 1970.
The Mask Shop. London, Hale, 1970.
The Summer Visitors. London, Hale, 1971.
Journey with Doctor Godley. London, Hale, 1973.
Shadows in the Park. London, Hale, 1973.
The White Zig-Zag Path. London, Hale, 1974.
Ali and the Little Camel. London, Hale, 1975.
The Private Prisoners. London, Hale, 1975.
The Devil of the Lake. London, Hale, 1976.
The Egyptian Woman. London, Hale, 1976.
Suspicion. London, Hale, 1978.
Syrilla Black. London, Hale, 1978.
Justin and the Witch. London, Hale, 1979.
The Secretary. London, Hale, 1979.
Homeward Bound. London, Hale, 1980.
The Secret Dancer. London, Hale, 1981.
The Spell of the Hanged Man. London, Hale, 1981.
That Year at the Office. London, Hale, 1981.
The Face in the Leaves. London, Hale, 1982.
Night Talk. London, Hale, 1982.
Chidori's Room. London, Hale, 1983.
The Office Party—and After. London, Hale, 1984.
Love and Death. London, Hale, 1985.
After School Hours. London, Hale, 1988.
Inside. London, Hale, 1988.

Play

The Man Who Collected Beauty. London, Leonard, 1955.

*   *   *

Rosemary Timperley was the author of over 60 novels, in addition to her short fiction, editing, and work for radio and television. Born in London, she studied at King's College, London University, and went on to an initial career as a schoolteacher. The figures of well-educated, single, professional women pervade Timperley's writing, reflecting both Timperley's background and that of much of her readership. Timperley's ghosts often provide sympathetic relief to heroines trapped by their circumstances, and in a sense they helped her break out of teaching and into writing. Perhaps it is little wonder that her introductions to the "Ghost Book" series speak of ghosts as her friends, and sometimes thank them in the credits. Timperley approached writing via that well-worn path, journalism, and she began taking writing seriously in the 1950s, finally becoming a freelance author in 1959, aged 39.

Timperley edited a number of anthologies of ghost and supernatural stories. Some of her own stories have been adapted for broadcasting, appearing on Capital Radio's "Moment of Terror" and the BBC's "Haunted" series. As can be seen by her output, she concentrated on the novel as her primary work, and these ranged across romance, crime, mystery and horror. Although only about one in seven of her novels is clearly ghost or supernatural in theme, many of her other works have a strong element of terror. In *Miss X*, for example, a girl living in a boarding house loses her memory in an apartment explosion and fire, then has to face the world without possessions, identity or name. This theme of alienation is quite common in her ghost stories, sometimes as a result of, and sometimes causing, the supernatural encounters.

Her ghost and supernatural works could generally be described as chilling without being horrific, and having a 19th-century charm with mid-20th-century settings. Given Timperley's background as a teacher, it is no surprise that female teachers, children and schools feature heavily in her work. Even though she abandoned teaching, she appears to have generally had good relationships with her real-life students. Her fictional children are bright, sharp and sympathetically rendered, open to influences that adults have abandoned in the process of growing up and acquiring maturity. Thus Timperley's children can see into worlds that parallel ours and even intersect with it in places, yet cannot be accessed without the naivete that adults have lost. They can see the children's reactions, but not the stimulus. In contrast to the recent outpourings of Hollywood, her children are not malevolent monsters or pathetic victims. In a sense, ghosts are a normal feature of their childhood, and like toys they may be abandoned when they grow up. Typical of these stories is "Harry" (in *The Third Ghost Book*, edited by Cynthia Asquith, 1955) in which a woman complacently thinks that her adopted child has an imaginary friend. The "friend" is in fact the ghost of her brother, who died saving her life.

The ghosts in Timperley's stories often take inventive forms. In "Out of Sight, Out of Life" (in *The Second Bumper Book of Ghost Stories*, edited by Polly Parkin and James Hale, 1976) a child is unable to see people who are about to die, and on the day before her school exams she suddenly becomes a type of living ghost, unable to see herself in mirrors. Much to the relief of the reader she persuades her mother to keep her at home, but as her mother leaves to go shopping, a crippled aircraft falls out of the sky and annihilates the house. "The Man with the Flute" (in *The 13th Fontana Book of Great Ghost Stories*, edited by R. Chetwynd-Hayes, 1977) begins rather ominously with a girl left alone at home during the term holidays meeting a mysterious flute-player, yet this benevolent ghost merely re-unites two separated branches of her family. The ghost of "The Mistress in Black" (in *The Fifth Ghost Book*, edited by Timperley, 1969) is posthumously trying to clear her name of murder, as the school mistress of the title is supposed to have killed one of her students then committed suicide. A new teacher is guided to the dead student's desk, where she finds a note showing that the girl's death was an accident.

Timperley was well attuned to the life of educated, urban British women, and although her ghosts show great variety, her principal characters are mostly female. Whether lonely, single professionals having affairs with married men, or married women raising children at home and longing for something more exciting, they are vulnerable to supernatural intervention—for better or worse. Others of her more notable short stories include "The Private Torture Chamber" (in *The Fourth Ghost Book*, edited by James Turner, 1965); "Walk on Water" (in *The Eighth Ghost Book*, edited by Timperley, 1972); "Sister Varden" (in *The Ninth Ghost Book*, edited by Timperley, 1973; "Little Girl Lost" (in *The Bumper Book of Ghost Stories*, edited by Aiden Chambers, 1974); "To Keep Him Company" (in *The 10th Fontana Book of Great Ghost Stories*, edited by R. Chetwynd-Hayes, 1974); "From Another World" (in *The 12th Fontana Book of Great Ghost Stories*, edited by R. Chetwynd-Hayes, 1976); "The Tunnel" (in *Tales of Unknown Horror*, edited by Peter Haining, 1978); "No Living Man So Tall" (in *The 15th Fontana Book of Great Ghost Stories*, edited by R. Chetwynd-Hayes, 1979); "On the Theatre Steps" (in *More Tales of Unknown Horror*, edited by Peter Haining, 1979); "Some Travellers Return" (in *New Tales of Terror*, edited by Hugh Lamb, 1980); and "Mandragora" (in *The 26th Pan Book of Horror Stories*, edited by Clarence Paget, 1985).

As a thriller writer Timperley also retained a perspective from her own background. Set on the savannah of Guyana, "Masks and Voices" (in *The 14th Fontana Book of Great Ghost Stories*, edited by R. Chetwynd-Hayes, 1978) incorporates ghost, thriller and murder-mystery themes, and shows Timperley in a different gear. Kate is on the run after murdering her rather insufferable husband during their honeymoon in Paris. Voices begin calling to her, from a shaman in a trance, from a snatch of a radio play on the BBC World Service, even from overheard conversations in bars. Like Pollock in H. G. Wells's "Pollock and the Porroh Man," she is driven to suicide by a ghost that might not exist outside her own imagination. Like many of Timperley's characters, most notably Susan in the rather harrowing prison novel *Inside*, Kate has fled from reality and society, only to lose all the buffers and handholds that they include.

As a window on the lives, attitudes and circumstances of many career women in postwar Britain, Timperley's works can provide some valuable insights, but in a way she was also an exception. She broke out into a more fulfilling career, and the good-natured optimism of much of her work reflects this.

—Steven Paulsen and Sean McMullen

TONKIN, Peter (Francis)

Nationality: British. **Born:** Limavady, Londonderry, Ireland, 28 January 1950. **Education:** Queen's University, Belfast, Northern Ireland, B.A. (with honors) 1973, M.A. 1974. **Family:** Married Charmaine May, 21 March 1980. **Career:** Schoolteacher; freelance writer since 1980. **Address:** c/o Severn House Publishers, 1st Floor, 9-15 High Street, Sutton, Surrey SM1 1DF, England.

HORROR, GHOST AND GOTHIC PUBLICATIONS

Novel

The Journal of Edwin Underhill. London, Hodder and Stoughton, 1981.

OTHER PUBLICATIONS

Novels

Killer. London, Hodder and Stoughton, and New York, Coward McCann, 1979.
The Coffin Ship. London, Headline, 1989; New York, Crown, 1990.
The Fire Ship. London, Headline, 1990; New York, Crown, 1992.
The Bomb Ship. London, Headline, 1993; North Pomfret, Vermont, Trafalgar, 1995.
Iceberg. London, Headline, 1994.
The Leper Ship. Thorndike, Maine, Thorndike Press, 1994.
The Pirate Ship. London, Headline, 1995; North Pomfret, Vermont, Trafalgar, 1997.
The Action. Sutton, Surrey, Severn House, 1996.
Meltdown. London, Headline, and North Pomfret, Vermont, Trafalgar, 1996.
The Zero Option. Sutton, Surrey, Severn House, 1997.
Tiger Island. London, Headline, 1997.

*   *   *

All of Peter Tonkin's novels are unashamedly melodramatic, and it can be argued that none of them is devoid of a significant element of horror. All save one are, however, primarily committed to other genres: his first, *Killer*, is more a criminological case-study than an out-and-out slasher story, while his more recent works have carved out their own distinctive sub-genre of nautical romance. The central motif of *The Coffin Ship* is more obviously Gothic than those of *The Fire Ship*, *The Pirate Ship* and so on but the stories contained in the novels in the loosely knit series are action-adventure thrillers rather than horror stories. *Iceberg* is similar, although its modern setting allows it to flirt with the conventions of the disaster story. Tonkin's one wholehearted horror novel, *The Journal of Edwin Underhill*, is strikingly different from the rest of his work and it is puzzling that it was not followed up in the public arena, despite the fact that he left the teaching profession in 1980 to pursue a career as a full-time writer. (In the event, he was forced to return to teaching, temporarily, in 1985.)

The Journal of Edward Underhill is a first-person account of vampiric metamorphosis—one of several such novels produced in the wake of Anne Rice's *Interview with the Vampire* (1976). The diary which forms the body of the text begins at midnight on New Year's Eve and ends as the following new year begins; in the meantime, ineffectual schoolmaster Edwin Underhill has undergone a slow and painful transmogrification into a self-confessed monster. The seed of the metamorphosis is sown when he flees in humiliation from the girl he loves, whose rejection of him has been observed by a crowd of hidden witnesses, and falls into a pit where his hand is impaled by the stake used to destroy a sixteenth-century vampire countess, Stana Etain (i.e., Satan Innate).

Edwin's awareness of his unfortunate process of transformation sends him scurrying to the library in search of enlightenment; his studies there stimulate and supplement his nightmarish dreams in leading him to a full understanding of his fate. The countess's spirit has returned to possess him—and perhaps, ultimately, to *dispossess* him from the empire of his own flesh—and he has become a plague-carrier, infecting further victims with vampiric lust. As in most other late-twentieth-century exercises in vampire existentialism, the process of Underhill's metamorphosis is represented by the text in ambivalent terms. It is an acquisition of a new freedom which might be triumphantly grasped if only the sharp pangs of conscience could be blunted. In becoming a vampire Edwin gradually loses all the stigmata of mortality and insignificance which led to his rejection as a lover. He becomes handsome and fascinating, all the more so as he is forced to shun the day—and the procession of diary entries records the displacement of his original personality by another which is far more robust and avidly eager to "shrug off vapid melancholia."

Alas, as every existentialist knows only too well, vapid melancholia is not something that can very easily be shrugged off, and it is not obvious to the anguished diarist that the maggot facing annihilation may find much solace in the prospect of its replacement by a very different kind of being. That, rather than its Gothic motif, is the essence of the *really* horrific element of the novel.

The Journal of Edwin Underhill failed to duplicate the success of *Interview with the Vampire*, although it contrived to avoid the obscurity into which Geoffrey Farrington's similarly ambitious *The Revenants* (1983) was subsequently to sink. It is not clear why it failed to capture the public imagination, although the contemporary British audience was presumably even less certain than Peter Tonkin as to whether it was yet ready to welcome an arrogantly unrepentant vampire. The privilege of its conversion was left to *The Vampire Lestat* (1985). In retrospect, however, *The Journal of Edwin Underhill* deserves attention, and some admiration, as a work slightly ahead of its time which is of more than merely historical interest.

—Brian Stableford

TREMAYNE, Peter

Pseudonym for Peter John Philip Berresford Ellis; also writes as Peter Berresford Ellis. **Other Pseudonym:** Peter MacAlan. **Nationality:** British. **Born:** Coventry, Warwickshire, 10 March 1943. **Education:** Brighton College of Art. **Family:** Married Dorothea Cheesmur in 1966. **Career:** Reporter, *Brighton Herald*; assistant editor, *Smith's Trade News*; deputy editor, *Irish Post*; editor, *Newsagent & Bookshop* magazine; freelance lecturer, historian, novelist and short-story writer from 1975. **Awards:** *Irish Post* award, 1989. **Member:** Celtic League (chairman, 1988-89); London Association for Celtic Education (chairman, 1989; vice-president, 1990-92). **Agent:** A. M. Heath, 79 St. Martin's Lane, London WC2N 4AA, England. Lives in London.

HORROR, GHOST AND GOTHIC PUBLICATIONS

Novels

Hound of Frankenstein. London, Mills and Boon, 1977.
Dracula Unborn. Folkestone, Kent, Bailey and Swinfen, 1977; as *Bloodright*, New York, Walker, 1979.
The Revenge of Dracula. Folkestone, Kent, Bailey and Swinfen, and West Kingston, Rhode Island, Grant, 1978.
The Vengeance of She. London, Sphere, 1978.
The Ants. London, Sphere, 1979.
The Curse of Loch Ness. London, Sphere, 1979.
Dracula, My Love. Folkestone, Kent, Bailey and Swinfen, 1980.

Zombie! London, Sphere, 1981.
The Morgow Rises! London, Sphere, 1982.
Snowbeast. London, Sphere, 1983.
Kiss of the Cobra. London, Sphere, 1984.
Angelus! London, Panther, 1985.
Swamp! London, Sphere, 1985.
Nicor! London, Sphere, 1987.
Trollnight. London, Sphere, 1987.
Dracula Lives! (omnibus; includes *Dracula Unborn, The Revenge of Dracula, Dracula, My Love*). London, Signet, 1993.

Short Stories

My Lady of Hy-Brasil, and Other Stories. West Kingston, Rhode Island, Grant, 1987.
Aisling and Other Irish Tales of Terror. Dingle, Ireland, Brandon, 1992.

Other

Editor, *Masters of Terror: William Hope Hodgson.* London, Corgi, 1977.
Editor, *Irish Masters of Fantasy.* Dublin, Wolfhound Press, 1979; as *The Wondersmith and Other Macabre Tales*, Dublin, Wolfhound Press, 1988.

OTHER PUBLICATIONS

Novels

The Fires of Lan-Kern. Folkestone, Kent, Bailey and Swinfen, 1980.
The Return of Raffles. London, Magnum, 1981.
The Destroyers of Lan-Kern. London, Methuen, 1982.
The Buccaneers of Lan-Kern. London, Methuen, 1983.
Raven of Destiny. London, Methuen, 1984.
Ravenmoon. London, Methuen, 1988; as *Bloodmist*, New York, Baen, 1988.
Island of Shadows. London, Mandarin, 1991.
Absolution by Murder. London, Headline, 1994; New York, St. Martin's Press, 1996.
Shroud for the Archbishop. London, Headline, 1995; New York, St. Martin's Press, 1996.
Suffer Little Children. London, Headline, 1995; New York, St. Martin's Press, 1997.
The Subtle Serpent. London, Headline, 1996.
The Spider's Web. London, Headline, 1997.

Novels as Peter Berresford Ellis

The Liberty Tree. London, Michael Joseph, 1982.
The Rising of the Moon. London, Methuen, 1987.

Novels as Peter MacAlan

The Judas Battalion. London, W. H. Allen, 1983.
Airship. London, W. H. Allen, 1984.
The Confession. London, W. H. Allen, 1985.
Kitchener's Gold. London, W. H. Allen, 1986.
The Valkyrie Directive. London, W. H. Allen, 1987.

The Doomsday Decree. London, W. H. Allen, 1988.
Fireball. Sutton, Surrey, Severn House, 1991.
The Windsor Protocol. Sutton, Surrey, Severn House, 1993.

Other as Peter Berresford Ellis

Wales—a Nation Again! N.p., Library 33, 1968.
The Creed of the Celtic Revolution. Medusa, 1969.
The Scottish Insurrection of 1820, with Seumas Mac a'Ghobhainn. London, Gollancz, 1970.
The Problem of Language Revival, with Seumas Mac a'Ghobhainn. Inverness, Club Lebhar, 1971.
The Story of the Cornish Language. Penryn, Cornwall, Tor Mark Press, 1971; revised edition, 1990.
A History of the Irish Working Class. London, Gollancz, 1972.
The Cornish Language and Its Literature. London, Routledge and Kegan Paul, 1974.
Hell or Cannaught! London, Hamish Hamilton, 1975.
The Boyne Water. London, Hamish Hamilton, 1976.
The Great Fire of London. London, New English Library, 1977.
H. Rider Haggard: A Voice from the Infinite. London, Routledge and Kegan Paul, 1978.
Caesar's Invasion of Britain. London, Orbis, 1978.
Macbeth: High King of Scotland 1040-57. London, Muller, 1980.
By Jove, Biggles! The Life of Captain W. E. Johns, with Piers Williams. London, W. H. Allen, 1981; revised edition, as *Biggles! The Life Story of Capt. W. E. Johns*, Godmanstone, Dorset, Veloce, 1993.
The Last Adventurer: The Life of Talbot Mundy, 1879-1940. West Kingston, Rhode Island, Grant, 1984.
Celtic Inheritance. London, Muller, 1985.
A Dictionary of Irish Mythology. London, Constable, 1987.
Revisionism in Irish Historical Writing. N.p., Connolly Association, 1989.
The Celtic Empire. London, Constable, 1990.
A Guide to Early Celtic Remains in Britain. London, Constable, 1991.
A Dictionary of Celtic Mythology. London, Constable, 1992.
The Cornish Saints. Penryn, Cornwall, Tor Mark Press, 1992.
Celt and Saxon. London, Constable, 1993.
The Celtic Dawn: Celtic Survival in the Modern World. London, Constable, 1993.
The Book of Deer, illustrated by Roy Ellsworth. London, Constable, 1994.
The Druids. London, Constable, 1994.
Celtic Women: Women in Celtic Society and Literature. London, Constable, 1995.
Celt and Greek: Celts in the Hellenic World. London, Constable, 1997.
The Un-Dead: The Legend of Bram Stoker and Dracula, with Peter Haining. London, Constable, 1997.

Editor, *James Connolly: Selected Writings.* London, Penguin, 1973.

*

Critical Study: "Peter Berresford Ellis" by Richard Dalby, *Book and Magazine Collector* (London), no. 108, March 1993.

*   *   *

When he was 14 years of age, Peter Tremayne (or Peter Berresford Ellis, as he still was) discovered Charles Maturin's *Melmoth the Wanderer* in his father's library. Although the boy was too young for the story's complexities, he had already formed a taste for a book's spooky bits, and he would skip to these as a matter of course. *Melmoth the Wanderer*—a tale of dungeons, castles, ghosts, cannibalism, monsters (both real and not real)—affected him deeply; and while this does not exactly explain Tremayne's fictional style (what single factor could?), it at least gives the reader a clue as to its formation. Tremayne thinks all aspiring writers should read Melmoth because "so many are substituting technicolor gore for more literary qualities, such as the slow build up of tension and psychological fear."

By the time Peter Tremayne first published, his *alter ego*, the historian Peter Berresford Ellis, had already published *Wales—A Nation Again!* and *A History of the Irish Working Class*. And again, this should give some clue as to the interests that Tremayne was to follow in his fiction. Reading Peter Tremayne's *oeuvre* is like turning the dial on a radio tuned to particularly long waves; one hears, at certain frequencies, broadcasts from very distinct countries. *Aisling*, for example, is a program being sent out from Ireland, and *Trollnight* is from Norway; both *The Curse of Loch Ness* and *Snowbeast* hail from Scotland; and the Dracula novels have their obvious origins. The voices and scenery, in all instances, are clear. Tremayne delivers everything he knows about a place—and that includes its attitudes and its pulse. Tremayne's technique is to lock on to a geographical location and broadcast without interference from any other of that country's stations. His work is full of national detail—whatever that nation may be—and Tremayne delights in exploring a location's myths, which shine through the prose or mumble beneath it: both styles have their successes.

In *Trollnight* some of the horror comes from dramatic irony—the reader knows exactly what is going on but the main characters do not. This is a novel rich in what might be termed "Norwegia," and one which would appeal to a somewhat discerning horror fan. The prose is thorough; occasionally, perhaps, a little fussy. Instead of the monster coming into the clan, the monsters have been there all along, and it takes the outsiders—who are exploring Norwegian heritage—to dig up the beasts, almost literally, while excavating. Tony has to enter the hardly-welcoming clan, and deal with the Trolls who would prefer buried truths stay asleep . . . Meanwhile, another part of the effectiveness of this novel is due to the locals' willful suspension of belief and fear; as the local lady, Girselda Surnadel, says, "Has not the village always believed that the Troll rests in the mound and a curse would fall on us if ever its sleep was disturbed?" Knowing this, it is unforgivable that the locals do not so much accept the presence of the beasts as they learn to deal with the fear of the creatures' existence; and that they would rather do either than help with the problem. *Trollnight's* trope is of a small community, trapped in the inevitability of the Trolls being released.

Snowbeast rumors the "Big Grey Man of Ben MacDhui—the Snowbeast" into life: a creature who (allegedly) haunted the upper slopes of the Scottish mountains. This novel introduces the frightening possibility of the snow-creatures being more intelligent than human beings. And the questions asked are those which are asked of all horror novels these days: Is the beast a natural or unnatural beast? And is there any room for human sympathy—reader sympathy?

The Curse of Loch Ness goes one step further: Tremayne establishes the beast in question with a well thought-out *modus op-*

erandi for the creature, and one which every reader will identify with: the compounded frustration caused by the equivalent of sexual jealousy and sexual loneliness. "The intelligence had once had a mate . . . in time, an egg was laid and there had been great joy that the wealth of knowledge would exist for another generation. But the man-things had come . . . with pointed sticks . . . . They discovered the egg and destroyed it in their fear and ignorance." The monster is oddly and effectively imbued with human characteristics; it weeps for its dead mate and for "the times when it had shown anger when it should have shown love; when it had shown indifference when it should have shown concern. Did the man-things ever feel such emotion? Or were primitive animals incapable of feeling such things?" Tremayne has created an underwater race as proud of its heritage as the clans on the surrounding banks and beyond are of theirs. In *The Curse of Loch Ness*, the rhythmic roll of the prose, and the repetitions, give rise to the idea that this tale had been intended to be read aloud.

Contributing to a fine tradition of Irish storytelling, the short-story collection *Aisling* is probably Peter Tremayne's *tour de force*: stories which dwell and breathe on the borders of consciousness and reality. If the term had not already been coined, we might say that we were discussing a Twilight Zone. At any rate, Tremayne's fiction delineates a hinterland, mental and physical, of possibilities and truths only kept alive by discussion and tale-repetition. These are tales of hauntings; as such, we can grasp for explanations that the characters, in their panic, cannot see. To Peter Tremayne's credit, it is rare that we wish to do so. Here we hear the rich Irish accent through the prose—even through the chatty, collusive sentences that seem to be curling a forefinger to summon us into the story's small world—and that is addictive enough, without wanting to know all the answers as well.

Tremayne's stories often take place in moments shortly after stressful changes: such as a broken marriage in "Samhain Feis," a holy man being posted to a godforsaken island in "Aisling," and moving house in "Deathstone." Amongst a swarm of images and ideas, the subject matter of these tales suits his cautious but solid style perfectly—unless it is, rather, the style which suits the subject matter. Whichever is the case, these tales are particularly successful in evoking atmosphere and emotional aroma. Take, for example, the eponymous tale. Introducing the notion of philosophy into horror, "Aisling" is a vision that the protagonist holy man sees; and the sight of himself is a Jungian moment of introspection and self-regulation. From the reader's point of view, it is an example of how horror fiction can address weighty themes (identity and sexual repression) as well as, or better than, the mainstream. In "My Lady of Hy-Brasil" (the name being a place), Tremayne's voice resonates with Irish fluidity; it is Joycean in its assumption of shared knowledge, experience, life. Though it is written in Tremayne's customarily careful prose, there is the warming notion as one reads that there is more behind the myth being described: this is prose under a perfectly dominant hand, the chills being released like a held breath that is leaked out in tiny hisses. It does not matter how painful holding the breath becomes; we know that Tremayne's every final set-piece exhalation, like our own, is worth the wait.

The ghost story is often like a palimpsest: beneath the immediate supernatural occurrence, normal lives are under way, but the supernatural elements often help to re-contextualize this so-called normality. That is, the ghost story often helps to describe existing tensions, strengths, wounds. In many cases, the ghost is emotion—changeable, indefinable, maybe—incarnate. Tales of ghosts and hauntings take for granted the existence of another plane, which is suddenly superimposed on our own. In Tremayne, and elsewhere, an existence of ghosts (and other agents of the supernatural) is accepted, and even their moral rights—to haunt, to be—are taken into consideration. As Alfred Hitchcock pointed out in *Ghostly Gallery*, being a ghost must be terribly lonely.

—David Mathew

TRYON, Thomas

Nationality: American. **Born:** Hartford, Connecticut, 14 January 1926. **Education:** Yale University, B.A. in Fine Arts 1949. **Military Service:** Served in the U.S. Navy at the end of World War II. **Career:** Set designer, Cape Playhouse, Cape Cod; actor on stage and in television and films until the late 1960s; novelist and screenwriter. **Died:** 4 September 1991.

HORROR, GHOST AND GOTHIC PUBLICATIONS

Novels

The Other. New York, Knopf, and London, Cape, 1971.
Harvest Home. New York, Knopf, and London, Cape, 1973.
The Night of the Moonbow. New York, Knopf, 1989; London, Hodder and Stoughton, 1990.
Night Magic (completed by Valerie Martin and John Cullen, uncredited). New York, Simon and Schuster, 1995.

OTHER PUBLICATIONS

Novels

Lady. New York, Knopf, 1974; London, Hodder and Stoughton, 1975.
Crowned Heads. New York, Knopf, and London, Hodder and Stoughton, 1976.
All That Glitters. New York, Knopf, and London, Hodder and Stoughton, 1986.
The Wings of the Morning. New York, Knopf, 1990.
Kingdom Come. New York, Knopf, 1992.

Plays

Screenplays: *The Other*, 1972; *The Dark Secret of Harvest Home*, 1978.

*

Film Adaptations: *The Other*, 1972; *The Dark Secret of Harvest Home* (television mini-series), 1978; *Fedora*, 1978, from a story in *Crowned Heads*.

*   *   *

In 1971 Thomas Tryon, a minor Hollywood actor, published *The Other*; to everyone's surprise, it became a bestseller. Two years later Tryon published *Harvest Home*. Had he written noth-

ing else, Tryon would have established himself as a significant voice, both historically and intrinsically, in modern horror literature; for it was the nearly simultaneous publication of *The Other* and William Peter Blatty's *The Exorcist*, and their domination of the bestseller lists for the better part of 1971, that largely created the horror "boom" of the 1970s and 1980s. But Tryon's works are worth considering for more than sociological reasons: they are, in fact, rather good.

What *The Exorcist* did for the tale of supernatural horror, *The Other* and *Harvest Home* did for the non-supernatural tale of psychological horror: they legitimized it and showed that in the hands of a master it formed a genuine sub-class of the weird tale. Tryon's two novels are emphatically non-supernatural and psychological— the horror is largely or wholly internal, a product of a disturbed mind—but they are also emphatically horrific. Indeed, few authors have *simulated* what might be called ontological horror (horror at the perception of some violation of natural law in the external world) better than Tryon.

The Other is based on a trick. To say this is not at all to say that it is somehow meretricious, for the "trick" is the whole focus of the novel and the source of Tryon's investigation of the psychology of his protagonist. In this tale of Niles and Holland Perry, twin boys growing up in rural Connecticut in the 1930s, we do not learn until about two-thirds through the novel that Holland is actually dead and that Niles, shattered by the loss of his twin brother, is desperately pretending that Holland is still alive. Neither the third-person narrator of the novel proper, nor the first-person narrator who introduces each of the three segments of the book (and who turns out to be Niles, speaking from a lunatic asylum), reveals the truth until Niles's grandmother Ada, who initially allowed him to continue pretending that Holland was alive but finally tires of it because of the tragedy it has caused, forces Niles to confront the spectacle of Holland's grave. It is one of the most powerful and shocking moments in all modern weird literature. And yet, a short time later we see Niles being unable to accept the truth of the situation, and he continues the pathetic charade that leads to still more horror and death, until he is finally put away.

The Other is, in effect, really a detective story; but it remains a work of horror because it pretends *not* to be a detective story. We have no reason to doubt Holland's guilt in the various gruesome crimes that are committed until it is revealed that Holland is dead. At this point, our increasingly horrified awareness of Holland's psychological aberrations is suddenly and cataclysmically transferred to Niles. Throughout the novel, random utterances that seem to have the most innocent implications—or, indeed, to have no implications at all—become, once the secret is known, full of loathsome suggestion.

It is not merely that Niles, heartbroken at the loss of his twin, seeks to keep him alive in his mind; it is that Niles is psychologically transferring his "evil" side to Holland. Niles cannot admit to himself that he, not Holland, has committed all the atrocities in the tale (and there are many of them). Interestingly, at one point the first-person narrator (who of course is Niles) actually remarks: "Believe me, Niles is not entirely the paragon he appears, nor Holland quite the knave." Of course, Holland really was the "bad boy" of the two, and he ultimately caused his own death when he tried to hang Ada's cat in the well but fell down it himself. This incident itself—the most deeply repressed event in Niles's psyche—is fragmentarily related several times throughout the novel until all the details finally come out.

There is one subsidiary element of the novel that might be considered quasi-supernatural: a "game" that Ada taught to Niles and Holland by Ada whereby their minds become psychologically united with some other being or object. Tryon needs this device both in order to establish the psychic unity of Niles and Holland and also to allow the truth to be revealed to the reader at critical points in the narrative.

Harvest Home is in some ways a still greater work than its predecessor, presenting a many-stranded tapestry of horror in which the diverse elements are all united in one of the most powerful denouements in the history of weird fiction. Like *The Other*, it is set in rural Connecticut, but in the present day; and yet, as we are introduced to the small, tightly knit village of Cornwall Coombe, we can imagine that we have entered some ageless agricultural community where the continual cycle of the planting, nurturing and harvesting of the corn is the eternal and perhaps the only reality. It is something that one of the villagers tells Ned and Beth Constantine shortly after they move into the town from New York: "The social unit here is not the family, it's the community. And the community is founded on corn."

Things seem tranquil enough as Ned, an artist, wins favour by drawing portraits of the villagers and Beth participates in a sewing circle and other village activities. But Ned's fortunes take a critical turn when he befriends a young man, Worthy Pettinger, who has been selected as the next Harvest Lord, a high honour in the eyes of the villagers; but he spurns the office and attempts to flee the community. Ned abets Worthy's attempts to escape and is ultimately detected. At the climax of the novel, Ned bursts in on the secret ceremony of Harvest Home, in which only the women of the village, along with the Harvest Lord, participate. That ceremony, involving ritualistic language that becomes increasingly archaic, involves nothing less than the death of the Harvest Lord after he has impregnated the Corn Maiden. It is this suggestion of the hoary antiquity of the ceremony, in addition to its barbaric violence, that lends a quasi-supernatural aura to the event. For his sin, Ned is blinded and his tongue is cut out. Only then do we realize that the entire novel has been a monumental flashback in which Ned has been telling the whole story after the fact.

Tryon's other novels are either only marginally weird or (as in the case of his novels and tales about Hollywood—*Crowned Heads* and *All That Glitters*—and his expansive historical sagas of Connecticut life) not weird at all. *Lady* is a winsome story of a charming but enigmatic and melancholy woman who, it turns out, killed her husband many years ago because she had fallen in love with her black servant. *The Night of the Moonbow* was marketed as a weird novel, but it is in fact a sensitive story of a boy's emotional maturation at a summer camp. Then there is the posthumously published *Night Magic*, a confused and unsatisfying novel about magic and sleight-of-hand that was evidently "finalized and polished" (according to the press release) by two other writers, Valerie Martin and John Cullen. The extent of Tryon's own contribution to the work is unknown.

—S. T. Joshi

TURNER, James (Ernest)

Nationality: British. **Born:** 16 January 1909. **Career:** Poet, novelist, editor and ghost-story writer. **Died:** 1975.

HORROR, GHOST AND GOTHIC PUBLICATIONS

Short Stories

Staircase to the Sea: Fourteen Ghost Stories. London, Kimber, 1974.
The Way Shadows Fall: Fourteen Ghost Stories. London, Kimber, 1975.

Other

Ghosts of the South West. Newton Abbott, David and Charles, n.d.

Editor, *The Fourth Ghost Book.* London, Barrie and Rockliff, 1965.
Editor, *The Unlikely Ghosts.* London, Cassell, 1967; New York, Taplinger, 1969.

OTHER PUBLICATIONS

Novels

Mass of Death. London, Fortune Press, 1937.
Murder at Landred Hall. London, Cassell, 1954.
A Death by the Sea. London, Cassell, 1955.
The Strange Little Snakes. London, Cassell, 1956.
The Frontiers of Death. London, Cassell, 1957.
The Crystal Wave. London, Cassell, 1957.
The Dark Index. London, Cassell, 1959.
The Deeper Malady. London, Cassell, 1959.
The Glass Interval. London, Cassell, 1961.
Condell. London, Cassell, 1961.
The Crimson Moth. London, Cassell, 1962.
The Nettle Shade. London, Cassell, 1963.
The Long Avenues. London, Cassell, 1964.
The Slate Landscape. London, Cassell, 1964.
The Blue Mirror. London, Cassell, 1965.
Requiem for Two Sisters. London, Cassell, 1968.
The Stone Dormitory. London, Cassell, 1971.

Poetry

Pastoral. N.p., n.d.
The Alien Wood. N.p., n.d.
The Hollow Vale. N.p., n.d.
The Interior Diagram and Other Poems. London, Cassell, 1960
The Accident and Other Poems. London, Cassell, 1966.

Other

My Life with Borley Rectory. London, Lane, 1950.
Rivers of East Anglia. London, Cassell, 1954.
The Dolphin's Skin. London, Cassell, 1956.
The Shrouds of Glory. London, Cassell, 1958.
Stella C. London, Souvenir Press, n.d.
Seven Gardens for Catherine (autobiography). London, Cassell, 1968.
Sometimes Into England (autobiography). London, Cassell, n.d.

Editor, *A Book of Gardens.* London, Cassell, 1963.
Editor, *Thy Neighbour's Wife.* London, Cassell, 1964.

Editor, *A Coin Has Two Sides*. N.p., n.d.
Editor, *Love Letters*. N.p., n.d.

*   *   *

The British James Turner is not to be confused with the American James Turner, who was the editor for Arkham House from 1971 to 1996. Although the British James Turner earned his living, for much of his life, as a market gardener, he also gained a reputation as a detective-fiction writer and a poet. He produced a long series of novels featuring the character of amateur sleuth Rampion Savage, starting with his first published novel, *Mass of Death*, before the Second World War, but the majority of his writing appeared in the 1950s and 1960s.

Turner's work features a mixture of emotions. Although he has a poet's eye for the subtle shades of life, his fiction tends to be imbued with a healthy scepticism verging on the sardonic. He remains open-minded about the supernatural. Even though he bought the site of the notorious Borley Rectory, supposedly the most haunted house in England, he witnessed no direct supernatural manifestations himself. Only in later years did he believe he saw a ghost, a very matter-of-fact flesh-and-blood being that he did not realize was a ghost until later. Turner believes many of us may have seen ghosts and not known it, and that they are likely to be as much a part of our world as any other everyday object. Our wish to make them something more than that is our desire for a belief in an afterlife, a theory that he expanded upon in his introduction to *The Fourth Ghost Book*. This series had been started by Lady Cynthia Asquith and it is appropriate that Turner, a very level-headed and objective author, should be commissioned to continue the series and ensure that the stories maintained the level of contemporary authenticity of the previous volumes.

Turner's main contributions to the world of supernatural fiction are his ghost stories, the best of which are collected in two slim volumes. While some of his novels verge on the strange and unreal, most notably *The Deeper Malady*, which explores, almost in the style of Oliver Onions, a decaying family living in the remoteness of East Anglia, with undertones of witchcraft and ancient rites, it is in his short fiction that he experiments with the supernatural. In almost all of these stories he elaborated upon his thesis in *The Fourth Ghost Book*, and in particular on how our desire to explore or relive the past, often for our own salvation, will bring back ghosts and memories best left undisturbed.

The past possessing the present is a common theme in Turner's ghost stories. Sometimes it is the spirits of the past who snare the trap, as in "Stratton," where a reincarnated spirit causes a man to relive a battle in the Civil War, or as in "Love Affair," where the spirit of a girl murdered in the 1840s captivates a man in the 1970s. Sometimes it is the curious of the present who become possessed by the past, as in "Naked We Came Into the World," where a man revisits the empty house of his childhood and becomes overwhelmed by its memories and ghosts. The story is powered by guilt and feelings of a lost childhood—the man has become possessed by his memories. There is a similar mood in "The St. Christopher Medallion," where a man continues to be haunted by memories of a tragedy that happened at school over 30 years before. The story has a strong autobiographical feel, and it is possible that Turner was exorcising some of his own memories.

Many of Turner's stories, especially those in *Staircase to the Sea*, are set in Cornwall, where he spent many of his last years.

Like many Cornish ghost stories, of which there are an inordinate number, they are fuelled by local legend and superstition, tales that Turner also collected for his book *Ghosts in the South West*. In Turner's case, however, the key to the haunting is always the individual. His stories are intensely personal, the events being wrapped within people's emotions. He likes to experiment with the variation on the theme of whether it is the supernatural which first sparks off the events, or whether the individual's emotional state is the key to the haunting. Typical of the former is "The Guardian" (in *The Fourth Ghost Book*, 1965), where an old house built upon a drained marsh is the focal point of powers that possess later occupants. An example of the latter is "Fly Away Home" (in *The Seventh Ghost Book*, 1971), where a painter with an emotional affinity for nature becomes engulfed by her surroundings.

All of Turner's ghost stories stem from the individual. He paints in a personal canvas and, as a consequence, the reader has a vivid experience of the events and hauntings described, making them powerful and memorable.

—Mike Ashley

TUTTLE, Lisa

Pseudonym: Maria Palmer. **Nationality:** American. **Born:** Houston, Texas, 16 September 1952. **Education:** Syracuse University, New York, B.A. in English 1973. **Career:** Editor of the fan magazine *Mathom*, 1968-70; television columnist, Austin *American Statesman*, Texas, 1976-79. **Awards:** John W. Campbell award, 1974; Nebula award, 1982. **Agents:** Howard Morhaim, 175 Fifth Avenue, Room 709, New York, NY 10010, USA; or, A. P. Watt Ltd., 20 John Street, London WC1N 2DL, England.

HORROR, GHOST AND GOTHIC PUBLICATIONS

Novels

Familiar Spirit. New York, Berkley, and London, New English Library, 1983.
Gabriel: A Novel of Reincarnation. London, Sphere, 1987; New York, Tor, 1988.
Lost Futures. New York, Dell Abyss, and London, Grafton, 1992.
Virgo: Snake Inside (as Maria Palmer; for children). London, Mammoth, 1995.
The Pillow Friend. Atlanta, Georgia, White Wolf, 1996.

Short Stories

A Nest of Nightmares. London, Sphere, 1986.
A Spaceship Built of Stone and Other Stories. London, Women's Press, 1987.
Memories of the Body: Tales of Desire and Transformation. Wallington, Surrey, and New York, Severn House, 1992.

Other

Editor, *Skin of the Soul: New Horror Stories by Women*. London, Women's Press, 1990; revised edition, New York, Pocket Books, 1991.

OTHER PUBLICATIONS

Novels

Windhaven, with George R. R. Martin. New York, Timescape,
  1981; London, New English Library, 1982.
Angela's Rainbow. Limpsfield, Surrey, Dragon's World, 1983.
Catwitch (for children). Limpsfield, Surrey, Dragon's World, and
  Garden City, New York, Doubleday, 1983.
Panther in Argyll (for children). London, Methuen, 1996.

Other

*Children's Literary Houses: Famous Dwellings in Children's Fic-
  tion,* with Rosalind Ashe. Limpsfield, Surrey, Dragon's World,
  and New York, Facts on File, 1984.
Encyclopedia of Feminism. Harlow, England, Longman, and New
  York, Facts on File, 1986.
Heroines: Women Inspired by Women. London, Harrap, 1988.
Mark Harrison's Dreamlands, with Mark Harrison. London, Pa-
  per Tiger, 1990.

*   *   *

Lisa Tuttle has written in many fields during her career and is
an extremely versatile writer. While her short stories cover science fiction, fantasy and horror, most of her novels have horrific
elements though the emphasis is on character-development rather
than gore. Numerous stories had seen print before *Windhaven*, her
collaboration with George R. R. Martin, was published. This is
science fiction, set on an alien world where communication between islands is by hang glider.

Her first solo novel, *Familiar Spirit*, has the same feel as many
of her stories. It is also a haunted-house story. The characters are
deftly sketched, there are no redundant descriptions and the story
develops rapidly. Sarah, afraid of being overwhelmed by her relationship with Brian, has tried to build a life apart and found she
has overestimated the amount of independence she can have and
still keep his love. He needs to be needed and as he has transferred his affections elsewhere she has to find somewhere to live
since she cannot continue to impose on the hospitality of her best
friend and her husband. The house she finds seems too good to be
true. It is large, cheap and available immediately. Almost as soon
as she moves in she begins to realize why the previous tenant,
Valerie, was so keen to move out. It appears to be haunted by a
demon intent on possessing her while offering her heart's desire.
In some ways the book is unsatisfying; but it is tidily written,
with just enough of each ingredient to keep the plot flowing without being overdramatic.

Tuttle herself has called her first story, "Stranger in the House"
(in *Clarion 2*) a "going home story." Many of her stories could be
described in this fashion as can the novel *Gabriel*. The narrator of
the latter, Dinah, had a brief, passionate marriage to an artist who
killed himself while under the influence of LSD. After ten years,
she returns to New Orleans, the city where she met and loved
Gabriel. Though much has changed there are people she once knew,
including Sallie who has borne Gabriel's son, Ben. Gabriel believed
strongly in reincarnation. As Dinah's relationship with the nine-
year-old Ben develops she begins to wonder if he is Gabriel reborn. The boy himself develops an unhealthy fixation for Dinah
and at times acts as if he is possessed, leading towards a chilling

climax. There is a degree of ambiguity as Dinah wants Gabriel
back, wishes Ben had been her child but realizes that she has to
look forward, not back—she cannot go home. Ben may be Gabriel
reborn, or he may simply have absorbed knowledge of him from
mother and grandparents.

The "going home" theme is present in the 1985 story "No Regrets" (collected in *A Spaceship Built of Stone*) in which poet
Miranda Ackerman returns to the university where she used to
be a student, this time as a visiting lecturer. By coincidence, the
house they have allocated her was the one she lived in before she
fled a potentially claustrophobic existence as a wife and mother.
The house is haunted by the future she might have had as she
begins to hear and see ghosts of her ex-lover and the child they
could have had. This idea of alternative lives is explored to a greater
extent in the novel *Lost Futures*. Clare Beckett is an accountant
who has walled herself into a comfortable niche where no one can
touch her. Then for no apparent reason the memories of her
brother's death and the guilt she feels as a result well up like evil
gases from a bog. Knocked off balance, she relives the past, creating gaps in her present life. The memories become might-have-
beens; the blanks are filled with the futures she once created for
herself. It is almost as if she is in touch with these other selves,
and if these futures exist, then there are pasts where her brother
didn't die. Clare's life crosses into fantasy—or begins the descent
into madness. Then Clare awakes from her dream of reality to
find herself staring at a blank wall. Everything she thought was
true turns out to be a lie. From being a horror novel, everything is
turned upside down and the central theme becomes science fiction. The elements of this novel are put together so skilfully that
reading it is a delight.

Tuttle's most recent adult novel, *The Pillow Friend*, re-explores
some of these elements, particularly the blurring between reality
and fantasy. At seven, Agnes Grey escapes into dreams to help
cope with her mother's erratic mood-swings. Her Aunt Marjorie
warns her to be careful about what she wishes for, but the child is
only interested in her made-up relationships which become more
real to her than her own life. As the novel progresses and Agnes
enters adulthood, the scenes become more bizarre and chilling.

Short stories are where Tuttle displays her greatest strengths
as a writer. She puts science fiction, fantasy and horror to good
use in exploring a number of themes. The majority of her stories
focus on vulnerable women, many of them are in or are emerging
from damaging relationships, others are still deeply affected by
events or circumstances of childhood or adolescence. "Flying to
Byzantium" (from *A Nest of Nightmares*), another "going home"
story, features Sheila Stoller, a writer of one fantasy novel who is
invited as guest of honour to a science-fiction convention. The
novel arose from Sheila's desires as an unattractive, unsociable child
to escape her mother's bullying tactics designed to make her conform. The convention is a nightmare in itself but Sheila finds herself trapped in the small American town of Byzantium by small-
minded people and reverting to the kind of person she thought
she had escaped becoming by leaving home.

Later stories can be regarded as overtly feminist, such as "Lizard Lust" (from *Memories of the Body*). This is also an allegory.
A bored librarian finds herself abducted to a world where, physically, there is no difference between the sexes. All are born female
but the "men" are those who have acquired lizards. All women
desire lizards and would do anything to get their hands on one—
or so the "men" say. Here a woman can become a "man" by fighting for and winning a lizard from someone else. Another story

from the same collection, "The Wound," explores the boundaries between genders. Olin is a downtrodden teacher who has been separated from his wife for several years. Seth is the new music teacher at the school and a friendship develops between them. After a while Olin realizes he is becoming a woman. Although this can be regarded as a science-fiction story it also suggests that gender is not necessarily to do with body form, but with attitude and particularly in the role played in a relationship. Both these stories are disturbing as they are intended to provoke a re-examination of preconceptions.

If anything, Tuttle spreads her talents too thinly. As well as her fiction, which includes work for children, she produces non-fiction and edits anthologies. Over the years the quality and depth of her work has improved in both her long and short fiction.

—Pauline Morgan

U-V

UPDIKE, John (Hoyer)

Nationality: American. **Born:** Shillington, Pennsylvania, 18 March 1932. **Education:** Attended public schools in Shillington; Harvard University, Cambridge, Massachusetts, A.B. (summa cum laude) 1954; Ruskin School of Drawing and Fine Arts, Oxford (Knox fellow), 1954-55. **Family:** Married 1) Mary Pennington in 1953 (marriage dissolved), two daughters and two sons; 2) Martha Bernhard in 1977. **Career:** Staff reporter, *New Yorker*, 1955-57. **Awards:** Guggenheim fellowship, 1959; Rosenthal award, 1960; National Book award, 1964; O. Henry award, 1966; Foreign Book prize (France), 1966; New England Poetry Club Golden Rose, 1979, MacDowell medal, 1981; Pulitzer prize, 1982, 1991; American Book award, 1982; National Book Critics Circle award, for fiction, 1982, 1991, for criticism, 1982; Union League Club Abraham Lincoln award, 1982; National Arts Club Medal of Honor, 1984; National Medal of the Arts, 1989. **Member:** American Academy, 1976. **Address:** 675 Hale Street, Beverly Farms, MA 01915, USA.

HORROR, GHOST AND GOTHIC PUBLICATIONS

Novel

The Witches of Eastwick. New York, Knopf, and London, Deutsch, 1984.

Short Stories

The Afterlife and Other Stories. New York, Knopf, and London, Hamish Hamilton, 1994.

OTHER PUBLICATIONS

Novels

The Poorhouse Fair. New York, Knopf, and London, Gollancz, 1959
Rabbit, Run. New York, Knopf, 1960; London, Deutsch, 1961
The Centaur. New York, Knopf, and London, Deutsch, 1963.
Of the Farm. New York, Knopf, 1965.
Couples. New York, Knopf, and London, Deutsch, 1968.
Rabbit Redux. New York, Knopf, 1971; London, Deutsch, 1972.
A Month of Sundays. New York, Knopf, and London, Deutsch, 1975.
Marry Me: A Romance. New York, Knopf, 1976; London, Deutsch, 1977.
The Coup. New York, Knopf, 1978; London, Deutsch, 1979.
Rabbit Is Rich. New York, Knopf, 1981; London, Deutsch, 1982.
Roger's Version. New York, Knopf, and London, Deutsch, 1986.
S. New York, Knopf, and London Deutsch, 1988.
Rabbit at Rest. New York, Knopf, 1990; London, Deutsch, 1991.
Memories of the Ford Administration. New York, Knopf, 1992; London, Hamish Hamilton, 1993.

Brazil. New York, Knopf, and London, Hamish Hamilton, 1994.
In the Beauty of the Lilies. New York, Knopf, and London, Hamish Hamilton, 1996.

Short Stories

The Same Door. New York, Knopf, 1959; London, Deutsch, 1962.
Pigeon Feathers and Other Stories. New York, Knopf, and London, Deutsch, 1962.
Olinger Stories: A Selection. New York, Knopf, 1964.
The Music School. New York, Knopf, 1966; London, Deutsch, 1967.
Penguin Modern Stories 2, with others. London, Penguin, 1969.
Bech: A Book. New York, Knopf, and London, Deutsch, 1970.
The Indian. Marvin, South Dakota, Blue Cloud Abbey, 1971.
Museums and Women and Other Stories. New York, Knopf, 1972; London, Deutsch, 1973.
Warm Wine: An Idyll. New York, Albondocani Press, 1973.
Couples: A Short Story. Cambridge, Massachusetts, Halty Ferguson, 1976.
Three Illuminations in the Life of an American Author. New York, Targ, 1979.
Too Far to Go: The Maples Stories. New York, Knopf, 1979; London, Deutsch, 1980.
The Chaste Planet. Worcester, Massachusetts, Metacom Press, 1980.
The Beloved. Northridge, California, Lord John Press, 1982.
Bech Is Back. New York, Knopf, and London, Deutsch, 1982.
Getting Older. Helsinki, Eurographica, 1985.
The Afterlife. Leamington, Warwickshire, Sixth Chamber Press, 1987.
Going Abroad. Helsinki, Eurographica, 1987
Trust Me. New York, Knopf, and London, Deutsch, 1987.
Baby's First Step. Huntington Beach, California, Cahill, 1993.

Plays

Three Tests from Early Ipswich: A Pageant. Ipswich, Massachusetts, 17th Century Day Committee, 1968.
Buchanan Dying. New York, Knopf, and London, Deutsch, 1974.

Poetry

The Carpentered Hen and Other Tame Creatures. New York, Harper, 1958; as *Hoping for a Hoopoe,* London, Gollancz, 1959.
Telephone Poles and Other Poems. New York, Knopf, and London, Deutsch, 1963.
Dogs Death. Cambridge, Massachusetts, Lowell House, 1965.
Verse. New York, Fawcett, 1965.
The Angels. Pensacola, Florida, King and Queen Press, 1968.
Bath after Sailing. Monroe, Connecticut, Pendulum Press, 1968.
Midpoint and Other Poems. New York, Knopf, and London, Deutsch, 1969.
Seventy Poems. London, Penguin, 1972.
Six Poems. New York, Aloe, 1973.
Query. New York, Albondocani Press, 1974.
Cunts (Upon Receiving the Swingers Life Club Memberships Solicitation). New York, Hallman, 1974.

Tossing and Turning. New York, Knopf, and London, Deutsch, 1977.

An Oddly Lovely Day Alone. Richmond, Virginia, Waves Press, 1979.

Sixteen Sonnets. Cambridge, Massachusetts, Halty Ferguson, 1979.

Five Poems. Cleveland Bits Press, 1980.

Spring Trio. Winston-Salem, North Carolina, Palaemon Press, 1982.

Jester's Dozen. Northridge, California, Lord John Press, 1984.

Facing Nature. New York, Knopf, 1985; London, Deutsch, 1986.

A Pear Like a Potato. Northridge, California, Santa Susana Press, 1986.

Two Sonnets. Austin, Texas, Wind River Press, 1987.

Collected Poems, 1953-1993. New York, Knopf, and London, Hamish Hamilton, 1993.

Other

The Magic Flute (for children), with Warren Chappell. New York, Knopf, 1962.

The Ring (for children), with Warren Chappell. New York, Knopf, 1964.

Assorted Prose. New York, Knopf, and London, Deutsch, 1965.

A Child's Calendar. New York, Knopf, 1965.

On Meeting Authors. Newburyport, Massachusetts, Wickford Press, 1968.

Bottom's Dream: Adapted from William Shakespeare's "A Midsummer Nights Dream" (for children). New York, Knopf, 1969.

A Good Place. New York, Aloe, 1973.

Picked-Up Pieces. New York, Knopf, 1975; London, Deutsch, 1976.

Hub Fans Bid Kid Adieu. Northridge, California, Lord John Press, 1977.

Talk from the Fifties. Northridge, California, Lord John Press, 1979.

Ego and Art in Walt Whitman. New York, Targ, 1980.

People One Knows: Interviews with Insufficiently Famous Americans. Northridge, California, Lord John Press, 1980.

Invasion of the Book Envelopes. Concord, New Hampshire, Ewert, 1981.

Hawthorne's Creed. New York, Targ, 1981.

Hugging the Shore: Essays and Criticism. New York, Knopf, 1983; London, Deutsch, 1984.

Confessions of a Wild Bore (essay). Newton, Iowa, Tamazunchale Press, 1984.

Emersonianism (lecture). Cleveland, Bits Press, 1984.

The Art of Adding and the Art of Taking Away: Selections from John Updike's Manuscripts, edited by Elizabeth A. Falsey. Cambridge, Massachusetts, Harvard College Library, 1987.

Just Looking: Essays on Art. New York, Knopf, and London, Deutsch, 1989.

Self-Consciousness: Memoirs. New York, Knopf, and London, Deutsch, 1989.

Odd Jobs: Essays and Criticism. New York, Knopf, and London, Deutsch, 1991.

Concerts at Castle Hill. Northridge, California, Lord John Press, 1993.

The Twelve Terrors of Christmas. New York, Gotham Book Mart, 1993.

A Helpful Alphabet of Friendly Objects (for children). New York, Knopf, 1995.

Golf Dreams: Writings on Golf. New York, Knopf, 1996.

Editor, *Pens and Needles,* by David Levine. Boston, Gambit, 1970.

Editor, with Shannon Ravenel, *The Best American Short Stories 1984.* Boston, Houghton Mifflin, 1984; as *The Year's Best American Short Stories,* London, Severn House, 1985.

*

Film Adaptations: *Rabbit, Run,* 1970; *Too Far to Go,* 1982; *The Roommate* (TV movie), 1984; *The Witches of Eastwick,* 1987.

Bibliography: *John Updike: A Bibliography* by C. Clarke Taylor, Kent, Ohio, Kent State University Press, 1968; *An Annotated Bibliography of John Updike Criticism 1967-1973, and a Checklist of His Works* by Michael A. Olivas, New York, Garland, 1975; *John Updike: A Comprehensive Bibliography with Selected Annotations* by Elizabeth A. Gearhart, Norwood, Pennsylvania, Norwood Editions, 1978.

Manuscript Collection: Harvard University, Cambridge, Massachusetts

Critical Studies: *John Updike* by Charles T. Samuels, Minneapolis, University of Minnesota Press, 1969; *The Elements of John Updike* by Alice and Kenneth Hamilton, Grand Rapids, Michigan, Eerdmans, 1970; *Pastoral and Anti-Pastoral Elements in John Updike's Fiction* by Larry E. Taylor, Carbondale, Southern Illinois University Press, 1971; *John Updike: Yea Sayings* by Rachael C. Burchard, Carbondale, Southern Illinois University Press, 1971; *John Updike* by Robert Detweiler, New York, Twayne, 1972, revised edition, 1984; *Rainstorms and Fire: Ritual in the Novels of John Updike* by Edward P. Vargo, Port Washington, New York, Kennikat Press, 1973; *Fighters and Lovers: Theme in the Novels of John Updike* by Joyce B. Markle, New York, New York University Press, 1973; *John Updike: A Collection of Critical Essays* by Suzanne H. Uphaus, New York, Ungar, 1980; *The Other John Updike: Poems/Short Stories/Prose/Play,* 1981, and *John Updike's Novels,* 1984, both by Donald J. Greiner, Athens, Ohio University Press; *John Updike's Images of America* by Philip H. Vaughan, Reseda, California, Mojave, 1981; *Married Men and Magic Tricks: John Updike's Erotic Heroes* by Elizabeth Tallent, Berkeley, California, Creative Arts, 1982; *Critical Essays on John Updike* edited by William R. Macnaughton, Boston, Hall, 1982; *John Updike* by Judie Newman, London, Macmillan, 1988; *Conversations with John Updike* edited by James Plath, Jackson, Mississippi, University Press, 1994.

*   *   *

John Updike is one of the most important figures in American post-war literature, renowned as a novelist, short-story writer, poet and essayist. One of his early novels, *The Centaur,* includes strong fantasy elements, in that there is a partly mythic structure counterpointing a realistic story; and one of his most recent, *Brazil,* also has strong mythic associations and a decidedly "magic realist" feel. Another of his novels, *The Witches of Eastwick* (one of the very few of his works to be adapted as a big-budget film), revolves around witchcraft and deviltry, while some of the pieces in his most recent collection, *The Afterlife and Other Stories,* are subtle "posthumous fantasies" or ghostly tales.

Variety, precision and poetry characterize Updike's prose. He normally writes about middle-class Americans in rural New England, cataloguing their hopes, tragedies and extramarital affairs, and *The Witches of Eastwick* is no exception to this. The only difference here is that the three main characters and viewpoints are all female.

This novel is principally realistic; that its three protagonists are a coven of witches is important to the story though does not prevent it being a literary novel of great merit. The witchcraft (unlike the fantasy in *The Centaur*) is meant to be believed, not simply a metaphor. Certainly the three witches themselves are confident of their powers, exercise them in a planned and scientific manner, and achieve a wide range of effects from the comic to the cruel and tragic. Obviously, it is also intended as a metaphor for the enhanced power of a divorced woman. Updike cannot seem to resist drawing out a metaphor from each circumstance he describes.

The plot describes twelve months in the small coastal town of Eastwick, Rhode Island, seen mostly through the eyes of the witches, each thirtysomething and divorced with children. They are Alexandra, a blonde who makes small sculptures and worries about the possibility of cancer; Jane, a brunette who teaches piano and plays cello; and Sukie, a redhead who does part-time reporting for the local newspaper. All of them have affairs with local husbands. When the rich and eccentric bachelor Darryl Van Horne buys a mansion on the edge of town, the three cannot stay away. They visit him separately (he helps Alexandra with her sculpture and Jane with her music) and together, being both attracted and repulsed by different aspects of his personality. A joint session in a hot tub leads to sexual encounters with him, but puts strains on the women's relationships with each other.

Sukie's boss kills his wife and commits suicide; one contributory factor is that the coven have been persecuting the wife, making feathers, pins and other small objects appear regularly in her mouth. The couple's two adult children return to the area to clear and sell the house; they are introduced to Van Horne by the pitying coven. But the daughter, Jennifer, commits the unforgivable sin of marrying Van Horne; she is made the subject of death magic and dies slowly of cancer. Her brother and Van Horne then start up a gay relationship and do a moonlight flit from Eastwick, leaving many bills unpaid.

Such a précis does far less than justice to the cleverness of the novel's construction, or to the great subtleties of plot advancement and information provision. Quite a few scenes are telephone conversations between two of the witches, dispensing with details of setting to imbue the story with a sense of added pace. Yet Updike's concern—almost a compulsion—for fine detail, leads him to comment, quite often, upon the way his characters speak, hissing an "s" or clipping an "r". At other times there are poetic descriptions of Eastwick at different seasons, establishing a sense of place in phrases that are succinct and arrestingly beautiful. The precision of his language is almost daunting, as he accurately isolates and describes thoughts and fragments of scenes which most other authors would lump into clichéd generalizations. There are slower and more trying passages here, just as there are longer and more convoluted sentences, yet most effects are achieved with a light touch.

This is a very entertaining novel, witty throughout via wry observations and self-deprecating thoughts, and sometimes extremely amusing, especially in the first half. While there is always variety, well orchestrated from scene to scene, the overall trend is from initial humour and the optimism felt by the witches at the arrival of Van Horne, through gradually more serious events, quarrels and the breakdown of relationships and ways of life, towards death, the sudden departure of Van Horne and the ending of the coven. (The renewed optimism of the last few pages, as the three women leave Eastwick, two of them happily with new partners,

is just a tailpiece.) This gradual descent into seriousness and tragedy is mirrored by the quality of the magic. In a big early scene, Alexandra is annoyed by the way the beach is seemingly in the grip of noisy young people, so she conjures up a thunderstorm to send "the offending youths" scurrying for cover. This is played for laughs; so is the way she causes an old lady's string of pearls to break in order to escape from a boring conversation; similarly the game of tennis between the witches and Van Horne, in which the ball magically becomes a bat and then a toad. But later the editor's wife is driven to distraction by magic inflicted by Sukie and Jane, Alexandra casually uses magic to kill a neighbour's dog simply because it barks at night, and the three of them conspire, credibly and horrifically, to kill Van Horne's bride.

If *The Witches of Eastwick* is often lighthearted, it must never be considered lightweight. Updike is full of epigrams, aphorisms and basic truths. "Boredom in a wife is part of the social contract, but boredom in a mistress undermines a man." He intends his characters to be microcosms of us all. And it is very convincing; the witches are so believable in everything else that the reader wants to believe in their magic, too, and if the excess of female sexuality written (very perceptively) by a man seems just a trifle too deliberate and lascivious, well, put it down to entertainment.

A final problem is Van Horne, who has too many hidden talents, who remains mysterious and enigmatic to the end, whose viewpoint is never used. Subtle signs, including the way in which he, a scientist, seems to accept magic without comment, and the ever-present whiff of sulphur in the doorway of his house, suggest that he may be the greatest black magician of them all, and that he may, like the author, have controlled the whole year's worth of events in Eastwick.

—Chris Morgan

VANCE, Steve

Nationality: American. **Born:** Steven Edward Vance, in Brunswick, Georgia, 13 July 1952. **Career:** Writer since 1978; contributor of short stories to *Isaac Asimov's Science Fiction Magazine, Unearth, Chillers, The Magazine of Fantasy & Science Fiction, Tesseract, Mind's Eye, Affinity, American Inventor* and other publications. Not to be confused with the illustrator Steve Vance. **Address:** 1049 Good Hope Road, Dalton, Georgia 30721-7544, USA.

HORROR, GHOST AND GOTHIC PUBLICATIONS

Novels

The Hyde Effect. New York, Leisure, 1986.
The Abyss. New York, Leisure, 1989.
Spook. New York, Soho Press, 1990.
Shapes. New York, Leisure, 1991.

OTHER PUBLICATIONS

Novels

Planet of the Gawfs. New York, Leisure, 1978.
All the Shattered Worlds. New York, Manor, 1979.

The Reality Weavers. Davenport, Florida, Laura, 1979.
The Hybrid. New York, Tower, 1981.
The Asgard Run. New York, Leisure, 1990.
The Price of Darkness: A Shane King Mystery Thriller, edited by Todd Kelly. New Orleans, Louisiana, Serenity, 1996.

*   *   *

The world has paid little attention to the career of Steve Vance, and, when one considers his work during his first decade of publishing, that indifference seems wholly justifiable. Still, teachers are always urged to never give up on their slower students, since some may be late bloomers who will eventually display their true talents; and there is at least one powerful piece of evidence to suggest that horror readers may have given up on Steve Vance too quickly.

After a trio of mediocre science-fiction novels—the first one, *Planet of the Gawfs*, humiliatingly published without cover art as a generic-style "Inflation Fighter"—Vance shifted to mediocre horror novels with *The Hyde Effect*. One character in the novel, Allen Blake Corbett, is a horror novelist who regrets agreeing to produce a routine thriller that he is struggling to finish, and it is easy to discern some autobiographical significance in this. Recalling an article by a college professor called "The Hyde Effect" positing that lycanthropy is actually a very rare and poorly understood illness, Corbett, a newspaper columnist, and a freelance occult researcher team up to prove that a series of gruesome murders, always occurring on the first night of the full moon, were in fact perpetrated by a werewolf. The simplicity of the unfolding plot is suggested by the novelist's initials, A. B. C.—the professor turns out to be the werewolf, infected with the disease by a vengeful old Native American—and, as the ensuing manhunt for the professor begins to marginalize the purported protagonists, Vance abruptly folds his tent halfway through the novel, arranges for the professor to be easily captured in a few pages, and embarks upon a second story: after the villain is held for observation in a fortified research centre, a series of breathtakingly idiotic bureaucratic decisions allow the transformed professor to escape and go on a lethal rampage through the sealed-off facility until Corbett finally contrives to decapitate him with a car. A potentially interesting minor character—a deluded patient at the centre who goes off to attack the werewolf while imagining himself the hero of a fantasy novel—suggests an intent to achieve some sort of grand combination of horror, science fiction and fantasy, but the science-fiction and fantasy elements in *The Hyde Effect* only interrupt the story without really contributing to it.

In Vance's second, and even worse, horror novel, *The Abyss*, a character considers the forbidding York Mansion and remarks, "This place is like something out of Stephen King!" But many other writers also come to mind while reading this stale drama about two outsiders probing the sinister mystery of the small town of Euphrata, Indiana, where visitors have an odd tendency to vanish or turn up dead. It turns out that the conspiratorial residents are addicted to, and hiding the secret of, a powerful healing gas that is improving their health and longevity; their dynamic leader, who presides over the inevitable boring rituals, also engages in novel experiments like brain transplants, one of which may have involved the heroine's dead brother. In the end, while pale victims return from the abyss where they were tossed to attack the evildoers, another ally of the outsiders brilliantly decides to burn their house down to end the whole business. To explain *The Abyss*, readers

might reasonably theorize that Vance kept tossing in various poorly-integrated ideas simply to ensure that the work achieved a certain length, and this is just about the worst impression that a writer could convey.

Then, after these clumsy and deficient efforts, it is with a sense of genuine astonishment—and even wonder—that one encounters the evocative and absolutely marvellous *Spook*. Casting aside the phoney stage-sets of his previous novels, Vance goes to a place he knows well, rural Georgia, and offers a persuasive and refreshingly un-stereotypical picture of life in such communities; and, as if invigorated by this environment, Vance for the first time creates characters that seem like real people, and his story unfolds in a focused and cohesive manner. Lola Aragon, a Mexican-American woman who arrives to take control of the school district, learns about and attempts to help MaryAnn Nelson, a 16-year-old girl, horribly disfigured since birth, who has been kept at home all her life by her harsh and embittered mother. Known as "Spook," she is derided and taunted by other children, yet she also shows signs of intelligence and striking artistic ability. When the discovery of some brutally murdered people indicates that she has become monstrous in her actions as well as her appearance, residents band together to hunt down the girl; yet nothing is as it seems, and Vance skilfully proceeds to a surprising yet satisfactory denouement. With only mildly supernatural overtones and minimal graphic violence, *Spook* is a powerful parable about just how cruel people can be, and just how horribly people can suffer because of others' cruelty; and, had it come from a writer with a stronger track record, it might have been acclaimed as a true masterpiece of the genre.

Instead, however, *Spook* was generally ignored, and after publishing one more, hard-to-find horror novel, *Shades*, Vance apparently abandoned the field. It is hard to predict what he might produce if he returns: certainly, he could return to churning out undistinguished hackwork, but if he ever again matches the excellence of *Spook*, Vance just might manage to attract some serious attention.

—Gary Westfahl

VANDERMEER, Jeff

Nationality: American. **Born:** 1968. **Career:** Editor, *Jabberwocky*, and contributor to other small-press magazines. **Awards:** International Rhysling Award for poetry, 1994. Lives in Tallahassee, Florida.

HORROR, GHOST AND GOTHIC PUBLICATIONS

Novel

Dradin, in Love. Tallahassee, Florida, Buzzcity Press, 1996.

Short Stories

The Book of Frog. Gainesville, Florida, Ministry of Whimsy Press, 1989.
The Book of Lost Places. Concord, California, Dark Regions Press, 1996.

*

Jeff VanderMeer comments:

My work often features a bittersweet tension between an appreciation for the beauty, the complexity, of our world and the sadness that we who live within it are mortal and will one day pass from it. In this context, "horror" serves an important function in my fiction, especially the horror of mortality and the horror of what we sometimes do to each other, against all reason, against the miraculous reality of our surroundings. Horror also plays a part in an ongoing concern of mine—the nature of morality and courage (especially explored in three novellas set in the same milieu as my short novel *Dradin, In Love*). Often these explorations are set against a backdrop of war or personal suffering. Only in such extremes can we find definitive and intrinsic proofs of humankind's potential for both grace and atrocity.

For these reasons, I am uninterested in the build-up to the "scare" that has traditionally formed the backbone of horror fiction. In this sense, I am a mimic—like the butterfly that pretends to be the Monarch—as I prefer to use horror tropes for dislocation, for disorientation, and to shock the reader out of his or her comfortable assumptions about the world. In horror I find the pursuit of beauty *in extremis*, of the strangeness and the sadness which make us truly human. Horror to me, therefore, exists most powerfully when not confined to publishers' marketing labels, i.e., books like Ian McEwan's *The Innocent* or Cormac McCarthy's *Blood Meridian*.

*   *   *

Like Thomas Ligotti and D. F. Lewis, Jeff VanderMeer launched his literary career by becoming a prolific contributor to small-press magazines, although his activity in the field has also extended to editing such publications. His magazine *Jabberwocky* published early work by Kathe Koja as well as stories by small-press stalwarts Mark Rich and Wayne Allen Sallee. VanderMeer has published a good deal of poetry—"Flight . . ." won the 1994 International Rhysling Award—and numerous short stories, which range from quirky comedies to striking *contes cruels* and vividly surreal horror stories.

The most horrific of the early tales collected in *The Book of Frog* are the two set in New Orleans, both of which make reference to a drinking-den called A Fresh Bucket of Blood. "The Color of Chance Is Green," in which a matter of life and death is settled in the aptly named establishment—though not as expected—by maze-running frogs and toads, provided VanderMeer with an early professional sale when it was reprinted in the British magazine *Fear*. VanderMeer also published "So the Dead Walk Slowly" and "Flesh" in *Fear*, and won that magazine's annual award for the "Best Short Story by an Established Author" in 1991. Among later stories set in A Fresh Bucket of Blood is "Welcome to the Masque" (1991), a *fin de siècle* story set as the midnight chimes of New Year's Day 1900 die away, in which the bar's regulars catch a glimpse of the coming reality of Black Power in the exotic person of Jean Claude Rimbaud. Jean Claude Rimbaud's "twin" Jean Luc plays a prominent role in "The Game of Lost and Found," one of two works-in-progress included in *The Book of Frog*.

No complete version of "The Game of Lost and Found" has yet appeared, but the other unfinished story in *The Book of Frog*, the surreal fantasy "Greensleeves," was effectively carried through to its conclusion in a version reprinted in *The Book of Lost Places*. Various inhabitants of a library—who include a number of derelicts and an eagle imprisoned in a glass dome as well as the spinster librarian—are liberated from their existential stasis by the magician Cedric Greensleeves, though not without difficulty and a measure of destruction. Although it is not a horror story this colourful work retains a dark element, which imports a Decadent sensibility into its breezy bizarrerie. VanderMeer's most extended exercise in this kind of sardonic fabulation is the novella *Dradin in Love*, in which an out-of-work missionary returns to the exotic city of Ambergris as Festival time approaches, unwisely enlisting the roguish dwarf Dvorak Nibelung to act as a go-between in paying court to a lovely woman glimpsed through a high window. Dradin's romantic delusions are swiftly and systematically shattered by the wilderness of excessive artifice which he finds in Ambergris—a city far more Decadent than New Orleans ever was, even at the height of its most extravagant Mardi Gras. The book's dedication to "the late Angela Stalker" (i.e., Angela Carter) acknowledges a key influence on VanderMeer's contemporary fables; he has written several essays on her work.

Most of the stories in *The Book of Lost Places* are *contes cruels*. "Black Duke Blues" returns yet again to New Orleans—here called Nawlins because the tale is told in a broad southern dialect—but no supernatural embellishments are required to spice up the protagonist's awful encounter in The Fresh Bucket o' Blood, here reincarnate as a jazz club. The fantasy element in "Falling into the Arms of Death He Found a Beautiful Place," in which an American soldier loses his bearings in a Third World theatre of war, is marginal and hallucinatory but no less striking for that. "Mahout" is an extended meditation on the death of a circus elephant in Tennessee in 1916. "The Sea, Mendeho, and Moonlight" is similar in spirit, its sombre tone reminiscent of the "graveyard poetry" which enjoyed a brief vogue in mid-18th-century England. Although the protagonist of "The Ministry of Butterflies" shares a surname with the protagonist of "The Sea, Mendeho, and Moonlight" the story is of a different kind, employing butterflies as a symbol of metamorphosis in an account of the fateful meeting of a female revolutionary and a retired general. All these stories display VanderMeer's evolving mastery of ornate language and the increasing sensitivity of his treatment of mortality and disillusionment.

The finest stories in *The Book of Lost Tales* are "The Emperor's Reply" and "The Bone-Carver's Tale," both of which combine a remarkable delicacy of style with a keen appreciation of the horrors left in the train of military adventures and both of which employ a crucial element of fantasy to heighten their response to actual events. "The Emperor's Reply" describes the fate of the last emperor of the Incas, Tupac Amaru, employing the symbolism of metamorphosis in a fashion similar to, but more delicate than, "The Ministry of Butterflies." "The Bone-Carver's Tale" is set in Kampuchea in the wake of one of that nation's many military atrocities, describing the nightmarish spiritual odyssey of the bone-carver Sajit Xuan-Ti, whose talent for shaping beautiful objects from the relics of once-living creatures proves an inadequate distancing device when he goes in search of the corpse of the lovely *serunai* player Prei Chen. Together with *Dradin, in Love* these two stories suggest that VanderMeer's fledgling career should proceed from strength to strength, and that he will make a major contribution to the field of neo-Decadent dark fantasy.

—Brian Stableford

VISIAK, E(dward) H(arold)

Pseudonym of Edward Harold Physick. **Nationality:** British. **Born:** London, 20 July 1878. **Career:** Indo-European Telegraph

Company, 1897-1914; teacher, 1914-24(?); writer. **Died:** 30 August 1972.

HORROR, GHOST AND GOTHIC PUBLICATIONS

Novels

The Haunted Island. London, Elkin Mathews, 1910.
Medusa: A Story of Mystery and Ecstacy and Strange Horror. London, Gollancz, 1929.
"The Shadow" in *Crimes, Creeps and Thrills*, edited by John Gawsworth. London, E. H. Samuel, 1936.

Poetry

The Phantom Ship. London, Elkin Mathews, 1912.

OTHER PUBLICATIONS

Poetry

Buccaneer Ballads. London, Elkin Mathews, 1910.
Flints and Flashes. London, Elkin Mathews, 1911.
The Battle Fiends. London, Elkin Mathews, 1916.
Brief Poems. London, Elkin Mathews, 1919.
E. H. Visiak, edited by John Gawsworth. London, Richards Press, 1936.

Other

The War of the Schools, with C. V. Hawkins. London, Elkin Mathews, 1912.
Milton Agonistes. London, A. M. Philpot, 1922.
The Animus Against Milton. Derby, Grasshopper Press, 1945.
The Mirror of Conrad. London, Laurie, 1955; New York, Philosophical Library, 1956.
The Portent of Milton. London, Laurie, 1958; New York, Humanities Press, 1958.
Life's Morning Hour (autobiography). London, John Baker, 1968.
Machen and Myself. London, Twyn Barlwm Press, 1963.

Editor, *Complete Poetry and Selected Prose of John Milton.* London, Nonesuch Press, and New York, Random House, 1938.

*

Critical Study: "Terror and Enchantment: E. H. Visiak's Fiction" by Hugh Lamb, in *All Hallows* #3, 1991.

*   *   *

E. H. Visiak was the leading expert on the poetry of John Milton, but in his fiction he was fascinated with the lure and power of the sea. Many of his poems and his three novel-length works explore the mystical and metaphysical aspects of the sea. Although outwardly they may appear to be adventure novels in the style of Robert Louis Stevenson and Jules Verne, both of whose works Visiak devoured as a child, at their heart they are unique, personalized visions of the unrelenting sea. It is possible that Visiak also enjoyed the fiction of William Hope Hodgson, as there are occasional parallels.

His first novel, *The Haunted Island*, was a relatively straightforward excursion into uncharted waters. Although set in the 17th century and involving a strange island with arcane scientific knowledge, it was essentially an adventure novel and had none of the mystique of *Medusa*, his second and most famous novel-length work. *Medusa* is Visiak's premier achievement, one of those rare, indescribable novels of personal vision (comparable in some ways to David Lindsay's fantasy masterpiece *A Voyage to Arcturus* [1920]; Lindsay was a friend of Visak's). It is narrated by Will Harvell, the orphaned son of a sea captain, who befriends John Huxtable whose own son has been kidnapped by pirates. Will joins Huxtable in his search for his son; and soon he experiences visions of a ghastly face, both before their voyage and on board ship. As the voyage continues so rumours of a ghost begin to circulate and they encounter a man-fish bearing the hideous face of Will's visions. Only gradually do we learn of a lost civilization that has fractured the barriers between our world and another, leaving this world open to experimentation from the other world. At one level *Medusa* may be interpreted as science fiction, but Visiak was exploring deeper levels than this, probing into the human psyche and what influences us. The novel (as with all of Visiak's work) requires more than one reading to understand and for the reader to benefit from Visiak's strength of vision and purpose.

Visiak himself continued to explore the theme of alien control and perceptions beyond reality. "Medusan Madness" (*New Tales of Horror*, 1934) plucks at the same strings in depicting a man driven mad by a vision. "The Uncharted Islands" (*Crimes, Creeps and Thrills*, 1936) could well be an excised chapter from *Medusa*, as it relates a separate exploratory voyage of one of the sailors in that novel to an island where the natives are haunted by some vast supernatural being. A constant theme throughout Visiak's books are dreams of huge man-like beings, not necessarily god-like but certainly having a supernatural power over humanity.

Visiak's third novel, "The Shadow," was not published separately but was incorporated in John Gawsworth's anthology *Crimes, Creeps and Thrills*. Again we have a brooding influence from beyond our normal perceptions. Several generations ago Hamond Layton had been an evil and vicious smuggler; the two aspects of Hamond live on in two modern characters, the demonic artist Reginald Thurston, and the young boy Edmund Shear who is sensitive to Hamond's influence and who must in some way redeem the evil. The novel follows the battle of psychic wills between Shear and Thurston under the overwhelming evil shadow of Layton, until the final cataclysmic vision of Layton's phantom ship.

Visiak was a competent writer with a remarkable psychological vision much of which was too personal to express adequately in his fiction. His work requires an intense sympathy from its readers to gauge Visiak's own intent, but such will be rewarded by some of strangest work in supernatural fiction.

—Mike Ashley

W-Z

WAKEFIELD, H(erbert) Russell

Nationality: British. **Born:** Elham, Kent, 9 May 1888. **Education:** Marlborough College; University College, Oxford. **Family:** Married 1) Barbara Standish Waldo in 1920 (divorced 1936); 2) Jessica Sidney Davey in 1946. **Career:** Private Secretary to Lord Northcliffe, 1911-14; war service, 1914-18; publisher's editor, 1920-30; full-time writer, 1930-45; civil servant, 1945-53. **Died:** 2 August 1964.

HORROR, GHOST AND GOTHIC PUBLICATIONS

Short Stories

They Return at Evening. London, Philip Allan, and New York, Appleton Century, 1928.
Old Man's Beard. London, Geoffrey Bles, 1929; as *Others Who Returned*, New York, Appleton Century, 1929.
Imagine a Man in a Box. London, Philip Allan, and New York, Appleton Century, 1931.
Ghost Stories. London, Cape, 1932; New York, Arno Press, 1976.
A Ghostly Company. London, Cape, 1935.
The Clock Strikes Twelve. London, Jenkins, 1940; enlarged edition, Sauk City, Wisconsin, Arkham House, 1946; abridged edition, as *Stories from The Clock Strikes Twelve*, New York, Ballantine, 1961.
Strayers from Sheol. Sauk City, Wisconsin, Arkham House, 1961.
The Best Ghost Stories of H. Russell Wakefield, edited by Richard Dalby. London, Murray, 1978; Chicago, Academy Chicago, 1982.

OTHER PUBLICATIONS

Novels

Gallimaufry. London, Philip Allan, 1928.
Hearken to the Evidence. London, Geoffrey Bles, 1933.
Belt of Suspicion. London, Collins, 1936.
Hostess of Death. London, Collins, 1938.

Other

The Green Bicycle Case. London, Philip Allan, 1930.
Landru, the French Bluebeard. London, Duckworth, 1936.

*   *   *

Although H. R. Wakefield wrote over 60 ghost stories his work became neglected even in his own lifetime and remains so, despite a small but avid following. Yet he was one of the master writers of the ghost story of the first half of this century. He was one of the few English writers whose work spanned the period from the heyday of supernatural fiction in the 1920s to its re-emergence in the early 1960s. Unfortunately, due to the paucity of markets, Wakefield wrote little during the 1950s and what remained unpublished he destroyed shortly before his death.

By profession Wakefield was a journalist and editor, after spending some years as a private secretary. He was an editor for the publisher Philip Allan and worked with Charles Birkin on the Creeps Library of books. He did not start out with the intention of producing primarily ghost stories. Early on he wrote a humorous society novel, *Gallimaufry*, and became well known in the 1930s for his studies of real-life crimes, and for a few crime novels. But it is his ghost stories that have kept his name alive and will probably ensure his lasting reputation.

His work falls into two main periods. His early stories, collected in *They Return at Evening, Old Man's Beard* and *Imagine a Man in a Box*, and his later work collected in *The Clock Strikes Twelve* and *Strayers from Sheol*, with a few stories scattered between and after. This division also delineates a change in mood in Wakefield's fiction. The early tales are more in the vein of traditional ghost stories, whilst the later ones become more complex and subjective, radiating a mood of the unusual without necessarily featuring a direct manifestation of the supernatural. Both of these groupings also sub-divide. There are, to begin with, the basic haunted-house stories. It was Wakefield's own supernatural vision at a house that inspired his first story, "The Red Lodge," about a house haunted by the slimy spirit of a suicide by drowning. Another suicide haunts by nightmares in "A Peg on Which to Hang," whilst yet another reappears annually in "The Dune." In "That Dieth Not" the vengeful ghost of a murdered wife causes her husband to commit suicide. Suicide or murder is the usual cause of Wakefield's early hauntings as featured in "Old Man's Beard," "Look Up There!" and "The Frontier Guards," which rank amongst his most atmospheric ghost stories.

Even at this early stage, however, Wakefield tried to ring the changes. A few of his stories do show the influence of M. R. James. "He Cometh and He Passeth By," for instance, about a black magician who kills his victims by sending them cut-out paper figures, is clearly based on "Casting the Runes." "The Seventeenth Hole at Duncaster" is unusual in being a ghostly golf story but has unmistakeable Jamesian imagery in its vision of the guardian of an ancient Druidic site where the golf course was built. Even "Damp Sheets" may owe some inspiration to James in that Agatha, who has caused her uncle to die of pneumonia by making his bed with damp sheets, is in turn smothered by damp linen.

Like E. F. Benson, who also enjoyed intermingling the supernatural with new gadgets, Wakefield describes a machine capable of reviving the dead in "The Lazaroid," and uses the radio as a new medium for supernatural communication in "Surprise Item." "Mr. Ash's Studio" is somewhat reminiscent of H. G. Wells's "The Moth" in that both deal with a haunting by moths that no one else can see.

Some of these early stories, though, are distinctly Wakefield's own and are most creative. "Professor Pownall's Oversight" explores the rivalry between two chess-players and how even murder and suicide do not stop the desire to win. "The Central Figure" is an excellent portrayal of madness and guilt. "Colonel Humpit of the Fourth Musketeers" is an ironic twist on the concept of the Unknown Soldier. In this case it is a traitor whose body is used as the symbolic soldier and the traitor's ghost is pursued by the ghosts of those he betrayed. One of Wakefield's most unusual stories may feel Jamesian but has a special twist: "The Last to Leave" tells of a man who so loves the old house in which he lives that he is saved by the house's ghosts, represented by two cowled carved figures. The story may also be viewed as a reversal of the House of Usher theme.

Wakefield's interest in real-life crime and murder mysteries impinged on a few of his later writings where he uses supernatural means to explore cases of murder, though always with an extra twist. For example, in "I Recognised the Voice" a psychic solves a murder that has not yet been committed whilst in "Farewell Performance" guilt-transference allows a ventriloquist's dummy to betray its owner. Wakefield occasionally uses animals in his stories, and he was evidently anti-hunting. In "Present at the End" an avid hunter undergoes a conversion and is haunted by the spirit of the rabbit his dogs mutilated. In "Death of a Poacher" a hunter kills a were-hyena and is tracked down and killed himself. In "Masrur" a man kills his wife's cat because it hunts creatures, but is haunted thereafter by the cat's cry, whilst in "Immortal Bird" the vision of an albino blackbird continues to haunt one man after he arranges the death of a rival.

The stories of Wakefield's later years are generally darker and more sinister. Two of them touch on the subject of child abuse: "The Gorge of the Churels" (*Fantasy & Science Fiction*, 1951), where the ghosts of women steal babies, and "Monstrous Regiment" where a young boy is trapped by his governess until helped by the spirit of his mother. Wakefield's ghosts tend to be malevolent or more tangible, especially in the evocation of smells. There are particularly nasty manifestations in "Ingredient X" and "The Middle Drawer." He also had the experiences of two World Wars to draw upon for his fiction. Just as "Corporal Humpit of the Fourth Musketeers" and "Day-Dream in Macedon" drew their cynicism from the First World War so "The Caretaker," "The Sepulchre of Jasper Sarasen" (*Fantastic Universe*, 1953) and his last story, "Death of a Bumble-Bee" (*Travellers by Night*, 1967) consider effects arising from the Second World War.

Wakefield was an inventive and adaptable writer. While he remoulded influences from writers he admired he also generated ideas of his own, always willing to build into his stories current ideas and possibilities. Although many of his stories looked to the crimes of the past, Wakefield also considered the possibilities of the present and future. As a result the best of his work remains alive and as effective as when it was written.

—Mike Ashley

WALKER, Robert W(ayne)

Pseudonyms: Geoffrey Caine; Glenn Hale; Stephen Robertson.
Nationality: American. **Born:** 1948.

HORROR, GHOST AND GOTHIC PUBLICATIONS

Novels (series: Dr. Jessica Coran; Dr. Dean Grant; Abraham Stroud, in the books as by Geoffrey Caine; Ryne Lanark, in the books as by Stephen Robertson)

Brain Watch. New York, Leisure, 1985.
Salem's Child. New York, Leisure, 1987.

Aftershock. New York, St. Martin's Press, 1987.
Dead Man's Float. New York, Pinnacle, 1988.
Disembodied. New York, St. Martin's Press, 1988.
Decoy (as Stephen Robertson). New York, Pinnacle, 1989.
Razor's Edge (Grant). New York, Pinnacle, 1989.
Burning Obsession (Grant). New York, Pinnacle, 1989.
Dying Breath (Grant). New York, Pinnacle, 1989.
Blood Ties (as Stephen Robertson). New York, Pinnacle, 1989.
The Handyman (as Stephen Robertson). New York, Pinnacle, 1990.
Curse of the Vampire (as Geoffrey Caine). New York, Diamond, 1991.
Dr. O (as Glenn Hale on cover only). New York, Zebra, 1991.
Wake of the Werewolf (as Geoffrey Caine). New York, Diamond, 1991.
Legion of the Dead (as Geoffrey Caine). New York, Diamond, 1992.
Killer Instinct (Coran). New York, Diamond, 1995.
Primal Instinct (Coran). New York, Diamond, 1995.
Pure Instinct (Coran). New York, Diamond, 1996.
Fatal Instinct (Coran). New York, Diamond, 1996.
Darkest Instinct (Coran). New York, Jove, 1996.
Cutting Edge. New York, Jove, 1997.

OTHER PUBLICATIONS

Novels

Sub-Zero! New York, Belmont, 1979.
Search for the Nile. New York, Bantam, 1986.

* * *

Robert W. Walker's career in horror fiction has been extensive though in large part invisible, partly because he has written under at least three different names, partly because most of his fiction that could be included in the genre was marketed as straight suspense or even detective fiction. His first overt horror novel, *Brain Watch*, borrowed from the popularity of medical thrillers. Through a combination of drugs and computer assistance, a brilliant but possibly deranged researcher has found a way to infiltrate and control the brains of others. The protagonists who discover the plot and eventually bring the experimentation to a halt are hampered by the fact that clandestine organizations within the government are secretly sponsoring the research because of its military applications. This is a blend of horror and science fiction that has its moments, but which is too derivative and predictable to be memorable.

Walker's next horror novel, *Salem's Child*, was even more formulaic, though more effectively delivered. A young boy becomes the conduit through which the uneasy spirits of the executed witches of Salem return to the modern world. With his assistance, they infect the living, and give fresh life to a demon living buried beneath the earth. *Aftershock* ignored the supernatural and turned to misguided science for its menace. A devastating earthquake has destroyed Los Angeles so thoroughly that rescue efforts are virtually impossible. In the aftermath, a strange new plague breaks out, released from a secret laboratory, but also on the prowl is a monstrously malformed human being with a taste for blood. A handful of survivors attempting to free themselves from imprisonment in the wreckage discover that they are being stalked. Much more effective than its two predecessors, *Aftershock* presents one crisis after another in a plot filled with shocks and surprises. *Dis-*

embodied is the most interesting of Walker's horror novels. A psychic investigator is killed and his body destroyed by an insane killer, but he survives on the astral plane. With the help of his still living assistant, he sets out to find the supernatural entity that controlled his killer.

As Geoffrey Caine (not to be confused with the British writer Jeffrey Caine, born 1944, who also has written a small amount of horror fiction), Walker wrote three far more conventional horror novels featuring Abraham Stroud, a psychic detective. In *Curse of the Vampire* Stroud suspects foul play when the children of a small town begin to disappear. He tracks the menace to the local hospital, where a handful of vampires have taken control of that institution in order to develop ways to conceal their existence, even walk in the daylight. Stroud foils their plans and survives to encounter another classic monster in *Wake of the Werewolf*. In this case, a brutal, possibly insane killer is leaving half-devoured bodies in his wake as he travels across country. Stroud sets out to track him down, whether the killer is just insane or an actual lycanthrope, and nearly underestimates the danger by not realizing that there may be more than one of the killers. Nevertheless, he's back in the third and final volume, *Legion of the Dead*, this time investigating a mysterious burial vault discovered in New York City. A creature escapes from the vault, and begins spreading a deadly disease which not only kills those who contract it, but causes them to rise from their graves as zombies, enslaved by the creature. Stroud triumphs again, ending what might have been an interesting series had it continued.

Although most of Walker's other fiction appears to be detective stories or thrillers, there are elements of horror scattered throughout most of them. As Stephen Robertson, he wrote the "Decoy" series about Ryne Lanark, an actor turned police officer. Although the format is a blend of tough detective and police-procedural, there are distinct horror motifs as well. In the opening volume, *Decoy*, the villain is a serial killer who drains his victims' blood vampire-style. There's another serial killer in *Blood Ties* who mutilates the bodies of his victims, and yet another in *The Handyman*, best in the series, a psychotic who amputates and collects the hands of those he slays.

Under his own name, Walker wrote a similar series about coroner Dr. Dean Grant. As with the Decoy series, the novels are contemporary suspense, but filled with scenes more commonly found in horror fiction. A serial killer makes a practice of burning his victims to death in *Burning Obsession*, another specializes in asphyxiation in *Dying Breath*, and the villain of *Razor's Edge* collects the scalps of his prey. The Dr. Jessica Coran series is very similar in tone. There's another vampire killer in *Killer Instinct*, a nasty contemporary variation of Jack the Ripper in *Fatal Instinct*, and yet more serial killers in *Primal Instinct*, *Pure Instinct* and *Darkest Instinct*. Walker started yet another series featuring a police psychiatrist with *Cutting Edge*, which features a killer inspired by computer games to stalk and claim other players in the real world.

Because of the way in which Walker's books have been marketed, he is not generally seen as a significant writer in the horror field. But the bulk of his fiction thematically resembles that of Thomas Harris and Michael Slade, whose work is claimed by horror and mystery enthusiasts alike. If the dark content of his detective novels was better known, it is likely that Walker would be able to lure new readers from the horror genre as well as maintaining the audience he has already developed.

—Don D'Ammassa

WALPOLE, Horace

Pseudonym: William Marshal. **Nationality:** British. **Born:** London, 24 September 1717; son of the prime minister, Sir Robert Walpole. **Education:** Eton College; King's College, Cambridge. **Career:** Member of Parliament, 1741-67; writer and man of letters, 1757-97; proprietor, from 1757, of the Strawberry Hill press, one of the first notable private presses; became fourth Earl of Orford, 1791. **Died:** 2 March 1797.

HORROR, GHOST AND GOTHIC PUBLICATIONS

Novels

The Castle of Otranto (as William Marshal, translating from the Italian of Onuphrio Muralto). London, Thomas Lownds, 1764.
The Mysterious Mother. Twickenham, Strawberry Hill, 1768.

Short Stories

An Account of the Giants Lately Discovered. Twickenham, Strawberry Hill, 1766.
Hieroglyphic Tales. Twickenham, Strawberry Hill, 1785; expanded edition, edited by Kenneth W. Gross, 1982.

OTHER PUBLICATIONS

Other

The Lessons for the Day. London, 1742.
The Beauties: An Epistle to Mr. Eckhardt, the Painter. London, 1746.
Epilogue to Tamerlane, on the Suppression of the Rebellion. London, 1746.
Aedes Walpolianae; or, A Description of the Collection of Pictures at Houghton Hall in Norfolk, the Seat of the Right Honourable Sir Robert Walpole, Earl of Orford. London, 1747.
The Original Speech of Sir W(illia)m St(anho)pe. London, 1748.
The Speech of Richard White-Liver Esq; in Behalf of Himself and His Brethren. London, 1748.
A Letter from Xo Ho, a Chinese Philosopher at London, to His Friend Lien Chi at Peking. London, Graham, 1757.
A Catalogue of Royal and Noble Authors of England. Twickenham, Strawberry Hill, 1758; expanded as *A Catalogue of the Royal and Noble Authors of England, Scotland and Ireland*, edited by Thomas Park, J. Scott, 5 vols., 1806.
Fugitive Pieces in Verse and Prose. Twickenham, Strawberry Hill, 1758.
A Dialogue Between Two Great Ladies. London, Cooper, 1760.
Catalogue of Pictures and Drawings in the Holbein-Chamber, at Strawberry-Hill. Twickenham, Strawberry Hill, 1760.
Catalogues of the Pictures of the Duke of Devonshire, General Guise, and the Late Sir Paul Methuen. Twickenham, Strawberry Hill, 1760.
Anecdotes of Painting in England. Twickenham, Strawberry Hill, 4 vols., 1762-1771.
The Opposition to the Late Minister Vindicated. Twickenham, Strawberry Hill, 1763.

Catalogue of Engravers in England. Twickenham, Strawberry Hill, 1763.

A Counter-Address to the Public, on the Late Dismission of a General Officer. Twickenham, Strawberry Hill, 1764.

The Magpie and Her Brood. Twickenham, Strawberry Hill, 1764.

Historic Doubts on the Life and Reign of King Richard the Third. Twickenham, Strawberry Hill, 1768.

Reply to Dean Milles. Twickenham, Strawberry Hill, 1770.

A Description of the Villa of Horace Walpole at Strawberry-Hill, near Twickenham. Twickenham, Strawberry Hill, 1774; revised edition, 1784.

Essay on Modern Gardening. Twickenham, Strawberry Hill, 1785.

Postscript to the Royal and Noble Authors. Twickenham, Strawberry Hill, 1786.

Works, edited by Mary Berry. London, Robinson, 8 vols., 1798-1822.

Letters to George Montague, edited by John Martin. London, Robinson, 1818.

Letters to the Rev. William Cole, and Others, edited by John Martin. London, Robinson, 1818.

Memoires of the Last Ten Years of the Reign of George the Second, edited by Lord Holland. London, John Murray, 2 vols., 1822.

Letters to the Earl of Hertford, edited by John Wilson Croker. London, Knight, 1825.

Letters to Sir Horace Mann, edited by Lord Dover. New York, Dearborn, 3 vols., 1833.

Letters, edited by John Wright. London, Bentley, 6 vols., 1840.

Memoires of the Reign of King George the Third, edited by Sir Denis le Marchant. London, Bentley, and Philadelphia, Lea and Blanchard, 1845.

Letters Addressed to the Countess of Ossory, edited by R. Vernon Smith. London, Bentley, 2 vols., 1848.

Letters, edited by Peter Cunningham. London, Bentley, 9 vols., 1857-59.

Journal of the Reign of King George the Third from the Year 1771 to 1783, edited by John Doran. London, Bentley, 2 vols., 1859.

Some Unpublished Letters, edited by Sir Spencer Walpole. London and New York, Longmans Green, 1902.

Letters, edited by Paget Toynbee. Oxford, Clarendon Press, 16 vols., 1903-05.

Supplement to the Letters, edited by Paget Toynbee. Oxford, Clarendon Press, 3 vols., 1918-25.

A Selection of the Letters, edited by W. S. Lewis, New York, Harper, 2 vols., 1926.

Miscellaneous Antiquities, edited by W. S. Lewis. Farmington, Connecticut, privately printed, 16 vols., 1927.

Correspondence, edited by W. S. Lewis and others. New Haven, Yale University Press, 48 vols., 1937-81.

Memoirs and Portraits 1786-1795, edited by Matthew Hodgart. London, Batsford, 1963.

Selected Letters, edited by W. S. Lewis. New Haven, Yale University Press, 1973.

Horace Walpole's Miscellany, edited by Lars E. Troide. New Haven, Connecticut, Yale University Press, 1978.

Editor, *Memoires du Comte de Grammont*, by Anthony Hamilton, Twickenham, Strawberry Hill, 1772.

*

Bibliography: *A Bibliography of Horace Walpole* by Allen T. Hazen, New Haven, Yale University Press, 1948.

Critical Study: *Horace Walpole* by W. S. Lewis, New York, Pantheon Books, 1961.

*   *   *

Horace Walpole's reputation is divided between two great legacies. On the one hand he was a great epistolarian. He knew all the magnates and luminaries of his day and his vast correspondence is a mine of information. On the other hand he was a devotee of the Renaissance and of medievalism and it was through this that he inspired a revival in gothic architecture and instigated the gothic novel. His novel *The Castle of Otranto* began a whole new movement in literature and captured and redirected the public taste. While it would be excessive to state that Walpole's novel was the sole perpetrator of this revolution, since there had been a rekindling of interest in historical fiction after decades of fascination for the oriental tale, Walpole's fiction rapidly became the figurehead of the movement and has remained so to this day.

The novel contains all the elements that later came to signify, and almost to parody, gothic fiction. It tells of the fate of Manfred, grandson of the usurper of Otranto, whose own son, Conrad, is killed on his wedding day by the mysterious fall of a giant helmet, which seems to belong to the statue of Alfonso, the former lord of Otranto. Manfred seeks to continue his line by marrying his son's betrothed, Isabella, but he is thwarted by all manner of supernatural manifestations. At the climax, part of the castle falls about him as the mighty ghost of Alfonso rises into the heavens declaring that Theodore, whom Manfred has imprisoned, is the true heir of Otranto. As in all gothic novels, the core is retribution, either by supernatural or mock-supernatural means.

It had not been Walpole's intention to start a new vogue in literature. He had simply sought to share his interest in the Middle Ages. He was already a respected scholar and man-of-letters, though some had started to regard him as something of an eccentric since he had built his mock gothic castle at Strawberry Hill in Twickenham, which he began in 1750. Walpole had a sensitive disposition and did not like to be mocked. At the same time he also had a sense of humour and delighted in hoaxes. When he first issued *Otranto* to his readers he treated it as a translation by one William Marshal of a medieval Italian manuscript by "Onuphrio Muralto." However its success allowed Walpole to admit his authorship in the second edition issued four months later, in April 1765. The Castle of Otranto itself was modelled wholly on Walpole's Strawberry Hill, and much of the inspiration for the story came from a dream and from his own bouts of melancholy while ensconced alone in his vast edifice. The novel can, in fact, be interpreted on two levels: the immediate one of the historical events, but at a psychological level of a man trapped by his own guilt and the sins of his fathers. It is the precursor of the House-of-Usher theme that Edgar Allan Poe would so effectively develop.

Although Walpole did not write a second fully gothic novel, he came close with *The Mysterious Mother*, which focused on the aspect of sin and the effects upon a family of their discovery of the curse of incest. Meanwhile, Walpole became quite possessive about his original gothic novel, *Otranto*, and disliked Clara Reeve's attempt at a rationalized imitation, *The Champion of Virtue*, in 1777.

Walpole produced a few further works of imaginative fiction, though none of them is gothic. A short selection of fairy tales, showing the influences of other cultures, noticeably the Arabian or Oriental fantasy, was issued as *Hieroglyphic Tales*. His energies, however, were directed mostly to his correspondence and to cataloguing works of art. *The Castle of Otranto*, therefore, may be regarded as a solitary excursion into the extravagant, but one directed by a fervid and passionate mind. Its uniqueness at the time contributed to its popularity and it was some years before the romantic movement caught up with Walpole's experiment, and the real gothic romance was ushered in by Ann Radcliffe's *The Mysteries of Udolpho*.

—Mike Ashley

WALPOLE, (Sir) Hugh (Seymour)

Nationality: British. **Born:** Auckland, New Zealand, 13 March 1884, of English parents. **Education:** King's School, Canterbury, Kent, and Durham School; Emmanuel College, Cambridge, 1903-06, B.A. (honours) in history 1906. **Military Service:** Russian Red Cross in Galicia, 1914-16; director, Anglo-Russian Propaganda Bureau, Petrograd, 1916-17. **Career:** Lay minister, Mersey Mission to Seamen, 1906; travelled in France and Germany, 1907; assistant master, Epsom College, Surrey, 1908; full-time writer, in London, from 1909; became a friend of Henry James and Arnold Bennett; gave lecture tours in the United States, from 1919; Rede lecturer, Cambridge University, 1925; first chair of the Selection Committee, Book Society, London, from 1929; first chair, Society of Bookmen (now National Book League). **Awards:** James Tait Black memorial prize, 1919, 1920. Fellow, Royal Society of Literature. CBE (Commander, Order of the British Empire), 1918. Knighted, 1937. **Died:** 1 June 1941.

HORROR, GHOST AND GOTHIC PUBLICATIONS

Novels

The Killer and the Slain: A Strange Story. London, Macmillan, and New York, Doubleday, 1942.

Short Stories

The Silver Thorn. London, Macmillan, and New York, Doubleday, 1928.
All Souls' Night. London, Macmillan, and New York, Doubleday, 1933.

Other

Editor, *A Second Century of Creepy Stories*. London, Hutchinson, 1937.

OTHER PUBLICATIONS

Novels

The Wooden Horse. London, Smith Elder, 1909; New York, Doran, 1915.
Maradick at Forty: A Transition. London, Smith Elder, 1910; New York, Duffield, 1911.

Mr. Perrin and Mr. Traill: A Tragi-Comedy. London, Mills and Boon, 1911; as *The Gods and Mr. Perrin*, New York, Century, 1911.
The Prelude to Adventure. London, Mills and Boon, and New York, Century, 1912.
Fortitude, Being the True and Faithful Account of the Education of an Explorer. London, Secker, and New York, Doran, 1913.
The Duchess of Wrexe, Her Decline and Death: A Romantic Commentary. London, Secker, and New York, Doran, 1914.
The Dark Forest. London, Secker, and New York, Doran, 1916.
The Green Mirror: A Quiet Story. New York, Doran, 1917; London, Macmillan, 1918.
Jeremy. London, Cassell, and New York, Doran, 1919.
The Secret City. London, Macmillan, and New York, Doran, 1919.
The Captives. London, Macmillan, and New York, Doran, 1920.
The Young Enchanted: A Romantic Story. London, Macmillan, and New York, Doran, 1921.
The Cathedral. London, Macmillan, and New York, Doran, 1922.
Jeremy and Hamlet. London, Cassell, and New York, Doran, 1923.
The Old Ladies. London, Macmillan, and New York, Doran, 1924.
Portrait of a Man with Red Hair: A Romantic Macabre. London, Macmillan, and New York, Doran, 1925.
Harmer John: An Unworldly Story. London, Macmillan, and New York, Doran, 1926.
Jeremy at Crale. London, Cassell, and New York, Doran, 1927.
Wintersmoon. London, Macmillan, and New York, Doubleday, 1928.
Farthing Hall, with J. B. Priestley. London, Macmillan, and New York, Doubleday, 1929.
Hans Frost. London, Macmillan, and New York, Doubleday, 1929.
Rogue Herries. London, Macmillan, and New York, Doubleday, 1930.
Above the Dark Circus. London, Macmillan, 1931; as *Above the Dark Tumult*, New York, Doubleday, 1931.
Judith Paris. London, Macmillan, and New York, Doubleday, 1931.
The Fortress. London, Macmillan, and New York, Doubleday, 1932.
Vanessa. London, Macmillan, and New York, Doubleday, 1933.
Captain Nicholas. London, Macmillan, and New York, Doubleday, 1934.
The Inquisitor. London, Macmillan, and New York, Doubleday, 1935.
A Prayer for My Son. London, Macmillan, and New York, Doubleday, 1936.
John Cornelius. London, Macmillan, and New York, Doubleday, 1937.
The Joyful Delaneys. London, Macmillan, and New York, Doubleday, 1938.
The Sea Tower: A Love Story. London, Macmillan, and New York, Doubleday, 1939.
The Bright Pavilions. London, Macmillan, and New York, Doubleday, 1940.
The Blind Man's House. London, Macmillan, and New York, Doubleday, 1941.
Katherine Christian (unfinished). New York, Doubleday, 1943; London, Macmillan, 1944.

Short Stories

The Golden Scarecrow. London, Cassell, and New York, Doran, 1915.

The Thirteen Travellers. London, Hutchinson, and New York, Doran, 1921.
Cathedral Carol Service. London, Faber, 1934.
Head in Green Bronze and Other Stories. London, Macmillan, and New York, Doubleday, 1938.
Mr. Huffam and Other Stories. London, Macmillan, 1948.

Plays

Robin's Father, with Rudolf Besier (produced Liverpool, 1918).
The Cathedral, adaptation of his own novel (produced London, 1932). London, Macmillan, 1937.
The Young Huntress (produced London, 1933).
The Haxtons (produced Liverpool, 1939). London, Deane, and Boston, Baker, 1939.

Screenplays: *David Copperfield*, with Howard Estabrook, 1934; *Vanessa: Her Love Story*, 1935; *Little Lord Fauntleroy*, 1936.

Radio Serial: *Behind the Screen*, with others, 1930.

Other

Joseph Conrad. London, Nisbet, and New York, Holt, 1916; revised edition, Nisbet, 1924.
The Art of James Branch Cabell. New York, McBride, 1920.
A Hugh Walpole Anthology. London, Dent, and New York, Dutton, 1921.
The Crystal Box. Privately printed, 1924.
The English Novel: Some Notes on Its Evolution (lecture). Cambridge, University Press, 1925.
Reading: An Essay. London, Jarrolds, and New York, Harper, 1926.
A Stranger (for children), with *Red Pepper*, by Thomas Quayle. Oxford, Blackwell, 1926.
Anthony Trollope. London and New York, Macmillan, 1928.
My Religious Experience. London, Benn, 1928.
The Apple Trees: Four Reminiscences. Waltham St. Lawrence, Berkshire, Golden Cockerell Press, 1932.
A Letter to a Modern Novelist. London, Hogarth Press, 1932.
Extracts from a Diary. Privately printed, 1934.
Works (Cumberland Edition). London, Macmillan, 30 vols, 1934-40.
Claude Houghton: Appreciations, with Clemence Dane. London, Heinemann, 1935.
Roman Fountain (travel). London, Macmillan, and New York, Doubleday, 1940.
A Note . . . on the Origins of the Herries Chronicle. New York, Doubleday, 1940.
The Freedom of Books. London, National Book Council, 1940.
Open Letter of an Optimist. London, Macmillan, 1941.
Women Are Motherly. London, Todd, 1943.

Editor, *The Waverley Pageant: The Best Passages from the Novels of Sir Walter Scott.* London, Eyre and Spottiswoode, 1932.
Editor, *Essays and Studies 18.* London, English Association, 1933.
Editor, with Wilfred Partington, *Famous Stories of Five Centuries.* New York, Farrar and Rinehart, 1934.
Editor, with others, *The Nonesuch Dickens.* London, Nonesuch Press, 23 vols, 1937-38.

*

Film Adaptations: *Vanessa: Her Love Story*, 1935; *Mr. Perrin and Mr. Traill*, 1948.

Manuscript Collections: Fitz Park Museum, Keswick, Cumberland; King's School, Canterbury, Kent; British Library, London; Berg Collection, New York Public Library; Library of Congress, Washington, D.C.

Critical Studies: *Hugh Walpole: A Study* by Marguerite Steen, London, Nicholson and Watson, and New York, Doubleday, 1933; *Hugh Walpole: A Biography* by Rupert Hart-Davis, London and New York, Macmillan, 1952; *Hugh Walpole* by Elizabeth Steel, New York, Twayne, 1972.

*   *   *

Hugh Walpole's literary work seems to be almost entirely uninfluenced by the work of his august ancestor Horace, whose lurid account of *The Castle of Otranto* launched the Gothic novel into late-18th-century fashionability. Hugh Walpole was an unashamedly commercial writer and his horror fiction is in a distinctly modern vein, shunning the exaggerated aristocratic sensibility and the blatant kinds of supernatural apparatus employed by his ancestor.

There is an element of horror in the Buchanesque thriller *Portrait of a Man with Red Hair*, which was undoubtedly intended as a mere pot-boiler—Walpole characterized it as an adventure in "romantic macabre"—but caught the imagination of the contemporary public. The red-haired villain is a deceptive but monstrous sadist who is only prevented from perpetrating all manner of horrors upon the heroine by the pluck and clever brinkmanship of the hero. The author's later exercises in the same sub-genre, of which the best is *Above the Dark Circus*, failed to recapture the effect of *Portrait of a Man with Red Hair* but were reprinted along with it in the inaptly-named *Four Fantastic Tales*. Meanwhile, Walpole became a regular contributor to the series of anthologies compiled by Cynthia Asquith begun with *The Ghost Book* (1926) and became increasingly adventurous in the writing of brief "shockers." He was eventually invited to follow Asquith's example; he is credited as the editor of *A Second Century of Creepy Stories* and may also have compiled the first in the series, which foregrounded his four contributions but carried no editorial credit. Even if he was only responsible for the second selection he proved therein that he was at least as competent an anthologist as the compilers of the many rival volumes that appeared in the period between the wars.

There are only a few stories with any horrific content in *The Silver Thorn*, mostly in the same vein of exaggerated but non-supernatural melodrama as *Portrait of a Man with Red Hair*. Although Walpole's *The Ghost Book* story of murder supernaturally avenged, "Mrs. Lunt," is omitted, the very similar "The Tarn" (from *The Black Cap*, 1927) is included, along with the more interesting delusional fantasy "The Tiger." *All Souls' Night* is, however, entirely given over to weird tales. "Mrs. Lunt" is reprinted here, alongside other accounts of far more subtle hauntings, but the most oft-reprinted—and most frequently dramatized—item in the book is "The Silver Mask," in which an impulsive act of charity opens the door to the inexorable and ruthless parasitization of a well-to-do woman by a family of deceptively sinister ne'er-do-wells, who reduce her by degrees from a state of contented independence to one of utter helplessness. Everett Bleiler has characterized the story as an archetypal account of "social vampirism."

It is typical of Walpole's outlook and narrative method that evil is almost always the prerogative of living men—whose victims are usually women—while supernatural intervention is usually revealing or benevolent. In "The Staircase" an impersonally haunted house extends its protection to a potential victim, but the visionary moments in "Tarnhelm, or the Death of my Uncle Robert" and "A Seashore Macabre: A Moment's Experience" merely serve to make evil manifest. When female figures of evil are employed, as they are in "The Oldest Tallant" and "The Snow," they tend to be markedly less powerful than their male counterparts; in the latter story it is a revenant first wife who comes to save her ex-husband from the stifling grip of her successor. The later collection *Head in Green Bronze and Other Stories* includes two light fantasies—the title story and "The Conjurer"—and two horror stories; "The Fear of Death" is a meditative *conte cruel* and "Field with Five Trees" an effective delusional fantasy.

The Killer and the Slain was Walpole's only supernatural novel. It is much more subtle than *Portrait of a Man with Red Hair* and far more effective, although it never attained the same popularity as the earlier novel. The ineffectual and repressed narrator is continually mocked by the subtly insulting bonhomie of an uninhibited sensualist and becomes terrified that the false friend intends to seduce his wife. In order to remove the imagined threat he murders his tormentor, but then begins gradually to take on the psychological and physical characteristics of the dead man, to the extent that he finds a victim to tease and torment exactly as he was teased and tormented. The process of infection—metaphorically represented as the transference of a sadistic "evil spirit"—is eventually completed, securing a truly horrible fate which is not without an element of ironic justice. The propensity to make the life of others a misery seems always to have been Walpole's "ultimate horror"; all his best stories bring such propensities into sharp focus but *The Killer and the Slain* is the only one which examines its operation most minutely, from both points of view. Although it would be overstating its merits to describe the novel as a classic it is certainly a work which deserves more attention than it has previously received.

Hugh Walpole achieved his greatest critical and commercial successes in other genres, and as a thoroughgoing professional he naturally chose to concentrate his efforts in the areas he found most rewarding. Like many a writer in that position he indulged his interest in horror and the supernatural mainly by writing short stories, most of which qualify as amusements. He was, however, capable of producing a powerful paranoid intensity even in short narratives and his best works are outstanding contributions to the British tradition of horror fiction.

—Brian Stableford

WALTER, Elizabeth (Margaret)

Nationality: British. **Born:** London, 1930s. **Career:** Publishers' editor, 1961-93.

HORROR, GHOST AND GOTHIC PUBLICATIONS

Short Stories

Snowfall and Other Chilling Events. London, Harvill Press, 1965; New York, Stein and Day, 1966.
The Sin Eater and Other Scientific Impossibilities. London, Harvill Press, 1967; New York, Stein and Day, 1968.

Davy Jones's Tale and Other Supernatural Stories. London, Harvill Press, 1971.
Come and Get Me and Other Uncanny Invitations. London, Harvill Press, 1973.
Dead Woman and Other Haunting Experiences. London, Harvill Press, and New York, St. Martin's Press, 1975.
In the Mist and Other Uncanny Encounters. Sauk City, Arkham House, 1979.

OTHER PUBLICATIONS

Novels

The More Deceived. London, Jonathan Cape, 1960.
The Nearest and Dearest. London, Harvill Press, 1963.
A Season of Goodwill. London, Harvill Press, 1986; New York, Scribner, 1987.
Homeward Bound. London, Headline, 1990; New York, St. Martin's Press, 1990.

Other

A Christmas Scrapbook. London, Collins, 1979
Season's Greetings. London, Collins, 1980
A Wedding Bouquet. London, Collins, 1981.

Translator, *A Scent of Lilies* by Claire Gallois. London, Collins, 1971; New York, Stein and Day, 1971.
Translator, *Lord of the River* by Bernard Clavel. London, Collins, 1973; Boston, Little, Brown, 1974.
Translator, *A Matter of Feeling* by Janine Boissard. London, Hodder and Stoughton, 1979; Boston, Little, Brown, 1980.

*

Elizabeth Walter comments:

I grew up in Herefordshire, still the most rural of English counties and one from which my family have come for over two centuries. Much of my childhood was spent during the wartime blackout. These things have combined to give me a feeling for locale, an abiding interest in the weather (I cannot bear to be anywhere where I cannot see the sky) and an interest also in the superstitions and stories with which I grew up. Forty years in London have done nothing to diminish any of this.

My own three favourites among my stories are "The Street of the Jews," "Davy Jones's Tale" and "The Drum," but the three most technically innovative have always seemed to me to be "Dearest Clarissa," "Exorcism" and "Dual Control," the last being my most anthologized story.

I am currently engaged in compiling an anthology of supernatural verse.

* * *

Although respected as a writer and editor, and having received awards for her translations, Elizabeth Walter keeps herself to herself and, as a consequence, is not automatically listed in the front rank of British ghost-story writers. She has not produced a book of new stories in over 20 years. Previous to that, between 1966 and 1975, she produced five books, with a total of 31 stories, most of novelette length. Three of these have been adapted for television. All five collections received much critical acclaim, and almost half of the stories have been reprinted in anthologies of note. And yet Elizabeth Walter still does not have the reputation she deserves within the ghost-story field.

On the surface her stories seem traditional: there is a fair share of haunted houses, mist-covered moors and ancient curses. But that is where it ends. Although one reviewer stated that she indulged in "old-fashioned hauntings" that is not true. Walter brings a modern treatment to all her stories. Even where a story may seem to start traditionally, as in the title piece of her first collection, "Snowfall," where the protagonist is caught in the snow and must seek refuge in an isolated house, matters soon take a different course. Bellamy, the victim of that story, does encounter Rees, the inhabitant of that house, though he appears as hale and hearty as the next man. When Rees is suddenly killed in an accident the locals don't believe Bellamy, because Rees was away in the West Indies, but Bellamy's insistence causes the police to suspect Bellamy of the crime himself. The lack of a body, however, impedes investigations, but as the story unravels Bellamy discovers that Rees had been a ghost, or at least an astral projection of the real Rees, who was fleeing vengeance from the natives in the Caribbean.

Walter makes especially effective use of the elements in her stories. Snow, wind and rain are as haunting as the ghosts themselves. In "The New House" a couple find that their house is bedevilled by the spirit of a young girl who had been hanged on the site when it used to be Gibbet Hill in the last century. The story comes to a climax in a terrific storm when the wind, rain and maniacal laughter of the ghost combine to possess the house and its youngest inhabitant. Yet the story is not as gothic as that description might suggest. Maniacal laughter is also the first intimation of a ghost in "Come and Get Me," one of Elizabeth Walter's best stories, which is part-supernatural, part-detective. The ghost is that of a young soldier who had deserted during the war. This so shamed his father that the son was locked up in a room and never released, though the locals were led to believe he had drowned himself in the lake. It is only when the army arrives at the old house, now deserted and being used for manouevres, that the spirit is reawakened with dire consequences. One of the most effective elements in the story is Walter's use of a parrot which is able to talk in the voices of those long-dead and which acts as a catalyst to invoke old memories.

Elizabeth Walter makes considerable use of lonely and remote places, where nature imposes its own rules, in order to create the atmosphere for her hauntings. Where nature has already staked its claim, the supernatural cannot be far behind. Thus the rugged coastlines of Cornwall and Wales, lashed by the sea and winds and already hostile, became the settings for reawakened horrors in "The Concrete Captain" and "Davy Jones's Tale." The mist-enshrouded Yorkshire moors are the setting for a ghostly encounter with former RAF bombers in "In the Mist." A lonely island with a deserted house off the coast of Brittany is the setting for a very powerful story of a malicious haunting, "The Island of Regrets." The remote inaccessibility of the Harz Mountains provides background for witchcraft and black magic in "The Hare." It is evident that Walter relies heavily on the power of the location to build the atmosphere for her tales, a process which can be seen in the story where the very title is proof enough, "The Spirit of the Place." Set in Italy, it is the story of a fresco and of an encounter with a young boy whose image is later seen in the fresco. A re-

viewer of *Come and Get Me*, the book in which "The Spirit of the Place" appeared, referred to Elizabeth Walter as "an M. R. James-style believer," and he probably had that story in mind. Generally her stories are not like those by James. They are certainly not antiquarian, and her ghosts are seldom corporeal, but they are often vengeful.

If Walter's work must be likened to any classic author, her sense of place gives her an affinity with Algernon Blackwood, but her characterization and skewed perspective of hauntings is closer to the approach of Walter de la Mare. It is only when Elizabeth Walter moves from this formula to create something simple that her ghost stories are less successful, as in "The Travelling Companion," where a young lady, mourning the loss of her lover in a car accident, only discovers in the story's climax that it is she who is dead. Walter gives this old idea as good a treatment as it can get, but it is still suffers from the hoariness of the concept.

A representative sample of her best fiction was published in the United States as *In the Mist*, but a more complete omnibus of her work, together with unpublished material that she has to hand, is long overdue.

—Mike Ashley

WANDREI, Donald

Nationality: American. **Born:** 1908. **Family:** Brother of artist and writer Howard Wandrei. **Military Service:** Served in U.S. Army from 1942. **Career:** Contributor to poetry journals, pulp magazines and occasionally to *Esquire*, from the mid-1920s; cofounder, Arkham House publishing company, 1939. **Awards:** World Fantasy Life Achievement award, 1984 (declined). **Died:** 1987.

HORROR, GHOST AND GOTHIC PUBLICATIONS

Novels

The Web of Easter Island. Sauk City, Wisconsin, Arkham House, 1948; London, Consul, 1961.

Short Stories

The Eye and the Finger. Sauk City, Wisconsin, Arkham House, 1944.
Strange Harvest. Sauk City, Wisconsin, Arkham House, 1965.
Colossus: The Collected Science Fiction of Donald Wandrei. Minneapolis, Fedogan and Bremer, 1989.

Poetry

Ecstasy and Other Poems. N.p., 1928.
Dark Odyssey. N.p., 1931.
Poems for Midnight. Sauk City, Wisconsin, Arkham House, 1964.

Other

Editor, with August Derleth, *The Outsider and Others* by H. P. Lovecraft. Sauk City, Wisconsin, Arkham House, 1939.

Editor, with August Derleth, *Beyond the Wall of Sleep* by H. P. Lovecraft. Sauk City, Wisconsin, Arkham House, 1943.
Editor, with August Derleth, *Marginalia* by H. P. Lovecraft. Sauk City, Wisconsin, Arkham House, 1944.
Editor, with August Derleth, *Selected Letters I: 1911-1924* by H. P. Lovecraft. Sauk City, Wisconsin, Arkham House, 1965.
Editor, with August Derleth, *Selected Letters II: 1925-1929* by H. P. Lovecraft. Sauk City, Wisconsin, Arkham House, 1968.
Editor, with August Derleth, *Selected Letters III: 1929-1931* by H. P. Lovecraft. Sauk City, Wisconsin, Arkham House, 1971.

*   *   *

Donald Wandrei was a moderately prolific contributor to the science-fiction and horror pulps during the 1930s. He was associated with the Lovecraft circle but his early work—much of which was poetry of an imaginative stripe—was far more heavily influenced by Clark Ashton Smith than by Lovecraft himself. He helped August Derleth to establish the specialist publisher Arkham House, for which he wrote his only substantial contribution to the Lovecraftian Cthulhu Mythos, *The Web of Easter Island*.

Wandrei's earliest prose publications were prose poems which appeared in the *Minnesota Quarterly* in 1926. "The Messengers" and "The Pursuers" are brief visionary fantasies attempting to strike that "note of cosmic horror" which—according to Lovecraft—was Clark Ashton Smith's forte. "A Fragment of a Dream" is an extended essay of the same kind, whose unnamed protagonist ploughs a lone furrow through a desolate landscape in futile pursuit of an inaccessible ideal.

Wandrei made his debut in *Weird Tales* the following year with a highly melodramatic fantasy of the far future, "The Red Brain," in which the inhabitants of the last shining star make their final desperate attempt to halt the inexorable advance of the Cosmic Dust. In *The Eye and the Finger* the story is coupled with "On the Threshold of Eternity," a meditative sequel in which the surviving Great Brain witnesses the consequent end of the universe. Although superior to the earlier work in several ways this story presumably proved unsaleable when first written and Wandrei did not begin to publish stories in the pulp magazines on a regular basis until 1930, when he finally consented to develop a much more conventional narrative strategy. This was displayed in such present-set stories as "The Green Flame," a brief tale of a biter supernaturally bit.

Although he was now prepared to produce such standard *Weird Tales* fare as "The Tree-Men of M'Bwa," a routine account of monstrous metamorphosis, Wandrei retained his affection for dramatic escalations of scale. "The Lives of Alfred Kramer" is a romance of reincarnation which reaches back into a remoter past than most stories of that kind, but *Astounding Stories* provided far more scope for such adventures than *Weird Tales* and Wandrei became a prolific contributor to that magazine between 1933 and 1936 (it was he who placed Lovecraft's "The Shadow out of Time" and "At the Mountains of Madness" with *Astounding*). Although such tales as the macrocosmic fantasy "Colossus" allowed Wandrei to give fee rein to his taste for wild adventures of the imagination the element of horror became increasingly peripheral to his work. Wandrei regarded his *Astounding* stories as potboilers—just as Clark Ashton Smith seems to have regarded his contributions to *Wonder Stories*—and only included a handful in *The Eye and the Finger* (which would otherwise have been a very short book). "The Nerveless Man" and "A Scientist Divides" are Frankensteinian

fables; "The Blinding Shadows" describes an invasion of Earth by four-dimensional beings; "Earth-Minus" and "Finality Unlimited" are catastrophe stories concerning unwise experiments with atomic power.

The more orthodox weird tales in *The Eye and the Finger* include "The Lady in Gray," a dream-fantasy employing Freudian symbolism, and "It Will Grow on You," about a tumorous growth with similar symbolic implications. The latter is one of three stories reprinted from the "slick" magazine *Esquire*; two others are from *Argosy*, including an intriguing account of altered perception, "The Witch-Makers." Although Arkham House subsequently issued a second collection of Wandrei's pulp stories, *Strange Harvest*, the material in it was considerably less interesting; "The Chuckler" and "Uneasy Lie the Drowned" are very minor supernatural horror stories, but "The Man Who Never Lived" draws some horrific effect from its account of time-travel beyond the beginning of the universe and "Strange Harvest" is the best of Wandrei's accounts of catastrophes caused by incautious scientific experimentation.

The Web of Easter Island begins as a typical Lovecraftian tale of an archaeologist whose strange discoveries lead him to the heart of an awful mystery. The mystery here concerns dormant "titans" whose re-emergence from their long slumber would bring about the end of mankind. Lovecraft usually closed his tales with the moment of terrible realization but Wandrei was not content with that; his hero goes on to take an active part in combating the alien threat, achieving a highly unlikely success and eventually taking on a quasi-Messianic role which arguably takes the work way beyond he boundaries of the sub-genre of Lovecraftian horror fiction. Although it is not ineffective as pulpish melodrama, *The Web of Easter Island* remains an uncomfortably hybrid work which cannot please Lovecraftian purists although it is unlikely to hold overmuch appeal for anyone else. Wandrei wrote very little after publishing this novel, but he did provide a kind of philosophical summary of his work in the Stapledonian future-historical essay "Requiem for Mankind," published in the Arkham House anthology *Dark Things* (1971).

Wandrei never quite succeeded, in his poetry or his prose, in his attempt to cultivate an ornamented style comparable to the one that was the hallmark of his first idol, Clark Ashton Smith. Nor was his awe in the face of cosmic magnitude ever as sensitively paranoid as that of H. P. Lovecraft. There is a certain casualness about his work that always reduces its effects—including, of course, its horrific effect wherever one is intended. In the introduction to *The Eye and the Finger* he suggested that horror stories seem to their writers "as natural as malted milk at the drugstore, as familiar as a radio program, as vivid as the war headlines"—and that was, perhaps his problem. To him, horror was indeed something natural and familiar—vivid, but essentially tame. His best work does succeed in striking a note of cosmic horror which is only slightly false, but he was always outshone by those of his contemporaries who could bring a little better artistry and far more conviction to their task.

—Brian Stableford

WATSON, Ian

Nationality: British. **Born:** North Shields, Northumberland, 20 April 1943. **Education:** Tynemouth School, 1948-59; Balliol College, Oxford, 1960-65, B.A. (honours) in English 1963, B.Litt. 1965, M.A. 1966. **Family:** Married Judith Jackson in 1962; one daughter. **Career:** Lecturer, University College, Dar es Salaam, Tanzania, 1965-67, and Tokyo University of Education, 1967-70; lecturer, 1970-75, and senior lecturer in Complementary Studies, 1975-76, Birmingham Polytechnic Art and Design Centre; features editor and regular contributor, *Foundation,* London, 1975-90; writer-in-residence, Nene College, Northampton, 1984. Since 1983, European editor, *Science Fiction Writers of America Bulletin.* **Awards:** Prix Apollo (France), 1975; Orbit award, 1976; British Science Fiction Association award, 1978; Southern Arts Association bursary, 1978. **Address:** Daisy Cottage, Moreton Pinkney, near Daventry, Northamptonshire, NN11 6SQ, England.

HORROR, GHOST AND GOTHIC PUBLICATIONS

Novels

The Power. London, Headline, 1987.
Meat. London, Headline, 1988.
The Fire Worm. London, Gollancz, 1988.

Short Stories

Evil Water and Other Stories. London, Gollancz, 1987.
Salvage Rites and Other Stories. London, Gollancz, 1989.
Stalin's Teardrops and Other Stories. London, Gollancz, 1991.
The Coming of Vertumnus and Other Stories. London, Gollancz, 1994.

OTHER PUBLICATIONS

Novels

The Embedding. London, Gollancz, 1973; New York, Scribner, 1975.
The Jonah Kit. London, Gollancz, 1975; New York, Scribner, 1976.
Orgasmachine. Paris, Editions Champ Libre, 1976.
The Martin Inca. London, Gollancz, and New York, Scribner, 1977.
Alien Embassy. London, Gollancz, 1977; New York, Ace, 1978.
Miracle Visitors. London, Gollancz, and New York, Ace, 1978.
God's World. London, Gollancz, 1979; New York, Carroll and Graf, 1990.
The Gardens of Delight. London, Gollancz, 1980; New York, Timescape, 1982.
Under Heaven's Bridge, with Michael Bishop. London, Gollancz, 1981; New York, Ace, 1982.
Deathhunter. London, Gollancz, 1981; New York, St. Martin's Press, 1986.
Chekhov's Journey. London, Gollancz, 1983; New York, Carroll and Graf, 1989.
The Book of the Black Current. Garden City, New York, Doubleday, 1986.
The Book of the River. London, Gollancz, 1984; New York, DAW, 1986.
The Book of the Stars. London, Gollancz, 1984; New York, DAW, 1986.
The Book of Being. London, Gollancz, 1985; New York, DAW, 1986.

Converts. London, Panther, 1984; New York, St. Martin's Press, 1985.
Queenmagic, Kingmagic. London, Gollancz, and New York, St. Martin's Press, 1988.
Whores of Babylon. London, Grafton, 1988.
The Flies of Memory. London, Gollancz, 1990; New York, Carroll and Graf, 1991.
Inquisitor. Brighton, East Sussex, Games Workshop, 1990.
Space Marine. London, Boxtree, 1993.
Lucky's Harvest: The First Book of Mana. London, Gollancz, 1993.
The Fallen Moon: The Second Book of Mana. London, Gollancz, 1994.
Harlequin. London, Boxtree, 1994.
Chaos Child. London, Boxtree, 1995.
Hard Questions. London, Gollancz, 1996.

Short Stories

Japan Tomorrow. Osaka, Bunken, 1975.
The Very Slow Time Machine: Science Fiction Stories. London, Gollancz, and New York, Ace, 1979.
Sunstroke and Other Stories. London, Gollancz, 1982.
The Book of Ian Watson (includes nonfiction). Willimantic, Connecticut, Ziesing, 1985.
Slow Birds and Other Stories. London, Gollancz, 1985.
Nanoware Time, with *The Persistence of Vision,* by John Varley. New York, Tor, 1991.

Other

Japan: A Cat's Eye View (for children). Osaka, Bunken, 1969.

Editor, *Pictures at an Exhibition.* Cardiff, Greystoke Mobray, 1981.
Editor, with Pamela Sargent, *Afterlives: An Anthology of Stories about Life after Death.* New York, Vintage, 1986.
Editor, with Michael Bishop, *Changes: Stories of Metamorphosis: An Anthology of Speculative Fiction about Startling Metamorphoses, Both Psychological and Physical.* New York, Ace, 1983.

*

Manuscript Collection: Science Fiction Foundation, University of Liverpool.

*   *   *

Ian Watson is primarily known as a science-fiction writer but there is a substantial minority of his short stories which aims to excite a horrified response; he has written two novels which are pure horror stories and a third which is a horror/sf hybrid. His science fiction is unusually wide-ranging in its visionary scope and he has a particular propensity for writing unfettered metaphysical extravaganzas which readily take aboard elements more familiar in supernatural fantasy. *Deathhunter* involves a fanciful re-personalization of Death and a highly original vision of the afterlife, which includes many wildly melodramatic flourishes and builds to a blackly ironic climax. *The Gardens of Delight* is highly colourful fantasy of evolution which, although strictly rationalized in a conscientiously science-fictional manner, involves the fleshly incarnation of all the monsters featured in Hieronymous Bosch's famous painting of the Garden of Earthly Delights and a dynamic version of the alchemical symbolism supposedly encoded within it. There are also significant horrific elements in *Converts*, the trilogy begun with *The Book of the River*, and the two-volume novel commenced with *Lucky's Harvest*.

The incorporation of mythological imagery into science fiction, often with horrific effect, was manifest in some of Watson's earliest short fiction, including "Thy Blood Like Milk" (1973) and the subtly disturbing "My Soul Swims in a Goldfish Bowl" (1978). His second collection, *Sunstroke and Other Stories*, demonstrated an increasing interest in science-fictional *contes cruels*; "Nightmares," "Peace," "The Thousand Cuts" and the title story all belong to that category. The introduction to *Slow Birds and Other Stories* argues that fantastic fiction "often has its roots in the fear and madness of the present day" and points out the particular fears embodied in many of the stories—but it was *Evil Water and Other Stories* which included the first of Watson's tales to jettison science-fictional logic altogether and employ the supernatural in a forthright and unashamed manner. "Cold Light" is more ironic than horrific but the title story is a fine tale of effective witchcraft, elaborately dressed with sinister symbolism of an unusual stripe.

"Evil Water" was originally published in the same year as *The Power*, the first of the novels Watson wrote for Headline in the hope of cultivating a secondary career as a horror writer. The title is ambiguous, referring both to the power of the atomic weapons held in the American air base near the English village where the story is set and to the power of the mysterious ancient entity that lies dormant beneath its fields. When nuclear war devastates the world it is the ancient entity which preserves the population of the village from annihilation—but it does so only in order to tease and torment them in all kinds of gruesome ways. The story is calculatedly gross, the nastiest of its inventions being the invasive "toilet-thing" which infects the heroine with a time-reversed pregnancy and must eventually be conceived in necrophiliac perversity.

The same calculated grossness is further extrapolated in *Meat*, which similarly underlines a contemporary political agenda—in this case that of the Animal Liberation Front—with the exploits of an avid supernatural entity. The gruesome activities of the monster in *Meat* serve to heighten sensitivity to the plight of prisoners in various kinds of "animal Auschwitz"; the cleaver-wielding meatman is an ironic reflection of the journalistic cliché which represents serial killers as "butchers." Watson's attempt to politicize schlock-horror seems, however, to have been commercially unsuccessful and his association with Headline proved short-lived. His third horror novel appeared from his long-time publisher Gollancz, apologetically jargonized into science fiction although its monster is derived from the folktale of the Lambton Worm. Written with greater sophistication than the Headline novels, *The Fire Worm* is Watson's most effective horror novel, subtly and cleverly combining the occult lore of ancient alchemy with science-fictional ideas of the alien. The prefatory sequence, separately published as "Jingling Geordie's Hole," offers an understated but profoundly unsettling account of a schoolboy's unnatural "pregnancy" with the monster's offspring.

Watson's continuing interest in supernatural fiction was subsequently confined to his short-story collections, where horror continued to play an increasingly loud second fiddle to science fic-

tion. *Salvage Rites and Other Stories* includes such blackly humorous *contes cruels* as "The Mole Field," "Lost Bodies" and "The Resurrection Man" as well as invoking classical supernatural motifs in "Samathiel's Summons" and "Aid for a Vampire"—although the most effective story in the book is the quietly surreal "The Emir's Clock." The title story of *The Coming of Vertumnus and Other Stories* is a fine novella about the revival of an ancient entity far more elliptical in its effects than those featured in *The Power* and *Meat*, while "The Bible in Blood" is a graphic account of the unexpected consequences of a hideous Nazi experiment. *Stalin's Teardrops* includes the *conte cruel* "In Her Shoes" and the angrily but deftly politicized horror story "The Eye of the Ayatollah."

Watson's great strength as a writer has always been his exceptionally prolific and vivid imagination. The ideas on which his stories are based are uncommonly wild and his development of them unusually flamboyant. His science fiction is driven by a fervent curiosity intent on exploring the hitherto-unrevealed consequences of following various trains of thought to their logical conclusions, and although the general tenor of his work is constructive he is never averse to exploiting the shock value of horrific imagery. In his short fiction he has always been enthusiastic to deploy exotic imagery to its best effect, and even his most orthodox *contes cruels* tend to be exalted by moments of visionary extravagance. Such moments remain stubbornly exultant even when the characters experiencing them obtain news of their certain and painful annihilation. Watson has a talent for phantasmagoria that few of his contemporaries can match, and although he usually directs its produce to other ends it has served the cream of his horror fiction very well.

—Brian Stableford

WEINBERG, Robert (Edward)

Nationality: American. **Born:** Newark, New Jersey, 29 August 1946. **Family:** Married Phyllis Horsky in 1973; one son. **Education:** Stevens Institute of Technology, B.S. 1968; Fairleigh Dickinson University, M.S. 1970; Illinois Institute of Technology. **Career:** Freelance writer, editor, publisher and bookseller; proprietor, Weinberg Books, Inc. **Awards:** World Fantasy award for non-fiction, 1978 and 1989; Horror Writers of America Bram Stoker award for non-fiction, 1989, and special award, 1997. **Address:** c/o Weinberg Books, 1515 Oxford Drive, Oak Forest, IL 60452, USA.

HORROR, GHOST AND GOTHIC PUBLICATIONS

Novels (series: Jack Collins; Kaufman and Lane; Masquerade of the Red Death; Alex Warner)

The Devil's Auction (Alex Warner). Philadelphia, Owlswick Press, 1988.
The Armageddon Box (Alex Warner). Newark, New Jersey, Wildside Press, 1991.
The Black Lodge (Kaufman and Lane). New York, Pocket, 1991.
The Dead Man's Kiss (Kaufman and Lane). New York, Pocket, 1992.

A Logical Magician (Jack Collins). New York, Ace, 1993; as *A Modern Magician*, London, Raven, 1995.

A Calculated Magic (Jack Collins). New York, Ace, 1994; London, Raven, 1995.

Blood War (Masquerade). Clarkston, Georgia, White Wolf, 1995.

Unholy Allies (Masquerade). Clarkston, Georgia, White Wolf, 1995.

The Unbeholden (Masquerade). Clarkston, Georgia, White Wolf, 1996.

The Road to Hell. Clarkston, Georgia, White Wolf, 1997.

Graphic Novel

Vampire Diary: The Embrace, with Mark Rein-Hagen. N.p., 1995.

Other

Editor, *Revelry in Hell: Pulp Classics 3.* Oak Lawn, Illinois, Weinberg, 1974.

Editor, *Dr. Satan: Pulp Classics 6.* Oak Lawn, Illinois, Weinberg, 1974.

Editor, *Far Below, and Other Horrors.* West Linn, Oregon, FAX Collector's Editions, 1974.

Editor, *Devils in the Dark.* Chicago, Weinberg, 1979.

Editor, with Stefan R. Dziemianowicz and Martin H. Greenberg, *Weird Tales: 32 Unearthed Terrors.* New York, Bonanza, 1988.

Editor, *The Eighth Green Man (and Other Strange Folk).* Mercer Island, Washington, Starmont House, 1989.

Editor, with Martin H. Greenberg, *Lovecraft's Legacy.* New York, Tor, 1990.

Editor, with Stefan R. Dziemianowicz and Martin H. Greenberg, *Rivals of Weird Tales: 30 Great Fantasy & Horror Stories from the Weird Fiction Pulps.* New York, Bonanza, 1990.

Editor, with Stefan R. Dziemianowicz and Martin H. Greenberg, *Famous Fantastic Mysteries: 30 Great Tales of Fantasy and Horror from the Classic Pulp Magazines Famous Fantastic Mysteries & Fantastic Novels.* New York, Gramercy, 1991.

Editor, with Stefan R. Dziemianowicz and Martin H. Greenberg, *Weird Vampire Tales.* New York, Gramercy, 1992.

Editor, with Stefan R. Dziemianowicz and Martin H. Greenberg, *A Taste for Blood.* New York, Dorset, 1992.

Editor, with Stefan R. Dziemianowicz and Martin H. Greenberg, *The Mists from Beyond.* New York, Roc, 1993.

Editor, with Stefan R. Dziemianowicz and Martin H. Greenberg, *Nursery Crimes.* New York, Barnes and Noble, 1993.

Editor, with Stefan R. Dziemianowicz and Martin H. Greenberg, *100 Ghastly Little Ghost Stories.* New York, Barnes and Noble, 1993.

Editor, with Stefan R. Dziemianowicz and Martin H. Greenberg, *To Sleep, Perchance to Dream . . . Nightmare.* New York, Barnes and Noble, 1993.

Editor, with Stefan R. Dziemianowicz and Martin H. Greenberg, *100 Creepy Little Creature Stories.* New York, Barnes and Noble, 1994.

Editor, with Stefan R. Dziemianowicz and Martin H. Greenberg, *100 Wild Little Weird Tales.* New York, Barnes and Noble, 1994.

Editor, with Stefan R. Dziemianowicz and Martin H. Greenberg, *Between Time and Terror.* New York, Roc, 1995.

Editor, with Martin H. Greenberg and Jill Morgan. *Great Writers and Kids Write Spooky Stories.* N.p., 1995.

Editor, with Stefan R. Dziemianowicz and Martin H. Greenberg, *100 Vicious Little Vampire Stories.* New York, Barnes and Noble, 1995.

Editor, with Stefan R. Dziemianowicz and Martin H. Greenberg, *100 Wicked Little Witches.* New York, Barnes and Noble, 1995.

Editor, with Martin H. Greenberg, *Miskatonic University.* N.p., 1996.

Editor, with Stefan R. Dziemianowicz and Martin H. Greenberg, *Rivals of Dracula.* N.p., 1996.

Editor, with Stefan R. Dziemianowicz and Martin H. Greenberg, *Virtuous Vampires.* N.p., 1996.

Editor, with Stefan R. Dziemianowicz and Martin H. Greenberg, *100 Astounding Little Alien Stories.* New York, Barnes and Noble, 1996.

Editor, with Stefan R. Dziemianowicz and Martin H. Greenberg, *100 Tiny Terror Tales.* New York, Barnes and Noble, 1996.

Editor, with John Betancourt, *The Best of Weird Tales.* New York, Barnes and Noble, 1997.

Editor, with Stefan R. Dziemianowicz and Martin H. Greenberg, *100 Fiendish Little Frightmares.* New York, Barnes and Noble, 1997.

Editor, with Stefan R. Dziemianowicz and Martin H. Greenberg, *Girls' Night Out: Twenty-Nine Female Vampire Stories.* New York, Barnes and Noble, 1997.

OTHER PUBLICATIONS

Other

Reader's Guide to the Cthulhu Mythos, with Edward P. Berglund. Hillside, New Jersey, Weinberg, 1969; revised edition, Albuquerque, New Mexico, Silver Scarab Press, 1973.

A Tribute to Unknown Worlds, with Joel Frieman. Newark, New Jersey, Frieman, 1969.

The Hero-Pulp Index, with Lohr McKinstry. Hillside, New Jersey, Weinberg, 1970; revised edition, Evergreen, Colorado, Opar Press, 1971.

Lester Dent: The Man Behind Doc Savage. Oak Lawn, Illinois, Weinberg, 1974.

Annotated Guide to Robert E. Howard's Sword & Sorcery. West Linn, Oregon, Starmont House, 1976.

The Weird Tales Story. West Linn, Oregon, FAX Collector's Editions, 1977.

A Biographical Dictionary of Science Fiction and Fantasy Artists. Westport, Connecticut, Greenwood Press, 1988.

The Louis L'Amour Companion. N.p., 1992.

Editor, *WT50: A Tribute to Weird Tales.* Oak Lawn, Illinois, Weinberg, 1974.

*   *   *

Robert Weinberg is a member of the select fraternity of fan-collectors turned professional weird-fiction writers. Owner of one of the largest collections ever assembled of horror, fantasy and science fiction, author of *The Weird Tales Story* and many other reference works, and editor (sometimes anonymously, in his role as publisher) of over one hundred anthologies and collections of popular fiction, he is regarded as one of the world's leading authorities on pulp magazines and fantasy art. His novels and short stories reflect his interests as a collector and scholar. They show a familiarity with the panorama of fantastic fiction produced in the twentieth century, both in their eclectic combinations of well-known motifs and their clever variations on classic themes.

Weinberg's novel-length works are memorable for complex plots that synthesize textbook history, current events and literary references, and for their engaging series characters. *The Devil's Auction* and *The Armageddon Box* feature the husband-and-wife team of Valerie Lancaster, a practising witch, and Alex Warner, a professor of history who has mastered the black arts through his association with Valerie's warlock father. *The Black Lodge* and *The Dead Man's Kiss* are both adventures of Chicago police detectives Moe Kaufman and Calvin Lane, and introduce several characters who appear in Weinberg's shorter fiction, notably psychic detective Sid Taine and voodoo houngan Papa Benjamin and his apprentice Ape Largo. Jack Collins, a graduate student in mathematics, is the hero of his comic fantasies, *A Logical Magician* and *A Calculated Magic*, and a huge recurring cast of human and supernatural beings dominate the events of his "Masquerade of the Red Death" trilogy. Although their adventures differ markedly, each of these novels is set in a fully realized world where occult conspiracies and the eternal struggle between forces of Good and Evil take place secretly behind the everyday.

The plots of both *The Devil's Auction* and *The Armageddon Box* are built around quests for a magic talisman. *The Devil's Auction* concerns an exclusive black-magic auction run by the mysterious Ashmedai, "king of Hebrew demons." Only a half dozen of the most renowned black magicians were invited to it any of the four times it was held since 1895, and although none of the losing bidders ever lived to discuss its details, the talisman up for auction is presumed so powerful that other practitioners of the black arts will kill to obtain an invitation. When Valerie's father is murdered for his, she determines to attend the auction in his place, setting in motion a series of confrontations with a werewolf, a golem, and other supernatural monsters mobilized by her competitors. These horrors keep the story's action moving at breakneck pace, and also build considerable suspense by suggesting a talisman (the true identity of which is not revealed until the novel's final line) with even more extraordinary powers than those that they represent.

In *The Devil's Auction*, Weinberg establishes his trademark narrative pattern of interleaving illuminating discussions of occult arcana (both genuine and imagined) among his characters with action sequences involving supernatural menaces. Because his multiethnic casts of good guys each contributes some bit of information to the stew of occult wisdom simmering in the background—Shintoism, Kabbalism, Gnosticism, biblical scholarship, data on mystical splinter groups, and little known curiosities of history—they are never entirely sure how that knowledge fits together, or what its relationship is to the threats they face, until the climactic final chapters. Weinberg works this formula to perfection in *The Armageddon Box*, which begins with a battle between a scourge of the Nazi death camps named Dietrich Vril and a paramilitary team revealed to be a radical Christian group known as the Circumcellions over a rare book that has fallen into Alex Warner's possession. The book, a copy of Hans Heinz Ewers's *Alraune*, is a clue for readers familiar with its story of a human born of black magic, as is Ewers's known association with the Nazis. But both prove only the beginning of a string of widely dissociated hints and portents that include a legendary race of vampires known as the Very Old Folk, Nazi medical experiments, biblical apocrypha, and the anecdotal history of Attila the Hun's meeting with Pope Leo in the fifth century—all of which Alex, Valerie and their confidantes must put together to understand the true nature of the horror they are fighting.

Their ancient folklore and occasional pulp elements notwithstanding, Weinberg's stories are noticeably modern. Most are set in contemporary Chicago and use aspects of late-twentieth-century life to give inventive twists to classic themes. "The Midnight El" is a deal-with-the-devil story set aboard a commuter train. "Ro Erg" features a doppelganger whose identity is contrived from a misspelled name on a piece of junk mail. "Dial Your Dreams" builds a traditional biter-bit story around the idea of the more unusual services a telephone talk-line might offer clients. *The Black Lodge* and *The Dead Man's Kiss* both incorporate the stuff of the daily headlines into their plots: in the former, a demonic entity wreaks havoc on the Chicago drug trade, which proves to be a major source of funding for a cabal of businessmen who practise black magic; in the latter, a white supremacist schemes to bring his vision of a New World Order into being through an alliance with the resurrected mummy of an Egyptian sorcerer.

Weinberg's most imaginative modern flourishes can be found in *A Logical Magician* and *A Calculated Magic*, a diptych written in the logical-fantasy tradition pioneered by the groundbreaking pulp magazine *Unknown Worlds*. In the world of these novels, creatures of classic fantasy and mythology have adapted to modern times, and thus can only be fought with equally modern variations on the defences and counterspells normally used to manage them. Jack Collins, who has been chosen by the powers of goodness for his prowess in mathematics and his encyclopedic knowledge of fantasy and horror fiction, spends most of his time contriving new ways to kill old monsters: exposing a vampire to an ultraviolet sun lamp, for example, and dispatching the story's worst supernatural heavy with the ordered light of a helium-neon laser beam, "the ultimate icon of order versus chaos."

Weinberg's most ambitious work to date is his "Masquerade of the Red Death Trilogy," comprised of *Blood War*, *Unholy Allies* and *The Unbeholden*. Set in an alternative world ruled by warring vampire clans, the series folds elements of supernatural horror into a thickly layered plot with overtones of both the hard-boiled detective drama and the multi-generation crime saga. It abounds with references to the work of Edgar Allan Poe and a sufficient number of other weird-fiction writers to make it read like a road map for twentieth-century horror and fantasy fiction. It also features imaginative embellishments on standard plot devices, not the least of which is a monster so horrifying that even a vampire civilization fears it. Like all of Weinberg's writing, the series pays tribute to the weird-fiction tradition even as it explores hitherto undiscovered possibilities in the tradition's most sacred icons.

—Stefan Dziemianowicz

WELDON, Fay

Nationality: British. **Born:** Fay Birkinshaw in Alvechurch, Worcestershire, 22 September 1931; grew up in New Zealand. **Education:** Girls' High School, Christchurch; Hampstead Girls' High School, London; University of St. Andrews, Fife, 1949-52, M.A. in economics and psychology 1952. D. Litt, University of Bath, 1988, University of St. Andrews, 1992. **Family:** Married Ron Weldon in 1960; four sons. **Career:** Writer for the Foreign Office and *Daily Mirror*, both London, late 1950s; later worked in advertising. Lives in London. **Awards:** Writers Guild award, for radio play, 1973; Giles Cooper award, for radio play, 1978;

Society of Authors travelling scholarship, 1981; Los Angeles *Times* award, for fiction, 1989. **Agent:** Ed Victor, 6 Bayley St., London WC1B 3HB; Casarotto Company, National House, 62-66 Wardour Street, London W1V 3HP, England.

HORROR, GHOST AND GOTHIC PUBLICATIONS

Novels

The Life and Loves of a She-Devil. London, Hodder and Stoughton, 1983; New York, Pantheon, 1984.
Growing Rich. London, HarperCollins, 1992.

Short Stories

Watching Me, Watching You. London, Hodder and Stoughton, and New York, Summit, 1981.
The Rules of Life (novella). London, Hutchinson, and New York, Harper, 1987.

OTHER PUBLICATIONS

Novels

The Fat Woman's Joke. London, MacGibbon and Kee, 1967; as *And the Wife Ran Away,* New York, McKay, 1968.
Down among the Women. London, Heinemann, 1971; New York, St. Martin's Press, 1972.
Female Friends. London, Heinemann, and New York, St. Martin's Press, 1975.
Remember Me. London, Hodder and Stoughton, and New York, Random House, 1976.
Words of Advice. New York, Random House, 1977; as *Little Sisters,* London, Hodder and Stoughton, 1978.
Praxis. London, Hodder and Stoughton, and New York, Summit, 1978.
Puffball. London, Hodder and Stoughton, and New York, Summit, 1980.
The President's Child. London, Hodder and Stoughton, 1982; New York, Doubleday, 1983.
The Shrapnel Academy. London, Hodder and Stoughton, 1986; New York, Viking, 1987.
The Heart of the Country. London, Hutchinson, 1987; New York, Viking, 1988.
The Hearts and Lives of Men. London, Heinemann, 1987; New York, Viking, 1988.
Leader of the Band. London, Hodder and Stoughton, 1988; New York, Viking, 1989.
The Cloning of Joanna May. London, Collins, 1989; New York, Viking, 1990.
Darcy's Utopia. London, Collins, 1990; New York, Viking, 1991.
Life Force. London, HarperCollins, and New York, Viking, 1992.
Affliction. London, HarperCollins, 1994; as *Trouble,* New York, Viking, 1994.
Splitting. London, HarperCollins, and New York, Grove Atlantic, 1994.
Worst Fears. London, HarperCollins, and New York, Grove Atlantic, 1996.

Short Stories

Polaris and Other Stories. London, Hodder and Stoughton, 1985; New York, Penguin, 1989.
Moon over Minneapolis. London, HarperCollins, 1991.

Plays

Permanence, in *We Who Are about to . . .,* later called *Mixed Doubles* (produced London, 1969). London, Methuen, 1970.
Time Hurries On, in *Scene Scripts,* edited by Michael Marland. London, Longman, 1972.
Words of Advice (produced London, 1974). London, French, 1974.
Friends (produced Richmond, Surrey, 1975).
Moving House (produced Farnham, Surrey, 1976).
Mr. Director (produced Richmond, Surrey, 1978).
Polaris (broadcast 1978). Published in *Best Radio Plays of 1978,* London, Eyre Methuen, 1979.
Action Replay (produced Birmingham, 1978; as *Love among the Women,* produced Vancouver, 1982). London, French, 1980.
I Love My Love (broadcast 1981; produced Richmond, Surrey, 1982). London, French, 1984.
After the Prize (produced New York, 1981; as *Word Worm,* produced Newbury, Berkshire, 1984).
Jane Eyre, adaptation of the novel by Charlotte Brontë (produced Birmingham, 1986).
The Hole in the Top of the World (produced Richmond, Surrey, 1987).
Someone Like You, music by Petula Clark and Dee Shipman (produced London, 1990).

Radio Plays: *Spider,* 1973; *Housebreaker,* 1973; *Mr. Fox and Mr. First,* 1974; *The Doctor's Wife,* 1975; *Polaris,* 1978; *Weekend,* 1979; *All the Bells of Paradise,* 1979; *I Love My Love,* 1981; *The Hole in the Top of the World,* 1993.

Television Plays: *Wife in a Blonde Wig,* 1966; *A Catching Complaint,* 1966; *The Fat Woman's Tale,* 1966; *What about Me,* 1967; *Dr. De Waldon's Therapy,* 1967; *Goodnight Mrs. Dill,* 1967; *The 45th Unmarried Mother,* 1967; *Fall of the Goat,* 1967; *Ruined Houses,* 1968; *Venus Rising,* 1968; *The Three Wives of Felix Hull,* 1968; *Hippy Hippy Who Cares,* 1968; *£13083,* 1968; *The Loophole,* 1969; *Smokescreen,* 1969; *Poor Mother,* 1970; *Office Party,* 1970; *On Trial* (Upstairs, Downstairs, series), 1971; *Old Man's Hat,* 1972; *A Splinter of Ice,* 1972; *Hands,* 1972; *The Lament of an Unmarried Father,* 1972; *A Nice Rest,* 1972; *Comfortable Words,* 1973; *Desirous of Change,* 1973; *In Memoriam,* 1974; *Poor Baby,* 1975; *The Terrible Tale of Timothy Bagshott,* 1975; *Aunt Tatty,* from the story by Elizabeth Bowen, 1975; *Act of Rape,* 1977; *Married Love* (Six Women series), 1977; *Act of Hypocrisy* (Jubilee series), 1977; *Chickabiddy* (Send in the Girls series), 1978; *Pride and Prejudice,* from the novel by Jane Austen, 1980; *Honey Ann,* 1980; *Life for Christine,* 1980; *Watching Me, Watching You* (Leap in the Dark series), 1980; *Little Mrs. Perkins,* from a story by Penelope Mortimer, 1982; *Redundant! or, The Wife's Revenge,* 1983; *Out of the Undertow,* 1984; *Bright Smiles* (Time for Murder series), 1985; *Zoe's Fever* (Ladies in Charge series), 1986; *A Dangerous Kind of Love* (Mountain Men series), 1986; *The Life and Loves of a She-Devil,* 1986; *Heart of the Country,* 1987; *Growing Rich,* 1992.

Other

Simple Steps to Public Life, with Pamela Anderson and Mary Stott. London, Virago Press, 1980.
Letters to Alice: On First Reading Jane Austen. London, Joseph, 1984; New York, Taplinger, 1985.
Rebecca West. London and New York, Viking, 1985.
Wolf the Mechanical Dog (for children). London, Collins, 1988.
Sacred Cows. London, Chatto and Windus, 1989.
Party Puddle (for children). London, Collins, 1989.

Editor, with Elaine Feinstein, *New Stories 4.* London, Hutchinson, 1979.

*

Film Adaptations: *She-Devil*, 1989, from the novel *The Life and Loves of a She-Devil*; *The Cloning of Joanna May* (television serial), 1991.

*   *   *

Fay Weldon's chief stock-in-trade is anti-romantic fiction. Her work subjects the myth of romance to an analysis intimate enough to qualify as vivisection, aiming to reveal that the throbbing heart which is the cardinal symbol of romance is ragged and leaky, its afferent arteries clogged up with cholesterol. It is only natural that such an endeavour, if long enough sustained, should lead to flamboyant satirical exaggeration. It is natural, too, that the satirical exaggeration in question should adopt fantastic devices in order that its scalpels and probes should dig deeper and cut more painfully. (In this kind of literary analysis, if it isn't hurting, it isn't working).

To this end, Weldon's earliest and most sombre short stories, collected in *Watching Me, Watching You,* often take the form of *contes cruels* and sometimes invoke bleak hauntings. In "Angel, All Innocence" (1977) ghostly footsteps in the attic serve as one abandoned woman's warning to another. In "Breakages" (1978) a poltergeist measures out the disintegration of a relationship. The *genius loci* of "Spirit of the House" (1980) is a home-breaker of a nastier kind. As with so many writers whose ghosts perform symbolic functions, however, Weldon's stories are even more horrific when there is no hypothetical entity to deflect the moral debit; the *contes cruels* "Alopecia" (1976), "Man with No Eyes" (1977) and "Geoffrey and the Eskimo Child" (1980) are bleaker than any of her ghost stories.

A writer who begins to map a phenomenon with the aid of stark tragedy has little scope for extrapolative development; if she does not mellow, her only further recourse is black comedy. Weldon did both; her later short fiction is generally much lighter in tone, and its primary instrument is cunning sarcasm. The revenant in the future-set novella *The Rules of Life* comes neither to warn nor to bear witness but to offer cynically subversive advice to those still engaged in the eternal struggle. Weldon's later short stories very rarely dabble in the supernatural, although "A Good, Sound Marriage" (1991) and "Through a Dustbin, Darkly" (1992)—both reprinted in *Wicked Women*—invoke a ghostly grandmother and an insistently chilly shadow in order to impress upon their heroines an awareness of their folly. The *contes cruels* produced in parallel with these stories are defiantly flippant.

Although there is an element of horror in *Puffball* it was not until *The Life and Loves of a She-Devil* that Weldon recruited fantastic devices to a novel. Here the myth of romance is personified by the beautiful novelist Mary Fisher, who steals the husband of the much less-favoured Ruth—whose minutely plotted and meticulously executed revenge concludes with her triumphant metamorphosis into the image of her rival. Like much feminist fantasy the story is a resentful inversion of a traditional tale, which brings an ugly sister to centre stage instead of Cinderella and follows the process of self-mutilation by which she fits herself to the glass slipper which symbolizes victory in the war of the sexes. Although widely hailed as a parable of female empowerment (and twice filmed, as a successful British television serial and as a less-successful Hollywood movie) it is a deeply ambivalent book, which can discover no other moral than "if you can't beat 'em, join 'em."

Growing Rich, which describes the harassment of three adolescent girls by a Mephisphelean devil—who has promised one of them as a prize to the wealthy businessman with whom he has made a Faustian pact—seems to be casting around for a different moral, but cannot in the end discover one. The demon in question is incarnate as the businessman's chauffeur and is thus referred to as the Driver, which makes the novel's presiding proverb "needs must when the devil drives"—and the luckless Carmen cannot in the end avoid his driving. She withstands his temptations easily enough—although her friends Annie and Laura are not nearly so fortunate—but she cannot prevail against his nastier threats. In the end, the fact that she is not required to yield everything demanded by his blackmail cannot conceal the fact that she has no option but to yield. The Driver is, however, a fascinating literary creation: a very apt devil for the modern age, whose acid observations reveal as strong a kinship with le Sage's Asmodeus as with Marlowe's Mephistopheles.

Growing Rich is so exuberantly good-humoured that its comedy is little more than black-edged, and the same is true of the marginal Gothic elements in two of its recent predecessors, the mock-Dickensian melodrama *The Hearts and Lives of Men* and the mock-science-fictional *The Cloning of Joanna May*. It was not until unfortunate events in Weldon's own life jolted her out of her good humour that her work regained its old ferocity in *Affliction*. Whether this will result in the production of more dark fantasy remains to be seen, but it does seem probable that the next Fury to emerge from her imaginary Hell will be a good deal more scornful than the mercurial Driver.

Fay Weldon is the grand-daughter of Edgar Jepson, a close friend of Arthur Machen who flirted briefly with the production of Decadent fantasies and occult mysteries before settling down to write calculatedly lightweight romances and crime novels for the sake of an easy income. Although he kept his sarcasm under a tight rein in his fiction, Jepson gave his natural inclinations much freer range in a magnificently cynical two-volume autobiography which Weldon probably read, if only for curiosity's sake. It is doubtful whether a talent for sarcasm can possibly have any genetic component, but it may run in families nevertheless. Jepson would undoubtedly have loved Fay Weldon's fiction; its penetrating accuracy and defiant subversiveness might well have made him ashamed of his own capitulation with the demands of the contemporary marketplace and its imbecilic myths.

—Brian Stableford

WELLS, H(erbert) G(eorge)

Nationality: British. **Born:** Bromley, Kent, 21 September 1866. **Education:** Mr. Morley's Bromley Academy until age 13: certificate in bookkeeping; apprentice draper, Rodgers and Denyer, Windsor, 1880; pupil-teacher at a school in Wookey, Somerset, 1880; apprentice chemist in Midhurst, Sussex, 1880-81; apprentice draper, Hyde's Southsea Drapery Emporium, Hampshire, 1881-83; student/assistant, Midhurst Grammar School, 1883-84; studied at Normal School (now Imperial College) of Science, London (editor, *Science School Journal*), 1884-87; teacher, Holt Academy, Wrexham, Wales, 1887-88, and at Henley House School, Kilburn, London, 1889; B.Sc. (honours) in zoology 1890, and D.Sc. 1943, University of London. **Family:** Married 1) his cousin Isabel Mary Wells in 1891 (separated 1894; divorced 1895); 2) Amy Catherine Robbins in 1895 (died 1927), two sons; had one daughter by Amber Reeves, and one son by Rebecca West, the writer Anthony West. **Career:** Tutor, University Tutorial College, London, 1890-93; full-time writer from 1893; theatre critic, *Pall Mall Gazette,* London, 1895; member of the Fabian Society, 1903-08; Labour candidate for Parliament, for the University of London, 1922, 1923; lived mainly in France, 1924-33. International president, PEN, 1934-46, D. Lit.: University of London, 1936. Honorary fellow, Imperial College of Science and Technology, London. **Died:** 13 August 1946.

HORROR, GHOST AND GOTHIC PUBLICATIONS

Novels

The Island of Doctor Moreau. London, Heinemann, and New York, Stone and Kimball, 1896.
The Invisible Man: A Grotesque Romance. London, Pearson, and New York, Arnold, 1897.
The War of the Worlds. London, Heinemann, and New York, Harper, 1898.
Mr. Blettsworthy on Rampole Island. London, Benn, and New York, Doubleday, 1928.
The Croquet Player: A Story. London, Chatto and Windus, 1936; New York, Viking Press, 1937.

Short Stories

The Stolen Bacillus and Other Incidents. London, Methuen, 1895.
The Plattner Story and Others. London, Methuen, 1897.

OTHER PUBLICATIONS

Novels

The Time Machine: An Invention. London, Heinemann, and New York, Holt, 1895; as *The Definitive Machine: A Critical Edition of H. G. Wells's Scientific Romance,* edited by Harry M. Geduld, Bloomington, Indiana University Press, 1987.
The Wonderful Visit. London, Dent, and New York, Macmillan, 1895.
The Wheels of Chance. London, Dent, and New York, Macmillan, 1896.
When the Sleeper Wakes. London and New York, Harper, 1899; revised edition, as *The Sleeper Awakes,* London, Nelson, 1910.
Love and Mr. Lewisham: A Story of a Very Young Couple. New York, Stokes, and London, Harper, 1900.
The First Men in the Moon. Indianapolis, Bowen-Merrill, and London, Newnes, 1901.

The Sea Lady: A Tissue of Moonshine. London, Methuen, and New York, Appleton, 1902.
The Food of the Gods, and How It Came to Earth. London, Macmillan, and New York, Scribner, 1904.
A Modern Utopia. London, Chapman and Hall, and New York, Scribner, 1905.
Kipps: A Monograph. New York, Scribner, and London, Macmillan, 1905.
In the Days of the Comet. London, Macmillan, and New York, Century, 1906.
The War in the Air, and Particularly How Mr. Bert Smallways Fared While It Lasted. London, Bell, and New York, Macmillan, 1908.
Tono-Bungay. New York, Duffield, 1908; London, Macmillan, 1909.
Ann Veronica. London, Unwin, and New York, Harper, 1909.
The History of Mr. Polly. London, Nelson, and New York, Duffield, 1910.
The New Machiavelli. New York, Duffield, 1910; London, Lane, 1911.
Marriage. London, Macmillan, and New York, Duffield, 1912.
The Passionate Friends. London, Macmillan, and New York, Harper, 1913.
The World Set Free: A Story of Mankind. London, Macmillan, and New York, Dutton, 1914.
The Wife of Sir Isaac Harman. London and New York, Macmillan, 1914.
Boon: The Mind of the Race, the Wild Asses of the Devil, and the Last Trump (as Reginald Bliss). London, Unwin, and New York, Doran, 1915.
Bealby: A Holiday. London, Methuen, and New York, Macmillan, 1915.
The Research Magnificent. London and New York, Macmillan, 1915.
Mr. Britling Sees It Through. London, Cassell, and New York, Macmillan, 1916.
The Soul of a Bishop. London, Cassell, and New York, Macmillan, 1917.
Joan and Peter. London, Cassell, and New York, Macmillan, 1918.
The Undying Fire. London, Cassell, and New York, Macmillan, 1919; with nonfiction as *The Undying Fire, and Philosophical and Theological Speculations,* London, Unwin, 1925.
The Secret Places of the Heart. London, Cassell, and New York, Macmillan, 1922.
Men Like Gods. London, Cassell, and New York, Macmillan, 1923.
The Dream. London, Cape, and New York, Macmillan, 1924.
Christina Alberta's Father. London, Cape, and New York, Macmillan, 1925.
The World of William Clissold. London, Benn, 3 vols., and New York, Doran, 2 vols., 1926.
Meanwhile: The Picture of a Lady. London, Benn, and New York, Doran, 1927.
The King Who Was a King: The Book of a Film. London, Benn, and New York, Doubleday, 1929.
The Adventures of Tommy (for children). London, Harrap, and New York, Stokes, 1929.
The Autocracy of Mr. Parham: His Remarkable Adventures in This Changing World. London, Heinemann, and New York, Doubleday, 1930.
The Bulpington of Blup. London, Hutchinson, 1932; New York, Macmillan, 1933.
The Shape of Things to Come: The Ultimate Revolution. London, Hutchinson, and New York, Macmillan, 1933.

Stories of Men and Women in Love (omnibus). London, Hutchinson, 1933.

Brynhild. London, Methuen, and New York, Scribner, 1937.

Star Begotten: A Biological Fantasia. London, Chatto and Windus, and New York, Viking Press, 1937.

The Camford Visitation. London, Methuen, 1937.

Apropos of Dolores. London, Cape, and New York, Scribner, 1938.

The Brothers. London, Chatto and Windus, and New York, Viking Press, 1938.

The Holy Terror. London, Joseph, and New York, Simon and Schuster, 1939.

Babes in the Darkling Wood. London, Secker and Warburg, and New York, Alliance, 1940.

All Aboard for Ararat. London, Secker and Warburg, 1940; New York, Alliance, 1941.

You Can't Be Too Careful: A Sample of Life 1901-1951. London, Secker and Warburg, 1941; New York, Putnam, 1942.

The Desert Daisy (for children), edited by Gordon N. Ray. Urbana, University of Illinois Press, 1957.

The Wealth of Mr. Waddy, edited by Harris Wilson. Carbondale, Southern Illinois University Press, 1969.

Short Stories

Select Conversations with an Uncle (Now Extinct) and Two Other Reminiscences. London, Lane, and New York, Merriman, 1895.

Thirty Strange Stories. New York, Arnold, 1897.

Tales of Space and Time. London, Harper, and New York, Doubleday, 1899.

A Cure for Love: A Story of the Days to Come (Anno Domini 2090). New York, Scott, 1899.

The Vacant Country: A Story of the Days to Come. New York, Kent, 1899.

Twelve Stories and a Dream. London, Macmillan, 1903; New York, Scribner, 1905.

The Country of the Blind and Other Stories. London, Nelson, 1911; revised edition of *The Country of the Blind,* London, Golden Cockerel Press, 1939.

The Door in the Wall and Other Stories. New York, Kennerley, 1911; London, Richards, 1915.

The Star. London, Simplified Speling Sosieti, 1912(?).

Tales of the Unexpected [of Life and Adventure; of Wonder], edited by J. D. Beresford. London, Collins, 3 vols., 1922-23.

The Short Stories of H. G. Wells. London, Benn, 1927; Garden City, New York, Doubleday, 1929; as *Famous Short Stories of H. G. Wells,* Garden City, New York, Doubleday, 1938; as *The Complete Short Stories of H. G. Wells.* London, Benn, and New York, St. Martin's Press, 1987.

The Favorite Short Stories of H. G. Wells. Garden City, New York, Doubleday Doran, 1937.

28 Science Fiction Stories. New York, Dover, 1952.

Selected Short Stories. London, Penguin, 1958.

The Valley of Spiders. London, Fontana, 1964.

The Cone; Another Collection of Horror Stories. London, Fontana, 1965.

Best Science Fiction Stories of H. G. Wells. New York, Dover, 1966.

The Man with the Nose and the Other Uncollected Short Stories, edited by J. R. Hammond. London, Athlone Press, 1984.

The H. G. Wells Science Fiction Treasury. New York, Chatham River, 1984.

Plays

Kipps, with Rudolf Besier, adaptation of the novel by Wells (produced London, 1912).

The Wonderful Visit, with St. John Ervine, adaptation of the novel by Wells (produced London, 1921).

Hoopdriver's Holiday, adaptation of his novel *The Wheels of Chance,* edited by Michael Timko. Lafayette, Indiana, Purdue University English Department, 1964.

Screenplays: *H. G. Wells Comedies (Bluebottles, The Tonic, Daydreams),* with Frank Wells, 1928; *Things to Come,* 1936; *The Man Who Could Work Miracles,* 1936.

Other

Text-Book of Biology. London, Clive, 2 vols., 1893.

Honours Physiography, with R. A. Gregory. London, Hughes, 1893.

Certain Personal Matters: A Collection of Material, Mainly Autobiographical. London, Lawrence and Bullen, 1897.

Anticipations of the Reaction of Mechanical and Scientific Progress upon Human Life and Thought. London, Chapman and Hall, 1901; New York, Harper, 1902.

The Discovery of the Future (lecture). London, Unwin, 1902; New York, Huebsch, 1913; revised edition, London, Cape, 1925.

Mankind in the Making. London, Chapman and Hall, 1903; New York, Scribner, 1904.

The Future in America: A Search after Realities. London, Chapman and Hall, and New York, Harper, 1906.

Faults of the Fabian (lecture). Privately printed, 1906.

Socialism and the Family. London, Fifield, 1906; Boston, Ball, 1908.

Reconstruction of the Fabian Society. Privately printed, 1906.

This Misery of Boots. London, Fabian Society, 1907; Boston, Ball, 1908.

Will Socialism Destroy the Home? London, Independent Labour Party, 1907.

New Worlds for Old. London, Constable, and New York, Macmillan, 1908; revised edition, London, Constable, 1914.

First and Last Things: A Confession of Faith and Rule of Life. London, Constable, and New York, Putnam, 1908; revised edition, London, Cassell, 1917; London, Watts, 1929.

Floor Games (for children). London, Palmer, 1911; Boston, Small Maynard, 1912.

The Labour Unrest. London, Associated Newspapers, 1912.

War and Common Sense. London, Associated Newspapers, 1913.

Liberalism and Its Party. London, Good, 1913.

Little Wars (children's games). London, Palmer, and Boston, Small Maynard, 1913.

An Englishman Looks at the World, Being a Series of Unrestrained Remarks upon Contemporary Matters. London, Cassell, 1914; as *Social Forces in England and America,* New York, Harper, 1914.

The War That Will End War. London, Palmer, and New York, Duffield, 1914; reprinted in part as *The War and Socialism,* London, Clarion Press, 1915.

The Peace of the World. London, Daily Chronicle, 1915.

What Is Coming? A Forecast of Things after the War. London, Cassell, and New York, Macmillan, 1916.

The Elements of Reconstruction. London, Nisbet, 1916.

War and the Future. London, Cassell, 1917; as *Italy, France, and Britain at War,* New York, Macmillan, 1917.

God the Invisible King. London, Cassell, and New York, Macmillan, 1917.

A Reasonable Man's Peace. London, Daily News, 1917.

In the Fourth Year: Anticipations of a World Peace. London, Chatto and Windus, and New York, Macmillan, 1918; abridged edition, as *Anticipations of a World Peace,* Chatto and Windus, 1918.

British Nationalism and the League of Nations. London, League of Nations Union, 1918.

History Is One. Boston, Ginn, 1919.

The Outline of History, Being a Plain History of Life and Mankind. London, Newnes, 2 vols., and New York, Macmillan, 2 vols., 1920 (and later revisions).

Russia in the Shadows. London, Hodder and Stoughton, 1920; New York, Doran, 1921.

The Salvaging of Civilisation. London, Cassell, and New York, Macmillan, 1921.

The New Teaching of History, with a Reply to Some Recent Criticisms of "The Outline of History." London, Cassell, 1921.

Washington and Hope of Peace. London, Collins, 1922; as *Washington and the Riddle of Peace,* New York, Macmillan, 1922.

The World, Its Debts, and the Rich Men. London, Finer, 1922.

A Short History of the World. London, Cassell, and New York, Macmillan, 1922; revised edition, London, Penguin, 1946.

Socialism and the Scientific Motive (lecture). Privately printed, 1923.

The Story of a Great Schoolmaster, Being a Plain Account of the Life and Ideas of Sanderson of Oundle. London, Chatto and Windus, and New York, Macmillan, 1924.

The P.R. Parliament. London, Proportional Representation Society, 1924.

A Year of Prophesying. London, Unwin, 1924; New York, Macmillan, 1925.

Works (Atlantic Edition). London, Unwin, and New York, Scribner, 28 vols., 1924.

A Forecast of the World's Affairs. New York, Encyclopaedia Britannica, 1925.

Works (Essex Edition). London, Benn, 24 vols., 1926-27.

Mr. Belloc Objects to "The Outline of History." London, Watts, 1926.

Democracy under Revision (lecture). London, Hogarth Press, and New York, Doran, 1927.

Wells' Social Anticipations, edited by H. W. Laidler. New York, Vanguard Press, 1927.

In Memory of Amy Catherine Wells. Privately printed, 1927.

The Way the World Is Going: Guesses and Forecasts of the Years Ahead. London, Benn, 1928; New York, Doubleday, 1929.

The Open Conspiracy: Blue Prints for a World Revolution. London, Gollancz, and New York, Doubleday, 1928; revised edition, London, Hogarth Press, 1930; revised edition, as *What Are We to Do with Our Lives?,* London, Heinemann, and New York, Doubleday, 1931.

The Common Sense of World Peace (lecture). London, Hogarth Press, 1929.

Imperialism and the Open Conspiracy. London, Faber, 1929.

The Science of Life: A Summary of Contemporary Knowledge about Life and Its Possibilities, with Julian Huxley and G. P. Wells. London, Amalgamated Press, 3 vols., 1930; New York, Doubleday, 4 vols., 1931; revised edition, as *Science of Life Series,* London, Cassell, 9 vols., 1934-37.

The Problem of the Troublesome Collaborator. Privately printed, 1930.

Settlement of the Trouble Between Mr. Thring and Mr. Wells: A Footnote to The Problem of the Troublesome Collaborator. Privately printed, 1930.

The Way to World Peace. London, Benn, 1930.

The Work, Wealth, and Happiness of Mankind. New York, Doubleday, 2 vols., 1931; London, Heinemann, 1 vol., 1932; revised edition, Heinemann, 1934; as *The Outline of Man's Work and Wealth,* Doubleday, 1936.

After Democracy: Addresses and Papers on the Present World Situation. London, Watts, 1932.

What Should Be Done—Now. New York, Day, 1932.

Experiment in Autobiography: Discoveries and Conclusions of a Very Ordinary Brain (since 1866). London, Gollancz-Cresset Press, 2 vols., and New York, Macmillan, 1 vol., 1934.

Stalin-Wells Talk: The Verbatim Record, and A Discussion, with others. London, New Statesman and Nation, 1934.

The New America: The New World. London, Cresset Press, and New York, Macmillan, 1935.

The Anatomy of Frustration: A Modern Synthesis. London, Cresset Press, and New York, Macmillan, 1936.

The Idea of a World Encyclopaedia. London, Hogarth Press, 1936.

World Brain. London, Methuen, and New York, Doubleday, 1938.

Travels of a Republican Radical in Search of Hot Water. London, Penguin, 1939.

The Fate of Homo Sapiens: An Unemotional Statement of the Things That Are Happening to Him Now and of the Immediate Possibilities Confronting Him. London, Secker and Warburg, 1939; as *The Fate of Man,* New York, Alliance, 1939.

The New World Order, Whether It Is Obtainable, How It Can Be Obtained, and What Sort of World a World at Peace Will Have to Be. London, Secker and Warburg, and New York, Knopf, 1940.

The Rights of Man; or, What Are We Fighting For? London, Penguin, 1940.

The Common Sense of War and Peace: World Revolution or War Unending? London, Penguin, 1940.

The Pocket History of the World. New York, Pocket Books, 1941.

Guide to the New World: A Handbook of Constructive World Revolution. London, Gollancz, 1941.

The Outlook for Homo Sapiens (revised versions of *The Fate of Homo Sapiens* and *The New World Order*). London, Secker and Warburg, 1942.

Science and the World-Mind. London, New Europe, 1942.

Phoenix: A Summary of the Inescapable Conditions of World Reorganization. London, Secker and Warburg, 1942; Girard, Kansas, Haldeman Julius, n.d.

A Thesis on the Quality of Illusion in the Continuity of Individual Life of the Higher Metazoa, with Particular Reference to the Species Homo Sapiens. Privately printed, 1942.

The Conquest of Time. London, Watts, 1942.

The New Rights of Man. Girard, Kansas, Haldeman Julius, 1942.

Crux Ansata: An Indictment of the Roman Catholic Church. London, Penguin, 1943; New York, Agora, 1944.

The Mosley Outrage. London, Daily Worker, 1943.

'42 to '44: A Contemporary Memoir upon Human Behavior during the Crisis of the World Revolution. London, Secker and Warburg, 1944.

Marxism vs. Liberalism (interview with Stalin). New York, Century, 1945.

The Happy Turning: A Dream of Life. London, Heinemann, 1945.
Mind at the End of Its Tether. London, Heinemann, 1945.
Mind at the End of Its Tether, and The Happy Turning. New York, Didier, 1945.
Henry James and H. G. Wells: A Record of Their Friendship, Their Debate on the Art of Fiction, and Their Quarrel, edited by Leon Edel and Gordon N. Ray. Urbana, University of Illinois Press, and London, Hart Davis, 1958.
Arnold Bennett and H. G. Wells: A Record of a Personal and Literary Friendship, edited by Harris Wilson. London, Hart Davis, 1960.
George Gissing and H. G. Wells: Their Friendship and Correspondence, edited by Royal A. Gettman. London, Hart Davis, 1961.
Journalism and Prophecy 1893-1946, edited W. Warren Wagar. Boston, Houghton Mifflin, 1964; revised edition, London, Bodley Head, 1965.
Early Writings in Science and Science Fiction, edited by Robert M. Philmus and David Y. Hughes. Berkeley, University of California Press, 1975.
H. G. Wells's Literary Criticism, edited by Patrick Parrinder and Robert M. Philmus. Brighton, Sussex, Harvester Press, and Totowa, New Jersey, Barnes and Noble, 1980.
H. G. Wells in Love, edited by G. P. Wells. London, Faber, 1984.
The Discovery of the Future, with The Common-Sense of World Peace and The Human Adventure, edited by Patrick Parrinder. London, PNL, 1989.
Bernard Shaw and H. G. Wells, edited by J. Percy Smith (correspondence). Toronto, University of Toronto Press, 1995.

Editor, with G. R. S. Taylor and Frances Evelyn Warwick, *The Great State: Essays in Construction.* London, Harper, 1912; as *Socialism and the Great State,* New York, Harper, 1914.

*

Film Adaptations (selection): *The Island of Lost Souls,* 1932, *The Island of Dr. Moreau,* 1977, 1996, all from the novel *The Island of Dr. Moreau; The Invisible Man,* 1933, 1984 (TV serial); *Things to Come,* 1935, from the novel *The Shape of Things to Come; The Man Who Could Work Miracles,* 1936, from the short story; *Kipps,* 1941, 1960 (TV serial); *The History of Mr. Polly,* 1949, 1959 (TV serial), 1979 (TV serial); *The War of the Worlds,* 1953; *The Door in the Wall,* 1956, from the short story; *The Time Machine,* 1960, 1978 (TV movie); *The First Men in the Moon,* 1963; *Love and Mr. Lewisham,* 1972 (TV serial).

Bibliography: *H. G. Wells: A Comprehensive Bibliography,* London, H. G. Wells Society, 1966, revised editions, 1968, 1986; *Herbert George Wells: An Annotated Bibliography of His Works* by J.R. Hammond, New York, Garland, 1977; *H. G. Wells: A Reference Guide* by William J. Scheick and J. Randolf Cox, Boston, 1988.

Manuscript Collection: University of Illinois, Urbana.

Critical Studies (selection): *The World of H. G. Wells* by Van Wyck Brooks, New York, Mitchell Kennerley, and London, T. Fisher Unwin, 1915; *H. G. Wells: A Biography,* London, Longman, 1951; *The Early H. G. Wells: A Study of the Scientific Romances* by Bernard Bergonzi, Manchester, Manchester University Press, 1961, and *H. G. Wells: A Collection of Critical Essays* edited by Bergonzi, Englewood Cliffs, New Jersey, Prentice Hall, 1976; *H. G. Wells: An Outline by F. K. Chaplin,* London, P. R. Macmillan, 1961; *H. G. Wells and the World State* by W. Warren Wagar, New Haven, Connecticut, Yale University Press, 1961; *The Life and Thought of H. G. Wells* by Julius Kagarlitsky (translated by Moura Budberg), London, Sidgwick and Jackson, 1966; *H. G. Wells* by Richard Hauer Costa, New York, Twayne, 1967, revised edition, 1985; *H. G. Wells: His Turbulent Life and Times* by Lovat Dickson, London, Macmillan, 1969; essay in *A Soviet Heretic* by Yevgeny Zamyatin (translated by Mirra Ginsburg), Chicago, University of Chicago Press, 1970; *H. G. Wells* by Patrick Parrinder, Edinburgh, Oliver and Boyd, 1970, New York, Capricorn, 1977, and *H. G. Wells: The Critical Heritage* edited by Parrinder, London, Routledge, 1972; *The Time Traveller: The Life of H. G. Wells* by Norman and Jeanne Mackenzie, London, Weidenfeld and Nicolson, 1973, as *H. G. Wells: A Biography,* New York, Simon and Schuster, 1973; *H. G. Wells: Critic of Progress* by Jack Williamson, Baltimore, Mirage Press, 1973; *H. G. Wells and Rebecca West* by Gordon N. Ray, New Haven, Connecticut, Yale University Press, and London, Macmillan, 1974; *The Scientific Romances of H. G. Wells* by Stephen Gill, Cornwall, Ontario, Vesta, 1975; *Anatomies of Egotism: A Reading of the Last Novels of H. G. Wells* by Robert Bloom, Lincoln, University of Nebraska Press, 1977; *H. G. Wells and Modern Science Fiction* edited by Darko Suvin and Robert M. Philmus, Lewisburg, Pennsylvania, Buckness University Press, 1977; *H. G. Wells: A Pictorial Biography* by Frank Wells, London, Jupiter, 1977; *The H. G. Wells Scrapbook* edited by Peter Haining, London, New English Library, 1978; *Who's Who in H. G. Wells* by Brian Ash, London, Elm Tree, 1979.

H. G. Wells, Discoverer of the Future: The Influence of Science on His Thought by Roslynn D. Haynes, New York, New York University Press, and London, Macmillan, 1980; *H. G. Wells: Interviews and Recollections* edited by J. R. Hammond, London, Macmillan, 1980; *The Science Fiction of H. G. Wells: A Concise Guide* by P. H. Niles, Clifton Park, New York, Auriga, 1980; *The Science Fiction of H. G. Wells* by Frank McConnell, New York, Oxford University Press, 1981; *H. G. Wells and the Culminating Ape: Biological Themes and Imaginative Obsessions* by Peter Kemp, London, Macmillan, and New York, St. Martin's Press, 1982; *The Logic of Fantasy: H. G. Wells and Science Fiction* by John Huntington, New York, Columbia University Press, 1982; *H. G. Wells* by Robert Crossley, Mercer Island, Washington, Starmont House, 1984; *The Splintering Frame: The Later Fiction of H. G. Wells* by William J. Scheick, Victoria, University of Victoria English Literary Studies, 1984; *H. G. Wells: Aspects of a Life* by Anthony West, London, Hutchinson, and New York, Random House, 1984; *H. G. Wells* by John Batchelor, London, Cambridge University Press, 1985; *H. G. Wells: Desperately Mortal: A Biography* by David C. Smith, New Haven, Connecticut, Yale University Press, 1986; *H. G. Wells: Reality and Beyond* edited by Michael Mullin, Champaign, Illinois, Public Library, 1986; *The Prophetic Soul: A Reading of Things to Come* by Leon Stover, Jefferson, North Carolina, and London, McFarland, 1987; *H. G. Wells* by Michael Draper, London, Macmillan, and New York, St. Martin's Press, 1987; *H. G. Wells* by Christopher Martin, Hove, Wayland, 1988; *H. G. Wells under Revision* edited by Patrick Parrinder and Christopher Rolfe, Selinsgrove, Pennsylvania, and London, Susquehanna University Presses, 1990; *H. G. Wells* by

Brian Murray, New York, Continuum, 1990; *Critical Essays on H. G. Wells* edited by John Huntington, Boston, G. K. Hall, 1991; *H. G. Wells and the Short Story* by J. R. Hammond, New York, St. Martin's Press, 1992; *The Invisible Man: The Life and Liberties of H. G. Wells* by Michael Coren, New York, Random House, 1993; *A Critical Edition of The War of the Worlds: H. G. Wells's Scientific Romance* edited by David Hughes and Harry M. Geduld, Bloomington, Indiana University Press, 1993; *The Critical Response to H. G. Wells* edited by William J. Scheick, Westport, Greenwood Press, 1995.

*   *   *

H. G. Wells was the founding father of the British genre of scientific romance, and hence became the most important practitioner of science fiction *avant la lettre*, but his early works in that vein have a powerful component of horror. Like Mary Shelley and Robert Louis Stevenson before him Wells became a significant inspiration of Hollywood shockers, the success of James Whale's *Frankenstein* (1931) and Reuben Mamoulian's *Dr. Jekyll and Mr. Hyde* (1932) being followed in 1933 by Whale's version of *The Invisible Man* and Erle C. Kenton's *Island of Lost Souls* (based on *The Island of Dr. Moreau*).

Wells's early short stories include several relevant works. *The Stolen Bacillus and Other Incidents* includes "The Flowering of the Strange Orchid," about a vampiric plant, and the excellent *conte cruel* "The Lord of the Dynamos." The title story of *The Plattner Story and Others* is a weird fantasy about the protagonist's temporary displacement into the fourth dimension. The latter collection also includes a disturbing account of personality-exchange, "The Story of the Late Mr. Elvesham," which Wells later expanded into an unproduced film script (published in *The Man with the Nose and Other Uncollected Short Stories*) and several other notable horror stories. "Under the Knife" is a visionary fantasy experienced under surgical anaesthetic; "Pollock and the Porroh Man" is an ironic tale of black magic; "The Red Room" is an interesting story in which fear is externalized as a supernatural force; "The Cone" is another graphic *conte cruel*.

The Island of Doctor Moreau is an allegory of religion and evolution, in which the creatively-talented Moreau uses surgery to give animals human form but finds it more difficult to make them behave properly. The law which they are forced by fear of violence to obey, based in a set of taboos, eventually proves useless in controlling their bestial instincts. Although the man cast away on Moreau's island escapes the slaughter which follows the rebellion of the beast-men he is henceforth unable to see human society as anything but Moreau's petty empire writ large. *The Invisible Man* is a cautionary tale rather than an outright horror story, the luckless scientist being more a victim of misfortune than a villain, although he is driven to violence in the end. More recent adaptations of the basic idea have tended to employ their invisible men as heroes rather than villains and even Whale's version is more thriller than horror movie. *The War of the Worlds* is, however, the archetypal science-fiction horror story, which established a template for thousands of other accounts of the invasion of earth by monstrous aliens.

The Martians of *The War of the Worlds* were designed to terrify, and so was the tale itself—so much so that Orson Welles' Mercury Theater radio broadcast of Halloween 1938 caused a panic which spread across the United States. The aliens were compounded out of the most repugnant features of various arthropodal, crustacean and molluscan species, with the addition of huge staring eyes calculated to induce a special paranoia. That image has been replicated, with only slight variations, by countless pulp melodramas and B-movies—and the huge eyes continue to recur in all fearful images of extraterrestrial life, including those enshrined in the modern mythology of UFO visitations and "alien abductions." The second part of Wells's novel, which describes the exemplary responses of the Curate and the Artilleryman to the victory of the Martians, provides a savage mockery of the frailty of human illusions and aspirations. Cavor's adventures among the Selenites in *The First Men in the Moon* sound a calculated echo of *The War of the Worlds*, but it is only an echo; the horror of his laconic reports is of a much quieter and more insidious quality.

Although Wells's early supernatural fantasies, *The Wonderful Visit* and *The Sea Lady*, are both tragedies they are not at all horrific—and if one sets aside the horrors of war as described in such novels as *The War in the Air* the element of horror was absent from his work for a long time after 1898. Of the fantasies collected in *Twelve Stories and a Dream* only the conspicuously half-hearted "The Stolen Body" qualifies as a marginal horror story, although "The Inexperienced Ghost" is a neat black comedy. The giant insects in *The Food of the Gods* produce a few scary moments early in the text but are soon forgotten. Wells's transfiguration of the Book of Job in *The Undying Fire* inevitably piles on the agony but never comes close to matching the extravagant horrors of M. P. Shiel's transfiguration of the same Biblical text in *The Purple Cloud* (1901). The visionary fantasy *Mr. Blettsworthy on Rampole Island* is effective in its description of the hero's life among the tradition-bound savages who turn out, in the end, not to be what they seem, but the real point of the story's horrific imagery is satirical.

By far the most interesting of Wells's later works, in the context of horror fiction, is the novella *The Croquet Player*. In this story the "ghosts" haunting the symbolically-named region of Cainmarsh are the brutish aspects of human nature, which the hallucinating protagonist is trying to exorcise from his civilized soul. The ideative links with *The Island of Doctor Moreau* are obvious, all the more so when a secondary level of psychoanalysis re-reads the hallucination as the plight of the whole world as it marches steadfastly towards a new world war. Such real horrors had entirely displaced the purely hypothetical horrors of *The War of the Worlds* in Wells's imagination—as might be expected of the one man who foresaw with some degree of accuracy the appalling mess that World War I turned out to be—and then had to live for 28 more years with the troublesome awareness that the awful lessons offered by that terrible conflict had not been properly learned.

—Brian Stableford

WELTY, Eudora (Alice)

Nationality: American. **Born:** Jackson, Mississippi, 13 April 1909. **Education:** Mississippi State College for Women, Columbus, 1925-27; University of Wisconsin, Madison, B.A. 1929; Columbia University School for Advertising, New York, 1930-31. **Career:** Part-time journalist, 1931-32; publicity agent, Works Progress Administration (WPA), 1933-36; staff member, *New York Times Book Review*, during World War II. Honorary Consultant in American Letters, Library of Congress, Washington, D.C., 1958.

Awards: Bread Loaf Writers Conference fellowship, 1940; O. Henry award, 1942, 1943, 1968; Guggenheim fellowship, 1942, 1948; American Academy grant, 1944, Howells Medal, 1955, and gold medal, 1972; Ford fellowship, for drama; Brandeis University Creative Arts award, 1965; Edward MacDowell medal 1970; Pulitzer prize, 1973; National Medal for Literature, 1980; Presidential Medal of Freedom, 1980; American Book award, for paperback, 1983; Bobst award, 1984; Common Wealth award, 1984; Mystery Writers of America award, 1985; National Medal of Arts, 1987; National Endowment for the Arts Award, 1989; National Book Foundation Medal, 1991; Charles Frankel prize, 1992. D.Litt.: Denison University, Granville, Ohio, 1971; Smith College, Northampton, Massachusetts; University of Wisconsin, Madison; University of the South, Sewanee, Tennessee; Washington and Lee University, Lexington, Virginia. **Member:** American Academy, 1971; Chevalier, Order of Arts and Letters (France), 1987.

HORROR, GHOST AND GOTHIC PUBLICATIONS

Short Stories

A Curtain of Green. New York, Doubleday, 1941; London, Lane, 1943.
The Wide Net and Other Stories. New York, Harcourt Brace, 1943; London, Lane, 1945.

OTHER PUBLICATIONS

Novels

The Robber Bridegroom. New York, Doubleday, 1942; London, Lane, 1944.
Delta Wedding. New York, Harcourt Brace, 1946; London, Lane, 1947.
The Ponder Heart. New York, Harcourt Brace, and London, Hamish Hamilton, 1954.
Losing Battles. New York, Random House, 1970; London, Virago Press, 1982.
The Optimist's Daughter. New York, Random House, 1972; London, Deutsch, 1973.

Short Stories

Music from Spain. Greenville, Mississippi, Levee Press, 1948.
The Golden Apples. New York, Harcourt Brace, 1949; London, Lane, 1950.
Selected Stories. New York, Modern Library, 1954.
The Bride of Innisfallen and Other Stories. New York, Harcourt Brace, and London, Hamish Hamilton, 1955.
Thirteen Stories, edited by Ruth M. Vande Kieft. New York, Harcourt Brace, 1965.
The Collected Stories of Eudora Welty. New York, Harcourt Brace, 1980; London, Boyars, 1981.
Moon Lake and Other Stories. Franklin Center, Pennsylvania, Franklin Library 1980.
Retreat. Jackson, Mississippi, Palaemon Press, 1981.

Poetry

A Flock of Guinea Hens Seen from a Car. New York, Albondocani Press, 1970.

Other

Short Stories (essay). New York, Harcourt Brace, 1949.
Place in Fiction. New York, House of Books, 1957.
Three Papers on Fiction. Northampton, Massachusetts, Smith College, 1962.
The Shoe Bird (for children). New York, Harcourt Brace, 1964.
A Sweet Devouring (on children's literature). New York, Albondocani Press, 1969.
One Time, One Place: Mississippi in the Depression: A Snapshot Album. New York, Random House, 1971.
A Pageant of Birds. New York, Albondocani Press, 1975.
Fairy Tale of the Natchez Trace. Jackson, Mississippi Historical Society, 1975.
The Eye of the Story: Selected Essays and Reviews. New York, Random House, 1978; London, Virago Press, 1987.
Ida M'Toy (memoir). Urbana, University of Illinois Press, 1979.
Miracles of Perception: The Art of Willa Cather, with Alfred Knopf and Yehudi Menuhin. Charlottesville, Virginia, Alderman Library, 1980.
Conversations with Eudora Welty, edited by Peggy Whitman Prenshaw. Jackson, University Press of Mississippi, 1984.
One Writer's Beginnings. Cambridge, Massachusetts, Harvard University Press, 1984; London, Faber, 1985.
Photographs. Jackson, University Press of Mississippi, 1989.
A Worn Path (for children). Mankato, Minnesota, Creative Education, 1991.
A Writer's Eye: Collected Book Reviews, edited by Pearl Amelia McHaney. Jackson, University Press of Mississippi, 1994.

Editor, with Ronald A. Sharp, *The Norton Book of Friendship.* New York, Norton, 1991.

*

Bibliography: In *Mississippi Quarterly* (Mississippi State), Fall 1973, and *Eudora Welty—A Bibliography of Her Work,* Jackson, University Press of Mississippi, 1994, both by Noel Polk; *Eudora Welty: A Reference Guide* by Victor H. Thompson, Boston, Hall, 1976; *Eudora Welty: A Critical Bibliography* by Bethany C. Swearingen, Jackson, University Press of Mississippi, 1984; *The Welty Collection: A Guide to the Eudora Welty Manuscripts and Documents at the Mississippi Department of Archives and History* by Suzanne Marrs, Jackson, University Press of Mississippi, 1988.

Manuscript Collection: Mississippi Department of Archives and History, Jackson.

Critical Studies (selection): *Eudora Welty* by Ruth M. Vande Kieft, New York, Twayne, 1962, revised edition, 1986; *A Season of Dreams: The Fiction of Eudora Welty* by Alfred Appel, Jr., Baton Rouge, Louisiana State University Press, 1965; *Eudora Welty* by Joseph A. Bryant, Jr., Minneapolis, University of Minnesota Press, 1968; *The Rhetoric of Eudora Welty's Short Stories* by Zelma Turner Howard, Jackson, University Press of Mississippi, 1973; *A Still Moment: Essays on the Art of Eudora Welty* edited by John F. Desmond, Metuchen, New Jersey, Scarecrow Press, 1978; *Eudora Welty: Critical Essays* edited by Peggy Whitman Prenshaw, Jackson, University Press of Mississippi, 1979; *Eudora Welty: A Form of Thanks* edited by Ann J. Abadie and Louis D. Dollarhide,

Jackson, University Press of Mississippi, 1979; *Eudora Welty's Achievement of Order* by Michael Kreyling, Baton Rouge, Louisiana State University Press, 1980; *Eudora Welty* by Elizabeth Evans, New York, Ungar, 1981; *Tissue of Lies: Eudora Welty and the Southern Romance* by Jennifer L. Randisi, Boston, University Press of America, 1982; *Eudora Welty's Chronicle: A Story of Mississippi Life* by Albert J. Devlin, Jackson, University Press of Mississippi, 1983, and *Welty: A Life in Literature* edited by Devlin, University Press of Mississippi, 1988; *With Ears Opening Like Morning Glories: Eudora Welty and the Love of Storytelling* by Carol S. Manning, Westport, Connecticut, Greenwood Press, 1985; *Eudora Welty* by Louise Westling, London, Macmillan, 1989; *Eudora Welty: Eye of the Storyteller* edited by Dawn Trouard, Kent, Ohio, Kent State University Press, 1989; *Serious Daring from Within: Female Narrative Strategies in Eudora Welty's Novels* by Franziska Gygax, New York, Greenwood, 1990; *Eudora Welty: Seeing Black and White* by Robert MacNeil, Jackson, University Press of Mississippi, 1990; *The Heart of the Story: Eudora Welty's Short Fiction* by Peter Schmidt, Jackson, University Press of Mississippi, 1991; *The Critical Response to Eudora Welty's Fiction* by Laurie Champion, Westport, Connecticut, Greenwood Press, 1994; *Daughter of the Swan: Love and Knowledge in Eudora Welty's Fiction* by Gail Mortimer (Gail Linda), Athens, University of Georgia Press, 1994; *The Dragon's Blood: Feminist Intertextuality in Eudora Welty's "The Golden Apples"* by Rebecca Mark, Jackson, University Press of Mississippi, 1994; *Eudora Welty's Aesthetics of Place* by Jan Nordby Gretlund, Newark, University of Delaware Press, 1994; *The Still Moment* by Paul Binding, London, Virago, 1994.

* * *

Eudora Welty is widely regarded as one of the pre-eminent American literary figures of the 20th century. A short-story writer by nature and choice, coming to the full-length novel later, Welty first published her tales in magazines such as *The Southern Review* and *Manuscript* in the 1930s.

Early assessments of Welty's work, in the critical shorthand of the day, quickly categorized her stories as Southern Gothic, following a long regional tradition. Time, persistence, continued publication, and a small group of dogged supporters—Katherine Ann Porter and Robert Penn Warren among them—helped elevate Welty's work beyond the regional and genre designations that it received in the beginning.

Welty's early short stories were often dismissed as dense, grotesque or inscrutable, due in part to her raw, sometimes plain, subject matter and her moody, ethereal descriptive power. Although her success with the smaller and regional markets came early, she later enlisted the aid of a New York agent, Diarmuid Russell, the son of Irish poet and playwright "A.E." (George Russell), in her approach to the national markets.

With Russell's assistance, and the championing of her work by John Woodburn of Doubleday, Welty published her first collection, *A Curtain of Green*, in 1941. This rare event, a short-story collection from a writer without a novel, was a remarkable feat, and was followed up with several more collections in the next few years.

The pieces in *A Curtain of Green*, and in the following collection, *The Wide Net and Other Stories*, include some of the best examples of Welty's work that can be claimed by the horror genre. Though her mastery of mood and place in her stories are evident throughout all of her work, these early works display an unusually gentle handling of the grotesque, death, and the despair of failure and loneliness.

Several stories in *A Curtain of Green* stand out. "A Piece of News" deals with a woman who has received a newspaper clipping reporting her own death, as she awaits the inevitable, haunted by the violence that will come with the arrival of her husband. "The Petrified Man" deals with a common Welty theme, the travelling freak show, in which one of the exhibits might be a notorious local rapist, with this fact hidden in the dialogue of a group of women in a beauty parlour. Another travelling-carnival story, "Keela, the Outcast Indian Maiden," reaches into the history of a small, nearly mute black man who was once forced to eat live chickens and drink their blood for a sideshow. Three views of the act, guilt, disbelief and acceptance, come through a barrage of noncommunication. In these and many of her stories, the vacillation of perceptual reality is in play, with the characters struggling against some sort of limited or heightened ability—imagination, mental acuity, or self delusion—to discern the real from the imagined. This is the case in "Clytie," where upon seeing the face that she has spent her life hunting in fear, her own, the title character drowns herself in a rain-barrel. "Flowers for Marjorie" tells of the desperate murder of a loved one during times so bad, death seems like a gift to both the murderer and the recipient. "In Death of a Travelling Salesman" a man ponders the loneliness of his life, much too late, lost at the end of a lonely dirt road, and at his own end. In "Powerhouse" a lively story of a travelling blues revue, a cryptic telegram tells of a death that seems too well imagined by the recipient. Welty fashions these and the other stories in the collection with an elegant and gentle voice, and with an understated, wry, and very Southern sense of humour. The title story in *A Curtain of Green* is perhaps the collection's most powerful—and most reserved—piece, a story of the power of life and its command over death, however fleeting.

A lifelong fascination with the Natchez Trace, and the possibilities along the historical trail through her native Mississippi, shaped the second collection as well as many later stories. *The Wide Net and Other Stories* opens with "First Love," the story of a young man who lost his parents, and his awakening to life without them. The collection's title story deals with the search for a drowning victim, in which the search is the important thing, and the victim, if there is one, is the least consequential aspect of the event. This collection also contains "The Purple Hat," which Welty wanted to be nothing more than a "playful ghost story," but which transcends the form as a typical Welty *tour de force*—a ghost story in which the ghost never appears.

Her focus on the grim and the grotesque in these collections became somewhat muted in a later collection, *The Bride of Innisfallen and Other Stories*. With these pieces, we see a maturing of Welty's voice, as well as stories of greater length, which would eventually lead to novel-length works. Even in her gentle novella, *The Ponder Heart*, Welty manages, within what is possibly her funniest work, as well as a narrative masterpiece, to zero in on the internal emotional and delusional capacity of the human mind, which permeates even the most bizarre of her stories. This is one of the best examples, along with "Why I Live at the PO" of Welty's sure-footed comic sense.

Her voice is uniquely southern, and always female. Touches of gothic, old and new, abound in her stories, from the rundown, worn, heavy familiarity of an old family home, to the internal misjudgments of her characters, elevating the simple everyday object, or statement or action, to proportions determining life or death. Welty honours the imagination in fiction, above all, and has frequently counted Chekhov as one of her most profound literary kinships.

Although not strictly a genre writer in any sense, Eudora Welty is a writer of tremendous talent, depth, and vision.

—Tom Winstead

WHARTON, Edith (Newbold)

Nationality: American. **Born:** Edith Newbold Jones, New York City, 24 January 1862. **Education:** Private; travelled in Italy, Spain, and France as a child. **Family:** Married Edward Wharton in 1885 (divorced 1913). Lived in Newport, Rhode Island, after her marriage, and in Europe from 1907; close friend of Henry James. **Career:** Helped organize the American Hostel for Refugees, and the Children of Flanders Rescue Committee, during World War I. **Awards:** Pulitzer Prize, 1921; American Academy gold medal, 1924. Litt.D.: Yale University, New Haven, Connecticut, 1923; Chevalier, Legion of Honor (France), 1916, and Order of Leopold (Belgium), 1919. **Member:** American Academy, 1930. **Died:** 11 August 1937.

Horror, Ghost and Gothic Publications

Short Stories

Tales of Men and Ghosts. New York, Scribner, and London, Macmillan, 1910.
Here and Beyond. New York, Appleton, 1926.
Ghosts. New York, Appleton Century, 1937.
The Ghost Stories of Edith Wharton. New York, Scribner, 1973; London, Constable, 1975.
The Ghost-Feeler: Stories of Terror and the Supernatural, edited by Peter Haining. London, Peter Owen, and Chester Springs, Pennsylvania, Dufour, 1996.

Other Publications

Novels

The Touchstone. New York, Scribner, 1900; as *A Gift from the Grave*, London, Murray, 1900.
The Valley of Decision. New York, Scribner, and London, Murray, 1902.
Sanctuary. New York, Scribner, and London, Macmillan, 1903.
The House of Mirth. New York, Scribner, and London, Macmillan, 1905.
Madame de Treymes (novella). New York, Scribner, and London, Macmillan, 1907.
The Fruit of the Tree. New York, Scribner, and London, Macmillan, 1907.
Ethan Frome (novella). New York, Scribner, and London, Macmillan, 1911.
The Reef. New York, Appleton, and London, Macmillan, 1912.
The Custom of the Country. New York, Scribner, and London, Macmillan, 1913.

Summer. New York, Appleton, and London, Macmillan, 1917.
The Marne: A Tale of the War. New York, Appleton, and London, Macmillan, 1918.
The Age of Innocence. London and New York, Appleton, 1920.
The Glimpses of the Moon. New York, Appleton, 1922; London, Macmillan, 1923.
A Son at the Front. New York, Scribner, and London, Macmillan, 1923.
The Mother's Recompense. London and New York, Appleton, 1925.
Twilight Sleep. London and New York, Appleton, 1927.
The Children. New York, Appleton, 1928; as *The Marriage Playground*, New York, Grosset and Dunlap, 1930.
Hudson River Bracketed. London and New York, Appleton, 1929.
The Gods Arrive. London and New York, Appleton, 1932.
The Buccaneers (incomplete). London and New York, Appleton, 1938; revised, completed by Marion Mainwaring, New York, Viking Press, and London, Fourth Estate, 1993.
Novels (Library of America; includes *The House of Mirth, The Reef, The Custom of the Country, The Age of Innocence*), edited by R. W. B. Lewis. New York, Viking Press, 1986.

Short Stories

The Greater Inclination. New York, Scribner, and London, John Lane, 1899.
Crucial Instances. New York, Scribner and London, Murray, 1901.
The Descent of Man and Other Stories. New York, Scribner, and London, Macmillan, 1904.
The Hermit and the Wild Woman, and Other Stories. New York, Scribner, and London, Macmillan, 1908.
Xingu and Other Stories. New York, Scribner, and London, Macmillan, 1916.
Old New York: False Dawn (The 'forties). The Old Maid (The 'fifties). The Spark (The 'sixties). New Year's Day (The 'seventies). New York, Appleton, 1924.
Certain People. New York, Appleton, 1930.
Human Nature. New York, Appleton, 1933.
The World Over. New York, Appleton, 1936.
The Collected Short Stories, edited by R. W. B. Lewis. New York, Scribner, 1968.
Quartet: Four Stories. New York, Allen Press, 1975.
Fast and Loose: A Novelette, edited by Viola Hopkins Winner. 1977.
The Stories of Edith Wharton, edited by Anita Brookner. New York, Simon and Schuster, 2 vols., 1988-89.
The Muse's Tragedy and Other Stories, edited by Candace Waid. New York, New American Library, 1990; London, Penguin, 1992.
Novellas and Other Writings, edited by Cynthia Griffin Wolff. New York, Viking Press, 1990.

Plays

The Joy of Living, from a play by Hermann Sudermann (produced 1902). New York, Scribner, 1909.
The House of Mirth, with Clyde Fitch, from the novel by Wharton (produced 1906). Edited by Glenn Loney, Cranbury, New Jersey, Associated Universities Press, 1981.

Poetry

Verses (as Edith Newbold Jones). Newport, Rhode Island, privately printed by C. E. Hammett, 1878.

Artemis to Actaeon and Other Verse. New York, Scribner, and London, Macmillan, 1909.

Twelve Poems. London, Medici Society, 1926.

Other

The Decoration of Houses, with Ogden Codman, Jr. New York, Scribner, 1897.

Italian Villas and Their Gardens. New York, Century, and London, John Lane, 1904.

Italian Backgrounds. New York, Scribner, and London, Macmillan, 1905.

A Motor-Flight through France. New York, Scribner, and London, Macmillan, 1908.

Fighting France: From Dunkerque to Belfort. New York, Scribner, and London, Macmillan, 1915.

French Ways and Their Meaning. New York, Appleton, and London, Macmillan, 1919.

In Morocco. New York, Scribner, and London, Macmillan, 1920.

The Writing of Fiction. New York, Scribner, 1925.

A Backward Glance (autobiography). New York, Appleton Century, 1934; London, Constable, 1972.

An Edith Wharton Treasury. New York, Appleton Century Crofts, 1950.

The Letters of Edith Wharton, edited by R. W. B. and Nancy Lewis. New York, Simon and Schuster, 1988.

Letters 1900-1915, with Henry James, edited by Lyall H. Powers. London, Weidenfeld and Nicolson, 1989.

Editor, *Le Livre des sans-foyer.* N.p., 1915; as *The Book of the Homeless: Original Articles in Verse and Prose,* New York, Scribner, and London, Macmillan, 1916.

Editor, with Robert Norton, *Eternal Passion in English Poetry.* New York, Appleton Century, 1939.

Translator, *The Joy of Living* by Hermann Sudermann. New York, Scribner, 1902.

*

Film Adaptations: *The Glimpses of the Moon,* 1923; *The Age of Innocence,* 1924, 1934, 1993; *The Marriage Playground,* 1929, from the novel *The Children; The Old Maid,* 1939; *Ethan Frome* (television movie), 1992; *The Buccaneers* (television serial), 1995.

Bibliography: *Wharton: A Bibliography* by Vito J. Brenni, 1966; *Wharton and Kate Chopin: A Reference Guide* by Marlene Springer, 1976; *Wharton: A Descriptive Bibliography* by Stephen Garrison, 1990; *Wharton: An Annotated Secondary Bibliography* by Kristin O. Lauer and Margaret P. Murray, 1990.

Critical Studies: *Wharton: A Study of Her Fiction* by Blake Nevius, 1953; *Wharton: Convention and Morality in the Work of a Novelist* by Marilyn Jones Lyde, 1959; *Wharton,* 1961, and *Wharton: A Woman in Her Time,* 1971, both by Louis Auchincloss; *Wharton: A Collection of Critical Essays* edited by Irving Howe, 1962; *Wharton and Henry James: The Story of Their Friendship* by Millicent Bell, 1965; *Wharton: A Critical Interpretation* by Geoffrey Walton, 1971, revised edition, 1982; *Wharton: A Biography* by R. W. B. Lewis, 1975; *Wharton and the Novel of*

Manners by Gary Lindberg, 1975; *Wharton* by Margaret B. McDowell, 1976, revised edition, 1991; *Wharton* by Richard H. Lawson, 1977; *A Feast of Words: The Triumph of Wharton,* 1977, and *Wharton's Prisoners of Shame: A New Perspective on Her Neglected Fiction,* 1991, both by Cynthia Griffin Wolff; *The Frustrations of Independence: Wharton's Lesser Fiction* by Brigitta Lüthi, 1978; *Wharton's Argument with America* by Elizabeth Ammons, 1980; *The Female Intruder in the Novels of Wharton* by Carol Wershoven, 1982; *Wharton: Orphancy and Survival* by Wendy Gimbel, 1984; *Wharton: Traveller in the Land of Letters* by Janet Goodwyn, 1989; *Wharton and the Art of Fiction* by Penelope Vita-Finzi, 1990; *Verging on the Abyss: The Social Fiction of Kate Chopin and Wharton* by Mary E. Papke, 1990; *The House of Mirth: A Novel of Admonition* by Linda Wagner-Martin, 1990; *Wharton and the Unsatisfactory Man* by David Holbrook, 1991; *Wharton's Letters from the Underworld: Fictions of Women and Writing* by Candace Waid, 1991.

*   *   *

From her childhood Edith Wharton (then Edith Jones) became entranced by the idea of the supernatural and used to terrify herself with the feeling that she was being followed. This caused her to look for safety in society, but it was this feeling of possible ostracism and a fear of being unprotected that began to drive her more powerful fiction, starting with *The House of Mirth* in 1905 which tore at the fabric of New York high society. Thereafter Wharton began to break down the barriers of tradition that created a sense of isolation. While none of her novels can be described as horror or supernatural, a sense of the gothic does start to pervade *Ethan Frome,* certainly her most tragic novel, fuelled by its characters' desire for self-destruction in what should be the homely landscape of New England but which, in Wharton's perception, has become an isolated, almost alien, land.

It is this sense of alienation and foreboding that enabled Wharton to create some of the best ghost stories of her age. She wrote some 16 or so stories of the supernatural, the best being collected in her omnibus volume, *Ghosts.* One of her earliest excursions into short fiction, "The Fullness of Life" (*Scribner's,* 1893) was a ghost story, an afterlife fantasy in the vein of Elizabeth Stuart Phelps. The spirit of a deceased wife finds herself attracted to another spirit but decides she must wait for her husband. A greater sense of foreboding intrudes upon "A Journey" (1899). A married couple are travelling across American by train; *en route* the husband dies and the wife, rather than have the journey disrupted, pretends he is still alive until the end of the journey when, due to the stress, she also collapses, hits her head and dies.

With "The Moving Finger" (*Harper's,* 1901) Wharton moved fully into the genre of the macabre. A man decides that he wants the painting of his dead wife aged so that the two can age together. He perceives this as the wish of his dead wife, but as time proceeds the painting changes again with the wife's realization of her husband's impending death. The best of these early ghost stories is "The Lady's Maid's Bell" (*Scribner's* 1902), in which the ghost of a former maid continues to serve like a guardian angel to the ailing but sexually active lady of the house.

However it was not until she moved to France that Wharton could view her life and her inner fears more objectively and thereafter she produced a series of rounded, cleverly observed supernatural stories. The best of these share some common ground with those by Henry James, of whom Wharton was a close friend. Both saw the supernatural as an extension of the subconscious which may be projected by either guilt or fear and is often stimulated by a breakdown in human relationships. In "Afterward" (*Century*, 1910) we have the ghost of guilt. The story explores the concept of a ghost that is not recognized for what it is until afterward, which has its parallels in the protagonist's (Boyne) treatment of a young man whom he strips of his fortune. The ghost of the young man returns to visit Boyne with his new-made wealth. "The Eyes" (*Century*, 1910) is a more personalized story and may be related to Wharton's own hallucinations in her youth. A man is haunted by a pair of eyes that he sees whenever he undertakes an act which possibly harms others. He realizes that these are the eyes of the conscience of his elder self looking back at the indiscretions of youth. In "The Triumph of Night" (*Scribner's*, 1914) Faxon is plagued by guilt for failing to help his friend Rainer following a vision in which he realizes that Rainer's death is being planned by his greedy uncle Lavington. Both this story and "Kerfol" (*Scribner's*, 1916) are rather more gothic than Wharton's other fiction emphasizing the mood of alienation and despair that had struck her in war-torn Europe. "Kerfol" depicts a ruined French estate haunted by the spirits of dogs murdered by the previous owner in revenge for what he wrongly believed was his wife's adultery. This mood had passed by the time Wharton wrote "Miss Mary Pask" (*Pictorial Review*, 1925), where there is a more jubilant feeling in the narrator's meeting with an old friend whom he only belatedly realizes has died.

In her old age Wharton produced two of her best ghost stories. "Mr. Jones" (*Ladies Home Journal*, 1928) is her most Jamesian piece (Henry James, that is). It tells of a house which is dominated by the spirit of a former caretaker whose rule was so formidable that it continues to control the house and those living in it. "Pomegranate Seed" (*Saturday Evening Post*, 1931) tells of a man who continues to receive letters from his dead wife.

In all of these stories Wharton is able to use the supernatural to project aspects of the human psyche ranging from fear and guilt to joy and longing. The only times her work veered off the mark were when she tried to write stories of witchcraft or black magic, as in "Bewitched" (*Pictorial Review*, 1925) and "All Souls'" (first published in *Ghosts*), where the atmosphere is strong but the plot lacks conviction. Wharton was always at her best when dealing with the projection of human and spiritual emotions.

—Mike Ashley

WHEATLEY, Dennis (Yates)

Nationality: British. **Born:** London, 8 January 1897. **Education:** Dulwich College, London, 1908; H.M.S. Worcester, 1909-13; privately in Germany, 1913. **Family:** Married 1) Nancy Robinson in 1923 (divorced 1931), one son; 2) Joan Gwendoline Johnstone in 1931. **Military Service:** Served in the Royal Field Artillery, City of London Brigade, 1914-17; 36th Ulster Division, 1917-19 (invalided out); recommissioned in Royal Air Force Volunteer Reserve, 1939; member, National Recruiting Panel, 1940-41; member, Joint Planning Staff of War Cabinet, 1941-44; Wing Commander, 1944-45; U.S. Army Bronze Star. **Career:** Joined his father's wine business, Wheatley & Son, London, 1914; worked in the business, 1919-26; sole owner, 1926-31. Received Livery

of Vintners' Company, 1918, and Distillers' Company, 1922. Editor, Dennis Wheatley's Library of the Occult, Sphere Books, London, from 1973 (over 40 volumes). **Member:** Fellow, Royal Society of Arts, and Royal Society of Literature. **Died:** 11 November 1977.

HORROR, GHOST AND GOTHIC PUBLICATIONS

Novels (series: Molly Fountain; Duke de Richleau; Gregory Sallust)

The Devil Rides Out (Richleau). London, Hutchinson, 1934; New York, Bantam, 1967; abridged for younger readers by Alison Sage, London, Hutchinson, 1987.
Strange Conflict (Richleau). London, Hutchinson, 1941.
The Haunting of Toby Jugg. London, Hutchinson, 1948.
To the Devil—a Daughter (Fountain). London, Hutchinson, 1953; New York, Bantam, 1968.
The Black Magic Omnibus (includes *The Devil Rides Out*, *Strange Conflict*, *To the Devil—a Daughter*). London, Hutchinson, 1956.
The Ka of Gifford Hillary. London, Hutchinson, 1956.
The Satanist (Fountain). London, Hutchinson, 1960; New York, Bantam, 1967.
They Used Dark Forces (Sallust). London, Hutchinson, 1964.
Unholy Crusade. London, Hutchinson, 1967.
The White Witch of the South Seas (Sallust). London, Hutchinson, 1968.
Gateway to Hell (Richleau). London, Hutchinson, 1970; New York, Ballantine, 1973.
The Irish Witch. London, Hutchinson, 1973.
The Devil Rides Out, Gateway to Hell (omnibus). London, Chancellor Press, 1992.

Short Stories

Gunmen, Gallants, and Ghosts. London, Hutchinson, 1943; revised edition, London, Arrow, 1963.

Other

The Devil and All His Works. London, Hutchinson, and New York, American Heritage Press, 1971.

Editor, *A Century of Horror Stories*. London, Hutchinson, 1935; Freeport, New York, Books for Libraries, 1971; selection as *Quiver of Horror* and *Shafts of Fear*, London, Arrow, 2 vols., 1965; as *Tales of Strange Doings* and *Tales of Strange Happenings*, Hutchinson, 2 vols., 1968.
Editor, *Uncanny Tales*. London, Sphere, 2 vols., 1974.
Editor, with Stan Nicholls (uncredited), *The Dennis Wheatley Library of the Occult*. London, Sphere, 44 vols., 1974-76.

OTHER PUBLICATIONS

Novels

The Forbidden Territory. London, Hutchinson, and New York, Dutton, 1933.
Such Power Is Dangerous. London, Hutchinson, 1933.

Black August. London, Hutchinson, and New York, Dutton, 1934.

The Fabulous Valley. London, Hutchinson, 1934.

The Eunuch of Stamboul. London, Hutchinson, and Boston, Little Brown, 1935.

They Found Atlantis. London, Hutchinson, and Philadelphia, Lippincott, 1936.

Murder Off Miami, with J. G. Links. London, Hutchinson, 1936; New York, Rutledge Press, 1981; as *File on Bolitho Blane,* New York, Morrow, 1936.

Contraband. London, Hutchinson, 1936.

The Secret War. London, Hutchinson, 1937.

Who Killed Robert Prentice?, with J. G. Links. London, Hutchinson, 1937; as *File on Robert Prentice,* New York, Greenberg, 1937.

Uncharted Seas. London, Hutchinson, 1938.

The Malinsay Massacre, with J. G. Links. London, Hutchinson, 1938; New York, Rutledge Press, 1981.

The Golden Spaniard. London, Hutchinson, 1938.

The Quest of Julian Day. London, Hutchinson, 1939.

Herewith the Clues!, with J. G. Links. London, Hutchinson, 1939; New York, Mayflower, 1982.

Sixty Days to Live. London, Hutchinson, 1939.

The Scarlet Impostor. London, Hutchinson, 1940; New York, Macmillan, 1942.

Three Inquisitive People. London, Hutchinson, 1940; New York, Macmillan, 1942.

Faked Passports. London, Hutchinson, 1940; New York, Macmillan, 1943.

The Black Baroness. London, Hutchinson, 1940; New York, Macmillan, 1942.

The Sword of Fate. London, Hutchinson, 1941; New York, Macmillan, 1944.

"V" for Vengeance. London, Hutchinson, and New York, Macmillan, 1942.

The Man Who Missed the War. London, Hutchinson, 1945.

Codeword—Golden Fleece. London, Hutchinson, 1946.

Come into My Parlour. London, Hutchinson, 1946.

The Launching of Roger Brook. London, Hutchinson, 1947.

The Shadow of Tyburn Tree. London, Hutchinson, 1948; New York, Ballantine, 1973.

The Rising Storm. London, Hutchinson, 1949.

The Second Seal. London, Hutchinson, 1950.

The Man Who Killed the King. London, Hutchinson, 1951; New York, Putnam, 1965.

Star of Ill-Omen. London, Hutchinson, 1952.

Curtain of Fear. London, Hutchinson, 1953.

The Island Where Time Stands Still. London, Hutchinson, 1954.

The Dark Secret of Josephine. London, Hutchinson, 1955.

The Prisoner in the Mask. London, Hutchinson, 1957.

Traitors' Gate. London, Hutchinson, 1958.

The Rape of Venice. London, Hutchinson, 1959.

Vendetta in Spain. London, Hutchinson, 1961.

Mayhem in Greece. London, Hutchinson, 1962.

The Sultan's Daughter. London, Hutchinson, 1963.

Bill for the Use of a Body. London, Hutchinson, 1964.

Dangerous Inheritance. London, Hutchinson, 1965.

The Wanton Princess. London, Hutchinson, 1966.

Evil in a Mask. London, Hutchinson, 1969.

The Ravishing of Lady Mary Ware. London, Hutchinson, 1971.

The Strange Story of Linda Lee. London, Hutchinson, 1972.

Desperate Measures. London, Hutchinson, 1974.

Short Stories

Mediterranean Nights. London, Hutchinson, 1942; revised edition, London, Arrow, 1963.

Play

Screenplay: *An Englishman's Home (Madmen of Europe),* with others, 1939.

Other

Old Rowley: A Private Life of Charles II. London, Hutchinson, 1933; as *A Private Life of Charles II,* 1938.

Red Eagle: A Life of Marshal Voroshilov. London, Hutchinson, 1937.

Invasion (war game). London, Hutchinson, 1938.

Blockade (war game). London, Hutchinson, 1939.

Total War. London, Hutchinson, 1941.

The Seven Ages of Justerini's. London, Riddle Books, 1949; revised edition, as *1749-1965: The Eight Ages of Justerini's,* Aylesbury, Buckinghamshire, Dolphin, 1965.

Alibi (war game). London, Geographia, 1951.

Stranger Than Fiction. London, Hutchinson, 1959.

Saturdays with Bricks and Other Days Under Shell-Fire. London, Hutchinson, 1961.

The Time Has Come: The Memoirs of Dennis Wheatley. London, Arrow, 1981.

The Young Man Said 1897-1914. London, Hutchinson, 1977.

Officer and Temporary Gentleman 1914-1919. London, Hutchinson, 1978.

Drink and Ink 1919-1977, edited by Anthony Lejeune. London, Hutchinson, 1979.

The Deception Planners: My Secret War, edited by Anthony Lejeune. London, Hutchinson, 1980.

Editor, *A Century of Spy Stories.* London, Hutchinson, 1938.

*

Film Adaptations: *The Forbidden Territory,* 1934; *The Secret of Stamboul,* 1936, from the novel *The Eunuch of Stamboul; The Devil Rides Out (The Devil's Bride),* 1968; *The Lost Continent,* 1968, from the novel *Uncharted Seas; To the Devil—A Daughter (Child of Satan),* 1975.

*   *   *

The prolific Dennis Wheatley was a highly popular, best-selling author of rip-roaring adventure in various genres: historical romance, thrillers, tales of war and espionage, and his sometimes loosely linked "Black Magic" stories. There is a sense in which these occult yarns are not deeply felt supernatural fiction. Instead, they tend to plug supernatural devices into an adventure-thriller template. Nazi villains may be replaced or supplemented by evil adepts, and McGuffins like treasure or secret plans by such occult plot tokens as the Talisman of Set. But Wheatley's vigorous if uninventive narrative pattern of revelations, confrontations, pursuits, captures and escapes remains much the same.

Nevertheless the formula can be effective. Its advantages over more traditional ghost/horror fiction are the excitement of slam-bang action on two complementary levels, physical and occult;

and the fact that evil magicians of the Left-Hand Path are villains of human scale with human weaknesses, who may plausibly be defeated. Dr. Saturday in *Strange Conflict*, for example, must eventually sleep and become astrally vulnerable.

The sequence opens with the energetic *The Devil Rides Out*, in which the wise Duke de Richleau and his younger friends (established in the non-supernatural *The Forbidden Territory*) cross swords with forces of Satanism, led by the adept Mocata. Two striking scenes which transferred well to the movie version involve an open-air Sabbat where the massed power of darkness is broken by the brilliance of car headlight beams, and the lengthy siege of a defensive pentacle constructed by de Richleau—within which his party stands off various unpleasant manifestations, culminating with the Angel of Death. The ritual preparation of this "astral fortress" is described with a panache which foreshadows Ian Fleming's spy thrillers and their knowing use of brand names: the eclectic occult name-dropping runs from Ancient Egypt through Hebrew *gematria*, the karmic wheel, paganism, early Christianity, the Cabbala, astrology, folklore, and even a detectable steal from William Hope Hodgson's *Carnacki the Ghost-Finder*. After a final pursuit, Mocata gains the evilly all-potent Talisman of Set (the Egyptian god's mummified penis) and reduces his opponents to helplessness; the tables are turned by divine intervention.

In *Strange Conflict*, Wheatley added a heavily Spiritualist dimension to World War II, with a hostile adept spying from the astral plane on British convoy-route orders. De Richleau rather implausibly contrives to be enlisted as an astral counter-espionage agent—as his War Cabinet contact puts it, "in those slender hands of yours lies the Victory or Defeat of Britain." There follow lively etheric scenes as the Duke conducts night-time security checks on such possible suspects as an Admiral whose sleeping life includes much intangible copulation with dusky maidens. When the black-magician spy is traced to the Caribbean, de Richleau and cronies journey there physically to confront the local perils of voodoo, poison, zombification, and—incongruously—an evil summoning of Pan. But virtue triumphs: "As long as Britain stands the Powers of Darkness cannot prevail. On Earth the Anglo-Saxon race is the last Guardian of the Light, and [. . .] our island will prove the Bulwark of the World." The chief disappointment of *Strange Conflict* is that large chunks of occult exposition, including the detailed construction of a pentacle, are reproduced almost verbatim from *The Devil Rides Out*.

The Haunting of Toby Jugg is a more claustrophobic exercise in paranoid horror, with the crippled, bedridden title character tormented by "irrational" fears and visions. These are in fact diabolical in origin, conjured up by a sinister guardian doctor—in particular, a spider-demon whose shadow crawls and dances nightly at the hapless invalid's window. The aim is to break his mind and sequester his family fortune to support the international "Brotherhood" of communist Satanists, with Jugg either a brainwashed convert or consigned to the asylum. Although Wheatley's notions of political nightmare now seem badly dated (and not without embarrassing touches of anti-semitism), useful tension is wrung from our hero's immobile situation: struggling against overwhelming evil and the constant threat of madness, armed with only will-power and ingenuity. Unfortunately the author's own ingenuity fails towards the Black Mass finale, resorting to a multiple *deus ex machina* which includes the miraculous healing of Jugg's paralysed legs.

Wheatley returns to his more standard formula in *To The Devil—a Daughter*, though with new characters, led by the redoubtable mystery novelist Molly Fountain. The shadow of evil lies over a mysterious young woman who proves to be unwittingly consecrated to Satan. Each night, as darkness falls, she is possessed and transformed from a "nice girl" to an amoral and mildly promiscuous one . . . the Satanists, however, are keeping her virgin for a sacrifice (intended, for no clear reason, to complete the manufacture of a repellent homunculus) while the young male hero is incorruptible. An unpleasant expedition to a demon-infested crypt is characteristically saved from disaster when lightning strikes the evil altar: "God had intervened." Finally the ceremony of sacrifice is disrupted at the last minute of the eleventh hour and the chief Satanist killed by his own homunculus—while Molly Fountain irrepressibly disposes of the remaining evil congregation with a Mills bomb.

The Ka of Gifford Hillary rings the changes slightly as Sir Gifford Hillary is reduced to a spirit attempting to expose his own murderer. His faithless wife's lover has killed him with an experimental death ray (the background contains much voluminous exposition and advocacy of Cold War arms escalation). Eventually, after lurking helplessly and intangibly behind the scenes of the thriller plot, Hillary reanimates his own corpse and re-enters the story to find himself accused of murder.

The books continued. *The Satanist* revisits now-familiar formula material, as does *Gateway to Hell*. *They Used Dark Forces* makes minor use of occult tropes—astrology, numerology, thought-transference—in an over-long spy story featuring Wheatley's series character Gregory Sallust, sent into Hitler's Germany towards the end of World War II and aided by an adept. *The White Witch of the South Seas*, hardly even borderline-supernatural, is another Sallust caper which uses firewalking and voodoo curses as incidental local colour. *The Irish Witch* introduces the established historical-adventure series character Roger Brook to some mild supernatural elements.

Wheatley's narratives are too often burdened with expository lumps and arguments for his own political and military views. The charm of the Black Magic sequence was a spice of wickedness that particularly appealed to adolescents. Its once great popularity has waned with the widespread availability of stronger meat, more skilfully prepared, in the modern horror genre.

—David Langford

WHITEHEAD, Henry S(t. Clair)

Nationality: American. **Born:** Elizabeth, New Jersey, 5 March 1882. **Education:** Harvard University, graduated 1904; Berkeley Divinity School, Middletown, Connecticut. **Career:** Newspaper editor, Point Chester, New York; commissioner of the American Athletic Union; entered Episcopal Church, 1909; ordained a deacon, 1912; archdeacon to the Virgin Islands, 1921-29; contributor of short stories to *Weird Tales* and other magazines; rector in Dunedin, Florida, in his last years. **Died:** 23 November 1932.

HORROR, GHOST AND GOTHIC PUBLICATIONS

Short Stories

Jumbee and Other Uncanny Tales. Arkham House, Sauk City, Wisconsin, 1944.
West India Lights. Arkham House, Sauk City, Wisconsin, 1946.

OTHER PUBLICATIONS

Other

The Invitations of Our Lord. N.p., n.d.
Neighbours of the Early Church. N.p., n.d.
Good Manners in Church. N.p., n.d.

*   *   *

The stories of Henry S. Whitehead are regarded as highly as those of H. P. Lovecraft, Clark Ashton Smith, Robert E. Howard and other alumni of what Robert H. Barlow, in his introduction to Whitehead's collection *Jumbee and Other Uncanny Tales*, dubbed "the serious *Weird Tales* school." Yet Whitehead's renown as a weird fiction writer seems due as much to serendipity as to his storytelling skills. An Episcopal deacon who lived most of his life in the Northeastern United States, he took up fiction writing for his personal enjoyment in 1922. His first dozen stories were a mixed bag of supernatural and adventure fiction that appeared in a variety of publications including *Adventure*, *Black Mask* and *Weird Tales* (which he broke into in 1924). Competent but undistinguished, their themes range from fortune-telling ("Tea Leaves") to ghosts ("The Door"), weird diseases ("The Sea Change"), Asian funeral customs ("The Gladstone Bag") and frontier law ("The Cunning of the Serpent"), and their settings from the American South ("The Fireplace") to the Canadian wilderness ("The Thin Match"). All are relatively short, save for his 1923 novella "The Intarsia Box," a tale of piracy in the Caribbean whose blend of adventure and history portended greater things to come.

"Jumbee," published in the September 1926 issue of *Weird Tales*, marked a turning point in Whitehead's writing. A nearly plotless account of native superstitions in the West Indies, it was the first of Whitehead's supernatural tales drawn from his experiences as acting archdeacon in the Virgin Islands (a post he held throughout the 1920s). He followed it in the October issue with "The Projection of Armand Dubois," which introduces Gerald Canevin, a American writer of popular fiction clearly modelled on himself. Over the next six years Whitehead established the West Indies as the outpost of his imagination, setting nearly three dozen stories there, all nominally (if not explicitly) featuring Canevin as their narrator. In the annals of weird fiction, these stories are virtually unmatched for the vividness with which they convey the awe and mystery of their exotic locale.

Whitehead's West Indies are, as he writes in "West India Lights," "a land of the imagination." Although settled by the Dutch, French and English, and engaged in trade with most other developed nations, the islands have a native culture that has yet to assimilate completely with western civilization. "Among the West Indian black population," he remarks in "Black Tancrede," "occurs every belief, every imaginable practice of the occult, which is interwoven closely into their lives and thoughts." In Whitehead's view, the mystical beliefs of the West Indian native are not a sign of primitivism, but the signature of a culture shaped by a reality inscrutable to the western mind. White settlers who refuse to tolerate this cultural difference are not long for the islands. Even the Christian clergy adapt to the environment, and learn from their island experiences to revere God (as a priest acknowledges in "Black Terror") as "Creator *of all things* visible and invisible!" (emphasis Whitehead's).

Only a handful of Whitehead's West Indian tales are genuinely horrifying. The majority read like travel anecdotes in which the supernatural is inextricably bound up with local colour and historical fact. As Barlow notes, "Whitehead wrote as a realist; a reporter." His stories have a casual as-told-to-me style that made them as welcome in adventure magazines as in the weird fiction pulps. However, the most obvious influences on his writing were modern masters of the weird tale. Edward Lucas White's "Lukundoo" and "Amina" were obvious inspirations for, respectively, "The Lips" and "The Chadbourne Episode." Whitehead explicitly mentions William Hope Hodgson in "The Shut Room," and he secured Lovecraft's assistance to revise "The Trap" after it was rejected by *Weird Tales*. He tempered the lessons of these and other mentors with a gentle sense of humour that gives his tales an uncommon buoyancy and charm.

Whitehead's West Indies tales can be divided nearly equally into two categories. Some are built around basic supernatural themes that might have been developed in any setting. "The Shadows," for example, is set in a haunted room which plays out nightly the ordeal of a deceased former occupant. "Cassius" tells of an undeveloped siamese twin who becomes animated after he is surgically removed from his fully developed host. "Mrs. Lorriquer" is an amusing fantasy of supernatural possession in which a woman is taken over by the spirit of a card cheat every time she sits down to a game of bridge. "Seven Turns in a Hangman's Rope," a pirate adventure leavened with elements of voodoo, actually passed through two early published drafts—the non-supernatural "The Intarsia Box" and the mildly supernatural "West India Lights"—before becoming one of Whitehead's weird masterpieces. Whitehead seems to have been aware that the West Indian setting wasn't integral to all his tales, for he sent Canevin to England in "The Napier Limousine" and "The Shut Room," and to rural Connecticut in "The Trap" and "The Chadbourne Episode."

His most powerful stories, however, are those steeped in the lore and legends of the islands. In "The Tree-Man," he spins a peculiar superstition of an agrarian native tribe into an eerie parable of intolerance and its consequences. "The Passing of a God" is a challenging rumination on the varieties of religious experience in which a cancerous growth proves to be the earthly incarnation of a native deity. Whitehead tackled a wide array of themes in these stories, but none engaged his imagination so fully as miscegenation. In "The Black Beast" and "Sweet Grass," sexual intimacy between whites and blacks opens the door to a host of supernatural reprisals. This idea gets pushed to the extreme in "Williamson," a sympathetic portrait of a man whose mixed animal and human heritage arouses instinctive loathing in everyone he meets.

"The Great Circle," one of the last stories published in his lifetime, suggests that Whitehead was growing anxious to explore realms beyond the West Indies. A lost-race tale with sword-and-sorcery elements, it revealed an enduring interest in a story type he had attempted as far back as 1929 in "The People of Pan," a saga of the survivors of Atlantis. Atlantis was also the theme of "Bothon" and "Scar Tissue," both published posthumously. Had Whitehead lived longer, he might have made a name for himself as a writer of heroic fantasy. Fortunately for the weird fiction field, he lived long enough to make an indelible mark through his tales of magic and mystery in the West Indies.

—Stefan Dziemianowicz

WHITTEN, Leslie H(unter)

Nationality: American. **Born:** Jacksonville, Florida, 21 February 1928. **Education:** Lehigh University, B.A. 1950. **Family:** Married Phyllis Webber in 1951; three sons. **Career:** Journalist; news editor, Radio Free Europe, 1952-57; newsman, United Press International, 1958; reporter, *Washington Post*, 1958-62; reporter, Hearst Newspapers, 1962-69; chief associate, Jack Anderson column, from 1969. **Agent:** Curtis Brown Ltd., 10 Astor Place, New York, NY 10003, USA.

HORROR, GHOST AND GOTHIC PUBLICATIONS

Novels

Progeny of the Adder. New York, Doubleday, 1965; London, Hodder and Stoughton, 1966.
Moon of the Wolf. New York, Doubleday, 1967; as *Death of a Nurse*, London, Hale, 1969.
The Alchemist. New York, Charter House, 1973.
Moon of the Wolf/Progeny of the Adder (omnibus). New York, Leisure, 1992.
The Fangs of Morning/The Alchemist (omnibus; "The Fangs of the Morning" original to the volume). New York, Leisure, 1994.

OTHER PUBLICATIONS

Novels

A Killing Pace. New York, Atheneum, 1983; London, Severn House, 1985.
A Day without Sunshine. New York, Atheneum, 1985; London, Severn House, 1986.

* * *

Vampire novels have grown increasingly popular since the late 1980s, but the form has undergone a considerable number of changes during that period. Currently we have vampire detectives, suave vampire lovers, humorous vampires, literate vampires, vampires with *angst*, vampire teens, vampire gangs feuding with one another, even vampire romance novels. The old-fashioned, vile, walking-dead bloodsucker has gone out of style, and readers who long for the days when there was no question about the vampire's nature are forced to look in used bookstores for stories of the nosferatu. One such story, one of the best, is *Progeny of the Adder*, Leslie Whitten's first horror novel.

Harry Picard is a police officer assigned to the case of two women found floating dead in the Potomac River. All three experienced traumatic throat wounds and each body is notably emaciated, as though the victims were starved for a period prior to their death. He discovers that one of the women was lured from her normal lifestyle by a mysterious figure, that she seemed distracted and troubled by contradictory feelings, and was never seen again after the man appeared. Picard suspects, but cannot prove, that there is a link between the two murders. The discovery of a third victim, confirming this time that the blood was artificially drained from their bodies, convinces him, though not his superiors. And there are other complications as well, because one of the dead women is the daughter of a prominent foreign diplomat.

Picard manages to trace the mystery man's car and learns that it was purchased under peculiar circumstances by a foreigner named Sebastian Paulier. But Paulier's present location is unknown, and a check of his background reveals a long and convoluted trail stretching across the world. Eventually a lead pans out and they learn the address of some property rented by Paulier, but they find a deserted house, with no trace of the man or his victims. They grow even more puzzled by Paulier's living arrangements, which seem to include neither food nor fresh clothing. Lying in wait, they surprise Paulier when he returns to reclaim his coffin, but they are surprised in turn when he overcomes several attackers, shrugging off multiple bullet wounds in the process.

Picard is still reluctant to accept the fact that he is dealing with a genuine vampire, and his superiors won't even consider the possibility. But there is mounting evidence that this is the case, and if true, conventional police methods will not suffice. When Paulier attacks the woman Picard loves, the situation becomes even more personal, and the detective ultimately makes the decision to act outside normal police channels in order to destroy the vampire. Whitten's blend of police-procedural with supernatural horror was groundbreaking at the time, though now commonplace. But the relentless pursuit of Paulier and the gripping confrontations still hold a power that most subsequent vampire novels lack.

Whitten turned to the werewolf legend for his second novel, *Moon of the Wolf*, and once again his treatment is anything but conventional. Ellie Burrifous is a bright young woman whose mysterious death upsets the quiet style of life usually practised in the small town of Stanley, Mississippi. Her body is found in a field, literally torn apart, but it's unclear whether the tragedy came by human hand or during an attack by wolves. There is additional tension when it is revealed that Ellie was pregnant, and racial prejudice stirs after rumours that a black man might have been involved. Whitten does a superb job creating his small-town setting, and his fairly large cast of characters are quickly established as distinct individuals.

Ellie's brother is one of the suspects, but he is clearly terrified following an odd encounter with his father, who mentions the loup-garou, the werewolf. At the same time, a party of hunters sets out to destroy any wild dogs or wolves that might have strayed into the area, but the protagonist believes from the outset that there's a human agency involved. The plot thickens when the brother is killed in a manner similar to that of his sister, even though he is in custody at the time. That eliminates the possibility that a wild animal is responsible, but it is hard to believe that a man could commit such brutal crimes. The atmosphere of violence in Stanley grows worse before the guilty party is identified, a man whose transformation to wolfish nature appears to be entirely psychological, though no less deadly to his victims. Just before his death, he admits that he blacks out during the attacks, and regrets what he has done, but he is still incapable of controlling the violent urges that take possession of his mind and body. Whitten's message is clear; the demons that live within ordinary humans can be just as terrifying, and deadly, as the supernatural, and in fact many of the ordinary citizens of Stanley are transformed into monsters of a sort as hatred and fear take control of their lives. A taut, thoughtful suspense story that avoids the clichés of most werewolf fiction.

Whitten's third novel, *The Alchemist*, is only peripherally horror. It's primarily the story of a corrupt lawyer who gets involved in various sexual escapades as well as financial manoeuvring, but he also practices black magic. None of the magic really works, but some of the sequences are creepy enough to make this of minor interest to horror readers. Unfortunately, Whitten never returned to the genre, a great loss considering the powerful impact of his first two novels.

—Don D'Ammassa

WILLIAMS, Mary

Pseudonym: Marianne Harvey. **Nationality:** British. **Born:** 1925(?). **Family:** Married Mr. Williams. **Career:** Columnist, *St. Ives Times*; wrote children's programmes for BBC Wales for six years; prolific short-story writer and romantic novelist; has also written a number of mainstream novels under the pseudonym Marianne Harvey. Has lived in Cornwall since 1947. **Address:** c/o Piatkus Books, 5 Windmill St., London W1P 1HF, England.

HORROR, GHOST AND GOTHIC PUBLICATIONS

Short Stories

The Dark Land. London, Kimber, 1975.
Chill Company. London, Kimber, 1976.
Where Phantoms Stir. London, Kimber, 1976.
They Walk at Twilight. London, Kimber, 1977.
Unseen Footsteps. London, Kimber, 1977.
Where No Birds Sing. London, Kimber, 1977.
The Haunted Valley. London, Kimber 1978.
Ghostly Carnival. London, Kimber, 1980.
The Dark God. London, Kimber, 1980.
The Haunted Garden. London, Kimber, 1986.
Haunted Waters. London, Kimber, 1987.
Whisper in the Night. London, Kimber, 1988(?).
Ravenscarne and Other Ghost Stories. London, Piatkus, 1991.
Creeping Fingers. London, Hale, 1992.

OTHER PUBLICATIONS

Novels

Carnecrane. London, Kimber, 1979.
Trenhawk. London, Kimber, 1980.
Heronsmere. London, Kimber, 1980.
Return to Carnecrane. London, Kimber, 1981.
Louise. London, Kimber, 1981.
The Granite King. London, Kimber, 1982.
The Tregallis Inheritance. London, Kimber, 1982.
The Stuart Affair. London, Kimber, 1983.
Forest Heritage. London, Kimber, 1983.
Castle Carnack. London, Kimber, 1983.
Merlake Towers. London, Kimber, 1984.
Mistress of Blackstone. London, Kimber, 1984.
Tarnefell. London, Kimber, 1985.
Folly's End. London, Kimber, 1985.
Portrait of a Girl. London, Kimber, 1986.

Destiny's Daughter. London, Kimber, 1987.
Stormy Heritage. London, Kimber, 1987.
Dark Flame. London, Kimber, 1988.
The Secret Tower. London, Kimber, 1988.
Tangled Roots. London, Piatkus, 1990.
Duke's Gold. London, Piatkus, 1992.

*   *   *

There is a long tradition of ghost stories set in Cornwall. The most south-westerly English county, it is relatively mild, dry and rocky, with a small permanent population and surrounded on three sides by the sea. It is covered with prehistoric burial mounds and has dozens of small rocky coves, many of which have been used by smugglers. Sir Arthur Quiller-Couch and Daphne du Maurier have employed it as a wonderfully supernatural setting for fiction, and Denys Val Baker has put together a couple of anthologies of Cornish ghost stories.

Mary Williams is one of the most prolific of all ghost-story writers, and the vast majority of her 150 or so tales are set in Cornwall. She fictionalizes her place names, but tends to make great use of the area between Penzance and Land's End. Her fiction is studded with appropriately atmospheric names like Tyzarne, Zillack, Penderrick and Penjust. A long-time resident of Cornwall, and still probably regarded as a "furriner," she writes about the locals who were born there (using their unique dialect in dialogue) and about the incomers, mainly those of an artistic nature, or people retiring there. Her stories are all supernatural, involving ghostly personages or feelings; there is almost no horror content. Mostly her work is undistinguished and unoriginal.

While all her ghost books are collections, some of the stories are almost of novel-length. "The Dark God" is an example of this, describing a group of incomers who live in and around the village of Magswikk in western Cornwall. They are youngish and they are all influenced by Manfred Hearne, a powerful man who admits to pagan beliefs and who organizes parties for Beltane (May 1st) and Samain (November 1st). He plays haunting tunes on the piano, owns an intimidatingly large black cat, and has amorous desires for some of the women in the group. It is never made clear whether Hearne has any supernatural powers or whether his attitude merely attracts spirits to the area. Certainly, several of the group experience something frightening: blackness in the air and inexplicable movements. And there is a local legend concerning three 17th-century witches hanged in the area. The main characters are a strange trio, Adam and Lucinda who are a young married couple, and her half-sister Aleyne who had been engaged to Adam, a situation which leads to much emotional strain. Hearne persuades both Lucinda and another of the group, Yvonne, to have sex with him, and he fails to persuade Aleyne. Lucinda and Yvonne die at the Samain party, presumably drained of their life-force by evil spirits, and Hearne goes mad. There are strong suggestions that Hearne's servant, who seemed to be a teenage gypsy boy, may have been the supernatural controller of events. After this, Adam and Aleyne still have to take action against evil relics in the village's former rectory. This is a short novel overcrowded with ingredients and characters.

More characteristic are stories like "Poppies in December" or "Anna" or "Poor Kate," in which the narrator sees a person they have not seen for years, but looking just the same as before—a clear sign of a ghost. Always the person wants something, either to show the narrator their grave, as in "Poor Kate," or to take over the narrator's unexciting wife just occasionally, investing her with sexiness, as in "Anna."

Other themes recur, too, such as somebody staying in Cornwall for a few weeks to recuperate from an illness. In Wayne Cartwright's case, in "The Other Side," he forces his weakened body to climb to the top of the adjacent moors because he has an obsession to see what is on the other side. His landlady and his fiancée try to dissuade him, but he perseveres and, instead of seeing the poor scrubland falling away towards the village of Skarle, he sees the figure of Death waiting for him. And in the case of Nigel in "The Road," who normally lives in London with his wife Theodora, he is recovering from depression and doing a little oil-painting, but he is seduced by a ghostly view of an idyllic scene; he vanishes into another reality.

There is humour in some of the pieces. In "Unseen Footsteps," for example, the elderly narrator keeps on finding that her comfortable slippers have moved to another part of her flat. She investigates and discovers that the cause is a ghostly pair of legs which want to be reunited with their owner, who has just died. And "Nemesis" concerns the wives of a multiple bigamist, one of whom pursues her supposed husband from beyond the grave, causing him to have a fatal heart attack.

Williams integrates Cornish legends into a few of her stories. "Pookan," set partly in a cove of that name, is about a seal-woman who lures people to their deaths on a cliff. In "The Dark Thing" Jenny Crane knows that her husband is having an affair, and she offers herself to a "gigantic dark man in his stone hut, standing and watching under the grim summit of Men-an-Hawk," a local tor. She is found dead the next day, crushed by fallen rocks. "Green Man" features a town carnival led by a pagan Green Man, except that the usual man who takes the part is ill and somebody else has dressed in the costume and carried out a sacrifice by the standing stone above the town.

One of Williams's best stories is "They Walk at Twilight." Here, again, the protagonist (and narrator) is recovering from a serious illness and her parents have chosen to move to the Cornish moors for her health. She, Jessica, is only 17. But she keeps on glimpsing ghosts on the empty upper floor of the large house they have taken. Gradually she discovers that these are all youngish people, even if they are ghosts. They are a lot more fun to live with than her elderly parents, and she goes to join them. Now it is her parents who seem to be ghosts, occasionally to be glimpsed, calling for her. Another exceptional tale is "The Pit," in which a retired librarian, Miss Twilley, moves down to Cornwall to buy a mansion in the hopes of running it as a guest house for summer visitors. When she tries to tidy up the gazebo and rockery she encounters ghosts. But she persists and they kill her, with the help of Adam, the gardener, who seems to be in the control of his previous (now deceased) employer.

These are generally fairly cosy and undemanding stories, full of supernatural entities but never shocking or even very surprising.

—Chris Morgan

WILLIAMSON, Chet

Nationality: American. **Born:** Chester Carlton Williamson, in Lancaster, Pennsylvania, 1948. **Family:** Married; one son. **Career:** Teacher of English; writer of short stories for magazines and anthologies since 1981. Lives in Elizabethtown, Pennsylvania.

HORROR, GHOST AND GOTHIC PUBLICATIONS

Novels

Soulstorm. New York, Tor, 1986; London, Headline, 1987.
Ash Wednesday. New York, Tor, 1987; London, Headline, 1988.
Lowland Rider. New York, Tor, and London, Headline, 1988.
Dreamthorp. Arlington Heights, Illinois, Dark Harvest, 1989.
Reign. Arlington Heights, Illinois, Dark Harvest, 1990.
Second Chance. Baltimore, Maryland, CD Publications, 1994.
Atmosfear. Rocklin, California, Prima, 1995.
The Crow: City of Angels (novelization of screenplay). New York, Boulevard, and London, Boxtree, 1996.

Short Stories

The House of Fear: A Study in Comparative Religions. Round Top, New York, Footsteps Press, 1989.

OTHER PUBLICATIONS

Novels

McKain's Dilemma. New York, Doherty, 1988.
Ravenloft: Mordenheim. Lake Geneva, Wisconsin, TSR, 1994.
Hell: A Cyberpunk Thriller. Rocklin, California, Prima, 1995.
Forgotten Realms: Murder in Cormyr. Lake Geneva, Wisconsin, TSR, 1996.

*   *   *

In Chet Williamson's novel *Soulstorm* a man contrives an ingenious ploy to deceive a supernatural entity that has taken possession of him: he obsesses so intently upon the evil thoughts that first made him vulnerable to the entity that he is able to overwhelm it and turn its power against it. It is a significant moment that crystallizes the concerns of much of Williamson's writing. Like many of his contemporaries, Williamson uses the horror story as a vehicle for exploring the nature of Evil. But though monsters of supernatural evil abound in his stories, ultimately they only mirror an aspect of the struggle between good and evil taking place within his human characters.

Williamson's characters are not monsters themselves. Most are caring family people and conscientious members of the small communities (usually in suburban Pennsylvania) where they live and work. Some have known personal tragedy, but rarely of a magnitude that sets them apart from their neighbours. A great strength of Williamson's fiction is his sympathetic portrayal of ordinary people whose hopes and fears exist in an equilibrium that allows them to live at peace with themselves and others. Once that equilibrium is upset, however, they find themselves wrestling with moral dilemmas, and confronting hitherto unacknowledged evil tendencies. In his short story "A Scent of the Soul" a doctor turns murderer upon discovering the extraordinary sensory rush a patient's death provides. In "Confessions of St. James" a priest is tempted to literal consumption of the body and blood symbolized by the Eucharist. In "Dr. Joe" a kindly physician involved in an insurance scam rationalizes the under-diagnosis of disease in terminally ill patients whose insurance benefits pay for the upkeep of his practice.

In his novel-length fiction, Williamson uses the supernatural to externalize these deeply personal conflicts. His first novel, *Soulstorm*, lays the moral foundations for nearly all of his fiction. A variant on the haunted-house theme, it concerns three individuals—a disgraced businessman, an officer fired from the police force for his brutality, and a soldier of fortune—lured to the Pines, a house with a history of lethal hauntings. With a nod to Shirley Jackson's *The Haunting of Hill House* and Richard Matheson's *Hell House*, Williamson endows the Pines with a malevolent personality that plays upon the weaknesses of those trapped inside it. But his house is more than Jackson and Matheson's repositories of psychic residues left by former inhabitants: built on a "psychic lodestone" that has drawn evil to it since time immemorial, it dominates its victims by manipulating their own potential for evil. "Every man has evil within, but often the good overbalances it," notes the spiritual entity infesting the house. "It is different here." The entity is particularly cruel to George McNeely, a mercenary who has undergone a change of heart about his work since discovering his soulmate in the wife of the house's owner. When it informs McNeely, who is homosexual, that it has given him the ability to make love to the woman but will withdraw it if he does not do its bidding, the man asks the question that many of Williamson's protagonists find themselves pondering: "How could anything that brings me so much good be truly evil?"

Although thoroughly grounded in the secular, Williamson's explorations of Good and Evil are rich with theological implications. The quasi-religious character of some of his horror fiction gives it a weight and substance that distinguishes it from most genre fare. *Ash Wednesday* and *Lowland Rider* are structured like theodicies, in which characters search for a rationale that will make sense of the good and bad in their lives and the world. In *Ash Wednesday*, the town of Merrivale awakens one day to find the ghosts of all who have died there materialized as transparent blue spectres frozen in their death agonies. For some of the townspeople, the phenomenon provides an epiphany that leads to soul-searching and self-improvement. The majority, however, respond with behaviour that only highlights their pettiness and mean-spiritedness. The novel is less a horror story than a tale of despair at the human condition, summed up by the local pastor: "I thought, when this all started, I thought that we'd learn more, we were lucky, we were chosen, that by, by staring death in the face so openly, we'd learn to live better. Knowing, you see, knowing that death's waiting would make us value living so much more that we'd be better, be kinder to each other. But we weren't."

Lowland Rider echoes another quasi-religious text, Dante's *Inferno*, in its metaphoric rendering of a man's descent into a spiritual hell. Its protagonist, Jesse Gordon falls victim to a gang of thugs who murder his wife and child. When he kills a gang member who has returned to save him from the certain death they have left him to, he realizes that "now he was no better than those who had hurt him . . . . The killing had dehumanized him, and he felt filthy, as though he would never be clean again, regardless of whether or not the blood would come off his hands. He felt soulless. He felt dead." The random violence of the whole experience horrifies him with its suggestion of "an unstructured universe" in which "there's no reason for anything." Seeking penance, and a purpose for his tragedy, Jesse retreats to the crime-ridden subways, where he befriends the homeless (depicted as fellow lost souls) and fights a corrupt transit cop who preys upon them. His exploits eventually bring him face to face with Enoch, the god of this particular underworld, who demands of its denizens horrifying crimes not unlike those that destroyed Jesse's family. In a surprising twist, Williamson reveals Enoch to be not the Satanic emissary he seems, but a servant of God, whose job it is to "feed the evil so the good can survive . . . if it was not fed, not satisfied, held at bay, it would overcome the world."

The bleakness of these stories notwithstanding, Williamson is an optimist. His characters are capable of achieving the self-awareness necessary to save their souls as well as others. In *Dreamthorp*, the honesty of the hero and heroine toward one another proves a catalyst for exorcising the demonic spirit that permeates their town. In *Reign*, actor Dennis Hamilton realizes that his denial of his baser impulses has split them off and given them independent life as a bloodthirsty doppelganger. Only by confronting and mastering them—in a fight that puts him at risk of life and limb—is he able to put an end to the murders that are decimating his theatrical troupe. The extreme sacrifices Williamson's characters make to do right by themselves and others is typified by Woody, the hero of *Second Chance*. By means of fantasy-fuelled wish-fulfilment, Woody is able to prevent the explosion that took the life of the lover he still pines for during his student protest days a quarter-century before. When it turns out that her survival also means the survival of a mutual friend whose eco-terrorist activities threaten the entire world, Woody recants his wish—recapitulating, through his denial of personal fulfilment for the greater good of humanity, the very spirit that defined his generation's selfless idealism. Ultimately, there is no horror in Williamson's fiction that cannot be understood in such fundamentally human terms, and at the heart of his horrors, there lies—a heart.

—Stefan Dziemianowicz

WILLIAMSON, J(erry) N(eal)

Pseudonym: Julian Shock. **Nationality:** American. **Born:** Gerald Neal Williamson, 1932. **Family:** Married in 1960; two children and four stepchildren. **Career:** Numerous jobs, including singing with his parents' professional dance-band from the age of 16; short-story writer since the early 1960s; novelist since 1979. **Awards:** Balrog award for anthology, 1985. Lives in Indianapolis.

HORROR, GHOST AND GOTHIC PUBLICATIONS

Novels (series: Martin Ruben; Lamia Zacharius)

The Ritual (Ruben). New York, Leisure, 1979.
The Houngan. New York, Leisure, 1980; as *Profits*, Leisure, 1984.
Queen of Hell. New York, Leisure, 1981.
Premonition (Ruben). New York, Leisure, 1981.
The Tulpa. New York, Leisure, 1981.
Horror House. Chicago, Playboy, 1981.
Ghost Mansion. New York, Zebra, 1981.
Death-Angel (Zacharius). New York, Zebra, 1981.
The Banished. Chicago, Playboy, 1981.
Death-Coach (Zacharius). New York, Zebra, 1981.
Extraterrestrial (as Julian Shock). New York, Zebra, 1982.
The Evil One. New York, Zebra, 1982.
Horror Mansion. New York, Zebra, 1982.
Death-School (Zacharius). New York, Zebra, 1982.

Death-Doctor (Zacharius). New York, Zebra, 1982.
Playmates. New York, Leisure, 1982.
Brotherkind (Ruben). New York, Leisure, 1982.
The Dentist. New York, Dell, 1983.
Ghost. New York, Leisure, 1984.
The Offspring. New York, Leisure, 1984.
Babel's Children. New York, Dell, 1984.
The Longest Night. New York, Leisure, 1985.
Wards of Armageddon, with John Maclay. New York, Leisure, 1986.
Evil Offspring. New York, Leisure, 1987.
Noonspell. New York, Leisure, 1987.
Dead to the World. New York, Leisure, 1988.
The Black School. New York, Dell, 1989.
Shadows of Death. New York, Dell, 1989.
Hell Storm. New York, Dell, Dell, 1991.
The Night Seasons. New York, Zebra, 1991.
The Monastery. New York, Zebra, 1992.
Don't Take Away the Light. New York, Zebra, 1993.
Bloodlines. New York(?), Longmeadow, 1994.
The Book of Webster's. New York(?), Longmeadow, 1995.

Short Stories

The Naked Flesh of Feeling. Eugene, Oregon, Pulphouse, 1991.
The Fifth Season. Seattle, Washington, Detours, 1994.

Other

Editor, *Masques: All-New Works of Horror and the Supernatural*. Baltimore, Maryland, Maclay, 1984; London, Futura, 1989.
Editor, *Masques II: All-New Stories of Horror and the Supernatural*. Baltimore, Maryland, Maclay, 1987; London, Orbit, 1989.
Editor, *The Best of Masques*. New York, Berkley, 1988.
Editor, *Masques III: All-New Works of Horror and the Supernatural*. New York, St. Martin's Press, 1989; as *Flesh Creepers*, London, Robinson, 1990.
Editor, *Masques IV: All-New Works of Horror & the Supernatural*. Baltimore, Maryland, Maclay, 1991.

OTHER PUBLICATIONS

Other

The New Devil's Dictionary: Creepy Clichés and Sinister Synonyms. Buffalo, New York, Ganley, 1985.

Editor, *How to Write Tales of Horror, Fantasy & Science Fiction*. Cincinnati, Ohio, Writer's Digest, 1987; London, Robinson, 1991.

*   *   *

J. N. Williamson flooded the paperback horror market in the early 1980s, producing over 20 novels in five years. Although several of these seemed hastily done and unpolished, others were quite ably written and his continuing popularity indicates that most were well received by readers. Most of Williamson's novels were variations of familiar horror themes, ghosts, vampires, voodoo and the like, but he also wrote about aliens from other worlds and other less frequently used devices.

His greatest success was with the haunted-house story. *Ghost Mansion* and its sequel, *Horror Mansion*, are both set in Minnifield Place, a classic haunted house. The estate has been long abandoned when the new tenants move in, to be greeted by the usual assortment of strange visions and inexplicable noises. Another unsuspecting family runs into trouble in the sequel. There's not much mystery in this type of novel, which has become a cliché in terms of plot, but Williamson provides a steady parade of sufficiently weird events to maintain the suspense. A somewhat similar novel, *Horror House*, uses some of the same devices, but provides a new twist. The building in this case was the site of experiments by Thomas Edison to communicate with the dead, and although he believed himself to have failed, he wakened an angry presence that still prowls those halls. The protagonist of *Ghost* is recently dead, but refuses to accept the new state of affairs until two mortals help him make the transition.

Williamson's later ghost stories are considerably more sophisticated. In *Dead to the World* we learn that ghosts are all around us, frequently visible though we don't recognize them for what they actually are. When the protagonist discovers the truth, he attracts the unwelcome attention of those who have lingered in our world after their time has passed. A young woman moves into a new home on what is supposed to be a temporary basis, and discovers that her predecessors have been experimenting with a weak spot in the veil that separates the living from the dead. And there is a unique aspect of her personality that makes her the key with which the door might be completely opened. The ghosts of murdered prostitutes refuse to accept that they are dead in *The Longest Night*, and are instrumental in bringing their killer to justice. The best of Williamson's ghost stories, and the most subtle, is *Don't Take Away the Light*. A child with an abusive mother finds friends in a most unlikely place, the world of the dead.

Williamson explored the vampire legend with a four-volume series that opened with *Death-Coach*. Lamia Zacharius is an ageless, satisfyingly evil vampire who dominates the remote town of Thessaly, eventually destroying it. Unlike the sympathetic, reluctant, or doubting vampires of much modern horror fiction, Williamson's creation is foul, nasty, and ruthless. Surviving the first round of attempts on her continued existence, she returns to foil another group of enemies in *Death-Angel*, poses as a school teacher in *Death-School*, and then as a physician in *Death-Doctor*. The final novel in the series was the best, involving an attempt to create a vampire child sexually rather than through the usual process, and although it was the last in the series, Williamson left his villaness's future as uncertain as in the others. More than a decade later, Williamson would pick up the vampire theme in one of his very best novels, *Bloodlines*. The daughter of a man who became a vampire tries to track down her missing brother, convinced that the disorder is hereditary and that he will become a bloodsucker eventually if he does not seek help.

Another of the author's recurring themes is satanism and secret societies. His first published novel, *The Ritual*, concerned the efforts of a parapsychologist to investigate what appears to be a genuine demonic possession. The novel introduced Martin Ruben, who would briefly be a recurring character in Williamson's work. In *The Houngan* an advertising writer takes a job with a new agency, only to discover that there is a clannishness about his fellow workers that is very disconcerting. It turns out they are in the thrall of a voodoo witch-doctor. Similarly, Martin Ruben's visit to a health resort in *Premonition* becomes a source of danger when he discovers that the residents have obtained a sort of quasi-immortality by selling their souls to an evil force. All three of these novels are competent and readable, but so routine that there is little real suspense in any of them.

That was not the case with three later novels that used similar devices. A mystical book of great power is discovered in *Hell Storm*, and its owner seeks allies to prevent it from falling into the hands of Satan himself. *The Black School* is a secret cult that kidnaps the protagonist's daughter, and his subsequent attempts to rescue her are complicated by the fact that this group has actually opened a doorway to hell. One of Williamson's best novels is *The Monastery*, in which a family takes shelter at a secluded monastery during a storm. The inhabitants seem friendly, although they have a disturbingly casual attitude toward sexual matters, but their new guests become suspicious when they discover their hosts are the remnants of a bizarre cult that was chased out of Europe.

Williamson's occasional attempts to blend science fiction and horror were not particularly successful. Children are kidnapped by a ball of light in *The Banished*, and Men in Black persecute one of Martin Ruben's clients in *Brotherkind*. *Extraterrestrial* is a very disappointing alien-invasion story. Although Williamson is not one of the many horror writers who concentrated on children-in-jeopardy variations, he does use the theme occasionally. The best of these is *Playmates*, in which a child's imaginary playmates come to life. Twins use mental powers to kill their enemies in *Babel's Children*, there's a plot to kill children in their wombs in *Wards of Armageddon*, and another child is possessed by a demonic creature in *The Offspring*.

Of his remaining work, the most interesting novel is *The Night Seasons*, in which an innocent man is caught up in a series of horrible murders. There's a nicely devised curse in *Noonspell*, and one of the author's more interesting protagonists. A discorporate creature from a prehistoric civilization wakens in *Evil Offspring* and we see what happens when an insane woman possesses psychic powers in *The Evil One*. Of less interest are *The Dentist*, where pain can be traded for occult satisfactions, *The Tulpa*, in which a man discovers that he has become the vessel for an evil force, and *Queen of Hell*, featuring a young woman who discovers she is a reincarnation of the witch Hecate.

Williamson has also written many short stories, some of the best of which are "Hildekin and the Big Diehl," "The Land of Second Chance," "The Girl of My Dreams" and "The Gap Nearly Closed Today." Although several of his early novels were comparatively pedestrian, his later work shows a noticeable increase in maturity and skill, and the development of a lighter hand that is, for the most part, far more effective.

—Don D'Ammassa

WILSON, Colin (Henry)

Nationality: British. **Born:** Leicester, 26 June 1931. **Education:** Gateway Secondary Technical School, Leicester, 1942-47. **Military Service:** Served in the Royal Air Force, 1949-50. **Family:** Married 1) Dorothy Betty Troop in 1951 (divorced 1952), one son; 2) Pamela Joy Stewart in 1960, two sons and one daughter. **Career:** Laboratory assistant, Gateway School, 1948-49; tax collector, Leicester and Rugby, 1949-50; labourer and hospital porter in London, 1951-53; salesman for the magazines *Paris Review* and *Merlin,* Paris, 1953. Since 1954 full-time writer. British Council lecturer in Germany, 1957; writer-in-residence, Hollins College, Virginia, 1966-67; visiting professor, University of Washington, Seattle, 1968; professor, Institute of the Mediterranean (Dowling College, New York), Majorca, 1969; visiting professor, Rutgers University, New Brunswick, New Jersey, 1974. **Agent:** David Bolt Associates, 12 Heath Drive, Ripley, Surrey GU23 7EP. **Address:** Tetherdown, Trewallock Lane, Gorran Haven, Cornwall PL26 6NT, England.

Horror, Ghost and Gothic Publications

Novels (series: Gerard Sorme)

Ritual in the Dark (Sorme). London, Gollancz, and Boston, Houghton Mifflin, 1960.
Man without a Shadow: The Diary of an Existentialist (Sorme). London, Barker, 1963; as *The Sex Diary of Gerard Sorme,* New York, Dial Press, 1963.
The Mind Parasites. London, Barker, and Sauk City, Wisconsin, Arkham House, 1967.
The God of the Labyrinth (Sorme). London, Hart Davis, 1970; as *The Hedonists,* New York, New American Library, 1971.
The Philosopher's Stone. London, Barker, 1969; New York, Crown, 1971.
The Space Vampires. London, Hart Davis MacGibbon, and New York, Random House, 1976; as *Life Force,* New York, Warner, 1985.

Short Story

The Return of the Lloigor. London, Village Press, 1974.

Other Publications

Novels

Adrift in Soho. London, Gollancz, and Boston, Houghton Mifflin, 1961.
The World of Violence. London, Gollancz, 1963; as *The Violent World of Hugh Greene,* Boston, Houghton Mifflin, 1963.
Necessary Doubt. London, Barker, and New York, Simon and Schuster, 1964.
The Glass Cage: An Unconventional Detective Story. London, Barker, 1966; New York, Random House, 1967.
The Killer. London, New English Library, 1970; as *Lingard,* New York, Crown, 1970.
The Black Room. London, Weidenfeld and Nicolson, 1971; New York, Pyramid, 1975.
The Schoolgirl Murder Case. London, Hart Davis MacGibbon, and New York, Crown, 1974.
The Janus Murder Case. London, Granada, 1984.
The Personality Surgeon. London, New English Library, and San Francisco, Mercury, House, 1986.
Spider World: The Tower. London, Grafton, 1987; in 3 vols., as *Spider World 1: The Desert,* New York, Ace, 1988, *Spider World 2: The Tower,* New York, Ace, 1989, *Spider World 3: The Fortress,* New York, Ace, 1989.
Spider World: The Delta. London, Grafton, 1987; as *Spider World 4: The Delta.* New York, Ace, 1990

The Magician from Siberia. London, Hale, 1988.
Spider World: The Magician. London, HarperCollins, 1992.

Plays

Viennese Interlude (produced Scarborough, Yorkshire, and London, 1960).
Strindberg (as *Pictures in a Bath of Acid,* produced Leeds, Yorkshire, 1971; as *Strindberg: A Fool's Decision,* produced London, 1975). London, Calder and Boyars, 1970; New York, Random House, 1971.
Mysteries (produced Cardiff, 1979).
Mozart's Journey to Prague. Nottingham, Paupers' Press, 1992.
The Metal Flower Blossom and Other Plays. San Bernardino, California, Borgo Press, 1993.

Other

The Outsider. London, Gollancz, and Boston, Houghton Mifflin, 1956.
Religion and the Rebel. London, Gollancz, and Boston, Houghton Mifflin, 1957.
The Age of Defeat. London, Gollancz, 1959; as *The Stature of Man,* Boston, Houghton Mifflin, 1959.
Encyclopaedia of Murder, with Patricia Pitman. London, Barker, 1961; New York, Putnam, 1962.
The Strength to Dream: Literature and the Imagination. London, Gollancz, and Boston, Houghton Mifflin, 1962.
Origins of the Sexual Impulse. London, Barker, and New York, Putnam, 1963.
Rasputin and the Fall of the Romanovs. London, Barker, and New York, Farrar Straus, 1964.
Brandy of the Damned: Discoveries of a Musical Eclectic. London, Baker, 1964; as *Chords and Discords: Purely Personal Opinions on Music,* New York, Crown, 1966; augmented edition as *Colin Wilson on Music,* London, Pan, 1967.
Beyond the Outsider: The Philosophy of the Future. London, Baker, and Boston, Houghton Mifflin, 1965.
Eagle and Earwig (essays). London, Baker, 1965.
Introduction to the New Existentialism. London, Hutchinson, 1966; Boston, Houghton Mifflin, 1967; as *The New Existentialism,* London, Wildwood House, 1980.
Sex and the Intelligent Teenager. London, Arrow, 1966; New York, Pyramid, 1968.
Voyage to a Beginning (autobiography). London, Cecil and Amelia Woolf, 1966; New York, Crown, 1969.
Bernard Shaw: A Reassessment. London, Hutchinson, and New York, Atheneum, 1969.
A Casebook of Murder. London, Frewin, 1969; New York, Cowles, 1970.
Poetry and Mysticism. San Francisco, City Lights, 1969; London, Hutchinson, 1970.
The Strange Genius of David Lindsay, with E. H. Visiak and J. B. Pick. London, Baker, 1970; as *The Haunted Man,* San Bernardino, California, Borgo Press, 1979.
The Occult. New York, Random House, and London, Hodder and Stoughton, 1971.
New Pathways in Psychology: Maslow and the Post-Freudian Revolution. New York, Taplinger, and London, Gollancz, 1972.
Order of Assassins: The Psychology of Murder. London, Hart Davis, 1972.

L'Amour: The Ways of Love, photographs by Piero Rimaldi. New York, Crown, 1972.
Strange Powers. London, Latimer New Dimensions, 1973; New York, Random House, 1975.
Tree by Tolkien. London, Covent Garden Press-Inca, 1973; Santa Barbara, California, Capra Press, 1974.
Hermann Hesse. London, Village Press, and Philadelphia, Leaves of Grass Press, 1974.
Wilhelm Reich. London, Village Press, and Philadelphia, Leaves of Grass Press, 1974.
Jorge Luis Borges. London, Village Press, and Philadelphia, Leaves of Grass Press, 1974.
A Book of Booze. London, Gollancz, 1974.
The Unexplained. Lake Oswego, Oregon, Lost Pleiade Press, 1975.
Mysterious Powers. London, Aldus, and Danbury, Connecticut, Danbury Press, 1975; as *They Had Strange Powers,* New York, Doubleday, 1975; revised edition, as *Mysteries of the Mind,* with Stuart Holroyd, London, Aldus, 1978.
The Craft of the Novel. London, Gollancz, 1975.
Enigmas and Mysteries. Danbury, Connecticut, Danbury Press, and London, Aldus, 1976.
The Geller Phenomenon. London, Aldus, 1976.
Mysteries: An Investigation into the Occult, The Paranormal, and the Supernatural. London, Hodder and Stoughton, and New York, Putnam, 1978.
Science Fiction as Existentialism. Hayes, Middlesex, Bran's Head, 1978.
The Search for the Real Arthur, with *King Arthur Country in Cornwall,* by Brenda Duxbury and Michael Williams. Bodmin, Cornwall, Bossiney, 1979.
Starseekers. London, Hodder and Stoughton, 1980; New York, Doubleday, 1981.
The War Against Sleep: The Philosophy of Gurdjieff. Wellingborough, Northamptonshire, Aquarian Press, and York Beach, Maine, Weiser, 1980; revised edition Aquarian Press, 1986.
Frankenstein's Castle. Sevenoaks, Kent, Ashgrove Press, 1980; Salem, New Hampshire, Salem House, 1982.
Anti-Sartre, with an Essay on Camus. San Bernardino, California, Borgo Press, 1981.
The Quest for Wilhelm Reich. London, Granada, and New York, Doubleday, 1981.
Witches. Limpsfield, Surrey, Dragon's World, 1981; New York, A and W, 1982.
Poltergeist! A Study in Destructive Haunting. London, New English Library, 1981; New York, Putnam, 1982.
Access to Inner Worlds: The Story of Brad Absetz. London, Rider, 1983.
Encyclopaedia of Modern Murder 1962-82, with Donald Seaman. London, Barker, 1983; New York, Putnam, 1985.
Psychic Detectives: The Story of Psychometry and the Paranormal in Crime Detection. London, Pan, 1984; San Francisco, Mercury House, 1985.
A Criminal History of Mankind. London, Granada, and New York, Putnam, 1984.
Lord of the Underworld: Jung and the Twentieth Century. Wellingborough, Northamptonshire, Aquarian Press, 1984.
The Essential Colin Wilson. London, Harrap, 1985.
The Bicameral Critic, edited by Howard F. Dossor. Bath, Avon, Ashgrove Press, 1985

Rudolf Steiner: The Man and His Vision. Wellingborough, Northamptonshire, Aquarian Press, 1985.

Afterlife: An Investigation of the Evidence of Life After Death. London, Harrap, 1985; New York, Doubleday, 1987.

The Laurel and Hardy Theory of Consciousness. Mill Valley, California, Brigg, 1986.

Scandal! An Encyclopaedia, with Donald Seaman. London, Weidenfeld and Nicolson, and New York, Stein and Day, 1986; as *An Encyclopedia of Scandal,* London, Grafton, 1987.

An Essay on the "New" Existentialism. Nottingham, Pauper Press, 1986.

The Encyclopaedia of Unsolved Mysteries, with Damon Wilson. London, Harrap, 1987; Chicago, Contemporary Books, 1988; as *Unsolved Mysteries,* New York, Galahad, 1992; as *Unsolved Mysteries Past and Present,* Chicago, Contemporary Books, 1992; London, Headline, 1993.

Jack the Ripper: Summing Up and Verdict, with Robin Odell, edited by Joe Gaute. London and New York, Bantam, 1987.

Aleister Crowley: The Nature of the Beast. Wellingborough, Northamptonshire, Aquarian Press, 1987.

The Musician as "Outsider." Nottingham, Pauper Press, 1987.

The Misfits: A Study of Sexual Outsiders. London, Grafton, 1988; New York, Carroll and Graf, 1989.

Beyond the Occult. London, Bantam, 1988; New York, Carroll and Graf, 1989.

Autobiographical Reflections. Nottingham, Pauper Press, 1988.

Written in Blood: A History of Forensic Detection. Wellingborough, Northamptonshire, Equation, 1989; as *Written in Blood: Detectives and Detection,* New York, Warner, 1991.

Existentially Speaking: Essays on the Philosophy of Literature. San Bernardino, California, Borgo Press, 1989.

The Untethered Mind (essays), edited by Howard F. Dossor. Bath, Avon, Ashgrove Press, 1989.

The Decline and Fall of Leftism. Nottingham, Pauper's Press, 1989.

The Serial Killers: A Study in the Psychology of Violence, with Donald Seaman. London, W. H. Allen, 1990; revised edition, London, True Crime, 1992.

Music, Nature and the Romantic Outsider. Nottingham, Paupers' Press, 1990.

Marriage and London, with Paris, Leicester, London Again. Nottingham, Paupers' Press, 1991.

The Strange Life of P. D. Ouspensky. London, Aquarian Press, 1993.

Editor, *Colin Wilson's Men of Mystery.* London, W. H. Allen, 1977; as *Dark Dimensions: A Celebration of the Occult,* London, Everest House, 1978.

Editor, with John Grant, *The Book of Time.* Newton Abbot, Devon, Westbridge, 1980.

Editor, with John Grant, *The Directory of Possibilities.* Exeter, Webb and Bower, and New York, Rutledge Press, 1981; as *Mysteries: A Guide to the Unknown, Past, Present, Future,* London, Chancellor, 1994.

Editor, with Christopher Evans, *The Book of Great Mysteries.* London, Robinson, 1986; New York, Dorset, 1990.

Editor, with Ronald Duncan, *Marx Refuted: The Verdict of History.* Bath, Avon, Ashgrove Press, 1987.

Editor, *The Mammoth Book of True Crime 1-2.* London, Robinson, and New York, Carroll and Graf, 2 vols., 1988-90.

Editor, with Damon Wilson, *Murder in the 1930s.* London, Robinson, and New York, Carroll and Graf, 1992.

Editor, with Damon and Rowan Wilson. *World Famous Murders.* London, Robinson, 1993; as *World Famous Crimes,* New York, Carroll and Graf, 1995.

Editor, with Damon Wilson, *Murder in the 1940s.* London, Robinson, and New York, Carroll and Graf, 1993.

*

Film Adaptation: *Life Force,* 1985, from the novel *The Space Vampires.*

Bibliography: *The Work of Colin Wilson: An Annotated Bibliography & Guide* by Colin Stanley, San Bernardino, California, Borgo Press, 1990.

Manuscript Collection: University of Texas, Austin.

Critical Studies: *The Angry Decade* by Kenneth Allsop, London, Peter Owen, 1958; *The World of Colin Wilson* by Sidney Campion, London, Muller, 1963; *Colin Wilson* by John A. Weigel, New York, Twayne, 1975; *Colin Wilson: The Outsider and Beyond* by Clifford P. Bendau, San Bernardino, California, Borgo Press, 1979; *The Novels of Colin Wilson* by Nicolas Tredell, London, Vision Press, 1982; *An Odyssey of Freedom: Four Themes in Colin Wilson's Novels* by K. Gunnar Bergström, Uppsala, University of Uppsala, 1983; *Colin Wilson: The Man and His Mind* by Howard F. Dossor, London, Element, 1990; *Colin Wilson: The Positive Approach* by Michael Trowell, Nottingham, Paupers' Press, 1990; *The Guerilla Philosopher: Colin Wilson and Existentialism* by Tim Dalgleish, Nottingham, Paupers' Press, 1993; *Two Essays on Colin Wilson: World Rejection and Criminal Romantics, and, From Outsider to Post-Tragic Man* by Gary Lachman, Nottingham, Paupers' Press, 1994.

*   *   *

Colin Wilson's supernatural stories form only a tiny fraction of his voluminous and popular output, much of which is non-fiction (some of it potboiling). His own strongly held occult and paranormal beliefs may not be his greatest fictional asset, since they can occasionally lead to taking such matters for granted rather than weaving a spell of narrative plausibility. But his extensive knowledge of occult lore and historical oddity provides a fund of corroborative detail—where M. R. James would invent a sinister legend or manuscript, Wilson likes to make creative use of a genuine source. Above all, he has a personal philosophical agenda which interestingly resonates through his better novels.

Wilson's career began with literary philosophy in the initially over-praised and then (in a critical backlash) over-reviled *The Outsider,* exploring the alienated "Outsider" figure through a ragbag of quotations and sources. His first novel *Ritual in the Dark* features a modern Jack the Ripper, an Outsider, violently murdering women in Whitechapel: these horrors are filtered through abstract discussions of sadism and of the possibility that murder might somehow be a creative, spiritually liberating act. The existentialist viewpoint character Gerard Sorme reappears in later novels such as *Man without a Shadow.*

The author's probing, intellectual approach to themes of supernatural terror is well suited to H. P. Lovecraft's brand of "cosmic fear," as in the explicitly Lovecraftian *The Mind Parasites.* This strange curate's egg of a novel mingles extensive archaeological and Cthuloid research (an aged August Derleth appears as a character), some shambolic science-fictional props and patter which are best not scrutinized, and several episodes of intense, deliberately paranoid dread. On one level the eponymous parasites are foul Cthulhu-mythos entities which feed on human neurosis, encouraging mental stagnation and routinely driving those who discover their existence towards madness or suicide. "Real" evidence for the creatures is marshalled from copious (though selective) examples of humanity's spiritual decay, from de Sade to Hitler.

These malign psychic vampires are intangible, dwelling in the deeps of the mind; an insubstantiality which makes them no less loathsome. They are, in fact, mental cancers. Metaphorically, they represent all the negative factors in the human psyche: slimy, sluglike, octopoid-seeming personifications of laziness, cowardice, self-doubt, self-hatred and despair. Wilson's subtext is that the chief obstacles to humanity's mental development are such tumours within the mind itself. The narrator's rocky spiritual progress from helpless parasite-host to independence and true sanity (and then beyond) is considerably more fascinating than the book's incidental sf apparatus of vast cyclopean cities beneath Turkish deserts, global war fostered by the parasites to distract us from the truth, the Moon's baleful influence, etc.

Wilson returned to Lovecraftian themes in *The Philosopher's Stone*, which, although more rambling and discursive than *The Mind Parasites*, is ultimately a more satisfying work. The hero is much possessed by death, and gropes towards a philosopher's stone of literal immortality—to be achieved, as was freedom from the parasites, by transcendent efforts of will. (Philosophical echoes of Nietzsche and the George Bernard Shaw of *Back to Methuselah* recur throughout Wilson's works.) This mental self-discipline through self-understanding duly leads to the development of psychic abilities. There are interesting psychometric glimpses of Shakespearean and Classical Greek times; in one dramatic occult-detective episode, the narrator disperses a claustrophobic tangle of repressed family emotions which have spawned a poltergeist.

Experimenting with his growing powers, our hero stumbles into psychic traps and safeguards left by the Lovecraftian monstrosities who dwelt on Earth before us, and who for aeons have lain in coma after a disaster resulting from racial hubris. ("That is not dead which can eternal lie. . . .") Wilson's heady mix of ingredients includes not only the Cthulhu Mythos but Theosophy, a dash of *Forbidden Planet*, various real-world sources like the mysterious Voynich Manuscript, and a revisionist history of the Lovecraftian monstrosities which passes through horror and out on the other side. It is up to humanity to develop its full potential so that when the almost infinitely powerful Elder Ones wake again, we shall meet them as equals. . . .

The novella *The Return of the Lloigor* is a rather more conventional Lovecraftian chiller which outlines the eponymous and slowly growing psychic menace through an accretion of sinister incidents and hints, halting on the brink of worse things to come.

Also of genre interest is *The God of the Labyrinth* (alias *The Hedonists*), the third in the loosely connected "Gerard Sorme" series but the first with real supernatural content. Here, however, the approach varies. Just as Wilson adapted the paraphernalia of supernatural horror for his own purposes in the Lovecraftian novels, he now uses conventions of pornography as an alternative route to his familiar transcendental vision. The lead character Sorme becomes entangled with a centuries-old erotic cult which—in a sly allusion to Jorge Luis Borges—is known as the Sect of the Phoenix. Naturally there is a good deal of sex, much of it less

than pleasant. Sorme is amicably possessed by the spirit of a long-dead rake and adept, somewhat reducing his personal responsibility for later sexual excess. Here, the characteristic Wilsonian escape from mundane habits of mind and gaining of psychic abilities (including astral travel) comes from strenuously and, one might think, impossibly prolonged orgasm.

An occult detective who sees clues to crime in visions plays a small part (indeed, is consulted by the official police investigator) in Wilson's otherwise non-supernatural crime novel *The Schoolgirl Murder Case*. Speculations on energy vampires in *The Space Vampires* are of science-fictional rather than supernatural interest: the book is a homage to A. E. van Vogt's similarly themed 1942 science-fiction story "Asylum." The "Spider World" science-fantasy sequence, though featuring something very like the Shavian Life Force to which Wilson often alludes, is still more remote from the supernatural tradition. *The Strength to Dream*, a polemical critical work on "Literature and the Imagination," interestingly discusses—among others—de Sade, Gogol, Hoffmann, M. R. James, Le Fanu and Lovecraft.

Colin Wilson hops without prejudice from genre to genre, and may yet revisit supernatural horror.

—David Langford

WILSON, F(rancis) Paul

Pseudonym: Colin Andrews. **Nationality:** American. **Born:** Jersey City, New Jersey, 17 May 1946. **Family:** Married Mary Murphy in 1969; two daughters. **Career:** Since 1974, physician, Cedar Bridge Medical Group, Bricktown, New Jersey. **Awards:** Prometheus award for novel, 1979. **Agent:** Albert Zuckerman, Writers House, 21 West 26th Street, New York, NY 10010, USA.

HORROR, GHOST AND GOTHIC PUBLICATIONS

Novels (series: Nightworld)

The Keep (Nightworld). New York, Morrow, 1981; London, New English Library, 1982.
The Tomb (Nightworld). Binghamton, New York, Whispers Press, 1984; London, New English Library, 1985.
The Touch (Nightworld). New York, Putnam, and London, New English Library, 1986.
Black Wind. New York, Tor, 1988; London, Michael Joseph, 1989.
Reborn: A Novel (Nightworld). Arlington Heights, Illinois, Dark Harvest, and London, New English Library, 1990.
Reprisal: A Novel (Nightworld). Arlington Heights, Illinois, Dark Harvest, and London, New English Library, 1991.
Sibs. Arlington Heights, Illinois, Dark Harvest, 1991; as *Sister Night,* London, New English Library, 1993.
Nightworld: A Novel. London, New English Library, and Arlington Heights, Illinois, Dark Harvest, 1992.

Short Stories

Soft and Others: 16 Stories of Wonder and Dread. New York, Tor, 1989.
Ad Statum Perspicuum. Eugene, Oregon, Pulphouse, 1990.
Midnight Mass. Eugene, Oregon, Axolotl Press, 1990.

Pelts. Round Top, New York, Footsteps Press, 1990.
Buckets. Eugene, Oregon, Pulphouse, 1991.
The Barrens. Newark, New Jersey, Wildside Press, 1992.

Editor, *Freak Show.* New York, Pocket Books, 1992.
Editor, *Diagnosis: Terminal.* New York, Tor, 1996.

OTHER PUBLICATIONS

Novels

Healer. New York, Doubleday, 1976; London, Sidgwick and Jackson, 1977.
Wheels within Wheels: A Novel of the LaNague Federation. New York, Doubleday, 1979; London, Sidgwick and Jackson, 1980.
An Enemy of the State. New York, Doubleday, 1980.
The LaNague Chronicles (omnibus; includes *Healer, Wheels within Wheels, An Enemy of the State).* Riverdale, New York, Baen, 1992.
The Select (as Colin Andrews). London, Headline, 1993; as F. Paul Wilson, New York, Morrow, 1994.
Implant (as Colin Andrews). London, Headline, 1995; as F. Paul Wilson, New York, Tor, 1995.
Mirage, with Matthew J. Costello. London, Headline, 1996.

Short Stories

Dydeetown World. Norwich, Connecticut, Easton Press, 1989.
The Tery. New York, Baen, 1990.

*

Film Adaptation: *The Keep*, 1983.

*   *   *

F. Paul Wilson writes in a number of genres, including horror which probably displays his talents at their best. Supernatural, mythical and physically gory elements all feature in his novels but not necessarily in every one.

The early volumes in the sequence of novels brought together under the Nightworld banner do not, at first, seem to have any connection and to yoke them together may well have been a later, marketing decision. The initial book in the series, *The Keep*, brought Wilson to the attention of the wider world and was filmed in 1983. It has an atmosphere reminiscent of that generated by Dennis Wheatley in his World War II black-magic novels, partly because *The Keep* utilizes the same kind of setting. The eponymous building is set high on a mountainside overlooking a pass in the Transylvanian region of Romania. A detachment of the German army captained by an old-school career soldier is sent to occupy the site. His men start dying, horribly. An arrogant, ambitious SS officer is sent to sort out the problem and an elderly Jewish scholar is dragged in merely because he has visited the keep in the past. From this point, it begins to appear that if what has been released is not an actual vampire, then it is the creature which gave rise to the legends. The novel could at this point have become a tired, familiar story but Wilson is cleverer than that, introducing another element. A red-haired man appears bearing an ancient sword, and the story develops into a battle between the millennia-old forces of dark and light personified as Rasalom and Glaeken.

It could have ended there, but *Reborn* was hailed as the sequel to *The Keep*, and sequentially it is. On the day that Rasalom was defeated, his soul was transmuted into a foetus growing in America. Jim Stevens has no soul of his own as he is a clone (it seems techniques only recently publicized for cloning sheep were being used in 1941). Until 1968, when the novel is set, he has led a relatively ordinary life, is married to Carol and is attempting to make a living as a writer. Then he inherits a fortune and discovers his origins. Just as the reader begins to think that the book is a traditional tale of possession by an evil entity, Jim is killed. A small religious sect, to which Carol's aunt, Grace, belongs are convinced that Jim's unborn child is evil incarnate and must be aborted. In the background, Glaeken, now an old man, hovers as an observer.

Reprisal opens out the action initiated in *Reborn*, with its principal characters fleeing the township of Monroe where most of *Reborn* took place. It gives time for the characters to grow up before the events of *Nightworld* are set in motion. It also gives Wilson space to develop characters like William Ryan (calling himself Will Ryerson in the early chapters) who was a boyfriend of Carol Stevens before he acknowledged his calling to the priesthood. Carol's son, a precocious child, has set out to destroy the priest who, by his faith, nearly destroyed him. Anyone precious to him becomes a victim and the way the youth obtains his revenge provides the horror element.

At first sight, neither *The Tomb* or *The Touch* has any connection to the Nightworld series. *The Tomb* introduces Repairman Jack, whose line of work has much in common with that of the character portrayed by Edward Woodward in *The Equalizer* television series: Jack fixes things for people. He is asked to recover a necklace stolen in a mugging; simultaneously, his ex-girlfriend asks him to look into the disappearance of her aunt. Outwardly the two events are unconnected but Kusum Bahkti, who hired Jack, is also the man responsible for abducting Grace Westphalen. He has a ship-load of rakoshi (Indian demons) which he is using to extract vengeance on the descendants of the man who killed his parents. Jack would never have discovered the connection if Kusum's sister, Kolabati, had not decided to show Jack how grateful she was for his swift recovery of the necklace. *The Touch* involves a wandering spirit in Indochina called Dat-tay-vao: when it lodges inside a human it conveys the ability to heal with a touch. Alan Bulmer, a physician practising in Monroe, innocently becomes the host. Although he can heal with a touch every time he uses the power, part of his brain is destroyed.

By the time of the events of *Nightworld*, the Dat-tay-vao is lying dormant in the body of a child, Bulmer's last cure, who lives in the township of Monroe. Rasalom has decided it is time to make his bid for enslavement of the world, and an entity as powerful as he is can change the laws of physics. The first sign of something amiss is that the sun rises late and sets early. Then a bottomless hole opens in Central Park and flesh-eating things emerge from it during the hours of darkness. The only hope is for Glaeken to remake the sword that he used to kill Rasalom in *The Keep*. Repairman Jack is sent to find Kolabati and get from her the necklaces that have kept her young for over a century; Bill Ryan goes to the gorge beneath the Keep to recover fragments of the original sword, and the Dat-tay-vao is needed to activate it. Events come full circle and Glaeken once again has to wield the instrument of light against that of darkness.

Wilson is equally good at writing short horror stories. One, first published in *Night Visions IV* (1988) is linked obliquely to the Nightworld series. The detective investigating a series of grisly murders in which the victims have their faces chewed off, discovers that the perpetrator is a deformed girl from his home town of Monroe (a number of children were born with gross deformities, including his sister, nine months after the events in *Reborn*).

A number of Wilson's novellas have been printed as limited-edition chapbooks. *Buckets*, written in 1985, was originally collected in *Soft and Others*. It concerns a doctor who, on Halloween, is visited by children carrying metal buckets. The buckets contain blood and gobbets of flesh. The children are what the foetuses he aborted in the course of his work would have become; and they are looking for revenge. *Midnight Mass* is a vampire story; as in Richard Matheson's novel *I am Legend*, vampires dominate the world, and the surviving humans hide during the hours of darkness, hoping to remain undiscovered. Father Joe Cahill has resigned himself to the idea that sooner or later he will become a victim. Then an old friend, Rabbi Zev Wolpin, arrives to tell him that his former church has been taken over. Against his better judgement Cahill goes to see and is coerced into making a stand. Although the gesture may be futile, delaying the inevitable, Wilson uses it to make a statement about faith, friendship and human nature. Wilson donated the royalties from *Pelts* to Friends of Animals and, as might be expected, makes a political point in the story: in it the people who exploit animals for the fur are destined to die horribly.

The novel *Black Wind* has only slight horror elements. It looks at both sides of the events leading up to both the attack on Pearl Harbor and the dropping of the first atomic bomb. On one side is Frank Skinner who loves a Japanese woman, on the other is his boyhood friend whose brother is determined that Japan will win the conflict. The horror element is provided by the Black Wind which is generated by mutilating children horribly and which, once released, destroys every living thing. In comparison, *Sibs* is a slight novel: in it Kara returns to New York after ten years since the death of her twin sister, Kelly, and discovers that not only has Kelly lived a double life but she appears to have had a split personality. This could be classified as a romantic thriller except for the supernatural explanation of events.

Wilson is a fine writer who has developed his craft over the years. The descriptions of the horrific elements tend to be factual. He does not linger over the gory details, and his tales are more effective as a result.

—Pauline Morgan

WISMAN, Ken(neth)

Nationality: American. **Born:** New York City, 7 July 1947. **Education:** Fairleigh Dickinson University and the University of Michigan. **Family:** Married Lois Wisman; one son. **Career:** Worked in a succession of jobs in the United States and Europe before settling down to the production of technical manuals. **Address:** Applewood Village, 91 Cortland Lane, Boxborough, MA 01719, USA.

HORROR, GHOST AND GOTHIC PUBLICATIONS

Short Stories

Weird Family Tales: A Journal of Familial Maledictions. Parma, Ohio, Earth Prime, 1993.

Frost on the Window: Fourteen Stories of Christmas. Eugene, Oregon, Pulphouse, 1995.
Weird Family Tales II: The Curse Continues. Concord, Dark Regions Press, 1995.

*

Ken Wisman comments:

I have been writing and publishing stories consistently since that wonderful moment when the first ones were bought. To keep my son in designer sneakers, I write technical manuals during the day—documents for operating MRI systems and centrifuges, or for servicing image-setters and storage devices. To keep myself sane, I write imaginative fiction at night. The realms of Lord Dunsany and Tolkien, the worlds of Le Guin and Bradbury, ever remain the ones where I feel most at home.

*   *   *

Despite having no full-length published work to his name, Ken Wisman has crafted a special mythos all of his own through a series of engaging and often surreal short stories.

Wisman is not the first to concentrate on the short form for his literary creations: both Harlan Ellison and Ray Bradbury before him have made their reputations—particularly in the case of Ellison—primarily through their short fiction output. But it is Bradbury's early short run of stories featuring a family of supernatural beings ("Uncle Einar," etc) and Lord Dunsany's eerie short tales which seem to have served as inspiration for Wisman's own dysfunctional literary family . . . and a remarkably extensive gathering it is, too.

Wisman's world-view is that of a child, and he frequently uses children as protagonists—as, of course, does Bradbury . . . and that other great fantasist, Rod Serling—recognizing that a child's attitude to the world is more tolerant of occasional aberrations in the firmament of normality and logic, and of those nameless images that seem to dwell on the very periphery of our vision. But Wisman's "grownups" too soon fall under the spell, sometimes willingly and sometimes without even realizing that it's happening.

Although Wisman's tales have appeared in a wide and varied selection of magazines and anthologies, primarily in the United States, he has two exceptional collections to his credit.

One of these, *Frost on the Window*, pulls together 14 stories of Christmas, heartfelt and poignant, sometimes chilling and always amazing in their fantastic view of the world. The leading title story, a paean to lost innocence in which a young girl first encounters death with the loss of her beloved grandmother, sets the scene and the tone for all the stories that follow. In this respect, and particularly in this collection, Wisman perhaps wears his heart a little too much on his literary sleeve. For while the stories are very traditional in their approach to that Holiday, told with a simplicity that is highly effective, the occasionally overdone religious undertones can prove to be irritating.

Nevertheless, *Frost on the Window* is a wonderful book, particularly if its stories are consumed only one or two at a time . . . and ideally at Christmas, perhaps read aloud to younger members of the family. Magical seasonal wishes and the fairy spirits of trees cut down for family hearthsides share shoulder space with talking toys—some of which are delightfully malevolent—and ghosts of loved ones whose lives re-enact themselves in the frosted tapestries left on Christmas Eve window panes. A very unique, mysterious and highly satisfying collection.

But it is in the two volumes of his *Weird Family Tales*, featuring the most supernaturally (Wisman refers to it in olde-world parlance as "preternatural") blighted family in existence, that Wisman's style and creativity come blissfully together in perfect union.

The "Weird Family" is massive, introduced to us in a seemingly endless procession of aunts, uncles, cousins and siblings by an unnamed narrator who usually travels to some desolate spot in response to a mysterious letter or telephone call. Once there, some decidedly strange goings-on must be faced.

For example, in the first volume, we meet "Brother Senechelle," a composer whose piano is constructed from an old tree in which a wood nymph has made her home; "Brother Endle," an eight-foot-tall dentist who falls hopelessly in love with the inhabitant of a large cocoon which appears in his room; "Uncle Endrick," a globe-trotting drifter who learns the Himalayan art of matter materialization, only to discover that he is being pursued by a mysterious figure in a monk's habit; Grandm (yes, Grandm) Sessy, who introduces the narrator to "Captain Seofon" and a magical bed constructed of whalebone which transports its occupants to a dark, metaphysical sea and its lone inhabitant, a constantly size-doubling "Null" shark; and the twin cousins "Septima/Septimus," whose Parallux Windows, a carefully placed pair of facing mirrors, permit the entering of thousands of alternate worlds and realities . . . with the only problem that the journeys become dangerously addictive.

In volume two, Wisman and his narrator introduce readers to yet another brother, "Brother Estevan," who has discovered a way to enter into a singularly hellish domain hidden within Hieronymous Bosch's haunting *Garden of Earthly Delights* triptych; the narrator's own offspring, "Eryc, Son," who takes him to a world where trees have a very special significance; "Niece Enyva," a little girl who projects her madness into the world at large; "Great Uncle Seweyne," who finds a long-lost staircase beneath the still waters of his pond; and Aunt "Em," behind whose blank house wall sits a secret door leading to a long tunnel which contains an endlessly spinning man.

Many more stories have appeared but have not yet been collected. Wisman is a natural storyteller, blending the style and techniques of Lord Dunsany with a yearning for the simplicity of the past so perfectly captured by Bradbury. His stories brim with affection and warmth, both for his craft and for humanity itself, with all its attendant gods, fables and beliefs. Into his work, these taller-than-tall tales, where the worlds of faery, space and the supernatural are constantly at odds with contemporary society, he mixes the mundane and the magical with consummate ease. One can only look forward to his first full-length work with eager anticipation.

—Peter Crowther

WOOD, Bari

Nationality: American. **Born:** 1936. **Career:** Worked for the American Cancer Service; novelist. Not to be confused with the British-born romantic novelist Barbara Wood (born 1947), some of whose novels, such as *Yesterday's Child* (1979), have ghostly themes. **Awards:** Putnam award for first novel, 1975. **Address:** c/o William Morrow and Company, Inc., 1350 Avenue of the Americas, New York, NY 10019, USA.

HORROR, GHOST AND GOTHIC PUBLICATIONS

Novels

The Killing Gift. New York, Putnam, 1975.
Twins, with Jack Geasland. New York, Putnam 1977; as *Dead Ringers*, London, Sphere, 1988.
The Tribe. New York, New American Library, and London, New English Library, 1981.
Amy Girl. New York, New American Library, 1987; London, Michael Joseph, 1988.
Doll's Eyes. New York, Morrow, 1993.
The Basement. New York, Morrow, 1995.

OTHER PUBLICATIONS

Novel

Lightsource. New York, New American Library, 1984; London, Macdonald, 1985.

*

Film Adaptation: *Dead Ringers*, from the novel *Twins*, 1988.

*   *   *

Bari Wood's career was launched immediately after Stephen King's, but it is highly unlikely that *The Killing Gift* could actually have been influenced by *Carrie*, which had appeared the previous year and still languished in relative obscurity. Indeed, *The Killing Gift*—which won Putnam's "first novel award"—might well have seemed the more promising work to contemporary reviewers. Although Wood's subsequent novels have usually reached best-seller status, however, she has been comprehensively upstaged and overshadowed by King, many of whose works are similar in spirit and method to hers but rather more effective.

The heroine of *The Killing Gift* discovers that she can wish people dead and cannot help indulging her thirst for justice, even though she kanows that such punishments tend to be excessive. Others sensing her power draw away from her, with the exception of a homicide detective who becomes fascinated by her—because rather than in spite of the fact that she can never be connected to her vengeful acts by any evidence acceptable to a court of law. Any book of this kind penned by a female writer on the verge of 40 inevitably invites the suspicion that it is a self-indulgent wish-fulfilment fantasy but the theme is handled with a reasonable degree of even-handed objectivity.

Twins is an idiosyncratic study of the destructive mutual dependence of twin gynaecologists who are physically but not psychologically identical. Its innate peculiarity was further exaggerated when David Cronenberg filmed it as *Dead Ringers*, but its most interesting aspect is its commentary on the psychological hardships experienced by doctors specializing in cancer treatment, which draws on the legacy of Wood's long service with the American Cancer Service as well as co-author Jack Geasland's experience as a medical writer. It is the most distinctive of her works, strengthened in its realism by the marginalization of the paranormal aspects of the bond between the brothers.

The Tribe detaches a vengeful spirit similar to that deployed in *The Killing Gift* from its beneficiaries, a Jewish family who have found refuge in Minnesota after a harrowing history which reached its nadir in the extermination camps of World War II. In this context the supernatural avenger is linked—appropriately, if not inevitably—with the myth of the golem, defender of Medieval Jews against the "blood libel" used to excuse persecutions and pogroms. As in *The Killing Gift* the author's own committed sympathies do not prevent her treating this hypothesis with a degree of moral care unusual in a horror novel. It is the most intense of Wood's novels and it is significant that she switched genres thereafter to produce the frenetic chase thriller *Lightsource*, in which an odd assortment of hitmen and psychopaths is despatched by evil oil barons to exterminate scientists who have stumbled across the secret of nuclear fusion.

Wood's subsequent works are all conventional exercises in genre horror which recapitulate key elements of her early novels without ever recovering their power. *Amy Girl* is an indignant but rather slow-moving case-study of an abused child who acquires a killing gift. Like King's *Carrie*—but unlike the heroine of Wood's first novel—Amy has no idea what is happening to her as she is driven by measured degrees from the poisoned sanctuary to which she has been removed after the murder of her mother.

Doll's Eyes is also a "case-study" novel, similarly featuring a good-hearted policeman as its main viewpoint character, but it offers a much nastier and far more convoluted account of an emotionally-anaesthetized doctor whose attempts to understand his condition entice him into a career as a serial killer. When the killer discovers that a psychic woman has "seen" one of his crimes he begins to stalk her, equally intent on removing the threat to his freedom and employing her talent to reach the deeply-buried psychological roots of his problem.

The Basement features a querulous Connecticut socialite whose haunted basement stubbornly resists the assaults of a crack team of interior decorators and a rather comical exorcism before conferring a disconcerting but perversely welcome killing gift upon her. The novel is lacklustre; even the anti-anti-Semitic rhetoric incorporated into one of the minor narrative threads seems oddly tokenistic, never capturing the least vestige of the heartfelt fervour of *The Tribe*.

Viewed as a set, *Amy Girl*, *Doll's Eyes* and *The Basement* seem to display a gradual retreat into a more mechanical kind of production. None of the three comes close to duplicating the seemingly-authentic conviction of *The Killing Gift* and *Lightsource*, let alone *Twins* and *The Tribe*. The slightly condescending manner in which the heroine of *The Basement* is characterized, and the ironic verdict offered by the text regarding the future utility of her ability to serve as an avenging angel, might be regarded as a lapse into tired cynicism. It seems probable, though, that the incapacity of these works to push the genre buttons with sufficient force is a reflection of the author's inability to cultivate the kind of quasi-sadistic glee with which more wholehearted gore-mongers approach the task of grossing out their readers.

Wood is perhaps more accurately perceived as a best-seller who happened to get stuck in the horror fiction rut than as a dedicated horror writer who contrived to attain best-seller status. Her later work gives the impression that she might have preferred not to be typecast, and would have been happier moving on to fresh fields. Although her books have always sold well and Stephen King has provided several ringing endorsements of her work in the form of cover quotes, Wood has not received much attention from genre insiders. Such insiders tend to be more sensitive to—and more critical of—half-hearted artifice and contrivance than general readers, and in spite of its conscientious efforts her later work has little to offer hardened connoisseurs of supernatural mayhem and brutal homicide. *Twins* and *The Tribe* are, however, genuinely disturbing works written with deep feeling and authentic psychological insight. It is on those two books that Wood's reputation ought to rest, and they are sufficient to establish her as a writer of considerable power and artistry.

—Brian Stableford

WOODS, Stuart

Nationality: American. **Born:** Stuart Lee (legally changed to stepfather's surname in 1955), Manchester, Georgia, 9 January 1938. **Education:** University of Georgia, B.A. 1959. **Military Service:** U.S. Air National Guard, 1960-68, active duty, 1961; served in Germany. **Career:** Advertising writer and creative director with firms in New York, 1960-69, including Batten, Barton, Durstine & Osborne, Paper, Koenig & Lois, Young & Rubicam, and J. Walter Thompson; creative director and consultant with firms in London, 1970-73, including Grey Advertising and Dorland; consultant to Irish International Advertising and Hunter Advertising, both in Dublin, both 1973-74; free-lance writer, 1973—. Past member of board of directors of Denham's, Inc. **Awards:** Mystery Writers of America Edgar Allan Poe award for first novel, 1982. **Address:** 4340 Tree Haven Dr. N.E., Atlanta, Georgia 30342. **Agent:** Peter Shepherd, Harold Ober Associates, Inc., 40 East 49th St., New York, New York 10017, USA.

HORROR, GHOST AND GOTHIC PUBLICATIONS

Novel

Under the Lake. New York, Simon and Schuster, and London, Heinemann, 1987.
Dead Eyes. New York, Harper, 1994; London, HarperCollins, 1995.

OTHER PUBLICATIONS

Novels

Chiefs. New York, Norton, 1981; London, Norton, 1982.
Run Before the Wind. New York, Norton, 1983.
Deep Lie. New York, Norton, and London, Heinemann, 1986.
Grass Roots. New York, Simon and Schuster, 1989; London, HarperCollins, 1991.
Palindrome. New York, Harper, and London, HarperCollins, 1991.
Santa Fe Rules. New York, Harper, and London, HarperCollins, 1992.
L. A. Times. New York, Harper, and London, HarperCollins, 1993.
Heat. New York, Harper, and London, HarperCollins, 1994.
Imperfect Strangers. New York, Harper, 1995; London, HarperCollins, 1996.
Choke. New York, Harper, 1995; London, HarperCollins, 1997.
Dirt. New York, Harper, 1996.
Dead in the Water. New York, Harper, 1997.

Short Stories

White Cargo. New York, Simon and Schuster, 1988; London, Century, 1989.
New York Dead. New York, Harper, 1991; London, HarperCollins, 1992.

Other

Blue Water, Green Skipper. New York, Norton, 1977.
Stanford Maritime. N.p., 1977.
A Romantic's Guide to the Country Inns of Britain and Ireland. N.p., n.d.

*

Film Adaptation: *Chiefs* (television mini-series), 1983.

*   *   *

Stuart Woods is a respected writer of crime and mystery novels. His single work of supernatural horror is *Under the Lake*, a splendidly original novel set in rural Georgia in the summer of 1976. John Howell is a first-rate journalist who, since winning a Pulitzer Prize, has tried to write novels but has only succeeded in becoming an alcoholic with a failing marriage. Salvation comes in the shape of a lucrative contract to ghost-write the autobiography of a man (not Colonel Sanders) who has made millions out of fried-chicken restaurants. And Howell's lawyer (and brother-in-law), who has brokered the deal, lends him a very isolated lakeside cabin to work in.

So Howell moves to the cabin, on Lake Sutherland, near the small town of Sutherland, for a three-month stay. But he is too well known as a newspaperman, and those locals with something to hide—especially Eric Sutherland, who owns the lake and the town, and Bo Scully, the sheriff—believe that he has come to investigate them. But Scully still goes out of his way to meet Howell and form an acquaintance with him. More than that, Howell is instrumental in saving Scully's life when Scully is trying to arrest some store-robbers. In fact, the investigatory journalist is Scotty Miller, a young woman previously known to Howell, who has got herself a job in Scully's office.

What Scotty is trying to investigate is a tip that the sheriff is involved in drugs. But Howell wonders about a mystery from 25 years before, when Sutherland bought out lots of homesteaders in the valley so that it could be flooded to create the lake, which is the essential part of a hydro-electric power scheme. The last home-owner, Donal O'Coineen, who suddenly agreed to sell and move after a long period of refusal, has not been seen since, and has never touched the money paid into a bank account for him.

The situation quickly grows more complicated. Howell experiences several supernatural hallucinations, in particular seeing the valley as it used to be before flooding. He begins an affair with Scotty, and a séance at the cabin involving both of them and a quartet of summer visitors suggests that Scotty and the O'Coineens are involved in the mystery. Another complicating factor is Howell's peculiar neighbours at another cabin a few hundred yards away, the dying Mama Kelly and her brood of grown-up children: two simple-minded, one a blind albino piano-tuner and the fourth a beautiful young woman named Leonie who heals Howell's backache and later has sex with him. (The novel contains quite a bit of casual sex.)

While Scotty gathers information on Scully's illegal activities, Howell tries to discover more about the O'Coineens and whether the house he sometimes sees under the lake is theirs. He breaks into Sutherland's office, gaining valuable information but also leaving a clue (a flexible plastic storecard used to open a bolt) which leads back to Scotty.

In a few final, violent scenes, Howell discovers Sutherland shot dead (apparently a suicide), Scully's latest drug-delivery (flown in to an adjacent landing strip) ends up with a shooting match, and the true story of how the O'Coineen family were all killed 25 years before is revealed. There are chapters full of revelations. Scully, it transpires, is the illegitimate son of Sutherland, while Scotty is the illegitimate daughter of Scully. At the end, not only does Scully drown in the lake, but Scotty gets rich and Howell finishes his book and signs up as a journalist again.

This is a highly entertaining novel, very fast-paced and satisfying to read, despite a couple of drawbacks. The scenes often seem a little too brief, rather lacking in atmosphere. (Stephen King would have made this plot into a novel twice as long.) And the welter of revelations at the end are just a little too coincidental and contrived, even though the whole subject of casual sex (even incest) and illegitimacy is central to the novel and to the way of life in the Sutherland area in past times.

The characters are sharply defined and entertaining, especially Howell (a laid-back man with too much integrity for his own good), Scully and Scotty, but also some of the town characters. Some, like McAuliffe the lawyer, Benny Pope the simple-minded handyman and Mama Kelly, are under-used.

The supernatural elements are well employed, though not dwelt upon for long enough. The lights of houses under the lake, the old 1940 Lincoln Continental which nobody owns any more (but which Sutherland used to own back in 1951), the player piano which will only play "I'll Take You Home Again, Kathleen," and the girl whom Howell sees in his cabin looking out at the lake, are all fine ghostly images. This rural Georgian background is very plausible, a quiet and peaceful setting with all kinds of trouble boiling up underneath the facade. And the use of the phrase "under the lake" by Sutherland residents as a euphemism for "dead" is both clever and chilling.

At least one of Woods's later novels, *Dead Eyes*, may qualify as horror fiction of the non-supernatural sort. It is the tale of a young woman threatened by a stalker, in which the heroine's plight is heightened by the fact that she is temporarily blinded. Her menacing "admirer" sends her a dog's head, and at one point even tattoos her hand—before he eventually gets his come-uppance in a conventional thriller-ish denouement.

—Chris Morgan

WRIGHT, T(errance) M(ichael)

Pseudonym: F. W. Armstrong. **Nationality:** American. **Born:** 1947. **Address:** c/o Tor Books, 175 Fifth Avenue, New York, NY 10010, USA.

HORROR, GHOST AND GOTHIC PUBLICATIONS

Novels

Strange Seed. New York, Everest House, 1978; London, Gollancz, 1993.

The Woman Next Door. Chicago, Playboy Press, 1981.
The Playground. New York, Tor, 1982.
Nursery Tale. Chicago, Playboy Press, 1982; London, Gollancz, 1994.
The Children of the Island. New York, Jove, 1983.
Carlisle Street. New York, Tor, 1983.
A Manhattan Ghost Story. New York, Tor, 1984; London, Gollancz, 1990.
The People of the Dark. New York, Tor, 1985.
The Changing (as F. W. Armstrong). New York, Tor, 1985.
The Waiting Room. New York, Tor, 1986; London, Gollancz, 1990.
The Devouring (as F. W. Armstrong). New York, Tor, 1987.
The Island. New York, Tor, 1988; London, Gollancz, 1989.
The Place. New York, Tor, 1989; London, Gollancz, 1991.
The School. New York, Tor, 1990; London, Gollancz, 1991.
Boundaries. New York, Tor, 1990; London, Gollancz, 1992.
The Last Vampire. London, Gollancz, 1991.
Little Boy Lost. New York, Tor, 1992; London, Gollancz, 1993.
Goodlow's Ghosts. New York, Tor, and London, Gollancz, 1993.
Sleepeasy. London, Gollancz, 1993.
The Ascending. New York, Tor, 1994.
Erthmun. London, Gollancz, 1995.

*   *   *

T. M. Wright's horror novels characteristically involve the confrontation of his characters with the realization that the world isn't quite the way they thought it was, that the border between life and death isn't quite so distinct, that strange creatures live in familiar woods, making them alien, and that nothing else is quite what it seems either. Wright established this in his very first novel, *Strange Seed.* Rachel has recently married and moved to a new home, a house surrounded by woods. But as the days pass, her husband seems to grow more and more self-involved, retreating from the world, and Rachel spots strange children playing in the woods—or at least they look like children.

Equally eerie, though more conventional in theme, is *The Woman Next Door.* Marilyn's life seems to be going just as she hoped it would until she acquires a new next-door neighbour, a mysterious woman whose influence quickly infects Marilyn's family. Suddenly her son's imaginary playmate seems entirely too real, her husband has become involved with another woman, and the next-door neighbour seems to know much more than she's supposed to. *Nursery Tale* is virtually a sequel to *Strange Seed.* Years after a couple die mysteriously in a wooded area, the trees are cleared and the area developed as a housing project. Janice and her husband move in, and almost immediately she begins to see things invisible to everyone else. Janice would like to believe that they are simply illusions brought on my her pregnancy, but then neighbourhood children start to disappear and a ghost warns her that the other things she sees aren't ghosts at all. They're something much worse.

The Playground continues the theme of evil children. Goode's Crossing is a town whose population includes a large number of mystics and would-be magicians. Many of them have been experimenting with the occult. Unfortunately, they aren't skilled enough to be in control of the powers they have unleashed, and several of the local children become possessed by a demonic force. The childlike figures of *Strange Seed* are back again in *The Children of the Island,* this time revealed as an ancient race that preceded humanity and which once dwelt on Manhattan. And now they've decided to reclaim their birthright at the expense of the unaware invaders. Their presence in the urban setting is nicely creepy.

Carlisle Street is another novel in the same vein, ghostly children prowling the streets. Wright's gift for subtle horror and strange atmosphere can't quite carry this one, however, which seems to stagger rather than rush toward its conclusion. Far better was *A Manhattan Ghost Story,* an episodic but frequently chilling story of the spirits of the dead active in modern New York City, interacting with the living in deadly ways. This is one of Wright's best works, carefully utilizing his talent for evoking strange images with traditional narrative values.

The People of the Dark is a haunted-place story. An entire suburban neighbourhood was deserted years earlier after a series of unsolved murders. Jack and Erika move into a nearby house and are troubled by the disturbed spirits of the dead, and of the evil forces that caused their deaths. *The Waiting Room* is another Manhattan ghost story, and probably Wright's best novel. The protagonist learns that one of his acquaintances has inadvertently crossed the border between the living and the dead while still alive, and doesn't know how to return. He tries to help his friend, and instead attracts the attention of the decidedly unfriendly creatures that dwell on that other plane.

Wright uses the bad place theme again in *The Island,* this time locating it in a remote lake. The uneasy dead lie at the bottom of the lake, waiting for the ice to thaw so that they can emerge and vent their anger on the living. Despite the melodramatic theme, the actual story is restrained and atmospheric rather than graphically horrifying. *The Place* is very atypical, the story of a man whose wife and son are kidnapped by a maniac. Search parties can find no trace of them, but the protagonist's daughter is psychically linked to the kidnapper, who is also a serial killer. An odd diversion for Wright, and a not particularly successful one.

Wright's interest in exploring the world of the dead was resumed in *Boundaries.* David Case is traumatized when his sister is murdered, after which the killer took his own life. Case uses an experimental drug that allows his consciousness to leave his body and enter the world of the dead, but what he finds there is both frightening and puzzling. There's a similar situation in *Goodlow's Ghosts,* wherein the ghost of a murdered man returns to solve the mystery of his own death, a plot device that Hollywood seems to have adopted widely of late. But in Wright's novel, some of the living have crossed the barrier between life and death in the opposite direction, and the distinction between the two states has grown unclear. In *Little Boy Lost* an archaeologist is dismayed by the disappearance of his wife and son, and grows convinced that they have somehow travelled to a mystical otherworld that has survived since ancient times as a kind of parallel universe.

Wright also wrote two far more conventional horror novels as F. W. Armstrong. *The Changing* is a werewolf novel, interesting primarily because it is set in the upper strata of the business world and presents some startling contrasts. *The Devouring* is a vampire variation, although the monster encompasses demons, vampires and many other legendary creatures. Her opponent is a psychic detective whose lover is destined to become a victim unless he can destroy the creature. One short story, "A World without Toys," is worth mentioning, a surreal piece about a house full of toys washed away by a violent storm, and pursued by a woman convinced that it has some mystical importance. Wright shares with Charles L. Grant the gift of writing a truly frightening story that relies on subtlety and mood rather than overt horror themes.

—Don D'Ammassa

YARBRO, Chelsea Quinn

Pseudonyms: Terry Nelson Bonner; Vanessa Pryor. **National-ity:** American. **Born:** Berkeley, California, 15 September 1942. **Education:** Attended San Francisco State College, 1960-63. **Family:** Married Donald P. Simpson in 1969 (divorced 1982). **Career:** Theatre manager and playwright, Mirthmakers Children's Theatre, San Francisco, 1961-64; children's counsellor, 1963; cartographer, C. E. Erickson and Associates, Oakland, California, 1963-70; composer; card and palm reader, 1974-78. **Member:** Secretary, Science Fiction Writers of America, 1970-72; president, Horror Writers of America, 1988-89. **Agent:** Ellen Levine Literary Agency, 15 East 26th Street, Suite 1801, New York, NY 10010, USA.

HORROR, GHOST AND GOTHIC PUBLICATIONS

Novels (series: Atta Olivia Clemens; Saint-Germain)

Hôtel Transylvania: A Novel of Forbidden Love (Saint-Germain). New York, St. Martin's Press, 1978; London, New English Library, 1981.
The Palace: A Historical Horror Novel (Saint-Germain). New York, St. Martin's Press, 1978; London, New English Library, 1981.
Blood Games: A Novel of Historical Horror (Saint-Germain). New York, St. Martin's Press, 1979.
Dead and Buried (novelization of screenplay). New York, Warner, and London, Star, 1980.
Sins of Omission. New York, New American Library, 1980.
Path of the Eclipse: A Historical Horror Novel (Saint-Germain). New York, St. Martin's Press, 1981.
Tempting Fate (Saint-Germain). New York, St. Martin's Press, 1982.
The Godforsaken. New York, Warner, 1983.
Nomads (novelization of screenplay). New York, Bantam, 1984.
A Mortal Glamour. New York, Bantam, 1985.
Firecode. New York, Popular Library, 1987.
A Flame in Byzantium (Clemens). New York, Tor, 1987.
Crusader's Torch (Clemens). New York, Tor, 1988.
A Candle for D'Artagnan (Clemens). New York, Tor, 1989.
Out of the House of Life (Saint-Germain). New York, Tor, 1990.
Better in the Dark (Saint-Germain). New York, Tor, 1993.
Darker Jewels (Saint-Germain). New York, Tor, 1993.
Mansions of Darkness (Saint-Germain). New York, Tor, 1996.
Writ in Blood (Saint-Germain). New York, Tor, 1997.

Short Stories (series: Saint-Germain)

The Saint-Germain Chronicles. New York, Pocket Books, 1983.
Signs and Portents. Santa Cruz, California, Dream Press, 1984.
The Spider Glass (Saint-Germain). Eugene, Oregon, Pulphouse, 1991.

OTHER PUBLICATIONS

Novels

Ogilvie, Tallant, and Moon (as C. Q. Yarbro; Moon). New York, Putnam, 1976; as *Bad Medicine,* New York, Jove, 1990.

Time of the Fourth Horseman. Garden City, New York, Doubleday, 1976; London, Sidgwick and Jackson, 1980.
False Dawn. Garden City, New York, Doubleday, 1978; London, Sidgwick and Jackson, 1979.
Music When Sweet Voices Die (as C. Q. Yarbro; Moon). New York, Putnam, 1979; as *False Notes,* New York, Berkley, 1990.
Ariosto. New York, Pocket Books, 1980.
A Taste of Wine (as Vanessa Pryor). New York, Pocket Books, 1982.
Hyacinths. Garden City, New York, Doubleday, 1983.
The Making of Australia 5: The Outback (as Terry Nelson Bonner). New York, Dell, 1983.
Locadio's Apprentice (for children). New York, Harper, 1984.
Four Horses for Tishtry (for children). New York, Harper, 1985.
To the High Redoubt. New York, Popular Library, 1985.
Floating Illusions (for children). New York, Harper, 1986.
A Baroque Fable. New York, Berkley, 1986.
Taji's Syndrome. New York, Popular Library, 1988.
Beastnights. New York, Warner, 1989.
The Law in Charity. Garden City, New York, Doubleday, 1989.
Poison Fruit (as C. Q. Yarbro; Moon). New York, Jove, 1991.
Cat's Claw (as C. Q. Yarbro; Moon). New York, Jove, 1992.
Charity, Colorado. New York, M. Evans, 1993.
Crown of Empire. New York, Baen, 1994.

Short Stories

Cautionary Tales. Garden City, New York, Doubleday, 1978; expanded edition, New York, Warner, and London, Sidgwick and Jackson, 1980.
On Saint Hubert's Thing. New Castle, Virginia, Cheap Street, 1982.

Other

CQY. New Castle, Virginia, Cheap Street, 1982.
Messages from Michael on the Nature of the Evolution of the Human Soul. Chicago, Playboy Press, 1979.
More Messages from Michael. New York, Berkley, 1986.
Michael's People. New York, Berkley, 1988.

Editor, with Thomas N. Scortia, *Two Views of Wonder.* New York, Ballantine, 1973.

*   *   *

Changes in the United States book-publishing and distribution system in the 1990s had a significant, negative impact on genre fiction, and horror fiction was dealt a particularly strong blow as publisher after publisher eliminated the category from their lists. Despite this trend, vampire novels grew in popularity, sustaining the careers of writers as diverse as Anne Rice, Les Daniels and Chelsea Quinn Yarbro.

Yarbro's Count Saint-Germain made his debut in *Hotel Transylvania,* a suave aristocratic figure in mid-18th-century France, actually a vampire who has forsworn the taking of human life for the sake of blood, and who has succeeded in blending into the world of the living. Saint-Germain falls in love with a beautiful young woman who is menaced by debauched noblemen with a taste for the occult as well as the first stirrings of the French Revolution. Yarbro was one of the first to exploit the inherent sexuality of the vampire and anticipated Anne Rice by using historical settings and a strong romantic element.

Saint-Germain returned in *The Palace*, this time in Renaissance Florence. Once again it is the human characters who practice evil rather than the vampire, who is again seeking a woman who can become his partner through the ages. The series continues to jump back and forth from one time-period to another, but the gaps are large enough that it makes little difference in which order the individual volumes are read. Saint-Germain visits Nero's Rome in *Blood Games*, wherein he is forced to rescue his friends and the woman he loves from sacrifice in the Circus. He is forced to make the woman, Olivia, into a vampire in order to save her life—and she was featured in a less successful spinoff series.

In *Path of the Eclipse*, Saint-Germain visits the land of Genghis Khan where he champions the cause of an oppressed people and becomes involved with two women, one a dangerous temptress. Despite his superhuman powers, he is remarkably ineffective in the face of such overwhelming odds. Yarbro carefully avoids transforming Saint-Germain into a comic-book superhero throughout the series. Rather, he is a well-intentioned man with extraordinary powers, but also prone to errors of judgment and subject to the limitations of his kind. *Tempting Fate* is chronologically the most recent of the novels, with Saint-Germain living in Germany and watching with increasing horror the rise to power of the Nazi Party. When they kill the woman he currently loves, Saint-Germain strikes back, but as before, he is incapable of more than a token strike.

A Flame in Byzantium is the first of three novels that featured Olivia, no longer Saint-Germain's companion. In the first, she flees from Rome to Constantinople seeking a new patron. Like Saint-Germain, she seeks to survive without taking human lives, but the tumultuous political upheavals in her new homeland make life just as perilous there as they were in Rome. She returns to that city during the Crusades in *Crusader's Torch*, but only to have a perilous journey. Her final appearance is in *A Candle for D'Artagnan*, in the 17th century. There she meets the dashing young swordsman of the title and is once more plunged into a world of political intrigue and personal danger. The Olivia series never enjoyed the popularity of Saint-Germain, although both series share meticulously researched settings and Yarbro's superb talent for creating the feel of the various historical periods about which she writes.

Saint-Germain returned in *Out of the House of Life*, this time to show us the earliest period of his life, while he still lived in Egypt. A demonic force has been conjured and imprisoned, but for how long? The story line alternates with a more modern tale of another of his lovers, this one determined to unearth the secrets of his past. Saint-Germain is shipwrecked and brought to a beleaguered 10th-century fortress in *Better in the Dark*, a stronghold whose future is in doubt because it is ruled by a young woman, and her dwindling forces are restive and disheartened. Ivan the Terrible almost causes Saint-Germain to die his final death in *Darker Jewels*, but once again he escapes into exile. He flees the Inquisition and finds a new home in the Americas in *Mansions of Darkness*, but when he becomes sympathetic to the flight of a woman defending the Aztec civilization from Spanish plunder, he alienates his current hosts. In *Writ in Blood* Saint-Germain becomes a spy in the service of the Tsar of Russia in the days immediately preceding the First World War. Five shorter adventures are collected in *The Saint-Germain Chronicles*, the best of which is "The Spider Glass." He also makes a brief appearance in the short story "Advocates."

Yarbro has written other horror fiction not involving vampires. *Dead and Buried* and *Nomads* are both film novelizations, but unusually good ones based on source material that involved un-usual concepts, in one case a mortician who can revive the dead, though with some unpleasant side-effects, in the other the investigation of mysterious street people who turn out to be something other than human. *Firecode* concerns a series of supernaturally caused fires, an elemental creature inadvertently summoned into our world. *The Godforsaken* is another historical horror novel set during the time of the Inquisition and involving a curse; and a woman struggles to harness her psychic abilities in *Sins of Omission*. Yet another historical novel, *A Mortal Glamour*, involves evil secrets within a 14th-century convent.

Yarbro has also written a respectable number of short stories, among the best of which are "Confession of a Madman," "Creatures That Walked in Darkness," "Do I Dare Eat a Peach?," "Lapses," "Novena" and "Such Nice Neighbors." Several of her stories were brought together in the volume *Signs and Portents*, but many of her best remain uncollected.

Yarbro has written in other genres as well, including science fiction, fantasy and detective stories, but is identified primarily with her vampire fiction. Although the Saint-Germain stories are certainly the books for which Yarbro is most famous, their horror content has grown thinner through the years, and they might more properly be called historical romances with supernatural overtones. However they may be labelled, they enjoy a continued popularity that is not likely to fade with the passage of time.

—Don D'Ammassa

ZELL, Steve

Nationality: American. **Born:** Arizona. **Career:** Editorial cartoonist for *The Tombstone Epitaph*; session vocalist; writer. **Address:** c/o St. Martin's Press, 175 Fifth Avenue, New York, NY 10010, USA. Lives in Los Angeles.

HORROR, GHOST AND GOTHIC PUBLICATIONS

Novels

Wizrd. New York, St. Martin's, and London, Headline, 1994.

*   *   *

Imagine an unlikely test of horror-lore knowledge. You are given a list of countries, and quite simply all you have to do is write down next to them the type of horror that is most often traditionally associated with them in most people's minds, stereotypically or no. Quite possibly next to England you might suggest the haunted house, regardless of the fact that such stories are declining in popularity. Next to many of the Eastern European countries might be the bat-infested castle on the hill. For Wales, see the sin-eater; for Ireland the *sidhe*, or any other of its legendary spirits. Next to America (these days) most likely the answer would be the serial killer. But say that for the American question more detail is required: to the point of specifying individual states. Almost certainly the answer for Arizona would be the idea of sacred Indian ground, Indian curses, or haunted mines.

Steve Zell, who hails from that state, where he grew up "surrounded by the ghost towns and Indian lore of Arizona," builds on the tradition of such stories. *Wizrd* is Zell's only published novel to date, and the word is so spelled by ill-educated Arizona mining folk in the novel's flashback scenes—with reference to the Wizard mines that form the backdrop for most of the action. Before writing the novel Steve Zell was involved in cartoons; and now he is a singer. Quite a leap, surely, from cartoons to a first novel; cartoons depending as they do on ostensible brevity. Of course, cartoons are a way of condensing complex ideas or emotions into bite-sized pockets suitable for mass comprehension; a good cartoon is a difficult trick to pull off. *Wizrd* uses very little of such condensation.

One of the factors that make the novel something of a slow burn to begin with is the remarkable amount of detail that Zell goes into to show us how the life of the family that has moved from the Big City to a small town in Arizona has been uprooted and changed. Microscopically we see all of the unpacking, the children's exploring of the new terrain, and (most interestingly of all) the thwarted creative processes of the family's father, he being an artist. (Pretty soon we get to see that the father is doing a lot more drinking than drawing.) Everything being divulged in this way has a sort of bullying effect: we are clearly not going to get to the good stuff until the scene has been meticulously set.

Wizrd holds to its bosom with some considerable pride the trope of the Ghost Town. The abandoned Wizard mines (which once upon a time gleefully threw up vast quantities of copper, gold and marble) are inevitably the source of all childish fascination. Bryce and Meg find the caves. Nearby, a boy drowns after flash-floods, and shortly afterwards Meg, from the New York family, starts to see (and believe to be real) certain apparitions: boys "dressed like kids in a western." The ghost town's ghosts are waking: "As much as the facades looked like cutouts, Pinon Rim was no candy-ass movie set. Pinon Rim was the Old West, always would be, and it didn't matter how many shiny new cars prowled its streets. It had real ghosts. If you couldn't see them, you felt them." Or, presumably, you did if you were susceptible to these things; a high level of denial takes place in Arizona small towns, apparently.

So what is the nature of the curse? In a word: demonomania. Bryce's friend Cody explains: "They told me the rest of the legend, but they still won't believe it. It's gonna drive everybody kill-crazy. It needs someone to start it off, then it's like British Bulldog: that one gets the next one, then those two get someone else. Man, you were right. Your sister's it!"

Welcome to Helldorado! This is the name of the town's annual celebration of Halloween, only this year the jubilations do not go strictly according to plan. *Wizrd* changes its spots, or at least a few of them, as it becomes a novel with the sensibilities of the Western. Very quickly the good townsfolk are finding themselves desirous of protection from all outsiders. Except that these outsiders will not be any mean rustlers dressed in black; they will be much worse. Oddly enough, by this point, *Wizrd* also resembles the Old English poem *Beowulf* (some argue that this was the first horror story): the tribe is in the Mead Hall, not knowing that the monster is planning its attack. *Mystery of the Haunted Mine* by Gordon D. Shirreffs (1962, original title: *The Haunted Treasure of the Espectros*) was another possible source of inspiration for Steve Zell—a tale of the Espectros, a range of haunted mountains in Arizona, and what two men will do to solve the mystery ("Gary and Tuck refuse to believe that ghosts use live ammunition").

Perhaps what led to Zell's execution of *Wizrd* is irrelevant, although one school of thought has it that horror should be a lineal genre, with forefathers clearly visible. All that is important to mention is that *Wizrd* is an impressive debut: a novel that builds slowly and lets out a large held breath in the final quarter. His next offering should be looked forward to with anticipation.

—David Mathew

FOREIGN-LANGUAGE WRITERS

BERNANOS, Michel (1924-1964)

Nationality: French. **Selected Publications:** Novel: *La Montagne morte de la vie*, 1967; as *The Other Side of the Mountain*, Boston, Houghton Mifflin, 1968.

* * *

Michel Bernanos's only novel, *The Other Side of the Mountain*, was completed shortly before his death and published posthumously. It owes an obvious debt to Edgar Allan Poe's *Narrative of Arthur Gordon Pym* (the text carries a headquote from Poe's French translator, Charles Baudelaire) and some further inspiration to the work of the French symbolists who were Poe's most accomplished artistic heirs. It also has a good deal in common with the marine horror stories of William Hope Hodgson, although this is less likely to be due to direct influence.

The protagonist of the novel is a young man shanghaied aboard a French galleon in the 17th century. He is direly mistreated by the crew but finds a protector in the ship's cook, Toine. When the ship is becalmed in mid-Atlantic and its supplies are exhausted the crewmembers mutiny and turn to cannibalism. The wind finally returns but its velocity quickly increases to storm force and tears the vessel apart. Toine and the narrator lash themselves to a mast and drift helplessly among monstrous medusae until they are thrown on to a rust-coloured shore whose fine sand turns the surrounding shallows blood-red.

The castaways make their way through caves filled with enigmatic statues of beasts and men to the silent, heavily-wooded interior of the strange land. The forest creepers are mobile and predatory and there are gigantic carnivorous flowers; even the riverbeds open hungry mouths when the castaways attempt to bathe. A muted pulse, reminiscent of a heartbeat, is tangible within the ground. During a brief luminescent interlude which interrupts each night the trees of the forest bow down in the direction of a distant mountain-peak. As they approach the mountain—which seems to be the source of the continent's pulse—the castaways find that their skin is becoming encrusted with a stony substance. As they climb the mountain they find the petrified relics of other men. Some have been broken, apparently by virtue of falling from the upper slopes, but all are gradually being absorbed into the mountain-side.

The narrator's metamorphosis is nearly complete by the time he reaches the rim of the crater at the mountain's summit, but he nevertheless contrives to look over the edge. What he sees, before rolling back down the slope to begin his own fusion with the body of the mountain, is a gigantic staring eye afloat on a lake of blood.

The novel's original title—which translates into English as "The Dead Mountain of Life"—strongly implies that the text is allegorical, but its meaning is far from obvious. At one point Toine advises the narrator that he should not look for a solution to the mystery posed by the alien land, but he is not necessarily functioning as the author's mouthpiece when he does so. If one ignores Toine's advice, the story lends itself most readily to interpretation as a posthumous fantasy in which the strange continent is a post-Dantean afterworld. In that decoding the narrator's journey to the mountain becomes a kind of rite of passage by means of which he becomes able to accept death meekly and reverently. Other interpretations are, however, possible—and perhaps more likely.

Michel Bernanos was the son of George Bernanos, the author of several philosophical novels—including *The Star of Satan*, which is cast as a supernatural horror story—and many polemical essays. The perennial complaint of the elder Bernanos was that the vast majority of people deliver themselves to Satan—and, in consequence, ultimately to Hell—in their first moment of disillusionment, after which they hide from their true spiritual nature and live "inauthentically." Michel Bernanos must have been very familiar with this thesis—but he must also have been familiar with the very different notion of "inauthenticity" popularized by the French existentialist philosophers, who associated it with the cowardly denial of personal freedom. Seen in this light, *The Other Side of the Mountain* might be interpreted as an anti-existentialist fable, which denies at every turn the effectiveness of human freedom, representing life (and perhaps afterlife too) as a desperate struggle for survival aboard a Ship of Fools. Such a struggle can have no conceivable conclusion but a confrontation with the bleak accusing eye of God, whose metastasizing judgment is final and eternal.

Whichever interpretation one prefers, the novel is one of the most powerful and most memorable of all surreal fantasies.

—Francis Amery

BULGAKOV, Mikhail (1891-1940)

Nationality: Russian. **Selected Publications:** Novels: *The Master and Margarita*, London, Collins and Harvill Press, 1967. *The Heart of a Dog*, London, Collins and Harvill Press, 1968. Short Stories: *Diaboliad and Other Stories*, edited by Elleanda Proffer and Carl R. Proffer, Bloomington, Indiana University Press, 1972. *The Heart of a Dog and Other Stories*, Moscow, Raduga, 1990.

* * *

Mikhail Bulgakov, torn between careers in medicine and literature, eventually opted for the latter. It was a bad move, which he probably came to regret very deeply, although not as deeply as he might have done had it not been for the stroke of luck that led Josef Stalin to see and be deeply touched by the opening performance of his play *The Day of the Turbins* (based on the novel *The White Guard*) in 1926. But for the moral credit accumulated that evening, the lifelong harassment to which Bulgakov was subject by virtue of being a "bourgeois writer" would have been even worse. *The Master and Margarita*, which became a masterpiece partly by virtue of being written in such difficult circumstances, might never have been written at all had it not been for Stalin's sentimentality; it is the only literary work in existence of which one can say that.

Bulgakov's troubles began with *Diaboliad*, a collection of satirical stories issued in the same year as *The White Guard*, 1925. The title story is a surreal sketch parodying Soviet bureaucratic inefficiency, while the centrepiece of the book is the long novella "The Fatal Eggs," a science-fictional black comedy which borrows the theme of H. G. Wells's *The Food of the Gods* in the service of a blistering satirical demolition of Stalin's beloved Five Year Plan. The eggs in question are reptile eggs mistakenly substituted for chicken eggs in an experiment with magical rays that is intended to turn their hatchlings into giants; the resultant monsters run riot.

Although they are supposedly comedies all but one of the stories in *Diaboliad* end with a fatality, and hence with an implicit switch to tragedy—sardonic twists which made Bulgakov's work even less endearing to the bureaucrats he was mocking—but in "The Fatal Eggs" the killing goes on and on, transforming the narrative into an authentic horror story whose jocular surface only serves to amplify that effect.

Bulgakov followed "The Fatal Eggs" with another Wellsian novella, *The Heart of a Dog*, which adapts the central motif of *The Island of Doctor Moreau* to a political satire in which a famous Moscow surgeon transforms a stray dog into the image of a man. Alas, image is not enough; the essential bestiality of the creature continues to make life a misery for everyone. When the surgeon's assistant suggests that the experiment should be swiftly concluded, the bureaucratic niceties of so doing prove annoyingly complicated, with the result that the dog-made-man moves his anarchic career on to a further stage. The blatant allegory of the miscarried revolution was too much for the authorities, who refused to allow the story's publication. Bulgakov spent the rest of his life writing numerous unproduced plays and a single unpublished novel. The novel, on which he worked throughout the 1930s, is an agonized allegory of his own life and predicament: *The Master and Margarita*.

The Master is the author of a philosophical novel which revises the orthodox account of Pontius Pilate's condemnation of the Messiah Yeshua (chapters from which make up one of the narrative strands of the novel). The suppression of this novel by the authorities has driven the Master mad and led to his confinement in a lunatic asylum. There he meets the struggling poet Ivan Bezdomny, who has been incarcerated after a bizarre encounter with a "professor" who claims to have been present when Pilate condemned Yeshua to death and seems to be able to foretell the future. The Master tells Bezdomny that he has undoubtedly met the Devil—and so he has. Professor Woland, aided by the demons Azazello and Faggot, the black cat Behemoth and the witch Hella, has arrived to raise merry Hell in Moscow while preparing to hold the latest in a long series of extravagant balls, which he puts on so that his loyal subjects may pay him the homage that is his due.

As his human hostess for this magnificent occasion Woland selects the lovely but somewhat heart-broken Margarita Nikolayevna, the wife of a scientist and one-time mistress of the Master. As her fee for providing this service Margarita asks to be reunited for a brief while with her old lover, in the tawdry love-nest they shared—the place where the Master burned his masterpiece and went mad. (Bulgakov had burned his own manuscripts in 1929 by way of lending emphasis to his plea to be allowed to emigrate; Stalin refused to let him go.) It is the Devil who resurrects the lost manuscript so that it can take its place within the broader text. The Devil also responds to a further plea—made on the author's behalf by the one and only actual disciple with whom Yeshua is credited in the Master's novel, Matthew the Levite—far more generously than Stalin had responded to Bulgakov's.

One might argue that *The Master and Margarita* is not a horror story at all, by virtue of the fact that the reader is invited to rejoice in every cruelty and humiliation—especially the homicidal ones—that the Devil inflicts upon the mean-minded bureaucrats of 1930s Moscow. The rest of the narrative is horrific only in the sense that all tragedy is painful, and even that is lightened by the Devil's climactic gesture of benevolence. Nor can the novel sensibly be reckoned Gothic, although it certainly features a truly mag-nificent and charismatic villain. It is, however, one of the great classics of the revisionist tradition of Literary Satanism, whose roots were deeply embedded in Gothic Romanticism. Its Satan may not be the Satan of the horror-story tradition—the Satan of *The Monk* and *The Exorcist*—but he is definitely Satanic in the sense that he is the Adversary and the Rebel against oppressive Authority. If he has become heroic, dashing, liberating and merciful it is only because the Authority whose adversary he is has been revealed, in its every earthly manifestation, as corrupt, parsimonious, tyrannical and merciless—and if that is not a truly horrific thought, what is?

—Francis Amery

BUZZATI, Dino (1906-1972)

Nationality: Italian. **Selected Publications:** Novel: *Il Grande Ritratto*, Arnoldo Mondadori, 1960; as *Larger Than Life*, London, Secker and Warburg, 1962. Short Stories: *Catastrophe*, London, Calder and Boyars, 1965. *Restless Nights*, San Francisco, North Point, 1983. *The Siren*, San Francisco, North Point, 1984.

* * *

Dino Buzzati once wrote in his notebook that, "Every writer and artist, however long he may live, says only one thing." He considered this to be inevitable, because any other state of affairs would amount to insincerity. Buzzati's work is more various than one might expect were this judgment to be taken too literally, but if there is one underlying note sounding there in perpetuity it is the Existentialist conviction that human life is, after all, futile: that all hopes of achievement come to nothing in the end. That is the implication of his first publication, the novella "Barnabo of the Mountains" (1933). It is also the implication of his first novel, *The Tartar Steppe*, in which the soldiers waiting to mount a heroic defence of the frontier against a Tartar invasion never encounter any self-justifying action (a failure made even more acute by the novel's publication during World War II). His fabular short stories so often become horrific because they have exactly the same nihilistic bent.

The stories in *Catastrophe*, originally published between 1949 and 1958, are indeed replete with images of collapse and desolation. In the title story passengers on a train begin to see signs of panic in the towns through which they pass, which slowly escalate as they hurry on to the eerily deserted terminus. In "The Landslide" a city journalist searches a remote mountain region for the site of a recent disaster, only to find that the local notion of "news" does not correspond with his own. (Buzzati made his living as a journalist and published many of his stories in newspapers; this meant that brevity was a always a priority, if not an absolute necessity, and that different perceptions of "news" were always of interest to him.) The protagonist of "The Collapse of the Baliverna" must live with the guilt of having accidentally precipitated a disaster, while the protagonist of "The Epidemic" must wrestle with the suggestion that the influenza he has just caught might be selecting out the morally defective.

Paranoia is as important an element in Buzzati's work as catastrophe. "And Yet They Are Knocking at Your Door" is a political parable as well as a paranoid nightmare but the awful outcomes of "Oversight," "The Alarming Revenge of a Domestic Pet," "The Monster" and "Something Beginning with 'L'" afflict perfectly ordinary folk. "Seven Floors" is an unusually detailed and acute parable of paranoia, and the most disturbing story in the whole volume is the striking *conte cruel* "Just the Very Thing They Wanted." "The Slaying of the Dragon," in which the last surviving dinosaurs are ruthlessly hunted down and their progeny slaughtered, is a bitter allegory declaring that ignorance is not merely destructive but self-destructive too.

Restless Nights and *The Siren* select materials spanning the entirety of Buzzati's career from 1933 to 1971; the former collection—which has the items of first choice—is by far the better of the two. "The Seven Messengers" (1942) is a neat account of a quest which can have no end, a theme repeated and further elaborated in "The Walls of Anagoor" (1955), "The Bewitched Jacket" (1966) and "The Eiffel Tower" (1966). It is noticeable, however, that "The Ubiquitous" (1966), "The Scriveners" (1971) and "What Will Happen on October 12th" (1971) are far more intimate and ironic in their attempts to capture the same sensibility. It is also noticeable that "The Count's Wife" (1971) and "The Bogeyman" (1971) are much lighter in tone; in the former fable the good woman who grows angel's wings is lucky enough to discover a countervailing influence, while in the latter, the extinction of the fabular haunter by order of the city council is an occasion for mourning. Buzzati's ironic sympathy for the figures we appoint to carry our fearful anxieties is also evident in "The Colomber" (1966), a fine account of a wonderful sea-monster.

The most notable items in *The Siren* include "The Five Brothers" (1954), a mock folk tale in which a dishonest warning wrecks the lives of the princes of an imaginary kingdom, and "The Flying Carpet" (1955), one of several Buzzati tales about miraculous devices which lie unused because their owners are paralysed by fear of opportunity. "The Prohibited Word" (1958) is an exceptionally clever parable about the power of conformity.

Buzzati's narrative extrapolations of Existentialist angst reach their most feverish pitch in his futuristic fantasies and science-fiction stories. In "The Saucer Has Landed" (1954) the priest who makes first contact with sinless and joyful extraterrestrials is decidedly unimpressed by their intellectual achievements—although "Appointment with Einstein," published the same year, is a seeming endorsement of the notion that at least some scientific knowledge is impressive by virtue of being diabolically inspired. "The Time Machine" (1955) describes an attempt to prolong life by slowing down time, which ends with appalling suddenness when the machine malfunctions. *Larger than Life* is about the construction of a huge computer with a human personality, which begins to overwhelm those around it; although it is eventually robbed of its voice it cannot be stopped, for the day of its mechanical dominion has arrived. "Elephantiasis" (1971)—which recapitulates and updates the theme of "The Plague" (1958)—details the absurd but catastrophic effects of an infection which overtakes all plastics, subjecting civilization to a "universal tumour" whose invasive proliferation "annihilat[es] man's happy paradise."

Buzzati's work has obvious methodological links with the short stories produced by such writers of the following generation as Italo Calvino and Primo Levi, who may well have taken some inspiration from his work; the polite but devastating temper of the satirical exercises produced by all three writers has a distinctive feel to it. Buzzati's imagination is nowhere near as far-ranging as Calvino's, and he has not such a tragically painful field of experience to draw on as Levi—both of which observations may be relevant to the fact that they are far more careful than he in the care and conservation of hope and wonder—but he does have a unique narrative dexterity which makes him a master of the very short story. His *modus operandi* is perfectly suited to the production of *contes cruels* of both the brutal and slick varieties, but his black humour is never merely casual. His best work has a profound depth of feeling, which serves to remind his readers that although all human endeavour might, at the end of the day, be devoid of meaning, there is an authentic heroism in steadfast attempts to prove otherwise.

—Brian Stableford

CAZOTTE, Jacques (1719-1792)

Nationality: French. **Selected Publications:** Novel: *Le Diable amoureux*, 1772; as *The Devil in Love*, London, Heinemann, 1925.

* * *

Almost all of Jacques Cazotte's literary work was lightweight and fanciful, written with tongue in cheek to amuse his readers. He wrote fairy tales and satires, fables and Oriental fantasies, and a mock-chivalric romance. *The Devil in Love* cannot really be said to stand apart from all the rest, given that it too is an essentially amiable flight of fancy, but it is possessed by a certain fugitive seriousness that none of his other works has. Cazotte does seem to have intended it as a horror story of sorts, although many readers would argue that it turned out in the end to be something altogether different. It is, at any rate, a work shot through with fascinating contradictions.

Cazotte's interest in the fantastic and the occult extended in the latter part of his life to a close involvement with the Martinists, an Illuminist sect claiming affiliation to the Rosicrucian Order and Weishaupt's Bavarian Illuminati. After the founder of the sect, Martinez de Pasqualis, died in 1768 he was succeeded by the self-styled Saint-Martin, whose close associate Madame la Croix became a member of Cazotte's household, collaborating with him in séances and other occult experiments. The occult apparatus of *The Devil in Love* does not seem to be taken very seriously, but Cazotte's reputation as an occultist led many contemporary readers to regard it with undue suspicion or reverence—both of which contributed to the novel's reputation and influence.

The story relates how a group of young men, including the protagonist Alvare, issue a sarcastic summons to the Devil. They do so merely as a lark—but the Devil comes, at first in bizarrely ominous form but subsequently preferring the guise of a winsome female, Biondetta. While patiently working in quasi-Mephistophelean fashion to secure Alvare's damnation, however, Biondetta seemingly conceives a genuine affection for him.

Cazotte admitted that the work as originally envisaged would have had two parts, the first describing Alvare's seduction and the second following his subsequent career as the devil's minion. He explained the non-publication of the second part (which, if it ever existed, has been lost) by saying that it was too dark to be welcomed by an audience in search of amusement and distraction. The removal of the second part was initially compounded by a softening of the ending of the first part; in the first edition Biondetta does not complete her seduction but gives away her true nature by her calmness in the face of a storm, and is commanded to vanish—which she does, after briefly showing her true form for a second time. This abrupt conclusion apparently failed to satisfy the audience, so Cazotte added an extra episode in which Alvare yields to Biondetta's temptations—but this is a recomplication rather than a clarification, and it makes morality of the story distinctly murky, given that Alvare still seems to be saved from damnation in spite of his fall from grace.

The danger to young men posed by demonic succubi, who used eroticism as an instrument of temptation, had long been preached by the church. It had also received a good deal of publicity in pious chivalric romances, which placed a high value on knightly chastity. The myth had presumably arisen from—and remained connected with—erotic dreams, and Alvare does wonder whether his entire adventure might have been delusory. Cazotte seems to have been uncertain as to how best to resolve this issue and never really does; although many of Alvare's exploits are dismissed as purely subjective experiences there seems to be no doubt that Biondetta is real, and that her attendance upon the hero extends over a long period.

Had Cazotte stuck to his original plan and let Alvare become a living servant of the devil his story would have become an important prototype of Gothic fantasy. Even in its truncated form it does seem to have influenced a number of Gothic writers. Because it appears that Biondetta does the hero no real harm, though, *The Devil in Love* is more readily associated with daringly sceptical works which gradually muster more and more sympathy for the supposed agents of evil—such works as Théophile Gautier's "La morte amoureuse" (1836; usually translated as "Clarimonde"), whose title may well carry a deliberate echo of Cazotte's, and Anatole France's *The Revolt of the Angels* (1914). In such stories as these the pleasure-denying morality of the Church is severely questioned, and ultimately condemned. Although this was not probably Cazotte's aim it is easy enough to believe that—like Milton, according to William Blake—he was "of the devil's party without knowing it." The modern reader who follows Alvare's affair with the ever-obliging Biondetta can hardly help but find her charming even while refusing to be duped by the blatantly false explanation of her nature which she offers to him.

Ironically, if the imagery of Cazotte's tale lent inspiration to those who wanted to argue that the Devil was not as black as the Church painted him, it also offered some inspiration for those who wanted to believe that all seductive women had a little of the devil in them. Baudelaire sometimes invoked Cazotte while lamenting his unhappy relationships with the opposite sex, and there is a calculated echo of *The Devil in Love* in Barbey d'Aurevilly's misogynistic collection *Les diaboliques* (1874; usually translated as *The She-Devils*).

So many tales of diabolical bargains have been published since 1772 that *The Devil in Love* cannot help but seem pale, hesitant and confused by comparison with the best of them, but its pallor, its hesitancy and its confusion are its most intriguing and rewarding characteristics. The complexity of the tale might well have arisen from the author's inability to figure out exactly what he meant to do and how best to do it, but it is all the more revealing for that. If Cazotte made the Devil a heroine in spite of his intention and determination to do otherwise, that surely provides a better advertisement for the Devil's innate heroism than any that was ever carefully wrought by a fully-committed Literary Satanist.

—Francis Amery

ECO, Umberto (1932-)

Nationality: Italian. **Selected Publications:** Novels: *Il nom della rosa*, Fabbri-Bompiani, 1980; tr. by William Weaver, as *The Name of the Rose*, New York, Harcourt Brace Jovanovich, 1983; London, Martin Secker & Warburg, 1983. *Il pendolo di Foucault*, Fabbri-Bompiani, 1988; tr. by William Weaver, as *Foucault's Pendulum*, New York, Harcourt Brace Jovanovich, 1989; London, Martin Secker and Warburg, 1989. Other: *Postille a Il nome della rosa*, 1983; tr. by William Weaver, as *Reflections on The Name of the Rose*, New York, Harcourt Brace Jovanovich, 1984; London, Martin Secker and Warburg, 1984.

*   *   *

Umberto Eco, a professor at the University of Bologna with a considerable academic reputation as a postmodern philosopher, historian and literary critic, came to international bestselling fame with his first novel, *The Name of the Rose*. This could be called a medieval detective story, but the essential reasonableness of detection and revelation is undermined by dark and indeed horrific elements. Deductive logic here labours in the shadow of apocalypse and is opposed by the terrible unreason of too-blind faith.

The richly described setting is a large Italian abbey in the year 1327, a year (like so many) of religious upheaval, clashing heresies, and bitter debates about spiritual versus temporal power. To this abbey comes the English monk William of Baskerville—a cognate of Sherlock Holmes, as obliquely hinted in his name and emphasized by his physical appearance, showy displays of deduction, fits of characteristic indolence, etc. William's attendant novice Adso tells, but does not always comprehend, the twisted tale that follows.

Several intertwined strands emerge. There is corruption within the abbey: intellectual and physical lusts, homosexual encounters, smuggled-in women. A developing pattern of deaths seems to echo the sequence of tribulations in the Apocalypse of *Revelation* (re-echoed in the monastery's carvings and the magnificent collection of Apocalypses in its great locked library). The first four angels' trumpets bring disaster from on high, transformation of the sea to blood, death of sea-creatures, and the smiting of the heavens themselves—and dead monks are duly found fallen from a great height, immersed in a tub of pig's blood, immersed again in the balneary or bathhouse, struck down with a celestial armillary sphere. Linking the deaths is a mysterious book which virtually everyone conspires to keep William from inspecting. The spiritual core of evil seems to lie in the forbidden library atop the great tower or Aedificium, a library which is both labyrinth and cryptogram, and which "defends itself" with mirrors, frightening sounds, hallucinogenic vapours, and an inaccessible secret room towards which William slowly maps his way during terrifying nightly explorations.

Meanwhile, the political-theological struggle between corrupt Pope and Holy Roman Emperor also shakes the abbey. The Inquisition arrives, with torture and ruthless questioning that condemns the relatively innocent—like the idiot monk who has attempted a grisly but useless piece of black magic that begins with digging out a cat's eyes, and a beautiful young woman brought in for various monks' pleasure (with whom poor Adso has also had a fling). Although the apocalyptic pattern of crime proves part accidental and part fraudulent, it is left for William to hunt down the truly guilty monk who remains, and who is motivated by a grim fanaticism that despises laughter and reason as cheapening the true faith. The book that he regards as deadly, and has made so by impregnating the pages with poison (recalling the book of the seventh and last angel in *Revelation*), is the lost second volume of Aristotle's *Poetics*—which deals approvingly with humour.

Reason—aided by chance, and insights from Adso's visions and dreams—has lit the way to the heart of the maze and an uncovering of its horrors. But unreason triumphs in the resulting holocaust, in which the entire priceless library is consumed. The final horror is that reason has not been enough.

Densely textured historical detail and sensuous descriptions add to the book's phantasmagoric power. A later pendant, the slim essay *Reflections on The Name of the Rose*, is interestingly illustrated with apocalyptic art and carvings inspired by *Revelation*—that hallucinated prophetic nightmare which underlies the story.

Eco's professional expertise in semiotics is detectable in *The Name of the Rose*, as narrative disquiet is craftily intensified by the unreliability of clues and the elusiveness of truth. The name of the rose is distinct from the rose itself, the sign from the signified, the map from the territory.

This insight pervades *Foucault's Pendulum*, which is steeped in occult lore—all the accumulated garbage from millennia of credulity. The tale escalates from jokiness to horror as the occult's signs and symbols prove to be potent triggers of terror, pain and death, irrespective of whether they relate to anything "real". As one of John Crowley's characters remarks in *Aegypt* (1987): "Secret societies have not had power in history, but the *notion* that secret societies have had power in history *has* had power in history." Some notions—and the argument is dismayingly plausible—are dangerous even to play with.

Our hero Casaubon is an amused dabbler who enjoys the fly-blown conspiracy theories of the occult fringe: the endless intellectual mazes surrounding the legends of Templars, Rosicrucians, Jesuits, Assassins and a hundred more. Much entertainment flows from the game of supposing that it's all true. But ambiguous and sinister notes repeatedly intrude. Early on, an eccentric colonel proposes a ramifying theory about the Templars as secret masters of history—and is soon reported dead, garrotted. An acquaintance hints that he is an immortal adept, like the legendary Comte de Saint-Germain. Casaubon's girlfriend joins the game and laughs with him at cultists—only to become "possessed" at a Brazilian quasi-voodoo ceremony.

Nevertheless Casaubon and two friends, editors at a publishing company that exploits the occult, continue to play in the labyrinth-cum-minefield of esoterica. They delightedly programme a computer to permute random fragments of "lore," from "The Templars have something to do with everything" to "Minnie Mouse is Mickey's fiancée." From this comes a wonderful Plan, a gloriously elaborate lie which cross-links every aspect of the occult. It is so gaudily convincing that cultists who believe themselves on the verge of ultimate secrets become convinced that the friends hold *the* final secret. In a fearful yet still ambiguous ceremony (is the ectoplasmic horror magic, fraud, or incense-induced delirium?) one companion is horridly killed rather than utter the secret which he cannot reveal, for it does not exist. The imaginary labyrinth contains real monsters.

Foucault's Pendulum is perhaps too long, too stuffed with the fruits of interminable esoteric research. Its bitter core remains effective and chilling.

—David Langford

EWERS, Hanns Heinz (1871-1943)

Nationality: German. **Selected Publications:** Novels: *Die Zauberlehrling*, 1907; as *The Sorcerer's Apprentice*, New York, John Day, 1927. *Alraune*, 1911; New York, John Day, 1929. *Vampir*, 1921; as *Vampire*, New York, John Day, 1934. Short Stories: *Blood*, New York, Heron Press, 1930.

*   *   *

Hanns Heinz Ewers was for a while a performer in one of the literary cabarets which were eventually to be established in the Anglo-American mind, courtesy of Bob Fosse's 1972 film *Cabaret*, as the paradigmatic locus of German Decadence. That was in the period before World War I, in which Ewers also produced his most famous literary works. By the time war broke out he had become a great traveller; his work as an enthusiastic propagandist for the German cause in the United States resulted in his internment there when America entered the war on the other side. This experience served to deepen the passion of his nationalism, but his subsequent alliance with the ideals of the Nazi party—which extended to writing a biography of the political "martyr" Horst Wessel and scripting an unproduced film version—eventually ran into trouble. His works were banned in 1935 and he was forbidden to publish anything further.

The arrival of literary Decadence in Berlin was a trifle late, missing the *fin de siècle* years, and such dandified poseurs as Ewers were obvious imitations of French originals. Ewers—who was Villiers de l'Isle Adam's German translator—tried to compensate for this belatedness by defining a quintessentially Germanic Decadent anti-hero who might carry the cause which had already begun to flag in France to a new extreme. Wagner and Nietzsche, the principal German sources of inspiration for the French Decadents, provided models for the artistic tastes and philosophy of Frank Braun, Ewers's fictitious alter ego. In *The Sorcerer's Apprentice* Braun becomes contemptuously fascinated with the raw religiosity of a small Alpine village and hypnotizes a girl whom he has previously debauched into believing that she is a saint. She carries off the imposture with unexpected flair, becoming the focus of a fervent cult before deciding that the proper moment for her martyrdom has arrived—after which Braun is lucky to escape with his life.

Alraune begins in an earlier phase of Braun's career when, as a penniless student, he enters into an unholy alliance with his uncle to conduct an experiment in selective breeding which will combine all the worst elements of degenerate humanity. (The experiment was presumably suggested by Max Nordau's best-selling exercise in alarmism *Entartung*, translated into English as *Degeneration*.) The use of a mandrake root—*alraune* is the German term for the mandrake—in the experiment is purely symbolic, although the nature and career of the progeny in question reflect the dark legends connected with the root. The story resumes 20 years later, when Alraune—the orphan offspring of a vulgar whore and a sadistic murderer—has become a lovely but utterly corrupt *femme fatale*. Her sexual magnetism is infallible but everyone who comes into contact with her is reduced to abject misery before perishing from disease, accident or suicide. As a self-appointed *ubermensch*, Braun thinks that he can resist the effects of her curse, and dares to hope that her love for him might be her salvation, but the iron hand of Fate is far too powerful. In the end, Alraune brings him even closer to the brink of disaster than his previous apprentice.

By the time Ewers completed the Frank Braun trilogy in *Vampire* he was an older and perhaps wiser man, and he was becoming more interested in the development of the German cinema—to which he was later to contribute several Expressionist scripts—than the media with which he had previously been involved. The novel is mostly content to dramatize a chastened Braun's attempts to win support in the United States for the German cause in World War I. Yet again there is a *femme fatale* whose attentions threaten to bring about his destruction but she is peripheral to the quasi-autobiographical record of the hero's travails, and probably ought to be seen as a symbol of the gradual weakening of the German nation while trench warfare sucked up the blood of an entire generation. Although John Day released a translation of *Vampire* in the wake of its two predecessors, it appeared without the gorgeously Decadent decorations by Mahlon Blaine which made the earlier volumes so spectacular, and it was not rendered into English by Guy Endore, whose flamboyant translation of *Alraune* might be reckoned a masterpiece in its own right.

Ewers's other translated works help to emphasize the slavishness of his Decadent affiliations; they include a long and reverent study of Edgar Allan Poe and a book on ants which is solidly in the tradition of Maurice Maeterlinck's philosophical studies. *Blood* is a collection of three *contes cruels*, although none is quite as cruel as his factually-based account of "The Execution of Damiens." Another striking *femme fatale* story, in which Ewers is careful to acknowledge the influence of Théophile Gautier, is "The Spider," which can be found in the Dashiell Hammett anthology *Creeps by Night* (1931). By far the greater number of his many short stories still remain untranslated.

Ewers's reputation has not worn well, partly due to the fact that those critics least likely to be offended by his Decadent pretensions are most likely to be offended by his attempts to curry favour with the Nazis, and vice versa. Although an eclectic collection of his short fiction appeared in Germany in 1964 his literary endeavours have not been fully rehabilitated there, let alone in the English-speaking world. He was, however, a more able, more versatile and more interesting writer than commentators annoyed by his flirtation with Nazism sometimes imply. *Alraune* deserves recognition as the most extreme of all *femme fatale* stories, and together with its predecessor it really did succeed in the mission that Ewers temporarily adopted as his own: to create a distinctively Germanic subspecies of Literary Decadence.

—Brian Stableford

GOGOL, Nikolai (Vasilievich) (1809-1852)

Nationality: Russian. **Selected Publications:** Short Stories: *Vechera na khutore bliz Dinkan'ki*, 1831-2; as *Evenings on a Farm Near Dikanka*, London, Chatto & Windus, 1926. *Mirgorod*, 1835; as *Mirgorod; Being a Continuation of Evenings in a Village Near Dikanka*, New York, Knopf, 1929. *The Mantle and Other Stories*, New York, Stokes, 1915. *The Overcoat and Other Stories*, New York, Knopf, 1923. *The Collected Tales and Plays of Nikolai Gogol*, New York, Pantheon, 1964.

* * *

Nikolai Gogol's early stories masquerade as folk tales, and he made a habit of insisting that he was only their recorder, not their author, but that only adds an extra layer to their intrinsic deceptiveness. Most of the tales in the two volumes of *Evenings on a Farm Near Dikanka* are supernatural, ironic and gloomy. "Sorochinsky Fair" is a love story which ends, as convention dictates, with a marriage—but the fair takes place on haunted ground, and the same is tacitly true of virtually everything Gogol wrote.

When the dead return, as they do in "St. John's Eve" and "A May Night," they come in search of reparation for sins committed against them by the living, and in Gogol's literary cosmos judgment is never mild. "A Terrible Vengeance" alleges that even God's stern notions of appropriate punishment cannot serve to discharge the moral debts that some sinners owe. When the Devil interferes in the course of human affairs, as he does in "The Lost Letter," "Christmas Eve" and "A Bewitched Place," he can sometimes be thwarted but usually finds an opportunity to bounce back after the tables have been turned. "Christmas Eve" is an exceptionally convoluted tale in which the Devil's malevolent intentions towards a pious blacksmith are subverted by his own passion for a witch who turns out to be the blacksmith's mother.

The four very various novellas assembled in *Mirgorod* include the horror story "Viy" (also reprinted as "The Viy" in *The Mantle and Other Stories*), in which three seminary students going home for a holiday are unwise enough to beg overnight shelter from an old witch. When she unleashes her malice against one of them, riding him like a horse, he is able to fight back with the power of prayer—and once he has forced her to appear in her true form as a beautiful young woman he is able to repay her in kind. Alas, when he is later dispatched from the safety of the seminary to pray by the bedside of a dying girl he discovers that the advantage has turned the witch's way again. She rises from her crypt to join with a host of demons in harrying him unmercifully; this time, the power of prayer can only delay the climax in which Viy, the king of the gnomes, completes the luckless novice's ignominious destruction.

Gogol's later works include "The Portrait," an allegory about the demotivation which artists suffer if they are paid too well, and "Diary of a Madman," a bizarre tale of obsessive love. His two masterpieces of short fiction are, however, the fabular novellas "The Nose" (1836) and "The Overcoat" (1842). "The Nose" belongs to an academic named Kovalev (or Kovalyov, according to the orthographic tastes of the translator), which is thrown into a river by his barber after its mysterious detachment. When it returns, costumed as a high-ranking civil servant, it refuses to acknowledge its former owner. Kovalev demands that the police intervene to thwart its attempts to flee the country; they oblige him, but he still has considerable difficulty restoring it to its proper place. Although this pioneering exercise in absurdism is not particularly horrific in matters of detail, its calculated nonsensicality becomes strangely disturbing.

"The Overcoat"—also known as "The Mantle" and "The Cloak" in various different translations—is so devoutly coveted by the clerk who must save to buy it that the quest lends new meaning to his life, and when it is stolen he dies of grief. Mere death is, however, insufficient to lay his shattered self-image to rest. His reanimated corpse returns to lash out at all those who scorned him in the days before his determination to possess the overcoat taught him what life was all about. The story earned Gogol a reputation as the champion of the downtrodden, although that seems an overly naive interpretation of the tale's implications.

"The Nose" appeared in the same year as Gogol's classic satirical drama *The Inspector General*, while "The Overcoat" appeared in the same year as the first part of his most famous novel, *Dead Souls*, whose protagonist carries out a macabre trade in the title-deeds to dead serfs. The anarchic but assertive spirit of the former pair is replaced in the latter two by a thoroughly Russian nihilism, and it is hardly surprising the author's plan to transform *Dead Souls* into his own version of the *Divine Comedy*—initially by providing a companion piece that would transform and regenerate its sinful characters in purgatorial fashion—eventually came to nothing. This failure serves to emphasize the fact that the element of horror in Gogol's work was always intensely personal, incapable of reinterpretation in terms of some general allegory of the human predicament. Its fantastic elements have frequently been subjected to psychoanalysis as if they were neurotic symptoms; orthodox Freudians have, of course, had a whale of a time with "The Nose," and much has also been made of the supposed displays of Oedipal anxieties in "Christmas Eve" and "Viy."

It is easy enough to link the preoccupation of Gogol's fiction with doomed love affairs and the paradoxical character of witches to the blasted hopes and persistent guilt feelings laid out with such painful exactitude in his *Confessions*, but it is not inconceivable that such links arise as much out of the literary dishonesty of his memoirs as the neurotic quality of his dark fantasies. He is a more robust fantasist and a more ingenious inventor than any simple-minded psychoanalytic decoding of his work could detect. If, in the end, he did waste away to premature death because he could not escape the grip of his own psychotic fears, he probably expected to return to claim his existential due—and although his reanimated corpse has rarely, if ever, been sighted, his work lives on to do his haunting for him.

—Francis Amery

GRABINSKI, Stefan (1877-1936)

Nationality: Polish. **Selected Publications:** Short Stories: *The Dark Domain*, tr. by Miroslaw Lipinsi, Sawtry, Cambridgeshire, Dedalus, 1993.

*   *   *

The career of Stefan Grabinski appears to have run along much the same lines as many other pioneering writers of supernatural fiction. He worked in lonely isolation, was commercially unsuccessful and was largely ignored by critics. He was gradually weakened and eventually destroyed by poor health—in his case by tuberculosis—while being sustained in his idiosyncratic labours by stubborn determination and by the sheer intensity of his esoteric preoccupations. He published five collections of stories, most of which were horrific or blackly ironic, between 1918 and 1922, then switched to novels of a more diffuse and mystical character, which were even less well-received. His passing was virtually unnoticed in a country that was about to be plunged into a catastrophe on a far grander scale than anything a compiler of tales of individual psychological disaster could ever have imagined. The 1970s saw a revival of interest in his work when a collection of his best stories was edited by the prestigious Polish writer Stanislaw Lem, and his work then began to be translated into other languages so that his status could at last be measured against the giants of his field.

The most striking features of the work assembled in the eclectic collection *The Dark Domain* are the author's obsessively repetitive use of doppelgänger figures and his fascination with trains. His characters are prone to haunt themselves by unwittingly dislodging fragments of their own personality, which then become independently incarnate. These distorted doubles usually become hated adversaries, as they do in the grotesque "Strabismus" and "Saturnin Sektor." "Szamota's Mistress"—whose incarnation is even more problematic than the others—is unusual in taking the form of an elusive *femme fatale*. Sometimes, the alienated part of the self manifests itself in a very different form, as it does in "The Area," which refers to a magical space where the blocked artistic creativity of the protagonist is free to run riot.

Even when it fails to achieve a consistently solid secondary manifestation the leaching away of an aspect of the self can be severely discomfiting to Grabinski's characters. In "The Glance" such a loss eventually brings about a fatal confrontation; in "The Vengeance of the Elementals" it opens the way for a deadly demonic possession. In all of his stories of personal fragmentation Grabinski implies that the process embodies a kind of poetic justice, although it is difficult to say what crime any of his protagonists is supposed to have committed. The fire-chief in "The Vengeance of the Elementals" seems to be a heroic benefactor of mankind, and yet the impression remains that the fire elementals who come to plague him are somehow entitled to their cruel and unusual revenge. It seems that Grabinski, like many writers of a similar stripe, was no great admirer of his fellow men, nor even of himself.

As with all writers of psychological horror stories, Grabinski is at his most powerful when his narratives are at their most intimate. He is by no means a clinical writer, and his work becomes less interesting when the narrative viewpoint is more objective. "Fumes" is yet another tale of personality fragmentation, but the protagonist is merely an observer, albeit an erotically entangled one. "A Tale of the Gravedigger" is a story of exotic possession, but the case study of the enigmatic gravedigger is too oblique to command an involvement of the reader as wholehearted as that demanded by "The Vengeance of the Elementals." "The Wandering Train" is the least of the three railway stories in the collection because the apparition in question must be watched from the sidelines. The other train stories, by contrast, make much of the supposedly delicious sensation of being on a fast-moving train, exaggerating it to extraordinary effect.

"The Motion Demon" is yet another tale of metamorphic doppelgängers, more effective than "Fumes" though it lacks the eroticism of the latter story. Even more effective still is the account of a meek man driven to sexual and murderous excess, while temporarily in the possessive grip of a train's thrust and momentum, that is contained in "In the Compartment." The translator of the tales in *The Dark Domain*, Miroslaw Lipinski, suggests that Grabinski's supernaturalization of the experience of riding on a train is linked to his fascination with the philosophical works of Henri Bergson and the notion of *élan vital*; one suspects that Sigmund Freud would offer a rather different interpretation, although Freud might well have preferred it if Grabinski's sexual displays had not been so forthrightly literal.

The influence of Bergson's classic analysis of *Time and Free Will* does show up unambiguously in the phantasmagoric "Saturnin

Sektor," in which the dissociated personality-fragments of the narrator embody contrary theories of time, so that the inevitable climactic murder becomes overtly symbolic of a supposedly imminent shift in the popular conceptualization of time. This is the most complicated tale in the collection, and perhaps the most interesting, although its philosophical pretensions do detract somewhat from its effectiveness as a horror story.

Grabinski was a highly accomplished writer whose work deserves to be firmly established within the international canon of supernatural fiction. As with most Eastern European stalwarts of the canon, his work is surreal and blackly comic rather than direct and gruesome, but it possesses an uncommon element of casual carnality which adds to its dramatic effect. It is to be hoped that more of his work will soon be translated into English.

—Brian Stableford

HOFFMANN, E(rnst) T(heodor) A(madeus) (1776-1822)

Nationality: German. **Selected Publications:** Novels: *Die Serapionsbrüder* (4 vols., 1819-21, tr. by Alexander Ewing as *The Serapion Brethren*, London, George Bell, 2 vols., 1886, 1891. *Die Elixiere des Teufels* (1816), tr. by R. P. Gillies as *The Devil's Elixir*, Edinburgh, Blackwood, 1824. Short Stories: *Fantasiestücke in Callots Manier* (4 vols., 1814-15). *Nachtstücke* (2 vols., 1816-17). *The Tales of Hoffmann*, New York, Heritage Press, 1943. *The Best Tales of Hoffmann*, edited by E. F. Bleiler, New York, Dover, 1967. *Selected Writings of E. T. A. Hoffmann*, edited by Leonard J. Kent and Elizabeth C. Knight, Chicago, University of Chicago Press, 2 vols., 1969. *The Golden Pot and Other Tales*, edited and translated by Ritchie Robertson, Oxford University Press, 1992.

*   *   *

Hoffmann is one of the seminal German fantasists, although his work has suffered in translation and he tends to be remembered outside Germany more for its adaptations in music and ballet than for the original stories themselves. It is only in the last 30 years that serious efforts have been made to render Hoffmann's work more accurately into English and the editions by E. F. Bleiler and Elizabeth Knight are those best acquired, though they are still incomplete.

Hoffmann's early aspirations were towards music and painting; he only drifted towards writing in middle life, and most of his best work was the product of his last ten years, before his early death following an illness at the age of 46. His work was heavily influenced by the German romantic movement and reveals a welcome shift away from the oppressive gothicism of the previous 20 or 30 years. He was one of the earliest writers to present new tales (albeit some based on legend) in the short-story form rather than as novels. This approach had an enormous influence outside Germany, particularly in the United States, where Hoffmann's work affected the writings of Washington Irving, Nathaniel Hawthorne and Edgar Allan Poe.

Hoffmann's earliest work was directed by his musical interests and grew out of his role as Germany's foremost music critic. His first weird tale was "Ritter Gluck" (1809), which juxtaposes interpretations of madness and possession in a musician who believes that he is the composer Gluck. Hoffmann created an *alter ego* in the form of an imaginary musician, Johannes Kreisler, to pursue his interpretations of music, and in his musical criticism collected under the generic title of "Kreisleriana" (written between 1812 and 1820) we find Hoffmann pursuing an alternative perception which later influenced his avowed fantasies. This became most marked in "Don Juan" (1813) in which a hotel guest undergoes a supernatural experience while watching a performance of Mozart's *Don Giovanni*. Mozart's ghost is able to exert an influence through his music. Other stories influenced by Hoffmann's musical background include "Councillor Krespel" ("Rat Krespel," 1816; sometimes published as "Antonia" or "The Cremona Violin"), in which a delicate young girl dies when encouraged to produce the perfect voice, and "Der Kampf der Sänger" ("The Singers' Contest," 1818), based on a 13th-century tale, in which the great minnesingers come together for a contest, one of them with the devil on his side.

Traditional tales, either based on legends, or created by Hoffmann in their likeness, became his trademark later in life, and were subsequently treated as fairy tales. They emerged following the success of "Nutcracker and the Mouse King" (1816), in which an ensorcelled young man in the form of a nutcracker, fights the evil mouse-king to protect a young girl. Thereafter Hoffmann wrote a series of stories for children about the fight between good and evil. Most are fairly light, although they do challenge the use and misuse of good fortune, but others, like "Ignaz Denner" (1816), while sometimes collected amongst Hoffmann's fairy tales, are not tales for children at all. This story, which is not usually rated as one of Hoffmann's best, tells of Andres, a gamekeeper, and his family, who find themselves in debt of gratitude to the evil bandit Denner who has helped cure Andres's wife. Denner is in league with the devil and needs Andres's children as a sacrifice to his master.

"Ignaz Denner" is a rare reversion in Hoffmann's writings to Germany's gothic roots. His best work in this vein was the novel *The Devil's Elixir*, which is Hoffmann's homage to M. G. Lewis's *The Monk*. As with Lewis's work, it follows the degradation of a monk, Medardus, who falls victim to drinking the elixir with which the devil had sought to tempt St. Anthony, and which has been in the family's possession for centuries. Medardus becomes (in his eyes) a murderer (though his victims remarkably escape death), and there is an interesting interplay with Medardus's exact double, who turns out to be a long-lost half-brother.

This marks the re-emergence of the doppelgänger motif from Hoffmann's earliest fictions. Along with his tales of possession it indicates that Hoffmann had a strong desire for an alternative life, regarding himself as something of a failure because he had not succeeded as a composer. Alternate personalities, or their shallow equivalents, may be found in the stories that followed. In "A New Year's Eve Adventure" ("Die Abenteuer der Silvester-Nacht," 1815; sometimes called "The Lost Reflection"), a man meets both the shadowless Peter Schlemihl (from the story by Adelbert von Chamisso) and Erasmus Spikher, who has lost his reflection. In "Fascination" ("Der Magnetiseur," 1814), Alban, who has hypnotic powers, subdues Maria to his will. It transpires that Alban has a pact with the devil and can assume different personalities after death.

The clash of personalities is also evident in what many regard as Hoffmann's three best stories. "The Golden Pot" ("Der Goldne Topf," 1814) is an allegorical story of the battle between the artistic world and the philistine. Anselmus is a young, somewhat clumsy student, whose existence operates on two spheres, and parallel confrontations run between the everyday world and Anselmus's invoked dreamworld or alternate reality. In "The Sandman" (1816), Nathanael, since his childhood, has associated the lawyer Coppelius with the evil Sandman, the bringer of sleep. In adulthood, Nathanael confuses Coppelius with the instrument-maker, Coppola. He falls in love with Olimpia, whom he believes is the daughter of Professor Spalanzani, only to discover that she is an automaton. Nathanael, tormented by his inability to understand or even distinguish reality from fantasy, is driven to madness and suicide. "Madame Scuderi" ("Das Fräulein von Scuderi," 1819) is a non-supernatural murder mystery which nevertheless explores the fate of the obsessive Cardillac, who is a highly regarded citizen and goldsmith by day but at night becomes a criminal who will go to any lengths to recover his own work.

Hoffmann's fiction represents the first great flowering of the horror and fantasy short story. He took themes from his gothic and romantic antecedents and imbued them with his own fascination for possession and personality-changes to create the foundation of the modern horror story. This juxtaposition of personalities may also be viewed as a transition from the traditional German roots into a modern, more scientific world, which Hoffmann viewed with an uncertain fascination.

—Mike Ashley

HUYSMANS, Joris-Karl (1848-1907)

Nationality: French. **Selected Publications:** Novel: *Là-Bas*, 1891; as *Down There*, New York, Boni, 1924.

*　　*　　*

There are some striking elements of horror in Joris-Karl Huysmans's archetypal Decadent novel *A Rebours*—most notably the passage where Des Esseintes dreams of the progress of syphilis down the ages and is welcomed into the embrace of a *femme fatale* whose genitalia are made in the image of a Venus flytrap—but that book requires attention in the context of the present volume primarily for its celebration of the perverse delights to be obtained from the contemplation of horrific works of art. It built on groundwork laid by Gautier and Baudelaire in explaining and celebrating the aesthetics of horror but it did not seek to put its conclusions into practice; that task was left to *Là-Bas*, the first of Huysmans's novels to feature his fictional alter ego Durtal.

In *Là-Bas* Durtal decides to write a biography of Gilles de Rais, the French marshal briefly associated with Joan of Arc, who had been the subject of a famous sorcery trial in 1440. His friend des Hermies tells him that the kind of Satanism of which de Rais was accused is still rife in contemporary Paris, but Durtal is sceptical until he begins an affair with Hyacinthe Chantelouve, an intimate of the active Satanist Canon Docre. Durtal is also aided in his research by a pious bell-ringer, Louis Carhaix, and Gvingey, an expert on occultism who was once brought to the brink of damnation by Docre. Madame Chantelouve is eventually persuaded to take Durtal to a Black Mass conducted by Docre, but he finds the experience disappointing. In subsequent discussions Carhaix argues that the prevalence of Satanism is proof of the decadence

of modern society, as the 19th century moves to an ignominious end beneath "storm-clouds of foul abomination." Durtal agrees that the world is indeed sick, and breaks off his affair with Madame Chantelouve, but he remains unable to embrace Carhaix's simple faith.

Là-Bas is, of course, an uneasy debate rather than an orthodox novel, but it is more a debate about aesthetics than a debate about morals. Durtal's flirtation with Satanism and Madame Chantelouve is distinctly half-hearted—and in the end, the worst charge he can bring himself to lay against Satanism is not that it is evil, but merely that it is inefficient and tawdry. Durtal finds the Black Mass lacking in aesthetic excitement as well as demonic power—and that, to one who had formerly cultivated a Decadent sensibility, if only at second hand (Huysmans worked by day as a clerk for the Sûreté while he wrote *A Rebours* by night), is by far the more significant failure.

Là-Bas was researched as conscientiously by Huysmans as its imaginary biography of Gilles de Rais is by Durtal, and some commentators have been tempted to see it as a roman à clef. *Fin-de-siècle* Paris was indeed full of occultists, some of whom are mentioned in the text. Most took their inspiration from the career of "Eliphas Lévi" (Alphonse Louis Constant), who had successfully posed as a practitioner of magic a generation before; the most famous was Josephin Péladan, whose Rosicrucian lodge was loudly advertised in his many novels railing against the decadence of the age. Whether Huysmans ever saw a Black Mass is, however, doubtful; Satanism was then—as it is now and always has been—a product of the lurid fantasies of the devout rather than the active practices of the unholy.

The likelihood is that Gilles de Rais was innocent of all the charges bought against him; like all the other victims of famous sorcery trials he was almost certainly framed by his enemies, who used the same vicious slanders to discredit and destroy him as the English had earlier used to discredit and destroy his companion-in-arms Joan of Arc. Huysmans presumably knew that, or suspected it very strongly. It is significant that the flights of fancy upon which Durtal and his two friends continually embark are forever being brought down to earth by the kindly attentions of Madame Carhaix, who is always bustling around with ready supplies of good hot food. She, rather than the devout bellringer, is the novel's paragon of common sense and virtue—and her unobtrusive presence within the plot is testimony to the fact that Huysmans never lost touch with reality while he was in pursuit of his temporary obsession.

The methodology of Durtal's historical researches is explicitly modelled on that of Jules Michelet, who had written a book of his own about the witch-hunts and sorcery trials of the Middle Ages: *La Sorcière* (1862). There Michelet represented accused witches as heroic rebels against the tyranny of an autocratic and misogynistic Church, suggesting (with tongue in cheek) that they might indeed have elevated their folk-medicine into a kind of Satanism by way of ideological resistance. Michelet's book became the parent of all the modern scholarly fantasies which insist, falsely, that there was indeed a witch-cult, albeit one that was misunderstood and misrepresented by the Church. Durtal's conclusion that Gilles de Rais was eventually driven to madness and remorse by the knowledge that there were no further depths of evil to be plumbed is a fantasization exactly similar to Michelet's, arising from the calculated error of putting a thoroughly modern Decadent consciousness into a situation to which it cannot and does not belong.

As a horror story *Là-Bas* is too contemplative to be wholly successful, and its conclusion that Satanism is trivial rather than evil is hardly calculated to boost its melodramatic quality. As a philosophical novel debating the status and worth of religious faith in the decadent Paris of the 1890s, however, it is a thoroughly fascinating work. It explores extremes of faith and feeling that no one else had ever treated with such scrupulous even-handedness. However false it may be as a record of contemporary Satanism it remains a remarkably intense examination of the possible utility of Satanism as creed and ritual. Its conclusion—that Satanism can never be anything but a hollow sham, incapable of delivering any kind of aesthetic or material gratification to an intelligent man—is surely secure, no matter how convoluted the argument was that led Durtal and Huysmans to its achievement.

—Francis Amery

KAFKA, Franz (1883-1924)

Nationality: Czech. **Selected Publications:** Novels: *Der Prozess*, Berlin, Die Schmiede, 1925; as *The Trial*, New York, Knopf, and London, Gollancz, 1937. *Das Schloss*, Munich, Wolff, 1926; as *The Castle*, New York, Knopf, and London, Secker, 1930. Short stories: "Die Verwandlung," 1916; as "Metamorphosis" in *Metamorphosis and Other Stories*, London, Secker, 1933; "In der Strafkolonie," 1919; as "In the Penal Settlement" in *Metamorphosis and Other Stories*, London, Secker, 1933.

*   *   *

Franz Kafka was an unassuming and neurotic Jewish Bohemian who died young and whose most noted work was published posthumously. His name has been used to categorize the sub-genre of bureaucratic nightmare which he created: "Kafkaesque," which has connotations of the bizarre, the surrealistic, the absurd. *The Trial* and *The Castle* are acknowledged as two of the greatest novels of the 20th century, perhaps symbolizing our paranoid times better than any other works of literature. Neither novel is regarded as complete, and they were among the papers which Kafka asked to be burnt after his death.

The interpretations and intentions of both novels have been the subject of intense debate ever since their publication. It is suggested that their meaning remained enigmatic even to Kafka himself (even though they are partly autobiographical), though this in no way lessens their importance. The fact that both novels seem to be open to a whole range of justifiable interpretations adds strength to their classic status. Also, they have been extremely influential upon later writers; though Kafka was not the first to employ paranoid and dreamlike elements within an otherwise realistic novel, he is the best known exponent of the technique. Some areas of horror fiction and, in particular, dark fantasy, owe a tremendous debt to Kafka's work. Many contemporary horror writers, notably Ramsey Campbell and Jonathan Carroll, show Kafka's influence. The wonderful examples of surrealism in the novels have been influential upon another group of writers, especially Samuel Beckett.

In *The Trial*, the bank clerk Joseph K. wakes on his 30th birthday to find that he is being arrested. (Kafka was a 30-year-old bank clerk when he was writing this.) K.'s situation quickly becomes absurd, just as if he is in a dream or in a country where logic works differently. He never learns what his offence is. He never understands the peculiar system of justice under which he is examined and tried; but neither does the lawyer, Huld, whom he finds to handle his case. The system (K. learns from Huld's mistress) seems to be that all accused are found guilty, with some cases drawn out over years and a concealing blanket of secrecy placed over all court proceedings. But another character, Titorelli the Court painter, tells K. that he will never be acquitted though he may be able to postpone his trial indefinitely. In fact, through all these odd events, K. is not kept in custody; he continues to work at the bank and to assert his innocence; yet his life has been ruined. And on the evening before his 31st birthday he is collected from his lodgings by two men, taken to a quarry and executed.

The protagonist of *The Castle* is also known as K. One winter's night he arrives in the village below the Castle and announces that he is a Land Surveyor, summoned by the Count. But he has no permit, without which no one is allowed to stay in the village. K. tries to obtain a permit, to explain himself and ultimately to get to the Castle, and he is thwarted at every turn by circumstances or petty officials. Even when the assistant Land Surveyors for whom he is waiting arrive nothing becomes clearer, for their stories conflict, and they do not recognize each other. His firm resolve is gradually worn down by the unhelpful attitude of the villagers and by his inability to obtain any useful answers from the direction of the Castle. In particular he tries to get into contact with Klamm, Chief of the Castle's Department X, who seems to be the only one senior enough to provide definite answers. There are scenes of black farce. In one instance, K. accidentally confronts an official from the Castle by entering his room at one of the inns—but although he does obtain a helpful assurance he also falls asleep. Later on, K., having fallen in love with a girl from the village, and having taken on a job as caretaker of the local school, sets up home with her in one of the two classrooms and is forced to move rooms often, as lessons must take precedence. It all ends without resolution, though not completely without hope. Anecdotal evidence suggests that Kafka intended K. to be exhausted by his struggles, learning on his death-bed that although his claim for a permit was not valid, he would nevertheless be allowed to remain in the village, the sort of enigmatic solution one might expect.

While the Joseph K. of *The Trial* is a victim, the K. of *The Castle* is an aggressor, but neither strategy works: both protagonists are ground down by the system, and both systems—the law-courts and the village and Castle respectively—are meant to be microcosms of the world. So the novels may be pessimistic views of the chances of survival of an Everyman figure. This is a simple interpretation, though it is certainly the one picked up and emphasized by both Arthur Koestler in *Darkness at Noon* and George Orwell in *Nineteen Eighty-Four*, two of the more important novels influenced by Kafka.

Kafka's friend and biographer Max Brod, as well as his first translators into English Willa and Edwin Muir, considered the two novels to be allegories concerned with divine grace: suffering brings its own reward. But they (especially Brod) were in a good position to see that many of Kafka's own concerns were being aired in the novels, particularly his difficult relationship with his father, whom he saw, partly, as an authority figure whom he was letting down, leading to feelings of guilt. Different interpreters have found different messages here, even a prediction of the upsurge of the Nazis.

Still sharper and more explicit examples of horror are to be found in two of Kafka's most important shorter stories, "Metamorphosis" and "In the Penal Settlement." The former, in which young Gregor Samsa wakes up one morning to find himself transformed into a beetle, may be taken as a study of alienation and also as another example of Kafka's guilt over his relationship with his father. (Samsa is the family's breadwinner, and he feels ashamed and very guilty that he can no longer go off to work.) "In the Penal Settlement" contains gruesome descriptions of an instrument of torture, like a man-sized sewing machine, which writes the lesson the condemned man must learn (such as "HONOUR THY SUPERIORS"), all across his naked body, ever deeper until death intervenes—except that, in true Kafkaesque style, the prisoner is never told of his sentence; he must *feel* the words as they are written. The points being made include suggestions that punishment demeans the punishers and that redemption is never certain. But, like all of Kafka's writings, the tale is ambiguous.

—Chris Morgan

KAST, Pierre (1920-1984)

Nationality: French. **Selected Publications:** Novel: *Les Vampires de l'Alfama*, 1975; as *The Vampires of Alfama*, London, W. H. Allen, 1976.

*   *   *

Pierre Kast's *Les Vampires de l'Alfama* began life as a short animated film in 1963, placing it way ahead of the boom in revisionist vampire stories that struck America in the mid-1970s, earlier even than Jane Gaskell's pioneering representation of a virtuous vampire in *The Shiny Narrow Grin* (1964). The novel, which provides a dramatic elaboration of the idea, is even more fervently erotic and far more ideologically radical than Anne Rice's *Interview with the Vampire*, which was published a year later. In beginning the new crusade that would establish vampires as heroic outsiders battling against moral tyrannies based in unreasoning fear, Kast was also carrying forward a rich French tradition of literary Satanism which had begun with the poet Charles Baudelaire and the historian Jules Michelet and had been brought to its most extravagant fruition by Anatole France in *The Revolt of the Angels* (1914).

The hero of Kast's novel, Joao, Duke of Queluz, is a mid-18th century prime minister of Portugal. Although he is a cardinal he is a freethinker, extraordinarily liberal in both the political and the sexual senses of the term. His endeavours are dedicated to the cause of progress, but in a world where tyranny is the norm and the Church is avid to exterminate all dissent his efforts must be clandestine. His principal rival in the struggle for political power is the chief of police, the brutal Marquis da Silva, whose lustful designs on Joao's niece Alexandra are unlikely to bear fruit while she has any say in the matter.

In the Alfama—the rogues' quarter of Lisbon, which plays host to social dissidents of all kinds—a scholarly sorceress named Clara offers shelter to a family of refugees headed by Count Kotor. Kotor has attained a problematic kind of longevity by virtue of becoming a vampire but he is searching desperately for the secret of true immortality. Ever since his resurrection to undeath 285 years before, however, he has been handicapped in his pursuit of this goal by the attention of the Inquisition, in whose eyes he is an instrument of Satan. The inhabitants of the Alfama, by contrast, soon recognize Kotor as an ally. They bring their sick relatives to him so that he may help them stave off death, and they are glad to offer their blood in return—but rumours of his activities attract the attention of the secret police.

Clara seeks Joao's protection on Kotor's behalf and Joao immediately offers to lend what help he can, even though it endangers his own position. He becomes more deeply committed to the Count's cause when he falls in love with Kotor's daughter Barbara. At the same time, Alexandra becomes enamoured of Kotor's son Laurent. Informed of what is happening by the secret police, the Marquis da Silva employs torture and bribery to build a case against the prime minister. Having done so, he unleashes a bloody invasion of the Alfama. His troops burn the coffins in which the vampires must rest by day and slaughter their human allies wholesale—but Joao manages to escape and to save Barbara, while Clara and Kotor ship out for the New World. Da Silva does manage to trap Laurent and Alexandra, but destroying them leads him to his own doom.

The Duke of Queluz is far more wholeheartedly modern in his attitudes than such real heroes of the Portuguese Enlightenment as Father Luis Verney and the Marquis de Pombal, not merely in his politics but in his connoisseur attitude to sexual pleasure. In his own way, he is almost as exotic an intrusion into the actual pattern of European history as Count Kotor. Unlike Louis, the problematic hero of Rice's *Interview with the Vampire*, Kotor is no troubled introvert obsessed with his own peculiar brand of existential angst. He is, instead, a modern Prometheus whose desire is to find a means that will enable humankind to advance to a higher state of being—and he pursues this selfless quest in spite of the fact that those who presently hold power in the human world are determined to destroy him and obliterate his ambiguous kind from the face of the earth. The would-be tyrants of Church and State are, of course, correct to see Kotor as an enemy—if he were to succeed he would be able to offer his fellows a kind of immortality which would be in direct competition with religion's main stock-in-trade—but that only serves to demonstrate the awful extent of their own selfish stupidity.

The extent to which the Church's promises of an afterlife had been undermined by the Age of Enlightenment is measured by Kast's confident assertion that all sensible people would rather be undead than dead—but he accepts that they might have difficulty admitting the fact in a world full of people who have a superstitious fear of the "unnatural." By selecting Kotor and the Duke of Queluz as his twin heroes of the Age of Enlightenment Kast admits that the cause of progress has always been best served by men who work quietly and stealthily. Although Joao holds a position of power he must pursue his goals in secret, while Kotor must labour under the perpetual threat of persecution—but those are the costs of attempting to liberate and empower the downtrodden. The Marquis da Silva, by contrast, is the abject slave of his desires; it is not surprising that he and others like him have no purpose but to enslave others.

Kast is uncompromising in linking intellectual, political and sexual liberation; unlike some subsequent works, however, his does not load the dice by promising some form of "ultimate orgasm" available to vampires but unattainable by mere mortals. His allegory remains steadfastly responsible to actual human aspirations; however unconventional his central motif may be, and however unashamedly melodramatic his methods, the ideals he wishes to promote are those of science, freedom and love. There is a certain delicious irony in the fact that the vehicle he chose to convey this message is a neo-Gothic novel staffed with horror-story stereotypes—but there is a good deal of sense in his tacit recognition that the kinds of thinking and feeling which have to be staked through the heart if science, freedom and love are to prosper are those which have long animated Gothic dread and horror-story stereotypy.

—Francis Amery

LEROUX, Gaston (1868-1927)

Nationality: French. **Selected Publications:** Novels: *La Double vie de Théophraste Longuet*, Paris, Flammarion, 1903; as *The Double Life*, New York, Kearney, 1909; as *The Man with the Black Feather*, London, Hurst & Blackett, 1912. *Le Fantôme de l'Opéra*, Paris, Lafitte, 1910; as *The Phantom of the Opera*, London, Mills & Boon, 1911. *Le Coeur cambriol*, Paris, Lafitte, 1922; as *The Burgled Heart*, London, Long, 1925. *Le Fauteuil hanté*, Paris, Lafitte, 1911; as *The Haunted Chair*, New York, Dutton, 1931. *La Poupée sanglante*, Paris, Tallandier, 1924; as *The Kiss That Killed*, New York, Macaulay, 1934. *La Machine assassiner*, Paris, Tallandier, 1924; as *The Machine to Kill*, New York, Macaulay, 1935. Short Stories: *The Gaston Leroux Bedside Companion*, edited by Peter Haining, London: Gollancz, 1980.

*   *   *

Gaston Leroux was a prolific *feuilletonist*, producing two dozen newspaper serials—sometimes running two or even three at a time—between 1903 and 1927 as well as many shorter works and seven plays. Most of his serials seem to have been made up as he went along, and the necessity to spice them with anything up to a hundred narrative hooks lends their book versions a feverish quality. All of them are thrillers of one kind or another, usually involving fanciful crimes and even more fanciful investigators. Desperation caused Leroux to employ many fantastic devices but he was always hesitant in his employment of supernatural devices, preferring rational explanations for apparently supernatural phenomena whenever possible—although it has to be admitted that some of his "rational" explanations seem infinitely less likely than supernatural ones (the enigma of the disappearing train in *The Double Life* is a cardinal example.)

The Double Life is a story of split personality whose unlucky protagonist is continually "possessed"—perhaps by virtue of some kind of hereditary memory—by the intelligence of a famous criminal of yore. Most of the other novels by Leroux that were translated into English are also crime stories, reflecting the fact that his reputation in the UK and the USA was long based on his claim to have laid down a highly significant precedent (the locked-room murder mystery) in his detective story *The Mystery of the Yellow Room. The Haunted Chair* is a slightly fantasized detective story, and although the pair of mysteries translated as *The Kiss that Killed* and *The Machine to Kill* feature a vampire and a robot as murderers the stories remain straightforward accounts of lengthy pursuits and eventual captures. The only full-blown supernatural story of Leroux's to be translated for book publication

was the novella *The Burgled Heart*, in which the astral body of a French woman is seduced by an English artist, much to the distress of her husband.

Leroux's short fiction was mostly modelled on the *Grand Guignol* productions of Maurice Level, although only one of his theatrical adaptations was actually staged at the Théâtre du Grand-Guignol. *The Gaston Leroux Bedside Companion* reprints four translations from *Weird Tales* and three from contemporary British magazines plus one of more recent provenance, the most interesting being "In Letters of Fire," about a deal with the Devil. The collection also includes, but misattributes, the introduction to *The Phantom of the Opera*, the work on which Leroux's continuing fame is now based.

The Phantom of the Opera was one of three newspaper serials Leroux produced in 1910. It is presented as a story carefully pieced together from interviews with the parties involved, 30 years after the events took place, offering a "true" history of the Opera Ghost. The "ghost" in question was a mysterious figure with a face like a death's head, whose appearances became more frequent—and the demands which he made upon the Opera's managers more forceful—immediately before his abrupt disappearance.

What the reporter gradually reveals is a plot whose key elements have become almost as well-known as the plots of *Frankenstein* and *Dracula*. Raoul, Vicomte de Chagny, is in love with the singer Christine Daaé, but Christine is forbidden to respond to his advances by a mysterious tutor she never sees, who claims to be the Angel of Music about which her father used to tell her when she was a child. This enigmatic individual and the Opera Ghost are, of course, one and the same. The recalcitrance of the theatre managers leads the Ghost to spoil a performance by a diva who refuses to make way for Christine, sending the great chandelier which lights the auditorium crashing down upon the audience. The Ghost then takes Christine to his abode on the shore of a lake in the catacombs beneath the Opera, where he composes his own music. There she snatches away his mask and sees his horrible face—but she persuades him that she loves him in spite of his appearance so that he will not feel the need to kill Raoul. During a masked ball where he appears as Edgar Allan Poe's Red Death, however, the Ghost eavesdrops on a rooftop meeting between Christine and Raoul and learns that they plan to elope.

In the novel the Opera Ghost is a stonemason named Erik, whose career and morals have been utterly blighted by his horrific deformities. He has helped in the reconstruction of the cellars of the Opera, incorporating many trapdoors into the edifice so that he might "haunt" it. Erik was, however, too much for subsequent adaptors of the plot to swallow, and they mostly substituted some other vengeful figure. Oddly enough, although a dozen of Leroux's novels were filmed in France during his lifetime it was left to Hollywood to produce a version of *The Phantom of the Opera* in 1925, with Lon Chaney in the lead. It was Nelson Eddy who first realized the potential of the plot as a musical vehicle, and the 1943 version—in which Claude Rains played the Phantom—foregrounds his singing. The story was given a spectacular new lease of life in Andrew Lloyd Webber's stage musical, first produced in 1987.

Were it not for the films and stage musicals *The Phantom of the Opera* would have been forgotten, but it was the text that provided the key scenes which have kept the story alive in the public imagination. One must also remember, though, that it was the actual Paris Opera which provided the inspiration for the text; Paris really is set above a network of catacombs so extensive as not to have been fully explored in 1910, and Leroux was not the only Parisian writer to be fascinated with them. The fact that the focal point of French "high culture" was situated above a dark labyrinth provided a golden opportunity for striking symbolism, which the novel and all its subsequent adaptations gladly seized. It is for that reason that *The Phantom of the Opera* transcended the dulling influence of Leroux's hackwork habits and became established as a significant modern myth.

—Francis Amery

MAUPASSANT, Guy de (1850-1893)

Nationality: French. **Selected Publications:** Short Stories: *Contes Fantastiques Complets*, edited by Anne Richter, Paris, Marabout, 1984. *The Dark Side: Tales of Terror and the Supernatural*, edited by Arnold Kellett, London, Xanadu, and New York, Carroll and Graf, 1989.

* * *

Guy de Maupassant's horror fiction consists of some 30 stories, only a tenth of his total. It is claimed that all his fiction came from his own experiences; he may have fictionalized true occurrences or tales told to him, but there is meant to be some truth in them all. As a short-story writer he is of the very greatest importance, not just in French literature but worldwide. Building upon the work of Gustave Flaubert, Maupassant created his own spare, highly controlled style of story, frequently only ten pages long. Most of his stories are narrated in the first person or are tales told by a named character. He was influential upon such 20th-century masters of the short story as W. Somerset Maugham and O. Henry. Indeed, so much has he been imitated that it is difficult to imagine the originality of his stories and to understand their impact when they first appeared during the 1880s.

It is easy to divide up Maupassant's horror fiction into three groups: supernatural, non-supernatural or *grand guignol*, and psychological. While there is some overlap, the division makes analysis easier.

Of these, the psychological are the most fascinating, for they express the personal thoughts and fears of Maupassant himself. It is impossible to separate the man from the stories, and they present a vivid, frightening picture of a disturbed mind, of a man who was a misanthrope and who possessed a morbid fear of becoming mad. It was a justified fear, for his mind was afflicted by advanced syphilis and, after a few years of deteriorating control and an unsuccessful attempt to cut his throat, he died in an asylum at the age of 42.

Critics have charted Maupassant's developing madness through his semi-autobiographical stories of abnormal psychology. An early instance is "He?," in which the narrator feels himself uneasy, then agitated, then menaced in his own flat over a period of months by something he cannot see or explain. Only once does he believe that he sees something—a person sitting in one of his own chairs by the fire—but the next moment the person has gone. In his desperation, the narrator decides to get married in the hope that company (which he also detests) will keep the even more dreadful "he" away. Another story, "Was He Mad?," a reminiscence of the moody Jacques Parent who can hypnotize dogs and

claims even more terrible powers, suggests a growing struggle within Maupassant's mind. The story opens with the prophetic news that Parent has just died in an asylum.

Being possessed is the theme of Maupassant's longest and best-known horror story, "The Horla." It consists of diary entries, cataloguing the narrator's descent into madness, and the Horla is the name he gives to the alien creature whom he believes is stalking him. By the end of the story he realizes that neither travel abroad nor locked doors will keep the creature away, and that it cannot be killed even by fire (he sets his own house alight with the creature inside). The only solution is suicide.

Madness of this kind is a recurring theme in the stories. "Mad" contains a protagonist who is insanely jealous of the horse his loved one rides; he shoots the horse and her. In "A Woman's Hair," the narrator discovers, by accident, a lock of hair and from it imagines the woman of his dreams; his obsession causes him to be locked up in an asylum. "A Night in Paris" is a paranoid nightmare as its narrator feels compelled to walk the streets, alone and with increasing desperation, until time stops for him and he begins to walk into the Seine, knowing that his time is nearly over. A late story, "Who Knows?," shows a very disturbed narrator, subject to massive delusions about the furniture in his house, which disappears and reappears. In the end he enters a private mental hospital, just as the author was to do three years later.

Relatively few of Maupassant's stories are supernatural. The best, often anthologized in one or other of its versions, is "The Hand," about a severed human hand which, despite being chained up, escapes and strangles its owner. There are other tales of spectres seen (with some sightings leading to death) including "The Phantom Hag," "Apparition" and "The Drowned Man." Perhaps the greatest strength of this group of stories is that Maupassant never tries to explain his phenomena or to account for the actions of ghosts; he simply presents the bones of the story.

The non-supernatural stories are sometimes breathtakingly nasty. For example, in "The Mother of Monsters" we have a peasant woman who, when she was young and harvesting crops, got herself pregnant and tried to conceal the fact by tightly binding herself. The resulting baby was so malformed that she was able to sell him to a showman, and she has since given birth to eleven other monsters by the same means, from which she receives a very useful income. The story is, in fact, a satire on corsets. In "A Madman," a judge commits murder, just for the experience, and condemns an innocent man to death for the crime. "The Inn" is frequently reprinted. It describes how an inn high up in the French Alps is able to be reached only for six months of the year. For the rest of the time it is inhabited only by a couple of caretakers and a mountain dog. After the older caretaker goes missing, presumed dead, while out hunting, the younger, believing himself haunted, loses his reason. It is a fruitful idea, taken up and much enlarged by Stephen King in *The Shining*.

Terror (which one must assume drove the caretaker mad) is a theme to which Maupassant often returned. In a story of the same name he quotes the Russian novelist Turgenev as saying, "We are truly afraid only of the things we do not understand." It is an aphorism which Maupassant proves by example in several stories and which was later echoed by H. P. Lovecraft in the famous opening sentence of *Supernatural Horror in Literature*: "The oldest and strongest emotion of mankind is fear, and the oldest and strongest kind of fear is fear of the unknown."

Arguably the most unpleasant of Maupassant's non-supernatural pieces is "The Spastic Mannerism," in which a father relates how his teenage daughter died and was laid to rest in a coffin in the family vault. After a couple of days, she returned to life, ringing the bell of the house for entrance and covered in blood. The family's faithful old servant had cut off one of her fingers in order to steal a ring, and this had revived her. Its matter-of-fact style in just six pages makes it as horrifying as anything written today.

—Chris Morgan

MEYRINK, Gustav (1868-1932)

Nationality: Austrian. **Selected Publications:** Novels: *Der Golem*, 1915; as *The Golem*, London, Gollancz, 1928. *Der Engel vom westlichen Fenster*, 1927; as *The Angel of the West Window*, Sawtry, Cambridgeshire, Dedalus, 1991. *Das grune Gesicht*, 1916; as *The Green Face*, Sawtry, Cambridgeshire, Dedalus, 1992. *Walpurgisnacht*, 1917; as *Walpurgisnacht*, Sawtry, Cambridgeshire, Dedalus, 1993. *Der weisse Dominikaner*, 1921; as *The White Dominican*, Sawtry, Cambridgeshire, Dedalus, 1994. Short Stories: *The Opal (and Other Stories)*, Sawtry, Cambridgeshire, Dedalus, 1994.

*   *   *

Gustav Meyrink's literary career began when he became a regular contributor to the satirical weekly *Simplicissimus*. The brief tales he produced for the magazine—samples of which are included in *The Opal (and Other Stories)*—are as calculatedly bizarre as they are calculatedly bitter. Meyrink had plenty to be bitter about, having suffered insult, injury and discrimination by virtue of his illegitimate birth. His early business career had been ruined by malicious charges of fraud and he was eventually driven into exile from his beloved native city of Prague. Before turning his resentments to constructive purposes he had come close to suicide, but had been deflected by his growing fascination with occultism; he sought out and joined all the secret societies he could find, actively cultivating the outsider status that others were so enthusiastic to thrust upon him. Although he could never make up his mind how seriously occultism ought to be taken—his exposure to so many rival theses prevented his capture by any one faith—his scholarly investigations lasted throughout his life and provided the raw materials for all his best literary works.

The occult fantasies in *The Opal* are mostly flippant and trivial. "The Violet Death" and "The Black Ball" are ironic apocalyptic fantasies. The title story is a mock-horrific tale of a curse, while "The Man in the Bottle" advertises its lightweight Decadent credentials by invoking the name of Aubrey Beardsley. It is only in the later stories, including "Chimera" and "A Suggestion" that the element of comedy is overtaken by a frisson of authentic horror. Meyrink's first novel, however, marked a very dramatic shift of emphasis. *The Golem* is a nightmarish visionary fantasy in which a man who accidentally puts on another man's hat becomes privy to the inmost secrets of Athanasius Pernath, a late-19th-century jeweller in the Prague ghetto. The distressed Pernath, having been framed as a murderer, experiences visions of the golem: the man of clay animated by the legendary rabbi Judah Loew in order to combat the blood libel (the malicious accusation of child-murder and cannibalism used by Christians to justify pogroms launched against the Jews). The solution to Pernath's practical problems

has to be based in a more fundamental kind of self-healing, which requires a special mystical insight—a fantastic mirroring of Meyrink's reinterpretation of his own predicament.

The Green Face is more closely akin to Meyrink's short fiction. Set in Amsterdam—which is here considered, however inaptly, a uniquely decadent city—it describes the bizarre events following the central character's first encounter with Chidher Green's Hall of Riddles. Chidher Green never puts in an unambiguous appearance, nor is it ever clear exactly who he is; he is supposedly the Wandering Jew, but the symbolism of that particular legend is complicated by other patterns of significance. In addition to serving as a living witness to the reality of Christ's crucifixion, awaiting merciful redemption, Chidher Green is a seed of renewal, a promise of the new order which is to be raised from the ruins of the old after the Apocalypse.

Walpurgisnacht is similar in spirit but more economical in execution. The setting reverts to Prague and the apocalyptic awareness of the novel is much sharpened by virtue of its composition while the Austro-Hungarian Empire was actually in the grip of its death-throes. Walpurgisnacht is one of the two nights in the year (the other being Halloween) when the evil spirits of paganism allegedly return to plague Christendom; in the novel Czech rebels against Germanic authority seek to symbolize their historical release in appropriately mystical fashion—but as in *The Green Face* the new order remains an unactualized hope.

The White Dominican is a less melodramatic and more constructive novel than its predecessors, tracking a quest for enlightenment which eventually reaches a conclusion. Here, although the path to wisdom is strewn with many distractions, there really is an authentic secret order which possesses that which all the others merely pretend to have. The introduction to the novel conveys the implication that Meyrink really thought that he had achieved some such enlightenment, or at least stood on its threshold, but if that was not simple literary dishonesty he soon began to doubt the conclusion.

The Angel of the West Window—which probably ought to be reckoned Meyrink's masterpiece, although *The Golem* has always been more famous—offers a far more ambivalent account of occult ambitions and delusions. The narrator of *The Angel of the West Window* is a descendant of John Dee who comes into possession of various documents relating to his ancestor, including fragments of his diary. By virtue of his perusal of these documents—and his evolving relationships with three other characters who have mysterious affinities with key figures in Dee's life—he gradually discovers that he is in some sense the same individual as Dee, charged with the duty of taking up the thread of the Elizabethan mage's appointed mission and attempting to bring it to a proper conclusion.

Meyrink's Dee is the sponsor of the revolutionary Ravenheads and their amazing leader Bartlett Greene, to whose imprisonment and torture he is a reluctant witness. It is Greene who introduces Dee to the ultimate *femme fatale*, Black Isas, planting a seed which comes to fruition when Dee—who is ambitious to become the husband of the future Elizabeth I—creates an imitative succubus. After this, Dee can never escape the grip of the goddess; his subsequent career in England and in Prague—where he meets Rabbi Loew, the golem-maker—is constantly blighted, but his damnation is never quite completed. As the novel progresses, the past and the present become increasingly and dangerously entangled, until the climax of Dee's career becomes the narrator's own personal crisis. The narrator must decide whether he will take_up

Dee's cause, and face in his turn the threats and temptations of Black Isas, in the hope of completing the difficult task of his salvation.

The Angel of the West Window combines all the best features of Meyrink's work: the vivid melodrama, the philosophical urgency and the ironic insight. It is something of a patchwork, stylistically so uneven that a few critics have alleged that some of its chapters might be the work of another hand, but it is fascinating nevertheless. Meyrink's work carries forward the German tradition of hallucinatory and allegorical fantasy instituted a century before by E. T. A. Hoffmann, bringing it decisively into the period between the two world wars and abandoning it—with almost perfect timing—on the eve of Hitler's rise to power. In retrospect, its distinctive combination of phantasmagoric apocalyptic anxiety and desperate hopefulness seem exceptionally prescient.

—Brian Stableford

OWEN, Thomas (1910-)

Nationality: Belgian. **Selected Publications:** Short Stories: *The Desolate Presence*, London, Kimber, 1984.

*   *   *

A lawyer, journalist, and member of the Belgian Académie Royale de Langue et de Littérature Françaises, Thomas Owen (real name Gérard Bertot) has also been an art critic, and has published a number of detective novels. Of greater interest to present readers, he has written several volumes of "strange tales."

Horror is at its core a personal, individualized experience—the emotion of fear pushed to its extreme. Though a crowd can express fear, only an individual can have the internal experience of intense, personalized fear—i.e., horror. Owen knows this; as is true of several of the best writers of horror stories, he typically confines his tale to a single character. Life is reduced to the individual and his immediate needs; the unexpected, sometimes sudden, perversion of those requirements can be horrifying indeed, and that is his focus. He carefully and subtly develops his tales with a sparse, graceful style emphasizing the individual's inescapable need to complete some action that most often results in the collapse (or even loss) of his life. The elegance of his language is matched by the dark intelligence of his ideas.

This is shown most effectively in, among other stories, "The Black Ball." Here a man in the ostensible safety of his house, initially sensing the movement of an unusual object from the corner of his eye, ultimately devolves, becoming the replacement for this strange fibrous object he destroys just before his transformation. Similarly, in "The Desolate Presence," a lonely man wandering in "a hostile and deserted countryside," happens on an isolated farmhouse. Briefly glimpsing a face behind a barred window, he decides to investigate and, entering the forlorn place, eventually becomes that face behind the window, waiting an indeterminate span of time for the next hapless wanderer to replace him.

Owen's short tales are ultimately saddening; it is often the uselessness of one man's attempt at fulfilling even the slightest of expectations or accomplishments that informs his work. In "The Death of Alexis Balakine," an isolated man dreams of the death of the title character and, finding a wallet with the man's name, is

finally overcome with despair when details of his dream begin to invade his immediate surroundings. The character in an Owen story faces the inevitable consequences of an innocent quest for understanding, or of a carrying out of his normal activity. Unfortunately, these consequences are inevitably far removed from what he desires. In "The Hunter" a female vampire, relishing the fresh blood of her current male victim, a hunter, misjudges his profession. After partially draining him, she's dealt a fatal thrust from his exactly-placed knife. He is indeed a hunter—a vampire hunter. And in "The Park," a young girl who must cross a nearby municipal park has to change her carefree walk to decidedly more wary movement when a woman is assaulted in the very area the girl traverses. Against her parents' wishes that she choose another path, she arms herself with her brother's hunting knife and continues her same daily walk. Suspecting a small old man she regularly sees in the park of the misdeed, when he finally approaches her one night, after only being seen from afar, she kills him—and is then immediately grabbed and murdered for her trouble by the real killer.

One of Owen's favourite themes is an encounter with a seemingly real person who is revealed by story's conclusion to be a ghost. In these tales, such as "The Castellan," "The Girl in the Rain" and "The Passing of Dr. Babylon," it is the narrator's chance meeting with the title character that creates the need in the narrator for some form of amplified contact with the other. When that need is ultimately subverted by the revelation of the other's ghostly existence, the narrator is left emotionally stranded. Here again the twisting of expectations results in a partial collapse of the main character's life.

Owen is morbid, solemn, bitterly ironic. With only one of his six collections of stories translated into English—and even that published by a relatively small British house—his work is hard to find. But it is certainly worth seeking out as a superior example of how horror and gracefulness of style are faultlessly melded.

—Lawrence Greenberg

PAVIC, Milorad (1929-)

Nationality: Serbian. **Selected Publications:** Novels: *Dictionary of the Khazars*, 1984. *Landscape Painted with Tea*, 1990. *The Inner Side of the Wind*, 1993. Short Stories: *The Russian Wolfhound*, 1979. Poetry: *The Iron Curtain*, 1973. *St. Mark's Horses*, 1978. *The Inverted Glove*, 1989.

*   *   *

Although horrific, ghostly and gothic episodes play subservient roles in his work, Milorad Pavic's highly original treatment of supernatural themes has profoundly influenced the dark genres. One of the most inventive of all modern writers, he specializes in merging realism and fantasy in complex books which owe their forms to puzzles and conundrums. His multi-layered narratives are monumental tricks, parts of which must be disbelieved by any reader who wishes to decipher them. Enormously convoluted, each text is allegory, satire and thanatopsis: a purée of historical fact, rococo allusion and unique fabrication. Philosophical vignettes and scholarly digressions rub footnotes with passages of sombre intrigue and diabolic comedy. The stench of sulphur is never far away, but Pavic smothers it with attar of roses. When his devils do break through, they are sullen aesthetes with a culture and politics of their own, masters of disguise and lute-players, frequently giving themselves away by using ten fingers and a tail to pluck impossible chords.

Growing up in pre-war Belgrade, Pavic absorbed the convoluted folk tales and myths of the Balkans. He taught at the Paris Sorbonne and also in Germany before returning to Yugoslavia to accept a professorship. He soon consolidated his position as a leading expert on his country's extensive history and literature, publishing articles on the poetry of the Serbian Baroque. In 1967 his own verses began to attract attention from critics, though his international reputation grew slowly. Lyrics such as "Rejoice Eleventh Finger Reckoner of Stars," "But I'm the One to Whom Others Spit in the Hand When He Works," "Rejoice You Who Sleep With a Finger in Your Ear" and "But I'm the One From Whom They Stole a Button From His Trouser Leg" hint at his peculiar phraseology and penchant for startling similes and paradoxical images. The extreme compression of his songs served as a model for his short stories, which started appearing in 1973. Controlled and erudite, these pieces smoothly blend the grotesque with the prosaic, twisting motifs from conventional gothic sources into conveyances for an urbane poignancy beyond naturalism.

A number of such texts, linked together by the framing device of a reconstructed lexicon, comprise Pavic's first novel. *Dictionary of the Khazars* takes accounts of an obscure Caucasian people as its foundation, alternating between three separate eras with a set of characters in each who choose to involve themselves with the mystical tribe. The lexicon, a volume burned by the Inquisition and existing only in two copies, one of which has been printed with poisoned ink, is divided into three partisan interpretations, all of which must be cross-referenced to filter out the truth. To further the confusion, the novel itself comes in two versions, a male and female edition, which differ by one crucial paragraph. Though both are coherent when unravelled individually, they supposedly combine into a third, even more momentous, riddle. This is misleading—a typical Pavician joke and an attempt at involving his readers in the structure of the lexicon's metafictional coda.

Study of the entries, which employ literary techniques ranging from existential farce to eschatological poetics, eventually reveals the core plot: the Khazar Dream-Hunters and their efforts to attach themselves to the body of the angel ancestor of mankind, who oscillates between Heaven and Hell like a celestial ferry-service. To succeed in this futile quest the Hunters have to track and capture every dream that has ever existed, for this angel's substance is made from dreams. The dangers they face in the venture to harness angelic propulsion are insurmountable. A plethora of thaumaturgics harry them at every turn. The vampire-drenched lands of Central and Eastern Europe set the stage for myriad weird encounters. There is the golem so lifelike it is devoured by cannibals; the man who drowns when his head falls off into a bowl of soup; the messenger whose tattoos describe the history of the Khazar nation and who must submit to amputations whenever it is rewritten; the painter who can sing colours. *Dictionary of the Khazars* is a hybrid of two traditions, a descendant of the philosophical essay as well as the huge, nested novels of the gothic revival. The opposing voices mesh perfectly, *guignol* events carrying the abstractions on their hunched backs.

Pavic's second novel, *Landscape Painted with Tea*, is less sweeping in its effects, though just as fantastic. An architect whose designs are never constructed seeks his father, who disappeared while

fighting Nazis in Greece. His journey becomes entwined with the legends of Mouth Athos, the theocratic peninsula where menace and ecstasy dominate society. The plot is constructed like a cryptic crossword, with chapters which can be read "down" or "across." If anything, Pavic's writing has improved: his characters are pioneers in a psychological thought-experiment where past events intrude on the present to synthesize new futures. Again, although his interests are manifold, there are enough paranormal elements, demons included, to satisfy the most insatiable devotees of horror fiction. Almost alone among European writers, Pavic is capable of demonstrating how alien our Western traditions can be. The Gormenghastly monasteries where Atanas Svilar learns the differences between quiet and silence are repositories of our prodigal dreams, the final echoes of a time when men were shaved by looks as well as razors and professional devils were free to defect from one Hell to another.

This ability to disturb and enchant with hermetic ideas reaches an apotheosis with *The Inner Side of the Wind*, a retelling of the Hero and Leander story, which weaves parallel improvisations on the theme into a rope to strangle familiarity. Printed back-to-back, the dual texts meet in the middle and resolve difficult questions in the original myth which only Pavic seems to have noticed. The sheer strangeness of his language might remain an obstacle to the attainment of a wide popularity, but the eerie beauty of this twice-told tale is certain to spawn some imitators. Very slowly but effectively Pavic is mapping a new direction for modern speculative writing, a direction that, though it runs across mainstream, historical and experimental territory, mostly takes its bearings from all the morbid and spectral literatures.

—Rhys Hughes

QUIROGA, Horacio (1878-1937)

Nationality: Uruguayan. **Selected Publications:** Short Stories: *Cuentos de amor, de locura y de muerte*, 1917; as *The Decapitated Chicken and Other Stories*, 1976. *Los desterrados*, 1926; as *The Exiles*, 1987.

*   *   *

One of the best unknown international writers of darker stories, Horacio Quiroga, sadly achieved his most widespread recognition many years after his untimely suicide at the age of 58. With Jack London, Quiroga was probably the greatest writer of *natural* horror stories, chronicling the terror that can occur when man finds himself in the midst of a natural environment he cannot understand or cope with. For London, these surroundings are most often the barren ice-covered plains of the far North. For Quiroga, they're typically the creature-infested wilds of the Amazon.

Quiroga is nothing if not terse. Few of his stories run longer than 10 pages, yet he manages to pack a lethal punch in many of them, owing, at least in part, to lessons learned from having extensively read Poe, Chekhov and de Maupassant. Quiroga can move from the subtle suggestion of nuance to the intensity of stark terror flawlessly. In "Drifting" (also called "In the Current"), a man bitten by a deadly snake tries to remedy his situation by boating downstream to medical care but soon after being pulled into shore by a friend, succumbs; the last line of the story, in fact, is "And he stopped breathing." It's the matter-of-fact description of the man's increasingly severe symptoms, the sudden, unexpected, and relentless seizure by death of this man, that gives the story its fearsome power. In "The Decapitated Chicken," the four "idiot sons" of a bitterly disappointed middle-class couple watch in stupefied fascination as the family servant beheads a chicken for their dinner. The boys love bright colours, as a result of which their unfortunate normal younger sister suffers the same fate as the chicken. And in "The Feathered Pillow," a newly-married woman begins to waste away inexplicably until, after her demise five days later, her husband makes a startling discovery inside her unusually heavy pillow—a bloodsucking thing "so swollen one could scarcely make out its mouth."

Even with the suggestion of the supernatural, as in "The Feathered Pillow," Quiroga depicts his characters and settings with so realistic a style it is difficult to believe there is anything noticeably out of the ordinary. He often pinpoints the cold intensity of death by contrasting it with the warm vibrancy of life. In "The Dead Man," a field worker who daily cuts away excess foliage with his machete slips on some wet bark and fatally impales himself. As his life fades, he cannot help but sense the grass, the sky, the birds surrounding him, and hear the voice of his son calling him, until finally, a nearby horse passes by "the fallen man—who has rested now." This juxtaposition of life and death is seen even more dramatically in "The Son" in which a grey-haired, weak-sighted father trusts his 13-year-old son with a shotgun to hunt game for dinner. The boy goes off; not long after, "a sharp crack sounds." The man imagines his son has accidentally killed himself; he mentally replays the sight of his dead son several times, only to see, at last, the boy emerge from the woods, alive and whole. They converse briefly and the man smiles. But the smile is one of hallucinated happiness, for "his beloved son, dead since ten o'clock in the morning, lies in the sun." It is the unrelieved crushing presence, the ruthless inevitability of death that makes these stories more horrific than others featuring characters who meet their ends for whatever reason.

There are two volumes of Quiroga's stories translated into English; both testify to the dark power of terse prose that horrifies us with its depiction of Nature's ceaseless, uncaring universe, whose details cannot help but overwhelm the frail humans who try to live within it. Quiroga, like Jack London, is a writer who forces his readers to confront their own mortality head on. This, perhaps more than any other thematic content, is the essence of horror.

—Lawrence Greenberg

RAY, Jean (1887-1964)

Nationality: Belgian. **Selected Publications:** Novel: *Malpertuis*, 1943. Short Stories: *Ghouls in My Grave*, New York, Berkley, 1965.

*   *   *

Jean Ray (real name Raymond Jean Marie de Kremer, who also wrote as "John Flanders") was a Belgian journalist remembered for his numerous works of fantastic fiction. Like Thomas Owen,

his fellow Belgian, he wrote horror stories. But unlike Owen, Ray revels in the wide-open terror faced by those who throw themselves into life lived with the people around them. While Owen typically focuses on the quiet internalized terror of the individual psyche, Ray, in true pulp fashion, presents someone caught in the grip of horrific forces generated by his interaction with others.

In "The Cemetery Watchman," a man taken on as one of three mausoleum guards discovers his colleagues are not as benevolent as they appear, then ultimately confronts the vampiric duchess whose grave he was hired to protect. In "Mr. Glass Changes Direction," the title character, a murderous shopkeeper, slaughters ungrateful customers, then meets a nondescript man, Mr. Sheep, responsible for a newsworthy series of killings not unlike the unreported ones committed by Mr. Glass himself. The two exchange pleasantries about their mutual transgressions. Mr. Glass finally murders his "colleague," then continues in the same spirit, randomly dispatching fellow citizens until early autumn when, after winning a lottery, he is killed in bed for his newfound riches.

As befitting pulp fiction, Ray's stories are more coarsely written than Owen's, but they are also marked with the bite of black humour Owen rarely if ever shows. The main character in a Ray story goes about his life somewhat mindlessly; there's little if any reflection on the meaning of what he encounters, why he finds himself in a given situation, or, for that matter, who he is. The humour, black as it is, comes from the juxtaposition of the obviously mundane day-to-day events and/or superficial musings of Ray's main characters with the often suddenly-appearing fantastical occurrences that hit them out of the blue, obviously more profound than the mental scope of those they affect.

In his longer stories, Ray gives himself the room to stretch out and develop atmosphere, more cursorily created in his shorter works. The narrator of "The Mainz Psalter," a dying captain, relates the bizarre events that befell him and his crew on a voyage to Icelandic waters involving a schoolmaster obsessed with a 15th-century book and encounters with strangely-coloured waters, enormous shadowy monsters, and unseen death. The sailors try battling the obviously supernatural things, but there is little they can do. All succumb save the captain, who ultimately dies soon after finishing his tale. Interestingly, the story veers off from traditional pulp fiction at its conclusion—there is no pat resolution; indeed, a weird event near the end generates a question additional to those already raised, none of which are really explained.

In Europe, Ray's best-known work is *Malpertuis*, a novel whose subject, the confrontation of modern-day humans with the gods of ancient Greece, seems to give the lie to the author's penchant for more populist themes found in his short stories. The novel was filmed in 1972 by Harry Kuemel and proved too convoluted to follow easily for at least some critics. A dying sea captain, played by Orson Welles, discovers the pantheon of Greek deities. He succeeds in capturing and bringing them back to the unusual mansion he inhabits, Malpertuis, filled with passages that occasionally lead to unexpected dimensional spaces. There he enlists the services of a taxidermist to "stuff" the gods into the bodies of normal-looking people. Subsequently a hapless sailor wanders into the mansion and proceeds to fall in love with a beautiful maiden who is actually the Gorgon. Studiously avoiding his gaze, she eventually has no choice but to look at him and he is permanently transfixed in stone. Other strange events ensue based on supernatural beings having ordinary appearances, but as in "The Mainz Psalter," there is no definitive ending. In fact, there are three of them and all are inconclusive. Another more obscure film, *Le Grande Frousse*, was also based on Ray's writing.

Ray published several collections of short stories and one novel. Unfortunately, only one book was translated into English, *Ghouls in My Grave*, a selection of his short stories, currently out of print. The book is worth seeking out for an intriguing look at one of Continental Europe's more versatile and enjoyable horror writers.

—Lawrence Greenberg

RENARD, Maurice (1875-1940)

Nationality: French. **Selected Publications:** Novels: *Le Docteur Lerne, sous-dieu*, Paris, Mercure de France, 1908; as *New Bodies for Old*, New York, Macaulay, 1923. *Le Mains d'Orlac*, Paris, Nilson, 1921; as *The Hands of Orlac*, New York, Dutton, 1929; more accurate translation, London, Souvenir Press, 1970. *Le Singe*, with Albert Jean, Paris, Crès, 1925; as *Blind Circle*, New York, Dutton, 1928.

* * *

Maurice Renard was a prolific writer of horror fiction, much of it employing science-fictional devices. Very little of his short fiction has been translated into English, perhaps because of his inordinate fondness for working at novella length. His earliest exercises in this vein were four of the items collected in *Fantômes et fantoches* (*Phantoms and Puppets*, 1905); seven more were reprinted in *Le Voyage immobile* (*The Motionless Voyage*, 1909) and a further five in *Monsieur d'Outremort et autres histoires singulières* (*Mister Beyond-Death and Other Singular Stories*, 1913).

Renard's first novel, *New Bodies for Old*, is a wild tale of surgical experimentation presumably inspired by H. G. Wells's *The Island of Dr. Moreau* (the novel is fulsomely dedicated to Wells). The brains of a young Frenchman and a bull are briefly transposed by the would-be *sous-dieu*, or subgod, Dr. Lerne—whose body, it subsequently transpires, is now animated by the villainous brain of a German colleague, Klotz. Not content with transplant techniques, Klotz/Lerne is trying to master the art of transferring his personality telepathically. His experiments in that line are brought to an end, however, when he becomes the animating spirit of a motor car and is trapped within its mechanism.

Most of Renard's other novels were produced for serialization in the daily newspaper *L'Intransigeant*, and they bear the usual hallmarks of that kind of fiction, proceeding by means of an extended series of narrative hooks which become unduly dense and exaggerated when the story is read in volume form. The science-fiction thriller *Le Péril bleu* (*The Blue Peril*) appeared in *L'Intransigeant* in 1912, and he returned to its pages after World War I with the novel that was to become his most famous, *The Hands of Orlac*. It was first filmed in 1924 then remade as a talkie in 1935, retitled *Mad Love* and starring Peter Lorre; a British/French co-production using the original title followed in 1960. The famous pianist Stephen Orlac is badly injured in a train crash but is saved by the experimentally-inclined surgeon Professor Cerral. Subsequently, however, Orlac and his wife are disturbed by dreams of a recently-executed serial killer named Vasseur, whose fingerprints are found at the scenes of crimes for which Orlac has no

alibi. The plot thickens when it transpires that Cerral has transplanted Vasseur's hands to replace Orlac's own, which were crushed in the accident—but there are further surprises in store.

Blind Circle is another murder mystery with fantastic embellishments, evidently inspired by the widely-publicized exploits of France's most famous serial killer, Landru. A womanizing salesman with a weak heart turns up dead not once but several times. The multiplicity of identical corpses causes severe distress to his brother, who is involved with a religious sect that holds strong views regarding the physical resurrection of the body on Judgement Day. It turns out, after a police investigation, that the salesman had been living a double life as one "Pantu," inhabiting a medieval tower strewn with human bones—the results of his experiments in the production of artificial corpses. Just when the case seems to be wrapped up, however, further complications set in; the salesman begins communicating from the world of the dead, so that the secret of his process will not be lost. As in *The Hands of Orlac*, there is an extra twist which takes the plot even further into the hinterlands of extreme unlikelihood.

Apart from *Le Maître de la lumière* (*The Master of Light*, 1933; reprinted in book form, 1947) Renard's later newspaper serials were all *policiers* or mundane adventure stories, but he did produce one other full-length fantasy—the remarkable microcosmic fantasy *Un Homme chez les microbes* (*A Man Among the Microbes*, 1928)—and numerous shorter pieces, including the short novel *L'Homme truqué* (*The Fake Man*, 1921). Although his crucial contribution to the evolution of science fiction and horror fiction in France was acknowledged by the production of a huge (1,247-page) omnibus issued by Robert Laffont in 1990, Renard's reputation outside his own country continues to be marred by the relative dearth of translations and the inadequacy of the earlier ones that were made (the unsigned rendition of *New Bodies for Old* is execrable and Florence Crewe-Jones's version of *The Hands of Orlac* is extensively rewritten).

Renard's work for newspapers was heavily influenced by that of Gaston Leroux, who had been at his most prolific a decade in advance of him. It is perhaps unfortunate that he adopted some of Leroux's worst habits and silliest tricks for use in his novels, but his shorter fiction demonstrates that he was a far better and more ingenious writer than Leroux ever was; it is a shame that his virtuosity and versatility have never been made properly apparent to English-language readers.

—Francis Amery

SEIGNOLLE, Claude (1917-)

Nationality: French. **Selected Publications:** Short Stories: *The Accursed*, New York, Coward-McCann, 1967. *The Night Charmer and Other Tales*, Texas A&M University Press, 1983.

* * *

One of the best-known writers of horror stories in his native country, Claude Seignolle began his writing career chronicling the French folk tales that became the basis for much of his subsequent fiction. This ethnologic background informs many of his stories; they can be simple and earthy, combining elements of the supernatural with the pragmatic, keen-eyed perspective of a commoner. At the same time they are also clever and ironic enough to leave a greater impact than would a straightforward retelling of such folk tales. His blend of events that defy rational explanation or that hint of madness with O. Henry-like twists of fate generates shudders felt from the fear of an unforeseen and malevolent intelligence that never fails to intrude at precisely the wrong moment.

In "Starfish" (originally titled "The Mirror"), a beautiful actress who has suffered a traumatic accident disfiguring her face has been through an operation to repair it and still wears the requisite bandages during the healing process. She comes to a small seaside village inn to recuperate, deciding that the bandages have finally served their purpose. Because of impaired vision from prolonged visual blockage, she does not realize that the hideous visage she sees in her mirror after unwrapping herself is not her own face, but that of a long-unused mannequin somehow left in her room, whose decay from exposure to the sea has resulted in swollen, misshapen features. She drowns herself in despair. A common fisherman finds her body; the caretaker of the inn discovers the fatal dummy after her drowning. Though the main character is not herself of humble origin, it's commoners who underline the story's most important actions.

In "The Healer" the title character, Glaude, a simple gardener, prides himself on his ability to take on the symptoms of villagers afflicted with various ailments and rid both himself and the sufferer of the physical problem after one or two nights of sleep. But an encounter with a stranger from an unknown locale proves too much for him. For the stranger is troubled not with warts, pneumonia, or rheumatism, but with obsessive, unending lust that will not leave him alone for a moment. Glaude has, in the past, reversed the taking on of an undesirable ailment by returning the villager's money. This time, however, the tormented man who has transferred his affliction has hanged himself.

Though Seignolle's stories have a decidedly 19th-century feel, they also share the intense grimness of many 20th-century stories in the genre. In "The Last Rites" (originally "But Who is the Stronger?"), an older farmer prays to the locally-revered figure of worship, Hubertine—a woman dead at an early age and thought to be a paragon of virtue in his village—for the return of his young, and obviously unfaithful, wife. Because of his fervent imploring, he is at last visited, in the middle of the night, by a woman he believes is his wife, but who is significantly more skilled in the amatory arts than ever before. This he attributes to her adulterous trysts. Unfortunately the woman's ardour is far greater than even he can cope with, and he succumbs to a demonic passion. His wife, as it happens, was not the nocturnal visitor at all; it was the spirit of Hubertine, who is revealed at story's end to be a minion of the Devil.

And in "Night Horses," one of the more traditionally Gothic of Seignolle's tales, the narrator travels to rural France to visit his fiancée. An educated man, he is somewhat out of his element, surrounded by the farmers and villagers the author so frequently depicts. Thus he does not believe the local legend of the Ankou, the death labourer—he who drives a carriage through the countryside to collect those about to die. The unnamed narrator has seen the carriage, its driver, and the two attendants, said by locals to be servants of the netherworld. At first he dismisses the nervous words of his host and his host's wife as so much foolishness. But their continuing entreaties are so fraught with terror he cannot help but feel there is truth in what they say. And the Ankou is coming for Joceline, the narrator's betrothed. He spirits her back to Paris

which he deems safe, but soon after is shocked to hear the sound of hoofbeats in the dead of night. It is the Ankou. In the dark, quickly pushing her into a closet to protect her, he discovers too late that rather than a closet, it is a window he has pushed her from—to her death.

In his longer works, Seignolle delves more deeply into the lives and mores of the peasants he is so drawn to. Interestingly, the presence of the supernatural is muted, significantly more implicit than in his shorter works. What matters more is how collective village psychology transforms the protagonist from a figure with suspected negative influence to one of (supposedly) outright evil. Horror in these longer works is defined by the tragedy that befalls the main character based on his neighbours' growing distrust and hatred of him.

In both "The Outlander" and "Marie the Wolf" the title character is perceived initially as an outsider, then further reviled after forming an attachment to a more accepted member of the community. In both tales, this attachment triggers the display of the villagers' baser instincts. Both stories end not with the death of the protagonist, but with that of the one to whom the protagonist is emotionally linked. Though the main characters in both works are said to be allied with the Devil, the feelings they experience, especially with the killing of their lovers, reveal them as possessing more humanity than their accusers.

Of the two books of Seignolle's work available in English by far the better is Eric Deudon's translation of eight pieces, *The Night Charmer and Other Tales*. Seignolle occupies a nearly unique place in 20th-century horror literature. Along with American author Manly Wade Wellman and perhaps one or two others, he effectively portrays many of the most deeply ingrained fears and beliefs of the rural commoner.

—Lawrence Greenberg

SOLOGUB, Fyodor (1863-1927)

Pseudonym for Fyodor Kuzmich Teternikov. **Nationality:** Russian. **Selected Publications:** Novels: *Bad Dreams*, 1896. *The Little Demon*, 1907. *The Created Legend Trilogy*, 1908-12. Short Stories: *The Sting of Death*, 1904. *Mouldering Masks*, 1907. *A Book of Enchantments*, 1909. *The Sweet-Scented Name and Other Fairy Tales, Fables and Stories*, 1915. *The Old House and Other Tales*, 1915. Poetry: *The Fiery Circle*, 1908. Plays: *The Triumph of Death*, 1907. *The Gift of the Wise Bees*, 1907. *Vanka the Butler and the Page Jehan*, 1909. *Hostages of Life* 1912.

*   *   *

The eccentric (some might say demented) Fyodor Sologub shares with Ivan Goncharov the dubious distinction of adding a disreputable noun to the Russian language. "Peredenovism" is used to describe the brutal face of petty officialdom. Peredenov himself, the main character of *The Little Demon*, Sologub's major work, is one of the most original sadists in modern literature, a dull-witted and plodding schoolmaster who seeks to lower his profession to new depths of malevolent banality. Relentlessly misanthropic, the novel demonstrates Sologub's light handling of gothic images, which increase in strangeness when rendered in his clear prose. Like Lautréamont, he often insults his readers, treating them as agents of his loneliness. His venom and obsession with inverse morality is too total to be purely fictive: when his wife, a noted lyrical poet, killed herself, the act seemed the apotheosis of his career—in much the same way that Lautréamont's death at the hands of the Parisian secret police was a logical conclusion to his work.

Born in St. Petersburg, Sologub studied and taught at the Teacher's Institute before the success of *The Little Demon* enabled him to take up fiction full-time. He wrote for many years without publishing material, though his first poems appeared in *The Northern Herald* in 1892. Hasty and sometimes ludicrous, these early verses betray an insecure grasp of symbolist aesthetics, though he was to improve steadily until he became one of the movement's leading lights. At times, his professed Diabolism parallels that of Beerbohm's invented decadent, Enoch Soames, with prim acceptance of Satanic forces and evil defined simply as a style. "I Was Languishing in Lunar Magic" and "I Love to Wander Over a Quagmire" both extol the virtues of escapism, though from polar extremes: the first is a melodic flight of mystic whimsy, the second is a Schopenhauerian rant in which the narrator, endlessly reborn as a variety of entities, seeks to cheat conscious suffering by reincarnating himself out of the bottom of existence, rather than upward to Nirvana, an end which can be gained only by tormenting other creatures.

Sologub's first novel, the semi-autobiographical *Bad Dreams*, was a failure on publication, but he salvaged parts of it to form the core of *The Little Demon*, whose scenes are grounded in the reality Sologub knew in his capacity as a district inspector of schools (he later claimed the book formed the memoirs not of himself but of his critics). Peredenov beats his pupils, abuses his landlady and cook. The demon of the title is his inclination toward vice, which manifests itself as a furry Nedotykomka, a being which pursues him through arson and murder into the depths of a lunatic asylum. Peredenov's decline is balanced by the doomed purity of the beautiful schoolboy Sasha, a contrast which breaks down as Sasha is manipulated by the author for reasons of perverse sensuality. Like Géza Csáth, Sologub is keen to juxtapose children and evil, partly to convey a sense of innocence corrupted by contact with the real world, but also to satisfy a hidden agenda of unhealthy eroticism. His pedant's eye for the details of psychological fragmentation, his stress on the timing of paranoia, are qualities largely absent in the madhouse stories of other symbolists, for whom the asylum exerted a powerful fascination. Sologub perfected the Grand-Guignol format of the theme and in doing so made it redundant: after him, fictional explorations of mental illness began to replace the centrifuge with the couch.

More ambitious and awkward, *The Created Legend* is a trilogy fusing genuine Satanism with deliberate pedestrianism. The bizarre exploits of Trirodov, a Prospero-like magician, epitomize all that is unique in the author's style: the intrusion of the fantastic into the bland in such a way that the marvels are less startling than the mundanity. As the plot moves from the Russia of the nihilists to a sequence of invented Aegean islands, the structure of the work disintegrates. *The Created Legend* is almost a negative of *The Little Demon*—whereas Sologub exerted control over Peredenov's lunacy, maintaining an ironic distance between himself and the psychosis, Trirodov seems to be manipulating his creator to the same effect. In the earlier novel, the character is mad while the prose is sane: the trilogy is an odd reversal of this condition. A failure as a whole, the work contains some scenes reminiscent of Sologub's shorter fiction, where the ostentatious invention has been straitjacketed and can thrash in one direction only.

Sologub published 16 volumes of short stories, though many of the individual pieces are more properly vignettes. His Manichean belief in the dual world—the grotesque reality developed by God and the cool realm of imagination created by Satan—finds lyrical expression in the wonderful "Turandina," which concerns a princess who levers herself out of a fairy tale to bear a prosaic lawyer children before vanishing back into non-existence. Sacrifice and liberation, debauchery and purity are confused in "The Red-Lipped Guest," a religious-vampiric tale, and also in "Beyond the Meirur River," a piece which can best be described as an anterior post-catastrophe fantasy. In contrast, "A Little Man" takes an obvious metaphor to its limit: the protagonist obtains a medicine which is guaranteed to reduce the dimensions of his gargantuan wife to normal proportions, mistakenly drinks it himself and dwindles away to nothing. Sologub's methodology extends the approach of Poe: the neglected Poe of peculiar comedies and absurdist satires.

Less overtly horrific, his works for the theatre stressed the need for actors to perform mechanically, fully aware of the play as fiction, a requirement which did not endear him to the thespian hierarchy. *Vanka the Butler and the Page Jehan* is a complex retelling of a folk tale, in which two main plots, mirroring each other through the centuries, serve to contrast Russian barbarism with French quasi-refinement. *Hostages of Life* is an attempt to examine realist issues from a mythic perspective by delivering natural dialogue from the mouths of fantastic characters. These plays are seldom performed and Sologub's reputation relies on his novels. These remain a navigable bridge between the gothic romanticism of Poe, Hoffmann and Potocki and the self-conscious visceral modernism of Cendrars, Bataille and Leiris.

—Rhys Hughes

SUE, Eugène (1804-1857)

Nationality: French. **Selected Publications:** Novels: *The Wandering Jew*, New York, Harper, 1844. *The Gold Sickle; or, Hena, the Virgin of the Isle of Sen*, New York, Labor News, 1904. *The Brass Bell; or, The Chariot of Death*, New York, Labor News, 1907. *The Iron Collar; or, Faustina and Syomara*, New York, Labor News, 1909. *The Infant's Skull; or, The End of the World*, New York, Labor News, 1904. *The Iron Pincers; or, Mylio and Karvel*, New York, Labor News, 1909.

*   *   *

Eugène Sue's earliest publications were melodramatic tales of the sea, some of which—including the novella *Atar-Gull* (1831; translated as *Atar-Gull; or, the Slave's Revenge* and as *The Negro's Revenge; or, Brulart the Black Pirate*)—already exhibited the taste for horrific scenes of violence which were to make his work notorious. *Lautréamont* (1838), a historical novel set in the days of Louis XIV, was extravagant enough for the name of its lead character to be borrowed as a pseudonym by Isidore Ducasse, the author of the infamous *Les Chants du Maldoror* (1868). *Le Morne-au-diable* (1842: translated as *The Female Bluebeard* and as *The Refugees of Martinique*) is an extravagant account of the cruel exploits of a female pirate. Sue found his true métier, however, in the 1840s, when the editors of daily newspapers began using serial fiction as a weapon in their circulatory wars. Sue and

Alexandre Dumas soon became the most popular exponents of this exacting craft, whose potential was first demonstrated by Sue's *Les Mystères de Paris*, which ran in *Le Journal des Débats* from 19 June 1842 to 15 October 1843.

The Mysteries of Paris is a sprawling thriller of great complexity whose horrific element is mostly derived from the exploits of its neo-Gothic villains: the miserly notary, Jacques Ferrand; the monstrous whoremistress La Chouette ["Screech-Owl"]; and a multiple murderer with a mutilated face known as Le Maitre d'école ["Schoolmaster"]. Such scenes as the deliberate blinding of Le Maitre d'école and the eventual destruction of La Chouette led Sue's detractors to accuse him of sadism, but what such scenes actually strive for is an appropriate expression of an outrage so profound that nothing but extremes of horror can possibly assuage it.

The same method is employed in the even more massive tale of *The Wandering Jew*, whose second part brings to the fore the most menacing of all Sue's neo-Gothic villains: the Jesuit clerk Rodin, who intends to secure the Wandering Jew's treasure (swollen over the centuries by compound interest) even if it requires the incarceration or murder of its dozen legitimate heirs. In one of the most extreme examples of French anti-clericalism the Society of Jesus is here represented as an organization bent on world domination at any cost. The Wandering Jew and his female counterpart Herodias function in the plot as symbolic figures, reflecting the plight of working men and women beneath the tyranny of Church and State. The Radical sympathies given strident voice within the plot—which caused a minor panic when several serial versions of the story began running in English penny papers—came increasingly to the fore in Sue's later works, and he continued to employ non-supernatural horror as a means of sharpening his message whenever it seemed appropriate.

Cruel episodes recur throughout *Les Sept péchés capitaux* (1847-48) translated for English periodicals as *The Seven Deadly Sins*, and in *Martin l'enfant trouvé; ou les mémoires d'un valet de chambre* (1846), translated as *Martin the Foundling*, but it was the huge family saga *Les mystères de peuple* (1849-52)—a sprawling series of novellas and short novels Sue considered to be his magnum opus—that provided the most abundant and extreme opportunities. A translation of the early episodes was issued in England as *The Rival Races; or, the Sons of Joel* (1863) but the only full translation was organized by the noted American socialists Daniel and Solon de Leon, whose New York Labor News Company issued it in 19 volumes (out of chronological order) under the collective title of *The Mysteries of the People: The History of a Proletarian Family Across the Ages* between 1904 and 1911.

The early items in this series are the most vividly violent. *The Gold Sickle* is a tale of druids and human sacrifice. *The Brass Bell* is an account of Caesar's bloody invasion of Gaul. *The Iron Collar* displays the iniquities of Roman slavery and the horrors of the arena. The most horrific of the later volumes include *The Infant's Skull*, which recapitulates the popular myth that crops went unplanted throughout Europe in the year 999 because the world was expected to end before the harvest, and *The Iron Pincers*, a bloodcurdling account of the persecution of the Albigensian heretics. These tales confirmed Sue's reputation for sadism, while the intermediate volumes presented quieter analyses of the historical evolution of socialist ideals. His commitment to such ideals made Sue avidly enthusiastic to play a role when the revolution of 1848 began (the Communist rising in Paris occurred on 15 May, the day after *Les Sept péchés capitaux* concluded its serial-

ization in *Le Constitutionnel*). The new Republican constitution was promulgated in November, and in the following year Sue was elected a Socialist deputy for the Seine. Unfortunately, the new constitution lasted only three years before the duly elected president, Louis Napoleon, abolished it in the wake of his coup d'état. Sue conscientiously opposed the coup, with the consequence that he was exiled from the city whose miseries and mysteries had moved him to such outrage, and he was never able to return. He died in exile, his career in ruins.

Sue's contribution to the genre of horror fiction is marginal but by no means insignificant. His work can be regarded as a continuation of the "political Gothic" tradition and must be numbered among the precursors of Grand Guignol fiction. He helped to set the initial pattern for the *roman feuilleton*, which was modified by such later writers of exaggerated thrillers as Gaston Leroux and Maurice Renard, and which deserves recognition as the remotest ancestor of television soap operas.

—Francis Amery

SÜSKIND, Patrick (1949-)

Nationality: German. **Selected Publications:** Novels: *Perfume: The Story of a Murderer*, New York, Knopf, and London, Hamilton, 1986. *The Pigeon*, New York, Knopf, and London, Hamilton, 1988.

*   *   *

The term *tour de force* might have been created with Patrick Süskind's novel *Perfume* in mind. It is difficult to classify and might be horror or fantasy or science fiction or an historical account or a parable. Certainly it is an obsessive novel about an obsessive character, audaciously overwritten to the extent that the reader will recognize it as a memorable triumph but will not know whether to laugh or cry.

Jean-Baptiste Grenouille is born in Paris in 1738, the illegitimate son of a fishseller. He is soon an orphan. He has the peculiarity of having no personal odour, which causes a wet-nurse to describe him as "possessed by the devil" and other orphans to avoid him. But as a child of three he begins to realize that the world is composed of scents, and he can smell them all. This means that, by the time he is six, he can find his way in the dark by smell alone, can find lost or hidden objects by their scents, can identify people some minutes before they arrive. He never forgets or confuses a scent. Aged eight, he is sold to a tanner, one of the most odiferous of trades, besides being dangerous for its workers.

At 15, Grenouille catches the faintest whiff of an astoundingly wonderful scent. He follows it across Paris and discovers it to be a person, a girl of about his own age. He strangles her at once, for no better reason than that it affords him the opportunity to strip her and smell her all over, capturing her scent.

Soon after, Grenouille is delivering some goatskins from his master to a perfumer, M. Baldini, and he takes the chance to ask for a job there. He knows nothing of the technique of perfume-making, yet he can recognize all the ingredients of any perfume, and even their proportions, and he knows that he has the best nose in Paris. He is tested by Baldini, who can scarcely believe Grenouille's talent. Quickly, Baldini buys Grenouille from the tanner and uses him to create new perfumes of such quality that Baldini becomes rich and famous, and Grenouille learns all that Baldini knows about the trade. After three years, Grenouille secures his freedom, ostensibly to travel south and study the different methods employed by perfumers in the area of Grasse. But *en route* he becomes sickened by humanity and spends seven years alone in a remote cave high in the Massif Central, from where even with his ability he cannot scent another human being.

He leaves to rejoin the human race only when he realizes that he cannot smell himself and must somehow remedy this. With some help from a friendly marquis with crackpot ideas, he creates a perfume for himself which does "not smell like a scent, but like a human being who *gives off* scent" (Süskind's italics). So the acquisition of a body scent becomes a concern of his. He joins a perfumer in Grasse and learns the techniques of obtaining perfume from fresh petals by heat, by cold and by oil, and of refining scents to their essence. In his spare time he prepares a variety of special scents for himself, and he begins to commit murder.

Already he has identified a young girl with the perfect scent and is waiting for her to mature. Meanwhile he practises by killing young women and capturing their scents carefully in tallow-impregnated rags. He kills 25 young women including, finally, the one with the perfect scent. So terrorized is the neighbourhood that scientific principles are applied and Grenouille is arrested and convicted. He is due to be executed in a particularly barbaric fashion, but the perfume he wears for the occasion so enamours the waiting crowds that they are driven to ecstasy, full of feelings of love for him and desire for each other. Grenouille is aided by his last victim's father; he returns to Paris where, wearing that same perfume, he is torn apart by an over-enthusiastically loving crowd in the year 1766, a few weeks short of his 28th birthday.

So Grenouille is a monster; his special ability gives rise to obsession and is counterbalanced by a misanthropy and an emotionlessness so intense that he is never concerned with morals; so far as he is concerned, his ends always justify the means. He is as unsympathetic as a character can be, and yet his progress through life in this *bildungsroman* is so astonishing that the reader is too fascinated not to read on. There is no direct suggestion (apart from the comment of that wet-nurse) that Grenouille might be a supernatural creature sent by the devil, yet everybody who has dealings with him suffers badly: his mother is guillotined for child neglect and infanticide; the master tanner gets drunk on the money for selling him, falls in the Seine and drowns; Baldini is killed when his premises collapse the night after Grenouille has departed; his employer at Grasse is convicted of the murder of the 25 young women and hanged.

Süskind piles irony upon irony. Grenouille, born to a fishseller in a hot summer fishmarket, becomes a cold fish. The man with the greatest sense of smell the world has ever known has no personal odour. While he could have used his talent to become a very rich man through perfumery, Grenouille seems to have no use for money. When he gets close to attractive young women he has no thoughts except to kill them for their scent. And finally, the man who has been avoided or reviled all his life is killed by an excess of public love in a conclusion which is inevitable, tragic and comic all at once.

The atmosphere which Süskind builds up is no less obsessive than his character. His long descriptions of Paris at its worst, of the tanning trade, of the uses of perfumes, of the creation of perfumes, of Grenouille's grandiose daydreams, are all so intense and compelling as to mark out the novel as a one-off, the summit of originality.

Süskind's novella *The Pigeon* is similar though much milder in its treatment of a much less dangerous obsessive. Jonathan Noel is a bank security guard in his 50s, a loner set in his ways. One day he is terrified (for no good reason that the reader can see) and his life turned upside down by the glassy stare of a pigeon which has become trapped on the landing outside his apartment. The story shows how one moment of horror can change a man's attitude to life.

—Chris Morgan

VILLIERS de L'ISLE ADAM, (Jean Marie-Mathias-Philippe-Auguste) Comte de (1840-1889)

Nationality: French. **Selected Publications:** Novels: *L'Eve future*, 1886; as *Tomorrow's Eve*, Urbana, University of Illinois Press, 1982. *Claire Lenoir*, 1887; New York, Boni, 1925. Short Stories: *Contes cruels*, Paris, 1883; as *Sardonic Tales*, New York, Knopf, 1927; as *Cruel Tales*, Oxford, Oxford University Press, 1963.

*   *   *

Villiers de l'Isle Adam gave a name to an entire sub-genre of fiction when he published his first book of *Contes cruels* in 1883, collecting together items which had been appearing in periodicals since 1867. The majority of the tales are set solidly in the tradition of Poe—not unnaturally, considering that Villiers saw himself as the principal living example of the species of impoverished, enfeebled and decadent descendants of aristocratic families that featured so prominently in Poe's work. Even in the cruellest of Poe's tales, however, such figures had preserved a residual dignity in their obstinate pride while ensconced in their Gothic piles, and a sentimental if somewhat terrorized regard for their *femmes fatales*; Villiers had lost his dignity along with his home and the consistent failure of his attempts to marry for money had turned him into a diehard misogynist.

The degraded Romanticism of Poe still shows in a few of Villiers' tales—notably "Occult Memories," which is headed by a passage misquoted from "Eleanora"—but in the main his pieces are more pointed and more cynical. "The Sign" recalls "The Fall of the House of Usher" but the Abbé who presses a haunted cloak upon the protagonist is probably a version of Villiers' own uncle. Only the bittersweet "Véra," the most oft-reprinted of the tales in the first collection, could pass muster as a vehicle for the unadulterated spirit of Poe, although the even-more-widely reprinted "The Torture of Hope," which appeared in a supplementary volume, is a tale of the Inquisition more subtle—and perhaps more effective—than "The Pit and the Pendulum."

"The Duke of Portland" is among the most widely-imitated of the *contes cruels*, its climactic revelation echoed in Marcel Schwob's "The King in the Golden Mask" and Dino Buzzati's "Something Beginning with 'L'," among others. "The Desire to be a Man" also stands, less obtrusively, at the head of a considerable tradition, deftly infiltrating the *conte cruel* with an existentialist *conte philosophique* whose moral is recapitulated in dozens of meditative posthumous fantasies and earnest literary ghost stories. "The Apparatus for the Chemical Analysis of the Last Breath" anticipates many quasi-science-fictional tales of the attempted domestication of the soul, and casts a sarcastic shadow over all of them. The most effective of the remaining tales are "The Eleventh-Hour Guest," a jocular account of a nobleman whose secret fascination with death makes him the "guillotine's sweetheart" and "torture's hobbyist," and "The Messenger," a sonorously bleak Biblical fantasy.

Tomorrow's Eve is a phantasmagoric, allegorical science-fiction story in which a young English nobleman, rendered heartsick by the awful perfidy of womankind, is rescued from despair by the American inventor Thomas Edison, who volunteers to build him an android from which all the imperfections of the human female have been carefully omitted. The young man falls in love with the android, who claims to be more than a mere automaton, but she is lost in a fire aboard the ship which carries them back across the Atlantic. The story is, in essence, an inflated *conte cruel* whose padding is sometimes as inelegant as it is bizarre, but the story itself is fascinatingly different from such predecessors as E. T. A. Hoffmann's "The Sandman" and such successors as Hanns Heinz Ewers's *Alraune*. If it is not a horror story—and its relentless philosophizing certainly serves to minimize its horrific quality—it can nevertheless be placed in interesting juxtaposition with some classics of the horror genre.

Claire Lenoir is also an unduly inflated *conte cruel*, but a much weaker one, whose philosophical pretensions are not seriously intended even as satire. The narrator, Dr. Tribulat Bonhomet, causes the death of his friend Lenoir, whose final words declare that adultery is the only unforgivable sin. Bonhomet has already heard a British naval officer confess that he is in love with Madame Lenoir, and he later hears that the officer has been killed by cannibals. When he attends the dying Madame Lenoir she tells him that it was her husband's spirit that took possession of the officer's murderer, and offers him proof in the form of the last image imprinted by death upon her retina. The then-popular superstition which held that a man's eyes might somehow preserve the last vision experienced in life is here ironically extended to a supernatural extreme, losing even the remotest probability by virtue of that extension.

In 1887 Villiers was, of course, still to produce his masterpiece, the tragic drama *Axel*, in which the scion of a noble family finds an escapee from a nunnery in the vaults beneath his castle, and eventually makes a suicide pact with her. That was the work which measured out the full extent of his cynicism and despair, shorn in the end of all its dark humour.

Although his career began some time before he turned to *contes cruels*, with steadfastly Parnassian poems and Romantic plays, Villiers was never a prolific writer. Had he contrived to be more prolific he might have made a living from his pen—but had he made a living from his pen, he could not then have cultivated the awesome resentment of his low-fallen position which made his work unique. He was one of those paradoxical souls whose artistic success was firmly rooted in personal failure, and in his sharp awareness of the magnitude of that failure. No one who does not share that kind of sharp awareness can properly reproduce in a literary medium the special kind of cruelty which invests *contes cruels*. There were to be later dabblers in that sub-genre more gifted than Villiers, but none with quite the same motive force; that is why his heirs have never succeed in relegating him to the status of a mere pioneer.

—Francis Amery

NAME INDEX

The following index lists all entrants alphabetically by last name and includes pseudonyms with cross-references to main entrant names.

Freeman, Mary E. Wilkins
Frost, Mark

G

Gaiman, Neil
Gallagher, Stephen
Garton, Ray
Gilchrist, R. Murray
Gilman, Charlotte Perkins
Gilmer, Anne
    See Ross, Marilyn
Godwin, William
Gogol, Nikolai (appendix)
Golding, William
Gordon, John
Gorman, Ed
Grabinski, Stefan (appendix)
Grant, Charles L.
Grant, Kathryn
    See Ptacek, Kathryn
Grave, Stephen
    See Schow, David J.
Gray, Alasdair
Gresham, Stephen
Gronmark, Scott
    See Sharman, Nick

H

Hague, G. M.
Hallahan, William H.
Hamilton, Alex
Harbinson, W. A.
Hargrave, Leonie
    See Disch, Thomas M.
Harold, Clive
    See Hutson, Shaun
Harris, Joanne
Harris, Steve
Harris, Thomas
Harrison, M. John
Hart, Veronica
    See Kelleher, Victor
Hartley, L. P.
Harvey, W. F.
Hautala, Rick
Hawthorne, Julian
Hawthorne, Nathaniel
Heard, H. F.
Hearn, Lafcadio
Herbert, James
Heron-Allen, Edward
    See Blayre, Christopher
Hichens, Robert
Hill, Susan
Hjortsberg, William
Hodgson, William Hope
Hoffmann, E. T. A. (appendix)
Hogg, James
Holder, Nancy

Holdstock, Robert
Holland, Tom
Honeycombe, Gordon
Hood, Robert
Housman, Clemence
Hughes, Rhys
Hunt, Violet
Hutson, Shaun
Huysmans, Joris-Karl (appendix)
Hyde, Christopher

J

Jackson, Shirley
Jacobi, Carl
Jacobs, W. W.
James, G. P. R.
James, Henry
James, M. R.
James, Peter
Jeter, K. W.
Joyce, Graham

K

Kafka, Franz (appendix)
Kalogridis, Jeanne
Kast, Pierre (appendix)
Kay, Susan
Kaye, Marvin
Kelleher, Victor
Keller, David H.
Kelly, Richard
    See Laymon, Richard
Kennett, Rick
Kerruish, Jessie Douglas
Kersh, Gerald
Ketchum, Jack
Kilpatrick, Nancy
King, Stephen
Kirk, Russell
Klein, T. E. D.
Kneale, Nigel
Knight, Amarantha
    See Kilpatrick, Nancy
Knight, Harry Adam
Knye, Cassandra
    See Disch, Thomas M.
Koja, Kathe
Konvitz, Jeffrey
Koontz, Dean
Kosinski, Jerzy

L

Laing, Alexander
Lake, Simon
    See Grant, Charles L.
Lambert, S. H.
    See Bell, Neil
Lamsley, Terry

Lane, Joel
Lansdale, Joe R.
Laski, Marghanita
Lawrence, Margery
Laws, Stephen
Laymon, Richard
Lecale, Errol
    See Saxon, Peter
Lee, Vernon
Leech, Ben
Le Fanu, J. Sheridan
Leiber, Fritz
Leroux, Gaston (appendix)
Leven, Jeremy
Levin, Ira
Lewis, D. Francis
Lewis, Deborah
    See Grant, Charles L.
Lewis, M. G.
Leyton, E. K.
    See Campbell, Ramsey
Ligotti, Thomas
Lindsey, David L.
Little, Bentley
Locke, Joseph
    See Garton, Ray
Long, Frank Belknap
Long, Margaret Campbell
    See Bowen, Marjorie
Lory, Robert
Lovecraft, H. P.
Lovegrove, James
Lucas, Tim
Luke, Thomas
    See Masterton, Graham
Lumley, Brian

M

MacAlan, Peter
    See Tremayne, Peter
Macardle, Dorothy
MacEoin, Dennis
    See Aycliffe, Jonathan
Machen, Arthur
Maginn, Simon
Marsh, Geoffrey
    See Grant, Charles L.
Marsh, Richard
Martens, Paul
    See Bell, Neil
Martin, David
Martin, George R. R.
Martin, Jack
    See Etchison, Dennis
Massie, Elizabeth
Masterton, Graham
Matheson, Richard
Matheson, Richard Christian
Maturin, Charles R.
Maupassant, Guy de (appendix)

McCammon, Robert R.
McDowell, Michael
McEwan, Ian
McGrath, Patrick
McKenney, Kenneth
McNally, Clare
McNeilly, Wilfred
    See Saxon, Peter
Metcalfe, John
Meyrink, Gustav (appendix)
Middleton, Richard B.
Miller, Rex
Millhiser, Marlys
Molesworth, Mary L.
Monahan, Brent
Monteleone, Thomas F.
Morlan, A. R.
Morrell, David
Morris, Mark
Morrow, W. C.
Munby, A. N. L.
Munn, H. Warner
Munro, H. H.
    See Saki

N

Navarro, Yvonne
Neiderman, Andrew
Nesbit, E.
Neville, Robert
    See Hutson, Shaun
Newman, Gavin
    See Smith, Guy N.
Newman, Guy
    See Smith, Guy N.
Newman, Kim
Nichols, Leigh
    See Koontz, Dean
Nisbet, Hume
Nye, Robert

O

Oates, Joyce Carol
O'Donnell, Elliott
Oliphant, Mrs.
Onions, Oliver
O'Sullivan, Vincent
Owen, Thomas (appendix)

P

Paget, Violet
    See Lee, Vernon
Paige, Richard
    See Koontz, Dean
Palmer, Jessica
Palmer, Maria
    See Tuttle, Lisa
Parkinson, T. L.

Partridge, Norman
Pavic, Milorad (appendix)
Paye, Robert
    See Bowen, Marjorie
Piccirilli, Tom
Pike, Christopher
Poe, Edgar Allan
Polidori, John
Popescu, Petru
Praed, Mrs. Campbell
Preedy, George
    See Bowen, Marjorie
Prest, Thomas Peckett
Prichard, K. & Hesketh
Pritchard, John
Ptacek, Kathryn

Q

Quiller-Couch, Arthur
Quinn, Seabury
Quinn, Simon
    See Smith, Martin Cruz
Quiroga, Horacio (appendix)

R

Radcliffe, Ann
Ramsay, Jay
    See Campbell, Ramsey
Randolph, Ellen
    See Ross, Marilyn
Ransom, Daniel
    See Gorman, Ed
Raucher, Herman
Ray, Jean (appendix)
Reeves-Stevens, Garfield
Renard, Maurice (appendix)
Reynolds, G. W. M.
Rhodes, Daniel
Rice, Anne
Rickman, Phil
Riddell, Mrs. J. H.
Robbins, Tod
Robertson, Stephen
    See Walker, Robert W.
Rodgers, Alan
Rohmer, Sax
Rolt, L. T. C.
Ross, Adrian
Ross, Clarissa
    See Ross, Marilyn
Ross, Dana
    See Ross, Marilyn
Ross, Marilyn
Roszak, Theodore
Rousseau, Victor
Royle, Nicholas
Russell, Ray
Russell, W. Clark
Russo, John

Ryan, Alan
Ryan, R. R.
Rymer, James Malcolm

S

Saberhagen, Fred
Sackett, Jeffrey
St. Clair, David
Saki
Sarban
Sarrantonio, Al
Saul, John
Saxon, Peter
Schow, David J.
Scott, A. G.
    See Sharman, Nick
Scott, Michael
Scott, Walter
Seignolle, Claude (appendix)
Seltzer, David
Sharman, Nick
Shearing, Joseph
    See Bowen, Marjorie
Shelley, Mary
Shepard, Lucius
Shiel, M. P.
Shirley, John
Shock, Julian
    See Williamson, J. N.
Siddons, Anne Rivers
Silva, David B.
Simmons, Dan
Simons, Les
    See Ptacek, Kathryn
Sinclair, Iain
Sinclair, May
Singer, Isaac Bashevis
Siodmak, Curt
Skal, David J.
Skipp, John
Slade, Michael
Sloane, William M.
Smith, Clark Ashton
Smith, Guy N.
Smith, Lady Eleanor
Smith, Martin Cruz
Smith, Michael Marshall
Smith, Rosamond
    See Oates, Joyce Carol
Sologub, Fyodor (appendix)
Somtow, S. P.
Southwold, Stephen
    See Bell, Neil
Spector, Craig
    See Skipp, John and Craig Spector
Spencer, William Browning
Stableford, Brian
Stallman, Robert
Steele, V. M.
    See Fortune, Dion

Stenbock, Eric
Stevenson, Robert Louis
Stewart, Fred Mustard
Stine, R. L.
Stoker, Bram
Stout, Tim
Straczynski, J. Michael
Straub, Peter
Strieber, Whitley
Sturgeon, Theodore
Sucharitkul, Somtow
    See Somtow, S. P.
Sue, Eugène (appendix)
Süskind, Patrick (appendix)
Suster, Gerald
Swanson, Logan
    See Matheson, Richard

T

Talbot, Michael
Taylor, Bernard
Taylor, Frank
    See Hutson, Shaun
Taylor, Lucy
Tem, Melanie
Tem, Steve Rasnic
Tessier, Thomas
Theroux, Paul
Thomas, D. M.
Timperley, Rosemary
Tonkin, Peter
Tremayne, Peter
Tryon, Thomas
Turner, James
Tuttle, Lisa

U

Updike, John

V

Vance, Steve
Vandermeer, Jeff

Villiers de l'Isle Adam, Comte de (appendix)
Visiak, E. H.

W

Wakefield, H. Russell
Walker, Robert W.
Wall, John W.
    See Sarban
Walpole, Horace
Walpole, Hugh
Walter, Elizabeth
Wandrei, Donald
Watson, Ian
Weinberg, Robert
Weldon, Fay
Wells, H. G.
Welty, Eudora
West, Owen
    See Koontz, Dean
Wharton, Edith
Wheatley, Dennis
Whitehead, Henry S.
Whitten, Leslie H.
Wilkins, Mary E.
    See Freeman, Mary E. Wilkins
Williams, Mary
Williamson, Chet
Williamson, J. N.
Wilson, Colin
Wilson, F. Paul
Wisman, Ken
Wood, Bari
Woods, Stuart
Wright, T. M.

Y

Yarbro, Chelsea Quinn
Yeovil, Jack
    See Newman, Kim
Young, Axel
    See McDowell, Michael

Z

Zell, Steve

NATIONALITY INDEX

American

Conrad Aiken
V. C. Andrews
Robert Arthur
Gertrude Atherton
Scott Baker
Charles Beaumont
Peter Benchley
Stephen Vincent Benét
Ambrose Bierce
William Peter Blatty
Robert Bloch
Jay R. Bonansinga
Douglas Borton
Randall Boyll
Ray Bradbury
Scott Bradfield
Gary Brandner
Joseph Payne Brennan
Alan Brennert
Poppy Z. Brite
Charles Brockden Brown
Edward Bryant
Arthur J. Burks
William S. Burroughs
Michael Cadnum
Jack Cady
Lisa W. Cantrell
Jonathan Carroll
David Case
Hugh B. Cave
Robert W. Chambers
Fred Chappell
Suzy McKee Charnas
Joseph Citro
Mary Higgins Clark
Douglas Clegg
Leonard Cline
Nancy A. Collins
Robin Cook
Dennis Cooper
Matthew J. Costello
Sean Costello
Mary Elizabeth Counselman
John Coyne
F. Marion Crawford
Brian D'Amato
Don D'Ammassa
Les Daniels
Ron Dee
Frank De Felitta
August Derleth
Thomas M. Disch
Katherine Dunn
Max Ehrlich
Bret Easton Ellis
Harlan Ellison
P. N. Elrod
Guy Endore
Elizabeth Engstrom
Dennis Etchison

Ken Eulo
John Farris
Mary E. Wilkins Freeman
Mark Frost
Ray Garton
Charlotte Perkins Gilman
Ed Gorman
Charles L. Grant
Stephen Gresham
William H. Hallahan
Thomas Harris
Rick Hautala
Julian Hawthorne
Nathaniel Hawthorne
William Hjortsberg
Nancy Holder
Shirley Jackson
Carl Jacobi
Henry James
K. W. Jeter
Jeanne Kalogridis
Marvin Kaye
David H. Keller
Gerald Kersh
Jack Ketchum
Stephen King
Russell Kirk
T. E. D. Klein
Kathe Koja
Jeffrey Konvitz
Dean Koontz
Jerzy Kosinski
Alexander Laing
Joe R. Lansdale
Richard Laymon
Fritz Leiber
Jeremy Leven
Ira Levin
Thomas Ligotti
David L. Lindsey
Bentley Little
Frank Belknap Long
Robert Lory
H. P. Lovecraft
Tim Lucas
David Martin
George R. R. Martin
Elizabeth Massie
Richard Matheson
Richard Christian Matheson
Robert R. McCammon
Michael McDowell
Clare McNally
Rex Miller
Marlys Millhiser
Brent Monahan
Thomas F. Monteleone
A. R. Morlan
David Morrell
W. C. Morrow
H. Warner Munn

Yvonne Navarro
Andrew Neiderman
Joyce Carol Oates
Vincent O'Sullivan
Jessica Palmer
T. L. Parkinson
Norman Partridge
Tom Piccirilli
Christopher Pike
Edgar Allan Poe
Petru Popescu
Kathryn Ptacek
Seabury Quinn
Herman Raucher
Daniel Rhodes
Anne Rice
Tod Robbins
Alan Rodgers
Theodore Roszak
Victor Rousseau
Ray Russell
John Russo
Alan Ryan
Fred Saberhagen
Jeffrey Sackett
David St. Clair
Al Sarrantonio
John Saul
David J. Schow
David Seltzer
Lucius Shepard
John Shirley
Anne Rivers Siddons
David B. Silva
Dan Simmons
Isaac Bashevis Singer
Curt Siodmak
David J. Skal
John Skipp
William M. Sloane
Clark Ashton Smith
Martin Cruz Smith
Craig Spector
William Browning Spencer
Robert Stallman
Fred Mustard Stewart
R. L. Stine
J. Michael Straczynski
Peter Straub
Whitley Strieber
Theodore Sturgeon
Michael Talbot
Lucy Taylor
Melanie Tem
Steve Rasnic Tem
Thomas Tessier
Paul Theroux
Thomas Tryon
Lisa Tuttle
John Updike
Steve Vance

Jeff Vandermeer
Robert W. Walker
Donald Wandrei
Robert Weinberg
Eudora Welty
Edith Wharton
Henry S. Whitehead
Leslie H. Whitten
Chet Williamson
J. N. Williamson
F. Paul Wilson
Ken Wisman
Bari Wood
Stuart Woods
T. M. Wright
Chelsea Quinn Yarbro
Steve Zell

Australian
Guy Boothby
Gary Crew
Terry Dowling
G. M. Hague
Robert Hood
Rick Kennett
Harry Adam Knight
Mrs. Campbell Praed

Austrian
Gustav Meyrink

Belgian
Thomas Owen
Jean Ray

British
Peter Ackroyd
Robert Aickman
Joan Aiken
W. Harrison Ainsworth
Grant Allen
Kingsley Amis
Michael Arlen
Cynthia Asquith
Peter Atkins
Jonathan Aycliffe
Denys Val Baker
J. G. Ballard
Iain Banks
Maurice Baring
Clive Barker
William Beckford
Neil Bell
E. F. Benson
R. H. Benson
Anne Billson
Margaret Bingley
Charles Birkin
Campbell Black
John Blackburn
Algernon Blackwood

Caroline Blackwood
Christopher Blayre
Marjorie Bowen
M. E. Braddon
Chaz Brenchley
David Britton
J. W. Brodie-Innes
Owen Brookes
D. K. Broster
Rhoda Broughton
John Buchan
Edward Bulwer-Lytton
John Burke
Mark Burnell
A. M. Burrage
Arthur Calder-Marshall
Ramsey Campbell
Bernard Capes
Mark Chadbourn
R. Chetwynd-Hayes
Simon Clark
A. E. Coppard
Basil Copper
John Keir Cross
Aleister Crowley
Peter Crowther
Roald Dahl
M. P. Dare
Walter de la Mare
Charles Dickens
Joe Donnelly
John Douglas
Arthur Conan Doyle
H. B. Drake
Daphne du Maurier
J. Meade Falkner
Dion Fortune
Christopher Fowler
John Fowles
Neil Gaiman
Stephen Gallagher
R. Murray Gilchrist
William Godwin
William Golding
John Gordon
Alex Hamilton
W. A. Harbinson
Joanne Harris
Steve Harris
M. John Harrison
L. P. Hartley
W. F. Harvey
H. F. Heard
James Herbert
Robert Hichens
Susan Hill
William Hope Hodgson
James Hogg
Robert Holdstock
Tom Holland
Gordon Honeycombe

Clemence Housman
Rhys Hughes
Violet Hunt
Shaun Hutson
W. W. Jacobs
G. P. R. James
Henry James
M. R. James
Peter James
Graham Joyce
Susan Kay
Victor Kelleher
Jessie Douglas Kerruish
Nigel Kneale
Terry Lamsley
Joel Lane
Marghanita Laski
Margery Lawrence
Stephen Laws
Vernon Lee
Ben Leech
D. Francis Lewis
M. G. Lewis
James Lovegrove
Brian Lumley
Arthur Machen
Simon Maginn
Richard Marsh
Graham Masterton
Ian McEwan
Patrick McGrath
John Metcalfe
Richard B. Middleton
Mary L. Molesworth
Mark Morris
A. N. L. Munby
E. Nesbit
Kim Newman
Hume Nisbet
Robert Nye
Mrs. Oliphant
Oliver Onions
John Polidori
Thomas Peckett Prest
K. & Hesketh Prichard
John Pritchard
Arthur Quiller-Couch
Ann Radcliffe
G. W. M. Reynolds
Phil Rickman
Sax Rohmer
L. T. C. Rolt
Adrian Ross
Nicholas Royle
W. Clark Russell
R. R. Ryan
James Malcolm Rymer
Saki
Sarban
Peter Saxon
Walter Scott

Nick Sharman
Mary Shelley
M. P. Shiel
Iain Sinclair
May Sinclair
Guy N. Smith
Lady Eleanor Smith
Michael Marshall Smith
Brian Stableford
Robert Louis Stevenson
Bram Stoker
Tim Stout
Gerald Suster
Bernard Taylor
D. M. Thomas
Rosemary Timperley
Peter Tonkin
Peter Tremayne
James Turner
E. H. Visiak
H. Russell Wakefield
Horace Walpole
Hugh Walpole
Elizabeth Walter
Ian Watson
Fay Weldon
H. G. Wells
Dennis Wheatley
Mary Williams
Colin Wilson

Canadian
Nancy Baker
Robertson Davies
Christopher Hyde
Nancy Kilpatrick
Garfield Reeves-Stevens
Marilyn Ross
Michael Slade

Czech
Franz Kafka

Danish
Isak Dinesen

Estonian
Eric Stenbock

Fiji Islander

Kenneth McKenney
French
Michel Bernanos
Jacques Cazotte
Joris-Karl Huysmans
Pierre Kast
Gaston Leroux
Guy de Maupassant
Maurice Renard
Claude Seignolle
Eugène Sue
Comte de Villiers de l'Isle Adam

German
Hanns Heinz Ewers
E. T. A. Hoffmann
Patrick Süskind

Irish
Elizabeth Bowen
Lafcadio Hearn
J. Sheridan Le Fanu
Dorothy Macardle
Charles R. Maturin
Elliott O'Donnell
Mrs. J. H. Riddell
Michael Scott

Italian
Dino Buzzati
Umberto Eco

Polish
Stefan Grabinski

Russian
Mikhail Bulgakov
Nikolai Gogol
Fyodor Sologub

Scottish
Alasdair Gray

Serbian
Milorad Pavic

Thai
S. P. Somtow

Uruguayan
Horacio Quiroga

TITLE INDEX

The following list includes the titles of all novels, short stories (designated "ss") and plays cited as horror, ghost and gothic publications. The name in parenthesis is meant to direct the user to the appropriate entry, where full publication information is given. The term "series" indicates a recurring distinctive word or phrase (or name) in the titles of the entrant's books; series characters are also listed here, even if their names do not appear in specific titles of works.

1-900-Killer (Garton), 1994
3 Tales of Horror (ss, Lovecraft), 1967
7 Steps to Midnight (Matheson, Richard), 1993
'48 (Herbert), 1996
76 Short Stories (ss, Saki), n.d.
99 Fear Street (Stine), from 1994
472 Cheyne Walk (ss, Kennett), 1992
668: The Neighbor of the Beast (Grant), 1992

Abbot (Scott, W.), 1820
Abominable Snowman of Pasadena (Stine), 1995
Abomination (Smith, G.), 1986
Abominations of Yondo (ss, Smith, C.), 1960
Abracadabra (Gresham), 1988
Abracadabra (Kennett), 1997
Absence of Light (Lindsey), 1994
Absences: Charlie Goode's Ghosts (ss, Tem, S.), 1991
Absolute Power (Russell, R.), 1992
Abyss (Vance), 1989
Academy of Terror (Grant), 1986
Acceptable Risk (Cook), 1995
Account of the Giants Lately Discovered (ss, Walpole, Horace), 1766
Accursed (Smith, G.), 1983
Accursed (appendix; ss, Seignolle), 1967
Ace of Cads and Other Stories (ss, Arlen), 1927
Across the Stream (Benson, E.), 1919
Act of Providence (Brennan), 1979
Ad Statum Perspicuum (ss, Wilson, F.), 1990
Adam and Eve and Pinch Me (ss, Coppard), 1921
Addison House (McNally), 1988
Adelmorn, the Outlaw (play, Lewis, M.), 1801
AdventureLand (Harris, S.), 1990
Adventures of Jules de Grandin (ss, Quinn), 1976
Adventures of Lucius Leffing (ss, Brennan), 1990
Adventures of Meng & Ecker (Britton), 1997
Adversary (Rhodes), 1989
Affinities (Praed), 1885
After Alice (Bingley), 1989
After Alice Died (Bingley), 1986
After Life (Neiderman), 1993
After Silence (Carroll), 1992
After Sundown (Boyll), 1989
Afterage (Navarro), 1993
Afterlife and Other Stories (ss, Updike), 1994
Aftershock (Walker), 1987
Agnes Day (Grant), 1987
Agonizing Resurrection of Victor Frankenstein & Other Gothic Tales (ss, Ligotti), 1994
Ah, Sweet Mystery of Life (ss, Dahl), 1988
Aisling and Other Irish Tales of Terror (ss, Tremayne), 1992
Alabaster Hand, and Other Ghost Stories (ss, Munby), 1949

Alarums (Laymon), 1993
Albigenses (Maturin), 1824
Alchemist (James, P.), 1996
Alchemist (Whitten), 1973
Alien Flesh (Quinn), 1977
Alien Invasion (Pike), 1997
Aliens in the Sky (Pike), 1996
Aliens: Music of the Spears (Navarro), 1996
All Around the Town (Clark, M.), 1992
All Fall Down (Saul), 1991
All Heads Turn When the Hunt Goes By (Farris), 1977
All Souls' Night (ss, Walpole, Hugh), 1933
All That Glitters (Neiderman, as Andrews), 1995
All That Money Can Buy (play, Benét), 1943
All the Lies That Are My Life (ss, Ellison), 1980
All the Sounds of Fear (ss, Ellison), 1973
Allhallows Eve (Laymon), 1985
Alligators (Smith, G.), 1987
All-Night Party (Stine), 1997
Almira's Curse (Prest), 1849
Almost Adam (Popescu), 1996
Alone Against Tomorrow (ss, Ellison), 1971
Alone in the Wild Forest (Singer), 1971
Alone with the Horrors (ss, Campbell), 1993
Alpha and Omega (ss, Bell), 1946
Alraune (appendix; Ewers), 1911
Amarantha Knight Reader (ss, Kilpatrick, as Knight), 1996
Ambrosio (Lewis, M.), 1798
American Chills: Ghost Harbor (Massie), 1992
American Gothic (Bloch), 1974
American Psycho (Ellis), 1991
Amethyst of Tears (Ross, M.), 1975
Among the Dead and Other Events Leading to the Apocalypse (ss, Bryant), 1973
Among the Lost People (ss, Aiken, C.), 1934
Amulet (McDowell), 1979
Amulet (Morlan), 1991
Amy Girl (Wood), 1987
Anastasia Syndrome and Other Stories (ss, Clark, M.), 1989
Ancestral Hunger (Baker, S.), 1995
Ancient Echoes (Holdstock), 1996
Ancient Images (Campbell), 1989
Ancient Sorceries and Other Stories (ss, Blackwood, A.), 1968
Ancient Sorceries and Other Tales (ss, Blackwood, A.), 1927
And Afterward, the Dark (ss, Copper), 1977
And Love Survived (Chetwynd-Hayes), 1979
And Now the Screaming Starts. . . (Case), 1973
"And the Dead Spake—" (ss, Benson, E.), 1923
Anecdotes of Destiny (ss, Dinesen), 1958
Angel and Other Stories (ss, McGrath), 1995
Angel of Mons: The Bowmen and Other Legends of the War (ss, Machen), 1915

Angel of Pain (Benson, E.), 1905
Angel of Pain (Stableford), 1991
Angel of the West Window (appendix; Meyrink), 1991
Angelina (Prest), 1849
Angels (Harris, S.), 1993
Angels & Visitations (ss, Gaiman), 1993
Angels of Mourning (Pritchard), 1995
Angelus! (Tremayne), 1985
Angry Candy (ss, Ellison), 1988
Animal Planet (Bradfield), 1995
Animals (Skipp), 1993
Annabelle Says (ss, Clark, S.), 1995
Annabelle Says (ss, Laws), 1995
Anno Dracula (Newman), 1992
Anno Dracula series (Newman), from 1992
Antibodies (Skal), 1988
Ants (Tremayne), 1979
Ape, the Idiot and Other People (ss, Morrow), 1897
Apocalypse (Konvitz), 1979
Apology for Tales of Terror (poetry, Scott, W.), 1799
Apparition (Prest), 1846
Apparition (Rymer), 1846
Apple Tree (ss, du Maurier), 1952
Approaching Oblivion (ss, Ellison), 1974
Arabian Tale, from an Unpublished Manuscript (Beckford), 1786
Archibald Malmaison (Hawthorne, J.), 1879
Arm of Mrs. Egan and Other Stories (ss, Harvey), 1951
Arm of Mrs. Egan and Other Strange Stories (ss, Harvey), 1952
Armageddon Box (Weinberg), 1991
Armageddon Rag (Martin, G.), 1983
Armorica (Somtow), 1994
Art in the Blood (Elrod), 1991
Arthur Gordon Pym (Poe), 1841
Arthur Mervyn (Brown), 1799-1800
"As a Watch in the Night" (Praed), 1901
As One Dead (Kilpatrick), 1993
Ascending (Wright), 1994
Ash, David series (Herbert), from 1988
Ash Wednesday (Williamson, C.), 1987
Ashes to Ashes (Saul), 1997
Asmodeus at Large (Bulwer-Lytton), 1833
Assassin (Hutson), 1988
Asylum (McGrath), 1996
Asylum (Saul), 1997
At a Winter's Fire (ss, Capes), 1899
At the Mountains of Madness (Lovecraft), 1990
At the Mountains of Madness and Other Novels (ss, Lovecraft), 1964
At the Rainbow's End and Other Stories (ss, Baker, D.), 1983
At the Sea's Edge and Other Stories (ss, Baker, D.), 1979
Atmosfear (Williamson, C.), 1995
Atoms and Evil (ss, Bloch), 1962
Attack of the Beastly Baby-Sitter (Stine), 1997
Attack of the Jack-O'-Lanterns (Stine), 1996
Attack of the Mutant (Stine), 1994
Aubrey House series (Kaye), from 1983
Audrey Rose (De Felitta), 1975
Auriol (Ainsworth), 1850
Awakening (Chetwynd-Hayes), 1980
Awakening (Russo), 1983
Axman Cometh (Farris), 1989

Baal (McCammon), 1978
Babel's Children (Williamson, J.), 1984
Baby-Sitter (Stine), 1989
Baby-Sitter II (Stine), 1991
Baby-Sitter III (Stine), 1993
Baby-Sitter IV (Stine), 1995
Babysitter (Gorman, as Ransom), 1989
Back Home (play, Sloane), 1931
Bad Blood (Farris), 1989
Bad Brains (Koja), 1992
Bad Dreams (Newman), 1990
Bad Dreams (appendix; Sologub), 1896
Bad Dreams (Stine), 1994
Bad Hare Day (Stine), 1996
Bad Intentions (ss, Partridge), 1996
Bad Moonlight (Stine), 1994
Bad Place (Koontz), 1990
Bag and Baggage (ss, Capes), 1913
Baily's Bones (Kelleher), 1988
Bamboo Guerillas (Smith, G.), 1977
Bane (Donnelly), 1989
Banished (Williamson, J.), 1981
Banished Dreams (ss, Simmons), 1990
Banshee (Scott, M.), 1990
Bargain Bumper Treble (Smith, G.), 1991
Barking Ghost (Stine), 1995
Barn (ss, Crew), 1996
Barnabas Collins (Ross, M.), 1968
Barnabas Collins and Quentin's Demon (Ross, M.), 1970
Barnabas Collins and the Gypsy Witch (Ross, M.), 1970
Barnabas Collins and the Mummy's Curse (Ross, M.), 1970
Barnabas Collins and the Mysterious Ghost (Ross, M.), 1970
Barnabas Collins versus the Warlock (Ross, M.), 1969
Barnabas, Quentin, and Dr. Jekyll's Son (Ross, M.), 1971
Barnabas, Quentin, and the Avenging Ghost (Ross, M.), 1970
Barnabas, Quentin, and the Body Snatchers (Ross, M.), 1971
Barnabas, Quentin, and the Crystal Coffin (Ross, M.), 1970
Barnabas, Quentin, and the Frightened Bride (Ross, M.), 1970
Barnabas, Quentin, and the Grave Robbers (Ross, M.), 1971
Barnabas, Quentin, and the Haunted Cave (Ross, M.), 1970
Barnabas, Quentin, and the Hidden Tomb (Ross, M.), 1971
Barnabas, Quentin, and the Mad Magician (Ross, M.), 1971
Barnabas, Quentin, and the Magic Potion (Ross, M.), 1971
Barnabas, Quentin, and the Nightmare Assassin (Ross, M.), 1970
Barnabas, Quentin, and the Scorpio Curse (Ross, M.), 1970
Barnabas, Quentin, and the Sea Ghost (Ross, M.), 1971
Barnabas, Quentin, and the Serpent (Ross, M.), 1970
Barnabas, Quentin, and the Vampire Beauty (Ross, M.), 1972
Barnabas, Quentin, and the Witch's Curse (Ross, M.), 1970
Barrens (ss, Wilson, F.), 1992
Barrett, Jonathan, series (Elrod), from 1993
Bars on Satan's Jailhouse (ss, Partridge), 1995
Basement (Wood), 1995
Bat Flies Low (Rohmer), 1935
Batman: Captured by the Engines (Lansdale), 1991
Batman: Terror on the High Skies (Lansdale), 1992
Bats Out of Hell (Smith, G.), 1978
Battle of the Singing Men (ss, Kersh), 1944
Battle That Ended the Century (Ms. Found in a Time Machine) (ss, Lovecraft), 1934
Be Careful What You Wish For (Stine), 1993

Beach House (Stine), 1992
Beach Party (Stine), 1990
Beam of Malice (ss, Hamilton), 1966
Beast (Benchley), 1991
Beast (Konvitz), 1983
Beast (Stallman), 1982
Beast from the East (Stine), 1996
Beast House (Laymon), 1986
Beast in Holger's Woods (Derleth), 1968
Beast That Shouted Love at the Heart of the World (ss, Ellison), 1969
Beast with Five Fingers and Other Tales (ss, Harvey), 1928
Beasts and Super-Beasts (ss, Saki), 1914
Beautiful Strangers (ss, Tem, M.), 1992
Beautiful Strangers (ss, Tem, S.), 1992
Beauty (D'Amato), 1992
Beckoning Hand and Other Stories (ss, Allen), 1887
Bedlam (Knight), 1992
Beetle (Marsh), 1897
Beginning and Other Stories (ss, de la Mare), 1955
Beginning of Sorrows (Martin, D.), 1987
Behind Locked Shutters (Ross, M.), 1968
Behind the Purple Veil (Ross, M.), 1973
Beleaguered City (Oliphant), 1879
Beleaguered City and Other Stories (ss, Oliphant), 1988
Bell in the Fog and Other Stories (ss, Atherton), 1905
Bell Witch (Monahan), 1997
Bellefleur (Oates), 1980
Beneath Still Waters (Costello, M.), 1989
Beneath the Moors (Lumley), 1974
Bent Back Bridge (ss, Crew), 1995
Bertram (play, Maturin), 1816
Best Friend (Stine), 1992
Best Ghost Stories (ss, Blackwood, A.), 1973
Best Ghost Stories of H. Russell Wakefield (ss, Wakefield), 1978
Best Ghost Stories of J. S. Le Fanu (ss, Le Fanu), 1964
Best Ghost Stories of M. R. James (ss, James, M.), 1944
Best Horror Stories (ss, Le Fanu), 1970
Best Horror Stories of Arthur Conan Doyle (ss, Doyle), 1988
Best of Beaumont (ss, Beaumont), 1982
Best of D. F. Lewis (ss, Lewis, D.), 1993
Best of Gerald Kersh (ss, Kersh), 1960
Best of H. P. Lovecraft (ss, Lovecraft), 1982
Best of Robert Bloch (ss, Bloch), 1977
Best Short Stories of M. P. Shiel (ss, Shiel), 1948
Best Stories of Walter de la Mare (ss, de la Mare), 1942
Best Supernatural Stories of H. P. Lovecraft (ss, Lovecraft), 1945
Best Supernatural Tales of Algernon Blackwood (ss, Blackwood, A.), 1973
Best Supernatural Tales of Arthur Conan Doyle (ss, Doyle), 1979
Best Tales of Hoffmann (appendix; ss, Hoffmann), 1967
Bestsellers Guaranteed (ss, Lansdale), 1993
Bethany's Sin (McCammon), 1980
Betrayal (Stine), 1993
Better in the Dark (Yarbro), 1993
Betty's Visions and Mrs. Smith of Longmains (ss, Broughton), 1886
Between the Minute and the Hour (ss, Burrage), 1967
Beware My Love! (Ross, M.), 1965
Beware of the Kindly Stranger (Ross, M.), 1970
Beware of the Purple Peanut Butter (Stine), 1996

Beware, the Snowman (Stine), 1997
Beware! (Laymon), 1985
Beyond (ss, Sturgeon), 1960
Beyond the Shroud (Hautala), 1996
Beyond the Wall of Sleep (ss, Lovecraft), 1943
Bid for Fortune, or Dr. Nikola's Vendetta (Boothby), 1895
Bid Time Return (Matheson, Richard), 1975
Bidden (Leech), 1994
Big Thunder (Atkins), 1997
Billy (Strieber), 1990
Biofire (Garton), 1996
Birds, and Other Stories (ss, du Maurier), 1977
Birthday (ss, Morris), 1992
Birthstone series (Ross, M.), from 1975
Bishop of Hell and Other Stories (ss, Bowen, M.), 1949
Bite (Laymon), 1996
Bitter/Sweet (ss, Cave), 1996
Black Ambrosia (Engstrom), 1988
Black Angel (Masterton), 1991
Black Carousel (Grant), 1995
Black Castle (Daniels), 1978
Black Cat (Russo), 1982
Black Charade (Burke), 1977
Black Christmas (Black, as Altman), 1983
Black Cocktail (Carroll), 1990
Black Crusade (ss, Machen), 1966
Black Death (Copper), 1991
Black Doctor and Other Tales of Terror and Mystery (ss, Doyle), 1925
Black Dogs (McEwan), 1992
Black Dragon (Hyde), 1992
Black Druid, and Other Stories (ss, Long), 1975
Black Dwarf (Scott, W., as Cleishbotham), 1816
Black Fedora (Smith, G.), 1991
Black Fox (Heard), 1950
Black House (Theroux), 1974
Black Leather Required (ss, Schow), 1994
Black Lightning (Saul), 1995
Black Lodge (Weinberg), 1991
Black Magic (Strieber), 1982
Black Magic: A Tale of the Rise and Fall of Antichrist (Bowen, M.), 1909
Black Magic Omnibus (Wheatley), 1956
Black Mariah (Bonansinga), 1994
Black Medicine (ss, Burks), 1966
Black Monk (Rymer), 1844
Black Orchid (Gaiman), 1991
Black Oxen (Atherton), 1923
Black Reaper (ss, Capes), 1989
Black River Falls (Gorman), 1996
Black Rock (Harris, S.), 1996
Black School (Williamson, J.), 1989
Black Spaniel and Other Stories (ss, Hichens), 1905
Black Throne (Saberhagen), 1990
Black Water (Oates), 1992
Black Wind (Wilson, F.), 1988
Black Wine (ss, Campbell), 1986
Black Wine (ss, Grant), 1986
Blackstone Chronicles (Saul), from 1997
Blackthorne, Lincoln, series (Grant, as Marsh), from 1984
Blind Circle (appendix; Renard), 1928

Bridge (Skipp), 1991
Brief Lives (Gaiman), 1994
Bright Messenger (Blackwood, A.), 1921
Brighton Monster and Others (ss, Kersh), 1953
Bring Me Children (Martin, D.), 1992
Broken Date (Stine), 1988
Broken Hearts (Stine), 1993
Bronze King (Charnas), 1985
Brood of the Witch-Queen (Rohmer), 1918
Brother of the Shadow (Praed), 1886
Brotherkind (Williamson, J.), 1982
Brownie of Bodsbeck and Other Tales (Hogg), 1818
Brownstone (Eulo), 1980
Buckets (ss, Wilson, F.), 1991
Bundle of Nerves (ss, Aiken, J.), 1976
Bureau of Lost Souls (ss, Fowler), 1989
Burgled Heart (appendix; Leroux), 1925
Burial (Masterton), 1992
Burning (Masterton), 1991
Burning (Stine), 1993
Burning and Other Stories (ss, Cady), 1973
Burning Baby and Other Ghosts (ss, Gordon), 1992
Burning Obsession (Walker), 1989
Burrowers Beneath (Lumley), 1974
Bury Him Darkly (Blackburn), 1969
Bury Me Deep (Pike), 1991
Businessman (Disch), 1984
Butcher (Miller), 1994
By Bizarre Hands (ss, Lansdale), 1989
By the Time I Get to Nashville (Grant), 1994
Bye-Ways (ss, Hichens), 1897

Cabal (ss, Barker), 1988
Cabal: The Nightbreed (Barker), 1989
Cadaver of Gideon Wyck, by a Medical Student (Laing), 1934
Cage of Night (Gorman), 1996
Cages (ss, Gorman), 1995
Calculated Magic (Weinberg), 1994
Caleb (Crew), 1996
Caleb Williams (Godwin), 1970
California Gothic (Etchison), 1995
Call Waiting (Stine), 1994
Caller of the Black (ss, Lumley), 1971
Calling All Creeps (Stine), 1996
Calling Home (Cadnum), 1991
Camaralzaman (play, James, G.), 1848
Cameron Castle (Ross, M.), 1975
Cameron's Closet (Brandner), 1987
Cameron's Terror (Brandner), 1988
Camp (Smith, G.), 1989
Campbell Wood (Sarrantonio), 1986
Can Such Things Be? (ss, Bierce), 1893
Canal Dreams (Banks), 1989
Candle for D'Artagnan (Yarbro), 1989
Candlemas Eve (Sackett), 1988
Candlenight (Rickman), 1991
Cannibal Cult (Smith, G.), 1983
Cannibal Dwight's Special Purpose (ss, Holder), 1992
Cannibals (Smith, G.), 1986
Captain of the Polestar and Other Tales (ss, Doyle), 1890

Captain Quad (Costello, S.), 1991
Captain's Woman and Other Stories (ss, Bell), 1955
Captive (Stallman), 1981
Captives (Hutson), 1991
Caracal (Smith, G.), 1980
Caravan of Crime (ss, O'Donnell), 1946
Carlisle Street (Wright), 1983
Carmilla and Other Classic Tales of Mystery (ss, Le Fanu), 1996
Carnacki, The Ghost Finder (ss, Hodgson), 1913
Carnacki, The Ghost Finder, and a Poem (ss, Hodgson), 1910
Carnival of Destruction (Stableford), 1993
Carnivore (Smith, G.), 1990
Carnosaur (Knight), 1984
Carrie (King), 1974
Carrion (Brandner), 1986
Carrion Comfort (Simmons), 1989
Cartoonist (Costello, S.), 1990
Carwin the Biloquist and Other American Tales and Pieces (ss, Brown), 1822
Case Against Satan (Russell, R.), 1962
Case of Charles Dexter Ward (Lovecraft), 1951
Casebook of Jules de Grandin (ss, Quinn), 1976
Casebook of Lucius Leffing (ss, Brennan), 1973
Casket (Burks), 1973
Cast a Cold Eye (Ryan, A.), 1984
Casteel-Tatterton Saga (Andrews), from 1985
Casting the Runes, and Other Ghost Stories (ss, James, M.), 1987
Castle (appendix; Kafka), 1930
Castle Barebane (Aiken, J.), 1976
Castle d'Or (du Maurier), 1962
Castle d'Or (Quiller-Couch), 1962
Castle of Ehrenstein (James, G.), 1847
Castle of Otranto (Walpole, Horace, as Marshal), 1764
Castle on the Cliff (Ross, M.), 1967
Castle on the Hill (Ross, M., as Randolph), 1964
Castle Spectre (play, Lewis, M.), 1798
Castledoom (Saxon, as Lecale), 1974
Castles of Athlin and Dunbayne (Radcliffe), 1789
Cat (Stine), 1997
Cat Jumps and Other Stories (ss, Bowen, E.), 1934
Cat People (Brandner), 1982
Cat with the Tulip Face (ss, Morlan), 1991
Catacombs (Farris), 1981
Catastrophe (appendix; ss, Buzzati), 1965
Catch Your Death and Other Ghost Stories (ss, Gordon), 1984
Catmagic (Strieber), 1986
Cats (Sharman), 1977
Cats of Ulthar (ss, Lovecraft), 1935
Cauldron of Evil (Ross, M.), 1977
Celestial Inventory (ss, Tem, S.), 1991
Cell (ss, Case), 1969
Cell and Other Tales of Horror (ss, Case), 1969
Cellar (Laymon), 1980
Cellars (Shirley), 1982
Cement Garden (McEwan), 1978
Centaur (Blackwood, A.), 1911
Ceremonies (Klein), 1984
Certain Man (Onions), 1931
Chain Letter (Pike), 1986
Chain Letter 2: The Ancient Evil (Pike), 1992
Chain Letter series (Pike), from 1986

Chained Together (Pike), 1994
Chaingang (Miller), 1992
Chaingang series (Miller), from 1987
Chalice (Rickman), 1997
Challenge from Beyond (ss, Long), 1954
Challenge to Dracula (Lory), 1975
Chamber of Horrors (ss, Bloch), 1966
Chandal series (Eulo), from 1980
Changeling (McKenney), 1985
Changing (Wright, as Armstrong), 1985
Charles Beaumont (ss, Beaumont), 1988
Charles Dickens' Christmas Ghost Stories (ss, Dickens), 1992
Charmed Life (Taylor, B.), 1991
Charnel House (Masterton), 1978
Chase (Koontz, as Dwyer), 1972
Cheater (Stine), 1993
Cheetah Girl (ss, Blayre), 1923
Chicago Loop (Theroux), 1990
Chicken Chicken (Stine), 1997
Child Across the Sky (Carroll), 1989
Child in the Dark (ss, Timperley), 1956
Child in Time (McEwan), 1987
Child of Darkness (Silva), 1986
Child of Shadows (Coyne), 1990
Child of the Night (Kilpatrick), 1996
Child Possessed (St. Clair), 1979
Child's Play (Neiderman), 1985
Child's Play 2 (Costello, M.), 1990
Child's Play 3 (Costello, M.), 1991
Childmare (Sharman), 1980
Children of the Island (Wright), 1983
Children of the Night (Bingley), 1985
Children of the Night (Blackburn), 1966
Children of the Night (Simmons), 1992
Children of the Pool and Other Stories (ss, Machen), 1936
Children of the Shroud (Reeves-Stevens), 1987
Children of the Storm (Koontz, as Dwyer), 1972
Children of the Vampire (Kalogridis), 1995
Children of the Wind (Drake), 1954
Children's Hour (Clegg), 1995
Chill Company (ss, Williams), 1976
Chiller (Boyll), 1992
Chimera (Gallagher), 1982
Chimes (Dickens), 1844
China Shadow (Ross, M.), 1974
Chosen Child (Masterton), 1997
Christine (King), 1983
Christmas Books (Dickens), 1852
Christmas Carol, in Prose (Dickens), 1843
Christmas Stories (Dickens), 1868
Christopher's Mansion (Ross, M.), 1969
Chromosome 6 (Cook), 1997
Chronicle of Golden Friars and Other Stories (ss, Le Fanu), 1896
Chronicles of Clovis (ss, Saki), 1911
Chronicles of Golden Friars (ss, Le Fanu), 1871
Chronicles of Lucius Leffing (ss, Brennan), 1977
Chronicles of the Canongate (ss, Scott, W.), 1827
Chui Chai (ss, Somtow), 1995
Cipher (Koja), 1991
Cities of the Red Night (Burroughs), 1981
Citizen Vampire (Daniels), 1981

City Come A-Walkin' (Shirley), 1980
City Jitters (ss, Fowler), 1986
City of Masques (Brennert), 1978
City of the Singing Flame (ss, Smith, C.), 1981
City: The Rats Saga Continues (Herbert), 1994
Claire Lenoir (appendix; Villiers), 1887
Clara Reeve (Disch, as Hargrave), 1975
Classics of the Macabre (ss, du Maurier), 1987
Clavering Grange series (Chetwynd-Hayes), from 1985
Claw (Campbell, as Ramsay), 1983
Claw (Campbell), 1992
Cleanup (Skipp), 1987
Clemens, Atta Olivia, series (Yarbro), from 1987
Clive Barker's Books of Blood, Volume One (ss, Barker), 1984
Clive Barker's Books of Blood, Volume Two (ss, Barker), 1984
Clive Barker's Books of Blood, Volume Three (ss, Barker), 1984
Clive Barker's Books of Blood, Volume Four (ss, Barker), 1985
Clive Barker's Books of Blood, Volume Five (ss, Barker), 1985
Clive Barker's Books of Blood, Volume Six (ss, Barker), 1985
Clock of Dreams (Lumley), 1978
Clock Strikes Twelve (ss, Wakefield), 1940
Clorinda Walks in Heaven (ss, Coppard), 1922
Close to the Bone (ss, Morris), 1995
Close to the Bone (ss, Taylor, L.), 1993
Cockatrice Boys (Aiken, J.), 1996
Cold Blue Light (Kaye), 1983
Cold Blue Midnight (Gorman), 1995
Cold Chills (ss, Bloch), 1977
Cold Fire (Koontz), 1991
Cold Hand in Mine (ss, Aickman), 1976
Cold Mind (Lindsey), 1983
Cold Moon Over Babylon (McDowell), 1980
Cold Night (Sarrantonio), 1989
Cold One (Pike), 1995
Cold People (Pike), 1996
Cold Print (ss, Campbell), 1985
Cold Terror (ss, Chetwynd-Hayes), 1973
Cold Turkey (ss, Collins), 1992
Cold Whisper (Hautala), 1991
Colin (Benson, E.), 1923
Colin II (Benson, E.), 1925
Collapsing Cosmoses (ss, Lovecraft), 1977
Collected Ghost Stories (ss, Freeman), 1974
Collected Ghost Stories of E. F. Benson (ss, Benson, E.), 1992
Collected Ghost Stories of M. R. James (ss, James, M.), 1931
Collected Ghost Stories of Oliver Onions (ss, Onions), 1935
Collected Short Stories of L. P. Hartley (ss, Hartley), 1968
Collected Short Stories of Roald Dahl (ss, Dahl), 1991
Collected Tales and Plays of Nikolai Gogol (appendix; ss, Gogol), 1964
Collected Tales of Walter de la Mare (ss, de la Mare), 1950
Collector (Fowles), 1963
College Weekend (Stine), 1995
Collins, Barnabas/Dark Shadows series (Ross, M.), from 1966
Collins, Jack, series (Weinberg), from 1993
Colonel Markesan and Less Pleasant People (ss, Derleth), 1966
Colossus (ss, Wandrei), 1989
Colour Out of Space and Others (ss, Lovecraft), 1964
Coma (Cook), 1977
Come and Get Me and Other Uncanny Invitations (ss, Walter), 1973

Dance with the Devil (Koontz, as Dwyer), 1973
Dancing Bears (Saberhagen), 1995
Dancing Floor (Buchan), 1926
Dandelion Wine (Bradbury), 1957
Dare (Stine), 1994
Dark (Herbert), 1980
Dark Angel (Andrews), 1986
Dark Ann and Other Stories (ss, Bowen, M.), 1927
Dark Beasts and Eight Other Stories from The Hounds of Tindalos
    (ss, Long), 1964
Dark Brotherhood and Other Pieces (Lovecraft), 1966
Dark Carnival (ss, Bradbury), 1947
Dark Chamber (Cline), 1927
Dark Channel (Garton), 1992
Dark Chateau and Other Poems (poetry, Smith, C.), 1951
Dark Companions (ss, Campbell), 1982
Dark Corner (Pike), 1996
Dark Country (ss, Etchison), 1982
Dark Cry of the Moon (ss, Grant), 1986
Dark Domain (appendix; ss, Grabinski), 1993
Dark Dominion (Little), 1995
Dark Dreaming (Cady, as Franklin), 1991
Dark Enchantment (Macardle), 1953
Dark Entries (ss, Aickman), 1964
Dark Father (Piccirilli), 1990
Dark Feasts (ss, Campbell), 1987
Dark God (ss, Williams), 1980
Dark Gods (ss, Klein), 1985
Dark Half (King), 1989
Dark Harbor Haunting (Ross, M.), 1975
Dark Harbor series (Ross, M.), from 1965
Dark Is My Shadow (Ross, M.), 1976
Dark Journey (Morlan), 1991
Dark Land (ss, Williams), 1975
Dark Lullaby (Palmer), 1991
Dark Man (Chetwynd-Hayes), 1964
Dark Matter (Reeves-Stevens), 1990
Dark Menace (ss, Birkin), 1968
Dark Mountain (Laymon), 1992
Dark Odyssey (poetry, Wandrei), 1931
Dark of Summer (Koontz, as Dwyer), 1972
Dark of the Eye (Clegg), 1994
Dark of the Moon (Ross, M.), 1968
Dark of the Woods (Koontz), 1970
Dark One (Smith, G.), 1995
Dark Places (Black, as Altman), 1984
Dark Returners (ss, Brennan), 1959
Dark Rivers of the Heart (Koontz), 1994
Dark Seeker (Jeter), 1987
Dark Shadows (Ross, M.), 1966
Dark Side (appendix; Maupassant), 1989
Dark Silence (Hautala), 1992
Dark Sister (Joyce), 1992
Dark Stars over Seacrest (Ross, M.), 1972
Dark Street (Stine), 1995
Dark Symphony (Koontz), 1970
Dark Tower: The Gunslinger (King), 1982
Dark Tower II: The Drawing of Three (King), 1987
Dark Tower III: The Waste Lands (King), 1991
Dark Tower series (King), from 1982
Dark Towers of Fog Island (Ross, M.), 1975

Dark Twilight (Citro), 1991
Dark Villa of Capri (Ross, M.), 1968
Dark Ways to Death (Saxon), 1968
Dark Whispers (ss, Gorman), 1993
Darkborn (Costello, M.), 1992
Darker (Clark, S.), 1996
Darker Angels (Somtow), 1997
Darker Jewels (Yarbro), 1993
Darker Passions (ss, Bryant), 1992
Darker Passions series (Kilpatrick, as Knight), from 1993
Darkest Day (Fowler), 1993
Darkest Hour (Neiderman, as Andrews), 1993
Darkest Instinct (Walker), 1996
Darkest Night (Saxon), 1966
Darkfall (Koontz), 1984
Darkfall (Laws), 1992
Darklings (Garton), 1985
Darkman (Boyll), 1990
Darkman series (Boyll), from 1990
Darkness (Saul), 1991
Darkness Comes (Koontz), 1984
Darkness, Tell Us (Laymon), 1991
Darkside (Etchison), 1986
Daughter of Darkness (Grant), 1992
David Poindexter's Disappearance and Other Tales (ss,
    Hawthorne, J.), 1888
Davy Jones's Tale and Other Supernatural Stories (ss, Walter),
    1971
Dawn (Neiderman, as Andrews), 1990
Dawn of All (Benson, R.), 1911
Day and Night Stories (ss, Blackwood, A.), 1917
Day Care (Russo), 1985
Day of Creation (Ballard), 1987
Day of Forever (ss, Ballard), 1967
Day of Reckoning (Saul), 1997
Day of the Dead (Russo), 1988
Day the World Ended (Rohmer), 1930
Day-dreaming on Company Time (ss, Hood), 1988
de Grandin, Jules, series (Quinn), from 1976
de Richleau, Duke, series (Wheatley), from 1934
Dead and Buried (Yarbro), 1980
Dead Beat (Bloch), 1960
Dead End (Smith, G.), 1996
Dead End (Stine), 1995
Dead Eyes (Woods), 1994
Dead Fingers Talk (Burroughs), 1963
Dead Girlfriend (Stine), 1993
Dead in the Water (Holder), 1994
Dead in the West (Lansdale), 1986
Dead Lifeguard (Stine), 1994
Dead Lines (Skipp), 1989
Dead Man's Float (Walker), 1988
Dead Man's Kiss (Weinberg), 1992
Dead of Light (Brenchley), 1995
Dead Riders (O'Donnell), 1952
Dead Ringers (Wood), 1988
Dead Smile (ss, Crawford), 1986
Dead to the World (Williamson, J.), 1988
Dead Voices (Hautala), 1990
Dead White (Ryan, A.), 1983
Dead Woman and Other Haunting Experiences (ss, Walter), 1975

Dead Zone (King), 1979
Deadhead (Hutson), 1993
Deadly Communion (Brookes), 1984
Deadly Experiments of Dr. Eeek (Stine), 1996
Deadly Eyes (Herbert), 1983
Deadly Fire (Stine), 1995
Deadly Past (Pike), 1996
Deadly Relations (Garton, as Locke), 1994
Deadrush (Navarro), 1995
Deadtime Story (Bingley), 1990
Dealings of Daniel Kesserich (Leiber), 1997
Dean R. Koontz (Koontz), 1992
Death and the Maiden (Elrod), 1994
Death Box (Saxon, as Lecale), 1974
Death Cycle (Grant), 1993
Death Dream (Masterton), 1988
Death Grasp (Prest), 1842
Death Instinct (Little, as Emmons), 1992
Death Masque (Elrod), 1995
Death of a Nurse (Whitten), 1969
Death of a Sadist (Ryan, R.), 1937
Death of Methuselah and Other Stories (ss, Singer), 1988
Death of the Office Witch (Millhiser), 1993
Death Poems (poetry, Brennan), 1974
Death Rocks the Cradle (Bell, as Martens), 1933
Death Ship (Prest), 1846
Death Ship (Russell, W.), 1888
Death Spore (Knight), 1990
Death Stalks the Night (ss, Cave), 1995
Death: The High Cost of Living (Gaiman), 1994
Death Trance (Masterton), 1986
Death Walkers (Brandner), 1980
Death's Dark Music (Ross, M.), 1977
Death-Angel (Williamson, J.), 1981
Death-Coach (Williamson, J.), 1981
Death-Doctor (Williamson, J.), 1982
Death-School (Williamson, J.), 1982
Deathbell (Smith, G.), 1980
Deathbell 2: Demons (Smith, G.), 1987
Deathbird Stories (ss, Ellison), 1975
DeathBite (Monahan), 1979
Deathday (Hutson), 1987
Deathsong (Borton), 1989
Deathstone (Eulo), 1982
Decapitated Chicken and Other Stories (appendix; ss, Quiroga), 1976
December (Rickman), 1994
Decoded Mirrors (ss, Tem, S.), 1992
Decoy (Walker, as Robertson), 1989
Deep (Benchley), 1976
Deep in the Jungle of Doom (Stine), 1996
Deep Trouble (Stine), 1994
Deep Trouble III (Stine), 1997
Deep Waters (ss, Hodgson), 1967
Del-Del (Kelleher), 1991
Delicate Dependency (Talbot), 1982
Deliver Us from Evil (Holland), 1997
Delta Flame (Ross, M.), 1978
Demogorgon (Lumley), 1987
Demon (Sackett), 1991
Demon and Other Tales (ss, Oates), 1996
Demon Child (Koontz, as Dwyer), 1971

Demon Knight (Boyll), 1995
Demon Lover (Fortune), 1927
Demon Lover and Other Stories (ss, Bowen, E.), 1945
Demon Night (Straczynski), 1988
Demon of Barnabas Collins (Ross, M.), 1969
Demon of Darkness (Ross, M.), 1975
Demon Seed (Koontz), 1973
Demon with a Glass Hand (ss, Ellison), 1986
Demon's Eye (Gresham), 1989
Demons by Daylight (ss, Campbell), 1973
Demons of the Sea (ss, Hodgson), 1992
Dentist (Williamson, J.), 1983
Deptford Trilogy (Davies), 1983
Der Reisefuhrer/The Guide (ss, Campbell), 1994
Descent (Dee), 1991
Desirable Residences and Other Stories (ss, Benson, E.), 1991
Desmodus (Tem, M.), 1995
Desolate Presence (appendix; ss, Owen), 1984
Desperation (King), 1996
Detention (Stine), 1997
Deus X (Citro), 1994
Devil and Daniel Webster (ss, Benét), 1937
Devil and the Floral Dance (Thomas), 1978
Devil Daddy (Blackburn), 1972
Devil in Love (appendix; Cazotte), 1925
Devil in the Pulpit (O'Donnell), 1932
Devil on May Street (Harris, S.), 1997
Devil Rides Out (Wheatley), 1934
Devil Rides Out, Gateway to Hell (Wheatley), 1992
Devil Rocked Her Cradle (St. Clair), 1987
Devil Snar'd (ss, Bowen, M., as Preedy), 1932
Devil's Advocate (Neiderman), 1990
Devil's Auction (Weinberg), 1988
Devil's Bride (Quinn), 1976
Devil's Child (Bingley), 1983
Devil's Elixir (appendix; Hoffmann), 1824
Devil's Footsteps (Burke), 1976
Devil's Maze (Suster), 1979
Devil's Mirror (ss, Russell, R.), 1980
Devil's Mistress (Brodie-Innes), 1915
Devil's Numbers (Hague), 1997
Devil's Shelter (Ryan, R.), 1937
Devil's Spawn (ss, Birkin), 1936
Devils of D-Day (Masterton), 1978
Devouring (Wright, as Armstrong), 1987
Dew Claws (Gresham), 1986
Dhampire (Baker, S.), 1982
Diaboliad and Other Stories (appendix; ss, Bulgakov), 1972
Diagnosis: Terminal (ss, Wilson, F.), 1996
Dialing the Wind (Grant), 1988
Diaries of the Family Dracul series (Kalogridis), from 1994
Diary of a Mad Mummy (Stine), 1996
Dictionary of the Khazars (appendix; Pavic), 1984
Die Softly (Pike), 1991
Diego series (Grant, as Fenn), from 1993
"Dies Irae" (Oliphant), 1895
Different Seasons (ss, King), 1982
Ding Dong Bell (ss, de la Mare), 1924
Disappearance of Mr. Jeremiah Redworth (Riddell), 1878
Disappeared (Silva), 1995
Disaster Area (ss, Ballard), 1967

Disaster Area (Lucas), 1994
Disciples of Dread (Cave), 1988
Disclosures in Scarlet (ss, Jacobi), 1972
Disembodied (Walker), 1988
Disoriented Man (Saxon), 1966
Dispossession (Brenchley), 1996
Dissertation Upon Second Fiddles (ss, O'Sullivan), 1902
Disturbing Affair of Noel Blake (Bell), 1932
Djinn (Masterton), 1977
Dr. Caspian series (Burke), from 1976
Dr. Chaos, and The Devil Snar'd (ss, Bowen, M., as Preedy), 1933
Dr. Grimshaw's Secret (Hawthorne, N.), 1883
Dr. Haggard's Disease (McGrath), 1993
Dr. Jekyas Knightll and Mr. Hyde (Kilpatrick), 1995
Dr. Jekyll and Mr. Hyde and Other Stories of the Supernatural (ss, Stevenson), 1963
Dr. Nikola (Boothby), 1896
Dr. Nikola Returns (Boothby), 1976
Dr. Nikola series (Boothby), from 1895
Dr. Nikola's Experiment (Boothby), 1899
Dr. O (Walker, as Hale), 1991
Dr. Terror's House of Horrors (Burke), 1965
Dog Syndrome & Other Sick Puppies (Piccirilli), 1997
Dolan's Cadillac (ss, King), 1989
Doll and One Other (ss, Blackwood, A.), 1946
Doll Maker (Sarban), 1960
Doll Maker and Other Tales of the Uncanny (ss, Sarban), 1953
Doll Who Ate His Mother (Campbell), 1976
Doll's Eyes (Wood), 1993
Doll's House (Gaiman), 1990
Dollenganger Family series (Andrews), from 1979
Dolliver Romance and Other Pieces (ss, Hawthorne, N.), 1876
Dolores Claiborne (King), 1993
Domain (Herbert), 1984
Dominion (Little), 1996
Dominion (Saberhagen), 1982
Dominique (Chetwynd-Hayes), 1979
Don Sebastian Vampire Chronicles (Daniels), 1994
Donovan's Brain (Siodmak), 1943
Don't Go to Sleep! (Stine), 1997
Don't Look Behind You (Ross, M.), 1973
Don't Look Now (ss, du Maurier), 1971
Don't Take Away the Light (Williamson, J.), 1993
Doom That Came to Sarnath (ss, Lovecraft), 1971
Doomflight (Smith, G.), 1981
Doomsdeath Chronicles (ss, Stout), 1980
Doomstalker (Brandner), 1989
Door to December (Koontz), 1985
Dormant (Nesbit), 1911
Dorothea Dreams (Charnas), 1986
Double Date (Stine), 1994
Double Delight (Oates, as Smith), 1997
Double Edge (Etchison), 1996
Double God (Kelleher, as Hart), 1994
Double Life (appendix; Leroux), 1909
Double Shadow and Other Fantasies (ss, Smith, C.), 1933
Down River (Gallagher), 1989
Down There (appendix; Huysmans), 1924
Downriver (Sinclair, I.), 1991
Doyle, Sean, series (Hutson), from 1991
Dozen Black Roses (Collins), 1996

Dracula (Kilpatrick), 1993
Dracula (Stoker), 1897
Dracula in Love (Shirley), 1983
Dracula Lives! (Tremayne), 1993
Dracula, My Love (Tremayne), 1980
Dracula: Prince of Darkness (Burke), 1967
Dracula Returns! (Lory), 1973
Dracula series (Lory), from 1973
Dracula series (Saberhagen), from 1975
Dracula Tape (Saberhagen), 1975
Dracula Unborn (Tremayne), 1977
Dracula's Brother (Lory), 1973
Dracula's Children (ss, Chetwynd-Hayes), 1987
Dracula's Daughter (Campbell, as Dreadstone), 1977
Dracula's Disciple (Lory), 1975
Dracula's Gold (Lory), 1973
Dracula's Guest and Other Weird Stories (ss, Stoker), 1914
Dracula's Lost World (Lory), 1974
Dradin, in Love (Vandermeer), 1996
Dragon Tears (Koontz), 1992
Dragon under the Hill (Honeycombe), 1972
Dragonfly (Koontz, as Dwyer), 1975
Dragons and Nightmares (ss, Bloch), 1969
Draught of Eternity (Rousseau, as Egbert), 1924
Drawing Blood (Brite), 1993
Dread of Night (ss, O'Donnell), 1945
Dream Country (Gaiman), 1991
Dream Cycle of H. P. Lovecraft (ss, Lovecraft), 1995
Dream Demon (Billson), 1989
Dream Maker (Harbinson), 1991
Dream of the Wolf (ss, Bradfield), 1990
Dream-Detective (ss, Rohmer), 1920
Dream-Quest of Unknown Kadath (Lovecraft), 1955
Dreamer (James, P.), 1989
Dreamhouse (Borton), 1989
Dreaming Jewels (Sturgeon), 1950
Dreamland (Reeves-Stevens), 1985
Dreamlands series (Lumley), from 1986
Dreams and Fancies (ss, Lovecraft), 1962
Dreams with Sharp Teeth (ss, Ellison), 1991
Dreamside (Joyce), 1991
Dreamthorp (Williamson, C.), 1989
Dreamwatcher (Roszak), 1985
Dressed to Kill (Black), 1980
Drifthaven (Ross, M.), 1974
Drive-By (Lansdale), 1993
Drive-In 2: Not Just One of Them Sequels (Lansdale), 1990
Drive-In: A "B"-Movie with Blood and Popcorn, Made in Texas (Lansdale), 1988
Druid Connection (Smith, G.), 1983
Drums of Dracula (Lory), 1974
Drums of the Dark Gods (Saxon, as Ballinger), 1966
Dualitists (ss, Stoker), 1986
Dunwich Horror (ss, Lovecraft), 1945
Dunwich Horror and Others (ss, Lovecraft), 1963
Duplicates (Neiderman), 1994
Durrell Towers (Ross, M.), 1965
Dusk (Dee), 1991
Dweller on the Threshold (Hichens), 1911
Dwellers in Darkness (ss, Derleth), 1976
Dying Breath (Walker), 1989

E Pluribus Unicorn (ss, Sturgeon), 1953
Early Fears (ss, Bloch), 1994
Early Long (ss, Long), 1975
Earth Wire and Other Stories (ss, Lane), 1994
Earthbound (Matheson, Richard, as Swanson), 1982
Earthman, Go Home (ss, Ellison), 1964
East of Samarinda (ss, Jacobi), 1989
Eating Pavlova (Thomas), 1994
Ebony and Crystal (poetry, Smith, C.), 1923
Echo of a Curse (Ryan, R.), 1939
Echoes from the Macabre (ss, du Maurier), 1976
Ecstasy and Other Poems (poetry, Wandrei), 1928
Eden (Harbinson), 1987
Eden's Eyes (Costello, S.), 1989
Edgar Huntly (Brown), 1799
Edge (ss, Beaumont), 1966
Edge of Running Water (Sloane), 1939
Edge of the World (Gordon), 1983
Edges of Night (poetry, Brennan), 1974
Edgeworks (ss, Ellison), 1996-97
Egg Monsters from Mars (Stine), 1996
Egypt Green (Hyde), 1989
Eight Tales (ss, de la Mare), 1971
Elect (Suster), 1980
Electric Gumbo (ss, Lansdale), 1994
Elemental (ss, Chetwynd-Hayes), 1974
Elementals (McDowell), 1981
Ellice Quentin and Other Stories (ss, Hawthorne, J.), 1880
Ellison Wonderland (ss, Ellison), 1962
Elm Haven series (Simmons), from 1991
Elysia: The Coming of Cthulhu! (Lumley), 1989
Embarrassments (ss, James, H.), 1896
Embrace of the Wolf (Cady, as Franklin), 1993
Empire of Fear (Stableford), 1988
Empty House and Other Ghost Stories (ss, Blackwood, A.), 1906
Encounters (ss, Bowen, E.), 1923
Endless Night (Laymon), 1993
Ends of the Earth (ss, Shepard), 1991
Enemy Within (Grant), 1987
Enter Dr. Nikola! (Boothby), 1975
Entity (De Felitta), 1978
Entombed (Smith, G.), 1982
Entropy's Bed at Midnight (ss, Simmons), 1990
Episodes of Vathek (ss, Beckford), 1912
Erebus (Hutson), 1984
Ernestus Berchtold (Polidori), 1819
Erthmun (Wright), 1995
Escape from Camp Run-for-Your-Life (Stine), 1997
Escape from the Carnival of Horrors (Stine), 1995
Escardy Gap (Crowther), 1996
Escardy Gap (Lovegrove), 1996
Espedair Street (Banks), 1987
Essential Ellison (ss, Ellison), 1987
Eternal (Chadbourn), 1996
Eternal Enemy (Pike), 1993
Eve of the Hound (Grant), 1977
Even More Tales to Give You Goosebumps (ss, Stine), 1995
Evening Advances (poetry, Brennan), 1978
Evenings on a Farm Near Dikanka (appendix; ss, Gogol), 1926
Events at Poroth Farm (ss, Klein), 1990
Everville: The Second Book of the Art (Barker), 1994

Evil (Cave), 1981
Evil Always Ends (Brennan), 1982
Evil Deeds (Little), 1994
Evil Intent (Taylor, B.), 1994
Evil Moon (Stine), 1995
Evil of Dark Harbor (Ross, M.), 1975
Evil Offspring (Williamson, J.), 1987
Evil One (Williamson, J.), 1982
Evil Seed (Harris, J.), 1992
Evil That Christy Knows (McNally), 1995
Evil Water and Other Stories (ss, Watson), 1987
Ex Oblivione (ss, Lovecraft), 1969
Excavation (Tem, S.), 1987
Exiles (appendix; ss, Quiroga), 1987
Exorcist (Blatty), 1971
Exorcist III: Legion (Blatty), 1990
Expiation, and Naboth's Vineyard (ss, Benson, E.), 1924
Exploded Heart (ss, Shirley), 1996
Exquisite Corpse (Brite), 1996
Extraterrestrial (Williamson, J., as Shock), 1982
Eye and the Finger (ss, Wandrei), 1944
Eye for an Eye (Saul), 1997
Eyelidiad (Hughes), 1996
Eyes of Darkness (Koontz, as Nichols), 1981
Eyes of the Beast (Harris, S.), 1993
Eyes of the Dragon (King), 1984
Eyes of the Panther (ss, Bierce), 1928

Fables & Fantasies (ss, Stableford), 1996
Fables and Reflections (Gaiman), 1993
Fabulists (ss, Capes), 1915
Face (ss, Benson, E.), 1924
Face (Stine), 1996
Face in the Mirror (ss, Baker, D.), 1971
Face in the Pond (Ross, M.), 1968
Face in the Shadows (Ross, M.), 1973
Face of Fear (Koontz), 1977
Face of Fear and Other Poems (poetry, Counselman), 1984
Face That Must Die (Campbell), 1979
Faces of Fear (ss, Masterton), 1996
Fair to Middling (Calder-Marshall), 1959
Fairy Water (Riddell), 1873
Fairytales (ss, Tem, S.), 1990
Fall Into Darkness (Pike), 1990
Fall of the House of Usher (Kilpatrick), 1995
Fallen Country (Somtow, as Sucharitkul), 1986
Fallen Hearts (Neiderman, as Andrews), 1988
Falling Angel (Hjortsberg), 1978
Familiar Spirit (Tuttle), 1983
Family Portrait (Masterton), 1985
Famine (Masterton), 1981
Famous Monsters (ss, Newman), 1995
Fangs of Morning/The Alchemist (Whitten), 1994
Fangs of the Hooded Demon (Grant, as Marsh), 1988
Fantasies of Harlan Ellison (ss, Ellison), 1979
Fantasma (Monteleone), 1989
Fantastic Fables (ss, Bierce), 1899
Fantastic Failures (play, Hood), 1989
Fantastic Summer (Macardle), 1946
Fantastic World of Kamtellar (ss, Chetwynd-Hayes), 1980
Fantastics and Other Fancies (ss, Hearn), 1914

Fantastique (Kaye), 1992
Far Away and Never (ss, Campbell), 1996
"Farewell, Nikola" (Boothby), 1901
Fatal Cure (Cook), 1994
Fatal Fiddle (ss, Blayre, as Heron-Allen), 1890
Fatal Instinct (Walker), 1996
Fatal Revenge (Maturin, as Murphy), 1807
Fate of Mary Rose (Blackwood, C.), 1981
Fates (Tessier), 1978
Father of Stones (ss, Shepard), 1989
Faust (Nye), 1980
Faust (Reynolds), 1845-46
Fear (ss, Nesbit), 1910
Fear and Trembling (ss, Bloch), 1989
Fear Hall: The Beginning (Stine), 1997
Fear Hall: The Conclusion (Stine), 1997
Fear No More (play, Aiken, C.), 1949
Fear Street Cheerleaders series (Stine), from 1992
Fear Street: Fear Hall series (Stine), from 1997
Fear Street: Fear Park series (Stine), from 1996
Fear Street Saga series (Stine), from 1993
Fear Street series (Stine), from 1989
Fear Street Super Chillers series (Stine), from 1991
Fear Street: The Cataluna Chronicles series (Stine), from 1995
Fear Today—Gone Tomorrow (ss, Bloch), 1971
Fearful Pleasures (ss, Coppard), 1946
Fearsome Inn (Singer), 1967
Feast (Masterton), 1988
Feasting Dead (Metcalfe), 1954
Feeding Frenzy (Hood), 1997
Fengriffen (Case), 1970
Fengriffen and Other Stories (ss, Case), 1971
Festering (Smith, G.), 1989
Fetch (Bowen, M., as Shearing), 1942
Fetch (Holdstock), 1991
Fetish (ss, Bryant), 1991
Fever (Cook), 1982
Fever Dream and Other Fantasies (ss, Bloch), 1970
Fevre Dream (Martin, G.), 1982
Fiddling for Waterbuffaloes (ss, Somtow), 1992
Fiend (Smith, G.), 1988
Fiends (Farris), 1990
Fiends (ss, Laymon), 1997
Fiery Circle (appendix; poetry, Sologub), 1908
Fifth Business (Davies), 1970
Fifth Season (ss, Williamson, J.), 1994
Figures of Julian Ashcroft (Crew), 1996
Final Friends series (Pike), from 1989
Final Grade (Stine), 1995
Final Harbor (Martin, D.), 1984
Final Impact (Navarro), 1997
Fine Feathers and Other Stories (ss, Benson, E.), 1994
Finishing Touches (Tessier), 1986
Fire (Rodgers), 1990
Fire Cloud (McKenney), 1979
Fire from the Wine-Dark Sea (ss, Somtow, as Sucharitkul), 1983
Fire Game (Stine), 1991
Fire in the Blood (Elrod), 1991
Fire Mask (Grant), 1991
Fire of Driftwood (ss, Broster), 1932
Fire of the Witches (Long), 1971

Fire Worm (Watson), 1988
Firebug (Bloch), 1961
Firecode (Yarbro), 1987
Fires of Eden (Simmons), 1994
Firestarter (King), 1980
First Date (Stine), 1992
First Evil (Stine), 1992
First Horror (Stine), 1994
First Light (Ackroyd), 1989
First Love (Oates), 1996
First Love, Last Rites (ss, McEwan), 1975
First Scream (Stine), 1996
Fistful of Stories (ss, Lansdale), 1997
Fit of Shivers (ss, Aiken, J.), 1990
Five Jars (James, M.), 1922
Flame in Byzantium (Yarbro), 1987
Flames: A London Phantasy (Hichens), 1897
Flaw in the Crystal (ss, Sinclair, M.), 1912
Flesh (Laymon), 1988
Flesh and Blood (Masterton), 1994
Flesh Artist (ss, Taylor, L.), 1994
Flesh Wounds (ss, Fowler), 1995
Flicker (Roszak), 1991
Flies on the Wall (ss, Hamilton), 1972
Flights of Fear (ss, Masterton), 1995
Flint Knife (ss, Benson, E.), 1988
Floater (Brandner), 1988
Floating Café and Other Stories (ss, Lawrence), 1936
Floating Dragon (Straub), 1982
Flood (McDowell), 1983
Flowers in the Attic (Andrews), 1979
Fluke (Herbert), 1977
Flute-Player (Thomas), 1979
Flying Dutchman (Russell, W.), 1888
Foe of Barnabas Collins (Ross, M.), 1969
Fog (Etchison), 1980
Fog (Herbert), 1975
Fog and the Stars (Ross, M., as Gilmer), 1963
Fog Heart (Tessier), 1997
Fog Island Secret (Ross, M.), 1975
Fog Island series (Ross, M.), from 1971
Fogbound (Ross, M.), 1967
Foghorn (ss, Atherton), 1934
Follower (Gallagher), 1984
Folsom Flint, and Other Curious Tales (ss, Keller), 1969
Fools of Chem and Their History (Singer), 1973
Foot in the Grave (ss, Aiken, J.), 1989
Footsteps (ss, Ellison), 1989
For Fear of Little Men (Blackburn), 1972
For Fear of the Night (Grant), 1988
For Love of Audrey Rose (De Felitta), 1982
For Maurice (ss, Lee), 1927
For Satan's Sake (O'Donnell), 1904
For the Blood Is the Life (ss, Crawford), 1996
For the Soul of a Witch: A Romance of Badenoch (Brodie-Innes), 1910
Forbidden Zone (Strieber), 1993
Force (Suster), 1984
Forest of the Night (Somtow), 1992
Forest Plains (ss, Crowther), 1996
Forget-Me-Knots (Brookes), 1985

Ghoul (Slade), 1987
Ghoul Man (Hood), 1996
Ghoul Warning and Other Omens (poetry, Lumley), 1982
Ghouls in My Grave (appendix; ss, Ray), 1965
Giant Under the Snow (Gordon), 1968
Gideon (Laws), 1993
Gift of the Wise Bees (appendix; play, Sologub), 1907
Gifts (ss, Singer), 1985
Gila! (Ptacek, as Simons), 1981
Gilray's Ghost (Gordon), 1995
Gimme a Kiss (Pike), 1989
Gimpel the Fool and Other Stories (ss, Singer), 1957
Girl in the Photograph and Other Stories (ss, Baker, D.), 1982
Girl Next Door (Ketchum), 1989
Girl of the Sea of Cortez (Benchley), 1982
Girl Who Cried Monster (Stine), 1993
Girlfriend (Stine), 1991
Give Yourself a Fright (ss, Aiken, J.), 1989
Give Yourself Goosebumps series (Stine), from 1995
Glass Centipede (Laing), 1936
Glass Mender and Other Stories (ss, Baring), 1910
Glimpse into Terror (Ross, M.), 1971
Glittering Savages (Burnell), 1995
Glow of Candles and Other Stories (ss, Grant), 1981
Go Eat Worms! (Stine), 1994
Goat Dance (Clegg), 1989
Goat-Foot God (Fortune), 1936
Goblins (Grant), 1994
God Game (Suster), 1997
God of the Labyrinth (Wilson, C.), 1970
God Project (Saul), 1982
Godforsaken (Yarbro), 1983
Godplayer (Cook), 1983
Gods of Hell (Boyll), 1994
Godsend (Taylor, B.), 1976
Gold Sickle (appendix; Sue), 1904
Golden (Shepard), 1993
Golden Helix (ss, Sturgeon), 1979
Golden Pot and Other Tales (appendix; ss, Hoffmann), 1992
Golem (appendix; Meyrink), 1928
Golem (Singer), 1982
Golgotha Falls: An Assault on the Fourth Dimension (De Felitta),
    1984
Gollan (ss, Coppard), 1929
Gone South (McCammon), 1992
Good Omens (Gaiman), 1990
Good, Secret Place (ss, Laymon), 1993
Goodlow's Ghosts (Wright), 1993
Goodnight Kiss (Stine), 1992
Goodnight Kiss 2 (Stine), 1996
Goodnight, Sweet Angel (McNally), 1996
Goose on Your Grave (ss, Aiken, J.), 1987
Goosebumps series (Stine), from 1992
Gorilla Gunslinger (Partridge), n.d.
Graduation (Pike), 1989
Grange (Chetwynd-Hayes), 1985
Grant, Dr. Dean, series (Walker), from 1989
Grasshopper (Gordon), 1987
Grave (Grant), 1981
Graveyard Vultures (Smith, G.), 1982
Great Amen (Burks), 1938

Great and Secret Show: The First Book of the Art (Barker), 1989
Great Fog (ss, Heard), 1946
Great Fog and Other Weird Tales (ss, Heard), 1944
Great God Pan and The Inmost Light (ss, Machen), 1894
Great Granny Webster (Blackwood, C.), 1977
Great Mirror (Burks), 1952
Great Return (ss, Machen), 1915
Great Secret (Nisbet), 1895
Great Taboo (Allen), 1890
Great White Space (Copper), 1974
Green Eyes (Shepard), 1984
Green Face (appendix; Meyrink), 1992
Green Flames of Aries (Lory), 1974
Green Flash and Other Tales of Horror, Suspense, and Fantasy
    (ss, Aiken, J.), 1971
Green Man (Amis), 1969
Green Mile (King), 1996
Green Piper (Kelleher), 1984
Green Round (Machen), 1933
Green Tea and Other Ghost Stories (ss, Le Fanu), 1945
Greetings from Earth (ss, Bradfield), 1993
Grey Face (Rohmer), 1924
Grey Weather: Moorland Tales of My Own People (ss, Buchan),
    1899
Grim Tales (ss, Nesbit), 1893
Grimscribe (ss, Ligotti), 1991
Grotesque (McGrath), 1989
Growing Rich (Weldon), 1992
Guardian (Konvitz), 1979
Guardian (Saul), 1993
Guardian Angels (Citro), 1988
Guardians series (Saxon), from 1968
Gunmen, Gallants, and Ghosts (ss, Wheatley), 1943
Gunslinger (King), 1988
Guttersnipe (ss, Kersh), 1954

H. P. Lovecraft in the "Eyrie," (ss, Lovecraft), 1979
Haiti Circle (Ross, M.), 1976
Half a Minute's Silence and Other Stories (ss, Baring), 1925
Half in Shadow (ss, Counselman), 1964
Half Moon Down (Gresham), 1985
Halfway House (play, Blackwood, A.), 1921
Halloween II (Etchison), 1981
Halloween III: Season of the Witch (Etchison), 1982
Halloween Night (Stine), 1993
Halloween Night II (Stine), 1994
Halloween Party (Stine), 1991
Halloween Tree (Bradbury), 1972
Hallows (Scott, M.), 1995
Hammer Horror Omnibus 1 (ss, Burke), 1966
Hammer Horror Omnibus 2 (ss, Burke), 1967
Hand of Dracula (Lory), 1973
Hand of Kornelius Voyt (Onions), 1939
Hands of Orlac (appendix; Renard), 1929
Handyman (Walker, as Robertson), 1990
Hanging Man & Other Strange Suspensions (Piccirilli), 1996
Hangman (Boyll), 1994
Hangman (Smith, G., as Newman), 1994
Hard Shoulder (Douglas), 1996
Harlan Ellison's Chocolate Alphabet (ss, Ellison), 1978
Harlan Ellison's Dream Corridor Special (ss, Ellison), 1995

Harmful Intent (Cook), 1990
Harps in the Wind (Hichens), 1945
Harrigan's File (ss, Derleth), 1975
Harvest Home (Tryon), 1973
Hashish-Eater (poetry, Smith, C.), 1989
Haunted (Herbert), 1988
Haunted (ss, Oates), 1994
Haunted (Stine), 1991
Haunted and Hunted (ss, O'Donnell), 1946
Haunted and the Haunters (ss, Bulwer-Lytton), 1859
Haunted Castles (ss, Russell, R.), 1985
Haunted Cave (Pike), 1995
Haunted Chair (appendix; Leroux), 1931
Haunted Garden (Timperley), 1966
Haunted Garden (ss, Williams), 1986
Haunted Grange (Chetwynd-Hayes), 1988
Haunted House, and Calderon the Courtier (ss, Bulwer-Lytton), 1882
Haunted House at Latchford (Riddell), 1975
Haunted Island (Visiak), 1910
Haunted Man (O'Donnell), 1917
Haunted Man and the Ghost's Bargain (Dickens), 1848
Haunted Mask (Stine), 1993
Haunted Mask II (Stine), 1995
Haunted Pampero (ss, Hodgson), 1993
Haunted River (Riddell), 1877
Haunted School (Stine), 1997
Haunted Station and Other Stories (ss, Nisbet), 1894
Haunted Valley (ss, Williams), 1978
Haunted Vintage (Bowen, M.), 1921
Haunted Waters (ss, Williams), 1987
Haunter of the Dark and Other Tales of Horror (ss, Lovecraft), 1951
Haunting of Alan Mais (Saxon), 1969
Haunting of Clifton Court (Ross, M.), 1972
Haunting of Hill House (Jackson), 1959
Haunting of Lamb House (Aiken, J.), 1991
Haunting of Low Fennel (ss, Rohmer), 1920
Haunting of Toby Jugg (Wheatley), 1948
Hauntings (ss, Lee), 1890
Hauser's Memory (Siodmak), 1968
Havock Junction (Donnelly), 1995
Hawk Moon (Gorman), 1995
Hawksmoor (Ackroyd), 1985
Haydon, Stuart series (Lindsey), from 1983
He Told Me To (Grant), 1993
Headhunter (Slade), 1984
Headless Ghost (Stine), 1995
Headpiece, a Tailpiece, and an Intermezzo (ss, Allen), 1899
Hear the Children Calling. . . (McNally), 1990
Hearse for Dark Harbor (Ross, M.), 1974
Heart of a Dog (appendix; Bulgakov), 1968
Heart of a Dog and Other Stories (appendix; ss, Bulgakov), 1990
Hearts of Earth (poetry, Brennan), 1950
Heat from Another Sun (Lindsey), 1984
Heathen (Hutson), 1992
Heatseeker (ss, Shirley), 1989
Heaven (Andrews), 1985
Hedonists (Wilson, C.), 1971
Height of the Scream (ss, Campbell), 1976
Heirloom (Masterton), 1981

Hell Candidate (Masterton), 1980
Hell House (Matheson, Richard), 1971
Hell Is What You Make It (ss, Chetwynd-Hayes), 1994
Hell! Said the Duchess: A Bed-Time Story (Arlen), 1934
Hell Ships of Many Waters (ss, O'Donnell), 1946
Hell Storm (Williamson, J.), 1991
Hellborn (Brandner), 1981
Hellbound Heart (Barker), 1991
Hellfire (Saul), 1986
Hellfire Club (Straub), 1996
Hellfire Files of Jules de Grandin (ss, Quinn), 1976
Hell's Gate (Koontz), 1970
Her Pilgrim Soul, and Other Stories (ss, Brennert), 1990
Herbert West, the Reanimator (ss, Lovecraft), 1977
Here and Beyond (ss, Wharton), 1926
Here Be Daemons (ss, Copper), 1978
Hero of Dreams (Lumley), 1986
Heroes and Horrors (ss, Leiber), 1978
Hexes (Piccirilli), 1995
Hexing (Holdstock, as Faulcon), 1984
Hexing and The Labyrinth (Holdstock, as Faulcon), 1989
Hidden Beast (Pike), 1996
Hidden Chapel (Ross, M., as Ames), 1967
Hidden Jewel (Neiderman, as Andrews), 1995
Hide and Seek (Ketchum), 1984
Hideaway (Koontz), 1992
Hieroglyphic Tales (ss, Walpole, Horace), 1785
High Spirits (ss, Davies), 1982
High Tide (Stine), 1997
High-Rise (Ballard), 1975
Hill of Dreams (Machen), 1907
History of Luminous Motion (Bradfield), 1989
History of the Caliph Vathek (Beckford), 1868
Hit and Run (Stine), 1992
Hitchhiker (Stine), 1993
Hobgoblin (Coyne), 1981
Hole of the Pit (Ross, A.), 1914
Holiday (ss, Matheson, Richard Christian), 1988
Hollow Laughter (ss, Stout), 1978
Hollow Man (Simmons), 1992
Hollowing (Holdstock), 1993
Holmes-Dracula File (Saberhagen), 1978
Holy Terrors (ss, Machen), 1946
Homing (Black, as Campbell), 1980
Homing (Saul), 1994
Hoodoo Man (Harris, S.), 1992
Hope (Lovegrove), 1990
Horrible Dummy and Other Stories (ss, Kersh), 1944
Horror at Camp Jellyjam (Stine), 1995
Horror at Oakdeene and Others (ss, Lumley), 1977
Horror Chambers of Jules de Grandin (ss, Quinn), 1977
Horror Club (Morris), 1991
Horror Expert (Long), 1961
Horror from the Hills (Long), 1963
Horror Horn (ss, Benson, E.), 1974
Horror House (Williamson, J.), 1981
Horror in the Burying Ground and Other Tales (ss, Lovecraft), 1975
Horror in the Museum and Other Revisions (ss, Lovecraft), 1970
Horror Mansion (Williamson, J.), 1982
Horror of Fog Island (Ross, M.), 1978

In the Mist and Other Uncanny Encounters (ss, Walter), 1979
In the Moons of Borea (Lumley), 1979
In the Realm of Terror (ss, Blackwood, A.), 1957
In the Shadow of Evil (Saul), 1997
In the Flesh (ss, Barker), 1986
Inagehi (Cady), 1994
Incarnate (Campbell), 1983
Incarnations (play, Barker), 1995
Inception (Harbinson), 1991
Incredible Adventures (ss, Blackwood, A.), 1914
Incredible Shrinking Man (Matheson, Richard), 1988
Incubus (Donnelly), 1996
Incubus (Russell, R.), 1976
Indian Mystery (Allen), 1902
Infant's Skull (appendix; Sue), 1904
Influence (Campbell), 1988
Inhabitant of the Lake, and Less Welcome Tenants (ss, Campbell), 1964
Inheritance (Brookes), 1980
Inheritor (Benson, E.), 1930
Inhuman (Russo), 1986
Inhuman Condition (ss, Barker), 1986
Inner Side of the Wind (appendix; Pavic), 1993
Innocent (McEwan), 1990
Innsmouth Heritage (ss, Stableford), 1992
Insane Root (Praed), 1902
Insanity of Jones and Other Stories (ss, Blackwood, A.), 1966
Inside the Works (Piccirilli), 1997
Insomnia (King), 1994
Intensity (Koontz), 1995
Intercessor and Other Stories (ss, Sinclair, M.), 1931
Interview with the Vampire (Rice), 1976
Intimate Knowledge of the Night (ss, Dowling), 1995
Into the Silence (Copper), 1983
Intruder (Black, as Altman), 1985
Intruders (ss, Burrage), 1995
Intrusions (ss, Aickman), 1980
Invaders from Mars (Garton), 1986
Invasion (Cook), 1997
Inverted Glove (appendix; poetry, Pavic), 1989
Invisible Man (Wells), 1897
Irish Ghost Stories of Sheridan Le Fanu (ss, Le Fanu), 1973
Irish Ghosts and Hauntings (ss, Scott, M.), 1994
Irish Witch (Wheatley), 1973
Iron Collar (appendix; Sue), 1909
Iron Curtain (appendix; poetry, Pavic), 1973
Iron Pincers (appendix; Sue), 1909
Is the Devil a Gentleman? (ss, Quinn), 1970
Island (Benchley), 1979
Island (Laymon), 1995
Island (Smith, G.), 1988
Island (Wright), 1988
Island Nights' Entertainments (ss, Stevenson), 1893
Island of Doctor Moreau (Wells), 1896
Isle of Devils (poetry, Lewis, M.), 1827
It (King), 1986
It (ss, Sturgeon), 1948
It Came from Beneath the Sink! (Stine), 1995
Italian (Radcliffe), 1797
It's All in Your Mind (Bloch), 1971
Ivan Greet's Masterpiece (ss, Allen), 1893
Ivy Gripped the Steps and Other Stories (ss, Bowen, E.), 1946

Jackals (Grant), 1994
Jago (Newman), 1991
Jaguar Hunter (ss, Shepard), 1987
Jaws (Benchley), 1974
Jekyll Legacy (Bloch), 1990
Jericho Falls (Hyde), 1986
Jewel of Seven Stars (Stoker), 1903
Jig of Forslin: A Symphony (poetry, Aiken, C.), 1916
Jimbo: A Fantasy (Blackwood, A.), 1909
John Silence, Physician Extraordinary (ss, Blackwood, A.), 1908
Johnny Pye and the Fool-Killer (ss, Benét), 1938
Joining Charles (ss, Bowen, E.), 1929
"Jolly Roger" (Nisbet), 1893
Jonah (Herbert), 1981
Jonah Hex: Two Gun Mojo (Lansdale), 1993
Jonah Watch (Cady), 1981
Jonathan Barrett, Gentleman Vampire (Elrod), 1996
Jonathan Bradford (Prest), 1851
Joseph and Koza (Singer), 1970
Journal of Edwin Underhill (Tonkin), 1981
Joyride (Ketchum), 1994
Judas and Other Stories (ss, Metcalfe), 1931
Judas Glass (Cadnum), 1996
Judgment Day (Sharman), 1982
Julia (Straub), 1975
Julia Roseingrave (Bowen, M., as Paye), 1933
Juliet (Timperley), 1974
Julius LeVallon (Blackwood, A.), 1916
Jumbee and Other Uncanny Tales (ss, Whitehead), 1944
Just an Ordinary Day (ss, Jackson), 1996

Ka of Gifford Hillary (Wheatley), 1956
Kachina (Ptacek), 1986
Kalee's Shrine (Allen), 1886
Kalimantan (Shepard), 1990
Kane (Borton), 1990
Karma and Other Stories (ss, Hearn), 1918
Katie (McDowell), 1982
Kaufman and Lane series (Weinberg), from 1991
Kecksies and Other Twilight Tales (ss, Bowen, M.), 1976
Keep (Wilson, F.), 1981
Keeper of the Children (Hallahan), 1978
Kent Montana and the Once and Future Thing (Grant), 1991
Kent Montana and the Really Ugly Thing from Mars (Grant), 1990
Kent Montana and the Reasonably Invisible Man (Grant), 1991
Kepple (Chetwynd-Hayes), 1992
Key to Midnight (Koontz, as Nichols), 1979
Khai of Ancient Khem (Lumley), 1981
Kidnapper (Bloch), 1954
Kildhurm's Oak (ss, Hawthorne, J.), 1889
Kill (Ryan, A.), 1982
Kill Riff (Schow), 1988
Kill the Teacher's Pet (Garton, as Locke), 1991
Killer and the Slain (Walpole, Hugh), 1942
Killer Crabs (Smith, G.), 1978
Killer Instinct (Walker), 1995
Killer's Kiss (Stine), 1997
Killing Bone (Saxon), 1969
Killing Bottle (ss, Hartley), 1932
Killing Gift (Wood), 1975

Kindly Ones (Gaiman), 1996
Kindness of Strangers (Taylor, B.), 1985
Kindred Passions (Oates, as Smith), 1988
Kindred Spirits (Brennert), 1984
King Blood (Clark, S.), 1997
King in Yellow (ss, Chambers), 1895
King in Yellow and Other Horror Stories (ss, Chambers), 1970
King of Satan's Eyes (Grant, as Marsh), 1984
King of Terrors (ss, Bloch), 1977
King's Ghost (Chetwynd-Hayes), 1985
Kink (Koja), 1996
Kiss Daddy Goodbye (Black, as Altman), 1980
Kiss, Kiss (ss, Dahl), 1960
Kiss Me Again, Stranger (ss, du Maurier), 1953
Kiss of Death (ss, Birkin), 1964
Kiss of Death (Garton, as Locke), 1992
Kiss of Death (Rhodes), 1990
Kiss of the Cobra (Tremayne), 1984
Kiss That Killed (appendix; Leroux), 1934
Knife (Stine), 1992
Knife Edge (Hutson), 1997
Knight in Screaming Armor (Stine), 1996
Knighton Vampires (Smith, G.), 1993
Koko (Straub), 1988
Kwaidan (ss, Hearn), 1904

Labyrinth (Holdstock, as Faulcon), 1987
Lady of Frozen Death and Other Stories (ss, Cline), 1992
Lady of the Barge and Other Stories (ss, Jacobs), 1902
Lady of the Island (ss, Boothby), 1904
Lady of the Shroud (Stoker), 1909
Ladygrave (Burke), 1978
Lady's Walk (ss, Oliphant), 1883
Lair (Herbert), 1979
Lair of the White Worm (Stoker), 1911
Laird's Luck and Other Fireside Tales (ss, Quiller-Couch, as Q), 1901
Lanark: A Life in Four Books (Gray), 1981
Lanark, Ryne, series (Walker, as Robertson), from 1989
Lancashire Witches (Ainsworth), 1849
Land of Darkness (ss, Oliphant), 1888
Land of Laughs (Carroll), 1980
Land of Mist (Doyle), 1926
Landscape Painted with Tea (appendix; Pavic), 1990
Larger Than Life (appendix; Buzzati), 1962
Lasher (Rice), 1993
Last Act (Pike), 1988
Last Aerie (Lumley), 1993
Last Alien (Grant), 1987
Last Bouquet (ss, Bowen, M.), 1932
Last Call of Mourning (Grant), 1979
Last Circle (ss, Benét), 1946
Last Incantation (ss, Smith, C.), 1982
Last Magician (ss, Keller), 1978
Last Man (Shelley), 1826
Last of the Fairies (James, G.), 1847
Last Rite (ss, Lumley), 1992
Last Rites (Dee, as Darke), 1996
Last Scream (Stine), 1996
Last Tales (ss, Dinesen), 1957
Last Vampire (Pike), 1994

Last Vampire (Wright), 1991
Last Vampire 2: Black Blood (Pike), 1994
Last Vampire 3: Red Dice (Pike), 1995
Last Vampire 4: Phantom (Pike), 1996
Last Vampire series (Pike), from 1992
Last Wave (Popescu), 1977
Late Breakfasters (Aickman), 1964
Late Show (Douglas), 1994
Laughing Mill and Other Stories (ss, Hawthorne, J.), 1879
Laughter of a Ghoul: What Every Young Ghoul Should Know (ss, Bloch), 1977
Lavondyss: Journey to an Unknown Region (Holdstock), 1988
Leffing, Lucius, series (ss, Brennan), from 1973
Legacy (Coyne), 1979
Legacy of Evil (Long), 1973
Legacy of Terror (Koontz, as Dwyer), 1971
Legend of the Lost Legend (Stine), 1996
Legend of the Werewolf (Holdstock, as Black), 1976
Legion (Blatty), 1983
Legion of the Dead (Cave), 1979
Legion of the Dead (Walker, as Caine), 1992
Lemoyne Heritage (Long), 1977
Lesson of the Master and Other Stories (ss, James, H.), 1892
Let Me Call You Sweetheart (Clark, M.), 1995
Let's Get Invisible! (Stine), 1993
Letters from the Dead (Black), 1985
LeVallon, Julius, series (Blackwood, A.), from 1916
Levee (McDowell), 1983
Lie to Me (Martin, D.), 1990
Life and Death of My Lord Gilles de Rais (Nye), 1990
Life and Loves of a She-Devil (Weldon), 1983
Life During Wartime (Shepard), 1987
Life Everlasting, and Other Tales of Science, Fantasy, and Horror (ss, Keller), 1947
Life Force (Wilson, C.), 1985
Lifeblood (Elrod), 1990
Light at the End (Skipp), 1986
Light Errant (Brenchley), 1997
Light Invisible (ss, Benson, R.), 1903
Light of Eden (Harbinson), 1987
Lightning (Koontz), 1988
Lights Out (Stine), 1991
List of Seven (Frost), 1993
Listener and Other Stories (ss, Blackwood, A.), 1907
Listeners (Pike), 1994
Listening Child (ss, Timperley), 1956
Little Boy Lost (Wright), 1992
Little Brothers (Hautala), 1988
Little Comic Shop of Horrors (Stine), 1997
Little Demon (appendix; Sologub), 1907
Little People (Pike), 1996
Little Pilgrim in the Unseen (ss, Oliphant), 1882
Live Girls (Garton), 1987
Lives of the Twins (Oates, as Smith), 1987
Living Dark (Gresham), 1991
Living Dead series (Russo), from 1974
Living Demons (ss, Bloch), 1967
Living Things (Russo), 1988
Loaves and Fishes (ss, Capes), 1906
Loch Sinister (Ross, M.), 1974
Locked Corridor (Ross, M.), 1965

Loco-Zombies (Hood), 1996
Locusts (Smith, G.), 1979
Lodge Sinister (Ross, M.), 1975
Lodger (ss, Chappell), 1993
Logical Magician (Weinberg), 1993
Lone Cottage (Prest), 1845
Lonesome Places (ss, Derleth), 1962
Long Black Dress (Timperley), 1972
Long Lost (Campbell), 1993
Long Midnight (Gorman, as Ransom), 1993
Long Night of Fear (Ross, M.), 1972
Long Night of the Grave (Grant), 1986
Long Walk (King, as Bachman), 1979
Longbarrow (Morris), 1997
Longest Night (Williamson, J.), 1985
Longest Single Note and Other Strange Compositions (ss, Crowther), 1998
Look Back on Laurel Hills (poetry, Brennan), 1989
Look Behind You! (ss, Burks), 1954
Lord Horror (Britton), 1989
Lord of the Dead (Holland), 1996
Lord of the Flies (Golding), 1954
Lord of the Hollow Dark (Kirk), 1979
Lord of the Vampires (Kalogridis), 1996
Lord of the World (Benson, R.), 1907
Lori (Bloch), 1989
Lost (Aycliffe), 1996
Lost Angels (ss, Schow), 1990
Lost Cavern and Other Tales of the Fantastic (ss, Heard), 1948
Lost Futures (Tuttle), 1992
Lost in Time and Space with Lefty Feep (ss, Bloch), 1987
Lost Lake (ss, Kirk), 1966
Lost Mind (Pike), 1995
Lost Souls (Brite), 1992
Lost Stradivarius (Falkner), 1895
Lost Valley and Other Stories (ss, Blackwood, A.), 1910
Lost Worlds (ss, Smith, C.), 1944
Lot Lizards (Garton), 1991
Lottery (ss, Jackson), 1949
Loudest Scream (Stine), 1996
Love Ain't Nothing But Sex Misspelled (ss, Ellison), 1968
Love Child (Neiderman), 1986
Love Me to Death (Martin, D.), 1993
Love, Sleep and Dreams (poetry, Stenbock), 1881
Love Throbbing Bob (ss, Collins, as Regalia), 1990
Lovedeath (ss, Simmons), 1993
Lovers' Meeting (Smith, L.), 1940
Loves Music, Loves to Dance (Clark, M.), 1991
Low-Flying Aircraft and Other Stories (ss, Ballard), 1976
Lower Deep (Cave), 1990
Lowland Rider (Williamson, C.), 1988
Lucifer's Eye (Cave), 1991
Luck of the Vails (Benson, E.), 1901
Lucy's Child (Hutson), 1995
Lurker at the Threshold (Derleth; Lovecraft), 1945
Lurkers (Smith, G.), 1982
Lurking Fear and Other Stories (ss, Lovecraft), 1947
Lust of Hate (Boothby), 1898
Lydyard, David, series (Stableford), from 1990
Lyre of Orpheus (Davies), 1988
Lyrica (Monteleone), 1987

M.D. (Disch), 1991
Ma Qui, and Other Phantoms (ss, Brennert), 1991
Macabre (Laws), 1994
Machine to Kill (appendix; Leroux), 1935
Mad Moon of Dreams (Lumley), 1987
Madam Crowl's Ghost, and Other Tales of Mystery (ss, James, M.; Le Fanu), 1923
Madeleine (Taylor, B.), 1987
Madonna of Seven Moons (Lawrence), 1931
Maggot (Fowles), 1985
Magic Cottage (Herbert), 1986
Magic Man—and Other Science-Fantasy Stories (ss, Beaumont), 1965
Magic Mirror (ss, Blackwood, A.), 1989
Magic of Shirley Jackson (ss, Jackson), 1966
Magic Wagon (Lansdale), 1986
Magician of Lublin (Singer), 1960
Magnificent Gallery (Monteleone), 1987
Magus (Fowles), 1965
Mailman (Little), 1991
Majestic (Strieber), 1989
Majorettes (Russo), 1979
Maker of Moons (ss, Chambers), 1896
Making Love (Holder; Tem, M.), 1993
Mall Time (Brenchley), 1991
Malpertuis (appendix; Ray), 1943
Man in the Moss (Rickman), 1994
Man of the Future (ss, Bryant), 1990
Man Overboard! (ss, Crawford), 1903
Man That Was Used Up (ss, Poe), 1843
Man Upstairs (Parkinson), 1991
Man Who Lost Red (ss, Dowling), 1995
Man with the Black Feather (appendix; Leroux), 1912
Man with the Broken Nose and Other Stories (ss, Arlen), 1927
Man with the Beard (Timperley), 1977
Man without a Shadow (Wilson, C.), 1963
Manhattan Ghost Story (Wright), 1984
Manhunter (Harris, T.), 1986
Mania (Smith, G.), 1989
Maniac Father (Prest), 1842
Manitou (Masterton), 1975
Manitou Doll (Smith, G.), 1981
Manitou series (Masterton), from 1975
Manse (Cantrell), 1987
Mansions of Darkness (Yarbro), 1996
Manstopper (Borton), 1988
Manticore (Davies), 1972
Mantis (Jeter), 1987
Mantle and Other Stories (appendix; ss, Gogol), 1915
Manuscripts from the Diary of a Physician (Rymer), 1844
Maracot Deep and Other Stories (ss, Doyle), 1929
Marble Faun (Hawthorne, N.), 1860
Marginalia (ss, Lovecraft), 1944
Mark of the Moderately Vicious Vampire (Grant), 1992
Mark of the Werewolf (Sackett), 1990
Markheim (ss, Stevenson), 1925
Marta (Ross, M.), 1973
Marvels and Mysteries (ss, Marsh), 1900
Mask (Koontz), 1981
Mask, and Other Stories (ss, Chambers), 1929
Mask of Cthulhu (ss, Derleth), 1958
Mask of Evil (Ross, M.), 1977

Masquerade of the Red Death series (Weinberg), from 1995
Master (Smith, G.), 1988
Master and Margarita (appendix; Bulgakov), 1967
Master of Fallen Years (ss, O'Sullivan), 1995
Master of Lies (Masterton), 1992
Master of Murder (Pike), 1992
Master of Murder (Robbins), 1933
Master of Shadows (ss, Lawrence), 1959
Master of the Fallen Years (ss, O'Sullivan), 1990
Masterpieces of Shirley Jackson (Jackson), 1996
Matrix (Aycliffe), 1994
Matter of Taste (Saberhagen), 1990
Matter of the Heart (Royle), 1997
Max Hensig (play, Blackwood, A.), 1929
Maxwell's Train (Hyde), 1985
May Fair, in Which Are Told the Last Adventures of These
    Charming People (ss, Arlen), 1925
Maybe I'll Call Anna (Spencer), 1990
Mayfair Witches series (Rice), from 1990
Maynard's House (Raucher), 1980
Mazel and Shlimazel (Singer), 1967
McDowell's Ghost (Cady), 1982
Meat (Watson), 1988
Medusa (ss, Campbell), 1987
Medusa (Visiak), 1929
Mefisto in Onyx (ss, Ellison), 1993
Melmoth the Wanderer (Maturin), 1820
Melody (Neiderman, as Andrews), 1996
Memnoch the Devil (Rice), 1995
Memoirs of Elizabeth Frankenstein (Roszak), 1995
Memories of the Body (ss, Tuttle), 1992
Memory (ss, Lovecraft), 1969
Men without Bones and Other Stories (ss, Kersh), 1955
Meng & Ecker (Britton), 1989-95
Mephisto Waltz (Stewart), 1969
Mercy (Lindsey), 1990
Merlin's Wood, or The Vision of Magic (Holdstock), 1994
Merry Men and Other Tales and Fables (ss, Stevenson), 1887
Meshugah (Singer), 1994
Metamorphosis and Other Stories (appendix; ss, Kafka), 1933
Methods of Confinement (Maginn), 1996
Methods of Madness (ss, Garton), 1990
Midnight (Koontz), 1989
Midnight (Russo), 1980
Midnight Blue: The Sonja Blue Collection (Collins), 1995
Midnight Boy (Gresham), 1987
Midnight Club (Pike), 1994
Midnight House and Other Tales (ss, Harvey), 1910
Midnight Mass (ss, Wilson, F.), 1990
Midnight Place series (Grant, as Lake), from 1992
Midnight Pleasures (ss, Bloch), 1987
Midnight Sun (Campbell), 1990
Midnight Tales (ss, Harvey), 1946
Midnight Tales (ss, Stoker), 1990
Midnight Whispers (Neiderman, as Andrews), 1992
Midnight's Lair (Laymon, as Kelly), 1988
Midsummer (Costello, M.), 1990
Milesian Chief (Maturin), 1812
Millennium (Harbinson), 1995
Mind Fields (ss, Ellison), 1994
Mind Parasites (Wilson, C.), 1967

Mind Reader (Stine), 1994
Mindbend (Cook), 1985
Mine (McCammon), 1990
Mine to Kill (St. Clair), 1985
Miracleman: Book 4: The Golden Age (Gaiman), 1993
Mirage (Costello, M.), 1996
Mirgorod (appendix; ss, Gogol), 1929
Mirror (Masterton), 1988
Mirror (Millhiser), 1978
Mirror of Shalott (ss, Benson, R.), 1907
Misery (King), 1987
Miss X (Timperley), 1979
Missing (Stine), 1990
Missing Pieces (Hague), 1997
Mist in the Mirror (Hill), 1992
Mr. Arcularis (play, Aiken, C.), 1957
Mr. Bad Face (Morris), 1996
Mr. Barrett's Secret and Other Stories (ss, Amis), 1993
Mr. Blettsworthy on Rampole Island (Wells), 1928
Mr. Dunton's Invention and Other Stories (ss, Hawthorne, J.),
    1896
Mr. Fox and Other Feral Tales (ss, Partridge), 1992
Mr. George and Other Odd Persons (ss, Derleth, as Grendon),
    1963
Mr. Murder (Koontz), 1993
Mrs. Carteret Receives and Other Stories (ss, Hartley), 1971
Mrs. de Winter (Hill), 1993
Mrs. God (ss, Straub), 1990
Mistress of Moorwood Manor (Ross, M.), 1972
Mistress of Ravenswood (Ross, M.), 1966
Mists of Dark Harbor (Ross, M.), 1974
Mixed Pickles (ss, Bell), 1935
Model (Aickman), 1987
Modern Magician (Weinberg), 1995
Monastery (Scott, W.), 1820
Monastery (Williamson, J.), 1992
Mongster (Boyll), 1991
Monk (Hallahan), 1983
Monk (Lewis, M.), 1796
Monkey's Paw (play, Jacobs), 1910
Monkey's Paw and Other Stories (ss, Jacobs), 1994
Monster (Pike), 1992
Monster: A Tale of Loch Ness (Konvitz), 1982
Monster Blood (Stine), 1992
Monster Blood II (Stine), 1994
Monster Blood III (Stine), 1995
Monster Club (ss, Chetwynd-Hayes), 1975
Monster of the Prophecy (ss, Smith, C.), 1983
Montana, Kent, series (Grant, as Fenn), from 1988
Moods and Tenses (ss, Harvey), 1933
Moon (Herbert), 1985
Moon Dance (Somtow), 1990
Moon Endureth (ss, Buchan), 1912
Moon Lake (Gresham), 1982
Moon Magic (Fortune), 1956
Moon of the Wolf (Whitten), 1967
Moon Witch (Grant), 1980
Moonbane (Sarrantonio), 1989
Moonbog (Hautala), 1982
Moonchasers and Other Stories (ss, Gorman), 1996
Moonchild (Crowley), 1929

Moonchild (McKenney), 1978
Moonchild series (McKenney), from 1978
Moondeath (Hautala), 1980
Moonlight Becomes You (Clark, M.), 1996
Moon's Revenge (Aiken, J.), 1987
Moonwalker (Hautala), 1989
Moorstone (Taylor, B.), 1988
Moorstone Sickness (Taylor, B.), 1982
Morag the Seal (Brodie-Innes), 1908
More and More Tales to Give You Goosebumps (ss, Stine), 1997
More City Jitters (ss, Fowler), 1988
More Ghost Stories of an Antiquary (ss, James, M.), 1911
More Nightmares (ss, Bloch), 1962
More Shapes Than One (ss, Chappell), 1991
More Spook Stories (ss, Benson, E.), 1934
More Tales of the Frightened (ss, Lory), 1975
More Tales of the Uneasy (ss, Hunt), 1925
More Tales of the Unexpected (ss, Dahl), 1980
More Tales to Give You Goosebumps (ss, Stine), 1995
More Than Once Upon a Time (ss, Kersh), 1964
Morgow Rises! (Tremayne), 1982
Morningstar, or The Vampires of Summer (Atkins), 1992
Mortal Fear (Cook), 1988
Mortal Glamour (Yarbro), 1985
Mortal Immortal (ss, Shelley), 1996
Mortuary (ss, Smith, C.), 1971
Mosses from an Old Manse (ss, Hawthorne, N.), 1846
Motherfuckers: The Auschwitz of Oz (Britton), 1996
Mother's Boys (Taylor, B.), 1988
Motives of Nicholas Holtz, Being the Weird Tale of the Ironville Virus (Laing), 1936
Mouldering Masks (appendix; ss, Sologub), 1907
Mountain King (Hautala), 1996
Mountain Witch (Grant), 1980
Mummy (Rice), 1989
Mummy's Purse (play, Hood), 1991
Murder at Moot Point (Millhiser), 1992
Murders in the Rue Morgue (ss, Poe), 1843
Murgunstrumm and Others (ss, Cave), 1977
Murther and Walking Spirits (Davies), 1991
Music Room (Ross, M.), 1971
Mutation (Cook), 1989
My Best Friend Is Invisible (Stine), 1997
My Cousin Geoffrey (Metcalfe), 1956
My Hairiest Adventure (Stine), 1994
My Lady of Hy-Brasil, and Other Stories (ss, Tremayne), 1987
My Name Is Death and Other New Tales of Horror (ss, Birkin), 1966
My Pretty Pony (ss, King), 1989
My Sweet Audrina (Andrews), 1982
My Uncle Oswald (Dahl), 1979
Myrtle, Rue and Cypress (poetry, Stenbock), 1883
Mysteries of the Worm: All the Cthulhu Mythos Stories of Robert Bloch (ss, Bloch), 1981
Mysteries of Udolpho (Radcliffe), 1794
Mysteries of Winterthurn (Oates), 1984
Mysterious House (ss, Blackwood, A.), 1987
Mysterious Martin (Robbins), 1912
Mysterious Mother (Walpole, Horace), 1768
Mystery (Straub), 1990
Mystery of Choice (ss, Chambers), 1897
Mystery of Cloomber (Doyle), 1888

Mystery of Collinwood (Ross, M.), 1968
Mystery of Edwin Drood (Dickens), 1870
Mystery of Fury Castle (Ross, M.), 1967
Mystery of the Beetle (Marsh), 1912
Mystery Walk (McCammon), 1983
Mystery Woman (Praed), 1913
Mythago series (Holdstock), from 1984
Mythago Wood (Holdstock), 1984
Myths of the Near Future (ss, Ballard), 1982

Naftali the Storyteller and His Horse, Sus, and Other Stories (Singer), 1976
Nailed by the Heart (Clark, S.), 1995
Naked Flesh of Feeling (ss, Williamson, J.), 1991
Naked Lunch (Burroughs), 1959
Name of the Rose (appendix; Eco), 1983
Nameless (Campbell), 1981
Nameless One (Timperley), 1978
Nameless Sins (ss, Collins), 1994
Naomi's Room (Aycliffe), 1991
Nap and Other Stories (ss, de la Mare), 1936
Narrative of Arthur Gordon Pym of Nantucket (Poe), 1838
Nathaniel (Saul), 1984
Near Death (Kilpatrick), 1994
Nebulon Horror (Cave), 1980
Necromancer (Holdstock), 1978
Necromancer (Reynolds), 1851-52
Necromancers (Benson, R.), 1909
Necropolis (Copper), 1980
Necroscope (Lumley), 1986
Necroscope II (Lumley), 1988
Necroscope III: The Source (Lumley), 1989
Necroscope IV: Deadspeak (Lumley), 1990
Necroscope V: Deadspawn (Lumley), 1991
Necroscope: Resurgence (Lumley), 1996
Necroscope: The Lost Years (Lumley), 1995
Necroscope: The Lost Years, Volume II (Lumley), 1996
Necroscope series (Lumley), from 1986
Need (Neiderman), 1992
Needful Things (King), 1991
Needing Ghosts (Campbell), 1990
Neither Man nor Dog (ss, Kersh), 1946
Neither the Sea nor the Sand (Honeycombe), 1969
Nella Waits (Millhiser), 1974
Nemesis (Hutson), 1989
Nemesis (Oates, as Smith), 1990
Neon Twilight (ss, Bryant), 1990
Neophyte (Smith, G.), 1986
Nero and Other Poems (poetry, Smith, C.), 1937
Nest of Nightmares (ss, Tuttle), 1986
Nestling (Grant), 1982
Neverland (Clegg), 1991
Nevermore (Hjortsberg), 1994
Neverwhere (Gaiman), 1996
New Arabian Nights (ss, Stevenson), 1882
New Bodies for Old (appendix; Renard), 1923
New Boy (Stine), 1994
New Evil (Stine), 1994
New Fear (Stine), 1996
New Girl (Stine), 1989
New Life for the Dead (ss, Rodgers), 1991

Off Season (Cady), 1995
Off Season (Ketchum), 1980
Offering (Suster), 1982
Offspring (Ketchum), 1991
Offspring (McKenney), 1990
Offspring (Williamson, J.), 1984
Oktober (Gallagher), 1988
Old as the World (Brodie-Innes), 1909
Old Fires and Profitable Ghosts (ss, Quiller-Couch, as Q), 1900
Old Friend of the Family (Saberhagen), 1979
Old House and Other Tales (appendix; ss, Sologub), 1915
Old House of Fear (Kirk), 1961
Old Lady Mary (Oliphant), 1884
Old Love (ss, Singer), 1979
Old Man's Beard (ss, Wakefield), 1929
Omega Man: I Am Legend (Matheson, Richard), 1971
Omen (Seltzer), 1976
On an Odd Note (ss, Kersh), 1958
On Getting to the Heart of the Monster, or the Reviewer's Revenge (play, Hood), 1983
On the Edge (ss, de la Mare), 1930
On the Far Side of the Cadillac Desert with the Dead Folks (ss, Lansdale), 1991
Once Upon a Time in the East (Grant), 1993
One Day at Horrorland (Stine), 1994
One Evil Summer (Stine), 1994
One o'Clock! or, The Knight and the Wood Daemon (play, Lewis, M.), 1811
One Rainy Night (Laymon), 1991
One Safe Place (Campbell), 1995
Only Child (Ketchum), 1995
Only Forward (Smith, Michael MArshall), 1994
Opal (appendix; ss, Meyrink), 1994
Open Door, and The Portrait (ss, Oliphant), 1885
Opener of the Way (ss, Bloch), 1945
Orchard (Grant), 1986
Orgy of the Blood Parasites (Newman, as Yeovil), 1994
Origin of the Crabs (Smith, G.), 1979
Original Dr. Shade and Other Stories (ss, Newman), 1994
Ormond (Brown), 1799
Ornaments in Jade (ss, Machen), 1924
Orphan (Stallman), 1980
Orpheus in Mayfair and Other Stories and Sketches (ss, Baring), 1909
Other (Tryon), 1971
Other Dimensions (ss, Smith, C.), 1970
Other Passenger (ss, Cross), 1944
Other Side (ss, Chetwynd-Hayes), 1988
Other Side of the Mountain (appendix; Bernanos), 1968
Others Who Returned (ss, Wakefield), 1929
OtherSyde (Straczynski), 1990
Otherworld (Harbinson), 1984
Our Lady of Darkness (Leiber), 1977
Our Lady of Pain (Blackburn), 1974
Out Are the Lights (Laymon), 1982
Out of My Head (ss, Bloch), 1986
Out of Space and Time (ss, Smith, C.), 1942
Out of the House of Life (Yarbro), 1990
Out of the Mouths of Graves (ss, Bloch), 1979
Out of the Storm (ss, Hodgson), 1975
Outbreak (Cook), 1987

Outside the Dog Museum (Carroll), 1991
Outsider and Others (ss, Lovecraft), 1939
Outward Walls (Burke), 1952
Over the Edge (ss, Ellison), 1970
Overcoat and Other Stories (appendix; ss, Gogol), 1923
Overloaded Man (ss, Ballard), 1967
Overnight (Stine), 1990
Oxrun Station series (Grant), from 1977

Paingod and Other Delusions (ss, Ellison), 1965
Paint it Black (Collins), 1995
Painted Bird (Kosinski), 1965
Painted Devils (ss, Aickman), 1979
Painted Face (ss, Onions), 1929
Palace (Yarbro), 1978
Pale Ape and Other Pulses (ss, Shiel), 1911
Pandora (Rodgers), 1994
Panic Hand (ss, Carroll), 1995
Pan's Garden (ss, Blackwood, A.), 1912
Panther! (Ryan, A.), 1981
Paradise (Brenchley), 1994
Parasite (Campbell), 1980
Parasite (ss, Doyle), 1894
Pariah (Masterton), 1983
Partaker (Chetwynd-Hayes), 1980
Particle Theory (ss, Bryant), 1981
Partners in Wonder (ss, Ellison), 1971
Party (Pike), 1989
Party Summer (Stine), 1991
Passionate Pilgrim and Other Tales (ss, James, H.), 1875
Passions and Other Stories (ss, Singer), 1975
Patch of the Odin Soldier (Grant, as Marsh), 1987
Path of the Eclipse (Yarbro), 1981
Pavilion of Frozen Women (ss, Somtow), 1995
Payne, Robert, series (Gorman), from 1994
Pearl in the Mist (Neiderman, as Andrews), 1994
Pelts (ss, Wilson, F.), 1990
Penguin Complete Ghost Stories of M. R. James (ss, James, M.), 1984
Penitent (Singer), 1983
People of the Dark (Wright), 1985
Perfect Date (Stine), 1996
Perfect Little Angels (Neiderman), 1989
Perfume: The Story of a Murderer (appendix; Süskind), 1986
Peril of Barnabas Collins (Ross, M.), 1969
Pet (Grant), 1986
Pet Sematary (King), 1983
Petals on the Wind (Andrews), 1980
Petrified (Garton, as Locke), 1991
Phantom (Kay), 1990
Phantom (Tessier), 1982
Phantom and Barnabas Collins (Ross, M.), 1969
Phantom Death and Other Stories (ss, Russell, W.), 1895
Phantom Fighter (ss, Quinn), 1966
Phantom Husband (Timperley), 1977
Phantom Lover (ss, Lee), 1886
Phantom of Edgewater Hall (Ross, M.), 1980
Phantom of Fog Island (Ross, M.), 1971
Phantom of Glencourt (Ross, M.), 1972
Phantom of the 13th Floor (Ross, M.), 1975
Phantom of the Auditorium (Stine), 1994
Phantom of the Opera (appendix; Leroux), 1911

Phantom of the Snow (Ross, M.), 1977
Phantom of the Swamp (Ross, M.), 1972
Phantom Ship (poetry, Visiak), 1912
Phantom Wedding (Ross, M.), 1976
Phantoms (Koontz), 1983
Pharos, the Egyptian (Boothby), 1899
Philosopher's Stone (Wilson, C.), 1969
Phobia (Masterton, as Luke), 1980
Phobia (Smith, G.), 1990
Phoenix (Harbinson), 1995
Piano Lessons Can Be Murder (Stine), 1993
Picture of Evil (Masterton), 1985
Pictures at an Exhibition (Thomas), 1993
Pieces of Hate (ss, Garton), 1995
Piercing (Coyne), 1979
Pigeon (appendix; Süskind), 1988
Pilgrims of the Rhine (ss, Bulwer-Lytton), 1834
Pillow Friend (Tuttle), 1996
Pin (Neiderman), 1981
Pincher Martin (Golding), 1956
Piper (Black), 1986
Place (Wright), 1989
Place of Dead Roads (Burroughs), 1983
Place to Fear (Hague), 1994
Plague (Masterton), 1977
Plague Chronicles (Smith, G.), 1993
Plant (ss, King), 1982
Plants (McKenney), 1976
Plattner Story and Others (ss, Wells), 1897
Playground (Wright), 1982
Playmates (Neiderman), 1987
Playmates (Williamson, J.), 1982
Pleasant Dreams—Nightmares (ss, Bloch), 1960
Please Don't Feed the Vampire! (Stine), 1997
Plots (ss, Capes), 1902
Pluto Pact (Smith, G.), 1982
Poems (poetry, Lewis, M.), 1812
Poems for Midnight (poetry, Wandrei), 1964
Poems in Prose (poetry, Smith, C.), 1964
Poor Things (Gray), 1992
Pope Jacynth and Other Fantastic Tales (ss, Lee), 1907
Portent (Herbert), 1992
Portrait of Dorian Gray (Kilpatrick), 1996
Portrait of Gideon Power (Bell, as Lambert), 1944
Portraits in Moonlight (ss, Jacobi), 1964
Portraits of His Children (ss, Martin, G.), 1987
Possession (James, P.), 1988
Possession of Immanuel Wolf and Other Improbable Tales (ss, Kaye), 1981
Power (Watson), 1987
Power of Light (Singer), 1980
Powers of Darkness (ss, Aickman), 1966
Prayers to Broken Stones (ss, Simmons), 1990
Precious Porcelain (Bell), 1931
Preludes and Nocturnes (Gaiman), 1991
Premonition (Williamson, J.), 1981
Presence (Saul), 1997
Presence (Silva), 1994
Pretend You Don't See Her (Clark, M.), 1997
Prey (Masterton), 1992
Price of Fear (Boyll), 1994

Priest (Disch), 1994
Primal Instinct (Walker), 1995
Primal Land series (Lumley), from 1989
Prince Alcouz and the Magician (ss, Smith, C.), 1977
Prince of Darkness (ss, Russell, R.), 1971
Prince Saroni's Wife, and The Pearl Shell Necklace (ss, Hawthorne, J.), 1882
Princess Daphne (Blayre), 1885
Princess of All Lands (ss, Kirk), 1979
Prisoners and Other Stories (ss, Gorman), 1992
Private Life, The Wheel of Time, Lord Beaupré, The Visits, Collaboration, Owen Wingrave (ss, James, H.), 1893
Private Memoirs and Confessions of a Justified Sinner (Hogg), 1824
Private School series (Grant, as Charles), from 1986
Prodigal (Tem, M.), 1991
Profane Men (Miller), 1989
Professor's Sister (Hawthorne, J.), 1888
Profits (Williamson, J.), 1984
Progeny of the Adder (Whitten), 1965
Projekt Saucer series (Harbinson), from 1980
Prom Queen (Stine), 1992
Prophecy (James, P.), 1992
Prophecy (Seltzer), 1979
Psychamok! (Lumley), 1985
Psychic Detective (Chetwynd-Hayes), 1993
Psycho (Bloch), 1959
Psycho II (Bloch), 1982
Psycho House (Bloch), 1990
Psycho series (Bloch), from 1959
Psychomech (Lumley), 1984
Psychomech series (Lumley), from 1984
Psychosphere (Lumley), 1984
Psychoville (Fowler), 1995
Punish the Sinners (Saul), 1978
Purcell Papers (ss, Le Fanu), 1880
Pure Instinct (Walker), 1996
Purple Cloud (Shiel), 1901
Purple Sapphire and Other Posthumous Papers (ss, Blayre), 1921

Q's Mystery Stories (ss, Quiller-Couch, as Q), 1937
Quadriphobia (ss, Ryan, A.), 1986
Quake (Laymon), 1995
Quatermass (Kneale), 1979
Quatermass II (play, Kneale), 1960
Quatermass and the Pit (play, Kneale), 1960
Quatermass Experiment (play, Kneale), 1959
Queen of Hell (Williamson, J.), 1981
Queen of the Damned (Rice), 1988
Quelling Eye (Gordon), 1986
Quest for the White Duck series (Grant, as Fenn), from 1986
Question of Time (Saberhagen), 1992
Quiet Night of Fear (Grant), 1981
Quintana Roo (Brandner), 1984
Quiver of Ghosts (ss, Chetwynd-Hayes), 1984
Quorum (Newman), 1994

Radon Daughters (Sinclair, I.), 1994
Rage (King, as Bachman), 1977
Raging (Stout), 1987
Raiders of the Lost Ark (Black), 1981

Rain (Gallagher), 1990
Rain (McDowell), 1983
Ralph the Bailiff and Other Tales (ss, Braddon), 1862
Ranger of the Tomb (Prest), 1845
Rapture (Tessier), 1987
Rare Breed (Leech), 1996
Rat Heads (Hood), 1997
Rats (Herbert), 1974
Rats series (Herbert), from 1974
Raven (Grant), 1993
Raven and the Phantom (Ross, M.), 1976
Ravenhurst (Ross, M.), 1975
Ravenna and Her Ghosts (ss, Lee), 1962
Ravens' Brood (Benson, E.), 1934
Ravens of the Moon (Grant), 1978
Ravenscarne and Other Ghost Stories (ss, Williams), 1991
Raymond and Agnes (ss, Lewis, M.), 1820
Razor's Edge (Walker), 1989
Real Thing and Other Tales (ss, James, H.), 1893
Re-Animator (ss, Lovecraft), 1991
Reaping (Taylor, B.), 1980
Rebecca (du Maurier), 1938
Rebel Angels (Davies), 1981
Reborn (Wilson, F.), 1990
Red (Ketchum), 1995
Red Bride (Fowler), 1992
Red Death (Elrod), 1993
Red Dragon (Harris, T.), 1981
Red Dreams (ss, Etchison), 1984
Red, Red Robin (Gallagher), 1995
Reflection (Neiderman), 1987
Reflection (Scott, M.), 1992
Reflections on The Name of the Rose (appendix; Eco), 1984
Refuge (Brenchley), 1989
Reginald and Reginald in Russia (ss, Saki), 1921
Reginald in Russia (ss, Saki), 1910
Regulators (King, as Bachman), 1996
Rehearsal Night (Long), 1981
Reign (Williamson, C.), 1990
Reincarnation in Venice (Ehrlich), 1979
Reincarnation of Peter Proud (Ehrlich), 1974
Relics (Hutson), 1986
Reluctant Ghost-Hunter (ss, Kennett), 1991
Remedy (Drake), 1925
Remember Me (Clark, M.), 1994
Remember Me (Pike), 1989
Remember Me 2: The Return (Pike), 1994
Remember Me 3: The Last Story (Pike), 1995
Remember Me series (Pike), from 1989
Rendezvous in Averoigne (ss, Smith, C.), 1988
Renegades (Hutson), 1991
Rent in the Veil (Lawrence), 1951
Reprisal (Wilson, F.), 1991
Requiem (Joyce), 1995
Requiem for a Glass Heart (Lindsey), 1996
Residence Afresh (Lawrence), 1969
Restless Nights (appendix; ss, Buzzati), 1983
Résumé with Monsters (Spencer), 1995
Resurrected (Smith, G.), 1991
Resurrection Dreams (Laymon), 1988
Resurrectionist (Monteleone), 1995

Return (de la Mare), 1910
Return of Count Electric and Other Stories (ss, Spencer), 1993
Return of the Deep Ones, and Other Mythos Tales (ss, Lumley), 1994
Return of the Howling (Brandner), 1979
Return of the Living Dead (Russo), 1978
Return of the Lloigor (ss, Wilson, C.), 1974
Return of the Mummy (Stine), 1994
Return of the Werewolf (Smith, G.), 1977
Return of Uncle Walter (ss, Baker, D.), 1948
Return to Harken House (Aiken, J.), 1988
Revelation (Harbinson), 1982
Revelation (Little), 1989
Revelations in Black (ss, Jacobi), 1947
Revenant (Tem, M.), 1994
Revenge of Dracula (Tremayne), 1978
Revenge of Taurus (Lory), 1974
Revenge of the Lawn Gnomes (Stine), 1995
Revenge of the Manitou (Masterton), 1979
Reverbstorm (Britton), 1994-95
Rhoda Broughton's Ghost Stories and Other Tales of Mystery and Suspense (ss, Broughton), 1995
Rich Girl (Stine), 1997
Richard Matheson (ss, Matheson, Richard), 1989
Riddle and Other Tales (ss, de la Mare), 1923
Ride the Wind (Gordon), 1989
Ridge (Cantrell), 1989
Right to Kill (Ryan, R.), 1936
Rim of Morning (Sloane), 1964
Rim of the Unknown (ss, Long), 1972
Ring of Roses (Blackburn), 1965
Ringstones (Sarban), 1961
Ringstones and Other Curious Tales (ss, Sarban), 1951
Ripper (Slade), 1994
Rita Hayworth and Shawshank Redemption (ss, King), 1983
Ritual (Masterton), 1988
Ritual (Williamson, J.), 1979
Ritual in the Dark (Wilson, C.), 1960
Rivals (Prest), 1847
River Witch (Grant), 1979
Riverrun (Somtow), 1991
Riverrun series (Somtow), from 1991
Riverrun Trilogy (Somtow), 1996
Road Kill (Ketchum), 1994
Road to Hell (Weinberg), 1997
Road to Nowhere (Pike), 1993
Roads (Quinn), 1948
Roadwork (King, as Bachman), 1981
Roald Dahl Selection (ss, Dahl), 1980
Roald Dahl's Tales of the Unexpected (ss, Dahl), 1979
Romance of the Forest, Interspersed with Some Pieces of Poetry (Radcliffe), 1791
Romance with Capsicum (Hughes), 1995
Romantic Tales (ss, Lewis, M.), 1808
Roofworld (Fowler), 1988
Rook (Masterton), 1996
Rook series (Masterton), from 1996
Rookwood (Ainsworth), 1834
Room in the Tower and Other Stories (ss, Benson, E.), 1912
Rose Madder (King), 1995
Rose Royal (Nesbit), 1912

Rosemary's Baby (Levin), 1967
Rothby (Ross, M.), 1978
Round the Fire Stories (ss, Doyle), 1908
Round the Red Lamp, Being Facts and Fancies of Medical Life
    (ss, Doyle), 1894
Ruben, Martin, series (Williamson, J.), from 1979
Ruby (Neiderman, as Andrews), 1991
Rules of Life (ss, Weldon), 1987
Runagates Club (ss, Buchan), 1928
Runaway (Gresham), 1988
Runaway (Stine), 1997
Rune (Fowler), 1990
Runner in the Dark (Gorman), 1996
Runner in the Snow (play, Sloane), 1931
Running Man (King, as Bachman), 1982
Running Wild (Ballard), 1988
Rushing to Paradise (Ballard), 1994
Russian Wolfhound (appendix; ss, Pavic), 1979

Sabat series (Smith, G.), from 1982
Sacrament (Barker), 1996
Sacred Fount (James, H.), 1901
Sacrifice (Masterton), 1985
Sad Road to the Sea (ss, Kersh), 1947
Safety of Unknown Cities (Taylor, L.), 1995
Sagittarius (ss, Russell, R.), 1971
Saint-Germain Chronicles (ss, Yarbro), 1983
Saint-Germain series (Yarbro), from 1978
St. Leon (Godwin), 1799
St. Mark's Horses (appendix; poetry, Pavic), 1978
Saint Peter's Wolf (Cadnum), 1991
Salem's Child (Walker), 1987
'Salem's Lot (King), 1975
Sallust, Gregory, series (Wheatley), from 1964
Salome and the Head (Nesbit), 1909
Salvage Rites and Other Stories (ss, Watson), 1989
Samaritan (Brenchley), 1988
Sandalwood (poetry, Smith, C.), 1925
Sandman series (Gaiman), from 1990
Saquaro Riptide (Partridge), 1997
Sardonic Tales (appendix; ss, Villiers), 1927
Sardonicus and Other Stories (ss, Russell, R.), 1961
Satan in Goray (Singer), 1955
Satan Whispers (Ross, M.), 1981
Satan: His Psychotherapy and Cure by the Unfortunate Dr.
    Kassler, J.S.P.S (Leven), 1982
Satanist (Wheatley), 1960
Satanists (Holdstock, as Black), 1978
Satan's Child (Saxon), 1967
Satan's Circus and Other Stories (ss, Smith, L.), 1932
Satan's Island (Ross, M.), 1975
Satan's Serenade (Monahan), 1989
Satan's Snowdrop (Smith, G.), 1980
Savage (Laymon), 1993
Savant (Miller), 1994
Sawney Bean, the Man-Eater of Midlothian (Prest), 1851
Saxophone Dreams (Royle), 1996
Say Cheese and Die (Stine), 1992
Say Cheese and Die—Again! (Stine), 1996
Say You Love Satan (St. Clair), 1987
Scalehunter's Beautiful Daughter (ss, Shepard), 1988

Scar (Suster), 1981
Scare Tactics (ss, Farris), 1988
Scarecrow Walks at Midnight (Stine), 1994
Scared Stiff: Tales of Sex and Death (ss, Campbell), 1987
Scarf (Bloch), 1947
Scarf of Passion (Bloch), 1948
Scarlet Boy (Calder-Marshall), 1961
Scarlet Letter (Hawthorne, N.), 1850
Scars, and Other Distinguishing Marks (ss, Matheson, Richard
    Christian), 1987
Scavenger Hunt (Pike), 1989
Scavengers (Skal), 1980
Scent of New-Mown Hay (Blackburn), 1958
Schamyl (Prest), 1856
School (Wright), 1990
Scissorman (Chadbourn), 1997
Scourge (Sharman, as Scott), 1980
Scream (Skipp), 1988
Scream and Scream Again (Saxon), 1967
Scream at Midnight (ss, Brennan), 1963
Scream of the Evil Grave (Stine), 1997
Screams (Bloch), 1989
Sea Demons (Rousseau), 1924
Sea Priestess (Fortune), 1938
Sea Whispers (ss, Jacobs), 1926
Sea-Kissed (ss, Bloch), 1945
Séance and Other Stories (ss, Singer), 1968
Seance for a Vampire (Saberhagen), 1994
Search for Joseph Tully (Hallahan), 1974
Searing (Coyne), 1980
Season of Mists (Gaiman), 1992
Season of Passage (Pike), 1992
Sebastian, Don, series (Daniels), from 1978
Second Chance (Williamson, C.), 1994
Second Child (Saul), 1990
Second Evil (Stine), 1992
Second Horror (Stine), 1994
Second Roald Dahl Selection (ss, Dahl), 1987
Second Wish, and Other Exhalations (ss, Lumley), 1995
Secret (Stine), 1993
Secret Admirer (Stine), 1996
Secret Agent Grandma (Stine), 1997
Secret Bedroom (Stine), 1991
Secret Corridor (Gordon), 1990
Secret Glory (Machen), 1922
Secret Life of Houses (ss, Bradfield), 1988
Secret of Anatomy (Morris), 1994
Secret of Barnabas Collins (Ross, M.), 1969
Secret of Mallet Castle (Ross, M.), 1966
Secret of the Pale Lover (Ross, M.), 1969
Secret Path (Pike), 1996
Secret Place and Other Cornish Stories (ss, Baker, D.), 1977
Secret Sin of Septimus Brope, and Other Stories (ss, Saki), 1995
Secret Songs (ss, Leiber), 1968
Secret Strangers (Tessier), 1990
Secrets of Dr. Taverner (ss, Fortune), 1926
Secrets of the Morning (Neiderman, as Andrews), 1991
Sedalia (ss, Schow), 1991
Seductions (Garton), 1984
See You Later (Pike), 1990
Seeds of Evil (Bingley), 1988

Seeds of Yesterday (Andrews), 1984
Seeing Red (ss, Schow), 1990
Seeker to the Dead (Burrage), 1942
Seen and the Unseen (ss, Marsh), 1900
Selected Short Stories of Algernon Blackwood (ss, Blackwood, A.), 1945
Selected Short Stories of the Supernatural (ss, Oliphant), 1985
Selected Stories (ss, Dahl), 1970
Selected Stories (ss, Kersh), 1943
Selected Stories and Sketches (ss, Hogg), 1982
Selected Stories of Robert Bloch (ss, Bloch), 1987
Selected Tales (ss, Blackwood, A.), 1964
Selected Tales: Stories of the Supernatural and the Uncanny (ss, Blackwood, A.), 1942
Selected Works of Elizabeth Massie (Massie), 1993
Selected Writings of E. T. A. Hoffmann (appendix; ss, Hoffmann), 1969
Sense of the Past (James, H.), 1917
Sentinel (Konvitz), 1974
Sentinel II (Konvitz), 1979
Septimius Felton (Hawthorne, N.), 1872
Sepulchre (Herbert), 1987
Serapion Brethren (appendix; Hoffmann), 1886
Serpent's Kiss (Gorman, as Ransom), 1992
Servant of the Bones (Rice), 1996
Servants of Twilight (Koontz), 1988
Seven Gothic Tales (ss, Dinesen), 1934
Seven Short Stories (ss, de la Mare), 1931
Seven Spears of the W'dch'ck (Grant), 1988
Seventh Guest (Costello, M.), 1995
Severed Hand (Saxon, as Lecale), 1974
Sex & Blood (ss, Dee), 1994
Sex and the Single Vampire (ss, Kilpatrick), 1994
Sex Diary of Gerard Sorme (Wilson, C.), 1963
Shackled (Garton), 1997
Shade (Dee, as Darke), 1994
Shades of Dracula (ss, Stoker), 1982
Shades of Evil (Cave), 1982
Shades of Night (Hautala), 1995
Shadow (Visiak), 1936
Shadow Child (Citro), 1987
Shadow Dance (Palmer), 1994
Shadow Dreams (Massie), 1996
Shadow Games (Gorman), 1993
Shadow Guests (Aiken, J.), 1980
Shadow Man (Gresham), 1986
Shadow of Death (poetry, Stenbock), 1893
Shadow on the Doorstep (ss, Bryant), 1987
Shadow out of Time and Other Tales of Horror (ss, Derleth; Lovecraft), 1968
Shadow over Emerald Castle (Ross, M.), 1975
Shadow over Innsmouth (ss, Lovecraft), 1936
Shadow over Denby (Ross, M.), 1976
Shadow Play (ss, Beaumont), 1964
Shadoweyes (Ptacek), 1984
Shadowfires (Koontz, as Nichols), 1987
Shadowings (ss, Hearn), 1900
Shadowland (Straub), 1980
Shadowman (Etchison), 1993
Shadows (Hutson), 1985
Shadows (Saul), 1993

Shadows of Death (Williamson, J.), 1989
Shadows with Eyes (ss, Leiber), 1962
Shadowy Thing (Drake), 1928
Shaft (Schow), 1990
Shape of Fear (Long), 1971
Shapes (Vance), 1991
Shapes in the Fire (ss, Shiel), 1896
Shapes of Midnight (ss, Brennan), 1980
Shards (Piccirilli), 1996
Sharper Knives (ss, Fowler), 1992
Sharpness on the Neck (Saberhagen), 1996
Shatterday (ss, Ellison), 1980
Shattered (Koontz, as Dwyer), 1973
She Wakes (Ketchum), 1989
She Who Sleeps (Rohmer), 1928
Shee (Donnelly), 1991
Sheep (Maginn), 1994
Shepherd's Calendar (ss, Hogg), 1829
Sheridan Le Fanu: The Diabolic Genius (ss, Le Fanu), 1959
Shining (King), 1977
Shining Pyramid (ss, Machen), 1923
Ship of Dreams (Lumley), 1986
Shock! (ss, Matheson, Richard), 1961
Shock 1 (ss, Matheson, Richard), 1979
Shock 2 (ss, Matheson, Richard), 1964
Shock 3 (ss, Matheson, Richard), 1966
Shock 4 (ss, Matheson, Richard), 1980
Shock Waves (ss, Matheson, Richard), 1970
Shocker on Shock Street (Stine), 1995
Shocks (ss, Blackwood, A.), 1935
Shockwaves (Tessier), 1983
Shooting Star (Bloch), 1958
Shores of Space (ss, Matheson, Richard), 1957
Short Friday and Other Stories (ss, Singer), 1964
Short Stories (ss, Saki), 1976
Short Stories of Saki (ss, Saki), 1930
Short Stories of To-Day and Yesterday (ss, Blackwood, A.), 1930
Shrewd Todie and Lyzer the Miser and Other Children's Stories (Singer), 1994
Shrike (Donnelly), 1994
Shrine (Herbert), 1983
Shrine (Holdstock, as Faulcon), 1984
Shrinking Man (Matheson, Richard), 1956
Shroud (Coyne), 1983
Shudders and Shivers (ss, Chetwynd-Hayes), 1995
Shunned House (ss, Lovecraft), 1928
Shuttered Room and Other Pieces (Lovecraft), 1959
Shuttered Room and Other Tales of Horror (ss, Derleth; Lovecraft), 1970
Sibs (Wilson, F.), 1991
Sicilian Romance (Radcliffe), 1790
Sick (Bonansinga), 1995
Sickness of the Soul (Maginn), 1995
Sight Unseen (Neiderman), 1987
Signal to Noise (Gaiman), 1992
Signalman and Other Ghost Stories (ss, Dickens), 1990
Signs and Portents (ss, Yarbro), 1984
Signs of Life (Harrison), 1997
Silence of the Lambs (Harris, T.), 1988
Silent Night (Clark, M.), 1995
Silent Night (Stine), 1991

Silent Night 2 (Stine), 1993
Silent Night 3 (Stine), 1996
Silent, White and Beautiful, and Other Stories (ss, Robbins), 1920
Silver Bullet (King), 1985
Silver Pillow (ss, Disch), 1987
Silver Skull (Daniels), 1979
Silver Thorn (ss, Walpole, Hugh), 1928
Sin Eater and Other Scientific Impossibilities (ss, Walter), 1967
Sineater (Massie), 1992
Sinful Ones (Leiber), 1953
Sinister Garden (Ross, M.), 1972
Sins of Omission (Yarbro), 1980
Siren (appendix; ss, Buzzati), 1984
Sister Night (Wilson, F.), 1993
Sister, Sister (Neiderman), 1992
Six Messiahs (Frost), 1995
Six-Cent Sam's (ss, Hawthorne, J.), 1893
Sixty Selected Poems (poetry, Brennan), 1985
Skeleton Closet of Jules de Grandin (ss, Quinn), 1976
Skeleton Clutch (Prest), 1842
Skeleton Crew (ss, King), 1985
Skeleton Key (Grant), 1986
Skeletons (Sarrantonio), 1992
Ski Weekend (Stine), 1991
Skin (Koja), 1993
Skull (Hutson), 1982
Skull of the Marquis de Sade and Other Stories (ss, Bloch), 1965
Skyscape (Cadnum), 1994
Slayer of Souls (Chambers), 1920
Sleep No More (ss, Rolt), 1948
Sleep, Pale Sister (Harris, J.), 1994
Sleep Tight (Costello, M.), 1987
Sleepeasy (Wright), 1993
Sleeping in Flame (Carroll), 1988
Sleepless (Masterton), 1993
Sleepwalk (Saul), 1990
Sleepwalker (Cadnum), 1991
Sleepwalker (Stine), 1991
Slice (Miller), 1990
Slime Beast (Smith, G.), 1975
Slime Zone (Hood), 1996
Slimer (Knight), 1983
Slippage (ss, Ellison), 1997
Slipping into Darkness (Partridge), 1994
Sliver (Levin), 1991
Slob (Miller), 1987
Slow (ss, Campbell), 1985
Slugs (Hutson), 1982
Slugs series (Hutson), from 1982
Slumber Party (Pike), 1985
Slumming in Voodooland (ss, Stableford), 1991
Small Assassin (ss, Bradbury), 1962
Smell of Evil (ss, Birkin), 1965
Smoke of the Snake (ss, Jacobi), 1994
Smoking Leg and Other Stories (ss, Metcalfe), 1925
Snake Eyes (Oates, as Smith), 1992
Snake Lady and Other Stories (ss, Lee), 1954
Snakes (Smith, G.), 1986
Snowbeast (Tremayne), 1983
Snowfall and Other Chilling Events (ss, Walter), 1965
Snow-Image and Other Twice-Told Tales (ss, Hawthorne, N.), 1851

Snowman (Stine), 1991
So Dark a Heritage (Long), 1966
So Pale, So Cold, So Fair (ss, Birkin), 1970
Soft and Others (ss, Wilson, F.), 1989
Soft Machine (Burroughs), 1961
Soft Side (ss, James, H.), 1900
Soft Whisper of the Dead (Grant), 1982
Sole Survivor (Koontz), 1997
Solitary Hunters, and The Abyss (Keller), 1948
Solomon Organization (Neiderman), 1993
Some Chinese Ghosts (ss, Hearn), 1887
Some Ghost Stories (ss, Burrage), 1927
Some of Your Blood (Sturgeon), 1961
Some Stories (ss, de la Mare), 1962
Some Women of the University, Being a Last Selection from the
    Strange Papers of Christopher Blayre (ss, Blayre), 1934
Somebody Come and Play (McNally), 1987
Someone in the Dark (ss, Derleth), 1941
Someone in the Room (ss, Burrage, as Ex-Private X), 1931
Someone Like You (ss, Dahl), 1953
Someone's Watching (Neiderman), 1983
Something about Cats and Other Pieces (ss, Lovecraft), 1949
Something Near (ss, Derleth), 1945
Something Stirs (Grant), 1991
Something Wicked This Way Comes (Bradbury), 1962
Something's Watching (Grant), 1993
Somewhere in Time (Matheson, Richard), 1980
Somewhere South of Midnight (Laws), 1996
Son of the Endless Night (Farris), 1985
Son of the Morning (Oates), 1978
Son of the Werewolf (Smith, G.), 1978
Song of Kali (Simmons), 1985
Song of Stone (Banks), 1997
Songs of a Dead Dreamer (ss, Ligotti), 1986
Sonja Blue series (Collins), from 1989
Sons of Noah and Other Stories (ss, Cady), 1992
Sorcerer's Apprentice, Day (appendix; Ewers), 1927
Sorcery Club (O'Donnell), 1912
Sorcery in Shad: Tales of the Primal Land, Volume Three (ss,
    Lumley), 1991
Sorme, Gerard, series (Wilson, C.), from 1960
Soul Eater (Jeter), 1983
Soul of Countess Adrian (Praed), 1891
Soul-Mate (Oates, as Smith), 1989
Soulstorm (Williamson, C.), 1986
Sound of His Horn (Sarban), 1952
Sound of Midnight (Grant), 1978
Space Vampires (Wilson, C.), 1976
Spaceship Built of Stone and Other Stories (ss, Tuttle), 1987
Spanky (Fowler), 1994
Spares (Smith, Michael MArshall), 1996
Spawn (Hutson), 1983
Spawn of Satan (ss, Birkin), 1971
Spawn of the Winds (Lumley), 1978
Spear (Herbert), 1978
Specialist series (Saxon, as Lecale), from 1973
Species (Navarro), 1995
Specters (Kalogridis, as Dillard), 1991
Spectral Bride (Bowen, M.), 1942
Spectral Mist (Ross, M.), 1972
Spectre (Laws), 1986

Spectre of the Camera (Hawthorne, J.), 1888
Spellbound (Pike), 1988
Spells and Philtres (poetry, Smith, C.), 1958
Sphinx (Masterton), 1978
Spider (McGrath), 1990
Spider Glass (ss, Yarbro), 1991
Spiderweb (Bloch), 1954
Spinach, and Reconciliation (ss, Benson, E.), 1924
Spinoza of Market Street and Other Stories (ss, Singer), 1961
Spiral (Lindsey), 1986
Spire (Golding), 1964
Spirit (Masterton), 1995
Spitfire Grave and Other Stories (ss, Gordon), 1979
Spook (Vance), 1990
Spook Stories (ss, Benson, E.), 1928
Spooksville series (Pike), from 1995
Square Egg and Other Sketches, with Three Plays (ss, Saki), 1924
Stage Fright (McNally), 1995
Staircase to the Sea (ss, Turner), 1974
Stake (Laymon), 1990
Stalin's Teardrops and Other Stories (ss, Watson), 1991
Stalking (Holdstock, as Faulcon), 1987
Stalking the Nightmare (ss, Ellison), 1982
Stallion Gate (Smith, Martin Cruz), 1986
Stand (King), 1978
Stanley Brereton (Ainsworth), 1881
Star Child (Stewart), 1974
Star Stalker (Bloch), 1968
Star-Treader and Other Poems (poetry, Smith, C.), 1912
Statement of Randolph Carter (ss, Lovecraft), 1976
Stay Out of the Basement (Stine), 1992
Steel Gods (Sharman, as Gronmark), 1990
Steel Valentine (ss, Lansdale), 1991
Step (ss, Benson, E.), 1930
Step into Terror (Ross, M.), 1973
Stepford Wives (Levin), 1972
Stephen King's Skeleton Crew (ss, King), 1985
Steppin' Out, Summer '68 (ss, Lansdale), 1992
Stepsister (Stine), 1991
Stepsister 2 (Stine), 1995
Stewards of Stormhaven: Cellars of the Dead (Ross, M.), 1976
Stiff Lips (Billson), 1996
Still Life (Donnelly), 1993
Still More Tales to Give You Goosebumps (ss, Stine), 1996
Stillwatch (Clark, M.), 1984
Sting of Death (appendix; ss, Sologub), 1904
Stinger (McCammon), 1988
Stir of Echoes (Matheson, Richard), 1958
Stitch (Morris), 1991
Stolen Angels (Hutson), 1996
Stolen Bacillus and Other Incidents (ss, Wells), 1895
Stolen Souls (Sackett), 1987
Stone (Donnelly), 1990
Stone Dragon and Other Tragic Romances (ss, Gilchrist), 1894
Stone Shadow (Miller), 1989
Store (Little), 1996
Stories by Mama Lansdale's Youngest Boy (ss, Lansdale), 1991
Stories for Children (Singer), 1984
Stories from The Clock Strikes Twelve (ss, Wakefield), 1961
Stories from The Other Passenger (ss, Cross), 1961
Stories of Darkness and Dread (ss, Brennan), 1973

Stories of the Seen and Unseen (ss, Oliphant), 1889
Stories of the Supernatural (ss, James, H.), 1970
Stories Weird and Wonderful (ss, Nisbet), 1900
Storyman (Kelleher), 1996
Strange and the Damned (ss, Baker, D.), 1964
Strange Angels (Koja), 1994
Strange Case of Dr. Jekyll and Mr. Hyde (Stevenson), 1886
Strange Conflict (Wheatley), 1941
Strange Dream and Other Stories (ss, Broughton), 1881
Strange Eons (Bloch), 1979
Strange Harvest (ss, Wandrei), 1965
Strange Highways (ss, Koontz), 1995
Strange Journeys (ss, Baker, D.), 1969
Strange Objects (Crew), 1990
Strange Papers of Dr. Blayre (ss, Blayre), 1932
Strange Seed (Wright), 1978
Strange Shadows (ss, Smith, C.), 1989
Strange Stories (ss, Allen), 1884
Strange Stories (ss, Blackwood, A.), 1929
Strange Story (Bulwer-Lytton), 1862
Strange Things and Stranger Places (ss, Campbell), 1993
Strange Wine (ss, Ellison), 1978
Strange World of Arthur Machen (ss, Machen), 1960
Stranger (Timperley), 1976
Stranger Is Watching (Clark, M.), 1978
Strangers (Koontz), 1986
Strangers at Collins House (Ross, M.), 1967
Stranglehold (Ketchum), 1995
Stratagem and Other Stories (ss, Crowley), 1929
Stray Leaves from Strange Literature (ss, Hearn), 1884
Strayers from Sheol (ss, Wakefield), 1961
Striker (Suster), 1984
String of Pearls (James, G.), 1832
String of Pearls (Prest), 1846-48
Stroud, Abraham, series (Walker, as Caine), from 1991
Student (ss, Bulwer-Lytton), 1835
Studies of Death (ss, Stenbock), 1894
Stunts (Grant), 1990
Styx (Hyde), 1982
Sub Rosa (ss, Aickman), 1968
Subjugated Beast (Ryan, R.), 1939
Succumb (Dee), 1994
Such Stuff as Screams Are Made Of (ss, Bloch), 1979
Suckers (Billson), 1993
Sucking Pit (Smith, G.), 1975
Suffer the Children (Saul), 1977
Suicide Club, and Other Stories (ss, Stevenson), 1970
Summer of Night (Simmons), 1991
Summer of the Shaman (Ross, M.), 1982
Summoning (Little), 1993
Sunburn (Stine), 1993
Sundial (Jackson), 1958
Sunglasses after Dark (Collins), 1989
Supernatural Short Stories of Robert Louis Stevenson (ss, Stevenson), 1976
Supernatural Stories of Sir Walter Scott (ss, Scott, W.), 1977
Supernatural Tales (ss, Lee), 1955
Supernatural Tales of Sir Arthur Conan Doyle (ss, Doyle), 1988
Superstitious (Stine), 1995
Supping with Panthers (Holland), 1996
Surly, Sullen Bell (ss, Kirk), 1962

Surprise Party (Stine), 1990
Surrogate (Sharman), 1980
Surrogate Child (Neiderman), 1988
Surrounded (Koontz, as Coffey), 1974
Survivor (Herbert), 1976
Survivor and Others (ss, Derleth; Lovecraft), 1957
Swamp! (Tremayne), 1985
Swamp Foetus (ss, Brite), 1993
Swan Song (McCammon), 1987
Sweeney Todd, The Demon Barber of Fleet Street (Prest), 1878
Sweet Heart (James, P.), 1990
Sweet Nothings (Lucas), 1988
Sweet William (Palmer), 1995
Sweetheart, Sweetheart (Taylor, B.), 1977
Sweetman Curve (Masterton), 1979
Sweet-Scented Name and Other Fairy Tales, Fables and Stories (appendix; ss, Sologub), 1915
Switch (Sharman), 1984
Switch Bitch (ss, Dahl), 1974
Switch on the Night (Bradbury), 1955
Switched (Stine), 1995
Synchronicity, or Something (ss, Lumley), 1988
Synthetic Man (Sturgeon), 1957

Tail of the Arabian, Knight (Grant, as Marsh), 1986
Taking It (Cadnum), 1995
Tale of an Empty House, and Bagnell Terrace (ss, Benson, E.), 1925
Tale of the Body Thief (Rice), 1992
Tale of the Empty House and Other Ghost Stories (ss, Benson, E.), 1986
Tale of Three Wishes (Singer), 1976
Tales and Fantasies (ss, Stevenson), 1905
Tales and Sketches of the Ettrick Shepherd (ss, Hogg), 1837
Tales before Midnight (ss, Benét), 1939
Tales for Christmas Eve (ss, Broughton), 1872
Tales from Beyond (ss, Chetwynd-Hayes), 1982
Tales from the Dark Lands (ss, Chetwynd-Hayes), 1984
Tales from the Haunted House (ss, Chetwynd-Hayes), 1986
Tales from the Hidden World (ss, Chetwynd-Hayes), 1988
Tales from the New Twilight Zone (ss, Straczynski), 1989
Tales from the Nightside: Dark Fantasy (ss, Grant), 1981
Tales from the Other Side (ss, Chetwynd-Hayes), 1983
Tales from the Shadows (ss, Chetwynd-Hayes), 1986
Tales from Underwood (ss, Keller), 1952
Tales in a Jugular Vein (ss, Bloch), 1965
Tales of Algernon Blackwood (ss, Blackwood, A.), 1938
Tales of Chinatown (ss, Rohmer), 1922
Tales of Darkness (ss, Chetwynd-Hayes), 1981
Tales of East and West (ss, Rohmer), 1932
Tales of Fear and Fantasy (ss, Chetwynd-Hayes), 1977
Tales of Hoffmann (appendix; ss, Hoffmann), 1943
Tales of Horror and the Supernatural (ss, Machen), 1948
Tales of Love and Death (ss, Aickman), 1977
Tales of Men and Ghosts (ss, Wharton), 1910
Tales of Science and Sorcery (ss, Smith, C.), 1964
Tales of Secret Egypt (ss, Rohmer), 1918
Tales of Soldiers and Civilians (ss, Bierce), 1891
Tales of Terror (ss, Nesbit), 1983
Tales of Terror and Darkness (ss, Blackwood, A.), 1977
Tales of Terror and Mystery (ss, Doyle), 1922

Tales of Terror and the Unknown (ss, Blackwood, A.), 1965
Tales of the Grotesque and Arabesque (ss, Poe), 1840
Tales of the Mysterious and Macabre (ss, Blackwood, A.), 1967
Tales of the Supernatural (ss, Blackwood, A.), 1983
Tales of the Uncanny and Supernatural (ss, Blackwood, A.), 1949
Tales of the Uneasy (ss, Hunt), 1911
Tales of the Werewolf Clan, Volume 1 (ss, Munn), 1979
Tales of the Werewolf Clan, Volume 2 (ss, Munn), 1979
Tales of Wonder (poetry, Lewis, M.), 1801
Tales to Give You Goosebumps (ss, Stine), 1994
Talisman (Holdstock, as Faulcon), 1983
Talisman (King; Straub), 1984
Taltos: Lives of the Mayfair Witches (Rice), 1994
Tap, Tap (Martin, D.), 1994
Tarnished Gold (Neiderman, as Andrews), 1996
Tarra Khash: Hrossak! Tales of the Primal Land, Volume Two (ss, Lumley), 1991
Taste and Other Tales (ss, Dahl), 1979
Tattoo and Other Stories (ss, Cady), 1978
Tea Party (Grant), 1985
Teacher's Pet (Neiderman), 1986
Technique of the Ghost Story and Three Short Stories (ss, Benson, E.), 1993
Temple (ss, Benson, E.), 1925
Tempter (Collins), 1990
Tempting Fate (Yarbro), 1982
Ten Minute Stories (ss, Blackwood, A.), 1914
Ten Ounce Siesta (Partridge), 1998
Ten Tales Tall and True (ss, Gray), 1993
Tenant and Other Stories (ss, Baker, D.), 1985
Tender, Loving Care (Neiderman), 1984
Tendrils (Knight, as Childer), 1986
Tengu (Masterton), 1983
Tenth Crusade (Hyde), 1983
Terminal (Cook), 1993
Terminal Beach (ss, Ballard), 1964
Terminations and Other Stories (ss, James, H.), 1895
Terraces of Night, Being Further Chronicles of the Club of the Round Table (ss, Lawrence), 1932
Terribly Wild Flowers (ss, Kersh), 1962
Terror (Bloch), 1962
Terror: A Fantasy (Machen), 1917
Terror at Dark Harbor (Ross, M.), 1975
Terror by Night (ss, Chetwynd-Hayes), 1974
Terror in the Night and Other Stories (ss, Bloch), 1958
Terrors of the Sea (ss, Hodgson), 1996
Testament (Morrell), 1975
Tethered (Martin, D.), 1979
There He Keeps Them Very Well (McNally), 1994
There Is a Serpent in Eden (Bloch), 1979
Thermals of August (ss, Bryant), 1992
These Charming People (ss, Arlen), 1923
They Return at Evening (ss, Wakefield), 1928
They Thirst (McCammon), 1981
They Used Dark Forces (Wheatley), 1964
They Walk at Twilight (ss, Williams), 1977
Thief of Always (Barker), 1993
Thin Ghost, and Others (ss, James, M.), 1919
Thing in the Cellar (ss, Keller), 1940
Things as They Are (Godwin), 1794
Thinner (King, as Bachman), 1984

Third Evil (Stine), 1992
Third from the Sun (ss, Matheson, Richard), 1955
Third Grave (Case), 1981
Third Horror (Stine), 1994
Third Specter (Ross, M.), 1967
Thirst (Smith, G.), 1980
Thirst 2: The Plague (Smith, G.), 1987
Thirteen Ghost Stories (ss, James, M.), 1935
Thirteen O'Clock: Stories of Several Worlds (ss, Benét), 1937
This Evil Village (Ross, M.), 1977
This Mortal Coil (ss, Asquith), 1947
This Shrouded Night (Ross, M.), 1975
Thorn (Saberhagen), 1980
Thrawn Janet (ss, Stevenson), 1906
Three Freaks (Robbins), 1934
Three Impostors (ss, Machen), 1895
Threshold (Millhiser), 1984
Thrill Club (Stine), 1994
Thrills, Chills, and Nightmares (Pike), 1987
Throat (Straub), 1993
Throat Sprockets (Lucas), 1987
Through Channels (Matheson, Richard), 1989
Through the Dark Curtain (Saxon), 1968
Through the Walls (ss, Campbell), 1981
Throwback (Smith, G.), 1985
Tick Tock, You're Dead! (Stine), 1995
Tick-Tock (Koontz), 1995
Ticket That Exploded (Burroughs), 1962
Tides (Tem, M.), 1996
Tiger Skin (ss, Hunt), 1924
Tigerman of Terrahpur (Saxon, as Lecale), 1973
Tight Little Stitches on a Dead Man's Back (ss, Lansdale), 1992
Time and Chance (Brennert), 1990
Time of the Eye (ss, Ellison), 1974
Time Terror (Pike), 1997
Time: The Semi-Final Frontier (Grant), 1994
Titus Crow (Lumley), 1996
Titus Crow series (Lumley), from 1974
Titus Crow, Volume Two (Lumley), 1997
To the Dark Tower (Long), 1969
To the Devil—a Daughter (Wheatley), 1953
To Wake the Dead (Campbell), 1980
To Walk the Night (Sloane), 1937
Toady (Morris), 1989
Todd Dossier (Bloch, as Young), 1969
Tom Ossington's Ghost (Marsh), 1898
Tomato Cain, and Other Stories (ss, Kneale), 1949
Tomb (Wilson, F.), 1984
Tomb and Other Tales (ss, Lovecraft), 1969
Tomb from Beyond (ss, Jacobi), 1977
Tommyknockers (King), 1987
Tomorrow's Eve (appendix; Villiers), 1982
Tongues of Conscience (ss, Hichens), 1900
Tongues of Fire and Other Sketches (ss, Blackwood, A.), 1924
Tooth and Claw (Masterton), 1997
Tooth Fairy (Joyce), 1996
Toplin (McDowell), 1985
Topsy-Turvy Emperor of China (Singer), 1971
Torched! (Knight), 1986
Torments (Cantrell), 1990
Tortuga Hill Gang's Last Ride (ss, Collins), 1991

Torturer (Saxon), 1966
Totem (Morrell), 1979
Totentanz (Sarrantonio), 1985
Touch (Wilson, F.), 1986
Touch of Chill (ss, Aiken, J.), 1979
Tower (ss, Laski), 1974
Tower of Oblivion (Onions), 1921
Toy Terror: Batteries Included (Stine), 1997
Toys in the Attic (Gorman, as Ransom), 1986
Toys of Peace and Other Papers (ss, Saki), 1919
Trade Secrets (Garton), 1990
Tragical Comedy or Comical Tragedy of Mr. Punch (Gaiman), 1994
Trail of Cthulhu (Derleth), 1962
Transformation (Hawthorne, N.), 1860
Transition of H. P. Lovecraft (ss, Lovecraft), 1996
Transition of Titus Crow (Lumley), 1975
Transylvania Mon Amour (Lucas), 1989
Trapped in Bat Wing Hall (Stine), 1995
Travelling Companions (ss, James, H.), 1919
Travelling Grave, and Other Stories (ss, Hartley), 1948
Tread Softly (Laymon, as Kelly), 1987
Tree of Heaven (ss, Chambers), 1907
Trial (appendix; Kafka), 1937
Trial of Elizabeth Cree (Ackroyd), 1995
Tribe (Wood), 1981
Tribe of the Dead (Brandner), 1984
Trilobyte: An Easter Treasure (ss, Bryant), 1987
Triumph of Death (appendix; play, Sologub), 1907
Trollnight (Tremayne), 1987
True Bride (Black, as Altman), 1982
True Story of a Vampire (ss, Stenbock), 1989
Truth (James, P.), 1997
Truth or Dare (Stine), 1995
Tulpa (Williamson, J.), 1981
Turn of the Screw (James, H.), 1898
Turning (ss, Dee), 1993
Twenty-Nine Kisses from Roald Dahl (ss, Dahl), 1969
Twice Dead (Ross, M.), 1978
Twice-Told Tales (ss, Hawthorne, N.), 1837
Twilight (James, P.), 1991
Twilight (Koontz, as Nichols), 1984
Twilight Eyes (Koontz), 1985
Twilight Stories (ss, Broughton), 1879
Twilight Time (Hautala), 1994
Twilight Web (Ross, M.), 1968
Twilight Zone: The Movie (ss, Bloch), 1983
Twilight's Child (Neiderman, as Andrews), 1992
Twins (Wood), 1977
Twist of Fate (Saul), 1997
Twisted (Stine), 1987
Twisted Images (ss, D'Ammassa), 1995
Twisted Tale of Tiki Island (Stine), 1997
Twitchy Eyes (Donnelly), 1997
Two Deaths of Christopher Martin (Golding), 1957
Two Fables (ss, Dahl), 1986
Two for the River and Other Stories (ss, Hartley), 1961
Two Ghost Stories (ss, Rolt), 1994
Two Magics (James, H.), 1898
Two Obscure Tales (ss, Campbell), 1993
Two Sides of the Face (ss, Quiller-Couch, as Q), 1903
Two Stories of the Seen and Unseen (ss, Oliphant), 1885

Two Tales: The Green-Room, The Connoisseur (ss, de la Mare), 1925

Ugly Face of Love and Other Stories (ss, Kersh), 1960
Unbeholden (Weinberg), 1996
Unbidden (ss, Chetwynd-Hayes), 1971
Uncanny Stories (ss, Sinclair, M.), 1923
Uncanny Tales (ss, Crawford), 1911
Uncanny Tales (ss, Molesworth), 1896
Uncle Silas (Le Fanu), 1864
Undead (Smith, G.), 1983
Under the Crust: Supernatural Tales of Buxton (ss, Lamsley), 1993
Under the Lake (Woods), 1987
Under the Magician's Spell (Stine), 1996
Under the Sunset (ss, Stoker), 1881
Underground (Chadbourn), 1993
Undying Monster (Kerruish), 1922
Uneasy Freehold (Macardle), 1941
Unexpurgated Clark Ashton Smith (ss, Smith, C.), 1987-88
Unforeseen (Macardle), 1946
Unholy Allies (Weinberg), 1995
Unholy Crusade (Wheatley), 1967
Unholy Fire (Strieber), 1992
Unholy Relics (ss, Dare), 1947
Unholy Three (Robbins), 1917
Unholy Trinity (Bloch), 1986
Unholy Trinity (ss, Russell, R.), 1967
Uninhabited House (Riddell), 1875
Uninvited (Farris), 1982
Uninvited (Macardle), 1942
University (Little), 1995
University of Cosmopoli series (ss, Blayre), from 1923
Unknown Depths (O'Donnell), 1905
Unknown Regions (Holdstock), 1996
Unknown Sea (Housman), 1898
Unlikely Stories, Mostly (ss, Gray), 1983
Unlimited Dream Company (Ballard), 1979
Unloved (Saul), 1988
Unnatural Acts and Other Stories (ss, Taylor, L.), 1994
Unpaying Guests (ss, Burrage), 1989
Unquiet Corpse (Sloane), 1956
Unquiet Dead (Bingley), 1987
Unseen (Citro), 1990
Unseen (Smith, G.), 1990
Unseen Footsteps (ss, Williams), 1977
Unsettled Dust (ss, Aickman), 1990
Untold Tales (ss, Smith, C.), 1984
Unwanted (Saul), 1987
Upper Berth (ss, Crawford), 1894
Uprising (Monahan), 1992
Usher's Passing (McCammon), 1984

Valdmer the Viking (Nisbet), 1893
Valentine (Somtow), 1992
Valentine series (Somtow), from 1992
Valley of Lights (Gallagher), 1987
Vampir (appendix; Ewers), 1921
Vampire (appendix; Ewers), 1934
Vampire Breath (Stine), 1996
Vampire Chronicles (Rice), from 1976

Vampire Contessa, from the Journal of Jeremy Quentin (Ross, M.), 1974
Vampire Diary: The Embrace (Weinberg), 1995
Vampire Files series (Elrod), from 1990
Vampire Heart (Garton, as Locke), 1994
Vampire Junction (Somtow), 1984
Vampire Lestat (Rice), 1985
Vampire Lovers and Other Stories (ss, Le Fanu), 1970
Vampire Stories of R. Chetwynd-Hayes (ss, Chetwynd-Hayes), 1996
Vampire Tapestry (Charnas), 1980
Vampire World series (Lumley), from 1992
Vampire's Beautiful Daughter (Somtow), 1997
Vampire's Moon (Saxon), 1970
Vampires of Alfama (appendix; Kast), 1976
Vampires of Finistère (Saxon), 1970
Vampyre (Holland), 1995
Vampyre: A Tale (ss, Polidori), 1819
Vanishment (Aycliffe), 1993
Vanitas (Somtow), 1995
Vanka the Butler and the Page Jehan (appendix; play, Sologub), 1909
Varney the Vampire (Rymer), 1845-47
Vathek (Beckford), 1816
Vengeance (Garton, as Locke), 1994
Vengeance of She (Tremayne), 1978
Venus Hunters (ss, Ballard), 1980
Vermilion Sands (ss, Ballard), 1971
Vic and Blood (ss, Ellison), 1989
Victim (Suster), n.d.
Victims (Hutson), 1987
Victoria Winters (Ross, M.), 1967
Victorian Chaise Longue (Laski), 1953
Videodrome (Etchison), 1983
Village of Satan (Bingley), 1990
Violent Cases (Gaiman), 1987
Virgin of the Seven Daggers (ss, Lee), 1962
Virgins and Martyrs (Maginn), 1995
Virgo: Snake Inside (Tuttle, as Palmer), 1995
Visible and Invisible (ss, Benson, E.), 1923
Vision (Koontz), 1977
Vision: Liber Veritatis (ss, Beckford), 1930
Visions and Venturers (ss, Sturgeon), 1978
Visitor (Pike), 1995
Vital Signs (Cook), 1991
Voice of Our Shadow (Carroll), 1983
Voice of the Night (Koontz), 1980
Voices (Aiken, J.), 1988
Voices of Doom (ss, Copper), 1980
Voices of Evil (Hague), 1996
Voices of Time (ss, Ballard), 1984
Voices out of Time (Grant), 1977
Voodoo Dawn (Russo), 1987
Voyages into Darkness (ss, Laws; Morris), 1993

Wagner, the Wehr-Wolf (Reynolds), 1846-47
Wailing Well (ss, James, M.), 1928
Waiting Darkness (Bingley), 1984
Waiting in the Shadows (Ross, M.), 1976
Waiting Room (Wright), 1986
Wake of the Werewolf (Walker, as Caine), 1991

Waking Nightmares (ss, Campbell), 1991
Walk to San Michele (Timperley), 1971
Walkers (Brandner), 1980
Walkers (Masterton), 1989
Walking Dead (Smith, G.), 1984
Walking on Glass (Banks), 1985
Walking Wolf (Collins), 1995
Wall of Masks (Koontz, as Coffey), 1975
Walpurgisnacht (appendix; Meyrink), 1993
Wandering Ghosts (ss, Crawford), 1911
Wandering Heath (ss, Quiller-Couch, as Q), 1895
Wandering Jew (appendix; Sue), 1844
Wanting (Black), 1986
War (McDowell), 1983
War Fever (ss, Ballard), 1990
War of the Worlds (Wells), 1898
Wards of Armageddon (Williamson, J.), 1986
Warhead (Smith, G.), 1981
Warlock (Garton), 1989
Warner, Alex, series (Weinberg), from 1988
Warning to the Curious, and Other Ghost Stories (ss, James, M.), 1925
Warning Whispers (ss, Burrage), 1988
Wasp Factory (Banks), 1984
Watch the Birdie (ss, Campbell), 1984
Watcher and Other Weird Stories (ss, Le Fanu), 1894
Watcher by the Threshold and Other Tales (ss, Buchan), 1902
Watchers (Koontz), 1987
Watchers at the Strait Gate (ss, Kirk), 1984
Watchers Out of Time and Others (ss, Derleth; Lovecraft), 1974
Watching Me, Watching You (ss, Weldon), 1981
Water Rites (Smith, G.), 1996
Waterfall Box (Gordon), 1978
Watertower (Crew), 1994
Watseka: America's Most Extraordinary Case of Possession and Exorcism (St. Clair), 1977
Wave (Hyde), 1979
Way Shadows Fall (ss, Turner), 1975
We Are for the Dark (ss, Aickman), 1951
We Have Always Lived in the Castle (Jackson), 1962
Weavers and Weft and Other Tales (ss, Braddon), 1877
Weaveworld (Barker), 1987
Web of Defeat (Grant), 1987
Web of Dreams (Neiderman, as Andrews), 1990
Web of Easter Island (Wandrei), 1948
Webs (Baker, S.), 1989
Webs of Time (poetry, Brennan), 1979
Weekend (Pike), 1986
Weep No More, My Lady (Clark, M.), 1987
Weird Family Tales (ss, Wisman), 1993
Weird Family Tales II: The Curse Continues (ss, Wisman), 1995
Weird Romance (play, Brennert), 1993
Weird Shadow over Innsmouth and Other Stories of the Supernatural (ss, Lovecraft), 1944
Weird Stories (ss, Riddell), 1882
Weirdmonger's Tales (ss, Lewis, D.), 1994
Welcome to Camp Nightmare (Stine), 1993
Welcome to Dead House (Stine), 1992
Welcome to the Wicked Wax Museum (Stine), 1996
Well (Cady), 1980
Well (ss, Crew), 1996

Wells of Hell (Masterton), 1980
Were-Wolf (ss, Housman), 1896
Werewolf Among Us (Koontz), 1973
Werewolf by Moonlight (Smith, G.), 1974
Werewolf of Fever Swamp (Stine), 1993
Werewolf of Paris (Endore), 1933
Werewolf of Ponkert (ss, Munn), 1958
Werewolf series (Smith, G.), from 1974
Werewolf Skin (Stine), 1997
Werewolves of London (Stableford), 1990
Wes Craven's Shocker (Boyll), 1990
West India Lights (ss, Whitehead), 1946
Western Lands (Burroughs), 1987
Wetbones (Shirley), 1991
What About the Baby? (McNally), 1983
What Dreams May Come (ss, Asquith), 1951
What Dreams May Come (Matheson, Richard), 1978
What Holly Heard (Stine), 1996
What the Moon Brings (ss, Lovecraft), 1970
What's Bred in the Bone (Davies), 1985
What's Wrong with America (Bradfield), 1994
Wheel of Time (ss, James, H.), 1893
When Chaugnar Wakes (ss, Long), 1978
When Darkness Loves Us (Engstrom), 1985
When Footsteps Echo (ss, Copper), 1975
When Graveyards Yawn (ss, Derleth), 1965
When Shlemiel Went to Warsaw and Other Stories (Singer), 1968
When the Wind Blows (Saul), 1981
When We Were Good (Skal), 1981
Where Are the Children? (Clark, M.), 1975
Where No Birds Sing (ss, Williams), 1977
Where Phantoms Stir (ss, Williams), 1976
Where Terror Stalked and Other Horror Stories (ss, Birkin), 1966
While My Pretty One Sleeps (Clark, M.), 1989
Whirlwind (Grant), 1995
Whisper in the Night (ss, Aiken, J.), 1982
Whisper in the Night (ss, Williams), 1988(?)
Whisper of Death (Pike), 1991
Whispering Gallery (Ross, M.), 1970
Whisperland (Hyde), 1987
Whispers (Koontz), 1980
Whispers in the Dark (Aycliffe), 1992
Whispers in the Night (Ross, M.), 1972
Whit, or Isis Among the Unsaved (Banks), 1995
White Chappell, Scarlet Tracings (Sinclair, I.), 1987
White Demon (Daniels), forthcoming
White Dominican (appendix; Meyrink), 1994
White Ghost (Hutson), 1994
White Hotel (Thomas), 1981
White Lies (Hyde), 1990
White Magic (play, Blackwood, A.), 1921
White Shark (Benchley), 1994
White Sybil (ss, Smith, C.), 1935(?)
White Wand and Other Stories (ss, Hartley), 1954
White Witch of the South Seas (Wheatley), 1968
White Wolf and Other Fireside Tales (ss, Quiller-Couch, as Q), 1902
Who Walk in Fear (ss, Bell), 1953
Who Wants a Green Bottle? and Other Uneasy Tales (ss, Robbins), 1926
Why I'm Afraid of Bees (Stine), 1994

Wicked Cat (Pike), 1996
Wicked Heart (Pike), 1994
Wicked Stepmother (McDowell, as Young), 1983
Widdershins (ss, Onions), 1911
Wide Net and Other Stories (ss, Welty), 1943
Widow of Ratchets (Brookes), 1979
Widow of Westwood (Ross, M.), 1976
Wieland (Brown), 1798
Wild (Strieber), 1991
Wild Animals (Straub), 1984
Wild Blood (Collins), 1993
Wild Boys: A Book of the Dead (Burroughs), 1971
Wild Irish Boy (Maturin), 1808
Wilding (Tem, M.), 1992
Wildwood (Farris), 1986
Will to Kill (Bloch), 1954
Willows and Other Queer Tales (ss, Blackwood, A.), 1932
Wind Blows Over (ss, de la Mare), 1936
Wind in the Rose-Bush and Other Stories of the Supernatural (ss, Freeman), 1903
Wind of Time (poetry, Brennan), 1961
Winds of Change (Ross, M., as Gilmer), 1965
Windscreen Weepers and Other Tales of Horror and Suspense (ss, Aiken, J.), 1969
Windsor Castle (Ainsworth), 1843
Wine-Dark Sea (ss, Aickman), 1988
Winged Bull (Fortune), 1935
Winter Evening Tales (ss, Hogg), 1820
Winter Sleepwalker and Other Stories (ss, Aiken, J.), 1994
Winter Wake (Hautala), 1989
Winter's Tales (ss, Dinesen), 1942
Wishing Stone (Pike), 1996
Witch (Pike), 1990
Witch of Bralhaven (Ross, M.), 1972
Witch of Goblin's Acres (Ross, M.), 1975
Witch of Prague (Crawford), 1891
Witch Spell (Smith, G.), 1993
Witch Tree (Long), 1971
Witch Wood (Buchan), 1927
Witches of Eastwick (Updike), 1984
Witching Hour (Pritchard), 1997
Witching Hour (Rice), 1990
Witching Lands (ss, Cave), 1962
Witching of Dracula (Lory), 1974
Witchlight (Holder; Tem, M.), 1996
Witch's Cove (Ross, M.), 1974
Witch's Eye (Grant), 1986
Witch's Revenge (Pike), 1995
Without Sorcery (ss, Sturgeon), 1948
Wizard's Son (Oliphant), 1883
Wizrd (Zell), 1994
Wolf Flow (Jeter), 1992
Wolf Moon (Gorman), 1993
Wolf Tracks (Case), 1980
Wolfcurse (Smith, G.), 1981
Wolfen (Strieber), 1978
Wolfman (Campbell, as Dreadstone), 1977
Wolf's Hour (McCammon), 1989
Wolves of God and Other Fey Stories (ss, Blackwood, A.), 1921
Woman in Black (Hill), 1983

Woman in the House (Hichens), 1945
Woman Next Door (Wright), 1981
Wonderful Adventures of Arthur Gordon Pym (Poe), 1861
Wonderland (Oates), 1971
Wood (Smith, G.), 1985
Wood Daemon (play, Lewis, M.), 1807
Woods Are Dark (Laymon), 1981
World of Wonders (Davies), 1975
World, the Flesh and the Devil (Braddon), 1891
World's End (Gaiman), 1995
World's End and Other Stories (ss, Theroux), 1980
Worlds of Theodore Sturgeon (ss, Sturgeon), 1972
Worlds without End (ss, Baker, D.), 1945
Worm (Knight, as Childer), 1987
Worming the Harpy, and Other Bitter Pills (Hughes), 1995
Worms (Sarrantonio), 1985
Wrath of Fu Manchu and Other Stories (ss, Rohmer), 1973
Wreath of Roses (Blackburn), 1965
Writ in Blood (Yarbro), 1997
Writer of the Purple Rage (ss, Lansdale), 1994
Wrong (ss, Cooper), 1992
Wrong Envelope, and Other Stories (ss, Molesworth), 1906
Wrong Number (Stine), 1990
Wrong Number II (Stine), 1995
Wulf (Harris, S.), 1991
Wurm (Costello, M.), 1991
Wyoming Sun (ss, Bryant), 1980
Wyrm (Laws), 1987

X-Files series (Grant), from 1994
Xlucha and Others (ss, Shiel), 1975

Year of the Sex Olympics and Other TV Plays (play, Kneale), 1976
Yellow Fog (Daniels), 1986
Yellow Wallpaper (ss, Gilman), 1899
Yellow-Cap (ss, Hawthorne, J.), 1880
Yesteryear Phantom (Ross, M.), 1971
You Can't Catch Me (Oates, as Smith), 1995
You Can't Scare Me! (Stine), 1994
Young Blood (Stableford), 1992
Young, Sister Rachel and Razoxane, series (Pritchard), from 1993
Your Secret Admirer (Laymon), 1980
You're All Alone (ss, Leiber), 1972
You're Next! (Sharman), 1986
Yours Truly, Jack the Ripper (ss, Bloch), 1962

Zacharius, Lamia, series (Williamson, J.), from 1981
Zanoni (Bulwer-Lytton), 1840
Zero at the Bone (Cadnum), 1996
Zlateh the Goat and Other Stories (Singer), 1966
Zod Wallop (Spencer), 1995
Zombie (Oates), 1995
Zombie (Saxon, as Lecale), 1975
Zombie (Slade), 1996
Zombie! (Tremayne), 1981
Zoo Event (Douglas), 1997
Zoroaster (play, Lewis, M.), 1811
Zothique Hyperborea Xiccarph Poseidonis (ss, Smith, C.), 1970-73

READING LIST

Aguirre, Manuel. *Closed Space: Horror Literature and Western Symbolism.* Manchester, Manchester University Press, 1990.

Ashley, Mike. *Who's Who in Horror and Fantasy Fiction.* London, Elm Tree, 1977.

Ashley, Mike, and William G. Contento. *The Supernatural Index: A Listing of Fantasy, Supernatural, Occult, Weird, and Horror Anthologies.* Westport, Connecticut, Greenwood Press, 1995.

Badley, Linda. *Film, Horror, and the Body Fantastic.* Westport, Connecticut, Greenwood Press, 1995.

Badley, Linda. *Writing Horror and the Body: The Fiction of Stephen King, Clive Barker, and Anne Rice.* Westport, Connecticut, Greenwood Press, 1996.

Bansak, Edmund G. *Fearing the Dark: The Val Lewton Career.* Jefferson, North Carolina, McFarland, 1995.

Barclay, Glen St. John. *Anatomy of Horror: The Masters of Occult Fiction.* London, Weidenfeld and Nicolson, and New York, St. Martin's Press, 1978.

Barker, Martin. *A Haunt of Fears: The Strange History of the British Horror Comics Campaign.* London, Pluto Press, 1984.

Barron, Neil, ed. *Horror Literature: A Reader's Guide.* New York, Garland, 1990.

Benton, Mike. *Horror Comics: The Illustrated History.* Dallas, Texas, Taylor, 1991.

Birkhead, Edith. *The Tale of Terror: A Study of the Gothic Romance.* London, Constable, 1921.

Bleiler, Everett F. *The Checklist of Fantastic Literature: A Bibliography of Fantasy, Weird and Science Fiction Books Published in the English Language.* Chicago, Shasta, 1948; revised edition, as *The Checklist of Science Fiction and Supernatural Fiction*, Glen Rock, New Jersey, Firebell, 1978.

Bleiler, Everett F., ed. *The Guide to Supernatural Fiction: A Full Description of 1,775 Books from 1750 to 1960.* Kent, Ohio, Kent State University Press, 1983.

Bleiler, Everett F., ed. *Supernatural Fiction Writers: Fantasy and Horror.* New York, Scribner, 2 vols., 1985.

Bloom, Clive, ed. *Creepers: British Horror and Fantasy in the Twentieth Century.* London, Pluto Press, 1993.

Bloom, Harold, ed. *Modern Horror Writers.* New York, Chelsea House, 1995.

Briggs, Julia. *The Night Visitors: The Rise and Fall of the English Ghost Story.* London, Faber, 1977.

Brosnan, John. *The Horror People.* London, Joseph, and New York, St. Martin's Press, 1976.

Bussing, Sabine. *Aliens in the Home: The Child in Horror Fiction.* Westport, Connecticut, Greenwood Press, 1987.

Butler, Ivan. *Horror in the Cinema.* New York, Paperback Library, 1971.

Carpenter, Lynette, and Wendy K. Kolmar, eds. *Haunting the House of Fiction: Feminist Perspectives on Ghost Stories by American Women.* Knoxville, Tennessee, University of Tennessee Press, 1991.

Carroll, Noel. *The Philosophy of Horror, or Paradoxes of the Heart.* London and New York, Routledge, 1989.

Carter, Margaret L. *Shadow of a Shade: A Survey of Vampirism in Literature.* Gordon Press, 1975.

Carter, Margaret L. *Specter or Delusion?: The Supernatural in Gothic Fiction.* Ann Arbor, Michigan, UMI Research Press, 1987.

Carter, Margaret L. *The Vampire in Literature: A Critical Bibliography.* Ann Arbor, Michigan, UMI Research Press, 1989.

Clarens, Carlos. *An Illustrated History of the Horror Film.* New York, Putnam, 1967; as *Horror Movies: An Illustrated Survey*, London, Secker and Warburg, 1968.

Clemit, Pamela. *The Godwinian Novel: The Rational Fictions of Godwin, Brockden Brown, Mary Shelley.* Oxford, Clarendon Press, 1993.

Clover, Carol J. *Men, Women, and Chain Saws: Gender in the Modern Horror Film.* Princeton, New Jersey, Princeton University Press, 1992.

Coates, Paul. *The Gorgon's Gaze: German Cinema, Expressionism and the Image of Horror.* Cambridge, Cambridge University Press, 1991.

Copper, Basil. *The Vampire in Legend, Fact and Art.* London, Hale, 1973.

Copper, Basil. *The Werewolf in Legend, Fact and Art.* New York, St. Martin's Press, 1977.

Cornwell, Neil. *The Literary Fantastic: From Gothic to Postmodernism.* London, Harvester/Wheatsheaf, 1990.

Cox, Greg. *The Transylvanian Library: A Consumer's Guide to Vampire Fiction.* San Bernardino, California, Borgo Press, 1993.

Crane, Jonathan L. *Terror and Everyday Life: Singular Moments in the History of the Horror Film.* Thousand Oaks, California, Sage, 1994.

Cummiskey, Gary R. *The Changing Face of Horror: A Study of the Nineteenth-Century French Fantastic Short Story.* New York, Peter Lang, 1992.

Daniels, Les. *Living in Fear: A History of Horror in the Mass Media.* New York, Scribner, 1975; as *Fear: A History of Horror in the Mass Media*, London, Paladin, 1977.

Davis, Richard, ed. *The Octopus Encyclopedia of Horror.* London, Octopus, 1981.

Day, William Patrick. *In the Circles of Fear and Desire: A Study of Gothic Fantasy.* Chicago, University of Chicago Press, 1985.

DeLamotte, Eugenia C. *Perils of the Night: a Feminist Study of Nineteenth-Century Gothic.* New York, Oxford University Press, 1990.

Derleth, August. *Thirty Years of Arkham House, 1939-1969: A History and Bibliography.* Sauk City, Wisconsin, Arkham House, 1970.

Derry, Charles. *Dark Dreams: The Horror Film from Psycho to Jaws.* Cranbury, New Jersey, Barnes, 1977.

Dika, Vera. *Games of Terror: Halloween, Friday the 13th, and the Films of the Stalker Cycle.* N.p., 1990.

Docherty, Brian, ed. *American Horror Fiction: From Brockden Brown to Stephen King.* London, Macmillan Press, 1990.

Douglas, Adam. *The Beast Within. "A History of the Werewolf."* London, Chapmans, 1992.

Drake, Douglas. *Horror!* New York, Macmillan, 1966.

Dresser, Norine. *American Vampires: Fans, Victims, Practitioners.* New York, Norton, 1989.

Dutt, Sukumar. *The Supernatural in English Romantic Poetry 1780-1830.* University of Calcutta, 1938.

Dyson, Jeremy. *Bright Darkness: The Lost Art of the Supernatural Horror Film.* London, Cassell, 1997.

Eisner, Lotte H. *The Haunted Screen.* Berkeley and Los Angeles, University of California Press, 1973.

Ellis, Kate Ferguson. *The Contested Castle: Gothic Novels and the Subversion of Domestic Ideology.* Urbana and Chicago, University of Illinois Press, 1989.

Ellis, Reed. *A Journey Into Darkness: The Art of James Whale's Horror Films.* New York, Arno Press, 1980.

Everson, William K. *Classics of the Horror Film.* Secaucus, New Jersey, Citadel, 1974.

Fiedler, Leslie A. *Freaks: Myths and Legends of the Secret Self.* New York, Simon and Schuster, 1978.

Fiedler, Leslie A. *Love and Death in the American Novel.* New York, Criterion, 1960; second edition, New York, Stein and Day, 1966; London, Cape, 1967.

Fisher, Benjamin Franklin, IV. *The Gothic's Gothic: Study Aids to the Tradition of the Tale of Terror.* New York, Garland, 1988.

Fleenor, Juliann E., ed. *The Female Gothic.* Montreal, Eden Press, 1983.

Flynn, John L. *Cinematic Vampires: The Living Dead on Film and Television, from The Devil's Castle (1896) to Bram Stoker's Dracula (1992).* Jefferson, North Carolina, McFarland, 1992.

Frank, Frederick S. *The First Gothics: A Critical Guide to the English Gothic Novel.* New York, Garland, 1987.

Frank, Frederick S. *Gothic Fiction: A Master List of Twentieth Century Criticism and Research.* Westport, Connecticut, Meckler, 1988.

Frank, Frederick S. *Guide to the Gothic: An Annotated Bibliography of Criticism.* Metuchen, New Jersey, Scarecrow Press, 1984.

Frank, Frederick S. *Through the Pale Door: A Guide to and Through the American Gothic.* New York, Greenwood Press, 1990.

Frayling, Christopher, ed. *Vampyres: Lord Byron to Count Dracula.* London, Faber, 1992.

Frost, Brian J. *The Monster with a Thousand Faces: Guises of the Vampire in Myth and Literature.* Bowling Green, Ohio, Bowling Green State University Popular Press, 1989.

Geary, Robert F. *The Supernatural in Gothic Fiction: Horror, Belief and Literary Change.* Lewiston, New York, Mellen, 1992.

Gelder, Ken. *Reading the Vampire.* London, Routledge, 1994.

Gifford, Denis. *A Pictorial History of Horror Films.* London, Hamlyn, 1973.

Golden, Christopher, ed. *Cut! Horror Writers on Horror Film.* New York, Berkley, 1992.

Goldsmith, Arnold L. *The Golem Remembered, 1909-1980: Variations of a Jewish Legend.* Detroit, Michigan, Wayne State University Press, 1981.

Gordon, Mel. *The Grand Guignol: Theatre of Fear and Terror.* New York Amok Press, 1988.

Graham, Kenneth W., ed. *Gothic Fictions: Prohibition/Transgression.* New York, AMS Press, 1989.

Grant, Barry K., ed. *Planks of Reason: Essays on the Horror Film.* Metuchen, New Jersey, Scarecrow Press, 1988.

Grixti, Joseph. *Terrors of Uncertainty: The Cultural Contexts of Horror Fiction.* London, Routledge, 1989.

Gross, Louis S. *Redefining the American Gothic: From Wieland to Day of the Dead.* Ann Arbor, Michigan, UMI Research Press, 1988.

Grudin, Peter D. *The Demon-Lover: The Theme of Demoniality in English and Continental Fiction of the Late Eighteenth and Early Nineteenth Centuries.* N.p., 1987.

Haggerty, George E. *Gothic Fiction/Gothic Form.* N.p., 1989.

Haining, Peter, ed. *The Penny Dreadful.* London, Gollancz, 1975.

Haining, Peter. *A Pictorial History of Horror Stories: 200 Years of Spine-Chilling Illustrations from the Pulp Magazines.* London, Souvenir Press, 1976; new edition, London, Treasure Press, 1985.

Hanke, Ken. *A Critical Guide to Horror Film Series.* New York, Garland, 1991.

Hardy, Phil, ed. *The Aurum Film Encyclopedia: Horror.* London, Aurum Press, 1985; as *The Encyclopedia of Horror Movies*, New York, Harper and Row, 1986.

Harris, Anthony. *Witchcraft and Magic in Seventeenth Century English Drama.* Manchester, Manchester University Press, 1980.

Hearn, Marcus, and Alan Barnes. *The Hammer Story.* London, Titan, 1997.

Heller, Terry. *The Delights of Terror: An Aesthetics of the Tale of Terror.* Urbana and Chicago, Illinois, University of Illinois Press, 1987.

Herdman, John. *The Double in Nineteenth-Century Fiction: The Shadow Life.* London, Macmillan, 1990; New York, St. Martin's Press, 1991.

Hogan, David J. *Dark Romance: Sex and Death in the Horror Film.* Jefferson, North Carolina, McFarland, 1986; Wellingborough, Equation, 1988.

Howells, Coral Ann. *Love, Mystery, and Misery: Feeling in Gothic Fictions.* London, Athlone Press, 1978.

Hoyt, Olga Gruhzit. *Lust for Blood: The Consuming Story of Vampires.* New York, Stein and Day, 1984.

Hughes, Winifred. *The Maniac in the Cellar: Sensation Novels of the 1860s.* Princeton, New Jersey, Princeton University Press, 1980.

Huss, Roy, and T. J. Ross, eds. *Focus on the Horror Film.* Englewood Cliffs, New Jersey, Prentice-Hall, 1972.

Hutchings, Peter. *Hammer and Beyond: The British Horror Film.* N.p., 1993.

Iaccino, James F. *Psychological Reflections on Cinematic Terror: Jungian Archetypes in Horror Films.* Westport, Connecticut, Praeger, 1994.

Inverso, Marybeth. *The Gothic Impulse in Contemporary Drama.* Ann Arbor, Michigan, UMI Research Press, 1990.

Jaffery, Sheldon R. *Horrors and Unpleasantries: A Bibliographical History & Collectors' Price Guide to Arkham House.* Bowling Green, Ohio, Bowling Green State University Popular Press, 1982; revised as *The Arkham House Companion: Fifty Years of Arkham House: A Bibliographical History*, Mercer Island, Washington, Starmont House, 1989.

Jaffery, Sheldon R., and Fred Cook. *The Collector's Index to Weird Tales.* Bowling Green, Ohio, Bowling Green State University Popular Press, 1985.

Jones, Robert K. *The Shudder Pulps: A History of the Weird Menace Magazines of the 1930's.* West Linn, Oregon, Fax, 1975.

Jones, Stephen. *The Illustrated Vampire Movie Guide.* London, Titan, 1993.

Jones, Stephen. *The Illustrated Werewolf Movie Guide.* London, Titan, 1996.

Jones, Stephen, and Kim Newman, eds. *Horror: 100 Best Books.* London, Xanadu, 1988; revised edition, London, New English Library, 1992.

Joshi, S. T. *The Weird Tale.* Austin, Texas, University of Texas Press, 1990.

Kendrick, Walter. *The Thrill of Fear: 250 Years of Scary Entertainment.* New York, Grove Press, 1991.

Kerr, Howard, J. W. Crowley and C. L. Crow, eds. *The Haunted Dusk: American Supernatural Fiction, 1820-1920.* Athens, Georgia, University of Georgia Press, 1983.

Kiely, Robert. *The Romantic Novel in England.* Cambridge, Massachusetts, Harvard University Press, 1972.

Kies, Cosette. *Presenting Young Adult Horror Fiction.* New York, Twayne, 1992.

Kies, Cosette, *Supernatural Fiction for Teens: More Than 1300 Good Paperbacks to Read for Wonderment, Fear, and Fun.* 2nd ed. Englewood, Colorado, Libraries Unlimited, 1992.

Kilgour, Maggie. *The Rise of the Gothic Novel.* London and New York, Routledge, 1995.

King, Stephen. *Stephen King's Danse Macabre.* New York, Everest House, and London, Macdonald, 1981.

Kinnard, Roy. *Horror in Silent Films: A Filmography, 1896-1929.* Jefferson, North Carolina, McFarland, 1995.

Kracauer, Siegfried. *From Caligari to Hitler: A Psychological History of the German Film.* Princeton, New Jersey, Princeton University Press, 1947.

Lea, Sydney L. W. *Gothic to Fantastic: Readings in Supernatural Fiction.* New York, Arno Press, 1980.

Lloyd-Smith, Allan G. *Uncanny American Fiction: Medusa's Face.* New York, St. Martin's Press, 1989.

Lovecraft, H. P. *Supernatural Horror in Literature.* New York, Abramson, 1945.

McAndrew, Elizabeth. *The Gothic Tradition in Fiction.* New York, Columbia University Press, 1979.

McCarty, John, ed. *The Fearmakers: The Screen's Directorial Masters of Suspense and Terror.* New York, St. Martin's Press, 1994.

McCarty, John. *Movie Psychos and Madmen: Film Psychopaths from Jekyll and Hyde to Hannibal Lecter.* Secaucus, New Jersey, Carol, 1993.

McCarty, John. *The Official Splatter Movie Guide.* New York, St. Martin's Press, 1989.

McCarty, John. *Psychos: Eighty Years of Mad Movies, Maniacs, and Murderous Deeds.* New York, St. Martin's Press, 1986.

McCarty, John. *Splatter Movies: Breaking the Last Taboo of the Screen.* New York, St. Martin's Press, 1984.

McNutt, Dan J. *The Eighteenth-Century Gothic Novel: An Annotated Bibliography of Criticism and Selected Texts.* New York, Garland, 1975.

Magistrale, Tony, and Michael A. Morrison, eds. *A Dark Night's Dreaming: Contemporary American Horror Fiction.* Columbia, University of South Carolina Press, 1996.

Mank, Gregory W. *Hollywood Cauldron: Thirteen Horror Films from the Genre's Golden Age.* Jefferson, North Carolina, McFarland, 1993.

Massé, Michelle A. *In the Name of Love: Women, Masochism, and the Gothic.* Ithaca, New York, Cornell University Press, 1992.

Melton, J. Gordon. *The Vampire Book: The Encyclopedia of the Undead.* Detroit, Gale Research, 1994.

Messent, Peter B., ed. *Literature and the Occult: A Collection of Critical Essays.* Englewood Cliffs, New Jersey, Prentice-Hall, 1981.

Miles, Robert. *Gothic Writing 1750-1820: A Genealogy.* London and New York, Routledge, 1993.

Millbank, Alison. *Daughters of the House: Modes of the Gothic in Victorian Fiction.* N.p., 1992.

Miller, Karl. *Doubles: Studies in Literary History.* Oxford, Oxford University Press, 1985.

Milne, Tom, and Paul Willeman, eds. *Encyclopedia of Horror Movies.* New York, Harper, 1987.

Monleon, José B. *A Specter is Haunting Europe: A Sociohistorical Approach to the Fantastic.* Princeton, New Jersey, Princeton University Press, 1990.

Naha, Ed. *Horrors: From Screen to Scream.* New York, Avon, 1975.

Napier, Elizabeth R. *The Failure of Gothic: Problems of Disjunction in an Eighteenth-Century Literary Form.* Oxford, Oxford University Press, 1987.

Newman, Kim, ed. *The BFI Companion to Horror.* London, Cassell/British Film Institute, 1996.

Newman, Kim. *Nightmare Movies: A History of the Horror Film, 1968-1988.* London, Bloomsbury, 1988.

Nicholls, Stan. *Wordsmiths of Wonder: Fifty Interviews with Writers of the Fantastic.* London, Orbit, 1993.

Northey, Margot. *The Haunted Wilderness: The Gothic and Grotesque in Canadian Fiction.* Toronto, University of Toronto Press, 1976.

Parish, James Robert. *Ghosts and Angels in Hollywood Films: Plots, Critiques, Casts and Credits for 264 Theatrical and Made-for-Television Releases.* Jefferson, North Carolina, McFarland, 1994.

Parnell, Frank H., and Mike Ashley. *Monthly Terrors: An Index to the Weird Fantasy Magazines Published in the United States and Great Britain.* Westport, Connecticut, Greenwood Press, 1985.

Paul, William. *Laughing Screaming: Modern Hollywood Horror and Comedy.* New York, Columbia University Press, 1994.

Penzoldt, Peter. *The Supernatural in Fiction.* London, Peter Nevill, 1952.

Pirie, David. *A Heritage of Horror: The English Gothic Cinema, 1946-1972.* London, Fraser, and New York, Avon, 1973.

Pirie, David. *The Vampire Cinema.* London, Hamlyn, 1977.

Prawer, S. S. *Caligari's Children: The Film as Tale of Terror.* Oxford, Oxford University Press, 1980.

Praz, Mario. *The Romantic Agony.* Oxford, Oxford University Press, 1933; second edition, 1951.

Proulx, Kevin. *Fear to the World: Eleven Voices in a Chorus of Horror.* Mercer Island, Washington, Starmont House, 1992.

Punter, David. *The Literature of Terror: A History of Gothic Fictions from 1765 to the Present Day.* London, Longman, 1980.

Radcliffe, Elsa J. *Gothic Novels of the Twentieth Century: An Annotated Bibliography.* Metuchen, New Jersey, Scarecrow Press, 1979.

Railo, Eino. *The Haunted Castle: A Study of the Elements of English Romanticism.* London, Routledge, and New York, Dutton, 1927.

Reed, Toni. *Demon-Lovers and Their Victims in British Fiction.* Lexington, Kentucky, University Press of Kentucky, 1988.

Riccardo, Martin V. *Vampires Unearthed: The Complete Multi-Media Vampire and Dracula Bibliography.* New York, Garland, 1983.

Ringe, Donald A. *American Gothic: Imagination and Reason in 19th-Century Fiction.* Kentucky University Press, 1982.

Roberts, Marie E. *Gothic Immortals: The Fiction of the Brotherhood of the Rosy Cross.* London and New York, Routledge, 1990.

Robillard, Douglas, ed. *American Supernatural Fiction: From Edith Wharton to the Weird Tales School.* New York, Garland, 1996.

Rudwin, Maximilian J. *The Devil in Legend and Literature.* N.p., 1931.

Sadleir, Michael. *The Northanger Novels: A Footnote to Jane Austen.* N.p., 1927.

Sage, Victor, ed. *The Gothic Novel: A Casebook.* London, Macmillan, 1990.

Sage, Victor. *Horror Fiction in the Protestant Tradition.* London, Macmillan, 1988.

Scarborough, Dorothy. *The Supernatural in Modern English Fiction.* New York, Putnam, 1917.

Schiff, Gert. *Images of Horror and Fantasy.* New York, Abrams, 1978.

Schneider, Kirk J. *Horror and the Holy: Wisdom Teachings of the Monster Tale.* Chicago, Open Court, 1993.

Schoell, William. *Stay Out of the Shower: The Shocker Film Phenomenon.* New York, Dembner, 1985.

Schweitzer, Darrell, ed. *Discovering Classic Horror Fiction 1.* Mercer Island, Washington, Starmont House, 1992.

Schweitzer, Darrell, ed. *Discovering Modern Horror Fiction.* Mercer Island, Washington, Starmont House, 1985.

Schweitzer, Darrell, ed. *Discovering Modern Horror Fiction II.* Mercer Island, Washington, Starmont House, 1988.

Schweitzer, Darrell. *Speaking of Horror: Interviews with Writers of the Supernatural.* San Bernardino, California, Borgo Press, 1994.

Sedgwick, Eve Kosofsky. *The Coherence of Gothic Conventions.* London, Methuen, 1986.

Senf, Carol A. *The Vampire in 19th-Century English Literature.* Bowling Green, Ohio, Bowling Green State University Popular Press, 1988.

Sevastakis, Michael. *Songs of Love and Death: The Classical American Horror Film of the 1930s.* Westport, Connecticut, Greenwood Press, 1993.

Siebers, Tobin. *The Romantic Fantastic.* Ithaca, New York, Cornell University Press, 1984.

Silver, Alain, and James Ursini. *The Vampire Film.* Cranbury, New Jersey, Barnes, 1975.

Skal, David J. *The Monster Show: A Cultural History of Horror.* New York, Norton, 1993; London, Plexus, 1994.

Slethaug, Gordon E. *The Play of the Double in Postmodern American Fiction.* Carbondale, Southern Illinois University Press, 1993.

Smith, Guy N. *Writing Horror Fiction.* London, A. and C. Black, 1996.

Spacks, Patricia Myer. *The Insistence of Horror: Aspects of the Supernatural in Eighteenth Century Poetry.* Cambridge, Massachusetts, Harvard University Press, 1962.

Spector, Robert Donald. *The English Gothic: A Bibliographic Guide to Writers from Horace Walpole to Mary Shelley.* Westport, Connecticut, Greenwood Press, 1984.

Stuart, Roxana. *Stage Blood: Vampires of the 19th-Century Stage.* N.p., 1995.

Sullivan, C. W., III, ed. *The Dark Fantastic: Selected Essays from the Ninth International Conference on the Fantastic in the Arts.* Westport, Connecticut, Greenwood Press, 1997.

Sullivan, Jack. *Elegant Nightmares: The English Ghost Story from Le Fanu to Blackwood.* Athens, Ohio, Ohio University Press, 1978.

Sullivan, Jack, ed. *The Penguin Encyclopedia of Horror and the Supernatural.* New York, Viking, 1986.

Summers, Montague. *A Gothic Bibliography.* London, Fortune Press, 1941; New York, Russell and Russell, 1964.

Summers, Montague. *The Gothic Quest: A History of the Gothic Novel.* London, Fortune Press, 1938.

Summers, Montague. *The Vampire: His Kith and Kin.* London, Kegan Paul, 1928; New York, Dutton, 1929.

Sutton, David, ed. *Voices From Shadow.* Birmingham, Shadow Publishing, 1994.

Testa, Carlo. *Desire and the Devil: Demonic Contracts in French and European Literature.* New York, Peter Lang, 1991.

Thompson, G. Richard, ed. *The Gothic Imagination: Essays in Dark Romanticism.* Pullman, Washington State University Press, 1974.

Thornburg, Mary K. Patterson. *The Monster in the Mirror: Gender and the Sentimental/Gothic Myth in Frankenstein.* Ann Arbor, Michigan, UMI Research Press, 1987.

Tohill, Cathal, and Pete Tombs. *Immoral Tales: European Sex and Horror Movies, 1956-1984.* New York, St. Martin's Press, 1995.

Tompkins, J. M. S. *The Popular Novel in England, 1770-1800.* London, Constable, 1932.

Tracy, Ann B. *The Gothic Novel, 1790-1830: Plot Summaries and Index to Motifs.* Lexington, Kentucky, University Press of Kentucky, 1982.

Tropp, Martin. *Images of Fear: How Horror Stories Helped Shape Modern Culture (1818-1918).* Jefferson, North Carolina, McFarland, 1991.

Tudor, Andrew. *Monsters and Mad Scientists: A Cultural History of the Horror Movie.* Oxford, Blackwell, 1989.

Twitchell, James B. *Dreadful Pleasures: An Anatomy of Modern Horror.* New York, Oxford University Press, 1985.

Twitchell, James B. *The Living Dead: A Study of the Vampire in Romantic Literature.* Durham, North Carolina, Duke University Press, 1981.

Tymn, Marshall B. *Horror Literature: A Core Collection and Reference Guide.* New York, Bowker, 1981.

Tymn, Marshall B., and Mike Ashley, eds. *Science Fiction, Fantasy, and Weird Fiction Magazines.* Westport, Connecticut, Greenwood Press, 1985.

Ursini, James, and Alain Silver. *More Things Than are Dreamt Of: Masterpieces of Supernatural Horror, from Mary Shelley to Stephen King, in Literature and Film.* New York, Limelight, 1994.

Varma, Devendra P. *The Gothic Flame: Being a History of the Gothic Novel in England.* London, Barker, 1957.

Varnado, S. L. *Haunted Presence: The Numinous in Gothic Fiction.* University of Alabama, 1987.

Waller, Gregory A., ed. *American Horrors: Essays on the Modern American Horror Film.* Urbana, Illinois, University of Illinois Press, 1987.

Waller, Gregory A. *The Living and the Undead: From Stoker's Dracula to Romero's Dawn of the Dead.* Champaign, Illinois, University of Illinois Press, 1986.

Warren, Bill. *Set Visits: Interviews with 32 Horror and Science Fiction Filmmakers.* Jefferson, North Carolina, McFarland, 1997.

Watt, William Whyte. *Shilling Shockers of the Gothic School: A Study of the Chapbook Gothic Romances.* Cambridge, Massachusetts, Harvard University Press, 1932.

Weinberg, Robert, and Edward P. Berglund. *Reader's Guide to the Cthulhu Mythos,* with Edward P. Berglund. Albuquerque, New Mexico, Silver Scarab Press, 1973.

Weinberg, Robert. *The Weird Tales Story.* West Linn, Oregon, Fax, 1977.

Wiater, Stanley. *Dark Dreamers: Conversations with the Masters of Horror.* Columbia, Pennsylvania, Underwood-Miller, 1990.

Wiater, Stanley. *Dark Visions: Conversations with the Masters of the Horror Film.* New York, Avon, 1992.

Wilt, Judith. *Ghosts of the Gothic: Austen, Eliot and Lawrence.* Princeton, New Jersey, Princeton University Press, 1980.

Williamson, J. N. *How to Write Tales of Horror, Fantasy & Science Fiction.* Cincinnati, Ohio, Writer's Digest, 1987; London, Robinson, 1991.

Wilson, Colin. *The Strength to Dream: Literature and the Imagination.* London, Gollancz, and Boston, Houghton Mifflin, 1962.

Winter, Douglas E. *Faces of Fear: Encounters with the Creators of Modern Horror.* New York, Berkley, 1985; revised edition, London, Pan, 1990.

Wolf, Leonard. *Horror: A Connoisseur's Guide to Literature and Film.* New York, Facts on File, 1990.

Wolff, Robert Lee. *Strange Stories: Explorations in Victorian Fiction—The Occult and the Neurotic.* Boston, Gambit, 1971.

Wolstenholme, Susan. *Gothic (Re) Visions: Writing Women as Readers.* Albany, New York, State University of New York, 1993.

Wright, Gene. *Horrorshows: The A-Z of Horror in Film, TV, Radio, & Theater.* New York, Facts on File, 1986.

NOTES ON
ADVISERS AND CONTRIBUTORS

ADRIAN, Jack. Freelance writer. Editor of many anthologies for Oxford University Press, J. M. Dent and other publishers, and widely recognized as one of Britain's foremost experts on popular fiction. **Essays:** E. F. Benson; D. K. Broster; A. M. Burrage; Walter de la Mare; W. W. Jacobs; Jessie Douglas Kerruish; Sax Rohmer.

AMERY, Francis. Pseudonym of Brian Stableford, used for translations from the French; see his own entry. **Essays:** Michel Bernanos; Mikhail Bulgakov; Jacques Cazotte; Nikolai Gogol; Joris-Karl Huysmans; Pierre Kast; Gaston Leroux; Maurice Renard; Eugene Sue; Villiers de l'Isle Adam.

ASHLEY, Mike. Editor, bibliographer and critic. Author or editor of numerous books, including *The History of the Science Fiction Magazine* (4 vols.), 1974-78, *Who's Who in Horror and Fantasy Fiction*, 1977; *Science Fiction, Fantasy and Weird Fiction Magazines* (with Marshall B. Tymn), 1985, *The Mammoth Book of Short Horror Novels*, 1988, and *The Supernatural Index: A Listing of Fantasy, Supernatural, Occult, Weird, and Horror Anthologies* (with William G. Contento), 1995. **Essays:** Robert Arthur; R. H. Benson; Algernon Blackwood; Christopher Blayre; Mary E. Braddon; Rhoda Broughton; Simon Clark; Basil Copper; M. P Dare; Dion Fortune; W. F. Harvey; Lafcadio Hearn; E. T. A. Hoffmann; Violet Hunt; G. P. R. James; Sheridan Le Fanu; Matthew Gregory Lewis; Robert Lory; Richard Middleton; Mary Molesworth; A. N. L. Munby; Elliott O'Donnell; Thomas Peckett Prest; Mrs J. H. Riddell; L. T. C. Rolt; Marilyn Ross; James Malcolm Rymer; James Turner; E. H. Visiak; H. Russell Wakefield; Horace Walpole; Elizabeth Walter; Edith Wharton.

CAMPBELL, Ramsey. See his own entry. **Essays:** Terry Lamsley; R. R. Ryan.

COUZENS, Gary. Writer; contributor of stories to *Fantasy & Science Fiction, Interzone* and other magazines. Lives in Hampshire, England. **Essay:** Joyce Carol Oates.

CROWTHER, Peter. See his own entry. **Essays:** Neil Gaiman; Ed Gorman; Stephen Laws; Ken Wisman.

D'AMMASSA, Don. See his own entry. **Essays:** Margaret Bingley; Campbell Black; John Blackburn; Jay R. Bonansinga; Douglas Borton; Randall Boyll; Gary Brandner; Owen Brookes; Lisa W. Cantrell; Suzy McKee Charnas; Joseph Citro; Douglas Clegg; Matthew J. Costello; Sean Costello; John Coyne; Ron Dee; P. N. Elrod; Elizabeth Engstrom; Ken Eulo; John Farris; Ray Garton; Charles L. Grant; Stephen Gresham; William H. Hallahan; Rick Hautala; James Herbert; Nancy Holder; K. W. Jeter; Jeffrey Konvitz; Richard Laymon; Michael McDowell; Kenneth McKenney; Clare McNally; George R. R. Martin; Graham Masterton; Brent Monahan; Thomas F. Monteleone; Yvonne Navarro; Andrew Neiderman; Kathryn Ptacek; Daniel Rhodes; John Russo; Jeffrey Sackett; Al Sarrantonio; John Skipp & Craig Spector; Michael Slade; Whitley Strieber; Bernard Taylor; Robert W. Walker; Leslie H. Whitten; J. N. Williamson; T. M. Wright; Chelsea Quinn Yarbro.

DI FILIPPO, Paul. Novelist and short-story writer. Author of *The Steampunk Trilogy* (1995), *Ribofunk* (1996) and *Fractal Paisleys* (1997). Regular book reviewer for *Asimov's Science Fic-*

tion. Lives in Providence, Rhode Island. **Essays:** Scott Bradfield; Alasdair Gray; Russell Kirk; Ian McEwan; Lucius Shepard.

DZIEMIANOWICZ, Stefan. Critic, and editor of numerous anthologies. Co-editor, *Necrofile: The Review of Horror Fiction.* Lives in Union City, New Jersey. **Essays:** Charles Beaumont; Robert Bloch; Ray Bradbury; Joseph Payne Brennan; Arthur J. Burks; Hugh B. Cave; Fred Chappell; Mary E. Counselman; August Derleth; Dennis Etchison; Brian Hodge; Carl Jacobi; Kathe Koja; Fritz Leiber; Frank Belknap Long; Robert R. McCammon; Richard Matheson; Richard Christian Matheson; H. Warner Munn; Alan Ryan; Clark Ashton Smith; Robert Weinberg; Henry S. Whitehead; Chet Williamson.

GARRATT, Peter T. Clinical psychologist and short-story writer. Contributor to *Interzone* and various anthologies. Lives in Brighton, Sussex, England. **Essays:** Peter Ackroyd; W. A. Harbinson; Brian Lumley; Jessica Palmer; Iain Sinclair.

GILMORE, Chris. Freelance editor, critic and short-story writer; regular book reviewer for *Interzone* magazine. Lives in Bedford, England. **Essays:** Peter Crowther; James Lovegrove; Anne Rice.

GRANT, John. Pseudonym for Paul Barnett, who lives in Devon, England. Author of numerous fantasy and science-fiction novels; reference-book editor, including *The Encyclopedia of Fantasy* (with John Clute), 1997. **Essays:** Jonathan Aycliffe; Iain Banks; Ira Levin; Theodore Roszak.

GREENBERG, Lawrence. New York-based freelance writer of short stories, poetry and book reviews in various anthologies, the *Washington Post*, the *Cleveland Plain Dealer*, etc. **Essays:** Dennis Cooper; Thomas Owen; T. L. Parkinson; Horacio Quiroga; Jean Ray; Claude Seignolle; Paul Theroux.

HUGHES, Rhys. See his own entry. **Essays:** Milorad Pavic; Fyodor Sologub.

JOHNSTONE, Will. Scottish writer; occasional contributor of stories and reviews to British fanzines. **Essay:** Rhys Hughes.

JOSHI, S. T. Editor, critic and bibliographer. Winner of the Horror Writers of America Bram Stoker award for his criticism. Author of *The Weird Tale*, 1990, *Lord Dunsany: A Bibliography* (with Darrell Schweitzer), 1993, *H. P. Lovecraft: A Life*, 1996, and numerous other books. **Essays:** Robert Aickman; Ambrose Bierce; William Peter Blatty; Ramsey Campbell; F. Marion Crawford; Les Daniels; Thomas Harris; L. P. Hartley; William Hjortsberg; Shirley Jackson; T. E. D. Klein; H. P. Lovecraft; Peter Straub; Thomas Tryon.

KENNEDY, Ann. Software engineer, and editor and publisher of *The Silver Web* magazine and Buzzcity Press First Editions. **Essay:** Jack Ketchum.

KIES, Cosette. Teacher. Author of *Presenting Young Adult Horror Fiction*, 1992, and other books. **Essay:** Marlys Millhiser.

LANE, Joel. See his own entry. **Essays:** M. John Harrison; Graham Joyce; Ben Leech; D. F. Lewis; Mark Morris; Nicholas Royle; Michael Marshall Smith.

LANGFORD, David. Freelance fiction-writer and computer-software writer; winner of thirteen Hugo awards as best science-fiction fan-writer and for best fanzine (*Ansible*). Book reviewer and columnist for various magazines. Lives in Reading, England. **Essays:** Kingsley Amis; Roald Dahl; Robertson Davies; Umberto Eco; John Fowles; John Gordon; M. R. James; Gerald Kersh; Saki; Dennis Wheatley; Colin Wilson.

MATHEW, David. Regular book reviewer for *Interzone* magazine. **Essays:** Nancy A. Collins; Frank De Felitta; Mark Frost; Shaun Hutson; Christopher Hyde; Dean Koontz; Jerzy Kosinski; David L. Lindsey; Bentley Little; David Martin; Rex Miller; Christopher Pike; Garfield Reeves-Stevens; Phil Rickman; David St Clair; Peter Saxon; David Seltzer; Nick Sharman; David B. Silva; David J. Skal; Guy N. Smith; D. M. Thomas; Peter Tremayne; Steve Zell.

McMULLEN, Sean. Computer systems analyst, novelist and short-story writer. Lives in Melbourne, Australia. **Essays** (all in collaboration with Steve Paulsen): Conrad Aiken; Gary Crew; Terry Dowling; G. M. Hague; Robert Hood; Victor Kelleher; Rick Kennett; Isaac Bashevis Singer; Rosemary Timperley.

MEYER, Adam. Reviewer and interviewer for various publications, including *The Armchair Detective* and the Barnes and Noble Website. **Essays:** David Morrell; Tom Piccirilli; Steve Rasnic Tem.

MORGAN, Chris. Writer. Author of *The Shape of Futures Past*, 1980, *Future Man*, 1980, *Facts and Fallacies* (with David Langford), 1981; editor of *Dark Fantasies*, 1989. Frequent contributor to *Science Fiction and Fantasy Book Review Annual*. Lives in Birmingham, England. **Essays:** Cynthia Asquith; Peter Atkins; Denys Val Baker; Scott Baker; Clive Barker; Anne Billson; Charles Birkin; Caroline Blackwood; Chaz Brenchley; Charles Brockden Brown; John Burke; Mark Burnell; David Case; R. Chetwynd-Hayes; Brian D'Amato; Isak Dinesen; Max Ehrlich; Bret Easton Ellis; Stephen Gallagher; Susan Hill; Gordon Honeycombe; Peter James; Franz Kafka; Susan Kay; Harry Adam Knight; Joel Lane; Marghanita Laski; Patrick McGrath; Simon Maginn; Charles R. Maturin; Guy De Maupassant; Robert Nye; Petru Popescu; K. & Hesketh Prichard; John Pritchard; Arthur Quiller-Couch; Ann Radcliffe; Herman Raucher; G. W. M. Reynolds; Ray Russell; Sir Walter Scott; Curt Siodmak; Robert Stallman; Fred Mustard Stewart; Patrick Suskind; Gerald Suster; Thomas Tessier; John Updike; Mary Williams; Stuart Woods.

MORGAN, Pauline. Writer. Frequent contributor to *Science Fiction and Fantasy Book Review Annual*. Lives in Birmingham, England. **Essays:** Joan Aiken; Nancy Baker; Mark Chadbourn; Joe Donnelly; John Douglas; Christopher Fowler; Joanne Harris; Steve Harris; Jeanne Kalogridis; Michael Scott; Brian Stableford; Melanie Tem; Lisa Tuttle; F. Paul Wilson.

PAULSEN, Steve. Australian writer and editor. **Essays** (all in collaboration with Sean McMullen): Conrad Aiken; Gary Crew; Terry Dowling; G. M. Hague; Robert Hood; Victor Kelleher; Rick Kennett; Isaac Bashevis Singer; Rosemary Timperley.

PRINGLE, David. Editor and publisher of the monthly magazine *Interzone*, Brighton, England. Author of *Science Fiction: The 100 Best Novels*, 1985, *Modern Fantasy: The 100 Best Novels*, 1988, and several other books; editor, *St James Guide to Fantasy Writ-*

ers, 1st ed., 1996. **Essays:** J. G. Ballard; William S. Burroughs; Don D'Ammassa; William Golding.

ROYLE, Nicholas. See his own entry. **Essay:** Alex Hamilton.

SAWYER, Andy. Administrator, Science Fiction Foundation Library, University of Liverpool, England. Book reviewer for *Vector*, *Foundation* and other journals. **Essays:** V. C. Andrews; Tim Stout.

SCHWEITZER, Darrell. Novelist and critic, resident in Philadelphia, Pennsylvania. Editor, *Discovering Modern Horror Fiction*, 2 vols, 1985-89, *Discovering Classic Horror Fiction*, 1992, and numerous other books. **Essays:** Michael Cadnum; Jack Cady; Leonard Cline; H. B. Drake; Marvin Kaye; Joe R. Lansdale; Elizabeth Massie; Alan Rodgers; Lady Eleanor Smith; Michael Talbot.

STABLEFORD, Brian. See his own entry. **Essays:** W. Harrison Ainsworth; Grant Allen; Michael Arlen; Gertrude Atherton; Maurice Baring; William Beckford; Neil Bell; Stephen Vincent Benet; Guy Boothby; Marjorie Bowen; Poppy Z. Brite; David Britton; J. W. Brodie-Innes; John Buchan; Edward Bulwer-Lytton; Dino Buzzati; Arthur Calder-Marshall; Bernard Capes; Jonathan Carroll; Robert W. Chambers; A. E. Coppard; Aleister Crowley; Charles Dickens; Thomas M. Disch; A. Conan Doyle; Guy Endore; Hans Heinz Ewers; J. Meade Falkner; Mary E. Wilkins Freeman; R. Murray Gilchrist; William Godwin; Stefan Grabinski; Julian Hawthorne; Nathaniel Hawthorne; H. F. Heard; Robert Hichens; William Hope Hodgson; James Hogg; Tom Holland; Clemence Housman; David H. Keller; Alexander Laing; Margery Lawrence; Vernon Lee; Jeremy Leven; Thomas Ligotti; Dorothy Macardle; Arthur Machen; Richard Marsh; John Metcalfe; Gustav Meyrink; A. R. Morlan; W. C. Morrow; E. Nesbit; Hume Nisbet; Margaret Oliphant; Oliver Onions; Vincent O'Sullivan; Edgar Allan Poe; John Polidori; Mrs Campbell Praed; Seabury Quinn; Tod Robbins; Adrian Ross; Victor Rousseau; W. Clark Russell; Fred Saberhagen; Sarban; M. P. Shiel; Anne Rivers Siddons; May Sinclair; William Sloane; Count Eric Stenbock; Robert Louis Stevenson; Bram Stoker; Theodore Sturgeon; Peter Tonkin; Jeff VanderMeer; Hugh Walpole; Donald A. Wandrei; Ian Watson; Fay Weldon; H. G. Wells; Bari Wood.

TUTTLE, Lisa. See her own entry. **Essays:** Elizabeth Bowen; Daphne du Maurier; Charlotte Perkins Gilman; Robert Holdstock; Henry James.

VANDERMEER, Jeff. See his own entry. **Essay:** Katherine Dunn.

WESTFAHL, Gary. Lecturer at the University of California, Riverside. Prolific contributor to *Extrapolation, Foundation, Science-Fiction Studies* and other journals. **Essays:** Peter Benchley; Alan Brennert; Edward Bryant; Robin Cook; John Keir Cross; Harlan Ellison; Stephen King; Nigel Kneale; Kim Newman; John Saul; David J. Schow; Mary Shelley; Dan Simmons; Martin Cruz Smith; S. P. Somtow; R. L. Stine; J. Michael Straczynski; Steve Vance.

WINSTEAD, Tom. Writer, resident in Huntsville, Alabama. Contributor of stories to *The Silver Web, Aberrations, Tales From the Fringe* and *The Virtual Times*. His reviews, essays and interviews have appeared in *Tangent* and elsewhere. **Essays:** Mary Higgins Clark; Nancy Kilpatrick; Tim Lucas; John Shirley; William Browning Spencer; Lucy Taylor; Eudora Welty.